THE GENEALOGIST'S ADDRESS BOOK

THE GENEALOGIST'S ADDRESS BOOK

4th Edition

Elizabeth Petty Bentley

Library of Congress Catalogue Card Number 92-640686
International Standard Book Number 0-8063-1580-6
Made in the United States of America

INTRODUCTION

The information in each edition of *The Genealogist's Address Book* is based largely upon data received in response to direct-mail questionnaires, supplemented by information from printed and Internet sources. In my letters to libraries, archives, genealogical and historical societies, publishers, and other vendors across the country, I requested name and address correction; telephone and FAX numbers; e-mail and web site addresses; contact person (with title); hours of operation (local time); periodical title, frequency of publication, and cost of subscription; membership and search fees; and comments regarding the organization's specialty. Of course, some responses were more expansive than others, and some organizations did not respond, presumably because the information was correct as it appeared in the letter. Readers can determine which organizations responded to questionnaires by the asterisks next to their names in the general index.

Naturally, all information is subject to change—addresses, personnel, hours of operation (local time), telephone numbers, and even the names of organizations and their publications. Area codes pose an ever-growing problem, owing to the multiplication of communications devices such as FAX machines, pagers, cellular phones, and computer modems, which have gobbled up available phone numbers at an unprecedented rate. Many new area codes are being introduced throughout the country each year; in California alone, there are almost a dozen area code splits scheduled for 1998 and 1999. I have done my best in tracking down the most current codes. If you do encounter a telephone number in this book that doesn't work, you should check the area code for that state to see if there has been a change.

I'm glad to note that very few new organizations requested that their addresses be withheld, and some which had requested so previously have changed their policy. In particular, The Church of Jesus Christ of Latter-day Saints, which continues to oppose commercial publication of the names and mailing addresses of the various branch libraries (Family History Centers) throughout the world, has released the phone numbers of selected centers, which are included here in the state-by-state listings. Still, a few organizations, especially religious archives, cited the inability of their limited staffs to cope with the mounting demands of genealogists—hobbyists, in their view, rather than serious scholars. Others seem to be discouraging inquiries, either by citing exorbitant search fees or by simply referring queries directly to professional researchers who charge hourly fees plus travel time and expenses. To avoid having even more facilities resort to these tactics, all mail inquiries should be as brief and concise as possible, asking only for specific information, and should include either a self-addressed, stamped envelope and a donation to offset copying, postage, and research costs or a request for an estimate or fee schedule before any work is undertaken.

I'm grateful to the thousands of correspondents who generously took the time to answer my own inquiries. I'm especially indebted to Marian R. Hoffman, who spent many a tedious hour checking and verifying data, and to Dr. Michael Tepper, who originally perceived a need for this book and its companion volumes, and provided me the opportunity to have a part in compiling it.

I'd appreciate it if readers who find omissions or errors in the text would send any additions or corrections to me in care of the publisher.

Elizabeth Petty Bentley

CONTENTS

Part 1. National Addresses

Part 2. State Addresses

Each state includes the following categories, where applicable:

Archives and Libraries with Holdings in Genealogy: State Archives and Libraries •
State Historical Societies • City, County and Regional Archives and Libraries

Historical Societies—Local and Regional

LDS Family History Centers

Genealogical Societies: State Genealogical Societies • Regional Genealogical Societies

Independent Publications and Miscellany

Part 2A. American Trust Territories

Part 3. Ethnic and Religious Organizations and Research Centers

Religious Archives and Organizations

Part 4. Special Resources

THE GENEALOGIST'S ADDRESS BOOK

Part 1. National Addresses

NATIONAL ARCHIVES

National Archives and Records Administration

Seventh Street and Pennsylvania Avenue, N.W.
Washington, DC 20408
(202) 501-5400; (202) 523-3218; (202) 523-3286
E-mail: webmaster@nara.gov
http://www.nara.gov; http://www.nara.gov/genealogy/soundex/soundex.html (form provides any surname's Soundex code)
Hours: Research Room: Mon & Wed 8:45–5:00, Tue & Thur–Fri 8:45 A.M.–9:00 P.M.; Sat 8:45–4:45; Exhibits: Mon–Sun (1 Apr–Labor Day) 10:00–9:00, Mon–Sun (winter) 10:00–5:30
Pub. *Prologue*, quarterly, $15.00 per year subscription; *News from the Archives*; *Guide to Genealogical Research in the National Archives* (Washington, D.C., rev. ed., 1985)

National Archives and Records Administration

Public Affairs Office (NXI)
Seventh Street and Pennsylvania Avenue, N.W.
Washington, DC 20408
(202) 501-5525 (Civil Reference Branch: State, BIA, Judicial, etc.); (202) 501-5390 (Military Reference Branch: old military)
Shirley Clarkson, Director, Public Affairs Office
Hours: Mon–Fri 8:00–4:30; Research Room: Mon & Wed 8:45–5:00, Tue & Thur–Fri 8:45 A.M.–9:00 P.M.; Sat 8:45–4:45
Pub. *National Archives Calendar of Events*, monthly, free
(pictorial calendar of events, including genealogical workshops, courses, and presentations)

National Archives and Records Administration—Archives II

The National Archives at College Park
(8601 Adelphi Road, College Park, MD 20740-6001—location)
Seventh and Pennsylvania Avenue, N.W. (mailing address)
Washington, DC 20408
(301) 713-6800 (User Services); (301) 713-7040 (Cartographic Reference Branch)
Hours: Mon–Fri 8:45–5:00; Research Rooms: Mon & Wed 8:45–5:00, Tue & Thur–Fri 8:45–9:00 P.M., Sat 8:45–4:45
Pub. *Archives II Researcher Bulletin*, quarterly

(Some records from the Washington, D.C., and Suitland, MD, archives buildings have been transferred to this new facility. There are no genealogy records here. Archives II reference branches include Nixon Presidential Materials; Research Rooms; Center for Electronic Records; Cartographic Reference Branch; Motion Picture, Sound, and Video Branch; and Still Picture Branch.)

Regional Records Services Facilities

(formerly known as Regional Branches and/or Archives Records Centers)

Anchorage

NARA's Pacific Alaska Region (Anchorage)
654 West Third Avenue
Anchorage, AK 99501-2145
(907) 271-2443; (907) 271-2442 FAX
E-mail: archives@alaska.nara.gov
Area served: AK

Atlanta (East Point)

NARA's Southeast Region
1557 St. Joseph Avenue
East Point, GA 30344-2593
(404) 763-7477; (404) 763-7033 FAX
E-mail: archives@atlanta.nara.gov
Area served: Alabama, Florida, Georgia, Kentucky, Mississippi, North Carolina, South Carolina, Tennessee

Boston (Waltham)

NARA's Northeast Region (Boston)
380 Trapelo Road
Waltham, MA 02154-6399
(781) 647-8100; (781) 647-8460 FAX
E-mail: archives@waltham.nara.gov
Area served: Connecticut, Maine, Massachusetts, New Hampshire, Rhode Island, Vermont

Chicago

NARA's Great Lakes Region (Chicago)
7358 South Pulaski Road
Chicago, IL 60629-5898
(773) 581-7816; (312) 353-1294 FAX
E-mail: archives@chicago.nara.gov
Area served: Illinois, Indiana, Michigan, Minnesota, Ohio, and Wisconsin

Dayton

NARA's Great Lakes Region (Dayton)
3150 Springboro Road
Dayton, OH 45439-1867
(937) 225-2852; (937) 225-7236 FAX
E-mail: center@dayton.nara.gov
Area served: Indiana, Michigan, Minnesota, and Ohio

Denver

NARA's Rocky Mountain Region
Building 48, Denver Federal Center
Denver, Colorado 80225
P. O. Box 25307
Denver, CO 80225-0307
(303) 236-0804; (303) 236-9297 FAX
E-mail: center@denver.nara.gov
Area served: Colorado, Montana, New Mexico, North Dakota, South Dakota, Utah, Wyoming

Fort Worth

NARA's Southwest Region
501 West Felix Street, Building 1
Fort Worth, Texas 76115-3405
P. O. Box 6216
Fort Worth, TX 76115-0216
(817) 334-5525; (817) 334-5621 FAX
E-mail: archives@ftworth.nara.gov
Area served: Arkansas, Louisiana, Oklahoma, Texas

Kansas City

NARA's Central Plains Region
2312 East Bannister Road
Kansas City, MO 64131-3011
(816) 926-6272; 816-926-6982 FAX
E-mail: archives@kansascity.nara.gov
Area served: Iowa, Kansas, Missouri, Nebraska

Laguna Niguel, California

NARA's Pacific Region (Laguna Niguel)
24000 Avila Road, First Floor-East Entrance
Laguna Niguel, CA 92677-3497
P. O. Box 6719
Laguna Niguel, CA 92607-6719
(949) 360-2641; (949) 360-2624 FAX
E-mail: center@laguna.nara.gov
Area served: Arizona, southern California, and Clark County, Nevada

Lee's Summit, Missouri

NARA's Central Plains Region (Lee's Summit, Missouri)
200 Space Center Drive
Lee's Summit, MO 64064-1182
(816) 478-7079; (816) 478-7625 FAX
Area served: New Jersey, New York, Puerto Rico, and the U.S. Virgin Islands (temporary records)

New York City

NARA's Northeast Region (New York City)
201 Varick Street
New York, NY 10014-4811
(212) 337-1300; (212) 337-1306 FAX
E-mail: archives@newyork.nara.gov
Area served: New Jersey, New York, Puerto Rico, the U.S. Virgin Islands (permanent records)

Philadelphia (Center City)
NARA's Mid Atlantic Region (Center
City Philadelphia)
Ninth and Chestnut Streets
Philadelphia, PA 19107-4292
(215) 597-3000; (215) 597-2303 FAX
E-mail: archives@philarch.nara.gov
Area served: Delaware, Maryland,
Pennsylvania, Virginia, and West
Virginia

NARA's Mid Atlantic Region (Northeast Philadelphia)
14700 Townsend Road
Philadelphia, PA 19154-1025
(215) 671-9027; (215) 671-8001 FAX
E-mail: center@philadelphia.nara.gov
Area served: Delaware, Maryland,
Pennsylvania, Virginia, and West
Virginia

Pittsfield, Massachusetts
NARA's Northeast Region (Pittsfield)
10 Conte Drive
Pittsfield, MA 01201-8230
(413) 445-6885; (413) 445-7599 FAX
E-mail: archives@pittsfield.nara.gov

San Francisco
NARA's Pacific Region (San Francisco)
1000 Commodore Drive
San Bruno, CA 94066-2350
(650) 876-9009; (650) 876-9233 FAX
E-mail: center@sanbruno.nara.gov
Area served:Northern California, Guam,
Hawaii, Nevada (except Clark
County), American Samoa, Trust
Territory of the Pacific Islands

Seattle
NARA's Pacific Alaska Region (Seattle)
6125 Sand Point Way NE
Seattle, WA 98115-7999
(206) 526-6507; (206) 526-4344 FAX
E-mail: archives@seattle.nara.gov
Area served: Idaho, Oregon, Washington

St. Louis
NARA's National Personnel Records
Center
Civilian Personnel Records
111 Winnebago Street
St. Louis, MO 63118-4199
(314) 425-5719 FAX
E-mail: center@cpr.nara.gov

NARA's National Personnel Records Center
Military Personnel Records
9700 Page Avenue
St. Louis, MO 63132-5100
(314) 538-4005 FAX
E-Mail: center@stlouis.nara.gov

Suitland, Maryland
Washington National Records Center
4205 Suitland Road
Suitland, MD 20746-8001
(301) 457-7000; (301) 457-7117 FAX
E-mail: center@suitland.nara.gov

Area served: Washington, D.C., area,
Maryland, Virginia, and West Virginia

GOVERNMENT DEPARTMENTS AND AGENCIES

Bureau of Indian Affairs
Department of the Interior
Muskogee Area Office
Federal Building
125 South Main Street
Muskogee, OK 74401

Bureau of Indian Affairs
Department of the Interior
1849 C Street, N.W.
Washington, DC 20240
(202) 343-1334; (202) 343-1334 FAX

Bureau of Land Management
Department of the Interior
1849 C Street, N.W.
Washington, DC 20240
(202) 343-9435; (202) 343-4152 FAX

Bureau of Land Management
Department of the Interior
1474 Rodeo Road
PO Box 27115
Santa Fe, NM 87502-0115
(505) 438-7400
(has microfiche of New Mexico, Kansas
and Oklahoma public land records,
including original patents, tract books
and survey plats)

Bureau of Land Management
Eastern States Office
General Land Office (GLO) Automated
Records System
7450 Boston Boulevard
Springfield, VA 22153-3121
(703) 440-1600; (703) 440-1609 FAX
E-mail: tmayfiel@es.blm.gov
Tony Mayfield, Public Contact Specialist
Hours: Mon–Fri 8:00–4:30
Pub. *Federal Land Patents 1787–1960*
(has automated patent index 1820–1908
for Alabama, Arkansas, Florida,
Louisiana, Michigan, Minnesota,
Mississippi, Ohio, Indiana and
Wisconsin, and can locate documents
through any one of six categories: land
description, patentee name, patent
authority, land office, certificate
number, or county; has brochure on
how researchers can use their
resources; collection includes federal
land surveys and field notes, and land
patents from the late 1820s to 1908)

Bureau of the Census
Personal Census Search Unit
(1201 East Tenth Street, Building 48—
location)

PO Box 1545 (mailing address)
Jeffersonville, IN 47131-0001
(812) 285-5314
http://www.census.gov/genealogy/www/
agesearch.html
Mary Lee Eldridge, Processing
Resources Section Chief
Hours: Mon–Fri 7:00–4:30
$40.00 per search

Department of State
Passport Correspondence Branch
1111 Nineteenth Street, N.W., Suite 510
Washington, DC 20522-1705
William Crawford, Branch Chief
(certification of report of birth, consular
report of death, certificate of witness
to marriage, certification of citizenship
at birth of persons born abroad, $10.00
each)

Department of the Interior
U.S. Geological Survey
Earth Science Information Center
(ESIC)
507 National Center
Reston, VA 20192
(800) USA-MAPS (24-hour message
recording system)
Hours: Mon–Fri 8:00–4:00

Department of the Interior
U.S. Geological Survey (USGS)
Earth Science Information Center
Department of the Interior Building,
Room 2650
1849 C Street, N.W.
Washington, DC 20240
(202) 208-4047; (800) HELP-MAP;
(202) 202-4693 FAX
http://mapping.usgs.gov/esic/
mapprice.html (price list of maps)
Hours: Mon–Fri 8:00–4:00
(over-the-counter sales of U.S.G.S.
topographic maps)

Department of the Treasury
U.S. Customs Service
1301 Constitution Avenue, N.W.
Washington, DC 20002
(202) 566-2321; (202) 633-7645 FAX

Freedom of Information and Privacy Acts Unit (FOIA/PA)
Administrative Center, Dallas
Southern Regional Office
7701 North Stemmons Freeway
Dallas, TX 75247-9998

National Park Service
Office of Library, Archives and Graphics
Research
Harpers Ferry Center
Harpers Ferry, WV 25425-0050
(304) 535-6261; (304) 535-6492 FAX
David Nathanson, Chief
Hours: Mon–Fri 8:00–4:30
(employees and alumni of the National
Park Service)

United States Geological Survey
Field Records Library

United States Geological Survey
  Photographic Library
Building 20, Room C-2006
Denver Federal Center
MS 914, Box 25046, Federal Center
Denver, CO 80225-0046
(303) 236-1005 (Field Records Library);
  (303) 236-1010 (Photographic
  Library); (303) 236-0998 TTY
Hours: Mon–Fri 8:00–4:00
("Both collections reflect earth science
  research activities of the U.S.
  Geological Survey; Photo Library
  includes extensive portraits collection
  of USGS personnel only.")

United States Geological Survey

Map Distribution Center
Federal Center Building 810
Box 25286
Denver, CO 80225-0286
(303) 236-7477
Hours: 8:00–4:00
(for "Quadrangles" of states; first order a
  free "Index Map" of the state)

Immigration and Naturalization Service Regional, District and Local Offices

Immigration and Naturalization Service

U.S. Department of Justice
INS Historical Reference Library and
  Reading Room Section
Chester Arthur Building, 425 I Street,
  N.W., Room 1100A
Washington, DC 20536
(202) 514-2837 (Historical Office/
  Library); (202) 514-3278 (FOIA/PA
  Unit); (202) 633-3296 FAX
E-mail: mrnsmith@ix.netcom.com
Marian L. Smith, INS Historian
Hours: Mon–Fri 8:00–4:30
(The INS has duplicate records of all
  naturalizations that occurred after 26
  September 1906, has records
  documenting the arrival and later
  naturalization of millions of American
  immigrants. Requests for information
  must be made through a Freedom of
  Information Act and Privacy Act
  request, sent to the attention of "FOIA/
  PA" at the INS District Office where
  the records are maintained, if known,
  or to the office serving the area where
  you live. Form G-639 is available
  from the FOIA/PA Unit, Second Floor
  ULLB. For naturalization records,
  supply full name, date and country of
  birth. For arrival records, supply port
  and date of arrival and, if possible, the
  name of the ship.)

Immigration and Naturalization Service

Regional Office, Western Region
24000 Avila Road
Laguna Niguel, CA 92677

Immigration and Naturalization Service

Regional Office, Central Region
Administrative Center, Dallas
7701 North Stemmons Freeway
Dallas, TX 75247-9998
Susie A. Hood, Branch Manager, Files
  and Forms Management
(The Freedom of Information and
  Privacy Acts require federal agencies
  to make their records promptly
  available upon receipt of a request
  from any U.S. citizen or permanent
  resident.)

Immigration and Naturalization Service

Regional Office, Eastern Region
70 Kimball Avenue
Burlington, VT 05403-6813
(800) 755-0777; (802) 951-6658
James W. Buckley, Director, Office of
  Records and Information
(an administrative office, not housing
  alien records)

Immigration and Naturalization Service

Twin Cities Administrative Center
Bishop Henry Whipple Federal Building,
  Room 400
1 Federal Drive
Fort Snelling, MN 55111-4007

Immigration and Naturalization Service

620 East Tenth Avenue, Suite 102
Anchorage, AK 99501
(907) 271-4953

Immigration and Naturalization Service

2035 North Central Street
Phoenix, AZ 85004
(602) 379-3122

Immigration and Naturalization Service

300 North Los Angeles Street
Los Angeles, CA 90012

Immigration and Naturalization Service

880 Front Street, Suite 1234
San Diego, CA 92101-8834

Immigration and Naturalization Service

Appraisers Building
630 Sansome Street, Room 232
San Francisco, CA 94111-2280

Immigration and Naturalization Service

4730 Paris Street
Denver, CO 80239
(303) 371-3041

Immigration and Naturalization Service

450 Main Street
Hartford, CT 06103
(860) 240-3171

Immigration and Naturalization Service

4420 North Fairfax Drive
Arlington, VA 22203
(serves the District of Columbia)

Immigration and Naturalization Service

7880 Biscayne Boulevard
Miami, FL 33138

Immigration and Naturalization Service

5390 Bear Road
Orlando, FL 32812

Immigration and Naturalization Service

MLK Federal Building
77 Forsyth Street, S.W., Room 117
Atlanta, GA 30303

Immigration and Naturalization Service

(595 Ala Moana Boulevard, Honolulu,
  HI 96813—location)
PO Box 461 (mailing address)
Honolulu, HI 96809
(808) 543-1479

Immigration and Naturalization Service

10 West Jackson Boulevard
Chicago, IL 60604
(312) 353-7334

Immigration and Naturalization Service

Gateway Plaza
950 North Meridian, Suite 400
Indianapolis, IN 46204
(317) 226-6009

Immigration and Naturalization Service

601 West Broadway, Gene Snyder
  Building
Louisville, KY 40202
(502) 582-6375
Hours: walk-in: 8:00–1:00, phone: 2:00–
  4:00

Immigration and Naturalization Service

Postal Service Building
Room T-8011
701 Loyola Avenue
New Orleans, LA 70113

Immigration and Naturalization Service
176 Gannett Drive
South Portland, ME 04106

Immigration and Naturalization Service
NationsBank Center
Tower One
100 South Charles Street
Baltimore, MD 21201
(410) 962-2065
Hours: 7:30–4:30

Immigration and Naturalization Service
John Fitzgerald Kennedy Federal
    Building
Room 1700
Boston, MA 02203

Immigration and Naturalization Service
Federal Building
333 Mount Elliott Street
Detroit, MI 48207-4381

Immigration and Naturalization Service
2901 Metro Drive, Suite 100
Bloomington, MN 55424
(612) 854-7754

Immigration and Naturalization Service
9747 North Conant Avenue
Kansas City, MO 64153
(816) 891-9312

Immigration and Naturalization Service
1222 Spruce Street
Saint Louis, MO 63103-2815
(314) 539-2532

Immigration and Naturalization Service
2800 Skyway Drive
Helena, MT 59601
(406) 449-5288

Immigration and Naturalization Service
3736 South 132nd Street
Omaha, NE 68144
(402) 697-9155

Immigration and Naturalization Service
1351 Corporate Boulevard
Reno, NV 89502
(702) 784-5427

Immigration and Naturalization Service
Peter Rodino Federal Building
970 Broad Street
Newark, NJ 07102
(973) 645-4400

Immigration and Naturalization Service
Room 220
U.S. Post Office and Courthouse
445 Broadway
Albany, NY 12207

Immigration and Naturalization Service
130 Delaware Avenue
Buffalo, NY 14202

Immigration and Naturalization Service
26 Federal Plaza, Room 14-102
New York, NY 10278

Immigration and Naturalization Service
210 East Woodlawn Road, Building 6,
    Suite 138
Charlotte, NC 28217
(704) 523-1704
Hours: 7:30–2:00

Immigration and Naturalization Service
550 Main Street, #8525
Cincinnati, OH 45202-3212

Immigration and Naturalization Service
FOIA/PA Officer
Anthony J. Celebrezze Federal Office
    Building
1240 East Ninth Street, Room 1917
Cleveland, OH 44199-2085
(800) 375-5283; (800) 870-3676 (to
    request form G-639, genealogy
    requests by mail only)
Hours: 8:00–4:00

Immigration and Naturalization Service
Federal Office Building
511 North Broadway, Room 407
Portland, OR 97209

Immigration and Naturalization Service
1600 Callowhill Street, Room 100
Philadelphia, PA 19130
(215) 656-7144

Immigration and Naturalization Service
2130 Federal Building
100 Liberty Avenue
Pittsburgh, PA 15222

Immigration and Naturalization Service
8101 North Stemmons Freeway
Dallas, TX 75247
(972) 655-5384

Immigration and Naturalization Service
1545 Hawkins Boulevard
El Paso, TX 79925

Immigration and Naturalization Service
2102 Teege Avenue
Harlingen, TX 78550-4667

Immigration and Naturalization Service
126 North Point
Houston, TX 77060
(281) 847-7900
Hours: 7:15–3:00

Immigration and Naturalization Service
8940 Fourwinds Drive
San Antonio, TX 78239-1900

Immigration and Naturalization Service
5272 College Drive, #100
Salt Lake City, UT 84123-2611

Immigration and Naturalization Service
Federal Building
PO Box 328
Saint Albans, VT 05478

Immigration and Naturalization Service
Norfolk Federal Building
5280 Henneman Drive
Norfolk, VA 23513

Immigration and Naturalization Service
815 Airport Way South
Seattle, WA 98134

Immigration and Naturalization Service
691 U.S. Courthouse Building
Spokane, WA 99201

Immigration and Naturalization Service
U.S. District Court
Eastern District of Wisconsin
Room 186 Federal Building
517 East Wisconsin Avenue
Milwaukee, WI 53202

Immigration and Naturalization Service
801 Pacific News Building
238 O'Hara Street
Agana, GU 96910

Immigration and Naturalization Service
GPO Box 365068
San Juan, PR 00936

Department of Veterans Affairs and Regional Offices

810 Vermont Avenue, N.W.
Washington, DC 20420
(202) 273-5400
(Central Office, Marker Services,
provides military service markers)

Alabama
345 Perry Hill Road
Montgomery, AL 36109
(800) 827-1000

Alaska
2925 DeBarr Road
Anchorage, AK 99508
(907) 257-4700; (800) 827-1000

Arizona
3225 North Central Avenue
Phoenix, AZ 85012
(800) 827-1000

Arkansas
Building 65 Fort Roots
PO Box 1280
North Little Rock, AR 72215
(800) 827-1000

California
1301 Clay Street, Room 1300 North
Oakland, CA 94612
(800) 827-1000

Federal Building
11000 Wiltshire Boulevard
West Los Angeles, CA 90024
(800) 827-1000

Colorado
155 Van Gordon Street
Denver, CO 80225
(800) 827-1000

Connecticut
450 Main Street
Hartford, CT 06103
(800) 827-1000

Delaware
1601 Kirkwood Highway
Wilmington, DE 19805
(800) 827-1000

District of Columbia
1120 Vermont Avenue
Washington, DC 20421
(202) 418-4343

Florida
144 First Avenue, South
Saint Petersburg, FL 33731
(800) 827-1000

Georgia
730 Peachtree Street, N.E.
Atlanta, GA 30365
(800) 827-1000

Hawaii
PJKK Federal Building
300 Ala Moana Boulevard
PO Box 50188
Honolulu, HI 96850
(808) 566-1000; (800) 827-1000

Idaho
805 West Franklin Street
Boise, ID 83702
(800) 827-1000

Illinois
536 South Clark Street
Chicago, IL 60680
(800) 827-1000

Indiana
575 Pennsylvania Street
Indianapolis, IN 46204
(800) 827-1000

Iowa
210 Walnut Street
Des Moines, IA 50309
(800) 827-1000

Kansas
5500 E. Kellogg
Wichita, KS 67218
(800) 827-1000

Kentucky
545 South Third Street
Louisville, KY 40202
(800) 827-1000

Louisiana
701 Loyola Avenue
New Orleans, LA 70113
(800) 827-1000

Maine
1 VA Center
Toque, ME 04330
(800) 827-1000

Maryland
Federal Building
31 Hopkins Plaza
Baltimore, MD 21201
(800) 827-1000

Massachusetts
John Fitzgerald Kennedy Federal
Building
Government Center
Boston, MA 02203
(800) 827-1000

Michigan
Patrick V. McNamara Federal Building
477 Michigan Avenue
Detroit, MI 48226
(800) 827-1000

Minnesota
Federal Building
1 Federal Drive, Fort Snelling
Saint Paul, MN 55111
(800) 827-1000

Mississippi
1600 East Woodrow Wilson Avenue
Jackson, MS 39269
(800) 827-1000

Missouri
400 South Eighteenth Street
Saint Louis, MO 63103
(314) 342-1171; (800) 392-3761

Montana
Fort Harrison, MT 59636
(800) 827-1000

Nebraska
5631 South Forty-eighth Street
Lincoln, NE 68516
(800) 827-1000

Nevada
1201 Terminal Way
Reno, NV 89520
(800) 827-1000

New Hampshire
Norris Cotton Federal Building
275 Chestnut Street
Manchester, NH 03101
(800) 827-1000

New Jersey
20 Washington Place
Newark, NJ 07102
(800) 827-1000

New Mexico
Dennis Chavez Federal Building
500 Gold Avenue, S.W.
Albuquerque, NM 87107
(800) 827-1000

New York
Federal Building
111 West Huron Street
Buffalo, NY 14202
(800) 827-1000

245 West Houston Street
New York, NY 10014
(800) 827-1000

North Carolina
Federal Building
251 North Main Street
Winston-Salem, NC 27155
(800) 827-1000

North Dakota
2101 Elm Street
Fargo, ND 58102
(800) 827-1000

Ohio
Anthony J. Celebrezze Federal Building
1240 East Ninth Street
Cleveland, OH 44199
(800) 827-1000

Oklahoma
Federal Building
125 South Main Street
Muskogee, OK 74401
(800) 827-1000

Oregon
Federal Building
1220 S.W. Third Avenue
Portland, OR 97204
(800) 827-1000

Pennsylvania
PO Box 8079
5000 Wissahickon Avenue
Philadelphia, PA 19101
(800) 827-1000

1000 Liberty Avenue
Pittsburgh, PA 15222
(800) 827-1000

Rhode Island
330 Westminster Mall
Providence, RI 02903
(800) 827-1000

South Carolina
1801 Assembly Street
Columbia, SC 29201
(800) 827-1000

South Dakota
PO Box 5046
2510 West 22nd Street
Sioux Falls, SD 57117
(800) 827-1000

Tennessee
110 Ninth Avenue
Nashville, TN 37203
(800) 827-1000

Texas
6900 Almeda Road
Houston, TX 77030
(800) 827-1000

1 Veterans Plaza
701 Clay
Waco, TX 76799
(800) 827-1000

Utah
PO Box 11500
Federal Building
125 South State Street
Salt Lake City, UT 84147
(800) 827-1000

Vermont
215 North Maine Street
White River Junction, VT 05009
(800) 827-1000

Virginia
210 Franklin Road, S.W.
Roanoke, VA 24011
(800) 827-1000

Washington
Federal Building
915 Second Avenue
Seattle, WA 98174
(800) 827-1000

West Virginia
640 Fourth Avenue
Huntington, WV 25701
(800) 827-1000

Wisconsin
5000 West National Avenue
Building 6
Milwaukee, WI 53295
(800) 827-1000

Wyoming
2360 East Pershing Boulevard
Cheyenne, WY 82001
(800) 827-1000

Puerto Rico
GPO Box 364867
Carlos E. Chardon Street
Hato Rey
San Juan, PR 00936
(800) 827-1000

Philippines
1131 Roxas Boulevard
Manila 1000
022-632-521-7521

Federal Information Centers

Alaska
701 C Street
PO Box 33
Anchorage, AK 99513

California
300 North Los Angeles Street
Los Angeles, CA 90012
650 Capitol Mall
Sacramento, CA 95814
880 Front Street
San Diego, CA 92188
450 Golden Gate Avenue
PO Box 36082
San Francisco, CA 94102

Colorado
Federal Center
PO Box 25006
Denver, CO 80225

Florida
144 First Avenue South, Room 105
Saint Petersburg, FL 33701

Georgia
75 Spring Street, S.W.
Atlanta, GA 30303

Hawaii
300 Ala Moana Boulevard
PO Box 50091
Honolulu, HI 96850

Illinois
230 South Dearborn Street, 33rd Floor
Chicago, IL 60604

Massachusetts
McCormack P.O.C.H. Building,
   Room 812
Boston, MA 02109

Michigan
477 Michigan Avenue, Room M-25
Detroit, MI 48226

Missouri
1520 Market Street, Room 2616
Saint Louis, MO 63103

Nebraska
215 North 17th Street
Omaha, NE 68102

New York
111 West Huron
Buffalo, NY 14202
26 Federal Plaza, Room 2-110
New York, NY 10278

Ohio
550 Main Street
Cincinnati, OH 45202

Oregon
1220 S.W. Third Avenue, Room 321
Portland, OR 97204

Pennsylvania
Ninth and Market Streets, Room 4127
Philadelphia, PA 19107

Texas
819 Taylor Street
Fort Worth, TX 76102
515 Rusk Avenue
Houston, TX 77002

VITAL RECORDS OFFICES

Alabama Department of Public Health
Center for Health Statistics
PO Box 5625
Montgomery, AL 36130-5625
(334) 206-5418

Alaska Department of Health and Social Services
Bureau of Vital Statistics
(350 Main Street, Room 114, Juneau, AK
   99801—location)
PO Box 110675 (mailing address)
Juneau, AK 99811-0675
(907) 465-3392; (907) 465-3391
   (recorded message)
Hours: Mon–Fri 8:00–4:30
Pub. *Annual Report* (statistical analysis)
("Birth records are strictly confidential
   for 100 years; marriage, divorce and
   death records are strictly confidential
   for 50 years.")
$10.00 per certified copy of birth,
   marriage, divorce or death

Arizona Department of Health Services
Office of Vital Records
2727 West Glendale Avenue
PO Box 3887
Phoenix, AZ 85030-3887
(602) 255-3260

Arkansas Department of Health
Division of Vital Records
4815 West Markham Street
Little Rock, AR 72205-3867
(501) 661-2336

California Department of Health Services
Office of the State Registrar of Vital Statistics
304 S Street
PO Box 730241
Sacramento, CA 94244-0241
(916) 445-2684

Colorado Department of Health and Environment
Vital Records Division, HSVRD-VR-A1
4300 Cherry Creek Drive South
Denver, CO 80222-1530
(303) 756-4464 General Information; (303) 692-2224 Phone orders (Visa, MasterCard, Discover); (800) 423-1108 FAX orders
E-mail: linda.eisnach@state.co.us
http://www.state.co.us/gov_dir/cdphe_dir/hs/cshom.html (Application forms)
Hours: 8:30–4:30

State of Connecticut Department of Public Health
Certifications Unit
(150 Washington Street, First Floor, Vital Records, Hartford, CT 06106-4476—location)
PO Box 340308, MS#: 11VRS (mailing address)
Hartford, CT 06134-0308
(860) 509-7896
Hours: Public service counter: 8:30–4:30
("Because birth certificates are 'Confidential' in Connecticut, a full certified copy of a certificate can be obtained only by registrant 18 or over, parent, legal representative, or member of a legally incorporated genealogical society which is registered with the Secretary of State and authorized to do business in Connecticut. A copy of the current, signed membership card and a copy of a photo ID must accompany all requests from genealogists for requests for certificates.")

Office of Vital Statistics
Division of Public Health
(Corner of Federal and William Penn Streets—location)
PO Box 637 (mailing address)
Dover, DE 19903-0637

(302) 739-4721; (302) 739-6617 FAX
Michael L. Richards, Vital Statistics Director
Hours: Mon–Fri 8:00–4:20
(has births from 1925, deaths from 1957, marriages from 1957, and divorces from 1976; however the records are confidential and the office may only confirm whether a divorce has taken place, or it may issue birth and marriage records only to the individual named in them, or a death record only to a family member of someone named in it, or to an attorney or to someone who demonstrates "the need to obtain said records"; vital records through the early twentieth century are open to the public at the Delaware Public Archives, Hall of Records; divorce records prior to 1976 are obtained from the county seat where the divorce was granted)
$6.00 for five-year search and certified copy

District of Columbia
Department of Human Services
Vital Records Branch
c/o Research
800 Ninth Street, S.W., #100
Washington, DC 20024-2480
(202) 727-5314
Carl W. Wilson, Registrar
Hours: 8:30–3:30

State of Florida Department of Health and Rehabilitative Services
Vital Statistics
(1217 Pearl Street—location)
PO Box 210 (mailing address)
Jacksonville, FL 32231-0042
(904) 359-6900 (Information); (904) 359-6911 (Rush or credit card orders)

Georgia Department of Human Resources
Vital Records Service
Room 217-H
47 Trinity Avenue, S.W.
Atlanta, GA 30334-1201
(404) 656-4750

Hawaii State Department of Health
Research and Statistics Office
Vital Records Section
(1250 Punchbowl Street, Room 103, Honolulu, HI 96813—location)
PO Box 3378 (mailing address)
Honolulu, HI 96801
(808) 961-7327; (808) 586-4539; (808) 586-4542

Center for Vital Statistics and Health Policy (Idaho)
(450 West State, Boise, ID 83702—location)
PO Box 83720 (mailing address)
Boise, ID 83720-0036
(208) 334-5988 (recorded message)
Hours: Mon–Fri 8:00–5:00
(requires signature of person named in birth or marriage records)

Illinois Department of Public Health
Division of Vital Records
605 West Jefferson Street
Springfield, IL 62702-5097
(217) 782-6553
Hours: 8:30–5:00
$15.00 for full certified copies of births or deaths from 1916 (birth certificates available only to the person named, a parent or other legal representative, or upon court order), $5.00 for verifications of marriages or divorces

Indiana State Department of Health
2 North Meridian Street
Indianapolis, IN 46206-1964
(317) 233-2700

Iowa Department of Public Health
Vital Records Bureau
Lucas State Office Building
Des Moines, IA 50319-0075
(515) 281-4944 (credit card orders, 7:00–4:45); (515) 281-4956 (Supervisor)
E-mail: webmaster@idph.state.ia.us
http://www.state.ia.us/pa/vr.htm
Pat McClure, Supervisor
Hours: 7:00–5:00

Kansas Department of Health and Environment
Office of Vital Statistics
Landon State Office Building
900 S.W. Jackson, Room 151
Topeka, KS 66612-2221
(785) 296-1400
http://www.ink.org/public/kdhe/ovs.html
Hours: Mon–Fri 9:00–4:00
$10.00 for five-year search and certified copy of births and deaths from 1 July 1911 and marriages and divorces from 1 May 1913 (if not an immediate family member, proof of direct interest is required by the OVS, but marriage and divorce records can be obtained from the county where the event occurred without restriction)

Commonwealth of Kentucky Department for Health
Vital Statistics Branch
275 East Main Street
Frankfort, KY 40621-0001
(502) 564-4212; (502) 227-0032 FAX
Barbara F. White, State Registrar
Hours: Mon–Fri 8:00–4:30
(births and deaths from 1911, marriages and divorces from June 1958)
Births $9.00; deaths, marriages and divorces $6.00

Vital Records Registry
(325 Loyola Avenue, Room 102, New Orleans, LA 70112—location)
PO Box 60630 (mailing address)
New Orleans, LA 70160-0630
(504) 568-5152 (Information); (504) 568-5172; (504) 568-8353; (504) 568-5391 FAX

Lorraine A. Stuart, Archivist
Hours: Mon–Fri 8:00–4:00
(holds one hundred years of birth records
and fifty years of deaths and Orleans
Parish marriages; records are
confidential and require statement of
relationship or a release)
$9.00 for birth card, $15.00 for long
form of births, $5.00 for deaths or
Orleans marriages, $25.00 for
adoption, correction or delay (only
certified copies issued)

Maine Department of Human Services

Office of Vital Statistics
(221 State Street—location)
State House, Station 11 (mailing address)
Augusta, ME 04333-0011
(207) 287-3181; (207) 287-1907 FAX
Hours: Mon–Fri 9:00–4:00
births, deaths and marriages from 1892:
$6.00 for search two years before and
after event (includes non-certified
copy), $10.00 for search and certified
copy, $2.00 for each additional year
searched, $2.00 for each additional
non-certified copy, $4.00 for each
additional certified copy, $5.00 for
orders placed through Vitalcheck
Network using a credit card, $15.50
for next-day delivery, payable to
Treasurer, State of Maine

State of Maryland Department of Health and Mental Hygiene

Division of Vital Records
4201 Patterson Avenue
PO Box 68760
Baltimore, MD 21215-0020
(410) 764-3036
David L. Johnson, Deputy Chief
Hours: Mon–Fri & third Sat 8:00–4:00
(birth and marriage records are generally
available only to the individual(s)
named in the record, or to a person
designated in writing as a
representative of the individual(s)
named; city births from 1875, county
births from 1898, marriages from June
1951, divorces from July 1961, county
deaths from 1911 to 1968, city deaths
from 1950 to the present)

Registry Division (City of Boston)

1 City Hall Square, Room 213
Boston, MA 02201
(617) 743-4177

Registry of Vital Records and Statistics

470 Atlantic Avenue, Second Floor
Boston, MA 02210-2224
(617) 753-8600
(records from 1901)

Michigan Department of Public Health

Office of the State Registrar
3423 North Logan Street

PO Box 30195
Lansing, MI 48909
(517) 335-8656
Hours: Mon–Fri 8:00–5:00

Minnesota Department of Health

Section of Vital Statistics Registration
717 Delaware Street, S.E.
PO Box 9441
Minneapolis, MN 55440-9441
(612) 623-5121
Hours: 8:00–4:00
(births from 1900 and deaths from 1908
for the entire state; marriages and
divorces available only from Clerk,
County District Court of county where
marriage took place)
search: $11.00 for births (includes
certified copy), $8.00 for deaths
(includes certified copy), $8.00 for
verification of information or for a
non-certified copy of birth or death

Mississippi State Department of Health

Public Health Statistics Division
(2423 North State Street, Jackson, MS
39216—location)
PO Box 1700 (mailing address)
Jackson, MS 39215-1700
(601) 960-7960
five-year search of records: $6.00,
special search (genealogy): $20.00 per
hour, $10.00 minimum, certified birth
record $12.00 (abstract $7.00), death
and marriage records $10.00

Missouri Department of Health

Bureau of Vital Records
(Broadway State Office Building, 930
Wildwood, Jefferson City, MO
65101—location)
PO Box 570 (mailing address)
Jefferson City, MO 65102-0570
(573) 751-6400; (573) 526-3846 FAX
http://www.health.state.mo.us/cgi-bin/
uncgi/birthanddeathrecords
Gary L. Shipley, Vital Records
Administrator
Hours: Mon–Fri 8:00–5:00
no search without fees required by law:
$10.00 for births or deaths since 1910
(includes five-year search and
certificate) to Fee Receipts Unit

Records Management and Archives Service

Office of the Secretary of State
1001 Industrial Drive
PO Box 778
Jefferson City, MO 65102
(573) 751-3280
Mary Beck, Archivist
Hours: Mon–Fri 8:00–5:00, Thur 8:00–
9:30, Sat 8:30–3:30
(microfilm copies of county vital
statistics, especially 1883–1893 and
some others from before 1910)

Montana Department of Health and Environmental Sciences

Vital Records and Statistics Bureau
111 North Sanders
PO Box 4210
Helena, MT 59604
(406) 444-4228

Health Records Management (Vital Records)

(301 Centennial Mall, South, Lincoln,
NE 68508—location)
PO Box 95065 (mailing address)
Lincoln, NE 68509-5066
(402) 471-2872
Hours: Mon–Fri 8:00–5:00
(births and deaths from 1904, marriages
from 1909)
births $10.00 each, deaths, marriages and
divorces $9.00 each

Nevada State Department of Human Resources

State Health Division
Section of Vital Statistics
505 East King Street
Carson City, NV 89710-4761
(702) 687-4480

New Hampshire Bureau of Vital Records

6 Hazen Drive
Concord, NH 03301-6527
(603) 271-4650; (800) 735-2964 TDD
Stephen Wurtz, Supervisor Vital Records
Hours: Mon–Fri 8:30–4:00
(births before 1901, deaths, marriages
and divorces before 1938; application
can also be made to the town in which
the event took place)
$10.00 for certified copy (includes
search), plus $6.00 for each additional
copy ordered at the same time

New Jersey State Bureau of Vital Statistics

CN 370
Trenton, NJ 08625-0370
(609) 292-4087; (609) 392-4292 FAX
Donald L. Lipira, State Registrar of Vital
Statistics
Hours: 8:30–5:00
$4.00 per record for search when the
exact year is known

New Mexico Department of Health

Bureau of Vital Records and Health
Statistics
(Harold Runnels Building, 1190 Saint
Francis Drive, Santa Fe, NM 87502—
location)
PO Box 26110 (mailing address)
Santa Fe, NM 87504-6110
(505) 827-2321; (505) 827-2338
(recorded message)
Hours: 8:00–5:00; counter hours: 9:00–
4:00
Pub. *Selected Health Statistics*, annually
("New Mexico's records are restricted
access.")

Archives Division

Department of Records and Information Services
31 Chambers Street
New York, NY 10007
(212) 374-4781
(New York City births prior to 1910 and deaths prior to 1949, marriages from 1847 to 1865, except Brooklyn records)

New York City Department of Health

Division of Vital Records
(125 Worth Street—location)
PO Box 3776, Church Street Station (mailing address)
New York, NY 10007
(212) 619-4530 (recorded message)
(births from 1910, deaths from 1949 in Manhattan, Brooklyn, Bronx, Queens and Staten Island boroughs)
$15.00 for births and deaths

City Clerk's Office

1780 Grand Concourse
Bronx, NY 10457
(Bronx Borough marriages from 1866 to 1907, and after 1907 if the borough was the bride's residence or if the license of non-residents was obtained in the borough)
$10.00 each

City Clerk's Office

Municipal Building
Brooklyn, NY 11201
(Brooklyn Borough marriages from 1866 to 1907, and after 1907 if the borough was the bride's residence or if the license of non-residents was obtained in the borough)
$10.00 each

City Clerk's Office

Municipal Building
New York, NY 10007
(Manhattan Borough marriages from 1866 to 1907, and after 1907 if the borough was the bride's residence or if the license of non-residents was obtained in the borough)
$10.00 each

City Clerk's Office

120-55 Queens Boulevard
Kew Gardens, NY 11424
(Queens Borough marriages from 1866 to 1907, and after 1907 if the borough was the bride's residence or if the license of non-residents was obtained in the borough)
$10.00 each

City Clerk's Office

Staten Island Borough Hall
Staten Island, NY 10301
(Staten Island Borough [no longer called Richmond Borough] marriages from 1866 to 1907, and after 1907 if the borough was the bride's residence or if the license of non-residents was obtained in the borough)
$10.00 each

New York State Department of Health

Vital Records Section
Corning Tower
The Governor Nelson A. Rockefeller Empire State Plaza
Albany, NY 12237-0023
(518) 474-3077
L. Julien Rivers, Genealogy Unit, Vital Records Section
(vital records for New York State, exclusive of New York City; births 1881–1922, marriages 1881–1947, deaths 1881–1947, otherwise applicant must be a direct descendant of the person named in the record; processing time is six months for genealogy requests, but may be obtained more rapidly from the local registrar/clerk of the district where the event occurred)
$11.00 for a three-year search (includes an uncertified copy, if found), $21.00 for a four-to-ten year search, and $10.00 for each additional decade searched

National Archives—Northeast Region, New York Office

201 Varick Street
New York, NY 10014-4811
(212) 337-1300
Hours: Mon–Fri 8:00–4:30, third Sat (microfilm only, not naturalization records) 8:30–4:00
(Serves New Jersey, New York, Puerto Rico, and the Virgin Islands; federal census records for all states and New York passenger arrivals on microfilm, also naturalization records for New York, New Jersey, and Puerto Rico; houses microfiche guides to the older vital records of New York State (except New York City): births 1880–1921, deaths and marriages from 1880 to 1946)

North Carolina Department of Environment, Health, and Natural Resources

Vital Records Section
PO Box 29537
Raleigh, NC 27626-0537
(919) 733-3526 (credit card order accepted)
(births from 1913, marriages from 1962, deaths from 1930 and divorces from 1958)

North Dakota State Department of Health and Consolidated Laboratories

Division of Vital Records
State Capitol
600 East Boulevard Avenue
Bismarck, ND 58505-0200
(701) 224-2360
Hours: Mon–Fri 7:30–5:00

Ohio State Department of Health

Bureau of Vital Statistics, Certifications
PO Box 15098
Columbus, OH 43215-0098
(614) 466-2531
Hours: Mon–Fri 7:45–4:00
(county health departments also issue certified birth and death records)

Oklahoma Department of Health

Bureau of Vital Records
(1000 N.E. Tenth Street, Oklahoma City, OK 73117—location)
PO Box 53551 (mailing address)
Oklahoma City, OK 73152-3551
(405) 271-4040
Hours: Mon–Fri 8:00–4:00

Oregon Vital Records

(800 N.E. Oregon Street, Suite 205, #23, Portland, OR 97232—location)
PO Box 14050 (mailing address)
Portland, OR 97293-0050
(503) 731-4095 (recorded message); (503) 731-4108 (operator); (503) 731-8417 FAX
http://www.ohd.hr.state.or.us
Hours: Mon–Fri 8:00–4:30
$15.00 for certified copies of births (available to immediate family, including grandchildren), deaths or marriages, includes a five-year search, additional search for $1.00 per year, non-certified copies available for births over 100 years old or deaths over 50 years old

Pennsylvania Department of Health

Division of Vital Records
(101 South Mercer Street—location)
PO Box 1528 (mailing address)
New Castle, PA 16103-1528
(724) 656-3100
Hours: 8:00–4:30
(birth and death records (except for Erie, Scranton, Philadelphia and Pittsburgh) from 1906; request marriage records from County Clerk at the County Courthouse of the county in which the marriage took place)
births: $4.00 plus SASE, deaths: $3.00 plus SASE

Division of Vital Records

1910 West 26th Street
Erie, PA 16508-1148
(birth and death records from 1906; request marriage records from County Clerk at the County Courthouse)
births: $4.00 plus SASE, deaths: $3.00 plus SASE

Division of Vital Records

1400 West Spring Garden Street, Room 1009
Philadelphia, PA 19130-4090

(birth and death records from 1906; request marriage records from County Clerk at the County Courthouse)
births: $4.00 plus SASE, deaths: $3.00 plus SASE

Division of Vital Records
300 Liberty Avenue, Room 512
Pittsburgh, PA 15222-1210
(birth and death records from 1906; request marriage records from County Clerk at the County Courthouse)
births: $4.00 plus SASE, deaths: $3.00 plus SASE

Division of Vital Records
100 Lackawanna Avenue
Scranton, PA 18503-1928
(birth and death records from 1906; request marriage records from County Clerk at the County Courthouse)
births: $4.00 plus SASE, deaths: $3.00 plus SASE

State of Rhode Island and Providence Plantations Department of Health
Division of Vital Records
Cannon Building
3 Capitol Hill, Room 101
Providence, RI 02908-5097
(401) 277-2812; (401) 277-2506 TDD
Roberta A. Chevoya, State Registrar, Vital Records
Hours: Mon, Wed & Fri 8:30–4:00 (for in-person application for certified copies)
(births and marriages from 1895, deaths from 1945; may also be obtained from the town in which the event occurred)
$15.00 for two-year search and one certified copy (if found), 50¢ for each additional year searched, $10.00 for each additional certified copy ordered at the same time, payable to General Treasurer, State of Rhode Island

South Carolina Department of Health and Environmental Control
Office of Vital Records and Public Health Statistics
2600 Bull Street
Columbia, SC 29201-1797
(803) 799-0301
JoAnn Gooding, Director of Vital Records
Hours: 8:30–4:30

South Dakota Department of Health
Center for Health Statistics
445 East Capitol
Pierre, SD 57501-3185
(605) 773-4961
search for birth, death, marriage or divorce record: $7.00 (includes certified copy, if found)

State of Tennessee Department of Health
Central Services Building, First Floor

421 Fifth Avenue North
Nashville, TN 37247-0350
(615) 741-1763; (615) 726-2559 FAX
Hours: Mon–Fri 8:00–4:30
(marriage, divorce and death records from the past fifty years only, and birth records)
$10.00 for verification of information on certificate, which is public information and available to anyone

Texas Department of Health
Bureau of Vital Statistics
PO Box 12040
Austin, TX 78711-2040
(512) 458-7111 (for fee verification only)
Hours: Mon–Fri 8:00–5:00
(For birth records less than fifty years old or death records less than twenty-five years old, "If the requester is not an immediate family member or properly qualified applicant, an authorization from the registrant or an immediate family member must also be enclosed." Indexes to deaths 1903–1976, and delayed birth indexes may be borrowed through interlibrary loan from the Texas State Library, and the library will consult the index of births for a fee.)

Utah Department of Health
Bureau of Vital Records and Health Statistics
(288 North 1460 West, Salt Lake City, UT 84145-0500—location)
PO Box 142855 (mailing address)
Salt Lake City, UT 84114-1021
(801) 538-3013
John E. Brockert, Bureau Director
Hours: Mon–Fri 8:00–5:00

Vermont Department of Health
Vital Records Unit
108 Cherry Street
PO Box 70
Burlington, VT 05401
(802) 863-7275
Hours: 7:45–4:15
(records up to ten years old)
$5.00 per certified copy

Vermont General Services Department
Public Records Division
(U.S. Route 2, Middlesex—location)
PO Drawer 33 (mailing address)
Montpelier, VT 05633-7601
(802) 828-3286; (802) 828-3710 FAX
Randy Hurlburt, Records Research Specialist
Hours: Mon–Fri 8:00–4:00
(records more than ten years old)
search fees: $2.00, certified copies: $5.00

Virginia Department of Health
Division of Vital Records
James Madison Building
PO Box 1000
Richmond, VA 23208-1000

(804) 786-6228
Hours: Mon–Fri 8:30–4:00

Washington State Department of Health
Center for Health Statistics
1112 S.E. Quince Street
PO Box 9709
Olympia, WA 98507-9709
(360) 753-5936
Philip Freeman, Manager, Customer Services
Hours: 8:00–4:30

Vital Registration Office (West Virginia)
Capitol Complex, Building 3, Room 516
Charleston, WV 25305
(304) 558-2931; (304) 558-1051 FAX
Hours: 8:00–4:00
$5.00 per year search

State of Wisconsin Department of Health and Family Services
Division of Health
(1 West Wilson Street, Room 158, Madison, WI 53702—location)
PO Box 309 (mailing address)
Madison, WI 53701-0309
(608) 266-1371 (recording); (608) 266-1372
Hours: Mon–Fri 8:00–4:15

Wyoming State Vital Records Services
Hathaway Building
Cheyenne, WY 82002
(307) 777-7591
births, deaths and marriages: $11.00 each

LIBRARIES

(Major Research Libraries with National Focus)

Allen County Public Library
Fred J. Reynolds Historical Genealogy Department
900 Webster Street
PO Box 2270
Fort Wayne, IN 46802
(219) 424-7241, ext. 3315
http://www.acpl.lib.in.us/genealogy/genealogy.html
Curt B. Witcher, Manager
Hours: Mon–Thur 9:00–9:00, Fri–Sat 9:00–6:00, Sun 1:00–6:00 (Labor Day–Memorial Day)
Pub. *Periodical Source Index* (PERSI), annually, $40.00 per year subscription
(North American genealogy and local history: 183,000 volumes, 123,470 pieces of microtext, approximately 3,500 periodicals)
$50.00 per year membership

The Burdick International Ancestry Library
2317 Riverbluff Parkway, #249
Sarasota, FL 34231-5032
(941) 922-7931
Frank P. Mueller, Executive Director and Editor
Hours: daily 9:00–4:00

Clayton Library, Center for Genealogical Research
a unit of the Houston Public Library
5300 Caroline
Houston, TX 77004-6896
(713) 284-1999
http://sparc.hpl.lib.tx.us/hpl/clayton.html
Margaret J. Harris, Manager
Hours: Mon–Wed 9:00–9:00, Thur–Sat 9:00–5:00
(a nationwide genealogical collection with some foreign materials; complete collection of federal census through 1920 and Soundex through 1910, plus indexes to federal military service and pensions through Spanish American War; county, state and federal records, passenger lists, lineage material from many patriotic societies, family histories, vertical files, periodicals, maps, finding aids)

Cleveland Public Library
325 Superior Avenue
Cleveland, OH 44114-1271
(216) 623-2864
Jo Ann Petrello, Head of History and Geography Department
Hours: Mon–Sat 9:00–6:00

College of William and Mary
Omohundro Institute of Early American History and Culture
Earl Gregg Swem Library Building
PO Box 8781
Williamsburg, VA 23187-8781
(757) 221-1126 (*Quarterly*); (757) 221-3508 (Reference and Information Department, Swem Library); (757) 221-1110 (Omohundro Institute); (757) 221-1047 FAX (Omohundro Institute)
E-mail: pvhigg@facstaff.wm.edu; ieahc1@facstaff.wm.edu (Omohundro Institute)
Pat Higgs, Office Manager; Beverly Smith, Secretary to the Director
Hours: Mon–Fri 8:30–5:30
Pub. *The William and Mary Quarterly: A Magazine of Early American History and Culture*, 3rd series (emphasis is no longer on Virginia history or genealogy), quarterly, $30.00 per year subscription, $4.00 surcharge for foreign address, $15.00 per year subscription for students; *Uncommon Sense*, two times per year, not available by subscription
(not a historical society but maintains a small library and is devoted to the publication of scholarly articles and books in the field of early American studies from discovery to approximately 1815)
$50.00 per year Associate membership for individuals, $25.00 per year Associate membership for students.

Dallas Public Library
Genealogy Section
1515 Young Street
Dallas, TX 75201
(214) 670-1433; (214) 670-1434
Lloyd DeWitt Bockstruck, F.N.G.S., Supervisor, Genealogy Section
Hours: Mon–Thur 9:00–9:00, Fri–Sat 9:00–5:00, Sun 1:00–5:00

National Society, Daughters of the American Revolution Library
1776 D Street, N.W.
Washington, DC 20006-5392
(202) 879-3229
http://www.dar.org
Eric G. Grundset, Library Director
Hours: Mon–Fri 8:45–4:00, Sun 1:00–5:00 (closed Sun before holiday, and closed to the public in mid-Apr)
(collection includes "all periods of U.S. history and records for the entire country")
entrance fee to non-members

Denver Public Library
Genealogy Division
Western History Collection
10 West Fourteenth Avenue Parkway
Denver, CO 80204-2731
(303) 571-2190; (303) 571-2171; (303) 571-2009 (Western History Collection)
James K. Jeffrey, Genealogy Collection Specialist; Eleanor Gahres, Manager, Western History Collection
Hours: Mon–Wed 10:00–9:00, Thur–Sat 10:00–5:30, Sun 1:00–5:00
(national in scope; specialty: Colorado, Rocky Mountains, Hispanic)

Detroit Public Library
Burton Historical Collection
5201 Woodward Avenue
Detroit, MI 48202
(313) 833-1480; (313) 832-0877
E-mail: nvangor@cms.cc.wayne.edu
http://www.detroit.lib.mi.us/special_collections.htm
Noel VanGorden, Chief of the Burton Collection
Hours: Tue & Thur–Sat 9:30–5:30, Wed 1:00–9:00

Family History Library of The Church of Jesus Christ of Latter-day Saints
Genealogical Society of Utah
35 North West Temple
Salt Lake City, UT 84150
(801) 240-2331; (801) 240-5551
http://www.lds.org/Welcome_to_FamHist/Welcome_to_FamHist.html
Jimmy B. Parker, Manager
Hours: Mon 7:30 A.M.–6:00 P.M., Tue–Sat 7:30 A.M.–10:00 P.M.
(The Genealogical Society of Utah is the acquisitions arm of the Family History Library. Membership is limited to employees of the Church's corporation. No individual research services are provided by the Society. At the present time Church policy is opposed to commercial publication of the names and mailing addresses of the various branch libraries [Family History Centers] throughout the world, but has released the phone numbers of selected centers, which are included below in the state-by-state listings. A partial list of centers is available upon request from the Family History Library. The location of the nearest library, where microfilm copies of the Family History Library's holdings can be viewed, may be obtained by phoning local LDS church representatives, usually listed in the yellow pages of the phone book. Accredits professional genealogists.)

Genealogical Center Library
PO Box 71343
Marietta, GA 30007-1343
Barbara A. Geisert, Director
(over 9,000 books and periodicals, mail order only)
$25.00 for membership in GUILD, includes book catalog and book loan forms; $3.00 per book plus $2.50 handling fee per order of up to five books

Library of Congress
Local History and Genealogy Reading Room
Humanities and Social Sciences Division
Thomas Jefferson Building, Room LJ 20
10 First Street, S.E.
Washington, DC 20540-5554
(202) 707-5537
E-mail: lcweb@loc.gov
http://lcweb.loc.gov/rr/genealogy (Reading Room)
Judith P. Austin, Head
Hours: Mon & Wed–Thur 8:30–9:30, Tue & Fri–Sat 8:30-5:00, Sun (winter) 1:00–5:00
(published genealogies and U.S. local histories)

Los Angeles Public Library
History and Genealogy Department
630 West Fifth Street
Los Angeles, CA 90071
(213) 228-7400; (213) 228-7000 (to verify hours)
Michael Kirley, Genealogy Librarian
Hours: Mon & Thur–Sat 10:00–5:30, Tue–Wed noon–8:00, Sun 1:00–5:00, hours subject to change

Mid-Continent Public Library

North Independence Branch/Genealogy
   and Local History Department
(317 West 24 Highway—location)
15616 East 24 Highway (mailing
   address)
Independence, MO 64050
(816) 252-0950
http://www.ge@mcpl.lib.mo.us
Martha L. Henderson, Department Head
Hours: Mon–Thur 9:00–9:00, Fri 9:00–
   6:00, Sat 9:00–5:00
(national in scope, includes circulating
   collection)

National Genealogical Society (NGS)

4527 17th Street, North
Arlington, VA 22207-2399
(703) 525-0050; (703) 525-0052 FAX
Jean K. Findeis, Executive Director;
   Dereka Smith, Librarian
Hours: Library: Mon & Wed 10:00–9:00,
   Fri–Sat 10:00–4:00; Offices: daily
   8:30–5:00
Pub. *National Genealogical Society
   Quarterly*; *NGS Newsletter*,
   bimonthly; *NGS/CIG Digest*,
   bimonthly
$35.00 per year membership for
   individuals, $10.00 per year
   membership for spouse, $30.00 per
   year membership for senior citizens

The New England Historic Genealogical Society

101 Newbury Street
Boston, MA 02116-3007
(888) 286-3447 (Education, Membership
   and Sales); (617) 536-5740, ext. 214;
   (617) 536-7307 FAX
E-mail: membership@nehgs.org
http://www.nehgs.org
Tom Downard, Membership and
   Marketing Manager
Hours: Tue & Fri–Sat 9:00–5:00 (closed
   Sat before Mon holiday), Wed–Thur
   9:00–9:00
Pub. *The New England Historical and
   Genealogical Register*, quarterly;
   Nexus, bimonthly; *The Computer
   Genealogist*, $30.00 per year
   subscription for non-members, $20.00
   per year subscription for members;
   Great Migration Newsletter, bimonthly,
   $10.00 per year subscription
(New England and eastern Canadian
   history and genealogy primarily, but
   generally strong in all aspects of
   genealogy)
$50.00 per year membership for
   individuals (includes *Register* only),
   $70.00 per year membership for
   families, $20.00 per year membership
   for students, $250.00 per year
   Contributing membership, $500.00 per
   year Sustaining membership,
   $2,000.00 life membership, $5,000 life
   Benefactor membership; Enquiry

service: $40.00 per hour for non-
   members, $25.00 per hour for
   members, $50.00 per hour for
   corporate clients (rush and FAX
   service additional); copies: 35¢ each,
   maximum of 35 copies, plus $5.00
   service fee for members, $10.00 for
   non-members

The New York Public Library

The Research Libraries
U.S. History, Local History and
   Genealogy Division
Fifth Avenue and 42nd Street
New York, NY 10018
(212) 930-0828 (U.S. History, Local
   History and Genealogy Division);
   (212) 930-0587 (Map Division); (212)
   930-0801 (Rare Books and
   Manuscripts)
http://www.nypl.org/research/chss/lhg/
   genea.html
Ruth A. Carr, Division Chief
Hours: Tue 11:00–7:30, Wed 11:00–6:00,
   Thur–Sat 10:00–6:00

Newberry Library

60 West Walton Street
Chicago, IL 60610-3305
(312) 943-9090; (312) 255-3506
   (Reference); (312) 255-3512
   (Genealogy)
http://www.newberry.org/
David T. Thackery, Curator of Local and
   Family History
Hours: Tue–Thur 10:00–6:00, Fri–Sat
   9:00–5:00
Pub. *Newberry Newsletter*, quarterly;
   *Origins: A Newsletter of the Local &
   Family History Section and the Family
   & Community Center at the Newberry
   Library*, quarterly
("North American local and family
   history; non-genealogical areas of
   strength include history of cartography
   and history of Native Americans.")

Saint Louis Public Library

History and Genealogy Department
1301 Olive Street
Saint Louis, MO 63103
(314) 539-0386; (314) 539-0393 FAX
E-mail: cmillar@slpl.lib.mo.us
http://www.slpl.lib.mo.us.
Cynthia Millar, Genealogy Librarian
Hours: Mon 10:00–9:00, Tue–Fri 10:00–
   6:00, Sat 9:00–5:00
photocopies 15¢ from paper copy, 25¢
   from microfilm, $1.00 postage and
   handling per order

Samford University

American Genealogical Society
   Depository and Headquarters
Harwell Goodwin Davis Library
Special Collection Department
800 Lakeshore Drive
Birmingham, AL 35229
(205) 870-2749

Elizabeth C. Wells, Librarian
Hours: Mon 8:00–9:00, Tue–Fri 8:00–4:30

Seattle Public Library

Genealogy Section, Humanities
   Department
1000 Fourth Avenue
Seattle, WA 98104
(206) 386-4629 (Genealogy); (206) 386-
   4625 (Humanities)
Darlene E. Hamilton, Humanities
   Librarian-Genealogy
Hours: Mon–Thur 9:00–9:00, Fri–Sat
   9:00–6:00
(Genealogy Collection covers U.S., with
   some regions stronger than others;
   library also has a separate Northwest
   History Collection)

Genealogical Research Center and Library of Southeast Texas

Rt. 1, Box 405
Kountze, TX 77625
Pub. *International Genealogical
   Exchange*, monthly, $12.00 per year
   subscription

The State Historical Society of Wisconsin

816 State Street
Madison, WI 53706-1488
(608) 264-6535 (Reference Librarian);
   (608) 264-6460 (Reference Archivist)
http://www.wisc.edu/shs-library/; http://
   www.wisc.edu/shs-archives
James L. Hansen, Reference Librarian
Hours: when University of Wisconsin is
   in session: Mon–Thur 8:00–9:00, Fri–
   Sat 8:00–5:00; when university is not
   in session: Mon–Sat 8:00–5:00;
   Archives: Mon–Fri 8:00–5:00, Sat
   9:00–4:00
Pub. *Wisconsin Magazine of History*,
   quarterly; *Columns—Newsletter of the
   State Historical Society of Wisconsin*,
   bimonthly
(library has a strong collection with
   emphasis on North American
   genealogy; archives serves as Area
   Research Center for Columbia, Dane
   and Sauk counties)
$27.50 per year membership for
   individuals, $32.50 per year
   membership for families, $22.50 per
   year membership for individual senior
   citizens, $27.50 per year membership
   for senior citizen families, $30.00 per
   year membership for institutions

Tree Trackers Library

(between Golden, MO, and Eagle Rock,
   MO—location)
HCR-01, Box 1210 (mailing address)
Eagle Rock, MO 65641
(417) 271-3532
E-mail: tedphylerfries@juno.com
Phyllis Eldridge Friesner, Owner/
   Librarian

Hours: by appointment
("35-year collection open to the public as a `labor of love' in retirement; Books, film, fiche from all states and Norway, many family histories, lots of periodicals.")
donations for reimbursement of postage, copies, film rental

The University of Texas at Austin
Eugene C. Barker Texas History Center
The Center for American History
Sid Richardson Hall 2.101
Austin, TX 78712
(512) 495-4515; (512) 495-4542 FAX
http://www.lib.utexas.edu/Libs/CAH/cah.html
Dr. Don E. Carleton, Director; Reference Librarian
Hours: Mon–Sat 9:00–5:00
Pub. *Center for American History Newsletter*, irregularly
(a national collection with emphasis on Texas, southern and southwestern U.S., and the Rocky Mountain west)
charges for photocopying and photographs and other duplication of materials

The Western Reserve Historical Society Library
10825 East Boulevard
Cleveland, OH 44106-1777
(216) 721-5722; (216) 721-5702 FAX
http://www.wrhs.org/
Kermit J. Pike, Library Director
Hours: Tue & Thur–Sat 9:00–5:00, Wed 9:00–9:00
Pub. *The Western Reserve Historical Society Genealogical Committee Bulletin*, quarterly, $5.00 per year subscription
(235,000 books, 25,000 volumes of newspapers, 30,500 rolls of microfilm, 1,000,000 prints and photographs, and more than 3,000 collections of manuscripts and archives which comprise more than six million items from New England to Georgia and west to the Mississippi River; also regional African American and ethnic archives, Ohio Labor history and urban archives; member of the Ohio Network of American History Research Centers, the designated repository for local government records and historical manuscript materials from Ashtabula, Cuyahoga, Geauga, Lake, Lorain and Medina counties)
$4.00 per year membership; admission: $6.00 for adults, $5.00 for senior citizens, $6.00 for three-month student pass, $4.00 for children (ages 6–12), members free; search service: $30.00 per hour (half-hour minimum), includes up to ten photocopies, $10.00 for each additional ten photocopies, plus postage and handling

HISTORICAL SOCIETIES

(National Focus)

American Antiquarian Society
185 Salisbury Street
Worcester, MA 01609-1634
(508) 755-5221, ext. 136; (508) 753-3311 FAX
E-mail: mel@nwa.org
Marie E. Lamoureux, Assistant Director of Reference Services
Hours: Mon–Fri 9:00–5:00 (closed stacks, readers need to complete an application and show two forms of identification)
Pub. *American Antiquarian Society Newsletter*, irregularly; *Proceedings of the American Antiquarian Society*, semiannually, $45.00 per year subscription
(American history and culture through 1876, strong collections of genealogies on early North American lines of descent, United States and Canadian local histories)
membership is by election

College of William and Mary
Omohundro Institute of Early American History and Culture
Earl Gregg Swem Library Building
PO Box 8781
Williamsburg, VA 23187-8781
(757) 221-1126 (*Quarterly*); (757) 221-3508 (Reference and Information Department, Swem Library); (757) 221-1110 (Omohundro Institute); (757) 221-1047 FAX (Omohundro Institute)
E-mail: pvhigg@facstaff.wm.edu; ieahc1@facstaff.wm.edu (Omohundro Institute)
Pat Higgs, Office Manager; Beverly Smith, Secretary to the Director
Hours: Mon–Fri 8:30–5:30
Pub. *The William and Mary Quarterly: A Magazine of Early American History and Culture*, 3rd series (emphasis is no longer on Virginia history or genealogy), quarterly, $30.00 per year subscription, $4.00 surcharge for foreign address, $15.00 per year subscription for students; *Uncommon Sense*, two times per year, not available by subscription
(not a historical society but maintains a small library and is devoted to the publication of scholarly articles and books in the field of early American studies from discovery to approximately 1815)
$50.00 per year Associate membership for individuals, $25.00 per year Associate membership for students.

National Trust for Historic Preservation Library Collection
McKeldin Library
University of Maryland
College Park, MD 20742
(301) 405-6320
E-mail: NT_Library@umail.umd.edu
Sally Sims Stokes, Curator
Hours: Mon–Fri 10:00–5:00 (appointment suggested)
(materials on certain historic landmarks)

The New England Historic Genealogical Society
101 Newbury Street
Boston, MA 02116-3007
(888) 286-3447 (Education, Membership and Sales); (617) 536-5740, ext. 214; (617) 536-7307 FAX
E-mail: membership@nehgs.org
http://www.nehgs.org
Tom Downard, Membership and Marketing Manager
Hours: Tue & Fri–Sat 9:00–5:00 (closed Sat before Mon holiday), Wed–Thur 9:00–9:00
Pub. *The New England Historical and Genealogical Register*, quarterly; *Nexus*, bimonthly; *The Computer Genealogist*, $30.00 per year subscription for non-members, $20.00 per year subscription for members; *Great Migration Newsletter*, bimonthly, $10.00 per year subscription
(New England and eastern Canadian history and genealogy primarily, but generally strong in all aspects of genealogy)
$50.00 per year membership for individuals (includes *Register* only), $70.00 per year membership for families, $20.00 per year membership for students, $250.00 per year Contributing membership, $500.00 per year Sustaining membership, $2,000.00 life membership, $5,000 life Benefactor membership; Enquiry service: $40.00 per hour for non-members, $25.00 per hour for members, $50.00 per hour for corporate clients (rush and FAX service additional); copies: 35¢ each, maximum of 35 copies, plus $5.00 service fee for members, $10.00 for non-members

The Urban History Association
c/o Department of History
Lake Forest College
Lake Forest, IL 60045
Michael H. Ebner, Executive Secretary

GENEALOGICAL SOCIETIES

(National Focus)

American Family Records Association (AFRA)
PO Box 15505
Kansas City, MO 64106-0505
(816) 373-6570
Nita Neblock
Hours: Mid-Continent Public Library, North Independence Branch, Independence, MO: Mon–Thur 9:00–9:00, Fri 9:00–6:00, Sat 9:00–5:00
Pub. *Family Records Today, The Journal of American Family Records*, quarterly; *Interlibrary Loan Catalog* (about 3,000 titles in circulating collection), $5.00 postpaid
$27.00 per year membership

The Augustan Society, Inc.
PO Box P
Torrance, CA 90508-0210
(310) 326-8603; (310) 326-4446 FAX
Sir Rodney Hartwell, KtB(Y), Director
Hours: Tue–Sat 8:00–4:00
Pub. *The Augustan* (heraldry, chivalry, ancient and medieval history, European research, royal and noble genealogy, colonial U.S., ancient Egypt, etc.), quarterly; *Journal of Royal and Noble Genealogy*, irregularly; *Heraldry*, irregularly; *Chivalry*, irregularly

National Society, Daughters of the American Revolution (D.A.R.)
1776 D Street, N.W.
Washington, DC 20006-5392
(202) 879-3229
http://www.dar.org
Eric G. Grundset, Library Director
Hours: Mon–Fri 8:45–4:00, Sun 1:00–5:00 (closed Sun before holiday, and closed to the public in mid-Apr)
Pub. *Daughters of the American Revolution Magazine*, ten times per year, $12.00 per year subscription; *Continental Columns*, quarterly (reprinted in *DAR Magazine*)
(collection includes "all periods of U.S. history and records for the entire country")
entrance fee to non-members

Federation of Genealogical Societies
PO Box 830220
Richardson, TX 75083-0220
http://www.fgs.org
Pub. *The FGS Forum*, quarterly, $9.00 per year subscription to individuals who belong to an FGS member society, $15.00 per year subscription to individuals who do not belong to an FGS member society
membership for organizations or

institutions based on size of the organization

National Genealogical Society (NGS)
4527 17th Street, North
Arlington, VA 22207-2399
(703) 525-0050, ext. 225; (703) 525-0052 FAX; (800) 473-0060
E-mail: 76702.2417@compuserve.com
Francis J. Shane, Executive Director
Hours: Library: Mon & Wed 10:00–9:00, Fri–Sat 10:00–4:00; Offices: daily 9:00–5:00
Pub. *NGS Quarterly*; *NGS Newsletter*, bimonthly; *NGS/CIG Digest*, bimonthly
(extensive family files and Bible records collection)
$40.00 per year membership for individuals, $10.00 per year membership for spouse, $35.00 per year membership for senior citizens

The New England Historic Genealogical Society
101 Newbury Street
Boston, MA 02116-3007
(888) 286-3447 (Education, Membership and Sales); (617) 536-5740, ext. 214; (617) 536-7307 FAX
E-mail: membership@nehgs.org
http://www.nehgs.org
Tom Downard, Membership and Marketing Manager
Hours: Tue & Fri–Sat 9:00–5:00 (closed Sat before Mon holiday), Wed–Thur 9:00–9:00
Pub. *The New England Historical and Genealogical Register*, quarterly; *Nexus*, bimonthly; *The Computer Genealogist*, $30.00 per year subscription for non-members, $20.00 per year subscription for members; *Great Migration Newsletter*, bimonthly, $10.00 per year subscription
(New England and eastern Canadian history and genealogy primarily, but generally strong in all aspects of genealogy)
$50.00 per year membership for individuals (includes *Register* only), $70.00 per year membership for families, $20.00 per year membership for students, $250.00 per year Contributing membership, $500.00 per year Sustaining membership, $2,000.00 life membership, $5,000 life Benefactor membership; Enquiry service: $40.00 per hour for non-members, $25.00 per hour for members, $50.00 per hour for corporate clients (rush and FAX service additional); copies: 35¢ each, maximum of 35 copies, plus $5.00 service fee for members, $10.00 for non-members

INDEPENDENT PUBLICATIONS

(Unrelated to a Geographic Region)

American Association for State and Local History
530 Church Street, #600
Nashville, TN 37219-2325
(615) 255-2971; (615) 255-2979 FAX
John-Paul Richiuso, Director of Publications and Archives
Hours: 9:00–5:00
Pub. *History News*, bimonthly; *History News Dispatch*, monthly, $55.00 per year subscription (includes both *History News* and *History News Dispatch*); *Directory of Historical Organizations in the United States and Canada*, about every four years
("AASLH is a non-profit, membership organization providing educational assistance to professionals and amateurs doing local and state history.")
$30.00 per year membership (does not include *Directory*)

The American College of Heraldry
PO Box 11084
Tuscaloosa, AL 35486-0025
Dr. David Pittman Johnson, President
Hours: various
Pub. *The Armiger's News*, quarterly; *The Heraldic Register of America*, occasionally, $7.00 per issue postpaid, special rates for libraries
(coats of arms rightfully borne in America, biographical listings of armigers)
$25.00 per year membership, includes only *The Armiger's News*.

AGLL
(PO Box 40, Orting, WA 98360-0040, Editorial Offices location)
PO Box 329 (Subscription Department mailing address)
Bountiful, UT 84011-0329
(801) 298-5358 (Subscription Department); (801) 298-5446 (Sales); (801) 298-1712 (Customer Service); (435) 770-0551 (Editorial Offices); (800) 760-AGLL (Orders); (801) 298-5468 FAX
E-mail: sales@agll.com
http://www.heritagequest.com (Editorial Offices); http://www.agll.com (Sales)
Leland K. Meitzler, Executive Editor; Steve Williams, Vice President Marketing
Hours: Editorial Offices: Mon–Fri 9:00–5:00; Sales: 8:00–4:00
Pub. *Heritage Quest* (U.S. and international research articles, how-to, queries, book reviews), bimonthly, $28.00 per year subscription; *Genealogy Bulletin*, $12.00 per year subscription

(over 250,000 titles on microfilm and microfiche for rent; microfilming of books, documents, newspapers; microfilm and microfiche duplication in both silver and diazo)
$47.50 membership

The American Genealogist (TAG)
PO Box 398
Demorest, GA 30535
(706) 865-6440 phone or FAX
David L. Greene, C.G., F.A.S.G., Co-editor and Publisher
Pub. *The American Genealogist*, quarterly, $25.00 per year subscription, $48.00 for two years, $70.00 for three years (plus $1.00 for libraries which require invoices)
(Colonial U.S.; "We focus on critical problem-solving articles and short compiled genealogies.")

American Name Society
Modern Languages
Baruch College
Modern Languages Box G-1224
New York, NY 10010
(212) 387-1570; (212) 387-1591 FAX
E-mail: wayne_finke@baruch.cuny.edy
Wayne H. Finke, Executive Secretary/ Treasurer
Hours: 9:00–5:00
Pub. *Names*, quarterly
$35.00 per year membership for individuals in the U.S., $36.00 per year membership for individuals in Canada, $40.00 per year membership for individuals elsewhere

American Society/French Legion of Honor
22 East 60th Street
New York, NY 10022-1077
Pub. *Laurels*, three times per year
$10.00 per year membership

American Studies Association
1120 19th Street, N.W., Suite #301
Washington, DC 20036
(202) 467-4783; (202) 467-4786 FAX; (800) 548-1784 (The Johns Hopkins University Press)
http://www.georgetown.edu/crossroads
John F. Stephens, Executive Director
Hours: 9:00–5:00
Pub. *American Quarterly* (March, June, September, December), $69.00 per year subscription for institutions, $18.00 per issue (from The Johns Hopkins University Press, Journals Publishing Division, 2715 North Charles Street, Baltimore, MD 21218-4319)
$15.00 per year membership for individuals with income under $12,000, $30.00 per year membership for individuals with income between $12,000 and $19,999, $30.00 per year membership for individuals with income between $20,000 and $31,999,

$40.00 per year membership for individuals with income between $32,000 and $44,999, $50.00 per year membership for individuals with income over $45,000, $60.00 per year joint membership (with only one subscription to *AQ*), $100.00 per year membership for institutions, $1,000.00 life membership

A.G.E.S. (Ancestral Genealogical Endexing Schedules, Inc.)
PO Box 2127
Bountiful, UT 84010
Ronald Vern Jackson, Senior Archivist
(958 U.S. and state census volumes, marriages, land, military, will indexes; database not on line)
search fee: $5.00 per surname, per year, per state

Ancestry, Inc.
PO Box 476
Salt Lake City, UT 84110-0476
(800) ANCESTRY (262-3787); (800) 531-1790 (*Genealogical Computing*); (801) 531-1798 FAX
http://www.ancestry.com
Dean R. Zimmerman, Director of Marketing and Sales; Dennis Sampson, Editor, *Genealogical Computing*
Hours: 8:00–5:00
Pub. *Ancestry* (instructional, international genealogy, how-to articles, regular columns), bimonthly, $4.95 per issue for non-members, $21.00 per year subscription for non-members, $38.00 two-year subscription for non-members, $54.00 three-year subscription for non-members; *Genealogical Computing*, quarterly, $25.00 per year subscription
$24.95 membership in Ancestry Research Club (includes subscription)

AntiqueWeek
Mayhill Publications, Inc.
(27 North Jefferson Street—location)
PO Box 90 (mailing address)
Knightstown, IN 46148-9900
(765) 345-5133; (800) 876-5133
Tom Mayhill, Publisher
Pub. *AntiqueWeek*, weekly, Eastern Edition $3.70 for eight-week subscription, $12.20 for thirty-week subscription, $22.70 for sixty-week subscription

Armchair Publications
810 McDonough Road
Rt. 2, Box 895
Hampton, GA 30228
Joel Dixon Wells
Pub. *Armchair Researcher*, quarterly, $12.50 per subscription; *Florida Armchair Researcher*, quarterly, $15.00 per year subscription; *Georgia Armchair Researcher*, quarterly, $15.00 per year subscription

Association for Gravestone Studies
278 Main Street, Suite 207
Greenfield, MA 01301-3230
Pub. *Association for Gravestone Studies Newsletter*, quarterly; *Markers— Journal of the Association for Gravestone Studies*, annually, $20.00 per issue to members, $25.00 per issue to non-members
$20.00 per year membership for individuals, $25.00 per year membership for institutions

Association for the Promotion of Scholarship in Genealogy, Ltd.
255 North Second West
Salt Lake City, UT 84103-4545
(801) 521-4732
Neil D. Thompson, Ph.D., F.A.S.G., Executive Director

Association of One-Name Studies
2509 Placid Place
Virginia Beach, VA 23456-3743
(757) 468-5829
E-mail: clbarkle@leo.vsla.edu
http://www.mediasoft.net/scottc/aans.htm
Carolyn L. Barkley, Secretary
Pub. *Association of One-Name Studies Newsletter*, quarterly; *Directory of One-Name Studies and Surname Genealogists*, annually
$20.00 membership includes registration of up to five variants of one surname, additional surnames at $5.00 each

The Augustan Society, Inc.
PO Box P
Torrance, CA 90508-0210
(310) 326-8603; (310) 326-4446 FAX
Sir Rodney Hartwell, KtB(Y), Director
Hours: Tue–Sat 8:00–4:00
Pub. *The Augustan* (heraldry, chivalry, ancient and medieval history, European research, royal and noble genealogy, colonial U.S., ancient Egypt, etc.), quarterly; *Journal of Royal and Noble Genealogy*, irregularly; *Heraldry*, irregularly; *Chivalry*, irregularly

Cemetery Q & A's
PO Box 8003
Janesville, WI 53547-8003
Peggy Gleich, Editor
Pub. *Cemetery Q & A's (Queries & Anecdotes)*, four times per year, (March, June, September, December), $20.00 per year subscription in the U.S., $30.00 per year subscription outside the U.S., $3.00 plus LSASE for sample
(regarding cemeteries anywhere in the world, tips on copying, cleaning, gravestone rubbings, special columns by well-known cemetery enthusiasts, etc.)
queries free to subscribers

Center for Historical Population Studies
211 Carlson Hall
Salt Lake City, UT 84112
Pub. *Center for Historical Population Studies Newsletter*, annually

Claudette's
3962 Xenwood Avenue South
Saint Louis Park, MN 55416-2842
Claudette Atwood Maerz
Pub. *Current Genealogical Publications*, annually

Clements Library Associates
University of Michigan
William L. Clements Library
909 South University Avenue
Ann Arbor, MI 48109-1190
(734) 764-2347; (734) 647-0716
E-mail: clements.library@umich.edu
http://clements.umich.edu/associates.html
Pub. *American Magazine and Historical Chronicle*, semiannually

Communal Studies Association
PO Box 122
Amana, IA 52203
(319) 622-6446 phone and FAX
E-mail: csa@netins.net
http://www.ic.org/csa/
Susan Shoup, Office Manager
Pub. *Communal Societies*, annually, $15.00 per year subscription
$25.00 per year membership for individuals, $50.00 per year membership for institutions

Cowles Magazines
6405 Flank Drive
PO Box 8200
Harrisburg, PA 17105-8200
(717) 657-9555
Ed Holm, Editor
Pub. *American History Illustrated*, bimonthly, $20.00 per year subscription; *Civil War Times Illustrated*, bimonthly, $20.00 per year subscription

Datatrace Systems
PO Box 1587
Stephenville, TX 76401
(254) 965-6979
James Pylant, Editor
Hours: Mon–Fri 9:00–5:00
Pub. *American Genealogy Magazine*, quarterly (March, June, September, December), $22.50 per year subscription, $43.00 for two-year subscription, $3.75 sample issue (Texas residents add 8.25% sales tax)
(Indian records, pension files, Black Dutch ancestry; also transmitted electronically on nationwide satellite)

The Everton Publishers, Inc.
(3223 South Main Street, Nibley, UT—location)
PO Box 368 (mailing address)

Logan, UT 84323-0368
(435) 752-6022; (800) 443-6325; (435) 752-0425 FAX
http://www.everton.com
Bob Arbon, Manager
Hours: Mon–Fri 8:00–5:00
Pub. *Everton's Genealogical Helper*, bimonthly, $4.50 per issue, $24.00 per year subscription
(queries, classified advertisements; directories of genealogical researchers, periodical publications, etc.; computerized database of ancestor data: Computerized "Roots Cellar"; computerized Family File; computerized Pedigree Library)
Roots Cellar registration: $5.00 for one name, $1.00 for each additional name

Family Photo Quarterly
6431 Hanover Crossing Drive, #F
Mechanicsville, VA 23111-3953
Katharine Harbury
Pub. *Family Photo Quarterly*

Footprints of Our Past
1940 New Jersey Street
Fairfield, CA 94533
(707) 425-2711; (707) 426-2859 FAX
E-mail: footprints@juno.com
http://vader.castles.com/ftprints/index.html
Don P. Wright, Editor
Pub. *Footprints of Our Past: Our Ancestors and Their Descendants* (nationwide coverage), quarterly, $6.00 per issue, $20.00 per year subscription

Gangster Chronicles
13509 Pendleton Street
Oxon Hills, MD 20022
Shannon Bridget Murphy
Pub. *Gangster Chronicles*, quarterly, $14.00 per year subscription

Genealogical Heritage, Ltd.
2006 South Ninth East
Salt Lake City, UT 84105
Pub. *Family Tree*, bimonthly

Genealogical Institute
Family History World
(875 North 300 East, Tremonton, UT—location)
PO Box 22045 (mailing address)
Salt Lake City, UT 84122
(801) 250-6717 phone and FAX; (435) 245-0256; (801) 829-4030
E-mail: eakle@xmission.com
Arlene H. Eakle; JoAnn Jackson, Office Manager
Hours: Mon–Fri 9:00–5:00
Pub. *Research News*, occasionally, $3.00 per issue plus postage and handling; *Immigration Digest* (English and Southern research), occasionally, $13.50 per issue plus postage and handling

Genealogical Queries Magazine
169 Melody Lane
Tonawanda, NY 14150
Robert J. Wilson, Editor
Pub. *Genealogical Queries Magazine*

Genealogical Research Directory
3324 Crail Way
Glendale, CA 91206-1107
(818) 790-2642; (818) 952-3462 FAX
http://www.ozemail.com.au/~grdxxx
Mrs. Jan Jennings, U.S. Agent
Pub. *Genealogical Research Directory*, annually, $29.75 postpaid for current year
(150,000 surname entries worldwide with names and addresses of worldwide listing of libraries and archives and genealogical societies)

Genealogy Digest Magazine
PO Box 15861
Salt Lake City, UT 84115
Pub. *Genealogy Digest Magazine*, quarterly, $18.00 per year subscription

Genee's Exchange
Rt. 4
West Chester, PA 19380
Helen Pierrard, Editor
Pub. *Genee's Exchange*

The Great Lakes Historical Society
480 Main Street
PO Box 435
Vermilion, OH 44089
(440) 967-3467
Martha Long, Business Manager
Hours: 10:00–5:00
Pub. *Inland Seas* (Great Lakes history), quarterly
$35.00 per year membership

Heritage Books, Inc.
1540-E Pointer Ridge Place
Bowie, MD 20716
(800) 398-7709 (credit card orders only, Mon–Fri 10:00–4:00); (800) 276-1760 FAX
Laird C. Towle, Editor; Leslie Towle, Marketing Director
Pub. *Genealogical Periodical Annual Index*, annually, costs vary

Heritage Papers
PO Box 7776
Athens, GA 30604-7776
(770) 613-0030
Mary B. Warren, Editor
Pub. *Family Puzzlers*, weekly, $30.00 per year subscription (Georgia residents add $1.50 tax)

Heritage Quest Research Library
(220 Bridge Street S.W.—location)
PO Box 1119 (mailing address)
Orting, WA 98360-1119
(360) 893-2799
E-mail: famlyhistn@aol.com
Betty Leonard, Director

Hours: Mon–Tue & Thur–Fri 1:00–5:00,
Wed 9:00–9:00
Pub. *Heritage Quest Researcher*, four
times per year
(specializes in Germanic records, family
books, regional U.S. books, census
films, assorted film and fiche)
$30.00 per year membership; admission:
$4.00 per day for non-members

Hunterdon House
38 Swan Street
Lambertville, NJ 08530
(609) 397-2523
E-mail: tombwilson@aol.com
Thomas B. Wilson, General Manager

**International Genealogy and
Heraldry Fellowship of Rotarians**
I.F.R. Genealogy
10 Fox Tail Lane
Brookfield, CT 06804
James R. High
Pub. *Roto-Gene*, quarterly, $15.00 per
year subscription

Journal of the West, Inc.
1531 Yuma
PO Box 1009
Manhattan, KS 66502-4228
(785) 539-1888
Carol A. Williams, Publisher
Hours: Mon–Fri 9:00–4:00
Pub. *Journal of the West*, quarterly
$38.00 per year membership for
individuals, $48.00 per year
membership for institutions

Kids' Genes
PO Box 8003
Janesville, WI 53547-8003
Peggy Gleich, Editor
Pub. *Cemetery Q & A's*, four times per
year
(includes how-to articles, samples, book
reviews, forms, specialized topic
columns from beginner to
intermediate)

*Lost and Found National
Genealogical Query Newsletter*
PO Box 207
Wathena, KS 66090
(785) 989-3117
Ethel M. Weber, Publisher/Editor
Pub. *Lost and Found National
Genealogical Query Newsletter*,
bimonthly, $15.00 per year
subscription
(U.S. and Canada)

**Martin/Barnett Genealogical
Company, Inc.**
4314 Nenana
Houston, TX 77035
Pub. *Genealogical Compendium of
Books and Articles in Print*,
semiannually, $12.50 per issue, $20.00
per year subscription

National Council on Family Relation
55 Old Post Road
PO Box 1678
Greenwich, CT 06836-1678
Pub. *Journal of Family History*,
quarterly, $80.00 per year subscription

National Council on Public History
327 Cavanaugh Hall, IUPUI
425 University Boulevard
Indianapolis, IN 46202-5140
(317) 274-2716; (317) 274-2347
E-mail: ncph@iupui.edu
David G. Vanderstel, Ph.D., Executive
Director
Pub. *The Public Historian*, quarterly;
Public History News
(historic preservation, oral history;
museums, archives, historical
societies)
$47.00 per year membership for
individuals, $21.00 per year
membership for students, $73.00 per
year membership for institutions

*National Genealogy and History
News*
Rt. 3, Box 65
Chandler, OK 74834-8504
R. D. Bradshaw, Editor
Pub. *National Genealogy and History
News*

Oral History Association
1093 Braxton Avenue
Los Angeles, CA 90024
Pub. *Oral History Association Annual
Report and Membership Directory*,
annually

Oral History Association
(Old Capitol Annex—location)
PO Box H (mailing address)
Frankfort, KY 40601
(502) 564-3016
Kim Lady Smith, Manager
Hours: 8:00–4:30
Pub. *Oral History Review*, semiannually,
$20.00 per year subscription

Pentref Press
65–67 Main Street
Machias, ME 04654
Rosemary E. Bachelor, Publisher and
Editor; Joanna W. Foust, Business
Manager
Pub. *The Second Boat*, bimonthly, $25.00
per volume (colonial American
genealogy); *The Dinghy*, bimonthly,
$25.00 per volume (a supplement to
The Second Boat)

Pioneer Genealogy Society
PO Box 11488
Salt Lake City, UT 84147
Michel L. Call, President
(specializes in royal ancestry,
Mayflower, New England colonial and
pre-colonial, Mormon pioneer
ancestry)

$2.00 plus SASE for list of colonists
with royal descent and price list for
indexes and other services

Plantation Society in the Americas
University of New Orleans/University of
South Florida
Department of History
University of New Orleans
New Orleans, LA 70148-2550
(504) 280-6886; (504) 286-5505 FAX
Professor Edward Lazzerini
Hours: daily
Pub. *Plantation Society in the Americas*,
two or three times per year, three
issues per volume
(West Indies, plantations, families,
Creole studies, Southern U.S.,
Caribbean, Mississippi Valley, Afro-
American)
$25.00 per year membership to
individuals in the U.S., $50.00 per
year membership for institutions

Progenitor Genealogical Society
PO Box 16422
Salt Lake City, UT 84116-0422
(801) 328-8128
Ron Bremer, President
Pub. *Roots Digest*, occasionally
(seminars, lectures, workshops,
databases, Internet genealogical
research services through parent
company, Kindred Konnections)

Reunions Magazine
PO Box 11727
Milwaukee, WI 53211-1727
(414) 263-4567; (414) 263-6331 FAX
E-mail: reunions@execpc.com
http://www.execpc.com/~reunions
Carol Burns, Editor; Edith Wagner,
Publisher
Hours: Mon–Fri 9:00–5:00
Pub. *Reunions Magazine* (reunions—
family, class, military—genealogy and
others), quarterly (1 March, 1 June, 1
September, 1 December); *Workbook*,
annually; $24.00 per year subscription
for both, $10.00 for *Workbook* and
catalog only

**Society for Preservation of Covered
Bridges**
1611 Sandcastle Road
Sanibel, FL 33957
David A. Topham, Treasurer
Pub. *Covered Bridge Topics*, quarterly
$15.00 per year membership

**Society of History of the Early
American Republic**
Department of History
Purdue University
1358 University Hall
West Lafayette, IN 47907-1358
(765) 494-4135; (765) 496-1755 FAX
E-mail: jer@sla.purdue.edu
John A. Larson, Editor; Michael
Morrison, Editor

Hours: various

Pub. *Journal of the Early Republic*, quarterly

(history and culture 1789–1850)

$15.00–$30.00 per year membership for individuals, $40.00 per year membership for institutions

Steamboat Masters and Associates, Inc.

(2316 Northwestern Parkway, Louisville, KY 40212-1024—location)

PO Box 3046 (mailing address)

Louisville, KY 40201-3046

(502) 778-6784; (502) 776-9006 FAX

Sandra Miller Custer, President

Hours: Mon–Fri 9:00–5:00 by appointment only

Pub. *The Egregious Steamboat Journal*, bimonthly, $5.00 per issue, $20.00 per year U.S. subscription, $24.00 per year Canadian subscription, $40.00 per year foreign subscription

(extensive library and archives of books, indices, model plans, and videos pertaining to steamboating, history of steamboats and the people who worked and traveled on them, on the inland rivers of America)

will quote price for finding information; catalogue of resources: $4.00

Steward University System Library

Rt. 5, Box 109

Piedmont, AL 36272-8709

(205) 447-2939

Mrs. Frank Ross Stewart, Sr.

Hours: 8:00–5:00

Pub. *numeroos*, irregularly, free

(county, family, church, etc., worldwide)

Tapestry Press

PO Box 3647

Princeton, NJ 08543

Pub. *American Family History*, quarterly, $25.00 per year subscription

Part 2. State Addresses

Archives and Libraries with Holdings in Genealogy

State Archives and Library

Alabama Department of Archives and History
(624 Washington Avenue—location)
PO Box 300100 (mailing address)
Montgomery, AL 36130-0100
(334) 242-4435 (Reference Room)
E-mail: archref@dsmd.dsmd.state.al.us
http://www.asc.edu/archives/agis.html
Frazine Taylor, Head, Ready Reference
Hours: Reference Room: Tue–Fri 8:00–
   5:00, Sat 9:00–5:00, closed Sun &
   Mon
$15.00 out-of-state research fee for mail
   requests

State Historical Society

Alabama Historical Association
The University of Alabama Press
(address withheld upon request)
Pub. *The Alabama Review: A Quarterly
   Journal of Alabama History*, quarterly
   (January, April, July, October), $20.00
   per year subscription for non-member
   individuals, $25.00 per year
   subscription for libraries or foreign
   individuals; *Newsletter*
$25.00 per year membership for
   individuals, $35.00 per year
   membership for families, $30.00 per
   year membership for institutions or
   foreign members, $15.00 per year
   membership for students; no research
   staff, facilities, archives library, or
   resources for genealogical research

City, County and Regional Archives and Libraries

Abbeville Memorial Library
History Room
301 Kirkland Street
Abbeville, AL 36310
(334) 585-2818
Linda Floyd, Director
Hours: Mon–Fri 9:00–5:00, Sat 9:00–
   12:00

Andalusia Public Library
212 South Three Notch Street
Andalusia, AL 36420
(205) 222-6612

Howard Strevel, Director; Elizabeth
   Starr, Library Administrator
Hours: Mon–Fri 9:00–5:30, Sat 9:00–
   12:00
$2.00 charge for requested searches and
   limited copying

Ashville Museum and Archives
(Saint Clair County Courthouse—
   location)
PO Box 1570 (mailing address)
Ashville, AL 35953
(205) 594-2128
Charlene Simpson, Archivist
Hours: Mon–Fri 8:00–noon & 1:00–5:00

Auburn University
Auburn University Archives
Auburn, AL 36849-5637

Auburn University
Special Collections
Ralph Brown Draughon Library
231 Mell Street
Auburn, AL 36849-5606
(334) 844-1700
E-mail: fostecd@lib.auburn.edu
http://www.lib.auburn.edu/special
Dale Foster, Head of Special Collections
Hours: Mon–Thur 7:45–midnight, Fri
   7:45–10:00, Sat 9:00–6:00, Sun 1:00–
   midnight (fall hours: closed Fri & Sun
   7:45–6:00)

Birmingham Public Library
Tutwiler Collection of Southern History
   and Literature
2100 Park Place
Birmingham, AL 35203
(205) 226-3665; (205) 226-3663
E-mail: sou@bham.lib.al.us
http://www.bham.lib.al.us
Anne F. Knight, Coordinator for
   Research Services
Hours: Mon–Tue 9:00–8:00, Wed–Sat
   9:00–6:00, Sun 2:00–6:00

**H. Grady Bradshaw-Chambers
County Library and Cobb Memorial
Archives**
3419 20th Avenue
Valley, AL 36854
(334) 768-2161
Miriam Ann K. Syler, Archivist Assistant
   to Director
Hours: Mon–Fri 10:00–6:00, Sat 10:00–
   5:00

Brent-Centreville Public Library
153 Walnut Street
Centreville, AL 35042
(205) 926-4736
Flo Franklin, Librarian
Hours: Mon 9:00–8:00, Tue–Fri 9:00–
   5:00, Sat 9:00–12:00
(genealogy section, microfilm of early
   county records, newspapers, census)

**Chattahoochee Valley Community
College**
Learning Resources Center
2606 Savage Drive
Phenix City, AL 36867
(334) 291-4979
Cathy Woolbright, Director, Learning
   Resources Center
Hours: Mon–Thur 8:00–9:00, Fri 8:00–
   5:00, Sun (except summer) 2:00–6:00
("self-directed research only; a research
   assistant is not available at this time")

Cullman County Public Library
200 Clarke Street, N.E.
Cullman, AL 35055

Discovery Place of Birmingham
1320 22nd Street, South
Birmingham, AL 35205

The Carl Elliott Regional Library
Genealogy Department
Jasper, AL 35502
(205) 221-2568

Florence-Lauderdale Public Library
Genealogy-Local History Room
218 North Wood Avenue
Florence, AL 35630
(205) 764-6563
Dr. Darrel A. Russel
Hours: Mon & Wed 10:00–6:00, Tue &
   Thur 10:00–7:00, Fri–Sat 9:00–5:00,
   Sun 1:00–4:00
(northwest Alabama)

**Gadsden-Etowah County Public
Library**
254 College Street
Gadsden, AL 35999
(205) 549-4699, ext. 30 (Genealogy);
   (205) 549-4699, ext. 29 (Reference)
Barbara Reed, Reference Librarian
Hours: Mon–Thur 8:00–8:00, Fri–Sat
   9:00–5:00, Sun 1:00–5:00; summer:
   Mon–Thur 8:00–7:00

Hacksma House Genealogy Library
(see Washington)

Heritage Hall
PO Box 1118
Talladega, AL 35160
Mary Nelson

**Historic Mobile Preservation
Society, Inc.**
300 Oakleigh Place
Mobile, AL 36604
(334) 432-6161
Carole M. Perez, Executive Director
(2,000 books in Archives)

Houston-Love Memorial Library
212 West Burdeshaw Street
PO Box 1369
Dothan, AL 36302

(334) 793-9767
Susan Veasey, Reference Librarian
Hours: Mon–Thur 9:00–9:00, Fri 9:00–
6:00, Sat 9:00–5:00, Sun 1:00–5:00
(southern states genealogy and history)
15¢ per photocopy, minimum $3.00
prepaid

Huntsville-Madison County Public Library
(915 Monroe Street, S.W., Huntsville,
AL 35801—location)
PO Box 443 (mailing address)
Huntsville, AL 35804
(205) 532-5969; (205) 532-5997 FAX
Annewhite T. Fuller, Department Head,
Heritage Room
Hours: Mon–Thur 9:00–9:00, Fri–Sat
9:00–6:00, Sun 2:00–6:00
(library deals with eastern U.S.,
especially the southeast; archives deals
with northern Alabama and the Civil
War)
photocopies $3.00 minimum, list of local
researchers available

Jackson George Regional Library System
(see Mississippi)

Landmarks of DeKalb County, Inc.
Landmarks of DeKalb Museum, Inc.
500 Gault Avenue, North
PO Box 518
Fort Payne, AL 35967
Walter Weatherly, President
Pub. *Landmarks Bulletin*, biannually
(genealogical services)
$10.00 per year membership, $125.00
life membership, $150.00 life
memorial membership

Liles Memorial Library
Public Library of Anniston and Calhoun
County
Alabama Room
108 East Tenth Street
PO Box 308
Anniston, AL 36202
(205) 237-8501
Thomas B. Mullins
Hours: Mon–Fri 9:00–5:00, Sat 12:00–
4:00, Sun (winter only) 2:00–5:00

Limestone County Department of History and Archives
310 West Washington Street
Athens, AL 35611
(205) 233-6404
Philip Reyer, Archivist
Hours: Mon–Fri 8:00–4:30
("publish census records, indexes, and
abstracts")

Museums of the City of Mobile
355 Government Street
Mobile, AL 36602
(334) 434-7569
Charles Torrey, Museum Researcher

Hours: Research: Mon–Fri 9:00–5:00;
Three museums: Tue–Sat 9:00–5:00,
Sun 1:00–5:00
free admission

Mobile Public Library
Local History and Genealogy
704 Government Street
Mobile, AL 36602
(334) 434-7093
George H. Ewert, Manager
Hours: Mon–Sat 9:00–6:00

Monroe County Heritage Museums
(Old Monroe County Courthouse—
location)
PO Box 1637 (mailing address)
Monroeville, AL 36461-1637
(334) 575-7433; (334) 575-7934 FAX
Dawn Crook, Assistant Director
Hours: Mon–Fri 8:00–noon & 1:00–4:00,
Sat 10:00–2:00
Pub. *Legacy*, biannually, $20.00 per year
subscription
$35.00 per year museum membership

Ohoopee Regional Library
(see Georgia)

Red Mountain Museum
1421 22nd Street, South
Birmingham, AL 35205-4199

Samford University
American Genealogical Society
Depository and Headquarters
Harwell Goodwin Davis Library
Special Collection Department
800 Lakeshore Drive
Birmingham, AL 35229
(205) 870-2749
Elizabeth C. Wells, Librarian
Hours: Mon 8:00–9:00, Tue–Fri 8:00–
4:30

Scottsboro-Jackson Heritage Center
208 South Houston Street
PO Box 53
Scottsboro, AL 35768
(205) 259-2122
Melanie Bradford, Director
Hours: Tue–Fri 11:00–4:00
(records dating as far back as 1820, such
as Orphan's Court, Deed Books,
Commissioner's Court, Chancery
Court and Circuit Court, many medical
and store ledgers)

Troy Public Library
Troy, AL 36081
(334) 566-1314
Hours: Mon–Fri 8:00–5:00, Sat 8:00–
12:00
("Genealogy Room: largest collections
on Alabama, Georgia, North Carolina,
South Carolina and Virginia")

Tuscaloosa Public Library
1801 River Road
Tuscaloosa, AL 35401
(205) 345-5820

Glen A. Johnson
Hours: Mon–Thur 9:00–9:00, Fri–Sat
9:00–5:00, Sun 2:00–6:00

University of Alabama
Hoole Special Collections Library
PO Box 870266
Tuscaloosa, AL 35487-0266
(205) 348-0500
E-mail: awatson@ualvm.ua.edu
http://www.ua.edu

University of Southern Alabama
History Department
Humanities Building 344, USA
Mobile, AL 36688
(334) 460-6210; (334) 460-6750 FAX
Dr. Michael Thomason, Editor
Pub. *Gulf Coast Historical Review*,
semiannually, $14.00 per year
subscription, $25.00 for two years
(focuses on Gulf Coast history, Florida to
Texas)

Wallace State Community College Library
Family and Regional History Program
801 Main Street
PO Box 2000
Hanceville, AL 35077-2000
(205) 352-6403 (office); (205) 352-9641
(home)
Robert Scott Davis, Jr., M.Ed., Director
Hours: Mon–Thur 7:30 A.M.-8:30 P.M.,
Fri 7:30-4:00
(Alabama and surrounding states,
Confederate records; houses collection
of North Central Alabama
Genealogical Society; also offers
college courses and research field trips
in genealogy)

Washington County Museum
Washington County Courthouse
PO Box 52
Chatom, AL 36518
Dr. Claire W. Duncan, Chairman,
Museum Board

Historical Societies— Local and Regional

Aliceville Historical Preservation, Inc.
103 Fourth Avenue, N.E.
Aliceville, AL 35442
(205) 373-6364

Arab Historical Society
Rt. 4, Box 418C
Arab, AL 35016

Arlington Historical Association
15 Woodhill Road
Birmingham, AL 35213

Auburn Heritage Association
159 North College Street
PO Box 2248
Auburn, AL 36830

Autauga County Heritage Association
102 East Main Street
Prattville, AL 36067-3114
(334) 361-0961

Baldwin County Historical Society
PO Box 69
Stockton, AL 36579
(334) 937-9464

Bibb County Heritage Association
Rt. 1, Box 147
Brierfield, AL 35035
(205) 665-1856

Birmingham Historical Society
1 Sloss Quarters
Birmingham, AL 35222
(205) 251-1880
Marjorie L. White, Chairman
Pub. *Birmingham Historical Society Journal*, semiannually

Blount County Historical Society
PO Box 45
Oneonta, AL 35121
(205) 625-6905
E-mail: blountal@aol.com
C. Warren Weaver, Archivist
Hours: various
Pub. *BCHS Newsletter*, quarterly
$10.00 per year membership

Bullock County Historical Society
PO Box 563
Union Springs, AL 36089
Judy Rutland, President
Pub. *Quarterly Newsletter*
$5.00 per year membership

Butler County Historical and Genealogical Society
309 Fort Dale
Greenville, AL 36037
(334) 382-3216
Judy Taylor, Historical Librarian and Editor
Pub. *Butler County Historical and Genealogical Quarterly*
$8.00 per year membership for individuals, $10.00 per year membership for families

Chattahoochee Valley Historical Society, Inc.
H. Grady Bradshaw-Chambers County Library and Cobb Memorial Archives
3419 20th Avenue
Valley, AL 36854
(334) 768-2161 (Library-Archives); (334) 768-7272 FAX
Miriam Ann K. Syler, Society Representative and Archivist Assistant to Director

Hours: Library-Archives: Mon–Fri 10:00–6:00, Sat 10:00–5:00 (appointments preferred on Sat)
Pub. *The Voice*, quarterly
(Chattahoochee Valley, Chambers and surrounding counties, Alabama, Troup and Harris counties, Georgia)
$10.00 per year membership

Chilton County Historical Society and Archives, Inc.
Chilton/Clanton Public Library
PO Box 644
Clanton, AL 35045
(205) 755-1768
B. D. Roberts; Marian Mills
Pub. *Quarterly*
$12.00 per year membership

Choctaw County Historical Society
Rt. 1, Box 320
Butler, AL 36904
(205) 459-3888
Charles A. Heffernan, Treasurer
Pub. *Newsletter*, annually
$5.00 per year regular membership, $25.00 per year Sustaining membership, $50.00 per year Sponsor membership, $100.00 per year Patron membership

Citronelle Historical Preservation Society
18990–19000 South Center Street
PO Box 384
Citronelle, AL 36522
(334) 866-7730
Nell Fisher, President
$10.00 per year membership

Coosa County Historical Society
PO Box 5
Rockford, AL 35136
Pub. *Coosa Heritage*, bimonthly
$10.00 per year membership

Coosa River Valley Historical and Genealogical Society
PO Box 295
Centre, AL 35960
(205) 447-2939

Covington Historical Society
PO Box 1582
Andalusia, AL 36420

Eleventh Circuit Historical Society, Inc.
(see Georgia)

Escambia County Historical Society
PO Box 276
Brewton, AL 36427
Barbara Jones, Editor of Publications
Hours: Jefferson Davis Community College Library: 8:00–4:00; summer: Mon–Thur 7:30-6:30, Fri 7:30–1:30
Pub. *Escambia County Historical Society Journal*, semiannually (July and December); *Escambia Echoes*, monthly
$7.50 per year membership

Fayette County Historical Society
PO Box 309
Fayette, AL 35555-0309
(205) 932-3255

Fayette County Memorial Library
326 Temple Avenue North
Fayette, AL 35555
(205) 932-6625; (205) 932-4152 FAX
Gwendolyn Lacey, Director
Hours: Mon–Tue & Thur 9:00–6:00, Fri 9:00–5:00, Sat 9:00–1:00

Forney Historical Society
(3084 Sterling Road—location)
Samford University, S-215 (mailing address)
Birmingham, AL 35229
(205) 870-2784

Free State of Winston Historical Society
PO Box 26
Double Springs, AL 35553-0026

Greene County Historical Society
PO Box 746
Eutaw, AL 35462

Henry County Historical Society
(Abbeville Memorial Library, History Room, 301 Kirkland Street—location)
PO Box 222 (mailing address)
Abbeville, AL 36310
(334) 585-3020
William W. Nordan, Executive Director
Hours: Library: Mon–Fri 9:00–5:00, Sat 9:00–12:00
Pub. *Henry County Historical Society Newsletter*, monthly
(Henry County was formed from Alabama territory and comprised all of southeast Alabama, now known as the "Wiregrass," and produced all or parts of nine other counties: Barbour 1832, Bullock 1866, Coffee 1841, Covington 1822, Crenshaw 1866, Dale 1824, Geneva 1868, Houston 1903, Pike 1821)
limited membership presently closed

Historic Chattahoochee Commission
211 North Eufaula Avenue
PO Box 33
Eufaula, AL 36072-0033
(334) 687-9755; (334) 687-6631 phone and FAX
Douglas C. Purcell, Executive Director
Hours: Mon–Fri 8:00–5:00
Pub. *Chattahoochee Tracings*, quarterly
(history, art, architecture, preservation of lower Chattahoochee Valley of Alabama and Georgia)
free memberships available

Jackson County Genealogical Society
PO Box 1494
Scottsboro, AL 35768

Pub. *Jackson County Chronicles*, quarterly
$10.00 per year membership

Jackson County Historical Association
Rt. 1
Langston, AL 35755

Jefferson County Historical Commission
2027 First Avenue North, Suite 801
Birmingham, AL 35203
(205) 324-0988
Barbara B. King, Executive Secretary
Hours: Tue–Thur

Lawrence County Archives and Historical Commission, Inc.
698 Main Street
PO Box 728
Moulton, AL 35650
(205) 974-1757; (205) 974-2538
E-mail: lchc35650@aol.com
http://members.aol.com/lchc35650
Myra Borden, Archivist
Hours: Mon–Fri 9:00–4:00
Pub. *Old Lawrence Reminiscences*, quarterly
(family files, vertical files, census, court records, library section and a large collection of microfilm)
$15.00 per year membership for individuals, $20.00 per year membership for families; marriage license research only, $5.00 each for out-of-town members, $7.00 for non-members

Lee County Historical Society
PO Box 206
Loachapoka, AL 36865
Pub. *Trails in History*, quarterly

Limestone County Historical Society
PO Box 82
Athens, AL 35612
Doyle Lovelace, President
Pub. *Limestone Legacy*, quarterly
$15.00 per year membership

Lowndes County Historical Society
Rt. 1, Box 408
Fort Deposit, AL 36032
Pub. *Lowndes County Historical Society Publications*, quarterly
$6.00 per year membership

Marengo County Historical Society
407 North Commissioner Avenue
PO Box 159
Demopolis, AL 36732
(334) 289-1666
Mrs. J. C. P. Turner, President
Pub. *MCHS Newsletter*, biannually

Pea River Historical and Genealogical Society
(108 South Main—location)
PO Box 310628 (mailing address)
Enterprise, AL 36331

(334) 393-2901
Clayton G. Metcalf, President and Editor
Hours: Mon–Fri 10:00–4:00
Pub. *Pea River Trails*, quarterly
$15.00 per year membership

Piedmont Historical and Genealogical Society
PO Box 47
Spring Garden, AL 36275

Pike County Historical and Genealogical Society
Rt. 2, Box 272
Goshen, AL 36035
(334) 484-3314; (334) 566-1314 (Library)
Mrs. Henry W. Folmar, Treasurer and Book Committee Chairman; Karen Bullard, Assistant Reference Librarian
Hours: Troy Public Library: Mon–Fri 8:00–5:00, Sat 8:00–12:00
Pub. *Pike County Historical and Genealogical Society Papers*, usually semiannually (April and October)
$10.00 per year local membership, $13.00 per year membership outside local area

Pleasant Grove Historical Commission
501 Park Road
Pleasant Grove, AL 35127

Russell County Historical Commission
801 Dillingham Street
Phenix City, AL 36867
(334) 298-9735

Saint Clair County Historical Society
PO Box 125
Odenville, AL 35120

St. Clair Historical Society
11975 U.S. Highway 411
Odenville, AL 35120
Pub. *Cherish*, quarterly

Selma-Dallas County Historic and Preservation Society
Old Cahawba Archaeological Park
9518 Canaba Road
Orrville, AL 36767
(334) 872-8058 (Park); (334) 875-2529 (Manager)
http://www.olg.com/selma/cahawba.html
Linda Derry, Park Manager/Site Archaeologist
Hours: Park: Mon–Sun 9:00–5:00; Office: 9:00–5:00
Pub. *Old Cahawba Newsletter*, irregularly
(manager maintains research file on historic families and soldiers; Alabama's first state capital 1820–1826, Dallas County seat 1819–1866, Civil War prison)

$10.00 per year membership; free search of Cahawba family files

Shelby County Historical Society
Shelby County Museum and Archives
1854 Courthouse, Main Street
PO Box 457
Columbiana, AL 35051
(205) 669-3912
Madine Evans, Archivist
Hours: Mon–Fri 8:00–4:00
Pub. *The Quarterly*
$15.00 per year membership for individuals or couples, $2.50 per year membership for students

Society of Pioneers of Montgomery, Inc.
PO Box 413
Montgomery, AL 36101

Southern Studies Institute
(see Louisiana)

Talladega County Historical Association
106 Broome Street
Talladega, AL 35160
(205) 362-2219
Pub. *Talladega County Historical Association Newsletter*
$10.00 per year membership

Tennessee Valley Historical Society
PO Box 149
Sheffield, AL 35660
E-mail: sheridanrc@aol.com
Richard C. Sheridan, Editor
Pub. *Newsletter*, quarterly; *Journal of Muscle Shoals History*, occasionally, price varies
(northwest Alabama)
$5.00 per year membership (includes *Newsletter* but not *Journal*)

West Jefferson County Historical Society, Inc.
(1740 Eastern Valley Road, Bessemer, AL 35020—location)
PO Box 184 (mailing address)
Bessemer, AL 35021
(205) 426-6604
Pub. *Journal of History*, semiannually
$10.00 per year membership

LDS Family History Centers

Birmingham
(205) 967-7279

Dothan
(334) 793-7425

Mobile
(334) 344-6051

Montgomery
(334) 269-9041

Genealogical Societies

State Genealogical Societies

Alabama Genealogical Society, Inc. (AGS)
Samford University
American Genealogical Society Depository and Headquarters
Harwell Goodwin Davis Library
Special Collection Department
800 Lakeshore Drive
Birmingham, AL 35229
(205) 870-2749 (Library)
Elizabeth C. Wells, Librarian
Hours: Library: Mon 8:00–9:00, Tue–Fri 8:00–4:30
Pub. *Alabama Genealogical Society Newsletter*, quarterly; *Alabama Genealogical Society Magazine*, quarterly
$20.00 per year membership

Southern Society of Genealogists, Inc.
Stewart University
PO Box 295
Centre, AL 35960
(205) 447-2939

Regional Genealogical Societies

AlaBenton Genealogical Society
Liles Memorial Library
Public Library of Anniston and Calhoun County
Alabama Room
108 East Tenth Street
PO Box 308
Anniston, AL 36202
(205) 237-8501 (Library)
Thomas B. Mullins
Hours: Library: Mon–Thur 9:00–5:00, Sat 9:00–4:00, Sun 1:00–5:00
Pub. *AlaBenton Genealogical Society Quarterly*
$15.00 per year membership

Autauga Genealogical Society
PO Box 668
Prattville, AL 36067

Baldwin County Genealogical Society
c/o Foley Public Library
319 East Laurel Avenue
Foley, AL 36535
(334) 943-7665
Jeanette Bornholt, Library Aide and Genealogical Society Member
Hours: Mon & Wed 9:00–9:00, Tue & Thur 1:00–9:00, Fri–Sat 9:00–6:00
$10.00 per year membership for individuals, $12.00 per year membership for couples

Birmingham Genealogical Society, Inc.
PO Box 2432
Birmingham, AL 35201
Pub. *Pioneer Trails*, quarterly; *Birmingham Genealogical Society Newsletter*, monthly
$10.00 per year membership

Butler County Historical and Genealogical Society
309 Fort Dale
Greenville, AL 36037
(334) 382-3216
Judy Taylor, Historical Librarian and Editor
Pub. *Butler County Historical and Genealogical Quarterly*
$8.00 per year membership for individuals, $10.00 per year membership for families

Central Alabama Genealogical Society
PO Box 125
Selma, AL 36702-0125
Prissy Odom, President; June Carter, Treasurer
Hours: Mon–Sat 9:00–5:00
Pub. *Central Alabama Genealogical Society*, biannually
$20.00 per year membership

Coosa River Valley Historical and Genealogical Society
PO Box 295
Centre, AL 35960
(205) 447-2939

Delta Genealogical Society (northeast Alabama)
(see Georgia)

The Genealogical Society of East Alabama, Inc.
(909 Avenue A, Opelika, AL 36801—location)
PO Box 2892 (mailing address)
Opelika, AL 36803
James Noel Baker, President
Pub. *Tap Roots*, quarterly (April, July, October, January)
("Bible records, family histories, cemeteries, church histories, items of community interest, tax and courthouse records; serving Chambers, Lee, Macon, Russell, and Tallapoosa counties")
$15.00 per year membership for individuals, $20.00 per year membership for husband and wife

Marion County Genealogical Society
Winfield Public Library
PO Box 360
Winfield, AL 35594
(205) 487-2484
Loree Lindsey, Editor; Joel Palmer, President

Hours: Mon–Fri 9:00–5:00
Pub. *Marion County Alabama Tracks*, quarterly
$15.00 per year membership

Mobile Genealogical Society, Inc.
(Woman's Club House, 1200 Government Street—location)
PO Box 6224 (mailing address)
Mobile, AL 36660
(334) 626-6573
Dolores F. "Dee" Rhodes, President
Hours: Mon 11:00–2:00, Thur noon–4:00, second Sat
Pub. *Deep South Genealogical Quarterly* (February, May, August, November); *Deep South Genealogical Society Newsletter*, monthly
$20.00 per year membership for individuals, families, libraries or societies; research for members only: $15.00 per hour

Montgomery Genealogical Society, Inc.
PO Box 230194
Montgomery, AL 36123-0194
Pub. *Montgomery Genealogical Society Quarterly*
$10.00 per year membership for individuals, $15.00 per year membership for families

Natchez Trace Genealogical Society
PO Box 420
Florence, AL 35631-0420
Darrell A. Russel, Ph.D., Publications Chairperson
Pub. *Natchez Trace Newsletter*, quarterly, $20.00 per year subscription; *Natchez Trace Traveler*, five times per year
(Colbert, Franklin, and Lauderdale counties, Alabama)

North Alabama Genealogical Society
3327 Danville Road, S.W.
Decatur, AL 35603-9027

North Central Alabama Genealogical Society
PO Box 13
Cullman, AL 35056-0013
Carolina Nigg, Editor and Vice President
Hours: Wallace State Community College Library: Mon–Thur 7:30 A.M.–8:30 P.M., Fri 7:30–4:00
Pub. *Alabama Family History and Genealogy News*, quarterly, $15.00 per year subscription
(Blount, Cullman, Marshall, Walker, and Winston counties, and Alabama families)
$15.00 per year membership for individuals or families

Northeast Alabama Genealogical Society, Inc.
PO Box 8268
Gadsden, AL 35902-8268
Jane Keenum, Librarian

Hours: Thur 10:00–3:00, first & third Sat 9:00–1:00
Pub. *Northeast Alabama Settlers*, quarterly (July, October, January, April)
$15.00 per year membership if paid before 15 June, $18.00 thereafter

Pea River Historical and Genealogical Society
(108 South Main—location)
PO Box 310628 (mailing address)
Enterprise, AL 36331
(334) 393-2901
Clayton G. Metcalf, President and Editor
Hours: Mon–Fri 10:00–4:00
Pub. *Pea River Trails*, quarterly
$15.00 per year membership

Pickens County Genealogical Society
PO Box 38
Gordo, AL 35466
(205) 364-7830 (President)
Kathleen S. Brown, President
Hours: Mon–Fri by appointment
$5.00 per year membership; copying charge

Piedmont Historical and Genealogical Society
PO Box 47
Spring Garden, AL 36275

Pike County Historical and Genealogical Society
Rt. 2, Box 272
Goshen, AL 36035
(334) 484-3314; (334) 566-1314 (Library)
Mrs. Henry W. Folmar, Treasurer and Book Committee Chairman; Karen Bullard, Assistant Reference Librarian
Hours: Troy Public Library: Mon–Fri 8:00–5:00, Sat 8:00–12:00
Pub. *Pike County Historical and Genealogical Society Papers*, usually semiannually (April and October)
$10.00 per year local membership, $13.00 per year membership outside local area

Southeast Alabama Genealogical Society
PO Box 246
Dothan, AL 36302-0246
(334) 794-7480
Mrs. Ceya Minder, Corresponding Secretary
Hours: meeting third Tue except December
Pub. *Southeast Alabama Genealogical Society Quarterly*, unavailable by subscription
(southeast Alabama counties, upper bordering counties of Florida and lower bordering counties of Georgia)
$12.00 per year Associate membership

Tennessee Valley Genealogical Society
PO Box 1568
Huntsville, AL 35807-0567
(205) 728-2788; (205) 532-5969 (Library); (205) 532-5997 FAX (Library)
http://iquest.com/~rwhite/tvgs/tvgs
Hours: Huntsville-Madison County Public Library, Heritage Room: Mon–Thur 9:00–9:00, Fri–Sat 9:00–6:00, Sun 2:00–6:00
Pub. *Valley Leaves*, quarterly; *TVGS News* (meeting announcements only)
(nine north Alabama counties that border on the Tennessee River)
$18.00 per year membership

Morning Group Tuscaloosa Genealogical Society
29 DuBois Terrace
Tuscaloosa, AL 35401
Mrs. Billie Lockard, Research
Hours: Tuscaloosa Public Library: first Thur 10:00
Pub. *Roots and Branches*, three times per year
$8.00 per year membership

Tuscaloosa Genealogical Society
Night Group
PO Box 020802
Tuscaloosa, AL 35406

Walker County Genealogical Society
PO Box 3408
Jasper, AL 35502

Independent Publications and Miscellany

Alabama Heritage
500 Margaret Drive
Tuscaloosa, AL 35487-0342
(205) 348-7434
Sara Martin, Marketing/Advertising Director
Hours: 8:00–4:45
Pub. *Alabama Heritage* (Alabama and the South), quarterly, $16.95 per year subscription, $28.95 for two-year subscription, $38.95 for three-year subscription
"Genealogy in Alabama" queries: $30.00 for 50-word listing

AlGenWeb
Part of U.S. GenWeb Project
E-mail: al@usgenweb.com
http://www.rootsweb.com/ algenweb/
(links to other Alabama resources)

Ancestor Files Library
PO Box 249
Lanett, AL 36863-0249
(334) 576-2797

Lynda S. Eller, Heard County, Georgia, Historian
Hours: by appointment
Pub. *Heard Heritage, Heard County, Georgia*, semiannually (May and November), $8.00 per year subscription
(covers Clay, Cleburne, Randolph, Talladega, and Tallapoosa counties, Alabama; Carroll, Chambers, Coweta, Harris, Heard, Meriwether, and Troup counties, Georgia)

Arkansas Ancestors
(see Arkansas)

Baldwin County Historic Development Commission
(1100 Fairhope Avenue, Fairhope, AL 36532—location)
PO Box 86 (mailing address)
Montrose, AL 36559
(334) 928-3002; (334) 580-2590 FAX
Jack Thomas, chairman
Hours: Mon–Fri 8:00–4:30
(preserving and protecting historic districts and the maintenance of the distinctive characters of these districts)

Clayton Historical Preservation Authority
PO Box 385
Clayton, AL 36016
(334) 775-3542

Colbert County Historical Landmarks Foundation, Inc.
1004 East Third Street
Tuscumbia, AL 35674
(205) 383-8466

Genealogical Institute
(see Virginia)

Genealogy Books and Consultation
(see Texas)

Historic Huntsville Foundation, Inc.
PO Box 786
Huntsville, AL 35804
(205) 837-2925
Pub. *Historic Huntsville: Quarterly of Local Architecture and Preservation*
minimum $20.00 per year membership

Hunting for Bears Genealogical and Historical Society
(3878 West 3200 South, Salt Lake City, UT 84120-2154—location)
PO Box 25593 (mailing address)
Salt Lake City, UT 84125-0593
(801) 966-1611; (801) 957-1612 FAX
E-mail: genealogy@juno.com
http://www.cc.utah.edu/ dm6055/ hfb.html
Dixie Murray
Hours: various
Pub. *Bear Tracks* (an electronic newsletter), monthly, free
(Alabama, Arkansas, Georgia, Kentucky, Indiana, Illinois, Louisiana, Maryland,

Mississippi, Missouri, Ohio, North Carolina, South Carolina, Tennessee, Texas and Virginia; marriage records) surname search of marriage records on a statewide basis: $5.00 per search

MLH Research
3916 Bramble Road
Anniston, AL 36201
MariLee Beatty Hagness, Owner
Pub. *Alabama-Georgia Queries*, bimonthly, $16.00 per year subscription
(queries, court records, Bible records, military listings, limited to Alabama and Georgia surnames)
search fees: $10.00 per hour

Mobile DAR
15 Gaywood Circle
Birmingham, AL 35213
Alice Merchant

Mountain Press
(see Tennessee)

Society of Alabama Archivists
Auburn University
Auburn University Archives
Auburn, AL 36849-5637
(334) 826-4465
Dwayne Cox, President

Somerville Courthouse Preservation Commission
PO Box 153
Somerville, AL 35670
(205) 778-8277
Imogene Williams, Town Clerk
Hours: 8:00–5:00

The Source Historical and Adventure
PO Box 656
Russellville, AL 35653
Pub. *The Source Historical and Adventure*, $5.00 per year subscription

Southern Genealogist's Exchange Society
(see Florida)

Surnames Ltd.
(see Mississippi)

Tracking Your Roots
E-mail: genweblisa@aol.com
http://members.aol.com/genweblisa/
Lisa R. Franklin, R.N.
(links to other Alabama resources)

Tracks
280 Sierra Vista
Mobile, AL 36607
Pub. *Tracks*, quarterly, $15.00 per year subscription

ALASKA

Archives and Libraries with Holdings in Genealogy

State Archives and Library

Alaska Collection and Archives
4101 University Drive
Anchorage, AK 99508
(907) 561-1265

Alaska State Archives
Reference Desk
141 Willoughby Avenue
Juneau, AK 99801-1720
(907) 465-2270; (907) 465-2465 FAX
E-mail: archives@educ.state.ak.us; archives@muskox.alaska.edu
http://www.educ.state.ak.us/lam/ home.hyml
Hours: Mon–Fri 9:00–5:00
(Alaska State and Territorial Government Agency records)
minimal photocopy charge

Alaska State Library, Alaska Historical Collections
Historical Reference
(State Office Building, Eighth Floor— location)
PO Box 110571 (mailing address)
Juneau, AK 99811-0571
(907) 465-2925; (907) 465-2990 FAX
E-mail: asl@muskox.alaska.edu
http://www.educ.state.ak.us/lam/library/ hist.html
Kathryn H. Shelton, Librarian III, Head of Historical Collections
Hours: Mon–Fri 1:00–5:00
(book and print collection, newspapers and periodicals, maps, photographs, manuscripts, microfilm, etc.)

State Historical Societies

Alaska Association for Historic Preservation
645 West Third Avenue
Anchorage, AK 99501-2124
(907) 272-2119
Bill Coghill, Executive Director
Pub. *The Alaska Association for Historic Preservation*, quarterly
(not primarily genealogical)
$15.00 per year membership for individuals, $25.00 per year membership for families, $25.00 per year membership for non-profit organizations, $50.00 per year Contributor membership, $100.00 per year Friend membership, $250.00 per year Sponsor membership, $500.00 per year Benefactor membership

Alaska Historical Society
(1489 C Street, Suite 202—location)
PO Box 100299 (mailing address)
Anchorage, AK 99510-0299
(907) 276-1596 phone and FAX
Nancy Gross, Assistant to the President
Hours: by appointment
Pub. *Alaska History*, semiannually, $12.00 per year subscription; *Alaska History News*, quarterly
$305.00 per year membership for individuals

City, County and Regional Archives and Libraries

Anchorage Municipal Libraries
Z. J. Loussac Public Library
3600 Denali Street
Anchorage, AK 99503
(907) 261-2975
Peg Thompson, Social Sciences Librarian
Hours: Mon–Thur 11:00–9:00, Fri–Sat 10:00–6:00, Sun 1:00–5:00

Clausen Memorial Museum
203 Fram Street
PO Box 708
Petersburg, AK 99833
(907) 772-3598
Michale Edgington, Director

Duncan Cottage Museum
Duncan Street
PO Box 282
Metlakatla, AK 99926

Heritage Library and Museum
301 West Northern Lights
Anchorage, AK 99510
(907) 265-2834
Lea Worcester, Curator/Librarian

Juneau-Douglas City Museum
(Fourth and Main Streets—location)
155 South Seward Street (mailing address)
Juneau, AK 99801
(907) 586-3572; (907) 586-3203 FAX
E-mail: mary_pat_wyatt@mail.ci.juneau.ak.usa
Mary Pat Wyatt, Curator
Hours: summer: daily; winter: Fri–Sat
(reference assistance, cemetery and records, high school yearbooks, telephone books, vital statistic newspaper records; local Juneau-Douglas, Alaska, information)

Kotzebue Museum, Inc.
PO Box 73
Kotzebue, AK 99752

Carrie M. McLain Memorial Museum
PO Box 53
Nome, AK 99762
(907) 443-2566

Janet Williams, Museum Director
Hours: Tue–Sat 10:00–5:00
(bibliography of famous people, early
    twentieth century, all copies of *Nome
    Nugget*, oldest newspaper in Alaska;
    gold mining, native culture)
no search fees

Museum Society of Petersburg
Second and F Street
PO Box 708
Petersburg, AK 99833
(907) 772-3598

National Park Service
Cultural Resources Division, Alaska
    Region
2525 Gambell Street
Anchorage, AK 99503-2892
(907) 257-2543
Leslie Starr Hart, Chief, Cultural
    Resources

Elmer E. Rasmuson Library
Alaska and Polar Regions Department
University of Alaska Fairbanks
PO Box 756800
Fairbanks, AK 99701
(907) 474-7261
David Hales, Head
Hours: Mon–Fri 9:00–5:00
("Rare books, archives, manuscripts, rare
    maps, oral histories, archival films,
    historical photographs; materials deal
    with Alaska and Polar regions")

Sheldon Museum and Cultural Center
(11 Main Street, just above boat
    harbor—location)
PO Box 269 (mailing address)
Haines, AK 99827
(907) 766-2366; (907) 766-2368 FAX
E-mail: sheldmus@seaknet.alaska.edu
Cynthia Jones, Director/Curator
Hours: winter: Mon, Wed & Sun 1:00–
    4:00, Tue & Thur–Fri 3:00–5:00;
    summer: daily 1:00–5:00
(pioneer history, Tingit Indian art and
    culture)
museum admission: $3.00; photocopies
    25¢ per page

Tongass Historical Museum
629 Dock Street
Ketchikan, AK 99901
(907) 225-5600
Roxana Adams, Museum Director

Trail of '98 Museum
Spring Street
PO Box 415
Skagway, AK 99840
(907) 983-2420

University of Alaska, Anchorage
Consortium Library
3211 Providence Drive
Anchorage, AK 99508
(907) 786-1874 (Government
    Documents); (907) 786-1849
    (Archives and Manuscripts)

Professor Alden Rollins, Government
    Documents Librarian; Dennis Walle,
    Archivist
Hours: call ahead, hours vary with
    university calendar
(national scope collection of biographies,
    journals, diaries, local histories,
    gazetteers, plus archival and
    manuscript collections on Alaska, the
    northern Pacific area and the Arctic,
    with an emphasis on southcentral and
    southwestern Alaska, also pre-1900
    Canadiana)

University of Alaska Fairbanks
College of Arts and Science
University of Alaska Museum
907 Yukon Drive
Fairbanks, AK 99701
(907) 474-7505

The Valdez Museum and Historical Archive
(217 Egan Drive—location)
PO Box 8 (mailing address)
Valdez, AK 99686-0008
(907) 835-2764; (907) 835-4597 FAX
E-mail: vldzmuse@alaska.net
http://www.alaska.net/vldzmuse/
    index.html
M. Joseph Leahy, Director
Hours: 9:00–5:00
(Valdez, Prince William Sound, Copper
    River Valley regional history; gold
    rush 1898–1910)
search fee: hour free, $20.00 per hour
    thereafter

Wrangell Museum
318 Church Street
PO Box 1050
Wrangell, AK 99929
(907) 874-3770; (907) 874-3785 FAX
Theresa Thibault, Director/Curator
Hours: winter: Tue–Fri 10:00–4:00;
    summer: Mon–Fri 10:00–5:00, Sat
    1:00–5:00
(over 3,000 photos relating to Wrangell
    and the immediate surrounding area)
search fees: $5.00 minimum, $10.00 per
    hour after the first half-hour; photo
    reproduction fees vary

Yugtarvik Regional Museum
PO Box 388
Bethel, AK 99559
(907) 543-2098

Historical Societies— Local and Regional

Bristol Bay Historical Society
PO Box 36
Naknek, AK 99633
(907) 246-4406
John Knutsen, President

Chilkat Valley Historical Society
c/o Sheldon Museum and Cultural Center
(11 Main Street, just above boat
    harbor—location)
PO Box 269 (mailing address)
Haines, AK 99827
(907) 766-2366; (907) 766-2368 FAX
E-mail: sheldmus@seaknet.alaska.edu
Jim Heaton, President
Hours: Museum: winter: Mon, Wed &
    Sun 1:00–4:00, Tue & Thur–Fri 3:00–
    5:00; summer: daily 1:00–5:00
Pub. *Chilkat Valley Historical Society
    Newsletter*, quarterly
$10.00 per year membership for
    individuals, $20.00 per year
    membership for families, $100.00 life
    membership; museum admission:
    $3.00

Circle District Historical Society, Inc.
Circle District Museum
Mile 127 Steese Highway
PO Box 1893
Central, AK 99730
(907) 520-1893
Hannelore Wilde, Secretary
Hours: Memorial Day–Labor Day: noon–
    5:00
Pub. *Newsletter*, annually
(mining history, gold display 1893–
    1950+)
$5.00 per year membership for
    individuals, $1.00 per year
    membership for children (under 14
    years), free membership for senior
    citizens (over 70 years)

Cook Inlet Historical Society
Anchorage Museum of History and Art
121 West Seventh Avenue
Anchorage, AK 99501
(907) 343-6189 (Archives); (907) 343-
    6149 FAX
http://www.ci.anchorage.ak.us
M. Diane Brenner, Museum Archivist
Hours: Museum: Mon–Fri 10:00–noon,
    afternoons by chance or appointment

Copper Valley Historical Society
Mile 101 Rich Highway
PO Box 84
Copper Center, AK 99573
(907) 822-5285
Fred T. Williams, President
Hours: Mon–Sat (1 Jun–1 Sept) 1:00–
    5:00

Cordova Historical Society, Inc.
First Street-Centennial Building
PO Box 391
Cordova, AK 99574
(907) 424-6665; (907) 424-6000 FAX
Cathy Sherman, Museum Director
Hours: Tue–Sat 1:00–5:00
Pub. *The Discoverer*, somewhat quarterly
(specializes in information on Cordova,
    Katalla, Kennicott, Prince William
    Sound)

$10.00 per year membership for individuals, $25.00 per year membership for families, $5.00 per year membership for students

Eagle Historical Society
(Third and Chamberlain—location)
PO Box 23 (mailing address)
Eagle City, AK 99738
(907) 547-2230; (907) 547-2232 FAX
E-mail: escott@aol.com
Elva Scott, President
Pub. *Eagle Wireless*, three times per year
$10.00 per year membership for individuals; research: $15.00 per hour

Kenai Historical Society, Inc.
PO Box 1348
Kenai, AK 99611
(907) 283-7618

Kodiak Historical Society
101 Marine Way
Kodiak, AK 99615
(907) 486-5920; (907) 486-3166 FAX
Marian Johnson, Director
Hours: winter 11:00–3:00 (five days); summer: Mon–Sun 10:00–4:00

Resurrection Bay Historical Society Museum
336 Third Avenue
PO Box 55
Seward, AK 99664
(907) 224-3902
Lee E. Poleske, President
Hours: 1 May–30 Sept: 10:00–5:00, and by appointment
Pub. *Resurrection Bay Historical Society Newsletter*, nine times per year
$10.00 per year membership

Sitka Historical Society
Isabel Miller Museum
330 Harbor Way
Sitka, AK 99835
(907) 747-6455
Dr. Orriene First Denslow
Hours: summer: daily 8:00–5:00; winter: Tue–Sat 10:00–4:00
Pub. *SHS Newsletter*
$25.00 per year membership for individuals, $35.00 per year membership for families, $10.00 per year Associate membership (out-of-town)

Talkeetna Historical Society
(First Alley and Village Airstrip—location)
PO Box 76 (mailing address)
Talkeetna, AK 99676
(907) 733-2487; (907) 733-2484 FAX
Alice Johannewes-Tobiason, Museum Coordinator
Hours: Jan & Dec: Sat 11:00–5:00; Feb–Mar & Oct–Nov: Sat–Sun 11:00–5:00; Apr & Sept: Fri–Sat 11:00–6:00, Sun 11:00–5:00; May–Aug: Mon–Sun 10:00–6:00

Pub. *Newsletter*, annually
(oral history projects, humanities research and projects, state and local history; books, documents, photos, scrapbooks and newspapers)
$10.00 per year regular membership, $2.00 per year charter membership, $100.00 life membership; museum admission, Memorial Day–Labor Day: $1.00 for adult non-members (over 12 years of age)

Tanana-Yukon Historical Society
PO Box 71336
Fairbanks, AK 99707
(907) 455-TYHS
E-mail: tyhs@polarnet.com
http://www2.polarnet.com/ tyhs/
Renee Blahuta, President
Pub. *TYHS Newsletter*, monthly, $12.00 per year subscription
(local history/historic preservations)
$10.00 per year membership for individuals (includes newsletter), $15.00 per year membership for families, $50.00 per year Contributing membership, $200.00 life membership

Valdez Historical Society, Inc.
"Archives Alive"
(705 North Glacier Drive—location)
PO Box 6 (mailing address)
Valdez, AK 99686
(907) 835-4367
Dorothy I. Clifton, Director
Hours: 9:00–5:00
(Valdez from earliest dates)
$5.00 per year membership

Wasilla-Knik-Willow Creek Historical Society
323 Main Street
Wasilla, AK 99687
(907) 376-2005
Dorothy Page, President

LDS Family History Centers

Anchorage
(907) 277-8433

Wasilla
(907) 376-9774

Genealogical Societies

State Genealogical Society

Alaska Genealogical Society
7030 Dickerson Drive
Anchorage, AK 99504

Regional Genealogical Societies

Anchorage Genealogical Society
PO Box 212265
Anchorage, AK 99521-2265
(907) 337-6377
Elizabeth J. Blair, President
Pub. *Newsletter*, monthly; *Quarterly* (August, November, February, May)
$15.00 per year membership for individuals, $25.00 per year membership for families

Fairbanks Genealogical Society
PO Box 60534
Fairbanks, AK 99706-0534
http://www.polarnet.com/users/fgs
Gigi Lemoine, President; Susan Gibson, Vice President; Charity Delana, Corresponding Secretary
Hours: meetings: fourth Thur 7:00 P.M.– 9:00 P.M.
Pub. *The Taproot*, nine times per year (monthly, September–May)
$15.00 per year membership; search fees vary

Forget-Me-Not Genealogical Society
(705 North Glacier Drive—location)
PO Box 6 (Secretary-Treasurer's mailing address)
PO Box 830 (Board Member's mailing address)
Valdez, AK 99686
(907) 835-4367 (Secretary-Treasurer); (907) 835-4451 (Board Member)
Dorothy I. Clifton, Secretary-Treasurer; Minnie La Page, Board Member
Hours: 9:00–5:00
$5.00 per year membership

Gastineau Genealogical Society
3270 Nowell Avenue
Juneau, AK 99801
(907) 586-3695
O. R. Kent, President
no membership dues

Kenai Totem Tracers
Kenai Community Library
163 Main Street Loop
PO Box 4380
Kenai, AK 99611
(907) 283-4378
Emily Deforest
Hours: Mon–Thur 8:30–8:00, Fri–Sat 8:30–5:00

Genealogical Society of Southeast Alaska
PO Box 6313
Ketchikan, AK 99901
Hours: monthly meetings
Pub. *Genealogical Society of Southeast Alaska Newsletter*, monthly
$15.00 per year membership

Wrangell Genealogical Society
PO Box 928EP
Wrangell, AK 99929

Independent Publications and Miscellany

AkGenWeb
Part of U.S. GenWeb Project
E-mail: ak@usgenweb.com
http://www.rootsweb.com/ akgenweb/
(links to other Alaska resources)

Alaska State Museum
395 Whittier Street
Juneau, AK 99801-1718
(907) 465-2901
E-mail: brucek@educ.state.ak.us
http://ccl/alaska.edu/local/museum/home/
    html
Bruce Kato, Chief Curator
Hours: summer (mid-May to mid-Sept)
    Mon–Fri 9:00–6:00, Sat–Sun 10:00–
    6:00; winter: Tue–Sat 10:00–4:00
admission up to $3.00

Ghosts of the Klondike Gold Rush
Pan for Gold Database
http://gold-rush.org

ARIZONA

Archives and Libraries with Holdings in Genealogy

State Archives and Library

Arizona Department of Library, Archives and Public Records
State Capitol
1700 West Washington
Phoenix, AZ 85007
(602) 542-3942; (602) 542-4500 FAX
E-mail: archive@dlapr.lib.az.us
http://www.dlapr.lib.az.us
James Lovell, Genealogy Librarian
Hours: Mon–Fri 8:00–5:00 (closed state
    holidays)
(national scope)

State Historical Societies

Arizona Historical Society
949 East Second Street
Tucson, AZ 85719
(520) 617-1157; (520) 628-5695 FAX
E-mail: azhist@azstarnet.com
Riva Dean, Library/Archives
    Co-manager
Hours: Mon–Fri 10:00–4:00, Sat 10:00–
    1:00
Pub. *Journal of Arizona History*,
    quarterly
$40.00 per year membership

Arizona Historical Society— Flagstaff Branch
North Fort Valley Road
Rt. 4, Box 705
Flagstaff, AZ 86001
(520) 774-6272

Arizona Historical Society/Pioneer Museum
2340 North Fort Valley Road
Flagstaff, AZ 86001
(520) 774-6272
Joseph M. Meehan, Director; Bonnie
    Greer, Archivist
Hours: Mon–Sat 9:00–5:00; Archives,
    Cline Library Special Collections,
    Northern Arizona University: Mon–Fri
    8:00–5:00, Sat 10:30–1:00
$25.00 per year membership (includes
    the Arizona Historical Society's
    Journal of Arizona History)

Arizona Historical Society—Yuma Branch
Century House Museum
240 South Madison Avenue
Yuma, AZ 85364
(520) 782-1841
Megan Reid, Director; Carol Brooks,
    Curator

Hours: Museum: Tue–Sat 10:00–4:00;
    Library: by appointment
Pub. *Newsletter*, bimonthly
("Lower Colorado River, including Yuma
    County, Arizona, southeast Imperial
    County, California, and Sonora,
    Mexico; we have photos, maps, family
    histories, voter registers, tax records,
    business directories, phone books,
    coroner's records, high school
    yearbooks.")
$40.00 per year membership (includes
    the Arizona Historical Society's
    Journal of Arizona History)

City, County and Regional Archives and Libraries

The Arizona Historical Foundation
Charles Trumbull Hayden Library,
    Fourth Floor
Arizona State University
Tempe, AZ 85287
(602) 966-8331; (602) 965-3283
E-mail: archives@asuvm.inre.asu.edu
Dr. Evelyn Cooper, Director
(research facility and archives; primary
    and secondary sources for Arizona and
    southwest history)
$20.00 per year membership for
    individuals, $45.00 per year
    membership for families, $10.00 per
    year membership for students, $200.00
    per year membership for corporations

Bisbee Mining and Historical Museum
5 Copper Queen Plaza
PO Box 451
Bisbee, AZ 85603
(520) 432-7071

Flagstaff City-Coconino County Public Library
300 West Aspen Avenue
Flagstaff, AZ 86001
(520) 779-7670; (520) 774-9573 FAX
Kay Whitaker, Public Services Manager
Hours: Mon–Thur 10:00–9:00, Fri
    10:00–7:00, Sat 10:00–6:00, Sun
    noon–7:00
(extensive U.S. genealogy collection of
    1,500 volumes, and Arizona research
    collection of 11,000 volumes; also
    City of Flagstaff Archives of 300
    cubic feet)

Fort Lewis College
(see Colorado)

Mohave Museum of History and Arts
400 West Beale Street
Kingman, AZ 86401
(520) 757-2019
Norma Bailey, Director
(genealogical services)

Mojave River Valley Museum Association
(see California)

Phoenix Museum of History
105 North Fifth Street
Phoenix, AZ 85004
(602) 253-2734
Cindy Myers, Executive Director
Hours: Wed–Sun 11:00–4:00
Pub. *Phoenix Museum of History Newsletter*, quarterly
$15.00–$1,000.00 per year membership

Phoenix Public Library—Central Library
Arizona Room
1221 North Central Avenue
Phoenix, AZ 85004
(602) 262-4636
Fay Freed, Arizona Room Librarian
Hours: Library: Mon–Wed 9:00–9:00,
Thur–Sat 9:00–6:00, Sun 1:00–5:00;
Arizona Room: Tue 5:00–9:00, Wed &
Sat 10:00–6:00
(materials on Arizona; James H.
McClintock Collection)
fee-based research available at library
through Facts To Go

Prescott Public Library
215 East Goodwin
Prescott, AZ 86303
(520) 445-8110
Toni Kaus, Assistant Director
Hours: Mon & Fri–Sat 9:00–5:30, Tue–
Thur 9:00–9:00

Saint Michaels Historical Museum
PO Box 680
Saint Michaels, AZ 86511
(520) 871-4172

Scottsdale Public Library
3839 Civic Center Plaza
Scottsdale, AZ 85251
(602) 994-2476; (602) 994-2320
Becky Henry, Reference Coordinator
Hours: Mon–Thur 10:00–9:00, Fri–Sat
10:00–6:00, Sun 1:00–5:00

State Capitol Museum
Arizona Department of Library, Archives
and Public Records
1700 West Washington
Phoenix, AZ 85007
(602) 542-4675 (Museum Division);
(602) 542-4690 FAX
E-mail: micarma@dlapr.lib.az.us
Michael D. Carman, Museum Division
Director
(no genealogy function)

Sun City Library
16828 99th Avenue
Sun City, AZ 85351

Tempe Historical Museum
809 East Southern Avenue
Tempe, AZ 85282
(602) 350-5100

Scott Solliday, Curator of History
Hours: Mon–Thur 10:00–5:00
(Tempe and Arizona history)
photocopies: 10¢ per page

Historical Societies— Local and Regional

Apache County Historical Society
180 West Cleveland
PO Box 146
Saint Johns, AZ 85936
(520) 337-4737; (520) 337-2000 FAX
Ethel Smith, Director/Curator
Hours: Mon–Fri 9:00–5:00, and by
appointment
$5.00 per year membership for
individuals, $10.00 per year
membership for families

Arizona Archaeological and Historical Society
Arizona State Museum, University of
Arizona
Tucson, AZ 85721
(520) 621-3656
Tobi Taylor, Editor
Pub. *Kiva: The Journal of Southwestern
Anthropology and History*, quarterly
(archaeology, anthropology, history)
$40.00 per year membership for
individuals, $30.00 per year
membership for students

Arizona Historical Society, Central Division
1300 North College
Tempe, AZ 85281
Andrew E. Masich, Director

Casa Grande Valley Historical Society, Inc.
110 West Florence Boulevard
Casa Grande, AZ 85222
Craig Ringer, Executive Director
Hours: Mon–Fri 9:00–noon
Pub. *Historical Happenings*, one to two
times per month

Chandler Historical Society
Chandler Museum
178 East Commonwealth Avenue
PO Box 926
Chandler, AZ 85244
(602) 786-2842

Chloride Historical Society
PO Box 294
Chloride, AZ 86431
(520) 565-3619
Joyce Herbst, President

Cochise County Historical and Archaeological Society
1116 G Avenue
PO Box 818
Douglas, AZ 85607

(520) 364-5226
Cindy Hayostek, President
Hours: 2:00–4:00, and some mornings by
appointment
Pub. *Cochise County Historical and
Archaeological Society Newsletter*,
irregularly; *Cochise Quarterly*
$15.00 per year membership

Eastern Arizona Museum and Historical Society
(2 North Main Street—location)
PO Box 274 (mailing address)
Pima, AZ 85543
(520) 485-9400
Edres Bryant Barney, Curator/Manager
Hours: Wed–Fri 2:00–4:00, Sat 1:00–
5:00
$5.00 per year membership, $100.00 life
membership

El Paso County Historical Society
(see Texas)

Gila County Historical Society
1330 North Broad Street
PO Box 2891
Globe, AZ 85501
(520) 425-7385
W. A. Haak, President
Hours: Mon–Fri 10:00–4:00
$25.00 per year membership

Glendale Arizona Historical Society
PO Box 2544
Glendale, AZ 85301

Graham County Historical Society
808 Eighth Avenue
Safford, AZ 85546

Jerome Historical Society
200 Main Street
PO Box 156
Jerome, AZ 86331
(520) 634-1066; (520) 634-7349
Jeannette Duke, Director
Hours: Museum: Mon–Fri 9:00–5:00
Pub. *Chronicle*, quarterly
(history of town of Jerome)
$15.00 per year membership for
individuals, $25.00 per year
membership for families, $50.00 per
year membership for businesses,
$100.00 per Patron membership,
$500.00 per year Benefactor
membership

Maricopa County Historical Society
21 North Frontier Street
PO Box 1446
Wickenburg, AZ 85358
(520) 684-2272
Cheryl A. Taylor, Director
Hours: Mon–Sat 10:00–4:00, Sun 1:00–
4:00

Mohave County Historical Society
Library Archives
400 West Beale Street
Kingman, AZ 86401

(520) 753-3195
Mona Cochran and Karin Goudy, Library
    Staff
Hours: Mon & Fri 10:00–4:00

Navajo County Historical Society
Holbrook Branch Museum
100 East Arizona
Holbrook, AZ 86025
(520) 524-6558
Garnette Franklin, Museum Director/
    President
Pub. *NCHS Newsletter*

Northern Arizona University
Center for Colorado Plateau Studies
PO Box 5613
Flagstaff, AZ 86011
(520) 523-2562

Oracle Historical Society, Inc.
Acadia Ranch Museum
PO Box 10
Oracle, AZ 85623
(520) 896-9609; (520) 896-9037
    (President)
Evaline J. Auerbach, President
Hours: Sat 1:00–5:00, except holidays

Pimeria Alta Historical Society
(126 Grand Avenue, Nogales, AZ
    85621—location)
PO Box 2281 (mailing address)
Nogales, AZ 85628-2281
(520) 287-4621
Patricia B. Molina, Museum
    Administrator
Hours: Museum: Fri 10:00–5:00, Sat
    10:00–4:00, Sun 1:00–4:00; Office:
    Mon–Fri 9:00–5:00

Pinal County Historical Society, Inc.
Pinal County Historical Society Museum
715 South Main Street
PO Box 851
Florence, AZ 85232
Alma Yost, Conservator
Hours: Wed–Sun (1 Apr–31 Oct) 12:00–
    4:00; Wed–Sun (1 Dec–31 Mar)
    11:00–4:00
Pub. *Our Heritage*, monthly
("Extensive research library for Pinal
    County")
$8.00 per year membership for
    individuals, $15.00 per year
    membership for couples, $100.00 life
    membership for individuals, $150.00
    life membership for couples

Prescott Historical Society
Sharlot Hall Museum
415 West Gurley
Prescott, AZ 86301
(520) 445-3122
http://www.bslnet.com/accounts/jclraig/
    www/sharlot.html
Michael Wurtz, Archivist
Hours: Tue–Fri 10:00–5:00
Pub. *New Directions*, bimonthly; *Cactus
    on a Pine*, annually
$20.00 per year membership for
    individuals

**San Pedro Valley Arts and Historical
Society**
(180 South San Pedro Street—location)
PO Box 1090 (mailing address)
Benson, AZ 85602
(520) 586-2844
Lucille Kowalczyk, President
Hours: winter: Tue–Sat 10:00–4:00;
    May–Sept: Tue–Sat 10:00–2:00
(artifacts and history of Benson and the
    San Pedro Valley in southeast Arizona)
$10.00 per year membership

Scottsdale Historical Society, Inc.
Scottsdale Historical Museum
(7333 Scottsdale Mall, Scottsdale, AZ
    85251—location)
PO Box 143 (mailing address)
Scottsdale, AZ 85252
(602) 945-4499
JoAnn Handley, Secretary
Hours: Sept–Jun: Wed–Sat 10:00–5:00,
    Sun noon–4:00
Pub. *Scottsdale Historical Society
    Newsletter*, five times per year
(artifacts, documents and photographs
    about the history of Scottsdale and the
    surrounding area)

Sun Cities Area Historical Society
10801 Oak Mont Drive
Sun City, AZ 85351
(602) 974-2568
Jane Freeman
Hours: Tue–Sat 1:30–3:30
("limited to Sun Cities area")

**Superstition Mountain Historical
Society**
PO Box 1535
Apache Junction, AZ 85220

Tubac Historical Society
PO Box 3261
Tubac, AZ 85646
(520) 398-2919

**White Mountain Historical Society
and Historical Park**
PO Box 12
Springerville, AZ 85938
(520) 333-3322
Ginger Williams, President

**LDS Family History
Centers**

Casa Grande
(520) 836-7519

Flagstaff
(520) 774-2930

Mesa
(602) 964-1200

Phoenix
(see Mesa)

Prescott
(520) 778-2311

Safford
(520) 428-7927

Sun City
(602) 974-2749

Tucson
(520) 298-0905

Yuma
(520) 782-6364

Genealogical Societies

**State Genealogical
Societies**

Genealogical Society of Arizona
Hobson
Tempe, AZ 85282
(602) 964-1200
Pub. *Genealogical Society of Arizona
    Quarterly*
$10.00 per year membership

Arizona Society of Genealogists
6565 East Grant Road
Tucson, AZ 85715

Arizona State Genealogical Society
PO Box 42075
Tucson, AZ 85733-2075
(520) 885-7714 FAX
http://www.goodnet.com/
    ~eb43571.asgs.html
Ann Day, President
Pub. *Copper State Journal*, quarterly
$19.00 per year membership (beginning
    1 July)

Family History Society of Arizona
PO Box 63094
Phoenix, AZ 85082-3094
E-mail: jeannie@getnet.com
http://www.getnet.com/charity/fhs
Pub. *Family Connections*, quarterly
$15.00 per year membership

**Regional Genealogical
Societies**

Apache Genealogy Society
Sierra Vista Public Library
Maria Bishop Room
PO Box 1084
Sierra Vista, AZ 85636-1084
(520) 458-7770
Bonnie Temple Blackwell, President
(specializes in Tombstone, Arizona and
    Cochise County marriages; how to do
    Hispanic research)
Pub. *The Genealogist*, quarterly
$5.00 per year membership

Cochise Genealogical Society

(Douglas Williams House, 1001 D
Avenue, Douglas, AZ 85607—
office/library location)
PO Box 68 (mailing address)
Pirtleville, AZ 85626
(520) 364-3372 (Library Director); (520)
364-8297 (President)
Natalie Orozco, Library Director; Joan
Findlay, President
Hours: Wed 9:00–4:00, Thur & Sun
1:00–4:00, and by appointment
Pub. *Tombstone*, semiannually
(specializes in southwest Arizona and
Cochise County)
$7.50 per year membership for
individuals, $10.00 per year
membership for families; free queries
for members; no search fee for limited
research for members

Genealogical Workshop of Mesa, Inc.

PO Box 6052
Mesa, AZ 85206-6052
(602) 985-0250 (recorded message);
(602) 985-0250 (Statutory Agent)
Doris Miller-Redwine, Statutory Agent
Hours: mid-Sept to mid-May: second &
fourth Fri 8:15–11:45
$12.00 per year membership for
individuals, $15.00 per year
membership for couples

Green Valley Genealogical Society

PO Box 1009
Green Valley, AZ 85622
(520) 625-3065
Lou Anne Bunnel, Secretary
Hours: meetings at Church of Jesus Christ
of Latter-day Saints, 17699 Comino de
la Quintas, Schuarite, AZ: Oct–Apr
Pub. *Past Tracks*, quarterly
$10.00 per year membership

Lake Havasu Genealogical Society, Inc.

(2283 Holly Drive—location)
PO Box 953
Lake Havasu City, AZ 86405-0953
(520) 855-7105; (520) 855-3607
E-mail: wb7alo@juno.com
Gloria Harrington, Acting Librarian
Hours: Library: Wed 1:00–5:00, Thur
9:00–1:00; meetings: third Fri 7:00
Pub. *Newsletter*, three times per year
(local cemetery listings; member
surname cards)
$15.00 per year membership

Mohave County Genealogical Society

400 West Beale Street
Kingman, AZ 86401

Northern Arizona Genealogical Society

PO Box 695
Prescott, AZ 86302
(520) 776-8745

E-mail: jony@goodnet.com
John Paulsen, Editor
Hours: Sharlot Hall Museum: Tue–Fri
9:00–4:00
Pub. *The Bulletin*, quarterly
$12.00 per year membership for
individuals, $20.00 per year
membership for couples; search fee:
on contract basis with individual
members

Northern Gila County Genealogical Society, Inc.

(708 South Ponderosa Street, Payson, AZ
85541—location)
PO Box 952 (mailing address)
Payson, AZ 85547-0952
(520) 474-0747 (Thur–Sat 1:00–4:00)
Lettie B. Cole, President
Hours: Oct–Apr: Thur–Sat 1:00–4:00;
May–Sept: 9:00–noon
Pub. *Gila Heritage*, quarterly, $8.00 per
year subscription
$10.00 per year membership

Ohio Genealogical Society

Arizona Chapter
(see Ohio)

Phoenix Genealogical Society

6220 North 35th Drive
Phoenix, AZ 85019
(602) 841-0739
Frances Hortsch, President

Sedona Genealogy Club

PO Box 4258
Sedona, AZ 86340
Pub. *Newsletter*, nine times per year
(monthly January–June & September–
November)
$10.00 per year membership for
individuals, $15.00 per year
membership for families

Sun Cities Genealogical Society

(12600 113th Avenue, Suite C-6,
Youngtown—library location)
PO Box 1448 (mailing address)
Sun City, AZ 85372-1448
(602) 933-4945; (602) 974-3415
(Administrator)
Lorraine Menich, Library Administrator
Hours: Tue & Thur–Fri 9:00–4:00, Sat
9:00–noon
Pub. *Sun City Genealogist Quarterly*;
Tidbits, nine times per year (monthly,
September–May)
("frequent genealogical workshops;
computer-use groups")
$20.00 per year membership for
individuals, $25.00 per year
membership for families

Tri-State Genealogical Society

PO Box 6045
Mohave Valley, AZ 86440

Genealogical Society of Yuma, Arizona

3117 West 17th Street
PO Box 2905
Yuma, AZ 85364
(520) 783-7982 (President's home)
Earl Mathews, President
Hours: Family History Center: Tue &
Wed 9:00–4:00 & 6:30–9:00, Thur
6:30–9:00, Fri–Sat 9:00–1:00
Pub. *Newsletter*, four to six times per
year
(specializes in Germans to America,
index of local newspaper, *Arizona
Sentinel*, 1872–1899)
$10.00 per year membership for
individuals, $5.00 per year
membership for spouse

Independent Publications and Miscellany

AzGenWeb

Part of U.S. GenWeb Project
E-mail: az@usgenweb.com
http://www.rootsweb.com/ azgenweb/
(links to other Arizona resources)

Center for Southwest Research

(see New Mexico)

State Board on Geographic and Historic Names

Arizona Department of Library, Archives
and Public Records
State Capitol
1700 West Washington
Phoenix, AZ 85007
E-mail: aznames@dlapr.lib.az.us

University of Arizona Press

1230 North Park Avenue, Suite 102
University of Arizona
Tucson, AZ 85721
(520) 621-2484
Karen E. Seger, Managing Editor (JSW)
Pub. *Journal of the Southwest* (multi-
disciplinary, southwest U.S. and
northern Mexico), quarterly; *Arizona
Quarterly*, $6.00 per issue
$18.00 per year membership for
individuals, $24.00 per year
membership for institutions, additional
$3.00 per year for all foreign mailings

Tucson Corral of the Westerners

(1937 East Blacklidge Drive, Tucson, AZ
85719—office location)
4968 East South Regency Circle (mailing
address)
Tucson, AZ 85711-3040
(520) 745-2793; (520) 745-2830 FAX
Maurice F. Guptill, Editor
Hours: meetings: first Mon (Oct–May),
second Mon (Sept)

Pub. *Smoke Signal*, semiannually, $2.00
for the first copy, 50¢ for each
additional copy
(the southwest)
$10.00 per year corresponding
membership (calendar year)

ARKANSAS

Archives and Libraries with Holdings in Genealogy

State Archives and Library

Arkansas History Commission
1 Capitol Mall
Little Rock, AR 72201
(501) 682-6900
http://www.state.ar.us:80/ahc/index.htm
John L. Ferguson, State Historian
Hours: Mon–Sat 8:00–4:30
(Arkansas history and genealogy)

Arkansas State Library
Department of Education
1 Capitol Mall
Little Rock, AR 72201-1081
(501) 682-1527
http://www.state.ar.us/html/
ark_library.html
John A. Murphy, Jr., State Librarian

State Historical Society

Arkansas Historical Association
Department of History, Old Main #416
University of Arkansas
Fayetteville, AR 72701
(501) 575-5884
Jeannie M. Whayne, Secretary-Treasurer
and Editor; Gretchen Gearhardt,
Assistant Editor
Hours: 8:00–4:30
Pub. *Arkansas Historical Quarterly*;
*Arkansas Historical Association
Newsletter*, quarterly
(no library, archives or research staff,
specializes in "Arkansas and the
region")
$16.00 per year membership, $30.00 for
two-year membership

City, County and Regional Archives and Libraries

Arkadelphia Public Library
609 Caddo Street
Arkadelphia, AR 71923

Arkansas State University Museum
Museum/Library Building
PO Box 490
Jonesboro, AR 72467-0490
(870) 972-2074; (870) 972-2793
E-mail: cjones@choctaw.astate.edu
Charlott Jones, Ph.D., Director
Hours: Mon–Fri 9:00–4:00, Sat–Sun
1:00–4:00
Pub. *A Different Drummer*, two times per
year

(specializes in Arkansas history and
American Indians)
$25.00 per year membership for
individuals, $40.00 per year
membership for families

Ashley County Library
211 East Lincoln
Hamburg, AR 71646-3217
(870) 853-2078; (870) 853-2079 FAX
Henrietta Thompson, Director
Hours: Mon–Fri 9:00–5:30

Bentonville Public Library
125 West Central
Bentonville, AR 72712

Boone County Public Library
221 West Stephenson Street
Harrison, AR 72601
(870) 741-5913
MariLyn Smith, Genealogy
Hours: Tue–Wed & Fri–Sat 10:00–5:00,
Thur 10:00–7:00

Booneville Public Library
419 North Kennedy
Booneville, AR 72927
(501) 675-2735; (501) 675-2735 FAX
Patricia L. Curry, Librarian
Hours: Mon 11:00–7:00, Tue–Thur 9:00–
5:00
(Logan County history and genealogy)
search fee: $3.00 plus copies and postage

**Richard C. Butler, Sr. Center For
Arkansas Studies**
Central Arkansas Library System
100 Rock Street
Little Rock, AR 72201
(501) 918-3056
E-mail: arkinfo@fones.cals.lib.ar.us
http://www.cals.lib.ar.us
Tom W. Dillard, Curator of Special
Collections; Timothy G. Nutt, Deputy
Curator of Special Collections
Pub. *Arkansian* (journal), *Butler Center
Banner* (newsletter)

Central Arkansas Library System
100 Rock Street
Little Rock, AR 72201
(501) 370-5952; (501) 375-7451 FAX
E-mail: arkansas@fones.cals.lib.ar.us;
timn@fones.cals.lib.ar.us
Timothy G. Nutt, Arkansiana Librarian
Hours: Mon–Tue & Thur 9:00–8:00,
Wed & Fri–Sat 9:00–6:00
(Arkansas and southern states)

Corning Library
613 Pine Street
Corning, AR 72422
(870) 857-3453 phone and FAX
Hours: Mon–Tue & Thur 9:00–6:00,
Wed & Fri 9:00–5:00

Crowley Ridge Regional Library
Craighead County-Jonesboro Public
Library
Information Services
315 West Oak Avenue
Jonesboro, AR 72401

(870) 935-5133; (870) 935-7987 FAX
Hours: Mon 11:30–8:30, Tue–Fri 9:30–
6:00, Sat 9:30–5:00, Sun 1:00–5:00

Desha County Museum Society
Highway 165, East
PO Box 141
Dumas, AR 72639
(870) 382-4222

East Arkansas Community College
Forrest City, AR 72335-9598

Fayetteville Public Library
Grace Keith Genealogy Collection
217 East Dickson Street
Fayetteville, AR 72701
(501) 442-2242; (501) 442-5723 FAX
Mary Jo Godfrey, Chief Genealogical
Librarian
Hours: Library: Mon–Sat 9:00–5:00;
Genealogy Department: Mon–Sat
9:00–5:00
(microfilm of federal censuses, Arkansas
1830–1920, all states 1910 and 1920;
4,000 microfilms and 10,000 books
focus on Arkansas and states on
migration trails to Arkansas)
correspondence search fee: $2.50 per hour,
limit two hours, plus 25¢ per copy

Fort Smith Public Library
61 South Eighth Street
Fort Smith, AR 72901
(501) 783-0229
http://www.fspl.lib.ar.us
Sheila M. Brushes, Genealogy Librarian
Hours: Genealogy Room: Mon & Wed–
Sat 9:00–5:30, Tue 9:00–9:00
research: $10.00 per hour (minimum
$5.00 in advance), copies 25¢ per page
from paper original, 50¢ per page from
microform original

The Gann Museum of Saline County
218 South Market Street
Benton, AR 72015
(501) 778-5513
Mrs. Ike Sharp, Director
Hours: Tue–Sat 10:00–2:00, Sun 1:30–
4:00
Pub. *Newsletter*
(genealogical services)

Hacksma House Genealogy Library
(see Washington)

Hempstead County Library
Fifth and Elm Streets
Hope, AR 71801
(870) 777-4564
Judy Sooter, Librarian
Hours: Mon noon–9:00, Tue–Fri 9:00–
5:30, Sat 9:00–noon

**S. S. Lipscomb Arkansas History
and Genealogy Room**
Northeast Arkansas Regional Library
Greene County Library
120 North 12th Street
Paragould, AR 72450

(870) 236-8711 (no extension in
genealogy room; no research queries
taken by phone, only basic questions
about holdings); (501) 236-1442 FAX
http://www.cswnet.com/ michael/
greene.html
Kitty Sloan
Hours: Library: Mon–Thur 9:00–7:00,
Fri–Sat 9:00–5:00; Lipscomb Room
open same hours as library but not
always staffed, usually staffed by
volunteers 1:00–4:00
(extensive section on Greene County
with census, marriage and tombstone
indexes, family and community
histories, and local newspapers on
microfilm; rest of collection focuses
on Arkansas and southeastern states
from which early settlers migrated,
especially Tennessee)
queries regarding indexed materials will
be answered by volunteers from the
Greene County Historical and
Genealogical Society as time permits
for SASE & copy costs at 20¢ per
page

Lum and Abner Museum
Highway 88
PO Box 38
Pine Ridge, AR 71966
(870) 326-4442 phone and FAX
E-mail: ns@hsnp.com
Kathryn Stucker, Owner/Operator
Hours: Mar 1–Nov 1: Tue–Sun 9:00–5:00

Lyon College
Regional Studies Center
Mabee Library
Batesville, AR 72501
(870) 698-4330
Nancy S. Griffith, Director
Hours: Mon–Fri 8:00–3:00
("Collection focuses on Arkansas history
and genealogy, particularly
Independence and neighboring
counties.")
free admission, photocopies 10¢ per page

Marianna-Lee County Museum
PO Box 584
Marianna, AR 72360
(870) 295-2469

Phillips County Library
Phillips County Museum
623 Pecan Street
Helena, AR 72342
(501) 338-3537; (501) 338-7732 FAX
E-mail: hplib@deltanet.org
Susan Hamilton, Helena Head Librarian
Hours: Mon–Sat 9:00–5:00

Piggott Public Library
361 West Main Street
Piggott, AR 72454
Gay Johnson, Librarian
Hours: Mon–Tue & Thur–Fri 9:00–5:00,
Sat 9:00–12:00

**Pine Bluff and Jefferson County
Public Library**
200 East Eighth Avenue
Civic Center Complex
Pine Bluff, AR 71601
(870) 534-4802
Hours: Mon–Sat 10:00–5:00

Pope County Library
Russellville Heritage Room
116 East Third
Russellville, AR 72801
(501) 968-4368
Katie Murdoch, Local History Librarian
Hours: Mon–Wed & Fri 8:30–5:30, Thur
1:00–8:30, Sat 8:30–noon

Randolph County Library
111 West Everett Street
Pocahontas, AR 72455-3316
(870) 892-5617; (870) 892-1142 FAX
Hours: Mon–Tue 10:00–7:00, Wed–Fri
9:00–5:00, Sat 10:00–2:00

Rector Public Library
PO Box 252
Rector Library
PO Box 252
Rector, AR 72461

Rogers Historical Museum
322 South Second Street
Rogers, AR 72756
(501) 621-1154
Gaye Bland, Director
Hours: Tue–Sat 10:00–4:00

Searcy County Museum
(Center—location)
PO Box 233 (mailing address)
Marshall, AR 72650
(870) 448-5786
Veda Clemons, Director
Pub. *Marshall Mountain Wave*

Shiloh Museum
118 West Johnson
Springdale, AR 72764
(501) 750-8165
Hours: Mon–Sat 10:00–5:00
(seven buildings, including 22,000
square foot main building)
free admission

**Southwest Arkansas Regional
Archives (SARA)**
Old Washington Historic State Park
PO Box 134
Washington, AR 71862
(870) 983-2633
Hours: Mon–Sun 9:00–4:00
$5.00 per year membership

Texarkana Museums System
(see Texas)

University of Arkansas
Special Collections Division
University of Arkansas Libraries
Mullins Library
Fayetteville, AR 72701-1201

(501) 575-5577; (501) 575-6656 FAX
http://www.uark.edu/campus-resources/
    libinfo/ (Library); http://
    cavern.uark.edu/libinfo/speccoll/
    index.html (Special Collections
    Division)
Andrea Cantrell, Head of Research
    Services
Hours: Mon–Fri 8:00–5:00, Sat 9:00–
    1:00 (hours vary at holidays and
    between semesters)
Pub. *Books and Letters*, semiannually
$25.00 per year membership in Friends
    of the Library; no extensive search
    services

**University of Central Arkansas
Archives and Special Collections**
Torreyson Library
Conway, AR 72032
(501) 450-3418
http://www2.uca.edu/archives/main-
Tom W. Dillard, Director
Hours: Mon–Fri 8:00–5:00
(Faulkner County genealogy)

Van Buren County Library
(Highway 65—location)
Rt. 6, Box 193 (mailing address)
Clinton, AR 72031
(501) 745-5860
Karla Fultz, Branch Manager
Hours: Mon 9:00–7:00, Tue–Fri 9:00–
    5:00, Sat 9:00–3:00
(microfilm and a few publications put
    out by historical society)

Historical Societies— Local and Regional

**Arkansas River Historical Society
Museum**
(see Oklahoma)

Ashley County Historical Society
Museum
300 North Cherry Street
Hamburg, AR 71646
(870) 853-5796
J. Edward White, Chairman

**Baxter County Historical and
Genealogical Society**
1505 Mistletoe
Mountain Home, AR 72653
(870) 425-0405
http://www.geocities.com/Athens/2101/
    bchgs.htm
Margie Garr
Pub. *Baxter County History*, quarterly
$10.00 per year membership for
    individuals, additional $2.50 per year
    membership for spouse

**Bella Vista Historical Society and
Museum**
1885 Bella Vista Way
Bella Vista, AR 72714

(501) 855-2335
Durand Young, President
Hours: Mar–Nov: daily 1:00–4:00
Pub. *BVHSM Newsletter*, bimonthly
    (February, April, June, August,
    October, December)
$10.00 per year membership; no research
    help except on Bella Vista topics

Benton County Historical Society
400 South Walton Boulevard
PO Box 1034
Bentonville, AR 72712
(501) 273-3890
Win Logue, President
Hours: Mon, Wed & Fri 1:30–4:00
Pub. *Benton County Pioneer*, quarterly
$10.00 per year membership for
    individuals (calendar year), $15.00 per
    year Contributing membership, $25.00
    per year Sustaining membership,
    $100.00 life membership after age 65

**Boone County Historical and
Railroad Society, Inc.**
Boone County Heritage Museum
Corner of Central and Cherry
PO Box 1094
Harrison, AR 72601
(870) 741-3312
Virginia Phillips, Corresponding
    Secretary for Historical and Genealogy
    Affairs
Hours: Mon–Fri 10:00–4:00 (Mar–Nov);
    Thur 10:00–4:00 (Dec–Feb)
Pub. *Boone County Historian*, quarterly
$15.00 per year membership; $2.00
    admission to museum

**Carroll County Historical Society
and Heritage Center**
1880 Court House
PO Box 249
Berryville, AR 72616
(870) 423-6312
Pub. *Carroll County Historical Society
    Quarterly*
$12.00 per year membership

Clark County Historical Society
Ouachita Baptist University
Riley-Hickingbotham Library
Special Collections
PO Box 516
Arkadelphia, AR 71923
(870) 245-5332
Wendy Richter, Archivist
Hours: Mon–Fri 8:00–4:00
Pub. *Clark County Historical Journal*,
    annually
$10.00 per year membership

Cleveland County Historical Society
PO Box 342
Rison, AR 71665

Craighead County Historical Society
PO Box 1011
Jonesboro, AR 72403-1011
(870) 935-6838

Mrs. Frank F. Sloan, Corresponding
    Secretary
Pub. *Craighead County Historical
    Quarterly* (January, April, July,
    October)
("History and some genealogies of
    Craighead County, formed 1859 from
    Greene, Mississippi, and Poinsett
    counties.")
$10.00 per year regular membership,
    $15.00 per year Contributing
    membership, $25.00 per year
    Corporate membership, $200.00 life
    membership, $500.00 Permanent
    membership; queries free to members,
    $7.00 to non-members

Crawford County Historical Society
PO Box 1317
Van Buren, AR 72956
(501) 474-2218
Doris West, President
Pub. *The Heritage*, annually
$10.00 per year membership

**Crittenden County Historical
Society, Inc.**
401 Gibson
West Memphis, AR 72301
(870) 735-1659
Melanie Newton Sims, Past President

Cross County Historical Society
(Cross County Courthouse, 705 East
    Union—office location)
PO Box 943 (mailing address)
Wynne, AR 72396-0943
Mrs. Jimmie S. James, Secretary
Hours: Mon–Fri 11:00–4:00
("Census records of Cross County,
    histories, newspaper files for past and
    present Cross County")
$4.00 per year membership

Drew County Historical Society
404 South Main
Monticello, AR 71655
Roy A. Grizzell, Ph.D., Chairman of the
    Board
Pub. *Drew County Historical Journal*

Faulkner County Historical Society
PO Box 731
Conway, AR 72032
Pub. *Faulkner County Historical Society
    Newsletter*, quarterly; *Faulkner Facts
    and Fiddlings*, quarterly
$10.00 per year membership

Fort Smith Historical Society, Inc.
c/o Fort Smith Public Library
61 South Eighth Street
Fort Smith, AR 72901
(501) 783-1237
Amelia Martin, Editor
Hours: Library, Genealogy Room: Mon
    & Wed–Sat 9:00–5:30, Tue 9:00–9:00
Pub. *Journal*, semiannually
$15.00 per year membership

Garland County Historical Society
222 McMahan Drive
Hot Springs, AR 71913-6243
(501) 623-6766 phone and FAX
E-mail: bsmclane@direclynx.net
Bobbie Jones McLane, Editor
Hours: Tue & Thur 8:00–noon, and by
appointment
Pub. *The Record*, annually
(primarily Hot Springs and Garland
County)
$17.00 per year membership

Grand Prairie Historical Society
203 South Monroe Street
DeWitt, AR 72042
Ellen West, Editor
*Grand Prairie Historical Society
Bulletin*, semiannually

**Greene County Historical and
Genealogical Society**
120 North 12th Street
Paragould, AR 72450
(870) 239-4328 (President)
Frances Morris, President
Hours: Greene County Library: Mon–
Tue 9:00–8:00, Wed–Sat 9:00–5:00; S.
S. Lipscomb Arkansas History and
Genealogy Room open same hours as
library but not always staffed, usually
staffed by volunteers 1:00–4:00
Pub. *The Greene County Historical and
Genealogical Quarterly*; *The GCHGS
Newsletter*, nine times per year
(monthly September-May)
$20.00 per year membership for families,
$35.00 Sponsor and Corporate
membership; indexed material
researched: cost of photocopies plus
postage

**Hempstead County Historical
Society**
PO Box 1257
Hope, AR 71802-1257
(870) 777-2491 (Editor)
E-mail: turnermn@arkansas.net
Mary Nell Turner, Treasurer-Editor
Pub. *The Journal of the HCHS*, annually
$10.00 per year membership; some
search service

**Hot Spring County, Arkansas,
Historical Society**
PO Box 674
Malvern, AR 72104
(501) 337-7488
Bonnie J. Stanley, Past President
Hours: Hot Spring County Public
Library: 8:30–5:00, until 8:30 on
certain evenings
Pub. *The Heritage*, annually, $22.50
postpaid per issue for non-members
(specializes in Hot Springs County,
Arkansas, history and genealogy)

**Independence County Historical
Society**
201 Library Building
PO Box 2036
Batesville, AR 72501
(870) 793-2383
A. C. McGinnis, Editorial Committee;
Wilson Powell, Secretary-Treasurer
Hours: 8:00–4:00
Pub. *The Independence County
Chronicle*, quarterly
$10.00 per year membership

**The Izard County Historical and
Genealogical Society**
PO Box 306
Pineville, AR 72566
Juanita Stowers, Editor
Pub. *The Izard County Historian*,
quarterly (January, April, July,
October)
$15.00 per year membership for
individuals and spouse (calendar year),
$200.00 life membership for
individuals; queries and surnames
researching for members

Jackson County Historical Society
7 Pickens Street
Newport, AR 72112
(870) 523-5150
Wayne Boyce, Editor
Hours: 9:00–5:00
Pub. *Stream of History*, quarterly
(specializes in Jackson County history)
$10.00 per year membership, $25.00 per
year Patron membership

Johnson County Historical Society
PO Box 505
Clarksville, AR 72830
(501) 754-8539
Annita M. Powell, Editor
Hours: Johnson County Library: Mon
1:30–8:30, Tue–Fri 9:30–5:30, Sat
9:00–noon
Pub. *Johnson County Historical Society
Journal*, semiannually (April and
October)
$15.00 per year membership

Lafayette County Historical Society
(201 Hope Road, Stamps, AR 71860—
location)
PO Box 91 (mailing address)
Lewisville, AR 71845
(870) 921-4785
Eugene D. Smith, President
Pub. *Lafayette Lookback*, semiannually
$7.00 per year membership

Lawrence County Historical Society
PO Box 93
Powhatan, AR 72458
Pub. *Lawrence County Historical
Journal*, semiannually
$10.00 per year membership

Logan County Historical Society
PO Box 40
Magazine, AR 72943
Patricia L. Curry, Secretary
Pub. *Wagon Wheels*, quarterly; *LCHS
Newsletter*, monthly
$15.00 per year membership; search fee:
$3.00 plus copies

Lonoke County Historical Society
PO Box 14
Lonoke, AR 72086
(501) 676-6988 (Ruby Gagliano)
Pub. *Lonoke County Historical Society
Newsletter*, three times per year
$10.00 per year membership

**Madison County Genealogical and
Historical Society**
(corner of Highway 74 West and
Mitchusson Park Road—location)
PO Box 427 (mailing address)
Huntsville, AR 72740
(501) 738-6408
Joy Russell, Treasurer
Hours: 10:00–3:00
Pub. *The Madison County Musings*,
quarterly
$12.50 per year membership

**Marion County, Arkansas, Historical
and Genealogical Society**
Marion County Library
PO Box 554
Yellville, AR 72687

**Montgomery County Historical
Society**
(Highway 270—location)
PO Box 520 (mailing address)
Mount Ida, AR 71957
(870) 867-3121
Debbie Baldwin, President
Hours: various
(updating county cemetery records)
$10.00 per year membership

**Nevada County Depot Museum
Association**
400 West First Street, South
PO Box 10
Prescott, AR 71857
(870) 887-5821
http://wolfden.swsc.k12.ar.us/
depot_museum
J. W. Teeter and Mrs. Jim Miner, Board
Members
Hours: Mon–Fri 10:00–noon & 2:00–
5:30
Pub. *News Letter—Events & Projects*,
quarterly
(family histories [written and audio
tapes], cemetery records 1790–1950,
photographs, letters, documents,
school and church histories, Civil War
Battle of Prairie De Ann; some
material online)
$10.00 per year membership; SASE for
information, no fees

Newton County Historical Society/ Bradley House Museum

(corner of Clark and Daniel Street— location)
PO Box 360 (mailing address)
Jasper, AR 72641
(870) 446-6247
Diana Nelson, Secretary-Hostess
Hours: Mon–Fri 1:00–5:00
Pub. *Newton County Historical Society Newsletter*, quarterly
$10.00 per year membership (calendar year); hourly charge for research

Ouachita County Historical Society

926 Washington, N.W.
Camden, AR 71701
Pub. *Ouachita County Historical Society Quarterly*
$12.00 per year membership

Phillips County Historical Society

Helena Public Library
623 Pecan Street
Helena, AR 72342
(870) 338-3271; (870) 338-3481
Ivey S. Gladin and Nancee James, Editors
Hours: Library: Mon–Sat 9:00–5:00
Pub. *Phillips County Historical Review*, semiannually (spring and fall), $5.00 per issue plus mailing
(history of eastern Arkansas)
$10.00 or $15.00 per year membership

Pope County Historical Association

4200 A Street
Little Rock, AR 72205-4046
(501) 663-3301
Elaine Weir Cia, Editor
Pub. *Pope County Historical Quarterly*
$10.00 per year membership

Pope County Historical Foundation (Pottsville)

c/o Pope County Library
Russellville Heritage Room
116 East Third
Russellville, AR 72801
(501) 968-4368
Katie Murdoch, Local History Librarian
Hours: Russellville Heritage Room: Mon–Wed & Fri 8:30–5:30, Thur 1:00–8:30, Sat 8:30–noon

Prairie County Historical Society

PO Box 451
Hazen, AR 72064
(870) 255-4522

Saline County Historical Commission

The Gann Museum of Saline County
218 South Market Street
Benton, AR 72015
(501) 778-5513
Ann Wheat Bryan, Librarian, Saline County History and Heritage Society, Bryant, AR
Hours: Tue–Sat 10:00–2:00, Sun 1:30–4:00

Pub. *Newsletter: The Gann Museum of Saline County*, quarterly

Saline County History and Heritage Society, Inc.

PO Box 221
Bryant, AR 72022-0221
(501) 847-0402; (501) 778-5513 (Library)
Eddie G. Landreth, Editor; Ann Wheat Bryan, Librarian
Hours: Library: The Gann Museum, Benton, Arkansas: Tue–Sat 10:00–2:00, Sun 1:30–4:00
Pub. *The Saline*, quarterly
$15.00 per year membership

Scott County Historical and Genealogical Society

(West Second Street—location)
PO Box 1560 (mailing address)
Waldron, AR 72958-1560
(501) 637-2466
Betty Leeper, President
Hours: Mon 10:00–5:00
Pub. *Echoes*, four times per year
(publishes Scott County records: census, marriages, obituaries, etc.)

Sevier County Historical Society

717 Maple Street
PO Box 288
DeQueen, AR 71832
(870) 642-6642 (Museum)
June King, Museum Director
Hours: Tue–Sat 10:00–4:00, Sun 2:00–4:00
Pub. *Sevier County Historical Society Newsletter*, about quarterly
$5.00 per year membership

Sharp County Historical Society

PO Box 185
Ash Flat, AR 72513
(870) 257-2323
Rose Thompson, Secretary
Hours: not open to the public
Pub. *Sharp County Historical Society Newsletter*, quarterly
(historical events, towns and people; "We answer what queries we can, or point them in the direction of someone who may be able to help them.")
$10.00 per year membership (includes *Newsletter* and any new *Journal* published)

South Sebastian County Historical Society

PO Box 523
Greenwood, AR 72936
Roger W. McConnell, Secretary-Treasurer
Pub. *The Key*
$10.00 per year membership

Southern Studies Institute

(see Louisiana)

Stone County Historical Society

PO Box 284
Mountain View, AR 72560

Pub. *Heritage of Stone*, semiannually
$6.00 per year membership

Van Buren County Historical Society

PO Box 1023
Clinton, AR 72031-1023
Wilda Jones, President
Hours: Mon–Fri 10:00–4:00
Pub. *Van Buren County Historical Journal*, quarterly
$10.00 per year membership

Washington County Historical Society

118 East Dickson Street
Fayetteville, AR 72701
(501) 521-2970
Ann Sugg, President
Hours: usually Thur 1:00–4:00, Sat 10:00–noon (call to confirm hours)
Pub. *Flashback & Flashforward*, quarterly
(specializes in Fayetteville, Washington County, and northwest Arkansas books and products)
$15.00 per year membership for individuals (calendar year), $25.00 per year membership for families; research requests referred to Genealogy Section, Fayetteville Public Library

White County Historical Society

PO Box 537
Searcy, AR 72143
(501) 268-8726
Cloie Presley
Pub. *White County Heritage*, annually
$12.00 per year membership; queries accepted

White River Valley Historical Society

(see Missouri)

Yell County Arkansas Historical and Genealogical Association

PO Box 622
Dardanelle, AR 72834
Pub. *Yell County Historical and Genealogical Association Bulletin*, quarterly
$10.00 per year membership

LDS Family History Centers

Fort Smith
(501) 484-5373

Jacksonville
(501) 985-2501

Little Rock
(501) 455-4998

Rogers
(501) 636-8090

Genealogical Societies

State Genealogical Society

Arkansas Genealogical Society, Inc.
(1411 Shady Grove Road, Hot Springs,
AR 71901—shipping location)
PO Box 908 (mailing address)
Hot Springs, AR 71902-0908
(501) 262-4513 (phone or FAX)
Margaret Harrison Hubbard, Editor
Pub. *Arkansas Family Historian*,
quarterly
$15.00 per year membership (calendar
year)

Regional Genealogical Societies

Ancestors Unknown
PO Box 164
Conway, AR 72033
(501) 329-2868 (weekdays); (501) 329-
3404 (evenings); (501) 329-3093 FAX
E-mail: evatt@cswnet.com
Linda Evatt, Treasurer
Hours: meetings at Faulkner County
Library, 1900 Tyler, Conway, AR:
second Mon 6:30
Pub. *Ancestors Unknown Newsletter*,
monthly
$15.00 per year membership for
individuals, $20.00 per year
membership for couples

**Ark-La-Tex Genealogical
Association, Inc.**
Randle T. Moore Senior Citizen Center
PO Box 4462
Shreveport, LA 71134-0462
(318) 868-0036 (President)
E-mail: aga@softdisk.com
http://www.softdisk.com/comp/aga
Reed Mathews, President
Hours: meetings at the Randle: second
Sat (Sept–Jul) 1:00
Pub. *The Genie*, quarterly
(Arkansas, Louisiana and Texas)
$12.50 per year membership for
individuals, $15.00 per year
membership for husband and wife

Ashley County Genealogical Society
PO Drawer R
Crossett, AR 71635
(501) 364-2885
Mary Spainhour, President
Pub. *Kin Kollecting*, quarterly, $6.50
postpaid per issue; *News, Etc.*,
monthly
$20.00 per year membership for families,
$150.00 life membership

Batesville Genealogical Society
PO Box 3883
Batesville, AR 72503-3883

Pub. *Bits of Bark from the Family Tree*,
quarterly
$10.00 per year membership

**Baxter County Historical and
Genealogical Society**
1505 Mistletoe
Mountain Home, AR 72653
(870) 425-0405
http://www.geocities.com/Athens/2101/
bchgs.htm
Margie Garr
Pub. *Baxter County History*, quarterly
$10.00 per year membership for
individuals, additional $2.50 per year
membership for spouse

**Carthage Genealogical Society and
Southwest Missouri Genealogical
Library**
(see Missouri)

Clay County Genealogy Club
Piggott Public Library
361 West Main Street
Piggott, AR 72454
(870) 598-3666 FAX
Gay Johnson, Librarian; Camilla Cox,
Editor
Hours: Library: Mon–Tue & Thur 9:00–
6:00, Wed & Fri 9:00–5:00; meetings:
fourth Sun 2:00
Pub. *Quarterly Newsletter*
$7.00 per year membership (calendar
year)

**Crawford County Genealogical
Society**
(314 Fayetteville Street—location)
PO Box 276 (mailing address)
Alma, AR 72921
Lucille Titsworth, President
Hours: Tue & Thur 9:00–3:00
Pub. *Panning for Nuggets of Old*, two
times per year (spring and fall)
$15.00 per year membership

**Crowley's Ridge Genealogical
Society**
14515 Wunderlich Drive, #211
Houston, TX 77069-2614
Mr. Hames

**Frontier Researchers Genealogical
Society**
PO Box 2123
Fort Smith, AR 72902-2123
Sherrell Buchanan, Corresponding
Secretary
Hours: Fort Smith Public Library,
Genealogy Room: Mon & Wed–Sat
9:00–5:30, Tue 9:00–9:00
Pub. *Frontier Research*, annually
(emphasis on Oklahoma and Arkansas)
$15.00 per year membership

**Greene County Historical and
Genealogical Society**
120 North 12th Street
Paragould, AR 72450
(870) 239-4328 (President)

Frances Morris, President
Hours: Greene County Library: Mon–
Tue 9:00–8:00, Wed–Sat 9:00–5:00; S.
S. Lipscomb Arkansas History and
Genealogy Room open same hours as
library but not always staffed, usually
staffed by volunteers 1:00–4:00
Pub. *The Greene County Historical and
Genealogical Quarterly*; *The GCHGS
Newsletter*, nine times per year
(monthly September–May)
$20.00 per year membership for families,
$35.00 Sponsor and Corporate
membership; indexed material
researched: cost of photocopies plus
postage

**Hempstead County Genealogical
Society**
PO Box 1158
Hope, AR 71801
Pub. *Hempstead Trails*, semiannually
$10.00 per year membership

**The Heritage Seekers Genealogical
Club**
William F. Laman Public Library
2800 Orange Street
North Little Rock, AR 72114
Arlene Ryan, Secretary
Hours: fourth Mon 7:00 P.M.–9:00 P.M.
$5.00 per year membership

Howard County Heritage Club
218 West Howard Street
Nashville, AR 72852
John Reuther

**The Izard County Historical and
Genealogical Society**
PO Box 306
Pineville, AR 72566
Juanita Stowers, Editor
Pub. *The Izard County Historian*,
quarterly (January, April, July,
October)
$15.00 per year membership for
individuals and spouse (calendar year),
$200.00 life membership for
individuals; queries and surnames
researching for members

**Jefferson County Genealogical
Society**
PO Box 2215
Pine Bluff, AR 71613

**Madison County Genealogical and
Historical Society**
(corner of Highway 74 West and
Mitchusson Park Road—location)
PO Box 427 (mailing address)
Huntsville, AR 72740
(501) 738-6408
Joy Russell, Treasurer
Hours: 10:00–3:00
Pub. *The Madison County Musings*,
quarterly
$12.50 per year membership

Marion County, Arkansas, Historical and Genealogical Society
Marion County Library
PO Box 554
Yellville, AR 72687

Melting Pot Genealogical Society
(223A Hazel Street—location)
PO Box 936
Hot Springs National Park, AR 71901
(501) 624-0229 (Library); (501) 767-5831 (Librarian)
Barbara Stainback, Librarian
Hours: Mon, Fri & second Sat 10:00–2:00, second & 4th Mon 4:30–8:00; meetings at Garland County Library, Williams Hall: fourth Tue (Sept–May) 1:30
Pub. *The Melting Pot Genealogical Society Quarterly* (April and November)
$15.00 per year membership

Northeast Arkansas Genealogical Association
North Central Arkansas Genealogical Society
314 Vine Street
Newport, AR 72112
Pub. *Arkansas Genealogical Register*, quarterly

Northwest Arkansas Genealogical Society
(400 South Walton, Bentonville, AR—location)
PO Box 796 (mailing address)
Rogers, AR 72757
(501) 273-3890
Mary Crabtree, Corresponding Secretary
Hours: Tue–Sat 10:00–4:00
Pub. *The Backtracker*, quarterly
(Benton, Washington, Madison and Carroll counties)
$12.50 per year membership (calendar year)

Ouachita-Calhoun Genealogical Society
PO Box 2092
Camden, AR 71701
(870) 836-5083 (Library)
Hours: Tue–Fri 9:30–5:30, Sat 9:00–12:00
Pub. *Researchin' Ouachita-Calhoun Counties, Arkansas*, semiannually
$10.00 per year membership

Polk County Genealogical Society
PO Box 12
Hatfield, AR 71945
Pub. *Polk County Genealogical Society Quarterly*
$12.00 per year membership

Sevier County Genealogical Society, Inc.
717 North Maple Street
PO Box 288
DeQueen, AR 71832

Pub. *Footprints*, quarterly
$12.00 per year membership; no research services

Southwest Arkansas Genealogical Society
523 East Union
Magnolia, AR 71753
Pub. *SO-WE-AR*, semiannually (Columbia County)
$7.50 per year membership

Stone County Genealogical Society
PO Box 1477
Mountain View, AR 72560

Texarkana U.S.A. Genealogy Society
(see Texas)

Tri-County Genealogical Society
(Davidson Civic Center, 406 South Midway Street—location)
PO Box 580 (mailing address)
Marvell, AR 72366-0580
(870) 829-2772
E-mail: r_c_white@deltanet.org.
Rose White, Treasurer; Carrie Davison, Librarian
Hours: Library: Thur 1:00–4:00, Sun 2:00–5:00
Pub. *Tri-County Genealogy*, three times per year, $5.00 per issue
(Monroe, Lee and Phillips counties)
$15.00 per year membership for individuals, $20.00 per year membership for families, $150.00 life membership; queries accepted

Union County Genealogical Society
Barton Library
200 East Fifth
El Dorado, AR 71730
(870) 863-5447; (870) 862-3944 FAX
Nancy Arn, Librarian
Hours: Mon, Wed & Fri 9:30–5:30, Tue & Thur 1:00–9:00, Sat 1:00–5:00
Pub. *Tracks and Traces*, semiannually
$10.00 per year membership for individuals, $15.00 per year membership for families

Yell County Arkansas Historical and Genealogical Association
PO Box 622
Dardanelle, AR 72834
Pub. *Yell County Historical and Genealogical Association Bulletin*, quarterly
$10.00 per year membership

Independent Publications and Miscellany

ArGenWeb
Part of U.S. GenWeb Project
E-mail: ar@usgenweb.com

http://www.rootsweb.com/ argenweb; http://bl-12.rootsweb.com/~argenweb/ (links to other Arkansas resources)

Arkansas Ancestors
222 McMahan Drive
Hot Springs, AR 71913-6243
(501) 623-6766 phone and FAX
E-mail: bsmclane@direclynx.net
Bobbie Jones McLane, Publisher
Hours: daily 8:00–4:00
(books on Arkansas and Alabama)

Arkansas Department of Heritage Services
1500 Tower Building
Little Rock, AR 72201
(501) 324-9150; (501) 324-9154 FAX
E-mail: info@dah.state.ar.us
http://www.heritage.state.ar.us/ dahhome.html

Arkansas Genealogical Research
805 East Fifth Street
Russellville, AR 72801
(501) 967-7792
E-mail: rsnorris@cswnet.com
Rhonda S. Norris, C.G.R.S.
("Arkansas research, specializing in Pope County, Arkansas")

Arkansas Internet Project
http://www.compnetar.com/~billc/

Arkansas Municipal League
PO Box 38
North Little Rock, AR 72115
(501) 374-3484; (501) 374-0541
E-mail: hhamner@aristotle.net
http://www.aiea.ualr.edu/dina/mleague/ publications/publications.html

Arkansas Records Association
314 Vine Street
Newport, AR 72112
Pub. *Arkansas Record Survey*, three times per year

Arkansas Research
PO Box 303
Conway, AR 72033
(501) 470-1120 phone and FAX
E-mail: desmond@intellinet.com
http://biz.ipa.net/arkresearch/
Desmond Walls Allen, Editor
(publishes death record indexes, census transcriptions, county records, military records, family histories, marriage records, newspaper abstracts, etc.)
free catalog

Counts Genealogical Research and Publishing
3812 Glenmere Road
North Little Rock, AR 72116
Pub. *Arkansas Genealogical Research Aid*, irregularly

Elk River Current
(see Missouri)

Genealogical Institute
(see Virginia)

Genealogy Books and Consultation
(see Texas)

**Hunting for Bears Genealogical and
Historical Society**
(see Alabama)

The Looking Glass
PO Box K
Murfreesboro, AR 71958
Pub. *The Looking Glass* (Ouachita),
monthly, $12.00 per year subscription

Mountain Press
(see Tennessee)

The Old Time Chronicle
PO Box 15
Antoine, AR 71922
Karron Cot, Editor
Hours: 8:00–5:00
Pub. *The Old Time Chronicle* (Pike
County; folk history), bimonthly,
$14.50 per year in-state subscription,
$16.00 per year out-of-state
subscription, $22.00 (U.S.) per year
Canadian subscription

Pike County Archives
RR 1, Box 443
Delight, AR 71940
DeWayne Gray, President

**Professional Genealogists of
Arkansas, Inc.**
PO Box 1807
Conway, AR 72033
(501) 470-1120 phone and FAX
E-mail: desmond@intellinet.com
http://biz.ipa.net/arkresearch/
Desmond Walls Allen, Editor
Pub. *Arkansas Historical and
Genealogical Magazine*, bimonthly
(odd-numbered months)
("PGA is a loose network of
genealogists, family historians,
researchers, teachers, librarians,
archivists, publishers, and
professionals interested in promoting
the field of genealogy in Arkansas.")
$12.00 per year membership

*Searcy County Ancestor Information
Exchange*
2333 East Oaks Drive
Fayetteville, AR 72703
(501) 442-3691
E-mail: johnston@ipa.net
James J. Johnston
Pub. *Searcy County Ancestor
Information Exchange*, bimonthly,
$10.00 per year subscription
(beginning in June)
(sponsors North Arkansas Ancestor Fair)

Seeking Your Heritage
4511 North Schaer Street
PO Box 2074

North Little Rock, AR 72115-2074
(501) 758-8351 phone and FAX
Arlene Ryan, Editor/Publisher
Hours: Mon–Fri 8:00–5:00
Pub. *Seeking Your Heritage*, quarterly
(October, January, April, July), $15.00
per year subscription

**Southern Genealogist's Exchange
Society**
(see Florida)

CALIFORNIA

Archives and Libraries with Holdings in Genealogy

State Archives and Libraries

California State Archives
Office of the Secretary of State
1020 "O" Street
Sacramento, CA 95814
(916) 653-2246; (916) 653-7363 FAX
E-mail: archivesweb@ss.ca.gov
http://www.ss.ca.gov/archives/
archives_home.htm
John F. Burns, Director, Archives and
Museum
Hours: Mon–Fri 9:30–4:00
photocopies: 25¢ per page

California State Library
California History Room
(900 N Street, Room 200, Sacramento,
CA 95814—location)
PO Box 942837 (mailing address)
Sacramento, CA 94237-0001
(916) 654-0174 (Library); (916) 654-
0176 (California History Room); (916)
654-8777 FAX
E-mail: cslcal@library.ca.gov
Kathleen A. Correia, Supervising
Librarian
Hours: Mon–Fri 9:30–4:00
Pub. *New Arrivals in Californiana* (a
selected guide to sources for
genealogy in the California History
Section), irregularly, free
list of private researchers available

Sutro Library
Branch of the California State Library
480 Winston Drive
San Francisco, CA 94132-1777
(415) 731-4477; (415) 557-0421; (415)
557-9325 (Card Catalog)
http://nick.sfpl.lib.ca.us/gencoll/
gencolsu.htm
Clyde Janes, Director; Frank Glover,
Reference Librarian
Hours: Library: Mon–Fri 10:00–5:00
(collection covers whole U.S.)

State Historical Societies

California Historical Society
678 Mission Street
San Francisco, CA 94105
(415) 357-1848, ext. 10; (415) 357-1850
FAX
E-mail: info@calhist.org
http://www.calhist.org
Judith Deaton, Director of Operations
Hours: Library: by appointment only;
Other: Tue–Sat 11:00–5:00

Pub. *California Chronicle*, quarterly; *California History*, quarterly
$40.00 per year membership; library use: $5.00 for non-members

Conference of California Historical Societies
University of the Pacific
Stockton, CA 95211
(209) 946-2169; (209) 946-2578 FAX
Ronald Limbaugh, Executive Director
Hours: 8:30 A.M.–12:30 P.M.
Pub. *California Historian*, quarterly, $20.00 per year subscription
$25.00 per year Associate membership for individuals or out-of-state organizations or area associations, $35.00 per year Associate membership for two adults at the same address, $10.00 per year Associate membership for students (under age 20), $15.00 per year Associate membership for young historian organizations, $300.00 Associate life membership for individuals, beginning at $25.00 per year Active membership for societies

City, County and Regional Archives and Libraries

The American Victorian Museum
325 Spring Street
PO Box 328
Nevada City, CA 95959
(530) 265-5804
David S. Osborn, President
(not primarily genealogical)

Anderson Valley Historical Museum
Highway 128 North
PO Box 676
Boonville, CA 95415
(707) 895-3207

Arcadia Public Library
20 West Duarte Road
Arcadia, CA 91006
(626) 821-5567; (626) 447-8050 FAX
Mary Beth Hayes, Librarian
Hours: Mon–Thur 10:00–9:00, Fri–Sat 10:00–6:00
(Arcadia history)

Archival Center
The Diocese of Los Angeles
15151 San Fernando Mission Boulevard
Mission Hills, CA 91345
(818) 365-1501; (818) 365-3276 FAX
Kevin Feeney, Adjunct Archivist and Records Manager
Hours: Mon–Fri 8:30–4:30

Mary M. Arron Memorial Museum Association
704 D Street
Marysville, CA 95901
(530) 743-1004

Auburn-Placer County Library
350 Nevada Street
Auburn, CA 95603
(530) 889-4111
James R. Hickson, Reference Librarian
Hours: Mon & Thur 10:00–6:00, Tue & Wed 10:00–8:00, Fri–Sat 10:00–5:00
(Placer County history; genealogy department within the library organized and operated by Placer County Genealogical Society)

Autry Museum of Western Heritage
4700 Western Heritage Way
Los Angeles, CA 90027-1462
(213) 667-2000; (213) 666-9030 FAX
Joanne D. Hale, President and CEO
Hours: Tue–Sun 10:00–5:00
Pub. *Spur* (not primarily genealogical, emphasis on the history and myth of the American West)

R. C. Baker Memorial Museum, Inc.
297 West Elm Street
Coalinga, CA 93210
(209) 935-1914
Helen Cowan, Curator
Hours: Mon–Fri 10:00–noon & 1:00–5:00, Sat 11:00–5:00, Sun 1:00–5:00

Beale Library
Genealogical Room
701 Truxtun Avenue
PO Box 2214
Bakersfield, CA 93303
Hours: Mon–Sat 1:00–4:00
(houses Kern County Genealogical Society's collection of books, microfiche and periodicals)

Bruggemeyer Memorial Library
City of Monterey Park
318 South Ramona Avenue
Monterey Park, CA 91754
(626) 307-1368; (626) 288-4251
http://www.mcls.org/bin/entity/41
Dana Lubow, Reference/Adult Services
Hours: Mon–Tue 12:00–9:00, Wed 10:00–9:00, Thur–Fri 10:00–6:00, Sat 9:00–5:00
Pub. *Footnotes*, quarterly

Butte County Library
1820 Mitchell Avenue
Oroville, CA 95966
(530) 538-7642
Nancy Brower
Hours: Tue & Sat 10:00–5:00, Wed 2:00–9:00, Thur 2:00–5:00, Sat 10:00–4:00

Calaveras County Archives
(Fricot Building, 46 North Main Street—location)
PO Box 1281 (mailing address)
San Andreas, CA 95249
(209) 754-6513
Lorrayne Kennedy, Archivist

Hours: Mon & Thur–Fri 8:30–4:30 by appointment
(early Goldrush history, 1852–present, Calaveras County; many official records not previously available for research)
research: $10.00 per hour plus copies and postage

California Heritage Museum
2612 Main Street
Santa Monica, CA 90405
(310) 392-8537
Tobi Smith, Director
Hours: Wed–Sat 11:00–4:00, Sun 10:00–4:00
(archives/library, historical decorative arts exhibitions)

California History Center Foundation
21250 Stevens Creek Boulevard
Cupertino, CA 95014
(408) 864-8712; (408) 864-5486 FAX
Kathi Peregrin, Director
Hours: Mon–Thur 8:30–noon & 1:00–4:30
Pub. *The Californian*, three times per year
$30.00 per year membership; $3.00 daily archive admission fee for non-students or non-members

California State University
Meriam Library, Special Collections
First and Hazel Streets
Chico, CA 95929-0295
(530) 898-5710
http://www.csuchico.edu
William A. Jones, Head
Hours: Mon–Fri (Sept–Dec & Feb–May) 9:00–3:00
(northeastern California archives)

California State University, Fresno
Special Collections Department
Henry Madden Library
Fresno, CA 93740
E-mail: specialc@listserv.csufresno.edu
http://duchess.lib.csufresno.edu/specialcollections/english collection.html
June English, Local History and Genealogy Collection

California State Univeristy, Los Angeles, Library
5151 State College Drive
Los Angeles, CA 90032

California State University, Northridge
Special Collections Department
Oviatt Library, Room 4
Northridge, CA 91330-1600
(818) 677-2832
E-mail: tgardner@csun.edu
http://www.csun.edu/ spcoll/ hbspcoll.html

California State University, Stanislaus
Library
801 West Monte Vista Avenue
Turlock, CA 95382
(209) 667-3233; (209) 667-3164 FAX
E-mail: bsantos@toto.csustan.edu
http://www.library.csustan.edu
Bob Santos, University Archivist
Hours: Library: Mon–Thur 7:30–11:00,
Fri 7:30–5:00, Sat 9:00–5:00, Sun
1:00–9:00; Archives: Mon–Fri 8:00–
5:00
(regional history; CSUS history)

Campbell Historical Museum
51 North Central Avenue
Campbell, CA 95008
(408) 866-2119
Peggy R. Coats, Historical Resources
Supervisor

Carlsbad City Library
1250 Carlsbad Village Drive
Carlsbad, CA 92008-1991
(760) 434-2931
http://www.compuology.com/nsdcgs/
Everett B. Ireland, President
Hours: Mon–Thur 9:00–9:00, Fri–Sat
9:00–5:00
(36,000 volumes, genealogy and local
history collection)

Carmichael Regional Library
Capital Area Joint Genealogical Library
Genealogy Room
5605 Marconi Avenue
Carmichael, CA 95608
(916) 483-6055
Mary Pitts, Librarian, Root Cellar;
Lorraine Lineer, Librarian, Genealogical
Association of Sacramento
Hours: Mon & Thur 12:00–9:00, Tue
10:00–9:00, Wed 10:00–6:00, Fri &
Sat 1:00–5:00

Catalina Island Museum Society, Inc.
Cassino Building
1 Casino Way
PO Box 366
Avalon, Santa Catalina Island, CA 90704
(310) 510-2414
http://www.catalina.com/museum.html
Patricia Anne Moore, Director/Curator

Chabot College
South County Community College District
25555 Hesperian Boulevard
Hayward, CA 94545
(510) 786-6764; (510) 786-6600
Hours: Mon–Thur 7:45–10:00, Fri 7:45–
5:00, Sat 9:30–2:00

Chaffey Communities Cultural Center and Cooper History Museum
(525 West 18th Street and 217 East A
Street—location)
PO Box 772 (mailing address)
Upland, CA 91785-0772

(909) 982-8010
http://www.culturalcenter.org
Max A. van Balgooy, Curator
Hours: by appointment only
Pub. *Record*, quarterly
("Records, photographs, and artifacts
related to Upland, Ontario, Rancho
Cucamonga, Montclair, Mount Baldy,
California, from 1880–1980; museum
and archive catalogue available on
History Database.")
$15.00 per year membership for
individuals; search fee: $25.00 per hour

City of San Buenaventura
PO Box 99
Ventura, CA 93002
(805) 654-7837

Clarke Memorial Museum, Inc.
240 East Street (at Third)
Eureka, CA 95501
(707) 443-1947
Raymond W. Hillman, Director/Curator
Pub. *Members News*

Colton Hall Museum and Old Monterey
Pacific Street Between Madison and
Jefferson
Monterey, CA 93940
(831) 375-9944
Donna Penwell, Museum Manager
Pub. *Historic Monterey* (not primarily
genealogical)

Columbia State Historic Park
PO Box 151
Columbia, CA 95310
(209) 532-4301
E-mail: sherrin@goldrush.com
http://www.sierra.parks.state.ca.us
Sherrin Grout, Ranger
Hours: 8:00–5:00
(collection includes documents on
nineteenth-century inhabitants)

Colusa County Free Library
738 Market Street
Colusa, CA 95932
(530) 458-7671; (530) 458-7358 FAX
Hours: Mon–Tue noon–5:00, Thur noon–
8:00, Fri 10:00–1:00

Compton Public Library
240 West Compton Boulevard
Compton, CA 90220
(310) 637-0202
Joanne N. Eldridge, Community Library
Manager
Hours: Mon–Tue noon–8:00, Wed 1:00–
8:00, Sat noon–5:00
("Our library is no longer the site of the
Black Resource Center, a.k.a. Afro-
American Resource Center. We still
carry a substantial amount of Black
titles, however they are general
interest and not necessarily for
scholarly research.")

Corona Public Library
Heritage Room
650 South Main Street
Corona, CA 91720-3417
(909) 736-2386; (909) 736-2499 FAX
http://www.ci.corona.ca.us/library/
index.htm
Gloria Freel, Heritage Room Librarian
Hours: Mon–Tue 5:00–9:00, Wed–Thur
& Sat 1:00–5:00
(Corona/Riverside County history books,
pamphlets and memorabilia; Southern
California history)
photocopies: 15¢ per page

Downey City Library
11121 Brookshire Avenue
Downey, CA 90241
(562) 904-7358
Maury McCord, Senior Librarian
Hours: Mon–Thur 10:00–8:00, Fri–Sat
10:00–5:00

Eastern California Museum
155 Grant Street
PO Box 206
Independence, CA 93526
(760) 878-0364; (760) 878-0258
William Michael, Director
Hours: Mon & Wed–Sun 10:00–4:00
(county subject and family history files,
regional reference library)

El Dorado County Library
345 Fair Lane
Placerville, CA 95667
(530) 621-5540; (530) 622-3911 FAX
E-mail: lib-pl@spider.lloyd.com
http://www.el-dorado.ca.us/ lib-pl/
welcome.shtml
Bonnie Battaglia, Reference Librarian
Hours: Mon–Wed 1:00–8:00, Thur–Sat
10:00–5:00
(California, gold rush era, local history)

El Dorado County Museum
104 Placerville Drive
Placerville, CA 95667
(530) 621-5865; (530) 621-6644 FAX
Denis Witcher, Director
Hours: Mon–Sat 10:00–4:00
(research library; probate, early court
records, naturalizations, voting
registers, county directories)
copies: 25¢ per page plus postage and
donation

El Segundo Public Library
111 West Mariposa Avenue
El Segundo, CA 90245
(562) 322-4121
Debra Brighton
Hours: Mon–Thur 9:00–9:00, Fri 9:00–
6:00, Sat 9:00–5:00

Eureka Humboldt County Library
1313 Third Street
Eureka, CA 95501-0533
(Humboldt County history)

Falkirk Community Cultural Center
Robert Dollar Estate
1408 Mission Street
PO Box 60
San Rafael, CA 94915
(415) 485-3328

Ferndale Museum, Inc.
Shaw and Third Streets
PO Box 431
Ferndale, CA 95536
(707) 786-4466 phone and FAX
Jerry Lesandro, Director
Hours: Tue (summer) 11:00–4:00, Wed–
Sat 11:00–4:00, Sun 1:00–4:00
("Ferndale Enterprise on microfilm 1878
to present, Ferndale Cemetery register
on microfilm.")
search fees: $7.50 per hour plus copy
costs

Fillmore Historical Museum
(350 Main Street, Fillmore, CA 93015—
location)
PO Box 314
Fillmore, CA 93016
(805) 524-0948; (805) 524-0516 FAX
Rochelee Mekinnon, Executive Director;
Ynez Haase, Historian
Hours: Mon–Fri 9:00–noon
Pub. *Newsletter*, quarterly
membership and research fees vary

Fortuna Depot Museum
3 Park Street
Fortuna, CA 95540
(707) 725-7645
http://www.springville.com/ fortuna/
museum.htm
Caroline Weed, Curator
Hours: Jun–Aug: Mon–Sun 9:00–4:30;
Sept–May: Wed–Sun noon–4:30
(research material: Fortuna, Eel River
Valley, Humboldt County)
free admission; research copies: 10¢
each

Fresno County Free Library
California History and Genealogy Room
2420 Mariposa
Fresno, CA 93721
(209) 488-3195
Linda Sitterding, County Historian
Hours: California History and Genealogy
Room: Mon–Wed & Fri noon–
6:00, Thur noon–8:00, Sat 10:00–5:00

**Friends of La Canada-Flintridge
Library**
4545 Oakwood Avenue
La Canada-Flintridge, CA 91011

City of Gilroy Historical Museum
195 Fifth Street
Gilroy, CA 95020
(408) 847-2685
Patricia Baldwin Snar, Director
(houses the South Santa Clara Valley
Archives)

Gold Discovery Museum—Marshall
Gold Discovery State Historic Park
310 Back Street
PO Box 265
Coloma, CA 95613
(530) 622-3470
Matthew S. Sugarman, Park
Superintendent
(collection includes diaries and letters of
gold rush pioneers)

Haggin Museum
Alameda May Petzinger Library of
Californiana
1201 North Pershing Avenue
Stockton, CA 95203-1699
(209) 462-4116
Tod Ruhstaller, Curator of History
Hours: Tue–Sat 1:30–4:30 by
appointment only

Harrison Memorial Library
Local History Department
Park Branch, Sixth at Mission
PO Box 800
Carmel, CA 93921
(831) 624-1615
Letitia Bennett, Archivist
Hours: Tue–Fri noon–4:00, and by
appointment
("Carmel, California history;
photographs, books, periodicals,
artwork, personal papers,
memorabilia")

**Holt-Atherton, Department of
Special Collections**
University of the Pacific Library
Stockton, CA 95211
(209) 946-2404
Daryl Morrison, Department Head
Hours: Mon–Fri 10:00–5:00
Pub. *Library Associates Newsletter*,
quarterly, $5.00 per year subscription

Homestead Museum
15415 East Don Julian Road
City of Industry, CA 91745-1029
(626) 968-8492; (626) 968-2048 FAX
E-mail: info@homesteadmuseum.org
http://homesteadmuseum.org
Karen Graham Wade, Director
Hours: Tours: Tue–Fri 1:00–4:00, Sat–
Sun 10:00–4:00, closed fourth
weekend and major holidays; group
tours by appointment
Pub. *Homestead*, quarterly, $5.00 per
year subscription; *San Gabriel Valley
Historian*, annually
(specializes in southern California,
California and U.S. from 1830–1930,
plus history of Workman and Temple
families)

The Honnold/Mudd Library
Special Collections
800 North Dartmouth Avenue
Claremont, CA 91711-3991
(909) 621-8045; (909) 621-8681

Jean Beckner, Special Collections
Librarian
Hours: Mon–Fri 9:00–noon & 1:00–5:00
(history only; serves as the central library
for the five undergraduate colleges and
the Claremont Graduate School;
genealogy is not a subject taught at
any of the colleges, so the library does
not collect in that area)

Humboldt State University Library
Humboldt County Collection
Arcata, CA 95521
(707) 826-3419
Erich F. Schimps, Special Collections
Librarian
Hours: Mon–Fri 9:00–5:00, Mon & Thur
6:00–9:00, Sun (during academic year)
1:00–5:00
(northwestern California, especially Del
Norte and Humboldt counties)

Huntington Beach Public Library
7111 Talbert Avenue
Huntington Beach, CA 92648-1296

Huntington Library
(address withheld upon request)
(historical collection; does not, as a
general policy, allow genealogists
access to the library)

Johnston House Foundation
Higgins-Purissima Road
PO Box 789
Half Moon Bay, CA 94019
(415) 641-9102

Jurnpa Mountains Cultural Center
7621 Granite Hill Drive
Riverside, CA 92509
(909) 685-5818

Kern County Museum
3801 Chester Avenue
Bakersfield, CA 93301
(805) 861-2132; (805) 322-6415 FAX
http://www.kruznet.com/kcmuseum/
Jeff Nickell, MA, Curator
Hours: General operating: Mon–Fri 8:00–
5:00, Sat 10:00–5:00, Sun noon–5:00
Pub. *Newsletter*, quarterly
(photograph collection of over 250,000
photo images, Kern County)
$50.00 per year membership; search fees
for photos only under $20.00 plus cost
of reproduction

Kings County Library
401 North Douty
Hanford, CA 93230
(209) 582-0261
Janet Harader, Head, Reference
Department
Hours: Mon–Wed 10:00–8:00, Thur
10:00–6:00, Fri–Sat noon–5:00

Klamath National Forest
1312 Fairlane Road
Yreka, CA 96097
(530) 842-6131

Gilbert W. Davies
(maintains historical research library)

Landmark Conservators
d.b.a. Cabot's Old Indian Pueblo
    Museum
67-616 East Desert View Avenue
PO Box 1267
Desert Hot Springs, CA 92240
(760) 329-7610
Colbert H. Eyraud, Curator
Hours: Oct–Jun: Wed–Sun 10:00–4:00;
    Jul–Sept: Sat–Sun 10:00–4:00
$20.00 per year membership for
    individuals, $35.00 per year
    membership for families, $10.00 per
    year membership for students

Lompoc Public Library
501 East North Avenue
Lompoc, CA 93436
(805) 736-3477; (805) 736-6440 FAX
E-mail: lref@rain.org
Hours: Mon–Wed noon–8:00, Thur
    10:00–8:00, Fri-Sun 1:00–5:00

Long Beach Public Library
101 Pacific Avenue (Ocean at Pacific
    Avenue)
Long Beach, CA 90822-1097
(562) 570-7500
Robert Brasher, Volunteer
Hours: Mon 10:00–8:00, Tue–Sat 10:00–
    5:30, Sun 12:00–5:00; volunteer
    hours: Wed & Sat 1:00–5:00
(2,700 books and other items;
    "Genealogical collection supported by
    Questing Heirs Genealogical
    Society.")

Los Angeles Public Library
History and Genealogy Department
630 West Fifth Street
Los Angeles, CA 90071
(213) 228-7400; (213) 228-7000 (to
    verify hours)
http:///www.lapl.org
Michael Kirley, Genealogy Librarian
Hours: Mon & Thur–Sat 10:00–5:30,
    Tue–Wed noon–8:00, Sun 1:00–5:00,
    hours subject to change

Marin County Library
Anne Kent California Room
Civic Center
San Rafael, CA 94903
(415) 499-7419
Jocelyn A. Moss
Hours: Mon & Wed–Fri 10:00–6:00, Tue
    10:00–8:30

**Mariposa Museum and History
Center, Inc.**
5119 Jessie Street
PO Box 606
Mariposa, CA 95338
(209) 966-2429
Muriel L. Powers, Curator/Executive
    Secretary

Hours: Nov–Dec & Feb: Sat–Sun 10:00–
    4:00; Mar–Oct: Mon–Sun 10:00–4:30
Pub. *Dear Charlie Letters*
    (49er local history)
$10.00 per year active membership,
    $5.00 per year membership for senior
    citizens, $25.00 per year membership
    for businesses or Patron membership,
    $150.00 life membership

Maturango Museum
100 East Las Flores
Ridgecrest, CA 93555
(760) 375-6900; (760) 375-0479 FAX
E-mail: matmus@ridgecrest.ca.us
http://www.ridgecrest.ca.us/ matmus/
Richard L. Senn, Administrator
Hours: Wed–Sun 10:00–5:00
Pub. *Maturango News*, eleven times per
    year
$30.00 per year membership for
    individuals, $40.00 per year
    membership for families, $25.00 per
    year membership for senior citizen
    individuals (age 55), $35.00 per year
    membership for senior citizen families,
    $10.00 per year membership to the
    Historical Society of the Upper
    Mojave Desert

Mendocino County Museum
Mendocino County Heritage Network
400 East Commercial
Willits, CA 95490
(707) 459-2736; (707) 459-7836 FAX
E-mail: museum@zapcom.net
Daniel Taylor, Director/Coordinator
Hours: Wed–Sun 10:00–4:30
(Mendocino County archives)

Merced County Library
2100 O Street
Merced, CA 95340
(209) 385-7597
Catherine McCullough, Reference
    Librarian
Hours: Mon–Thur 9:00–9:00, Fri–Sat
    9:00–6:00

Mill Valley Public Library
History Room
375 Throckmorton Avenue
Mill Valley, CA 94941
(415) 388-2190; (415) 388-8929 FAX
Joyce Crews, Reference Librarian
Hours: Mon–Thur & Sat 10:00–noon &
    2:00–4:00, Mon–Thur 7:00–9:00, Fri
    2:00–4:00 (hours depend on docent
    available)

Ralph L. Milliken Museum
PO Box 2294
Los Banos, CA 93635

**Mojave River Valley Museum
Association**
(southwest corner of Barstow Road at
    Virginia Way—location)
PO Box 1282 (mailing address)
Barstow, CA 92312-1282

(760) 252-4681 (for history and
    genealogy); (760) 256-5452 (MRVM,
    specialty old data)
Germaine L. Moon, Historian/Researcher
Hours: 11:00–4:00
Pub. *Monthly Newsletter*
(specializes in entire Mojave Desert of
    San Bernardino County, also parts of
    southern Nevada and western Arizona)
$20.00 per year membership; research
    fee: copies at 25¢–$1.00 per sheet plus
    postage and donation appreciated

Monrovia Public Library
Reference Desk
321 South Myrtle Avenue
Monrovia, CA 91016
(626) 358-0174
Hours: winter: Mon–Wed 10:00–9:00,
    Thur–Sat 10:00–5:00; summer: Mon
    10:00–9:00, Tue–Wed 10:00–6:00,
    Thur–Sat 10:00–5:00
(Monrovia archives/history)

Monterey County Free Libraries
26 Central Avenue
Salinas, CA 93901
(408) 424-3244; (408) 755-5839 FAX
Martha Clark, Librarian
Hours: Mon–Fri 8:00–5:00

Morgan Hill Museum
40 El Toro Avenue
Morgan Hill, CA 95037
(408) 779-5755; (408) 778-0355
Mary Dutra, Curator

Museum of Art and History
The McPherson Center
705 Front Street
Santa Cruz, CA 95060-4508
(408) 429-1964; (408) 429-1954 FAX
E-mail: mah@cruzio.com
Rachel McKay, Research Librarian
Hours: Museum: Tue–Thur & Sat–Sun
    noon–5:00, Fri noon–7:00; Archives
    Library: Tue–Thur noon–5:00
Pub. *Calendar*, quarterly; *Santa Cruz
    County History Journal*, annually,
    $14.95 per issue
(Evergreen Cemetery files, a Protestant
    cemetery, started in 1850s; clipping
    files on places and people; early voter
    registration records, Porter family
    papers, Knight family papers; books
    on Santa Cruz County)
$35.00 per year membership; research:
    donation plus 10¢ per photocopy

Museum of History and Art, Ontario
225 South Euclid Avenue
Ontario, CA 91761
(909) 983-3198
Lou Ann Svenson, Director
Hours: four afternoons per week

Napa City-County Library
1150 Division Street
Napa, CA 94559-3396
(707) 253-4235

Hours: Mon, Tue, Fri 10:00–5:30, Wed–
Thur 10:00–9:00, Sat 10:00–5:00, Sun
1:00–5:00

Nevada County Library
(Local History Branch, 211 North Pine
Street—location)
980 Helling Way (mailing address)
Nevada City, CA 95959
(530) 265-4606; (530) 265-1407
Dorothy Boettner, Library Technician
Hours: Mon–Wed 1:00–4:00
(emphasis on California with a focus on
Nevada County)

Oakland Museum of California
1000 Oak Street
Oakland, CA 94607
(510) 238-6579
Deborah Cooper, Collections Manager
Pub. *The Museum of California*, four
times per year, $5.00 per issue
$25.00 per year membership for
individuals

Oakland Public Library
Oakland History Room
125 14th Street (14th and Oak Streets)
Oakland, CA 94612
(510) 238-3222; (510) 238-2232 FAX
William W. Sturm, Librarian
Hours: Mon–Tue & Sat 10:00–5:30,
Wed–Thur noon–8:00, Fri noon–5:30,
Sun 1:00–5:00
(city directories, voting registers, county
histories, Oakland births and deaths,
etc.)

Occidental College
Department of History
Los Angeles, CA 90041
(213) 259-2751
Maryanne Horowitz, Ph.D., Chair of the
Department
(diverse library collection in Occidental
College Library)

Oceanside Public Library
330 North Coast Highway
Oceanside, CA 92054
(619) 966-4690
Deborah Polich, Assistant Library Director

Old Mission San José Museum
43300 Mission Boulevard
PO Box 3159
Fremont, CA 94539
(510) 657-1797
Dolores Ferenz, Administrator
Hours: daily 10:00–5:00
(small reference library; also stories of
the local Ohlone natives; "our
genealogy (church) records are not
open, but we will research as time
allows.")
search fee: $10.00 per hour

Ontario City Library
Model Colony History Room
215 East C Street
Ontario, CA 91764

(909) 988-8481
Terry Carter, Library Assistant
Hours: Tue–Sat 1:00–5:00, Tue 5:30–
8:30

Palm Springs Public Library
300 South Sunrise Way
Palm Springs, CA 92262
(760) 323-8294; (760) 320-8294 FAX
E-mail: 74111.3302@compuserve.com
Josette McNary, Reference Coordinator
Hours: Mon–Tue 9:00–8:00, Wed–Thur
& Sat 9:00–5:30, Fri 10:00–5:30

Palos Verdes Library District
Local History Room
(2400 Via Campesina, Palos Verdes
Estates—location)
650 Deep Valley Drive, PO Box 8000
(mailing address)
Rolling Hills Estates, CA 90274
(562) 377-9584, ext. 250
Lenore M. Blume
Hours: Tue–Thur 1:00–7:00, Sat 10:00–
5:00

Pasadena Public Library
Pasadena Centennial Room
285 East Walnut Street
Pasadena, CA 91101
(626) 405-4052; (626) 796-3818
http://www.ci.pasadena.ca.us/library
Carolyn L. Garner, Librarian II
Hours: Mon–Thur 9:00–9:00, Fri–Sat
9:00–6:00, Sun 1:00–5:00

Petaluma Museum and Historical Library
20 Fourth Street
Petaluma, CA 94952
(707) 778-4398

Governor Pico Mansion Society
14216 Neargrove Road
La Mirada, CA 90638

Placer County Archives
11437 D Avenue West, DeWitt Center
Auburn, CA 95603
(530) 889-7994
http://www.placer.ca.gov/museum/
archives.htm
Hours: Mon–Tue noon–4:00
(mining records, court case files,
assessment rolls and maps, record of
wills, board of supervisors,
naturalization-citizenship, estrays,
marks and brands, deed books, great
register of voters, water rights
appropriations, newspapers, plus a
Finding Aid for accessing the records,
available only at the Archives)

Placer County Department of Museums
Placer County Museum
101 Maple Street
Auburn, CA 95603
(530) 889-6500; (530) 889-6510 FAX

http://www.placer.ca.gov/museum/
Jerry Rouillard, Director; Doris Parker-
Coons, Administrative Curator
Hours: Tue–Sun 10:00–4:00
(besides Placer County Museum
location, includes Gold Country
Museum (mining), 1273 High Street,
Auburn, CA 95603, (530) 887-0690,
Tue–Sun 10:00–4:00; Bernhard
Museum Complex (winery), 291
Auburn-Folsom Road, Auburn, CA
95603, (530) 888-6891, Tue–Fri
10:30–3:00, Sat-Sun 12:00–4:00;
Griffith Quarry Museum (granite),
corner of Taylor and Rock Springs
Road, Penryn, CA, (530) 663-1837,
Sat–Sun 12:00–4:00; Golden Drift
Museum (mining and railroads), 32820
Main Street, Dutch Flat, CA, (530)
389-2126, Memorial Day through mid-
Sept: Wed & Sat–Sun noon–4:00; and
Forest Hill Divide Museum (local
history of Foresthill and Iowa Hill
Divides), 24601 Harrison Street,
Foresthill, CA, (530) 367-3988, Sat–
Sun noon–4:00)

Pleasanton Library
400 Old Bernal Avenue
Pleasanton, CA 94566
Judy Person, Librarian
Hours: Mon–Tue 1:00–8:00, Wed–Thur
10:00–6:00, Sat 2:00–6:00, Sun 1:00–
5:00

Plumas County Museum Association, Inc.
500 Jackson Street
PO Box 10776
Quincy, CA 95971
(530) 283-6320
Scott Lawson, Director
Hours: Mon–Fri 8:00–5:00
Pub. *Association Newsletter*, quarterly
(regional and local history)
$10.00 per year membership for
individuals; search fee: $5.00
minimum

Pomona Public Library
Special Collections Department
625 South Garey Avenue
PO Box 2271
Pomona, CA 91766

Porterville Historical Museum
(257 North D Street—location)
36 West Cleveland (mailing address)
Porterville, CA 93257
(209) 784-2053
Beverly Faul, Curator
Hours: Tue–Sat 10:00–4:00
Pub. *Porterville Historical Museum
Newsletter*, quarterly
$20.00 per year membership for
individuals, $35.00 per year
membership for families, $60.00 per
year Contributing membership,
$100.00 per year Sustaining
membership, $500.00 per year

Sponsorship membership; museum admission for non-members: $1.00 for adults, 50¢ for students, children under six free

Potrero-East County Museum Society
PO Box 70
Potrero, CA 92063

Ramona Museum of California History
4580 North Figueroa Street
Los Angeles, CA 90065
(213) 222-0012

Rancho Cordova Library
9845 Folsom Boulevard
Sacramento, CA 95827

Redding Museum and Art Center
(56 Quartz Hill Road, Redding, CA 96003—location)
PO Box 427 (mailing address)
Redding, CA 96099
(916) 225-4155
Keith Foster, Director
(local history)

Redwood City Public Library
Local History Collection
1044 Middlefield Road
Redwood City, CA 94063-1868
(650) 780-7030; (650) 780-7069 FAX; (650) 780-7000 (Library); (650) 780-7026 (Library Reference); (650) 780-7225 (Library) FAX
E-mail: thivierg@pls.lib.ca.us
http://www.ci.redwood-city.ca.us/library/rcpl.html
Jeanne Thivierge, Local History Specialist
Hours: Mon–Thur 10:00–9:00, Fri–Sat 10:00–5:00, Sun 1:00–4:00; Local History Room: Tue & Thur 1:00–5:00, Wed 5:00–9:00
Pub. *Archives Committee Newsletter*, quarterly
$5.00 per year membership for individuals

Richmond Museum Association
400 Nevin Avenue
PO Box 1267
Richmond, CA 94802
(510) 235-7387; (510) 620-6842
Kathleen Rupley, Administrator

Richmond Public Library
325 Civic Center Plaza
Richmond, CA 94804
(510) 620-6561
Emma Clark, Head, Reference Department
Hours: Mon–Thur 9:00–9:00, Fri–Sat 9:00–6:00, Sun 1:00–5:00

Rio Vista Museum Association
16 North Front Street
Rio Vista, CA 94571
(707) 374-5169
Hours: Sat–Sun 1:30–4:30

City of Riverside Municipal Museum
3580 Mission Inn Avenue
Riverside, CA 92501
(909) 782-5273; (909) 369-4970 FAX
http://www.museumpress.com
Vince Moses, Curator of History
Hours: Mon 9:00–1:00, Tue–Fri 9:00–5:00, Sat 10:00–5:00, Sun 11:00–5:00
Pub. *Newsletter of the Riverside Museum Associates*, monthly
$10.00 per year membership for individuals, $20.00 per year membership for families

Riverside Public Library
Local History Office
3581 Mission Inn Avenue
Riverside, CA 92501
(909) 782-5202
http://co.riverside.ca.us/community/rccpl/
William M. A. Swafford, Local History Librarian
Hours: Mon–Wed 10:00–9:00, Thur–Sat 10:00–6:00

Rosemead Library
8800 Valley Boulevard
Rosemead, CA 91770
(626) 573-5220; (626) 280-8523 FAX
Lisa Castaneda, Library Manager
Hours: Tue–Wed noon–8:00, Thur 10:00–6:00, Fri noon–5:00, Sat 11:00–5:00

Roseville Public Library
225 Taylor Street
Roseville, CA 95678
(916) 781-0231
Hours: Mon–Thur 9:00–9:00, Fri 9:00–6:00, Sat 9:00–5:00, Sun 1:00–5:00

Sacramento Archives and Museum Collection Center
551 Sequoia Pacific Boulevard
Sacramento, CA 95814-0229
(916) 264-7072
Charlene Gilbert Noyes, Archivist
Hours: Wed–Fri 8:15–noon by appointment
(Sacramento city and county)

Sacramento Branch Genealogical Library
5343 Halsted Avenue
Carmichael, CA 95608
Verl F. Weight
Pub. *Sacramento Branch Genealogical Library Newsletter*, monthly

Sacramento City Cemetery Archives
Old City Cemetery Committee
1000 Broadway
Sacramento, CA 95818
(916) 448-5665; (916) 554-7508 FAX
John Bettencourt, Volunteer Staff Coordinator
Hours: Mon–Fri 10:00–3:00
(deaths and burials 1850–1927, cemetery records from 1927)

Sacramento Public Library
Special Collections, Central Library, Sacramento Room
828 I Street
Sacramento, CA 95814
(916) 264-2920; (916) 264-2854 FAX
Ruth Ellis, Sacramento Room Librarian
Hours: Tue–Thur & Sun 1:00–5:00
("Collection includes Sacramento and California history, a local authors collection, Sacramento city directories and a book arts collection; genealogy collection is presently housed at the Carmichael Regional Branch of the Sacramento Public Library.")

Sacramento Valley Museum
(1491 "E" Street—location)
PO Box 1437 (mailing address)
Williams, CA 95987
(530) 473-2978
Ms. Bobbie Burlingame, Curator
Hours: Thur (Apr–Oct) & Fri–Sat 10:00–4:00, and by appointment
Pub. *Newsletter*, two times per year
(no genealogy, but historical records in and of the Colusa County area)
$10.00 per year membership for individuals, $15.00 per year membership for families, $25.00 per year membership for businesses, $100.00 per year Sponsor membership, $250.00 per year Patron membership, $500.00 per year Benefactor membership

San Bernardino County Archives
777 East Rialto Avenue
San Bernardino, CA 92415-0795
(909) 387-2030
James D. Hofer, Archivist/Records Manager
Hours: Mon–Fri 9:00–5:00
("official records of San Bernardino County, 1853–present")

San Bernardino County Law Library
401 North Arrowhead Avenue
San Bernardino, CA 92401

San Bernardino County Museum
2024 Orange Tree Lane
Redlands, CA 92374
(909) 798-8570
Allen D. Griesemer, Ph.D., Director
Hours: Tue–Thur 9:00–5:00
Pub. *Museum Quarterly*, $40.00 per year subscription
(cultural and natural history)

San Diego Public Library
Genealogy Room
820 E Street
San Diego, CA 92101-6478
(619) 236-5834
Mary Allely, Section Supervisor
Hours: Mon–Thur 10:00–9:00, Fri–Sat 9:30–5:30, Sun 1:00–5:00

("DAR Materials, census microfilm, original 13 colonies")
photocopies 15¢ per page (book or microfilm)

San Francisco Maritime National Historical Park
J. Porter Shaw Library
Building E, Fort Mason Center
San Francisco, CA 94123
(415) 556-0793; (415) 556-1659; (415) 556-1624 FAX; (415) 556-9870 (Library)
Lynn Cullivan, Publications
Hours: Park: Mon–Sat 8:00–5:00; Library: Tue 5:00–8:00, Wed–Fri 1:00–5:00, Sat 10:00–5:00 by appointment
Pub. *Sea Letter*, semiannually
(major research library: 22,000 volumes, including backruns of 500 periodicals (including *Lloyds, Record of American and Foreign Shipping* and *Merchant Vessels of the United States* from 1764 into the 1980s), and over 100 bibliographies, 400 oral history interviews, and ephemeral collection of 50,000 items, also west coast commercial maritime history)
free admission to library

Museum of the City of San Francisco
2801 Leavenworth Street
San Francisco, CA 94133-1117
(415) 928-0289
E-mail: curator@sfmuseum.org
http://www.sfmuseum.org
Hours: Wed–Sun 10:00–4:00
(San Francisco history)

San Francisco Public Library
Genealogy Collection
Civic Center
San Francisco, CA 94102
(415) 557-4400
E-mail: ennism@sfpl.lib.ca.us
http://sfpl.lib.ca.us/

San Francisco State University
Library
480 Winston Drive
San Francisco, CA 94132-1719
(415) 564-4010; (415) 564-3606 FAX
E-mail: larc@sfsu.edu
http://www.sfsu.edu
(labor archives and research center)

San Jacinto Valley Museum Association, Inc.
181 East Main Street
PO Box 922
San Jacinto, CA 92383
Madenia Freitas, President
Hours: Tue–Sat noon–4:00
$10.00 per year membership

San Jose Historical Museum Archives
1600 Senter Road
San Jose, CA 95112-2599

(408) 287-2290; (408) 277-3890 FAX
Leslie Masunaga, Archivist
Hours: Archives: Mon–Fri by appointment, Wed 1:00–4:00
(San Jose, Santa Clara Valley, New Almaden Mines)
museum admission: $4.00 for adults, $3.00 for senior citizens; photocopies 15¢ per page

San Jose Public Library
California Room
180 West San Carlos Street
San Jose, CA 95113
(408) 277-4867; (408) 277-4868 FAX
E-mail: bob.johnson@ci.sj.ca.us
http://www.lib.ci.sj.ca.us/home/california.htm
Bob Johnson, Reference Librarian
Hours: Mon & Thur 2:00–5:00, Tue–Wed 3:00–9:00, Fri 10:00–1:00, Sat 1:00–6:00
(local history, but no specialized genealogy collection)
photocopies: $3.00 for one to three pages, 75¢ for each additional page

San Leandro Community Library
Californiana Room
300 Estudillo Avenue
San Leandro, CA 94577
(510) 577-3491
Janet Prince, Librarian
Hours: collection available by appointment during regular library hours
(San Leandro history; San Leandro historical photo collection; Alameda County history; California history)

San Rafael Public Library
1100 E Street
San Rafael, CA 94901
(415) 485-3321
Catherine Wright, Reference Librarian
Hours: Tue–Thur 10:00–9:00, Fri–Sat 10:00–5:00

Santa Ana Public Library
Santa Ana History Room
26 Civic Center Plaza
Santa Ana, CA 92701
(714) 647-5280
Anne Harder
Hours: Tue, Thur & Sat 2:00–6:00
("Orange County, California, local history collection with Santa Ana materials; book collection on California history")
search fee: $10.00 for out-of-county inquiries

Santa Barbara Public Library
40 East Anapamu Street
PO Box 1019
Santa Barbara, CA 93102
(805) 962-7653
Hours: Mon–Thur 10:00–9:00, Fri–Sat 10:00–5:30, Sun 1:00–5:00
("We provide access to materials in

person; staff cannot answer research inquiries by mail.")

Santa Clara County Free Library
1095 North Seventh Street
San Jose, CA 95112

Central Branch Public Library
Local History and California Room
224 Church Street
Santa Cruz, CA 95060
(831) 429-3526
Hours: Tue–Thur 10:00–8:00, Fri–Sat 10:00–5:00

Santa Fe Springs Public Library
11700 Telegraph Road
Santa Fe Springs, CA 90670
Hours: Mon–Thur 10:00–9:00, Fri 10:00–6:00, Sat 10:00–5:00

Santa Maria Public Library
Genealogical Collection and California Room
420 South Broadway
Santa Maria, CA 93454
(805) 925-0994
Marcia Frasier, Principal Librarian
Hours: Mon–Wed noon–8:00, Thur–Sat 10:00–6:00
(passenger lists, general finding aids)

Searls Historical Library
214 Church Street
Nevada City, CA 95959
(530) 265-5910
Edwin L. Tyson
Hours: Mon–Sat 1:00–4:00
(Nevada County, California, with some material on adjoining areas)

Seaver Center for Western History Research
Natural History Museum of Los Angeles County
900 Exposition Boulevard
Los Angeles, CA 90007
(213) 744-3359 (Seaver Center); (213) 744-3301 (Museum)
Errol Stevens, Curator
Hours: Tue 1:00–4:00, Thur by appointment

Sharpsteen Museum
1311 Washington
PO Box 573
Calistoga, CA 94515
(707) 942-5911
Mary Elizabeth Cumpston, President

Shasta College Museum and Research Center
(1065 North Old Oregon Trail, Redding, CA 96001—location)
PO Box 496006 (mailing address)
Redding, CA 96049
(530) 225-4754
Edward Clewett, Director
Hours: Mon, Wed & Fri 11:00–2:00 (volunteer staff)
(northern California local history,

photographs, coroner records through the 1930s, etc.; special events)

Sherman Library and Gardens
(2647 East Coast Highway—location)
614 Dahlia Avenue (mailing address)
Corona Del Mar, CA 92625
(949) 673-1880

Siskiyou County Public Library
719 Fourth Street
Yreka, CA 96097
(530) 841-4175; (530) 842-7001 FAX
E-mail: sislib@snowcrest.net
http://www.snowcrest.net/fueston/
    index.html
Kathy Fueston, Reference
Hours: Mon 10:00–7:00, Tue–Wed
    10:00–6:00, Thur noon–5:00, Sat
    (school year) 1:00–5:00

Jedediah Smith Society
Holt-Atherton Pacific Center for Western
    Studies
University of the Pacific
Stockton, CA 95211
(209) 946-2169; (209) 946-2578 FAX;
    (650) 432-1552 FAX
http://www.uop.edu
Dr. Clover, Executive Secretary
Hours: Mon–Fri 9:00–12:00 A.M.
Pub. *Castor Canadensis*, quarterly
(collection emphasizes the Mountain
    Man era)
$10.00 per year membership, $25.00 per
    year Donor membership, $100.00 per
    year Patron membership

Sonoma County Library
Third and E Streets
Santa Rosa, CA 95404
(707) 545-0831, ext. 562
Audrey Herman, Local History/
    Genealogy Librarian
Hours: Mon noon–9:00, Tue & Thur–Sat
    9:30–6:00, Wed 10:00–6:00, Sun
    2:00–6:00
(Sonoma County history/archives,
    genealogy)

Sonoma State University
Finley McFarling Genealogy Collections
Special Collections
Library
1801 East Cotati Avenue
Rohnert Park, CA 94928-3609
(707) 664-2861
E-mail: lisastrawter@sonoma.edu;
    sandrawalton@sonoma.edu
http://www.sonoma.edu/library/special/
    finley.html

South San Francisco Public Library
South San Francisco History Room
Grand Avenue Branch Library
306 Walnut Avenue
South San Francisco, CA 94080
(650) 877-8533; (650) 877-8530
Kathleen Kay, Historian
Hours: Mon–Fri 1:00–4:00

Stanislaus County Free Library
1500 I Street
Modesto, CA 95354
(209) 558-7814; (209) 558-8097 FAX
E-mail: refquest@scfl.lib.ca.us
Hours: Mon–Thur 10:00–9:00, Fri–Sat
    10:00–5:00, Sun noon–5:00

Stockton-San Joaquin County Public Library
605 North El Dorado Street
Stockton, CA 95202-1999
(209) 937-8221
Karen Ramos, Reference Librarian
Hours: Mon–Thur 10:00–8:00 (closed
    second Wed), Fri 10:00–6:00, Sat
    10:00–5:00
(local history, general American
    genealogy collection)

Tehama County Museum Foundation, Inc.
275 C Street
PO Box 275
Tehama, CA 96090
(530) 384-2420

Tomales Regional Local History Center
(26700 Highway 1—location)
PO Box 262 (mailing address)
Tomales, CA 94971
(707) 878-2398
Lois Parks, President
Hours: by appointment
Pub. *Bulletin*, quarterly
(photographs, North Pacific Coast
    Railroad, family histories)
$15.00 per year membership; search:
    $5.00 per hour plus copies at 10¢ per
    page

Tulare County Free Library Headquarters
c/o Annie Mitchell Local History Room
200 West Oak Street
Visalia, CA 93291
(209) 733-6954; (209) 730-2524 FAX
CAL GEN WEBB: telnet
    gilgamesh.sjvls.lib.ca.us (login:
    library)
Mary Anne Terstegge, Historical
    Research Librarian
Hours: History Room: Mon–Thur 1:00–
    5:00, Tue 10:00 A.M.–noon, Wed 6:00
    P.M.–8:00 P.M.
(emphasis on Tulare County, San Joaquin
    Valley and Sequoia National Park;
    "Our 'archival' material is strictly
    Tulare County [and Kern and Kings
    counties, which came off Tulare
    County]; book material encompasses
    all California.")
copies/search: $1.00 or 15¢ per sheet (if
    seven or more copies are made)

Tulare Public Library
113 North F Street
Tulare, CA 93274

(209) 685-2342
Ronad W. Gilstrap, Genealogy Librarian
Hours: Mon & Wed 10:00–6:00, Tue &
    Thur 10:00–8:30, Sat 10:00–2:00
$4.50 per surname for out-of-town
    research requests

Tuolumne County Library
480 Greenley Road
Sonora, CA 95370
(209) 533-5507
Joan Rutty, Librarian Assistant I
Hours: Mon 10:00–9:00, Tue & Thur
    10:00–6:00, Wed 12:00–9:00, Fri
    12:00–6:00, Sat 10:00–5:00
(Tuolumne County only)
copies 15¢ per page

University of California—Berkeley
The Bancroft Library
(address withheld upon request)
http://www.lib.berkeley.edu/banc
(does not collect general genealogical
    works; has some resources which may
    be used to carry out research,
    especially on western North America;
    pictorial collection, oral history,
    archival collections, newspaper and
    periodical indexes)

University of California—Davis
Department of Special Collections
Shields Library
Davis, CA 95616-5292
(530) 752-1621; (530) 752-3148 FAX
E-mail: jlskarstad@ucdavis.edu
http://www.lib.ucdavis.edu/speccoll/
    index.html
(history collection, manuscripts)

University of California—Los Angeles
University Research Library
405 Hilgard Avenue
West Los Angeles, CA 90024

University of California—Riverside
Department of History
Riverside, CA 92521
(909) 787-5403
Ronald C. Tobey, Ph.D., Professor of
    History
(special collections)

University of California—Santa Barbara
Department of History
Graduate Program in Public Historical
    Studies
Public History Information Unit
Santa Barbara, CA 93106
(805) 961-2224
Otis L. Graham, Ph.D., Director/Editor
Pub. *The Public Historian*
(not primarily genealogical, maintains
    archive)

University of California—Santa Cruz

Special Collections Library
Santa Cruz, CA 95064
(831) 459-2547
Hours: school year: Mon–Sun 10:00–12:00 & 1:00–4:00; quarter break & summer: by appointment only

University of La Verne

Wilson Library
2040 Third Street
La Verne, CA 91750
(909) 593-3511, ext. 4300
Hours: academic year: Mon–Fri 8:00–5:00; summer: Mon–Fri 8:30–4:30, except as posted

University of Washington Libraries

(see Washington)

Vacaville Museum, A Center for Solano County History

213 Buck Avenue
Vacaville, CA 95688
(707) 447-4513; (707) 447-2661 FAX
E-mail: vacmuseum@aol.com
Ruth Gardner Begell, Museum Director
Hours: Wed–Sun 1:00–4:30
Pub. *Vacaville Museum News & Notes*, quarterly
(Solano County history)
$20.00 per year membership for individuals, $30.00 per year membership for families

Ventura County Museum of History and Art

100 East Main Street
Ventura, CA 93001
(805) 653-0323
Charles Johnson, Librarian
Hours: Mon–Fri 10:00–5:00, Sat 10:00–1:00

Vintage Hall, Inc.

473 Main Street
Saint Helena, CA 94574
(707) 963-7411

Whittier College Library

7031 Founders Hills Road
Whittier, CA 90602

Whittier Public Library

7344 South Washington Avenue
Whittier, CA 90602
(562) 698-8949
Cynthia Birt
Hours: Mon–Wed 10:00–9:00, Thur–Fri 10:00–6:00, Sat 10:00–5:00

Yolo County Archives and Record Center

226 Buckeye Street
Woodland, CA 95695
(530) 666-8010; (530) 666-8006 FAX
http://www.compuology.com/cagenweb/yolcty.htm
Marylin Thompson, Archives Co-ordinator

Hours: Tue 9:00–noon & 12:30–3:00, and by appointment
(Yolo County history from 1850)

Yolo County Historical Museum

512 Gibson Road
Woodland, CA 95695
(530) 666-1045
Antonina "Monika" Stengert, Director/Curator
Hours: Mon–Tue 9:00–5:00, Sat–Sun 12:00–4:00
(archival material; northern California, Yolo County)

Yosemite National Park Research Library

PO Box 577
Yosemite National Park, CA 95389
(209) 372-4461, ext. 280

Yuba County Library

California Room
303 Second Street
Marysville, CA 95901

Historical Societies— Local and Regional

Alameda County Historical Society

5461 Fernhoff Road
Oakland, CA 94619-3111

Alameda Historical Society

2264 Santa Clara Avenue
Alameda, CA 94501

Alpine County Museum and Historical Society of Alpine County

(1 School Street—location)
PO Box 24 (mailing address)
Markleeville, CA 96120
(530) 694-2317; (530) 694-2102 (Director's home); (530) 694-2102
E-mail: nthornburg@telis.org
Nancy C. Thornburg, Director
Hours: Memorial Day weekend through October: Mon & Wed–Sun 12:00–5:00, and by appointment
$10.00 per year membership for individuals, $15.00 per year membership for families, $200.00 life membership

Amador County Historical Society

18708 Clinton Road
PO Box 761
Jackson, CA 95642

Amador-Livermore Valley Historical Society

603 Main Street
PO Box 573
Pleasanton, CA 94566
(510) 462-2766

American Historical Association, Pacific Coast Branch

Department of History
Loyola Marymount University
Los Angeles, CA 90045
(310) 338-2805; (310) 338-7662
Lawrence J. Jelinek, Secretary-Treasurer
Pub. *Pacific Historical Review*, quarterly (specializes in "frontier West, post frontier West, Pacific rim")
$21.00 per year membership for individuals, $42.00 per year membership for institutions, $14.00 per year membership for students

Association for Northern California Records and Research

PO Box 3024
Chico, CA 95927
Clarence F. McIntosh, President
Pub. *ANCRR Newsletter*

Atascadero History Society

6600 Palma
PO Box 1047
Atascadero, CA 93423
(805) 466-1811
Marj Mackey, Curator
Hours: Mon–Sat 1:00–4:00
$10.00–$15.00 per year membership

Azusa Historical Society, Inc.

City Hall Complex
213 East Foothill Boulevard
Azusa, CA 91702

Berkeley Historical Society

(1325 Grant Street, Berkeley, CA 94703—location)
PO Box 1190 (mailing address)
Berkeley, CA 94701
(510) 524-9880
Carl C. Wilson, President

Big Bear Valley Historical Society

(In the northeast portion of Big Bear City Park, east of the airport—location)
PO Box 513 (mailing address)
Big Bear City, CA 92314
(909) 585-8100
Thomas H. Core, President
Hours: May 30–Oct 15: Sat 10:00–4:00, Sun 11:00–2:00
$7.50 per year membership for individuals

Bishop Museum and Historical Society

(Laws Narrow Gauge Railroad Museum, off Silver Canyon Road, Laws, CA—location)
PO Box 363 (mailing address)
Bishop, CA 93515
(760) 873-5950
Alice J. Boothe, Administrator
Hours: daily 10:00–4:00
(has quite a lot of pioneer information for the area)

Buena Park Historical Society
7842 Whitaker Street
Buena Park, CA 90621

Butte County Historical Society
Ehmann Home
1480 Lincoln Street
PO Box 2195
Oroville, CA 95965
(530) 533-5316
Hours: flexible
Pub. *Diggin's*, quarterly; *Butte County
    Historical Society Slickens*, irregularly
$15.00 per year membership

Cabrillo Historical Association
Cabrillo National Monument
1800 Cabrillo Memorial
San Diego, CA 92106

Calaveras County Historical Society
30 North Main Street
PO Box 721
San Andreas, CA 95249
(209) 754-1058
W. P. Fuller, Jr., Director
Hours: Mon–Fri 8:30–4:30
Pub. *Las Calaveras*, quarterly
$8.00 per year membership

**Carpinteria Valley Historical Society
and Museum of History**
956 Maple Avenue
Carpinteria, CA 93013
(805) 684-3112
David W. Griggs, Director/Curator
Pub. *Grapevine*, bimonthly
(includes Native American collection
    [Chumash] and items from Mexican
    rancho period—1800–1840)
$20.00 per year membership

**Historical Society of Centinela
Valley**
7634 Midfield Avenue
Los Angeles, CA 90045
(213) 649-6272
L. R. Utter, President
Hours: Wed & Sun 2:00–4:00
Pub. *Historical Society News Letter*,
    monthly
(Inglewood history, Machado family
    history and Daniel Freeman history;
    large collection of prominent early
    settlers in the area)
$20.00 per year membership; search
    fees: $17.00 per hour per person

**Century House Museum (Imperial
County, CA)**
(see Arizona, Arizona Historical
    Society—Yuma Branch)

Chino Valley Historical Society
5493 B Street
PO Box 972
Chino, CA 91708
(909) 627-6464
Hours: Old Schoolhouse Museum: first
    Wed & first Sat 1:30–4:00
(local history)

**City of San Bernardino Historical
and Pioneer Society**
796 North D Street
PO Box 875
San Bernardino, CA 92402
(909) 384-5211

Claremont Heritage, Inc.
590 West Bonita Avenue
PO Box 742
Claremont, CA 91711
(909) 621-0848
Ginger Elliott, Executive Director
Pub. *Heritage News*

Colusa County Historical Society
Rt. 1, Box 510
Glen, CA 95943

**Contra Costa County Historical
Society**
(1700 Oak Park Boulevard, Room C-5,
    Pleasant Hill, CA 94523—
    location)
PO Box 821 (mailing address)
Concord, CA 94522
(510) 939-9180
Betty J. Maffei, Director
Hours: Mon–Fri 9:00–3:00
Pub. *CCCHS Bulletin*, quarterly
(court records, obituaries, maps, photos)
$15.00 per year membership for
    individuals, $25.00 per year
    membership for couples

Costa Mesa Historical Society
(1870 Anaheim Avenue—location)
PO Box 1764 (mailing address)
Costa Mesa, CA 92628
(949) 631-5918
Alvin "Bud" Anderson, SAPAB Wing;
    Charles Beecher, President; Gladys
    Refakes, Secretary
Hours: Thur 10:00–3:00, and by
    appointment
Pub. *Fairview Register*, ten times per
    year (monthly, except July and
    August); *Santa Ana Army Air Base
    CADET*, two or three times per year
("We have a few old directories and we
    keep finding things for people who
    phone and write.")
$10.00 per year membership; search fee:
    donation accepted

Covina Valley Historical Society, Inc.
125 East College Street
Covina, CA 91723

**Cypress College Local History
Association**
Cypress, CA 90630
(714) 826-2220, ext. 294

The Diocese of San Diego
Mission San Diego de Alcala—Archive-
    Library
10818 Mission San Diego Road
San Diego, CA 92108
(619) 283-6338; (619) 490-8200
    (Diocesan Archives)

Sister Catherine Louise La Coste, C.S.J.,
    Archivist-Librarian
Hours: Tue & Thur 10:00–noon;
    Diocesan Archives is not staffed and is
    closed to research except by
    appointment (PO Box 85728, San
    Diego, CA 92186)
Pub. *Newsletter—Mission San Diego
    Historical Society Quarterly*
(not only religious, lots of California
    history and original documents, also
    Spanish, Mexican and American
    history, San Diego history from 1769
    onward, and lots of Indian history for
    California and the California missions)
$10.00 per year membership for
    individuals, $15.00 per year
    membership for couples, $200.00 life
    membership; copy costs: 5¢ per page

**Downey Historical Society/Downey
History Center**
12540 Rives Avenue
PO Box 554
Downey, CA 90241
(562) 862-2777
Barbara Callarman, Director
Hours: Wed–Thur 9:00–2:00, third Sat
    10:00–3:00, and by appointment
Pub. *DHS Newsletter*, ten times per year
    (monthly, September–June)
("local history and genealogy; large
    photo collection")
$10.00 per year membership for
    individuals, $15.00 per year
    membership for families

**Duarte Historical Society, Museum,
and Friends of the Duarte Library**
777 Encanto Parkway
PO Box 263
Duarte, CA 91009
(626) 357-3419
Claudia Heller, President; Jim Kirchner,
    Editor; Irwin Margiloff, Curator
Hours: Wed 1:00–3:00, Sat 1:00–4:00
Pub. *The Branding Iron*, bimonthly
$10.00 per year membership for senior
    citizens, teachers or students, $25.00
    per year membership for families

Eagle Rock Valley Historical Society
2035 Colorado Boulevard
Eagle Rock, CA 90041

El Cajon Historical Society
Magnolia and Park
PO Box 1173
El Cajon, CA 92022
(619) 444-3800
Dorothy Maranda, President
Hours: Tue & Thur 11:00–3:30, Sun
    1:00–3:30
Pub. *The Heritage*, quarterly
$10.00 per year membership for
    individuals, $15.00 per year
    membership for families, $35.00 per
    year membership for businesses,
    $200.00 life membership

El Monte Historical Society
3150 North Tyler Avenue
El Monte, CA 91731
(626) 444-3813
Helen E. Huffines, Museum Curator
Pub. *The Landmark*, quarterly
$6.00 per year membership

Elk Grove Historical Society
PO Box 562
Elk Grove, CA 95759-0562
(916) 687-7713
Dorothy Hrepich
Hours: meetings second Mon at Elk
  Grove Hotel, Elk Grove

Encino Historical Society
16756 Moorpark Street
Encino, CA 91436

Escondido Historical Society
321 North Broadway
PO Box 263
Escondido, CA 92025
(530) 743-8207
Margaret K. Trussell, Executive Director

Fair Oaks Historical Society
PO Box 2044
Fair Oaks, CA 95628
(916) 961-0637; (916) 961-6912

Fallbrook Historical Society
PO Box 1375
Fallbrook, CA 92028

Folsom Historical Society
Wells Fargo Building Museum
823 Sutter Street
Folsom, CA 95630
(916) 985-2707 (Museum)
June Hose, Manager
Hours: Wed–Sun 11:00–4:00; meetings
  third Tue 7:00

Fontana Historical Society
PO Box 426
Fontana, CA 92334

Fort Crook Historical Society
Fort Crook Avenue
PO Box 397
Fall River Mills, CA 96028
(530) 336-5110

Fresno City and County Historical Society
(7160 West Kearney Boulevard, Fresno,
  CA 93706—location)
PO Box 2029 (mailing address)
Fresno, CA 93718
(209) 441-0862
Zelma Barrett Smith, Executive Director
Pub. *Fresno—Past & Present*, quarterly,
  $9.00 per year subscription; *Grape
  Vine Newsletter*, bimonthly, $9.00 per
  year subscription

Galt Historical Society
PO Box 782
Galt, CA 95632

Glendora Historical Society
Glendora Historical Society Museum
314 North Glendora Avenue
PO Box 532
Glendora, CA 91740
(626) 963-6485 (Society); (626) 963-
  0419 (Museum)
Kay Hall, Co-curator; Linda Price,
  Co-curator
Hours: Sun 1:00–4:00, and by
  appointment
Pub. *Newsletter*, bimonthly, free

Goleta Valley Historical Society
304 North Los Carneros Road
Goleta, CA 93117
(805) 964-4407
Ron Nye, President
Hours: by appointment
Pub. *Goleta Valley History*, two times per
  year; *Newsletter*, quarterly
(some Santa Barbara County records)
$25.00 per year membership for
  individuals, $35.00 per year
  membership for families, $50.00 per
  year Sustaining membership, $100.00
  per year Patron membership

Hayward Area Historical Society
22701 Main Street
Hayward, CA 94541
(510) 581-0223
Bernard Golumb, Librarian
Hours: Museum: Mon–Fri 11:00–4:00,
  Sat 12:00–4:00; Library: Mon 11:00–
  4:00, and by appointment
Pub. *Adobe Trails*, quarterly
("Hayward, Castro Valley, and San
  Lorenzo [Eden Township]; our
  archive/library is not dedicated to
  genealogical research but we have
  many resources (both primary and
  secondary) which genealogists find
  useful [i.e. cemetery records for
  several local cemeteries].")
$12.00 per year membership, $18.00 per
  year membership for families, $35.00
  per year Supporting membership,
  $50.00 per year Company, Fraternal
  and Club membership, $100.00 per
  year Sustaining membership, $200.00
  per year Patron membership, $500.00
  life membership

Healdsburg Museum and Historical Society
Healdsburg Museum
221 Matheson Street
Healdsburg, CA 95448
(707) 431-3325
Marie Djordjevich, Curator
Hours: Tue–Sun 11:00–4:00
Pub. *Russian River Recorder*, four times
  per year
("newspapers indexed, genealogical
  research by mail, photograph archive,
  family ephemera files, history of
  northern Sonoma County")

$20.00 per year membership for
  individuals; museum admission: free;
  research: $5.00

Held-Poage Research Library
Mendocino County Historical Society
603 West Perkins Street
Ukiah, CA 95482-4726
(707) 462-6969; (707) 462-2039
Lila J. Lee, Director
Hours: Tue, Thur & Sat 1:30–4:00, and
  by appointment
Pub. *Newsletter (Mendocino County
  Historical Society)*, quarterly
  (February, May, July, October)
$15.00 per year membership; research:
  donation plus 15¢ per photocopy

Heritage Association of El Dorado County, Inc.
PO Box 62
Placerville, CA 95667
(530) 622-8388

Humboldt County Historical Society
(703 Eighth Street, Eureka, CA 95501—
  location)
PO Box 8000 (mailing address)
Eureka, CA 95502-8000
(707) 445-4342; (707) 445-4146 FAX
E-mail: hchs@reninet.com
Matina Kilkenny, Research and
  Collections Manager
Hours: Tue–Wed & Fri noon–4:00, Thur
  4:00–8:00
Pub. *The Humboldt Historian*, quarterly
  (research library—local history; also
  historical book publisher)
$25.00 per year membership

Irvine Historical Society and Museum
5 Rancho San Joaquin
Irvine, CA 92715
(949) 786-4112

Julian Historical Society
PO Box 513
Julian, CA 92036
(760) 765-0436
John Mattias, Treasurer
Hours: various
Pub. *Julian Historical Society Reporter*,
  bimonthly
$10.00 per year membership

Kern County Historical Society
PO Box 141
Bakersfield, CA 93302
John Ludeke, President
Pub. *Historic Kern*, quarterly, $3.00 per
  year subscription; *Kern Grapevine*,
  irregularly

Kern River Valley Historical Society
PO Box 651
Kernville, CA 93238

La Habra Old Settlers Historical Society
2310 Vista Road
La Habra, CA 90631

La Jolla Historical Society
7846 Eads Avenue
PO Box 2085
La Jolla, CA 92038
(619) 459-5335 phone and FAX
Sandra Zarcades, Archivist
Hours: Tue & Thur noon–4:00
Pub. *La Jolla Historical Society Quarterly Newsletter*, quarterly
(photographs and documents relating to La Jolla's history, dating from the 1860s)
$20.00 per year membership for individuals, $25.00 per year membership for families, $50.00 per year business and professional membership

La Mesa Historical Society
(8369 University Avenue, La Mesa, CA 92041—location)
PO Box 882 (mailing address)
La Mesa, CA 92044
(619) 460-3726
Donna Regan, President

La Puente Valley Historical Society
(16021 East Gale Avenue, City of Industry, CA 91748—location)
PO Box 522 (mailing address)
La Puente, CA 91747
(626) 336-7644; (626) 336-2382
Harold Rogers, President
Hours: Museums: first and third Wed & Sun
Pub. *The Bridge*, bimonthly
$6.00 per year membership

Lafayette Historical Society
PO Box 133
Lafayette, CA 94549
Bill Wakeman
$10.00 per year membership for families

Lake County Historical Society
PO Box 1011
Lakeport, CA 95453
(707) 279-4466
Pub. *POMO Bulletin*, quarterly
$7.50 per year membership

Lake Tahoe Historical Society
(3058 Lake Tahoe Boulevard—location)
PO Box 404 (mailing address)
South Lake Tahoe, CA 96156
(530) 541-5458
Bob Corkill, President
Hours: winter: Sat–Sun 12:00–4:00; summer: daily 11:00–4:00
Pub. *Lake Tahoe Historical Society Quarterly*
(Lake Tahoe archives, artifacts, photos, books, oral histories)
$25.00 per year membership

Las Virgenes Historical Society
30473-50 Mulholland Highway
PO Box 124
Agoura, CA 91301
(818) 889-0836

Lassen County Historical Society
105 North Weatherlow Street
PO Box 321
Susanville, CA 96130

Leisure World Historical Society of Laguna Hills
23522 Paseo de Valencia
PO Box 2220
Laguna Hills, CA 92654
(949) 951-2330
Claire Still, President
Pub. *LWHSLH Newsletter*

Little Landers Historical Society
(Bolton Hall Museum, 10110 Commerce Avenue, Tujunga, CA 91042—location)
PO Box 203 (mailing address)
Tujunga, CA 91043-0203
(818) 352-3420
Joan Conrad, President
Hours: Tue & Sun 1:00–4:00, and by appointment
Pub. *Newsletter*, monthly
$15.00 per year membership for individuals, $25.00 per year membership for couples, $50.00 per year Sponsor or Donor membership (business or group)

Livermore Heritage Guild
Third and K Streets
PO Box 961
Livermore, CA 94550
(510) 443-3272

Lomita Historical Society
(City Hall, 24300 Narbonne Avenue—location)
24016 Benhill Avenue (mailing address)
Lomita, CA 90717

Lompoc Valley Historical Society, Inc.
207 North L Street
PO Box 88
Lompoc, CA 93438
(805) 735-4626; (805) 736-5304
Myra Manfrina, Historian
Hours: Mon & Thur 9:00–11:00
Pub. *Lompoc Legacy*, quarterly, $1.00 per issue
(genealogical files, local history and genealogy of old families)
search fees: $5.00, printing family genealogy $10.00–$20.00, up to $50.00

Historical Society of Long Beach
(418 Pine Avenue—location)
PO Box 1869 (mailing address)
Long Beach, CA 90801
(562) 495-1210; (562) 495-1281
Julie Bartolotto, Executive Director
Pub. *History Is Happening in Long Beach*, quarterly
$25.00 per year membership, limited research: $3.50

Los Altos Hills Historical Society
27200 Elena Road
Los Altos Hills, CA 94022
(650) 948-8470
Daniel Alexander, President
Pub. *LAHHS Newsletter*

Los Altos Historical Commission
1 North San Antonio Road
Los Altos Hills, CA 94022
(650) 948-1491

Los Angeles City Historical Society
PO Box 41046
Los Angeles, CA 90041
Hours: Southern California Genealogical Society Library: Mon & Wed–Sat 10:00–4:00, Tue 10:00–9:00, first & second Sun 10:00–4:00
Pub. *Newsletter* (not genealogical in content), quarterly
$15.00 per year membership

Madera County Historical Society
(210 West Yosemite, Madera, CA 93637—location)
PO Box 478 (mailing address)
Madera, CA 93639
(209) 673-0291
Bill Coats, President
Pub. *Madera County Historian*

Marin County Historical Society
1125 B Street
San Rafael, CA 94901
(415) 454-8538; (415) 499-3017 FAX
Jocelyn A. Moss, Librarian
Hours: Mon, Wed & Fri 10:00–6:00, Tue & Thur 10:00–9:00, Sat 1:00–5:00
Pub. *Marin County Historical Society Magazine*, annually; *MCHS Bulletin*, biannually; *Newsletter*, quarterly
(Marin newspapers, photographs, San Quentin, Louise Boyd)
$20.00 per year membership; research fee: $15.00

Mayo Hayes O'Donnell Library (of the Monterey History and Art Association)
(155 Van Buren Street—location)
5 Custom House Plaza (mailing address)
Monterey, CA 93940
(831) 372-2608; (831) 626-9364 FAX (Chairperson)
Faye Messinger, Chairperson
Hours: Wed & Fri–Sun 1:30–3:45
Pub. *Noticias del Puerto de Monterey*, quarterly (for Association)
(2,000 books on maritime history, 2,200 books on local history)
$35.00 per year Association membership for individuals; library open to the public; copies: 50¢ each

McHenry Museum and Historical Society
1402 I Street
Modesto, CA 95354-1402
(209) 577-5366

Wayne A. Mathes, Cultural Services
   Manager
Hours: Tue–Sun noon–4:00
Pub. *Stanislaus Stepping Stones*, quarterly
$10.00 per year membership

Merced County Historical Society
Merced County Courthouse Museum
Old County Courthouse
21st and N Streets
Merced, CA 95340
(209) 385-7426
Andrea Metz, Director
Hours: Wed–Sun 1:00–4:00
Pub. *For the Record*, quarterly
(Jail registers 1900–40, assessor records
   1880s–1950, some funeral records,
   school registers 1890s–1950s; "our
   research room is just in progress.")
search fees: $10.00 donation

Mill Valley Historical Society
Mill Valley Public Library, History Room
375 Throckmorton Avenue
Mill Valley, CA 94941
(415) 388-2190 (Library); (415) 388-
   8929 FAX (Library)
Ron Olson, President; Joyce Crews,
   Reference Librarian
Hours: History Room: Mon–Thur & Sat
   10:00–noon & 2:00–4:00, Mon–Thur
   7:00–9:00, Fri 2:00–4:00 (hours
   depend on docent available)
Pub. *Mill Valley Historical Review* (Mill
   Valley and Marin County), annually,
   $5.00 per issue
$12.00 per year membership

Millbrae Historical Society
(621-A Magnolia, Constitution Square—
   location)
PO Box 511 (mailing address)
Millbrae, CA 94030
(650) 697-5786
Alma Massolo, Curator
Hours: Sat noon–4:00

**Modoc County Historical Society
and Museum**
600 South Main Street
Alturas, CA 96101
(916) 233-2944
Ann Odgers, Curator
Pub. *Modoc County Historical Society
   Journal*, annually
$6.50 per year membership

Mohave Historical Society
PO Box 163
Victorville, CA 92393

Montecito History Committee
1469 East Valley Road
Montecito, CA 93108
(805) 969-1597

Monterey County Historical Society
(333 Boronda Road, Salinas, CA
   93906—location)
PO Box 3576 (mailing address)
Salinas, CA 93912

(831) 757-8085
Mona Gudgel, Administrator
Pub. *MCHS Newsletter*

**The Historical Society of Monterey
Park, Inc.**
(781 South Orange Avenue—museum
   location)
PO Box 272 (mailing address)
Monterey Park, CA 91754
(626) 281-3015
Bea Rexius, President
Hours: Museum: Sat–Sun 2:00–4:00
Pub. *Newsletter*, nine times per year
   (monthly, except July–August &
   December)
from $10.00 per year membership to
   $100.00 life membership

Moraga Historical Society
PO Box 103
Moraga, CA 94556
Pub. *Moraga Historical Society
   Newsletter*, quarterly
$7.00 per year membership

Morgan Hill Historical Society, Inc.
PO Box 1258
Morgan Hill, CA 95037
(408) 779-5755
Susan Locarnini, President
Pub. *Historically Speaking*

Mount Lassen Historical Society
PO Box 291
Shingletown, CA 96088
(530) 474-3061

**Mountain View Historical
Association**
(Mountain View Library—location)
PO Box 252 (mailing address)
Mountain View, CA 94042
(650) 968-6595
Barbara Kinchen, City Historian
Hours: meetings at the Mountain View
   Senior Center, Escuela Avenue: first
   Sun (Feb, May, Aug, Nov)
Pub. *M.V. Historical Newsletter*,
   quarterly
$7.00 per year membership for
   individuals, $10.00 per year
   membership for families, $100.00 life
   membership

Napa County Historical Society
Goodman Library Building, 1219 First
   Street
Napa, CA 94559
(707) 224-1739; (707) 224-5933 FAX
Diane S. Ballard, Executive Director
Hours: Tue & Thur noon–4:00; special
   tours by appointment
Pub. *Tidings*, monthly
$12.00 per year membership for
   individuals, $20.00 per year
   membership for families, $30.00 per
   year Contributing membership, $50.00
   per year Patron membership, $200.00
   life membership; free museum and
   library admission

Nevada County Historical Society
214 Main Street
PO Box 1300
Nevada City, CA 95959
(530) 265-5468; (530) 265-3754
   (President)
Jim Rose, President
Hours: Mon–Sun 11:00–4:00
Pub. *Nevada County Historical Society
   Bulletin*, quarterly; *Newsletter*
(pre-gold rush and gold rush mining
   history; operates three museums and
   two research libraries)
$12.00 per year membership

North Lake Tahoe Historical Society
(130 West Lake Boulevard—location)
PO Box 6141 (mailing address)
Tahoe City, CA 96145
(916) 583-1762; (916) 583-8992 FAX
Miriam Biro, Director Museums
Hours: May 1–Oct 1: 11:00–5:00
Pub. *NLTHS Newsletter*, quarterly, not
   available by subscription
$15.00 per year Contributing
   membership for senior citizens or
   juniors, $35.00 per year Sustaining
   membership, $75.00 per year Sponsor
   membership, $100.00+ per year Patron
   membership

**Ojai Valley Museum and Historical
Society**
(130 West Ojai Avenue—location)
PO Box 204
Ojai, CA 93024
(805) 640-1390
Sherry Smith, Director
Hours: Wed–Sun 1:00–4:00, and
   mornings by appointment
Pub. *OVMHS Newsletter*, quarterly
$20.00 per year membership for
   individuals, $25.00 per year
   membership for families

Orange County Historical Society
(Dr. Howe-Waffle Victorian House, 120
   Civic Center Drive West, Santa Ana,
   CA 92701—office location)
PO Box 10984 (mailing address)
Santa Ana, CA 92711
(714) 543-8282; (714) 525-4879
E-mail: vvigus@ix.netcom.com
Betsy Vigus, Newsletter Editor; Richard
   Vining, President
Hours: by appointment only
Pub. *County Courier*, ten times per year
   (monthly, September–June)
(local history and education, publishing
   program)
$15.00 per year membership (beginning
   in June); no genealogy research done
   but will answer inquiries if
   information is available

Pacific Grove Heritage Society
Laurel Avenue at 17th Street
PO Box 1007
Pacific Grove, CA 93950
(831) 372-2898

Hours: Sat 1:00–4:00
Pub. *Board and Batten*, bimonthly
$10.00 per year membership

Pacific Palisades Historical Society
PO Box 1299
Pacific Palisades, CA 90272
Fred Blum, Treasurer
Pub. *PPHS Newsletter*

Pajaro Valley Historical Association
William H. Volck Memorial Museum
261 East Beach Street
Watsonville, CA 95076
(831) 722-0305
Albert Schadel, Archivist
Hours: Tue–Thur 11:00–3:00
Pub. *Pajaro Valley Historical Association Newsletter*, quarterly
$25.00 per year Donor membership, $50.00 per year Sponsor membership, $100.00 per year Supporter membership, $250.00 per year Benefactor membership, $500.00+ per year Patron membership; research fee: $10.00 per hour, $10.00 minimum; copies 20¢ per 8$^{1}/_{2}$" x 11" page

Palm Springs Historical Society
(Village Green Heritage Center, 221 South Palm Canyon Drive, Palm Springs, CA 92262—location)
PO Box 1498 (mailing address)
Palm Springs, CA 92263
(760) 323-8297
Sally Hall McManus, Director/Curator
Hours: Wed & Sun noon–3:00, Thur–Sat 10:00–4:00
Pub. *Whispering Palms*, quarterly
$10.00 per year membership for individuals, $25.00 per year membership for families, $50.00 per year Sustaining membership, $100.00 per year Patron membership, $1,000.00 life membership; research: $25.00 per hour; admission free to members, 50¢ per home general admission, children or students free with an adult

Palo Alto Historical Association
(1213 Newell Road, Palo Alto, CA 94303—location)
PO Box 193 (mailing address)
Palo Alto, CA 94302
(650) 329-2664
Steven Staiger, Historian
Hours: Tue 6:00–9:00, Thur 2:00–5:00
Pub. *Tall Tree*, ten times per year (monthly, September–June)
$15.00 per year membership

Paradise Historical Society
PO Box 1696
Paradise, CA 95967
(530) 873-0769
Lois McDonald, Editor
Pub. *Tales of Paradise Ridge*, semiannually
$9.00 per year membership

Pasadena Historical Society Research Library
470 West Walnut Street
Pasadena, CA 91103
(626) 577-1660
Tim Gregory, Archivist
Hours: Thur–Sun 1:00–4:00
Pub. *Newsletter*, quarterly
no library use fee

Patterson Township Historical Society
PO Box 15
Patterson, CA 95363
(209) 892-6882

Pioneer Historical Society of Riverside
PO Box 246
Riverside, CA 92502
(909) 684-4074 (President)
Alan Curl, President
Pub. *Journal of the Riverside Historical Society*, annually, $5.00 per issue
$10.00 per year membership

Plumas County Historical Society
500 Jackson Street
PO Box 695
Quincy, CA 95971
(530) 283-4379
Edward C. Brown, Director
Pub. *Plumas Memories*, annually
$5.00 per year regular membership (beginning 1 July), $3.00 per year membership for students, $12.00 per year Sustaining membership, $100.00 life membership

Historical Society of Pomona Valley
1569 North Park Avenue
Pomona, CA 91768
(909) 623-2198
E-mail: Historical<gallivan@worldnet.att.net
http://www.osb.net/Pomona
Beth Page, President
Pub. *News Notes*, four to five times per year
(society maintains three historical sites and a pioneer cemetery, refers genealogical inquiries to Special Collections Department, Pomona Public Library)
$7.50 per year membership, $100.00 life membership

Poway Historical and Memorial Society
(Old Poway Park, Poway, CA 92064—location)
PO Box 19 (mailing address)
Poway, CA 92074
(619) 679-8587 (Sat–Sun only); (619) 748-3700 (Secretary's home)
Cecilia Burr, Secretary
Hours: Sat 10:00–2:00, Sun 11:00–2:00
Pub. *Newsletter*, monthly
$15.00 per year membership for

individuals, $17.00 per year membership for families, $30.00 per year Corporate membership

Ramona Pioneer Historical Society and Guy B. Woodward Museum
(645 Main Street—location)
PO Box 625 (mailing address)
Ramona, CA 92065
(760) 789-1062
Geneva Woodward, President

The City of Rancho Cucamonga Historical Program
(10500 Civic Center Drive—location)
PO Box 807 (mailing address)
Rancho Cucamonga, CA 91729
(909) 477-2750; (909) 477-2847 FAX
Larry Henderson, Principal Planner

Redlands Area Historical Society, Inc.
Genealogical Branch
PO Box 1024
Redlands, CA 92373
(909) 307-6060
Liz Beguelin, President and Genealogist
Pub. *R.A.H.S. Newsletter*, ten times per year (monthly, September–June)
$10.00 per year membership

Reedley Historical Society
1752 Tenth Street
PO Box 877
Reedley, CA 93654
(209) 638-1913

Rialto Historical Society
205 North Riverside Avenue
Rialto, CA 92377
(909) 875-1750
Elizabeth Hughbanks, President
Pub. *RHS Newsletter*

Rio Linda/Elverta Historical Society
PO Box 478
Rio Linda, CA 95673-0478
(916) 332-0355
Martha Glidden
Hours: meetings at Calvary Lutheran Church, Fifth and L Streets, Rio Linda: third Sun (except Aug & Nov)
Pub. *The Eggspress*, semiannually
(building an extensive collection of historical material, with a great deal of genealogical material included in this collection; museum expected to open in 1999)
$15.00 per year membership for individuals, $20.00 per year membership for families

Riverside County Historical Commission
4600 Crestmore Drive
PO Box 3507
Riverside, CA 92519
(909) 787-2551
Diana L. Seider, History Division Director

Roseville Historical Society
c/o Carnegie Museum
557 Lincoln Street
Roseville, CA 95678
(916) 773-3003
Hours: meetings third Sat 10:00

Sacramento County Historical Society
PO Box 160065
Sacramento, CA 95816-0065
(916) 443-6265
Melinda A. Peak, President
Pub. *Golden Notes*, quarterly; *Golden Nuggets* (newsletter)
$25.00 per year membership for individuals

Sacramento River Delta Historical Society
PO Box 41
Ryde, CA 95680
(916) 776-1390
Leonard Souza
Hours: meetings third Mon 7:30

Genealogical and Historical Council of Sacramento Valley
PO Box 214749
Sacramento, CA 95821-0749
(916) 331-4349; (916) 332-4359
E-mail: llarson@foothill.net
http://feefhs.org/ghcsv/frgghcsv.html
Marilyn Larson, Corresponding Secretary
Hours: meetings at the Sacramento Family History Center, 2745 Eastern Avenue, Sacramento
Pub. *Council News Coordinator*, bimonthly
(speakers list, list of local organizations; public service telephone—anyone may call for information such as addresses, meeting and seminar information, how-to information, etc.)
$15.00 per year membership for individuals (calendar year), $25.00 per year membership for organizations

Saddleback Area Historical Society
PO Box 156
El Toro, CA 92630
(949) 586-8488

San Antonio Valley Historical Association
(216 Grove Place, King City, CA 93930—location)
PO Box 184 (mailing address)
Lockwood, CA 93932
(831) 385-3587

San Benito County Historical Society (Museum)
(498 Fifth Street—location)
PO Box 357 (mailing address)
Hollister, CA 95023
(831) 635-0335
Sharlene Van Rooy, Museum Director

Hours: Thur 7:00–9:00, Sat–Sun 2:00–4:30, and by appointment; meetings at Dunne Park clubhouse: last Wed
(historical museum with access to county records, audio history, coroner's reports, vital records, court listings, maps, and other documents)
$20.00 per year membership for individuals, $50.00 per year premier membership; research for cost of photocopies

San Clemente Historical Society
PO Box 283
San Clemente, CA 92672
(949) 492-4716
Jim Kempton, President

San Diego Historical Society
Research Archives
(1649 El Prado, Balboa Park—location)
PO Box 81825 (mailing address)
San Diego, CA 92138-1825
(619) 232-6203
http://edweb.sdsu.edu/sdhs/histsoc.html
Richard W. Crawford, Archivist and Editor
Hours: Thur–Sat 10:00–4:00
Pub. *Journal of San Diego History*, quarterly; *SDHS Times*, quarterly
$40.00 per year membership

San Gabriel Historical Association
546 West Broadway
San Gabriel, CA 91776
(626) 308-3223
Hours: Museum: Wed & Sat–Sun 1:00–4:00
Pub. *San Gabriel Historical News*, five times per year (January, March, May, September, November)
(local history, Gabrielino Indians, California missions, etc.)
$5.00 per year membership for individuals, $10.00 per year membership for families, $35.00 per year membership for businesses

San Joaquin County Historical Society and Museum
(11793 North Micke Grove Road, Lodi, CA 95240—location)
PO Box 30 (mailing address)
Lodi, CA 95241-0030
(209) 331-2055; (209) 331-2057 FAX
Michael W. Bennett, Director
Hours: Wed–Sun 1:00–4:45
Pub. *News and Notes*; *San Joaquin Historian*, quarterly
(indexed newspaper, reclamation district and county records, business records)
$4.00 per year membership; search fees: $25.00 per hour for non-members

San Joaquin Pioneer and Historical Society
The Haggin Museum
1201 North Pershing Avenue
Stockton, CA 95203
(209) 462-4116
Tod Ruhstaller, Director

San Juan Bautista Historical Society
308 Third Street
PO Box 1
San Juan Bautista, CA 95045
(831) 623-4542

San Luis Obispo County Historical Society Museum
696 Monterey Street
San Luis Obispo, CA 93401
(805) 543-0638; (805) 543-6659 FAX
Linda Field, Director
Hours: Wed–Sat 10:00–4:00
$20.00 per year membership

San Marino Historical Society
2701 Huntington Drive
PO Box 80222
San Marino, CA 91108
(626) 568-0119
Peggy Winkler, Librarian; Lillian Colle-Campbell, President
Hours: by appointment
Pub. *Grape Vine*, semiannually
$15.00 per year membership; no research fees unless extensive

San Mateo County Historical Association and Museum
College of San Mateo Campus
1700 West Hillsdale Boulevard
San Mateo, CA 94402
(650) 574-6441; (650) 574-6468 FAX
Marion C. Holmes, Archivist
Hours: Mon–Thur 9:30–4:30, Sun 12:30–4:30
Pub. *La Peninsula*, semiannually
(San Mateo County history)
$35.00 per year active membership for individuals or families, $20.00 per year membership for senior citizens or students, $50.00 per year Contributor membership, $250.00 per year Patron membership, $500.00 per year Historian membership, $1,000.00 per year Benefactor membership

San Pablo Historical and Museum Society
Alvarado Adobe
1 Alvarado Square
San Pablo, CA 94806
(510) 236-7373
Ann Roberts, Curator
(local history reference service)

San Ramon Valley Historical Society
PO Box 521
Danville, CA 94526
(510) 837-0369
Mary Anne Iarussi, President
Pub. *Record*, five times per year, *Roster*, annually
$10.00 per year membership

Santa Barbara Historical Society
136 East De La Guerra Street
PO Box 578
Santa Barbara, CA 93102
(805) 966-1601; (805) 966-1603 FAX

Michael Redmon, Librarian
Hours: Tue–Sat 10:00–5:00, Sun noon–
   5:00; Gledhill Library: Tue–Fri 10:00–
   4:00, first Sat 10:00–1:00
Pub. *Noticias*, quarterly; *Santa Barbara
   Historical Museum Newsletter*,
   monthly
$40.00 per year membership

Santa Clara County Historical and Genealogical Society

Santa Clara Central Library
2635 Homestead Road
Santa Clara, CA 95051-5387
(408) 984-3236
Micki Mistretta, President
Hours: Library: Mon–Thur 9:00–9:00,
   Fri–Sat 9:00–6:00, Sun 1:00–5:00;
   Society: third Thur (except Aug and
   Dec) 7:00
Pub. *Santa Clara County Connections*,
   semiannually, $5.00 per year
   subscription; *Newsletter*, monthly
   (except Aug and December)
   (international genealogy collection)
$15.00 per year membership for
   individuals, $20.00 per year
   membership for two people at the
   same address, $25.00+ per year
   Contributing membership; research
   fees vary

Santa Clara County Historical Heritage Commission

70 West Hedding Street
San Jose, CA 95110
(408) 299-4321
Janis Kuechenmeister, Deputy Clerk of
   the Board

Santa Clarita Valley Historical Society

(24107 San Fernando Road, Newhall,
   CA 91321—location)
PO Box 221925 (mailing address)
Newhall, CA 91322-1925
(805) 259-4669

Santa Fe Springs Historical Committee

(Santa Fe Springs Public Library, 11710
   Telegraph Road—location)
10146 Gridley Road (mailing address)
Santa Fe Springs, CA 90670
(562) 864-4538

Santa Maria Valley Historical Society

616 South Broadway
PO Box 584
Santa Maria, CA 93454
(805) 922-3130

Santa Monica Historical Society and Museum

1539 Euclid Street
PO Box 3059, Will Rogers Station
Santa Monica, CA 90408
(310) 394-2605
Louise Gabriel, President

Hours: second & fourth Sun 1:00–4:30,
   library and group tours by
   appointment
Pub. *Santa Monica Historical Society
   Newsletter*, bimonthly
("Resource library (California and Santa
   Monica-Westside history), photo
   archives (7,000 photos, 3,000 slides);
   our library also has a collection of
   early phone directories and early street
   maps.")
$20.00 per year membership

Santa Ynez Valley Historical Society

3596 Sagunto
PO Box 181
Santa Ynez, CA 93460
(805) 688-7889
Richard S. Sims, Executive Director
Pub. *The Gates of Memory*

Saratoga Historical Foundation

20450 Saratoga Los Gratos Road
PO Box 172
Saratoga, CA 95071
(408) 867-4311
Louise Cooper, President
Hours: Wed–Sun 1:00–4:00
$30.00 per year membership for families

Sausalito Historical Society

(420 Litho Street, Sausalito, CA 94965—
   location)
PO Box 352 (mailing address)
Sausalito, CA 94966

Searles Valley Historical Society

(13193 Main Street, corner of Main and
   Searles Streets—location)
PO Box 630 (mailing address)
Trona, CA 93592
(760) 372-4800; (760) 372-4884
Marydith Haughton, President
Hours: Sat 11:00–1:00, and by
   appointment
Pub. *Ol Timer*, quarterly
$10.00 per year membership

Shafter Historical Society

150 Central Valley Highway
PO Box 1088
Shafter, CA 93263
(805) 746-1557
Helen Gaede, President
Hours: first Sat 10:00–2:00, and by
   appointment
("Museum is a restored Santa Fe Depot
   built in 1917; railroad artifacts, farm
   equipment")
$10.00 per year membership for
   individuals, $15.00 per year
   membership for families, $5.00 per
   year membership for students (through
   college)

Shasta Historical Society

Redding Museum of Art and History
(56 Quartz Hill Road—location)
PO Box 990277 (mailing address)
Redding, CA 96099-0277

(530) 225-4155
Hazel McKim, Librarian
Hours: when Museum is open, and by
   appointment
Pub. *Covered Wagon* (Shasta County
   pioneers), annually, price varies by
   edition
("Shasta County pioneers; material
   limited to Shasta County and
   California related")

Sierra County Historical Society

Kentucky Mine Museum, Highway 49
PO Box 260
Sierra City, CA 96125
(916) 862-1310 phone and FAX
Karen Donaldson, Museum Curator
Hours: Wed–Sun 10:00–5:00, weekends
   in Oct, closed till Memorial Day
Pub. *The Sierran*, semiannually
$10.00 per year membership for
   individuals, $15.00 per year
   membership for families or schools/
   libraries, $25.00 per year membership
   for businesses, $50.00 per year
   Sustaining membership, $250.00 life
   membership

Sierra Madre Historical Society

PO Box 202
Sierra Madre, CA 91024

Simi Valley Historical Society

Strathearn Historical Park
137 Strathearn Place
PO Box 351
Simi Valley, CA 93065
(805) 526-6453
Patricia Havens, Museum Director
Hours: Office: Tue–Fri 9:00–1:00
Pub. *Mail Cart*

Siskiyou County Historical Society and Museum

910 South Main Street
Yreka, CA 96097
(530) 842-3836
Michael Hendryx, Museum Director
Hours: Tue–Sat 9:00–5:00 (no research
   on Wed)
Pub. *Nuggets—Siskiyou County
   Historical Society*, irregularly; *The
   Siskiyou Pioneer*, annually
$15.00 per year membership for
   individuals, $25.00 per year
   membership for institutions, $50.00+
   per year Sponsor membership,
   $450.00 life membership (under age
   65), $200.00 life membership (over
   age 65)

Solano County Historical Society

PO Box 922
Vallejo, CA 94590

Sonoma County Historical Society

PO Box 1373
Santa Rosa, CA 95402
(707) 539-1786 (Archivist)
H. A. Lapham, Archivist

Pub. *The Journal of the Sonoma County Historical Society*, quarterly
$10.00 per year membership for individuals, $15.00 per year membership for families

Sonoma Valley Historical Society
PO Box 861
Sonoma, CA 95476
Pub. *Sonoma Valley Notes*, bimonthly

South Humboldt Historical and Genealogical Society
PO Box 656
Garberville, CA 95440
Pub. *Southern Humboldt Roots and Trails*, quarterly
$5.00 per year membership

Historical Society of Southern California
200 East Avenue 43
Los Angeles, CA 90031
(213) 222-0546
Pub. *Southern California Quarterly*; *Southern Californian*, quarterly, $35.00 per year subscription for both periodicals

Spanishtown Historical Society
PO Box 62
Half Moon Bay, CA 94019
(650) 728-5027

Sunnyvale Historical Society and Museum Association
235 East California
PO Box 61301
Sunnyvale, CA 94088
(408) 749-0220
Jan Camp, President
Hours: Tue & Thur 12:30–3:30, Sun 1:00–4:00, and by appointment
Pub. *SHSMA Newsletter*, monthly (local history resources, museum)
$15.00 per year membership for individuals, $25.00 per year membership for families, $8.00 per year membership for senior citizens (age 60+) and students, $15.00 per year membership for senior citizen families, $45.00 per year membership for businesses and organizations

Surveyors' Historical Society
10324 Newton Way
Rancho Cordova, CA 95670

Surveyors' Historical Society
31457 Hugh Way
Hayward, CA 94544
(510) 471-3905

Sutter County Historical Society
PO Box 1004
Yuba City, CA 95992
(530) 673-2721
Linda Leone, Treasurer/Co-editor
Pub. *SCHS News Bulletin*, quarterly (January, April, July, October)
$15.00 per year membership for

individuals, $10.00 per year membership for students, senior citizens or libraries

Tehama Genealogical and Historical Society
PO Box 415
Red Bluff, CA 96080
Pub. *Memories*, annually, $10.00 per issue (yearbook on County of Tehama history)

Torrance Historical Society
1345 Post Avenue
Torrance, CA 90501

Trinity County Historical Society
508 Main Street
PO Box 333
Weaverville, CA 96093-0333
(530) 623-5211
Hal Goodyear, Museum Director
Hours: May–Oct: 10:00–5:00; Apr & Nov: noon–4:00
Pub. *Trinity County Historical Society Yearbook*, annually (December), $4.95 per issue
$10.00 per year membership for individuals, $15.00 per year membership for families, $150.00 life membership

Truckee-Donner Historical Society, Inc.
PO Box 893
Truckee, CA 95734
(530) 587-2876

Tulare County Historical Society
(Tulare County Museum, Mooney Grove, 27000 Mooney Boulevard, Visalia—museum location)
PO Box 295 (mailing address)
Visalia, CA 93279
(209) 732-5829
E-mail: histerry@lightspeed.net
Terry L. Ommen, President
Pub. *Los Tulares*, quarterly
(extensive historical information on families, events and places in Tulare County)
$15.00 per year membership for individuals, $200.00 life membership

Tuolumne County Historical Society
158 West Bradford Avenue
PO Box 695
Sonora, CA 95370
(209) 532-1317
Lyle R. Scott, Treasurer
Hours: Mon–Sat 9:30–4:00
Pub. *Chispa*, quarterly, $2.00 per issue; *Historian*, monthly
$15.00 per year membership

Twentynine Palms Historical Society
6760 National Park Drive
PO Box 1926
Twentynine Palms, CA 92277
(760) 367-2366

Margot Spangenberg, Board President
Hours: Museum and Gift Shop: Wed– Sun 1:00–4:00
Pub. *News & Notes*, quarterly (March, June, September, December)
(Morongo Basin area historical society)
$12.50 per year Contributing or Business membership, $25.00 per year membership for families, $5.00 per year Pioneer (before 1940) membership, $50.00 per year Patron membership, $100.00 per year Benefactor membership, $300.00 life membership

Historical Society of the Upper Mojave Desert
Maturango Museum
100 East Las Flores
Ridgecrest, CA 93555
(760) 375-5249 (Membership)
http://www.ridgecrest.ca/us/ matmus/ Hist.html
Fred Weals, Membership
Hours: meetings: third Tue 7:30
Pub. *Newsletter*; *Bulletin*
$10.00 per year membership per address (calendar year to Fred Weals, Treasurer, 554 East Dana, Ridgecrest, CA 93555)

Ventura County Historical Society
Ventura County Museum of History and Art
100 East Main Street
Ventura, CA 93001
(805) 653-0323
Charles Johnson, Librarian
Hours: Museum: Mon–Fri 10:00–5:00, Sat 10:00–1:00
Pub. *Heritage and History*, monthly; *The Ventura County Historical Society Quarterly*, $4.00 per issue
$35.00 per year membership for individuals

Walnut Creek Historical Society
Shadelands Ranch Historical Museum
2660 Ygnacio Valley Road
Walnut Creek, CA 94598
(925) 935-7871
Elizabeth Isles
Hours: Office: Mon–Thur 9:00–4:00, Sun 1:00–4:00; Museum: Wed–Thur 11:30–4:00, Sun 1:00–4:00
Pub. *Shadelands Newsletter*, quarterly (Walnut Creek history)
$10.00 per year membership for individuals, $15.00 per year membership for families, $150.00 life membership

Washington Township Historical Society
(43263 Mission Boulevard, Fremont, CA 94538—location)
PO Box 3045 (mailing address)
Fremont, CA 94539
(510) 656-3761

Western Sonoma County Historical Society

261 South Main Street
Sebastopol, CA 95472
(707) 829-6711; (707) 829-7041 FAX
Jan King, Museum Director
Hours: Research Room: Thur–Sun 1:00–
4:00 and by appointment
Pub. *Apple Press*, monthly
$10.00 per year membership for
individuals, $15.00 per year
membership for families, $30.00 per
year Sustaining membership, $50.00
per year Patron membership

Whittier Historical Society

6755 Newlin Avenue
Whittier, CA 90601
(562) 945-3871
Rosalie Dannenbaum, President
Hours: Tue–Fri 9:00–3:00, Sat–Sun
1:00–4:00
Pub. *Whittier Gazette*, quarterly

Windsor Square-Hancock Park Historical Society

137 North Larchmont Boulevard, #135
Los Angeles, CA 90004
(213) 243-8182
Fluff McLean, President

Yolo County Historical Society

PO Box 1447
Woodland, CA 95776-1447
(530) 661-2212 (information line only)
Pub. *YCHS Newsletter*, ten times per
year
(local history books, church records)
$12.00 per year membership for
individuals, $8.00 per year membership
for senior citizens (over 65)

LDS Family History Centers

Anaheim
(714) 533-2772

Bakersfield
(805) 831-2036; (805) 322-1975

Chico
(916) 343-6641

Concord
(510-686) 1766

El Cajon
(619) 588-1426

Fresno
(209) 431-3759; (209) 431-4759

Glendale
(818) 241-8763

Hemet
(909) 658-8104

Huntington Beach
(714) 536-4736

Lancaster
(805) 943-1670

Los Angeles (Visitors' Center)
(310) 474-2202

Menlo Park
(415) 325-9711

Mission Viejo
(714) 364-2742

Modesto
(209) 571-0370; (209) 545-4814

Moreno Valley
(909) 247-8839

Oakland (Visitors' Center)
(510) 531-3905

Orange
(714) 997-7710

Pasadena
(818) 351-8517

Riverside
(909) 784-1918; (909) 360-8547

Sacramento
(916) 487-2090

San Bernardino
(909) 881-5355

San Diego
(619) 584-7668

San Francisco
(see Menlo Park or Oakland)

San Jose
(408) 274-8592

Santa Barbara
(805) 682-2092

Santa Clara
(408) 241-1449

Santa Maria
(805) 928-4722

Santa Rosa
(707) 525-0399

Seaside
(408) 394-1124

Simi Valley
(805) 581-2456

Stockton
(209) 951-7060

Thousand Oaks
(805) 241-9316

Ventura
(805) 643-5607

Vista
(619) 945-6053

Genealogical Societies

State Genealogical Societies

California Genealogical Society

(300 Brannan Street—location)
PO Box 77105 (mailing address)
San Francisco, CA 94107-0105
(415) 777-9936; (415) 777-0932 FAX
http://members.aol.com/calgensoc/home/
home.htm
Manuel A. Pacheco, Office Manager
Hours: Wed–Thur & Sat 9:00–4:00
Pub. *CGS News*, bimonthly; *The Nugget*
(general genealogy), semiannually
(specializes in California and San
Francisco)
$30.00 per year membership for
individuals, $45.00 per year
membership for families; research:
$12.00 per hour for members, $15.00
per hour for non-members

California State Genealogical Alliance

PO Box 3113
Danville, CA 94526-0113
(714) 993-1168 (President's home);
(714) 278-3474 (President's office);
(714) 278-2101 FAX
E-mail: welliott@ccvax.fullerton.edu
http://feefhs.org/csga/frg-csga.html
Wendy L. Elliott, C.G., President
Pub. *CSGA Newsletter*, monthly; *CSGA
Speakers Director*, biannually;
*California County Recorders Source
Book*, biannually; *CSGA Society
Directory*, annually
(statewide organization with annual
meetings in conjunction with
seminars)
Regions: **South San Joaquin Valley**
(Fresno, Inyo, Kern, Kings, Madera,
Mono and Tulare counties), Valerite V.
Howland, (209) 227-8569, Lea
Mitchem, (209) 226-7993, E-mail:
ccspca@ix21.ix.netcom.com; **San
Francisco Bay** (Alameda, Contra
Costa, Marin, San Francisco, Santa
Clara and San Mateo counties), Betty
Timmers, (510) 283-8864, Susan
Swindell, (510) 372-6996, E-mail:
swindell@value.net; **East LA/Orange
County** (Orange County and Los
Angeles County, east of Highway
605), Michelle Amsbury, (714) 447-
3009; **Sacramento Valley** (Alpine,
Amador, El Dorado, Nevada, Placer,
Sacramento, Solano and Yolo
counties), Iris Carter Jones, (916) 682-
3381, E-mail: ijones@ns.net; **North
San Joaquin Valley** (Calaveras,
Mariposa, Merced, San Joaquin,
Stanislaus and Tuolumne counties),
David & Jolene Abrahams, (510) 447-

9386, E-mail: drabraha@ccnet.com;
San Diego/Imperial (Imperial and
San Diego counties), Everett Ireland,
(619) 485-7684, E-mail:
everett.ireland@internetMCI.com,
Joan Lowrey, (619) 454-7046, E-mail:
jlowrey@connectnet.com; **Riverside/
San Bernardino** (Riverside and San
Bernardino counties), Janet Meservy,
(909) 681-5720, E-mail:
janta@earthlink.net, Nancy Gies,
(909) 923-2268, E-mail:
negdag@genesisnetwork.net,
negdag@aol.com; **South Central
Coast** (Montery, San Benito and Santa
Cruz), Barbara Clark, (831) 426-6298,
E-mail: marygra@redshift.com; **Tri-
counties** (San Luis Obispo, Santa
Barbara and Ventura counties), Emma
Lee Price, (805) 497-8293, E-mail:
hkxn84b@prodigy.com, Jean
Nepsund, (818) 991-9475, E-mail:
NEPSUND@aol.com; **Los Angeles
County** (Los Angeles County, west of
Highway 605, south of San Fernando
Valley), Sandy Bourassa, (310) 540-
6230, E-mail: SeNiDiA@aol.com,
Michael Reagan, (310) 540-6230, E-
mail: MahGaLee@aol.com; **San
Fernando Valley**, John/Nillah O'Neill,
(818) 846-2532, E-mail:
chooch@pacbell.net; **North West** (Del
Norte, western Siskiyou, Humboldt
and western Trinity counties); **North
Bay** (Lake, Mendocino, Napa and
Sonoma); **North Corridor** (eastern
Siskiyou, Shasta and eastern Trinity
counties); **North Central Valley**
(Butte, Colusa, Glenn, Tehama, Sutter
and Yuba counties); **North East**
(Lassen, Modoc, Plumas and Sierra
counties)
$20.00 per year membership

**Professional Genealogists of
California**
5048 J Parkway
Sacramento, CA 95823

**Southern California Chapter
Association of Professional
Genealogists**
PO Box 9486
Brea, CA 92822-9486
E-mail: tkashuba@aol.com;
    barbzr@msn.com
http://www.compuology.com/sccapg

Regional Genealogical
Societies

Antelope Valley Genealogical Society
PO Box 1049
Lancaster, CA 93584-1049
(805) 256-1646 (President's home)
E-mail: leslie@hughes.net
Leslie A. Harrington, President

Pub. *Prospector Quarterly*, $8.00 per
year subscription; *Antelope Valley
Genealogical Society Surname Index*,
annually
$12.00 per year membership for
individuals, $15.00 per year
membership for families

Chester Genealogy Club
PO Box 107
Chester, CA 96020

**Clan Diggers Genealogical Society,
Inc., of the Kern River Valley (Kern
County)**
PO Box 531
Lake Isabella, CA 93240
Pub. *Clan Gleanings Newsletter*,
quarterly

**Genealogical Society of Coachella
Valley**
PO Box 124
Indio, CA 92202
(760) 342-3725 (Editor)
Pat Westcott, Newsletter Editor
Hours: meetings at Indio Library: last Sat
Pub. *Desert Diggins'*, monthly
$15.00 per year membership for
individuals, $20.00 per year
membership for families

**Colorado River-Blythe-Quartzite
Genealogical Society**
411 South Fifth Street
Blythe, CA 92225-2816

**Conejo Valley Genealogical Society,
Inc.**
PO Box 1228 (mailing address)
Thousand Oaks, CA 91358-0228
(805) 497-8293 (Corresponding
Secretary)
Emma Lee Price, Corresponding
Secretary; Lois Burlo, President
Hours: Thousand Oaks Library, E Janss
Road, Thousand Oakes: Mon–Thur
10:00–9:00, Sat 10:00–5:00, Sun
1:00–5:00; meetings: second Tue;
Computer Interest Group meetings:
first Tue
Pub. *Rabbit Tracks*, quarterly, $3.00 per
issue; *The Genealogist* (events and
information of interest to members),
monthly
(Ventura County censuses and voter
registration, ahnentafel charts and
family histories)
$15.00 per year membership for
individuals, $20.00 per year
membership for families, plus one-
time fee of $4.00 for registration and
information packet

**Contra Costa County Genealogical
Society**
PO Box 910
Concord, CA 94522
(925) 937-5774

Kathy Castro, Corresponding Secretary
Pub. *Diablo Descendants* (Contra Costa
County, California), monthly
$15.00 per year membership; queries
accepted

Davis Genealogy Club and Library
Davis Senior Center
646 A Street
Davis, CA 95616
(530) 753-2672
Clarence Barry
Hours: Mon, Wed & Fri 1:00–4:00;
meetings last Mon 1:00

Delta Genealogical Interest Group
PO Box 157
Knightsen, CA 94548
Carolyn Sherfy

East Bay Genealogical Society
(405 14th Street, Terrace Level—library
location)
PO Box 20417 (mailing address)
Oakland, CA 94620-0417
(510) 451-9599 (Library)
Gretchen Kohl, President
Hours: Library: Mon 9:00–4:00
Pub. *The Live Oak*, bimonthly
$12.50 per year membership for
individuals, additional $6.25 for each
family member

East Kern Genealogical Society
PO Box 961
North Edwards, CA 93523
(619) 769-4345; (619) 769-4166
Ray Young, President; Penny Kailer,
Vice President
Hours: Library: Tue 5:00–9:00, Wed
9:00–1:00 & 5:00–9:00, Thur–
Fri 9:00–1:00; meetings: second Sat
9:00–noon
Pub. *Tortoise Tracks*, monthly
$10.00 per year membership for
individuals, $15.00 per year
membership for couples

Escondido Genealogical Society, Inc.
PO Box 2190
Escondido, CA 92033-2190
(760) 480-7369
Jacqueline S. Veen, President
Hours: meetings at Escondido Public
Library: third Sat (Sept–Jun) 10:00
Pub. *Escondido Genealogical Society
Newsletter*, bimonthly; *Hidden Valley
Journal*, annually (November), $8.00
per issue
$18.00 per year membership (includes
both publications)

Fresno Genealogical Society
PO Box 1429
Fresno, CA 93716-1429
(209) 488-3195 (option 5)
Hours: Fresno County Free Library,
California History and Genealogy
Room: Mon–Wed & Fri noon–6:00,
Thur noon–8:00, Sat 10:00–5:00;

meetings first Tue 6:30–9:00
Pub. *Ash Tree Echo*, two times per year
(March and September); *The Jotted
Line*, monthly
$15.00 per year membership for
individuals, $20.00 per year
membership for families, $200.00 life
membership for individuals, $225.00
life membership for families

Genealogical Society of North Orange County California (GSNOCC)

PO Box 706
Yorba Linda, CA 92885-0706
(714) 993-2448
E-mail: ricega@aol.com
Grace Rice, President
Hours: meetings at Bradford House, 136
Palm Circle, Placentia, CA 92870:
third Wed (Jan–Nov) 7:00 (beginners
and computer help at 6:30)
Pub. *GSNOCC Newsletter*, eleven times
per year
$15.00 per year membership for
individuals or families

Glendora Genealogy Group

PO Box 1141
Glendora, CA 91740
Pat Chavarria, President
Hours: meetings: fourth Tue
Pub. *Newsletter*, monthly
$12.00 per year membership for
individuals, $20.00 per year
membership for couples

Glenn Genealogy Group

1121 Marin
Orland, CA 95963

HEFA Kinseekers

PO Box 3310
Fullerton, CA 92634

Hayward Area Genealogical Society

PO Box 754
Hayward, CA 94543

Hemet-San Jacinto Genealogical Society

(1779 East Florida Avenue, Unit C-4,
Hemet, CA 92544—location)
PO Box 2516 (mailing address)
Hemet, CA 92546-2516
(909) 658-6153; (909) 658-1962
(Library)
Mary Allred, Librarian
Hours: Library-Headquarters: Mon–Wed
& first & third Sat 10:00–3:00
Pub. *Pastfinder*, four times per year
(August, October, January, May)
(approximately 10,000 quarterlies and
3,000 hardbound books in library)
$15.00 per year membership for
individuals (beginning in June),
$21.00 per year membership for
husband and wife

Hi Desert Genealogical Society

PO Box 1271
Victorville, CA 92392
Pub. *Desert Diggings*, quarterly
$10.00 per year membership

Imperial County Genealogical Society

1573 Elm Street
El Centro, CA 92243-3133

Indian Wells Valley Genealogical Society

131 Los Flores
PO Box 2047
Ridgecrest, CA 93555

Kern County Genealogical Society

PO Box 2214
Bakersfield, CA 93303
(805) 831-7527 (Librarian's home)
Joyce Bayless, Librarian
Hours: meetings at Beale Library: third
Tue 1:00–3:00
Pub. *Kern-Gen*, quarterly
$12.00 per year membership for
individuals, $14.00 per year
membership for couples

Laarveld House

PO Box 56
El Dorado, CA 95623
(530) 622-9434
Betty C. Laarveld, Owner
Hours: Mon–Fri 9:00 A.M.–10:00 P.M.,
Sat–Sun noon–6:00
(El Dorado cemeteries 1850–present;
deed indexes from 1850; federal
census)
research fees: $15.00 per hour

Lake County Genealogical Society

Lake County Museum
255 North Main Street
PO Box 1323
Lakeport, CA 95453
(707) 263-4555
E-mail: kgene@jps.net
Kathleen Alvey, Vice President/Librarian
Hours: Wed–Sun 11:00–4:00
Pub. *Lake County Genealogical Society
Newsletter*, bimonthly
(California genealogy and Lake County
genealogy)
$7.50 per year membership for
individuals, $10.00 per year
membership for families

Lake Elsinore Genealogical Society "Legs"

PO Box 807
Lake Elsinore, CA 92531-0807
(909) 674-5776
Imogene Lewellen, President
Pub. *LEGS*, monthly
$10.00 per year membership

Leisure World Genealogical Workshop

Leisure World Library
PO Box 2069
Seal Beach, CA 90740
Susan Montgomery, President
Hours: Mon–Thur 9:00–6:00, Fri–Sat
9:00–5:00
$2.00 per year membership

Livermore-Amador Genealogical Society (LAGS)

(Pleasanton Library, 400 Old Bernal
Avenue, Pleasanton, CA 94566—
location)
PO Box 901 (mailing address)
Livermore, CA 94551
(510) 846-6972
http://www.california.com/~lags/lags.html
Judy Person, President
Hours: Library: Mon–Tue 1:00–8:00,
Wed–Thur 10:00–6:00, Sat 2:00–6:00,
Sun 1:00–5:00
Pub. *Roots Tracer*, quarterly
(web page has surname index, registers
of local cemeteries)
$18.00 per year membership for
individuals, $25.00 per year membership
for families; search fee: $1.00

Los Angeles Westside Genealogical Society

PO Box 10447
Marina Del Rey, CA 90291
Pub. *Newsletter*, eleven times per year
(monthly, except December)
$18.00 per year membership

Los Banos Genealogical Society, Inc.

16778 South Place
PO Box 2525
Los Banos, CA 93635
(209) 826-4882 (Library); (209) 826-
7161 (President); (209) 826-0763
(Secretary)
Betty Bettencourt, Librarian; Barbara
Mitchell, President; Josie Bosworth,
Secretary
Hours: by appointment
Pub. *The Tree Shakers*, monthly
$15.00 per year membership

Genealogical Society of Madera County

(Madera County Main Library, across
from courthouse—library location)
PO Box 495 (mailing address)
Madera, CA 93639-0495
Sandra Williams, Editor
Pub. *Madera Heritage Quarterly*
(February, May, August, November)
(cemetery records of Madera County;
genealogical books and publications)
$12.00 per year membership for
individuals, $17.00 per year
membership for couples

Maidu Genealogical Society
Maidu Community Center
1550 Maidu Drive
Roseville, CA 95661
(916) 786-0186
E-mail: pbdallas@jps.net
Pamela Dallas, President
Hours: meetings: second Tue 12:30 &
    fourth Tue 1:00–3:00
Pub. *Maidu Genealogical Society
    Newsletter*, monthly

Marin County Genealogical Society
PO Box 1511
Novato, CA 94948-1511
(415) 435-2310
Pat Friesen
Pub. *Marin Kin Tracer*, quarterly
$15.00 per year membership for
    individuals, $20.00 per year
    membership for families; research:
    $10.00 per hour

**Mendocino Coast Genealogical
Society**
PO Box 762
Fort Bragg, CA 95437
Alice Holmes, Editor
Hours: Wed–Sat 10:00–4:30 by
    appointment
Pub. *Under Construction*, quarterly
    (February, May, August, November),
    $7.50 per year subscription
$15.00 per year full membership

Merced County Genealogical Society
PO Box 3061
Merced, CA 95344
(209) 723-9019
Lois Jimenez
Hours: Merced County Library:
    Mon–Thur 9:00–9:00, Fri–Sat 9:00–
    6:00
Pub. *The Family Snoop*, monthly
$10.00 per year membership for
    individuals

Mission Oaks Genealogy Club
(Mission Oaks Community Center, 4701
    Gibbons Drive, Carmichael—
    location)
PO Box 216 (mailing address)
Carmichael, CA 95609-0216
(916) 482-8531
Elizabeth Kohler
Hours: meetings third Thur 1:00; PAF™
    User's Group meetings first Thur
    1:00–4:00
Pub. *Mission Oaks Genealogy Club
    Newsletter*, quarterly

**Mojave Desert Genealogical
Society**
PO Box 1320
Barstow, CA 92311

**Genealogical Society of Morongo
Basin**
PO Box 234
Yucca Valley, CA 92284

Mount Diablo Genealogical Society
1938 Tice Boulevard
PO Box 4654
Walnut Creek, CA 94596
(510) 932-4423
A. Maxim Coppage, Newsletter Editor
Hours: Contra Costa County Library:
    third Thur 1:00–3:00
Pub. *Mount Diablo Genealogical Society
    Newsletter*, monthly
$10.00 per year membership

**Napa Valley Genealogical and
Biographical Society**
1701 Menlo
Napa, CA 94559
(707) 252-2252
Dolores Melby Hibbert, Librarian;
    Virginia Bromage Wakeman, Research
Hours: Tue 10:00–9:00, Wed–Thur
    10:00–4:00, second & fourth Sat
    10:00–2:00
Pub. *Wine Press Monthly Newsletter*,
    monthly
$25.00 per year membership for
    individuals; research: $10.00 per hour

Nevada County Genealogical Society
PO Box 176
Cedar Ridge, CA 95924
(530) 272-2119
Maria Brower, Founder and Editor
Hours: meetings at Nevada County
    Library
Pub. *Kith & Kin*, monthly
(early mining records and maps, great
    registers, Nevada County records
    resource guide)
$12.00 per year membership

Newberry Springs Genealogy Club
701 Montara Road, #27
Barstow, CA 92311-5742

**North San Diego County
Genealogical Society, Inc.**
(Carlsbad City Library, 1250 Carlsbad
    Village Drive, Carlsbad, CA 92008-
    1991—location)
PO Box 581 (mailing address)
Carlsbad, CA 92018-0581
Hours: Carlsbad City Library: Mon–Thur
    9:00–9:00, Fri–Sat 9:00–5:00
Pub. *Paths to the Past*, monthly
$15.00 per year membership

Ohio Genealogical Society
Southern California Chapter
(see Ohio)

**Orange County California
Genealogical Society (OCCGS)**
(Huntington Beach Public Library, 7111
    Talbert Avenue, Huntington Beach, CA
    92648-1296—location)
PO Box 1587 (mailing address)
Orange, CA 92856-1587
Pub. *OCCGS Journal*, two times per
    year, $12.00 per year subscription for

members, $15.00 per year subscription
    for non-members
$14.50 per year membership for
    individuals, $22.00 per year joint
    membership

Pajaro Valley Genealogical Society
53 North Drive
Freedom, CA 95019
Grace Marie Hackwell

Palm Springs Genealogical Society
(Palm Springs Public Library—
    collection location)
PO Box 2093 (mailing address)
Palm Springs, CA 92263
E-mail: editormt@aol.com
Margaret M. Turlo, President
Hours: meetings first Sat (Oct–May)
    10:00 at Palm Springs Public Library
Pub. *Pedigree Searchers*, eight times per
    year (monthly, except June–
    September)
$12.00 per year membership

Paradise Genealogical Society
PO Box 460
Paradise, CA 95969-0460
(530) 877-2330
http://www.joshuanet.com/~pargenso
Earl Cowden, Membership Chair
Hours: Mon & Wed 10:00–4:00, Sat
    10:00–2:00
Pub. *Goldmine*, semiannually
$23.00 per year membership for
    individuals, $28.00 per year
    membership for families

Pasadena Genealogy Society
1080 North Holliston Avenue
Pasadena, CA 91104-3014
Hours: meetings quarterly
$10.00 per year membership for
    individuals, $12.00 per year
    membership for families

Placer County Genealogical Society
PO Box 7385
Auburn, CA 95604-7385
http://www.webcom.com/gunruh/
    pogs.html
Barbara Leak, Library and Research
    Chairman
Hours: meetings fourth Thur 7:00; study
    group: first Tue 10:00
Pub. *Placer Trails*, nine times per year
$7.50 per year membership for
    individuals, $10.00 per year
    membership for families

Pomona Valley Genealogical Society
PO Box 286
Pomona, CA 91768-0286
(909) 593-6786
E-mail: jcbh98a@prodigy.com
Anne Larkin, Newsletter Editor
Hours: Meetings: second Tue (Sept–
    May) 6:30
Pub. *Pomona Valley Genealogical
    Society Newsletter*, nine times per year
    (monthly, September–May)

(publications from California State Assembly Records from 1851 on)

$12.00 per year membership for individuals, $15.00 per year membership for couples (monies and donations support Genealogical Collection of the Pomona Public Library); queries free for members, $1.00 for non-members; research: $10.00 donation requested

Questing Heirs Genealogical Society, Inc.

PO Box 15102
Long Beach, CA 90815-0102
Pub. *Questing Heirs Genealogical Society, Inc., Newsletter*, monthly, $12.00 per year subscription
$18.00 per year membership for individuals, $27.00 per year membership for families

Redlands Area Historical Society, Inc.

Genealogical Branch
PO Box 1024
Redlands, CA 92373
(909) 307-6060
Liz Beguelin, President and Genealogist
Pub. *R.A.H.S. Newsletter*, ten times per year (monthly, September–June)
$10.00 per year membership

Redwood Genealogical Society, Inc.

(Community Center Building, Rohner Park, #5 Park Way—location)
PO Box 645 (mailing address)
Fortuna, CA 95540
(707) 725-3791 (Board Member); (707) 725-3791 (Secretary)
Evelyn Deike, Board Member; Nina Winfrey, Corresponding Secretary
Hours: Wed 9:00–10:00, and by appointment
Pub. *Redwood Researcher*, quarterly (February, May, August, November)
$12.00 per year membership for individuals, $15.00 per year membership for families; queries welcome; research fees: costs of copies and postage

Renegade Root Diggers

9171 Fargo Avenue
Hanford, CA 93230

Genealogical Society of Riverside

PO Box 2557
Riverside, CA 92516
Hours: Riverside Public Library
Pub. *Lifeliner*, quarterly, $10.00 per year subscription
$15.00 per year membership

Genealogical Association of Sacramento

(Belle Cooledge Library, 5600 South Lane Park Drive, Sacramento—location)

PO Box 292145 (mailing address)
Sacramento, CA 95829-2145
(916) 682-8004 (President)
Esther McAllister, President
Hours: Mon & Thur 12:00–9:00, Tue–Wed 10:00–9:00, Fri–Sat 1:00–5:00; meetings third Wed (except July–Aug & Dec) 12:30 at Belle Cooledge Library, 5681 Freeport Boulevard, Sacramento
Pub. *G.A.S. Lites*, semiannually; *Lamplighter*, monthly
$15.00 per year membership for individuals, $20.00 per year membership for couples

Sacramento Genealogical Society— Root Cellar

(California State Archives, 1020 "O" Street, Sacramento—collection location)
PO Box 265 (mailing address)
Citrus Heights, CA 95611-0265
(916) 481-4930 (Library Chair)
Sammie Hudgens, Library Chair
Hours: Archives: Mon–Fri 9:30–4:00; meetings at Citrus Heights Elementary School, 7085 Auburn Building, Citrus Heights: second Wed (Sept–Jun) 6:30
Pub. *Root Cellar Preserves*, quarterly (worldwide holding and large periodical collection)
$15.00 per year membership for individuals (beginning 1 October), $22.50 per year membership for couples, $12.50 per year membership for senior citizen individuals, $20.00 per year membership for senior citizen couples

Genealogical and Historical Council of Sacramento Valley

PO Box 214749
Sacramento, CA 95821-0749
(916) 331-4349; (916) 332-4359
E-mail: llarson@foothill.net
http://feefhs.org/ghcsv/frgghcsv.html
Marilyn Larson, Corresponding Secretary
Hours: meetings at the Sacramento Family History Center, 2745 Eastern Avenue, Sacramento
Pub. *Council News Coordinator*, bimonthly
(speakers list, list of local organizations; public service telephone—anyone may call for information such as addresses, meeting and seminar information, how-to information, etc.)
$15.00 per year membership for individuals (calendar year), $25.00 per year membership for organizations

San Bernardino Valley Genealogical Society

(Norman Feldheyon Library, Mary Kellogg Room—location)
PO Box 2220 (mailing address)
San Bernardino, CA 92406-2220

(909) 883-7468
Blanche Tompkins, President
Hours: first Sat 10:00–12:00
Pub. *Valley Quarterly* (local history)
$10.00 per year membership for individuals, $15.00 per year membership for families; search fee: $5.00 per hour

San Diego County Genealogical Association

PO Box 422
Ramona, CA 92065
(619) 789-2534
Jacqueline Beck, President
$10.00 per year membership

San Fernando Valley Genealogical Society

20387 Londeliuss
Canoga Park, CA 91306

San Gorgonio Genealogical Society

1050 Brinton Avenue
Banning, CA 92220
Joan Carpenter Covington, President

San Joaquin Genealogical Society

PO Box 4817
Stockton, CA 95204-0817
http://www.rootsweb.com/~sjgs/
Cheri A. Pillsbury, President
Hours: Mon–Sat 10:00–9:00; meetings third Thur 1:30 at Stockton Public Library, Park and Oak Streets, Stockton
Pub. *San Joaquin Genealogical Society*, five times per year
$10.00 per year membership for individuals, $15.00 per year membership for families; research: $10.00 per hour

San Luis Obispo County Genealogical Society, Inc.

PO Box 4
Atascadero, CA 93423-0004
(805) 927-8172 (President); (805) 927-4025 FAX (President); (805) 238-6421 (Atascadero Librarian); (805) 489-7409 (Arroyo Grande Librarian)
http://www.slonet.org/~rmiklas/slogen/genweb1.html
Beverly Krause Blum, President; Michele McCaffrey, Atascadero Librarian; Jean James, Arroyo Grande Librarian
Hours: Atascadero Library, City Administration Building, Palma and West Mall, Room 104B: Tue 1:00–9:00, Wed 10:00–4:00, Fri & third Sat 1:00–4:00; Arroyo Grande Library, South County Regional Center, 800 West Branch in the County Library: Mon 6:00–8:00, Tue 10:00–5:00
Pub. *Bulletin*, quarterly, $10.00 per year subscription; *Newsletter*, bimonthly
(publishes records of San Luis Obispo County)

$18.00 per year membership for individual membership, $22.00 per year membership for couples, $200.00 life membership; research: $7.50 per hour plus copies at 10¢ per page for members, $10.00 per hour plus copies for non-members

San Mateo County Genealogical Society

PO Box 5083
San Mateo, CA 94402
Doris M. Newbery, President
Hours: Wed & Sat 1:00–4:00
Pub. *Newsletter*, ten times per year (monthly except August and December)
$15.00 per year membership (calendar year)

San Ramon Valley Genealogical Society

(Danville, CA—location)
PO Box 305 (mailing address)
Diablo, CA 94528
(925) 837-8858
Ed O'Donnell, Membership
Pub. *San Ramon Valley Genealogical Society Newsletter*, ten times per year
$15.00 per year membership for individuals, $20.00 per year membership for families

Santa Barbara County Genealogical Society

(711 Santa Barbara Street—library location)
PO Box 1303 (mailing address)
Santa Barbara, CA 93116-1303
(805) 965-7423
http://www.compuology.com/sbarbara/
Janice G. Cloud, President
Hours: library: Tue, Thur–Fri & Sun 1:00–4:00
Pub. *Ancestors West*, quarterly; *Tree Tips, Newsletter*, monthly
$17.00 per year membership for individuals, $24.00 per year membership for couples

Santa Clara County Historical and Genealogical Society

Santa Clara Central Library
2635 Homestead Road
Santa Clara, CA 95051-5387
(408) 984-3236
Micki Mistretta, President
Hours: Library: Mon–Thur 9:00–9:00, Fri–Sat 9:00–6:00, Sun 1:00–5:00; Society: third Thur (except Aug and Dec) 7:00
Pub. *Santa Clara County Connections*, semiannually, $5.00 per year subscription; *Newsletter*, monthly (except Aug and December)
(international genealogy collection)
$15.00 per year membership for individuals, $20.00 per year membership for two people at the

same address, $25.00+ per year Contributing membership; research fees vary

Genealogical Society of Santa Cruz County

Central Branch Public Library
(224 Church Street, Santa Cruz, CA 95060—location)
PO Box 72 (mailing address)
Santa Cruz, CA 95063
(831) 429-3530
Hours: Library: Tue–Thur 10:00–8:00, Fri–Sat 10:00–5:00
Pub. *Newsletter—The Genealogical Society of Santa Cruz County*, bimonthly (odd-numbered months)
(sponsors speakers program, annual seminar, compilation of local records)
$15.00 per year membership for individuals, additional $8.00 for each family member

Santa Maria Valley Genealogical Society

PO Box 1215
Santa Maria, CA 93456
(805) 925-4093
Mary McBride Munding, President
Hours: Meetings at Oak Knolls Haven, 4845 South Bradley Road, Santa Maria: third Thur 3:30
Pub. *Santa Maria Valley Genealogical Society Quarterly* (spring, summer, fall, winter)
(Santa Maria Valley early births, deaths, marriages; Knights of Pythias records; local pioneer families)
$15.00 per year membership for individuals, $20.00 per year membership for families; research for donation

Sequoia Genealogical Society, Inc.

Tulare Public Library
113 North F Street
Tulare, CA 93274-3803
(209) 685-2342 (Library)
Mary De Luz, Library Assistant
Hours: Tulare Public Library: Mon & Wed 10:00–6:00, Tue & Thur 10:00–8:30, Sat 10:00–2:00
Pub. *Sequoia Genealogical Society, Inc., Newsletter*, eight times per year (monthly, March–November)
$15.00 per year membership for individuals, $18.00 per year membership for couples

Shasta County Genealogical Society

PO Box 994652
Redding, CA 96099-4652
$10.00 per year membership

Genealogical Society of Siskiyou County

PO Box 225
Yreka, CA 96097
(530) 842-6018 (President)

Sharon Youngs, President
Hours: meetings: last Tue 7:30
Pub. *Heir Lines*, quarterly
$12.00 per year membership (beginning in June), $18.00 per year membership for families

Sloughhouse Area Genealogical Society

Rancho Murietta, CA 95683
(916) 354-2807
Ruthena Grimes

Solano County Genealogical Society

(Old Town Hall, 620 East Main Street, Vacaville—location)
PO Box 2494 (mailing address)
Fairfield, CA 94533
(707) 446-6869 (Library)
Kathy Mercurio, Librarian
Hours: Mon & third Sat 10:00–2:00, except federal holidays; meetings fourth Thur 7:00 at Senior Center, 1200 Civic Center Drive, Fairfield
Pub. *Solano County Genealogical Society Newsletter*, ten times per year (monthly, except July and August); *The Root Digger*, quarterly
$10.00 per year membership

Sonoma County Genealogical Society

(Santa Rosa, CA—location)
c/o 8330 Blue Spruce Way (mailing address)
Windsor, CA 95492
(707) 838-1311; (707) 838-3635
E-mail: chuckadoo@aol.com
Charles H. Warner, President
Hours: daily 9:00–5:00
Pub. *The Sonoma Searcher*, quarterly, $10.00 per year subscription
("Special interest groups: British, German, Irish, southern states, computers")
$15.00 per year membership; non-member queries: $2.00

South Humboldt Historical and Genealogical Society

PO Box 656
Garberville, CA 95440
Pub. *Southern Humboldt Roots and Trails*, quarterly
$5.00 per year membership

Southern California Genealogical Society, Inc.

417 Irving Drive
Burbank, CA 91504
(818) 843-7247
http://www.cwire.com/scgs/
John M. O'Neill, President; Jennifer Weber, Editor
Hours: Mon & Wed–Fri 10:00–4:00, Tue, first & second Sun, third & fourth Sat 9:00–4:00
Pub. *The Searcher*, monthly

("Research Team: Revolutionary War, colonial wars, Irish famine immigrants, Virginia ancestry, Massachusetts town vital records"; Turner Collection; 18,000 books, *The American Genealogist* and many state periodicals, CDs, annual jamboree) $22.00 per year membership for individuals; search fees vary

The Genealogical Society of Stanislaus County, Inc.
(1600 Carver Road—location)
PO Box 4735 (mailing address)
Modesto, CA 95352-4735
(209) 522-2880 (President)
Dorothy Jenkinson, President
Hours: Book Nook (private home): Fri 10:00–3:00; Special Collection Room, Stanislaus County Free Library: Mon–Wed 10:00–3:00, Thur–Sat 10:00–5:00; meetings third Mon 7:00 at Morris Community Center
Pub. *Stanislaus Researcher*, monthly (cemetery listings)
$15.00 per year membership for individuals, $22.50 per year membership for families

TRW Genealogical Society
One Space Park S-1156
Redondo Beach, CA 90278
(310) 813-6171
E-mail: snminer@aol.com
Mike O'Rell, President
Pub. *Montage*, quarterly
membership limited to employees and family members of TRW

Taft Area Genealogical Society
PO Box 1411
Taft, CA 93268
Hours: monthly business meeting
$12.00 per year membership

Tehama Genealogical and Historical Society
PO Box 415
Red Bluff, CA 96080
Pub. *Memories*, annually, $10.00 per issue (yearbook on County of Tehama history)

Tule Tree Tracers
Porterville Public Library
41 West Thurman Avenue
Porterville, CA 93257
(209) 784-0177
Melanie Wells
Hours: Genealogy: Mon–Sat 9:00–5:00; Local History: Mon–Thur 10:00–12:00

Tuolumne County Genealogical Society
158 West Bradford Street
PO Box 3956
Sonora, CA 95370
(209) 532-1317 (Secretary)
Metta Schafft, Librarian; Nell Holloway, Secretary

Hours: Tue & Thur 10:00–4:00, Sat 10:00–3:00
Pub. *Golden Roots of the Mother Lode*, quarterly, $2.50 per issue; *Gold Digger*, six times per year
(Tuolumne County and other Mother Lode counties; gold rush history and genealogy)
$18.00 per year membership for individuals, $30.00 per year membership for family, additional $4.00 per year for overseas membership; research for donation

Vandenberg Genealogical Society
(LDS Church, 1312 West Prune—location)
PO Box 81 (mailing address)
Lompoc, CA 93438-0081
(805) 686-1707
Richard Hunter, President
Hours: third Tue 7:00–9:00
Pub. *SearchNotes*, monthly
$12.00 per year membership for individuals, $18.00 per year membership for families

Ventura County Genealogical Society
E. P. Foster Branch
The Ventura County Library Services Agency
651 East Main
PO Box D.N.
Ventura, CA 93002
(805) 648-2715 (Library); (805) 642-1242 (Society President)
Betty Johnsen, President
Hours: Mon–Thur 10:00–9:00, Fri–Sat 10:00–5:00, Sun 1:00–4:00
Pub. *Ventura County Genealogical Society Quarterly*
$12.00 per year membership

Whittier Area Genealogical Society
(13502 Suite "J," Quad Shopping Center, Whittier Boulevard and Central—location)
PO Box 4367 (mailing address)
Whittier, CA 90607-4367
(562) 946-1758 (President)
Bonnie Jean Sell, President
Hours: Santa Fe Springs Public Library: Mon–Thur 10:00–9:00, Fri 10:00–6:00, Sat 10:00–5:00
Pub. *Whittier Area Genealogical Society Newsletter*, monthly
$15.00 per year membership, additional $7.50 per year membership for family members, $250.00 life membership, $125.00 life membership for senior citizens

Yucaipa Valley Genealogical Society
PO Box 32
Yucaipa, CA 92399
Pub. *Yucaipa Valley Family Finders Quarterly*
$5.00 per year membership

Independent Publications and Miscellany

Anderson Marsh State Historic Park
Clear Lake District
5300 Soda Bay Road
Kelseyville, CA 95451
(707) 994-0688
Stephen Hill, District Superintendent

Belvedere-Tiburon Landmarks Society
Esperanza Street
PO Box 134
Belvedere-Tiburon, CA 94920
(415) 435-1853
(archives department)

CaGenWeb
Part of U.S. GenWeb Project
E-mail: ca@usgenweb.com
http://www.compuology.com/cagenweb/
(links to other California resources)

California Council for the Humanities
312 Sutter Street, Suite 601
San Francisco, CA 94108
(415) 391-1474
Morton Rothstein, Chair; James Quay, Executive Director

California Council for the Promotion of History
PO Box 221476
Sacramento, CA 95822
Pub. *California History Action*, quarterly (public history and history action in California, professional organization)
$35.00 per year membership

California Department of Parks and Recreation
San Joaquin Valley District
PO Box 205
Friant, CA 93626
(209) 822-2332

California Pioneers of Santa Clara Valley
PO Box 8208
San Jose, CA 95155
Pub. *Trailblazer*, quarterly
$4.00 per year membership

California Views
Pat Hathaway Collection of Historical Photos
469 Pacific Street
Monterey, CA 93940-2702
(831) 373-3811
E-mail: hathaway@mbay.net
http://www.caviews.com/

Center for San Diego Studies
Department of History/Political Science
2900 Lomaland Drive
San Diego, CA 92106
(619) 221-2200

Dwayne Little, Department Chair
(historical databases)

Center for Southwest Research
(see New Mexico)

H-California
http://h-net2.msu.edu/~cal/
(history network)

Huntington Westerners
PO Box 80241
San Marino, CA 91118
(626) 284-2130
Midge Sherwood, Editor and Founder
(authentic history of the American
   frontier west, 1850–1900)
$20.00 per year membership

The K.A.R.D. Files
19305 S.E. 243rd Place
Kent, WA 98042-4820
(425) 432-1659
Judy K. Dye, Owner/Compiler
Pub. *Siskiyou County, California, Series*,
   irregularly

**Labor Archives and Research
Center**
San Francisco State University
480 Winston Drive
San Francisco, CA 94132
(415) 564-4010
Lynn A. Bonfield, Director

**Los Californianos, Hispanic
Ancestors of Alta California**
4530 LaCrosse Avenue
San Diego, CA 92117
(619) 273-2260
Alice Thomson, Membership Chairman
Hours: quarterly meetings at various
   locations: Sat & Sun
Pub. *Antepasados*, annually; *Noticias*,
   quarterly
(descendants of Hispanics in Alta
   California before February 1848)
regular membership subject to approval
   of Genealogy Committee, spouses also
   eligible, historians and libraries
   (corresponding) eligible with approval
   of board

**Los Fundadores, The Founders and
Friends of Santa Clara County**
(City of Santa Clara Civic Center, 1509
   Warburton Avenue, Santa Clara, CA
   95050—location)
1053 South White Road (mailing
   address)
San Jose, CA 95127
(408) 926-1165; (408) 248-ARTS (24-
   hour message)
Hours: meetings: first Sun
Pub. *Los Fundadores* (California's
   Spanish/Mexico period, genealogy of
   early California; articles about the
   Hispanic progenitors of California;
   early American pioneers, recognition
   of Native Americans), quarterly

$11.00 per year membership for
   individuals, $16.50 per year
   membership for families or societies;
   free queries for members

Los Pobladores 200
2830 East 56th Way
Long Beach, CA 90805

Marin Heritage
PO Box 1432
San Rafael, CA 94902
(415) 457-9280

Mendocino Historical Research, Inc.
Kelley House Museum
45007 Albion Street
PO Box 922
Mendocino, CA 95460
(707) 937-5791
Pat Turner, Executive Director
Hours: Museum: Fri–Mon 1:00–4:00;
   Office: Tue–Fri 9:00–4:00
Pub. *Mendocino Historical Review*,
   annually, $15.00 per issue
(Mendocino Coast, Mendocino and
   adjacent coastal towns; archival
   materials, genealogical records)
$35.00 per year membership

Modern Ancestors
PO Box 1217
Salida, CA 95368
(209) 521-9830
Susan K. Park

Mother Colony Household, Inc.
(685 North Helena, Anaheim, CA
   92805—location)
PO Box 3246 (mailing address)
Anaheim, CA 92803
(949) 854-1115
Harold Bastruf, President
Pub. *The Grapefine*, three times per year
(preserves Anaheim history by support of
   museums, history rooms, history
   programs, construction of historical
   place markers)
$240.00 membership

**William Penn Mott, Jr., Training
Center**
837 Asilomar Boulevard
PO Box 699
Pacific Grove, CA 93950
(831) 649-2954

Oregon-California Trails Association
(see Miscellaneous)

Petaluma Adobe State Historic Park
3325 Adobe Road
Petaluma, CA 94952
(707) 762-4871
Larry Costa, State Park Ranger I
Hours: 10:00–5:00
(not primarily genealogical)

Roots Investigators
PO Box 3261
Beaumont, CA 92223
Lila Hubbard

Pub. *Pass Genealogical Reporter
   Quarterly*

**Sacramento Trust for Historic
Preservation**
710 Coronado Boulevard
Sacramento, CA 95825

San Francisco History
http://www.zpub.com/sf/history/

Society of California Archivists
ASUC Store, Box 605, Telegraph
   Avenue and Berkeley Way
Berkeley, CA 94720-4510
(626) 405-2206
E-mail: dlewis@huntington.org
Dan Lewis, Ph.D., Publications Chair
Hours: Mon–Fri 8:30–5:00
Pub. *Directory of Archival and
   Manuscript Repositories in California*
   (lists more than 1,000 repositories
   throughout the state), about every five
   years, $49.00 postpaid for fourth
   edition, allow four to six weeks for
   delivery

**Sourisseau Academy for California
State and Local History**
San Jose State University
San Jose, CA 95192
(408) 924-6510
E-mail: glaffey@email.sjsu.edu
Glory Anne Laffey, Executive Secretary
Hours: by appointment

University of Arizona Press
Journal of the Southwest
(see Arizona)

University of California Press
2120 Berkeley Way
Berkeley, CA 94720
(800) 822-6657 (Orders); (415) 642-4262
   (Customer Service); (415) 642-4247
   (Office); (415) 643-7127 FAX
Judy Lucietta, Customer Service
   Manager
Pub. *Pacific Historical Review*, quarterly

Los Angeles Corral of Westerners
1506 Linda Rosa Avenue
Los Angeles, CA 90041

**San Francisco Corral, Westerners
International**
201 Homer Avenue
Palo Alto, CA 94301
(650) 327-2717

Stockton Corral of Westerners
PO Box 1315
Stockton, CA 95201
Joseph C. Elliff, Jr., Sheriff
Pub. *The Far Westerner*

COLORADO

Archives and Libraries with Holdings in Genealogy

State Archives and Library

Division of Archives and Public Records
Department of Personnel
1313 Sherman Street, Room #1B-20
Denver, CO 80203
(303) 866-2358; (303) 866-2390
http://www.state.co.us/gov_dir/gss/
archives/index.html
Terry Ketelsen, State Archivist
Hours: Mon–Fri 9:00–4:45 except
holidays
search fees: $25.00 for first item, $10.00
for each additional item, plus copying
costs

Colorado State Library
State Office Building, 201 East Colfax
Avenue
Denver, CO 80203-1799
(303) 866-6728; (303) 830-0793 FAX
http://www.aclin.org (Office of Library
and Adult Services)
Maureen K. Crocker, State Publications
Librarian
Hours: Mon–Fri 8:00–5:00
(not a statewide library or archives, does
not have materials of use to
genealogists; refer to Division of
Archives and Public Records)

State Historical Society

Colorado Historical Society
Stephen H. Hart Library
1300 Broadway
Denver, CO 80203-2137
(303) 866-2305
Rebecca Lintz, Assistant Director,
Collections Services
Hours: Tue–Sat 10:00–4:30
Pub. *Colorado Heritage*, quarterly;
Colorado History News, monthly;
*Essays and Monographs in Colorado
History*, irregularly
$30.00 per year membership for
individuals, $40.00 per year
membership for families, $18.00 per
year membership for students, $25.00
per year membership for senior
citizens (65+), $35.00 per year
membership for senior citizen couples;
search fees: $5.00 for 1/2 hour search
time and up to five photocopies,
additional copies 35¢ per page (up to
50 copies)

City, County and Regional Archives and Libraries

Adams State College Library
San Luis Valley Room
First and Edgemont
Alamosa, CO 81102
(719) 587-7781
Dianne Machado, Library Director
Hours: Mon–Thur 8:00–10:00, Fri 8:00–
5:00, Sat 10:00–6:00, Sun 1:00–9:00
(Colorado, San Luis Valley, northern
New Mexico)

Arvada Center for the Arts and Humanities Museum
6901 Wadsworth Boulevard
Arvada, CO 80003
(303) 431-3080

Auraria Library
Lawrence at 11th Street
Denver, CO 80204
(303) 556-8373; (303) 556-3528 FAX
E-mail: ftapp@carbon.cudenver.edu
http://www.cudenver.edu/public/library/
(archives and special collection;
manuscript collections)

Aurora History Museum
15001 East Alameda Drive
Aurora, CO 80012
(303) 360-8545

Aurora Public Library
14949 East Alameda Drive
Aurora, CO 80012
(303) 340-2290
Bette Yager, Information Services
Librarian
Hours: Mon–Thur 10:00–10:00, Fri–Sat
10:00–6:00, Sun 12:30–6:00

Bemis Public Library
6014 South Datura Street
Littleton, CO 80120
(303) 795-3996 FAX
E-mail: phyll.sl@csn.net
Phyllis Larison, Head of Adult Services
Mon–Thur 9:00–9:00, Fri–Sat 9:00–5:00
(genealogy collection includes books,
microfilm, periodicals)

Berthoud Public Library
(236 Welch Avenue—location)
PO Box 1259 (mailing address)
Berthoud, CO 80513
(970) 532-2757; (970) 532-4372 FAX
Roberta Depp, Director
Hours: Mon–Tue & Thur–Fri noon–6:00,
Wed 10:00–8:00, Sat 10:00–2:00
(local history, local newspaper on
microfilm)

Carnegie Branch Library for Local History
1125 Pine Street
Boulder, CO 80302
(303) 441-3110 phone and FAX
E-mail: hallw@boulder.lib.co.us

Wendy Hall, Manager
Hours: Mon 1:00–9:00, Tue & Thur–Sat
11:00–5:00, Wed 9:00–5:00
(local Boulder County history; houses
collection of Boulder Genealogical
Society)

Colorado Springs Museum
215 South Tejon Street
Colorado Springs, CO 80903
(719) 578-6650; (719) 578-6718
E-mail: cosmuseum@aol.com
Leah M. Davis, Archivist
Pub. *Update*
(35,000 historic photographs; manuscript
repository)

Cripple Creek District Museum, Inc.
Fifth and Bennett Avenue
PO Box 1210
Cripple Creek, CO 80813
(719) 689-2634
Erik C. Swanson, Director
Hours: summer 9:30–5:50; winter:
weekends only
("County cemetery records, city
directories: Cripple Creek, Victor,
Teller County")
research done for a donation

Denver Public Library
Genealogy Division
Western History Collection
10 West Fourteenth Avenue Parkway
Denver, CO 80204-2731
(303) 640-6200; (303) 640-6291
(Western History Collection)
http://www.denver.lib.co.us/
James K. Jeffrey, Genealogy Collection
Specialist; Eleanor Gahres, Manager,
Western History Collection
Hours: Mon–Wed 10:00–9:00, Thur–Sat
10:00–5:30, Sun 1:00–5:00
(national in scope; specialty: Colorado,
Rocky Mountains, Hispanic)

Lula W. Dorsey Museum
(2515 Tunnel Road, Estes Park, CO
80517—location)
PO Box 597 (mailing address)
Estes Park, CO 80511
(970) 586-3341, ext. 1137

El Pueblo Museum
324 West First Street
Pueblo, CO 81003

Fort Collins Public Library—Local History Section
201 Peterson Street
Fort Collins, CO 80524-2990
(970) 221-6688 (Local Historian); (970)
221-6398 FAX
Rheba Massey, Local History Coordinator
Hours: by appointment Mon noon–4:30
& 6:00–9:00, Tue–Fri 9:30–11:30 &
1:00–5:00
(specializes in Fort Collins, Larimer
County, and Colorado history: city
directories, newspapers, oral history

transcripts, historic photograph collection, biographical and subject files, historical maps, Colorado books and magazines, cemetery records, obituary/anniversary files, yearbooks, tax assessor records)
copies: 5¢ each ($2.00 minimum)

Fort Lewis College
Center of Southwest Studies
1000 Rim Drive
Durango, CO 81301-3999
(970) 247-7456
E-mail: ellison_t@flc.colorado.edu
Richard N. Ellis, Ph.D., Archivist/ Assistant Professor
Hours: Mon–Thur 11:00–8:00, Fri 11:00–4:00, Sun 3:00–7:00 (more limited hours during academic breaks, May–Aug)
("Collection strengths include ethnographic and historic records and artifacts relating to Native Americans (especially their U.S. government relations) and other peoples of the southwest; local and regional historic newspapers, U.S. census records for the Four Corners States, census records for Indians of North America, and records of businesses and organizations of southwest Colorado; center's holdings include over 13,000 volumes of published research material concerning the southwest, over 1,200 linear shelf feet of manuscripts and unbound printed materials, over 5,000 rolls of historic microfilm, and more than 15,000 historic photos; we require a weekday's advance notice for retrieval of microfilm materials")

Fort Morgan Museum
414 Main Street
PO Box 184
Fort Morgan, CO 80701
(970) 867-6331
Marne Jurgemeyer, Director
Pub. *Museum Monitor*
(genealogical services)

Gem Village Museum
Rt. 1
Bayfield, CO 81122
(970) 884-2811

Golden Library Branch of Jefferson County Public Library
1019 Tenth Street
Golden, CO 80401
(303) 279-4585
Hours: Mon–Thur 10:00–9:00, Fri–Sat 10:00–5:00, Sun 12:00–5:00
("local newspaper, *Golden Transcript*, on microfilm, holdings back to 1867")

City of Greeley Museums
City Complex at Seventh Street
Greeley, CO 80631
(970) 350-9220

Peggy Ford, Acting Supervisor
(genealogical services)

Greeley Public Library
919 Seventh Street
Greeley, CO 80631
(970) 350-9210 (Circulation); (970) 350-9212 (Reference)
Shirley Soenksen, Reference Librarian
Hours: Mon–Thur 9:00–9:00, Fri–Sat 9:00–5:00, Sun 1:00–5:00 (closed Jun–Aug)

Lakewood Library
Jefferson County Public Library
10200 West 20th Avenue
Lakewood, CO 80215
(303) 232-7833
Hours: Mon–Thur 10:00–9:00, Fri–Sat 10:00–5:00, Sun 12:00–5:00
(collection supported by Foothills Genealogical Society of Colorado)

Lakewood's Historical Belmar Village
797 South Wadsworth Boulevard
Lakewood, CO 80226
(303) 987-7850
Sheila A. Smyth, Supervisor, Heritage and Culture
Hours: Mon–Fri 8:00–5:00, Sat 1:00–5:00
(historical museum)
no admission charge

Littleton Historical Museum
6028 South Galleys
Littleton, CO 80120
(303) 795-3850
Robert McQuarie, Director
(reference library)

Longmont Public Library
409 Fourth Avenue
Longmont, CO 80501
(303) 651-8470
E. A. Brewer, Library Director
Hours: Mon–Thur 9:00–9:00, Fri–Sat 9:00–6:00
(Longmont and Saint Vrain Valley)

Loveland Museum/Gallery
Fifth and Lincoln
Loveland, CO 80537
(970) 962-2410; (970) 962-2910 FAX
Susan P. Ison, Director of Cultural Services
Hours: Tue–Wed & Fri 10:00–5:00, Thur 10:00–9:00, Sat 10:00–4:00, Sun noon–4:00

Loveland Public Library
300 North Adams
Loveland, CO 80537
(970) 962-2665; (970) 962-2905 FAX
E-mail: aslpl@webaccess.net
Carol Hammang, Reference Librarian
Hours: Mon–Thur 10:00–9:00, Fri–Sat 10:00–6:00, Sun (Sept–May) 1:00–5:00

McAllister House Museum
National Society of the Colonial Dames, Colorado
423 North Cascade Avenue
Colorado Springs, CO 80903
(719) 635-7925

Mesa County Public Library District
530 Grand Avenue
PO Box 20000-5019
Grand Junction, CO 81502-5019
(970) 241-5251; (970) 243-4744 FAX
http://www.colosys.net/mcpld
Kay Oxer, Head Reference Librarian
Hours: Mon–Thur 9:00–9:00, Fri–Sat 9:00–5:00, Sun (Sept–May) 1:00–5:00

Phillips S. Miller Branch Library
961 South Plum Creek Boulevard
Castle Rock, CO 80104

Montrose Library District
434 South First
Montrose, CO 81401

Museum of Northwest Colorado
590 Yampa Avenue
Craig, CO 81625
(970) 824-6360; (970) 824-7175 FAX
http://www.nadga.com/museum
Dan Davidson, Director
Hours: Mon–Sat 10:00–5:00
(local history museum; obituaries, marriages, some births, some land records, photos)

Museum of the Great Plains
(see Oklahoma)

Museum of Western Colorado
Archives and Library
(233 South Fifth, Grand Junction, CO 81501—location)
PO Box 20000-5020 (mailing address)
Grand Junction, CO 81502-5020
(970) 242-0971; (970) 242-3960 FAX
E-mail: judypa@colosys.net
http://www.colosys.net.uranium; http://www.mwc.mus.co.us
Judy A. Prosser-Armstrong, Librarian/ Archivist; Janice V. McLean, Director
Hours: Tue–Sat 10:00–4:00, and by appointment
Pub. *Museum Times*, monthly
(genealogy and western Colorado history)
$25.00 per year membership for individuals, $50.00 per year membership for families, $22.50 per year membership for senior citizen individuals (over 60 years), $40.00 per year for senior citizen families

Pikes Peak Library District
Local History and Genealogy
Penrose Public Library—Palmer Wing
20 North Cascade
PO Box 1579
Colorado Springs, CO 80901
(719) 531-6333, ext. 2252
Ree Mobley, Local History and Genealogy Librarian

Hours: Mon–Thur 10:00–9:00, Fri–Sat
10:00–6:00
(Colorado Springs, El Paso County,
Pikes Peak region and Colorado)
copies: 10¢ each for 8½" x 10" sheets,
20¢ each for 11" x 14" or 11" x 17"
sheets, plus postage and handling

Pueblo Library District
100 East Abriendo Avenue
Pueblo, CO 81004
(719) 543-9601; (719) 543-9610 FAX
Noreen Riffe, Special Collections
Librarian
Hours: Library: Mon–Thur 9:00–9:00,
Fri–Sat 9:00–6:00; Western Research
Room: Tue–Fri 1:00–6:00, Tue & Thur
7:00–9:00
(specializes in southern Colorado
history)

Rio Grande County Museum and Cultural Center
Sixth and Oak Street
Del Norte, CO 81132
(719) 657-2847; (719) 657-2627 FAX
Mark W. Allison, Director
Hours: Mon–Fri (winter) 11:00–4:00;
Mon–Sat (summer) 10:00–5:00

San Luis Museum Cultural and Commercial Center
401 Church Place
San Luis, CO 81152
(719) 672-3611
Juanita Gurule, Director
(research center)

Charles Leaming Tutt Library
Special Collections and Archives
Colorado College
1021 North Cascade
Colorado Springs, CO 80903
(719) 389-6668; (719) 389-6859 FAX
E-mail: vkiefer@cc.colorado.edu
http://www.cc.colorado.edu/library/
specialcollections/special.html
Virginia R. Kiefer, Curator
Hours: weekdays 9:00–noon & 1:00–
4:00
(specializes in "persons who have been
on the Colorado College faculty or in
some way connected to the Colorado
College"; Colorado and Pikes Peak
Region Collection)

University of Colorado, Boulder
University Libraries
Archives
Norlin Library
Campus PO Box 184
Boulder, CO 80309-0184
(303) 492-7242; (303) 492-3960 FAX
E-mail: montgomb@spot.colorado.edu
Hours: Mon–Fri 11:00–5:00
(Western American Collection collects
manuscript material on the settlement
and growth of the west; Labor

Collection; Politics Collection;
University of Colorado Archives)

University of Northern Colorado
James A. Michener Library
Archives and Special Collections
Greeley, CO 80639
(970) 351-2854; (970) 351-2540
E-mail: mlinscom@mail.univnorthco.edu
http://www.univnorthco.edu/library/
archives.htm

Weld County Library
Weld Library District
2227 23rd Avenue
Greeley, CO 80631
(970) 330-7691
Hours: Mon–Sat 9:00–9:00

Historical Societies— Local and Regional

Adams County Historical Society
Adams County Museum and Cultural
Center
9601 Henderson Road
Brighton, CO 80601
(303) 659-7103
Patricia Erge, Administrator
Hours: 10:00–4:30
Pub. *Hi-Story News*, bimonthly

Arkansas River Historical Society Museum
(see Oklahoma)

Arvada Historical Society
PO Box 419
Arvada, CO 80001
Robert C. Walker, Secretary
Pub. *Arvada Historian*, quarterly
$10.00 per year membership for families,
$25.00 per year membership for
businesses

Aspen Historical Society
620 West Bleeker Street
Aspen, CO 81611
(970) 925-3721
Carl Bergman, President, Board of
Directors
Pub. *AHS Newsletter*
(Pitkin County)

Aurora Historical Society
415 Oswego Street
Aurora, CO 80010
(303) 360-8545
Gladys Metcalf
Pub. *AHS Newsletter*

Berthoud Historical Society, Inc.
The Little Thompson Valley Pioneer
Museum
PO Box N
Berthoud, CO 80513
(970) 532-2149
Preston Barrowman, President

Boulder Historical Society and Museum
1206 Euclid Avenue
Boulder, CO 80302
(303) 449-3464; (303) 938-8322 FAX
Thomas Meier, Director
Hours: Tue–Fri 11:00–4:00, Sat–Sun
noon–4:00
Pub. *Newsletter*, quarterly
("Select photographs and manuscripts
from the Boulder Historical Society's
remarkable collections are displayed in
Museum's exhibits; however, the bulk
of these collections are housed at the
Carnegie Branch Library for Local
History.")
$20.00 per year membership for
individuals, $30.00 per year
membership for families, $15.00 per
year membership for senior citizens,
$50.00 per year membership for
families; $50.00 per year Contributor
membership, $100.00 per year
Supporting membership, $500.00 per
year Patron membership, $1,000.00
Benefactor membership; $1.00
suggested donation for museum
admission

Buena Vista Heritage
109 West Main
PO Box 1414
Buena Vista, CO 81211
(719) 395-2572
Suzanne Kelley, Treasurer

Kit Carson Museum and Historical Society
(Bent and Ninth Streets—location)
PO Box 68 (mailing address)
Las Animas, CO 81054
(719) 456-0829

Cherry Creek Valley Historical Society, Inc.
4950 South Laredo Street
Aurora, CO 80015
(303) 699-5145
Michael McCarthy, President
Hours: by appointment
Pub. *The Quill*, quarterly
$5.00 per year membership

Clear Creek Canyon Historical Society of Chaffee County, Inc.
PO Box 2181
Granite, CO 81228
(719) 486-2942

Columbine Genealogical and Historical Society, Inc.
(Bemis Public Library—location)
PO Box 2074 (mailing address)
Littleton, CO 80161
(303) 688-9652; (303) 688-3388
Earl King, President; Sharon Lee, First
Vice President
Hours: meetings at Library: second &
third Tue 1:00

Pub. *Newsletter*, quarterly
$10.00 per year membership for
individuals, $12.50 per year
membership for couples

Comanche Crossing Historical Society
PO Box 647
Strasburg, CO 80136-0647
(303) 622-4668

Creede Historical Society
PO Box 608
Creede, CO 81130
Janis Jacobs, President
Hours: Library: Tue 10:00–2:00, Wed
(summer) 10:00–2:00, and by
appointment; Museum: Memorial
Day–Labor Day: Mon–Sun 10:00–
4:00
(Creede and Mineral County)
$10.00 per year membership for
individuals, $15.00 per year
membership for families; search fee:
donation

Deer Trail Pioneer Historical Society
PO Box 176
Deer Trail, CO 80105
(303) 769-4577
Clara Hanks, Curator

Delta County Historical Society
Delta County Courthouse
251 Meeker Street
Delta, CO 81416
(970) 874-8721
Lucy Hodgin, President
Hours: May–Sept: Tue–Fri 10:00–4:00,
Sat 10:00–1:00; Oct–Apr: Wed & Sat
1:00–4:00

Douglas County Historical Society
620 Lewis
Castle Rock, CO 80104

Eagle Valley Historical Society
PO Box 192
Eagle, CO 81631
(970) 845-7741
E-mail: japotter@vail.net
Joann Potter, Genealogist for Three Bells
Genealogy and Eagle Valley Historical
Society
Pub. *Eagle Valley Enterprise*

East Yuma County Historical Society
205 East Third Street
PO Box 161
Wray, CO 80758
(970) 332-5063
Patricia E. Walborn, Director
Hours: Tue–Sat 10:00–5:00
Pub. *Pictorgraph*, bimonthly
$5.00 per year membership, additional
$5.00 per year membership in
genealogical society; admission: $1.00
for adults, 50¢ for children under 12
years of age

Eastern Colorado Historical Society (Cheyenne County)
85 West Second Street
c/o 43433 Road CC
Cheyenne Wells, CO 80810
(719) 767-5907
Karlene McKean, Librarian
Hours: afternoons, Memorial Day
through Labor Day

Estes Park Area Historical Museum
200 Fourth Street
PO Box 1691
Estes Park, CO 80517
(970) 586-6256
E-mail: epmuseum@juno.com
http://estes-on-line.com/epmuseum
Betty Kilsdonk, Director
Hours: May–Oct: daily, and by
appointment
Pub. *Museum Pieces*, quarterly
$15.00 per year membership for
individuals, $25.00 per year
membership for families; photocopy
fees

Florence Pioneer Museum and Historical Society
Price Pioneer Museum
Pikes Peak Avenue and Front Street
Florence, CO 81226

Fort Sedgewick Historical Society
PO Box 69
Julesburg, CO 80737

Fremont-Custer Historical Society, Inc.
PO Box 965
Canon City, CO 81212

Friends of Historic Trinidad, Inc.
1208 Logan
Denver, CO 80203
(303) 832-7165

Frisco Historical Society
120 Main Street
PO Box 820
Frisco, CO 80443
(970) 668-3428
Karen Mack, Museum Manager
Hours: Tue–Sat 11:00–4:00, Sun (after
Memorial Day) 11:00–4:00
Pub. *Frisco Historical Society
Newsletter*, quarterly
$10.00 per year membership for
individuals, $25.00 per year
membership for families, $100.00 life
membership

Frontier Historical Society (Garfield County)
1001 Colorado Avenue
Glenwood Springs, CO 81601
(970) 945-4448
Ann Roberts, Director
Hours: winter: Mon & Thur–Sat 1:00–
4:00; May 1–Oct 1: Mon–Sat 11:00–
4:00

Pub. *Frontier Historical Society
Newsletter*, quarterly
$15.00 per year membership for
individuals, $25.00 per year
membership for families, $5.00 per
year membership for senior citizens

The Gilpin County Historical Society
Gilpin County Museum
PO Box 247
Central City, CO 80427-0247
(303) 582-5283
James J. Prochaska, P.E., Executive
Director
Hours: Memorial Day–Labor Day: Mon–
Sun 11:00–4:00; winter: Mon & Fri
8:00–6:00

Grand County Historical Association
110 Byers Avenue
PO Box 165
Hot Sulphur Springs, CO 80451
(970) 725-3939
Lesley Allen, Administrative Assistant
Hours: summer: daily 10:00–5:00;
winter: Tue–Sat 10:00–5:00
Pub. *Grand County Historical
Association Journal*, annually
("historic buildings, history exhibits,
photo collection")
$20.00–$100.00 per year membership;
search fees dependent on subject

Grand Lake Area Historical Society
Pitkin Street
PO Box 656
Grand Lake, CO 80447
(970) 627-9277
Dr. Richard Leinbach, President
Hours: Memorial Day to Labor Day:
11:00–5:00
Pub. *GLAHS Newsletter*, annually
$5.00 per year membership for
individuals, $15.00 per year
membership for businesses, $50.00 per
year Sustaining membership, $100.00
life membership

Gunnison County Pioneer and Historical Society
(South Adams Street—location)
696 County Road 16 (mailing address)
Gunnison, CO 81230
(970) 641-0740
Gus Grosland, President
Hours: summer 9:00–5:00
("family research-limited; we do not
have staff for general research")
search fee: expenses only

Hinsdale County Historical Society
Second and Silver Streets
PO Box 353
Lake City, CO 81235

Hotchkiss-Crawford Historical Society
(Second and Hotchkiss Avenue—location)
PO Box 727 (mailing address)
Hotchkiss, CO 81419

(970) 872-4858
Julie Littlefield, President
Hours: summer: Fri 1:00–4:00; tours by
    appointment
$10.00 per year membership for
    individuals; $10.00 admission

Huerfano County Historical Society
PO Box 428
Laveta, CO 81055
Christine R. Schmidt, President, Board
    of Directors
("We have no staff who specifically do
    genealogy; requests are done by
    volunteers when available; we cannot
    offer this service as always
    available.")

Jefferson County Historical Commission
PO Box 659
Morrison, CO 80468
Pub. *Historically Jeffco*, semiannually

Jefferson County Historical Society
(Hiwan Homestead Museum, 4208 South
    Timbervale Drive—location)
PO Box 703 (mailing address)
Evergreen, CO 80439
(303) 674-5934; (303) 674-6262
    (Museum)
Jo Ann Dunn, President; Jennifer Karber,
    Museum Administrator
Hours: Wed–Thur (Jun–Aug) 10:00–
    2:00; Museum: Tue–Sun 12:00–5:00,
    Tue–Sun (summer) 11:00–5:00
Pub. *The Record*, quarterly
$10.00 per year membership for
    individuals, $15.00 per year
    membership for couples

La Plata County Historical Society
Animas Museum
31st Street and West Second Avenue
PO Box 3384
Durango, CO 81302
(970) 259-2402
Robert McDaniel, Museum Director
Hours: May–Oct: Mon–Sat 10:00–6:00;
    Oct–Apr: by appointment
Pub. *Artifacts*, quarterly
(photo archives and research library:
    Durango, La Plata County, southwest
    Colorado; gift shop specializing in
    used, out-of-print and rare books)
$150.00–$1500.00 per year membership;
    negotiable research fees; museum
    admission: adults $1.75, children free

Lake County Civic Center Association, Inc.
100–102 East Ninth Street
PO Box 962
Leadville, CO 80461
(719) 486-1878

Leadville Historical Association
206 West Third Street
PO Box 909
Leadville, CO 80461

(719) 486-0425
Leroy Wingenbach, President
Hours: 1:00–4:00; meetings every fifth
    Monday during the year at 7:00
$5.00 per year membership for
    individuals

Lincoln County Historical Society
Lincoln County Museum
615 Third Avenue
PO Box 626
Hugo, CO 80821
(719) 743-2209

Logan County Historical Society, Inc.
(21053 County Road 26-5/10—location)
PO Box 4000 (mailing address)
Sterling, CO 80751
(970) 522-3895 (Museum); (970) 521-
    0632 FAX
Anna Mae Hagemeier, Superintendent
Hours: 1 Apr–31 Oct: Sat 9:00–5:00, Sun
    10:00–5:00; 1 Nov–31 Mar: Tue–Sat
    10:00–4:00
("Have some pioneer files and
    newspapers; local history museum and
    files on local pioneers")

Lyons Historical Society
(d.b.a. Lyons Redstone Museum)
340 High Street
PO Box 9
Lyons, CO 80540
(303) 823-6692; (303) 823-5271; (303)
    443-0084 FAX
LaVern M. Johnson, President
Hours: Jul–Sept: Mon–Sat 9:30–4:30,
    Sun 12:30–4:30
("Files of the area of Lyons, Colorado;
    we are continually working on them
    and hope to have more each year.")
$10.00 per year membership; search fee:
    $10.00 for first half hour, $20.00 per
    hour thereafter; copies: 50¢ each

Manitou Springs Historical Society, Inc.
Miramont Castle Museum and
    Conference Center
9 Capitol Hill Avenue
Manitou Springs, CO 80829
(719) 685-1011
Robert Yager, Executive Director
Hours: summer: 10:00–5:00; spring &
    fall: 11:00–4:00; winter: noon–3:00

Marble Historical Society
Marble Historical Museum
412 West Main Street
Marble, CO 81623
(970) 945-2824
Oscar D. McCollum, President
Pub. *Marble Chips*, quarterly
(Gunnison County)

Mesa County Historical Society
PO Box 841
Grand Junction, CO 81502
E-mail: jmoston@aol.com

K. Don Thompson, 1997 President;
    Juanita Moston, 1998 President
Pub. *Mesa County Historical Society
    Newsletter*, bimonthly
$7.50 per year membership for
    individuals or families, $15.00 per
    year membership for businesses,
    $100.00 life membership

North Fork Historic Preservation Society
(1600 Highway 187—location)
PO Box 622 (mailing address)
Paonia, CO 81428
(970) 527-3970
Judy Livingston, President
Hours: Tue & Thur–Fri 1:00–4:00, and
    by appointment
$7.50 per year membership for
    individuals, $10.00 per year
    membership for families, $15.00 per
    year membership for businesses

Palmer Lake Historical Society
PO Box 662
Palmer Lake, CO 80133
Emory Hightower, President

Prowers County Historical Society
Big Timbers Museum
7515 U.S. Highway 50
PO Box 362
Lamar, CO 81052
Jeanne Clark, Curator
Hours: Mon–Sun 1:30–4:30, and by
    appointment
$7.00 per year membership for
    individuals, $10.00 per year
    membership for families, $100.00 life
    membership

Pueblo County Historical Society
217 South Grand Avenue
Pueblo, CO 81003
Pat Crum, Museum Director
Hours: Tue–Sat 1:00–4:00
Pub. *Lore*, monthly
$20.00 per year membership for
    individuals

Rimrock Historical Society of West Montrose County
PO Box 305
Naturita, CO 81424
(970) 864-7837
L. S. Zatterstrom, Curator

Saint Vrain Historical Society, Inc.
(312 Terry Street, Longmont, CO
    80501—location)
PO Box 705 (mailing address)
Longmont, CO 80502-0705
(303) 776-1870
Mrs. Dale S. Bernard, Executive Director
Hours: Mon–Thur 8:30–12:30
(specializes in historical preservation;
    "We do not have genealogical research
    materials.")
$10.00 per year membership for
    individuals, $25.00 per year
    membership for families

San Juan County Historical Society
1567 Greene Street
PO Box 154
Silverton, CO 81433
(970) 387-5838
Allen Nossaman, Archive Director
Hours: Mon 1:00–6:00, Wed noon–6:00,
and by appointment (recommended)
("General archive and research facility
for San Juan County, Colorado, only")

**San Miguel County Historical
Society**
PO Box 476
Telluride, CO 81435

South Park Historical Foundation
South Park City Museum
100 Fourth Street (Fourth and Front
Streets)
PO Box 634
Fairplay, CO 80440
(719) 836-2387
Carol Davis, Director/Curator
Hours: Mon–Fri (May 15–Oct 15) 9:00–
5:00
(specializes in Park County, Colorado)

Summit Historical Society
403 LaBonte Street
PO Box 747
Dillon, CO 80435
(970) 468-6079
Rebecca Waugh, Museum Administrator

Trinidad Historical Society
1102 Corant Avenue
PO Box 176
Trinidad, CO 81082

LDS Family History Centers

Aurora
(303) 367-0570

Colorado Springs
(719) 634-0572

Denver
(see Aurora or Littleton)

Fort Collins
(303) 226-5999

Grand Junction
(970) 243-2782

Littleton
(303) 798-6461

Pueblo
(719) 564-0793

Genealogical Societies

State Genealogical Societies

**Colorado Council of Genealogical
Societies**
PO Box 24379
Denver, CO 80224-0379
(303) 688-9652
Lily W. Budd, President
Pub. *Colorado Council of Genealogical
Societies Newsletter*, quarterly, $10.00
per year subscription
(a cooperative organization of many
Colorado groups, does not offer direct
services to genealogists)
$10.00 per year Associate membership
(open to all genealogical and historical
societies in Colorado)

Colorado Genealogical Society
PO Box 9218
Denver, CO 80209-0218
(303) 571-1535
E-mail: genealogist@cogensoc.org
http://www.cogensoc.org/cgs/cgs-
home.htm
Vern Tomkins, President
Hours: Denver Public Library,
Genealogy Division: Mon–Wed
10:00–9:00, Thur–Sat 10:00–5:30, Sun
1:00–5:00
Pub. *The Colorado Genealogist*,
quarterly; *Colorado Genealogical
Society Newsletter*, ten times per year
$20.00 per year membership for
individuals, $25.00 per year
membership for families and
institutions

Regional Genealogical Societies

Ancestor Seekers Genealogy Society
c/o Columbine Genealogical and
Historical Society, Inc.
PO Box 2074
Littleton, CO 80161
Hours: Phillips S. Miller Branch Library:
fourth Tue (except Jun–Aug & Sept)
Pub. *Newsletter*, three times per year
$7.50 per year membership

**Archuleta County Genealogical
Society**
PO Box 1611
Pagosa Springs, CO 81147
(970) 264-2645
Margo Butner
Hours: Sisson Public Library, Pagosa
Springs, Genealogy Section: Mon–Fri
10:00–5:00
$10.00 per year membership from
individuals, $15.00 per year
membership for families

**The Aurora Genealogical Society of
Colorado**
1298 Peoria Street
PO Box 31732
Aurora, CO 80041-0732
(303) 363-8257 (Secretary)
Paul Rawls, Corresponding Secretary
Hours: Wed 10:00–4:00; summer and
holidays: Wed 10:00–1:00
Pub. *The Aurora Genealogical Society of
Colorado Newsletter*, five times per
year
("*Aurora Democrat Newspaper* indexed;
we maintain library")
$8.00 per year membership for
individuals, $10.00 per year
membership for couples

Boulder Genealogical Society
(Carnegie Branch Library for Local
History, 1125 Pine Street, Boulder, CO
80302—library location)
PO Box 3246 (mailing address)
Boulder, CO 80307-3246
(303) 441-3110 (Library)
Lewis Headrick, President
Hours: Carnegie Branch Library for
Local History: Mon 1:00–9:00, Tue &
Thur–Sat 11:00–5:00, Wed 9:00–5:00;
meetings at Mountain View Methodist
Church, 355 Ponca Place, Boulder, CO
80301
Pub. *Boulder Genealogical Society
Quarterly*; *Boulder Genealogical
Society Newsletter*, quarterly
(worldwide genealogical research)
$12.00 per year membership for
individuals, $14.00 per year
membership for families

Boulder Genealogy Group
856 Applewood Drive
Lafayette, CO 80026
Vella May Blazzard

Brighton Genealogical Society
343 South 21st Avenue
Brighton, CO 80601

**Columbine Genealogical and
Historical Society, Inc.**
(Bemis Public Library—location)
PO Box 2074 (mailing address)
Littleton, CO 80161
(303) 688-9652; (303) 688-3388
Earl King, President; Sharon Lee, First
Vice President
Hours: meetings at Library: second &
third Tue 1:00
Pub. *Newsletter*, quarterly
$10.00 per year membership for
individuals, $12.50 per year
membership for couples

Estes Park Genealogy Society
Longs Peak Route
Estes Park, CO 80517
Larry Carpenter
$11.00 per year membership for
individuals, $13.00 per year
membership for couples

Foothills Genealogical Society of Colorado, Inc.
PO Box 150382
Lakewood, CO 80215-0382
(303) 642-7262; (303) 642-3646 FAX
Donna J. Porter, President; Patricia A. Kemper, Past President and Editor
Pub. *Newsletter*, five times per year; *The Inquirer*, quarterly
(emphasis on Clear Creek, Gilpin, Jefferson and Park counties)
$10.00 per year membership for individuals or institutions, $12.50 per year membership for families

Fore-Kin Trails Genealogical Society
4458 North Townsend
Montrose, CO 81401
(970) 249-8140
Fay Brewer, Corresponding Secretary
Pub. *Fore-Kin Trails Quarterly* (February, May, August and November), $1.50 per issue
(Montrose County, Colorado)
$12.50 per year membership for individuals, $17.50 per year membership for families)

High Country Genealogical Society
601 Willow Wood Lane
Delta, CO 81416-3037
Nadine Lillpop

High Plains Heritage Genealogical Society (Morgan County)
Morgan County Genealogical Society
5775 East El Camino Quinto
Apache Junction, AZ 85219-8808
Elaine V. Rouse-Haskin, President

Historic Georgetown, Inc.
PO Box 667
Georgetown, CO 80444
(303) 569-2840 Denver Metro Live; (303) 674-2625
E-mail: histgtwn@sprynet.com
Jonathan Held, Curator, Collections and Properties
Hours: Mon–Fri 9:00–4:00
(local, county, regional, family, property, genealogical research)

Larimer County Genealogical Society
(Masonic Temple, 225 West Oak— location)
PO Box 9502 (mailing address)
Fort Collins, CO 80524
(970) 226-6146 (answering machine)
Karen Helt, Corresponding Secretary
Pub. *Larimer County Genealogical Society Newsletter*, bimonthly
$12.00 per year membership for individuals, $18.00 per year membership for families; search: $10.00

Liberal Area Genealogical Society
(see Kansas)

Logan County Genealogical Society
PO Box 294
Sterling, CO 80751
Evelyn Camblin

Longmont Genealogical Society
PO Box 6081
Longmont, CO 80501-2077
Harry Ross, President, Karl Stone, Queries
Hours: meetings at Bethlehem Lutheran Church, 1000 15th Avenue, Longmont: second Wed 1:00
Pub. *Longmont Heritage*, quarterly
$10.00 per year membership for individuals, $12.00 per year membership for families; queries free to members, $10.00 to non-members; search requests limited to Longmont or Boulder County for expenses plus donation

Mesa County Genealogical Society
PO Box 1506
Grand Junction, CO 81502
Pub. *Mesa Dwellers*, quarterly
$10.00 per year membership

Ohio Genealogical Society
Colorado Chapter
(see Ohio)

Pikes Peak Genealogical Society
PO Box 1262
Colorado Springs, CO 80901
Marjorie Rapp, President
Pub. *Pikes Peak Genealogical Society Newsletter*, quarterly
$5.00 per year membership for individuals, $8.00 per year membership for families, $75.00 life membership; search fee: donation to book fund

Prowers County Genealogical Society
(Big Timers Museum and Historical Society, 7515 U.S. Highway 50— location)
PO Box 928 (mailing address)
Lamar, CO 81052-0928
(719) 336-2472
Jeanne Clark, Member/Curator
Hours: Mon–Sun 1:30–4:30 (closed Good Friday, Thanksgiving, Christmas and New Years)
Pub. *Prowers County Genealogical Society Newsletter*, quarterly
$10.00 per year membership for individuals, $15.00 per year membership for families, $7.00 per year membership for senior citizens

San Luis Valley Genealogical Society
PO Box 911
Alamosa, CO 81101-0911
(719) 589-6592
Dorothy Wilson, Librarian
Hours: Tue–Sat 9:00–5:00
Pub. *San Luis Valley Genealogical Journal*, semiannually
(Conejos, Costilla, Alamosa, Rio Grande, Mineral and Saguache counties)
$10.00 per year membership

Seeley Genealogical Society
PO Box 1231
Allenspark, CO 80510

Southeastern Colorado Genealogical Society, Inc.
PO Box 4207
Pueblo, CO 81003-0207
(719) 564-2479 (President)
Esther Nesslage, President
Hours: meetings at McClelland Library, 100 East Abriendo, Pueblo, CO: fourth Sat 2:00–4:00
Pub. *Pinon Whispers*, quarterly, $12.00 per year subscription for members, $20.00 per year subscription for non-members
("alphabetized cemeteries, marriages, 1885 Colorado State Census, alphabetized deaths in *Pueblo Chieftain*, 1940–1992")
research: $5.00 per hour

Weld County Genealogical Society
PO Box 278
Greeley, CO 80632
Jackie Glavinick, Editor
Hours: Weld County Library: Tue & Thur 9:00–12:00 & 1:00–4:00
Pub. *Weld County Genealogical Society Quarterly* (August, November, February and May)
$12.50 per year membership for individuals, $15.00 per year membership for families

Western Trails Genealogical Society
1570 South Knox Court
Denver, CO 80219

White River Trace Genealogical Society
425 12th Street
Meeker, CO 81641
Ola Keller

Independent Publications and Miscellany

CoGenWeb
Part of U.S. GenWeb Project
E-mail: co@usgenweb.com
http://www.rootsweb.com/~cogenweb/ comain.htm
(links to other Colorado resources)

Genealogical Advisor
PO Box 535
Farmington, MI 48332
Andrew J. Morris
Pub. *Genealogical Advisor*

CONNECTICUT

Archives and Libraries with Holdings in Genealogy

State Archives and Library

Connecticut State Archives
231 Capitol Avenue
Hartford, CT 06106
(860) 566-5650
http://www.cslnet.ctstateu.edu/
archives.htm
Mark Jones, State Archivist
Hours: Mon–Fri 9:30–5:00; Archives
Research Area within the History and
Genealogy Reading Room: Mon–Fri
10:00–1:00 & 2:00–4:15
(records from more than 70 state
agencies, manuscripts, photographs,
posters, postcards)

Connecticut State Library
History and Genealogy Unit
231 Capitol Avenue
Hartford, CT 06106-1537
(860) 566-3690; (860) 566-3692; (860)
566-4452 (to arrange for handicapped
parking and access)
http://www.cslnet.ctstateu.edu/
indexsch.htm (search form request);
http://www.cslnet.ctstateu.edu/list.htm
(list of professional genealogists
familiar with the library's collections)
Richard C. Roberts, Unit Head
Hours: Mon–Fri 9:30–5:00; Archives
Research Area within the History and
Genealogy Reading Room: Mon–Fri
10:00–1:00 & 2:00–4:15
(Barbour Collection of town vital
records, family and Bible records,
federal and state censuses, newspaper
marriage and death notice abstracts,
Hale Collection of cemetery
inscriptions, church records abstracts,
probate estate papers, extensive
collection of local histories and
genealogies, most town vital, land and
probate record books to the early
1900s, church records on microfilm,
naturalization papers index on
microfilm, atlases and maps, city
directories, passenger lists, etc.)
a limited genealogical index search
service for an individual name in the
seven major indexes in the collection,
plus up to ten pages of photocopying:
$5.00 for Connecticut residents,
$15.00 plus long SASE for non-
Connecticut residents, additional
photocopy charges will be billed (no
inquiries by phone, allow six weeks
for a response)

State Historical Societies

Connecticut Historical Commission
59 South Prospect Street
Hartford, CT 06106-1901
(860) 566-3005; (860) 566-5078 FAX
John W. Shannahan, Director
Hours: Mon–Fri 8:30–4:30
(Connecticut architecture, historic
landscapes, women's history, no
archives or library)

**The Connecticut Historical Society
(CHS)**
1 Elizabeth Street at Asylum Avenue
Hartford, CT 06105
(860) 236-5621; (860) 236-2664 FAX
E-mail: cthist@ix.netcom.com
http://www.hartnet.org/chs/main.htm
Judith Ellen Johnson, Reference
Librarian and Genealogist; David M.
Kahn, Director
Hours: Library: Tue–Sat 9:00–4:45
Pub. *The Connecticut Historical Society
Bulletin*, semiannually, $16.00 ($20.00
foreign) per year subscription to
members, $20.00 ($25.00 foreign) per
year subscription to individual non-
members and to institutions;
*Connecticut Historical Society Annual
Report*; *Connecticut Historical Society
Collections*, irregularly; *Notes and
News*, three times per year; *Loan
Catalog* (16,000 volume Loan
Collection available to members of
The Connecticut Historical Society or
The Society of Mayflower
Descendants in the State of
Connecticut), $7.00 postpaid
(Connecticut residents add 30¢ tax)
$30.00 per year membership for
individuals, $45.00 per year
membership for families, $25.00 per
year membership for students, senior
citizens, institutions, and out-of-state
individuals, $40.00 per year
membership for senior citizen couples,
$150.00 per year Sustaining
membership, $500 per year Standing
Order membership, $5,000 life
membership (reduced three-year
membership rates, membership
includes *CHS Annual Report* and
Notes and News, and access to Loan
Collection); $3.00 per day library and
museum user's fee for non-members;
research service for a nominal charge

**Connecticut League of Historical
Societies**
2105 Chester Village West
Chester, CT 06412-1040
Janet G. Jainschigg
Pub. *League Bulletin*

City, County and Regional Archives and Libraries

Abington Social Library
536 Hampton Road
Abington, CT 06230-0118
(860) 974-0415
Hours: Mon 3:00–5:30, Tue & Thur
6:00–9:00, Sat 10:00–noon
(almost no genealogical holdings, and
staff is not able to do genealogical
research)

**Beardsley and Memorial Library of
Winsted**
40 Munro Place
Winsted, CT 06098
(860) 379-6043 (Library); (860) 379-
2158 (Genealogy Librarian)
E-mail: bmlstaff@nai.net (Library);
newman@esslink.com (Genealogy
Librarian)
Dr. Newman A. Hall, Genealogy
Librarian; Mary Pitt, History Research
Assistant
Hours: Library: Tue–Thur 10:30–8:00,
Fri 10:30–4:00, Sat 10:00–1:00;
Genealogy Library: Thur 10:30–12:00,
and by appointment
(focus on Connecticut and western
Massachusetts; correspondence
inquiries welcomed)

Berkshire Athenaeum
(see Massachusetts)

James Blackstone Memorial Library
758 Main Street
Branford, CT 06405
(203) 488-1441
E-mail: jbml@connix.com
http://www.connix.com/~jbml
Barbara Cangiano
Hours: Mon–Thur 9:00–8:00, Fri–Sat
9:00–5:00, Sat (Jul–Aug) 9:00–
12:00

Cyrenius H. Booth Library
25 Main Street
Newtown, CT 06470
(203) 426-4533
Beryl Harrison, Reference Librarian
Hours: Mon–Tue 10:00–8:00, Wed–Thur
10:00–6:00, Fri 12:00–5:00, Sat
10:00–5:00, Sun 1:00–5:00
(family histories of many Fairfield
County people)

Bridgeport Public Library
Historical Collections
925 Broad Street
Bridgeport, CT 06603
(203) 576-7417; (203) 576-8255 FAX
http://bridgeport.lib.ct.us/bpl/hc/
hchp2.htm
Mary K. Witkowski, Head
Hours: Mon–Sat (call for hours); closed
Sat from late Jun to Labor Day

(includes P.T. Barnum and circus collection; Family Search on CD, census microfilm for Connecticut 1790–1920, plus Soundex)

Bristol Public Library
Bristol History Room
5 High Street
PO Box 730
Bristol, CT 06010
(860) 584-7787
Robert G. Robles, Historical Research Librarian
Hours: Library: Mon–Thur 8:30–8:00, Fri–Sat 8:30–5:00; Bristol History Room: Tue 2:00–4:00, Wed 6:00–7:45
(City of Bristol archives)

Silas Bronson Library
Public Library of Waterbury, Connecticut
267 Grand Street
Waterbury, CT 06702
(203) 574-8222; (203) 574-8055 FAX
http://www.biblio.org/bronson/silas.htm
Ellen Gambini, Head, Main Reading Room
Hours: Mon–Wed 9:00–9:00, Thur–Fri 9:00–5:30, Sat 9:00–5:00, Sun 1:00–5:00; closed Sat & Sun in summer
(genealogy and local history of New England states)

Cheshire Public Library
104 Main Street
Cheshire, CT 06410
(203) 272-2245; (203) 272-7714 FAX
http://www.cheshirelib.org
Mary Beeckman, Co-Head, Reference Department
Hours: Mon–Thur 10:00–9:00, Fri–Sat 10:00–5:00

Connecticut College Library
(address withheld upon request)

Connecticut Valley Historical Museum
(see Massachusetts)

Danbury Public Library
170 Main Street
PO Box 1160
Danbury, CT 06810
(203) 797-4527
Diana Nolan, Reference Librarian
Hours: Library and Local History Room: Mon & Thur 9:00–8:00, Tue & Fri–Sat 9:00–5:00, Wed 1:00–5:00, Sun (Labor Day–Memorial Day) 1:00–5:00
(Local History Room specializing in Danbury history and local genealogy: microfilm, periodicals, atlases, maps, town and county histories)

East Hartford Public Library
840 Main Street
East Hartford, CT 06108

Eastern Connecticut State University
Center for Connecticut Studies
J. Eugene Smith Library
Willimantic, CT 06226
(860) 456-2231, ext. 443

Fairfield Public Library
1080 Old Post Road
Fairfield, CT 06430
(203) 256-3160
Carol Alexander, Head of Reference
Hours: Mon–Thur 9:00–9:00, Fri 9:00–6:00, Sat 9:00–5:00
("We refer all genealogy questions to either our local Historical Society or the Pequot Library in Southport.")

The Farmington Library
6 Monteith Drive
PO Box 407
Farmington, CT 06034-0407
(860) 673-6791; (860) 675-7148 FAX
Ann J. Arcari, Farmington Room Librarian
Hours: Mon–Tue & Thur 9:00–9:00, Wed 10:00–9:00, Fri 9:00–5:30, Sat 9:00–5:00, Sat (summer) 9:00–1:00, Sun 1:00–4:00; (call in advance of visit)
(archives and history of Farmington and daughter towns: Avon, Berlin, Bristol, Burlington, New Britain, Plainville and Southington)
can answer only brief questions over the phone, send letter for more: $5.00 per half-hour

The Ferguson Library
Adult Services Department
1 Public Library Plaza
Stamford, CT 06904
(203) 964-1000; (203) 357-0660 FAX
E-mail: comments@ferg.lib.ct.us
http://www.ferglib.org/ferg
Carolyn Karwoski, Local History Librarian
Hours: Mon–Thur 10:00–9:00, Fri 10:00–6:00, Sat 10:00–5:00, Sun (Sept to mid–May) 1:00–5:00
(Stamford, Connecticut and New England collection of history and genealogy)
limited research for mail requests

Friends of Boothe Park, Inc.
(Main Street and Putney—location)
PO Box 902 (mailing address)
Stratford, CT 06497
(203) 381-2046
Bessie Burton, Director of Volunteers
Hours: Tue & Fri 8:30–1:30, and tour hours
Pub. *Boothe Museum Newsletter*, two times per year
$10.00 per year membership for individuals, $25.00 per year membership for families

Godfrey Memorial Library
134 Newfield Street
Middletown, CT 06457
(860) 346-4375
Doris Post, Director
Hours: Mon–Fri 10:00–3:00
Pub. *American Genealogical-Biographical Index*, four volumes per year, $270.00 per year subscription
(specializing in New England, but does have material on most states in the U.S.)

Greenwich Library
101 West Putnam Avenue
Greenwich, CT 06830
(203) 622-7900
Richard Hart, Local History/Genealogy Librarian
Hours: Mon–Fri 9:00–9:00, Sat 9:00–5:00, Sun (except summer) 1:00–5:00
$15.00 for locating, copying, and sending obituaries, articles, etc.

Groton Public Library
52 Route 117, Newtown Road
Groton, CT 06340
(860) 441-6750; (860) 448-0363 FAX
E-mail: groton.public.lib@snet.net
http://www.state.ct.us/munic/groton/library.htm
Barbara Clark-Greene, Reference Librarian
Hours: Mon–Thur 9:00–9:00, Fri 9:00–5:30, Sat 9:00–5:00, Sun (Sept–Jun) 12:00–5:00

Gunn Memorial Library and Museum
(5 Wykeham Road—location)
PO Box 1273
Washington, CT 06793
(860) 868-7756 (Museum); (860) 868-7586 (Library); (860) 868-7247 FAX
E-mail: gunnlib@nai.net (Library)
Sarah Griswold, Curator; Kristine Dyson, Librarian
(some family and local histories, photos, archival material; library has the Connecticut Room, a reference library with published genealogies, histories, etc.)

Hartford Public Library
500 Main Street
Hartford, CT 06103

Hill-Stead Museum
(671 Farmington Avenue, Farmington, CT 06032—location)
PO Box 353 (mailing address)
Farmington, CT 06034
(860) 677-4787

Kent Memorial Library
50 North Main Street
Suffield, CT 06078
(860) 668-3896
Anne W. Borg, Assistant

Hours: Library: Tue–Thur 10:00–8:30, Fri 10:00–6:00, Sat 10:00–5:00, Sat (Jul–Aug) 10:00–1:00; Historical Room: by appointment
(Suffield genealogy and local history)

Manchester Community College
Institute of Local History
60 Bidwell Street
Manchester, CT 06040
(860) 647-6101

Mattatuck Museum
144 West Main Street
Waterbury, CT 06702
(203) 753-0381; (203) 7565-6283 FAX
Carey McDougall, Assistant Curator
Hours: Tue–Sat 10:00–5:00, Sun (except Jul–Aug) noon–5:00
(history specific to the greater Waterbury region)
research: $25.00 per hour

Meriden Public Library
(105 Miller Street—location)
PO Box 868 (mailing address)
Meriden, CT 06450
(203) 238-2344, ext. 1
Janis L. Franco, Local History Librarian
Hours: Mon–Wed 10:00–9:00, Thur–Sat 10:00–5:00

Mystic Seaport Museum
G. W. Blunt White Library
75 Greenmanville Avenue
PO Box 6000
Mystic, CT 06355
(860) 572-0711 (Main Desk); (860) 572-5367 (Library); (860) 572-5394 FAX; (860) 572-5319 TDD
http://www.mysticseaport.org; http://www.mystic.org/welcome.html
Hours: Mon–Sat 10:30–5:00
Pub. *Log of Mystic Seaport*, quarterly
(some abstracts of manuscript collections and ships plans on the web)
research: $20.00 per hour

New Britain Public Library
Local History Room
20 High Street
New Britain, CT 06051-4226
(860) 224-3155, ext. 16; (860) 223-6729 FAX
E-mail: aplamer@connect.crlc.org
http://www.nbpl.lib.ct/
Arlene C. Palmer, Curator
Hours: Local History Room: open Mon–Fri or Mon–Thur & Sat on alternate weeks (call to verify hours): Mon noon–5:00 & 6:00–8:00, Tue 9:00–1:00 & 2:00–6:00 (or 5:00 on weeks open on Sat), Wed 1:00–noon, Thurs 9:00–1:00 & 2:00–6:00, Fri 9:00–1:00 & 2:00–5:00 or Sat 10:00–1:00 & 2:00–4:00
$10.00 for any search requiring more than hour , photocopying 50¢ per page plus $1.00 processing for 1–5 pages, 25¢ per page plus $2.00 processing for 6 or more pages

New Haven Free Public Library
Local History Department
133 Elm Street
New Haven, CT 06510-2033
(203) 946-8130 Local History Department; (203) 946-7430
Janet Zigadto, Reference Librarian
Hours: Mon–Thur 9:00–9:00, Fri–Sat 9:00–5:00 (patrons must have identification to get into the room when it's not staffed)

The Public Library of New London
Genealogy and History Room
63 Huntington Street
New London, CT 06320
Hours: Mon–Thur 9:00–9:00, Fri–Sat 9:00–5:00 (closed Sat during schools' summer vacation, Jun–Labor Day); reference assistance is available in the room Tue–Fri 9:00–3:00
(genealogy and local history of southeastern Connecticut; "single query answered by mail only, for a fee")

Norfolk Historical Museum
13 Village Green
Norfolk, CT 06058
(860) 542-5761
Hours: Sat–Sun (Jun–Sept) 1:00–4:00 by appointment
(museum and research library/archives)

Old Lyme-Phoebe Griffin Noyes Library
(address withheld upon request)
(southeastern Connecticut, particularly Lyme and Old Lyme, genealogy and local history)
no longer has staff to support genealogical searches

Otis Library
261 Main Street
Norwich, CT 06360
(860) 889-2365, ext. 13; (860) 886-4744 FAX
E-mail: dnorman@otis.lib.ct.us
http://www.otis.lib.ct.us
Diane Norman, Assistant Reference Librarian
Hours: Oct–Apr: Mon–Thur 8:30–8:30, Fri–Sat 8:30–5:00, Sun 1:00–5:00; summer: Mon & Thur 8:30–8:30, Tue–Wed & Fri 8:30–5:00
(New London County and Norwich history and genealogy, NLC census; architectural, industrial history of Norwich)

The Pequot Library
720 Pequot Avenue
Southport, CT 06490
(203) 259-0346; (203) 259-5602
Mary Freedman, Director
Hours: winter: Mon & Wed 9:00–8:30, Tue & Thur–Fri 9:00–5:30, Sat 9:00–5:00, Sun 1:00–5:00; summer (4 Jul–Labor Day): Mon–Tue & Thur–Fri

9:00–5:30, Wed 9:00–8:30, Sat 9:00–1:00
Pub. *Bookmark*, quarterly, free
(Americana, New England local history)

Rathbun Free Memorial Library
36 Main Street
East Haddam, CT 06423
(860) 873-8210
Martha T. Monte, Library Director
Hours: Tue–Wed & Fri 10:00–5:00, Thur 10:00–7:00, Sat (except summer) 10:00–12:00
(genealogies, town history, cemetery records, church records, scrapbooks, account books, and old photographs; "known over the entire U.S.A. for having the most complete material on East Haddam")

E. C. Scranton Memorial Library
801 Boston Post Road
PO Box 631
Madison, CT 06443
(203) 245-7365
Marcia Sokolnicki
Hours: Mon & Wed 9:00–9:00, Tue & Thur–Fri 9:00–5:30, Sat 9:00–5:00; summer: closed Mon at 5:30, closed Sat at noon

Seymour Public Library
46 Church Street
Seymour, CT 06483
(203) 888-3903
Hours: Mon–Wed 9:30–8:00, Thur–Fri 9:30–5:00, Sat 10:00–4:00

South Windsor Public Library
1550 Sullivan Avenue
South Windsor, CT 06074
(860) 644-1541; (860) 644-7645 FAX
Hours: Mon–Thur 9:00–9:00, Fri 9:00–4:30, Sat (school year) 9:00–4:30, Sat (Jul–Aug) 9:00–1:00, Sun (Oct–May) 1:00–4:30

Southington Public Library
255 Main Street
Southington, CT 06489
(860) 628-0947
Hours: Mon–Tue 9:15–9:00, Fri–Sat 9:15–5:00 (closed Sat, Jul–Aug)

Stanley-Whitman House
37 High Street
Farmington, CT 06032
(860) 677-9222
Deborah Feinstein, Curator/Director
$15.00 per year membership for individuals

Stratford Library Association
Reference Department
2203 Main Street
Stratford, CT 06497
(203) 385-4164
Hours: variable

Tree Farm Archives
272 Israel Hill Road
Shelton, CT 06484

(203) 929-0126
Philip H. Jones
Hours: 9:00–5:00
(archive of human interest, historical
    letters)

Wallingford Public Library
200 North Main Street
Wallingford, CT 06492
(203) 265-6754
Hours: Mon–Fri 10:00–9:00, Sat 10:00–
    5:00 (except summer)
("Collection includes books, pamphlets
    and clippings on Wallingford and
    Connecticut; the Connecticut
    Collection is not open for browsing;
    materials will be retrieved for patron
    use outside the room.")

Noah Webster House
227 South Main Street
West Hartford, CT 06107
(860) 521-5362
Sally Whipple, Executive Director
Hours: House: Mon–Fri 8:00–4:00, and
    weekends by appointment; researchers
    call for appointment
(archival material about West Hartford;
    Webster genealogy, West Hartford
    probate records)

Welles-Turner Memorial Library
2407 Main Street
Glastonbury, CT 06033
(860) 652-7720; (860) 652-7721 FAX
http://www.wtmlib.com
Barbara Bailey, Reference Librarian
Hours: Mon–Tue & Thur 9:00–9:00,
    Wed 12:00–9:00, Fri 9:00–6:00, Sat
    9:00–5:00, Sun 1:00–5:00; summer:
    Sat 9:00–1:00
(specializes in Glastonbury history)

West Hartford Public Library
(address withheld upon request)
(some materials of interest to local
    genealogists)
no search services

Western Connecticut State College
181 White Street
Danbury, CT 06810

**Henry Whitfield State Historical
Museum**
Old Whitfield Street
PO Box 210
Guilford, CT 06437-0210
(203) 453-2457
Michael A. McBride, Curator
Hours: by appointment
(small history/genealogy library)

Wilton Library Association, Inc.
Friends of the Wilton Library
137 Old Ridgefield Road
Wilton, CT 06897-3000
(203) 762-3950; (203) 834-1166 FAX
Carol Russell, Archivist
Hours: Mon–Wed & Fri 10:00–6:00,
    Thur 10:00–9:00, Sat 10:00–5:00, Sun
    (Oct–Apr) 1:00–5:00

(Wilton, Connecticut, families)
contributions accepted

Yale University Libraries
PO Box 208240
New Haven, CT 06520

Historical Societies— Local and Regional

**Amity and Woodbridge Historical
Society**
Thomas Darling House
Litchfield Turnpike
Woodbridge, CT 06525
Don Menzies, President
Hours: Jun–Oct: Sun 2:00–4:00

Andover Historical Society
Bunker Hill Road
Andover, CT 06232
(860) 742-6796

**Aspinock Historical Society of
Putnam, Inc.**
(206 School Street—location)
PO Box 465 (mailing address)
Putnam, CT 06260
(860) 928-6128
Robert J. Miller, Town Historian; Robert
    Chicoine, President
Pub. *Aspinock Newsletter*, three or four
    times per year
$10.00 per year membership

Bantam Historical Society, Inc.
PO Box 436
Bantam, CT 06750-0436
R. C. Schele, Chairman of Board

Barkhamsted Historical Society, Inc.
PO Box 94
Pleasant Valley, CT 06063

Beacon Falls Historical Commission
10 Maple Avenue
Beacon Falls, CT 06403
(203) 729-4340
Leonard Damico, First Selectman
Pub. *Beacon Falls Historical
    Commission*

Branford Historical Society
124 Main Street
PO Box 504
Branford, CT 06405
(203) 488-4828
Marjorie B. Dill, President

Bridgewater Historical Society
Main Street
Bridgewater, CT 06752

Brookfield Historical Society, Inc.
Whisconier Road
PO Box 5231
Brookfield, CT 06804
(203) 740-8140

Marilyn Whittlesey, Town Historian
Hours: Sat noon–4:00, 1st Sun noon–
    4:00, and by appointment May–Dec,
    by appointment only Dec–Apr
Pub. *Brookfield Historical Society
    Newsletter*, quarterly
$10.00 per year membership for
    individuals, $15.00 per year
    membership for families; limited
    research for donation

Brooklyn Historical Society
PO Box 90
Brooklyn, CT 06234
(860) 774-7728
Elaine R. Knowlton, President
$5.00 per year membership for
    individuals, $10.00 per year
    membership for families

Canton Historical Society
11 Front Street
Collinsville, CT 06022
(860) 693-2793
Jane Goedecke, Librarian
Hours: Wed–Sun 1:00–4:00 (weekends
    only, Dec–Mar), call for appointment
    if a librarian's help is required
(printed and pictorial material dealing
    with the history of Canton and
    Collinsville)
$10.00 per year membership; admission
    for non-members: $2.00 for adults,
    $1.00 for senior citizens and children

**Chatham Historical Society of East
Hampton, Connecticut**
Bevin Boulevard
East Hampton, CT 06424
Walter Olsen, President

Chester Historical Society
PO Box 204
Chester, CT 06412
Dawn Burr, President

Colchester Historical Society
243 Old Hebron Road
Colchester, CT 06415
(860) 537-2925 (President); (860) 537-
    2253) (Town Historian)
Jennie Boluck Lenkiewicz, President;
    Stanley Moroch, Colchester Town
    Historian

Colebrook Historical Society, Inc.
558 Colebrook Road
PO Box 85
Colebrook, CT 06021
Hours: weekends (Memorial Day–
    Columbus Day) 2:00–4:00
(Colebrook-related only)
from $2.00 per year membership,
    $100.00 life membership

**The Columbia Historical Society,
Inc.**
486 Route 66
Columbia, CT 06237
(860) 228-9385
Belle Robinson, President

Cornwall Historical Society
Pine Street
PO Box 115
Cornwall, CT 06753

Coventry Historical Society, Inc.
South Street
PO Box 307
Coventry, CT 06238

Danbury Scott-Fanton Museum and Historical Society, Inc.
43 Main Street
Danbury, CT 06810
(860) 743-5200 phone & FAX
Kathleen Zuris, Assistant Director
Hours: Wed–Sun 2:00–5:00; Office: Tue–Fri 10:00–5:00
Pub. *The Scott-Fanton Museum Newsletter—The Pahquidque Packet*, quarterly
(Danbury local history, published genealogies, genealogy files, city directories, cemetery inscriptions, etc., hatting, Charles Ives)
$15.00 per year membership for individuals, $25.00 per year membership for families, $10.00 per year membership for senior citizens, $5.00 per year membership for students, $50.00 per year Fellowship membership, $100.00 per year Special Friend membership, $200.00 per year Patron membership, $500.00 per year Corporate membership, $1,000.00 life membership

Darien Historical Society
45 Old Kings Highway North
Darien, CT 06820
(203) 655-9233
Madeline Hart, Executive Director
Hours: Tue–Fri 9:00–2:00; tours of house museum: Thur & Sun 2:00–4:00
Pub. *Darien Historical Society Annual*
(archival material pertaining to Darien and its residents; local history in addition to quilt and costume collections)
$25.00 per year membership

The Denison Society, Inc.
(120 Pequotsepos Road—location)
PO Box 42 (mailing address)
Mystic, CT 06355
(860) 536-9248 phone & FAX
E-mail: deniso29@mail.idt.net
Kitty Von Rump, Administrative Assistant; Wayne L. Denison, President
Hours: Office: Mon–Fri 4–5 hours per day; Museum: Memorial Day–Columbus Day: Thur–Sun 1:00–4:00
$15.00 per year membership (application required); admission: $4.00 for non-members

Derby Historical Society, Inc.
(37 Elm Street, Ansonia, CT 06401—location)

PO Box 331 (mailing address)
Derby, CT 06418
(203) 735-1908

Durham Historical Society
Main Street
PO Box 345
Durham, CT 06422

East Haddam Historical Society
PO Box 27
East Haddam, CT 06423

East Haven Historical Society
133 Main Street
PO Box 120052
East Haven, CT 06512
(203) 467-1766
William Anderson, Genealogist
Hours: Wed 11:00–2:00

East Windsor Historical Society, Inc.
(115 Scantic Road—location)
PO Box 551 (mailing address)
East Windsor, CT 06088
Bobbi Mazvrek, Vice President
Hours: by appointment

Eastford Historical Society
Eastford, CT 06242
Pub. *Eastford Historical Society Quarterly*
$4.00 per year membership

Historical Society of Easton, Inc.
(Easton Center in Public Library—location)
PO Box 121 (mailing address)
Easton, CT 06612
(203) 261-2090
Jerry L. Gabert, President
Hours: by appointment
Pub. *The Schoolhouse Sentinel*, quarterly
(only relating to the Town of Easton; open for "independent research but no staff to handle searches")
$25.00 per year membership

Enfield Historical Society, Inc.
1294 Enfield Street
Enfield, CT 06082
(860) 745-1729
Anthony Secondo, President

Essex Historical Society, Inc.
Hills Academy
Prospect Street
PO Box 261
Essex, CT 06426
(860) 767-8269
E-mail: essexct@aol.com
Donald Malcarne, President
Pub. *Quarterly Newsletter*, quarterly
$15.00 per year membership for individuals, $25.00 per year membership for families

Fairfield Historical Society
636 Old Post Road
Fairfield, CT 06430
(203) 259-1598; (203) 255-2716 FAX

Barbara E. Austen, Librarian/Archivist
Hours: Mon–Fri 9:30–4:30, Sat–Sun 1:00–5:00
Pub. *Chronicle*, quarterly
$25.00 per year membership for individuals, $35.00 per year membership for families; queries: $10.00 plus photocopies and postage

Falls Village-Canaan Historical Society
Main Street
PO Box 206
Falls Village, CT 06031
(860) 824-0707
Marion L. Stock, Curator
Hours: Fri 2:00–4:00
(local history, some genealogical materials)
donation

Farmington Historical Society
PO Box 1645
Farmington, CT 06034

Franklin Historical Society
Rt. 32
North Franklin, CT 06254

The Historical Society of Glastonbury
1944 Main Street
PO Box 46
Glastonbury, CT 06033
(860) 633-6890 phone & FAX
Nancy W. Berlet, Executive Director
Hours: Mon & Thur 10:00–4:00, and by appointment
Pub. *The Publick Post*, annually
(Connecticut, Glastonbury [central Connecticut River Valley towns] genealogy, recent search for descendants of Glastonbury founders complete and computerized)
$12.00 per year membership for individuals, $20.00 per year membership for families, $8.00 per year membership for individual senior citizens (62 and up), $12.00 per year membership for senior citizen families, $35.00 per year Contributing membership; research for members: $8.00 for up to two hours, $4.00 for each additional hour, plus photocopies at 10¢ per page; research for non-members: $12.00 for up to two hours, $6.00 for each additional hour, plus photocopies at 25¢ per page; admission: $2.00 per day for non-members

Goshen Historical Society
21 Old Middle Street
Goshen, CT 06756-2001
(860) 491-9610
N. Terry Hall, President
Hours: Tue 10:00–noon, and by appointment; volunteer workshops: Tue 10:00–noon; presentations: Sat afternoon during summer and early fall

The Greater Bristol Historical Society, Inc.
54 Middle Street
PO Box 1393
Bristol, CT 06010
(860) 583-6309
Laurie Larue, President

The Historical Society of the Town of Greenwich
39 Strickland Road
Cos Cob, CT 06807
(203) 869-6899; (203) 869-6727 FAX
Mrs. Meriwether Schmid, Genealogy;
 William E. Finch, Jr., Town Historian;
 Susan Richardson, Archivist
Hours: Tue & Thur 10:00–4:00
Pub. *HSTG Post*, six times per year;
 Greenwich History, annually
$30.00 per year membership for
 individuals, $45.00 per year
 membership for families

Guilford Keeping Society, Inc.
171 Boston Street
PO Box 363
Guilford, CT 06437

Haddam Historical Society, Inc.
(14 Hayden Hill Road—location)
PO Box 97 (mailing address)
Haddam, CT 06438-0097
(860) 345-2400
Jan Sweet, Director
Hours: Mon–Wed 10:00–5:00, Thur–Fri
 10:00–noon, call for appointment
$15.00 per year membership

Hamden Historical Society, Inc.
(The Hamden Historical Society Library,
 Miller Memorial Cultural Center, 2901
 Dixwell Avenue—location)
PO Box 5512 (mailing address)
Hamden, CT 06518-0512
(203) 248-8001; (203) 562-1483
Ann Reddington
Hours: by appointment only
(volunteer by project/no staff)

Hampton Antiquarian and Historical Society
Main Street
PO Box 12
Hampton, CT 06247

Hartland Historical Society, Inc.
(Route 20, West Hartland, CT 06091—
 location)
PO Box 221 (mailing address)
East Hartland, CT 06027
(860) 379-9722; (860) 653-3055
 (President)
Joan Stoltze, President
Hours: first Sun 2:00–4:00, and by
 appointment
Pub. *The Chronicler*, three times per year
$5.00 per year membership for
 individuals, $10.00 per year
 membership for families, $2.00 per
 year membership for senior citizens

Harwinton Historical Society, Inc.
(Hungerford Memorial Library, 50
 Burlington Road—location)
PO Box 84 (mailing address)
Harwinton, CT 06791
(860) 485-1202; (860) 485-0610
Marion Bentley Thierry and Beverly
 Mosher, Co-Curators
Hours: by appointment

Lebanon Historical Society
PO Box 151
Lebanon, CT 06249

Litchfield Historical Society
Corner East and South Street
Litchfield, CT 06759
(860) 567-4501
Catherine Keene, Director
Pub. *The Portico*

Lyme Historical Society, Inc.
96 Lyme Street
Old Lyme, CT 06371
(860) 434-5542
Jeffrey W. Andersen, Director
Pub. *Lyme Ledger*

Madison Historical Society
853 Boston Post Road
PO Box 17
Madison, CT 06443
(203) 245-4567
E-mail: achard@cshore.com
A. M. Chard, President
Hours: Wed & Fri–Sat (28 May–27 Sept)
 1:00–4:00, and by appointment
Pub. *Madison Now & Then*, five times
 per year
(Madison, Connecticut, history, houses,
 genealogy)
$12.00 per year membership for
 individuals, $20.00 per year
 membership for couples, $100.00 life
 membership

Manchester Historical Society, Inc.
106 Hartford Road
Manchester, CT 06040
(860) 643-5588

Mansfield Historical Society
(954 Storrs Road, Route 195—location)
PO Box 145 (mailing address)
Storrs, CT 06268
(860) 429-6575
Ann Galonska, Museum Director
Hours: Jun–Sept: Thur & Sun 1:30–4:30,
 and by appointment
(genealogical and archival materials
 relating to Mansfield history)

The Marlborough Historical Society
PO Box 281
Marlborough, CT 06447
(860) 295-8106 (President's home)
Sandra Soucy, President
$5.00 per year membership for
 individuals, $7.50 per year
 membership for families

Massacoh Plantation/Simsbury Historical Society
800 Hopmeadow Street
PO Box 2
Simsbury, CT 06070
(860) 658-2500; (860) 658-9591 FAX
Evan Woolacott, President; Lois W.
 Calvert, Managing Director
Hours: Phelps House: open all year;
 Tours: (1 May–31 Oct) 1:00–4:00
Pub. *The Signpost*, irregularly
admission: $5.00 for adults, $4.00 for
 senior citizens, $2.50 for students

Middlesex County Historical Society
151 Main Street
Middletown, CT 06457
(860) 346-0746
Ms. Dione Longley, Director
Hours: Tue–Thur by appointment only
Pub. *Historical Observer*, bimonthly
$15.00 per year membership for
 individuals, $25.00 per year
 membership for families

Milford Historical Society
34 High Street
Milford, CT 06460
(203) 874-2664
Arthur W. Stowe, President
Pub. *Wharf Lane Newsletter*

Monroe Historical Society, Inc.
Wheeler and Old Tannery Roads
Monroe, CT 06468

Morris Historical Society, Inc.
(12 South Street—location)
PO Box 234 (mailing address)
Morris, CT 06763
(860) 567-1776
Marilyn Birkett, President; Walter
 France, Historian
Hours: Sat (first weekend in Jun–last
 weekend in Sept) 1:00–4:30, and by
 appointment
Pub. *MHS Newsletter*

Mystic River Historical Society, Inc.
(74 High Street—location)
PO Box 245 (mailing address)
Mystic, CT 06355
(860) 536-4779
Janet Burrows Godwin, Archives
 Manager
Hours: William A. Downes Archives:
 Tue 10:00–noon, Thur 1:00–3:00;
 Portersville Academy: May–Oct: Tue
 10:00–noon, Thur 1:00–3:00, first &
 third Sat 11:00–3:00
Pub. *Newsletter*, eight times per year
 (monthly from Sept to May, combined
 issue in November/December)
(Mystic history and genealogy, Mystic
 schools and businesses, collections of
 Mary Jobe Akeley, Capt. George Gates
 and John L. Allyn Family Papers and
 Photographs)
$5.00 per year membership for
 individuals, $10.00 per year

membership for families, $4.00 per year membership for senior citizens

Naugatuck Historical Society
(87 Church Street, Naugatuck Savings Bank—location)
PO Box 317 (mailing address)
Naugatuck, CT 06770
(203) 729-3235
Ann Simons, President
Hours: Thur 2:00–5:00
Pub. *Naugatuck Historical Society News*, bimonthly
(artifacts and material from many early local industries, large manuscript and picture files, early maps, original bound newspapers, local census, city directories, high school yearbooks, memorabilia, books)
$10.00 per year membership (calendar year)

New Canaan Historical Society
13 Oenoke Ridge
New Canaan, CT 06840
(203) 966-1776
Marilyn T. O'Rourke, Librarian
Hours: Tue–Sat 9:30–12:30 & 2:00–4:30 (genealogical research by appointment)
Pub. *New Canaan Historical Annual*, biannually [sic]
(primarily New Canaan local history, not genealogical, but features Silliman, Noyes, Weed surname collections)
$25.00 per year membership for individuals, $30.00 per year membership for families

The New England Historic Genealogical Society
(see Massachusetts)

New Fairfield Historical Society, Inc.
(Lower level of New Fairfield Public Library, Rt. 39—location)
PO Box 8156 (mailing address)
New Fairfield, CT 06812
(203) 746-3289; (203) 775-3223
Linda Decker and Carol Ballard, Co-Curators
Hours: Wed 1:00–4:00
("Our files include information about early residents of New Fairfield as well as history of town to date.")
$10.00 per year membership

New Haven Colony Historical Society
Whitney Library
114 Whitney Avenue
New Haven, CT 06510-1025
(203) 562-4183
James W. Campbell, Librarian and Curator of Manuscripts
Hours: Tue–Fri & first Sat 1:00–4:45
Pub. *New Haven Colony Historical Society Journal*
$35.00 per year membership; admission: $2.00 per day for non-members, $15.00 per year for students

New London County Historical Society
11 Blinman Street
New London, CT 06320
(860) 443-1209
Alice D. Sheriff, Director/Curator
Hours: Wed–Fri 1:00–4:00, Sat 10:00–4:00, by appointment for research

New Milford Historical Society, Inc.
6 Aspetuck Avenue
PO Box 566
New Milford, CT 06776
(860) 354-3069
Elizabeth Michelson, Curator
Hours: Apr–Nov: Thur–Sat 1:00–4:00, and by appointment
("We have extensive genealogical files on New Milford people.")

Newington Historical Society and Trust, Inc.
679 Willard Avenue
Newington, CT 06111
(860) 666-7118
Pamela Toma, Director/Curator

Newtown Historical Society
44 Main Street
PO Box 189
Newtown, CT 06470
(203) 426-5937; (203) 426-3313 FAX
Sallie S. Meffert, President
Hours: Sun (May–Jun & Sept–Oct) 2:00–5:00, and by appointment
Pub. *The Rooster's Crow*, five times per year
$10.00 per year membership for individuals, $15.00 per year membership for families, $100.00 life membership; search fee by arrangement

Noank Historical Society, Inc.
(17 Sylvan Street—museum location Latham-Chester Store Exhibition Hall, 108 Main Street—location)
PO Box 9454 (mailing address)
Groton, CT 06340
(860) 536-3021; (860) 536-3960 (President)
James Giblin, President
Hours: summer: Wed & Sat–Sun 2:00–5:00, and by appointment
Pub. *NHS Newsletter*
$5.00 per year membership for individuals

North Haven Historical Society
27 Broadway
North Haven, CT 06473
(203) 239-7722
Sylvia M. Garfield, President
Hours: winter: Tue & Thur 1:00–4:30; summer: Thur 1:00–4:30
Pub. *Newsletter*, two or three times per year
(archives and museum of local history, including family history of North Haven only)

$7.00 per year membership for individuals, $10.00 per year membership for families, $40.00 per year Supporting membership

North Stonington Historical Society, Inc.
(1 Wyassup Road—location)
PO Box 134
North Stonington, CT 06359-0134
(860) 535-9448 (Library)
Hours: Library: Tue 2:00–4:00
Pub. *Newsletter*, nine times per year (monthly except July–August & December)
$10.00 per year membership for individuals, $15.00 per year membership for families, $5.00 per year membership for youth, $200.00 life membership

Norwalk Historical Commission
141 East Avenue
Norwalk, CT 06851
(203) 866-0202
Ralph C. Bloom, Curator
Hours: Mon–Fri 9:00–noon & 1:00–5:00
("All written and visual forms of local history")
copy costs, research fees if required, donations accepted

Norwalk Historical Society
PO Box 335
Norwalk, CT 06852
(203) 853-4228
James R. Cunningham, President

The Old Bethlehem Historical Society, Inc.
North Main Street, The Green
Bethlehem, CT 06751
(203) 266-5188
Doris B. Nicholls, President

Old Post Road Association
PO Box 581
Fairfield, CT 06430

The Old Saybrook Historical Society
Archival Section
(Gen. Wm. Hart House, 350 Main Street—location)
PO Box 4 (mailing address)
Old Saybrook, CT 06475
(860) 388-2622
Hours: Hart House library: Wed (seasonally) 10:30–noon; Archives, Main Street School: Fri 9:30–noon, and by appointment
(Archives consists of printed and manuscript data on the history and genealogy of the Saybrook Plantation, which became the Connecticut towns of Old Saybrook, Essex, Deep River, Chester, and Westbrook; Hart House library has bound books on Connecticut and Saybrook history)

Old Woodbury Historical Society
PO Box 705
Woodbury, CT 06798
Vera T. Elsenboss, President

Orange Historical Society
615 Orange Center Road
PO Box 784
Orange, CT 06477
(203) 795-3106; (203) 795-9466
(President)
Harry W. Jones, President
Hours: Sun (Apr–Oct) 1:00–3:00, and by
appointment
Pub. *OHS Newsletter*, five times per year
$4.00 per year membership

Oxford Historical Society, Inc.
154 Bowers Hill Road
Oxford, CT 06478
(203) 888-0363
Jane Fertig

Plainville Historical Society, Inc.
Plainville History Center
Farmington Canal Room
29 Pierce Street
Plainville, CT 06062
(860) 747-6577
Ruth Hummel, President
Hours: May through mid–Dec: Wed &
Sat noon–3:30; Office: usually Wed–
Fri mornings
(before 1869 was part of Farmington,
which has older holdings)
$6.00 per year Active membership for
individuals, $10.00 per year Active
membership for families (any
number), $100.00 Active life
membership, $10.00 per year
Sustaining membership for
individuals, $25.00–$100.00 per year
Sustaining membership for families or
businesses

Plymouth Historical Society
(572 Main Street—location)
PO Box 176 (mailing address)
Plymouth, CT 06782
(860) 283-8229
Marie MacDermid, Registrar
Hours: by appointment

Pomfret Historical Society, Inc.
(11 Town House Road—location)
PO Box 152 (mailing address)
Pomfret Center, CT 06259
(860) 974-3950 FAX
Elizabeth Carter, President; Mary G.
Page, Municipal Historian
Hours: various
search fee depending on scope of search

Portland Historical Society, Inc.
PO Box 98
Portland, CT 06480

Prospect Historical Society
(Center Street—location)
6 Maria Hotchkiss (mailing address)
Prospect, CT 06712

Redding Historical Society, Inc.
Redding Center, CT 06875

**Ridgefield Library and Historical
Association**
Historical Collection
472 Main Street
Ridgefield, CT 06877
(203) 438-2282
Anita T. Daubenspeck, Director
Hours: Mon, Wed & Fri 10:00–6:00, Tue
& Thur 10:00–9:00

Rowayton Historical Society
177 Rowayton Avenue
PO Box 106
Rowayton, CT 06853
Frank E. Raymond

Roxbury Historical Society
Blue Stone Ridge
Roxbury, CT 06783

**Salisbury Association (Historic
Group)**
Scoville Library History Room
38 Main Street
PO Box 516
Salisbury, CT 06068-0516
(860) 435-9440
Virginia Moskowitz, Salisbury Town
Historian
Hours: by appointment
search fee depends on requests and what
is involved

Salmon Brook Historical Society
208 Salmon Brook Street
Granby, CT 06035
(860) 653-9713
http://www.harborside.com/home/p/
p2241/sbhs.html
Carol Laun, Genealogist-Curator
Hours: Thur 9:00–noon, and by
appointment
Pub. *Heritage of Granby*
(genealogy of Granby-Simsbury families,
Granby history)
search fee: copying and mailing costs
plus donation

**Saybrook Colony Founders
Association, Inc.**
PO Box 1635
Old Saybrook, CT 06475-1000
(860) 388-2234; (860) 395-3123
Elaine F. Staplins, President
Pub. *Hear-Saye*, quarterly
(genealogical services; social history of
Saybrook Colony)
$12.00 per year membership

Seymour Historical Society
59 West Street
Seymour, CT 06483
(203) 888-7471; (203) 888-0037
David Kummer, President; Alese
Kummer, Curator
Hours: Museum: first Sun; Office: Mon
$5.00 per year Active membership, $3.00

per year Student membership, $10.00
per year Contributing membership

Shelton Historical Society
(70 Ripton Road—location)
PO Box 2155 (mailing address)
Shelton, CT 06484
(203) 925-1803
Mary Solomon, Director
Hours: Mon 10:00–4:00, seasonally two
Sun per month, and by appointment
Pub. *Shelton Historical Society News*,
quarterly
(local history of the City of Shelton,
small genealogical collection)
$15.00 per year membership for
individuals, $20.00 per year
membership for families; search fee:
$8.00 plus copies at 25¢ per page

Sherman Historical Society
(David Northrop House Museum—
location)
10 Route 37 Center (mailing address)
Sherman, CT 06784
(860) 354-3083; (860) 350-1187 FAX
Gloria Thorne, President
Hours: May–Oct: Sat–Sun 1:00–4:00,
and by appointment
Pub. *S.H.S. Newsletter*, quarterly
(local genealogy and resource library)
from $15.00 per year membership

**South Windsor Historical Society,
Inc.**
PO Box 216
South Windsor, CT 06074

Southbury Historical Society, Inc.
PO Box 124
Southbury, CT 06488
(203) 264-2993
Richard C. Perry, President
Pub. *SHS Newsletter*, bimonthly
(local history and genealogy)
$10.00 per year membership for
individuals, $15.00 per year
membership for families

Southington Historical Society
Southington Historical Center
239 Main Street
Southington, CT 06489
(860) 621-4811

Sprague Historical Society
1 Main Street
Baltic, CT 06330

Stafford Historical Society, Inc.
(2 Main Street, Haymarket Square,
Stafford Springs, CT 06076—
location)
PO Box 56 (mailing address)
Stafford Springs, CT 06075
David Bartlett, President
Hours: Sept–Jun: second Sun 2:00–4:00;
Jul–Aug: Thur 2:00–4:00
Pub. *Newsletter*, quarterly
(local history, some regional and state
history)

$5.00 per year membership for individuals, $8.00 per year membership for families, $50.00 life membership

The Stamford Historical Society

1508 High Ridge Road
Stamford, CT 06903
(203) 329-1183; (203) 322-1607 FAX
http://www.cslnet.ctstateu.edu/stamford/
   index.html
Ron Marcus, Librarian
Hours: Tue–Sun noon–4:00
$35.00 per year membership for individuals, $25.00 per year membership for students or senior citizens; $25.00 suggested contribution for research

The Stonington Historical Society

(Capt. Nathaniel B. Palmer House, 40 Palmer Street—location)
PO Box 103 (mailing address)
Stonington, CT 06378-0103
(860) 535-1131; (860) 535-0888 (Librarian); (860) 535-8445 (Palmer House); (860) 535-1440 (Lighthouse)
Michael H. Davis, President; Mary Thacher, Librarian; Connie Colon, N. B. Palmer House-Manager; Louise Pittaway, Lighthouse Museum Curator
Hours: Palmer House: Tue–Sun (May–Nov) 10:00–4:00; Lighthouse: Mon (Jul–Aug) & Tue–Sun (May–Nov) 10:00–5:00; Library: Wed 1:00–5:00, by appointment
Pub. *Historical Footnotes*, quarterly ("Genealogy and history of the Stonington area; also operate The Old Lighthouse Museum in Stonington.")
$10.00 per year membership for individuals, $15.00 per year membership for families, $20.00 per year Contributing membership; admission charge

The Stratford Historical Society

967 Academy Hill
PO Box 382
Stratford, CT 06497
(203) 378-0630
Hiram Tindall, Curator
Hours: Tue 9:00–1:00
Pub. *SHS Newsletter*, bimonthly (Stratford genealogy, manuscripts, photos, history of Stratford; "Very small library may be used for reference only; books not available for circulation.")
$10.00 per year membership for individuals, $7.00 per year membership for senior citizens

Suffield Historical Society

232 South Main Street
Suffield, CT 06078
(860) 668-5256
Roger C. Loomis, President

Thomaston Historical Society, Inc.

Town Hall, 158 Main Street
Thomaston, CT 06787
(860) 283-2159
Joseph Wassong, Curator
Hours: by appointment
$10.00 per year membership

The Thompson Historical Society

(339 Thompson Road—location)
PO Box 47 (mailing address)
Thompson, CT 06277
(860) 928-5874
Jane Vercelli, President; Georgia Ballard, Genealogist
donations accepted

Tolland Historical Society, Inc.

PO Box 107
Tolland, CT 06084

Torrington Historical Society, Inc.

192 Main Street
Torrington, CT 06790
(860) 482-8260
Mark McEachern, Executive Director
Pub. *THS Newsletter*

Municipal Historian

City Hall, Room 209
140 Main Street
Torrington, CT 06790
Ernest Ceder

Totoket Historical Society, Inc.

1605 Foxon Road
PO Box 563
North Branford, CT 06471
(203) 488-0423

Trumbull Historical Society

65 Woolsley Avenue
Trumbull, CT 06611
(203) 268-3545; (203) 377-6620 (answering machine)
http://pages.prodigy.com/sakal/ths.htm
Dorothy M. Hawley, Genealogist
Hours: by appointment Thur 10:00–1:00, Sun 2:00–4:00
Pub. *Gristmill*, four times per year (Sept, Nov, Jan, May)
$10.00 per year membership for individuals, $7.50 per year membership for senior citizens

Union Historical Society, Inc.

(Town Hall Road—location)
1099 Buckley Highway (mailing address)
Union, CT 06076
(860) 684-7078
Jeannine M. Upson, President
Hours: by appointment
$3.00 per year membership

Wallingford Historical Society

(180 South Main Street—location)
PO Box 73 (mailing address)
Wallingford, CT 06492
(203) 294-1996
Robert N. Beaumont, President

Hours: Sun (Memorial Day–Labor Day) 2:00–4:30, and by appointment
$5.00 per year membership for individuals, $8.00 per year membership for families; search fee: donation plus expenses

Waterford Historical Society, Inc.

Jordan Green, Rope Ferry Road
PO Box 117
Waterford, CT 06385
Pub. *Crier*, irregularly

Watertown Historical Society, Inc.

22 DeForest Street
Watertown, CT 06795

Weston Historical Society

104 Weston Road
PO Box 1092
Weston, CT 06883

Westport Historical Society

25 Avery Place
Westport, CT 06880
(203) 221-0981
Sheila O'Neill, Executive Director
Hours: Office: Mon–Fri 9:00–5:00; Museum: Tue–Sat 10:00–3:00
Pub. *News Notes*

Wethersfield Historical Society

150 Main Street
Wethersfield, CT 06109
(860) 529-7656; (860) 529-1905 FAX
Brenda Milkofsky, Director
Hours: Tue–Fri 10:00–4:00, Sat 1:00–4:00
Pub. *Wethersfield Newsletter*, quarterly (Wethersfield events, historical articles)
$23.00 per year membership for individuals, $35.00 per year membership for couples

Dorothy Whitfield Historic Society, Inc.

84 Boston Street
PO Box 229
Guilford, CT 06437

Willington Historical Society

48 Red Oak Hill
West Willington, CT 06279
(860) 429-2656
Isabel Weigold, Historian
Hours: 9:00–5:00
Pub. *Hourglass*, quarterly (Willington's early families, also Tolland County vital records and history)
$3.50 per year membership; search fee: $7.50 per hour

Wilton Historical Society

(Wilton History Room at the Wilton Library, 137 Old Ridgefield Road—location)
249 Danbury Road (mailing address)
Wilton, CT 06897
(203) 762-3950; (203) 762-7257
Marilyn Gould, Director

Hours: Wilton Library: Mon–Wed & Fri
9:00–5:30, Thur 9:00–9:00, Sat 9:00–
5:00, Sun (Oct–Apr) 1:00–5:00
(local history and genealogy)

The Windsor Historical Society, Inc.
96 Palisado Avenue
Windsor, CT 06095
(860) 688-3813
Robert T. Silliman, Director
Hours: 1 Apr–31 Oct: Tue–Sat 10:00–
4:00; 1 Nov–31 Mar: Mon–Fri 10:00–
4:00
Pub. *Windsor Historical Society News*,
bimonthly
$8.00 per year membership for
individuals, $12.00 per year
jointmembership, $16.00 per year
Sustaining membership for
individuals, $24.00 per year joint
Sustaining membership; $120.00 life
membership for individuals, $160.00
joint life membership

**Windsor Locks Historical Society,
Inc.**
(Noden-Reed Park, 58 West Street—
location)
PO Box 733 (mailing address)
Windsor Locks, CT 06096
(860) 623-4143
Mickey Danyluk, Curator
Hours: Wed & Sun (May–Oct) 1:00–5:00
Pub. *Windsor Locks Journal*
$5.00 per year membership; search fees:
donation

Wintonbury Historical Society, Inc.
21 Westbrook Road
Bloomfield, CT 06002

Woodstock Historical Society
PO Box 65
Woodstock, CT 06281

LDS Family History Centers

Bloomfield
(203) 242-1607

Hartfield
(see Bloomfield)

Genealogical Societies

State Genealogical Society

**Connecticut Society of Genealogists,
Inc.**
(175 Maple Street, East Hartford, CT
06118—location)
PO Box 435 (mailing address)
Glastonbury, CT 06033-0435

(860) 569-0002
http://www.fgs.org/~fgs/soc0034.htm
Helen H. Hodge, Office Manager
Hours: Mon–Fri 9:30–4:00
Pub. *The Connecticut Nutmegger*,
quarterly; *Connecticut Society of
Genealogists Newsletter*, bimonthly
(publishes *Connecting to Connecticut*)
$3.00 registration fee, $32.00 per year
membership for individuals
nationwide, $14.00 per year
membership for libraries (includes
Nutmegger only)

Regional Genealogical Societies

**American-Canadian Genealogical
Society**
(see New Hampshire)

Connecticut Ancestry Society, Inc.
PO Box 249
Stamford, CT 06904-0249
(914) 764-5014 (Vice President)
Marian Otis, Vice President
Pub. *Connecticut Ancestry*, quarterly
(computer column)
$25.00 per year membership

**Descendants of the Founders of
Ancient Windsor**
(see Lineage and Hereditary Societies)

Middlesex Genealogical Society
PO Box 1111
Darien, CT 06820-1111
(203) 655-2734
E-mail: sfpr48a@prodigy.com;
dbowley@concentric.net
http://www.darien.lib.ct.us/mgs/
default.htm
Pub. *Middlesex Genealogical Society*

**Minnesota Genealogical Society,
Yankee Branch**
(see Massachusetts)

**The New England Historic
Genealogical Society**
(see Massachusetts)

**Palm Beach County Genealogical
Society, Inc.**
(see Florida)

Southington Genealogical Society
Southington Historical Center
239 Main Street
Southington, CT 06489
(860) 628-7831
E-mail: bahai999@aol.com
Raymond L. Thomas, President
Hours: fourth Tue 7:30 P.M. (about two
hours)
Pub. *SGS Newsletter*, semiannually
$5.00 per year membership

Independent Publications and Miscellany

**Association for the Study of
Connecticut History**
Emerson College
100 Beacon Street
Boston, MA 02116
Pub. *Association for the Study of
Connecticut History Newsletter*,
quarterly; *Connecticut History*,
annually, $10.00 per issue

**Association of Northeastern
Connecticut Historical Societies**
PO Box 104
Central Village, CT 06332
Alvin P. Ridgway, Jr., President
Pub. *News and Notes*
(publishes information about area
history)

**Canton Historic District
Commission**
Town Hall
Collinsville, CT 06022

CtGenWeb
Part of U.S. GenWeb Project
E-mail: ct@usgenweb.com
http://www.99main.com/ jrothgeb/
ctgenweb.htm
(links to other Connecticut resources)

**Indian and Colonial Research
Center**
The Eva Butler Library
Main Street, Route 27
PO Box 525
Old Mystic, CT 06372
(860) 536-9771
Kathleen Greenhalgh, Librarian
Hours: Apr–Nov: Tue, Thur & Sat 2:00–
4:00
Pub. *ICRC Newsletter*, quarterly
$10.00 per year membership for
individuals, $15.00 per year
membership for families, $25.00 per
year Contributing membership or
membership for organizations or clubs,
$50.00 per year Sustaining
membership, $100.00 per year Patron
membership, $250.00 life
membership; free admission, in-house
genealogy research for $10.00 per
surname plus 25¢ per copy

The New England Quarterly
(see Massachusetts)

Old State House Association
800 Main Street
Hartford, CT 06103

Society for the Preservation of New England Antiquities—Archives
(see Massachusetts)

Trumbull Bicentennial Page
E-mail: auria@worldnet.att.net
http://trumbull.ct.us/history

DELAWARE

Archives and Libraries with Holdings in Genealogy

State Archives and Library

Delaware Public Archives
(Corner of Duke of York and Legislature Avenues, Dover, DE 19901—location)
Hall of Records, PO Box 1401 (mailing address)
Dover, DE 19903
(302) 739-5318; (302) 739-2578 FAX
http://www.archives.state.de.us (Archives); http://www.lib.de.us/archives (Library)
Joanne Mattern, Deputy State Archivist
Hours: Mon–Fri 8:30–4:15
(holdings include records collected by the Office of Vital Statistics and its predecessor from the mid-nineteenth century until 1925 for births and 1957 for deaths and marriages)

Delaware State Library
Delaware Division of Libraries
Department of Community Affairs
43 South Dupont Highway
Dover, DE 19901
(302) 736-4748; (302) 739-6948 FAX
E-mail: webmaster@lib.de.us
http://www.lib.de.us/

State Historical Society

Historical Society of Delaware
505 North Market Street
Wilmington, DE 19801-3091
(302) 655-7161; (302) 655-7844 FAX
E-mail: hsd@dca.net
http://www.hsd.org
Hours: Mon 1:00–9:00, Tue–Fri 9:00–5:00
Pub. *Delaware History*, semiannually
(Delaware and Delaware families)
$25.00 per year membership; $20.00 genealogy search fee plus copying costs, if any

City, County and Regional Archives and Libraries

Dover Public Library
45 South State Street
Dover, DE 19901

Old Swedes' Foundation
Holy Trinity (Old Swedes') Church Foundation, Inc.
Hendrickson House Museum and Old Swedes' Church
606 Church Street
Wilmington, DE 19801

(302) 652-5629; (302) 652-8615 FAX
E-mail: oldswedes@aol.com
Jo Thompson, Curator/Business Manager
Hours: Mon, Wed & Fri–Sat 1:00–4:00
Pub. *Old Swedes' Foundation Newsletter*, annually
(genealogy/history; Swedish/Finnish)
$25.00 per year membership for individuals (year beginning in June), $45.00 per year membership for families, $15.00 per year membership for senior citizens or students, $100.00 per year Patron membership, $500.00 life membership; search for baptism, marriage or burial of one individual: $10.00 (includes photocopies of the event from printed copies of the church records, but a letter attesting to the information is $5.00 extra), determining if and when members of a certain family were buried in the church yard: $10.00 (includes a photocopy of records, where possible, and a letter attesting to the information), researching records on some of the early Swedish families for a specific name and making photocopies: $10.00 plus 20¢ per page

University of Delaware
Morris Library
South College Avenue (Route 896)
Newark, DE 19717-5267
(302) 831-2965 (Reference); (302) 831-BOOK (Library); (302) 831-6952 (Special Collections Department); (302) 831-1046 FAX
E-mail: timothy.murray@mvs.udel.edu; lrjm@udel.edu
(collection available for on-site use, no individualized genealogical assistance available)

Wilmington Library
Tenth and Market Streets
Wilmington, DE 19801
(302) 571-7416; (302) 654-9132 FAX
Hours: Mon–Thur 9:00–8:00, Fri–Sat 9:00–5:00
copies: 15¢ each from paper originals, 25¢ each from microfilm originals

Historical Societies— Local and Regional

Duck Creek Historical Society
(11 South Main Street—museum location)
(227 East Mount Vernon Street—museum mailing address)
PO Box 335 (mailing address)
Smyrna, DE 19977
(302) 653-8844; (302) 653-7023 (Museum)
George L. Caley, Secretary; Katherine D. Bailey, Museum

Hours: Sat 1:00–4:00, and by
appointment
$10.00 per year membership for
individuals

Fort Delaware Society
PO Box 1251
Wilmington, DE 19899
(302) 658-7897

**The Greater Harrington Historical
Society**
(108–110 Fleming Street—location)
PO Box 64 (mailing address)
Harrington, DE 19952
(302) 398-3698
Grace C. Welch, Museum Manager
Hours: Mon–Fri 9:00–5:00, and by
appointment
Pub. *Newsletter*, semiannually
(a small but growing genealogy section)
$5.00 per year membership

The Laurel Historical Society, Inc.
PO Box 102
Laurel, DE 19956
(302) 875-5678
Kendal T. Jones, President

Milford Historical Society
501 N.W. Front Street
PO Box 352
Milford, DE 19963
David W. Kenton, President
Pub. *Milford Historical Society
Newsletter*, semiannually (spring and
fall), not available by subscription
(house museum only, no research
archives)

New Castle Historical Society
2 East Fourth Street
New Castle, DE 19720
(302) 322-2794
Kathleen Bidwell, Director

Seaford Historical Society, Inc.
Ross Mansion
Rt. 1, Box 393
PO Box 715
Seaford, DE 19973
(302) 628-9500
Claudia Melson, President
Hours: by appointment

LDS Family History Centers

Wilmington
(302) 654-1911

Genealogical Societies

State Genealogical Society

Delaware Genealogical Society
505 North Market Street
Wilmington, DE 19801-3091
http://www.delgensoc.org
Hours: Historical Society of Delaware:
Mon 1:00–9:00, Tue–Fri 9:00–5:00
Pub. *Delaware Genealogical Society
Journal*, semiannually, $20.00
subscription for four issues; *Delaware
Genealogical Society Newsletter*, five
times per year (January, March, May,
September, November); *Delaware
Genealogical Guide*, $11.50 postpaid
for non-members
$15.00 per year membership for
individuals, $18.00 per year
membership for families (includes
both publications)

Regional Genealogical Society

**Lower Delmarva Genealogical
Society**
(see Maryland)

Independent Publications and Miscellany

DeGenWeb
Part of U.S. GenWeb Project
E-mail: de@usgenweb.com;
crossd@cyberia.com
http://www.geocities.com/Heartland/
8074/state_de.htm
(links to other Delaware resources)

**Delaware Society for the
Preservation of Antiquities**
606 Stanton-Christiana Road
Newark, DE 19713
(302) 998-3792

Family Line Publications
(see Maryland)

Hagley Museum and Library
(298 Buck Road East—location)
PO Box 3630 (mailing address)
Wilmington, DE 19807
(302) 658-2400; (302) 658-0568 FAX
Hours: Mon–Fri 8:30–4:30, second Sat
9:00–4:30
(regional business and industrial records)

DISTRICT OF COLUMBIA

Archives and Libraries with Holdings in Genealogy

District Archives and Libraries

District of Columbia Archives
1300 Naylor Court, N.W.
Washington, DC 20001-4225
(202) 727-2054
Dorothy Provine, Archivist
Hours: by appointment
(D.C. original wills; marriage records)

Suitland Reference Branch
Washington National Records Center
4205 Suitland Road
Suitland, MD 20746
(301) 457-7000
(houses temporary records for
Washington, D.C. area, Maryland,
Virginia, and West Virginia)

District Historical Societies

U.S. Capitol Historical Society
200 Maryland Avenue, N.E.
Washington, DC 20002
(202) 543-8919
(no archives, no records of genealogical
interest)

**The Historical Society of
Washington, D.C.**
1307 New Hampshire Avenue, N.W.
Washington, DC 20036-1507
(202) 785-2068; (202) 887-5785 FAX
Gail Redmann, Reference Librarian
Hours: Wed–Sat 10:00–4:00, Thur
12:00–4:00 (members only)
Pub. *Washington History*, two times per
year, $7.95 per issue
(over 14,000 volumes, vertical files,
microform collection, over 500
individual manuscript collections,
photographs, prints, maps)
$40.00 per year membership for
individuals, $55.00 per year
membership for families, $25.00 per
year membership for students, $100.00
per year Contributing membership,
$200.00 per year Sustaining
membership; admission: $3.00 per
visit for non-members, $1.50 per visit
for non-member students and senior
citizens, $3.00 for three-month student
pass; research: $30.00 per hour (half-
hour minimum), including up to 20
photocopies; copies: 20¢ per exposure
from paper originals for non-members

(15¢ for members), 50¢ per exposure from microform originals (40¢ for members), plus minimum $5.00 postage and handling

City and Regional Archives and Libraries

National Society, Daughters of the American Revolution (D.A.R.)
1776 D Street, N.W.
Washington, DC 20006-5392
(202) 879-3229
http://www.dar.org
Eric G. Grundset, Library Director
Hours: Mon–Fri 8:45–4:00, Sun 1:00–5:00 (closed Sun before holiday, and closed to the public in mid–Apr)
Pub. *Daughters of the American Revolution Magazine*, ten times per year, $12.00 per year subscription; *Continental Columns*, quarterly (reprinted in *DAR Magazine*)
(collection includes "all periods of U.S. history and records for the entire country")
entrance fee to non-members

Folger Shakespeare Library
201 East Capitol Street, S.E.
Washington, DC 20003-1094
(202) 544-4600
(seventeenth-century immigration lists)

Martin Luther King Memorial Library
Washingtoniana Division
901 G Street, N.W.
Washington, DC 20001
(202) 727-1213
Roxanna Deane
Hours: Mon–Thur 9:00–9:00, Fri–Sat 9:00–5:30, Sun (Sept to mid–Jun) 1:00–5:00

LDS Family History Centers

District of Columbia
(see Kensington, Maryland, or Falls Church, Virginia)

Genealogical Society

Regional Genealogical Society

Ohio Genealogical Society
National Capital Buckeye Chapter
(see Ohio)

Independent Publications and Miscellany

Advisory Council on Historic Preservation
1100 Pennsylvania Avenue, N.W., Suite 809
Washington, DC 20004

DCGenWeb
Part of U.S. GenWeb Project
E-mail: dc@usgenweb.com
http://www.members.aol.com/DCGenWeb/index.html
(links to other DC resources)

Family Line Publications
(see Maryland)

FLORIDA

Archives and Libraries with Holdings in Genealogy

State Archives and Library

Florida State Archives
Bureau of Archives and Records Management
Division of Library and Information Services
R. A. Gray Building
500 South Bronough Street
Tallahassee, FL 32399-0250
(904) 487-2073 (State Archives); (904) 488-4894 FAX
E-mail: barm@mail.dos.state.fl.us
http://www.dos.state.fl.us/dlis/barm/archives.html
David Coles, Reference Supervisor
Hours: Mon–Fri 8:00–5:00, Sat 9:00–3:00 (closed on state holidays and holiday weekends)

State Library of Florida
Florida Collection
Division of Library and Information Services
R. A. Gray Building, Second Floor
500 South Bronough Street
Tallahassee, FL 32399-0250
(904) 487-2651 (State Library); (904) 488-2746 (Florida Collection)
http://www.dos.state.fl.us/sos/divisions/dlis/dlis.html
Elaine Martin Dickinson, Librarian Specialist
Hours: Mon–Fri 8:00–5:00

WebLUIS!
Florida Center for Library Automation
E-mail: fclmmd@nervm.nerdc.ufl.edu
http://www.fcla.edu/cgi-bin/cgiwrap/fclwptl/webportal
(statewide online library catalog)

State Historical Societies

Florida Historical Society
1320 Highland Avenue
Melbourne, FL 32935
(407) 259-0947
http://www.lib.usf.edu/spccoll/fhs/fhs.html
Hours: *Florida Historical Quarterly*; *Florida Historical Society Report*
Pub. $25.00 per year membership for individuals, $30.00 per year membership for families; research $5.00 per hour or part thereof, plus 10¢ per copy for first 50 copies and 5¢ per copy over 50 copies, plus postage, invoiced prior to shipment of materials

Florida History Associates
R. A. Gray Building
500 South Bronough Street
Tallahassee, FL 32399-0250
(904) 488-1484
M. Diane Lewis, Secretary
Pub. *Newsletter*

City, County and Regional Archives and Libraries

Alachua County Library District
401 East University Avenue
Gainesville, FL 32601
(352) 352-3900
http://www.acld.lib.fl.us
Bobby Ruth Powell, Librarian
Hours: Mon–Thur 10:00–9:00, Fri–Sat
  10:00–5:00, Sun 1:00–5:00

Amelia Island Museum of History
Research Room for Florida and Georgia
  Family History
233 South Third Street
Fernandina Beach, FL 32034
(904) 261-7378
Deon L. Jaccard, Director and President
  of Board of Directors

Birmingham Public Library
(see Alabama)

Bonita Springs Public Library
26876 Pine Avenue
Bonita Springs, FL 33923

Boynton Beach City Library
208 South Seacrest Boulevard
Boynton Beach, FL 33435
(561) 738-7495
William Coup
Hours: Mon–Thur 9:00–8:30, Fri–Sat
  9:00–5:00

Bradford County Public Library
105 East Jackson Street
Starke, FL 32091-3396
(904) 964-6400
E-mail: bradplib@daccess.net
Phalbe Henriksen, Director
Hours: Mon 9:00–8:00, Tue–Thur 9:00–
  7:00, Fri–Sat 9:00–5:00

Collier County Museum
Collier County Government Center
3301 Tamiami Trail East
Naples, FL 34112
(941) 774-8476; (941) 774-8580 FAX
Carrie Lee Welch, Curator of Collections
Hours: Museum: Mon–Fri 9:00–5:00;
  Library: by appointment only
(documents from the pioneer era and
  Seminole Indian culture)

Collier County Public Library
650 Central Avenue
Naples, FL 33940
(941) 263-7768
Elizabeth Nagengast, Reference
  Librarian

Hours: Mon–Thur 9:00–9:00, Fri–Sat
  9:00–5:00
(growing genealogy collection)

DeSoto Correctional Institution Library
PO Box 1072
Arcadia, FL 33821

Florida Folklife Archives
500 South Bronough Street
Tallahassee, FL 32399-0250

Florida State Museum
Museum Drive
Gainesville, FL 32611
(352) 392-1721

Fort Myers Historical Museum
2300 Peck Street
Fort Myers, FL 33901
(941) 322-5955
Patricia Bartlett, Director

Fort Myers-Lee County Public Library
2050 Lee Street
Fort Myers, FL 33901
(941) 479-4635; (941) 479-4634
  (Librarian)
Bryan L. Mulcahy, Librarian
Hours: Mon–Thur 9:00–9:00, Fri–Sat
  9:00–6:00
(basic research materials covering states
  east of the Mississippi River;
  consolidated collections formerly in
  Lee County Branches in Cape Coral,
  Pine Island and Lehigh Acres)

Heritage Museum, Inc.
115 Westview Avenue
PO Box 488
Valparaiso, FL 32580-0488
(904) 678-2615 phone and FAX
Mrs. Christian S. LaRoche, Museum
  Director
Hours: Tue, Thur & Sat 1:00–4:00, and
  by appointment
Pub. *Heritage*, bimonthly
(local history, Florida history, family
  history)

Helen B. Hoffman Library
501 North Fig Tree Lane
Plantation, FL 33317
Hours: Mon 6:30–8:00, Wed–Thur 9:00–
  1:00, Sat 10:00–2:00

Indian River County Main Library
Florida History and Genealogy
  Department
1600 21st Street
Vero Beach, FL 32960
(561) 770-5060
E-mail: phall@iu.net
Pamela J. Hall, Genealogy Librarian
Hours: Mon–Thur 10:00–8:00, Fri
  10:00–5:00, Sat 10:00–4:00
(specializes in states east of the
  Mississippi, extensive microform
  collection)

Jacksonville Public Libraries
Main Library, Florida and Genealogy
  Room
122 North Ocean Street
Jacksonville, FL 32202
(904) 630-2409 (Genealogy); (904) 630-
  2410 (Florida Collection);
  jpl.itd.ci.jax.fl.us/
Mr. Carol Harris, Florida Curator; Arden
  Brugger, Genealogy Librarian
Hours: Mon 10:00–8:00, Tue–Thur
  10:00–5:30, Fri–Sat 10:00–6:00

Jefferson County Public Library
260 North Cherry Street
Monticello, FL 32344
(904) 997-3712
Mary Laverty, Director
Hours: Tue 11:00–8:00, Wed–Fri 9:00–
  5:30, Sat 9:00–3:00
("All of our genealogy information
  collection, etc., has been turned over
  to Keystone Genealogy Society.")

Lakeland Public Library
Special Collections (Lakeland) Room
100 Lake Morton Drive
Lakeland, FL 33801
(941) 284-4269; (941) 284-4327 FAX
Hal Hubener, Special Collections
  Librarian
Hours: Mon–Fri 9:00–5:00, and by
  appointment

Leesburg Public Library
204 North Fifth Street
Leesburg, FL 34748
(352) 728-9790
Nancy Ellen Flint, Director
Hours: Mon–Thur 9:00–9:00, Fri 9:00–
  6:00, Sat 9:00–3:00, Sun 1:00–5:00
(collection includes local history and
  genealogy material on Leesburg and
  Lake County, Florida; also material on
  Sumter and Marion County, Florida,
  federal census for Florida through
  1920; reference collection focuses on
  all states east of the Mississippi)

Manatee County Central Library
Eaton Florida History Room
1301 Barcarrota Boulevard
Bradenton, FL 34205
(941) 748-5555
Pamela N. Gibson, Eaton Room
  Librarian
Hours: Mon–Thur 9:00–9:00, Fri–Sat
  10:00–5:00
(Florida and local Manatee County
  history, description and travel; books,
  maps, magazines, 25,000 archival
  negatives, microfilm of old
  newspapers and Florida census; main
  concentration is on both the area
  covered by Old Manatee County,
  stretching to the Peace River and Lake
  Okeechobee, and the history taking
  place within the current boundaries of
  the county)

Manatee County Historical Records Library
1405 Fourth Avenue, West
Bradenton, FL 34205
(941) 741-4070
Cathy Slusser, Supervisor
Hours: 8:30–5:00
(houses all of Manatee County's governmental records from 1855 to the mid-1970s and into the 1990s)

Melbourne Public Library
540 East Fee Avenue
Melbourne, FL 32901

Miami Beach Public Library
2100 Collins Avenue
Miami, FL 33139
(305) 673-7535

Miami-Dade Public Library
Genealogy Collection
101 West Flagler Street
Miami, FL 33130-1523
(305) 375-5580
Renee Pierce, Genealogy Librarian
Hours: Mon–Wed & Fri–Sat 9:00–6:00, Thur 9:00–9:00, Sun (Oct–May) 1:00–5:00

Monroe County-May Hill Russell Library
Florida Reference Room
700 Fleming Street
Key West, FL 33040
(305) 292-3595; (305) 295-3626 FAX
Lynda Hambright, Genealogist
Hours: Mon 11:00–8:00, Tue & Thur–Sat 10:00–6:00, Wed 9:00–8:00
(specializes in Florida Keys and Bahamas)

Museum of Florida History
Florida Museum Association
R. A. Gray Building
500 South Bronough Street
Tallahassee, FL 32399-0250
(904) 488-1484; (904) 921-2503 FAX
http://www.dos.state.fl.us./dhr/museum
Wanda Richey, Publicity Coordinator
Hours: Mon–Fri 9:00–4:30, Sat 10:00–4:30, Sun noon–4:30
Pub. *The Associate*, bimonthly
(history of Florida)

North Brevard Public Library
2121 South Hopkins Avenue
Titusville, FL 32780-4726
(407) 269-7323; (407) 264-5030 FAX
Nancy C. Sieck, Volunteer Genealogist
Hours: Mon–Thur 9:00–9:00, Fri–Sat 9:00–5:00, Sun 1:00–5:00; volunteer on duty Tue 10:00–2:00
(genealogy collection)

Orange County Library System
Genealogy Department
101 East Central Boulevard
Orlando, FL 32801
(407) 425-4694

http://www.ocls.lib.fl.us/index.htm
Gregg B. Gronlund, Department Head
Hours: Mon–Thur 9:00–9:00, Fri–Sat 9:00–6:00, Sun 1:00–6:00
(all 1790–1920 federal census (no Soundex), passenger list indexes, the state DAR collection, southeastern U.S. and New England states; includes the former Orlando Public Library)

Palm Harbor Library
2330 Nebraska Avenue
Palm Harbor, FL 34683
(813) 784-3332
Lauren Stokes, Reference Manager
Hours: Mon–Thur 10:00–8:00, Fri–Sat 10:00–5:00

Polk County Historical and Genealogical Library
Historic Courthouse—East Wing
100 East Main Street
Bartow, FL 33830-4629
(941) 534-4380
Joseph E. Spann, Jr., Library Manager
Hours: Tue–Sat 10:00–4:00; closed first Tue
(over 15,000 books, 7,000 microfilms on southeastern United States only)
photocopies: 15¢ per page from paper originals, 50¢ per page from microform originals

Putnam County Archives and History
(216 Reid Street, Palatka, FL 32177—location)
PO Box 1976 (mailing address)
Palatka, FL 32178-1976
(904) 329-0330
Janice S. Mahaffey, Archivist
Hours: Mon–Fri 8:00–5:00 (EST)
(Putnam County history, cemetery listings, biographical information)
$5.00 research fee, plus cost of copying

Safety Harbor Museum of History and Fine Arts
329 South Bayshore Boulevard
Safety Harbor, FL 33572

Saint Lucie County Library System
124 North Indian River Drive
Fort Pierce, FL 34950
(561) 468-1615; (561) 466-4150 (dial-in catalog, 2400-9600 baud, 8 bits, 1 stop bit, no parity, full duplex)
Allardyce A. Hamill, Reference Coordinator
Hours: Mon–Wed 9:00–8:30, Thur–Fri 9:00–6:00, Sat 9:00–5:00

Sanford Museum
(520 East First Street, Sanford, FL 32771—location)
PO Box 1788 (mailing address)
Sanford, FL 32772-1788
(407) 302-1000; (407) 330-5666 FAX
Alicia Clarke, Curator
Hours: Tue–Fri 11:00–4:00, Sat 1:00–4:00

(local history; Henry S. Sanford papers of the Civil War, the U.S. State Department, Belgian Congo, Florida development, Swedish American colony)

Selby Public Library
1001 Boulevard of the Arts
Sarasota, FL 34236
(941) 951-5501
Hours: Mon–Tue & Thur 9:00–9:00, Wed & Fri–Sat 9:00–6:00

Seminole County Historical Museum
Genealogical Group
PO Box 2148
Casselberry, FL 32707

South Florida Museum
201 Tenth Street, West
Bradenton, FL 34205
Jennifer M. Hamilton

Suwannee River Regional Library
207 Pine Avenue
Live Oak, FL 32060
(904) 362-5779
Hours: Mon 8:00–9:00, Tue–Fri 8:00–5:30, Sat 8:00–4:00

Tampa-Hillsborough County Public Library System
Special Collections Department
900 North Ashley Drive
Tampa, FL 33602
(813) 273-3652, ext. 6
http://scfn.thpl.lib.fl.us/thpl/thpl.htm
Abby Connor
Hours: Mon–Thur 9:00–9:00, Fri 9:00–5:00, Sat 1:00–5:00
("Genealogical holdings include southeastern U.S., the original thirteen colonies, and those states bordering the Mississippi River; collection also includes Florida history and Burgert Brothers Photographic Collection.")

Tampa Museum
601 Doyle Carlton Drive
Tampa, FL 33602-4395
R. Andrew Maass

University of Florida Libraries
404 Library West
Gainesville, FL 32611
(352) 392-0319
Elizabeth Alexander, Librarian/Chair
(Florida and the southeast)

University of Florida
P. K. Yonge Library of Florida History
210 Smathers Library
Gainesville, FL 32611
(352) 392-0319
E-mail: jeingr@nervm.nerdc.ufl.edu
http://www.ufl.edu/
(biographical materials, church records, manuscripts, maps)

University of South Florida
USF Library, LIB 407
Special Collections Department
4202 East Fowler Avenue
Tampa, FL 33620-5400
(813) 974-2731; (813) 974-5153 FAX
E-mail: tomkemp@lib.usf.edu
http://www.lib.usf.edu/spccoll/ (Special
   Collections); http://www.lib.usf.edu/
   spccoll/genea.html (Genealogy
   Resources)

University of South Florida
Oral History Center
4202 East Fowler Avenue
Tampa, FL 33620

University of Southern Alabama
Gulf Coast Historical Review
(see Alabama)

University of Miami
Archives and Special Collections
   Department
Richter Library
Coral Gables, FL 33124
(305) 284-3247; (305) 665-7352 FAX
E-mail: wbrown@miami.ir.miami.edu
http://www.miami.edu/archives/
   intro.html
(also Cuban collection)

University of West Florida
John C. Pace Library
Special Collections Department
11000 University Drive
Pensacola, FL 32514-5750
(904) 474-2213; (904) 474-3338 FAX
E-mail: ddebolt@uwf.edu
Dean DeBolt, University Librarian
Hours: Mon–Fri 8:00–noon & 12:30–
   4:30; Mon–Thur 5:00–9:00
(Florida Panhandle; west Florida, 1559–
   present; Gulf Coast; Florida; the
   South; "This is an archives of papers
   of families and individuals, businesses,
   churches, organizations, etc.; many
   family records include genealogical
   research files and materials about the
   family throughout the U.S.")
minimal costs for photocopying or
   photograph reproduction

University School Library
7500 S.W. 36th Street
Fort Lauderdale, FL 33066

Venice Archives and Area Historical Collection
351 South Nassau Street
Venice, FL 34285
(941) 486-2487
Dorothy Korwek, Director of Historical
   Resources
Hours: Mon & Wed 10:00–4:00

Vizcaya Museum and Gardens
3251 South Miami Avenue
Miami, FL 33129
(305) 579-2708

Volusia County Archives
252 South Beach Street
Daytona Beach, FL 32014
(904) 254-4647
James M. Wheeler, Director

Volusia County Library Center
City Island
Daytona Beach, FL 32114
(904) 255-3765
Mary E. Gasparry, Reference Librarian
Hours: Mon & Fri–Sat 9:00–5:00, Tue–
   Thur 9:00–9:00

West Florida Regional Library System
200 West Gregory Street
Pensacola, FL 32501-4878
(904) 435-1763
http://www.rootsweb.com.1~f/lscamb/
   index.htm
Dolly Pollard, Librarian
Hours: Tue–Thur 9:00–8:00, Fri–Sat
   9:00–5:00
(northwest Florida and Native American
   genealogy, mainly Creek and
   Cherokee tribes)
no extensive research service

West Palm Beach Public Library
100 Clematis Street
West Palm Beach, FL 33402
Lorraine M. Lentsch, Librarian
Hours: Mon–Sat 10:00–4:00

Historical Societies—
Local and Regional

Alachua County Historical Commission
(30 East University Avenue, Gainesville,
   FL 32601—location)
PO Box 17 (mailing address)
Gainesville, FL 32602-0017
(352) 374-5260; (352) 377-4217
Melanie Barr
Hours: Mon–Fri 9:00–5:00
Pub. *Historical Driving Tours of Alachua
   County*, irregularly, free
(Alachua County and Gainesville history;
   also places historic markers; the
   Historical Commission is appointed by
   the County Commission to oversee the
   historical aspects of the county)

Apalachicola Area Historical Society
PO Box 75
Apalachicola, FL 32320
(904) 653-9524

Archer Historical Society, Inc.
(Corner of Magnolia and West Main
   Street—location)
PO Box 39 (mailing address)
Archer, FL 32618
Jane Behringer, President
Hours: Archer Depot: third Thur

Baker County Historical Society
PO Box 856
MacClenny, FL 32063
Alice Williams, President
Hours: Tue noon–5:00, Sat 3:00–7:00
$10.00 per year membership

Beaches Area Historical Society
PO Box 50646
Jacksonville Beach, FL 32250

Boca Raton Historical Society
71 North Federal Highway
Boca Raton, FL 33432-3919
(561) 395-6766; (561) 395-4049 FAX
Peg McCall, Archivist; Kristen Hamre,
   Director
Hours: Office, gift shop, exhibit: Tue–Fri
   9:00–4:00 (archivist available Mon &
   Thur 1:00–5:00, and by appointment)
Pub. *Spanish River Papers*, irregularly,
   $1.50 plus postage per copy
("local history, pioneer settlers, buildings
   and general area history, oral histories,
   some genealogical information,
   especially on early settlers (1895))
search fees: cost of copies and postage,
   and an hourly rate for extensive
   searches

Bradford County Historical Board of Trustees
West Call and Court Streets
PO Drawer A
Starke, FL 32091
(904) 964-6305
E. L. Matthews, Chairman
Hours: Mon–Fri 9:00–5:00
Pub. *Bradford County Telegraph*,
   weekly, $10.17 for six-month
   subscription, $18.19 for one-year
   subscription

Broward County Historical Commission
151 S.W. Second Street
Fort Lauderdale, FL 33301
(954) 765-4670
Dorothy Bryan, Administrative Secretary
Hours: 8:00–4:30
Pub. *Broward Legacy*, semiannually,
   $6.00 plus 6% tax per year
   subscription
("Research collection includes
   microfilm, oral history tapes,
   photographs, documents, manuscripts,
   library, artifacts and maps")

Calusa Valley Historical Society
439 Hickpochee
PO Box 818
LaBelle, FL 33935
(941) 675-1616

Cedar Key Historical Society
Second Street at State Road 25
PO Box 222
Cedar Key, FL 32625
(352) 543-5549
Dorothy Tyson, President
Pub. *The Beacon*

Citrus County Historical Society, Inc.
The Old Courthouse, Room 111
1 Courthouse Square
Inverness, FL 34450-4802
(352) 637-9928
D. Dale Hughes, Public Relations

The Coastal Heritage Preservation Foundation, Inc.
203 Sanford Road
Andalusia, AL 36420-4113
Mr. Cory
Pub. *CHPF Newsletter*

Collier County Historical Society
137 Twelfth Avenue, South
PO Box 201
Naples, FL 33939
(941) 261-8164
Charles J. Dauray, President
Hours: tours Mon–Fri 2:00–4:00
Pub. *Collier County Historical Society Membership Directory*, annually; *The Timepiece*, semiannually
(southwest Florida history and artifacts)
$3.00 per year membership

Delray Beach Historical Society
5 N.W. First Street
Delray Beach, FL 33444
(561) 243-0223
Margie Miller, Executive Director
Pub. *The Quarterly Newsletter*

Duncan Lamont Clinch Historical Society
PO Box 7
Fernandina Beach, FL 32034

East Hillsborough Historical Society
The Quintilla Geer Bruton Archives Center
605 North Collins Street
Plant City, FL 33566-3321
(813) 757-9226; (813) 754-7031 (Volunteer Director); (813) 757-9252 FAX
Shelby R. Bender, Volunteer Director; Adrienne M. Shoffstall, Historic Site Administrator
Hours: Tue 10:00–8:00, Wed–Fri 1:00–5:00, Sat 1:00–5:00
Pub. *The Pen & Quill*, bimonthly
$10.00 per year membership for individuals, $25.00 per year membership for businesses, $100.00 life membership, $1,000.00 one-time Patron membership

Eleventh Circuit Historical Society, Inc.
(see Georgia)

Florida Supreme Court Historical Society
(Florida Supreme Court Building, Room 268D—location)
PO Box 11344 (mailing address)
Tallahassee, FL 32302

(904) 222-3703; (904) 222-2865
Nancy Dobson, Executive Director
Hours: Mon–Fri 9:00–4:30
Pub. *Review*
$25.00 per year membership for individuals, $100.00 per year Contributing membership, $500.00 per year Patron membership, $1,000 life membership

Fort Lauderdale Historical Society
(219 S.W. Second Avenue, Fort Lauderdale, FL 33301—location)
PO Box 14043 (mailing address)
Fort Lauderdale, FL 33302
(954) 463-4431
Daniel T. Hobby, Executive Director
Pub. *New River News*

Geneva Historical and Genealogical Society
PO Box 145
Geneva, FL 32732

Glades Historical Society
530 South Main Street
Belle Glade, FL 33430

Gulf Coast Heritage Association, Inc.
(337 North Tamiami Trail—location)
PO Box 846 (mailing address)
Osprey, FL 34229
(941) 966-5214; (941) 966-1355 FAX
Karen Whitehair, Curator
Hours: Mon–Fri 9:00–5:00 by appointment only
Pub. *Vision Newsletter*, quarterly
(regional history, environment, archaeology, no genealogical records)
$25.00 per year membership for individuals, $40.00 per year membership for families

Gulfport Historical Society
5301 28th Avenue, South
Gulfport, FL 33707
Keith Hickman, President

Halifax Historical Society Museum
252 South Beach Street
Daytona Beach, FL 32114
(904) 255-6976
Elizabeth B. Baker, Director
Hours: Tue–Sat 10:00–4:00
Pub. *Halifax Historical Herald*, quarterly; *Halifax Historical Society Newsletter*, bimonthly
(local archives, over 10,000 early photos, documents, etc.)
$20.00 per year membership for individuals; $10.00 research fee; $2.00 museum admission

Hillsborough County Historical Museum and Library
3705 West San Rafael Street
Tampa, FL 33629-5124
Elizabeth Jones, Treasurer
Hours: Mon–Fri 10:00–4:00

(early Florida material and families, special local history
limited research is free, charges for copies

Historic Lake Wales Society, Inc.
Depot Museum
Lake Wales Museum and Cultural Center
325 South Scenic Highway
Lake Wales, FL 33853
(941) 676-5443
Janet M. Collins, Assistant Director
Pub. *Across the Track*
(Lake Wales and Polk County)

Historical Society and Avon Park Museum
PO Box 483
Avon Park, FL 33825
(941) 453-3938

Indian River County Historical Society, Inc.
(Vero Station, 2336 14th Avenue—location)
PO Box 6535 (mailing address)
Vero Beach, FL 32961
(561) 778-3435
Carolyn Short, Executive Director
Hours: Wed 10:00–3:00, Sat 10:00–noon, Sun 2:00–4:00
Pub. *IRCHS Newsletter*
$15.00 per year membership for individuals, $20.00 per year membership for families, $50.00 per year Sustaining/club/group/organization membership, $100.00 per year Patron membership, $500.00 per year Benefactor membership

Jefferson County Historical Association
PO Box 496
Monticello, FL 32344
(904) 997-2565

Key West Art and Historical Society
East Martello Museum
3501 South Roosevelt Boulevard
Key West, FL 33040
(305) 296-3913; (305) 296-6206 FAX
Susan Olsen, Director
Hours: daily 9:30–5:00
Pub. *Martello*, quarterly
$25.00 per year membership

Lake County Historical Society, Inc.
(Main Street—location)
PO Box 7800 (mailing address)
Tavares, FL 32778-7800
(352) 343-9802; (352) 343-9814 FAX
Donna Jean Hayes, Office Manager, Secretary
Hours: Mon–Fri 9:00–4:00
Pub. *Tangelo*, quarterly
$10.00 per year membership for individuals, $15.00 per year membership for families, $125.00 life membership

Largo Area Historical Society
805 South Palm Drive
Largo, FL 33541
(813) 584-3480

Lemon Bay Historical and Genealogical Society
PO Box 1245
Englewood, FL 34295-1245

Loxahatchee Historical Society, Inc.
805 North U.S. Highway 1
Jupiter, FL 33477
(561) 747-6639
Eva Cambell

Manatee County Historical Commission, Inc.
604 15th Street, East
Bradenton, FL 34208
(941) 749-7165
Peggy Somerville, Coordinator
Hours: Mon–Fri 8:30–4:30, Sun 1:30–4:30
free admission to museum and eight restored buildings

Manatee County Historical Society
604 15th Street, East
Bradenton, FL 34208
$8.00 per year membership

Marion County Historical Society
801 N.E. Sanchez Avenue
Ocala, FL 34470-5821
Pub. *MCHS Newsletter*

Historical Society of Martin County
825 N.E. Ocean Boulevard
Stuart, FL 34996-1696
(561) 225-1961; (561) 255-2333 FAX

Oakland Park Historical Society
3976 N.E. Sixth Avenue
Oakland Park, FL 33334
(954) 566-4284
Midge Turpen, Historian

Orange County Historical Museu m
Orange County Historical Society, Inc.
Orlando Loch Haven Park
812 East Rollins Street
Orlando, FL 32803-1214
(407) 897-6350; (407) 897-6409 FAX
Frank Mendola, Librarian
Hours: Museum: Mon–Sat 9:00–5:00, Sun noon–5:00; Library: Tue–Thur 1:00–2:00
Pub. *Orange County Historical Museum Quarterly Newsletter: Historic Times*, quarterly
(Floridiana, central Florida history)
$25.00 per year membership; search fee: $10.00 per hour plus 25¢ per photocopy page

Osceola County Historical Society, Inc.
Museum
Spence-Lanier Pioneer Enrichment Center
1750 Palmetto Drive
Kissimee, FL 32743-8960
Andrew W. Herrmann, Curator
Pub. *The Osceola Journal*

Pensacola Historical Society
Lelia Abercrombie Historical Library
117 East Government Street
Pensacola, FL 32501
(904) 433-1559
Sandra Johnson, Curator
Hours: Tue–Thur & Sat 10:00–noon & 1:00–3:00
Pub. *Pensacola History Illustrated*, two times per year (no scheduled times)
$25.00 per year membership for individuals, $35.00 per year membership for families, $15.00 per year membership for students

Pinellas County Historical Society
Heritage Park—Pinellas County Historical Museum
11909 125th Street, North
Largo, FL 34644
(813) 462-3474
Ernest F. Dibble, Ph.D., President; Kendrick T. Ford, Museum Director
Pub. *Punta Pinal*

Polk County Historical Association
(180 North Central Avenue—location)
PO Box 2749 (mailing address)
Bartow, FL 33831-2749
(941) 533-3710
Freddie T. Wright, President
Pub. *Polk County Historical Quarterly* (March, June, September, December); *Newsletter, Polk County Historical Association*, twelve times per year
$20.00 per year membership for individuals, $25.00 per year membership for families

Saint Augustine Historical Society
271 Charlotte Street
Saint Augustine, FL 32084
(904) 824-2872
E-mail: sahs@aug.com
Charles Tingley, Reference Librarian
Hours: Mon–Fri 9:00–noon & 1:00–5:00
Pub. *East Florida Gazette*, quarterly; *El Escribano*, annually
(Spanish, Saint Augustine, Saint Johns County, Florida)
$35.00 per year membership for individuals, $10.00 per year membership for students

Saint Lucie County Historical Society
Saint Lucie County Historical Museum
Saint Lucie Historical Commission
414 Seaway Drive
Fort Pierce, FL 34949

(561) 462-1795 (Museum); (561) 464-6635 (Commission)
http://www.st-lucie.lib.fl.us/museum.htm
Richard Schmidt, President; Edward C. Swanson, Superintendent of Museums
Hours: Tue–Sat 10:00–4:00, Sun noon–4:00
Pub. *Historical Quarterly*

Saint Petersburg Historical Society
335 Second Avenue, N.E.
Saint Petersburg, FL 33701
(813) 894-1052
Pub. *Sea Breeze*, quarterly
$20.00 per year membership

South Brevard Historical Society
PO Box 1064
Melbourne, FL 32902-1064
(407) 723-6835 (Chair)
B. Preece, Chair

South Brevard Historical Society, Inc.
Kellersberger Fund
PO Box 5847 F.I.T.
Melbourne, FL 32901
(407) 723-6835
Betty Preece, Chair

Historical Museum of Southern Florida
101 West Flagler Street
Miami, FL 33130
(305) 375-1492
E-mail: hasf@ix.netcom.com
Natalie Brown, Marketing Director
Hours: Mon–Sat 10:00–5:00, Thur 5:00–9:00, Sun noon–5:00
Pub. *Currents-Historical Museum of Southern Florida*, quarterly; *South Florida History Magazine*, quarterly; *Tequesta*, annually
(southern Florida and Caribbean history; research center, archives and exhibitions)
$35.00 per year membership for individuals or institutions, $45.00 per year membership for families

Historical Association of Southern Florida
Society of Florida Archivists
14220 Leaning Pine Drive
Miami Lakes, FL 33014
E-mail: baltman@mailer.fsu.edu
http://mailer.fsu.edu/~baltman/sfa.html

Southern Studies Institute
(see Louisiana)

Southwest Florida Historical Society, Inc.
(1001 McGregor Boulevard, Fort Myers, FL 33919—location)
PO Box 1381 (mailing address)
Fort Myers, FL 33902-1381
(941) 939-4044
Jean Meola, President
Hours: Wed (Sept–May) 10:00–noon, and by appointment

Pub. *PastFinder*, quarterly
$12.00 per year membership for
individuals, $20.00 per year
membership for famillies

Tallahassee Historical Society
History Department
Florida State University
Tallahassee, FL 32306
E-mail: jdbarret@mailer.fsu.edu
Julie Barrett
Pub. *Apalachee*, semiannually
$2.70 per year membership

LDS Family History Centers

Boca Raton
(407) 395-6644

Fort Lauderdale
(see Boca Raton or Plantation)

Fort Myers
(813) 275-0001

Hialeah
(see Plantation)

Jacksonville
(904) 272-1150; (904) 743-0527

Lake Mary
(407) 333-0137

Largo
(813) 399-8018

Miami
(see Plantation)

Orlando
(see Lake Mary)

Palm Beach Gardens
(407) 626-7989

Pensacola
(904) 969-1254

Plantation
(954) 472-0524

Saint Petersburg
(see Largo)

Tallahassee
(904) 222-8870

Tampa
(813) 971-2869

Winter Haven
(941) 299-1691

Genealogical Societies

State Genealogical Societies

Florida Genealogical Society, Inc.
PO Box 18624
Tampa, FL 33679-8624
Mrs. Ceta Armitage, Editor
Pub. *Journal*, semiannually (March and
October); *Newsletter*, five times per
year (February, April, June, August,
December), $10.00 per year
subscription
$15.00 per year membership for
individuals, $20.00 per year
membership for families or for
overseas individuals

Florida Society for Genealogical Research
8461 54th Street, North
Pinellas Park, FL 33565
(813) 391-2914

Florida State Genealogical Society, Inc.
PO Box 10249
Tallahassee, FL 32302-2249
http://www.fgs.org/~fgs/soc0275.htm
Leslie Jeffcoat Maddocks, Membership
Pub. *The Florida Genealogist*, quarterly;
*Florida State Genealogical Society
Newsletter*, irregularly (four to eight
times per year)
$18.00 per year membership for
individuals, $4.00 per year for each
additional member at the same address

Regional Genealogical Societies

Alachua County Genealogical Society
PO Box 12078
Gainesville, FL 32604
(352) 332-2065
Jack Wood, President
Hours: Alachua County Public Library:
Mon–Thur 10:00–9:00, Fri–Sat 10:00–
5:00, Sun 1:00–5:00
Pub. *'Latchua County News*, quarterly;
'Latchua Notes, as needed (newsletter)
$18.00 per year membership for
individuals, $20.00 per year
membership for families

Amelia Island Genealogical Society
PO Box 6005
Fernandina Beach, FL 32035-6005
(904) 261-2139 (President); (904) 277-
7365 (Library)
Winkie Robinson, President
Hours: Fernandina Library: Mon, Wed &
Fri 10:00–noon
Pub. *The Geneline*, ten times per year;

The Nassau Genealogist, quarterly
(winter, spring, summer, fall)
$15.00 per year membership (Oct 1–Sep
30), $20.00 per year membership for
families (two members)

Bay County Genealogical Society
PO Box 662
Panama City, FL 32402-0662
(904) 872-9882; (904) 872-9057 FAX
Berniece Loper, President
Hours: Bay County Library Meeting
Room: first Sat
Pub. *The County Line*, quarterly (March,
June, September, December)
$15.00 per year membership; search fees
vary; queries accepted

Bonita Springs Genealogical Club
25311 Paradise Road
Bonita Springs, FL 33923-7620
Mrs. Cecil D. Harvard, Secretary

Brevard Genealogical Society
PO Box 1123
Cocoa, FL 32922
(407) 632-6570
Hilda Mayo, Corresponding Secretary
Hours: 9:00–9:00
Pub. *Newsletter*, quarterly
$12.00 per year membership

Genealogical Society of Broward County, Inc.
PO Box 485
Fort Lauderdale, FL 33302
Hours: Helen B. Hoffman Library: Mon
6:30–8:00, Wed–Thur 9:00–1:00, Sat
10:00–2:00
Pub. *Imprints*, quarterly (January, April,
July, October), $12.00 per year
subscription
$15.00 per year membership

Central Florida Genealogical Society, Inc.
PO Box 177
Orlando, FL 32802-0177
(407) 894-8518; (407) 228-4842 FAX
E-mail: lknorr@magicnet.net
Lynne Knorr, President
Pub. *Buried Treasures*, quarterly;
Treasure Chest News, ten times per
year
$20.00 per year membership for
individuals, $25.00 per year
membership for families of two or
more at one address

Charlotte County Genealogical Society
PO Box 2682
Port Charlotte, FL 33949-2682
(941) 766-1985
Web site in process
Jo Sommerville, Editor
Hours: Port Charlotte Library: Mon–Wed
9:00–9:00 (Mon nights during summer
only), Thur 1:00–5:00, Fri–Sat 9:00–
5:00

Pub. *Geneagram*, ten times per year (monthly except Jul–Aug)
$12.00 per year membership for individuals, $18.00 per year membership for families

Citrus County Genealogical Society
PO Box 2211
Inverness, FL 34451-2211
(352) 746-0027 (President); (352) 637-6482 FAX
Robbie Joiner, Recording Secretary, Dr. Bernie O'Neil, President
Hours: 9:00–5:00
Pub. *CCGS Newsletter*, four times per year (February, April, October, December), $10.00 per year subscription
$10.00 per year membership for individuals, $15.00 per year membership for families

Clay County Genealogical Society
PO Box 1071
Green Cove Springs, FL 32043

Genealogical Society of Collier County
PO Box 7933
Naples, FL 33941
(941) 793-1066
W. R. "Bob" Holbrook, President
$10.00 per year membership

Geneva Historical and Genealogical Society
PO Box 145
Geneva, FL 32732

Genealogical Society of Greater Miami, Inc.
PO Box 162905
Miami, FL 33116-2905
Deborah Baker, President
Hours: Miami-Dade Public Library: Mon–Wed & Fri–Sat 9:00–6:00, Thur 9:00–9:00, Sun (Oct–May) 1:00–5:00
Pub. *The Heritage*, quarterly
$15.00 per year membership

The Genealogy Society of Hernando County
PO Box 1793
Brooksville, FL 34605-1793
(352) 796-1623
Kathleen Marsh, Corresponding Secretary
Hours: fourth Tue 6:30
Pub. *Links and Bridges*, monthly
$15.00 per year active membership for individuals, $25.00 per year membership for families, $12.00 per year associate membership; free queries

Highlands County Genealogical Society
Avon Park Library
100 North Museum Avenue
Avon Park, FL 33825
(941) 382-4112 (Genealogical Society); (941) 453-4842 (Library)
Janis Grove, President
Hours: Library: Mon 9:30–8:00, Tue–Thur 9:30–5:30, Fri 9:30–3:30, Sat 9:30–noon
Pub. *Highlands County Genealogical Society Newsletter*, four times per year (Jan, Mar, May, Nov)
$12.00 per year membership for individuals, $15.00 per year membership for couples

Historic Ocala/Marion County Genealogical Society
18 S.E. 14th Avenue
PO Box 1206
Ocala, FL 32678-1206
Marguerite L. Dillman, Secretary
Pub. *Past Times*
$15.00 per year membership

Huxford Genealogical Society, Inc.
(see Georgia)

Imperial Polk Genealogical Society
(Lakeland, FL—location)
PO Box 10 (mailing address)
Kathleen, FL 33849-0045
Pub. *IPGS Newsletter*, monthly
$7.50 per year membership for individuals

Indian River Genealogical Society
(Indian River County Main Library—location)
PO Box 1850 (mailing address)
Vero Beach, FL 32961
(561) 770-5060, ext. 18 (Library)
George Gross, President
Hours: second Tue (Sept–May) 10:00–noon; Advanced BK/PAF® Users Group: first Thur
Pub. *IRGS Newsletter*, nine times per year (monthly September through May)
$15.00 per year membership for individuals or families

Jacksonville Genealogical Society, Inc.
PO Box 60756
Jacksonville, FL 32205-0756
Robert Carlton Smith, Editor
Pub. *Jacksonville Genealogical Society Newsletter*, quarterly; *Jacksonville Genealogical Society Quarterly*, $5.00 per issue plus postage subscription for non-members

Keystone Genealogical Society
950 East Washington
PO Box 50
Monticello, FL 32344
(904) 997-2559
Donna Jean Wiehaus, President
Pub. *Keystone Kin*, quarterly (Jefferson County and surrounding counties in FL and GA)
$12.00 per year membership

Kinseekers Genealogical Society of Lake County
PO Box 492711
Leesburg, FL 32749-2711
Mrs. Buddy Brokaw
Hours: Mon–Thur 9:00–9:00, Fri 9:00–6:00, Sat 9:00–3:00, Sun 1:00–5:00
Pub. *Kinseekers Quarterly*
$10.00 per year membership

Lee County Genealogical Society, Inc.
PO Box 150153
Cape Coral, FL 33914
Pub. *Lee County Genealogical Society Newsletter*, quarterly
$15.00 per year membership for individuals, $20.00 per year membership for families

Lehigh Acres Genealogical Society
(Homestead Road—location)
PO Box 965 (mailing address)
Lehigh Acres, FL 33970-0965
(941) 369-1050
Hours: Lehigh Acres Public Library: Mon, Wed & Fri 10:00–5:00, Tue & Thur 9:00–8:00, Sat 9:00–1:00; Heritage Room: second Tue 1:00–3:00
(Lee County)
$2.00 per year membership for individuals, $3.00 per year membership for families at same address

Lemon Bay Historical and Genealogical Society
PO Box 1245
Englewood, FL 34295-1245

The Manasota Genealogical Society, Inc.
Manatee County Historical Records Library
1405 Fourth Avenue, West
Bradenton, FL 34205
(941) 749-7162
Fran Carter, Vice President
Hours: 9:00–5:00
Pub. *Cracker Crumbs*, quarterly (Manatee County)
$12.00 per year membership

Martin County Genealogical Society, Inc.
c/o Martin County Public Library
701 East Ocean Boulevard
Stuart, FL 34994
(561) 288-4606
E-mail: rshep70683@aol.com
Lawrence I. Shepard, President
Hours: Martin County Public Library, Stokes Room: third Fri (Jan–Nov) 1:00
Pub. *Martin County Genealogical Society Newsletter*, three to four times per year, $12.00 per year subscription for individuals
(Martin County cemetery project in process)

$12.00 per year membership for individuals, $18.00 per year membership for couples, $17.00 per year membership for institutions

Genealogical Society of North Brevard (GSNB)
PO Box 897
Titusville, FL 32781-0897
http://www.webshopper.com/
brevardgenweb
Nancy C. Sieck, President
Hours: first Tue
Pub. *The Register*, monthly
$10.00 per year membership for individuals, $15.00 per year membership for families

Ohio Genealogical Society
Florida Chapter
(see Ohio)

Genealogical Society of Okaloosa County
PO Drawer 1175
Fort Walton Beach, FL 32549
(904) 689-1535
Florence Lembeck, President
Pub. *A Journal of Northwest Florida*, three times per year
$12.00 per year membership

Genealogical Society of Okeechobee
PO Box 371
Okeechobee, FL 34973-0371
(941) 467-1400 (Secretary); (941) 467-2482 (President)
E-mail: maryk@okeechobee.com (Secretary)
Mary E. Kelchner, Secretary; Joy Morley, President
Hours: Presbyterian Church: second Mon 1:30
Pub. *Okeechobee Genealogist*, quarterly
$10.00 per year membership

Palm Beach County Genealogical Society, Inc.
West Palm Beach Public Library
100 Clematis Street
PO Box 1746
West Palm Beach, FL 33402
(561) 832-3279
Lorraine M. Lentsch, Librarian
Hours: Library: Mon–Sat 10:00–4:00
Pub. *Ancestry*, quarterly (January, April, July, October), $15.00 per year subscription
(specializes in Massachusetts, Connecticut, Pennsylvania, Virginia, North Carolina; 1920 Florida census, Florida marriage and divorce records 1927–1991, Florida death records 1877–1991)
$25.00 per year membership for individuals, $35.00 per year membership for families; search fee: $10.00 minimum, one name, one year, one copy

Putnam County Genealogical Society
(Putnam County Library Headquarters, 601 College Road—location)
PO Box 2354 (mailing address)
Palatka, FL 32177
Bobby B. Morris, President
Pub. *Putnam County Genealogical Society Newsletter*, monthly; *Putnam County Genealogical Society Journal*, quarterly
$25.00 per year membership, c/o PO Box 1305, Palatka, FL 32078

Ridge Genealogical Society
PO Box 477
Babson Park, FL 33827
(941) 638-1616
Virginia Johnston, President
Hours: Lake Wales Public Library: second Thur (Sept–May)
Pub. *The Root Digger*, three times per year (January, May, September)
$3.00 per year membership for individuals, $5.00 per year membership for families

Saint Augustine Genealogical Society
Saint Johns County Public Library
1960 North Ponce de Leon Boulevard
Saint Augustine, FL 32084

Genealogical Society of Sarasota, Inc.
PO Box 1917
Sarasota, FL 34230-1917
(941) 923-7791
Maxine L. Colgate, President
Hours: Oct–May: once a month
Pub. *Genealogical Society of Sarasota, Inc., Newsletter*, quarterly
$12.00 per year membership for individuals, $20.00 per year membership for two people of the same family

Genealogical Society of South Brevard County
(Melbourne Public Library—location)
PO Box 786 (mailing address)
Melbourne, FL 32902-0786
Sarah McCarthy, Corresponding Secretary
Pub. *The Bulletin*, quarterly
(Melbourne cemetery project; *Hartford Times* index)
$15.00 per year membership; search fee: $4.00

South Georgia Genealogical Society
(see Georgia)

Southeast Alabama Genealogical Society
(see Alabama)

Suncoast Genealogy Society, Inc.
PO Box 1294
Palm Harbor, FL 34682
(813) 785-5167

Linda Carpenter, President
Hours: Palm Harbor Library: fourth Mon
Pub. *Suncoast Searcher*, monthly
(serving northern Pinellas County, researching all areas)
$15.00 per year membership for individuals, $20.00 per year membership for families

Tallahassee Genealogical Society, Inc.
PO Box 4371
Tallahassee, FL 32315-4371
(904) 878-2900
Nellie Bird Mims, President
Pub. *The Tallahassee Genealogist*, quarterly; *TGS Bulletin*, monthly
$15.00 per year membership for individuals, $20.00 per year membership for households

Treasure Coast Genealogical Society
PO Box 12582
Fort Pierce, FL 34979-2582
Pub. *Treasure Coast Genealogical Society Bulletin*, quarterly
$10.00 per year membership

Volusia County Genealogical Society, Inc.
(Volusia County Library Center, City Island—location)
PO Box 2039 (mailing address)
Daytona Beach, FL 32015
(904) 255-3765
Louise Schutt, President
Hours: Mon–Sat 10:00–5:00, Tue & Thur 5:00–8:00

West Florida Genealogical Society
PO Box 947
Pensacola, FL 32594-0947
Pub. *West Florida Footprints*, irregularly
$6.00 per year membership

West Pasco County Genealogical Society
(First Christian Church, 6219 River Road, New Port Richey, FL 34653—location)
PO Box 1142 (mailing address)
Port Richey, FL 34673
E-mail: hvgr74a@prodigy.com
Debbe Ann Hagner, President
Hours: last Wed 2:00–4:00
$7.00 per year membership for individuals, $10.50 per year membership for couples

Roots and Branches Genealogical Society of West Volusia County
DeLand Public Library
130 East Howry Avenue
DeLand, FL 32724
(904) 734-2424
Charles Baker, President
Hours: Mon, Wed & Fri–Sat 10:00–5:00, Tue & Thur 10:00–8:00
Pub. *Newsletter*, three times per year

Independent Publications and Miscellany

Armchair Publications
810 McDonough Road
Rt. 2, Box 895
Hampton, GA 30228
Joel Dixon Wells
Pub. *Armchair Researcher*, quarterly,
$12.50 per year subscription; *Florida
Armchair Researcher*, quarterly,
$15.00 per year subscription; *Georgia
Armchair Researcher*, quarterly,
$15.00 per year subscription

FlGenWeb
Part of U.S. GenWeb Project
E-mail: fl@usgenweb.com
http://www.rootsweb.com/~flgenweb/
index.html
(links to other Florida resources)

Florida Historical Research Foundation
2301 East 148th Avenue
Lutz, FL 33549
(813) 971-2968

Genealogical Institute
(see Virginia)

Genealogy Books and Consultation
(see Texas)

Kingdom of the Sun
4911 N.E. Seventh Street
Ocala, FL 32671
(904) 236-4740

Mountain Press
(see Tennessee)

Osceola County Department
Genealogical Research
326 Eastern Avenue
Saint Cloud, FL 32769
Marjorie B. Bright

Sarasota County Department of Historical Resources
701 North Tamiami Trail
Sarasota, FL 34236-4899
(941) 316-1115; (941) 316-1117 FAX
Ann Shank, Historical Librarian; Mark
Smith, Archivist
Hours: Office: Mon–Fri 8:00–5:00;
Research: Mon–Thur 9:00–4:00
(indexed obituary file, newspapers,
journals, maps, plats, architectural
drawings, photographs, family and
organization manuscript files related to
Sarasota County history)

Southern Genealogist's Exchange Society, Inc.
(1580 Blanding Boulevard, Jacksonville,
FL 32210—location)
PO Box 2801 (mailing address)
Jacksonville, FL 32203
(904) 387-9142

Sally S. Baldwin, President
Hours: Tue–Thur 10:00–4:00, Sat 1:00–
5:00
Pub. *Southern Genealogist's Exchange
Quarterly*, $20.00 per year
subscription
(southeastern U.S.: Alabama, Arkansas,
Georgia, Louisiana, Mississippi, North
Carolina, South Carolina, Tennessee,
Virginia)
$25.00 per year membership for
individuals, $30.00 per year
membership for families, $300.00 life
membership for individuals, $350.00
life membership for families; search
fee: $5.00 minimum plus expenses

University of South Florida
College of Arts and Sciences
Department of History
4202 East Fowler Avenue, SOC 107
Tampa, FL 33620-8100
(813) 974-2807
Gail Smith, Administrative Assistant
Hours: Mon–Fri 8:00–5:00
Pub. *Tampa Bay History*, semiannually
(June and December)
(general history of central and southwest
Florida, including the fifteen counties
surrounding Tampa: Charlotte, Collier,
DeSoto, Glades, Hardee, Hendry,
Hernando, Highlands, Hillsborough,
Lee, Manatee, Pasco, Pinellas, Polk
and Sarasota counties)
$18.00 per year membership

GEORGIA

Archives and Libraries with Holdings in Genealogy

State Archives and Library

Georgia Department of Archives and History
Office of Secretary of State
330 Capitol Avenue, S.E.
Atlanta, GA 30334
(404) 656-2393 (Information); (404)
656-2350 (Reference); (404) 657-8427
FAX
http://www.sos.state.ga.us
Joanne Smalley, Reference Service
Manager
Hours: Mon–Fri 8:00–4:45, Sat 9:30–
3:15
index check, $15.00 for Georgia
residents, $25.00 for out-of-state
requests

Georgia State Law Library
(244 Washington Street—location)
40 Capitol Square (mailing address)
Atlanta, GA 30334
(404) 656-3468
Martha Lappé, State Law Librarian
Hours: Mon–Fri 8:30–5:00
(strictly Georgia law and legal history, no
genealogy materials)

Georgia Division of Public Library Services
156 Trinity Avenue, S.W.
Atlanta, GA 30303-3652
(404) 656-2461
http://galileo.gsu.edu/homepage.cgi;
http://www.peachnet.edu/galileo/
libraries.html (links to Georgia
libraries)

State Historical Society

Georgia Historical Society
501 Whitaker Street
Savannah, GA 31499
(912) 651-2128; (912) 651-2831 FAX
http://www.savannah-online.com/ghs
Hours: Wed–Fri 10:00–5:00, Sat 9:00–
3:00
Pub. *Georgia Historical Quarterly*;
G.H.S. Footnotes
$35.00 per year membership (includes
both publications)

City, County and Regional Archives and Libraries

Amelia Island Museum of History
(see Florida)

Andrew College Archives
Pitts Library
413 College Street
Cuthbert, GA 31740
(912) 732-2171
Karan Ann Berryman, Director of
  Library Services
Hours: Mon–Fri 8:30–12:00
(Southwest Georgia, Andrew College)
photocopy charge

Armstrong State College
Center for Low Country Studies
11935 Abercorn Street
Savannah, GA 31419-1997
Peter Scardino

Athens Regional Library
(Corner of Baxter Street and Dudley
  Drive—location)
2025 Baxter Street (mailing address)
Athens, GA 30606
(706) 613-3650; (706) 613-3661 FAX
Laura W. Carter, Heritage Room
  Specialist
Hours: Mon–Thur 9:00–9:00, Fri–Sat
  9:00–6:00, Sun 2:00–6:00
(specializes in Athens, Clarke County
  and the Civil War, local African-
  American history and genealogy)

Atlanta History Center
Library/Archives
3101 Andrews Drive, N.W.
Atlanta, GA 30305
(404) 814-4040
E-mail: webmaster@atlhist.org
http://www.atlhist.org/; http://
  www.atlhist.org/html/civilgu.htm
  (Civil War Manuscript Collections)
Anne Salter, Director of Library/Archives
Hours: Tue–Fri 9:00–5:00, Sat 10:00–
  5:00
Pub. *Atlanta History: A Journal of
  Georgia and the South*, quarterly
  $20.00 per year membership

Atlanta University Center
Special Collections and Archives
Robert W. Woodruff Library
111 James P. Brawley Drive, S.W.
Atlanta, GA 30314
(404) 522-8980
Wilson Flemister, Sr., Head
Hours: Mon, Wed & Fri 9:00–5:00, Tue
  & Thur 9:00–7:00, Sat 2:00–5:00
(African-American archival collections)

Atlanta University Center
Theological Services
Robert W. Woodruff Library
111 James P. Brawley Drive, S.W.
Atlanta, GA 30314
Joseph E. Troutman

**Augusta-Richmond County Public
Library**
902 Greene Street
Augusta, GA 30901
(706) 821-2600; (706) 821-2629 FAX
E-mail: walker@csra.net
http://www.csra.net/publib
Alice O. Walker, Local History Librarian
Hours: Mon–Thur 9:00–9:00, Fri–Sat
  9:00–5:30, Sun 2:00–5:30
(Georgia local history)

Augusta State University
Reese Library
2500 Walton Way
Augusta, GA 30904-2200

Austell City Museum
2722 Broad Street
Austell, GA 30001
Rosa Mary Johnson

William and Evelyn Banks Library
601 Broad Street
La Grange, GA 30240
(706) 812-7233
Steve G. Weaver, Reference Librarian
Hours: 8:00–10:00 P.M.

**Bartow County Public Library
System**
429 West Main Street
Cartersville, GA 30120
(770) 382-4203
Lee Howington, Director
Hours: Mon, Wed & Fri 9:00–5:30,
  Tue & Thur 9:00–7:30,
  Sat 1:00–4:30

Bartow County/Roselawn Museum
PO Box 128
Cartersville, GA 30120
Mary Siniard

Bartow History Center
(13 Wall Street—location)
PO Box 1239 (mailing address)
Cartersville, GA 30120
(770) 382-3818; (770) 382-0288 FAX
Michele Rodgers, Director
Hours: Tue–Sat 10:00–4:00
(a Bartow County, Georgia, history
  museum, with exhibits and archives;
  houses some local county records:
  wills, deeds, letters, personal papers,
  photographs, etc.)

Birmingham Public Library
(see Alabama)

W. C. Bradley Memorial Library
Genealogical and Historical Room
1120 Bradley Drive
Columbus, GA 31995
(706) 649-0780
John Lassiter
Hours: Mon–Thur 9:00–9:00, Fri–Sat
  9:00–6:00, Sun 1:30–6:30

**Brunswick-Glynn Regional
Library**
Reference Department
208 Gloucester Street
Brunswick, GA 31520-7007
(912) 267-1212
Hours: Mon–Tue & Thur 10:00–8:00,
  Wed & Fri–Sat 10:00–5:00

**Chatham-Effingham-Liberty
Regional Library**
(Thunderbolt Branch Library, 2708
  Mechanics Avenue, Savannah, GA
  31404—temporary 1997–99 location)
2002 Bull Street (permanent location and
  mailing address)
Savannah, GA 31499-4301
(912) 234-5127; (912) 354-5864
  (Thunderbolt Branch Library)
Erick Erickson, Head of Reference
Hours: Thunderbolt Branch Library:
  Mon–Tue 10:00–8:00, Wed–Thur
  10:00–6:00, Fri 2:00–6:00, Sat 1:00–
  5:00; call for hours at permanent
  location after renovation period
Pub. *Savannah Morning News Index*,
  annually, $50.00 per issue

**Chattahoochee Valley Regional
Library**
1120 Bradley Drive
Columbus, GA 31995
Myretta Holden

Chattooga County Library
201 Farrar Drive
Stone Mountain, GA 30747

Cherokee Regional Library
Georgia History and Genealogy Room
(LaFayette-Walker County Library,
  305 South Duke Street—location)
PO Box 707 (mailing address)
LaFayette, GA 30728
(706) 638-2992
Danette Mullinax, Georgia Room
  Guardian
Hours: Mon & Wed 9:00–6:00, Tue &
  Thur 9:00–8:00, Fri–Sat 9:00–5:00
$5.00 for 30 minutes research, 25¢ each
  for copies

**Chipley Historic Center of Pine
Mountain**
PO Box 1055
Pine Mountain, GA 31822
Franklin Davenport

**Clarkesville/Habersham County
Library**
(178 East Green Street—location)
PO Box 2020 (mailing address)
Clarkesville, GA 30523
(706) 754-4413
Frances Black
Hours: Mon 9:00–8:00, Tue–Fri 9:00–
  5:00, Sat 9:00–1:00

Clayton County Library System Headquarters
865 Battlecreek Road
Jonesboro, GA 30236
(770) 473-3850
Hours: Mon–Thur 9:00–9:00, Fri 9:00–
6:00, Sat 9:00–5:00

Cobb County Public Library
Central Library
Georgia Room
266 Roswell Street, S.E.
Marietta, GA 30060-2004
(770) 528-2333
Carolyn M. Crawford
Hours: Mon–Thur 9:00–9:30, Fri–Sat
9:00–6:00
fees for photocopy and postage

Collections of Life and Heritage
135 Auburn Avenue, N.E.
Atlanta, GA 30308
Deborah Strahorn

Collins-Callaway Library
1235 Fifteenth Street
Augusta, GA 30910-2799
(706) 821-8253
Cassandra M. Norman, Head Librarian
Hours: 7:45–10:00

Columbus College
Chattahoochee Valley Historical
Collections and Columbus College
Archives
School Library
Columbus, GA 31993
(706) 568-2247
Craig Lloyd, Ph.D., Associate Professor
of History/Archives

Dahlonega Courthouse Gold Museum
Department of Natural Resources
Public Square
PO Box 2042
Dahlonega, GA 30533
(706) 864-2257
Sharon Johnson, Superintendent
Hours: Mon–Sat 9:00–5:00, Sun 10:00–
5:00
(genealogical and mining files)
museum admission fee; donation charged
for research material that is available

Decatur-DeKalb Library
215 Sycamore Street
Decatur, GA 30030
(404) 370-3070; (404) 370-3073 FAX
E-mail:
starkeyb@mail.dekalb.public.lib.ga.us
http://www.dekalb.public.lib.ga.us
Beth Starkey, Special Collections
Librarian
Hours: Mon–Thur 9:00–9:00, Fri–Sat
9:00–5:00, Sun 1:00–5:00
$45.00 per year for non-residents, free to
residents

Dougherty County Public Library
300 Pine Avenue
Albany, GA 31701
(912) 430-1900
James F. Forsyth, Genealogical
Reference Librarian
Hours: Mon–Wed 10:00–9:00, Thur–Sat
10:00–6:00

Eagle Tavern Welcome Center
Main Street
PO Box 321
Watkinsville, GA 30677
Carol A. Puryear

Emory University
Robert W. Woodruff Library
Special Collections Department
540 Asbury Circle
Atlanta, GA 30322
(404) 727-6887
Linda M. Matthews, Head, Special
Collections Department
(Georgia and the south, the Civil War,
and Methodists)

Fitzgerald-Ben Hill County Library
123 North Main Street
Fitzgerald, GA 31750-2591
(912) 423-3642
Lee Ann Shain, Director
Hours: Mon, Wed & Fri–Sat 9:00–6:00,
Tue & Thur 9:00–9:00

Fulton County/Atlanta-Fulton Public Library
1 Margaret Mitchell Square
Corner of Carnegie Way and Forsythe
Atlanta, GA 30303
(404) 688-4636, ext. 212 and 292
Janice W. Sikes, Curator; Joyce E. Jelks,
Assistant Curator
Hours: Mon & Fri 9:00–6:00, Tue–Thur
9:00–8:00, Sat 10:00–6:00, Sun 2:00–
6:00

Georgia College
Old Governor's Mansion
120 South Clark Street, CPO 092
Milledgeville, GA 31061
Mary Jo Thompson

Georgia College
Ina Dillard Russell Library
(231 West Hancock Street—location)
PO Box 43 (mailing address)
Milledgeville, GA 31061
(912) 453-5573; (912) 454-0988; (912)
453-4047 FAX
E-mail: scinfo@mail.gac.peachnet.edu
http://peacock.gac.peachnet.edu/
Nancy Davis Bray
Hours: Library: Mon–Thur 7:30–10:00,
Fri 7:30–5:00, Sat 12:00–5:00, Sun
1:00–10:00; Special Collections:
Mon–Fri 9:00–12:00 & 1:00–4:00
(Baldwin County and surrounding
counties)

Georgia Institute of Technology
Archives Department
Price Gilbert Memorial Library
Atlanta, GA 30332
Anne Bartlow

Georgia Southern College
Georgia Humanities Resource Center
PO Box 8074
Statesboro, GA 30460-8074
Alan L. Kaye

Georgia Southern College
Henderson Library
PO Box 8074
Statesboro, GA 30460-8074
Julius F. Ariail

Gwinnett History Museum
Lawrenceville Female Seminary
Building
455 Perry Street, S.W.
Lawrenceville, GA 30245
(770) 822-5178; (770) 237-5612 FAX
Angela Trigg, Director
Hours: Mon–Thur 10:00–4:00, Sat noon–
5:00
Pub. *Gwinnett Muse*, quarterly
(history museum dedicated to the history
of Gwinnett County and its people;
small, growing archives)
$15.00 per year membership for
individuals, $25.00 per year
membership for families, $20.00 per
year membership for non-profit
organizations, $8.00 per year
membership for students or senior
citizens; $1.00 museum admission

Hacksma House Genealogy Library
(see Washington)

Hall County Library System
127 Main Street, N.W.
Gainesville, GA 30505
(770) 532-3311; (770) 532-4305 FAX
Ruth Sanders, Library Assistant
Hours: Labor Day–Memorial Day: Mon–
Thur 9:00–9:00, Fri–Sat 9:00–5:30,
Sun 1:30–5:30; summer: Mon, Wed &
Fri–Sat 9:00–5:30, Tue & Thur 9:00–
9:00
(microfilm of Georgia census for all
counties to 1920; microfilm of
newspapers for Gainesville, Dahlonega
and several surrounding counties;
microfilm of local church records and
court records; some General Longstreet
papers in photocopy form; and many
family histories in vertical files)

Hamburg State Park Museum
Rt. 1, Box 233
Mitchell, GA 30820
(706) 552-2393
Russell Hinson, Site Manager
Hours: 8:00–5:00; Museum: daily tours
but only grinding on an as-needed basis
(operating grist mill and museum)
$2.00 parking fee

Houston County Public Library

1201 Washington Avenue
Perry, GA 31069
(912) 987-3050
Hours: Mon & Wed–Sat 9:00–6:00, Tue
9:00–9:00

Indian Springs State Park Museum

Rt. 2, Box 447
Jackson, GA 30233
Louis Taylor

Jefferson County Library System

306 East Broad Street
Louisville, GA 30434
(912) 625-3751
John K. Hadden, Director
Hours: Mon 9:00–5:30, Tue–Fri 8:30–
5:30, Sat 9:00–1:00

Jefferson Davis Memorial Museum and Park

(Irwinville, GA 31760—location)
823 West Sixth Street (mailing address)
Ocilla, GA 31774
(912) 831-2335; (912) 468-7630
Mrs. Oscar Powell, Chairman
Hours: Tue–Sat 9:00–noon & 1:00–5:00,
Sun 1:00–5:00
(genealogical services; War Between the
States memorabilia)

Jekyll Island Museum

375 Riverview Drive
Jekyll Island, GA 31527
(912) 635-2119; (912) 635-4420
Hours: Mon–Fri 8:00–5:00

Kennesaw State College

Kennesaw College Library
PO Box 444
Marietta, GA 30061
(770) 423-6186
Robert Williams
Hours: Mon–Thur 7:00 A.M.–midnight,
Fri 7:00–5:00, Sat 8:00–6:00, Sun
2:00–10:00
Pub. *Recent Acquisitions*, semiannually,
free

Lake Blackshear Regional Library

307 East Lamar Street
Americus, GA 31709
(912) 924-8091
Jeanine Bruce, Genealogy Clerk
Hours: Mon–Sat 10:00–6:00, Tue 10:00–
8:00

Bryan Lang Historical Library

PO Box 725
Woodbine, GA 31569
(912) 576-5841
John H. Christian, Librarian
Hours: Mon–Fri 8:00–5:00

Lee-Steizer Heritage Research Museum

372 Sisson Avenue, N.E.
Atlanta, GA 30317
M. L. Walker

Neva Lomason Memorial Library

710 Rome Street
Carrollton, GA 30117
(770) 836-6711; (770) 836-4787 FAX
Roni L. Willis, Assistant Director
Hours: Mon–Thur 9:00–8:00, Fri 9:00–
5:30, Sat 9:00–4:30, Sun 2:00–6:00

Lumpkin County Library— Chestatee Regional System

342 Courthouse Hill
Dahlonega, GA 30533
(706) 864-3668; (706) 864-3937 FAX
Sallie Sorohan, Assistant Manager
Hours: Mon, Wed & Fri 10:00–6:00, Tue
& Thur 10:00–8:00, Sat 10:00–2:00

Madison-Morgan Cultural Center

434 South Main Street
Madison, GA 30650
(706) 342-4743; (706) 342-1154 FAX
Cassandra E. Baker, Executive Director
Hours: Tue–Sat 10:00–4:30, Sun 2:00–
5:00
Pub. newsletter, quarterly
(Piedmont, Georgia, History Museum)
$20.00 per year membership for
individuals, $30.00 per year
membership for families, $10.00 per
year membership for students

Massie Heritage Interpretation Center

207 East Gordon Street
Savannah, GA 31401
(912) 651-7022
Francis W. Smith, Heritage Education
Teacher

Medical College of Georgia

Special Collections Program
Medical College of Georgia Library
Laney-Waler Boulevard
Augusta, GA 30912-0300
Dorothy H. Mims

Mercer University

Tift College Archives
1400 Coleman Avenue
Macon, GA 31207
Ann G. Park

Middle Georgia College

Roberts Memorial Library
Cochran, GA 31014
Raj Ambardekar

Midway Museum, Inc.

U.S. Highway 17
PO Box 195
Midway, GA 31320

Mountain Regional Library

(698 Miller Street—location)
PO Box 159 (mailing address)
Young Harris, GA 30582
(706) 379-3732; (706) 379-2047 FAX
E-mail:
haymoret@mail.towns.public.lib.ga.us
Teresa Haymore, Director

Hours: Mon–Fri 8:30–5:00, Sat 10:00–
2:00
(local Georgia and special Appalachian
collections)

North Georgia College

Old North Georgia College Museum
Student Center
Dahlonega, GA 30597
Alan Theriault

Northwest Georgia Regional Library

310 Cappes Street
Dalton, GA 30720
(706) 278-4507
Linda Litton, Reference Librarian
Hours: Mon–Thur 9:00–8:00, Fri 9:00–
6:00, Sat 9:00–5:00

Ocmulgee Regional Library System

505 Second Avenue
PO Box 4369
Eastman, GA 31203
(912) 374-5646
E-mail:
swhigham@mail.dodge.public.lib.ga.us
Stephen Whigham, Computer Services
Librarian
Hours: Mon & Wed 9:00–5:00, Tue &
Thur 9:00–8:00, Fri 9:00–4:00, Sat
10:00–2:00
(special collections)

Oconee County Library

(1080 Experiment Station Road—
location)
PO Box 837 (mailing address)
Watkinsville, GA 30677
(706) 769-3950
Janet Murphy, Reference
Hours: Mon–Thur 10:00–9:00, Fri–Sat
10:00–6:00, Sun 2:00–4:00

Ellen Payne Odom Genealogy Library

(204 Fifth Street, S.E., Moultrie, GA
31768—location)
PO Box 2828 (mailing address)
Moultrie, GA 31776-1110
(912) 985-6540; (912) 985-0936 FAX
http://www.teleport.com/~binder/
famtree.html (Internet edition)
Beth Gay, FSA SCOT, Public Relations
Director and Editor
Hours: Mon–Sat 8:30–5:00
Pub. *The Family Tree: The Ellen Payne
Odom Genealogy Library*, bimonthly,
no charge (postage contributions
appreciated)
(includes Scots Clan archival and
genealogical material; "now home to
more than ninety Scots Clans")

Ohoopee Regional Library

John E. Ladson, Jr., Genealogical and
Historical Foundation Library Branch
(119 Church Street—location)
PO Box 584 (mailing address)
Vidalia, GA 30475
(912) 537-8186

Emilie K. Hartz, Branch Manager
Hours: Mon–Fri 9:00–1:00 & 2:00–6:00,
Sat 9:00–1:00
(21,000 monographs and 2,863
microfilm items with concentrations in
New Hampshire, Massachusetts, New
York, Pennsylvania, Virginia,
Alabama, North Carolina, South
Carolina, Georgia and Tennessee)

Okefenokee Regional Library
401 Lee Avenue
PO Box 1669
Waycross, GA 31501
(912) 287-4978
James Britton, Reference Librarian
Hours: Mon & Thur 10:00–9:00, Tue–
Wed 10:00–6:00, Fri–Sat 10:00–
4:00

Oxford College of Emory University
O'Kelley Memorial Library
Oxford, GA 30267
Margaret McPherson

Pine Mountain Regional Library
PO Box 709
218 Perry Street
Manchester, GA 31816
(706) 846-2186
Charles B. Gee, Director
Hours: Mon–Wed & Fri 8:30–5:00, Thur
8:30–8:00, Sat 9:00–1:00
photocopies $.25 per page

**Preservation Library and Resource
Center**
498 South Main Street
Madison, GA 30650
Marcia Miller

Roddenbery Memorial Library
310 North Broad Street
Cairo, GA 31728

Rome-Floyd County Library
Special Collections Department
205 Riverside Parkway
Rome, GA 30161
(706) 236-4607
E-mail:
broomes@mail.floyd.public.lib.ga.us
Sandra Broome, Curator
Hours: Mon–Thur 8:30–8:30, Fri 8:30–
6:00, Sat 9:00–4:00, Sun 1:30–5:30
("Will respond to brief mail queries.")

San Souci Library
PO Box 167
Adairsville, GA 30103

Satilla Regional Library
Genealogy and Local History
Department
201 South Coffee Avenue
Douglas, GA 31533
(912) 384-6450
Winifred Merier Gourley
Hours: Mon–Thur 10:00–6:00, Fri
10:00–3:00

(local and Georgia family history, local
archives)

Sequoyah Regional Library
116 Brown Industrial Parkway
Canton, GA 30114
(770) 479-3090; (770) 479-3069 FAX
http://www.mindspring.com/~tede/
cherokee_ga/library_links.html
Emma Ingle, ILL/Genealogy Coordinator
Hours: Mon–Thur 9:00–8:00, Fri–Sat
9:00–5:00

South Georgia Regional Library
300 Woodrow Wilson Drive
Valdosta, GA 31602
(912) 333-5285; (912) 333-5286
Roddelle B. Folsom, Director
Hours: Mon–Thur 10:00–9:00, Fri–Sat
10:00–5:30, Sun 2:30–5:30

**Southern College of Technology
Library**
1112 Clay Street
Marietta, GA 30060
John W. Pattillo

Statesboro Regional Library
Genealogy Department
124 South Main Street (Main Street
South and Grady)
Statesboro, GA 30458
(912) 681-0940
Henrietta Royal, Genealogy Librarian
Hours: Mon–Thur 9:00–8:00, Fri–Sat
9:00–6:00

Stone Mountain Park
Memorial Hall Museum
Antebellum Plantation
PO Box 778
Stone Mountain, GA 30086
Jack Bearden

Thomas County Museum of History
(725 North Dawson Street, Thomasville,
GA 32792—location)
PO Box 1922 (mailing address)
Thomasville, GA 31799
(912) 226-7664
Charles T. Hill, Curator
Hours: Mon–Fri 9:00–5:00, Sat 10:00–
5:00, Sun 2:00–5:00
$20.00 per year membership for
individuals, $25.00 per year
membership for families

Thomaston-Upson Archives
(301 South Center Street—location)
PO Box 1137 (mailing address)
Thomaston, GA 30286-0015
(706) 646-2437; (706) 646-3524 FAX
Winston E. Walker, III, Archivist
Hours: Mon–Fri 8:00–5:00, Sat 9:00–
1:00
Pub. *The Hickory Nut*, bimonthly; *Upson
Vigil*, six times per year
no fee for limited research requests only,
more in-depth requests referred to
local independent researchers

**Thomasville Cultural Center
Library**
600 East Washington Street
PO Box 1597
Thomasville, GA 31799
(912) 377-1311; (912) 226-9640
Pearl Thomas, Librarian
Hours: Mon–Fri 9:00–noon & 1:00–5:00
Pub. *Origins Georgia*, quarterly
$20.00 per year membership with
quarterly, $15.00 per year membership
without quarterly

Troy Public Library
(see Alabama)

University of Georgia
Hargrett Rare Book and Manuscript
Library
Athens, GA 30602
(706) 542-7123; (706) 542-4144 FAX
E-mail: web_editor@mail.libs.uga.edu
http://www.libs.uga.edu/hargrett/
speccoll.html
Linda Aaron, Archivist
Hours: Mon–Fri 8:00–5:00, Sat 9:00–
5:00

University of Georgia
Instructional Resources Center
South P-J Auditorium
Athens, GA 30602
John R. Stephens, Jr.

University of Georgia
Map Collection
Science Library
Athens, GA 30602
John Sutherland

University of Georgia Libraries
Richard B. Russell Memorial Library
Athens, GA 30602
(706) 542-5788
Sheryl B. Vogt, Department Head

Valdosta State College
Archives of Contemporary South
Georgia History
Valdosta, GA 31698
Jay Evatt

Mary Vinson Memorial Library
North Jefferson Street
Milledgeville, GA 31061
(genealogy room)

Washington Memorial Library
Stevens-Davis Memorial Collection
Middle Georgia Regional Library
Middle Georgia Archives
1180 Washington Avenue
Macon, GA 31201-1794
(912) 744-0821 (Genealogy
Department); (912) 744-0820; (912)
744-0851 (Archives)
Willard L. Rocker, Chief of Genealogy
Hours: Mon 9:00–9:00, Tue–Sat 9:00–
6:00

(20,000 volumes and 7,500 microfilms on the thirteen original colonies; British and pre-colonial history and genealogy; J. W. Burke imprints)

Wesleyan College
Willet Library
Forsyth Road
Macon, GA 31297
Tena Roberts

West Georgia College
A. B. Weaver Special Collections
Ingram Library
Carrollton, GA 30118
Myron W. House

Wynne-Russell House
City of Lilburn
76 Main Street
Lilburn, GA 30247
Jean Cole

Young Harris College
Duckworth Libraries
PO Box 39
Young Harris, GA 30582
Bob Richardson

Historical Societies— Local and Regional

Albany-Daugherty Historic Area Commission
1108 Maryland Drive
Albany, GA 31707
Mackey R. Saunders

Historical Society of Alma-Bacon County
PO Box 2026
Alma, GA 31510
(912) 632-8450

Alpharetta and Old Milton County Historical and Genealogical Society
1355 Bethany Court
Alpharetta, GA 30201
Jere Hook
Pub. *Alpharetta and Old Milton County Historical and Genealogical Quarterly*

Ansley Park Civic Association
PO Box 7775, Station "C"
Atlanta, GA 30357
Jane P. Harmon

Arts and Heritage Council of Pelham
415 West Railroad Street
PO Box 389
Pelham, GA 31779

Athens-Clarke Heritage Foundation
Fire Hall 2
489 Prince Avenue
Athens, GA 30601
(706) 353-1801

Athens Historical Society
PO Box 7745
Athens, GA 30604-7745

Banks County Historical Society
PO Box 473
Homer, GA 30547
(706) 677-2108
Richard Chambers
Hours: Mon–Fri 10:00–4:00

Barnesville-Lamar County Historical Society
888 Thomaston Street
Barnesville, GA 30204
(770) 358-1289

Barrow County Historical Society
Barrow County Museum
Athens Street
PO Box 277
Winder, GA 30680
(404) 307-1183
C. Fred Ingram, President
Hours: 9:00–noon & 1:00–4:00

Beach Institute Historic Neighborhood Association
9520 Ferguson Avenue
Savannah, GA 31405
W. W. Law

Bleckley County Historical Society
Middle Georgia College
Cochran, GA 31014
(912) 934-6221

Blue and Gray Memorial Association
(Blue and Gray Museum—location)
Municipal Building (mailing address)
Fitzgerald, GA 31750
(912) 423-5375
Beth M. Davis, Executive Director
Hours: 1 Mar–31 Oct: Mon–Fri 2:00–5:00
(museum mirrors the history of this former Union veterans' colony in former Confederate territory)
$5.00 per year membership

Bowdon Area Historical Society
PO Box 277
Bowdon, GA 30108
Jackie Jackson

Brooks County Historical Society
PO Box 676
Quitman, GA 31643
Wilma G. Knight

Bulloch County Historical Society
PO Box 42
Statesboro, GA 30459
(912) 681-1956
Dr. N. Kemp Mabry
Pub. *Our Birthright and Heritage*, monthly; *Readings in Bulloch County History*, annually
$15.00 per year membership for individuals, $20.00 per year

membership for husband and wife, $150.00 life membership

Burke County Historical Association
Quaker Road
Waynesboro, GA 30830
Mrs. Alden Dye

Burke County Historical Society
Burke County Museum
536 Liberty Street
Waynesboro, GA 30830
(706) 554-4889 (Museum); (706) 554-4815 FAX
E-mail: bcmuseum@csranet.com
Robert L. Hammond, Sr., Curator
Hours: Museum: Wed–Fri 10:00–5:00, Sat 10:00–4:00, Sun 1:00–4:00
(historical information, genealogical information—Burke County and Georgia; private database of many local families)

Butts County Historical Society
PO Box 215
Jackson, GA 31233
(770) 775-6734
Mrs. Deryle Lamb, President

Carroll County Historical Society
PO Box 1308
Carrollton, GA 30117
Myron W. House, President

Catoosa County Historical Society
PO Box 113
Ringgold, GA 30736
Mary D. Humphreys, President
Hours: second Mon 7:00–8:30
Pub. *Catoosa County Historical Society Newsletter*, monthly
$5.00 per year membership for individuals, $7.50 per year membership for couples

Cave Spring Historical Society, Inc.
PO Box 715
Cave Spring, GA 30124
Mary Jo Posey

Charlton County Historical Society Library
100 Cypress Street
PO Box 575
Folkston, GA 31537-0575
(912) 496-4578
Lois B. Mays, President
Hours: by appointment
(Charlton County local history, pioneer family histories; abstracts of 1908–1929 *Charlton County Herald*, weekly county paper; microfilm census of county)
$5.00 per year membership

Chattahoochee Valley Historical Society, Inc.
(see Alabama)

Chattooga County Historical Society
119 East Washington Street
Summerville, GA 30747

Steven Strickland, President
Pub. *The Chattooga County Historical Society Quarterly*
$8.00 per year membership for individuals or families

Cherokee County Historical Society, Inc.
PO Box 1287
Canton, GA 30114
(770) 479-4741
Mary H. Free, Genealogist
Pub. *Crescent Chronicle*, monthly
$15.00 per year membership

Coastal Georgia Historical Society
101 Twelfth Street
Saint Simons Island, GA 31522
(912) 638-4666

Coastal Heritage Society, Inc.
303 Martin Luther King, Jr., Boulevard
Savannah, GA 31401
(912) 651-6840; (912) 651-6971 FAX
Sandra Godwin, Director's Assistant
Hours: Mon–Fri 9:00–5:00
Pub. *CHS Update*, quarterly
(Savannah's history, Georgia railroad history, military history, especially Civil War)
$25.00 per year membership

Cobb Landmarks and Historical Society
145 Denmeade Street
Marietta, GA 30060
Ginger B. McPherson, Director

Colbert Improvement Club
PO Box 245
Colbert, GA 30628
(706) 788-2904
Barbarianne Russell, President
(publishes local history)

College Park Historical Society, Inc.
3336 East Main Street
PO Box F
College Park, GA 30337

Colquitt County Historical Society
Moultrie-Colquitt County Library
204 Fifth Street, S.E.
Moultrie, GA 31776
Scott Morris
Hours: Library: Mon–Sat 8:30–5:00

Columbia County Historical Society
PO Box 203
Appling, GA 30802
Julia D. Prather

Cook County Historical Society
Rt. 1
Sparks, GA 31647
Dillard Ensley

Cordele Carnegie Library
115 East 11th Avenue
Cordele, GA 31015
Jane Hendrix

Cordele-Crisp County Historical Society
Rt. 2, Box 995
Cordele, GA 31015
Sarah Summers

Coweta Chatter Genealogical and Historical Society
8031 Highway 54, Rt. 1
Sharpsburg, GA 30277
Norma Gunby

Crawford County Historical Society
PO Box 1028
Roberta, GA 31078
Sara W. Paravis

Dade County Historical Society, Inc.
PO Box 604
Trenton, GA 30752
Claude E. Owens, Jr.

Dahlonega Club, Inc.
Vickery House Museum
(West Main and Vickery Drive—location)
PO Box 785 (mailing address)
Dahlonega, GA 30533
(706) 864-4197; (706) 864-3365
Helyn Brooks, President
Hours: 4 Jul, first week of Dec, and by appointment

Dahlonega Historical Commission
106 Moores Drive
Dahlonega, GA 30533
Steve Gallant

Dawson County Historical Society
PO Box 303
Dawsonville, GA 30534
Mary Smith

Decatur County Historical Society
(119 West Water Street—museum location)
PO Box 682 (mailing address)
Bainbridge, GA 31718
(912) 248-1719
Jim Lillethun, President
Hours: Museum: Sat–Sun 1:00–5:00

DeKalb Historical Society, Inc.
101 East Court Square
Decatur, GA 30030
(404) 373-1088; (404) 373-3076
Robert J. Kothe, Executive Director
Pub. *DeKalb Historical Society Newsletter*
(family records, census records, some court records and some land records)

Early County Historical Society, Inc.
PO Box 564
Blakely, GA 31723
Chesley N. Wiger

East Point Historical Society, Inc.
City Hall Annex
2847 Main Street
East Point, GA 30344
(404) 767-4656

Eatonton-Putnam County Historical Society, Inc.
104 Church Street
Eatonton, GA 31024
(706) 485-6442 (home); (404) 679-5277 (work)
Jim Marshall, President and Primary Genealogical Researcher
Hours: by appointment
(compiling marked and unmarked graves/cemeteries index, published history of Putnam County which includes four surrounding county tidbits, maintains 300+ family files)
$10.00 per year membership; search fees at cost and donation

Elbert County Historical Society
1 Deadwyler Street
PO Box 1033
Elberton, GA 30635
J. W. Hyde, Chair-Executive Committee
Hours: monthly, except Jul–Aug
Pub. *Historic Echoes*, monthly
(located in a restored 1910 seaboard airline passenger depot)
$12.00 per year membership for individuals, $20.00 per year membership for couples

Eleventh Circuit Historical Society, Inc.
PO Box 1556
Atlanta, GA 30301
(404) 331-4605
Wanda W. Lamar
("Projects: videotaped oral histories of our federal judges; writing and publishing the histories of the district courts of Alabama, Florida, and Georgia, and the history of the Eleventh Circuit Court of Appeals")

Etowah Valley Historical Society
(Rt. 1, Cartersville, GA 30120—location)
Rt. 2 (mailing address)
Kingston, GA 30145

Fayette County Historical Society, Inc.
195 Lee Street
PO Box 495
Fayetteville, GA 30214
(770) 461-7152 (President); (770) 716-9230 FAX
E-mail: cccary@aol.com
Carolyn Cary, President, Co-founder, Official County Historian
Hours: Tue 6:00–9:00, Thur 10:00–1:00, Sat 9:00–1:00
("Fairly complete Civil War research section, 1,000 family file folders on Fayette Countians.")
$10.00 per year membership; search fee: 25¢ per page for photocopies

Forsyth County Heritage Foundation, Inc.
Forsyth County Government Building
PO Box 3121
Cumming, GA 30028
(770) 887-1626

Don L. Shadburn, County Historian and
Director
Hours: by appointment only
(historical/genealogical materials on
pioneer families, Cherokee mixed-
blood families, and Confederate
periods of Forsyth County)

Fort Gaines Historical Society, Inc.
308 East Jefferson Street
PO Box 6
Fort Gaines, GA 31751

**Fort Oglethorpe Preservation
Society**
PO Box 5321
Fort Oglethorpe, GA 30742

Franklin County Historical Society
Gainesville Street
PO Box 541
Carnesville, GA 30521
Anna Belle Tabor

Gainesville Heritage Group
Brenau College
Gainesville, GA 30501

**Gordon County Historical Society,
Inc.**
(335 South Wall Street—location)
PO Box 342 (mailing address)
Calhoun, GA 30701
(706) 629-4570 FAX
Mary Thomas, Secretary
Hours: Mon–Fri 10:00–4:00

Grady County Historical Society
Roddenbery Memorial Library
310 North Broad Street
Cairo, GA 31728
Wessie Connell

Greene County Historical Society
PO Box 238
Greensboro, GA 30642
V. T. Newsom

**Griffin Historical and Preservation
Society**
(633 Meriwether Street, Griffin, GA
30223—location)
PO Box 196 (mailing address)
Griffin, GA 30224
(770) 229-2432
Elizabeth L. Thomas, Executive Director

Guale Historical Society
PO Box 398
Saint Marys, GA 31558
(912) 882-4587 (Vice President)
Eloise Thompson, Vice President
Pub. *Guale News*, six times per year
$8.00 per year membership for
individuals, $15.00 per year
membership for families, $2.00 per
year membership for students

Guyton Historical Society
Central Boulevard
PO Box 15
Guyton, GA 31312
(912) 772-3344

Gwinnett Historical Society, Inc.
(185 Clayton Street, Lawrenceville, GA
30245—location)
PO Box 261 (mailing address)
Lawrenceville, GA 30246
(770) 822-5174
Frances Johnson, President
Hours: Mon–Fri 9:30–1:30
Pub. *The Heritage*, quarterly
(history and genealogy of Gwinnett and
surrounding counties)
$15.00 per year membership for
individuals, $20.00 per year
membership for families

Hall County Historical Society
PO Box 1640
Gainesville, GA 30501
Eula Pierce

**Hancock County Foundation for
Historic Preservation**
703 Burwell Street
Sparta, GA 31087
Larry Gulley

Hapeville Historical Society, Inc.
PO Box 82055
Hapeville, GA 30354
Gene Norton

**Haralson County Historical Society,
Inc.**
Van Wert Street
PO Box 383
Buchanan, GA 30113
(770) 646-3369
Daisy H. Sargent, President

**Hart County, Georgia Historical
Society**
40 Bailey Place Road
Lavonia, GA 30553-9561
(706) 377-5612
Travis Parker, President
Hours: 9:00–4:00
Pub. *Pioneers of Hart County, Georgia*,
quarterly
(Hart, Franklin, and Elbert counties,
Georgia; records before 1865)
$21.00 per year membership, includes
periodical and free search of all
Historical Society records by surname

**Hawkinsville-Pulaski County
Chamber of Commerce**
100 Lumpkin Street
PO Box 447
Hawkinsville, GA 31036
(912) 783-1717; (912) 783-1700 FAX
E-mail: hawkins@gnat.net
http://www.gnat.net/hawkinsville.html
Chris Clark, Executive Director
Hours: Mon–Fri 9:00–5:00

("This is the Chamber office and we do
make referrals as needed.")

Heard County Historical Society
Heard County Historical Center and
Museum
(161 Shady Street—location)
PO Box 990 (mailing address)
Franklin, GA 30217
(706) 675-6507 (Museum); (706) 675-
0819 FAX
Selma Bowen, Museum Coordinator;
Lela Craft, Museum Coordinator
Hours: Museum: Tue & Thur 8:30–5:00,
and by appointment
Pub. *Heard and Scene*, quarterly
(January, April, July, October)
$15.00 per year membership for
individuals, $25.00 per year
membership for families, $10.00 per
year membership for college students
or senior citizens, $5.00 per year
membership for high school or
elementary students

Historic Chattahoochee Commission
(see Alabama)

Historic Effingham Society
PO Box 999
Springfield, GA 31329
Milton H. Rahn

Jackson County Historical Society
Crawford W. Long Museum
28 College Street
Jefferson, GA 30549
(706) 367-5307 phone and FAX
Tina Harris, Treasurer and Museum
Director
Hours: Tue–Sat 10:00–4:00
Pub. *Jackson County Historical Society
News*, quarterly
(genealogy, history, library, archives)
$10.00 per year membership for
individuals, $15.00 per year
membership for families; research fee:
$10.00 per hour

**Jasper County Historical
Foundation, Inc.**
College Street
Monticello, GA 31064
(706) 468-6637
Marcia Carnes, President

Jenkins County Historical Society
PO Box 67
Perkins, GA 30822
Leonard Hawes

**Johnson County Historical Society,
Inc.**
PO Box 86
Wrightsville, GA 31096

Keystone Genealogical Society
(see Florida)

King-Tisdell Cottage Foundation, Inc.

514 East Huntingdon Street
Savannah, GA 31401
(912) 234-8000
W. W. Law, President
(Gullah areas of coastal Georgia and South Carolina)

Laurens County Historical Society

Dublin-Laurens Museum
(Bellevue and Academy at Church, Dublin, GA 31021—location)
PO Box 1461 (mailing address)
Dublin, GA 31040
(912) 272-9242
John N. Ross, Director
Hours: Tue–Fri 1:00–4:30
Pub. *LCHS Newsletter*, quarterly
(Laurens County history and genealogy)
$25.00 per year membership

Lee County Historical Society

PO Box 393
Leesburg, GA 31763

Lincoln County Historical Society, Inc.

2357 Highway 220 East
Lincolnton, GA 30817
Marion M. Glover

Lower Altamaha Historical Society

PO Box 1405
Darien, GA 31305
(912) 437-4687
Buddy Sullivan, President; Mattie R. Gladstone, Genealogist
Hours: Ida Hilton Public Library: third Thur except Dec
Pub. *Altamaha Echoes*, biannually; *LAHS Newsletter*, quarterly
(Scots of McIntosh [list of original settlers], McIntosh County cemeteries)
$10.00 per year membership for individuals, $15.00 per year membership for families

Lowndes County Historical Society

305 West Central Avenue
PO Box 434
Valdosta, GA 31601
(912) 247-4780
Albert Pendleton, Curator
Hours: Mon–Fri 2:00–5:00
Pub. *Newsletter—LCHS*, monthly
(Lowndes County history)
$25.00 per year membership for individuals, $40.00 per year membership for families

Macon County Historical Society

PO Box 571
Montezuma, GA 31063
Betty Anne Souter

Madison County Heritage Foundation, Inc.

PO Box 74
Danielsville, GA 30633
Albert L. Stone, Jr.

Marble Valley Historical Society

PO Box 815
Jasper, GA 30143
$10.00 per year membership for individuals, $15.00 per year membership for families

Mechanicsville Community Association of Gwinnett County

35 South Peachtree Street
Norcross, GA 30071
Herbert Green

Meriwether Historical Society

PO Box 741
Greenville, GA 30222
Nan F. Tidwell

Metcalfe Historical Society

Rt. 4, Box 219
Thomasville, GA 31792
Sarah C. Johnson

Middle Georgia Historical Society, Inc.

(Sidney Lanier Cottage, 935 High Street, Macon, GA 31201—location)
PO Box 13358 (mailing address)
Macon, GA 31208-3358
(912) 743-3851
Katherine C. Oliver, Executive Director
Hours: Mon–Fri 9:00–1:00 & 2:00–4:00, Sat 9:30–12:30
Pub. *MGHS Newsletter*, quarterly
(Sidney Lanier, Macon, Georgia)
$15.00 per year membership for individuals, $20.00 per year membership for couples; all requests for genealogy turned over to Willard Rocker at Washington Memorial Library, where society's collection is kept

Monroe County Historical Society

Old Train Depot
Tift College Drive
Forsyth, GA 31029
(912) 994-5070
Saundra Cleveland, Manager
Hours: Tue–Fri 10:00–5:00
(genealogy files and museum, also two members who will help with genealogy for SASE)
$5.00 per year membership

Original Montgomery County Historical Society, Inc.

PO Box 105
Mount Vernon, GA 30445
(912) 583-4401
Dwight Newsome, President

Moreland Community Historical Society

PO Box 128
Moreland, GA 30259
Sara T. Skinner, President

Morgan County Historical Society, Inc.

277 South Main Street
Madison, GA 30650
(706) 342-9627
June Whittaker, Director
Hours: Mon–Sat 10:00–4:30, Sun 1:30–4:30
Pub. *Heritage News*, nine times per year

Newnan-Coweta Historical Society

Male Academy Museum
(30 Temple Avenue, Newnan, GA 30263—location)
PO Box 1001 (mailing address)
Newnan, GA 30264
(770) 251-0207
Daniel R. Dietz, President
Hours: Tue–Thur 10:00–noon & 1:00–3:00, Sat–Sun 2:00–5:00

Northeast Georgia Historical and Genealogical Society

PO Box 907643
Gainesville, GA 30501
Bob Conner, President
Pub. *Newsletter*, quarterly
$10.00 per year membership

Northwest Georgia Historical and Genealogical Society, Inc.

PO Box 5063
Rome, GA 30162-5063
http://www.rootsweb.com/~ganwhags/index.html
Pat Millican, President and Editor
Hours: Rome-Floyd County Library: Mon–Thur 8:30–8:30, Fri 8:30–6:00, Sat 9:00–4:00, Sun 1:30–5:30
Pub. *Northwest Georgia Historical and Genealogical Society Quarterly*
(people, newspaper excerpts, church histories, queries, scannings of exchange publications, five-generation charts, community histories, Confederacy, Indians, schools)
$15.00 per year membership for individuals, $10.00 for topical index; free queries

Oglethorpe University Library

4484 Peachtree Road, N.E.
Atlanta, GA 30319
George G. Stewart

Okefenokee Heritage Center

(North Augusta Avenue—location)
Rt. 5, Box 406A (mailing address)
Waycross, GA 31501
(912) 285-0733; (912) 285-4260
Lin Owen, Executive Director
Pub. *OHC Newsletter*

Old Campbell County Historical Society, Inc.

Courthouse, East Broad Street
Po Box 153
Fairburn, GA 30213

Old Capital Historical Society
PO Box 4
Milledgeville, GA 31061
Ray Olivier
(museum house, no genealogy
 department)
$10.00 per year membership for
 individuals, $15.00 per year
 membership for families, $200.00 life
 membership

Old Clinton Historical Society, Inc.
RFD 5, Box 143
Gray, GA 31032-9207
(912) 986-3384
Earlene Hamilton, President

Paulding County Historical Society
Box 232
Dallas, GA 30132
Charlotte Clonts

Pebble Hill Foundation, Inc.
PO Box 830
Thomasville, GA 31799
Joseph Kitchens

Perry Area Historical Society
1138 Macon Street
Perry, GA 31069
(912) 987-2588 (home answering
 machine); (912) 987-1823 (office,
 8:30–5:30)
Pauline Lewis, Past President

Pioneer Historic Society
815 College Street
McRae, GA 31055
(912) 868-6377
Ruth Mizell

Polk County Historical Society
(205 North College Street—location)
PO Box 203 (mailing address)
Cedartown, GA 30125
(770) 749-0073; (770) 748-5276
 (President)
Mary Brewster, President
Hours: fourth Sun 2:00–5:00, and special
 occasions
$10.00 per year membership

Portal Heritage Society
Rt. 1, Box 318
Moultrie, GA 31768-9711
Denver Hollingsworth

Rabun County Historical Society
PO Box 155
Dillard, GA 30537
Sue B. Pennington

Randolph Historical Society, Inc.
7150 West Highway UU
Columbia, MO 65203-9298
Gail Carty

Richmond County Historical Society
c/o Reese Library, Augusta State
 University
2500 Walton Way
Augusta, GA 30904-2200

(706) 737-1532
Vicki H. Greene, Executive Director
Hours: Mon–Tue & Thur–Fri 9:30 A.M.–
 12:30 P.M.
Pub. *Richmond County Journal*,
 semiannually, $6.50 per issue, $15.00
 per year subscription
(Richmond County archives)
$25.00 per year membership for
 individuals, $45.00 per year
 membership for families

Rockdale County Historical Society
PO Box 351
Conyers, GA 30207

Rome Area Heritage Foundation
PO Box 6181
Rome, GA 30162-6181
Mary J. McGuffey, President
$25.00 per year membership

Roopville Historical Society and Archives
(Highway 27 South—location)
PO Box 165 (mailing address)
Roopville, GA 30170
(770) 854-4460
Nancy Bell

Roswell Historical Society/City of Roswell Research Library and Archives
Roswell Municipal Auditorium Building
Roswell, GA 30075
(770) 594-6405
Darlene Walsh and Louise DeLong, Co-
 Chairmen
Hours: Mon & Thur 1:00–4:30
Pub. *Historic Roswell: Roswell
 Historical Society Newsletter*
("materials concerning the history and
 genealogy of Roswell, Georgia, and
 environs")

San Souci Club
San Souci Historical Committee
San Souci Library
PO Box 167
Adairsville, GA 30103
Carol Adams

Schley County Preservation Committee
Ellaville, GA 31806
Virginia Whaley

Screven County Historical and Genealogical Society
239 Sylvan Circle
Sylvania, GA 30467
Elizabeth Lee

Seminole County Historical Society
PO Box 566
Donalsonville, GA 31745
Stan Johnson

Senoia Area Historical Society
PO Box 301
Senoia, GA 30276
Jack Thompson

Seven Springs Historical Society Museum
PO Box 4
Powder Springs, GA 30073
Sarah F. Miller

Shellman Historical Commission
PO Box 55
Shellman, GA 31786
Gary Martin

Smyrna Historical and Genealogical Society
825 Austin Drive
Smyrna, GA 30082-3305
(770) 435-7549; (770) 431-2858
Harold Smith, Executive Director
Hours: Smyrna Museum: Tue 10:00–
 4:00, Wed & Fri 10:00–noon, Sat
 10:00–2:00
Pub. *Lives and Times*, bimonthly
$20.00 per year membership for
 individuals, $25.00 per year
 membership for families

Southern Studies Institute
(see Louisiana)

Southwest Georgia Regional Library System
Gilbert H. Gragg Library
Shotwell and Monroe Streets
Bainbridge, GA 31717
(912) 248-2665; (912) 248-2670 FAX
Susan S. Whittle, Director
Hours: Mon 10:00–7:00, Tue–Fri 9:00–
 6:00, Sat 10:00–4:00
(with branches: James W. Merritt Library
 in Colquitt and Seminole County
 Library in Donalsonville)

Stephens County Historical Society
Rt. 4, Box 208
Toccoa, GA 30577
Ray Ward

Stewart County Historical Commission
Corner Broad and Cotton Streets
PO Box 817
Lumpkin, GA 31815
(912) 838-4201

Stewart County Historical Society
PO Box 818
Lumpkin, GA 31815
W. E. Cannington

Sweetwater Historical Society
2910 Bankhead Highway
Lithia Springs, GA 30057
Gleda James

Taliaferro County Historical Society, Inc.
Broad Street
PO Box 32
Crawfordville, GA 30631
(706) 456-2339; (706) 456-2294
Ian Macfie, President
Hours: varies

Pub. *Taliaferro County, Georgia, Records & Notes*, quarterly
(locally significant old photos, papers, periodicals, and artifacts)
$5.00 per year membership

Tattnall County Historical Society
705 Virginia Avenue
Glennville, GA 30427
Paul Oliver

Taylor County Historical Society
Butler, GA 31006
Richard Turk

Thronateeska Heritage Center
100 Roosevelt Avenue
Albany, GA 31701
(912) 432-6955
Joseph H. Kitchens, Executive Director
Hours: Mon–Fri 10:00–4:00, Sat noon–4:00
Pub. *Journal of Southwest Georgia History*, annually, $15.00 per year subscription
$20.00 per year membership for individuals, $30.00 per year membership for families, $15.00 per year membership for teachers, $10.00 per year membership for students, $100.00 per year Patron membership, $250.00 per year Partnership membership, $500.00 per year Landmark membership, $1,000.00 Benefactor membership

Towns County Historical and Genealogical Society
PO Box 101
Young Harris, GA 30582
Jerry A. Taylor

Treutlen County Historical Society, Inc.
Treutlen County Courthouse
Soperton, GA 30457
(912) 529-6711
J. Clayton Stephens, Jr., President

Troup County Historical Society—Archives
136 Main Street
PO Box 1051
La Grange, GA 30241
(706) 884-1828; (706) 884-1838 FAX
E-mail: kaye@mentor.lgc.peachnet.edu
http://www.lgc.peachnet.edu/archives/tcarchiv.htm
Kaye Laning Minchew, Director
Hours: Archives: Mon & Wed–Fri 9:00–5:00, Tue 9:00–8:00, Sat 9:00–1:00
Pub. *Newsletter*, quarterly

Turner County Historical Society
PO Box 647
Ashburn, GA 31714
Floyd H. Wardlow, Jr.

Tybee Island Historical Society
30 Meddin Drive
PO Box 366
Tybee Island, GA 31328

(912) 786-5801
Robert Adkins, Acting Director
Hours: summer: 10:00–6:00; winter (Oct–Mar): noon–4:00

Union County Historical Society
PO Box 35
Blairsville, GA 30512
(404) 745-5441
Maurice Farabee, President
Hours: Jun–Oct: Wed–Sat 10:00–4:00
Pub. *Union County Historical Society Newsletter*, quarterly
$10.00 per year membership

Upson Historical Society
PO Box 363
Thomaston, GA 30286-0005
(706) 647-3425
Hours: Thomaston-Upson Archives: Mon–Fri 8:00–5:00, Sat 9:00–1:00
Pub. *Newsletter*, about eight times per year
$15.00 per year membership for individuals

Vineville Neighborhood Association
PO Box 2894
Macon, GA 31203
Alexandra Klingelhofer

Walker County GA Historical Society
PO Box 707
LaFayette, GA 30728
David Boyle, President; Margaret McWhorter, Corresponding Secretary
Pub. *Walker County Historical Society Newsletter*, quarterly
$8.00 per year membership

Historical Society of Walton County, Inc.
238 North Broad Street
Monroe, GA 30655

Washington-Wilkes Historical Foundation, Inc.
308 East Robert Toombs Avenue
Washington, GA 30673
(706) 678-2105

Weston Woman's Club
PO Box 127
Weston, GA 31832
(912) 828-2555
Mrs. C. R. Merritt, President
(family histories, cemeteries, communities, census, churches, memorials, early history)

White County Historical Society
Town Square
PO Box 1139
Cleveland, GA 30528

Whitfield-Murray Historical Society, Inc.
Crown Garden and Archives
715 Chattanooga Avenue
Dalton, GA 30720
(706) 278-0217 phone and FAX

Marcelle White, Director
Hours: Tue–Fri 10:00–5:00, Sat 10:00–1:00
Pub. *Whitfield-Murray Historical Quarterly*
(Whitfield and Murray counties and some northwest Georgia materials)
$15.00 per year membership for individuals, $20.00 per year membership for families

LDS Family History Centers

Atlanta
(see Jonesboro, Powder Springs or Tucker)

Augusta
(see Evans)

Columbus
(706) 563-7216

Evans
(706) 860-1024

Jonesboro
(770) 477-5985

Powder Springs
(770) 943-1983

Roswell
(770) 594-1706

Savannah
(912) 927-6543

Tucker
(770) 723-9941

Genealogical Societies

State Genealogical Society

Georgia Genealogical Society
PO Box 54575
Atlanta, GA 30308-0575
(770) 475-4404
E-mail: georgiagen@gnn.com
http://members.gnn.com/georgiagen/index.htm
Pub. *Georgia Genealogical Society Quarterly*; *Georgia Genealogical Society Newsletter*, quarterly
$25.00 per year membership for individuals, $30.00 per year membership for couples, additional $15.00 per year for foreign delivery

Regional Genealogical Societies

Alpharetta and Old Milton County Historical and Genealogical Society
1355 Bethany Court
Alpharetta, GA 30201
Jere Hook
Pub. *Alpharetta and Old Milton County Historical and Genealogical Quarterly*

Augusta Genealogical Society, Inc.
1025 Chafee Avenue
PO Box 3743
Augusta, GA 30904-3743
(706) 738-2241
Corrie M. Adamson, Honorary President
Hours: Mon & Wed 9:00–4:00, Sat 9:00–1:00, Sun 2:00–5:00
Pub. *Ancestoring*, semiannually, $6.50 per issue; *Echoes*, monthly, $10.00 per volume
$25.00 per year membership for individuals, $30.00 per year membership for families

Bartow County Genealogical Society
(425 West Main Street, the yellow brick building behind the Public Library—location)
PO Box 993 (mailing address)
Cartersville, GA 30120-0993
(770) 382-6676; (770) 606-0706
E-mail: bcgs@innerx.net
Jean Belew, Board Chairman
Hours: Mon–Wed & Fri 10:00–3:30, Wed 5:00–7:00, Thur 1:00–4:00, and by appointment
Pub. *Bartow County Quarterly* (March, June, October, December)
$20.00 per year membership (calendar year)

Carroll County Genealogical Society
PO Box 576
Carrollton, GA 30117
(770) 832-7746
http://members.aol.com./carrollgen/
Mary F. Word, Corresponding Secretary
Pub. *Carroll County Genealogical Quarterly*
$20.00 per year membership; queries for members

Central Georgia Genealogical Society, Inc.
(Warner Robins, GA—location)
319 North Houston Lake Boulevard (mailing address)
Centerville, GA 31028
(912) 953-3114
Addie P. Howell, Corresponding Secretary and Membership
Pub. *Central Georgia Genealogical Society Quarterly*
$20.00 per year membership for individuals, $25.00 per year membership for families

Clarke-Oconee Genealogical Society of Athens, Georgia
PO Box 6403
Athens, GA 30604
Pub. *COGS Quarterly*
$10.00 per year membership

Coastal Georgia Genealogical Society
PO Box 21863
Saint Simons Island, GA 31522
(912) 638-4383
Jim C. Wroton, Jr., President
Hours: Wesley United Methodist Church, Saint Simons Island opposite Fort Frederica: second Sun 3:00
Pub. *CGGS NewsLetter*, monthly
$12.00 per year membership for individuals, $15.00 per year membership for couples

Cobb County Genealogical Society, Inc.
PO Box 1413
Marietta, GA 30061-1413
(770) 434-0507
http://www2.vivid.net/~chuck/ccgs.html
Sharon Thomas, President
Pub. *Family Tree Newsletter*, monthly (except December); *Family Tree Quarterly*
$25.00 per year membership for individuals (calendar year)

Coweta Chatter Genealogical and Historical Society
8031 Highway 54, Rt. 1
Sharpsburg, GA 30277
Norma Gunby

Coweta County Genealogical Society
(32 Clark Street, corner of Clark and Kellogg Streets—location)
PO Box 1014 (mailing address)
Newnan, GA 30264
Ruby Johnston, President
Hours: Mon–Thur 10:00–4:00
Pub. *The Coweta Courier*, quarterly (information for Coweta and Campbell counties)
$15.00 per year membership for individuals, $18.00 per year membership for families, $20.00 per year membership for organizations or Associate membership; no charge for simple research

Delta Genealogical Society
c/o Rossville Public Library
504 McFarland Avenue
Rossville, GA 30741
James Douthat, President; Betty P. Corliss, Corresponding Secretary
Hours: Library: Mon–Wed 9:00–5:00, Thur 1:00–8:00, Fri–Sat 9:00–12:00
Pub. *Southern Roots and Shoots*, quarterly
(northwest Georgia, northeast Alabama, southeast Tennessee)

$12.00 per year membership for individuals, $15.00 per year membership for families, student and life memberships available; free queries

Genealogy Unlimited Society, Inc.
2511 Churchill Drive
Valdosta, GA 31602-2547
(912) 244-0464
Lillian Newham McRee, Founder and Past President
Pub. *Genealogy Unlimited Society Newsletter*, monthly
$15.00 per year membership

The Genealogical Society of Henry and Clayton Counties, Inc.
Henry County Historical Society Building
71 Macon Street
PO Box 1296
McDonough, GA 30253
(770) 366-3686; (770) 954-1456; (770) 474-8465 (President)
R. Swann, President
Hours: Mon, Wed & Fri 10:00–3:00
Pub. *Ancestor Update*, quarterly
$15.00 per year membership; search fee: $10.00

Huxford Genealogical Society, Inc.
(Homerville Municipal Complex Building—location)
PO Box 595 (mailing address)
Homerville, GA 31634
(912) 487-2310
Mary Day, Librarian; Cindy Sirmans, Librarian
Hours: Mon–Fri 9:00–5:00, Sat 10:00–4:00
Pub. *Huxford Genealogical Society Quarterly*, $20.00 per year subscription
(emphasis on Georgia, South Florida, North and South Carolina, etc.)
$25.00 per year membership; research fee: $10.00 plus 15¢ per copy for non-members

Muscogee Genealogical Society
PO Box 761
Columbus, GA 31902
Pub. *Muscogiana: Journal of the Muscogee Genealogical Society*, semiannually
(Columbus/original Muscogee County, Georgia, area consisting of Harris, Talbot, Marion, Chattahoochee and current Muscogee counties)
$15.00 per year membership for individuals, $20.00 per year membership for families and libraries, $300.00 life membership

Northeast Georgia Historical and Genealogical Society
PO Box 907643
Gainesville, GA 30501
Bob Conner, President

Pub. *Newsletter*, quarterly
$10.00 per year membership

Northwest Georgia Historical and Genealogical Society, Inc.
PO Box 5063
Rome, GA 30162-5063
http://www.rootsweb.com/~ganwhags/
index.html
Pat Millican, President and Editor
Hours: Rome-Floyd County Library:
Mon–Thur 8:30–8:30, Fri 8:30–6:00,
Sat 9:00–4:00, Sun 1:30–5:30
Pub. *Northwest Georgia Historical and Genealogical Society Quarterly*
(people, newspaper excerpts, church histories, queries, scannings of exchange publications, five-generation charts, community histories, Confederacy, Indians, schools)
$15.00 per year membership for individuals, $10.00 for topical index; free queries

Savannah Area Genealogical Society
PO Box 15385
Savannah, GA 31416
(periodical "in planning stages")
$15.00 per year membership for individuals, $5.00 per year assoc. and youth

Savannah River Valley Genealogical Society
Hart County Library
110 Benson Street
Hartwell, GA 30643
(706) 376-6372 (Founder and Genealogist); (706) 376-4655 (Library)
Shirley Kaufhold, Founder and Genealogist; Donna Long, President
Hours: Mon–Fri 8:00–5:00, Sat 9:00–12:00
Pub. *Savannah River Valley Genealogical Society Newsletter*, monthly
$10.00 per year membership

Screven County Historical and Genealogical Society
239 Sylvan Circle
Sylvania, GA 30467
Elizabeth Lee

Smyrna Historical and Genealogical Society
825 Austin Drive
Smyrna, GA 30082-3305
(770) 435-7549; (770) 431-2858
Harold Smith, Executive Director
Hours: Smyrna Museum: Tue 10:00–4:00, Wed & Fri 10:00–noon, Sat 10:00–2:00
Pub. *Lives and Times*, bimonthly
$20.00 per year membership for individuals, $25.00 per year membership for families

South Georgia Genealogical Society
(Thomasville, GA—location)

PO Box 246 (mailing address)
Ochlocknee, GA 31773
(912) 574-5349
James A. Rollins, Treasurer and Editor
Pub. *Pine Barrens*, quarterly
(genealogical source information for south Georgia and bordering Florida)
$10.00 per year membership for individuals, $15.00 per year membership for families (one issue to same address); limited research for members

Southeast Alabama Genealogical Society
(see Alabama)

Southwest Georgia Genealogical Society, Inc.
(Dougherty County, Central Library—location)
PO Box 4672 (mailing address)
Albany, GA 31706
(912) 430-1918
Mrs. Leonard DeLamar, Editor
Hours: Mon–Wed 10:00–9:00, Thur–Sat 10:00–6:00
Pub. *Genealogy Gazette*, quarterly
$15.00 per year membership for individuals, $20.00 per year membership for families

Towns County Historical and Genealogical Society
PO Box 101
Young Harris, GA 30582
Jerry A. Taylor

West Central Georgia Genealogical Society, Inc.
PO Box 2291
La Grange, GA 30241
Mr. Julian Harris, President
Pub. *West Central Georgia Genealogical Society Newsletter*, quarterly

Independent Publications and Miscellany

Ancestor Files Library
(see Alabama)

Andersonville Guild
(114 Church Street—location)
PO Box 6 (mailing address)
Andersonville, GA 31711
(912) 924-2558
Peggy Sheppard, President
Hours: 9:00–5:00; festivals: Memorial Day weekend and first full weekend of October
$10.00 per year membership

National Society of Andersonville
305 Ellaville Street
Andersonville, GA 31711
(912) 924-7228

Armchair Publications
810 McDonough Road
Rt. 2, Box 895
Hampton, GA 30228
Joel Dixon Wells
Pub. *Armchair Researcher*, quarterly, $12.50 per year subscription; *Florida Armchair Researcher*, quarterly, $15.00 per year subscription; *Georgia Armchair Researcher*, quarterly, $15.00 per year subscription

Austell Historic Preservation Society
Austell City Hall
Broad Street
Austell, GA 30001
Rosa Mary Johnson

Bartram Trail Society
6688 Marsh Avenue
Lithia Springs, GA 30057

Bethesda Home for Boys
Bethesda Museum
Cunningham Historic Center
9520 Ferguson Avenue
Savannah, GA 31499
Lorane H. Minis

Brasstown Bald Visitor Information Center
PO Box 9
Blairsville, GA 30514
Frances Mason

Emanuel Historic Preservation Society
PO Box 1101
Swainsboro, GA 30401

Foxfire Fund, Inc.
PO Box 541
Mountain City, GA 30562-0541

GaGenWeb
Part of U.S. GenWeb Project
E-mail: ga@usgenweb.com
http://www.rootsweb.com/~gagenweb/
gaindex.htm
(links to other Georgia resources)

Genealogical Institute
(see Virginia)

Genealogy Books and Consultation
(see Texas)

Georgia Association of Historians
Clayton State College
Morrow, GA 30260
Bradley R. Rice

The Georgia Salzburger Society
2889 Ebenezer Road
Rincon, GA 31326-3716
(912) 754-7001
Frank L. Perry, Jr., President
Hours: 12 March and Labor Day
Pub. *The Georgia Salzburger Society Newsletter* (perpetuates the memory of Lutherans who emigrated from Salzburg and Germany from 1734–

1752 to the Colony of Georgia, and updates the genealogy of their descendants; settled by General Edward Oglethorpe thirty miles north of Savannah on the Savannah River as a buffer with the Uchee Indians)

Historic Acworth
4468 Dallas Street
Acworth, GA 30101
Scott Evans

Historic Augusta, Inc.
(111 Tenth Street, Augusta, GA 30901—location)
PO Box 37 (mailing address)
Augusta, GA 30903
(706) 724-0436; (706) 724-3083 FAX
Erick Montgomery, Executive Director
Hours: Mon–Fri 9:00–5:00
Pub. *Historic Augusta Newsletter*, quarterly
(maintains files of historic buildings in Augusta and Richmond County, Georgia)
$35.00 per year membership for individuals, $45.00 per year membership for families

Historic Cobbham Foundation, Inc.
PO Box 534
Athens, GA 30603
Phinizy Spalding

Historic Decatur
726 South Candler Street
Decatur, GA 30030
Lyn Deardoff

Historic Oakland Cemetery, Inc.
248 Oakland Avenue, S.E.
Atlanta, GA 30312
Nancy L. Jacobus

Historic Oglethorpe County, Inc.
PO Box 1793
Lexington, GA 30648
Jerry Titus

Historic Preservation Society of Social Circle
PO Box 772
Social Circle, GA 30279
Jane McDaniel

Historic Talbotton
Rt. 1, Box 101
Talbotton, GA 31827
Gary D. Page

Historical Jonesboro, Inc.
PO Box 922
Jonesboro, GA 30236

Hunting for Bears Genealogical and Historical Society
(see Alabama)

In-Town Renaissance Association
224 Dixie Street
Carrollton, GA 30117
Stanley Lovvorn

MLH Research
(see Alabama)

Mountain Press
(see Tennessee)

Old Athens Cemetery Foundation, Inc.
145 Pendleton Drive
Athens, GA 30606
Patricia Cooper

Old Town Brunswick Preservation Association
1229 Newcastle Street
Brunswick, GA 31520
Phyllis Taunton

Plains Historic Preservation Trust, Inc.
PO Box 136
Plains, GA 31780
P. J. Wise

Root Hunters
PO Box 546
Thomasville, GA 31799
Pub. *Root Hunters*, quarterly

Roswell Historic Preservation Commission
City of Roswell
PO Box 1309
Roswell, GA 30075
Barbara S. Gross

Saint Marys Historic Preservation Commission
418 Osborne Street
Saint Marys, GA 31558
(912) 882-6926
Loretta Conner, Planning Director
Hours: 8:00–5:00

Society of Georgia Archivists
PO Box 80631
Athens, GA 30608-0631
(706) 542-7123
http://library.gac.peachnet.edu/~sga/index.html
Linda Aaron, SGA Administrative Assistant
Pub. *Provenance*, semiannually; *SGA Newsletter*, quarterly
(scholarly articles of archival issues, news of educational opportunities, meetings)
$15.00 per year membership

Southern Genealogist's Exchange Society
(see Florida)

Southern Historical Press
(375 West Broad Street, Greenville, SC 29601—location)
PO Box 1267 (mailing address)
Greenville, SC 29602-1267
(864) 233-2346; (800) 233-0152; (864) 233-2349 FAX
LaBruce M. S. Lucas

Hours: Mon–Fri 9:00–5:00
Pub. *The Georgia Genealogical Magazine*, quarterly, $35.00 per year subscription

Sumter Historic Trust
(318 East Church Street—location)
PO Box 961 (mailing address)
Americus, GA 31709
Malcolm Argo, Executive Vice President
Pub. *Views from the Verandah*, quarterly

Tattnall County Historic Preservation, Inc.
PO Box 392
Reidsville, GA 30453
(912) 557-4802

Terrell County Council for Historic Preservation
PO Box 779
Dawson, GA 31742
Edgar W. Duskin

Victorian Society of America, Savannah Chapter
10 West Jones Street
Savannah, GA 31401
Dean Owens

HAWAII

Archives and Libraries with Holdings in Genealogy

State Archives and Library

Hawaii State Archives
Iolani Palace Grounds
Honolulu, HI 96813
(808) 586-0329; (808) 586-0316; (800) 486-4644 (in Hawaii only); (808) 586-0330 FAX
http://www.htdc.org/ hsa/
Hours: Mon–Fri 7:45–4:30

Hawaii State Library
Hawaii and Pacific Section
478 South King Street
Honolulu, HI 96813-2901
(808) 586-3535
http://www.hcc.hawaii.edu/hspls/
Joyce Miyamoto, Section Head
Hours: Mon, Wed & Fri–Sat 9:00–5:00, Tue & Thur 9:00–8:00
(specializing in "Hawaii genealogy of long resident families, especially Hawaiian ethnic group")

Hawaii State Library
Language, Literature and History Section
478 South King Street
Honolulu, HI 96813
(808) 586-3499
Sandra Ann Kolloge, Section Head
Hours: Mon, Wed & Fri–Sat 9:00–5:00, Tue & Thur 9:00–8:00
(material for tracing family lines internationally with emphasis on early U.S. immigrants into the colonies and original states; "especially eastern U.S., British and western European ancestry")

State Historical Society

Hawaiian Historical Society
560 Kawaiahao Street
Honolulu, HI 96813
(808) 537-6271
E-mail: edunn@lava.net
http://www.aloha.com/ mem/ hhshome.html
Barbara Dunn, Administrative Director
Hours: Library Reading Room: Mon–Fri 10:00–4:00
Pub. *The Hawaiian Journal of History*, annually, $12.00 per issue; *Hawaiian Historical Society Newsletter*; *Annual Report*
(Library collection includes early voyages to Hawaii and the Pacific, Hawaiian-language books, over 64 newspapers, manuscript collections, photographs, maps, broadsides,

pamphlets, journals and periodicals, newspaper clipping file, etc.)
$25.00 per year membership, $20.00 per year membership for educational institutions; research fee: $5.00 plus photocopies

City, County and Regional Archives and Libraries

Alu Like, Inc. (Native Hawaiian Library Project)
567 South King Street, Suite 400
Honolulu, HI 96813-3036
(808) 535-6750; (808) 524-2776
E-mail: nhlp@pixi.com
Mahealani Merryman, Project Administrator
Hours: Mon–Fri 8:00–5:00

Bernice Pauahi Bishop Museum Library
1525 Bernice Street
Honolulu, HI 96817-0916
(808) 848-4147; (808) 848-4148; (808) 845-4133 FAX
E-mail: library@bishop.bishop.hawaii.org
http://www.bishop.hawaii.org
Duane Wenzel, Library Chairman
Hours: Tue–Fri 1:00–4:00, Sat 9:00–noon, except holiday weekends

Brigham Young University
Hawaii Campus
Joseph F. Smith Library
55-220 Kulanui Street
Laie, HI 96762
(808) 293-3850; (808) 237-8826 FAX
Rex Frandsen, Director
Hours: Mon–Thur 7:00 A.M.–midnight, Fri 7:00–6:00, Sat 10:00–9:00
Pub. *Pacific Studies* (emphasis on Pacific islands and Mormonism), semiannually
$5.00 per year membership

Hanalei Museum
PO Box 91
Hanalei, HI 96714
(808) 826-7387

Hawaiian Mission Children's Society Library
553 South King Street
Honolulu, HI 96813
(808) 531-0481
Marilyn L. Reppun, Librarian
Hours: Mon–Fri 10:00–4:00
("19th century Hawaiiana; Congregational Church records beginning 1820; unpublished letters, journals, reports of Protestant missionaries to Hawaii, personal as well as business; Hawaiian-language books; Micronesian-language books; early voyages to Hawaii and the

Pacific; early photographs and drawings of Hawaii")
no library admission fees

Hawaiian Sugar Planters Association
99-193 Aiea Heights Road
PO Box 1057
Aiea, HI 96701-1057
(808) 487-5561

Kauai Museum Association, Ltd.
4428 Rice Street
PO Box 248
Lihue, HI 96766
(808) 245-6931
Margaret Lovett, Collections Curator
Hours: Mon–Fri 9:00–4:00, Sat 10:00–4:00
$15.00 per year membership for individuals, $25.00 per year membership for families, $50.00 per year Contributing membership, $75.00 per year Sustaining membership, $100.00 per year Patron membership, $350.00 per year Corporate membership

Lyman House Memorial Museum
276 Haili Street
Hilo, HI 96720
(808) 969-7685
E-mail: lymanwks@interpac.net
Charlene Dahlquist, Librarian
Hours: Mon–Wed 9:00–4:00, and by appointment
(publications, photos, newspapers, manuscripts, maps; depository for Hawaii County Genealogical Society's collection)

Municipal Reference and Records Center Archives
City Hall Annex
Honolulu, HI 96813
(808) 523-4044
Anne K. Pulfrey, Records Management Analyst

University of Hawaii at Manoa
Center for Oral History
2424 Maile Way
Porteus Hall 724
Honolulu, HI 96822
(808) 956-6259; (808) 956-9794 FAX
E-mail: wnishimo@hawaii.edu
http://www2.soc.hawaii.edu/css/oral-hist/index.html
Warren S. Nishimoto, Center Director
Hours: 8:00–4:30
Pub. *Oral History Recorder*, quarterly

University of Hawaii at Manoa
Hamilton Library
Hawaiian Collection
2550 The Mall
Honolulu, HI 96822
(808) 956-7203; (808) 956-8264; (808) 956-5968 FAX
E-mail: speccoll@hawaii.edu; jimc@hawaii.edu
http://www2.hawaii.edu/~speccoll/hawaii.html

James F. Cartwright, University Archivist
Hours: Mon–Thur 9:00–5:00, Fri 9:00–
    4:45

Wailoa Center–State of Hawaii
200 Piopio Street
PO Box 936
Hilo, HI 96720
(808) 933-4360; (808) 967-4240 FAX
Mrs. Pudding Lassiter, Director
Hours: Mon–Tue & Thur–Fri 8:00–4:30,
    Wed noon–8:30, Sat 9:00–3:00
(a wide range of culture and art in
    Hawaii)

Historical Societies— Local and Regional

Kona Historical Society
(Kona District, Hawaii Island/Kalu
    Kalu—location)
PO Box 398 (mailing address)
Captain Cook, HI 96704
(808) 323-3222; (808) 323-2398 FAX
Jill R. Olson, Executive Director; Sheree
    Chase, Curator
Hours: Mon–Fri 9:00–3:00, Sat 9:00–1:00
Pub. *Newsletter*, three times per year
(extensive photo archives, land use
    records, artifact collection, library;
    historic site)
$20.00 per year membership for
    individuals, $30.00 per year
    membership for families, $50.00
    Sustaining membership

Maui Historical Society Museum
Bailey House
2375-A Main Street
PO Box 1018
Wailuku, HI 96793
(808) 244-3326
Hokulani Holt-Padilla, Administrative
    Assistant
Hours: Mon–Fri 9:00–4:00
Pub. *Maui News Index*
("We assist people in starting
    genealogical work but retain only the
    family genealogy of Edward &
    Caroline Bailey; we have no
    unpublished genealogical information
    nor are we a repository of any family,
    county, or state records.")
$10.00 per year membership for
    individuals, $15.00 per year
    membership for families

Mormon Pacific Historical Society
Brigham Young University
Hawaii Campus
PO Box 1887
Laie, HI 96762
(808) 393-3837
Dr. Lance D. Chase, Executive Secretary
Hours: 9:00–6:00
Pub. *MPHS Proceedings*, annually,
    $10.00 per issue
$5.00 per year membership

LDS Family History Centers

Hilo, Hawaii
(808) 935-0711

Honolulu, Oahu
(808) 955-8910

Kahului, Maui
(808) 871-8841

Laie, Oahu
(808) 293-2133

Mililani, Hawaii
(808) 623-1712

Genealogical Societies

State Genealogical Societies

**The Sandwich Islands Genealogical
Society**
PO Box 235039
Honolulu, HI 96823-3500
Roland F. Perkins, Librarian III
Pub. *Ke Ku'Auhau: The Genealogist*,
    quarterly

Hawaii County Genealogical Society
Lyman House Memorial Museum
276 Haili Street
Hilo, HI 96720
(808) 969-7685 (Museum)
E-mail: lymanwks@interpac.net
Charlene Dahlquist, Librarian
Hours: Library: Mon–Wed 9:00–4:00,
    and by appointment

Independent Publications and Miscellany

D.A.R. Memorial Library
1914 Makiki Heights Drive
Honolulu, HI 96822
(808) 949-7256
Mary Louise Cloyd, Librarian
Hours: Thur 9:00–noon, Sat 9:00–4:00
(colonial and pre-1850 American
    genealogy, some Hawaiian)

HiGenWeb
Part of U.S. GenWeb Project
E-mail: hi@usgenweb.com
http://www.rootsweb.com/~higenweb
(links to other Hawaii resources)

University of California Press
Pacific Historical Review
(see California)

IDAHO

Archives and Libraries with Holdings in Genealogy

State Archives and Library

The Idaho State Historical Society
Library and Archives
450 North Fourth Street
Boise, ID 83702
(208) 334-3356
Gene Williams, CGRS, Genealogist;
    Sarah Theme, Librarian
Hours: Tue–Sat 9:00–5:00
(houses genealogy collections)

Idaho State Library
325 West State Street
Boise, ID 83702
(208) 334-2150, (208) 334-4016 FAX
E-mail: webteam@isl.state.id.us
http://www.state.id.us/isl/hp.htm
(no collections of historical or
    genealogical value; see The Idaho
    State Historical Society, Library and
    Archives)

State Historical Society

**Idaho State Historical Society
(Genealogy Library)**
(325 West State Street—location)
450 North Fourth Street (mailing
    address)
Boise, ID 83702
(208) 334-3357; (208) 334-3198 FAX
Gene F. Williams, CGRS, Librarian
Hours: Tue–Sat 9:00–5:00
Pub. *Idaho Yesterdays: A Quarterly
    Journal of Idaho and Northwest
    History*, $25.00 per year subscription;
    *The Mountain Light: A Newsletter of
    the Idaho State Historical Society*,
    quarterly
research: $100.00 per hour plus 25¢ per
    photocopy

City, County and Regional Archives and Libraries

Boise Public Library
715 South Capitol Boulevard
Boise, ID 83702
(208) 384-4023; (208) 384-4021 FAX
E-mail: bwilson@pobox.ci.boise.id.us
William J. Wilson, Librarian, Idaho
    Room
Hours: Mon & Fri 10:00–6:00, Tue–Thur
    10:00–9:00, Sat 12:00–5:00, Sun
    (Sept–May) 12:00–5:00
research: cost of photocopies at 10¢ per
    page, plus postage

Boise State University
Albertsons Library
Special Collections Department
1910 University Drive
Boise, ID 83725
http://library.idbsu.edu
(Idaho history)

Castle Museum
Second and State Street
PO Box 454
Juliaetta, ID 83535
(208) 276-3081
Onal or Donna Cope
Hours: by appointment, closed Oct 1–
Mar 1

College of Idaho Library
Caldwell, ID 83605

College of Saint Gertrude Library
Cottonwood, ID 83522

College of Southern Idaho Library
Twin Falls, ID 83301

Grangeville Centennial Library
215 West North
Grangeville, ID 83530
Hours: Mon, Wed & Fri 12:00–5:00, Tue
& Thur 12:00–7:00

Heritage Hall Museum
(Reynolds Street, Old Highway 91,
Dubois, ID 83423—location)
HC 62, Box 41 (mailing address)
Dubois, ID 83446
(208) 374-5359; (208) 374-5799 FAX
E-mail: joy.myers@mci2000.com
Joy Myers, Secretary
Hours: by appointment; summer: Fri
afternoons
(family histories of the settlers of the
Silver Sage, Clark County; numerous
scrapbooks, pictures, etc.)

Idaho State University Library
Pocatello, ID 83209-0009
(208) 236-3249
Gary Domitz
Hours: Mon–Fri 8:00–4:30

Community Library (Ketchum)
Regional History Department
415 Spruce Avenue, North
PO Box 2168
Ketchum, ID 83340
(208) 726-3493
Sandra Hofferber, Regional History
Librarian
Hours: Mon & Wed 9:00–5:00, Tue &
Thur–Sat 1:00–5:00

Lewis-Clark State College Library
500 Eighth Avenue
Lewiston, ID 83501
(208) 799-2230; (208) 799-2831
E-mail: jboyd@lcsc.edu/
http://www.lcsc.edu
JoAnn Boyd, Assistant to the Director
Hours: vary with school year and
holidays

(back files of local daily newspaper,
Lewiston Morning Tribune; Idaho and
Pacific Northwest history)

Lewiston Public Library
Pioneer Park
101 Fifth Street
Lewiston, ID 83501

McCall Public Library
218 Park Street
McCall, ID 83638
(208) 634-5522
Gloria Cantrell, Librarian
Hours: Mon–Fri 11:00–6:00

Museum of North Idaho
(115 Northwest Boulevard—location)
PO Box 812 (mailing address)
Coeur d'Alene, ID 83816-0812
(208) 664-3448
Dorothy Dahlgren, Director
Hours: Tue–Sat 10:00–5:00
Pub. *Museum of North Idaho Newsletter*,
quarterly
$15.00 per year membership

Nampa Public Library
101 11th Avenue, South
Nampa, ID 83651
(208) 465-2263
Pam Purcell, Reference Librarian
Hours: Mon–Thur 10:00–8:00, Fri–Sat
10:00–5:00
(collects Nampa, Canyon County, and
Idaho history, not specifically
genealogical material)

North Idaho College Library
Coeur d'Alene, ID 83814

North Idaho History Center
1000 West Garden Avenue—Fort
Sherman Officers' Quarters
Coeur d'Alene, ID 83814
(208) 769-3300
Judith A. Sylte, Director

Ricks College
McKay Library
525 South Center
Rexburg, ID 83460-0405
(208) 356-2377
Blaine R. Bake, Archivist
Hours: winter: Mon–Fri 7:00–10:00, Sat
9:00–6:00, Sun 3:00–7:00; summer:
Mon & Fri 8:00–5:00, Tue–Thur 8:00–
9:00, Sat 10:00–2:00, Sun 3:00–6:00
(LDS church material, especially
southeast Idaho; also Idaho local
history)

Snake River Heritage Center
2295 Paddock Avenue
PO Box 307
Weiser, ID 83672
(208) 549-0205
Carol Odoms, Manager
Hours: by appointment only
Pub. *Snake River Heritage Center
Newsletter*, quarterly

("Our research library contains only
materials donated to the museum,
therefore, it is not a complete library.")
$15.00 per year membership for
individuals, couples and families

University of Idaho
University Library
Special Collections
Rayburn Street
Moscow, ID 83844-2351
(208) 885-7951; (208) 885-6817 FAX
E-mail: tabraham@uidaho.edu
http://www.lib.uidaho.edu/special-
collections
Terry Abraham, Head, Special
Collections
Hours: summer: Mon–Fri 8:00–5:00
(Repositories of Primary Sources lists
over 2,500 Web sites, worldwide,
describing holdings of manuscripts,
archives, rare books, historical
photographs, and other primary
sources for the research scholar)

Wallace District Mining Museum
509 Bank Street
PO Box 469
Wallace, ID 83873
(208) 556-1592
John Amonson, Executive Director
Hours: summer: Mon–Sun 8:00–8:00;
spring & fall: Mon–Sun 8:00–6:00,
winter: Mon–Sat 9:00–4:00
("We are in the process of accumulating
cemetery records and maps, payroll
records, etc.; research time is very
limited.")
museum admission: $1.50 for adults
(ages 16–54), $1.00 for senior citizens
(over 55); no admission fee for
archives

Winchester Museum
Rt. 2, Box 28
Winchester, ID 83524
(208) 924-7772

Historical Societies—
Local and Regional

Adams County Historical Society
PO Box 352
New Meadows, ID 83654

Bannock County Historical Society
3000 Alvord Loop
PO Box 253
Pocatello, ID 83204-0253
(208) 233-0434
Mary Lien, Curator
Hours: Memorial Day–Labor Day: daily
11:00–6:00; Labor Day–Memorial
Day: Tue–Sat 10:00–2:00

(local and county history)
$10.00 per year membership for
  individuals

Bonner County Historical Society
PO Box 1063
Sandpoint, ID 83864
(208) 263-4949
$10.00 per year membership

Bonneville County Historical Society
(Corner of Northeastern Avenue and
  Elm—location)
PO Box 1784 (mailing address)
Idaho Falls, ID 83401
(208) 522-1400
Mary Jane Fritzen, Archivist
Hours: Mon–Fri 10:00–5:00, Sat 1:00–
  5:00
(Idaho Falls area)
$10.00 per year membership for
  individuals, $15.00 per year
  membership for couples; search fees
  by the hour done by private
  arrangement with Ms. Fritzen

Boundary County Historical Society
PO Box 808
Bonners Ferry, ID 83805

Camas County Historical Society
PO Box 125
Fairfield, ID 83327

Canyon County Historical Society
Canyon County Historical Museum
1200 Front Street
PO Box 595
Nampa, ID 83651
(208) 467-7611

Caribou Historical Society, Inc.
2253 Lago-Liberty Road
Grace, ID 83241
(208) 427-6274

Cassia County Historical Society, Inc.
Highland and Main Streets
PO Box 331
Burley, ID 83318
(208) 678-7172
Hours: 1 Apr–15 Nov: Tue–Sat 10:00–
  5:00

Clearwater County Historical Society
Clearwater County Historical Museum
315 College Avenue
PO Box 1154
Orofino, ID 83544
(208) 476-5033
Evelyn Welter, Director
Hours: Tue–Sat 1:30–4:30
("We do not have a lot of genealogy
  information here, but do have some
  old records and newspapers—also old
  photos.")

Elmore County Historical Foundation
180 South Third East
PO Box 204
Mountain Home, ID 83647
(208) 587-9041 (City Hall)
Patti McGrath, President
Hours: Mon–Tue 11:00–4:30, Fri–Sat
  1:30–4:30
Pub. *Heritage*, quarterly
$4.00 per year membership

Gem County Historical Society
501 East First
PO Box 312
Emmett, ID 83617
(208) 365-9530, (208) 365-2990
Jessie Goodwin, Co-ordinator
Hours: Sat–Sun (Jun–Sept) 2:00–5:00;
  group and private tours

Gooding County Historical Society
(North Main—location)
PO Box 580 (mailing address)
Gooding, ID 83330
Sharon Kelley, Secretary
Hours: summer: Fri–Sat 1:00–5:00
$5.00 per year membership; research for
  Gooding, Lincoln and Twin Falls
  counties

Hagerman Valley Historical Society
PO Box 86
Hagerman, ID 83332

Jefferson County Historical Society
110 North State
PO Box 284
Rigby, ID 83442
(208) 745-8423
Gae Lynne Hinckley, President

Jerome County Historical Society
(220 North Lincoln—location)
PO Box 50 (mailing address)
Jerome, ID 83338
(208) 324-2711 phone and FAX
Clair K. Ricketts, President
Hours: Tue–Sat 1:00–5:00
Pub. *Jerome County Historical Society
  Monthly Newsletter*
$5.00 per year membership for
  individuals, $10.00 per year
  membership for couples, $12.00 per
  year membership for families, $25.00
  per year Sustaining membership,
  $50.00 per year Supporting
  membership, $100.00 life membership

Latah County Historical Society
327 East Second Street
Moscow, ID 83843
(208) 882-1004
Joann Jones, Curator
Hours: Tue–Fri 9:00–noon & 1:00–5:00
Pub. *Latah Legacy*, semiannually
$10.00 per year membership for
  individuals, $15.00 per year
  membership for families, $25.00 per
  year membership for businesses

Lemhi County Historical Society
PO Box 645
Salmon, ID 83467

Lewis County Historical Society
Rt. 2, Box 512
Kamiah, ID 83536
Mildred Ivie, Secretary

Minidoka County Historical Society, Inc.
100 East Baseline
PO Box 21
Rupert, ID 83350
(208) 436-0336

Nez Perce County Historical Society
0306 Third Street
Lewiston, ID 83501
(208) 743-2535
Lora Feucht, Registrar
Hours: Tue–Sat 10:00–4:00
Pub. *The Golden Age*, semiannually
(operates the Luna House Museum;
  limited genealogical resources)
$20.00 per year basic membership; in-
  house research: $5.00 per hour

Nez Perce Historical Society
PO Box 86
Nezperce, ID 83542

Old Fort Boise Historical Society
Old Fort Boise Park
PO Box 942
Parma, ID 83660
(208) 722-5138 (Mayor Patricia
  Romanko, City Hall); 722-5573
  (President)
Shirley Huff, President
Hours: Museum: Fri–Sun 1:00–4:00
  (Jun–Aug), and by appointment (May–
  Sept)
$1.00 admission to Museum for adults,
  children free if accompanied by an
  adult

Owyhee County Historical Society
Owyhee County Historical Complex
PO Box 67
Murphy, ID 83650
(208) 495-2319
Byron W. Johnson, Director
Hours: Wed–Fri 10:00–4:00
Pub. *Owyhee Outpost*, irregularly
$10.25 per year membership

Pacific Northwest Historians Guild
(see Washington)

Payette County Historical Society
PO Box 476
Payette, ID 83661

Sawtooth Interpretive and Historical Association
(Highway 75—location)
PO Box 75 (mailing address)
Stanley, ID 83278
(208) 774-3517
Ruth Niece, President

Hours: Memorial Day weekend through
Sept 15: Mon–Fri & Sun 11:00–5:00,
Sat 11:00–6:00

**South Bannock County Historical
Center and Museum**
110 East Main Street
PO Box 387
Lava Hot Springs, ID 83246
(208) 776-5254
Ruth Ann Olson, Director
Hours: daily noon–5:00
(files of family history available for
research, local and South Bannock
County area)

**South Custer County Historical
Society**
PO Box 355
Mackay, ID 83251

Spirit Lake Historical Society
PO Box 186
Spirit Lake, ID 83869

**Upper Snake River Valley Historical
Society**
51 North Center
PO Box 244
Rexburg, ID 83440
(208) 356-9101
Bonnie Curtis, Assistant Director
Hours: Mon–Fri 11:00–4:00
Pub. *Snake River Echoes*, biannually
(local history)
$10.00 per year membership

LDS Family History Centers

Blackfoot
(208) 785-5022; (208) 684-3784

Boise
(208) 338-3811; (208) 376-0452

Coeur D'Alene
(208) 765-0150

Idaho Falls
(208) 524-5291; (208) 524-1038

Nampa
(208) 467-5827

Pocatello
(208) 232-9262

Rexburg
(208) 356-2377

Twin Falls
(208) 733-8073

Genealogical Societies

State Genealogical Society

The Idaho Genealogical Society, Inc.
9846 Westview Drive
Boise, ID 83704
E-mail: dyingst@rmci.net
http://www.rmci.net/idaho/genidaho/
index.htm
Pub. *Idaho Genealogical Society
Quarterly*
(sponsors Oregon Trail Project:
certificates given to descendants of
Oregon Trail pioneers (families who
came west 1811–1911), to descendants
of pioneers (residing in Idaho on or
before July 3, 1890), and to
descendants of early settlers (settled in
Idaho between July 4, 1890 and
December 31, 1900)
$10.00 per year membership for
individuals, $12.50 per year
membership for couples; $10.00
application fee for Oregon Trail
certificate; research $10.00 per hour

Regional Genealogical Societies

Bonner County Genealogical Society
(Sandpoint, ID—location)
PO Box 27 (mailing address)
Dover, ID 83825-0027
(208) 263-4949
Teena Weisz, Secretary-Treasurer
Pub. *Bonner County Genealogical
Society Newsletter*, ten times per year
(monthly, January–October)
$10.00 per year membership; reasonable
research requests free to members

Caldwell Genealogy Group
3504 South Illinois Street
Caldwell, ID 83605
Carol A. Murphy

Kamiah Genealogical Society
PO Box 322
Kamiah, ID 83536

**Kootenai County Genealogical
Society**
8385 North Government Way
Hayden Lake, ID 83835-9280
(208) 772-5778 (Secretary's home)
Lelah Achey, Corresponding Secretary
Hours: Mon–Sat 9:00–5:00
("census for the state of Idaho,
obituaries, over fifty research books,
history books, old newspapers for four
northern counties of Idaho, etc.")
$10.00 per year membership for
individuals, $12.00 per year
membership for couples, $8.00 per
year Supporting membership; research
fees vary

Latah County Genealogical Society
327 East Second Street
Moscow, ID 83843
(208) 882-5943
Dorothy Schell, Editor
Pub. *Latah County Genealogical Society
Quarterly*
$8.00 per year membership for
individuals, $10.00 per year
membership for families

**Pocatello Branch Genealogical
Society**
PO Box 4272
Pocatello, ID 83201

**Shoshone County Genealogical
Society**
PO Box 183
Kellogg, ID 83837
Oradell Triplett, President (PG)
Hours: Osburn Public Library
$5.00 per year membership

Twin Rivers Genealogical Society
PO Box 386
Lewiston, ID 83501
Margaret Nell Longeteig

Valley County Genealogical Society
(Cascade Library, 105 Front Street—
location)
PO Box 697 (mailing address)
Cascade, ID 83611
(208) 382-4757
E-mail: casclib@cyberhighway.net
Ruth Redmon, Secretary; Bea Snyder,
President
Hours: Mon–Fri 12:00–6:00, Sat 10:00–
2:00
Pub. *Valley County Heritage*,
semiannually (January and July)
("Valley County courthouse records,
news clippings, etc.")
$10.00 per year membership (calendar
year); queries free to members, 10¢
per word for non-members

Independent Publications and Miscellany

IdGenWeb
Part of U.S. GenWeb Project
E-mail: id@usgenweb.com
http://www.rootsweb.com/~idgenweb/
(links to other Idaho resources)

Northwest Pioneer
(see Washington)

ILLINOIS

Archives and Libraries with Holdings in Genealogy

State Archives and Library

Illinois State Archives
Office of the Secretary of State
Margaret Cross Norton Building
Capitol Complex
Springfield, IL 62756-0001
(217) 782-4682; (217) 782-3556; (217) 524-3930 FAX
http://www.sos.state.il.us/depts/archives/arc_home.html
John Daly, Director
Hours: Mon–Fri 8:00–4:30, Sat 8:00–3:30 (except holiday weekends)
Pub. *Newsletter of the Illinois State Archives*, semiannually, free to institutions and societies

Illinois State Library
300 South Second Street
Reference Department
Springfield, IL 62701-1796
(217) 782-7596; (217) 524-0041 FAX
http://www.library.sos.state.il.us/
Hours: Mon–Fri 8:00–4:30
(circulating collections of state and federal documents; no genealogy section)

State Historical Societies

Illinois State Historical Library
1 Old State Capitol Plaza
Springfield, IL 62701-1507
(217) 524-7216; (217) 524-6358 (genealogical reference)
E-mail: kathrynh@alpha1.rpls.lib.il.us
http://www.state.il.us/hpa/lib
Kathryn M. Harris, Director, ISHL; Jane Ehrenhart, Supervisor, Reference and Technical services
Hours: Mon–Fri 8:30–5:00
(family histories, county histories, and indexes to vital records held elsewhere)
search fee: $5.00 for non-Illinois residents

Illinois State Historical Society
(210 South Sixth Street, Suite 210—location)
1 Old State Capitol Plaza (mailing address)
Springfield, IL 62701-1507
(217) 782-2635; (217) 524-8042 FAX
E-mail: ishs@eosinc.com
http://www.prairienet.org/ishs
Jon Austin, Executive Director
Hours: 9:00–5:00
Pub. *Dispatch/News*, quarterly; *Illinois Historical Journal*, quarterly

(promotes research, writing and participation in Illinois history)
$25.00 per year membership

Association of Illinois Museums and Historical Societies (AIMHS)
(210 South Sixth Street, Suite 210—location)
1 Old State Capitol Place (mailing address)
Springfield, IL 62701-1507
(217) 524-7080; (217) 782-4286; (217) 524-8042; (217) 785-7937 FAX
E-mail: mturner@midwest.net; ishs@eosinc.com
http://www.prairienet.org/ishs
Mary Turner, Coordinator; Karen E. Everingham, Programs Assistant
Hours: 8:30–4:30
Pub. *IAM News*, quarterly; *Directory of Illinois Museums*, biannually, free
(statewide association of Museums, Historical and Genealogical Societies; directory lists about 900 agencies and institutions)
$30.00 per year membership

Illinois Historic Preservation Agency
Old State Capitol
1 Old State Capitol Plaza
Springfield, IL 62701-1507
(217) 524-6045
Evelyn Taylor, Managing Editor
Hours: Mon–Fri 8:30–5:00
Pub. *Illinois Historical Journal*, quarterly, $20.00 per year subscription

City, County and Regional Archives and Libraries

Jane Addams' Hull House Museum at University of Illinois—Chicago
800 South Halsted Street
Chicago, IL 60607-7017
(312) 413-5354
Mary Johnson, Director
Hours: Mon–Fri 10:00–4:00, Sun noon–5:00
(local history, women's history)

Alton Area Historical Society Research Library
Alton Museum of History and Art
121 East Broadway
Alton, IL 62002-6217
(618) 462-0595; (618) 462-2763 (Museum)
Shirley Durie, Librarian
Hours: Museum: Thur–Sat 11:00–3:00, Sun 1:00–4:00; Library: Thur–Sun 1:00–4:00, and by appointment
Pub. *Newsletter*, three times per year
$5.00 per year membership

Alton Museum of History and Art, Inc.
121 East Broadway
Alton, IL 62002-6217
(618) 462-2763

Diana Taylor, Museum Director
Hours: Thur–Sat 11:00–3:00, Sun 1:00–4:00

Arlington Heights Memorial Library
500 North Dunton Avenue
Arlington Heights, IL 60004-5966
(847) 392-0100 (Local History/Genealogy); (847) 506-2639 (Library); (847) 392-0136 FAX (Library)
http://www.ahml.lib.il.us/
Carol Blohm, Local History/Genealogy Librarian
Hours: Mon–Fri 9:00–10:00, Sat 9:00–5:00, Sun noon–5:00
(Illinois and midwest states, German ancestry)

Assumption Public Library
131 North Chestnut
PO Box 227
Assumption, IL 62510-0227

Atlanta Library and Museum
100 Race Street
PO Box 526
Atlanta, IL 61723-0526
(217) 648-2003; (217) 648-2112
Weldon Cheek
Hours: Tue–Wed & Fri 12:30–4:30, Thur 12:30–8:00, Sat 9:00–1:00
(local history)

Augustana College Library
Special Collections
Seventh Avenue and 35th Street
Rock Island, IL 61201-2210
(309) 794-7317
E-mail: alijb@augustana; alidh@augustana.edu
http://www.augustana.edu
Judy Belan, Special Collections Librarian/Archivist

Barrington Area Library
505 North Northwest Highway
Barrington, IL 60010
(847) 382-1300; (847) 382-1261 FAX
E-mail: mthomas@bal.alibrary.com
http://www.bal.alibrary.com
Rose M. Faber, Head, Adult Services; Marie Thomas, Reference Librarian
Hours: Mon–Fri 9:00–9:00, Sat 9:00–5:00, Sun 1:00–5:00
(Barrington genealogy and local history information; the *Barrington Courier-Review* indexed for births, deaths, marriages, 1890–1929, 1994–1996 on home page site)

Belleville Public Library
121 East Washington Street
Belleville, IL 62220-2205
(618) 234-0441 (ask for Archives); (618) 234-9474 FAX
Lou Ann James, Archives Librarian
Hours: Mon–Thur 9:00–9:00, Fri–Sat 9:00–5:00
(emphasis on Illinois and family history; oldest continuing library in Illinois)

Bellwood Public Library
600 Bohland Avenue
Bellwood, IL 60104
(708) 547-7393
Hours: Mon–Thur 9:30–9:00, Fri 9:30–
6:00, Sat 9:30–4:00

Benton Public Library
502 South Main Street
Benton, IL 62812
(618) 438-7511; (618) 439-4476
Mary Eubanks, Society for the Historic
Preservation of Franklin County

Bishop Hill State Historic Site
Village of Bishop Hill
PO Box 104
Bishop Hill, IL 61419-0104
(309) 927-3345
Martha Jane Downey, Site Manager
Hours: Mar–Oct 9:00–5:00; Nov–Feb:
9:00–4:00

Bloomington Public Library
(205 East Olive Street, Bloomington, IL
61701—location)
PO Box 3308 (mailing address)
Bloomington, IL 61702-3308
(309) 828-6091
Lois Wood, Library Associate II (Local
History)
Hours: Mon–Thur 9:00–9:00, Fri–Sat
9:00–5:00, Sun 1:00–5:00 (Sept–May)
(specializes in Bloomington-Normal,
Illinois, McLean County, Illinois, and
Illinois state local history, as opposed
to genealogy)
research: $5.00 minimum plus 15¢ per
copy

Blue Island Public Library
2433 York Street
Blue Island, IL 60406-2011
(708) 388-1078; (708) 388-1143 FAX
Lynne Ingersoll, Reference Librarian
Hours: Mon–Thur noon–8:00, Fri–Sat
9:00–5:00
(history of Blue Island, Illinois)

Gail Borden Public Library District
200 North Grove Avenue
Elgin, IL 60120
(847) 742-2411; (847) 742-0485 FAX
E-mail: wblohm@nslsilus.org
http://www.elgin.lib.il.us/
William R. Blohm, Reference Librarian
Hours: Mon–Thur 9:00–9:00, Fri–Sat
9:00–5:30, Sun 1:00–5:30; summer:
Mon–Thur 9:00–9:00, Fri–Sat 9:00–5:30
(Elgin and Kane County genealogy and
history)
$5.00 for basic search and photocopies
from microfilm

**Louisa H. Bowen University
Archives and Special Collections**
Lovejoy Library
Southern Illinois University at
Edwardsville
Box 1063, SIUE
Edwardsville, IL 62026-1063

(618) 692-2665
Dr. Stephen Kerber
Hours: Mon–Fri by appointment
(Madison County naturalization records)

Bradley University
Special Collections Center/Cullum Davis
Library
1501 W. Bradley
Peoria, IL 61625
(309) 677-2822; (309) 677-2823; (309)
677-2827 FAX
Charles Frey
Hours: Mon–Fri 9:00–noon & 1:00–4:30

**C. E. Brehm Memorial Public
Library District**
Genealogy Department
101 South Seventh
Mount Vernon, IL 62864-4187
(618) 242-6322; (618) 242-0810 FAX
Maggie Kirwan, Interlibrary Loan-
Genealogy Librarian
(emphasis on southern Illinois, $5.00 for
loans to libraries outside Illinois, who
should address requests to Shawnee
Library System)

Brenner Library of Quincy College
1800 College Avenue
Quincy, IL 62301-2670
(217) 228-5350; (217) 228-5354 FAX
Patricia Tomczak, Librarian
Hours: Mon–Thur 8:00 A.M.–11:00 P.M.,
Fri 8:00–8:00, Sat 11:00–5:00, Sun
1:00–11:00
(local history collection)

Bridgeview Public Library
7840 West 79th Street
Bridgeview, IL 60455-1496
Elsie Mikrut
(708) 458-2880
Hours: Mon–Thur 9:00–8:00, Fri–Sat
9:00–5:00, Sun 10:00–2:00

**Mr. & Mrs. Alfred A. Brown
Memorial Museum**
128 West Main Street
Sparta, IL 62286
(618) 443-2897
Fred Gerlach, Chair
Hours: Wed & Sat 2:00–4:00
(local history)

Bryan-Bennett Library
217 West Main
Salem, IL 62881

Byron Museum District
110 North Union
PO Box 186
Byron, IL 61010-0186
(815) 234-5031; (815) 234-7114 FAX
Jim Jennings
Hours: Tue–Fri 9:00–3:00, weekends &
evening by appointment
(history of region)

Cairo Public Library
1609 Washington Avenue
PO Box 151
Cairo, IL 62914-0151
(618) 734-1840; (618) 734-9346 FAX
Monica L. Smith
Hours: Mon–Fri 10:00–5:00, Sat 9:00–
noon

Canton Museum
(100 Block North Main—location)
129 East Oak (mailing address)
Canton, IL 61520-3042
(309) 647-9121
Dick Strode
Hours: by appointment
(local history)

Carthage Public Library District
538 Wabash
Carthage, IL 62321
(217) 357-3232; (217) 357-2392 FAX
Diana Robison, Director
Hours: Summer: Mon–Thur noon–6:00,
Fri noon–5:00, Sat 9:00–5:00; fall–
spring: Mon–Thur noon–9:00, Fri
noon–5:00, Sat 9:00–5:00
(local history)

**Champaign County Historical
Museum, Inc.**
111 East University Avenue
Champaign, IL 61820
(217) 356-1010
E-mail: cchmus@c-u.net
http://www.m-crossroads.org/cchmus/
index.html
Barbara Peckham, President
Hours: None, collection in temporary
storage
$15.00 per year membership for
individuals, $30.00 per year
membership for families

Charleston Public Library
Genealogy Room
712 Sixth Street
Charleston, IL 61920
(217) 345-4913
Sheryl Snyder, Director
Hours: Mon–Thur 10:00–8:00, Fri–Sat
10:00–6:00
(houses the collection of the Coles
County, Illinois, Genealogical Society)

Chicago Heights Free Public Library
15th and Chicago Road
Chicago Heights, IL 60411
(708) 754-0323
Barbara Paul
Hours: Mon–Thur 9:00–9:00, Fri–Sat
9:00–5:00, Sun (during the school
year) 1:00–5:00

Chicago Maritime Museum
North Pier Chicago
465 East Illinois Street
Chicago, IL 60611-4305
(312) 836-4343
Barton Updike, Executive Director

Hours: Tue–Sun noon–5:00
(archives)

Chicago Public Library
Special Collections and Preservation
  Division
9N-15, 400 South State Street
Chicago, IL 60605-1203
(312) 747-4876; (312) 747-4887 FAX
http://www.chipublib.org/
John P. Chalmers, Curator
Hours: Mon–Tue & Thur noon–6:00,
  Wed & Fri–Sat noon–4:00, Sun 1:00–
  5:00
(Civil War; Chicago area history)

Collinsville Historical Museum
Collinsville Memorial Public Library
408 West Main Street
Collinsville, IL 62234-3018
(618) 233-7989; (618) 344-5637; (618)
  345-6401 FAX
Floyd Sperino, Curator
Hours: Wed & Fri–Sat 2:00–4:30 by
  appointment
(Collinsville and adjacent area of
  Madison and Saint Clair counties)

Cook Memorial Public Library
413 North Milwaukee Avenue
Libertyville, IL 60048
(847) 362-2330
Aileen Hapke, Genealogy; Eileen
  Kloberdanz, Local History
Hours: Mon–Thur 9:00–9:00, Fri–Sat
  9:00–5:00, Sun (during school year)
  1:00–5:00

**J. T. & E. J. Crumbaugh Memorial
Public Library**
405 East Center Street
PO Box 129
LeRoy, IL 61752-0129
(309) 962-3911
Lois Evans, Librarian
Hours: Mon–Sat 10:00–5:00
Pub. *Tracing Your Roots*, every two
  years, $1.00 for postage and handling
(local history and genealogy)

Danville Public Library
319 North Vermilion Street
Danville, IL 61832-4787
(217) 477-5228; (217) 477-5230 FAX
E-mail: rdallen@prairienet.org;
  dpl@prairienet.org
Roberta D. Allen, Director of Reference
  and Director of Archives
Hours: Mon–Thur 9:00–8:00, Fri–Sat
  9:00–5:30
(emphasis on Vermilion County, Illinois)

Decatur Public Library
Local History Room
247 East North Street
Decatur, IL 62523
(217) 424-2900; (217) 423-5741 FAX
E-mail: bhackney@decaturnet.org;
  dirwin@decaturnet.ort
http://www.decaturnet.org/dpl
Bev Hackney, Periodicals Librarian;

Dayle Irwin, Local History Library
  Assistant
Hours: Mon–Thur 9:00–5:00, Mon 6:00–
  8:00, Sat 10:30–noon & 1:00–3:00
  (staffing may depend on volunteer
  availability, call first)
(newspaper microfilm from the 1860s,
  obituary index from 1868, city
  directories from the 1870s,
  biographical and historical information
  focusing on Decatur)
search fee: $5.00 plus 50¢ per photocopy

DeKalb Public Library
309 Oak Street
DeKalb, IL 60115
(815) 756-9568; (815) 756-7837 FAX
E-mail: efulton@mail.nibcomp.com
Elaine Fulton, Adult Services Librarian
Hours: Mon–Thur 9:00–9:00, Fri 9:00–
  6:00, Sat 9:00–5:00, Sun (Sept–May)
  1:00–4:00

DeWitt County Museum Association
219 East Woodlawn Street
Clinton, IL 61727-1052
(217) 935-6066 (after 1:00)
Jill Fostervold, Resident Manager
Hours: 1 Apr–31 Dec: Tue–Sun 1:00–5:00

Downers Grove Historical Museum
831 Maple Avenue
Downers Grove, IL 60515-4904
(630) 963-1309; (630) 963-0496 FAX
Mark S. Harmon, Museum Supervisor
Hours: Office/Research: Mon–Fri 8:30–
  4:30
Pub. *The Plank*, quarterly
(family history, atlases, census records; a
  special facility of the Downers Grove
  Park District)
$10.00 per year membership

Dundee Township Library
55 Barrington Avenue
Dundee, IL 60118
(847) 428-3661
Abbey LaVell, Local History
Hours: Mon–Thur 9:00–9:00, Fri–Sat
  9:00–5:30

Early American Museum
(Route 47 North, Lake of the Woods
  Park—location)
PO Drawer 1040 (mailing address)
Mahomet, IL 61853
(217) 586-2612
http://www.mah-online.com/early/
Cheryl Kennedy, Director
Hours: weekends (May & Sept) 10:00–
  5:00; daily (Jun–Aug) 10:00–5:00
(east central Illinois)
$15.00 per year membership for
  individuals, $30.00 per year
  membership for families; $3.50
  admission for adults

Edgar County Genealogy Library
408 North Main (Edgar County
  Historical Museum Complex)
Paris, IL 61944-1549

(217) 463-4209
Barbara Hammond, Director
Hours: Wed–Fri 9:00–4:00, Wed–Fri
  (Dec 1–Mar 31) 10:00–3:00, second,
  third & fourth Sat 10:00–2:00
(Holdings include Illinois marriages,
  public domain land records, Paris
  newspapers, county cemetery records,
  family and county histories, military
  records, vertical files, scrapbooks,
  surname exchange files, and computer
  databases, including LDS
  FamilySearch)
SASE for searches and fee schedule

Eisenhower Public Library District
4652 North Olcott Avenue
Harwood Heights, IL 60656
(708) 867-7828
Hours: Mon–Thur 10:00–9:00, Fri
  10:00–6:00, Sat 10:00–5:00
(stronger in local history than genealogy)

**Ellwood House Museum (DeKalb
County)**
509 North First Street
DeKalb, IL 60115-3232
(815) 756-4609; (815) 756-4645 FAX
Gerald J. Brauer, Executive Director

Elmhurst Historical Museum
120 East Park Avenue
Elmhurst, IL 60126-3420
(630) 833-1457; (630) 833-1326 FAX
Brian F. Bergheger, Director
Hours: Tue–Sun 1:00–5:00, and by
  appointment

Elmwood Park Public Library
4 Conti Parkway
Elmwood Park, IL 60635-4506
(708) 453-7645
Russell Parker, Librarian
Hours: Mon–Thur 9:00–9:00, Fri 9:00–
  6:00, Sat 9:00–5:00
(emphasis on Elmwood Park, Galewood,
  Montclare and Chicago)

Evanston Public Library
(address withheld upon request)

Forest Park Library
7555 Jackson Avenue
Forest Park, IL 60130

Fossil Ridge Public Library
386 Kennedy Road
Braidwood, IL 60408
(815) 458-2187
Beverley Craig
Hours: Mon–Thur 9:00–9:00, Fri 9:00–
  6:00, Sat 9:00–3:00, Sun (Oct–May)
  1:00–5:00
(emphasis on local and Illinois history/
  genealogy; house library collection of
  Will/Grundy Counties (IL)
  Genealogical Society)

Gladys Fox Museum
Lockport Township Park District
1911 South Lawrence
Lockport, IL 60441-4498

(815) 838-1183; (815) 838-4974 FAX
Robert Paddock
Hours: Tue–Wed & Fri 11:00–3:00, Sun
    1:00–4:00
(local history)

**Franklin Park Public Library
District**
10311 West Grand Avenue
Franklin Park, IL 60131
(847) 455-6016; (847) 455-6299 FAX
E-mail: mjohnson@vax.linc.lib.il.us
Mark Johnson, Head of Local History
    Department
Hours: Mon–Thur 9:00–9:00, Fri–Sat
    9:00–5:00, Sun 1:00–5:00
(Franklin Park, some Leyden Township)

Freeport Public Library
314 West Stephenson Street
Freeport, IL 61032
(815) 233-3000
John Locascio
Hours: Mon–Thur 9:00–9:00 (summer
    9:00–8:00), Fri 9:00–6:00, Sat 9:00–
    5:00, Sun (during the school year)
    1:00–4:00

Galena Public Library
Historical Collections Room
601 South Bench Street
Galena, IL 61036
(815) 777-0200
H. Scott Wolfe, Historical Librarian
Hours: Mon–Fri 3:00–5:00, Sat 1:00–
    4:00, or by special appointment
(history and genealogy of the upper
    Mississippi lead region)

Galesburg Public Library
40 East Simmons Street
Galesburg, IL 61401
(309) 343-6118
Enid Hanks, Reference Librarian
Hours: Mon–Thur 9:00–9:00, Fri–Sat
    9:00–5:00, Sun (Sept–May) 1:00–5:00

**G.A.R. Memorial and Veterans'
Military Museum**
23 East Downer Place
PO Box 1865
Aurora, IL 60507-1865
(630) 897-7221
Art Stiegleiter, Director
Hours: Mon, Wed & Fri noon–4:00, and
    by appointment
(local history, genealogy, military)

Geneva Public Library District
127 James Street
Geneva, IL 60134
(630) 232-0780
Jeanne Hintz, Director
Hours: Mon–Thur 9:00–9:00, Fri–Sat
    9:00–5:00, Sun (Sept–May) noon–4:00
charge for photocopies

Glenview Public Library
1930 Glenview Road
Glenview, IL 60025

(847) 729-7682; (847) 729-7682 FAX
http://www.glenview.lib.il.us
Sally E. Morris, Reference Librarian
Hours: Mon–Fri 9:00–9:00, Sat 9:00–
    5:00, Sun 1:00–5:00

Granite City Public Library District
2001 Delmar Avenue
Granite City, IL 62040
(618) 452-6238
Jeanette L. Kampen, Assistant Director
Hours: Sept–May: Mon–Thur 9:00–9:00,
    Fri–Sat 9:00–5:00; Jun–Aug: Mon &
    Wed 9:00–9:00, Tue & Thur–Sat 9:00–
    5:00

**Grayslake Historical Municipal
Museum**
164 Hauley Street
PO Box 185
Grayslake, IL 60030-0185
(847) 223-4978; (847) 223-6888
Charles Clow, President
(local history)

Greenville Public Library
414 West Main
Greenville, IL 62246
(618) 664-3115
Ted Thies, Library Director
Hours: Mon–Thur noon–8:00, Fri 10:00–
    6:00, Sat 10:00–5:00

**Gretna Station and Caboose
Museums**
391 Illini Drive
Carol Stream, IL 60188
(630) 260-7863; (630) 665-2311; (630)
    665-9045 FAX
Mary Brosious
Hours: various
(Railroad memorabilia, Fire Protection
    District display, bicentennial display)
free tours

Gridley District Library
PO Box 370
Gridley, IL 61744-0370
Perry Klopfenstein

Hacksma House Genealogy Library
(see Washington)

Harvey Public Library District
155th Street and Turlington Avenue
Harvey, IL 60426
(708) 331-0757
Jay Kalman, Reference Librarian
Hours: Mon–Thur 9:00–8:00, Fri–Sat
    9:00–5:00
(Harvey local history)

Haynor Public Library District
Main Library
326 Belle Street
Alton, IL 62002
(618) 462-0651
Katherine Bouman, Adult Services
    Librarian
Hours: Mon–Thur 8:00–8:00, Fri 8:00–
    5:00, Sat 9:00–5:00, Sun (Sept–May)
    2:00–5:00

Heritage Cultural Center
(125 South Webster—location)
200 West Douglas (mailing address)
Jacksonville, IL 62650-2012
(217) 243-7488
Hours: Wed 1:00–4:00 by appointment
(local history)

Historic Pullman Foundation
Pullman Historic District
11111 South Forrestville Avenue
Chicago, IL 60628-4649
(312) 785-3828; (312) 785-8181; (312)
    785-8182 FAX
John Paul Vega, Executive Director
Hours: Hotel Florence Museum: Mon–
    Fri 11:00–2:00, Sat 8:00–12:30, Sun
    10:00–3:00; Historic Pullman
    Foundation Visitor Center: Sat 11:00–
    2:00, Sun noon–3:00
(history)

Homewood Public Library
17917 Dixie Highway
Homewood, IL 60430
(708) 798-0121
Cindy Rauch, Administrator
Hours: Mon–Fri 9:30–9:00, Sat 9:30–
    5:00

Illinois State University
The University Museum
301 South Main Street
Normal, IL 61761
(309) 438-8800
Marcia D. Young, Ph.D., Acting Director
(local history collection)

Joiner History Room
DeKalb County Courthouse
133 West State Street
Sycamore, IL 60178
(815) 895-7271
Phyllis Kelley, County Historian
Hours: Thur 1:00–4:00
(Atlases, maps, plat books, cemetery
    records, church histories, city
    directories, county and township
    histories, printed census, Civil War
    discharges, commissioner's papers
    1837–1935, miscellaneous school
    records, nurse's registry 1877–1983,
    poll books 1859–1872, poor farm
    records, family files and genealogies,
    Grand Army of the Republic Roster
    Book, Illinois Adjutant General's
    reports, obituaries 1860–1930, photo
    collection, manuscript materials,
    newspapers 1867–1965; "A
    cooperative effort of the DeKalb
    County Board, DeKalb County
    Judiciary, DeKalb County Clerk's
    Office, DeKalb County Central Plant,
    DeKalb County Sesquicentennial
    Committee, DeKalb County
    Historical-Genealogical Society, and
    the DeKalb County citizens concerned
    with safeguarding their heritage as
    represented by the historical
    documents in the collection.")

Kankakee Public Library
304 South Indiana Avenue
Kankakee, IL 60901
Hours: Mon–Thur 9:00–9:00, Fri 9:00–
6:00, Sat 9:00–5:00

Keithsburg Museum
(14th and Washington—location)
PO Box 79 (mailing address)
Keithsburg, IL 61442-0079
(309) 374-2659
Sharon Reason
Hours: Mon–Fri & Sat 1:00–5:00, and by
appointment
(local history)

LaGrange Public Library
10 West Cossitt
LaGrange, IL 60525
(specializes in La Grange, Illinois)

Lake County Museum
(At 176 and Fairfield Road—location)
27277 North Forest Preserve Drive
(mailing address)
Wauconda, IL 60084-2016
(847) 525-7878; (847) 526-0024 FAX
Janet Gallimore
Pub. *The Postcard Journal* (not
genealogical: popular culture)
(regional history archives)

Lake Villa Public Library District
1001 East Grand Avenue
Lake Villa, IL 60046
(847) 356-7711
Michael Chatlien, Librarian
Hours: Mon–Thur 9:00–9:00, Fri–Sat
9:00–5:00, Sun (except summer) 1:00–
5:00
(local history)

**Lewis University Canal and
Regional History Special Collection**
Rt. 53 Lewis University
Romeoville, IL 60446-2298
(815) 838-0500, ext. 5579
John Lamb, Director
Hours: Mon–Thur 2:00–4:00, and by
appointment
Pub. *Annual Newsletter*
("Material on canals, photos,
correspondence, annual reports, also
local histories of northern Illinois and
other materials such as complete files
of local Chamber of Commerce and
regional Chamber of Commerce.")
$10.00 per year membership; searches
$5.00 plus $1.00 per page
photoduplication

Lincoln Courtroom and Museum
101 West Third Street
Beardstown, IL 62618-1142
(217) 323-4191
Kermit Pilger
Hours: weekends by appointment
(local history)

**Lincoln Library-Sangamon Valley
Collection**
326 South Seventh Street
Springfield, IL 62701-1621
(217) 753-4900
Edward J. Russo, City Historian
Hours: Mon–Thur 9:00–9:00, Fri 9:00–
6:00, Sat 9:00–5:00
(central Illinois)

Lincolnwood Public Library District
4000 West Pratt Avenue
Lincolnwood, IL 60646
(847) 677-5277
Ruth Whitney
Hours: Mon–Fri 10:00–5:00

Litchfield Carnegie Public Library
400 North State Street
Litchfield, IL 62056-0212
(217) 324-4841
Hours: Mon–Thur 10:00–8:00; Fri
10:00–5:00, Sat 10:00–2:00
("Repository of the collection of the late
Walter R. Sanders, some 20,000 pages
of research on the Sanders-Saunders
family and on Montgomery County,
Illinois, and surrounding area.")

Lyons Public Library
4209 Joliet Avenue
Lyons, IL 60534-1597
(708) 447-3577; FAX (708) 447-3589
Denise E. Ard, Director
Hours: Mon–Fri 10:00–9:00, Sat 10:00–
4:00, Sun (during school year) 1:00–
4:00
(Illinois, local history/New England
genealogy/passenger lists)

Matson Public Library
109 Park Avenue West
Princeton, IL 61356
Hours: Mon–Thur noon–9:00, Fri 9:00–
5:00, Sat noon–5:00; summer: Tue–
Thur noon–6:00
(houses collection of the Bureau County
Genealogical Society)

Helen Matthes Library
100 Market Street
Effingham, IL 62401
(217) 342-2464; (217) 342-2464 FAX
Normalie Strickland, Director
Hours: winter: Mon–Thur 10:00–9:00,
Fri 10:00–5:00, Sat 10:00–4:00;
summer: Mon–Thur 10:00–8:00, Fri
10:00–5:00, Sat 10:00–1:00;
genealogy assistance: Tue 1:00–3:00,
Thur 10:00–noon
(emphasis on local and Illinois
genealogy, and houses DAR and
genealogical society collections)

Mattoon Public Library
(1600 Charleston Avenue—proposed
Local History Room location)
PO Box 809 (mailing address)
Mattoon, IL 61938
(217) 234-2621; (217) 234-2660 FAX

Melinda Matthews, Library Assistant
Hours: Library: Sept–May: Mon–Fri
9:00–8:00, Sat 9:00–5:00; Library:
Jun–Aug: Mon–Sat 9:00–5:00; Local
History Room: Mon–Sat noon–5:00,
and by appointment
(limited access to items during temporary
relocation for renovation)
search fees: $2.00 minimum, 15¢ per
copy made from paper original, 25¢
per copy made from microfilm
original

Mitchell Museum at Cedarhurst
Richview Road
PO Box 923
Mount Vernon, IL 62864
(618) 242-1236; (618) 242-9530 FAX
Liz Hinman, Communications/Grants
Hours: Tue–Sat 10:00–5:00, Sun 1:00–
5:00

Moline Public Library
Reference Department
504 17th Street
Moline, IL 61625
(309) 762-6883; (309) 797-0484 FAX
E-mail: refmpl@libby.rbls.lib.il.us

Morris Area Public Library
604 Liberty Street
Morris, IL 60450
(815) 942-6880; (815) 942-6415 FAX
Deborah Steffes
Hours: Mon–Fri 10:00–9:00, Sat 10:00–
4:00
("We collect basically information
relative to Grundy County, Illinois.")

John Mosser Public Library
106 West Meek Street
Abingdon, IL 61410

Mount Prospect Public Library
10 S. Emerson St.
Mount Prospect, IL 60056
Hours: Mon–Fri 9:00–9:00, Sat 9:00–
5:00, Sun noon–5:00, volunteer on
duty Mon & Fri 9:00–noon

**Museum Association of Douglas
County**
Douglas County Museum
700 South Main Street
Tuscola, IL 61953-1822
(217) 253-2535
Lynnita Sommer, Administrator
Hours: Mon–Sat 9:00–4:00, Sun 1:00–
4:00
Pub. *Cabin Chatter*, quarterly
(Douglas County history; genealogical
materials and research assistant
available; Korean War oral history
interviews)
$15.00 per year membership for
individuals, $25.00 per year
membership for families, $6.00 per
year Junior membership, $10.00 per
year membership for senior citizens,
$35.00 per year Corporate or Civic
membership, $250.00 life membership

Naperville Public Libraries

Nichols Library
200 West Jefferson Avenue
Naperville, IL 60540-5351
(630) 961-4100
Margaret A. Brown, Head of Reference
 Services
Hours: Mon–Fri 9:00–9:00, Sat 9:00–
 5:00, Sun 1:00–5:00

Newberry Library

60 West Walton Street
Chicago, IL 60610-3305
(312) 943-9090; (312) 255-3506
 (Reference); (312) 255-3512
 (Genealogy)
http://www.newberry.org/
David T. Thackery, Curator of Local and
 Family History
Hours: Tue–Thur 10:00–6:00, Fri–Sat
 9:00–5:00
Pub. *Newberry Newsletter*, quarterly;
 *Origins: A Newsletter of the Local &
 Family History Section and the Family
 & Community Center at the Newberry
 Library*, quarterly
("North American local and family
 history; non-genealogical areas of
 strength include history of cartography
 and history of Native Americans.")

North Park College

Archives Department
Library
3225 West Foster Avenue
Chicago, IL 60625
(312) 244-6224; (312) 267-2362 FAX
E-mail: tjohnsol@gumby.npcts.edu
http://www.northpark.edu/

Northern Illinois University

Regional History Center
Swen Parson Hall 155
DeKalb, IL 60115-2854
(815) 753-1779
Glen A. Gildemeister, Ph.D., Director
(history, genealogy, local government
 records)

Heritage League of Northwest Illinois

c/o Stockton Public Library-Lower level
140 West Benton Street
Stockton, IL 61085-1312
(815) 947-2435; (815) 947-2030
 (Library)
Patricia Nagel, Curator
Hours: Sat 1:00–3:00, and by
 appointment

Oak Lawn Public Library

9427 South Raymond Avenue
Oak Lawn, IL 60453
(708) 422-4990

Oak Park Public Library

834 Lake Street
Oak Park, IL 60301
(708) 383-8200
William Jerousek

Hours: Mon–Fri 9:00–9:00, Sat 9:00–
 5:00, Sun (Sept–May) 1:00–5:00

Odell Public Library

Whiteside County Genealogy Room
307 South Madison Street
Morrison, IL 61270
(815) 772-READ
Hours: Mon–Sun

Oregon Public Library

Genealogy Room
Oregon, IL 61061
(815) 732-2724
Hours: Mon–Thur 9:00–8:00, Fri–Sat
 9:00–4:00
(houses material from the Ogle County
 Genealogical Society)

Park Forest Public Library

400 Lakewood Boulevard
Park Forest, IL 60466-1684
(708) 748-3731; (708) 748-8829 FAX
Gretchen Falk, Head, Reference
 Department
Hours: Mon–Thur 10:00–9:00, Fri
 10:00–6:00, Sat 10:00–5:00, Sun
 (Sept–May) 2:00–5:00

Parlin-Ingersoll Library

205 West Chestnut Street
Canton, IL 61520
(309) 647-0328
Hours: Mon–Fri 9:00–8:00, Sat 9:00–
 4:00, Sun 1:00–4:00

Pekin Public Library

301 South Fourth Street
Pekin, IL 61554-4284
(309) 347-7111; (309) 347-6587 FAX
Laurie Hartshorn
Hours: Mon–Thur 9:00–9:00, Fri 9:00–
 6:00, Sat 9:00–5:00; Jun–Aug: Mon–
 Thur 9:00–8:00, Fri 9:00–6:00; Jun–
 Jul: Sat 9:00–1:00
(emphasis on Tazewell County)
$5.00 fee for searches, but "extensive
 genealogical research is not available
 via mail"

Peoria Public Library

107 N.E. Monroe Street
Peoria, IL 61602
(309) 672-8858
Susan Kaufman, Genealogy Librarian
Hours: Mon–Thur 9:00–9:00, Fri–Sat
 9:00–6:00; summer: closed weekends
(Peoria and area history and genealogy
 collections)

Piatt County Museum

315 West Main
Monticello, IL 61856
(217) 762-4731
Lila Miller, Vice President
Hours: Jun–Oct: Sat–Sun 1:00–4:00
$15.00 per year membership for
 individuals, $25.00 per year
 membership for families

Poplar Creek Public Library

1405 South Park Avenue
Streamwood, IL 60107
(630) 837-6800
Hours: Mon–Thur 9:00–9:30, Fri–Sat
 9:00–5:00, Sun 12:00–5:00
(a small genealogical collection with a
 few local histories, no archival
 materials)

Quincy Museum

1601 Maine Street
Quincy, IL 62301-4264
(217) 224-7669; (217) 218-2817
Steve Adams
(county history)

Quincy Public Library

526 Jersey Street
Quincy, IL 62301
(217) 223-1309; (217) 222-3052 FAX
Nancy Dolan, Head, Reference
 Department
Hours: Tue after Labor Day to Sat before
 Memorial Day: Mon–Thur 9:00–9:00,
 Fri–Sat 9:00–6:00, Sun 1:00–5:00;
 Jun–Aug: Mon 9:00–9:00, Tue–Sat
 9:00–6:00

Randolph County Archives and Museum

1 Taylor Street
Chester, IL 62233-0332
(618) 826-3743; (618) 826-3750 FAX
Emily B. Lyons, Curator
Hours: Mon, Thur–Fri & Sun 12:30–3:30
 by appointment
(Kaskaskia manuscripts, Native
 American, town and county artifacts)

Raupp Memorial Museum

(901 Dunham Lane—location)
530 Bernard Drive (mailing address)
Buffalo Grove, IL 60089
(847) 459-2318; (847) 459-5700, ext.
 116; (847) 459-5741 FAX
Lynne Mickle
Hours: Wed 2:00–5:00, second Wed
 7:00–8:30, Sun 1:00–4:00, by
 appointment

Rend Lake College

Southern Illinois Room
Learning Resource Center
RR 1
Ina, IL 62845-9801
(618) 437-5321, ext. 275
David Patton
Hours: Mon–Thur 7:45 A.M.–9:30 P.M.,
 Fri 7:45–4:30, Sat 8:00–noon

Richland Heritage Museum Foundation

Carnegie Building Museum
401 East Main Street
PO Box 153
Olney, IL 62450-1548
(618) 395-3893; (618) 397-5491
E. L. Bosomworth, President
(local and midwest artifacts history)

Robinson Public Library District
606 North Jefferson Street
Robinson, IL 62454
(618) 544-3273; (618) 544-7172 FAX
Marilyn Manning
Hours: Mon–Thur 10:00–8:00, Fri–Sat
    10:00–5:30; summer: Mon 10:00–
    8:00, Tue–Sat 10:00–5:30
("A large collection of source materials
    for Crawford County, Illinois,
    including county histories, census,
    family histories, historical folders, and
    a significant number of books for
    other states.")

Rock Island Public Library
401 19th Street
Rock Island, IL 61201-8143
(309) 788-7627; (309) 788-6591 FAX
http://www.rbls.lib.il.us/rbls/index.html
Katy Powers, Reference
Hours: winter: Mon–Thur 9:00–9:00,
    Fri–Sat 9:00–5:30; summer: Mon–
    Wed 9:00–9:00, Fri 9:00–5:30, Sat
    9:00–1:00
search fees: $10.00 per hour plus copies
    and postage

Rockford Public Library
215 North Wyman Street
Rockford, IL 61101
(815) 965-6731, ext. 163
John L. Molyneaux
Hours: Mon–Wed & Fri 9:00–12:00 &
    1:00–6:00, Thur 12:00–5:00 & 6:00–
    9:00, Sat 1:00–5:00
(specializes in Illinois and the U.S., east
    of the Mississippi)

**Saint Charles Public Library
District**
1 South Sixth Avenue
Saint Charles, IL 60174
(630) 584-0076
Virginia L. Champion, Reference
    Librarian
Hours: Mon–Thur 9:00–9:00, Fri 9:00–
    6:00, Sat 9:00–5:00, Sun (except
    summer) 1:00–5:00
(emphasis on Saint Charles, Kane
    County, and Illinois)

Sangamon State University
Illinois Regional Archives Depository
Brookens Library, Room 144
Shepherd Road
Springfield, IL 62794-9243
(217) 786-6520
Thomas J. Wood, University Archivist
Hours: Mon–Fri 9:00–5:00
(University archives, local government
    records, local history)

Sangamon Valley Collection
(see Lincoln Library)

**Sauk Valley Community College
(SVCC)**
Learning Resource Center (LRC)
173 Illinois Route 2
Dixon, IL 61021-9112

(815) 288-5511, ext. 306 or 247; (815)
    288-5651 FAX
Robert Thomas, Coordinator
(local history)

Schuyler Jail Museum
Schuyler County Historical Museum and
    Genealogical Center
200 South Congress
Rushville, IL 62681
(217) 322-6975
Evelyn Eifert, President
Hours: Apr 1–Nov 1: Mon–Sun 1:00–5:00;
    Nov 1–Apr 1: Sat–Sun 1:00–5:00
Pub. *The Schuylerite*, quarterly
(much genealogical information on
    Schuyler County, other counties and
    many states)
$15.00 per year membership; search:
    $5.00 per hour

Matthew T. Scott House
227 North First Street
Chenoa, IL 61726-1019
(815) 945-4555
Elaine Augspurgen, caretaker
Hours: Thur & Sun 2:00–4:00, and by
    appointment
(local history)

**Shabbona-Lee-Rollo Historical
Museum**
119 West Comanche
Shabbona, IL 60550
(815) 824-2759; (815) 824-2745
Mary DeBolt
Hours: Tue–Thur 9:00–11:00 & 1:00–
    3:00
(local history)

Shawnee Library System
511 Greenbriar Road
Carterville, IL 62918-1621
(618) 985-3711
James Ubel, Executive Director
Hours: Mon–Fri 8:30–5:00

Southern Illinois University
Morris Library Special Collections
    (SIU-C)
Carbondale, IL 62901
(618) 458-3516; (618) 453-3451; (618)
    453-6851 (American Conference for
    Irish Studies)
E-mail: dkoch@lib.siu.edu
http://www.lib.siu.edu/
David V. Koch, Curator, Special
    Collections
Hours: Mon–Fri 8:30–4:30
Pub. *I Carbs*

Staunton Public Library
George and Santina Sawyer Genealogy
    Room
306 West Main
Staunton, IL 62088
Hours: Mon–Thur 1:00–8:00, Fri–Sat
    9:00–5:00

Suburban Library System
(address withheld upon request)

Conrad Sulzer Regional Library
Historical Room
4455 North Lincoln Avenue
Chicago, IL 60625-2192
(312) 744-7616; (312) 744-2899 FAX
Glenn E. Humphreys, Special
    Collections Librarian
Hours: by appointment
(emphasis on north side communities
    that once made up the townships of
    Jefferson and Lake View, annexed to
    Chicago in 1889, and those
    neighborhoods further north and west
    that were annexed a few years later,
    such as Rogers Park, Edison Park, and
    Norwood Park)

Thomson Depot Museum
Main Street
PO Box 392
Thomson, IL 61285-0392
(815) 259-2155
Marian McKee
Hours: 23 May–31 Oct: Sat–Sun 1:00–
    4:00 by appointment
(historical library)

Three Rivers Public Library District
Local History Collection
Minooka Branch Library
109 North Wabena
PO Box 370
Minooka, IL 60447
(815) 467-1600; (815) 467-1632
E-mail:
    mhouchens@starbase1.htls.lib.il.us
Michele Houchens, Local History Clerk
("Collection consists of information from
    the local area only: Aux Sable
    Township, Grundy County, Channahon
    Township, Will County, and the
    villages of Minooka and Channahon.")

University of Illinois
Illinois Historical Survey
Library 346
1408 West Gregory Drive
Urbana, IL 61801
(217) 333-1777
Hours: Mon–Fri 8:30–5:00

Urbana Free Library
Champaign County Historical Archives
201 South Race Street
Urbana, IL 61801-3283
(217) 367-4025; (217) 367-4061 FAX
Jean E. Koch, Archives Director
Hours: Mon–Sat 9:00–5:00, Sun 1:00–
    5:00
Pub. *Champaign County Historical
    Archives Historical Publications
    Series*, irregularly
(local history and genealogy, especially
    of east-central Illinois)

Vermilion County Museum
116 North Gilbert Street
Danville, IL 61832-8506
(217) 442-2922
Susan E. Richter, Curator

Hours: Tue–Sat 10:00–5:00, Sun 1:00–5:00

Pub. *Vermilion County Museum Society Newsletter*, bimonthly; *Heritage of Vermilion County Illinois*, quarterly

(local county history; Lincoln site on National Register)

$15.00 per year membership

Village of Bethalto
213 North Prairie
Bethalto, IL 62010
(618) 377-8723
Arvel Fowler
Hours: Sat afternoons by appointment
(local history)

Warren County Public Library
60 West Side Square
Monmouth, IL 61462

Warren-Newport Public Library
224 North O'Plaine Road
Gurnee, IL 60031
(847) 244-5150
Ms. Lourdes Mordini, Head of Adult Services
Hours: Mon–Thur 9:00–9:00, Fri–Sat 9:00–5:00

West Chicago City Museum
132 Main Street
West Chicago, IL 60185-2835
(630) 231-3376
Sally DeFauw, Archivist
Hours: Mon–Fri 8:00–4:30, research by appointment
(specializes in greater West Chicago area: selected individual family genealogy, obituary files, cemetery transcriptions, Civil War records, railroad workers information, some census material, newspapers)

Western Illinois University Library
Archives and Special Collections Unit
1 University Circle
Macomb, IL 61455-1391
(309) 298-2717
Gordana Rezab, University Archivist and Special Collections Librarian
Hours: Mon–Fri 8:00–4:30

Western Illinois University
Western Museum
900 West Adams Street
Macomb, IL 61455-1396
(309) 298-1808
Mary McMullen, Supervisor
Hours: Mon–Fri 9:00–noon & 1:00–4:00
(local and university history)

Wheaton Public Library
225 North Cross Street
Wheaton, IL 60187
(630) 668-1374
http://www.wheaton.lib.il.us
Nelva Hamelink, Reference Librarian
Hours: Mon–Fri 9:00–9:00, Sat 9:00–5:00, Sun 1:00–5:00 (Sept–May)

Willard Library
(see Indiana)

Wilmette Public Library
1242 Wilmette Avenue
Wilmette, IL 60091
(847) 256-5025
http://www.wilmette.lib.il.us
Ellen B. Clark, Head of Adult Services
Hours: Mon–Fri 9:00–9:00, Sat 9:00–5:00, Sun 1:00–5:00 (during school year)

Wilmington Public Library
201 South Kankakee Street
Wilmington, IL 60481
(815) 476-2834; (815) 476-7805
Mary Jane Anderson, Library Director
Hours: Mon–Thur 9:00–8:30, Fri–Sat 9:00–5:00
(Illinois Collection contains genealogical materials, microfilm file of local newspaper with index to obituaries)

Winnetka Public Library District
768 Oak Street
Winnetka, IL 60093
Hours: Mon–Thur 9:00–9:00, Fri–Sat 9:00–5:00, Sun 1:00–5:00 (during school year)

Zion-Benton Public Library
2400 Gabriel Avenue
Zion, IL 60099-2296
Hours: Mon–Thur 9:00–9:00, Fri 9:00–6:00, Sat 9:00–5:00

Historical Societies— Local and Regional

Addison Historical Society
Historical Museum of Addison
131 West Lake Street
Addison, IL 60101-2774
Adele Larsen, Historical Commission Member
Hours: Museum: Sat 10:00–2:00, except holiday weekends, and by appointment
Pub. *Salt Creek Tattler*, ten times per year (monthly, except July and August)
("Some family genealogies of this area, census books for DuPage County 1840–70, Soul registry from old Lutheran churches, old county record books and atlases, etc.")
$5.00 per year membership research fee to be arranged with Mrs. Gerace

Alton Area Historical Society, Inc
(239 West Elm Street—location)
PO Box 971 (mailing address)
Alton, IL 62002-0971
(618) 466-5853 (President)
Maitland A. Timmermiere, President
Pub. *AAHS Newsletter*, three times per year
$5.00 per year membership

Andover Historical Society
(418 Locust Street—location)
340 Fourth Street, Box 197 (mailing address)
Andover, IL 61233-0197
(309) 476-8378; (309) 476-8501
Doris L. Anderson
Hours: Jun–Aug: Sun 1:00–4:00, and by appointment

Historical Society and Museum of Arlington Heights
Arlington Heights Historical Museum
(110 West Fremont Street, Arlington Heights 60004-5912—museum location)
500 North Vail Avenue (society location and mailing address)
Arlington Heights, IL 60004
(847) 255-1225 (Historical Society); (847) 255-1893 (Museum); (847) 255-1570 FAX (Museum)
Susan P. English, Museum Administrator
Hours: Library: Thur 1:00–4:00, Fri 9:00–12:00
Pub. *Dunton Post*, monthly
$10.00 per year membership for individuals, $25.00 per year membership for families

Augustana Historical Society
Augustana College Library
Seventh Avenue and 35th Street
Rock Island, IL 61201-2210
(309) 794-7266
Loryann Eis, President
Pub. *Augustana Historical Society Publications* (monograph series); *AHS Newsletter*

Aurora Historical Society and Museum
(305 Cedar Street, corner of Oak and Cedar Streets, Aurora, IL 60506—location)
317 Cedar Street (mailing address)
Aurora, IL 60507
(630) 897-9029
John Jaros, Director
Hours: Wed & Sat–Sun 1:00–5:00, and by appointment
Pub. *McCarty Mills Gazette*
$35.00 per year membership

Avon Historical Society
(Avcom Park—North Edge of Avon—location)
PO Box 483 (mailing address)
Avon, IL 61415-0483
(309) 465-3189; (309) 465-3043
Margaret Hickerson, President
Hours: first two weekends of Oct 9:00–5:00

Barrington Area Historical Society
The Heritage Research Center
212 West Main Street
Barrington, IL 60010
(847) 381-1730

Michael J. Harkins, Executive Director;
Dean Maiben, Director Heritage
Research Center
Hours: Office: Mon–Fri 9:00–4:00 by
appointment; Museum: Thur–Fri
10:00–4:00, Sat 10:00–1:00
Pub. *Landmark Living Journal*
(area family and institutional
manuscripts)

Bartlett Historical Society
228 South Main Street
PO Box 8257
Bartlett, IL 60103-8257
Thomas Perkins, Jr.
Hours: Memorial Day–Labor Day: Mon–
Fri 8:30–4:30, Sat 9:00–noon
(local history of Bartlett, Ontarioville
and some of Elgin)

Batavia Historical Society
Batavia Depot Museum, 155 Houston
Street
PO Box 14
Batavia, IL 60510-0014
(630) 406-5274 Historical Society);
(630) 879-5235 (Museum); (630) 879-
9537 FAX (Museum)
Carla Hill
Hours: Mar–30 Nov: Mon, Wed & Fri–
Sun 2:00–4:00 by appointment
Pub. *Historic Batavia*
(local history)

Beecher Community Historical Society
(Washington Township Museum, 673
Penfield—location)
PO Box 1469 (mailing address)
Beecher, IL 60401-1469
(708) 946-2198 (Society); (708) 946-
6218 (Museum)
Paula Franke, President; Virginia Bath,
Museum
Hours: Wed 6:00 P.M.–8:00 P.M., Sat
9:00–11:00
(local history)

Bellflower Genealogical and Historical Society
(Latcha Street—location)
Rt. 1, Box 17 (mailing address)
Bellflower, IL 61724
(309) 722-3467 (President); (309) 722-
3757 (Bellflower Village and
Museum)
Dorothy Woliung, President
Hours: by appointment
Pub. *Bellflower Highlights*, annually
(July), subscription by donation

Bensenville Historical Society
(900 West Wood—location)
c/o Bensenville Library, 200 South
Church Road (mailing address)
Bensenville, IL 60106-2303
(630) 595-3742; (630) 766-4642
(Historical Commission)
Patricia Johnson

Berwyn Historical Society
Piper School, 2435 Kenilworth
PO Box 479
Berwyn, IL 60402-0479
(708) 484-0020
Sue Svec, President
Hours: by appointment
(local history)

Bishop Hill Heritage Association
Bishop Hill Heritage Museum
103 North Bishop Hill Street
PO Box 92
Bishop Hill, IL 61419-0092
(309) 927-3899; (309) 927-3010 FAX
Crystle D. Clark, Museum Director
Hours: Mon–Fri 10:00–4:00
Pub. *Heritage Newsbulletin*, three to four
times per year
("Information on Bishop Hill and the
Swedish immigrants who founded it;
we have a library and an archives
which contains many documents and
photographs.")
$25.00–$500.00 membership; search fees
vary by time involved

Bloomingdale Historical Society
(Bloomingdale Public Library, 101
Fairfield Way—location)
241 Driftwood Lane (mailing address)
Bloomingdale, IL 60108-1902
(630) 529-0787
Dolores P. Howe
Hours: Mon–Thur 9:00–9:00; Sept–May
Fri–Sat 9:00–5:00, 1:00–5:00

Blue Island Historical Society
Blue Island Public Library
2433 York Street
Blue Island, IL 60406-2094
(708) 371-8546; (708) 388-1078
(Library)
Richard May
Hours: Library: Mon–Thur noon–8:00,
Fri–Sat 9:00–5:00
(history of Blue Island, Illinois)

Bolingbrook Historical Society
162 North Canyon Drive
Bolingbrook, IL 60440-1526
(630) 759-4974
Philip Hanson, President

Bond County Historical Society
1014 Asbury
Greenville, IL 62246-0172
(618) 664-3054
Dean Anthony, President
Hours: Library: Mon–Thur 2:00–8:00,
Fri noon–6:00, Sat 10:00–5:00
(Bond County, Illinois, research)
$10.00 per year membership for families
of two

Boone County Historical Society
311 Whitney Boulevard
Belvidere, IL 61008-3609
(815) 544-8391 (Tue & Thur)
George A. Thomas, Museum Coordinator

Hours: Museum: Tue & Thur 9:00–3:00;
May–Oct: third Sun 2:00–5:00

Bourbonnais Grove Historical Society
(Stratford Drive at Illinois Route 102—
location)
PO Box 311 (mailing address)
Bourbonnais, IL 60914-0311
(815) 933-2308; (815) 933-6452
James V. Johnson
Hours: first & third Sun 1:00–4:00 by
appointment
(French-Canadian heritage, county
pioneer history)

Brimfield Historical Society
Brimfield Public Library
111 South Galena
Brimfield, IL 61517
(309) 446-3631; (309) 446-3670
Alfred Arnold
Hours: Tue–Fri 3:00–6:00, Wed 9:00–
noon & 3:00–7:00, Thur 3:00–7:00

Brookfield Historical Society
8820 Brookfield Avenue
Brookfield, IL 60513
(708) 485-3420
Hours: Sun 1:00–4:00; summer: second
& fourth Sun
Pub. *Grossdale Gazette*, quarterly
$7.50 per year membership for
individuals, $5.00 per year
membership for senior citizens

Bureau County Historical Society
109 Park Avenue, West
Princeton, IL 61356-1927
(815) 875-2184
Barbara Hansen, Museum Director
Hours: Mon & Wed–Sun 1:00–5:00,
closed Dec 24–Jan 31, Easter,
Mother's Day, Thanksgiving

Bushnell Historical Society
Bushnell Recreation and Cultural Center
300 Miller Street
Bushnell, IL 61422
(309) 772-3782; (309) 772-3612
Donna Tracy, President
Hours: Mon–Fri 9:00–4:00 by
appointment

Cairo Historical Association
Magnolia Manor
826 Charles Street
Cairo, IL 62914-1458
(618) 734-0201; (618) 734-3807
Carolyn Mayberry
Hours: Wed–Sat 9:00–5:00, Sun 1:00–
5:00

Calhoun County Historical Society
(County Road, Second Floor of Farm
Bureau Building—location)
PO Box 46 (mailing address)
Hardin, IL 62047
(618) 576-2660 (after 5 P.M.)
Tina Pluester, Secretary-Treasurer
Hours: Wed 9:00–3:00

Pub. *Newsletter*; quarterly
$5.00 per year membership; research:
$5.00 per hour

Calumet City Historical Society Museum
760 Wentworth Avenue
PO Box 1917
Calumet City, IL 60409-3515
(708) 862-8662
Florence Steffel, President
Hours: Tue–Thur 1:00–4:00 by
appointment

Cambridge Historical Society
RR 2, Box 96
Cambridge, IL 61238-9633
(309) 937-2233 (Library)
Deb Edmund
Hours: meetings: last Wed

Carroll County Historical Society
(107 West Broadway—location)
PO Box 65 (mailing address)
Mount Carroll, IL 61053
(815) 244-3474
Susan Appel, President
Hours: Mon–Fri 10:00–2:00, Sat 10:00–
3:00, Sun noon–3:00

Cass County Illinois Historical/ Genealogical Society
PO Box 11
Virginia, IL 62691-0011
Janice L. Fox, President
Pub. *Cass County, Illinois, Historian Newsletter*, quarterly
(Cass County marriages, cemeteries, land
records, 1840, 1850 and 1880
censuses, etc.)
$7.00 per year membership (beginning in
July)

Catlin Historical Society
Catlin Heritage Museum
210 North Paris Street
PO Box 658
Catlin, IL 61817-0658
(217) 427-5766
Shirley Nesbitt, Museum Director
Hours: Mon, Wed & Sat 9:00–noon &
1:00–4:00
Pub. *Catlin Historical Society Newsletter*, quarterly
(much genealogical information on the
local level: obituaries, pictures, oral
histories, history of people in the area,
etc.)
$10.00 per year membership for
individuals, $15.00 per year
membership for families, $5.00 per
year membership for youths under 18
years of age, $8.00 per year
membership for senior citizens over 65
years of age, $12.00 per year
membership for senior citizen couples,
$150.00 life membership for
individuals, $250.00 life membership
for families

Cedarville Area Historical Society
Cherry Street
PO Box 46
Cedarville, IL 61013-0046
(815) 563-4523
Jane Goodspeed
Hours: Apr–Nov: Sat–Sun 1:00–4:00
(local history library)

Champaign County Historical Society
Urbana Free Library
201 South Race Street
Urbana, IL 61801-3283
(217) 367-4025 (Library)
Jean Gordon
Hours: Library: Mon–Sat 9:00–5:00, Sun
1:00–5:00

Chapin Community Historical Society
Superior Street
Chapin, IL 62628
(217) 472-6216
Mary Smith
Hours: by appointment
(local and family history)

Chatsworth Historical Society
424 East Locust Street
PO Box 755
Chatsworth, IL 60921-0755
(815) 635-3124
Richard A. Pearson, Chairman/President

Chicago and Northwestern Historical Society
8703 North Olcott Avenue
Niles, IL 60648-2023
(847) 794-5633
Walter Feret, Chair
(local history and genealogy)

Chicago Heights Historical Society
Chicago Heights Free Public Library
15th and Chicago Road
Chicago Heights, IL 60411
(708) 754-0323 (Library)
Barbara Paul
Hours: Library: Mon–Thur 9:00–9:00,
Fri–Sat 9:00–5:00, Sun (during the
school year) 1:00–5:00

Chicago Historical Society
1601 Clark Street at North Avenue
Chicago, IL 60614-9990.
(312) 642-4600; (312) 642-5035, ext.
356; (312) 266-2077 FAX
E-mail: ziemer@chicagohs.org
http://www.chicagohs.org/
Hours: Library: Tue–Sat 9:30–4:30,
subject to change, call for current
hours
Pub. *Chicago History*, quarterly
$30.00 per year membership for
individuals (only very limited
genealogical reference services via
mail requests, but may change policy
to discontinue this service)

Chicago Lawn Historical Society
(Chicago Lawn Library, 6120 South
Kedzie Avenue—location)
4043 West 63rd Street (mailing address)
Chicago, IL 60629-4638
(312) 582-8778; (312) 434-4790
Jack Klaus

Chillicothe Historical Society
(Old Rock Island Depot, Cedar and
Third Street—location)
PO Box 181
Chillicothe, IL 61523-0181
(309) 274-2247; (309) 274-3440
Tom Landes
Hours: Mar–Dec: first Sat–Sun 1:00–
4:00

Christian County Historical Society
(Route 29 and Route 48 East—location)
PO Box 254 (mailing address)
Taylorville, IL 62568-0254
(770) 824-6922; (770) 824-5807
Mary Ann E. Durbin, President
Hours: Apr–Nov: Wed–Sat 10:00–4:00,
Sun 1:00–4:00

Historical Society of Cicero
2423 South Austin Boulevard
Cicero, IL 60650-2695
(708) 652-8305; (708) 652-0156
Norma F. Zbasnik
Hours: by appointment during school
hours, 8:30–2:30

Clark County Historical Society and Museum
Fourth and Maple
PO Box 207
Marshall, IL 62441-0207
(217) 826-6027; (217) 826-8089
Eleanor Macey
Hours: mid–May to mid–Sept: Sun 1:00–
4:00

Clinton County Historical Society
1091 Franklin Street
Carlyle, IL 62231-1820
Hours: Memorial Day–Labor Day:
second, third & fourth Thur 10:00–
3:00, Sun 1:00–4:00
Pub. *Clinton County Historical Society Quarterly*; *Museum Newsletter*,
quarterly
$8.00 per year membership

Coles County Historical Society
Greenwood School Museum
800 Hayes Avenue
PO Box 225
Charleston, IL 61920-3449
(217) 345-6690; (217) 581-3310
Robert E. Hennings, President
Hours: Apr–May: Sat–Sun 1:00–3:00
Pub. *CCHS Newsletter*

Columbia Historical Society, Inc.
11562 Bluff Road
Columbia, IL 62236
(618) 281-5734; (618) 939-6652

Linda Maus, President

Crawford County Historical Society, Inc.

(North Lincoln Trail College Campus, on Prison Road—location)
PO Box 554 (mailing address)
Robinson, IL 62454-0554
(618) 544-3087; (618) 592-4474 (President)
Sue Jones, President
Hours: Sun 2:00–4:00, and by appointment
Pub. *Ole Crawford*, quarterly
$10.00 per year membership

Cumberland County Historical and Genealogical Society of Illinois

PO Box 393
Greenup, IL 62428
Pub. *Happy Hunter*, semiannually

Arnold Damen Historical and Preservation Society

1076 West Roosevelt Road
Chicago, IL 60608-1519
(312) 421-5900
Donald F. Rowe, President
Hours: by appointment
(archives)

Danvers Historical Society

118 West Park
Danvers, IL 61732
(309) 392-2042
Robert McAllister

Darien Historical Society

7422 Cass Avenue
Darien, IL 60561
(630) 969-5171, (630) 969-8257, (630) 964-7033
Edward Miller, President
Hours: first Sun 2:00–4:00
Pub. *Newsletter*, quarterly
("Official center of City of Darien"; one-room schoolhouse)
$6.00 per year membership for individuals, $10.00 per year membership for families, $100.00 life membership for individuals, $150.00 life membership for families

Deerfield Area Historical Society

450 Kipling Place
PO Box 520
Deerfield, IL 60015
(847) 948-0680
Barbara McMahon
(local history, genealogy)

DeKalb County Historical-Genealogical Society

PO Box 295
Sycamore, IL 60178-0295
Phyllis Kelley, Corresponding Secretary
Pub. *"Cornsilk" of DeKalb County, Illinois*, quarterly
(Society works with the Joiner History Archives in the county courthouse)

$15.00 per year membership

DeLavan Community Historical Society

Locust Street
DeLavan, IL 61734-0612
(309) 244-7321
Glenn Allen
(local history)

Des Plaines Historical Society

Museum
789 Pearson Street
Des Plaines, IL 60016
(847) 391-5399; (847) 297-1710
Joy A. Matthiessen, Director
Hours: Mon–Fri 9:00–4:00, Sun 1:00–4:00
Pub. *Cobweb*, bimonthly
(City of Des Plaines and Maine Township in Cook County, Illinois)
$12.50 per year membership for individuals

Dundee Township Historical Society, Inc.

426 Highland Avenue
Dundee, IL 60118-1225
(847) 428-6996 phone and FAX
Jack Wendt
Hours: Wed & Sun 2:00–4:00
$15.00 per year membership

DuPage County Historical Society

DuPage County Historical Museum
102 East Wesley Street
Wheaton, IL 60187-5321
(630) 682-7343
Patricia A. Wallace, Director
Pub. *DuPage Roots*

Dwight Historical Society

120 East Chippewa
PO Box 7
Dwight, IL 60420-1302
(815) 584-1865; (815) 584-2091
Tony Thorsen

Earlville Community Historical Society

(Earl Township Public Library, 205 Winthrop Street—location)
PO Box 420 (mailing address)
Earlville, IL 60518-0420
(815) 246-9543; (815) 246-9543 FAX
Maureen Corrigan, Librarian
(local history)

East Side Historical Society

(James P. Fitzgibbons Historical Museum, 9800 Avenue and Calumet Park Fieldhouse—location)
3658 East 106th Street (mailing address)
Chicago, IL 60617-6611
(312) 721-7948; (312) 221-7349
Frank W. Stanley
Hours: Thur 1:00–4:00

Edgar County Historical Society

408-414 North Main Street
Paris, IL 61944-1549

(217) 463-5305
Linda A. Cary, President
Hours: Wed–Fri 9:00–4:00, Sun 1:30–3:30
Pub. *Tense Past Present Future*, quarterly (spring, summer, fall, winter)
$7.50 per year membership for individuals, $10.00 per year membership for families, $25.00 per year membership for businesses, $100.00 life membership for individuals, $150.00 life membership for couples

Edgebrook Historical Society

6173 North McClellan
Chicago, IL 60646-4013
(312) 631-2854; (312) 774-3914; (312) 631-2379 FAX
Janet Stessl

Edgewater Historical Society

1112 West Bryn Mawr
Chicago, IL 60660-4410
(312) 334-5609; (312) 439-3994
Kathy Gemperle

Edwards County Historical Society

Edwards County Genealogical Society
212 West Main Street
Albion, IL 62806
(618) 445-2631
Terry L. Harper, President
Hours: Thur 6:00 P.M.–10:00 P.M.
Pub. *Edwards County Historical Society Publication*, quarterly
$7.00 per year membership for individuals, $8.00 per year membership for couples

Effingham Regional Historical Society

PO Box 1352
Effingham, IL 62401-1352
(217) 342-6280
Phil Lewis

Elburn and Countryside Historical Society

525 North Main
PO Box 115
Elburn, IL 60119-0115
(630) 365-6655 (Community Center)
Larry Kelly

Elgin Area Historical Society

360 Park Street
Elgin, IL 60120-4455
(847) 742-4248
Ann-Macon Smith, Museum Director
Hours: Wed–Sat 12:00–4:00; group tours and research requests by appointment
Pub. *Crackerbarrel*, bimonthly
$20.00 per year membership for individuals, $30.00 per year membership for families; cost of reproduction of photographs or documents provided upon specific request

Elk Grove Historical Society
399 Biesterfield Road
Elk Grove, IL 60007-3625
(847) 439-3994
Philip H. Barry, Chairman
Pub. *EGHS Newsletter*

Elkhart Historical Society
(116 North Latham—location under
restoration)
PO Box 225
Elkhart, IL 62634-0225
(217) 947-2238
Gillette Ransom

Elmwood Historical Society
Lorado Taft Museum
302 North Magnolia
Elmwood, IL 61529
(309) 742-7791; (309) 742-2431
Gene Shissler, President
Hours: Wed noon–4:00
$10.00 per year membership, $250.00
life membership

Historical Society of Elmwood Park
Elmwood Park Public Library
4 Conti Parkway
Elmwood Park, IL 60707-4506
(708) 453-7645
Edwin P. Emmerling, Director Archivist
Hours: Library: Mon–Thur 9:00–9:00,
Fri 9:00–6:00

Evanston Historical Society
Charles Gates Dawes House
225 Greenwood Street
Evanston, IL 60201-4713
(847) 475-3410; (847) 475-3599 FAX
Joan M. Costello, Director; Eden Juron
Pearlman, Collections Manager
Hours: House: Wed–Sun 1:00–5:00;
Research: Wed–Sat 2:00–5:00
Pub. *Time Lines*, quarterly
(Evanston newspapers from 1872, city
directories 1879–1963, manuscript
collections, city records)
$25.00 per year membership for
individuals, $35.00 per year
membership for families, $50.00 per
year Contributor membership, $100.00
per year Sustaining membership,
$250.00 per year Patron membership,
$500.00 per year Benefactor
membership, $1,000.00 life
membership; $5.00 house admission,
$3.00 admission for senior citizens and
students; research fee: $5.00

Evergreen Park Historical Society
3538 West 98th Street
Evergreen Park, IL 60642
Mathilda May

Fairmount-Jamaica Historical Society
116 South Main Street
Fairmount, IL 61841-9601
(217) 288-9278; (217) 733-2171
Edna Underwood, President

Farmer City Genealogy and Historical Society
(Franklin School, 400 East Market—
location)
PO Box 173 (mailing address)
Farmer City, IL 61842-0173
(309) 928-9547; (309) 928-2113
Sharon Stiger

Fayette County Genealogical and Historical Society
Evans Public Library
215 South Fifth Street
PO Box 177
Vandalia, IL 62471-0177
(618) 423-2625
Linda Hanabarger, Editor
Hours: Mon–Thur 10:00–7:00, Fri–Sat
10:00–5:00
Pub. *Fayette Facts*, quarterly
$5.00 per issue to members, $6.00 per
issue to non-members, $15.00 per year
membership

Fern Dell Historic Association
502 Chicago Road
PO Box 254
Newark, IL 60541-0254
(815) 695-5328
Ole W. Duvick, President
Pub. *FHA Newsletter*

Flagg Creek Historical Society
PO Box 227
Burr Ridge, IL 60558
(708) 246-6169; (708) 246-7365; (708)
246-4142 (for seasonal hours)
Martha Mees, President
Hours: Museum: first & third Sat 10:00–
1:00

Flagg Township Historical Society and Museum
(Sixth Street and Fourth Avenue—
location)
1060 Westview Drive (mailing address)
Rochelle, IL 61068-1204
(815) 562-7423; (815) 562-4693
David Guest, President; Marguerite
Thomas
Hours: Memorial Day–Labor Day: Sun
2:00–4:30, and by appointment

Ford County Historical Society
PO Box 213
Paxton, IL 60957
(217) 379-4133
Dr. W. W. Sauer, Executive Director
Pub. *FCHS Newsletter*, bimonthly
(Ford County obituaries and microfilm of
newspapers from 1859)
$3.00 per year membership, $15.00 per
year Sustaining membership, $100.00
life membership; research: contact
Florence Elliott, 351 South Market
Street, Paxton, IL 60937, (217) 379-
4192

Historical Society of Forest Park
(7555 Jackson Boulevard—location)
519 Jackson Boulevard (mailing address)
Forest Park, IL 60130-1896
(708) 771-7716
Frank Orland, President

Historical Society of the Fort Hill Country
(Fort Hill Heritage Museum, 601 Noel
Drive—location)
PO Box 582 (mailing address)
Mundelein, IL 60060
(847) 526-7566
Leonard J. Schmitt, President
Hours: Sat 1:00–4:00, and by
appointment
Pub. *Newsletter*, monthly
(specializes in local history of the Fort
Hill area and other history: all of
Fremont Township, parts of Avon
Township and Libertyville Township)
$5.00 per year membership for
individuals, $10.00 per year
membership for families, $3.00 per
year membership for students, $100.00
life membership

Fort LaMotte Genealogical and Historical Society
Palestine Public Library
116 South Main
Palestine, IL 62451-1244
(618) 586-5580
Hours: Tue–Fri 9:00–4:30, Sat 8:30–
10:30

Frankfort Area Historical Society and Museum
2000 East Saint Louis Street
West Frankfort, IL 62896-1647
(618) 932-6159 (Museum); (618) 937-
4458 (Home)
Mary Alyce Kern
Hours: 16 Dec–31 Jan: Wed–Thur 9:00–
4:00, Sun 1:30–4:00

Frankfort Area Historical Society of Will County
(132 Kansas Street—location)
PO Box 546 (mailing address)
Frankfort, IL 60423-0546
(815) 469-4534; (815) 469-6541
Judy K. Herder, President
Pub. *Frankfort Newsletter*

Franklin County Historical Society
803 North McLeansboro Street
Benton, IL 62812-2732
(618) 435-6947
Bobbie Armstrong, Secretary
(materials are in storage at this time)

Franklin Grove Area Historical Society
110 West Front
Mount Morris, IL 61054
(815) 734-6905
Lynn Asp

Freeburg Historical and Genealogical Society

PO Box 69
Freeburg, IL 62243-0069
(618) 539-5771
Frank X. Heiligenstein
Hours: 9:00–noon
Pub. *Quarterly*

Fulton County Historical and Genealogical Society

45 North Park Drive
Canton, IL 61520
(309) 647-0771
E-mail: mbordner@netins.net
Marjorie R. Bordner, Ph.D., President
Hours: Parlin-Ingersoll Library: Mon–Fri
    9:00–8:00, Sat 9:00–4:00, Sun 1:00–
    4:00
Pub. *Fulton County Historical and
    Genealogical Society Newsletter*,
    quarterly, $12.00 per year subscription
("Long list of published records
    available.")

Galena/Jo Daviess County Historical Society and Museum

211 South Bench Street
Galena, IL 61036-2297
(815) 777-9129; (815) 777-9131 FAX
Daryl Watson, Ph.D., Executive Director
Hours: Museum: Mon–Sun 9:00–4:30
Pub. *Miners' Journal*, quarterly
(no research facilities, most genealogical
    research materials kept at the Galena
    Public Library)
$15.00 per year membership for
    individuals, $25.00 per year
    membership for families, $12.00 per
    year membership for senior citizens

Galesburg Historical Society, Inc.

(586 North Academy Street—location)
1166 North Prairie (mailing address)
Galesburg, IL 61401-2758
(309) 344-2139
Raleigh Barnstead, President

Galewood-Mont Clare Historical Society

1705 North Nashville Avenue
Chicago, IL 60707-3904
(312) 237-8960; (708) 453-4671 FAX
Russell N. Parker, Director
Hours: by appointment
(Chicago neighborhood history)

Gallacia Historical Society

PO Box 489
Gallacia, IL 62935
Jonathan Russell

Gallatin County Historical Society

PO Box 693
Shawneetown, IL 62984
(618) 269-3716
Lucille Lawler, Executive Director and
    Secretary
Pub. *Gallatin County History and
    Families*

Galva Historical Society/Wiley House Museum

906 West Division Street
PO Box 4
Galva, IL 61434-0004
(309) 932-2100
George Swank, President
Hours: May–Sept: Sun 1:00–4:30, and
    by appointment

Garden Prairie Genealogical and Historical Society

PO Box 115
Garden Prairie, IL 61038-0115
(815) 597-1109
Carla Vassmer

Garfield Heritage Society

444 South LaGrange Road
LaGrange, IL 60525-2448
(847) 584-8485
Jerome Johnson, Executive Director
(local history)

Geneseo Historical Association

212 South State Street
Geneseo, IL 61254-1455
(309) 944-3043; (309) 944-3248
    (Curator's home)
Donald Stocks, Curator
Hours: Mar–Dec: Sat–Sun 1:30–4:30,
    and by appointment

Geneva Historical Society

(400 Wheeler Drive—location)
PO Box 345 (mailing address)
Geneva, IL 60134-0345
(630) 232-4951; (630) 232-4561
Lockett Ford Ballard, Jr., Executive
    Director
Hours: Apr–Oct: Wed–Sun 1:00–4:00;
    Research Library: Mon–Fri 9:00–4:00

Glen Ellyn Historical Society

(557 Geneva Road, Glen Ellyn, IL
    60137—location)
PO Box 283 (mailing address)
Glen Ellyn, IL 60138
(630) 858-8696 phone and FAX
    (Museum); (630) 469-1867 (Archives)
http://www.glenellyn.com/historical/
Keith McClow, Executive Director
Hours: Museum: Tue, Wed & Sun 1:30–
    4:30; Archives: Wed 1:00–5:00, Thur
    7:00–9:00, and by special appointment
Pub. *The Messenger*, five times per year
(An 1850s-era museum called "Stacys
    Tavern")
$15.00 per year membership for
    individuals, $25.00 per year
    membership for families, $10.00 per
    year membership for senior citizens

Glencoe Historical Society

(305 Randolph Street—location)
999 Green Bay Road (mailing address)
Glencoe, IL 60022-1263
(847) 835-4935; (847) 835-2638
Alice Glicksberg
Hours: Sept–Apr: second Sun 2:00–4:00;

May: third Sun 2:00–4:00, and by
    appointment

Glenview Area Historical Society

1121 Waukegan Road
Glenview, IL 60025
(847) 724-2235
Hours: Tue 1:00–3:00, Sun 1:00–4:00
(Glenview area history only, limited
    genealogy information; Naval Air
    Station-Glenview, history when it was
    Curtiss-Wright, 1929–1937, and as
    Naval Air Station, 1937–1995)
$15.00/$30.00/$50.00 per year
    membership, $300.00 life
    membership; search fees: $25.00 to
    $100.00

Golden Historical Society

PO Box 148
Golden, IL 62339-0148
(217) 696-4672; (217) 696-2583
    (Curator)
Lois Reason, President
Hours: Jun–early Sept: Sun 1:00–4:00,
    and by appointment

Goode-Barren Historical-Genealogical Society

201 East Callie Street
PO Box 1024
Sesser, IL 62884-0944
(618) 625-2851; (618) 625-5762
Clara Brown
Hours: Mon 10:00–1:00, Wed 10:00–
    3:00 by appointment

Greater Harvard Area Historical Society (McHenry County)

308 North Hart Street
PO Box 505
Harvard, IL 60033-0505
(815) 943-6141
Elaine Fiducci, Curator; Selma
    Davidson, President
Hours: May 18–Nov 16: Wed 9:30–
    11:30, Sun 1:30–4:00
Pub. *Newsletter*, semiannually
$10.00 per year membership for
    individuals

Historical Society of Greater Peotone

213 West North Street
Peotone, IL 60468-9153
(708) 258-3436; (708) 258-3320
Michael R. Morrison, President
search fee: donation plus copying

Greene County Historical and Genealogical Society

221 North Fifth Street
PO Box 137
Carrollton, IL 62016-0137
Barbara B. Daum, President
Hours: Wed & Fri 9:00–2:00
Pub. *Greene County Historical and
    Genealogical Society Newsletter*,
    quarterly
$10.00 per year membership

Griggsville Area Genealogical and Historical Society
PO Box 22
Griggsville, IL 62340-0022
(217) 833-2308; (217) 285-6672
June Johnson
Hours: Mon–Fri 1:00–5:00, and by
appointment

Grundy County Historical Society
PO Box 224
Morris, IL 60450-2329
Henry Barschdorf, President

Hamilton County Historical Society
205 North Washington Street
McLeansboro, IL 62859-1048
(618) 643-4203
Eugene Van Winkle
Hours: Museum on second floor of
McCoy Memorial Library: Fri 1:00–
4:00, and by appointment
(local history and genealogy)

Hampton Historical Society
(601 First Avenue—location)
PO Box 68 (mailing address)
Hampton, IL 61256
(309) 755-0362
Merlin A. Nelson, President
Hours: Museum: Sat–Sun (summer)
2:30–4:30
Pub. *Hampton Historical Society News*,
quarterly
$10.00 per year membership for
individuals, $15.00 per year
membership for families

Hancock County Historical Society
Hancock County Courthouse
PO Box 68
Carthage, IL 62321-0068
Donald Parker, Correspondent
Hours: daily 9:00–3:00 when courthouse
is open
Pub. *Hancock County Historical Society
Newsletter*, quarterly
(local history and genealogy)
$5.00 per year membership; search:
$4.00 per hour plus 25¢ per copy

**The Hanover Park Ontarioville
Historical Commission**
2121 West Lake Street
Hanover Park, IL 60103-4398
(630) 372-4200
Cathy-Ann Romero, Assistant to the
Village Manager

**Hardin County Historical and
Genealogical Society**
PO Box 72
Elizabethtown, IL 62931-0072
(618) 287-2361
Noel E. Hurford, Secretary
$9.00 per year membership

**Henderson County Historical
Society Museum**
RR 1, Box 130
Oquawka, IL 61469-9711

Bill Allaman
Hours: Memorial Day–Labor Day: Sun
& 4 Jul 1:30–4:40
(local history and genealogy)

Henry County Historical Society
PO Box 48
Bishop Hill, IL 61419-9999
(309) 927-3528
Maurice Martin, President
Hours: Museum: Mon–Sun 10:00–4:00

**Henry Historical and Genealogical
Society**
610 North Street
Henry, IL 61537-1226
(309) 364-3272
Connie Swanson, President
Hours: City Library: Mon–Sat 1:00–
5:00, Wed 1:00–8:00
Pub. *Newsletter*, quarterly
(specializes in Marshall County,
especially city of Henry)
$5.00 per year membership

Highland Historical Society
(1739 Broadway and 1464 Old Trenton
Road—location)
PO Box 51
Highland, IL 62249-0051
(618) 654-6781; (618) 654-4259
Lynn Rehberger, President

Highland Park Historical Society
326 Central Avenue
PO Box 56
Highland Park, IL 60035-0056
(847) 432-7090
Betty M. Mills, Executive Director
Hours: Tue–Fri 10:00–3:00, Sat–Sun
2:00–4:00
(local history)
$25.00 per year membership; research
fees vary

Hinsdale Historical Society
15 South Clay
PO Box 336
Hinsdale, IL 60521-0366
(630) 789-2600
Sandy Williams, Archives Chairman
Hours: Wed 11:00–2:00
(people, places and events in Hinsdale)
search fee: donation

Historic Elsah Foundation
(51 Mills Street—location)
PO Box 117 (mailing address)
Elsah, IL 62028-0117
(618) 374-1059
Hours: Thur–Sun (Apr–Nov) 1:00–4:00
Pub. *Elsah History*, biannually
(no genealogy focus)
$10.00 per year membership

Homer Historical Society
(105 North Main Street—location)
RR 1 (mailing address)
Homer, IL 61849-9801
(217) 896-2538
Crystal Allen, President

Homewood Historical Society
(2035 West 183rd Street—location)
PO Box 1144
Homewood, IL 60430-1044
(708) 799-1896 (Museum); (708) 798-
9535 (Home)
Gerald Egdorf; Elaine Egdorf
Hours: Tue & Sat 1:00–3:00 by
appointment

Hoopeston Historical Society
617 East Washington
Hoopeston, IL 60942-1659
(217) 283-7898
Tommy McMillan

Hyde Park Historical Society
5529 South Lake Park
Chicago, IL 60637-1718
(312) 493-1893; (312) 643-8053
Stephen A. Treffman, Archivist
Hours: Sat–Sun 2:00–4:00
Pub. *Hyde Park History*

**Illiana Genealogical and Historical
Society**
(19 East North—location)
PO Box 207 (mailing address)
Danville, IL 61834-0207
(217) 431-8733
Sally Powell, President
Hours: Mon & Wed–Sat 10:00–4:00, Tue
10:00–8:00
Pub. *Illiana Genealogist*; quarterly
(March, June, September, December)
(includes bordering counties of
Vermilion County, IL)
$15.00 per year membership for
individuals, $15.50 per year
membership for couples; research:
$18.00 for two hours

Iroquois County Historical Society
Old Courthouse Museum
103 West Cherry Street
Watseka, IL 60970-1524
(815) 432-2215
Marie Hanford, Executive Secretary
Hours: Mon–Fri 10:30–4:30, Sat–Sun
1:00–4:00
Pub. *Iroquois County Historical Society
Newsletter*, monthly; *The Iroquois
Stalker*, quarterly
(Iroquois County Genealogical Society is
a division of the Iroquois County
Historical Society.)
$5.00 per year membership individuals
(in Historical Society only), additional
$2.00 per year Canadian membership,
additional $10.00 per year other
foreign membership, $7.00 per year
membership for families (includes
spouse and children to 18 years old),
$25.00 per year commercial
membership, $100.00 life membership
for husband and wife

Irving Park Historical Society
4122 North Kedvale
Chicago, IL 60641-2245

(312) 736-2143
William Tyre
(local history)

Itasca Historical Society

Itasca Historical Depot Museum
101 North Catalpa Avenue
Itasca, IL 60143-2050
(630) 773-3363; (630) 773-2257
  (Society); (630) 250-7938 (Museum)
Joan Stinton, Curator
Hours: Summer: Sun 1:00–4:00; Sept–
  May: Sun 1:00–3:00, and by
  appointment

Jackson County Historical Society

1401 Walnut—Lower Level
PO Box 7
Murphysboro, IL 62966-0007
(618) 684-3455
Cliff Swafford, Director
Hours: Wed–Fri 12:00–3:00, Thur 6:30–
  9:00
Pub. *Jacksonian Ventilator*, quarterly
$12.00 per year membership for
  individuals

Jacksonville Area Genealogical and Historical Society

(203 South Fayette Street—library and
  office location)
416 South Main Street (mailing address)
Jacksonville, IL 62650-2904
(217) 673-4241 (Librarian); (217) 245-
  5911 (for appointment)
Mary Frances Alkire, Volunteer Librarian
Hours: weekdays by appointment, Sat
  10:00–4:00
Pub. *Jacksonville Illinois Genealogical
  Journal*, quarterly
$14.00 per year membership (calendar
  year)

Jasper County Historical and Genealogical Society

Newton Public Library
100 South Van Buren Street
Newton, IL 62448-1559
(618) 783-8141 (Library)
Patty Huston, Membership Secretary;
  Mary A. Miller, Editor and
  Corresponding Secretary
Hours: Mon–Sat 10:00–5:00
Pub. *Our Heritage*, monthly
$13.00 per year membership

Jefferson County Historical Society

PO Box 106
Mount Vernon, IL 62864-0106
(618) 242-5423; (618) 242-4337
John Howard

Jersey County Historical Society

108 North Lafayette Street
Jerseyville, IL 62052-1612
(618) 498-2465; (618) 498-3511
Fred Easley, President
Hours: Wed & Sun 1:00–4:00

Joliet Area Historical Society and Museum

17 East Van Buren Street
PO Box 477
Joliet, IL 60431-1211
(815) 722-7003; (815) 726-7171
Dale T. Evans, President
Hours: Tue–Fri noon–3:00, Sat 10:00–
  2:00

Kankakee County Historical Society Museum

801 South Eighth Avenue
Kankakee, IL 60901-4744
(815) 932-5279; (815) 932-9501
Anne L. Chandler
Hours: Mon–Thur 9:30–4:30, Sat–Sun
  1:00–4:00

Kendall County Historical Society

(105 West Center—location)
PO Box 123 (mailing address)
Yorkville, IL 60560-0123
(630) 553-6777
Marilyn Seaton, Librarian
Hours: Wed 9:00–noon
Pub. *Historical Notes, The Newsletter of
  the KCHS*, quarterly, not available by
  subscription
$10.00 per year membership for
  individuals, $15.00 per year
  membership for families; research
  fees: first hour $5.00, each additional
  hour $8.00, plus 15¢ per copy

The Kenilworth Historical Society

415 Kenilworth Avenue
PO Box 181
Kenilworth, IL 60043-1134
(847) 251-2565
Harriet Carlson, Executive Secretary
Hours: Mon 9:00–4:30, Thur 9:00–12:00
  (history of village and early inhabitants,
  not a genealogical collection, no
  family records)

Kewanee Historical Society, Inc.

211 North Chestnut Street
Kewanee, IL 61443-2019
(309) 854-9701; (309) 853-1914
Marcella Richards, Curator
Hours: Fri–Sat 1:30–4:00

Kishwaukee Valley Heritage Society

(700 West Park Avenue, Highway 72
  West—location)
PO Box 59 (mailing address)
Genoa, IL 60135-0059
(815) 784-5498
JoAnn Watson, President
Hours: by appointment

LaGrange Area Historical Society

444 South LaGrange Road
LaGrange, IL 60525-2448
(708) 482-4248
Alice Petrik
Hours: Wed 9:30–noon, last Sun 1:00–
  4:00

LaHarpe Historical and Genealogical Society

East Main Street
PO Box 289
LaHarpe, IL 61450
Ada Hubbard, Vice President; Lois
  Bradshaw, Secretary
Hours: Museum: Mon & Sat 9:00–11:00
  & 1:00–4:00
Pub. *Historical Society Newsletter*,
  quarterly
$5.00 per year inactive membership,
  $9.00 per year active membership

Lake County Historical Society Collection

Donnelley Library, Special Collections
  Department
Lake Forest College
5555 North Sheridan Road
Lake Forest, IL 60045-2396
(847) 234-3100 (Mon–Fri 8:30–5:00)
Arthur Miller, Librarian

Lake Forest-Lake Bluff Historical Society

Gorton Community Center
400 East Illinois Road
PO Box 82
Lake Forest, IL 60045-0082
(847) 234-3133; (847) 234-5253
Elizabeth E. Brown, President
Hours: Tue & Thur 9:00–noon, and by
  appointment

Lakes Region Historical Society

PO Box 240
Antioch, IL 60002-0240
(847) 395-0048
Betty Williams
Hours: Sat 11:00–3:00

Lansing Historical Museum and Society

2750 Indiana Avenue
PO Box 1776
Lansing, IL 60438-2226
(708) 474-6160; (708) 474-9384
Betty Humphrey, Curator; Richard W.
  Tereba, President
Hours: Mon 6:00–8:00, Wed 10:00–
  noon, Sun (Sept–May) 10:00–noon

LaSalle County Historical Society

(Museum, Canal and Union Streets,
  along Illinois/Michigan Canal—
  location)
PO Box 278 (mailing address)
Utica, IL 61373-0278
(815) 667-4861
Mary Toraason, Director
Hours: Winter: Fri–Sun noon–4:00;
  summer: Wed–Fri 10:00–4:00, Sat–
  Sun noon–4:00
(library)

Lawrence County Historical Society

Eleventh and State
PO Box 511
Lawrenceville, IL 62439-0511

(618) 943-2300
Michael Neal, President
$3.00 per year membership for
individuals, $5.00 per year
membership for couples

Lebanon Historical Society
309 West Saint Louis Street
Lebanon, IL 62254-1516
(618) 537-4498
Harrison Church

Lee County Historical Society
(Boyd Street near Galena Street
Bridge—location)
PO Box 58
Dixon, IL 61021-0058
(815) 284-3157; (815) 288-6099
Stella Grobe

**Lemont Area Historical Society
Museum**
306 Lemont Street
PO Box 126
Lemont, IL 60439-0126
(630) 257-2972
Sonia Kallick
Hours: Tue–Sat 10:00–2:00, Sun 1:00–
4:00
(local history, genealogy)

Lena Area Historical Society
427 West Grove Street
PO Box 620
Lena, IL 61048
(815) 369-2215; (815) 369-4555
Wieland Kayser; Margaret Scholtz
Hours: Sat–Sun 1:00–4:00 by
appointment

LeRoy Historical Society
301 East Cedar
LeRoy, IL 61752
John Tompkins, President
Pub. *Heritage of the Prairie*

**Lexington Genealogical and
Historical Society**
318 West Main Street
Lexington, IL 61753-1328
(309) 365-4591
Verda Gerwick, President
Hours: Tue–Sat 9:00–4:00
(McLean, Livingston and Woodford
County, Illinois, cemetery records)
$20.00 per year membership

Leyden Historical Society
PO Box 506
Franklin Park, IL 60131
(847) 678-1929; (847) 455-4269
Daniel Pritchett

**Libertyville-Mundelein Historical
Society, Inc.**
Cook Memorial Library
413 North Milwaukee Avenue
Libertyville, IL 60048-2280
(847) 362-2330; (847) 362-3130
Douglass D. Getchell, Jr.
Hours: Sun (Jun–Aug) 2:00–4:00, first
two weekends in Dec 1:00–5:00

Pub. *Newsletter*, monthly
(interested in The Ansel B. Cook
Victorian Museum)
from $5.00 per year membership for
senior citizens to $100.00 life
membership

The Lisle Heritage Society
Lisle Station Park
919 Burlington
Lisle, IL 60532
(630) 968-2747
Edgar L. Land, President

Livingston County Historical Society
(Jones House, 314 East Madison Street
and Catherine V. Yost Museum, 298
West Water Street—location)
PO Box 680 (mailing address)
Pontiac, IL 61764-0999
(815) 844-3457
Laura Sellmyer, President

**Logan County Genealogical and
Historical Society**
(11 Arcade Building—location)
PO Box 283 (mailing address)
Lincoln, IL 62656
(217) 732-3988; (217) 732-7148
Mildred Wickline, President

Lombard Historical Society
23 West Maple Street
Lombard, IL 60148-2512
(630) 629-1885; (630) 629-9927 FAX
http://www.tccafe.com/apeck6/
peck0.html
Lorri Mahoney, Interim Director
Hours: staffed full-time; Tours: Wed–Sat
& Sun 1:00–4:00, and by appointment
Pub. *Lombard Historical Society
Newsletter*, quarterly
$10.00 per year membership for
individuals, $15.00 per year
membership for families of two, $1.00
per year membership for students

Long Grove Historical Society
(Historical Lane—location)
RFD, Box 3110 (mailing address)
Long Grove, IL 60047
(847) 634-6155
Hours: May–Dec: second Wed & third
Sun 10:00–2:00

Lyndon Historical Society
405 First Street
PO Box 112
Lyndon, IL 61261-0112
(815) 778-4511
L. Gene Harrington, President

Lyons Historical Commission
3910 Barry Point Road
PO Box 392
Lyons, IL 60534-0392
(708) 447-5815
Lloyd Adamski, President
Hours: Mar–Nov: first Sun 1:00–4:00
(local history)

Mackinaw Historical Society
RR 1, Box 260
Mackinaw, IL 61755-9637
(309) 359-4001
Ross Coil, President

Macon County Historical Society
5580 North Fork Road
Decatur, IL 62521-1859
(217) 422-4919
Mary C. Talbott, Director
Hours: Museum: Tue–Sun 1:00–4:00;
Office: Mon–Fri 8:00–4:30
Pub. *MCHS Newsletter*, monthly
(Macon County and Decatur)
$15.00 per year membership for
individuals

Macoupin County Historical Society
(Breckenridge Street—location)
PO Box 432 (mailing address)
Carlinville, IL 62626-0432
(217) 854-3939; (217) 854-8916
Lucy Klaus
Hours: Wed (Mar–Nov) 10:00–2:00, Sun
(Jun–Aug) 1:00–5:00

**Madison County Historical Society
Museum and Library**
715 North Main Street
Edwardsville, IL 62025
(618) 656-7562
Mrs. Marion Sperling, Librarian
Hours: Wed–Fri 9:00–4:00, Sun 1:00–
4:00, and groups by appointment
Pub. *Museum News*, two times per year
(Madison County area history and
genealogy)
$10.00 per year membership in
Historical Society, $100.00 per year
membership in James Madison Society

Maine West Historical Society
Main West High School
Social Science Department
1755 South Wolf Road
Des Plaines, IL 60018-1994
(847) 827-6176

**Manhattan Township Historical
Society**
(Manhattan Public Library, 240
Whitson—location)
PO Box 53
Manhattan, IL 60442-0053
(815) 478-3374; (815) 478-3987
Janet Werner, President
Hours: Mon–Fri 9:00–4:00

Manito Historical Society
PO Box 304
Manito, IL 61546-0304
(309) 968-6985
Donna Thompson, President
Pub. *Jail House Key*, monthly
$5.00 per year membership

Manteno Historical Society
192 West Third
Manteno, IL 60950-1104

(815) 468-3480; (815) 468-8002
Wendell Marr, President
Hours: by appointment
(local history and genealogy)

Maquon Historical Association
(South end of West Street—location)
PO Box 93 (mailing address)
Maquon, IL 61458-0093
(309) 875-3481; (309) 875-3342
Beulah Donaldson, Secretary; Robert
   Bird

**Marion County Genealogical and
Historical Society**
(Bryan-Bennett Library, 217 West
   Main—location)
PO Box 342 (mailing address)
Salem, IL 62881
Wanda Fatheree, Archivist
Hours: Archives: Wed noon–4:00, and by
   appointment when library is open
Pub. *Footprints in Marion County*,
   quarterly
$15.00 per year membership (beginning
   in July); free queries

**Marissa Historical and Genealogical
Society**
(610 South Main Street—location)
PO Box 47 (mailing address)
Marissa, IL 62257-0047
(618) 295-2562
Elda L. Jones, President
Hours: Wed 1:00–4:00, and anytime by
   appointment
Pub. *Branching Out from Saint Clair
   County, Illinois*, quarterly (November,
   February, May, August)
$15.00 per year membership (beginning
   in Oct)

Marshall County Historical Society
314 Fifth Street
Lacon, IL 61540
(309) 246-2349; (309) 246-6565
Eleanor H. Bussell, Curator
Hours: weekdays through Friday:
   mornings
Pub. *Newsletter*, quarterly
(genealogy searches for Marshall
   County)
$10.00 per year membership

Mascoutah Historical Society
(3 West Main Street—location)
504 North Jefferson Street (mailing
   address)
Mascoutah, IL 62258-1421
Carol Klopmeyer, President
Pub. *Newsletter*, intermittently

**Mason County Genealogical and
Historical Society**
PO Box 246
Havana, IL 62644

Massac County Historical Society
23 Chick Street
Metropolis, IL 62960
Paul Fellows

Matteson Historical Society
813 School Avenue
Matteson, IL 60443-1849
(708) 748-3033; (708) 748-2326 FAX
E-mail: lrmathis@lincolnnet.net
Deanna M. Lovell, Director
Hours: Mon–Tue 9:00–5:00, Sat 1:00–
   3:00
Pub. *The Matteson Bell*, four times per
   year
$7.50 per year membership for
   individuals, $10.00 per year
   membership for husband/wife, $25.00
   per year Contributing membership,
   $50.00 per year Supporting
   membership, $125.00 life membership

Maywood Historical Society
202 South Second Avenue
Maywood, IL 60153-2304
(708) 344-4282
A. Becker, President

**McDonough County Historical
Society**
(address withheld upon request)

McHenry County Historical Society
6422 Main Street
PO Box 434
Union, IL 60180-0434
(815) 923-2267; (815) 923-2271 FAX
Nancy J. Fike, Museum Administrator
Hours: Library: Tue–Fri 9:00–4:30 by
   appointment; Museum (May–Oct):
   Tue–Fri & Sun 1:00–4:00
Pub. *The Tracer*, quarterly
("Strictly McHenry County history and
   genealogy: obituary files, biography
   files, maps, pictures, abstracts, Bibles,
   club/organization history, diaries.")
$12.50 per year membership for
   individuals, $20.00 per year
   membership for families, $7.50 per
   year membership for senior citizens
   (60+); non-member use of library:
   $1.00 per hour plus copy costs; no
   extensive genealogy research by mail

McLean County Historical Society
Genealogical Library
Old Courthouse, 200 North Main Street
Bloomington, IL 61701-3912
(309) 827-0428; (309) 827-0100 FAX
E-mail: mchs@dave-world.net
http://www.dave-world.net/community/
   mchs/mchs.html
Greg Koos, Executive Director
Hours: Mon & Wed–Sat 10:00–5:00, Tue
   10:00–9:00

Melrose Park Historical Society
(1000 North 25th Avenue, Melrose Park,
   IL 60160—location)
PO Box 1453 (mailing address)
Melrose Park, IL 60161

Menard County Historical Society
125 South Seventh Street
Petersburg, IL 62675-1554

(217) 632-7363; (217) 636-8310
Melody Grossbaier; Eddie Dirks
Hours: Mon–Fri 9:00–noon; Jun–Aug
   Mon–Fri 9:00–noon, Tue–Sat 12:30–
   4:30

**Mendota Museum and Historical
Society**
901 Washington Street
PO Box 901
Mendota, IL 61342
(815) 539-6507; (815) 539-6025 FAX

Mercer County Historical Society
1406 S.E. Second Avenue
Aledo, IL 61231-2504
(309) 582-2280; (309) 582-7463
   (Curator)
Ruth Giffin, Curator
Hours: Apr–Oct: Wed & Sat–Sun 1:00–
   5:00, and by appointment
$5.00 per year membership

Meredosia Area Historical Society
(Main Street—location)
PO Box 304 (mailing address)
Meredosia, IL 62665-0304
(217) 584-1356; (217) 584-1281; (217)
   584-1571 FAX
Dora Dawson
Hours: Tue–Wed & Fri–Sun 1:00–5:00

Midlothian Historical Society
(14609 Springfield—location)
14801 Pulaski (mailing address)
Midlothian, IL 60445
(708) 389-0200; (708) 389-0055; (708)
   389-0255 FAX
Deborah J. McAdams
Hours: first & third Sat 11:00–2:00

Monroe County Historical Society
700 South Church Street
PO Box 48
Waterloo, IL 62298-0048
(618) 939-3088; (618) 782-4592; (618)
   939-4633 FAX
Michael J. Wightman, President
Hours: by appointment
(local history and genealogy)

**Historical Society of Montgomery
County**
Solomon Harkey House
(South Broad Street—location)
904 South Main (mailing address)
Hillsboro, IL 62049-1738
(217) 532-3329; (217) 532-2958
Idabel Evans

Morgan County Historical Society
PO Box 1033
Jacksonville, IL 62651-1033
(217) 245-7019
William B. Ricks, Treasurer
("We are not involved in genealogical
   research.")
$5.00 per year membership

Morrison Historical Society

(219 East Main Street—museum
location)
PO Box 1 (mailing address)
Morrison, IL 61270-0001
(815) 772-3287
E-mail: cgronner@essex1.com
Curt J. Gronner, DDS, President
Hours: Sat–Sun 1:00–4:00, and by
appointment
(most of genealogical collection is
duplicated by Odell Public Library)
$5.00 per year membership for
individuals (calendar year), $100.00
per year Patron membership

Morrisonville Historical Society

606 Carlin Street
PO Box 227
Morrisonville, IL 62546-0227
(217) 526-3543
Dorothy Bullard, President
Hours: by appointment

Morton Grove Historical Society

Morton Grove Historical Museum
(Haupt-Yehl House)
Harrer Park, 6240 Dempster Street
PO Box 542
Morton Grove, IL 60053-2946
(847) 965-7185; (847) 965-7447 (Park)
Fred N. Huscher, Coordinator
Hours: Wed 11:00–3:00, Sun 2:00–4:00

Moultrie County Historical and Genealogical Society

Moultrie County Historical and
Genealogical Research Library
Heritage Center, 117 East Harrison
PO Box 588
Sullivan, IL 61951-0588
(217) 728-4085
Sue Durbin, Genealogist
Hours: Mon & Sat 1:00–5:00
Pub. *Moultrie County Heritage*,
quarterly; *Moultrie County Historical
and Genealogical Society Newsletter*,
monthly
$9.00 per year membership for
individuals, $12.00 per year
membership for families of two, $1.00
per year membership for each
additional family membership

Mound City Civic and Historical Association

314 Main Street
Mound City, IL 62963-1128
Frederick Winkler

Mount Greenwood Historical Society

11010 South Kedzie Avenue
Chicago, IL 60655-2222
(312) 239-2805
Bonnie Azeling, President
(local history library)

Mount Prospect Historical Society Museum

(1100 South Linneman Road and 101
South Maple—location)
PO Box 81 (mailing address)
Mount Prospect, IL 60056-0081
(847) 392-9006; (847) 956-6777
Michelle Oberly

Mount Pulaski Township Historical Society

(108 South Washington Street—museum
location)
PO Box 12 (mailing address)
Mount Pulaski, IL 62548-0012
Phyllis Bryson, President; Tom and
Waneta Stephens, Editors
Hours: Sept–May: Thur–Sat 1:00–4:00;
Jun–Aug: Tue–Sat 1:00–4:00
Pub. *Mt. Pulaski Township Historical
Society*, quarterly
$15.00 per year membership for
individuals, $25.00 per year
membership for couples, $150.00 life
membership, $225.00 life membership
for couples; free queries

Moweaqua Area Historical Society

(100 Block of East Main Street—
location)
103 Birch Street (mailing address)
Moweaqua, IL 62550-1301
(217) 768-3228; (217) 768-3019
(Museum)
Howard Knight; Bruce Sarver
Hours: meetings at Moweaqua Coal
Mine Museum, 129 South Main Street,
Moweaqua, IL 62550-1028: third Tue
7:00

Mulkeytown Area Historical Society

PO Box 485
Mulkeytown, IL 62865
Sarah Furlow, Secretary

Nauvoo Historical Society

1380 Mulholland Street
PO Box 69
Nauvoo, IL 62354-0338
(217) 453-2528
Mary Logan, President
Hours: May 1–Oct 31: 9:00–5:00
Pub. *Nauvoo Historical Society
Newsletter*, quarterly
(operates three facilities: restored home
museum, Resource Center, and a
museum undergoing restoration)
$5.00 per year membership; research:
$4.00 per hour

New Boston Historical Society and Museum

202 Main Street
PO Box 284
New Boston, IL 61272-0284
(309) 587-8640; (309) 587-8181 phone
and FAX
Peggie Puckett; Cindy Marston
Hours: Apr–Oct: Sat–Sun 1:00–5:00

New Lenox Area Historical Society

c/o New Lenox Public Library
516 South Cedar Road
New Lenox, IL 60451-1796
(815) 485-9139
Wendy Elliot-Manheim

Newport Township Historical Society

Wadsworth Road
PO Box 98
Wadsworth, IL 60083-0098
(847) 623-0939
Grace Shields, President

Niles Historical Society

8970 Milwaukee Avenue
Niles, IL 60714-1737
(847) 390-0160; (847) 647-0185
Marilyn Brown
Hours: Wed & Fri 10:30–3:00

The North Eastern Illinois Historical Council (NEIL)

7007 Fargo Avenue
Niles, IL 60714-3719
(847) 390-0160; (847) 647-0185
(Chairman)
Marilyn Brown, Chairman
("An organization of societies and
libraries who gather in an attempt to
learn more in order to create better
historical societies with amateur or
volunteer help and little money; it
does not serve the genealogist's needs
though individual members may.")

Northbrook Historical Society

1776 Walters Avenue
PO Box 2021
Northbrook, IL 60065
(847) 998-1322; (847) 564-1824
Janis L. Harman; Martha Brand
Hours: first Sun 2:00–4:00

Northern Illinois Historical Society

505 South Midlothian Road
Mundelein, IL 60060-2633
(847) 949-1776
Richard F. Johnson, President
Pub. *Northern Illinois Record*

Norwood Park Historical Society

5624 North Newark Avenue
Chicago, IL 60631-3533
(773) 631-4633
Thomas P. Spenny, President
Hours: Sat 12:00–4:00, and by
appointment
Pub. *The Journal of the Norwood Park
Historical Society*, quarterly
$15.00 per year membership for
individuals, $50.00 per year
membership for businesses

Oak Brook Historical Society

PO Box 3821
Oak Brook, IL 60522-3821
(708) 654-2982; (708) 833-8154
Arlene Birkhahn, President

Oak Forest Historical Society

15440 South Central Avenue
Oak Forest, IL 60452-2104
(708) 687-4050
LaVerne Schultz

Oak Lawn Historical Society

(9526 South Cook Avenue—location)
4332 West 109th Street (mailing address)
Oak Lawn, IL 60453

Historical Society of Oak Park and River Forest

(217 Home Avenue, Oak Park, IL
    60302—location)
PO Box 771 (mailing address)
Oak Park, IL 60303-0771
(708) 848-6755
Frank Lipo, Executive Director
Hours: Research: Tue & Thur; Tours:
    Thur–Sun P.M.
Pub. *Village Yesteryears*, bimonthly
$25.00 per year membership

Oakland Historical Foundation

(Corner of Washington and Walnut
    Streets—location)
PO Box 431 (mailing address)
Oakland, IL 61943-0431
(217) 346-3274; (217) 346-3365
June Johnson; Zora Moore
Hours: May–Sept: Sat–Sun 1:00–4:00,
    and by appointment
(history from churches)

Odell Prairie Trails Genealogical and Historical Society

PO Box 82
Odell, IL 60460-0082
(815) 998-2324
Lorraine Hare, Secretary
Hours: by appointment
(Livingston and local history)
$5.00 per year membership

O'Fallon Historical Society

PO Box 344
O'Fallon, IL 62269-0344
(618) 632-5216 (President)
Berneice T. Reidelberger, President

Ogle County Historical Society

Sixth and Franklin Streets
PO Box 183
Oregon, IL 61061-0183
(815) 732-6876 (Mrs. Wood)
Mrs. Leonard Wood, Board Member
Hours: May–Oct: Thur 9:00 A.M.–11:00
    A.M., Sun 1:00–4:00; tours by request
Pub. *Ogle County Historical Society
    "Gazette,"* quarterly
$10.00 per year membership for
    individuals, $200.00 life membership;
    search fees: $5.00 plus copy costs

Oglesby Historical Society

(128 West Walnut Street—location)
100 Oak Street (mailing address)
Oglesby, IL 61348
(815) 883-3619
Evelyn Moyle

Hours: Mon, Wed & Fri 10:00–5:00,
    Tue, Thur & Sat 12:30–5:00, Tue–
    Thur 6:00–8:00

Old Six Mile Historical Society

3279 Maryville Road
PO Box 483
Granite City, IL 62040-0483
Georgia Engelke, Curator
Hours: Sun 1:00–4:00, special tours by
    appointment

Olmsted Historical Society

PO Box 64
Olmsted, IL 62970-0064
(618) 342-6416; (618) 742-8194
Jeanne Edwards

Orland Historical Society

PO Box 324
Orland Park, IL 60462-0324
(708) 349-0065
Don Gee

Oswegoland Heritage Association

(72 Polk Street—location)
PO Box 23 (mailing address)
Oswego, IL 60543
(630) 554-2999
Judith A. Wheeler, President of the
    Board
(collection for genealogical research on
    Kendall County families; Oswego
    history and genealogy, school
    material)
$5.00 per year membership

Palatine Historical Society

(Clayson House Museum, 224 East
    Palatine Road, Palatine, IL 60067—
    location)
PO Box 134 (mailing address)
Palatine, IL 60078-0134
(847) 991-6460
Marilyn Pedersen, Museum Coordinator
Hours: Tue & Thur 10:00–4:00, Sun
    1:30–4:30
Pub. *Palatine Palaver*, four times per
    year
$10.00 per year membership for
    individuals, $15.00 per year
    membership for families, $5.00 per
    year membership for individuals over
    60 or under 19 years of age

Palestine Historical Society

413 South Lincoln
Palestine, IL 62451

Palos Heights Historical Society

City of Palos Heights
7607 College Drive
Palos Heights, IL 60463

Palos Historical Society

c/o Palos Park Library
12330 Forest Glen Boulevard
Palos Park, IL 60464
(708) 361-3118; (708) 448-1410
John Rogers, Curator

Hours: Tue 9:00–1:00, and by
    appointment
$7.50 per year membership

Park Forest Historical Society

Park Forest Public Library
400 Lakewood Boulevard
Park Forest, IL 60466-1684
(708) 748-3731 (Library); (708) 748-
    8829 FAX (Library)
Jane Nicoll, Archivist; Mr. Magne B.
    Olson, President
Hours: Library: Mon–Thur 10:00–9:00,
    Fri 10:00–6:00, Sat 10:00–5:00, Sun
    (Sept–May) 2:00–5:00
Pub. *Prologue*, occasionally
$10.00 per year membership

Park Ridge Historical Society

41 Prairie
Park Ridge, IL 60068
(847) 696-1973
Hours: Mar–Dec: Sat 10:00–1:00
$10.00 per year membership for
    individuals, $15.00 per year
    membership for families, $100.00 life
    membership

Pecatonica Historical Society

PO Box 298
Pecatonica, IL 61063-0599
Jane Nabor, Treasurer

Peoria Historical Society

c/o Bradley University
Special Collections Center/Cullum Davis
    Library
1501 W. Bradley
Peoria, IL 61625
(309) 677-2822; (309) 677-2823; (309)
    677-2827 FAX
Charles Frey
Hours: Mon–Fri 9:00–noon & 1:00–4:30
Pub. *PHS Newsletter*

Perry County Historical Society

(Perry County Jail Museum, 108 W.
    Jackson Street, Pinkneyville, IL
    62274—location)
PO Box 1013 (mailing address)
DuQuoin, IL 62832-5013
(618) 357-2225
Jean Ibendahl
Hours: Thur 4:00–6:00, Sat 10:00–4:00,
    Sun 1:00–4:00

Piatt County Historical and Genealogical Society

(Courthouse Annex—location)
PO Box 111 (mailing address)
Monticello, IL 61856-0111
Betty Varner, Librarian
Hours: Mon & Wed 1:00–4:00
Pub. *Piatt County Historical and
    Genealogical Society Newsletter*,
    quarterly
$8.00 per year membership

Pike County Historical Society and Museum

(400 Block of East Jefferson—location)
PO Box 44 (mailing address)
Pittsfield, IL 62363-0044
(217) 285-4618
Elizabeth L. Lacy, Museum Director
Hours: May–Oct 31: 1:30–4:00
Pub. *Pike County Historical Society Newsletter* ("does not cover genealogy at this time")
$5.00 per year membership; donation for search (not included in membership)

Piper City Community Historical Society

39 West Main
Piper City, IL 60959
(815) 686-2414; (815) 686-2374
Skip Fincklin
Hours: first Sat 9:30–11:30

Plainfield Historical Society Museum

217 East Main Street
PO Box 291
Plainfield, IL 60544
(815) 436-4073
Miette Rutten, Museum Director
Hours: Sat 1:00–4:00

Polo Historical Society

125 North Franklin Street
Polo, IL 61064-1506
(815) 946-2716
Keith McGuire, President

Pope County Historical Society

Main Street
PO Box 387
Golconda, IL 62938-0387
(618) 683-7551; (618) 683-3050
Paul Trovillion; Mabel Trovillion

Prairie Historians

PO Box 301
Waltonville, IL 62894
Hours: meetings in the Waltonville Universalist Church: fourth Tue (Mar, Jun & Sept) 7:30 P.M., first Tue (Dec) 7:30 P.M.
Pub. *Prairie Historian*, quarterly (March, June, September, December)
$6.00 per year membership

Historical Association of Princeville

130 North Walnut
PO Box 608
Princeville, IL 61559-9535
(309) 385-2394
Finch Stowell
Hours: May–Oct: Sat 9:00–11:00, and by appointment

Prophetstown Area Historical Society

320 Washington Street
Prophetstown, IL 61277
(815) 537-2818; (815) 537-2668
Dick Sommers; Mary Sommers

Hours: Sat 10:00–noon by appointment
(local history and genealogy)

Putnam County Historical Society

Rt. 26 and Power Road
Hennepin, IL 61327
(815) 925-7560
Julia S. Edgerley, President
Hours: 9:00–3:00
Pub. *Putnam Past Times*, quarterly
(30,000 indexed names for genealogists)
$10.00 per year membership; search fee: $5.00 per hour

Historical Society of Quincy and Adams County

425 South 12th Street
Quincy, IL 62301-4303
(217) 222-1835
Philip Germann, Executive Director
Hours: Mon–Fri 10:00–2:00

Randolph County Historical Society

104 Hillcrest Drive
Chester, IL 62233-2250
(618) 826-2667 phone & FAX
Emily B. Lyons, Curator, Randolph County Archives and Museum
Hours: by appointment
Pub. *Footprints*
(Charter Oak School; Fr & Am Creole House in Prairie du Rocher)
$10.00 per year membership for individuals, $20.00 per year membership for families, $200.00 life membership; search fees: donation if possible

Ravenswood-Lake View Historical Association

Conrad Sulzer Regional Library
Historical Room
4455 North Lincoln Avenue
Chicago, IL 60625-2192
(312) 744-7616; (312) 744-2899 FAX
Glenn E. Humphreys, Special Collections Librarian
Hours: by appointment
Pub. *RLVHA Newsletter*, irregularly
(history of neighborhoods on Chicago's North Side)
$3.00 per year general membership

Richland County Illinois Genealogical and Historical Society

(Olney Central College, Anderson Library—library location)
PO Box 202 (mailing address)
Olney, IL 62450-0202
(618) 869-2425 (Editor)
Jan Doan, President
Hours: when college library is open: Mon–Thur 8:00–7:30, Fri 8:00–4:00
Pub. *Footprints Past and Present*, quarterly; *Richland County Genealogical Society Newsletter*, bimonthly
$15.00 per year membership

Ridge Historical Society

10621 South Seeley Avenue
Chicago, IL 60643-2618
(773) 881-1675 (recorded message)
Sue H. Delves, President
Hours: Thur & Sun: 2:00–5:00, and by appointment
Pub. *RHS NewsLetter*, bimonthly
(stories of people in Beverly/Morgan Park in Chicago's far southwest corner, 1850 onward; research into community's rich architectural heritage)
from $20.00 per year membership

River Grove Historical Commission

(2621 Thatcher Avenue—location)
2561 North Budd Street (mailing address)
River Grove, IL 60171-1736
(708) 453-8000
Loretta Page

Riverdale Historical Society

c/o Riverdale Library
208 West 144th Street
Riverdale, IL 60627-2788
(708) 841-3311
Mary Thillman
Hours: Mon & Wed–Thur 9:30–8:00, Tue 10:00–2:00, Fri 9:30–6:00, Sat 9:30–4:00, Sun 11:00–3:00

Riverside Historical Commission

Riverside Historical Museum
27 Riverside Road
Riverside Village, IL 60546-2264
(708) 447-2542 (Museum); (708) 447-6228 FAX
Ann Nowotarski, Chairman R.H.C.
Hours: Sat 10:00–2:00

Robbins Historical Society

13822 South Central Park Avenue
PO Box 1561
Robbins, IL 60472-1561
(708) 389-5393; (708) 385-8940
Tyrone Haymore
Hours: 10:00–4:30

Rock Island County Historical Society

Rock Island County Historical Research Library
822 11th Avenue
PO Box 632
Moline, IL 61266-0632
(309) 764-8590
Lloyd Efflandt, President; N. Lucille Sampson, Archivist
Hours: Mon & Thur–Sat 9:00–5:00, Sun (last Sun in May through first Sun in Dec) 1:30–4:30, closed Christmas and New Year's weeks
Pub. *Rock Island County Historical Society Newsletter*, semiannually
("John H. Hauberg Collection, Belgian Book Collection, oral tapes, photographs, family collections, books and manuscripts that fit our purpose:

to collect, preserve and disseminate Rock Island County history.")
$15.00 per year membership for individuals; $10.00 per hour research plus photocopying

Rockford Historical Society
Rockford Museum Association
6799 Guilford Road
Rockford, IL 61107-2613
(815) 962-6993
Eldora Ozanne, Secretary

Rockton Township Historical Society
PO Box 22
Rockton, IL 61072
(815) 624-4541
Hester Bigelow
Hours: 1 Jun–15 Sep: Sun 1:00–4:00; Dec: first Sun by appointment

Rogers Park/West Ridge Historical Society
6424 North Western
Chicago, IL 60645-5422
(312) 764-4078; (312) 764-2401; (312) 274-7297 FAX
Mary Jo Doyle, Executive Director
Hours: Mon, Wed & Fri 10:00–5:00, Thur 7:00 P.M.–9:00 P.M.

Romeoville Historical Society
Fountaindale Library
Romeo Road
PO Box 504 R
Romeoville, IL 60441
Dorothy Hassert
Hours: first & 4th Thur 7:00 P.M.–9:00 P.M., and by appointment

Roselle Historical Foundation
102 South Prospect Street
Roselle, IL 60172-2026
(630) 351-5300; (630) 351-5417
Joseph L. Devlin, Administrator
Hours: 10:00–3:00; Museum: Sun 2:00–4:00, and by appointment
Pub. *Etched in Time*, every five to six years, $20.00 per issue for hardcover, $12.00 per issue for paperback

Rossville Historical Society
108 West Attica Street
PO Box 263
Rossville, IL 60963
(217) 748-6194 (President); (217) 748-6625 (First Vice President)
Eva V. Neeland, President; Tom Cornell, First Vice President
Hours: Tue–Sat noon–4:00; monthly meetings
Pub. *Ross/South Ross Ramblings*, quarterly
(family local histories, cemetery books)
$2.00 per year regular membership, $10.00 per year Sustaining membership, $100.00 life membership for husband and wife; free queries for members; search fees: $5.00 per hour

Saint Charles Heritage Center
(Dunham Hunt Museum of the Saint Charles Heritage Center, 304 Cedar Avenue—location)
2 East Main Street (mailing address)
Saint Charles, IL 60174
(630) 584-6967; (630) 443-6733 (Museum); (630) 377-4487 FAX
Karen Ponton, Administrator
Hours: Tue–Sun (Jun–Aug) noon–4:00, and by appointment
Pub. *The Charlemange* [sic], quarterly
$25.00 per year membership for individuals, $40.00 per year membership for families, $10.00 per year membership for senior citizens and students, $125.00 per year Patron membership; Junior Historical Society for children aged 7–14 years, free with family membership, or $10.00 per year; free admission; local historical research service: $100.00–$150.00 minimum

Saint Clair County Historical Society
(602 Fulton Street—location)
Victorian Museum-Home
701 East Washington Street (mailing address)
Belleville, IL 62220-3846
(618) 234-0600
Norma Walker, Office Administrator
Hours: Museum: Mon–Fri 10:00–2:00, Sun 2:00–4:00
Pub. *Saint Clair County Historical Society Journal*

Sandwich Historical Society
Lafayette and Railroad Streets
PO Box 82
Sandwich, IL 60548
(815) 786-7936; (815) 786-2092
Roger Peterson, President
Hours: May–Oct: Sun 1:00–4:00

Sangamon County Historical Society
308 East Adams
Springfield, IL 62701
(217) 522-2500

Schiller Park Historical Society
(4200 Old River Road—location)
9526 Irving Park Road (mailing address)
Schiller Park, IL 60176
(847) 671-8513; (847) 678-6444; (847) 678-0567 FAX
June Oulund
Hours: Mon 9:00–noon by appointment, second Sun 1:00–5:00

Scott County Historical Society
PO Box 85
Winchester, IL 62694-0085
(217) 742-5575
John Rutherford
Hours: 10:00–4:00

Sheffield Historical Society
Washington and Cook Streets
Sheffield, IL 61361

(815) 454-2788; (815) 454-2686
Margaret B. Schmitt
Hours: Tue–Sun noon–4:00

Shelby County Historical and Genealogical Society
151 South Washington Street
PO Box 286
Shelbyville, IL 62565
(217) 774-2260
E-mail: shgensoc@bmmhnet.com
http://www.bmmhnet.com/shgensoc
June McCain, Vice President and Librarian
Hours: Apr–Oct: Mon–Sat 10:00–4:00; Nov–Mar: Mon & Fri–Sat 10:00–4:00
Pub. *Shelby County Ancestors*, quarterly; *Shelby County Historical and Genealogical Society Newsletter*, four times per year
$15.00 per year membership for individuals (calendar year), $17.00 per year membership for husband and wife, $150.00 life membership for individuals, $200.00 life membership for husband and wife

Sidell Community Historical Society
PO Box 42
Sidell, IL 61876
(217) 288-9030
Clifford Guthrie
Hours: by appointment

Sidney Historical Society
PO Box 87
Sidney, IL 61877-0087
(217) 688-2974
Kevin Erb
Hours: by appointment

Skokie Historical Society
8031 Floral Avenue
Skokie, IL 60077
(847) 673-1888
Hours: Tue–Sat noon–4:00
Pub. *Bell Ringer*, quarterly
search fee: $10.00 per hour

South Beloit Historical Society
440 Oak Grove Avenue
South Beloit, IL 61080-1949
Charles Novachek

South Holland Historical Society
16250 Wausau Avenue
PO Box 48
South Holland, IL 60473-0096
(708) 596-2722
Pauline Schaap, President
Hours: Sat 1:00–4:00
Pub. *Ohionskin*, quarterly
$5.00 per year membership for individuals

South Suburban Genealogical and Historical Society
320 East 161st Place
PO Box 96
South Holland, IL 60473-0096
(708) 333-9474

http://www.rootsweb.com/saveall.gif
Alice DeBoer, Librarian
Hours: Mon, Wed & Fri 10:00–4:00, Tue
1:00–9:00, Sat 11:00–4:00
Pub. *Where the Trails Cross*, quarterly;
Newsletter, monthly
(Pullman Car Company employment
records, ca 1890–1940)
$15.00 per year membership

The South Suburban Heritage Association
17130 67th Court
PO Box 716
Tinley Park, IL 60477-3450
(708) 614-8713
June M. Staackmann, Executive Director
Pub. *The Heritage Trail*, semiannually
(for the "preservation and dissemination
of the history and heritage of
Chicago's south and southwest
suburbs")
$15.00 per year membership for
individuals, $20.00 per year
membership for not-for-profit
agencies, $45.00 per year Institutional
and Corporate membership, $60.00 per
year Contributing membership,
$100.00–$499.00 per year Sustaining
membership, $500.00–$999.00 Patron
membership, $1,000.00 per year
Benefactor membership

Stark County Historical Society
318 West Jefferson Street
PO Box 524
Toulon, IL 61483
(309) 286-7139; (309) 896-4532
Norman Black
Hours: Jun–Aug: Sun 1:00–5:00 by
appointment
(historical home)

Stephenson County Historical Society
1440 South Carroll Avenue
Freeport, IL 61032-6530
(815) 232-4819
Lyall Taubert, President
Hours: Fri–Sun 1:00–4:00
(museum only, no archives)

Stephenson County Historical Society
Genealogical Committee
110 Coates Place
Freeport, IL 61032

Sterling-Rock Falls Historical Society Museum
1005 East Third Street
PO Box 65
Sterling, IL 61081-0065
(815) 625-9019
Terence Buckaloo, Museum Curator;
Ronald Koster, President of Society
Hours: Museum: Tue, Thur & Sat 10:00–
12:00 & 1:00–4:00, Sun 1:00–5:00
Pub. *Newsletter*, monthly (except
December and summer)

(Whiteside County history)
$5.00 per year membership for
individuals, $10.00 per year
membership for families, $100.00 life
membership

Stone Park Historical Association
1629 North Mannheim Road
Stone Park, IL 60165-1118
(708) 345-2272
George Danda, Chair
(local history)

Streatorland Historical Society, Inc.
306 South Vermillion Street
Streator, IL 61364-2940
(815) 672-2443
Patricia Breen, Director
Hours: Mon–Fri 10:00–3:00, Sun 1:00–
4:00
Pub. *Unionville Dispatch*, monthly
from $12.00 per year membership

Sugar Grove Historical Society
214 Main Street
PO Box 102
Sugar Grove, IL 60554-0102
(630) 466-4382; (630) 466-4616
Ruth Frantz, Treasurer
Hours: by appointment
(local history and genealogy)

Tazewell Genealogical and Historical Society
(719 North 11th Street—location)
PO Box 312 (mailing address)
Pekin, IL 61555-0312
(309) 477-3044; (309) 579-2732
(President)
Margaret Bush, President
Hours: Wed 1:00–4:00, Thur 9:00–12:00,
Sun 2:00–4:30 (closed holiday
weekends)
Pub. *Tazewell Genealogical and
Historical Monthly*
(specializes in Tazewell County and
surrounding counties)
$12.00 per year membership for
individuals, $12.00 per year
membership for families, $15.00 per
year Canadian membership, $150.00
life membership

Tazewell County Historical Association
PO Box 636
Pekin, IL 61554

Thebes Historical Society
PO Box 14
Thebes, IL 62990-0014
(618) 764-2600

Thornton Township Historical Society
Genealogical Section
(154 East 154th Street, Harvey, IL
60426—location)
66 Water Street (mailing address)
Park Forest, IL 60466

(708) 596-2000, ext. 356; (708) 481-
6628
Dave Bartlett, President
Hours: Oct–Jun: first Sat
$5.00 per year membership for adult
individuals, $10.00 per year
membership for families

Tilton Historical Society
201 West Fifth Street
Tilton, IL 61833-7427
(217) 442-9309
Betty Montgomery, President
Hours: Thur 9:00–noon by appointment
(local history and genealogy)

Tinley Park Historical Society
(formerly Bremen Historical Society of
Tinley Park)
6727 West 174th Street
PO Box 325
Tinley Park, IL 60477-0325
(708) 429-4210
E-mail: lrtphist@lincolnnet.net
Brad L. Bettenhausen, President
Hours: Wed 10:00–2:00, and by
appointment
Pub. *New Bremen News* (formerly *Tinley
Towne Crier*), quarterly
("Museum and research materials related
primarily to the history of the Village
of Bremen (a.k.a. New Bremen, now
Tinley Park) and surrounding area in
Bremen, Orland, and Rich townships
in Cook County, and Frankfort
Township in Will County.")
$20.00 per year membership

Tremont Museum and Historical Society
Madison and South Sampson Streets
PO Box 738
Tremont, IL 61568-0738
(309) 925-5262; (309) 925-3453
Mrs. David Lee
Hours: second & fourth Sun 2:00–4:00,
and by appointment
(archives)

Tri-Township Heritage Association
306 Lime Street
Albany, IL 61230
Helen Hanson, Secretary
(genealogical services)

Triton Community History Organization
Triton College
2000 Fifth Avenue
River Grove, IL 60171-1995
(708) 456-0300, ext. 245
Florence Weese
Hours: Mon–Fri 8:00–4:00
(local history, college archives)

Union County Historical and Genealogy Society
104 Clemens
Cobden, IL 62920
Patrick Brumleve, President

Pub. *Friends of the Union County Historical and Genealogy Society*, three times per year
$7.00 per year membership

Vandalia Historical Society
307 North Sixth
Vandalia, IL 62471-2236
(618) 283-0024
Mary Burtschi, Vice President

Versailles Area Genealogical and Historical Society
113 West First Street
PO Box 92
Versailles, IL 62378
(217) 225-9091 (President); (217) 225-3227 (Second Vice President)
Joyce Workman, President; Rose Cooper, Second Vice President
Hours: Mon, Wed & Fri 1:30–5:00 (weather permitting); winter: Wed & Fri only
Pub. *The Versailles Area Genealogical & Historical Society Newsletter*, quarterly (March, June, September, December), contribution for subscription
(many family histories, census, marriages, obituaries, cemeteries, maps, scrapbooks, photo albums; research center, historical library, and museum)
$10.00 per year membership for individuals, $11.00 per year membership for couples

Villa Park Historical Society, Inc.
220 South Villa Avenue
Villa Park, IL 60181-2222
(630) 941-0223; (630) 834-9278
Gail McGrew
Hours: Tue–Fri 2:00–6:00, Sat–Sun 10:00–4:00

Village of Thornton Historical Society
208 Schwab Street
PO Box 34
Thornton, IL 60476-0034
(708) 877-9394; (708) 877-8942
Freda Rietveld, Curator
Hours: May–Oct: Sat 1:00–4:00 by appointment

Warren County Historical Society Museum
Route 116 East
Roseville, IL 61473
(309) 426-2231; (309) 426-2304
Austin Felt
Hours: 30 May–1 Sep: Mon–Sun 1:00–5:00 by appointment

Warrenville Historical Society
3 South 530 Second Street
PO Box 311
Warrenville, IL 60555-0311
(630) 393-3335
Marge Duller

Hours: Mar–Dec: Wed & Sat–Sun 1:00–4:00; Jan–Feb: by appointment

Warsaw Historical Society and Museum
401 Main Street
Warsaw, IL 62379-1246
Martha Zumwalt, President; Helen Seggelke, Secretary
Hours: Apr 1–Nov 1: 2:00–5:00, and special occasions, and by appointment
$3.00 per year membership for individuals, $1.00 per year membership for students, $100.00 life membership for individuals, $150.00 life membership for couples

Historical Society of Washington County
326 South Kaskaskia Street
PO Box 9
Nashville, IL 62263-0009
(618) 327-8953
Harrl Beatty

Washington Historical Society
101 and 105 Zinser Place
PO Box 54
Washington, IL 61571
(309) 444-4239; (309) 444-2668
Marguerite Lucas, President
Hours: Wed–Sat 10:00–4:00

Wauconda Township Historical Society
711 North Main Street
PO Box 256
Wauconda, IL 60084-0256
(847) 526-9303
Helen Funk, President
Hours: Sun afternoons in summer by appointment
Pub. *WTHS Newsletter*
(Lake County, Illinois, history)
$10.00 per year membership

Waukegan Historical Society
(The Haines Museum, 1917 North Sheridan Road, Waukegan, IL 60087—location)
PO Box 857 (mailing address)
Waukegan, IL 60079-0857
(847) 336-1859 (Museum); (847) 360-4772 (Research Library)
Deb Fandrei, Volunteer Coordinator
Hours: Museum: Wed–Fri 10:00–2:30, third weekend 1:00–3:00
Pub. *Historically Speaking*, quarterly
(also large photo archives)
$15.00 per year membership for individuals, $7.00 per year membership for students or senior citizens; photocopies: 25¢ per page; research time free

Waverly Genealogical and Historical Society
(Congregational Church, Waverly—location)
359 East Tremont (mailing address)
Waverly, IL 62692-1026

(217) 435-4961
Myra Martin, Historian
Hours: every other Mon, and by appointment
Pub. *Newsletter*, quarterly
$6.00 per year membership for individuals

Wayne County Historical Society
300 S.E. Second Street
Fairfield, IL 62837
(618) 842-4701 (evening); (618) 842-5323
Carl Meeks

West Chicago Historical Society
Kruse House Museum
527 Main Street
PO Box 246
West Chicago, IL 60186
(708) 231-0564; (708) 231-8472
Merle L. Burleigh, Public Relations Coordinator
Hours: Sat (May–Sept) 11:00–3:00 ("House Museum—Kruse/Burchert Families")
$7.00 per year membership for individuals, $10.00 per year membership for families

Westchester Historical Society
10332 Bond Street
Westchester, IL 60154-4361
(708) 865-1972
Luella Seida

Western Springs Historical Society
(Tower Green, 840 Hillgrove Avenue—museum location; Grand Avenue School—archives location)
PO Box 139 (mailing address)
Western Springs, IL 60558-0139
(708) 246-9230
Ann Vance, Office Manager
Hours: Museum: Sat 11:00–1:00, first Sun 1:00–3:00
(local history, photos, tapes, slides, genealogy)
$10.00 per year membership for individuals, $25.00 per year membership for families, $30.00 per year membership for businesses, $50.00 per year Sustaining membership; $100.00 per year Patron membership, $500.00 or more life membership

Westmont Historical Society
William L. Gregg House Museum
(115 South Linden Avenue—location)
75 East Richmond Street (mailing address)
Westmont, IL 60559-1894
(630) 960-3392
Silvia Baranek, Curator
Hours: Wed & Sun 1:00–3:00
(history of Westmont area)
$10.00 per year membership for individuals or families, $5.00 per year membership for senior citizens

Wheeling Historical Society

Wheeling Park District
251 North Wolf Road
PO Box 3
Wheeling, IL 60090-0003
(847) 537-0327; (847) 537-2930 (Park District)
Betty Barrie, Curator
Pub. *WHS Newsletter*

White County Historical Society

216 East Main Street
PO Box 121
Carmi, IL 62821-0121
Janet Armstrong, Director
Hours: Genealogy Library: Wed 11:00–5:00, except holidays
(maintains four museums: the Robinson-Stewart House, The L. Haas Store Museum, the Ratcliff Inn, and Matsel Cabin)
$15.00 per year membership for individuals (calendar year), $25.00 per year membership for families, $50.00 per year Sustaining membership, $100.00 per year Patron membership; $1,000.00 life membership

Will County Historical Society

(Off Route 7, 1 block west of 171—location)
803 South State Street (mailing address)
Lockport, IL 60441-3433
(815) 838-5080
Rose Bucciferro, Director
Pub. *WCHS Quarterly*; *Newsletter*, nine times per year
$25.00 per year subscription without membership, $5.00 per year membership for individuals, $1.00 per year membership for students, $10.00 per year Contributing membership, $25.00 per year membership for businesses, $50.00 per year Sustaining membership, $100.00 life membership; research by mail for $10.00 per surname

Williamson County Historical Society

105 South Van Buren Street
Marion, IL 62959-2509
(618) 997-5863 (Museum)
Connie Hudson Cram, Membership Chair
Hours: Thur (Apr–Dec) 9:00–3:00, and by appointment; meetings: third Sun (Apr–Nov) 2:00
Pub. *Williamson County Historical Society Newsletter*, eight times per year (monthly, April–November)
$15.00 per year membership; research: $7.50 per hour plus copy costs

Wilmette Historical Society

The Wilmette Historical Museum
609 Ridge Road
Wilmette, IL 60091
(847) 256-5838; (847) 256-5895 FAX

Kathy Hussey-Arntson, Museum Director
Hours: Tue–Thur 9:30–noon & 1:30–4:00, Sat 2:00–5:00
Pub. *Ouilmette Heritage*, quarterly (archives focus on Wilmette and Gross Point)

Wilmington Area Historical Society

100 North Water Street
PO Box 1
Wilmington, IL 60481-0001
(815) 476-6330
Dorthea Smith, Curator
Hours: Sat–Sun 1:00–4:00

Winfield Historical Society

(555 Winfield Road—location)
PO Box 315 (mailing address)
Winfield, IL 60190
(630) 653-1489; (630) 665-0358
Adrienne Rose
Hours: by appointment

Winnetka Historical Society

Winnetka Historical Museum
1140 Elm Street
PO Box 142
Winnetka, IL 60093-0142
(847) 501-6025
Carol Meeske, President; Jeannette Scott, Museum Director
Hours: Tue, Thur & Sat 1:00–4:00, and by appointment

Wood Dale Historical Society

850 North Wood Dale Road
PO Box 13
Wood Dale, IL 60191-0013
(630) 595-8777; (630) 766-1768
Robert H. Doane, Curator

Woodford County Historical Society

615 West Maple
Eureka, IL 61530-1340
Don Pioletti

Woodridge Area Historical Society

2628 Mitchell Drive
Woodridge, IL 60517-2929
(630) 985-9423
Joanie Mimhaugh

Wyanet Historical Society

109 East Main Street
PO Box 169
Wyanet, IL 61379-0169
(815) 699-2531
Maxine Trotter, President and Curator
Hours: by appointment
Pub. *Newsletter*, annually
(cemetery book, newspapers, high school alumni book 1879–1976, display of canal, railroad, military memorabilia, hotel register 1875–1879, Civil War diary of Emmerson Pomeroy, minutes and pictures, records of Wyanet War Mothers, slide presentation of early businesses)
$5.00 per year membership, $25.00 life membership; search: minimum $5.00 donation per person or place

Zion Historical Society

1300 Shiloh Boulevard
Zion, IL 60099
(847) 746-2427; (847) 746-2427
Alice Marshall

LDS Family History Centers

Buffalo Grove
(847) 913-5387

Chicago
(see Buffalo Grove, Naperville, Schaumburg or Wilmette)

Naperville
(708) 505-0233

Nauvoo
(217) 453-6347

Peoria
(309) 682-4073

Schaumburg
(847) 885-4130

Wilmette
(847) 251-9818

Genealogical Societies

State Genealogical Societies

Illinois State Genealogical Society

(Margaret Cross Norton Building, Second and Edwards—location)
PO Box 10195 (mailing address)
Springfield, IL 62791-0195
(217) 789-1968 (Business Office)
http://www.tbox.com/isgs/
A. Joyce Brown, President
Pub. *Illinois State Genealogical Society Quarterly*; *Illinois State Genealogical Society Newsletter*, bimonthly
(does not maintain a research facility)
$25.00 per year membership for individuals, $30.00 per year joint membership (two people living at the same address), $500.00 life membership for individuals; genealogist on staff to answer research letters

Council of Northeastern Illinois Genealogical Societies

3629 West 147th Place
Midlothian, IL 60445-3505
Loretta Szuks
(coordinates society activities)

Regional Genealogical Societies

Bellflower Genealogical and Historical Society

(Latcha Street—location)
Rt. 1, Box 17 (mailing address)
Bellflower, IL 61724
(309) 722-3467 (President); (309) 722-3757 (Bellflower Village and Museum)
Dorothy Woliung, President
Hours: by appointment
Pub. *Bellflower Highlights*, annually (July), subscription by donation

Blackhawk Genealogical Society of Rock Island and Mercer Counties, Illinois

PO Box 3912
Rock Island, IL 61204-3912
(309) 787-1826
E-mail: bfrancque@delphi.com
http://www.rootsweb.com/~ilrockis/
Judy Rueckert, President; Lorraine Hathaway, Editor
Hours: collection housed at the Rock Island Public Library
Pub. *Blackhawk Genealogical Society Quarterly*
$15.00 per year membership

Bond County Genealogical Society

PO Box 172
Greenville, IL 62246-0172
(618) 664-3054 (President)
Dean Anthony, President
Hours: 8:00–5:00; collection housed in the Greenville Public Library: Mon–Thur noon–8:00, Fri 10:00–6:00, Sat 10:00–5:00
Pub. *BCGS News*, quarterly
(census, family histories, probate records, cemetery records, veterans records, etc.)
$10.00 per year membership; search fees: $5.00 per hour plus copies and postage

Bureau County Genealogical Society

PO Box 402
Princeton, IL 61356-0402
E-mail: genmus@theramp.net
Carol Shipp, Board Member
Hours: Matson Public Library: Mon–Thur noon–9:00, Fri 9:00–5:00, Sat noon–5:00; summer: Tue–Thur noon–6:00; meetings at First United Methodist Church, 316 South Church Street (corner of East Peru and South Church Streets), Princeton, IL (not a mailing address): fourth Thur 7:00 p.m.
Pub. *Bureau County Genealogical Society*, bimonthly
(Bureau County records, extensive marriage, cemetery and church records)

$8.00 per year membership for individuals (calendar year), $10.00 per year membership for families at one address; search fee: $6.00 per hour for members, $10.00 per hour for non-members

Carroll County Genealogical Society

Savanna Public Library, History Room
326 Third Street
PO Box 354
Savanna, IL 61074-0347
(815) 273-3707 (President)
Mrs. Wilma Brunner, Secretary/Treasurer
Hours: by appointment only
Pub. *Carroll County Genealogical Society Newsletter*, four times per year
(Carroll County histories, cemeteries, censuses)
$10.00 per year membership (calendar year); search fee: $5.00 per hour, 25¢ per copy

Cass County Illinois Historical/Genealogical Society

PO Box 11
Virginia, IL 62691-0011
Janice L. Fox, President
Pub. *Cass County, Illinois, Historian Newsletter*, quarterly
(Cass County marriages, cemeteries, land records, 1840, 1850 and 1880 censuses, etc.)
$7.00 per year membership (beginning in July)

Champaign County Genealogical Society

Urbana Free Library
201 South Race Street
Urbana, IL 61801-3283
(217) 367-4025 (Library)
Hours: Library: Mon–Sat 9:00–5:00, Sun 1:00–5:00
Pub. *Champaign County Genealogical Society Quarterly*; *Champaign County Genealogical Society Newsletter*, quarterly
$15.00 per year membership

Chicago Genealogical Society

(120 Berteau Avenue, Elmhurst, IL 60126—library location)
PO Box 1160 (mailing address)
Chicago, IL 60690-1160
(312) 725-1306 (recorded message); (312) 834-7491 (library)
Kathy O'Leary, Editor, *Newsletter*; Mildred R. Smith, Librarian
Hours: Library: by appointment, for use by members only
Pub. *Chicago Genealogist*, quarterly; *Newsletter of the Chicago Genealogical Society*, eleven times per year
(Cook County and Chicago, Illinois)
$16.00 per year membership for individuals

Christian County Genealogical Society

PO Box 28
Taylorville, IL 62568
Nelvin Sloman, President
Pub. *Christian County Genealogical Quarterly*; *Christian County Genealogical Society Newsletter*, quarterly
$10.00 per year membership

Clark County Genealogical Society

309 Maple
PO Box 153
Marshall, IL 62441-0153
(217) 826-2864; (217) 826-5925
Betty L. Turner, Vice President
Hours: Thur–Sat 12:30–3:00
Pub. *Clark County Genealogical Newsletter*, quarterly

Clay County Genealogical Society

(West side of square—location)
PO Box 94
Louisville, IL 62858-0094
(618) 665-4544
Hours: second Mon 12:00–4:00, Sat 9:00–4:00
Pub. *Clay Roots*, quarterly

Coles County, Illinois, Genealogical Society

PO Box 592
Charleston, IL 61920-0592
Karen Zike, Corresponding Secretary
Hours: Charleston Public Library: Mon–Thur 10:00–8:00, Fri–Sat 10:00–6:00
Pub. *Among the Coles*, bimonthly
$10.00 per year membership for individuals

Crawford County Genealogical Society

803 North Madison
Robinson, IL 62454
Sue Jones, Secretary; King Schmalhausen, President
Hours: Robinson Public Library District: Mon–Thur 10:00–8:00, Fri–Sat 10:00–5:30; summer: Mon 10:00–8:00, Tue–Sat 10:00–5:30
Pub. *Crawford County Genealogical Society Newsletter*, semiannually
(state census of Illinois, DAR lineage books, cemetery records, marriages, obituaries, U.S. censuses of Crawford and surrounding counties; Crawford County history and records)
$8.00 per year membership

Genealogical Society of Cumberland and Coles County

1816 Walnut
Mattoon, IL 61938

Cumberland County Historical and Genealogical Society of Illinois

PO Box 393
Greenup, IL 62428
Pub. *Happy Hunter*, semiannually

Decatur Genealogical Society

(356 North Main Street—location)
PO Box 1548 (mailing address)
Decatur, IL 62526-1548
(217) 429-0135
Mary Lou Eckart
Hours: Mon 10:00–6:00, Wed & Sat
10:00–4:00, Sun 1:00–4:00
Pub. *Central Illinois Genealogical
Quarterly*; *Decatur Genealogical
Society Newsletter*
$15.00 per year membership

DeKalb County Historical-Genealogical Society

PO Box 295
Sycamore, IL 60178-0295
Phyllis Kelley, Corresponding Secretary
Pub. *"Cornsilk" of DeKalb County,
Illinois*, quarterly
(Society works with the Joiner History
Archives in the county courthouse)
$15.00 per year membership

DeWitt County Genealogical Society

(Warner Library—location)
PO Box 632 (mailing address)
Clinton, IL 61727-0632
Nettie Davenport, President
Hours: Mon–Thur 9:00–9:00, Fri 9:00–
6:00, Sat 9:00–4:00
Pub. *DeWitt County Genealogical
Quarterly*
$15.00 per year membership for
individuals, $16.00 per year
membership for families; research:
$5.00 per surname

Douglas County Genealogical Society

PO Box 113
Tuscola, IL 61953-0113
(217) 253-4635; (217) 268-3551
Mary Nater, Corresponding Secretary;
Tracy Carpenter
Pub. *Douglas Trails and Traces*,
quarterly
$7.50 per year membership for
individuals, $8.50 per year
membership for two people

Dubuque County-Key City Genealogical Society Chapter (IGS)

(see Iowa)

Dunton Genealogical Society

Arlington Heights Memorial Library
500 North Dunton Avenue
Arlington Heights, IL 60004-5966
(847) 392-0100 (Local History/
Genealogy); (847) 506-2639 (Library);
(847) 392-0136 FAX (Library)
http:www.ahml.lib.il.us (Library)
Everett and Joan Huff, Genealogy
Volunteers
Hours: Library: Mon–Fri 9:00–10:00, Sat
9:00–5:00, Sun noon–5:00
(Illinois and midwest states, German
ancestry)

DuPage County Genealogical Society

PO Box 133
Lombard, IL 60148-0133
http://www.dcgs.org
Jeff Bockman, President; Lynn Tucker,
Corresponding Secretary
Hours: third Wed 7:30 at Wheaton Public
Library
Pub. *The Review*, eight times per year
(bimonthly plus summer and winter)
$12.00 per year membership for
individuals, $15.00 per year
membership for families, $1.00 per
year junior membership

Edgar County, Illinois Genealogical Society

PO Box 304
Paris, IL 61944-0304
(217) 463-4209
Linda Cary, Editor
Hours: Edgar County Genealogy Library:
Wed–Fri 9:00–4:00, second & fourth
Sat 10:00–1:00
Pub. *Edgar County Genealogical Society
Quarterly* (July, October, January,
April)
$12.50 per year membership for
individuals, $150.00 life membership

Edwards County Genealogical Society

Edwards County Historical Society
212 West Main Street
Albion, IL 62806
(618) 445-2631; (618) 445-3969
E-mail: melrose@wworld.com
Terry L. Harper, President
Hours: Thur 6:00 P.M.–10:00 P.M.
Pub. *Edwards County Historical Society
Publication*, annually
$7.00 per year membership for
individuals, $8.00 per year
membership for couples

Effingham County Genealogical Society

(Helen Matthes Library, 100 Market
Street—location)
PO Box 1166 (mailing address)
Effingham, IL 62401-1166
(217) 342-2210
Arnetia Osborn, Corresponding Secretary
Hours: Library: winter: Mon–Thur
10:00–9:00, Fri 10:00–5:00, Sat
10:00–4:00; summer: Mon–Thur
10:00–8:00, Fri 10:00–5:00, Sat
10:00–1:00; genealogy assistance: Tue
1:00–3:00, Thur 10:00–noon
Pub. *Crossroad Trails*, quarterly;
*Effingham County Genealogical
Society Newsletter*, monthly
$10.00 per year membership

Elgin Genealogical Society

PO Box 1418
Elgin, IL 60121-1418
(847) 697-5683
Daniel DuBois

Pub. *Newsletter—Elgin Genealogical
Society Quarterly*
(research of probation records of Elgin)
$10.00 per year membership for
individuals, $15.00 per year
membership for families

Genealogical Forum of Elmhurst, Illinois

Elmhurst Historical Museum
120 East Park Avenue
Elmhurst, IL 60126-3420
(630) 833-1457 (Museum)
Hours: meetings first Sun (odd-numbered
months) 3:00–5:00
Pub. *Newsletter of the Genealogical
Forum of Elmhurst*, five times per year
(August, October, December,
February, April)
(Elmhurst cemeteries prior to 1916)
$10.00 per year membership, search fees:
$5.00 and up, free to members

Farmer City Genealogy and Historical Society

(Franklin School, 400 East Market—
location)
PO Box 173 (mailing address)
Farmer City, IL 61842-0173
(309) 928-9547; (309) 928-2113
Sharon Stiger

Fayette County Genealogical and Historical Society

Evans Public Library
215 South Fifth Street
PO Box 177
Vandalia, IL 62471-0177
(618) 423-2625
Linda Hanabarger, Editor
Hours: Mon–Thur 10:00–7:00, Fri–Sat
10:00–5:00
Pub. *Fayette Facts*, quarterly
$5.00 per issue to members, $6.00 per
issue to non-members, $15.00 per year
membership

Fort LaMotte Genealogical and Historical Society

Palestine Public Library
116 South Main
Palestine, IL 62451-1244
(618) 586-5580
Hours: Tue–Fri 9:00–4:30, Sat 8:30–
10:30

Frankfort Area Genealogy Society

1200 East Saint Louis Street
PO Box 427
West Frankfort, IL 62896-0427
Mary Rea Eubank, President
Pub. *Facts and Findings*, quarterly
$10.00 per year membership

Freeburg Historical and Genealogical Society

PO Box 69
Freeburg, IL 62243-0069
(618) 539-5771
Frank X. Heiligenstein

Hours: 9:00–noon
Pub. *Quarterly*

Fulton County Historical and Genealogical Society
45 North Park Drive
Canton, IL 61520
(309) 647-0771
E-mail: mbordner@netins.net
Marjorie R. Bordner, Ph.D., President
Hours: Parlin-Ingersoll Library: Mon–Fri 9:00–8:00, Sat 9:00–4:00, Sun 1:00–4:00
Pub. *Fulton County Historical and Genealogical Society Newsletter*, quarterly, $12.00 per year subscription ("Long list of published records available.")

Genealogical Questers
Des Plaines Historical Society
789 Pearson Street
Des Plaines, IL 60016-4506
Hours: temporarily not meeting on a regular basis

Goode-Barren Historical-Genealogical Society
201 East Callie Street
PO Box 1024
Sesser, IL 62884-0944
(618) 625-2851; (618) 625-5762
Clara Brown
Hours: Mon 10:00–1:00, Wed 10:00–3:00 by appointment

Great River Genealogical Society
Quincy Public Library
526 Jersey Street
Quincy, IL 62301-3996
(217) 222-0226
http://www.outfitters.com/~grgs
Hours: Library: Tue after Labor Day to Sat before Memorial Day: Mon–Thur 9:00–9:00, Fri–Sat 9:00–6:00, Sun 1:00–5:00; Jun–Aug: Mon 9:00–9:00, Tue–Sat 9:00–6:00
Pub. *The Yellowjacket*, quarterly
(Adams County indexes to deaths, land records, cemeteries, surname index; Quincy newspapers on microfilm 1838 to date; German-American Historical Papers; tax lists, will indexes, coroners inquests indexes, and divorce index)
$10.00 per year membership for individuals, $8.00 per year membership for senior citizens

Green Hills Genealogical Society
Green Hills Public Library
8611 West 103rd Street
Palos Hills, IL 60465
(708) 598-8446
Darline Filis
Hours: Mon–Fri 9:00–8:30, Sat 9:00–5:00 (except Jun–Aug: Sat 9:00–3:00)

Greene County Historical and Genealogical Society
221 North Fifth Street
PO Box 137
Carrollton, IL 62016-0137
Barbara B. Daum, President
Hours: Wed & Fri 9:00–2:00
Pub. *Greene County Historical and Genealogical Society Newsletter*, quarterly
$10.00 per year membership

Griggsville Area Genealogical and Historical Society
PO Box 22
Griggsville, IL 62340-0022
(217) 833-2308; (217) 285-6672
June Johnson
Hours: Mon–Fri 1:00–5:00, and by appointment

Hardin County Historical and Genealogical Society
PO Box 72
Elizabethtown, IL 62931-0072
(618) 287-2361
Noel E. Hurford, Secretary
$9.00 per year membership

Henry County Genealogical Society
(102 South Tremont Street—location)
PO Box 346 (mailing address)
Kewanee, IL 61443-0346
E-mail: cornish@starcourier
Alice Neirynck, President
Hours: Mon, Wed & Sat 1:00–5:00; meetings at the First Methodist Church, 108 East Central Boulevard, Kewanee, IL: fourth Mon
Pub. *Henry County Genie*, quarterly; *Newsletter*, monthly
(how-to materials; U.S. general, foreign, family surnames, U.S. by state and county; issues Pioneers of Henry County, Illinois Certificates for direct descendants)
$14.00 per year membership for individuals, $15.00 per year membership for families, $125.00 life membership for individuals, $175.00 life membership for families; send SASE for research information

Henry Historical and Genealogical Society
610 North Street
Henry, IL 61537-1226
(309) 364-3272
Connie Swanson, President
Hours: City Library: Mon–Sat 1:00–5:00, Wed 1:00–8:00
Pub. *Newsletter*, quarterly
(specializes in Marshall County, especially city of Henry)
$5.00 per year membership

Illiana Genealogical and Historical Society
(19 East North—location)
PO Box 207 (mailing address)
Danville, IL 61834-0207
(217) 431-8733
Sally Powell, President
Hours: Mon & Wed–Sat 10:00–4:00, Tue 10:00–8:00
Pub. *Illiana Genealogist*; quarterly (March, June, September, December) (includes bordering counties of Vermilion County, IL)
$15.00 per year membership for individuals, $15.50 per year membership for couples; research: $18.00 for two hours

Iroquois County Genealogical Society
A Division of the Iroquois County Historical Society
Old Courthouse Museum
103 West Cherry Street
Watseka, IL 60970-1524
(815) 432-3730
Cheryl Gocken, Librarian/Researcher
Hours: Mon–Fri 12:30–4:30
Pub. *The Iroquois Stalker*, quarterly; *Newsletter*, monthly
("Also states of the migration path to Illinois")
$18.00 per year membership; searches: $5.00 per hour

Jacksonville Area Genealogical and Historical Society
(203 South Fayette Street—library and office location)
416 South Main Street (mailing address)
Jacksonville, IL 62650-2904
(217) 673-4241 (Librarian); (217) 245-5911 (for appointment)
Mary Frances Alkire, Volunteer Librarian
Hours: weekdays by appointment, Sat 10:00–4:00
Pub. *Jacksonville Illinois Genealogical Journal*, quarterly
$14.00 per year membership (calendar year)

Jasper County Historical and Genealogical Society
Newton Public Library
100 South Van Buren Street
Newton, IL 62448-1559
(618) 783-8141 (Library)
Patty Huston, Membership Secretary; Mary A. Miller, Editor and Corresponding Secretary
Hours: Mon–Sat 10:00–5:00
Pub. *Our Heritage*, monthly
$13.00 per year membership

Jefferson County Genealogical Society
c/o C. E. Brehm Memorial Library
101 South Seventh Street
Mount Vernon, IL 62864-4187

(618) 242-6322 (Library); (618) 242-6322 (Genealogy)
Linda Capps Clark
Hours: Library: Mon–Thur 9:00–8:00, Fri 9:00–5:00, Sat 12:00–6:00, Sun 1:00–5:00

Kane County Genealogical Society
PO Box 504
Geneva, IL 60134-0504
E-mail: bowl12x@aol.com
Susan Lye, Editor/President
Hours: meetings at The Kane County Chronicle Building, 1000 Randall Road, Geneva, IL 60134: fourth Thur
Pub. *The Kane County Chronicles*, quarterly
(emphasis on Saint Charles, Kane County, and Illinois; database containing over 500,000 names from Kane County resources)
$8.00 per year membership for individuals, $10.00 per year membership for families; search of database: $10.00 per husband/wife couple

Kankakee Valley Genealogical Society
PO Box 442
Bourbonnais, IL 60914-0442
(815) 939-4564
Marcia Stang, President
Hours: Kankakee Public Library: Mon–Thur 9:00–9:00, Fri 9:00–6:00, Sat 9:00–5:00
Pub. *The-a-Kiki*, quarterly
$10.00 per year membership

Kendall County Genealogical Society
83 Brockway
Oswego, IL 60543
(630) 554-8342
Mickie Meegan, President
Pub. *The Homestead*, annually; *Newsletter*, monthly
$12.00 per year membership

Kishwaukee Genealogists
PO Box 5503
Rockford, IL 61125-0503
(815) 874-2706
Stacia Gibson, Recording Secretary
Hours: meetings at North Suburban Library, Loves Park: second Sat (Sept–May) 1:30
Pub. *Kishwaukee Genealogists Newsletter*, five times per year
(Boone and Winnebago counties)
$7.00 per year membership

Knox County Genealogical Society
PO Box 13
Galesburg, IL 61402-0013
(309) 343-1466
Kathy Hale, President
Hours: meetings: second Mon
Pub. *Knox County Genealogical Society Quarterly* (March, June, September, December)

$10.00 per year membership; research: $12.50

Lake County (IL) Genealogical Society
PO Box 721
Libertyville, IL 60048-0721
Michael Wynn, President
Pub. *Lake County (IL) Genealogical Society Quarterly*
$15.00 per year membership for individuals, $16.00 per year membership for families

LaSalle County Genealogy Guild
(115 Glover Street—location)
PO Box 2134 (mailing address)
Ottawa, IL 61350-6734
Carole Wenzel, President
Hours: Mon 9:00–4:00, Sat 9:30–3:30
Pub. *Pastfinder*, three times per year; *Gene View*, bimonthly
$10.00 per year membership for individuals, $12.00 per year membership for two people in same household

Lawrence County Genealogical Society
Rt. 1, Box 44
Bridgeport, IL 62417
(618) 945-7181
Geraldine Satterthwaite, Corresponding Secretary
Pub. *Lawrence County Genealogical Society Newsletter*, quarterly
(books of obituaries from Lawrence County area)
$10.00 per year membership

Lee County Genealogical Society
(Family Tree Center, 213 South Peoria Avenue—location)
PO Box 63 (mailing address)
Dixon, IL 61021-0063
(815) 288-6702
http://www.rootsweb.com/~illee/lcgs.htm
Millie Dutchoff, President; Bob Boward, Vice President
Hours: Tue & Sat 9:00–3:00, Thur 5:00–8:00, and by appointment
Pub. *Lee County Genealogical Society Newsletter*, monthly
(information on Lee, Whiteside, Ogle and other surrounding counties)
$10.00 per year membership for individuals (calendar year); search fee: $10.00 for initial search, plus $10.00 per hour for extensive research plus copy costs

Lewis and Clark Genealogical Society
PO Box 485
Godfrey, IL 62035-0485
(618) 372-3997
Loraine Watt

Lexington Genealogical and Historical Society
318 West Main Street
Lexington, IL 61753-1328
(309) 365-4591
Verda Gerwick, President
Hours: Tue–Sat 9:00–4:00
(McLean, Livingston and Woodford County, Illinois, cemetery records)
$20.00 per year membership

Little Rock Township Public Library Genealogical Group
Little Rock Township Library
North Center Street
Plano, IL 60545

Logan County Genealogical and Historical Society
(11 Arcade Building—location)
PO Box 283 (mailing address)
Lincoln, IL 62656
(217) 732-3988; (217) 732-7148
Mildred Wickline, President

Macoupin County Genealogical Society
PO Box 95
Staunton, IL 62088-0095
(618) 635-8506 (Secretary's home); (618) 635-3852 (Library)
Cindy Leonard, Corresponding Secretary
Hours: Staunton Public Library: Mon–Thur 1:00–8:00, Fri–Sat 9:00–5:00; meetings at First United Baptist Church, 604 North Franklin, Staunton: third Mon (except Dec) 7:30
Pub. *Macoupin County Searcher*, quarterly
$10.00 per year membership

Madison County Genealogical Society
PO Box 631
Edwardsville, IL 62025-0631
(618) 656-2299 (MCGS Librarian)
Elsie M. Wasser, Librarian
Hours: Edwardsville Public Library, 112 South Kansas: Mon–Thur 9:00–9:00, Fri–Sat 9:00–5:00, Sun 1:00–5:00
Pub. *Madison County Genealogical Society Newsletter*, nine times per year; *Madison County Genealogical Society Stalker*, quarterly
("Early birth, death, marriage, probate printed indexes 1810–1920, census records, biographical index of all history books.")
$15.00 per year membership for individuals, families or institutions, $150.00 life membership

Marion County Genealogical and Historical Society
(Bryan-Bennett Library, 217 West Main—location)
PO Box 342 (mailing address)
Salem, IL 62881
Wanda Fatheree, Archivist

Hours: Archives: Wed noon–4:00, and by appointment when library is open

Pub. *Footprints in Marion County*, quarterly

$15.00 per year membership (beginning in July); free queries

Marissa Historical and Genealogical Society

(610 South Main Street—location)
PO Box 47 (mailing address)
Marissa, IL 62257-0047
(618) 295-2562
Elda L. Jones, President
Hours: Wed 1:00–4:00, and anytime by appointment
Pub. *Branching Out from Saint Clair County, Illinois*, quarterly (November, February, May, August)
$15.00 per year membership (beginning in Oct)

Mason County Genealogical and Historical Society

PO Box 246
Havana, IL 62644

McDonough County Genealogical Society

(Macomb District Public Library—location)
PO Box 202 (mailing address)
Macomb, IL 61455-0202
(309) 837-4558
Sarah Semonis
Hours: Library: Mon–Tue, Thur & Sat 9:00–6:00, Wed & Fri 9:00–9:00
Pub. *McDonough County Genealogical Society News Quarterly*
$10.00 per year membership

McHenry County Illinois Genealogical Society (MCIGS)

(McHenry Library, 1011 Green Street, McHenry, IL 60050—location)
PO Box 184 (mailing address)
Crystal Lake, IL 60039-0184
(815) 385-0686
E-mail: cphist@ais.net
Craig Pfarmkuche, Corresponding Secretary
Pub. *McHenry County Illinois Connection*, quarterly
$15.00 per year membership

The McLean County Genealogical Society

(Second Floor, McLean County Courthouse, 200 North Main, Bloomington, IL 61701-3912—location)
PO Box 488 (mailing address)
Normal, IL 61761-0488
Joy Craig, Corresponding Secretary; Laurel Quaid, Quarterly Editor
Hours: Mon & Wed–Sat 10:00–5:00, Tue 10:00–9:00
Pub. *Gleanings from the Heart of the Cornbelt*, quarterly; *McLean County*

Genealogical Society Newsletter, monthly
$15.00 per year membership

Monroe County Research Group

6104 State Route 156
Waterloo, IL 62298
Mr. Weilbacker

Montgomery County Genealogical Society

(Litchfield Carnegie Public Library, 400 North State Street—library location)
PO Box 212 (mailing address)
Litchfield, IL 62056-0212
Nola M. Eskra, President
Hours: Library: Mon–Thur 10:00–8:00; Fri 10:00–5:00, Sat 10:00–2:00
Pub. *Montgomery County Genealogical Society Quarterly*
$12.50 per year membership for individuals, $15.00 per year membership for families, $100.00 life membership

Morgan County Genealogical Association

PO Box 84
Jacksonville, IL 62651-0084
Florence Hutchison, Corresponding secretary
Pub. *Star Genealogical Journal*, quarterly
$10.00 per year membership

Moultrie County Historical and Genealogical Society

Moultrie County Historical and Genealogical Research Library
Heritage Center, 117 East Harrison
PO Box 588
Sullivan, IL 61951-0588
(217) 728-4085
Sue Durbin, Genealogist
Hours: Mon & Sat 1:00–5:00
Pub. *Moultrie County Heritage*, quarterly; *Moultrie County Historical and Genealogical Society Newsletter*, monthly
$9.00 per year membership for individuals, $12.00 per year membership for families of two, $1.00 per year membership for each additional family membership

Mount Vernon Genealogical Society

c/o C. E. Brehm Memorial Library
101 South Seventh Street
Mount Vernon, IL 62864-4187
(618) 242-6322 (Library)
Hours: Library: Mon–Thur 9:00–8:00, Fri 9:00–5:00, Sat 12:00–6:00, Sun 1:00–5:00
Pub. *Newsletter*, quarterly
$5.00 per year membership

North Central Illinois Genealogical Society

PO Box 4635
Rockford, IL 61110-4635

Hours: meetings second Sat (Sept–May)
Pub. *Twigs and Branches*, quarterly
$12.50 per year membership; search fees: $7.50 per hour

North Suburban Genealogical Society

Winnetka Public Library District
768 Oak Street
Winnetka, IL 60093-2583
(847) 446-7220
Rosalie Clary, President
Hours: Library: Mon–Thur 9:00–9:00, Fri–Sat 9:00–5:00, Sun 1:00–5:00 (during school year)
Pub. *Newsletter*, bimonthly
$10.00 per year membership

Northwest Suburban Council of Genealogists

PO Box AC
Mount Prospect, IL 60056-9019
(847) 398-8565
Rita Hodgetts, President
Pub. *News from the Northwest*, five times per year
$10.00 per year membership for individuals, $12.00 per year membership for families, $3.00 per year membership for students, $100.00 life membership

Northwest Territory Genealogical Society

(see Indiana)

Odell Prairie Trails Genealogical and Historical Society

PO Box 82
Odell, IL 60460-0082
(815) 998-2324
Lorraine Hare, Secretary
Hours: by appointment
(Livingston and local history)
$5.00 per year membership

Ogle County Illinois Genealogical Society

PO Box 251
Oregon, IL 61061-0251
(815) 734-6818 (Secretary)
Ruth Baker, Corresponding Secretary
Hours: Lower Level, Oregon Public Library: Mon–Thur 9:00–8:00, Fri–Sat 9:00–4:00
Pub. *Ogle County Links*, quarterly (January, April, July, October)
$5.00 per year membership for individuals, $6.00 per year membership for families

Peoria County Genealogical Society

PO Box 1489
Peoria, IL 61655-1489
(309) 692-9758 BBS (settings of N. 8+1)
Donna Neuhaus, Corresponding Secretary
Hours: Peoria Public Library: Mon–Thur 9:00–9:00, Fri–Sat 9:00–6:00; summer: closed weekends

Pub. *Prairie Roots*, quarterly; *Newsletter*, monthly
(specializes in Peoria County)
$17.00 per year membership for individuals, $15.00 per year membership for senior citizens aged 65 and older

Piatt County Historical and Genealogical Society
(Courthouse Annex—location)
PO Box 111 (mailing address)
Monticello, IL 61856-0111
Betty Varner, Librarian
Hours: Mon & Wed 1:00–4:00
Pub. *Piatt County Historical and Genealogical Society Newsletter*, quarterly
$8.00 per year membership

Pike and Calhoun Counties Genealogical Society
(207 North Main Street—location)
PO Box 104 (mailing address)
Pleasant Hill, IL 62366-0104
(217) 734-2221 (Office); (217) 734-2736 (President)
Virginia R. Hart, President and Editor
Pub. *A Peek at Pike*, quarterly
$10.00 per year membership

Randolph County Genealogical Society
First State Bank Building, 600 State Street, Room 306
Chester, IL 62233-1633
(618) 826-3807 (Mon–Tue); (618) 763-4427 (President); (573) 547-1881 (Vice President)
Virginia Mansker, President; Lola Crowder, Vice President
Hours: Mon–Tue 9:00–2:30
Pub. *The Trails*, quarterly (March, June, September, December), $4.50 per issue
$20.00 per year membership

Richland County Illinois Genealogical and Historical Society
(Olney Central College, Anderson Library—library location)
PO Box 202 (mailing address)
Olney, IL 62450-0202
(618) 869-2425 (Editor)
Jan Doan, President
Hours: when college library is open: Mon–Thur 8:00–7:30, Fri 8:00–4:00
Pub. *Footprints Past and Present*, quarterly; *Richland County Genealogical Society Newsletter*, bimonthly
$15.00 per year membership

Saint Clair County Genealogical Society
(Saint Luke's Parish Center—location)
PO Box 431 (mailing address)
Belleville, IL 62222-0431
Dennis Hermann, President

Hours: collection housed at Belleville Public Library: Mon, Wed & Fri 9:00–9:00, Tue, Thur & Sat 9:00–5:00; meetings at Saint Luke's
Pub. *Saint Clair County Genealogical Society Quarterly*; *Saint Clair County Genealogical Society Newsletter*, monthly
$16.00 per year membership

Saline County Genealogical Society
(Room 24, City Hall—location)
PO Box 4 (mailing address)
Harrisburg, IL 62946-0004
(618) 252-1216 (Treasurer); (618) 252-1096
E-mail: kstill@midamer.net
Karen Stilley, Treasurer
Hours: fourth Tue 9:00–3:00, and by appointment
Pub. *The Shawnee*, quarterly, $4.00 per issue; *Newsletter*, monthly
$12.00 per year membership for individuals or families

Sangamon County Genealogical Society
PO Box 1829
Springfield, IL 62705-1829
(217) 529-0542
Daniel W. Dixon, President
Pub. *Circuit Rider*, quarterly
(Sangamon County genealogical interest)
$12.00 per year membership for individuals (calendar year), $1.00 per year membership for each additional family member at the same address, $20.00 per year Contributing membership, $125.00 life membership

Shelby County Historical and Genealogical Society
151 South Washington Street
PO Box 286
Shelbyville, IL 62565
(217) 774-2260
E-mail: shgensoc@bmmhnet.com
http://www.bmmhnet.com/shgensoc
June McCain, Vice President and Librarian
Hours: Apr–Oct: Mon–Sat 10:00–4:00; Nov–Mar: Mon & Fri–Sat 10:00–4:00
Pub. *Shelby County Ancestors*, quarterly; *Shelby County Historical and Genealogical Society Newsletter*, four times per year
$15.00 per year membership for individuals (calendar year), $17.00 per year membership for husband and wife, $150.00 life membership for individuals, $200.00 life membership for husband and wife

South Suburban Genealogical and Historical Society
320 East 161st Place
PO Box 96
South Holland, IL 60473-0096
(708) 333-9474

http://www.rootsweb.com/saveall.gif
Alice DeBoer, Librarian
Hours: Mon, Wed & Fri 10:00–4:00, Tue 1:00–9:00, Sat 11:00–4:00
Pub. *Where the Trails Cross*, quarterly; *Newsletter*, monthly
(Pullman Car Company employment records, ca 1890–1940)
$15.00 per year membership

The Genealogy Society of Southern Illinois
c/o John A. Logan College
Rt. 2, Box 145
Carterville, IL 62918-9599
(618) 985-6213
Tullyne Oliver, Membership Chair
Hours: subject to college hours
Pub. *Newsletter*, monthly; *Saga of Southern Illinois*, quarterly
$16.00 per year membership for individuals, $2.00 additional per year for each additional family member, $25.00 per year Sustaining membership, $5.00 additional per year foreign membership

Stark County Genealogical Society
(207 West Main—location)
PO Box 32 (mailing address)
Toulon, IL 61483
Hours: Tue 1:00–4:00, Sat 10:10–noon, and by appointment
Pub. *Stark County Genie Quarterly*
(local history, indexed scrapbooks, diaries, letters, newspapers, oral history)
$12.00 per year membership

Stephenson County Genealogical Society
PO Box 514
Freeport, IL 61032-0514
Norma Fluechtling, Corresponding Secretary
Hours: Freeport Public Library: Mon–Thur 9:00–9:00 (summer 9:00–8:00), Fri 9:00–6:00, Sat 9:00–5:00, Sun (during the school year) 1:00–4:00
Pub. *Stephenson County SWOGHEN*, quarterly
$8.00 per year membership

Tazewell Genealogical and Historical Society
(719 North 11th Street—location)
PO Box 312 (mailing address)
Pekin, IL 61555-0312
(309) 477-3044; (309) 579-2732 (President)
Margaret Bush, President
Hours: Wed 1:00–4:00, Thur 9:00–12:00, Sun 2:00–4:30 (closed holiday weekends)
Pub. *Tazewell Genealogical and Historical Monthly*
(specializes in Tazewell County and surrounding counties)
$12.00 per year membership for individuals, $12.00 per year

membership for families, $15.00 per year Canadian membership, $150.00 life membership

Tri-County Genealogical Society
PO Box 355
Augusta, IL 62311-0355
(217) 392-2211; (217) 392-2626
Michael Scott, President
Hours: Mon–Tue & Thur–Fri 1:00–5:30, Wed 9:00–noon & 1:00–5:30, Sat 1:00–5:00

Tri-State Genealogical Society
(see Indiana)

Union County Historical and Genealogy Society
104 Clemens
Cobden, IL 62920
Patrick Brumleve, President
Pub. *Friends of the Union County Historical and Genealogy Society*, three times per year
$7.00 per year membership

Versailles Area Genealogical and Historical Society
113 West First Street
PO Box 92
Versailles, IL 62378
(217) 225-9091 (President); (217) 225-3227 (Second Vice President)
Joyce Workman, President; Rose Cooper, Second Vice President
Hours: Mon, Wed & Fri 1:30–5:00 (weather permitting); winter: Wed & Fri only
Pub. *The Versailles Area Genealogical & Historical Society Newsletter*, quarterly (March, June, September, December), contribution for subscription
(many family histories, census, marriages, obituaries, cemeteries, maps, scrapbooks, photo albums; research center, historical library, and museum)
$10.00 per year membership for individuals, $11.00 per year membership for couples

Vogel Genealogical Research Library
305 North First Street
PO Box 132
Holcomb, IL 61043-0132
(815) 393-4110
Doris Glade Vogel, C.G.R.S., Librarian
Hours: by appointment
(Ogle County, Illinois)

Warren County Illinois Genealogical Society
PO Box 761
Monmouth, IL 61462-0761
(309) 734-2763
Ethel Trego, Researcher
Hours: 8:30–5:00

Pub. *Prairie Pioneer*, quarterly, $2.50 per issue
$9.00 per year membership

Waverly Genealogical and Historical Society
(Congregational Church, Waverly—location)
359 East Tremont (mailing address)
Waverly, IL 62692-1026
(217) 435-4961
Myra Martin, Historian
Hours: every other Mon, and by appointment
Pub. *Newsletter*, quarterly
$6.00 per year membership for individuals

Whiteside County Genealogists Society
PO Box 145
Sterling, IL 61081-0145
(815) 625-8750
Ruby J. Isley, President
Hours: Sterling Public Library: Mon–Fri 9:00–8:00, Sat 8:00–5:00
Pub. *Whiteside Genealogical News*, quarterly
$8.00 per year membership

Will/Grundy Counties (IL) Genealogical Society
(Fossil Ridge Public Library, 386 Kennedy Road, Braidwood, IL 60408—location)
PO Box 24 (mailing address)
Wilmington, IL 60481-0024
(815) 458-2187 (Library)
Alice Dinger, Genealogist
Hours: Mon–Thur 9:00–9:00, Fri 9:00–6:00, Sat 9:00–3:00, Sun (Oct–May) 1:00–5:00
Pub. *Will/Grundy Counties Genealogical Society Newsletter*, monthly; *Will/Grundy Genealogical Society Quarterly*
(gathering and publishing local records and statistics)
$15.00 per year membership; research in our collection free, county research for a fee plus expenses

Winnebago/Boone Counties Genealogical Society
PO Box 10166
Rockford, IL 61131-0166
Ruth N. Lunde, Corresponding Secretary
Pub. *Newsletter*, five times per year
$10.00 per year membership

Zion Genealogical Society
Zion-Benton Public Library
2400 Gabriel Avenue
Zion, IL 60099-2296
(847) 360-0360
Joanne Layne
Hours: Library: Mon–Thur 9:00–9:00, Fri 9:00–6:00, Sat 9:00–5:00
Pub. *The Illuminator*, quarterly
(emphasis on southern research)

$10.00 per year membership for individuals, $11.00 per year membership for families

Independent Publications and Miscellany

Cottonwood Hill Publishing Company
PO Box 82
Benton, WI 53803
Stephen Calvert, Editor
Pub. *Galena Genealogy* (Galena and Jo Daviess County, Illinois), quarterly; $13.95 per year subscription

Family Tree Resource Network, Inc.
(312 First Grand Avenue—location)
PO Box 107 (mailing address)
Cowden, IL 62422-0107
(800) 881-2574
Helen Cox Tregillis, CEO
Hours: Mon–Fri 1:00–5:00
Pub. *Illinois Sources/Resources*, published on demand, costs vary

Hunting for Bears Genealogical and Historical Society
(see Alabama)

IlGenWeb
Part of U.S. GenWeb Project
E-mail: il@usgenweb.com
http://www.rootsweb.com/~ilgenweb
(links to other Illinois resources)

Illinois Association for the Advancement of History
Northern Illinois University
Department of History
DeKalb, IL 60115-2302
(815) 753-6818
Otto Olsen, Secretary/Treasurer
Hours: Mon–Fri 8:30–4:30

Illinois Genealogy and History News
Rt. 3, Box 65
Chandler, OK 74834-8504
R. D. Bradshaw, Editor
Pub. *Illinois Genealogy and History News*

Mason County History Project
14454 North State Route 78
Havana, IL 62644
Hugh McHarry
(primarily deals with Mason County)

Masonic Lodge, Office of the Grand Secretary
PO Box 4147
Springfield, IL 62708
send SASE

Mississippi Valley French Research
PO Box 502
Cambria, IL 62915-0502
(618) 985-6857

Eugene Beckett, Genealogist
Hours: after 5:30 P.M.
Pub. *Hello Cousins*, monthly, $22.00 per
year subscription
(Includes Missouri and Illinois, "as most
Mississippi Valley French were in
these states.")

Poplar Creek Newsletter
63 Golfview Lane
Carpentersville, IL 60110
Pub. *Poplar Creek Newsletter*, quarterly

Reppert Publications
(112 Lafayette Street—location)
PO Box 529 (mailing address)
Anna, IL 62906
(618) 833-2158; (618) 833-5813 FAX
E-mail: reppert@midwest.net
Mike Newell, Editor
Hours: 8:00–5:00
Pub. *Antique and Collectible News*,
monthly, $12.00 per year subscription
(covers Illinois, Indiana, Kentucky,
Missouri, and Tennessee)

Carl Sandburg College
2232 South Lake Storey Road
Galesburg, IL 61401
(309) 344-2518
http://csc.techcenter.org/~mcneill/
csc.html
(genealogy classes and workshops)

Weaver Genealogical Publications
Rt. 3, Box 279
Petersburg, IL 62675
(217) 632-3543
E-mail: jdcweaver@aol.com;
members@aol.com/jdcweaver/
index.html
Jeanne Crain Weaver, Editor-Owner
Hours: Office: 8:00–7:00
Pub. *Menard County Heritage
Newsletter*, quarterly (separate yearly
index), $9.00 per year subscription,
free queries for subscribers
(publishes county and court records,
cemetery records, etc.)
will research Nenard County references/
court records for a fee

**Frances Willard Historical
Association**
1730 Chicago Avenue
Evanston, IL 60201-4585
(847) 864-1396; (847) 864-1397
Rachel Kelly
(women of Illinois in the latter half of
the nineteenth century)

INDIANA

Archives and Libraries with Holdings in Genealogy

State Archives and Library

Indiana State Archives
State Library and Historical Building
140 North Senate Avenue, Room 117
Indianapolis, IN 46204-2296
(317) 232-3660; (316) 233-1085 FAX
http://www.ai.org/acin/icpr/index.html
Alan F. January, Head
Hours: Mon–Fri 8:00–4:30
Pub. *Archives/Current: Newsletter of the
Friends of the Indiana State Archives*,
quarterly
(25,000 cubic feet of records dating from
the territorial period to the present)
research: $10.00 per half-hour for out-of-
state residents; photocopies: from 25¢
each from paper originals, $1.00 each
from microform originals

Society of Indiana Archivists
State Library and Historical Building
140 North Senate Avenue
Indianapolis, IN 46204-2296
(317) 232-2537
E-mail: cawley.1@nd.edu
http://cawley.archives.nd.edu/sia/

Indiana State Library
140 North Senate Avenue
Indianapolis, IN 46204-2296
(317) 232-3689 (Genealogy Division);
(317) 232-7763 TDD (Genealogy
Division); (317) 232-3664 (Newspaper
Section); (317) 232-3670 (Indiana
Reference Section); (317) 232-3671
(Manuscript Section); (317) 232-7763
TDD
http://www.statelib.lib.in.us
Diane Sharp, Coordinator, Genealogy
Division; Cynthia Faunce, Consultant/
Senior Subject Specialist, Indiana
Division
Hours: Genealogy Division: Mon, Wed
& Fri 8:00–4:30, Tue & Thur 8:00–
8:00, Sat 8:30–4:00 (call to confirm
hours); Indiana Division (housing the
Newspaper, Manuscript and Indiana
Reference sections): Mon–Fri 8:00–
4:30
("The Genealogy Section contains many
items pertaining to family history
useful to genealogists. Most of the
materials relate to families in Indiana
although material from the eastern
seaboard and southern states is also
collected. The staff is not able to
perform research but can assist those
who come in to use the collections.
The Newspaper Section contains
newspapers from around the state,

both historical and present day. The
Reference Section contains many
volumes pertaining to the history of the
state of Indiana and biographical
information about Indiana people. It
also includes the depository for state
documents. The Manuscript Section
holds unpublished items relating to
Indiana people, places and events.
Civil War materials are one strength of
the collection.")
photocopy charge, postage charge

State Historical Societies

Indiana Historical Society
Indiana State Library and Historical
Building
315 West Ohio Street
PO Box 88255
Indianapolis, IN 46202
(317) 233-3157 (Editor); (317) 232-1879
(Library); (317) 232-1874; (317) 233-
3109 FAX
E-mail: rboomhower@statelib.lib.in.us;
agressitt@statelib.lib.in.us;
ldarbee@statelib.lib.in.us
http://www.ihs1830.org/
Ruth Dorrel, Editor
Hours: Mon–Fri 8:00–4:30, Sat (Sept–
May) 8:30–4:00
Pub. *The Hoosier Genealogist*, quarterly
(for members only, no subscription)
(library specializes in Indiana and The
Old Northwest)
$20.00 per year membership

Indiana Historical Bureau
State Library and Historical Building
140 North Senate Avenue, Room 408
Indianapolis, IN 46204-2296
(317) 232-2535; (317) 232-3728 FAX;
(317) 232-7763 TDD
E-mail: ihb@statelib.lib.in.us
http://www.statelib.lib.in.us/www/ihb/
ihb.html
Judy A. Rippel, Administrative Assistant
Hours: Mon–Fri 8:00–4:30
Pub. *Indiana History Bulletin*, quarterly,
$5.00 per year subscription (calendar
year); *The Indiana Historian*,
quarterly, $5.00 per year subscription
(calendar year)

City, County and Regional Archives and Libraries

Alexandrian Public Library
115 West Fifth Street
Mount Vernon, IN 47620
(812) 838-3286; (812) 838-9639 FAX
Jas Holman, Director
Hours: Mon–Thur 9:00–8:00, Fri–Sat
9:00–5:00, Sun 1:00–5:00
(Posey County, Indiana, local history and
genealogy)

Allen County Public Library

Fred J. Reynolds Historical Genealogy
Department
900 Webster Street
PO Box 2270
Fort Wayne, IN 46802
(219) 424-7241, ext. 3315
http://www.acpl.lib.in.us/genealogy/
genealogy.html
Curt B. Witcher, Manager
Hours: Mon–Thur 9:00–9:00, Fri–Sat
9:00–6:00, Sun 1:00–6:00 (Labor
Day–Memorial Day)
Pub. *Periodical Source Index* (PERSI),
annually, $40.00 per year subscription
(North American genealogy and local
history: 183,000 volumes, 123,470
pieces of microtext, approximately
3,500 periodicals)
$50.00 per year membership

Anderson Public Library

Local History and Genealogy
Department
Indiana Room
111 East 12th Street
Anderson, IN 46013
(765) 641-2442
E-mail: beth@apl.acsc.net
Beth E. Oljace, Local History and
Genealogy Librarian
Hours: Mon–Thur 9:00–9:00, Fri–Sat
9:00–5:30, Sun 1:00–5:00
(Madison and Wayne counties, Indiana)

Bartholomew County Public Library

Fifth and Lafayette Streets
Columbus, IN 47201
(812) 379-1266
Hours: Mon–Thur 8:30–9:00, Fri–Sat
8:30–6:00, Sun (Sept–Apr) 1:00–4:00
Pub. *Footnotes*, quarterly

Bedford Public Library

1323 K Street
Bedford, IN 47421
(812) 275-4471; (812) 277-1145 FAX
http://www.bedlib.org
Andrea Pedigo, Reference Specialist
Hours: Mon–Thur 9:00–8:00, Fri–Sat
9:00–5:00, Sun 1:00–5:00
(local newspaper on microfilm, not
indexed)
search fee: 10¢ per page for copies, plus
postage

Bell Memorial Public Library

306 North Broadway
PO Box 368
Mentone, IN 46539
(219) 353-7234
Eileen Bowser, Librarian's Assistant
Hours: Mon–Wed & Fri–Sat 9:00–5:00,
Thur 9:00–8:00

Bloomfield-Eastern Greene County Public Library

125 South Franklin Street
Bloomfield, IN 47424
(812) 384-4125; (812) 384-0820
E-mail: c.konnert@bloomfield.lib.in.us
Carolyn Konnert, Library Director
Hours: Mon–Thur 10:00–8:00, Fri–Sat
10:00–5:00

Bluffton-Wells County Public Library

220 West Washington
Bluffton, IN 46714
(219) 824-2315
Barbara Elliott
Hours: Mon–Thur 9:00–8:00, Fri 9:00–
6:00, Sat (Jun–Oct) 9:00–5:00, Sat
(Sept–May) 9:00–12:00

Brookville Library

919 Main Street
Brookville, IN 47012
(317) 647-4031
Hours: Mon–Fri 10:00–8:00, Sat 10:00–
1:00

Charlestown-Clark County Public Library

Sellersburg Library
Indiana Room
430 North Indiana
Sellersburg, IN 47172
(812) 246-4493; (812) 246-4382 FAX
Carol Haas
Hours: Mon–Thur 9:00–8:00, Fri–Sat
9:00–5:00
(mainly local history plus cemetery and
church listings)

Charlestown-Clark County Public Library

51 Clark Road
Charlestown, IN 47111
(812) 256-3337; (812) 256-3890 FAX
Susan Bennett, Researcher; Linda
Lossner, Researcher
Hours: Mon–Thur 9:00–8:00, Fri–Sat
9:00–5:00
(main genealogy source for the county)

Crawford County Indiana Museum

Rt. 1
Leavenworth, IN 47137

Crawfordsville District Public Library

222 South Washington Street
Crawfordsville, IN 47933

Crown Point Community Library

214 South Court Street
Crown Point, IN 46307
(219) 663-0270
Elizabeth Anstak
Hours: Mon–Thur 9:00–8:00, Fri–Sat
9:00–5:00
(specializes in Indiana, especially Crown
Point history)

Culbertson Mansion State Historic Site

914 East Main Street
New Albany, IN 47150
(812) 944-9600
Bill Brockman, Curator
Hours: Tue–Sat 9:00–5:00, Sun 1:00–
5:00
(genealogical services)
donations accepted

Danville Public Library

101 South Indiana Street
Danville, IN 46122
(317) 745-2604; (317) 745-0756 FAX
Becky Gramling, Historical Department
Hours: Mon–Thur 9:00–8:00, Fri–Sat
9:00–5:00, Sun 2:00–5:00

Daughters of the American Revolution

Francis Vigo Chapter DAR Genealogical
Library
3 West Scott Street
Vincennes, IN 47592
(812) 882-2096
Jane Prather Niehaus, Librarian
Hours: Thur 10:00–4:00
(early Knox County, Indiana, genealogy
and history)
photocopies: 10¢ each

East Chicago Public Library

2401 East Columbus Drive
East Chicago, IN 46312
(219) 397-2453
Eileen Cvitkovich, MLS Archivist
Hours: Mon–Thur 9:00–8:00, Fri–Sat
9:00–5:30; East Chicago History
Room: Mon & Wed–Fri 9:00–5:00

Eckhart Public Library

603 South Jackson
Auburn, IN 46706
(219) 925-2414
Janelle Graber, Director
Hours: Mon–Thur 9:00–9:00, Fri 9:00–
7:00, Sat 9:00–5:00

Elkhart Public Library

300 South Second Street
Elkhart, IN 46516
(219) 522-5669; (219) 293-9213 FAX
Marsha J. Eilers, Associate Director,
Reference Services
Hours: Mon–Thur 9:00–9:00, Fri–Sat
9:00–6:00
("Collection development centers on
Elkhart and surrounding counties.")

Evansville Museum of Arts and Science

411 S.E. Riverside Drive
Evansville, IN 47713
(812) 425-2406
John W. Streetman, III, Director
(local and regional history collection)

Evansville-Vanderburgh County Public Library
22 S.E. Fifth Street
Evansville, IN 47708
(812) 428-8218
Judith Hanefeldt, Head Reference Department
Hours: Sept–Jun: Mon–Wed 8:30–7:00, Thur–Sat 8:30–5:30; Jun–Sept: Mon–Sat 8:30–5:30
(small DAR collection, available to the public on Friday afternoons)

Fayette County Public Library
828 Grand Avenue
Connersville, IN 47331-2098
(765) 827-0883; (765) 825-4592 FAX
Paulette Hayes, Local History/Genealogy
Hours: Mon–Fri 9:00–8:00, Sat 9:00–5:00

Frankfort Community Public Library
208 West Clinton Street
Frankfort, IN 46041
(317) 654-8746; (317) 654-8747
E-mail: fcpl@accs.net
Helen E. Grove, Genealogist
Hours: Mon–Thur 9:00–8:00, Fri–Sat 9:00–5:00
(genealogy of Clinton County and the surrounding area)

Franklin College Library
501 East Monroe Street
Franklin, IN 46131-2598
(317) 738-8162; (317) 736-6030 FAX
Mary A. Medlicott, Archivist
Hours: fall and spring semesters: Mon–Thur 8:00–midnight, Fri 8:00–5:00, Sat 1:00–5:00, Sun 1:00 P.M.–midnight; winter term (January) and summer hours are shortened
("Archives, American Baptist churches of Indiana; Archives, Franklin College; David Demaree Banta Indiana History Collection.")
fee for photocopies mailed to patrons

Gary Public Library
220 West Fifth Avenue
Gary, IN 46402
(219) 886-2484
Hours: Mon–Thur 9:30–8:00, Fri–Sat 9:30–5:00

Hacksma House Genealogy Library
(see Washington)

Huntington City-Township Public Library
Indiana Room
200 West Market Street
Huntington, IN 46750
(219) 356-0824
Joan Keefer, Department Head—Indiana Room
Hours: Mon–Thur 9:00–8:00, Fri–Sat 9:00–5:00
(extensive local history and genealogy)

Indiana State University
Cunningham Memorial Library
Department of Rare Books-Special Collections
Terre Haute, IN 47809
(812) 237-2610
Pub. *Friends of the Library Newsletter*

Indiana University-Purdue University at Fort Wayne
Walter E. Helmke Library
2101 East Coliseum Boulevard
Fort Wayne, IN 46805-1499
(219) 481-6514; (219) 481-6509 FAX
http://www-lib.ipfw.indiana.edu/index.html

Indianapolis-Marion County Public Library
Social Sciences Service Section
(40 East Saint Clair, Indianapolis, IN 46204—location)
PO Box 211 (mailing address)
Indianapolis, IN 46206
(317) 269-1700; (317) 269-5229 FAX
http://www.imcpl.lib.in.us
Hours: Mon–Fri 9:00–9:00, Sat 9:00–5:00, Sun 1:00–5:00
Pub. *Reading in Indianapolis*, monthly
(only basic, introductory guides to doing genealogical research)

Jay County Public Library
(315 North Ship Street—location)
131 East Walnut Street (mailing address)
Portland, IN 47371-2192
(219) 726-7890; (219) 726-7317 FAX
Marcia Ford, Adult Services Librarian
Hours: Mon–Fri 8:00–8:00, Sat 8:00–5:00
(specializes in Jay County history)
search fee: $10.00 per hour

Jeffersonville Township Public Library
211 East Court Avenue
PO Box 1548
Jeffersonville, IN 47131
(812) 282-7765
Ilona Franck, Manager, Adult Services
Hours: Mon–Thur 9:00–9:00, Fri 9:00–5:30, Sat 9:00–5:00
(Clark County)

Johnson County Public Library
401 South State Street
Franklin, IN 46131
(317) 738-2833; (317) 738-9635 FAX
E-mail: frlref1@infodepo.jcpl.lib.in.us
Terri Frank, Reference/Historical Room Librarian
Hours: Mon–Thur 9:00–8:00, Fri 9:00–6:00, Sat 9:00–5:00, Sun (Labor Day–Memorial Day) 1:00–5:00
(Johnson County, Indiana, archives)

Knox County Public Library Historical Collection
502 North Seventh Street
Vincennes, IN 47591

(812) 886-4380; (812) 886-0342
E-mail: bspangle@kcpls1.vinu.edu
http://birch.palni.edu/~bspangle/histcoll.htm
Brian Spangle, Historical Collection Administrator
Hours: Mon & Thur 8:30–5:30, Tue 5:00–9:00, Wed & alternate Fri & Sat 1:30–5:30

Knox County Records Library
819 Broadway
Vincennes, IN 47591
(812) 885-2557
http://birch.palni.edu/~bspangle/reclib.htm
Brian Spangle, Librarian
Hours: Mon & Wed–Sat 8:30–12:30 (closed Fri or Sat on alternate weeks), Tue 12:00–4:00

Kokomo-Howard County Public Library
Genealogy-Local History Room
220 North Union Street
Kokomo, IN 46901-4614
(765) 457-3242; (765) 457-3683 FAX
E-mail: mmcnabb@kokomo.lib.in.us
http://www.kokomo.lib.in.us
Michele McNabb, Genealogy and Local History Coordinator
Hours: Mon–Thur 9:00–9:00, Fri–Sat 9:00–5:30, Sun (Labor Day–Memorial Day) 2:00–5:30
research: $2.00 plus photocopies at 10¢ per page

Lawrenceburg Public Library
123 West High Street
Lawrenceburg, IN 47025
(812) 537-2775
Eleanor Ewbank, Director
Hours: Mon–Thur 10:00–8:00, Fri–Sat 10:00–5:00
("Have family histories, county histories, cemetery records, census records, local newspapers from 1819.")
enclose SASE with written inquiry, copies 25¢ per page from paper original, 50¢ per page from microfilm original

Lewis Historical Library
LRC-22
Vincennes University
Vincennes, IN 47591
(812) 888-4330
E-mail: gstevens@vunet.vinu.edu
Robert R. Stevens, Director
Hours: Mon–Fri 8:30–4:30

Logansport Public Library
616 East Broadway
Logansport, IN 46947
(219) 753-6383
Hours: Mon–Fri 9:00–9:00, Sat 9:00–5:00

Madison-Jefferson County Public Library
420 West Main Street
Madison, IN 47250
(812) 265-2744
Janice Barnes, Library Assistant
Hours: Mon–Thur 9:00–8:00, Fri–Sat 9:00–6:00
$5.00 search fee per surname or subject for non-residents, copies 10¢ for non-residents

Marion Public Library
Indiana Room
600 South Washington Street
Marion, IN 46953-1992
(765) 668-2900; (765) 668-2911
Barbara Love, Head of Indiana History, Genealogy, and Museum Services
Hours: Mon, Wed & Fri 9:00–5:30; Tue & Thur 9:00–9:00, Sat 9:00–5:00, Sun 1:00–5:00; summer: Mon, Wed & Fri 9:00–5:30, Tue & Thur 9:00–8:00, Sat 1:00–5:00
(Marion and Grant County history)
handling $1.00, photocopies 10¢ each from paper originals, 15¢ each from microfilm originals, plus postage

William Hammond Mathers Museum
601 East Eighth Street
Bloomington, IN 47405
(812) 335-6873

Alameda McCollough Library
909 South Street
Lafayette, IN 47901
(765) 742-8411
Nancy L. Weirich, Librarian and Tippecanoe County Historian
Hours: Tue & Thur–Fri 1:00–5:00, Wed 1:00–7:00, third Sat (Feb–Nov)1:00–5:00, closed Jan

Mennonite Historical Library
Goshen College
Goshen, IN 46526
(219) 535-7418; (219) 535-7438 FAX
E-mail: anetss@goshen.edu
John D. Roth, Director
Hours: Mon–Fri 8:00–5:00, Sat 9:00–1:00
Pub. *Mennonite Quarterly Review* (a scholarly historical publication), $24.00 per year subscription
(strong in genealogy of Amish and Mennonite families from Switzerland, Germany, The Netherlands, West Prussia and Russia; U.S., European and Canadian records)
$30.00 per year membership in Mennonite Historical Society includes periodical

Michigan City Public Library
One Library Plaza
Michigan City, IN 46360-3393
(219) 873-3063

Vivianne L. Crowley, Library Genealogist
Hours: Library: Mon–Thur 9:00–8:00, Fri–Sat 9:00–6:00, Sun 1:00–5:00; Genealogy: Wed & Fri–Sat 12:00–5:00
(Michigan City and Indiana family history)

Middletown Public Library
880 High
Middletown, IN 47356

Minnetrista Cultural Center
1200 North Minnetrista Parkway
Muncie, IN 47303-2925
(317) 282-4848
Karen Vincent, Director of Collections
Hours: Library: Mon–Sat 10:00–5:00
(archival material from east central Indiana)

Mishawaka-Penn Public Library
209 Lincoln Way, East
Mishawaka, IN 46544
(219) 259-5277
Olga Nazaroff
Hours: winter: Mon–Fri 9:00–9:00, Sat 9:00–6:00; summer: Mon–Thur 9:00–9:00, Fri 9:00–6:00, Sat 9:00–1:00

Monroe County Public Library
Indiana Room
303 East Kirkwood Avenue
Bloomington, IN 47408
(812) 349-3080
http://www.monroe.lib.in.us
Reann Lydick, Indiana Room Librarian
Hours: Mon–Thur 9:00–9:00, Fri 9:00–6:00, Sat 9:00–5:00, Sun 1:00–5:00
(Local history, genealogy, Indiana history; "We have Bloomington/Monroe County newspapers microfilmed 1824–present, vital statistics, cemetery records, census records.")

Morgan County Public Library
110 South Jefferson Street
Martinsville, IN 46151
(317) 342-3451
E-mail: morglib@scican.net
http://www.scican.net/~morglib/libweb.html
Janice Kistler, Reference Librarian
Hours: Mon–Thur 9:00–8:30, Fri–Sat 9:00–5:30, Sun 1:00–5:00

Morrisson-Reeves Library
80 North Sixth Street
Richmond, IN 47374
(317) 966-8291
Marilyn Nobbe, Reference Librarian
Hours: Sept–May: Mon–Thur 9:00–9:00, Fri–Sat 9:00–5:30; Jun–Aug: Mon–Thur 9:00–7:00, Fri–Sat 9:00–5:30
("This is a relatively small collection which focuses on Wayne and

contiguous counties; index of Richmond newspapers from 1822.")
copies 10¢ each plus cost of mailing

Muncie Public Library
301 East Jackson Street
Muncie, IN 47305
(317) 747-8200
Marie Ann Coil, Head Reference Librarian
Hours: Mon–Fri 8:00–7:00, Sat 9:00–6:00

New Albany-Floyd County Public Library
Stuart Barth Wrege Indiana History Room
180 West Spring Street
New Albany, IN 47150-3692
(812) 949-3527
Benita K. Mason, Department Head
Hours: Mon–Thur 9:00–8:30, Fri–Sat 9:00–5:30
(Floyd County history and southern Indiana genealogy)

New Castle-Henry County Public Library
376 South 15th Street
PO Box J
New Castle, IN 47362
(765) 529-0362; (765) 521-3581 FAX
http://www.nchcpl.lib.in.us
Bertha Snell, Genealogy Librarian
Hours: Mon–Thur 8:30–9:00, Fri 8:30–6:00, Sat 8:30–5:00, Sun (Sept–May) 1:00–5:00
photocopies 10¢ per page

New Harmony Workingmen's Institute Library and Museum
407 West Tavern Street
PO Box 368
New Harmony, IN 47631
(812) 682-4806
Bonnie Smith, Director
Hours: Tue–Sat 10:00–4:30
("Extensive local history file.")
search fee: $4.00

Noble County Public Library
813 East Main
Albion, IN 46701
(219) 636-7197
Linda J. Shultz, Director
Hours: Mon–Thur 8:30–8:30, Fri 8:30–5:30, Sat 8:30–3:30

Noblesville-Southeastern Public Library
Indiana Room
1 Library Plaza
Noblesville, IN 46060
(317) 773-1384; (317) 773-0578
E-mail: masseyn@nspl.lib.in.us
http://www.nspl.lib.in.us/referenc.html
Nancy Massey, Indiana Room Clerk

Hours: Mon–Thur 9:30–8:30, Fri–Sat
9:30–5:30, Sun 1:30–5:30
(emphasis on Hamilton County histories
and genealogical records)

Ohio Township Public Library System

23 West Jennings Street
Newburgh, IN 47630
(812) 853-5468
Janet Weideman, Local History/
Genealogy Librarian
Hours: Mon 12:00–4:00, Tue–Fri 9:00–
5:00, Sat 10:00–5:00

Paoli Public Library

10 East Court
Paoli, IN 47454
(812) 723-3841
Carol Vance, Librarian
Hours: Mon & Thur–Fri 12:30–5:30, Tue
11:00–7:00, Sat 9:00–1:00

Plainfield Public Library

Guilford Township Historical Collection
1120 Stafford Road
Plainfield, IN 46168-2230
(317) 839-6602; (317) 839-4044 FAX
Susan Miller Carter, Department Head
Hours: Mon–Thur 12:00–5:00 & 6:00–
8:30, Sat 9:00–noon & 1:00–5:00

Plymouth Public Library

201 North Center Street
Plymouth, IN 46563
(219) 936-2324
Lillian Sherwood, Reference Librarian
Hours: Mon–Thur 9:00–9:00, Fri 9:00–
8:00, Sat 9:00–5:30, Sun (Oct–Apr)
1:00–5:00
(repository for the Pioneer Society of
Marshall County lineages)
search: $2.00 minimum, includes
photocopies up to that amount at 15¢
per sheet, over $2.00 you will be
notified of extra charges, please
include SASE

Porter County Public Library System

107 East Jefferson Street
Valparaiso, IN 46383
(219) 462-0524
Larry J. Clark, Genealogy Department
Head
Hours: Mon–Fri 9:00–9:00, Sat 9:00–
5:00
(Indiana, Midwest, eastern and
southeastern United States, Canada)

Pulaski County Public Library

121 South Riverside Drive
Winamac, IN 46996
(219) 946-3432
Lynda Irving
Hours: Mon 9:00–8:00, Tue–Sat 9:00–
6:00

Spencer County Public Library

210 Walnut Street
Rockport, IN 47635-1398
(812) 649-4866, ext. 12; (812) 649-4018
FAX
E-mail: scpl@pscl.net
http://www.rockport-spco.lib.in.us/
Becky Middleton, Genealogy Room
Librarian
Hours: Mon & Fri 9:00–5:00, Tue–Thur
9:00–9:00, Sat 9:00–3:00
(microfilm copies of probate records
November 1833–December 1921,
guardianships 1871–1885, wills 1833–
1933, marriages March 1818–
December 1921, naturalizations July
1852–1903, indentures 1836–1855,
deeds November 1818–1886, grantor/
grantee indexes 1818–1888, index of
birth records 1882–1920, death records
1882–1936)

Rockville Public Library

106 North Market Street
Rockville, IN 47872
(765) 569-5544
Hours: Mon–Fri 9:00–6:00, Sat 9:00–
2:00

Saint Joseph County Public Library

304 South Main
South Bend, IN 46601
(219) 282-4621; (219) 282-4679 FAX
http://sjcpl.lib.in.us
Mary Waterson, Local History/
Genealogy
Hours: Mon–Thur 9:00–9:00,
Fri–Sat 9:00–6:00, Sun (Oct–Apr)
1:00–5:00

Seymour Public Library

Second and Walnut Streets
Seymour, IN 47274
Hours: Mon–Fri 8:30–8:30, Sat 9:00–
5:00, Sun 1:00–5:00

Shelbyville-Shelby County Public Library

57 West Broadway
Shelbyville, IN 46176
(317) 398-7121; (317) 398-4480
(Reference); (317) 835-2653 FAX;
(317) 398-4430 FAX (Reference)
E-mail: annems@shelbynet.net
http://sscpl.lib.in.us
Ann Herold-Short, Director
Hours: Mon–Thur 9:00–9:00, Fri 9:00–
7:00, Sat 9:00–5:00

Sullivan County Public Library

Genealogy/Local History Department
100 South Crowder Street
Sullivan, IN 47882
(812) 268-4957; (812) 268-5370 FAX
Donna K. Adams, Sullivan County
Historian and Head of Genealogy/
Local History Department
Hours: Mon–Fri 9:00–5:00, Sat noon–
5:00

Tippecanoe County Public Library

Reference Department
627 South Street
Lafayette, IN 47901
(317) 429-0100
Joel Robinson, Director
Hours: Mon–Thur 9:00–9:00, Fri–Sat
9:00–6:00, Sun 1:00–6:00
$3.00 for search of newspapers from
1854 (must have exact dates)

Tipton County Public Library

127 East Madison Street
Tipton, IN 46072
(765) 675-8761; (765) 675-4475 FAX
Julie Brown, Head of Information
Services
Hours: Mon–Thur 9:30–8:00, Fri–Sat
9:30–5:00

University of Notre Dame

Rare Books and Special Collections
102 Hesburgh Library
Notre Dame, IN 46556
(219) 631-5636; (219) 631-6772
E-mail: library.rarebook.1@nd.edu
http://www.nd.edu/

University of Southern Indiana

David L. Rice Library
Special Collections/University Archives
8600 University Boulevard
Evansville, IN 47712-3595
(812) 464-1896
Gina Walker, Certified Archivist
Hours: Mon–Fri 8:00–noon & 1:00–4:30

Vigo County Public Library

Special Collections/Archives
1 Library Square
Terre Haute, IN 47807
(812) 232-1113, ext. 212 or 292
http://vax1.vigo.lib.in.us
Nancy Sherrill, Genealogy; Susan
Dehler, Archives
Hours: Mon–Thur 9:00–9:00, Fri 9:00–
6:00, Sat 9:00–5:00, Sun 1:00–5:00
(Labor Day–Memorial Day)

Wabash Carnegie Public Library

188 West Hill Street
Wabash, IN 46992
(219) 563-2972; (219) 563-0222 FAX
E-mail: wcpl@ctlnet.com
Helen M. Bruss, Technical Services
Hours: Mon–Thur 9:00–8:00, Fri–Sat
9:00–5:00; summer: Mon–Thur 9:00–
6:00, Fri–Sat 9:00–5:00
(Wabash County history and archives)

Warrick County Museum, Inc.

117 South First Street
PO Box 581
Boonville, IN 47601
(812) 897-3100
Virginia S. Allen, Director
Hours: Mon–Thur 11:00–2:00, Sun 1:00–
4:00
free admission, tours arranged

Warsaw Community Public Library
315 East Center Street
Warsaw, IN 46580
(219) 267-6011
Joni L. Brookins, Assistant Director
Hours: Mon–Wed & Fri 9:00–9:00, Thur
& Sat 9:00–6:00
(materials on Kosciusko County,
Indiana)

Willard Library
Regional and Family History Center
21 First Avenue
Evansville, IN 47710
(812) 425-4309; (812) 425-4303 FAX
Lyn Martin, Special Collections
Hours: Tue 9:00–8:00, Wed–Fri
9:00–5:30, Sat 9:00–5:00,
Sun 1:00–5:00
(Clark, Crawford, Daviess, Dubois,
Floyd, Gibson, Greene, Harrison,
Jefferson, Knox, Lawrence, Martin,
Orange, Perry, Pike, Posey, Scott,
Spencer, Sullivan, Vanderburgh,
Warrick and Washington counties,
Indiana; Alexander, Clay, Edward,
Franklin, Gallatin, Hamilton, Hardin,
Jackson, Jefferson, Johnson,
Lawrence, Massac, Pope, Pulaski,
Richland, Saline, Union, Wabash,
Wayne, White and Williamson
counties, Illinois; Ballard,
Breckinridge, Butler, Caldwell,
Christian, Crittenden, Daviess,
Grayson, Hancock, Hardin,
Henderson, Hopkins, Livingston,
Logan, Lyon, McCracken, McLean,
Meade, Muhlenberg, Ohio, Todd,
Trigg, Union and Webster counties,
Kentucky)

Worthington-Jefferson Township Public Library
26 North Commercial Street
Worthington, IN 47471
(812) 875-3815; (812) 875-3815 FAX
E-mail: markle@uno.com
Lori Markle, Director
Hours: Mon & Wed noon–4:00, Tue &
Thur noon–8:00, Fri 9:00–4:00, Sat
10:00–2:00

Historical Societies— Local and Regional

Adams County Historical Society
(420 West Monroe Street—location)
PO Box 262 (mailing address)
Decatur, IN 46733-0262
(219) 724-2341
E-mail: historian@decaturnet.com
Gordon Gregg, President,
Hours: Sun (Jun–Sept) 1:00–4:00, and by
appointment
Pub. *The Trumpeter*, quarterly

$10.00 per year membership for
individuals, $15.00 per year
membership for couples, $25.00 per
year Sustaining membership

Alexandria Monroe Township Historical Society
313 North Harrison Street
Alexandria, IN 46001-1624
Pub. *Alexandria Monroe Township
Historical Society Newsletter*

Allen County-Fort Wayne Historical Society
302 East Berry Street
Fort Wayne, IN 46802
(219) 426-2882
William J. Decker, Director
Hours: Feb–Dec: Tue–Fri 9:00–5:00,
Sat–Sun 12:00–5:00
Pub. *Allen County-Fort Wayne Historical
Society Bulletin*, bimonthly; *The Old
Fort News*, annually
$25.00 per year membership

Allen County Historian
220LN 201A
Lake George
Fremont, IN 46737
Michael Westfall

Anson Wolcott Historical Society
(500 North Range Street—location)
PO Box 417 (mailing address)
Wolcott, IN 47995-0417
(219) 279-2123; (219) 279-2167 FAX
Richard Wheeler, President
Hours: by appointment
Pub. *AWHS News*, annually, free

Bartholomew County Historical Society
McEwen-Samuels-Marr House
524 Third Street
Columbus, IN 47201
(812) 372-3541
John Hamblem, Volunteer Librarian;
Laura Moses, Director
Hours: Tue & Thur 2:00–4:00, and by
appointment
Pub. *Quarterly Connection*, quarterly
$15.00 per year membership for
individuals, $25.00 per year
membership for families

Beiger Heritage Corporation
317 Lincoln Way, East
Mishawaka, IN 46544
(219) 256-0365

Benton County Historian
711 East Third Street
Fowler, IN 47944-2343
(765) 884-1764
Freeman Harold Furr
Hours: Mon–Fri 8:00–4:00

Benton County Historical Society
711 East Third Street
Fowler, IN 47944

(765) 884-1848
Myrtle E. Stone, President

Blackford County Historian
321 North High Street
PO Box 264
Hartford City, IN 47348
Dwight Mikkelson

Blackford County Historical Society
321 North High Street
PO Box 264
Hartford City, IN 47348
Sinuard Castelo, President
Hours: Sun 1:00–4:00, and by
appointment
(houses the Cecil Beeson Genealogical
Library)
$2.00 per year membership for
individuals, $5.00 per year
membership for families, $25.00 life
membership

Boone County Historian
2202 Roselawn Drive
Lebanon, IN 46052
Rosemary Peterman

Boone County Historical Society, Inc.
(105 West Main Street—location)
PO Box 141 (mailing address)
Lebanon, IN 46052
Marilyn Wall, Treasurer
Pub. *Boone County Historical Society
Newsletter*, three to four times per year
$10.00 per year membership (beginning
July)

Brown County Historian
PO Box 668
Nashville, IN 47448
Bart Updike

Brown County Historical Society, Inc.
Brown County Historical Society Log
Museum
Museum Lane, Highway 135 North of
Nashville
PO Box 668
Nashville, IN 47448
(812) 988-4297; (812) 988-6089
Helen Reeve, Genealogist
Hours: by appointment
Pub. *Newsletter*, quarterly

Carroll County Historian
Carroll County Historical Society
(Museum)
(Carroll County Courthouse,
101 West Main Street,
Ground Floor—location)
PO Box 277 (mailing address)
Delphi, IN 46923
(765) 564-3152; (765) 564-3634
Phyllis Davis Moore, Curator
Hours: Museum: Mon–Tue & Thur–Fri
8:00–5:00, Wed 8:00–noon & 1:00–
5:00, and by appointment

Carroll County Historical Society (Museum)

(Carroll County Courthouse,
101 West Main Street,
Ground Floor—location)
PO Box 277 (mailing address)
Delphi, IN 46923-0277
(765) 564-3152; (765) 564-3634; (765) 564-4851
Phyllis Davis Moore, Curator
Hours: Mon–Tue & Thur–Fri 8:00–5:00, Wed 8:00–noon & 1:00–5:00, and by appointment
Pub. *Newsletter*, quarterly
$5.00 per year active membership, $1.00 per year Junior membership (under 18), $25.00 per year Patron membership, $100.00 life membership

Cass County Historian

2732 East Broadway
Logansport, IN 46947
Hubert Leslie

Cass County Historical Society

1004 East Market Street
Logansport, IN 46947
(219) 753-3866
Bruce Stuart, Curator
Hours: Tue–Sat 1:00–5:00
(Cass County information only)
search fee for donation

Clark County Historian

Charlestown Clark Libraries
Sellersburg Library
430 North Indiana
Sellersburg, IN 47172
(812) 246-4493; (812) 246-4382 FAX
Carol Haas

Clark County Historical Society and Howard Steamboat Museum, Inc.

1101 East Market Street
PO Box 606
Jeffersonville, IN 47131-0606
(812) 283-3728; (812) 283-6049 FAX
Yvonne B. Knight, Administrator
Hours: Museum: Tue–Sat 10:00–3:00, Sun 1:00–3:00; Library: by appointment
(steamboats, Ohio River history, the Howards of Jeffersonville, steamboat builders)
$15.00 per year membership for individuals; admission charged for mansion tour

Clay County Historian

130 North Washington
Brazil, IN 47834
Robert T. Moore

Clinton County Historical Society, Inc.

Historical Museum
301 East Clinton Street
Frankfort, IN 46041
(765) 654-7773

Nancy Hart, Registrar/Curator and Director
Hours: Mon–Fri 8:00–4:00
Pub. *Historical Notes*, bimonthly
$15.00 per year membership

Clinton County, Indiana, Historian

4641 East County Road 250N
Frankfort, IN 46041-8256
(765) 249-2616
Mary Ellen Mattingly

Crawford County Historical and Genealogical Society

PO Box 133
Leavenworth, IN 47137
Sharon Morris, Secretary/Treasurer
Pub. *Crawford Countian*, quarterly
$10.00 per year membership

Daviess County Historian

812 East National Highway
Washington, IN 47501
L. Rex Myers

Daviess County Historical Society

PO Box 2341
Washington, IN 47501

Dearborn County Historian

136 Tebbs Avenue
Lawrenceburg, IN 47025
Doris W. Marple

Historical Society of Decatur County, Inc.

222 North Franklin Street
PO Box 163
Greensburg, IN 42740
(812) 663-2478 (President)
Pub. *Historical Society of Decatur County Bulletin*, quarterly
$5.00 per year membership

DeKalb County Historian

DeKalb County Historical Society
PO Box 686
Auburn, IN 46706-0686
(219) 925-4560; (219) 925-4563
John Martin Smith

DeKalb County Historical Society

PO Box 686
Auburn, IN 46706-0686
(219) 925-4560; (219) 925-4563
John Martin Smith, DeKalb County Historian
free search, but donations accepted

Delaware County Historical Alliance

(120 East Washington—location)
PO Box 1266 (mailing address)
Muncie, IN 47308
(765) 282-1550
E-mail: dcha@iquest.net
http://www.iquest.net/~dcha/
Angi Weiss, Executive Director Interim
Hours: Mon–Fri 9:00–5:00; Heritage Library: Mon–Tue 10:00–4:00, and by appointment

Pub. *Delaware County Genealogist*, quarterly, $13.00 per year subscription; *Delaware County Heritage*, bimonthly
("Goal is the preservation of our local history, family history, and our architectural heritage.")
$20.00 per year membership for individuals (includes only *Delaware County Heritage*), $30.00 per year membership for families, $5.00 per year membership for students; research: $15.00 per hour, one-hour minimum

DuBois County Historian

1529 Jackson Street
Jasper, IN 47546
Lillian Doane

DuBois County Historical Society, Inc.

737 West Eighth Street
Jasper, IN 47546
(812) 482-3074
John J. Fierst, Secretary

East Chicago Historical Society

East Chicago Public Library
East Chicago History Room
2401 East Columbus Drive
East Chicago, IN 46312
(219) 397-4253 (Library)
Jennifer Beiriger, MLS Archivist
Hours: Library: Mon–Fri 9:00–5:00, Sat 9:00–5:30; East Chicago History Room: Mon & Wed–Fri 9:00–5:00
Pub. *Memory Lane* (department newsletter), seasonally, free

Elkhart County Historian

71346 State Highway 19
Nappanee, IN 46550
John Stahly

Elkhart County Historical Society, Inc.

Elkhart County Historical Museum
304 West Vistula
PO Box 343
Bristol, IN 46507
(219) 848-4322 (Museum); (219) 848-5703 FAX
E-mail: echm@juno.com
Tina Mellott, Director/Curator
Hours: Museum: Wed–Fri 10:00–4:00, Sun 1:00–5:00
Pub. *Elkhart County Historical Society Newsletter*, bimonthly
$5.00 per year membership for individuals, $7.50 per year membership for families, $100.00 life membership

Fayette County Historian

610 Marion Street
Connersville, IN 47331
(765) 825-5325
Harry M. Smith
Hours: by appointment

Ferdinand Historical Society
PO Box 194
Ferdinand, IN 47532
(812) 367-1803 (President)
Phyllis A. Johanneman, President

Floyd County Historian
3308 Norwood Drive
New Albany, IN 47150
Ann Robison

Floyd County Historical Society
PO Box 455
New Albany, IN 47150
Stephen Pierce
$20.00 per year membership

Fountain County Historian
3219 East New Richmond Road
Wingate, IN 47994
(765) 295-2604
Robert Quirk

Fountain County Historical Society
3219 East New Richmond Road
Wingate, IN 47994
(765) 295-2604
Robert Quirk, Fountain County Historian
Pub. *Fountain County History*

Franklin County Historian
650 East Eighth Street
Brookville, IN 47012
Martha Shea

Franklin County Historical Society
(Fifth and Mill Streets—location)
PO Box 342 (mailing address)
Brookville, IN 47012
Martha Shea, President
Hours: by appointment
$8.00 per year membership

Fulton County Historian
Fulton County Historical Society, Inc.
(4 miles north of Rochester on U.S. 31—
  location)
37 East 375 North (mailing address)
Rochester, IN 46975
(219) 223-4436 (Historical Society)
Shirley Ogle Willard, President and
  Museum Director
Hours: Historical Society: Mon–Sat
  9:00–5:00

**Fulton County Historical Society,
Inc.**
(4 miles north of Rochester on U.S. 31—
  location)
37 East 375 North (mailing address)
Rochester, IN 46975
(219) 223-4436
Shirley Ogle Willard, President and
  Museum Director
Hours: Mon–Sat 9:00–5:00
Pub. *Fulton County Folk Finder*,
  quarterly, $6.00 per year subscription;
  Fulton County Images, annually,
  $15.00 per year subscription
(specializes in Potawatomi Indians)

Garrett Historical Society
Quincy and Franklin Streets
PO Box 225
Garrett, IN 46738
(219) 357-5575; (219) 357-5582

Gibson County Historian
530 West Washington Street
Oakland City, IN 47660
Alvetta S. Wallace

Gibson County Historical Society
PO Box 516
Princeton, IN 47670
Kanda Walden, Editor
Pub. *Gibson County Lines*, monthly
("Gibson County family genealogy as
  well as history of county.")
$10.00 per year membership (calendar
  year); queries $3.00

Goshen Historical Society, Inc.
(132 South Main Street—location)
PO Box 701 (mailing address)
Goshen, IN 46526
(219) 533-1053; (219) 642-4516
Earlene Nofziger, President
Pub. *Goshen Historical Society
  Newsletter*, bimonthly
$7.00 per year membership for
  individuals, $12.00 per year
  membership for families, $5.00 per
  year membership for senior citizens,
  $25.00 per year membership for
  organizations, $100.00 life
  membership; no research available by
  mail

Grant County Historian
113 East South A Street
Gas City, IN 46933
Leslie Neher

Greene County Historical Society
PO Box 301
Bloomfield, IN 47424-0301
Mildred Uland, President
Pub. *Newsletter*, quarterly (April, June,
  August, October)
$5.00 per year membership, $100.00 life
  membership

**Guilford Township Historical
Society**
100 East Lincoln Street
Plainfield, IN 46168
James V. Gilbert, President
$2.00 per year membership

Hamilton County Historian
384 North 11th Street
Noblesville, IN 46060
(317) 773-3454
Joe H. Burgess
Hours: daytime

Hamilton County Historical Society
818 Conner Street
PO Box 397
Noblesville, IN 46061
Irving M. Heath, Treasurer

Hours: Noblesville-Southeastern Public
  Library: Mon–Thur 9:30–8:30, Fri–Sat
  9:30–5:30, Sun 1:30–5:30; Museum,
  810 Conner Street: Sat 9:00–2:00
Pub. *Newsletter*, bimonthly
$10.00 per year membership, $12.50 per
  year membership for families, $2.00
  per year membership for students,
  $15.00 per year individual or family
  Sustaining membership, $100.00 life
  membership

Hammond Historical Society
564 State Street
Hammond, IN 46320
(219) 931-5100
Kathryn Thegze, Information Services
  Librarian
Hours: Mon & Wed 1:00–4:00
Pub. *Hammond Historical Society
  Newsletter*, (Jan–May, Sept–Nov)
(Hammond area history)
$5.00 per year membership for
  individuals, $10.00 per year
  membership for institutions

Hancock County Historian
710 South Brook Street, Lot 8
Greenfield, IN 46140
Joe Skvarenina

Hancock County Historical Society
28 North Apple Street
PO Box 375
Greenfield, IN 46140
(317) 462-7780
Joseph L. Skvarenina, President
Hours: Sat–Sun (March 1–Dec 1)
  1:00–5:00
Pub. *Old Log Chain*, biannually
$10.00 per year membership

Harrison County Historian
116 East Walnut
PO Box 446
Corydon, IN 47112
Frederick P. Griffin

Hendricks County Historian
Plainfield Public Library
Guilford Township Historical Collection
1120 Stafford Road
Plainfield, IN 46168-2230
E-mail: scarter.plpl@incolsa.palni.edu
Susan Miller Carter

Hendricks County Historical Society
Hendricks County Museum
170 South Washington
Danville, IN 46122
(317) 745-9229
Dorothy Kelley, Curator
Hours: Tue 9:30–3:30
Pub. *Hendricks County Historical
  Society Bulletin*, quarterly (February,
  May, August, November)
$10.00 per year membership

Henry County Historian
303 South Pearl Street
Spiceland, IN 47385
Richard P. Ratcliff

Henry County Historical Society
614 South 14th Street
New Castle, IN 47362
(765) 529-4028
John Paul, Museum Curator
Hours: Mon–Sat 1:00–4:30 (closed Mon,
    Jan–Mar)
Pub. *Henry County Historical Log*,
    semiannually
$6.00 per year membership

Highland Historical Society, Inc.
2611 Highway Avenue
Highland, IN 46322

Hobart Historical Society, Inc.
706 East Fourth Street
PO Box 24
Hobart, IN 46342
(219) 942-0970 (no long distance return
    calls)
Dorothy Ballantyne, Museum Director
Hours: Sat 10:00–3:00
Pub. *Hobart History News*, three times
    per year; *Hobart History Advocate*,
    irregularly
(specializes in Hobart and Hobart
    Township information)
research: contribution for postage and
    copying costs

Howard County Historian
6070 East Center Road, 300 S
Kokomo, IN 46902-9742
(765) 628-7567
E-mail: ebrjr@aol.com
Ed Riley

Howard County Historical Society
1200 West Sycamore Street
Kokomo, IN 46901
(765) 452-4314
Kelly Thompson, Executive Director
Hours: Museum: Tue–Sun 1:00–4:00;
    Office: Mon–Fri 9:00–4:00
Pub. *Museum Highlights*
$20.00 per year membership; museum
    admission: $2.00

Huntington County Historian
(County Courthouse, Fourth Floor—
    location)
1041 South Jefferson (mailing address)
Huntington, IN 46750
(219) 356-5874
William Abbott

**Huntington County Historical
Society**
(County Courthouse, Fourth Floor—
    location)
1041 South Jefferson (mailing address)
Huntington, IN 46750
(219) 356-5874
William Abbott, President
Hours: Tue–Fri 1:00–4:00

Pub. *Newsletter*, monthly
$10.00 per year membership

**Illiana Genealogical and Historical
Society**
(see Illinois)

Indiana Covered Bridge Society, Inc.
725 Sanders Street
Indianapolis, IN 46203-1856
(317) 632-3081
John Sechrist, Treasurer-Editor
Hours: Mon–Fri 8:00–3:00
Pub. *Indiana Covered Bridge Society
    Newsletter*, quarterly (January, April,
    July, October)
(information on Indiana covered bridges,
    current events, histories associated
    with them, and other related subjects)
$10.00 per year membership

Indiana University Northwest
Calumet Regional Archives
3400 Broadway
Gary, IN 46408
(219) 980-6628
Stephen G. McShane, Archivist/Curator
Hours: Mon–Fri 8:00–4:30
Pub. *CRA Newsletter*; *Steel Shavings*,
    annually, $5.00 per year subscription
(northwest Indiana history)

Jackson County Historian
401 East Walnut Street
Brownstown, IN 47220
(812) 358-2182
Loren W. Noblitt, Ph.D.
Hours: 9:00–3:00

Jackson County Historical Society
401 East Walnut Street
Brownstown, IN 47220
(812) 358-2182
Loren W. Noblitt, Ph.D., Vice President
Hours: 9:00–3:00
(county/national history and genealogical
    charts)
$20.00 per year membership;
    professional research: $10.00 per hour

Jasper County Historian
128 South Augusta Street
Rensselaer, IN 47978
(219) 866-5433
Beulah Arnott

Jasper County Historical Society
475 North Van Rensselaer Street
Rensselaer, IN 47978
(219) 866-5433
Beulah Arnott, Jasper County Historian

Jay County Historical Society, Inc.
903 East Main Street
PO Box 1282
Portland, IN 47371
(219) 997-6749 (President)
Roseamond Scott, President
Hours: Museum: by appointment
$5.00 per year membership; no search
    fees at this time

Jefferson County Historian
PO Box 157
Hanover, IN 47243
Frank S. Baker

Jefferson County Historical Society
615 West First Street
Madison, IN 47250
(812) 265-2335
Lee Rogers, Chairman, Local History
Hours: Mon–Fri 10:00–4:30
("We have the county archives.")

Jennings County Historian
PO Box 313
North Vernon, IN 47265
Helen Horstman

**Jennings County Historical Society,
Our Heritage, Inc.**
Brown and Pike Streets
PO Box 335
Vernon, IN 47282
(812) 346-8989
Chris Asher, President
Hours: Mon–Fri 11:00–4:00
(historical museum)

Johnson County Historian
1070 West Jefferson Street, #206-W
Franklin, IN 46131-2179
Rachel S. Henry

Johnson County Museum of History
135 North Main Street
Franklin, IN 46131
(317) 736-4655; (317) 736-5451 FAX
E-mail: map@inetdirect
Mary Ann Plummer, Director
Hours: Mon–Fri 9:00–4:00; second Sat
    10:00–3:00
Pub. *Nostalgia News*, quarterly
$10.00 per year membership for
    individuals

Knox County Historian
Lewis Historical Library
LRC-22
Vincennes University
Vincennes, IN 47591
(812) 888-4330 (Library)
E-mail: gstevens@vunet.vinu.edu
Robert R. Stevens
Hours: Library: Mon–Fri 8:30–4:30

Kosciusko County Historian
1010 North Huntington
Syracuse, IN 46567
Ronald Sharp

**Genealogy Section, Kosciusko
County Historical Society**
Kosciusko County Historical Museum
    and Library
(Corner of Indiana and Main Street—
    location)
PO Box 1071 (mailing address)
Warsaw, IN 46581-1071
(219) 267-6955
http://culture.kconline.com/kchs/

Susan Zellers, Genealogy Chairman; Douglas Mayer, President; Caroline Fawley, Librarian
Hours: Thur–Sat 10:00–4:00, Sun 1:00–4:00
Pub. *Our Missing Links*, quarterly, $10.00 per year subscription; *Kosciusko County Newsletter*
(emphasis on Kosciusko County, county records repository, large genealogy holdings, volunteer researchers)
$10.00 per year membership (includes newsletter only)

LaGrange County Historian
(MacKan House Museum, 405 Poplar Street—location)
3630 South 200 East (mailing address)
LaGrange, IN 46761
(219) 463-2632
J. Scott McKibben
Hours: Sun (summer) 2:00–4:00, and year-round by appointment

LaGrange County Historical Society, Inc.
(MacKan House Museum, 405 Poplar Street—location)
3630 South 200 East (mailing address)
LaGrange, IN 46761
(219) 463-2632
J. Scott McKibben, President
Hours: Sun (summer) 2:00–4:00, and year-round by appointment
Pub. *LaGrange County Historical Society Newsletter*, quarterly
$5.00 per year membership

Lake County Historian
3606 Belshaw Road
Lowell, IN 46356
Rebecca Crabb

Lake County Historical Society/ Museum
(Court House Square, Crown Point, IN 46307—location)
5131 Canterbury Avenue (mailing address)
Portage, IN 46368
(219) 662-3975
Bruce L. Woods, President
Hours: Museum: May–Oct: Thur–Sat 1:00–4:00; meetings second Sat (even-numbered months)
$5.00 per year membership

LaPorte County Historian
5817 West Johnson Road
LaPorte, IN 46350-8586
Fern Eddy Schultz

LaPorte County Historical Society
LaPorte County Complex
LaPorte, IN 46350-3430
(219) 326-6808, ext. 276
Fern Eddy Schultz, President
Hours: Mon–Fri 10:30–4:00
Pub. *The Oldletter*, quarterly

$2.50 per year active membership, $5.00 per year Sustaining membership, $10.00 per year Patron membership

Lawrence County Historian
Rural Route 15, Box 1328
Bedford, IN 47421
(812) 275-5165 (home); (812) 275-7637 (work)
Maxine Kruse
(Lawrence County history, cemeteries, limestone carvings and famous Lawrence county people)

Lexington Historical Society, Inc.
(8060 East State Road 356—location
Highway 203, Cherry Street, next to the Post Office, corner of Walnut Street, in the Penny Pincher Shoppe—museum location)
PO Box 238 (mailing address)
Lexington, IN 47138-0238
(812) 889-2044 (Editor)
Jeannie Noe Carlisle, Secretary, Treasurer and Editor
Hours: meetings fourth Mon (except May, Nov & Dec) 7:00 P.M.; Museum: by appointment only
Pub. untitled newsletter, quarterly
(specializes in Scott County, Indiana, Lexington Township area)
$5.00 per year membership (calendar year); free museum admission

Madison County Historian
2113 Silver Street
Anderson, IN 46012-1615
Howard I. Eldon

Madison County Historical Society, Inc.
PO Box 523
Anderson, IN 46015-0523
(765) 641-2442 (Library)
Phyllis Leedom, President
Hours: Library: Mon–Thur 9:00–9:00, Fri–Sat 9:00–5:30, Sun 1:00–5:00
Pub. *Madison County Historical Gazette*, ten times per year; *Searchlight* (for adoptees in search); *Camp Stilwell* (on the Civil War)
$4.00 per year membership

Marion County Historian
4451 Central Avenue
Indianapolis, IN 46205
Harriet O'Connor

Marion County/Indianapolis Historical Society
735 Woodruff Place, East Drive
Indianapolis, IN 46201
(317) 635-7278
Ray Brown, President
Pub. *The Circular*

Marshall County Historian
430 Clark Street
Plymouth, IN 46562
Linda Lou Rippy

Marshall County Historical Society, Inc.
123 North Michigan Street
Plymouth, IN 46563-2132
(219) 936-2306
Judy McCollough, Research Librarian
Hours: Museum: Mon–Fri 9:00–5:00, Sat 10:00–2:00, Sun 1:00–4:00 (research library is not always open on weekends, call to confirm)
Pub. *Musings*, quarterly; *Marshall County Historical Society Quarterly*
$10.00 per year museum membership; a per-hour search fee in research library at musuem

Martin County Historian
Rural Route 1, Box 271-1
Loogootee, IN 47553-9714
Robert B. Green

Martin County Historical Society, Inc.
PO Box 564
Shoals, IN 47581
(812) 247-2351

Miami County Historian
101 West Ohio Street, #200
Indianapolis, IN 46204-1906
Horace D. Cook

Miami County Historical Society
Miami County Museum
51 North Broadway
Peru, IN 46970
(765) 473-9183; (765) 473-3880 FAX
Catherine Powell, Director
Hours: Museum: Tue–Sat 9:00–5:00
Pub. *Historical Bulletin of Miami County*, monthly
$10.00 per year membership for individuals

Michigan City Historical Society, Inc.
Old Lighthouse Museum
Heisman Harbor Road, Washington Park
PO Box 512
Michigan City, IN 46360-0512
(219) 872-6133
Pub. *Old Lighthouse Museum News*
(no longer answers genealogical queries)

Monroe County Historical and Genealogical Society
202 East Sixth Street
Bloomington, IN 47408
(812) 339-0728
Ron Baldwin, President; Mary Schroeder, Museum Director and Newsletter Editor
Hours: Mon–Fri 1:00–4:00, Sat 10:00–2:00
Pub. *Monroe County Historian*, quarterly
(specializes in Monroe County history)
$10.00 per year membership

Montgomery County Historian
2005 State Road 55, North
Crawfordsville, IN 47933
Stephen Jay Thompson

Montgomery County Historical Society
Genealogy Section
212 South Water Street
Crawfordsville, IN 47933
(765) 362-3416

Morgan County Historian
PO Box 1728
Martinsville, IN 46151
(765) 349-9936
Sam Cline

Morgan County History & Genealogy Association
PO Box 1012
Martinsville, IN 46151-0012
(765) 349-9936
http://www.rootsweb.com/~inmchaga/
mchagai.html
Sam Cline, President
Pub. *Morgan County History & Genealogy*, quarterly
$12.00 per year membership; queries with Morgan County connections free to members, $3.00 for non-members; research in Morgan County records: $8.00 per hour for members, $12.00 per hour for non-members

Newton County Historian
PO Box 320
Goodland, IN 47948
Velma Jean Dart

Newton County Historical Society, Inc.
County Courthouse
Kentland, IN 47951
John Yost, President
$5.00 per year membership for individuals, $8.00 per year membership for couples

Noble County Historian
PO Box 11
Albion, IN 46701
Robert C. Gagen, Jr.

Noble County Historical Society
(Old Jail Museum, East Main Street—location)
PO Box 152 (mailing address)
Albion, IN 46701
Debbie Sieber, President
Hours: Jail: Sun (Jun–Labor Day weekend) 1:30–4:30
Pub. *Pioneer Echoes*, quarterly (January, April, July, October)
$5.00 per year membership for adults, $1.00 per year membership for students

North Manchester Historical Society, Inc.
PO Box 361
North Manchester, IN 46962
(219) 982-4706
Robert J. Nelson, Jr., President
Pub. *NMHSI Newsletter*

Northern Indiana Historical Society
808 West Washington
South Bend, IN 46601
(219) 235-9664
Cheryl Taylor, Director
Hours: Tue–Fri 10:00–5:00
Pub. *Saint Joseph Valley Record* (not specifically genealogical), semiannually
$35.00 per year membership for individuals

Ohio County Historical Society, Inc.
3773 State Road 56 North
Rising Sun, IN 47040-9342
Dillon R. Dorrell, President
Pub. *Newsletter*, annually
$5.00 per year membership, $100.00 life membership

Orange County Historian
311 West Main Street
Paoli, IN 47454
Wilma Davis

Osceola Historical Society
PO Box 14
Osceola, IN 46561-0014
(219) 674-9410
Kaye Solliday, President

Owen County Historian
35 West Hillside
Spencer, IN 47460
Linda Simmerman

Parke County Historian
411 Jackson
Rockville, IN 47872
William E. Davis

Parke County Historical Society
PO Box 332
Rockville, IN 47872

Perry County Historian
Highway 37
Tell City, IN 47586
Mike Rutherford

Perry County Historical Society
General Delivery
Rome, IN 47574
Mrs. James J. Groves

Pike County Historian
413 South Fifth Street
Petersburg, IN 47567
Sandra McBeth

Pike County Historical Society and Museum
PO Box 216
Petersburg, IN 47567

Sandy McBeth, Secretary
Hours: Sat 10:00–3:00
Pub. *Pike County Historical Society Newsletter*, bimonthly
(Pike county history and genealogy)
$7.00 per year membership

Historical Society of Porter County, Inc. (Old Jail Museum)
153 Franklin Street
Valparaiso, IN 46383
(219) 465-3595
Bonnie Cuson, Curator
Hours: Tue–Wed & Fri 1:00–4:00
Pub. *Muse News*, quarterly
(naturalization books 1854–1955, marriage index 1836-1905, 1880 census)
$5.00 per year membership for individuals, $10.00 per year Contributing membership, $5.00 per year membership for businesses or organizations

Posey County Historian
9016 Schroeder Court
Mount Vernon, IN 47620
Glenn Curtis

Posey County Historical Society
PO Box 171
Mount Vernon, IN 47620
Wanda L. Griess, President
Pub. *The Posey*, quarterly
$10.00 per year membership for individuals; research: $10.00 per hour plus copy costs

Pulaski County Historian
Pulaski County Public Library
121 South Riverside Drive
Winamac, IN 46996
(219) 946-3432 (library)
Lynda Irving
Hours: Library: Mon 9:00–8:00, Tue–Sat 9:00–6:00

Pulaski County Historical Society, Inc.
(123 South Riverside—museum location)
PO Box 135 (mailing address)
Winamac, IN 46996
(219) 946-3712
Christine Smith
Hours: Museum: Fri 1:00–4:00
$5.00 per year membership

Putnam County Historian
704 Highwood Avenue
Greencastle, IN 46135
John J. Baughman

Randolph County Historian
2212 East Greenville Pike
Winchester, IN 47394
(765) 584-4323 (evenings); (765) 584-1155, ext. 10 (days)
Monisa Wisener

Randolph County Historical/ Genealogical Society
2212 East Greenville Pike
Winchester, IN 47394
(765) 584-4323 (evenings); (765) 584-1155, ext. 10 (days)
Monisa Wisener, Randolph County Historian
Hours: Society Collection in the Office of the County Health Department, Vital Records, 211 South Main Street, Winchester: Mon–Fri 8:00–4:00
Pub. *Historical and Genealogical Society of Randolph County Newsletter*, irregularly (two to four times per year) (genealogical library and museum)
$10.00 per year membership (beginning in June); records search: postage, copies and expenses for members

Randolph Southern Historical Society
PO Box 127
Lynn, IN 47355
(765) 874-2267
Linda L. Black

Ripley County Historian
PO Box 83
Holton, IN 47023
Beatrice Boyd

Ripley County Historical Society, Inc.
(Main and Water Street—location)
PO Box 525 (mailing address)
Versailles, IN 47042
(812) 689-3031
E-mail: rchslib@seidata.com
Hours: Mon–Fri 1:00–4:00
Pub. *Ripley County Historical Society Bulletin*, quarterly
$10.00 per year membership (calendar year), $100.00 life membership; search fee: per hour basis

Rush County Historian
Rt. 1, Box 199
Rushville, IN 46173
James S. Scott

Rush County Historical Society
Rt. 1, Box 199
Rushville, IN 46173
James S. Scott

Saint Joseph County Historian
59215 High Pointe Drive
South Bend, IN 46614
Mary Renshaw
refers genealogical queries to South Bend Area Genealogical Society

Scott County Historian
PO Box 25
Lexington, IN 47138
Joe Gibson

Scott County Historical Society
(Scottsburg Heritage Station, Archive Room, Suite D, 90 North Main Street—location)
PO Box 245
Scottsburg, IN 47170-0245
Hours: Mon 10:00–1:30, and by appointment

Shelby County Historian
330 Shelby Street
Shelbyville, IN 46176
Martha Ann Creed

Shelby County Historical Society
52 West Broadway
Shelbyville, IN 46176
(317) 392-4634
June Barnett, Director
Hours: Fri–Sun 1:00–4:00
Pub. *Echos of Old Shelby (Newsletter)*, quarterly
$10.00 per year membership

Sheridan Historical and Genealogical Society
308 Main Street
Sheridan, IN 46069
(317) 758-5765
James H. Pickett, President
Hours: Tue & Fri 1:00–4:00

Southwestern Indiana Historical Society
435 South Spring Street
Evansville, IN 47714-1550
(812) 477-6777
Vivian M. Taylor, Secretary-Treasurer
(not a genealogical group)
research: $10.00 per hour

Spencer County Historian
615 Main Street
Rockport, IN 47635
Ellen J. S. Brown

Spencer County Historical Society
Rockport Library
210 Walnut Street
Rockport, IN 47635-1398
(812) 649-4866, ext. 12 (Library)
Steve Sisley, President; Leta Alley, Treasurer; Becky Middleton, Genealogy Room Librarian
Hours: Library: Mon & Fri 9:00–5:00, Tue–Thur 9:00–9:00, Sat 9:00–3:00
Pub. *Newsletter*, quarterly
(Spencer County and surrounding area)
$10.00 per year membership (beginning in August); search fee: $5.00 per hour plus cost of copies

Starke County Historian
3750 East 500 North
Knox, IN 46534
(219) 772-4311
Melba Shilling

Starke County Historical Society
3750 East 500 North
Knox, IN 46534
(219) 772-4311
Melba Shilling, Starke County Historian
Hours: Museum, 401 South Main, Knox, IN: afternoons

Steuben County Historian
127 Powers Street
Angola, IN 46703
Charles D. Skove

Sullivan County Historian
Genealogy/Local History Department
100 South Crowder Street
Sullivan, IN 47882
(812) 268-4957 (Library)
Donna K. Adams

Sullivan County Historical Society
Sullivan County Genealogical Society
Historical Museum
(10 South Court—location)
PO Box 326 (mailing address)
Sullivan, IN 47882
(812) 268-6253
E-mail: imrzip@aol.com
Dola Vickery Braner, President; Donna Adams, Sullivan County Historian
Hours: Mon–Fri 10:00–4:00
Pub. *Sullivan County Historical Society Newsletter*, bimonthly
$10.00 per year membership

Switzerland County Historian
59 Knox Ford Road
Vevay, IN 47043
Janet Hendricks

Switzerland County Historical Society
(Main and Market—location)
PO Box 201 (mailing address)
Vevay, IN 47043
(812) 427-3560; (812) 427-3921 (Secretary)
E-mail: akern@venus.net
Ellyn Kern, Secretary
Hours: Mon–Fri noon–4:00, Sat 10:00–4:00
Pub. *The Grapevine*, two times per year, 25¢ per copy
$8.00 per year membership for individuals, $12.00 per year membership for couples; search service for donation

Tell City Historical Society
PO Box 728
Tell City, IN 47586

Three Creeks Historical Association
c/o Lowell Library
Lowell, IN 46356
(219) 696-9234
Richard C. Schmal, President and Historian
Pub. *Pioneer History*

Tippecanoe County Historian
Tippecanoe County Historical
 Association (TCHA)
Wetherill Historical Resource Center
Alameda McCollough Library
909 South Street
Lafayette, IN 47901
(765) 742-8411 (Library)
Nancy L. Weirich, Librarian and
 Tippecanoe County Historian
Hours: Library: Tue & Thur–Fri 1:00–
 5:00, Wed 1:00–7:00, third Sat (Feb–
 Nov) 1:00–5:00, closed Jan

Tippecanoe County Historical
Association (TCHA)
Wetherill Historical Resource Center
Alameda McCollough Library
909 South Street
Lafayette, IN 47901
(765) 742-8411 (Library)
Nancy L. Weirich, Librarian and
 Tippecanoe County Historian
Hours: Library: Tue & Thur–Fri 1:00–
 5:00, Wed 1:00–7:00, third Sat (Feb–
 Nov) 1:00–5:00, closed Jan
Pub. *Weatenotes*, monthly

Tipton County Historian and
Genealogist
124 North Conde
Tipton, IN 46072
(765) 675-7781
E-mail: de@netusa1.net
Donna Jean Ekstrom

Tipton County Historical Society
4161 South 200 East
Atlanta, IN 46031
(765) 292-2451
Margaret Miller, President
$5.00 per year membership; search fees
 vary

Union County Historian
107 East Union Street
Liberty, IN 47353
Marcellene O'Toole

Union County Indiana Historical
Society
Railroad Street
PO Box 9
Liberty, IN 47353
Marcellene O'Toole, Union County
 Historian
Hours: Sun (Apr–Oct) 2:00–4:00
$5.00 per year local membership, $50.00
 life membership

Upper Whitewater Historical
Association
302 East Main
Cambridge City, IN 47327

Vanderburgh County Historical
Society
201 N.W. Fourth Street, Room 105
Evansville, IN 47712
Dr. Darrel E. Bigham

Vermillion County Historian
PO Box 166
Dana, IN 47847
Martha W. Helt

Vigo County Historian
520 Francis Avenue Court
Terre Haute, IN 47804
Dorothy J. Clark

Vigo County Historical Society
1411 South Sixth Street
Terre Haute, IN 47802
(812) 235-9717
David M. Buchanan, Executive Director
Pub. *Leaves of Thyme*
("We combined all of our resources with
 the Vigo County Public Library.")

Vincennes Historical and
Antiquarian Society
PO Box 487
Vincennes, IN 47591
(812) 735-3800
Dr. Alan Snyder, President
Pub. *Knox County History*

Wabash County Historian
574 Ferry Street
Wabash, IN 46992
Ronald L. Woodward

Wabash County Historical Society
Wabash County Historical Museum
Memorial Hall, 89 West Hill Street
Wabash, IN 46992
(219) 563-0661, ext. 55
Jack M. Miller, Curator
Hours: Tue–Sat 9:00–1:00
Pub. *Wabash County Historical
 Newsletter*, quarterly
$5.00 per year membership for
 individuals, $2.00 per year
 membership for senior citizens

Warren County Historian
1959 South 775 West
West Lebanon, IN 47991-8069
Helen Baum

Warren County Historical Society
PO Box 176
Williamsport, IN 47993
Pub. *Warren County Reflections*,
 quarterly
$3.00 per year membership

Warrick County Historian
6000 Lincoln Avenue
Evansville, IN 47715
Kay F. Lant

Washington County Historian
407 West Market Street
Salem, IN 47167
Willie Harlen

Washington County Historical
Society, Inc.
Stevens Museum
307 East Market Street
Salem, IN 47167

(812) 883-6495
Martha Bowers
Hours: Library: Tue–Sat 9:00–5:00
Pub. *Newsletter*, quarterly
$10.00 per year membership for
 individuals or couples, $2.00 non-
 member admission for research

Wayne County Historian
PO Box 14
Centerville, IN 47330
Dr. Gertrude L. Ward

Wayne County Historical Museum
1150 North A Street
Richmond, IN 47374
(765) 962-5756
Michele Bottorff, Director
Hours: Tue–Fri 9:00–4:00, Sat–Sun
 1:00–4:00

Wells County Historical Society
420 West Market Street
PO Box 143
Bluffton, IN 46714

Western Wayne Heritage, Inc.
(800 National Road—location)
PO Box 254 (mailing address)
Cambridge City, IN 47327
(765) 478-5993
Jack O'Malley, President
Hours: daytime

White County Historian
Rt. 1, Box 147
Idaville, IN 47950
William E. Parrish

White County Historical Society and
Museum
101 South Bluff Street
Monticello, IN 47960-2308
(219) 583-7281

Whiting-Robertsdale Historical
Society Museum
1610 119th Street
Whiting, IN 46394-1702
(219) 659-1432
Elizabeth Gehrke, Director
Hours: Tue–Wed & Sat 1:00–4:00
Pub. *Whiting-Robertsdale Historical
 Society Newsletter*, quarterly (fall,
 winter, spring, summer)
(Whiting newspapers from 1894,
 obituaries from 1894, city directories
 and telephone directories, artifacts and
 vertical files)
$5.00 per year membership

Whitley County Historian
2930 East Muncie Road
Columbia City, IN 46725
Barbara Brindle

Whitley County Historical Museum
108 West Jefferson Street
Columbia City, IN 46725
(219) 244-6372; (219) 244-6384 FAX
Susan Richey, Curator

Hours: Mon–Wed 9:00–2:00, and by appointment
Pub. *The Bulletin of the Whitley County Historical Society*, quarterly
$12.00 per year membership; search fees by donation.

LDS Family History Centers

Bloomington
(812) 333-0050

Indianapolis
(317) 888-6002

Genealogical Societies

State Genealogical Society

Indiana Genealogical Society, Inc.
PO Box 10507
Fort Wayne, IN 46852-0507
http://www.fgs.org/~fgs/soc0087.htm
Pub. *Indiana Genealogist*, quarterly; *Indiana Genealogical Society Newsletter*, bimonthly
$20.00 per year membership for individuals, $25.00 per year joint membership

Regional Genealogical Societies

Allen County Genealogical Society of Indiana
PO Box 12003
Fort Wayne, IN 46862
Pub. *Allen County Lines*, quarterly
$15.00 per year membership for individuals, $18.00 per year membership for families

Bartholomew County Genealogical Society
PO Box 2455
Columbus, IN 47202
Ronald P. Bulthuis, President; Imogene Weisner, Editor
Pub. *Bartholomew County (Indiana) Ancestors*, quarterly
$10.00 per year membership

Benton County Genealogical Society
711 East Third Street
Fowler, IN 47944-2343
(765) 884-1764
Freeman Harold Furr, Benton County Historian
Hours: Mon–Fri 8:00–4:00

(war veterans of Benton County, from the Revolutionary War to the Gulf War; vital records, cemeteries, wills and deeds, etc.)

Brown County Genealogical Society
PO Box 1202
Nashville, IN 47448
(812) 988-4297
Peggy Scrougham, President
Hours: meetings at Brown County Public Library, Nashville
Pub. *Brown County Genealogical Society Newsletter*, quarterly, $1.00 per issue for non-members
("Focus is on Brown County families.")
$10.00 per year membership for individuals, $12.00 per year membership for families

Cass County Genealogical Society
PO Box 373
Logansport, IN 46947

Clay County Genealogical Society, Inc.
(309 Main Street—location)
PO Box 56 (mailing address)
Centerpoint, IN 47840-0056
(812) 835-5005
Patricia Wilkinson, President
Hours: Wed & Sat 1:00–4:00
Pub. *The Researcher*, quarterly
$12.00 per year membership for individuals, $20.00 per year membership for families; queries printed; research: $5.00 per hour

County Seat Genealogical Society
52 West Broadway
Danville, IN 46122
Pub. *County Seat Scraps*, quarterly
(Hendricks County)
$12.00 per year membership for individuals, $9.00 per year membership for organizations

Crawford County Historical and Genealogical Society
PO Box 133
Leavenworth, IN 47137
Sharon Morris, Secretary/Treasurer
Pub. *Crawford Countian*, quarterly
$10.00 per year membership

DuBois County Genealogical Society
(Jasper, IN—location)
PO Box 84 (mailing address)
Ferdinand, IN 47532-0084
Allen Englert
Hours: meetings at Jasper Public Library: first Mon
Pub. *Newsletter*, quarterly
$10.00 per year membership for individuals, $13.00 per year membership for couples

Elkhart County Genealogical Society
1812 Jeanwood Drive
Elkhart, IN 46514

Thomas Ruhling, President
Pub. *Michiana Searcher*, quarterly
$8.00 per year membership

Grant County Genealogy Club
1419 West 11th Street
Marion, IN 46953
June Shields, President
Pub. *Grant County Beacon*, quarterly
$8.00 per year membership for individuals, $12.00 per year membership for husband and wife, $10.00 per year Contributing membership, $20.00 per year Sustaining membership, $50.00 per year Patron membership, $100.00 life membership; research: for contribution

Hendricks County Genealogical Society
Danville Public Library
101 South Indiana Street
Danville, IN 46122
(317) 745-2604 (Library); (317) 745-0756 FAX (Library)
Becky Gramling, Historical Department
Hours: Library: Mon–Thur 9:00–8:00, Fri–Sat 9:00–5:00, Sun 2:00–5:00

Howard County Genealogical Society
(Kokomo-Howard County Public Library, Genealogy-Local History Room, 220 North Union Street, Kokomo, IN 46901-4614—location)
PO Box 2 (mailing address)
Oakford, IN 46965-0002
(765) 457-3242 (Library)
E-mail: mmcnabb@kokomo.lib.in.us
http://www.kokomo.lib.in.us/genealogy.html; http://www.rootsweb.com/-inhoward/county.html
Hertha White, President
Hours: Library: Mon–Thur 9:00–9:00, Fri–Sat 9:00–5:30, Sun (Labor Day–Memorial Day) 2:00–5:30
Pub. *Howard County (IN) Genealogical Society Newsletter*, quarterly
(Indiana counties, Howard County, Indiana)
$10.00 per year membership for individuals or families; free queries in newsletter

Illiana Genealogical and Historical Society
(see Illinois)

Jackson County Genealogical Society, Inc.
415 South Poplar Street
Brownstown, IN 47220-1939
Hours: by appointment
Pub. *Genealogy Jottings*, quarterly
$10.00 per year membership; send SASE with inquiry

Jasper-Newton Counties Genealogical Society

Rt. 1, Box 307
Wheatfield, IN 46392
Kathy Lund
Pub. *Jasper-Newton Counties Genealogical Society—Genealogy Trails*, quarterly

Jennings County Genealogical Society

PO Box 863
North Vernon, IN 47265
Hours: meetings at Farm Bureau Insurance Building, North Vernon: fourth Mon (Jan–Nov) 7:00
Pub. *Newsletter*, annually
$10.00 per year membership; search for donation

Kosciusko County Area Genealogist Researchers

1134 South Ferguson
Warsaw, IN 46580
Mrs. Willodean Metzger Andrew (Mayer, Warren and Andrew Family Association)

Genealogy Section, Kosciusko County Historical Society

Kosciusko County Historical Museum and Library
(Corner of Indiana and Main Street—location)
PO Box 1071 (mailing address)
Warsaw, IN 46581-1071
(219) 267-6955
http://culture.kconline.com/kchs/
Susan Zellers, Genealogy Chairman; Douglas Mayer, President; Caroline Fawley, Librarian
Hours: Thur–Sat 10:00–4:00, Sun 1:00–4:00
Pub. *Our Missing Links*, quarterly, $10.00 per year subscription; *Kosciusko County Newsletter*
(emphasis on Kosciusko County, county records repository, large genealogy holdings, volunteer researchers)
$10.00 per year membership (includes newsletter only)

LaPorte County Genealogical Society

LaPorte County Public Library
904 Indiana Avenue
LaPorte, IN 46350-3464
(219) 362-6156; (219) 326-6458
Hours: Library: Mon–Thur 9:00–9:00, Fri–Sat 9:00–6:00
Pub. *Newsletter*, quarterly
("Not affiliated with Indiana Genealogical Society.")
$7.00 per year membership for individuals

Lawrence County Genealogical Society

204032 Plaza Drive, #309
Bedford, IN 47421
Louis Ingle

Marshall County Genealogical Society

Marshall County Historical Society
123 North Michigan Street
Plymouth, IN 46563-2132
(219) 936-2306 (Historical Society)
Judy McCollough, Secretary-Editor
Hours: meetings: monthly except Aug & Dec
Pub. *Marshall County Roots and Branches*, quarterly
$8.00 per year membership

Miami County Genealogical Society

PO Box 542
Peru, IN 46970
(765) 985-3435 (President)
http://www.netusa1.net/~beheler/index.html
Jean A. Musselman, President
Pub. *Miami County Trakker*, quarterly
$5.00 per year membership

Monroe County Historical and Genealogical Society

202 East Sixth Street
Bloomington, IN 47408
(812) 339-0728
Ron Baldwin, President; Mary Schroeder, Museum Director and Newsletter Editor
Hours: Mon–Fri 1:00–4:00, Sat 10:00–2:00
Pub. *Monroe County Historian*, quarterly
(specializes in Monroe County history)
$10.00 per year membership

Genealogical Society of Montgomery County

Crawfordsville District Public Library
222 South Washington Street
Crawfordsville, IN 47933
Pub. *Balhinch Gazette*, quarterly

Morgan County History & Genealogy Association

PO Box 1012
Martinsville, IN 46151-0012
(765) 349-9936
http://www.rootsweb.com/~inmchaga/mchagai.html
Sam Cline, President
Pub. *Morgan County History & Genealogy*, quarterly
$12.00 per year membership; queries with Morgan County connections free to members, $3.00 for non-members; research in Morgan County records: $8.00 per hour for members, $12.00 per hour for non-members

Noble County Genealogical Society, Inc.

Noble County Public Library
813 East Main
Albion, IN 46701
(219) 636-7197 (Library); (219) 636-3321 FAX
Linda J. Shultz, Executive Secretary
Hours: Library: Mon–Thur 8:30–8:30, Fri 8:30–5:30, Sat 8:30–3:30
Pub. *The Noble News*, semiannually (June and December)
$5.00 per year membership for individuals, $7.50 per year membership for families, $1.00 per year membership for students, $20.00 per year Benefactor membership, $50.00 per year life membership

North Central Indiana Genealogical Society

1404 Zartman Road
Kokomo, IN 46902-3263
R. Tetrick

Northwest Indiana Genealogical Society

(Valparaiso-Porter County Public Library—location)
103 Jefferson Street (mailing address)
Valparaiso, IN 46383
Nancy Shepler Howell, Second Vice President
Pub. *Twigs*, bimonthly
(various publications available for Lake and Porter counties)
$8.00 per year membership for individuals, $9.00 per year membership for families, $1.00 less if two-year membership

Northwest Territory Genealogical Society

Lewis Historical Library
LRC-22
Vincennes University
Vincennes, IN 47591
(812) 885-4330 (Library)
E-mail: dbeeson@vunet.vinu.edu
Donna Beeson, Editor
Hours: Library: Mon–Fri 8:30–4:30
Pub. *Northwest Trail Tracer*, quarterly
(Northwest Territory: Illinois, Indiana, Michigan, Ohio, Wisconsin and part of Minnesota; specializes in Knox County, Indiana, genealogical listings)
$12.00 per year membership

Orange County Genealogical Society

(301 West Main Street—location)
PO Box 344 (mailing address)
Paoli, IN 47454
(812) 723-3437
Everett or Wilma Davis
Hours: by appointment
Pub. *Orange Peelings*, quarterly (March, June, September and December)
$10.00 per year membership

Pulaski County Genealogy Society
Pulaski County Public Library
121 South Riverside Drive
Winamac, IN 46996
Lynda Irving
Hours: 8:00–6:00
Pub. *Pulaski County Genealogical Newsletter*, quarterly
$5.00 per year membership

Randolph County Historical/ Genealogical Society
2212 East Greenville Pike
Winchester, IN 47394
(765) 584-4323 (evenings); (765) 584-1155, ext. 10 (days)
Monisa Wisener, Randolph County Historian
Hours: Society Collection in the Office of the County Health Department, Vital Records, 211 South Main Street, Winchester: Mon–Fri 8:00–4:00
Pub. *Historical and Genealogical Society of Randolph County Newsletter*, irregularly (two to four times per year) (genealogical library and museum)
$10.00 per year membership (beginning in June); records search: postage, copies and expenses for members

Scott County Genealogical Society
5764 South State Road 203
Lexington, IN 47138-8365
(812) 889-2044 phone and FAX
E-mail: jeannie@hsonline.net
Jeannie Noe Carlisle, Secretary and Editor
Hours: meetings at Courthouse, 1 East McClain Avenue, Scottsburg, IN 47170: first Thur 6:30
Pub. *The Scott County Genealogical Society Newsletter*, quarterly
$10.00 per year membership for individuals (calendar year), $12.00 per year membership for husband and wife, $5.00 per year membership for students in first 12 grades of school, $100.00 lifetime membership for individuals, $150.00 lifetime membership for husband and wife, additional $5.00 for foreign membership; newsletter queries free to members and non-members

Shelby County, Indiana Genealogical Society
PO Box 434
Shelbyville, IN 46176-0434
Marjorie Roberts, Secretary-Treasurer
Hours: meetings at Grover Museum, 52 West Broadway, Shelbyville, IN 46176-1256: third Sat 10:00 A.M.
Pub. *Fore Bears Paws*, quarterly (February, May, August, November)
$10.00 per year membership (calendar year)

Sheridan Historical and Genealogical Society
308 Main Street
Sheridan, IN 46069
(317) 758-5765
James H. Pickett, President
Hours: Tue & Fri 1:00–4:00

South Bend Area Genealogical Society
PO Box 1222
South Bend, IN 46624-1222
(219) 234-6747
Jackie Eufemi, Membership Chairman
Hours: meetings at First Christian Church of South Bend, 1101 East Jefferson Boulevard: fourth Mon (except June–Aug & Dec) 7:00
Pub. *South Bend Area Genealogical Quarterly*
$12.00 per year membership for individuals (calendar year), $14.00 per year membership for families at one mailing address; new members may receive two hours of free research

Southern Indiana Genealogical Society
PO Box 665
New Albany, IN 47151
Mary Stauble, President
Hours: New Albany-Floyd County Public Library: Mon–Thur 9:00–8:30, Fri–Sat 9:00–5:30
Pub. *Southern Indiana Genealogical Society Quarterly*, $4.00 per back issue; *Southern Indiana Genealogical Society Newsletter*, irregularly
(covers only Floyd, Clark, Harrison, Washington, Crawford, Scott and Perry counties)
$12.00 per year membership; non-member query, $2.00 per fifty words

Starke County Genealogical Society
152 West Culver Road
Knox, IN 46534
Peg Brettin, President

Sullivan County Genealogical Society
Sullivan County Historical Society Historical Museum
(10 South Court—location)
PO Box 326 (mailing address)
Sullivan, IN 47882
(812) 268-6253
E-mail: imrzip@aol.com
Dola Vickery Braner, President; Donna Adams, Sullivan County Historian
Hours: Mon–Fri 10:00–4:00
Pub. *Sullivan County Historical Society Newsletter*, bimonthly
$10.00 per year membership

Tippecanoe County Area Genealogical Society (TIPCOA)
Wetherill Historical Resource Center
Alameda McCollough Library
909 South Street
Lafayette, IN 47901
(765) 476-8420; (765) 476-8414 FAX
Nancy Weirich, Librarian
Hours: Library: Tue & Thur–Fri 1:00–5:00, Wed 1:00–7:00, third Sat (Feb–Nov) 1:00–5:00, closed Jan
Pub. *TIPCOA Newsletter*, quarterly
$8.00 per year membership

Tri-State Genealogical Society
Willard Library
21 First Avenue
Evansville, IN 47710
(812) 425-4309
George Wolf, President
Hours: Library: Tue 9:00–8:00, Wed–Fri 9:00–5:30, Sat 9:00–5:00, Sun 1:00–5:00; meetings second Tue (Sept–Jun)
Pub. *Tri-State Packet*, quarterly
(southwestern Indiana, western Kentucky, southeastern Illinois; "We conduct an annual genealogical seminar, provide help sessions monthly.")
$12.00 per year membership

Wabash County Genealogical Society
PO Box 825
Wabash, IN 46992
Ronald L. Woodward, President
Pub. *Family Branches*, monthly
$10.00 per year (beginning in June)

Wabash Valley Genealogical Society
2906 East Morris Avenue
Terre Haute, IN 47805-2123
Hours: Tue–Thur 1:00–4:00 & 7:00–9:00
Pub. *Sycamore Leaves*, quarterly
$10.00 per year membership (beginning in July)

Wayne County, Indiana, Genealogical Society
Wayne County Historical Museum
1150 North A Street
Richmond, IN 47374
(765) 935-0614 (late evenings)
Arnold Dean, President
Hours: Museum: Tue–Fri 9:00–4:00, Sat–Sun 1:00–4:00
Pub. *Family Pathways*, quarterly (March, June, September and December)
(Wayne County, Indiana and Preble and Darke counties, Ohio)
$15.00 per year membership for individuals, $20.00 per year membership for couples

White County Genealogical Society

White County Historical Society and
Museum
101 South Bluff Street, Basement
Monticello, IN 47960-2308
(219) 583-3998; (219) 583-7281
(Historical Society)
Hours: Mon, Wed & Fri 8:00–2:00
genealogical research: $5.00 per hour

Independent Publications and Miscellany

Canal Society of Indiana

(304 East Berry Street, Fort Wayne, IN
46802—location)
PO Box 40087 (mailing address)
Evansville, IN 46804
(219) 432-0279
E-mail: indcanal@aol.com
http://user.centralnet.net/zepp/canal.html
Carolyn Schmidt, Editor
Hours: Mon–Sat: 8:00–5:00
Pub. *Indiana Canals*, quarterly, $15.00
per year subscription; *Newsletter*,
monthly

Historic Genealogical Magazine

1240 Vineland Road, Apartment S 7
Winter Garden, FL 34787-4318
(407) 654-1847
Joan C. Bohm, Genealogist
Pub. *Historic Genealogical Magazine*,
semiannually (spring & summer, fall
& winter), $20.00 per year
subscription
(specializing in Boone and Clinton
counties, Indiana)
research fee: $10.00 plus postage and
copies

Hoosier Journal of Ancestry

(7718 Franklin Bottoms Road,
Scottsburg, IN 47170—location)
PO Box 33 (mailing address)
Little York, IN 47139
(812) 752-2051
Naomi Keith Sexton, Editor
Pub. *Hoosier Journal of Ancestry*, three
times per year (mid-March, mid-July,
mid-November), $17.50 per year
subscription, Indiana residents add 88¢
state tax
(source records from thirty counties of
southeastern Indiana)

Hunting for Bears Genealogical and Historical Society

(see Alabama)

Indiana Society, Sons of the American Revolution

1598 Constitution Row
Crawfordsville, IN 47933-7605
William R. Hawley, Editor
Pub. *Hoosier Patriot*, quarterly

Indiana University Folklore Institute

504 North Fess
Bloomington, IN 47408-3890
(812) 855-1027; (812) 855-4008 FAX
E-mail: raaten@indiana.edu
http://www.indiana.edu/~folklore
Ruth Aten, Administrative Secretary
Hours: 8:00–5:00
Pub. *Journal of Folklore Research*, three
times per year
$18.00 per year membership for
individuals, $25.00 per year
membership for institutions, $15.00
per year membership for students

InGenWeb

Part of U.S. GenWeb Project
E-mail: in@usgenweb.com
http://www.rootsweb.com/~ingenweb
(links to other Indiana resources)

Jefferson County and Switzerland County, Indiana, Internet Site

http://www.seidata.com/~bhoggatt/ruth/
ingenweb/spiry.html

Montgomery County Magazine

(PO Box 82, Waveland, IN 47989—
location)
119 North Green Street (mailing address)
Crawfordsville, IN 47933
E-mail: zacho@wico.net
Karen Zach
Pub. *Montgomery County Magazine*,
monthly, $6.00 per year subscription
(Montgomery and surrounding counties)
queries free

Old Northwest Corporation

PO Box 1979
Vincennes, IN 47591
(812) 885-4173
Richard Day, President
Pub. *ONC Newsletter*

Reppert Publications

Antique and Collectible News
(see Illinois)

The Researchers

PO Box 39063
Indianapolis, IN 46239
(317) 862-6133
Carley Gioe, Owner
(publisher of over 250 genealogy books)

IOWA

Archives and Libraries with Holdings in Genealogy

State Archives and Library

State Archives of Iowa

State Historical Society of Iowa
State of Iowa Historical Building
600 East Locust, Capitol Complex
Des Moines, IA 50319-0290
(515) 281-3007; (515) 282-0502 FAX
http://www.uiowa.edu.8080/~shsi
Gordon O. Hendrickson, State Archivist
Hours: Library: Tue–Sat 9:00–4:30
(except state holidays and Saturdays
preceding or following state holidays);
Archives: Tue–Fri 9:00–4:30
(Iowa government records, statewide
history sources)

State Library of Iowa

East 12th and Grand Streets
Des Moines, IA 50319
(515) 281-4102; (515) 281-3384 FAX;
(515) 281-6191 FAX
E-mail: nhaigh@mail.lib.state.ia.us;
siloweb@www.silo.lib.ia.us
http://www.silo.lib.ia.us/

State Historical Societies

State Historical Society of Iowa

Library/Archives Bureau
State of Iowa Historical Building
600 East Locust, Capitol Complex
Des Moines, IA 50319-0290
(515) 281-6200 (Library); (515) 281-
3007 (Archives)
http://www.uiowa.edu/~shsi/library/
library.htm
Ruth Bartels, Lead Reference Librarian
Hours: Library: Tue–Sat 9:00–4:30
(except state holidays and Saturdays
preceding or following state holidays);
Archives: Tue–Fri 9:00–4:30
Pub. *The Iowa Heritage Illustrated*,
quarterly (free to active members);
The Annals of Iowa, quarterly, $20.00
per year subscription ($18.00 per year
subscription to active members); *The
Goldfinch*, quarterly, $10.00 per year
subscription ($9.00 per year
subscription to active members); *Iowa
Historian*, bimonthly, (free to all
members)
$50.00–$59.00 per year basic
membership

State Historical Society of Iowa

Library/Archives
Centennial Building
402 Iowa Avenue
Iowa City, IA 52240-1806

(319) 335-3916
Karen Laughlin, Reference Librarian
Hours: Tue–Sat 9:00–4:30 (except state
 holidays and Saturdays preceding or
 following state holidays)
Pub. *The Palimpsest*, quarterly, $15.00
 per year subscription (free to active
 members); *The Annals of Iowa*,
 quarterly, $20.00 per year subscription
 ($18.00 per year subscription to active
 members); *The Goldfinch*, quarterly,
 $10.00 per year subscription ($9.00
 per year subscription to active
 members); *Iowa Historian*, bimonthly,
 (free to all members)
$20.00–$59.00 per year basic
 membership

City, County and Regional Archives and Libraries

Ames Public Library
515 Douglas Avenue
Ames, IA 50010
(515) 233-2115
Mike Quinn, Information Services
Hours: Mon–Thur 9:00–9:00, Fri–Sat
 9:00–6:00, Sun 1:30–5:00 (Sept–May)

Burlington Public Library
501 North Fourth Street
Burlington, IA 52601
(319) 753-1647; (319) 753-5316 FAX
http://www.burlington.lib.ia.us
Kay Weiss, Director
Hours: Mon–Thur 9:00–9:00, Fri–Sat
 9:00–5:00, call for holiday and
 summer hours
(Burlington, Iowa, and Des Moines
 County, Iowa, history)

Carnegie-Evans Library
203 Benton Avenue, East
Albia, IA 52531-2036
Hours: Mon–Fri 12:00–6:00, Sat 10:00–
 4:00

Carnegie-Stout Public Library
(11th and Bluff Streets—location)
360 West 11th Street (mailing address)
Dubuque, IA 52001
(319) 589-4227; (319) 589-4217 FAX
Betty Baule, Adult Services Librarian
Hours: Mon–Thur 9:00–9:00, Fri 9:00–
 6:00, Sat 9:00–5:00

Carroll Public Library
118 East Fifth Street
Carroll, IA 51401
(712) 792-3432
Gordon S. Wade
Hours: Mon–Thur 10:00–8:30, Fri
 10:00–6:00, Sat 10:00–5:00
(local newspaper on microfilm, 1870 to
 the present)
search fee: $5.00 per request

Cedar Falls Public Library
524 Main Street
Cedar Falls, IA 50613
(newspapers on microfilm, county
 histories, local history)

Cedar Rapids Public Library
500 First Street, S.E.
Cedar Rapids, IA 52401-2095
(319) 398-5123
Hours: Mon–Thur 9:30–9:00, Fri–Sat
 9:30–5:00, Sun 1:00–5:00

Chariton Public Library
803 Braden
Chariton, IA 50049
(515) 774-5514; (515) 774-8695 FAX
Roberta Reynolds, Director
Hours: noon–6:00

Cherokee Area Archives, Inc.
(228 West Main—location)
215 South Second (mailing address)
Cherokee, IA 51012
(712) 225-6414
Hours: Nov–Apr: Mon, Wed & Fri 2:00–
 4:00, May–Oct: Mon–Fri 2:00–4:00
(local history and genealogy material)

Clermont Historical Society Museum
PO Box 372
Clermont, IA 52135
(319) 423-7173
Henry Follett, Site Manager

Davenport Public Library
321 Main Street
Davenport, IA 52801
(319) 326-7902; (319) 326-7809 FAX
E-mail: agroskop@libby.rbls.lib.il.us
Amy Groskopf, Archivist and Special
 Collections Supervisor
Hours: Mon–Thur 9:00–8:30, Fri–Sat
 9:00–5:00, Sun (winter only) 1:00–
 3:30
call for information about search fees

Public Library of Des Moines
100 Locust
Des Moines, IA 50309-1791
(515) 283-4152
http://www.pldminfo.org/
M. J. Scott, Research Requests
Hours: Mon–Wed 10:00–9:00, Thur–Fri
 10:00–6:00, Sat 10:00–5:00
(Polk County, Des Moines, history, plus
 National Bar Association Archives)
research: $90.00 per hour plus 25¢ per
 page for photocopies, payable in
 advance, $10.00 minimum per request

Dexter Historical Museum
Dexter, IA 50070

Donnellson Public Library
Family History Department
Donnellson, IA 52625

Eckles Memorial Library
East Pottawattamie County
207 South Highway
Oakland, IA 51560
(712) 482-6668
Hours: Mon & Thur 1:00–5:00, Tue
 9:00–12:00 & 1:00–5:00, Fri 7:00–
 9:00, Sat 1:00–5:00
$5.00 per year membership

Mamie Doud Eisenhower Birthplace Museum and Library
709 Carroll Street
PO Box 55
Boone, IA 50036

Elgin Public Library
250 Center Street
Elgin, IA 52141
(319) 426-5313 phone and FAX
Kathy Chapman, Library Director
Hours: Tue 1:00–5:00, Wed 9:30–11:30
 & 1:00–5:00, Thur 6:30–8:30, Fri
 1:00–5:30, Sat 9:00–2:00
(*Elgin Echo* newspaper on microfilm
 from September 1891)

Ericson Public Library
702 Greene Street
Boone, IA 50036
(515) 432-3727; (515) 432-1103 FAX
Cynthia Watson, Director
Hours: Mon–Thur 10:00–8:30, Fri
 10:00–6:00, Sat 10:00–5:00
(Boone, Iowa, history)
$5.00 per hour research fee

Fort Dodge Public Library
605 First Avenue, North
Fort Dodge, IA 50501
(515) 573-8167
Hours: Mon–Thur 10:00–9:00 (summer
 until 8:00), Fri–Sat 10:00–5:30
("Iowa archives; Webster County
 histories; *Fort Dodge Messenger* on
 microfilm")

Garner Public Library
416 State Street
Garner, IA 50438
(515) 923-2850
Hours: winter: Mon 10:00–5:30 & 7:00–
 8:00, Tue–Wed 10:00–5:30, Thur
 noon–8:00, Fri noon–4:00, Sat 10:00–
 noon & 1:00–3:00; summer: Mon–
 Wed 10:00–5:00 & 7:00–8:00, Thur
 noon–8:00, Fri noon–4:00, Sat 10:00–
 noon

Gibson Memorial Library
310 North Maple
Creston, IA 50801
Hours: winter: Mon–Tue & Thur–Fri
 10:00–8:00, Wed 10:00–6:00, Sat
 10:00–4:00; summer: Mon–Tue &
 Thur–Fri 10:00–6:00, Wed 10:00–
 4:00, Sat 9:00–12:00

Glenwood Public Library
109 North Vine Street
Glenwood, IA 51534-1516
(712) 527-5252 (Library)
Betty Jo Budd, Interlibrary Loan and
    Genealogy Department
Hours: Mon–Tue & Thur–Fri 10:00–
    6:00, Wed 10:00–8:00, Sat 10:00–4:00
("Will do research for Mills County,
    Iowa")

Grand Meadow Heritage Center
Rt. 1, Box 45
Washta, IA 51061
(712) 375-5117

Grinnell Historical Museum
(1125 Broad Street—location)
616 Broad Street, #213 (mailing address)
Grinnell, IA 50112
(515) 236-5005
Elizabeth H. Ernst, Archivist
Hours: 1 Jun–31 Aug: Tue–Sun 2:00–
    4:00; 1 Sept–31 May: Sat 2:00–4:00
no admission charge

**Grout Museum of History and
Science**
503 South Street
Waterloo, IA 50701
(319) 234-6357
Jan Taylor, Archivist/Volunteer
    Coordinator
Hours: winter: Tue–Sat 1:00–4:30;
    summer: Tue–Fri 10:00–4:30, Sat
    1:00–4:30
(genealogy, Iowa history, local history)

Hacksma House Genealogy Library
(see Washington)

Public Library (Humboldt)
30 Sixth Street North
Humboldt, IA 50548

Iowa State University
Parks Library, Room 403
Ames, IA 50011
(515) 294-6672; (515) 294-5525 FAX
E-mail: twalters@iastate.edu
http://www.iastate.edu/spcl/spcl.html
    (Special Collections Department)
Hours: Mon–Fri 8:00–11:50 & 1:00–5:00

Keokuk Museum Commission
(Johnson Street—location)
226 High Street (mailing address)
Keokuk, IA 52632
(319) 524-4765

Keokuk Public Library
210 North Fifth Street
Keokuk, IA 52632
(319) 524-1483; (319) 524-2320 FAX
E-mail: ddsystem@interl.net
Shirley Dick, Director
Hours: Mon–Thur 9:30–9:00, Fri–Sat
    9:30–6:00

Lamoni Public Library
Lamoni, IA 50140

Le Mars Public Library
46 First Street, S.W.
Le Mars, IA 51031
Hours: Mon–Thur 10:00–8:00, Fri–Sat
    10:00–5:00

John L. Lewis Commission, Inc.
John L. Lewis Mining and Labor
    Museum
102 Division Street
PO Box 3
Lucas, IA 50151
(515) 766-6831; (515) 766-6443
Jean Hager, President
Hours: mid-Apr to mid-Oct: Tue–Sat
    9:00–3:00, and by appointment
("Many photographs, artifacts and
    documents pertaining to Mr. Lewis,
    mining and labor")
$1.00 admission

Loras College
Center for Dubuque History
PO Box 178
Dubuque, IA 52004-0178
(319) 588-7163
Michael D. Gibson, Archivist
Hours: various, call in advance
(specializes in Dubuque and Dubuque
    County, Iowa)
search fees: write for details

Lucas County Museum
17th Street and Braden Avenue
Chariton, IA 50049
(515) 774-4464

Marshalltown Public Library
36 North Center Street
Marshalltown, IA 50158
(515) 754-5738
Melissa Hauelka
Hours: Sept–May: Mon–Thur 9:00–7:30,
    Fri–Sat 9:00–5:00, Sun 1:00–4:00;
    Jun–Aug: Mon–Sat 9:00–6:00

Mason City Public Library
Mason City, IA 50401

Merry Brook School Museum
210 Lincoln Way
Woodbine, IA 51579
Hours: Thur & Fri 1:00–4:40
(houses collection of the Harrison
    County Genealogical Volunteers
    Chapter, Iowa Genealogical Society)

Musser Public Library
304 Iowa Avenue
Muscatine, IA 52761
(319) 263-3472; (319) 264-1033
E-mail: mus@libby.rbls.lib.il.us
Diane Mayer Day, Library Assistant
Hours: Mon–Thur 10:00–9:00, Fri
    10:00–6:00, Sat 10:00–4:00
(Muscatine City and County history)

New Hampton Public Library
Genealogy Section
New Hampton, IA 50659

Nishna Heritage Museum
(117–119 North Main—location)
3878 Hickory Road (mailing address)
Oakland, IA 51560
Merle Davis, Curator
Hours: 6 days per week
Pub. *Curator*
(history and preservation)
admission: $2.00 per person

Nodaway Valley Historical Museum
(420 South 16th Street—location)
PO Box 393 (mailing address)
Clarinda, IA 51632
(712) 542-3073
Betty J. Ankeny, Curator
Hours: daily 1:00–5:00
(good area genealogy library)
research: $10.00 per hour plus copies
    and postage

Northwestern College
Ramaker Library
101 Seventh Street
Orange City, IA 51041
(712) 737-4821
Cornelia B. Kennedy, Curator
Hours: Mon–Sat 8:00 A.M.–midnight
    (closes at 4:30 during holidays)

Oskaloosa Public Library
301 South Market Street
Oskaloosa, IA 52577
(515) 673-0441
Randy Bellinger, Director
Hours: Mon–Thur 10:00–8:00, Fri–Sat
    10:00–4:00

Ottumwa Public Library
102 West Fourth
Ottumwa, IA 52501
(515) 682-7563
Mary Ann Lemon, Adult Services
    Librarian
Hours: winter: Mon–Thur 8:30–8:30,
    Fri–Sat 9:00–5:00, Sun 1:00–5:00;
    summer: Mon–Wed 9:00–6:00, Thur
    9:00–9:00, Fri–Sat 9:00–5:00

**Plymouth County Historical
Museum**
335 First Avenue, S.W.
Lemars, IA 51031
(712) 546-7002
Delores Burkard, Director
Hours: Tue–Sun 1:00–5:00

**Prairie Trails Museum of Wayne
County Iowa**
(Highway 2, East Jefferson Street—
    location)
PO Box 104 (mailing address)
Corydon, IA 50060
(515) 872-2211; (515) 872-2483; (515)
    872-2037
Wilma West, Librarian; Mrs. Jan
    Winslow, President

Hours: Apr 15–Oct 15: Mon–Sun 1:00–5:00
("Cemetery records, obituary books, county newspaper clippings, census records, county marriages, Dr. Hinkle's birth and death records 1880–1920, historical articles, microfilms; the Mormon Trail crossed Wayne County 1846; sesquicentennial of Mormon Trail and Iowa Statehood in 1996; big Mormon exhibit at museum.")
$3.00 per year membership; $2.00 museum entrance fee; answers letters of search during winter also

Putnam Museum
1717 West 12th Street
Davenport, IA 52804
(319) 324-1933
Michael J. Smith, Director

Rashid Memorial Library
3421 Avenue L
Fort Madison, IA 52627
Hours: Mon, Wed & Fri noon–5:00, Tue & Thur noon–8:00, Sat 9:00–1:00
(houses Iowa and genealogy collection)

Red Oak Public Library
400 North Second Street
Red Oak, IA 51566
(712) 623-6516; (712) 623-6518 FAX
E-mail: redoak00@iren.net
Karen McClendon, Library Director
Hours: Mon–Thur 10:00–8:00, Fri–Sat 10:00–5:00
(good regional archives and local history collection, some biographies)
no research done by library staff, will supply list of individual researchers

Richardson-Sloane Genealogical Library
(1019 Mound Street, Suite 301, Davenport, IA 52803-3923—location)
PO Box 4077 (mailing address)
Davenport, IA 52808-4077
(319) 383-0007; (800) 828-4363; (319) 383-0008 FAX
L. Ted or Alice R. Sloane
Hours: Mon–Fri 10:00–4:00, by appointment only
(all federal census indexes and all Illinois censuses 1850–1920; IGI, SS death index, military, US phone listings, approximately 11,000 volumes in area's major genealogical resource library)
$1.00 per year for library use; copies: 10¢ each plus $1.00 annual library users charge requested

Sioux Center Public Library
327 First Avenue, N.E.
Sioux Center, IA 51250
(712) 722-2138
Hours: Mon–Fri 10:00–9:00, Sat 10:00–5:00

Public Library, Sioux City
529 Pierce Street
Sioux City, IA 51101-1203
(712) 255-2933; (712) 279-6432 FAX
Nancy A. Neumann, Local History and Genealogy Librarian
Hours: Mon–Thur 9:00–9:00, Fri–Sat 9:00–5:00, Sun (Sept–May) 1:00–5:00
(local history collection with an emphasis on northwest Iowa, genealogy collection with an emphasis on Woodbury and surrounding counties)
20¢ per copy, $1.00 handling fee, plus postage if SASE not enclosed

Spencer Public Library
Charlotte Brett Memorial Collection of Genealogical Books and Magazines
21 East Third Street
Spencer, IA 51301
(712) 264-7290
Vicki Myron, Director; Esther Connell, Secretary, Iowa Lakes Genealogical Society Chapter (IGS)
Hours: Mon–Thur 9:00–9:00, Fri–Sat 9:00–5:00

Public Library, Storm Lake
609 Cayuga Street
Storm Lake, IA 50588
Hours: Sept–May: Mon–Thur 9:00–8:00, Fri–Sat 9:00–5:00; Jun–Aug: Mon 12:00–5:30, Tue–Wed 10:00–5:30, Thur 10:00–9:00, Fri 10:00–5:00, Sat 10:00–2:00

Tama County Historical Museum Library
200 North Broadway Street
Toledo, IA 52342
(515) 484-6767
Joan Bidwell, President
Hours: Tue–Sat 1:00–4:30
Pub. *Tama County Museum News*, quarterly, $10.00 per year subscription
(extensive genealogical library)

University of Iowa
100 Main Library
Iowa City, IA 52242-1420
(319) 335-5921 (Archives)
E-mail: earl-rogers@uiowa.edu
http://www1.arcade.uiowa.edu/

University of Northern Iowa Library
Special Collections and University Archives
Rod Library, Third Floor
Cedar Falls, IA 50613-3675
(319) 273-6307; (319) 273-2913 FAX
E-mail: gerald.peterson@uni.edu
http://www.uni.edu
(Iowa census, Cedar Falls, Waterloo and Des Moines newspapers on microfilm, county history books for most counties, excellent collection of maps)

Urbandale Public Library
7305 Aurora Avenue
Urbandale, IA 50322
(515) 278-3946
Virginia Gee, Librarian
Hours: Mon–Thur 9:30–9:00, Fri–Sat 9:30–5:30

Washington Public Library
120 East Main Street
Washington, IA 52353
(319) 653-2726
Hours: Mon & Wed 10:00–8:00, Tue & Thur 10:00–8:00, Fri–Sat 10:00–5:00

Waterloo Public Library
West Park and Commercial
Waterloo, IA 50701
(federal and state census, newspapers and city directories, county histories, maps, genealogical books)

Historical Societies— Local and Regional

Adair County Historical Society
Highway 92 West
PO Box 214
Greenfield, IA 50849
(515) 743-2232; (515) 743-2022
Marjorie Sublett, President

Adel Historical Society
Rt. 2, Box 136
Adel, IA 50003
(515) 993-4124

Albert City Historical Association, Inc.
(212 North Second Street—location)
2226 510 Street (mailing address)
Albert City, IA 50510
(712) 843-5684
Marilyn Bolte, Registrar/Curator

Allamakee County Historical Society
(North Allamakee Street—location)
400 Fourth Avenue, S.W. (mailing address)
Waukon, IA 52172
(319) 568-4680

Amana Heritage Society
PO Box 81
Amana, IA 52203
(319) 622-3567
Lanny Haldy, Executive Director

Audubon County Historical Society
1745 160th Street
Audubon, IA 50025
(712) 563-3984
Betty Sievers, Secretary
Hours: Sun P.M., and by appointment at museums

(two museums: Court House Museum at Exira and Nathaniel Hamlin Park and Museum at Audubon)
$2.00 per year membership, $10.00 life membership

Benton County Historical Society
204 Riverview Drive
Vinton, IA 52349

Big Sioux River Valley Historical Society
1934 410th Street
Hawarden, IA 51023
(712) 552-2985
Diana Oldenkamp, President

Bloomfield Historical Society
Castalia, IA 52133
(319) 567-8470
Gwenn R. Koenig
Hours: 8:00 A.M.–8:00 P.M.

Boone County Historical Society
602 Story Street
Boone, IA 50036
(515) 432-1907
Charles W. Irwin, Director of Museums
Hours: Nov–Apr: Tue–Sun 1:00–5:00; May–Oct: Tue–Sun 10:00–5:00
Pub. *Trail Tales*, three times per year
$20.00 per year membership

Bremer County Historical Society
(Waverly, IA 50677—museum location)
PO Box 218 (mailing address)
Plainfield, IA 50666-0218
(319) 276-4674
J. W. "Bill" Lynes, Sr., President
Hours: Tue–Fri 1:30–4:00, Sun 2:00–4:00

Buena Vista County Historical and Genealogical Society Chapter (IGS)
Buena Vista Museum
214 West Fifth Street
Storm Lake, IA 50588-2346
(712) 732-4955
Tina Donath; Lois McConkey, President
Hours: Mon–Fri 9:00–12:00, and by appointment
Pub. *The Rootdigger*, quarterly
(genealogical research available, historical museum and genealogical library)
$8.00 per year membership; research: $5.00 per hour plus costs

Butler County Historical Society
420 West Jefferson Street
Clarksville, IA 50619
(319) 278-4479; (319) 267-2255 (Ms. Poppen for appointments)
Betty Jane McElhaney, President; Judy Poppen
Hours: by appointment

Calhoun County Historical Society
(150 High Street—museum location)
858 Lake (mailing address)
Rockwell City, IA 50579

(712) 297-8139 (Museum); (712) 297-8307 (Curator)
Judy Webb, Curator
Hours: Mon–Thur 8:00–11:30, Tue, Thur & Sat–Sun (May–Oct) 1:30–5:00, and by appointment
("plat maps 1884 & 1901, histories, cemetery records, obituaries, personal stories")
$5.00 per year membership, $50.00 life membership

Camanche Historical Society
(12th Avenue and Second Street—location)
City Hall, Second Street (mailing address)
Camanche, IA 52730
(319) 259-1268

Carroll County Historical Society
126 East Sixth
Carroll, IA 51401

Cass County Historical Society and Museum
(Corner of Main and Cass Street—location)
PO Box 254 (mailing address)
Griswold, IA 51535
(712) 778-2695 (President); (712) 778-4182 (Vice President)
Marjorie Sothman, President; Bob Brandt, Vice President
Hours: Sun 1:30–4:30, and by appointment
(Cass County history books and old atlases, local school books)
$5.00 per year membership

Cedar County Historical Society
607 Orange Street
Tipton, IA 52772
(319) 886-2740 (9:00 A.M.–8:00 P.M.)
Dorothy Stout, Corresponding Secretary
Hours: 8:00–4:00
Pub. *The Cedar County Review*, annually (July)
(local history)
$11.00 per year membership (includes book, add $1.50 if mailed)

Cedar Falls Historical Society
(308 West Third Street—location)
303 Franklin Street (mailing address)
Cedar Falls, IA 50613
(319) 266-5149; (319) 268-1812 FAX
Hours: Office: Mon–Fri 8:00–noon & 1:00–5:00; Library/archives: by appointment
("Cedar Falls history, Bess Streeter Aldrich memorabilia and writings, probate records of Black Hawk County 1852–1932")
copy fee, search fee as necessary

Central Community Historical Society
(628 Sixth Avenue—location)
2503 340th Avenue (mailing address)
De Witt, IA 52742
(319) 659-3686
Ann Soenksen, President
Hours: Mar–Dec: 1:00–4:30
("Reference for Clinton County, Iowa")
$5.00 per year membership for individuals, $12.50 per year membership for families; donations accepted

Cherokee County Historical Society
(105 East Front Street—location)
PO Box 247 (mailing address)
Cleghorn, IA 51014-0247
(712) 436-2624
Ann Wilberding, President
Hours: by appointment only
Pub. *Cherokee County Historical Society Newsletter*, sporadically
("The Cherokee County Chapter (IGS), known as the Tree Stumpers, is a part of the Cherokee County Historical Society.")

Chickasaw County Historical Society
Rural Route
Nashua, IA 50658
(515) 435-4701

Clarke County Historical Society
Rt. 4, Box 5
Osceola, IA 50213
(515) 342-4246

Clinton County Historical Society
PO Box 3135
Clinton, IA 52732
(319) 242-1201
Don Ketelsen
Hours: Wed 1:00–3:00, Sat–Sun 1:30–4:30
$10.00 per year membership for individuals, $15.00 per year membership for families

Community Historical Society
Maxwell, IA 50161
(515) 387-1380

Crawford County Historical Society
2134 Rocky Run
Denison, IA 51442

Davis County Historical Society
(302 East Franklin Street—location)
Rt. 6 (mailing address)
Bloomfield, IA 52537
(515) 664-2408
Hours: summer hours, and by appointment

Decatur County Historical Society
Main Street
Leon, IA 50144
(515) 446-4186

Delaware County Historical Society
PO Box 70
Hopkinton, IA 52237-0070
(319) 926-2639
Kene Bacon, President

Des Moines County Historical Society
The Apple Trees
1616 Dill Street
Burlington, IA 52601
(319) 753-2449 phone and FAX
Debra S. Olson, Executive Secretary
Hours: Office: Mon–Fri 9:00–noon; The
  Apple Trees: May–Oct: Wed & Sun
  1:30–4:30; Phelps House Museum,
  521 Columbia Street, Burlington:
  May–Oct: Sat–Sun 1:30–4:30;
  Hawkeye Log Cabin, 2915 South
  Main Street, Crapo Park, Burlington:
  May–Sept: Wed & Sun 1:30–4:30
$8.00 per year membership for
  individuals, $15.00 per year
  membership for families, $25.00 per
  year membership for businesses

Dickinson County Historical Society and Dickinson County Museum, Inc.
507 11th Street
Milford, IA 51351
(712) 338-2138
Faye Peterson, Secretary and Museum
  Curator

Dyersville Historical Society
120 Third Street S.E.
Dyersville, IA 52040
(319) 875-2504
Hours: Mon & Thur 10:00–4:00
$5.00 per year membership

Elkader Historical Society
Elkader, IA 52043
(319) 245-2622

Emmet County Historical Society, Inc.
1720 Third Avenue, South
PO Box 101
Estherville, IA 51334
David L. Kaltved, President
Hours: Mon–Sun (Jun–Aug) 2:00–5:00
$5.00 per year membership, $50.00 life
  membership

Fayette County Helpers Club and Historical Society
Fayette County Genealogical Society
  Chapter (IGS)
100 North Walnut Street
West Union, IA 52175
(319) 422-5797
Frances R. Graham, Administrator
Hours: Mon–Fri (May–Oct) 10:00–4:00,
  Mon–Fri (Nov–Apr) 10:00–3:00
Pub. *Newsletter*, quarterly
(Fayette County historical and
  genealogical material)
$5.00 per year membership in
  Genealogical Society, $5.00 per year

membership in Historical Society;
  search fees: $2.00 for non-members,
  search fee by center personnel, $5.00
  per surname plus copies

Floyd County Historical Society Museum
500 Gilbert Street
Charles City, IA 50616
(515) 228-1099 (Museum and Library)
E-mail: fchs@fia.net
Frank McKinney, Director; Mary Ann
  Townsend, Collections Manager
Hours: Museum: winter: Tue–Fri 9:00–
  4:30; summer: Tue–Fri 9:00–4:30,
  Sat–Sun 1:00–4:00
Pub. *Floyd County Heritage Newsletter*
  (not genealogical), quarterly
$7.50 per year membership for
  individuals, $15.00 per year
  membership for families

Franklin County Historical Society
PO Box 114
Hampton, IA 50441
Virginia Fredericks, President
Pub. *Franklin County Historical
  Newsletter*

Fremont County Historical Society
(East side of Square—location)
Sidney, IA 51652 (mailing address)
(712) 374-2719
Winifred Rhoades, Treasurer
Hours: Memorial Day Weekend and Sun
  (Jun–Aug) 1:00–4:00, special hours
  during Rodeo in Aug
$3.00 per year membership, $20.00 per
  year life membership

Garnavillo Historical Society
Garnavillo, IA 52049

Gowrie Historical Society
(Beek Street—location)
PO Box 297 (mailing address)
Gowrie, IA 50543
Yvonne Lungren, President
Hours: Sun (May 30–Sept 7) 2:00–4:00
$2.00 per year membership, $50.00
  memorial membership or life
  membership

Grafton Heritage Depot
Main Street
Grafton, IA 50440
(515) 748-2337
Connie Bruesewitz, Director
Hours: Sun 1:30–5:00; tours during the
  week
no charge

Greene County Historical Society
106 East State Street
Jefferson, IA 50129
(515) 386-8544 (Museum); (515) 386-
  9322 (Voice mail)
Bessie McClelland, Curator; Valeir
  Ogren, President
Hours: 18 April–24 Dec: Wed–Sat 2:00–
  5:00, Sun 2:00–4:00

$5.00 per year membership for
  individuals, $7.50 per year
  membership for families

Grundy County Historical Society
Rt. 1
Grundy Center, IA 50638
(319) 824-3585

Guthrie County Historical Society
901 Grand
Guthrie Center, IA 50115
(515) 747-3403

Hardin County Historical Society
(1603 South Washington Street—
  location)
PO Box 187 (mailing address)
Eldora, IA 50627
Gene Farmer, Curator
Hours: by appointment

Harrison County Historical Society
119 West Fourth Street
Logan, IA 51546
(712) 644-2941
Faye Marie Dow, Secretary
Pub. *Harrison County Historical Society*

Henry County Historical Society
(Mount Pleasant, IA—location)
Rt. 1, Box 224 (mailing address)
New London, IA 52645
(319) 367-5157

Honey Creek Church Preservation Group
30293 O Avenue
New Providence, IA 50206-8008
(515) 497-5458
Vera Cutler, Historian, Library
Hours: by appointment
(local Iowa history, Quaker records,
  genealogy; Honey Creek Friends
  Meetinghouse on Registry of National
  Historic Places)

Howard County Historical Society
(324 Fourth Avenue, West—location)
Rt. 1, Box 208 E (mailing address)
Cresco, IA 52136
(319) 547-5593
Raymond W. Morrison, President
Hours: by appointment

Humboldt County Historical Association
(East edge of Dakota City— museum
  location)
PO Box 162 (mailing address)
Humboldt, IA 50548
(515) 332-5280
Hours: Mon–Tue & Thur–Sat 10:00–
  4:30, Sun (Jun–Sept) 1:30–4:30
$5.00 per year membership

Ida County Historical Society
(Grant Center School, Moorehead
    Pioneer Park, Ida Grove, IA 51445—
    location)
Rural Route, Box 38 (mailing address)
Galva, IA 51020
(712) 364-3605

Iowa County Historical Society
Pioneer Heritage Museum
(675 East South Street—location)
PO Box 288 (mailing address)
Marengo, IA 52301
Janet Dains, President; Donna Martinson,
    Corresponding Secretary

Jackson County Historical Society
(Pearson Memorial Center, Fair
    Grounds—location)
PO Box 1245 (mailing address)
Maquoketa, IA 52060
(319) 652-5020
Mrs. Toni Kracke, Curator
Hours: Tue–Fri 10:00–4:00, Sat–Sun
    noon–4:00
Pub. *Timelines*, quarterly
$15.00 per year membership for
    individuals, $20.00 per year
    membership for families, $5.00 per
    year membership for students, $50.00
    per year Contributor membership,
    $300.00 life membership

**Jasper County Historical Society of
Iowa**
Jasper County Historical Museum
1700 South 15th Avenue, West
PO Box 834
Newton, IA 50208
(515) 792-9118
Hans J. Brosig, Museum Director
Hours: Mon–Fri business hours
Pub. *The Newsletter*, five times per year
    (Jasper County, Iowa, history only)
$5.00 per year membership for
    individuals, $10.00 per year
    membership for families

Jefferson County Historical Society
304 East Broadway
Fairfield, IA 52556
(515) 472-8071
Scott Reneker, Treasurer
Hours: second Tue 7:00 P.M.
$5.00 per year membership for
    individuals, $100.00 life membership

Johnson County Historical Society
Heritage Museum
(310 Fifth Street—location)
PO Box 5081 (mailing address)
Coralville, IA 52241
(319) 351-5738; (319) 351-5310 FAX
Laurie Robinson, Executive Director
Hours: Museum: Wed–Sat 1:00–5:00,
    Sun 1:00–4:00
Pub. *Newsletter*, bimonthly
from $15.00 per year membership;
    genealogical inquiries are referred to
    Iowa City Genealogical Society

Jones County Historical Society
301 North Chestnut
Monticello, IA 52310
C. L. Norlin

Kellogg Historical Society
218 High Street
PO Box 295
Kellogg, IA 50135-0295
(515) 526-8734
Judy Parsons, Secretary
Hours: Memorial Day–Labor Day: Mon–
    Fri 9:00–4:00, Sun 1:30–5:00, and by
    appointment
Pub. *The Kellogg Enterprise*, quarterly
    (January, April, July, October)
(houses library with genealogy and
    cemetery records)
$10.00 per year membership; search fees
    vary

Keokuk County Historical Society
(East and Elm—location)
PO Box 324 (mailing address)
Sigourney, IA 52591
(515) 622-3300
Hours: Wed–Thur 9:00–4:00
(obituary files, historical subject,
    miscellaneous records)
$5.00 per year membership; research
    available by mail

Kingsley Historical Society
Kingsley, IA 51028
(712) 378-2636
Helen K. Hager
Hours: summer and fall weekends, and
    summer holidays

Lee County Iowa Historical Society
(318 North Fifth Street—location)
PO Box 125 (mailing address)
Keokuk, IA 52632
(319) 524-7283 (answering machine)
Linda Bradley, President; Douglas
    Atterberg, Archivist
Hours: summer Sat–Sun afternoon, and
    by appointment
(Mark Twain and family, Civil War,
    Medical College, River history; topical
    and family history requests expedited)
research: by donation

**Lewis and Clark Historical
Association of Sioux City, Iowa**
(101 Pierce Street, Sioux City, IA
    51101—location)
PO Box 1804 (mailing address)
Sioux City, IA 51102
(712) 255-0107
Stan Swanson, President, Warren Nelson,
    Secretary/Treasurer

Linn County Historical Society
(101 Eighth Avenue, S.E., Cedar Rapids,
    IA 52401—location)
PO Box 175 (mailing address)
Cedar Rapids, IA 52406
(319) 369-1501
William R. Kreuger, Executive Director

Hours: Mon–Fri 9:00–4:00, Sat–Sun
    1:00–4:00
Pub. *Communique*, monthly
$15.00 per year membership for
    individuals, $20.00 per year
    membership for families, $50.00–
    $249.00 per year Contributor
    membership, $250.00–$499.00 per
    year Friend membership

Lowden Historical Society
(Main Street next to City Hall—location)
2199 155th Street (mailing address)
Lowden, IA 52255-9543
Virgil Kruckenberg, President
Hours: by appointment
Pub. *Lowden Historical Society Annual
    Report*
(local history and newspaper pictures)
$5.00 per year membership

Lyon County Historical Society
Rock Rapids, IA 51246

Madison County Historical Society
815 South Second Avenue
PO Box 15
Winterset, IA 50273
(515) 462-2134
Wendell Spencer, Manager
Hours: May 1–Oct 31: Mon–Sat 11:00–
    4:00, Sun 1:00–5:00

Mahaska County Historical Society
PO Box 578
Oskaloosa, IA 52577
(515) 672-2989
Hours: May 12–Oct 12: 9:30–4:30, and
    by appointment in winter
Pub. *NCHS Newsletter*

**Marble Rock Historical Society
Museum**
313 Bradford Street
Marble Rock, IA 50653
(515) 397-2216 (President)

Marion County Historical Society
Marion County Park
Rt. 3
Knoxville, IA 50138

**Historical Society of Marshall
County**
202 East Church Street
PO Box 304
Marshalltown, IA 50158
(515) 752-6664
Michael W. Vogt
Hours: Wed–Sat 10:00–noon & 1:00–
    5:00
Pub. *Then & Now*, bimonthly
(specializes in historical items)
$10.00 per year membership

McGregor Historical Society
(254 Main Street—location)
217 Ann Street (mailing address)
McGregor, IA 52157
(319) 873-3450

Mae Huebsch, Curator
Hours: regular summer hours, winter by
appointment

Mitchell County Historical Society

Rt. 1, Box 185
Osage, IA 50461
(515) 732-3059
Dave Biederman

Monona Historical Society

302 South Egbert Street
PO Box 434
Monona, IA 52159
(319) 539-2689
Hours: Memorial Day–Oct: Sun 1:00–
4:00, and by appointment

Monroe County Historical Society

114-116A Avenue, East
Albia, IA 52531
(515) 932-7046
E. St. Clair Gantz, President
Hours: Sat–Sun (May–Sept) 1:00–4:00,
and by appointment
("We have a modest library.")

Moulton Historical Society

Rt. 1
Moulton, IA 52572
(515) 642-3770 (President)
Lois Harris, President
Hours: 1 Jun–Labor Day by appointment
$3.00 per year membership, $25.00 life
membership

North Iowa Historical Society

Kinney Pioneer Museum
Highway 18 West, Airport Entrance
PO Box 421
Mason City, IA 50402-0421
(515) 423-1258; (515) 357-2980
(off-season)
Fran Tagesen, Director
Hours: Wed–Fri & Sun (May–Sept)
noon–5:00; Sat (Jun–Aug) noon–5:00
$10.00 per year membership for
individuals, $20.00 per year
membership for families

North Lee County Historical Society

Historic Museum
Ninth and Avenue H
PO Box 285
Fort Madison, IA 52627-0285
(319) 372-7661
Nellie Foster, President

O'Brien County Historical Society

(First Street, N.E., and Heritage Park
Road—location)
PO Box 385 (mailing address)
Primghar, IA 51245
(712) 757-1511
Kurt Brown, President
Hours: Sun (May–Aug) 2:00, and by
appointment
(historical library)

Oelwein Area Historical Society

(900 Second Avenue, S.E.—location)
PO Box 445 (mailing address)
Oelwein, IA 50662
(319) 283-5322
David Moore, President
Hours: first weekend in Jun–first
weekend in Oct: Sun 1:00–4:00
$10.00 per year membership for
individuals

Osceola County Historical Society

McCallum Museum
724 Third Avenue
Sibley, IA 51249
(712) 754-3882
E-mail: verstoff@rconnect.com
Jan Stofferan, Museum Curator
Hours: Memorial Day–Labor Day: Sun
1:30–4:30 (call ahead)

Parker Historical Society of Clay County

PO Box 91
Spencer, IA 51301
(712) 262-9800

Pella Historical Society

507 Franklin
Pella, IA 50219
(515) 628-2409

Pioneer Historical Society, Inc.

203 South Fourth Street
Farmington, IA 52626

Pocahontas County Historical Society

Rt. 2, Box 12
Rolfe, IA 50581
(712) 848-3342
Florence MacVey, President
Pub. *PCHS Newsletter*

Polk County Historical Society

317 S.W. 42nd Street
Des Moines, IA 50312
(515) 255-6657
LeRoy G. Pratt, Editor
Pub. *PCHS Newsletter*, ten times per
year (monthly, except July and
August)
(no genealogical library)
$7.00–$12.00 per year membership

Postville Historical Society

205 West Williams Street
Postville, IA 52162
(319) 864-3818
Edward W. Kozelka, Register Agent

Poweshiek County Historical and Genealogical Society Chapter (IGS)

206 North Mill Street
PO Box 280
Montezuma, IA 50171
(515) 623-3322 (Office); (515) 236-6407
Ferne Hart Norris, President
Hours: Mon & Thur 9:00–4:00, and by
appointment
Pub. *The Searcher*, quarterly

$10.00 per year membership for adults,
$2.00 per year membership for
students; search fee: donation of $6.00
per hour plus costs

Ringgold County Historical Society, Inc.

Mount Ayr, IA 50854
(515) 464-2140

Shelby County Historical Society

(Morse and Pine Streets—location)
837 Orange Road (mailing address)
Harlan, IA 51537
(712) 755-2437
Thelma Heflin, Public Relations
Secretary
Hours: Sun (Jun–Aug) 2:00–5:00, and by
appointment
Pub. *Wagon Tracks on Prairie Trails*,
quarterly
$3.00 per year membership

Sheldon Historical Society

Prairie Museum
Sheldon, IA 51201

Sioux City Public Museum and Historical Association

2901 Jackson Street
Sioux City, IA 51104
(712) 279-6174; (712) 252-5615 FAX
Craig R. Olson
Hours: Mon–Sat 9:00–5:00, Sun 2:00–
5:00
(museum archives/research library)

Sloan Historical Society

Sloan, IA 51055

Strawberry Point Historical Society

Strawberry Point, IA 52076
(319) 933-4461

Taylor County Historical Society

(Bedford, IA 50833—location)
PO Box 8 (mailing address)
Gravity, IA 50848
(712) 539-2475
Helen Janson

Taylor County Museum

Rt. 1, Box 13A
Bedford, IA 50833
(712) 523-2041 (Museum)
Helen Janson, President
Hours: Tue–Sun (Apr 1–Dec 25) 1:00–
5:00

Union County Historical Society

1101 North Vine Street
Creston, IA 50801
(515) 782-4247
Marcella M. Howe, Secretary and
Treasurer
Hours: Mon–Sun 1:00–5:00
$1.00 per year membership, $25.00 life
membership, $20.00 life membership
for senior citizens

Wapello County Historical Society

Wapello County Historical Museum
Amtrak Depot
201 West Main
Ottumwa, IA 52501

Washington County Historical Society

(903 East Washington—museum
location)
PO Box 364 (mailing address)
Washington, IA 52353
(319) 653-3125
Mary Levy, President
Hours: Sun (Jun–Aug) 1:00–5:00, first
two weekends in Dec 1:00–5:00
(Washington County history artifacts, no
genealogy)

West Bend Historical Society

4473 550th Avenue
West Bend, IA 50597
(515) 887-3241 (Treasurer)

West Des Moines Historical Society

Historic Jordan House
2001 Fuller Road
West Des Moines, IA 50265
(515) 225-1286
Joyce Grabinski, President
Hours: May–Oct: Wed & Sat–Sun, and
private group tours
admission $2.00 for adults, 50¢ for
children

John Whitmer Historical Association

Graceland College
700 College Avenue
Lamoni, IA 50140
E-mail: alblair@netins.net
A. R. Blair, Executive Secretary
Pub. *John Whitmer Historical
Association Journal*, annually
(September; *Newsletter*, irregularly
(not genealogical, scholarly historical
articles on Mormon history, especially
the "minor" historical groups)
$15.00 per year membership

Winnebago Historical Society

(336 North Clark Street—location)
PO Box 27 (mailing address)
Forest City, IA 50436

Winneshiek County Historical Society

Decorah Public Library
Decorah, IA 52101
(319) 382-1009
Shan Thomas, President
Hours: Tue–Sat 9:00–noon & 1:00–5:00
(local county historical documents and
records, includes county governmental
records)

Wright County Historical Society

615 Fifth Avenue
Clarion, IA 50525
(515) 532-3669

Wright County Historical Society, Eagle Grove Chapter

(Broadway and North Iowa Streets—
location)
917 West Broadway (mailing address)
Eagle Grove, IA 50533
(515) 448-4220

Wright County Historical Society

Rt. 2, Box 337
Goldfield, IA 50542
(515) 825-3641

LDS Family History Centers

Ames
(515) 232-3634

Davenport
(319) 386-7547

Des Moines
(see West Des Moines)

Sioux City
(712) 255-9686

West Des Moines
(515) 225-0416

Genealogical Societies

State Genealogical Society

Iowa Genealogical Society (IGS)

6000 Douglas
PO Box 7735
Des Moines, IA 50322-7735
(515) 276-0287
E-mail: igs@digiserve.com
http://www.digiserve.com/igs/igs.htm
Rhonda Q. Riordan, Office Coordinator
Hours: Mon & Fri–Sat 10:00–4:00, Tue–
Thur 10:00–9:00
Pub. *Hawkeye Heritage*, quarterly; *Iowa
Genealogical Society Newsletter*,
bimonthly
$25.00 per year membership for
individuals, $29.00 per year
membership for families

IGS Chapters

Adair County Chapter (IGS)

Greenfield Library
PO Box 328
Greenfield, IA 50849
Pub. *Newsletter*, quarterly
("Extensive collection of family histories
and microfilm")

$4.00 per year membership for
individuals, $5.00 per year
membership for couples

Adams County Genealogical Society Chapter (IGS)

PO Box 117
Prescott, IA 50859
(515) 335-2352
Cathy Eggleston, Vice President
Hours: Mon–Tue & Thur 9:00–4:00,
Wed 9:00–6:30, Fri 9:00–12:00
Pub. *Treetender*, quarterly
$5.00 per year membership for
individuals, $7.50 per year
membership for families

Ankeny Area Chapter (IGS)

Bondurant, IA 50035
Barbara Crum
(Polk County)

Appanoose County Genealogical Society Chapter (IGS)

1020 Shamrock Lane, Apartment 107
Centerville, IA 52544-1147
(515) 437-4077
Loretta Crow, Vice President
Hours: Oct–Jun: 12:00–8:00, Jul–Sept
12:00–6:00, Sat 10:00–6:00
Pub. *Pages from the Past*, quarterly
$5.00 per year membership for
individuals, $7.50 per year
membership for couples

Audubon County Chapter (IGS)

511 Tracy Street
Audubon, IA 50025
Lois A. Olsen

Boone County Genealogical Society

PO Box 453
Boone, IA 50036
Bruce Kelly, President
Hours: Boone County Historical Society,
Historical Building, Lower Level,
Research Room: by appointment
Pub. *Boone County Genealogical Society
Newsletter*, quarterly
$7.50 per year membership for
individuals, $10.00 per year
membership for couples; free queries
for members, $2.00 each for non-
members

Botna Valley Chapter (IGS)

PO Box 633
Oakland, IA 51560
(712) 482-3209
Opal Palmer, President
Hours: Mon–Tue, Thur & Sat 1:00–5:00,
Tue 9:00–12:00, Fri 7:00–9:00
Pub. *Botna Valley Genealogical Society
News*, quarterly
(Pottawattamie County)
$5.00 per year membership for
individuals, $7.00 per year
membership for couples, $1.00 per
year junior membership

Bremer County Genealogical Society Chapter (IGS)

1378 Badger Avenue
Plainfield, IA 50666-9772
(319) 276-3234
Nancy S. Robinson, Corresponding
Secretary/Editor
Pub. *Bremer County Browsings*,
quarterly (usually February, May,
August, November)
$6.00 per year membership for
individuals (calendar year), $8.00 per
year membership for couples

Buena Vista County Historical and Genealogical Society Chapter (IGS)

221 West Railroad
Storm Lake, IA 50588
(712) 732-7111
E-mail: bucogen@ncn.net
Janice Danielson, President
Hours: Mon–Fri 9:00–12:00, and by
appointment
Pub. *The Rootdigger*, quarterly
(genealogical research available,
historical museum and genealogical
library)
$10.00 per year membership; research:
$5.00 per hour plus costs

Calhoun County Chapter (IGS)

Carnegie Public Library
426 Fifth Street
Rockwell City, IA 50579

Carroll County Genealogical Society Chapter (IGS)

(Genealogical Library at Lidderdale—
location)
PO Box 21 (mailing address)
Carroll, IA 51401
Neoma Hagge, Corresponding Secretary
Hours: Library: Wed 9:00–4:00, some
Saturday mornings; meetings at
Methodist Church in Carroll: second
Mon 7:30
Pub. *Carroll County Genealogical
Society Newsletter*, bimonthly
$8.00 per year membership (calendar
year); free queries

Central Iowa Genealogical Society Chapter (IGS)

PO Box 945
Marshalltown, IA 50158
Jo Ann Naumann, President
Pub. *Central Iowa Genealogical Society*,
irregularly
(Marshall County)
$5.00 per year membership

Cherokee County Chapter (IGS)

Tree Stumpers
(105 East Front Street—location)
PO Box 247 (mailing address)
Cleghorn, IA 51014-0247
(712) 436-2624
Pat Behrens, Cherokee County Historical
Society Treasurer and Tree Stumpers
Chairman

Hours: by appointment in summer
(part of the Cherokee County Historical
Society)

Chickasaw County Chapter (IGS)

Chickasaw County Genealogical Society
PO Box 434
New Hampton, IA 50659-0434
(515) 394-4343
Carol Bottin, Editor
("Maintains society library at the New
Hampton Public Library")
Pub. *Chickasaw County Genealogical
Society Newsletter*, quarterly
$6.00 per year membership; research:
$5.00 per hour, $5.00 minimum

Clayton County Chapter (IGS)

Clayton County Genealogical Society
PO Box 846
Elkader, IA 52043
(319) 245-1418
Myra Voss, Corresponding Secretary
Hours: Elkader Public Library: Mon &
Wed 10:00–12:00 & 2:00–5:00, Tue &
Thur 2:00–5:00, Fri 10:00–5:00, Sat
9:30–2:00

Clinton County Gateway Genealogical Society Chapter (IGS)

618 14th Avenue
Camanche, IA 52730
(319) 259-1285
Ruth Evans
Hours: Library: by appointment only
Pub. *Clinton County Gateway
Genealogical Society Newsletter*
$8.00 per year membership

Crawford County Chapter (IGS)

c/o Norelius Community Library
1403 First Avenue South
Denison, IA 51442
Dawn Boettger, President
Pub. *Crawford County Iowa
Genealogical Society Newsletter*,
quarterly
$5.00 to $7.50 per year membership

Dallas County Chapter (IGS)

(Dallas Center Library—location)
PO Box 264 (mailing address)
Dallas Center, IA 50063
(515) 992-3185; (515) 992-3003
Lorna Baldner Grow, Query Chair
Hours: Mon & Fri 9:00–noon & 1:00–
5:00, Tue–Thur 9:00–noon & 1:00–
7:00, Sat 9:00–noon
(holdings include card index to Dallas
County newspapers for births, deaths,
marriages, published Dallas County
cemeteries, probate index 1850–1990)
$5.00 per year membership

Davis County Genealogical Society Chapter (IGS)

(Bloomfield Public Library—location)
PO Box 94 (mailing address)
Bloomfield, IA 52537-0094
Pat Howk, President

Hours: Library: Tue–Fri 11:00–5:00, Sat
11:00–2:00
Pub. *Davis County Genealogical Society
Newsletter*, quarterly
$7.50 per year membership; search fee:
$6.00 per hour

Decatur County Chapter (IGS)

c/o Lamoni Public Library
Lamoni, IA 50140

Delaware County Chapter (IGS)

823 Howard Street
Manchester, IA 52057

Des Moines County Genealogical Society Chapter (IGS)

PO Box 493
Burlington, IA 52601
Phyllis Rothlauf, President
Pub. *The Quarterly* (February, May,
August, November)
$8.00 per year membership for
individuals, $10.00 per year
membership for families

Dubuque County-Key City Genealogical Society Chapter (IGS)

PO Box 13
Dubuque, IA 52004-0013
Hours: Society Library: members only,
and by appointment
Pub. *Dubuque County-Key City
Genealogical Society Newsletter*,
quarterly (March, June, September,
December)
(Dubuque County, Iowa, Jo Daviess
County, Illinois, and Grant County,
Wisconsin; publishing cemetery
readings for Dubuque County)
$8.00 per year membership (beginning in
March); queries free to members,
$2.00 to non-members (maximum of
two per issue)

Fayette County Genealogical Society Chapter (IGS)

Fayette County Helpers Club and
Historical Society
100 North Walnut Street
West Union, IA 52175
(319) 422-5797
Frances R. Graham, Administrator
Hours: Mon–Fri (May–Oct) 10:00–4:00,
Mon–Fri (Nov–Apr) 10:00–3:00
Pub. *Newsletter*, quarterly
(Fayette County historical and
genealogical material)
$5.00 per year membership in
Genealogical Society, $5.00 per year
membership in Historical Society;
search fees: $2.00 for non-members,
search fee by center personnel, $5.00
per surname plus copies

Franklin County Chapter (IGS)

PO Box 335
Chapin, IA 50427

Judy Dannen
Pub. *Newsletter*, quarterly
$6.00 per year membership

Fremont County Chapter (IGS)
PO Box 337
Sidney, IA 51652
Winnie Rhoades

Greater Sioux County Genealogical Society Chapter (IGS)
Sioux Center Public Library
327 First Avenue, N.E.
Sioux Center, IA 51250
Jennie Den Besten, President; Wilma J. Vande Berg, Corresponding Secretary
Hours: meetings in the Robert Frost Room (lower level) of the library: fourth Monday (except May & Dec) 7:30
(Lyon, Sioux and O'Brien counties and Dutch genealogy)
$5.00 per year membership for individuals, $6.00 per year membership for couples; search fee: donation

Grundy County Genealogical Society Chapter (IGS)
811 Pioneer Road
PO Box 2
Reinbeck, IA 50669
Barbara McMartin, President
Hours: Conrad Public Library, Conrad, IA: summer: Mon–Tue & Thur–Fri 2:00–8:00, Wed 9:00–12:00 & 5:30–8:00; fall/winter: Sat 9:00–12:00
$8.50 per year membership

Guthrie County Genealogical Society Chapter (IGS)
PO Box 96
Jamaica, IA 50128-0096
(515) 429-3362; (515) 429-3362 FAX
Dana Lowry, Librarian
Hours: Mon–Wed 1:00–6:00, Thur 9:00–11:00
Pub. *Guthrie County Genealogical Society Newsletter*, quarterly
$7.00 per year membership

Hamilton Heritage Hunters Chapter (IGS)
(Kendall Young Public Library, 943 First Street, Webster City, IA 50595-2001—library location)
PO Box 364 (mailing address)
Webster City, IA 50595
(515) 832-5784 (President); (515) 832-9100 (Library)
Norma Jeane Bell, President
Hours: Library: Mon–Thur 10:00–8:00, Fri 10:00–6:00, Sat 10:00–5:00
Pub. *Hamilton Heritage Hunters Newsletter*, quarterly (March, June, September, December)
(genealogy in Hamilton County)

$7.00 per year membership; research: $5.00 per hour

Hancock County Genealogical Society Chapter (IGS)
PO Box 81
Klemme, IA 50449
(515) 587-2324 (President and Researcher); (515) 923-2850 (Library)
Gail C. Linahon, President and Researcher
Hours: Garner Public Library: winter: Mon 10:00–5:30 & 7:00–8:00, Tue–Wed 10:00–5:30, Thur noon–8:00, Fri noon–4:00, Sat 10:00–noon & 1:00–3:00; summer: Mon 10:00–5:00 & 7:00–8:00, Tue–Wed 10:00–5:00, Thur noon–8:00, Fri noon–4:00, Sat 10:00–noon
$5.00 per year membership; research $5.00 per hour plus expenses

Harrison County Genealogical Volunteers Chapter (IGS)
(Merry Brook School Museum, 210 Lincoln Way—location)
2810 190th Train (mailing address)
Woodbine, IA 51579
(712) 647-2454; (712) 647-2593
E-mail: hcgs51579@aol.com
http://www.rootsweb.com/ iaharris
Linda Dickman, Corresponding Secretary
Hours: Museum: Thur 1:30–4:30, Fri–Sat by appointment
Pub. *Harrison County Happenings*, quarterly
("3,000 early 1890s obituaries handwritten for Harrison County, Iowa, newspapers, *Missouri Valley Times*, *Woodbine Twiner*, and *Logan Observer*")
$10.00 per year membership, research fee: $5.00 per hour

Henry County Chapter (IGS)
Henry County Genealogical Society
PO Box 81
Mount Pleasant, IA 52641-0081
Doris Sharp, President
Pub. *HCGS Newsletter*, quarterly
$8.00 per year membership for individuals, $10.00 per year Mr. & Mrs. membership, $1.00 per year membership for students

Iowa Lakes Genealogical Society Chapter (IGS)
600 West 11th Street
Spencer, IA 51301
Esther Connell, Vice President
Hours: Spencer Public Library: Mon–Sat 9:00–5:00
Pub. *ILGS Teaser*, quarterly
(Clay County)
$5.00 per year membership

Jackson County Genealogical Chapter (IGS)
(Jackson County Historical Museum, Pearson Memorial Center, Fair Grounds—location)
PO Box 1065 (mailing address)
Maquoketa, IA 52060
(319) 652-5020 (Museum)
Hours: Museum: Tue–Fri 10:00–4:00, Sat–Sun noon-4:00; genealogists available: Tue & Fri 10:00–4:00, Sat–Sun noon-4:00; meetings: third Mon 1:30
Pub. *Genie Gems*, quarterly
$5.00 per year membership (calendar year); free queries for members; research: $5.00 per hour plus copies at 10¢ each for members, 25¢ each for non-members

Jasper County Genealogical Society Chapter (IGS)
(Basement of the Jasper County Courthouse—location)
PO Box 163 (mailing address)
Newton, IA 50208
(515) 792-1522
Hours: Tue–Thur 9:30–noon & 1:00–3:30, and by appointment
Pub. *Jasper County Gleaner*, quarterly
$10.00 per year membership for individuals, $12.00 per year membership for families, $2.50 per year membership for youths (under 18); research: $5.00 per hour (two surnames), plus copy costs and SASE

Iowa City Genealogical Society
Johnson County Chapter (IGS)
PO Box 822
Iowa City, IA 52244
http://www.rootsweb.com/~iajohnso/ icgensoc.htm
Peter J. Seaba, President
Pub. *I.C.G.S. Newsletter*, ten times per year
$10.00 per year membership for individuals, $11.00 per year membership for families

Jones County Genealogical Society Chapter (IGS)
(209 West Main—location)
PO Box 174 (mailing address)
Anamosa, IA 52205
LaVerta Langenberg, Treasurer
Hours: Tue 9:00–1:00, and by appointment
Pub. *News & Notes*, bimonthly
$10.00 per year membership; search fees: $7.00 per hour for members, $10.00 per hour for non-members

Keo Mah Genealogical Society Chapter (IGS)
(Penn Central Mall—location)
PO Box 616 (mailing address)
Oskaloosa, IA 52577
(515) 673-6507

Mabel Daniels, Corresponding Secretary/ Librarian
Hours: Penn Central Mall: Mon–Fri 10:00–5:00, Sat 10:00–2:00
Pub. *Tracers*, quarterly
(Keokuk and Mahaska counties; collection consists of other counties in Iowa and other states, also DAR material, microfilm newspapers, census on various counties; publishes local records)
$7.00 per year U.S. membership (calendar year), $9.00 per year foreign membership; free queries

Laurens Genies Chapter (IGS)
273 North Third Street
Laurens, IA 50554-1215
(Pocahontas County)

Lee County Genealogical Society of Iowa Chapter (IGS)
PO Box 303
Keokuk, IA 52632-0303
(319) 524-4121
Frances E. Sprunger, Corresponding Secretary
Hours: Library: Mon–Thur 9:30–9:00, Fri–Sat 9:30–6:00; meetings fourth Thur at Keokuk Public Library, Round Room
Pub. *Gleanings, The Lee County Genealogical Society of Iowa Newsletter*, quarterly
("Census microfilm; Clark, Lee, Hancock; courthouse records; marriages, obituaries, scrapbooks, etc.")
$8.00 per year membership for individuals, $10.00 per year membership for families; search fee: $6.00 per hour plus copies and postage

Lime Creek Chapter (IGS)
115 East L Street
Forest City, IA 50436
(Winnebago County)

Genealogical Society of Linn County, Iowa, Chapter (IGS)
(101 Eighth Avenue, S.E.—location)
PO Box 175 (mailing address)
Cedar Rapids, IA 52406
(319) 362-0022
Marilyn J. Walsh, President
Hours: Tue–Sat 10:00–4:00
Pub. *Linn County Heritage Hunters*, quarterly
$12.50 per year membership for individuals, $15.00 per year membership for families

Lucas County Chapter (IGS)
Lucas County Genealogical Society
c/o Chariton Public Library
Eighth and Braden Avenue
Chariton, IA 50049
(515) 774-5514 (Library); (515) 535-2704 (Secretary)
Betty Cross, Corresponding Secretary

Hours: Library: noon–6:00
("Many indexed resources, all available local censuses on microfilm, newspapers on microfilm, large obituary file, many family histories and much more; our files are open for research all library hours, with limited help for searchers; more extended research done for reasonable fees by contacting the society.")
$2.00 per year membership; $5.00 basic research of printed indexes

Madison County Chapter (IGS)
PO Box 26
Winterset, IA 50273
(515) 462-1731 (Winterset Public Library); (515) 462-4318 (Corresponding Secretary)
Lorraine Kile, Corresponding Secretary
Hours: Mon–Sat 10:00–5:00, Wed 10:00–8:00; meetings at a meeting room: first Tue 7:30
Pub. *Newsletter*, quarterly
$5.00 per year membership for individuals, $8.00 per year membership for families; $8.00 per hour research fee plus postage and copies

Marion County Genealogical Society Chapter (IGS)
PO Box 385
Knoxville, IA 50138
(515) 842-0585
E-mail: jean2gen@se-iowa.net
Jean Leeper, President and Newsletter Editor
Hours: Knoxville Public Library: Mon–Thur 10:00–8:00, Fri 10:00–5:00, Sat 10:00–3:00
Pub. *Marion County Newsletter*, quarterly
$10.00 per year membership

Mills County Chapter (IGS)
Mills County Genealogical Society
c/o Glenwood Public Library
109 North Vine Street
Glenwood, IA 51534-1516
(712) 527-5252 (Library)
Linda Rose, President
Hours: Library: Mon–Tue & Thur–Fri 10:00–6:00, Wed 10:00–8:00, Sat 10:00–4:00
Pub. *Mills County Genealogical Society Newsletter*, quarterly
$4.00 per year membership

Monona County Chapter (IGS)
901 12th Street
PO Box 16
Onawa, IA 51040
Emma Stanislav

Monroe County Genealogical Society Chapter (IGS)
Carnegie-Evans Library
203 Benton Avenue, East
Albia, IA 52531-2036

(515) 932-5477 (Editor); (515) 932-2593 (Secretary)
Vivian Shelquist, Editor; Sarah Hindman, Correspondence Secretary
Hours: Library: Mon–Fri 12:00–6:00, Sat 10:00–4:00
Pub. *Monroe County Genealogical Society News*, quarterly
$8.00 per year membership (calendar year)

Montgomery County Chapter (IGS)
901 Washington Avenue
Red Oak, IA 51566
Jean Schaffer

Muscatine County Chapter (IGS)
323 Main Street
Muscatine, IA 52761
Gladys Mittman

Nishnabotna Genealogical Society Chapter (IGS)
847 Road M 56
Harlan, IA 51537
(712) 782-3400
Margaret Anderson, President; Anabelle Petersen, Secretary
Hours: Harlan Community Library: Mon–Sat 9:30–5:30
(Shelby County marriage records, 1853–1880, and some cemeteries; records in Library and in Museum in Harlan)
$2.00 per year membership

Northeast Iowa Genealogical Society Chapter (IGS)
c/o Grout Museum of History and Science
503 South Street
Waterloo, IA 50701
(319) 234-6357
Michael J. Magee, Secretary; Mrs. Richard Dean, President
Hours: winter: Tue–Sat 1:00–4:30; summer: Tue–Fri 10:00–4:30, Sat 1:00–4:30
Pub. *Cedar Tree Branches*, quarterly
(Black Hawk County only; "indexes for most cemeteries, early probates, naturalizations, early marriages, deaths.")
$7.00 per year membership for individuals, $9.00 per year membership for husband/wife; $6.00 per hour research

Northwest Iowa Genealogical Society Chapter (IGS)
Le Mars Public Library
46 First Street, S.W.
Le Mars, IA 51031
(712) 546-5004
John L. Winterringer, President
Hours: Library: Mon–Thur 10:00–8:00, Fri–Sat 10:00–5:00
Pub. *Northwest Iowa Root Diggers*, quarterly
(provides research for Plymouth County and a few surrounding counties)

$7.50 per year membership for individuals or couples; research fee: $10.00 per hour plus postage and photocopies

Oelwein Area Genealogical Society Chapter (IGS)
c/o Oelwein Public Library
Oelwein, IA 50662
(319) 283-5601
Viola Sims, Treasurer; Hazel Short, President
Pub. *Newsletter*, quarterly
(Fayette County; material at Oelwein Public Library)
$5.00 per year membership for individuals, $6.00 per year membership for husband and wife; research: $5.00 per hour plus copy costs

Old Fort Chapter (IGS)
Old Fort Genealogical Society, Inc.
PO Box 1
Fort Madison, IA 52627
(319) 372-2987 (President)
Betty Haas, President
Hours: Rashid Memorial Library: Mon, Wed & Fri noon–5:00, Tue & Thur noon–8:00, Sat 9:00–1:00
Pub. *Quarterly*
(North Lee County)
$8.00 per year membership for individuals, $10.00 per year membership for families

Pioneer Sons and Daughters Chapter (IGS)
PO Box 13133
Des Moines, IA 50310
Pub. *Pioneer Trails*, quarterly
(Polk County records)
$6.00 per year membership for individuals, $8.00 per year membership for families

Poweshiek County Historical and Genealogical Society Chapter (IGS)
206 North Mill Street
PO Box 280
Montezuma, IA 50171
(515) 623-3322 (Office); (515) 236-6407
Ferne Hart Norris, President
Hours: Mon & Thur 9:00–4:00, and by appointment
Pub. *The Searcher*, quarterly
$10.00 per year membership for adults, $2.00 per year membership for students; search fee: donation of $6.00 per hour plus costs

Ringgold County Genealogy Society Chapter (IGS)
Rt. 2, Box 67 C, 301 Amy Lane
Mount Ayr, IA 50854
(515) 464-3594
Earle M. Schad
Hours: meetings fourth Wed (except Dec)

Pub. *Ringgold Roots*, quarterly
$5.00 per year membership

Scott County Iowa Genealogical Society, Chapter (IGS)
PO Box 3132
Davenport, IA 52808-3132
Pub. *Scott County Iowan*, quarterly (collection placed with local library)
$12.00 per year membership for individuals, $16.00 per year membership for families

Story County Chapter (IGS)
c/o Chamber of Commerce
205 Clark Avenue
Ames, IA 50010
(515) 292-3283
Lucille Wahrenbrock, Librarian
Pub. *Newsletter*
$5.00 per year membership

Tama County Tracers Genealogical Society Chapter (IGS)
Tama County Historical Museum Library
200 North Broadway Street
Toledo, IA 52342
(515) 484-6767
Hours: Museum Library: Tue–Sat 1:00–4:30, and by appointment
Pub. *Tama County Museum News*, quarterly
$10.00 per year membership

Taylor County, Iowa Genealogical Society Chapter (IGS)
(102 Washington—location)
PO Box 8 (mailing address)
Gravity, IA 50848
(712) 539-2475 (President); (712) 523-2041 (Museum)
Helen Janson, President
Hours: Taylor County Museum: Tue–Sun (Apr 1–Dec 25) 1:00–5:00
Pub. *Taylor County, Iowa Genealogical Society*, semiannually
$4.00 per year membership (calendar year)

Tree Shakers Chapter (IGS)
1009 Woodland Ridge Court
Louisville, KY 40245-5209
Judy Stacey
(Polk County)

Union County Chapter (IGS)
Gibson Memorial Library
310 North Maple
Creston, IA 50801
Irma M. Miller, Query Coordinator
Hours: Library: winter: Mon–Tue & Thur–Fri 10:00–8:00, Wed 10:00–6:00, Sat 10:00–4:00; summer: Mon–Tue & Thur–Fri 10:00–6:00, Wed 10:00–4:00, Sat 9:00–12:00
Pub. *Union Roots*, quarterly
$5.00 per year membership for individuals, $7.00 per year membership for families; research: $6.00 per hour plus copies and postage

Van Buren County Genealogy Society Chapter (IGS)
Keosauqua Public Library
First and Van Buren
PO Box 158
Keosauqua, IA 52565
(319) 293-3766
Shirley Aldrich, President
Hours: Mon–Wed & Fri 1:00–5:00, Thur 10:00–5:00, Sat 10:00–3:00
Pub. *Van Buren County Quill*, quarterly ("Surname card file, obituary file, cemetery inscriptions, county-wide")
$7.50 per year membership for individuals, $10.00 per year membership for families

Wapello County Genealogical Society Chapter (IGS)
PO Box 163
Ottumwa, IA 52501
(515) 682-8676
E-mail: dhull@franklin.se-iowa.net
http://www.rootsweb.com/~iawapegs
Mary Clark, President
Hours: Tue–Fri noon–3:30, Sat 10:00–3:30, Sun 1:00–3:30
Pub. *Wapello County Genealogical Society Newsletter*, quarterly
$10.00 per year membership; search fee: $5.00 per name for members, $10.00 per name for non-members

Warren County Genealogical Society Chapter (IGS)
306 West Salem Street
Indianola, IA 50125
(515) 961-4409
Thelma Pehrson, Corresponding Secretary
Pub. *Warren County Genealogical Society Newsletter*, bimonthly
$6.00 per year membership

Washington County Chapter (IGS)
(Washington Public Library, 120 East Main Street—location)
PO Box 446 (mailing address)
Washington, IA 52353
(319) 653-2726 (Library)
Cindy S. Juhl, President; Wilma Atkinson, Corresponding Secretary; Sally Reighard, Editor
Hours: Library: Mon–Thur 10:00–8:00, Fri–Sat 10:00–5:00
Pub. *Newsletter*, quarterly
(Washington County records, several records for surrounding counties)
$8.00 per year membership for individuals

Wayne County Genealogical Society Chapter (IGS)
LeCompte Memorial Library
110 South Franklin
Corydon, IA 50060-1518
(515) 872-1621
E-mail: lecompte@netins.net
Roberta Amdor, President

Hours: Mon–Fri 12:30–5:00, Sat 10:00–2:00

Pub. *Wayne County Genie News*, quarterly

$5.00 per year membership (calendar year; research: $5.00 minimum

Webster County Genealogical Society Chapter (IGS)

PO Box 1584
Fort Dodge, IA 50501
Pub. *Genie Gleaners*, quarterly
$10.00 per year membership; research: $10.00 per hour plus costs

Woodbury County Genealogical Society Chapter (IGS)

PO Box 624
Sioux City, IA 51102-0624
Janet P. Jolin
Hours: Public Library, Sioux City: Mon–Thur 9:00–9:00, Fri–Sat 9:00–5:00, Sun (Sept–May) 1:00–5:00
Pub. *Waukaw*, quarterly
$12.00 per year membership; search fee: $10.00 per hour

Wright County Genealogical Searchers Chapter (IGS)

PO Box 225
Clarion, IA 50525
Ann Hines, Researcher
(Wright and Clarion counties)
$5.00 per year membership for individuals, $7.00 per year double membership; search: $5.00 per hour, plus copying costs and postage

Regional Genealogical Societies

Adair County Anquestors Genealogical Society

Genie Bug Club Genealogical Society
2787 335th Street
Menlo, IA 50164
(515) 524-5110
Sherry Foresman

Buchanan County Genealogical Society

(331 First Street East, Basement of City Hall, side entrance—location)
PO Box 4 (mailing address)
Independence, IA 50644-0004
Nina Hickey, President
Hours: Mon 10:00–2:00, first & third Thur 4:00–7:00, and by appointment
Pub. *Newsletter*, biannually
("Focus: Buchanan County; outstanding collection of obituary files; probates from 1850s; all census records for the county and the surrounding counties; extensive microfilm collection of newspapers from 1867; cemetery book, etc.")

$7.50 per year membership; search fee: $10.00 per hour plus copy fees; $5.00 donation to open during unscheduled hours

Butler County Genealogical Society

PO Box 177
Parkersburg, IA 50665
Patricia Atteberry
Pub. *Butler Branches*, quarterly

Calhoun County Genies

(150 High Street—museum location)
226 North Grant (mailing address)
Rockwell City, IA 50579
(712) 297-7237 (President); (712) 297-8307 (Museum Curator)
Beverly Courter, President
Hours: by appointment
(only Calhoun County records)
$5.00 per year membership

Cass County, Iowa Genealogical Society

706 Hazel Street
Atlantic, IA 50022
(712) 781-2227
Marietta Petresen, President
Hours: meetings at the Atlantic Library: fourth Thur (Feb–Nov) 7:00
Pub. *Cass County Newsletter*, quarterly
$5.00 per year membership; search fee: $5.00 per hour, $1.00 for non-member queries

Decorah Genealogy Association

Decorah Public Library
202 Winnebago
Decorah, IA 52101
(319) 382-8559; (319) 382-4524 FAX
E-mail: stan8@juno.com
Stan Jeffers, President
Hours: Library: Mon–Sat 10:00–5:00
Pub. *Decorah Area Diggers*, quarterly (genealogy, northeast Iowa)
$6.00 per year membership (calendar year); research: $5.00 per year plus copies and postage

Delaware County Genealogical Society

300 North Franklin
Manchester, IA 52057

Franklin County Genealogical Society of Hampton, Iowa

Rt. 1
PO Box 119
Geneva, IA 50633
Mrs. Fred Abbas
Pub. *Franklin Record*, quarterly
$6.00 per year membership

Greene County Genealogical Society

PO Box 133
Jefferson, IA 50129-0133
Valerie Ogren, Registrar
Hours: Jefferson Public Library, Reference Room: Wed 2:00–5:00, Sat 9:00–1:00

Pub. *Greene Gleanings*, six times per year
(county history, county vital statistics and cemeteries)
$5.00 per year membership for individuals, $7.50 per year membership for families, $2.00 per year membership for students

Humboldt County Genealogical Society

c/o Public Library
30 Sixth Street North
Humboldt, IA 50548
(515) 332-1439 (Secretary)
Charlotte Marvin, Corresponding Secretary; Marilyn Hundertmark, President
Hours: 9:30–4:00
Pub. *Humboldt County Genealogical Society Newsletter*, three to four times per year
("GEDCOM in/out; cemetery records, indexed census, obituary file, indexed county history 1963 & 1884")
$5.00 per year membership with one free research; search fee: $5.00 per hour in advance

Iowa City Genealogical Society

Johnson County Chapter (IGS)
PO Box 822
Iowa City, IA 52244
http://www.rootsweb.com/~iajohnso
Peter J. Seaba, President
Pub. *I.C.G.S. Newsletter*, ten times per year
$8.50 per year membership for individuals, $11.00 per year membership for families

Iowa County Genealogy Society

(Pioneer Heritage Museum, 675 East South Street—location)
PO Box 372 (mailing address)
Marengo, IA 52301
(319) 642-7018 (Museum); (319) 668-2401 (Secretary)
Netha M. Meyer, Corresponding Secretary
Hours: Thur–Sat 1:00–4:00, and by appointment
Pub. *Iowa County Byways*, quarterly
(queries, articles pertaining to Iowa County)
$8.00 per year membership (calendar year); search fees: donation

Jefferson County Genealogical Society

2791 240th Street
Fairfield, IA 52556-8518
(515) 472-4667
Verda Baird, Corresponding Secretary
$5.00 per year membership; research fee: $8.00 per hour; send SAE for list of county publications

172

Marion County Genealogical Society
1017 West Marion Street
Knoxville, IA 50138

Monona County Genealogist
Onawa Public Library
Genealogy Department
707 Iowa Avenue
Onawa, IA 51040
(712) 423-1167
Ariel E. Wonder, Historian and
   Genealogist
Hours: Mon–Fri 1:00–5:00

**North Central Iowa Genealogical
Society**
(225 Second Street, S.E., Mason City, IA
   50401—location)
PO Box 237 (mailing address)
Mason City, IA 50402-0237
Beth McBride, President
Hours: Public Library: Mon, Wed & Fri
   9:00–noon & 1:00–4:00, Mon 6:00–
   8:00, Sat 9:00–noon
Pub. *The Genie Bug*, quarterly
(Cerro Gordo County)
$7.00 per year membership for
   individuals, $8.00 per year
   membership for families; research
   charges vary

Sac County Genealogical Society
PO Box 54
Sac City, IA 50583
(712) 662-4094
Janice Larsen, President
Hours: by appointment
Pub. *SACOGE News*, quarterly
$5.00 per year membership

**Winneshiek County Genealogical
Society**
PO Box 344
Decorah, IA 52101
George Pfester, President
Pub. *Winneshiek County Genealogical
   Society Newsletter*, four times per year
$5.00 per year membership for
   individuals, $7.50 per year
   membership for families

Independent Publications and Miscellany

**Audubon County, Iowa Genealogical
Research Services**
1019 Tekamah Lane
Papillion, NE 68128-6245
(402) 339-7291; (402) 339-0051
Donna M. Christensen Thomas
(publishes compilations of local records)

Sherry Foresman Library
Rt. 1, Box 23
Menlo, IA 50164
Sherry Foresman
(30-day book rentals, $.75 for catalog)

IaGenWeb
Part of U.S. GenWeb Project
E-mail: ia@usgenweb.com
http://www.rootsweb.com/~iagenweb/
   iowa.htm
(links to other Iowa resources)

New Sweden, Iowa, Descendants
3623 North 37th Street
Arlington, VA 22207-4821
(703) 276-8228; (703) 276-8236 FAX
E-mail: BAnnMunsey@aol.com
Bernice Wilson Munsey
(assisting those beginning to search their
   own families)

Pages from Our Past
Rt. 2
Clarinda, IA 51632
B. Hartman and B. Ankenny, Editors
Pub. *Pages from Our Past*

Peterson Heritage, Inc.
PO Box 222
Peterson, IA 51047
(712) 295-6401
Judy Bang, President
$5.00 per year membership

Pioneer Village Commission
City Hall
Cedar Rapids, IA 52401
(319) 398-5104

**Spillville Historic Action Group, Inc.
(SHAG)**
PO Box 187
Spillville, IA 52168-0187
(319) 562-3186 (Secretary)
Juanita J. Loven, Secretary
(Spillville history, including Antonin
   Dvorak in Spillville, and Spillville's
   Czech heritage)
$5.00 per year membership

**Victorian Society in America, Iowa
Chapter**
2940 Cottage Grove
Des Moines, IA 50311
(515) 274-4996 (evenings and weekends)
Patrice Beam, Executive Director
Pub. *Hope & Glory*, annually;
   Newsletter, quarterly

KANSAS

Archives and Libraries with Holdings in Genealogy

State Archives and Library

Kansas State Library
State Capitol Building, Third Floor
Topeka, KS 66612
(785) 296-3296; (800) 432-3919 (from
   within Kansas); (785) 296-6650 FAX
E-mail: ksst13lb@ink.org (Cindy Roupe)
http://skyways.lib.ks.us/kansas
Duane Johnson, State Librarian

State Historical Society

Kansas State Historical Society
6425 S.W. Sixth Avenue
Topeka, KS 66615-1099
(785) 272-8681; (785) 272-8682 FAX;
   (913) 272-8683 TTY
E-mail: webmaster@hspo.wpo.state.ks.us
http://history.cc.ukans.edu/heritage/kshs/
   kshs1.html
Patricia Michaelis, Head of Library and
   Archives Division
Hours: Mon–Sat 9:00–4:30
Pub. *Kansas History: A Journal of the
   Central Plains*, quarterly; *Kansas
   Heritage*, quarterly
(Kansas newspapers, census, family
   histories, photographs, maps, state
   archives, manuscripts)
$25.00 per year membership for
   individuals

City, County and Regional Archives and Libraries

Arkansas City Public Library
120 East Fifth Avenue
Arkansas City, KS 67705
(316) 442-1280
Lesly M. Smith, Head Librarian
Hours: Mon–Thur 9:00–8:00, Fri–Sat
   9:00–6:00

Ashland Public Library
Dorothy Berryman Collection
604 Main
PO Box 86
Ashland, KS 67831
(316) 635-2589
Eldora McMinimy, Director
Hours: daily 1:30–5:30

Atwood Public Library
102 South Sixth Street
Atwood, KS 67730
(785) 626-3805
Hours: Mon–Fri 9:00–5:00, Wed 7:00–
   8:30, Sat 9:00–1:00

Boot Hill Museum
Front Street
Dodge City, KS 67801
(316) 227-8188; (316) 227-7673 FAX
David Kloppenborg, Curator; Shirley
McLoughlin, President and CEO
Hours: Mon–Fri 9:00–5:00
(Ford County District Court records
(except probate records which have
been returned to the county); historic
photographs; archives)
copies: 25¢ each

Frank Carlson Library
702 Broadway
Concordia, KS 66901
(785) 243-2250 (Library); (785) 243-
4618 (Archivist's Home)
Denise DeRochefort-Reynolds, Head
Librarian; Jeanne M. Chubbuck, Cloud
County Genealogical Society Archivist
and Researcher
Hours: Mon–Thur 9:00–9:00, Fri–Sat
9:00–5:00; Jun–Aug: Mon & Thur
9:00–8:00, Tue–Wed 9:00–5:30, Fri–
Sat 9:00–5:00
(genealogy archives of Cloud County
Genealogical Society; newspaper
microfilm of all towns of Cloud
County, 1870–1950)

Center for Great Plains Studies
Emporia State University
1200 Commercial
Emporia, KS 66801-5087
(316) 341-5574
E-mail: johnsonj@esumail.emporia.edu
http://www.emporia.edu/S/www/cgps/
grplsst.htm
Julie Johnson, Managing Editor
Hours: Mon, Wed & Fri 8:00–4:00
Pub. *Heritage of the Great Plains*,
semiannually, $7.00 per year
subscription
(refereed journal dealing with Great
plains topics; Kansas, Montana,
Nebraska, North Dakota, Oklahoma,
South Dakota, Texas)

Center for Great Plains Study
(see Nebraska)

Cherokee Strip Land Rush Museum
(South Summit Street Road—location)
PO Box 1002 (mailing address)
Arkansas City, KS 67005
(316) 442-6750
Hours: Tue–Sun
(Cowley County genealogy library)
admission: $2.50 for adults, $2.25 for
senior citizens (55 or over), $1.00 for
children 6–12, free for children 5 and
under

Chisholm Trail Museum Corporation
502 North Washington
Wellington, KS 67152
(316) 326-2174

Douglass Historical Museum
(312–314 South Forest Street—location)
PO Box 35
Douglass, KS 67039
(316) 747-2319
Jean Valentine, Curator
Hours: Mon–Wed & Fri 10:30–2:00,
most Thur
(Town of Douglass, people of Douglass
and area; family history files, cemetery
records, some birth and death records
of the City, local newspaper, *The
Douglass Tribune*, 1884–1977 on
microfilm)

Emporia Public Library
110 East Sixth
Emporia, KS 66801
(316) 342-6524; (316) 342-2633 FAX
E-mail: commerfk@computer-
services.com
Katharine Commerford, Genealogist
Hours: Mon–Thur 9:00–9:00, Fri 9:00–
6:00, Sat 9:00–5:00, Sun 2:00–5:00;
Memorial Day–Labor Day: closes at
6:00 on Mon–Tue & Thur
(genealogy of Lyon County, general
genealogy)

Fort Hays State University
Western Kansas Archives
Forsyth Library
600 Park Street
Hays, KS 67601-4099
(785) 628-5901
Hours: Library: Mon–Fri 8:00–4:30;
closed during university vacations

Friends University
Fellow-Reeve Museum of History and
Science
2100 University Avenue
Wichita, KS 67213
(316) 261-5800, ext. 794
Philip Nagley, Director
Pub. *Museum Chatter*

Galena Mining and Historical Museum Association, Inc.
(319 West Seventh Street—location)
PO Box 367 (mailing address)
Galena, KS 66739
(316) 783-2192 (Museum)
Gene Russell, President
Hours: May 1–Nov 1: 9:00–11:30 &
1:00–3:00
(museum contains mining tools, artifacts,
paintings and pictures of mines,
smelter and mineral specimens, horse
drawn hearse, etc.)

Galena Public Library
Fifth and Main Streets
Galena, KS 66739

Garden City Public Library
605 East Walnut
Garden City, KS 67846

Geneseo City Museum
Silver Avenue
Geneseo, KS 67444
Earl Alexander, President of Board

Girard Public Library
128 West Prairie Avenue
Girard, KS 66743
Joan House, Staff Genealogist
Hours: six days per week
(a separate, staffed genealogy room with
an extensive obituary card index and
many local genealogical and historical
materials, mostly for Girard and
Crawford counties)

Goodnow House Museum and Historical Site
c/o The Riley County Historical Society
and Museum
(2301 Claflin—location)
2309 Claflin Road (mailing address)
Manhattan, KS 66502-3421
(785) 565-6490
D. Cheryl Collins, Director-Curator,
RCHM
Hours: Sat–Sun 2:00–5:00, and by
arrangement
(Goodnow family related artifacts)
no charge for tour

Grant County Library
215 East Grant Street
Ulysses, KS 67880
(316) 356-1433
Norma Jean Bricker, Adult Librarian
Hours: Mon–Sat 9:30–5:30

Harper Public Library
1002 Oak
Harper, KS 67058-1233
(316) 896-2959
Imogene Van Dolah, Librarian

Haun Museum
Jetmore, KS 67854
(316) 357-6181

Hays Public Library
Kansas Room
1205 Main
Hays, KS 67601
(785) 625-9014
Mary Ann Thompson, Kansas Room
Librarian
Hours: winter: Mon–Thur 9:00–9:00, Fri
9:00–6:00, Sat 9:00–5:00, Sun 1:00–
5:00; summer: Mon–Thur 9:00–7:00,
Fri 9:00–6:00, Sat 9:00–5:00
(Kansas, Western U.S., genealogy)

Hesperian Library
802 Locust Street (second floor of City
Building)
Cawker City, KS 67430
(785) 781-4925 (for appointment only,
no research over the phone)
Celia Norton Kincheloe, Librarian
Hours: Mon, Thur & Sat 1:00–5:00, Tue
10:00–noon, Wed 1:00–7:00

High Plains Museum
1717 Cherry
Goodland, KS 67735
(785) 899-4595
Linda Holton, Director
(primarily Sherman County)

Hutchinson Public Library
901 North Main Street
Hutchinson, KS 67501
(316) 663-5441; (316) 663-1583 FAX
http://www.hplsck.org
Cheryl L. Canfield, Head of Reference
Hours: Mon–Fri 9:00–9:00, Sat 9:00–
6:00, Sun 1:00–5:00
limited research

Public Library, Independence
220 East Maple Street
Independence, KS 67301
(316) 331-3030; (316) 331-3912 FAX
E-mail: indlib@horizon.hit.net
Hours: Mon & Wed 9:00–8:00, Tue &
Thur 9:00–6:00, Fri noon–5:00, Sat
9:00–1:00
(DAR, Kansas independent newspapers
and census, city directories, marriage
licenses)
search: $5.00 minimum per search

**Johnson County Archives and
Records Management**
Johnson County Administration Building
111 South Cherry Street, Suite 500
Olathe, KS 66061-3441
(913) 764-8484, ext. 6174; (913) 791-
5000 FAX
Gina Alvarez, Archivist Technician
Hours: 9:00–4:30

Johnson County Library
9875 West 87th Street
PO Box 2933
Shawnee Mission, KS 66201-1333
(913) 495-2400; (913) 495-2480 FAX
http://www.jcl.org
Barbara Baker, Local History and
Genealogy Supervisor
Hours: Mon–Thur 9:00–9:00, Fri 9:00–
6:00, Sat 9:00–5:00, Sun 1:00–5:00
(a collection of items pertaining to the
history of Johnson County, Kansas; the
Otham Meeker Papers, the Isaac
McCoy Papers, Johnson County state
and federal census films, individual
histories of Johnson County cities, and
the Johnson County Obituary file from
1977)

Johnson County Museum of History
6305 Lackman Road
Shawnee Mission, KS 66217
(913) 631-6709; (913) 631-6359 FAX
Janet Bruce Campbell, Director
Hours: Tue–Sat 10:00–4:00,
appointments recommended
(Johnson County manuscripts and
printed materials)
from $25.00 per year membership

Public Library, Kansas City
625 Minnesota
Kansas City, KS 66101-2872
(913) 551-3280
Eleanor Fox, Reference Librarian
Hours: Mon–Fri 3:00–5:00, and by
appointment
("A part of the William E. Connelley
manuscript collection that pertains to
the Wyandotte Indians and early local
history.")

**Kingman County Historical
Museum**
400 North Main
Po Box 281
Kingman, KS 67068
(316) 532-5274
June Walker, Curator
Hours: Fri 9:00–4:00, and by
appointment
$10.00 per year membership for
individuals, $20.00 per year Sustaining
membership, $75.00 life membership

Kinsley Public Library
208 East Eighth Street
Kinsley, KS 67547
(316) 659-3341
Beverly J. Craft, Director; Rosetta Graff,
Assistant Librarian
Hours: Mon & Wed 9:30–11:00 & 1:00–
8:00, Tue & Thur–Fri 9:30–11:00
& 1:00–5:00, Sat 1:00–5:00
(Kinsley newspapers)
limited research if specific information is
given (date within a month, name,
etc.), send SASE & cost of copies at
25¢ each

Lawrence Public Library
707 Vermont
Lawrence, KS 66044
(785) 843-3833
Cecilia Jecha May, Head, Reference
Department
Hours: Mon–Fri 9:30–9:00, Sat 9:30–
6:00, Sun 2:00–5:00

Leavenworth Public Library
417 Spruce
Leavenworth, KS 66048
(913) 682-5666; (913) 682-1248 FAX
Hours: Mon–Thur 9:00–9:00, Fri–Sat
9:00–5:00, Sun (Sept–May) 1:00–4:00

Liberal Memorial Library
519 North Kansas
Liberal, KS 67901
(316) 626-0180; (316) 626-0182 FAX
Natalie Randall, Genealogy Research
Manager
Hours: Mon–Thur 10:00–8:00, Fri–Sat
10:00–5:00, Sun 1:00–5:00
("Seward County newspapers from 1886
to present on microfilm, Seward
County rural school records on
microfilm")
search fee: $10.00 per hour (one hour
minimum), plus 25¢ per photocopy

Lyndon Carnegie Library
127 East Sixth
Lyndon, KS 66451

McPherson Museum
1130 East Euclid
McPherson, KS 67460
(316) 241-5977
Rachel Goering, Director
(member of the Kansas Council of
Genealogical Societies)

Museum of the Great Plains
(see Oklahoma)

Northwest Kansas Library System
PO Box 446
Norton, KS 67654-0046
(785) 877-5148
Linda Keith, Reference
Hours: Mon–Fri 8:00–5:00

Oakley Public Library
700 West Third
Oakley, KS 67748
Hours: 10:00–5:00

Oketo Community Museum
Oketo, KS 66518
(785) 744-3516
Mrs. Marvin Argo
Hours: Apr–Nov: by appointment
(early photographs)

Olathe Public Library
201 East Park Street
Olathe, KS 66061
(913) 764-2259
Valerie Vogt, Library Assistant
Hours: Mon–Thur 9:00–9:00, Fri 9:00–
6:00, Sat 9:00–5:00, Sun 1:00–5:00
"Prefer written request of specific
information, no fees, donations
accepted"

Osborne Public Library
307 West Main Street
Osborne, KS 67473-2425

Phillipsburg City Library
888 Fourth
Phillipsburg, KS 67661
(785) 543-5325; (785) 543-5374 FAX
E-mail: phill1b@ruraltel.net
http://skyways.lib.ks.us/kansas/towns/
Phillipsburg/library.html
Carolyn Little, Director
Hours: Mon–Fri 10:00–6:00, Sat 10:00–
4:00
("Area newspapers on microfilm from
1800s, obituary clippings,
approximately 400 volumes in the
Marjorie Goode Collection on New
England; also Kansas collection of
historical materials.")
copying charges and postage appreciated

Pittsburg Public Library
308 North Walnut
Pittsburg, KS 66762
(316) 231-8110

Ms. Pat Clement, Librarian
Hours: Mon–Sat opens 9:00 A.M.

Pottowatomie-Wabaunsee Regional Library
306 North Fifth
Saint Marys, KS 66536
(785) 437-2278
Freda J. Dobbins, Director
Hours: Mon–Wed & Fri 8:30–5:00, Thur 8:30–8:00, Sat 9:00–1:00
(historical records relating to the Jesuit St. Mary's College fromcirca 1870–1930)

W. A. Rankin Memorial Library
502 Indiana
Neodesha, KS 66757
(316) 325-3275 (Library)
Barbara Shoop, Librarian Director
Hours: Mon 9:30–8:00, Tue–Fri 9:30–5:30, Sat 9:00–noon
(index to Wilson County census, 1885 and 1895; estate records, 1866–1912, obituaries, *Neodesha Register*, 1883–1911; tax lists 1890)
search fee: $5.00 plus copies at 20¢ each

Saint Mary College
Special Collections
De Paul Library
4100 South 4th Street
Leavenworth, KS 66048-5082
(913) 682-5151, ext. 200; (913) 682-2406 FAX
Sister Therese Deplazes, SCL Special Collections Librarian
Hours: Mon–Fri 9:00–3:00, Sat–Sun by appointment
(Heritage Collection includes Kansas history)

Salina Public Library
Campbell Room of Kansas Research
301 West Elm
Salina, KS 67401
(785) 825-4624; (785) 823-0706 FAX
Judy Lilly, Kansas Librarian
Hours: Mon–Fri 12:00–5:00, Wed 6:00–9:00, Sat 1:00–5:00
(Kansas and Saline County history collection includes vertical files on Saline County people and subjects, Saline County newspapers, Kansas census)

Smoky Hill Museum
(211 West Iron Avenue—location)
PO Box 101 (mailing address)
Salina, KS 67402-0101
(785) 826-7460
E-mail: tompf@midusa.net
Tom Pfannenstiel, Director
Hours: Tue–Fri 12:00–5:00, Sat 10:00–5:00, Sun 1:00–5:00
Pub. *Heritage Express*, bimonthly, free

Southeast Kansas Library System
218 East Madison
Iola, KS 66749

(316) 365-5136; (316) 365-5137 FAX
E-mail: rogerc@midusa.net
http://skyways.lib.ks.us/kansas/sekls/
Roger Carswell, Director
Hours: Sept–May: Mon–Thur 9:30–8:00, Fri–Sat 9:00–5:00; Jun–Aug: Mon–Thur 9:30–5:30, Fri–Sat 9:00–5:00
$1.50 per item for interlibrary loan out-of-state (genealogy bibliography available)

Stevens County Gas and Historical Museum
PO Box 87
Hugoton, KS 67951
(316) 544-8751

Thomas County Museum
75 West Fourth Street
Colby, KS 67701
(785) 462-6301

Tonganoxie Public Library
303 Bury
Tonganoxie, KS 66086
(913) 845-3281
Winifred Turner, Librarian
Hours: Mon & Fri 9:00–noon & 1:00–5:00, Wed 9:00–noon & 2:00–7:00, Sat 9:00–1:00

Topeka Public Library
1515 West Tenth Street
Topeka, KS 66604
(785) 233-2040
Warren E. Taylor
Hours: Mon–Fri 9:00–9:00, Sat 9:00–6:00, Sun (during school year) 2:00–6:00

University of Kansas
Kansas Heritage Center for Family and Local History
Kansas Data and Links
Lawrence, KS 66045-2800
E-mail: lhnelson@ukanaix.cc.ukans.edu; chinn@ctrvax.vanderbilt.edu
http://history.cc.ukans.edu/hertiage/heritage_main.html

University of Kansas
Thomas R. Smith Maps Collection
Level 1, Anschutz Library
Lawrence, KS 66045-2800
(785) 864-4420; (785) 864-5380 FAX
E-mail: maps-ref@ukans.edu
http://kuhttp.cc.ukans.edu/cwis/units/kulib/maps/collect.html

University of Kansas
Kansas Collection
Spencer Research Library, Room 220
Lawrence, KS 66045-2800
(785) 864-4274; (785) 864-3855 FAX
E-mail: lhnelson@rave.cc.ukans.edu; husker@sky.net; susancs@awod.com
http://kuhttp.cc.ukans.edu/carrie/kancoll/index.html

Wichita Public Library
223 South Main Street
Wichita, KS 67202
(316) 262-0611, ext. 262
Marsha Stenholm, Library Assistant
Hours: Mon–Thur 10:00–9:00, Fri–Sat 10:00–5:30, Sun 1:00–5:00
(U.S. genealogy and Kansas history)

Wichita/Sedgwick County Historical Museum Association
204 South Main Street
Wichita, KS 67202
(316) 265-9314
Robert A. Puckett, Director
Pub. *Heritage*
(local history archives)
$10.00 per year membership

Historical Societies— Local and Regional

Albany Historical Society
415 Grant
Sabetha, KS 66534
(785) 284-3323
Marvin Moore, Treasurer
Hours: Memorial Day through Labor Day: Sat–Sun 1:00–4:00, and by appointment
(local history)

Allen County Historical Society
207 North Jefferson
Iola, KS 66749
(316) 365-3051
Betsy C. Pyle, Curator/Director
Pub. *Gaslight*

Anderson County Historical Society
Rt. 3
PO Box 134
Garnett, KS 66032
(785) 448-5962
Ona Mae Hunt, President
Pub. *Anderson County Historical Society*

Argonia and West Sumner County Historical Society and Museum
Argonia, KS 67004
(316) 435-6733

Arkansas River Historical Society Museum
(see Oklahoma)

Atchison County Historical Society
200 South 10th Street
PO Box 201
Atchison, KS 66002
(913) 367-6238
James McCellen, President
Hours: Mon–Fri 9:00–5:00, Sat 10:00–4:00, Sun 1:00–4:00, and by appointment

Augusta Historical and Genealogical Society
303 State Street
Augusta, KS 67010
(316) 775-5655
Doylene Foreman
Hours: Mon–Sat 11:00–3:00, Sun 1:00–4:00
$5.00/$10.00/$25.00 per year membership

Barton County Historical Society
PO Box 1091
Great Bend, KS 67530
(316) 793-9831

Baxter Springs Historical Society
(Eighth and East Avenue—location)
Rt. 2, Box 314 (mailing address)
Baxter Springs, KS 66713
(316) 856-9860

Butler County Historical Society
383 East Central
PO Box 696
El Dorado, KS 67042
(316) 321-9333
Robert Burgess, Director
Hours: Mon–Sat 9:00–noon & 1:00–5:00, Sun 1:00–5:00
Pub. *The Crown Block*
$5.00 per year membership

Butterfield Trail Association and Historical Society of Logan County, Kansas, Inc.
(315 Hilts—location)
PO Box 383 (mailing address)
Russell Springs, KS 67755-0383
(785) 751-4242
Joye Rogge, Curator
Hours: first Tue of May through first Tue of Sept: Tue–Sat 9:00–noon & 1:00–5:00, Sun 1:00–5:00
(a few family histories on file and some old photographs and school memorabilia, besides the usual pioneer artifacts)
$10.00 per year membership, $100.00 life membership

Caney Valley Historical Society
Rt. 1
Caney, KS 67333
(316) 874-2938
Ivan L. Pfalser, President

Cedar Vale Historical Society
600 Cedar Street
Cedar Vale, KS 67024

Chase County Historical Society, Inc.
301 Broadway
PO Box 375
Cottonwood Falls, KS 66845
(316) 273-8500
Whitt E. Laughridge, President

Hours: Tue–Wed & Fri–Sun 1:00–5:00
quotes will be made on inquiry of information needed

Cherokee County Kansas Genealogical-Historical Society, Inc.
100 South Tennessee
PO Box 33
Columbus, KS 66725-0033
(316) 429-2992
Helen Kelley, Librarian
Hours: Mon–Sat 1:00–5:00
Pub. *Relatively Seeking*, two times per year
(Cherokee County history and genealogy)
$10.00 per year membership

Cheyenne County Historical Society
Cheyenne County Museum
PO Box 611
Saint Francis, KS 67756
(785) 332-2504
Marilyn Holzwarth
Hours: Mon–Fri 1:00–4:00
Pub. *Newsletter*
("Cheyenne County family genealogy")
$2.00 per year membership

Clark County Historical Society
d.b.a. Pioneer-Krier Museum
430 West Fourth Street, Highway 160 West
PO Box 862
Ashland, KS 67831-0862
(316) 635-2227 (afternoons only)
Floretta Rogers, Curator
Hours: Apr–Oct: 1:00–5:00; Nov–Mar: 1:00–4:00; Jan–Mar: closed Sun
(member of the Kansas Council of Genealogical Societies)
$10.00 life membership; search fees: $10.00 plus copies

Clay County Historical Society Museum
2021 Seventh Street
Clay Center, KS 67432
(785) 632-3786
(has some naturalization records from 1869, marriages from 1867, court records from 1889)

Clinton Lake Historical Society, Inc.
Rt. 2, Box 99
Overbrook, KS 66524
(785) 748-9836
Martha J. Parker, Director

Cloud County Historical Society and Museum
635 Broadway
Concordia, KS 66901
(785) 243-2866
Brad Chapin, Curator
Hours: Tue–Sat 1:00–5:00
Pub. *Cloud Comments*, quarterly
$5.00 per year membership for individuals, life memberships depending on age of member

Coffey County Historical Society
1101 Neosho
Burlington, KS 66839
(316) 364-2653
Glenda Rodgers, Director
Pub. *Dob's and Data*

Coffeyville Historical Society, Inc.
PO Box 843
Coffeyville, KS 67337
(316) 251-0550
Gary Misch, President

Cowley County Historical Society
1011 Mansfield Street
Winfield, KS 67156
(316) 221-4811; (316) 221-0793 (Director)
Mrs. Frankie Cullison, Museum Director
Hours: Sat–Sun 2:00–5:00
("We are a pioneer museum housing articles, items used, and documents for the period from approximately 1869 to the present showing the history of the development of this county.")
$10.00 per year active membership; donation appreciated for search

Crawford County Historical Society and Museum
651 South 69 Highway
Pittsburg, KS 66762
(316) 231-1440
Hours: Wed–Sun
Pub. *Pioneer Times*

Dickinson County Historical Society
412 South Campbell
Abilene, KS 67410-2905
(785) 263-2681; (785) 263-0380 FAX
Jeff Sheets, Director
Hours: Mon–Fri 9:00–4:00
Pub. *The Gazette*, quarterly
$10.00 per year membership

Douglas County Historical Society
Elizabeth M. Watkins Community Museum
1047 Massachusetts Avenue
Lawrence, KS 66044
(785) 841-4109
Dr. Steven Jansen, Director
Hours: Tue–Sat 10:00–4:00, Sun 1:30–4:00
Pub. *Douglas County Historical Society Newsletter*, bimonthly
(Douglas County genealogical research and Quantrill's Raid research material)
$10.00 per year membership for individuals, $25.00 per year membership for families

Historical Society of the Downs Carnegie Library
504 South Morgan Avenue
Downs, KS 67437-2019
(member of the Kansas Council of Genealogical Societies)

$5.00 per year membership for individuals, $7.50 per year membership for families; search: $7.00 per hour

Elk County Historical Society
PO Box 1033
Howard, KS 67349
(316) 374-2266

Ellis County Historical Society
100 West Seventh Street
Hays, KS 67601-4429
(785) 628-2624
Jerome Waltner, Executive Director
Hours: Tue–Fri 10:00–noon & 1:00–4:00
Pub. *Homesteader*, quarterly
(member of the Kansas Council of Genealogical Societies)
$15.00 per year membership for individuals, $20.00 per year membership for families, $10.00 per year membership for students, $35.00 per year Benefactor membership, $50.00 per year Patron membership, $100.00+ per year Contributor membership, $250.00 life membership

Ellsworth County Historical Society
PO Box 144
Ellsworth, KS 67439-0144
(785) 472-3059
Hours: Tue–Sat 9:00–noon & 1:00–5:00, Sun (1 May–1 Oct) 1:00–5:00
Pub. *Sharing History*, quarterly
$7.50 per year membership for individuals, $15.00 per year membership for families, $25.00 per year membership for businesses; research: $5.00 donation and SASE

Eudora Area Historical Society
Eudora Public Library
PO Box 370
Eudora, KS 66025
(785) 542-2496; (785) 542-2298
Hours: six days a week
Pub. *Eudora Area Newsletter*

Everest Community Historical Society
Seventh and Chestnut Streets
Everest, KS 66424
(785) 548-7792
Dorothy Selland, Treasurer
Hours: by appointment
(a small group of volunteers, running a small community museum in a small town)

Finney County Historical Society
(403 South Fourth Street—location)
PO Box 796 (mailing address)
Garden City, KS 67846-0796
(316) 272-3664
Mary Regan Wildeman, Executive Director
Hours: winter: 1:00–5:00; summer: 10:00–5:00, Sun 1:00–5:00
Pub. *The Sequoyan*, quarterly

$10.00 per year membership for individuals, $15.00 per year membership for families, $50.00 per year membership for businesses

Florence Historical Society
(221 Marion—location)
408 West Seventh Street (mailing address)
Florence, KS 66851
(316) 878-4296
Pub. *Florence*, quarterly

Ford County Historical Society, Inc.
112 East Vine
PO Box 131
Dodge City, KS 67801
(316) 227-6791
Charles Wycoff, President
Hours: Mon–Sat 9:00–5:00, Sun (Jun–Aug) 2:00–5:00
$6.00 per year membership

Fort Larned Historical Society, Inc.
Rt. 3
Larned, KS 67550
(316) 285-2054; (316) 285-7491 FAX
Alan Hitz, Archivist/Education Director
Hours: Mon–Sun 9:00–5:00, closed Mon Labor Day to Memorial Day
(Larned and Pawnee County, Kansas, history; Civil War records; complete set of *War of the Rebellion*, complete *Records of the North & South for the War Between the States*)

Franklin County Historical Society, Inc.
PO Box 145
Ottawa, KS 66067-0145
(785) 242-1232
Hours: by appointment only

Geary County Historical Society and Museum
530 North Adams Street
PO Box 1161
Junction City, KS 66441-1161
(785) 238-1666
Marilyn Heldstab, Director
Hours: Tue–Sun 1:00–4:00
Pub. *Geary Glimmers*, monthly
(Member of the Kansas Council of Genealogical Societies; "Preserving Geary (Davis) County and Junction City history; docent tours on request, research room, museum displays.")
$10.00 per year membership for individuals, $15.00 per year membership for families, $5.00 per year membership for senior citizens; research: $5.00 plus copy fees

Gove County Historical Association
Gove, KS 67736

Graham County Historical Society
414 North West Street
Hill City, KS 67642

Grant County Historical Society, Inc.
Grant County Museum
300 East Oklahoma
Ulysses, KS 67880
(316) 356-3009
Ginger Anthony, Director
Hours: Tue–Fri 10:00–5:00, Sat–Sun 1:00–5:00
(County history, early county records; member of the Kansas Council of Genealogical Societies)

Greeley County Historical Society
(Horace Greeley Museum, 214 East Harper—location)
PO Box 231 (mailing address)
Tribune, KS 67879-0231
(316) 376-4996
Nadine Cheney, Curator
Hours: 10:00–4:00 by appointment
(census, newspaper, homestead, school, county school, cemetery records; member of the Kansas Council of Genealogical Societies)
$6.00 per year membership, $75.00 life membership

Greenwood County Historical Society, Inc.
120 West Fourth
Eureka, KS 67045-1445
(316) 583-6682
Helen Bradford; Jeff Hoakanson
Hours: Mon–Sat 9:00–noon & 1:00–4:00
Pub. *News Letter*, semiannually (June and December)
(family histories; best source for Greenwood County information)
$5.00 per year membership for individuals, $8.00 per year membership for couples, $10.00 per year membership for institutions, $25.00 per year Sustaining membership, $75.00 life membership; donations accepted for research

Harvey County Historical Society
203 Main Street
PO Box 4
Newton, KS 67114
(316) 283-2221 (Society's answering machine); (316) 283-7511 (Interim Director)
Jane Jones, Archivist; Ron Dietzel, Interim Director
Hours: Fri–Sun 1:00–4:00, except holiday weekends
Pub. *Historical Notes*, bimonthly
(Harvey County history: tax records, census, marriage licenses (1872–1913), county newspapers through 1930, Newton City directories; Santa Fe Railroad collection and memorabilia as pertains to Newton, once a rail hub for SFRR)
research: $10.00 for the first hour, $5.00 for each additional hour, plus copy costs

The Haskell County Historical Society and Museum
(North side of Haskell County Fairgrounds—location)
PO Box 101 (mailing address)
Sublette, KS 67877
(316) 675-8344
Janice McClure, Curator
Hours: Wed–Sun 1:00–5:00
(local history of Haskell County)
$5.00 per year membership, $15.00 per year Sustaining membership, $100.00 life membership; no research services but visitors welcome

Hillsboro Historical Society and Museum
501 South Ash Street
Hillsboro, KS 67063
(316) 947-3775
David F. Wiebe, Director
Hours: Mar–Dec: daily
(Dutch/German research center)

Jackson County Historical Society
4th Street and New York Avenue
PO Box 104
Holton, KS 66436
(785) 364-2087
Anna Wilhem, Board Member; Mildred E. Francis, Volunteer Director
Hours: Fri–Sat 10:00–4:00, Sun 2:00–4:00; tours by appointment
Pub. *JCHS Newsletter*, quarterly
("Jackson County history and all nine cities; genealogy work.")
$10.00 per year Active membership, $25.00 per year Sustaining membership, $150.00 life membership; search fee: $25.00 for first two hours, $8.00 for each hour thereafter

Jefferson County Historical Society
(Highway 59—location)
PO Box 146 (mailing address)
Oskaloosa, KS 66066
(785) 863-2070
Hours: May–Sept: Sat 1:00–5:00, Sun 1:30–5:00
Pub. *Yesteryears*, semiannually (April and October)
$10.00 per year membership, $150.00 life membership

Kansas Heritage Center
PO Box 1275
Dodge City, KS 67801
(316) 227-1616
Jeanie Covalt
Hours: Mon–Fri 8:00–5:00

Kearny County Historical Society
101–111 South Buffalo
PO Box 329
Lakin, KS 67860
(316) 355-7448
Patricia Heath, Museum Director
10¢ per page for copies

Lake Region Historical Society
Lake Region RCGD Area Office
121 East Second Street
Ottawa, KS 66067
(785) 242-2073
Hours: 8:00–5:00
Pub. *Lake Region Historical Society Association Newsletter*, quarterly

Lane County Historical Society
Lane County Historical Museum
333 North Main Street
PO Box 821
Dighton, KS 67839
(316) 397-5652
Virginia Johnston, Director
Hours: Tue–Sat 1:00–5:00
Pub. *Friends of the Museum*, quarterly
("newspapers from 1880 to the present, census, cemetery books, some marriage licenses, county history books and family histories; working on book of obituaries for the county")
$10.00 per year membership for individuals; research fee: $10.00 per hour plus 15¢ per page for copies

Lanesfield School Historical Society
(Rt. 1, Edgerton, KS 66021—location)
Rt. 1, Box 156 (mailing address)
Gardner, KS 66030
(913) 882-6645

Lansing Area Historical Society
PO Box 32
Lansing, KS 66043

Leavenworth County Historical Society and Museum
1128 Fifth Avenue
Leavenworth, KS 66048-3213
(913) 682-7759; (913) 682-2089 FAX
http://leavenworth-net.com/lchs
Robert A. Holt, Museum Administrator
Hours: Sept–Apr: Mon–Sun 1:00–4:30; May–Aug: Mon–Sat 10:30–4:30, Sun 1:00–4:30 and by appointment
Pub. *Historical Society Gazette*, quarterly
$10.00 per year membership for individuals; research: $10.00 per hour, limit of two hours

Lecompton Historical Society
Rt. 1
Lecompton, KS 66050
(785) 887-6285
Paul M. Bahnmaier, President
Hours: Sun (Mar–Nov) 1:00–4:00
Pub. *Bald Eagle*, quarterly
("Museum contains artifacts from the Territorial Period through the Lane University era.")
$6.00 per year membership

Lenexa Historical Society
14907 West 87th Street Parkway
Lenexa, KS 66215-4135
(member of the Kansas Council of Genealogical Societies)

Lincoln County Historical Society
(214 West Lincoln Avenue—location)
PO Box 85 (mailing address)
Lincoln, KS 67455
(785) 524-4614
Ruby Ahring, President
Hours: Sun (May 30–Sept 1) P.M., and by appointment
Pub. *Newsletter*, annually
$5.00 per year membership for individuals, $10.00 per year membership for families; search fee: $5.00

Linn County Historical and Genealogical Society
Linn County Museum
History/Genealogy Library
Dunlap Park
PO Box 137
Pleasanton, KS 66075-0137
(913) 352-8739
Ola May Earnest, President
Hours: winter: Tue & Thur 9:00–5:00, Sat–Sun 1:00–5:00; summer: Tue–Thur 9:00–5:00, Fri–Sun 1:00–5:00
Pub. *Kin in Linn*, quarterly; *Linn County Historical Society Newsletter*, quarterly
(holdings include state and federal census records, mortality schedules, all Linn County newspapers from 1864, funeral records from 1910, cemetery records, military records, vital statistics, D.A.R. lineage books, index to probate court records)
$2.00 per year membership in Historical Society, $8.00 per year membership in Genealogical Society

Lyon County Historical Society
Lyon County Historical Museum
118 East Sixth Avenue
Emporia, KS 66801
(316) 342-0933
Carol Miguelino, M.L.S., Librarian/Archivist
Hours: Tue–Sat 9:30–5:00, call for appointment on weekends
Pub. *Lyon County Lines*, quarterly
$10.00 per year membership

Marshall County Historical Society
1207 Broadway
Marysville, KS 66508
(785) 562-5012
Barbara Fenstermacher, Librarian
Hours: Mon–Tue & Thur–Sat 9:00–noon & 1:00–4:00, Wed & Sun 1:00–4:00
Pub. *Magpie*, quarterly
(specializes in Marshall County genealogy)
$5.00 per year membership (calendar year); research: cost of copies

McPherson County Historical Society, Inc.
540 East Hill Street
McPherson, KS 67460-3527

(316) 241-2699
Mr. Linn Peterson, President
$10.00 and $25.00 per year membership,
$1.00 per year minimum

Meade County Historical Society
200 East Carthage
Meade, KS 67864

Miami County Historical Society
PO Box 393
Paola, KS 66071
(913) 294-2663
Virginia Bundy, President
Hours: Apr–Nov: Mon 1:00–4:00, Thur
5:00–8:00, Sat 9:00–noon

Midwest Historical and Genealogical Society
1203 North Main
PO Box 1121
Wichita, KS 67201-1121
(316) 264-3611
Sherry Weir, Librarian
Hours: Tue & Sat 9:00–4:00, second Sat
9:00–12:30
Pub. *Midwest Historical and Genealogical Register*, quarterly
$20.00 per year membership for individuals, $15.00 per year membership for libraries

Milan Historical Association
Monroe and Market Streets
PO Box 144
Milan, KS 67105
(316) 435-6423

Montgomery County Historical Society
PO Box 100
Independence, KS 67301
(316) 331-3770
Mary Stuckey, Curator

Mulvane Historical Society
(Mulvane Historical Museum, 300 West Main—location)
PO Box 117 (mailing address)
Mulvane, KS 67110
(316) 777-0506 (Museum)
Martha Wright, President
Hours: Tue–Sat 10:00–4:00
Pub. *Mulvane Historical Society News*, semiannually or quarterly
(Sumner County, Kansas)
$5.00 per year membership, $50.00 life membership

Nemaha County Historical Society, Inc.
Sixth and Nemaha
Seneca, KS 66538
(785) 336-3645 (Editor); (785) 336-3160 (President)
E-mail: explorer@parod.com
http://www.ukans.edu/kansas/seneca/histsoc/nemcohis.html
Marcia Philbrick, Editor; Lillian Engelken, President

Hours: Museum: Memorial Day weekend–Labor Day weekend: Mon–Fri afternoons, Sat by appointment
Pub. *Pioneer Press*, quarterly
(museum located in sheriff's home/county jail)
$5.00 per year membership

Ness County Historical Society
Ness County Historical Museum
123 South Pennsylvania Avenue
Ness City, KS 67560
(785) 798-3298
Margery Frusher, President
Hours: Tue–Sun 1:00–5:00, Thur–Fri
1:00–7:00
(Ness county history and genealogical information; member of the Kansas Council of Genealogical Societies)
$25.00 life membership

Norman #1 Oil Well and Museum Historical Society
109 Mill
Neodesha, KS 66757
(316) 325-5316
Nancy J. Wilson, President

Northwest Kansas Genealogical and Historical Society
Oakley Public Library
700 West Third Street
Oakley, KS 67748-1256
(785) 672-4389
Lillian Martin, President
Hours: Library: 10:00–5:00
(Logan County newspapers on film)

Norton County Historical Society
PO Box 303
Norton, KS 67654
(785) 877-2475

Onaga Historical Society
310 East Second Street
Onaga, KS 66521
Marjorie Labbe, President
Hours: by appointment

Osage County Historical Society
631 Topeka Avenue
Lyndon, KS 66451
(785) 828-4844 (Secretary); (785) 528-4960 (Ms. Hawley)
Florence Stout, Secretary; Margaret Hawley
Hours: Tue–Thur 1:00–4:00
Pub. *The Hedge Post*, quarterly
$5.00 per year membership for individuals, $7.00 per year membership for families

Osawatomie Historical Society
420 16th Street
Osawatomie, KS 66064
(913) 755-4330 (Fisher Law Office)
Richard Fisher, President
Hours: Mon–Fri 9:00–5:00
Pub. *Osawatomie and Its People*, biannually, $6.00 postpaid per issue

("Most of our records are at the Osawatomie Public Library, 527 Brown Street, as well as county cemetery listings, mortuary listings, and other county and state records, including local newspaper microfilm, census records—state and federal for Miami County.")
$5.00 per year membership

Osborne County Genealogical and Historical Society
213 North First
Osborne, KS 67473
Pub. *Leaves of Lineage*, quarterly; *Osborne County Genealogical Society Quarterly*
$10.00 per year membership

The Peabody Historical Society
RR 2
Peabody, KS 66866
(316) 983-2815 (President); (316) 983-2174 (City Hall)
Marilyn Jones, President
Hours: Thur–Sun (Jun–Aug) 1:00–4:00, and by appointment
Pub. *The Peabody Historical Society Newsletter*, semiannually
$10.00 per year membership for individuals, $15.00 per year membership for families

Pratt County Historical Society
208 South Ninnescah
Pratt, KS 67124
Dorothy Giannangelo, Office Manager
Hours: Mon–Sun 2:00–4:00, and by appointment
Pub. *P.C.H.S. Newsletter*, bimonthly
(genealogical information on settlers in Pratt County)

Rawlins County Historical Society
308 State Street
Atwood, KS 67730

Frederic Remington Area Historical Society
Frederic Remington High School
PO Box 133
Whitewater, KS 67154
Theodore J. Regier, President

Reno County Historical Society
100 South Walnut Street
PO Box 664
Hutchinson, KS 67504
(316) 662-1184
Jay S. Smith, Director
Hours: Tue–Sat 10:00–4:30, Sun 1:00–4:00
Pub. *Legacy: The Journal of the Reno County Historical Society*, quarterly, $5.00 per year subscription

Republic County Historical Society
(2726 Highway 36—location)
PO Box 218 (mailing address)
Belleville, KS 66935-0218

(785) 527-5971
Patricia Walter, Curator
Hours: Mon–Fri 1:00–5:00, Sat (spring–fall) 1:00–5:00, Sun 1:30–5:00
Pub. *Illumination*, bimonthly
(Republic County cemetery grave marker list; member of the Kansas Council of Genealogical Societies)
$5.00 per year membership for individuals, $10.00 per year membership for families, $25.00 per year membership for businesses; donation for search, free queries for members

Rice County Historical Society, Inc.
Coronado-Quivira Museum
105 West Lyon
Lyons, KS 67554-2703
(316) 257-3941
Janel Cook, Museum Director
Hours: Mon–Fri 9:00–5:00, Sun 1:00–5:00
(archive resources; member of the Kansas Council of Genealogical Societies)
$10.00 per year membership for individuals; search fee: $6.00 per hour plus copies at 25¢ each

The Riley County Historical Society and Museum
2309 Claflin Road
Manhattan, KS 66502-3421
(785) 537-2210
D. Cheryl Collins, Director-Curator
Hours: Tue–Fri 8:30–5:00, Sat–Sun 2:00–5:00; Library: by appointment
Pub. *RCHS Newsletter*, ten times per year
(member of the Kansas Council of Genealogical Societies)
$5.00 to $125.00 per year membership, no charge for library use

Rock Creek Valley Historical Society and Museum
(Sixth and State Streets—location)
PO Box 13 (mailing address)
Westmoreland, KS 66549
(785) 457-3578
Rose Wahl
Hours: by appointment

Rooks County Historical Society
(921 South Cedar—location)
PO Box 43 (mailing address)
Stockton, KS 67669
(785) 425-7217
Vinta Butler, Curator
Hours: Mon–Wed 9:00–4:00; meetings: third Sun (Jan–Nov) 2:00–4:00
(genealogical services)
$5.00 per year membership

Russell County Historical Society
PO Box 245
Russell, KS 67665
(785) 483-3637

E-mail: jmccoy@media-net.net
Jeff McCoy, President
Hours: Memorial Day weekend–Labor Day weekend: 1:00–4:00, and by appointment

Saint Marys Historical Society
710 Alma Street
Saint Marys, KS 66536
(785) 437-6387 (President)
Rita Muckenthaler, President

Saline County Historical Society
PO Box 32
Salina, KS 67402
Dale Weis

Santa Fe Trail Historical Society
1314 Eighth Street
PO Box 443
Baldwin City, KS 66006
(785) 594-6595
John C. Doudna
Pub. *Santa Fe Trail Rider*, semiannually
$10.00 per year membership

Scott County Historical Society
211 College Street
Scott City, KS 67871
(316) 872-3708

Seward County Historical Society, Inc.
567 East Cedar
Liberal, KS 67901
(316) 624-7624

Shawnee County Historical Society
PO Box 2201
Topeka, KS 66601-2201
Dr. Bill Wagnon, Treasurer
Pub. *The Shawnee County Historical Society Newsletter*; *Shawnee County Historical Society Bulletin*, annually
$15.00 per year regular membership, $25.00 per year Sustaining membership, $50.00 per year Friend membership, $100.00 per year Patron membership

Shawnee Historical Society, Inc.
Old Shawnee Town
11501 West 57th Street
PO Box 3042
Shawnee Mission, KS 66203
(913) 268-8772

Sheridan County Historical Society, Inc.
(1224 Oak Avenue—location)
PO Box 274 (mailing address)
Hoxie, KS 67740
(785) 675-3501
Marilyn Carder, Office Director
Hours: Tue–Fri 8:30–noon & 1:30–4:00
Pub. *Newsletter*, annually
(births, marriages, deaths, homestead, school, mortuary, etc.)
$7.50 per year membership for individuals, $15.00 per year

membership for families, $25.00 per year membership for businesses, $150.00 life membership; research: $7.50 per hour

Sherman County Historical and Genealogical Society
PO Box 684
Goodland, KS 67735
Clarence Scheopner, President Historical Society
Hours: 10:00–7:00
Pub. *Quarterly*
$5.00 per year membership

Stafford County Historical and Genealogical Society
(100 South Main, corner of Main and Broadway—location)
PO Box 249 (mailing address)
Stafford, KS 67578-0249
Adelaid H. Thole
Pub. *Reflections*

Stanton County Historical Society
Stanton County Museum
104 East Highland
PO Box 806
Johnson, KS 67855
(316) 492-1526
Katie Herrick, Curator
Hours: Mon–Fri 9:00–5:00
("County records are at Museum and Registrar of Deeds at Stanton County Courthouse.")

Stevens County History Association
PO Box 417
Hugoton, KS 67951

Sumner County Historical Society
PO Box 213
Mulvane, KS 67110
(316) 777-1434
Ruth Swan, President
Hours: meetings at Wellington Steakhouse, Wellington: fourth Mon (Jan–Apr & Aug–Nov) 6:30
(land patents, Sumner County story)
$2.00 per year membership, $15.00 life membership; some family research for donation

Thomas County Historical Society
1905 South Franklin Street
PO Box 465
Colby, KS 67701-0465
(785) 462-4590
Sue Ellen Taylor, Director
Hours: Tue–Fri 9:00–5:00, Sat–Sun 1:00–5:00, extended summer hours
Pub. *Prairie Winds*, quarterly
(Member of the Kansas Council of Genealogical Societies; "We are a historical society but we do handle written or first person requests about our county; history of Thomas County, some assistance with surrounding counties.")

$10.00 per year membership for individuals, $15.00 per year membership for families; donations accepted for research

Tonganoxie Community Historical Society

PO Box 325
Tonganoxie, KS 66086
(913) 845-2102
John C. Lenahan, Sr., President
Hours: Mon–Sat 8:00–5:00
$3.00 per year membership

Trading Post Historical Society

Trading Post Historical Museum
(U.S. 69 Highway, 96 milemarker 6 miles north of Pleasanton, KS—location)
Rt. 2, Box 145A (mailing address)
Trading Post, KS 66075-9479
(913) 352-6441
Alice Widner, Curator and Researcher
Hours: Tue–Sat 9:00–5:00, Sun 1:00–5:00
(Member of the Kansas Council of Genealogical Societies; specializes in Valley Township, Linn County, Kansas, history and other areas as well; many old records and access to county records.")
research fee: $6.00 per hour, 25¢ per mile, plus copying costs

Trego County Historical Society

(Trego County Fairgrounds, Wakeeney, KS 67672—location)
614 Chase (mailing address)
Wakeeney, KS 67672-1713
(785) 743-2964
Nadine Kroeger, Curator
Hours: Tue & Fri 1:00–4:00, Sun 1:30–4:30; meetings fourth Sun 2:30
(member of the Kansas Council of Genealogical Societies)

Tri-County Historical Society

800 South Broadway
PO Box 9
Herington, KS 67449
(785) 258-2842
Virginia Brunner, Director
Hours: 10:00–noon & 1:15–4:00
Pub. *Tri-County Newsletter*, quarterly
$5.00 per year membership for individuals, $10.00 per year membership for families; search fee: $2.00-$5.00

Valley Center Historical and Cultural Society

112 North Meridian
PO Box 173
Valley Center, KS 67147
(316) 755-0275
Blondie Roark, President
$5.00 per year membership for individuals, $10.00 per year membership for families

Wabaunsee County Historical Society Museum

227 Missouri
PO Box 387
Alma, KS 66401
(785) 765-2200
Lila Beasterfeld, Curator
Hours: Tue–Sat 10:00–4:00, Sun 1:00–4:00, closed holidays
Pub. *Wabaunsee County Historical Society Newsletter*, annually (spring)
("1928 Reo Firetruck, Indian Artifacts, Main St. U.S.A., Marine General Walt Display, Old Farm Implements.")
$10.00 per year membership, $100.00 life membership; genealogy search fee: $5.00 donation

Wamego Historical Society

Old Dutch Mill Museum Complex
PO Box 84
Wamego, KS 66547
(785) 456-2040
Jan Nicklus
Hours: third weekend in Apr–Labor Day: Mon–Sat 9:30–3:30, Sun 12:30–3:30; Labor Day–31 Oct: Mon–Fri 1:00–4:00, Sat 10:00–4:00, Sun 1:00–4:00, and by appointment
Pub. *WHS Newsletter*

Washington County Historical Society

208 Ballard
PO Box 31
Washington, KS 66968-0031
(785) 325-2198
Blaine Wells, President
Pub. *Past & Present*
(member of the Kansas Council of Genealogical Societies)

Wilson County Historical Society and Genealogical Chapter

420 North Seventh Street
Fredonia, KS 66736-1315
(316) 378-3965
Hours: Mon–Fri 1:00–4:30
Pub. *Wilson County Historical Society Newsletter*, quarterly
("We have a Wilson County obituary index from 1873 to the present time.")
$7.00 per year membership in Historical Society, $10.00 per year membership in Historical Society and Genealogical Chapter; research: $10.00 per hour plus cost of copies

Wyandotte County Historical Society and Museum

631 North 126th Street
Bonner Springs, KS 66012
(913) 721-1078; (913) 721-1394 FAX
R. Barber, Executive Director
Hours: Tue–Sat 10:00–5:00

| LDS Family History Centers |

LDS Family History Centers

Kansas City
(see Olathe)

Olathe
(913) 829-1775

Topeka
(913) 271-6818

Wichita
(316) 683-2951

Genealogical Societies

State Genealogical Societies

Kansas Council of Genealogical Societies, Inc.

PO Box 3858
Topeka, KS 66604-6858
C. Jean Vorhees, President
Pub. *The Kansas Review*, quarterly
(sponsors a state certificate program to honor the settlers of Kansas and the *Forgotten Settlers of Kansas* series: Territorial Certificate for direct descendants of ancestors who lived in Kansas prior to 29 January 1861, Pioneer Certificate for direct descendants of ancestors who lived in Kansas between 29 January 1861 and 31 December 1880, and Early Settler Certificate for direct descendants of ancestors who lived in Kansas between 1 January 1881 and 31 December 1900)
$10.00 per year voting membership for genealogical or historical organizations in Kansas, $10.00 per year affiliate membership for any person or organization interested in genealogy

Kansas Genealogical Society, Inc.

(Village Square Mall-Lower Level, 2601 Central—location)
700 Avenue G at Vine Street, PO Box 103 (mailing address)
Dodge City, KS 67801-0103
(316) 225-1951
Doris D. Rooney, Executive Manager
Hours: Mon–Fri 1:30–5:00, first Sat (Sept–May) 10:45-4:00
Pub. *The Treesearcher*, quarterly
$15.00 per year membership for individuals, $20.00 per year membership for families, $12.00 per year membership for public libraries

Regional Genealogical Societies

Atchison County Kansas Genealogical Society
Atchison Public Library
401 Kansas Avenue
Atchison, KS 66002-2495
(913) 367-1902
Cora Chambers, President
Hours: Mon–Fri 10:30–8:30, Sat 10:00–5:00, Sun 1:30–5:00
Pub. *The Atchison Connection*, quarterly
$10.00 per year membership

Augusta Historical and Genealogical Society
303 State Street
Augusta, KS 67010
(316) 775-5655
Doylene Foreman
Hours: Mon–Sat 11:00–3:00, Sun 1:00–4:00
$5.00/$10.00/$25.00 per year membership

Barton County Genealogical Society, Inc.
PO Box 425
Great Bend, KS 67530-0425
(316) 793-7304
Cathy Grover, President
Pub. *The Quarterly* (winter, spring, summer, fall)
$10.00 per year membership, $12.50 per year membership with mailed *Quarterly*; research services available

Bluestem Genealogical Society
PO Box 582
Eureka, KS 67045-0582
Peggy Rickey, Corresponding Secretary
Hours: meetings second Fri
Pub. *Bluestem Root Diggers*, quarterly
$12.00 per year membership

Branches and Twigs Genealogical Society
c/o Kingman Carnegie Library
455 North Main Street
Kingman, KS 67068-1395
(316) 532-3061 (Library)
E-mail: ospec@websurf.net
http://www.kingman.ks.net
Opal Specht, President; Letha Mitchell, Corresponding Secretary
Hours: Mon–Thur 10:00–7:00, Fri 10:00–6:00; meetings: first Wed (Sept–May)
(Kingman County marriage books, obituary index, many county publications, all Kingman newspapers on microfilm, most county papers)
$5.00 per year membership; research: donation

Chanute Genealogical Society
1000 South Allen Street
Chanute, KS 66720-2639

(316) 431-1563
Dee Fouch, Corresponding Secretary
Hours: Chapman Library, College Campus: Sept–May: 8:00–9:00; summer: 8:00–5:00
("We have probate records 1860s to 1960s, newspaper obituary index from 1910, birth and death records 1892–1905, marriage index 1864–1915, cemetery index, Neosho County, 1864–1976.")
$3.00 per year membership for individuals, $4.00 per year membership for families

Cherokee County Kansas Genealogical-Historical Society, Inc.
100 South Tennessee
PO Box 33
Columbus, KS 66725-0033
(316) 429-2992
Helen Kelley, Librarian
Hours: Mon–Sat 1:00–5:00
Pub. *Relatively Seeking*, two times per year
(Cherokee County history and genealogy)
$10.00 per year membership

Cloud County Genealogical Society
(Frank Carlson Library, 702 Broadway—location)
PO Box 202 (mailing address)
Concordia, KS 66901
(785) 243-4618 (Archivist's Home)
Jeanne M. Chubbuck, Archivist and Researcher
Hours: Library: Mon–Thur 9:00–9:00, Fri–Sat 9:00–5:00
Pub. *Cloud County (KS) Genealogical Society Newsletter*, quarterly
(Cloud County and French-Canadian settlements in eastern Cloud County)
$5.00 per year membership for individuals, $6.00 per year membership for families; research: $5.00 per hour plus costs

Coffey County Genealogical Society
1110 Merrimac Street, #3
Burlington, KS 66839-2157
Kevin Bailey
Pub. *Coffey County Footprints*, quarterly

Coffeyville Genealogical Group
1607 West Fifth
Coffeyville, KS 67337

Cowley County Genealogical Society
1518 East 12th Street
Winfield, KS 67156-3923
(316) 221-4591
Clarie Utt, Secretary-Treasurer
Hours: Cherokee Strip Living Museum, Arkansas City: May–Sept: Tue-Sat 10:00–5:00, Sun 1:00–5:00; Oct–Apr: Tue–Sun 1:00–4:00
$11.00 per year membership; research: $6.00 per hour plus copying costs and postage

Crawford County Genealogical Society
c/o Pittsburg Public Library
308 North Walnut
Pittsburg, KS 66762-4797
Dorothy Benskin, Society Librarian
Hours: Library: Mon 9:00–8:00, and other hours to be announced
Pub. *Seeker*, quarterly
$10.00 per year membership

Decatur County Genealogy Society
Decatur County Museum
258 South Penn Avenue
Oberlin, KS 67749-2245
(785) 475-2712 (Museum)
Fonda Farr, President
Hours: 10:00–5:00
Pub. *Ancestree Kinnection*, quarterly
$10.00 per year membership

Douglas County Kansas, Genealogical Society
PO Box 3664
Lawrence, KS 66044-0664
Lawrence Cybervillage
Mary Burchill, President
Hours: Lawrence Public Library: Mon–Fri 9:30–9:00, Sat 9:30–6:00, Sun 2:00–5:00
Pub. *The Pioneer*, quarterly
$15.00 per year membership; search fee: $5.00

Finney County Genealogical Society
(Finney County Public Library, Genealogy Room—location)
PO Box 592 (mailing address)
Garden City, KS 67846-0592
Patricia D. Smith, Research Query Chairman
Hours: Mon–Thur 9:00–8:30, Fri–Sat 9:00–6:00, Sun 1:00–6:00
Pub. *FCGS Newsletter*, quarterly, $10.00 per year subscription
search fee: $10.00 per hour

Flint Hills Genealogical Society
PO Box 555
Emporia, KS 66801-0555
Pub. *FHGS Newsletter*, quarterly
(Lyon County and adjoining areas; indexed newspapers, marriage licenses and cemeteries for Lyon County)
$7.00 per year membership; research: $10.00 per hour

Fort Hays Kansas Genealogical Society
Fort Hays State University
Forsyth Library, Room 122
600 Park Street
Hays, KS 67601-4099
(785) 628-5901
Marc Campbell, Librarian; Esta Lou Riley
Hours: Library: Mon–Fri 8:00–4:30; closed during university vacations
$5.00 per year membership

Four State Genealogical Society
805 Galena Avenue
Galena, KS 66739
Helen L. E. Hays, President
Pub. *Prospectors, Diggers and Doers*

Franklin County Genealogical Society, Inc.
PO Box 145
Ottawa, KS 66067-0145
(785) 242-5383

Harper County Genealogical Society
Harper Public Library
1002 Oak
Harper, KS 67058-1233
(316) 896-2959 (Library)

Haskell County Tracers
PO Box 547
Sublette, KS 67877-0547

Heritage Genealogical Society
W. A. Rankin Memorial Library
502 Indiana
Neodesha, KS 66757
(316) 325-3275 (Library)
Kathryn Howell, Librarian Director
Hours: Library: Mon–Fri 10:30–5:30, Sat 10:30–3:00
Pub. *Heritage Genealogical Society Quarterly*
$8.00 per year membership

Hodgeman County Genealogical Society
PO Box 441
Jetmore, KS 67854-0441
(316) 357-8568
Twila Smidt, President
$5.00 per year membership for individuals, $7.50 per year membership for families

Jefferson County Genealogical Society, Inc.
Research Center
Highway 59, Old Jefferson Town
PO Box 174
Oskaloosa, KS 66066-0174
(785) 863-2070
Mary Ann Caskey, President
Hours: Jan–Dec: Sat 1:00–5:00; Apr–Dec: Mon 7:00 P.M.-8:30, Sun 1:30–5:00
Pub. *Yesteryears*, semiannually; *Jefferson County Genealogical Society Newsletter*
$10.00 per year membership, $150.00 life membership

Johnson County Genealogical Society and Library, Inc.
(Johnson County Library—location)
PO Box 12666 (mailing address)
Shawnee Mission, KS 66282-2666
(913) 383-2368

http://raven.cc.ukans.edu/heritage/society/jcgs/jcgs_main.html.
Bill Hawkins, President
Hours: Library: Mon–Thur 9:00–9:00, Fri 9:00–6:00, Sat 9:00–5:00, Sun 1:00–5:00
Pub. *The Johnson County Genealogist*, quarterly (March, June, September, December)
$12.50 per year membership for individuals, $17.50 per year membership for families; queries: free to members, $2.00 each for non-members

Labette Genealogical Society
PO Box 826
Parsons, KS 67357
Tina Rice

LaCygne Genealogical Society
Linn County Library, District 2
210 North Commercial
PO Box 127
LaCygne, KS 66040
(913) 757-2151; (913) 757-2405
E-mail: lacygilb@midusa.net
Janet Reynolds
Hours: Mon–Tue & Thur 9:00–6:00, Wed & Fri 9:00–5:00, Sat 9:00–12:00
(LaCygne and some Linn County records)

Leavenworth County Genealogical Society, Inc.
(Leavenworth Public Library—collection location)
PO Box 362 (mailing address)
Leavenworth, KS 66048-0362
(913) 682-8641 (President)
Robert A. Holt, President
Hours: Library: Mon–Thur 9:00–9:00, Fri–Sat 9:00–5:00
Pub. *Rooting Around*, quarterly (January, April, July, October)
$15.00 per year membership (calendar year)

Liberal Area Genealogical Society
PO Box 1094
Liberal, KS 67905-1448
(316) 626-0181
Florence Palmer Herring, Special Collections/Genealogist
Hours: Library: Mon–Thur 10:00–8:00, Fri–Sat 10:00–5:00, Sun 1:00–5:00
Pub. *Windy Times*, quarterly (March, June, September, December)
(local information and research; Kansas panhandle, Oklahoma, Texas and Colorado)
$10.00 per year membership for individuals, $15.00 per year membership for families; search fee: $5.00

Linn County Historical and Genealogical Society
Linn County Museum
History/Genealogy Library
Dunlap Park
PO Box 137
Pleasanton, KS 66075-0137
(913) 352-8739
Ola May Earnest, President
Hours: winter: Tue & Thur 9:00–5:00, Sat–Sun 1:00–5:00; summer: Tue–Thur 9:00–5:00, Fri–Sun 1:00–5:00
Pub. *Kin in Linn*, quarterly; *Linn County Historical Society Newsletter*, quarterly
(holdings include state and federal census records, mortality schedules, all Linn County newspapers from 1864, funeral records from 1910, cemetery records, military records, vital statistics, D.A.R. lineage books, index to probate court records)
$2.00 per year membership in Historical Society, $8.00 per year membership in Genealogical Society

McPherson County Genealogical Society
(McPherson College Library, 1600 East Euclid—holdings location)
PO Box 1402 (mailing address)
McPherson, KS 67460-1402
(316) 241-0731, ext. 1213; (316) 241-1649 FAX
Rowena Olsen, Librarian
Hours: Library: Mon–Thur 7:30 A.M.–10:00 P.M., Fri 7:30–5:00, Sat 8:00–5:00, Sun 2:00–10:00; meetings at the Senior Center
Pub. *Leaves to Taproots*, ten times per year (monthly, September–June)
$10.00 per year membership

Miami County Genealogy Society
(North Side Square—location)
PO Box 123 (mailing address)
Paola, KS 66071-0123
(913) 294-3529 (President); (913) 533-2485 (Treasurer); (913) 837-5216 (Secretary)
Helen Gilliland, President; Betty, Treasurer and Librarian; Kathy, Corresponding Secretary
Hours: Apr–Nov: Mon 1:00–4:00, Thur 5:00–8:00, Sat 9:00–12:00, and by appointment
Pub. *MICOGESOQU*, quarterly
$9.00 per year membership; research fee: $5.00 per hour

Midwest Historical and Genealogical Society
1203 North Main
PO Box 1121
Wichita, KS 67201-1121
(316) 264-3611
Sherry Weir, Librarian
Hours: Tue & Sat 9:00–4:00, second Sat 9:00–12:30

Pub. *Midwest Historical and Genealogical Register*, quarterly
$20.00 per year membership for individuals, $15.00 per year membership for libraries

Montgomery County Genealogical Society
311 West Tenth
PO Box 444
Coffeyville, KS 67337-0444
(316) 251-5265; (316) 251-0716
Carol Duvall, President
Hours: winter: 10:00–8:00, summer: 9:00–6:00
Pub. *The Descender*, semiannually
$8.00 per year membership

Morris County Genealogical Society
210 West Grant Street
White City, KS 66872
(785) 349-2987
Hours: Fri 1:00–4:00
Pub. *Bits and Pieces of the Past*
$12.00 per year membership

Nemaha County Genealogical Society
Sixth and Nemaha
Seneca, KS 66538
(785) 336-2494
E-mail: mphil@parod.com
http://www.ukans.edu/kansas/seneca/gensoc/gensoc.html
Marcia Philbrick, Editor
Hours: Seneca Free Public Library, Sixth and Main: Mon–Thur 10:00–8:00, Fri 10:00–5:00, Sat 10:00–2:00
Pub. *Nemaha County Genealogical Society Newsletter*, quarterly
$10.00 per year membership; research: hourly fee plus copying costs

North Central Kansas Genealogical Society
(Hesperian Library, 802 Locust Street, Second Floor of City Building—location)
PO Box 251 (mailing address)
Cawker City, KS 67430-0251
(785) 781-4925 (Hesperian Library, for appointment only, no research over the phone); (785) 781-4343 (Librarian, weekdays); (785) 781-4303 (Ms. Reling)
Celia Norton Kincheloe, North Central Kansas Genealogical Society Librarian; Dorothy Reling
Hours: Library: Mon, Thur & Sat 1:00–5:00, Tue 10:00–noon, Wed 1:00–7:00
Pub. *Waconda Roots and Branches*, quarterly
$8.00 per year membership for individuals, $9.00 per year membership for two people (beginning in September); research $5.00 and up, plus SASE, for records of Jewell and Mitchell counties, principally, but can refer to researchers of Cloud, Smith, Osborne and Saline counties, Kansas

Northwest Kansas Genealogical and Historical Society
Oakley Public Library
700 West Third Street
Oakley, KS 67748-1256
(785) 672-4389
Lillian Martin, President
Hours: Library: 10:00–5:00
(Logan County newspapers on film)

Norton County Genealogical Society
1 Washington Square
PO Box 446
Norton, KS 67654-0446
Fleta Hanlon, President
Hours: Mon–Thur 10:00–8:00, Fri–Sat closed early
Pub. *Norton County Tracer*, quarterly (births, deaths, marriages, obituaries, old papers, census records, area newspapers)
$8.00 per year membership

Old Fort Genealogical Society of Southeast Kansas, Inc.
502 South National Avenue
Fort Scott, KS 66701-1327
Georgia L. Wood, Librarian
Hours: Mon–Sat 1:00–4:00
Pub. *Old Fort Log*, three times per year (southeastern Kansas; "local area information")
$14.00 per year membership for individuals, $16.00 per year membership for families

Osage County Genealogical Society
Lyndon Carnegie Library
PO Box 563
126 East Sixth
Lyndon, KS 66451
Pub. *Osage County Genealogical Society Quarterly*

Osborne County Genealogical and Historical Society
213 North First
Osborne, KS 67473
Pub. *Leaves of Lineage*, quarterly; *Osborne County Genealogical Society Quarterly*
$10.00 per year membership

Phillips County Genealogical Society
(Phillipsburg City Library, 888 Fourth—location)
PO Box 114 (mailing address)
Phillipsburg, KS 67661-0114
(785) 543-5325 (Library); (785) 543-6550 (President); (785) 543-5680 (Research)
http://skyways.lib.ks.us/kansas/genweb/phillips/queries1.html;http://skyways.lib.ks.us/kansas/genweb/phillips/plgensoc.html; http://skyways.lib.ks.us/kansas/towns/Phillipsburg/library.html (Library)
Darlene Johnson, President; Katie Davis, Research

Hours: Genealogy Room: Mon–Fri 10:00–6:00, Sat 10:00–4:00
Pub. *Tree Tracker*, quarterly
$7.50 per year membership for individuals who pick up their newsletters, $15.00 per year membership for individuals or families who have their newsletters mailed

Rawlins County Genealogical Society
(102 South Sixth—location)
PO Box 203 (mailing address)
Atwood, KS 67730-0203
(785) 626-3850
E-mail: atwoolb@ruraltel.net
Delores Luedke, Researcher
Hours: meetings at Atwood Public Library
Pub. *Rawlins County Chronicle*, quarterly
("family files, newspapers, obituaries, burial records, cemeteries, births, weddings, old tax and court records, scrapbooks, all indexed on database at Rawlins County Historical Society")
$3.00 per year membership; research by donation

Reno County Genealogical Society
PO Box 5
Hutchinson, KS 67504-0005
(316) 663-2804
Ruth Filbert, Editor
Hours: Hutchinson Public Library: Mon–Fri 9:00–9:00, Sat 9:00–6:00, Sun 1:00–5:00; meetings at Hutchinson Public Library
Pub. *The Sunflower*, quarterly
$10.00 per year membership; research: $5.00 per hour plus expenses

Republic County Genealogical Society
(Republic County Historical Museum, Highway 36—location)
PO Box 31 (mailing address)
Belleville, KS 66935
(785) 527-5826
Ruth Rahe, Genealogical Chairman
Hours: Mon–Fri 1:00–5:00
Pub. *Quarterly Newsletter*
$5.00 per year membership

Riley County Kansas Genealogical Society and Computer Interest Group
2005 Claflin Road
Manhattan, KS 66502-3415
(785) 565-6495
E-mail: rcgs@flinthills
Jane Brown, President
Hours: Tue, Thur & Sat 10:00–4:00, Wed 1:00–4:00 & 7:00–9:00, Sun 2:00–5:00
Pub. *Kansas Kin*, quarterly, $10.00 per year subscription
(genealogy publications on 105 Kansas counties)
$21.00 per year membership; search for donation

Santa Fe Trail Genealogical Society
PO Box 528
Syracuse, KS 67878
(316) 384-7614
Ruth Schibbelhut
Hours: 9:00–5:00

Sherman County Historical and Genealogical Society
PO Box 684
Goodland, KS 67735
Clarence Scheopner, President Historical Society
Hours: 10:00–7:00
Pub. *Quarterly*
$5.00 per year membership

Smoky Valley Genealogical Society and Library, Inc.
211 West Iron, Suite 205
Salina, KS 67401-2613
(785) 825-7573
Hours: Mon–Thur & Sat noon–4:00
Pub. *Tree Climber*, quarterly; *Smoky Valley Genealogical Society and Library Newsletter*, bimonthly
$15.00 per year membership

Southeast Kansas Genealogical Society
(Southeast Kansas Library System, 218 East Madison—location)
PO Box 393 (mailing address)
Iola, KS 66749
(316) 365-5136 (Library)
Joan B. Beck, Corresponding Secretary
Hours: Library: Sept–May: Mon–Thur 9:30–8:00, Fri–Sat 9:00–5:00; Jun–Aug: Mon–Thur 9:30–5:30, Fri–Sat 9:00–5:00; meetings first Sat 1:30 at Library
Pub. *Treebark*, quarterly (January, April, July, October)
(state and federal census, 1855–1925; marriages of Allen County, 1856–1925; deaths from *Iola Reg.*, 1900–1996; births from Iola City Hall, 1895–1935)
$15.00 per year membership for individuals, $20.00 per year membership for families; research: hourly fee plus copy cost

Stafford County Historical and Genealogical Society
(100 South Main, corner of Main and Broadway—location)
PO Box 249 (mailing address)
Stafford, KS 67578-0249
(316) 234-5664
Ruth Shocklee, Executive Secretary
Hours: Tue–Thur 1:30–3:30, Sat 2:00–4:00
Pub. *Reflections*, two times per year
(excellent collection of family histories)

Stevens County Genealogical Society
HC 01, Box 12
Hugoton, KS 67951

Tonganoxie Genealogical Society
PO Box 354
Tonganoxie, KS 66086
(913) 845-2905
Connie Putthoff, President
Hours: Mon & Fri 9:00–5:00, Tue & Thur 2:00–7:00, Wed 9:00–7:00, Sat 9:00–1:00

Topeka Genealogical Society
(2717 Indiana—location)
PO Box 4048 (mailing address)
Topeka, KS 66604-0048
(785) 233-5762
William Cope, Corresponding Secretary
Hours: Wed–Thur & Sat 1:00–4:00, first & third Thur 5:30–8:30
Pub. *Topeka Genealogical Society Quarterly*; *Topeka Genealogical Society Newsletter*, quarterly
$15.00 per year membership for individuals, $18.00 per year membership for families, $25.00 per year Sustaining membership

Washington County Genealogical Society
Washington County Historical Society
208 Ballard
PO Box 31
Washington, KS 66968

Wichita Genealogical Society
PO Box 3705
Wichita, KS 67201-3705
http://history.cc.ukans.edu/kansas/wgs/wgs.html
Pub. *The Ark Valley Crossroads*, quarterly; *On the Trail* (current events, single-sheet newsletter), quarterly
(local and area cemeteries and mortuaries, obituaries and other newspaper extractions; a support group to the Genealogy Department of the Wichita Public Library)
$15.00 per year membership for individuals, $20.00 per year membership for couples; research: $5.00 (one-hour maximum) plus copy costs, list of professional researchers available on request; queries published free for members, $2.00 each for non-members

Wilson County Historical Society and Genealogical Chapter
420 North Seventh Street
Fredonia, KS 66736-1315
(316) 378-3965
Hours: Mon–Fri 1:00–4:30
Pub. *Wilson County Historical Society Newsletter*, quarterly
("We have a Wilson County obituary index from 1873 to the present time.")
$7.00 per year membership in Historical Society, $10.00 per year membership in Historical Society and Genealogical Chapter; research: $10.00 per hour plus cost of copies

Wyandotte County Genealogical Society
150 North 38th Street
Kansas City, KS 66102-3759
Pub. *Bear Tracks*

Independent Publications and Miscellany

Center for Mennonite Brethren Studies
Tabor College
400 South Jefferson
Hillsboro, KS 67063
(316) 947-3121, ext. 342; (316) 947-3121, ext. 318
Peggy Goertzen, Director
Hours: Mon–Fri 9:00–noon & 1:30–4:00, and by appointment
Pub. *Newsletter*, annually
("Mennonite Brethren historical records: congregational, conference, photographs, manuscripts, as well as materials on Mennonites in general and Germans from Russia, also strong collection of Marion County, Kansas records.")

Historic Merriam
9516 Hocker Drive
Shawnee Mission
Merriam, KS 66203
(913) 831-9339

Kanhistique
220 Court Avenue
Ellsworth, KS 67439
Edna M. Lee, Editor
Pub. *Kanhistique*, monthly, $12.00 per year subscription

Kansas Press Association
5423 S.W. Seventh
Topeka, KS 66606
(785) 271-5304
E-mail: cwright@kspress.com
http://www.kspress.com/
(directory of Kansas newspapers)

KsGenWeb
Part of U.S. GenWeb Project
E-mail: ks@usgenweb.com
http://www.skyways.lib.ks.us/kansas/genweb/index.html
(links to other Kansas resources)

Mountain Press
(see Tennessee)

KENTUCKY

Archives and Libraries with Holdings in Genealogy

State Archives and Library

Kentucky State Archives
Kentucky Department for Libraries and Archives
Public Records Division
Archives Research Room
300 Coffee Tree Road
PO Box 537
Frankfort, KY 40602-0537
(502) 564-8300, ext 346/347; (502) 564-8704 (inquiries regarding research guidelines)
http://www.kdla.state.ky.us/
James M. Prichard, Research Room Supervisor
Hours: Archives Research Room: Tue–Sat 8:00–4:00; State Library Reference: Mon–Fri 8:00–4:30
Pub. *Friends of Public Archives, Inc. Newsletter*, quarterly
(collects Kentucky's public records: city, county and state, supplemented by Kentucky Genealogical Society Library)
search fees: $3.00 minimum plus copying costs for Kentucky residents, no prepayment required, $8.00 non-refundable prepayment for out-of-state residents, covering thirty minutes of research time and three photocopies from microform originals or six copies from paper originals, additional copies to be billed

State Historical Societies

Historical Confederation of Kentucky
(Kentucky Historical Society—location)
PO Box 1792 (mailing address)
Frankfort, KY 40602-1792
(502) 564-3016; (502) 564-4701 FAX
E-mail: knichols@mis.net
Karla Nicholson
Hours: 8:00–4:30
Pub. *Circuit Rider*, quarterly
$9.50 per year membership

Kentucky Historical Society Library
(300 West Broadway, Old Capitol Annex, Frankfort, KY 40601—location)
PO Box 1792 (mailing address)
Frankfort, KY 40602-1792
(502) 564-3016; (502) 564-4701 FAX
http://www.state.ky.us/agencies/khs/
Anne McDonnell, Librarian; Tom Stephens, Editor

Hours: Mon–Sat 8:00–4:00, Sat 9:00–4:00
Pub. *Kentucky Ancestors*, quarterly; *Register of the Kentucky Historical Society*, quarterly; *Bulletin of Kentucky Historical Society*, bimonthly
$25.00 per year membership for individuals (includes *Bulletin* and a choice of the *Register* or *Kentucky Ancestors*), $35.00 per year Contributing membership (includes all three periodicals), $50.00 per year Friend membership

City, County and Regional Archives and Libraries

Adair County Public Library
Kentucky History and Genealogy Section
307 Greensburg Street
Columbia, KY 42728
(502) 384-2472
Hours: Mon, Wed & Fri 8:00–4:30, Tue & Thur 8:00–6:00, Sat 8:00–noon

Anchorage Civic Club Archives
City Hall
PO Box 23266
Anchorage, KY 40223
(502) 245-4654; (502) 245-5651 FAX
Peggy Revell, Director
Hours: Wed 10:00–noon, and by appointment
Pub. *Civic Club Newsletter*, quarterly
(little involving genealogy, but all city and school records, various organizations, maintains a file of names and where they can be found in document boxes)

Ballard-Carlisle-Livingston Public Library
Genealogy Section
132 North Fourth Street
Wickliffe, KY 42087
Hours: Wed 3:00–6:00, Fri 9:00–4:00

Behringer-Crawford Museum
1600 Montague Road
Devou Park, PO Box 67
Covington, KY 41012
(606) 491-4003
Hours: Tue–Fri 10:00–5:00, Sat–Sun 1:00–5:00 by appointment only

Belcher History Center
U.S. 460 East
PO Box 10
Belcher, KY 41513
(606) 754-8876
Fon R. Belcher, Ed.D., Director
Pub. *Belcher Bulletin*

Berea College
Hutchins Library
Campus Drive
Berea, KY 40404
(606) 986-9341, ext. 5260
Sidney Farr, Editor

Hours: Mon–Fri 8:00–noon & 1:00–5:00
Pub. *Appalachian Heritage* (a literary magazine), quarterly, $18.00 per year subscription
(southern Appalachian region life and work)

Boone County Public Library
7425 U.S. 42
Florence, KY 41042
(606) 371-6222
E-mail: info@bcpl.org
http://www.bcpl.org
Patricia Yannarella, Information Services Coordinator
Hours: Mon–Thur 9:00–9:00, Fri 9:00–6:00, Sat 9:00–5:00; Sun 1:00–5:00
(Boone County history)

Boyd County Public Library
Minnie Winder Genealogy and Local History Collection
1740 Central Avenue
Ashland, KY 41101
(606) 329-0090
James C. Powers, Resident Historian
Hours: Mon–Thur 10:00–8:30, Fri 10:00–5:30, Sat 10:00–5:00; Sun 1:00–5:00

Breathitt County Museum
Broadway Street, Senior Citizens Building
Jackson, KY 41339
(606) 666-4159
Donna Stivers, Director

Breckinridge County Public Library
Special Collections
Hardinsburg, KY 40143

Buchanan County Public Library
(see Virginia)

Campbell County Public Library
Fourth and Monmouth Streets
Newport, KY 41071
(606) 291-4770
Aileen Hurst, Reference
Hours: Mon–Thur 10:00–8:00, Fri 10:00–6:00, Sat 10:00–5:00

Casey County Public Library
Genealogical Research Center
238 Middleburg Street
Liberty, KY 42529
(606) 787-9381; (606) 787-7720 FAX
(includes family files, books, maps, oral history tapes, microfilm of court records, and VCR tapes of guest speakers to the Bicentennial Heritage Corporation; includes publications on Maryland, Pennsylvania, Virginia, North and South Carolina, Georgia, Tennessee, Kentucky, Indiana, Missouri, Texas and all known early publications on Casey County and surrounding counties)

Centre College
Special Collections
600 West Walnut Street
Danville, KY 40422
(606) 238-5272; (606) 236-7925
http://www.centre.edu/academic/library/
archives/archives.html

Clark County Public Library
109 South Main Street
Winchester, KY 40391
(606) 744-5661; (606) 744-5993 FAX
Kelle Hoskins, Adult Services Librarian
Hours: Mon–Thur 9:00–8:00, Fri 9:00–
5:30, Sat 9:00–5:00

George Coon Public Library
PO Box 230
114 South Harrison Street
Princeton, KY 42445
(502) 365-2884; (502) 365-2892 FAX
Judy Boaz, Director
Hours: Mon–Thur 9:00–6:00, Fri–Sat
9:00–5:00

Eastern Kentucky University
Crabbe Library, Special Collections and
Archives
Library 126
Richmond, KY 40475-3121
(606) 622-1792; (606) 622-1174 FAX
E-mail: archive@acs.eku.edu
http://www.library.eku.edu/sca/
scahome.htm
Mrs. Jerry Parrish Dimitrov, Curator
Hours: Mon–Tue & Thur–Fri 8:00–5:00,
Wed 8:00–8:00
(Madison county, Kentucky, genealogy,
early Boonesborough; limited staff
research, local researchers list
available)
photocopies 20¢ each

Eastern Kentucky University
Jonathan Truman Dorris Museum
Richmond, KY 40475
(606) 622-5585

Eastern Kentucky University
Eastern Kentucky University Archives
Cammack Building
Richmond, KY 40475
(606) 624-2760

John Fox Jr. Memorial Library
Duncan Tavern, DAR Shrine and
Historic Center
323 High Street
Paris, KY 40361
(606) 987-1788
Melissa Gibson, Librarian
Hours: Thur–Sat 10:00–noon & 1:00–
4:00
(DAR records, one-of-a-kind
publications and manuscripts)
$2.00 admission for all non-Kentucky
DAR members

Fulton Public Library
312 Main Street
Fulton, KY 42050

(502) 472-3439
E-mail: fultonlib@kih.net
Elaine Allen, Director
Hours: Tue 10:30–5:00 & 6:00–8:00,
Fri–Sat 9:00–11:30 & 12:30–5:00
(Civil War collection, genealogical
collection)

Gallatin Public Library
PO Box 258
Warsaw, KY 41095

Grayson County Public Library
130 East Market Street
Leitchfield, KY 42754
(502) 259-5455; (502) 259-4552
E-mail: library@creative-net.net
Karen Gillespie, Director
Hours: Mon & Thur 9:00–7:00, Tue–
Wed & Fri–Sat 9:00–5:00

Greenup County Public Library
614 Main Street
Greenup, KY 41144
(606) 473-6514 phone and FAX
Dorothy K. Griffith, County Library
Director
Hours: Mon–Tue & Thur–Fri 9:00–5:00,
Wed 9:00–8:00, Sat 9:00–2:00
(genealogy and local history collection)

Hacksma House Genealogy Library
(see Washington)

Hancock County Archives
Old Court House, Third Floor
Hawesville, KY 42348
(502) 927-8095
Claribel Phillips, Archivist

Hardin County Library
South Logsdon Parkway
Radcliff, KY 40160

Hardy Memorial Museum
296 South Main
Logan, KY 42276

Henderson County Public Library
101 South Main Street
Henderson, KY 42420
(502) 826-3712; (502) 827-4226 FAX
Debra Mayhew, Reference Librarian
Hours: Mon–Thur 9:00–8:00, Fri–Sat
9:00–5:00, Sun 1:30–5:00

Historic Russellville
PO Box 116
Russellville, KY 42276
(502) 726-9501
E-mail: jbasham@logantele.com
Pat Basham, Secretary
Hours: meetings at the Woman's Club
Building, 145 East Fifth Street,
Russellville: fourth Thur 5:00
Pub. *Newsletter*, annual
$10.00 per year membership for
individuals, $15.00 per year
membership for families

Johnson County Public Library
Main Street
Paintsville, KY 41240

Kenton County Public Library
Fifth and Scott Streets
Covington, KY 41011
(606) 491-7610; (606) 655-7956 FAX
Charles D. King, Local History Librarian
Hours: Mon–Thur 10:00–9:00, Fri
10:00–6:00, Sat 10:00–5:00, Sun
1:00–5:00
(Kentucky history, emphasis on northern
Kentucky; on-line newspaper index
covering 1835–1930 and 1984 to the
present)
search fee: $10.00 per hour plus copies)

Kentucky Highlands Museum
PO Box 1494
Ashland, KY 41105
Pub. *Highlands Highlights*

Kentucky Military History Museum
(Kentucky Historical Society, 300
Broadway, Old Capitol Annex,
Frankfort, KY 40601—location)
PO Box H (mailing address)
Frankfort, KY 40602-2108
(502) 564-3265
Thomas W. Fugate, Museum Curator
Hours: Mon–Fri 9:00–4:00 by
appointment (at least 24 hours ahead)

Kentucky State University Archives
Blazer Library
Frankfort, KY 40601
(502) 227-6852
Jane A. Minder, Archives and Records
Manager

Laurel County Public Library
116 East Fourth Street
London, KY 40741

Leslie County Public Library
PO Box 498
Hyden, KY 41749
(606) 672-2460
Mason Collett, Director
Hours: Mon–Fri 8:00–5:00, Sat 8:00–
2:00

Lexington Public Library
Kentucky Room
140 East Main Street
Lexington, KY 40507-1376
(606) 231-5520
Robin Rader, Kentucky Reference
Librarian
Hours: Mon–Thur 9:00–9:00, Fri–Sat
9:00–5:00, Sun 1:00–5:00
no costs

Logan County Public Library
201 West Sixth Street
Russellville, KY 42276

City of Louisville Archives
970 South Fourth Street
Louisville, KY 40203

(502) 574-3508; (502) 574-4318 FAX
E-mail: sarece01@ulkyvh.louisville.edu
Sharon Receveur, Assistant Director,
Office of Information Services
Hours: 9:00–5:00
(only City of Louisville government
records, also a records center for non-
current, non-permanent records)
copies: 25¢ each, no search fee charged

Louisville Free Public Library
Fourth and York Streets
Louisville, KY 40203
(502) 561-8600
Hours: Mon–Thur 9:00–9:00, Fri–Sat
9:00–5:00
10¢ per copy from paper original, 20¢
per copy from microfilm, plus
handling charges for mailing: $2.00
(1–10 pp.), $3.00 (11–20 pp.), $4.00
(21–30 pp.), $5.00 maximum

Lyon County Library
Eddyville, KY 42038
(has a genealogy section and family file
for researchers, but does not answer
queries)

**Madisonville-Hopkins County Public
Library**
31 South Main Street
Madisonville, KY 42431

Marshall County Public Library
1003 Poplar Street
Benton, KY 42025
(502) 527-9969; (502) 527-0506 FAX
Barbara Serls, Director
Hours: Mon 9:00–8:00, Tue–Sat 9:00–
5:00
(genealogical collection)

**Muhlenberg County Public
Libraries**
Genealogy and Local History Annex
117 South Main Street
Greenville, KY 42345
(502) 338-5388
Barry W. Edwards, Annex Manager
Hours: Mon 9:00–8:00, Tue–Fri 9:00–
5:00, Sat 9:00–1:00
(Western Kentucky)

Murray State University
Forrest C. Pogue Special Collections
Library
1 Murray Street
Murray, KY 42071-3309
(502) 762-6152; (502) 762-4998
Keith M. Heim, Ph.D., Head, Special
Collections and Archives
Hours: Mon–Fri 8:00–4:30, Sat 10:00–
3:00 (schedule varies with school
year)
(Kentucky and southeast U.S. genealogy
and local history)

Murray State University
Wrather West Kentucky Museum
Murray, KY 42071-3308
(502) 762-4771

Northern Kentucky University
Christopher Gist Historical Society
Collection
Special Collections and Archives
Department
Library
Highland Heights, KY 41099-6101
(606) 572-6158; (606) 572-5390 FAX
E-mail: adamsr@nku.edu
http://www.nku.edu/~refdept/gist.html

**Owensboro-Daviess County Public
Library**
Kentucky Room: Local History and
Genealogy
450 Griffith Avenue
Owensboro, KY 42301
(502) 684-0211, ext. 24
Shelia E. Heflin, Supervisor, Kentucky
Room
Hours: Mon–Fri 9:00–12:00 & 1:00–
9:00, Sat 9:00–12:00 & 1:00–6:00,
Sun 2:00–5:00

Paducah Public Library
555 Washington Street
Paducah, KY 42003-1735
(502) 442-2510; (502) 444-6436 FAX
Vonnie Shelton
Hours: Mon–Thur 9:00–9:00, Fri–Sat
9:00–6:00, Sun 1:00–6:00

Pennyroyal Area Museum
217 East Ninth Street
Hopkinsville, KY 42240
(502) 887-4270

Perry County Public Library
High Street
Hazard, KY 41701

Pikeville Public Library
210 Pike Avenue
Pikeville, KY 41501

Portland Museum
2308 Portland Avenue
Louisville, KY 40212
(502) 776-7678
Nathalie Andrews, Executive Director
Pub. *Kicks*

Don F. Pratt Museum
G3/DPTM 101st ABN DIV (ASSLT) &
Fort Campbell
5702 Tennessee Avenue
Fort Campbell, KY 42223-5335
(502) 798-3215
Rex Boggs, Curator/Director
Hours: 9:30–4:30 (guided tours upon
request, 36 hours notice)

Rowan Public Library
First Street
Morehead, KY 40351

Scott County Public Library
230 East Main
Georgetown, KY 40324
(502) 863-3566
Earlene H. Arnett, Director

Hours: Mon–Thur 10:00–8:00, Fri
10:00–5:30, Sat 9:00–5:30
(local history collection)

John L. Street Library
244 Main Street
Cadiz, KY 42211
(502) 522-6301; (502) 522-1107 FAX
E-mail: trigglib@kih.net
Pam Metts, Director; Ann McAtee,
Volunteer
Hours: Library: Mon 9:00–8:00, Tue–Fri
9:00–5:30, Sat 9:00–noon; Volunteer:
Tue 12:30–5:30, Fri 12:30–5:00

Union County Public Library
126 South Morgan
Morganfield, KY 42437
(502) 389-1696; (502) 389-3925 FAX
Laura Wildey, Director
Hours: Mon–Tue & Thur–Fri 9:00–5:00,
Wed 9:00–6:00, Sat 9:00–2:00

University of Kentucky
Kentucky Humanities Council
Ligon House
Lexington, KY 40506-0442
(606) 257-5932

University of Kentucky
Margaret I. King Library
Department of Special Collections and
Archives
Lexington, KY 40506-0039
(606) 257-8611
E-mail: wjmars01@ukcc.uky.edu
http://www.uky.edu/Libraries/Special
Ms. B. J. Gooch, Public Services
Coordinator
Hours: Mon–Fri 8:00–4:30, Wed (when
university is in session) 4:30–9:00, Sat
8:00–12:00, Sun (when university is in
session) 2:00–5:00

University of Kentucky Libraries
Photographic Archives
111 Margaret I. King Library North
500 South Limestone Street
Lexington, KY 40506
(606) 257-8379
Bill Marshall, Director
Hours: Mon–Fri 8:00–5:00, Sat 8:00–
noon

University of Louisville
University Archives and Records Center
Louisville, KY 40292
(502) 852-6674
William J. Morison, Ph.D., Director

University of Louisville
Special Collections—Rare Books and
Photographic Archives
William F. Ekstrom Library
Belknap Campus
Louisville, KY 40292
(502) 852-6752; (502) 852-8734 FAX
http:/www.louisville.edu/library
Delinda Stephens Buie, Curator; James
C. Anderson, Curator

Hours: Mon–Fri 10:00–4:00, Thur 4:00–8:00, and by appointment
Pub. *Library Review*, annually (but slightly irregularly), $25.00 per year subscription
(publication of friends of the libraries group, The Library Associates, including articles researched in Special Collections)

Washington County Public Library
210 East Main Street
Springfield, KY 40069
(606) 336-7655; (606) 336-0256 FAX
Lisa K. Jones, Library Director
Hours: Mon 10:00–8:00, Tue & Thur–Fri 10:00–5:00
no research assistance available

Wayne County Public Library
159 South Main Street
Monticello, KY 42633
(606) 348-8565
Hours: Mon–Tue & Thur–Fri 8:00–4:30, Wed & Sat 8:00–4:00

Western Kentucky University
Kentucky Museum and Library
(1442 Kentucky Street—location)
1 Big Red Way (mailing address)
Bowling Green, KY 42101-3576
(502) 745-5083 (Reading Room, Second Floor); (502) 745-6086 (Folklife Archives, Room E-216); (502) 745-2592 (Museum); (502) 745-6264 FAX
Constance A. Mills, Kentucky Library Coordinator
Hours: Reading Room: Mon–Fri 8:00–4:30, Sat 9:30–4:00 (hours may vary during holidays, semester breaks and summer semester)
Pub. *The Fanlight*, irregularly
(Kentucky, with emphasis on south-central region of the state and Shakers at South Union, Kentucky)
$15.00 per year Museum membership for individuals, $25.00 per year membership for families, $3.00 per year membership for Junior members, $6.00 per year membership for students; requests for specific records only will be considered and a list of professional researchers is available upon request

Willard Library
(see Indiana)

Historical Societies— Local and Regional

Ancestral Trails Historical Society, Inc.
(Vine Grove Optimist Club, 127 West Main Street—location)
PO Box 573 (mailing address)
Vine Grove, KY 40175
E-mail: aths@kvnet.org
http://www.kvnet.org/aths
Paul W. Urbahns, President
Pub. *Ancestral News*, quarterly
(Breckinridge, Bullitt, Edmonson, Grayson, Hardin, Hart, Jefferson, LaRue, Meade and Nelson counties)
$10.00 per year membership

Auburn Historical Society
(433 West Main Street—location)
PO Box 114 (mailing address)
Auburn, KY 42206
(502) 542-4677
Eloise Hadden, President
Hours: meetings at the Auburn Museum: first Tue (even-numbered months) 7:00
Pub. *Newsletter*
(Logan County)
$5.00 per year membership

Ballard-Carlisle Historical-Genealogical Society
PO Box 279
Wickliffe, KY 42087
(502) 628-3468
E-mail: ccscotts@apex.net
http://www.ballardconet.com/bchgs/
Joe K. Scott, President
Hours: meetings: second Sun (except Dec) 2:00
Pub. *The Root Diggers*, semiannually (March and August)
(books, newspapers, microfilm, pictures, and private papers housed in the genealogy section of the Ballard-Carlisle-Livingston Public Library)
$10.00 per year membership for individuals, libraries or organizations (calendar year), $12.00 per year membership for families; free queries to Lois M. Scott, Corresponding Secretary or via E-mail

Bell County Historical Society
PO Box 1344
Middlesboro, KY 40965
(606) 248-5304
Virginia T. Green, Corresponding Secretary
Hours: Mon–Thur 10:00–8:00, Fri 10:00–7:00, Sat 10:00–4:00 (closes one hour earlier in summer)
Pub. *Gateway*, quarterly
$15.00 per year membership

Big Sandy Valley Historical Society
319 F.M. Stafford Avenue
Paintsville, KY 41240
Betty Hazelette, Secretary
Hours: meetings at Kenova, WV: second Sat of Apr; at Breaks Interstate Park, second Sat of Sept at Paintsville: second Sat of Jul; at Louisa: second Sat of November
Pub. *Sandy Valley Heritage*, quarterly
$10.00 per year membership

Boyd County Historical Society
Boyd County Public Library
Minnie Winder Genealogy and Local History Collection
1740 Central Avenue
Ashland, KY 41101
(606) 329-0090
James C. Powers, Resident Historian
Hours: Library: Mon–Thur 10:00–8:30, Fri 10:00–5:30, Sat 10:00–5:00; Sun 1:00–5:00
(specializes in Kentucky, Virginia and Pennsylvania)

Bracken County Historical Society
302 East Fourth
Augusta, KY 41002
(606) 756-2409
George Cummins, President
Pub. *Bracken County Historical Society*, monthly
$7.50 per year membership

The Breathitt County Historical and Genealogical Society
121 Turner Drive
Jackson, KY 41339
Hours: meetings in the Breathitt Public Library: third Mon 7:00
Pub. *The Record*, quarterly
$7.00 per year membership

Breckinridge County Historical Society
PO Box 498
Hardinsburg, KY 40143
Hours: meetings: fourth Mon

Butler County Historical and Genealogical Society, Inc.
PO Box 435
Morgantown, KY 42261
(502) 526-4408
E-mail: cjsouth@tcsx.net
Carole J. Southerland, Secretary/Treasurer
Hours: Butler County Library: 9:00–4:00
Pub. *Kentucky Traces*, quarterly, $2.00 per issue
$10.00 per year membership (calendar year)

Campbell County Historical and Genealogical Society
19 East Main Street
Alexandria, KY 41001
(606) 635-6417
Hours: meetings: second Thur 7:30
Pub. *Campbell County History News*
$8.00 per year membership

Christian County Historical Society
PO Box 890
Hopkinsville, KY 42240
(502) 886-3921
William T. Turner, Official City-County Historian
Hours: Mon–Fri 8:00–4:30
(social history, Edger Cayce, The Night Riders)

Clay County Genealogical and Historical Society
PO Box 394
Manchester, KY 40962
Pub. *Clay County Ancestral News*,
  quarterly
$15.00 per year membership

Clinton County Historical Society
Albany, KY 42602
(606) 387-5519 (President)

Crittenden County Historical Society, Inc.
West Carlisle Street
PO Box 25
Marion, KY 42064
(502) 965-9257

Danville-Boyle County Historical Society
PO Box 1122
Danville, KY 40422

Daviess County Historical Society
c/o Owensboro-Daviess County Public
  Library
Kentucky Room: Local History and
  Genealogy
450 Griffith Avenue
Owensboro, KY 42301
(502) 684-0211, ext. 24
Shelia E. Heflin, Secretary
Hours: Kentucky Room: Mon–Fri 9:00–
  12:00 & 1:00–9:00, Sat 9:00–12:00 &
  1:00–6:00, Sun 2:00–5:00
$7.00 per year membership

Edmonson County Historical Society
8621 Brownsville Road
Brownsville, KY 42210
(502) 597-3140
Ricky L. Carroll, President
Pub. *Newsletter*, quarterly
$10.00 per year membership

Estill County Historical and Genealogical Society
PO Box 221
Ravenna, KY 40472-0221
Hours: meetings at the Estill County
  Public Library, Irvine: first Tue
  (except Jul) 7:00
Pub. *Estill County Historical and
  Genealogical Society Newsletter*,
  eleven times per year
$10.00 per year membership

The Filson Club Historical Society
1310 South Third Street
Louisville, KY 40208
(502) 635-5083; (502) 635-5086 FAX
Mark V. Wetherington, Director
Hours: Mon–Fri 9:00–5:00, Sat 9:00–
  12:00
Pub. *Filson Club History Quarterly*,
  $35.00 per year subscription; *Filson
  Club Publications*, irregularly
(excellent research collections for
  Kentucky history and genealogy)

$35.00 per year membership; user fee:
  $3.00 per day for non-members

Floyd County Historical and Genealogical Society
PO Box 982
Prestonsburg, KY 41653
Hours: meetings in the Floyd County
  Library conference room: third Mon
  7:00
$20.00 per year membership

Gallatin County Historical Society
Hawkins-Kirby House
PO Box 405
Warsaw, KY 41095
(606) 567-4591
Sue Bogardus, Vice President
Pub. *Year Book*, annually

Garrard County Historical Society
208 Danville Street
Lancaster, KY 40444
Pub. *Garrard County Historical Society
  Bulletin*, semiannually; *On the
  Garrard County Line*, semiannually
$5.00 per year membership

Grant County Historical Society, Inc.
12 Charlotte Heights
Williamstown, KY 41097
(606) 824-5357
Betty Barnes, Corresponding Secretary
Hours: by appointment only
Pub. *Grant County Historical Society
  Newsletter*, quarterly
$5.00 per year membership (beginning in
  July)

Grayson County Historical Society
PO Box 84
Leitchfield, KY 42755

Green County Historical Society
PO Box 276
Greensburg, KY 42743
William DeSpain, President
Pub. *Green County Review*, quarterly
$10.00 per year membership

Hancock County Historical Society
Old Court House
Hawesville, KY 42348

Hatfield-McCoy Historical Society (Ky.-W.Va.)
PO Box 2676
South Williamson, KY 41503
(606) 237-4646
Tom Atkins
Pub. *Feud Country*, biannually
$20.00 per year membership

Hardin County Historical Society
128 North Main Street
Box C
Elizabethtown, KY 42701
(502) 769-2301

Harrodsburg Historical Society
Genealogical Committee
Morgan Row House
220 South Chiles Street
PO Box 316
Harrodsburg, KY 40330
(606) 734-5985
James H. Miller, President
Hours: summer: Tue–Fri 1:00–5:00, Sat
  1:00–4:00; Nov–Mar: Tue 10:00–4:00,
  Wed–Sat 1:00–4:00
Pub. *Olde Towne Ledger*, bimonthly
(Mercer County and central Kentucky
  history)
$15.00 per year membership (1 May–30
  April); library use for non-members:
  $3.00 for first hour, $1.00 for each
  additional hour or portion thereof;
  research by committee: $10.00 per
  hour

Hart County Historical Society
(109 Main Street—location)
PO Box 606 (mailing address)
Munfordville, KY 42765-0606
(502) 524-0101
http://www.ovnet.com/userpages/
  feenerty/history.html
Mary W. Branstetter, Clerk
Hours: Mon–Fri 10:00–2:00
Pub. *Quarterly*
(early Hart County history and artifacts,
  Civil War period, and family
  genealogical records)
$12.00 per year membership

Henderson County Genealogical and Historical Society, Inc.
(1041 Fourth Street—location)
PO Box 303 (mailing address)
Henderson, KY 42420-0303
(502) 830-7514
E-mail: netta@hcc-uky.campus.mci.net
Netta Mullin, First Vice President
Hours: meeting at Henderson County
  Public Library, Multi-Purpose Room:
  first Thur 7:00
Pub. *The Legacy*, quarterly (March, June,
  September and December), $3.00 per
  issue
$12.00 per year membership for
  individuals (calendar year); research:
  $15.00 per hour plus copies at 20¢ per
  page

Hickman County Historical Society
Rt. 1, Box 70
Clinton, KY 42031

Historical Society of Hopkins County
107 South Union Street
Madisonville, KY 42431
(502) 821-3986
J. Harold Utley, President
Hours: Mon–Fri 1:00–5:00
Pub. *Historical Society of Hopkins
  County Yearbook*, annually, $20.00
  plus shipping and handling to non-
  members

Jackson Purchase Historical Society
1202 Joe Creason Drive
Benton, KY 42025
(502) 527-3705

Jefferson County Genealogical and Historical Society
PO Box 960
Shepherdsville, KY 40165-0960
Pub. *Jefferson County Genealogical and Historical Society Quarterly* (July, October, January, April)
$10.00 per year membership (beginning in June)

Jeffersontown and Southeast Jefferson County Historical Society
2432 Merriwood Drive
Jeffersontown, KY 40299
(502) 267-1715

Jessamine Historical Society
501 South Third Street
Nicholasville, KY 40356-1811
Mr. Hager

Johnson County Historical Society
444 Main Street
PO Box 788
Paintsville, KY 41240
(606) 789-4355; (606) 789-6758 FAX
Pat Patton, Corresponding Secretary
Hours: Mon, Wed & Fri 9:30–5:00, Tue & Thur 9:30–8:00, Sat 9:00–2:00
Pub. *Highland Echo*, quarterly (March, June, September, December)
$10.00 per year membership (calendar year)

Kenton County Historical Society
PO Box 641
Covington, KY 41012
(606) 292-2188 (President); (606) 261-2807 (Editor)
John Boh, President; Karl Lietzenmayer, Editor
Pub. *KCHS Bulletin*, monthly; *Northern Kentucky Heritage*, biannually, $15.00 per year subscription for non-members, $30.00 per year subscription for institutions
(local history and genealogy, especially, but not exclusively, for Boone, Campbell, Carroll, Gallatin, Grant, Kenton, Owen, and Pendleton counties of northern Kentucky, also Bracken, Mason and other associated counties; has index of Kenton County federal censuses)
$22.00 per year membership

Knott County Historical Society
PO Box 1023
Hindman, KY 41822
Hours: meetings at the Knott County Court House, Hindman: last Thurs evening
Pub. *Journal*, quarterly
$15.00 per year membership

Laurel County Historical Society
Old City Hall Building, Broad Street
PO Box 816
London, KY 40743-0816
(606) 864-0607
E-mail: lchistsoc@kih.net
Shirley McCowan, Librarian
Hours: Wed–Sat 10:00–4:00; monthly meetings second Thur 7:00
Pub. *Branches of Laurel*, quarterly
$15.00 per year membership (calendar year); $25.00 for initial search

Leslie County Historical Society
Leslie County Public Library
PO Box 498
Hyden, KY 41749
(606) 672-2460
Hours: Library: Mon–Fri 8:00–5:00, Sat 8:00–2:00

Letcher County Historical and Genealogical Society
PO Box 312
Whitesburg, KY 41858
Hours: meetings at the Harry M. Caudill Memorial Library, Whitesburg: second Tue 5:30
Newsletter

Lewis County Historical Society
(318 Lexington Avenue—location)
PO Box 212 (mailing address)
Vanceburg, KY 41179-0212
(606) 796-3778 (Corresponding Secretary)
Bettye B. Dillow, Corresponding Secretary and Treasurer; Joan Godfrey, President
Hours: Fri–Sat 11:00–4:00
Pub. *Shakin' and Diggin'*, quarterly (March, June, September, December)
$10.00 per year membership (calendar year); research: $5.00 per hour, four-hour minimum

Lewisburg/North Logan Historical Commission
PO Box 239
Lewisburg, KY 42256
(502) 755-4828
Mayor Gwyneth McKinney
Hours: meetings at the Dr. Sutton Building, Front Street, Lewisburg: second Thurs 10:00

Lincoln County Historical Society
11475 Brodhead Road
Crab Orchard, KY 40419-9608
(606) 355-2204
Martha Scott

Logan County Genealogical Society, Inc.
(West Fourth Street in Archive Building—location)
PO Box 853 (mailing address)
Russellville, KY 42276
(502) 726-8179

Hours: Mon–Fri 8:30–3:00
send SASE with query

Lyon County Historical Society, Inc.
Lyon County Museum
PO Box 811
Eddyville, KY 42038
(502) 388-9986; (502) 388-7322
Odell Walker, Lyon County Historian
Hours: Museum: Wed–Sun (May 15–Oct 15) 1:00–4:00, and by appointment
$5.00 per year museum and society membership for individuals, $10.00 per year membership for families, $100.00 life membership; $2.00 museum admission for non-members (children free)

Madison County Historical Society
(Madison County, KY—location)
PO Box 5066 (mailing address)
Richmond, KY 40476-5066
(606) 623-1398
David C. Greene, Treasurer
Pub. *Heritage Highlights*, quarterly (genealogical and historical society; queries welcomed)
$10.00 per year membership for individuals, $15.00 per year membership for families

Magoffin County Historical Society
(213 South Church Street—location)
PO Box 222 (mailing address)
Salyersville, KY 41465
(606) 349-1607; (606) 349-1353 FAX
http://www.geocities.com/heartland/1621
Connie Wireman, Director
Hours: Mon–Sat, and by appointment
Pub. *Journal of the Magoffin County Historical Society*, quarterly
(maintains a genealogy library, Magoffin County Kentucky Museum, and a Log Cabin Pioneer Village, sponsors an annual Founders Day Festival each Labor Day weekend)
$12.00 per year membership

Marshall County Genealogical and Historical Society
(County Courthouse—location)
PO Box 373 (mailing address)
Benton, KY 42025
(502) 527-4749
E-mail: marcoky@vci.net
Clara Creason, Secretary
Hours: County Archives: Mon & Wed–Thur 9:00–3:00
Pub. *Marshall County Genealogical and Historical Society Newsletter*, quarterly, $8.00 per year subscription
("Our organization 'mans' the County Archives.")
$10.00 per year membership

Mason County Historical Society
PO Box 13
Maysville, KY 41056
(606) 564-0900; (606) 564-7974 FAX
David Stumpf, President

Mason County Museum
215 Sutton Street
Maysville, KY 41056
(606) 564-5865; (606) 564-4372 FAX
http://www.trib.com/maysville
Sue Ellen Grannis, Curator
Hours: Apr–Dec: Mon–Sat 10:00–4:00;
   Jan–Mar: Tue–Sat 10:00–4:00
Pub. *Mason County Museum Newsletter*,
   quarterly
(extensive collection of family files)
$20.00 per year membership for
   individuals, $25.00 per year
   membership for families; research:
   $15.00 per hour

McCracken County Historical and Genealogical Society
(Paducah Public Library, 555
   Washington Street, Paducah, KY
   42003-1735—location)
PO Box 7651 (mailing address)
Paducah, KY 42002
(502) 442-2510 (Library); (502) 898-
   8168 (Past President's home)
Roy F. Olson, Jr., Past President
Hours: 8:00 A.M.–10:00 P.M.
Pub. *McCracken County, Kentucky,
   Newsletter*, several times per year
$10.00 per year membership (calendar
   year)

Metcalfe County Historical Society
Rt. 1, Box 371
Summer Shade, KY 42166
(502) 428-3391
Kay Harbison

Montgomery County Historical Society
30 East Main Street
PO Box 861
Montgomery, KY 40353
(606) 498-1413
Helene Perkins, President
Hours: Mon, Wed & Fri 11:00–3:00
$3.00 per year membership for
   individuals, $5.00 per year
   membership for families

Mount Washington Historical Society
PO Box 212
Mount Washington, KY 40047-0212
Mr. Smith
no research assistance, address
   genealogical queries to Bullitt County
   Genealogical Society

Nelson County Historical Society
The Jacob Rizer House
PO Box 743
Bardstown, KY 40004
(502) 348-8559
Dixie Hibbs, President
Pub. *The Nelson County Pioneer*,
   quarterly

(Nelson County records, mostly abstracts
   of official county clerk records since
   1785, formation date)
$10.00 per year membership

Northern Kentucky Heritage League
PO Box 104
Fort Mitchell, KY 41017

Northern Kentucky Historical Society, Inc.
PO Box 151
Fort Thomas, KY 41075-9998
(606) 441-7000
L. K. Patton, Past President

Ohio County Historical Society, Inc.
415 Mulberry Street
PO Box 44
Hartford, KY 42347
(502) 298-3177; (502) 298-7452
Dorothy Gentry, President; Anna Laura
   Duncan
Hours: Mon–Sun (Apr–Aug) 1:00–4:00
$10.00 per year membership

Owen County Historical Society
(Main Street—location)
PO Box 84 (mailing address)
Owenton, KY 40359
(502) 463-2633
E-mail: kmgibson@kih.net
Katie Gibson, President
Pub. *The Bulletin*, two times per year
$5.00 per year membership; search fees
   vary, including 15¢ per page copies
   and postage

Pendleton County Historical and Genealogical Society
Rt. 5, Box 280
Falmouth, KY 41040
Hours: meetings at the Public Library,
   Falmouth: third Sat 2:00
Pub. *Newsletter*, quarterly
$10.00 per year membership

Perry County Genealogical and Historical Society, Inc.
(Perry County Public Library—
   upstairs—location)
148 Chester Street (mailing address)
Hazard, KY 41701-1947
(606) 436-5829
Helen P. Horne, Editor and Treasurer
Hours: Library: Mon–Fri 8:00–5:00, Sat
   8:00–1:00
Pub. *Perry County Genealogical and
   Historical Society Newsletter*, three
   times per year (April, August,
   December)
$18.00 per year membership; research
   fees from Tabatha L. Farler, PO Box
   365, Happy, KY 41746

Pike County Society for Historical and Genealogical Research
PO Box 97
Pikeville, KY 41502

(606) 432-9371 (Library) (606) 432-4904
   (Ms. Warrix's home)
Connie Maddox, President; Sharon D.
   Warrix
Hours: Special Collections, Allara
   Library, Pikeville College: Mon–Fri
   noon–4:00, and by appointment
Pub. *Pike County Historical Review*,
   quarterly
(Pike County genealogy and local
   history)
$20.00 per year membership; free
   queries for members

Pulaski County Historical Society
Public Library Building
(107 North Main Street—location)
PO Box 36 (mailing address)
Somerset, KY 42501
(606) 679-8401
Jerri Brown, Office Manager
Hours: Tue–Sat 1:00–4:00
Pub. *Newsletter*, semiannually
$3.00 per year membership

Red River Historical Society
Main Street
PO Box 195
Clay City, KY 40312
(606) 663-2555
Hours: meetings at Red River History
   Museum, Clay City: third Thurs 7:00
(Powell County)

Rockcastle County Historical Society
Library—Ford Street
PO Box 698
Mount Vernon, KY 40456
(606) 256-2388 (Library); (606) 256-
   2397 (Home)
Juanita Witt, President; Geraldine
   Robbin, Librarian
Hours: Mon–Wed & Fri 10:00–5:00,
   Thur noon–8:00, Sat 10:00–4:00
Pub. *Rockcastle Reminiscence*, quarterly,
   $5.00 per year subscription (includes
   query)

Otto Rothert Historical Society
(Broad Street, Central City, KY 42330—
   location)
Rt. 1, Box 198-A (mailing address)
Drakesboro, KY 42337
Alexander Cather

Rowan County Historical Society
6770 U.S. Highway 60 E
Morehead, KY 40351-9035

The Russell County Historical Society
PO Box 544
Jamestown, KY 42629
Hours: meetings in the community room
   of Jamestown Public Library: first
   Mon 6:30
Pub. *Newsletter*, quarterly
$10.00 per year membership for
   individuals, $15.00 per year
   membership for families

Shelby County Historical Society
PO Box 444
Shelbyville, KY 40066-0444
Pub. *Shelby County Historical Society Newsletter*, approximately six times per year
$15.00 per year membership

Simpson County Historical Society, Inc.
Simpson County Archives and Museum
206 North College Street
Franklin, KY 42134
(502) 586-4228
Sue F. Groves Cooper, Director
Hours: Archives: Mon–Fri 9:00–4:00, Sat by appointment
Pub. *Jailhouse Journal*, quarterly (January, April, July, October)
(repository for Simpson County court records, genealogical library, some Tennessee)
$10.00 per year membership for individuals, $15.00 per year membership for families; research by mail: $5.00 plus SASE plus copying and postage

South Central Kentucky Historical/ Genealogical Society
PO Box 157
Glasgow, KY 42142-0157
Martha P. Reneau, Editor
Pub. *Traces*, quarterly
(historical, genealogical, Bible records, new book reviews)
$10.00 per year membership

Southern Kentucky Past Finders
1095 Sportsman Club Road
Russellville, KY 42276
(502) 726-6604
David Guion
Hours: Meetings at Logan County Public Library: third Tue (odd-numbered months)
(historical research, archeology, Civil War)
$10.00 per year membership

Taylor County Historical Social
204 North Columbia
PO Box 14
Campbellsville, KY 42719
(502) 465-3400 (not at location)
Gwynette Sullivan, Vice President
Hours: by appointment only
Pub. *Central Kentucky Researcher*, quarterly
$10.00 per year membership (calendar year)

Trimble County Historical Society
Rt. 1, Box 127A
Pendleton, KY 40055-9511
Violet Jennings, President
Hours: monthly meeting third Sat (Apr–Nov) 1:30
$5.00 per year membership

University of Louisville
University Photographic Archives
Louisville, KY 40292
(502) 588-6752

Van Lear Historical Society
PO Box 12
Van Lear, KY 41265

Wayne County Historical Society
PO Box 320
Monticello, KY 42633
Pub. *Overview*, quarterly
$15.00 per year membership

Webster County Genealogical and Historical Society
(Webster County Courthouse—location)
PO Box 215 (mailing address)
Dixon, KY 42409
(502) 639-5170
http://www.dsenter.com/-cpalmer/index.htm
Betty J. Branson, Editor and Corresponding Secretary
Hours: Wed–Fri 1:00–4:00
Pub. *Webster's Wagon Wheel*, quarterly
$10.00 per year membership

The Wise County Historical Society
The Appalachian Quarterly
(see Virginia)

Woodford County Historical Society
121 Rose Hill
Versailles, KY 40383
(606) 873-6786
Hours: Tue–Sat 9:00–4:00
Pub. *Woodford Heritage News*, quarterly
$10.00 per year membership

LDS Family History Centers

Lexington
(606) 269-2722

Louisville
(502) 426-8174

Genealogical Societies

State Genealogical Society

Kentucky Genealogical Society, Inc.
PO Box 153
Frankfort, KY 40602
(502) 875-4452
http://members.aol.com/bdharney2
Hours: Research Room, Kentucky State Archives: Tue–Sat (except Sat immediately preceding or following state holidays) 8:00–4:00

Pub. *Bluegrass Roots*, quarterly
(three million entries in Kentucky Genealogical Index)
$15.00 per year membership

Regional Genealogical Societies

Adair County Genealogical Society
(Adair County Public Library, 307 Greensburg Street—location)
PO Box 613 (mailing address)
Columbia, KY 42728
(502) 384-2472
Beverly A. England, President
Hours: Library: Mon, Wed & Fri 8:00–4:30, Tue & Thur 8:00–6:00, Sat 8:00–noon
Pub. *Adair County Review*, quarterly (spring, summer, fall, winter)
(marriage bonds, cemetery records, family folders, census records)
$10.00 per year membership

Ballard-Carlisle Historical-Genealogical Society
PO Box 279
Wickliffe, KY 42087
(502) 628-3468
E-mail: ccscotts@apex.net
http://www.ballardconet.com/bchgs/ (see also http://www.ballardconet.com/genweb/carlisle.html and http://www.ballardconet.com/genweb/ballard.html)
Joe K. Scott, President
Hours: meetings: second Sun (except Dec) 2:00
Pub. *The Root Diggers*, semiannually (March and August)
(books, newspapers, microfilm, pictures, and private papers housed in the genealogy section of the Ballard-Carlisle-Livingston Public Library)
$10.00 per year membership for individuals, libraries or organizations (calendar year), $12.00 per year membership for families; free queries to Lois M. Scott, Corresponding Secretary or via E-mail

Bicentennial Heritage Corporation
148 Wolford Street
Liberty, KY 42539
(606) 787-6194; (606) 787-9381 (Library); (606) 787-7720 FAX (Library)
Gladys Cotham Thomas, President
Hours: Casey County Public Library: Mon–Thur & Fri 10:00–6:00, Sat 9:00–3:00; meetings: fourth Mon (Mar, Apr, May, Jun, Oct, Nov)
Pub. *Casey County, Ky. Kinfolk*, quarterly
$10.00 per year membership

Big Sandy Valley Genealogical Society
1215 Stafford Avenue
Paintsville, KY 41240
(606) 789-3416

Boyle County Genealogical Association
321 Springhill Drive
Danville, KY 40422
Kathryn Roller
Pub. *Danville Constitution*
$7.00 per year membership

The Breathitt County Historical and Genealogical Society
121 Turner Drive
Jackson, KY 41339
Hours: meetings in the Breathitt Public Library: third Mon 7:00
Pub. *The Record*, quarterly
Dues $7.00 per year membership

Breathitt County Genealogical Society
Breathitt County Public Library
1024 College Avenue
Jackson, KY 41339
Pub. *Looking for Leads*, semiannually

Bullitt County Genealogical Society
(Ridgway Memorial Library on Walnut Street, just south of the courthouse annex—location)
PO Box 960 (mailing address)
Shepherdsville, KY 40165-9998
(502) 538-6428; (502) 538-8743
Doris C. Owen, President
Hours: Library: Mon–Sat 9:00–5:00, Tue 5:00–7:00; meetings third Thur 7:45
Pub. *Wilderness Road*, quarterly
(county records and family charts; "We are dedicated to preserving our history and helping others.")
$15.00 per year membership

Butler County Historical and Genealogical Society, Inc.
PO Box 435
Morgantown, KY 42261
(502) 526-5290 (Secretary)
Lois Russ, Editor; Christine Coleman, Secretary-Treasurer
Hours: Butler County Library: 9:00–4:00
Pub. *Kentucky Traces*, quarterly, $2.00 per issue
$6.00 per year membership

Campbell County Historical and Genealogical Society
19 East Main Street
Alexandria, KY 41001
(606) 635-6417
Hours: meetings: second Thur 7:30
Pub. *Campbell County History News*
$8.00 per year membership

Christian County Genealogical Society
1101 Bethel Street
Hopkinsville, KY 42240
(502) 887-4262
D. D. Cayce, President
Hours: 11:00–8:00
Pub. *Tree Builders*, quarterly
$11.00 per year membership

Clay County Genealogical and Historical Society
PO Box 394
Manchester, KY 40962
Pub. *Clay County Ancestral News*, quarterly
$15.00 per year membership

Corbin Genealogy Society
McBurney Building, Barbourville Street
PO Box 353
Corbin, KY 40701
(606) 878-8074 (President)
Carol Pace, President
Hours: by appointment only
Pub. *Our Heritage*, quarterly
(Knox, Laurel and Whitley counties)
$15.00 per year membership

Eastern Kentucky Genealogical Society
PO Box 1544
Ashland, KY 41105-1544
(606) 329-0090 (Library)
James C. Powers, Corresponding Secretary
Hours: Minnie Winder Genealogical and Local History Collection, Boyd County Public Library: Mon–Thur 10:00–8:30, Fri 10:00–5:30, Sat 10:00–5:00, Sun 1:00–5:00
Pub. *Treeshaker*, quarterly
$6.00 per year membership

Estill County Historical and Genealogical Society
PO Box 221
Ravenna, KY 40472-0221
Hours: meetings at the Estill County Public Library, Irvine: first Tue (except Jul) 7:00
Pub. *Estill County Historical and Genealogical Society Newsletter*, eleven times per year
$10.00 per year membership

Fayette County (KY) Genealogical Society
PO Box 8113
Lexington, KY 40533-8113
(606) 278-9966
Melvin E. Hurst, Editor
Pub. *The Fayette County (KY) Genealogical Society Quarterly* (March, June, September, December), $3.00 per issue
(includes area which was in Fayette County when it was formed in 1780 from Kentucky County, Virginia)

$10.00 per year membership for individuals, $15.00 per year membership for families, $200.00 life membership; 50-word queries accepted from members only

Floyd County Historical and Genealogical Society
PO Box 982
Prestonsburg, KY 41653
Hours: meetings in the Floyd County Library conference room: third Mon 7:00
$20.00 per year membership

Fulton County Genealogical Society
PO Box 1031
Fulton, KY 42041-1031
E-mail: fultonlib@kih.net
Elaine Allen, President
Hours: Fulton Public Library: Tue 10:30–5:00 & 6:00–8:00, Fri–Sat 9:00–11:30 & 12:30–5:00
Pub. *Fulton-Hickman County Journal*, semiannually
$10.00 per year membership

Graves County Genealogical Society
PO Box 245
Mayfield, KY 42006
Pub. *Journey into the Past*, semiannually
$10.00 per year membership

Genealogical Society of Hancock County, Kentucky
(Old Court House, Third Floor—location)
PO Box 667 (mailing address)
Hawesville, KY 42348
(502) 927-8095
E-mail: archives@juno.com
Dorothy Watkins, President; George Gibbs, Editor and Archivist
Hours: Mon–Fri 8:00–4:00
Pub. *Forgotten Pathways of Hancock County Kentucky*, quarterly
(marriage books of Hancock County)
$10.00 per year membership; research fee: $4.50 per hour, half-hour minimum, plus copies at 15¢ each

Harlan Heritage Seekers
PO Box 853
Harlan, KY 40831
Pub. *Harlan Mountain Roots*, quarterly
$15.00 per year membership

Henderson County Genealogical and Historical Society, Inc.
(1041 Fourth Street—location)
PO Box 303 (mailing address)
Henderson, KY 42420-0303
(502) 830-7514
E-mail: netta@hcc-uky.campus.mci.net
http://www.comsource.net/~kyseeker/index/html
Netta Mullin, First Vice President
Hours: meeting at Henderson County Public Library, Multi-Purpose Room: first Thur 7:00

Pub. *The Legacy*, quarterly (March, June, September, December), $3.00 per issue

$12.00 per year membership for individuals (calendar year); research: $15.00 per hour plus copies at 20¢ per page

Hopkins County Genealogical Society, Inc.

(Madisonville-Hopkins County Public Library—location)
PO Box 51 (mailing address)
Madisonville, KY 42431
Debbie Hammonds, Corresponding Secretary
Hours: inquire
Pub. *Yesterday's Tuckaways*, quarterly
$15.00 per year (calendar year)

Jefferson County Genealogical and Historical Society

PO Box 960
Shepherdsville, KY 40165-0960
Pub. *Jefferson County Genealogical and Historical Society Quarterly* (July, October, January, April)
$10.00 per year membership (beginning in June)

Knox County Genealogical Society

2603 Aintree Way
Louisville, KY 40220
(502) 459-8718
Maxine Humfleet Jones, President
Hours: by appointment
Pub. *Knox County Kentucky Kinfolk*, quarterly
$15.00 per year membership for individuals, $10.00 per year membership for senior citizens (65 or older)

KYOWVA Genealogical Society

(see West Virginia)

Letcher County Historical and Genealogical Society

PO Box 312
Whitesburg, KY 41858
Hours: meetings at the Harry M. Caudill Memorial Library, Whitesburg: second Tue 5:30
Pub. *Newsletter*
$12.00 per year membership

Louisville Genealogical Society

(Church of Jesus Christ of Latter-day Saints, Hurstbourne Lane and Linn Station Road—location)
PO Box 5164 (mailing address)
Louisville, KY 40205-0164
(502) 894-0629
Philip A. Wagner, Jr., Treasurer
Hours: second & fourth Tue 1:00, second Thur 7:30 P.M.

Pub. *Lines-and-By-Lines*, quarterly
$12.00 per year membership for individuals (beginning in January), $15.00 per year membership for families

Marshall County Genealogical and Historical Society

(County Courthouse—location)
PO Box 373 (mailing address)
Benton, KY 42025
(502) 527-4749
E-mail: marcoky@vci.net
Clara Creason, Secretary
Hours: County Archives: Mon & Wed–Thur 9:00–3:00
Pub. *Marshall County Genealogical and Historical Society Newsletter*, quarterly, $8.00 per year subscription ("Our organization 'mans' the County Archives.")
$10.00 per year membership

Mason County Genealogical Society

PO Box 266
Maysville, KY 41056
(606) 759-7257; (606) 759-5370 FAX
E-mail:eryan@May–uky.campus.mci.net
Edith Ryan, Corresponding Secretary
Hours: anytime; meetings at 8031 Day Pike, Maysville, KY 41056: first Mon 7:00
Pub. *Mason County Genealogical Society Newsletter*, quarterly
$10.00 per year membership

McCracken County Historical and Genealogical Society

(Paducah Public Library, 555 Washington Street, Paducah, KY 42003-1735—location)
PO Box 7651 (mailing address)
Paducah, KY 42002
(502) 442-2510 (Library); (502) 898-8168 (Past President's home)
Roy F. Olson, Jr., Past President
Hours: 8:00 A.M.–10:00 P.M.
Pub. *McCracken County, Kentucky, Newsletter*, several times per year
$10.00 per year membership (calendar year)

Muhlenberg County Genealogical Society

PO Box 758
Greenville, KY 42345
(502) 338-3713; (502) 338-5388 (Library)
Carol Brown, President
Hours: Muhlenberg County Public Libraries, Genealogy and Local History Annex: Mon 9:00–8:00, Tue–Fri 9:00–5:00, Sat 9:00–1:00
Pub. *The Heritage*, quarterly
$10.00 per year membership (calendar year)

Nelson County Genealogical Roundtable

(Nelson County Public Library, 90 Court Square—location)
PO Box 409 (mailing address)
Bardstown, KY 40004-0409
(502) 348-3714
Pub. *The Genealogist*, quarterly
$10.00 per year membership

Pendleton County Historical and Genealogical Society

Rt. 5, Box 280
Falmouth, KY 41040
Hours: meetings at the Public Library, Falmouth: third Sat 2:00
Pub. *Newsletter*, quarterly
$10.00 per year membership

Perry County Genealogical and Historical Society, Inc.

(Perry County Public Library—upstairs—location)
148 Chester Street (mailing address)
Hazard, KY 41701-1947
(606) 436-5829
Helen P. Horne, Editor and Treasurer
Hours: Library: Mon–Fri 8:00–5:00, Sat 8:00–1:00
Pub. *Perry County Genealogical and Historical Society Newsletter*, three times per year (April, August, December)
$18.00 per year membership; research fees from Tabatha L. Farler, PO Box 365, Happy, KY 41746

Pike County Society for Historical and Genealogical Research

PO Box 97
Pikeville, KY 41502
(606) 432-9371 (Library) (606) 432-4904 (Ms. Warrix's home)
Connie Maddox, President; Sharon D. Warrix
Hours: Special Collections, Allara Library, Pikeville College: Mon–Fri noon–4:00, and by appointment
Pub. *Pike County Historical Review*, quarterly
(Pike County genealogy and local history)
$20.00 per year membership; free queries for members

Scott County Genealogical Society

Scott County Public Library
230 East Main
Georgetown, KY 40324
(502) 863-3566 (Library)
Doris B. Reed, President
Hours: Library: Mon–Thur 10:00–8:00, Fri 10:00–5:30, Sat 9:00–5:30
Pub. *Scott County Genealogical Society Newsletter*, quarterly
$10.00 per year membership

South Central Kentucky Historical/ Genealogical Society

PO Box 157
Glasgow, KY 42142-0157
Martha P. Reneau, Editor
Pub. *Traces*, quarterly
(historical, genealogical, Bible records, new book reviews)
$10.00 per year membership

South Kentucky Genealogical Society

Rt. 1, Box 3332
Franklin, KY 42134

Southern Kentucky Genealogical Society

PO Box 1782
Bowling Green, KY 42102-1782
(502) 843-9452
Betty Lyne, Corresponding Secretary
Hours: Kentucky Library: Mon–Fri 8:00–4:30, Sat 9:00–4:30
Pub. *The Longhunter*, quarterly
$15.00 per year membership

Tri-State Genealogical Society

(see Indiana)

Tug Valley Genealogical Society (Ky.-W.Va.)

PO Box 2676
South Williamson, KY 41503
(606) 237-4646
O. T. Atkins
Pub. *Tug Valley Heritage*, biannually
$20.00 per year membership

Webster County Genealogical and Historical Society

(Webster County Courthouse—location)
PO Box 215 (mailing address)
Dixon, KY 42409
(502) 639-5170
http://www.dsenter.com/-cpalmer/index.htm
Betty J. Branson, Editor and Corresponding Secretary
Hours: Wed–Fri 1:00–4:00
Pub. *Webster's Wagon Wheel*, quarterly
$10.00 per year membership

West-Central Kentucky Family Research Association

(722 Harvard Drive—Library-Workroom location)
PO Box 1932 (mailing address)
Owensboro, KY 42302
(502) 684-4150
Margaret Alford, *The Bulletin* Editor; Diane Morris, *Kentucky Family Records* Editor
Hours: Kentucky Room, Owensboro-Daviess County Public Library: Mon–Fri 9:00–12:00 & 1:00–9:00, Sat 9:00–12:00 & 1:00–6:00, Sun 2:00–5:00; Library-Workroom: Wed 9:00–noon, and by appointment

Pub. *The Bulletin*, quarterly; *Kentucky Family Records*, quarterly
$15.00 per year membership (calendar year)

Independent Publications and Miscellany

Alice Lloyd College Library— Special Collections

Appalachian Oral History Project
Pippa Passes, KY 41844
(606) 368-2101, ext. 7001
Tom Graham, Assistant Library Director
Hours: Mon–Fri 8:00–4:30, Sun 5:00–9:30
(Special Collections and Appalachian Oral History Project mostly deal with the history of the southeast Kentucky region)

Appalachian Roots

(see West Virginia)

Steven A. Birchfield Publications

3201 Hardmoney Road
Paducah, KY 42003-1058
(502) 554-9579
Steven A. Birchfield
Hours: 9:00–9:00
(specializes in McCracken County cemeteries and funeral home records)

Certified Genealogist

2400 Lysle Lane
Norwood, OH 45212-1222
Sandra Evans Smith, C.G.
(author specializing in genealogical and historical books and articles on Kentucky and East Tennessee)

The East Kentuckian

305 Albany Road
Lexington, KY 40503-2625
(606) 277-4569
Clayton R. Cox, Owner
Pub. *The East Kentuckian: A Journal of Genealogy and History*, quarterly (March, June, September, December), $10.00 per year subscription

Genealogical Institute

(see Virginia)

Historic Middletown, Inc.

PO Box 43013
Middletown, KY 40245
Blaine A. Guthrie, Jr.
Hours: Sun 1:00–3:00
(a small group concerned with the history of the Middletown area)

Hunting for Bears Genealogical and Historical Society

(see Alabama)

Kentucky Cabinet for Economic Development

Map Sales
133 Holmes Street
Frankfort, KY 40601
(502) 564-4715; (502) 564-4083 FAX
Jeff Rarden, Office Supervisor
Hours: Mon–Fri 8:00–4:00
Pub. *Kentucky Deskbook of Economic Statistics*, annually, $17.00 postpaid per issue
(source for state-made county and city maps, river charts, fishing maps, community profiles and brochures and geologic publications regarding minerals, coal, water and oil and gas and recreational type maps, as well as the Geological Quadrangle maps)

Kentucky Civil War, Confederate States of America, Orphan Brigade

E-mail: orphans1@mc.net; walden@octagon.tacom.army.mil
http://bl-12.rootsweb.com/~orphanhm/

Kentucky Explorer

PO Box 227
Jackson, KY 41339
(606) 666-5060; (606) 666-7018
E-mail: kyexgen@harold.eastky.com
http://www.win.net/kyexmag/KEhome.html

Kentucky Genealogy and History News

Rt. 3, Box 65
Chandler, OK 74834-8504
R. D. Bradshaw, Editor
Pub. *Kentucky Genealogy and History News*, semiannually, $15.00 per year subscription

Kentucky Oral History Commission

300 Coffee Tree Road
PO Box 537
Frankfort, KY 40602-0537
(502) 564-7644
Kim Lady Smith, Executive Director
Pub. *Oral History in Kentucky*

Kentucky Tree-Search

PO Box 22621
Lexington, KY 40522
Gwendolyn G. Tippie, Editor
Pub. *Kentucky Kinfolk*, quarterly, $17.00 per year subscription

Kin Hunters Genealogical Publications and Research

PO Box 151
Russellville, KY 42276-0151
Montgomery Vanderpool
Pub. *Kin Hunters*, quarterly (January, April, July, October), $16.00 for four-issue subscription, $30.00 for eight-issue subscription
(Logan, Todd, Simpson, Butler, Warren and Muhlenberg counties)
free queries

KyGenWeb
Part of U.S. GenWeb Project
E-mail: ky@usgenweb.com
http://www.rootsweb.com/~kygenweb/
(links to other Kentucky resources)

Lexington Cemetery Company, Inc.
833 West Main Street
Lexington, KY 40508-2094
(606) 255-5522
Daniel R. Scalf, General Manager
Hours: Mon–Sat 8:00–4:00, Sun 1:00–
4:00
(over 60,000 interments)
search fee depends on research time

Military Records and Research Branch
Kentucky Department of Military Affairs
Division of Veterans Affairs
1121 Louisville Road
Frankfort, KY 40601-6169
(502) 564-4883; (502) 564-4437 FAX
C. L. McDaniels, Manager
Hours: 8:30–4:30
no charge

The Mountain Empire Genealogical Quarterly
(see Virginia)

Mountain Press
(see Tennessee)

Name Game Enterprises
Tennessee and Kentucky Queries
(see Tennessee)

Old News from Kentucky
PO Box 1164
Madisonville, KY 42431
Pub. *Old News from Kentucky*, quarterly

Reppert Publications
Antique and Collectible News
(see Illinois)

Silent Footsteps
306 Sequoia Drive
Leitchfield, KY 42754
Pub. *Silent Footsteps*, quarterly, $8.00
per year subscription

Simmons Historical Publications
(2015 SR 2192, near Metser, Boaz, KY
42027—location)
PO Box 66 (mailing address)
Melber, KY 42069-0066
(502) 856-3552
Don Simmons, Owner
(publishes books on genealogical
records, deeds, wills, marriage records,
etc., from Kentucky, North Carolina,
Tennessee and Virginia)

Virginia Settlers
(see Virginia)

LOUISIANA

Archives and Libraries with Holdings in Genealogy

State Archives and Library

Le Comité des Archives de la Louisiane
PO Box 44370, Capitol Station
Baton Rouge, LA 70804
(504) 355-9906; (504) 387-4264
(President)
Judy Riffel, Treasurer and Editor
Pub. *Le Raconteur*, three times per year,
$15.00 per year (plus $2.00 after
March 1) subscription

Louisiana Archives and Manuscripts Association
PO Box 51213
New Orleans, LA 70151-1213
http://home.gnofn.org/~nopl/links/
archives/lama.htm
Pub. *Newsletter*

State Archives and Records
Office of the Secretary of State
3851 Essen Lane
PO Box 94125
Baton Rouge, LA 70804-9125
(504) 922-1207
http://www.sec.state.la.us/arch-1.htm
Selena A. Baker, Archivist
Hours: Mon–Fri 8:00–4:30, Sat 9:00–
5:00, Sun 1:00–5:00

State Library of Louisiana
760 North Third Street
PO Box 131
Baton Rouge, LA 70821-0131
(504) 342-4914
E-mail: ladept@pelican.state.lib.la.us
http://smt.state.lib.la.us/statelib.htm
Judith D. Smith, Head, Louisiana Section
Hours: Mon–Fri 8:00–4:30
Pub. *Searching for Your Ancestors . . .
And all that jazz*, biannually (every
two years), free (available on
homepage)
photocopies: 25¢ per page

State Historical Societies

Louisiana Genealogical and Historical Society
PO Box 82060
Baton Rouge, LA 70884-2060
Nell T. Boersma, Editor; Jane G. Aprill,
President
Pub. *The Louisiana Genealogical
Register*, quarterly
$25.00 per year membership

Louisiana Historical Society
Maritime Building
New Orleans, LA 70130
(504) 588-9044
Richard C. Bell, President
$10.00 per year membership

City, County and Regional Archives and Libraries

L. W. Anderson Genealogical Library
(see Mississippi)

Assumption Parish Library
104 Franklin Avenue
Napoleonville, LA 70390
(504) 369-7070
Mary G. Judice, Librarian
Hours: Mon & Wed–Thur 8:30–5:30,
Tue 8:30–7:00

Avoyelles Parish Library
104 North Washington Street
Marksville, LA 71351
(318) 253-7559; (318) 253-6361 FAX
Susan Guidry, Associate Librarian
Hours: Mon–Tue & Thur–Fri 8:00–5:00,
Wed 9:00–6:00, Sat 9:00–1:00

Beauregard Parish Library
Genealogical Resources
E-mail: jamey@beaulib.dtx.bet
http://www.beaulib.dtx.net/genie.htm

Centenary College of Louisiana
Magale Library, Cline Room
2911 Centenary Boulevard
Shreveport, LA 71104
Carolyn Garison, Collection
Development

East Baton Rouge Parish Library
Bluebonnet Regional Branch
9200 Bluebonnet Boulevard
Baton Rouge, LA 70810
(504) 763-2283
Hours: Mon–Thur 9:00–9:00, Fri–Sat
9:00–6:00, Sun 2:00–6:00
(covers all Southern states)

Gallier House Museum
820 Saint Louis Street
New Orleans, LA 70112-3416
Pub. *Gallier House Museum Quarterly*

Iberville Parish Library
1501 J. Gerald Berret Boulevard
PO Box 736
Plaquemine, LA 70764
(504) 687-4397; (504) 687-2520; (504)
344-6948

Jefferson Parish Library
3420 North Causeway Boulevard
PO Box 7490
Metairie, LA 70010
(504) 838-1100

Dianne Bordelon, Reference Librarian
Hours: Mon–Fri 9:00–8:00, Sat 9:00–
5:00

Lafayette Public Library
(301 West Congress Street, Lafayette,
LA 70501—location)
PO Box 3427
Lafayette, LA 70502
(318) 261-5787
Suzanne Pomerleau, Special Collections
Librarian
Hours: winter: Mon–Thur 9:00–9:00, Fri
9:00–6:00, Sat 9:00–5:00; summer:
Mon–Wed 9:00–7:00, Thur 9:00–9:00,
Fri 9:00–6:00, Sat 9:00–5:00

Lafourche Parish Public Library
303 West Fifth Street
Thibodaux, LA 70301
(504) 446-1163
Cathy Richard, Library Associate
Hours: Mon–Fri 9:00–4:00

Lasalle Parish Library
Highway 127
Jena, LA 71342
Gloria Rambo, Librarian
Hours: 8:30–5:00
(extensive genealogy, cemeteries,
marriages, death notices [local paper],
census, etc.)

Lincoln Parish Library
509 West Alabama
Ruston, LA 71270
(318) 255-1920
Marsha Clinton, Librarian
Hours: Mon–Fri 9:00–6:00

Louisiana State Museum
Louisiana Historical Center Library
(Old U.S. Mint, 400 Esplanade
Avenue—location)
751 Chartres Street (mailing address)
New Orleans, LA 70176
(504) 568-8214
Kathryn Page, Curator of Maps and
Manuscripts
Hours: Tue–Fri 9:00–5:00 by
appointment
(colonial Louisiana)

**Louisiana and Lower Mississippi
Valley Collections**
Special Collections, Hill Memorial
Library
Louisiana State University
Baton Rouge, LA 70803
(504) 388-6501; (504) 334-1695 FAX
E-mail: gmcmull@unix1.sncc.lsu.edu
http://www.lib.lsu.edu/special
Glenn L. McMullen, Curator
Hours: Mon–Fri 9:00–5:00, Sat 9:00–
1:00
(Louisiana and the Lower Mississippi
Valley, including Mississippi and
Arkansas; French-language manuscript
resources)
limited research, charges for copies

Louisiana State University
Middleton Library, Department of
Archives and Manuscripts
Room 202
Baton Rouge, LA 70803
(504) 388-2240

Louisiana State University—Eunice
LeDoux Library
PO Box 1129
Eunice, LA 70535
(318) 457-7311, ext. 64
Jean B. Forester
Hours: Mon–Thur 7:30–7:00, Fri 7:30–
5:00

**Louisiana State University—
Shreveport**
Noel Memorial Library
Archives and Special Collections
1 University Place
Shreveport, LA 71115-2399
(318) 797-5378; (318) 797-5156 FAX
E-mail: lstreet@pilot.lsus.edu
Laura B. Street, Acting Archivist
Hours: Mon–Tue & Thur–Fri 8:00–4:30,
Wed 8:00–9:00
(Louisiana and Northwest Louisiana
history

**Louisiana State University—
Shreveport**
Pioneer Heritage Center
1 University Place
Shreveport, LA 71115
(318) 797-5332; (318) 797-5237
E-mail: pilot1@iamerica.net
Marguerite R. Plummer, Director
Hours: by appointment
("A Regional History Museum; The
Pioneer Heritage Center has
transferred photographs and
documents to Noel Memorial
Library.")

**Louisiana State University—
Shreveport**
Red River Regional Studies Center
1 University Place
Shreveport, LA 71115
E-mail: pilot1@iamerica.net
Marguerite R. Plummer
Pub. *Red River Review*

Loyola University Library
6363 Saint Charles Avenue
New Orleans, LA 70118
(504) 865-3346

Military Library, Jackson Barracks
Building 53
New Orleans, LA 70146-0330
(504) 278-8241

The Historic New Orleans Collection
Williams Research Center
410 Chartres Street
New Orleans, LA 70130
(504) 598-7171; (504) 598-7168 FAX
http://www.hnoc.org

Hours: Tue–Sat 10:00–4:30
Pub. *The Historic New Orleans
Collection Quarterly*, no charge

New Orleans Public Library
Louisiana Division
219 Loyola Avenue, Third Floor
New Orleans, LA 70112-2044
(504) 596-2610; (504) 596-2609
http://home.gnofn.org/ nopl
Collin B. Hamer, Jr., Head, Louisiana
Division
Hours: Mon–Thur 10:00–6:00, Sat
11:00–5:00 (use of Special Collections
after 4:30 or anytime on Sat by
appointment only)
(all types of printed, manuscript, graphic,
and oral resources relating to the study
of Louisiana and its citizens; other
areas of interest include the
Mississippi River, the Gulf of Mexico,
and the South; is the official City
Archives of New Orleans and is also
the official repository for the pre-1928
records of the Civil Courts and the
pre-1932 records of the Criminal
Courts of Orleans Parish)
photocopies of exact references: $2.00
per page (limit of five items) plus
SASE; search services: from $1.00 to
$3.00 per name, maximum of ten
names per search (send SASE for
detailed list)

Nicholls State University Library
Thibodaux, LA 70310
(504) 466-8111

The Orleans Notarial Archives
Civil District Courts Building
421 Loyola Avenue
New Orleans, LA 70112
(504) 568-8577; (504) 568-8599
E-mail: skrnona@gnofn.org
Sally K. Reeves, Archivist
Hours: Mon–Fri 9:00–4:00
(notorial acts, New Orleans and
Louisiana and the south, from 1731 to
the present)

Ouachita Parish Public Library
1800 Stubbs Avenue
Monroe, LA 71201
(318) 327-1490
Miss Wheeler, Genealogy Department
Hours: Mon–Fri 9:00–5:30, Sat 9:00–
5:00, Sun 2:00–5:00
(strong Southern states collection)

Rapides Parish Library
Main Branch
411 Washington Street
Alexandria, LA 71301
(318) 442-1840
Wesley H. Saunders, Reference
Coordinator
Hours: Mon–Sat 9:00–6:00
(specializes in Louisiana history and
genealogy)

Saint James Parish Library
1879 West Main Street
Lutcher, LA 70071
(504) 869-3618
Sarah B. Byrd, Reference Librarian
Hours: Mon–Thur 8:30–6:00, Fri 8:30–
5:00, Sat 8:30–1:00

Saint John the Baptist Parish Library
1334 West Airline Highway
La Place, LA 70068-3721
(504) 652-6857
Michael Maurin, Reference
Hours: Mon–Thur 8:30–9:00, Fri–Sat
8:30–5:30

Saint Martin Parish Library
(201 Porter Street—location)
PO Box 79 (mailing address)
Saint Martinville, LA 70582
(318) 394-2207; (318) 394-2248 FAX
Jeanne Essemier
Hours: Mon–Thur 8:00–8:00, Fri–Sat
8:00–5:00

Shreve Memorial Library
424 Texas Street
PO Box 21523
Shreveport, LA 71120-1523
(318) 226-5890; (318) 226-4780 FAX
Julia Gahagan, Special Collections
Librarian
Hours: Mon–Thur 9:00–7:00, Mon–Thur
(Labor Day–Memorial Day) 9:00–
9:00, Fri–Sat 9:00–6:00, Sun 1:00–
5:00
(emphasis is on the South, also a
Louisiana Collection which is
primarily history)

Southeastern Lousiana University Library
Western Avenue
Hammond, LA 70402
(504) 549-2194

Tangipahoa Parish Library
739 West Oak
Amite, LA 70422
(504) 748-7151; (504) 748-5476
Hours: Mon–Fri 8:30–5:30, Sat 8:30–
3:00

Terrebonne Parish Public Library
Main Branch
424 Roussell Street
Houma, LA 70360
(504) 876-5864
Dorotha Horvath, Genealogical Assistant
Hours: Mon–Thur 9:00–8:00, Fri–Sat
9:00–5:00

Tulane University
Howard-Tilton Memorial Library
7001 Freret Street at Newcomb Place
New Orleans, LA 70118-5682
(504) 865-5685 (Manuscripts/Special
Collections); (504) 865-5643
(Louisiana Collection); (504) 865-
6773 (Louisiana Collection) FAX:

(504) 865-5605 (Reference); (504)
865-5681 (Latin American Archives)
E-mail:
meneray@mailhost.tcs.tulane.edu
(Special Collections Division);
lmiller@mailhost.tcs.tulane.edu
(Manuscripts Department)
http://www.tulane.edu
Leon C. Miller, Manuscripts; Joan
Caldwell, Louisiana Collection
Hours: General Library: Mon–Fri 8:30–
12:45, Sat 8:30–9:45, Sun 10:00–
12:45 during school session;
Manuscripts: Mon–Fri 8:30–5:00, Sat
9:00–1:00; Louisiana Collection:
Mon–Fri 8:30–5:00, Sat 1:00–5:00

University of New Orleans
Earl K. Long Library/Louisiana and
Special Collections
Lakefront Campus
New Orleans, LA 70148
(504) 280-6543
http://www.uno.edu/Welcome.shtml
Florence M. Jumonville, Head of
Louisiana and Special Collections
Hours: Louisiana and Special
Collections: Mon–Fri 8:00–4:30, Sat
(when classes are in session) 10:00–
4:00 (some collections available by
appointment only)
(specializes in Lutheran records, ethnic
groups of New Orleans, preservation
groups, Louisiana Supreme Court legal
archives, business records, Orleans
Parish School Board records, records
of civic organizations)

University of Southern Alabama
Gulf Coast Historical Review
(see Alabama)

The University of Southwestern Louisiana
Louisiana Room, Dupre Library
(302 East Saint Mary Boulevard,
Lafayette, LA 70503-2038—location)
PO Box 40199 (mailing address)
Lafayette, LA 70504-0199
(318) 482-6031; (318) 482-5841 FAX
E-mail: jsk8711@usl.edu
http://www.usl.edu/departments/library
Jean S. Kiesel, Louisiana Room
Librarian
Hours: Mon–Tue 7:30 A.M.–9:00 P.M.,
Wed–Fri 7:30–4:30, Sat 10:00–2:00
("We do not have the staff to do
genealogical research for patrons.")

Vernon Parish Library
301 East Courthouse Street
Leesville, LA 71446
(318) 239-2027; (800) 737-2231; (318)
238-0666 FAX
Hours: Mon, Wed, Fri & Sat 8:00–5:30,
Tue & Thur 8:00–7:30
(participates in interlibrary loan, will
only do simple search)

Washington Parish Library System
825 Free Street
Franklinton, LA 70438
(504) 839-5336 (Franklinton); (504) 735-
1961 (Bogalusa)
Veronica Westbrook, Circulation
(Franklinton); Alecia Applewhite,
Branch Assistant (Bogalusa)
Hours: Mon–Fri 10:00–5:00, Sat 10:00–
1:00 (Franklinton); Mon 10:00–6:00,
Tue–Fri 10:00–5:00, Sat 10:00–3:00
(Bogalusa)

Branch: **Bogalusa Branch**, c/o 304
Avenue F, Bogalusa, LA 70427

West Baton Rouge Parish Library
830 North Alexander
Port Allen, LA 70767
(504) 342-7920; (504) 342-7918 FAX
E-mail: pawbr1@unix1.sncc.lsu.edu
Hours: Mon, Wed & Fri 8:30–5:30, Tue
& Thur 8:30–8:00, Sat 9:00–5:00

Historical Societies— Local and Regional

The Alexandria Historical and Genealogical Library and Museum
503 Washington Street
PO Box 4133
Alexandria, LA 71301
(318) 487-8556
Gic Kraushaar, President and Museum
Director
Hours: Tue–Sat 10:00–4:00
$10.00 per year membership; free
admission

Allen Genealogical and Historical Society
PO Box 789
Kinder, LA 70648

Attakapas Historical Association
The University of Southwestern
Louisiana
PO Box 4-3010
Lafayette, LA 70504
(318) 231-6029
Glenn R. Conrad, Secretary-Treasurer
Pub. *Attakapas Gazette*, quarterly
$8.00 per year membership

Baton Rouge Genealogical and Historical Society
PO Box 80565, S.E. Station
Baton Rouge, LA 70895-0565
(504) 765-7369
Stella Williamson, President; Karen
Strawn, Editor
Hours: meetings third Sat 1:30 at East
Baton Rouge Parish Library,
Bluebonnet Regional Branch
Pub. *le Baton Rouge*, quarterly
$20.00 per year membership

Brimstone Historical Society and Museum
800 Picard Road
Sulphur, LA 70663
(318) 527-7142
Nell Pickens, Director
Hours: Mon–Fri 9:30–5:00
$10.00 per year membership for individuals, $20.00 per year membership for families, $50.00 per year Special membership, $100.00 per year Corporate membership, $1,000.00 life membership

Commission des Avoyelles, Inc.
PO Box 26
Hamburg, LA 71339
(318) 964-2675

De Soto Historical and Genealogical Society
PO Box 523
Mansfield, LA 71052
(318) 872-1591
Raymond E. Powell, Past President and Board Member
Hours: Mon–Fri 8:00–4:00
Pub. *De Soto Plume*, quarterly
$10.00 per year membership

East Ascension Genealogical and Historical Society
PO Box 1006
Gonzales, LA 70707-1006
(504) 644-4547; FAX (504) 647-2987
James M. Templeton, Jr., President
Pub. *Journal of the East Ascension Genealogical and Historical Society*, quarterly
$10.00 per year membership

Evangeline Genealogical and Historical Society
PO Box 664
Ville Platte, LA 70586
Ramona Smith, Treasurer
Hours: Mon–Fri 9:00–5:00, Sat 9:00–12:00
Pub. *La Voix des Prairies*, quarterly (emphasis on Louisiana and southwest genealogy)
$10.00 per year membership; free queries

Franklin Parish Genealogical and Historical Society
Rt. 4, Box 150
PO Box 84
Winnsboro, LA 71295

French Settlement Historical Society
PO Box 365
French Settlement, LA 70733
Mercy Lobell
Hours: Creole House Museum: Apr–Aug: Sun (except Mother's Day) 1:00–4:00; Sept–Mar: second Sun 1:00–4:00

Pub. *Newsletter*, quarterly
$5.00 per year membership; free admission to museum

Friends of Cabildo
701 Chartres Street
New Orleans, LA 70115
(504) 523-3939

German-Acadian Coast Historical and Genealogical Society
PO Box 517
Destrehan, LA 70047
Pub. *Les Voyageurs*, quarterly
$10.00 per year membership

Jackson Assembly, Inc.
PO Box 494
Jackson, LA 70748
(504) 634-7155

LaFourche Heritage Society
PO Box 913
Thibodaux, LA 70302-0913
Dorothy Naquin

Lasalle Art Association and Genealogical Association
Rt. 1, Box 234
Trout, LA 71371
(318) 992-6210
Louise DeMars Windham, Past President

Lincoln Parish Museum and Historical Society
609 North Vienna Street
PO Drawer F
Ruston, LA 71270
(318) 251-0018

Edward Livingston Historical Association
PO Box 67
Livingston, LA 70754
Pub. *E.L.H.A. Gram*, quarterly

Louisiana Historical Association
Center for Louisiana Studies
The University of Southwestern Louisiana
PO Box 40831, USL
Lafayette, LA 70504
(318) 231-6029
Pub. *Louisiana History*, quarterly, $18.00 per year subscription; *Louisiana History Newsletter*, quarterly

Madison Parish Historical Society, Inc.
400 North Mulberry Street
PO Box 268
Tallulah, LA 71284
(318) 574-3542
Glenn Booth, President
(genealogical records of Madison residents)
$15.00 per year membership for individuals, $50.00 per year Associate membership, $100.00 per year Patron membership, $1,000.00 per year Corporate membership

Natchitoches Genealogical and Historical Association
PO Box 1349
Natchitoches, LA 71458-1349
(318) 357-2235
E-mail: ngha@wolf.nat.k12.la.u
http://www.rootsweb.com/~lanatchi.htm
Theophile Scott, President
Hours: Mon–Fri 9:00–4:00, Sat 10:00–4:00
Pub. *Natchitoches Genealogists*, two times per year, $6.00 per issue
$15.00 per year membership

North Louisiana Historical Association
PO Box 6701
Shreveport, LA 71136-6701
(318) 797-5355; (318) 797-5122 FAX
E-mail: athompso@pilot.lsus.edu
Dr. Alan Thompson, Editor
Hours: Mon, Wed & Fri 10:00–11:00 & 1:00–3:00, Tue & Thur 9:00–noon & 1:00–3:00
Pub. *North Louisiana Historical Association Journal*, three times per year
$12.00 per year membership

River Road Historical Society
9999 River Road
PO Box 5
Destrehen, LA 70047
(504) 764-9315
Irene Tastet, Administrator
Hours: 9:30–4:00
Pub. *Le Communique*, quarterly

Saint Charles Avenue Association
5801 Saint Charles Avenue
New Orleans, LA 70115

Saint Tammany Historical Society, Inc.
Saint Tammany History Library
310 West 21st Avenue
Covington, LA 70433
(504) 893-6280; (504) 893-6281 FAX
John T. Hunley, Corresponding Secretary

Southeast Louisiana Historical Association
Southeastern Louisiana University
PO Box 789
Hammond, LA 70402
Pub. *Southeast Louisiana Historical Association Papers*, annually
$5.00 per year membership

Southern Historical Association
Tulane University
New Orleans, LA 70118
(504) 865-6201

Southern Studies Institute
Northwestern State University
Natchitoches, LA 71497
(318) 357-5507
E-mail: taylor@alpha.nsula.edu
Dr. Maxine Taylor

Pub. *Southern Studies Journal*, quarterly, $20.00 per year subscription

Terrebonne Historical and Cultural Society, Inc.
(Louisiana Highway 311 at Saint Charles Street—location)
PO Box 2095 (mailing address)
Houma, LA 70361
(504) 873-8832
Christian L. Olivier, Jr., President
Hours: Mon–Sun 10:00–4:00
Pub. *THCS Newsletter*, quarterly
$7.50 per year membership

West Baton Rouge Historical Association
845 North Jefferson
Port Allen, LA 70767
(504) 336-2422; (504) 336-2448 FAX
Roddey Peebles, Jr., Curator
Hours: Mon 10:00–4:30 by appointment, Tue–Sat 10:00–4:30
Pub. *Ecoutez*, bimonthly

West Feliciana Historical Society
PO Box 338
Saint Francisville, LA 70775
(504) 635-6330
("We do not do any genealogical work and have no records.")

LDS Family History Centers

Baton Rouge
(504) 769-8913

Metairie
(504) 885-3936

Shreveport
(318) 868-5169

Genealogical Societies

State Genealogical Society

Louisiana Genealogical and Historical Society
PO Box 82060
Baton Rouge, LA 70884-2060
Nell T. Boersma, Editor; Jane G. Aprill, President
Pub. *The Louisiana Genealogical Register*, quarterly
$25.00 per year membership

Regional Genealogical Societies

Alexandria Historical and Genealogical Library
503 Washington Street
Alexandria, LA 71301
Constance Henderson

Allen Genealogical and Historical Society
PO Box 789
Kinder, LA 70648

Ark-La-Tex Genealogical Association, Inc.
(see Arkansas)

Baton Rouge Genealogical and Historical Society
PO Box 80565, S.E. Station
Baton Rouge, LA 70895-0565
(504) 765-7369
Stella Williamson, President; Karen Strawn, Editor
Hours: meetings third Sat 1:30 at East Baton Rouge Parish Library, Bluebonnet Regional Branch
Pub. *le Baton Rouge*, quarterly
$20.00 per year membership

Central Louisiana Genealogical Society
PO Box 12206
Alexandria, LA 71315-2206
David Manning, President
Hours: meetings: first Sun 2:00–4:30
Pub. *Central Louisiana Genealogical Society Quarterly* (January, April, July, October)
(family charts, Bible records, original record abstracts)
$15.00 per year membership (calendar year); free 50-word queries for members, $2.50 for non-members

De Soto Historical and Genealogical Society
PO Box 523
Mansfield, LA 71052
(318) 872-1591
Raymond E. Powell, Past President and Board Member
Hours: Mon–Fri 8:00–4:00
Pub. *De Soto Plume*, quarterly
$10.00 per year membership

East Ascension Genealogical and Historical Society
PO Box 1006
Gonzales, LA 70707-1006
(504) 644-4547; FAX (504) 647-2987
James M. Templeton, Jr., President
Pub. *Journal of the East Ascension Genealogical and Historical Society*, quarterly
$10.00 per year membership

Evangeline Genealogical and Historical Society
PO Box 664
Ville Platte, LA 70586
Ramona Smith, Treasurer
Hours: Mon–Fri 9:00–5:00, Sat 9:00–12:00
Pub. *La Voix des Prairies*, quarterly (emphasis on Louisiana and southwest genealogy)
$10.00 per year membership; free queries

Franklin Parish Genealogical and Historical Society
Rt. 4, Box 150
PO Box 84
Winnsboro, LA 71295

Friends of Genealogy, Inc.
PO Box 17835
Shreveport, LA 71138-0835
(318) 424-7648; (318) 636-7798
E-mail: lhduffy@prysm.net
Laura H. Duffy, President; Janine J. Dunlap, Editor
Hours: 8:00–8:00
Pub. *The Journal*, quarterly
$15.00 per year membership; free queries to members and non-members

German-Acadian Coast Historical and Genealogical Society
PO Box 517
Destrehan, LA 70047
Pub. *Les Voyageurs*, quarterly
$10.00 per year membership

Jefferson Genealogical Society
PO Box 961
Metairie, LA 70004-0961
Dwight Duplessis, President
Pub. *Jefferson Genealogical Society Newsletter*, bimonthly
$10.00 per year membership for individuals, $15.00 per year membership for families; queries

Natchitoches Genealogical and Historical Association
PO Box 1349
Natchitoches, LA 71458-1349
(318) 357-2235
E-mail: ngha@wolf.nat.k12.la.u
http://www.rootsweb.com/ lanatchi.htm
Theophile Scott, President
Hours: Mon–Fri 9:00–4:00, Sat 10:00–4:00
Pub. *Natchitoches Genealogists*, two times per year, $6.00 per issue
$15.00 per year membership

Genealogical Research Society of New Orleans
PO Box 51791
New Orleans, LA 70151
(504) 488-1660
Pub. *New Orleans Genesis*, quarterly (January, April, July, October)
$25.00 per year membership

North Louisiana Genealogical Society
Lincoln Parish Library
509 West Alabama
Ruston, LA 71270
(318) 251-5030
Denise Hodge
Hours: Library: Mon–Fri 9:00–6:00
Pub. *North Louisiana Genealogical Journal*, quarterly
$15.00 per year membership for individuals, $8.00 per year membership for libraries

Ouachita Genealogical Society
221 Riverbend
West Monroe, LA 71291
Agatha Burkett

Plaquemines Parish Genealogical Society
203 Highway 23 South
Buras, LA 70041

Saint Bernard Genealogical Society, Inc.
PO Box 271
Chalmette, LA 70044
(504) 271-0896
Shirley C. Bourquard, C.G., Editor
Pub. *L'Heritage*, quarterly
$20.00 per year membership

Saint Tammany Genealogical Society
Rt. 4, Box 332
Covington, LA 70433
Brenda Martina

Southwest Louisiana Genealogical Society, Inc.
PO Box 5652
Lake Charles, LA 70606-5652
(318) 477-3087
Mrs. Pat Huffaker, President
Pub. *Kinfolks*, quarterly
$12.00 per year membership for individuals (calendar year), $17.00 per year membership for husband and wife, $22.00 per year Patron membership

Terrebonne Genealogical Society
PO Box 295, Station 2
Houma, LA 70360
E-mail: pchau@cajun.net
http://www.rootsweb.com/ laterreb/ laterreb.htm
Phil Cauvin, President; Jess Bergeron, Corresponding Secretary
Hours: Terrebonne Parish Library: Mon–Thur 9:00–7:00, Fri–Sat 9:00–5:00
Pub. *Terrebonne Life Lines*, monthly; *Terrebonne Genealogical Society Newsletter*, monthly
$20.00 per year membership

Vermilion Genealogical Society
PO Box 117
Abbeville, LA 70511-0117

(318) 893-1363 (Secretary's office); (318) 893-4965 (Secretary) FAX
Aline Meaux, President; Mary Broussard, Secretary
Hours: meetings bimonthly
Pub. *Echoes of the Past*, annually
$10.00 per year membership

West Baton Rouge Genealogical Society
PO Box 1126
Port Allen, LA 70767-1126
(504) 343-8417
Ann R. Newman, President
Hours: daily 9:00–4:00
Pub. *West Baton Rouge Genealogical Society Newsletter*, quarterly
$10.00 per year membership

Independent Publications and Miscellany

Acadian House Publishing
PO Box 52247
Lafayette, LA 70505
(318) 235-7919; (318) 235-8851; (318) 235-9925 FAX
Trent Angers, Publisher
Hours: Mon–Fri 8:00–5:00
Pub. *Acadiana Profile, the Magazine of the Cajun Country*, bimonthly, $17.00 six-issue subscription, $33.00 per twelve-issue subscription, $49.00 per eighteen-issue subscription, $65.00 per twenty-four issue subscription
(south Louisiana, "Cajun Country") free catalog available on request

Ancestor Research and Analysis
13727 North Amiss Road
Baton Rouge, LA 70810-5042
(504) 766-0140; (504) 766-3018
Danell Spillman and Barbara Comeaux Strickland, Owners
Hours: Mon–Sat 8:00–5:00

Comité Louisiane Française
2717 Massachusetts Avenue
Metairie, LA 70003
(504) 469-2555

Courier Publications
PO Box 1320
Winnfield, LA 71483-1320
Pub. *Louisiana State Courier*, quarterly, $20.00 per year subscription

Genealogical Institute
(see Virginia)

Genealogy Books and Consultation
(see Texas)

Genealogy West, Inc.
West Bank of the Mississippi River
5644 Abby Drive
New Orleans, LA 70131-3808
(504) 393-8565

Marjorie H. Lessentine, Query Chairman and Founder
Pub. *Genealogy West Newsletter*, ten times per year (monthly, September–May and July)
$10.00 per year membership for individuals, $15.00 per year membership for couples

Greater New Orleans Archivists
The Amistad Research Center
Tilton Memorial Hall, Tulane University
6823 Saint Charles Avenue
New Orleans, LA 70118-5698
(504) 865-5535
Rebecca Hankins, Newsletter Editor
Pub. *Greater New Orleans Archivists Newsletter*, three times per year (activities of New Orleans Area professional archivists and their institutions, not open to non-professionals)

Hunting for Bears Genealogical and Historical Society
(see Alabama)

J & W Publications
PO Box 19443
Shreveport, LA 71149-0443
(318) 686-5089
Wanda Head, Editor
Pub. *Claiborne Parish Trails* (north Louisiana), quarterly, $14.00 per year subscription

LaGenWeb
Part of U.S. GenWeb Project
E-mail: la@usgenweb.com
http://www.goldenbranches.com/la-state/
(links to other Louisiana resources)

Mountain Press
(see Tennessee)

Save Our Cemeteries, Inc.
2520 Prytania Street
New Orleans, LA 70130

Southern Genealogical Institute
9418 Shartel Drive
Shreveport, LA 71118

Southern Genealogist's Exchange Society
(see Florida)

Southwest Mississippi and the Boot
School Library, 7024 Morgan Road
Greenwell Springs, LA 70739
Serena Abbess Haymon, Editor and Genealogist
Pub. *Newsletter*
(publishes books on Mississippi and West Florida Parishes, Louisiana)

U.S. District Court
Boggs Building, 500 Camp Street
New Orleans, LA 70130
(504) 589-4471

MAINE

Archives and Libraries with Holdings in Genealogy

State Archives and Library

Maine State Archives
L.M.A. Building
State House Station, Number 84
Augusta, ME 04333-0084
(207) 287-5795; (207) 287-5739 FAX
E-mail: jbrown@saturn.caps.maine.edu
http://www.state.me.us/sos/arc/general/
    admin/mawww001.htm
Jeffrey Brown, Archivist
Hours: Mon–Fri 8:00–11:30 & 12:30–
    4:00
(Maine state government records, county
    court records)

Maine State Library
L.M.A. Building
State House Station, Number 64
Augusta, ME 04333
(207) 287-5600; (207) 287-5615 FAX
E-mail: slgnich@state.me.us;
    sldwhit@state.me.us
http://www.state.me.us/msl/mslhome.htm
Susan McCarthy, Reference Librarian
Hours: Mon–Fri 9:00–5:00, Sat (during
    school year) noon-5:00
(New England, Atlantic Canada)

Maine State Museum
L.M.A. Building
Augusta, ME 04333
(207) 289-2301
Paul E. Rivard, Director

State Historical Society

Maine Historical Society
485 Congress Street
Portland, ME 04101
(207) 774-1822
http://www.mainehistory.com
Nicholas Noyes, Librarian
Hours: Tue–Fri 10:00–4:00, second &
    fourth Sat (except holiday weekends)
    10:00–4:00
Pub. *Maine History*, quarterly
(New England and Maritimes)
$30.00 per year membership for
    individuals; $10.00 daily research fee,
    $25.00 for a four-day pass

City, County and Regional Archives and Libraries

Auburn Public Library
49 Spring Street (Court and Spring
    Streets)
Auburn, ME 04210
(207) 782-3191

Sarah Sabasteanski, Reference Librarian
Hours: winter: Mon & Thur 9:00–8:00,
    Tue–Wed & Fri 9:00–6:00, Sat 9:00–
    5:00; summer: Mon 9:00–8:00, Tue–
    Fri 9:00–6:00

Bangor Public Library
145 Harlow Street
Bangor, ME 04401
(207) 947-8336
Hours: winter: Mon–Thur 9:00–9:00,
    Fri–Sat 9:00–5:00; summer: Mon–
    Thur 9:00–7:00, Fri 9:00–5:00

L. C. Bates Museum of Good Will-Hinckley Homes
Hinckley Home-School-Farm
Route 201
Hinckley, ME 04944
(207) 453-4894 (Museum); (207) 453-
    7335 (School Office)
Deborah Staber, Museum Staff
Hours: Wed–Sat 10:00–4:30, Sun 1:00–
    4:30
Pub. *Beaver Paw Press*, four times per
    year (publication of Museum); *Good
    Will-Record*, four times per year
    (publication of Good Will-Hinckley
    Home Association)
(archives and library: material about
    Hinckley family and students who
    have attended Good Will-Hinckley
    School)
$10.00 per year membership for
    individuals

Belfast Museum, Inc.
6 Market Street
Belfast, ME 04915
Andrew Kuby, President
Hours: Thur & Sun (summer) 1:00–4:00
    by appointment
(Belfast history only)
donation

Burnham Tavern Museum
Hannah Weston Chapter, D.A.R.
(Main Street—location)
2 Free Street (mailing address)
Machias, ME 04654
(207) 255-4432
Valdine C. Atwood, Chairman
Hours: Mon–Fri (Jun–Oct) 9:00–5:00,
    and by appointment

Castine Scientific Society
(Wilson Museum, John Perkins House,
    The Blacksmith Shop, Hearse House,
    all on Perkins Street—location)
PO Box 196 (mailing address)
Castine, ME 04421
(207) 326-8753
Patricia Hutchins
Hours: Wilson Museum: Tue–Sun 2:00–
    5:00 (May 27–Sept 30); research by
    appointment only
Pub. *Wilson Museum Bulletin*, three
    times per year, $5.00 per year
    subscription

Connecticut Valley Historical Museum
(see Massachusetts)

Curtis Memorial Library
23 Pleasant Street
Brunswick, ME 04011-2295
(207) 725-5242
http://www.curtislibrary.com
Larua Bean, Reference Librarian
Hours: Mon–Wed 9:30–8:00, Thur–Fri
    9:30–6:00, Sat (winter) 9:30–5:00,
    Sat (summer) 9:30–1:00
(two leaflets for SASE: *Information
    Sources on Genealogy at Curtis
    Memorial Library* and *Brunswick
    History: A Guide to Basic Sources*)

Neal Dow Memorial
714 Congress Street
Portland, ME 04102
(207) 773-7773

Dyer Library Association
371 Main Street
Saco, ME 04072
(207) 283-3861
Caroline Pinkham, Administrative
    Assistant
Hours: Library: Tue & Thur 10:00–8:00,
    Wed & Fri 10:00–5:00; Historical
    Room: Tue 1:00–3:00, Thur 10:00–
    noon & 1:00–4:00, and by
    appointment
20¢ per photocopy, plus $2.50 shipping
    and handling

The Fishermen's Museum
(Pemaquid Point—location)
HC 61, Box 332 (mailing address)
New Harbor, ME 04554
(207) 677-2494; (207) 677-2726
Mary Norton Orrick, Director
Hours: Memorial Day–Columbus Day:
    weekdays 10:00–5:00, Sun 11:00–5:00
(artifacts, charts, old photographs,
    lighthouse memorabilia)

Friendship Museum, Inc.
Route 220
PO Box 321
Friendship, ME 04547
(207) 832-4221
Mary Carlson, Secretary
Hours: Mon–Sat 1:00–4:00, Sun (Jul–
    Aug) 2:00–4:00
(memorabilia of the town)
$5.00 per year membership for
    individuals, $8.00 per year
    membership for couples

Grand Banks Schooner Museum Trust
(100 Commercial Street, Boothbay
    Harbor, ME 04538—location)
PO Box 123 (mailing address)
Boothbay, ME 04537
(207) 633-4727
Robert Ryan, Director

Kennebunk Free Library
112 Main Street
Kennebunk, ME 04043
(207) 985-2173
Hours: Mon, Wed & Fri 1:00–8:00, Tue,
Thur & Sat 9:30–5:00
(has back copies of the local newspaper,
York County Coast Star)

Lewiston Public Library
200 Lisbon Street
Lewiston, ME 04240
(207) 784-0135; (207) 784-3011
E-mail: lleveill@avcnet.lpl.org
http://www.avcnet.lpl.org/lpl
Lizette R. Leveille, Reference Librarian
Hours: winter: Mon–Thur 9:00–8:00,
Fri–Sat 9:00–5:00; summer: Mon–
Thur 9:00–8:00, Fri 9:00–5:00, Sat
9:00–2:00
(Franklin Company Papers collection)

McArthur Library
270 Main Street
Biddeford, ME 04005
(207) 284-6841

Nylander Museum
393 Main Street
PO Box 1062
Caribou, ME 04736
(207) 493-4474; (207) 498-3098

Old Town Museum
(138 South Main Street—location)
PO Box 375 (mailing address)
Old Town, ME 04468
(207) 827-7256
William A. Osborne, Treasurer
Hours: 1:00–5:00

Patten Free Library in the Park
Sagadahoc History and Genealogy Room
33 Summer Street
Bath, ME 04530-2687
(207) 443-5141
Hours: History Room: Sept–Jun: Tue–
Sat noon-4:00, Sat 11:00–3:00; Jul–
Aug: Mon–Fri noon-4:00

Penobscot Marine Museum
Stephen Phillips Memorial Library
Church Street
PO Box 498
Searsport, ME 04974-0498
(207) 548-2529; (207) 548-2520
Robert D. Farwell, Director; Paige S.
Lilly, Librarian and Archivist
Hours: Apr–Nov: Mon–Fri 9:00–4:00;
Dec–Mar: Tue–Fri 9:00–4:00
Pub. *Bay Chronicle*
(genealogical materials)

Ruggles House Society
Columbia Falls, ME 04623
(207) 288-3597

**The Mark and Emily Turner
Memorial Library**
39 Second Street
Presque Isle, ME 04769

(207) 764-2571; (207) 768-5756 FAX
E-mail:
turner.memorial.library@msln.net
Marilyn Clark, Librarian
Hours: Mon–Thur 10:00-8:00, Fri 10:00–
5:30, Sat (winter) 10:00–4:00
(Presque Isle newspapers from 1853)
non-resident borrowers card: $15.00 for
individuals, $25.00 for families

United Society of Shakers
The Shaker Library at Sabbathday Lake
Route 26
New Gloucester, ME 04260
Poland Spring, ME 04274
(207) 926-4597
Anne Gilbert, Librarian/Archivist
Hours: Mon–Fri 8:30–4:30,
appointments preferred
Pub. *The Shaker Quarterly*, $4.00 per
issue, $15.00 per year subscription
(Shakers and other radical Christian
groups; Shaker manuscript collection;
Index Nominum of over 15,000 names
with biographical data; library
collection brochure available on
request)
$15.00 per year membership

University of Maine
Special Collections Department
5729 Fogler Library
Orono, ME 04469-5729
(207) 581-1686; (207) 581-1653 FAX
E-mail: muriels@ursus1.ursus.maine.edu
http://www.umaine.edu/;
http://libraries.maine.edu/umaine/
speccoll/speccol.htm

Walker Memorial Library
800 Main Street
Westbrook, ME 04092

Waterville Public Library
73 Elm Street
Waterville, ME 04901
(207) 873-4779
Richard Sibley, Librarian
Hours: Mon–Fri 9:00–9:00, Sat 9:00–
1:00 (closed Sat in summer)

York Institute Museum
375 Main Street
Saco, ME 04072
(207) 282-3031

Historical Societies— Local and Regional

**Alexander-Crawford Historical
Society**
216 Pokey Road
Alexander, ME 04694
(207) 454-7476
John Dudley, Archivist
Hours: by appointment

Pub. *A-CHS Newsletter*, quarterly
(Downeast Maine history and genealogy)
$5.00 per year membership

Andover Historical Society
Andover, ME 04216

Androscoggin Historical Society
(County Building—location)
2 Turner Street (mailing address)
Auburn, ME 04210-5978
(207) 784-0586
E-mail: itigapa@aol.com (Mr. Young)
http://www.rootsweb.com/~meandrhs
Michael Lord, Executive Secretary;
David Young
Hours: Wed–Fri 9:00–noon & 1:00–5:00
(except Fri till 4:00 in winter)
Pub. *Androscoggin History*, three to four
times per year
(genealogical resources)
$5.00 per year membership, $10.00 per
year Contributing membership, $50.00
life membership; search fee: $10.00
per hour after the first hour, plus
photocopies at 15¢ per page

Bangor Historical Society
Penobscot Heritage Museum of Living
History
159 Union Street
Bangor, ME 04401
(207) 942-5766
Susan Joy Sager, Executive Director
Hours: Tours: Tue–Fri noon–4:00 (call
for current hours)
(history of Bangor and the Penobscot
Valley Region; small library with
books, city directories, as well as
primary source material)
$25.00 per year membership for
individuals, $50.00 per year per
household, $100.00 per year
Contributing membership; research or
admission: donation

Bar Harbor Historical Society
34 Mount Desert Street
Bar Harbor, ME 04609
(207) 288-4245
Deborah M. Dyer, Curator
Hours: Mon–Sat 1:00–4:00 (15 Jun–1
Oct), after 1 Oct by appointment
Pub. *Newsletter*, quarterly
$10.00 per year membership for
individuals, $100.00 life membership

Bath Historical Society
Sagadahoc History and Genealogy Room
Patten Free Library in the Park
33 Summer Street
Bath, ME 04530-2687
(207) 443-5141; (207) 443-3514 FAX
Denise R. Larson, Manager
Hours: History Room: Tue–Sat noon–
4:00, Sat (Oct–May) noon–4:00
Pub. *The Bath Historical Society
Newsletter*, bimonthly; *The Times of
Bath*, three times per year

$20.00 per year membership for individuals, $30.00 per year membership for families, $10.00 per year membership for students, $50.00 per year membership for businesses, $100.00 per year Sponsor membership, $1,000.00 life membership; research: $10.00 per hour

Berwick Historical Society, Inc.
PO Box 904
Berwick, ME 03901-0904

Bethel Historical Society, Inc.
14 Broad Street
PO Box 12
Bethel, ME 04217-0012
(207) 824-2908; (800) 824-2910
Randall H. Bennett, Curator of Collections
Hours: Mon–Fri 1:00–4:00, and by appointment
Pub. *The Bethel Courier*, quarterly
(historical and genealogical data for western Maine and the White Mountain area of New Hampshire; *Guide to Research* available for SASE)
$10.00 per year membership for individuals, $5.00 per year membership for senior citizens, over 55 years

The Biddeford Historical Society
(McArthur Library, 270 Main Street—location)
PO Box 200 (mailing address)
Biddeford, ME 04005-0200
(207) 284-6841 (Library)
Charles L. Butler, Jr., Secretary and Genealogist
Hours: Thur 11:00–noon
Pub. *Annual Report* (April)
(a secondary depository for Biddeford records, 1653–1891)
$5.00 per year membership; research: donation

Border Historical Society
Barracks Museum
(74 Washington Street—location)
1 Capen Avenue (mailing address)
Eastport, ME 04631
Ruth McInnis, Board of Director
Hours: Jul–Aug: Tue–Sat 1:00–4:00
$5.00 per year membership

Bradford Heritage: Museum and Historical Society
(John B. Curtis Free Public Library, Main Street—location)
RR 1, Box 362 (mailing address)
Bradford, ME 04410
(207) 327-1246 (President)
Muriel S. Parker, President and Librarian
Hours: Sat 9:00–3:00, and by appointment

(Bradford history scrapbook, tax records from 1852, some vital records from 1860, news clipping scrapbooks, miscellaneous photos and documents)

Brewer Historical Society
199 Wilson Street
Brewer, ME 04412
(207) 989-7825

The Bridgton Historical Society
Gibbs Avenue Museum
PO Box 44
Bridgton, ME 04009-0044
(207) 647-3699
E-mail: bhs@megalink.net
Ned Allen, Executive Director
Hours: Jul–Aug: Tue–Fri 10:00–4:00; Sept–Jun: Tue & Thur 1:00–4:00, and by appointment
Pub. *Bridgton Historical Society Newsletter*, quarterly
(local history and genealogy; narrow gauge Bridgton & Saco River Railroad)
$10.00 per year membership for individuals; research $10.00 per hour

Bucksport Historical Society, Inc.
Main Street
Bucksport, ME 04416
(207) 469-2591

Bustins Island Historical Society
(Bustins Island, ME 04013—location)
PO Box 118 (mailing address)
South Freeport, ME 04078

Cherryfield-Narraguagus Historical Society
Main
PO Box 96
Cherryfield, ME 04622
Margery Brown, President
Pub. *Newsletter*, semiannually
$3.00 per year membership

China Historical Society
(Maine Street, China, ME 04330—location)
PO Box 245 (mailing address)
China, ME 04926

Cumberland Historical Society
Rt. 2, Box 479-A
Cumberland Center, ME 04021

Deer Isle-Stonington Historical Society
PO Box 464
Deer Isle, ME 04627

Dexter Historical Society
(Off Main Street, signs on Route 7—location)
PO Box 481 (mailing address)
Dexter, ME 04930
(207) 924-5721 (summer only); (207) 924-3043 (Ms. Feurtado)
Richard M. Whitney, Curator; Carol Feurtado

Hours: mid-Jun to mid-Sept: Mon–Fri 10:00–4:00, Sat 1:00–4:00
(much information on Dexter families)

Dover-Foxcroft Historical Society
Blacksmith Shop Museum
Chandler Road
Dover-Foxcroft, ME 04426
(207) 564-8618
Dave Lockwood, Curator
Hours: 8:00–5:00

East Machias Historical Society
PO Box 658
East Machias, ME 04654-0658

Ellsworth Historical Society
PO Box 355
Ellsworth, ME 04605

Fort Kent Historical Society
(Market Street—location)
PO Box 181
Fort Kent, ME 04743
(207) 834-3933
Annette Daigle, President
Hours: Mid-Jun to 31 Jul: 1:00–4:00

Frenchboro Historical Society and Museum
Frenchboro, ME 04635
(207) 334-2929
Vivian Lunt, President
Hours: 30 May–30 Sept: noon–7:00
Pub. *Newsletter*, semiannually
$5.00 per year membership

Greene Plantation Historical Society
(Belmont, ME—location)
Rt. 1, Box 2040 (mailing address)
Morrill, ME 04952-9729
(207) 342-5208
Isabel Morse Maresh, Secretary
Hours: by appointment
Pub. *Greene Plantation Newsletter*, monthly
(The society has a one-room schoolhouse at Greer's corner, but because of vandalism, holdings—genealogies, Waldo County census records, etc.— can be seen only by appointment at the secretary's house.)

Hampden Historical Society
(Kinsley House, 83 Main Road, South—location)
PO Box 456 (mailing address)
Hampden, ME 04444
Gary Mock, President; Alan Ritchie, Treasurer
Hours: Apr–Nov: Tue 10:00–4:00, and by appointment
Pub. *Newsletter*, monthly
(history of Hampden and surrounding towns)
$10.00 per year membership

Harpswell Historical Society
Rt. 1
South Harpswell, ME 04079

Hawthorne Community Association

Hawthorne Road
Raymond, ME 04077

Islesboro Historical Society

Main Road
PO Box 301
Islesboro, ME 04848
(207) 734-6733
Ms. Rowland Logan, Archivist
Hours: varies, summer only, by
    appointment
("We are a small volunteer organization
    . . . we do try to answer our mail—
    providing information if we can."

Jay Historical Society

Holmes-Crafts Homestead
(Jay Hill, Jay, ME—location)
Rt. 1, Box 3915 (mailing address)
Wilton, ME 04294
(207) 645-2723

The Kennebunkport Historical Society

(The School House, 125 North Street and
    The Nott House, 8 Maine Street—
    location)
PO Box 1173
Kennebunkport, ME 04046
(207) 967-2751; (207) 967-1205 FAX
Ellen Driscoll Moy, Executive Director
Hours: The School House: Wed–Fri
    10:00–4:00; The Nott House: mid-Jun
    to mid-Oct: Tue–Fri 1:00–4:00;
    Research: Thur–Fri afternoons, by
    appointment
Pub. *The Log*, quarterly
(Kennebunkport history, photograph
    collection)
$25.00 per year membership for
    individuals, $35.00 per year
    membership for families, $100.00 per
    year membership for businesses;
    search fee: free to members, $2.00 for
    non-members; The Nott House
    admission: $3.00; The School House
    admission: free

Knox Memorial Association

(High Street—location)
33 Knox Street (mailing address)
Thomaston, ME 04861
Mrs. L. French

Leeds Historical Commission

PO Box 1
North Leeds, ME 04263
Constance Buckley

Lewiston Historical Commission

36 Oak Street
Lewiston, ME 04240

L'Heritage-Vivant—Living Heritage

(The Acadian Village, 5 miles north of
    Van Buren—location)
PO Box 165 (mailing address)
Van Buren, ME 04785
(207) 868-2691; (207) 868-5042
    (summer)

Anne L. Roy, President
Hours: 15 June–15 Sept: noon–5:00
(sixteen buildings dating from 1800 to
    early 1900)

Lincoln County Cultural and Historical Association

Federal Street
PO Box 61
Wiscasset, ME 04578
(207) 882-6817

Lincolnville Historical Society and School House Museum

(Route 173, Lincolnville Beach—
    location)
PO Box 211 (mailing address)
Lincolnville Center, ME 04850
(207) 789-5445 (School House Museum,
    seasonal); (207) 763-4332 (Treasurer)
E-mail: loonmere@midcoast.com
http://www.booknotes/lhs
Peggy S. Bochkay, Treasurer
Hours: Jun–Oct: Mon–Fri noon–3:00,
    Sat–Sun 1:00–3:00
Pub. *L.H.S. Newsletter*, biannually
(very large photo collection of family
    members along with the genealogical
    background)
$5.00 per year membership for
    individuals; search fee: $10.00 plus
    costs

Stewart M. Lord Memorial Historical Society

c/o Cummings Health Care
PO Box 367
Howland, ME 04448-0367

Machiasport Historical Society

Machiasport, ME 04655
(207) 255-8461

Madawaska Historical Society

Library Building, Main Street
Madawaska, ME 04756
(207) 738-4272

Moosehead Historical Society

(Pritham Avenue—location)
PO Box 1116 (mailing address)
Greenville, ME 04441
(207) 695-2909
E-mail: eparker@moosehead.net
Everett L. Parker, Executive Director
Hours: Mar–Jun: 7:00–1:00; Jul–Sept:
    Wed–Fri 1:00–4:00
Pub. *Insight*, three times per year
(genealogy records, cemetery records)
$5.00 per year membership for
    individuals, $10.00 per year
    membership for families

Morrill Historical Society

(Morrill, ME 04952—location)
RR 1, Box 5845, Tufts Road (mailing
    address)
Belfast, ME 04915
(207) 338-1405; (207) 338-5383
    (President); (207) 338-1405
    (Secretary)

F. Eleanor Warner, President; Josephine
    Grady, Secretary

Mount Carmel Cultural and Historical Center

PO Box 155
L'Ille, ME 04749-0155

Mount Desert Island Historical Society

(1119 Main Street—location)
PO Box 653 (mailing address)
Mount Desert, ME 04660
(207) 288-3723
E-mail: jroths@acadia.net
Jaylene Roths, Director
Hours: 1 Jun–15 Oct: Tue–Sat 10:00–
    5:00
(primarily information on Somes family)
$10.00 per year membership for
    individuals

The New England Historic Genealogical Society

(see Massachusetts)

New Gloucester Historical Society

Cobb's Bridge Road
New Gloucester, ME 04260

New Sweden Historical Society

(Capitol Hill Road—location)
RR 1, Box 8 (mailing address)
New Sweden, ME 04762
(207) 896-3018; (207) 896-5841; (207)
    896-3120 FAX
Mabel E. Todd, Secretary
Hours: Tue–Sun 1:00–4:00, and by
    appointment
Pub. *Newsletter*, three times per year
(Swedish heritage artifacts of New
    Sweden)
$10.00 per year membership; admission:
    donation

North Yarmouth Historical Society

Old North Yarmouth Townhouse, 1853,
    Route 9
Cumberland Center, ME 04021
Hours: Archives: by appointment;
    monthly programs

Norway Historical Society

(232 Main Street—location)
PO Box 167 (mailing address)
Norway, ME 04268
(207) 743-7377
Irene B. Campbell, Curator
Hours: summer only
Pub. *Pennesseewassee Sketches*,
    irregularly
$5.00 per year membership for
    individuals, $50.00-$150.00 life
    membership

Old Berwick Historical Society

Corner of Main and Liberty Street
PO Box 296
South Berwick, ME 03908
(207) 384-8041; (207) 384-5162; (207)
    384-0000

Paul Colburn, President; Wendy Pirsig,
Archivist
Hours: Jul & Aug: Sat P.M., and by
appointment
(limited resource of local cemetery
inventories and a few family histories
and genealogies, but not professionally
oriented)

Old Carratunk Historical Society
PO Box 303
Bingham, ME 04920

Old York Historical Society
207 York Street
PO Box 312
York, ME 03909
(207) 363-4974
Virginia S. Spiller, Librarian
Hours: Thur–Fri 9:00–noon & 1:00–5:00
(local genealogies, manuscripts, 18th-
century Maine history)
free library use, research facilities only

Pejepscot Historical Society
159 Park Row
Brunswick, ME 04011
(207) 729-6606; (207) 729-6012 FAX
E-mail: phs@biddeford.com;
pejepscot@acornbbs.com
http://www.curtislibrary.com/
pejepscot.htm
Amy Poland, Curator; Erik C. Jorgensen,
Director
Hours: Research Room and Archives:
Mon–Fri 9:00–4:30, Sat (Jun–Sept)
9:00–4:30
Pub. *Cupola* (non-genealogical
newsletter), quarterly
(historical information on the Brunswick,
Topsham and Harpswell areas)
$15.00 per year membership for
individuals; research service: free for
members, $10.00 for non-members

Pemaquid Historical Association
Rt. 2, Box 4000-314
Damariscotta, ME 04543-9766

Phippsburg Historical Society, Inc.
(Phippsburg Center—location)
PO Box 21 (mailing address)
Phippsburg, ME 04562
Ada M. Haggett
Hours: 1:00–4:00

Rangeley Lakes Region Historical Society
PO Box 521
Rangeley, ME 04970

Raymond-Casco Historical Society
Casco, ME 04015
(207) 627-4220

Readfield Historical Society
(Route 17—location)
PO Box 354 (mailing address)
Readfield, ME 04355-0354
(207) 685-4424; (207) 685-9877
(President)

David Giroux, President
Hours: summer: one day a week 10:00–
3:00; and by appointment
Pub. *Newsletter*

Rumford Area Historical Society
Rumford Municipal Building
Congress Street
Rumford, ME 04276
Myrtle McKenna, Secretary/Historian
Hours: Thur 9:00–2:00
(histories of Rumford and surrounding
towns, some genealogy)

Sagadahoc Preservation, Inc.
804 Washington Street
PO Box 322
Bath, ME 04530

Sainte Agathe Historical Society
PO Box 237
Saint Agatha, ME 04772
(207) 543-6364
David Raymond, President
Hours: Mon (after Labor Day–15 Jun)
1:00–4:00, Tue–Sat 1:00–4:00
Pub. *Annual Newsletter*
(emphasis on local Saint John Valley,
Maine, genealogy and history)
$2.50 per year membership, $40.00 life
membership

Sanford Historical Committee
263 Main Street
Sanford, ME 04073

Sedgwick-Brooklin Historical Society
(Rt. 1, Box 4570—location)
PO Box 171 (mailing address)
Sedgwick, ME 04676
(207) 359-8977 (President)
R. M. Sargent, President
Hours: Jul–Aug: Sun 2:00–4:00
Pub. *Newsletter*, irregularly
(local history, library, some genealogy)

South Portland-Cape Elizabeth Historical Society
(Braeburn Avenue—location)
PO Box 2623 (mailing address)
South Portland, ME 04106
(207) 799-1977
Lenora Bangert, President
Hours: Apr–Nov: Sat 1:00–4:00
$5.00 per year membership

Southern Aroostook Historical Society
Aroostook Historical and Art Museum
109 Main Street
Houlton, ME 04730

Standish Historical Society
Old Red Church, Oak Hill Road
Standish, ME 04084
(207) 642-3216; (207) 642-4443
Joline Webber, President; Myke Waite,
Curator
Hours: summer: Tue & Thur 10:00–2:00

Stockholm Historical Society
(Lake and South Main Streets—location)
PO Box 37 (mailing address)
Stockholm, ME 04783
Albertine Dufour, President

Sullivan-Sorrento Historical Society
PO Box 67
West Sullivan, ME 04689
(207) 422-6253 (Curator)

Vassalboro Historical Society
(Route 32—location)
PO Box 62 (mailing address)
East Vassalboro, ME 04935-0062
(207) 923-3505 (Museum); (207) 923-
3533 (Curator)
Betty Taylor, Secretary and Curator
Hours: various

The Vinalhaven Historical Society
High Street
PO Box 339
Vinalhaven, ME 04863
(207) 863-4410
E-mail: vhhissoc@midcoast.com
http://www.midcoast.com/~vhhissoc
Roy Van N. Heisler, Secretary
Hours: Museum: 15 Jun–13 Sept: 11:00–
3:00, and by appointment
$3.00-$25.00 per year membership,
$100.00 life membership; search fee:
$12.00 per hour after the first half-
hour

Waldoboro Historical Society
Route 220 South
PO Box 110
Waldoboro, ME 04572
William Travers, President
Hours: Jul–Labor Day: Mon–Sun 1:00–
4:30
Pub. *WHS Newsletter*, one or two times
per year
from $4.00 per year membership

Warren Historical Society
PO Box 11
Warren, ME 04864

Waterborough Historical Society
Rt. 5
East Waterboro, ME 04030
(207) 247-5878

Waterford Historical Society
Mary Gage Rice Museum—Waterford
Village
North Waterford, ME 04267
Norman Rust
Pub. *Waterford Echoes*, quarterly

Weld Historical Society, Inc.
Wilton Road
Weld, ME 04285
Susan Stowell, President
Pub. *WHS Newsletter*

Historical Society of Wells and Ogunquit

Post Road
PO Box 801
Wells, ME 04090
(207) 646-4775
Joan B. Adams, Chairperson of Board
Pub. *Waves & Furrows*

Wilton Historical Society

Farm and Home Museum
Kineowatha Park
PO Box 33
Wilton, ME 04294

Windham Historical Society, Inc.

(234 Windham Center Road—location)
22 Montgomery Road (mailing address)
Windham, ME 04062
(207) 892-1433 (Thursdays); (207) 892-6589 (Historian)
Elizabeth R. Barto, Historian
Hours: Thur 10:00–2:00, and by appointment
Pub. *Windham Historical Society Newsletter*, eleven times per year (monthly except December)
(Windham history and genealogy)
$3.00 per year membership for individuals, $50.00 life membership; search fee: donation

Winslow Historical Society

(Lithgow Street—location)
16 Benton Avenue (mailing address)
Winslow, ME 04902

Winter Harbor Historical Society

Main Street
PO Box 400
Winter Harbor, ME 04693
(207) 963-7461

Winterport Historical Association

PO Box 342
Winterport, ME 04496-0342
$3.00 per year membership

Winthrop Historical Society

PO Box 111
East Winthrop, ME 04343

LDS Family History Centers

Augusta
(see Farmingdale)

Bangor
(207) 942-7310

Cape Elizabeth
(207) 767-5000

Farmingdale
(207) 582-1827

Portland
(see Cape Elizabeth)

Genealogical Societies

State Genealogical Society

Maine Genealogical Society

PO Box 221
Farmington, ME 04938-0221
Clayton Adams, President; Lauralee Clayton, Newsletter Editor
Pub. *The Maine Genealogist*, quarterly; *Maine Genealogical Society Newsletter*, quarterly
$15.00 per year membership for individuals (beginning in January), $5.00 new member fee; free queries for members

Regional Genealogical Societies

American-Canadian Genealogical Society
(see New Hampshire)

Broad Bay Family History Projects

(Waldoboro, ME 04572-0010—location)
6094 South Glen Oaks Drive (mailing address)
Murray, UT 84107
W. W. "Will" Whitaker, Editor
Pub. *Old Broad Bay Bund und Blatt*
(includes the 100+ families which established a German colony in Broad Bay [Waldoboro, Maine] in 1740–1753)

Le Club Calumet

Genealogical Section
PO Box 110
Augusta, ME 04330-0110

Minnesota Genealogical Society, Yankee Branch
(see Massachusetts)

The New England Historic Genealogical Society
(see Massachusetts)

York County Genealogical Society

PO Box 431
Eliot, ME 03903-0431
Pub. *Journal*, quarterly; *Newsletter*, irregularly
$12.00 per year membership for individuals, $10.00 per year membership for libraries and institutions

---

Independent Publications and Miscellany

Cumberland and Oxford Canal Association

36 Lester Drive
Portland, ME 04103
(207) 797-2745

Jonathan Fisher Memorial, Inc.

PO Box 537
Blue Hill, ME 04614
(207) 374-2780

Maine League of Historical Societies and Museums

Stone House
Phippsburg, ME 04562
Dorris Isaacson, President

Maine Old Cemeteries Association

2 Sylvan Road
Farmingdale, ME 04344
Catherine Allen, Corresponding Secretary
Pub. *MOCA Newsletter*, quarterly
$3.00 per year membership

MeGenWeb

Part of U.S. GenWeb Project
E-mail: me@usgenweb.com
http://www.rootsweb.com/~megenweb
(links to other Maine resources)

New England Old Newspaper Index Project

PO Box 152
Danville, ME 04223
(207) 786-2129; (207) 786-2129 FAX
E-mail: neonipme@aol.com
http://www.geocities.com/heartland/hills/1460
David Colby Young
(compiles and publishes vital records and genealogical and historical information from Maine newspapers, also supports microfilming of newspapers)
no costs, send resume with SASE to offer help

The New England Quarterly
(see Massachusetts)

Society for the Preservation of New England Antiquities—Archives
(see Massachusetts)

Sunrise Research Institute

PO Box 156
Whitneyville, ME 04692

Victoria Society of Maine

The Victoria Manson
109 Danforth Street
Portland, ME 04101
(207) 772-4841

MARYLAND

Archives and Libraries with Holdings in Genealogy

State Archives and Library

Maryland State Archives
Hall of Records Building
350 Rowe Boulevard
Annapolis, MD 21401-1686
(410) 974-3914; (410) 974-3916; (800)
235-4045 (in Maryland); (410) 974-2525 FAX
E-mail:
archives@mdarchives.state.md.us
http://www.mdarchives.state.md.us/msa/
homepage/html/homepage.html
Edward C. Papenfuse, Ph.D., State
Archivist and Records Administrator;
Douglas P. McElrath, Director of
Education and Outreach
Hours: Tue–Fri 8:00–4:30, Sat 8:30–12:00 & 1:00–4:30
Pub. *Maryland Manual*
$15.00 search fee for mail reference,
schedule of charges for photocopies

Maryland State Law Library
Robert C. Murphy Court of Appeals
Building
361 Rowe Boulevard
Annapolis, MD 21401-1697
(410) 974-3395; (410) 974-2063
E-mail: mdlawstf@epfl2.epflbalto.org
Shirley Rittenhouse, Librarian III;
Michael S. Miller, Director
Hours: Mon, Wed & Fri 8:00–4:30, Tue
& Thur 8:00–9:00, Sat 9:00–4:00
(Maryland history)

State Historical Society

Maryland Historical Society
201 West Monument Street
Baltimore, MD 21201
(410) 685-3750, ext. 359; (410) 385-2105 FAX
E-mail: @mdhs.org (individual staff)
http://www.mcps.k12.md.us/curriculum/
socialstd/ft/md_historic_soc.html
Francis P. O'Neill, Reference Librarian
Hours: Tue–Fri 10:00–4:30; Sat 9:00–4:30
Pub. *Maryland Historical Magazine*,
quarterly; *News and Notes of MHS*,
five times per year
$40.00 per year membership for
individuals; $4.00 non-member
admission; search fees vary for
members and non-subscribers, simple
or complex research

City, County and Regional Archives and Libraries

Allegany College of Maryland Library
Appalachian Collection
12401 Willowbrook Road, S.E.
Cumberland, MD 21502-2596
(301) 724-7700, ext. 294 (Coordinator)
E-mail: mona@ac.cc.md.us
Mona Clites, Coordinator of Library
Services
Hours: usually Mon–Thur 8:00–10:00,
Fri 8:00–4:30, Sat 10:00–2:00, Sun
2:00–6:00 (hours may vary)
(local history and genealogy for western
Maryland and surrounding counties in
West Virginia and Pennsylvania; more
than 1400 historical and genealogical
books, about 300 oral history
recordings, plus pamphlet and
photograph file)
donation requested

Allegany County Library System
31 Washington Street
Cumberland, MD 21502-2981
(301) 777-1200; (301) 777-1200 FAX
http://www.alle.lib.md.us
Jane Rustin, Director
Hours: Mon–Thur 9:00–9:00, Fri–Sat
9:00–5:00, Sun 1:00–5:00

Anne Arundel County Public Library
Annapolis Area Branch
1410 West Street
Annapolis, MD 21401
(410) 222-1750
http://web.aacpl.lib.md.us
Ellen Berkov, Annapolis Area Reference
Librarian
Hours: Mon–Thur 9:00–9:00, Fri–Sat
9:00–5:00, Sun 1:00–5:00
(includes Maryland Gold Star Collection,
a non-circulating collection of titles on
Maryland history and genealogy)

C. Burr Artz Library
Maryland Room
110 East Patrick Street
Frederick, MD 21701
(301) 631-3757
James W. Lowry
Hours: Library: Mon–Thur 10:00–9:00,
Fri–Sat 10:00–5:00; Maryland Room:
Mon–Wed 1:00–4:00, Thur–Sat
10:00–1:00
(specializes in Frederick County history
and genealogy)

Baltimore City Archives and Records Management Office
211 East Pleasant Street, Room 201
Baltimore, MD 21202
(410) 396-4861
Thomas L. Hallowak, City Archivist and
Records Management Officer

Hours: Tue–Fri 9:00–4:00
search fee: $25.00 per hour

Baltimore County Public Library
Catonsville Area Branch
1100 Frederick Road
Catonsville, MD 21228
(410) 887-0951; (410) 788-8166 FAX
Evangeline Benner, Branch Manager
Hours: Mon–Thur 10:00–9:00, Fri–Sat
10:00–5:30

Baltimore County Public Library
Reisterstown Branch
Cockeys Mill Road
Reisterstown, MD 21136
(410) 887-1165; (410) 833-8756 FAX
http://204.255.212.10/branchpgs/re/
rehome.html
Grace Jonke, Branch Manager
Hours: Mon–Thur 10:00–9:00, Fri–Sat
9:00–5:30

Baltimore County Public Library
Towson Area Branch
320 York Road
Towson, MD 21204
(410) 887-6166; (410) 887-6100
E-mail: webmaster@mail.bcpl.lib.md.us
http://204.255.212.10/centers/history/
history.html
Cornelia M. Ives, Branch Manager
Hours: Mon–Thur 10:00–9:00, Fri–Sat
10:00–5:30, Sun noon–5:00

Caroline County Public Library
100 Market Street
Denton, MD 21629
(410) 479-1343; (410) 479-1443 FAX
Deborah Bennett, Assistant
Administrator
Hours: Mon & Fri 10:00–8:00, Tue–Thur
& Sat 10:00–5:30

Carroll County Public Library
50 East Main Street
Westminster, MD 21157
(410) 876-6018
Janet R. Colburn, Adult Services
Specialist
Hours: Mon–Thur 9:30–8:45, Fri–Sat
9:30–5:00
(all genealogical services are now
provided by Carroll County
Genealogical Society at this location)

Cecil County Public Library
Information Services
301 Newark Avenue
Elkton, MD 21921
(410) 996-5600
Hours: Mon–Thur 10:00–9:00, Fri–Sat
10:00–5:00
no search services available

Charles County Public Library
PO Box 490
Charles and Garrett Streets
La Plata, MD 20646
(301) 934-9001

Louise C. Crouse, Reference
Hours: Mon–Thur 9:00–8:00, Fri 12:00–
5:00, Sat (closed summers) 9:00–5:00

City Hall Museum and Cultural Center
110 West Church Street
PO Box 884
Salisbury, MD 21801
(410) 546-9007

Research Center for Delmarva History and Culture
Power Professional Building—Salisbury
State University
Salisbury, MD 21801
(410) 543-6312
G. Ray Thompson, Ph.D., Co-director
Hours: Mon–Fri (during University
sessions) 9:00–4:00

Dorchester County Public Library
303 Gay Street
Cambridge, MD 21613
(410) 228-7331
Cheryl Michael, Adult Services
Department Head
Hours: Mon, Wed & Fri 10:00–6:00, Tue
& Thur 10:00–8:00, Sat 9:00–5:00

The Ruth Enlow Library of Garrett County
6 North Second Street
Oakland, MD 21550
(301) 334-3996
Emily Ferren, Director
Hours: Mon & Wed 9:15–8:00, Tue &
Thur–Fri 9:15-5:30, Sat 9:00–4:00
no fees

Office of Historic Alexandria
5613 Belmont Avenue
Chevy Chase, MD 20815
Jean Taylor Federico

Johns Hopkins University
Milton S. Eisenhower Library
3400 North Charles Street
Baltimore, MD 21218
(410) 516-8348; (410) 516-7202
E-mail: james.stimpert@jhu.edu
http://archives.mse.jhu.edu:8000/
(early Americana collections, maps,
special collections and archives)

Menno Simons Historical Library
(see Virginia)

Ocean City Museum Society
Ocean City Life-Saving Station Museum
Boardwalk at the Inlet
PO Box 603
Ocean City, MD 21842
(410) 289-4991 (Museum)
E-mail: ocmuseum@beachin.net
Sandra D. Hurley, Assistant Manager
Hours: Jun–Sept: daily 11:00–10:00;
May–Oct: daily 11:00–4:00
Pub. *Newsletter Scuttlebutt*, quarterly
(Ocean City history; some genealogy
sources, contacts to other sources)

$2.00 per year membership for students,
$5.00 per year membership for
individuals, $10.00 per year
membership for couples, $15.00 per
year membership for families, $50.00
per year Supporting membership,
$100.00 per year Sustaining
membership, $50.00 life membership;
$2.00 admission for adults, $1.00
admission for children aged 12 and
under

Enoch Pratt Free Library
Maryland Department
400 Cathedral Street
Baltimore, MD 21201
(410) 396-5468
Hours: Mon–Wed 10:00–8:00, Thur &
Sat 10:00–5:00
("Pratt does not have a genealogical
collection, local history collection
only.")

Queen Anne's County Free Library
121 South Commerce Street
Centreville, MD 21617
(410) 758-0980
Kimberly Baklarz, Assistant
Administrator
Hours: Mon–Thur 10:00–8:00, Fri–Sat
9:00–5:00

Riversdale—Calvert Mansion
4811 Riverdale Road
Riverdale, MD 20737
(301) 864-0420
Joyce McDonald, Facility Manager
(genealogical services)

Rockville Regional Library
Montgomery County Public Libraries
99 Maryland Avenue
Rockville, MD 20850
(301) 279-1953
Patricia Burt
Hours: Mon–Thur 9:00–9:00, Fri–Sat
9:00–5:00, Sun (during schoolyear)
1:00–5:00

Saint Mary's College of Maryland Library
Saint Mary's City, MD 20686
(301) 862-0264 (Circulation)
http://www.smcm.edu/library/index.htm
Deloris Bomarc, Head of Public Services
Hours: School semester: Mon–Thur
8:00 A.M.–midnight, Fri 8:00 A.M.–
9:00 P.M., Sat 9:00–9:00, Sun noon–
midnight

Southern Maryland Studies Center
Charles County Community College
Mitchell Road
PO Box 910
La Plata, MD 20646-0910
(301) 934-2251, ext. 7110 (local); (301)
870-3008, ext. 7110 (Washington
metro area); (301) 884-8131, ext. 7110
(Saint Mary's County)
Sarah L. Barley, Coordinator

Hours: Reading Room: Mon–Thur 8:00
A.M.–10:00 P.M., Fri 8:00–4:00, Sat
9:00–4:00 (hours vary between college
sessions); Documents Room: Mon–Fri
1:00–4:00

Talbot County Free Library
Maryland Room
100 West Dover Street
Easton, MD 21601
(410) 822-1626
Ms. Scotti Oliver, Curator
Hours: Mon & Thur 9:00–9:00, Tue–
Wed & Sat 9:00–1:00; summer: Mon
9:00–9:00, Tue–Thur 9:00–5:00, Sat
9:00–1:00

University of Maryland
McKeldin Library
Marylandia and Rare Book Department
Archives and Manuscript Department
College Park, MD 20742
(301) 405-9212; (301) 405-9058
http://www.itd.umd.edu/ums/umcp/rare/
797hmpg.html
Timothy Pyatt, Curator, Marylandia and
Rare Book Department; Mr. Lauren
Brown, Archives and Manuscript
Department
Hours: Mon–Fri 10:00–5:00
("Our resources are primarily non-
genealogical in nature.")

University of Maryland, Baltimore County
Albin O. Kuhn Library
5401 Wilkens Avenue
Catonsville, MD 21228
(410) 455-2232
Simmona E. Simmons-Hodo
Hours: Mon–Thur 8:00 A.M.–11:00 P.M.,
Fri 8:00–6:00, Sat 12:00–6:00, Sun
12:00–8:00

Washington College
Clifton M. Miller Library
300 Washington Avenue
Chestertown, MD 21620-1192
(410) 778-7292; (410) 778-7288 FAX
E-mail: judith_hymes@washcoll.edu
Judith I. Hymes, Director of Technical
Services
Hours: Mon–Thur 8:30–midnight, Fri
8:30–10:00, Sat 10:00–10:00, Sun
noon–midnight

Washington County Free Library
Western Maryland Room
100 South Potomac Street
Hagerstown, MD 21740
(301) 739-3250, ext. 158; (301) 739-
5839 FAX
John C. Frye, Director
Hours: Mon 2:00–9:00, Tue & Fri 9:00–
5:00
(western Maryland and adjacent areas)
free room use, free parking

Wicomico County Free Library
122–126 South Division Street
PO Box 4148
Salisbury, MD 21801
(410) 749-5171
Joanne Doyle, Head of Reference
Hours: Mon–Thur 10:00–9:00, Fri–Sat
    10:00–5:00

Worcester County Library
Worcester Room
307 North Washington Street
Snow Hill, MD 21863
(410) 632-2600
Lisa Harrison, Coordinator of
    Community Services; Fay Brooks,
    Volunteer Genealogical Researcher
Hours: Mon & Wed 10:00–8:00, Tue &
    Thur–Fri 10:00–6:00, Sat 9:00–1:00
(local history and genealogy)

Historical Societies—Local and Regional

Allegany County Historical Society, Inc.
History House
218 Washington Street
Cumberland, MD 21502
(301) 777-8678
Sharon Nealis, Administrator
Hours: Tue–Sat 9:00–4:00, Sun 1:30–
    4:00 (Jun–Oct)
Pub. *Newsletter*, quarterly
(very small genealogy collection)
$20.00 per year membership for couples

Baltimore County Historical Society
Agriculture Building
9811 Van Buren Lane
Cockeysville, MD 21030
(410) 666-1876
Marjorie Shipley, Librarian
Hours: Wed 1:00–4:00, Sat 10:00–3:00
Pub. *History Trails*, quarterly, $5.00
    subscription (for libraries only)
(cemetery inscriptions, family histories,
    newsletters, newspaper clippings,
    obituaries)
$20.00 per year membership; search fee:
    $10.00

Berlin Heritage Foundation, Inc.
(208 North Main Street—location)
PO Box 351 (mailing address)
Berlin, MD 21811
(410) 641-1019
Susan Taylor, Administrator
Hours: Memorial Day weekend through
    September: Mon, Wed & Fri–Sat
    1:00–4:00
Pub. *BHF Newsletter*, three or more
    times per year
(operates a historic house museum of
    local history)

$10.00 per year membership for
    individuals, $15.00 per year
    membership for families, $50.00 per
    year membership for businesses

History Division (Bladensburg)
4302 Baltimore Avenue
Bladensburg, MD 20710
(301) 779-2011
Catherine Wallace Allen, Historian III

Boyds-Clarksburg-Germantown Historical Society, Inc.
16112 Barnesville Road
Boyds, MD 20841
(301) 972-3452

Brunswick History Commission
City Hall, 20 "A" Street
Brunswick, MD 21716
(301) 834-7500
Mary Margrabe, President
Hours: Wed 10:00–noon

Calvert County Historical Society, Inc.
Genealogy Section
(30 Duke Street—location)
PO Box 358 (mailing address)
Prince Frederick, MD 20678
(410) 535-2452
Linda M. Collins, Curator
Hours: Tue–Thur 10:00–3:00
Pub. *News and Notes*, semiannually
    (spring and fall); *The Calvert
    Historian*, semiannually (spring and
    fall), $4.00 per issue to non-members
(includes Maryland and county history
    and genealogy records)
$20.00 per year membership

Caroline County Historical Society, Inc.
(The Courthouse Green—location)
PO Box 514 (mailing address)
Denton, MD 21629
(410) 482-8072
Jean L. Kelly, Secretary
Hours: by appointment
$10.00 per year membership for
    individuals, $15.00 per year
    membership for families

Carroll County Genealogical Society
Carroll County Public Library
(50 East Main Street, Westminster, MD
    21157—location)
PO Box 1752 (mailing address)
Westminster, MD 21158
(410) 876-6018 (Library)
E-mail: ccgs@ccpl.carr.lib.md.us
Mary Ann Ashcraft, President
Hours: Library: Mon–Thur 9:30–8:45,
    Fri–Sat 9:30–5:00
Pub. *Carrolltonian*, quarterly
(includes Maryland history, local history,
    church and cemetery records)
$10.00 per year membership

Historical Society of Carroll County, Inc.
210 East Main Street
Westminster, MD 21157-5225
(410) 848-6494
Jay A. Graybeal, Director
Hours: Tue–Fri 9:30–4:00, Sat 9:00–
    12:00
Pub. *Carroll County History Journal*,
    quarterly
(includes file cards, drawings, surveyors'
    books and maps of early land patents
    and settlement patterns in Western
    Maryland (Baltimore, Carroll,
    Frederick and Washington counties),
    journals, ledgers, maps, scrapbooks,
    family papers, photographs, files on
    the history of local churches, and local
    newspapers: *The Democratic Advocate*
    [1842–1972], *The Carrolltonian*
    [1833–1844], *Union Bridge Pilot*
    [1899–1972], *American Sentinel*
    [1855–1928], and *Carroll County
    Times* [1911–present])
$20.00 per year membership for
    individuals, $30.00 per year
    membership for families, $15.00 per
    year membership for senior citizens

Catoctin Furnace Historical Society
12320 Auburn Road
Thurmont, MD 21788
(301) 271-2306
Clement E. Gardiner, President

Catonsville Historical Society, Inc.
Genealogical Section
1824 Frederick Road
PO Box 9311
Catonsville, MD 21228
(410) 744-3034
Hours: by appointment
$5.00 per year membership in Historical
    Society, $2.00 additional per year for
    membership in Genealogical Section

The Historical Society of Cecil County
135 East Main Street
Elkton, MD 21921
(410) 398-1790
Michael Dixon, President
Hours: Mon 12:00–4:00, Tue 6:00–8:30,
    Thur 10:00–4:00, fourth Sat 10:00–
    2:00
Pub. *The Bulletin of the Historical
    Society of Cecil County*, three times
    per year (April, September, December)
(Cecil County history)
$10.00 per year membership for
    individuals, $15.00 per year
    membership for couples, $100.00 life
    membership; no fees for searches, but
    donation appreciated

The Historical Society of Charles County, Inc.
PO Box 261
Port Tobacco, MD 20677

212

(301) 934-2251, ext. 610
Mrs. George C. Dyson, Chair Genealogy
and Research Committee
Hours: volunteer hours
Pub. *News and Notes from the Historical
Society of Charles County*, quarterly;
*Historical Society of Charles County
Record*, quarterly
(Charles County history and genealogy)
$10.00 per year membership for
individuals, $12.00 per year
membership for families, $100.00 life
membership for individuals

Chevy Chase Historical Society
(address withheld upon request)

**Clear Spring District Historical
Association**
PO Box 211
Clear Spring, MD 21722
(301) 842-2342

Downs Park Historical Society
8311 John Downs Loop
Pasadena, MD 21122
(410) 222-6230
Rick Holt, Park Superintendent

**Dundalk-Patapsco Neck Historical
Society**
(4 Center Place—location)
PO Box 21781 (mailing address)
Dundalk, MD 21222
(410) 284-2331
Eleanor Lukanich, President
Hours: Mon 10:00–2:00, Tue–Wed 9:00–
noon, Thur–Fri 1:00–5:00, and
evenings & weekends by appointment
Pub. *Society Newsletter*, monthly
(historical and genealogical information
on Dundalk Patapsco Neck area)
$5.00 per year membership; no charge
for search, copy fee only

Emmitsburg Historical Society
PO Box 463
Emmitsburg, MD 21727
J. R. Marsden, President
Hours: quarterly meetings: March, May,
September, November
Pub. *Bits & Pieces*, quarterly
(Emmitsburg and central Maryland)
$10.00 per year membership

**Heritage Society of Essex and
Middle River, Inc.**
516 Eastern Boulevard
Essex, MD 21221
(410) 574-6934
Paul Michael Blitz, Archivist
Hours: Museum: Sun 1:00–4:00, and
weekdays by appointment for group
tours; Archives: by appointment only
$5.00 per year membership for
individuals, $8.00 per year
membership for husband and wife,
$15.00 per year membership for
families, $25.00 per year membership

for businesses, $100.00 life
membership for individuals; admission
by donation

**The Historical Society of Frederick
County, Inc.**
24 East Church Street
Frederick, MD 21701
(301) 663-1188; (301) 663-0526 FAX
Marie Washburn, Librarian; Barbara F.
Johnson, Executive Director
Hours: Library: Tue–Sat 10:00–4:00;
Museum: Mon–Sat 10:00–4:00, Sun
1:00–4:00
Pub. *Newsletter*, quarterly (members
only); *Journal*, semiannually, $10.00
subscription for two years or $5.00 per
issue
(Frederick County history and
genealogical research)
$20.00 per year membership for
individuals, $30.00 per year
membership for couples; museum
tours: $2.00; library fee: $2.00; $40.00
for research

**Garrett County Historical Society,
Inc.**
(123 Center Street—location)
111 East Oak Street (mailing address)
Oakland, MD 21550
(301) 334-3226; (301) 334-3403
(Curator)
Charlotte Friend, Curator
Hours: Jun–Aug: Mon–Fri 10:00–4:00
Pub. *Glades Star*, quarterly
$10.00 per year membership

Greenbelt Historical Society
204 Lastner Lane
Greenbelt, MD 20770-1617
(301) 474-5156
Emory A. Harman, President

**The Historical Society of Harford
County, Inc.**
143 North Main Street
PO Box 366
Bel Air, MD 21014-3539
(410) 838-7691
E-mail: harchis@aol.com
Marlene Magness, President; Margaret S.
Bishop, Chair, Genealogy
Hours: Court Records: Tue 10:00–noon
and 1:00–2:30; Archives: Wed 8:00–
2:00; Research Library and Genealogy
Library: Thurs 9:00–3:00, fourth Sat
10:00–2:00 (call to confirm hours)
Pub. *Newsletter of the Historical Society
of Harford County, Inc.*, six times per
year; *Harford Historical Bulletin*,
quarterly
$20.00 per year membership for
individuals; first half-hour research
free

**Howard County Historical Society,
Inc.**
(8328 Court Avenue, Ellicott City, MD
21043—Museum location
8324 Court Avenue—Library location)
PO Box 109 (mailing address)
Ellicott City, MD 21041
(410) 461-1050 (Museum); (410) 750-
0370 (Library)
E-mail:
mkmannix@welchlink.welch.jhu.edu
Phyllis Knill, Museum Director; Mary K.
Mannix, Library Director; Robin E.
Emrich, Archivist
Hours: Museum: Tue & Sat 1:00–5:00,
and by appointment; Library: Tue
12:00–8:00, Sat noon–5:00
Pub. *Legacy*, quarterly
(Howard County and Maryland history)
$15.00 per year membership for
individuals, $20.00 per year
membership for families

Historical Society of Kent County
101 Church Alley
PO Box 665
Chestertown, MD 21620
(410) 778-3499
Nancy Nunn, Executive Director
Hours: The Geddes-Piper House: Nov–
Apr: Mon 9:00–3:00, Wed–Thur 9:00–
11:30; May–Oct: Sat–Sun 1:00–4:00
Pub. *Old Kent*, quarterly
$15.00 per year membership for
individuals, $25.00 per year
membership for families

Middletown Valley Historical Society
305 West Main Street
PO Box 294
Middletown, MD 21769-0294
(301) 293-6816 for appointments only
Kathleen Rudesill, President
Hours: Library: Jun–Aug: Sun 2:00–
5:00, and by appointment
(emphasis on Middletown Valley,
Frederick County)
$10.00 per year membership for
individuals, $25.00 per year
membership for families, $100.00 life
membership

**Montgomery County Historical
Society**
103 West Montgomery Avenue (Beall-
Dawson House)
Rockville, MD 20850
(301) 340-2974; (301) 762-1492
Jane C. Sween, Librarian
Hours: Tue–Sat 12:00–4:00, first Sun
2:00–5:00
Pub. *Line Upon Line*, ten times per year
$15.00 per year ($30.00 joint with
Genealogical Club of the MCHS)
membership for individuals, $20.00
per year membership for couples

Newtown Association, Inc.
PO Box 543
Salisbury, MD 21801
(410) 543-2111

Port Deposit Heritage Corporation
PO Box 101
Port Deposit, MD 21904
(301) 378-3866

Prince George's County Historical Society
(Marietta, 5626 Bell Station Road, Glenn Dale, MD—location)
PO Box 14 (mailing address)
Riverdale, MD 20737
(301) 464-0590
Frederick S. De Marr, Historian
Hours: Sat 12:00–4:00
Pub. *News and Notes*, monthly
$10.00 per year membership for individuals, $15.00 per year membership for couples

Queen Anne's County Historical Society
PO Box 62
Centreville, MD 21617
Mrs. Lee Brookes, President

Records Management Division
7275 Waterloo Road, Routes 175 and U.S. 1
PO Box 275
Jessup, MD 20794
(301) 799-1930
William E. Taylor, State Records Administrator
Hours: 8:00–4:30
("RMD doesn't provide information to the general public.")

Saint Mary's County Historical Society
11 Court House Drive
PO Box 212
Leonardtown, MD 20650
(301) 475-2467
Bleecker S. Harrison, Executive Secretary
Hours: Tue–Sat 10:00–4:00
Pub. *Chronicles of Saint Mary's*, quarterly
$20.00 per year membership

Shady Side Rural Heritage Society, Inc.
(1418 E.W. Shady Side Road—location)
PO Box 89 (mailing address)
Shady Side, MD 20764
(410) 867-4486
Mavis and George Daly, Co-presidents
Hours: March through December: Sun 1:00–4:00, and by appointment
Pub. *SSRHS Newsletter*, quarterly
$15.00 per year membership for individuals; $10.00 per year for full time students and adults over 65;

$30.00 per year membership for families (up to five members); $35.00 per year Sustaining membership

Somerset County Historical Society
Treackle Mansion
PO Box 181
Princess Anne, MD 21853

Takoma Park Historical Society
Municipal Building
7500 Maple Avenue
Takoma, MD 20012
(301) 585-3542

Historical Society of Talbot County, Inc.
25 South Washington Street
PO Box 964
Easton, MD 21601
(410) 822-0773; (410) 322-7911 FAX
Linda Prochaska
Hours: Tue–Sat 10:00–4:00; Library: by appointment

University of Maryland
History Department
College Park, MD 20742
Pub. *Maryland Historian*, semiannually
$10.00 per year membership

Washington County Historical Society
Jamieson Memorial Library
The Miller House
135 West Washington Street
Hagerstown, MD 21740
(301) 797-8782
Peggy Bledsoe, Library Consultant
Hours: Mon & Fri 9:00–4:00, Wed 12:00–4:00
(Washington and Frederick counties)
search fee: $15.00 per surname

Washington Grove Heritage Committee
PO Box 5
Washington Grove, MD 20880
(301) 926-4786
R. Carole Huberman, Chairman

Wicomico County Historical Trust, Inc.
517 Parker Road
Salisbury, MD 21801
(301) 742-7733
James L. Jackson, President
Pub. *Wicomico County Historical Trust, Inc.*
(genealogical services)

Worcester County Historical Society
PO Box 111
Snow Hill, MD 21863-0111
Julia Robertson

LDS Family History Centers

Baltimore
(see Lutherville)

Frederick
(301) 698-0406

Kensington
(301) 587-0042

Lutherville
(410) 821-0044

Genealogical Societies

State Genealogical Society

Maryland Genealogical Society (MGS)
201 West Monument Street
Baltimore, MD 21201
(410) 685-3750, ext. 360 (MGS)
Ella Rowe, Corresponding Secretary
Hours: Tue–Fri 10:00–4:30, Sat 9:00–4:30
Pub. *Maryland Genealogical Society Bulletin*, quarterly; *MGS Newsletter*, quarterly
$20.00 per year membership for husband and wife or two in the same household ($43.00 joint membership with Maryland Historical Society)

Regional Genealogical Societies

Genealogical Society of Allegany County
PO Box 3103
La Vale, MD 21502
Hours: Mon–Tue & Thur–Sat 12:00–8:00 (members only)
Pub. *Old Pike Post*, quarterly
$10.00 per year membership, $7.00 per year (subscription)

Anne Arundel Genealogical Society
(3 Crain Highway, S.E., Glen Burnie—library location)
PO Box 221 (mailing address)
Pasadena, MD 21123-0221
(410) 760-9679 (Library)
Hours: Thur–Sat 10:00–4:00
Pub. *Anne Arundel Speaks*, quarterly
$15.00 per year membership

Baltimore County Genealogical Society, Inc.
(8601 Harford Road, Parkville, MD—location)
PO Box 10085 (mailing address)
Towson, MD 21285-0085

(410) 256-4028
http://www.serve.com/bcgs/bcgs.html
Ken Zimmerman, President
Hours: fourth Sun at regular meetings;
second Tuesday 5:00–9:00, second
Thursday & second Saturday 10:00–
2:00
Pub. *The Notebook*, quarterly
$15.00 per year membership for
individuals, $20.00 per year
membership for families of two

Calvert County Genealogy Society
PO Box 9
Sunderland, MD 20689
(410) 535-0839
Jerry and Mildred Bowen O'Brien,
Editors
Hours: 9:00–5:00
Pub. *Calvert County Genealogy
Newsletter*, monthly
(includes southern Maryland's old
families in Anne Arundel, Charles,
Montgomery, Prince George's, and St.
Mary's counties)
$15.00 per year membership

Catonsville Historical Society, Inc.
Genealogical Section
1824 Frederick Road
PO Box 9311
Catonsville, MD 21228
(410) 744-3034
Hours: by appointment
$5.00 per year membership in Historical
Society, $2.00 additional per year for
membership in Genealogical Section

Genealogical Society of Cecil
County, Inc.
(Colonial Charlestown, Inc., 343 Market
Street—location)
PO Box 11 (mailing address)
Charlestown, MD 21914
(410) 287-8793
E-mail: murp6391@zeus.dpnet.net
Joanne Daly, President
Hours: first Saturday of the month, and
by appointment
Pub. *Genealogical Society of Cecil
County Newsletter*, quarterly
(includes surname files)
$8.00 per year membership for
individuals, $10.00 per year
membership for couples

Frederick County Genealogical
Society (FRECOGS)
(LDS Family History Center, 199 North
Place, Frederick, MD 21701—
location)
PO Box 234 (mailing address)
Monrovia, MD 21770
(301) 831-5781
E-mail: sjcx93a@prodigy.com
Trudie Davis Long, Newsletter/
Membership
Hours: Tue 9:00–4:00, Wed 9:00–3:00,
Thur 10:00–2:00, Sat 9:00–1:00, Tue–
Fri 7:00 P.M.–9:00 P.M.

Pub. *Frecogs Newsletter*, bimonthly
(microfilm series of Holdcraft collection)
$15.00 per year membership for
individuals, $20.00 per year
membership for families

Harford County Genealogical
Society
PO Box 15
Aberdeen, MD 21001
Hours: Harford County Historical
Society Library: Thurs 9:00–3:15;
Genealogy Room: second and fourth
Sat 10:00–2:00
Pub. *Newsletter*, bimonthly
$10.00 per year membership

Howard County Genealogical
Society
PO Box 274
Columbia, MD 21045
(410) 465-6696
Duane Smith, President
Hours: Tue 1:00–8:00, Sat 1:00–5:00
Pub. *The Family Tree*, ten times per year
$10.00 per year membership

Lower Delmarva Genealogical
Society
PO Box 3602
Salisbury, MD 21802-3602
(410) 742-3501 (Membership/Surname
Chairman); (410) 546-0314 (Vice
President)
http://bay.intercom.net/ldgs/index.html
Peggie Lauridsen, Membership/Surname
Chairman; Pat Taylor, President
Hours: Maryland Room of the Wicomico
County Library: Thur 1:00–5:00
Pub. *More from the Shore*, semiannually
(March and September)
(primarily the Eastern Shore of
Maryland, also Delaware and Virginia)
$15.00 per year membership for
individuals or families; queries free to
members, short queries $5.00 for non-
members; simple search (one date):
$5.00 plus SASE, professional
researchers available for longer
inquiries

Genealogical Club of the
Montgomery County Historical
Society
103 West Montgomery Avenue (Beall-
Dawson House)
Rockville, MD 20850
(301) 340-2974; (301) 762-1492
Jane C. Sween, Librarian
Hours: Tue–Sat 12:00–4:00, first Sun
2:00–5:00
Pub. *Line Upon Line*, ten times per year
$15.00 per year ($30.00 joint with
MCHS) membership for individuals,
$20.00 per year membership for
couples

National Capital Buckeye Chapter
(OGS)
(see Ohio)

Prince George's County
Genealogical Society
(12219 Tulip Grove Drive—location)
PO Box 819 (mailing address)
Bowie, MD 20718-0819
(301) 262-2063
http://his.com/-krutar/pgcgs/
Karen D. Miles, Archivist
Hours: Wed 10:00–dusk, first Wed
10:00–1:00, last Sat 1:00–5:00
Pub. *Prince George's County
Genealogical Society Bulletin*, ten
times per year (monthly September–
June), $2.00 per issue
("Research Center holdings include
3000+ volumes, large periodical
collection with 49 of 50 states
represented, family surname files,
maps, Bible records, microforms, and
manuscript material.")
$12.00 per year membership; free
admission; research fee: $10.00 per
hour

Saint Mary's County Genealogical
Society, Inc.
PO Box 1109
Leonardtown, MD 20650-1109
(301) 373-8458; E-mail:
ehayden@pastracks.com
http://www.win.net/~ehayden/smcgs/
welcome.html
Lorraine Bliss Wallace, President;
Loranna Gray, Treasurer
Pub. *The Generator*, ten times per year
$10.00 per year membership

Upper Shore Genealogical Society of
Maryland
PO Box 275
Easton, MD 21601
(410) 745-2785
Irma S. Harper, President
Hours: Trinity Cathedral, Easton, MD:
monthly meetings
Pub. *Chesapeake Cousins*, semiannually
(eastern shore of Maryland genealogy;
published tombstone records of Kent,
Queen Anne, Caroline and Talbot
counties)
$10.00 per year membership

Independent Publications
and Miscellany

Appalachian Roots
(see West Virginia)

Catoctin Press
Western Maryland Genealogy
PO Box 505
New Market, MD 21774-0505
(301) 620-0157; (301) 620-1817 FAX
E-mail: ghmj48a@prodigy.com
Donna Valley Russell, Editor/Publisher
Hours: 9:00–5:00

Pub. *Western Maryland Genealogy*,
quarterly
(includes western Maryland only)
$19.00 per year membership

Colonial Charlestown, Inc.
(343 Market Street—location)
PO Box 11 (mailing address)
Charlestown, MD 21914
(410) 287-8793
E-mail: murp6391@zeus.dpnet.net
Nelson H. McCall, President
Hours: by appointment
(Town of Charlestown records—Land,
Minutes, Ledge and Death)

Dorchester County Genealogical Magazine
1058 Taylors Island Road
Madison, MD 21648
(410) 228-5442
Debra S. Moxey, Editor
Pub. *Dorchester County Genealogical
Magazine*, bimonthly, $14.00 per year
subscription

Family Historians
c/o Civilian Welfare
9800 Savage Road
Fort George G. Meade, MD 20755-6000
Marvin D. Muhlhansen, President
Pub. *Rootbound*, bimonthly
$7.00 per year membership (activities
and meetings, first Tue, not open to
the public)

Family Line Publications
Rear 63 East Main Street
Westminster, MD 21157
(410) 876-6101; (800) 876-6103 FAX
E-mail: famline@cot.infi.net
http://pages.prodigy.com/strawn/
family.htm
F. Edward Wright, Owner
Hours: Mon–Sat 10:00–5:00
Pub. *Genealogical Source Books for
Delaware, Maryland, New Jersey,
Pennsylvania, Virginia, and
Washington, D.C.*, semiannually
(spring and fall), free; *Pocket Guide to
Genealogical Centers of the Mid-
Atlantic*, annually, $4.50 per issue
postpaid

Genealogical Institute
(see Virginia)

Historic Medley District, Inc.
PO Box 232
Poolesville, MD 20837
(301) 972-8588
Perry Kephart, President
Hours: John Poule Store and Seneca
Schoolhouse in Poolesville, museums:
Sun Apr–Oct
Pub. *HMD Newsletter*, occasionally
$10.00 per year membership for
individuals, $15.00 per year
membership for families, from $25.00
per year Patron membership

Hunting for Bears Genealogical and Historical Society
(see Alabama)

MLH Research
3916 Bramble Road
Anniston, AL 36201
MariLee Beatty Hagness, Owner
Pub. *Maryland Connections Queries*,
bimonthly, $17.00 per year
subscription
(parish records, court records)
search fees: $10.00 per hour; queries

Maryland Roots and Branches
200 Weatherby Drive
Greenville, SC 29615-9731
Pub. *The Wye Oak Tree Newsletter*

MdGenWeb
Part of U.S. GenWeb Project
E-mail: md@usgenweb.com
http://www.rootsweb.com/~mdgenweb/
mdstate.html
(links to other Maryland resources)

Mountain Press
(see Tennessee)

Preservation Association for Tudor Hall, Inc. (P.A.T.H., Inc.)
Tudor Hall
Bel Air, MD 21014
(410) 838-0466
Dorothy E. Fox, Secretary
Pub. *Pathways*, quarterly, $15.00 per
year subscription
(genealogical services)

Society for the Preservation of Maryland Antiquities
2335 Marriottsville Road
Marriottsville, MD 21104
(301) 442-1772

Somerset County Historical Trust, Inc.
10380 Anderson Road
Princess Anne, MD 21853
(410) 651-0788
Mrs. Howard Yerges, Chairman
Hours: Mon–Fri 9:00–4:00
Pub. *Maryland Historical Trust
Newsletter*
(genealogical services)
$15.00 per year membership for
individuals, $25.00 per year
membership for couples, $250.00 life
membership for individuals; search
requests turned over to Meredith
Johnson, Princess Anne, $6.00 per
hour

MASSACHUSETTS

Archives and Libraries with Holdings in Genealogy

State Archives and Library

Archives of the Commonwealth
Reference Desk
220 Morrissey Boulevard (Columbia
Point)
Boston, MA 02125
(617) 727-2816; (617) 288-4505
http://www.magnet.state.ma.us/sec/arc
Hours: Mon–Fri 9:00–5:00, Sat (except
holiday weekends) 9:00–3:00

The Commonwealth of Massachusetts
Military Division History Research and
Museum
Massachusetts National Guard Supply
Depot, Building 2
143 Speen Street
Natick, MA 01760-2599
(508) 651-5700
James Fahey, Archivist
Hours: Mon–Fri 9:00–4:00

Massachusetts Department of Public Health
Central Library
150 Tremont Street
Boston, MA 02111-1197
(617) 727-0201

Supreme Judicial Court
Division of Archives and Records
Preservation
(Judicial Archives, Archives of the
Commonwealth, 220 Morrissey
Boulevard, Boston, MA 02125—
location)
1300 New Court House (mailing
address)
Boston, MA 02108
(617) 727-2816 (Judicial Archives);
(617) 557-1082 (Archivist)
Elizabeth C. Bouvier, Head of Archives
Hours: Archives: Mon–Fri 9:00–5:00,
Sat (except holiday weekends) 9:00–
3:00
(locating and preserving inactive,
historically important judicial records)

State Library of Massachusetts
George Fingold Library
State House, Room 341
Beacon Street
Boston, MA 02133
(617) 727-2590
Hours: Mon–Fri 9:00–5:00
("The State Library staff cannot
undertake personal research projects.
Researchers are welcome to visit and
use the Library's collections; staff

members are available to guide researchers. The Library is open to the public and charges no fees for use of the collections. Coin copiers are available.")

Massachusetts Board of Library Commissioners
648 Beacon Street
Boston, MA 02215
(617) 267-9400; (800) 952-7403 (in Massachusetts); (617) 421-9833 FAX
E-mail: info@mlin.lib.ma.us
http://www.mlin.lib.ma.us/mblc.htm

State Historical Society

Massachusetts Historical Society
1154 Boylston Street
Boston, MA 02215
(617) 536-1608
Virginia Smith, Reference Librarian
Hours: Library: Mon–Fri 9:00–4:45
Pub. *Proceedings*, annually
(manuscript repository, referring most genealogical queries to The New England Historic Genealogical Society)

City, County and Regional Archives and Libraries

Acton Historical Commission
377 Central Street
Acton, MA 01720
(978) 263-7081
Anita Dodson, Chairperson

Acton Memorial Library
486 Main Street
Acton, MA 01720
(978) 264-9641
Susan J. Paju, Reference Librarian
Hours: Mon–Thur 9:00–9:00, Fri 9:00–5:00, Sat (fall–spring) 10:00–5:00, Sat (summer) 9:00–1:00
Pub. *The Good Word*, quarterly

Acushnet Historical Commission
Town Hall
Acushnet, MA 02743
(508) 763-2488
Erwin Marks, Co-Chairperson
Hours: Sat–Sun & holidays (May 30–Oct 12)
50¢ admission

Agawam Public Library
750 Cooper Street
Agawam, MA 01001
(413) 789-1550
Hours: Mon–Thur 9:00–9:00, Fri 10:00–6:00, Sat (closed summers) 9:00–5:00

Amesbury Public Library
149 Main Street
Amesbury, MA 01913
(978) 388-8148; (978) 388-2662

E-mail: mam@mvlc.lib.ma.us
Hours: Mon–Thur 10:00–9:00, Fri–Sat 10:00–5:00, Sat (summer) 10:00–1:00

Amherst Historical Commission
Town Hall
Amherst, MA 01002
(413) 253-3944
Mary Elizabeth Bernhard, Chairperson

Atheneum Society of Wilbraham
450 Main Street
Wilbraham, MA 01095
(413) 596-4097
Martha D. Williams, President
Hours: various
Pub. *The Peppercorn*, four times per year
$7.50 per year membership for individuals, $10.00 per year membership for families

Attleboro Public Library
Reference Department
74 North Main Street
Attleboro, MA 02703
(508) 222-0157; (508) 222-0157; (508) 226-3326 FAX
Hours: Labor Day to mid-Jun: Mon–Thur 8:30–8:30, Fri–Sat 8:30–4:30; summer: Mon & Wed–Fri 8:30–4:30
(local history)

Barre Historical Commission
281 Old State Road
Barre, MA 01005
(978) 355-2327
Audrey Stevens, Chair

Bartlett Museum
PO Box 692
Amesbury, MA 01913-0016
(978) 388-4528; (978) 388-1879
Evelyn Woodman, Secretary
Hours: Tue–Sun 1:00–5:00 (Jun–Oct)

Beardsley and Memorial Library of Winsted
(see Connecticut)

Becket Historical Commission
Becket Town Hall, Main Street
Becket, MA 01223
(413) 623-8934 (Town Hall); (413) 623-5506 (Chair)
Constance Mulholland, Chair
Hours: meetings: every three months, second Wed 7:00 P.M.

Bedford Free Public Library
Mudge Way
Bedford, MA 01730
(781) 275-9440
Hours: Mon–Thur 9:00–9:00, Fri–Sat 9:00–5:00, Sun (Sept–May) 2:00–5:00

Lucius Beebe Memorial Library
Main Street
Wakefield, MA 01880
(781) 246-6334
Charlotte Thompson

Hours: Mon–Thur 9:00–9:00, Fri 9:00–6:00, Sat 9:00–5:00 (closed Sat in the summer)

Bellingham Historical Commission
Town Hall
Bellingham, MA 02019
(508) 966-1373
Florence McCracken, Chairperson
Pub. *Crimpville Comments*

Belmont Memorial Library
335 Concord Avenue
Belmont, MA 02178
(617) 489-2000; (617) 489-5725
Duane Crabtree, Coordinator of Public Services
Hours: Mon–Thur 9:00–9:00, Fri–Sat 9:00–5:00, Sun (Oct–Apr) 1:00–5:00

Bentley College
Solomon R. Baker Library Archives
17 South Forest Street
Waltham, MA 02154-4705
(781) 891-2308
John D. Cathcart

The Berkshire Athenaeum
Local History and Genealogy Department
1 Wendell Avenue
Pittsfield, MA 01201-6385
(413) 499-9486
Katharine Westwood, Supervisor
Hours: winter (Sept to mid-Jun): Mon–Thur 9:00–9:00, Fri 9:00–5:00, Sat 10:00–5:00; summer (mid-Jun through Labor Day):Mon, Wed & Fri 9:00–5:00, Tue & Thur 9:00–9:00, Sat 10:00–1:00
(over 8,000 volumes in historical collections, vital records, church and cemetery records, census, newspapers, family history file, periodicals, indexes; Massachusetts local and New England regional historical and genealogical information)

Library of the Boston Athenaeum
10 Beacon Street
Boston, MA 02108
(617) 227-0270; (617) 227-5266 FAX
Trevor J. Johnson, Reference Librarian
Hours: Mon–Fri 9:00–5:30, Sat (Oct–May) 9:00–4:00
Pub. *Athenaeum Items*, quarterly
(New England state and local history and genealogy; researchers requested to call in advance for information)
$100.00 per year membership for individuals, $150.00 per year membership for families, $50.00 per year junior membership (under 35 years of age)

Boston College
The John J. Burns Library
140 Commonwealth Avenue
Chestnut Hill, MA 02167
(617) 552-3282

Robert K. O'Neill, Ph.D., Librarian
(local Boston history, West African and
Caribbean history, the American
Catholic Church and Jesuitana)

Boston College
University Archives
140 Commonwealth Avenue
Chestnut Hill, MA 02167
(617) 552-3248
Paul A. Fitzgerald, S.J., Director

Boston Public Library
Social Sciences Department
700 Boylston Street
PO Box 286
Boston, MA 02117
(617) 536-5400, ext. 261
http://www.bpl.org/
Mary Frances O'Brien, Curator of Social
Sciences
Hours: Mon–Thur 9:00–9:00, Fri–Sat
9:00–5:00, Sun (Oct–May) 1:00–5:00
(strong collections in New England
genealogy and history)
The staff cannot undertake genealogical
or heraldic research; nor can it check
our holdings to determine if they
contain passages on sections of
genealogies pertinent to a particular
family. The staff cannot search
shipping records, passenger lists, or
city directories unless a specific year
is given. Arrangements can bemade to
photocopy pages of certain of our
published genealogies and armories,
but only if citations to author, title, and
specific pages are provided. The staff
cannot search the index to, nor provide
abstracts from the genealogical
columns of the *Boston Evening
Transcript*. Inquirers having specific
citations to items in the *Transcript*
may request photocopies of these
items from the Library. Charges for
this service are available upon request.
Requests for photocopies must be
made in person or in writing

Bourne Archives
The Jonathan Bourne Historical Center
30 Keene Street
Bourne, MA 02532
(508) 759-6928
Patricia K. McAliece, Chairman
Hours: Tue 9:00–3:00
(responsible for custody, preservation
and management of the permanently
valuable, non-current records of the
town; histories of town and its
villages, Cape Cod Canal, genealogies,
schools, industries, organizations,
maps, pictures, etc.)
only charge is for photocopies

Braintree Historical Commission
132 Middle Street
Braintree, MA 02184
(781) 843-5091

Ronald F. Frazier, Chairman
(operates out of the Braintree Historical
Society)

Bridgewater Public Library
15 South Street
Bridgewater, MA 02324
(508) 697-3331
http://www.ultranet.com/~bwpl
Elizabeth L. Gregg, Associate Director,
Public Services
Hours: Library: Mon–Thur 9:00–8:00,
Fri 9:00–5:00, Sat (except summer)
9:00–2:00; Historical Room: Tue
2:00–4:00, Thur 2:00–4:00, and by
appointment

Brockton Public Library
304 Main Street
Brockton, MA 02401
(508) 580-7860
Lucia Shannon, Head of Adult Services
Hours: Mon–Wed 9:00–8:00, Thur–Sat
9:00–5:00 (closed Fri, Sept–Jun;
closed Sat, Jun–Aug)

Brookline Historical Commission
Town Hall
2333 Washington Street
Brookline, MA 02146
(617) 232-9000, ext. 246
Judith Selwyn, Chairperson

Public Library of Brookline
361 Washington Street
Brookline, MA 02146
(617) 730-2370; (617) 232-7146 FAX
E-mail: cbattis@mln.lib.ma.us
Cynthia Battis, Collection Development
Librarian
Hours: Mon–Thur 10:00–9:00, Fri–Sat
10:00–5:00, Sun 1:00–5:00 (closed
Sat–Sun mid-June to Labor Day)

Brooks Free Library
739 Main Street
Harwich Center, MA 02645

Burlington Historical Commission
Town Hall, Center Street
Burlington, MA 01803
(781) 272-2708
Pauline R. Keans, President

Cambridge Historical Commission
831 Massachusetts Avenue
Cambridge, MA 02139
(617) 349-4683; (617) 349-6165 FAX
Charles M. Sullivan, Executive Director
Hours: Mon–Fri 9:00–5:00
(about 26,000 photographs and extensive
local history collection)

Cambridge Public Library
449 Broadway
Cambridge, MA 02138
(617) 498-9080; (617) 868-2938 FAX
Donald York, Assistant Director
Hours: Mon–Fri 9:00–9:00, Sat 9:00–
5:00

Carlisle Historical Commission
Town Hall
Carlisle, MA 01741
(978) 369-6136

Cary Memorial Library
1874 Massachusetts Avenue
Lexington, MA 02173
(781) 862-6288
http://link.ci.lexington.ma.us
Julie Triessl, Curator
Hours: Mon–Thur 9:00–9:00, Fri–Sat
9:00–5:00, Sun (Jun–Aug) 1:00–5:00
(local history)

Chelmsford Public Library
25 Boston Road
Chelmsford, MA 01824
(978) 256-5521; (978) 256-2344
Linda Webb, Interlibrary Loan
Department
Hours: Mon–Thur 9:00–9:00, Fri–Sat
9:00–5:30, Sun (Oct–May) 1:00–5:00

Chelsea Historical Archives
Chelsea Public Library
569 Broadway
Chelsea, MA 02150
(617) 884-0270; (617) 884-2335
(Library)
N. J. Minadakis, Director
Hours: Library: Mon–Fri 10:00–5:00

Chelsea Public Library
569 Broadway
Chelsea, MA 02150
(617) 884-2335
Hours: Mon–Fri 10:00–5:00

Cheshire Historical Commission
(Church Street—location)
120 North Street, PO Box 73 (mailing
address)
Cheshire, MA 01225
(413) 743-2669 (Chairperson)
Eileen Nuttall, Chairperson

Chester Historical Commission
(Old Jail, Route 20, Jacob's Ladder
Trail—location)
4 William (mailing address)
Chester, MA 01011-0114
(413) 354-7820
Fay M. Piergiovanni, Chairperson
Pub. *Quarterly Newsletter*
$3.00 per year membership

Cohasset Historical Commission
179 South Main Street
Cohasset, MA 02025
(781) 383-0234
Noel A. Ripley, Chairman

The Commonwealth Museum
220 Morrissey Boulevard (Columbia
Point)
Boston, MA 02125
(617) 727-9268
Theodore Z. Penn, Director

Concord Antiquarian Museum
200 Lexington Road
PO Box 146
Concord, MA 01742
(978) 369-9609
Dennis Fiori, Director
Hours: Mon–Sat 10:00–4:30, Sun 1:00–4:30

Concord Free Public Library
129 Main Street
Concord, MA 01742
(978) 371-6242; (978) 371-6244 FAX
Leslie Nilson, Curator
Hours: Mon–Fri 9:00–1:00, Sat (Sept–Jun) 9:00–1:00, and by appointment
Tue–Thur 1:00–5:00
(county history and literature, municipal records, genealogy)

Connecticut Valley Historical Museum
Research Library and Archives
194 State Street (rear)
Springfield, MA 01103
(413) 263-6800, ext. 230; (413) 263-6898 FAX
http://www.spfldlibmus.org
Margaret Humberston, Supervising Librarian
Hours: Wed–Sun noon-4:00
(history of greater Springfield area, Massachusetts and New England history, and New England genealogy)
research: $15.00 per hour; admission: $4.00 (includes all museums)

Conway Historical Commission
PO Box 187
Conway, MA 01341
(413) 369-4654
Gladys Graves, Chairperson

Cummington Historical Commission
Kingman Tavern Historical Museum
(41 Main Street—location)
50 Main Street (mailing address)
Cummington, MA 01026
(413) 634-5335
Merrie Bergmann, Chair
Hours: Sat 2:00–5:00 (Jul–Aug), and by appointment
donations suggested

Dalton Historical Commission
462 Main Street
Dalton, MA 01226
Mary Ellen Shea, Chairperson
Hours: by appointment
(museum; records of local interest)

Danvers Historical Commission
c/o Town Hall, Sylvan Street
Danvers, MA 01923
(978) 777-2821
Toni E. Collins, Director
Hours: Mon–Fri 9:00–2:00

Historical Records of Dukes County, Massachusetts
RR 2, Box 247
Vineyard, MA 02568
E-mail:cbaer@vineyard.net
http://www.vineyard.net/vineyard/history/

Duxbury Historical Commission
c/o Rockland Trust
2036 Washington Street, #FURNES
Hanover, MA 02339-1617
Jean Poindexter Colby, Chairman

Dyer Memorial Library
28 Centre Avenue
PO Box 2245
Abington, MA 02351
(781) 878-8480
Marion Delaney, Curator and Librarian
Hours: Tue–Fri 1:00–5:00, second & fourth Sat noon–4:00
(private library, open to the public; town histories, vital records to 1850, some family histories)

East Bridgewater Historical Commission
418 Plymouth Street
East Bridgewater, MA 02333
(508) 378-7775

East Bridgewater Public Library
32 Union Street
East Bridgewater, MA 02333
(508) 378-1616
Hours: Mon–Tue 9:00–8:00, Wed–Thur 9:00–5:00, Fri 1:00–5:00, Sat 9:00–1;00

East Longmeadow Historical Commission
Center Square
East Longmeadow, MA 01028
(413) 525-3305

Eastham Public Library
190 Samoset Road
Eastham, MA 02642
(508) 240-5950; (508) 240-0786 FAX
Sue Lederhouse, Director
Hours: Summer: Mon & Fri–Sat 10:00–4:00, Tue & Thur 10:00–8:00; winter: Wed & Fri–Sat 10:00–4:00, Tue & Thur 10:00–8:00

Easthampton Historical Commission
Town Hall, Main Street
Easthampton, MA 01027
(413) 527-2211
Edward J. Dwyer, Chair
Hours: by appointment
(archives, various publications, general information)

Easton Historical Commission
Easton Town Office
Easton, MA 02356
(508) 238-9966
John J. Kent, Secretary

Egremont Historical Commission
PO Box 127
Egremont, MA 01252
(413) 528-5226
Ann M. Van Deusen, Member
Hours: Archives Room in Academy Building: first Sat 10:00–noon

Eldredge Public Library
The Edgar Francis Waterman Memorial Genealogical Collection
564 Main Street
Chatham, MA 02633
(508) 945-0274
Mrs. Fitzhugh McMaster, Genealogy Department
Hours: Tue & Thur 1:00–5:00
no charge

Fairhaven Historical Commission
PO Box 212
Fairhaven, MA 02719
(508) 993-1707 (Business); (508) 993-3114 (Home)
Louis A. Veilleux, Chairperson

Fitchburg Historical Commission
City Hall, 718 Main Street
Fitchburg, MA 01420
(978) 345-9550
Stephen A. Svolis, Chairperson

J. V. Fletcher Library
50 Main Street
Westford, MA 01886
(978) 692-5555; (978) 692-4418 FAX
Virginia Moore, Local History Librarian
Hours: Mon–Thur 10:00–9:00, Fri 1:00–5:00, Sat 10:00–5:00
(Westford history and genealogy)
photocopies: 15¢ per page

Forbes Library
20 West Street
Northampton, MA 01060

Forbush Memorial Library
110 Main Street
Westminster, MA 01473
(978) 874-2172
Betsy Hannula, Curator
Hours: Thur 3:00–5:00, and by appointment

Foxborough Historical Commission
Memorial Hall
Foxborough, MA 02035
(508) 543-5301

Framingham Historical Commission
Memorial Building
150 Concord Street
Framingham, MA 01701
(508) 877-4333
Stephen W. Herring, Chair

Franklin Historical Commission
Washington Street
PO Box 212
Franklin, MA 02038
(508) 528-0867
D. Arnold, Chairperson

Fruitlands Museums, Inc.
Four Museums of American Art and
  History
102 Prospect Hill Road
Harvard, MA 01451
(978) 456-3924
E-mail: frutland@usa1.com
http://www1.usa1.com/frutland
Robert S. Farwell, Director; Michael
  Volmar, Curator
Hours: Library: Tue–Sun 10:00–5:00,
  and by appointment
Pub. *Mulberry Tree*, quarterly
  (transcendentalism, Shaker, American
  Indian, 19th century portraiture of the
  Hudson River School)
$40.00 per year membership for
  individuals, $65.00 per year
  membership for families, $25.00 per
  year membership for senior citizens or
  students, $125.00 per year Patron
  membership, $350.00 per year Sears
  Benefactor membership

Gloucester Lyceum and Sawyer Free
Library
(address withheld upon request)

Goodnow Library
(Sudbury Town Hall—temporary
  location)
21 Concord Road (mailing address)
Sudbury, MA 01776
(978) 443-1035; (978) 443-1036 FAX
E-mail: sudref@mln.lib.ma.us
Jennifer Root, Reference Librarian
Hours: Mon–Wed 10:00–8:30, Thur–Sat
  10:00–5:00, Sat (summer) 10:00–1:00,
  Sun (Oct–May) 2:00–5:00

Grafton Historical Commission
23 Keith Hill Road
Grafton, MA 01519
(508) 839-2245
Mrs. Benjamin S. Bean

Greenfield Historical Commission
Town Hall, 14 Court Square
Greenfield, MA 01301
(413) 774-5363
Peter S. Miller, Chairman
Hours: evenings
("early vital records and general
  Greenfield history, knows where to
  find answers to Greenfield's history")

Greenfield Public Library
402 Main Street
Greenfield, MA 01301
(413) 772-1545; (413) 772-1589 FAX
Pam Murray, Interlibrary Loan and
  Assistant Reference
Hours: Mon & Fri 10:00–5:00, Tue–Thur
  10:00–8:00
(local town histories, vital records to
  1850, Town of Greenfield and
  Montague street listings 1891 to
  present, local newspaper microfilm
  1792 to present)

search fees: photocopying plus postage,
  extra charge if search is lengthy

Hammond Castle Museum, Inc.
80 Hesperus Avenue
Gloucester, MA 01930
(978) 283-2080

Harvard University
Peabody Museum of Archaeology and
  Ethnology
11 Divinity Avenue
Cambridge, MA 02138
(617) 495-2254; (617) 495-2248
  (General Information)
C. C. Lamberg-Karlovsky, Director
Hours: Mon–Sat 9:00–4:30, Sun 1:00–
  4:30

Harwich Historical Commission
617 Main Street
Harwich Port, MA 02646
(508) 432-2210
Mrs. Leslie V. Nickerson, Secretary

Haverhill Public Library
99 Main Street
Haverhill, MA 01830
(978) 373-1586
Gregory H. Laing, Curator of Special
  Collections
Hours: Special Collections: Mon–Wed
  10:00–1:00, 2:00–5:00 & 6:00–9:00,
  Thur 10:00–1:00 & 2:00–5:00, Sat
  10:00–1:00 & 2:00–5:00
(microfilm of Massachusetts vital records
  1841–1900, and the Massachusetts
  D.A.R. library materials, including
  7,000 volumes of Haverhill history,
  8,250 volumes in Pecker genealogy
  and local history collections, 500
  volumes of military history, full runs
  of many periodicals)

Hawley Historical Commission
Middle Road
Hawley, MA 01339
(413) 339-5513
Harrison Parker, Chairman
(Hawley local history)

Hingham Public Library
66 Leavitt Street
Hingham, MA 02043
(781) 741-1406
Walter T. Dziura, Director
Hours: Mon–Thur 10:00–9:00, Sat 9:00–
  5:00, Sun (winter only) 2:00–5:00

Hinsdale Historical Commission
PO Box 58
Hinsdale, MA 01235
(413) 655-2060
Peter White, Chairman
Hours: Library: Sat 10:00–12:00 & 2:00–
  4:00 (Memorial Day through Labor
  Day)

Holyoke Public Library
335 Maple Street
Holyoke, MA 01040

(413) 534-2211; (413) 532-4230 FAX
Maria G. Pagán, Director; Paul Graves,
  History Room Assistant
Hours: Holyoke History Room: Tue
  9:00–5:00, Thur 9:00–5:00, Sat (after
  Labor Day to before Memorial Day
  weekend) 9:00–4:00

Hopedale Historical Commission
c/o Community House
43 Hope Street
Hopedale, MA 01747
(508) 473-0867
Olga Till, Chairman

Huntington Historical Commission
PO Box 103
Huntington, MA 01050-0103
Hours: Library: 1:00–4:00 (Jun through 1
  Sept by appointment

Immigrant City Archives, The
Historical Society of Lawrence and
Its People
6 Essex Street
PO Box 1638
Lawrence, MA 01842
(978) 686-9230
Eartha Dengler, Executive Director
Hours: Mon–Fri 9:00–4:30 by
  appointment only
(local history, especially ethnic, labor,
  urban planning, and history of
  immigrants to New England; large
  collection of photographs and oral
  history interviews)
$15.00 per year membership for
  individuals, $25.00 per year
  membership for families; $5.00 per
  year membership for senior citizens;
  $10.00 per year membership for
  students

The Jackson Homestead
527 Washington Street
Newton, MA 02158
(617) 552-7238
Susan D. Abele, Curator of Documents
Hours: winter: Mon–Thur 8:30–5:00,
  Sun 2:00–5:00; summer: Mon–Thur
  8:30–4:00
Pub. *Jackson Homestead Newsletter*
(local history and history of abolition
  activities)

James Library
24 West Street
PO Box 164
Norwell, MA 02061
(781) 659-7100
Vivian Perry, Librarian
Hours: Mon–Fri 2:00–5:00, Sat 10:00–
  1:00

Jones Library
43 Amity Street
Amherst, MA 01002
Daniel J. Lombardo, Curator of Special
  Collections

Lancaster Historical Commission
Town Hall, Town Green
Lancaster, MA 01523
(978) 368-4355
Phyllis A. Farnsworth, Chairman
Hours: Tue 9:00–1:00

Lawrence Public Library
Information Services Coordinator
51 Lawrence Street
Lawrence, MA 01841
(978) 682-1727
Hours: Mon & Fri 10:00–5:00, Tue–Thur
10:00–8:00, Sat (Oct–May) 10:00–
5:00

Lenox Historical Commission
Lenox Academy Building
75 Main Street
Lenox, MA 01240
(413) 637-1880
Marcia B. Brown, Chairman

Leominster Historical Commission
City Hall, 25 West Street, Room 13
Leominster, MA 01453
(978) 537-3684; (978) 534-7519
Evelyn B. Hachey

Leyden Historical Commission
27 Eden Trail
Leyden, MA 01337
(413) 773-7336
Edith Fisher, Chairperson
(collection of artifacts, papers, clothing,
etc., held in town safe)

Lincoln Historical Commission
Town Offices
Lincoln, MA 01773
(781) 259-2610
Colin Smith, Chairman
(town archives)

Lowell University
1 University Avenue
Billerica, MA 01821
Hours: Summer: Mon & Thur 8:00–5:00,
Tue–Wed 8:00–9:00; School year:
Mon–Fri 8:00–10:00, Sat 8:00–5:00

Lynn Public Library
5 North Common Street
Lynn, MA 01902
(781) 595-0567; (781) 592-5050
E-mail: lynnlib@shore.net
Nadine M. Mitchell, Head of Reference
Hours: Mon & Wed 1:00–9:00, Tue
9:00–9:00, Thur–Sat 9:00–5:00

Lynnfield Public Library
Genealogy Room
18 Summer Street
Lynnfield, MA 01940
(781) 334-5411
Hours: Mon–Thur 9:00–9:00, Fri–Sat
9:00–5:00

Malden Historical Commission
200 Pleasant Street, Room 623
Malden, MA 02148
(781) 324-6600, ext. 210
Barbara L. Tolstrup, Chairperson

Malden Public Library
36 Salem Street
Malden, MA 02148
(781) 324-0218
Hours: Mon–Thur 9:00–9:00, Fri–Sat
9:00–6:00 (closed Sat mid-Jun to mid-
Sept)

Mansfield Historical Commission
265 Pratt Street
Mansfield, MA 02048
(508) 339-9492
Maureen Cooke, Chairperson

Marlborough Public Library
35 West Main Street
Marlborough, MA 01752
(508) 624-6900
http://www.marlborough.com/
library.html
Barbara Oberlin, Reference Librarian
Hours: Mon–Thur 9:00–8:30, Fri noon–
5:00, Sat 9:00–5:00

Mashpee Historical Commission
(13 Great Neck Road, North—location)
Mashpee Town Hall, 16 Great Neck
Road, North (mailing address)
Mashpee, MA 02649
(508) 539-1438
Joanne M. Ferragamo, Chairperson
Hours: Thur 10:00–4:00, Wed 7:00 P.M.–
9:00 P.M., and by appointment
(town history, Wampanoag history,
Native Americans of the northeast)

Medfield Historical Commission
Town Hall
Medfield, MA 02052
(508) 359-8505
Burgess P. Standley, Chairman

Melrose Historical Commission
76 Linden Road
Melrose, MA 02176
(781) 665-5010
Arnold W. Williams, Chairman

Melrose Public Library
69 West Emerson Street
Melrose, MA 02176
(781) 665-2313
Jane M. D'Alessandro
Hours: Mon–Thur 9:00–9:00, Fri–Sat
9:00–5:00, Sun 1:00–5:00 (closed
weekends Jul–Aug)

Memorial Hall Library
Elm Square
Andover, MA 01810
(978) 475-6960
Shirley McGrath, Assistant Director

Hours: Mon–Thur 9:00–9:00, Fri 9:00–
5:30, Sat 9:00–5:00, Sun 2:00–5:00;
closed weekends during summer
(local history and genealogy)

The Memorial Libraries
Memorial Street
PO Box 53
Deerfield, MA 01342
(413) 774-5581, ext. 125
David Bosse, Librarian
Hours: Mon–Fri 8:30–5:00
Pub. *Research at Deerfield*, infrequently
(Historic Deerfield Library: history,
museum studies; Pocumtuck Valley
Memorial Association Library:
genealogy, local history, manuscripts,
family papers, account books, town
papers, diaries, church records, etc.)

Middlefield Historical Commission
Skyline Trail
Middlefield, MA 01243
(413) 623-8904
Marjorie Batorski, Chairperson

Milford Historical Commission
(Memorial Hall, School Street—location)
2 Nicholas Road (mailing address)
Milford, MA 01757
(508) 473-7327
Marilyn Lovell, Secretary

Milford Town Library
80 Spruce Street
Milford, MA 01757
(508) 473-2145
Reference Librarian
Hours: Mon–Thur 9:00–9:00, Fri 9:00–
6:00, Sat (Sept–Jun) 9:00–5:00

Milton Public Library
476 Canton Avenue
Milton, MA 02186
(617) 698-5757
Daniel Haacker, Branch Librarian
Hours: Library: Mon–Thur 9:00–9:00,
Fri 1:00–5:30, Sat (Sept–Jun) 9:00–
5:00; Historical Collection: Sat (Sept–
Jun) 9:00–12:00
(Milton history/genealogy)

Morrill Memorial Library
Walpole Street
PO Box 220
Norwood, MA 02062
(781) 769-0200
Hours: Mon–Fri 9:00–9:00, Sat 9:00–
5:00, Sun 1:00–5:00; closed Sat & Sun
4 Jul–Labor Day

Morse Institute Library
14 East Central Street
Natick, MA 01760
(508) 651-7300
Carol Coverly, Reference
Hours: Mon–Thur 9:00–9:00, Fri–Sat
9:00–5:00
(Natick, Massachusetts, archives)
10¢ per page for copies

Mount Washington Historical Commission

(Town Hall—location)
RD 3, Box 67A (mailing address)
Mount Washington, MA 01258
William D. Miles, Chairman

Needham Free Public Library

1139 Highland Avenue
Needham, MA 02194
(781) 455-7559; (781) 455-7591 FAX
Arian Schuster, Archivist
Hours: Library: Mon–Thur 10:00–9:00,
Fri 10:00–5:30, Sat 9:00–5:00, Sun
(Sept–May) 1:00–5:00; Genealogy
Room: open when library is open;
Archives: by appointment
(Massachusetts; Needham; town
archives)
copies 10¢ per page ($2.00 minimum)

New Bedford Free Public Library

613 Pleasant Street
New Bedford, MA 02740
(508) 991-6275, ext. 15
Paul Cyr
Hours: Mon & Wed 9:00–9:00, Tue &
Fri–Sat 9:00–5:00

Newburyport Public Library

Hamilton Room
94 State Street
Newburyport, MA 01950
(978) 465-4428; (978) 463-0394 FAX
http://www.mvlc.org
Hours: Library: Mon–Thur 9:00–8:00,
Fri–Sat 9:00–5:00; Hamilton Room:
call in advance
(Newbury/Newburyport family
genealogies)

Newton Free Library

330 Homer Street
Newton, MA 02158-1423
(617) 552-7152
Georgina J. Flannery, Newton Collection,
Reference Department
Hours: Mon–Thur 9:00–9:00, Fri 9:00–
6:00, Sat 9:00–5:00, Sun (except
summer) 1:00–5:00
Pub. *Newtoniana*, irregularly
(Newton archives; library does not do
genealogical research)

Newton Historical Commission

City Hall, 1000 Commonwealth Avenue
Newton, MA 02159
(617) 552-7135
Barbara Thibault, Chairman

North Attleborough Historical Commission

Town Hall
43 South Washington Street
North Attleboro, MA 02760
(508) 699-0100 (Selectmen's office to
leave a message)
Hours: by appointment
(several sources of information for
research, maps and books)

Northampton Historical Commission

Planning Office, City Hall
210 Main Street
Northampton, MA 01060
(413) 586-0138
Dorothy Chapin, Chairperson

Northborough Free Library

34 Main Street
Northborough, MA 01532
(508) 393-5025
Daniel Finneran, Reference Librarian
Hours: Mon–Thur 9:30–8:30, Fri–Sat
9:30–5:00

Northfield Historical Museum

(Pine Street—location)
PO Box 159 (mailing address)
Northfield, MA 01360-0159
(413) 498-5565
Rosa S. Johnston, Registrar
Hours: Jul–Aug: 1:00–3:00
(local history and genealogy)

Ohoopee Regional Library

(see Georgia)

Old South Meeting House

310 Washington Street
Boston, MA 02108
(617) 482-6439
Meredith Devine, Assistant to Director
Hours: Apr–Oct Mon–Sun 9:30–5:00;
Nov–Mar: Mon–Fri 10:00–4:00, Sat–
Sun 10:00–4:00
(limited amount of material on members
of the Third Church [Congregational]
in Boston, 1669–1870)

Orleans Historical Commission

Town Hall
Orleans, MA 02653
(508) 255-2658
Charles H. Thomsen, Chairperson

Palmer Historical Commission

Town Administration Building
Main Street
Palmer, MA 01069
(413) 283-5061
Marion Lis
Hours: 9:00–4:30

Peabody Essex Museum of Salem

(see Phillips Library, Peabody Essex
Museum)

Peabody Institute Library

Danvers Archival Center
15 Sylvan Street
Danvers, MA 01923
(978) 774-0554
Richard B. Trask, Town Archivist
Hours: Mon 1:00–7:30, Wed–Thur &
first Sat 9:00–noon & 1:00–5:00,
second & fourth Fri 1:00–5:00, call or
write before traveling
(emphasis on Danvers, Salem Village
and colonial witchcraft; printed
materials on local history and
genealogy, 75,000 manuscripts)

Phillips Library

Peabody Essex Museum
East India Square
Salem, MA 01970-3773
(978) 745-1876; (978) 744-0036 FAX
William T. La Moy, James Duncan
Phillips Librarian
Hours: call for hours
Pub. *Peabody Essex Museum
Collections*, annually, $25.00 per year
subscription within the U.S., $30.00
per year subscription outside the U.S.
(Massachusetts and New England history
and culture)
$40.00 per year membership for
individuals, $60.00 per year
membership for households, $30.00
per year membership for senior
citizens and students, $100.00 per year
Sponsor membership, $250.00 per
year Patron membership, $500.00 per
year Benefactor membership

Plymouth Public Library

Plymouth Collection
132 South Street
Plymouth, MA 02360
(508) 830-4250
http://www2.pcix.com/~ppl
Ms. Lee Regan, Head of Adult Services;
Beverly Ness, History Room Assistant
Hours: Mon–Wed 10:00–9:00, Thur
10:00–6:00, Fri–Sat 10:00–5:30
Pub. *Plymouth Collection Newsletter*,
irregularly (generally four times per
year); *Genealogical and Local History
Resources Available in Plymouth*,
$6.00 plus shipping and handling
(over 1,200 items relating to local
history, the descendants of the
Mayflower Pilgrims and other
immigrants who came to the Plymouth
area in the 17th through 20th
centuries, including individual family
histories, local town histories,
genealogical journals, vital records of
many Massachusetts communities,
pamphlet collection, vertical file, and
photographs)
mail and phone queries: 10¢ per page
plus shipping and handling

Pollard Memorial Library

401 Merrimack Street
Lowell, MA 01852
(978) 970-4120; (978) 970-4117 FAX
Peter Alexis, Local History
Hours: Mon 1:00–9:00, Tue–Wed & Fri
1:00–4:30, Thur 9:30–9:00

Provincetown Heritage Museum

Town Hall, 356 Commercial Street
Provincetown, MA 02657
(508) 487-7098
Josephine DelDeo, Curator; David
Colburn, Chairman
Hours: daily (14 Jun–12 Oct) 10:00–6:00

Randolph Historical Commission
54 South Street
Randolph, MA 02368
(781) 963-4385
Major Raymond P. MacGerrigle,
Chairman
Hours: Ladies Library Association
(Belcher House): by appointment

Reading Historical Commission
16 Lowell Street
Reading, MA 01867
(781) 942-0500
Sharon K. Ofenstein, Chairman

Reading Public Library
64 Middlesex Avenue
Reading, MA 01867-2550
(781) 944-0840; (781) 942-1021 FAX
E-mail: readingpl@noblenet.org
Sally McDonald, Reference Librarian
Hours: Mon–Thur 10:00–9:00, Fri–Sat
10:00–5:30, Sun 1:00–5:00
("Will answer brief questions regarding
Reading history and vital records.")

Revere Historical Commission
City Hall, c/o Law Department
Revere, MA 02151
(781) 284-3600, ext. 140
Frederick Sannella, Chairman

Rochester Historical Commission
661 Walnut Plain Road
Rochester, MA 02770
(508) 763-8959
Naida Parker, Chairperson

Rockland Memorial Library
366 Union Street
Rockland, MA 02370
(781) 878-1236
Evelyn M. Hinde, Assistant Director
Hours: Mon–Thur 10:00–8:00, Fri–Sat
10:00–5:00 (closed Sat in summer)
Pub. *Library News*, quarterly with
occasional monthly updates (not
genealogical)

Salem Public Library
370 Essex Street
Salem, MA 01970
(978) 744-0860
Elizabeth M. Armand, Reference
Librarian
Hours: Mon–Thur 9:00–9:00, Fri–Sat
9:00–5:00

Salisbury Historical Commission
PO Box 5464
Salisbury, MA 01950
(978) 465-5546
Carol Sargent, Chairperson
Hours: three days per week during the
summer, and by appointment

Salisbury Public Library
Elm Street
Salisbury, MA 01952
(978) 465-5071
Gail Lyon, Director

Hours: Mon & Wed 10:00–5:00, Tue
12:00–8:00, Thur 10:00–8:00

**Sandwich Archives and Historical
Center**
145 Main Street
Sandwich, MA 02563
Barbara J. Walling, Chairperson

Sandwich Historical Commission
145 Main Street
Sandwich, MA 02563
(508) 888-4200

Savoy Historic Commission
720 Main Road
Savoy, MA 01256

Scituate Town Archives
Town Hall
600 Chief Justice Cushing Highway
Scituate, MA 02066
(781) 545-8745
Dorothy Clapp Langley, Town Archivist
Hours: Mon 10:00–2:00, Wed 10:00–
noon
(vital statistics, old Plymouth Colony and
Massachusetts Bay Colony records
from 1633, maps, church records,
property records, assessors' records,
genealogies and local histories, town
meeting records, militia data, etc.)
research fee: donation; certified copies:
$5.00

Scituate Town Library
85 Branch Street
Scituate, MA 02066
(781) 545-6700
Hours: Mon–Wed 9:00–9:00, Thur 1:00–
9:00, Sat 9:00–5:00, Sun (Oct–May)
1:00–5:00

Sharon Historical Commission
41 Bay Road
Sharon, MA 02067
(781) 784-5532
Chandler W. Jones, Chairman

Sharon Public Library
11 North Main Street
Sharon, MA 02067
(781) 784-5974
Hours: Tue–Thur 9:30–9:00, Fri–Sat
9:30–5:30

Sherborn Historical Commission
(Room in Town Offices Building, 19
Washington Street, Route 16—
location)
PO Box 186 (mailing address)
Sherborn, MA 01770-0186
(508) 651-7850 (Selectmen's Office, for
messages)
Elizabeth Johnson, Chairman
Hours: third Wed 7:30 at Town Offices,
and by appointment

Shrewsbury Public Library
609 Main Street
Shrewsbury, MA 01545

(508) 842-0081
http://www.ci.shrewsbury.ma.us/
libtop.htm
Hours: Mon & Fri 10:00–6:00, Tue–Thur
10:00–9:00, Sat 10:00–5:00
(history and biography)

Simmons College
Library
300 The Fenway
Boston, MA 02115
(617) 521-2440
E-mail: beatley@artemis.simmons.edu
http://www.simmons.edu/
(archives, special collections,
manuscripts)

**Henry E. Simonds Memorial
Archives of the Town of Winchester**
15 High Street
Winchester, MA 01890
(781) 721-7146
Evelyn M. Hinde, Historical Services
Coordinator
Hours: Library/Archives: Sept–Jun: Tue
9:00–noon, Wed 11:00–6:00 & 7:00–
9:30; Jul: Mon & Wed 5:30–10:00

Somerville Public Library
79 Highland Avenue
Somerville, MA 02144
(617) 623-5000
Alix Minton Quan
Hours: Mon–Thur 9:00–9:00, Fri 9:00–
6:00, Sat (school year) 9:00–5:00

South Hadley Historical Commission
55 North Main Street
South Hadley, MA 01075
(413) 532-1879
James B. Allen

Southampton Historical Commission
PO Box 59
Southampton, MA 01073-0059
Susan Kozub, Recording and
Corresponding Secretary

Southbridge Historical Commission
236 Main Street
Southbridge, MA 01550
(508) 764-8121
Helen E. Walkowiak, Secretary

Spencer Historical Commission
25 Pleasant Street
Spencer, MA 01562
(508) 885-3675
Anna Marie Hughes, Chairperson

Stockbridge Library Association
Historical Room
Main Street
Stockbridge, MA 01262
(413) 298-5501
Pauline D. Pierce, Curator
Hours: Tue–Fri 9:00–5:00, Sat 9:00–4:00

Stoneham Historical Commission
Stoneham, MA 02180
(781) 438-6250
Gus Niewenhous, Chairperson

Stow Historical Commission
Town Office Building
Stow, MA 01775
(978) 897-2787; (978) 897-2808
John Makey, Chair; Linda Hathaway-
Smart, Secretary

Sturbridge Historical Commission
Town Hall
Sturbridge, MA 01566
(508) 347-3000

The Sturgis Library
3090 Main Street
PO Box 606
Barnstable, MA 02630
(508) 362-6636
http://www.capecod.net/sturgis
Susan R. Klein, Chief Librarian
Hours: Mon & Thur 10:00–2:00, Tue–
Wed 1:00–9:00, Fri 1:00–5:00, Sat
10:00–4:00
(Cape Cod genealogy material)
use of genealogy room: $5.00 per day or
$25.00 per year for non-residents of
one of seven communities within the
town of Barnstable

Sudbury Historical Commission
Town Hall
Sudbury, MA 01776
(978) 443-8205
Lyn MacLean, Chairman
Hours: Hosmer House: Memorial Day, 4
Jul, Columbus Day, & first weekend in
Dec

Swampscott Historical Commission
Administration Building
Swampscott, MA 01907
(781) 596-8850; (781) 596-8870 FAX;
(781) 596-8851 FAX
Louis A. Gallo, Chairman
(street listings, birth and death cards)

Swansea Free Public Library
69 Main Street
Swansea, MA 02777
(508) 674-9609; (508) 675-5444 FAX
E-mail: spl@ultranet.com
Kevin Lawton, Director
Hours: Mon–Thur & Sat 10:00–5:00,
Mon–Tue & Thur 6:30–8:30

Taft Public Library
Main Street
PO Box 35
Mendon, MA 01756
Hours: Mon–Thur 9:00–8:00, Fri 9:00–
5:00, Sat 9:00–2:00

The Thoreau Lyceum
156 Belknap Street
Concord, MA 01742
(978) 369-5912

Townsend Historic Commission
181 Fitchburg Road
Townsend, MA 01469
(978) 597-2668
Elsie Therrien

Tyringham Historical Commission
George Canon Road
Tyringham, MA 01264
(413) 243-0416
Clinton Elliot, Chairman
Hours: Library: Mon

University of Massachusetts at Boston
Joseph P. Healy Library
Harbor Campus
100 Morrissey Boulevard
Dorchester, MA 02125-3393
(617) 287-5944
Elizabeth R. Mock, Archivist
Hours: Library: winter: Mon–Thur 8:00–
10:00, Fri 8:00–6:00, Sat 9:00–5:00,
Sun 1:00–8:00; summer: Mon–Thur
8:00–6:00, Fri 8:00–5:00, Sat 9:00–
5:00; Archives Department: Mon–Fri
9:00–5:00

Uxbridge Historical Commission
Town Hall, South Main Street
Uxbridge, MA 01569
(508) 278-5544
J. Francis Cove, III, Chairman

Ventress Memorial Library
Library Plaza
Marshfield, MA 02050
(781) 834-5535
Bruce Brigell, Reference Librarian
Hours: Mon–Tue 10:00–9:00, Wed–Thur
10:00–5:30, Sat 9:30–5:30

Ware Historical Commission
PO Box 201
Middleborough, MA 02346
(508) 947-4433
George C. Decas, Chairperson

Watertown Free Public Library
123 Main Street
Watertown, MA 02172
(617) 972-6431 (General); (617) 972-
6436 (Reference)
Katherine A. Gardner-Westcott,
Reference/Genealogy Librarian
Hours: Mon–Wed 9:00–9:00, Thur 1:00–
9:00, Fri 9:00–5:00, Sat (winter) 9:00–
5:00
(local history/genealogy; written
inquiries must include SASE,
donations welcomed)

Wayland Historical Commission
41 Cochituate Road
Wayland, MA 01778
Dorothy Walsh, Chairperson

Wayland Public Library
5 Concord Road
Wayland, MA 01778
(508) 358-2311
Phoebe Homans
Hours: Mon–Thur 9:00–9:00, Fri 9:00–
6:00, Sat (Oct–May) 10:00–5:00, Sun
(Oct–May) 2:00–5:00

Wellesley Historical Commission
31 Curve Street
Wellesley, MA 02181
(781) 237-9247
William J. Toy

Wendell Historic Commission
(45 Depot Road—location)
PO Box 112 (mailing address)
Wendell, MA 01379
(978) 544-7502
Jean S. Forward, Ph.D., Co-Chair
Hours: by appointment

Wenham Public Library
138 Main Street
Wenham, MA 01984-1598
(978) 468-5527; (978) 468-5535 FAX
E-mail: mwn@mvlc.lib.ma.us
Doris L. Gallant, Director
Hours: Mon & Wed 1:30–9:00, Tue &
Thur 9:30–5:30 & 7:00–9:00, Fri
1:30–5:30, Sat 9:30–5:00, Sat
(summer) 9:30–1:00
(local authors, local history and
genealogy)

West Springfield Historical Commission
200 Park Street
West Springfield, MA 01089
(413) 732-7230
E-mail: fblally@k12s.phast.umass.edu
F. Bernard Lally, Chairperson

Westborough Public Library
55 West Main Street
Westborough, MA 01581
Hours: Mon–Thur 10:00–9:00, Fri
10:00–6:00, Sat 10:00–5:00, Sun
(Oct–May) 1:00–5:00
(Reed Collection)

Westfield Athenaeum
6 Elm Street
Westfield, MA 01085
(413) 562-0716
Joan B. Ackerman, Reference Librarian
Hours: Mon–Thur 8:30–8:00, Fri 8:30–
5:00, Sat (fall–spring) 8:30–5:00
(local history and genealogy)
research: $5.00 minimum plus copies at
10¢ per page

Weston Public Library
356 Boston Post Road
Weston, MA 02193
(781) 893-4090
Roberta Rothwell, Technical Services
Librarian
Hours: Mon & Wed 9:00–9:00, Tue
1:00–9:00, Thur–Fri 9:00–6:00, Sat
9:00–5:00, Sun 2:00–5:00

Whitman Historical Commission
Town Hall
Whitman, MA 02382
(781) 447-3267
Helen Clancy, Chairman
Hours: fourth Thur of month

Williams College

Williams College Archives and Special
  Collections
Stetson Hall
Williamstown, MA 01267
(413) 597-2568; (413) 597-3931 FAX
E-mail: archives@williams.edu
Sylvia Kennick Brown, College
  Archivist/Special Collections Librarian
Hours: Archives and Special Collections:
  Mon–Fri 9:00–noon & 1:00–4:30
(genealogy and biography of Williams
  alumni)

Williams College

Chapin Library
Stetson Hall, Second Floor
PO Box 426
Williamstown, MA 01267
(413) 597-2462; (413) 597-2929 FAX
E-mail: robert.l.volz@williams.edu
Robert L. Volz, Custodian
Hours: Chapin Library: Mon–Fri 10:00–
  noon & 1:00–5:00
(important historical collections, but little
  actual genealogical material, registers,
  diaries, etc.)
free, except costs of photocopying

Williamstown House of Local History

Milne Library Building, 1095 Main
  Street
Williamstown, MA 01267
(413) 458-2160
Nancy Burstein, Curator
Hours: by appointment
Pub. *Williamstown House of Local
  History News*, two times per year
(history of the town of Williamstown,
  Massachusetts, only)
$5.00 per year membership for
  individuals, $15.00 per year
  membership for families, $25.00 per
  year Friend membership, $50.00 per
  year Patron membership, $100.00 per
  year Benefactor membership

Wilmington Historical Commission

Town Hall, Glen Road
Wilmington, MA 01887
(978) 658-3311

Winchester Historical Commission

Henry E. Simonds Memorial Archives of
  the Town of Winchester
15 High Street
Winchester, MA 01890
(781) 721-7146
Susan Keats
Hours: Library/Archives: Sept–Jun: Tue
  9:00–noon, Wed 11:00–6:00 & 7:00–
  9:30; Jul: Mon & Wed 5:30–10:00
(Winchester, Massachusetts, history and
  genealogies)

Winchester Public Library

80 Washington Street
Winchester, MA 01890
(781) 721-7171
Julie Kinchla, Head of Reference

Hours: Mon–Tue 9:30–9:00, Wed 1:30–
  9:00, Thur & Sat 9:30–5:30, Fri 1:30–
  5:30

Woburn Historical Commission

33 Elm Street
Woburn, MA 01801
(781) 935-3561
L. Harmon, Chairman

Woburn Public Library

45 Pleasant Street
PO Box 298
Woburn, MA 01801
(781) 933-0148
Sylvia C. Pope, Archivist
Hours: Mon–Thur 9:00–9:00, Fri–Sat
  9:00–5:00

Woods Hole Library

Woods Hole Historical Collection and
  Museum
(573 Woods Hole Road, Woods Hole,
  MA 02543—location)
PO Box 185 (mailing address)
Woods Hole, MA 02543
(508) 548-7270
Jennifer Stone Gaines, Archivist
Hours: Archives: Tue & Thur 10:00–
  2:00; Exhibits: summer: Tue–Sat
  10:00–4:00
Pub. *Spritsail*, biannually
(local history with a *little bit* of
  genealogy included, also museum
  exhibits in the summer; Woods Hole is
  in the Town of Falmouth)
$20.00 per year membership

Worcester Historical Museum

30 Elm Street
Worcester, MA 01609
(508) 753-8278
Hours: Library: Tue–Sat 10:00–4:00
Pub. *Worcester Historical Museum
  Newsletter*, semiannually
(Worcester and Worcester County)
$5.00 per year membership for
  individuals, $35.00 per year
  membership for families, $15.00 per
  year membership for seniorcitizens or
  students; museum admission $2.00
  suggested contribution for non-
  members

Worcester Public Library

3 Salem Square
Worcester, MA 01608-2074
(508) 799-1655
Nancy E. Gaudette, Librarian, Worcester
  Collection; Jean W. Missud, Worcester
  Collection
Hours: Mon & Wed noon–9:00, Tue
  10:00–9:00, Thur–Fri 10:00–5:30, Sat
  (Sept–Jun) 10:00–5:30
("Call or write before coming; staff
  coverage limited.")

Wrentham Historical Commission

677 South Street
PO Box 841
Wrentham, MA 02093-0006

(508) 384-2461
Earle T. Stewart, Chairman
Hours: by appointment
(Cemeteries, religious, military, schools,
  documents, vitals; "Always willing to
  help!")

Yarmouth Port Library

297 Main Street
Yarmouth Port, MA 02675
(508) 362-3717 phone & FAX
Virginia M. Gifford, Librarian
Hours: Tue–Thur 1:00–5:00, Wed 6:00–
  8:00, Sat 10:00–1:00

Yesteryears Museum Association, Inc.

Main and River Streets
PO Box 609
Sandwich, MA 02563
(508) 888-1711
Diane Costa, Director
Hours: Mid-May through Oct 31: Mon–
  Sat 10:00–4:00
Pub. *Yesteryears Museum News*, annually
$15.00 per year membership for
  individuals, $25.00 per year
  membership for families; $50.00 per
  year Patron membership

Historical Societies— Local and Regional

Acton Historical Society, Inc.

PO Box 2389
Acton, MA 01720
(978) 264-0690
Pub. *AHS Newsletter*

Adams Historical Society

McKinley Square
Adams, MA 01220
Eugene Michalenko
Hours: by appointment
Pub. *Adams Historical Society
  Newsletter*, eight times per year
("We don't have the staff to answer mail
  from researchers; we regret this and
  hope it will change in the future.")
$5.00 per year membership

American Antiquarian Society

185 Salisbury Street
Worcester, MA 01609-1634
(508) 755-5221, ext. 136

Amesbury History Committee

Lion's Mouth Road
Amesbury, MA 01913
(978) 388-1420
Margaret S. Rice, Director

Andover Historical Society

97 Main Street
Andover, MA 01810
(978) 475-2236; (978) 470-2671 FAX
Barbara Thibault, Director

Hours: Tue–Fri 9:00–5:00, Sat (Sept–Jun) 9:00–5:00, Mon by appointment
Pub. *Andover Historical Society Newsletter*, quarterly
(emphasis on Andover history, genealogy and architecture; Charlotte Helen Abbot genealogies)
library admission: $4.00 for general admission, $2.00 for students or senior citizens; research: $10.00 per hour; copies: 50¢ per page for mailed photocopies, 25¢ per page for in-house photocopies

Annawan Historical Society of Rehoboth
PO Box 71
Rehoboth, MA 02769
(508) 669-6464

The Arlington Historical Society and Smith Museum
7 Jason Street
Arlington, MA 02174
(781) 648-4300
Tina Dorr; Richard E. Erickson, President
Hours: Library: Tue–Sat 1:00–5:00 (Apr–Oct); Archives: Mon–Fri 9:00–4:30 by appointment

Ashburnham Historical Society, Inc.
Main Street
Ashburnham, MA 01430

The Ashfield Historical Society
Main Street
PO Box 277
Ashfield, MA 01330
(413) 628-4541; (413) 628-3962 (Helen Hall, Howes Brothers collection)
Hours: Jul–Sept: Sun 2:00–5:00, and by appointment
Pub. *Newsletter*, quarterly
(archival photographic and genealogical material on Ashfield families; Howes Brothers photographic collection: 24,000 glass negatives, ca 1885–1907, of Connecticut River Valley area, viewable on microfilm at museum)
$15.00 per year membership for individuals, $35.00 per year membership for families

Ashland Historical Society
2 Myrtle Street
PO Box 145
Ashland, MA 01721
Catherine Powers, Curator
Hours: Wed 7:00–9:00, Fri 10:00–4:00, Sat 9:00–noon
Pub. *Newsletter*, monthly
(Ashland history and genealogy)
$5.00 per year membership

Athol Historical Society
1307 Main Street
PO Box 21
Athol, MA 01331

(978) 249-4890; (978) 249-6598 (Curator)
Dexter Gleason, Curator; Howard Wilson, President
Hours: Jun–Jul: Sun 2:00–4:00, and by appointment
(few genealogical files)
$5.00 per year membership, $25.00 life membership

Auburn Historical Society
PO Box 413
Auburn, MA 01501
(508) 832-9449
George A. Furst, President

Historical Society of the Town of Barnstable, Inc.
(3353 Main Street—location)
General Delivery (mailing address)
Barnstable, MA 02630
(508) 362-2092

The Barre Historical Society, Inc.
18 Common Street
PO Box 755
Barre, MA 01005
(978) 355-4978; (978) 355-2810
Rita M. Robinson, President
Hours: Jun–Aug: Wed 2:00–4:00 & 7:00–9:00, and by appointment
$5.00 per year membership for individuals, $10.00 per year membership for families

Beacon Hill Civic Association
74 Joy Street
Boston, MA 02114
(617) 227-1922; (617) 227-7959 FAX
E-mail: bhcivic@aol.com
Tanya M. Holton, Executive Director; Kristine Glynn, Director of Public Relations and Marketing
Hours: 9:00–5:00
Pub. *BHCA News*, monthly
$40.00 per year membership for individuals, $35.00 per year nonprofit membership, $50.00 per year business membership

The Bedford Historical Society
PO Box 702
Bedford, MA 01730
(781) 275-9427
Mary S. Hafer, Curator
Hours: various
Pub. *Bedford Banner*, nine times per year
$8.00 per year membership for individuals

Belchertown Historical Association
(20 Maple Street—location)
PO Box 1211 (mailing address)
Belchertown, MA 01007
(413) 323-6573
Doris M. Dickinson, Curator
Hours: Library: about May 15 through October 15: Wed & Sat 2:00–5:00, and by appointment

Belmont Historical Society
Belmont Room (Local History Collection)
336 Concord Avenue
PO Box 125
Belmont, MA 02178
(617) 489-2000
Madaline Marshall, Curator
Hours: Belmont Room: Mon, Wed & Fri 2:00–4:00, and by appointment
Pub. *Belmont Historical Society Newsletter*, quarterly

Berkley Historical Society
725 Berkley Street
Berkley, MA 02779
(508) 824-5367
Blanche E. Trzcinski, Curator

Berkshire County Historical Society
Arrowhead
780 Holmes Road
Pittsfield, MA 01201
(413) 442-1793
Carolyn E. Banfield, Director
Hours: 9:00–4:00
Pub. *Berkshire History*, irregularly; *News and Notes*, bimonthly
$20.00 per year for general membership, $30.00 per year Supporting membership, $50.00 per year Sustaining membership, $100.00 (or more) Donor membership, $500.00 (or more) Patron membership, $1,000,00 (or more) life membership

The Berkshire Museum
39 South Street
Pittsfield, MA 01201
(413) 443-7171
Gary Burger, Director
Hours: Tue–Sat 10:00–5:00, Sun 1:00–5:00; Mon 10:00–5:00 (Jul–Aug)

Beverly Historical Society
117 Cabot Street
Beverly, MA 01915
(978) 922-1186
Daniel J. Hoisington, Director
Hours: Library at Cabot House: Wed–Sat 10:00–4:00, Sun (May 20–Oct 15) 1:00–4:00

Billerica Historical Society
(Clara Sexton House, 36 Concord Road—location)
PO Box 381 (mailing address)
Billerica, MA 01821
(978) 663-8769
Marion Potter, President

Blandford Historical Society
North Street
Blandford, MA 01008
(413) 848-2787
Hap Bush, President
Hours: by appointment only

Bolton Historical Society, Inc.
Great Road
Bolton, MA 01740

The Bostonian Society
(1713 Old State House and 15 State Street, Third Floor—locations)
206 Washington Street (mailing address)
Boston, MA 02109-1773
(617) 720-1713 (Society); (617) 720-3285 (Library); (617) 720-3290 (Old State House Museum)
Douglas Southard, Librarian
Hours: daily 9:30–4:30

Bourne Historical Society, Inc.
Aptucxet Trading Post Museum Comples, 24 Aptucxet Road—location)
PO Box 3095 (mailing address)
Bourne, MA 02532-0795
(508) 759-9487; (508) 759-6928 (Bourne Historical Center)
Eleanor A. Hammond, Curator/Site Interpreter; Martha Hossell, Accessions Chairman
Hours: Mon (Jul–Aug & holidays), Tue–Sat (1 May through Columbus Day) 10:00–5:00, Sun 2:00–5:00; collection housed in The Jonathan Bourne Historical Center, 22 Keene Street, Bourne: Tue 9:00–3:00
Pub. *Post Scripts*, quarterly (1 March, 1 June, 1 September, 1 December), not available by subscription
$5.00 per year membership for families, $150.00 life membership

Boxford Historical Society
PO Box 281
Boxford, MA 01921
(978) 887-9545
Peter Loring, President

Boylston Historical Society, Inc.
7 Central Street
PO Box 459
Boylston, MA 01505-0459
(508) 869-2720
Norman H. French, Curator
Hours: Tue 9:00–noon, and by appointment
(extensive real estate transactions 1730–1930, photo collection)
$10.00 per year membership; search fee: $25.00 plus expenses

The Braintree Historical Society, Inc.
31 Tenney Road
Braintree, MA 02184-6512
(781) 848-1640
Marjorie Maxham, Librarian/Archivist
Hours: Tue–Wed 10:00–4:00 by appointment
(official custodian of the Penniman Family Records)
$15.00 per year membership for individuals, $25.00 per year membership for families

Brewster Historical Society
PO Box 1146
Brewster, MA 02631

(508) 896-3058
Marion H. Wylie, President
Hours: Library: Wed–Fri 1:00–4:00 (summer)

Brighton Historical Society
68 North Beacon Street
PO Box 163
Brighton, MA 02135
(617) 254-6955
William P. Marchione, Curator
(primarily Allston-Brighton communities within Boston)

Brockton Historical Society
216 North Pearl Street
Brockton, MA 02401
(508) 583-1039
E-mail: gerrb@ici.net
http://www.brocktonma.com
Gerald Beals, Acting Curator
Hours: Sun 2:00–4:00, and by appointment
Pub. *Brockton Historical Quarterly*
$10.00 per year membership

Brookline Historical Society
347 Harvard Street
Brookline, MA 02146
(617) 566-5747
Helen C. McIntosh, Curator
Pub. *Brookline Historical Society Proceedings*

Buckland Historical Society
Upper Street
Buckland, MA 01338
(413) 625-6619
Helen Roberts, President

Burlington Historical Society, Inc.
Town Hall, Center Street
Burlington, MA 01803
(781) 272-4840
Pauline R. Keans, President

Cambridge Historical Society
159 Brattle Street
Cambridge, MA 02138-3300
(617) 547-4252; (617) 661-1623 FAX
Warren M. Little, Ed.D., Executive Director
Hours: Tue & Thur 2:00–5:00
Pub. *Proceedings*, infrequently, $10.00 per issue

Canton Historical Society
1400 Washington Street
Canton, MA 02021
(781) 828-4962

Cape Ann Historical Association
27 Pleasant Street
Gloucester, MA 01930
(978) 283-0455
Ellen Nelson, Librarian
Hours: Library: Wed & Sat 10:00–1:00, Thur 10:00–3:00, Fri 10:00–1:00 & 2:00–5:00; Museum: Tue–Sat 10:00–5:00

Pub. *Cape Ann Historical Association Newsletter*, quarterly
(fisheries/maritime, art history, Cape Ann local history)
$20.00 per year membership

Centerville Historical Society
Centerville Historical Society Museum
513 Main Street
PO Box 491
Centerville, MA 02632
(508) 775-0331
Nancy Lee Nelson, Director
Hours: Library: Wed–Sun (June to mid-Sept)
(part of the town of Barnstable)

Charlton Historical Society
PO Box 252
Charlton, MA 01507
(508) 248-3202
Hours: by appointment

The Chatham Historical Society, Inc.
347 Stage Harbor Road
PO Box 381
Chatham, MA 02633
Daniel L. Buckley, President
Hours: mid-June through Sept: Tue–Fri 1:00–4:00
(history or genealogical books pertaining to Chatham)
$10.00 per year membership for individuals, $15.00 per year membership for families

Chelmsford Historical Society, Inc.
40 Byam Road
Chelmsford, MA 01824
(978) 256-2311
Hours: second & fourth Sun (June–Sept) 2:00–4:00
$10.00 per year membership for individuals, $18.00 per year membership for families, $6.00 per year membership for senior citizens and students; search fees: $5.00 plus postage

Chesterfield Historical Society
Edwards Museum
North Street
Chesterfield, MA 01012
(413) 296-4759
Ruth Z. Temple, Museum Curator
Hours: Sat 2:00–4:00 (Jul–Aug)
(historical, not genealogical)

Clinton Historical Society
210 Church Street
Clinton, MA 01510
(978) 368-0084; (978) 365-4877

Cohasset Historical Society
Caleb Lothrop House
14 Summer Street
Cohasset, MA 02025
(781) 383-6930
David H. Wadsworth, Senior Curator
Pub. *Historical Highlights Newsletter*

Colonial Society of Massachusetts
87 Mount Vernon Street
Boston, MA 02108
(617) 227-2782
John W. Tyler, Editor of Publications
Hours: various
Pub. *Publications of the Colonial Society
of Massachusetts*, annually, priced
from $35.00–$85.00 each
(publishes documents and records, but
maintains no library or collection,
membership is by nomination)

Colrain Historical Society
91 East Catamount Hill Road
Colrain, MA 01340-9514

Cuttyhunk Historical Society
PO Box 165
Cuttyhunk, MA 02713
(508) 971-0932 (summer)
Peter C. Coope, President
Hours: 4 Jul to Labor Day: Tue & Fri–
Sun 10:00–4:00
Pub. *Historical Papers*, semiannually
(an island in the Elizabeth Islands chain,
part of the Town of Gosnold, Dukes
County)

Danvers Historical Society
13 Page Street
PO Box 381
Danvers, MA 01923
(978) 777-1666
Sarah E. Symmes, President
Pub. *Danvers Historical Collections*,
irregularly
$10.00 per year membership

Dedham Historical Society
(612 High Street—location)
PO Box 215 (mailing address)
Dedham, MA 02027
(781) 326-1385; (781) 326-5762 FAX
E-mail: dhs@dedham.com
http://www.c9.com/dhs/dhs.htm
Ronald F. Frazier, Executive Director
and CEO
Hours: Tue–Thur 9:00–4:00, even-dated
Sat 1:00–4:00
Pub. *Dedham Historical Society
Newsletter*, bimonthly
(an extensive genealogical and historical
library)
$25.00 per year membership for
individuals, $35.00 per year
membership for families; $5.00 per
day library use for non-
members

Dennis Historical Society
(1736 Josiah Dennis Manse, Nobscusset
and Whig Street, Dennis, MA 02638
and 1801 Jericho-Trotting Park and
Main, West Dennis, MA 02670—
locations)
PO Box 607 (mailing address)
South Dennis, MA 02660
(508) 394-0017
Phyllis Horton, Curator

Hours: Jericho: Jul–Aug: Mon, Wed &
Fri 2:00–4:00; DHS library at Josiah
Dennis Manse: Jul–Sept: Tue & Thur
2:00–4:00
Pub. *Dennis Historical Society
Newsletter*, monthly (Dennis history)
$10.00 per year membership for
individuals, $15.00 per year
membership for families, $2.00 per
year membership for students, $100.00
life membership

Dighton Historical Society
1217 Williams
Dighton, MA 02715
(508) 669-5514
Elaine Varley, Curator
Hours: by appointment
(history and documents of Dighton and
surrounding area)
$4.00 per year membership for
individuals, $6.00 per year
membership for families

Dorchester Historical Society
The William Clapp House
195 Boston Street
Dorchester, MA 02125
(617) 436-8367
Anthony M. Sammarco, Curator
Hours: by appointment
Pub. *Newsletter*, bimonthly
$6.00 per year membership for
individuals, $10.00 per year
membership for families

Douglas Historical Society, Inc.
(The E. N. Jenckes Store Museum, 283
Main Street—location)
PO Box 176 (mailing address)
East Douglas, MA 01516-0176
(508) 476-3856
Mrs. Marieta G. Howard, President
Hours: Memorial Day weekend through
the first weekend in Dec: Sat–Sun
1:00–4:00
Pub. *The Ledger*, three or four times per
year
$6.00 per year membership for
individuals, $10.00 per year
membership for families, $2.00 per
year membership for students, $25.00
per year Contributing membership,
$50.00 per year Sustaining
membership, $100.00 per year Patron
membership

Dover Historical Society
(Sawin Museum, 80 Dedham Street and
Caryl House, 107 Dedham Street—
locations)
PO Box 534 (mailing address)
Dover, MA 02030
(508) 785-1832
Emily Bertschey, Curator; Pamela
Kunkemueller, President
Hours: Sat (spring and fall) 1:00–4:00,
and by appointment

(focus on history of Dover,
Massachusetts, and its citizens)
$10.00 per year membership for
individuals, $15.00 per year
membership for families; no search fee

Dracut Historical Society, Inc.
1660 Lakeview Avenue
Dracut, MA 01826
(978) 957-1701
Norma Taplin, President
Hours: Sun 1:00–3:00
$5.00 per year membership for
individuals, $10.00 per year
membership for families

Duxbury Rural and Historical Society, Inc.
685 Washington Street
PO Box 2865
Duxbury, MA 02331
(781) 934-6106
Marcia Solberg, Executive Director
Hours: Mon–Fri 9:00–5:00
Pub. *Newsletter*

Eastham Historical Society, Inc.
PO Box 8
Eastham, MA 02642
(508) 255-4968
Phil Ryder, Public Relations Director

Easton Historical Society
(North Easton Railroad Station, 80
Mechanic Street—location)
PO Box 3 (mailing address)
North Easton, MA 02356
(508) 238-7774
Dorothy Berry, Curator
Hours: second Sun 2:00–4:00, and by
appointment
Pub. *Families—Chaffin's Early Easton
Families*
$7.00 per year membership for
individuals

Elbow Plantation Historical Society
40 Converse Street
Palmer, MA 01069
(413) 283-6130
Frances T. Fulton, Secretary

Erving Historical Society
(Main Street, Erving, MA 01344—
location)
9 Moore Street (mailing address)
Millers Falls, MA 01349

Essex County Historical Association
Phillips Library
Peabody Essex Museum
East India Square
Salem, MA 01970-3773
(978) 468-2377
Eleanor E. Thompson, President
(confederation of historical societies with
no public facilities)

Essex County Historical Association
23 Bancroft Avenue
Beverly, MA 01915
(978) 927-0138

Essex Historical Society and Shipbuilding Museum
28 Main Street
PO Box 277
Essex, MA 01929
(978) 768-7541
Diana H. Stockton, Administrator
Hours: Thur–Sun (May 15 through Oct 15) 10:00–4:00, and year-round by appointment
("We have a wealth of papers from Essex families, including Andrews, Burnham and Story.")
50¢ per page for genealogical and headstone transcription information

Everett Historical Society
Town Hall
Everett, MA 02149
(617) 387-7059
Ciro R. Yannaco

Fall River Historical Society
451 Rock Street
Fall River, MA 02720
(508) 679-1071
Michael Martins, Curator
Hours: Tue–Fri (Apr–Dec) 9:00–4:30, Sat–Sun (June-Sept) 1:00–5:00
Pub. *The Fall River Historical Society Quarterly Report*
(history of Fall River, Massachusetts, including Lizzie Borden)
$20.00 per year membership for individuals, $35.00 per yearmembership for families

Falmouth Historical Society
(55–65 Palmer Avenue, Falmouth, MA 02540—location)
PO Box 174 (mailing address)
Falmouth, MA 02541
(508) 548-4857
Joyce S. Pendery, CGRS, Genealogist
Hours: Archives and Office: Mon–Thur 9:00–1:00, Fri 9:00–4:00, and by appointment; Museum: 15 Jun–15 Sept: Wed–Sun 2:00–5:00
Pub. *Spritsail*, biannually; *Newsletter*, irregularly
(Falmouth and related families)
$10.00 per year membership for individuals (not including journal), $20.00 per year membership for individuals (including journal) or for families (not including journal), $30.00 per year membership for families (including journal) or Contributing membership (not including journal), $40.00 per year Contributing membership (including journal), $50.00 per year membership, $100.00 per year Patron membership,

$200.00 life membership; non-member museum admission: $2.00 for adults, 50¢ for children

Fitchburg Historical Society
50 Grove Street
PO Box 953
Fitchburg, MA 01420
(978) 345-1157
Eleanora F. West, Executive Director
Hours: Museum: Mon–Thur 10:00–4:00, Mon 6:00–9:00, Sun (Sept–June) 2:00–4:00
Pub. *Newsletter* (no genealogical information)

Foxborough Historical Society
PO Box 437
Foxborough, MA 02035

Framingham Historical Society
(Corner of Vernon and Grove Streets—location)
PO Box 2032 (mailing address)
Framingham, MA 01703-2032
(508) 872-3780
http://www.framingham.com
Carolyn Maguire, Director
Hours: Wed–Thur & Sat 10:00–4:00
Pub. *Newsletter*, quarterly
(genealogies of local families)
$15.00 per year membership for individuals, $25.00 per year membership for families, $10.00 per year membership for senior citizens and students, $15.00 per year membership for senior citizen couples, $250.00 life membership for individuals, $400.00 life membership for couples; admission: $2.00

Franklin Historical Society
Ray Memorial Library
21 School Street
Franklin, MA 02038
(508) 528-2684 (Home); (508) 528-9110 (Office)
Alfred D. Nicholson, President

Freetown Historical Society Museum
(1 Slab Bridge Road—location)
PO Box 253 (mailing address)
Assonet, MA 02702
(508) 644-5310 (Mondays)
Melanie J. Dodenhoff, Curator
Hours: Mon 10:00–4:00
(large local genealogical library, computerized finding aid)

Georgetown Historical Society
Brocklebank House Museum
108 East Main Street
PO Box 376
Georgetown, MA 01833
(978) 352-8372
Rosemary Morse, Curator
Hours: 4 Jul through Columbus Day: Sun 2:00–5:00

$6.00 per year membership for individuals

Grafton Historical Society, Inc.
Grafton, MA 01519
(508) 839-2063
George Carroll, President

Historical Society of Greenfield
43 Church Street
PO Box 415
Greenfield, MA 01302
(413) 772-6992
Tim Blagg, Curator
Hours: by appointment
$15.00 per year membership for individuals; research sub-contracted to a professional

Groveland Historical Society, Inc.
Uptack Road, Rt. 4
Groveland, MA 01834
(978) 372-6216
Mildred C. Esty, Secretary

Hamilton Historical Society
577 Bay Road
PO Box 108
Hamilton, MA 01936
Arthur H. Crosbie, Jr., President
Hours: Thur 1:00–4:00, and by appointment
$6.00 per year membership for individuals, $10.00 per year membership for couples, $4.00 per year membership for students

Historical Society of the Town of Hampden, Inc.
616 Main Street
PO Box 363
Hampden, MA 01036
(413) 566-3466
Mrs. Gerald Doten, Curator
Hours: fourth Sun (May–Oct) 2:00–4:00, and by appointment
(Hampden local history, some genealogy)
$5.00 per year membership for individuals

Hanover Historical Society
Stetson House, 514 Hanover Street
PO Box 156
Hanover, MA 02339
(781) 826-9575 (Wednesdays); (781) 826-3736 (President)
Carol Franzosa, President
Hours: Wed 2:00–4:00, and by appointment; open house: first weekend Dec
Pub. *The Hanover Historian*, four times per year
(Hanover history, South Shore genealogy, shipbuilding, North River)
$7.50 per year membership for individuals, $15.00 per year membership for families; search fees: donation

Hanson Historical Society
417 High Street
Hanson, MA 02341
David Clemons

Hardwick Historical Society
Hardwick, MA 01037
(413) 477-6635
Elizabeth Reilly, President

Harvard Historical Society
(215 Still River Road, Still River, MA—
location)
PO Box 542 (mailing address)
Harvard, MA 01451
(978) 456-8285
Joyce M. Verrando, Curator
Hours: Tue 10:00–noon, and by
appointment
Pub. *Harvard Historical Newsletter*, two
times per year (spring and fall)
$15.00 per year membership for
individuals, $20.00 per year
membership for families, $50.00 per
year Patron membership, $500.00 life
membership

Harwich Historical Society
80 Parallel Street
PO Box 5217
Harwich, MA 02645
(508) 432-8089
E-mail: hhs@tiac.net
http://www.tiac.net/users/hhs
James Brown, Director
Hours: Wed & Fri–Sat 1:00–4:00, Thur
1:00–7:00
Pub. *Powder House Quarterly*
(vital records of Harwich, copies of
Harwich Independent 1872–1948,
photographs, several privately
compiled genealogical collections,
etc.)

Hatfield Historical Society
PO Box 168
Hatfield, MA 01038
(413) 247-5545
Eugene Proulx, President

Heath Historical Society
Brunelle Road, R.F.D.
Charlemont, MA 01339
William Thane, Curator

Hingham Historical Society
(Old Derby Acadamy, 34 Main Street—
location)
PO Box 434 (mailing address)
Hingham, MA 02043
Gene Chamberlain, President
Pub. *News and Notes Out of the
Ordinary*, irregularly
$15.00 per year membership

Holden Historical Society, Inc.
(Hendricks House, 1157 Main Street—
location)
PO Box 421 (mailing address)
Holden, MA 01520-0421
(508) 793-3448

Ross W. Beales, Jr., Membership
Secretary
Hours: Sat 9:00–noon, and by
appointment
Pub. *Newsletter*, three times per year
$6.00 per year membership for
individuals, $10.00 per year
membership for families, $25.00 per
year Patron membership, $100.00 life
membership

Hubbardston Historical Society
(Jonas Clark Buliding, Main Street—
location)
PO Box 119 (mailing address)
Hubbardston, MA 01452-0119
Joyce Green, Secretary
Hours: by appointment
$4.00 per year membership

Hyde Park Historical Society
Weld Hall-Hyde Park Branch, Boston
Public Library
30 Ayles Road
Hyde Park, MA 02136
(617) 361-4398
Nancy Hannan, President
Hours: by appointment
(archival material pertaining to Hyde
Park people and history)
$5.00 per year membership

**Jones River Village Historical
Society**
PO Box 22
Kingston, MA 02364
(781) 585-1664
Scot E. Lyall, President
$15.00 per year membership for
individuals, $25.00 per year
membership for families

**Lancaster League of Historical
Societies**
56 Manchester Street
Leominster, MA 01453
(978) 537-3684
Evelyn B. Hachey, President

Lenox Historical Society
Lenox Academy Building
(75 Main Street—location)
PO Box 1856 (mailing address)
Lenox, MA 01240
Nancy D. Marasco, Curator
Hours: by appointment only
Pub. *Lenox Historical Society
Newsletter*, quarterly
$12.00 per year membership for
individuals, $15.00 per year
membership for families, $30.00 per
year membership for businesses

Leominster Historical Society
17 School Street
Leominster, MA 01453
(978) 534-5375
David Wilson, Trustee; Paul J. Benoit,
Trustee

Hours: Mon–Fri 9:00–2:00, Sat 9:00–
noon
Pub. *Newsletter*, 10 times per year
$5.00 per year membership

Lexington Historical Society
PO Box 514
Lexington, MA 02173-0005
(781) 862-1703
George Comtois, Executive Director
Hours: Library: Mon–Sat 10:00–5:00,
Sun (19 Apr–31 Oct) 1:00–5:00;
Archives: by appointment;
Administration: Mon–Fri 9:00–2:00

Lincoln Historical Society
Lincoln, MA 01773
(781) 259-8958

Littleton Historical Society
Houghton Memorial Building
4 Rogers Street
PO Box 721
Littleton, MA 01460-2721
(978) 486-8202 (message recorder)
Nancy Bradbury, Curator
Hours: Wed 1:00–4:00, second Sun
2:00–4:00
(Littleton vital records and history)
$5.00 per year membership for families
(includes two voting memberships),
$25.00 per year Supporting
membership, $100.00 per year Patron
membership; $1,000.00 life
membership; research for donation;
photocopies: 10¢ per page

Longmeadow Historical Society
697 Longmeadow Street
Longmeadow, MA 01106
(413) 567-3600; (413) 567-5432
(appointments); (413) 567-5432
(Curator)
Mabel Crosmon Swanson, Curator
Hours: Library: Wed–Thur 9:00–noon,
and by appointment
(genealogical records)
$6.00 per year membership for
individuals, $10.00 per year
membership for families

Lowell Historical Society
Boott Cotton Mill Museum
(400 Foot of John Street, Lowell, MA
01852—location)
PO Box 1826 (mailing address)
Lowell, MA 01853
(978) 970-5180 (President); (978) 934-
4998 (Librarian)
Louise Hunt, President; Martha Mayo,
Librarian
Hours: Tue–Wed 1:00–4:00
$10.00 per year membership for
individuals, $25.00 per year Donor
membership, $50.00 per year Sponsor
membership, $100.00 per year
Associate membership, $250.00 per
year Patron membership

Lynn Historical Society
Museum and Library
125 Green Street
Lynn, MA 01902
(781) 592-2465
Fay Greenleaf, Administrative Assistant
Hours: Mon–Fri 9:00–4:00
(Lynn history, Lynn genealogy
manuscripts, vital records for most of
Massachusetts)
$15.00 per year membership

Lynnfield Historical Society
PO Box 274
Lynnfield, MA 01940
(781) 334-4899; (781) 334-5411
(Library); (781) 334-3814 (President)
Shirley Northrup, President
Hours: Lynnfield Public Library: Mon–
Thur 9:00–9:00, Fri–Sat 9:00–5:00
Pub. *Historical Lynnfield*, quarterly
$3.00 per year membership

Malden Historical Society
Malden Public Library
36 Salem Street
Malden, MA 02148
(781) 324-0218 (Library)
Hours: Library: Mon–Thur 9:00–9:00,
Fri–Sat 9:00–6:00 (closed Sat mid-
June to mid-Sept)
(society not open to the public,
publications available at the Malden
Public Library)
$15.00 per year membership

Manchester Historical Society
10 Union Street
Manchester, MA 01944
(978) 526-7230
Lotte Calnek, Curator
Hours: Jul–Aug: Sat 10:00–4:00, Sun
noon–4:00, and by appointment
Pub. *MHS Newsletter*, quarterly

Mansfield Historical Society, Inc.
(53 Rumford Avenue—location)
21 Hodges Street (mailing address)
Mansfield, MA 02048
(508) 339-7398; (508) 285-4048
George Yelle, President
Hours: Mon 7:30–9:00; meetings Oct–
Jan & Mar–May: second Monday 7:30
Pub. *The M.H.S. Newsletter*, seven times
per year
$10.00 per year membership for
individuals, $15.00 per year
membership for families, $25.00 per
year Supporting membership, $200.00
life membership

Marblehead Historical Society
161 Washington Street
PO Box 1048
Marblehead, MA 01945
(781) 631-1762
Janice Rideout, Historian; Karen
MacInnis, Research
Hours: Library: Mon–Fri 10:00–4:00

Pub. *MHS Newsletter*, three times per
year
(Marblehead history and genealogy)
$20.00 per year membership for
individuals; staff-done research:
$10.00 per hour

Marlborough Historical Society
(377 Elm Street—location)
PO Box 513 (mailing address)
Marlborough, MA 01752
(508) 838-0479
Virginia H. Johnson, Curator
Hours: Archives: Mon 10:00–noon, and
by appointment; Museum House:
Sept–Jun: third Tue
Pub. *Newsletter*
$10.00 per year membership

Marshfield Historical Society
Webster and Careswell Streets
PO Box 1244
Marshfield, MA 02050
(781) 834-7236

**Martha's Vineyard Historical
Society**
Vineyard Museum
59 School Street
PO Box 827
Edgartown, MA 02539-0827
(508) 627-4441; (508) 693-2725
(Genealogist); (508) 627-4436 FAX
E-mail: islebyte@max.tiac.net
(Genealogist)
Bruce Andrews, Director; Catherine
Merwin Mayhew, Genealogist
Hours: Gale Huntington Library of
History: mid-Sept through mid-June:
Wed–Fri 1:00–4:00, Sat 10:00–4:00;
mid-June through mid-Sept: Tue–Sat
10:00–4:30
Pub. *The Dukes County Intelligencer*,
quarterly (February, May, August,
November) (emphasis on Martha's
Vineyard history); *Martha's Vineyard
Historical Society Messenger*,
quarterly (society news only)
$30.00 per year membership for
individuals, $50.00 per year
membership for families; research:
$20.00 per hour

Mattapoisett Historical Society
Mattapoisett Museum and Carriage
House
(5 Church Street—location)
PO Box 535 (mailing address)
Mattapoisett, MA 02739
(508) 758-2844
Bette A. Roberts, Curator
Hours: Sept–Jun: Tue–Wed & Fri 9:00–
noon; Jul–Aug: Tue–Sat 1:00–4:30

Maynard Historical Society
Town Building, Main Street
Maynard, MA 01754
(978) 897-9696
Paul V. Boothroyd, Curator

Hours: daytime by appointment only
$5.00 per year membership

Medfield Historical Society
6 Pleasant Street
PO Box 233
Medfield, MA 02052
Al Clark, President
Hours: Sat 9:00–1:00
Pub. *Bulletin*
$5.00 per year membership for
individuals; $1.50 per year Junior
membership; $10.00 per year
Contributing family membership,
$25.00 per year Sustaining family
membership, $100.00 individual life

Medford Historical Society
(10 Governors Avenue—location)
34 Summit Road (mailing address)
Medford, MA 02155
(781) 395-7863; (781) 391-8739
Michael F. Bradford, Curator; Dr. Joseph
V. Valeriani, President
Hours: Sun 2:00–4:00, and by
appointment
(emphasis on Massachusetts, Civil War,
the slave trade, shipbuilding and rum
distilling)
$8.00 per year membership for
individuals, $10.00 per year
membership for families

Melrose Historical Society, Inc.
131 West Emerson Street
PO Box 301
Melrose, MA 02176
(781) 665-5010
Arnold W. Williams, Chairman

Mendon Historical Society
Mendon Historical Museum
(3 Main Street at Founders' Park—
location)
PO Box 196 (mailing address)
Mendon, MA 01756
(508) 473-7672 (Curator's home)
Alice Pickering Palladini, Curator
Hours: May 30 through Sept: Sat–Sun
(two times per month) 2:00–4:00, Tue
(once a month) 6:30–8:00
(history and genealogy of Mendon and
area towns)
$4.00 per year membership; search fees:
20¢ per copy, plus postage; free
museum admission, donations
accepted

**Middleborough Historical
Association, Inc.**
Jackson Street
PO Box 304
Middleborough, MA 02346
(508) 947-1969; (508) 866-4414
(President); (508) 947-7120 (Director)
Robert M. Beals, President; Marsha
Manchester, Director
Hours: Museum: first–fourth Wed–Fri
(Jul–Aug), first & second Sun (Sept)
1:00–4:00

Pub. *The Middleborough Antiquarian*, three times per year

$10.00 per year membership for individuals

Milton Historical Society

Suffolk Resolves House
1370 Canton Avenue
Milton, MA 02186
(617) 333-0644
Mr. and Mrs. Wesley J. Merritt, Curators
Hours: Library: by appointment; Archives in Milton Public Library

Monson Historical Society, Inc.

1 Green Street
PO Box 114
Monson, MA 01057
(413) 267-4292
Grace Makepeace, Historian
Hours: by appointment

Montague Historical Society, Inc.

34 Central Street
Montague, MA 01351
(413) 367-2216

Monterey Historical Society

Monterey, MA 01245
(413) 528-3044
Mrs. John Fijux, President

Nantucket Historical Association

PO Box 1016
Nantucket, MA 02554
(508) 228-1894
John N. Welch, Administrator
Pub. *Historic Nantucket*, quarterly; *GAM*
$25.00 per year membership, includes both periodicals

Natick Historical Society and Museum

Bacon Free Library
58 Eliot Street
South Natick, MA 01760
(508) 647-4841; (508) 653-6730 FAX
E-mail: elliot@ma.ultranet.com
http://www.ultranet.com/~elliot/
Anne K. Schaller, Director
Hours: Tue 6:00 P.M.–8:30 P.M., Wed 2:00–4:30, Sat (16 Sept–14 June) 10:00–12:30
Pub. *The Arrow*, two or three times per year
$10.00 per year membership for individuals (beginning 1 May), $20.00 per year membership for families, $8.00 per year membership for senior citizens, $30.00 per year Contributing membership, $50.00 per year Sponsoring membership, $100.00 per year Sustaining membership; research: $10.00 per hour plus postage and copies

Needham Historical Society, Inc.

53 Glendoon Road
Needham, MA 02192
(781) 444-3181
Henry Hicks, President

The New England Historic Genealogical Society

101 Newbury Street
Boston, MA 02116-3007
(888) 286-3447 (Education, Membership and Sales); (617) 536-5740, ext. 214; (617) 536-7307 FAX
E-mail: membership@nehgs.org
http://www.nehgs.org
Tom Downard, Membership and Marketing Manager
Hours: Tue & Fri–Sat 9:00–5:00 (closed Sat before Mon holiday), Wed–Thur 9:00–9:00
Pub. *The New England Historical and Genealogical Register*, quarterly; *Nexus*, bimonthly; *The Computer Genealogist*, $30.00 per year subscription for non-members, $20.00 per year subscription for members; *Great Migration Newsletter*, bimonthly, $10.00 per year subscription
(New England and eastern Canadian history and genealogy primarily, but generally strong in all aspects of genealogy)
$50.00 per year membership for individuals (includes *Register* only), $70.00 per year membership for families, $20.00 per year membership for students, $250.00 per year Contributing membership, $500.00 per year Sustaining membership, $2,000.00 life membership, $5,000 life Benefactor membership; Enquiry service: $40.00 per hour for non-members, $25.00 per hour for members, $50.00 per hour for corporate clients (rush and FAX service additional); copies: 35¢ each, maximum of 35 copies, plus $5.00 service fee for members, $10.00 for non-members

North Andover Historical Society

153 Academy Road
North Andover, MA 01845
(978) 686-4035
Carol Machado, Executive Director
Hours: Mon–Fri 9:00–5:00 (closed state holidays and the Friday after Thanksgiving)
research fee for non-members

North Reading Historical and Antiquarian Society, Inc.

(Bow Street—location)
PO Box 354 (mailing address)
North Reading, MA 01864
(978) 664-1066
Thomas W. Parker, Curator
Hours: Spring & fall: Wed & Sun afternoons
Pub. *Newsletter*, irregularly
(historic house, artifacts, library)
$10.00 per year membership for individuals, $15.00 per year membership for families

Northampton Historical Society

(doing business as Historic Northampton)
46 Bridge Street
Northampton, MA 01060
(413) 584-6011
E-mail: hstnhamp@javanet.com
http://www.virtual-valley.com/histnhamp
Kerry Buckley, Executive Director
Hours: Mar–Dec: Tue–Fri 10:00–4:00, Sat–Sun noon–4:00
Pub. *The Weathervane Newsletter*, quarterly
(Northampton, Massachusetts, history)
$30.00 per year membership for individuals, $50.00 per year membership for families, $20.00 per year membership for senior citizens; written research inquiry: $15.00

Northborough Historical Society, Inc.

52 Main Street
Northborough, MA 01532

Northbridge Historical Society

183 Cooper Road
Northbridge, MA 01534
(508) 234-5110
John Rogers, President

Norton Historical Society

(18 West Main Street, Route 123—location)
PO Box 1711 (mailing address)
Norton, MA 02766-0909
(508) 285-7070 (Wednesdays); (508) 285-4048 (President)
George Yelle, President
Hours: Wed 9:00–noon & 7:00–9:00; meetings: Sept–Nov & Jan–May: third Tue 8:00
Pub. *Meeting Notice Letter*, eight times per year
$5.00 per year membership for individuals, $8.00 per year membership for families, $25.00 per year Supporting membership, $100.00 life membership

Norwell Historical Society, Inc.

Main Street
PO Box 693
Norwell, MA 02061
(781) 659-1888
Gertrude Daneau, President
Hours: various
Pub. *Newsletter*, six times per year
$10.00 per year membership for individuals, $15.00 per year membership for families, $200.00 life membership; limited research for donation to the society, but will refer to professional researchers on request

Norwood Historical Society

93 Day Street
Norwood, MA 02062
(781) 762-9197

Barbara J. Rand, President
Hours: Library: by appointment

Historical Society of Old Abington
Dyer Memorial Library
Centre Avenue
PO Box 22
Abington, MA 02351
Hours: Library: Mon–Tue & Thur–Fri
    1:00–5:00

Old Bridgewater Historical Society
162 Howard Street
PO Box 17
West Bridgewater, MA 02379
(508) 559-1510
Diana Lothrop, President
Hours: Wed 10:00–4:00, Sat 1:00–4:00
    (Apr–Oct)
Pub. *Newsletter*, monthly
$12.00 per year membership

Old Colony Historical Society
66 Church Green
Taunton, MA 02780
(508) 822-1622
Katheryn P. Viens, Director
Hours: Tue–Sat 10:00–4:00 (closed
    holidays and Sat before Mon holidays)
Pub. *Newsletter*, quarterly
(southeastern Massachusetts)
$25.00 per year membership for
    individuals, $35.00 per year
    membership for families of two;
    research by mail: $19.00 per hour, plus
    copies; admission for genealogical
    research: $5.00 per day; museum
    admission: $2.00 for adults and $1.00
    for children aged 12–18 and senior
    citizens

Old Dartmouth Historical Society
Whaling Museum Library
18 Johnny Cake Hill
New Bedford, MA 02740
(508) 997-0046
Virginia M. Adams, Librarian
Hours: weekdays 10:00–12:00 & 1:00–
    4:00
Pub. *Bulletin from Johnny Cake Hill*,
    three times per year
(history of American whaling and of
    southeastern Massachusetts,
    particularly the New Bedford area)
$15.00 per year membership for
    individuals

Historical Society of Old Newbury
98 High Street
Newburyport, MA 01950
(978) 462-2681; (978) 462-0134 FAX
Clifford Bonney, President
Hours: Library: Tue–Sat 10:00–4:00 by
    appointment only
(Newbury, Newburyport, and West
    Newbury families)
search fee: $10.00 per hour

Historical Society of Old Yarmouth
(11 Strawberry Lane—location)
PO Box 11 (mailing address)
Yarmouth Port, MA 02675
(508) 362-3021
Barbara Ryan, Director
Hours: by appointment
Pub. *Newsletter*, two times per year
$15.00 per year membership

Orange Historical Society, Inc.
(41 North Main Street—location)
80 Fountain Street (mailing address)
Orange, MA 01364
Irene Ballou, President
Hours: Sun 2:00–4:00 (June–Aug), and
    by appointment
Pub. *Orange Historical Society, Inc.*

Orleans Historical Society
Margaret Stranger House
(3 River Road—location)
PO Box 353 (mailing address)
Orleans, MA 02653
(508) 240-1329
Jon Howard, Director
Hours: Mon & Fri 9:00–4:30; Jul–Aug:
    Mon–Fri noon–4:00
$5.00 per year membership

Osterville Historical Society
West Bay and Parker Road
PO Box 3
Osterville, MA 02655
(508) 428-5861
John M. Groff, Director
(part of the town of Barnstable)

Peabody Historical Society
35 Washington Street
Peabody, MA 01960
(978) 531-0805
Neil T. Corning, President
Hours: Library: Tue 7:00–9:00

Pelham Historical Society
(Amherst Road, Pelham, MA 01002—
    location)
40 South Valley Road (mailing address)
Amherst, MA 01002
(413) 253-3970 (President); (413) 253-
    2739 (Genealogy)
Elva Anderson, President; Robert Lord
    Keyes, Genealogist
Hours: Museum: Sun (May–Sept) 1:30–
    4:30
Pub. *Newsletter*, annually
(Pelham and Prescott, Massachusetts;
    Shay's Rebellion, 1786–1787)
$5.00 per year membership; queries free,
    but would like to trade information if
    possible

Petersham Historical Society, Inc.
10 North Main Street
Petersham, MA 01366
(978) 724-3380
Delight Gale Haines, Curator and
    Librarian

Hours: Library: summer: Sun 3:00–5:00,
    and by appointment
(Daniel Shays; local history and families)
$5.00 per year membership for
    individuals, $7.50 per year
    membership for families, $75.00 life
    membership

The Pilgrim Society
Pilgrim Hall Museum
75 Court Street
Plymouth, MA 02360-3891
(508) 746-1620
Peggy M. Timlin, Curator of Manuscripts
    and Books
Hours: daily 9:30–4:30
("dedicated to preserving the artifacts
    and the legacy of the Pilgrims
    themselves; membership open to all
    interested parties; some of our
    resources could be used profitably by
    a knowledgeable genealogist")

The Plainfield Historical Society, Inc.
344 Main Street
Plainfield, MA 01070
(413) 634-5417 (President)
Arvilla L. Dyer, President
Hours: Museum: by appointment

Princeton Historical Society
PO Box 199
Princeton, MA 01541-0199
Katherine L. Poor, President

Quincy Historical Society
Adams Academy Building
8 Adams Street
Quincy, MA 02169
(617) 773-1144
Elliott W. Hoffman, Ph.D., Director
Hours: Library: Mon–Fri 9:30–3:30, Sat
    12:30–3:30
Pub. *Quincy History*

Ramapogue Historical Society
(70 Park Street, West Springfield, MA
    01089—location)
PO Box 826 (mailing address)
West Springfield, MA 01090
(413) 732-8049
Emily W. Delaney, Curator
Hours: Sat–Sun (mid-June to mid-Oct)
    1:00–5:00

Randolph Historical Society
360 North Main Street
Randolph, MA 02368
(781) 963-3142
Henry M. Cooke, IV, President

Reading Antiquarian Society
(Parker Tavern, 103 Washington Street—
    location)
PO Box 842 (mailing address)
Reading, MA 01867
(781) 944-4030
Eleanor Dustin, President
Hours: Sun (May–Oct) 2:00–5:00
(local history)

Rehoboth Antiquarian Society
Bay State Road
PO Box 2
Rehoboth, MA 02769

Roslindale Historical Society
PO Box 356
Boston, MA 02131
Sandra MacKinnon, President

Rowe Historical Society, Inc.
(Zoar Road—location)
PO Box 456 (mailing address)
Rowe, MA 01367
(413) 339-5598
Alan Bjork
Pub. *Rowe Historical Society Bulletin*,
three times per year, $5.00 per year
subscription, $15.00 per three-year
subscription, $25.00 per year
Contributing subscription, $75.00 life
subscription; *Rowe Massachusetts
Yearbook*, annually

Rowley Historical Society
Main Street
Rowley, MA 01969
(978) 948-3381

Roxbury Historical Society, Inc.
Dillaway-Thomas House at Roxbury
Heritage State Park
183 Roxbury Street, John Eliot Square
Dudley Station, PO Box 5
Roxbury, MA 02119
(617) 445-3399; (617) 445-3397
Renita L. Martin, Program Coordinator
Hours: Wed–Fri 10:00–4:00, Sat–Sun
noon-5:00
Pub. *The Roxbury Heritage News*

Royalston Historical Society
(The Common, Royalston, MA 01368—
location)
Fernald Road (mailing address)
South Royalston, MA 01331
(978) 249-4964

Village Improvement and Historical Society of Royalston, Inc.
Society Building
Royalston, MA 01368
(978) 249-2598; (978) 249-2018
Haines J. Kirkman, President; Patricia C.
Poor, Curator

Sandisfield Historical Society
SR 66, Box 96
Sandisfield, MA 01255
Hours: second Sat 10:00

Sandwich Historical Society, Inc.
Glass Museum
129 Main Street
PO Box 103
Sandwich, MA 02563
(508) 888-0251; (508) 888-4941 FAX
Lynne Horton, Curator of History
Hours: by appointment
Pub. *The Acorn*, annually, $12.95
postpaid

Sandy Bay Historical Society and Museums, Inc.
(40 King Street—location)
PO Box 63 (mailing address)
Rockport, MA 01966
(978) 546-9533
Cynthia A. Peckham, Curator
Hours: Mon 9:00–1:00; mid-Jun to mid-
Sept: Tue–Sun 2:00–5:00
(local history and genealogy)
$10.00 per year membership; search:
$3.00; copies: 10¢ each

Historical Society of Santuit and Cotuit, Inc.
PO Box 1484
Cotuit, MA 02635-1484
(508) 428-3895; (508) 428-8008
William G. Morse, Jr., Treasurer
Hours: Thur & Sun 4:00–6:00 (last Sun
in June through Labor Day)
(part of town of Barnstable)

The Saugus Historical Society, Inc.
(59 Water Street, Saugus, MA 01906—
location)
21 Lovell Road (mailing address)
Lynnfield, MA 01940
(781) 233-1191

Scituate Historical Society
Scituate Town Archives
Town Hall
600 Chief Justice Cushing Highway
Scituate, MA 02066
(781) 545-0474
Hours: Library: Mon, Wed & Fri 10:00–
4:00; Wed–Sat (June–Sept) 2:00–5:00,
and by appointment
Pub. *Scituate Historical Society Bulletin*,
semiannually
$5.00 per year membership

Sharon Historical Society
30 Crest Road
Sharon, MA 02067
(781) 784-5137
Irving Post

Family History Center of the Sheffield Historical Society
(Main Street—location)
PO Box 747 (mailing address)
Sheffield, MA 01257-0747
(413) 229-3682
James Miller, Archivist
Hours: Mon & Fri 1:30–4:00, and by
appointment
(Sheffield area genealogy, social and
house history)
donation for research

Shelburne Historical Society, Inc.
(33 Severance Street—location)
PO Box 86 (mailing address)
Shelburne, MA 01370
(413) 625-6150
Pub. *Mount Massaemet Shadows*,
quarterly

Sherborn Historical Society
(Room in Town Offices Building, 19
Washington Street, Route16—
location)
PO Box 186 (mailing address)
Sherborn, MA 01770-0186
(508) 651-7850 (Selectmen's Office, for
messages)
Betsy Johnson, Curator; Faith Tiberio,
President
Hours: Mon 10:00–2:00, and by
appointment
(Sherborn history, families, artifacts)
$7.50 per year membership for
individuals, $10.00 per year
membership for families; search fee:
copy costs plus donation

Shirley Historical Society
PO Box 217
Shirley, MA 01464
(978) 425-9328; (978) 425-4513
Meredith Marcinkewicz, Curator
Hours: Sat 10:00–1:00, and by
appointment
(with special collections on MacKaye
family and Shirley Shaker community)
$5.00 per year membership; copies: 25¢
per page

Shrewsbury Historical Society
Church Street
Shrewsbury, MA 01545

Sippicorn Historical Society
PO Box 541
Marion, MA 02738
Ellen Stone
Hours: Wed & Sat 11:30–5:00 (closed in
the winter)
(local history)
$10.00 per year membership

Somerville Historical Society
Somerville Historical Museum
1 Westwood Road
Somerville, MA 02143
(617) 666-9810
Constance B. Fuller, Director, Museum
Services

South Gardner Historical Society
55 Union Street
Gardner, MA 01440
(978) 632-5118
Warren M. Sinclair, President

Southborough Historical Society
PO Box 364
Southborough, MA 01772
(508) 485-5089
Mrs. Raymond R. Allen
$3.00 per year membership

Sterling Historical Society, Inc.
7 Pine Street
PO Box 356
Sterling, MA 01564
Ruth M. Hopfmann, Curator
Hours: Tue 9:00–1:00, and by
appointment with Curator

Pub. *SHS Newsletter*, quarterly
donation requested

Stoneham Historical Society, Inc.
36 William Street
Stoneham, MA 02180-3845
(781) 438-4185 or (781) 438-4542
Mary K. Marchant, Curator; Joanne B.
  Harriman, President
Hours: by appointment
Pub. *Stoneham Historical Society*, two
  times per year
search fee: voluntary contribution

Stoughton Historical Society
6 Park Street
PO Box 542
Stoughton, MA 02072
(781) 344-5456
Aina M. McMann, President
Hours: Tue 2:00–4:00, Thur 7:00–9:00,
  and by appointment
Pub. *Stoughton Historical Society*
  Newsletter, five times per year
$6.00 per year membership for
  individuals, $10.00 per year
  membership for families, $100.00 life
  membership for individuals

Stow Historical Society
PO Box 261
Stow, MA 01775
(978) 897-5996
Barbara P. Sipler, President
Hours: by appointment
(files on Gardner, Randall; local history)

Sudbury Historical Society
Loring Parsonage
Old Sudbury Road
PO Box 233
Sudbury, MA 01776
(978) 443-6672
Hilda A. Whitney, Clerk

Sutton Historical Society, Inc.
4 Uxbridge Road
Sutton, MA 01590
(508) 865-2010
Daniel Griffith, President
Pub. *Bulletin*

Swampscott Historical Society
99 Paradise Road
Swampscott, MA 01907
(781) 598-4894; (781) 592-8566
Joseph Balsama, President
Hours: by appointment

Swansea Historical Society, Inc.
Old Warren Road
PO Box 67
Swansea, MA 02777
(508) 379-0972
Carl Becker, President
Hours: Sun (Jul–Aug) 2:00–5:00

**Swift River Valley Historical Society,
Inc.**
(40 Elm Street, North—location)
PO Box 22 (mailing address
New Salem, MA 01355
(978) 544-6885 (Jun–Aug); (978) 544-
  6207 (President)
Elizabeth L. Peirce, President
Hours: Library: 25 Jun–30 Aug: Wed &
  Sun 1:00–4:00; 1 Sep–12 Oct: Sun
  1:00–4:00
Pub. *Newsletter*, quarterly
(museum created to remember the towns
  of Dana, Greenwich, Enfield, Prescott,
  and part of New Salem, which were
  destroyed to create Quabbin
  Reservoir)
$5.00 per year membership

Topsfield Historical Society
(1 Howlett Street—location)
PO Box 323 (mailing address)
Topsfield, MA 01983
(978) 887-3998
Norman J. Isler, President
Hours: Wed, Fri & Sun (June 15 through
  Sept 15) 1:00–4:30, and by
  appointment
(Old Topsfield families)
$10.00 per year membership for
  individuals; search fees vary with
  degree of difficulty

Truro Historical Society
Truro Historical Museum
(Lighthouse Road, North Truro, MA
  02652—museum location)
PO Box 486 (mailing address)
Truro, MA 02666
(508) 497-3397 (summer); (508) 349-
  2809 (winter)
Elizabeth J. Allen, Curator
Hours: June 15–Sept 15: Mon–Sun
  10:00–5:00
Pub. *News Letter*, annually
(materials on families Coan, Lombard,
  Rich, Snow, etc.)
$7.50 per year membership for
  individuals; museum or
  archivesadmission: $2.00

Upton Historical Society
PO Box 171
Upton, MA 01568
(508) 529-6200
Ashley Perkins, President; Carol
  Blomquist, House Committee
  Chairman
Hours: Building, Second Floor Rooms:
  Wed 9:00–noon; meetings: last Fri
Pub. *Newsletter*, monthly
$5.00 per year membership, $50.00 life
  membership

Walpole Historical Society
33 West Street
PO Box 1724
Walpole, MA 02081
(508) 668-0449 (Secretary)

Karl West, Secretary
Hours: by appointment
(some local histories and genealogies)
$5.00 per year membership

Wareham Historical Society, Inc.
(8 Elm Street—location)
PO Box 211 (mailing address)
Wareham, MA 02571
(508) 295-3227
Betty Wright, Curator
Hours: Jul–Aug: Thur–Sun 1:00–4:00

Warwick Historical Society
(Morse Building, Athol Road, Warwick
  Center—location)
625 Winchester Road (mailing address)
Warwick, MA 01378
(978) 544-3461
Charles A. Phelps, President and
  Director/Curator)
Hours: by appointment

The Historical Society of Watertown
Edmund Fowle House
28 Marshall Street
Watertown, MA 02172
(617) 923-6067
Lou Allegro, President
Hours: Mon–Fri 10:00–2:00
Pub. *The Town Crier*, quarterly
$5.00 per year membership

Wayland Historical Society
PO Box 56
Wayland, MA 01778
(508) 358-7959
John B. Wilson, President
Pub. *WHS Newsletter*

Webster Dudley Historical Society
(School Street—location)
43 Union Count Road (mailing address)
Webster, MA 01570
(508) 943-1965
Bertha A. Hart, President

Wellesley Historical Society
229 Washington Street
PO Box 81142
Wellesley Hills, MA 02181
(781) 235-6690
Barbara Gorely Teller, Director/Curator
Hours: Library: Mon & Sat 2:00–4:30
Pub. *WHS Newsletter*
(Civil War books)
$15.00 per year membership

**The Wellfleet Historical Society
Museum**
Main Street
PO Box 58
Wellfleet, MA 02667
(508) 349-9157
Joan Hopkins Coughlin, Curator
Hours: Tue–Sat (late June through Aug)
  2:00–5:00
Pub. *Beacon*, annually
$3.50 per year membership; $1.00
  admission to museum (over 12 years
  of age)

Wenham Historical Association and Museum, Inc.
132 Main Street
Wenham, MA 01984
(978) 468-2377; (978) 468-1763 FAX
Marilyn Corning, Librarian
Hours: Mon–Fri 10:00–4:00, Sat–Sun
 1:00–4:00
Pub. *Wenham Museum Newsletter*,
 bimonthly; *Annual Report* (April/May)
(Wenham history, dolls, dolls' houses,
 model railroads; local genealogy in
 research library, papers on early
 Wenham, ice trade)
$25.00 per year membership for
 individuals, $40.00 per year
 membership for families, $20.00 per
 year membership for senior citizens

West Boylston Historical Society, Inc.
PO Box 201
West Boylston, MA 01583
(508) 853-1947

West Brookfield Historical Commission
Town Hall
Main Street
West Brookfield, MA 01585
(508) 867-2006; (508) 867-6011
(collection of manuscripts and
 unpublished genealogies, published
 histories, some church histories, 1st
 Precinct Parish Records from 1754 to
 1826, many town reports and valuation
 and taxes books)

West Newbury Historical Association
PO Box 332
West Newbury, MA 01985
(978) 465-8046
Beatrice Downey, President

West Roxbury Historical Society
1961 Centre Street
Boston, MA 02132
(617) 325-3147
Daniel Cantwell
Hours: winter: Sat 9:00–5:00; summer:
 Mon & Thur 12:00–8:00, Tue, Wed &
 Fri 9:00–5:00

Westborough Historical Society (and Archives)
(13 Parkman Street—location)
PO Box 149 (mailing address)
Westborough, MA 01581-1911
(508) 898-0975; (508) 366-2351
 (Curator's home)
Kenneth Housman, President
Hours: third Thursday
Pub. *Newsletter*, monthly
(maps, letters, wills, deeds, etc., of
 residents and business/industry from
 1717; birthplace of Eli Whitney)

$15.00 per year membership for
 individuals, $25.00 per year Patron
 membership; $100.00 life
 membership; search: hourly fee plus
 cost of copies to Jacqueline C.
 Tidman, Curator

Western Hampden Historical Society
Dewey House
PO Box 256
Westfield, MA 01086
(413) 562-3657
Barbara Bush, Chairperson, Board of
 Trustees

Westford Historical Society, Inc.
2 Boston Road
PO Box 411
Westford, MA 01886
(978) 692-8513
Alexander Belida, President

Westminster Historical Society
(110 Main Street—museum location)
PO Box 177 (mailing address)
Westminster, MA 01473
(978) 874-5569
Betsy Hannula, Curator
Hours: Library: Mon 7:00–9:00, and by
 appointment
Pub. *Newsletter*, four times per year
(artifacts and documents pertaining to the
 history of Westminster; General
 Nelson A. Miles)
$15.00 per year membership for
 individuals

Weston Historical Society
PO Box 343
Weston, MA 02193
(781) 237-1447 (Curator's home); (781)
 237-1471 (Curator's home) FAX;
 (781) 891-4662 (President)
Dr. Vera Laska, Curator; Mrs. Lee
 Marsh, President
Hours: Wed 10:00–noon, and by
 appointment
Pub. *Weston Historical Society Bulletin*,
 two times per year (spring and fall)
$10.00 per year

Westport Historical Society, Inc.
(25 Drift Road—location)
PO Box 3031 (mailing address)
Westport, MA 02790-0700
(508) 636-6011
Lincoln S. Tripp, Director
Hours: Tue–Wed 9:00–noon & 1:00–
 4:00, and by appointment
Pub. *The Harbinger*, bimonthly
$10.00 per year membership for
 individuals, $20.00 per year
 membership for families, $50.00 per
 year Contributing membership,
 $150.00 per year Sustaining
 membership, $200.00 per year
 membership for businesses; search fee:
 donation from non-members

Weymouth Historical Society
PO Box 56
Weymouth, MA 02190
Candace A. Wright, President

Winchendon Historical Society, Inc.
50 Pleasant Street
Winchendon, MA 01475
(978) 297-0300 (Library)
Julia White, Co-curator
Hours: Tue evening (Jul–Aug)

Winchester Historical Society
PO Box 127
Winchester, MA 01890
(781) 721-7146
Mrs. Robert Bairnsfather, Chair of
 Genealogy Group
Hours: various (call first)
Pub. *Black Horse Bulletin*, quarterly
$15.00 per year membership for
 individuals, $20.00 per year
 membership for families

Winthrop Improvement and Historical Association
40 Shirley Street
Winthrop, MA 02152
(617) 846-0684
G. David Hubbard, II, President
Hours: by appointment only
Pub. *Newsletter*, monthly
$12.00 per year membership

Worthington Historical Society
(6 Williamsburg Road—location)
PO Box 12 (mailing address)
Worthington, MA 01098
(413) 238-5363
Edward Claydon, President
Hours: various
$5.00 per year membership

Wrentham Historical Society
PO Box 300
Wrentham, MA 02093
(508) 384-7151
Jean Nall, President
Pub. *Newsletter*, about every five weeks
(vital statistics 1673–1930, with few
 exceptions)
$10.00 per year membership for
 individuals, $18.00 per year
 membership for families

LDS Family History Centers

Boston
(see Weston)

Springfield
(see Bloomfield, Connecticut)

Weston
(617) 235-2164

Genealogical Societies

State Genealogical Societies

Massachusetts Genealogical Council
PO Box 5393
Cochituate, MA 01778
Gratia Mahony, Secretary
Pub. *MGC Newsletter*, quarterly
$7.50 per year membership for
individuals, $10.00 per year
membership for organizations, $15.00
per year Sponsor membership

M.S.O.G. Chapters

**The Massachusetts Society of
Genealogists, Inc. (M.S.O.G.)**
705 Southbridge Street
Worcester, MA 01610
(508) 792-5066
Katherine A. Gardner-Westcott, Librarian
Hours: Wed 11:00–3:00, Sat 10:00–4:00
(subject to change)
Pub. *MASSOG: A Genealogical
Magazine for the Commonwealth of
Massachusetts*, quarterly
$19.00 per year membership for
individuals, $24.00 per year
membership for families, $30.00 per
year membership for institutions;
queries free to members, $2.00 to non-
members; research requests: $6.00 per
hour (half-hour minimum) for
members, $10.00 per hour for non-
members, plus photocopies at 15–25¢
each, to be billed by Sylvia I.
Bockstein, Research Coordinator, 172
Jackson Street, Jefferson, MA 01522-
1469 or Research Committee, c/o
MSOG Library

Bristol County Chapter (M.S.O.G.)
(address withheld upon request)
all queries should be sent to the parent
organization

Hampden Chapter (M.S.O.G.)
6 Ridgewood Road
Wilbraham, MA 01095
Roy Powers
Pub. *Hampden Chapter Newsletter*,
monthly

Middlesex Chapter (M.S.O.G.)
244 Flanders Road
Westborough, MA 01581
(508) 485-3275
Bob Cumming
Pub. *The News Mix*, nine times per year
$19.00 per year membership for
individuals, $24.00 per year
membership for families, $30.00 per
year membership for institutions

Worcester Chapter (M.S.O.G.)
27 Brigham Hill Road
Grafton, MA 01519
Mary Ann Hall

Regional Genealogical Societies

**Berkshire Family History
Association**
PO Box 1437
Pittsfield, MA 01201-1437
(413) 445-5521; (413) 623-5267
Donald L. Lutes, Jr., President
Hours: Berkshire Athenaeum: winter
(Sept to mid-June) Mon–Thur 9:00–
9:00, Fri 9:00–5:00, Sat 10:00–5:00;
summer (mid-June through Labor
Day): Mon, Wed & Fri 9:00–5:00, Tue
& Thur 9:00–9:00, Sat 10:00–5:00
Pub. *Berkshire Genealogist*, quarterly
(western Massachusetts, Berkshire
County and nearby)
$12.00 per year membership for
individuals, $14.00 per year
membership for families, $5.00 per
year membership for students

Cape Cod Genealogical Society
PO Box 906
Brewster, MA 02631
(508) 896-3434
Mary Ella Jones Parrott, President
Pub. *Cape Cod Genealogical Society
Bulletin*, quarterly
(Cape Cod and Massachusetts
genealogy)
$15.00 per year membership for
individuals or families

**Central Massachusetts Genealogical
Society**
(American Legion Post 129, Elm Street,
Gardner, MA 01440—location)
PO Box 811 (mailing address)
Westminster, MA 01473-0811
(978) 874-2505
Ruth Wellner, Founder/First President
Hours: Mount Wachusett Community
College, Room 113, Green Street,
Gardner, MA: fourth Tue (Jan–Nov)
7:00
Pub. *The Searchers*, bimonthly
$12.00 per year membership, $17.00 per
year membership for families, $10.00
per year membership for individuals,
$20.00 per year membership for
organizations

Essex Society of Genealogists, Inc.
PO Box 313
Lynnfield, MA 01940-0313
(781) 664-9279
Nancy C. Hayward, Secretary
Pub. *The Essex Genealogist* (*TEG*),
quarterly (February, May, August,
November), $4.50 per issue; *The*

Newsletter of the ESOG, quarterly
(March, June, September, December)
(Essex County, Massachusetts, also all
eastern Massachusetts, New England,
and the Maritime Provinces of
Canada)
$18.00 per year membership for
individuals (beginning in January,
includes both publications), $21.00 per
year membership for families, $16.00
per year membership for libraries, add
$8.50 per year for first class mail
within the U.S. or foreign membership

Falmouth Genealogical Society
PO Box 2107
Teaticket, MA 02536
Hours: meetings at the Falmouth Public
Library: second Sat 10:00

Genealogical Roundtable
20 Loblolly Lane
Wayland, MA 01778-1429
Shirley Barnes
Hours: fourth Mon (except June–Aug &
Dec) 1:00 at Concord Free Public
Library
Pub. *New Newsletter for Roundtable*
(genealogy, history and literature)
$8.00 per year membership

**Minnesota Genealogical Society,
Yankee Branch**
(1650 Carroll Avenue, Saint Paul, MN
55104—location)
PO Box 16069 (mailing address)
Saint Paul, MN 55116-0069

**The New England Historic
Genealogical Society**
101 Newbury Street
Boston, MA 02116-3007
(888) 286-3447 (Education, Membership
and Sales); (617) 536-5740, ext. 214;
(617) 536-7307 FAX
E-mail: membership@nehgs.org
http://www.nehgs.org
Tom Downard, Membership and
Marketing Manager
Hours: Tue & Fri–Sat 9:00–5:00 (closed
Sat before Mon holiday), Wed–Thur
9:00–9:00
Pub. *The New England Historical and
Genealogical Register*, quarterly;
Nexus, bimonthly; *The Computer
Genealogist*, $30.00 per year
subscription for non-members, $20.00
per year subscription for members;
Great Migration Newsletter,
bimonthly, $10.00 per year
subscription
(New England and eastern Canadian
history and genealogy primarily, but
generally strong in all aspects of
genealogy)
$50.00 per year membership for
individuals (includes *Register* only),
$70.00 per year membership for
families, $20.00 per year membership

for students, $250.00 per year
Contributing membership, $500.00 per year Sustaining membership, $2,000.00 life membership, $5,000 life Benefactor membership; Enquiry service: $40.00 per hour for non-members, $25.00 per hour for members, $50.00 per hour for corporate clients (rush and FAX service additional); copies: 35¢ each, maximum of 35 copies, plus $5.00 service fee for members, $10.00 for non-members

Palm Beach County Genealogical Society, Inc.
(see Florida)

Plymouth County Genealogists, Inc.
60 Sheridan Street
Brockton, MA 02402-2852
(508) 583-6106
James E. Hoban, President
Hours: first Sat (Sept–June) 1:00
Pub. *The Genealogical Inquirer*, ten times per year (monthly, except July and August)
(Plymouth County research only, not the entire state of Massachusetts)
$10.00 per year membership for individuals, $12.50 per year membership for families

The South Shore Genealogical Society
PO Box 396
Norwell, MA 02061
John C. Murray, President
Hours: Mon–Sat 10:00–5:00; meetings: second Sat (Sept–Jun)
Pub. *Newsletter*, bimonthly
(research New England, mid-west U.S., Nova Scotia, maintains surname file)
$10.00 per year membership; accepts inquiries

Western Massachusetts Genealogical Society, Inc.
PO Box 80206, Forest Park Station
Springfield, MA 01108
Claudia Chicklas, President
Hours: meetings at Connecticut Valley Historical Museum: first Wed (except Jul–Aug) 5:00–9:00
Pub. *The American Elm*, quarterly
$10.00 per year membership for individuals, $12.50 per year membership for families, $25.00 per year Sustaining membership for individuals, $35.00 per year Sustaining membership for families, $100.00 life membership for individuals, $125.00 life membership for families

Independent Publications and Miscellany

Ancient Free and Accepted Masons Library
Grand Lodge of Massachusetts
186 Tremont Street (corner of Boylston Street)
Boston, MA 02111
(617) 426-6040, ext. 131
Roberta A. Hankamer, Library Director
Hours: Mon–Fri 9:00–5:00; Sept–June: Thur 9:00–7:00 also
(emphasis on freemasonry, especially in Massachusetts)

Archive Publishing
4 Mayfair Circle
Oxford, MA 01540-2722
(508) 987-0881
DeLene Holbrook, Owner
(New England original records, mostly on fiche, with currentemphasis on Massachusetts, including original Massachusetts vital records, 1620–1905, for over 250 cities and towns; transcripts to 1850 for 179 towns)

Committee for a New England Bibliography, Inc.
233 Bay State Road
Boston, MA 02215
(617) 266-9706

Friends of the Blue Hills Trust (F.B.H.)
(F.B.H. Quarry-Granite Railway and Rock Climbing Museum—location)
1894 Canton Avenue (mailing address)
Milton, MA 02186
(617) 326-0079 (F.B.H. 24-hour hot line information)
David P. Hodgdon, Executive Director and Museum Curator
Hours: activities on weekends and holidays
Pub. *FBH Newsletter*, bimonthly; *Your Blue Hill Reservation*, $3.00 postpaid
(preservation of historical resources)
$25.00 membership for individuals, $35.00 per year membership for families, $20.00 per year membership for senior citizens (60 years or more), $10.00 per year Junior membership (through age 17), $45.00 per year Sustaining membership, $80.00 per year Patron membership, $200.00 per year Sponsor membership, $400.00 life membership, $50.00 per year Agency membership, $100.00 per year Institutional membership

Goethe Institute
170 Beacon Street
Boston, MA 02116
(617) 262-6050
Hans-Ulrich Kaup, Librarian
Hours: Sept–June: Tue–Wed & Fri 12:00–6:00, Thur 12:00–8:00

Historic Salem, Inc.
Old Town Hall, Derby Square
PO Box 865
Salem, MA 01970
(978) 745-6470

Institute for Boston Studies
Boston College
Chestnut Hill
Boston, MA 02167
(617) 552-8458
Sharlene Voogd Cochrane, Director
Hours: Resource Center: by appointment during school year

Institute for Massachusetts Studies
Westfield State College
Western Avenue
Westfield, MA 01086
(413) 572-5344
Martin Kaufman, Ph.D., Editorial Director
Hours: 9:00–4:00
Pub. *Historical Journal of Massachusetts*, semiannually (Winter and Summer), $7.00 per year subscription
(history of Massachusetts)

Little Red Schoolhouse Association, Inc.
(Concord Avenue, Brockton, MA 02401—location)
PO Box 3036 (mailing address)
Brockton, MA 02404-3036
(508) 559-8871
Sal Madonna, Clerk
Hours: seasonal
Pub. *Newsletter*, quarterly
$5.00 per year membership

MaGenWeb
Part of U.S. GenWeb Project
E-mail: ma@usgenweb.com
http://www.rootsweb.com/~magenweb
(links to other Massachusetts resources)

The New England Quarterly
Meserve Hall 243
Northeastern University
Boston, MA 02115
(617) 373-4445; (617) 373-2661 FAX
Professor William M. Fowler, Jr., Editor
Pub. *The New England Quarterly*, $25.00 per year subscription
(one of America's oldest scholarly journals, focuses on New England's history and literature)

Society for the Preservation of New England Antiquities—Archives

Harrison Gray Otis House
141 Cambridge Street
Boston, MA 02114
(617) 227-3956
Ellie Reichlin; Lorne Condon
Hours: Tue–Fri 9:30–5:00 by
appointment only
Pub. *SPNEA News*

Tales of Cape Cod, Inc.

(3046 Main Street—location)
PO Box 41 (mailing address)
Barnstable, MA 02630
Mrs. Gene D. Gardner, President
(produces historical publications,
summer lecture series, weekly cable
T.V. historic program; maintains pre-
Revolutionary courthouse)
$15.00 per year membership

Victorian Society in America, New England Chapter

137 Beacon Street
Boston, MA 02116
(617) 267-6338
Peter Ambler, President

MICHIGAN

Archives and Libraries with Holdings in Genealogy

State Archives and Library

State Archives of Michigan

Michigan Historical Center
Department of State
717 West Allegan Street
Lansing, MI 48918-1800
(517) 373-1408; (517) 241-1658 FAX
http://www.sos.state.mi.us/history/
archive/archive.html
LeRoy Barnett, Reference Archivist
Hours: Mon–Fri 10:00–4:00

Library of Michigan

Michigan and Genealogy Special
Collection
(717 West Allegan Street—location)
PO Box 30007 (mailing address)
Lansing, MI 48909-7507
(517) 373-1300
http://www.libofmich.lib.mi.us
Hours: Mon–Fri 8:00–6:00, Sat 9:00–
5:00, Sun 1:00–5:00

State Historical Societies

Michigan Historical Commission

505 State Office Building
Lansing, MI 48913

Historical Society of Michigan

2117 Washtenaw Avenue
Ann Arbor, MI 48104
(734) 769-1828
Thomas L. Jones, Executive Director
Hours: Mon–Fri 9:00–5:00
Pub. *Chronicle*, quarterly; *HSM
Newsletter*, bimonthly; *Michigan
Historical Review*, semiannually
("Center for teaching Michigan history;
conferences, books, publications, no
archives but small library for
teachers.")
$25.00 per year membership

City, County and Regional Archives and Libraries

Adrian Public Library

143 East Maumee Street
Adrian, MI 49221
(517) 265-2265
Jule J. Fosbender, Director
Hours: Mon–Tue & Thur 10:00–9:00,
Wed & Fri 10:00–5:30, Sat 9:30–5:30
(Adrian and Lenawee County)

Albion Public Library

501 South Superior Street
Albion, MI 49224

Ann Arbor Hands-On Museum

219 East Huron Street
Ann Arbor, MI 48104
(734) 995-5439

Bacon Memorial District Library

45 Vinewood
Wyandotte, MI 48192
(734) 246-8357; (734) 282-1540 FAX
E-mail: whayden@tln.lib.mi.us
Wallace Hayden, Local History Librarian
Hours: Mon–Thur 10:00–9:00, Fri–Sat
10:00–5:00
(downriver area genealogy and local
history, southern suburbs of Detroit)

Baldwin Public Library

(300 West Merrill Street, Birmingham,
MI 48009—location)
PO Box 3002 (mailing address)
Birmingham, MI 48012-3002
(248) 647-1700, ext. 27; (248) 647-6393
FAX
http://metronet.lib.mi.us/BALD/bpl.html
James Moffet, Head, Reference
Department
Hours: Mon–Thur 9:30–9:00, Fri–Sat
9:30–5:30, Sun 1:00–5:00

Bay City Branch Library

Bay County Library System
708 Center Avenue
Bay City, MI 48708
(517) 893-9566
Mary McManman, Head of Reference
Department
Hours: Mon–Thur 10:00–9:00, Fri–Sat
10:00–5:00, Sun (Sept–May) 1:00–
4:00

Benton Harbor Public Library

213 East Wall Street
Benton Harbor, MI 49022

Boyne City Public Library

201 East Main Street
Boyne City, MI 49712
(616) 582-7861
Nancy Fulkerson, Assistant Librarian

Branch County Library

10 East Chicago Street
Coldwater, MI 49036
(517) 278-2341
Shirley Pascal
Hours: Mon 10:00–8:00, Tue–Wed & Fri
9:00–5:00, Thur 9:00–8:00, Sat 9:00–
4:00

Cadillac-Wexford Public Library

411 South Lake Street
Cadillac, MI 49601
(616) 775-6541
Hours: Sept–May: Mon–Thur 8:30–8:30,
Fri–Sat 8:30–5:30; Jun–Aug: Mon &
Wed 8:30–8:30, Tue & Thur–Fri 8:30–
5:30, Sat 8:30–12:30

Cass District Library
Local History Branch
(145 North Broadway—location)
319 M-62 North (mailing address)
Cassopolis, MI 49031-1099
(616) 445-3400; (616) 445-8795 FAX
E-mail: cass@monroe.lib.mi.us
Amy Druskovich, Local History
    Librarian
Hours: Mon–Tue 10:00–3:00, Wed–Thur
    10:00–5:00
(county history, genealogies of families
    in county)
searches done on a donation basis,
    photocopy fees charged

**Central Michigan University
Library**
Clarke Historical Library
Mount Pleasant, MI 48858
(517) 774-3352; (517) 774-2179 FAX
http://www.lib.cmich.edu/clarke/
    clarke.htm
Evelyn Leasher, Public Services
    Librarian
Hours: Mon–Fri 8:00–5:00, Sat 9:00–
    1:00
Pub. *Annual Report of the Clarke
    Historical Library*, annually; *Clarke
    Historical Library Newsletter*,
    semiannually
free

Cheboygan Public Library
107 South Ball Street
Cheboygan, MI 49721
(616) 627-2381; (616) 627-2381
E-mail: cheboy1@northland.lib.mi.us
Sue Ver Wys, Library Director
Hours: Mon–Thur 10:00–8:00, Fri
    10:00–5:00, Sat 10:00–3:00

Clawson Historical Museum
(41 Fisher Court—location)
425 North Main (mailing address)
Clawson, MI 48017
(248) 588-9169

Comstock Township Library
6130 King Highway
PO Box 25
Comstock, MI 49041
(616) 345-0136; (616) 345-0138 FAX
Mark Crum, Reference Librarian
Hours: Mon–Thur 10:00–9:00, Fri
    10:00–6:00, Sat 10:00–4:00
("Modest holdings in Comstock history;
    houses Kalamazoo Valley
    Genealogical Society collection")

Con Foster Museum
(Grandview Parkway—location)
400 Boardman Avenue, PO Box 592
    (mailing address)
Traverse City, MI 49685-0592
(616) 941-2332

Cranbrook Archives
(1221 North Woodward Avenue—
    location)
PO Box 801 (mailing address)
Bloomfield Hills, MI 48303-0801
(248) 645-3581; (248) 645-3029
E-mail: mark_coirdcc@cranbrook.edu
http://www. cranbrook.edu
Mark Coir, Director
Hours: Mon–Fri 8:00–5:00

**Marguerite DeAngeli Branch
Library**
921 West Nepessing Street
Lapeer, MI 48446
(810) 664-6971
Hours: Mon–Thur 9:00–9:00, Fri 9:00–
    5:00, Sat 9:00–4:00

Detroit Public Library
Burton Historical Collection
5201 Woodward Avenue
Detroit, MI 48202
(313) 833-1480; (313) 832-0877
E-mail: nvangor@cms.cc.wayne.edu
http://www.detroit.lib.mi.us/
    special_collections.htm
Noel VanGorden, Chief of the Burton
    Collection
Hours: Tue & Thur–Sat 9:30–5:30, Wed
    1:00–9:00

Grace A. Dow Library
1710 West Saint Andrews Drive
Midland, MI 48640
(517) 835-7157
Joan Somerville, Library Employee
Hours: Mon–Fri 10:00–9:00, Sat 10:00–
    5:00, Sun (winter) 1:00–5:00

Elk Rapids Historical Museum
(401 River Street—location)
PO Box 2 (mailing address)
Elk Rapids, MI 49629
(616) 264-8886
Marjorie Kinery, Corresponding
    Secretary
Hours: summer: Tue, Thur & Sat–Sun
    2:00–4:00; winter: Sat–Sun 2:00–4:00

Flint Public Library
1026 East Kearsley Street
Flint, MI 48502
(810) 232-7111, ext. 253; (810) 232-
    8360 FAX
http://www.flint.lib.mi.us/fpl.html
Angie Wesch, Librarian
Hours: Mon–Thur 9:00–9:00, Fri–Sat
    9:00–6:00

Fort Saint Joseph Museum
City of Niles History Department
508 East Main Street
Niles, MI 49120
(616) 683-4702
Carol Bainbridge, Director
Hours: Wed–Sat 10:00–4:00

Grand Rapids Public Library
Michigan and Family History
    Department
60 Library Plaza, N.E.
Grand Rapids, MI 49503-3093
(616) 456-3640
Hours: Mon–Wed 9:00–9:00, Thur–Sat
    9:00–5:30
Research fee of $10.00 per hour for all
    written inquiries

Hackley Public Library
316 West Webster Avenue
Muskegon, MI 49440
Hours: Sept–May: Tue–Wed 9:00–8:00,
    Thur 9:00–6:00, Sat 9:00–5:00;
    summer hours vary

Herrick Public Library
300 River Avenue
Holland, MI 49423
Hours: winter: Mon–Thur 9:00–9:00,
    Fri–Sat 9:00–6:00, Sun 2:00–5:00;
    summer: Mon–Thur 9:00–9:00, Fri
    9:00–6:00, Sat 9:00–1:00
(specializes in Dutch genealogy, Holland,
    Michigan, genealogy)

Howell Area Archives
c/o Howell Carnegie District Library
314 West Grand River Avenue
Howell, MI 48843
(517) 546-0720, ext. 129
Milton E. Charboneau, Curator
Hours: Wed, Fri & Sat 1:00–5:00
(houses most written material for all
    Livingston County; history and
    genealogy)

Howell Carnegie District Library
314 West Grand River Avenue
Howell, MI 48843
(517) 546-0720
Diane McKee, Administrative Assistant
Hours: Mon–Thur 10:00–8:00, Fri
    12:00–5:00, Sat 10:00–5:00

Hoyt Public Library
Eddy Historical Collection
505 Janes Avenue
Saginaw, MI 48605
(517) 755-0904
Anna Mae Maday, Eddy Room
Hours: Eddy Room: Mon–Thur 9:00–
    9:00, Fri–Sat 9:00–5:00, Sun (Oct–
    May) 1:00–5:00
(Saginaw and Michigan genealogy)
photocopy fee, staff research limited to
    indexed resources

Huron City Museum
7930 Huron City Road
Port Austin, MI 48467
(517) 428-4123

Iosco-Arenac District Library
951 Turtle Road
Tawas City, MI 48763
(517) 362-2651; (517) 362-6056 FAX

Stephanie Mallak Olson
Hours: Mon–Fri 8:00–4:30

Iosco County Historical Museum
405 West Bay
PO Box 135
East Tawas, MI 48730
(517) 362-8911
Barbara Ericksen, Executive Secretary
Hours: Office: daily except Wed 10:00–
1:00; Public hours: Sat–Sun 1:00–
4:00; genealogists available by
appointment

Jackson District Library
Reference Department
244 West Michigan Avenue
Jackson, MI 49201
(517) 788-4316
Nancy Buckland; Elaine Piper
Hours: Sept–May: Mon–Thur 9:30–8:30,
Fri 9:30–6:00, Sat 9:30–5:00; Jun–
Aug: Mon–Thur 9:30–7:00, Fri 9:30–
6:00, Sat 9:30–1:30

Kalamazoo Public Library
Clarence L. Miller Family Local History
Room
315 South Rose Street
Kalamazoo, MI 49007
(616) 342-5745; (616) 342-9837, ext.
245
E-mail: kazoodesk@kpl.gov
Catherine A. Larson, Local History
Specialist
Hours: Mon–Thur 9:00–9:00, Fri 9:00–
6:00, Sat 9:00–5:00, Sun 1:00–5:00
during school year, closed Thur
evening in summer
(emphasis on Kalamazoo County)
charges for copying and postage

Kalamazoo Valley Museum
(230 North Rose Street—location)
PO Box 4070
Kalamazoo, MI 49003-4070
(616) 373-7984; (616) 373-7997 FAX;
(616) 373-7988 (Director)
Patrick Norris, Ph.D., Museum Director;
Thomas Dietz, Curator of Research
Hours: Mon–Tue & Thur–Sat 10:00–
6:00, Wed 10:00–9:00, Sun 1:00–5:00
(history/science museum, phono/photo
collection, very limited genealogical
information)

Lake Superior State University
Kenneth J. Shouldice Library
Sault Sainte Marie, MI 49783
(906) 635-2167
Mary M. June, Public Services Librarian
Hours: when classes are in session:
Mon–Thur 7:30 A.M.–10:30 P.M., Fri
7:30–6:00, Sat 10:00–5:00, Sun 11:00–
10:30; summer: Mon–Thur 7:30 A.M.–
9:00 P.M., Fri 7:30–5:00, Sat 10:00–
2:00
(specializes in Michigan history)

Livonia Historical Commission
Greenmead Historic Site
38125 Eight Mile Road
Livonia, MI 48152
(300-volume library)

Manistee County Historical Museum
425 River Street
Manistee, MI 49660
(616) 723-5531
Steve Harold, Museum Director
Hours: Tue–Sat 10:00–5:00
(40,000 file cards on local residents)
$1.50 admission; no research by mail

Manistee County Library
95 Maple Street
Manistee, MI 49660
(616) 723-2519; (616) 723-8270 FAX
Pamela Spoor, Reference Librarian
Hours: winter: Tue–Wed 10:00–8:30,
Thur–Fri 10:00–5:00, Sat 10:00–3:00;
summer: Mon–Wed 10:00–8:30, Thur–
Fri 10:00–5:00

**Mason County Genealogical,
Historical Resource Center**
Rose Hawley Museum
White Pine Village
1687 South Lakeshore Drive
Ludington, MI 49431
Hours: closed winters

Michigan Historical Museum
717 West Allegan Street
Lansing, MI 48918
(517) 373-3559; (517) 373-1645
(magazine); (800) 366-3703 (museum
and magazine)
E-mail:
webspinners@sosmail.state.mi.us
http://www.sos.state.mi.us/history/
museum/explore/explore.html
Basil Hedrick, Ph.D., Director, Division
of Museums, Archaeology and
Publications
Pub. *Michigan History Magazine*

Michigan State University
Archives and Historical Collections
101 Conrad Hall
East Lansing, MI 48824-1327
(517) 355-2330; (517) 353-9319 FAX
E-mail: honhart@pilot.msu.edu
http://pilot.msu.edu/unit/msuarhc/
Frederick L. Honhart, Ph.D., Director
Hours: Mon–Fri 8:00–noon & 1:00–5:00

Michigan State University Museum
Michigan State University
West Circle Drive
East Lansing, MI 48824-1045
(517) 355-2370; (517) 432-2846 FAX
C. Kurt Dewhurst, Ph.D., Director
Hours: Mon–Wed & Fri 9:00–5:00, Thur
9:00–9:00, Sat 10:00–5:00, Sun 1:00–
5:00
Pub. *Michigan Folklife*, annually;
Associate, quarterly
(archeology, folklife, AG history)

Monroe County Historical Museum
Monroe County Historical Commission
Archives
126 South Monroe
Monroe, MI 48161
(734) 243-7137; (734) 243-7362 FAX
Christine Kull, Archivist
Hours: summer (May–Sept): Mon–Sun
10:00–5:00; winter (Oct–Apr): Wed–
Sun 10:00–5:00, weekends by
appointment
(Monroe County history and genealogy)
Jun–Aug: $2.00 admission; research:
first half-hour free, $11.00 per hour
thereafter, plus photocopies at 25¢ per
page

Monroe County Library System
Ellis Reference and Information Center
3700 South Custer Road
Monroe, MI 48161
(734) 241-5277; (734) 242-9037 FAX
http://www.monroe.lib.mi.us/
Carl Katafiasz, Head of Ellis Reference
Hours: Mon–Thur 9:00–9:00, Fri 9:00–
6:00, Sat 9:00–5:00
(southeast Michigan and northwest Ohio)

Montague Museum
(Church Street at Meade Street—
location)
8679 Sheridan Street (mailing address)
Montague, MI 49437
(616) 893-4585; (616) 894-6813
John Leddick, Treasurer
Hours: Memorial Day–Labor Day: Sat–
Sun 1:00–5:00, and by appointment

Mount Clemens Public Library
150 Cass Avenue
Mount Clemens, MI 48043
(810) 469-6200
Deborah J. Mowat, Adult Services
Librarian
Hours: Mon–Thur 9:30–9:00, Fri–Sat
9:30–5:30

**MTU Archives and Copper County
Historical Collections**
Michigan Technological University
1400 Townsend Drive
Houghton, MI 49931-1295
(906) 487-2505; (906) 487-2357 FAX
E-mail: copper@mtu.edu
http://www.lib.mtu.edu/jrvp/index.htm
Hours: Mon–Fri 8:00–5:00
(U.S. and Michigan census, Polk
directories, copper mining records;
predominantly Houghton and
Keweenaw counties, Michigan, but
also Ontonagon, Baraga, Iron and
Gogebic counties)

Muskegon County Museum
430 West Clay Avenue
Muskegon, MI 49440-1002
(616) 722-0278; (616) 728-4119 FAX
Barbara L. Martin, Historian/Librarian
Hours: Mon–Fri 9:30–4:30

Pub. *The Muser*, quarterly
(specializes in "lumbering, shipping,
Muskegon County history [cultural,
industrial, natural]; over 10,000
photographic images of people and
places of Muskegon County")
$15.00 per year membership

Northwestern Michigan College
Mark and Helen Osterlin Library
1701 East Front Street
Traverse City, MI 49684
(616) 922-1060
Douglas Campbell, Public Services
Librarian
Hours: academic term: Mon–Thur 8:00
A.M.–10:00 P.M., Fri 8:00–5:00, Sat
11:00–5:00, Sun 1:00–5:00; summer:
Mon & Thur–Fri 8:30–4:30, Tue–Wed
8:30 A.M.–9:30 P.M.

Novi Public Library
45245 West Ten Mile Road
Novi, MI 48050
(248) 349-0720
Barbara Louie
Hours: Mon–Thur 10:00–9:00, Fri–Sat
10:00–5:00

Ogemaw District Library
107 West Main
PO Box 427
Rose City, MI 48654
Hours: Mon 10:00–8:00, Tue–Fri 10:00–
5:00, Sat 10:00–12:00

Orion Township Public Library
825 Joslyn Road
Lake Orion, MI 48362
Hours: Mon–Thur 10:00–9:00, Fri–Sat
10:00–5:00

Plymouth Historical Museum
155 South Main Street
Plymouth, MI 48170
(734) 455-8940
Beth Stewart, Director
Hours: Wed–Thur & Sat 1:00–4:00, Sun
2:00–5:00
Pub. *Newsletter*
(Michigan history and genealogy, Civil
War history)
$15.00 per year membership for
individuals, $25.00 per year
membership for families; $5.00
research fee

Presque Isle County Historical Museum
176 West Michigan Avenue
PO Box 175
Rogers City, MI 49779
(517) 734-4121
Laural Maldonado Curator
Hours: 1 Jun–31 Oct: Mon–Fri noon–
4:00
(Presque Isle County *Advance* and
Onaway, Michigan, *Outlook*
newspapers on microfiche for the past
100 years)
$10.00 per year membership

Rochester Hills Museum at Van Hoosen Farm
1005 Van Hoosen Road
Rochester Hills, MI 48309
(248) 608-8198
Patrick J. McKay, Supervisor of
Interpretive Services
Hours: Wed–Sun 1:00–4:00
(local history, Stoney Creek Village,
local archaeology)

Rochester Hills Public Library
500 Olde Towne Road
Rochester, MI 48307-2043
Diane Burgeson
Hours: Mon–Thur 9:30–9:00, Fri 9:30–
5:30, Sat 9:30–5:00

Rosa Public Library
401 South Capitol Avenue
Lansing, MI 48933-2037
(517) 325-6413
Judy Forester, Head of Adult Services
Hours: Local History Room: Tue & Thur
noon–3:00; Library: Mon & Wed
9:30–8:30, Tue & Thur 9:30–5:30, Fri
9:30–5:00, Sat 9:30–4:30 (if the Local
History Room is closed, reference
librarian will retrieve limited local
history materials for patrons for in-
library use)

Roseville Public Library
29777 Gratiot Avenue
Roseville, MI 48066

Royal Oak Public Library
222 East Eleven Mile Road
PO Box 494
Royal Oak, MI 48068-0494
(248) 541-1470; (248) 545-6220 FAX
P. Gosik, Head of Reference
Hours: Mon–Tue & Thur 10:00–9:00,
Wed & Fri–Sat 10:00–6:00

Saint Clair County Library
210 McMorran Boulevard
Port Huron, MI 48060
(810) 987-7323; (810) 987-7327 FAX
E-mail: bking@netra.stclair-ph.lib.mi.us
http://www.stclair-ph.lib.mi.us
Barbara King, Reference Librarian,
Michigan Room
Hours: Michigan Room: Mon 9:30–8:30,
Tue–Thur 9:00–4:30 by appointment;
Library: Mon–Fri 9:00–9:00, Sat
9:00–5:30
(emphasis on Saint Clair County and
Port Huron)
search fees: $7.50 minimum, $14.00 for
searches of hour or more, $2.00 for
first photocopy, 25¢ for each
additional copy, including mailing

Saint Joseph Public Library
Maud Preston Palenske Memorial
Library
500 Market Street
Saint Joseph, MI 49085
(616) 983-7167; (616) 983-5804

E-mail: kwsmith@qtm.net
Katherine W. Smith, Public Services/
Reference Librarian
Hours: Mon–Thur 10:00–9:00, Fri–Sat
10:00–6:00, Sun (Oct–May) 1:00–5:00

Sault Sainte Marie Foundation for Culture and History
209 East Portage Avenue
PO Box 627
Sault Sainte Marie, MI 49783
(906) 632-1999
Hours: May 15–Oct 15: Mon–Sat 10:00–
5:00, Sun noon–5:00

Ella Sharp Museum Association of Jackson
3225 Fourth Street
Jackson, MI 49203
(517) 787-2320

Alfred P. Sloan Museum
1221 East Kearsley Street
Flint, MI 48503
(810) 760-1169
James Johnson, Interim Director
Pub. *Sloan News*
(genealogical services)

South Side Branch Library
311 Lafayette Street
Bay City, MI 48706

Southwest Michigan College Museum
58900 Cherry Grove Road
Dowagiac, MI 49047
(616) 782-7800
Michael Breza, Curator of History; Craig
R. Olson, Director
Hours: Tue–Sat 10:00–5:00
Pub. *SMC Museum News*, quarterly
$15.00 per year membership for
individuals, $25.00 per year
membership for families, $5.00 per
year membership for senior citizens,
$10.00 per year membership for senior
citizen couples

Sturgis Public Library and Information Center
130 North Nottawa at West Street
Sturgis, MI 49091
(616) 651-7907 (for hours); (616) 651-
3687 (for assistance)
Karla Weidner, Technical Services
Hours: winter: Mon–Thur 9:30–8:00, Fri
9:30–5:30, Sat 9:30–2:00, Sun 12:30–
3:30; summer: Mon & Thur 9:30–
8:30, Tue–Wed & Fri 9:30–5:30, Sat
9:30–12:00

Tri-Cities Historical Museum
1 North Harbor
PO Box 234
Grand Haven, MI 49417
(616) 842-0700; (616) 842-3698 FAX
Elizabeth Kammeraad
Hours: Tue–Fri 10:00–5:00
Pub. *The Packet*
(local history)

Troy Public Library
510 West Big Beaver Road
Troy, MI 48084
(248) 524-3538
E-mail: rutledgm@lcm.macomb.lib.mi.us
http://web.macomb.lib.mi.us/troy
Marcia Rutledge, Head of Adult Services
Hours: Mon–Thur 10:00–9:00, Fri–Sat
10:00–6:00, Sun 1:00–6:00

Union Township Library
221 North Broadway
Union City, MI 49094

The University of Michigan
Bentley Historical Library
Michigan Historical Collections
1150 Beal Avenue
Ann Arbor, MI 48109-2113
(734) 764-3482; (734) 936-1333 FAX
E-mail: bentley.ref@umich.edu
http://www.umich.edu/~bhl/
Nancy Bartlett, Reference Archivist
Hours: Mon–Fri 8:30–5:00; Sat (Sept–
Apr) 9:00–12:30
(no resources specifically devoted to
genealogy)

University of Michigan-Dearborn
4901 Evergreen Road
Dearborn, MI 48128-1491
E-mail: rfraser@umich.edu
http://www.umd.umich.edu/

Van Buren County Library
Webster Memorial Library
200 North Phelps Street
Decatur, MI 49045
(616) 423-4771; (616) 423-8373 FAX
Toni I. Benson, Librarian
Hours: Mon–Thur 9:00–8:00, Fri 9:00–
5:00, Sat 9:00–3:00

West Branch Public Library
119 North Fourth Street
West Branch, MI 48661
(517) 345-2235
Marsha Boyd, Director
Hours: Mon 3:00–7:00, Tue & Thur–Fri
9:00–5:00, Wed 9:00–7:00, Sat 9:00–
1:00

Western Michigan University
Archives and Regional History
Collections
111 East Hall, East Campus
Kalamazoo, MI 49008-5081

White Pine Library Cooperative
1840 North Michigan, Suite 114
Saginaw, MI 48602-5590

Peter White Public Library
217 North Front Street
Marquette, MI 49855
(906) 228-9510; (906) 228-7315 FAX
http://lib.up.net/pwpl/pwpl_home.htm
Caroline Jordan, Collection
Development/Reference Librarian

Hours: Mon–Thur 10:00–9:00, Fri
10:00–6:00, Sat 10:00–5:00, Sun
(winter) 1:00–5:00

The Wilkinson Heritage Museum
15300 Red Arrow Highway
Lakeside, MI 49116
(616) 469-2090
Nadra D. Kissman, President
Hours: Mon–Sun 10:00–6:00
donations accepted

Willard Library
7 West Van Buren Street
Battle Creek, MI 49017
(616) 968-8166
Helen Jo Emerson, Reference Head
Librarian; Marlene A. Steele
Hours: Mon–Thur 9:00–9:00, Fri–Sat
9:00–5:00

Ypsilanti District Library
229 West Michigan
Ypsilanti, MI 48197
(734) 482-4110
Paula Drummond, Reference Department
Hours: Mon 10:00–8:00, Tue–Thur 9:00–
8:00, Fri–Sat 9:00–5:30

Historical Societies— Local and Regional

Albion Historical Society
The Gardiner House Museum
500 South Eaton Street
Albion, MI 49224
(517) 629-5100
Frank Passic, Curator of Local History
Hours: Apr–Oct: Sat–Sun 1:00–4:00, and
by appointment
Pub. *Albion Historical Society
Newsletter*, quarterly
$5.00 per year regular membership,
$2.00 per year junior (16−)
membership, $3.00 per year senior
(65+) membership

Alger County Historical Society
203 West Onota Street
PO Box 201
Munising, MI 49862
(906) 387-4186
Pub. *Alger Footprints*, semiannually
$5.00 per year membership

Allegan County Historical Society
(13 Walnut Street—location)
536 Trowbridge Street (mailing address)
Allegan, MI 49010
(616) 673-8292 (Tuesdays); (616) 673-
4853
Marguerite Miller, Director

Arenac County Historical Society
Michigan Avenue
PO Box 272
Au Gres, MI 48703
(517) 846-9967

Arvon Township Historical Society
PO Box 151
Skanee, MI 49962
(906) 524-6934

Au Sable-Oscoda Historical Society
110 State Street
Oscoda, MI 48750
(517) 739-3178
Edward Glotfelty, President
$1.00 per year membership

Au Sable River Valley Historical Society
PO Box 304
Mio, MI 48647

Historical Society of Battle Creek
165 North Washington Avenue
Battle Creek, MI 49017
(616) 965-2613
T. Zoe Kimmel, Executive Director
Hours: Mon–Fri 9:00–noon
Pub. *Heritage Battle Creek*, two to four
times per year, $7.00 to $9.00 per year
subscription, with a 20% discount for
members
from $20.00 per year membership

Bay County Historical Society and Historical Museum of Bay County
321 South Washington Avenue
Bay City, MI 48708
(517) 893-5733
Gay McInerney, Director; Ron
Bloomfield, Curator of Collections and
Research
Hours: Mon–Sat 10:00–5:00, Sun 1:00–
5:00

Bay Mills-Brimley Historical Research Society
PO Box 273
Brimley, MI 49715
(906) 248-3665

Beaver Island Historical Society
(The Mormon Print Shop, 26250 Main
Street, corner of Forest and Main
Streets—location)
PO Box 263 (mailing address)
Beaver Island, MI 49782
(616) 448-2254; (616) 448-2106 FAX
Phyllis Gregg Moore, Director
Hours: Memorial Day–Labor Day: Mon–
Sat 11:00–5:00, Sun noon–3:00
Pub. *Journal of Beaver Island History*,
irregularly
$10.00 per year membership for
individuals, $100.00 per year
Sustaining membership; search fees:
$10.00 per hour plus copying costs

Bellaire Area Historical Society
202 North Bridge Street
PO Box 646
Bellaire, MI 49615
(616) 533-8631
Carol Boros

Hours: 1 Jun–1 Sept: Mon–Fri 11:00–3:00, and by appointment
Pub. *News Letter*, annually
$5.00 per year membership for adult individuals, $7.00 per year membership for families, $10.00 per year membership for businesses

Bellevue Area Historical Society
212 North Main Street
Bellevue, MI 49021
(616) 763-3369; (616) 763-3440
Bernard J. Geyer, President
Hours: Mon–Fri 1:00–5:00
Pub. *Newsletter*, quarterly
$5.00 per year membership

Benzie Area Historical Society
Benzie Area Historical Museum
6941 Traverse Avenue
PO Box 185
Benzonia, MI 49616
(616) 882-5539
Debbra Kerby, Museum Manager
Hours: May–Dec: Mon–Sat 10:00–4:00
Pub. *Benzie Heritage*, quarterly
$25.00 per year membership for individuals, $30.00 per year membership for families, $20.00 per year membership for senior citizens; search fee: $10.00 per hour

Bernard Historical Society and Museum
7135 West Delton Road
Delton, MI 49046
(616) 623-5451

Berrien County Historical Association, Inc.
1839 Courthouse Museum
313 North Case Street
PO Box 261
Berrien Springs, MI 49103
(616) 471-1202; (616) 471-7412 FAX
Robert Myers, Curator
Hours: Tue–Fri 9:00–4:00, Sat–Sun 1:00–5:00
Pub. *The Docket*, quarterly; *Berrien County Historical Association Annual Report*, annually
(indexes to Berrien County marriage records 1831–94, death records 1867–1914, probate court files 1831–1930, naturalization applications 1840–1894, and miscellaneous records)
$15.00 per year membership for individuals, $25.00 per year membership for families

Blissfield Historical Society
Blissfield Historic Depot Museum
7148 East Weston Road
Blissfield, MI 49228
Shelby Jean Raines, President
Hours: Sat–Sun noon–5:00, weekdays in the summer; meetings: third Tue; Victorsville School House, 424 Adrian Street: by appointment only

$5.00 per year membership for individuals, $20.00 per year membership for businesses

Branch County Historical Society
27 South Jefferson Street
PO Box 107
Coldwater, MI 49036
(517) 278-2871
Thomas Oxenham, Curator
Hours: Museum: Wed–Sun 1:00–5:00, and by appointment
Pub. *Newsletter*, monthly

Historical Society of Bridgeport
6190 Dixie Highway
PO Box 337
Bridgeport, MI 48722
(517) 777-5230; (517) 777-3328
William W. Schomaker, State Representative and Curator
Hours: Tue 1:00–4:00, Thur 1:00–4:00 & 7:00–9:00
Pub. *Business Directory*; *News Letter* (artifacts, family history)
$2.50 per year membership for individuals, $3.50 per year membership for families, $1.00 per year membership for senior citizens (65 and older) or youth (under 16); fees: postage and handling donation

Canton Historical Commission
46870 Cherry Hill
Canton, MI 48187
(734) 981-0087

Canton Historical Society and Museum
(Corner of South Canton Center and Proctor (Heritage) Drive—location)
PO Box 87362 (mailing address)
Canton, MI 48187
(734) 397-0088
Marta McCabe, Museum Chair
Hours: Mar–Dec: Tue 1:00–3:00, Sat 1:00–4:00
Pub. *Canton Crossroads*, bimonthly ("Museum collection focuses mainly on Canton.")
$10.00 per year membership for individuals, $20.00 per year membership for families, $25.00 per year membership for businesses, $100.00 life membership for individuals; free museum admission; research fees: 20¢ per photocopy plus postage

Cass County Historical Commission
24010 Hospital Street, Apartment 105
Cassopolis, MI 49031-9690

Historical Society of Cheboygan County, Inc.
Corner Huron and Court
PO Box 5005
Cheboygan, MI 49721
(616) 627-5448
Quincy Leslie, President

Chippewa County Historical Society, Inc.
The Johnston and Schoolcraft Houses
PO Box 342
Sault Sainte Marie, MI 49783
(906) 635-5170

Clarkston Historical Society
6085 South Main Street
Clarkston, MI 48016
Dennis Spande

Clinton County Historical Commission
8565 Grange
Portland, MI 48875
(517) 587-6839
Evelyn Weiland

Clinton County Historical Society
(Brook Road, Lansing, MI—Archives location)
PO Box 174 (mailing address)
Saint Johns, MI 48879-1740
Hours: Mon–Tue 9:00–4:00
$6.00 per year membership for individuals (includes membership in The Genealogists of the Clinton County Historical Society), $10.00 per year membership for couples

Community Historical Society and Museum (Colon)
(217 and 219 North Blackstone Avenue—location)
PO Box 136 (mailing address)
Colon, MI 49040-0136
(616) 432-3804 (President); (616) 432-2462 (Treasurer)
Joe Ganger, President; David J. Farrell, Treasurer
Hours: 1 Jun–Labor Day: Tue, Thur & Sun 2:00–4:30
$5.00 per year membership, $100.00 life membership

Commerce Township Area Historical Society (CTAHS)
207 Liberty Street
PO Box 264
Walled Lake, MI 48390
(248) 624-2554; (248) 624-2309
Pub. *CTAHS Newsletter*, nine times per year (monthly, September–May)

Copper Range Historical Society
PO Box 507
Painesdale, MI 49931
(906) 523-4770
Robert Bergdahl, President

Dearborn Historical Commission
Dearborn Historical Museum
915 South Brady
Dearborn, MI 48124
(313) 565-3000; (313) 565-4848 FAX
William K. McElhone, Curator of Research

Hours: Museum: Mon–Fri 9:00–5:00, Sat
(May–Nov) 9:00–5:00, Sat (Nov–
May) 1:00–5:00
Pub. *Dearborn Historian*, quarterly

Detroit Historical Society
5401 Woodward Avenue
Detroit, MI 48202
(313) 833-7934
Michael W. R. Davis, Executive Director
Pub. *Detroit Historical Society Bulletin*

**Dexter Area Historical Society and
Museum**
3443 Inverness Street
Dexter, MI 48130
(734) 426-2519
E-mail: dexmuseum@aol.com
Nancy J. Van Blaricum, Genealogist
Hours: May–Dec: Fri–Sat 1:00–3:00
Pub. *Dexter Area Historical Society
Newsletter*, irregularly
("We have photocopies of early church
records for most Dexter Protestant
churches.")
$3.00 per year membership for
individuals; search fees vary with
requests

Drummond Island Historical Society
(Drummond Island Historical Museum,
Old Mill Drive—location)
PO Box 293
Drummond Island, Mi 49726
(906) 493-5746 (Museum); (906) 493-
5224
Kathryne B. Lowe, Curator
Hours: daily (mid-May to Oct 1) 1:00–
5:00
Pub. *Chimney Chatter*, irregularly
("Early Island history, township records,
scrapbooks and family albums.")

Elk Rapids Area Historical Society
(Elk Rapids Historical Museum, 401
River Street—location)
PO Box 2 (mailing address)
Elk Rapids, MI 49629
(616) 264-8024; (616) 264-6354
Adam Schuler, Co-chairman; Glenn
Newmann, Co-chairman
Hours: Elk Rapids Historical Museum:
meetings

Elsie Historical Society
145 West Main Street
PO Box 125
Elsie, MI 48831-0125
Hours: Historical Room: Wed 2:00–5:00
(local history and genealogy)

**Farmington Hills Historical
Commission**
31555 Eleven Mile Road
Farmington Hills, MI 48336
(248) 474-6115

Farmington Historical Commission
23600 Liberty Street
Farmington, MI 48335

(248) 474-4608
Kathryn Briggs, Chairman
Hours: 8:30–4:30

**Flat River Historical Society and
Museum**
213 North Franklin Street
PO Box 188
Greenville, MI 48838
(616) 754-5296
Hours: by appointment

Flat Rock Historical Society
(Munger Lane, behind City Hall, corner
of Gibralter and Evergreen—location)
PO Box 337 (mailing address)
Flat Rock, MI 48134
(734) 782-5220; (734) 782-1269
(Secretary)
Lila Fedokovitz, Secretary
Hours: second Sun 1:00–4:00
Pub. *Newsletter*, quarterly
$5.00 per year membership for
individuals, $15.00 per year
membership for families, $7.00
inactive membership

Flint Historic Commission
1101 South Saginaw Street
Flint, MI 48506
(810) 766-7426

The Flushing Area Historical Society
431 West Main Street
PO Box 87
Flushing, MI 48433
(810) 732-1024
Lois Bettesworth, Editor and Treasurer
Hours: 9:00–5:00
Pub. *Flushing Area Historical Society
Newsletter*, monthly
from $2.00 per year membership,
$150.00 life membership

Franklin Historical Society
PO Box 7
Franklin Village, MI 48025

Friends of Historic Meridian
(5151 Marsh Road, Okemos, MI
48864—location)
PO Box 155 (mailing address)
Okemos, MI 48805
(517) 349-1993
Elaine C. Davis, President
Pub. *The Toll-gate Keeper*

**Friends of the Krause Memorial
Library**
Krause Memorial Library
140 East Bridge Street
Rockford, MI 49341
(616) 866-2352
Nancy Schellenberg, President
$10.00 per year membership for families

Garden City Historical Commission
6000 Middlebelt
Garden City, MI 48135
(734) 421-1262

**Grand Blanc Heritage Association
and Museum**
203 East Grand Blanc Road
Grand Blanc, MI 48439-1303
(810) 694-7274
Clare Hatten, Director
Hours: Wed 10:00–2:00, and by
appointment
Pub. *Newsletter*, bimonthly
(local history and genealogy and
artifacts; family histories, diaries,
ledgers, obituaries, cemetery records)
$7.00 per year membership for
individuals, $10.00 per year
membership for families, $1.00 per
year membership for students, $15.00
per year Contributing membership,
$25.00 per year Sustaining
membership, $60.00 life membership
for individuals, $100.00 life
membership for couples; museum
admission free; free genealogical help
for Grand Blanc only

Grand Ledge Area Historical Society
(The Museum, 118 West Lincoln
Street—location)
PO Box 203 (mailing address)
Grand Ledge, MI 48837-0203
(517) 627-3149 (Museum); (517) 627-
4949 (Library); (517) 627-5170
(Library)
Neil Miller, President
Hours: Museum: Sun 2:00–4:00, and by
appointment; Archival collection at the
Grand Ledge Public Library, 131 East
Jefferson, Grand Ledge, MI 48837
$10.00 per year membership for families

Grand Rapids Historical Society
Grand Rapids Public Library
Michigan and Family History
Department
60 Library Plaza, N.E.
Grand Rapids, MI 49503-3093
(616) 456-3640
David Wier, President
Hours: Library: Mon–Wed 9:00–9:00,
Thur–Sat 9:00–5:30
Pub. *Grand River Valley Review*

**Grandville Historical Association
and Museum**
3195 Wilson Avenue, S.W.
PO Box 124
Grandville, MI 49418
(616) 534-2687; (616) 538-1145
(Chairperson)
Marilyn DeVries, Chairperson
Hours: first Thur 1:00–5:00

**Gratiot County Historical and
Genealogical Society**
228 West Center Street
Ithaca, MI 48847-1415
(517) 875-4974 (Museum)
Georgiana Peet Miller, Chair,
Genealogical Group

Hours: Genealogy: Tue 1:00–5:00;
Museum: Thur (Jun–Nov) 11:00–3:00
& 7:00–9:00
Pub. *Pages from the Past*, monthly
(genealogical material four times per
year)
(primarily Gratiot County research, but
also some state and national)
$10.00 per year membership for
individuals, $12.00 per year
membership for families, $75.00 per
year Sustaining membership, $200.00
life membership; research: $5.00 per
hour, $10.00 minimum, plus LSASE
and 10¢ per page for copies

Greater West Bloomfield Historical Society
PO Box 5024
Orchard Lake, MI 48033

Green Oak Township Historical Society
(Gage Museum, 6440 Kensington
Road—location)
PO Box 84 (mailing address)
Brighton, MI 48116
Cleo Moran, President
Hours: Jun–Aug: weekends 1:00–4:00,
and by appointment
Pub. *Green Oak Historian*, four times
per year
(early township families)
$7.00 per year membership for families,
$10.00 per year for businesses and
professions, $25.00 per year Patron
membership; search fee: reproduction
and mailing costs plus contribution
appreciated

Grosse Ile Historical Society
East River Road and Parkway
PO Box 131
Grosse Ile, MI 48138
(734) 675-1250
Hours: Apr–Dec: Thur 10:00–noon, Sun
1:00–4:00
Pub. *GIHS Newsletter*

Hackley Heritage Association, Inc.
(484 West Webster Avenue, Muskegon,
MI 49440—location)
PO Box 32 (mailing address)
Muskegon, MI 49443-0032
(616) 722-7578; (616) 759-2505

Henika Public Library
Main Street
Wayland, MI 49348
Hours: 10:00–3:00 except Thur

Heritage Hill Association
126 College Avenue, S.E.
Grand Rapids, MI 49503
(616) 459-8950

Homer Historical Society
505 Grandview
Homer, MI 49245
(517) 568-3116

JoAnne Miller, Vice President
Hours: by appointment
Pub. *Homer Historical Society
Newsletter*, two times per year

Houghton County Historical Society
5500 Highway M-26
PO Box 127
Lake Linden, MI 49945
(906) 296-4121; (906) 296-9191 FAX
William Barkell, Secretary
Hours: seasonal museum
$10.00 per year membership for
individuals, $20.00 per year
membership for families, $200.00 life
membership

Houghton Lake Area Historical Society
(1625 West Houghton Lake Drive,
Prudenville, MI 48651—location)
PO Box 146 (mailing address)
Houghton Lake Heights, MI 48630
(517) 422-5074
R. W. Carman

Huron County Historical Society
Bad Axe Historical Society Chapter
223 Willis Street
Bad Axe, MI 48413
(517) 269-8165

Ionia County Historical Society
(John C. Blanchard House, 253 East
Main Street—location)
PO Box 1776 (mailing address)
Ionia, MI 48846
Ralph Bartlett, President of the Board
Hours: May 30–Labor Day: Sun noon–
4:00
$10.00 per year membership

Iron County Historical and Museum Society
PO Box 272
Caspian, MI 49915
(906) 265-2617; (906) 265-3942 (off-
season)
Harold O. Bernhardt, President/
Administrator
Pub. *Past Present Prints*

Ironwood Historical Society
PO Box 553
Ironwood, MI 49938
(906) 932-0287
Ray Maurin, Curator
Hours: Memorial Day–Labor Day: noon–
4:00, and by appointment

Kalamazoo County Historical Society
PO Box 1623
Kalamazoo, MI 49005
Jean Bright, President

Kalamo Township Historical Society
8889 Spore Highway
Vermontville, MI 49096
(517) 726-0408

Kalkaska County Historical Society
4360 Spencer Road, S.E.
Kalkaska, MI 49646-9621
(616) 258-8285
Geraldine Montgomery, Secretary
Hours: Jun–Aug 1:00–4:00
donations accepted

Keweenaw County Historical Society
HC-1, Box 265L
Eagle Harbor, MI 49950
(906) 296-2561
Clarence J. Monette, Secretary
Pub. *Superior Signal*, quarterly, not
available by subscription
(no genealogical files, only local
Keweenaw County history)

Lake Odessa Area Historical Society
(Emerson Street—Depot Museum
location)
Page Memorial Building, 839 Fourth
Avenue (mailing address)
Lake Odessa, MI 48849
(616) 374-8698
John Waite, President
Hours: meetings at the Emerson Manor,
Lake Odessa: second Thur 7:30
Pub. *Bonanza Bugle*, quarterly (February,
May, August, November)
(accumulated obituaries, microfilm of
Ionia County census 1870–1920,
microfilm of local newspapers 1891–
1948)
$10.00 per year membership

Leelanau Historical Society, Inc.
Leelanau Historical Museum
203 East Cedar Street
PO Box 246
Leland, MI 49654-0246
(616) 256-7475
Laura J. Quackenbush, Curator/
Administrator
Hours: Archives: by appointment only
Pub. *Leemuse*, semiannually
(local history collection)
$15.00 per year membership for
individuals, $25.00 per year
membership for families

Lenawee County Historical Society, Inc.
Lenawee County Historical Museum
110 East Church Street
PO Box 511
Adrian, MI 49221
(517) 265-6071
Doris Conklin Trowbridge, Archivist;
Charles N. Liquist, Ph.D., Curator
Pub. *From the Tower*, five times per year
$10.00 per year membership, $100.00
life membership

Les Cheneaux Historical Association: Meridian Road
Les Cheneaux Historical Museum and
Maritime Museum
PO Box 301
Cedarville, MI 49719

(906) 484-2821
Annegret Goehring, Curator
Hours: May & Oct: by appointment; Jun
& Sept: Tue–Sat 11:00–4:00; Jul–Aug:
Mon–Fri 10:00–4:00, Sun 1:00–4:00

Lincoln Park Historical Museum and Society
1335 Southfield
Lincoln Park, MI 48146
(313) 386-3137
Daniel Beggs, Curator
Hours: Tue–Thur & Sat 1:00–5:00
Pub. *Historical Society Newsletter*, four
times per year
(genealogy library, collection of local
newspapers)
$5.00 per year membership for
individuals, $7.50 per year
membership for couples, $25.00 per
year Patron membership, $200.00 life
membership

Linden Mills Historical Society
PO Box 551
Linden, MI 48451

Little Traverse Regional Historical Society
Water Front Park
PO Box 162
Petoskey, MI 49770
(616) 347-2620

Livonia Historical Society
Greenmead Historic Site
38125 Eight Mile Road
Livonia, MI 48152

Luce County Historical Society
Luce County Historical Museum
110 East McMillan Avenue
Newberry, MI 49868-1555
(906) 293-5946
Lillian A. Waite

Mackinac Associates
PO Box 1800
Mackinac Island, MI 49757
(906) 847-3328 (summer); (517) 373-
4296 (winter)
Carl R. Nold, Administrative Agent
Hours: 9:00–5:00
Pub. *Curiosities*, quarterly
("Association to assist Mackinac State
Historic Parks with its educational
mission and help preserve Mackinac's
heritage.")
$40.00 per year membership for
individuals, $70.00 per year
membership for families, $150.00
Sustaining membership, $350.00
Patron membership, $500.00
Commandant's Circle membership

Macomb County Historical Society
Crocker House
15 Union
Mount Clemens, MI 48043
(810) 465-2488

Madeline Page, President
Hours: Mar–Dec: Tue–Fri 10:00–4:00,
first Sun 1:00–4:00
Pub. *Newsletter, Macomb County
Historical Society*, monthly
(obituaries of former residents of the
area)
$20.00 per year membership

Marquette County Historical Society and Museum
J. M. Longyear Research Library
213 North Front Street
Marquette, MI 49855
(906) 226-3571
Linda K. Panian, Librarian; Frances
Porter, Executive Director
Hours: Mon–Fri 10:00–noon & 1:00–
5:00, third Thur till 9:00
Pub. *Harlow's Wooden Man* (a journal of
general regional history, not
genealogy), quarterly
(has biographical card file, census
information, city directories,
gazetteers, pamphlets, vital records,
cemetery records, military records,
photos, maps, manuscripts,
periodicals, local history collection)
$20.00 per year membership for
individuals, $30.00 per year
membership for families or Supporting
membership for individuals, $55.00
per year Supporting membership for
families, $500.00 life membership for
individuals; library admission: $5.00
per project for non-members, $2.00
per project for university students;
staff research: $15.00 per hour, plus
$3.50 minimum postage and handling,
plus copies at 25¢ each from paper
originals or 50¢ each from microform
originals

Marshall Historical Society, Inc.
PO Box 68
Marshall, MI 49068

Mason County Historical Society
1687 South Lake Shore Drive
Ludington, MI 49431
(616) 843-4808; (616) 843-7089 FAX
Ronald M. Wood, Director
Hours: summer: Tue–Sun 11:00–4:30;
spring & fall: Tue–Fri 11:00–4:00
Pub. *Epoch*, monthly; *Mason Memories*,
quarterly
$35.00 per year membership for
individuals or families, $100.00 per
year membership for businesses,
organizations or government entities;
library admission: $4.00 for non-
members; research: $10.00 per hour,
$5.00 (half-hour) minimum plus
copies at 20¢ per 8½" x 11" page

Mason Historical Society
122 Walnut Court
Mason, MI 48854
(517) 676-2209
Virginia Schlichter, President

Mayville Area Museum of History and Genealogy
(on Highway M 24, mile east of
Mayville—location)
PO Box 242 (mailing address)
Mayville, MI 48744
(517) 843-6712 (President)
Howard J. Brumley, President
Hours: weekends during summer months
(Obituary file, family genealogies, births,
historical events)
$5.00 per year membership, $100.00 life
membership

Menominee County Historical Society
908 11th Avenue
Menominee, MI 49858
(906) 863-2797 (President)
Roger Seidl, President

Midland County Historical Society
Midland Center for the Arts
1801 West Saint Andrews Drive
Midland, MI 48640
(517) 835-7401
Gary F. Skory, Director
Hours: Mon–Fri 9:00–noon & 1:00–5:00
Pub. *The Midland Log*, annually, $5.00
per issue
$25.00 per year membership for
individuals, $35.00 per year
membership for families, $20.00 per
year membership for senior citizens

Montrose Area Historical Society
Montrose Historical and Telephone
Pioneer Museum
144 East Hickory Street
PO Box 577
Montrose, MI 48457
(810) 639-6644 (Director/Secretary,
A.M.); (810) 639-6217 (Treasurer, P.M.)
Karrie Morrissett, Director/Secretary;
Elizabeth Lea, Treasurer
Hours: Sat–Sun 1:00–5:00; Director:
Mon–Fri 9:00–1:00, call ahead to book
tours
Pub. *Memory Lane Gazette*, quarterly
(spring, summer, fall, winter), $6.00
per year subscription; *Montrose
Historical and Pioneer Telephone
Museum News*, free
$3.00 per year membership for
individuals, $5.00 per year
membership for families, $25.00 life
membership, $15.00 sponsorship of
Gazette issue

New Baltimore Historical Society and Museum
51065 Washington
New Baltimore, MI 48047
(810) 725-4755; (810) 725-7987
Carmen Eggert, Curator; Ed Anne,
President
Hours: Wed noon–2:00, Sat 11:00–1:00
Pub. *New Baltimore Historical Society
Newsletter*, monthly

(genealogy and local history room)
$10.00 per year membership for
individuals, $15.00 per year
membership for families, $100.00 life
membership

Newaygo County Society of History and Genealogy
1038 East Wilcox
PO Box 68
White Cloud, MI 49349
(616) 689-6631; (616) 689-6699
E-mail: wclibrary@ncats.net
Allen Bradley, President
Hours: Evans Historical Collection:
various
Pub. *NCSHG Newsletter*, bimonthly
$10.00 per year membership, $150.00
life membership; specific documents
found and mailed for $1.00 per copy,
extensive searches referred to qualified
area genealogists

North Berrien Historical Society
PO Box 207
Coloma, MI 49038
(616) 468-4228

Northville Historical Society
Griswold Road
PO Box 71
Northville, MI 48167
(248) 348-1845
Diann Dupuis, Office Manager
Hours: Mon–Fri 9:00–1:00; Archives:
Wed 9:00–11:00
Pub. *Mill Race Quarterly*
(includes information on early
settlement, community history and
some residents on microfilm)
from $10.00 per year membership

Northwest Oakland County Historical Society
(306 South Saginaw—location)
1755 Tannock Drive (mailing address)
Holly, MI 48422
Josephine A. Spencer, Genealogical
Records Chairman
Hours: by appointment
Pub. *Lantern Lite*, no set time
no set membership fee

Oakland County Pioneer and Historical Society
Pine Grove Historical Museum
Governor Moses Wisner Historic House
405 Oakland Avenue
Pontiac, MI 48342
(248) 338-6732
Charles H. Martinez, Operations
Manager
Hours: Office: Mon–Fri 9:00–4:00;
Library: Mon–Fri 9:00–3:00
Pub. *Oakland Gazette*, quarterly
(local, state, family histories, genealogy;
Howlett Collection of local history on
specific families, Avery Collection of
marriages, births, deaths of Oakland

County families; 2500 books, 1500
bound periodical volumes, vertical file
of photographs)
from $20.00 per year membership; no
search fees but donations accepted

Oakland Township Historical Society
4393 Collins Road
Rochester, MI 48307
Delores Burkhart, Secretary-Treasurer
$6.00 per year membership for
individuals, $10.00 per year
membership for families

Oceana County Historical and Genealogical Society
114 Dryden Street
Hart, MI 49420
(616) 873-2600
Esther Moul, Corresponding Secretary
Hours: Wed 10:00–5:00
Pub. *Newsletter*, quarterly
(obituary files, cemetery census, old
school records, maps, atlases, county
newspaper microfilm, etc.)
$10.00 per year membership for
individuals, $15.00 per year Sustaining
membership, $50.00 per year
Corporate membership, $100.00 life
membership

Ogemaw Genealogical and Historical Society
Ogemaw County Museum
PO Box 734
West Branch, MI 48661-0734

Ontonagon County Historical Society
422 River Street
PO Box 92
Ontonagon, MI 49953
(906) 884-6165
Ruth Ristola, Manager
Hours: Mon–Sat 9:00–5:00
("Ontonagon County history; we have
quite a bit of genealogy and family
trees on a computer that we have
access to.")
$2.00 museum admission, copy fees only
on materials

Pinckney Area Historical Society
PO Box 606
Pinckney, MI 48169

Pontiac Area Historical and Genealogical Society
(60 East Pike, Pontiac, MI 48342—
location)
PO Box 430901 (mailing address)
Pontiac, MI 48343-0901
(248) 334-9929; (248) 334-3418
Joseph P. Lafnear, Sr., President
Hours: Pontiac Public Library, Lower
Level: second Thur 7:30 P.M.
Pub. *Connections*

Rockwood Area Historical Society
PO Box 68
Rockwood, MI 48173

Romeo Historical Society
132 Church Street
PO Box 412
Romeo, MI 48065
(810) 752-4111
Thelma Huet, Administrator
Hours: Wed 10:00–noon, and by
appointment
$12.00 per year membership for
individuals, $18.00 per year
membership for families

Romulus Historical Society
11121 Wayne Road
Romulus, MI 48174
(734) 941-0775

Rose City Area Historical Society, Inc.
Ogemaw District Library
107 West Main
PO Box 427
Rose City, MI 48654
(517) 685-3300
Roberta Willett, Corresponding Secretary
Hours: Library: Mon 10:00–8:00, Tue–
Fri 10:00–5:00, Sat 10:00–12:00
Pub. *Rose City Area Historical Society
Newsletter*, three times per year
(Michigan and Ogemaw County history,
Ogemaw County newspapers and
censuses on microfilm; "Our society is
indexing the Ogemaw County
newspapers.")
$5.00 per year membership

Roseville Historical and Genealogical Society
Roseville Public Library
29777 Gratiot Avenue
Roseville, MI 48066

Saginaw County Historical Society
County Castle Building
500 Federal Avenue
PO Box 390
Saginaw, MI 48606
(517) 752-2861
Pub. *Saginaw County Historian*

Saint Clair Shores Historical Commission
Saint Clair Shores Public Library
22500 Eleven Mile Road
Saint Clair Shores, MI 48081-1399
(810) 771-9020; (810) 771-8935
Arthur Woodford, Director
Hours: winter: Mon–Thur 9:00–9:00, Sat
9:00–5:00; summer: Mon–Thur 9:00–
9:00, Fri 9:00–5:00
Pub. *Muskrat Tales*, two times per year,
$3.00 per issue; *Newsletter*, six times
per year, $3.00 per issue
(Great Lakes and Michigan historical
collections)
$12.50 per year membership

Sanford Historical Society
North Saginaw at Smith Street
PO Box 243
Sanford, MI 48657
(517) 687-2771

Sanilac County Historical Society
Sanilac Historical Museum
228 South Ridge
PO Box 158
Port Sanilac, MI 48469
(810) 622-9946
Nancy Marvin, Administrator
Hours: Museum: Jun–Sept: Tue–Sun
10:00–4:30; Sept–Jun: Tue–Wed
noon–4:00
(history of Sanilac County only, and
some Marine)
$10.00 per year membership, $50.00 life
membership; search fee: $5.00
minimum

Schoolcraft Historical Society
16278 Prairie Rhonda
Schoolcraft, MI 49087
Earl Christiansen

Shepherd Area Historical Society
314 Maple Street
PO Box 505
Shepherd, MI 48883
(517) 828-5881
Rose I. Cohoon, President
Hours: by appointment
$3.00 per year membership

**Shiawassee County Historical
Society**
Shiawassee County Archives
224 Curwood Castle Drive
Owosso, MI 48867
(517) 725-7891; (517) 288-3058
(Archivist)
Margaret Zdunic, Archivist
Hours: by appointment
Pub. *Shiawassee Gazette*, quarterly
$10.00 per year membership

**South Lyon Area Historical Society,
Inc.**
300 Dorothy Street
PO Box 263
South Lyon, MI 48178

South Lyon Historical Commission
214 West Lake Street
PO Box 263
South Lyon, MI 48178

**Sterling Heights Genealogical and
Historical Society**
Sterling Heights Public Library
40255 Dodge Park Road
Sterling Heights, MI 48078-4496
(810) 977-6267
Julia Santini
Hours: Mon–Thur 9:30–8:30, Fri–Sat
9:30–5:00 (closed Sat insummer)
Pub. *Ancestral Tree*, quarterly
$8.00 per year membership

Trenton Historical Commission
Trenton Historical Museum
(306 Saint Joseph—location)
2800 Third Street (mailing address)
Trenton, MI 48183
(734) 675-2130
Alfred Sidebottom, Chairman

Troy Historical Society
Troy Museum and Historical Village
60 West Wattles Road
Troy, MI 48098
(248) 524-3570 (Museum)
Jan Mecoli Klco, Museum Director
Hours: Tue–Sat 9:00–5:30, Sun 1:00–
5:00
Pub. *Troy Village Press*

Van Buren County Historical Society
(6215 East Red Arrow Highway, East—
location)
PO Box 452 (mailing address)
Hartford, MI 49057
(616) 621-2188
$10.00 per year membership; search fee:
$10.00

Vicksburg Historical Society
7683 East YZ Avenue
Vicksburg, MI 49097-9714
(616) 649-2876; (616) 649-1733
(Museum, to leave a message)
Bonnie Holmes, President
Hours: Vicksburg Depot Museum, 300
North Richardson, Vicksburg, MI
49097: Sat 1:00–4:00, and by
appointment; meetings third Tue 7:30
Pub. *Depot Review*, semiannually
$5.00 per year membership

**Washtenaw County Historical
Society**
Museum on Main Street: A Museum of
County Life
(500 North Main at Beakes Street—
location not yet open)
PO Box 3336 (mailing address)
Ann Arbor, MI 48106-3336
(734) 662-9092
Pub. *Washtenaw Impressions*, seven
times per year
$15.00 per year general membership,
special rates for students and senior
citizens

**Washtenaw County History District
Commission**
(c/o Washtenaw County Metropolitan
Planning Commission, 100 North
Fourth Avenue—location)
PO Box 8645 (mailing address)
Ann Arbor, MI 48107
(734) 994-2435
Ina Hanel, Staff Representative
Hours: meetings: first Thur; office: 8:30–
5:00

Waterloo Area Historical Society
PO Box 37
Stockbridge, MI 49285

(517) 596-2254
Agnes Dikeman, President
Hours: summer: Tue–Sun 1:00–4:00;
Sept: Sat–Sun 1:00–4:00 (last tour
3:30)
Pub. *Quarterly Newsletter*
$5.00 per year membership

Wayne Historical Society
Wayne Historical Commission
1 Town Square
Wayne, MI 48184
(734) 722-0113

Wexford County Historical Society
127 Beech Street
PO Box 124
Cadillac, MI 49601
(616) 775-1717
Linda Boyer, President
Hours: Wed–Fri (Memorial Day–Labor
Day) noon–4:00, Sat noon–4:00, Sun
(autumn) noon–4:00
$10.00 per year membership for
individuals, $25.00 per year
membership for families, $250.00 life
membership

White Lake Area Historical Society
Montague, MI 49437

Wyandotte Historical Society
Wyandotte Museum
2610 Biddle Avenue
Wyandotte, MI 48192
(734) 246-4520
Marc M. Partin, Site Supervisor
Hours: Mon–Fri 9:00–5:00
Pub. *Wyandotte Historical Society
Newsletter* (not genealogical), monthly
$10.00 per year membership

**Wyoming Historical and Cultural
Commission**
PO Box 905
Wyoming, MI 49509
(616) 534-7671

Ypsilanti Historical Society Museum
220 North Huron Street
Ypsilanti, MI 48197
(734) 482-4990; (734) 483-7481 FAX
Mrs. Billie Zolkosky, Archivist
Hours: 9:00–noon
Pub. *Ypsilanti Gleanings*, quarterly
$5.00 per year membership

Zeeland Historical Society
37 East Main Avenue
Zeeland, MI 49464
(616) 772-4079
William S. Tuinstra, President
Hours: Dekker Huis Museum: mid-
March to mid-October: Thur 10:00–
4:00, Sat 10:00–1:00
Pub. *Timeline*, quarterly; *Year Book*,
annually
(a few histories of local families for
Holland-Zeeland area)
minimum $10.00 per year membership

LDS Family History Centers

Bloomfield Hills
(810) 647-5671

Detroit
(see Bloomfield Hills or Westland)

East Lansing
(517) 332-2932

Flint
(see Grand Blanc)

Grand Blanc
(810) 694-2964

Grand Rapids
(see East Lansing)

Kalamazoo
(616) 342-1906

Westland
(313) 459-4570

Genealogical Societies

State Genealogical Society

Michigan Genealogical Council
PO Box 80953
Lansing, MI 48908-0953
Pub. *Michigan Genealogical Council Newsletter*, three times per year
$6.00 per year membership

Regional Genealogical Societies

Bay County Genealogical Society
PO Box 27
Essexville, MI 48732
(517) 892-5951
E-mail: ddolsen989@attworldnet.net
Donald F. Dolsen, President
Hours: by appointment
Pub. *Clarion*, five times per year
(specializes in Bay County and Michigan)
$8.00 per year membership for individuals, $10.00 per year membership for families

Berrien County Genealogical Society
PO Box 8808
Benton Harbor, MI 49023-8808
E-mail: bcgensoc@aol.com
http://www.qtm.net/bcgensoc
Brenda Sears, Corresponding Secretary; Harold Atwood, Librarian; Joyce Hudak, Research Director
Pub. *Pastfinder*, quarterly
(cemetery listings)

$10.00 per year membership; free queries with Berrien County connection

Branch County Genealogical Society
PO Box 443
Coldwater, MI 49036
$5.00 per year membership for individuals, $7.50 per year membership for couples; research in Branch County only: $6.00 for first hour, $5.00 for each hour thereafter

Calhoun County Genealogical Society
PO Box 777
Marshall, MI 49068
(616) 962-3498
Nancy Hibiske, President
Hours: meetings at VFW Hall: fourth Tue (Sept–Jun) 7:00
Pub. *Generations*, bimonthly
(cemetery transcriptions)
$12.00 per year membership (beginning in October)

Charlevoix County
Boyne District Library
201 East Main Street
Boyne City, MI 49712
(616) 582-7861 (Library); (616) 582-2998 (Library) FAX
http://www.rootsweb.com/~micharle/charleux.htm
Nancy Fulkerson, President
Pub. *Back-tracking Pa's Roots*, quarterly, $5.00 per year subscription
(specializes in Charlevoix County only)
$10.00 per year membership; no search services, but will send list of professional researchers

Cheboygan County Genealogical Society
PO Box 51
Cheboygan, MI 49721
Julia Hinds, President
Hours: meetings at Family House Restaurant: third Tue 7:30; meetings at LDS Family History Center: second Wed 9:30 A.M.
Pub. *Rivertown Roots*, quarterly
$10.00 per year membership

The Genealogists of the Clinton County Historical Society
(Brook Road, Lansing, MI—Archives location)
PO Box 23 (mailing address)
Saint Johns, MI 48879-0023
(517) 482-1291, ext. 147
Maralyse Brooks, President
Hours: Mon–Tue 9:00–4:00, Thur–Fri 2:00–6:00
Pub. *Clinton County Trails*, quarterly
$6.00 per year membership for individuals (includes membership in Clinton County Historical Society), $10.00 per year membership for couples; research: $6.00 per hour

Dearborn Genealogical Society
The McFadden-Ross House/Dearborn Historical Museum
(915 South Brady, Dearborn, MI 48124—location)
PO Box 1112 (mailing address)
Dearborn, MI 48121-1112
(313) 565-3000 (Museum)
Eunyce Fina, President
Hours: Museum: Mon–Fri 9:00–5:00
Pub. *Dearborn Genealogical Society Newsletter*, quarterly
$10.00 per year membership for individuals, $15.00 per year membership for families

Delta County Genealogical Society
314 North 20th Street
Escanaba, MI 49829
(906) 786-1893
Marguerite Larsen, Librarian
Pub. *Delta Pedigree Press*, quarterly
$7.00 per year membership

The Detroit Society for Genealogical Research, Inc.
Detroit Public Library
Burton Historical Collection
5201 Woodward Avenue
Detroit, MI 48202-4093
(313) 833-1480 (Library)
http://www.fgs.org/~fgs/soc0042.htm
David L. Curtis, President
Hours: Library: Tue & Thur–Sat 9:30–5:30, Wed 1:00–9:00
Pub. *Detroit Society for Genealogical Research Magazine*, quarterly; *Detroit Society for Genealogical Research Newsletter*, quarterly
$15.00 per year membership for individuals, $17.00 per year membership for families, $20.00 Contributing membership, $25.00 Sustaining membership, $5.00 additional for Canadian postage, $10.00 additional for overseas postage

Dickinson County Genealogical Society
Dickinson County Public Library
401 Iron Mountain Street
Iron Mountain, MI 49801
(906) 774-1218; (906) 774-4079 FAX
John Alquist, President
Hours: Library: winter: Mon–Fri 9:00–9:00, Sat 9:00–5:00, Sun 1:00–4:00; summer: Mon–Fri 9:00–8:00, Sat 9:00–1:00
Pub. *Dickinson Diggins*, quarterly
$8.00 per year membership

Downriver Genealogical Society
(1335 Southfield Road—location)
PO Box 476 (mailing address)
Lincoln Park, MI 48146
(313) 382-3229 (President)
E-mail: shuntin348@aol.com
Sherry Huntington, President

Hours: Tue–Thur & Sat 1:00–5:00; meetings at Saint John's Church, Fourth and Chestnut Streets, Wyandotte, MI: third Wed 7:30 P.M.
Pub. *Downriver Seeker*, quarterly
$10.00 per year membership for individuals or families

Eaton County Genealogical Society, Inc.
(100 West Lawrence Avenue, 1885 Historical Courthouse—location)
PO Box 337 (mailing address)
Charlotte, MI 48813
(517) 543-8792; (517) 543-6999 FAX
http://www.sojourn.com/ mmgs
Drouscella Halsey, Secretary
Hours: Mon–Fri 10:00–2:00, Mon 6:00–9:00; meetings: third Wed (Jan–May & Sept–Oct) 7:00, second Wed (Nov) 7:00
Pub. *Eaton County Quest*, $4.50 per issue
$15.00 per year membership for individuals (calendar year, includes rental privileges in AGLL, $7.00 per year membership for families, $10.00 per year membership for families without rental privileges, $5.00 per year membership for individuals without periodical or rental privileges; free queries for members

Elkhart County Genealogical Society
(see Indiana)

Farmington Genealogical Society
Farmington Community Library
Farmington Branch
23500 Liberty Street
Farmington, MI 48335-3570
(313) 474-7770
Myra Burger, Corresponding Secretary
Hours: Mon–Thur 10:00–9:00, Fri–Sat (during school year) 10:00–5:00
Pub. *Newsletter*, eight times per year (monthly, September–May, except December)
$10.00 per year membership for individuals, $12.00 per year membership for couples

Flint Genealogical Society
PO Box 1217
Flint, MI 48501-1217
Jack O. Briggs, Registrar
Hours: Mon–Fri 10:00–9:00
Pub. *Flint Genealogical Quarterly*, three times per year; *Flint Genealogical Society Newsletter*, monthly
(has Genesee County obituaries)
$15.00 per year membership for individuals, $20.00 per year membership for families

Four Flags Area Genealogical Society
(Niles Community Library Meeting Room—location)
PO Box 414 (mailing address)
Niles, MI 49120
(616) 463-4696
Carole Kiernan, President
Hours: 9:00–8:00
Pub. *Four Flags Tracer* (Berrien and Cass counties)
$14.00 per year membership for families

Friends of the Mitchell Public Library Research Committee
PO Box 873
Hillsdale, MI 49242-0873
(especially Hillsdale County area families)

Gaylord Fact-Finders Genealogical Society
PO Box 1524
Gaylord, MI 49735-5534
(616) 584-2625
Donna M. Marrs, President
Hours: meetings: third Wed (Jan–Jun & Aug–Nov) 7:00–9:00
Pub. *The Keystone Newsletter*, quarterly (January, April, July, October)
(Otsego County, Michigan, newspapers)
$10.00 per year membership for individuals, $12.00 per year membership for families; queries: $2.00 for non-members; research fee: $5.00 per hour plus expenses

Genealogy Group
Benzie Area Historical Society
Benzie Area Historical Museum
6941 Traverse Avenue
PO Box 185
Benzonia, MI 49616
(616) 882-5539 (Museum)
Florence Bixby, Curator

Grand Haven Genealogical Society
Loutit Library
407 Columbus
Grand Haven, MI 49417

Grand Traverse Genealogical Society
(430 South Airport Road, East, Traverse City, MI 49685—location)
PO Box 2015 (mailing address)
Traverse City, MI 49684
http://members.aol.com/vivilson577/gtogs.html
Jan Novak
Pub. *Kinship Tales*, quarterly (February, May, August and November)
(census, cemetery books; collection of books and film housed at Northwestern Michigan College's Mark and Helen Osterlin Library)
$10.00 per year membership for individuals or married couples; research: $5.00 per hour plus expenses

Gratiot County Historical and Genealogical Society
228 West Center Street
Ithaca, MI 48847-1415
(517) 875-4974 (Museum)
Georgiana Peet Miller, Chair, Genealogical Group
Hours: Genealogy: Tue 1:00–5:00; Museum: Thur (Jun–Nov) 11:00–3:00 & 7:00–9:00
Pub. *Pages from the Past*, monthly (genealogical material four times per year)
(primarily Gratiot County research, but also some state and national)
$10.00 per year membership for individuals, $12.00 per year membership for families, $75.00 per year Sustaining membership, $200.00 life membership; research: $5.00 per hour, $10.00 minimum, plus LSASE and 10¢ per page for copies

Hillsdale County Genealogical Society
PO Box 61
Hillsdale, MI 49242

Holland Genealogical Society
Herrick Public Library
300 River Avenue
Holland, MI 49423
(616) 355-1400
Don Johnson, President
Hours: Library: winter: Mon–Thur 9:00–9:00, Fri–Sat 9:00–6:00, Sun 2:00–5:00; summer: Mon–Thur 9:00–9:00, Fri 9:00–6:00, Sat 9:00–1:00
Pub. *Family Ties*, three times per year
$15.00 per year membership

Huron Shores Genealogical Society
1050 North Skeel Avenue
Oscoda, MI 48750
(517) 739-9581
Rosemary Klenow, President
Hours: Mon & Fri 10:30–5:00, Tue–Thur 10:30–8:00, Sat 9:00–5:00
Pub. *Huron Shores Genealogical Society Newsletter*, monthly
$7.00 per year membership

Huron Valley Genealogical Society
1100 Atlantic
Milford, MI 48042

Ionia County Genealogical Society
13051 Ainsworth Road Route 3
Lake Odessa, MI 48849
(616) 374-3141
E-mail: pkswiler@juno.com
Pamela K. Swiler, Founder
Hours: meetings at the Lake Odessa Historical Society Depot Museum: second Sat 1:00

Jackson County Genealogical Society

c/o Jackson District Library
244 West Michigan Avenue
Jackson, MI 49201
(517) 787-8105
Doris Littebrant, Research Coordinator
Hours: Library: Sept–May: Mon–Thur
9:30–8:30, Fri 9:30–6:00, Sat 9:30–
5:00; Jun–Aug: Mon–Thur 9:30–7:00,
Fri 9:30–6:00, Sat 9:30–1:30
Pub. *Lexicon*, quarterly
$12.00 per year membership

Kalamazoo Valley Genealogical Society

(Comstock Township Library, 6130 King
Highway, Lower Floor—collection
location)
PO Box 405 (mailing address)
Comstock, MI 49041
(616) 665-9697
E-mail: magrindol@juno.com
http://www.rootsweb.com/~mikvgs/
Mary Grindol, Editor
Hours: Library: Mon–Thur 10:00–9:00,
Fri 10:00–6:00, Sat 10:00–4:00;
Genealogy Room: Fri 10:00–6:00 for
the public, same hours as library for
authorized society members
Pub. *The Kalamazoo Valley Heritage*,
monthly
(Kalamazoo County and southwestern
Michigan)
$12.00 per year membership for
individuals (beginning in September),
$1.00 per year Associate membership
(at member's address); research: $5.00
for first hour

Kalkaska Genealogical Society

PO Box 353
Kalkaska, MI 49646

Lapeer County Genealogical Society

Marguerite DeAngeli Branch Library
921 West Nepessing Street
Lapeer, MI 48446
Keitha VerPlanck, President
Hours: Library: Mon–Thur 9:00–9:00,
Fri 9:00–5:00, Sat 9:00–4:00
Pub. *Lapeer Legacy*, quarterly
$12.00 per year membership for
individuals, $15.00 per year
membership for families

Lenawee County Genealogical Committee

Lenawee County Historical Society, Inc.
Lenawee County Historical Museum
110 East Church Street
PO Box 511
Adrian, MI 49221
(517) 265-6071
Doris Conklin Trowbridge, Archivist;
Charles N. Liquist, Ph.D., Curator
Pub. *From the Tower*, five times per year
$10.00 per year membership, $100.00
life membership

Lewiston Genealogical Society

701 West Main Street
Lewiston, MI 49756

Livingston County Genealogical Society

PO Box 1073
Howell, MI 48844-1073
Pub. *Newsletter*, quarterly
$10.00 per year membership for
individuals, $13.00 per year
membership for couples

Lyon Township Genealogical Society

Lyon Township Public Library
27005 Milford Road
PO Box 326
New Hudson, MI 48165
(248) 437-8800
Mary Canfield, Library Director
Hours: Mon & Fri 10:00–5:00, Tue &
Thur 10:00–9:00, Sat 10:00–3:00

Macomb County Genealogy Group

Mount Clemens Public Library
150 Cass Avenue
Mount Clemens, MI 48043
(810) 469-6200
Deborah J. Larsen, Assistant Library
Director
Hours: Library: Mon–Thur 9:30–9:00,
Fri–Sat 9:30–5:30

Marquette County Genealogical Society

Peter White Public Library
217 North Front Street
Marquette, MI 49855
(906) 228-9510 (Library); (906) 228-
7315 FAX
http://www.fgs.org/~fgs/soc0119.htm
Sherrye Woodworth, Corresponding
Secretary
Hours: Library: Mon–Wed 10:00–9:00,
Thur–Fri 10:00–6:00, Sat 11:00–5:00,
Sun (winter) 1:00–5:00
Pub. *Lake Superior Roots*, three times
per year
$10.00 per year membership for
individuals

Mid-Michigan Genealogical Society

(Valley Court Community Center, 201
Hillside Court, East Lansing, MI—
location)
PO Box 16033 (mailing address)
Lansing, MI 48901-6033
Ruth Z. Lewis, C.G.R.S., Chairman,
Research Committee
Hours: meetings fourth Wed (Jan–May &
Sept–Nov) 7:15-9:00
Pub. *Newsletter*, quarterly (1 March, 1
June, 1 September, 1 December)
$5.00 per year membership (beginning 1
May); research: $10.00 per three
hours, queries accepted from members
only

Midland Genealogical Society

Grace A. Dow Library
1710 West Saint Andrews Drive
Midland, MI 48640-2695
(517) 835-7151 (Library reference desk);
(517) 835-7157 (Library office)
http://members.mdn.net/billword/
mgs.htm
Joanne Brines, President
Hours: Library: Mon–Fri 9:00–9:00, Sat
10:00–5:00, Sun (winter) 1:00–5:00
Pub. *Pioneer Record*, four times per year,
$4.50 per year subscription
("Midland County research and
publications: cemeteries, obituaries,
marriages, church records, census;
volunteers to help with library
research and inquiries five afternoons
per week.")
$10.00 per year membership for
individuals, $12.50 per year
membership for couples; search: $3.00
minimum, plus cost of copies and
postage, $5.00 per hour

Genealogical Society of Monroe County

PO Box 1428
Monroe, MI 48161
Rick Grassley, President
Pub. *Record*, quarterly
$12.00 per year membership for
individuals, $5.00 per year
membership for senior citizens (over
62 years of age)

Muskegon County Genealogical Society

Hackley Public Library
316 West Webster Avenue
Muskegon, MI 49440
(616) 722-7276
Kay Cross Deuster, President
Hours: Library: Sept–May: Tue–Wed
9:00–8:00, Thur 9:00–6:00, Sat 9:00–
5:00; summer hours vary
Pub. *Family Tree Talk*, quarterly
$15.00 per year membership for
individuals, $18.00 per year
membership for families; free queries
for members and non-members, two
hours research done for nominal fee to
cover postage and cost of copies

Newaygo County Society of History and Genealogy

1038 East Wilcox
PO Box 68
White Cloud, MI 49349
(616) 689-6631; (616) 689-6699
E-mail: wclibrary@ncats.net
Allen Bradley, President
Hours: Evans Historical Collection:
various
Pub. *NCSHG Newsletter*, bimonthly
$10.00 per year membership, $150.00
life membership; specific documents

found and mailed for $1.00 per copy, extensive searches referred to qualified area genealogists

North Oakland Genealogical Society
Orion Room
Orion Township Public Library
825 Joslyn Road
Lake Orion, MI 48362
(248) 693-3001
Hours: Library: Mon–Thur 10:00–9:00, Fri–Sat 10:00–5:00, Sun (fall–spring) 1:00–5:00, closed holiday weekends; meetings: third Thur (Feb–May & Sept–Nov) 7:00
Pub. *Heirlines*, monthly
$15.00 per year membership (calendar year) to Ella Mae Schultz, Membership Chairperson, 1440 Hemingway Road, Lake Orion, MI 48360, $20.00 per year membership for families in the same household, $10.00 per year membership for societies and organizations

Northeast Michigan Genealogical Society
Jesse Besser Museum
491 Johnson Street
Alpena, MI 49707
(517) 595-2384; (517) 354-8689; (517) 595-2593 (President)
http://www//members.aol.com/alpenaco/migenweb
Janet Romas, President
Hours: Museum: 10:00–5:00; meetings third Thur 6:30
Pub. *Roots and Branches*, quarterly
$10.00 per year membership (calendar year); no research available by mail

Northville Genealogical Society
PO Box 932
Northville, MI 48167-0932
(248) 348-1857
Gloria J. Collins, President
Pub. *Northville Genealogy Society Newsletter*, bimonthly
$8.00 per year membership; research fee: $10.00

Northwest Territory Genealogical Society
(see Indiana)

Oakland County Genealogical Society
(Baldwin Public Library, 300 West Merrill Street, Birmingham, MI 48009—location)
PO Box 1094 (mailing address)
Birmingham, MI 48012
(248) 335-4061
John Beedle-Gee, President
Hours: meetings: first Tue (Oct–Jun) 7:00
Pub. *Quarterly, Acorns to Oaks*, quarterly (December, March, June, September)

$10.00 per year membership for individuals (beginning in October), $12.00 per year membership for families, $3.00 additional for Canadian membership, $5.00 additional for foreign membership

Oakland County Pioneer and Historical Society
Pine Grove Historical Museum
Governor Moses Wisner Historic House
405 Oakland Avenue
Pontiac, MI 48342
(248) 338-6732
Charles H. Martinez, Operations Manager
Hours: Office: Mon–Fri 9:00–4:00; Library: Mon–Fri 9:00–3:00
Pub. *Oakland Gazette*, quarterly
(local, state, family histories, genealogy; Howlett Collection of local history on specific families, Avery Collection of marriages, births, deaths of Oakland County families; 2500 books, 1500 bound periodical volumes, vertical file of photographs)
from $20.00 per year membership; no search fees but donations accepted

Oceana County Historical and Genealogical Society
114 Dryden Street
Hart, MI 49420
(616) 873-2600
Esther Moul, Corresponding Secretary
Hours: Wed 10:00–5:00
Pub. *Newsletter*, quarterly
(obituary files, cemetery census, old school records, maps, atlases, county newspaper microfilm, etc.)
$10.00 per year membership for individuals, $15.00 per year Sustaining membership, $50.00 per year Corporate membership, $100.00 life membership

Ogemaw Genealogical and Historical Society
Ogemaw County Museum
PO Box 734
West Branch, MI 48661-0734

Pontiac Area Historical and Genealogical Society
(60 East Pike, Pontiac, MI 48342—location)
PO Box 430901 (mailing address)
Pontiac, MI 48343-0901
(248) 334-9929; (248) 334-3418
Joseph P. Lafnear, Sr., President
Hours: Pontiac Public Library, Lower Level: second Thur 7:30 P.M.
Pub. *Connections*

Reed City Area Genealogical Society
(780 North Park Street—location)
PO Box 27 (mailing address)
Reed City, MI 49677
(616) 832-5431

Betsy Randall, President
Hours: May 1–Oct 1: Mon–Sun 1:00–4:00, and by appointment
Pub. *RCAGS Reader*, semiannually
$7.00 per year membership for individuals, $8.00 per year membership for couples

Roseville Historical and Genealogical Society
Roseville Public Library
29777 Gratiot Avenue
Roseville, MI 48066

Saginaw Genealogical Society, Inc.
Hoyt Public Library
Eddy Historical Collection
505 Janes Avenue
Saginaw, MI 48605
(517) 755-0904 (Eddy Room)
Darlene A. Hudson, Corresponding Secretary
Hours: Eddy Room: Mon–Thur 9:00–9:00, Fri–Sat 9:00–5:00, Sun (Oct–May) 1:00–5:00; meetings second Tue (Sept–Nov & Jan–Apr) 6:30 in Auditorium
Pub. *Timbertown Log*, quarterly (fall, winter, spring, summer); *Newsletter*, monthly
(collection devoted first to Saginaw, then Michigan, but contains info for most of the world; largest collection north of Detroit)
$15.00 per year membership for individuals, $17.00 per year membership for families, $17.00 per year membership for individuals outside the U.S., $19.00 per year membership for families outside the U.S.

Saint Clair Family History Group Inc.
PO Box 611483
Port Huron, MI 48060-1483
(810) 982-0441 (President)
Jim Muir, President
Hours: Saint Clair County Library: meeting fourth Wed
Pub. *Blue Water Family Backgrounds*, quarterly
(genealogy and local history)
$10.00 per year membership; search fee: $10.00 per name

The Searchers
14300 "V" Avenue
Vicksburg, MI 49097
(616) 778-3712
Lucille Pierson, President

Shiawassee County Genealogical Society
PO Box 841
Owosso, MI 48867
(517) 725-8549
Mrs. R. J. Couzynse, Corresponding Secretary

Hours: Mon–Thur 10:00–9:00, Fri–Sat
10:00–5:00
Pub. *Shiawassee Steppin' Stones*,
quarterly
$10.00 per year membership

Southern Michigan Genealogical Society
239 East Chicago Road
Allen, MI 49227

Sterling Heights Genealogical and Historical Society
Sterling Heights Public Library
40255 Dodge Park Road
Sterling Heights, MI 48078-4496
(810) 977-6267
Julia Santini
Hours: Mon–Thur 9:30–8:30, Fri–Sat
9:30–5:00 (closed Sat in summer)
Pub. *Ancestral Tree*, quarterly
$8.00 per year membership

Three Rivers Genealogy Club
13724 Spence Road
Three Rivers, MI 49093
Mrs. Robert Shingledecker

Tri-County Genealogical Society
21715 Brittany
Eastpointe, MI 48021-2503
(810) 774-7953
E-mail: rfred27240@aol.com;
redtag@juno.com
Randy Ferrari
(serves Michigan and Ontario, Canada;
also conducting genealogy research in
Michigan)

Tri-State Genealogical Society
30874 U.S. #12
Sturgis, MI 49091

Tuscola County Genealogical Society
1658 West Gilford Road
Caro, MI 48723
Pub. *Tuscola County Genealogical
Society Newsletter*, bimonthly
$6.00 per year membership

Union City Genealogical Society
(210 Charlotte Street—location)
123 Barry Street (mailing address)
Union City, MI 49094
(517) 741-3597
E-mail: waitebc@orion.branch.-
co.lib.mi.us
Bradley C. Waite, Treasurer
Hours: by appointment
$6.00 per year membership for families

Van Buren Regional Genealogical Society
Van Buren County Library
Webster Memorial Library
200 North Phelps Street
PO Box 143
Decatur, MI 49045
(616) 423-4771
Toni I. Benson, Librarian

Hours: Library: Mon–Wed 9:00–8:00,
Thur 9:00–6:00, Fri 9:00–5:00, Sat
9:00–2:00
Pub. *Van Buren Echoes*, quarterly
(local history, family history; "We also
serve Allegan, Berrien, Cass, and
Kalamazoo counties.")
$10.00 per year membership for
individuals, $13.00 per year
membership for families, $7.00 per
year membership for students, $15.00
per year foreign membership

Genealogical Society of Washtenaw County, Michigan, Inc.
PO Box 7155
Ann Arbor, MI 48107-7155
(734) 483-2799
http://www.hvcn.org/info/gswc/
Marcia C. McCrary, President
Pub. *Family History Capers*, quarterly;
*Genealogical Society of Washtenaw
County Newsletter*, quarterly
$14.00 per year membership for
individuals, $15.00 per year
membership for families, $12.00 per
year membership for senior
individuals, $13.00 per year
membership for senior families,
$10.00 per year membership for
organizations; research: $10.00
donation

Wayland Tree Tracers Genealogy Society
Henika Public Library
129 West Cedar Street
Wayland, MI 49348
(616) 792-2891
Donna L. Benedict, Corresponding
Secretary
Hours: Library: 10:00–3:00 except Thur
(specializes in eastern Allegan County)
donations accepted

Western Michigan Genealogical Society
Grand Rapids Public Library
Michigan and Family History
Department
60 Library Plaza, N.E.
Grand Rapids, MI 49503-3093
(616) 456-3640 (Library)
Rita A. Smith, Corresponding Secretary
Hours: Library: Mon–Wed 9:00–9:00,
Thur–Sat 9:00–5:30; meetings first Sat
(Sept–Jun)
Pub. *Michigana*, quarterly (March, June,
September, December), $10.00 per
year subscription; *Western Michigan
Genealogical Society Newsletter*,
irregularly
$16.00 per year membership (calendar
year); searches, c/o Search Committee:
$10.00 per hour ($5.00 minimum,
$30.00 maximum, includes up to five
photocopies and postage in the U.S.)

Western Wayne County Genealogical Society
PO Box 530063
Livonia, MI 48153-0063
(734) 425-8832
Pub. *The Society Page*, quarterly;
Messenger Newsletter, four to five
times per year
$10.00 per year membership for
individuals (beginning in May),
$12.00 per year membership for
families of two; queries published in
quarterly

Independent Publications and Miscellany

A.U.W. Genealogy Colloquium
1830 Washtenaw Avenue
Ann Arbor, MI 48104

Coppertown USA
(Red Jacket Road—location)
1197 Calumet Avenue (mailing address)
Calumet, MI 49913
(906) 337-4579

Ingham County Commission on History
(Ingham County Courthouse, 121 East
Maple Street—location)
PO Box 319 (mailing address)
Mason, MI 48854-0319
(517) 676-7213; (517) 676-7230 FAX
Thomas G. Clinton, County Historian
Hours: Courthouse: Mon–Fri 8:00–5:00;
tours by appointment
("Government facility, oldest County
Historical Commission in the state; we
do government research only, no
public research is done except for
informational services.")

Kent County Council for Historic Preservation
115 College Avenue, S.E.
Grand Rapids, MI 49503
(616) 458-2422

Kinseeker Publications
(5697 Old Maple Trail—location)
PO Box 184 (mailing address)
Grawn, MI 49637
E-mail: kinseeker6@aol.com
http://www.angelfire.com/biz/kinseeker/
index.html
Vicki Wilson, Owner

Lenawee County Researchers
1100 South Main, Lot 61
Adrian, MI 49221
Sherrann Lynn Nichols
Pub. *Lenawee County Researchers*,
quarterly, $8.00 per year subscription

Livonia Historic Preservation Commission
(Greenmead Historic Site, 38125 Eight Mile Road, Livonia, MI 48152—location)
2050 Newburgh (mailing address)
Livonia, MI 48152
(248) 477-7375; (248) 477-6921 FAX
Marian Renaud
Hours: Mon–Fri 9:00–5:00

Marine Historical Society of Detroit
29825 Joy Road
Westland, MI 48185
(313) 421-6130

MiGenWeb
Part of U.S. GenWeb Project
E-mail: mi@usgenweb.com
http://www.rootsweb.com/~migenweb/
(links to other Michigan resources)

MINNESOTA

Archives and Libraries with Holdings in Genealogy

State Archives and Library

Minnesota Historical Society Research Center
345 Kellogg Boulevard, West
Saint Paul, MN 55102-1906
(612) 296-2143; (612) 297-7436 FAX
http://www.mnhs.org
Denise Carlson, Head of Reference
Hours: Mon–Wed & Fri–Sat 9:00–5:00, Thur 9:00–9:00
Pub. *Research Center Gazette*, quarterly, free

Department of Library Services
Department of Minnesota Children, Families and Learning
Capitol Square Building
550 Cedar Street
Saint Paul, MN 55101
(612) 296-6104
E-mail: children@state.mn.us
http://www.sos.state.mi.us/history/archive/archive.html

Minnesota Library Association
1315 Lowry Avenue North
Minneapolis, MN 55411-1398
(612) 521-1735; (612) 529-5503
E-mail: mnla@augsburg.edu
http://www.lib.mankato.msus.edu:2000/

State Historical Societies

Minnesota Historical Society
345 Kellogg Boulevard, West
Saint Paul, MN 55102-1906
(612) 296-6126; (612) 297-7436 FAX
http://www.mnhs.org
Denise Carlson, Head of Reference
Hours: Mon–Wed & Fri–Sat 9:00–5:00, Thur 9:00–9:00
Pub. *Minnesota History*, quarterly, $10.00 per year subscription; *Roots*, quarterly, $5.00 per year subscription

Minnesota State Archaeologist's Office
Fort Snelling History Center
Saint Paul, MN 55111
Mark Dudzik, State Archaeologist
(listing of all cemetery sites older than 50 years within the state)

Central Minnesota Historical Center
Saint Cloud State University
Centennial Hall, Room 14B
Saint Cloud, MN 56301
(320) 255-3254
Calvin W. Gower, Ph.D., Director

Northeast Minnesota Historical Center
University of Minnesota
Duluth, MN 55812
(218) 726-8526
E-mail: pmaus@d.umn.edu
Patricia Maus, Administrator/Curator of Manuscripts
Hours: Mon–Fri 8:00–noon & 1:15–4:30
(archives for northeast Minnesota history: St. Louis, Lake, Cook and Carlton counties)

Northwest Minnesota Historical Center
Moorhead State University
Livingston Lord Library
1104 Seventh Avenue South
Moorhead, MN 56563
(218) 236-2343
E-mail: shoptaug@mhdli.moorhead.msus.edu
Dr. Terry L. Shoptaugh
Hours: Mon–Fri 8:00–noon & 1:00–4:30

Southern Minnesota Historical Center
Mankato State University
Mankato, MN 56001
(507) 389-1029
William E. Lass, Ph.D., Director

Southwest Minnesota Historical Center
Southwest State University
Marshall, MN 56258
(507) 532-7373
Jan Louwagie, coordinator
Hours: afternoons, during academic calendar, by appointment

West Central Minnesota Historical Center
University of Minnesota
Fourth and College Streets
Morris, MN 56267
(320) 589-2211, ext. 6172
Professor John Quinn Imholte
Hours: 20 hours per week
(Big Stone, Chippewa, Douglas, Grant, Pope, Stevens, Swift and Traverse counties records and manuscripts)

City, County and Regional Archives and Libraries

Austin Public Library
323 Fourth Avenue, N.E.
Austin, MN 55912-3370

Duluth Public Library
520 West Superior Street
Duluth, MN 55802
(218) 723-3802
David Ouse, Head, Reference; Don Johnson, Reference Librarian I
Hours: Mon–Thur 10:00–8:30, Fri 12:00–5:30, Sat (Oct–May) 10:00–4:00

1877 Peterson Station Museum
Mill and Centennial Streets
PO Box 233
Peterson, MN 55962
(507) 895-2551

Folke Bernadette Memorial Library
Gustavus Adolphus College
Saint Peter, MN 56082
(507) 933-7572
Hours: 8:00 A.M.–midnight
(includes church records of five earlier
conferences of the Lutheran Church,
basically those based in Minnesota)

Hay Lake School Museums
Country Road 3 and Old Marine Trail
PO Box 123
Scandia, MN 55073
Hazel Gronquist, Executive Director
Hours: Sat–Sun (May–Nov 1) 1:30–4:30
Pub. *Historical Whisperings*, quarterly
(genealogical services)
$10.00 per year membership

Heritage-Hjemkomst Interpretive Center
202 First Avenue, North
Moorhead, MN 56560
(218) 233-5604
Beverly Woodward, Executive Director
Pub. *Hjemkomst Interpretive Center*
(genealogical services)

Iron Range Research Center Library and Archives
A Division of the Iron Range Resources
and Rehabilitation Board
Highway 169 West
PO Box 392
Chisholm, MN 55719
(218) 254-3325; (218) 254-4938 FAX
Tom Sersha, Director
Hours: winter: Mon–Sat 9:00–4:00;
summer: Mon–Sun 10:00–7:00

Lake Superior Marine Museum Association
PO Box 177
Duluth, MN 55801
(218) 727-2497
C. Patrick Lasadie, Corresponding
Secretary
Hours: 7:00–4:00
Pub. *The NorEaster*, bimonthly, $20.00
per year subscription
(maritime industry and history)

Minneapolis Public Library and Information Center
300 Nicollet Avenue
Minneapolis, MN 55401-1992
(612) 372-6547 (Humanities
Department); (612) 372-6648 (Special
Collections, Local History, no research
by phone); (612) 372-6623 FAX
http://www.mpls.lib.mn.us
Betsy Williams, Humanities Department
Head—Genealogy; Edward Kukla,

Special Collections Department
Head—Local History
Hours: Humanities Department: Mon–
Thur 9:00–9:00, Fri 9:00–5:30, Sat
10:00–5:30 (genealogist on duty Wed
1:00–3:00); Special Collections: Mon–
Fri 9:00–5:30, Sat 10:00–5:30
(Minneapolis local history)

Murphy's Landing
2187 East Highway 101
Shakopee, MN 55379
(612) 445-6900

Olivia Historic Preservation Corporation
PO Box 148
Olivia, MN 56277
(320) 523-1322
Don Walser, President
(collects local historical documents)

Owatonna Public Library
105 North Elm
PO Box 387
Owatonna, MN 55060
(507) 451-4660; (507) 451-3909 FAX
E-mail: bonnie@selco.lib.mn.us
Bonnie Krueger, Reference Librarian
Hours: Mon–Thur 9:00–9:00, Fri–Sat
9:00–5:00
research: nominal donation based on
request

Rochester Public Library
101 Second Street, S.E.
Rochester, MN 55904
(507) 285-8002
Louise Moe, Reference Librarian
Hours: Mon–Wed 9:30–9:00, Fri 9:30–
5:30, Sat 9:00–5:00 (summer: 9:00–
1:00)

Roseau County Historical Museum and Interpretive Center
110 Second Avenue, N.E.
Roseau, MN 56751
(218) 463-1918
E-mail: roseau@roseau.polaristel.net
Ardyce Stein, Director
Hours: Tue–Sat 9:00–4:00
(local and area history resource center,
archives; vital records indexes,
newspapers, census, cemeteries, school
records, assessment, court records,
printed histories, maps, vertical files.
etc.)
$5.00 per year membership for
individuals, $10.00 per year
membership for families, $25.00 per
year membership for businesses,
$50.00 per year Sponsor membership,
$100.00 per year Sustaining
membership; research: $8.00 per hour
plus 30¢ per copy; admission: $1.00
for adults, 50¢ for children

Saint Paul Public Library
90 West Fourth Street
Saint Paul, MN 55102

(612) 292-6307 (Reference Room)
Carol Martinson, Librarian II
Hours: Mon 11:30–8:00, Tue–Wed & Fri
9:00–5:30, Thur 9:00–8:00, Sat 11:00–
4:00
("Our main strength is newspaper
clippings; because of budget cuts we
can only provide a little assistance
over the phone or through the mail.")

South Saint Paul Public Library
106 Third Avenue, North
South Saint Paul, MN 55075
(612) 451-1093
Carol Johnson, Director
Hours: Mon & Thur 9:00–8:00, Tue–
Wed & Fri 9:00–6:00, Sat (school
year) 9:00–4:00

Southdale-Hennepin Area Library
Information Services
7001 York Avenue, South
Edina, MN 55435-4287
(612) 830-4933; (612) 830-4976 FAX
Roseanne Byrne, Coordinating Librarian
Hours: Mon–Thur 10:00–9:30, Fri–Sat
10:00–5:00, Sun (Oct–May) noon–
5:00

University of Minnesota Libraries
Manuscript Division
826 Berry Street
Saint Paul, MN 55114
(612) 624-3855
E-mail: a-lathl@vml.spcs.umn.edu
http://www.umn.edu/tc/

University of Minnesota
Department of History
269 A. B. Anderson Hall
Duluth, MN 55812
Roger A. Fischer, Chair
Pub. *Upper Midwest History*, annually

University of Saint Thomas
Archbishop Ireland Memorial Library
2260 Summit Avenue
Saint Paul, MN 55105
(612) 962-5453
E-mail: j9malcheski@stthomas.edu;
memartin@al.stthomas.edu

University of Saint Thomas
Department of Special Collections
O'Shaughnessy-Frey Library
2115 Summit Avenue
PO Box 5004
Saint Paul, MN 55105-1096
(612) 962-5467
E-mail: jbdavenport@stthomas.edu
http://www.lib.stthomas.edu/
Dr. John Davenport, Head of Special
Collections
Hours: Mon–Fri 1:00–4:30, third Sat
10:00–noon & 1:00–5:00, and by
appointment
Pub. *Varia*, one or two times per year
(Luxembourg; Celtic nations: Ireland,
Scotland, Wales; Isle of Man,
Cornwall, and Brittany)
photocopies: 10¢ per page

Vermilion College
Vermilion Interpretive Center
1900 East Camp Street
Ely, MN 55731
(218) 365-3256

Waseca-LeSueur Regional Library
408 North State
Waseca, MN 56093
(507) 835-2910
Sue Nelson, Acquisitions
Hours: Mon–Thur 9:00–8:30, Fri 9:00–
5:00

Winnebago Area Museum
36 North Main Street
Winnebago, MN 56098
(507) 893-3196

Historical Societies— Local and Regional

Afton Historical Society
Museum
3165 Saint Croix Trail
PO Box 178
Afton, MN 55001
(612) 436-8895
Gloria L. Haslund, President
Hours: Sun (Memorial Day weekend to
mid-Oct) 1:00–4:00, and by
appointment
$7.00 per year membership for
individuals, $10.00 per year
membership for families, $25.00 per
year Sustaining membership, $50.00
per year Supporting membership,
$100.00 per year Patron membership

Albany Heritage Society
Rt. 2, Box 266
Albany, MN 56307
(320) 845-2344
Bert Schunighamer, President
(genealogical services)

Anoka County Historical Society
1900 Third Avenue South
Anoka, MN 55303-2421
(612) 421-0600
Jean Smith or Vickie Wendel, Co-
Directors
Hours: Tue–Fri 12:30–4:00; first Sat
9:30–12:30
Pub. *Colonial Hall Crier Newsletter*, five
times per year
(Anoka County, Civil War)
$8.00 per year membership for
individuals, $16.00 per year
membership for families, $5.00 per
year membership for senior citizens,
$1.50 per year membership for
students (ages 6–17), $35.00 per year
Sustaining membership; mail research:
$10.00 per hour

Bay Area Historical Society
PO Box 33, Outer Drive
Silver Bay, MN 55614
(218) 226-4870
Ed Macki, Jr., Liaison
(early history of Lake County and
commercial fishing)

**Becker County Historical Society
and Museum**
(Corner of Summit Avenue and West
Front—location)
PO Box 622 (mailing address)
Detroit Lakes, MN 56501
(218) 847-2938
Harriet Davis, Director
Hours: Mon–Fri 8:00–4:30
Pub. *Newsletter*, quarterly
$10.00 per year membership for families,
$5.00 per year membership for senior
citizens, $25.00 per year membership
for businesses and organizations

Beltrami County Historical Society
(7301 Frontage Road N.W., Bemidji,
MN 56601—location)
PO Box 683 (mailing address)
Bemidji, MN 56619
(218) 751-7824
Wanda Hoyum, Director
Hours: Mon–Thur 9:00–2:00
Pub. *Centennial Gazette*, quarterly
$7.50 per year membership for
individuals, $12.50 per year
membership for families, $25.00 per
year Sponsor membership, $50.00 per
year Benefactor membership, $100.00
per year Sustaining membership;
research: $5.00 per half-hour for
members, $10.00 for non-members

Benton County Historical Society
PO Box 245
Sauk Rapids, MN 56379-0245
(320) 253-9614
Dorothy Milnor, Executive Director
Hours: various
Pub. *Benton Newsline*, quarterly
$25.00 per year membership for families;
research: varies with each request

Bertha Historical Society, Inc.
Main Street and Second Avenue, West
Bertha, MN 56437
(218) 924-4095
Laura Foster, President
Pub. *Bertha Historical Society, Inc.*

**Blue Earth County Historical
Society**
415 Cherry Street
Mankato, MN 56001
(507) 345-5566
Carol Oney, Archivist
Hours: Tue–Sat 10:00–4:00
Pub. *Newsletter*, bimonthly
$20.00 per year membership for
individuals, $30.00 per year
membership for families, $15.00 per

year membership for students;
research: $10.00 per hour plus 25¢ per
photocopy; admission $2.00 per day
for non-members

Brooklyn Historical Society
3824 58th Avenue, North
Brooklyn Center, MN 55429
(612) 537-2218
Barbara Sexton, Secretary
write for flyer

Brown County Historical Society
2 North Broadway
New Ulm, MN 56073
(507) 354-2016; (507) 354-1068 FAX
Darla Gebhard, Research Librarian
Hours: Research Library: Mon–Fri
10:00–5:00, Sat 1:00–5:00
Pub. *News Notes*, quarterly
$20.00 per year membership; library
admission: $2.00 for non members;
research: $10.00 per letter

Browns Valley Historical Society
PO Box 334
Browns Valley, MN 56219
(320) 695-2110

**Paul Bunyon Historical Society and
Museum**
Main Street
Akeley, MN 56433
(218) 652-2725 (President); (218) 652-
2575 (Curator)
Joyce Gunkel, President; Fran Lamb,
Curator
Hours: summer months only, and by
appointment with Curator
(emphasis on logging)

Carlton County Historical Society
Carlton County History and Heritage
Center
406 Cloquet Avenue
Cloquet, MN 55720
(218) 879-1938
Marlene Wisuri, Director
Hours: Museum: Mon–Fri 9:00–4:00
Pub. *Society News*, quarterly
$10.00 per year membership for
individuals, $15.00 per year
membership for families, $3.00 per
year membership for students, $25.00
per year membership for organizations
or businesses, $50.00 per year Friend
membership, $75.00 per year Sponsor
membership, $100.00 per year Patron
membership; research: $10.00 per hour
for telephone or written requests

Carver County Historical Society
119 Cherry Street
Waconia, MN 55387
(612) 442-4234
Leanne Brown, Executive Director

Cass County Museum/Cass County Historical Society

(Minnesota and Second Street—location)
PO Box 505 (mailing address)
Walker, MN 56484
(218) 547-7251
Renee Geving, Director
Hours: May–Sept: Mon–Fri 10:00–5:00,
and by appointment during winter
months
(obituary file 1894–1985)

Center City Historical Society

Center City, MN 55012
(612) 257-6818

Chatfield Historical Society

314 South Main Street
Chatfield, MN 55923

Chippewa County Historical Society

(151 Pioneer Drive, Highways 7 and
59—location)
PO Box 303 (mailing address)
Montevideo, MN 56265
(320) 269-7636
E-mail: cchs.june@juno.com
June Lynne, Executive Director
Hours: Mon–Fri 9:00–5:00
Pub. *Pioneer Crier*, monthly
$10.00 per year membership for
individuals, $15.00 per year
membership for families

Chisago County Historical Society

PO Box 146
Lindstrom, MN 55045-0146
Hours: Mon–Fri 8:00–4:30
Pub. *Chisago Heritage Newsletter*,
bimonthly
("county cemetery transcriptions,
newspapers on microfiche,
biographical information on county
pioneers")
$10.00 per year membership for
individuals, $15.00 per year
membership for families

Chisago County Historical Society

Taylors Falls Chapter
Taylors Falls, MN 55084
(612) 465-3125

Clay County Historical Society and Museum

(202 First Avenue, North—location)
PO Box 501 (mailing address)
Moorhead, MN 56560
(218) 233-4604; (218) 233-6209 FAX
E-mail: mpeihl/@delphi.com
Margaret Ristvedt, Office Manager
Hours: Mon–Sat 9:00–5:00, Thur 9:00–
9:00, Sun noon–5:00
Pub. *Clay County Historical Society
Newsletter*, bimonthly
(museum and archives)
$15.00 per year membership for
individuals, $35.00 per year
membership for families; admission
free to the public

Clearwater County Historical Society

(Highway 2 West, Shevlin, MN 56676—
location)
PO Box 241 (mailing address)
Bagley, MN 56621
(218) 785-2000
Tamara Edevold, Executive Director
Hours: May–Sept: Tue–Fri noon–7:00,
Sat 10:00–3:00, Sun noon–3:00; Sept–
May: Tue–Fri noon–5:00, Sat 10:00–
3:00
Pub. *Clearwater History News*, six times
per year
$10.00 per year membership; search fee:
$5.00 initial cost

Cokato Historical Society

94 West Fourth Street
PO Box 269
Cokato, MN 55321
(320) 286-2427; (320) 286-5876 FAX
E-mail: cokatomuseum@cmgate.com
http://www.cokato.mn.us
Mike Worcester, Museum Director
Hours: Mon–Fri 9:00–4:30, Sat–Sun
1:00–4:00
Pub. *In the Midst*, quarterly
("Complete obituary index to local paper,
Cokato Enterprise; state and federal
census schedules for Wright County;
other information indexed from local
paper")
research: $10.00 per hour, copies 50¢
each

Community Historical Society

115 North Broadway
Alden, MN 56009
(507) 874-3462 (Treasurer)
E-mail: ruben@deskmedia.com
Ruben F. Schmidt, M.D., Treasurer
Hours: Memorial Day to Labor Day:
Wed & Fri 10:00–4:00, and by
appointment
$2.00 per year membership

Cook County Historical Society

(12 South Broadway—location)
PO Box 1293 (mailing address)
Grand Marais, MN 55604-1293
(218) 387-1678

Coon Rapids Historical Commission

1313 Coon Rapids Boulevard
Coon Rapids, MN 55433
(612) 755-2880
Gaylord Aldinger, Staff Liaison

Cottonwood County Historical Society

812 Fourth Avenue
Windom, MN 56101
(507) 831-1134
Christine Thompson, Administrator
Hours: Mon–Fri 8:00–4:00
Pub. *Newsletter*, quarterly
(computer database of county tax
records, family history files, obituaries,

etc.; comprehensive research library
pertaining to Cottonwood County)
$15.00 per year membership for
individuals; research: $10.00 per hour
donation

Crosslake Historical Society Museum

PO Box 155
Crosslake, MN 56442
(218) 692-3731
Paul Fruth, Curator
Pub. *Crosslake Historical Society
Museum*

Crow Wing County Historical Society

320 Laurel Street
PO Box 722
Brainerd, MN 56401-0722
(218) 829-3268
Mary Lou Moudry, Executive Director
Hours: Labor Day–Memorial Day: Mon–
Fri 1:00–5:00, Sat 9:00–1:00;
Memorial Day–Labor Day: Mon–Fri
9:00–5:00, Sat 9:00–1:00
Pub. *Historian*, quarterly
$10.00 per year membership for
individuals, $20.00 per year
membership for families; research:
donation plus charge for copies

Cuyuna Range Historical Society

(101 First Avenue—location)
PO Box 128 (mailing address)
Crosby, MN 56441
(218) 546-6178 (summer); (218) 546-
5435 (winter)
Elsi Mooers, President
Hours: Mon–Sat (Jun–Aug) 10:00–4:00
("Cuyuna Range iron ore history, early
town and pioneer histories, artifacts,
memorabilia, some genealogical
information")
$5.00 per year membership, $10.00 per
year Sustaining membership, $100.00
life membership

Dakota County Historical Society

Dakota County Historical Museum
130 Third Avenue, North
South Saint Paul, MN 55075
(612) 451-6260
Rebecca Snyder, Research Librarian
Hours: Tue–Wed & Fri 9:00–5:00, Thur
9:00–8:00, Sat 10:00–3:00
Pub. *Society Happenings*, quarterly; *Over
the Years*, semiannually
$20.00 per year membership for
individuals, $10.00 per year
membership for those on fixed
income; research: $10.00 per hour;
copies: 20¢ or 25¢ each

Dakota County Historical Society

Mendota-West Saint Paul Chapter
370 G Street
Mendota, MN 55150
Sharon Bruestle, Custodian
Pub. *The Little Historian*

Dodge County Historical Society
615 North Main Street
PO Box 433
Mantorville, MN 55955-0433
(507) 635-5508 (seasonal)
Idella Conwell, Director
Hours: 1 May–15 Oct: Tue–Sun 1:00–
5:00; 16 Oct–30 Apr: Thur–Sat 1:00–
4:00
Pub. *Dodge County Chronicle*, quarterly
$10.00 per year membership; research:
$8.00 per hour

Douglas County Historical Society
1219 Nokomis Street
Alexandria, MN 56308
(320) 762-0382; (320) 762-9062 FAX
Barbara Grover, Executive Director
Hours: Mon–Fri 8:00–5:00

**Edina Historical Society and
Museum**
4711 West 70th Street
Edina, MN 55435
(612) 920-8952
Marian Hansen, Administrator
Hours: Thur 9:00–noon, Sat 10:00–noon
Pub. *Newsletter*, quarterly
$10.00 per year membership for
individuals, $15.00 per year
membership for families, $7.50 per
year membership for senior citizens

Ely-Winton Historical Society
c/o Vermilion College
Vermilion Interpretive Center
1900 East Camp Street
Ely, MN 55731
(218) 365-3226
Lillian Hren, Manager

England Prairie Pioneer Club
Rt. 1, Box 36
Verndale, MN 56481
(218) 631-1770
Denny Richter, President

Esko Historical Society
(Highway 61 West—location)
PO Box 83 (mailing address)
Esko, MN 55733
(218) 879-4400

**Excelsior-Lake Minnetonka
Historical Society**
(Village Hall, Third Street—location)
PO Box 305 (mailing address)
Excelsior, MN 55331
(612) 474-5880

Faribault County Historical Society
The Wakefield House
405 East Sixth Street
Blue Earth, MN 56013
(507) 526-5421
Constance Helgeson, President
Hours: Tue–Sat 2:00–4:00, and by
appointment
Pub. *FCHS Newsletter*, two times per
year

$3.00 per year membership, $10.00 life
membership for individuals, $15.00
life membership for families; search
fee: donation

Fillmore County Historical Society
Fillmore County History Center,
Museum and Genealogy Library
(202 County Road #8—location)
Rt. 1, Box 81D (mailing address)
Fountain, MN 55935
(507) 268-4449
Jerry Henke, Executive Director
Hours: Mon–Fri 9:00–4:00
Pub. *Rural Roots Newsletter* (non-
genealogical), quarterly
$10.00 per year membership for
individuals, $16.00 per year
membership for families

Finland Historical Society
PO Box 583
Finland, MN 55603
(218) 353-7393
Dave Geist
(specializes in Finnish immigrants)

Freeborn County Historical Society
1031 Bridge Avenue
Albert Lea, MN 56007
(507) 373-8003
Linda Evenson, Librarian
Hours: Museum: Apr–Dec: Tue–Fri
10:00–5:00, Sat–Sun 1:00–5:00
Pub. *FCHS Newsletter*, quarterly
$12.00 per year membership; research
fees: $7.50 per hour

Fulda Heritage Society
(Corner of Front Street and Saint Paul
Avenue—location)
PO Box 275 (mailing address)
Fulda, MN 56131
(507) 425-2583
Howard E. Anderson, President
Hours: during Fulda Wood Duck
Festival, last weekend of Jun, and by
appointment
Pub. *Fulda Heritage Society*
$5.00 per year membership, $100.00 life
membership

Goodhue County Historical Society
1166 Oak Street
Red Wing, MN 55066
(612) 388-6024
Mary Maronde, Director
Hours: Museum: Tue–Fri 10:00–5:00,
Sat–Sun 1:00–5:00; Research library:
Tue–Fri, and by appointment
Pub. *Goodhue County Historical News*,
three times per year; *Museum Briefs*,
three times per year
$15.00 per year membership for
individuals, $25.00 per year
membership for families, $10.00 per
year membership for students;
research by mail or phone: free for the
first 30 minutes, then $5.00 per half-
hour plus copy fees

**Goodridge Area Historical Society,
Inc.**
Goodridge, MN 56725
(218) 378-4380; (218) 378-4280 FAX
Norma Hanson, President
Hours: Fri 1:00–5:00, Sat 11:00–4:00,
Sun 1:00–4:00
$2.00 per year membership, $1.00 per
year membership for senior citizens

Grant County Historical Society
(Highway 79 East—location)
PO Box 1002 (mailing address)
Elbow Lake, MN 56531
(218) 685-4864
Patricia Benson, Curator
Hours: Mon–Fri 10:00–noon & 1:00–
4:00, Sat (Memorial Day weekend
through Sept) 10:00–noon & 1:00–
4:00
(index to obituaries and marriages in
local newspapers)
$5.00 per year membership, $8.00 per
year membership for families;
research: $5.00 per hour plus copies at
10¢ or 25¢ per page

Hennepin County Historical Society
Hennepin History Museum
2303 Third Avenue, South
Minneapolis, MN 55414
(612) 870-1329
Dorothea Guiney, Director
Hours: Tue–Sat 12:00–5:00
Pub. *Hennepin History*, quarterly
$25.00 per year membership

Hibbing Historical Society
21st Street and Fourth Avenue, East
Hibbing, MN 55746
(218) 262-3486
Pub. *Hibbing Historical Society
Newsletter*, quarterly

Historic Heartland Association, Inc.
PO Box 1
Brainerd, MN 56401
(218) 963-2218; (218) 277-7294

Hopkins Historical Society
1010 First Street, South
Hopkins, MN 55343
(612) 938-7315
Dean Empanger, President

Houston County Historical Society
(1212 East Main Street, Caledonia, MN
55921—location)
PO Box 173 (mailing address)
Houston, MN 55943
(507) 724-3884; (507) 896-3546 (Media
Generalist); (507) 498-3318 (Ms.
Rosendahl); (507) 896-3794 (Mr. Witt)
Anita Palmquist, Media Generalist;
Georgia Rosendahl; Mason Witt
Hours: Mon–Wed 10:00–4:00, Sat–Sun
(Jun–Sept) 1:00–4:00
Pub. *Houston County Historical Society
Newsletter*, quarterly
$5.00 per year membership

Iron Range Historical Society
Old Gilbert City Hall
PO Box 786
Gilbert, MN 55741-0786
(218) 749-3150 (1 May–30 Sept)
Kathy Bergan, Researcher
Hours: Mon–Tue 9:00–2:00, Wed & Sat
   10:00–1:00
Pub. *Range Reminiscing*, quarterly
   (March, June, September, December)
   (Eveleth, Minnesota, newspapers from
   1902 to 1978, Gilbert newspapers
   from 1923, family history)
$10.00 per year membership for
   individuals, $20.00 per year
   membership for clubs, 35.00 per year
   membership for businesses, $100.00
   life membership; research for non-
   membership: $5.00 per hour plus
   copies at 25¢ each and postage

**Historical Committee of the Isabella
Community Council**
PO Box 500
Isabella, MN 55607
(218) 323-7738

Isanti County Historical Society
PO Box 525
Cambridge, MN 55008
(612) 689-4229
Valorie Arrowsmith, Director
Hours: Tue 9:00–4:30, Thur–Fri by
   appointment
Pub. *Isanti Cuttings*, quarterly
$15.00 per year membership for
   individuals, $35.00 per year Sustaining
   membership

Itasca County Historical Society
(Central School, 105th Street, N.W.—
   location)
PO Box 664 (mailing address)
Grand Rapids, MN 55744
(218) 326-6431
Jodi Maki, Executive Director
Hours: Mon–Fri 9:30–5:00, Sat 9:30–
   4:00
Pub. *Itasca History News*, quarterly
$20.00 per year membership for
   individuals, $30.00 per year
   membership for families

Jackson County Historical Society
(307 North Highway 86—location)
PO Box 238 (mailing address)
Lakefield, MN 56150-0238
(507) 662-5505
Judy Nelson, Museum Manager
Hours: Tue & Thur (Sept–Apr) 10:00–
   4:00; Mon–Fri (May–Aug) 10:00–4:00
Pub. *JCHS Jottings Newsletter*, three
   times per year (March, July,
   November)
$20.00 per year membership for
   individuals, $30.00 per year
   membership for families, $50.00 per
   year membership for businesses;

research: $10.00 per hour plus copy
charges, including $5.00 non-
refundable deposit on all requests

**Kanabec County Historical Society
and History Center**
805 West Forest Avenue
PO Box 113
Mora, MN 55051
(320) 679-1665; (320) 679-1673 FAX
Edna Cole, Executive Director
Hours: Mon–Sat 10:00–4:30, Sun &
   holidays 12:30–4:30
Pub. *News*, quarterly
$20.00 per year membership for
   individuals, $35.00 per year
   membership for families (including
   students K–12 living at home), $50.00
   per year Family Plus membership
   (includes guest accompanied by adult
   family member), $100.00 per year
   Century membership, $150.00 per year
   Sponsor membership; general
   admission: $3.00 for adults, $1.00 for
   students (K–12), $8.00 for families,
   free to members; research fee: $5.00
   plus photocopies at 25¢ per page

Kandiyohi County Historical Society
Lawson Memorial Research Center
610 N.E. Highway 71
Willmar, MN 56201
(320) 235-1881
Mona Nelson-Balcer, Director
Hours: Mon–Fri 9:00–5:00
Pub. *Kandi Express*, quarterly
   (local history and biography)
$10.00 per year membership for
   individuals, $20.00 per year
   membership for families

**Kittson County History Center and
Museum**
(East Main Street—location)
PO Box 100 (mailing address)
Lake Bronson, MN 56734
(218) 754-4100
Cindy A. Adams, Museum Director
Hours: Mon–Fri 9:00–5:00, Sat & Sun
   (summer) 1:00–5:00
Pub. *Kittson County Historical Society
   Newsletter*, two or three times per year
   (microfilm newspapers from 1882,
   cemetery records, census records,
   obituary files)
$5.00 per year Sustaning membership,
   $25.00 per year Patron membership;
   no search fees, donations accepted

**Koochiching County Historical
Society**
Koochiching County Historical Museum
(214 Sixth Avenue—location)
PO Box 1147 (mailing address)
International Falls, MN 56649-1147
(218) 283-4316
Sarah Williams, Executive Director
Hours: Museum: Mon–Fri 11:00–5:00,
   Sat–Sun & holidays 1:00–5:00;

Research Facilities and Historical
Society Office: Mon–Fri (May 24–
Sept 24) 9:00–5:00, Mon–Tue (Sept
25–May 23) 9:00–4:00
Pub. *Koochiching Chronicle*, eight times
   per year
$7.50 per year membership for
   individuals, $10.00 per year
   membership (husband and wife and
   any children of school age or
   younger), $35.00 per year Sustaining
   membership, $100.00 life
   membership; museum admission:
   $3.00 for adults, $1.00 for children
   (K–12), preschoolers and members of
   the Historical Society free

**Lac qui Parle County Historical
Society**
250 Eighth Avenue, South
Madison, MN 56256
(320) 598-7678
Gerda Dolman, Curator
Hours: May–Sept
Pub. *Bulletin*, annually
   ("3000 books and pamphlets,
   catalogued")

**Lake County Historical Society and
Railroad Museum**
Depot Building
PO Box 313
Two Harbors, MN 55616
(218) 834-4898
Rachelle King, Director
Pub. *Lake County Historical Society
   Newsletter*, quarterly
   (railroad history, lighthouse, 3M
   museum)
$15.00 per year membership for
   individuals

Lake of the Woods Historical Society
Eighth Avenue, S.E.
PO Box 808
Baudette, MN 56623
(218) 634-1200
Marlys Hirst, Curator
Hours: Tue–Sat (May–Sept) 10:00–4:00
Pub. *LOW County Newsletter*, annually

**LeSueur County Historical Society,
Museum, and Genealogy Center**
(Fourth and Frank Streets—location)
PO Box 240 (mailing address)
Elysian, MN 56028
(507) 267-4620
David Wollin, Director-Museum; Shirley
   Zimprich, Coordinator-Genealogy
   Center
Hours: Memorial Day through Labor
   Day: Wed–Sun 1:00–5:00; May:
   weekends only

LeSueur Historians
(709 North Second Street—location)
208 North Main Street (mailing address)
LeSueur, MN 56058
(507) 665-2050
Helen Meyer, President

Hours: Mon–Sun (Jun–Aug) 1:00–4:30,
and by appointment
("We have a Genealogy Section.")
search fees: copying costs

Lincoln County Historical Society
Lincoln County Pioneer Museum
610 West Elm
Hendricks, MN 56136
(507) 275-3537
Mrs. Allen S. Johnson, Museum Director

Lyon County Historical Society
c/o Courthouse
607 West Main Street
Marshall, MN 56258
(507) 532-4694
Ellayne Conyers, Museum Director
Hours: 12:30–4:30
(Lyon County and southwest Minnesota
history)
$20.00 per year membership for
individuals, $25.00 per year
membership for couples; 50¢ per page
for photocopies

Mahnomen County Historical Society
Courthouse
PO Box 123
Mahnomen, MN 56557
(218) 935-5490
Grace Rock, Museum Aide
Hours: Mon & Wed 9:00–11:00 & noon–
4:00, Fri 8:00–11:00 & noon–4:00
Pub. *Mahnomen County Historical
Society Newsletter*, semiannually

Marine Historical Society
PO Box 84
Marine on Saint Croix, MN 55047

Marshall County Historical Society
East Johnson Avenue
PO Box 103
Warren, MN 56762
(218) 745-4803
Elaine Olson, Curator
Hours: May–Sept 9:00–5:00

Martin County Historical Society, Inc.
304 East Blue Earth Avenue
Fairmont, MN 56031
(507) 235-5178
Roy Levik, President
Hours: May–Sept: Mon 6:30 P.M.–8:30
P.M., Tue–Sat 1:00–4:30
Pub. *Newsletter*, biannually
$10.00 life membership; research: $7.50
per hour plus postage, and copies at
25¢ each

McLeod County Historical Society
McLeod County Heritage and Cultural
Center
380 School Road, North
Hutchinson, MN 55350
(320) 587-2109
Patsy R. Prieve, Administrator
Pub. *MCHS Newsletter*

Meeker County Historical Society
GAR Hall—Meeker County Museum
308 Marshall Avenue, North
Litchfield, MN 55355
(320) 693-8911
E-mail: garhall@willmar.net;
oakhaven@hutchtel.net
http://+ccn.com/mn.tourism/exp/
at1448.html
Paula Nelson, Director
Hours: Museum: Tue–Sun noon–4:00
Pub. *Meeker County Historical Society
Newsletter*, quarterly
$10.00 per year membership

Milaca Area Historical Society and Museum
Milaca Community Library and Museum
145 Central Avenue South
Milaca, MN 56353
(320) 983-3677
Hours: Museum: Thur 1:00–4:00, Sat
10:00–1:00; archives during library
hours: Tue–Wed & Fri 11:00–5:00,
Thur 1:00–8:00, Sat 10:00–1:00
(Milaca newspapers, Mille Lacs County
census on microfilm, Mille Lacs
County cemetery records)
$5.00 per year membership for
individuals, $8.00 per year
membership for families, $3.00 per
year membership for senior citizens,
$30.00 per year membership for
businesses

Mille Lacs Lake Historical Society
Main Street
PO Box 42
Isle, MN 56342

Minnesota Lake Area Historical Society
Kremer House Library and Museum
317 Main
Minnesota Lake, MN 56068
(507) 462-3420
Mary E. Herbst, President

Minnetonka Historical Society
13209 McGinty Road East
Minnetonka, MN 55305
(612) 933-1611; (612) 938-0901
(President's home)
Maxine Dickson, President
Hours: phone inquiries only
Pub. *Minnetonka Mill Wheel Newsletter*,
quarterly
(specializes in the city of Minnetonka)
$8.00 per year membership

Monongalia Historical Society
(220 Norwood Street S.W., one block
west of Millpond on Second Avenue,
one block south on Norwood Street—
location)
18946 Highway 9 N.E. (mailing address)
New London, MN 56273
(320) 354-2557 (President)
Jean E. Kalevik, President

Hours: Memorial Day–Labor Day: Tue–
Sun 1:00–4:00

Morrison County Historical Society
(1600 South Lindbergh Drive—location)
PO Box 239 (mailing address)
Little Falls, MN 56345
(320) 632-4007
Jan Warner, Executive Director
Hours: Tue–Sat 10:00–5:00, Sun (May–
Sept) 1:00–5:00
Pub. *Morrison County Historical Society
Newsletter*, quarterly
(emphasis on family history)
$15.00 per year membership for
individuals, $20.00 per year
membership for families

Mower County Historical Society
(Mower County Fairgrounds, 1303 Sixth
Avenue, S.W.—office location)
PO Box 804 (mailing address)
Austin, MN 55912
(507) 437-6082
Monica Lonergan, Chairman
Hours: Genealogy Room: Sept–May:
Mon–Fri 1:00–4:00; Jun–Aug: Tue–
Sun 11:00–4:00; and by appointment
("Research library, especially Mower
County")
$5.00 per year membership, $50.00 life
membership

Murray County Historical Society/ Museum
2655 Linden Avenue
Slayton, MN 56172
(507) 836-6533
Char Larson, Museum Director
Hours: Mon–Fri 1:00–5:00
(microfilm newspapers, naturalization
records, census, family histories)
$5.00 per year membership; search fees:
$8.00 per hour

New Brighton Area Historical Society
1786 Glenview Avenue
Saint Paul, MN 55112
(612) 633-6991
Pub. *NBAHS Newsletter*

New Prague Historical Society
Rt. 3, Box 37
New Prague, MN 56071
(612) 758-2201

Nicollet County Historical Society and Museum
Treaty Site History Center
1851 North Minnesota Avenue
Saint Peter, MN 56082
(507) 931-2160; (507) 931-0172 FAX
John W. Hans, Director
Hours: Mon–Sat 10:00–4:00, Sun 1:00–
4:00
Pub. *The Crossing*, quarterly
(Nicollet County history; Treaty of
Traverse des Sioux)

$20.00 per year membership for individuals, $30.00 per year membership for families, $10.00 per year membership for students, $50.00 Sustaining membership, $100.00 Patron or Business membership, $500.00 life membership

Nobles County Historical Society
407 12th Street, Suite 2
Worthington, MN 56187
(507) 376-4431
E-mail: tzishlca@rconnect.com
Thomas Zishka, Museum Director
Hours: Mon–Fri 1:00–5:00
Pub. *Nobles County Historical Society Newsletter*, quarterly
$15.00 per year membership for individuals, $30.00 per year membership for families

North Saint Paul Historical Society
2666 East Seventh Avenue
North Saint Paul, MN 55109
(612) 779-6402
Priscilla Olson, Secretary; Betty Lyon, Museum Curator
Hours: Fri 1:00–4:00, Sat 10:00–1:00
$7.50 per year membership for individuals, $10.00 per year membership for families

Northfield Historical Society
(408 Division Street—location)
PO Box 372 (mailing address)
Northfield, MN 55057
(507) 645-9268
Susan Garwood, Executive Director
Hours: Tue–Sat 10:00–4:00, Sun 1:00–4:00
Pub. *Scriver Scribbler*, quarterly
("Minnesota history, Jesse James, Northfield history")
$25.00 per year membership for individuals, $35.00 per year membership for families, $5.00 per year membership for students, $15.00 per year membership for individuals on fixed income, $50.00 per year Patron membership, $100.00 per year Sustaining membership, $500.00 life membership

Olmsted County Historical Society
1195 County Road 22, S.W.
Rochester, MN 55902-6619
(507) 282-9447
E-mail: sweetman@millcomm.com
http://www.millcomm.com/~gzimmer/ochs.html
Sherry Sweetman, Archivist/Librarian
Hours: Tue–Sat 9:00–noon & 1:00–5:00
Pub. *Olmsted Historian*
(printed county histories, plat maps, local newspapers, city directories, census, vertical files, books and periodicals, cemetery transcripts, probate records, guardianship records, grantor-grantee books, vital records)

$25.00 per year membership; admission: $2.00 for non-members; research by mail: $15.00 per hour (one-hour minimum), copies: 20¢ to 50¢ per page from paper originals, 40¢ per page from microform originals

Otter Tail County Historical Society
1110 West Lincoln Avenue
Fergus Falls, MN 56537
(218) 736-6038 (Museum)
LeAnn Neuleib, Office Manager
Hours: Library: Mon–Fri 9:00–5:00; Museum: Mon–Fri 9:00–5:00, Sat (Jan–Dec) 1:00–4:00, Sun (Jun–Sept) 1:00–4:00
Pub. *Otter Tail County Historical Society Newsletter*, bimonthly; *Otter Tail Record*, quarterly
$20.00 per year membership for individuals, $35.00 per year membership for families, $50.00 per year Booster membership, $100.00 per year Sustaining membership, $150.00 per year Sponsor membership, $250.00 per year Patron membership; search fee: $10.00 per hour

Paynesville Historical Society
(543 River Street—location)
329 Washbune Ave (mailing address)
Paynesville, MN 56362
(320) 243-4433
Bertha Zniewski, Executive Secretary
$10.00 per year membership, $25.00 life membership; admission: $1.00

Pine County Historical Society
Askov, MN 55704
(320) 838-3792
Elizabeth Espointour, President
Hours: Museum: Memorial Day–Labor Day: Tue–Sun 1:00–4:00
$10.00 per year membership

Pipestone County Historical Society and Museum
113 South Hiawatha Avenue
Pipestone, MN 56164
(507) 825-2563
E-mail: pipctymu@rconnect.com
http://www.pipestone.mn.us/museum/homepa~1.htm
David C. Rambow, Director of Museum
Hours: Mon–Sun 10:00–5:00, expanded hours during Hiawatha Pageant (last two weekends of Jul and first weekend of Aug)
(non-lending volumes of local newspapers, other Pipestone County related data, obituaries, birth, marriage notices)
$10.00 per year membership for individuals, $5.00 per year membership for senior citizens; $2.00 per person, free for ages 12 and under; research: $5.00 plus 50¢ per copy

Polk County Historical Society
(719 East Robert—location)
PO Box 214 (mailing address)
Crookston, MN 56716
(218) 281-1038
Ed Melby, President
Hours: May 20–Sept 15: noon–5:00
Pub. *Newsletter*, three times per year (January, May, September)
$5.00 per year membership for individuals, $10.00 per year membership for families, $20.00 per year Patron membership

Pope County Historical Society and Museum
809 South Lakeshore Drive
Glenwood, MN 56334
(320) 634-3293
Merlin Peterson, Administrator
Hours: Tue–Sat 10:00–5:00
Pub. *PCHS Newsletter*, quarterly
("County historical artifacts and county genealogy; 40,000+ files on personal events, businesses, organizations, newspapers indexed from 1891")
$10.00 per year membership, $50.00 life membership; non-member search: $3.00; admission: $3.00

Ramsey County Historical Society
323 Landmark Center
75 West Fifth Street
Saint Paul, MN 55102
(612) 222-0701; (612) 223-8539
Julie Wyman, Research Assistant
Hours: Mon–Fri 9:00–5:00
Pub. *Ramsey County History*, quarterly
("Ramsey County history; Saint Paul city directories, 1885–1959)
$30.00 per year membership; research fees vary

Red River Valley Historical Society
PO Box 157
Moorhead, MN 56561-0157
Pub. *Heritage Press*, bimonthly
$15.00 per year membership

Rice County Historical Society
1814 N.W. Second Avenue
Faribault, MN 55021
(507) 332-2121
James Lundgren, Executive Director
Hours: fall, winter, spring: Mon–Fri 9:00–4:00; summer: Tue–Fri 9:00–4:00, Sat–Sun 1:00–4:00
Pub. *The Rice County Historian*, quarterly
("Rice County burial records, 1882 & 1910 history books, city directories, plat maps, family genealogies, newspaper records")
$15.00 per year membership; research by donation

Richfield Historical Society
Bartholomew House Museum
(69th and Lyndale Avenue, South—
  location)
PO Box 23304 (mailing address)
Richfield, MN 55423
(612) 861-2049
Ruthann Clay, President
Hours: May–Sept by appointment
Pub. untitled newsletter, about seven
  times per year
("Reference library, photos, family
  history, schools, churches")
$8.00 per year membership for
  individuals, $10.00 per year
  membership for families, $15.00 per
  year membership for businesses,
  $50.00 per year Friend of the Society

Roseville Historical Society
1114 Woodhill Drive
Roseville, MN 55113
(612) 490-2280
Kay Korupp, President

Royalton Historical Society
Center Street
Royalton, MN 56373
(320) 584-5641; (320) 584-5417

Saint Louis County Historical Society
506 West Michigan Street
Duluth, MN 55802
(218) 722-8011
Lawrence J. Sommer, Director
Pub. *Saint Louis County Historical
  Society Newsletter*, quarterly

Saint Louis Park Historical Society
6210 West 37th Street
Saint Louis Park, MN 55416
(612) 929-9486
Marie U. Hartmann, Board Chairman

Sherburne County Historical Society
13122 First Street
Becker, MN 55308
(612) 261-4433
Kurt Kragness, Executive Director
Hours: 8:00–5:00
Pub. *Historically Speaking*, quarterly

Sibley County Historical Society, Inc.
(Sibley County Historical Museum, 700
  Main Street—location)
PO Box 407 (mailing address)
Henderson, MN 56044-0407
(507) 248-3434; (507) 248-3687
Sharon Haggenmiller, Secretary
Hours: Memorial Day through October:
  Sun 2:00–5:00, and by appointment
Pub. *Sibley County Historical Society
  Newsletter*, quarterly
$6.00 per year membership for
  individuals, $10.00 per year
  membership for families, $25.00 per
  year membership for businesses,

$500.00 per year membership for
  corporations; admission and search
  fees: donation

Spring Valley Community Historical Society, Inc.
221 West Courtland
Spring Valley, MN 55975
(507) 346-7659; (507) 346-2206
  (Genealogist)
Mary Jo Dathe, Secretary; Sharon Jahn,
  Genealogist
("Complete genealogical research for
  Spring Valley area")
$8.00 per year membership

Stearns County Historical Society
Stearns County Heritage Center
235 33rd Avenue, South
PO Box 702
Saint Cloud, MN 56302-0702
(320) 253-8424; (320) 253-2172 FAX
John Decker, Archivist
Hours: Mon–Sat 10:00–4:00, Sun noon–
  4:00
Pub. *Crossings*, bimonthly
$25.00 per year membership for
  individuals, $40.00 per year
  membership for families; research:
  $4.00 minimum, $16.00 per hour plus
  30¢ per copy; admission: $4.00
  minimum for adults, $2.00 for children
  (ages 5–16), free for children under 5,
  $10.00 for families

Steele County Historical Society
1448 Austin Road
Owatonna, MN 55060-4018
(507) 451-1420
Marlene Knutson, Director/Curator
Hours: Oct 1–Apr 30: Mon–Fri 1:00–
  5:00; May 1–Sept 30: daily 1:00–5:00
("Steele County burial files and
  obituaries, history, Indian and
  military")
$10.00 per year membership for
  individuals, $7.50 per year
  membership for senior citizens; search
  fee: $5.00 per hour

Stevens County Historical Society
Stevens County Genealogical Society
Nevada Avenue and Sixth Street
Morris, MN 56267
(320) 589-1719 (Historical Society);
  (320) 589-2190 (President)
Dennis Warnes, President
Hours: Historical Society: Mon–Fri
  9:00–noon & 1:00–5:00, Sun (summer
  only) 1:30–4:30
Pub. *Stevens County Genealogical
  Society Newsletter*, quarterly
  (February, April, June and October)
("funeral records, researching")
$10.00 per year membership for
  individuals (in both Genealogical and
  Historical societies), $17.00 per year
  membership for families

Swift County Historical Society
(On west Highway 12 in Benson—
  location)
2135 Minnesota Avenue, Building 02
  (mailing address)
Benson, MN 56215-9304
(320) 843-4467
Marlys Gallagher, Executive Director
Hours: Tue–Fri 10:00–4:30, Sat 10:00–
  3:00
Pub. *Echo*, six times per year
(obituary file for one-time residents of
  Swift County, census files for Swift
  County, county newspapers dating
  back to 1876)
$5.00 per year membership for
  individuals, $8.00 per year
  membership for families; research:
  $5.00 per hour for non-members
  ($5.00 minimum), plus charge for
  copies to both members and non-
  members

Todd County Historical Society, Inc.
33 Central Avenue
Long Prairie, MN 56347
Wilma Finseth, Museum Administrator
Hours: Mon–Fri 10:00–noon & 1:00–
  4:00
Pub. *Todd County Historical Society, Inc.*

Traverse County Historical Society
Broadway
Wheaton, MN 56296

Upsala Area Historical Society
(Main Street—location)
PO Box 35 (mailing address)
Upsala, MN 56384
(320) 573-4208
Carol Gerads, President
Hours: summer holidays, and by
  appointment
Pub. *UAHS Newsletter*

Verndale Historical Society
(North Farwell Street—location)
Rt. 2 Box 11 (mailing address)
Verndale, MN 56481
(218) 445-5745
Wilbur Desrocher, President
Hours: by appointment
Pub. *Newsletter*, annually (January)
$3.00 per year membership for
  individuals, $5.00 per year
  membership for families

Virginia Area Historical Society
Heritage Center Museum
(800 Olcott Park, Ninth Avenue North—
  location)
PO Box 736 (mailing address)
Virginia, MN 55792
(218) 741-1136
Jan Nelson, Secretary
Hours: 1 May–30 Sept: Tue–Sat 11:00–
  4:00; 1 Oct–31 Dec: Thur–Sat 11:00–
  4:00
Pub. *Heritage News*, quarterly
$5.00 per year membership

Wabasha County Historical Society
3243 60th Avenue, S.W.
Rochester, MN 55902
Hours: daily 1:00–5:00

Wadena County Historical Society
603 North Jefferson
Wadena, MN 56482-2336
(218) 631-9079
Tom Schrader; Joyce Bach
Hours: Tue–Thur 9:00–3:00, Fri 9:00–
4:00
Pub. *Wadena County Historical Society
Quarterly Newsletter*, quarterly
$10.00 per year membership for
individuals, $20.00 per year
membership for families, $5.00 per
year membership for senior citizens or
students, $15.00–$49.00 per year
Friend membership, $20.00–$49.00
per year Business membership,
$50.00–$99.00 per year Patron
membership, $100.00 or more per year
Sponsor membership; research fee:
donations accepted

Wanamingo Historical Society
Main Street
Wanamingo, MN 55983
(507) 824-2556
Mavis Kyllo, Vice President
Hours: Sun (summer) 1:00–4:00 by
appointment
("Historic Log House on Main Street")
$2.50 per year membership

Warroad Historical Society
Main Street
Warroad, MN 56763
(218) 386-1283
Mrs. Cal Marvin, Vice President; Ruth
Stukel, President
Hours: Mon–Sun 1:00–5:00
(files on local families and subjects,
computer scanner and printer,
microform reader-printer, county
newspapers 1897–1990, Roseau
County census 1895–1920)

**Waseca County Historical Society
Museum**
PO Box 314.
Waseca, MN 56093
(507) 835-7700 (Historical Society)
Margaret Sinn, Executive Director of
Historical Society
Hours: Mon–Fri 8:00–12:00 & 1:00–
5:00, Sat (Memorial Day–Labor Day)
1:00–5:00
Pub. *Newsletter*, quarterly
$10.00 per year membership for
individuals, $20.00 per year
membership for families

**Washington County Historical
Society**
(602 North Main—location)
PO Box 167 (mailing address)
Stillwater, MN 55082
(612) 439-5956

Joan K. Daniels, Curator
Hours: Tue, Thur & Sat–Sun 2:00–5:00
Pub. *Historical Whisperings*, quarterly
(lumbering, Civil War, Indian artifacts)
$10.00 per year membership

Watonwan County Historical Society
(423 Dill Avenue, S.W.—location)
PO Box 126 (mailing address)
Madelia, MN 56062
(507) 642-3247
Ruth Anderson, Museum Director
Hours: Jun–Sept: Mon–Thur 9:00–4:00,
Sat–Sun 1:00–4:00; off season: Wed
1:00–3:00, and by appointment

**Western Hennepin County Pioneer
Association, Inc.**
(1953 West Wayzata Boulevard—
location)
PO Box 332 (mailing address)
Long Lake, MN 55356
(612) 473-6557
James R. Roehl, Archivist
Pub. *WHCPA Newsletter*

**White Bear Lake Area Historical
Society**
2350 Joy Avenue
White Bear Lake, MN 55110
(612) 429-5014

Wilkin County Historical Society
(704 Nebraska Avenue—location)
PO Box 212 (mailing address)
Breckenridge, MN 56520
(218) 643-1303
Ruth A. Poppel, Treasurer
Hours: Wed–Thur
$3.00 per year membership

**Winona County Historical Society,
Inc.**
160 Johnson Street
Winona, MN 55987
(507) 454-2723; (507) 454-0006
E-mail: wchs@uminet.net
Mark F. Peterson, Executive Director
Hours: Mon–Fri 9:00–5:00, Sat–Sun
noon–4:00
Pub. *Chronicles*, semiannually; *WCHSI
Memo*, semiannually
$25.00 per year membership for
individuals, $40.00 per year
membership for families, $20.00 per
year membership for senior citizens

Wright County Historical Society
2001 Highway 25 North
Buffalo, MN 55313
(612) 682-7323
Betty Dircks, Archivist
Hours: Oct–May: Mon–Fri 8:00–4:30;
Jun–Sept: Tue–Sat 8:00–4:30
Pub. *Wright County Historical Society
Newsletter*, monthly
$10.00 per year membership

**Yellow Medicine County Historical
Society and Museum**
(Junction Highways 23 and 67—
location)
PO Box 145 (mailing address)
Granite Falls, MN 56241-0145
(320) 564-4478
Mildred Washburn, Curator
Hours: Mid-May to mid-Oct: Tue & Fri
11:00–3:00, Sat–Sun 12:00–4:00
Pub. *Genealogy-history of Y.M. County
News Letters*, quarterly
(has complete county burial register, plus
obituary card file)
$5.00 per year membership for
individuals; free museum admission

LDS Family History Center

Rochester
(507) 281-6641

Genealogical Societies

State Genealogical Society

Minnesota Genealogical Society
(5768 Olson Memorial Highway
Golden Valley, MN 55422—location)
PO Box 16069 (mailing address)
(612) 595-9347
E-mail: mgsdec@mtn.org
http://www.mtn.org/mgs/
David E. Cross, President; Jean Jensen,
Library Committee Chair
Hours: Wed–Thur & Sat 9:00–3:00, Tue
& Thur 6:30–9:30
Pub. *Minnesota Genealogist*, quarterly,
$15.00 per year subscription;
*Minnesota Genealogical Society
Newsletter*, quarterly
Branches: Computer; Douglas County;
German (Germanic Genealogy
Society); Northwest Territory,
Canadian and French (Northwest
Territory, Canadian and French
Heritage Center); Irish (Irish
Genealogical Society, International);
Norwegian (Norwegian-American
Genealogical Association); Polish
(Polish Genealogical Society of
Minnesota); Scottish; Yankee; and
Scandinavian-American
(Scandinavian-American Genealogical
Society), with Danish, Finnish,
Icelandic and Swedish subgroups
$22.00 per year membership for
individuals, $28.00 per year
membership for families, additional
$7.00 per year foreign membership,

$50.00 per year Supporting membership, $100.00 per year Patron membership, $150.00 per year Benefactor membership

Regional Genealogical Societies

Anoka County Genealogical Society
1900 Third Avenue South
Anoka, MN 55303-2421
(612) 421-0600
Lucille Elrite, Vice President
Hours: Tue–Fri 12:30–4:00
Pub. *Anoka County, Minnesota, Genealogical Society Newsletter*, bimonthly
(research Anoka County pioneers)
$7.00 per year regular membership, $3.50 per year membership for students and seniors

Bemidji Genealogical Society
Bemidji Public Library
509 America Avenue N.W.
Bemidji, MN 56601

Genealogical Society of Carlton County
(Carlton County Historical Society, 406 Cloquet Avenue—location)
PO Box 204 (mailing address)
Cloquet, MN 55720
(218) 389-6229
E-mail: arpx27a@prodigy.com
Marlene Zalar
Hours: Mon–Fri 10:00–4:00
Pub. *Genealogical Society of Carlton County Quarterly*
$10.00 per year membership for individuals, $15.00 per year membership for families

Cottonwood/Jackson Genealogy Group
c/o Jackson County Historical Society
(307 North Highway 86—location)
PO Box 238 (mailing address)
Lakefield, MN 56150
H. Ed. Carlson, Co-chairperson

Crow Wing County Genealogical Society
(LDS Family History Center, 101 Buffalo Hills Lane West—location)
2103 Graydon Avenue (mailing address)
Brainerd, MN 56401
(218) 829-9738
E-mail: lkirk@brainerd.net
Lucille Kirkeby, Corresponding Secretary
Hours: Tue & Thur 10:30–8:30; meetings: third Thur of May, Sept, Nov. & Mar.
Pub. *Historian*, quarterly
$7.50 per year membership for individuals, $10.00 per year membership for families; research: varies with individuals

Dakota County Genealogical Society
PO Box 74
South Saint Paul, MN 55075
(612) 455-7080
Vicki Young Albu, President
Hours: Library at Dakota County Historical Society
Pub. *The Dakota County Genealogist*, quarterly
$10.00 per year membership

Dodge County Genealogical Society
PO Box 683
Dodge Center, MN 55927
Pub. *Dodge County Genealogical Society Newsletter*
$10.00 per year membership

Douglas County Genealogical Society
PO Box 505
Alexandria, MN 56308
(320) 763-3896 voice & FAX
E-mail: swarv01@att.com
Ginny Swartz, President
Pub. *Relatively Speaking*, quarterly
$10.00 per year membership (beginning in October)

Freeborn County Genealogical Society
1033 Bridge Avenue
Albert Lea, MN 56007-2205
(507) 373-9269
Jean R. Legried, Corresponding Secretary
Hours: Tue–Fri 1:00–5:00
Pub. *Freeborn County Tracer*, bimonthly
$10.00 per year membership

Heart O'Lakes Genealogical Society
(Becker County Museum, 714 Summit Avenue—location)
PO Box 622 (mailing address)
Detroit Lakes, MN 56501-2824
(218) 847-2938
Teresa Palmer, President; Julie M. Mastin, Corresponding Secretary
Hours: Mon–Tue & Thur–Fri 8:00–4:30, Wed 8:00 A.M.–8:30 P.M.
Pub. *Heart O'Lakes Genealogical Society*, four times per year
(Becker County, Minnesota, information)
$5.00 per year membership

Itasca County Genealogical Club
(Bovey Village Hall—library location)
PO Box 261 (mailing address)
Bovey, MN 55709
(218) 326-1329
Elizabeth Beckers, President
Hours: Library: Mon & Thur 9:30–8:00, Tue–Wed 12:00–8:00, Fri 11:00–5:00
Pub. *Itasca Genealogy Club Newsletter*, quarterly
$5.00 per year membership

Heritage Searchers of Kandiyohi County
PO Box 175
Willmar, MN 56201-0175
Pub. *Heritage HiLites*, bimonthly
("civil records, cemetery transcriptions for all of county, county history, newspaper indexes")
$10.00 per year membership for individuals (calendar year); research: donations accepted

Martin County Genealogical Society, Inc.
Martin County Library
110 North Park Street
Fairmont, MN 56031
(507) 238-4579 voice and FAX
E-mail: burkhart@polaristel.net
Sharon Burkhart, President
Hours: Mon & Thur 9:30–11:30, Wed 7:00–8:30 P.M., and by appointment; meetings: first Thur 9:00 A.M. (Jan–Mar 10:00 A.M.); Library: Mon & Wed–Thur 9:00–9:00, Tue 9:00–6:00, Fri–Sat 9:00–5:00
Pub. *Tree Climber*, quarterly (January, April, July, October)
(Martin County obituaries, city directories, census, funeral home records 1931–1981, cemeteries, vital records, newsletters/periodicals, history)
$8.00 per year membership (calendar year); search fees: $5.00 per hour plus copies and postage for members, $7.00 per hour plus copies and postage for non-members

Minnesota Genealogical Society, Douglas County Branch
(1650 Carroll Avenue, Saint Paul, MN 55104—location)
PO Box 16069 (mailing address)
Saint Paul, MN 55116-0069

Mower County Genealogical Society
PO Box 145
Austin, MN 55912
Hours: Library at Historical Center, Fairgrounds, Austin: Mon–Fri 11:00–4:00
Pub. *Mower County Genealogical News*, three times per year, $3.00 per year subscription
(cemetery records)
$8.00 per year membership

Nobles County Genealogical Society
407 12th Street, Suite 2
Worthington, MN 56187
Patrick Demuth
Hours: meetings: first Sat (Sept–Jun)
Pub. *Nobles County Genealogical Society Newsletter*, quarterly
$5.00 per year membership (includes limited research), $6.00 per year membership for families

Northfield/Rice County Genealogical Society
408 Division Street
Northfield, MN 55057

Northwest Territory Genealogical Society
(see Indiana)

Olmsted County Genealogical Society
(Olmsted County Historical Society, 1195 County Road 22, S.W.—location)
PO Box 6411 (mailing address)
Rochester, MN 55903
(507) 282-9447 (Historical Society)
Hours: Tue–Sat 9:00–5:00
Pub. *Olmsted County Genealogical Society Newsletter*, quarterly
$10.00 per year membership for households

Otter Tail County Genealogical Society
1110 West Lincoln Avenue
Fergus Falls, MN 56537
(218) 736-6038 (Museum)
Doloris Duncan
Hours: Library: Mon–Fri 9:00–5:00; Museum: Mon–Fri 9:00–5:00, Sat (Jan–Dec) 1:00–4:00, Sun (Jun–Sept) 1:00–4:00
Pub. *Otter Tail County Genealogical Newsletter*, quarterly
$8.00 per year membership, $10.00 per year membership with newsletter by mail; search fee: $15.00 per year

Pipestone County Genealogical Society
Pipestone County Museum
113 South Hiawatha Avenue
Pipestone, MN 56164
E-mail: coxfam@rconnect.com
(507) 825-2510 (President); (507) 825-2437 (Secretary/Treasurer)
Sheri Cox, President; Ruth Taylor, Secretary/Treasurer
Hours: Museum: Mon–Sun 10:00–5:00; meetings first Sat 2:00
Pub. *The Pipestem*, quarterly (spring, summer, winter, fall)
$7.50 per year membership (calendar year); queries free to members; search fee: charge to members, plus LSASE and copies at 25¢ per page from paper original and 50¢ per page from microfilm original; museum admission: $2.00 (students and children under 12, free)

Prairieland Genealogical Society
Southwest Minnesota Historical Center
Southwest State University
Marshall, MN 56258
(507) 532-7373
R. W. Taintor, M.D., President
Hours: 9:00–12:00 & 1:00–4:00

Pub. *Prairieland Pioneer*, quarterly
$12.00 per year membership

Range Genealogical Society
PO Box 388
Chisholm, MN 55719
Pub. *Northland Bulletin*, bimonthly; *Range Genealogical Society Newsletter*, quarterly

Renville County Genealogical Society
221 North Main Street
PO Box 331
Renville, MN 56284
(320) 329-8193
Mary Lou Smith, Librarian
Hours: Mon–Fri 12:00–5:30, Mon 6:30–8:00, and by appointment
Pub. *The Geneline—Renville County Genealogical Society Newsletter*, quarterly
(Renville County data)
$10.00 per year membership

Saint Cloud Area Genealogists, Inc.
PO Box 213
Saint Cloud, MN 56302-0213
E-mail: mstinson@tigger.stcloud.msus.edu
Dr. L. M. Stinson, President
Pub. *PasTimes*, bimonthly
$10.00 per year membership, $12.50 per year membership for families; research: $7.50 per hour

Stevens County Genealogical Society
Morris Public Library
102 East Sixth Street
Marvel Wagner, President
Hours: 9:00–9:00
Pub. *Stevens County Genealogical Society Newsletter*, quarterly (February, May, August and November)
(funeral records, cemetaries, obituaries)
$5.00 per year membership for individuals, $6.00 per year membership for families; search fee: $5.00 per hour plus copy costs

Traverse des Sioux Genealogical Society
815 Nicollet Avenue
North Mankato, MN 56002
(507) 387-2290
Janet M. Larson, Correspondent
no membership fee

Twin Ports Genealogical Society
PO Box 16895
Duluth, MN 55816-0895
Gerald Sime, President; Jackie Plunkett, Editor
Pub. *Branching Out*, quarterly (September, December, March, May)
(Duluth, Saint Louis County, Minnesota, and Superior, Douglas County, Wisconsin)

$10.00 per year membership for individuals, $15.00 per year membership for families

Waseca Area Genealogy Society (WAGS)
(a committee of the Waseca County Historical Society)
Waseca County Historical Society Museum
PO Box 314
Waseca, MN 56093
(507) 835-7700
Margaret Sinn, Executive Director
Hours: Waseca County Historical Society: Mon–Fri 8:00–12:00 & 1:00–5:00, Sat (Memorial Day–Labor Day) 1:00–5:00

White Bear Lake Genealogical Society
PO Box 10555
White Bear Lake, MN 55110
(612) 426-2705 (President's home)
Beverly Bosse, Board of Directors
Pub. *White Bear Lake Genealogical Society (Newsletter)*, quarterly
$8.00 per year membership, $12.00 per year membership for couples, $6.00 per year membership for senior citizens

Genealogy Guild of Wilkin County, Minnesota, and Richland County, North Dakota
(see North Dakota)

Winona County Genealogy Roundtable
(160 Johnson Street—location)
PO Box 363 (mailing address)
Winona, MN 55987-0363
Pub. *Table Talk*, quarterly
$5.00 per year membership (calendar year); search: $8.00 per hour

---

Independent Publications and Miscellany

Carver-on-the-Minnesota, Inc.
PO Box 281
Carver, MN 55315
(612) 448-4580
Barbara Swanson
volunteer staff, no facility open

Faribault Heritage Preservation Commission
208 N.W. First Avenue
Faribault, MN 55021
(507) 334-2222
Patricia Gustafson, Housing and Redevelopment Director
Hours: Mon–Fri 8:00–5:00
("videos, brochures, surveys, preservation, planning report, events,

tours, elementary education curriculum development, educational presentations, workshops, etc., preservation of materials generated by the HPC")

Historic Pipestone, Inc.
PO Box 470
Pipestone, MN 56164

Lanesboro Historical Preservation Association
105 Parkway, South
PO Box 345
Lanesboro, MN 55949
(507) 467-2177
Hours: Jun–Sept: 10:00–5:00
$3.00 per year membership for individuals, $5.00 per year membership for families, $100.00 life membership

Minnesota Obituaries
E-mail: bortsch@pconline.com
http://www.pconline.com/~bortsch/ mnobits/index.html

MnGenWeb
Part of U.S. GenWeb Project
E-mail: mn@usgenweb.com
http://www.rootsweb.com/~mngenweb/
(links to other Minnesota resources)

Park Genealogical Books
(626 Armstrong, Saint Paul, MN—office location)
PO Box 130968 (mailing address)
Roseville, MN 55113-0968
(612) 488-4416; (612) 488-2653
E-mail: mbakeman@parkbooks.com
http://www.parkbooks.com
Mary Bakeman, Owner
Hours: Mon 10:00–3:00
Pub. *Minnesota Genealogical Journal* (covers Minnesota and prior territories, many manuscript transcriptions, not available elsewhere), semiannually (March and September), $12.00 postpaid per issue, $14.00 postpaid per back issue, $20.00 per year subscription (Minnesota residents must include sales tax)

Society for the Preservation of Minnesota's Heritage
PO Box 157
Minneota, MN 56264

Upsala Obituary, Marriage and Cemetery Index
E-mail: johns@upstel.net
http://www.upstel.net/~johns/CemIndex/ CemIndex.html

MISSISSIPPI

Archives and Libraries with Holdings in Genealogy

State Archives and Library

Archives and Library Division
Mississippi Department of Archives and History
(100 South State Street, Jackson, MS 39201—location)
PO Box 571 (mailing address)
Jackson, MS 39205-0571
(601) 359-6876 (Division Director);
(601) 359-6964 FAX
H. T. Holmes, Division Director
Hours: Search Room: Mon–Fri 8:00– 5:00, Sat 8:00–1:00 (closed state holidays)
(Mississippiana, including private manuscripts and state government papers)
research $15.00 per hour plus copy costs for out-of-state residents (subject to change)

Historic Jefferson College
Mississippi Department of Archives and History
U.S. Highway 61 North
PO Box 700
Washington, MS 39190-0700
(601) 442-2901
Anne Gray, Historian; Jim Barnett, Director
Hours: by appointment only

Mississippi Library Commission
1221 Ellis Avenue
PO Box 10700
Jackson, MS 29289-0700
(601) 359-1036
http://www.mlc.lib.ms.us

Records Management Division
Mississippi Department of Archives and History
929 High Street
Jackson, MS 39202
(601) 354-7688
William J. Hanna, Director

State Historical Societies

Historical and Genealogical Association of Mississippi
618 Avalon Road
Jackson, MS 39206
(601) 362-3079
Jackie Ratcliffe, Editor, Secretary-Treasurer
Pub. *Family Trails*

Mississippi Historical Society
PO Box 571
Jackson, MS 39205-0571
(601) 359-6850
Elbert R. Hilliard, Secretary-Treasurer
Pub. *Journal of Mississippi History*, quarterly; *Mississippi History Newsletter*, monthly
$15.00 per year membership

City, County and Regional Archives and Libraries

L. W. Anderson Genealogical Library
PO Box 1647
Gulfport, MS 39502-1647
(228) 863-4975
Anne S. Anderson, Owner/Director
("While our Mississippi/Louisiana collections are large, other state collections are as large or larger; growing list of African-American material")
$2.00 per day per person for library use

Judge Armstrong Library
South Commerce Street
Natchez, MS 39120
Donna Jankey, Director of Library
Hours: Mon–Fri 9:00–6:00, Sat 9:00– 1:00

Attala County Library
201 South Huntington Street
Kosciusko, MS 39090
(601) 289-5141; (601) 289-9983
Ray Mikell, Jr., Genealogy Clerk
Hours: Mon–Fri 9:00–6:00, Sat 9:00– 5:00

Batesville Public Library
206 Highway 51 North
Batesville, MS 38606

Biloxi Public Library
PO Box 513
Biloxi, MS 39533

Birmingham Public Library
(see Alabama)

Bolivar County Library
104 South Leflore Avenue
Cleveland, MS 38732
(601) 843-2774; (601) 843-4701 FAX
Hours: Mon–Thur 9:00–8:00 (summer: 9:00–6:00), Fri 9:00–5:00, Sat 9:00– 5:00 (summer: 10:00–2:00)
(specializes in Bolivar County, Mississippi)

Carnegie Public Library of Clarksdale and Coahoma County
114 Delta Avenue
PO Box 280
Clarksdale, MS 38614
(601) 624-4461

Linda White, Reference Librarian
Hours: Mon 9:00–8:00, Tue–Thur 9:00–
5:30, Fri 9:00–5:00, Sat 10:00–2:00

Evans Memorial Library

105 North Long
Aberdeen, MS 39730
(601) 369-4601
Sara Myers, Librarian
Hours: Mon–Fri 9:00–4:30, Sat 9:00–
4:00

Greenwood-Leflore Public Library

Special Collections
405 West Washington
Greenwood, MS 38930
(601) 453-3634
Hours: Mon–Wed 8:30–7:30, Thur–Sat
8:30–5:30
(Mississippi and southeastern U.S.
genealogy)

Gulfport-Harrison County Public Library

14th Street and 21st Avenue
PO Box 4018
Gulfport, MS 39502
(228) 863-6411
Roy W. Fox
Hours: Mon–Thur 9:00–8:00, Fri–Sat
9:00–5:00

Hacksma House Genealogy Library

(see Washington)

Hattiesburg Public Library System

329 Hardy Street
Hattiesburg, MS 39401-3824
(601) 582-4461
Hours: Mon–Tue 9:00–8:30, Wed–Sat
9:00–5:30

Iuka Public Library

204 North Main Street
Iuka, MS 38852
(601) 423-6300
Fredda Sanderson, Librarian
Hours: Mon–Tue & Fri 10:00–6:00,
Wed–Thur 10:00–7:00, Sat 10:00–4:00
(mostly local interest)

Jackson George Regional Library System

3214 Pascagoula Street
Pascagoula, MS 39567
(228) 762-3060
Jean Strickland, Head, Genealogy and
Local History Department
Hours: Mon–Thur 9:00–8:00, Fri–Sat
9:00–5:00
(specializes in Mississippi and Alabama;
"large collection, excellent Genealogy
Department")

Laurel-Jones County Library— Genealogy

530 Commerce Street
Laurel, MS 39440
(601) 423-4313; (601) 428-4314
George Jaynes, Genealogy Librarian

Hours: Mon–Fri 10:00–noon & 2:00–
5:00, Sat 9:30–3:00
(much county and southern history
records)

Lee County Library

219 Madison Street
Tupelo, MS 38801
(601) 841-9029
Louann Hurst, Director
Hours: Mon–Thur 9:30–8:30, Fri 9:00–
5:00, Sat 9:00–5:00

Lincoln County Public Library

Local History and Genealogy Collection
100 South Jackson Street
PO Box 541
Brookhaven, MS 39601
(601) 833-3369; (601) 833-3381 FAX
Henry J. Ledet, Director
Hours: Mon & Wed 9:00–6:00, Tue &
Thur 9:00–8:00, Fri–Sat 9:00–5:00
(local history and genealogy of Lincoln,
Lawrence and Franklin counties)

Lowndes County Library System

314 North Seventh Street
Columbus, MS 39701
(601) 329-5304
Carolyn Neault, Local Historian; Mary
Bess Paluzzi, Archivist
Hours: Mon–Thur 9:00–8:00, Fri 9:00–
5:00, Sat 9:00–3:00

Marks-Quitman County Library

315 East Main
Marks, MS 38646

McCain Library and Archives

University of Southern Mississippi
Southern Station, Box 5148
Hattiesburg, MS 39406-5148
(601) 266-4345 (Reference desk)
http://www.lib.usm.edu/mccain.html
Hours: Mon–Thur 8:00–6:00, Fri 8:00–
5:00, Sat 10:00–2:00
(emphasis on southern U.S.)

Meridian-Lauderdale County Public Library

2517 Seventh Street
Meridian, MS 39305
(601) 693-6771
Carol James, Head of Genealogy
Department
Hours: Mon–Thur 9:00–9:00, Sat 9:00–
6:00

Millsaps College Archives

Millsaps-Wilson Library
Jackson, MS 39210
(601) 974-1077; (601) 974-1082 FAX
E-mail: mcintdw@okra.millsaps.edu
http://www.millsaps.edu/www/library/
archives/index.html
Debra McIntosh, College Archivist
Hours: Weekdays 8:30 A.M.–12:30 A.M.
(when the college is in session)

Mississippi College

Leland Speed Library
PO Box 51
Clinton, MS 39060-0051
(601) 925-3434
Rachel A. Pyron, Special Collections
Librarian
Hours: Mon–Fri 8:30–noon & 1:00–4:30
(except college holidays)

Mississippi State Historical Museum

Mississippi Department of Archives and
History
Old Capitol Restoration
100 South State Street
Jackson, MS 39201
(601) 354-6222
Patti Carr Black, Museum Director

Mississippi University for Women

Fant Memorial Library
PO Box W-1625
Columbus, MS 39701
(601) 329-7332; (601) 329-7348 FAX
http://www.muw.edu
Freda M. Davison, Professor and director
of Library Services
Hours: Mon–Fri 8:00–5:00 (extended
hours during semesters)
(University related historical archives
[alumni, etc.], Mississippi census and
newspapers on microfilm)
$10.00 per year for non-MUW affiliates

Mississippi University for Women

Fant Memorial Library
Columbus, MS 39701

Mitchell Memorial Library

Reference, Special Collections
(Mississippi State University—location)
PO Box 9570 (mailing address)
Mississippi State, MS 39762
(601) 325-7679
http://www.msstate.edu/library/spcoll
Hours: Mon–Fri 8:00–5:00, weekend and
evening hours during school terms
(do not confuse with the L. W. Anderson
Genealogical Library)

Northeast Regional Library

Corinth Public Library
1023 Fillmore Street
Corinth, MS 38834
(601) 287-2441
Mrs. Samuel Rea, Librarian
Hours: Mon–Thur 9:00–8:00, Fri–Sat
9:00–5:00

Oktibbeha County Heritage Museum

203 Fellowship Road
Starkville, MS 39759
(601) 323-0211
Dr. George R. Lewis, Director
Hours: Tue–Thur 1:00–4:00, and by
appointment
free admission, donations appreciated

Oxford-Lafayette County Public Library
401 Bramlett Boulevard
Oxford, MS 38655
Hours: Mon–Thur 9:30–8:00, Fri–Sat
9:30–5:00

Pike-Amite-Walthall Library System
114 State Street
McComb, MS 39648
(601) 684-2661
Katherine M. Niemeyer, Special Services
Librarian
Hours: Mon & Wed 8:30–5:30, Tue &
Thur 8:30–8:00, Fri–Sat 8:30–5:00

Jennie Stephens Smith Library
219 King Street
PO Box 846
New Albany, MS 38652
(601) 534-4331
Sissy Bullock, Director
Hours: Mon, Wed & Fri 9:00–5:30, Tue
& Thur 9:00–8:00, Sat 9:00–1:00

Sunflower County Library
201 Cypress Drive
Indianola, MS 38751-2415
(601) 887-1672 (Library); (601) 887-
2641 FAX (Library)
Anice Powell, Director; Jeff Weddle,
Assistant Director
Hours: Mon 9:00–8:00, Tue–Thur 9:00–
6:00, Fri 9:00–5:00, Sat 9:00–4:00
(regional and Mississippi materials)

Union County Library
PO Box 22
New Albany, MS 38652

Union Public Library
101 Peachtree Street
Union, MS 39365
(601) 774-5096; (601) 774-8735
Linda Hamm, Librarian
Hours: Mon–Fri 8:30–5:30

University of Mississippi
General Library
Archives and Special Collections
University, MS 38677
(601) 232-7408; (601) 232-5734 FAX
E-mail: ulverich@vm.cc.olemiss.edu;
ullandi@sunset.backbone.olemiss.edu
(Mississippi Collection)
http://www.olemiss.edu/

University of Southern Alabama
Gulf Coast Historical Review
(see Alabama)

Warren County-Vicksburg Public Library
Reference Department
700 Veto Street
Vicksburg, MS 39180
(601) 636-6411; (601) 634-4809 FAX
Rosemary Fairchild, Local History
Librarian
Hours: Mon–Thur 9:00–8:00, Fri–Sat
9:00–5:00

Washington County Library System
William Alexander Percy Memorial
Library
341 Main Street
Greenville, MS 38701
(601) 335-2331
Hours: Mon–Wed 9:00–8:00, Mon–Wed
(summer) 9:00–7:00, Thur–Fri 9:00–
6:00, Sat 1:00–5:00, Sun (except
summer) 1:00–5:00

The Waynesboro Municipal Library
712 Wayne Street
Waynesboro, MS 39367
(601) 735-2268
Patsy Brewer, Librarian
Hours: Mon, Wed & Fri 9:00–5:00, Tue
& Thur 9:00–8:00, Sat 9:00–noon
(substantial genealogical holdings)

Wilkinson County Museum
Woodville Civic Club, Inc.
(203 Boston Row—location)
PO Box 1055 (mailing address)
Woodville, MS 39669
(601) 888-3998 (Museum)
Ernesto Caldeira, Director
Hours: Museum: Mon–Fri 10:00–noon &
2:00–4:00, Sat 10:00–noon
Pub. *The Journal of Wilkinson County
History*, approximately annually

Historical Societies— Local and Regional

Amite County Foundation for Historic Preservation
Rt. 4, Box 226
Liberty, MS 39645
(601) 684-1281

Bolivar County Historical Society
1615 Terrace Road
Cleveland, MS 38732
(601) 843-8204
Pub. *Bolivar County Historical Society
Publications*, irregularly

Brice's Crossroads Museum
(Intersection of Highways 45 and 370—
location)
PO Box 100 (mailing address)
Baldwyn, MS 38824
(601) 365-2383; (601) 365-2274
Billy Roberson, Chairman, Brice's
Crossroads Museum Commission

Chickasaw County Genealogy and Historical Society
PO Box 42
Houston, MS 38851
(601) 456-4512
Kay Y. Griffin, Editor
Pub. *Chickasaw Times Past*, quarterly
(genealogical and historical information
of the original lands of Chickasaw
County, including Chickasaw,

Calhoun, Clay and Webster counties,
Mississippi)
$20.00 per year membership

The Columbus and Lowndes County Historical Society
(316 Seventh Street—location)
916 College Street (mailing address)
Columbus, MS 39701
(601) 328-5437

Hancock County Historical Society
(108 Cue Street—location)
PO Box 312 (mailing address)
Bay Saint Louis, MS 39520
(228) 467-4090 phone and FAX
http://datasync.copm/~history
Charles Gray, President
Hours: Mon–Fri 8:00–4:00
Pub. *Historian of Hancock County*,
monthly

Homochitto Valley Historical Society
PO Box 337
Crosby, MS 39633
(601) 639-4435

Itawamba County Historical Society
George Poteet History Center
(Church Street and Museum Drive—
location)
PO Box 7 (mailing address)
Mantachie, MS 38855
Bob Frankes
Hours: by appointment in winter months
Pub. *Itawamba Settlers*, quarterly
$20.00 per year membership

Jackson County Historical Society
4602 Fort Drive
Pascagoula, MS 39567
(228) 769-1505

Kosciusko-Attala Historical Society
200 North Huntington Street
PO Box 127
Kosciusko, MS 39090
(601) 289-5516
Mrs. George Thornton, Director
Hours: Mon–Fri 1:00–4:00

Marshall County Historical Society, Inc.
220 East College Avenue
PO Box 806
Holly Springs, MS 38635
(601) 252-4437

Mississippi Coast Historical and Genealogical Society
(Biloxi Library—location)
PO Box 513 (mailing address)
Biloxi, MS 39533
(228) 374-0330
Mary Louise Adkinson
Pub. *Mississippi Coast Historical and
Genealogical Journal*, three times per
year
$15.00 per year membership

Mississippi Junior Historical Society
William Carey College
Hattiesburg, MS 39401
(601) 582-5051

Monroe County Historical Society, Inc.
410 South Meridian Street
Aberdeen, MS 39730
(601) 369-8120
Mrs. Charles G. Hamilton, President
Pub. *The Journal of Monroe County History*

Natchez Historical Society
307 South Wall Street
Po Box 49
Natchez, MS 39120
Donna Jankey, Director of Library
Hours: Judge Armstrong Library: Mon–
Fri 9:00–6:00, Sat 9:00–1:00

Northeast Mississippi Historical and Genealogical Society
(Lee County Library, 219 Madison
Avenue—location)
PO Box 434 (mailing address)
Tupelo, MS 38802-0434
(601) 841-9013
Martis D. Ramage, Jr., Editor
Hours: Mon–Thur 9:30–8:30, Fri–Sat
9:00–5:00
Pub. *Northeast Mississippi Historical
and Genealogical Society Quarterly*
(Lee, Itawamba, Pontotoc, Monroe,
Tippah, Prentiss, Alcorn, Tishomingo
and Chickasaw counties)
$15.00 per year membership (beginning
in July)

Noxubee County Historical Society, Inc.
411 South Jefferson Street
PO Box 392
Macon, MS 39341
(601) 726-5218
E. G. Flora, Jr., President
Pub. *NCHS Bulletin*

'Pan Gens,' Historical and Genealogical Society of Panola County, Mississippi
210 Kyle Street
Batesville, MS 38606
Norma Riser, Corresponding Secretary
Pub. *Panola Story*, quarterly
$10.00 per year membership

Pass Christian Historical Society, Inc.
203 East Scenic Drive
PO Box 58
Pass Christian, MS 39571
W. C. Kidd, President
Hours: various

Rankin County Historical Society, Inc.
PO Box 841
Brandon, MS 39043
(601) 825-5937
Marjorie Steen, President
Hours: Museum: Sat–Sun 2:00–4:00
(Oct & May, approximately four or
five weekends each), and by
appointment
$5.00 per year membership for
individuals, $7.50 per year
membership for married couples,
$1.00 per year membership for
students, $2.00 per year Associate
membership; no cost to tour museum;
simple searches done for cost of
photocopies plus postage, extensive
search for $20.00 per hour

Skipwith Historical and Genealogical Society, Inc.
(Oxford-Lafayette County Public
Library—location)
PO Box 1382 (mailing address)
Oxford, MS 38655
(601) 234-7289
Annette Waite, President
Hours: Library: Mon–Thur 9:30–8:00,
Fri–Sat 9:30–5:00
Pub. *Lafayette County Heritage News*,
quarterly (October, January, April,
July)
$10.00 per year membership for
individuals, $12.00 per year
membership for families

Southern Studies Institute
(see Louisiana)

Sunflower County Historical Society, Inc.
Sunflower County Library
201 Cypress Drive
Indianola, MS 38751-2415
(601) 887-1672 (Library); (601) 887-
2641 FAX (Library); (601) 887-2153
phone and FAX (Headquarters); (601)
887-3758 (President)
Anice Powell, Treasurer; Sammy Ely,
President Director
Hours: Library: Mon 9:00–8:00, Tue–
Thur 9:00–6:00, Fri 9:00–5:00, Sat
9:00–4:00; Headquarters: Mon–Fri
8:00–5:00
(regional and Mississippi materials)
$5.00 per year membership for
individuals, $25.00 per year
membership for businesses or
institutions, $50.00 per year Sustaining
membership, $100.00 life membership

Tate County Genealogical and Historical Society
(307 Robinson Street—location)
PO Box 974 (mailing address)
Senatobia, MS 38668

(601) 562-0390
Syble Embrey, President
Hours: Thur–Fri 10:00–4:30
Pub. *Tate Trails*, quarterly
$15.00 per year membership (calendar
year)

Tippah County Historical and Genealogical Society
Ripley Public Library
308 North Commerce Street
Ripley, MS 38663
(601) 837-7773 phone and FAX
Tommy Covington, Librarian
Hours: Mon, Wed & Fri–Sat 9:00–5:00,
Tue & Thur 9:00–8:00
Pub. *News & Journal*, irregularly
$12.00 per year membership

Vicksburg and Warren County Historical Society
c/o Old Court House Museum
1008 Cherry Street
Vicksburg, MS 39180
(601) 636-0741
Gordon Cotton, Director; Blanche Terry,
Assistant Director
Hours: Mon–Fri 8:30–4:30
(holdings include Vicksburg and Warren
County marriage, funeral, census, etc.)
$2.00 fee per researcher

Webster County Historical Society
Rt. 3, Box 14
Eupora, MS 39744
(601) 258-6898

Winston County Historical and Genealogical Society
PO Box 428
Louisville, MS 39339

Yalobusha County Historical Society
PO Box 258
Coffeeville, MS 38922
Wade H. Johnson, Editor
Pub. *The Pioneer*, quarterly, $3.00 per
issue
$15.00 per year membership; no research

Yazoo Historical Society
332 North Main Street
Po Box 575
Yazoo City, MS 39194
(601) 746-2273

LDS Family History Centers

Clinton
(601) 924-2686

Jackson
(see Clinton)

Genealogical Societies

State Genealogical Societies

The Family Research Association of Mississippi
PO Box 13334
Jackson, MS 39205
Pub. *Newsletter*

Historical and Genealogical Association of Mississippi
618 Avalon Road
Jackson, MS 39206
(601) 362-3079
Jackie Ratcliffe, Editor, Secretary-Treasurer
Pub. *Family Trails*

Mississippi Genealogical Society
PO Box 5301
Jackson, MS 39296-5301
James E. Griffith, President
$10.00 per year membership

Regional Genealogical Societies

Genealogical Society of Adams County
PO Box 187
Washington, MS 39190
Mrs. V. L. Harker

Chickasaw County Genealogy and Historical Society
PO Box 42
Houston, MS 38851
(601) 456-4512
Kay Y. Griffin, Editor
Pub. *Chickasaw Times Past*, quarterly (genealogical and historical information of the original lands of Chickasaw County, including Chickasaw, Calhoun, Clay and Webster counties, Mississippi)
$20.00 per year membership

Genealogical Society of DeSoto County, Mississippi
(DeSoto County Courthouse—location)
PO Box 607 (mailing address)
Hernando, MS 38632
(601) 429-1310
Ozell D. Scott, President
Hours: Mon–Wed 10:00–4:00
Pub. *DeSoto Descendants*, quarterly
$15.00 per year membership for individuals and libraries, $20.00 per year membership for families

Jackson County Genealogical Society
PO Box 984
Pascagoula, MS 39567

(228) 762-7777
Tommy Wixon, Editor
Pub. *Journal of Jackson County Genealogical Society*, quarterly
$15.00 per year membership

Mississippi Coast Historical and Genealogical Society
(Biloxi Library—location)
PO Box 513 (mailing address)
Biloxi, MS 39533
(228) 374-0330
Mary Louise Adkinson
Pub. *Mississippi Coast Historical and Genealogical Journal*, three times per year
$15.00 per year membership

Northeast Mississippi Historical and Genealogical Society
(Lee County Library, 219 Madison Avenue—location)
PO Box 434 (mailing address)
Tupelo, MS 38802-0434
(601) 841-9013
Martis D. Ramage, Jr., Editor
Hours: Mon–Thur 9:30–8:30, Fri–Sat 9:00–5:00
Pub. *Northeast Mississippi Historical and Genealogical Society Quarterly*
(Lee, Itawamba, Pontotoc, Monroe, Tippah, Prentiss, Alcorn, Tishomingo and Chickasaw counties)
$15.00 per year membership (beginning in July)

'Pan Gens,' Historical and Genealogical Society of Panola County, Mississippi
210 Kyle Street
Batesville, MS 38606
Norma Riser, Corresponding Secretary
Pub. *Panola Story*, quarterly
$10.00 per year membership

Skipwith Historical and Genealogical Society, Inc.
(Oxford-Lafayette County Public Library—location)
PO Box 1382 (mailing address)
Oxford, MS 38655
(601) 234-7289
Annette Waite, President
Hours: Library: Mon–Thur 9:30–8:00, Fri–Sat 9:30–5:00
Pub. *Lafayette County Heritage News*, quarterly (October, January, April, July)
$10.00 per year membership for individuals, $12.00 per year membership for families

South Mississippi Genealogical Society
PO Box 15271
Hattiesburg, MS 39404
Elaine Bullock, President
Hours: monthly meetings
$10.00 per year (beginning in October)

Tate County Genealogical and Historical Society
(307 Robinson Street—location)
PO Box 974 (mailing address)
Senatobia, MS 38668
(601) 562-0390
Syble Embrey, President
Hours: Thur–Fri 10:00–4:30
Pub. *Tate Trails*, quarterly
$15.00 per year membership (calendar year)

Tippah County Historical and Genealogical Society
Ripley Public Library
308 North Commerce Street
Ripley, MS 38663
(601) 837-7773 phone and FAX
Tommy Covington, Librarian
Hours: Mon, Wed & Fri–Sat 9:00–5:00, Tue & Thur 9:00–8:00
Pub. *News & Journal*, irregularly
$12.00 per year membership

Vicksburg Genealogical Society
PO Box 1161
Vicksburg, MS 39181-1161
Ruth Land Hatten, C.G.R.S., Co-editor
Pub. *VGS Inc. Newsletter*, quarterly
$6.00 per year membership

The Wayne County Genealogical Organization
712 Wayne Street
Waynesboro, MS 39367
(601) 735-2268 (Library)
Betty Tiner, President
Hours: The Waynesboro Municipal Library: Mon, Wed & Fri 9:00–5:00, Tue & Thur 9:00–8:00, Sat 9:00–noon
Pub. *Tracts and Trails*, quarterly

Winston County Historical and Genealogical Society
PO Box 428
Louisville, MS 39339

Independent Publications and Miscellany

Courier Publications
PO Box 1320
Winnfield, LA 71483-1320
Pub. *Mississippi State Courier*, quarterly, $15.00 per year subscription

Genealogical Institute
(see Virginia)

Genealogy Books and Consultation
(see Texas)

Hunting for Bears Genealogical and Historical Society
(see Alabama)

Mississippi Memories
PO Box 18991
Shreveport, LA 71138-1991
(318) 686-3112
E-mail: jsbridg@aol.com
Joyce S. Bridges, Co-editor
Hours: 8:00–8:00
Pub. *Mississippi Memories*, quarterly
(February, May, August, November),
$15.00 per year subscription

Mountain Press
(see Tennessee)

MsGenWeb
Part of U.S. GenWeb Project
E-mail: ms@usgenweb.com;
rholler@insolwwb.net
http://www.rootsweb.com/~msgenweb/
(links to other Mississippi resources)

Pontotoc County Pioneers
207 North Main Street
Pontotoc, MS 38863
(601) 489-6748
Hazle Boss Neet,Editor

**Southern Genealogist's Exchange
Society**
(see Florida)

Surnames Ltd.
East 3725 Highway 53
Rathdrum, ID 83858
Pub. *Southern Roots—Mississippi-
Alabama*, $7.00 per issue

University of Southern Mississippi
Center for Oral History and Culture
Suite J, McClesky Hall
Hattiesburg, MS 39406-5175
(601) 266-4575
E-mail: cbolton@whale.st.usm.edu
http://www.usm.edu/~ocach/

MISSOURI

Archives and Libraries with Holdings in Genealogy

State Archives and Library

Missouri State Archives
(600 West Main Street—location)
PO Box 778 (mailing address)
Jefferson City, MO 65102
(573) 751-3280; (573) 526-7333 FAX
E-mail: archref@sos.state.mo.us
http://mosl.sos.state.mo.us
Patricia Luebbert, Senior Archivist
Hours: Mon–Fri 8:00–5:00, Thur 8:00–
9:00, Sat 8:30–3:30
no research fees, photocopies 10¢ per
page from paper originals, 25¢ per
page from microfilm originals

**Records Management and Archives
Service**
Office of the Secretary of State
1001 Industrial Drive
PO Box 778
Jefferson City, MO 65102
(573) 751-3280
Mary Beck, Archivist
Hours: Mon–Fri 8:00–5:00, Thur 8:00–
9:30, Sat 8:30–3:30
(microfilm copies of county vital
statistics, especially 1883–1893 and
some others from before 1910)

Missouri State Library
301 West High Street
PO Box 387
Jefferson City, MO 65102-0387
(573) 751-3615; (573) 751-3612 FAX
E-mail: sparker@mail.sos.state.mo.us
http://mosl.sos.state.mo.us/lib-ser/
libser.html

State Historical Societies

**The State Historical Society of
Missouri**
1020 Lowry Street
Columbia, MO 65201-7298
(573) 882-7083; (573) 884-4950 FAX
E-mail: shsofmo@ext.missouri.edu
James W. Goodrich, Ph.D., Executive
Director
Hours: Mon–Fri 8:00–4:30, Sat 9:00–
4:30 (closed holiday weekends)
Pub. *Missouri Historical Review*,
quarterly
(resources include 450,000 volumes of
monographs, serials, and state
government publications; Missouri
newspapers, 1808–the present;
microfilm census records; maps;

manuscript collections; photograph
collection)
$10.00 per year membership for
individuals

City, County and Regional Archives and Libraries

Adair County Public Library
1 Library Lane
Kirksville, MO 63501
(816) 665-6038
Hours: Mon–Wed 9:00–8:00, Thur–Fri
9:00–6:00, Sat 9:00–4:00

Albany Public Library
101 West Clay
Albany, MO 64402
(660) 726-5615
Helen Henton, Librarian
Hours: Mon–Sat 11:00–5:00

**Battle of Lexington State Historic
Site**
PO Box 6
North 13th Street
Lexington, MO 64067
(660) 259-4654
Janae Fuller, Administrator
Hours: Mon–Sat 10:00–4:00, Sun (Labor
Day–Memorial Day) noon–4:00, Sun
(Memorial Day–Labor Day) noon–
5:00, and by appointment
(emphasis on the Battle of Lexington
during the Civil War, also family and
local history)

Boonslick Regional Library
219 West Third Street
Sedalia, MO 63501
(816) 826-6195
Linda Allcorn, Director
(Benton, Cooper and Pettis counties)

Cape Girardeau Public Library
Reference Department
711 North Clark
Cape Girardeau, MO 63701
(573) 334-5279
Hours: Mon–Thur 9:00–9:00, Fri–Sat
9:00–5:00, Sun (Oct–Apr) 12:00–4:00
no staff available to answer research
questions on particular families

Carrollton Public Library
206 West Washington
Carrollton, MO 64633
(660) 542-0183
Charline Spangler, Librarian
(genealogy and local history)

Carthage Public Library
Genealogy Records
612 South Garrison
Carthage, MO 64836
(417) 358-2939

Cass County Public Library
400 East Mechanic
Harrisonville, MO 64701

(816) 884-6223; (816) 884-2301 FAX
Sharon Willey, Director
Hours: Mon–Wed 9:00–6:00, Thur noon–
8:30, Sat 9:00–5:00
(southeastern U.S. and Missouri)

Clay County Archives and Historical Library, Inc.
(210 West Franklin—location)
PO Box 99 (mailing address)
Liberty, MO 64069-0099
(816) 781-3611
Chad C. Means, President
Hours: Mon–Wed 10:00–4:00
Pub. *The Clay County Mosaic*, quarterly
(Collection includes probate files 1822–
1989, extensive but not complete
collection of abstracts obtained from
local companies, cemetery records and
obituaries, marriage records, family
histories, family files, the library of
the former Genealogical Society of
Liberty)
$10.00 per year membership for
individuals, $15.00 per year
membership for families; $5.00 per
day research fee for non-members

Columbia Public Library
Daniel Boone Regional Library
Reference Department
(100 West Broadway, Columbia, MO
65203—location)
PO Box 1267 (mailing address)
Columbia, MO 65205-1267
(573) 443-3161
Hours: Mon–Thur 9:00–9:00, Fri 9:00–
6:00, Sat 9:00–5:00, Sun (Sept–May)
1:00–5:00

Dulany Library
501 South Broadway
Salisbury, MO 65281
(660) 388-5712
Cheryl Springer, Librarian
Hours: Mon–Fri noon–5:00, Sat 8:00–
1:00
(material on Chariton County)

Dunklin County Museum
122 College
Kennett, MO 63857

Farmington Public Library
108 West Harrison Street
Farmington, MO 63640
(573) 756-5779; (573) 756-0614 FAX
Lynn Crites, Director
Hours: Mon & Fri 10:00–5:30, Tue–Thur
10:00–8:00, Sat 11:00–3:00
(large collection of miscellaneous
obituaries, good history of local area
and people)
no admission fee, copies 10¢ each, no
staff to do extensive research by mail

Fayette Public Library
201 South Main
Fayette, MO 65248
(660) 248-3348
Cathey Monckton

Hours: Mon–Fri 1:00–5:30, Sat 9:30–
3:00
(limited genealogical materials)

Gentry County Library
Second and Park
Stanberry, MO 64489
(816) 783-2335; (816) 783-2335
E-mail: tgn002@mail.connect.more.net
Norma Newman, Director
Hours: Mon–Fri 8:00–5:00, Sat 9:00–
12:00

Grundy County-Jewett Norris Library
1331 Main
Trenton, MO 64683
(660) 359-3577
Catheryn Higdon
Hours: Mon–Fri 9:00–5:00, Sat 9:00–
noon, and by appointment
(local history and genealogy)

Hacksma House Genealogy Library
(see Washington)

Henry County Public Library
123 East Franklin
Clinton, MO 64735-2199
(660) 885-2612
Liz Cashell, Director
Hours: Mon–Thur 8:00 A.M.–9:00 P.M.,
Sat 8:00–5:00

Friends of Historic Boonville
614 East Morgan
PO Box 1776
Boonville, MO 65233
(816) 882-7977; (816) 882-7977
E-mail: friendsart@vax1.rainis.net
Judy Shields, Administrator
Hours: Mon–Fri 9:00–5:00
Pub. *Friends Footnotes*, six times per
year
(a growing library of past, recent
genealogy requests; archives covers
Cooper County and Boonville
information)
$15.00 per year membership; search fee:
basic $5.00 plus 25¢ per copy, $10.00
additional for probate/deed/court
records

The History Museum for Springfield-Greene County
830 Boonville, City Hall
Springfield, MO 65802
(417) 869-1976; (417) 864-2019 FAX
Julie March, Curator
Hours: Tue–Sat 10:30–4:00
Pub. *The Herald*, quarterly
(significant collections of historic
regional photos, family collections,
business collections from southwest
Missouri)
$25.00 per year membership; suggested
donation: $3.00

Holden Public Library
101 West Third Street
Holden, MO 64040

(816) 732-4545
Vivian Ensley, Librarian
Hours: Tue–Fri 12:30–5:00, Sat 9:00–
noon
(small local genealogical collection)

William Jewell College
Curry Library
500 College Hill
Liberty, MO 64068-1896
(816) 781-7700, ext. 5465; (816) 415-
5027 FAX
E-mail: knaussb@william.jewell.edu
http://www.jewell.edu/

Joplin Public Library
Genealogy Department
300 Main Street
Joplin, MO 64801
(417) 623-7953; (417) 624-5465
Genealogy Department
Hours: Genealogy Department: Mon &
Thur 9:00–8:45, Tue–Wed & Fri–Sat
9:00–5:45, Sun 1:00–4:45

Kansas City Museum
3218 Gladstone Blvd.
Kansas City, MO 64123
(816) 483-8300; (816) 483-9912 FAX
Denise Morrison, Archivist
Hours: Mon–Fri 8:30–5:00, by
appointment only
(emphasis on Kansas City region from
the 1830s)

Kansas City Public Library
Missouri Valley Special Collections
311 East 12th Street
Kansas City, MO 64106
(816) 221-2698
E-mail: sc_kat@kcpl.lib.mo.us
Katherine Long, Department Manager
Hours: Mon–Thur 9:00–9:00, Fri–Sat
9:00–5:00, Sun 1:00–5:00
(a large collection of census index books
for the years 1790–1870; also Kansas
City, Missouri, city directories from
1859 to the present)

Keytesville Public Library
General Delivery
406 West Bridge Street
Keytesville, MO 65261
(816) 288-3204
Joe Hickey, Librarian
Hours: Mon, Wed & Fri 2:00–4:30
(census lists, cemetery records, and some
other records)
searches limited to library holdings as
time permits: 15¢ per photocopy plus
SASE, donations welcome

Liberty Memorial Museum of World War I
100 West 26th Street
Kansas City, MO 64108
(816) 221-1918
Lynn M. Ward

Hours: Museum: Wed–Sun 9:30–4:30,
please call for museum/offsite exhibit
hours; Archives: by appointment
(archives includes unit rosters of
individual war participants; if
researcher knows unit of individual
being studied, archives can identify the
battle activities of the unit and
possibly find the name of the
individual in a roster; archives has no
information regarding WW II)
photocopies: 10¢ per page; photograph
reproduction charges

The Linn Library
(902 East Oak Street, Princeton, MO
64673—location)
255 North El Cielo, #213 (mailing
address)
Palm Springs, CA 92262
(816) 748-3905
Joe Dale Linn
Hours: by appointment

Little Dixie Regional Libraries
111 North Fourth Street
Moberly, MO 65270
(816) 263-4426
Karen Hayden, Reference and Adult
Services Librarian
Hours: Mon–Wed & Fri 9:00–6:00, Thur
9:00–8:00, Sat 9:00–4:00
copies: 15¢ per page

Livingston County Library
450 Locust Street
Chillicothe, MO 64601-2597
(816) 646-0547; (816) 646-5504 FAX
http://vax2.rainis.net/~lclibrary/
index.html
Karen L. Hicklin, Director
Hours: Mon, Wed & Fri 9:00–6:00, Tue
& Thur 9:00–8:00, Sat 9:00–4:00
(some state and local history)

Lohefener House Museum and Gifts
710 Orange
PO Box 33
Concordia, MO 64020
(660) 463-7963
Lloyd and Nyla Shepard, Owners
Hours: Wed & Sat 10:00–4:00, and by
appointment
(death notices 1870–1910 in German,
1880 census [within city limits only],
some family histories, written
reminiscences and centennial history
book, lists of confirmations, baptisms,
marriages and funerals, 1840–1990,
local Lutheran Church, United Church
of Christ, confirmation programs of
church events and history of Saint
Paul's College [Lutheran Church—
Missouri Synod], from 1883)

Marshall Public Library
214 North Lafayette
Marshall, MO 65340
(660) 886-3391; (660) 886-2492 FAX
Ms. Wicky Sleight, Library Director

Hours: Mon–Thur 9:00–9:00, Fri 9:00–
6:00, Sat 9:00–5:00, Sun 1:00–5:00
(local history of Saline County and
genealogical material from Missouri
and eastern states from which
Missouri settlers came)

Maryville Public Library
509 North Main
Maryville, MO 64468
(660) 582-5281; (660) 582-2411 FAX
Margaret Kelley, Collection Coordinator
Hours: Mon–Wed 9:00–6:00, Thur 9:00–
7:00, Fri–Sat 9:00–6:00
Pub. None
(specializes in local history)

Mercer County Library
601 Grant
Princeton, MO 64673
Hours: Mon–Fri 9:00–5:00

Mid-Continent Public Library
North Independence Branch/Genealogy
and Local History Department
(317 West 24 Highway—location)
15616 East 24 Highway (mailing
address)
Independence, MO 64050
(816) 252-0950
http://www.ge@mcpl.lib.mo.us
Martha L. Henderson, Department Head
Hours: Mon–Thur 9:00–9:00, Fri 9:00–
6:00, Sat 9:00–5:00
(national in scope, includes circulating
collection)

Missouri Town 1855
22807 Woods Chapel Road
Blue Springs, MO 64015
(816) 524-8770; (816) 795-8200 (Friends
of Missouri Town 1855)

Missouri Western State College Library
4525 Downs Drive
Saint Joseph, MO 64507
(816) 271-4573
Julia Schneider, Dean LRC
Hours: Mon–Thur 7:30 A.M.–11:00 P.M.,
Fri 7:30–4:30, Sat 10:00–5:00, Sun
2:00–11:00; between semesters: Mon–
Fri 8:00–4:30; summer: Mon–Thur
7:30–7:00, Fri 7:30–4:30, Sun (while
school is in session) 1:00–6:00
(special collections on local history,
personal papers, university records,
women's materials)

Morgan County Library
102 North Fisher
Versailles, MO 65084
(573) 378-5319
Glenn D. Housworth, Librarian
Hours: Mon–Fri 9:00–5:00, Sat 9:00–
noon
(genealogy and local history)

Mound City Museum Association
104 East Seventh
Mound City, MO 64470
(816) 442-5635

Museum of Evangel College of Arts and Sciences
1111 North Glenstone
Springfield, MO 65802
(417) 865-2811
J. C. Holsinger, Ph.D., Director
Hours: when college is open
(Ozark Indian artifacts and pioneer
materials; also Eskimo and Near
Eastern objects)
free

Neosho-Newton County Library
201 West Spring
Neosho, MO 64850
(417) 451-4231; (417) 451-6438 FAX
Jack Wood, Director
Hours: Mon–Thur 9:00–9:00, Fri–Sat
9:00–5:30

Nevada Public Library
225 West Austin
PO Box B
Nevada, MO 64772
Marlene Hizer, Director
Hours: Mon–Wed & Fri 9:00–6:00, Thur
noon–8:00, Sat 9:00–4:00

Newton County Museum Library
121 North Washington Street
Neosho, MO 64850
Hours: Wed–Sun 12:30–4:30

Norborne Public Library
109 East 2nd Street
Norborne, MO 64668
(660) 594-3514
Doris Wightman, Librarian
Hours: Mon–Fri 8:00–noon & 1:00–5:00,
Sat 8:00–noon
(local history)

Northeast Missouri University Archives
(see Truman State University)

Owens Library
Northwest Missouri State University
Maryville, MO 64468
(816) 562-1536
Vickey Baumli, Serials Technical
Specialist
Hours: 8:00–4:00
(census of Nodaway County, most
Nodaway county newspapers)
search service: contact Vickey Baumli,
515 East Fourth, Maryville, MO
64468, fees vary

Powell Memorial Library
951 West College
Troy, MO 63379
(314) 528-7853
Sharon Hasekamp, Librarian

Hours: Mon noon–7:00, Tue–Fri 8:00–
7:00, Sat 9:00–1:00, except same
holidays as school district
not staffed to do research for people

Powers Museum
1617 Oak Street
PO Box 593
Carthage, MO 64836
(417) 358-2667
Michele Hansford, Director/Curator
Hours: Tue–Sat 10:00–5:00, Sun 1:00–
5:00
("Basically a local history resource, no
primary genealogical materials
(census, family books), etc.")

Purvines Genealogical Library
(112 North Fourth Street—location)
614 Clark Street (mailing address)
Canton, MO 63435
(573) 288-5713
Jean Purvines, Librarian
Hours: Mon–Fri 9:00–4:30, Sat by
appointment
(northeast Missouri genealogy)
$10.00 per year membership for
individuals

River Bluffs Regional Library
Reference Service
927 Felix Street
Saint Joseph, MO 64501
(816) 232-8151; (816) 232-7516 FAX
Hours: Mon–Thur 9:00–9:00, Fri–Sat
9:00–6:00, Sun 1:00–5:00
(local and county history)
costs being revised, please phone

Riverside Regional Library
204 South Union Avenue
PO Box 389
Jackson, MO 63755

Saint Clair County Library
Chestnut & Main
Box 370
Osceola, MO 64776
(417) 646-2214
Eleanor Ratliff, Director
Hours: Mon–Fri 8:00–5:00, Sat 8:00–
noon
(local history and genealogy)

Saint Joseph Museum
(1100 Charles, Saint Joseph, MO
64501—location)
PO Box 128 (mailing address)
Saint Joseph, MO 64502-0128
(816) 232-8471; (816) 232-8482 FAX
E-mail: sjm@stjosephmuseum.org
http://www.st.josephmuseum.org
Sarah Elder, Curator of History
Hours: Mon–Fri 9:00–4:00 by
appointment
Pub. *The Happenings*, bimonthly
photocopies: 10¢ per copy

Saint Louis County Library
Headquarters
1640 South Lindbergh Boulevard (at
Clayton Road)
Saint Louis, MO 63131-3598
(314) 994-3300 (Headquarters); (314)
994-9411, ext. 215 (Supervisor of
Reference); (314) 994-9411, ext. 287
FAX; (314) 994-9255 TTY-TDD
(Headquarters)
E-mail: hreference@slcl.lib.mo.us;
bmottin@slcl.lib.mo.us
http://www.slcl.lib.mo.us
Barbara A. Mottin, Supervisor of
Reference
Hours: Mon–Fri 8:30–9:00, Sat 8:30–
5:00, Sun (Sept–May) 1:00–5:00
(Saint Louis archdiocesan parish records
on microfilm and collection of the St.
Louis Genealogical Society: cemetery
and funeral home records, census and
Soundex, church records, city and
county directories, county histories,
family histories, immigration records,
land records, military records,
newspapers, periodicals, probate
records, vital records)

Saint Louis Mercantile Library Association
510 Locust Street, Sixth Floor
PO Box 633
Saint Louis, MO 63188
(314) 621-0670
Jerrold Lee Brooks, Ph.D., Executive
Director; John Neal Hoover, Special
Collections and Rare Books
Hours: Mon–Fri 8:30–4:30

Saint Louis Public Library
History and Genealogy Department
1301 Olive Street
Saint Louis, MO 63103
(314) 539-0386; (314) 539-0393 FAX
E-mail:cmillar@slpl.lib.mo.us
http://www.slpl.lib.mo.us.
Cynthia Millar, Genealogy Librarian
Hours: Mon 10:00–9:00, Tue–Fri 10:00–
6:00, Sat 9:00–5:00
photocopies: 15¢ from paper originals,
25¢ from microfilm originals, $1.00
postage and handling per order

Sedalia Public Library
311 West Third Street
Sedalia, MO 65301-4399
(816) 826-1314; (816) 826-0396 FAX
Donald G. Morton
Hours: winter: Mon–Thur 9:00–9:00, Fri
9:00–6:00, Sat 9:00–5:00, Sun 1:00–
5:00; summer: Mon 9:00–8:00, Tue–
Fri 9:00–6:00, Sat 9:00–4:00, Sun
1:00–5:00
(local history; Sedalia newspapers on
microfilm, 1870 to the present)
search fee: minimum $2.00, varies
according to time spent searching,
extensive research turned over to local
researcher

Shelbina Carnegie Public Library
102 North Center Street
PO Box 247
Shelbina, MO 63468
(573) 588-2271
Bonnie Wood, Assistant Librarian
Hours: Mon–Fri 11:00–6:00, Sat 9:00–
12:00
(Shelby County histories, newspaper
archives, cemetery records, censuses,
etc.)
photocopies: 25¢ per page

Slater Public Library
311 North Main
Slater, MO 65349
(660) 529-3100
Betty Jaeger
Hours: Mon–Fri 2:00–5:00
(genealogy and local history)

South Vernon Genealogical Library
Rt. 2, Box 10
Sheldon, MO 64784
(417) 884-2619
Wilma Lathrop, Historical Research and
Librarian
Hours: Mon–Fri by appointment
research in Barton and Vernon counties:
$10.00 per hour

Southeast Missouri State College
Kent Library
Cape Girardeau, MO 63701

Southwest Missouri Genealogical Library
(see Carthage Genealogical Society)

Springfield-Greene County Library
Shepard Room
397 East Central Street
PO Box 760
Springfield, MO 65801
(417) 869-4621
Michael Glenn, Local History Librarian
Hours: Mon–Thur 8:30–9:00, Fri–Sat
8:30–5:00, Sun (Sept–May) 1:00–5:00
(extensive newspaper indexing)
search fee (southwest Missouri or Greene
County): $3.00 plus copies at 25¢ each

Sullivan County Genealogy Library
Sullivan County Historical Society
North Water Street
Milan, MO 63556
(816) 265-3476
Mildred Baldridge
Hours: Tue (May–Oct) 9:00–noon &
1:00–4:00, and by appointment
(genealogy library and local
memorabilia)
donation for research

Sullivan County Public Library
109 East 2nd Street
Milan, MO 63556-1331
(660) 265-3911
Donna J. Sloan
Hours: Tue & Thur–Fri 9:00–5:00, Sat
9:00–3:00

Truman State University

Pickler Memorial Library
101 East Normal
Kirksville, MO 63501
(660) 785-4537; (660) 785-7368; (660) 785-4536 FAX
E-mail: emdoak@truman.edu
http://academic.truman.edu/~pickler/http/main.html
Elaine Doak, Special Collections Librarian/Archivist
Hours: Mon–Fri 8:00–5:00, Sat 1:00–5:00
(Missouri history—state, county, local; Northeast Missouri University Archives, Central Wesleyan College Archives)

University City Public Library

6701 Delmar
University City, MO 63130
(314) 727-3150; (314) 867-3876 (Librarian); (314) 343-7106 (Assistant Librarian)
Evelyn Brakensiek, Librarian; Beatrice Laws, Assistant Librarian
Hours: Mon–Fri 9:00–9:00, Sat 9:00–5:00, Sun 2:00–5:00

Washington Public Library

415 Jefferson Street
Washington, MO 63090
(314) 390-1070
Hours: Mon–Wed 8:00–8:00, Thur–Fri 8:00–6:00, Sat 9:00–1:00
(very little genealogy information)

Webster University

Eden-Webster Library
475 East Lockwood Avenue
Saint Louis, MO 63119
(314) 961-3627; (314) 961-9063 FAX
E-mail: edward@library2.websteruniv.edu
http://library2.websteruniv.edu/webdata/libhome.html

Western Historical Manuscript Collection

23 Ellis Library, University of Missouri—Columbia
Columbia, MO 65201
(573) 882-6028
E-mail: WHMC@ext.missouri.edu
Nancy Lankford, Associate Director
Hours: Mon & Wed–Fri 8:00–4:45, Tue 8:00 A.M.–9:00 P.M., when university is in session
("WHMC has branches on all four campuses of the University of Missouri system, and loans its holdings among them.")

Western Historical Manuscript Collection—Kansas City

University of Missouri
5100 Rockhill Road
302 Newcomb Hall
Kansas City, MO 64110-2499
(816) 235-1543; (816) 235-5500 FAX

E-mail: whmckc@smtpgate.umkc.edu
http://cctr.umkc.edu/dpt/whmckc/index.html
David L. Boutros, Associate Archivist and Associate Director of Western Historical Manuscript Collection
Hours: Mon–Fri 8:00–5:00

Western Historical Manuscript Collection—Rolla

(Room G-3, Library, UMR, Rolla, MO 65401-0249—location)
1870 Miner Circle (mailing address)
Rolla, MO 65409-0060
(573) 341-4874
E-mail: whmcinf0@umr.edu
http://www.umr.edu/~whmcinfo
Mark C. Stauter, Ph.D., Associate Director
Hours: Mon–Fri 8:00–5:00
("General historical manuscript repository for southern Missouri; access to Western Historical Manuscript Collection statewide holdings.")

Western Historical Manuscript Collection—Saint Louis and State Historical Society of Missouri Manuscripts Joint Collection

University of Missouri, Saint Louis
8001 Natural Bridge
Saint Louis, MO 63121
(314) 553-5143
Patricia L. Adams, Association Director

Westminster College

Winston Churchill Memorial and Library at Westminster College
331 West 7th Street
Fulton, MO 65251
(573) 642-3361; (573) 642-6648
Jane Duncan Flink, Director of External Relations

Westminster College

Reeves Library
501 Westminster Avenue
Fulton, MO 65251-1298
(573) 642-3361, ext. 247; (573) 642-6356 FAX
Lorna K. Mitchell, Head Librarian
Hours: Library: school year: Mon–Fri 8:00–5:00; summer and student break: Mon–Fri 8:00–11:00 A.M., Sat 1:00–5:00, Sun 1:00–11:00; Archives: Mon–Fri 8:00–5:00
(college archives and some materials on Fulton and Callaway counties)

Weston Historical Museum

601 Main Street
Weston, MO 64098
(816) 386-2977; (816) 386-2650 (President)
Mrs. John H. Gaskill, President
Hours: 16 Mar–14 Dec: Sat 1:00–4:00, Sun 1:30–5:00, and by appointment

Historical Societies— Local and Regional

Adair County Historical Society

Genealogy Study Group
211 South Elson
PO Box 342
Kirksville, MO 63501
(816) 665-6502
http://www.artcom.com/museums/nv/af/63501-03.htm (Museum)
Laura Cruse, Museum Director
Hours: Wed–Fri 1:00–4:00; Study Group meeting third Sun 2:00
Pub. *Adair County Historical Society Newsletter*, quarterly
$5.00 per year membership for individuals (includes membership in Study Group), $8.00 per year membership for families

Affton Historical Society

7801 Genesta
PO Box 28855
Saint Louis, MO 63123
(314) 352-5654; (314) 849-3859 FAX
Nancy Herndon, Conservator
Hours: third Sun (Mar–Nov), and by appointment
Pub. *Oakleaf*, quarterly
$10.00 per year membership

Andrew County Museum and Historical Society

(202 East Duncan Drive—location)
PO Box 12 (mailing address)
Savannah, MO 64485-0012
(816) 324-4720; (816) 324-5271 FAX
http://www.artcom.com/museums/
Patrick S. Clark, Director
Hours: Fri–Sat 9:00–4:00, Sun 1:00–4:00
Pub. *Diggin' History*, quarterly
(genealogy department in building)
$10.00 per year membership for individuals, $10.00 per year joint membership, $20.00 per year membership for families, $7.50 per year membership for students or senior citizens, $50.00 per year Patron membership, $100.00 per year Benefactor membership

Atchison County Historical Society

Tarkio, MO 64491

Audrain County Historical Society

501 South Musdrow Street
PO Box 3
Mexico, MO 65265
(573) 581-3910
Leta Hodge, Executive Director
Pub. *Graceland Gazette*

Barry County Historical Society

204 West Street
Cassville, MO 65625

Barton County Historical Society
Barton County Courthouse
PO Box 416
Lamar, MO 64759
(417) 682-3297

Bates County Historical Society
Museum of Pioneer History
100 West Fort Scot
Butler, MO 64730
Hours: May–Sept: 1:00–5:00

Belton Historical Society, Inc.
512 Main Street
PO Box 1144
Belton, MO 64012
(816) 331-2321
Thomas H. Keeney
Hours: Mon, Wed & Fri–Sat 1:00–4:00,
and by appointment
Pub. *BHS Newsletter*
requires donation for admission

Benton County Historical Society
(Warsaw, MO 65355—location)
1115 S.E. Z Highway (mailing address)
Deepwater, MO 64740
(816) 438-7590 (Historic Site and
Archivist)
Robert L. Salley, Historic Site and
Archivist of Benton County
$5.00 per year membership

Blue Springs Historical Society Archives
(Blue Springs City Hall—location)
1013 S.W. 21st (mailing address)
Blue Springs, MO 64015
(816) 229-1671
Karol R. Witthar, Archivist
Hours: by appointment
(local cemetery records, photos, family
histories, etc.)
photocopy fees

Bollinger County Historical Society
PO Box 402
Marble Hill, MO 63764
(573) 238-4304
Cathy Thompson, Chair-Genealogy
Committee
Pub. *Echo*, irregularly
$2.00 per year membership for
individuals (to Norma Bohnsack, RR
2, Box 1150, Marble Hill, MO 63764),
$5.00 per year Contributing
membership, $10.00 per year
Institutional/Corporate membership,
$50.00 per year Sustaining
membership, $100.00 life
membership; for genealogical inquiries
contact Cathy Thompson, 201
Mayfield Drive, Apartment 4, Marble
Hill, MO 63764

Boone-Duden Historical Society
3565 Mill Street
PO Box 82
New Melle, MO 63365
(314) 828-5887

E-mail: bdhissoc@norn.org
http://www.norn.org/pub/other-orgs/
bdhissoc
Lucille Wiechens, Historian
Hours: Sun 1:30–4:30
Pub. *Boone-Duden Historical Society
Newsletter*, bimonthly
$10.00 per year membership

Boonslick Historical Society
PO Box 324
Boonville, MO 65233
(816) 882-5938
Adolph Hilden, Historian
Pub. *Boone's Lick Heritage*, quarterly
$10.00 per year membership; queries
should include SASE

Butler County Historical Society, Inc
(1016 North Main—museum location)
PO Box 1526 (mailing address)
Poplar Bluff, MO 63901
(573) 785-7558
Thelma Sanders, President and Museum
Director
Hours: Sun 1:00–4:00, and by
appointment
Pub. *Butler County Historical Society
Newsletter*, quarterly
$10.00 per year membership; for
research contact Betty Hanks, PO Box
416, Poplar Bluff, MO 63901, (573)
686-2211

Cabool History Society
City Hall
Cabool, MO 65689
(417) 962-4775

Caldwell County Historical Society
PO Box 32
Kingston, MO 64650
(816) 586-3701 (Treasurer)
Lorene Carroll, Treasurer
Hours: daytime
$3.00 per year membership for
individuals, $5.00 per year
membership for families, $1.00 per
year membership for students, $50.00
life membership

Camden County Historical Society
(Highway V-Linn Creek—location)
PO Box 19 (mailing address)
Linn, MO 65052
(573) 346-7191
Daphne Jeffries, Society Secretary and
Museum Coordinator
Hours: Mon–Fri 10:00–4:00
Pub. *Camden County Historian*,
irregularly
$10.00 per year membership for
individuals, $12.00 per year
membership for families

Campbell Area Genealogical and Historical Society
PO Box 401
Campbell, MO 63933-0401

Pub. *Pipeline*, monthly
$8.00 per year membership

Carondelet Historical Society
6303 Michigan Avenue
Saint Louis, MO 63111
(314) 481-6303
Lois Waninger, Museum Coordinator
Hours: Tue–Wed & Fri 9:30–noon, Sat
10:30–2:00
Pub. *Carondelet Historical Society
Newsletter*, twice per year
(emphasis on Carondelet area and Susan
Blow)
$10.00 per year membership for
individuals

Cass County Historical Society, Inc.
Wade Archives
400 East Mechanic
PO Box 406
Harrisonville, MO 64701-0406
(816) 887-2393
Irene Webster, Treasurer
Hours: Office: Mon–Fri 9:00–5:00
Pub. *Newsletter—Cass County Historical
Society*, quarterly
(County courthouse records, tax, probate,
real estate)
$10.00 per year membership for
individuals, $15.00 per year
membership for families, $30.00 per
year membership for businesses,
$300.00 life membership; search:
$5.00

Cedar County Historical Society
Jackson Street (Museum)
PO Box 111
Stockton, MO 65785
Leila Ellis, Recording Secretary
Hours: Museum: last Sat 10:00–noon &
1:00–4:00
$2.00 per year membership for
individuals, $3.00 per year
membership for couples; will answer
some family history requests

Centralia Historical Society, Inc.
319 East Sneed Street
Centralia, MO 65240
(573) 682-5711
Hours: Tue–Fri 9:00–noon & 1:00–3:00
(historical museum concentrating on
local history)

Chariton County Historical Society
115 East Second Street
Salisbury, MO 65281
(816) 388-5941
Martha Fellows, President
Hours: May–Oct 1: Sat–Sun 2:00–4:00
by appointment
Pub. *Chariton County Newsletter*,
quarterly
$5.00 per year membership

Christian County Museum and Historical Society
(401 North Second Avenue, Ozark, MO 65721—location)
PO Box 12 (mailing address)
Nixa, MO 65714
(417) 485-2929

Clark County Historical Society and Museum
252 North Morgan
PO Box 202
Kahoka, MO 63445
(816) 727-1072
Edith Johnson, Secretary
Hours: Fri 10:00–4:00, Sun 1:00–4:00, and by appointment
(Missouri census, marriages, cemetery, probate, obituaries)
$4.00 per year membership for individuals, $5.00 per year membership for families; search fees: $6.00 per hour plus copies at 25¢ each

Clay County Museum and Historical Society
14 North Main Street
Liberty, MO 64068
(816) 792-1849
Ron Fuenfhausen, Curator
Hours: by appointment; Museum: Tue–Sat 1:00–4:00
Pub. *Our Clay Heritage*, quarterly
$8.00 per year membership for individuals (includes free admission to museum)

Clinton County Historical Society and Museum
509 Broadway
Plattsburg, MO 64477
(816) 539-2992
Karma Kay, President
Hours: Jun–Aug: Sun 1:00–5:00, and by appointment

Cole Camp Area Historical Society
Cole Camp Branch of Boonslick Regional Library
PO Box 206
Main Cole Camp, MO 65325
(660) 668-3887
Patricia Beckman, Librarian
Hours: Tue–Fri 1:00–5:00, Sat 9:00–noon

Cole County Historical Society
Cole County Historical Museum
109 Madison Street
Jefferson City, MO 65101
(573) 635-1850
Guy P. Barrett, Director
Hours: Tue–Fri 9:30–4:00
$15.00 per year membership for individuals, $25.00 per year membership for families, $10.00 per year membership for senior citizens

Crawford County Historical Society
(212 North Smith Street—location)
Rt. 2, Box 2700 (mailing address)
Cuba, MO 65453
(573) 885-7912
Dorothy Presson, President
$2.00 per year membership

Creve Coeur-Chesterfield Historical Society
(11631 Olive Boulevard, Creve Coeur, MO—location)
1222 Prinster (mailing address)
Saint Louis, MO 63141
(314) 434-5163

Crystal City Historical Society
130 Mississippi
Crystal City, MO 63019

Dade County Missouri Historical Society
207 McPherson
Greenfield, MO 65661
(417) 637-2744

Dallas County Historical Society
Dallas County Genealogical Society
HC 85, Box 291 B6
Buffalo, MO 65622-9805
(417) 345-7297
Leni Howe, Secretary
Hours: by appointment
Pub. *News Bulletin* (published by Historical Society only), semiannually
$5.00 per year membership for individuals

Daviess County Historical Society
c/o The Daviess County Library
306 West Grand Street
Gallatin, MO 64640
Jan Johnson, Librarian
Hours: Tue–Thur 9:00–6:00, Fri 9:00–5:00, Sat 9:00–1:00
all genealogy requests should be forwarded to the library

DeKalb County Historical Society
PO Box 467
Maysville, MO 64469
Ruth Owen, President
Hours: Apr–Oct: Mon–Fri 9:00–3:30
Pub. *DeKalb County Heritage*, quarterly (museum and genealogical library with DeKalb County Records Center)
$7.50 per year (beginning in Apr)

Dent County Historical Society
1210 Gertrude Street
Salem, MO 65560
(573) 729-5707

Douglas County Historical and Genealogical Society, Inc.
(200 block East Jefferson Street, on south side—location)
PO Box 986 (mailing address)
Ava, MO 65608
(417) 683-5799

Sharon Sanders, President
Hours: Sat 10:00–3:00, and by appointment
Pub. *Douglas County Historical and Genealogical Society Journal*, semiannually (May and December), $7.50 per year subscription
$15.00 per year membership; search fee depends on amount of search

Excelsior Springs Historical Society
Excelsior Springs Historical Museum
101 East Broadway
Excelsior Springs, MO 64024
(816) 630-3712; (816) 630-8063 phone and FAX
E-mail: starmktg@epsi.net
Victoria A. Bates, President
Hours: Mon–Fri 9:00–4:00; viewing tours and research by appointment
Pub. *The Phunn*, annually
$2.00 per year membership for individuals

Ferguson Historical Society
315 Darst Drive
Ferguson, MO 63135
(314) 521-0977

Florissant Valley Historical and Genealogical Society
(No. 1, Traille de Noyer, Florissant, MO 63031—location)
PO Box 298 (mailing address)
Florissant, MO 63032
(314) 524-1100
Pub. *Florissant Valley Quarterly*
$6.00 per year membership

Foundation for Restoration of Sainte Genevieve
70 South Third Street
Sainte Genevieve, MO 63670
(573) 883-2839

Gasconade County Historical Society
(105 South McFadden Street, Owensville, MO 65066—location)
PO Box 131 (mailing address)
Hermann, MO 65041
Ed Langenberg, President
Pub. *Gasconade County Historical Society Newsletter*, quarterly
$7.50 per year active membership, $25.00 per year Sustaining membership, $100.00 life membership

Graham Historical Society
(see Nodaway County Genealogical Society)

Grand River Historical Society and Museum
(Forrest and Irvin—location)
PO Box 154 (mailing address)
Chillicothe, MO 64601
(816) 646-4323; (816) 646-4433
Dr. Frank E. Stark, President
Hours: Apr–Oct: Tue & Sun 1:00–4:00

Pub. *Herald*, quarterly
$2.00 per year membership, $20.00 life
   membership

Historical Association of Greater Cape Girardeau, Inc.
325 South Spanish Street
Cape Girardeau, MO 63701
(573) 334-1177

Heritage League of Greater Kansas City
(Library Building 212, University of
   Missouri—location)
5100 Rockhill Road (mailing address)
Kansas City, MO 64110
(816) 276-1543

Historical Association of Greater Saint Louis
3601 Lindell Boulevard
Saint Louis, MO 63108
(314) 658-2588

Greene County Historical Society
Box 3466 GSS
Springfield, MO 65808
(417) 881-6147
E-mail: gsociety@mail.orion.org
http://www.rootsweb.com/~gcmohs
Hayward Barnett, Executive Secretary
Hours: Mon–Sat 8:00–5:00
Pub. *Greene County Historical Society
   Bulletin*, three times per year
$10.00 per year membership; will
   respond to queries for SASE, research
   for a fee (request details)

Grundy County Historical Society
1100 Mabel Drive
Trenton, MO 64683
(816) 359-9297

Harrison County Historical Society
1604 Fuller Street
Bethany, MO 64424
(816) 425-8360

Henry County Historical Society
203 West Franklin Street
PO Box 65
Clinton, MO 64735
(816) 885-8414
Marily Nold, Director; Mary Frances
   Abart, Genealogy Library
Hours: Apr–Dec: Tue–Sat: 11:00–4:00
Pub. *The Informer*, quarterly
$8.00 per year membership for
   individuals, $12.00 per year
   membership for families

Hickory County Historical Society
(Wheatland, MO 65779—location)
Hermitage, MO 65668 (mailing address)

Harvey J. Higgins Historical Society
1600 Main
Higginsville, MO 64037
(660) 584-3842
Don Smith, President

Hours: Mon–Fri 1:00–4:30, by
   appointment only
(emphasis on Higginsville and its
   founder, Harvey J. Higgins)

Huntsville, Missouri, Historical Society, Inc.
205 East Mulberry
Huntsville, MO 65259
(660) 277-3639
Myrtle Cairns, President
Hours: by appointment

Iron County Historical Society
123 West Wayne Street
Ironton, MO 63650-1327
(573) 546-3513
Elizabeth Holloman, Museum Director
Hours: May–Oct: Sat–Sun 1:00–4:00
Pub. *Iron County Historical Society
   Newsletter*, quarterly
$3.00 per year membership for
   individuals (beginning in April), $1.00
   membership for students, $5.00 per
   year Contributing membership, $10.00
   per year Sustaining membership

Jackson County Historical Society
(Archives and Research Library, 103
   Independence Square Courthouse—
   location)
112 West Lexington, Room 103 (mailing
   address)
Independence, MO 64050
(816) 252-7454
Jane Flynn, President; Kathleen Halcro,
   Director
Hours: Mon–Wed & Fri 10:00–4:00, Sat
   10:00–1:00
Pub. *Journal*, quarterly
("Strauss Peyton photographic collection,
   abstracts, personal diaries, business
   scrapbooks, and more)
$35.00 per year membership; fee
   admission; staff search: $10.00 per
   hour

Jasper County Historical Society
1718 South Garrison
Carthage, MO 64836
Eleanor Coffield

Jennings Historical Society
(8720 Jennings Road—location)
7028 Idlewild Avenue (mailing address)
Jennings, MO 63136
(314) 381-6650; (314) 381-7378 FAX
Linda Schmerber, President
(Jennings history, Jennings/Fairview
   High Yearbooks, twenty years of
   Jennings Progress newspapers,
   genealogy of James Jennings and Ann
   Bradley Montague Jennings of
   Cumberland County, Virginia)
$5.00 per year membership for
   individuals, $3.50 per year
   membership for senior citizens or
   students, $25.00 per year membership

for businesses, $100.00 life
   membership for individuals, $50.00
   life membership for senior citizens,
   aged 62 years and up

Johnson County Historical Society, Inc.
Heritage Library
302 North Main Street
PO Box 825
Warrensburg, MO 64093
(816) 747-6480
Vivian Richardson, Curator
Hours: Library: Mon–Sat 1:00–4:00;
   Museum and Courthouse: Mon–Sat
   1:00–4:00, Sun (Jun–Aug) 1:00–4:00
Pub. *Bulletin*, semiannually; *Johnson
   County Historical Society Journal*,
   semiannually; *Johnson County
   Historical Society Newsletter*
$5.00 per year membership for
   individuals, $8.00 per year
   membership for families

Joplin Historical Society
Schifferdecker Park
PO Box 555
Joplin, MO 64801
(417) 623-1180

Kimmswick Historical Society
6000 Third Street
PO Box 41
Kimmswick, MO 63053
(314) 464-TOUR
Darline A. Spink, President
Hours: Burgess-How House and
   Museum: Sun (Apr–Nov) 1:00–4:00
("At this time we are just getting into the
   genealogy; we have limited
   information.")
$2.00 museum admission (over 14 years
   of age)

Kingdom of Callaway Historical Society
Westminster College
Winston Churchill Memorial and Library
   at Westminster College
331 West 7th Street
Fulton, MO 65251
Barbara Huddleston, President;
   Rosemary Harris, Museum Director
Hours: Apr–30 Oct: Tue & Thur 1:00–
   4:00, and by appointment

Kirkwood Historical Society
(302 West Argonnee—location)
PO Box 3702 (mailing address)
Kirkwood, MO 63122
(314) 965-5151
Mrs. Keith Williams, Museum Curator
Hours: second & fourth Thur & Sun
   1:00–4:00, and selected holidays
Pub. *Kirkwood Historical Review*,
   quarterly
(documents pertaining to history of
   Kirkwood; some history of St. Louis
   and state of Missouri documents,
   primarily as they relate to Kirkwood;

books on history of Kirkwood to 1960, work in progress on history from 1960; works on Meremac Highlands resort area)

$25.00 per year membership, $75.00 per year Corporate membership, $500.00 life membership

Knox County Historical Society
PO Box 75
Edina, MO 63537
(816) 397-2349; (816) 397-3331 FAX
Brenton Karhoff, President
Hours: by appointment

Laclede County Historical Society
PO Box 1341
Lebanon, MO 65536
(417) 588-1485; (417) 532-2725 Geneva Harris; (417) 532-4141 Charlene Hopkins; (417) 532-5758 Dorothy Calton
Geneva Harris, Charlene Hopkins or Dorothy Calton

Lawrence County Historical Society
PO Box 406
Mount Vernon, MO 65712
Pub. *Lawrence County Historical Society Bulletin*, quarterly, $7.00 per year subscription

Lewis County Historical Society
Rt. 1, Box 72
Lewistown, MO 63452
(573) 497-2279

Lexington Library and Historical Association
PO Box 121
Lexington, MO 64067
(816) 259-2023

Macon County Historical Society
Rt. 1
Anabel, MO 63431
(816) 699-3548

The Historical Society of Maries County
PO Box 289
Vienna, MO 65582
(573) 422-3932
Mozelle Hutchison, Newsletter Editor
Hours: Research Room in the courthouse, Vienna: Wed 9:00–noon, and by appointment
Pub. *The Maries Countian*, quarterly
$10.00 per year membership; research $6.00 per hour

Marion County Historical Society
5021 College
Hannibal, MO 63401
(314) 248-1884

Mercer County Historical Society, Inc.
310 West Main Street
Princeton, MO 64673

Mine Au Breton Historical Society
105 State Street
Potosi, MO 63664
(573) 438-4973
http://www.geocities.com/heartland/4386/mabhs.html
Catherine Polete, President; Marie Edgar, Secretary
Hours: daily 8-hour service
$3.00 per year membership; genealogy inquiries answered for donation to MABHS

Mississippi County Historical Society
(403 North Main—location)
PO Box 312 (mailing address)
Charleston, MO 63834
(573) 683-3837; (573) 683-4348
Benj. Bird Moore, Curator
Hours: usually Tue 1:30–3:30, and by appointment

Missouri Alliance for Historical Preservation
(2505 Plymouth Rock Drive, Jefferson City, MO 65109—location)
PO Box 895 (mailing address)
Jefferson City, MO 65102
(573) 635-6877
Susan Hoefener, Executive Secretary
Hours: Mon–Fri 10:00–6:00
Pub. *Update: Preservation*, quarterly; *MAHP Bulletin*, bimonthly
$20.00 per year basic membership (two people at one address), $30.00 per year membership for families, $5.00 per year membership for students, $40.00 per year Sustaining membership, $100.00 per year Patron membership, $500.00 life membership for individuals, $30.00 per year Organization membership for correspondence only, $40.00 per year Organization membership with two representatives

Missouri Historical Society
Library and Research Center
(225 South Skinker—location)
PO Box 11940 (mailing address)
Saint Louis, MO 63112-0040
(314) 746-4500; (314) 454-3100 (Membership services); (314) 746-4599 (General information)
Emily Miller, Librarian
Hours: Tue–Fri 10:00–5:00
Pub. *Gateway Heritage*, quarterly; *Missouri Historical Society*, quarterly
(city and county directories; gazetteers; county, state and local histories; published transcripts and indexes to county records; family histories/genealogies; newspapers, maps, census, etc.; emphasis on St. Louis and regional history)
$45.00 per year membership for individuals, $35.00 per year

membership for senior citizens, $100.00 per year Contributing membership, $250.00 per year Sustaining membership, $500.00 per year Sponsoring membership; no search service or members' queries

Missouri River Heritage Association
Box 76, Station E
Saint Joseph, MO 64505

Moniteau County Missouri Historical Society
201 North High
California, MO 65018
(573) 796-3563 (during library hours only)
Della Huff, President; Betty Williamson, Secretary and Library/Genealogy Chairman
Hours: Thur–Sat (Apr–Oct) 2:00–5:00
Pub. *Moniteau County Historical Society Newsletter*, bimonthly
$5.00 per year active membership (attends meetings), $15.00 per year Sustaining (inactive) or Corporate/Business membership, $75.00 life membership; research: $5.00 deposit plus postage and cost of copies to be billed, in-depth research at $10.00 per hour (plus postage and copies) upon receipt of a $30.00 deposit

Montgomery County Historical Society
112 West Second Street
Montgomery City, MO 63361
Marjorie M. Miller, Member Board of Directors
Hours: by appointment
(Montgomery County information)
$2.00 per year membership

Morgan County Historical Society
(110 North Monroe—location)
202 South Van Buren (mailing address)
Versailles, MO 65084
E-mail: wmwwms@laurie.net (cemetery and marriage records)
K. Dornan; William W. Williams (for cemetery and marriage records)
(Morgan County cemetery listings indexed from 1830 to date, marriage records 1833–1909, census records)

Newton County Historical Society
(Newton County Museum Library, 121 North Washington Street—location)
PO Box 675 (mailing address)
Neosho, MO 64850
(417) 451-9743
James M. Taylor, President
Hours: Museum Library: Wed–Sun 12:30–4:30
Pub. *Newton County Saga*, quarterly
$10.00 per year membership

Nodaway County Heritage Collection

(Nodaway County Historical Society, 110 North Walnut—location)
PO Box 324 (mailing address)
Maryville, MO 64468
Margaret Kelley, Collection Curator
Hours: Mon–Fri & Sun 1:00–4:00
(Nodaway County and some northwest Missouri local history; family information)
free, open membership; search for postage, reimbursement for photocopies, donations welcome

Old Mines Area Historical Society

(Fertile, Washington County, MO—location)
Rural Route 1, Box 1466 (mailing address)
Cadet, MO 63630-9801
(573) 586-5171
Alice L. Widmer, President
Hours: Tue by appointment
("French, ethnic and historical data; artifacts, publications; incorporated in 1978 to keep alive and make better-known the old French-American-Indian culture in this area and Catholic Parish three times the size of the city of Saint Louis; first mining settlement in Missouri.")
$5.00 per year membership for individuals, $10.00 per year membership for families, $10.00 per year Patron membership, $100.00 life membership; searches $10.00 each, $3.00 for each additional family sheet

Old Trails Historical Society

Bacon Log Cabin
(Henry Avenue and Spring Meadow Drive, Ballwin, MO—location)
PO Box 852 (mailing address)
Manchester, MO 63011
(314) 227-5772
Til Keil, Secretary
Hours: Cabin: first Sun, and by appointment
Pub. *Newsletter*, monthly
$10.00 per year membership

Osage County Historical Society

402 East Main Street
PO Box 402
Linn, MO 65051
(573) 897-2932
Claudia Baker, Curator
Hours: Wed 10:00–noon & 1:00–4:00
Pub. *Osage County Historical Society Newsletter*, monthly
(history of Osage County and surrounding counties; microfilm of county records)
$10.00 per year membership for individuals; research: $7.00 per hour, minimum $21.00 for initial search; free library access for members

Overland Historical Society

9711 Lackland Road
Overland, MO 63114-3413
(314) 426-7027
LaVerne Dallas, President
Hours: by appointment
Pub. *Log House Gazette*, five times per year (September through June)
$10.00 per year membership for individuals, $15.00 per year membership for families; search fee: postage, donations accepted

Ozark County Genealogical and Historical Society

HCR 2, Box 2640
Isabella, MO 65676-9707
(417) 273-4817
Eloise Sletten, Vice President and Researcher
Hours: Mon–Fri 9:00–3:30
Pub. *The Old Mill Run*, quarterly
$10.00 per year membership

Park College Historical Society

Fishburn Archives
McAfee Library
8700 N.W. River Park Drive
PO Box 61
Parkville, MO 64152
(816) 741-2000, ext. 6285
Carolyn Elwess, Assistant Archivist
Hours: by appointment (call during business hours, Mon–Fri 8:00–4:30)
Pub. *Dusty Shelf*, quarterly
(records limited to Park Alumni, former students, faculty, Parkville and Platte County history, but no general genealogical information available)
$5.00 per year membership for individuals, $8.50 per year membership for families, $20.00 per year Sustaining membership, $50.00 per year Continuing membership

Pemiscot County Historical Society

(Archives Room, Presbyterian Church—location)
PO Box 604 (mailing address)
Caruthersville, MO 63830
(573) 333-4326 (President)
Mary Belle Poteet, President
Hours: by appointment, members only
Pub. *Pemiscot County Missouri Quarterly* (winter, spring, summer, fall)
$10.00 per year membership (beginning 1 May); research: cost of copies plus postage (members only)

Pettis County Historical Society

(Pettis County Courthouse—location)
Sedalia Public Library, 311 West Third Street (mailing address)
Sedalia, MO 65301-4399
(816) 826-1314
William B. Claycomb, President
Hours: Society: Mon–Fri 9:00–5:00;
Library: winter: Mon–Thur 9:00–9:00,
Fri 9:00–6:00, Sat 9:00–5:00, Sun 1:00–5:00; summer: Mon 9:00–8:00, Tue–Fri 9:00–6:00, Sat 9:00–4:00, Sun 1:00–5:00
Pub. *Newsletter*, five times per year (bimonthly, September to May)
$3.00 per year membership for individuals, $5.00 per year membership for families, $10.00 search fee

Phelps County Historical Society

37 Green Acres
Rolla, MO 65401
(573) 364-3877
Inez Bryant, President
Pub. *PCHS Newsletter*

Pioneer America Society

Southeast Missouri State University
Department of Earth Science
Cape Girardeau, MO 63701
(573) 651-2354
Michael Roark, Ph.D., Executive Director
Pub. *Material Culture*

Platte County Historical Society and Museum

(220 Ferrel Drive—location)
PO Box 103 (mailing address)
Platte City, MO 64079-0103
(816) 431-5121 (Museum); (816) 858-3599 (Office)
Betty Soper, Secretary
Hours: Mar–Oct: Tue–Sat 1:00–4:00, and by appointment
Pub. *Tri-mester*, three times per year
$12.00 per year membership for individuals, $15.00 per year membership for couples, $20.00 per year membership for families

Pleasant Hill Historical Society, Inc.

PO Box 31
Pleasant Hill, MO 64080
(816) 987-3248 (President)
Mary Margaret Ledwidge, President
Hours: by appointment only
donation required for use of collection

Polk County Historical Society

516 North Water Avenue
PO Box 298
Bolivar, MO 65613
(417) 236-7698
Pub. *Polk County Historama*, three times per year

Ralls County Historical Society

PO Box 375
New London, MO 63459
(573) 985-8211
Oliver N. Howard, President

Randolph County Historical Society

Historical Center
226 North Clark
Moberly, MO 65270
Carla Brockman, President

Hours: Museum/Library: Mon 10:00–
noon, Thur 1:00–3:00, Sat 9:00– noon
Pub. *Randolph County Historical Report*,
quarterly; *Old N' Newsletter*
$10.00 per year membership

Ray County Historical Society and Museum, Inc.

901 West Royle Street
PO Box 2
Richmond, MO 64085-0002
(816) 776-2305
Roy Fehlman, Caretaker
Hours: Wed–Sat 10:00–5:00
Pub. *News Letter—Looking Glass*,
quarterly
(museum and genealogical library)
$5.00 per year membership; send SASE
for search fee quotation

Reynolds County Genealogy and Historical Society, Inc.

(Ellington Library, 110 South Main—
location)
PO Box 281 (mailing address)
Ellington, MO 63638
(573) 663-2675 (Treasurer); (573) 663-
7289 (Library); (573) 663-3233
(Museum)
Lee Sylcox, Treasurer
Hours: Mon–Fri 9:00–5:00
Pub. *Kinfolks Search*, monthly
$10.00 per year membership for
individuals or families; $150.00 life
membership, $25.00 life membership
for spouse

Ripley County Historical Society

101 Washington Street
Doniphan, MO 63935
(573) 996-5298; (573) 875-2180
Phoebe Braschler, Corresponding
Secretary
Pub. *The Ripley County Heritage*,
quarterly
$15.00 per year membership

Saint Charles County Historical Society

101 South Main Street
Saint Charles, MO 63301
(314) 946-9828
Carol Wilkins, Archivist/Secretary
Hours: Mon, Wed & Fri 10:00–3:00, Sat
(May–Oct) 10:00–3:00
Pub. *Saint Charles Heritage Quarterly
Newsletter*
("Marriage, baptism, burial, census, land,
probate, naturalization records
available for research in Saint Charles
County.")
$10.00 per year membership for
individuals

Saint François Historical Society

PO Box 575
Farmington, MO 63640
Ruth Womack, Corresponding Secretary

The Scotland County Historical Society

Scotland County Museum
311 South Main
PO Box 263
Memphis, MO 63555

Shelby County Historical Society Museum

215 South Center Street
Shelbina, MO 63468
(573) 633-2206 (President)
E-mail: kwilham@nemonet.com
Kathleen Wilham, President
Hours: Fri (Jun–Aug) 1:00–3:00
$2.50 per year membership; search:
$10.00 per hour, four-hour minimum

Stoddard County Historical Society

(400 Center Street—location)
606 Guiling (mailing address)
Bloomfield, MO 63825
(573) 568-2163
Shannon J. Heilman, President
(cemetery book with index)
$5.00 per year membership

Sullivan County Historical Society

North Water Street
Milan, MO 63556
(816) 265-3476
Wayne Halter, President
Hours: by appointment
(genealogy library and local
memorabilia)
$10.00 life membership

Texas County Genealogical and Historical Society

PO Box 12
Houston, MO 65483
(417) 967-2946; (417) 967-3484
Shirley "Herndon" Wenger, President
Hours: Tue 10:00–3:00
Pub. *Ozark Happenings*, quarterly; *Texas
County Missouri Newsletter*
$10.00 per year membership

Tri-County Historical and Museum Society of King City, Inc.

508 North Grand Avenue and Junction
Highway 169
King City, MO 64463
(816) 535-4391
Danny Lewis, President
Hours: Memorial Day–Labor Day:
weekends: 1:00–4:00; Living History
Day: third Sat of Sept
(genealogical records of local families
available)
no entrance fee, donations accepted

Historical Society of University City

University City Public Library
6701 Delmar
University City, MO 63130
(314) 727-3150; (314) 645-1251
(Librarian); (314) 843-2763 (Assistant
Librarian)

Evelyn Brakensiek, Librarian; Beatrice
Laws, Assistant Librarian
Hours: Library: Mon–Fri 9:00–9:00, Sat
9:00–5:00, Sun 2:00–5:00

Vernon County Historical Society

Bushwhacker Museum
231 North Main Street
Nevada, MO 64772
(417) 667-5841; (417) 667-7108
Patrick Brophy, Curator and
Corresponding Secretary
Hours: Apr–Oct: Mon–Sat 10:00–5:00,
Sun 1:00–5:00
Pub. *Bushwhacker Musings* (includes a
genealogical section), quarterly
$10.00 per year membership; basic fee
for research: $10.00, basic research for
members at no extra cost

Walters-Boone County Historical Society

c/o Wilson-Wulff History and Genealogy
Library
3801 Ponderosa Drive
Columbia, MO 65201
(573) 443-8936
Tom Prater, Museum Curator, Harold C.
Edwards, President
Hours: Apr–Oct: Tue–Sun 1:00–5:00;
Nov–Mar: Wed & Sun 1:00–4:00
Pub. *BCHA Newsletter*

Warren County Historical Society

(Warren County Museum and Historical
Library, Market and Walton Streets—
location)
PO Box 12 (mailing address)
Warrenton, MO 63383
(314) 456-3820
Fred Vahle, Curator
Hours: third Sat of Apr through Oct: Sat
10:00–4:00, Sun 1:00–4:00
Pub. *Warren County Historical Society
Newsletter*, three times per year
(emphasis on Central Wesleyan College
and Central Wesleyan Orphans Home)
$3.00 per year membership for
individuals, $5.00 per year Sustaining
membership, $50.00 life membership;
research: cost of photocopies

Watkins Mill Association

Watkins Woolen Mill State Historic Site
26600 Park Road North
Lawson, MO 64062
(816) 296-3357
Ann M. Sligar, Site Administrator
Hours: Mon–Fri 8:00–4:00, and by
appointment
(some local history)

Webster County Historical Society

Marshfield, MO 65706
(417) 468-2284

Webster Groves Historical Society

1155 South Rock Hill Road
Webster Groves, MO 63119
(314) 968-1857

Charles F. Rehkopf, Archivist
Hours: Christopher Hawken House: weekends 1:00–4:00; Library and Archives: by appointment
Pub. *Webster Groves Historical Society Newsletter*, quarterly
("Kate Moody Papers, Laura Parker Papers, Esther Replogle programs and scrapbooks, records of the City of Webster Groves, local newspapers; probably one of the best collections of local history in Saint Louis County.")
$20.00 per year membership; research by archivist: $10.00 per hour

Westphalia Historical Society, Inc.
Westphalia, MO 65085
(573) 455-2337

Westport Historical Society
Harris Kearney House
4000 Baltimore
PO Box 10076, Westport Station
Kansas City, MO 64111
(816) 561-1821
Hours: Mon–Fri 10:30–3:00, weekends by appointment
Pub. *The Westporter*
(Westport and early Kansas City history, and tours of the historic house and museum)
$15.00 per year membership

White River Valley Historical Society
PO Box 555
Point Lookout, MO 65726-0555
(417) 334-4807 (Secretary-Treasurer)
Ionamae Rebenstorf, Secretary-Treasurer
Pub. *White River Valley Historical Quarterly*
(southwest Missouri and northwest Arkansas)
$14.00 per year membership (beginning in July)

Worth County Historical Society
Allendale, MO 64420
(816) 786-2318

LDS Family History Centers

Frontenac
(314) 993-2328

Independence
(816) 461-0245

Joplin
(417) 623-6506

Kansas City
(816) 941-7389

Saint Louis
(see Frontenac)

Springfield
(417) 889-8229

Genealogical Societies

State Genealogical Society

Missouri State Genealogical Association
PO Box 833
Columbia, MO 65205-0833
http://www.umr.edu/~mstauter/mosga/
Pub. *Missouri State Genealogical Journal*, quarterly; *Show Me State Genealogical News*, quarterly
$15.00 per year membership

Regional Genealogical Societies

Adair County Historical Society
Genealogy Study Group
211 South East Elson
Kirksville, MO 63501
(816) 665-6502
Laura Cruse, Museum Director
Hours: Wed–Fri 1:00–4:00; Study Group meeting third Sun 2:00
Pub. *Adair County Historical Society Newsletter*, quarterly
$5.00 per year membership for individuals (includes membership in Study Group), $8.00 per year membership for families

Audrain County Area Genealogical Society
c/o Mexico-Audrain County Library
305 West Jackson Street
Mexico, MO 65265
(573) 581-4939
Violet Lierheimer
Hours: Mon–Tue & Thur–Fri 9:00–4:00, Wed 2:00–8:00, Sat 2:00–4:00 (when volunteers can staff the room); meetings: third Sun (except Jul, Aug & Dec) 1:30
Pub. *Newsletter*, quarterly
(specializes in Audrain County, Missouri, genealogy, with some adjoining counties information; estimated 140,000 names in indexes)
$8.00 per year membership; search of indexes: $5.00 plus SASE

Barry County Genealogical Society
Rural Route
Cassville, MO 65625
Frances Dell

Genealogical Society of Butler County, Missouri, Inc.
PO Box 426
Poplar Bluff, MO 63901

(573) 686-8426
Mary Sue Beis, President
Pub. *Area Footprints*, semiannually (May and November), $17.00 for first year subscription, $12.00 per year subscription renewal
queries free to members, $1.00 for first 50 words, $2.00 for each additional 50 words for non-members

Campbell Area Genealogical and Historical Society
PO Box 401
Campbell, MO 63933-0401
Pub. *Pipeline*, monthly
$8.00 per year membership

Cape Girardeau County Genealogical Society
Riverside Regional Library
204 South Union Avenue
PO Box 389
Jackson, MO 63755
(573) 243-8141
Pub. *Collage of Cape County*, quarterly (emphasis on southeast Missouri genealogy)
$10.00 per year membership

Genealogical Society of Carter County
Rt. 1, Box 266
Ellsinore, MO 63937

Carthage Genealogical Society and Southwest Missouri Genealogical Library
Rt. 3, Box 117
Carthage, MO 64836
(417) 358-6494
Joan Kunkel, Genealogist and Librarian
Hours: by appointment
(Missouri and Arkansas research)

Genealogical Society of Central Missouri
(Boone County Historical Society Museum, 3801 Ponderosa, Columbia, MO 65203—location)
PO Box 26 (mailing address)
Columbia, MO 65205
(573) 443-8936
http://www.synapse.com/bocomogenweb
Charles and Laurie Shawver, Co-presidents
Hours: Boone County Historical Society Museum: Apr–Oct: Tue–Sun 1:00–5:00; Nov–Mar: Wed & Sat–Sun 1:00–4:00
Pub. *The Reporter*, six times per year
(serving Boone County, Missouri, and surrounding counties)
$12.50 per year membership for individuals, $15.00 per year membership for households

Dallas County Genealogical Society
Dallas County Historical Society
HC 85, Box 29186
Buffalo, MO 65622-9805

Leni Howe, Secretary
Hours: by appointment
Pub. *News Bulletin* (published by
  Historical Society only), semiannually
$5.00 per year membership for
  individuals

Douglas County Historical and Genealogical Society, Inc.

(200 block East Jefferson Street, on
  south side—location)
PO Box 986 (mailing address)
Ava, MO 65608
(417) 683-5799
Sharon Sanders, President
Hours: Sat 10:00–3:00, and by
  appointment
Pub. *Douglas County Historical and
  Genealogical Society Journal*,
  semiannually (May and December),
  $7.50 per year subscription
$15.00 per year membership; search fee
  depends on amount of search

Dunklin County Genealogical Society

Dunklin County Library
226 North Main Street
Kennett, MO 63857
(573) 888-3561
Jane Rogers, Editor; Patsy Fisher,
  Treasurer
Hours: 8:30–5:30
Pub. *Semo Record*, quarterly
$8.00 per year membership

Florissant Valley Historical and Genealogical Society

(No. 1, Traille de Noyer, Florissant, MO
  63031—location)
PO Box 298 (mailing address)
Florissant, MO 63032
(314) 524-1100
Pub. *Florissant Valley Quarterly*
$6.00 per year membership

Four Rivers Genealogical Society

314 West Main Street
PO Box 146
Washington, MO 63090

Genealogy Friends of The Library

(Neosho-Newton County Library, 201
  West Spring—location)
PO Box 314 (mailing address)
Neosho, MO 64850-0314
(417) 451-4231 (Library)
Doris McCleary, President
Hours: Mon–Thur 9:00–9:00, Fri 9:00–
  5:30, Sat 9:00–5:00
Pub. *Newton County Roots*, quarterly
$9.00 per year membership

Gentry County Genealogical Society

Albany Public Library
101 West Clay
Albany, MO 64402
(816) 726-5615
Hours: Library: Mon–Sat 11:00–5:00

Grundy County Genealogical Society

PO Box 223
Trenton, MO 64683
(816) 359-6512
Robert Greiner, President
Pub. *Grundy Gleanings*, quarterly, $2.50
  per issue
$10.00 per year membership

Harrison County Genealogical Society

2243 Central Street
Bethany, MO 64424
(816) 425-2459
Pearl James, Newsletter Editor
Hours: Tue & Thur 1:00–5:00, Sat 2:00–
  4:00
Pub. *Heritage Seeker*, quarterly
$7.50 per year membership

Heart of America Genealogical Society and Library, Inc.

c/o Kansas City Public Library
Missouri Valley Room
311 East 12th Street
Kansas City, MO 64106
(816) 221-2685, ext. 71; (816) 931-2373
  (Librarian)
Gladys Deever, Society Librarian
Hours: Mon–Sat 10:00–3:00, Sun 1:00–
  5:00
Pub. *The Kansas City Genealogist*,
  quarterly; *Heartlines*, bimonthly
$15.00 per year membership for
  individuals, $22.50 per year
  membership for households, $25.00
  per year Contributing membership,
  $50.00 per year Sustaining
  membership, $100.00 per year Patron
  membership, $250.00 life membership

Heritage Seekers

(417 South Main—location)
Rt. 1 (mailing address)
Palmyra, MO 63461
(320) 769-3076 (Memorial Day–Labor
  Day)
Mark Hoenes, President
Hours: 10:00–noon & 1:00–4:00
no genealogical research

Jackson County Genealogical Society

420 South Main (Library)
PO Box 2145
Independence, MO 64055
(816) 252-8128
James Hinkle, President
Hours: Tue, Thur 10:00–4:00, Sat 9:00–
  5:00
Pub. *Pioneer Trails*, monthly; *The
  Pioneer Wagon*, quarterly
(has tombstone readings of cemeteries,
  and marriage records)
$15.00 per year membership; research
  assistance by donation

Joplin Genealogical Society

(Joplin Public Library, 300 Main Street,
  Joplin, MO 64801—location)
PO Box 152 (mailing address)
Joplin, MO 64802
(417) 623-7953
Kay Heckmaster, President
Hours: Genealogy Department: Mon &
  Thur 9:00–8:45, Tue–Wed & Fri–Sat
  9:00–5:45, Sun 1:00–4:45
Pub. *Conestoga*, quarterly
(large collection on Jasper County and
  other counties)
$10.00 per year membership; search:
  $5.00 per name-per item (such as
  obituary)

Laclede County Genealogical Society

PO Box 350
Lebanon, MO 65536
Thomas C. Knight, President
Pub. *LCGS Newsletter*, quarterly
$10.00 per year membership

Genealogical Society of Liberty (Clay County, Missouri)

(see Clay County Archives and Historical
  Library, Inc.)

Lincoln County Genealogical Society

PO Box 192
Hawk Point, MO 63349
(314) 338-4639
Robert Monroe
Pub. *Newsletter*, quarterly
$5.00 per year membership

Linn County, Missouri Genealogy Researchers

771 Tomahawk
Brookfield, MO 64628
Audrey Stigall

Livingston County Genealogical Society

Livingston County Library
450 Locust Street
Chillicothe, MO 64601
(816) 646-5504 FAX
E-mail: travler1@aol.com (Editor)
http://vax2.rainis.net/~fwoods/
Robert Pigg, Newsletter Editor
Hours: Library: Mon, Wed & Fri 9:00–
  6:00, Tue & Thur 9:00–8:00, Sat 9:00–
  4:00
Pub. *Lifelines*, quarterly
(county atlases, cemetery indexes
$15.00 per year membership

Mercer County Genealogical Society

c/o Mercer County Library
601 Grant
Princeton, MO 64673
(816) 748-3725
Rosemary Beverage, Corresponding
  Secretary
Hours: Mon–Fri 9:00–5:00, Sat 9:00–
  12:00
Pub. *Pioneer Traces*, quarterly
$8.00 per year membership

Mid-Missouri Genealogical Society, Inc.
(Missouri State Archives, 600 West Main Street—location)
PO Box 715 (mailing address)
Jefferson, MO 65102
(573) 636-8856
Peter Schlup, President
Hours: meetings: first Wed
Pub. *Genealogia*, bimonthly
(Missouri regional and local genealogy; Civil War)
$15.00 per year membership

Mississippi County Genealogical Society
PO Box 5
Charleston, MO 63834
Nancy Raithel, Corresponding Secretary
Pub. *Muddy Roots*, quarterly
$14.00 per year membership; free queries for members

Nodaway County Genealogical Society
(Nodaway County Historical Society, 110 North Walnut—genealogical collection location)
PO Box 214 (mailing address)
Maryville, MO 64468
(816) 582-3254 (Treasurer)
E-mail: mowry@msc-net.com
Joan Eitel, Publications Chairman, Treasurer; Letha Marie Mowry, Files Secretary
Hours: Mon–Fri & Sun 1:00–4:00
Pub. *Smoke Signals*, quarterly
(emphasis on northwest Missouri, includes over 100,000 cards of information now being placed on computer for speeding response time; these files are not open to the public and are available only through correspondence; houses the files of the disbanded Graham Historical Society)
$10.00 per year membership; Nodaway County files $1.00 and up (postage in loose stamps) plus SASE, depending on size of file

Northeast Missouri Genealogical Society
614 Clark Street
Canton, MO 63435
Jean Purvines, Secretary-Treasurer
Pub. *Newsletter*
$10.00 per year membership

Northwest Missouri Genealogical Society and the Buchanan County Research Center
412 Felix Street
PO Box 382
Saint Joseph, MO 64502
(816) 233-0524
Hours: Tue 2:00–8:00, Wed–Fri 10:00–3:00, first & third Sat (summer) noon–4:00

Pub. *Northwest Missouri Genealogical Society Journal*, semiannually; *Northwest Missouri Genealogical Society Newsletter*, bimonthly
(serving Andrew, Atchison, Buchanan, Clinton, DeKalb, Gentry, Holt, Nodaway and Worth counties, as well as nearby counties in northeast Kansas)
$15.00 per year membership

Oregon County Genealogical Society
c/o Oregon County Courthouse
PO Box 324
Alton, MO 65606
Reva Baker, President
Hours: Thur 10:00–2:00
Pub. *Oregon County MO Newsletter*, quarterly
$5.00 per year membership for individuals (beginning in Oct), $7.00 per year membership for families, $3.00 per year membership for senior citizens

Ozark County Genealogical and Historical Society
HCR 2, Box 2640
Isabella, MO 65676-9707
(417) 273-4817
Eloise Sletten, Vice President and Researcher
Hours: Mon–Fri 9:00–3:30
Pub. *The Old Mill Run*, quarterly
$10.00 per year membership

Ozarks Genealogical Society, Inc.
(534 West Catalpa Street—OGS Library location)
PO Box 3945 (mailing address)
Springfield, MO 65808
(417) 831-2773 (OGS Library); (417) 889-5677 (President)
http://www.rootsweb.com/~osociety/
Luci Ortner, President
Hours: OGS Library: Tue (except third Tue) 6:00–8:30, third Tue 6:00–6:45, Wed 1:00–4:00, Sat 10:00–4:00; Springfield-Greene County Library: Mon–Thur 8:30–9:00, Fri–Sat 8:30–5:00, Sun (Sept–May) 1:00–5:00
Pub. *Ozar'kin: The People Who Settled the Missouri Ozarks* (covers southwest Missouri, south of the Osage River), quarterly, $15.00 per year subscription; *Newsletter*, ten times per year
$10.00 per year membership plus $10.00 initial registration

Phelps County Genealogical Society
PO Box 571
Rolla, MO 65402-0571
(573) 265-7401
E-mail: monahale@follanet.org
Mona Hale, Secretary
Hours: Saint James Memorial Library: Mon 10:00–8:00, Tue–Fri 10:00–5:00

Pub. *Phelps County Genealogical Society Quarterly* (January, April, July, October)
$18.00 per year membership

Pike County Genealogical Society
PO Box 364
Bowling Green, MO 63334
Pub. *Pike County Genealogical Society Quarterly*
$10.00 per year membership

Platte County Genealogical Society
(Platte County Historical Society, 220 Ferrell Drive—location)
PO Box 103 (mailing address)
Platte City, MO 64079-0103
(816) 431-5121 (Museum); (816) 858-3599 (Executive Secretary)
Betty Soper, Executive Secretary
Hours: Mar–Oct: Tue & Sat 1:00–4:00, and by appointment
Pub. *Tri-mester*, three times per year
$12.00 per year membership for individuals, $15.00 per year membership for couples, $20.00 per year membership for families

Genealogy Society of Pulaski County Missouri
PO Box 226
Crocker, MO 65452
(573) 736-2391
Joanna Christian, Secretary; Edna Christian, Vice President
Hours: call in advance
Pub. *Newsletter*
$7.50 per year membership (beginning Nov 1)

Ray County Genealogical Association
901 West Royle Street
Richmond, MO 64085-1545
(816) 776-2053
Sue Alexander, President; Sandra McKemy, Corresponding Secretary
Hours: Wed–Sat 10:00–5:00
Pub. *Ray County Reflections*, quarterly
$10.00 per year membership for individuals, $12.50 per year membership for families

Reynolds County Genealogy and Historical Society, Inc.
(Ellington Library, 110 South Main—location)
PO Box 281 (mailing address)
Ellington, MO 63638
(573) 663-2675 (Treasurer); (573) 663-7289 (Library); (573) 663-3233 (Museum)
Lee Sylcox, Treasurer
Hours: Mon–Fri 9:00–5:00
Pub. *Kinfolks Search*, monthly
$10.00 per year membership for individuals or families; $150.00 life membership, $25.00 life membership for spouse

Saint Charles County Genealogical Society

(100 North Third, Suite 106, Old Historic Courthouse—library location)
PO Box 715 (mailing address)
Saint Charles, MO 63302-0715
(314) 724-6668; (314) 946-0541
Wilma Jo Schnare, Librarian
Hours: Tue 9:00–2:00, last Tue 7:00–8:30 P.M.
Pub. *Tangled Roots*, quarterly
$10.00 per year membership for individuals, $15.00 per year membership for families; research: $5.00 per hour, $10.00 minimum

Saint Louis Genealogical Society

9011 Manchester Road, Suite #2
Saint Louis, MO 63144-2643
(314) 968-2763
http://www.rootsweb.com/~mostlogs/stinde.htm
Ann Fleming, President
Hours: Tue, Thur & Sat 9:00–noon
Pub. *S.L.G.S. Quarterly*; *News 'n' Notes*, monthly
(specializes in Saint Louis city and county)
$20.00 per year membership for individuals, $22.00 per year membership for households; search fee schedule being revised

Santa Fe Trail Researchers Genealogical Society

3096 State Road J
Franklin, MO 65250
(816) 248-1826 FAX
E-mail: kboggs@mail.coin.missouri.edu
Karen J. Boggs, Archivist

Shelbina Genealogical Society

Shelbina Carnegie Public Library
102 North Center Street
PO Box 247
Shelbina, MO 63468
(573) 588-2271 (Library)
Bonnie Wood, Assistant Librarian
Hours: Library: Mon–Fri 11:00–6:00, Sat 9:00–12:00

South Central Missouri Genealogical Society

(9 Court Square—library location)
939 Nichols Drive (mailing address)
West Plains, MO 65775
(417) 256-3769
Irene Kimberlin
Hours: Tue & Sat 9:00–12:00
Pub. *Newsletter*, quarterly
("Howell County, Missouri, cemeteries, courthouse records.")
$8.00 per year membership for individuals, $10.00 membership for two adults in the same household

Texas County Genealogical and Historical Society

PO Box 12
Houston, MO 65483

(417) 967-2946; (417) 967-3484
Shirley "Herndon" Wenger, President
Hours: Tue 10:00–3:00
Pub. *Ozark Happenings*, quarterly; *Texas County Missouri Newsletter*
$10.00 per year membership

Thrailkill Genealogical Society

2018 Gentry Street North
Kansas City, MO 64116

Vernon County Genealogical Society

Nevada Public Library
225 West Austin
Nevada, MO 64772
(417) 667-2831
Madge P. Baze, President
Hours: Library: Mon–Wed & Fri 9:00–6:00, Thur noon–8:00, Sat 9:00–4:00

Webb City Area Genealogy Society

101 South Liberty
Webb City, MO 64870
(417) 673-4326; (417) 673-5703 FAX
E-mail: wclibrary@clanjop.com
Lucille Kent, President
Hours: Mon–Fri 1:00–4:30, Sat 11:30–3:30
Pub. *The Miner*, quarterly
(Jasper County cemeteries, newspapers, census)
$7.50 per year membership

West Central Missouri Genealogical Society and Library, Inc.

125 North Holden
PO Box 435
Warrensburg, MO 64093
(816) 747-9664
Nadine Adams, Librarian
Hours: Sat 1:00–4:00
Pub. *The Prairie Gleaner*, quarterly
$10.00 per year membership for individuals

West Plains Genealogical Society

PO Box 138
West Plains, MO 65775
Larry Houf

Independent Publications and Miscellany

Elk River Current
PO Box 267
Southwest City, MO 64863
(417) 762-3270; (417) 762-3911 FAX
Bonnie Martin, Genealogy Writer
Hours: Office: Mon–Fri 8:00–5:00, Sat 8:00–12:00
Pub. *Elk River Current* (McDonald County, Missouri, Benton County, Arkansas, and Delaware County, Oklahoma), weekly, $18.59 per year subscription in Missouri, $17.50 per

year subscription in Arkansas and Oklahoma, $21.00 per year subscription elsewhere

Family Publications

5628 60th Drive, N.E.
Marysville, WA 98270-9509
E-mail: cxwp57a@prodigy.com
Rose Caudle Terry, Publisher
Pub. *Missouri Sources, Queries & Reviews*, two to four times per year, $8.95 per volume subscription, plus $1.50 postage per order

Family Tree Climbers

(D Hiway and Doniphan Street—location)
PO Box 422 (mailing address)
Lawson, MO 64062
Joyce Kindred, Secretary-Researcher
Hours: meetings second Wed 9:00 A.M. (mainly Ray County)
$3.00 per year membership

Friends of Florida

PO Box 132
Stoutsville, MO 65283
(573) 672-3330
Grace Hilbert, Treasurer

Friends of Keytesville, Inc.

304 Bridge Street
Keytesville, MO 65261

The Friends of Rocheport Museum

(First and Moniteau Streets—location)
120 North Clark (mailing address)
Rocheport, MO 65279
(573) 698-2835
JoAnn Moreau, President
Hours: Apr–Oct: Sat 2:00–4:00, Sun 1:00–5:00
admission: $1.00 donation

Hunting for Bears Genealogical and Historical Society

(see Alabama)

Mississippi Valley French Research

(see Illinois)

Missouri Ancestors

1002 Arthur Street
Burkburnett, TX 76354
Pub. *Missouri Ancestors*, irregularly

Missouri Territorial Pioneers

3929 Milton Drive
Independence, MO 64055-4043
(816) 373-5309
Robert L. Grover, President

MoGenWeb

Part of U.S. GenWeb Project
E-mail: mo@usgenweb.com
http://www.rootsweb.com/~mogenweb/mo.htm
(links to other Missouri resources)

Mountain Press

(see Tennessee)

Reppert Publications
Antique and Collectible News
(see Illinois)

Research and Publishing
RR 1, Box 150
Shelbyville, MO 63469
(573) 633-2206
E-mail: kwilham@nemonet.com
Kathleen Wilham
(publishes books on Adair, Audrain,
Callaway, Knox, Lewis, Macon,
Marion, Monroe, Ralls and Shelby
counties)
search fee: $10.00 per hour, four-hour
minimum

Saint Paul's College Historical Society
Concordia, MO 64020
(660) 463-2238
Richard Buesing
Hours: by appointment only
(collects materials documenting the
history of St. Paul's College; materials
concerning family and personal
papers, local history, and religion)

Seeking 'N Searching Ancestors
Rt. 1, Box 52
Saint Elizabeth, MO 65075
(573) 793-6998
Peggy Smith Hake, Editor
Pub. *Seeking 'N Searching Ancestors*
(Miller, Maries, Pulaski, Camden and
Cole counties), bimonthly, $7.00 per
year

Unterrified Democrat
300 East Main Street
PO Box 109
Linn, MO 65051
(573) 897-3150
Jerry Voss, Publisher
Pub. *Unterrified Democrat*, weekly
newspaper, $25.00 per year in-state
subscription, $27.00 per year out-of-
state subscription

Waterways Journal
650 Security Building
319 North Fourth Street
Saint Louis, MO 63102
(314) 241-7354
E-mail: waterwayj@aol.com
H. Nelson Spencer, III, Publisher
Hours: 8:00–4:30
Pub. *Waterways Journal*, weekly, $30.00
per year subscription
(emphasis on inland waterways)

Kansas City Possee—The Westerners
1250 West Gregory Boulevard
Kansas City, MO 64114
(816) 363-8174

MONTANA

Archives and Libraries with Holdings in Genealogy

State Archives and Library

Montana State Archives
Montana Historical Society
Memorial Building
225 North Roberts Street
Helena, MT 59620
(406) 444-4774 (Archives)
Kathryn Otto, State Archivist
Hours: Mon–Fri 8:00–5:00

Records Management Bureau
Secretary of State
PO Box 202801
Helena, MT 59620-2801
(406) 444-2716; (406) 444-3976 FAX
E-mail: sos@mt.gov
http://www.mt.gov/sos/
sectst.htm#anchor360717

Montana State Library
1515 East Sixth Avenue
PO Box 201800
Helena, MT 59620-1800
(406) 444-3115; (406) 444-5374
(Reference); (406) 444-5612 FAX
E-mail: mwhite@msl.mt.gov;
kstrege@msl.mt.gov
http://msl.mt.gov/
Hours: Mon–Fri 8:00–5:00
(not a genealogical library)

State Historical Society

Montana Historical Society
(Memorial Building, 225 North Roberts
Street, Helena, MT 59601—location)
PO Box 201201 (mailing address)
Helena, MT 59620
(406) 444-4702; (406) 444-2696 FAX
http://www.his.mt.gov
Angela Murray, Genealogical Reference
Hours: Mon–Fri 8:00–5:00, some Sat by
appointment
Pub. *Montana, the Magazine of Western
History*, quarterly; *Montana Post*,
quarterly
$40.00 per year membership

City, County and Regional Archives and Libraries

Big Horn County Historical Museum and Visitor Center
Rt. 1, Box 1206A
Hardin, MT 59034
(406) 665-1671
Pub. *On the Big Horn*

Butte-Silver Bow Public Archives
(17 West Quartz, Butte, MT 59701—
location)
PO Box 81 (mailing address)
Butte, MT 59703
(406) 723-8262, ext. 306
Ellen Crain, Director
Hours: Mon–Fri 9:00–5:00
(newspaper index, cemetery index,
obituary file, death and birth records,
city directories, census, maps, books,
photographs; written requests
welcome)
research fee: $7.00 per inquiry

Butte-Silver Bow Public Library
226 West Broadway
Butte, MT 59701
(406) 723-3361; (406) 782-1825 FAX
M. Andersen, Reference Librarian
Hours: Mon & Thur–Sat 10:00–5:00,
Tue–Wed 10:00–8:00

Cascade County Historical Museum and Archives
Paris Gibson Square
1400 First Avenue, North
Great Falls, MT 59401-3299
(406) 452-3462
Cindy Kittredge, Director
Hours: Tue–Fri 10:00–5:00, Sat by
appointment
Pub. *Western Genesis*, quarterly
(Montana history)
$15.00 per year membership; $5.00 for
each request, $20.00 per hour for
research

Center for Great Plains Studies
(see Kansas)

Center for Great Plains Study
(see Nebraska)

Copper Village Museum and Art Center
Anaconda City Hall Cultural Center
401 East Commercial Street
Anaconda, MT 59711
(406) 846-2422
Carol Jette, Director
(local history collection, genealogical
services)

Dawson County Library
Genealogy Room
200 South Kendrick
Glendive, MT 59330
(406) 365-3633
Gail Nagle
(room maintained by Dawson County
Tree Branches)

Garfield County Museum
PO Box 145
Jordan, MT 59337
(406) 557-2589

Public Library, Great Falls
Great Falls, MT 59401

Headwaters Heritage Museum
(Corner of Main and Cedar Streets—
    location)
PO Box 116 (mailing address)
Three Forks, MT 59752
(406) 285-3644
Robin Cadby-Sorensen, Curator
Hours: Mon–Sat 9:00–noon & 1:00–
    5:00, Sun 1:00–5:00
(genealogical services; small library for
    this area only)

Liberty County Museum Association
210 Second Street, East
PO Box 611
Chester, MT 59522
(406) 759-5256
Betty Frederickson, Treasurer
Hours: 28 May–15 Sept: daily: 2:00–
    5:00 & 7:00–9:00

Marias Museum of History and Art
206 12th Avenue, North
Shelby, MT 59474
(406) 434-2551

McCone County Museum
Circle, MT 59215-0334
(406) 485-2414

Mezzanine-Helena Public Library
120 South Last Chance Gulch
Helena, MT 59601-4133
(406) 442-2380
http://www.mth.mtlib.org/homepage.html
Hours: Tue–Wed 10:00–8:00, Thur–Sat
    10:00–5:00, Sun 1:00–4:00

Miles City Public Library
1 South Tenth Street
Miles City, MT 59301
(406) 232-1496
Reference/Research Librarian
Hours: Mon 10:00–8:00, Tue & Thur
    12:00–8:30, Wed 12:00–5:00, Fri
    10:00–5:00, Sat 11:00–5:00

Missoula Public Library
301 East Main
Missoula, MT 59802
(406) 721-2665
E-mail: mslaplib@ism.net
Paulette K. Parpart
Hours: Mon–Thur 10:00–9:00, Fri
    10:00–6:00, Sat (after Labor Day–
    Memorial Day, subject to change)
    10:00–6:00

Montana State University
Museum of the Rockies
South Seventh and Kagy Boulevard
Bozeman, MT 59717
(406) 994-2251

Montana State University
Special Collections and Archives
PO Box 17332
Bozeman, MT 59717-3320
(406) 994-4242; (406) 994-2851 FAX
http://www.lib.montana.edu/index.html

Museum of the Great Plains
(see Oklahoma)

Museum of the Yellowstone
146 Yellowstone Avenue
PO Box 411
West Yellowstone, MT 59758
(406) 646-7814

Musselshell Valley Historical Museum
524 First West
Roundup, MT 59072
(406) 323-1403
Ted Benes
Hours: Mon–Sun (May–Sept) 1:00–5:00

Northern Montana College
Northern Montana College Collections
Havre, MT 59501
(406) 265-7821, ext. 3285

Old Trail Museum
Teton Trail Village
Choteau, MT 59422
(406) 466-5332
John W. Brandvold, Director
(local history collection)

Park County Museum
118 West Chinook
Livingston, MT 59047
(406) 222-4184
Kristi Baukol
Hours: 10:00–5:00
Pub. *Park County Museum Library*
(cemetery records, Polk directories)
research: $5.00 per hour

Park County Public Library
228 West Callender Street
Livingston, MT 59047

Parmly Billings Library
510 North Broadway
Billings, MT 59101
(406) 657-8258 (Reference Desk)
Hours: Tue–Thur 10:00–9:00, Fri–Sat
    10:00–6:00, Sun 1:00–5:00

Pioneer Memorial Museum
(Highway 93, Council Park—location)
Rural Route (mailing address)
Darby, MT 59829

Powell County Museum
1199 Main Street
Deer Lodge, MT 59722
(406) 846-3294 (summer); (406) 846-
    3111 (winter)
James Haas, Curator
Hours: Jun–Aug: Mon–Fri noon–5:00
Pub. *Museum Post*, annually
(old photo archives)

Ronan City Library
203 Main Street, S.W.
Ronan, MT 59864
(406) 676-3682
Marilyn Koester, Library Director
Hours: Tue–Sat noon–6:00

George C. Ruhle Library
Glacier National Park
West Glacier, MT 59936
(406) 888-5441

The University of Montana
Mansfield Library
Missoula, MT 59812-1195
(406) 243-6860; (406) 243-6866
    (Reference); (406) 243-2060 FAX
E-mail: root@entity.lib.umt.edu;
    archives@selway.umt.edu (K. Ross
    Toole Archives);
    mullin@selway.umt.edu (Special
    Collections Department)
http://www.lib.umt.edu/
Hours: when school is in session: Mon–
    Thur 8:00 A.M.–11:00 P.M., Fri 8:00–
    6:00, Sat 9:00–6:00, Sun 9:00–11:00;
    when school is not in session: Mon–
    Fri 8:00–5:00

Western Heritage Center
2822 Montana Avenue
Billings, MT 59101
(406) 256-6809
Lynda Bourgue Moss, Director
Hours: Tue–Sat 10:00–5:00, Sun 1:00–
    5:00

Historical Societies— Local and Regional

Anaconda/Deer Lodge County Historical Society
401 East Commercial Street
Anaconda, MT 59711
(406) 563-2220
Jerry Hansen, Historical Consultant
Hours: Tue–Sat 1:00–4:00, and by
    appointment
Pub. *Historical Review*, quarterly
$10.00 per year membership for
    individuals, $15.00 per year
    membership for families, $7.50 per
    year membership for senior citizens,
    $100.00 per year Contributing
    membership, $250.00 life membership

Bitter Root Valley Historical Society
Ravalli County Museum
205 Bedford, Old Courthouse
Hamilton, MT 59840
(406) 363-3338 phone and FAX
Helen Ann Bibler, Director
Hours: Jun–1 Oct: Mon & Thur–Sat
    10:00–4:00, Sun 1:00–4:00
(all newspapers published in Valley,
    obits, etc., are catalogued)

Blaine County Historical Society
Blaine County Museum
501 Indiana
PO Box 927
Chinook, MT 59523
(406) 357-2590

Madelein M. Marsonette, Museum Manager
Hours: summer: Tue–Sat 8:00–5:00, Sun 2:00–4:00; winter: weekday afternoons

Butte Historical Society
(Butte-Silver Bow Public Archives, 17 West Quartz—location)
PO Box 3913 (mailing address)
Butte, MT 59701
(406) 723-8262, ext. 306 (Archives)
Ellen Crain, Director of Archives
Mon–Fri 9:00–5:00
$10.00 per year membership for individuals, $15.00 per year membership for families, $25.00 per year membership for businesses; research: $7.50 per inquiry, plus copy costs

Carbon County Historical Society
206 North Broadway
PO Box 881
Red Lodge, MT 59068
(406) 446-3667
Shirley Zupan, President
Hours: Mon–Fri 8:00–noon, and by appointment
Pub. *Cornerstones*, quarterly
$10.00 per year membership for individuals, $15.00 per year membership for families

Gallatin County Historical Society and Pioneer Museum
317 West Main Street
Bozeman, MT 59715
(406) 585-1311
Dennis Seibel, Executive Director
Hours: Jun–Sept: 10:00–4:30; Oct–May: 11:00–4:00, Sat 1:00–4:00
Pub. *Gallatin County Historical Society Newsletter*, quarterly
(regional history)
$10.00 per year membership

Madison County History Association
207 Mill Street
Sheridan, MT 59749
(406) 842-5410

Meagher County Historical Society
PO Box 389
White Sulphur Springs, MT 59645
(406) 547-3965

Mineral County Museum and Historical Society
(Library Building, 301 East Second Avenue—location)
PO Box 533 (mailing address)
Superior, MT 59872
(406) 822-4516; (406) 822-4078 (Curator); (406) 822-4626 (Researcher)
Deb Davis, Curator; Cathryn Strombo, Researcher
Hours: Mon & Thur–Sun 4:00–8:00

Pub. *Mullan Chronicles*, quarterly
(specializes in John Mullan and Mullan Road; Civil War veterans who came to Montana)
$5.00 per year membership

MonDak Historical and Arts Society
MonDak Heritage Center
PO Box 50
Sidney, MT 59270
(406) 482-3500

Powder River Historical Society
210 North Lincoln
PO Box 575
Broadus, MT 59317
(406) 436-2474
Jesse Barnhart, President

Richey Historical Society
Main Street
PO Box 218
Richey, MT 59259
(406) 773-5656
Betty B. Whiteman, Secretary-Treasurer
Hours: Mon, Wed & Fri (Memorial Day–Labor Day) 2:00–5:00

Rosebud County Historical Society
Museum
400 Woodrose
PO Box 430
Colstrip, MT 59323
Teresa Taylor, President
Pub. *RCHSM Newsletter*

Sun River Valley Historical Society
13847 Highway 200
Sun River, MT 59483
(406) 264-5572
Emma Toman, Agent
Hours: usually available
Pub. *SRVHS Newsletter*, annually (March)

Utica Museum and Historical Society
HC 81, Box 560
Hobson, MT 59452
(406) 423-5208
Barbara Twiford, Secretary
Hours: Memorial Day–Labor Day: 10:00–5:00
(local histories, artifacts of homestead era)
$3.00 per year membership

Wolf Point Area Historical Society
(200 Second Avenue, South—location)
PO Box 977 (mailing address)
Wolf Point, MT 59201-0977
(406) 653-1912 (Jun–Aug); (406) 653-1379 (Curator's home)
Alma Hall, Curator
Hours: Jun–Aug: 10:00–5:00

LDS Family History Centers

Billings
(406) 656-5559

Great Falls
(406) 453-1625

Helena
(406) 443-0713

Missoula
(406) 543-6148

Genealogical Societies

State Genealogical Society

Montana State Genealogical Society
PO Box 555
Chester, MT 59522
Pub. *Grains of Research*

Regional Genealogical Societies

Big Horn County Genealogical Society
PO Box 51
Hardin, MT 59034
Betty Whaley
("Good selection of research material for area")

Bitter Root Genealogical Society
Ravalli County Museum
205 Bedford, Old Courthouse
Hamilton, MT 59840

Broken Mountains Genealogical Society (Liberty County)
Liberty County Library
PO Box 261
Chester, MT 59522
(406) 759-5445 (Library)
Alice Shepherd, Corresponding Secretary
Hours: Library: Mon, Wed & Fri 8:00–12:00 & 1:00–5:00, Tue & Thur 1:00–5:00 & 7:00–9:00
Pub. *The Tri-County Searcher*, semiannually, $8.00 per year subscription
$10.00 per year membership for individuals, $15.00 per year membership for families

Butte Genealogical Society
1231 West Park Street
Butte, MT 59701
Vicki M. Miller
(Butte and southwest Montana)

Dawson County Tree Branches
PO Box 1275
Glendive, MT 59330-1275
(406) 365-4014
Rose Wyman, President
Pub. *The Tree Branch*, three times per
    year (annual current obituary index),
    $5.00 per year subscription
(maintains genealogy room at public
    library)
$6.00 per year membership; search:
    $2.00

Fort Assiniboine Genealogical Society
PO Box 321
Havre, MT 59501
(406) 265-4409
Bonnie Whittemore, President
Hours: Havre-Hill County Library: Mon–
    Thur 10:00–9:00, Fri 10:00–6:00, Sat
    12:00–5:00
Pub. *Smoke Signals*, quarterly, $4.00 per
    year subscription
$5.00 per year membership for
    individuals

Gallatin Genealogy Society
PO Box 1783
Bozeman, MT 59715
Hours: Tue & Thur 10:00–4:00 & 6:00–
    9:00
Pub. *Gallatin Trails*, quarterly, $2.00 per
    issue
$9.50 per year membership

Great Falls Genealogical Society
Paris Gibson Square
1400 First Avenue, North
Great Falls, MT 59401
(406) 727-3922
Larry D. Spicer, President
Hours: Tue–Fri 10:00–4:00, Tue–Fri
    (summer) 10:00–2:00, Sat 1:00–4:00
Pub. *Treasure State Lines*, quarterly; *The
    Falls Newsletter*, bimonthly
(Montana, Civil War, microform, CDs)
$20.00 per year membership for
    individuals, $25.00 per year
    membership for couples, $5.00 per
    year junior membership

Lewis and Clark Genealogical Society
(Mezzanine-Helena Public Library, 120
    South Last Chance Gulch, Helena, MT
    59601-4133—location)
PO Box 5313 (mailing address)
Helena, MT 59604
(406) 442-2380 (Library)
Eloyce Kockler, President
Hours: Tue–Thur 1:00–3:00 & 7:00–
    9:00, Sat 10:00–noon
Pub. *Faded Genes*, quarterly (March,
    June, September, December), $7.50
    per year subscription
$12.00 per year membership for
    individuals, $17.00 per year
    membership for families

Lewistown Genealogy Society, Inc.
701 West Main Street
Lewistown, MT 59457
Mary Ann Quiring, Quarterly Editor
Hours: Mon–Fri 1:00–4:00
Pub. *Central Montana Wagon Trails*,
    quarterly (February, May, August,
    November)
(Fergus County, Montana, census 1900–
    1920, census indexes, cemetery
    records, school census 1900–1920,
    taxpayers 1920, county history, most
    area newspapers on microfilm; records
    before 1920 include Judith Basin and
    Petroleum counties)
$15.00 per year membership, search:
    $5.00 plus 15¢ per page for copies

Miles City Genealogical Society
Miles City Public Library
1 South Tenth Street
Miles City, MT 59301
(406) 232-1496 (Library)
Reference/Research Librarian
Hours: Library: Mon 10:00–8:00, Tue &
    Thur 12:00–8:30, Wed 12:00–5:00, Fri
    10:00–5:00, Sat 11:00–5:00
$10.00 per year membership

Powell County Genealogical Society
912 Missouri Avenue
Deer Lodge, MT 59722

Root Diggers Genealogical Society
PO Box 249
Glasgow, MT 59230-0249
(406) 228-8507
E-mail: llind2326@aol.com
Lucille V. Lindgren, Secretary
Hours: 24
Pub. *Family History Newsletter*,
    quarterly
(Glasgow local research)
$12.00 per year membership (calendar
    year); research: will check local
    records for SASE and will make
    copies if payment is included

Western Montana Genealogical Society
PO Box 2714
Missoula, MT 59806-2714
Judith Field, Secretary
Hours: Missoula Public Library: Mon–
    Thur 10:00–9:00, Fri–Sat 10:00–6:00
Pub. *Western Montana Genealogical
    Society Newsletter*, nine times per year
    (monthly, September–May)
$11.00 per year membership for
    individuals (includes membership in
    Montana State Genealogical Society),
    $12.00 per year membership for
    families

Yellowstone Genealogy Forum
Parmly Billings Library
510 North Broadway
Billings, MT 59101
(406) 657-8258 (Reference Desk)

E-mail: mtheimer@imt.net
Myrle Theimer, President
Hours: Library: Tue–Thur 10:00–9:00,
    Fri–Sat 10:00–6:00, Sun 1:00–5:00
Pub. *The Gen-Bug News*, quarterly
$10.00 per year membership for
    individuals (beginning in September),
    $15.00 per year membership for
    families

Independent Publications and Miscellany

Fort Benton
711 21 Street, Apartment 114
Fort Benton, MT 59442
Joel F. Overholser, Historian
(card index on ancestry in Fort Benton)
search for SASE

The Last Leaf
1477 Highway 200 South
Glendive, MT 59330-9402
E-mail: boobear@midrivers.com
Sylvia Mickelson, Trust, Publisher;
    Margaret Basta, Editor
Pub. *The Last Leaf, Dawson County
    Historical & Genealogical Newsletter*,
    quarterly, $5.00 per year subscription

Montana Women's History Project
315 South Fourth Street, East
Missoula, MT 59801
(406) 728-3041

MtGenWeb
Part of U.S. GenWeb Project
E-mail: mt@usgenweb.com
http://www.imt.net/~corkykn/
    montana.htm
(links to other Montana resources)

Northwest Pioneer
(see Washington)

Tobacco Valley Historical Village
PO Box 301
Eureka, MT 59917
Barbara Larson, Board of History
    Chairman

NEBRASKA

Archives and Libraries with Holdings in Genealogy

State Archives and Library

Nebraska State Historical Society
Division of Library/Archives
(1500 R Street, Lincoln, NE 68508—
    location)
PO Box 82554 (mailing address)
Lincoln, NE 68501-2554
(402) 471-4771; (402) 471-4772; (402)
    471-4751; (402) 471-3600 FAX
E-mail: lanshs@inetnebr.com
Ann Billesbach, Head of Reference
    Services; Andrea I. Faling, Associate
    Director, Library/Archives
Hours: Mon–Fri 9:30–4:30, Sat 8:00–
    5:00, Sun 1:30–5:00 (closed state
    holidays and Sundays prior to a
    Monday holiday)
Pub. *Nebraska History*, quarterly;
    Historical Newsletter, monthly;
    Cornerstone, quarterly
$25.00 per year membership for
    individuals, $50.00 per year
    Supporting membership, $100.00 per
    year Contributing membership;
    $500.00 life membership

Nebraska Library Commission
(address withheld upon request)
http://www.nlc.state.ne.us/

Nebraska State Law Library
Statehouse, Third Floor South
PO Box 94926
Lincoln, NE 68502
(402) 471-3189

State Historical Societies

Nebraska State Historical Society
Division of Library/Archives
(1500 R Street, Lincoln, NE 68508—
    location)
PO Box 82554 (mailing address)
Lincoln, NE 68501-2554
(402) 471-4771; (402) 471-4772; (402)
    471-4751; (402) 471-3600 FAX
E-mail: lanshs@inetnebr.com
Ann Billesbach, Head of Reference
    Services; Andrea I. Faling, Associate
    Director, Library/Archives
Hours: Mon–Fri 9:30–4:30, Sat 8:00–
    5:00, Sun 1:30–5:00 (closed state
    holidays and Sundays prior to a
    Monday holiday)
Pub. *Nebraska History*, quarterly;
    Historical Newsletter, monthly;
    Cornerstone, quarterly

$25.00 per year membership for
    individuals, $50.00 per year
    Supporting membership, $100.00 per
    year Contributing membership,
    $500.00 life membership

Nebraska State Historical Society Room
Chadron State College
Chadron State Library
Chadron, NE 69337
Wayne Britt

City, County and Regional Archives and Libraries

Edith Abbott Memorial Library
Lue R. Spencer (DAR) and Ella Sprague
    Genealogical Collections
Second and Washington Streets
Grand Island, NE 68801

Alliance Knight Museum
(908 Yellowstone—location)
Drawer D (mailing address)
Alliance, NE 69301
(308) 762-2384
E-mail: alliance@btigate.com
Becci Thomas, Curator
Hours: 10:00–6:00
(compiling an extensive research library
    of area information)

Alliance Public Library
524 Box Butte Avenue
Alliance, NE 69301
(308) 762-1387; (308) 762-4148 FAX

Anna Palmer Museum
PO Box 403
York, NE 68467-0403
(402) 362-5549

Bayard Public Library
PO Box B
Bayard, NE 69334

Beatrice Public Library
100 North 16th Street
Beatrice, NE 68310-4100
(402) 223-3584; (402) 223-3913 FAX
E-mail: lriedesel@beatrice.lib.ne.us
Laureen Riedesel, Director
Hours: Mon–Thur 9:00–8:00, Fri–Sat
    9:00–6:00, Sun 2:00–5:00
("In addition to our own collection, we
    also have the Southeast Nebraska
    Genealogical Society and the
    Nebraska State Genealogical Society
    collections housed in our building.")

Beaver City Public Library
408 Tenth Street
Beaver City, NE 68926
(308) 268-4115
Hours: Mon & Fri 1:00–5:00, Wed 9:00–
    12:00 & 1:00–5:00, Thur 6:30–8:30,
    Sat 9:00–12:00

Big Springs Public Library
Big Springs, NE 69122

Blair Public Library
1665 Lincoln Street
Blair, NE 68008
Hours: Mon–Tue 10:00–5:30, Thur–Fri
    7:00–9:00

Bridgeport Public Library
722 Main
PO Box 940
Bridgeport, NE 69336
(308) 262-0326
Donna Nelson, Librarian
Hours: Tue–Fri 1:30–5:30

Broadwater Public Library
Broadwater, NE 69125

Burt County Museum
319 North 13th Street
PO Box 125
Tekamah, NE 68061-1415
(402) 374-1505
Bonnie Newell, Curator
Hours: Tue, Thur & Sat 1:00–5:00
Pub. *Burt County Museum Newsletter*,
    quarterly
("Our library includes cemetery listings
    and Tekamah newspapers 1800s–
    1900s.")
$6.00 per year membership; search:
    $10.00 per hour

Center for Great Plains Studies
(see Kansas)

Center for Great Plains Study
1214 Oldfather Hall
University of Nebraska
Lincoln, NE 68585
(402) 472-6058; (402) 472-0463
E-mail: gpq@unlinfo.unl.edu
Hours: Mon–Fri 8:00–4:30
Pub. *Great Plains Quarterly*, $15.00 per
    year subscription, $38.00 for two-year
    subscription
(Kansas, Montana, Nebraska, North
    Dakota, Oklahoma, South Dakota and
    Texas)

Chadron Public Library
Chadron, NE 69337

Chadron State College
Chadron State Library
Chadron, NE 69337

Chappell Public Library
PO Box 248
Chappell, NE 69129-0248

W. Dale Clark Library
Genealogy Department
215 South 15th Street
Omaha, NE 68102
(402) 444-4826 (History & Social
    Sciences)
Thomas Heenan, Head of History
    Department
Hours: winter: Mon–Fri 9:00–8:30, Sat
    9:00–5:30; summer: Mon & Wed–
    Thur 9:00–8:30, Tue & Fri–Sat 9:00–
    5:30

Columbus Public Library
2504 14th Street
Columbus, NE 68601
(402) 564-7116; (402) 563-3378 FAX
Robert Trautwein, Library Director
Hours: Mon–Thur 10:00–9:00, Fri
    10:00–5:00, Sat–Sun 1:30–5:00
(electronic obituary index of local
    newspaper, *Columbus Telegram*, from
    1970)

Cravath Memorial Library
PO Box 309
Hay Springs, NE 69347

Crawford Public Library
601 Second Street
Crawford, NE 69339

Creighton University
Carl M. Reinert/Alumni Memorial
    Library
2500 California Plaza
Omaha, NE 68178
(402) 280-2927; (402) 280-2435 FAX
E-mail: davids@creighton.edu
http://www.creighton.edu/

Crete Public Library
305 East 13th Street
PO Box 156
Crete, NE 68333
(402) 826-3809
Margaret Harding
Hours: Mon, Wed & Fri–Sat 10:00–5:30,
    Tue & Thur 10:00–7:30, Sun (Sept–
    May) 2:00–5:00
("We have many local records and work
    with the local genealogy group, but are
    not an 'official' genealogy group.")

Dalton Public Library
Dalton, NE 69131

Nancy Fawcett Memorial Library
Lodgepole, NE 69149

Gering Public Library
Gering, NE 69341

Gibbon Heritage Center
Court and Second
PO Box 27
Gibbon, NE 68840
(308) 468-5531
Avnelle Lauer, Secretary-Treasurer
Hours: first & second Sun 2:00–4:00,
    and by appointment
(Gibbon and Buffalo counties)

Gordon City Library
101 West Fifth Street
Gordon, NE 69343
(308) 282-1198
E-mail: gocili01@nd.org
Maria Kling, Director
Hours: Mon–Thur 2:00–8:00, Sat noon–
    6:00

Grand Island Public Library
211 North Washington
Grand Island, NE 68801

(308) 385-5333
Hours: Mon–Thur 10:00–9:00, Fri–Sat
    10:00–6:00, Sun 1:00–5:00

Hemingford Public Library
Hemingford, NE 69348

Holdrege Public Library
604 East Avenue
Holdrege, NE 68949

Jensen Memorial Library
443 North Kearney
Minden, NE 68959

**Kearney Public Library and
Information Center**
2020 First Avenue
Kearney, NE 68847
(308) 233-3282
Brenda Carroll, Director
Hours: Mon–Thur 9:00–9:00, Fri–Sat
    9:00–6:00

Kilgore Memorial Library
Sixth and Nebraska
York, NE 68467
(402) 362-3039
Hours: Mon–Thur 1:00–9:00, Fri 2:00–
    6:00, Sat 10:00–5:00

Kimball Public Library
208 South Walnut Street
Kimball, NE 69145

Lewellen Public Library
PO Box 58
Lewellen, NE 69147

Lexington Public Library
103 East Tenth Street
PO Box 778
Lexington, NE 68850
(308) 324-2151
Elberta Brummet, Assistant Director
Hours: Mon–Tue & Thur 10:00–8:30,
    Wed 10:00–6:00, Sat 10:00–3:30, Sun
    (winter) 2:00–5:00

Lincoln City Libraries
136 South 14th Street
Lincoln, NE 68508
(402) 441-8530
Rayma Shrader, Reference Department
Hours: Mon–Thur 9:00–9:00, Fri–Sat
    9:00–6:00, Sun 1:30–5:30
research: $1.00 plus 25¢ per page for
    copies

Lisco Library
Lisco, NE 69148

Lyman Public Library
Lyman, NE 69352

Merrick County Historical Museum
(211 E Street—location)
1111 17th Avenue (mailing address)
Central City, NE 68826
(308) 946-2867
Nancy B. Johnson, Historian
Hours: by appointment

Minatare Public Library
309 Main
PO Box 483
Minatare, NE 69356-0483
(308) 783-1414
Lana D. Hatcher, Head Librarian
Hours: Mon 9:00–noon, Mon & Wed
    1:30–4:30, Fri noon–6:00
("*Minatar Lake* and *Minatare Free Press*
    newspapers, along with books,
    magazines, cassettes, VHS, filmstrips,
    information")

Morrill Public Library
Morrill, NE 69358

**Museum Association of the
American Frontier**
(3 miles east of Chadron, on U.S. 20—
    location)
HC 74, Box 18 (mailing address)
Chadron, NE 69337
(308) 432-3843
Charles E. Hanson, Jr., Director
Pub. *Museum of the Fur Trade Quarterly*
("North American fur trade 1500–1900;
    emphasis is on objects as well as
    people.")
$6.00 per year membership; search fees:
    $10.00 per hour

Museum of Missouri River History
Brownville State Recreation Area
PO Box 38
Brownville, NE 68321
(402) 825-3341
Clay W. Kennedy, Curator
Hours: Memorial Day–Labor Day:
    10:00–5:00

Museum of the Great Plains
(see Oklahoma)

Nemaha Valley Museum, Inc.
Rt. 1, Box 43
Brock, NE 68320
Helen M. Nichols

Norfolk Public Library
308 Prospect Avenue
Norfolk, NE 68701
(402) 644-8711
Hours: Mon–Thur 10:00–9:00, Fri–Sat
    10:00–5:00, Sun (except holidays)
    1:30–4:30

North Platte Public Library
120 West Fourth Street
North Platte, NE 69101
(308) 535-8036
Hours: winter (Labor Day–Memorial
    Day): Mon–Thur 9:00–9:00, Fri–Sat
    9:00–6:00; summer (Memorial Day–
    Labor Day): Mon & Thur 9:00–9:00,
    Tue–Wed & Fri–Sat 9:00–6:00

Oshkosh Public Library
PO Box 140
Oshkosh, NE 69154-0140

Potter Public Library
333 Chestnut
PO Box 317
Potter, NE 69156
(308) 879-4345
Donna Aurich, Librarian
Hours: Wed 9:00–noon & 1:00–5:00, Sat
9:00–noon

Quivey Memorial Library
1449 Center Avenue
Mitchell, NE 69357

Ralston Public Library
7900 Park Lane
Ralston, NE 68127
(402) 331-7636; (402) 331-1168 FAX
E-mail: ralstlib@neoramp.com
Jan Gorman, Library Director
Hours: Mon–Thur 10:00–9:00, Fri–Sat
10:00–5:00
(houses the Nebraska Scottish Society's
library of over 100 Scottish items and
books on Scotland and Scottish
history, available on interlibrary loan;
very little on the history of Ralston,
vertical file folders of clippings,
archival documents and artifacts)

Reynolds Center
Stuhr Museum of the Prairie Pioneer
3133 West Highway 34
Grand Island, NE 68801
(308) 385-5316; (308) 385-5028 FAX
Russ Czaplewski, Historian
Hours: Mon–Fri 9:00–5:00
Pub. *Prairie Pioneer Press*, monthly
(Hall County settlement, especially
German settlers)

Rushville Public Library
PO Box 473
Rushville, NE 69360

Sac Museum Memorial Society
2510 Clay Street
Bellevue, NE 68005
(402) 292-2001

Scottsbluff Public Library
Scottsbluff, NE 69361

University of Nebraska
Archives and Special Collections
Department
South Love Library
Rooms 310–311
Lincoln, NE 68588-0410
(402) 472-2531
E-mail: infomail@unllib.unl.edu
http://iris.unl.edu

University of Nebraska
University Archives
University Library
Omaha, NE 68182
(402) 554-2362

Verdigre Heritage Museum
Verdigre, NE 68783

Wayne Public Library
410 Pearl
Wayne, NE 68787
(402) 375-3135; (402) 375-5772 FAX
Jolene Klein, Director
Hours: Mon–Fri 12:30–8:30, Sat 10:00–
6:00, Sun 2:00–5:00
(has *Wayne Herald* weekly from 1884 to
date with some exceptions; obituaries
for persons buried in Wayne County)

Lydia Bruun Woods Library
120 East 18th Street
Falls City, NE 68355
(402) 245-2913
Hours: Mon–Thur 12:00–8:00, Fri
12:00–6:00, Sat 11:00–4:00
no search fee, but most inquiries are
directed to the Tri-State Corners
Genealogical Society

Historical Societies—
Local and Regional

Adams County Historical Society
Hastings Museum
(1330 North Burlington Avenue,
Highway 281 at 14th Street—location)
PO Box 102 (mailing address)
Hastings, NE 68902
(402) 463-5838
Catherine Renschler, Director
Hours: Tue–Fri 9:00–5:00, Sat 10:00–
3:00
Pub. *Historical News*, bimonthly
$10.00 per year membership

Arthur County Historical Society
PO Box 134
Arthur, NE 69121-0134

Banner County Historical Society
General Delivery
Harrisburg, NE 69345
W. Stoddard

Blaine County Historical Society
HC 64, Box 4A
Brewster, NE 68821
(308) 547-2474
Alfred Schipporeit

Boone County Historical Society
Rt. 1, Box 135
Albion, NE 68620
Mr. O'Brien

Brown County Historical Society
(corner of Fifth Street and Old Highway
#7, one block north of Brock's Drive-
in [Café]—location)
339 North Ash (mailing address)
Ainsworth, NE 69210
(402) 387-2427
Marilyn A. Calver, Member
Hours: by appointment

$10.00 per year membership; research:
cost of photocopies plus postage

Brownville Historical Society
PO Box 1
Brownville, NE 68321
(402) 825-6001
Harold Davis, Vice President
Hours: May–Sept: 10:00–5:00
$8.00 per year membership

Buffalo County Historical Society
710 West 11th Street
PO Box 523
Kearney, NE 68847
(308) 234-3041; (308) 237-7858

Butler County Historical Society
Saint Joseph Villa
927 Seventh Street
David City, NE 68632
Mrs. C. Sargent

Cairo Roots Historical and
Genealogical Society
PO Box 308
Cairo, NE 68804
Opal Schnet
Hours: once a month

Cass County Historical Society
646 Main Street
Plattsmouth, NE 68048
(402) 296-4770
H. Margo Prentiss, Curator
Hours: Tue–Sat noon–4:00, Sun (Apr–
Oct) noon–4:00
Pub. *Newsletter*, quarterly
from $10.00 to $500.00 membership

Cedar County Historical Society
(Museum, 304 West Franklin—location)
PO Box 81 (mailing address)
Randolph, NE 68771
(402) 254-6597
Ernest Witte, President; Arnold
Anderson, Director
Hours: by appointment

Chase County Historical Society
(Chamfron, NE—location)
General Delivery (mailing address)
Imperial, NE 69033
(308) 882-5525
Anoma Hoffmeister
Hours: Mother's Day–Labor Day: 1:30–
4:30
$3.00 per year membership

Cherry County Historical Society
650 Essex Street
Valentine, NE 69201
(402) 376-2015
Marianne Beel, President

Cheyenne County Historical
Association
Cheyenne County Museum
Sixth and Jackson
PO Box 596
Sidney, NE 69162

(308) 254-2150
Hours: weekdays 1:00–4:00 (except Dec 25–Jan 1)

Cheyenne County Historical Society
PO Box 802
Sidney, NE 69162
Hours: Cheyenne County Museum, Sixth and Jackson Streets, Sidney, NE 69162: weekdays 1:00–4:00 (except Dec 25–Jan 1)

Chimney Rock Historical Society
Bayard Chamber of Commerce
PO Box 626
Bayard, NE 69334

Clarkson Historical Society
Clarkson, NE 68629
(402) 892-3629
Frances Hamernik, President

Clay County Historical Society
Inland, NE 68954-0218
(402) 463-8198
George Woolsey

Cozad Historical Society
503 Lake Avenue
Gothenburg, NE 69138
(308) 537-7217

Crawford Historical Society
127 Annin Street
Crawford, NE 69339

Cuming County Historical Society
780 North Holbrook Road
Coupeville, WA 98239-3111
James Konopik, Jr.

Custer County Historical Society
225 South Tenth Street
Broken Bow, NE 68822
(308) 872-2203
Mary Landkamer, Researcher
Hours: Mon–Fri 1:00–5:00
Pub. *Custer County Times*, semiannually
$15.00 per year membership

Dakota County Historical Society
PO Box 607
Dakota City, NE 68731
Lois Beermann, Secretary

Dawes County Historical Society Museum
(341 Country Club Road—location)
PO Box 1319 (mailing address)
Chadron, NE 69337
(308) 432-4999
Maggie Radcliffe, President; Belvadine Lecher, Curator
Hours: Mon–Sat 10:00–4:00, Sun & holidays 1:00–5:00
Pub. *Dawes County Historical Society Newsletter*, quarterly
(Dawes County historical items; extensive genealogical and historical research library)
$5.00 per year membership, $25.00 per year Colony membership, $100.00

Pioneer membership, $500.00 per year Homestead membership, $1,000.00+ Heritage membership; museum admission by donation; short queries for members

Dawson County Historical Society
Dawson County Museum
805 North Taft Street
PO Box 369
Lexington, NE 68850-0369
(308) 324-5340
Bob Wallace, Museum Director
Hours: Mon–Sat 9:00–5:00, Sun 1:00–5:00
Pub. *The Dawson County Banner*, quarterly
$7.50 per year membership for individuals, $10.00 per year membership for families, $15.00 per year Sustaining membership, $25.00 per year membership for businesses, $100.00 life membership, $150.00 joint life membership

Deuel County Historical Society
PO Box 324
Chappell, NE 69129
(308) 874-2865
Lester L. Becker, President

Dixon County Historical Society
PO Box 95
Allen, NE 68710-0095
Mrs. M. Greem

Dodge County Historical Society
1643 North Nye Avenue
PO Box 766
Fremont, NE 68025
(402) 721-4515; (402) 721-4515
Mary Hendrickson, Curator
Hours: Tue–Sun (Apr–Dec) 1:00–4:30
Pub. *Historical Society Newsletter*, bimonthly
(Fremont and Dodge County, Nebraska, history and information; Fremont City directories from 1891; Dodge County cemetery records)
$10.00 per year membership for individuals, $20.00 per year membership for families, $5.00 per year membership for students

Historical Society of Douglas County
(Library/Archives Center, Building 11A, Fort Omaha Campus, Metro Community College—location)
PO Box 11398 (mailing address)
Omaha, NE 68111-0398
(402) 451-1013; (402) 451-1394 FAX
E-mail: hsdc-lac@radiks.net
http://www.radiks.net/~hsdc-lac/
Roger L. Reeves, Director
Hours: Tue–Fri 10:00–4:00
Pub. *The Banner*, quarterly
$15.00 per year membership for individuals, $25.00 per year membership for families; $5.00 per day user fee for research center,

photocopies 35¢ per page, photographs $16.00 per 8" x 10" b&w print, $25.00 per color print; research: $12.00 per hour; search of database: $1.50 per minute plus 65¢ per kilobyte of information and 5¢ per printout page

Elkhorn Valley Historical Society
515 Queen City Boulevard
PO Box 1114
Norfolk, NE 68702-1114
Mary A. Voss, President
Pub. *Elkhorn Valley Historical Society Newsletter*, monthly
$10.00 per year membership for individuals, $20.00 per year membership for families, $7.50 per year membership for students or senior citizens, $25.00 per year Contributing membership, $50.00 per year Business and Professional membership; limited research done by EVHS library staff, send SASE for list of fees and services

Fillmore County Historical Society
633 North 11th
Geneva, NE 68361
Mrs. S. Ashby, Secretary

Franklin County Historical Society
Rt. 1, Box 157
Franklin, NE 68939
(308) 425-3030
Hours: Mon–Fri
("museum, genealogy, historical")

Furnas County Historical Society
401 Nebraska Avenue
PO Box 303
Arapahoe, NE 68922
(308) 962-5236
Weldon M. d'Allemand, Director
Hours: Sat (May–Sept) 2:00–5:00

Gage County Historical Society
Second and Court Street
PO Box 793
Beatrice, NE 68310-0793
(402) 228-1679
http://www4.infoanalytic.com/h/beatrice.html#gage
Kent Wilson, Administrator
Hours: Tue–Fri 9:00–noon & 1:00–5:00, Sat (Memorial Day–Labor Day) 9:00–noon & 1:00–5:00, Sun 1:30–5:00
Pub. *The Quarterly Express*, quarterly
$15.00 per year membership for individuals, $25.00 per year membership for families, $50.00+ per year Trailblazer membership (businesses included), $100.00+ per year Sodbuster membership, $250.00+ per year Homesteader membership

Historical Society of Garden County
(Second and Avenue G—location)
Rt. 1, Box 16 (mailing address)
Lewellen, NE 69147
(308) 772-4333
Mae Rose King, President

Hours: May 15–Aug: Mon–Sat 9:00–4:00, Sun 1:00–5:00
free admission

Garfield County Historical Society
737 H Street
PO Box 517
Burwell, NE 68823
(308) 346-5070

Genoa Historical Society
PO Box 425
Genoa, NE 68640-0425
A. Jarecke

Gothenburg Historical Society
520 Ninth Street
PO Box 153
Gothenburg, NE 69138
Virginia Hilton, President
Hours: summer, and by appointment
(local history and pony express history)
$5.00 per year membership

Grant County Historical Society
Grant County Courthouse
Hyannis, NE 69350
(308) 458-2226

Hamilton County Historical Society
Plainsman Museum
210 16th Street
Aurora, NE 68818
(402) 694-6531
Gwen Allen, Museum Director
Hours: Mon–Sat (Apr 1–Oct 31) 9:00–5:00, Mon–Sat (Nov 1–Mar 31) 1:00–5:00, Sun 1:00–5:00
Pub. *Plainsman News*, three times per year
$10.00 per year membership for individuals, $25.00 per year membership for families; research: usually $10.00-$20.00 depending on time required

Harlan County Historical Society
General Delivery
Orleans, NE 68966
Winnie Kuhl

Hay Springs Heritage Center
PO Box 236
Hay Springs, NE 69347

Hayes County Historical Society
General Delivery
Hayes Center, NE 69032
Lillian Fielding
SASE for information

High Plains Historical Society
423 Norris Avenue
McCook, NE 69001
(308) 345-3661
Donna Kanowicz

Hitchcock County Historical Society
313 East First Street
PO Box 511
Trenton, NE 69044
Angie Bowman, Director

Hours: Museum: Memorial Day weekend to Labor Day weekend: Thur & Sun 2:00–5:00
Pub. *Hitchcock County Historical Society Newsletter*, quarterly
$5.00 per year membership; genealogy research: $5.00 plus 20¢ per photocopy

Holt County Historical Society
401 East Douglas Street
O'Neill, NE 68763
(402) 336-2344
Carol Keyes, Curator
Hours: Mon–Thur 10:00–noon & 1:00–4:00
Pub. *Holt County Historical Society Newsletter*, quarterly
(over 3,000 family histories on site)
$8.00 per year membership, $10.00 Contributing membership, $100.00 life membership; search fee: $5.00 per hour plus copies and postage

Hooker County Historical Society
General Delivery
Mullen, NE 69152
Mrs. Glen Tompkins

Howard County Historical Society
823 Sherman Street
Saint Paul, NE 68873-1547
Florence Jacobsen

Humboldt Historical Society
734 Edwards Street
Humboldt, NE 68376
Mrs. H. D. Chilen

Jefferson County Historical Society
510 "D" Street
Fairbury, NE 68352

Johnson County Historical Society, Inc.
Third and Lincoln
Tecumseh, NE 68450
(402) 335-2671

Keya Paha County Historical Society
Star Rt. 4
Springview, NE 68778
(402) 497-2162
Betty Witter, Secretary-Director

Lincoln County Historical Museum and Society
Western Heritage Center
(2403 North Buffalo—location)
201 Circle Drive (mailing address)
North Platte, NE 69101
(308) 534-5640
Hours: Memorial Day–Labor Day: Mon–Sat 9:00–6:00, Sun 1:00–5:00; and by appointment
$10.00 per year membership

Lincoln/Lancaster Historical Society
Lincoln/Lancaster County Genealogical Society
PO Box 30055
Lincoln, NE 68503-0055
Pub. *Newsletter*, monthly
$7.00 per year membership

Logan County Historical Society
248 Main—Basement
PO Box 147
Stapleton, NE 69163
(308) 636-2461
Wilma Salisbury

Loup County Historical Society
(Fourth and Murry Streets—location)
PO Box 102 (mailing address)
Taylor, NE 68879
(308) 942-3403
Kevin Brown, President
Hours: summer weekends 1:00–5:00, and by appointment
$2.00 per year membership; search fee: $5.00 recommended donation

Madison County Historical Society
208 West Third Street
PO Box 708
Madison, NE 68748
(402) 454-3733
Carol Robertson, President
Hours: by appointment
(Madison County artifacts and history)
$3.00 per year membership for individuals, $5.00 per year membership for families

Mari Sandoz Heritage Society
Chadron State College
1000 Main Street
Chadron, NE 69337
(308) 432-6276
Dr. Donald E. Green, Dean, School of Liberal Arts
Hours: 8:00–4:30
Pub. *Mari Sandoz Heritage Society Newsletter*, three times per year; *Annual Distinguished Lecture* (monograph series)
$15.00 per year membership

Nance County Historical Society
(501 Broadway—location)
PO Box 10 (mailing address)
Fullerton, NE 68638-0010
(308) 536-2597
Henry Bigge, President
Hours: Sun (summer) 1:00–4:00, and by appointment
$2.50 per year membership for individuals, $10.00 per year membership for businesses, $75.00 lifetime membership for individuals

Niobrara Historical Society
Rt. 1, Box 24
Niobrara, NE 68760
Betty Swanson

North Central Nebraska Historical Society
General Delivery
Stuart, NE 68780
Lawrence Hamik

North Platte Historical Association, Inc.
(11th and J Streets, Oregon Trail Park— location)
PO Box 435 (mailing address)
Gering, NE 69341-0435
(308) 436-5411
Lillis E. Grassmick, Museum Director
Hours: Mon–Fri 8:30–5:00

Otoe County Historical Society
PO Box 175
Nebraska City, NE 68410
Sarah Whitten

Paradise Mills Historical Society
General Delivery
Waco, NE 68460
L. Murphy

Pawnee City Historical Society and Museum
(east edge on Highway 8—location)
1041 Fifth, Box 33 (mailing address)
Pawnee City, NE 68420
(402) 852-3121
Yvonne Dalluge, Treasurer
Hours: Apr–Oct: Tue–Fri 9:00–2:00, Sat 9:00–4:00, Sun 1:00–4:00
(alumni information, funeral cards, pictures, Nebraska and Pawnee County information)
search fee: $5.00 or more

Perkins County Historical Society
PO Box 731
Grant, NE 69140
Ruth Schumacher

Peru Historical Foundation
Fifth and California Street
PO Box 195
Peru, NE 68421
(402) 872-6875
Mary Ruth Wilson, President
Hours: Memorial Day–Labor Day: Sun 2:00–4:30
Pub. *Peru Historical Foundation News*, semiannually (spring and fall)
(Gage County books, city directories, cemetery lists)

Phelps County Historical Society
Holdrege Area Genealogy Club
(North on Highway 183, 1/2 mile— location)
PO Box 164 (mailing address)
Holdrege, NE 68949
(308) 995-5015 (Historical Society); (308) 995-6712 (President)
Sandra Slater, President of Historical Society and Librarian of Genealogy Club
Hours: weekdays 10:00–5:00, Sun 1:00– 5:00

Pub. *Phelps Helps*, quarterly
(specializes in Phelps County history and its residents)
$10.00 per year membership

Pierce County Historical Society
Gilman Park
104 East Willow
Pierce, NE 68767
(402) 329-6345
Greg Hoffman

Plains Historical Society
208 South Walnut
Kimball, NE 69145-0296
Betty Allen

Platte County Historical Society
PO Box 31
Columbus, NE 68601
Tim Terry, President

Polk County Museum Historical Society
Hawkeye Street
Osceola, NE 68651
(402) 747-7901
Ruth Lux, President and Director-Curator
Hours: Sun (1 Jun–1 Oct) 2:00–4:00, and by appointment

Ponca Historical Society
100 East Third Street
Ponca, NE 68770-0630
(402) 755-2202
Marilyn Mohr, President
Hours: Sat (Apr–Oct) 2:00–4:00, and by appointment
("Many scrapbooks on obituaries, weddings, schools, ads, and Ponca in general")
$2.50 per year membership for individuals, $10.00 per year Sustaining membership

Rock County Historical Society
PO Box 116
Bassett, NE 68714
(402) 684-3774
Clint Davis

Saline County, Nebraska, Historical Society, Inc.
1127 East Second Street
Friend, NE 68359-1113
(402) 947-2911
Norma Knoche, President
Hours: Sun 2:00–5:00, and by appointment
("Saline County and also Fillmore County for genealogy purposes.")
$1.00 per year membership; search: suggested donation with reply, depending on amount of information, time and expenses

Sarpy County Historical Society
2402 Clay Street
Bellevue, NE 68005
(402) 292-1880

Saunders County Historical Society-Museum
240 North Walnut
Wahoo, NE 68066-1858
(402) 443-3090 (Museum)
Raymond Screws, Curator
Hours: Museum: Nov–Mar: Tue–Fri 10:00–4:00; Apr–Oct: Tue–Sat 10:00– 4:00, Sun 1:30–4:30
Pub. *Saunders County Historical Society Newsletter*, four times per year
$7.50 per year membership for individuals, $10.00 per year membership for families, $150.00 life membership for individuals

Seven Valleys Historical Society
General Delivery
Callaway, NE 68825
(308) 836-2728
Wayne Hoag

Sheridan County Historical Society
East Highway 20
PO Box 274
Rushville, NE 69360
(308) 327-2961; (308) 327-2166 FAX
E-mail: rwbuchan@gpcom.net
Robert W. Buchan, Curator
Hours: Memorial Day–Labor Day: Mon–Fri 1:00–4:00

Sherman County Historical Society
433 South Seventh
PO Box 34
Loup City, NE 68853
Dorothy Richardson, Secretary
Hours: Sun 2:00–4:00, and by appointment
$5.00 per year membership, $7.50 per year membership for families

Sioux County Historical Society
General Delivery
Harrison, NE 69346
Hours: summer

Spalding Historical and Genealogical Society
Rt. 1, Box 13
Spalding, NE 68665
Mrs. L. J. Esch

Stanton County Historical Society
PO Box 149
Pilger, NE 68768-0146
Irene Wolverton

Table Rock Historical Society
General Delivery
Table Rock, NE 68447
Gordon Bethel

Thayer County Historical Society
Thayer County Museum
The Thayer County Historical and Genealogical Library Room
PO Box 387
Belvidere, NE 68315
(402) 768-7313; (402) 768-6845

Jacqueline J. Williamson, Curator of
Museum
Hours: May–Oct: Mon–Fri & Sun 1:00–
4:00, and by appointment

Thurston County Historical Society
(500 Ivan Street—location)
PO Box 624 (mailing address)
Pender, NE 68047
(402) 385-3210
Helen Johnson, Curator
Hours: Tue, Thur & Sat 8:00–4:00
two- and ten-year memberships
available, $100 life membership for
individuals, $150.00 double lifetime
membership

**Tobias Community Historical
Society**
(Main Street—location)
Rt. 1, Box 9 (mailing address)
Tobias, NE 68453
(402) 243-2356
Judith K. Rada, Treasurer
Hours: by appointment
(specializes in Saline County history)

Valley Community Historical Society
Valley Historical Museum
318 West Alexander
PO Box 685
Valley, NE 68064
(402) 359-2678 (Curator's home)
Mrs. Wayne Nielson, Curator and
Librarian

Valley County Historical Society
c/o Township Library
Ord, NE 68862
(308) 728-5256
Elsie Furtak, Secretary
Hours: Township Library: Mon–Sat
1:00–5:30, Tue & Thur 7:00–9:00;
meetings third Tue 7:30
("Our historical Society is inactive; no
museum; we do answer family
research inquiries")

**Washington County Historical
Association/Museum**
102 North 14th Street
PO Box 25
Fort Calhoun, NE 68023
(402) 468-5740
Agnes L. Smith, Curator
Hours: Mid-Mar to mid-Dec: Wed–Fri
8:30–4:30, Sat–Sun 1:30–4:30
Pub. *Washington County Historical
Association Newsletter*, quarterly
(spring, summer, fall, winter)
$5.00 per year membership

Wayne County Historical Society
Seventh and Lincoln Streets
PO Box 408
Wayne, NE 68787
(402) 375-3885
Leon Meyer, Treasurer

Webster County Historical Museum
721 West Fourth Avenue
PO Box 464
Red Cloud, NE 68970
(402) 746-2444
Helen Mathew, Director
Hours: Apr–Nov: daily 1:00–5:00; and
year-round by appointment
small search fee, varies with category of
need

**Weeping Water Valley Historical
Society**
Weeping Water, NE 68463
(402) 267-5447

LDS Family History Centers

Lincoln
(402) 423-4561

Omaha
(402) 393-7641

Papillion
(402) 339-0461

Genealogical Societies

State Genealogical Society

Nebraska State Genealogical Society
(Beatrice Public Library, 100 North 16th
Street, Beatrice, NE 68310—library
location
Rt. 2, Box 28, Exeter, NE 68351—NSGS
Librarian's location)
PO Box 5608 (mailing address)
Lincoln, NE 68505-0608
(402) 266-8881 (NSGS Librarian)
http://www.fgs.org/~fgs/soc0371.htm
Rose Marie Hulse, NSGS Librarian
Hours: Library: Mon–Thur 9:00–8:00,
Fri–Sat 9:00–6:00, Sun 2:00–5:00
Pub. *Ancestree*, quarterly; *The New Brass
Key Newsletter*, bimonthly
$15.00 per year membership

Regional Genealogical Societies

Adams County Genealogical Society
PO Box 424
Hastings, NE 68901
(402) 463-5838
Hours: Tue–Fri 9:30–5:00, Sat 10:00–
3:30
Pub. *Leafy Branches*, quarterly
$10.00 per year membership

**Boone-Nance County Genealogical
Society**
PO Box 231
Belgrade, NE 68623
(308) 358-0836
LaVerna Sauser, President
Hours: meetings at Boone County
Courthouse, Albion, NE
Pub. *The Scout*, quarterly
$8.00 per year membership; research:
$5.00 initial fee, maximum $5.00 per
hour plus 50¢ each for photocopies,
except $2.50 for a single marriage
license copy or $5.00 for three

Cairo Roots (Hall County)
PO Box 326
Cairo, NE 68824

**Cairo Roots Historical and
Genealogical Society**
PO Box 308
Cairo, NE 68804
Opal Schnet
Hours: once a month

Cass County Genealogy Club
1116 Third Avenue
Plattsmouth, NE 68048

Chase County Genealogical Society
PO Box 303
Imperial, NE 69033

**Cheyenne County Genealogical
Society**
Cheyenne County Historical Society
PO Box 802
Sidney, NE 69162
Joyce Luce, President
Hours: Cheyenne County Museum, Sixth
and Jackson Streets, Sidney, NE
69162: daily 1:00–4:00 (except Dec
25–Jan 1)
Pub. *Cheyenne County Genealogical
Newsletter*, semiannually
$10.00 per year membership; search fee:
$5.00 plus cost of copies

Cozad Genealogy Club
Cozad City Library
910 Meridian
Cozad, NE 69130
Norma Beans, President
Hours: meetings first Tue 7:30

Dakota County Genealogical Society
101 West Colonial Drive, Route 2
South Sioux City, NE 68776
Jody K. Boyd, President

**Eastern Nebraska Genealogical
Society**
PO Box 541
Fremont, NE 68025-0521
(402) 721-9553
Claire Mares, Editor
Hours: by appointment only
Pub. *Roots and Leaves*, quarterly;
Newsletter, monthly

$12.00 per year membership

Fillmore County Genealogical Society
Rt. 2, Box 28
Exeter, NE 68351
(402) 266-8881
$5.00 per year membership

Flatwater Genealogical Society
PO Box 373
Gibbon, NE 68840
(308) 468-5656; (308) 468-6142
Evelyn Vohland

Fort Kearney Genealogical Society
(Kearney Public Library and Information Center, 2020 First Avenue—library location)
PO Box 22 (mailing address)
Kearney, NE 68847
(308) 233-3282 (Library)
Hours: Library: Mon–Thur 9:00–9:00, Fri–Sat 9:00–6:00
Pub. *Buffalo Chips*, quarterly
$10.00 per year membership

Frontier County Genealogical Society
PO Box 289
Curtis, NE 69025
Mrs. Larry Sinn

Furnas County Genealogical Society
Beaver City Public Library
408 Tenth Street
PO Box 391
Beaver City, NE 68926-0391
(308) 268-4115 (Library); (308) 268-2641 (Society Librarian)
Eula Brown, Genealogical Society Librarian
Hours: Library: Mon & Fri 1:00–5:00, Wed 9:00–12:00 & 1:00–5:00, Thur 6:30–8:30, Sat 9:00–12:00; collection open by appointment with Society Librarian
Pub. *Furnas County Genealogical Society Newsletter*, quarterly
(Furnas County marriages, obituaries, family histories)
$5.00 per year membership; search: $5.00 per hour

Greater Omaha Genealogical Society
PO Box 4011
Omaha, NE 68104
Steve Hutchens
Hours: W. Dale Clark Library
Pub. *Westward into Nebraska*, ten times per year; *Remains to Be Found*
$15.00 per year membership

Greater York Area Genealogical Society
Kilgore Memorial Library
Sixth and Nebraska
York, NE 68467
(402) 363-2620
Ila Christensen, President

Hours: Library: Mon–Thur noon–9:00, Fri noon–5:00, Sat 10:00–5:00, Sun 2:00–5:00
Pub. *Newsletter—Greater York Area Genealogical Society*, quarterly
$2.00 per year membership for individuals, $3.50 per year membership for couples; search: $5.00 per hour plus cost of copies

Holdrege Area Genealogy Club
Phelps County Historical Society
(1 mile north of Holdrege on Highway 183—location)
PO Box 164 (mailing address)
Holdrege, NE 68949
(308) 995-5015 (Historical Society); (308) 995-6712 (President)
E-mail: rs.55453@navix.net
http://www.4w.com/pages/psimpson/phelpsgen.html
Sandra Slater, President of Genealogy Club
Hours: weekdays 10:00–5:00, Sun 1:00–5:00
Pub. *Phelps Helps*, quarterly
(specializes in Phelps County history and its residents; Nebraska federal and state censuses, Phelps County marriage records, Camp Atlanta P.W.W. German Archives)
$10.00 per year membership in the U.S., $15.00 per yearmembership outside the U.S.; research: $5.00 per hour plus photocopy costs and postage

Hooker County Genealogical Society
(Hooker County Library basement—location)
PO Box 280 (mailing address)
Mullen, NE 69152
(308) 546-2458; (308) 546-2756
Betty Fletcher Brown, President; Virginia Ericksen, Librarian
Hours: by appointment
Pub. *Hooker County Genealogical Quarterly*
("newspaper clippings from local newspapers of birth, deaths and marriages; alphabetical 3x5 card file of abstracts taken from local newspaper giving pertinent genealogical data")
$2.50 per year membership; search fee: $4.00 for original search, $4.00 per hour for extended search, plus $1.00 per photocopy

Jefferson County Genealogical Society
PO Box 163
Fairbury, NE 68352-0163
http://www.dsenter.com/ne/jefferson/jcgs1.html
Brenda Busing, President
Pub. *The Pioneer Trail*, quarterly
$9.00 per year membership; queries

Lexington Genealogical Society
Lexington Public Library
103 East Tenth Street
PO Box 778
Lexington, NE 68850
(308) 324-2151
John E. Wallace, President
Hours: Library: Mon–Tue & Thur 10:00–8:30, Wed 10:00–6:00, Sat 10:00–3:30, Sun (winter) 2:00–5:00
Pub. *Dawson County Genealogical Newsletter*, three times per year (winter, summer and fall)
$5.00 per year subscription

Lexington Genealogy Club
PO Box 66
Lexington, NE 68850

Lincoln/Lancaster County Genealogical Society
Lincoln/Lancaster Historical Society
PO Box 30055
Lincoln, NE 68503-0055
Pub. *Newsletter*, monthly
$7.00 per year membership

Madison County Genealogical Society
PO Box 1031
Norfolk, NE 68702-1031
Lottie Klein, President
Pub. *Quarterly*
$6.00 per year membership

North Central Nebraska Genealogical Society
PO Box 376
O'Neill, NE 68763-0376

North Platte Genealogical Society
PO Box 1452
North Platte, NE 69101
Hours: North Platte Public Library
Pub. *Railroad Ties*, quarterly
$8.00 per year membership

Northeastern Nebraska Genealogical Society (NENGS)
PO Box 169
Lyons, NE 68038-0169
Maxine Sandquist, Vice President
Pub. *NENGS Notes*, quarterly
(serves Burt County and also research queries in regard to Cuming and Thurston counties)
$10.00 per year membership (beginning September 1)

Northern Antelope County Genealogical Society
PO Box 56
Orchard, NE 68764
(402) 893-4565
Dorothy Zimmerman, President
$5.00 per year membership

Northern Nebraska Genealogical Society
PO Box 362
O'Neill, NE 68763

Northwest Genealogical Society
PO Box 6
Alliance, NE 69301-0006
(308) 762-3677
Neva Lewis, Treasurer
Pub. *Wagoner Journal*, semiannually,
$5.00 per issue
$12.50 per year membership

Nuckolls County Genealogy Society
PO Box 324
Superior, NE 68978

Perkins County Genealogical Society
PO Box 418
Grant, NE 69140
Mrs. Glen Keller

Plains Genealogical Society
Kimball Public Library
208 South Walnut Street
Kimball, NE 69145
Pub. *Newsletter of the Plains
Genealogical Society*
$5.00 per year membership

Platte Valley Kin Seekers
Columbus Area Genealogical Society
(Platte County Historical Museum, 2916
16th Street—location)
PO Box 153 (mailing address)
Columbus, NE 68601
(402) 564-5829; (402) 564-0644; (402)
564-3401
Frances Edwards, President; Kathirine
Smith, Treasurer
Hours: by appointment
Pub. *Quarterly*
$8.00 per year membership

**Prairie Pioneer Genealogical Society,
Inc.**
PO Box 1122
Grand Island, NE 68802
(308) 384-3218
Ruth McClurkin, President
Pub. *Prairie Pioneer Genealogical
Society* (Hall County), quarterly
$12.00 per year membership for
individuals, $15.00 per year
membership for families

**Ravenna Genealogical Society
(Buffalo County)**
105 Alba Street
Ravenna, NE 68869
Mrs. Robert Johnsten

Saline County Genealogical Society
PO Box 24
Crete, NE 68333
Pub. *County Lines*, quarterly, $2.50 per
issue
$10.00 per year membership

**Saunders County Genealogical
Seekers**
c/o Saunders County Historical Society-
Museum
240 North Walnut
Wahoo, NE 68066-1858
(402) 443-3090 (Museum)
Marlene McDonald, President
Hours: meetings third Tue (except
summer) evenings
Pub. *Newsletter*, bimonthly
$5.00 per year membership; research:
donation to microfilm fund, plus
copies and postage

Seward County Genealogical Society
(616 Bradford, basement of the Seward
Civic Center—location)
PO Box 72 (mailing address)
Seward, NE 68434
(402) 532-7635 (Editor)
Alta Krasser, Editor
Hours: Tue 10:00–4:00; meetings at
Seward Civic Center: third Tue 1:30
Pub. *The Log*, quarterly (January, April,
July, September)
$6.00 per year membership for
individuals (includes *The Log*),
however requests an additional
donation of $2.50 for postage;
research: $5.00 per surname

**South Central Nebraska
Genealogical Society**
c/o Jensen Memorial Library
443 North Kearney
Minden, NE 68959
Ms. Jerry M. Morris, Editor
Hours: Mon–Wed 11:00–8:00, Thur–Fri
11:00–5:30, Sat 10:00–4:00
Pub. *Leaves From Our Family Tree*,
quarterly
$7.50 per year membership

**Southeast Nebraska Genealogical
Society**
(Beatrice Public Library, 100 North 16th
Street—library location)
PO Box 562 (mailing address)
Beatrice, NE 68310
Pub. *Homesteader*, quarterly
$10.00 per year membership

**Southwest Nebraska Genealogical
Society**
(McCook Community College, 1205
East Third, Tipton Hall, Room 2—
location)
PO Box 156 (mailing address)
McCook, NE 69001
(308) 345-1738; (308) 345-4563
Hours: by appointment
Pub. *Ancestors Unlimited*, quarterly
(specializes in Red Willow, Hitchcock,
Hayes, and Frontier counties)
$12.00 per year membership for
individuals within 100 miles, $13.00
per year membership for couples,
$6.00 per year associate membership;

free queries; search fee: $5.00 per hour
plus cost of copies, SASE, and
mileage if applicable

**Spalding Historical and
Genealogical Society**
Rt. 1, Box 13
Spalding, NE 68665
Mrs. L. J. Esch

Thayer County Genealogical Society
Thayer County Museum
The Thayer County Historical and
Genealogical Library Room
PO Box 387
Belvidere, NE 68315
(402) 768-7313; (402) 768-6845
Jacqueline J. Williamson, Curator of
Museum
Hours: May–Oct: Mon–Fri & Sun 1:00–
4:00, and by appointment

Thayer Genealogical Society
345 Ninth Street
Hebron, NE 68370
Carol Burd

**Thomas County Genealogical
Society**
PO Box 136
Thedford, NE 69166
Mrs. Calvin E. Jones

**Tri-State Corners Genealogical
Society**
c/o Lydia Bruun Woods Library
120 East 18th Street
Falls City, NE 68355
(402) 245-2913 (Library); (402) 245-
5484
Dorothy Lewis
Hours: Library: Mon–Thur 12:00–8:00,
Fri 12:00–6:00, Sat 11:00–4:00
$5.00 per year membership for
individuals, $7.50 per year
membership for couples

Valley County Genealogical Society
619 South Tenth Street
Ord, NE 68862
(308) 728-3012
Patricia J. Tures, Researcher
Hours: Mon–Sat 1:00–5:30
(local families and history)

**Washington County Genealogical
Society**
Blair Public Library
1665 Lincoln Street
Blair, NE 68008
(402) 426-3617 (Library)
Hours: Library: Mon–Thur 10:00–5:00
& 6:00–8:00, Fri–Sat 10:00–4:00;
meetings: first Tue (Jan–Nov)
research for contribution

**Rebecca Winters Genealogical
Society**
PO Box 323
Scottsbluff, NE 69363-0323
Carole Tucker, Researcher

Pub. *Trail Seekers*, quarterly
(local records copied and indexed; Scotts
Bluff, Banner and Morrill counties)
$6.00 per year membership (beginning 1
June); free queries formembers; basic
search of indexes for SASE

Genealogical Society of York County
Rt. 1, Box 5
York, NE 68467
Carol McKenzie

Independent Publications and Miscellany

NeGenWeb
Part of U.S. GenWeb Project
E-mail: ne@usgenweb.com
http://www.rootsweb.com/~negenweb
(links to other Nebraska resources)

Western Heritage Society
801 South Tenth Street
Omaha, NE 68108

NEVADA

Archives and Libraries with Holdings in Genealogy

State Archives and Library

Nevada State Library and Archives
Division of Archives and Records
100 North Stewart Street
Carson City, NV 89701-4285
(702) 687-5210; (702) 687-8330 FAX
E-mail: jmkintop@clan.lib.nv.us
http://www.clan.lib.nv.us
Guy Louis Rocha, State Archives and
Records Administrator; Jeffrey M.
Kintop, State Archives Manager
Hours: Mon–Fri 8:00–5:00
research fee: $15.00 for Nevada
residents, $20.00 per hour for non-
residents

State Historical Societies

Nevada Historical Society
1650 North Virginia Street
Reno, NV 89503
(702) 688-1190
Lee Mortensen, Librarian
Hours: Tue–Sat noon–4:00
Pub. *Nevada Historical Society
Quarterly*
(Nevada and the Great Basin; "we are
not a genealogical library, but we do
have a lot of local history material.")
$25.00 per year membership

**Nevada State Museum and
Historical Society**
Department of Museums and History
700 Twin Lakes Drive
Las Vegas, NV 89107
(702) 486-5205
http://www.clan.lib.nv.us/docs/mus-
lv.htm
David Millman, Curator
Hours: Mon–Fri 8:30–4:30
$25.00 per year membership

Nevada State Museum
Division of Museums and History
600 North Carson Street
Carson City, NV 89701
(702) 687-4810; (702) 687-4168 FAX
Scott Miller, Administrator; Judy
Hendrix, Acting Director; Denise Sins,
Management Assistant II
Hours: Apr–Oct: 9:00–5:30; Nov–Mar:
8:30–4:30
Pub. *Nevada State Museum Newsletter*,
bimonthly
(history, geology, former U.S. mint,
ghost town, mine replica)

$25.00 per year membership for
individuals, $35.00 per year
membership for families

City, County and Regional Archives and Libraries

**Churchill County Museum and
Archives**
1050 South Maine Street
PO Box 1937
Fallon, NV 89406
(702) 423-3677 (Museum); (702) 423-
3662 FAX
Jane Pieplow, Museum Director/Curator
Hours: Jan–March: Mon–Sat 10:00–4:00,
Sun noon–4:00; Apr–Dec: Mon–Sat
10:00–5:00, Sun noon–5:00
Pub. *In Focus*, annually

Clark County Heritage Museum
1830 South Boulder Highway
Henderson, NV 89015
(702) 455-7955; (702) 455-7948 FAX
http://www.co.clark.nv.us
Mark Ryzdynski, Museum Administrator
Hours: Mon–Sun 9:00–4:30
admission: $1.50 for adults, $1.00 for
senior citizens and children

**Desert Research Institute—
Quaternary Sciences Center**
7010 Dandini Boulevard
PO Box 60220
Reno, NV 89506
(702) 673-7303

**Mojave River Valley Museum
Association**
(see California)

Northeastern Nevada Museum
1515 Idaho Street
PO Box 2550
Elko, NV 89801
(702) 738-3418

University of Nevada, Las Vegas
James R. Dickinson Library
Special Collections Department
4505 Maryland Parkway
Las Vegas, NV 89154-7010
(702) 895-3850 FAX
E-mail: michelp@nevada.edu
http://www.nscee.edu/unlv/libraries/
services/speccol/sc.html

University of Nevada, Reno
Special Collections Department
University Library/322
Reno, NV 89557-0044
(702) 784-6538
http://www.unr.edu/~specoll/index.html
Hours: Mon–Fri 8:00–5:00, Sat (Sept to
mid-Dec & Feb to mid-May) 1:00–
5:00

("Nevada and the Great Basin history, includes books, photos, maps and manuscripts; Great Basin Indians and women in the trans-Mississippi West")

Historical Societies— Local and Regional

Central Nevada Historical Society and Museum
Logan Field Road
PO Box 326
Tonopah, NV 89049
(702) 482-9676; (702) 482-5423 FAX
William J. Metscher, President
Hours: Apr–Sept: 9:00–5:00; Oct–Mar: 11:00–5:00
Pub. *Central Nevada's Glorious Past*, semiannually (May and November)
(central Nevada history of Nye and Esmeralda counties)
$15.00 per year membership

North Central Nevada Historical Society
Maple Avenue and Jungo Road
PO Box 819
Winnemucca, NV 89445
(702) 623-2912

Northeastern Nevada Historical Society
Northeastern Nevada Museum
1515 Idaho Street
PO Box 2550
Elko, NV 89801
Pub. *Northeastern Nevada Historical Society Quarterly*
$10.00 per year membership

Washoe County Historical Society
629 Jones Street
Reno, NV 89503

LDS Family History Centers

Boulder City
(702) 293-3304

Carson City
(702) 884-2064

Henderson
(702) 566-8190

Las Vegas
(702) 382-9695

Reno
(702) 826-1130

Genealogical Societies

State Genealogical Society

Nevada State Genealogical Society
PO Box 20666
Reno, NV 89515
Pub. *Nevada State Genealogical Society Newsletter*, monthly
$7.00 per year membership

Regional Genealogical Societies

Carson City Genealogical Society
1509 Sharon Drive
Carson City, NV 89701
Michael Wittmuss

Clark County Nevada Genealogical Society (CCNGS)
PO Box 1929
Las Vegas, NV 89125-1929
(702) 458-5540; (702) 225-5838 voice mail
Helen Smith, Editor
Hours: meetings: third Thur 7:00 P.M.– 9:00 P.M.
Pub. *The Prospector*, quarterly (January, April, July, October), $11.00 per year subscription
$16.00 per year membership for individuals, $19.00 per year membership for families, $200.00 life membership for individuals, $300.00 life membership for families; three free queries per issue for members, $1.00 per query per issue for non-members; research: $10.00

Humboldt County Genealogical Society
Humboldt County Library
85 East Fifth Street
Winnemucca, NV 89445

Northeastern Nevada Genealogical Society
Willow and College Parkway
Elko, NV 89801
Mrs. Primeaux, Archivist
Pub. *Chart and Quill*, quarterly

Town of Round Mountain, Nevada Genealogical Group
PO Box 330
Round Mountain, NV 89045

Independent Publications and Miscellany

NvGenWeb
Part of U.S. GenWeb Project
E-mail: nv@usgenweb.com
http://www.rootsweb.com/~nvgenweb/ nvstate.htm
(links to other Nevada resources)

NEW HAMPSHIRE

Archives and Libraries with Holdings in Genealogy

State Archives and Library

New Hampshire Division of Records Management and Archives
Department of State
71 South Fruit Street
Concord, NH 03301-2410
(603) 271-2236; (603) 271-2272 FAX
E-mail: fmevers@lilac.nhsl.lib.nh.us
Frank C. Mevers, Ph.D., Director and
    State Archivist
Hours: Mon–Fri 8:00–4:30
(census records: 1732, 1744, 1767, 1776,
    1880; court records: Inferior Court of
    Common Pleas to 1771, Rockingham
    County Court Records, 19th-century
    name change index; deed records: 224
    volumes to about 1824; military
    records: French and Indian War
    papers, Revolutionary War rolls, Civil
    War, Spanish-American War; petitions
    to the Executive and Council and to
    the General Court; probate records to
    1771; town papers, vital records)

New Hampshire State Library
20 Park Street
Concord, NH 03301-6314
(603) 271-6823 (Genealogy Desk); (603)
    271-6826 FAX
E-mail: tepare@lilac.nhsl.lib.nh.us
http://webster.state.nh.us/nhsl
Hours: Mon–Fri 8:00–4:30
Pub. *Genealogical Sources in New
    Hampshire*, irregularly (updated every
    two or three years), $1.00
(New Hampshire resources, including
    index to early town records, census
    indexes, town histories, family
    genealogies, etc.)

State Historical Societies

Association of Historical Societies of New Hampshire
14 Ironwood Lane
Atkinson, NH 03811-2706
Mrs. P. M. Ilsley, Corresponding
    Secretary
Hours: meetings: fourth Sat 10:00–3:00
Pub. *The Associate*, four times per year
    (April, June, August, October)
(includes most of the historical societies
    in New Hampshire)
$5.00 per year membership for
    individuals, $10.00 per year
    membership for societies

New Hampshire Division of Historical Resources
PO Box 2043
Concord, NH 03301
(603) 271-3483
R. Stuart Wallace, Ph.D., Director/State
    Historic Preservation Officer
(not genealogical)

New Hampshire Historical Society
30 Park Street
Concord, NH 03301-6384
(603) 271-2236; (603) 224-0463 FAX
E-mail: nhhslib@aol.com
http://newww.com/org/nhhs/
William Copeley, Librarian
Hours: Tue–Sat 9:30–5:00
Pub. *New Hampshire Historical Society
    Newsletter*, quarterly; *Historical New
    Hampshire*, quarterly
$30.00 per year membership; research:
    $20.00 per hour

City, County and Regional Archives and Libraries

Barrington Public Library
Community Building, Star Route
(Province Lane)
Barrington, NH 03825
(603) 664-9715
Hours: Mon & Wed 10:00–4:30 & 7:00–
    9:00, Tue & Thur–Fri 10:00–4:30, Sun
    2:00–4:30

G. H. Bixby Memorial Library
52 Main Street
Francestown, NH 03043

Bridge Memorial Library
Main Street
Walpole, NH 03608
(603) 756-3308 (Librarian/Historian)
Virginia H. Putnam
Hours: Wed & Sat 2:00–4:00, Sun (Jun–
    Sept) 2:00–4:00, and by appointment

Canterbury Shaker Village
288 Shaker Road
Canterbury, NH 03224

Conant Public Library
PO Box 6
Winchester, NH 03470
(603) 239-4331

Concord Public Library
45 Green Street
Concord, NH 03301
(603) 225-8670
Hours: winter: Mon–Wed 9:30–8:30,
    Thur–Sat 9:30–5:30, Sun 1:00–5:00;
    summer: Mon–Tue 9:30–8:30, Wed–
    Fri 9:30–5:30, Sat 9:30–2:00
(Concord history collection)

Connecticut Valley Historical Museum
(see Massachusetts)

Conway Public Library
Henney History Room
Main Street
PO Box 2100
Conway, NH 03818
(603) 447-5552; (603) 447-6921 FAX
E-mail: conwaypl@ncla.net
Margaret Marschner, Library Director
Hours: Mon–Thur 10:30–8:30, Fri–Sat
    10:30–5:30
(local history, town reports, family
    genealogies of the area: Androscoggin
    Valley, Brownfield, Gorham,
    Fryeburg, Saco and Biddeford,
    Limington, Old Kittery, and
    Parsonfield, Maine; Albany, Antrim,
    Bethlehem, Carroll County, Chester
    and Alburn, Concord, Coos County,
    Conway, Dover, Dublin, Dunbarton,
    Dunstable, Durham, Derry, Eaton,
    Freedom, Jackson (Gilman's
    Location), Henniker, Jefferson, Keene,
    Laconia, Lancaster, Londonderry,
    Madison, Manchester, Orford,
    Pembroke, Peterborough, Portsmouth,
    Randolf, Stratham, Tamworth,
    Waterville Valley, etc.)

Cook Memorial Library
93 Main Street
PO Box 249
Tamworth, NH 03886
(603) 323-8510; (603) 323-2077 FAX
Betty Parker, Librarian
Hours: Mon 10:00–noon, Tue–Wed
    2:00–8:00, Sat 10:00–2:00

Dartmouth College
Baker Memorial Library
Hinman Box 6025
Hanover, NH 03755-3590
(603) 646-2560 (Reference); (603) 646-
    2037 (Special Collections)
E-mail:
    baker.library.reference@dartmouth.edu
http://www.dartmouth.edu/
Robert D. Jaccaud, Genealogy
    Bibliographer; Anne M. Ostendarp,
    Archivist
Hours: Reference: Mon–Fri 8:00 A.M.–
    10:00 P.M., Sat 9:00–6:00, Sun 1:00–
    10:00 (hours change); Special
    Collections: Mon–Fri 8:00–4:30

Dover Public Library
73 Locust Street
Dover, NH 03820
(603) 743-6050
Carolyn Tremblay, Reference Librarian
Hours: Mon–Wed 9:00–8:30, Thur–Fri
    9:00–5:30, Sat (winter) 9:00–5:00, Sat
    (summer) 9:00–1:00
("Due to staffing limitations, we are
    unable to provide information by
    telephone or mail.")

Exeter Public Library
10 Chestnut Street
Founders Park
Exeter, NH 03833

(603) 772-3101
Pamela Gjettum, Head Librarian; Nancy
   C. Merrill, Reference Librarian
Hours: Mon–Thur 10:00–8:00, Fri–Sat
   10:00–5:00

George Gamble Library
(Route 104—location)
R.F.D. (mailing address)
Danbury, NH 03230

Gay-Kimball Public Library
10 South Main Street
PO Box 837
Troy, NH 03465
(603) 242-7743 phone & FAX
E-mail: troylibrary@top.monad.net
Darcy Doyle, Director
Hours: Tue–Thur 1:30–7:30, Sat 11:00–
   3:00

Harold Gilman Historical Museum
PO Box 428
Alton, NH 03809
A. Haase

Haynes Memorial Library
567 Washburn Road
Alexandria, NH 03222
(603) 744-8987

Keene Public Library
Wright Room
60 Winter Street
Keene, NH 03431
(603) 352-0157
David Howlett, Reference Librarian
Hours: Mon–Thur 9:00–9:00, Fri 9:00–
   6:00, Sat (winter) 9:00–5:00, Sat
   (summer) 9:00–1:00
(emphasis on New Hampshire genealogy
   and history; much of the Wright Room
   collection has been moved to the
   Historical Society of Cheshire County)

Keene State College
Mason Library
Preston Collection
Keene, NH 03431
(603) 352-1909, ext. 248
Robert J. Madden
Hours: various, call ahead

Laconia Public Library
695 Main Street
Laconia, NH 03246
(603) 524-4775
Betty Derby

Lane Memorial Library
2 Academy Avenue
Hampton, NH 03842-2280
(603) 926-3368; (603) 926-1348 FAX
E-mail: bteschek@hampton.lib.nh.us
http://www.hampton.lib.nh.us/

Leach Library
268 Mammoth Road
Londonderry, NH 03053
Hours: Research History Room: Mon–Fri
   9:00–8:00, Sat 9:00–5:00

Manchester City Library
New Hampshire Room
Carpenter Memorial Building
405 Pine Street
Manchester, NH 03104-6199
(603) 624-6550
Cynthia N. O'Neil
Hours: Labor Day to mid-Jun: Mon
   9:30–noon & 5:30–9:00, Tue 9:30–
   3:00, Wed 12:30–5:30, Thur 1:30–
   5:30, Fri 1:30–4:30, Sat 9:00–5:00;
   summer: 9:30–noon & 5:30–9:00, Tue
   9:30–5:30, Wed–Thur 12:30–5:30, Fri
   12:30–5:00
(emphasis on Manchester and New
   Hampshire local history and
   genealogy)

Mansfield Public Library
Main Street
PO Box 210
Temple, NH 03084
(603) 878-3100
Hours: Mon, Wed & Fri 1:30–5:00, Tue
   10:00–noon & 1:00–5:30, Wed 7:00–
   9:00, Sat 2:00–5:00

Byron Merrill Library
Rumney, NH 03266
(603) 786-9520
Hours: Tue & Thur 2:00–5:00 & 6:30–
   8:00, Sat 10:00–noon

Moultonboro Public Library
Main Street
PO Box 150
Moultonboro, NH 03254
(603) 476-8895
Hours: Mon & Wed 1:30–8:00, Fri 1:30–
   5:00, Sat 10:30–4:30
("We have some local history and
   genealogy information, which we are
   working to expand.")

Mount Caesar Union Library
628 Old Home Street
East Swanzey, NH 03431
(603) 357-0456
Ruth Palm, Director
Hours: Mon–Thur 1:00–5:00 & 6:30–
   9:00, Tue & Thur 9:30–11:30

Nashua Public Library
2 Court Street
Nashua, NH 03060-3475
(603) 594-3412; (603) 594-3457 FAX
Hours: Mon–Fri 8:30 A.M.–9:00 P.M., Sat
   (Sept–Jun) 8:30–5:30, Sun (Sept–Apr)
   1:00–5:00

Town of New Castle Archives and Records Committee
(Town Office, 49 Main Street—location)
PO Box 367 (mailing address)
New Castle, NH 03854
Eugene W. Morrill, Town Historian
Hours: by appointment only
(records dating from 1693, some
   incomplete; New Castle, formerly

Great Island, was the early site of New
   Hampshire provincial government)
inquiries answered as time is available,
   must be accompanied by SASE

New Durham Archives and Historical Collections
(Town Hall, Main Street, and New
   Durham Library, 2 Old Bay Road—
   location)
PO Box 207 (mailing address)
New Durham, NH 03855-0207
(603) 859-6881; (603) 859-2091 (Town
   Hall); (603) 859-2201 (Library)
Eloise Bickford, Town Historian
Hours: various
("New Durham genealogy and New
   Durham history, photos, Civil War
   letters from New Durham residents;
   the collection is stored in both the
   Town Hall vault and the New Durham
   Library.")
search fee: $5.00, depending on scope
   and quantity

New Hampshire Farm Museum, Inc.
PO Box 644
Milton, NH 03851

New Hampshire Votech College
Library
2020 Riverside Drive
Berlin, NH 03570
(603) 752-1113

North Hampton Public Library
Atlantic Avenue
North Hampton, NH 03862
(603) 964-6326

Ohoopee Regional Library
(see Georgia)

Old Store Museum Society of South Sutton
PO Box 462
South Sutton, NH 03273

Portsmouth Athenaeum
(6–8 Market Square—public entrance
   location)
9 Market Square (mailing address)
Portsmouth, NH 03801
(603) 431-2538
Jane Porter, Keeper
Hours: Tue & Thur 1:00–4:00, Sat
   10:00–4:00
(Piscataqua region history)

Portsmouth Public Library
8 Islington Street
Portsmouth, NH 03801
(603) 431-2000, ext. 252
Sherm Pridham, Director

Philip Read Memorial Library
1088 Route 12A
Plainfield, NH 03781
(603) 675-6866
E-mail: plfdlib@cyberportal.net
Nancy Norwalk, Librarian

Hours: Mon & Wed 7:00 P.M.–9:00 P.M.,
Wed & Fri 1:00–5:00, Sat 9:00–noon
(Plainfield genealogy and history; files
on Maxfield Parrish and other Cornish
Art Colony members)
copies 15¢ per page

Olivia Rodham Memorial Library
(Nelson, NH—location)
R.F.D. Nelson (mailing address)
Marlborough, NH 03455
(603) 847-3214

Silsby Public Library
Town Common
Acworth, NH 03601
(603) 835-2150
Barbara Davis, Administrator
Hours: Tue, Thur & Sun 1:00–4:00
(local history and genealogy)

Strawbery Banke Museum
454 Court Street
PO Box 300
Portsmouth, NH 03801-0300
(603) 422-7502; (603) 433-1115 FAX
http://wwwsc.library.unh.edu/specoll/
Sbanke/homepag.htm
Roberta L. Ransley, Librarian/Archivist
Hours: Tue 10:00–1:00, Thur 1:00–4:00,
and by appointment
(5,000 books, periodicals and
microfilms, emphasis on Portsmouth)

Sugar Hill Historical Museum
Village Green
Sugar Hill, NH 03585
(603) 823-5336
Jane L. Vincent, Curator
Hours: 1 Jul through late Oct: Thur &
Sat–Sun 1:00–4:00, and by
appointment
Pub. *Newsletter*, quarterly
(history of Sugar Hill and surrounding
towns, excellent library with
genealogical material relating to early
families)
$25.00 per year membership

Tucker Free Library
Henniker, NH 03242

University of New Hampshire
Special Collections
The University Library
18 Library Way
Durham, NH 03824-3592
(603) 862-2714; (603) 862-2637 FAX
E-mail: archives@unh.edu
http://wwwsc.library.unh.edu/specoll/
izaak.htm
Bill Ross
Hours: Mon–Fri 8:00–4:30, Sat (during
the semester) 1:00–5:00
(houses the Lamson Library of the
Piscataqua Pioneers)

Woodman Institute
PO Box 146
Dover, NH 03821-0146
(603) 742-1038

Historical Societies— Local and Regional

Acworth Historical Society
Silsby Public Library
Town Common
Acworth, NH 03601
(603) 835-2150 (Library)
Barbara Davis, Library Administrator
Hours: Library: Tue, Thur & Sun 1:00–
4:00

Alton Historical Society
PO Box 536
Alton, NH 03809

Historical Society of Amherst, New Hampshire
PO Box 717
Amherst, NH 03031
(603) 672-0411 (President); (603) 673-
5004 (Curators)
Ron Gerstenberger, President; Harold or
Bonnie Struss, Museum Curators
Hours: Museum: Sat (Jul–Aug) 10:00–
noon, and for special events
Pub. *Newsletter*, bimonthly
$10.00 per year membership, $100.00
life membership

Andover Historical Society
PO Box 167
Andover, NH 03216

Antrim Historical Society
63 Pleasant Street
Antrim, NH 03440
Nina M. Harding

Ashland Historical Society
Whipple House Museum
(Pleasant Street—location)
PO Box 175 (mailing address)
Ashland, NH 03217

Atkinson Historical Society
10 Academy Avenue
Atkinson, NH 03811
(603) 362-4760
Una M. Collins, President
Hours: Wed 2:00–4:00, and by
appointment
volunteer, free service

Auburn Historical Society
21 Deer Neck Road
Auburn, NH 03032
Joseph R. Higgins

Barrington Historical Society
49 Mallego Road
Barrington, NH 03825
(603) 664-9551
Andrea Calef Powell, Curator and
Society Genealogist
(Barrington/Strafford, New Hampshire,
families)
$5.00 per year membership

Bedford Historical Society
24 North Amherst Road
Bedford, NH 03110

Bennington Historical Society
PO Box 50
Bennington, NH 03442

Boscawen Historical Society, Inc.
King Street
PO Box 3067
Boscawen, NH 03303
Cynthia A. Houston, President
Hours: Sun 2:00–4:00
(history and local family genealogy;
published town histories with
genealogy section; maintains library
archives)
$5.00 per year membership, donations
accepted

Brentwood Historical Society
(Museum, 140 Crawley Falls Road,
Brentwood, NH 03833-6203—
location)
Town Office, Dalton Road (mailing
address)
Brentwood, NH 03833
(603) 642-8817 (Town Office); (603)
642-5394 (Secretary)
Ruth H. Brown, Secretary
Hours: third Sat 10:00–2:00, and by
appointment only in winter months
$5.00 per year membership

Bridgewater Historical Society
RFD 2, Box 390
Plymouth, NH 03264

Brookline New Hampshire Historical Society
Meetinghouse Hall
10 Main Street
Brookline, NH 03033
(603) 673-0543; (603) 673-2243 FAX
E-mail: brookliner@aol.com
Peter Cook

Campton Historical Society
RR 1, Box 1046
Campton, NH 03223
David Dearborn

Canaan Historical Society and Museum
Canaan Street
Canaan, NH 03741
(603) 523-4202
Judge Dan W. Fleetham, Chairman
Hours: 30 May–5 Oct: Sat 1:00–4:00

Candia Historical Society
PO Box 300
Candia, NH 03034

Canterbury Historical Society
Old Tilton Road
PO Box 81
Canterbury, NH 03224
(603) 783-9831; (603) 783-9955 (Town
offices)

Hours: last Sat in May–Columbus Day
weekend: 10:00–12:00, last Sat in Jul
10:00–4:00
$10.00 per year membership for
individuals or families, $25.00 per
year membership for businesses,
$100.00 life membership

Center Harbor Historical Society
PO Box 98
Center Harbor, NH 03226

Charlestown Historical Society
PO Box 253
Charlestown, NH 03603

**Historical Society of Cheshire
County**
Archive Center
246 Main Street
PO Box 803
Keene, NH 03431
(603) 352-1895
Alan F. Rumrill, Director
Hours: Mon–Tue & Thur–Fri 9:00–4:00,
Wed 9:00–9:00, Sat 9:00–noon
Pub. *Newsletter of Historical Society of
Cheshire County*, five times per year
(New Hampshire and New England
genealogical research library)
$20.00 per year membership for
individuals

Chester Historical Society
115 Hanson Road
PO Box 34
Chester, NH 03036
(603) 887-5767
Charles H. Frederick, Sr., President

Chesterfield Historical Society, Inc.
(Main Street—location)
PO Box 204 (mailing address)
Chesterfield, NH 03443-0204
(603) 363-8018
Cornelia Jenness, President
Hours: by appointment
(extensive genealogy files; published
Cemetery Book, reprinted 1881
History of Chesterfield by Oran
Randall)

Chichester Historical Society
Chichester Library
Main Street
Chichester, NH 03263

Claremont Historical Society, Inc.
26 Mulberry Street
Claremont, NH 03743

Colebrook Area Historical Society
PO Box 32
Colebrook, NH 03576

Conway Historical Society
PO Box 1949
Conway, NH 03818

Cornish Historical Society
RR 2, Box 416
Cornish, NH 03745

(603) 675-6003
James B. Atkinson, President
$5.00 per year membership

Deerfield Heritage Commission
60 South Road
Deerfield, NH 03037-1709
(603) 463-7151; (603) 463-7151
Laura C. Guinan, Chairman

Deerfield Historical Society
141 Middle Road
Deerfield, NH 03037
Ruth Sanborn

Derring Historical Society
(Derring, NH—location)
Rt. 1, Box 69 (mailing address)
Hillsboro, NH 03244
(603) 529-2441
Thomas J. Copadis, Treasurer

**Derry Historical Society and
Museum**
(West Broadway, Fire Station—location)
65 Birch Street (mailing address)
Derry, NH 03038
(603) 432-3188
Ralph S. Bonner, President
Hours: by appointment only
Pub. *Newsletter*, three times per year
$10.00 life membership; research: $20.00
per hour for work that takes more than
one hour

Dublin Historical Society
Main Street
PO Box 415
Dublin, NH 03444
(603) 563-8545
John Harris, Archivist; Nancy Campbell,
Assistant Archivist
Hours: usually five days per week 9:00–
noon by appointment
Pub. *DHS Newsletter*, quarterly
$20.00–$60.00 per year membership;
send donation plus copying and
mailing costs with information
requests

Dunbarton Historical Society
31 Mansion Road
Dunbarton, NH 03045
M. Mann

Durham Historic Association, Inc.
Corner of Route 108 at Main Street
PO Box 305
Durham, NH 03824
(603) 868-5560 (Curator); (603) 868-
5436 (Museum)
Mrs. John Hatch, Curator
Hours: Jun–Sept: Mon–Fri 2:00–5:00;
Sept–Jun: Tue & Thur 2:00–4:00, and
by appointment
Pub. *DHA Newsletter*, four to six times
per year
(genealogical material regarding
Durham, also history of Durham,
1900–1989)
search fees: cost of duplication plus mail

Effingham Historical Society
(Route 153, Effingham, NH—location)
PO Box 33 (mailing address)
South Effingham, NH 03882

Enfield Historical Society
(Route 4-A—location)
Rt. 2, Box 397 (mailing address)
Enfield, NH 03748
(603) 632-7486

Epping Historical Society
PO Box 348
Epping, NH 03042

Exeter Historical Society
47 Front Street
PO Box 924
Exeter, NH 03833-0924
(603) 778-2335
Edward S. Chase, Jr., President
Hours: Tue, Thur & Sat (Apr–Nov)
2:00–5:00, Tue, Thur & Sat (Dec–
Mar) 2:00–4:30; part-time staff usually
available Mon & Tue A.M., Wed & Fri
all day
Pub. *Exeter Historical Society
Newsletter*, three times per year
(maps, photographs, Exeter history)
photocopies 25¢ per page

Farmington Historical Society
Webster Street
Farmington, NH 03835
Ann Place

Fitzwilliam Historical Society
Amos J. Blake House, On the Common
PO Box 76
Fitzwilliam, NH 03447
Barbara Crutchley, President
Hours: Memorial Day through Columbus
Day: Sat 10:00–4:00, Sun 1:00–4:00,
and by appointment
$5.00 per year membership; search:
$10.00 minimum or $25.00 per hour

**Francestown Improvement and
Historical Society**
G. H. Bixby Memorial Library
52 Main Street
Francestown, NH 03043
(603) 547-2730; (603) 547-2856
Ellen Neilley
$5.00 per year membership for
individuals, $10.00 per year
membership for families

Franconia Area Heritage Council
PO Box 169
Franconia, NH 03580

Franklin Historical Society
PO Box 43
Franklin, NH 03235

Freedom Historical Society
Freedom, NH 03836

Fremont Historical Society
453 South Road
Fremont, NH 03044

(603) 895-4032
Matthew E. Thomas, President

Gilmanton Historical Society
PO Box 236
Gilmanton, NH 03237

Gilsum Historical Society
PO Box 205
Gilsum, NH 03448
(603) 352-8542

Goffstown Historical Society
PO Box 284
Goffstown, NH 03045

Goshen Historical Society, Inc.
RFD 2, Box 177
Newport, NH 03773
(603) 863-1509
D. W. Stephan

Greenland Historical Society
459 Portsmouth Avenue
Greenland, NH 03840

Hampton Historians, Inc.
3 Thomsen Road
Hampton, NH 03842
(603) 926-2111

Hampton Historical Association
40 Park Avenue
PO Box 1601
Hampton, NH 03842
(603) 929-0781
Susanne Falzone, President
Hours: Jun–Sept: Wed–Fri & Sun 1:00–
    4:00
(Hampton history, early families)
$10.00 per year membership for
    individuals, $15.00 per year
    membership for families, $5.00 per
    year membership for senior citizens

Hancock Historical Society
PO Box 138
Hancock, NH 03049

Hanover Historical Society
Webster Cottage
(32 North Main Street—location)
PO Box 142 (mailing address)
Hanover, NH 03755
(603) 643-3074 (Curator)
Joanne Pomeroy, Curator
Hours: Memorial Day to Columbus Day:
    Wed & Sat–Sun 2:30–4:30
(books and furnishings related to Daniel
    Webster; all genealogical and most
    historical requests are referred to
    Baker Memorial Library, Dartmouth
    College)
$10.00 per year membership for
    individuals, $15.00 per year
    membership for families, $30.00 per
    year Sustaining membership, $125 life
    membership

Haverhill Historical Society
Court Street, Haverhill Corner
Haverhill, NH 03765

(603) 989-3337
Mrs. John Klitgord, Curator
Hours: by appointment

Hawke Historical Society
PO Box 402
Danville, NH 03819
E-mail: nhwoods@nh.ultranet.com
Peter S. Meigs, President
Pub. *Reminiscences*, quarterly
(oral history, house histories,
    genealogies, maps, biographies of
    prominent citizens, pictures, veterans,
    vital statistics, traditions, journals,
    etc.)
$7.20 per year membership

Henniker Historical Society
5A Maple Street Academy Hall
PO Box 674
Henniker, NH 03242-0674
(603) 428-6267
Martha Taylor, Archives Chair
Hours: Thur & Sat 10:00–2:00, and by
    appointment
$5.00 per year membership

Hill Historical Society
PO Box 193
Hill, NH 03243

Hillsborough Historical Society, Inc.
East Washington Road
PO Box 896
Hillsboro, NH 03244
(603) 478-3165; (603) 478-3913 (to
    arrange for tour groups of Homestead)
Robert Charron, President
Hours: President Franklin Pierce
    Homestead (Routes 9 and 31): Jun:
    Sat–Sun; Jul–Aug: Mon–Sat 10:00–
    4:00, Sun 1:00–4:00; Sept–Columbus
    Day: Sat 10:00–4:00, Sun 1:00–4:00;
    open Memorial Day weekend, 4 Jul,
    and by appointment
$3.00 per year membership

Hinsdale Historical Society
RR 2, River Street, Box 9
Hinsdale, NH 03451

Holderness Historical Society
PO Box 319
Holderness, NH 03245

Hollis Historical Society
PO Box 754
Hollis, NH 03049

Hudson Historical Society, Inc.
Rt. 4, Derry Road
Hudson, NH 03051
(603) 882-7474; (603) 882-9522
Arlene MacIntyre, Clerk/Treasurer

Jackson Historical Society
PO Box 8
Jackson, NH 03846

Jaffrey Historical Society, Inc.
40 Main Street
Jaffrey Civic Center
Jaffrey, NH 03452
(603) 532-6527
Hours: Tue–Fri 1:30–5:00
Pub. *Newsletter*, bimonthly
(exhibits, archives at Civic Center)

Jefferson Historical Society
Rt. 2, Jefferson Hill
PO Box 5A-1
Jefferson, NH 03583
(603) 586-7004 (summer weekdays for
    volunteer docent)
Helen Merrill, President
Hours: Sun (Memorial Day–Columbus
    Day) 1:00–5:00

Kensington Historical Society
Public Library
126 Amesbury Road
Kensington, NH 03833

**Kingston Improvement and
Historical Society, Inc.**
(Church on the Plains, Main Street—
    location)
PO Box 663 (mailing address)
Kingston, NH 03848
(603) 642-5419
E-mail: txwr85a@prodigy.com
Joyce Davies, Secretary-Treasurer
Hours: by appointment
$5.00 per year membership for
    individuals, $10.00 per year
    membership for families; research for
    donation

Laconia Historical Society
PO Box 1126
Laconia, NH 03247
Warren D. Huse, Curator
Pub. *The Laconia Historian*, ten times
    per year (monthly, except July and
    August)
(general collection of photos and
    ephemera; has very little genealogical
    material, per se; however can usually
    locate information on persons
    prominent in business or professional
    life via microfilm copies of local
    newspapers)
$5.00 per year membership for
    individuals, $10.00 per year
    membership for families

Lancaster Historical Society
PO Box 473
Lancaster, NH 03584

Lebanon Historical Society, Inc.
40 Mascoma Street
Lebanon, NH 03766-2629
(603) 448-3118
Robert H. Leavitt, Curator and City
    Historian
(published *Lebanon 1761–1994*, $42.00
    postpaid)

Lee Historical Society
Lee Town Hall
7 Mast Road
Durham, NH 03824
Hours: varies
can't always answer inquiries

Lempster Historical Society
HCR 66, Box 875
Lempster, NH 03606
Emily Fairweather

Littleton Area Historical Society
Littleton Historical Museum
1 Cottage Street
Littleton, NH 03561
(603) 444-6435
Ardelle Hartford, President
Hours: Museum: Wed 1:30–4:30, and by
appointment

Londonderry Historical Society
PO Box 136
Londonderry, NH 03053
(603) 432-9619; (603) 432-1132 (Leach
Library)
Junie Vickers; Melvin Watts, Town
Historian
Hours: Research History Room at Leach
Library: Mon–Fri 9:00–8:00, Sat
9:00–5:00
$10.00 per year membership for
individuals, $25.00 per year
membership for families

Lyme Historical Society
Lyme, NH 03678

Madbury Historical Society
13 Town Hall Road
Madbury, NH 03820

Madison Historical Society
(East Madison Road-Madison Corner—
location)
PO Box 505 (mailing address)
Madison, NH 03849
Mary Lucy, President

Manchester Historic Association
129 Amherst Street
Manchester, NH 03101
(603) 622-7531
George S. Comtois, Director
Pub. *Reflections*
$25.00 per year membership

Marlborough Historical Society, Inc.
PO Box 202
Marlborough, NH 03455

Mason Historical Society
717 Greenville Road
Mason, NH 03048
(603) 878-2918

Meredith Historical Society
PO Box 920
Meredith, NH 03253
(603) 279-6136

Merrimack Historical Society
PO Box 1525
Merrimack, NH 03054

Milford Historical Society
6 Union Street
PO Box 609
Milford, NH 03055
William L. Dyer, President
Hours: second Sat & Sun 2:00–4:00
Pub. *M. H. S. Newsletter*, four times per
year

**Township of Milton Historical
Society**
PO Box 621
Milton, NH 03851

Moultonborough Historical Society
PO Box 659
Moultonboro, NH 03254

Nashua Historical Society
5 Abbott Street
Nashua, NH 03060
(603) 883-0015
Paul Taylor, Research and Records
Chair; Beth McCarthy, Curator
Pub. *Nashua Historical Society
Newsletter*, monthly
("Our library contains several great
sources for genealogical research as
well as historical research.")
$10.00 per year membership for
individuals, $25.00 per year
membership for families, $5.00 per
year membership for students and
senior citizens, $150.00 life
membership

**The New England Historic
Genealogical Society**
(see Massachusetts)

New Hampshire Antiquarian Society
(300 Main Street—location)
Rt. 3, Box 251 (mailing address)
Hopkinton, NH 03229
(603) 746-3825
Rosalind P. Hanson, President

New Hampton Historical Society
PO Box 422
New Hampton, NH 03256

New London Historical Society
(Little Sunapee Road—location)
PO Box 965 (mailing address)
New London, NH 03257
(603) 526-6564
Lynne Bell, President
Hours: free guided tours Jul–Aug: Wed
2:00–4:00; self-guided tours anytime

New Market Historical Society
Stone School Museum
(Granite Street—location)
51 North Main Street (mailing address)
Newmarket, NH 03857
(603) 659-7420

Sylvia Fitts Getchell, Curator
Hours: Memorial Day–Labor Day: Thur
2:00–4:00

Newbury Historical Society
PO Box 176
Newbury, NH 03255

Newfields Historical Society
PO Box 126
Newfields, NH 03856

Newington Historical Society
133 Fox Point Road
Newington, NH 03801
Dorothy M. Watson

**Newport Historic District
Commission**
15 Sunapee Street
Newport, NH 03773
(603) 863-1877; (603) 863-8008 FAX
Sharon H. Christie

Newport Historical Society, Inc.
Courthouse Square
PO Box 492
Newport, NH 03773
(603) 863-2079

North Hampton Historical Society
120 Walnut Avenue
North Hampton, NH 03862
Mrs. Earl H. Coffey

**Northam Colonists Historical
Society**
55 Applevale Dr.
Dover, NH 03820
B. Hennessey

Northwood Historical Society
PO Box 114
Northwood, NH

Nottingham Historical Society
Nottingham Square Schoolhouse
PO Box 241
Nottingham, NH 03290
(603) 679-1937
Joy Gannett, Co-president

Old Fort No. 4 Associates
PO Box 336
Charlestown, NH 03603

**Old Meetinghouse Historical
Association**
PO Box 27
Sandown, NH 03873

Ossipee Historical Society
(52 Route 16B, Center Ossipee, NH
03814—museum location)
PO Box 245 (mailing address)
Ossipee, NH 03864
(603) 539-2404
Doris W. Ashton, President
Hours: Museum: Jul–Aug: Tue, Thur &
Sat; meetings: Apr–Oct: third Tue
Pub. *Ossipee Almanac*, quarterly
$5.00 per year membership

Pelham Historical Society
8 Nashua Road
Pelham, NH 03076

Peterborough Historical Society
19 Grove Street
PO Box 58
Peterborough, NH 03458
(603) 924-3235
Ellen S. Derby, Executive Director
Hours: Mon–Fri 10:00–4:00
(Peterborough, New Hampshire, history)

Piermont Historical Society
High Street
PO Box 273
Piermont, NH 03779
Joe Medlicott, President
Pub. *Piermont Record*, occasionally
("Genealogical searches limited to
Piermont Town sources.")
$3.00 per year membership for
individual adults, $5.00 per year
membership for families, $1.00 per
year membership for students

Piscataqua Pioneers
9 Lindy Avenue
Claremont, NH 03743-2926
(603) 542-6513
Alice C. Haubrich, Curator
(Lamson Library of the Piscataqua
Pioneers is housed at University of
New Hampshire)

Pittsburg Historical Society
PO Box 128
Pittsburg, NH 03592

Pittsfield Historical Society
Pittsfield, NH 03263
R. C. Van Horn

Plainfield Historical Society
(Route 12A—location)
PO Box 107 (mailing address)
Plainfield, NH 03781
Nancy Norwalk, Archivist
Hours: by appointment only
(Plainfield history)
$3.00 per year membership

Plaistow Historical Society
PO Box 434
Plaistow, NH 03865

Plymouth Historical Society
RFD 1, Box 2695
Plymouth, NH 03264
Mrs. William Batchelder

Portsmouth Historical Society
State and Middle Streets
PO Box 728
Portsmouth, NH 03802-0728
(603) 436-8420 (Seasonal)
Carl W. Brage, Genealogical Coordinator
Hours: Jun–Oct: daily; Nov–May:
periodic

Raymond Historical Society, Inc.
PO Box 94
Raymond, NH 03077

Richmond Historical Society
480 Fitzwilliam Road
Richmond, NH 03470
N. Thibodeau

Rindge Historical Society
South Main Street
Rindge, NH 03461

Rochester Historical Society
PO Box 65
Rochester, NH 03867
(603) 332-4426
Florence Smith, Document Custodian
Hours: 2:00–4:00 & 6:00–9:00
Pub. *Newsletter*, annually
$3.00 per year membership for
individuals, $25.00 per year
membership for businesses

Rye Historical Society
PO Box 583
Rye, NH 03870

Salem Historical Society
PO Box 401
Methuen, NH 01844

Salisbury Historical Society
RFD 1, Box 1487
Racoon Hill Road
Salisbury, NH 03268
C. E. Hughes

Sanbornton Historical Society
PO Box 2
Sanbornton, NH 03269
(603) 286-7227; (603) 286-8490
(President)
Evelyn Auger, President
Hours: by appointment only; meetings
Apr–Oct: first Wed 7:30
(local history, limited early genealogy
information)
$10.00 per year membership for
individuals, $15.00 per year
membership for families

**Sandown Historical Society &
Museum**
PO Box 300
Sandown, NH 03873

Sandwich Historical Society
Maple Street
PO Box 106
Center Sandwich, NH 03227-0106
(603) 284-7412 phone and FAX
Robin Dustin, Director/Curator
Hours: Jun–Sept: Tue–Sat 11:00–5:00
Pub. *Sandwich Historical Society—
Annual Excursion Publication*,
annually, cost varies

Historical Society of Seabrook
PO Box 500
Seabrook, NH 03874
(603) 474-2232

Stoddard Historical Society
HCR 32, Box 551
Stoddard, NH 03464

Strafford Historical Society
PO Box 33
Center Strafford, NH 03815

Stratham Historical Society
PO Box 39
Stratham, NH 03885

Somersworth Historical Society
6 Drew Road
Somersworth, NH 03878

Sutton Historical Society
PO Box 503
South Sutton, NH 03273

Tamworth Historical Society
(22 Gregg's Way, Center of Village—
location)
PO Box 13 (mailing address)
Tamworth, NH 03886
Joan A. Casarotto, Curator and Vice
President
Hours: Jul–Aug: Tue 7:00–8:00 P.M., and
by appointment; meetings Apr–Oct:
third Wed 7:30 P.M.
$5.00 per year membership for
individuals, $8.00 per year
membership for families

Temple Historical Society
PO Box 114
Temple, NH 03084

Thompson Ames Historical Society
PO Box 252
Laconia, NH 03247

Tilton Historical Society
PO Box 351
Tilton, NH 03276

Tuftonboro Historical Society
PO Box 372
Melvin Village, NH 03850

**Wakefield-Brookfield Historical
Society**
(Mount Laural Road, Route 153,
Wakefield, NH—location)
PO Box 795 (mailing address)
Brookfield, NH 03872
(603) 522-3739
Hours: May–Oct: Tue 7:30 P.M.–9:00 P.M.

The Walpole Historical Society
Main Street
PO Box 220
Walpole, NH 03608
(603) 756-3449 (Jun–Sept); (603) 756-
3534; (603) 756-3308 (Librarian/
Historian)
Mervin Stevens, President; Virginia
Putnam, Librarian/Historian
Hours: Wed & Sat 2:00–4:00, Sun (Jun–
Sept) 2:00–4:00, and by appointment
Pub. *Walpole Historical Society
Newsletter*, two times per year

(excellent library/family histories made available on request for out-of-town visitors)

$10.00 per year membership for individuals, $25.00 per year membership for families, $50.00 per year Patron membership, $250.00 per year Sustaining membership

Warner Historical Society
PO Box 189
Warner, NH 03278
(603) 456-2437
Royal Latuch, President

Warren Historical Society
PO Box 114
Warren, NH 03279

Washington Historical Society
PO Box 90
Washington, NH 03280

Weare Historical Society
PO Box 33
Weare, NH 03281

Westmoreland Historical Society
PO Box 55
Westmoreland, NH 03467

Whitefield Historical Society
(Lower level, Fleet Bank Building, Kings Square—location)
PO Box 21 (mailing address)
Whitefield, NH 03598
(603) 837-2386 (Secretary)
Eleanor Mason, Secretary
Hours: Thur 2:00–4:00, and by appointment
Pub. *Annual Report*
(emphasis on Whitefield and the surrounding areas; the White Mountain region)
$5.00 per year membership for individuals, $8.00 per year membership for families

Wilmot Historical Society, Inc.
Town Office Building
Wilmot Flat, NH 03287

Wilton Historical Society
PO Box 845
Wilton, NH 03086
Gail Proctor

Windham Historical Society
PO Box 441
Windham, NH 03087

Wolfeboro Historical Society
PO Box 1066
Wolfeboro, NH 03894

LDS Family History Center

Nashua
(603) 594-8888

Genealogical Societies

State Genealogical Society

New Hampshire Society of Genealogists (NHSOG)
PO Box 2316
Concord, NH 03302-2316
E-mail: milliken@tiac.net
http://www.tiac.net/users/nhsog/
Pub. *New Hampshire Society of Genealogists' Newsletter*, quarterly; *The New Hampshire Genealogical Record*, quarterly, $20.00 per year subscription
$20.00 per year membership for individuals, $30.00 per year membership for households, $400.00 life membership

Regional Genealogical Societies

American-Canadian Genealogical Society
(Corner of South Elm Street and West Baker Street—location)
PO Box 6478 (mailing address)
Manchester, NH 03108-6478
(603) 622-1554; (603) 626-9812 FAX
E-mail: 102475.2260@compuserve.com; amperrault@juno.com (Editor)
http://ourworld.compuserve.com/homepages/acgs/
Anne-Marie Perrault, President
Hours: Wed & Fri 10:00–9:00, Sat 9:00–4:00, and by appointment
Pub. *American-Canadian Genealogist*, quarterly
(primarily French-Canadian and Franco-American resources, vital records from all New England and New York)
Chapter: **Father Leo Begin Chapter**, American-Canadian Genealogical Society, PO Box 2125, Lewiston, ME 04240
$25.00 per year membership for individuals, $12.50 for each additional person in the same household, $375.00 life membership, $30.00 per year institutional or foreign membership

Hancock Genealogy Committee
Hancock Historical Society
Main Street
PO Box 222
Hancock, NH 03449
Cynthia F. Dechert and Elizabeth Weston, Co-chairmen
Hours: varies
$15.00 basic search fee

Merrimack Valley Society of Genealogists
44 Pleasant Street
PO Box 1035
Concord, NH 03301
Mrs. James W. Moreland, President
Hours: fourth Tue (Jan, March, May, Sept, Nov)
Pub. *Family Traces*, quarterly
$6.00 per year membership for individuals, $9.00 per year membership for families

Minnesota Genealogical Society, Yankee Branch
(see Massachusetts)

The New England Historic Genealogical Society
(see Massachusetts)

North County Genealogical Society
PO Box 618
Littleton, NH 03561
(603) 444-2001
Elva M. Reeg, President

Rockingham Society of Genealogists
PO Box 81
Exeter, NH 03833-0081
(603) 436-5824
Carl W. Brage, Secretary
Pub. *Kinship Kronicle*, quarterly (March, June, September, December)
$6.50 per year membership for residents of the U.S.

Strafford County Genealogical Society
PO Box 322
Dover, NH 03820
(603) 742-6394 (President's home)
Beverly A. McCann, President
Hours: Dover Public Library: Mon–Wed 9:00–8:30, Thur–Fri 9:00–5:30, Sat (winter) 9:00–5:00, (summer) 9:00–1:00
Pub. *The Genealogical Record*, bimonthly
$12.00 per year membership

Independent Publications and Miscellany

Belknap Mill Society
Mill Plaza
Laconia, NH 03246
(603) 524-8813

Historic Harrisville, Inc.
Church Hill
Harrisville, NH 03450
(603) 827-3722 (to leave message)
Mary Meath, Archives Director

The New England Quarterly
(see Massachusetts)

New Hampshire Legacy Magazine
(603) 883-3344
E-mail: publisher@nh.com
http://www.nh.com/legacy/index.shtml

New Hampshire Old Graveyard Association (NHOGA)
8 Great Pond Road
Kingston, NH 03848-3747
(603) 642-5419
E-mail: txwr85a@prodigy.com
Joyce Davies, Corresponding Secretary
Pub. *Rubbings*, three times per year (May, July, September)
(has name and date records from a few New Hampshire towns, but can seldom assist with genealogical queries, but does have a good list of contacts in each town; published *Graveyard Restoration Handbook*, $2.00 postpaid)
$5.00 per year membership for individuals, $7.00 per year membership for organizations

NHGenWeb
Part of U.S. GenWeb Project
E-mail: nh@usgenweb.com
http://www.geocities.com/Heartland/5275/nh.htm
(links to other New Hampshire resources)

The Old Man of the Mountains
Cannon Mountain
Franconia Notch, NH 03580
(603) 823-5563
http://mutha.com/oldmanmt.html
(historic photographs)

Society for the Preservation of New England Antiquities—Archives
(see Massachusetts)

NEW JERSEY

Archives and Libraries with Holdings in Genealogy

State Archives and Library

New Jersey State Archives
185 West State Street
CN 307
Trenton, NJ 08625-0307
(609) 292-6260; (609) 396-2454 FAX
http://www.state.nj.us/state/darm/darmidx.html
Bette Epstein, Archivist II
Hours: Tue–Fri 8:30–4:30
transcripts of vital statistics, 1848–1878: $4.00 plus $1.00 per page for copies sent by mail

New Jersey State Library
Genealogy Section
(185 West State Street—location)
PO 520 (mailing address)
Trenton, NJ 08625-0520
(609) 292-6274; (609) 984-7901 FAX
http://www.state.nj.us/statelibrary/libgene.htm
Rebecca Colesar, Genealogy Librarian
Hours: Mon–Fri 8:30–5:00
(guides, indexes, how-to books, periodicals, county and local histories, family genealogies, some city directories, maps, and printed records, with a major emphasis on New Jersey and surrounding states)

State Historical Societies

New Jersey Historical Commission
20 West State Street
CN 305
Trenton, NJ 08625-0305
(609) 292-6062; (609) 633-8168 FAX
Richard Waldron, Executive Director
Hours: 8:30–4:30
Pub. *New Jersey Historical Commission Newsletter*, quarterly, $4.00 per year subscription
(ethnic history in New Jersey)

New Jersey Historical Society Library
52 Park Place
Newark, NJ 07102
(973) 596-8500, ext. 249
Elaine Harger, Head Librarian
Hours: Wed–Fri & first & third Sat 10:00–4:00
Pub. *New Jersey History*, two times per year
$25.00 per year membership for individuals (includes membership in

Genealogy Club of the Library of the New Jersey Historical Society)

Association of New Jersey County Cultural and Heritage Agencies
841 Georges Road
North Brunswick, NJ 08902
(732) 745-4489
Anna M. Aschkenes, President

League of Historical Societies of New Jersey
PO Box 909
Madison, NJ 07940
http://scils.rutgers.edu/ macan/leaguelist.html
(not genealogical)

City, County and Regional Archives and Libraries

Atlantic City Free Public Library
1 North Tennessee Avenue
Atlantic City, NJ 08401
(609) 345-2269, ext. 60
Dian Spitler, Senior Librarian, Reference; Marie Boyd, Heston Curator
Hours: Mon–Wed 10:00–8:00, Thur–Sat 9:00–5:00
(emphasis on east coast genealogy, Atlantic City history—Heston Collection)
free access to collection, copies $1.00 per page

Atlantic County Library
2 South Farragut Avenue
Mays Landing, NJ 08330
(609) 625-2776, ext. 310
Louisa C. Mazetis, Principal Librarian
Hours: Mon–Thur 9:00–9:00, Fri–Sat 9:00–5:00
(very limited collection)

Belleville
155 Main Street
Belleville, NJ 07109

Bloomfield Public Library
90 Broad Street
Bloomfield, NJ 07003

Bridgeton Free Public Library
150 East Commerce Street
Bridgeton, NJ 08302
(609) 451-2620
Patricia W. McCulley, Director
Hours: Mon–Thur 9:00–9:00, Fri 9:00–5:00, Sat 10:00–4:00 (Jun–Aug: 9:00–1:00)

Burlington County Library
5 Pioneer Boulevard
Westampton, NJ 08060
(609) 267-9660; (609) 267-4091 FAX
http://www.burlco.lib.nj.us
Molly Connor, Chief Librarian Adult Services

Hours: Mon–Thur 9:00–9:00, Fri–Sat
9:00–5:00, Sun 1:00–5:00

Camden County Cultural and Heritage Commission

Hopkins House, 250 South Park Drive
Haddon Township, NJ 08108
(609) 858-0040
Gail Greenberg, Executive Director
Hours: Mon–Fri 9:00–4:00 (review of
documents by appointment only,
through Executive Director, index
available)
(collection of original pioneer
documents, Camden County history)

Camden County Library

Echelon Urban Center
203 Laurel Road
Voorhees, NJ 08043
(609) 772-1636
Hours: Mon–Fri 10:00–9:00, Sat 10:00–
6:00, Sun 1:00–5:00 (Jul–Aug: closed
Sun)

Campbell Museum

Campbell Place
Camden, NJ 08103
(609) 342-6440

Cape May County Public Library

30 West Mechanic Street
Cape May Court House, NJ 08210
(609) 465-1042 (Reference)
Donna Soffe, Reference
Hours: winter: Mon–Fri 8:30 A.M.–9:00
P.M., Sat 9:00–4:30, Sun 1:00–5:00;
summer: Mon–Thur 8:30 A.M.–9:00
P.M., Fri 8:30–4:30, Sat 9:00–4:30

Centenary College

Taylor Memorial Learning Resource
Center
400 Jefferson Street
Hackettstown, NJ 07840
(908) 852-1400, ext. 243

Library of the Chathams

214 Main Street
Chatham, NJ 07928
(973) 635-0603
Hours: Mon–Thur 9:30–9:00, Fri 9:30–
6:00, Sat 9:30–5:00, Sun 2:00–5:00

Clark Public Library

303 Westfield Avenue
Clark, NJ 07066
(732) 388-5999
Elaine Wade, Reference Librarian
Hours: winter: Mon & Wed–Thur 10:00–
9:00, Tue & Fri 10:00–5:00, Sat
10:00–4:00; summer: Mon & Thur
10:00–9:00, Tue–Wed & Fri 10:00–
5:00
$25.00 fee for non-residents provides
restricted borrowing privileges

Dennis Library

101 Main Street
Newton, NJ 07860

East Brunswick Museum Corporation

16 Maple Street
PO Box 875
East Brunswick, NJ 08816
(973) 257-1508
John H. Runyon, President
Hours: Sat–Sun 1:30–4:00

East Orange Public Library

21 South Arlington Avenue
East Orange, NJ 07018
(973) 266-5613; (973) 674-1991 FAX
J. Robert Starkey
Hours: Mon–Tue & Thur 9:00–9:00,
Wed 9:00–6:00, Fri 10:00–6:00, Sat
9:00–5:00
(East Orange local history)

Edison Public Library

340 Plainfield Avenue
Edison, NJ 08817
(732) 287-2298
Judith Mansbach, Reference Librarian
Hours: winter: Mon–Thur 9:00–9:00,
Fri–Sat 9:00–5:00; summer: Mon–
Wed 9:00–9:00, Thur–Fri 9:00–5:00

Fairleigh Dickinson University

New Jersey Room
Messler Library
Madison, NJ 07940
(973) 443-8515 (Library); (973) 443-
8500 (Madison Campus)
Richard Goerner
Hours: Library: Mon–Thur 8:30 A.M.–
10:00 P.M., Fri 8:30–5:00, Sat 11:00–
5:00, Sun 1:00–9:00; New Jersey
Room: Mon 8:30 A.M.–9:00 P.M.,
Wed–Thur 8:30–6:00, Fri 8:30–5:00

Fort Lee Historic Park

Hudson Terrace
Fort Lee, NJ 07024
John Muller

Hackettstown Free Public Library

110 Church Street
Hackettstown, NJ 07840
(908) 852-4936; (908) 852-7850 FAX
Rona Mosler, Library Director
Hours: Mon–Thur 10:00–9:00, Fri
10:00–5:00, Sat 9:00–12:00
(local history)

Haddonfield Public Library

60 Haddon Avenue
Haddonfield, NJ 08033
(609) 429-1304; (609) 429-3760 FAX
Douglas B. Rauschenberger, Director
Hours: Mon–Fri 10:00–9:00, Sat 10:00–
5:00, Sun 1:00–5:00

Hamilton Township Public Library

1 Municipal Drive
Trenton, NJ 08619
(609) 890-3460
Hours: Mon–Thur 9:00–8:30, Fri–Sat
9:00–5:00

Hopewell Museum

28 East Broad Street
Hopewell, NJ 08525
(609) 466-0103

Hunterdon County Library

State Highway 12
Flemington, NJ 08822
(201) 788-1444
Amanda Philipp, Reference Supervisor
Hours: Mon–Fri 8:30 A.M.–9:00 P.M., Sat
9:00–5:00
(Jerseyana collection has approximately
700 volumes)

Hunterdon Historical Museum

(56 Main Street—location)
PO Box 5005 (mailing address)
Clinton, NJ 08809-0005
(908) 735-4101; (908) 735-0914 FAX
Jean Daly, Collections Manager
Hours: Mon–Fri 9:00–5:00 by
appointment
(has Hunterdon County business ledgers
and photographic archives)

Irvington Public Library

Civic Square
Irvington, NJ 07111-2498
(973) 372-6400; (973) 372-6860; (973)
372-6054
E-mail: qde@infolink.org
Joan Weiss, Head of Reference
Hours: Mon–Tue & Thur 9:00–9:00,
Wed & Fri 9:00–5:30, Sat (mid-Sept to
mid-Jun) 9:00–5:00

Jersey City Public Library

New Jersey Room
472 Jersey Avenue
Jersey City, NJ 07302
(201) 547-4503; (201) 547-4584
http://www.jclibrary.org
Kenneth French, Head Librarian, New
Jersey Room
Hours: Mon–Fri 10:00–5:00, Sat (Sept–
Jun) 10:00–5:00
(city directories, local newspaper index,
other local archives)

Johnson Free Public Library

275 Moore Street
Hackensack, NJ 07601
(201) 343-4169
Val Clark, Head of Reference
Hours: Mon–Thur 9:00–8:45, Fri–Sat
9:00–4:45

Kearny Museum

318 Kearny Avenue
Kearny, NJ 07032
(201) 997-6911

Lebanon Township Museum at New Hampton

57 Musconetcong River Road
Hampton, NJ 08827
(908) 537-6464
Joan Lucas, Curator
Hours: Tue & Thur 9:30–5:00, Sat 1:00–
5:00

Pub. *The Slate*, two times per year
(local genealogy)

Long Branch Free Public Library
Reference Department
328 Broadway
Long Branch, NJ 07740
(732) 222-3900
Muriel Scoles
Hours: Mon–Thur 10:00–8:00, Fri–Sat
    noon-5:00
(Monmouth County, New Jersey)

Long Branch Historical Museum
Saint James Episcopal Church
1260 Ocean Avenue
Long Branch, NJ 07740
(732) 229-0600; (732) 922-9879
Edgar N. Dinkelspiel, President
Hours: by appointment
free admission

Madison Public Library
39 Keep Street
Madison, NJ 07940
(973) 377-0722
Maria W. Fenton, Local Historian
Hours: Wed & Fri 9:00–6:00, Mon–Tue
    & Thur 9:00–9:00, Sat 9:00–5:00, Sun
    2:00–5:00

Meadowlands Museum
91 Crane Avenue
PO Box 3
Rutherford, NJ 07070
(201) 935-1175

Middletown Township Public Library
55 New Monmouth Road
Middletown, NJ 07748
(732) 671-3700
JoAnn B. Strano, Head of Reference
Hours: Mon–Thur 9:00–9:00, Fri 9:00–
    5:00, Sat 9:00–5:00 (closed Jul &
    Aug)
(Middletown, Monmouth County, and
    New Jersey history sources; "library
    does not do main-in research but will
    guide patrons in their research")

Midland Park Public Library
Franklin and Godwin Avenues
Midland Park, NJ 07432

Miller-Cory House Museum
614 Mountain Avenue
PO Box 455
Westfield, NJ 07091

Morris County Library
The New Jersey Collection
30 East Hanover Avenue
Whippany, NJ 07981
(973) 285-6974
E-mail: heagney@main.morris.org
http://www.gti.net/mocolib1/nj.html
Marie Heagney, Principal Librarian
Hours: Mon–Thur 9:00–9:00, Fri–Sat
    9:00–5:00, Sun (Sept–Jun) noon–5:00

The Joint Free Public Library of Morristown and Morris Township
Local History Department
1 Miller Road
Morristown, NJ 07960
(201) 538-3473; (201) 267-4064 FAX
E-mail: douthwaite@main.morris.org
http://www.makcom.com/jfpl/gene.htm
Lesley Douthwaite, Head
Hours: Mon–Thur 9:00–9:00, Fri 9:00–
    6:00, Sat 9:30–5:00 (Jul–Aug 10:00–
    2:00), Sun 1:00–5:00

New Jersey State Museum
Museums Council of New Jersey
205 West State Street
CN 530
Trenton, NJ 08625-0530
(609) 292-6464; (609) 599-4098 FAX
http://www.state.nj.us/state/museum/
    musidx.html
Leah P. Sloshberg, Director
Hours: Tue–Sat 9:00–4:45, Sun noon–
    4:45
Pub. *The Quarterly Calendar*
(collections and exhibitions and research
    in archaeology/ethnology, cultural
    history, etc.)
$40.00 per year membership

Newark Public Library
5 Washington Street
PO Box 630
Newark, NJ 07101-0630
(973) 733-7776
http://www.npl.org/
Charles Cummings, Assistant Director,
    Special Collections/NewJersey
Hours: Tue, Thur & Sat 9:00–5:00, Wed
    1:30–8:30, subject to change

Nutley Public Library
(address withheld upon request)

Ocean County Library
Bishop Building, 101 Washington Street
Toms River, NJ 08753
(201) 349-6200
E-mail: ljbrown@oceancounty.lib.nj.us
Lois Jane Brown, Senior Librarian
Hours: Mon & Wed 1:00–9:00, Tue &
    Thur–Sat 1:00–5:00
(New Jersey/Ocean County history and
    genealogy; all available federal
    censuses of New Jersey)

Paramus Public Library
East 116 Century Road
Paramus, NJ 07652
(201) 599-1305
E-mail: pararef@bccls.com
Sylvia Gaddi, Supervisor of Reference
    Services
Hours: Mon–Thur 9:30–9:00, Fri–Sat
    9:30–5:00, Sun 1:00–5:00

Paterson Museum
2 Market Street
Paterson, NJ 07501
(973) 881-3874

Phillipsburg Free Public Library
200 Frost Avenue
Phillipsburg, NJ 08865
(201) 454-3712

Princeton Public Library
65 Witherspoon Street
Princeton, NJ 08542
(609) 924-9529
Elba Barzelatto, Manager Information
    Services
Hours: Mon–Thur 9:00–9:00, Fri–Sat
    9:00–5:30, Sun (Sept–Jun) 1:00–5:30
(emphasis on Princetoniana, very limited
    genealogical material)

Princeton University Library
1 Washington Road
Princeton, NJ 08540
(609) 258-3184
E-mail:
    wljoyce@firestone.princeton.edu;
    mmsherry@princeton.edu
http://infoshare1.princeton.edu:2003/

Ramsey Free Public Library
30 Wyckoff Avenue
Ramsey, NJ 07446
(201) 327-1445
Leona F. Schauble
Hours: Mon–Sat (summer: closed Sat)

Ruth L. Rockwood Memorial Library
Robert H. Harp Drive
Livingston, NJ 07039
(973) 992-4600
Arlene Boland, Head of Reference
Hours: Mon & Wed–Thur 10:00–9:00,
    Tue & Fri 10:00–6:00, Sat 10:00–5:00
(local history information for the town of
    Livingston with some general New
    Jersey holdings for nearby areas)

Rowan University Library
Stewart Room
201 Mullica Hill Road
Glassboro, NJ 08028-0701
(609) 256-4967
William Garrabrant
Hours: during the semester: Mon–Thur
    8:00–midnight, Fri 8:00–9:00, Sat
    9:00–5:00, Sun noon–10:00
(emphasis on New Jersey genealogy,
    Indians, Quakers, and college
    archives)

Roxbury Public Library
103 Main Street
Succasunna, NJ 07876
(973) 584-2400
Hours: Mon–Thur 9:30–9:00, Fri 9:30–
    5:00, Sat (Sept–Jun) 9:30–3:00, Sat
    (Jul–Aug) 9:30–1:00, Sun (Sept–Jun)
    2:00–5:00

Rutgers University
Special Collections and University
 Archives
New Brunswick, NJ 08903
(732) 932-7510 (Reference); (732) 932-
 7012 FAX
http://www.rutgers.edu
Bonita Craft Grant, New Jersey
 Bibliographer
Hours: Special Collections: during the
 school year: Mon–Fri 9:00–5:00, Sat
 1:00–5:00; summer: Mon–Fri 9:00–
 5:00
(New Jersey history and genealogy,
 Rutgers University's archives and
 records/publications, rare books,
 manuscript materials; houses archives
 and records of the Genealogical
 Society of New Jersey and the DAR
 New Jersey Chapter)

Gardner A. Sage Library
21 Seminary Place
New Brunswick, NJ 08901
(732) 247-5243
Marsha Blake, Reference Librarian
Hours: Mon–Thur 10:00–10:00, Fri
 10:00–5:00, Sat 11:00–3:00
(emphasis on New York, New Jersey,
 Colonial Dutch, and Reformed Church
 in America)
search fee: $10.00 per day, $100.00 per
 year

Sandy Hook Museum
Gateway N.R.A., Sandy Hook Unit
PO Box 437
Highlands, NJ 07732
(973) 872-0115

Seton Hall University
Special Collections Center
Walsh Library
400 South Orange Avenue
South Orange, NJ 07079-2696
(973) 761-9476
E-mail: brownsam@pirate.shu.edu
http://www.shu.edu/library/speccoll.html
Msgr. William Field, Director; JoAnn
 Cotz, Associate Director
Hours: Mon–Fri 9:15–4:30 by
 appointment only
(New Jersey Roman Catholic history,
 sacramental records, 1850–1925)

Sparta Public Library
(address withheld upon request)

Sussex County Library
(Route 655, Frankford Township—
 location)
125 Morris Turnpike (mailing address)
Newton, NJ 07860
(973) 948-3660
Therese Erskine, Reference Librarian
Hours: Mon–Thur 8:30–8:30, Fri 8:30–
 6:00, Sat 9:00–5:00
no genealogical research services

Trenton City Museum
Trenton Museum Society
Cadwalader Park
Trenton, NJ 08606
(609) 989-3632

Free Public Library of Trenton
120 Academy Street
Trenton, NJ 08608
(609) 392-7188
Charles Webster, Historian
Hours: Mon & Wed–Thur 9:00–9:00,
 Tue & Fri–Sat 9:00–5:00

**University of Medicine and
Dentistry of New Jersey**
Department of Special Collections
30 12th Street
Newark, NJ 07103-2754
(973) 982-6293; (973) 982-7474
E-mail: irwin@umdnj.edu
http://www3.umdnj.edu/~libcwis/
 univlibs.html

Warren County Library
Second and Hardwick Streets
Belvidere, NJ 07823
(908) 475-6322; (908) 475-6359 FAX
Janet M. Davis, Reference Librarian
Hours: Mon–Thur 9:00–8:30, Fri 9:00–
 6:00, Sat 10:00–3:00

Washington Free Public Library
20 West Carlton Avenue
Washington, NJ 07882
(908) 689-0201
Carol McNeil, Senior Library Assistant
Hours: Mon–Fri 10:00–8:30, Sat 10:00–
 2:00
15¢ per photocopied page

Westfield Memorial Library
550 East Broad Street
Westfield, NJ 07090
(908) 789-4090
Hours: Mon–Fri 10:00–9:00, Sat (except
 Jul–Aug) 10:00–5:00

Willingboro Public Library
1 Salem Road
Willingboro, NJ 08046
(609) 877-6668
Janet Cheeseman, Reference Librarian
Hours: Mon–Thur 9:00–9:00, Fri–Sat
 9:00–5:00, Sun 1:00–5:00 (closed Sun
 in summer)
(Willingboro history and development)

Woodbridge Public Library
George Frederick Plaza
Woodbridge, NJ 07095
(201) 634-4450
Hours: winter: Mon–Thur 9:00–9:30, Fri
 9:00–9:00, Sat 9:00–5:00, Sun 1:00–
 5:00; summer: Mon–Thur 9:00–9:00,
 Fri–Sat 9:00–5:00

Yesteryear Museum
20 Harriet Drive (Regina Place and
 Harriet Drive)
Whippany, NJ 07981-1906

(973) 386-1920
Lee R. Munsick, President
Pub. *Yesteryear*

Historical Societies—
Local and Regional

Absecon Historical Society
618 Franklin Boulevard
Absecon, NJ 08201

**Alexandria Township Historical
Society**
174 Warsaw Road
Frenchtown, NJ 08825
Mary Ellen Sodalvin, President

**Allamuchy Township Historical
Society**
RD 1, Box 111
Great Meadows, NJ 07838
Harold Drake, President

Allendale Historical Society, Inc.
PO Box 294
Allendale, NJ 07401
(201) 327-0605
Pat Wardell
Pub. *Allendale History and Heritage*,
 monthly
$8.00 per year membership

**Allentown-Upper Freehold
Historical Society**
PO Box 328
Allentown, NJ 08501
(609) 259-3171

Alpine Historical Society
PO Box 59
Alpine, NJ 07620
(201) 768-1360

Historical Society of Andover Boro
189 Main Street
Andover, NJ 07821
(973) 786-6829
Beatrice D. Rush, President

Atlantic County Historical Society
907 Shore Road
PO Box 301
Somers Point, NJ 08244
(609) 927-5218
Sara Lee Sosy, Librarian
Hours: Wed–Sat 10:00–3:30
Pub. *Yearbook*, annually; *Atlantic County
 Historical Society Newsletter*,
 quarterly; *Atlantic Heritage*
(emphasis on New Jersey history and
 genealogy)
$12.00 per year membership for
 individuals; research: fee quoted on
 request

Atlantic Highlands Historical Society
22 Prospect Avenue, PO Box 108
Atlantic Highlands, NJ 07716
(732) 291-1861
Helen M. Marchette, President
Hours: Jun–Sept: Sun 1:00–4:00, and by
appointment
Pub. *Portland Poynts*, bimonthly
$5.00 per year membership for
individuals, $10.00 per year
membership for families

Audubon Historical Society
238 Washington Terrace
Audubon, NJ 08106
(609) 547-0586
Jack H. Taylor, Alternate Delegate

Barnegat Historical Society
PO Box 381
Barnegat, NJ 08005
(609) 698-9586
Gary Brower, President

The Barnegat Light Historical Society
(West Fifth Street and Boulevard—
location)
PO Box 386 (mailing address)
Barnegat Light, NJ 08006
(609) 494-8578
Mrs. Claire Ecker, President
Hours: weekends (Jun & Sept) 2:00–
5:00, Mon–Sun (Jul–Aug) 2:00–5:00
Pub. *A Museum at the Shore*, as needed,
$1.00 per issue
$10.00 per year membership for
individuals

Barrington Historical Society
9 Beaver Dr.
Barrington, NJ 08007
Mrs. Earl F. Shenk

Basking Ridge Historical Society
107 Dyckman Place
Basking Ridge, NJ 07920
(201) 766-3786

Batsto Citizens Committee
355 Mansion Avenue
Audubon, NJ 08106
(609) 547-6006
George C. Vail, Chairman

Battleground Historical Society
(Village Inn, 2 Water Street,
Englishtown, NJ 07726—location)
PO Box 61 (mailing address)
Tennent, NJ 07763
(732) 446-2825
Mauriello Kieke, President
Hours: by appointment
Pub. *Matchaponix Journal*, bimonthly
(some genealogy of owners of Village
Inn from 1726 and other associated
information)
$20.00 per year membership

Bay Head Historical Society
PO Box 127
Bayhead, NJ 08742
(732) 892-0223
Evalyn Shippee, President

Bayonne Historical Society
PO Box 3034
Bayonne, NJ 07002
(201) 823-4840

Beavertown Historical Society
94 Beaver Brook Road
Lincoln Park, NJ 07035
(973) 694-0640
George Shanoian, President

Belleville Historical Society
Belleville Public Library
221 Washington Avenue
Belleville, NJ 07109

Belvidere Historic Preservation Commission
Town of Belvidere
301 Second Street
Belvidere, NJ 07823
(908) 475-5331; (908) 475-2512
(Secretary)
Jane W. Ott, Secretary
(Belvidere, Warren County, New Jersey)

Bergen County Historical Society
194 Maplewood Avenue
Bogota, NJ 07603-1714
(201) 488-9463; (201) 343-4169
(Library)
Amy C. Northrup, President; Val Clark,
Head of Reference
Hours: Johnson Free Public Library:
Mon–Thur 9:00–8:45, Fri–Sat 9:00–
4:45
Pub. *Bergen County History*, annually; *In
Bergen's Attic*
$35.00 per year membership, includes
both periodicals

Bergenfield Museum Society
PO Box 95
Bergenfield, NJ 07621
(201) 385-4599
Betty Schmelz, President

Historical Society of Berkeley Heights
PO Box 237
Berkeley Heights, NJ 07922
(908) 464-0961
Helen Tyler, President

Bethlehem Township Historical Society
PO Box 56
Asbury, NJ 08802

Blackwells Mills Canal Historical Association
598 Elizabeth Street
Somerset, NJ 08873
(732) 873-2959
Eugene E. Howe

Blairstown Historical Society
Rt. 2, Box 2211
Columbia, NJ 07832
(201) 362-8523 (Secretary)
Arthur Dickison, President; Gloria
Grohowski, Secretary

Historical Society of Bloomfield
Bloomfield Public Library
90 Broad Street
Bloomfield, NJ 07003
(973) 566-6200
Richard West, President; Richard Pohli,
Vice President
Hours: Wed 2:00–4:45
Pub. *Newsletter*, four times per year, not
available by subscription
$5.00 per year membership; research fee:
voluntary donation

Blue Hills Historical Society
311 West End Ave.
North Plainfield, NJ 07060

Boonton Historical Society
619 Main Street
Boonton, NJ 07005

Historical Society of Boonton Township
Rt. 2, Box 152
Boonton, NJ 07005
Pub. *Historical Society of Boonton
Township, New Jersey Newsletter*

Bordentown Historical Society
13 Crosswicks Street
PO Box 182
Bordentown, NJ 08505
(609) 298-1740
Hours: by appointment

Bradley Beach Historical Society
Bradley Beach Library, 4th Avenue
Bradley Beach, NJ 07720
(732) 776-8446
Rae Biasi, President

Brick Township Historical Society, Inc.
(The Havens Homestead, 521
Herbertsville Road—proposed
location)
PO Box 160 (mailing address)
Brick, NJ 08723
(732) 477-4513
Jane Fabach, President
$10.00 per year membership for
individuals, $150.00 life membership

Bridgeton Antiquarian League
353 Roadstown-Greenwich Road
Bridgeton, NJ 08302
(609) 455-4100
Joseph C. DeLuca, President

Brigantine Historical Society
470 West Shore Drive
Brigantine, NJ 08203
Fritz Haneman

Burlington County Historical Society
Delia Biddle Pugh Library
(454 Lawrence Street—location)
457 High Street (mailing address)
Burlington, NJ 08016
(609) 386-4773; (609) 386-4828
E-mail: jflanphear@aol.com
Joan Lanphear, Librarian
Hours: Mon–Thur 1:00–4:00, Wed
    10:00–12:00, Sun 2:00–4:00
Pub. *Burlington County Historical
    Society Newsletter*, quarterly
(New Jersey history, especially
    Burlington County; Burlington County
    genealogies)
$15.00 per year membership

City of Burlington Historical Society
City Hall
Burlington, NJ 08016
(609) 386-3993

Byram Township Historical Society
3 Ghost Pony Road
Andover, NJ 07821
(973) 347-4585
Carl O. Johnson, President

Califon Historical Society
(The Old Stone Railroad Station, Route
    512 and Railroad Avenue—location)
PO Box 424 (mailing address)
Califon, NJ 07830
(908) 832-2266
Donald E. Philhower Freibergs, President
Hours: first & third Sun (May–Dec)
    1:00–3:00
(special collection of local history and
    artifacts pertaining to Califon and the
    surrounding area)
$15.00 per year membership

Camden County Historical Society
Park Boulevard and Euclid Avenue
Camden, NJ 08103
(609) 964-3333
http://www.cyberenet.net/~gsteiner/
    njgenweb/camdenhs.html
Paul W. Schopp, Executive Director
Hours: Library: Tue & Thur 12:30–4:30,
    Sun 1:00–5:00
Pub. *Communicator*, irregularly; *Camden
    County Historical Society Bulletin*,
    irregularly; *Camden County History
    Journal*, irregularly
$15.00 per year membership for
    individuals, $20.00 per year
    membership for families, $10.00 per
    year membership for students

Camden Preservation Trust
301 Cooper Street
Camden, NJ 08102

Campbell-Christie House Historical Society
530 James Street
New Milford, NJ 07646

Cape May County Historical and Genealogical Society
Route 9
Cape May Court House, NJ 08210
(609) 465-3535; (609) 465-4274 FAX
Ione E. Williams, Library
Hours: Tue–Wed & Fri 10:00–4:00, Sat
    by appointment
Pub. *Cape May County Magazine of
    History and Genealogy*, annually; *The
    Cape May County Crier*, quarterly
$10.00 per year membership for
    individuals, $15.00 per year
    membership for couples

Cedar Grove Historical Society
(903 Pompton Avenue—location)
PO Box 461 (mailing address)
Cedar Grove, NJ 07009
(973) 239-5414 (answering machine)
Mr. Christian Werndly, President

Chatham Historical Society
PO Box 682
Chatham, NJ 07928
Lester E. Lehman, Jr., President

Historical Society of Chatham Township
22 Papermill Road
Chatham, NJ 07928
(201) 635-1679
Robert D. Felch, President

Chester Historical Society
PO Box 376
Chester, NJ 07930
(973) 879-2761
Leonard J. Taylor, Chester Township
    Historian; Matt Koppinger, President
Pub. *Newsletter*, bimonthly
(publishes local history)
$8.00 per year membership for
    individuals, $15.00 per year
    membership for families, $5.00 per
    year Associate membership for
    students or senior citizens, $35.00 per
    year membership for businesses or
    Sustaining membership, $100.00 per
    year Benefactor membership

Chesterfield Township Historical Society
PO Box 86
Crosswicks, NJ 08515

Clark Historical Society
430 Westfield Avenue
Room 18, Municipal Building
Clark, NJ 07066
(201) 381-3081
Constance W. Brewer, President

Collingswood-Newton Colony Historical Society
Haddon and Frazer Avenue
Collingswood, NJ 08108
(609) 858-0649

Colts Neck Historical Society
16 Crusius Place
PO Box 101
Colts Neck, NJ 07722
(732) 462-1378

Cranbury Historical and Preservation Society
(Cranbury History Center, 6 South Main
    Street—location)
PO Box 77 (mailing address)
Cranbury, NJ 08512
(609) 860-1889; (609) 655-3736; (609)
    395-0420
Betty Wagner, Director, Cranbury
    History Center
Hours: Tue & Fri 9:30–noon, and by
    appointment
(genealogy collection restricted to
    Cranbury)
research: donation plus cost of copies

Cranford Historical Society
Hanson House Annex
38 Springfield Ave.
Cranford, NJ 07016
(908) 276-0082
Larry Fuhro, President
Pub. *Mill Wheel*, quarterly

Cumberland County Cultural and Heritage Commission
511 West Walnut Road
Vineland, NJ 08360
(609) 691-8572

Cumberland County Historical Society
Warren Lummis Library
PO Box 16
Greenwich, NJ 08323
(609) 455-8580
Hours: Mar–Nov: Wed 10:00–4:00, Sun
    2:00–5:00
Pub. *Cumberland Patriot*, quarterly
(history and genealogy of New Jersey
    and Cumberland County)
$8.00 per year membership for
    individuals

Dennis Township Historical Society
PO Box 109
South Dennis, NJ 08245

Denville Historical Society
Diamond Spring Road, Box 466
Denville, NJ 07834-0466
(973) 625-1165
Beverly Blanchard, President

Dover Area Historical Society
PO Box 609
Dover, NJ 07801
(973) 366-0786

Down Jersey Marine Historical Society
Box 1031
Delran, NJ 08075

Dunellen Historical Society
322 Whittier Avenue
Dunellen, NJ 08812

Eagleswood Historical Society
Route 9, Main Street
West Creek, NJ 08092
Helen Wisner

East Brunswick Historical Association
43 Sullivan Way
East Brunswick, NJ 08816
(732) 249-3522
Estelle Goldsmith, President

East Hanover Historical Society
181 Mount Pleasant Avenue
East Hanover, NJ 07936
(973) 884-0038

Eatontown Historical Committee
25 Cloverdale Avenue, PO Box 109
Eatontown, NJ 07724
(732) 542-5445
Patricia A. Collins, President

Edison Township Historical Society
328 Plainfield Avenue
Edison, NJ 08817
(732) 248-7310
David Sheehan

Egg Harbor City Historical Society
533 London Avenue
Egg Harbor City, NJ 08215

Elizabethtown Heritage Society
500 North Broad Street
Elizabeth, NJ 07207
(973) 558-3044

Elizabethtown Historical Foundation
PO Box 1
Elizabeth, NJ 07207
Stewart B. Kean

Elmwood Park Historical Society
210 Lee Street
Elmwood Park, NJ 07407
(201) 797-2109
Geraldine Mola

Englewood Historical Society
500 Liberty Road
Englewood, NJ 07631-1411
(201) 568-0678; (201) 568-2567
Eleanor S. Harvey, President
Hours: monthly meeting in the Mackay
 Room of the Englewood Public
 Library
Pub. *Newsletter*, as needed
(gathers autobiographical sketches,
 documents and artifacts in a resource
 center in City Hall)
$10.00 per year membership for
 individuals, $7.00 per year
 membership for students, $25.00 per
 year Contributing membership,
 $250.00 life membership

English Neighborhood Historical Society
656 Elm Street
Maywood, NJ 07607

Essex Fells Historical Society
96 Forest Way
Essex Fells, NJ 07021
Robert Holton

Evesham Historical Society
65 North Locust Avenue, PO Box 199
Marlton, NJ 08053
(609) 983-0395
Sylvia W. Bakley, President

Fair Haven Historical Society
(142 Lexington Avenue, Fairhaven, NJ
 07704-3040—location)
PO Box 72 (mailing address)
Fair Haven, NJ 07704-0072
(732) 842-4453
Timothy J. McMahon, President/
 Historian
Hours: by appointment only
(Fair Haven and surrounding areas)
$5.00 per year membership

Fairfield Historical Society
221 Hollywood Avenue
Fairfield, NJ 07006
Mary Scangarello

Farmingdale Historical Society
2 Goodenough Road
Farmingdale, NJ 07727
(732) 938-2008
Mildred Megill, President

Ferromonte Historical Society
11 Hillside Avenue, Mine Hill
Dover, NJ 07801
(973) 361-8813
Sherry Lenox

Historical Society of Florham Park
PO Box 193
Florham Park, NJ 07932
(973) 377-6291

Fort Lee Historical Society
Borough Hall, 309 Main Street
Fort Lee, NJ 07024
(201) 592-3580
Robert William

Fortescue Historical Society
Pier #1, Bayside
Fortescue, NJ 08321
Nicholas R. Beltrante, Esq.

Franklin Township Historical Society
84 Hillview Avenue
Franklin Park, NJ 08823
(973) 297-2641

Frelinghuysen Township Historical Society
PO Box 411
Johnsonburg, NJ 07846

(908) 852-7362
Debra Natyzak-Osadca, President

Frenchtown Historical Association
Borough Hall, Second Street
Frenchtown, NJ 08825

Galloway Township Historical Society
366 Upland Avenue
Absecon, NJ 08201
(609) 652-3049
Robert Reid

Garfield Historical Society
204 Outwater Lane
Garfield, NJ 07026
(973) 478-9022
Elizabeth Gray, President

Glen Ridge Historical Society
c/o Glen Ridge Congregational Church
PO Box 164
Glen Ridge, NJ 07028-0164
(973) 748-1784
Mrs. George Middleton, President

Glen Rock Historical and Preservation Society
Municipal Building, Borough Hall
Glen Rock, NJ 07452
(201) 447-2414
William Maynard, President

Gloucester County Historical Society
17 Hunter Street
PO Box 409
Woodbury, NJ 08096
(609) 845-4771
Edith Hoelle, Librarian
Hours: Mon–Fri 1:00–4:00, Fri 6:00–
 9:30, last Sun 2:00–5:00
Pub. *Bulletin of the Gloucester County
 Historical Society*, quarterly
(New Jersey history, South Jersey
 genealogy)
$8.00 per year membership

Gouldtown Historical Society
372 Magnolia Street
Salem, NJ 08079
Donald Pierce

Greater Cape May Historical Society
11 South Lafayette Street
Cape May, NJ 08204-5301
(609) 884-3115
Patricia P. Pocher

Great Egg Harbour Township Historical Society
3515 Bargaintown Road
Egg Harbor Township, NJ 08234
June Sheridan, Local Historian
Pub. *Origins*, monthly

Green Township Historical Society
PO Box 203
Tranquility, NJ 07879
(973) 383-5829; (908) 852-2186
Malcom Smith, President

Griggstown Historical Society
RD 1, Canal Road
Princeton, NJ 08554
Sue Rightmire, President

Hackettstown Historical Society
106 Church Street
Hackettstown, NJ 07840
(201) 852-8797
Helen G. Montfort, Co-Archivist; Ruth
   Scarborough, Co-Archivist
Hours: Wed, Fri & Sun 2:00–4:00
$10.00 per year membership; search fee:
   minimum $15.00

Haddon Heights Historical Society
Haddon Heights Library, Station Avenue
Haddon Heights, NJ 08035
(609) 547-7132
Robert Hunter, President

Haddon Township Historical Society
109 Emerald Avenue
Westmont, NJ 08108

Historical Society of Haddonfield
343 King's Highway, East
Haddonfield, NJ 08033
(609) 429-2462
Katherine Tossini, Librarian
Hours: Tue & Thur 9:30–11:30, first Sun
   1:00–3:00, and by appointment
Pub. *HSH Newsletter*, quarterly
(Library has family papers of many early
   Haddonfield families.)
$20.00 per year membership

Haddonfield Preservation Society
120 Warwick Road, PO Box 196
Haddonfield, NJ 08033
(609) 429-5486
Joan L. Aiken, Executive Director

**Township of Hamilton Historical
Society**
319 Clarktown Road
Mays Landing, NJ 08330
(609) 625-0805
Dottie Kinsey, President

**Historical Society of Hamilton
Township**
9 Benson Lane
Trenton, NJ 08610
(609) 585-5435
Dr. James Federici, President

Hammonton Historical Society
767 Central Avenue
Hammonton, NJ 08037
(609) 561-2830
Jeanette Feeley
Pub. *HHS Newsletter*

Hanover Township Historical Society
45 Whippany Road
Whippany, NJ 07981
Mrs. Donald Kitchell

Harding Township Historical Society
PO Box 1776
New Vernon, NJ 07976
Ellen Baumann, President

**Hardwick Township Historical
Society**
PO Box 722
Blairstown, NJ 07925
(908) 362-9462
Nan Horsfield. President

Hardyston Heritage Society
North Woods Trail, PO Box 434
Stockholm, NJ 07460
(973) 697-8733
Barbara Lacatena, President

Harrington Park Historical Society
10 Herring Street
Harrington Park, NJ 07640
(201) 768-5675

**Harrison Township Historical
Society**
(Routes 77 and 45—location)
PO Box 4 (mailing address)
Mullica Hill, NJ 08062
(609) 478-4949

Hazlet Township Historical Society
Municipal Offices, 319 Middle Road
Hazlet, NJ 07730

Helmetta Historical Society
60 Main Street
Helmetta, NJ 08828
(732) 521-2402

**Highland Park Historical
Commission**
PO Box 1330
Highland Park, NJ 08904
(732) 572-3400

Historical Society of Highlands
PO Box 13
Highlands, NJ 07732
(732) 291-4956
John Tomasulo, President

**Hightstown-East Windsor Historical
Society**
164 North Main Street
Hightstown, NJ 08520
(609) 371-9580
Richard S. Hutchinson, Editor,
   Genealogist
Hours: by appointment
Pub. *Hightstown-East Windsor Historical
   Society News*, five times per year
(large local area manuscript collection,
   photos; Hightstown-East Windsor
   families and local history)
$15.00 per year membership

Hillsborough Historical Society
PO Box 720
Neshanic, NJ 08853
(908) 369-3659
Harry B. Smith

**Hillsborough Township Historic
Commission**
(Planning Board Office, Municipal
   Annex—location)
Municipal Building, Amwell Road
   (mailing address)
Neshanic, NJ 08853
(201) 369-4313

The Hillside Historical Society, Inc.
111 Conant Street
Hillside, NJ 07205
(908) 353-8828; (908) 352-9270
Arnold H. McClow, President
Hours: Tours of Woodruff House
   Historical Museum: third Sun 2:00–
   4:00, and by appointment
Pub. *The Core*, occasionally
$5.00 per year membership

Historical Society of Millville
Second and Main Street
Millville, NJ 08332
(609) 825-0789

Historical Society of Somerset Hills
PO Box 136
Basking Ridge, NJ 07920
(908) 221-1770

Holland Township Historical Society
PO Box 434
Milford, NJ 08848
(908) 995-9197

Holmdel Historical Society
Stilwell Road
PO Box 282
Holmdel, NJ 07733
(201) 946-8618
Gerald Ceres, President

Hope Historical Society
High Street
PO Box 52
Hope, NJ 07844

Hopewell Valley Historical Society
124 South Main Street
Pennington, NJ 08534
(609) 737-8726
David Blackwell, President

Howell Historical Society
407 Lakewood-Farmingdale Road
Howell, NJ 07731
(732) 938-5868
Edith Smith, President

**Hunterdon County Historical
Society**
Hiram E. Deats Memorial Library
114 Main Street
Flemington, NJ 08822
(201) 782-1091
Roxanne K. Carkhuff, Librarian
Hours: Thur 1:00–3:00 & 7:00–9:00, and
   by appointment
Pub. *Hunterdon Historical Newsletter*,
   three times per year

(emphasis on Hunterdon County genealogy and local history, plus manuscript collection)

$15.00 per year membership for individuals, $18.00 per year membership for families

Indian Mills Historical Society
RD 5, Box 252, Atsion Road
Vincentown, NJ 08088
(609) 268-0439

Irvington Historical Society
34 Clinton Terrace
Irvington, NJ 07111-1417
(973) 374-7500
Harry Stevenson, President

Island Heights Cultural and Heritage Association
PO Box 670
Island Heights, NJ 08732
(201) 929-0695

Jamesburg Historical Association
203 Buckelew Avenue
Jamesburg, NJ 08831
(732) 521-0068
Nancy J. Luberecki, Acquisition Chairman
Hours: Sat 11:00–3:00; meeting first Wed 8:00 P.M.
Pub. *The House of Many Windows*, semiannually
$5.00 per year membership

Jefferson Township Historical Society
Dover-Milton Road, PO Box 1776
Oak Ridge, NJ 07438
(973) 697-8675
Clifford Williams, President

Kearny Cottage Historical Association
Kearny Cottage
63 Catalpa Avenue
Perth Amboy, NJ 08861
(732) 826-1826; (732) 826-3928 (President)
Jack M. Dudas, Esq., President
Hours: Tue & Thur 1:00–4:00, Sun by appointment
(house museum)
$10.00 per year membership

Kenilworth Historical Society
567 Kenilworth Blvd.
Kenilworth, NJ 07033
(908) 276-8449
Robert Woods

Keyport Historical Society
2 Broad Street
PO Box 312
Keyport, NJ 07735
(732) 739-6390; (732) 264-2102 (appointments); (732) 264-7822 (appointments); (732) 264-6119 (appointments)

Hours: May–Sept: Mon 10:00–noon, Sun 1:00–4:00 by appointment
Pub. *Steamboat Dock Museum Newsletter*, three or four times per year
(some genealogical information, birth, marriage and obituary index to *Matwen Journal* 1869–1928, some information on Green Grove Cemetery, Cedawood Cemetery, later called Raritan)
$5.00 per year membership for individuals, $10.00 per year membership for families, $3.00 per year membership for youths or senior citizens, $25.00 per year Contributing membership, $250.00 life membership

Kingwood Township Historical Society
Kingwood Township Municipal Building
PO Box 199
Baptistown, NJ 08803

Kinnelon Historical Commission
Municipal Building
Kinnelon Road
Kinnelon, NJ 07405

Lacey Township Historical Society
(Rt. 9—location)
PO Box 412 (mailing address)
Forked River, NJ 08731

Lake Hopatcong Historical Society
211 Park Heights Avenue
Dover, NJ 07801
(973) 366-2103
Martin Kane, President

Boro of Lakehurst Historical Society
300 Center Street
Lakehurst, NJ 08733
(732) 657-8864
Mary Scilex

Lambertville Historical Society
52 Bridge Street
PO Box 2
Lambertville, NJ 08530
(609) 397-0770

Lawnside Historical Society
231 Charleston Avenue
Lawnside, NJ 08045
(609) 547-8489
Linda Waller, President

Lawrence Historical Society
(Port Mercer Canal House, 4274 Quakerbridge Road, Princeton, NJ 08540—location)
PO Box 6025 (mailing address)
Lawrenceville, NJ 08648
(609) 243-9108
David Kimzey, Caretaker
Hours: Open house: second Sun Jun, second weekend Dec
Pub. *Newsletter*, semiannually (spring and fall)

Leonia Historical Society
199 Christie Street
Leonia, NJ 07605
(201) 947-5647
Milton Ehrlich

Linwood Historical Society
1014 Maple Avenue
Linwood, NJ 08221
Michael Everett, President
Pub. *LHS Newsletter*

Little Falls Historical Society
22 Crestmont Road
Little Falls, NJ 07424
(973) 256-1646
Clyde Meder, Alternate Delegate

Little Falls Township Historical Society
8 Douglas Drive
Little Falls, NJ 07424
(973) 256-3651
Clifford Swisher, President

Little Silver Historical Society
Borough Hall, Prospect Avenue
Little Silver, NJ 07739
(732) 842-2400
David Griffith, President

Livingston Historical Society
South Livingston Avenue
PO Box 220
Livingston, NJ 07039
Monte Caliman, President
Pub. *Livingston Historical Society Newsletter*, seven times per year
$6.00 per year membership

Long-A-Coming Historical Society
59 South White Horse Pike
Berlin, NJ 08009

Long Beach Island Historical Association
Engleside and Beach Avenue
PO Box 1222
Beach Haven, NJ 08008
(609) 492-0700
E-mail: smtg@juno.com
S. Mary T. Gruber, Genealogy Chairman
Hours: winter: Tue 1:00–4:00; summer: daily 2:00–4:00 & 7:00–9:00
Pub. *Museum Pieces*, quarterly
$10.00 per year membership for individuals, $20.00 per year membership for families, $30.00 per year Friend membership, $40.00 per year membership for merchants, $100.00 life membership

Long Hill Township Historical Society
1336 Valley Road
Stirling, NJ 07087
(908) 647-5762
Jennifer Lamson, President

Longport Historical Society
Borough Hall
Longport, NJ 08403
(609) 823-1115

Lower Alloways Creek Historical Society
736 Smick Road
Lower Alloways Creek, NJ 08079

Lumberton Historical Society
PO Box 22
Lumberton, NJ 08048
(609) 247-4067
Doris Priest, President

Lyndhurst Historical Society
PO Box 135
Lyndhurst, NJ 07071
(201) 804-2513; (201) 939-7639
Marilyn Romano, President

Madison Historical Society
PO Box 148
Madison, NJ 07940
(973) 377-3924

Madison Township Historical Society
Thomas Warne Historical Museum and Library
(Route 516, Old Bridge Township, NJ—location)
150 Morristown Road (mailing address)
Matawan, NJ 07747
(732) 566-0348
Mrs. Alvia D. Martin, Curator
Hours: Wed 9:30–noon, first Sun 1:00–4:00
Pub. *The Timepiece*, semiannually (spring/summer and fall/winter)
$10.00 per year membership

Magnolia Historical Society
208 Brooke Avenue
Magnolia, NJ 08049
(609) 783-8585
Helen Bradley, President

Mahwah Historical Society
310 Forest Road
Mahwah, NJ 07430
(201) 891-9049
William Lamoreaux, President

Manchester Historical Society
18 Bowie Dr.
Whiting, NJ 08759

Mansfield Township Historical Society
3121 Route 206
Columbus, NJ 08022-9530
(609) 298-4174

Mantua Historical Society
506 Buckingham Drive
Sewell, NJ 08080
Nancy Rotny

Maple Shade Historical Society
PO Box 368
Maple Shade, NJ 08052

Matawan Historical Society, Inc.
94 Main Street
PO Box 41
Matawan, NJ 07747
(732) 566-3817
Sarah Ellison, President; Helen Henderson, Director
Pub. *MHS Newsletter*

Maurice River Historical Society
PO Box 161
Mauricetown, NJ 08329
(no genealogical information)

Mauricetown Historical Society
Front Street
PO Box 1
Mauricetown, NJ 08329
(609) 785-0457

Maywood Historical Committee
652 Grant Avenue
Maywood, NJ 07607
(201) 843-1130
Betty A. Fetzer, President

Medford Historical Society
PO Box 362
Medford, NJ 08055
(609) 835-2652

Merchantville Historical Society
1 West Maple Avenue
Merchantville, NJ 08109
(609) 665-1819
Edith Silberstein, President
Hours: by appointment
Pub. *Merchantville Historical Society Newsletter*, annually
(collection of photographs)
$10.00 per year membership for individuals, $20.00 per year membership for families, $25.00 per year membership for businesses

Metuchen-Edison Regional Historical Society
PO Box 61
Metuchen, NJ 08840
(732) 906-0529

Middletown Township Historical Society
Leonardville Road and Chamone Avenue
PO Box 434
Middletown, NJ 07748
(201) 291-8739
Randall Gabrielan, President
Pub. *Newsletter of the MTHS*
refers genealogical queries to the Monmouth County HistoricalAssociation or the Shrewsbury Historical Society

Midland Park Historical Society
212 Park Avenue
Midland Park, NJ 07432
George Cook

Millbrook Village Society
Star Route/Fish Hill Road
Tannersville, PA 18372
(717) 629-0456
Bob Demarest, President

The Millburn-Short Hills Historical Society
(1 Station Plaza at the Short Hills Railroad Station—location)
PO Box 243 (mailing address)
Short Hills, NJ 07078
(973) 564-9519 phone and FAX
Lynne K. Ranieri, Vice President
Hours: Wed 2:00–4:00, and by appointment
Pub. *The Thistle*, one or two times per year
$10.00 per year membership for individuals

Milltown Historical Society
PO Box 96
Milltown, NJ 08850
(908) 828-0249
D. Bruce Schwendeman, President

Monmouth Beach Historical Society
23 Navesink Drive
Monmouth Beach, NJ 07750
(908) 222-2244
Mrs. Edwin L. Brower, President

Monmouth County Historical Association
70 Court Street
Freehold, NJ 07728-1795
(908) 462-1466
http://www.monmouth.com/~mcha
Carla Z. Tobias, Librarian/Archivist
Hours: Library: Wed–Sat 10:00–4:00
Pub. *Newsletter*, bimonthly
$25.00 per year membership for individuals, $35.00 per year membership for families, $20.00 per year membership for students and senior citizens; queries $1.00 through Monmouth County Genealogy Club membership

Monroe Area Historical Society
Dey Grove Road, RD 2, Box 60B
Englishtown, NJ 07726
Carol E. Dooley

Montague Association for the Restoration of Community History (MARCH)
320 River Road
Montague, NJ 07827
(973) 293-3106 (Wednesday); (973) 293-7360 (President)
Mario Gennarelli, President

Hours: Wed 10:00–noon (volunteers on duty); meetings: last Thur 7:30, tours: Jul–Aug: Sun 1:00–4:00
Pub. *Notes, News, and Nostalgia,* quarterly
$5.00 per year membership for individuals, $10.00 per year membership for families, $2.50 per year membership for students, $3.50 per year membership for senior citizens, $20.00 per year membership for businesses, $25.00 per year Supporting membership; research inquiries to Alicia Batko, Historian: SASE appreciated

Montclair Historical Society
108-110 Orange Road
Montclair, NJ 07042-2133
(973) 744-1796; (973) 783-9149 FAX
Karen Whitehaus, President
Hours: Office: 15 Sept–15 Jun: Mon–Fri 9:00–5:00; Crane House Museum: mid-Sept to mid-Jun: Sun 2:00–5:00; Terhune Library: by appointment
Pub. *Cranetown Crier,* ten times per year (monthly, September–June)
$25.00 per year membership for individuals, $35.00 per year membership for families, $50.00 per year Sustaining membership, $100.00 per year Patron membership, $250.00 per year Friend membership, $500.00 per year Benefactor membership, $1,000.00 Crane Circle (life) membership, plus optional $3.00 for first class mailing of all society information

Montville Historical Society
415 Boyd Street
PO Box 497
Boonton, NJ 07005
(973) 335-1970
Carol Catacchio, President

Historical Society of Moorestown
12 High Street
PO Box 477
Moorestown, NJ 08057
(609) 235-0353
John Coles, President
Hours: Tue 1:00–3:00
(local history and local genealogy)
$15.00 per year membership for individuals, $25.00 per year membership for families

Morris County Heritage Commission
(300 Mendham Road—location)
Morris County Courthouse, PO Box 900 (mailing address)
Morristown, NJ 07960-0900
(973) 829-8117
Mary Chalfant, Administrative Assistant
Hours: Mon–Fri 8:00–5:00

Pub. *County Circular,* three times per year
search fee: depends on information requested

Morris County Historical Society
18 Jeffrie Trail
Whippany, NJ 07891
(973) 672-7278
Mrs. Terry Schlatter, President
Pub. *The Morris Gazette*

Mount Holly Historical Society
307 High Street
PO Box 4081
Mount Holly, NJ 08060
(609) 267-8844

Mount Hope Historical Conservancy Inc.
32 Mountain Avenue
Rockaway, NJ 07866
(973) 625-2508
Joanna Wheeler Peak, President

Mount Laurel Historical Society
314 Union Mill Road
Mount Laurel, NJ 08054
Rena W. Hallett

Mount Tabor Historical Society
PO Box 137
Mount Tabor, NJ 07878-0137
(973) 625-8742
Natalie Rowell, President

Mountainside Historical Society
Mountainside Free Public Library
Watchung Avenue
Mountainside, NJ 07092

Munroe Township Historical Society
Main and Library Streets
PO Box 474
Williamstown, NJ 08094

Township of Neptune Historical Society
Neptune Township Historical Museum
25 Neptune Boulevard
PO Box 1125
Neptune, NJ 07754-1125
(732) 775-8241, ext. 306
Evelyn Stryker Lewis, Curator/Vice President
Hours: Museum: Tue–Fri 1:00–5:00
Pub. *Township of Neptune Historical Society Newsletter,* quarterly
(museum has a reference library with a genealogy section; Monmouth County, New Jersey, history)

New Brunswick Historical Club
278 George Street
New Brunswick, NJ 08901
(201) 247-1695

New Egypt Historical Society
PO Box 295
New Egypt, NJ 08533
Carol Reed, President

New Providence Historical Society
(1350 Springfield Avenue—museum location)
Municipal Center (mailing address)
New Providence, NJ 07974
(908) 464-0163
Ann Chovan, President
Hours: Museum: first & third Sun, and by appointment: Mason Room, New Providence Memorial Library: Tue & Thur 10:00–4:00
Pub. *Turkey Tracks,* quarterly
(New Providence genealogical and historical collection, photographs, maps, ledgers, etc.)
$10.00 per year membership

New Shrewsbury Historical Society
Wator Street
New Shrewsbury, NJ 07724
Mrs. Jack Branin

Newfield Historical Society
107 N.E. Boulevard
Newfield, NJ 08344
(609) 697-3811; (609) 697-1100

North Arlington Historical Society
89 Canterbury Ave.
North Arlington, NJ 07032
(201) 998-6290

North Brunswick Historical Society
690 Cranbury Crossroad
North Brunswick, NJ 08902

North Caldwell Historical Society
120 Grandview Avenue
North Caldwell, NJ 07006
(973) 228-7257
Sue Schlesinger, Vice President

North Jersey Highlands Historical Society
8 Stoney Lane
West Milford, NJ 07480
(973) 208-0034
Nancy Gibbs, President
Hours: by appointment
Pub. *The Highlander,* annually, $6.00 per year subscription
(good library for North Jersey, especially ironworking, but relatively little on genealogy)
$15.00 per year membership

Nutley Historical Society
22 Newman Avenue
Nutley, NJ 07110
(973) 667-9121
Tracy Scheckel, President

Oak Summit School Historical Society
190 Oak Summit Road
Frenchtown, NJ 08825
(908) 996-4633
Irene Leon, Treasurer

Oakland Historical Society
7 Fox River Crossing
Mahwah, NJ 07430
(201) 825-9049
Hugh T. Francis, President

Ocean County Historical Society
Strickler Research Library
Historical Research Department
(26 Hadley Avenue—location)
CN 2191 (mailing address)
Toms River, NJ 08754
(732) 341-1880
Corinne Murphy Lill, Director of
    Research
Hours: Research: Tue–Thur 1:00–4:00,
    Sat 10:00–1:00, and by appointment
Pub. *Society Scroll*, ten times per year
(Library of 8000 books on Ocean
    County, 500 family genealogies,
    vertical file, maps, rare books, census,
    computer, family files, microforms,
    vital statistics and other primary
    records)
$15.00 per year membership for
    individuals, $35.00 per year Patron
    membership; research: $10.00 per hour

Ocean Gate Historical Society
PO Box 342
Ocean Gate, NJ 08753
Pearl Greer

**Historical Society of Ocean Grove,
N.J.**
PO Box 446
Ocean Grove, NJ 07756
(201) 774-1869
Philip May, President; Elsalyn
    Palmisano-Drucker, Librarian/
    Archivist
Pub. *HSOG Newsletter*

**Township of Ocean Historical
Society**
342 Wells Avenue
Oakhurst, NJ 07755
(732) 531-0775
Kathleen Parrett, President

Oceanport Historical Society
20 Pemberton Avenue
Oceanport, NJ 07757
Helen Moffet

Ogdensburg Historical Society
15 Richards Street
Ogdensburg, NJ 07439
Wasco Hadowanetz

Old Bridge Historical Commission
1 Old Bridge Plaza
Old Bridge Township, NJ 08857
(201) 791-5600

Historical Society of Old Randolph
PO Box 1776
Ironia, NJ 07845
(973) 989-7095

**Old Schralenburgh Historical
Society**
43 Overlook Road
Dumont, NJ 07628

Old Wall Historical Society
(Allgor-Barkalow Homestead Museum,
    1701 New Bedford Road—location)
PO Box 1203 (mailing address)
Wall Township, NJ 07719
(201) 974-1430 (Sun); (201) 681-3806
    (President)
De Hearn, President
Hours: Sun 1:00–4:00, and by
    appointment
Pub. *Journal*, annually
(genealogy library, Wall Township and
    surrounding area)
$10.00 per year membership for
    individuals, $15.00 per year
    membership for families

Oldman Township Historical Society
Railroad Avenue, PO Box 158208
Pedricktown, NJ 08067
(609) 299-1743

Oxford Historical Society
(46 Kent Road—location)
PO Box 60 (mailing address)
Oxford, NJ 07863
(201) 453-2204
D. G. Cratch, President
$5.00 per year membership; currently
    has no resources for organized
    searches, inquiries are forwarded to
    other agencies

**Paramus Historical and Preservation
Society**
27 Sullivan Drive
Emerson, NJ 07630
(201) 262-8711
William Wassmann, President

Parsippany Historical Society
93 Intervale Road
Boonton, NJ 07005
(973) 334-2116
Roberta Chopko

Pascack Historical Society
(19 Ridge Avenue—location)
PO Box 285 (mailing address)
Park Ridge, NJ 07656
Katherine P. Randall, President
Pub. *Relics*, quarterly
$10.00 per year membership; refers
    genealogical inquiries to the Bergen
    County Historical Society

Passaic County Historical Society
Lambert Castle Museum and Library
Valley Road
Paterson, NJ 07509
(973) 357-1070
Andrew F. Shick, Acting Director
Hours: Mon–Fri by appointment only
Pub. *Castle Lite*, quarterly

(Passaic County families, New Jersey
    families)
$20.00 per year membership for
    individuals, $30.00 per year
    membership for families, $15.00 per
    year membership for senior citizens;
    search fees by letter: $8.00 for
    members, $15.00 for non-members

Pennsauken Historical Society
2506 Denby Avenue
Pennsauken, NJ 08109
(609) 663-1251
Robert Engelke, President

**Pennsville Township Historical
Society**
273 Fort Mott Road
Salem, NJ 08079
(609) 935-6538
Grace Alliegro, President

Perth Amboy Historical Society
1 Lewis Street
Perth Amboy, NJ 08861

**Phillipsburg Area Historical Society,
Inc.**
Municipal Building-Corliss Avenue
Phillipsburg, NJ 08865
(908) 454-3478
Carl Baxter, President
Hours: by appointment only
Pub. *Newsletter*, five times per year
    (September, November, January,
    March and May)
(local obituaries, weddings, births, etc.)
$3.00 per year membership for
    individuals, $5.00 per year
    membership for families, $2.00 per
    year membership for senior citizens or
    youths, $25.00 per year Supporter
    membership, $100.00 life
    membership; no facilities for research
    by mail

**Pilesgrove-Woodstown Historical
Society**
209 North Main Street
Woodstown, NJ 08098
(609) 769-3499
Ann W. Tatnall, President

**Piscataway Historical and Heritage
Society**
1001 Maple Avenue
Piscataway, NJ 08854
(732) 752-5252
Constance and John O'Grady, President

The Historical Society of Plainfield
Drake House
602 West Front Street
Plainfield, NJ 07060-1004
(908) 755-5831
Carol Davis, Genealogy Committee
    Chairperson
Hours: Sat 2:00–4:00
limited resources/search available: $5.00
    donation requested with response

Plainsboro Historical Society, Inc.
641 Plainsboro Road
PO Box 278
Plainsboro, NJ 08536-0278
(609) 799-0909
Phylllis DiFrancesco, President
Pub. *Reflections*

Pohatcong Heritage Commission
Rt. 1, Box 251
Phillipsburg, NJ 08865
(201) 995-7107
Frank Leary, Township Historian

Point Pleasant Historical Society
PO Box 1273
Point Pleasant Beach, NJ 08742

Port Republic Historical Society
PO Box 215
Port Republic, NJ 08241
(609) 652-1352
Doris Mollock

Historical Society of Princeton
158 Nassau Street
Princeton, NJ 08542
(609) 921-6748; (609) 921-6939 FAX
Gail F. Stern, Director
Hours: Tue–Sun noon–4:00 (winter
    hours vary)
Pub. *Princeton History*, annually, $5.00
    per issue
$25.00 per year membership for
    individuals; $3.00 daily fee for library
    use by non-members; written
    inquiries: $10.00 for members, $15.00
    for non-members

Rahway Historical Society, Inc.
(1632 Saint Georges Avenue—location)
PO Box 1842 (mailing address)
Rahway, NJ 07065
Linda McTeague, Director
(local history and genealogy)

John Ralston Historical Association
Box 301
Mendham, NJ 07945

Ramsey Historical Association
65 North Island Avenue
Ramsey, NJ 07446-2528
(201) 327-6467
William Irwin, President

Red Bank Historical Society, Inc.
PO Box 712
Red Bank, NJ 07701
Robert Parremore, President

Riverfront Historical Society
PO Box 175
Beverly, NJ 08010
(609) 871-0592
Claire Thoma, President

**Riverside Township Historical
Society**
220 Heulings Avenue
Riverside, NJ 08075
J. Robert Espenschied

**The Historical Society of Riverton,
Inc.**
405 Midway
Riverton, NJ 08077
(609) 829-6315
Betty B. Hahle, Historian
Pub. *Gaslight News*

Historical Society of the Rockaways
Box 100
Hibernia, NJ 07842
(973) 366-6730

Roebling Historical Society
119 Second Avenue
Roebling, NJ 08554
(609) 499-2415; (609) 499-8868 FAX
Donna McElrea, President
Hours: meetings at Florence Township
    Library, Roebling: third Mon 7:00
Pub. *Roebling Record*, quarterly
(Village of Roebling and John A.
    Roebling and Sons, Co.)
$7.00 per year membership

Roseland Historical Society
36 Buttonwood Road
Essex Fells, NJ 07021
(973) 226-2708
Mary Lou Rowe, Delegate

The Roselle Historical Society, Inc.
116 East Fourth Avenue
Roselle, NJ 07203
(908) 245-9010
William Frolich, President
(Roselle and New Jersey history; "We try
    to be cooperative with requests, but no
    guarantee."
$3.00 per year membership

Roselle Park Historical Society
PO Box 135
Roselle Park, NJ 07204
(908) 245-5422; (908) 245-9260
Patricia A. Pagnetti, Historian

**Roxbury Township Historical
Society**
PO Box 18
Succasunna, NJ 07876

Rumson Historical Society
Wilson Circle
Rumson, NJ 07760
(732) 842-0338
Nora Archibald, President

Salem County Historical Society
Alexander Grant House
79-83 Market Street
Salem, NJ 08079
(609) 935-5004
Alice G. Boggs, Librarian
Hours: Tue–Fri 12:00–4:00, second Sat
    12:00–4:00
Pub. *Newsletter*, quarterly
$20.00 per year membership for
    individuals, $30.00 per year
    membership for families or
    households, $10.00 per year

membership for students, $50.00 per
year membership for businesses or
Sustaining membership for
individuals, $200.00 per year
Benefactor membership for
individuals, $300.00 life
membershipfor individuals

Sayreville Historical Society
425 Main Street, PO Box 18
Sayreville, NJ 08872
(732) 257-0893
Helen Boehm, President

**Historical Society of Scotch Plains
and Fanwood**
(1840 Front Street—location)
PO Box 261 (mailing address)
Scotch Plains, NJ 07076
(908) 232-1199; (908) 232-2212 FAX
Richard A. Bousquet, President
Hours: first Sun 2:00–4:00
Pub. *Newsletter*, quarterly
$10.00 per year membership

Sewaren Historical Club
434 Cliff Street
Sewaren, NJ 07077

Shrewsbury Historical Society
(Museum, Education, and Research
    Center, 419 Sycamore Avenue—
    location)
PO Box 333 (mailing address)
Shrewsbury, NJ 07702
(732) 530-7974; (732) 741-9406
    (President)
J. Louise Jost, President
Hours: Tue & Thur 1:00–3:00, Sat
    10:00–4:00
$5.00 per year membership for
    individuals (beginning 1 June), $10.00
    per year membership for families,
    $25.00 per year Contributing
    membership, $50.00 per year
    membership for businesses and
    organizations, $200.00 life
    membership

Skylands Association
Box 302
Ringwood, NJ 07456
(201) 362-7527

Somers Point Historical Society
PO Box 517
Somers Point, NJ 08244

Somerset County Historical Society
(Van Veghten Drive, Bridgewater, NJ—
    location)
PO Box 632 (mailing address)
Somerville, NJ 08876
(908) 218-1281
Dorothy Stratford, Corresponding
    Secretary
Hours: Tue noon–3:00 & 7:00–9:00
Pub. *Newsletter*, ten times per year
$10.00 per year membership

Somerville Historical Society
16 East Summit Street
Somerville, NJ 08876

South Amboy Historical Society
109 Fletus Street
South Amboy, NJ 08879
Joseph Wojcieckowski

South Orange Historical and Preservation Society
162 Irving Ave.
South Orange, NJ 07079
(973) 761-5508
Katherine Flaxman, Delegate

South Plainfield Historical Society
PO Box 11
South Plainfield, NJ 07080
(908) 754-3503
Mary Mazepa, President

South River Historical Society
129 Main Street
South River, NJ 08882
(732) 257-2200

Southampton Historical Society
17 Mill Street
PO Box 2086
Vincentown, NJ 08088
(609) 859-4042
Joseph Laufer, President
Hours: by appointment
Pub. *Hello Central*, quarterly
$5.00 per year membership for
   individuals, $7.50 per year
   membership for husband and wife

Historic Speedwell
333 Speedwell Avenue
Morristown, NJ 07960
(973) 540-0211
Sarah E. Henrich, Delegate

Spring Lake Historical Society, Inc.
Municipal Building
PO Box 703
Spring Lake, NJ 07762
(732) 449-0772
Janice Sheehan, Vice President
Hours: Tue 10:00–noon, Sun 1:00–3:00
Pub. *Newsletter*, quarterly
(permanent museum and changing
   exhibit gallery)
$15.00 per year membership for
   individuals

Springfield Historical Society
133 Short Hills Avenue
Springfield, NJ 07081
(973) 379-2634
Janice P. Bongiovanni, President

Squan Village Historical Society
PO Box 262
Manasquan, NJ 08736
(732) 223-6770

Stafford Township Historical Society
87 Stafford Avenue
Manahawkin, NJ 08050

Stillwater Township Historical Society
PO Box 23
Stillwater, NJ 07855
(973) 383-4822
Mrs. Augustus Roof

Stratford Historical Society
201 South Atlantic Avenue
Stratford, NJ 08084
(609) 435-5901
Walt Baxter, President

Summit Historical Society
(Carter House, 90 Butler Parkway—
   location)
PO Box 464 (mailing address)
Summit, NJ 07901
(908) 277-1747
Arthur Cotterell, President
Hours: Tue 9:30–noon, Wed 1:30–4:00
Pub. *The Historian*, four times per year
(local history: Summit organizations,
   individuals, schools, churches,
   businesses, etc.)
$10.00 per year membership for
   individuals, $15.00 per year
   membership for couples

Sussex County Historical Society
82 Main Street
PO Box 913
Newton, NJ 07860
(973) 383-6010
Barbara Waskowich, Secretary-Curator
Hours: Fri 10:00–3:00
Pub. *Old Sussex Almanack*, quarterly
$10.00 per year membership

Swedesboro Historical Society
Swedesboro-Paulsboro Road
Swedesboro, NJ 08085
Elaine Roda, President

Tabernacle Historical Society
162 Carranza Road
Vincentown, NJ 08088
(609) 268-0473
Viola Sparagna, President
Hours: meetings at Town Hall: monthly
   evenings
(a small township historical society)

The Rockingham Association
175 Hun Road
Princeton, NJ 08540
(609) 924-3625
Jack K. Rimalover, President

The Tewksberry Historical Society
6 Saw Mill Road
Lebanon, NJ 08833
(908) 832-2562
Stephanie V. R. Koven, President

Trenton Historical Society
PO Box 1112
Trenton, NJ 08606-1112
(609) 883-7368 (President)
Harold W. Thompson, Jr., President

Tuckerton Historical Society
PO Box 43
Tuckerton, NJ 08087

Union County Historical Society
PO Box 3562, Chestnut Street Branch
Union, NJ 07083

Union Landing Historical Society
PO Box 473
Brielle, NJ 08730
(732) 528-5550
Candace Moore, President
Hours: meetings:; third Sun
Pub. *U.L.H.S. Newsletter*, monthly
$10.00 per year membership for
   individuals, $35.00 per year
   membership for families

Union Township Historical Society
The Caldwell Parsonage Museum
909 Caldwell Avenue
Union, NJ 07083
(908) 964-9047
Michael Yesenko
Hours: by appointment
(publishes local history)

United Railroad Historical Society
W-11 Avon Drive
East Windsor, NJ 08520-5647

Upper Saddle River Historical Society
245 Lake Street
Upper Saddle River, NJ 07458
(201) 327-6470
Bill Yeomans, President

Historical Preservation Society of Upper Township
859 South Shore Road
PO Box 659
Marmora, NJ 08223
(609) 628-3041

Van Harlingen Historical Society
Ludlow Avenue
Belle Mead, NJ 08502
(908) 359-2415
Jessie Havens

Vernon Township Historical Society
5 Sleepy Hollow Road
Sussex, NJ 07461
(973) 875-9562
Joan Magura, President
Pub. *VTHS Newsletter*

Verona Historical Society
31 Thomas Street
Wayne, NJ 07470
(973) 694-5835
Arthur Smith, President

Vineland Historical and Antiquarian Society
108 South Seventh Street
PO Box 35
Vineland, NJ 08360
(609) 691-1111
Patricia Stalhuth, Secretary-Genealogist
Hours: Tue–Sat 1:00–4:00 (closed July)
Pub. *Vineland Historical Magazine*, annually
$10.00 per year membership for individuals, $12.50 per year membership for couples, $5.00 junior membership (18 and under), $250.00 life membership

Voorhees Township Historical Society
820 Berlin Road
Voorhees, NJ 08043

Waldwick Historical Society
PO Box 273
Waldwick, NJ 07463

Walpack Historical Society
202 Stanhope Road
Sparta, NJ 07871
(973) 729-7392
Leonard R. Peck, President

Warren County Cultural and Heritage Commission
Shippen Manor, 8 Belvidere Avenue
Oxford, NJ 07863
(908) 453-4381; (908) 453-4981
E-mail: wcchc@nac.net
http://www.wcchc.org
George K. Warne, Chairman; Carol Cordes, Secretary
Hours: Mon–Fri 8:30–5:00
Pub. *The Furnace*, quarterly, free

Warren County Historical and Genealogical Society
(313 Mansfield Street—museum and library location)
PO Box 313 (mailing address)
Belvidere, NJ 07823-0313
(908) 475-2512; (908) 475-4246 (Museum recording machine); (908) 689-2993 (President)
V. A. Brown, Curator; Hattie M. Seiwell, President
Hours: Sun 2:00–4:00
Pub. *Oak Leaves*, three to four times per year
$7.50 per year membership

Warren Township Historical Society
5 Wychwood Way
Warren Township, NJ 07059
(732) 469-2318
Alan A. Siegal, President

Washington Township Historical Society
6 Fairview Avenue
PO Box 189
Long Valley, NJ 07853

(201) 876-9696
Hours: Sun 2:00–4:00
(Morris County)
$8.00 per year membership for individuals, $12.00 per year membership for families

Watchung Hills Historical Society
102 Old Army Road
Bernardsville, NJ 07924
Mrs. Marion J. Kennedy

Watchung Historical Society
105 Turtle Road
Watchung, NJ 07060
President

Wayne Township Historical Commission
533 Berdan Avenue
Wayne, NJ 07470
(973) 694-7192

Weehawken Historical Society, Inc.
212 Dodd Street
Weehawken, NJ 07087
(201) 867-2050

Wenonah Historical Society
206 South Princeton Avenue
Wenonah, NJ 08090
(609) 468-6594
Jean Ehlens

Historical Society of West Caldwell
(289 Westville Avenue—location)
PO Box 1701 (mailing address)
West Caldwell, NJ 07006
(973) 226-8976
Roxanne Douglas, President
$10.00 per year membership for individuals, $15.00 per year membership for families, $100.00 life membership for individuals

West Long Branch Historical Society
PO Box 151
West Long Branch, NJ 07764
Thomas D. Bazley, President

West Paterson Historical Society
556 BcBride Avenue
West Paterson, NJ 07424
(973) 345-1876
Alfred Baumann, President

West Portal Historical Society
PO Box 134
Asbury, NJ 08802

Historical Society of West Windsor
PO Box 38
Princeton Junction, NJ 08550
(609) 452-8598
Joan Parry

Westampton Township Historical Society
PO Box 132
Rancocas, NJ 08073-0132

Westfield Historical Society
PO Box 613
Westfield, NJ 07091
(201) 232-1776
Ralph H. Jones, Curator
Hours: Mon–Fri 9:30–noon (except holidays)
Pub. *Westfield Historical Society Newsletter*, quarterly
$10.00 per year membership for individuals, $15.00 per year membership for families, $50.00 per year Patron membership, $200.00 life membership

Wharton Historical Society
10 North Main Street, PO Box 424
Wharton, NJ 07885

White Township Historical Society
RD 1, Box 231, Sarepta Road
Belvidere, NJ 07823
Betty Jo King

Wildwood Crest Historical Society
Crest Borough Hall, 6101 Pacific Avenue
West Cape May, NJ 08210
Jesse Robert Coombs, President

Wildwood Historical Society, Inc.
George F. Boyer Historical Museum
3907 Pacific Avenue
Wildwood, NJ 08260
(609) 523-0277 (Museum); (609) 522-6285 (President)
Larry M. Lillo, President
Hours: summer: Mon–Sun 9:30–2:30, winter: Thur–Sun 10:30–2:30
Pub. *News Letter*, semiannually (fall-winter, spring-summer)
(historical museum, research room, National Marbles Hall of Fame)
$10.00 per year membership for individuals

Willingboro Historical Society
Municipal Complex
Willingboro, NJ 08046

Wood-Ridge History Committee
c/o Wood-Ridge Memorial Library
231 Hackensack Street
Wood-Ridge, NJ 07075
(201) 438-2455
Ruth Stumm

Historical Association of Woodbridge
23 East Green Street
Woodbridge, NJ 07095
(732) 636-5874
John P. O'Connor, President

Woodstown Historical Preservation Committee
250 Howard Avenue
Woodstown, NJ 08098
Robert Nathan

Wyckoff Historical Society
PO Box 73
Wyckoff, NJ 07481

LDS Family History Centers

Jersey City
(see North Caldwell or New York City, New York)

Morristown
(201) 539-5362

Newark
(see Morristown or North Caldwell)

North Caldwell
(201) 226-8975

Paterson
(see North Caldwell)

Genealogical Societies

State Genealogical Societies

Genealogical Society of New Jersey
PO Box 1291
New Brunswick, NJ 08903
(201) 356-6920 (Corresponding Secretary)
Dorothy A. Stratford, Corresponding Secretary
Hours: Rutgers University, New Jersey Room, Alexander Library, Special Collections and Archives: Mon–Fri 9:00–5:00, Sat 1:00–5:00
Pub. *The Genealogical Magazine of New Jersey*, three times per year; *Newsletter*, semiannually
(Bible records, gravestone inscriptions, surname data files, Revolutionary Soldier information files, abstracted records of New Jersey churches, etc.)
$15.00 per year membership

Genealogy Club of the Library of the New Jersey Historical Society
230 Broadway
Newark, NJ 07104
(973) 483-3939
Rosalind Libbey, Library Director
Hours: meetings: Sept–May: third Sat; Library: Tue–Fri & first & third Sat 10:00–4:00
Pub. *Newsletter*
$25.00 per year membership for individuals in Historical Society gives automatic membership in Genealogy Club

Regional Genealogical Societies

Genealogical Society of Bergen County
PO Box 432
Midland Park, NJ 07432
(201) 444-4319
Barbara Flurchick, President; Marion K. Armstrong, Library Committee Volunteer
Hours: Midland Park Public Library: Wed 10:30–12:30; meetings at Library: fourth Mon 7:00 P.M.
Pub. *Bergen County Genealogy Society Quarterly*; *The Archivist*, quarterly
$5.00 per year membership

Burlington County Genealogy Club
(Woodlane Road—location)
PO Box 2449, Rt. 2 (mailing address)
Mount Holly, NJ 08060-9754
(609) 267-0881
Elma Eckert
Hours: first & third Mon 7:00 P.M.–9:00 P.M.
("Library houses cemetery, towns, marriage, etc., records.")
search fee: $15.00 per hour plus cost of copies

Cape May County Historical and Genealogical Society
Route 9
Cape May Court House, NJ 08210
(609) 465-3535; (609) 465-4274 FAX
Ione E. Williams, Library
Hours: Tue–Wed & Fri 10:00–4:00, Sat by appointment
Pub. *Cape May County Magazine of History and Genealogy*, annually; *The Cape May County Crier*, quarterly
$10.00 per year membership for individuals, $15.00 per year membership for couples

Genealogy Club of the Metuchen-Edison Regional Historical Society
PO Box 61
Metuchen, NJ 08840

Monmouth County Genealogy Club
Monmouth County Historical Association
70 Court Street
Freehold, NJ 07728
(732) 462-1466
http://nj5.injersey.com/~kjshelly/mcgc.html
Bea Denman Howley, President
Hours: Library: Wed–Sat 10:00–4:00
Pub. *The Monmouth Connection*, bimonthly, $12.00 per year U.S. subscription
$25.00 per year membership in Historical Association for individuals, $35.00 per year membership for families, $20.00 per year membership for students and senior citizens

Morris Area Genealogy Society
PO Box 105, Convent Station
Convent Station, NJ 07961-0105
Bogert Holly, President
Pub. *Morris Area Genealogy Society Newsletter*, quarterly (June, September, December, March)
(genealogical information pertaining to the Morris area)
$15.00 per year membership for individuals (U.S. funds, beginning in June), $20.00 per year membership for families, $10.00 per year membership for institutions

Ocean County Genealogical Society
376B Lighthouse Drive
Manhawkin, NJ 08050-2327
Barbara Jackson, President
Pub. *Newsletter*, semiannually (summer and winter)

Passaic County, New Jersey Genealogy Club
Lambert Castle Museum and Library
Valley Road
Paterson, NJ 07509
(973) 357-1070
Andrew F. Shick, Acting Director
Hours: Mon–Fri by appointment only
Pub. *Castle Genie*, quarterly
(Passaic County families, New Jersey families)
$20.00 per year membership for individuals, $30.00 per year membership for families, $15.00 per year membership for senior citizens; search fees by letter: $8.00 for members, $15.00 for non-members

Warren County Historical and Genealogical Society
(313 Mansfield Street—museum and library location)
PO Box 313 (mailing address)
Belvidere, NJ 07823-0313
(908) 475-2512; (908) 475-4246 (Museum recording machine); (908) 689-2993 (President)
V. A. Brown, Curator; Hattie M. Seiwell, President
Hours: Sun 2:00–4:00
Pub. *Oak Leaves*, three to four times per year
$7.50 per year membership

Genealogical Society of the West Fields
c/o Westfield Memorial Library
550 East Broad Street
Westfield, NJ 07090
(908) 789-4090 (Library)
Frederick Bollinger, President
Hours: Library: Mon–Fri 10:00–9:00, Sat (except Jul–Aug) 10:00–5:00
Pub. *Gleanings from the West Fields*, bimonthly (February, April, June, August, October, December)

(New Jersey local history and genealogy)
$10.00 per year membership (beginning 1 June); research for non-members: $10.00

Independent Publications and Miscellany

Canal Society of New Jersey
(Waterloo Village, Stanhope—museum location)
PO Box 737 (mailing address)
Morristown, NJ 07963-0737
(908) 722-9556; (973) 875-1508
Robert H. Barth, President
Pub. *On the Level*, three times per year (information on New Jersey's historic canals)
$15.00 per year membership

Historic District Commission (Cape May)
643 Washington Street
Cape May, NJ 08204
(609) 884-8411

Family Line Publications
(see Maryland)

Historic Paulus Hook Association, Inc.
66 Sussex Street
Jersey City, NJ 07302
Steven B. Sanders, President

Jackson Heritage Preservation Society
Rt. 5, Box 70-D, Cooks Bridge Road
Jackson, NJ 08527
(201) 364-7448

New Jersey History Online
E-mail: macan@scils.rutgers.edu
http://scils.rutgers.edu/~macan/ nj.history.html

NJGenWeb
Part of U.S. GenWeb Project
E-mail: nj@usgenweb.com
http://www.cyberenet.net/~gsteiner/ njgenweb
(links to other New Jersey resources)

Somerset County Genealogical Quarterly
PO Box 6493
Bridgewater, NJ 08807
Pub. *Somerset County Genealogical Quarterly*, $15.00 per year subscription

South Jersey Magazine
1226 West Main Street
PO Box 847
Millville, NJ 08332
(609) 825-1615
Shirley R. Bailey, Editor

Hours: Mon–Sat 8:00–5:00, or by chance
Pub. *South Jersey Magazine*, quarterly, $10.00 per year second class subscription, $19.00 per year first class subscription

Union County Office of Cultural and Heritage Affairs
300 North Avenue, East
Westfield, NJ 07090

Victorian Society
Northern New Jersey Chapter
PO Box 717
Montclair, NJ 07042
(973) 744-8267

Warren County Morris Canal Commission
c/o Warren County Planning Board
Administration Building
Route 519
Belvidere, NJ 07823
(201) 475-8000, ext. 631
Dennis Bertland, Chair

NEW MEXICO

Archives and Libraries with Holdings in Genealogy

State Archives and Library

New Mexico Records Center and Archives
1205 Camino Carlos Rey
Santa Fe, NM 87505
(505) 476-7908; (505) 476-7909 FAX
http://www.state.nm.us/cpr/
Elaine Olah, State Records Administrator
Hours: Mon–Fri 8:00–5:00
Pub. *Quipu*, irregularly
(Spanish archives of New Mexico, 1621–1821)

New Mexico State Library
Southwest Room
325 Don Gaspar Avenue
Santa Fe, NM 87501-2777
(505) 827-3800; (505) 827-3805 (Southwest Room); (505) 827-3813 (Editor); (505) 827-3888 FAX
http://www.stlib.state.nm.us; http:// www.stlib.state.nm.us/hiker/ current.html (newsletter); http:// www.stlib.state.nm.us/sw.rm-info/ basic.html (suggested reference resources)
Hours: Mon–Fri 9:00–5:00
Pub. *The Hitchhiker: State Library's Weekly Newsletter*
(New Mexico history, New Mexico newspapers; slowly building a New Mexico genealogy section)

State Historical Societies

Historical Society of New Mexico
PO Box 1912
Santa Fe, NM 87504-1912
Pub. *La Cronica*, irregularly
$20.00 per year membership

Museum of New Mexico
History Library
110 Washington Avenue
PO Box 2087
Santa Fe, NM 87504-2087
(505) 827-6473; (505) 827-6472 (History Library); (505) 827-6521 FAX
Orlando Romero, History Librarian; Hazel Romero, History Librarian; Thomas A. Livesay, Director of Museum; Thomas E. Chavez, Ph.D., Director of The Palace of the Governors
Hours: Mon–Fri 1:00–5:00
Pub. *El Palacio*, quarterly
(a historical rather than a genealogical resource; no staff to conduct

genealogical searches, and refers questions to the Special Collections Branch at the University of New Mexico)

City, County and Regional Archives and Libraries

Alamogordo Public Library
920 Oregon Avenue
Alamogordo, NM 88310
(505) 439-4140; (505) 439-4108 FAX
Mary Leslie Schmitt, Reference Librarian
Hours: Mon–Thur 10:00–8:00, Fri–Sat 11:00–5:00, Sun 1:00–5:00

Albuquerque Public Library
Special Collections Library
423 Central Avenue, N.E.
Albuquerque, NM 87102
(505) 848-1376
http://www.cabq.gov/rgvls/specol.html
Laurel E. Drew, Manager
Hours: Tue & Thur 12:30–8:00, Wed & Fri–Sat 9:00–5:30
(New Mexico history and genealogy)

Artesia Historical Museum and Art Center
505 Richardson Avenue
Artesia, NM 88210
(505) 748-2390; (505) 746-3886 (Museum)
Nancy Dunn, Director
Hours: Tue–Sun 8:00–5:00, closed major holidays
(local and area history and family information)
search fee: occasional copy fees only or cost

Aztec Museum Association
125 North Main
Aztec, NM 87410
(505) 334-9829; (505) 334-9707 FAX
Deah Folk, Curator
Hours: winter: 10:00–4:00; summer: 9:00–5:00
Pub. *Aztec Museum Association Newsletter*, monthly
(area history, local genealogy, cemetery records, oil and gas, forty years of archives, local newspaper on microfilm from 1914 to 1989, intermittent from 1890)
$20.00 per year membership for individuals; search fee: $15.00 per hour

Thomas Branigan Memorial Library
200 East Picacho Avenue
Las Cruces, NM 88001
(505) 526-1047; (505) 647-9455 FAX
Marjory F. Day, Genealogy Librarian; Mark Pendleton, Reference Librarian; Carol Brey, Library Director
Hours: Mon–Thur 10:00–9:00, Fri–Sat 10:00–6:00, Sun (Sept–May) 1:00–5:00

Kit Carson Historic Museums
(222 LeDoux Street—main office location)
PO Drawer CCC (mailing address)
Taos, NM 87571
(505) 758-0505; (505) 758-5440 (Archives); (505) 758-0062 (Archives); (505) 758-0330 FAX
E-mail: wow_joan@laplaza.org (Registrar); nitkit@laplaza.org (Librarian)
http://www.nmculture.org
Skip Miller, Co-Director; Karen S. Young, Co-Director; Joan Phillips, Registrar/Archivist; Nita Murphy, Librarian
Hours: Museum sites: daily 9:00–5:00; Archives: by appointment only
Pub. *Taos Lightnin'*, quarterly, $15.00 per year subscription
(archives focus on Spanish Colonial and American territorial history; Carson family, Lucien and Ferdinand Maxwell family, James White Leal family and Don Antonio Severino Martinez family genealogies)
$25.00 per year membership for individuals, $50.00 per year membership for partners, $75.00 per year Contributing membership; search fee: $10.00 per hour, one-hour minimum; photocopies: 20¢ per page

Farmington Museum
302 North Orchard
Farmington, NM 87401-6227
(505) 599-1174
Catherine Davis, Collection's Manager
Hours: by appointment Tue–Fri noon–5:00, Sat 10:00–5:00
Pub. *Footnotes*, bimonthly
(publication is not historical; collection on history of San Juan County, photo archives, family documents)
price list and policy available for photocopies and reprints of photographs

Fort Lewis College
(see Colorado)

Lovington Public Library
115 South Main Street
Lovington, NM 88260
(505) 396-3144; (505) 396-7189
Mary Lee Smith, Director
Hours: Mon–Thur 9:30–7:30, Fri 9:30–5:30, Sat 9:30–1:30
(general genealogy collection, emphasizes southern and southwestern states)

Marshall Memorial Library
301 South Tin Avenue
Deming, NM 88030
(505) 546-8408
E-mail: demingpl@zianet.com
Margaret Becker, Director

Hours: Mon & Fri 9:00–5:00, Tue & Thur 9:00–8:00, Wed 9:00–6:00, Sat 9:00–1:00

General D. L. McBridge Museum
NMMI Campus
Roswell, NM 88201
(505) 622-3155

Menaul Historical Library of the Southwest
Menaul School, 301 Menaul Boulevard, N.E.
Albuquerque, NM 87107
(505) 345-7727, ext. 25
Nona Browne, Secretary, Advisory Board
Hours: Mon–Fri 9:15–4:15
("We are basically an archival research library.")

Mesa Public Library
Los Alamos County Library System
2400 Central Avenue
Los Alamos, NM 87544
(505) 662-8253
Kathy Bjorklund, Reference
Hours: Mon–Thur 10:00–9:00, Fri 10:00–6:00, Sat 9:00–5:00, Sun 11:00–5:00, selected holidays 11:00–5:00
(New Mexico history, basic genealogy tools; no primary genealogical resources, but a selection of indexes, bibliographies and catalogs to help the genealogist locate information and resources)

Million Dollar Museum
Carlsbad Caverns Highway
White's City, NM 88268
(505) 785-2291

Museum of the Great Plains
(see Oklahoma)

Portales Public Library
218 South Avenue B
Portales, NM 88130
(505) 356-3940; (505) 356-3964 FAX
Denise Burnett, Library Director
Hours: Mon–Wed 10:00–6:00, Thur 10:00–7:00, Fri 10:00–5:00, Sat 10:00–2:00
(southwest materials and small genealogy library)

Raton Museum
216 South First Street
Raton, NM 87740
(505) 445-8979
Shannon Morrow, Director
Hours: winter: Wed–Sat 10:00–4:00; Memorial Day–Labor Day: Tue–Sat 9:00–5:00
(large photo archive and donated family histories/genealogies)

Rio Grande Historical Collections
New Mexico State University Library
PO Box 30006, Department 3475
Las Cruces, NM 88003-0006
(505) 646-4727; (505) 646-7477 FAX

E-mail: archives@lib.nmsu.edu
Austin Hoover, University Archivist
Hours: Mon–Fri 8:00–noon & 1:00–4:30,
except university holidays
(specializes in New Mexico and the
Spanish borderlands; microfilm of the
Archivos Historicos del Arzobispado
de Durango)

Roswell Public Library
301 North Pennsylvania Avenue
Roswell, NM 88201
(505) 622-7101
Loretta Clark, Reference Librarian
Hours: Mon–Tue 9:00–9:00, Wed–Sat
9:00–6:00, Sun 2:00–6:00

**San Juan County Museum
Association**
San Juan County Archaeological
Research Center and Library
(6131 U.S. Highway 64, Farmington,
NM 87401—location)
PO Box 125 (mailing address)
Bloomfield, NM 87413
(505) 632-2013; (505) 632-1707 FAX
Larry L. Baker, Executive Director
Hours: daily 9:00–5:00
Pub. *Newsletter of the San Juan County
Museum Association*, quarterly
(collections specializing in regional
archaeological and historical research)
$15.00 per year membership

Silver City Museum Society
312 West Broadway
Silver City, NM 88061
(505) 538-5921; (505) 388-5721
E-mail: scmuseum@zianet.com
Susan M. Berry, Museum Director
Hours: Tue–Fri 9:00–4:30, Sat–Sun
10:00–4:00
Pub. *The Mansardian*, quarterly
(local history information: newspaper
indexes, biographical files, historic
buildings, local records, photo archive)
$20.00 per year membership for
individuals, $30.00 per year
membership for families, $15.00 per
year membership for students or senior
citizens; photocopies: 25¢ per page

Silver City Public Library
515 West College Avenue
Silver City, NM 88061
(505) 538-3672
Hours: Mon & Thur 9:00–8:00, Tue–
Wed 9:00–6:00, Fri 9:00–5:00, Sat
9:00–1:00

Tome Parish Museum
State Highway 47
PO Box 397
Tome, NM 87060
(505) 865-7497

**Truth or Consequences Public
Library**
325 Library Lane
Truth or Consequences, NM 87901

(505) 894-3027
Ellanie Sampson, Librarian
Hours: Mon–Fri 9:00–7:00, Sat 9:00–
noon

**University of New Mexico—General
Library**
Zimmerman Library
Albuquerque, NM 87131-1466
(505) 277-5761; (505) 277-7212
(Newspaper Project)
E-mail: zimref@unm.edu;
mfletch@unm.edu (Newspaper
Project)
http://www.unm.edu
Marilyn Fletcher (Newspaper Project)
Hours: 8:00–5:00
(has 457 newspaper titles from the 1840s
on microfilm)

**University of New Mexico—Map
and Geographic Information Center
(MAGIC)**
Centennial Science and Engineering
Library
Albuquerque, NM 87131-1466
(505) 277-4412

Historical Societies—
Local and Regional

Albuquerque Historical Society
PO Box 4552
Albuquerque, NM 87196
(505) 255-4595
Ann Johnson, Membership

**Artesia Historical and Genealogical
Society**
(Artesia Public Library—location)
PO Box 803 (mailing address)
Artesia, NM 88211-0803
(505) 746-4252 (Library); (505) 746-
3101 (Book Chairman)
Kay Peterson, Book Chairman
Hours: 9:00–6:00; meetings: third Mon
(Sept–May) 9:30–11:00
Pub. *Newsletter*, three or four times per
year
("Library staff does not do research.")
$10.00 per year membership for
individuals, $15.00 per year
membership

**Colonial New Mexico Historical
Foundation**
135 Camino Escondido
Santa Fe, NM 87501
(505) 982-5644

Columbus Historical Society, Inc.
(1902 Railroad Station Highway 9 &
11—location)
PO Box 562 (mailing address)
Columbus, NM 88029
(505) 531-2620

http://www.nmculture.org/
Marilyn B. Elliott, Curator
Hours: Sept–May: 11:00–4:00; summer:
Mon–Thur 10:00–1:00, Fri–Sun
10:00–4:00
$3.00 per year membership, $100.00 life
membership

Corrales Historical Society
PO Box 1051
Corrales, NM 87048
(505) 897-1150
Gay Betzer

El Paso County Historical Society
(see Texas)

**High Plains Historical Foundation,
Inc.**
313 Prairieview
Clovis, NM 88101
E-mail: hkilmer@etsc.net
Harold A. Kilmer, President

**Los Alamos County Historical
Society**
Los Alamos County Historical Museum
1921 Juniper Street
PO Box 43
Los Alamos, NM 87544-0043
(505) 662-6272 (Office); (505) 662-4493
(Museum); (505) 662-6312 FAX
htt://www.losalamos.com/lahistory
Hedy M. Dunn, Museum Director
Hours: summer: Mon–Sat 9:30–4:30,
Sun 11:00–5:00; winter: Mon–Sat
10:00–4:00, Sun 1:00–4:00
Pub. *Newsletter*, quarterly
(Manhattan District history [WW II era],
Los Alamos Ranch School [1918–
1942]; no "real" genealogical
database)

Luna County Historical Society, Inc.
Deming Luna Mimbres Museum
301 South Silver Avenue
Deming, NM 88030
(505) 546-2382
Dolly Shannon, Archivist
Hours: Museum: daily 9:00–5:00;
Archives: by appointment
("We operate chiefly as a museum,
specializing in southern New Mexico
and the Mimbres Indians; Genealogy
search as time permits.")
$3.00 per year membership; research fee:
donation

**Moriarty Historical Society and
Museum**
777 Central Avenue, S.W.
PO Box 1366
Moriarty, NM 87035
(505) 832-4087
Susie McComb, Director
Hours: summer: Mon–Sat 10:00–5:00;
winter: Mon–Fri 10:00–5:00, Sat
1:00–4:00
$10.00 for first-year membership, $7.00
per year renewal membership

Permian Historical Society
(see Texas)

Sacramento Mountains Historical Society, Inc.
U.S. Highway 82
PO Box 435
Cloudcroft, NM 88317
(505) 682-2932
Marie Wuersching, Museum Director
Hours: Tue–Sat 10:00–4:00

San Gabriel Historical Society
PO Box 1528
Santa Cruz, NM 87567
(505) 852-2112

Sandoval County Historical Society
PO Box 692
Bernalillo, NM 87004
(505) 867-2755
Martha Liebert

Sierra County Historical Society
211 Main
Truth or Consequences, NM 87901
(505) 894-6600
Ann Welborn, Director
Hours: Mon–Sat 9:00–5:00
$10.00 per year membership for individuals, $15.00 per year membership for couples

Sociedad Historica de la Tierra Amarilla
c/o General Delivery
Los Ojos, NM 87551
(505) 345-5147

Socorro County Historical Society
PO Box 923
Socorro, NM 87801
(505) 835-5242; (505) 835-0957
Spencer Wilson, Ph.D., Secretary

Historical Center for Southeast New Mexico, Inc.
(formerly Chaves County Historical Society, Inc.)
200 North Lea Avenue
Roswell, NM 88201
(505) 622-8333
David E. Orr, Administrator
Hours: Office: Mon–Fri 9:00–5:00; Archives: by appointment
("regional archival collections")

Southeastern New Mexico Historical Society
101 South Halagueno
Carlsbad, NM 88220
(505) 885-6776

Historical Society of Southwestern New Mexico
Western New Mexico University Museum
Silver City, NM 88061
(505) 538-6386

Taos County Historical Society
(121 C North Plaza, Old Courthouse—location)
PO Box 2447 (mailing address)
Taos, NM 87571
Andy Lindquist, President
Hours: Mon, Wed & Fri 1:00–3:00
Pub. *Ayer y Hoy en Taos*, biannually, $3.00 per issue
$15.00 per year membership for individuals, $20.00 per year membership for families, $30.00 per year Sustaining membership

Tucumcari Historical Research Institute
416 South Adams Street
Tucumcari, NM 88401
(505) 461-4201

Tularosa Basin Historical Society
1301 North White Sands Boulevard
PO Box 518
Alamogordo, NM 88310
(505) 434-4438
Kathy Gren, Museum Director/Curator
Hours: Mon–Sat 10:00–4:00, Sun 1:00–4:00, closed all Federalholidays
$6.00 per year membership

Tularosa Village Historical Society
(608 Central Avenue—location)
30 Dusty Lane (mailing address)
Tularosa, NM 88352
(505) 585-9597 (Museum); (505) 585-2057
Norma E. Cinert, Secretary
Hours: Mon–Sat 1:00–4:00
$6.00 per year membership for individuals, $6.00 per year membership for married couples, $10.00 per year Contributing membership, $100.00 life membership

Western History Association
University of New Mexico
Albuquerque, NM 87131

Western New Mexico University Museum
Silver City, NM 88061
(505) 538-6386

LDS Family History Centers

Albuquerque
(505) 266-4867; (505) 293-5610

Farmington
(505) 325-5813

Las Cruces
(505) 382-0618

Genealogical Societies

State Genealogical Society

New Mexico Genealogical Society
PO Box 8283
Albuquerque, NM 87198-8283
(505) 828-2514 (President); (505) 296-9759 (Editor)
E-mail: pjest@aol.com; pjest@juno.com
http://www.nmgs.org
Ernie Jaskolski, President; Patricia Black Esterly, Editor
Hours: meetings at Special Collections Branch, Albuquerque Public Library; third Sat 1:30
Pub. *New Mexico Genealogist*, quarterly (March, June, September, December)
$15.00 per year membership for individuals or households; research fee: $10.00 per hour (limit two hours paid in advance), plus copy charges at 25¢ per sheet, postage, and other expenses

Regional Genealogical Societies

Alamogordo Genealogical Society
PO Box 246
La Luz, NM 83337
(505) 434-1675
Joyce Taylor

The Genealogy Club of Albuquerque
11605 Hughes Avenue, N.E.
Albuquerque, NM 87112-1813
(505) 298-8018
Elizabeth Frost, President
Hours: meetings at Albuquerque Public Library, Special Collections Library: second Wed 10:00
Pub. *Genealogy Club Quarterly* (February, May, August and November)
(promotes genealogy, provides educational aid, supports the Albuquerque Public Library; The Genealogy Club consists primarily of members who are researching outside of New Mexico)
$10.00 per year membership for individuals, $15.00 per year membership for couples

Artesia Historical and Genealogical Society
(Artesia Public Library—location)
PO Box 803 (mailing address)
Artesia, NM 88211-0803
(505) 746-4252 (Library); (505) 746-3101 (Book Chairman)
Kay Peterson, Book Chairman
Hours: 9:00–6:00; meetings: third Mon (Sept–May) 9:30–11:00

Pub. *Newsletter*, three or four times per
year
("Library staff does not do research.")
$10.00 per year membership for
individuals, $15.00 per year
membership

Chaves County Genealogical Society
PO Box 1085
Roswell, NM 88202
Ken Lewis, President
Hours: meetings at the Roswell Adult
Center: fourth Tue (Sept–May) 7:00–
9:00
Pub. *Chaves County Roots and Branches
Newsletter*, nine times per year
(monthly, September–May)
$10.00 per year membership for
individuals, $15.00 per year
membership for families

Curry County Genealogy Society
c/o Clovis-Carver Public Library
701 Main Street
Clovis, NM 88101
(505) 762-5408
Wanda Dunn, President; Louise Reithel
Hours: meetings: first Mon 7:00

Eddy County Genealogical Society
Carlsbad Public Library
PO Box 461
Carlsbad, NM 88220
(505) 887-7167
Annette Price, President
Hours: Mon–Sat 10:00–8:00, Sun 2:00–
5:00; meetings: second Sun 2:00
Pub. *Pecos Trails*, semiannually
$8.00 per year active membership,
$10.00 per year associate membership

Grant County Genealogical Society
PO Box 1581
Silver City, NM 88062
(505) 538-2329
Barbara Holley Rock
(society no longer active, but Mrs. Rock
will assist with queries)

Las Vegas Genealogical Society
c/o Carnegie Public Library
500 National Avenue
Las Vegas, NM 87701-4399
(505) 454-1403; (505) 425-7175
Sue Parham
Hours: meetings: third Wed 7:00

Lea County Genealogical Society
(Bill McKibben Senior Center, 14 West
Avenue F—location)
PO Box 1044 (mailing address)
Lovington, NM 88260-1044
(505) 396-2608
Mrs. R. L. Binkley, President
Hours: meetings third Tue 1:30

Los Alamos Family History Society
(Mesa Public Library, 2400 Central
Avenue—location)
PO Box 900 (mailing address)
Los Alamos, NM 87544-0900

(505) 662-3381
Jodie C. Frye, Secretary
Hours: meetings: second Thur 7:00
Pub. *Los Alamos Family History Society
Newsletter*, quarterly, $8.00 per year
subscription

Roosevelt County Searchers
PO Box 474
Portales, NM 88130
(505) 359-0772
E-mail: jglocke@yucca.net
http://www.yucca.net/joyce
Joyce Gore Locke

Roswell Genealogical Society
Roswell Adult Center
807 North Missouri
Roswell, NM 88201
(505) 622-6725
Clarence Rollins, President
$6.00 per year membership for
individuals, $9.00 per year
membership for families

Roswell New Mexico Genealogical Group
2604 North Kentucky
Roswell, NM 88201

Santa Fe Genealogical Society
140 West Coronado Road
Santa Fe, NM 87501
Cora Mae Stumpff

Sierra County Genealogical Society
711 North Pershing
Truth or Consequences, NM 87901
(505) 744-5255
Jean George, President
Hours: meetings at Truth or
Consequences Public Library: third
Wed (Jun–Aug) 7:00–9:00

Southeastern New Mexico Genealogical Society
(Agnes Kastner Head Center, Room 115,
200 East Park Street, Hobbs, NM
88240—location)
PO Box 5725
Hobbs, NM 88241-5725
(505) 393-3658
Veta Blackburn, Assistant Librarian
Hours: Tue 2:00–4:00, Thur 6:00–9:00
Pub. *Newsletter*, monthly
$10.00 per year membership for
individuals, $15.00 per year
membership for couples

Southern New Mexico Genealogical Society
Thomas Branigan Memorial Library
200 East Picacho Avenue
Las Cruces, NM 88001
(505) 526-1047 (Library)
Marjory F. Day, Genealogy Librarian;
Mark Pendleton, Reference Librarian;
Carol Brey, Library Director
Hours: meetings: fourth Thur
(New Mexico genealogy and resources)

$5.00 per year membership for
individuals, $7.50 per year
membership for families

Tatah Tracers Genealogical Society
(Salmon Ruins Library and Museum,
Bloomfield Highway, Farmington, NM
87401—location)
PO Box 125 (mailing address)
Bloomfield, NM 87413-0125
(505) 632-3668
Ken Gomez, President
Hours: meetings at the Civic Center in
Farmingon: second Tue (Sept–May)
7:30
Pub. *Tatah Tracer*, irregularly
$15.00 per year membership

Independent Publications and Miscellany

Bandar Log, Inc.
Main Street
PO Box 86
Magdalena, NM 87825
(505) 854-2715

Center for Southwest Research
University of New Mexico—General
Library
Zimmerman Library
Albuquerque, NM 87131-1466
(505) 277-6451; (505) 277-6019 FAX;
(505) 272-2282 (Oral History
Program)
E-mail: cswrref@unm.edu;
oral@unm.edu (Oral History Program)
http://www.unm.edu/~cswrref
Dave Baldwin, Interim Director; Carols
Vasquez, Oral History Program
Director
Hours: 8:00–5:00
(has *Diligencias Matrimoniales* 1678–
1869 on microfilm, Dreesen extracts
of marriages from the seventeenth
through nineteenth century in the
middle Rio Grande Valley, and
Olmsted translation and abstraction of
Spanish Enlistment Papers of New
Mexico, 1732–1820)

Comgenes
PO Box 1581
Silver City, NM 88062
Barbara Holley Rock, Genealogy
Manager
Pub. *Grassroots Catalog*, semiannually
(January and July)
$20.00 per year membership

The New Mexico Historical Review
Mesa Vista Hall 1013
University of New Mexico
Albuquerque, NM 87131-1186
(505) 277-5839; (505) 277-6023 FAX
E-mail: nmhr@unm.edu
http://www.unm.edu/~nmhr

Elaine Carey, Managing Editor
Hours: Mon–Fri 9:00–3:00 (may vary)
Pub. *The New Mexico Historical Review*,
  quarterly (January, April, July,
  October), $26.00 per year subscription
  for individuals (calendar year), $16.00
  per year subscription for students,
  $36.00 per year subscription for
  institutions, $20.00 per year
  subscription for Historical Society of
  New Mexico (through their
  membership office)
(history of New Mexico and borderlands)

NMGenWeb
Part of U.S. GenWeb Project
(505) 299-7447
E-mail: nm@usgenweb.com; jo@us1.net
http://www.rootsweb.com/~nmgenweb/;
  http://www.abq.com/nmgenweb/
  index.htm
(links to other New Mexico resources)

**Southwest Field Office-National
Trust for Historic Preservation**
(see Texas)

Texas-New Mexico Field Office
500 Main Street, Suite 606
Fort Worth, TX 76102
(817) 334-2061

University of Arizona Press
Journal of the Southwest
(see Arizona)

NEW YORK

Archives and Libraries with Holdings in Genealogy

State Archives and Library

New York State Archives
New York Department of Education
Cultural Education Center, Room 11D40
Albany, NY 12230
(518) 474-8955; (518) 473-7573 FAX
E-mail: refserv@unix6.nysed.gov
http://www.sara.nysed.gov
Hours: Mon–Fri 9:00–5:00
(archival records of New York State
  government agencies, mostly
  administrative and not of use to
  genealogists)

New York State Library
Genealogy Section, Reference Services
Seventh Floor, Cultural Education Center
Empire State Plaza
Albany, NY 12230
(518) 474-5161; (518) 474-6282
E-mail: refserv@unix2.nysed.gov
http://www.nysl.nysed.gov/
Henry Ilnicki, Senior Librarian
Hours: Mon–Fri 9:00–5:00 (coverage is
  by members of the Capital District
  Genealogical Society, "call genealogy
  desk if coming long distance")
(New York State and Local History
  collection contains materials depicting
  all periods and aspects of New York
  State history from colonial times to the
  present; Genealogy Area includes an
  extensive collection of printed
  histories on individual families,
  national in scope with an emphasis on
  New York, Pennsylvania, New Jersey
  and New England), also DAR and
  Loyalist records, census, periodicals,
  probate, military, church and vital
  records)

State Historical Societies

The New York Historical Society
Library Office
170 Central Park West
New York, NY 10024-5194
(212) 873-3400
Hours: Mon–Fri 10:00–5:00

New York State Historian
3097 Cultural Education Center
Empire State Plaza
Albany, NY 12230
(518) 474-5353
Dr. Kenneth Ames, State Historian

**Association of Municipal Historians
of New York State**
Region I: Saint Lawrence-Champlain
  Region
Rt. 4, Hannawa
Potsdam, NY 13676
Betty Newton, President
(includes Clinton, Franklin, Jefferson,
  Lewis and Saint Lawrence counties)

**Association of Municipal Historians
of New York State**
Region II: Adirondacks-Upper Hudson
  Historical Federation
113 Vischers Ferry Road, Rt. 2
Rexford, NY 12148
John L. Scherer, President
(includes Essex, Hamilton, Saratoga,
  Warren and Washington counties)

**Association of Municipal Historians
of New York State**
Region III: Lower Hudson Region
PO Box 872
Monticello, NY 12701
Marjorie D. Smith, President
(includes Albany, Columbia, Dutchess,
  Greene, Orange, Putnam, Rensselaer,
  Rockland, Sullivan, Ulster and
  Westchester counties)

**Association of Municipal Historians
of New York State**
Region IV: Long Island-New York City
  Region
111-15 Queens Boulevard
PO Box 10
Forest Hills, NY 11375
(718) 268-2500
Charles G. Meyer, Jr., Chairman
(includes Nassau and Suffolk counties
  and the five boroughs of New York
  City)

**Association of Municipal Historians
of New York State**
Region V: Mohawk Valley Region
187 Bleecker Street
Gloversville, NY 12078
(518) 725-3073
Lewis G. Decker, President
(includes Fulton, Herkimer,
  Montgomery, Oneida, Schenectady
  and Schoharie counties)

**Association of Municipal Historians
of New York State**
Region VI: Ontario-Finger Lake Region
PO Box 91
Meridian, NY 13113
Mrs. Marion Dudley, President
(includes Cayuga, Monroe, Onondaga,
  Ontario, Oswego, Seneca, Steuben,
  Wayne and Yates counties)

**Association of Municipal Historians
of New York State**
Region VII: Southern New York Region
PO Box 336
Dryden, NY 13053

Ruth Sweetland, President
(includes Broome, Chemung, Chenango, Cortland, Delaware, Madison, Otsego, Schuyler, Tioga and Tompkins counties)

Association of Municipal Historians of New York State

Region VIII: Western New York Region
(7783 County Line Road, Arcade, NY 14009—location)
14407 Ridge Road West (mailing address)
Albion, NY 14411
(716) 589-4355
Delia Robinson, President
(includes Allegany, Cattaraugus, Chautauqua, Erie, Genesee, Livingston, Niagara, Orleans and Wyoming counties; no headquarters or library)

Regional Council of Historical Agencies

(Lake Road—location)
PO Box 28 (mailing address)
Cooperstown, NY 13326
(607) 547-4131 (answering machine)
E-mail: rchahist@wpe.com
Linda Norris, Projects Manager
Pub. *RCHA News*, quarterly
(serves Broome, Cayuga, Chemung, Chenango, Cortland, Delaware, Franklin, Hamilton, Herkimer, Jefferson, Lewis, Madison, Oneida, Onondaga, Ontario, Oswego, Otsego, Saint Lawrence, Schuyler, Seneca, Tioga, Tompkins and Wayne counties)
$25.00 per year membership for individuals, $35.00 per year membership for organizations; does not answer genealogical queries

New York State Historical Association

Fenimore House, West Lake Road
PO Box 800
Cooperstown, NY 13326-0800
(607) 547-1400 (Fenimore House Museum); (607) 547-1470 (Library); (607) 547-1405 FAX (Library)
E-mail: onet23@nsl.wpe.com
Wayne Wright, Associate Director of Research Library
Hours: Mon–Fri 9:00–5:00, Sat 10:00–5:00 (some evening hours during the school year), Sat (May–Aug) 1:00–5:00; Special Collections: Mon–Fri 1:00–5:00
Pub. *New York History*, quarterly, $20.00 per year subscription; *Heritage*, quarterly, $16.00 per year subscription
$35.00 per year membership for individuals (includes both periodicals)

City, County and Regional Archives and Libraries

Adriance Memorial Library/Greater Poughkeepsie Library District

93 Market Street
Poughkeepsie, NY 12601
(914) 485-3445
Myra Morales
Hours: by appointment only
(emphasis on Dutchess County and vicinity)

Albany County Hall of Records

250 South Pearl Street
Albany, NY 12202
(518) 447-4500
http://nyslgti.gen.ny.us/achor
Mary F. Wallen, Executive Director
Hours: 8:30–4:30

Albany Public Library

Pruyn Library
161 Washington Avenue
Albany, NY 12210
(518) 449-3380
Ellen K. Gamache, Local History Librarian
Hours: Mon–Thur 9:00–9:00, Fri 9:00–6:00, Sat 9:00–5:00, Sun (except summer) 1:00–5:00
(city and county of Albany)

Allegany County Department of History

Courthouse, Court Street
Belmont, NY 14813
(716) 268-9293; (716) 268-9446 FAX
Craig R. Braack, County Historian
Hours: Mon–Fri 9:00–5:00

Allegany County Museum

11 Wells Street
Belmont, NY 14813
(716) 268-9293
Craig R. Braack, County Historian
Hours: Mon–Fri 9:00–12:00 & 1:00–5:00
(census, land records, cemetery index)

Andes Society for History and Culture

Main Street
Andes, NY 13731

Babylon Public Library

24 South Carll Avenue
Babylon, NY 11702
(516) 669-1624
Patricia LaWare, Reference and Adult Services Librarian
Hours: Mon–Thur 9:30–9:00, Fri–Sat 9:30–5:00, Sun 1:00–5:00

Baldwinsville Public Library

33 East Genesee Street
Baldwinsville, NY 13027
(315) 635-5631; (315) 635-6760 FAX
E-mail: info@bville.lib.ny.us
http://www.bville.lib.ny.us

Margaret A. Van Patten, Head of Reference/Adult Services
Hours: Mon–Thur 10:00–9:00, Fri 10:00–5:00, Sat 10:00–4:00, Sun (Sept–Jun) 1:00–5:00
(emphasis on Baldwinsville, New York)

Ballston Spa Public Library

21 Milton Avenue
Ballston Spa, NY 12020
(518) 885-5022 phone and FAX
Virginia Humphrey, Director
Hours: winter: Tue & Fri 11:00–8:00, Wed–Thur 11:00–6:00, Sat 10:00–3:00; summer: Tue & Fri 11:00–8:00, Mon & Wed–Thur 11:00–5:00
(Saratoga County, New York; *Ballston Journal* partially indexed from 1847, various name indexes)
limited searches for only very specific requests: 15¢ per copy if more than six are requested

Historical Museum of the Darwin R. Barker Library

(20 East Main Street—entrance to location)
7 Day Street (mailing address)
Fredonia, NY 14063
(716) 672-2114
Jutta Rawcliffe, Curator; Julia Fairbanks, Genealogist
Hours: Tue & Thur–Sat 2:30–4:30, Thur 7:00–9:00
Pub. *Member's Newsletter Quarterly*; *Occasional Papers Series*
(local historical and genealogical library/archives)
$10.00 per year membership for individuals, $15.00 per year membership for families, $7.00 per year membership for seniors or students, $25.00 per year Contributor membership, $50.00 per year Donor membership, $100.00 Sponsor membership, over $100.00 Patron membership (may request dues be applied to Conservation Fund); search fee donation for genealogical research and copying, minimum $7.50

Glenn G. Bartle Library

Binghamton University
Vestal Parkway East, PO Box 6012
Binghamton, NY 13902-6012
(607) 777-2345 (Main Reference Desk); (607) 777-4844 (Special Collections)
Jeanne Eichelberger, Head, Special Collections; Ed Shephard, History/Genealogy Reference
Hours: Mon–Thur 8:00 A.M.–midnight, Fri 8:00 A.M.–9:00 P.M., Sat noon–9:00, Sun noon–midnight; Special Collections: Mon–Fri 11:00–3:00
(summer hours vary)

Frank J. Basloe Library

245 North Main Street
Herkimer, NY 13350
(315) 866-1733

Heidi L. Moody, Library Director
Hours: Mon–Thur 9:00–8:00, Fri 9:00–
5:00, Sat (Sept–Jun) 9:00–3:00

The Berkshire Athenaeum
(see Massachusetts)

Bethlehem Public Library
451 Delaware Avenue
Delmar, NY 12054
(518) 439-9314
http://www.crisny.org/libraries/capreg/
bethlehem
Marie S. Carlson, Reference Librarian,
Local History/Genealogy
Hours: winter: Mon–Fri 9:00–9:00, Sat
10:00–5:00, Sun (Sept–late Jun) 1:00–
5:00
("Growing collection—emphasizes local
genealogy, published records and
passenger lists")

Blauvelt Free Library
86 South Western Highway
Blauvelt, NY 10913
(914) 359-5366
Mary Behringer, Director
Hours: Mon–Thur 10:00–9:00, Fri
10:00–5:00, Sat 11:00–5:00 (summer
10:00–2:00), Sun 2:00–5:00 (except
summer)

Brentwood Public Library
Second Avenue and Fourth Street
Brentwood, NY 11717
(516) 273-7883
Carol Pomfrey
Hours: Mon–Tue & Thur–Fri 9:00–9:00,
Wed & Sat 9:00–5:00, Sun (Sept–
May) 12:00–4:00

Brooklyn College
Museum of the Borough of Brooklyn at
Brooklyn College
Bedford Avenue and Avenue H
Brooklyn, NY 11210
(718) 780-5152
(received part of the collection of the
former James A. Kelly Institute for
Local Historical Studies)

Brooklyn Public Library
Brooklyn Collection
Central Library
Grand Army Plaza
Brooklyn, NY 11238
(718) 780-7794
http://www.brooklyn.lib.ny.us
Judith Walsh, Local History Librarian
Hours: Mon–Fri 11:00–1:00 & 3:00–
5:00, Tue–Thurs 6:00–7:30, Sat
10:00–1:00 & 2:00–5:00, appointment
advisable
(*Brooklyn Daily Eagle* morgue clippings
ca 1904–1955, but very few other
genealogical materials)

Broome County Public Library
78 Exchange Street
Binghamton, NY 13901
(607) 778-6400; (607) 778-1441 FAX

E-mail: bcpl@spectra.net
Gerald R. Smith, Library Assistant
Hours: Mon–Thur 9:00–9:00, Fri–Sat
9:00–5:00
(Broome County, Binghamton, New
York, history

**Buffalo and Erie County Public
Library**
Lafayette Square
Buffalo, NY 14203
(716) 858-7103; (716) 858-6211 FAX
Robert M. Gurn, Head of Special
Collections
Hours: Mon–Wed & Fri–Sat 8:30–6:00,
Thur 8:30–8:00, Sun (during the
school year) 1:00–5:00
(strong focus on Buffalo and Erie County
history with some holdings for
Allegany, Cattaraugus, Chautauqua,
Genesee, Niagara, Orleans and
Wyoming counties)

**Canajoharie Library and Art
Gallery**
2 Erie Boulevard
Canajoharie, NY 13317
(518) 673-2314
E-mail: can_traha@sals.edu
James Crawford, Curator
Hours: Mon–Fri 10:00–4:45, Thur
10:00–8:30, Sat 10:00–1:30
(Montgomery County history and
families)

Cape Vincent Historical Museum
(James Street—location)
PO Box 376 (mailing address)
Cape Vincent, NY 13618
(315) 654-4400 (Office); (315) 654-3094
Jeanne Thompson, President of Board
Hours: 1 Jul–Labor Day: 10:00–4:00
(only artifacts from local area)

Historical Room—Town of Caroline
Town Hall, Slaterville Road
PO Box 36
Slaterville Springs, NY 14881
(607) 539-6464
Barbara B. M. Kone, Town Historian
Hours: Tue & Thur 6:30 P.M.–9:00 P.M.,
Fri (May–Sept) 1:00–4:00, and by
appointment
(local family histories, early town
records, family files; includes hamlets
of Caroline, Caroline Center,
Brooktondale, Slaterville Springs and
Speedsville)

**Cattaraugus County Memorial and
Historical Museum**
Court Street
Little Valley, NY 14755
(716) 938-9111, ext. 440
Lorna Spencer, Curator/Director
Hours: Mon–Fri 9:00–4:30
(genealogy center, operated by County;
local census, Civil War rolls,
cemeteries, newspapers)
$10.00 per search

Cayuga Community College
Norman F. Bourke Memorial Library
Franklin Street
Auburn, NY 13021
(315) 255-1743
Douglas O. Michael, Director
Hours: Mon–Thur 8:00 A.M.–9:30 P.M.,
Fri 8:00–5:00, Sun 3:00–9:30
free

Central Islip Public Library
33 Hawthorne Avenue
Central Islip, NY 11722
(516) 234-9333
Hours: Mon–Fri 10:00–8:30, Sat 10:00–
5:00, Sun 1:00–5:00 (closed Sun & Fri
evening in summer)

The Chapman Historical Museum
348 Glen Street
Glens Falls, NY 12801
(518) 793-2826; (518) 793-2831 FAX
Lori A. Fisher, Curator of Collections
Hours: Tue–Sat noon–5:00
Pub. *The Echo*; *Bridging the Years*
(a Regional History Center with a local
history library/archives component
relating to Glens Falls, the Town of
Queensbury, and Warren, Washington
and Saratoga counties)
fees for photocopies, photoreproduction
and the use of any materials for
publication

City History Center Library
City Hall, Top Floor
Schenectady, NY 12305
(518) 377-7061

Clermont State Historic Site
Rt. 1, Box 215
PO Box 215
Germantown, NY 12526
(518) 537-4240
Bruce E. Naramore, Historic Site
Manager
Hours: Tue–Sun 11:00–4:00
(genealogical services)

Cobblestone Society Museum
14393 Ridge Road
Albion, NY 14411
(716) 589-9013; (716) 589-9510

Crandall Public Library
City Park
251 Glen Street
Glens Falls, NY 12801-3539
(518) 792-6508; (518) 792-5251 FAX
Todd De Gormo, Director Center for
Folk Life, History and Cultural
Programs
Hours: winter: Mon–Tue & Thur–Fri
1:30–3:30, Wed 4:00–8:00, Sat 1:00–
4:00
(local history and genealogy, especially
Glens Falls, New York, and the Town
of Queensbury, New York, and nearby
communities, and to some extent the
rest of northern New York State,

Hudson River Valley, and other parts of New York State, some New England)

National Society, Daughters of the American Revolution

Hendrick Hudson Chapter
Robert Jenkins House and Museum
113 Warren Street
Hudson, NY 12534
(518) 851-9049
Marion F. Berntson, Curator
(genealogy library)

Charles Dawson History Center of Harrison

2 East Madison Street
White Plains, NY 10604
(914) 948-2550
Michael R. Casarella, Town Historian

Durham Center Museum, Inc.

(Route 145—location)
HC 1, Box 28 (mailing address)
East Durham, NY 12423-9608
(518) 239-4761; (518) 239-4313
Vernona Fleurent, Curator
Hours: Jun–Aug: Wed–Thur & Sat–Sun 1:00–4:00, and by appointment
(genealogical library: cemetery records, Bible records,genealogies)
search fee during off season: $2.00 per hour per person, donation for mailed requests

East Hampton Library

Pennypacker Long Island Collection
159 Main Street
East Hampton, NY 11937
(516) 324-0222; (516) 329-5947 FAX
E-mail: dking@suffolk.lib.ny.us
http://www.peconic.net/easthampton/library/
Dorothy T. King, Librarian
Hours: Mon–Wed & Sat 1:00–4:30, and mornings by appointment, closed when librarian is on vacation, so confirmation call advised
(Long Island history and genealogy: local histories on over 280 place names, family histories on over 680 Long Island families, extensive collection of over 100 Long Island newspapers, census returns, The Seversmith Collection, The Jeannette Edwards Rattray Collection, genealogical periodicals, and special indexes, etc.)

Edwards History Center

8 First Street
PO Box 100
Edwards, NY 13635
(315) 562-3511
Edith C. Duffy, Town Historian
Hours: by appointment only

Ellenville Public Library and Museum

40 Center Street
Ellenville, NY 12428
(914) 647-5530; (914) 647-3554 FAX
Pat Christian, Acting Director
Hours: Library: Mon & Thur–Fri 10:00–5:00; Museum: Apr–Dec: Wed & Fri–Sat noon–3:00
(local newspaper on microfilm from 1849, obituary file, books)

Erwin-Painted Post Museum

115 Water Street
Painted Post, NY 14870
Hours: 9:00–4:00
(local history and Indian artifacts)
free admission

Fenton Historical Center-Museum and Library

67 Washington Street
Jamestown, NY 14701
(716) 664-6256
Karen E. Livsey, Librarian/Archivist; Carl Belknap, Genealogist/Researcher; Barbara Cessna, Genealogist/Researcher; Frances TeCulver, Genealogist/Researcher
Hours: Mon–Sat 10:00–4:00
Pub. *Fenton History Center-Museum and Library Newsletter*, quarterly; *Annual Report*
(collections concentrate on Jamestown and southern Chautauqua County, but cover all of the county and include family history files, a card file for deaths and marriages from nineteenth century newspapers, printed family genealogies, county census records and indexes, Jamestown city directories, plus manuscript and photograph collections)
$25.00 per year membership for individuals, $15.00 per year membership for senior citizens or students, $100.00 per year Patron membership; research fee: $10.00

Field Library

4 Nelson Avenue
Peekskill, NY 10566
(914) 737-1212
Barbara J. Zimmer, Archives Librarian
Hours: Mon 9:30–2:00, Tue 10:30–2:30, Thur–Fri 9:30–1:30
(local history and genealogy; "We are very limited by time and staff to conduct research by mail.")

Floral Park Public Library

Tulip Avenue and Caroline Place
Floral Park, NY 11002
(516) 326-6330
Beverly DiGiulio, Reference Librarian
Hours: Mon–Tue & Thur 10:00–9:00, Wed & Fri 10:00–6:00, Sat 9:00–5:00

Roswell P. Flower Memorial Library

Genealogical Committee
229 Washington Street
Watertown, NY 13601
Mrs. Homer J. Perkins, Genealogist
Hours: 9:00–5:00; Genealogy Department: Mon, Wed & Fri 12:00–4:00

Fort Delaware-Museum of Colonial History

c/o Sullivan County DPW
Narrowsburg, NY 12764
(914) 252-6660
Ethel M. Poley, Director
(genealogical services)

Fryer Memorial Museum

(Williams Street—location)
PO Box 177 (mailing address)
Munnsville, NY 13409
(315) 495-5395
Olive S. Boylan, Museum Director and Town Historian
Hours: anytime, daytime or evenings, by appointment
(genealogy, local history, local Indian history, etc.; not handicap accessible)
no costs, no membership fees

Fulton Public Library

160 South First Street
Fulton, NY 13069
(315) 592-5981; (315) 592-4504 FAX
Joyce H. Cook, Library Director
Hours: Mon, Fri & Sat 10:00–5:00, Tue–Thur 10:00–8:00

Garden City Public Library

60 Seventh Street
Garden City, NY 11530
(516) 742-8405
Vincent F. Seyfried, Village Historian
Hours: winter: Mon–Thur 9:30–9:00, Fri 9:30–5:30, Sat 9:00–5:00; summer: Mon–Tue & Thur 9:30–9:00, Wed & Fri 9:30–5:30

Gates Public Library

1605 Buffalo Road
Rochester, NY 14624
(716) 247-6446; (716) 426-5733 FAX
http://www.ggw.org/freenet/g/GatesPublicLibrary
Judy MacKnight, Assistant Director
Hours: Mon–Fri 10:00–9:00, Sat 10:00–5:00
(small Rochester area local history collection)

Genesee County Museum

PO Box 310
Mumford, NY 14511-0310

Geneva Free Library

244 Main Street
Geneva, NY 14456

The Gilbertsville Free Library
Local History Collection
1 Bloom Street
PO Box 332
Gilbertsville, NY 13776
(607) 783-2832
E-mail: glibrary@tri-town.net
Leigh Eckmair, President
Hours: Library: Mon–Wed & Fri 2:45–
5:15, Wed 7:00 P.M.–8:30 P.M., Sat
10:00–4:00; Local History Collection:
Sat 10:30–12:30 (call ahead before
visiting), and by appointment
(Village of Gilbertsville and Town of
Butternuts family and genealogy files,
village and town structural inventory,
cemetery records, school records, tax
records, voting records, *Otsego
Journal* on microfilm, atlases,
blueprints, maps, church records,
census records, photographs, vital
statistics, scrapbooks)
mail requests answered

Glen Cove Public Library
4 Glen Cove Avenue
Glen Cove, NY 11542
(516) 676-2130
Jim Brown, Librarian
Hours: Mon–Fri 9:00–9:00, Sat (winter)
9:00–5:00, Sat (summer) 9:00–1:00
(also Long Island history)

Great Neck Library
Bayview Avenue at Grist Mill Lane
Great Neck, NY 11024
(516) 466-8055; (516) 829-8297 FAX
Risha Rosner, Reference Librarian
Hours: Mon–Tue & Thur–Fri 9:00–9:00,
Wed 10:00–9:00, Sat 1:00–6:00

Guernsey Memorial Library
Otis A. Thompson Local History Room
3 Court Street
Norwich, NY 13815
(607) 334-4034
Katheryn L. Barton, Head Researcher
Hours: Mon–Fri 1:00–5:00, Sat 9:00–
1:00, Sun (Labor Day–Memorial Day)
1:00–4:00
(emphasis on central New York
genealogy and local history)
30¢ per page charge for copies ($1.00
minimum)

Hamilton Public Library
13 Broad Street
Hamilton, NY 13346

The Museums at Hartwick
Hartwick College
Yager Hall
Oneonta, NY 13820
(607) 431-4480
Jane des Grange, Director
Hours: Mon–Sat 10:00–4:00, Sun 1:00–
4:00
(teaches genealogy to college students
and community special classes)

Haviland-Heidgerd Historical Collection
Elting Memorial Library
93 Main Street
New Paltz, NY 12561
(914) 255-5030
Marion W. Ryan, Director
Hours: Mon–Tue & Thur 1:00–5:30,
Wed & Fri 10:00–5:30
(Ulster County history and genealogy,
also Hudson Valley genealogy)
search fee on request

Hempstead Public Library
115 Nichols Court
Hempstead, NY 11550
(516) 481-6990
Susan J. Alessi, Head Reference
Department
Hours: photograph collection and Long
Island Collection by appointment only
(emphasis on Long Island and Village of
Hempstead)

Hinckley Foundation Museum
410 East Seneca Street
Ithaca, NY 14850
(607) 273-7053
Maeleah Carlisle, Director
Hours: Sat (Mar–Dec) 10:00–4:00, and
by appointment
("small library and archives (ephemera),
not much on specific families except
for Henry Noble Hinckley"; Ithaca
imprints)
$10.00–$500.00 per year membership

Historic Cherry Hill
523 South Pearl Street
Albany, NY 12202
(518) 434-4791
Anne W. Ackerson, Director
(5,000 books, 30,000 manuscripts, 3,000
photographs)

Homeville Museum
49 Clinton Street, Route 41
Homer, NY 13077-1024
(607) 749-3105
Kenneth M. Eaton, Director
Hours: May–Oct: Thur 7:00 P.M.–9:00
P.M., second & fourth Sun 1:00–4:00
(model railroad and military museum)
free admission, donations accepted

Huntington Memorial Library
New York Room
62 Chestnut Street
Oneonta, NY 13820
(607) 432-1980
http://lib.4cty.org/oneonta/index.html
Marie Bruni, Director
Hours: Library: Mon–Thur 9:00–9:00,
Fri–Sat 9:00–5:30; New York Room:
Mon–Fri 1:00–4:00, Tue–Wed & Fri
9:00–noon, Thur 6:00 P.M.–9:00 P.M.,
and by appointment

Huntington Public Library
Reference Department
338 Main Street
Huntington, NY 11743
(516) 427-5165; (516) 673-3351 FAX
Diana Navarro
Hours: Mon–Fri 9:00–9:00, Sat–Sun
9:00–5:00
(index to weekly *Long Islander*,
published since 1838)

Ilion Free Public Library
78 West Street
Ilion, NY 13357-1797
(315) 894-5028; (315) 894-9980 FAX
Christine Lozoski, Director/Head
Librarian
Hours: Mon–Tue & Thur 9:00–9:00,
Wed & Fri 9:00–6:00, Sat (Sept–May)
9:00–1:00; Local History Collection:
limited hours
(local history, local newspapers on
microfilm, files, city directories,
photos

Jericho Public Library
1 Merry Lane
Jericho, NY 11753
(516) 935-6790; (516) 433-9581 FAX
E-mail: merry2@lilrc.org
Betsey Murphy, Local History Librarian
Hours: Mon–Thur 9:00–9:00, Fri–Sat
9:00–5:00, Sun noon-5:00
Pub. *Long Island Forum*
(focus on Jericho area history and Long
Island history; small collection of
Hicks, Seaman and Underhill families,
oral history cassettes)

Jervis Public Library
613 North Washington Street
Rome, NY 13440
(315) 336-4570
Lori L. Esworthy, Local History/
Genealogy Librarian
Hours: Mon–Thur 9:30–9:00, Fri 9:30–
5:30, Sat (except Jul–Aug) 9:30–5:00
(Oneida County genealogy and local
history; John B. Jervis papers by
appointment only)

Johnstown Public Library
38 South Market Street
Johnstown, NY 12095
(518) 762-8317; (518) 762-9776 FAX
Deborah J. Callery, Co-ordinator
Hours: winter (local school district year):
Mon & Thur 1:00–8:00, Tue–Wed
10:00–8:00, Fri 10:00–5:00, Sat
10:00–1:00, Sun 1:00–4:00; summer:
Mon–Wed 10:00–8:00, Thur noon–
8:00, Fri 10:00–5:00
(federal census from 1790, Elizabeth
Cady Stanton and women's suffrage
history and Mohawk Valley history
beginning with Sir Wm. Johnson's
arrival in mid-1700s; "This collection
is primarily dedicated to the history of

Johnstown, with other information, such as the development of the Valley as available.")

Keene Valley Library Archives
Main Street
Keene Valley, NY 12943
(518) 576-4693
Dorothy W. Irving, Librarian for the Archives
Hours: Tue & Thur 9:00–noon
(news clippings, cemetery listings, photos, and genealogies)
charges vary according to materials

LaGuardia Community College
Fiorello H. LaGuardia Archives
31-10 Thomson Avenue
Long Island City, NY 11101
(718) 626-5078; (718) 482-5065
Richard K. Lieberman, Ph.D., Director
(history of 20th-century New York City)

Lehman College Library of the City University of New York
250 Bedford Park Boulevard, West
Bronx, NY 10468-1589
(718) 960-8577
E-mail: tbmlc@cunyvm.cuny.edu
Dr. Janet Butler Munch, Administrative Services Librarian
Hours: by appointment only
(Bronx research—Bronx Institute Archives)

Locust Valley Library
170 Buckram Road
Locust Valley, NY 11560
(516) 671-1837
Hours: Mon–Thur 10:00–9:00, Fri–Sat 10:00–5:00

Lorenzo State Historic Site
17 Rippleton Road (NY Route 13)
Cazenovia, NY 13035
(315) 655-3200; (315) 655-4304 FAX
Sharon M. Cooney, Interpretive Programs Assistant
Hours: Mon–Fri 8:00–4:00, weekends by appointment
(land records, cemetery and miscellaneous information; towns of Cazenovia, DeRuyter, Fenner, German, Lincklaen, Nelson, and Pitcher)

Lower East Side Tenement Museum
66 Allen Street
New York, NY 10002
(212) 431-0233
Anita Jacobson, Curator
Hours: Mon–Sun 10:00–5:00
Pub. *Tenement Times*, biannually, $2.00 per issue
$30.00 per year membership for individuals, $45.00 per year membership for couples, $60.00 per year membership for families

Mamaroneck Free Library
Library Lane
Mamaroneck, NY 10543
(914) 698-1250

Mannsville Museum
Lilac Park Drive
Mannsville, NY 13661
(315) 465-4049
Ellen B. Miller, President of Board of Trustees Library/Museum
(genealogical services)

Town of Massena Museum and Historian's Office
200 East Orvis Street
Massena, NY 13662
(315) 769-8571
Theresa Sharp, Town Historian
Hours: Mon–Fri 10:00–4:00 by appointment
(farming and lumbering community, turned industrial with Alcoa in early nineteen hundreds)
no charge for searches

Medaille College Library
18 Agassiz Circle
Buffalo, NY 14214
(716) 884-3281, ext. 283; (716) 884-9638 FAX

Mohawk Valley Museum
311 Main Street
Utica, NY 13501
(315) 724-2075

Montgomery County Department of History and Archives
Old Courthouse
Railroad Street
PO Box 1500
Fonda, NY 12068-1500
(518) 853-8186; (518) 853-8392 FAX
E-mail: murphyj@nyslgti.gen.ny.us
Jacqueline Murphy, Montgomery County Historian/RMO (Records Management Officer)
Hours: Sept–Jun: Mon–Fri 8:30–4:00; Jul–Aug: Mon–Fri 9:00–4:00
(county-funded department; third largest genealogical and historical research library and collection in New York State; Mohawk Valley civil and genealogy records)
$12.00 postpaid for catalog of genealogical and historical material; research: $15.00 per hour plus 25¢ per photocopy, $5.00 per certified copy

Moore Memorial Library
59 Genesee Street
Greene, NY 13778
(607) 656-9349
Scott Clark, Librarian
Hours: Mon & Wed noon–8:00, Tue & Thur 9:30–8:00, Fri 9:30–5:00, Sat 9:30–3:30
(copies of *Chenango American* from 1855)

Mount Vernon Public Library
Local History Room
28 South First Avenue
Mount Vernon, NY 10550
(914) 668-1840, ext. 315
Shannon E. Chandley, Curator
Hours: Mon–Fri 9:00–1:00, and by appointment

Museum Association of New York
189 Second Street
Troy, NY 12180
(518) 273-3460

Nassau County Museum
Division of Museum Services
1864 Muttontown Road
Syosset, NY 11791
(516) 364-1050

New City Library
The Rockland Room
220 North Main Street
New City, NY 10956
(914) 634-4997; (914) 634-0173 FAX
E-mail: spelleg@rcknet.com
http://www.newcitylibrary.org
Sally Pellegrini, Local History Librarian
Hours: Mon–Fri 9:00–9:00, Sat 9:00–5:00 (summer: 10:00–5:00), Sun 12:00–8:00 (summer: closed Sun)

New York City Department of Records and Information Services
Municipal Reference and Research Center (MRRC)
31 Chambers Street, Room 111
New York, NY 10007
(212) 788-8590
Joan Nichols, Acquisitions Librarian
Hours: Mon–Fri 9:00–4:30
(New York City government and history; MRRC is a library, not an archives)

The City of New York Department of Records and Information Services
Municipal Archives
31 Chambers Street, Room 103
New York, NY 10007
(212) 788-8580
Kenneth R. Cobb, Director
Hours: Archives: Mon–Thurs 9:00–4:30, Fri 9:00–1:00
(includes New York City vital records and other resources; received part of the collection of the former James A. Kelly Institute for Local Historical Studies)

The New York Public Library
The Research Libraries
U.S. History, Local History and Genealogy Division
Fifth Avenue and 42nd Street
New York, NY 10018
(212) 930-0828 (U.S. History, Local History and Genealogy Division); (212) 930-0587 (Map Division); (212) 930-0801 (Rare Books and Manuscripts)

http://www.nypl.org/research/chss/lhg/
genea.html
Ruth A. Carr, Division Chief
Hours: Tue 11:00–7:30, Wed 11:00–6:00,
Thur–Sat 10:00–6:00

Newburgh Free Library
124 Grand Street
Newburgh, NY 12550
(914) 561-1985, ext. 25; (914) 561-1985,
ext. 26
Hours: Mon–Thur 9:00–9:00, Fri–Sat
9:00–5:00, Sun 1:00–5:00

Niagara County Community College Library
3111 Saunders Settlement Road
Sanborn, NY 14132
(716) 731-3271, ext. 401; (716) 731-
7118 FAX
(Native American Collection, including
reference books, biography, history,
tribes, mythology, and periodicals e.g.
Native Peoples, *Journal of Cherokee
Studies*, *Northeast Indian Quarterly*,
Akwekon Journal, *Turtle Quarterly*,
and *Southern Indian Studies*)

Niagara Falls Public Library
Local History Department, Niagara
Room
Earl W. Brydges Library Building
1425 Main Street
Niagara Falls, NY 14305-2574
(716) 286-4899 (Local History); (716)
286-4912 FAX
Maureen Fennie, Manager; Daniel
Dumych, Local History Specialist
Hours: Mon 9:00–9:00, Tue–Fri 9:00–
5:00, second Sat (Sept–May) 9:00–
1:00 & 2:00–5:00
(Niagara Falls only, index of newspapers
for vital statistics prior to World War I
online since 1996 and scattered years
to date and for local events since
1854; Index of *Niagara Gazette*)

Town of Norfolk Historical Museum
39 Main Street
PO Box 645
Norfolk, NY 13667
(315) 384-4575; (315) 384-3223
Jean A. Young, Museum Director and
Norfolk Town Historian
Hours: Tue–Thur 2:00–5:00 (also most
Mon & Wed)
(Norfolk history and genealogy)
no charge for research if done in
museum, if outside research is
required, costs vary

North Merrick Public Library
1691 Meadowbrook Road
Merrick, NY 11566
(516) 378-7474
J. Jankolovits, Librarian
Hours: Mon–Thur 10:00–9:00, Fri
10:00–6:00, Sat 10:00–5:00, Sun
1:00–4:00
Pub. *Merrick Life*, weekly

North Tonawanda Public Library
505 Meadow Drive
North Tonawanda, NY 14120
(716) 693-4132
Hours: Mon–Thur 10:00–9:00, Fri–Sat
10:00–5:00
(local history, Niagara County census)

Ogdensburg Public Library
312 Washington Street
Ogdensburg, NY 13669
(315) 393-4325; (315) 393-4344 FAX
E-mail: franz@northnet.org
http://222.northnet.org/ogbpublib
David Franz, Library Director
Hours: Mon–Thur 9:00–9:00, Fri 10:00–
6:00, Sat 10:00–5:00, Sun 1:00–5:00
(closed Sat–Sun, Jul–Aug)

Ohoopee Regional Library
(see Georgia)

Old Merchants House of New York, Inc.
29 East Fourth Street
New York, NY 10003
(212) 777-1089

Oneida Library
220 Broad Street
Oneida, NY 13421

Onondaga County Public Library
Local History/Special Collections
447 South Salina Street
Syracuse, NY 13202-2400
(315) 435-1800
Mary Frances Smyth, Head of
Information Services
Hours: Mon & Thur–Sat 9:00–4:45,
Tue–Wed 9:00–8:15

Patterson Library
40 South Portage Street
Westfield, NY 14787
(716) 326-2154; (716) 326-2554 FAX
E-mail: wlibrar2@epix.net
http://www.cecomm.wm/wlibrary/
libfirst.htm
Mary S. Dibble, Town Historian
Hours: winter: Mon–Tue & Thur 9:00–
8:00, Wed & Fri–Sat 9:00–5:00;
summer: Mon & Wed–Fri 9:00–5:00,
Tue & Thur 9:00–8:00, Sat 9:00–1:00
(local history collection; no genealogical
services)
charges for copies and postage

Penfield Public Library
Penfield Local History Room
Division of Town Historian's Office
1985 Baird Road
Penfield, NY 14526
(716) 383-0500 (Library); (716) 383-
0557 (Local History Room)
Kathy Kanayer, Coordinator
Hours: Library: Mon–Thur 10:00–9:00,
Fri–Sat 10:00–5:00, Sun (Sept–Jun)
2:00–5:00; Local History Room:

Mon–Tue & Thur 1:00–5:00, Mon–
Tue 7:00–9:00, Sun (Sept–Jun) 2:00–
5:00, and by appointment

Pickering-Beach Historical Museum
West Main Street
Sacket Harbor, NY 13685
(315) 646-2052; (315) 646-3868

Plainview-Old Bethpage Public Library
999 Old Country Road
Plainview, NY 11803
Hours: Mon–Fri 9:00–9:00, Sat 9:30–
5:30, Sun 1:00–9:00

Port Chester Public Library
1 Haseco Avenue
Port Chester, NY 10573
(914) 939-6710; (914) 939-4735 FAX
http://www.wls.lib.ny.us
Mark Ross, Reference Librarian
Hours: Mon 9:00–9:00, Tue–Fri 9:00–
5:00 Sat (winter) 9:00–5:00

Port Washington Public Library
1 Library Drive
Port Washington, NY 11050
(516) 883-4400
Jerry McGee, Director; Priscilla
Ciccariello, Head of Information
Services
Hours: Mon–Fri 9:00–9:00, Sat 9:00–
5:00
Pub. *Port Washington Public Library
Newsletter*

Potsdam Public Museum
Civic Center, Park Street
Potsdam, NY 13676
(315) 265-6910
Betsy L. Travis, Director
Hours: Tue–Sat 2:00–5:00
Pub. untitled newsletter
(local history museum, small local
archives, no library)

James Prendergast Library Association
509 Cherry Street
Jamestown, NY 14701
(716) 484-7135
Kim Morris, Reference Librarian
Hours: Mon–Fri 9:00–9:00, Sat 9:00–
5:00, Sun (Nov–Apr) 1:00–4:00

Queens Library
Long Island Collection
89-11 Merrick Boulevard
Jamaica, NY 11432
(617) 990-0770
Charles F. J. Young, Curator

Margaret Reaney Memorial Library
19 Kingsbury Avenue
Saint Johnsville, NY 13452
(518) 568-7822; (518) 568-7822 FAX
Marta Zimmerman, Assistant Library
Director

Hours: Mon–Wed & Fri 9:30–5:00, Mon
& Fri 6:30–8:30, Thur 1:00–5:00, Sat
9:30–noon
(emphasis on Palatine Germans of the
Mohawk Valley)
search fee: $10.00 plus postage and
copies at 25¢ per page

Richmond Memorial Library
19 Ross Street
Batavia, NY 14020
(716) 343-9550
Kathleen Facer, Adult Services Librarian
Hours: Mon–Tue & Thur 9:00–9:00,
Wed 9:00–6:00, Fri–Sat 9:00–5:00
(closed Sat, Jul–Aug)
(Genesee County, New York)

Rochester Public Library
Local History Division
115 South Avenue
Rochester, NY 14604
(716) 428-7338 (general); (716) 428-
7338 (Local History and Genealogy
Department); (716) 428-7373 (dial-up
modem line for catalog)
Wayne K. Arnold, Head Librarian, Local
History Division
Hours: Mon & Thur 8:30–9:00, Tue &
Fri 8:30–6:00, Sat 8:30–5:00
Pub. *Rochester History*, quarterly, $6.00
per year subscription, $4.00 per year
subscription for senior citizens (over
age 55)
(collection of printed genealogies, county
and town histories, census, Rochester
directories from 1827, suburban
directories from 1932, maps,
newspapers indexed 1818–1902,
tombstone records, scrapbooks, etc.)

Rogers Memorial Library
9 Job's Lane
Southampton, NY 11968
(516) 283-0774
Sue Ann Taylor, Reference Librarian
Hours: Mon–Thur 10:00–9:00, Fri–Sat
10:00–5:00
(Long Island, especially Southampton;
"Staff is very limited and extended
searches not possible")

Gardner A. Sage Library
21 Seminary Place
New Brunswick, NJ 08901
(908) 247-5243
Marsha Blake, Reference Librarian
Hours: Mon–Thur 10:00–10:00, Fri
10:00–5:00, Sat 11:00–3:00
(emphasis on New York, New Jersey,
Colonial Dutch, and Reformed Church
in America)
search fee: $10.00 per day, $100.00 per
year

William K. Sanford Town Library
629 Albany-Shaker Road
Loudonville, NY 12211-1196
(518) 458-9274; (518) 438-0988; (518)
482-5441 FAX

Mary Hoefgen, Head of Reference
Services
Hours: Mon–Thur 9:00–9:00, Fri 9:00–
6:00, Sat 9:00–5:00, Sun (closed
summer) 1:00–5:00
(small collection of reference works, city
directories, maps, oral history tapes,
newspaper clipping file with an
emphasis on the Town of Colonie and
surrounding localities, including some
local church records and a few family
histories)

Scarsdale Public Library
Post and Olmsted Roads
Scarsdale, NY 10583
(914) 722-1300; (914) 722-1305 FAX
http://www.wls.lib.ny.us/libs/scarsdale/
welcome.html
Florence Sinsheimer, Reference
Librarian
Hours: Mon–Wed 10:00–9:00, Thur
10:00–6:00, Fri–Sat 9:00–5:00, Sun
1:00–5:00; summer hours differ
slightly
(weekly newspaper *Scarsdale Inquirer*
from 1901 with index; local history
collection, village reports from 1915,
biographical clippings, organizations,
phone books from 1931)

Schenectady County Public Library
99 Clinton Street
Schenectady, NY 12305-2083
(518) 382-4500; (518) 386-2241 FAX
Timothy McGowan, Head, Reference
and Adult Services
Hours: Mon–Thur 9:00–9:00, Fri–Sat
9:00–5:00, Sun (Oct–Apr) 1:00–5:00

Schenectady Museum
Nott Terrace Heights
Schenectady, NY 12308
(518) 382-7890

Skemesborough Museum
PO Box 238
Whitehall, NY 12887
(518) 499-0225; (518) 499-0754

Smithtown Library
Richard H. Handley Long Island History
Room
1 North Country Road
Smithtown, NY 11787
(516) 265-2072, ext. 38
Richard B. Hawkins, Librarian
Hours: Wed 1:00–5:00 & 6:00–9:00, Tue
& Thur–Fri 10:00–1:00 & 2:00–6:00,
Sat 9:00–1:00 & 2:00–5:00
(Smithtown Archives and Long Island
Special Collection)

State University of New York at Fredonia
Reed Library
Fredonia, NY 14063
(716) 673-3183; (716) 673-3185 FAX
E-mail: ericson@fredonia.edu
Jack T. Ericson, Archivist/Curator,

Special Collections
Hours: winter: Mon–Fri 1:00–5:00;
summer: Mon–Fri 1:00–4:00
(Chautauqua and Cattaraugus counties)

Penfield Library
State University of New York at Oswego
Oswego, NY 13126
(315) 341-3537; (315) 341-3567
E-mail: sturr@oswego.edu
http://www.oswego.edu/library/
Nancy Osborne, Coordinator of Special
Collections; Ed Vermue, Assistant
Coordinator
Hours: during the semester: Mon & Thur
1:30–4:30
(local history and college history)

State University of New York at Stony Brook
Long Island Archives Conference
Department of Special Collections
State University of New York Library
Stony Brook, NY 11794-3323
(516) 246-3615

Steele Memorial Library
101 East Church Street
Elmira, NY 14901
(607) 733-8602; (607) 733-9176 FAX
E-mail: ref@chstls
Rita Dery, Librarian
Hours: Mon–Thur 9:00–9:00, Fri 9:00–
5:00, Sat (except Jun–Sept) 9:00–5:00,
Sun (except Jun–Sept) 1:00–5:00
research: $12.00 per hour plus copy costs

Sullivan County Museum
PO Box 82
Woolbourne, NY 12788
Bernita Kimble, Museum Coordinator
Hours: Library: Tue & Thur 1:00–4:30,
Museum: daily 9:30–4:00
Pub. *The Observer*, monthly
$15.00 per year membership for
individuals, $20.00 per year
membership for couples, $25.00 per
year membership for families

Syosset Public Library
225 South Oyster Bay Road
Syosset, NY 11791
(516) 921-7161
Isabel Goldenkoff
Hours: winter: Mon–Fri 9:00–9:00, Sat
9:00–5:00, Sun 12:00–5:00; summer:
Mon–Fri 9:00–9:00, Sat 9:00–1:00

Didymus Thomas Library
Remsen, NY 13438

Trinity Museum
(Broadway and Wall Streets—location)
74 Trinity Place (mailing address)
New York, NY 10006
(212) 602-0872
David Jette, Verger
Hours: Mon–Fri 9:00–11:45 & 1:00–
3:45, Sat 10:00–3:45, Sun 1:00–3:45

Trocaire College Library
110 Red Jacket Parkway
Buffalo, NY 14220
(716) 826-1200; (716) 826-4704 FAX

Troy Public Library
100 Second Street
Troy, NY 12180
(518) 274-7071 (Reference); (518) 271-9154 FAX
http://www.global2000.net/troypl
Sarah K. Andrews, Reference, Local History and Genealogy Librarian
Hours: Mon–Tue 10:00–9:00, Wed–Sat 10:00–5:00, Sat (summer) 10:00–1:00
(local history and genealogy, Rensselaer County, City of Troy)
research: $25.00 for the first hour (including four copies and postage), $20.00 for each additional hour, 10¢ for each additional copy, plus additional postage if required (turnaround time about 2–3 months)

Union Street Public Library
Cobleskill, NY 12043

University at Buffalo Science and Engineering Library
Map Collection
316 Capen Hall
Buffalo, NY 14260
(716) 645-2946; (716) 645-3710 FAX

University at Buffalo
Special Collection Reading Room
420 Capen Hall
Buffalo, NY 14260
(716) 645-2916; (716) 645-3714 FAX
E-Mail: densmore@acsu.buffalo.edu
Christopher Densmore, Acting Director
Hours: Mon–Fri 9:00–5:00
(University Archives serves as the official repository of historically significant university records of the University at Buffalo, documenting the history of the University and its students, alumni, faculty, and administrators; also maintains a small local history collection and provides information about local sources available for research in the Buffalo area)

Utica Public Library
303 Genesee Street
Utica, NY 13501
(315) 735-2279; (315) 734-1034 FAX
Barbara Brookes, Reference Librarian
Hours: Mon–Tue 9:00–8:00, Wed–Fri 9:00–5:30, Sat (except summers) 9:00–5:00
search fees: $16.00 for inquiries from outside of the state, $10.00 for inquiries from outside of Mid-York Library System

Henry Waldinger Memorial Library
60 Verona Place
Valley Stream, NY 11582-3011
(516) 825-6422
Mamie Eng
Hours: Mon–Tue & Thur–Fri 10:00–9:00, Wed 10:00–5:30, Sat 10:00–4:00

Warner Library
121 North Broadway
Tarrytown, NY 10591
(914) 631-2189
Jonathan Tee, Reference Librarian
Hours: Mon & Thur 1:00–9:00, Tue–Wed & Fri–Sat 10:00–5:00
(collection of materials, chiefly books, pertaining to Tarrytown and North Tarrytown)

Waterford Historical Museum and Cultural Center
2 Museum Lane
PO Box 175
Waterford, NY 12188
(518) 238-0809 (answering machine)
Ida May Neary, President; Dennis Rivage, Town Historian, Merle Doud, Village Historian
Hours: Sat–Sun (spring–fall) 2:00–4:00, and by appointment
(no genealogy service)
$10.00 per year membership for individuals, $15.00 per year membership for families

West Islip Public Library
3 Higbie Lane
West Islip, NY 11795
(516) 661-7080; (516) 661-7037 FAX
Mary Scanlon, Head of Reference
Hours: Mon–Thur 10:00–9:00, Fri 10:00–6:00, Sat 9:00–5:00, Sun (Oct–May) 1:00–5:00

Pieter Claesen Wyckoff House Museum
Clarendon Road at Ralph Avenue
PO Box 100-376
New York, NY 11210
Alan J. Lipsky, Administrator
Pub. *PCWHM Bulletin*
(genealogical services)

Yorktown Museum Record Center
(3147 Old Yorktown Road—location)
2227 Crompond Road—mailing address
Yorktown Heights, NY 10598
(914) 962-0341; (914) 962-7282
Doris P. Auser, Town Historian
Hours: Mon & Fri 9:00–12:30
(genealogical and local history collection, cemetery records, census and documents)

Historical Societies— Local and Regional

(Note that New York's network of official government historians are not genealogists and have been advised by the State Historian not to focus on genealogical research, but they may be able to direct the researcher to sources and persons who can help with genealogical questions.)

Adirondack Genealogical-Historical Society
100 Main Street
Saranac Lake, NY 12983
(518) 891-2236
Spencer B. Newman, President
Hours: Mon–Fri 10:00–5:00, Sat 12:00–5:00

Albany County Historian
Albany County Office Building
Room 820
112 State Street
Albany, NY 12207
(518) 447-7057; (518) 447-7055 FAX
John N. Travis
Hours: 8:30–4:30
Municipal Historians: **City of Albany**: Virginia Bowers, 352 Second Avenue, Albany, NY 12209; **Village of Altamont**: Alice Begley, 27 Patricia Lane, Albany, NY 12203, (518) 356-1980; **Town of Berne**: Ralph Miller, 1136 Helderberg Trail, Berne, NY 12023; **Town of Bethlehem**: Joseph A. Allgaier, 15 Heather Lane, Delmar, NY 12054, (518) 439-2041; **Town of Coeymans**: Marvin D. Wolfe, Route 143, Coeymans Hollow, NY 12046, (518) 756-8166; **City of Cohoes**: William Horan, Waterford, NY 12188; **Town of Colonie**: Jean Olton, Memorial Town Hall, Newtonville, NY 12128; **Village of Colonie**: Linda Murphy, 14 Benjamin Lane, Albany, NY 12205; **Town and Village of Green Island**: Ginger Hewitt, Heatly School, 171 Hudson Avenue, Green Island, NY 12183; **Town of Guilderland**: Alice Begley, Village of Altamont Historian (see above); **Town of Knox**: Mrs. Austin Saddlemire, PO Box B, Knox, NY 12107, (518) 872-2551; **Village of Menands**: Kevin Franklin, Municipal Building, 250 Broadway, Menands, NY 12204; **Town of New Scotland**: Robert Parmenter, 82 Badgley Lane, Voorheesville, NY 12186, (518) 439-4889, ext. 5721; **Village of Ravena**: Mary McCabe, 171 Main Street, Ravena, NY 12143; **Town of Rensselaerville**: Porter Wright, 9 Fox Creek Road, Medusa, NY 12120, (518) 239-8483; **Village of Voorheesville**: Dennis Sullivan, 14

Voorheesville Avenue, Box 262, Voorheesville, NY 12186, (518) 765-2468; **City of Watervliet**: Craig Carlson, c/o City Hall, Watervliet, NY, 12189, (518) 447-4513; **Town of Westerlo**: Dennis Fancher, 350 County Route 402, Westerlo, NY 12193, (518) 797-3095

Albany County Historical Association
9 Ten Broeck Place
Albany, NY 12210
(518) 436-9826

Alden Historical Society
13213 Broadway
Alden, NY 14004
(716) 937-7606

Alexandria Township Historical Society
Market Street
Alexandria Bay, NY 13607
(315) 482-4586
Doris Langlois, Vice President
(no genealogical department or services)

Alfred Historical Society
PO Box 1137
Alfred, NY 14802
(607) 587-8886; (607) 587-4351 FAX (Hinkle Memorial Library, SUNY Alfred); (607) 587-8358 (President); (607) 587-4307 (Library Assistant)
Douglas Clarke, President; Galen Brooks, Library Assistant
Hours: Mon, Wed & Fri 11:00–4:00
(several genealogical books and collections of notes for Alfred area and Seventh Day Baptist families from Rhode Island west)

Allegany Area Historical Association
25 North Second Street
PO Box 162
Allegany, NY 14706
Stephen Eaton, President
Hours: May–Oct: Wed 1:00–4:00
Pub. *Newsletter*, five times per year
$5.00 per year membership

Allegany County Historian's Office and County Museum
Court Street
Belmont, NY 14813
(716) 268-9293 (Museum); (716) 268-9446 FAX
Craig R. Braack
Hours: Museum: winter: 9:00–5:00; Jun–Aug: 8:30–4:00
Municipal Historians: **Town of Alfred**: Jean Lang, Kenyon Road, Alfred, NY 14802; **Village of Alfred**: Peggy Rase, Alfred NY 14802; **Town of Allen**: Jane Andrews, County Road 15, Fillmore 14735; **Town of Alma**: Norman Ives, Piper Place, Wellsville, NY 14895; **Town of Almond**: Audrey Pettibone, c/o Hagadorn House,

Almond, NY 14804; **Village of Almond**: post vacant; **Town of Amity**: post vacant; **Town of Andover** and **Village of Andover**: Margaret Wood, 27 Dyke Street, Andover, NY 14806; **Town of Angelica** and **Village of Angelica**: post vacant; **Town of Belfast**: Paul Curcio, Belfast, NY 14711; **Village of Belmont**: post vacant; **Town of Birdsall**: post vacant; **Town of Bolivar** and **Village of Bolivar**: Doris June, RD 1, Bolivar, NY 14715; **Town of Burns**: Sherri Amers, Canaseraga, NY 14822; **Village of Canaseraga**: post vacant; **Town of Caneadea**: Larry Wilson, Houghton, NY 14744; **Town of Centerville**: Debbie Covert, Centerville, NY 14029; **Town of Clarksville**: Charlotte Gessel, West Clarksville, NY 14786; **Town of Cuba**: David Crowley, 44 South Street, Cuba, NY 14727; **Village of Cuba**: post vacant; **Village of Fillmore**: Margaret Hodnett, RD 2, Fillmore, NY 14735; **Town of Friendship**: Peggy Brown, 15 East Water Street, Friendship, NY 14739; **Town of Genesee**: Charles Barrett, 202 Main Street, Ceres, NY 114721; **Town of Granger**: Loreen Bentley, RD 1, Fillmore, NY 14735; **Town of Grove**: post vacant; **Town of Hume**: Margaret Hodnet, RD 2, Fillmore, NY 14735; **Town of Independence**: Velma Westlake, Whitesville, NY 14897; **Town of New Hudson**: Neva Gross, Black Creek, NY 14714; **Village of Richburg**: post vacant; **Town of Rushford**: Homer Norton, Rushford, NY 14777; **Town of Scio**: Phyllis Young, Scio, NY 14880; **Town of Ward**: Rose Main, RD 1, Belmont, NY 14813; **Town of Wellsville**: Diane Converso, 173 East State, Wellsville, NY 14895; **Village of Wellsville**: post vacant; **Town of West Almond**: Deborah Hoffman, Rural Delivery, Almond, NY 14804; **Town of Willing**: Tina Wightman, RD 1, Wellsville, NY 14895; **Town of Wirt**: Betty Bartoo, Richburg, NY 14774

Allegany County Historical Society
20 Willets Avenue
Belmont, NY 14813
(716) 268-7428
Bill Green, County Historian, Emeritus (census and land records)
nominal search fees

Almond Historical Society
7 Main Street
Almond, NY 14804
(607) 276-6465; (607) 276-6781
Charlotte K. Baker, President
Hours: Fri 2:00–5:00 plus various open houses
Pub. *AHS Newsletter*, bimonthly

Amityville Historical Society
(170 Broadway—location)
PO Box 764 (mailing address)
Amityville, NY 11701
(516) 598-1486
Seth Purdy, Curator
Hours: Tue, Fri & Sun 2:00–4:00
Pub. *Dispatch*, quarterly
$20.00 per year membership

Anderson Falls Historical Society
Community Center, Second Floor
Old High School Building
Main Street
Keeseville, NY 12944
James Hayes, President

Anthropology Museum of the People of New York
3801 23rd Avenue
Astoria, NY 11105
(718) 626-0307

Arcade Historical Society
The Gibby House
331 West Main Street
PO Box 237
Arcade, NY 14009
(716) 492-4466
Ann Drennan, Office Manager
Hours: Tue–Wed 10:00–4:00, and by appointment
Pub. *Arcade Historical Society News*, three times per year
$5.00 per year membership for individuals, $10.00 per year membership for families, $25.00 per year membership for businesses

Aurora Historical Society, Inc.
5 South Grove Street
East Aurora, NY 14052
(716) 652-7944
Donald H. Dayer, Town Historian
Hours: Wed 1:00–4:00

Austerlitz Historical Society
(Route 22—location)
PO Box 144 (mailing address)
Austerlitz, NY 12017
(518) 392-5933; (518) 392-5478 (President)
Phil Palladino, Director; Robert Herron, President
Pub. *Quarterly*
from $5.00 per year membership

Baldwin Historical Society and Museum
1980 Grand Avenue
Baldwin, NY 11510
(516) 223-6900
Glenn F. Sitterly, Curator
Hours: by appointment
Pub. *Baldwin Historical Society Newsletter*, bimonthly
(Baldwin local history)

Basket Historical Society of the Upper Delaware Valley
Rt. 11
Long Eddy, NY 12760
(914) 887-5417

Battle of Oriskany Historical Society
806 Utica Street
Oriskany, NY 13424
Robert H. Heeley, President

Bayport Heritage Association
PO Box 4
Bayport, NY 11705
(516) 472-4625

Bayside Historical Society
(Fort Totten—location)
PO Box 133 (mailing address)
Bayside, NY 11361
(718) 352-1548; (718) 352-3904 FAX
E-mail: bayside@donohue.com
http://www.donohue.com/bayside
Geraldine Spinella, President
Hours: Sat 10:00–3:00, evening events
Pub. *Society News*, quarterly
$25.00 per year membership for individuals, $35.00 per year membership for families, $20.00 per year membership for students and senior citizens, $100.00 per year Contributing membership, $250.00 per year membership for organizations, $500.00 life membership for individuals

Beacon Historical Society
The Howland Center, 477 Main Street
PO Box 89
Beacon, NY 12508
Nancy Siebert, President
Hours: Thur 10:00–noon, Sat 1:00–3:00
Pub. *Newsletter*, monthly
(deals with Beacon and its antecedents, Fishkill Landing and Matteawan, and the immediate surroundings)
$10.00 per year membership; donation for search

Beauchamp Historical Club
828 Fairway Circle
Baldwinsville, NY 13027
Joseph P. Uirkler, President

Bedford Historical Society
38 Village Green
PO Box 491
Bedford, NY 10506
(914) 234-9751
Lynne Ryan, Director of Development
Hours: Mon & Wed–Thur 9:00–noon, Tue 1:00–4:00
from $25.00 per year membership for individuals, $15.00 per year membership for students or senior citizens; genealogy inquiries handled by Town Historian

Historical Society of the Bellmores
32 Stratford Court
North Bellmore, NY 11710
(516) 221-4222
Ken Foreman, Curator
Hours: by appointment
(Long Island history)
$5.00 per year membership

Bellport-Brookhaven Historical Society
31 Bellport Lane
Bellport, NY 11713
(516) 286-9064
Richard Baldwin, Archivist
Hours: by appointment
$35.00 per year membership; search fee: $10.00 per year

Bergen Historical Society
(7547 South Lake Road—location)
6833 Pocock Road (mailing address)
Bergen, NY 14416
(716) 494-1511

Town of Berne Historical Society
Historical Center, Main Street
PO Box 34
Berne, NY 12023

Town of Bethlehem Historical Association
Old Cedar Hill Schoolhouse
Selkirk, NY 12158
(518) 767-9432

Big Flats Historical Society
(258 Hibbard Road—location)
PO Box 232 (mailing address)
Big Flats, NY 14814-0232
(607) 562-8773 (Curator), (607) 562-7460, (607) 562-3152
Glenn Bates, Curator
Hours: Tue 9:00–noon, Sun (Jul–Aug) 2:00–4:00
Pub. *Newsletter*, monthly
$6.00 per year membership for individuals

Big Springs Historical Society
Main Street
Caledonia, NY 14423
(716) 538-4473

Bowdoin Park Historical and Archeology Association
Bowdoin Park, 85 Sheafe Road
Wappinger Falls, NY 12590
(914) 297-1224
E. Russell Lang, President
Pub. *BPHAA Newsletter*

Bridge Hampton Historical Society
(Corwith Avenue and Main Street—location)
PO Box 977 (mailing address)
Bridgehampton, NY 11932
(516) 537-1088; (516) 537-4225 FAX
Margaret Stocker, Director

Hours: winter: Mon–Fri 9:00–3:00; summer: Mon–Wed 9:00–3:00, Thur–Sat 9:00–4:00

Brighton Historical Society
52 Kimbark Road
Rochester, NY 14610
(716) 381-6202
Roberta Lachiusa, President

The Bronx County Historical Society
Theodore Kazimiroff Library
3309 Bainbridge Avenue
Bronx, NY 10467
(718) 881-8900; (718) 881-4827 FAX
Laura Tosi, Associate Librarian
Hours: Mon–Fri 9:30–4:30
Pub. *The Bronx County Historical Society Journal*, semiannually; *The Bronx Historian Newsletter*
$20.00 per year membership for individuals, $25.00 per year membership for families, $15.00 for senior citizens and students

Official Bronx Historian
3930 Bailey Avenue
Bronx, NY 10463
(212) 549-5566
The Rev. Dr. William A. Tieck, Founder Kingsbridge Historical Society
Hours: by appointment
(emphasis on New York State and the American Revolution)

Brookfield Historical Society
Main Street
Brookfield, NY 13314
Gwendolyn Witter, Treasurer
Pub. *Bailyes Corner*

Brookfield Township Historical Society
Main Street
Brookfield, NY 13314
Edward McNamara
Hours: meeting fourth Tue (Apr–Nov)
Pub. *Beaver Gazette*, bimonthly
$5.00 per year membership

Brooklyn Historical Society
128 Pierpont Street, Corner Clinton Street
Brooklyn, NY 11201
(718) 624-0890
E-mail: bhs@parix.com
http://www.brooklynhistory.org
Michell Hackwelder, Head Librarian

Broome County Historian
Broome County Public Library
78 Exchange Street
Binghamton, NY 13901
(607) 778-2076; (607) 778-1441 FAX
E-mail: bcpl@spectra.net
Gerald R. Smith, County Historian; Margaret Shiel, Deputy County Historian
Hours: Thur 9:00–3:00 & 6:00–9:00
(Broome County, New York, history)

Municipal Historians: **Town of Barker**: Christine L. Gillett, Town Clerk, PO Box 66, Castle Creek, NY 13744; **City of Binghamton**: Gerald R. Smith, County Historian (see above); **Town of Binghamton**: Anne E. Lindsley, 1412 Hawleyton Road, Binghamton, NY 13903; **Town of Chenango**: Alice Ruby, Schoolhouse Museum, c/o 1137 Front Street, Binghamton, NY 13905; **Town of Colesville**: Minerva D. Flagg, 47 Flagg Road, Binghamton, NY 13904; **Town of Conklin**: Robert Barber, 543 Pierce Creek Road, Binghamton, NY 13903, (607) 723-1737; **Village of Deposit**: Mary Cable, 146 Front Street, Deposit, NY 13754; **Town of Dickinson**: Catherine McNally, 861 Chenango Street, Binghamton, NY 13901; **Village of Endicott**: Ted Warner, Endicott Village Office, 1009 East Main Street, Endicott, NY 13760; **Town of Fenton**: Dorothy Whiting, 1250 Cornell Avenue, Binghamton, NY 13901; **Village of Johnson City**: Janet A. Ottman, Your Home Public Library, 107 Main Street, Johnson City, NY 13790; **Town of Kirkwood**: Robert Cleary, 1105 Old State Road, Binghamton, NY 13904; **Town of Lisle** and **Village of Lisle**: Tressa Corcoran, Main Street, Lisle, NY 13797; **Town of Maine**: Ann Lewis, 2130 Bradley Creek Road, Johnson City, NY 13790; **Town of Nanticoke**: Leroy Youngs, Nanticoke Town Hall, Cherry Valley Hill Road, Star Route, Maine, NY 13802; **Village of Port Dickinson**: Catherine McNally, 7686 Chenango Street, Binghamton, NY 13901; **Town of Sanford**: Ann Parsons, 3 Lippencott, Deposit, NY 13754; **Town of Triangle**: Aleksandre Mesceda, 3276 Route 206 NY, Whitney Point, NY 13862; **Town of Union**: Suzanne Meredith, 3716 Maplehurst Drive, Endwell, NY 13760; **Town of Vestal**: Elizabeth Mae Bartlow, Vestal Public Library, 320 Vestal Parkway, Vestal, NY 13850; **Village of Whitney Point**: Juanita Aleba, 3124 Route 206 NY, Whitney Point, NY 13862; **Town of Windsor**: Bernard Osborne, 235 Old Route 17, Windsor, NY 13865; **Village of Windsor**: Charles English, 22 Chestnut Street, Windsor, NY 13865 out-of-state requests: $10.00 plus copies at 20¢ each

Broome County Historical Society
Roberson Museum and Science Center
30 Front Street
Binghamton, NY 13905-4779
(607) 772-0660
Charles J. Browne, Librarian
Hours: Tue–Fri 10:00–4:00
Pub. *Broome County Historical Society*

Newsletter, three times per year (large manuscript and photograph collection, genealogy files, etc.)
$20.00 per year membership for individuals, $30.00 per year membership for families, $45.00 per year membership in both Roberson Center and the Historical Society; search fee: $5.00 per hour, plus 25¢ per copy

General Jacob Brown Historical Society
Bronn Mansion
216 Brown Boulevard
Brownsville, NY 13615

Brunswick Historical Society
PO Box 1776
Cropseyville, NY 12052
(518) 279-4024; (518) 279-1215
Clara H. Steiner, President

The Bryant Library Local History Collection
Paper Mill Road
Roslyn, NY 11576
(516) 621-2240
Myrna L. Sloam, Archivist
Hours: by appointment
(history of Roslyn, New York, Long Island history; William C. Bryant, Christopher Morley Collections)

Buffalo and Erie County Historical Society
Research Library
25 Nottingham Court
Buffalo, NY 14216
(716) 873-9612; (716) 873-8754 FAX
Mary F. Bell, Director of Library and Archives
Hours: Wed–Fri 10:00–5:00, Sat 12:00–5:00
(local history, i.e. Buffalo and Erie County; "We do not do research that consists of more than fifteen minutes of time to look in published directories or indexes.")
$20.00 per year membership; $3.70 per day library use fee for non-members

Historical Association of the Town of Butternuts
Commercial Street and Marion Avenue
Gilbertsville, NY 13776
Winona Ferrara, Chair, Board of Trustees

Byron Historical Society
(Route 262—location)
PO Box 201 (mailing address)
Byron, NY 14422
Dora M. Jones, Town Historian
Hours: Jun–Aug: Sun 2:00–4:00
free admission

Cambria Historical Society
4159 Lower Mountain Road
Lockport, NY 14094
(716) 434-8937

Cambridge Historical Society
21 Broad Street
Cambridge, NY 12816
Audry Wallace, President
Hours: Museum: Sat 2:00–4:00 (Jul–Aug)

Town of Camillus Historical Society
4600 West Genesee Street
Syracuse, NY 13019
John W. Luebs, President
Pub. *Camillus Chronicle*, monthly
$5.00 per year membership for adults (includes periodical), $2.00 per year membership for children and students (does not include periodical)

Town of Carmel Historical Society
McAlpin Avenue
PO Box 808
Mahopac, NY 10541
(914) 628-0500
Alfred C. Eberhardt, Jr., President
Hours: Sun 2:00–4:00, and by appointment
Pub. *TCHS Newsletter*, quarterly (temporarily suspended)
$5.00 per year membership for individuals, $10.00 per year membership for families, $15.00 per year membership for businesses, $25.00 per year business membership, $100.00 life membership

Cattaraugus Area Historical Society
(23 Main Street—location)
Lover's Lane Road (mailing address)
Cattaraugus, NY 14719
(716) 257-9012

Cattaraugus County Historian
303 Court Street
Little Valley, NY 14755
(716) 938-9111, ext. 440
Kenneth Kysor
Hours: Tue & Wed 9:00–4:30, and by appointment
Municipal Historians: **Town of Allegany** and **Village of Allegany**: Harold Carls, 41 North Fifth Street, Allegany, NY 14706; **Town of Ashford**: B. Lynn Williams, Rt. 240, West Valley, NY 14171; **Village of Cattaraugus**: Kenneth Kysor, Lover's Lane Road, Cattaraugus, NY 14719; **Town of Coldspring**: Marcia Arrance, PO Box, Steamburg, NY 14783; **Town of Conewango**: Anna May Rhoades, Rt. 1, Cowen Road, Conewango Valley, NY 14726; **Town of Dayton**: Marilyn Turnbull, Rt. 1, Box 231, South Dayton, NY 14138; **Village of Delevan**: post vacant; **Town of East Otto**: Jean Fleckenstein, East Otto, NY 14729; **Village of East Randolph**: Dorothy Carnahan, Rt. 2, Randolph, NY 14772; **Town of Ellicottville**: Lois Siggelkow, Bryant Hill Road, Ellicottville, NY 14731; **Village of Ellicottville**: Paula Ayrhart, Registrar

of Vital Statistics, 1 West Washington Street, Ellicottville, NY 14731; **Town of Farmersville**: Alice Wright, Rogers Road, Franklinville, NY 14737; **Town of Franklinville** and **Village of Franklinville**: Mrs. Kaye Hall, 40 Maple Avenue, Franklinville, NY 14737; **Town of Freedom**: Lorna Spencer, 2372 Elton Road, Delevan, NY 14042; **Village of Gowanda**: Jean C. Hillis, Rt. 2, Box 66, Gowanda, NY 14070; **Town of Great Valley**: Roberta Stone, PO Box 35, Killbuck, NY 14748; **Town of Hinsdale**: Lila Cooper, 3819 Main Street, Hinsdale, NY 14743; **Town of Humphrey**: Mary Tyler, Bozard Hill Road, Star Route, Great Valley, NY 14741; **Town of Ischua**: Sally Pettengill, Ischua, NY 14746; **Town of Leon**: Bertha Millspaw, Rt. 1, West Road, Conewango Valley, NY 14726; **Village of Limestone**: Mary Haley, RVS, Killbuck, NY 14748; **Town of Little Valley**: Larry Gross, PO Box 15, Little Valley, NY 14755; **Village of Little Valley**: Patricia Isaman, RVS, Little Valley, NY 14755; **Town of Lyndon**: Gerry Emmons, 6458 Snyder Road, Cuba, NY 14727; **Town of Machias**: Gail Watkins, McKinstry Road, Machias, NY 14101; **Town of Mansfield**: Gail M. Burroughs, Rural Delivery, Box 22, Little Valley, NY 14755; **Town of Napoli**: Emmett Waite, Rural Delivery, Napoli, Little Valley, NY 14755; **Town of New Albion**: Kenneth Kysor, Lovers Lane Road, Cattaraugus, NY 14719; **City of Olean**: Josephine Weinman, Olean Municipal Building, Olean, NY 14760; **Town of Olean**: Margaret Kenney, 2634 Olean Hinsdale Road, Olean, NY 14760; **Town of Otto**: Medora Ball, Rt. 2, Ball Road, Cattaraugus, NY 14719; **Town of Perrysburg**: Lorraine Marvin, Rt. 2, Box 21, Gowanda, NY 14070; **Village of Perrysburg**: post vacant; **Town of Persia**: Jean C. Hillis, Rt. 2, Maltbie Road, Gowanda, NY 14070; **Town of Portville** and **Village of Portville**: Jane Miller, PO Box 253, Portville, NY 14770; **Town of Randolph** and **Village of Randolph**: Dorothy Carnahan, Rt. 2, Randolph, NY 14772; **Town of Red House**: Jane S. France, Rt. 1, Baystate Road, Salamanca, NY 14779; **City of Salamanca**: Joan M. Formica, 225 Wildwood Avenue, Salamanca, NY 14779; **Town of Salamanca**: post vacant; **Village of South Dayton**: Barbara Butcher, RVS, PO Box 9, South Dayton, NY 14138; **Town of South Valley**: Dorothy Bova, Rt. 1, Frewsburg, NY 14738; **Town of Yorkshire**: Naomi Baker, 57 Delevan Avenue, Delevan, NY 14042

Cayuga County Historian
Historic Old Post Office Building
157 Genesee Street
Auburn, NY 13021-3490
(315) 253-1300
Thomas G. Eldred
Hours: Mon–Fri 9:00–5:00
Pub. *Cayuga Gazette*, infrequently
Municipal Historians: **City of Auburn**: post vacant; **Town of Aurelius**: M. Ruth Probst, Rt. 1, Box 931, Cayuga, NY 13034; **Village of Aurora**: Edward Kabelac, Sherwood Road, Aurora, NY 13026; **Town of Brutus**: Howard Finley, 22 Bell Street, Weedsport, NY 13166; **Town of Cato**: Annie Backman, Rt. 2, Weedsport, NY 13166; **Village of Cato**: Letha Kelly, Mechanic Street, Cato, NY 13033; **Village of Cayuga**: Ruth Probst, Rt. 1, Box 931, Cayuga, NY 13034; **Town of Conquest**: Joani Lincoln, Rt. 2, Box 209, Port Byron, NY 13140; **Village of Fair Haven**: Erwin Fineout, Victory Street, Fair Haven, NY 13064; **Town of Fleming**: Sheila S. Tucker, Rt. 1, Auburn, NY 13021; **Town of Genoa**: Gordon Cummings, King Ferry, NY 13081; **Town of Ira**: Dorothy Southard, 3526 Dennison Road, Rt. 1, Box 200, Cato, NY 13033; **Town of Ledyard**: Edward Kabelac, Aurora, NY 13026; **Town of Locke**: Madeline Carey, Rt. 1, Box 133, Locke, NY 13092; **Town of Mentz**: Marie Van Detto, 32 Maiden Lane, Box 101, Port Byron, NY 13140; **Village of Meridian**: Mrs. Marion Dudley, PO Box 91, Meridian, NY 13113; **Town of Montezuma**: Horace Carner, Jr., PO Box 385, Montezuma, NY 13117; **Town of Moravia**: Robert J. Scarry, 18 Aurora Street, Moravia, NY 13118; **Village of Moravia**: Elsie Van Liew, 3 Congress Street, Moravia, NY 13118; **Town of Niles**: Rosemarie Tucker, Rt. 2, Box 35-A, Moravia, NY 13118; **Town of Owasco**: Laurel Auchampaugh, Rt. 2, Auburn, NY 13021; **Village of Port Byron**: Bruce Carter, Port Byron, NY 13140; **Town of Scipio**: Virginia Koon, Rural Delivery, Box 117, Union Springs, NY 13160; **Town of Sempronius**: Francis Armstrong, Rt. 3, Box 209, Moravia, NY 13118; **Town of Sennett**: Elaine Hutson, Rt. 4, Box 359, Auburn, NY 13021; **Town of Springport**: Jane Berry, Grove Street, Union Springs, NY 13160; **Town of Sterling**: Hallie A. Sweeting, Rt. 2, Box 245, Sterling, NY 13156; **Town of Summerhill**: Gregory Reed, Rt. 4, Cutler School Road, Cortland, NY 13045; **Town of Throop**: Hazel Humbert, Rt. 6, Box 283, Auburn, NY 13021; **Village of Union Springs**: Jane Berry, Grove Street, Union Springs, NY 13160;

Town of Venice: Dorothy Wiggans, Rt. 34, Rural Delivery, Aurora, NY 13027; **Town of Victory**: Evelyn Wood, Town Line Road, Cato, NY 13033; **Village of Weedsport**: Howard Finley, 22 Bell Street, Weedsport, NY 13166
$25.00 for all research

Cayuga County Historical Society
Cayuga Museum of History and Art
203 Genesee Street
Auburn, NY 13021
(315) 253-8051
Thomas G. Eldred, President
Pub. *Annual Summary of Programs*

Cayuga-Owasco Lakes Historical Society
Luther Research Center and Archives
14 West Cayuga Street
PO Box 247
Moravia, NY 13118
(315) 497-3206; (315) 497-3035 (evenings after 6:00)
E-mail: chipauch@baldcom.net
http://www.rootsweb.com/~nycayuga/colhs:htm#LUTHER
Laurel Auchampaugh, Owasco Town Historian
Hours: Mon & Sat 1:00–4:00; other days, evenings (off season) by appointment
Pub. *Newsletter*, quarterly
(750 family files; preserving the history of the twelve towns south of Auburn: Fleming, Genoa, Ledyard, Locke, Moravia, Niles, Owasco, Scipio, Sempronious, Springport, Summerhill and Venice))
$6.00 per year membership; research: $10.00 (local), $20.00 (extended)

Cedar Swamp Historical Society
(East of Hempstead Harbor, Long Island—location)
Cedar Swamp, LI, NY 11545 (mailing address)
(516) 671-6156
John G. Peterkin, Founder
Hours: Mon–Fri 10:00–4:00; annual Revolutionary War Ceremony at East Hillside Cemetery: second Sun of Sept 1:45
Pub. *Cedar Swamp Historical Society Newsletter*, irregularly, before events
(Cedar Swamp region of North Shore of "Long Iland," east of Hempstead Harbor, primarily 1592–1815; collection of over 1,100 books))
$15.00 per year membership for individuals living alone, $25.00 per year membership for families, $50.00 per year Patriot membership, $100.00 per year Benefactor membership, $500.00 Life membership

Charleston Historical Society
Rt. 1, Box 713
Esperance, NY 12066

(518) 875-6533
Edythe Meserand, Chair, Board of
Directors

Chautauqua County Historian
131 Center Street
Fredonia, NY 14063
Elizabeth Crocker
Municipal Historians: **Town of
Arkwright**: Beverly Smith, 2128
Route 83, Forestville, NY 14062;
Village of Bemus Point: Mary Jane
Stahley, 80 Lakeside Drive, Bemus
Point, NY 14712; **Village of Brocton**:
Edward Kurtz, PO Box H, Portland,
NY 14769; **Town of Busti**: post
vacant; **Town of Carroll**: June
Richards, PO Box 128, 26 Water
Street, Frewsburg, NY 14738; **Village
of Cassadaga**: Mr. W. Record Barris,
239 Maple Avenue, Cassadaga, NY
14718; **Village of Celoron**: Evelyn
Adams, Celoron, NY 14720; **Town of
Charlotte**: Donald Jordan, 8 Parkway
Drive, Sinclairville, NY 14782;
Chautauqua Institution: Alfreda
Irwin, Chautauqua Institution,
Chautauqua, NY 14722; **Town of
Chautauqua**: Lyle M. Staples,
Rollman Town Office Building, 11
South Erie Street, Mayville, NY
14757; **Town of Cherry Creek** and
Village of Cherry Creek: Joyce
Chase, PO Box 78, Cherry Creek, NY
14723; **Town of Clymer**: Suzanna
Rhebergen, 352 Mohawk
Street,Clymer, NY 14724; **City of
Dunkirk**: Mrs. Robert Dew, 720
Washington Avenue, Dunkirk, NY
14048; **Town of Dunkirk**: post
vacant; **Town of Ellery**: Lorraine C.
Smith, Rt. 1, Box 618, Bemus Point,
NY 14712; **Town of Ellicott**: Nancy
Anderson, 422 North Work Street,
Falconer, NY 14733; **Town of
Ellington**: Laurene Rice, Rt. 1,
Ellington-Gerry Road, Kennedy, NY
14747; **Village of Falconer**: Mrs.
Jerry Lyon, c/o Community Building,
101 West Main Street, Falconer, NY
14733; **Village of Forestville**: Mildred
Becker, 10960 Denison Road,
Forestville, NY 14062; **Village of
Fredonia**: Elizabeth Crocker, County
Historian (see above); **Town of
French Creek**: post vacant; **Town of
Gerry**: Jean Bedient, PO Box 111,
Gerry, NY 14740; **Town of Hanover**:
Vincent Martonis, 35 Monroe Street,
Silver Creek, NY 14136; **Town of
Harmony**: Irene Nagel, PO Box 32,
Panama, NY 14767; **City of
Jamestown**: B. Delores Thompson, 13
Lamont Street, Jamestown, NY 14701;
Town of Kiantone: Jean Brustrom, Rt.
5, Jamestown, NY 14701; **Village of
Lakewood**: Marie B. Burk, 120
Chautauqua Avenue, Lakewood, NY
14750; **Institutions Lily Dale**: Ms.

Paul Vogt, 11 Buffalo Street, Lily
Dale, NY 14718; **Village of Mayville**:
Dorothea Bertram, 53 South Portage
Street, Westfield, NY 14787; **Town of
Mina**: Sharon Scaren, PO Box 126,
Findley Lake, NY 14736; **Town of
North Harmony**: Robert Willsie, PO
Box 155, Stow, NY 14785; **Village of
Panama**: Irene Nagel, PO Box 32,
Panama, NY 14767; **Town of Poland**:
Roger Bish, Frewsburg Road,
Kennedy, NY 14747; **Town of
Pomfret**: Elizabeth Crocker, 131
Center Street, Fredonia, NY 14063;
Town of Portland: Edward Kurtz, PO
Box H, Portland, NY 14769; **Town of
Ripley**: Marie McCutcheon; **Town of
Sheridan**: Janet Dorsett, 3578 East
Main Road, Fredonia, NY 14063;
Town of Sherman and **Village of
Sherman**: Flora Hotchkiss, 117
Columbia Street, Sherman, NY 14781;
Village of Silver Creek: Agnes
Pfleuger, 12 Tew Street, Silver Creek,
NY 14136; **Village of Sinclairville**:
Donald Jordan, 8 Parkway Drive,
Sinclairville, NY 14782; **Town of
Stockton**: Helen Piersons, 14 East
Railroad Avenue, Stockton, NY 14784;
Town of Villenove: Barbara J. Wise,
Rt. 1, Box 72, South Dayton, NY
14138; **Town of Westfield** and **Village
of Westfield**: Mary S. Dibble, 42
Backman Avenue, Westfield, NY
14787

**Chautauqua County Historical
Society**
PO Box 7, Village Park
Westfield, NY 14787
(716) 326-2977
Michelle Henry, Museum Director
Hours: Tue–Sat 1:00–5:00, and by
appointment
Pub. *County History*, quarterly
$10.00 per year membership for
individuals, $25.00 per year
membership for families; research fee:
$10.00

Chemung County Historian
Municipal Historians: **Town of Ashland**:
Ethel Peck, Lowman, NY 14861;
Town of Baldwin: Vincent Little, Rt.
1, Lowman, NY 14861; **Town of Big
Flats**: Dorothy Burt, 449 Main Street,
PO Box 73, Big Flats, NY 14814;
Town of Catlin: Mable Gaboriault,
Murphy Hill Road, Rural Delivery,
Horseheads, NY 14845; **Town of
Chemung**: Joan B. Schafer, PO Box
113, Chemung, NY 14825; **City of
Elmira**: post vacant; **Town of Elmira**:
Thomas E. Byrne, 1448 West Water
Street, Elmira, NY 14905; **Village of
Elmira Heights**: Kenneth J. Erickson,
256 West 19th Street, Elmira Heights,
NY 14903; **Town of Erin**: Phyllis
Judson, Wilkinson Road, Rural

Delivery, Erin, NY 14838; **Town of
Horseheads**: post vacant; **Village of
Horseheads**: post vacant; **Village of
Millport**: post vacant; **Village of Pine
Valley**: post vacant; **Town of
Southport**: Nelda Holton, 985 Sebring
Avenue, Pine City, NY 14871; **Town
of Van Etten**: post vacant; **Village of
Van Etten**: William M. Gallow, Jr.,
PO Box 8, Hickory Grove Road, Van
Etten, NY 14889; **Town of Veteran**:
post vacant; **Village of Wellsburg**:
Miss Carol Dolan, 207 Main Street,
Wellsburg, NY 14894

**Chemung County Historical Society,
Inc.**
Mrs. Arthur W. Booth Memorial Library
415 East Water Street
Elmira, NY 14901
(607) 734-4167
Melissa Hollister, Registrar
Hours: Mon–Fri 9:00–5:00
Pub. *Chemung County Historical Society
Newsletter*, bimonthly; *Chemung
Historical Journal*, quarterly, $8.00
per year subscription
$15.00 per year membership; search
$5.00 and $10.00

**Chemung Valley Old Timers
Association**
(624 West Broad Street—location)
220 Sunnyfield Drive (mailing address)
Horseheads, NY 14845
(607) 739-1526

Chenango County Historian
Chenango County Historical Society
Museum
Research Facility
45 Rexford Street
Norwich, NY 13815
(607) 334-9227 FAX
Mrs. Dale Green, Historical Research
Assistant
Hours: Office: Mon–Fri 9:00–12:00 &
1:00–5:00
Pub. *Chenango County Historian's
Newsletter*, two times per year (April
and October)
Municipal Historians: **Town of Afton**
and **Village of Afton**: Charles J.
Decker, Rt. 2, Box 1267, East River
Road, Afton, NY 13730, (607) 639-
2720; **Town of Bainbridge**: Charles
D. Lord, 99 North Main Street,
Bainbridge, NY 13733, (607) 967-
4833; **Village of Bainbridge**: Floyd L.
Prouty, 20 Bixby Street, Bainbridge,
NY 13733, (607) 967-7435; **Town of
Columbus**: Barbara B. Avery, 40
Cushman Street, PO Box 191, New
Berlin, NY 13411, (607) 847-6498;
Town of Coventry: Louise Elliott, Rt.
3, Box 212, Greene, NY 13778, (607)
656-4286; **Town of German**: Claudia
C. White, Rt. 1, Box 708C, Greene,
NY 13778, (607) 656-8668; **Town of**

Greene and **Village of Greene**: Mildred Pixley, PO Box 421, 51 Genesee Street, Harbor Road, Greene, NY 13778, (607) 656-4191; **Town of Guilford**: Archibald Hubbard, Guilford, NY 13780, (607) 895-6441; **Town of Lincklaen**: Joy Barber, 9774 Lincklaen Road, PO Box 298, DeRuyter, NY 13052, (315) 852-6081; **Town of McDonough**: Cynthia L. Paul, RR 1, Box 203, McDonough, NY 13801; **Town of New Berlin**: Robert Gould, PO Box 508, New Berlin, NY 13411; **Village of New Berlin**: post vacant; **Town of North Norwich**: Janet Decker, Brookins Road, North Norwich, NY 13814, (607) 336-7013; **City of Norwich**: post vacant; **Town of Norwich**: Herbert S. Crumb, 48 Randall Avenue, Norwich, NY 13815, (607) 334-9167; **Town of Otselic**: Eloise Shuman, County Route 16, Plymouth, NY 13832, (315) 837-4631; **Town of Oxford** and **Village of Oxford**: Charlotte Stafford, 30 West State Street, PO Box 663, Oxford, NY 13830, (607) 843-9531; **Town of Pharsalia**: Joan Ortiz, Rt. 1, McDonough, NY 13801, (607) 863-3877; **Town of Pitcher**: Laura Catlin, Route 26, Pitcher, NY 13136, (607) 863-3385; **Town of Plymouth**: Mike Meyers, Bates Road, HC 67, Box 188, South Plymouth, NY 13832; **Town of Preston**: V. Peter Mason, RD 2, Oxford, NY 13830, (607) 334-4848; **Town of Sherburne**: Neva Conley, North Cross Road, Earlville, NY 13332, (315) 691-4884; **Village of Sherburne**: Village Clerk Treasurer, Municipal Building, Sherburne, NY 13460; **Town of Smithville**: Martha W. Rogers, Rt. 2, Box 659, Greene, NY 13778, (607) 656-4064; **Town of Smyrna**: Cynthia Kumatz, School Street, PO Box 14, Smyrna, NY 13464, (607) 627-6648; **Village of Smyrna**: Cynthia Kumatz, PO Box 14, Smyrna, NY 13464, (607) 627-6648

search: $5.00 per name or $2.00 per last name per 50 pages for printout

Chenango County Historical Society Museum
45 Rexford Street
Norwich, NY 13815
(607) 334-9227 FAX
Mae Smith, Chenango County Historian; Mrs. Dale Green, Recording Secretary
Hours: Library: by appointment; Museum: winter: Wed 1:00–4:00, summer: Wed & Sat–Sun 1:00–4:00; Historian's Office: Mon–Fri 9:00–12:00 & 1:00–5:00
Pub. *Newsletter*, semiannually (April and October)
(local history information)

$10.00 per year membership for individuals, $20.00 per year membership for families, $5.00 per year membership for senior citizens or students, $100.00 per year membership for corporations, $200.00 life membership

Cherry Valley Historical Association
49 Main Street
PO Box 115
Cherry Valley, NY 13320
(607) 264-3303
Marion J. Cornelia, Curator
Hours: Mon–Sun (Memorial Day through Oct 15) 10:00–5:00, and by appointment
upon request

Historical Society of the Town of Chester, Inc.
South Canada Drive
Chestertown, NY 12817
(518) 494-2711

Chili Historical Society
1365 Paul Road
Churchville, NY 14428
(716) 889-2823

Cincinnatus Area Heritage Society
PO Box 264
Cincinnatus, NY 13040
(607) 863-4251; (607) 863-4409

City Island Historical Society and Museum
190 Fordham Street
PO Box 82
Bronx, NY 10464
(718) 885-0008
Mauro De Candido, Vice President
Hours: Sun 1:00–5:00
(nautical, marine, sailing, boatbuilding history and City Island families)
$20.00 per year membership for individuals, $25.00 per year membership for families, $10.00 per year membership for senior citizens

Clay Historical Association
4591 Ver Plank Road
Clay, NY 13041
(315) 652-3288

Clayton Thousand Islands Area Historical Society
403 Riverside Drive
Clayton, NY 13624
(315) 686-5794

Clinton County Historian
Clinton County Government Center, First Floor
137 Margaret Street
Plattsburgh, NY 12901
(518) 565-4749 (Office); (518) 563-7178 (Home)
Addie L. Shields
Hours: by appointment

Municipal Historians: **Town of Altona**: Walter Coolidge, 77 Station Street, Altona, NY 12910, (518) 236-7420; **Town of Au Sable**: Helen Eagle, 71 Liberty Street, Keeseville, NY 12944, (518) 834-4614; **Town of Beekmantown**: Addie L. Shields, County Historian (see above); **Town of Black Brook**: Margaret L. Nolan, PO Box 526, Au Sable Forks, NY 12912, (518) 647-5936; **Town of Champlain**: Theresa Penfield, 30 Pratt Street, Rouses Point, NY 12979, (518) 297-6424; **Village of Champlain**: Richard Keddy, Prospect Street, Champlain, NY 12919, (518) 298-4127; **Town of Chazy**: Marie Gennett, 456 Route 191 East, Chazy, NY 12921, (518) 846-8395 (Office); **Town of Clinton**: Evelyn Watson, PO Box 14, Churubusco, NY 12923, (518) 497-6718; **Town of Dannemora**: Peggy Tolosky, 2970 Belmont, Lyon Mountain, NY 12952, (518) 735-4579; **Village of Dannemora**: Terrance Gilroy, 73 Smith Street, Dannemora, NY 12929, (518) 492-7000 (Village), (518) 492-7581 (Home); **Town of Ellenburg**: Donna Bohon, Bohon Road, Churubusco, NY 12923, (518) 497-6055; **Village of Keeseville**: Jim Blaise, 49 Liberty Street, Keeseville, NY 12944, (518) 834-7220; **Town of Mooers** and **Village of Mooers**: Mrs. Carol Nedeau, 85 Tappan Road, PO Box 13, Mooers, NY 12958, (518) 236-5665; **Town of Peru**: Nancy LaMar, 192 John Boswell Road, Peru, NY 12972, (518) 643-8679; **City of Plattsburgh**: James Bailey, 62 Prospect Avenue, Plattsburgh, NY 12901, (518) 563-7178; **Town of Plattsburgh**: John Scully, 204 Champlain Drive, Plattsburgh, NY 12901, (518) 561-8101; **Village of Rouses Point**: Dawn O'Boyle, 28 Pratt Street, Rouses Point, NY 12979, (518) 297-5502; **Town of Saranac**: Mrs. Jan Couture, 83 Ganong Drive, Saranac, NY 12981, (518) 293-8251; **Town of Schuyler Falls**: Michael Burgess, 135 Rabideau Street, Cadyville, NY 12918, (518) 293-8512
small fee for photocopies

Clinton County Historical Association
48 Court Street
Plattsburgh, NY 12901
(518) 561-0340
Jane E. Rupp, Director
Hours: Mon–Fri 9:00–4:00 by appointment only
Pub. *North Country Notes*, eleven times per year (monthly, except July/August combined); *The Antiquarian*, annually (October or November)
$15.00 per year regular membership, $25.00 per year Sponsor or Business/

Institution membership, $50.00 per year Patron membership, $100.00 per year Benefactor membership, $500.00 life membership

Clinton Historical Society
PO Box 42
Clinton, NY 13323
(315) 853-2097
Shirley Felt, President

Town of Cobleskill Historical Society
Union Street Public Library
Cobleskill, NY 12043

Cohocton Historical Society
14 Maple Avenue
PO Box 177
Cohocton, NY 14826
(716) 534-5317 (President)
Stacy Gilson, President
Hours: first Sat (May–Oct) 10:00–1:00
Pub. *Cohocton Journal*, bimonthly (even-numbered months), $5.00 per year subscription
(history and genealogy of Town of Cohocton, Steuben County, New York)

Historical Society of the Town of Colonie, Inc.
Memorial Town Hall
Newtonville, NY 12128
(518) 783-2713

Colton Historical Society
Main Street
PO Box 223
Colton, NY 13625
(315) 262-2524
Cynthia S. Hennessy, Director
Hours: Jun–Sept: 1:00–3:00, and by appointment
Pub. *CHS Newsletter*, four times per year, $4.00 per year subscription
(history of Colton, New York)

Columbia County Historian
(address withheld upon request)
Municipal Historians: **Town of Ancram**: Ethel Miller, Rt. 82, Ancramdale, NY 12503; **Town of Austerlitz**: Sarah B. Light, PO Box 17, Austerlitz, NY 12017; **Town of Canaan**: Anna Mary Dunton, PO Box 169, Canaan, NY 12029; **Town of Chatham**: Katherine Burgess, Rural Delivery, Box 35, Old Chatham, NY 12136-9705; **Village of Chatham**: Albert S. Callan, Jr., PO Box 58, Malden Bridge, NY 12115; **Town of Claverack**: Martin Miller, Philmont, NY 12565; **Town of Clermont**: Anne Poleschner, Rt. 3, Box 534, Germantown, NY 12526; **Town of Copake**: Olive Langdon, PO Box 26, Copake, NY 12516; **Town of Gallatin**: Siouxzanne Harris, Rt. 1,

Box 290, Red Hook, NY 12571; **Town of Germantown**: Elaine Liepshutz, Rt. 2, Box 6, Germantown, NY 12526; **Town of Ghent**: Esther French, PO Box 65, Ghent, NY 12075; **Town of Greenport**: David W. Hart, 22 Hart Road, Hudson, NY 12534; **Town of Hillsdale**: Margaret Hunt, Collins Street, Hillsdale, NY 12529; **City of Hudson**: Patricia Fenoff, 25 Cross Street, Hudson, NY 12534; **Town of Kinderhook** and **Village of Kinderhook**: Robert Monthie, Hudson Street, Kinderhook, NY 12106; **Town of Livingston**: Mary Howell, Rt. 2, Germantown, NY 12526; **Town of New Lebanon**: Rev. Ernest Smith, New Lebanon, NY 12125; **Village of Philmont**: post vacant; **Town of Stockport**: Viola Williams, PO Box 22, Stockport, NY 12171; **Town of Stuyvesant**: Priscilla B. Frisbee, Stuyvesant Falls, NY 12174; **Town of Taghkanic**: Millicent McKeon, Rural Delivery, Craryville, NY 12521; **Village of Valatie**: post vacant

Columbia County Historical Society
5 Albany Avenue
PO Box 311
Kinderhook, NY 12106

Concord Historical Society
(98 East Main Street, Springville, NY 14141—location)
12102 Vaughn Street
East Concord, NY 14055
(716) 592-5546
Margaret Mayerat, Vice President-Historian
Hours: Sun 2:00–4:00, and by appointment
Pub. *Concord Jottings*, three to four times per year
$10.00 per year membership for individuals, $5.00 per year membership for senior citizens, $50.00 life membership

Conklin Historical Society
(Town Hall, Conklin, NY—office location)
82 Pierce Creek Road (mailing address)
Binghamton, NY 13903
(607) 723-1737 (Historian)
Robert Barber, Conklin Town Historian
Hours: by appointment
$2.00 per year membership

Corning-Painted Post Historical Society
59 West Pulteney Street
Corning, NY 14830
(607) 937-5281; (607) 962-4865
Lois Janes, Historian
Hours: Mon–Sat 10:00–4:00

Pub. *Andaste Enquirer*, varies, $3.00 per issue; *CPPHS Newsletter*, monthly (local history)

Cortland County Historian
Cortland County Courthouse
PO Box 5590
Cortland, NY 13045-5590
(607) 753-5360
Yvonne J. Deligato
Hours: 9:00–5:00
Municipal Historians: **Town of Cincinnatus**: Rachel MacRae, Telephone Road Extension, PO Box 215, Cincinnatus, NY 13040-0215, (607) 863-4271; **City of Cortland**: Mary Ann Kane, Suggett House Museum/Kellogg Memorial Research Library, 25 Homer Avenue, Cortland, NY 13045-2056, (607) 756-6071; **Town of Cortlandville**: Alice P. Blatchley, 3475 Route 215, Cortland, NY 13045-9440, (607) 749-3944; **Town of Cuyler**: Ann Ludke, 4721 Bennett Road, Cuyler, NY 13058-9621, (607) 842-6781; **Town of Freetown**: Mr. Leslie Underwood, 2475 East Freetown Road, East Freetown, NY 13040-8703, (607) 849-6492; **Town of Harford**: Mary Ann Negus, RD 2, Box 204, Marathon, NY 13803-0204, (607) 844-9969; **Town of Homer**: Josephine Brown, 22 Cherry Street, Homer, NY 13077-1537, (607) 749-3944; **Village of Homer**: Nadyne Harris, 21 Cayuga Street, Homer, NY 13077-1307, (607) 749-2573; **Town of Lapeer**: Donald Barber, PO Box 533, Marathon, NY 13803-0533, (607) 849-3975; **Town of Marathon**: Eloise Couch, PO Box 607, Marathon, NY 13803-0606, (607) 849-6129; **Village of Marathon**: Marc Wheaton, 68 Cortland Street, Marathon, NY 13803-3712, (607) 849-6094; **Village of McGraw**: Mary Kimberly, PO Box 537, McGraw, NY 13101-0537, (607) 836-6738; **Town of Preble**: Pam Wright, 1965 Preble Road, Preble, NY 13141-9998, (607) 749-4207; **Town of Scott**: Kathy Barber, 7013 NYS Route 41, Homer, NY 13077-4461, (607) 749-4597; **Town of Solon**: Hazel Parsons, 3530 Stilwell Road, McGraw, NY 13101-9430, (607) 836-6638; **Town of Taylor**: Robert Pudney, 4484 Pudney Road, Cincinnatus, NY 13040-9636, (607) 863-3538; **Town of Truxton**: Donald McCall, 3703 Main Street, PO Box 98, Truxton, NY 13158-0098, (607) 842-6684; **Town of Virgil**: Frances Bays, 2208 Cortland Road, Route 215, Cortland, NY 13045-9431, (607) 835-6321; **Town of Willet**: Loma Wilkins, Box 2, 5556 Route 41, Willett, NY 13863-0002, (607) 863-4532
search fee: $10.00

Cortland County Historical Society, Inc.

(Suggett House Museum/Kellogg Memorial Research Library, Corner of Homer and Maple Avenues, entrance on Maple Avenue—location)
25 Homer Avenue (mailing address)
Cortland, NY 13045-2056
(607) 756-6071
Mary Ann Kane, Director
Hours: Tue–Sat 1:00–5:00
Pub. *Roots & Branches*, irregularly; *Cortland County Historical Society Bulletin*; *News Notes from the Suggett House*, irregularly
(county cemeteries, federal and state censuses indexed for Cortland County)
$15.00 per year membership; museum admission: $2.00 for adult non-members, children under 16 free; research library use: $3.00 for the first hour and $1.00 for each additional hour for non-members; research by mail: $10.00 per hour plus copies at 25¢ per copy, and postage

Covington Historical Society

(La Grange Road—location)
1088 Peoria Road (mailing address)
Pavilion, NY 14525
(716) 584-3254 (Historian)
Karen C. Milligan, Town Historian
Hours: by appointment

The Cow Neck Peninsula Historical Society

Sands-Willets House
336 Port Washington Boulevard
Port Washington, NY 11050
(516) 365-9074
Mary Vahey, Curator
Hours: Sun 2:00–4:00, and by appointment
Pub. *CNPHS Journal*, annually
$25.00 per year membership for individuals, $25.00 per year membership for families, $10.00 per year membership for students, $50.00 per year Sustaining membership, $100.00 per year Sponsor membership, $500.00 life membership; special research requests honored at $5.00

Croton Historical Society

(Croton Free Library—location)
Municpal Building, Van Wyck Street (mailing address)
Croton-on-Hudson, NY 10520
(914) 271-4574 (Historical Society)
Jane Northshield, Village Historian
Hours: Historical Society: Mon 9:00–1:00; Old Book Room: Thur–Sat 10:00–5:00, and by appointment
Pub. *Croton Historian*, four times per year
(Croton Dam and regional history, railroad, village history, some genealogy)

$8.00 per year membership for individuals, $10.00 per year membership for families

Cuba Historical Society

PO Box 200
Cuba, NY 14727
David H. Crowley, Town/Village Historian
Pub. *Cuba Historical Society Newsletter*, quarterly
$5.00 per year membership

Cutchogue-New Suffolk Historical Council

Village Green-Main Road
PO Box 714
Cutchogue, NY 11935
(516) 734-7122
Hallock E. Tuthill, President
Hours: Jun & Sept: Sat–Sun; Jul & Aug: Mon & Sat–Sun 2:00–5:00; May & Oct by appointment

Dansville Area Historical Society

PO Box 481
Dansville, NY 14437-0481

Davenport Historical Society

Town Hall
Davenport, NY 13751
(607) 278-5600
Mary Beardsley, President

Town of Dayton Historical Society

Route 62
PO Box 15
Dayton, NY 14041
$2.00 per year membership

Delaware County Historian

111 Main Street
Delhi, NY 13753
Clara H. Stewart
Municipal Historians: **Town of Andes**: Janis E. Reynolds, Box 143, Andes, NY 13731, (914) 676-3212; **Village of Andes**: post vacant; **Town of Bovina**: Charles LaFever, HC 85, Box 4, Bovina Center, NY 13740, (607) 832-4245; **Town of Colchester**: Jane Flannery, PO Box 336, Downsville, NY 13755, (607) 363-2212; **Town of Davenport**: Mary S. Briggs, RD 2, Box 444, Oneonta, NY 13820, (607) 278-5318; **Town of Delhi**: Billie Sturdevant, RD 2, Delhi, NY 13753, (607) 746-2731; **Village of Delhi**: Shirley Houck, 7 Division Street, Delhi, NY 13753, (607) 746-2857; **Town and Village of Deposit**: Mary S. Cable, 2 Elm Street, Deposit, NY 13754, (607) 467-2719; **Village of Fleischmanns**: post vacant; **Town and Village of Franklin**: Vernon Taylor, RD 1, Franklin, NY 13775, (607) 829-3872; **Town of Hamden**: Gabrielle

Buel, PO Box 67, Hamden, NY 13782, (607) 746-6625; **Town of Hancock**: Hancock-Chehocton Historical Association, 61 Wheeler Street, Hancock, NY 13783; **Village of Hancock**: post vacant; **Town of Harpersfield**: Evangeline MacLaury, Harpersfield, NY 13786, (607) 652-5152; **Village of Hobart**: Erma MacArthur, PO Box 177, Hobart, NY 13788, (607) 538-9179; **Town of Kortright**: Wilber Haynes, Roberts Road, Blommville, NY 13739, (607) 538-9227; **Village of Margaretville**: Willard F. Sanford, Main Street, Margaretville, NY 12455; **Town of Masonville**: Jean and Norman Jump, PO Box 86, Masonville, NY 13804, (607) 265-3383; **Town of Meredith**: Bernice Telian, HC 87, Box 341, Delhi, NY 13753-9311; **Town of Middletown**: George Hendricks, Southside Road, Margaretville, NY 12455, (914) 586-4566; **Town of Roxbury**: post vacant; **Town and Village of Sidney**: Sidney Historical Society, Civic Center, Liberty Street, PO Box 2217, Sidney, NY 13838; **Town and Village of Stamford**: Anne Willis, 10 Beaver Street, Stamford, NY 12167, (607) 652-7839; **Town of Tompkins**: Dorothy W. Brizzee, RR 4, Box 124, Walton, NY 13856, (607) 865-6265; **Town of Walton**: Walton Historical Society, Gardiner Place, Walton, NY 13856; **Village of Walton**: Frederica Cranston, 88 Townsend Street, Walton, NY 13856, (607) 865-4636

Delaware County Historical Association

RD 2, Box 201C
Delhi, NY 13753
(607) 746-3849
Helen Casey, Library Manager
Hours: Library: Mon–Tue 10:00–3:00
Pub. *The Chronicle-Times*, three times per year
$15.00 per year membership for individuals, $25.00 per year membership for families, $10.00 per year membership for senior citizens; research by mail: $15.00 per hour

The DeWitt Historical Society of Tompkins County

401 East State Street
Ithaca, NY 14850
(607) 273-8284; (607) 273-6107 FAX
E-mail: dhs@lakenet.org
Lorraine Johnson, Director
Hours: Tue, Thur & Sat 11:00–5:00
Pub. *Newsletter*, quarterly, $15.00 per year subscription
(Tompkins County, history)
$25.00 per year full membership; search fees: $11.50 per hour, two-hour minimum

Dobbs Ferry Historical Society
153 Main Street
Dobbs Ferry, NY 10522
(914) 693-7766
Tema Harnik, Director
Pub. *The Ferryman*

Dryden Historical Society
History House
36 West Main Street
PO Box 97
Dryden, NY 13053
(607) 844-9209; (607) 844-4691 (for
    appointment)
Gina Prentiss
Hours: Sat 10:00–2:00, and by
    appointment
Pub. *Newsletter*

Dundee Area Historical Society
PO Box 153
51 Center Street
Dundee, NY 14837

Dutchess County Historian
c/o Dutchess County Historical Society
549 Main Street
PO Box 88
Poughkeepsie, NY 12602
Municipal Historians: **Town of Amenia**:
    post vacant; **City of Beacon**: Joan
    VanVoorhis, Beacon City Hall, 427
    Main Street, Beacon, NY 12508;
    Town of Beekman: Lee Eaton,
    Beekman Town Hall, Poughquag, NY
    12570; **Town of Clinton**: Dr. William
    McDermott, Clinton Town Hall, PO
    Box 108, Centre Road, Clinton
    Corners, NY 12514; **Town of Dover**:
    Doris Dedrick, Dover Town Hall, Rt.
    2, Box 132, East Duncan Hill Road,
    Dover Plains, NY 12522; **Town of
    East Fishkill**: Everett Lee; East
    Fishkill Town Hall, 370 Route 376,
    Hopewell Junction, NY 12533; **Town
    of Fishkill**: Willa Skinner, Fishkill
    Town Hall, 401 Route 52, Fishkill, NY
    12524; **Village of Fishkill**: Rod
    Koopmans, Fishkill Village Hall, Main
    Street, Fishkill, NY 12524; **Town of
    Hyde Park**: Diane Boyce, Hyde Park
    Town Hall, PO Box 2002, Hyde Park,
    NY 12538; **Town of LaGrange**:
    Emily Johnson, LaGrange Town Hall,
    120 Stringham Road, LaGrangeville,
    NY 12540; **Town of Milan**: Norma
    Ingles, Milan Town Hall, Route 199,
    Box 42, Red Hook, NY 12571; **Village
    of Millbrook**: David Greenwood,
    Millbrook Village Hall, Millbrook, NY
    12548; **Village of Millerton**: Chester
    Eisenhuth, Simmons Street, Millerton,
    NY 12546; **Town of Northeast**:
    Chester Eisenhuth, North East Town
    Hall, Maple Avenue, Millerton, NY
    12546; **Town of Pawling**: Myrna
    Hubert, Pawling Town Hall, 160
    Charles Colman Boulevard, Pawling,
    NY 12564; **Village of Pawling**: post

vacant; **Town of Pine Plains**: Dyan
    Kilpatrick, Pine Plains Town Hall, PO
    Box 320, South Main Street, Pine
    Plains, NY 12567; **Town of Pleasant
    Valley**: Olive Doty, Pleasant Valley
    Town Hall, Route 44, Pleasant Valley,
    NY 12569; **City of Poughkeepsie**:
    Herbert Saltford, Poughkeepsie City
    Hall, PO Box 300, Poughkeepsie, NY
    12601; **Town of Poughkeepsie**: Mona
    Vaeth, Poughkeepsie Town Hall, Box
    3209, Dutchess Turnpike,
    Poughkeepsie, NY 12603; **Town of
    Red Hook**: J. Winthrop Aldrich, Red
    Hook Town Hall, 109 South
    Broadway, Red Hook, NY 12571;
    Village of Red Hook: Rosemary E.
    Coons, Red Hook Village Hall, 24
    South Broadway, Red Hook, NY
    12571; **Town of Rhinebeck**: Richard
    Crowley, Rhinebeck Town Hall, 80
    East Market Street, Rhinebeck, NY
    12572; **Village of Rhinebeck**: post
    vacant; **Town of Stanford**: Mrs. Irving
    Burdick, Stanford Town Hall, Box
    190, Route 82, Stanfordville, NY
    12581; **Village of Tivoli**: Richard C.
    Wiles, Tivoli Village Hall, 48-A
    Broadway, Tivoli, NY 12585; **Town of
    Unionvale**: Irena Stolarik, Union Vale
    Town Hall, Rt. 2, Box 180, Route 55,
    LaGrangeville, NY 12540; **Town of
    Wappinger**: Brenda Von Burg,
    Wappingers Town Hall, Box 324,
    Middlebush Road, Wappingers Falls,
    NY 12590; **Village of Wappingers
    Falls**: Vicki Kolb, Wappingers Falls
    Village Hall, 7 Spring Street,
    Wappingers Falls, NY 12590; **Town of
    Washington**: Carmine DiArpino,
    Washington Town Hall, PO Box 667,
    Millbrook, NY 12545

Dutchess County Historical Society
549 Main Street
PO Box 88
Poughkeepsie, NY 12602
(914) 471-1630
Eileen M. Hayden, Acting Director
Hours: Tue–Fri 10:00–3:00
Pub. *Yearbook*, annually, $10.00 per
    issue; *Dutchess Historian*, irregularly;
    *Dutchess County Historical Society
    Collections*, irregularly
$40.00 per year membership for
    individuals (includes *Yearbook*
    and*Dutchess Historian*); non-member
    library fee: $5.00; search fee: $45.00
    three hour minimum

**Historical Society of the Town of
East Bloomfield Academy Museum**
PO Box 212
East Bloomfield, NY 14443
Hours: Tue–Fri 10:30–5:00
Pub. *Academy Chronicles*, monthly
(local history, maps, articles on specific
    area families)

$10.00 per year membership for
    individuals, $15.00 per year
    membership for families, $6.00 per
    year membership for senior citizen
    individuals, $12.00 per year
    membership for senior citizen
    families; charge for searches

East Hampton Historical Society
101 Main Street
East Hampton, NY 11937
(516) 324-6850

Eastchester Historical Society
(388 California Road, Bronxville, NY
    10708—location)
PO Box 37 (mailing address)
Eastchester, NY 10709
(914) 793-1900
Madeline Schaeffer, Director of
    Education
Hours: by appointment only
(resource for lower Westchester County;
    school house museum 1835; 19th
    century collection of juvenile literature
    and textbooks; historical and
    genealogical reference library)
search fee: $10.00 for the first hour and
    $5.00 per hour thereafter

Elma Historical Society
1910 Bowen Road
PO Box 84
Elma, NY 14059-0084

**Elmira Heights Historical Society,
Inc.**
(266 East 14th Street—location)
PO Box 2084 (mailing address)
Elmira Heights, NY 14903
(607) 732-5167
Kenneth J. Erickson, Village Historian
Hours: third Wed 4:00–7:00, and by
    appointment

**Endicott Historical and Preservation
Society**
PO Box 52
Endicott, NY 13760
(607) 783-8373

Enfield Historical Society
398 Harvey Hill Road
Trumansburg, NY 14886
(607) 273-5369 (Editor); (607) 272-5930
    (President)
Wilma Fisher, Editor; Doris Rothermich,
    President
Pub. *Newsletter*

Erie County Historian
Buffalo and Erie County Historical
    Society
25 Nottingham Terrace
Buffalo, NY 14216
(716) 873-9644
Dr. William Siener, de facto Erie County
    Historian
Municipal Historians **Village of Akron**:
    Dorothy Webster, 8 John Street,
    Akron, NY 14001; **Village of Angola**:

post vacant; **Town of Aurora**: Donald H. Dayer, Aurora Historical Society, Inc., 5 South Grove Street, East Aurora, NY 14052; **Town of Amherst**: Dr. Andrea Shaw, 3069 Tonawanda Creek Road, North Tonawanda, NY 14120; **Town of Alden** and **Village of Alden**: Norma M. Sweet, 299 Exchange Street, Alden, NY 14006; **Village of Blasdell**: Nina Brown, 63 Pearl Street, Blasdell, NY 14219; **Town of Boston**: James J. Jehle, 9432 Boston State Road, Boston, NY 14025; **Town of Brant**: post vacant; **City of Buffalo**: post vacant; **Town of Clarence**: Laura Grenzebach, Clarence Town Hall, 1 Town Place, Clarence, NY 14031; **Town of Cheektowaga**: Julia Boyer Reinstein, 11 Danforth Street, Cheektowaga, NY 14227; **Town of Concord**: Lillian D. Geiger, 13153 Morton's Corners Road, Springville, NY 14141; **Town of Colden**: Mr. Julian Flackenstein, Heath Road, Colden, NY 14069; **Town of Collins**: Mrs. Richard Gaffney, Orchard Place, Collins, NY 14034; **Village of Depew**: Margaret Stock, 27 Litchfield Avenue, Depew, NY 14043; **Village of East Aurora**: Warren C. Moffett, 404 Oakwood Avenue, East Aurora, NY 14052; **Town of Eden**: Norma Hardy Webb, 2795 East Church Street, Eden, NY 14057; **Town of Elma**: Charlotte Yacabush, Elma Historical Society, 1910 Bowen Road, PO Box 84, Elma, NY 14059-0084; **Town of Evans**: Annette M. Frost, South Creek Road, North Evans, NY 14112; **Village of Farnham**: Mr. Christian Militello, Jr., Commercial Street, Farnham, NY 14061; **Town of Grand Island**: post vacant; **Town of Hamburg**: Joseph Streamer, 3697 Westview, Hamburg, NY 14075; **Town of Holland**: John Venner, 24 South Main Street, Holland, NY 14080; **Village of Kenmore**: post vacant; **City of Lackawanna**: William Emerling, 80 South Shore Boulevard, Lackawanna, NY 14218; **Town of Lancaster**: Dr. Harley Scott, Brookfield Place, Lancaster, NY 14086; **Village of Lancaster**: Edward Mikula, 88 Church Street, Lancaster, NY 14086; **Town of Marilla**: Laura E. Neumann, South 2755 Three Rod Road, East Aurora, NY 14052-9535; **Town of Newstead**: Dorothy Webster, 8 John Street, Akron, NY 14001; **Town of North Collins** and **Village of North Collins**: Grace Korthals, Shirley Road, North Collins, NY 14111; **Town of Orchard Park** and **Village of Orchard Park**: John N. Printy, 5800 Armor Duelles Road, Orchard Park, NY 14127; **Town of Sardinia**: Florence Rupert, Sardinia,

NY 14134; **Village of Sloan**: Beverly Sikova, 79 Jackson Street, Buffalo, NY 14212; **Village of Springville**: Lillian Geiger, 13153 Mortons Corners Road, Springville, NY 14141; **City of Tonawanda**: Willard B. Dittmar, 27 South Elmwood Park, Tonawanda, NY 14150; **Town of Tonawanda**: John W. Percy, 62 Devonshire Road, Tonawanda, NY 14223; **Town of Wales**: post vacant; **Town of West Seneca**: Carole Taylor, 93 Carmelite Drive, West Seneca, NY 14224; **Village of Williamsville**: Mary Jane Kibby, 24 Garrison Road, Williamsville, NY 14221

Erie County Historical Federation
11 Danforth Street
Cheektowaga, NY 14227
Pub. *ECHF Newsletter*
(loosely organized group of local historical societies and appointed town historians of Erie County, acting as a liaison between groups and providing a speakers bureau)

Esperance Historical Society and Museum
Church Street
PO Box 99
Esperance, NY 12066
(518) 875-6854
Hours: Memorial Day–Labor Day: weekends 1:00–5:00

Esquatak Historical Society
PO Box 151
Castleton-on-Hudson, NY 12033
(518) 732-2626

Essex County Historian
Adirondack Center Museum
Court Street
PO Box 428
Elizabethtown, NY 12932
(518) 873-6466
James A. Kinley, Director; Mary E. Bell, Ed. Director
Hours: by appointment
Municipal Historians: **Village of Bloomingdale**: Dorothy White, PO Box 16, Bloomingdale, NY 12913; **Town of Chesterfield**: post vacant; **Town of Crown Point**: Lydia Ross, Crown Point, NY 12928; **Town of Elizabethtown**: Conrad Hutchins, Water Street, Elizabethtown, NY 12932; **Town of Essex**: Ronald Jackson, Essex, NY 12936; **Town of Jay**: Mary Wallace, 30 Glen Road, Jay, NY 12941; **Town of Keene**: Anita Washburn, Keene, NY 12942; **Village of Lake Placid**: Mary MacKenzie, 30 Lakeview Street, Lake Placid, NY 12946; **Town of Lewis**: Mrs. Robert F. Sweatt, Rural Free Delivery, Elizabethtown, NY 12932; **Town of Minerva**: Mrs. Noelle Donahue, Minerva, NY 12851; **Town of**

Moriah: C. Eleanor Hall, 45 Spring Street, Port Henry, NY 12974; **Town of Newcomb**: Helen O'Donnell, Newcomb, NY 12852; **Town of North Elba**: Mary MacKenzie, 30 Lakeview Street, Lake Placid, NY 12946; **Town of North Hudson**: Lillian Nolette, North Hudson, NY 12853; **Village of Port Henry**: Eleanor Hall, 45 Spring Street, Port Henry, NY 12974; **Village of Saranac Lake**: Janet Decker, Coreys, NY 12986; **Town of Schroon**: Paul Stapley, Schroon Lake, NY 12870; **Town of Saint Armand**: Mary Gonyea, PO Box 766, Saranac Lake, NY 12983; **Town of Ticonderoga**: Sandy Hurlburt, Warner Hill Road, Ticonderoga, NY 12883; **Village of Ticonderoga**: Virginia R. Smith, 215 Champlain Avenue, Ticonderoga, NY 12883; **Town of Westport** and **Village of Westport**: Marjorie Lewis, Main Street, Westport, NY 12993; **Town of Willsboro**: Janice Allen, Mount View Road, Willsboro, NY 12996; **Town of Wilmington**: Marc V. Dubois, Wilmington, NY 12997

Essex County Historical Society
Brewster Memorial Library
Court Street
Elizabethtown, NY 12932
(518) 873-6466
Pat Casselman; Gayle Meaker
Hours: Tue & Thur 9:00–3:00
Pub. *Reveille*

Town of Evans Historical Society
(8351 Erie Road, Erie, County—location)
PO Box 7 (mailing address)
Angola, NY 14006
Jack Ehmke, President
(local history)
$5.00 per year membership

Farmingdale-Bethpage Historical Society
PO Box 500
Farmingdale, NY 11735

Fort Brewerton Historical Society
PO Box 392
Brewerton, NY 13029-0392
(315) 668-8801; (315) 676-7986
Erma Stallknecht, President
Hours: Jun–Oct: Fri & Sun 1:00–5:00, Sat 10:00–5:00; history-oriented lectures: fourth Mon (Mar–Nov) 7:30
Pub. *Newsletter*, monthly
$10.00 per year membership for individuals or families, $2.50 per year membership for students

Fort Edward Historical Association
(22 & 29 Broadway—location)
PO Box 106 (mailing address)
Fort Edward, NY 12828-0106
(518) 747-9600; (518) 747-8497
E-mail: oldforthousemuseum@juno.com

R. Paul McCarty, Director
Hours: genealogical queries: Wed 10:00–3:00
(genealogy and local history of Fort Edward and Hudson Falls, Washington County, New York)
from $10.00 per year membership; research fees based on time and copy work

Fort Hamilton Historical Society
Fort Hamilton, NY 11252
(617) 630-4349
(no genealogical materials)

Foundation Historical Association, Inc.
33 South Street
Auburn, NY 13021
(315) 252-1283

Four River Valleys Historical Society
PO Box 504
Carthage, NY 13619
(315) 773-5133

Franklin County Historian
Franklin County Historical and Museum Society
51 Milwaukee Street
Malone, NY 12953
(518) 483-2750
Virginia Anne Wolfe, Acting Contact Person
Hours: Sept–May: Sat 1:00–5:00; Jun–Aug: Tue–Sat 1:00–4:00
Municipal Historians: **Town of Altamont**: Louis J. Simmons, 12 Lake Street, Tupper Lake, NY 12986; **Town of Bangor**: Raymond Smith, North Bangor, NY 12966; **Town of Bellmont**: Addams Chase, Brainardsville, NY 12915; **Town of Bombay**: post vacant; **Village of Bombay**: Charles Reardon, Bombay, NY 12914; **Town of Brandon**: post vacant; **Town of Brighton**: Eilen Crary, Paul Smiths, NY 12970; **Village of Brushton**: Isabelle Dorey, PO Box 441, Brushton, NY 12916; **Town of Burke**: Beth Brand, RFD 1, Box 77, East Road, Burke, NY 12917, (518) 497-3162; **Village of Burke**: Ruth Legacy, Maple Street, Burke, NY 12917; **Town of Chateaugay**: John Bilow, 8 Grace Avenue, Plattsburgh, NY 12901; **Village of Chateaugay**: Olin Cook, 65 East Main Street, Chateaugay, NY 12920; **Town of Constable**: Mary Ann Tallon, PO Box 52, Constable, NY 12926; **Town of Dickinson**: Dorothy Jandrew, Nicholville NY 12965; **Town of Duane**: Linda Biesemeyer, HRC 1, Box 77, Malone, NY 12953; **Town of Fort Covington**: Carleen Burditt, Fort Covington, NY 12937; **Town of Franklin**: Betty Wilson, Vermontville, NY 12989; **Town of Harrietstown**: post vacant; **Town of Malone**: post vacant; **Village of Malone**: Franklin County Historical and Museum Society (see above); **Town of Moira**: Kermit A. Saxton, Saxton Road, Brushton, NY 12916; **Town of Santa Clara**: Roy Resenbarker, PO Box 146, Saranac Lake, NY 12983; **Village of Tupper Lake**: Louis J. Simmons, 12 Lake Street, Tupper Lake, NY 12986; **Town of Waverly**: Roland and Bonnie Drew, Conger Road, Saint Regis Falls, NY 12980; **Town of Westville**: Richard Avery, Rt. 1, Box 166, Constable, NY 12926

Franklin County Historical and Museum Society
51 Milwaukee Street
Malone, NY 12953
(518) 483-2750
Virginia Anne Wolfe, Acting Contact Person
Hours: Sept–May: Sat 1:00–5:00; Jun–Aug: Tue–Sat 1:00–4:00
Pub. *Franklin Historical Review*, annually
$15.00 per year membership for individuals, $25.00 per year membership for families

Franklin Square Historical Society
Museum at John Street School, Nassau Boulevard
PO Box 45
Franklin Square, NY 11010

French Creek Historical Society, Inc.
Rt. 2
Clymer, NY 14724
(716) 355-4101

Friends for Long Island's Heritage
1864 Muttontown Road
Muttontown, NY 11791
(516) 571-7600
Mildred MeLocoton
Hours: 9:00–4:45
Pub. *Long Island Forum*, quarterly, $20.00 for two-year subscription for non-members, $8.00 for two-year subscription for members

Friends of the Nyacks, Inc.
PO Box 384
Nyack, NY 10960
(914) 358-2113
Betti Schlyer, Chairperson
Hours: 9:00–5:00

Frontenac Historical Society
1 Foundry Street
Union Springs, NY 13160
(315) 889-7767

Fulton County Historian
187 Bleecker Street
Gloversville, NY 12078
(518) 725-3073
Lewis G. Decker
Municipal Historians: **Town of Bleecker**: Eleanor Brooks, Bleecker Stage, Box 161, Gloversville, NY 12078; **Town of Broadalbin** and **Village of Broadalbin**: Mr. Jay Nellis, 41 North Street, Broadalbin, NY 12025; **Town of Caroga**: Katherine Schmutz, PO Box 181 (Fisher Road), Caroga Lake, NY 12032; **Town of Ephratah**: Audrey Brundage, Rt. 1, Saint Johnsville, NY 13452; **City of Gloversville**: Lewis G. Decker, County Historian (see above); **City of Johnstown**: Robert E. Bedford, 205 Prindle Avenue, Johnstown, NY 12095; **Town of Johnstown**: Geraldine Becker, Rt. 1, Gloversville, NY 12078; **Town of Mayfield** and **Village of Mayfield**: Betty Tabor, 33 West Main Street, Mayfield, NY 12117; **Town of Northampton**: Terrance Warner, 251 South Main Street, Northville, NY 12134; **Village of Northville**: Terrance Warner, 251 South Main Street, Northville, NY 12134; **Town of Oppenheim**: Hector Allen, Rt. 1, Dolgeville, NY 13329; **Town of Perth**: May Yost, Rt. 1, Fort Johnson, NY 12070; **Town of Stratford**: Pearl Aubin, Star Route, Stratford, NY 13470

Historical Society of Fulton, N.Y.
117 South First Street
PO Box 157
Fulton, NY 13069
(315) 598-4616
Sandra Clarke, Director
Hours: by appointment
$12.50 per year membership for individuals or dual senior citizens, $25.00 per year membership for families or Sustaining membership, $7.50 per year membership for students or senior citizens, $50.00 per year Sponsoring membership, $100.00 per year Patron membership, $500.00 per year Benefactor membership, $1,000.00 per year Major Donor membership

Galen Historical Society
PO Box 43
Clyde, NY 14433

Genesee County Historian
Genesee County History Department
Records Management Officer
Holland Land Office
131 West Main Street
Batavia, NY 14020-2021
(716) 343-1164
Susan L. Conklin
Hours: History Department Club members: Mon–Fri 9:00–4:00; county history research: Mon–Thur 9:00–4:00; genealogy research with assistance: Mon–Tue 9:00–4:00, Wed

9:00–2:00; genealogy research without assistance: Wed 2:00–4:00, Thur 9:00–4:00

Municipal Historians: **Town of Alabama**: Jean Richardson, 7079 Maple Street, Basom, NY 14013-9770, (716) 948-9886; **Town of Alexander** and **Village of Alexander**: Katy Goodman, 10290 Goodman Road, Alexander, NY 14005-9737, (716) 591-1204; **City of Batavia**: Corrine Iwanicki, 41 Clinton Street, Batavia, NY 14020-2820, (716) 344-1633; **Town of Batavia**: Ruth Cobb, 3693 Galloway Road, Batavia, NY 14020-9434, (716) 343-8416; **Town of Bergen**: Wanda MacVean, PO Box 493, Bergen, NY 14416-0493, (716) 494-1177; **Village of Bergen**: F. E. "Tally" Almquist, 18 McKenzie Street, PO Box 417, Bergen, NY 14416-0417, (716) 494-1675; **Town of Bethany**: Ellen Kingdon, 10463 Bethany Center Road, East Bethany, NY 14054-9707, (716) 344-0210; **Town of Byron**: Dora M. Jones, 6148 Bird Road, Byron, NY 14422-0201, (716) 548-2252; **Village of Corfu**: Laura Fauth, PO Box 113, Corfu, NY 14036-0113, (716) 599-4840; **Town of Darien**: Elmer Heiman, 10709 Allegany Road, Darien Center, NY 14040, (716) 547-2294; **Town of Elba** and **Village of Elba**: Scott D. Benz, 39 Mechanic Street, Elba, NY 14058-9766, (716) 757-2553; **Town of LeRoy**: Irene Walters, 9306 Summit Street Road, LeRoy, NY 14482-8904, (716) 768-8376; **Village of LeRoy**: Myron Bancroft, 63 Clay Street, LeRoy, NY 14482, (716) 768-6993; **Town of Oakfield** and **Village of Oakfield**: Herbert Wolcott, 3559 Batavia-Oakfield Townline Road, Oakfield, NY 14125-9784, (716) 343-8022; **Town of Pavilion**: Virginia Rigoni, 9901 Roanoke Road, Pavilion, NY 14525-9731, (716) 768-6095; **Town of Pembroke**: Lois Brockway, Co-historian, 7905 Allegheny Road, Corfu, NY 14036-9724, (716) 762-8568, and Shirley Kern, Co-historian, 9036 South Lake Road, Corfu, NY 14036-9574, (716) 599-6465; **Town of Stafford**: Martha Heddon, 6684 Randall Road, LeRoy, NY 14482-9316, (716) 343-6699

fee for written requests

Geneva Historical Society and Museum
543 South Main Street
Geneva, NY 14456
(315) 789-5151; (315) 789-0314 FAX
Jennifer Walton, Archivist
Hours: Tue–Fri 1:30–4:30, and by appointment
(local and regional history)
$15.00 for initial search

Glen Haven Historical Society
7325 Fairhaven Road
PO Box 293 (mailing address)
Homer, NY 13077
(607) 749-7907
Hours: May–Sept: Sat 1:00–3:00 by appointment

Goshen Public Library and Historical Society
203 Main Street
Goshen, NY 10924
(914) 294-6606
Eulie Costello, Clerk, Historical and Genealogical Reference Room
Hours: Reference Room: Mon–Wed 10:00–6:00, Thur–Sat 10:00–2:00

Gowanda Area Historical Society
(Persia Town Hall, West Main Street—location)
PO Box 372 (mailing address)
Gowanda, NY 14070

Grafton Historical Society
Grafton, NY 12082

Grand Island Historical Society
Beaver Island State Park
PO Box 135
Grand Island, NY 14072

The Gravesend Historical Society
PO Box 1643, Gravesend Station
Gravesend, NY 11223
(718) 375-6831; (718) 375-6831 FAX
Eric J. Ierardi, President
Hours: 10:00–5:00
various memberships

Greater Milford Historical Association
Milford, NY 13807

Historical Society of Greater Port Jefferson
115 Prospect Street
PO Box 586
Port Jefferson, NY 11777
(516) 473-2665

Greater Ridgewood Historical Society
Queens Genealogy Workshop
Vander Ende-Onderdonk House
1820 Flushing Avenue
Ridgewood, NY 11385-1041
(718) 456-1776
George P. Miller, Archivist
Hours: by appointment
Pub. *Newsletter*, quarterly
(emphasis on Long Island history and genealogy; extensive surname files; "All inquiries must be by correspondence only.")
$15.00 per year membership in Historical Society, additional $10.00 per year membership in Queens Genealogy Workshop; no charge for surname searches, but donations (tax-deductible) appreciated

Historical Society of Greece, N.Y.
(595 Long Pond Road, Rochester, NY 14612—location)
PO Box 16249 (mailing address)
Rochester, NY 14616
(716) 225-7221
Lorraine Beane, President
Hours: Sun 2:00–4:30, and by appointment
Pub. *GHS Newsletter*, bimonthly
$5.00 per year membership for individuals, $10.00 per year membership for families, $25.00 per year membership for businesses

Greenbush Historical Society
PO Box 66
East Greenbush, NY 12144

Greene County Historian
Rt. 1, Box 10A
Coxsackie, NY 12051
(518) 731-1033; (518) 731-6822 (Home)
Raymond V. Beecher
Hours: Tue–Wed 10:00–2:00
Minority Historian: Charles B. Swain, U.S. Route 9-W, Athens, NY 12015
Municipal Historians: **Town of Ashland**: Helen E. Wier, Rt. 23, Ashland, NY 12407; **Town of Athens**: Edith Minerley, Rt. 1, Box 15, Athens, NY 12015; **Village of Athens**: Betty Jean Poole, 87 Second Street, Athens, NY 12015; **Town of Cairo**: Robert Uzzilia, Cairo, NY 12413; **Town of Catskill**: Betty D. Larsen, 532 Cairo Junction Road, Catskill, NY 12414; **Village of Catskill**: post vacant; **Town of Coxsackie**: Raymond Beecher, Beecher Road, Coxsackie, NY 12051; **Village of Coxsackie**: Margaret A. Chaloner, 66 Mansion Street, Coxsackie, NY 12051; **Town of Durham**: Thomas D. Uhll, Flinn Road, Cornwallville, NY 12418; **Town of Greenville**: Donald B. Teator, Rt. 1, Box 147, Freehold, NY 12431; **Town of Halcott**: post vacant; **Town of Hunter**: Justine Hommel, PO Box 129, Haines Falls, NY 12436; **Village of Hunter**: post vacant; **Town of Jewett**: Elwood Hitchcock, East Jewett, NY 12424; **Town of Lexington**: Margaret Lawrence, Lexington, NY 12452; **Town of New Baltimore**: Dr. Clesson Bush, PO Box 137, New Baltimore, MD 12124; **Town of Prattsville**: Muriel Pons, PO Box 398, Prattsville, NY 12468; **Village of Tannersville**: post vacant; **Town of Windham**: Patricia Morrow, PO Box 116, Maplecrest, NY 12454

Greene County Historical Society
(Vedder Research Library, Off Route 9W—location)
Rural Delivery (mailing address)
Coxsackie, NY 12051
(518) 731-1033; (518) 731-6822

Raymond V. Beecher, Librarian
Hours: Tue–Wed 10:00–4:00, first Sat
9:00–noon
Pub. *Quarterly Journal*
(extensive genealogical holdings for
Greene County; now housing
Surrogate Court records)
$10.00 per year membership; search fee:
$25.00

Greenlawn-Centerport Historical Association and Museum
31 Broadway
PO Box 354
Greenlawn, NY 11740
(516) 754-1180

Groton Historical Association
PO Box 142
Groton, NY 13073
(607) 898-5198; (607) 898-5787
Dr. Lucille S. Baker
Hours: Museum: Sat 10:00–2:00
Pub. *Newsletter*

The Half-Shire Historical Society
North Main Street
PO Box 73
Richland, NY 13144
(315) 298-2986
George O. Widrig, President

Hamburg Historical Society
(address withheld upon request)
(museum only, no genealogical services)

Hamilton County Historian
Lake Pleasant, NY 12108
Paul Wilbur
Municipal Historians: **Town of Arietta**:
Audrey Preston, Piseco, NY 12139;
Town of Benson: Harold E. Whitlock,
Rt. 2, Northville, NY 12134; **Town of
Hope**: Rudy F. Peters, Rt. 2,
Northville, NY 12134; **Town of
Indian Lake**: post vacant; **Town of
Inlet**: Peter Kallil, Inlet, NY 13360;
Town of Lake Pleasant: Ernest Virgil,
Lake Pleasant, NY 12108; **Town of
Long Lake**: Frances Seaman, Long
Lake, NY 12847; **Town of
Morehouse**: Earl Kreuzer,
Hoffmeister, NY 13353; **Village of
Speculator**: post vacant; **Town of
Wells**: Mr. and Mrs. Leon M. Perry,
Main Street, Wells, NY 12190

Hamlin Historical Society
731 Walker-Lake Ontario Road
Hilton, NY 14468
(716) 964-2101

Hancock-Chehocton Historical Association
61 Wheeler Street
Hancock, NY 13783
Pat Green, President
Hours: Mon 1:00–3:00, and by
appointment
Pub. *Point Mountain Press*, biannually

(limited to town of Hancock)
$5.00 per year membership for
individuals, $12.00 per year
membership for households, $100.00
life membership; donation for
searches, 15¢ per copy

Harrison Historical Society
PO Box 1696
Harrison, NY 10528

Hastings Historical Society
407 Broadway
Hastings-on-Hudson, NY 10706
(914) 478-2249
Mary Allison, Archivist
Hours: Mon 10:00–1:00, Thur 10:00–
2:00
Pub. *Hastings Historian*, quarterly
$15.00 per year membership; unable to
supply genealogical research and
doesn't publish anything of a
genealogical nature

Herkimer County Historian
(post vacant)
c/o Herkimer County Historical Society
400 North Main Street
Herkimer, NY 13350
(315) 866-6413
Susan R. Perkins, Administrative
Director
Municipal Historians: **Village of Cold
Brook**: post vacant; **Town of
Columbia**: Doris Huxtable, RD 1,
Box 284, West Winfield, NY 13491;
Town of Danube: Linda Welden, RD
3, Box 185A, Little Falls, NY 13365;
Village of Dolgeville: post vacant;
Town of Fairfield: Jane
Dieffenbacher, PO Box 1, Middleville,
NY 13406; **Town of Frankfort**: Gina
Bellino, 337 Second Avenue,
Frankfort, NY 13340; **Village of
Frankfort**: Vivian Sgroi, 247 West
Main Street, Frankfort, NY 13340;
Town of German Flatts: Francis
Cunningham, 374 Second Street, Ilion,
NY 13357; **Town of Herkimer**: James
Greiner, 318 Margaret Street,
Herkimer, NY 13350; **Village of
Herkimer**: post vacant; **Village of
Ilion**: George Hildebrant, 1 Shull
Street, Ilion, NY 13357; **Town of
Litchfield**: Elizabeth Ledda, Albany
Street, West Winfield, NY 13491; **City
of Little Falls**: Edwin J. Vogt, 78
Moreland Street, Little Falls, NY
13365; **Town of Little Falls**: Joan
Cotton, RD 2, Box 247, Little Falls,
NY 13365; **Town of Manheim**:
William C. Youker, 34 West State
Street, Dolgeville, NY 13329; **Village
of Middleville**: post vacant; **Village of
Mohawk**: Lillian Gaherty, 6 Marshall
Street, Mohawk, NY 13407; **Town of
Newport**: Muriel Fenner, Main Street,
Newport, NY 13416; **Village of
Newport**: Margery Foss, PO Box 237,

Newport, NY 13416; **Town of
Norway**: Elizabeth Agne, Kehli Road,
Newport, NY 13416; **Town of Ohio**:
Marion Williams, HCR, Cold Brook,
NY 13324; **Village of Poland**: Paula
Johnson, PO Box 21, Poland, NY
13431; **Town of Russia**: post vacant;
Town of Salisbury: Ann Schuyler, PO
Box 241, Salisbury Center, NY 13454;
Town of Schuyler: Betty Currier, RD
3, McGowan Road, Frankfort, NY
13340; **Town of Stark**: Leta Rickard,
RD 1, Fort Plain, NY 13339; **Town of
Warren**: Garry Aney, RD 1, Mohawk,
NY 13407; **Town of Webb**: Martha
Denio, Old Forge, NY 13420; **Town of
Winfield**: Steven Davis, RD 2, Route
20, West Winfield, NY 1391

Herkimer County Historical Society
400 North Main Street
Herkimer, NY 13350
(315) 866-6413
Susan R. Perkins, Administrative
Director
Hours: Mon–Fri 10:00–4:00 (request
appointment)
Pub. *Herkimer County Historical Crier*,
six times per year
$25.00 per year membership for
individuals, $40.00 per year
membership for families, $15.00 per
year membership for students, $55.00
per year Sustaining membership,
$300.00 per year Friend membership

Holland Purchase Historical Society
131 West Main Street
Batavia, NY 14020-2021
(716) 343-4727

Village of Honeoye Falls/Town of Mendon Historical Society
(1 Allen Park Drive—location)
50 East Street (mailing address)
Honeoye Falls, NY 14472
(716) 624-3810

Hoosick Township Historical Society
Louis Miller Museum
166 Main Street
PO Box 336
Hoosick Falls, NY 12090
(518) 686-4682
Edith Beaumont, Museum Director;
George Peer, HTHS President
Hours: Tue 1:00–4:00
(local history records; staffed completely
by volunteers)

Horicon Historical Society
Horicon Historical Society's Museum
Brant Lake, NY 12815
(518) 494-2804

Horseheads Cultural Center and Historical Society, Inc.
Zim Center
Horseheads, NY 14845
(607) 739-3938

Horseheads Historical Society and Museum

Old Pennsy Railroad Depot
312 West Broad
Horseheads, NY 14845
(607) 739-3938
Nadine Myers Ferraioli, President
Hours: Mon–Fri 10:00–1:00
Pub. *HHSM Newsletter*, four times per year
(village history [formerly named Fairport and North Elmira], Chemung Canal history, Indian collection, and cartoonist Eugene "Zim" Zimmerman)
$3.00 per year membership for individuals, $5.00 per year membership for families; request postage and donation for non-professional help

Hudson Mohawk Industrial Gateway

Foot of Polk Street
Troy, NY 12180

Huntington Historical Society

Resource Center and Archives
209 Main Street
Huntington, NY 11743
(516) 427-7064
Irene Sniffin, Library Registrar
Hours: Tue–Fri 1:00–4:00 (subject to change)
Pub. *The New Portico*, monthly
(emphasis on Huntington and Long Island history and genealogy)
$25.00 per year membership

Hyde Park Historical Association

PO Box 235
Hyde Park, NY 12538
(914) 229-9115

Hyde Park Historical Society

PO Box 182
Hyde Park, NY 12538

Interlaken Historical Society

Main Street
PO Box 323
Interlaken, NY 14847
(607) 532-4341
Maurice L. Patterson, President
Hours: Tue–Thur 2:30–5:00 & 7:00–8:30, Sat 10:00–1:00
Pub. *Between the Lakes*, quarterly
$5.00 per year membership for individuals, $6.00 per year membership for families, $4.00 per year membership for senior citizens and students, $100.00 life membership

Irondequoit Historical Office and Museum

877 Helendale Road
Rochester, NY 14609
Robert Gustafson

Irvington Historical Society

PO Box 1
Irvington-on-Hudson, NY 10533
(914) 591-7221

Ischua Valley Historical Society

9 Pine Street
Franklinville, NY 14737
Gertrude H. Schnell, President (Miner's Cabin)
Hours: Memorial Day–Labor Day: Sun 2:00–5:00, and by appointment
Pub. *Newsletter*, quarterly
(local history, artifacts, genealogy)
$5.00 per year membership for individuals, $10.00 per year Contributing membership, $25.00 per year Business or Professional membership, $100.00 life membership

Jefferson County Historian

c/o Jefferson County Planning Department
175 Arsenal Street
Watertown, NY 13601
Laura Lynne Scharer
Municipal Historians: **Town of Adams**: Mrs. John Herse, Rural Free Delivery, Adams Center, NY 13606; **Village of Adams**: Charles Clark, 10 East Church Street, Adams, NY 13605; **Town of Alexandria** and **Village of Alexandria Bay**: Hazel S. McMane, Goose Bay Road, Alexandria Bay, NY 13607; **Town of Antwerp**: Eleanor Jones, PO Box 41, Oxbow, NY 13671; **Village of Antwerp**: post vacant; **Village of Black River**: Carolyn Post, 172 Maple Street, Black River, NY 13612; **Town of Brownville**: June McCartin, West Main Street, Box 89, Brownville, NY 13615; **Village of Brownville**: post vacant; **Town of Cape Vincent**: Nina Comins, Rt. 2, Box 215, Clayton, NY 13624; **Village of Cape Vincent**: Mrs. Clarence Allen, PO Box 223, Cape Vincent, NY 13618; **Village of Carthage**: Laura Prievo, 307 Brown Street, Carthage, NY 13619; **Town of Champion**: Mrs. William Wiley, Rt. 2, Box 357, Carthage, NY 13619; **Village of Chaumont**: Charles Dunham, PO Box 367, Chaumont, NY 13622; **Town of Clayton** and **Village of Clayton**: Harold Kendall, 912 Strawberry Lane, Clayton, NY 13624; **Village of Deferiet**: Suzanne Wiley, Rt. 2, Box 357, Carthage, NY 13619; **Village of Dexter**: June McCartin, West Main Street, Brownville, NY 13615; **Town of Ellisburg** and **Village of Ellisburg**: William Eastman, PO Box 169, Ellisburg, NY 13636; **Village of Evan Mills**: post vacant; **Village of Glen Park**: post vacant; **Town of Henderson**: Gary L. Rhodes, Rt. 1, Box 668, Henderson, NY 13650; **Village of Herrings**: post vacant;

Town of Hounsfield: Mrs. G. Stanley Smith, 310 General Smith Drive, Sackets Harbor, NY 13685; **Town of Leray**: post vacant; **Town of Lorraine**: Wallace Corey, PO Box 8, Adams, NY 13605; **Town of Lyme**: Charles Dunham, Box 86, Water Street, Chaumont, NY 13622; **Village of Mannsville**: F. H. Clark, 952 Douglas Street, Mannsville, NY 13661; **Town of Orleans**: Dorothy Vaadi, Rt. 2, Box 658, LaFargeville, NY 13656; **Town of Pamelia**: Florence Salisbury, Rt. 1, Watertown, NY 13601; **Town of Philadelphia** and **Village of Philadelphia**: Gwendolyn Acheson, PO Box 46, Philadelphia, NY 13673; **Town of Rodman**: Dorothy Thomas, Rodman, NY 13682; **Town of Rutland**: Gayle Porter, Rt. 1, Box 301, Black River, NY 13612; **Village of Rutland**: Carolyne Post, 172 Maple Street, Black River, NY 13612; **Village of Sacketts Harbor**: Mrs. G. Stanley Smith, 310 General Smith Drive, Sackets Harbor, NY 13685; **Village of Stone Mills**: Rose Cullen, Rt. 1, Box 240, Lafargeville, NY 13656; **Town of Theresa** and **Village of Theresa**: Ronald Sinclair, Rt. 1, Theresa, NY 13691; **City of Watertown**: Junia Fitch-Stanton, Municipal Building, Watertown, NY 13601; **Town of Watertown**: Margaret Wilson, Plank Road, Star Route, Box 97, Watertown, NY 13601; **Village of West Carthage**: Ruth Bolan, 40 North Jefferson Street, Carthage, NY 13619; **Town of Wilna**: Laura Prievo, 307 Brown Street, Carthage, NY 13619; **Town of Worth**: Mrs. Henry Moreton, Rt. 1, Lorraine, NY 13659

Jefferson County Historical Society

228 Washington Street
Watertown, NY 13601
(315) 782-3491; (315) 782-2913 FAX
Elise D. Chan, Curator of Collections
Hours: Tue–Fri 10:00–5:00, Sat (May–Nov) noon–5:00
Pub. *Bulletin of the Jefferson County Historical Society*, two times per year
$20.00 per year membership for individuals, $25.00 per year membership for families, $10.00 per year membership for students or senior citizens, $35.00 per year Sustaining membership, $50.00 per year membership for institutions, $500.00 life membership; no genealogical research services, all inquiries referred to the Genealogy Department of Roswell P. Flower Memorial Library

Jewish Historical Society of New York, Inc.

(address withheld upon request)
Pub. *JHS Newsletter*

Johnstown Historical Society
17 North William Street
Johnstown, NY 12095
(518) 762-7076

Kent Historical Society
PO Box 123
Carmel, NY 10512
(914) 225-4882
Joyce Morin, President
Hours: by appointment
(Kent census figures, Sybil Ludington
    File)
$10.00 per year membership for
    individuals, $15.00 per year
    membership for families, $5.00 per
    year Associate membership

Kings County Historian
(address withheld upon request)

Kingsborough Historical Society
2001 Oriental Boulevard
Brooklyn, NY 11235
(212) 934-3122

Kingsbridge Historical Society
3930 Bailey Avenue
Bronx, NY 10463
(212) 549-5566
The Rev. Dr. William A. Tieck
Hours: by appointment

**Knickerbocker Historical Society,
Inc.**
166 Knickerbocker Road
PO Box 29
Schaghticoke, NY 12154
(518) 677-3807
E-mail: iseman7@aol.com
Stana Iseman, Project Director
Hours: 12 Jul–24 Aug: Sun 11:00–3:00
    and warm weather months by
    appointment
Pub. *Knickerbocker Mansion Newsletter*,
    quarterly; *The Knickerbocker*
    (genealogical newsletter), two times
    per year, $10.00 per year subscription
$10.00 per year membership (includes
    Knickerbocker Mansion Newsletter
    only)

Knox Historical Society
(Berne-Altamont Road, next to Fire
    Department—location)
PO Box 11 (mailing address)
Knox, NY 12107-0011
(518) 872-2551 (Town Hall)
Frieda Saddlemire, Town Historian;
    Virginia Quay, Treasurer
Hours: Jun–Sept: Sun 1:00–4:00, and by
    appointment
(ledgers, journals, church records, census
    information)
$2.00 per year membership; $5.00–
    $10.00 donation for search

Lake George Historical Association
Canada Street
PO Box 472
Lake George, NY 12845
(518) 668-5044

**Lake Placid-North Elba Historical
Society**
30 Lakeview Street
Lake Placid, NY 12946

**Lancaster New York Historical
Society**
40 Clark Street
Lancaster, NY 14086
(716) 681-7719
http://intotem.buffnet.net/lancasterpast/
    society
Terry Wolfe, President
Hours: Sun 2:00–5:00, and by
    appointment
Pub. *The Lancaster Legend*, monthly
$8.00 per year membership

Lansing Historical Association
PO Box 100
Lansing, NY 14882
Pub. *Newsletter*

Lansingburgh Historical Society
2 114th Street
PO Box 219
Lansingburgh, NY 12182
Alvin Thorne, Jr., President
Hours: by appointment only
(extensive manuscript collection)
$5.00 per year membership for
    individuals, $25.00 per year Sustaining
    membership, $100.00 life membership

Larchmont Historical Society
740 West Boston Post Road
Mamaroneck, NY 10543
(914) 381-2239
Bruce R. Allen, Archivist
Hours: Mon, Wed & Fri 1:00–3:00
Pub. *Gazebo Gazette*, monthly
$10.00 per year membership for
    individuals, $15.00 per year
    membership for families, $25.00 per
    year membership for institutions,
    $50.00 per year Sustaining
    membership, $150.00 life membership

LeRoy Historical Society
23 East Main Street
Leroy, NY 14482
(716) 768-7433
Lynne Belluscio, Director/Curator

Lewis County Historian
High Street
PO Box 277
Lyons Falls, NY 13368
(315) 348-8089
Lisa Becker, County Historian
Hours: Wed (year round) & Tue–Fri
    (1 Jun through mid-Oct) 10:00–3:00
Municipal Historians: **Village of
    Castorland**: post vacant; **Village of**

Constableville: Peter Payne, 6416
James Street, Constableville, NY
13325, (315) 397-2767; **Village of
Copenhagen**: Mary E. Boulio, PO
Box 201, Copenhagen, NY 13626,
(315) 688-2973; **Town of Croghan**:
Jack E. and Mary Sweeney, Rt. 1,
Castorland, NY 13620, (315) 346-
6201; **Village of Croghan**: post
vacant; **Town of Denmark**: Mary E.
Boulio, PO Box 201, Copenhagen, NY
13626, (315) 688-2973; **Town of
Diana**: Gladys Van Wyck, PO Box
321, High Street, Harrisville, NY
13648, (315) 543-2987; **Town of
Greig**: Randy Kerr, PO Box 87, Greig,
NY 13345, (315) 348-8016; **Town of
Harrisburg**: Madeline Bernat, Rt. 1,
Box 65, Lowville, NY 13367, (315)
376-7095; **Village of Harrisville**:
Gladys Van Wyck, Town of Diana
Historian (see above); **Town of Lewis**:
Rita Higby, PO Box 123, West
Leyden, NY 13489, (315) 942-4194;
Town of Leyden: Sally Riley, PO Box
29, Port Leyden, NY 13433, (315)
348-6264; **Town of Lowville** and
Village of Lowville: George R. Davis,
7641 Collins Street, Lowville, NY
13367, (315) 376-2437; **Village of
Lyons Falls**: Mary Teal, 7338
McAlpine Street, Lyons Falls, NY
13368, (315) 348-8216; **Town of
Lyonsdale**: Dorothy O'Brien, Rt. 1,
Box 172, Port Leyden, NY 13433,
(315) 942-4107; **Town of
Martinsburg**: Loretta Alexander, Rt.
2, Box 135, Lowville, NY 13367;
Town of Montague: post vacant;
Town of New Bremen: Fred J.
Schneider, Rt. 1, Box 86, Castorland,
NY 13620, (315) 376-3356; **Town of
Osceola**: Lola Moore, Rt. 3, Box 224,
Camden, NY 13316, (315) 599-8898;
Town of Pinckney: post vacant;
Village of Port Leyden: Alfred and
Erna Ward, PO Box 252, Port Leyden,
NY 13433, (315) 348-6190; **Town of
Turin**: Ada Mae Benedict, Box 43B,
East Road, Turin, NY 13473, (315)
348-8187; **Village of Turin**: Joy
Smith, PO Box 91, Turin, NY 13473,
(315) 348-8801; **Town of Watson**:
Charles Bunke, PO Box 2, Lowville,
NY 13367, (315) 376-3920; **Town of
West Turin**: Janice Klossner, High
Street, Constableville, NY 13325,
(315) 397-2570
25¢ per copy, no research charge

Lewis County Historical Society
High Street
PO Box 277
Lyons Falls, NY 13368
(315) 348-8089
Lisa Becker, Executive Director
Hours: Mid-May to Oct 15: 10:00–4:00
Pub. *Artifacts*, quarterly; *Lewis County
    Historical Society Journal*, annually

$5.00 per year membership for individuals, $6.00 per year membership for families, $25.00 per year Sustaining membership, $100.00 life membership for individuals

Historical Association and Society of Lewiston
Plain and Niagara Streets
PO Box 43
Lewiston, NY 14092
(716) 754-4214
Dorothy Cunningham, Acting Curator
Hours: Office: Wed 1:00–4:00; Museum: Wed–Sun (Jun–Aug) 1:00–4:00
Pub. *Historic Lewiston*, monthly
(Town and Village of Lewiston includes Sanborn, Dickersonvilleand part of Pekin)
$10.00 per year membership for individuals, $15.00 per year membership for families

Lima Historical Society
1850 Rochester Street
PO Box 532
Lima, NY 14485
(716) 263-2700
Kathryn Grover, President

Lindenhurst Historical Society
Old Village Hall Museum
215 South Wellwood Avenue
PO Box 296
Lindenhurst, NY 11757
(516) 957-4385
Evelyn Ellis, Village Historian
Hours: winter (1 Oct through 31 May): Wed, Fri–Sat & first Sun 2:00–4:00; summer (1 Jun through 30 Sept): Mon, Wed, Fri & first Sun 2:00–4:00

Little Nine Partners
The Historical Society
PO Box 243
Pine Plains, NY 12567

Little Red Schoolhouse Historical Society
PO Box 25
Coeymans Hollow, NY 12046
(518) 756-2562
Alice Christiana, Historian
Hours: Sun (Sept–Oct) 2:00–5:00

Livingston County Historian
(address withheld upon request)
Municipal Historians: **Town of Avon**: Maureen Kingston, Avon Town Hall, Genesee Street, Avon, NY 14414; **Village of Avon**: post vacant; **Town of Caledonia** and **Village of Caledonia**: Esther M. Hayward, Caledonia Town Hall, Main Street, Caledonia, NY 14423; **Town of Conesus**: Alice Pavlove, Conesus Town Hall, Conesus, NY 14435; **Village of**

Dansville: Quentin Masolotte, North Dansville Town Hall, Clara Barton Street, Dansville, NY 14437; **Town of Geneseo** and **Village of Geneseo**: David W. Parish, Geneseo Building, Main Street, Geneseo, NY 14454; **Town of Groveland**: Frances Teitsworth, Groveland Town Hall, Aten Road, Groveland, NY 14462; **Town of Leicester** and **Village of Leicester**: Velma Mahoney, Leicester Town Hall, Leicester, NY 14481; **Town of Lima**: Eileen Rawlins, Lima Town Hall, Main Street, Lima, NY 14485; **Village of Lima**: post vacant; **Town of Livonia**: Maurice Sweeney, Livonia Town Hall, Commercial Street, Livonia, NY 14487; **Village of Livonia**: post vacant; **Town of Mount Morris** and **Village of Mount Morris**: J. Frederick Beuerlein, Mount Morris Town Hall, 128 Main Street, Mount Morris, NY 14510; **Town of North Dansville**: Quentin Masolotte, North Dansville Town Hall, Clara Barton Street, Dansville, NY 14437; **Town of Nunda** and **Village of Nunda**: Sally D. Hall, Nunda Town Hall, Mill Street, Nunda, NY 14517; **Town of Ossian**: Alice Fenton, 10613 Sugar Creek Road, Dansville, NY 14437; **Town of Portage**: Elizabeth Thompson, Hunt, NY 14846; **Town of Sparta**: Leo Hendershott, Scottsburg, NY 14545; **Town of Springwater**: Dorothy Graham, Springwater Town Hall, Mill Street, Springwater, NY 14560; **Town of West Sparta**: David L. Palmer, Rt. 3, Bradner Hill Road, Dansville, NY 14437; **Town of York**: Patricia Stewart, York Town Hall, York, NY 14592

Lloyd Historical Society
38-A Bellevue Road
Highland, NY 12528
(914) 691-2145

Locust Valley Historical Society
Locust Valley Library
170 Buckram Road
Locust Valley, NY 11560
(516) 676-1837
Julia Clark, President
Hours: Library: Mon–Thur 10:00–9:00, Fri–Sat 10:00–5:00
(local history)
$10.00 per year membership

Lodi Historical Society
South Main Street
PO Box 279
Lodi, NY 14860
(607) 582-6016
Harry H. Curtin, President
Hours: various
$5.00 per year membership

Lower Hudson Conference of Historical Agencies and Museums
2199 Saw Mill River Road
Elmsford, NY 10523
(914) 592-6726; (914) 592-6946 FAX
http://www.purchase.edu/lhcmain.htm
Tema Harnik, Administrative Consultant
Hours: Mon–Fri 9:30–5:00
Pub. *Guide to Museums, Historical Organizations, Local Historians . . .*, irregularly; *Newsletter*, quarterly
(museum services organization)
$30.00 per year membership for individuals, $15.00 per year membership for students, $45.00 per year membership Professional/Consultant membership, $50.00 per year Supporting membership, $100.00 per year Sustaining membership, $30.00-$75.00 per year membership for non-profit organizations, $25.00 per year membership for businesses, $1,000.00 per year Corporate Sponsor membership

Macedon Historical Society, Inc.
(1185 Macedon Center Road—location)
PO Box 303 (mailing address)
Macedon, NY 14502
(315) 986-4845
David Taber
Hours: by appointment
Pub. *Pioneers of Macedon*
$2.00 per year membership for individuals, $3.00 per year membership for couples

Macomb Historical Association
Rt. 3
Hammond, NY 13646
(315) 578-2349

Madison County Historian
PO Box 188
Chittenango, NY 13037-0188
(315) 687-9222
Isabel Bracy
Municipal Historians: **Town of Brookfield**: Mrs. Donald Witter, Rt. 1, West Edmeston, NY 13485; **Village of Canastota**: post vacant; **Town of Cazenovia**: Peggy Ladd, Syracuse Road, Cazenovia, NY 13035; **Village of Cazenovia**: post vacant; **Village of Chittenango**: Richard F. Sullivan, 131 South Berkey Drive, Chittenango, NY 13037; **Town of DeRuyter**: Dick Burdick, 715 Division Street, DeRuyter, NY 13052; **Town of Eaton**: post vacant; **Town of Fenner**: Archie McEvers, Cody Road, Cazenovia, NY 13035; **Town of Georgetown**: Leona Goodrich, Rural Delivery, Erieville, NY 13061; **Town of Hamilton** and **Village of Hamilton**: Howard Williams, 60 Broad Street, Hamilton, NY 13346; **Town of Lebanon**: Gladys Bartlette, PO Box 15, Lebanon, NY 13085; **Town of Lenox**: Carolyn

Massarotte, 205 South Peterboro Street, Canastota, NY 13032; **Town of Lincoln**: Harlan Kilts, Timmerman Road, Clockville, NY 13043; **Town of Madison**: Anita Peckham, Augusta Road, Madison, NY 13402; **Village of Madison**: post vacant; **Village of Morrisville**: William Helmer, Morrisville, NY 13408; **Village of Munnsville**: Olive S. Boylan, ValleyMills Road, Box 177, Munnsville, NY 13409; **Town of Nelson**: Carol Stauring, Rt. 3, Nelson Road, Cazenovia, NY 13035; **City of Oneida**: Russell Hubbard, 212 East Elm Street, Oneida, NY 13421; **Town of Smithfield**: Carl Frank, PO Box 118, Peterboro, NY 13134; **Town of Stockbridge**: Olive Boylan, Valley Mills Road, Munnsville, NY 13409; **Town of Sullivan**: Carol Greene, Rt. 1, Bridgeport, NY 13030; **Village of Wampsville**: Teresa Bero, PO Box 86, Wampsville, NY 13163

Madison County Historical Society
435 Main Street
PO Box 415
Oneida, NY 13421
(315) 363-4136
Thomas Kernan, Director
Hours: Sept–May: Mon–Fri 9:00–4:00; Jun–Aug: Tue–Sat 9:00–4:00
Pub. *Heritage*, annually, $3.00 plus tax per volume
$15.00 per year membership for individuals, $12.00 per year membership for senior citizens; non-member research: $2.00

Mamaroneck Historical Society
PO Box 776
Mamaroneck, NY 10543
Gloria Pritts, Village Historian; Paula Lipsett, Town Historian
Hours: by appointment
Pub. *Newsletter*, monthly
$15.00 per year membership; search fees vary

Manhattan Borough Historian
1 Centre Street, Room 2035
New York, NY 10007
(212) 669-8089
Doris Rosenbaum
Hours: varies, usually Mon & Wed 10:00–1:00

Manlius Historical Society/Museum
109 Pleasant Street
Manlius, NY 13104
(315) 682-6660
Carrie Gannett, Director
Hours: Mon–Fri 8:00–4:00
Pub. *The Seraph*, quarterly
(town of Manlius history)

Marcellus Historical Society
(6 Slocombe—location)
PO Box 165 (mailing address)
Marcellus, NY 13108
(315) 673-3453
Hours: by appointment only

Marilla Historical Society
(2 Rock Road—location)
PO Box 36 (mailing address)
Marilla, NY 14102
(716) 652-7370
Hours: Museum: third Sun 2:00–4:00

Town of Maryland Historical Association
RR 1, Box 1038
Maryland, NY 12116
(607) 638-5436
E-mail: fieldeds@oneonta.edu
Dorothy Scott Fielder, President
Pub. *TMHA Newsletter*, annually
(no genealogical resources or resources to do genealogical research)
$3.00 per year membership

Historical Society of the Massapequas
(Merrick Road—location)
106 Toronto Avenue (mailing address)
Massapequa, NY 11758
(516) 779-4676
Arlene Goodenough, First Vice President
Hours: by appointment
Pub. *Newsletter*, five times per year
(Long Island; Major Thomas Jones family)
$7.00 per year membership; free help

Mattituck Historical Society
PO Box 766
Mattituck, NY 11952

Mayfield Historical Society
33 West Main Street
Mayfield, NY 12117
(518) 661-5085

Medina Historical Society
406 West Avenue
Medina, NY 14103
(716) 798-3006
Marian Perry, President

Historical Society of the Merricks
2279 South Merrick Avenue
Merrick, NY 11566
(516) 379-3476
Louis Kruh, President
Pub. *Memories of the Merricks*

Mid-Atlantic Regional Archives Conference
c/o Archives, Graymore
Garrison, NY 10524
(914) 424-3671

Middlebury Historical Society
Academy Street
Wyoming, NY 14591
(716) 495-6582 (Curator)
Marsha Morey, President

Town of Middlefield Historical Association
PO Box 348
Cooperstown, NY 13326
Evelyn Blanco, President
Hours: Jul–Aug: Sat, and by appointment
Pub. *Newsletter*, annually (June or late May), free
(photographic collection)
$3.00 per year membership for individuals, $5.00 per year membership for couples, $.50 per year membership for students, $10.00 per year Sustaining membership, $25.00 or more per year Patron membership

Historical Society of Middletown and Wallkill Precinct, Inc.
25 East Avenue
Middletown, NY 10940
(914) 343-6498
Charles L. Radzinsky, Curator
Hours: Wed 1:00–5:00, and by appointment
Pub. *Yearbook*, annually
$10.00 per year membership

Minerva Historical Society
Minerva, NY 12851
(518) 251-2146
Pub. *Minerva Historical Society Quarterly*
$5.00 per year membership

Minisink Valley Historical Society
(138 Pike Street—Archives location
131 West Main Street—Museum location)
PO Box 659 (mailing address)
Port Jervis, NY 12771
(914) 856-2375; (914) 856-1649
E-mail: muhs1889@magiccarpet.com
http://www.minisink.org
Peter Osborne, III, Executive Director
Pub. *Mennisenk*, quarterly
$15.00 per year membership for individuals, $20.00 per year membership for families, $50.00 per year membership for businesses

Office of the Monroe County Historian
Rundel Library
115 South Avenue
Rochester, NY 14604
(716) 428-7375
Carolyn S. Vacca
Hours: Mon–Fri 9:00–1:00, and by appointment
(no genealogical work for non-residents of the county)
Municipal Historians; **Town of Brighton**: Mary Jo Barone, 912 Landing Road North, Rochester, NY

14625, (716) 586-3009, (716) 473-8800; **Village of Brockport**: William Andrews, 80 State Street, Brockport, NY 14420, (716) 637-5342; **Town of Chili**: Jay Widener, Chili Town Hall, 3235 Chili Avenue, Rochester, NY 14624, (716) 889-4461; **Village of Churchville**: Ronald Balczak, 9 Ridgefield Drive, Churchville, NY 14428, (716) 293-3756; **Town of Clarkson**: Hazel Kleinbach, 34 Oak Drive, Hamlin, NY 14464, (716) 964-2152; **Village of East Rochester**: Mary Conners, 114 Woodbine Avenue, East Rochester, NY 14445, (716) 586-0057; **Village of Fairport**: David Taber, 57 East Avenue, Fairport, NY 14450, (716) 377-8208; **Town of Gates**: Jack Hart, Gates Town Hall, 1605 Buffalo Road, Gates, NY 14624, (716) 247-6100; **Town of Greece**: Lorraine Beane, Historical Society of Greece, N.Y., PO Box 16249, Rochester, NY 14616; **Town of Hamlin**: Mary E. Smith, 731 Walker-Lake Ontario Road, Hilton, NY 14468, (716) 964-2101 (home), (716) 964-7385 (office); **Town of Henrietta**: Helen Elam, 98 Tall Oak Lane, Pittsford, NY 14534, (716) 334-3860 (home), (716) 359-7092 (office); **Village of Hilton**: Mary Townsend, Hilton Community Center, 59 Henry Street, Hilton, NY 14468, (716) 392-4144; **Village of Honeoye Falls**: Anne Bullock, 5 East Street, Honeoye Falls, NY 14472, (716) 624-3232 (home), (716) 624-1711 (office); **Town of Irondequoit**: Patricia Wayne, 2180 East Ridge Road, Rochester, NY 14622, (716) 266-0456 (home); **Town of Mendon**: Diane Ham, 179 Plains Road, Honeoye Falls, NY 14472, (716) 624-3232 (home), (716) 624-1711 (office); **Town of Ogden**: Shirley Nixon, 388 Gillette Road, Spencerport, NY 14559, (716) 352-3672 (home); **Town of Parma**: Shirley Cox Husted, Parma Town Hall, 1300 Hilton Parma Road, Hilton, NY 14468, (716) 392-1915; **Town of Penfield**: Maude Frank, 1303 Sweets Corners Road, Penfield, NY 14526, (716) 377-3091; **Town of Perinton**: Susan Roberts, Perinton Town Hall, 1350 Turk Hill Road, Fairport, NY 14450, (716) 223-0770; **Town of Pittsford**: Audrey Johnson, 11 South Main Street, Pittsford, NY 14534, (716) 248-6245 (office), (716) 586-5608 (home); **Village of Pittsford**: post vacant; **Town of Riga**: Raymond Adams, 211 Riga-Mumford Road, Churchville, NY 14428, (716) 293-3658; **City of Rochester**: Ruth Naparsteck, 115 South Avenue, Rochester, NY 14604, (716) 428-7340; **Town of Rush**: post vacant; **Village of Scottsville**:

Florence Field, 341 South Road, Scottsville, NY 14546, (716) 889-3202; **Village of Spencerport**: Shirley Nixon, Town of Ogden Historian (see above); **Town of Sweden**: Mary Louise Henion, 4775 Sweden-Walker Road, Brockport, NY 14420, (716) 637-6408; **Town of Webster** and **Village of Webster**: Richard Batzing, 18 Lapham Park, Webster, NY 14580, (716) 265-3939 (home), (716) 265-3308 (office); **Town of Wheatland**: Florence Field, Village of Scottsville Historian (see above)

Montauk Historical Society
Montauk Highway
Montauk, NY 11954
Peggy Joyce, President

Heritage and Genealogical Society of Montgomery County
Old Court House
Railroad Street
PO Box 1500
Fonda, NY 12068-1500
(518) 853-8186 (Montgomery County Department of History and Archives); (518) 853-8392 FAX
E-mail: murphy5@nyslgti.gen.ny.us
Stephen Helmin, President
Hours: Montgomery County Department of History and Archives: Sept–Jun: Mon–Fri 8:30–4:00; Jul–Aug: Mon–Fri 9:00–4:00
Pub. *Catalogue of Genealogical and Historical Material*, annually, $12.00 postpaid (available in book form or on disk in Microsoft's Word)
("Friends" society to Montgomery County Department of History and Archives; third largest genealogical and historical research library and collection in New York State)

Montgomery County Historian
Old Court House
Railroad Street
PO Box 1500
Fonda, NY 12068-1500
(518) 853-8187; (518) 853-8186 (Montgomery County Department of History and Archives)
E-mail: murphyj@nyslgti.gen.ny.us
Jacqueline Murphy
Hours: Montgomery County Department of History and Archives: Sept–Jun: Mon–Fri 8:30–4:00; Jul–Aug: Mon–Fri 9:00–4:00
Municipal Historians: **Village of Ames**: Priscilla Smith, PO Box 644, Ames, NY 13317-0644, (518) 673-5793; **City of Amsterdam**: Dorothea N. Cooper, Rt. 4, Box 76A-81, Amsterdam, NY 12010, (518) 842-0583; **Town of Amsterdam**: Katherine Strobeck, R.D. Swart Hill Road, Amsterdam, NY 12010, (518) 843-2299; **Town of Canajoharie**: Kathleen Hanford, 24

Wheelock Street, Canajoharie, NY 13317, (518) 673-2379; **Village of Canajoharie**: Helena Glenar, Arkell Center, Apartment 109, 2 Maple Avenue, Canajoharie, NY 13317, (518) 673-3351; **Town of Charleston**: Lorraine Whiting, Box 741, Corbin Hill Road, Esperance, NY 12066, (518) 922-5867 (H), (518) 475-0291 (W); **Town of Florida**: Tim Seivers, 110 Abraham Road, Amsterdam, NY 12010, (518) 842-0719; **Village of Fonda**: Volkert Veeder, 4 Montgomery Terrace Ext., Fonda, NY 12068, (518) 853-4354; **Village of Fort Johnson**: Michael D. Mahoney, 7 Young Avenue, Fort Johnson, NY 12070, (518) 842-8806; **Village of Fort Plain**: Sandra Cronkhite, PO Box 278, 15 Berthoud Street, Nelliston, NY 13410, (518) 993-3805; **Village of Fultonville**: David Stone, PO Box 125, Fultonville, NY 12072, (518) 853-4901; **Town of Glen**: David Stone (see above); **Village of Hagaman**: Keith Schedlbauer, PO Box 226, Hagaman, NY 12086; **Town of Minden**: Mrs. Chris Eggleston, Airport Road, Fort Plain, NY 13339, (518) 993-4498; **Town of Mohawk**: Volkert Veeder, Village of Fonda Historian (see above); **Village of Nelliston**: Barbara Alkinburgh, 73 East Main Street, PO Box 307, Nelliston, NY 13410, (518) 993-4674; **Town of Palatine**: Sandra Cronkhite, Village of Fort Plain Historian (see above); **Village of Palatine Bridge**: post vacant; **Town of Root**: Carol Soodsma, 493 State Highway 162, Sprakers, NY 12166, (518) 673-2630; **Town of Saint Johnsville**: Anita Smith, 7 Center Street, Saint Johnsville, NY 13452, (518) 568-2910; **Village of Saint Johnsville**: Anita Smith, (see above)

Moriches Bay Historical Society
Main Street
Center Moriches, NY 11934

Mount Gulian Society
145 Sterling Street
Beacon, NY 12508
(914) 831-8172

Landmark and Historical Society of Mount Vernon
Mount Vernon Public Library
Local History Room
28 South First Avenue
Mount Vernon, NY 10550
(914) 668-1840 (Library)
Shannon E. Chandley, Library Curator
Hours: Library: Mon–Fri 9:00–1:00, and by appointment

Mountain Top Historical Society of Greene County, Inc.
Twilight Park
Haines Falls, NY 12436
(518) 589-5357

Nanticoke Valley Historical Society
PO Box 75
Maine, NY 13802
(607) 862-3243
Janet B. Bothwell, Curator

Naples Historical Society
PO Box 489
Naples, NY 14512

Nassau County Historian
Nassau County Museum
1864 Muttontown Road
Syosset, NY 11791
(516) 571-7605
Edward J. Smits, Director
Hours: Mon–Fri 9:00–5:00
Municipal Historians: **Village of Atlantic Beach**: post vacant; **Village of Baxter Estates**: Joyce C. Cailor, 2 Harbor Road, Port Washington, NY 11050; **Village of Bayville**: Gladys Mack, 34 School Street, Bayville, NY 11709; **Village of Bellerose**: Carol Mylod, 10 Massachusetts Boulevard, Bellerose Village, NY 11001; **Village of Brookville**: Rosemary Ahearn, Cedar Swamp Road, Brookville, NY 11545; **Village of Centre Island**: Charles G. Meyer, Jr., 518 Centre Island Road, Oyster Bay, NY 11771; **Village of Cove Neck**: Frances Roosevelt, Cove Neck Road, Oyster Bay, NY 11771; **Village of East Hills**: Charles Heckler, Jr., Deputy, 505 Glen Cove Road, East Hills, NY 11576; **Village of East Rockaway**: Mildred Roemer, 376 Atlantic Avenue, East Rockaway, NY 11518; **Village of East Williston**: Kathy Meyer, 29 Orchard Drive, East Williston, NY 11596; **Village of Farmingdale**: William J. Johnston, 42 Sherman Road, Farmingdale, NY 11735; **Village of Floral Park**: Hayden F. Allen, 29 Gladiolus Avenue, Floral Park, NY 11001; **Village of Flower Hill**: post vacant; **Village of Freeport**: Charles Zimmerman, Municipal Building, Freeport, NY 11520; **Village of Garden City**: Vincent F. Seyfried, 163 Pine Street, Garden City, NY 11530; **City of Glen Cove**: Daniel Russell, 44 Chestnut Street, Glen Cove, NY 11542; **Village of Great Neck**: Jane Martino, 115 Hampshire Road, Great Neck, NY 11023; **Village of Great Neck Estates**: Frieda Kessler, 1 Deepdale Drive, Great Neck, NY 11021; **Village of Great Neck Plaza**: Polly Whitehorn, PO Box 440, Gussack Plaza, Great Neck, NY 11021; **Town of Hempstead**: Tom Saltzman, Town Hall Plaza, Main Street, Hempstead, NY 11550; **Village of Hempstead**: James York, 99 Nichols Court, Hempstead, NY 11550; **Village of Hewlett Bay Park**: post vacant; **Village of Hewlett Harbor**: Mrs. Lee Kahan, 449 Pepperidge Road, Hewlett Harbor, NY 11557; **Village of Hewlett Neck**: Bertram Kalisher, 30 Piermont Avenue, Hewlett, NY 11557 **Village of Island Park**: post vacant; **Village of Kensington**: post vacant; **Village of Kings Point**: F. John Handler, 275 Kings Point Road, Kings Point, NY 11024; **Village of Lake Success**: post vacant; **Village of Lattingtown**: William Bales, 26 Wood Lane, Locust Valley, NY 11560; **Village of Laurel Hollow**: Mrs. William S. Smoot, 1270 Ridge Road, Syosset, NY 11791; **Village of Lawrence**: Mrs. Honor MacLean, 240 Causeway, Lawrence, NY 11559; **City of Long Beach**: Edward Graff, 260 West Walnut Street, Long Beach, NY 11561; **Village of Lynbrook**: Arthur Mattson, 28 Hart Street, Lynbrook, NY 11563; **Village of Malverne**: Jerry Janeske, 15 Wright Avenue, Malverne, NY 11565; **Village of Manorhaven**: Alice Peckelis, 33 Manorhaven Boulevard, Port Washington, NY 11050; **Village of Massapequa Park**: Florence Michel, 287 Illinois Avenue, Massapequa Park, NY 11762; **Village of Matinecock**: Dorothy H. McGee, PO Box 142, Locust Valley, NY 11560; **Village of Mill Neck**: post vacant; **Village of Mineola**: post vacant; **Village of Munsey Park**: Eileen Brennan, 1777 Northern Boulevard, Manhasset, NY 11030; **Village of Muttontown**: post vacant; **Village of New Hyde Park**: Florence Lisanti, 1420 Lincoln Avenue, New Hyde Park, NY 11040; **Town of North Hempstead**: Joan Kent, 220 Plandome Road, PO Box 3000, Manhasset, NY 11030; **Village of North Hill**: post vacant; **Village of Old Brookville**: post vacant; **Village of Old Westbury**: Richard Gachot, 1 Store Hill Road, Old Westbury, NY 11568; **Town of Oyster Bay**: Dorothy H. McGee, Town Hall, 54 Audrey Avenue, Oyster Bay, NY 11771; **Village of Oyster Bay Cove**: Paula Weir, 174 Cove Road, Oyster Bay, NY 11771; **Village of Plandome**: Grace Jayne, 2 Middle Drive, Plandome, NY 11030; **Village of Plandome Heights**: Arlene R. Hinkemeyer, 35 Cove Drive, Manhasset, NY 11030; **Village of Plandome Manor**: Beatrice Tusiani, PO Box 951, Plandome, NY 11030; **Village of Port Washington North**: George Williams, 1 Soundview Drive, Port Washington, NY 11050; **Village of Rockville Centre**: Barbara Smallback, 10 Allen Road, Rockville Centre, NY 11570; **Village of Roslyn**: Elizabeth H. Moger, 91 Remsen Avenue, Roslyn, NY 11576; **Village of Roslyn Estates**: Ruth Hinrichs, 3 Warner Avenue, Roslyn Heights, NY 11577; **Village of Roslyn Harbor**: Frank Harrington, 200 Scudders Lane, Roslyn Harbor, NY 11576; **Village of Russel Gardens**: Dr. William S. Grauer, 6 Melbourne Road, Great Neck, NY 11021; **Village of Saddle Rock**: post vacant; **Village of Sands Point**: Grace Frank, Sycamore Drive, Sands Point, NY 11050; **Village of Sea Cliff**: Frank O. Braynard, Sea Cliff Village Hall, Sea Cliff, NY 11579; **Village of South Floral Park**: post vacant; **Village of Stewart Manor**: John Ryan, 181 Fernwood Terrace, Stewart Manor, NY 11530; **Village of Thomaston**: post vacant; **Village of Upper Brookville**: Clarissa Watson, Wolver Hollow Road, Oyster Bay, NY 11771; **Village of Valley Stream**: Jack Sharkey, 5 Horton Road, Valley Stream, NY 11580; **Village of Westbury**: post vacant; **Village of Williston Park**: post vacant; **Village of Woodsburgh**: Robert Kullman, 30 Piermont Avenue, Hewlett, NY 11557

Nassau County Historical Society
PO Box 207
Garden City, NY 11530
Denward W. Collins, Jr., President
Pub. *Nassau County Historical Society Journal*, annually
(Long Island history)
$15.00 per year membership

National Temple Hill Association, Inc.
(1042 Route 94—location)
PO Box 315 (mailing address)
Valis Gate, NY 12584
(914) 561-5073
Hours: seasonal and by appointment; Jul–Sept: Sun 2:00–5:00
(The American Revolution; local history)
$15.00 per year membership for individuals, $25.00 per year membership for couples

New Castle Historical Society
(312 King Street—location)
PO Box 55 (mailing address)
Chappaqua, NY 10514
(914) 238-4666
Betsy Towl, Museum Director
Hours: Tue & Thur 9:00–noon, Wed 11:00–1:00
Pub. *Newsletter*, four times per year
("Extensive collection of Horace Greeley and family as well as local records of the Town of New Castle")
$15.00 per year membership for individuals, $25.00 per year

membership for families, $50.00 per year Patron membership, $100.00 Benefactor membership

The New England Historic Genealogical Society

(see Massachusetts)

New Hartford Historical Society

48 Genesee Street
PO Box 238
New Hartford, NY 13413
(315) 735-2332

Town of New Scotland Historical Association

Old New Salem Road
New Scotland, NY 12127
(518) 765-2071
Ann A. Eberle, President
Hours: by appointment; meetings first Tue (Feb–May & Oct–Dec)
Pub. *The Sentinel*, semiannually
$5.00 per year membership for individuals, $8.00 per year membership for couples, $25.00 per year Supporting membership, $100.00 life membership

New Woodstock Historical Society

New Woodstock, NY 13122

New York City Boroughs' Historians

(see Official Bronx Historian, Kings County Historian [Brooklyn], Manhattan Borough Historian [New York County], Queens County Historian, Richmond County Historian [Staten Island])

Newark Valley Historical Society

(Park Street, Municipal Building, Second Floor—location)
PO Box 222 (mailing address)
Newark Valley, NY 13811
(607) 642-9516; (607) 687-1337 FAX
Harriet Miller, Executive Director
Hours: by appointment
Pub. *Newsletter*, six times per year, plus annual report
(New York history)
$15.00 per year membership for individuals, $10.00 per year membership for senior citizens, membership categories up to $300.00 per year; library admission to members only

Historical Society of Newburgh Bay and the Highlands

189 Montgomery Street
Newburgh, NY 12550
(914) 5612585

Newfield Historical Society

541 Millard Hill Road
Newfield, NY 14867
(607) 564-3310
Florence Emery, President

Newstead Historical Society

PO Box 222
Akron, NY 14001
(716) 542-4369
Arlene Richardson, President
Pub. *Newstead Historical Society Newsletter*, four times per year
$6.00 per year membership for individuals, $10.00 per year membership for couples

Niagara County Historian

Niagara County Historian's Office
Civil Defense Building
139 Niagara Street
Lockport, NY 14094-2740
(716) 439-7324
Dorothy Rolling, Historian; Donna Barnes, Deputy Historian
Hours: Mon–Fri 9:00–5:00 by appointment
Municipal Historians: **Village of Barker**: Lorraine Wagner, 1116 Quaker Road, Barker, NY 14012, (716) 795-3575; **Town of Cambria**: Vernette Genter, 4280 Church Road, Lockport, NY 14094, (716) 434-8937, (716) 433-8829; **Town of Hartland**: Florence Arnold, 9035 Ridge Road, Gasport, NY 14067, (716) 735-7517, (716) 735-7179; **Town of Lewiston**: Richard Cary, Jr., 5235 Paddock Lane, Lewiston, NY, (716) 298-4027; **Village of Lewiston**: Paul Brucato, 225 North Water Street, Lewiston, NY 14092, (716) 754-8814; **City of Lockport**: Richard Dickenson, 161 Lock Street, Lockport, NY 14094, (716) 439-0985; **Town of Lockport**: Mary L. Newhard, 7122 North Ledge Drive, Lockport, NY 14094, (716) 434-0207; **Village of Middleport**: Anna Wallace, 8 Freeman Street, Middleport, NY 14105, (716) 735-9025; **Town of Newfane**: Judson Heck, 2538 Merritt Street, Newfane, NY 14108, (716) 778-8286; **Town of Niagara**: Dorothy Rolling, 7530 Packard Road, Niagara Falls, NY 14304, (716) 297-6601; **City of Niagara Falls**: Donald Loker, Local History Department, Niagara Falls Public Library, 1425 Main Street, Niagara Falls, NY 14305-2574, (716) 286-4899; **City of North Tonawanda**: Elizabeth Robson, 46 Niagara Street, Tonawanda, NY 14120, (716) 692-0538; **Town of Pendleton**: Benny Sobczyk, 5201 North Tonawanda Creek Road, North Tonawanda, NY 14120, (716) 692-3257; **Town of Porter**: Cora Gushee, 3452 East Avenue, Youngstown, NY 14174, (716) 745-7203; **Town of Royalton**: Donald Jerge, 8700 Slayton Settlement Road, Gasport, NY 14067, (716) 772-2974; **Town of Somerset**: Lorraine

Wayner, 1116 Quaker Road, Barker, NY 14012, (716) 795-3575; **Town of Wheatfield**: John Forcucci, 2552 Nicole Drive, Niagara Falls, NY 14304, (716) 731-2584; **Town of Wilson** and **Village of Wilson**: Eleanor Myers, 215 Lake Street, Box 98, Wilson, NY 14172, (716) 751-6053; **Village of Youngstown**: Donald Ames, 162 Jackson Street, Youngstown, NY 14174, (716) 745-3423

Niagara Falls Historical Society, Inc.

Niagara Falls Public Library
Local History Department, Niagara Room
Earl W. Brydges Library Building
1425 Main Street
Niagara Falls, NY 14305-2574
(716) 286-4899 (Library, Local History); (716) 286-4912 FAX (Library)
Donald E. Loker, President
Hours: Library: Mon 9:00–9:00, Tue–Fri 9:00–5:00, second Sat (Sept–May) 9:00–1:00 & 2:00–5:00
Pub. *Out of the Mist*

North Castle Historical Society

Smith's Tavern
440 Bedford Road
Armonk, NY 10504
(914) 273-4510
Sharon Tomback, Secretary
Pub. *North Castle History*, annually
$25.00 per year membership

North Collins Historical Society

2093 Shirley
North Collins, NY 14111
(716) 337-2215

Historical Society of the Town of North Hempstead

220 Plandome Road
Manhasset, NY 11030
(516) 627-0590

Northport Historical Society/ Museum

215 Main Street
PO Box 545
Northport, NY 11768
(516) 757-9859
Marguerite Mudge, Director

Norwood Historical Association and Museum

39 North Main Street
PO Box 163
Norwood, NY 13668
(315) 353-2751
Gerald Lacomb, Curator
Hours: Tue & Thur 2:00–4:00, and by appointment

Ogden Historical Society, Inc.

568 Colby Street
Spencerport, NY 14559

Ohio Historical Society

Rural Delivery
Cold Brook, NY 13324

Old Brutus Historical Society, Inc.

8943 North Seneca Street
PO Box 516
Weedsport, NY 13166
(315) 834-6779 (Historian)
Howard J. Finley, Historian

Old Onaquaga Historical Society

Saint Luke's Museum
PO Box 318
Harpursville, NY 13787
(607) 693-1298
(museum has very limited amount of
research material and is not open
regular hours)

Oneida County Historian

(post vacant)
Municipal Historians: **Town of
Annsville**: C. Harrison Ward, (Taberg,
NY 13471—location), 2 Second Street
(mailing address), Camden, NY
13316-1308, (315) 245-1213; **Town of
Augusta**: Helen Alberding, 124
Madison Street, Oriskany Falls, NY
13425; **Town of Ava**: Alson Castle, Rt.
1, Ava, NY 13303; **Town of
Barneveld**: Elizabeth Alger,
Barneveld, NY 13304; **Town of
Boonville**: James S. Pitcher, 507 Post
Street, Boonville, NY 13309; **Village
of Boonville**: post vacant; **Town of
Bridgewater**: Stanley Owens, Maple
Dale Road, Cassville, NY 13318;
Village of Bridgewater: post vacant;
Town of Camden: Gertrude Dillon,
Rt. 3, Box 170, Camden, NY 13316;
Village of Camden: Mrs. Elbert Peck,
13 Watkins Avenue, Camden, NY
13316; **Village of Clayville**: post
vacant; **Village of Clinton**: Philip
Munson, 6 Kirkland Avenue,
Apartment H23, Clinton, NY 13323-
1455; **Town of Deerfield**: Mrs. Bruce
Folts, Rt. 1, Roberts Road, Utica, NY
13502; **Town of Florence**: Gertrude
Dillon, Rt. 3, Box 170, Camden, NY
13316; **Town of Floyd**: Edwin C.
Evans, Rt. 4, Camroden Road, Rome,
NY 13440; **Town of Forestport**:
Elizabeth Ferjet, River Street,
Forestport, NY 13338; **Town of
Kirkland**: Mrs. Thomas Dever, 36
Williams Street, Clinton, NY 13323;
Village of Holland Patent: Mrs.
Edward Christiana, Steuben Street,
Holland Patent, NY 13354; **Town of
Lee**: post vacant; **Town of Marcy**:
Raymond Ball, 9975 Morgan Road,
Marcy, NY 13403; **Town of Marshall**:
Kenneth McConnell, Rt. 315,
Deansboro, NY 13328; **Town of New
Hartford**: post vacant; **Village of New
Hartford**: New Hartford Historical
Society, PO Box 238, New Hartford,

NY 13413; **Village of New London**:
Edith Pangburn, 6659, Rt. 46,
Durhamville, NY 13054; **Village of
New York Mills**: Mildred Szarek, 4
Clinton Street, New York Mills, NY
13417; **Village of Oneida Castle**:
Mrs. Frederick Hill, 56 Seneca
Avenue, Oneida Castle, NY 13421;
Village of Oriskany: Geraldine
Miller, 306 Miller Street, Oriskany,
NY 13424; **Village of Oriskany Falls**:
Helen Alberding, 124 Madison Street,
Oriskany Falls, NY 13425; **Town of
Paris**: Joe Tinker, 26 Church Road,
Clayville, NY 13322; **Village of
Prospect**: Sharon Pomicheter,
Prospect, NY 13435; **Town of
Remsen**: Lorena Jersen, Steuben
Street, Remsen, NY 13438; **Village of
Remsen**: post vacant; **City of Rome**:
post vacant; **Town of Sangerfield**:
Mrs. Martin Cleary, 125 White Street,
Waterville, NY 13480; **City of
Sherrill**: post vacant; **Town of
Steuben**: Myron Senchyna, Rt. 2,
Remsen, NY 13438; **Village of Sylvan
Beach**: Jack Henke, PO Box 175,
Brookfield, NY 13314; **Town of
Trenton**: Elizabeth Alger, Parker
Hollow Road, Barneveld, NY 13304;
City of Utica: post vacant; **Town of
Vernon**: Sadie Namminga, 9 North
Sconondoa Street, Vernon, NY 13476;
Village of Vernon: Ellen Murphy, 9N
Sconondoa Street, Vernon, NY 13476;
Town of Verona: Raymond P.
Ernenwein, Rt. 2, 5858 Germany
Road, Verona, NY 13478; **Town of
Vienna**: Vera Fowler, Rt. 2, Blossvale,
NY 13308; **Village of Waterville**:
Mrs. Martin Cleary, 125 White Street,
Waterville, NY 13480; **Town of
Western**: Dr. Russell Marriott, PO
Box 42, Westernville, NY 13486;
Town of Westmoreland: Gertrude
VanBenschoten, PO Box 45,
Westmoreland, NY 13490; **Town of
Whitestown**: Marilyn Collea, 2324
Arnold Avenue, Yorkville, NY 13495;
Village of Whitesboro: Charles
Sperry, 28 Brainard Street,
Whitesboro, NY 13492; **Village of
Yorkville**: Mrs. Robert Kohlbrenner, 2
Coventry Avenue, Yorkville, NY
13495

Oneida County Historical Society

1608 Genesee Street
Utica, NY 13502-5425
(315) 735-3642
Douglas M. Preston, Director
Hours: Tue–Fri 10:00–4:30
Pub. *Oniota*, six times per year
$25.00 per year membership for
individuals, $40.00 per year
membership for families, $5.00 per
day per person or couple library fee
for non-members, $15.00 minimum
contribution for mail research

Onondaga County Historian

(post vacant)
Municipal Historians: **Village of
Baldwinsville**: post vacant; **Town of
Camillus**: post vacant; **Town of
Cicero**: Lona Flynn, PO Box 296,
Cicero, NY 13039; **Town of Clay**:
Ferdinand Lepinske, 4834 Grange
Road, Clay, NY 13041; **Village of
Camillus**: post vacant; **Town of
DeWitt**: Frank J. Volcko, 501 Franklin
Park Drive, East Syracuse, NY 13057;
Village of East Syracuse: post vacant;
Town of Elbridge: Mrs. Harvey K.
Hudson, 45 Mechanic Street, Jordan,
NY 13080; **Village of Elbridge**: Jean
Schwartz, 822 Dumar Drive, PO Box
1033, Elbridge, NY 13060; **Town of
Fabius** and **Village of Fabius**:
Candace Svendsen, 1312 Keeney
Road, Fabius, NY 13063; **Village of
Fayetteville**: Mrs. Francis P. Rivette,
Rt. 1, Mycenae, Chittenango, NY
13037; **Town of Geddes**: post vacant;
Village of Jordan: Mrs. Harvey
Hudson, 45 Mechanic Street, Jordan,
NY 13080; **Town of LaFayette**: Rev.
Donald Moody, Rt. 1, PO Box 46,
Tully, NY 13159; **Village of
Liverpool**: Dorianne Gutierrez, 314
Second Street, Liverpool, NY 13088;
Town of Lysander: Robert F.
Nostrant, 6 Lock Street, Baldwinsville,
NY 13027; **Town of Manlius**: Mrs.
Francis P. Rivette, Rt. 1, Mycenae,
Chittenango, NY 13037; **Village of
Manlius**: post vacant; **Town of
Marcellus**: Lucy Sweet, 1 Park Street,
Marcellus, NY 13108; **Village of
Marcellus**: post vacant; **Village of
Minoa**: post vacant; **Village of North
Syracuse**: Jane Kimpland, Village
Hall, 600 South Bay Road, North
Syracuse, NY 13212; **Town of
Onondaga**: L. Jane Tracy, 4967
Carnarvon Road, Syracuse, NY 13215;
Town of Otisco: post vacant; **Town of
Pompey**: post vacant; **Town of Salina**:
Mrs. Joseph Ostuni, 200 Third Street,
Liverpool, NY 13088; **Town of
Skaneateles**: Helen Ionta, East Lake
Road, Skaneateles, NY 13152; **Village
of Skaneateles**: Catherine Barnes, 35
Academy Street, Skaneateles, NY
13152; **Village of Solvay**: Mrs.
Andrew R. March, 125 Charles
Avenue, Syracuse, NY 13209; **Town
of Spafford**: Bessie Turner, 3266
Becker Road, Skaneateles, NY 13152;
City of Syracuse: post vacant; **Town
of Tully**: Lynn M. Fisher, 22-24 State
Street, PO Box 22, Tully, NY 13159-
0022; **Village of Tully**: post vacant;
Town of Van Buren: post vacant

Onondaga Historical Association

Research Center
311 Montgomery Street
Syracuse, NY 13202-2098

(315) 428-1862
Judy Haven, Research Coordinator
Hours: Tue–Fri 1:00–4:30, Fri 9:30–noon
by appointment; Museum: Tue–Fri
noon-4:00, Sat 11:00–4:00
Pub. *History Highlights* (newsletter, not
genealogical), perhaps quarterly; *OHA
Annual Report*, annually
(Onondaga County history)
$30.00 per year membership for
individuals, $40.00 per year
membership for families, $25.00 per
year membership for senior citizens
(65 and over) or full-time students,
$50.00 per year Research membership,
$100.00 per year Archivist
membership, $250.00 per year Curator
membership, $500.00 per year
Historian membership, $1,000.00 per
year Scholar membership; search fee:
$20.00 minimum plus SASE, allow 8
weeks for response

Ontario County Historian
209 Davidson Avenue
Canandaigua, NY 14424
(716) 396-4034; (716) 394-8523
Dr. Preston E. Pierce
Hours: Tue & Thur 3:30–5:00
Pub. *Historian's Newsletter*, monthly,
$7.00 per year subscription
Municipal Historians: **Town of Bristol**:
Helen Fox, 4309 Route 64,
Canandaigua, NY 14424; **Town of
Canadice**: John T. Hopkins, 5624
County Road 37, Hemlock, NY 14466,
(716) 367-2823, (716) 396-4034; **City
of Canandaigua**: Dr. Marvin Rapp,
113 Cliffside Road, Bristol Harbour,
Canandaigua, NY 14424, (716) 394-
8124; **Town of Canandaigua**: Linda
McIlveen, 55 North Main Street,
Canandaigua, NY 14424, (716) 394-
4975; **Village of Clifton Springs**:
Frederick Gifford, 52 West Main
Street, Clifton Springs, NY 14432,
(315) 462-9657; **Town of East
Bloomfield**: Diane Wade, c/o Town
Clerk's Office, Box 85, East
Bloomfield, NY 14443, (716) 657-
6515; **Village of East Bloomfield**:
post vacant; **Town of Farmington**:
Margaret Hartsough, 128 County Road
8, Farmington, NY 14425; **City of
Geneva**: Stephen O'Malley, 543 South
Main Street, Geneva, NY 14456, (315)
789-5151; **Town of Geneva**: Mabel S.
Ansley, 371 Reed Road, Geneva, NY
14456, (315) 789-3922; **Town of
Gorham**: Mary O. Melious, Historian,
2655 Depew Road, Stanley, NY
14561, (315) 526-5882; **Village of
Holcomb**: post vacant; **Town of
Hopewell**: Adelbert Schutt, 2414
County Road 47, Canandaigua, NY
14424, (716) 394-2113; **Town of
Manchester**: Tim Record, Stafford
Road (Box 381), Manchester, NY
14504; **Village of Manchester**: Naomi

Warren, 92 Thad Chapin Street,
Canandaigua, NY 14424; **Town of
Naples**: William Vierhile, 32 West
Avenue, Naples, NY 14512, (716)
374-6440; **Village of Naples**: post
vacant; **Town of Phelps**: John
Parmelee, 23 Orchard Park, Phelps,
NY 14532, (315) 548-3522; **Village of
Phelps**: post vacant; **Town of
Richmond**: Peggy Treble, 30 Church
Street, Honeoye, NY 14471; **Village of
Rushville**: post vacant; **Town of
Seneca**: William Niles, PO Box 152,
Seneca Castle, NY 14547, (315) 526-
5525; **Village of Shortsville**: Ann
Walker, 12 High Street, Shortsville,
NY 14548; **Town of South Bristol**:
Roger S. Brahm, 5522 NYS Route 21
South, Canandaigua, NY 114424,
(716) 394-1505; **Town of Victor**:
Babette M. Huber, Town Hall, 85 East
Main Street, Victor, NY 14564;
Village of Victor: post vacant; **Town
of West Bloomfield**: Kurt Kleindienst,
PO Box 34, West Bloomfield, NY
14585, (716) 624-1888

Ontario County Historical Society
55 North Main Street
Canandaigua, NY 14424
(716) 394-4975 phone and FAX
Linda McIlveen, Director of Research
Hours: Research Room: Tue–Sat 10:00–
4:30, Wed 10:00–9:00; Museum: Tue–
Sat 10:00–5:00
Pub. *Chronicle*, quarterly
(Ontario County history and local
genealogy)
$20.00 per year membership for
individuals, $35.00 per year
membership for families; $1.00
general admission, $5.00 research
admission; mail-in research services:
$15.00 plus copy costs

**Town of Ontario Historical and
Landmark Preservation Society**
(Heritage Square at Brich Church
Corners—location)
PO Box 462 (mailing address)
Ontario, NY 14519
(315) 524-5356; (315) 524-0037
Thomas Treppa, President
Hours: six historic buildings: mid-May
through Sept: Sat–Sun 1:30–5:00
Pub. *Newsletter*, bimonthly
$5.00–$150.00 per year membership;
free admission

Orange County Historian
Goshen Public Library and Historical
Society
1841 Court House
101 Main Street
Goshen, NY 10924-1627
(914) 294-6644; (914) 294-5151, ext.
1745
Theodore W. Sly, County Historian
Hours: Library Reference Room: Mon–
Wed 10:00–6:00, Thur–Sat 10:00–2:00

Municipal Historians: **Town of
Blooming Grove**: Jean Versweyveld,
PO Box 38, Blooming Grove, NY
10914, (914) 496-7230; **Town of
Chester**: post vacant; **Village of
Chester**: Marjorie Nehrich, 22
Academy Avenue, Chester, NY 10918,
(914) 469-4405; **Town of Cornwall**:
Janet Dempsey, 7 Prospect Street,
Cornwall-on-Hudson, NY 12520,
(914) 534-5285; **Village of Cornwall-
on-Hudson**: Colette Fulton, 52 Spruce
Street, Cornwall-on-Hudson, NY
12520, (914) 534-2664; **Town of
Crawford**: Mary Smith, c/o Town
Hall, PO Box 109, Pine Bush, NY
12566, (914) 744-3946, or Jean T.
Vogelbach, Associate Historian,
Thompson Ridge, NY 10985, (914)
361-4386; **Town of Deerpark**: Dr.
Frank Simpson, 84 Neversink Drive,
Port Jervis, NY12771, (914) 856-
1914; **Village of Florida**: Gary
Randall, Route 94, 275 North Seward
Highway, Warwick, NY 10990, (914)
651-7466; **Town of Goshen**: Henry
Pomares, Axworthy Lane, Goshen, NY
10924, (914) 294-5236; **Village of
Goshen**: post vacant; **Town of
Greenville**: post vacant; **Village of
Greenwood Lake**: Wilbur E.
Christman, 16 Woodbine Avenue,
Greenwood Lake, NY 10925, (914)
477-2473; **Town of Greenville**:
Catherine Ardler, 124 County Route
35, Port Jervis, NY 12771, (914) 856-
3548; **Town of Hamptonburgh**:
Nancy H. Smit, Rt. 2, Box 131,
Campbell Hall, NY 10916, (914) 294-
6867, (914) 294-6111; **Village of
Harriman**: Evelyn McGarrah, PO
Box 258, Harriman, NY 10926;
Village of Highland Falls and **Town
of Highlands**: Stella Bailey, Box 28,
Mine Road, Fort Montgomery, NY
10922, (914) 446-2083; **Village of
Maybrook**: Roberta Petzold, PO Box
105, Maybrook, NY 12543; **City of
Middletown**: Peter Laskaris, 146 West
Main Street, Middletown, NY 10940;
Town of Minisink: Delmar S.
Dulaney, Rt. 1, Westtown, NY 10998,
(914) 726-3947; **Town of Monroe**:
James Nelson, 608 Arlin Road,
Monroe, NY 10950, (914) 783-3406;
Village of Monroe: Charles J. King,
Old Country Road, Monroe, NY
10950, (914) 783-3591 **Town of
Montgomery**: Robert L. Williams, 63
Union Street, Montgomery, NY 12549,
(914) 457-5182 (Home), (201) 345-
8220 (Work); **Village of
Montgomery**: Marion Wild, 42 Union
Street, Montgomery, NY 12549, (914)
457-5135; **Town of Mount Hope**:
Delores Hawkins, PO Box 471,
Otisville, NY 10963, (914) 386-5214;
Town of New Windsor: Donald C.
Gordon, 815 Blooming Grove

Turnpike, New Windsor, NY 12550, (914) 562-6397; **City of Newburgh**: Kevin Barrett Bilali, PO Box 357, Bloomingburg, NY 12721, (914) 733-1233; **Town of Newburgh**: Oliver E. Shipp, 343 A Forest Road, Wallkill, NY 12589, (914) 564-3677; **Village of Otisville**: Vivian Ketcham, 42 Mount Hope Avenue, Otisville, NY 10963, (914) 386-4532; **Village of Pine Island**: Frances Sodrick, Rt. 1, Box 10, Pine Island, NY 10969, (914) 258-4528; **City of Port Jervis**: Peter Osborne, PO Box 659, Port Jervis, NY 12771, (914) 856-2375; **Village of Prospect**: post vacant; **Town of Tuxedo** and **Village of Tuxedo**: Albert F. Winslow, Maplebrook, PO Box 444, Tuxedo Park, NY 10987, (914) 351-2623; **Village of Tuxedo Park**: post vacant; **Village of Unionville**: Donald Mavros, PO Box 547, Unionville, NY 10988, (914) 726-3501; **Village of Walden**: Marcus H. Millspaugh, Jr., 86 Ulster Avenue, Walden, NY 12586, (914) 778-7428; **Town of Wallkill**: Dorothy H. Nutt, 6 Lochinvar Lane, Middletown, NY 10940, (914) 692-4862; **Town of Warwick** and **Village of Warwick**: Florence P. Tate, 7 Clinton Avenue, Warwick, NY 10990, (914) 986-4420; **Village of Washingtonville**: Edward J. McLaughlin, III, 59 East Main Street, Washingtonville, NY 10992, (914) 496-3827; **Town of Wawayanda**: Emma Duvall, PO Box 84, New Hampton, NY 10958; **Town of Woodbury**: Leslie Rose, PO Box 30, Highland Mills, NY 10934, (914) 928-6479

Orchard Park Historical Society
(East Quaker Street—location)
5800 Armor Road (mailing address)
Orchard Park, NY 14127

Orleans County Historian
34 East Park Street
Albion, NY 14411
(716) 589-4174
C. Wilson Lattin
Hours: Mon, Wed & Fri 1:00–4:00
Municipal Historians: **Town of Albion**: Edith Anderson, Town Hall, 3665 Clarendon Road, Albion, NY 14411; **Village of Albion**: Dr. Neil Johnson, Village Hall, 35-37 East Bank Street, Albion, NY 14411; **Town of Barre**: Helen Mathes, Town Hall, 14317 West Barre Road, Albion, NY 14411; **Town of Carlton**: Lysbeth Hoffman, Town Hall, 14341 Waterport-Carlton Road, Albion, NY 14411; **Town of Clarendon**: Alan Isselhard, PO Box 145, Clarendon, NY 14429; **Town of Gaines**: Delia Robinson, Town Hall, 13941 Ridge Road, Albion, NY 14411; **Village of Holley**: Marsha DeFilipps,

Village Hall, 72 Public Square, Holley, NY 14470; **Town of Kendall**: Frank Clow, Town Hall, 1873 Kendall Road, Kendall, NY 14476; **Village of Lyndonville**: Virginia Cooper, Village Hall, 2 South Main Street, Lyndonville, NY 14098; **Village of Medina**: Elizabeth Childs, Village Hall, 600 Main Street, Medina, NY 14103; **Town of Murray**: Marsha DeFilipps, Town Hall, 3840 Route 31, Holley, NY 14470; **Town of Ridgeway**: Richard Nellist, Town Hall, 410 West Avenue, Medina, NY 14103; **Town of Shelby**: Alice Zacher, Town Hall, 11248 Maple Ridge Road, Medina, NY 14103; **Town of Yates**: Virginia Cooper, Town Hall, 8 South Main Street, Lyndonville, NY 14098

Orleans County Historical Association
13979 Allen Road
Albion, NY 14411
(716) 589-4690

Ossining Historical Society and Museum
196 Croton Avenue
Ossining, NY 10562
(914) 941-0001

Oswego County Historian
46 East Bridge Street
Oswego, NY 13126
(315) 342-8385; (315) 349-8383 FAX
Barbara J. Dix
Hours: County Clerk's Office: Mon–Fri 9:00–5:00; Historian: Mon–Fri 8:30–4:00
Municipal Historians: **Town of Albion**: Florence Gardner, 312 County Route 52, Altmar, NY 13302, (315) 298-5723; **Village of Altmar**: Florence Gardner, Town of Albion Historian (see above); **Town of Amboy**: Luceille Dunn, Route 1, Williamstown, NY 13493; **Town of Boylston**: Rita Rombach, 906 North Church Road, Lacona, NY 13083, (315) 387-5471; **Village of Central Square**: Irene Meyers, Rt. 3, Box 132, Central Square, NY 13036, (315) 668-2178; **Village of Cleveland**: post vacant; **Town of Constantia**: Joni Hinds, Clay Street, Cleveland, NY 13042, (315) 675-8611; **City of Fulton**: Mary Ellen Ross, 8 Riverview Drive, Fulton, NY 13069, (315) 598-4616; **Town of Granby**: John Byard, 100 Rochester Street, Apartment 206, Fulton, NY 13069, (315) 593-1306; **Town of Hannibal** and **Village of Hannibal**: Lowell Newvine, Auburn Street, Hannibal, NY 13074, (315) 564-5650; **Town of Hastings**: Irene Meyers, Village of Central Square Historian (see above); **Village of Lacona**: Marie Parsons, PO Box 178, Sandy Creek,

NY 13145-0178; **Town of Mexico** and **Village of Mexico**: Bonnie Shumway, PO Box 309, Mexico, NY 13114, (315) 963-7034; **Town of Minetto**: Katy Mantaro, West Fifth Street Road, Oswego, NY 13126, (315) 343-3025; **Town of New Haven**: Nancy Searles, Rt. 1, Box 263, Oswego, NY 13126, (315) 963-3159; **Town of Orwell**: Robert G. Pratt, Box 26, Orwell, NY 13426, (315) 298-2884; **City of Oswego**: Rosemary Nesbitt, 119 West Fourth Street, Oswego, NY 13126, (315) 343-1784; **Town of Oswego**: Dr. Charles Groat, Rt. 3, California Road, Oswego, NY 13126, (315) 343-0719; **Town of Palermo**: Beverly Beck, 139 Island Road, Phoenix, NY 13135, (315) 593-6825; **Town of Parish** and **Village of Parish**: Bridget Swartz, PO Box 145, Parish, NY 13131, (315) 625-7833; **Town of Phoenix**: post vacant; **Village of Phoenix**: post vacant; **Village of Pulaski**: Barbara Mandigo, Centerville Road, Pulaski, NY 13142, (315) 298-5417; **Town of Redfield**: Helen Anken, Rt. 2, McCaw Road, Williamstown, NY 13493, (315) 599-7737; **Town of Richland**: Mary E. Parker, 7384 Lake Street, Pulaski, NY 13142, (315) 298-5174; **Town of Sandy Creek** and **Village of Sandy Creek**: Marie Parsons, Village of Lacona Historian (see above); **Town of Schroeppel**: Peter Huntley, Rt. 3, Box 9A, Phoenix, NY 13135, (315) 668-3532; **Town of Scriba**: Charles D. Young, 2123 Candlewood Road, Rt. 8, Oswego, NY 13126, (315) 343-6871; **Town of Volney**: Fern E. Parsons, 2831 County Route 45, Fulton, NY 13069, (315) 598-3817, (315) 592-4177; **Town of West Monroe**: Lawrence Herbert, PO Box 25, West Monroe, NY 13167, (315) 668-2028; **Town of Williamstown**: Glenna Gorski, PO Box 54, Williamstown, NY 13493

Oswego County Historical Society
Richardson-Bates House Museum
135 East Third Street
Oswego, NY 13126
(315) 343-1342
Terrence M. Prior, Director
(city and rural directories, obituary indexes and county cemetery indexes)
research: $22.50 by mail

Otsego County Historian
Tuscan Road
Worcester, NY 12197
(607) 397-9705
Nancy Milavec
Municipal Historians: **Town of Burlington**: Walter F. Dauchy, Star Route 51, Burlington Flats, NY 13315; **Town of Butternuts**: Marion Webster, Black River Road, Gilbertsville, NY

13776; **Town of Cherry Valley** and **Village of Cherry Valley**: Helen Rury, Box 96, Main Street, Cherry Valley, NY 13320; **Village of Cooperstown**: Marjorie Tillapaugh, 28 Pioneer Street, Cooperstown, NY 13326; **Town of Decatur**: Mrs. Gene Schlierman, Rt. 2, Worcester, NY 12197; **Town of Edmeston**: Robert Nonenmacher, 59 South Street, Edmeston, NY 13335; **Town of Exeter**: John Stoltenborg, Rt. 1, Box 114, Hartwick, NY 13345; **Village of Gilbertsville**: Margaret P. Moore, 23 Spring Street, Gilbertsville, NY 13776; **Town of Hartwick**: Anita Harrison, Rt. 1, Box 37, Hartwick, NY 13348; **Town of Laurens**: post vacant; **Village of Laurens**: Richard Rose, Rural Delivery 3, Route 205, Oneonta, NY 13820; **Town of Maryland**: Dorothy Parmerter, PO Box 231, Schenevus, NY 12155; **Town of Middlefield**: Harriet Rogers, 63B Chestnut Street, Cooperstown, NY 13326; **Town of Milford** and **Village of Milford**: Sandra Bullard, Rt. 1, Milford, NY 13807; **Town of Morris**: Joyce Foote, PO Box 242, Morris, NY 13808; **Village of Morris**: post vacant; **Town of New Lisbon**: Virginia Schoradt, Rt. 1, Mount Vision, NY 13810; **City of Oneonta**: Floyd C. Allen, 15 Walling Boulevard, Oneonta, NY 13820; **Town of Oneonta**: Velma Green, West Oneonta, NY 13861; **Town of Otego**: Elma H. Mitchell, Rt. 1, Box 19, Otego, NY 13825; **Village of Otego**: Elma Mitchell, 26 Follett Street, Otego, NY 13825; **Town of Otsego**: Florence Michaels, Rt. 1, Box 32, Fly Creek, NY 13337; **Town of Pittsfield**: Barbara E. Lindholm, Rt. 3, Box 98, New Berlin, NY 13411; **Town of Plainfield**: Ida Bouck, Box 51, Lake Street, Richfield Springs, NY 13439; **Village of Richfield Springs**: Rose A. Agresti, Box 51, Lake Street, Richfield Springs, NY 13439; **Town of Roseboom**: Jeannette D. Smith, PO Box 65, Springfield Center, NY 13468; **Village of Schenevus**: Mildred Prager, 45 Main Street, Schenevus, NY 12155; **Town of Unadilla**: Shirley Goerlich, Rt. 3, Box 146-A, Bainbridge, NY 13733; **Village of Unadilla**: Patricia Sheret, 25 Main Street, Unadilla, NY 13849; **Town of Westford**: Elizabeth Harvard, Main Street, Westford, NY 13488; **Town of Worcester**: Winifred Bentley, Solar Bluffs, Worcester, NY 12197

Oyster Bay Historical Society
20 Summit Street
PO Box 297
Oyster Bay, NY 11771-0297
(516) 922-5032; (516) 922-6892 FAX
E-mail: obhistory@aol.com
http://members.aol.com/obhistory

Thomas A. Kuehhas, Director
Hours: Tue–Fri 10:00–2:00, Sat 9:00–1:00, Sun 1:00–4:00
Pub. *The Freeholder*, quarterly
(documents, deeds, letters, manuscripts of residents of Town of Oyster Bay from 1680 to the present, genealogies of local families; Theodore Roosevelt Collection)
$20.00 per year membership; search fee: $15.00 for members, $25.00 for nonmembers, includes five photocopies

Oysterponds Historical Society, Inc.
Box 844, Village Lane
Orient, NY 11957
(516) 323-2480
Courtney Burns, Director
Hours: Summer: Sat–Sun: 1:00–5:00, and all year by appointment
Pub. *OHS Newsletter*, quarterly
(east end of Long Island's North Fork; maritime and agricultural area, regional New York history, special exhibits and events)
$20.00 per year membership for individuals, $35.00 per year membership for families

Palatine Settlement Society
PO Box 183
Saint Johnsville, NY 13452
(518) 568-2346
Joyce Zbikowski, Secretary
Hours: by appointment
Pub. *Newsletter*, semiannually
(history of Mohawk Valley Palatines)
$10.00 per year membership for individuals, $17.00 per year membership for families, $5.00 per year membership for senior citizens

Parishville Historical Association
Parishville Museum
Main Street
PO Box 534
Parishville, NY 13672
(315) 265-7619
Emma Remington, Town Historian
Pub. *Parishville Museum*

Perinton Historical Society
18 Perrin Street
Fairport, NY 14450
(716) 223-3989; (716) 377-8208 (Director); (716) 388-0078 (Curator)
Matson Ewell, Museum Director; Imogene Blum, Museum Curator
Hours: Tue & Sun 2:00–4:00, Thur 7:00 P.M.–9:00 P.M.
Pub. *Perinton Historigram*, monthly
$10.00 per year membership for individuals, $8.00 per year membership for couples, $15.00 per year membership for families, $5.00 per year membership for senior citizens or students, $35.00 per year Patron membership; $50.00 per year Business or Professional membership

Town of Perth Historical Society
Rt. 6
Amsterdam, NY 12010
(518) 842-9497

Phelps Historical Society
PO Box 200
Phelps, NY 14532
John M. Parmelee, Town Historian

Pittstown Historical Society
Valley Falls, NY 12185

Plattekill Historical Society
PO Box 357
Clintondale, NY 12515

Poestenkill Historical Society
PO Box 140
Poestenkill, NY 12140-0140

Town of Pompey Historical Society
Pompey Town Hall
8354 Route 20
Manlius, NY 13104
(315) 677-9416
Lisa Moffa, Museum Chair; Dorothy De Angelo, Newsletter Editor
Hours: Museum: May–Sept: Sun 2:00–4:00, and by appointment; meetings: Apr–Oct
Pub. *Schoolhouse Happenings*, three times per year; *Town of Pompey Historical Society*, two times per year
(includes Delphi Falls, Oran, Pompey Center, Pompey Hill
$15.00 per year membership for individuals, $25.00 per year membership for families, $5.00 per year membership for students and senior citizens, $100.00 life membership; queries to Sylvia Shoebridge, Town Historian, Maple Hill Farm, 2327 Berry Road, Lafayette, NY 13084, (315) 677-3056

Pound Ridge Historical Society
The Pound Ridge Museum
Routes 137 and 172
PO Box 51
Pound Ridge, NY 10576
(914) 764-4333 (Museum)
Hours: Museum: Sat–Sun 2:00–4:00, and by appointment
Pub. *Pendulum*, four times per year
(history of Pound Ridge and its environs)
$15.00 per year membership; contact town historian (same address) for family history

Preserve It Now
PO Box 325
Fonda, NY 12068
(518) 922-7051

Princetown Historical Society
559 North Kelly Road
Schenectady, NY 12306
(518) 864-5218
Irma Mastrean, Princetown Historian
Hours: by appointment

Pultneyville Historical Society
PO Box 92
Pultneyville, NY 14538-0092
Ruth O. DeWitte, President
Pub. *Newsletter*, monthly

Putnam County Historian
Putnam County Office Facility
Myrtle Avenue
Mahopac Falls, NY 10542-0368
(914) 621-2302; (914) 628-0465 FAX
Municipal Historians: **Village of
Brewster**; Suzanne Truran, Village
Office, 208 East Main Street,
Brewster, NY 10509, (914) 279-3760,
or 42 Center Street, Brewster, NY
10509, (914) 279-2386; **Town of
Carmel**: Marilyn Cole Greene, Carmel
Town Hall, McAlpin Avenue,
Mahopac, NY 10541, (914) 628-1500,
or PO Box 367, Mahopac Falls, NY
10542-0367, (914) 628-0914; **Village
of Cold Spring**: Donald H.
MacDonald, Village Office, 87 Main
Street, Cold Spring, NY 10516, (914)
265-3611, or 72 Main Street, Cold
Spring, NY 10516, (914) 265-2756;
Town of Kent: Richard Muscarella,
Kent Town Offices, Route 52, Carmel,
NY 10512, (914) 225-2067, or 598
Horse Pound Road, Carmel, NY
10512, (914) 225-4882; **Village of
Nelsonville**: Village Office, 258 Main
Street, Nelsonville, NY 10516, (914)
265-2500; **Town of Patterson**:
Edward Scrivani, Patterson Town Hall,
Routes 311 and 164, Patterson, NY
12563, (914) 878-6500, or Rt. 3, Box
258, Patterson, NY 12563, (914) 878-
6897, (914) 279-5148 FAX; **Town of
Philipstown**: Donald H. MacDonald,
Philipstown Town Hall, 238 Main
Street, Cold Spring, NY 10516, (914)
265-3329, or 72 Main Street, Cold
Spring, NY 10516, (914) 265-2756;
Town of Putnam Valley: Stephen L.
Andersen, Putnam Valley Town Hall,
265 Oscawana Lake Road, Putnam
Valley, NY 10579, (914) 526-3280, or
PO Box 209, Putnam Valley, NY
10579-0209, (914) 528-4590; **Town of
Southeast**: Suzanne Truran, Southeast
Town Hall, 1 Main Street, PO Box O,
Brewster, NY 10509, (914) 279-2196,
or 42 Center Street, Brewster, NY
10509, (914) 279-2386

**Putnam County Historical Society
and Foundry School Museum**
63 Chestnut Street
Cold Spring, NY 10516
(914) 265-4010; (914) 265-2884 FAX
E-mail: pchs@highlands.com
Charlotte B. Eaton, Curator
Hours: Tue–Wed 10:00–4:00, Thur 1:00–
4:00, Sun 2:00–5:00 (research library
closed Sun)
Pub. *Newsletter*, semiannually

$25.00 per year membership for
individuals, $35.00 per year
membership for families, $10.00 per
year membership for students or senior
citizens, $50.00 per year Contributing
membership, $100.00 per year
Supporting membership, $250.00 per
year Sustaining membership

Putnam Valley Historical Society
301 Peekskill Hollow Road
PO Box 297
Putnam Valley, NY 10579
(914) 528-1024
Barbara Doyle, Director
Hours: Tue–Wed 10:00–3:00, and other
unscheduled times
Pub. *Potpourri*, three times per year
(genealogies of local families, not
verified; local history)
$10.00 per year membership for
individuals; donation for research use

**Historical Society Quaker Hill and
Pawling, Inc.**
(East Main Street—location)
PO Box 99 (mailing address)
Pawling, NY 12564
(914) 855-5891; (914) 855-1248
(Programs and Newsletter)
Betty Smith, Programs and Newsletter
Hours: Sat–Sun (May–Oct) 2:00–4:00
Pub. *Newsletter*, about four times per
year
no cost

**Carriage House Museum of the
Queen Village Historical Society**
2 North Park Street
PO Box 38
Camden, NY 13316
(315) 245-4652 (answering machine)
Elaine H. Norton, Vice President; Mary
Lou Park, Curator
Hours: 1 May–30 Oct: Tue–Wed & Fri–
Sat 1:00–4:00, and by appointment;
special exhibits May–Oct & Dec
(Camden area family histories and
photos on file, as well as histories of
area churches, schools, businesses,
services, maps)
$5.00 per year membership for
individuals, $10.00 per year
membership for families, $2.00 per
year membership for students, $25.00
life membership; no admission fee;
search fee: $5.00 to cover photocopies
and mailing

Queens County Historian
1543 150th Place
Whitestone, NY 11357
Henry Ludder

Queens Historical Society
Kingsland Homestead
143-35 37th Avenue
Flushing, NY 11363
(718) 939-0647; (718) 539-9885 FAX

Mary Cornell, Genealogy Research
Analyst
Hours: Mon–Sat 9:30–5:00 for office
assistance
Pub. *QHS Newsletter*
$15.00 per year membership for
individuals, $10.00 per year
membership for senior citizens and
students

Remsen-Steuben Historical Society
Prospect Street
PO Box 284
Remsen, NY 13438
(315) 831-5443
Leonard Wynne, President

Rensselaer County Historian
(post vacant, contact Rensselaer County
Historical Society, 59 Second Street,
Troy, NY 12180)
Municipal Historians: **Town of Berlin**:
Margaret Kinn, PO Box 314, South
Main Street, Berlin, NY 12022, (518)
658-2467; **Town of Brunswick**:
Sharon Zankel, 734 Pinewoods
Avenue Extension, Troy, NY 12180,
(518) 279-9714; **Village of Castleton-
on-Hudson**: Ellen Allen, 99 South
Main Street, Castleton, NY 12033,
(518) 732-4098; **Town of East
Greenbush**: Beverly Kennedy, East
Greenbush Town Hall, 225 Columbia
Turnpike, Rensselaer, NY 12144,
(518) 477-4614; **Town of Grafton**:
Irma Wagar, Grafton, NY 12082;
Town of Hoosick: Joseph Holloway,
95 Main Street, Hoosick Falls, NY
12090, (518) 686-9008; **Village of
Hoosick Falls**: George Peer, 24
Munsell Street, Hoosick Falls, NY
12090, (518) 686-9015;
Lansingburgh (unincorporated
village): post vacant; **Town of Nassau**:
Patricia Ann Davis, 29 Church Street,
Nassau, NY 12123, (518) 766-4449,
(518) 766-2343; **Village of Nassau**:
post vacant; **Town of North
Greenbush**: Karen Hartgen Fisher, 27
Jordan Road, Troy, NY 12180, (518)
283-0534; **Town of Petersburg**: Peter
Schaapok, 296 Potter Hill Road,
Petersburgh, NY 12138, (518) 658-
2963; **Town of Pittstown**: Ellen L.
Wiley, 35 Sherman Road, Valley Falls,
NY 12185, (518) 663-5601; **Town of
Poestenkill**: Florence Hill, PO Box
210, Poestenkill, NY 12140; **City of
Rensselaer**: post vacant; **Town of
Sand Lake**: Mary French, PO Box
221, Averill Park, NY 12018; **Town of
Schaghticoke**: Christina Kelly, 111
Roe Road, Northline Drive, Melrose,
NY 12121, (518) 235-5813; **Village of
Schaghticoke**: Richard Lohnes, 77
Main Street, Schaghticoke, NY 12154,
(518) 753-4721; **Town of Schodack**:
Irene R. Saganich, Schodack, Town of
Schodack, 1771 Columbia Turnpike,

Castleton, NY 12033, (518) 477-5421;
Town of Stephentown: post vacant;
City of Troy: post vacant; **Village of
Valley Falls**: Judy Hoag, State Street,
Valley Falls, NY 12185, (518) 753-
4936

Rensselaer County Historical Society
59 Second Street
Troy, NY 12180
(518) 272-7232; (518) 273-1264 FAX
E-mail: rchs@crisny.org
http://www.crisny.org/not-for-profit/rchs
Stacy P. Draper, Curator
Hours: Library: Tue–Fri 1:00–4:00, Sat
10:00–4:00; Museum: Feb–Dec: Tue–
Sat 1:00–4:00
Pub. *Newsletter: Current History*,
quarterly
(family history and local history)
$35.00 per year membership for
individuals, $50.00 per year
membership for families or Sustainer
membership, $15.00 per year
membership for students, $100.00 per
year Sponsor membership, $250.00
per year Patron membership, $500.00
per year Betsey Howard Hart
Company membership, $1,000.00 per
year Benefactor membership; search
fees: $20.00 per request

City of Rensselaer Historical Society
"The Agents House"
15 Forbes Avenue
Rensselaer, NY 12144

Rensselaerville Historical Society
(Grist Mill—location)
PO Box 8 (mailing address)
Rensselaerville, NY 12147
(518) 797-5154
Hours: by appointment only
Pub. *Rensselaerville Press*, quarterly
(Town of Rensselaerville and the
immediate area)
$5.00 per year membership for
individuals

Richmond County Historian
(post vacant)

Richville Historical Association
Gimlet Street
Richville, NY 13681

Rochester Historical Society
Genealogy Section
485 East Avenue
Rochester, NY 14607
(716) 271-2705
Elizabeth G. Holahan, President; Meghan
Lodge, Administrator
Hours: Reference: Mon–Fri 10:00–4:00;
Archives: by appointment
Pub. *News and Notes*, periodically
(local history and genealogy of the
pioneer families of Rochester)
$25.00 per year membership for
individuals; $2.00 admission for adults

**Official Historian of Rockland
County**
12 Ashwood Lane
Garnerville, NY 10923
(914) 942-3383 (Office); (914) 947-1231
(Home)
Thomas F. X. Casey
Municipal Historians: **Village of
Airmont**: Robert A. Goetschius, 100
Smith Hill Road, Monsey, NY 10952,
(914) 357-1611; **Village of Chestnut
Ridge**: Dr. Eudice Charney, 277 Old
Nyack Turnpike, Spring Valley, NY
10977; **Town of Clarkstown**: Robert
Knight, 18 Gilchrest Road, Congers,
NY 10920, (914) 268-3012 (Home),
(914) 364-3560 (Office); **Village of
Grand View-on-Hudson**: Anita Bell,
281 River Road, Grand View-on-
Hudson, NY 10960, (914) 398-0908;
Town of Haverstraw: Thomas F. X.
Casey; **Village of Haverstraw**: Jack
Berrian, 3 First Street, Haverstraw, NY
10927, (914) 429-7811; **Village of
Hillburn**: Chuck Stead, PO Box 915,
Hillburn, NY 10931, (914) 753-3667;
Village of Kasar: post vacant; **Village
of Montebello**: Craig Long, 120
Wayne Avenue, Suffern, NY 10901,
(914) 357-6383 (Home), (914) 357-
1882 (Office); **Village of New
Hempstead**: Stewart Schwartz, 189
Summit Park Road, Pomona, NY
10970, (914) 354-1122; **Village of
New Square**: Daniel Goldstein, New
Square Village, Spring Valley, NY
10977; **Village of Nyack**: Jean Pardo,
111 Sickles Avenue, Nyack, NY
10960, (914) 353-0851 or 12 First
Avenue, Nyack, NY 10960, (914) 358-
5229; **Town of Orangetown**: Mary
Cardenas, 66 Pine Tree Lane, Tappan,
NY 10983, (914) 359-1184; **Village of
Piermont**: Grace Meyer, Piermont
Public Library, 153 Hudson Terrace,
Piermont, NY 10968, (914) 359-4595;
Village of Pomona: post vacant, 85
Camp Hill Road, Pomona, NY 10970;
Town of Ramapo: Craig Long, 120
Wayne Avenue, Suffern, NY 10901,
(914) 357-6383 (Home), (914) 357-
1882 (Office); **Village of Sloatsburg**:
Harrison Bush, 6 Laurel Road,
Sloatsburg, NY 10974, (914) 753-
5990; **Village of South Nyack**: Myra
Starr, 146 South Broadway, South
Nyack, NY 10960, (914) 634-9629
(Office), (914) 358-2224 (Home);
Village of Spring Valley: Robert
Rubin, 2 Sky Lane Court, Suffern, NY
10901, (914) 368-3468 (Home); **Town
of Stony Point**: Stuart Gates, 29 Jay
Street, Stony Point, NY 10980, (914)
786-3861; **Village of Suffern**: Gardner
F. Watts, 15 Beech Road, Suffern, NY
10901, (914) 357-3667; **Village of
Upper Nyack**: Winston Perry, Jr., 319
North Broadway, Nyack, NY 10960,

(914) 358-0552; **Village of West
Haverstraw**: Cathy Grant, 1 Oldfield
Court, Garnerville, NY 10923, (914)
942-2773; **Village of Wesley Hills**:
Thomas C. France, 1 Wesley Chapel
Road, Suffern, NY 10901, (914) 354-
1830

**The Historical Society of Rockland
County**
20 Zukor Road
New City, NY 10956-4388
(914) 634-9629; (914) 634-8690 FAX
Marie Koestler, Genealogy Researcher
Hours: Tue–Fri 9:30–5:00, Sat–Sun
1:00–5:00
Pub. *Historical Society of Rockland
County News*, quarterly; *South of the
Mountains*, quarterly, $20.00 per year
subscription
queries

Rome Historical Society
200 Church Street
Rome, NY 13440
(315) 336-5870; (315) 336-5912 FAX
Kathleen Hynes-Bouska, Archivist and
Educator
Hours: Mon–Fri 9:00–4:00, and by
appointment
Pub. *Annals and Recollections*, quarterly,
$1.00 per issue
(Rome history, Erie Canal)
$10.00 per year membership; library
admission fee for non-members: $5.00
per day

Roxbury Burrough's Club
Main Street
Roxbury, NY 12474

Rye Historical Society
1 Purchase Street
Rye, NY 10580-3002
(914) 967-7588 (Society); (914) 967-
7595 (Director)
Jan Kelsey, Interim Director and Rye
City Historian
Hours: Office: Mon–Fri 9:00–5:00

Sachem Historical Society, Inc.
288 Gillette Avenue
Bayport, NY 11705
(516) 472-1559
$5.00 per year membership

Sacket Harbor Historical Society
Main Street
Sacket Harbor, NY 13685
(315) 646-3525

Saint Lawrence County Historian
Saint Lawrence County Historical
Association
3 East Main Street
PO Box 8
Canton, NY 13617
(315) 386-8133; (315) 386-8134 FAX
E-mail: slcha@northnet.org
Trent Trulock, Executive Director

Hours: Tue–Sat noon–4:00

Municipal Historians: **Town of Brasher**: Carl Goodrich, PO Box 132, Brasher Falls, NY 13613, (315) 389-5717; **Town of Canton** and **Village of Canton**: Linda Casserly, c/o Municipal Building, Canton, NY 13617, (315) 386-1633; **Town of Clare**: Claudia Griffin, 2467 CR 27, Russell, NY 13684, (315) 386-4233; **Town of Clifton**: Jeanne Reynolds, PO Box 640, Cranberry Lake, NY 12927, (315) 848-2900; **Town of Colton**: Dennis Eickoff, PO Box 109, Colton, NY 13625, (315) 262-2800; **Town of DeKalb**: Virginia Fischer or Bryan Thompson, PO Box 37, 15 School Street, DeKalb Junction, NY 13630, (315) 347-3554; **Town of Depeyster**: Adelaide Steele, 2212 SH 184, Heuvelton, NY 13654, (315) 344-7945; **Town of Edwards**: Edith C. Duffy or Katheryn Fuller, PO Box 100, 8 First Street, Edwards, NY 13635, (315) 562-3511; **Village of Edwards**: post vacant; **Town of Fine**: Jean Grimm, 536 Oswegatchie Trail Road, Box 915, Oswegatchie, NY 13670, (315) 848-2319, (315) 848-3152 FAX; **Town of Fowler**: Connie Bishop, 1499 CR 22, Gouverneur, NY 13642, (315) 287-2728; **Town of Gouverneur**: Dorothy Dillon, 4496 SH 58, Gouverneur, NY 13642, (315) 287-3693; **Village of Gouverneur**: Nelson B. Winters, PO Box 48, Gouverneur, NY 13642, (315) 287-0934; **Town of Hammond** and **Village of Hammond**: Valera Bickelhaupt, 320 Lake Street, Hammond, NY 13646; **Town of Hermon**: Carol Holly, (315) 347-2487; **Village of Hermon**: Mary H. Smallman, 138 Church Street, Hermon, NY 13652, (315) 347-3221; **Village of Heuvelton**: Persis Y. Boyesen, 5111 CR 6, Ogdensburg, NY 13669, (315) 393-1538; **Town of Hopkinton**: Addie Miller, 290 Wilson Road, Saint Regis Falls, NY 12980, (315) 328-4456; **Town of Lawrence**: Elizabeth Winn, PO Box 15, North Lawrence, NY 12967, (315) 389-4458; **Town of Lisbon**: Mrs. Terry Fischer, PO Box 216, Lisbon, NY 13658, (315) 393-7986; **Town of Louisville**: Paula Beattie, 611 CR 39, Massena, NY 13662, (315) 769-0379; **Town of Macomb**: Eloise Emrich, 6726 SH 58, Hammond, NY 13646, (315) 578-2247; **Town of Madrid**: Marian Bouchard, 2273 SH 310, Madrid, NY 13660, (315) 322-4419; **Town of Massena** and **Village of Massena**: Theresa Sharp, Town of Massena Museum and Historian's Office, 200 East Orvis Street, Massena, NY 13662, (315) 769-8571; **Town of**

Morristown and **Village of Morristown**: Lorraine Bogardus, 518 River Road East, Ogdensburg, NY 13669, (315) 375-6390; **Town of Norfolk**: Leon Burnap, 105 River Road, Norfolk, NY 13667; **Village of Norwood**: Susan Lyman or Patricia Veraldo, 38 Prospect Street, Norwood, NY 13668, (315) 353-4505; **City of Ogdensburg** and **Town of Oswegatchie**: Persis Y. Boyesen, 5111 CR 6, Ogdensburg, NY 13669, (315) 393-1538; **Town of Parishville**: Emma Remington, PO Box 534, Parishville, NY 13672, (315) 265-7619; **Town of Piercefield**: Stacy Gensel, 15 Circle Drive, Tupper Lake, NY 12986; **Town of Pierrepont**: Charlotte Regan, 5893 CR 24, Canton, NY 13617, (315) 386-8311; **Town of Pitcairn**: Pamela Conlin, 31 Edwards Road, Harrisville, NY 13648, (315) 543-2733; **Town of Potsdam**: Susan Lyman or Patricia Veraldo, 38 Prospect Street, Norwood, NY 13668, (315) 353-4505; **Village of Potsdam**: Betsy Travis, Potsdam Public Museum, Civic Center, Park Street, Potsdam, NY 13676, (315) 265-6910; **Village of Rensselaer Falls**: Dorothy Crane or Samuel McAdoo, PO Box 102, Rensselaer Falls, NY 13680, (315) 344-7911; **Village of Richville**: Stella Tamblin, PO Box 207, Richville, NY 13681, (315) 287-0182; **Town of Rossie**: Elwood Simons, 1403 CR 3, Rossie, NY 13646, (315) 324-5882; **Town of Russell**: Lochland Jeffries, PO Box 708, Russell, NY 13684, (315) 347-4666; **Town of Stockholm**: Mildred S. Jenkins, 2295 CR 47, Potsdam, NY 13676, (315) 353-4520; **Town of Waddington** and **Village of Waddington**: E. Jane Layo, 39 West Saint Lawrence Avenue, Box 277, Waddington, NY 13694, (315) 388-5967

The Saint Lawrence County Historical Association at the Silas Wright Museum
3 East Main Street
PO Box 8
Canton, NY 13617
(315) 386-8133; (315) 386-8134 FAX
E-mail: slcha@northnet.org
Trent Trulock, Executive Director
Hours: Tue–Sat noon–4:00
Pub. *The Quarterly*
$25.00 per year membership for individuals, $35.00 per year membership for families, $20.00 per year membership for students or senior citizens, $50.00 per year Contributing membership, $100.00 per year Sustaining membership, $250.00 per year Patron membership

Saint Nicholas Society of New York City
122 East 58th Street
New York, NY 10022-1939
Pub. *Weathercock*, quarterly

Salisbury Historical Society
Rt. 1
Dolgeville, NY 13329
(315) 429-3330
Dorothea S. Ives
Pub. *Salisbury Crier*

Sand Lake Historical Society
(Averill Park, NY 12018—location)
PO Box 492 (mailing address)
West Sand Lake, NY 12196
(518) 674-3127

Saratoga County Historian
40 McMaster Street
Ballston Spa, NY 12020
(518) 884-4749; (518) 884-4170 FAX
Karen Ufford Campola, Historian
Hours: Tue–Thur 9:00–4:00
Municipal Historians: **Village of Ballston** and **Town of Ballston Lake**: Katherine Briaddy, 4 Edward Road, Ballston Lake, NY 12019, (518) 399-4436; **Town of Ballston Spa**: Jean Puckhaber, 22 Hyde Boulevard, Ballston Spa, NY 12020, (518) 885-5809; **"Brookside"**: Chris Morley, 6 Charlton, Ballston Spa, NY 12020, (518) 885-4000; **Town of Charlton**: Laura Linder, 2115 Route 67, Charlton, NY 12019, (518) 882-6866; **Town of Clifton Park**: John L. Scherer, 113 Vischers Ferry Road, Rt. 2, Rexford, NY 12148, (518) 371-2619; **Town of Corinth** and **Village of Corinth**: Arthur Eggleston, 22 Mallery Street, PO Box 745, Corinth, NY 12822, (518) 654-6809; **Town of Day**: Nancy Norris, 82 Yates Hill Road, Hadley, NY 12835, (518) 696-3874; **Town of Edinburg**: Priscilla Edwards, 240 Tennantville Road, Edinburg, NY 12134, (518) 863-8337; **Town of Galway** and **Village of Galway**: Phyllis Keeler, R.D. 2, 6023 Crooked Street, Broadalbin, NY 12025, (518) 882-9765; **Town of Greenfield**: Mary DeMarco, R.D. 3, Daniels Road, Saratoga Springs, NY 12866, (518) 587-1927; **Town of Hadley**: Carolyn Weiss, 1057 Hunt Lake Road North, Corinth, NY 12822, (518) 696-2768; **Town of Halfmoon** and **Village of Halfmoon**: Ellen Kennedy, 15 Stone Quarry Road, Clifton Park, NY 12065, (518) 371-7410; **Town of Malta**: Ruth W. Roerig, 60 Round Lake Road, Ballston Lake, NY 12019, (518) 885-5296; **City of Mechanicville**: Paul Loatman, 607 Park Avenue, Mechanicville, NY 12118, (518) 664-7037; **Town of Milton**: Irene Wood, 111 Saratoga Avenue, Ballston Spa,

NY 12020, (518) 885-9111 (Work), (518) 885-9014 (Home); **Town of Moreau**: John Rafferty, 251 Gansevoort Road, Gansevoort, NY 12831, (518) 792-2824; **Town of Northumberland**: Georgia Ball, 6 Catherine Street, PO Box 195, Gansevoort, NY 12831, (518) 793-2017; **Town of Providence**: Mary Packer, 7189 Barkersville Road, Rt. 1, Middle Grove, NY 12850, (518) 882-6550; **Village of Round Lake**: Mary Hesson, PO Box 214, Round Lake, NY 12151, (518) 899-2800 (Home), (518) 899-2207 (Work); **Town of Saratoga**: Thomas N. Wood, III, 1104 Route 29, Schuylerville, NY 12871, (518) 695-6780 (evenings); **City of Saratoga Springs**: Martha Stonequist, 297 Broadway, Saratoga Springs, NY 12866, (518) 587-2358; **Village of Schuylerville**: Thomas N. Wood, III, Town of Saratoga Historian (see above); **Village of South Glens Falls**: John Rafferty, 10538 Tanglewood Drive, South Glens Falls, NY 12803; **Town of Stillwater** and **Village of Stillwater**: Linda Sanders, Box 700, Stillwater, NY 12170, (518) 664-4614 FAX (at Town Hall), (518) 664-6140; **Village of Victory**: Thomas N. Wood, III, Town of Saratoga Historian (see above); **Town of Waterford**: Dennis Rivage, 4 Third Avenue, Waterford, NY 12188, (518) 237-6733; **Village of Waterford**: Ms. Merle Doud, 46 South Street, Waterford, NY 12188, (518) 237-1844; **Town of Wilton**: Lorraine Westcott, 10 Waller Road, Gansevoort, NY 12831, (518) 584-2839
search fees: to $20.00

Saratoga County Historical Society
Brookside-Saratoga County History Center
6 Charlton Street
Ballston Spa, NY 12020
(518) 885-4000
Jennifer Ley, Director
Hours: Tue noon–8:00, Wed–Fri 10:00–4:00, Sat noon–4:00
Pub. *Columns*, bimonthly; *Grist Mill*, annually
(Saratoga County history and genealogy; genealogical research done by professional genealogist)
from $15.00 per year membership; research prices on request

Historical Society of Saratoga Springs
Casino Congress Park
PO Box 216
Saratoga Springs, NY 12866
(518) 584-6920

Sardinia Historical Society
(Savage Road, Sardinia, NY 14134—location)
3829 Creek Road (mailing address)
Chaffee, NY 14030
(716) 496-8847

Scarsdale Historical Society
937 Post Road
Scarsdale, NY 10583
(914) 723-1744
Kay Fiedler, Director

Schenectady County Historian
Schenectady County Office Building
620 State Street
Schenectady, NY 12305-2113
Larry W. Hart
Municipal Historians: **Village of Delanson**: Donna M. O'Connor, Delanson Village Hall, Delanson, NY 12053; **Town of Duanesburg**: Arthur Willis, Duanesburg Town Hall, Route 20, Quaker Street, NY 12050; **Town of Glenville**: Henrietta Vander Veer, Glenville Town Hall, 18 Glenridge Road, Scotia, NY 12302; **Town of Niskayuna**: Donald Hutchinson, Niskayuna Town Hall, 1335 Balltown Road, Schenectady, NY 12309; **Town of Princetown**: Irma Mastrean, Rt. 5, North Kelly Road, Schenectady, NY 12306; **Town of Rotterdam**: John Papp, Jr., Rotterdam Town Hall, Vinewood Avenue, Schenectady, NY 12306; **City of Schenectady**: Larry Hart, Schenectady City Hall, Jay Street, Schenectady, NY 12305; **Village of Scotia**: Michelle J. Norris, Scotia History Center, Scotia Village Hall, 4 North Ten Broeck Street, Scotia, NY 12302

Schenectady County Historical Society
32 Washington Avenue
Schenectady, NY 12305
(518) 374-0263
Elsie M. Maddaus, Archivist/Librarian
Hours: Mon–Fri 1:00–5:00, second Sat 9:00–1:00
Pub. *SCHS Newsletter*, bimonthly (local history and genealogy)
from $25.00 per year membership; research: $12.00 per hour, 20¢ per copy

Schoharie Colonial Heritage Association
PO Box 554
Schoharie, NY 12157
(518) 295-7505
Linda Feuz, President

Schoharie County Historian
c/o Armandine Handy, Town Historian, Town of Sharon
PO Box 335
Sharon Springs, NY 13459

Mildred L. Bailey
Municipal Historians: **Town of Blenheim**: Josephine Fuller, North Blenheim, NY 12131; **Town of Broome**: Betty Chichester, Rt. 2, Middleburgh, NY 12122; **Town of Carlisle**: Myron Brown, Rt. 1, Cobleskill, NY 12043; **Town of Cobleskill** and **Village of Cobleskill**: Mary Clist, Cobleskill Public Library, Cobleskill, NY 12043; **Town of Conesville**: Beatrice Mattice, Rt. 1, Gilboa, NY 12076; **Town of Esperance**: Kenneth Jones, Church Street, Esperance, NY 12066; **Village of Esperance**: Vernon Putnam, 417 South Main Street, Schoharie, NY 12157; **Town of Fulton**: Gladys Wayman, Fultonham, NY 12071; **Town of Gilboa**: Richard Lewis, Rt. 1, Gilboa, NY 12076; **Town of Jefferson**: Mildred L. Bailey (see above); **Town of Middleburgh** and **Village of Middleburgh**: Helene Farrell, 60 Prospect Street, Middleburgh, NY 12122; **Town of Richmondville**: Reginald Clay, 39 Summit Street, Richmondville, NY 12149; **Village of Richmondville**: post vacant; **Town of Schoharie**: Susan Kennedy, Schoharie, NY 12157; **Village of Schoharie**: post vacant; **Town of Seward**: Beryl Warner, Dorloo, NY 12099; **Town of Sharon**: Mrs. Armandine Handy, PO Box 335, Sharon Springs, NY 13459; **Village of Sharon Springs**: post vacant; **Town of Summit**: Mr.VanBuren Lamb, Summit, NY 12175; **Town of Wright**: Mrs. Frank Westfall, Rt. 2, Schoharie, NY 12157

Schoharie County Historical Society
(North Main Street—location)
Rt. 2, Box 30A (mailing address)
Schoharie, NY 12157
(518) 295-7192
Christine Palmatier, Librarian/Archivist; Martha Foland, Genealogy Volunteer
Hours: 1 May–31 Oct: Museum: Tue–Sat 10:00–5:00, Sun noon–5:00; Library: Tue–Sat 10:00–noon & 1:00–4:30, Sun 1:00–4:30
Pub. *Schoharie County Historical Review*, semiannually
(New York, Schoharie County history, folklore)
$25.00 per year membership for individuals, $40.00 per year membership for families, $20.00 per year membership for senior citizens, $50.00 per year Sustaining membership, $75.00 per year Supporting membership, $100.00 per year Benefactor membership; library use: free to members and county residents, $6.00 per day for all others; research requests by mail to

Genealogy Volunteer: $10.00 for the first hour, $8.00 for each additional hour

Schroeppel Historical Society
Corner Main and Volney Streets
Phoenix, NY 13135
Betty Thompson, President

Schroon-North Hudson Historical Society, Inc.
Main Street
Schroon Lake, NY 12870
Jack Richards, President
Pub. *SNHHS Newsletter*

Schuyler County Historian
3460 County Road 28
Watkins Glen, NY 14891
(607) 535-4577
Barbara H. Bell
Municipal Historians: **Village of Burdett**: post vacant; **Town of Catharine**: Carol Fagnan, 2351 Oak Hill Road, Alpine, NY 14850-9760; **Town of Cayuta**: Charlotte Collins, 1100 Conkrite Road, Cayuta, NY 14824; **Town of Dix**: Jean Kosty, Watkins Glen Municipal Building, North Franklin Street, Watkins Glen, NY 14891; **Town of Hector**: Sandra Bradford, 5588 Mark Taber Road, Trumansburg, NY 14886; **Town of Montour** and **Village of Montour Falls**: Louise Stillman, Box 366, Montour Falls, NY 14865; **Village of Odessa**: post vacant; **Town of Orange**: Marian Ellis, 3051 County Road 22, Watkins Glens, NY 14891; **Town of Reading**: Barbara H. Bell, County Historian (see above); **Town of Tyrone**: Colleen Howell, 3364 County Road 22, Bradford, NY 14815; **Village of Watkins Glen**: Mrs. Marian Boyce, 2470 County Road 16, Watkins Glen, NY 14891

Schuyler County Historical Society
108 North Catharine Street
PO Box 651
Montour Falls, NY 14865
(607) 535-4577
Belva Dickinson, Museum Director; Doris Gauvin, Director
Hours: Mon–Fri 10:00–4:00
Pub. *Schuyler County Historical Society Journal* (not genealogical), quarterly, $1.25 per issue for non-members
(ten exhibit rooms of local history, plus research library)
$10.00 per year membership for individuals, $15.00 per year double membership, $25.00 per year Sustaining membership; admission by donation for non members

Scotia History Center
Scotia Village Hall
4 North Ten Broeck
Scotia, NY 12302

Michelle J. Norris, Scotia Village Historian

Seaford Historical Society
(Waverly Avenue—location)
2234 Jackson Avenue (mailing address)
Seaford, NY 11783
(516) 781-5217

Seneca County Historian
1 Di Pronio Drive
Waterloo, NY 13165
(315) 539-5655, ext. 2068
Betty Auten
Municipal Historians: **Town of Covert**: Maurice Patterson, PO Box 323, Interlaken, NY 14847; **Town of Fayette**: Cynthia Black, 1439 Yellow Tevern Road, Waterloo, NY 13165; **Village of Interlaken**: Maurice Patterson, PO Box 323, Interlaken, NY 14847; **Town of Junius**: Irene Cottrell, Stone Church Road, Waterloo, NY 13165; **Town of Lodi**: Edith Brown, 8479 Maple Street, Lodi, NY 14860; **Village of Lodi**: Clayton Brown, 8479 Maple Street, Lodi, NY 14860; **Town of Ovid**: Mrs. John Holley, Center Road, Ovid, NY 14521; **Town of Romulus**: post vacant; **Town of Seneca Falls**: post vacant, send requests c/o Town Office, 10 Fall Street, Seneca Falls, NY 13148; **Village of Seneca Falls**: post vacant; **Town of Tyre**: Mrs. Lars Olufsen, Rt. 1, Box 1392, Seneca Falls, NY 13148; **Town of Varick**: Charmion Boyle Dinsmore, 2385 Willers Road, Seneca Falls, NY 13148; **Town of Waterloo**: Betty Auten, 1 Di PronioDrive, Waterloo, NY 13165, (315) 539-5655, ext. 2068; **Village of Waterloo**: Beatrice Contant, c/o Waterloo Historical Society, 31 East Williams Street, Waterloo, NY 13165

Seneca Falls Historical Society
55 Cayuga Street
Seneca Falls, NY 13148
(315) 568-8412
Frances T. Barbieri, Education Coordinator
Hours: Mon–Fri 9:00–5:00, Sat noon–4:00, Sun (Jun–Sept) noon–4:00
Pub. *S.F.H.S. Newsletter*, monthly (local history, New York, women's rights)
from $15.00 per year membership

Sharon Historical Society
Main Street
Sharon Springs, NY 13459
(518) 284-2350
Dorcas Comrie, Curator
Hours: 1 Jul–Labor Day, and by appointment
$5.00 per year membership; no genealogical research services, contact Armandine Handy, Town Historian, Box 335, Sharon Springs, NY 13459

Sidney Historical Association
Civic Center, Liberty Street
PO Box 2217
Sidney, NY 13838
(607) 563-1617 (President); (607) 563-9527 (Curator)
Neila C. Hayes, President
Hours: Tue 1:45–4:45
search fee: copies plus mailing costs

Silver Creek Historical Society
172 Central Avenue
Silver Creek, NY 14136
(716) 934-3240

Smithtown Historical Society
(5 North Country Road, Route 25A—location)
PO Box 69 (mailing address)
Smithtown, NY 11787
(516) 265-6768
Louise Hall, Director; Bradley L. Harris, President
Hours: Mon–Fri 9:00–4:00
(Smithtown history, Smith genealogy)

Snug Harbor Cultural Center
1000 Richmond Terrace
Staten Island, NY 10301
(718) 448-2500; (718) 442-8534 FAX
Celia Reilly, Director; Brian Rehr, Associate PR/Marketing Department
Hours: Gallery: Wed–Sun noon–5:00
Pub. *Newsletter-Columns*, bimonthly from $25.00 per year membership

Sodus Bay Historical Society
PO Box 94
Sodus Point, NY 14551
(315) 483-4013
Marjorie McCleery, President
Pub. *SDHS Newsletter*

Somers Historical Society
Elephant Hotel
PO Box 336
Somers, NY 10589
(914) 277-4977
Florence S. Oliver, Acting Archivist
Hours: by appointment

Historical Association of South Jefferson
9 East Church Street
Adams, NY 13605
(315) 232-2616

Southampton Colonial Society
17 Meeting House Lane
PO Box 303
Southampton, NY 11969
(516) 283-1612; (516) 283-0605
Hours: 12 Jun–15 Sept
(early Long Island history; Southampton Historical Museum [PO Box 805, Bridgehampton, NY 11932], Old Halsey Homestead, Pelletreau Silversmith Shop, Conscience Point)

Southold Historical Society
(54235 Main Street—location)
PO Box 1 (mailing address)
Southold, NY 11971
(516) 765-5500
Clara Bjerknes, Archives Chair
Hours: Archives: Mon, Wed & Fri 9:30–noon; Office: Mon–Fri 9:30–2:30
$10.00 per year membership

Spencer Historical Society
289 Fisher Settlement
Spencer, NY 14883
Laura C. Uhl, President
Hours: Memorial Day–Labor Day: Sun 2:00–5:00
Pub. *SHS Quarterly Newsletter*, quarterly (genealogies of Spencer residents)

Stanford Historical Society
Stanfordville, NY 12581

Staten Island Historical Society
411 Clarke Avenue
Staten Island, NY 10306
(718) 351-9414 (Education Department);
(718) 351-1611 (Museum)
Pub. *Richmondtown Restoration: Newsletter of the Staten Island Historical Society*; *Staten Island Historian*, quarterly, $9.00 per year subscription

Stephentown Historical Society
PO Box 11
Stephentown, NY 12168
(518) 733-6070; (518) 733-5235
Virginia Atwater, Genealogist
Hours: by appointment
search fee is voluntary

Sterling Historical Society
(104A at Sterling Center—location)
14412 Woods Road (mailing address)
Sterling, NY 13156
(315) 947-6461 (President)
Don H. Richardson, President
Hours: Museum: Jun–Oct: Sun 2:00–5:00
$3.00 per year membership for individuals, $5.00 per year membership for families, $50.00 life membership; queries to Hallie Sweeting, Genealogist and Historian, 876 State Route 104A, Sterling, NY 13156, (315) 947-5653

Steuben County Historian
Rt. 2, Box 228
Bath, NY 14810
(607) 569-2301
Richard G. Sherer
Municipal Historians: **Town of Addison** and **Village of Addison**: Larry Mundy, Rt. 1, Box 273, Addison, NY 14801; **Village of Arkport**: post vacant; **Town of Avoca**: Grace S. Fox, Rt. 1, Avoca, NY 14809; **Town of Bath**: James E. Hope, 88 Geneva Street, Rt. 2, Bath, NY 14810; **Village of Bath**:

Robert Dwyer, 112 East Steuben Street, Bath, NY 14810; **Town of Bradford**: Lilly Rizzon, 9693 Switzer Road, Bradford, NY 14815; **Town of Cameron**: Douglas Sherer, Rt. 1, Cameron, NY 14819; **Town of Campbell**: Adeline Brown, 8529 Main Street, Campbell, NY 14821; **Town of Canisteo**: Virginia Dickey, Rt. 1, Cameron, NY 14819; **Village of Canisteo**: post vacant; **Town of Caton**: Margaret Smyers, Caton Town Hall, Rt. 2, Corning,NY 14830; **Town of Cohocton**: Mr. W. Merle Wheaton, Rt. 2, Box 355, Cohocton, NY 14826; **Village of Cohocton**: post vacant; **City of Corning**: Lois Janes, 70 East Third Street, Corning, NY 14830; **Town of Corning**: Mrs. Marion Eberenz, Rt. 2, Davis Road, Corning, NY 14830; **Town of Dansville**: Sarah Gates, Rt. 2, Arkport, NY 14807; **Town of Erwin**: Joseph Kane, 108 Hamilton Circle, Painted Post, NY 14870; **Town of Fremont**: Joann Spencer, Rt. 2, Arkport, NY 14807; **Town of Greenwood**: Gerald Mullen, Rt. 2, Box 183, Andover, NY 14806; **Village of Hammondsport**: Gordon Herrick, 33 Main Street, Hammondsport, NY 14840; **Town of Hartsville**: Betty Caple, Rt. 1, Hornell, NY 14843; **Town of Hornby**: Lillian Adams, Rt. 3, Corning, NY 14830; **City of Hornell**: Mrs. Robert Oakes, 58 Bennett Street, Hornell, NY 14843; **Town of Hornellsville**: Mary Ann Rutski, 475 Cleveland Avenue, North Hornell, NY 14843; **Town of Howard**: Mary Kenny, Rt. 4, Bath, NY 14810; **Town of Jasper**: Twila J. Brotzman, Rt. 1, Box 53A, Canisteo, NY 14823; **Town of Lindley**: Wilma Welty, PO Box 8, Lindley, NY 14858; **Village of North Hornell**: Mary Ann Rutski, 475 Cleveland Avenue, North Hornell, NY 14843; **Village of Painted Post**: Joseph Kane, 108 Hamilton Circle, Painted Post, NY 14870; **Town of Prattsburg**: Elsie Moon, 9 Goff Stream Road, Penfield, NY 14526; **Town of Puleney**: Emily Radigan, Rt. 1, Box 160, Prattsburg, NY 14873; **Town of Rathbone**: Isabelle Risley, Rt. 3, Addison, NY 14801; **Village of Riverside**: post vacant; **Village of Savona**: Samuel Gauss, 31 Main Street, Savona, NY 14879; **Village of South Corning**: Althea O. Roll, 20 South Maple Street, Corning, NY 14830; **Town of Thurston**: Shirley Edsall, 7494 Thurston Road, Campbell, NY 14821; **Town of Troupsburg**: Clara Knowles, State Route 36, Troupsburg, NY 14885; **Town of Tuscarora**: Agnes Kane, Rt. 4, Box 182, Addison, NY 14801; **Town of Urbana**: Richard G.

Sherer, County Historian (see above); **Town of Wayland**: Marion Scott, 14 Pine Street, Wayland, NY 14572; **Village of Wayland**: Bunnie Schubmehl, 15 North Main Street, Wayland, NY 14572; **Town of Wayne**: Donald A. Rowland, 744 East Lake Road, Hammondsport, NY 14840; **Town of West Union**: Anna Cerrillo, Rt. 2, Box 10, Rexville, NY 14877; **Town of Wheeler**: Margelia P. Foster, 9057 Route 53, Bath, NY 14810; **Town of Woodhull**: Norma Crane, Rt. 2, Box 160, Addison, NY 14801; **Village of Woodhull**: Kathryn Andrews, PO Box 95, Woodhull, NY 14898

Steuben County Historical Society
PO Box 349
Bath, NY 14810-0349
Pub. *Steuben Echoes*, quarterly
$3.00 per year membership for individuals, $4.00 per year membership for couples

Stony Creek Historical Association
Lanfear Road
Stony Creek, NY 12878
(518) 696-3488

Suffern Village Museum
61 Washington Avenue
Suffern, NY 10901
(914) 357-2600

Suffolk County Historian
Division of Cultural and Historical Services
Suffolk County Department of Parks
PO Box 144, Montauk Highway
West Sayville, NY 11796
(516) 567-1487
J. Lance Mallamo
Municipal Historians: **Village of Amityville**: post vacant; **Village of Asharoken**: Joan G. Hauser, 483 Asharoken Avenue, Northport, NY 11768; **Town of Babylon**: Robert Mills Smith, 151 Phelps Lane, North Babylon, NY 11703; **Village of Babylon**: Stewart Aldrich, 75 Woodsome Road, Babylon, NY 11702; **Village of Belle Terre**: Daniel Cornish, PO Box 112, Port Jefferson, NY 11777; **Village of Bellport**: Mrs. Malcolm Johnson, 69 Country Club Road, Bellport, NY 11713; **Village of Brightwaters**: Rhoda Milligan, 467 Lombardy Boulevard, Brightwaters, NY 11718; **Town of Brookhaven**: David Overton, Town Hall, 215 South Ocean Avenue, Patchogue, NY 11772; **Village of Dering Harbor**: Helen Loper, PO Box K, Shelter Island, NY 11964; **Town of East Hampton**: Carleton Kelsey, Main Street, Amagansett, NY 11930; **Village of East Hampton**: N. Sherrill Foster, 4

Fireplace-Springs Road, East Hampton, NY 11937; **Village of Farmingdale**: Gary Hammond, 31 Lowell Drive, Farmingdale, NY 11735; **Village of Freeport**: post vacant; **Village of Greenport**: Jerome McCarthy, 151 Bay Avenue, Greenport, NY 11944; **Village of Head of the Harbor**: Barbara Van Liew, PO Box 416, Saint James, NY 11780; **Town of Huntington**: Rufus Langhans, 228 Main Street, Huntington, NY 11743; **Village of Huntington Bay**: Mrs. G. David Gudebrod, 230 Vineyard Road, Huntington, NY 11743; **Town of Islip**: Carl Starace, 214 Tahlulah Lane, West Islip, NY 11795; **Village of Lake Grove**: Mrs. Joseph Macchiarulli, 29 Long Street, Lake Grove, NY 11755; **Village of Lindenhurst**: Evelyn Ellis, 72Harrington Avenue, Lindenhurst, NY 11757; **Village of Lloyd Harbor**: David C. Fuchs, 32 Middle Hollow Road, Huntington, NY 11743; **Village of Nissequogue**: Louis Hall, PO Box 482, Saint James, NY 11780; **Village of North Haven**: George Finckenor, Shelter Island Avenue, North Haven, NY 11963; **Village of Northport**: Dorothy Walker, 180 Bayview Avenue, Northport, NY 11768; **Village of Ocean Beach**: Fred Charlton, 20 Ocean Road, Ocean Beach, NY 11770; **Village of Old Field**: Mildred Gillie, 105 Main Street, Port Jefferson Station, NY 11776-1001; **Village of Patchogue**: Mrs. Charles Miller, 8 Lake Court, Patchogue, NY 11772; **Village of Pine Valley**: post vacant; **Village of Poquott**: post vacant; **Village of Port Jefferson**: post vacant; **Village of Quogue**: Beatrice Marcks, PO Box 1165, Quogue, NY 11959; **Town of Riverhead**: Justine Wells, 102 Sound Avenue, Riverhead, NY 11901; **Village of Sag Harbor**: George A. Finckenor, Oakland Avenue, Sag Harbor, NY 11963; **Village of Saltaire**: Elizabeth Starkey, 109 West 77th Street, New York, NY 10024; **Town of Shelter Island**: Louise Green, Town Hall, Shelter Island, NY 11964; **Village of Shoreham**: post vacant; **Town of Smithtown**: Bradley Harris, Town Hall, Smithtown, NY 11787; **Town of South Salem**: post vacant; **Town of Southampton**: Robert Keene, Town Hall, Southampton, NY 11968; **Village of Southampton**: Richard A. Foster, 92 Post Crossing, Southampton, NY 11968; **Town of Southold**: post vacant; **Village of The Branch**: post vacant; **Village of Westhampton Beach**: Theodore Conklin, Jr., PO Box 991, Westhampton Beach, NY 11978

Suffolk County Historical Society

The Helen Raynor Hannah Memorial
  Library, Genealogy Section
300 West Main Street
Riverhead, NY 11901
(516) 727-2881
Mr. Wally Broege, Director
Hours: Wed–Thur & Sat 12:30–4:30, by
  appointment if coming from a distance
Pub. *Suffolk County Historical Society
  Register*, quarterly
(local/regional history museum and
  library, genealogical research library
  with both published and unpublished
  materials: wills, deeds, bills of sale,
  letters, account books, ledgers,
  journals, diaries, maps, atlases,
  photographs, scrapbooks, vertical files
  arranged by towns, periodicals and
  newspapers, photographic negatives,
  members' ancestor charts, application
  records of the disbanded Daughters of
  the Revolution of 1776)
$25.00 per year membership for
  individuals, $30.00 per year
  membership for families; library use
  fee for non-members: $2.00 per day

Sullivan County Historian

(post vacant)
c/o Sullivan County Museum
265 Main Street
PO Box 247
Hurleyville, NY 12747-0247
(914) 434-8044
Hours: Tue 9:30–4:00
Municipal Historians: **Town of Bethel**:
  Bert S. Feldman, PO Box 300, White
  Lake, NY 12786; **Village of
  Bloomingburg**: Loretta Franklin, PO
  Box 158, Bloomingburgh, NY 12721;
  Town of Callicoon: Jesse Abel, Main
  Street, Jeffersonville, NY 12748;
  Town of Cochecton: Aline Palmer,
  Lake Huntington, NY 12752; **Town of
  Delaware**: Mary Curtis, Callicoon,
  NY 12723; **Town of Fallsburg**: post
  vacant; **Town of Forestburgh**: post
  vacant; **Town of Fremont**: Elizabeth
  McCoo, Long Eddy, NY 12760;
  Village of Jeffersonville: Joseph Abel,
  Village Hall, Center Street, PO Box
  155X, Jeffersonville, NY 12748; **Town
  of Highland**: Austin Smith, Barryville,
  NY 12719; **Town of Liberty**: Delbert
  Van Etten, 120 North Main Street,
  Liberty, NY 12754; **Village of
  Liberty**: Delbert Van Etten, Municipal
  Building, Liberty, NY 12754; **Town of
  Lumberland**: Frank V. Schwarz, PO
  Box 1, Glen Spey, NY 12737; **Town
  of Mamakating**: Verdanna Lawrence,
  Rt. 1, Box 28C, Wurtsboro, NY
  12790; **Village of Monticello**: post
  vacant; **Town of Neversink**: Robert
  Dice, County Road 19, Claryville, NY
  12725; **Town of Rockland**: Wilmer E.
  Sipple, Town Office, Livingston

Manor, NY 12758; **Town of
  Thompson**: post vacant; **Town of
  Tusten**: Barbara Buckman, Town
  Office, Narrowsburgh, NY 12764;
  Village of Woodridge: James Slater,
  PO Box 655, Woodridge, NY 12789;
  Village of Wurtsboro: post vacant

Sullivan County Historical Society

Sullivan County Museum
PO Box 247
Hurleyville, NY 12747-0247
(914) 434-8044
Charlotte Osterhout, Genealogist; Mr. F.
  Hill, President
Hours: Tue, and by appointment
Pub. *Observer*, six issues per year
$15.00 per year membership

Taconic Valley Historical Society

Hilltop Road
PO Box 400
Berlin, NY 12022-0400

Tappantown Historical Society

PO Box 71
Tappan, NY 10983
(914) 359-5490

Historical Society of the Tarrytowns

1 Grove Street
Tarrytown, NY 10591
(914) 631-8374
Kim McCall, Administrator
Hours: Tue–Sat 2:00–4:00, Wed 1:00–
  4:00
Pub. *The Chronicle*, perhaps
  semiannually
$20.00 per year membership for
  individuals, $25.00 per year
  membership for families, $1.00 per
  year junior membership

Three Village Historical Society

(93 North Country Road—location)
PO Box 76 (mailing address)
East Setauket, NY 11733-0076
(516) 751-3730 phone and FAX
E-mail: tvhistsoc@aol.com
http://members.aol.com/tvhs1
Michele M. Morrisson, Director
Hours: three days per week, and by
  appointment
Pub. *The Three Village Historian:
  Journal of the Three Village Historical
  Society*, annually, $7.00 per issue for
  non-members, $5.50 per issue for
  members
(villages of Setauket, Stony Brook, and
  Old Field, in Town of Brookhaven;
  Long Island's North shore; ship
  building; Rhodes Collection/Historic
  Documents)
$20.00 per year membership for
  individuals, $30.00 per year
  membership for families, $40.00 per
  year Contributing membership, $50.00
  per year Corporate membership,
  $75.00 per year Sustaining
  membership, $125.00 per year Patron

membership, $250.00 per year
Benefactor membership, $500.00 per
year Major Donor membership

Ticonderoga Historical Society
Hancock House
Moses Circle
Ticonderoga, NY 12883
(518) 585-7868
Norma Dreimiller, Assistant Director
Hours: Wed–Sat 10:00–4:00
$10.00 per year membership

Tioga County Historian
Tioga County Office Building
56 Main Street
Owego, NY 13827
(607) 687-0100, ext. 29
Hours: Tue 3:30–5:00 and by
appointment
Municipal Historians: **Town of Barton**:
Louise Shallenberger, 102 Tracy Road,
Waverly, NY 14892; **Town of
Berkshire**: NancyHunt, Berkshire
Public Library and Museum,
Berkshire, NY 13736; **Town of
Candor** and **Village of Candor**:
Donald Weber, 64 Tuttle Hill Road,
Candor, NY 13743; **Town of Newark
Valley**: Tom Grant, 64 Elm Street,
Newark Valley, NY 13811; **Village of
Newark Valley**: post vacant; **Town of
Nichols**: William Caloroso, 192 East
River Road, Nichols, NY 13812;
Town of Owego: Emma Sedore,
Owego Town Hall, PO Box 248,
Owego, NY 13827; **Village of Owego**:
post vacant; **Village of Nichols**:
William Caloroso, 192 East River
Road, Nichols, NY 13812; **Town of
Richford**: Clarence Lacey, Main
Street, Richford, NY 13835; **Town of
Spencer** and **Village of Spencer**: Jean
Alve, Rt. 2, Box 302, Spencer, NY
14883; **Town of Tioga**: Carol
Tsleghardt, PO Box 175, Tioga Center,
NY 13845; **Village of Waverly**:
Pauline Perry, Waverly Village Office,
362 Broad Street, Waverly, NY 14892
copies 25¢ each

Tioga County Historical Society
Museum and Genealogical Committee
110–112 Front Street
Owego, NY 13827
(607) 687-2460
Jean Winnie Neff, Executive Director

Tompkins County Historian
The DeWitt Historical Society of
Tompkins County
401 East State Street
Ithaca, NY 14850
(607) 273-8284; (607) 273-6107 FAX
E-mail: dhs@lakenet.org
Gretchen Sachse
Hours: by appointment; general reference
services: Tue, Thur & Sat 11:00–5:00

Municipal Historians: **Town of Caroline**:
Barbara B. M. Kone, 36 Speed Hill
Road, Brooktondale, NY 14817, (607)
539-6464; **Village of Cayuga
Heights**: post vacant; **Town of Danby**:
Susan Hautala, 134 Hornbrook Road,
Ithaca, NY 14850, (607) 272-3287;
Town of Dryden: Harland Carpenter,
62 Beam Hill Road, Dryden, NY
13053, (607) 844-9674; **Village of
Dryden**: post vacant, refer questions
to Dryden Historical Society; **Town of
Enfield**: Susan Thompson, 487
Enfield Center Road, Ithaca, NY
14850, (607) 272-6412; **Village of
Freeville**: Joan Manning, 66 Main
Street, Freeville, NY 13068, (607)
844-9334; **Town of Groton**: Dorothy
Ostrander, 610 Elm Street, Groton, NY
13073, (607) 898-3401; **Village of
Groton**: Lee Shurtleff, 208 Cortland
Street, Groton, NY 13073, (607) 898-
3601; **City of Ithaca**: Susan Robey,
The DeWitt Historical Society of
Tompkins County (see above); **Town
of Ithaca**: The The DeWitt Historical
Society of Tompkins County
provideshistorical services under
contract (see above); **Town of
Lansing**: Louise Bement, 49 Myers
Road, Lansing, NY 14882, (607) 533-
4514; **Village of Lansing**: post vacant;
Town of Newfield: Alan Chaffee, 262
Van Kirk Road, Newfield, NY 14867,
(607) 564-7778; **Village of
Trumansburg** and **Town of Ulysses**:
Esther Northrup, Hector Street,
Trumansburg, NY 14886, (607) 387-
5855

Tonawanda-Kenmore Historical Society
100 Knoche Road
Tonawanda, NY 14150
(716) 873-5774
Marilyn Brown, President
Hours: Sun (Apr–Oct) 2:00–5:00
(local "Town of Tonawanda" history)

Historical Society of the Tonawandas, Inc.
113 Main Street
Tonawanda, NY 14150-2129
(716) 694-7406
Willard B. Dittmar, Executive Director
Hours: Wed–Fri 10:00–5:00
Pub. *The Lumber Shover*, monthly
(research library has census records and
genealogical information)
$6.00 per year membership for
individuals, $10.00 per year
membership for married couples

Tully Area Historical Society
22-24 State Street
PO Box 22
Tully, NY 13159-0022
(315) 696-4681
Eleanor L. Preston, President

Hours: Tue 9:30–noon, and by
appointment
Pub. *TAHS Newsletter*, quarterly
$5.00 per year membership for
individuals, $11.00 per year
membership for families; research:
$6.00 per hour

Tuxedo Historical Society
Route 17
PO Box 188
Tuxedo, NY 10987
(914) 351-5611

Ulster County Historian
4 Rita Street
New Paltz, NY 12561-2116
Kenneth E. Hasbrouck,Sr.
Hours: Wed–Fri 10:00–3:30
Municipal Historians: **Town of Denning**:
Jane Smith, Claryville, NY12725;
Village of Ellenville: Paul Ross,
Ellenville Central School, Ellenville,
NY 12428; **Town of Esopus**: Dorothy
R. Dumond, PO Box 5, Ulster Park,
NY 12487; **Town of Gardiner**:
Kenneth E. Hasbrouck, Sr., County
Historian (see above); **Town of
Hardenbergh**: Irene Barnhart,
Barnhart Road, HCR 1, Box 138, Lew
Beach, NY 12758; **Town of Hurley**:
Olive Clearwater, Rt. 7, Box 100,
Kingston, NY 12401; **City of
Kingston**: Edwin Ford, 58 Valentine
Avenue, Kingston, NY 12401; **Town
of Kingston**: Ann M. Ortloff, 51
Melissa Road, Kingston, NY 12401;
Town of Lloyd: Lindsay Sullivan, 30
Church Street, Highland, NY 12528;
Town of Marbletown: Dorothy E.
Pratt, Stone Ridge, NY 12484; **Town
of Marlborough**: John Matthews,
Milton Turnpike, Milton, NY 12547;
Town of New Paltz: Irene Martin, 45
North Oakwood Terrace, New Paltz,
NY 12561; **Village of New Paltz**:
Kenneth Hasbrouck, 401 Route 208,
New Paltz, NY 12561; **Town of Olive**:
Ruth Anne Muller, HCI Box 117A,
West Shokan, NY 12494; **Village of
Pine Hill**: post vacant; **Town of
Plattekill**: Muriel Obermeyer, PO Box
45, Modena, NY 12548; **Town of
Rochester**: Mrs. John Schoonmaker,
Accord, NY 12404; **Village of
Rosendale**: post vacant; **Town of
Saugerties**: Lloyd Loop, Glasco
Turnpike, Saugerties, NY 12477;
Village of Saugerties: post vacant;
Town of Shandaken: Nancy Smith,
Academy Street, Pine Hill, NY 12465;
Town of Shawangunk: Carole
Decker, Rt. 2, Box 237, Awosting
Road, Pine Bush, NY 12566; **Town of
Ulster**: Bruce Burgher, 32
Lawrenceville Street, Kingston, NY
12401; **Town of Warwarsing**: Mrs.
DeWitt Clinton, Laurel Terrace,
Ellenville, NY 12428; **Town of

Woodstock: Edgar C. Leaycraft, Historical Society of Woodstock, PO Box 841, Woodstock, NY 12498

Ulster County Historical Society
(Route 209, Town of Marbletown—location)
PO Box 3752 (mailing address)
Kingston, NY 12402
(914) 338-5614
Amanda C. Jones, Executive Director
Hours: Wed–Sun (Jun–Sept) 1:00–5:00
Pub. *Ulster County Gazette*, three times per year
$10.00 per year membership

Ulysses Historical Society
(South Street, Trumansburg, NY 14886—location)
PO Box 445 (mailing address)
Trumansburg, NY 14886-0445
(607) 387-7833; (607) 387-7262 (President)
Marion Hoffmire, Genealogist; Ruth Wolverton, President
Hours: May–Sept: Thur–Sat 2:00–4:00
$8.00 per year membership for individuals, $10.00 per year membership for families, $5.00 per year membership for students; search fee: cost of materials plus donation

Unadilla Valley Historical Society
7-AA Main Street
Mount Upton, NY 13809
(607) 764-8492

Upper Delaware Heritage Alliance
PO Box 143
Callicoon, NY 12723
(717) 685-4871 (Editor's residence in Pennsylvania)

Valley Historical Society
Main Street
Sinclairville, NY 14782
(716) 962-8520
Ruth I. Smith, President
Hours: summer: Sun 2:00–5:00, and by appointment
(cemetery, store, church, grange records to be examined in museum only)

Van Cortlandtville Historical Society
297 Locust Avenue
Peekskill, NY 10566-1308
(914) 737-7785
George Kummer, President
Hours: third Sat 2:00
Pub. *Historical Key*, quarterly
$10.00 per year membership for individuals, $15.00 per year membership for families, $5.00 per year membership for students

William K. Vanderbilt Historical Society
PO Box 433
Idle Hour, NY 11769
(516) 567-2277

Vernon Historical Society
PO Box 786
Vernon, NY 13476
(315) 768-7091
Jon Landers, President
$2.00 per year membership

Victor Historical Society
Valentown Museum
Valentown Square
Fishers, NY 14453
(716) 924-2645

Virgil Historical Society
(East State Road, Route 90—location)
Rt. 2 (mailing address)
Cortland, NY 13045

Historical Society of Walden and Wallkill Valley
PO Box 48
Walden, NY 12586
(914) 778-5862
Hours: by appointment

Warren County Historian
Warren County Municipal Center
1340 State Route 9
Lake George, NY 12845-9803
(518) 761-6544
Marjorie Swan
Hours: Tue & Thur 9:00–5:00
Municipal Historians: **Town of Bolton**: Kathleen Simmes or Patricia Steele, Bolton Town Hall, PO Box 698, Bolton Landing, NY 12814; **Town of Chester**: Phyllis Bogle, Town Hall, PO Box 423, Chestertown, NY 12817; **City of Glens Falls**: Dr. Robert King, 118 Crandall Street, Glens Falls, NY 12801; **Town of Hague**: Clifton West, Hague, NY 12836; **Town of Horicon**: Colleen Murtagh, PO Box 112, Brant Lake, NY 12815; **Town of Johnsburg**: Doris H. Patton, PO Box 126, Bakers Mills, NY 12811; **Town of Lake George**: Grace MacDonald, Ottawa Street, Lake George, NY 12845; **Village of Lake George**: Margaret A. Edwards, 72 Schuyler Street, Lake George, NY 12845; **Town of Lake Luzerne**: Beatrice Evans, Lake Avenue, Lake Luzerne, NY 12846; **Town of Queensbury**: Dr. Marilyn Van Dyke, Queensbury Town Office Building, Queensbury, NY 12804-5902; **Town of Stony Creek**: Cynthia Cameron, 91 Waite Road, Stony Creek, NY 12878; **Town of Thurman**: Robin Croissant, Mud Street, Box 72, Athol, NY 12810; **Town of Warrensburg**: Mabel Tucker, 88 River Street, Warrensburg, NY 12885

Town of Warren Historical Society
Main Street
Jordanville, NY 13407
(315) 858-1089

Warsaw Historical Society
45 Liberty Street
Warsaw, NY 14569
(716) 796-3422

Washington County Historian
Washington County Office Building
Upper Broadway
Fort Edward, NY 12828
(518) 747-3374
Doris McEachron
Hours: Wed 1:00–5:00
Municipal Historians: **Town of Argyle**: Doris McEachron, Municipal Building, Argyle, NY 12809; **Village of Argyle**: Mrs. Gordon McEachron, Municipal Building, Argyle, NY 12809; **Town of Cambridge** and **Village of Cambridge**: David Thornton, 14 Gilmore Avenue, Cambridge, NY 12816; **Town of Dresden**: Agnes Petersen, Box 1 B, Clemons, NY 12819; **Town of Easton**: Earline Houser, Rt. 1, Greenwich, NY 12834; **Town of Fort Ann**: Virginia Parrott, Rural Free Delivery, Fort Ann, NY 12828; **Village of Fort Ann**: post vacant; **Village of Fort Edward**: R. Paul McCarty, 22 Griffin Avenue, Fort Edward, NY 12828; **Town of Granville** and **Village of Granville**: James N. Ayres, 30 West Main Street, Granville, NY 12832; **Town of Greenwich**: Jane Haverley, 3 Cottage Street, Greenwich, NY 12834; **Town of Hampton**: Mildred Mashak, Rt. 1, Box 39, Hampton, NY 12837; **Town of Hartford**: Sylvia Van Anden, PO Box 35, Hartford, NY 12838; **Town of Hebron**: Drucille Craig, Rt. 1, Granville, NY 12832; **Village of Hudson Falls**: Paul Loding, Maple Street, Hudson Falls, NY 12839; **Town of Jackson**: Norma Skelly, Star Route, East Greenwich, NY 12826; **Town of Kingsbury**: Paul Loding, Town Hall, Hudson Falls, NY 12839; **Town of Putnam**: Rose Blood, Putnam Station, NY 12861; **Town of Salem** and **Village of Salem**: William A. Cormier, South Main Street, Salem, NY 12865; **Town of White Creek**: Marilyn B. Robinson, PO Box 150A, Eagle Bridge, NY 12057; **Town of Whitehall** and **Village of Whitehall**: Howard Bartholomew, 5 Elizabeth Street, Whitehall, NY 12887

Washington County Historical Society
Heritage Research Library
167 Broadway
Fort Edward, NY 12828
(518) 747-9108
Hours: Fri 1:00–4:00, and by appointment
no charge for admission to library

Waterloo Library and Historical Society
Terwilliger Museum
31 East Williams Street
Waterloo, NY 13165
(315) 539-0533
Beatrice Contant, Director of Museums
Hours: Mon 2:00–5:00, Wed 7:00–9:00
(Waterloo and area history and historical records, local genealogical records)
admission by donation; search fees $7.00–$15.00, depending on time

Waterloo Library and Historical Society
Waterloo Memorial Day Museum
31 East Williams Street
Waterloo, NY 13165
(315) 539-0533
Beatrice Contant, Director of Museums
Hours: Memorial Day weekend & Jul–Aug Mon & Thur 1:00–4:00, Sat 10:00–1:00
(all area war records and newspaper collections)

Watervliet Historical Society
PO Box 123
Watervliet, NY 12189
Eugene Burns, Treasurer

Wayne County Historian
Wayne County Office of Tourism and History
9 Pearl Street
PO Box 131
Lyons, NY 14489
(315) 946-5470; (315) 946-5978 FAX
E-mail: tourism@vivanet.com
http://www.tourism.co.wayne.ny.us
Marjory Allen Perez, Historian; Deborah J. Ferrell, Assistant Historian
Hours: Mon–Fri 9:00–noon & 1:00–5:00
Municipal Historians: **Town of Arcadia**: Robert Hoeltzel, 211 Moore Street, Newark, NY 14513; **Town of Butler**: Barbara Briscese, 4455 Spring Lake Road, Wolcott, NY 14590; **Village of Clyde**: post vacant; **Town of Galen**: post vacant; **Town of Huron**: Carol Flint, 11065 Ridge Road, Wolcott, NY 14590; **Town of Lyons**: post vacant; **Village of Lyons**: post vacant; **Town of Macedon**: Helen Burgio, 411 Canal Drive, East, Macedon, NY 14502; **Village of Macedon**: Anita Crowley, 17 Lapham Street, Macedon, NY 14502; **Town of Marion**: Carolyn Adriaansen, 4063 Maple Avenue, Marion, NY 14505; **Village of Newark**: Robert Hoeltzel, Town of Arcadia Historian (see above); **Town of Ontario**: Virginia Scully Hill, 5656 Walworth Road, Ontario, NY 14519; **Town of Palmyra** and **Village of Palmyra**: Robert Lowe, 222 Fayette Street, Palmyra, NY 14522; **Village of Red Creek**: Grace Frost, 6749 South Street, Red Creek, NY 13143; **Town

of Rose**: James Ryan, 10612 Salter Road, North Rose, NY 14516; **Town of Savannah**: John Spellman, High Street, Savannah, NY 13146; **Town of Sodus**: Richard Ransley, 19 Smith Street, Sodus, NY 14551; **Village of Sodus**: post vacant; **Village of Sodus Point**: post vacant; **Town of Walworth**: JohnTraas, 2219 Smith Hill Road, Walworth, NY 14568; **Town of Williamson**: Chester Peters, PO Box 63, Pultneyville, NY 14538; **Town of Wolcott**: Bill Armstrong, 6 Smith Street, Wolcott, NY 14590; **Village of Wolcott**: post vacant
research: $14.00 per hour, $7.00 minimum, plus copies at 10¢ each from paper originals or 25¢ each from microfilm originals

Wayne County Historical Society
PO Box 607
Lyons, NY 14489
Hours: Mon–Fri 9:00–4:00

Webster Museum and Historical Society
1000 Ridge Road
Webster, NY 14580
(716) 872-1000

Society for the Preservation of Weeksville and Bedford-Stuyvesant History/The Weeksville Society
1698 Bergen Street
PO Box 120, Saint Johns Station
Brooklyn, NY 11213
(718) 756-5250

West Seneca Historical Museum and Society
(919 Mill Road—location)
PO Box 2 (mailing address)
West Seneca, NY 14224-3038
(716) 674-4283
Laura Dulinawka, Secretary/Treasurer
Hours: Tue 9:00–5:00
Pub. *Just for Old Times Sake*, $4.00 per issue plus postage

Historical Society of the Westburys
454 Rockland Street
Westbury, NY 11590
(516) 333-0176

Westchester County Historian
Michaelian Office Building
Room 903
White Plains, NY 10601
(914) 285-2638
Susan Swanson, County Historian
Hours: Mon–Thur 10:00–4:00
Municipal Historians: **Village of Ardsley**: Daniel Kaufman, Ardsley Village Hall, 505 Ashford Avenue, Ardsley, NY 10502; **Town of Bedford**: Katharine Barrett Kelly, Bedford Town House, 321 Bedford Road, Bedford, NY 10507, (914) 666-4745, Tue & Thur 10:00–2:00; **Village

of Briarcliff**: post vacant, c/o Mayor, Municipal Building, 111 Pleasantville Road, Briarcliff Manor, NY 10510; **Village of Bronxville**: Mary Huber, Village Hall, Pondfield Road, Bronxville, NY 10708; **Village of Buchanan**: Anna Marie Burke, 188 Westchester Avenue, Buchanan, NY 10511; **Town of Cortlandt**: Maureen Erickson, Valeria 37, Cortlandt Manor, NY 10566; **Village of Croton-on-Hudson**: Jane Northshield, Municipal Building, Van Wyck Street, Croton-on-Hudson, NY 10520; **Village of Dobbs Ferry**: Judy Holzer, 186 Clinton Avenue, Dobbs Ferry, NY 10522; **Town of Eastchester**: Richard Forliano, 67 Archer Drive, Bronxville, NY 10708; **Town of Greenburgh**: Ann Blatt, 170 East 94th Street, Apartment 1B, New York, NY 10028; **Town of Harrison**: Michael R. Casarella, Charles Dawson History Center of Harrison, 2 East Madison Street, Harrison, NY 10528; **Village of Hastings-on-Hudson**: Barbara McManus, The Office Inc., 572 Warburton Avenue, Hastings-on-Hudson, NY 10706; **Village of Irvington**: Adele Warnock, 27 North Dutcher Street, Irvington, NY 10533; **Village of Larchmont**: Judith Spikes, 5 Maple Avenue, Larchmont, NY 10538; **Town of Lewisboro**: Maureen Koehl, Spring Street, Rt. 3, South Salem, NY 10590; **Town of Mamaroneck**: Paula Lipsett, Mamaroneck Historical Society, PO Box 776, Mamaroneck, NY 10543; **Village of Mamaroneck**: Gloria P. Pritts, 703 Palmer Court, Mamaroneck, NY 10543; **Village of Mount Kisco**: Oliver A. Knapp, 11 Valleyview Terrace, Mount Kisco, NY 10549; **Town of Mount Pleasant**: Wilfred V. Hurley, 21 Blemis Place, Valhalla, NY 10595; **City of Mount Vernon**: Dr. Larry Spruill, Mount Vernon High School, Mount Vernon, NY 10552; **Town of Mount Pleasant**: post vacant; **Town of New Castle**: Richard Neale, 4 Pondview Close, Chappaqua, NY 10514; **City of New Rochelle**: Thomas A. Hoctor, 1 Inverness Road, New Rochelle, NY 10804; **Town of North Salem**: Joan Hawley Bristol, Town House, Route 116, North Salem, NY 10560; **Village of North Tarrytown**: c/o Mayor, Village Hall, 28 Beekman Avenue, North Tarrytown, NY 10591; **Town of Ossining**: Greta Cornell, Town Hall, 16 Croton Avenue, Ossining, NY 10562; **Village of Ossining**: post vacant, c/o Greta Cornell (see above); **City of Peekskill**: John Kelly, 107 Overlook Avenue, Peekskill, NY 10566-3008; **Town of Pelham**: Susan

Swanson, Pelham Town House, 20 Fifth Avenue, Pelham, NY 10803; **Village of Pelham**: Kathleen Terkelsen, Village Hall, 195 Sparks Avenue, Pelham, NY 10803; **Village of Pelham Manor**: post vacant, c/o Susan Swanson (see above); **Village of Pleasantville**: John Crandall, PO Box 0236, 48 Wheeler Avenue, Pleasantville, NY 10570; **Village of Port Chester**: Goldie Solomon, 6 Puritan Drive, Port Chester, NY 10573; **Town of Pound Ridge**: Ethel Scofield, Pound Ridge Historical Society, The Pound Ridge Museum, Routes 137 and 172, PO Box 51, Pound Ridge, NY 10576; **City of Rye**: Jan Kelsey, 179 Grace Church Street, Rye, NY 10580; **Village of Rye Brook**: post vacant, c/o Mayor, 90 South Ridge Street, Rye Brook, NY 10573; **Village of Scarsdale**: Irving Sloan, 4 Tompkins Road, Scarsdale, NY 10583; **Town of Somers**: Florence Oliver, PO Box 245, Somers, NY 10589; **Town of South Salem**: post vacant; **Village of Tarrytown**: Thomas Dunnings, 154 Martling Avenue, Tarrytown, NY 10591; **Village of Tuckahoe**: Elizabeth Leckie, 6 McKinley Street, Bronxville, NY 10708; **City of White Plains**: Renoda Hoffman, 5 Belmont Street, White Plains, NY 10605; **Town of Yorktown**: Doris Auser, 2227 Crompond Road, Yorktown Heights, NY 10598, (914) 962-0341, (914) 962-7282

Westchester County Historical Society

2199 Saw Mill River Road
Elmsford, NY 10523
(914) 592-4323; (914) 592-4338; (914) 592-6481 FAX
Elizabeth Fuller, Librarian
Hours: Tue & Wed 9:00–4:00
Pub. *The Westchester Historian*, quarterly; *Westchester Historical Happenings*
$30.00 per year membership; research: $20.00–$30.00 per hour, depending on type of search

Western Monroe Historical Society

151 Main Street
Brockport, NY 14420
(716) 637-3645
Eunice Chesnut, Historian
Hours: Mon–Fri 9:00–noon; tours Sun (Apr–Nov) 2:00–4:00
Pub. *Newsletter*, monthly
(file of newspaper clippings, etc.)
$25.00 per year membership for families

Westport Historical Society

Barksdale Road
Westport, NY 12993
(518) 962-4809

Marcus Whitman Historical Society

PO Box 204
Gorham, NY 14461

Wilson Historical Society

PO Box 830
Wilson, NY 14172-0830

Worcester Historical Society

72 Main Street
PO Box 186
Worcester, NY 12197
Gynger O'Connor, President
Hours: Jun–Sept: Wed–Fri 1:00–3:00

Wyoming County Historian

Wyoming County Historian Office
26 Linwood Avenue
Warsaw, NY 14569
(716) 786-8818
Ray Barber, Historian; Doris Bannister, Deputy Historian
Hours: Mon–Fri 9:00–4:00
Pub. *Historical Wyoming*, quarterly (July, October, January, April), $7.50 per year for mailed subscription, $2.00 per issue at office, $2.50 per mailed issue
(history of Wyoming County, New York, biographies, cemetery lists, soldiers, etc.)
Municipal Historians: **Town of Arcade** and **Village of Arcade**: Jeffery C. Mason, 7783 County Line Road, Arcade, NY 14009, (716) 492-4742; **Town of Attica**: Lillian Merkle, 1680 Austin Road, Attica, NY 14011; **Village of Attica**: post vacant; **Town of Bennington**: Mrs. Alma Janish, 1784 Burrough Road, Cowlesville, NY 14037; **Town of Castile**: post vacant; **Town of Covington**: Karen C. Milligan, 1088 Peoria Road, Pavilion, NY 14525, (716) 584-3254; **Town of Eagle**: Frank Noble, Bliss, NY 14024; **Town of Gainesville**: Stanley Rutherford, 4344 Gainesville Road, Silver Springs, NY 14550; **Village of Gainesville**: post vacant; **Town of Genesee Falls**: Jean Totsline, 6940 River Road, Portageville, NY 14536; **Town of Java**: Ray Barber, Michigan Road, Arcade, NY 14009; **Town of Middlebury**: Doris Bannister, 872 Academy Street, Wyoming, NY 14591; **Town of Orangeville**: Mabel Spink, PO Box 538, Varysburg, NY 14167; **Town of Perry**: Norma Spencer, 6496 Oatka Road, Perry, NY 14530; **Village of Perry**: post vacant; **Town of Pike** and **Village of Pike**: Gladys Galton, PO Box 265, Pike, NY 14130; **Town of Sheldon**: Barb Durfee, 2348 Route 98, Varysburg, NY 14167; **Village of Silver Springs**: post vacant; **Town of Warsaw**: Lawrence Appleby, 260 North Main Street, Warsaw, NY 14569; **Village of Warsaw**: post vacant; **Town of**

Wethersfield: Wilma Ikeler, 2393 Route 98, Bliss, NY 14024; **Village of Wyoming**: post vacant

Wyoming Pioneer Historical Association

14 Covington Street
Perry, NY 14530
(716) 237-3458

Yates County Genealogical and Historical Society

Oliver House Museum
200 Main Street
Penn Yan, NY 14527
(315) 536-7318
Idelle Dillon, Executive Director
Hours: Mon–Fri 9:30–4:30, Sat by appointment
Pub. *Oliver House News*, monthly
$10.00 per year membership for individuals, $20.00 per year membership for families, $5.00 per year membership for students, $35.00 per year Patron membership, $100.00 per year Corporate membership

Yates County Historian

County Office Building, Room 3
110 Court Street
Penn Yan, NY 14527
(315) 536-5147; (315) 536-5170
E-mail: yatesco@vivanet.com
http://www.vivanet.com/~dumasm/
Frances Dumas, Historian
Hours: Office: Mon–Fri 8:00–noon
(complete county records, well-indexed, town and village records on microfilm, newspapers on microfilm, database of county's cemeteries and burials)
Municipal Historians: **Town of Barrington**: Wilfred Knapp, 2751 Knapp Road, Dundee, NY 14837; **Town of Benton**: Constance Murphy, 2230 Bellona Station Road, Penn Yan, NY 14527; **Village of Dresden**: Raymond Welker, 57 Main Street, Dresden, NY 14441; **Village of Dundee**: Mrs. Bruce Van Dyne, 51 Seneca Street, Dundee, NY 14837; **Town of Jerusalem**: Jane Davis, Italy Hill Road, Branchport, NY 14418; **Town of Italy**: Mrs. Robert Coons, Rt. 2, Naples, NY 14512; **Town of Middlesex**: Stuart J. Mitchell, 1309 Shay Road, Naples, NY 14512-9410; **Town of Milo**: Frances Dumas, 3798 Bath Road, Penn Yan, NY 14527; **Village of Penn Yan**: Catherine A. Spencer, 407 Liberty Street, Penn Yan, NY 14527; **Town of Potter**: Wilson Simmons, Jr., 1226 Phelps Road, Middlesex, NY 14507; **Village of Rushville**: Betty Clark, 4606 Fergusons Cross Road, Rushville, NY 14544; **Town of Starkey**: Mrs. Bruce Van Dyne, Village of Dundee Historian (see above); **Town of**

Torrey: Betty Smalley, Dresden, NY 14441
research: $10.00 per hour

Yonkers Historical Society
Yonkers City Hall, Room 415A
40 South Broadway
Yonkers, NY 10701
(914) 965-0401; (914) 965-0401 FAX
Marianne Winstanley, Director
Hours: Tue & Thur 10:00–4:00
Pub. *The Yonkers Historical Society Newsletter*, quarterly
$20.00 per year membership for individuals, $35.00 per year membership for husband and wife, $15.00 per year membership for students or senior citizens, $100.00 per year Contributor membership, $500.00 per year Corporate Sponsor membership, $1,000.00 per year Benefactor membership

---

LDS Family History Centers

Albany
(see Loudonville)

Buffalo
(see Williamsville)

Liverpool
(315) 457-5172

Loudonville
(518) 463-4581

New York City
(212) 873-1690

Plainview
(516) 433-0122

Rochester
(716) 271-5040

Syracuse
(see Liverpool)

Williamsville
(716) 688-6438

Yonkers
(see New York City)

Genealogical Societies

State Genealogical Society

New York Genealogical and Biographical Society Library
122 East 58th Street
New York, NY 10022-1939
(212) 755-8532

Joy Rich, Director of the Library
Hours: Tue–Sat 9:30–5:00 (closed for the three weeks preceding Labor Day and legal holidays)
Pub. *New York Genealogical and Biographical Record*, quarterly, $25.00 per year subscription; *New York Genealogical and Biographical Society Collections*; *NYG&B Newsletter*, quarterly, $2.00 per issue
(emphasis on New York city and state and the northeast, but collects materials for all states, and many countries)
$50.00 per year membership for individuals (includes *Record* and *Newsletter*), $60.00 per year membership for individuals who are residents of New York City, $75.00 per year membership for husband and wife, $85.00 per year membership for husband and wife who are residents of New York City; admission: non-members $15.00 donation per visit

New York State Council of Genealogical Organizations
PO Box 2593
Syracuse, NY 13220-2593
(518) 438-5115
E-mail: lufay@aol.com
Loren V. Fay, Editor
(membership limited to New York State organizations only)
Pub. *NYSCOGO Lifeline*, quarterly, $10.00 per year subscription; *Naturalization Records of New York State*, $13.00 postpaid, a county-by-county guide to records
$25.00 per year membership

Regional Genealogical Societies

Adirondack Genealogical-Historical Society
100 Main Street
Saranac Lake, NY 12983
(518) 891-2236
Spencer B. Newman, President
Hours: Mon–Fri 10:00–5:00, Sat 12:00–5:00

American-Canadian Genealogical Society
(see New Hampshire)

Brooklyn Historical Society
Genealogy Workshop
128 Pierpont Street, Corner Clinton Street
Brooklyn, NY 11201
(718) 624-0890; (718) 875-3869 FAX
E-mail: bhs@parix.com
http://www.brooklynhistory.org
Michell Hackwelder, Head Librarian

Broome County, The Southern Tier Genealogy Club
PO Box 680
Vestal, NY 13851-0680
http://www.spectra.net/~ann/stgs.htm
Pub. *News Letter*, three to four times per year
$7.00 per year membership

Capital District Genealogical Society
PO Box 2175, Empire State Plaza Station
Albany, NY 12220-0175
Hours: Volunteer Desk, New York State Library: Mon–Fri 9:00–5:00
Pub. *Capital District Genealogical Society Newsletter*, quarterly
$10.00 per year membership; surname index: $1.00 for members, $5.00 for non-members; index to all newsletter queries to 1996: $5.00

Central New York Genealogical Society
PO Box 104, Colvin Station
Syracuse, NY 13205
Harold J. Witter, Treasurer
Hours: bimonthly meetings at DeWitt Community Church, DeWitt, NY
Pub. *Tree Talks*, quarterly (March, June, September, December)
(includes Albany, Allegany, Broome, Cattaraugus, Cayuga, Chautauqua, Chemung, Chenango, Clinton, Columbia, Cortland, Delaware, Erie, Essex, Franklin, Fulton, Genesee, Greene, Hamilton, Herkimer, Jefferson, Lewis, Livingston, Madison, Monroe, Montgomery, Niagara, Oneida, Onondaga, Ontario, Orleans, Oswego, Otsego, Rensselaer, Saint Lawrence, Saratoga, Schenectady, Schoharie, Schuyler, Seneca, Steuben, Tioga, Tompkins, Warren, Washington, Wayne, Wyoming and Yates counties)
$20.00 per year membership for individuals or libraries, $25.00 per year membership for families, $38.00 per year Contributing membership (beginning in January)

Chautauqua County Genealogical Society (C.C.G.S.)
PO Box 404
Fredonia, NY 14063
(716) 672-2114 (Historical Museum)
E-mail: barris@netsync.net
http://www.rootsweb.com/~nygenweb
Valerie Veley Griffing, President; Norwood J. Barris, Membership Chairman
Pub. *The Chautauqua Genealogist*, quarterly (February, May, August, November)
(collection housed at Historical Museum of the D. R. Barker Library)
$9.00 per year membership for individuals (calendar year), $10.00 per year membership for families

Cortland County Genealogical Society
113 South Parkway
Groton, NY 13073
(607) 898-3381
E-mail: wiggit@aol.com
Wayne Thurston, President
Pub. *Newsletter*, quarterly
$7.00 per year membership

The Dutch Settlers Society of Albany
23 Dresden Court
Albany, NY 12203
(518) 456-7202
John Wemple, President
Pub. *Yearbook of the Dutch Settlers Society of Albany*, every two to three years
$25.00 regular or Associate membership the first year, $12.00 per year thereafter

The Dutchess County Genealogical Society
PO Box 708
Poughkeepsie, NY 12602
(914) 462-2361 (President)
Linda Koehler, Librarian
Hours: Tue & Thur 9:00–noon, Tue–Thur 6:30 P.M.–9:00 P.M., Fri noon–3:00
Pub. *The Dutchess*, quarterly
$15.00 per year membership; search fee: $10.00 per name—"only in our library"

Finger Lakes Genealogical Society
PO Box 581
Seneca Falls, NY 13148
J. E. Wood, President
Hours: Research Room, Mynderse Library: Mon–Fri 2:00–5:00 & 7:00–9:00, Wed noon–4:00, Sat 2:00–5:00
Pub. *Pathways*, four times per year
$10.00 per year membership

Genesee Area Genealogists
c/o Richmond Memorial Library
19 Ross Street
Batavia, NY 14020
(716) 343-9550 (Library)
Mary Van Abstyne, Editor; Dorothy H. Wilber, President; Kathleen Facer, Adult Services Librarian
Hours: Library: Mon–Tue & Thur 9:00–9:00, Wed 9:00–6:00, Fri–Sat 9:00–5:00 (closed Sat, Jul–Aug)
Pub. *The Family Tree is Growing*, four times per year (January, April, July, October)
(emphasis on western New York)
$5.00 per year membership; search fee: copy costs and SASE

Heritage Hunters
PO Box 1389
Saratoga Springs, NY 12866-0884
(518) 587-5852
E-mail: unlimitd1@juno.com
http://www.rootsweb.com/~nysarato/

Ruth Ann Messick, Founder
Hours: meetings at Community Room of the new Saratoga Springs Public Library: noon on the third Sat (Feb–Nov)
Pub. *Newsletter*, bimonthly
(interested in genealogy and history, especially in the preservation of genealogical and historical materials in and around Saratoga County)
$15.00 per year membership (calendar year), includes spring edition of Surname List

Kodak Genealogical Club
Kodak Park Activities Association
Eastman Kodak Company
Rochester, NY 14650

Livingston-Steuben County (NY) Genealogical Society
5 Elizabeth Street
Dansville, NY 14437-1719
$3.00 per year membership

Heritage and Genealogical Society of Montgomery County
Old Court House
Railroad Street
PO Box 1500
Fonda, NY 12068-1500
(518) 853-8186 (Montgomery County Department of History and Archives); (518) 853-8392 FAX
E-mail: murphy5@nyslgti.gen.ny.us
Stephen Helmin, President
Hours: Montgomery County Department of History and Archives: Sept–Jun: Mon–Fri 8:30–4:00; Jul–Aug: Mon–Fri 9:00–4:00
Pub. *Catalogue of Genealogical and Historical Material*, annually, $12.00 postpaid (available in book form or on disk in Microsoft's Word)
("Friends" society to Montgomery County Department of History and Archives; third largest genealogical and historical research library and collection in New York State)

The New England Historic Genealogical Society
(see Massachusetts)

Niagara County Genealogical Society
(2650 Hess Road, Appleton, NY 14008—office location)
215 Niagara Street (library location and mailing address)
Lockport, NY 14094-2605
(716) 778-7555 (Office); (716) 433-1033 (Library)
Nancy Balling Smith, Corresponding Secretary and Membership Chairman; Donald R. Jerge, Librarian
Hours: Library: Thur–Sat 1:00–5:00; Office: all hours
Pub. *The Niagara County Genealogical Society*, quarterly

(Niagara County, New York State, and the east)
$10.00 per year membership for individuals or families (January–December); free queries to members only; no individualized research conducted

Northeastern New York Genealogical Society
9 Lydia Street
South Glen Falls, NY 12803
Pub. *The Patents*, bimonthly
(Warren and Washington counties)
$10.00 per year membership

Northern New York American-Canadian Genealogical Society
(Community Center, Old High School Building, Main Street, Keeseville, NY—location)
PO Box 1256 (mailing address)
Plattsburg, NY 12901-1256
(518) 846-7707
Richard Ward, President
Hours: Community Center: May–Oct: Wed 1:00–7:00, Sat 10:00–4:00, and by appointment with two-weeks notice
Pub. *Lifelines*, two times per year
(southern Quebec, Northern New York, and Northern Vermont)
$20.00 per year membership for individuals ($25.00 outside the U.S.), $25.00 per year membership for families, libraries or institutions ($30.00 outside the U.S.), $7.50 per year membership for students ($10.00 outside the U.S.)

Nyando Roots Genealogical Society
PO Box 175
Massena, NY 13662
(315) 769-9914 (Massena Library)
John Kormanyos, President
Hours: Mon & Fri 10:00–5:00, Tue–Thur 10:00–9:00
Pub. *Nyando Roots*, quarterly
$10.00 per year membership

Ontario County Genealogical Society
Ontario County Historical Society Museum/Archives
55 North Main Street
Canandaigua, NY 14424
(716) 394-4975 phone and FAX
E-mail: bgen@sprynet.com
Bruce Stewart, Secretary
Hours: by appointment
Pub. *None*
(Ontario County manuscript collection, early records)
$5.00 per year membership for individuals

Orange County Genealogical Society
101 Main Street
Goshen, NY 10924-1627
Jeanne Krish, President

Hours: Mon 8:30–12:00, first Wed 9:00–
5:00, Fri 8:30–12:00, first Sat 11:30–
4:00, third Sat 9:00–4:00, and by
appointment by phoning (914) 294-
5871
Pub. *The Orange County Genealogical
Society Quarterly*
$10.00 per year membership

Queens Genealogy Workshop
Greater Ridgewood Historical Society
Vander Ende-Onderdonk House
1820 Flushing Avenue
Ridgewood, NY 11385-1041
(718) 456-1776
George P. Miller, Archivist
Hours: by appointment
Pub. *Newsletter*, quarterly
(emphasis on Long Island history and
genealogy; extensive surname files;
"All inquiries must be by
correspondence only.")
$15.00 per year membership in
Historical Society, additional $10.00
per year membership in Queens
Genealogy Workshop; no charge for
surname searches, but donations (tax-
deductible) appreciated

Rochester Genealogical Society
PO Box 10501
Rochester, NY 14610-0501
(716) 234-2584
http://www.vivanet.com/~halsey/rgs.html
Dick Halsey, Membership
Pub. *Hear-Ye Hear-Ye*, three times per
year
$15.00 per year membership

The Genealogical Society of
Rockland County
20 Zukor Road
New City, NY 10956-4388
(914) 634-9629 (Historical Society);
(914) 634-8690 FAX (Historical
Society)
Marie Koestler, Genealogy Researcher
Hours: The Historical Society of
Rockland County: Tue–Fri 9:30–5:00,
Sat–Sun 1:00–5:00
Pub. *Genealogical Society Newsletter*,
quarterly
$10.00 per year membership for
individuals, $15.00 per year
membership for families; search of
indexed records only

Saint Lawrence Valley Genealogical
Society
PO Box 341
Colton, NY 13625-0341
Pub. *SLVGS News*, bimonthly
(northern New York State, Ontario and
Quebec)
$7.00 per year membership

Tri-Town Genealogical Society
323 Kreag Road
Pittsford, NY 14534
Mrs. Elbert Gerritz

Twin Tier Genealogical Society, Inc.
(Steele Memorial Library, One Library
Plaza, Elmira, NY 14901—location)
PO Box 763 (mailing address)
Elmira, NY 14902-0763
(607) 732-0443 (Editor); (607) 733-8602
(Librarian)
Virginia Erle, President/Editor; Rita
Dery, Librarian
Hours: Library: Mon–Thur 9:00–9:00,
Fri 9:00–5:00, Sat (except Jun–Sept)
9:00–5:00, Sun (except Jun–Sept)
1:00–5:00
Pub. *Gemini*, quarterly
(Chemung, Schuyler, Steuben and
Tompkins counties, New York, and
Bradford and Tioga counties,
Pennsylvania)
$7.00 per year membership in the U.S.
and Canada, $10.00 per year
membership elsewhere; library search:
$10.00 per hour plus costs

Ulster County Genealogical Society
(Hurley Reformed Church—location)
PO Box 536 (mailing address)
Hurley, NY 12443
James Garde, President
Hours: third & fourth Mon (except Dec)
10:00–2:30, and by appointment
Pub. *Ulster Genie*, quarterly
(Ulster County, New York)
$12.00 per year membership

Westchester County Genealogical
Society
PO Box 518
White Plains, NY 10603-0518
(914) 941-9754 (Library)
http://pages.prodigy.com/hfbk19a/
wcgs.htm
Joanne Brogan, President
Hours: Library, LDS Church, Route 134,
Yorktown, NY: Tue–Thur 9:00–noon
& 7:00–9:00; meetings at Aldersgate
Methodist Church, Dobbs Ferry, NY:
second Sat 10:00 A.M.
Pub. *Westchester County Genealogical
Society Newsletter*, monthly;
Westchester Connections, biannually
(every other year); *Surname List*,
biannually (every other year)
$20.00 per year membership

Western New York Genealogical
Society, Inc.
PO Box 338
Hamburg, NY 14075-0338
Betty V. Walter, Library Committee
Chairperson
Pub. *Western New York Genealogical
Society Journal*, quarterly (June,
September, December, March)
(emphasis on eight western New York
counties: Allegany, Cattaraugus,
Chautauqua, Erie, Genesee, Niagara,
Orleans and Wyoming; collection
located in the Special Collections
Department of Downtown branch of

Buffalo and Erie County Public
Library)
$20.00 first-year membership for
individuals (beginning 1 May), $18.00
per subsequent-year membership for
individuals, $27.00 first-year
membership for families, $25.00 per
subsequent-year membership for
families, $350.00 life membership for
individuals, $500.00 life membership
for families, add $5.00 per year for
foreign membership; unable to do
genealogical research, queries
accepted from members only

Yates County Genealogical and
Historical Society
Oliver House Museum
200 Main Street
Penn Yan, NY 14527
(315) 536-7318
Idelle Dillon, Executive Director
Hours: Mon–Fri 9:30–4:30, Sat by
appointment
Pub. *Oliver House News*, monthly
$10.00 per year membership for
individuals, $20.00 per year
membership for families, $5.00 per
year membership for students, $35.00
per year Patron membership, $100.00
per year Corporate membership

Independent Publications and Miscellany

Bath Historic Committee
(Cameron Street—location)
5 Ellis Avenue (mailing address)
Bath, NY 14810

Berkshire Conference of Women
Historians
College of Staten Island (Cony)
Staten Island, NY 10301
(212) 390-7988

"Dear Cousin" Letter
1121 Linhof Road
Wilmington, OH 45177-2917
(513) 382-3803
William Brower Bogardus, Family
Representative
Hours: By appointment
Pub. *"Dear Cousin" Letter*, unscheduled
but usually at least twice per year, free
(extensive library permits research on
virtually all Colonial families of early
New York and New Jersey up to about
1800)

The Family Tree
(3290 South Eagle Road, Eagle, ID
83616—location)
PO Box 4311 (mailing address)
Boise, ID 83711
(208) 939-7141
E-mail: anasman@juno.com

Anna Nasman, Office Manager
Pub. *New York Pedigrees*, monthly, $7.00
per issue postpaid; *Genealogical
Journal of Jefferson County, New
York*, annually (April), $17.50 per
issue postpaid; *Genealogical Journal
of Oneida County, New York*, annually
(August), $17.50 per issue postpaid;
*Genealogical Journal of Essex County,
New York*, annually (November),
$17.50 per issue postpaid

Greene Genes
PO Box 116
Maplecrest, NY 12454-0116
(518) 734-3254
E-mail: greene-genes@msn.com
Patricia Morrow, Editor and Publisher
Pub. *Greene Genes: A Genealogical
Quarterly About Greene County, New
York*, quarterly, $20.00 per year
subscription, $5.00 per issue
(Greene County, New York; book
reviews, no advertising, queries)
unlimited free queries for subscribers
only

Heritage North
PO Box 205
Colton, NY 13625
Dennis E. Eickhoff, Director
(publishes records of northern New York
State, Ontario and Quebec)

Hofstra University
Long Island Studies Institute (LISI)
West Campus
Ninth Floor, Axinn Library
619 Fulton Avenue
Hempstead, NY 11550-1090
(516) 463-6409
Barbara M. Kelly, Ph.D., Curator
Hours: Mon–Fri 9:00–5:00
(New York State history)

Kinship—Sources for Kith and Kin
60 Cedar Heights Road
Rhinebeck, NY 12572
(914) 876-4592
Arthur C. M. Kelly,Editor
Hours: Mon–Sun 9:00–9:00
Pub. *The Capital* (Albany and Rensselaer
counties), quarterly, $14.00 per year
subscription; *The Columbia* (Columbia
County), quarterly, $14.00 per year
subscription; *The Mohawk*
(Montgomery and Schenectady
counties), quarterly, $14.00 per year
subscription; *The Saratoga* (Saratoga
County), quarterly, $14.00 per year
subscription
(vital records, queries)
back issues of all titles available, also
available in hardbound format

New Netherland Connections
1232 Carlotte View
Berkeley, CA 94707-2707
E-mail: dkoenig@library.berkeley.edu
Dorothy A. Koenig, Editor

Pub. *New Netherland Connections*,
quarterly (February, May, August and
November), $15.00 per year
subscription
(for those looking for Dutch Colonial
ancestors and their descendants)

New York State Queries
2206 West Borden Road
Spokane, WA 99224-9668
(509) 448-9263
http://www.cet.com/ weidnerc/
newyork.html
Carolyn Wilson Weidner
Pub. *New York State Queries* (queries
and book reviews on New York State,
and every-name index), irregularly,
$7.50 postpaid per issue

North Country Reference and Research Resources Council
7 Commerce Lane
Canton, NY 13617-9666
(315) 386-4560

NyGenWeb
Part of U.S. GenWeb Project
E-mail: ny@usgenweb.com
http://www.rootsweb.com/~nygenweb
(links to other New York resources)

Yesteryears Magazine
3 Seymour Street
Auburn, NY 13021
Malcolm O. Goodelle, Owner
Pub. *Yesteryears Magazine, A Quarterly
for New York State Historical and
Genealogical Research*, quarterly
$9.00 per year membership

NORTH CAROLINA

Archives and Libraries with Holdings in Genealogy

State Archives and Library

North Carolina State Archives
Department of Cultural Resources
Division of Archives and History
Archives and History—State Library
Building
109 East Jones Street
Raleigh, NC 27601-2807
(919) 733-3952; (919) 733-1354 FAX
Jesse R. Lankford, Jr., Assistant State
Archivist
Hours: Tue–Fri 8:00–5:30, Sat 9:00–5:00

State Library of North Carolina
Archives and History—State Library
Building
109 East Jones Street
Raleigh, NC 27601-2807
(919) 733-7222
http://www.dcr.state.nc.us/iss/gr/
genealog.htm
Mrs. Lee Albright, Head, Genealogical
Services
Hours: Mon–Fri 8:00–5:30, Sat 9:00–
noon & 1:00–5:00

State Historical Societies

**Federation of North Carolina
Historical Societies**
109 East Jones Street
Raleigh, NC 27601-2807
(919) 733-7305
Jo Ann Williford, Secretary-Treasurer
Hours: Mon–Fri 8:00–5:00
Pub. *Federation Bulletin*, quarterly
("This is a coalition of North Carolina
Historical Societies.")
$15.00 per year membership

North Carolina Society of Historians
PO Box 93
Sherrills Ford, NC 28673
Elizabeth Bray Sherrill, President

City, County and Regional Archives and Libraries

**Alamance County Historical
Museum**
4777 South N.C. 62
Burlington, NC 27215
(910) 225-8254
Dr. William M. Vincent
Hours: Tue–Fri 9:00–5:00, Sat 10:30–
5:00, Sun 1:00–5:00

("The Museum houses archival materials and maintains a smallgenealogical reference library.")

Anson County Library
120 South Greene Street
Wadesboro, NC 28170

Belhaven Memorial Museum, Inc.
Main Street
PO Box 220
Belhaven, NC 27810
(919) 943-6817; (919) 943-2242; (919) 943-6197; (919) 943-2357 FAX
Peg McKnight, President
Hours: Mon–Tue & Thur–Sun 1:00–5:00, closed major holidays
free admission

Bladen County Public Library
(111 North Cypress Street—location)
PO Box 1417 (mailing address)
Elizabethtown, NC 28337
(910) 862-6990; (910) 862-8777 FAX
Ms. Sherwin Rice, Library Director
Hours: Mon & Fri 8:30–5:30, Wed noon–5:30, Tue & Thur 8:30–5:30, Sat 8:30–3:30, Sun 2:00–4:30

Thomas Hackney Braswell Memorial Library
344 Falls Road
Rocky Mount, NC 27804
(919) 442-1951
Hours: Mon–Thur 9:00–9:00, Fri–Sat 9:00–5:00, Sun (Sept.–May) 1:00–5:00

Buchanan County Public Library
(see Virginia)

Burke County Public Library
204 South King Street
Morganton, NC 28655
(704) 437-5638
Lynda Garibaldi, Curator, North Carolina Room
Hours: Mon–Tue & Fri–Sat 8:30–6:00, Wed 8:30–12:00, Thur 8:30–8:30

Caldwell County Public Library
120 Hospital Avenue
Lenoir, NC 28645
(704) 757-1270; (704) 757-1413 FAX
E-mail: djustice@ncsl.dcr.state.nc.us
Diaana Justice, Reference Librarian
Hours: Mon, Wed & Fri 8:30–5:30, Tue & Thur 8:30–8:30, Sat 9:00–4:00

Charles A. Cannon Memorial Library
Local History Collection, Lore Room
27 Union Street, North
Concord, NC 28025
(704) 788-3167; (704) 784-3822 FAX
Kathryn L. Bridges, Local History Librarian
Hours: Local History Collection: Sept–May: Mon–Tue & Thur 9:00–12:00 & 1:00–5:00, Wed 1:00–4:00; Jun–Aug schedule varies, all out-of-town patrons call ahead for hours

(emphasis on Cabarrus County genealogy and local history)
search fee by mail: $10.00 (limited availability), photocopies 15¢ per page, microcopies 25¢ per page, some restrictions apply

Catawba County Library
115 West "C" Street
Newton, NC 28658
(704) 464-2421
Evelyn D. Rhodes, Genealogical Services Librarian
Hours: Mon–Thur 8:30–8:30, Fri–Sat 8:30–5:00

Public Library of Charlotte and Mecklenburg County
Robinson/Spangler Carolina Room
310 North Tryon Street
Charlotte, NC 28202-2176
(704) 336-2980, (704) 336-2677 FAX
E-mail: cbates@plcmc.lib.nc.us
http://www.plcmc.lib.nc.us/branch/main/carolina/
Christopher A. Bates, Curator and Manager
Hours: Mon–Thur 9:00–9:00, Fri–Sat 9:00–6:00, Sun 1:00–6:00

Charlotte Museum of History and Hezekiah Alexander Homesite
3500 Shamrock Drive
Charlotte, NC 28215
(704) 568-1774; (704) 566-1817 FAX
Lisa, Administrative Assistant
Hours: Tue–Fri 10:00–5:00, Sat–Sun 2:00–5:00
Pub. *Mecklenburg Courier*, quarterly (reference library (Lassiter Library); genealogy listings, monographs and publications, focus on Alexander families of Piedmont Carolinas and other regional families)
$35.00 per year membership in the Friends of the Charlotte Museum of History and H. Alexander Homesite

Cherokee County Historical Museum, Inc.
205 Peachtree Street
Murphy, NC 28906
(704) 837-6792
Alice D. White, Director
Hours: Mon–Fri 9:00–5:00
(genealogical services)

Cleveland County Memorial Library
104 Howie Drive
PO Box 1120
Shelby, NC 28150
(704) 487-9069; (704) 487-4856
Carol H. Wilson, Director
Hours: Mon–Thur 9:00–9:00, Fri 9:00–5:00, Sat 9:00–1:00
15¢ per page for photocopies from paper, 25¢ per page for photocopies from microform

Cumberland County Public Library
State and Local History Room
300 Maiden Lane
Fayetteville, NC 28301
(919) 483-3745
James Britton, State and Local History Librarian
Hours: Mon–Wed 9:00–9:00, Thur–Sat 9:00–6:00, Sun (Sept–May) 2:00–6:00

Currituck County Library
Star Route, Box 826, Highway 158
Barco, NC 27917
(919) 453-8345 (no calls for genealogical research)
Hours: Mon 9:00–8:00, Tue–Fri 9:00–6:00, Sat 10:00–4:00
SASE will be answered, copies 15¢ per page plus additional postage

Davidson County Historical Museum
(Old Courthouse on the Square—location)
2 South Main Street (mailing address)
Lexington, NC 27292
(704) 242-2035
Jeanette Wilson, Assistant

Davidson County Public Library
602 South Main Street
Lexington, NC 27292
(704) 242-2040
Jeanette Wilson, Genealogy Librarian
Hours: Mon–Thur 9:00–9:00, Fri–Sat 9:00–5:30

Davidson University
PO Box 1837
Davidson, NC 28036
(704) 892-2331; (704) 892-2625 FAX
http://www.davidson.edu/administrative/library/little.htm

Duke University
Special Collections Library
PO Box 90185
Durham, NC 27708-0185
(919) 660-5822; (919) 684-2855 FAX
E-mail: specoll@mail.lib.duke.edu
http://www.lib.duke.edu/

Durham County Library
300 North Roxboro
PO Box 3809
Durham, NC 27702
(919) 560-0171
E-mail: aberkley@ncsl.dcr.state.nc.us
Anne Berkley, North Carolina Reference Librarian
Hours: Mon–Thur 9:00–9:00, Fri 9:00–6:00, Sat 9:30–6:00, Sun (except Memorial Day–Labor Day) 2:00–6:00

East North Carolina University
J. Y. Joyner Library
Special Collections
Greenville, NC 27858-4353
(919) 328-6601; (919) 328-0268 FAX
http://fringe.lib.ecu.edu/JoynerLib/LibraryDepts/SpclColl/

Edgecombe County Memorial Library
Local History Collection
909 Main Street
Tarboro, NC 27886
(919) 823-1141
Hours: Mon–Thur 9:00–9:00, Fri 9:00–
6:00, Sat 9:30–5:00

Forsyth County Public Library
North Carolina Room
660 West Fifth Street
Winston-Salem, NC 27101
(919) 727-2152
Jerry R. Carroll, Head Librarian, North
Carolina Room
Hours: Mon–Thur 9:00–9:00, Fri 9:00–
6:00, Sat 9:00–5:00, Sun (Sept–May)
1:00–5:00

Gaston-Lincoln Regional Library
1555 East Garrison Boulevard
Gastonia, NC 28054
(704) 868-2168
Dianne Hollandsworth, Reference
Librarian
Hours: Mon–Thur 9:00–9:00, Fri–Sat
9:00–6:00, Sun (Sept–May) 2:00–6:00
(North Carolina materials, especially
Gaston and Lincoln County family
histories)

Greensboro Historical Museum
130 Summit Avenue
Greensboro, NC 27401-3004
(910) 373-2043; (910) 373-2204 FAX
Stephen Catlett Archivist
Hours: Tue–Sat 10:00–5:00, Sun 2:00–
5:00; Archivist: Mon–Fri 9:00–5:00
Pub. *GHM Journal* (not genealogical)

Hacksma House Genealogy Library
(see Washington)

Heritage Center
North Carolina Conference
Greensboro, NC 27411
(919) 379-7874

Heritage Place
Lenoir Community College
Learning Resources Center
(Highway 70 and 58 East—location)
PO Box 188 (mailing address)
Kinston, NC 28502
(919) 527-6223, ext. 508; (919) 527-
6223, ext. 501
Sue Rouse, Library Assistant
Hours: Mon–Thur 7:45–9:00, Fri 7:45–
4:00 (varies with college schedule)
(North Carolina local history museum)

Hertford County Library
Tryon Street
PO Box 68
Winton, NC 27986
(919) 358-7855; (919) 358-0368 FAX
Natalie Welker, Librarian
Hours: Mon & Wed–Fri 10:00–6:00, Tue
12:00–8:00, Sat 9:00–12:00

High Point Public Library
901 North Main Street
PO Box 2530
High Point, NC 27261-2530
(910) 883-3637; (910) 883-3657 FAX
E-mail: jackie.hedstrom@ci.high-
point.nc.us
Jacquelyn Browning Hedstrom
Hours: Mon–Thur: 8:00 A.M.–9:00 P.M.,
Fri 8:00–6:00, Sat 9:00–noon & 1:00–
6:00, Sun (Sept–May) 1:30–5:30 (call
ahead to verify hours)
Pub. *Newsletter for the North Carolina
Collection High Point Library*,
quarterly, free
(North Carolina genealogy and local
history, North Carolina census records,
Civil War history)
no in-depth correspondance research, but
responds to requests for copies of very
specific citations, $1.00 for the first
page, 50¢ each for pages 2–10, 30¢ for
each additional page

J. C. Holliday Memorial Library
Genealogy Department
217 Graham Street
Clinton, NC 28328

Iredell County Library
PO Box 1810
135 East Water Street
Statesville, NC 28677
(704) 878-3093
David A. Bunch
Hours: Mon–Thur 9:00–9:00, Fri–Sat
9:00–6:00, Sun 2:00–6:00

Elbert Ivey Memorial Library
420 Third Avenue, N.W.
Hickory, NC 28601
(704) 322-2905; (704) 322-3479 FAX
Jane L. Deal, R.G., Reference/Genealogy
Librarian
Hours: Mon–Thur 9:00–9:00, Fri–Sat
9:00–5:00, Sun (Sept–May) 2:00–5:00
(local historians: Hahn/Heffner
collections, UDC & DAR; "For a
library our size: medium, we have a
very good collection of local history,
genealogical, and state resources, plus
a very extensive vertical file on all
three areas.")
Catawba County residents free, out-of-
county $20.00 per year per family

Public Library of Johnston County and Smithfield
Johnston County Room
305 Market Street
Smithfield, NC 27577
Hours: Mon–Thur 9:00–9:00, Fri 9:00–
5:30, Sat 9:00–5:00

Lawrence Memorial Public Library
204 East Dundee Street
Windsor, NC 27983
(919) 794-4898
Nancy B. Hughes

Hours: Mon–Tue & Thur–Fri 10:00–
6:00, Wed 2:00–6:00, Sat 9:00–12:00

Macon County Public Library
45 Wayah Street
PO Box 822
Franklin, NC 28734
(704) 524-3600
Nancy Van Hook
Hours: Mon, Wed & Fri 11:00–5:30, Tue
& Thur 10:00–9:00, Sat 10:00–4:00

The Madison-Morgan Cultural Center
Museum Drive
Winston-Salem, NC 27105
David D. Bonney, II

Madison Public Library
a branch of Rockingham County Public
Library
140 East Murphy Street
Madison, NC 27025
(910) 548-6553; (910) 548-2010 FAX
Sarah Pell, Branch Librarian
Hours: Mon 10:00–8:00, Tue & Fri
10:00–6:00, Wed 9:00–6:00, Thur
noon–8:00, first, third and fifth Sat
9:00–4:00
(emphasis on Rockingham and Stokes
counties)

Mauney Memorial Library
100 South Piedmont
Kings Mountain, NC 28086
(704) 739-2371; (704) 734-4499 FAX
Rose Turner, Director
Hours: Mon–Thur 9:00–8:00, Fri 9:00–
5:00, Sat 9:00–1:00

May Memorial Library
Headquarters of Central North Carolina
Regional Library
342 South Spring Street
Burlington, NC 27215
(910) 229-3588; (910) 229-3592 FAX
E-mail: lkobrin@ncsl.dcr.state.nc.us
http://ils.unc.edu/nclibs/centralnc/
home.htm; http://www.netpath.net/~/
watson/alamance.htm (USGenWeb
homepage for Alamance County
genealogy information)
Lisa Kobrin, Reference Librarian
Hours: Mon–Thur 9:00–9:00, Fri–Sat
9:00–6:00, Sun (Labor Day–Memorial
Day) 1:00–5:00, reference assistance
not necessarily available at all times
(collection focuses on Alamance and
Orange counties, with some
information on surrounding counties)

McDowell County Public Library
100 West Court Street
Marion, NC 28752-3999
(704) 652-2098
E-mail: ehouse@ncsl.dcr.state.nc.us
Elizabeth House, Assistant Librarian
Hours: Mon, Wed & Fri–Sat 10:00–5:30,
Tue & Thur 9:30–8:30
no research by staff, but will supply the
names of area professionals

New Bern-Craven County Public Library
North Carolina Collection
400 Johnson Street
New Bern, NC 28560
(919) 638-7800
E-mail: vjones@ncsl.dcr.state.nc.us
Victor T. Jones, Jr.
Hours: Mon–Thur 9:00–9:00, Fri–Sat 9:00–6:00, Sun 2:00–6:00
(eastern North Carolina, particularly Craven, Pamlico, and Carteret counties)
costs of copying and postage: minimum of $2.00

New Hanover Public Library
Local History and Genealogy
201 Chestnut Street
Wilmington, NC 28401-3942
(910) 341-4394; (910) 341-4388 FAX
Beverly Tetterton, Special Collections Librarian
Hours: Mon–Thur 9:00–9:00, Fri 9:00–6:00, Sat 9:00–5:00, Sun 1:00–5:00
(vertical files, over 1,000 reels of microfilm of Wilmington newspapers from 1765, church records, African-American records, photographs, maps and books and pamphlets specializing in the local history and genealogy of southeastern North Carolina; special collection: Reaves Collection of Southeastern, North Carolina, families)

North Carolina Museum of History
5 East Edenton Street
Raleigh, NC 27601-1011
(919) 715-0200; (919) 733-8655 FAX
Dr. James C. McNutt, Director
Hours: Tue–Sat 9:00–5:00, Sun noon–5:00
Pub. *Tar Heel Junior Historian*, semiannually; *Cornerstone*, three times per year

Ohoopee Regional Library
(see Georgia)

Onslow County Public Library
Tucker Littleton Room
58 Doris Avenue East
Jacksonville, NC 28540
(910) 455-7350
Joan Dillemuth
Hours: Mon–Thur 9:00–9:00, Fri–Sat 9:00–6:00

Park Memorial Public Library
67 Haywood Street
Asheville, NC 28801
(704) 255-5203
Hours: Mon–Thur 10:00–9:00, Fri–Sat 10:00–6:00, Sun (Sept–May) 2:00–6:00

Person County Public Library
319 South Main Street
Roxboro, NC 27573

John Zika, Librarian
Hours: Mon–Thur 10:00–8:00, Fri 10:00–5:00, Sat 10:00–2:00

Reed Gold Mine Library
9621 Reed Mine Road
Stanfield, NC 28163

Robersonville Public Library
PO Box 1060
South Main Street
Robersonville, NC 27871
(919) 795-3359
Madge Partin
Hours: Mon–Fri 9:30–5:30, Sat 9:30–1:00

Robeson County Public Library
101 North Chestnut Street
PO Box 988
Lumberton, NC 28358
(919) 738-4859; (910) 739-8321 FAX
Barbara Allchin, Reference Librarian
Hours: Mon, Wed & Fri–Sat 9:00–6:00, Tue & Thur 9:00–9:00
(local history and genealogy collection)

Rowan Public Library
Edith M. Clark History Room
201 West Fisher Street
PO Box 4039
Salisbury, NC 28144-4039
(704) 638-3021
Kevin Cherry, Local History/Genealogy Librarian; Joe Barbee, Associate Local History/Genealogy Librarian
Hours: Mon–Thur 9:00–9:00, Fri 9:00–5:00, Sat 9:00–5:00, Sun (Sept–May) 1:00–5:00
(emphasis on North Carolina genealogy with holdings covering the southeastern and mid-Atlantic states: Pennsylvania, Maryland, Virginia, North Carolina, South Carolina, Georgia, Tennessee and Kentucky)

Sandhill Regional Library
1104 East Broad Avenue
PO Box 548
Rockingham, NC 28379

Scotland County Memorial Library
(312 West Church Street, Laurinburg, NC 28352—location)
PO Box 369 (mailing address)
Laurinburg, NC 28353
(919) 276-0563; (910) 276-4032
Robert Busko, Director
Hours: Mon, Wed & Fri 10:00–6:00, Tue & Thur 10:00–8:00, Sat 9:00–5:00, Sun 2:00–6:00
copies 20¢ per page, other fees depending on the request

Somerset Place State Historic Site
Rt. 1
PO Box 215
Creswell, NC 27928
(919) 797-4560
Leisa M. Brown, Site Manager
(genealogical services)

Stanly County Public Library
Margaret Johnston Heritage Room
133 East Main Street
Albemarle, NC 28001
(704) 983-7329
Lu J. Koontz, Research Assistant
Hours: Mon–Thur 9:00–8:00, Fri 9:00–5:00, Sat (school year) 9:00–5:00, Sat (summer) 9:00–1:00
(North Carolina local history and genealogy)

Sullivan County Library
(see Tennessee)

Richard H. Thornton Library
Main and Spring Streets
PO Box 339
Oxford, NC 27565
(919) 693-1121; (919) 693-2244 FAX
E-mail: fannm@hotmail.com
Fann Montague, Library Assistant
Hours: Library: Mon & Wed 9:00–6:00, Tue & Thur 9:00–8:00, Fri 9:00–5:00, Sat 10:00–2:00, Sun 2:00–5:00; Genealogy Room: Tue–Wed & ½ day on Thur

Troy Public Library
(see Alabama)

Union County Public Library
316 East Windsor Street
Monroe, NC 28110
(704) 283-8184
Daniel S. MacNeill, Director
Hours: Mon, Wed & Fri 9:00–6:00, Tue & Thur 9:00–8:00, Sat 9:00–5:00, Sun (Sept–May) 2:00–5:00

The University of North Carolina at Chapel Hill
North Carolina Collection
Wilson Library
Campus Box 3930
Chapel Hill, NC 27599-3930
(919) 933-1172; (919) 962-4452 FAX
H. G. Jones, Ph.D., Curator
Pub. *Annual Reports of the North Caroliniana Society, Inc. and the North Carolina Collection*, annually

The University of North Carolina at Chapel Hill
Southern Historical Collection and Manuscripts Department
Wilson Library
Campus Box 3926
Chapel Hill, NC 27514-8890
(919) 962-1345; (919) 962-4452 FAX
E-mail: mss@email.unc.edu
http://www.lib.unc.edu/mss/
Richard A. Shrader, Reference Archivist
Hours: Manuscripts Department: Mon–Fri 8:00–5:00, Sat 9:00–1:00

The University of North Carolina at Charlotte
Special Collections, Atkins Library
9201 University City Boulevard
Charlotte, NC 28223
(704) 547-2449
http://www.uncc.edu/lis/collections/
    special
Robin Brabham, Special Collections
    Librarian
(200+ manuscript collections, comprising
    approximately 1,000,000 items that
    document the social, political and
    architectural history of the greater
    Charlotte area; many of the collections
    contain material relevant to
    genealogical research)

Wayne County Public Library
1001 East Ash Street
Goldsboro, NC 27530
(919) 735-1824; (919) 731-2889 FAX
E-mail: pritty@ncsl.dcr.state.nc.us
Paul M. Ritty, Jr., Local History/
    Genealogy Librarian
Hours: Mon–Thur 9:00–9:00, Fri–Sat
    9:00–5:30, Sun (during school year)
    1:00–5:00

Wilson County Public Library
PO Box 400
Wilson, NC 27893
(919) 237-5355
Deborah Webb
Hours: Mon–Thur 9:00–9:00, Fri–Sat
    9:00–6:00

Historical Societies— Local and Regional

Alleghany Historical-Genealogical Society, Inc.
(Alleghany County Courthouse—
    location)
PO Box 817 (mailing address)
Sparta, NC 28675
(919) 372-4214
Irene R. Wagner
Pub. *Alleghany Historical-Genealogical
    Society, Inc., Bulletin*, quarterly
$5.00 per year membership

Anson County Historical Society
209 East Wade Street
PO Box 732
Wadesboro, NC 28170
(704) 694-6694
Lynda Garibaldi, President
Pub. *Newsletter*, bimonthly
$15.00 per year membership for
    individuals, $25.00 per year
    membership for families, $45.00 per
    year membership for businesses

The Appalachian Consortium
University Hall
Boone, NC 28608
(704) 262-2064; (704) 262-6564
E-mail: burlesonec@appstate.edu
Mike Epley, Executive Director
Hours: 8:00–4:30
(genealogical services)

Beaufort Historical Association
(100 Block Turner Street—location)
PO Box 1709 (mailing address)
Beaufort, NC 28516-0363
(919) 728-5225; (919) 728-4966 FAX
E-mail: bha@bmd.clis.com
Marilyn Collins, Executive Director
Hours: Apr–Oct: Mon–Sat 9:30–5:00
    Nov–Mar: Mon–Sat 10:00–4:00

Bladen County Historical Society
PO Box 848
Elizabethtown, NC 28337

Brunswick County Historical Society
PO Box 874
Shallotte, NC 28459
(919) 754-8445
Gwen Causey, President
Pub. *BCHS Newsletter*

Burke County Historical Society
Burke County Public Library
204 South King Street
PO Box 151
Morganton, NC 28655
(704) 437-3533
Joe Avery, Treasurer
Hours: Library: Mon–Tue & Fri–Sat
    8:30–6:00, Wed 8:30–12:00, Thur
    8:30–8:30

Camden County Historical Society
Camden, NC 27921
(919) 336-2747

Carteret County Historical Society, Inc.
Carteret County Museum of History and
    Art
100 Wallace Road
PO Box 481
Morehead City, NC 28557
(919) 247-7533 phone or FAX
E-mail: cchistry@bmd.clis.com
Jack Spencer Goodwin, Director of
    Library Services; Leslie A. Ewen,
    President CCHS; Michelle Stokes,
    Director CCMHA
Hours: Tue–Sat 1:00–4:00
Pub. *The Researcher*, quarterly
(Carteret County history and
    genealogies)
$20.00 per year membership for
    individuals, $25.00 per year
    membership for couples, $30.00 per
    year membership for families; charge
    for photocopies; accepts queries

Cary Historical Society
PO Box 134
Cary, NC 27512-0134
(919) 467-6989
Irene Kittinger, Treasurer
Pub. *CHS Newsletter*

Caswell County Historical Association, Inc.
PO Box 278
Yanceyville, NC 27379
(919) 694-6426
Sallie P. Anderson, Editor
Hours: Yanceyville Public Library:
    weekdays 9:00–5:00
Pub. *Newsletter*, quarterly (January,
    April, July, October)
$5.00 per year membership

Catawba County Historical Association, Inc.
(former Catawba County Courthouse, 15
    North College Avenue—location)
PO Box 73 (mailing address)
Newton, NC 28658-0073
(704) 465-0383; (704) 465-0928 FAX
Sidney Halma, Museum Director
Hours: Tue–Fri 9:00–4:00, Sat–Sun
    2:00–5:00
Pub. *Past Times*, quarterly
(primary sources)
$15.00 per year membership; free
    admission; search fees: $10.00 per
    hour

Chatham County Historical Association
PO Box 913
Pittsboro, NC 27312
(919) 542-3603
Jane Pyle, secretary
Pub. *Chatham Historical Journal*; *CCHA
    Newsletter*, occasionally (two to four
    per year)
$5.00 per year membership

Cleveland County Historical Association and Museum
Court Square
PO Box 1335
Shelby, NC 28150
(704) 482-8186
James D. Marler, Museum Director

Cumberland County Historical Society
312 DeVane Street
Fayetteville, NC 28305
(919) 484-5217

Davidson County Historical Association
1 South Main
PO Box 404
Lexington, NC 27292
(919) 476-7213

Duplin County Historical Society
Leora H. McEachern Library of Local
   History
314 East Main Street
PO Box 130
Rose Hill, NC 28458
(910) 289-2430 (Library, evenings only)
W. D. Herring, Librarian
Hours: 7:00 P.M.–midnight, and other
   times by appointment
Pub. *Footnotes*, quarterly
(genealogical collection)
$10.00 per year membership

**Eastern Cabarrus Historical Society
and Museum**
North Main Street
PO Box 1299
Mount Pleasant, NC 28124
(704) 436-6570 (President)

Edenton Historical Commission
505 South Broad Street
Edenton, NC 27932-1937
(919) 482-3663

**Edgecombe County Historical
Society**
130 Bridgers Street
Tarboro, NC 27886
(919) 823-4159
Meade B. Horne, Director, Blount-
   Bridgers House
Hours: 8:30–5:00
Pub. *Non Nulla*
(Blount, Bridgers families)

**Family Research Society of
Northeastern North Carolina**
106 South McMorrine Street, Suite 6
Elizabeth City, NC 27909
(919) 333-1640
Annette Williams, Research Co-ordinator
Hours: Tue, Thur & Sat 10:00–3:00
Pub. *Carolina Trees and Branches*,
   quarterly
(covers Camden, Currituck, Chowan,
   Dare, Gates, Pasquotank and
   Perquimans counties, part of the
   original Albemarle County)
$15.00 per year membership for
   individuals

**Gaston County Historical Society,
Inc.**
315 Union-New Hope Road
Gastonia, NC 28056
(704) 867-6712
Wilma Ratchford Craig, Editor
Pub. *Gaston County Historical Bulletin*

Gates County Historical Society
Old Gates County Courthouse
PO Box 98
Gates, NC 27937
(919) 357-1733
Edith Seiling, President
Hours: on request

Pub. *Gates County Historical Society
   Newsletter*, semiannually
$10.00 per year membership

**Halifax County Historical
Association**
PO Box 12
Halifax, NC 27839
(919) 583-7821; (919) 583-7831 FAX
J. Rivers Manning, Jr., Vice President

**Henderson County Genealogical and
Historical Society, Inc.**
432 North Main Street
PO Box 2616
Hendersonville, NC 28793-2616
(704) 693-1531
Evelyn Masden Jones
Hours: Mon–Fri 9:00–4:00, Sat 9:00–
   noon, and by appointment
Pub. *Henderson County North Carolina
   Genealogical and Historical Society
   Journal*, quarterly, $7.00 per issue
$20.00 per year membership

High Point Historical Society
High Point Museum
1859 East Lexington Avenue
High Point, NC 27262
(910) 885-6859; (910) 883-3284 FAX
Sherri Simon, Executive Director
Hours: Tue–Sat 10:00–4:30, Sun 1:00–
   4:30
Pub. *The Quill*, quarterly
(three galleries of local/regional North
   Carolina history, especially furniture
   and textiles, and three restored
   historical buildings adjacent to the
   Museum)
from $15.00 per year membership; free
   admission

Hillsborough Historical Society
Corbin Street
PO Box 871
Hillsborough, NC 27278
(919) 732-8648
Clarence D. Jones, Office Manager
Hours: mornings only
Pub. *Newsletter*, quarterly
$10.00 per year membership

Historic Jamestown Society, Inc.
PO Box 512
Jamestown, NC 27282
(919) 454-3819

**Hyde County Historical and
Genealogical Society**
Rt. 1, Box 74
Fairfield, NC 27826
(919) 926-4921
Betty S. Mann, Treasurer
Hours: Mon–Sat 1:00–8:00
Pub. *High Tides*, semiannually
(Hyde County and area history and
   genealogy)
$15.00 per year membership

Jones County Historical Society
PO Box 219
Trenton, NC 28585
(919) 448-3911

Kannapolis History Associates
PO Box 21
Kannapolis, NC 28102-0021

Lower Cape Fear Historical Society
126 South Third Street
Wilmington, NC 28402
(910) 762-0492; (910) 763-5869
   (Archives)
Jean S. Scott, Executive Director; Diane
   C. Cashman, Archivist
Hours: Society: Mon–Sat 10:00–4:00;
   Archives: Tue–Thur 10:00–12:30 and
   by appointment
Pub. *For the Record: Newsletter of the
   Lower Cape Fear Historical Society*;
   *Lower Cape Fear Historical Society
   Bulletin*, three times per year; *Lower
   Cape Fear Historical Society Journal*
(history of the Lower Cape Fear/
   southeastern North Carolina)
$20.00 per year membership for
   individuals (includes only *For the
   Record* and the *Bulletin*), $30.00 per
   year membership for families, $10.00
   per year membership for students,
   $50.00 per year Contributing
   membership for families, $100.00 per
   year Sustaining membership for
   families or Contributing membership
   for businesses, $250.00 per year
   Supporting membership for
   businesses, $500.00 per year Patron
   membership for families or Sustaining
   membership for businesses, $1,000.00
   per year Patron membership for
   businesses; research: copy costs,
   postage

Macon County Historical Society
(36 West Main Street, Franklin, NC
   28734—location)
PO Box 822 (mailing address)
Franklin, NC 28744
(704) 524-9758
http:///www.intertekweb.com/gpsbook/
   macon/index.htm/
Mia Rhodarmer, Director
Hours: Museum: Mon–Fri 10:00–4:00,
   Sat (May 1–Oct 31) 11:00–4:00
Pub. *Macon County Echoes*, quarterly
(Macon County history and families)
$15.00 per year membership for
   individuals (beginning in July); $25.00
   per year membership for families

Madison County Historical Society
PO Box 236
Marshall, NC 28753
(704) 689-1153

Malcolm Blue Historical Society
(Bethesda Road, Highway 5, South—location)
PO Box 603 (mailing address)
Aberdeen, NC 28315
(910) 692-8317
Paul Brill, President
Hours: Thur–Sat 1:00–4:00
Pub. *Blue Farm News*, quarterly

Martin County Historical Society
Francis M. Manning History Room
Martin County Community College Library
PO Box 468
Williamston, NC 27892
(919) 792-1521, ext. 296 (Library); (919) 792-4425 FAX
Doris L. Wilson, Chairman
Hours: College Library hours
(local and regional historical and genealogical materials)

Mecklenburg Historical Association
PO Box 35032
Charlotte, NC 28235
Robin Brabham, President
(has no staff or library and can only refer users to libraries)

Montgomery County Historical Society
PO Box 161
Mount Gilead, NC 27366

Moore County Historical Association
(Shaw House, Corner of Morganton and Broad—location)
PO Box 324 (mailing address)
Southern Pines, NC 28388
(910) 692-2051
Janet Cunningham, Director
Hours: Mid-Jan to Jul & Sept to mid-Dec: Fri–Sat 1:00–4:00
(history of Moore county)
$15.00 per year regular membership, $25.00 per year Contributing membership, $50.00 per year Supporting membership, $100.00 Patron and Corporate membership; no search fees but requests a donation for postage

Mordecai Square Historical Society
Capital Area Preservation (CAP)
Mordecai Historic Park
1 Mimosa Street
Raleigh, NC 27604
(919) 834-4844 (CAP)
Sally Poland, Executive Director
Hours: CAP Office: Mon–Fri 8:30–5:00
Pub. *Square Notes*; *Preservation Matters*, quarterly
$25.00 per year membership for individuals

Murfreesboro Historical Association
116 East Main Street
PO Box 3
Murfreesboro, NC 27855
(919) 398-4886

New Bern Historical Society
510 Pollock Street
PO Box 119
New Bern, NC 28563
(919) 638-8558; (919) 638-5773 FAX
Joanne Gwaltney, Executive Director
Hours: Mon–Fri 8:30–4:00
Pub. *Journal of the NBHS*, semiannually, $5.00 per year subscription; *NBHS Newsletter*

Onslow County (NC) Historical Society
PO Box 5203
Jacksonville, NC 28540
(910) 347-5287
JoAnn Stidger Becker, Secretary
$10.00 per year membership

Outer Banks History Center
(Roanoke Island Festival Park—location)
PO Box 250 (mailing address)
Manteo, NC 27954
(919) 473-2655; (919) 473-1483 FAX
E-mail: nsc0017@mail.interparth.com
http://www.ah.dcr.state.nc.us/obhc/default.htm
Wynne C. Dough, Curator
Hours: Mon–Fri 9:00–5:00, Sat 10:00–3:00 (call ahead)
Pub. *O.B.H.C. Associates Newsletter*, quarterly, $10.00 per calendar year subscription
(a non-lending regional library and manuscript repository of the North Carolina Department of Cultural Resources, Division of Archives and History; houses many types of genealogical resource materials, not entirely restricted to the coastal areas: more than 4500 U.S. Life Saving Service and U.S. Coast Guard wreck documents, more than 3000 photographs, more than 1300 serials, more than 700 original maps and charts, and a variety of clippings, recordings, microforms, engravings, and ephemera)
copying and postage fees for queries

Pasquotank Historical and Genealogical Society
PO Box 523
Elizabeth City, NC 27909
(919) 335-2041
Edna Shannonhouse, Historian
Pub. *Pasquotank Historical Society Newsletter*, quarterly
$5.00 per year membership

Person County Historical Society, Inc.
PO Box 887
Roxboro, NC 27573

Pitt County Historical Society
PO Box 5063
Greenville, NC 27834
(919) 752-3129

Randolph County Historical Society
(201 Worth Street, Asheboro, NC 27203—location)
PO Box 4355 (mailing address)
Asheboro, NC 27204
(919) 318-6815
L. McKay Whatley, President
Hours: Mon–Fri 9:00–5:00
$5.00 per year Associate membership for individuals, $10.00 per year regular membership for individuals, $15.00 per year membership for families, $25.00 per year Contributing membership, $50.00 per year Corporate membership; $100.00 life membership

Rockingham County Historical Society
PO Box 84
Wentworth, NC 27375
(910) 951-2595; (910) 342-5901 (Office)
Robert W. Carter, Jr., Editor
Hours: by appointment only
Pub. *Journal of Rockingham County History and Genealogy*, semiannually; *Newsletter*, quarterly
$12.00 per year membership

Sampson County Historical Society
PO Box 1084
Clinton, NC 28328

Southern Appalachian Historical Association, Inc.
PO Box 295
Boone, NC 28607
(704) 264-2120
William R. Winkler, III, Executive Producer

Southern Studies Institute
(see Louisiana)

Southport Historical Society
(Old Jail, Nash Street—location)
501 North Atlantic Avenue (mailing address)
Southport, NC 28461
(919) 457-6940
Susan S. Carson, Librarian; Cheryl R. Daniel, President
Hours: only on special occasions and by appointment
Pub. *The Whittlers' Bench*, bimonthly (includes a genealogy page)
$10.00 per year membership for individuals, $15.00 per year membership for husband and wife or institutions, $2.00 per year membership for students (through high school only)

Stokes County Historical Society
PO Box 250
Germanton, NC 27019
(919) 591-7969

Swain County Genealogical and Historical Society
PO Box 267
Bryson City, NC 28713
E. Proctor
Pub. *Bone Rattler*, quarterly
$16.00 per year membership

Wayne County Historical Association
PO Box 665
Goldsboro, NC 27530-0665
(919) 736-5011
Emily Weil, Association President
Hours: Archives in the Local History Room at Wayne County Public Library: Mon–Thur 9:00–9:00, Fri–Sat 9:00–5:30, Sun (during school year) 1:00–5:00; Wayne County Museum:
Pub. *WCHA Reflections*, periodically
(Wayne County Historical Association is a multifaceted umbrella organization composed of: Old Dobbs County Genealogical Society, Waynesborough Commission, Wayne County Museum, and Historical Association Revolving Fund; central eastern North Carolina, numerous publications about Wayne County and the former Dobbs County; owns and operates historic properties: the 1855 First Presbyterian Church, now called Town Meeting Hall, and the 1927 Goldsboro Woman's Club building, now the Wayne County Museum)
$10.00 per year membership for individuals in each component or a total of $40.00 for membership in all components, $15.00 per year membership for families in each component

Western North Carolina Historical Association, Inc.
283 Victoria Road
Asheville, NC 28801
(704) 253-9231
James C. McDonald, President
Pub. *WNCHA Newsletter*

The Wise County Historical Society
The Appalachian Quarterly
(see Virginia)

The Yadkin County Historical and Genealogical Society, Inc.
(The Tulbert House, 216 North Van Buren Street—location)
PO Box 1250 (mailing address)
Yadkinville, NC 27055-1250
(910) 679-2982
Andrew L. Mackie, President

Hours: Thur 10:00–4:00, and by appointment
Pub. *The Yadkin County Historical and Genealogical Society Journal*, quarterly
(Yadkin County, North Carolina, history, genealogy, historic preservation of properties, including abandoned cemeteries)
$15.00 per year membership for individuals or non-profit organizations, $20.00 per year membership for families; $25.00 per year membership for for-profit businesses; $150.00 life membership for individuals, $200.00 life membership for families; queries welcome

---

LDS Family History Centers

Chapel Hill
(919) 967-0988

Charlotte
(704) 535-0238

Fayetteville
(910) 860-1350

Greensboro
(see Chapel Hill)

Raleigh
(919) 878-7747

Genealogical Societies

State Genealogical Society

North Carolina Genealogical Society
PO Box 1492
Raleigh, NC 27602
E-mail: ncgs@earthlink.net
http://www.moobasi.com/genealogy/ncgs/homepage.html
Crestena Oakley, Secretary
Pub. *North Carolina Genealogical Society Journal*, quarterly; *NCGS News*, quarterly
$30.00 per year membership for individuals ($5.00 discount to renewing members if received before 1 January), $35.00 per year membership for families, $30.00 per year membership for institutions, $100.00 per year Patron membership, $500.00 life membership for individuals, $600.00 life membership for families

Regional Genealogical Societies

Alamance County Genealogical Society
PO Box 3052
Burlington, NC 27215-3052
Raymond D. Donnell, Past President
Pub. *Alamance Genealogist*, three times per year (May, September, January)
(emphasis on Alamance and Orange counties)
$10.00 per year membership for individuals or institutions, $2.50 per year membership for each additional member in a household, $25.00 per year overseas membership, $150.00 life membership

Albemarle Genealogical Society
Rt. 1, Box 15
Coinjock, NC 27923
Lois Meekins, Corresponding Secretary
Hours: meetings at Currituck County Library: second Tue (Jan, Apr, Jul, Oct) 7:30
Pub. *Genealogical Newsletter*, quarterly
(primarily Currituck, Dare and Pasquotank counties
$8.00 per year membership for individuals, $10.00 per year membership for couples; queries free, but members have priority as space permits

Alexander County Ancestry Association, Inc.
PO Box 241
Hiddenite, NC 28636
(704) 635-0064
Evelina Miller, President
Hours: Tue & Thur 9:00–3:00
Pub. *Kinfolk and Connections of Alexander County*, quarterly
$8.00 per year membership

Alleghany Historical-Genealogical Society, Inc.
(Alleghany County Courthouse—location)
PO Box 817 (mailing address)
Sparta, NC 28675
(919) 372-4214
Irene R. Wagner
Pub. *Alleghany Historical-Genealogical Society, Inc., Bulletin*, quarterly
$5.00 per year membership

Beaufort County Genealogical Society
PO Box 1089
Washington, NC 27889-1089
(919) 946-4212
Louise M. Cowell, Treasurer
Pub. *Pamteco Tracings*, semiannually, $6.00 per issue or $12.00 per year for back issues

$10.00 per year membership for individuals, $15.00 per year membership for two or more at one address

The Broad River Genealogical Society, Inc.
316 Dale Street
PO Box 2261
Shelby, NC 28151-2261
(704) 482-3016
E-mail: tombird@shelby.net
http://www.rootsweb.com/~ncclevel/clevel.htm
Tommy P. Bridges
Pub. *Eswau Huppeday (Line River in the Cherokee Languages)*, quarterly
$10.00 per year membership for individuals, $17.50 per year membership for families

Burke County Genealogical Society (BCGS)
PO Box 661
Morganton, NC 28655
(704) 437-5638 (Library)
Lynda Garibaldi, Curator, North Carolina Room; Robert Donaldson, President BCGS; Lori Rehberger, Vice President BCGS
Hours: Burke County Public Library: Mon–Wed & Fri–Sat 8:30–6:00,Thur 8:30–8:30
Pub. *The Burke Journal*, quarterly
$12.00 per year membership for individuals, $15.00 per year membership for families; search fee: $2.00 plus 25¢ per copy mailed out

Cabarrus Genealogy Society
PO Box 2981
Concord, NC 28025
E-mail: lhayer@concordnc.com
Larry Hayer, Vice President
Hours: Cabarrus Senior Center, 331 Corban Avenue, S.E., Concord, NC: second Tue 7:00 P.M.
Pub. *The Golden Nugget*, quarterly (March, June, September, December)
$15.00 per year membership for individuals, $17.00 per year membership for famiies living at one address, $7.00 per year membership for students under 18, $50.00 per year Sponsor membership, $200.00 life membership

Caldwell County Genealogical Society
PO Box 2476
Lenoir, NC 28645
(704) 757-1272
Hours: Mon, Wed & Fri 8:30–5:30, Tue & Thur 8:30–8:00, Sat 8:30–1:00
Pub. *Caldwell County Genealogical Society Journal*, quarterly
$10.00 per year membership

Carolinas Genealogical Society
Old Courthouse, on the Square
PO Box 397
Monroe, NC 28111
(704) 289-6737
Virginia Kendrick, President
Hours: Mon–Wed 10:00–3:00, Thur 1:00–4:00
Pub. *Bulletin of the Carolinas Genealogical Society*, quarterly; *Yearbook*, annually
(Piedmont section of North Carolina, upper-central South Carolina)
$15.00 per year membership for individuals, $18.00 per year membership for families

Catawba County Genealogical Society
PO Box 2406
Hickory, NC 28603
Lucille Fulbright, President
Pub. *Catawba Cousins*, quarterly
(Catawba County local and regional genealogy)
$10.00 per year membership for individuals, $15.00 per year membership for families

Coastal Genealogical Society
PO Box 1421
Swansboro, NC 28584
(910) 347-5287
JoAnn Stidger Becker, Secretary
Pub. *Coastal Genealogical Society*, quarterly
$10.00 per year membership

Cumberland County Genealogical Society
PO Box 53299
Fayetteville, NC 28305
(919) 484-5217
Mrs. W. D. Sherman, Corresponding Secretary
Hours: 7:00 A.M.–9:00 A.M. & 6:00 P.M.–9:00 P.M.
Pub. *Newsletter*, eight times per year
(Cumberland, Bladen and Robeson counties)
$8.00 per year membership

Genealogical Society of Davidson County
PO Box 1665
Lexington, NC 27292
(910) 242-2040; (910) 248-4122 FAX
Jeanette Wilson, Librarian
Hours: Mon–Thur 9:00–9:00, Fri–Sat 9:00–5:30
Pub. *The Genealogical Journal*, quarterly; *Newsletter*, quarterly
$15.00 per year membership

Durham-Orange Genealogical Society, Inc.
PO Box 4703
Chapel Hill, NC 27515-4703
E-mail: dogs@rtpnet.org

http://www.rtpnet.org/ dogs
Pub. *The Trading Path*, quarterly; *Newsletter*, eleven times per year (monthly, except June-July combined)
$15.00 per year membership; no charge for queries from members or non-members

Edgecombe County Genealogical Society
Edgecombe County Memorial Library
909 Main Street
Tarboro, NC 27886
(919) 827-4405; (919) 823-7241
Betty Reason, President
Hours: Pender Room: third Thur 7:00 (except December and July)
Pub. *Lines and Pathways*, monthly
$10.00 per year membership for individuals, $15.00 per year membership for couples; $3.00 donation per query plus copies

Family Finders Genealogical Society
410 Old Pollocksville Road
New Bern, NC 28562
(919) 633-4591
David Barteau, President
Hours: LDS Church: meetings second Tue 7:00 P.M.
Pub. *Family Finders*, bimonthly
$12.00 per year membership for individuals, $15.00 per year membership for families

Forsyth County Genealogical Society
(Forsyth County Public Library, 660 West Fifth Street, Winston-Salem, NC 27101—location)
PO Box 5715 (mailing address)
Winston-Salem, NC 27113-5715
(919) 724-0714
Cleo T. McBride, Treasurer
Pub. *Forsyth County Genealogical Society Journal*, quarterly; *Forsyth County Genealogical Society Newsletter*, monthly
(specializes in Forsyth, Stokes, Davie, Rowan and Surry counties)
$15.00 per year membership for individuals or institutions, $17.50 per year membership for families

The Guilford County Genealogical Society
PO Box 9693
Greensboro, NC 27429-0693
L. E. Jarrell, President
Hours: First Friends Meeting, 2100 West Friendly Avenue, Greensboro, NC: third Sat (Oct–Nov & Jan–May) 10:30 A.M.
Pub. *The Guilford Genealogist*, quarterly
$15.00 per year membership

Halifax County Genealogical Society
PO Box 447
Halifax, NC 27839
Pub. *Halifax County Genealogical Society Newsletter*

Harnett County Genealogical Society

(201 Leslie Campbell Avenue—location)
PO Box 219 (mailing address)
Buies Creek, NC 27506-0219
(910) 893-8786 FAX
Professor Eric Brodin, Treasurer
Pub. *Heirs & Ancestors*, quarterly
$14.00 per year membership

Henderson County Genealogical and Historical Society, Inc.

432 North Main Street
PO Box 2616
Hendersonville, NC 28793-2616
(704) 693-1531
Evelyn Masden Jones
Hours: Mon–Fri 9:00–4:00, Sat 9:00–
noon, and by appointment
Pub. *Henderson County North Carolina Genealogical and Historical Society Journal*, quarterly, $7.00 per issue
$20.00 per year membership

Huxford Genealogical Society, Inc.

(see Georgia)

Hyde County Historical and Genealogical Society

Rt. 1, Box 74
Fairfield, NC 27826
(919) 926-4921
Betty S. Mann, Treasurer
Hours: Mon–Sat 1:00–8:00
Pub. *High Tides*, semiannually
(Hyde County and area history and genealogy)
$15.00 per year membership

Genealogical Society of Iredell County

(Old Courthouse, Downtown, 200 South Center Street—location)
PO Box 946 (mailing address)
Statesville, NC 28677
(704) 878-5384
Nellie Gray Stimson, President
Hours: Tue & Fri 10:00–2:00
Pub. *Iredell County Tracks*, quarterly
(includes Homer Keever and Dr. P. F. Laugenour papers)
$10.00 per year membership; copies from files: 40¢ per page (plus $2.00 postage if over 50 pages)

Johnston County Genealogical Society

Public Library of Johnston County and Smithfield
305 Market Street
Smithfield, NC 27577
(919) 934-8146
Dr. Luby F. Royall, President
Hours: Johnston County Room: Mon–Thur 9:00–9:00, Fri 9:00–5:30, Sat 9:00–5:00
Pub. *Johnston County Genealogical Society Newsletter*, quarterly
$10.00 per year membership (beginning in January)

McDowell Genealogical Society

Rt. 1, Box 796
Nebo, NC 28761
(704) 652-5377
Peggy Silvers

Mecklenburg Genealogical Society

Olde Mecklenburg Genealogical Society
PO Box 32453
Charlotte, NC 28232
Pub. *Old Mecklenburg Genealogical Society Quarterly*; *Olde Mecklenburg Genealogical Society Newsletter*

Moore County Genealogical Society, Inc.

PO Box 1183
Pinehurst, NC 28370-1183
Pub. *Moore County Genealogical Society Newsletter*, quarterly
$12.00 per year membership for individuals, $15.00 per year membership for families and institutions

Old Buncombe County Genealogical Society, Inc.

#22 Innsbruck Mall
85 Tunnel Road
PO Box 2122
Asheville, NC 28802
(704) 253-1894
Zelma F. Smith, Business Manager
Hours: Mon 1:00–5:00 & 7:00–9:00, Tue–Fri 9:00–5:00, Sat 9:00–1:00
Pub. *A Lot of Bunkum*, quarterly
(Buncombe, Clay, Cherokee, Graham, Haywood, Henderson, Jackson, Macon, Madison, Transylvania, Swain and Yancey counties, and the western areas of McDowell, Rutherford and Polk counties)
$30.00 per year membership for individuals, $35.00 per year membership for families; search fee: $5.00 for members, $15.00 for non-members

Old Dobbs County Genealogical Society

PO Box 617
Goldsboro, NC 27533-0617
(919) 242-4772 (President)
Elizabeth Gordon Ellis, President
Hours: quarterly meetings at Western Sizzlin, Ash and Berkely Boulevard, Goldsboro, NC: fourth Sat (Jan, Apr, Jul, Oct)
Pub. *Old Dobbs Trail*, quarterly
(specializes in areas which were formerly Old Dobbs County, now Wayne, Greene, Lenoir and part of Wilson counties; vital statistics, land records, Bible records, etc.; limited research capability)
$10.00 per year membership for individuals, $15.00 per year membership for families; free queries for members

Old New Hanover Genealogical Society

PO Box 2536
Wilmington, NC 28402
(910) 452-9407
Sallie McClintock, Secretary
Hours: 3rd Tue (Sept–May) in Room 105, Bear Hall, University of North Carolina—Wilmington
Pub. *Clarendon Courier*, quarterly
(areas of interest: New Hanover, Bladen, Brunswick, Duplin, Onslow, Pender, Columbus counties)
$15.00 per year membership for individuals or institutions, $20.00 per year membership for families, $100.00 life membership

The Genealogical Society of Old Tryon County

2 West Main Street
PO Box 938
Forest City, NC 28043
(704) 248-4010
James O. Womack, President
Hours: Wed & Thur 9:30–2:00, Sat 1:30–4:30
Pub. *Bulletin of Old Tryon County, North Carolina*, quarterly
$17.50 per year membership

Onslow County Genealogical Society

PO Box 1739
Jacksonville, NC 28541-1739
(910) 347-5287
JoAnn Stidger Becker, President
Hours: Onslow County Public Library: Sept–May: first Tue
Pub. *Onslow County Genealogical Society Newsletter*, quarterly
$10.00 per year membership

Palm Beach County Genealogical Society, Inc.

(see Florida)

Pasquotank Historical and Genealogical Society

PO Box 523
Elizabeth City, NC 27909
(919) 335-2041
Edna Shannonhouse, Historian
Pub. *Pasquotank Historical Society Newsletter*, quarterly
$5.00 per year membership

Polk County North Carolina Genealogical Society

485 Hunting Country Road
Tryon, NC 28782
Frances N. Walker

Randolph County Genealogical Society

(Randolph County Historical Society, 201 Worth Street, Asheboro, NC 27203—location)
PO Box 4394 (mailing address)
Asheboro, NC 27204
(919) 318-6815

Ms. Jo Barrett, President
Hours: Mon–Fri 9:00–5:00, Sat staffed
   by volunteers
Pub. *Randolph County Genealogical
   Journal*, semiannually (March &
   October)
$10.00 per year membership before Feb
   15, $12.00 per year afterwards

Genealogical Society of Rockingham and Stokes Counties
PO Box 152
Mayodan, NC 27027

Genealogical Society of Rowan County
PO Box 4305
Salisbury, NC 28145-4305
June Clodfelter Watson, Editor
Pub. *Journal of the Genealogical Society
   of Rowan County*, quarterly
(includes Old Rowan and present-day
   Rowan County)
$15.00 per year membership for
   individuals, $20.00 per year
   membership for families

Southwestern North Carolina Genealogical Society
101 Blumenthal
Murphy, NC 28906
(704) 837-2417 (Murphy Library)
Becky Stiles, Library Director
Hours: Mon–Wed & Fri 9:00–6:00, Thur
   9:00–9:00, Sat 9:00–2:00
Pub. *Southwestern North Carolina
   Genealogical Quarterly*, $3.00 per
   issue
(Cherokee, Clay and Graham counties)
$12.00 per year membership

Stanly County Genealogical Society
PO Box 31
Albemarle, NC 28002-0031
Lucille C. Curlee, Secretary
Pub. *The Stanly County Genealogical
   Society Journal*, quarterly (January,
   April, July, October), $2.00 per issue
(Stanly County and North Carolina
   genealogical items)
$7.00 per year membership (beginning in
   May)

Surry County Genealogical Association
(Surry Community College, Dobson, NC
   27030—office location)
PO Box 997 (mailing address)
Dobson, NC 27017
(910) 786-7449
Robert B. Holder, President
Hours: anytime
Pub. *Surry County Genealogical
   Association Quarterly* (February, May,
   August, November), $5.00 plus
   postage per issue
$15.00 per year membership for
   individuals, $17.00 per year
   membership for families; limited
   research free

Swain County Genealogical and Historical Society
PO Box 267
Bryson City, NC 28713
E. Proctor
Pub. *Bone Rattler*, quarterly
$16.00 per year membership

Tar River Connections Genealogical Society
PO Box 8764
Rocky Mount, NC 27804
Pub. *Connector*
(covers the eastern North Carolina area
   known as the Tar River-Pamlico basin,
   which includes those counties through
   which the Tar River and its major
   tributaries flow: Person, Granville,
   Vance, Franklin, Nash, Edgecombe,
   Pitt and Beaufort counties; database of
   surnames)
$10.00 per year membership; three free
   queries per year to members, queries
   $5.00 each to non-members

VA-NC-Piedmont Genealogical Society
(see Virginia)

Wake County Genealogical Society
PO Box 17713
Raleigh, NC 27619
Hours: meetings fourth Tue
Pub. *Wake Treasures*, quarterly (spring,
   summer, fall, winter)
$20.00 per year membership (beginning
   in April)

Wilkes Genealogical Society, Inc.
Wilkes County Library
913 C Street
PO Box 1629
North Wilkesboro, NC 28659-1629
Nancy Simpson, Editor
Hours: Mon–Thur 8:00–8:30, Fri 8:00–
   5:00, Sat 8:00–3:00
Pub. *Wilkes County Genealogical Society
   Bulletin*, quarterly
$10.00 per year membership

The Yadkin County Historical and Genealogical Society, Inc.
The Tulbert House
216 North Van Buren Street
PO Box 1250
Yadkinville, NC 27055-1250
(910) 679-2982
Andrew L. Mackie, President
Hours: Thur 10:00–4:00, and by
   appointment
Pub. *The Yadkin County Historical and
   Genealogical Society Journal*,
   quarterly
(Yadkin County, North Carolina, history,
   genealogy, historic preservation of
   properties, including abandoned
   cemeteries)
$15.00 per year membership for
   individuals or non-profit organizations,
   $20.00 per year membership for

families; $25.00 per year membership
for for-profit businesses; $150.00 life
membership for individuals, $200.00
life membership for families; queries
welcome

Independent Publications and Miscellany

Anson County Heritage Book Committee
PO Box 417
Wadesboro, NC 28170
(published collection of family sketches)

Appalachian Roots
(see West Virginia)

Argyll Colony Plus
6716 Meadow Haven
Fort Worth, TX 76132
Scott Buie, Editor
Pub. *Argyll Colony Plus* (Highland Scots
   of North Carolina), quarterly, $20.00
   per year subscription

Center for Appalachian Studies
Berk Library
Appalachian State University
Boone, NC 28608
(704) 262-4072; (704) 262-2553 FAX
J. W. Williamson, Editor
Pub. *Appalachian Journal: A Regional
   Studies Review*, quarterly, $18.00 per
   year subscription
("We are a multi-disciplinary publication
   covering the entire Appalachian
   region.")

Central North Carolina Publications
PO Box 2681
Sanford, NC 27331-2681
James Vann Comer, Editor
Pub. *Central North Carolina Journal*,
   $7.50 per issue

Culbreth Associates
Rt. 2, Box 2987
Columbus, NC 28722
Pub. *For the Record: A Journal of Polk
   County History and Genealogy*,
   quarterly, $15.00 per year subscription

The 1850 Company
Rt. 4, Box 150
Whiteville, NC 28472
Pub. *Lower East Journal*, quarterly,
   $16.00 per year subscription

Friends of the Archives, Inc.
109 East Jones Street
Raleigh, NC 27601-2807
(919) 733-3952

Genealogical Institute
(see Virginia)

Genealogy Books and Consultation
(see Texas)

Granville Queries
3320 N.E. 120th Street
Okeechobee, FL 34972-7453
Frances (Scroggins) Wheeler, Publisher
Pub. *Granville Queries*, quarterly (May,
August, November and February),
$12.00 per year subscription (includes
the original Granville County, formed
in 1746 from Edgecombe County,
including the present-day counties of
Granville, Warren, Franklin, Vance,
Person, Caswell, Durham, Orange,
Rockingham and Alamance, as well as
Bute, which was abolished in 1779)
unlimited free queries to subscribers

Historic Cabarrus, Inc.
(65 Union Street, South, Concord, NC
28025—location)
PO Box 966 (mailing address)
Concord, NC 28026
(704) 786-8515
Elizabeth Bennett, Executive Director
Hours: Mon–Fri 9:00–noon

Historic Flat Rock, Inc.
PO Box 295
Flat Rock, NC 28731
(704) 693-1638

Historic Hamilton Commission, Inc.
(Front Street, Hamilton, NC 27840—
location)
508 Glenn Avenue (mailing address)
Rocky Mount, NC 27801
(919) 442-7941

Historical Publications Section
Archives and History—State Library
Building
109 East Jones Street
Raleigh, NC 27601-2807
Pub. *Carolina Comments*; *The North
Carolina Historical Review*, quarterly,
$25.00 per year subscription

Hunting for Bears Genealogical and Historical Society
(see Alabama)

The Mountain Empire Genealogical Quarterly
(see Virginia)

Mountain Press
(see Tennessee)

NCGenWeb
Part of U.S. GenWeb Project
E-mail: nc@usgenweb.com
http://www.goldenbranches.com/nc-state/
(links to other North Carolina resources)

North Carolina Genealogy and History News
Rt. 3, Box 65
Chandler, OK 74834-8504
R. D. Bradshaw, Editor
Pub. *North Carolina Genealogy and
History News*

North Carolina Museums Council
PO Box 2603
Raleigh, NC 27602
(910) 767-6730 (President)
Beverly Sanford, President
Pub. *NCMC Museum Directory*,
biannually
(the only organization to represent all of
North Carolina's museums: history,
science, art)

Robeson County Register
Doctor's Building, Suite 901
1012 South Kings Drive
Charlotte, NC 28283
(704) 333-1443
Dr. Morris F. Britt, Editor; JoAnn Britt,
Secretary
Hours: Office: Mon–Fri 9:00–5:00
Pub. *Robeson County Register*, quarterly,
$30.00 per year subscription
(Robeson, Bladen and Hoke counties;
genealogy and local history of
Robeson County, North Carolina)

Rowan County Register
403 Idlewood Drive
PO Box 1948
Salisbury, NC 28145-1948
(704) 633-3575
Jo White Linn, C.G., Editor
Pub. *Rowan County Register*, quarterly,
$25.00 per year subscription
(twenty-six North Carolina counties and
all of Tennessee formed from original
Rowan County, North Carolina)

Sherrill Investigations
PO Box 5
Sherrills Ford, NC 28673-0005
(704) 478-2469; (704) 478-2469
Elizabeth Bray Sherrill, R.G.
Hours: Mon–Thur 9:00–3:00
Pub. *Stepping Back in Time* (eastern
Catawba County—Mountain Creek,
Catawba and Caldwell townships—
Iredell and Lincoln counties),
annually, $25.00 per year subscription
search fee: $25.00 per hour plus
expenses

Simmons Historical Publications
(see Kentucky)

Society of North Carolina Archivists
PO Box 20448
Raleigh, NC 27619-0448

E-mail: paul_kiel@ncsu.edu
http://www.duke.edu/~rkoonts/index.htm
Ed Morris, Treasurer
(a professional organization of archivists
representing 130 North Carolina
public and private institutions and
corporations; no research facilities, but
publishes *Archival and Manuscript
Repositories in North Carolina: A
Directory*, $22.00 postpaid for non-
members)

Southern Genealogist's Exchange Society
(see Florida)

Virginia Settlers
(see Virginia)

Families of Yancey County, North Carolina
PO Box 1035
North Highlands, CA 95660-1035
(916) 991-4165
Sally Williams, Editor
Pub. *Families of Yancey County, North
Carolina*, quarterly, $15.00 per year
subscription

NORTH DAKOTA

Archives and Libraries with Holdings in Genealogy

State Archives and Library

State Archives and Historical Research Library
State Historical Society of North Dakota
North Dakota Heritage Center
612 East Boulevard Avenue
Bismarck, ND 58505
(701) 328-2668 (Division Office); (701) 328-2091 (Reference Desk); (701) 328-3710 FAX
Gerald Newborg, Division Director; Dolores Vyzralek, Chief Librarian
Hours: Mon–Fri 8:00–5:00

North Dakota State Library
Liberty Memorial Building
Capital Grounds
Bismarck, ND 58505
(701) 224-4622
http://www.sendit.nodak.edu/ndsl/index.html

State Historical Society

State Historical Society of North Dakota
State Archives and Historical Research Library
North Dakota Heritage Center
612 East Boulevard Avenue
Bismarck, ND 58505-0830
(701) 328-2668 (Division Office); (701) 328-2091 (Reference Desk); (701) 328-3710 FAX
http://www.state.nd.us./hist/
Gerald Newborg, Division Director; Dolores Vyzralek, Chief Librarian
Hours: Mon–Fri 8:00–5:00
Pub. *North Dakota History*, quarterly; *Plains Talk*, quarterly
(history of Dakota Territory, North Dakota, family history and genealogy; newspapers, census, naturalizations, index to deaths, marriages and divorces, index to naturalizations)
$30.00 per year membership; search fees: $5.00 per census, naturalization, obituary search, plus 25¢ per sheet for copies

City, County and Regional Archives and Libraries

Buffalo Trails Museum
PO Box 22
Epping, ND 58843

(701) 859-4361; (701) 859-3512
Elmer H. Halvorson, Curator
Hours: 9:00–5:00
(emphasis on regional history)
$5.00 per year membership

Carnegie Regional Library
Seventh and Griggs
Grafton, ND 58237
(701) 352-2754; (701) 352-2757 FAX
Garry Littlefield, MLS Director
Hours: Mon–Thur 10:00–6:00, Fri–Sat 10:00–5:00
(regional collection, genealogical resources limited)

Center for Great Plains Studies
(see Kansas)

Center for Great Plains Study
(see Nebraska)

Divide County Public Library
204 First Street, N.E.
PO Box 90
Crosby, ND 58730
(701) 965-6305
Dorene E. Wenstad, Director
Hours: Mon–Fri 8:30–5:00
(books on local cemeteries, deaths and indices of Divide County, also a few on Williams and Burke counties, inventory microfilms of most local newspapers, dating back to the early 1900s)

Fargo Public Library
102 North Third Street
Fargo, ND 58102
(701) 241-1492
Linda Clement-Sherman
Hours: Mon–Thur 9:00–9:00, Fri–Sat 9:00–6:00, Sun (Sept–May) 1:00–5:00

Frontier Museum
Rt. 2, Box 9
Williston, ND 58801
(701) 572-5009

Germans from Russia Heritage Society
1008 East Central Avenue
Bismarck, ND 58501-1936
(701) 223-6167
E-mail: grhs@btigate.com
http://www.teleport.com/nonprofit/grhs/
Rachel Schmidt, Office Manager
Hours: Mon–Fri 9:30–5:00
Pub. *Heritage Review*, quarterly
("The GRHS Library contains family histories, local histories, obituaries, pedigree charts, and passenger lists as well as other reference materials.")
Chapters: **British Columbia**, Pat Hagel, President, 2400 25th Street, Vernon, British Columbia V1T 4P5, Canada, (604) 542-2110; **First California Chapter**, c/o Tom Hoffman, 5070 Ducos Place, San Diego, CA 92124, (619) 277-9721; **Northern California**, Don Merton Schell, President, 6304

39th Avenue, Sacramento, CA 95824-1912, (916) 456-5035, *Northern California GRHS Chapter Newsletter*, quarterly; **Puget Sound**, Bob Schuh, Past President, 724 S.W. Hayter Street, Dallas, OR 97338-1845, (503) 623-5529, E-mail: rpschuh@teleport.com, *Puget Sound Chapter Newsletter*, quarterly
$25.00 per year membership; search fee: $10.00 per hour

Public Library, Grand Forks
2110 Library Circle
Grand Forks, ND 58201
(701) 772-8116
Hours: Mon–Thur 9:00–9:00, Fri–Sat 9:00–5:00, Sun 1:00–5:00

Hatton-Eielson Museum
PO Box 278
Hatton, ND 58240-0278
Hours: 9:00–4:00

Leach Public Library
417 Second Avenue, North
Wahpeton, ND 58075

Lewis and Clark Trail Museum
Alexander, ND 58331
(701) 828-3595
Evelyn Lebak, Manager
Hours: Sun (Memorial Day–Labor Day) 1:00–5:00

Minot Public Library
516 Second Avenue, S.W.
Minot, ND 58701
(701) 852-1045; (701) 852-2595
Jeanne Narum, Circulation Supervisor
Hours: Mon–Thur 9:00–9:00, Fri 9:00–6:00, Sat 10:00–4:00, Sun 1:00–5:00

Museum of the Great Plains
(see Oklahoma)

North Dakota State University
North Dakota Institute for Regional Studies
North Dakota State University Libraries
PO Box 5599
Fargo, ND 58105-5599
(701) 237-8914; (701) 231-7138 FAX
E-mail: mmmiller@badlands.nodak.edu
http://www.lib.ndsu.nodak.edu/ndirs/
John E. Bye, Archivist
Hours: Mon–Fri (academic year) 8:00–5:00; Mon–Fri (summer) 7:30–5:00
("Collects printed and manuscript material regarding North Dakota")

Reynolds Community Museum
PO Box 14
Reynolds, ND 58275

University of North Dakota
Elwyn B. Robinson Department of Special Collections
Chester Fritz Library
PO Box 9000
Grand Forks, ND 58202-9000

(701) 777-4625 (Special Collections);
(701) 777-3319 FAX
E-mail: slater@plains.nodak.edu
http://www.und.nodak.edu/dept/library/
Collections/spk.html
Sandra J. Slater
Hours: Mon–Thur 8:00–5:00, Fri 8:00–
4:30, Wed 8:00–9:00
Pub. *Guide to Norwegian Bygdeboker*,
annually; *Guide to Family History
Resources*, annually
(specializes in Norwegian ancestry, "825
vols. bygde boker")
research: $10.00 per hour plus 20¢ per
page for photocopies

Historical Societies— Local and Regional

Barnes County Historical Society, Inc.
2030 West Main
PO Box 661
Valley City, ND 58072
(701) 845-0966
Rebecca R. Heise, Secretary
Hours: Mar–May & Sept–Dec: Sun
1:00–4:00; Jun–Aug: Mon–Fri & Sun
1:00–4:00
Pub. *Barnes County History*
(local organization histories, town and
family histories)
$10.00 per year membership for
individuals; $15.00 per year
membership for families, $100.00 life
membership

Bismarck-Mandan Historical and Genealogical Society
2708 North Fourth Street
PO Box 485
Bismarck, ND 58501
(701) 223-2929
Pub. *Dakota Homestead Historical
Newsletter: Bismarck-Mandan
Historical and Genealogical Society*,
quarterly
$6.00 per year membership

Bottineau Historical Society
(North Main Street—location)
321 Alexander Street (mailing address)
Bottineau, ND 58318
Kenneth E. Johnson, President

Brenorsome Historical Society
PO Box 232
Tokio, ND 58379
(701) 294-3351
Louis Garcia, President
(Spirit Lake Dakota Nation, formerly
Devils Lake Sioux Tribe; genealogy,
history, customs, traditions; also local
county history, etc.)

Burke County Historical Society
HC 1, Box 196 (mailingaddress)
Powers Lake, ND 58773
(701) 464-5771
Larry Tenjum, President
Hours: occasional, special dates
Pub. *Local*
$1.00 per year membership, $25.00 life
membership

Cass County Historical Society
1351 West Main Avenue
PO Box 719
West Fargo, ND 58078
(701) 282-2822
Margo R. Lang, Administrative Manager
Hours: season, call for hours
Pub. *Bonanzaville Pioneer*, annually;
Quarterly Newsletter, quarterly

Cavalier County Historical Society
(Dresden, ND—museum location)
Rt. 1, Box 5 (mailing address)
Wales, ND 58281-9705
(701) 283-5284
Fannie Valentine, President
Hours: Library Day: first Sun (Jun–Sept)
2:00–5:00
Pub. *C.C. Museum Update*, semiannually
(spring and fall)
donations accepted

Coteau Hills Historical Center
Forbes, ND 58439
(701) 357-7011

Dunn County Historical Society
PO Box 86
Dunn Center, ND 58626
(701) 548-8111; (701) 225-3708
(President)
Dorothy Galyen, Chairman
Hours: various
Pub. *Tales and Trails*, three times per
year
$5.00 per year membership

Emmons County Historical Society
N.W. First and Oak
Linton, ND 58552
Ellen C. Woods, President
Pub. *ECHS Newsletter*

Flasher Historical Society
Fifth Avenue, East
PO Box 245
Flasher, ND 58535
(701) 597-3721
Howard VandeVenter, President

Fort Pembina Historical Society
245 South Second Street
Pembina, ND 58271
(701) 825-6209
Milfred D. Hart, President
("Ours is a historical society with
monthly meetings; no museum.")

Foster County Historical Society
480 McKenzie Avenue
Carrington, ND 58421

Geographical Center Historical Society
102 Highway 2 S.E.
Rugby, ND 58368-8801
(701) 776-6414
Pamela Schmitt, Curator
Hours: 1 May–1 Oct: Mon–Sat 8:00–
7:00, Sun 1:00–7:00

Glen Ullin Historical Society
Glen Ullin, ND 58631
(701) 348-3149

Golden Valley County Historical Society
PO Box 384
Beach, ND 58621-0384

Grand Forks County Historical Society
2405 Belmont Road
Grand Forks, ND 58201
(701) 775-2216

Grant County Historical Society
PO Box 135
Carson, ND 58551
(701) 622-3541

Griggs County Historical Society
Rt. 2, Box 85
Cooperstown, ND 58425
(701) 797-2267

Hebron Historical and Art Society
PO Box 123
Hebron, ND 58638
(701) 878-4486
Henry Mische; Lambert Kastrow; Saok
Hauser
Hours: holidays, and by appointment

Hettinger County Historical Society
Main Street
Regent, ND 58650
(701) 563-4547

Lansford Threshers and Historical Association, Inc.
Lansford, ND 58750
(701) 784-5422
Hours: Memorial Day–Labor Day by
appointment

Marmarth Historical Society
PO Box 518
Marmarth, ND 58643
(701) 279-5792
Evelyn Lecoe, President
Pub. *Marmarth Historical Society*

McIntosh County Historical Society
(101 Third Avenue, N.E.—location)
521 First Avenue, N.E., PO Box 10
(mailing address)
Ashley, ND 58413
(701) 288-3605

McKenzie County Museum and Historical Society, Inc.
PO Box 602
Watford City, ND 58854
(701) 842-5286

McLean County Historical Society
(700 Block, Main Street, Washburn, ND—location)
PO Box 84 (mailing address)
Garrison, ND 58540
(701) 463-2834
Dolores Staehr, President

Mercer County Historical Society
Seventh Street and Central Avenue
PO Box 1134
Beulah, ND 58523
Esther Scheidt, Secretary
Hours: summer: Sunday 1:00–4:00
Pub. *Bits and Pieces*, semiannually
$5.00 per year membership for individuals, $25.00 per year membership for businesses, $100.00 life membership

MonDak Historical and Arts Society
(see Montana)

Niagara Community Historical Society
Niagara, ND 58266
(701) 397-5774

Nome Community Historical Association
12730 51st Street, S.E.
Nome, ND 58062
(701) 924-8877 (Residence)
Ruth Christensen, Secretary

Oliver County Historical Society
(Center, ND—location)
New Salem, ND 58563 (mailing address)
(701) 794-3116

Ransom County Historical Society
Fort Ransom, ND 58033
(701) 973-2211

Richland County Historical Society
(Second Street and Seventh Avenue, Wahpeton, ND 58075—location)
PO Box 1326 (mailing address)
Wahpeton, ND 58075
(701) 642-3075
Hours: Tue, Thur & Sat–Sun 1:00–4:00, closed winters
small charge for search, depending on time

Theodore Roosevelt Nature and History Association
PO Box 167
Medora, ND 58645
(701) 623-4466

Stark County Historical Society
Taylor, ND 58656
(701) 974-3605

Steele County Historical Society
(Steele Avenue and Third Street—location)
PO Box 144 (mailing address)
Hope, ND 58046
(701) 945-2394
Russell Ford-Dunker, Director
Hours: Tue–Fri 9:00–5:00, Sun (summer) 2:00–5:00, and by appointment
("Archive Center-newspapers, family histories, records from 1883 on")
$5.00 per year membership; search fee: $10.00 per hour

Walsh County Historical Society
Minto, ND 58261

Ward County Historical Society
(North Dakota State Fairgrounds—location)
Rt. 5, Box 269 (mailing address)
Minot, ND 58701
(701) 839-0785
Stanley Saugstad, President

Wells County Historical Society
PO Box 554
Fessenden, ND 58438
(701) 547-3467
Pub. *Wells County History*
$5.00 per year membership

LDS Family History Centers

Bismarck
(701) 222-2794

Fargo
(701) 232-4003

GENEALOGICAL SOCIETIES

Regional Genealogical Societies

Bismarck-Mandan Historical and Genealogical Society
PO Box 485
Bismarck, ND 58502-0485
Pub. *The Dakota Homestead*, quarterly
$8.00 per year membership for individuals, $10.00 per year membership for families

McLean County Genealogical Society
PO Box 51
Garrison, ND 58540
(701) 463-2091 (Treasurer); (701) 337-5559 (Vice President)
Wanda G. Huettl, Treasurer; Betty Flath, Vice President
(cemetery records and obituary files)
$5.00 per year membership

Mouse River Loop Genealogical Society
PO Box 1391
Minot, ND 58702
Evelyn Zablotney, Board of Directors
Hours: Minot Public Library: Mon–Thur 9:00–9:00, Fri 9:00–6:00, Sat 10:00–3:00, Sun 1:00–5:00
Pub. *North Central North Dakota Genealogical Record*, quarterly
$7.50 per year membership for individuals, $10.00 per year membership for families and institutions, plus $4.00 postage and handling

Red River Valley Genealogical Society
(112 North University Drive, Suite L-116—location)
PO Box 9284 (mailing address)
Fargo, ND 58106-9284
(701) 239-4129
Linda Zeutschel, Librarian
Hours: Library: Tue–Wed 1:00–4:00, Sat 10:00–4:00
Pub. *Red River Valley Genealogical Society Newsletter*, quarterly
$10.00 per year membership for individuals, $15.00 per year membership for families

Genealogy Guild of Wilkin County, Minnesota, and Richland County, North Dakota
Leach Public Library
417 Second Avenue, North
Wahpeton, ND 58075
Don Karlsrud

Independent Publications and Miscellany

NDGenWeb
Part of U.S. GenWeb Project
E-mail: nd@usgenweb.com
http://www.rootsweb.com/~ndgenweb
(links to other North Dakota resources)

OHIO

Archives and Libraries with Holdings in Genealogy

State Archives and Library

Archives-Library Division
Ohio Historical Society
Interstate Route 71 and 17th Avenue
1982 Velma Avenue
Columbus, OH 43211-2497
(614) 297-2510; (614) 297-2546 FAX
http://winslo.ohio.gov/ohswww/
ohshome.html
Louise Jones, Head, Research Services
Hours: Tue–Sat 9:00–5:00
(member of the Ohio Network of
American History Research Centers,
the designated repository for local
government records and historical
manuscript materials from Delaware,
Fairfield, Fayette, Franklin, Knox,
Licking, Madison, Marion, Morrow,
Pickaway, and Union counties)

State Library of Ohio
65 South Front Street
Columbus, OH 43215-4163
(614) 644-6966
http://winslo.ohio.gov/
Petta Khouw, Head, Genealogy Section
Hours: Mon–Thur 8:00–5:00, Fri 9:00–
5:00
(includes Ohio, New England states,
Virginia, West Virginia and Kentucky)

State Historical Societies

Ohio Historical Society
Archives-Library Division
Interstate Route 71 and 17th Avenue
1982 Velma Avenue
Columbus, OH 43211-2497
(614) 297-2510 (Archives-Library);
(614) 297-2300 (OHS); (614) 297-
2340 (Local History Office); (614)
297-2411 FAX
E-mail: ohsref@winslo.ohio.gov;
ohswww@winslo.state.oh.us
http://winslo.ohio.gov/ohswww/
arch_lib.html
George Parkinson, Chief, Archives-
Library Division, and State Archivist;
Gary J. Arnold, Head of Reference
Services
Hours: Tue–Sat 9:00–5:00
Pub. *Echoes*, monthly, $5.00 per year
subscription; *Timeline*; *Ohio History*,
annually, $10.00 per year subscription

Ohio Association of Historical Societies and Museums (OAHSM)
1985 Velma Avenue
Columbus, OH 43211

(614) 297-2340 (Local History Office)
Richard Francaviglia, Ph.D., Executive
Secretary
Pub. *The Local Historian*, bimonthly
$30.00 per year membership

City, County and Regional Archives and Libraries

Ada Public Library Historical Annex
320 North Main Street
Ada, OH 45810
(419) 634-5246
(collection of local historical books,
newspapers, genealogical records, etc.)

Akron-Summit County Public Library
55 South Main Street
Akron, OH 44326-0001
(330) 643-9040
Marian Davies, Librarian
Hours: Mon–Thur 9:00–9:00, Fri 9:00–
6:00, Sat 9:00–5:00, Sun (winter)
1:00–5:00

Amos Memorial Public Library
230 East North Street
Sidney, OH 45365
(937) 492-8354
Hours: Mon–Thur 10:00–9:00, Fri
10:00–6:00, Sat 10:00–5:00, Sun
1:00–5:00 (summer: closed Sun)

Ashland Public Library
117 West Main Street
Geneva, OH 44041
Rita Kopp, Librarian
Hours: Mon–Thur 9:00–9:00, Fri–Sat
9:00–5:00; research help: first Tue
7:00–9:00, second Thur 1:00–3:00,
third Sat 10:00–noon; meetings third
Tue (Mar–Nov) 6:30–8:45

Aurora Public Library
Aurora Road
Aurora, OH 44202

Barberton Public Library
602 West Park Avenue
Barberton, OH 44203
(330) 745-1194; (330) 745-8261 FAX
Phyllis Taylor, Barberton History
Specialist
Hours: winter (mid-Sept to early May):
Mon–Fri 10:00–9:00, Sat 10:00–
6:00, Sun 1:00–5:00; summer:
Mon–Thur 10:00–9:00, Fri–Sat
10:00–6:00
(has published two books on Barberton)

Barnesville Hutton Memorial Library
308 East Main Street
Barnesville, OH 43713
(740) 425-1651
Jeff Scaggs, Director

Hours: summer: Mon & Thur 10:00–
8:00, Tue–Wed & Fri–Sat 10:00–5:00;
winter: Mon–Thur 10:00–8:00, Fri
10:00–6:00, Sat 10:00–5:00

Bellbrook Historical Museum
42 North Main Street
Bellbrook, OH 45305
(937) 848-2415
Joanne Taylor Caffrey, Museum Trustee
Hours: Wed & Sun 1:00–3:00, Sat (Feb–
Nov) 1:00–3:00
(a small local museum with some local
records available for research:
Bellbrook and Greene County)

Bellevue Public Library
224 East Main Street
Bellevue, OH 44811
(419) 483-4769
http://www.bellevue.lib.oh.us/
Theodore R. Allison, Director
Hours: Mon–Thur 9:00–8:30, Fri–Sat
9:00–5:00

Belpre Public Library
2012 Washington Boulevard
Belpre, OH 45714
(614) 423-8381
Hours: Mon–Wed & Fri–Sat 9:00–8:00

Bierce Library
The University of Akron
Archival Services
Buchtel Avenue
Akron, OH 44325-1702
(330) 972-7670; (330) 972-6383 FAX
John V. Miller, Jr., Director of Archival
Services
Hours: Archives: Mon–Fri 8:00–5:00
(emphasis on northeastern Ohio; member
of the Ohio Network of American
History Research Centers, the
designated repository for local
government records and historical
manuscript materials from Ashland,
Coshocton, Holmes, Portage,
Richland, Stark, Summit, Tuscarawas,
and Wayne counties)

Birchard Public Library
423 Croghan Street
Fremont, OH 43420

Bowling Green State University
Center for Archival Collections
Fifth Floor, Jerome Library
Bowling Green, OH 43403-0175
(419) 372-2411; (419) 372-0155 FAX
E-mail: scharte@bgnet.bgsu.edu
http://www.bgsu.edu/colleges/library/cac/
cac.html
Paul D. Yon, Director; Stephen Charter,
Reference Archivist
Hours: Mon 8:30–8:00, Tue–Fri 8:30–
4:30, Sun 4:00–8:00; summer: Mon–
Thur 8:00–4:30, Fri 8:00–11:00
Pub. *Archival Chronicle*, three times per
year, free subscription

(woman's history, labor history, Civil
War, church history; member of the
Ohio Network of American History
Research Centers, the designated
repository for local government
records and historical manuscript
materials from Allen, Crawford,
Defiance, Erie, Fulton, Hancock,
Hardin, Henry, Huron, Lucas, Ottawa,
Paulding, Putnam, Sandusky, Seneca,
Van Wert, Williams, Wood, and
Wyandot counties)

**Briggs Lawrence County Public
Library**
Phyllis Hamner Room for Local History
and Genealogy
321 South Fourth Street
Ironton, OH 45638
(614) 532-1124; (614) 532-4948 FAX
Naomi Deer, Librarian Assistant
Hours: Library: Mon–Thur 9:30–8:30,
Fri–Sat 9:00–5:30; Phyllis Hamner
Room for Local History and
Genealogy: Mon–Tue & Thur 9:30–
8:30, Wed 9:30–5:30, Fri–Sat 9:00–
5:30

Brooke-Gould Memorial Library
Preble County Room
301 North Barron Street
Eaton, OH 45320-1705
(937) 456-4331
Hours: Mon–Fri 9:00–8:00, Sat 9:00–
5:00, Sun 1:00–5:00

Bryan Public Library
107 East High Street
Bryan, OH 43506
(419) 636-6734
Jeff Yahraus, Circulation Supervisor
Hours: winter: Mon–Thur 10:00–8:30,
Fri 10:00–8:00, Sat 10:00–5:00;
summer: Mon–Fri 10:00–8:00, Sat
10:00–2:00

Burton Public Library
14588 West Park
PO Box 427
Burton, OH 44021
(440) 834-4466; (440) 834-0128 FAX
Pat Hauser, Adult Services Librarian
Hours: Mon–Thur 9:00–9:00, Fri–Sat
9:00–5:00, Sun (Sept–May) 1:00–5:00
(emphasis on Burton and Geauga County
history)

Caldwell Public Library
(517 Spruce Street—location)
PO Box 230 (mailing address)
Caldwell, OH 43724-0230
(614) 732-4506
Marilyn S. Blaney, Director
Hours: Mon–Wed 9:00–8:00, Thur–Fri
9:00–5:00, Sat 9:00–2:00
Pub. *Echoes*, bimonthly, free
(includes a room designated for
genealogy and local history with
family search CD-Rom)

Canal Fulton Public Library
Canal Fulton, OH 44614
(216) 854-4148
Jean Kindry, Director
Hours: Mon–Sat 9:00–9:00
(emphasis on Ohio and Erie Canal local
history)

Carnegie Public Library
219 East Fourth Street
East Liverpool, OH 43920
(330) 385-2048
Hours: Mon–Fri 10:00–8:00, Sat 9:00–
5:00

Carnegie Public Library
127 South North Street
Washington Court House, OH 43160
(614) 335-2540
Pam Waldrep, Adult Services
Hours: Mon–Thur 9:00–8:00, Fri–Sat
9:00–5:00; summer (Memorial Day–
Labor Day): Mon–Wed 9:00–8:00,
Thur–Fri 9:00–500, Sat 9:00–12:00

Champaign County Library
1060 Scioto Street
Urbana, OH 43078
(937) 653-3811; (937) 653-5679 FAX
Linda M. Gieser, Circulation Supervisor
Hours: Mon–Thur 9:00–8:00, Fri–Sat
9:00–5:00, Sun (during school year)
1:00–5:00
(mostly local and regional history)

Chardon Library
Anderson Allyn Room for Genealogical
Research
110 East Park Street
Chardon, OH 44024
Hours: Mon–Thur 9:00–9:00, Fri–Sat
9:00–5:00; Sun (after Labor Day–
before Memorial Day) 1:00–5:00

**Chillicothe and Ross County Public
Library**
140-146 South Paint Street
PO Box 185
Chillicothe, OH 45601
(614) 702-4145; (614) 702-4156 FAX
E-mail: chl0lib@winslo.ohio.gov
Vicky Frey, Genealogy Researcher
Hours: Mon–Thur 9:00–9:00, Fri–Sat
9:00–5:30

**Public Library of Cincinnati and
Hamilton County**
800 Vine Street
Library Square
Cincinnati, OH 45202-2071
(513) 369-6900; (513) 369-6905; (513)
369-6906 (Reference); (513) 369-6909
(Maps); (513) 369-6910 (Newspapers)
http://plch.lib.oh.us
Patricia M. Van Skaik, Head; Karen
Beiser, First Assistant
Hours: Mon–Fri 9:00–9:00, Sat 9:00–
6:00, Sun 1:00–5:00
free admission, fee for photocopies

Clark County Public Library
(201 South Fountain Avenue—location)
PO Box 1080 (mailing address)
Springfield, OH 45501-1080
(937) 328-6904
Hours: Mon–Fri 9:00–9:00, Sat 9:00–
6:00, Sun 1:00–5:00

Cleveland Public Library
325 Superior Avenue
Cleveland, OH 44114-1271
(216) 623-2864 (History); (216) 623-
2800 (Main library)
http://www.cpl.org
Jo Ann Petrello, Head of History and
Geography Department
Hours: Mon–Sat 9:00–6:00, Sun 1:00–
5:00

Columbus Metropolitan Library
Biography, History, Travel Division
96 South Grant Avenue
Columbus, OH 43215
(614) 645-2710
John Newman, Division Head
Hours: Mon–Thur 9:00–9:00, Fri–Sat
9:00–6:00, Sun (Sept–May) 1:00–
5:00
(houses Ohio materials such as county
histories and records of Ohio
genealogy and county historical
societies and Ohiocensus, but no
family histories)
15¢ per photocopy

The Mary L. Cook Public Library
Mary K. Current Ohioana Room
381 Old Stage Road
Waynesville, OH 45068
Linda Crane Swartzel, Reference/
Genealogy Librarian
(a core collection of genealogy books
for states from which people living in
this area may have migrated, local
Quaker records, Ohio county histories,
genealogical information on local
families, etc.; Warren County)

Coshocton Public Library
Miriam C. Hunter Local History Room
Reference Department
655 Main Street
Coshocton, OH 43824-1697
(614) 622-0956; (614) 622-4331 FAX
Linda Yoder, Library Assistant
Hours: Mon–Thur 9:30–9:00, Fri 9:30–
6:00, Sat 9:30–5:30, Sun (Jan–Mar)
1:00–5:00

Cuyahoga County Public Library
Fairview Park Regional Branch
4449 West 213 Street
Fairview Park, OH 44126
(440) 333-4700; (440) 333-0697 FAX
John Bellamy, II, History Specialist
Hours: Mon–Thur 9:00–9:00, Fri–Sat
9:00–5:30, Sun (Sept–May) 1:00–5:00
(regional library with genealogy
specialty)

Dayton and Montgomery County Public Library
215 East Third Street
Dayton, OH 45402-2103
(937) 227-9500; (937) 227-9528 FAX
E-mail: webmaster@dayton.lib.oh.us
http://www.dayton.lib.oh.us/
Carole Medlar, Genealogy Librarian
Hours: Mon–Fri 9:00–9:00, Sat 9:00–6:00, Sun (fall-spring) 1:00–5:00
Pub. *None*
(Montgomery County and Miami Valley records; strong southeast Pennsylvania and New England collections)
search fees: $1.00 out-of-state fee, 75¢ per page for photocopies

Defiance Public Library
320 Fort Street
Defiance, OH 43512-2186
(419) 782-1456
Mrs. Pat Little, Department Head
Hours: Ohioana Room: Mon–Fri 9:00–5:00, "evenings—on your own to 8:00 P.M."; Library: Mon–Thur 9:00–8:00, Fri–Sat 9:00–5:30 (summer: Sat 9:00–12:00)
Pub. *Holding the Fort*, monthly, free

Deshler Edwin Wood Memorial Library
208 North East Avenue
Deshler, OH 43516

Euclid Public Library
631 East 222 Street
Euclid, OH 44123
(216) 261-5300
Hours: Mon–Thur 9:00–9:00, Fri–Sat 9:00–5:00, Sun (Sept–May) 1:00–5:00

Fairfield County District Library
219 North Broad Street
Lancaster, OH 43130
(614) 653-2745
Joyce Harvey, Coordinator of Adult Services
Hours: Mon–Thur 9:00–9:00, Fri–Sat 9:00–5:00, Sun (Sept–May) 1:00–5:00

Findlay-Hancock County Public Library
206 Broadway
Findlay, OH 45840
(419) 422-1712; (419) 422-1737; (419) 422-0638 FAX
Dianne Wood, Local and Family History Librarian
Hours: Sept–Jun: Mon–Thur 9:30–8:30, Fri–Sat 9:30–5:00, Sun 1:00–5:00; Jul–Aug: Mon & Wed 9:30–8:30, Tue & Thur–Sat 9:30–5:00
(a source of history and genealogy for Ohio and the migration area into Ohio; Ohio census 1820–1920, Hancock courthouse records, newspaper collection from the 1850s, high school and college annuals for the city and county, and city directories from the 1890s)

Flesh Public Library
124 West Greene Street
Piqua, OH 45356
(937) 773-6753; (937) 773-5981 FAX
James C. Oda, Archivist
Hours: Mon–Thur 9:00–8:30, Fri–Sat 9:00–5:30
Pub. *Historical Register*

Fort Stephenson Museum
Birchard Public Library
423 Croghan Street
Fremont, OH 43420
(419) 334-7101

Geneva Public Library
Platt R. Spencer (Memorial) Special Collections and Archival Room
860 Sherman Street
Geneva, OH 44041-9101
(216) 466-4521, ext. 13; (216) 466-0162 FAX
Louise Legeza, Archivist
Hours: Mon 10:30–noon & 12:30–8:00, Tue–Wed 10:30–8:00, Thur 10:30–5:00, Fri 11:00–4:00, Sat (except summer) 10:30–4:00
(specializes in Geneva, Ohio, area history and Ashtabula County genealogy; Platt R. Spencer family and business interests; phonetic spelling movement books; old and rare books: U.S. and foreign history, Civil War, Mormon, medical, biography; photos)
search fees: photocopies 20¢ each, minimum $1.00, donation for services, but no extensive research undertaken

Grandview Heights Public Library
1685 West First Avenue
Columbus, OH 43212
(614) 486-2951
Hours: Mon–Fri 9:00–9:00, Sat 9:00–5:00; summer: Mon–Fri 9:00–9:00, Sat 9:00–3:00

Granville Public Library
217 East Broadway
Granville, OH 43023
(614) 587-0196
Hours: Mon–Thur 9:00–9:00, Fri–Sat 9:00–6:00

Greene Cou]nty Public Library
Greene County Room
76 East Market Street
PO Box 520
Xenia, OH 45385
(937) 376-4952; (937) 372-4673 FAX
E-mail: mkane@gcpl.lib.oh.us
Marianne Kane, Assistant
Hours: Mon–Thur 9:00–9:00, Fri–Sat 9:00–6:00, Sun (during school year) 1:00–5:00
free admission

Greenville Public Library
Genealogy Department
520 Sycamore Street
Greenville, OH 45331
(937) 548-3915; (937) 548-3837
E-mail: gplibrary@wesnet.com
Jennifer J. Hart, Library Associate
Hours: Mon–Fri 9:00–7:30, Sat 9:00–4:30
fees: copy cost and postage

Guernsey County District Public Library
800 Steubenville Avenue
Cambridge, OH 43725-2385
(614) 432-5946
Melissa L. Essex
Hours: Labor Day to Memorial Day: Mon–Thur 1:00–5:30, Fri 11:30–8:00, Sat 9:00–5:00; Memorial Day to Labor Day: Mon–Thur 1:00–5:30, Fri 9:00–5:30, Sat 9:00–1:00

Hamilton County Memorial Building
1225 Elm Street
Cincinnati, OH 45210
(513) 721-4506
(library includes local history and architecture)

Hancock Historical Museum
422 West Sandusky Street
Findlay, OH 45840
(419) 423-4433
Doramae O'Kelley, Director/Curator
Hours: Wed–Fri & Sun 1:00–4:00
Pub. *Centerpieces*, quarterly
$15.00–$1,000.00 per year membership; search fee: $15.00 per hour after the first half-hour

Hardin County Historical Museums, Inc.
(Sullivan-Johnson Museum, 223 North Main Street—headquarters location)
PO Box 521 (mailing address)
Kenton, OH 43326
(419) 673-7147
Charles M. Jacobs, Curator-Director
Hours: The Sullivan-Johnson Museum and The Dougherty House-Victorian Wedding Museum, 215 North Detroit Street, Kenton: Jan–Mar: Sat–Sun 1:00–4:00, Apr–Dec: Thur–Sun 1:00–4:00; Agricultural Museum Complex, 14344 County Route 140, south of Kenton: Jun–Aug: Sun 1:00–4:00
Pub. *Columns*, quarterly
(small library and archives, however most records are available through Mary Lou Johnson-Hardin County District Library)
$10.00 per year membership for individuals, $20.00 per year membership for families, $50.00 per year membership for businesses and professions, $10.00 per year

membership for corporations, $500.00 life membership

Harris-Elmore Public Library
PO Box 84
300 Toledo Street
Elmore, OH 43416
(419) 862-2482
Grace Luebke, Director
Hours: Mon–Thur 10:00–8:30, Fri–Sat 10:00–5:00
$18.00 per year membership

Rutherford B. Hayes Presidential Center Library
Spiegel Grove
1337 Hayes Avenue
Fremont, OH 43420-2796
(419) 332-2081; (419) 332-4952
E-mail: hayeslib@nwohio.com
http://www.rbhayes.org
Rebecca Hill and Barbara Paff, Head Librarians
Hours: Mon–Fri 9:00–5:00
(specializes in Ohio genealogy and local history, Civil War, nineteenth century history, President R. B. Hayes and Hayes family)

Henderson Memorial Library
54 East Jefferson Street
Jefferson, OH 44047-1198
(216) 593-2515

The Hudson Library and Historical Society
22 Aurora Street
Hudson, OH 44236
(330) 653-6658; (330) 650-4693 FAX
James F. Caccamo, Archivist
Hours: Library: Mon–Thur 9:00–9:00, Fri–Sat 9:00–5:00; Archives: Mon–Sat 9:00–5:00
$7.50 per year membership for individuals

Jackson City Library
21 Broadway Street
Jackson, OH 45640
(614) 286-2609
Hours: Mon–Wed 10:00–8:00, Thur–Fri 10:00–5:00, Sat 9:00–5:00

Mary Lou Johnson-Hardin County District Library
325 East Columbus Street
Kenton, OH 43326
(419) 673-2278; (419) 674-4321 FAX
E-mail: thaxtosa@oplin.lib.oh.us
Sandy Thaxton, Reference Librarian
Hours: Mon–Thur 9:00–8:00, Fri–Sat 9:00–5:00
(old newspapers and census records, passenger ship lists, Ohio soldiers' rosters)

Johnson-Saint Paris Library
East Main Street
Saint Paris, OH 43072
(513) 663-4349

Eleanor I. Jones Memorial Archives
1 Joy Lane
Camden, OH 45311
(937) 452-1238; (937) 452-3142
E-mail: iamjoyful@jano.com
Linda J. Rhoden
Hours: second Tue 9:00–11:00, and by appointment
(specializes in Camden, Ohio, history; Sherwood Anderson collection)

Junction City Branch Library
108 West Main Street
Junction City, OH 43748
(614) 987-7646
Evelyn Angle Wolfe, District Manager
Hours: Mon & Wed 10:00–7:00, Fri 10:00–6:00, Sat 9:00–1:00

Kent Free Library
312 West Main Street
Kent, OH 44240
(216) 673-4414
Hours: Mon–Fri 9:00–9:00, Sat 10:00–6:00, Sun (seasonally) 1:00–5:00

Kent State University Libraries
Department of Special Collections and Archives
1115 University Library, 12th Floor
Kent, OH 44242
(216) 672-2270
E-mail: nbirk@kentvm.kent.edu; jsomers@lms.kent.edu
http://www.library.kent.edu/speccoll/
Jeanne Somers, Acting Curator
Hours: Mon–Fri 1:00–5:00

Lakewood Public Library
15425 Detroit Avenue
Lakewood, OH 44107
(216) 226-8275; (216) 521-4327 FAX
E-mail: lpl@lkwdpl.org
http://www.lkwdpl.org
Kenneth Warren, Director
Hours: Mon–Fri 9:00–9:00, Sat 9:00–6:00, Sun 1:00–9:00

Lima Public Library
650 West Market Street
Lima, OH 45801
(419) 228-5113
Robert Bertrand, Reference Head
Hours: Mon–Thur 9:00–8:30, Fri–Sat 9:00–5:00, Sat (Memorial Day–Labor Day) 9:00–noon
(emphasis on Allen County)
research: minimum $5.00 per half-hour, 10¢ each for photocopies

Logan County District Library
220 North Main
Bellefontaine, OH 43311
(937) 599-4189; (937) 599-5503 FAX; loganco.lib.oh.us
Ellen V. Kelley, Reference Assistant
Hours: Mon–Fri 9:00–9:00, Sat 9:00–6:00

(Logan County birth and death indexes 1909 to present)
photocopies 20¢ per copy plus postage, obituary request $1.00

Lorain Public Library
351 Sixth Street
Lorain, OH 44052
(216) 244-1192
Joe Jeffries
Hours: Mon–Thur 9:00–8:30, Fri–Sat 9:00–6:00

Loudonville Public Library
122 East Main Street
Loudonville, OH 44842
(419) 994-5531
Hours: Mon–Fri 9:00–8:00, Wed & Sat 9:00–5:00, Sun (Oct–May) 1:00–4:00

Elizabeth M. MacDonell Memorial Library
620 West Market Street
Lima, OH 45801-4665
Anna B. Selfridge, Curator, Archives and Manuscripts; Ray Schuck, Director
Hours: Tue–Sat 1:00–5:00

Mansfield-Richland County Public Library
Sherman Room
43 West Third Street
Mansfield, OH 44902
(419) 521-3115; (419) 525-4750 FAX
Diane Daniels, Head of Adult Services; Karen Furlong, Sherman Room Assistant (Genealogy/Local History Collection)
Hours: Sherman Room: Mon–Thur 9:00–9:00, Fri–Sat 9:00–5:30, Sun 1:00–5:00

Marion Public Library
Ohio Room
445 East Church Street
Marion, OH 43302
(614) 387-0992; (614) 382-3951; (614) 382-2033 (online catalog, N-8-1: Login is HELLO PUBLIC. LIBRARY)
Lynda Williams, Head, Reference
Hours: Mon–Fri 9:00–9:00, Sat 9:00–5:30, Sun (mid-Sept to mid-May) 1:00–5:00

Marysville Public Library
(231 South Court Street—location)
PO Box 438 (mailing address)
Marysville, OH 43040-0438
(513) 642-1876
Mary Beth Merklin, President
Hours: Mon–Thur 10:00–8:00, Sat 10:00–5:00

McComb Public Library
113 South Todd Street
McComb, OH 45858
(419) 293-2425
Hours: Fall–spring: Mon–Thur 9:30–8:00, Fri–Sat 9:30–5:00

McKinley Memorial Library
40 North Main Street
Niles, OH 44446
(216) 652-1704
http://www.mckinley.lib.oh.us
Ann Yancura, Director
Hours: Mon–Thur 9:00–8:00, Fri 9:00–
5:30, Sat 9:00–5:30
(specializes in William McKinley, 25th
President)
$10.00–$100.00 membership in Friends
of the Library organization

**McKinley Museum of History,
Science and Industry**
Ramsayer Research Library
800 McKinley Monument Drive, N.W.
Canton, OH 44708
(216) 455-7043
W. J. Weber, Librarian
Hours: Tue–Wed & Fri 12:30–4:30
Pub. *Museum Highlights* (specializes in
McKinleyana), bimonthly

Menno Simons Historical Library
(see Virginia)

Middletown Public Library
125 South Broad Street
Middletown, OH 45044
(513) 424-1251 (Information and
Reference)
Deirdre Root, Reference Librarian
Hours: Mon–Fri 9:00–9:00, Sat 9:00–
5:00, Sun (except in summer) 1:00–
5:00

**Milan-Berlin Township Public
Library**
Church Street
PO Box 1550
Milan, OH 44846
(419) 499-4117; (419) 499-4697 FAX
Linda Gattshall, Genealogy Coordinator
Hours: 9:30–5:00; Sat 10:00–2:00

Milan Historical Museum
10 Edison Drive
PO Box 308
Milan, OH 44846
(419) 499-2968; (419) 499-9004 FAX
Ellen E. Maurer, Administrator
Hours: Office: daily 9:00–5:00; Museum:
Apr–Oct
Pub. *The New Milan Ledger*, two times
per year
(local Milan history, Western Reserve
history)

Monroe County Library System
(see Michigan)

Morley Library
184 Phelps Street
Painesville, OH 44077-3926
(216) 352-3383, ext. 04
Carl Engel, Local Historian
Hours: Mon–Thur 9:00–9:00, Fri 9:00–
6:00, Sat 9:00–5:00, Sun (mid-Oct to
Apr) 1:00–5:00
(emphasis on Lake County)

**Public Library of Mount Vernon
and Knox County**
201 North Mulberry Street
Mount Vernon, OH 43050
(614) 392-8671
E-mail: libref@knox.net
http://www.knox.net/knox/library/
welcome.htm
Hours: Mon–Fri 10:00–9:00, Sat 9:00–
5:00

John McIntire Library
220 North Fifth Street
Zanesville, OH 43702

Muskingum County Public Library
220 North Fifth Street
Zanesville, OH 43701
(614) 453-0391
Jeffrey Eling (Local History/Genealogy),
Reference Librarian
Hours: Mon–Thur 9:00–8:00, Fri–Sat
9:00–5:30, Sun (winter) 1:00–5:00

New London Public Library
67 South Main Street
New London, OH 44851
(419) 929-3981
Melissa Karnosh
Hours: Mon–Fri 9:00–5:00, Tue & Thur
7:00–8:30, Sat 10:00–5:00

Norwalk Public Library
46 West Main Street
Norwalk, OH 44857-1449
(419) 668-6063; (419) 663-2190 FAX
Laureen Drapp, Director
Hours: Mon–Thur 10:00–8:30; Fri–Sat
10:00–5:00

Oberlin College Archives
420 Mudd Center
Oberlin, OH 44074
(216) 775-8014, ext. 246
http://www.oberlin.edu/ archive/
Roland M. Baumann, Ph.D., Archivist
Hours: Mon–Fri 10:00–noon & 1:30–
4:30
Pub. *Annual Report*, annually
(records relating only to Oberlin students
and Oberlin faculty and staff)

Ohio Genealogy Center
104 East Stafford Avenue
Worthington, OH 43085
(614) 436-8674

Ohio University
Alden Library
Archives and Special Collections
Park Place
Athens, OH 45701-2978
(614) 593-2710; (614) 593-0138 FAX
E-mail: library@www.cats.ohiou.edu
http://www.library.ohiou.edu/libinfo/
depts/microforms/geneal.htm
(Genealogical Resources); http://
www.library.ohiou.edu/libinfo/depts/
archives/archspeccoll.htm (Special
Collections)

George W. Bain, Head, Archives and
Special Collections
Hours: Archives: Mon–Fri 8:00–5:00,
Sat (when university is in session)
noon–4:00; Microforms Department
open evenings, weekends when
university is in session
(member of the Ohio Network of
American History Research Centers,
the designated repository for local
government records and historical
manuscript materials from Athens,
Belmont, Gallia, Guernsey, Hocking,
Jackson, Lawrence, Meigs, Monroe,
Morgan, Muskingum, Noble, Perry,
Pike, Ross, Scioto, Vinton, and
Washington counties)
research fee: $20.00 per hour (prorated
to quarter hours) plus 10¢ per page for
copies

**Old Saint Mary's Historic
Community Center**
123 East 13th Street
Cincinnati, OH 45210
(513) 721-2298

Paulding County Carnegie Library
205 South Main Street
Paulding, OH 45879-1492
(419) 399-2032
Jean McMillen
Hours: Mon–Thur 9:00–8:00, Fri 9:00–
5:30, Sat (Sept–May) 9:00–3:00, Sat
(Jun–Aug) 9:00–noon

Pemberville Public Library
(375 East Front Street—location)
General Delivery (mailing address)
Pemberville, OH 43450
(419) 287-4012; (419) 287-4620
E-mail: kingla@oplin.lib.oh.us
http://library.norweld.lib.oh.us/
pemberville
Laura Zepernick King, Assistant
Director, Local and Family Historian
Hours: Mon & Tue 9:00–8:00, Wed
9:00–5:00, Thur 12:00–8:00, Fri
12:00–5:00, Sat 10:00–1:00
(emphasis on Wood County and Freedom
Township, German research)
10¢ per page for photocopies

**Peninsula Library and Historical
Society**
(6105 Riverview Road—location)
PO Box 236 (mailing address)
Peninsula, OH 44264-0236
(216) 657-BOOK
Randolph S. Bergdorf, Archivist
Hours: Mon–Thur 9:00–8:00, Fri–Sat
9:00–5:00
Pub. *PLHS Newsletter*, bimonthly
(Peninsula, Boston Township, and
Boston Heights)
$2.00 per year membership in Friends of
the Library

Pike Heritage Foundation
110 South Market Street
PO Box 663
Waverly, OH 45690
(614) 947-5281
Katherine Logan, Director
Hours: Sat–Sun 1:00–4:00

Portsmouth Public Library
Local History Department
1220 Gallia Street
Portsmouth, OH 45662
(614) 354-5304; (614) 353-1249 FAX
Betsy L. DeMent, Supervisor
Hours: Mon 10:00–6:30, Tue–Thur
10:00–7:00, Sat 9:00–5:30, Sun 1:00–
5:00
(county histories, early marriages, census
records, newspapers, early court
records, and cemetery records for
Scioto and nearby counties, also
surname and local history files)
copies: 10¢ per page from paper
originals, 20¢ per page from
microform originals

Princeton Museum of Education
515 Greenwood Avenue
Cincinnati, OH 45246
(513) 771-3824
Peggy Shardelow, Director
Hours: by appointment
(archives of records and historical
documents pertaining to the Princeton
City School District, located thirteen
miles north of Cincinnati)

Puskarich Public Library
200 East Market Street
Cadiz, OH 43907
(614) 942-2623
Hours: Mon–Tue & Thur 9:00–8:00,
Wed & Fri 9:00–6:00, Sat 9:00–5:00
(county histories, census indexes and
microfilm, Harrison County
newspapers and legal records on
microfilm)
copies 15¢ per page from paper, 25¢ per
page from microfilm

Putnam County District Library
525 North Thomas Street
PO Box 308
Ottawa, OH 45875-0308
(419) 523-3747; (419) 523-6477 FAX
Deborah Carder
Hours: Mon–Thur 9:00–8:00, Fri–Sat
(winter) 9:00–5:00
(Putnam County and neighboring
counties of Northwest Ohio)
first ½ hour research free, photocopies
15¢ each, include SASE with request,
list of professional researchers
available for more extensive research

Reed Memorial Library
Reference Department
167 East Main Street
Ravenna, OH 44266

(330) 296-2827; (330) 296-3780 FAX
E-mail: reedmem@ohionet.org
Marjorie Smith, Reference Librarian
Hours: Mon–Fri 10:00–9:00, Sat 10:00–
6:00
(emphasis on Portage County history)

Robbins Hunter Museum
221 East Broadway
PO Box 183
Granville, OH 43023
(614) 587-0430

Rodman Public Library
Reference Department
215 East Broadway Street
Alliance, OH 44601
(330) 821-2665; (330) 821-5053
E-mail: webref@roc.rodman.lib.oh.us
http://www.rodman.lib.oh.us/rpl/
Hours: Mon–Thur 9:00–9:00, Fri–Sat
9:00–5:30

Ida Rupp Public Library
310 Madison Street
Port Clinton, OH 43452-1921
(419) 732-3212; (419) 734-9867 FAX;
library.norweld.lib.oh.us/idarupp/
Natalie Bredbeck, Local History and
Genealogy Department
Hours: Mon–Thur 9:30–8:30, Fri–Sat
9:30–5:30, Sat (summer) 9:30–1:30,
Sun (Jan–Mar) 1:00–4:00
copies: 15¢ or 25¢ per page from paper
originals, 25¢ per page from
microform originals

Salem Public Library
Reference Department
821 East State Street
Salem, OH 44460
(216) 332-0042
http://www.salemohio.com/library
Ann Grimes, Reference Librarian
Hours: Mon–Thur 10:00–9:00, Fri–Sat
10:00–6:00

Sandusky Library
114 West Adams Street
Sandusky, OH 44870
(419) 625-3834
Molly Carver, Assistant Director,
Community Relations
Hours: Labor Day–Memorial Day: Mon–
Thur 9:00–8:30, Fri 9:00–6:00, Sat
9:00–5:00, Sun (Oct–Apr) noon–5:00;
Memorial Day–Labor Day: Mon–Wed
9:00–8:30, Thur–Sat 9:00–5:00
(Erie County history)

Sandusky Library Association
1154 West Adams Street
Sandusky, OH 44870
Julie Steinbrenner
Pub. *Follett House News*, quarterly

Kate Love Simpson Library
358 East Main Street
McConnelsville, OH 43756
(614) 962-2533

Verna Trayer, Corresponding Secretary,
Morgan County Chapter OGS
Hours: Mon–Thur 10:00–8:00, Fri–Sat
10:00–5:00

Smith Library of Regional History
A Department of Oxford Lane Public
Library
15 South College Avenue
Oxford, OH 45056
(513) 523-3035; (513) 523-6661 FAX
E-mail: velliott@ohionet.org
Valerie Elliott, Head
Hours: Mon–Fri 10:00–noon & 1:00–
5:00, Thur 6:00–9:00, Sat 10:00–1:00
(has materials on the history of the City
of Oxford and surrounding townships,
all of Butler Couty, Southwestern
Ohio, and for some topics, the entire
state of Ohio)

**South Central Ohio Preservation
Society, Inc.**
178 Church Street
Chillicothe, OH 45601
(614) 774-3510
Mrs. Joseph VanMeter, Coordinator
(archives/manuscripts collection for
southern Ohio)

Stark County District Library
Genealogy Collection, Humanities
Department
715 Market Avenue, North
Canton, OH 44702-1080
(330) 452-0665, ext. 252; (330) 452-
0665
Lauren K. Landis, Genealogist
Hours: Library: Mon–Thur 9:00–9:00,
Fri–Sat 9:00–5:00
(collection includes vital records, probate
records, guardianships, naturalizations,
land records, common pleas court
journals, land tax records, military
records, census, county histories,
atlases, cemetery records, newspapers,
city directories)

**Public Library of Steubenville and
Jefferson County**
Schiappa Memorial Branch Library
4141 Mall Drive
Steubenville, OH 43952
(614) 264-6166; (614) 264-7397 FAX
Sandy Day, Local Historian/Genealogist
Hours: Mon–Fri 9:00–9:00, Sat 9:00–
5:00, Sun 1:00–5:00
(Ohio local history and genealogy for
Ohio and a few other states; local
newspaper on microfilm from 1806)

Swanton Public Library
305 Chestnut Street
Swanton, OH 43558

Taylor Memorial Public Library
2015 Third Street
Cuyahoga Falls, OH 44221
(216) 928-2117

Kathleen Fenning, Head, Reference
Department; Virginia Bloetscher
Hours: Mon–Thur 10:00–9:00, Fri
10:00–6:00, Sat 10:00–5:00, Sun
(Oct–May) 1:00–5:00

Tiffin-Seneca Public Library
77 Jefferson Street
Tiffin, OH 44883
(419) 447-3751; ;(419) 447-3045 FAX
http://www.norweld.lib.oh.us/tiffin-
seneca/index.htm
Margaret Baker, Reference Assistant
Hours: Mon–Thur 10:00–9:00, Fri–Sat
10:00–5:30, Sun (during the school
year) 2:00–5:00

Toledo-Lucas County Public Library
Local History and Genealogy
Department
325 North Michigan Street
Toledo, OH 43624-1614
(419) 259-5233; (419) 255-1334
http://www.library.toledo.oh.us
James C. Marshall, Manager
Hours: Mon–Thur 9:00–9:00, Fri–Sat
9:00–5:30, Sun (Sept–May) 1:00–5:30
(Collections include local history of
Toledo and Lucas County, Ohio, and
genealogical materials covering all of
Ohio, plus the adjacent states and the
original thirteen states.)

Trenton Library
17 East State Street
Trenton, OH 45067
(513) 988-9050
Hours: Mon–Thur 1:00–8:00, Sat 9:00–
4:00

Union Township Library
7900 Cox Road
West Chester, OH 45069
(513) 777-3131
Hours: Mon–Fri 10:00–8:30, Sat 10:00–
5:00

University of Cincinnati
Univresity Libraries
Archives and Rare Books Department
PO Box 210113
Cincinnati, OH 45221-0113
(513) 556-1959; (513) 556-2113 FAX
Hours: Mon–Fri 8:00–5:00 (advance
correspondence recommended for
access to holdings, closed University
holidays)
(member of the Ohio Network of
American History Research Centers,
the designated repository for local
government records and historical
manuscript materials from Adams,
Brown, Butler, Clermont, Clinton,
Hamilton, Highland, and Warren
counties)
$5.00 minimum charge for copies by
mail

University of Toledo
Ward M. Canaday Center
2801 West Bancroft Street
Toledo, OH 43606
(419) 537-2443
Richard Oram, Director

**Upper Sandusky Community
Library**
Heritage Room
301 North Sandusky Avenue
Upper Sandusky, OH 43351
(419) 294-1345
Katherine Hull, Director
Hours: Mon–Fri 9:00–9:00, Sat 9:00–
1:00
(holdings include Wyandot County
information, census and indexed
booklets, family histories, county
histories, newspapers on microfilm,
etc.)

**Warren-Trumbull County Public
Library**
Local History and Genealogy
444 Mahoning Avenue, N.W.
Warren, OH 44483-4692
(330) 399-8807, ext. 120
http://www.wtcpl.lib.oh.us
Carol Willsey Bell, C.G., Department
Head
Hours: Local History and Genealogy
Department: Mon & Thur–Sat 9:00–
5:00, Tue–Wed 9:00–8:45
(emphasis on Trumbull County and
Warren, not Warren County;
Pennsylvania church records)
search fee: none, copy costs only

Washington County Public Library
(617 Fifth Street—location)
615 Fifth Street (mailing address)
Marietta, OH 45750-1973
(614) 373-1057, ext. 230; (614) 376-
2171 FAX
E-mail: aa727@big.seaorf.ohiou.edu
Ernest Thode, Manager, Local History
and Genealogy
Hours: Mon–Thur 9:00–8:30, Fri–Sat
9:00–5:00, Sun (Labor Day to
Memorial Day) 1:00–5:00

Willard V. Way Public Library
101 East Indiana
Perrysburg, OH 43551
(419) 874-3135; (419) 874-6129 FAX
Lynne Michalak, Local History Librarian
Hours: Mon–Thur 9:00–8:30, Fri–Sat
9:00–5:30, Sun (during school year)
1:00–5:00
(specializes in Perrysburg)

Wayne County Public Library
Genealogy Department
304 North Market Street
Wooster, OH 44691-3593
(330) 262-0916, ext. 225; (330) 262-
7313 FAX
Bonnie Knox, Genealogist

Hours: Mon–Fri 8:30 A.M.–9:00 P.M., Sat
9:00–6:00, Sun (during the school
year) 1:00–5:00
("We have a large collection, for a
county library, and have specialized in
the path of immigration from
Pennsylvania, Maryland and New
Jersey into our section of Ohio; we are
strong on the lower third of
Pennsylvania; we also are strong on
Wayne and surrounding counties.")
minor research by mail for cost of copies
with SASE; names of local researchers
supplied on request

**Mary H. Weir Public Library
(Jefferson County, Ohio)**
(see West Virginia)

West Alexandria Archive
6 North Main Street
West Alexandria, OH 45381
(937) 839-4915 (Archive); (937) 839-
4709 (Home)
Audrey Gilbert
Hours: Archive: Mon & Wed 2:00–4:00,
and by appointment
(emphasis on Preble County and nearby
counties)
free

Westlake-Porter Public Library
27333 Center Ridge Road
Westlake, OH 44145
(216) 871-2600; (216) 871-6969 FAX
Cynthia A. Hall, Assistant Coordinator of
Reference Services
Hours: Mon–Thur 9:00–9:00, Fri–Sat
9:00–5:00, Sun (after Labor Day to
before Memorial Day) 1:00–5:00
(for Westlake, Dover, Ohio; general
genealogy reference and circulating
collection; microfilm of local
newspaper, *Westlife*, from 1955)

Willard Memorial Library
6 West Emerald Street
Willard, OH 44890
(419) 933-8564; (419) 933-4783 FAX
Beverly Brandt, Reference Assistant
Hours: Mon–Thur 10:00–8:30, Fri–Sat
10:00–5:00

**Wilmington Public Library of
Clinton County**
268 North South Street
Wilmington, OH 45177
(937) 382-2417; (937) 382-1692 FAX
Judith K. Meyers, Director
Hours: Mon–Thur 10:00–8:00, Fri–Sat
10:00–5:00

**Wood County District Public
Library**
Local History Department
251 North Main Street
Bowling Green, OH 43402
(419) 352-5104; (419) 354-1134 FAX
E-mail: zenglema@oplin.lib.oh.us
http://www.wcnet.org/wcdpl

Marian L. Zengel, Local History
Librarian
Hours: Mon–Thur 9:00–8:30, Fri–Sat
9:00–5:00

Wright Memorial Public Library

1776 Far Hills Avenue
Dayton, OH 45419
(513) 294-7171
Hours: Mon–Fri 9:00–9:00, Sat 9:00–
5:00, Sun 1:00–5:00

Wright State University

Special Collections and Archives
Paul Laurence Dunbar Library
Dayton, OH 45435-0001
(513) 873-2092; (513) 873-2356 FAX
E-mail: archive@library.wright.edu
http://130.108.121.217/staff/dunbar/arch/
schome.htm
Dawne Dewey, Archivist
Hours: Mon–Fri 8:30–5:00, Tue & Wed
(academic quarter only) 7:00 P.M.–
10:00 P.M., Sun (academic quarter
only) 2:00–5:00
(member of the Ohio Network of
American History Research Centers,
the designated repository for local
government records and historical
manuscript materials from Auglaize,
Champaign, Clark, Darke, Greene,
Logan, Mercer, Miami, Montgomery,
Preble, and Shelby counties; also
houses a variety of family histories,
local newspapers on microfilm and
genealogical journals as well as a
special collection of over 2,000
published volumes pertaining to the
local and regional history of
southwestern Ohio)
research fees: $1.00 plus cost of copies
(10¢ each from paper, 20¢ each from
microfilm) and postage

Public Library of Youngstown and Mahoning County

Information Services Department
305 Wick Avenue
Youngstown, OH 44503
(330) 744-8636, ext. 25, (330) 744-8636,
ext 26; (330) 744-3355 FAX
Diane Vicarel, Supervisor
Hours: Mon–Thur 9:00–9:00, Fri–Sat
9:00–5:30

Youngstown Historical Center of Industry and Labor

(151 West Wood Street—location)
PO Box 533 (mailing address)
Youngstown, OH 44501
(330) 743-5934; (330) 743-2999
E-mail: yhcillibrary@cisnet.com
http://winslo.ohio.gov/ohswww/youngst/
arch_lib.html
Randall S. Gooden, Head, Archives-
Library
Hours: Tue–Sat 9:00–5:00

(member of the Ohio Network of
American History Research Centers,
the designated repository for local
government records and historical
manuscript materials from Carroll,
Columbiana, Harrison, Jefferson,
Mahoning, and Trumbull counties)

Youngstown State University

Maag Library
Wick Avenue
Youngstown, OH 44503

Historical Societies— Local and Regional

Adams County Historical Society

Adams County Heritage Center
State Route 247 North
PO Box 306
West Union, OH 45693
(937) 544-8522
Stephen Kelley, President
Hours: Thur & Sat noon–4:00
Pub. *The Centinel of the North-western
Territory*, bimonthly
$5.00 per year membership for
individuals, $10.00 per
yearmembership for families, $25.00
per year Contributing membership,
$100.00 life membership

Alexander Local Genealogical and Historical Society

2565 Pleasant Hill Road
Athens, OH 45701
M. L. Bowman

Alexandria Community Historical Society

23 West Main Street
Alexandria, OH 43001
Betty Duke, President
Hours: Sun 2:00–4:00

Allen County Historical Society

Elizabeth M. MacDonell Memorial
Library
620 West Market Street
Lima, OH 45801-4665
(419) 222-9426
http://www.worcnet.gen.oh.us/
acmuseum/
Anna B. Selfridge, Curator, Archives and
Manuscripts; Ray Schuck, Director
Hours: Library: Tue–Sat 1:00–5:00
Pub. *Allen County Historical Society
Newsletter*, bimonthly; *Allen County
Reporter*, three times per year
$10.00 per year membership for
individuals, $20.00 per year
membership for families, $50.00 per
year Patron membership, $200.00 life
membership

Alliance Historical Society

840 North Park
Alliance, OH 44601
(216) 823-4115
Cheryl Lundgren, President

Alpine Hills Historical Museum

106 West Main Street
PO Box 293
Sugarcreek, OH 44681
(216) 852-2223; (216) 852-4113
Les Raser, Curator
Hours: Apr–Nov: Mon–Sat 10:00–
4:30

Amalthea Historical Society

(975 South Sunbury Road—location)
483 Dempsey Road (mailing address)
Westerville, OH 43081
(614) 891-6363
Tim Milligan, Secretary
Pub. *Amalthea Chimes*, three times per
year
$3.00 per year membership

Amherst Historical Society

Quigley Museum
(Corner of South Lake and Milan
Avenue—museum location)
PO Box 272 (mailing address)
Amherst, OH 44001
(216) 988-7255
Valerie Jenkins, Museum Curator
Hours: Wed 9:00–3:00, and special
weekends
Pub. *AHS Newsletter*, three times per
year; *Quigley Quest*, three times
per year
(genealogy section; specializes in
Sandstone area history)
$10.00 per year membership for
individuals

Anderson Township Historical Society

6550 Clough Pike
Cincinnati, OH 45230
(513) 231-2114
Albert Wettstein, President
Pub. *Surveyor*

Ashland County Historical Society

Ashland County Historical Museum
414 Center Street
PO Box 484
Ashland, OH 44805
(419) 289-3111
Marybelle H. Landrum, Secretary/
Manager
Hours: Wed, Fri & Sun (Apr–Dec) 1:00–
4:00, Sun (Jan–Mar) 1:00–4:00
Pub. *County Crier*, three times per year
$7.50 per year membership for
individuals, $15.00 per year
membership for families, $25.00–
$49.00 per year Associate
membership, $50.00–$99.00 per year

Benefactor membership, $100.00 or more per year Distinguished membership, $1,000.00 life membership

Ashville Area Heritage Society
281 Randolph Street
Ashville, OH 43103
(614) 983-3166

Athens County Historical Society and Museum
65 North Court Street
Athens, OH 45701-2506
(614) 592-2280
http://www.searf.ohiou.edu/~xx023/
Joanne D. Prisley, Director
Hours: Mon–Fri 10:00–4:00, and by appointment
Pub. *Athens Historical Society and Museum Bulletin*, bimonthly
(Athens County history and genealogy; genealogical and history research library)
$10.00 per year membership; search fee: $10.00 per hour plus copies

Auglaize County Historical Society
223 South Main Street
Saint Marys, OH 45885
(419) 394-7069 (answering machine when museum is closed); (419) 394-5243 (President)
George Neargarder, President
Hours: by appointment
Pub. *Auglaize County Historical Society—Newsletter*, five times per year
$10.00 per year membership

Aurora Historical Society
Aurora Public Library
Aurora Road
PO Box 241
Aurora, OH 44202
Wallace Martel, Museum Director
Hours: Tue & Thur 1:00–4:00
Pub. *The Aurora Pioneer*, quarterly

Avon Historical Society
2940 Stoney Ridge Road
Avon, OH 44011
(216) 934-6106
Jean A. Fischer, President
Hours: by appointment

Bainbridge Historical Society
PO Box 424
Bainbridge, OH 45612

Barberton Historical Society
PO Box 666
Barberton, OH 44203
(216) 745-9383

Bath Township Historical Society
4655 Medina Road
Akron, OH 44321
Mrs. E. S. Stein

Bedford Historical Society, Inc.
30 South Park Street
PO Box 46282
Bedford, OH 44146
(216) 232-0796
Richard J. Squire, Director of Museum
Hours: Bedford Museum: Mon & Wed 7:30 P.M.–10:00 P.M., Thur 10:00–4:00, second Sun 2:00–5:00
Pub. *The Bedford Bee*, bimonthly (local and area genealogy resources, archives, reference library)
$7.50 per year membership

Bellevue Area Historical Commission
PO Box 304
Bellevue, OH 44811

Bellville Historical Society
Box 4511, Rule Road
Bellville, OH 44813
(419) 886-3680
http://www.angelfire.com/oh/bellville/

Belmont County Historical Society, Inc.
(532 North Chestnut Street—location)
PO Box 434 (mailing address)
Barnesville, OH 43713
(614) 425-2926
Howard LeMasters, Treasurer
Hours: May1–Oct 1: Thur–Sun 1:00–4:30, and all year by appointment
$15.00 per year membership for individuals, $20.00 per year membership for husband and wife, $25.00 per year Sustaining membership, $150.00 life membership for individuals, $200.00 per year membership for husband and wife

Belpre Area Historical Society
PO Box 731
Belpre, OH 45714
(614) 423-7382
Nancy M. Sams, President
Pub. *Farmers Castle Journal*, quarterly
$5.00 per year membership for individuals, $7.50 per year membership for families

Berea Area Historical Society
Mahler Museum & History Center
(118 East Bridge Street—location)
PO Box 173 (mailing address)
Berea, OH 44017
http://members.aol.com/bereahist/index.html
Hours: meetings: fourth Wed (Sept–May)
(history of Berea and Middleburg Township)
$15.00 per year membership for individuals, $20.00 per year membership for families, $25.00 per year Supporting membership for individuals, $35.00 per year Supporting membership for families, $50.00 per year Corporate membership

Bexley Historical Society
Bexley Historical Commission
2242 East Main Street
Bexley, OH 43209
(614) 235-8694
Betty Gearhart, Secretary
Pub. *Historical Herald*

Botkins Historical Society
(Shelby House Hotel Museum, West State Street—location)
PO Box 256 (mailing address)
Botkins, OH 45306
http://members.aol.com/BotkinsHS/history/bhshome/html
Brad Reed, President,
Hours: first & third Sun, and by appointment; meetings: first Thur
Pub. *Whistle Stop Newsletter*

Brewster-Sugar Creek Township Historical Society
45 South Wabash Avenue
Brewster, OH 44613
Hours: Sat–Sun 12:00–2:00
(specialty: Railroad Museum)
$4.00–$8.00 per year membership

Brooklyn Historical Society, Inc.
4442 Ridge Road
Brooklyn, OH 44144
(216) 749-2804
Barbara Stepic, President
Hours: Tue 10:00–2:00, Sun (Apr–Dec) 2:00–5:00, closed holiday weekends
(small library)
$4.00 per year membership for individuals, $6.00 per year membership for couples, $100.00 life membership

Brookville Historical Society
14 Market Street
PO Box 82
Brookville, OH 45309
(513) 833-3470

Brown County Historical Society
(Corner of Apple and Cherry Street, Old County Jail—location)
PO Box 238 (mailing address)
Georgetown, OH 45121
(937) 444-3521
Dorothy Helton
Hours: Thur & Sat 12:00–5:00
Pub. *Bits of Our Heritage*, quarterly (April, July, October, December)
$3.00 per year membership

Bucyrus Historical Society
202 South Walnut Street
PO Box 493
Bucyrus, OH 44820
(419) 562-6386
Linda Blicke, Curator
Hours: Mon (Mar–Dec) 1:00–4:00, Sun 2:00–4:00
Pub. *Scrogg's House News*, quarterly (Crawford County News)

Butler-Clear Fork Valley Historical Society

(43 Elm Street—location)
PO Box 186 (mailing address)
Butler, OH 44822
Tina Welty, Volunteer Curator
Hours: twenty hours per month
Pub. *The Clear Fork Grist*, quarterly, free

Butler County Historical Society and Museum

327 North Second Street
Hamilton, OH 45011
(513) 896-9930
Marjorie Brown, Curator
Hours: Tue–Sun 1:00–4:00
Pub. *Newsletter—Butler County Historical Society*, ten times per year
(Butler County history and surrounding area; genealogy room: many resource materials)
$10.00 per year membership for individuals, $15.00 per year membership for families, $8.00 per year membership for senior citizens, $12.00 per year membership for senior citizen families, $2.00 per year membership for students; $1.00 admission for non-members 12 years and older; search fee: 25¢ per photocopied page plus postage

Canal Fulton Heritage Society

Heritage House and Old Canal Days Museum
103 Tuscarawas Street, West
Canal Fulton, OH 44614-1044
(216) 854-3808
Ann A. McLaughlin, President
Hours: by appointment only
Pub. *The Canaler*, monthly

Carlisle Area Historical Society

453 Park Drive
Carlisle, OH 45005
Hours: by appointment
Pub. *Carlisle Area Historical Gazette*; *Newsletter*, three times per year
$10.00 per year membership for individuals, $100.00 life membership

Carroll County Historical Society

PO Box 174
Carrollton, OH 44615
(216) 735-2839

Centerville Historical Society

Centerville Historical Commission
Walton House
89 West Franklin Street
Centerville, OH 45459
(513) 433-0123
Lynn E. Russell, Administrator
Hours: Thur 1:00–4:00, and by appointment
Pub. *Newsletter*

$10.00 per year membership for individuals, $15.00 per year membership for families, $35.00 per year Sustaining membership, $50.00 per year membership for Patrons

Chagrin Falls Historical Society

Shute Memorial Building
21 Walnut
Chagrin Falls, OH 44022
(216) 247-4695
Mrs. Pat Zalba, Curator; Mrs. D. Pauly, Librarian
Hours: Thur 2:00–4:00, and by appointment
charges for postage and copying

Champaign County Historical Society

PO Box 65
Urbana, OH 43078-0065
(513) 653-6721

Cheviot Historical Society

3814 Harrison Avenue
Cheviot, Ohio 45211
(513) 481-9468
Elizabeth Nelson
E-mail: beth@cne.net
http://www.cheviot.org/
(history of the city of Cheviot)
$5.00 per year membership for individuals, $15.00 per yearmembership for families, $3.50 per year membership for students, $40.00 per year business membership, $50.00 per year Heritage membership

The Cincinnati Historical Society

The Cincinnati Historical Society Library and Museum Center
1301 Western Avenue
Cincinnati, OH 45203-1129
(513) 287-7097; (513) 287-7095 FAX
http://www.cincymuseum.org
Laura L. Chace, Director
Hours: Mon–Fri noon–5:00, Sat 9:00–5:00
Pub. *Queen City Heritage*, quarterly
(the Old Northwest Territory, southwestern Ohio and metropolitan Cincinnati)
free admission; research rates: 15¢ per exposure for photocopies, $5.00 minimum postage and handling, plus $25.00 per hour for non-members, $15.00 per hour (no charge for the first hour) for members and non-profit organizations, $35.00 per hour for commercial groups; copies: 15¢ per page plus service charge for orders of $25.00 or more, $5.00 minimum postage and handling

Clark County Historical Society

818 North Fountain
PO Box 2157
Springfield, OH 45504
Floyd Barmann, Director; Virginia Weygardt, Curator

Hours: Tue–Fri 10:00–4:00
Pub. *Champion City*, quarterly
$25.00 per year membership for individuals

The Clermont County Historical Society

PO Box 14
Batavia, OH 45103-0014
Ron Hill, Editor
Pub. *The Clermont Historian*, monthly

The Clinton County Historical Society

149 East Locust Street
PO Box 529
Wilmington, OH 45177-0529
(937) 382-4684
http://www.postcom.com/ccgshs
Joyce Thackston, Director
Hours: Mar–Dec: Wed–Sat 1:00–4:30
Pub. *Rombach Place*, four times per year
$15.00 per year membership for individuals, $25.00 per year membership for families, $100.00 per year membership for businesses

Clyde Heritage League, Inc.

PO Box 97
Clyde, OH 43410
Donald H. Hemminger, President
Pub. *CHL News*

Coalton Historical Society

552 Keystone Station Road
Jackson, OH 45640
Robert Ervin

Coleraine Historical Society

PO Box 39726
Cincinnati, OH 45239
(513) 541-8706
Ruth Wells, Editor and Curator
Pub. *Coleraine Pageant*, bimonthly
(Coleraine Township and greater Cincinnati area history)
$5.00 per year membership

College Hill Historical Society

5907 Belmont Avenue
Cincinnati, OH 45229
(513) 681-2470

Columbia Historical Society

PO Box 983
Columbia Station, OH 44028

Historical Society of Columbiana and Fairfield Township

10 East Park Avenue
Columbiana, OH 44408
Margaret Herrmann and Ada Wilhelm, Co-Chairmen of Genealogy Committee
Pub. *Quarterly*
$3.00 per year membership; research fee: $5.00 plus any additional costs for copying

County Line Historical Society of Wayne/Holmes
(Shreve Town House, 150 West McConkey Street—location)
PO Box 614 (mailing address)
Shreve, OH 44676
Carrie Brown, Secretary
Pub. *Newsletter*, every two or three months
$10.00 per year membership; search: $10.00 per specific search

Crestline Historical Society
(211 Thoman Street—location)
PO Box 456 (mailing address)
Crestline, OH 44827
(419) 683-3410
Ray Holland, President
Hours: by appointment, summer weekends
$6.00 per year membership

Dalton Community Historical Society
766 Mount Eaton Road
Dalton, OH 44618
Mrs. D. Rudy

Darke County Historical Society, Inc.
Garst Museum
205 North Broadway
Greenville, OH 45331-2222
(513) 548-5250
Judy Logan, Director
Hours: Garst Museum Library: Tue–Sat 11:00–5:00, Sun 1:00–5:00

Defiance County Historical Society
Au Glaize Village
(12296 Krouse Road—location)
PO Box 801 (mailing address)
Defiance, OH 43512
(419) 393-2662
Judy Butler, Public Relations
Hours: 7 Jun–1 Sept: Sat–Sun 11:00–4:00
(nineteenth century recreated rural village and farm museum)
$5.00 per year membership for individuals, $10.00 per year membership for families

Delaware County Historical Society
157 East William Street
PO Box 317
Delaware, OH 43015
(614) 369-3831
E-mail: dchsdcgs@midohio.net
http://206.31.169.201/dchsdcgs/
Marilyn M. Cryder
Hours: Sat 2:00–4:30, Thur 9:30–noon & 1:00–4:30
Pub. *Quarterly*
$10.00 per year membership for individuals

Delhi Township Historical Society
468 Anderson Ferry Road
Cincinnati, OH 45238

(513) 451-4313; (513) 251-1390
Shirley Althoff, Archivist
Hours: Tue, Thur & Sun noon–3:00, and by appointment
Pub. *Footprints*, monthly
(family history files with more than 14,000 listings, census records, family genealogies, some probate records)
$10.00 per year membership for individuals, $100.00 life membership; search fee: 5¢ per copy of material

Delphos Historical Association
309 West Second Street
Delphos, OH 45833
Ron Leonhart

Dover Historical Society
J. E. Reeves Home and Museum
325 East Iron Avenue
Dover, OH 44622
(216) 343-7040
James D. Nixon, Director; Cris Nixon, Assistant Director
Hours: Office: Mon–Fri 9:30–4:00; Museum: seasonal
Pub. *News Letter*, quarterly
museum admission: $3.00 per person

Dublin Historical Society, Inc.
6669 Coffman Road
PO Box 2
Dublin, OH 43017
(614) 764-9906
Elizabeth Myers, President

East Liverpool Historical Society
PO Box 476
East Liverpool, OH 43920
(330) 386-5964
Timothy R. Brookes, President
Hours: various
Pub. *The City of Hills and Kilns*, quarterly
$10.00 per year membership

East Palestine Historical Society
East Palestine, OH 44413

Otto E. Ehrhart-Paulding County Historical Society
City Hall
North Main Street
Antwerp, OH 45813
(419) 258-8161
James S. Temple, President
(genealogical services)

Enon Community Historical Society, Inc.
Genealogical Committee
45 Indian Drive
PO Box 442
Enon, OH 45323
(513) 864-7080
E-mail: echs@exinet.com
Hours: Tue & Wed 1:00–4:00, Wed 6:00–8:00, Sat 10:00–2:00
Pub. *Images*, quarterly

(some census CDs, marriage CDs, microfiche, etc.)
$7.00 per year membership for individuals, $10.00 per year membership for families; search fees: actual cost of research, copies, etc.

Erie County Historical Society
PO Box 944
Sandusky, OH 44870
(419) 625-4341
Janet A. Senne, President
Pub. *The Erie Chronicle*
("We have no genealogical holdings, however we are glad to provide information on places or people in the historical sense.")
$5.00 per year membership; search: depending on information needed, but no genealogical research

The Euclid Historical Society
21129 North Street
Euclid, OH 44117
(216) 383-8299
Roy R. Larick, Jr., President
Pub. *The Scroll*

Fairfield Heritage Association, Inc.
105 East Wheeling Street
Lancaster, OH 43130-3706
(614) 654-9923; (614) 654-9890 FAX
Mary Lou McCandlish, Executive Secretary
Hours: Tue–Fri 9:00–4:00
Pub. *Fairfield Heritage Quarterly*, $1.00 per issue
(area historical information but limited genealogical information)
$10.00 per year membership for individuals, $15.00 per year membership for families, $7.50 per year membership for students and senior citizens

Fairport Harbor Historical Society
Fairport Marine Museum
129 Second Street
Fairport Harbor, OH 44077
(216) 354-4825
Helen Kasari, Historian
Hours: Memorial Day–Labor Day weekend: Wed & Sat–Sun 1:00–6:00
Pub. *Through the Porthole*, quarterly
(Great Lakes shipping, Fairport history)
$5.00–$100.00 per year membership

Fairview Park Historical Society
21779 Seabury
Fairview Park, OH 44126
(216) 734-2067

Farmersville Historical Society, Inc.
PO Box 198
Farmersville, OH 45325
Mary P. Gisewite, President
Pub. *Farmersville Historical Society Newsletter*, quarterly

Fayette County Historical Society
Fayette County Museum
517 Columbus Avenue
Washington Court House, OH 43160
(614) 335-2953
http://www.washingtonch.com/faytrav/
museum.htm (Museum)
Carol Carey, Curator
Hours: Museum: Sat–Sun (May–Oct),
and by appointment
no admission charge; $5.00 per year
membership

**Firelands Historical Society
Research Center**
(9 Case Avenue—location)
PO Box 572 (mailing address)
Norwalk, OH 44857
(419) 668-6038
Henry R. Timman, Trustee
Hours: Apr–May & Sept–Nov: Sat–Sun
noon–4:00; Jun–Aug: Tue–Sun noon–
5:00
Pub. *Firelands Pioneer*, biannually
(every other year), $17.00 per issue,
$16.00 per year subscription to
members
(Firelands and Ohio history and
genealogy)
$10.00 per year membership (does not
include periodical)

Forest Area Historical Society
307 South Mary Street
Forest, OH 45843

Fort Loramie Historical Association
Main and Elm Street
PO Box 276
Fort Loramie, OH 45845
(937) 295-3855
Hours: Jun–Sept: Sun 1:00–4:00
Pub. *None*

**Fostoria Historical Society and
Museum**
122 West North Street
PO Box 142
Fostoria, OH 44830
George A. Gray, Program Chairman and
President

Franklin Area Historical Society
Harding Museum
302 Park Avenue
Franklin, OH 45005
(513) 746-8295; (513) 746-4466
Ann Squier, Manager
Hours: Sun (Apr–Nov) 2:00–5:00, and
year-round by appointment
Pub. *Franklin Area Historical Society
Newsletter*, five times per year
$15.00 per year membership for
individuals, $22.50 per year
membership for families, $225.00 life
membership

Franklin County Historical Society
(address withheld upon request)

Fulton County Historical Society
657 Meadow Lane
Wauseon, OH 43567

Gahanna Historical Society
(101 South High Street—location)
294 Villa Oaks Lane (mailing address)
Gahanna, OH 43230
(614) 475-3342
Mrs. LaRoux Mentz, Genealogist
Hours: by appointment
(has a continually growing file of early
Gahanna settlers)

Galion Historical Society, Inc.
955 Bucyrus Road
PO Box 125
Galion, OH 44833
(419) 468-5534
Douglas Osborne, President
Hours: three hours every Sun
$5.00 per year membership

Gallia County Chapter OGS
Gallia County Historical/Genealogical
Society
430 Second Avenue
PO Box 295
Gallipolis, OH 45631-0295
(614) 446-7200
Henrietta Evans, Corresponding
Secretary
Hours: Tue–Fri 10:00–4:00, Sat 10:00–
1:00
Pub. *Gallia County Historical/
Genealogical Society Newsletter*,
quarterly
(First Families of Gallia County files;
Revolutionary Soldiers Who Lived in
Gallia County files)
$15.00 per year membership

Gates Mills Historical Society
PO Box 191
Gates Mills, OH 44040-0191

Geauga County Historical Society
14653 East Park Street
PO Box 153
Burton, OH 44021
(440) 834-4012
Marlene Collins, Office Manager
Hours: by appointment
Pub. *The Quarterly*
$15.00 per year membership for
individuals, $10.00 per year
membership for senior citizens

**The Historical Society of
Germantown**
PO Box 144
Germantown, OH 45327-0144
Mary Anne Miletic, Coordinator
Hours: Mon–Wed 8:00–noon
Pub. *Newsletter*, bimonthly
$10.00 per year membership

Girard Historical Society
307 Churchhill Road
Girard, OH 44420
(330) 545-3893
Jane Harris

Gnadenhutten Historical Society
352 South Cherry Street
PO Box 396
Gnadenhutten, OH 44629-0396
(614) 254-4143
Barbara McKeown, Secretary/Treasurer
Hours: May–Aug: Mon–Sat 10:00–5:00,
Sun noon–5:00; Sept–Oct: weekends
noon–5:00, and by appointment
(history only, no genealogy records)

Grand Rapids Historical Society
PO Box 124
Grand Rapids, OH 43522
$2.00 per year membership

Granville, Ohio Historical Society
115 East Broadway
PO Box 129
Granville, OH 43023
(614) 587-3951
Hours: Sat–Sun (May–Oct) 1:00–5:00
Pub. *The Historical Times*, quarterly
$5.00 per year membership

**Greater Loveland Historical Society
Museum**
201 Riverside Avenue
Loveland, OH 45140
(513) 683-5692 phone and FAX
Jo Ann Richardson, Director
Hours: Fri–Sun 1:00–4:30, and by
appointment
Pub. *Reflections . . . then and now*,
bimonthly
$10.00 per year membership for
individuals, $15.00 per year
membership for families

**The Greene County Historical
Society**
74 West Church Street
Xenia, OH 45385
(937) 372-4606
Joan Baxter, Executive Secretary
Hours: Tue–Fri 9:00–noon & 1:00–3:30,
Sat–Sun (Jun–Aug) 1:30–4:00
Pub. *Our Heritage*, monthly
$10.00 per year membership for
individuals, discounted rates for
students and senior citizens

Greenfield Historical Society
671 South Washington Street
Greenfield, OH 45123-1646
George M. Waddell
Hours: by appointment
$5.00 per year membership for
individuals, $8.00 per year
membership for families

Guernsey County Historical Society
218 North Eighth Street
PO Box 741
Cambridge, OH 43725
(216) 439-4686

Harrison County Historical Society
Baker Institute for Local Studies
168 East Market Street
Cadiz, OH 43907
(614) 942-3900
Hours: Mon–Fri noon–3:00

The Heritage Commission Corporation
(Depot Office, 147 West Mound Street—first location
Opera House, 37 South Chillicothe Street—second location)
PO Box 457 (mailing address)
South Charleston, OH 45368
(937) 462-7236 (President's home)
George H. Berkhofer, President and Executive Director
Hours: Depot (museum and archives): second Sun 1:00–5:00, and by appointment
Pub. *Newsletter*, bimonthly
(print, manuscript and photographic collection; local history and genealogy)
$5.00 per year membership for individuals, $7.50 per year membership for families; search: $5.00

Highland County Historical Society
Highland House
151 East Main Street
Hillsboro, OH 45133
(937) 393-3392

Hiram Township Historical Society, Inc.
(Century House Museum, Garfield Road—location)
PO Box 1775 (mailing address)
Hiram, OH 44234
Monica W. Fratus, President
Hours: Hiram College Archives: Mon–Fri 9:00–5:00
Pub. *Newsletter*, quarterly
(specializes in Ohio, Connecticut Western Reserve, Disciples of Christ, Hiram College)
$10.00 per year membership

Historic Lyme Village Association
(5487 State Route 113—location)
PO Box 342 (mailing address)
Bellevue, OH 44811
(419) 483-4949
http://www.onebelevue.com/lymevillage/
Alvina Schaeffer, Village Curator/Co-ordinator
Hours: Tue–Sun (Jun–Aug) 1:00–5:00, Sun (May & Sept) 1:00–5:00
Pub. *Lyme Lines*, monthly
$10.00 per year membership for individuals, $15.00 per year

membership for couples, $25.00 per year membership for families, $6.00 per year membership for students, $10.00 per year Honorary membership, $40.00 per year Sustaining pass membership, $100.00 per year Patron membership, $200.00 life membership; $5.00 admission for adults, $2.50 admission for students, $4.50 admission for senior citizens or members of groups (12 or more)

Historic Southwest Ohio, Inc.
The John Hauck House Museum
812 Dayton Street
Cincinnati, OH 45214
(513) 721-3570
Janet H. Hauck, Manager of Hauck House
Hours: Fri–Sun 1:00–5:00, and by appointment
(a house museum in the nineteenth century townhouse of German brewer John Hauck)
$20.00 per year membership

Hocking County Historical Society
PO Box 262
Logan, OH 43138

Holmes County Historical Society
232 North Washington Street
PO Box 126
Millersburg, OH 44654
(330) 674-0022

Hudson Heritage Association
(34 North Main Street—location)
PO Box 2218 (mailing address)
Hudson, OH 44236
(330) 653-5024
Warren Wickes, President
Hours: Mon–Tue & Thur–Fri 11:00–1:00
Pub. *Hudson Heritage Newsletter*, monthly

The Hudson Library and Historical Society
22 Aurora Street
Hudson, OH 44236
(330) 653-6658; (330) 650-4693 FAX
James F. Caccamo, Archivist
Hours: Library: Mon–Thur 9:00–9:00, Fri–Sat 9:00–5:00; Archives: Mon–Sat 9:00–5:00
$7.50 per year membership for individuals

Indian Hill Historical Society
Indian Hill Historical Museum Association
8100 Given Road
Cincinnati, OH 45243
(513) 891-1873 phone and FAX
Peg Gillespie, President
Pub. *The Sampler*, monthly
(focus on local history)
$35.00 per year membership for individuals, $45.00 per year

membership for families, $80.00 per year Sustaining membership, $150.00 per year Patron membership

Jackson Center Historical Society
General Delivery
Jackson Center, OH 45334
Bernadine Heintz

Jackson Township Historical Society
(Massillon, OH 44646—location)
PO Box 35171 (mailing address)
Canton, OH 44735

Jefferson County Historical Association
Jefferson County Historical Museum and Genealogical Library
(Corner of North Fifth Street and Franklin Avenue—location)
PO Box 4268 (mailing address)
Steubenville, OH 43952
(614) 283-1133
Mary Hanlin, Volunteer Librarian; Marge Harris, Museum Director
Hours: Library: 10:00–3:00; Museum: by appointment only
Pub. *Newsletter Jefferson County Historical Association*, bimonthly
$10.00 per year membership; $2.00 museum admission

Kent Historical Society
Birkner Tower
5792 Glad Boulevard
PO Box 663
Kent, OH 44240
(330) 678-2712
Stephen Paschen, Director
Hours: Wed & Fri 12:30–4:30
Pub. *Newsletter*, quarterly
$10.00 per year membership for individuals, $15.00 per year membership for families, $35.00 per year membership for businesses, $2.50 per year membership for students, $50.00 per year silver membership, $100.00 golden membership, $1,000.00 life membership

Kettering-Moraine Museum and Historical Society
35 Moraine Circle South
Kettering, OH 45439

Kettlersville Historical Society
General Delivery
Kettlersville, OH 45336

Kidron Community Historical Society
Kidron-Sonnenberg Heritage Center
(13153 Emerson Road—location)
PO Box 234
Kidron, OH 44636-0234
(330) 857-9111; (330) 857-1475 (Director)
E-mail: bruce—i-db@juno.com (Director)

http://www.bright.net/~swisstea/
Bruce Detweiler Breckbill, Director
Hours: summer: Tue, Thur & Sat noon–
  4:00; winter: Thur & Sat noon–4:00
Pub. *Bit o' Vit*, quarterly
(access to over 500,000 names in
  different databases plus many books,
  primarily Swiss Mennonite, German/
  Russian Mennonite, and Amish in
  origin)
$10.00 per year regular membership for
  individuals, $15.00 per year regular
  membership for couples, $35.00 per
  year membership for organizations;
  $150.00 life membership for
  individuals; search fee: $1.00 per page
  printout plus donation for search time

Lake County Historical Society
8610 King Memorial Road
Mentor, OH 44060
(440) 255-8979; (440) 255-8980
Joan Kapsch, Executive Director
Hours: Tue–Fri 10:00–5:00
Pub. *Lake County History Review*, three
  times per year
$25.00 per year membership; research
  fees based on time

Lake Erie Islands Historical Society
E-mail: history@leihs.org
http://www.leihs.org

Lakeside Heritage Society, Inc.
Heritage Hall Museum and Archives
238 Maple Avenue
Lakeside, OH 43440
(419) 798-5719
Neil L. Allen, President
Hours: Memorial Day–Labor Day
Pub. *Lakeside Manifest-Newsletter*,
  quarterly
("Collections—memorabilia of Lakeside
  and the Marblehead Peninsula,
  Johnson Island artifacts, and Indian
  artifacts.")
$5.00 per year membership

Lakewood Historical Society
14710 Lake Avenue
Lakewood, OH 44107
(216) 221-7343
http://www.lkwdpl.org/histsoc/
Sandra L. Koozer, Curator
Hours: Wed 1:00–4:00, Sun 2:00–5:00
Pub. *LHS Newsletter*

Lawrence County Historical Society
(The Lawrence County Museum, 506
  South Sixth Street—location)
PO Box 73 (mailing address)
Ironton, OH 45638
(614) 532-1222
Sharon Kouns, President
Hours: Museum: Fri–Sun (Apr 1–Dec
  15) 1:00–5:00
Pub. *The Lawrence Countian*, six times
  per year

$10.00 per year membership for
  individuals, $15.00 per year
  membership for families, $2.00 per
  year membership for students, $50.00
  Friend membership, $100.00 Patron
  membership; $1,000.00 life
  membership

Leetonia Historical Society
Public Library
38027 Old 344
Leetonia, OH 44431
John C. Simonds

Lenox Historical Society, Inc.
3424 Lenox and New Lyme Road
Jefferson, OH 44047
(216) 294-2640

LeRoy Heritage Association
(Rt. 86, Brakeman Road—location)
12941 Girdled Road (mailing address)
Painesville, OH 44077
(440) 254-4955

Licking County Historical Society
(Sixth [Veterans] Park, Newark, OH
  43055—location)
PO Box 785 (mailing address)
Newark, OH 43058-0785
(614) 345-4898
Karen Dickman, Office Manager and
  Librarian
Hours: Tue–Fri 1:00–4:30
Pub. *The Licking County Historical
  Society Quarterly*, $10.00 per year
  subscription
("Museum and library containing
  information about people, industry and
  businesses of Licking County.")
$15.00 per year membership for
  individuals, $5.00 per year
  membership for students, $10.00 per
  year membership for senior citizen
  individuals, $25.00 per year
  membership for couples, $15.00 per
  year membership for senior citizen
  couples, $30.00 per year Sponsor
  membership, $35.00 per year Patron
  membership, $50.00 per year
  Contributing membership, $75.00 per
  year Supporting membership, $500.00
  life membership

Limaville Historical Society, Inc.
PO Box 13
Limaville, OH 44640

Lisbon Historical Society
100 East Washington Street
PO Box 191
Lisbon, OH 44432
(330) 424-1861
Jewyl Hina, Museum Curator
Hours: 1 Jun–15 Sept: Tue 10:00–3:00,
  Sun 1:00–4:00
Pub. *Preface*, quarterly
$10.00 per year membership

Liverpool Township Historical Society
Center Road
PO Box 399
Valley City, OH 44280
(330) 483-3994

The Logan County Historical Society and Museum
521 East Columbus Avenue
PO Box 296
Bellefontaine, OH 43311
(937) 593-7557
Corinne M. Dixon, Archives Library
Hours: May–Oct: Wed–Sun 1:00–5:00;
  Nov 1–May 1: 1:00–4:00
Pub. *Logan County Historical Society
  Newsletter*, bimonthly
(large museum with an Archives Library,
  also a Genealogical Library)
$10.00 per year membership for
  individuals, $15.00 per year
  membership for families; search fees:
  $7.00 per hour (limit two hours, unless
  directed otherwise), copies 20¢ per
  page

Lorain County Historical Society
Hicks Memorial Library
509 Washington Avenue
Elyria, OH 44035
(216) 322-3341
Karen Adinolfi, Executive Director
Hours: Tue–Fri 1:00–4:00
Pub. *Hickory Leaves*, quarterly
$25.00 per year membership for
  individuals, admission: $2.00 per visit;
  research: $10.00 per hour

Louisville Area Historical-Preservation Society
523 East Main Street
Louisville, OH 44641
(330) 875-4180

Lower Muskingum Historical Society
(Main and Park Street, Beverly, OH—
  location)
PO Box 191 (mailing address)
Waterford, OH 45786
(614) 984-2489; (614) 984-2141
Mary A. Irvin, Corresponding Secretary
Hours: weekends (Jun–Aug) 2:00–4:00
Pub. *Reflections Along the Muskingum*,
  quarterly
$3.00 per year membership for
  individuals, $5.00 per year
  membership for families, $1.00 per
  year membership for students, $100.00
  life membership

Lucasville Area Historical Society
PO Box 761
Lucasville, OH 45648
(614) 259-4392
Alice Moulton Barker
Hours: by appointment
$1.00 per year membership

Madison County Historical Society

260 East High Street
PO Box 124
London, OH 43140
(614) 852-2977
Gretchen Green, Director
Hours: first full weekend of each month
1:00–4:00, Wed 1:00–4:00
Pub. *Log Cabin Sentinel*, quarterly
$10.00 per year membership for
individuals

The Madison Historical Society

13 West Main Street
PO Box 91
Madison, OH 44057
Louanna M. Billington, Curator
Hours: Wed–Sat 11:00–4:00
Pub. *The Times*, monthly
$10.00 per year membership for
individuals, $12.00 per year
membership for couples, $25.00 per
year Sustaining membership, $50.00
per year Patron membership, $100.00
per year Angel membership

The Mahoning Valley Historical Society

The Arms Family Museum of Local
History
648 Wick Avenue
Youngstown, OH 44502-1289
(330) 743-2589; (330) 743-7210 FAX
H. William Lawson, Director; Pamela L.
Pletcher, Archivist
Hours: Archives: Tue–Fri 9:00–4:00, Sat
1:00–5:00
Pub. *Historical Happenings*, bimonthly
(history and genealogy of Mahoning
Valley watershed: Mahoning,
Columbiana, Portage and Stark
counties, Ohio, and Mercer and
Lawrence counties, Pennsylvania,
region; the Arms family; original
probate files and civil court files,
1846–1900, for Mahoning County)
$20.00 per year membership for
individuals, $30.00 per year
membership for families, $10.00 per
year membership for students; $50.00
per year Sustaining membership;
research fees available upon request,
members pay only for photocopies and
postage and have free admission to
archives

Maple Heights Historical Society

(5810 Dunham Road—location)
PO Box 37103 (mailing address)
Maple Heights, OH 44137
Frank Baloga, President; John Straka,
Treasurer
Hours: Mon & Wed (summer) 7:00–9:00,
second Sun (Jun & Sept) 1:00–4:00
$5.00 per year membership for
individuals, $15.00 per year
membership for families, $100.00 life
membership

Marion County Historical Society

Heritage Hall
169 East Church Street
Marion, OH 43302
(614) 387-4255
http://www.genealogy.org/~smore/
marion/
Dr. John D. Telfer, Executive Director
Hours: Reading Room (entrance on State
Street): Mon–Fri 9:00–1:00; Research
Library: by appointment; Museum:
summer: Wed–Sun 1:00–4:00, winter:
Sat–Sun 1:00–4:00
Pub. *Hallmarks*, quarterly
(emphasis on Marion County, Ohio;
Heritage Hall also includes "Wyandot
Popcorn Museum," Harding
Presidential Collections, and Marion
County Hall of Fame)
$7.50 per year membership for
individuals, $10.00 per year
membership for families

Marlboro Township Historical Society, Inc.

12205 Marlboro Avenue
Alliance, OH 44601
(330) 935-2229
Mary E. Devies, Treasurer
(an inactive group with no office, but has
Marlboro Township information
available and Heritage Handbook,
$10.00)

Martins Ferry Area Historical Society

Sedgwick Historical Museum
627 Hanover Street
PO Box 422
Martins Ferry, OH 43935
(614) 633-3134 (President)
Kay Ziegler, President
Hours: Tue–Sat (May–Oct) noon–4:00,
and by appointment
Pub. *Ferry Landing Newsletter*, three
times per year
(Martins Ferry City and Area Museum;
Imperial glass collection; Martins
Ferry is part of Northwest Territory
called "Seven Ranges.")
$5.00 per year membership for
individuals, $7.50 per year
membership for husband and wife;
search by request, no standard fee

Mason Historical Society

Alverta Green Museum
207 Church Street
PO Box 82
Mason, OH 45040
(513) 398-6750 (Museum); (513) 398-
6583
http://ww2.eos.net/edsale/cities/Mason/
museum/html
Lucy Gorsuch
Hours: Thur–Fri 1:00–4:00

Matamoras Area Historical Society, Inc.

200 Main Street
PO Box 1846
New Matamoras, OH 45767-1846
(614) 865-2171
Blanche Y. Brown, *Newsletter* Editor
Hours: Fri & Sat, and by appointment
Pub. *Newsletter*, quarterly
(maintains a museum of local history)
$10.00 per year membership (calendar
year); $150.00 life membership (which
becomes a memorial membership after
death); no search fees, "We are happy
to share our manuscripts and
genealogy materials"

Maumee Valley Historical Society

1031 River Road
Maumee, OH 43537
(419) 893-9602; (419) 893-3108 FAX
Marilyn Wendler, Curator
Pub. *Ohio Cues*, eight times per year,
$8.00 per year subscription; *Northwest
Ohio Quarterly*, semiannually (in two
double issues)
$29.00 per year membership

Mayfield Township Historical Society and Library

606 Som Center Road
Mayfield Village, OH 44143
(440) 461-0055
Jeanne Thompson Clough, Librarian
Hours: Mon & Sat 10:00–2:00
Pub. *Mayfield Township Historical
Society Newsletter*, quarterly
("Restored historical house; museum;
quilters; and historical and
genealogical library")
$5.00 per year membership for
individuals, $10.00 per year
membership for families; search fees
vary

Medina County Historical Society

206 North Elmwood
PO Box 306
Medina, OH 44258
(330) 722-1341
Kathryn Popio, Curator
Hours: Tue & Thur 9:00–5:00; meetings
second Mon 1:00–4:00; Open house:
first Sun
Pub. *Newsletter*, monthly
$8.00 per year membership for
individuals, $5.00 per year
membership for senior citizens

Meigs County Pioneer and Historical Society, Inc.

Meigs County Museum
(144 Butternut Avenue—location)
PO Box 145 (mailing address)
Pomeroy, OH 45769
(614) 992-3810
Margaret Parker, President
Hours: Tue–Sat 1:00–4:30

Pub. *Meigs County Historian*, quarterly
$7.50 per year membership, museum
   $1.00 donation

Mercer County Historical Society, Inc.

Mercer County Historical Museum
PO Box 512
Celina, OH 45822
(419) 586-6065
Joyce L. Alig, President
Hours: Wed–Thur & Fri 8:30–4:00, Sun
   1:00–4:00

Miami County Historical and Genealogical Society, Chapter OGS

PO Box 305
Troy, OH 45373-0305
Virginia L. Brown, Corresponding
   Secretary
Pub. *Miami Meanderings*, quarterly
$10.00 per year membership for
   individuals, $12.00 per year
   membership for families; research fees
   set by individuals

Miami Valley Council on Genealogy and History

4290 Honeybrook Avenue
Dayton, OH 45415
(937) 290-2811
Hours: Wright State University, Special
   Collections and Archives: Mon–Fri
   8:30–5:00, Tue & Wed (academic
   quarter only) 7:00 P.M.–10:00 P.M.,
   Sun (academic quarter only) 2:00–5:00
Pub. *The History Tree*, quarterly
$10.00 per year membership

Miamisburg Historical Society

(Miamisburg, OH 45342—location)
PO Box 774 (mailing address)
Miamisburg, OH 45343-0774
Connie Kline, Genealogist
(operates the Daniel Gebhart Tavern
   Museum; "Genealogy records are
   available through the local branch of
   the Montgomery County Library.")

Middletown Historical Society

(Titus Avenue at Veriety Parkway—
   location)
PO Box 312 (mailing address)
Middletown, OH 45042
(440) 422-4781
Everett W. Sherron, President
Hours: Sun (Apr–Oct) 2:00–4:00, and by
   appointment
Pub. *News Letter*, eight times per year
(Middletown history and Miami Erie
   Canal History)
$5.00 per year membership

Minerva Area Historical Society

(128 North Market—location)
103 Murray Avenue (mailing address)
Minerva, OH 44657
(330) 868-4287
Hours: Mon–Wed 9:00 A.M.–11:30 A.M.
(Minerva area history)

Minster Historical Society

PO Box 58
Minster, OH 45865

Mohican Historical Society

203 East Main Street
Loudonville, OH 44842

Monroe County Historical Society

(217 Eastern Avenue—location)
PO Box 538 (mailing address)
Woodsfield, OH 43793
(614) 472-1933
Mitchell Schumacher, President
Hours: Jun–Sept: Sun 2:00–5:00 and Fair
   Week
Pub. *Monroe County Heritage*, quarterly
$15.00 per year membership for
   individuals or families

The Montgomery County Historical Society

Old Court House Museum
7 North Main Street
Dayton, OH 45402
(937) 228-6271
Sarah J. Sessions, Curator of History and
   Collections
Hours: Museum: Tue–Fri 10:00–4:30,
   Sat noon–4:00
Pub. *Columns*, bimonthly
(specializes in Miami Valley,
   Montgomery County, Dayton local
   history (not genealogy); inventors:
   Wright Brothers, Patterson family of
   NCR)
research: $5.00 per hour for members,
   $7.50 per hour for non-members;
   photocopies: 10¢ each for letter size
   and 20¢ each for legal size for
   members, 25¢ and 30¢ each for non-
   members

Morgan County Historical Society

(126 East Main Street—location)
PO Box 524 (mailing address)
McConnelsville, OH 43756
(614) 962-4785
Betty White, Treasurer
Hours: Mon–Fri (summer) 1:00–3:00,
   Sat 10:00–noon
Pub. *Elk Eye*, quarterly
$5.00 per year membership for
   individuals, $8.00 per year
   membership for couples

The Morrow County Historical Society

PO Box 21
Mount Gilead, OH 43338
(419) 946-7264 (evenings)
James D. Miller, President
Hours: Sun 2:00–5:00, and by
   appointment
Pub. *Newsletter*, quarterly
$7.50 per year subscription

Mount Healthy Historical Society

1544 McMakin Avenue
Mount Healthy, OH 45231

(513) 522-3939
Marian Blum, Curator
Hours: Tue, Thur & Sat 9:00–noon
$5.00 per year membership, $100.00 life
   membership; pictures: $5.00 service
   fee plus cost of copy

Historical Society of Mount Pleasant, Ohio, Inc.

Union Street
Mount Pleasant, OH 43939
(614) 769-2893
Sherry Sawcheck, President
Hours: by appointment
Pub. *The Town Crier*, quarterly
(Quakers, Anti-slavery underground
   railroad)
$5.00 per year membership; research for
   hourly rate plus copy charges

Munroe Falls Historical Society

(83 Munroe Falls Avenue—museum
   location)
43 Munroe Falls Avenue (mailing
   address)
Munroe Falls, OH 44262
(330) 688-5878 (Curator)
Marilyn Lown, Curator
Hours: Sun 2:00–4:00
Pub. *Olde Heritage*, ten times per year
(museum of area artifacts, local history
   library)
$5.00 per year membership for
   individuals, $10.00 per year
   membership for families, $25.00
   Contributing membership, $100.00 life
   membership

Pioneer and Historical Society of Muskingum County

304 Woodlawn Avenue
PO Box 2201
Zanesville, OH 43701
Wendell Litt, Director
Pub. *Quarterly*
$7.50 per year membership

Muskingum Valley Archeological Survey

24 South Sixth Street
Zanesville, OH 43701
Pub. *Muskingum Annals*, irregularly
$10.00 per year membership

Navarre-Bethlehem Township Historical Society

(123 High Street—location)
PO Box 291
Navarre, OH 44662
(330) 879-5938
Don Cooke, President
Hours: by appointment only

New Albany-Plain Township Historical Society

4659 Reynoldsburg-New Albany Road
PO Box 219
New Albany, OH 43054
(614) 855-9809
Emily Eby, Editor

Pub. *New Albany Plain Township Historical Society Newsletter*, about nine times per year
("Most of our information is limited to New Albany and Plain Township, located in Franklin County, Ohio.")
from $2.50 to $35.00 per year membership

New Bremen Historic Association
Genealogy Department
(120 North Main Street—location)
PO Box 73 (mailing address)
New Bremen, OH 45869
Hours: Sun (Jun–Aug) 2:00–4:00 (initial inquiries by mail only)
Pub. *The Towpath*, quarterly
$5.00 per year membership; research: initial fee of $10.00 absolutely required for reply

Newcomerstown Historical Society
Old Temperance House Tavern Museum
(221 West Canal Street—location)
PO Box 443 (mailing address)
Newcomerstown, OH 43832
Barbara Scott, President
Hours: Memorial Day–Labor Day: Tue–Sun 10:00–4:00

Noble County Historical Society
PO Box 128
Caldwell, OH 43724
E-mail: smerry@earthlink.net
http://www.geocities.com/Heartland/6854/noble.html
Sigrid Merry
$8.00 per year membership for individuals, $10.00 per year membership for families, $15.00 per year Sustaining membership, $100.00 life membership

North Royalton Historical Society
11398 Royalton Road
North Royalton, OH 44133

Northampton Historical Society
783 West Bath Road
Cuyahoga Falls, OH 44223
Carrie Swain

Northwest Franklin County Historical Society
(Weaver Park—location)
PO Box 413 (mailing address)
Hilliard, OH 43026-0413
(614) 777-4852
Mary Fuller, President
Hours: by appointment only
Pub. *Northwest Chronicle*, five times per year (February, April, June, September, November)
$5.00 per year regular membership, $1.00 per year Student membership, $25.00 per year Supporting membership, $100.00 life membership; research fees vary; $1.00 admission per person

Oakwood Historical Society
1947 Far Hills Avenue
Dayton, OH 45419
(937) 299-3793
Kathy Ellis, Genealogy Chairman
Hours: Sat 10:00–noon
library use free to members, $1.00 per month for non-members

Historical Society of Old Northfield
(9390 Olde Eight Road, Northfield Center, OH 44067—location)
PO Box 99 (mailing address)
Northfield, OH 44067
Mildred A. McCarty, President
Hours: Palmer House Museum: second & fourth Sun (Apr–Dec) 3:00–5:00
Pub. *Historical Society of Olde Northfield*, three times per year
$5.00 per year membership for individuals, $8.00 per year membership for couples, $2.00 per year membership for children, $25.00 per year Contribution membership, $100.00 life membership

Old Northwest Historical Society
c/o Victoria Retirement Center
1500 Sherman Avenue
Cincinnati, OH 45212
E-mail: rrowan@fuse.net
Hours: meetings: second Sun 2:30
Pub. *The Old Northwest Historical Society "Trading Post"*
(The Tecumseh Club is a support organization to benefit the Loyal Shawnee Tribe of Oklahoma)

Oregon Jerusalem Historical Society of Ohio, Inc.
(3320 Starr Avenue—location)
3464 Starr Avenue (mailing address)
Oregon, OH 43616
(419) 691-7193

Ottawa County Historical Society
4392 East Ledge Avenue
PO Box 385
Port Clinton, OH 43452
$5.00 per year membership

Parma Area Historical Society
6975 Ridge Road
PO Box 29002
Parma, OH 44129
(440) 845-9770

Historical Society of Parma Heights
Town Hall
6281 Pearl Road
Parma Heights, OH 44130

John Paulding Historical Society Museum
(102 Fairground Drive—location)
James Sponsellar's Office, 200 North Williams Street (mailing address)
Paulding, OH 45879
Lesli Wiedenhamer, President

Hours: Tue 10:00–4:00
Pub. *Newsletter*, four times per year
$3.00 per year membership for individuals, $7.00 per year membership for families, $10.00 per year Supporting membership, $100.00 life membership; no admission charge

Pemberville-Freedom Area Historical Society
PO Box 802
Pemberville, OH 43450
(419) 287-4305
http://www.hcnet.org/organizations/p/pemhistsoc.html
Todd Sheets

Peninsula Library and Historical Society
(6105 Riverview Road—location)
PO Box 236 (mailing address)
Peninsula, OH 44264-0236
(216) 657-BOOK
Randolph S. Bergdorf, Archivist
Hours: Mon–Thur 9:00–8:00, Fri–Sat 9:00–5:00
Pub. *PLHS Newsletter*, bimonthly
(Peninsula, Boston Township, and Boston Heights)
$2.00 per year membership in Friends of the Library

Historical Society of Perry County
(105 South Columbus Street—location)
PO Box 746 (mailing address)
Somerset, OH 43783-0746
E-mail: pchs@netpluscom.com
http://www.netpluscom.com/~pchs/

Pickaway County Historical Society, Chapter OGS
Genealogical Library
(304 South Court Street—location)
PO Box 85 (mailing address)
Circleville, OH 43113
(614) 474-9144
Darlene Weaver, Library Director
Hours: Tue–Fri 1:00–4:00
Pub. *Pickaway Quarterly*
(Pickaway County obituaries 1826–1996)
$16.00 per year membership; research: $8.00 per surname

Portage County Historical Society, Inc.
6549 North Chestnut Street
Ravenna, OH 44266
(330) 296-3523
http://www2.clearlight.com/pchs
Raymond E. Wilson, President
Hours: Tue, Thur & Sun 2:00–4:00
Pub. *News/Views Portage County Historical Society*, quarterly
$7.00 per year membership for individuals, $12.00 per year membership for families, $4.00 per year membership for students and senior citizens

Preble County Historical Society
7693 Swartzel Road
Eaton, OH 45320
(937) 787-4256 phone and FAX
Jane Lightner, Executive Director
Hours: Library: Mon–Fri 9:00–8:00, Sat 9:00–5:00, Sun 1:00–5:00
Pub. *Telltales*, quarterly
$10.00 per year membership for individuals; donations for searches

Putnam County Historical Society
201 East Main Street
PO Box 264
Kalida, OH 45853
(419) 532-3008 (Office and Museum)
Ettie M. Rieman, Secretary
Hours: Wed 9:00–noon, Sun 1:00–4:00, except holidays
Pub. *Putnam County Heritage*, quarterly
$8.00 per year membership

Ragersville Historical Society, Inc.
(Sugarcreek, OH 44681—location)
1924 Dover Avenue (mailing address)
Dover, OH 44622

Reynoldsburg Truro Historical Society
PO Box 144
Reynoldsburg, OH 43068

Rocky River Historical Society
1600 Hampton Road
Rocky River, OH 44116
(440) 333-7610

Ross County Historical Society
45 West Fifth Street
Chillicothe, OH 45601
(614) 772-1936
Brian Hackett, Director
Pub. *Recorder*

Salem Historical Society and Museum
208 South Broadway
Salem, OH 44460
(330) 337-8514
Josephine Rupe, Director
Hours: by appointment
Pub. *The Bugle*, bimonthly
$8.00 per year membership

Sandusky County Historical Society
1337 Hayes Avenue
Fremont, OH 43420-2796

Scioto Society, Inc.
215 West Second Street
PO Box 73
Chillicothe, OH 45601
(614) 775-4100

Seneca County Historical Society
Seneca County Museum
28 Clay Street
Tiffin, OH 44883-2231
(419) 447-5955
Rosalie Adams, Director

Sharon Township Heritage Society
PO Box 154
Sharon Center, OH 44274
(330) 336-3832
Robert J. Remark, President
$6.00 per year membership for individuals, $9.00 per year membership for couples

Shelby County Historical Society
PO Box 376
Sidney, Ohio 45365-0376
E-mail: lodges@bright.net
http://www.bright.net/~richnsus/
Sherrie Casad-Lodge, Web Site Manager

Smithfield Historical Society
PO Box 484
Smithfield, OH 43948

Solon Historical Society
Solon Historical Museum
33975 Bainbridge Road
Solon, OH 44139
(440) 248-6419
Patricia W. Baumann, President
Hours: one hour prior to scheduled 8:00 P.M. meetings, second Wed 1:00–4:00, and by appointment

South Euclid Historical Society
5147 Cheltenham Boulevard
Lyndhurst, OH 44124
Ester Eich, Curator
Hours: Sat 1:00–4:00

Southern Lorain County Historical Society
Spirit of '76 Museum
(201 North Main Street—location)
PO Box 76 (mailing address)
Wellington, OH 44090
(440) 647-4367; (440) 647-4576 (President)
Charles Oney, President
Hours: Apr–Oct: Sat–Sun 2:30–5:00
$10.00 per year membership for couples

Stark County Historical Society
McKinley Museum of History, Science and Industry
Ramsayer Research Library
800 McKinley Monument Drive, N.W.
Canton, OH 44708
(330) 455-7043
W. J. Weber, Librarian
Hours: Library: Tue–Wed & Fri 12:30–4:30
no search fee, except postage plus copies at 25¢ each for 8 1/2" x 11" paper, 50¢ each for 11" x 17" paper

Stow Historical Society
Young Road
PO Box 1425
Stow, OH 44224
(330) 688-1718
Catherine Flower, President
Hours: Sun 1:00–4:00, and by appointment

Pub. *Heritage Reserve News*, monthly
$5.00 per year membership for individuals, $7.50 per year membership for families, $10.00 per year Contributing membership, $25.00 per year membership for businesses, $100.00 life membership

Strongsville Historical Society
13305 Pearl Road
Strongsville, OH 44136
(440) 572-0057
Carole L. Maatz, President
Hours: Apr–Nov: Wed & Sat–Sun 1:00–4:00, and by appointment
Pub. *Strongsville Historical Society Newsletter*, bimonthly
$15.00 per year membership for individuals, $25.00 per year membership for families, $10.00 per year membership for senior citizens, $50.00 per year Corporate membership, $300.00 life membership

Summit County Historical Society
550 Copley Road
Akron, OH 44320
(330) 535-1120; (330) 535-5164
Paula G. Moran, Executive Director
Hours: Tue–Sun 1:00–5:00
Pub. *Old Portage Trail Review*, bimonthly
$20.00 per year membership for families, $35.00 per year Sustaining membership, $50.00 per year Contributing membership, $100.00 per year Century Club membership, $250.000 per year Summit Sponsor membership, $500.000 per year Benefactor membership, $1,000.00 per year Perkins Patron membership; museum admission: $5.00 for adults

Swiss Community Historical Society
PO Box 5
Bluffton, OH 45817

Tallmadge Historical Society
PO Box 25
Tallmadge, OH 44278
(216) 630-9760
Richard L. Smith, President; Steve Brunot, Vice President
Hours: open on request
Pub. *Bulletin*, eight times per year (monthly October–May)

Three Rivers Historical Society
3289 Triplecrown Drive
North Bend, OH 45052
Marjorie Burress, Local Historian

Toronto Historical Society
326 Vollmer Street
Toronto, OH 43964

Trenton Historical Society
17-A East State Street
Trenton, OH 45067
(513) 988-9634; (513) 424-0740

Doris L. Page and JoAnn Howell,
Curators
Hours: first Sat (May–Aug) 1:00–4:00;
tours by appointment
$5.00 per year membership

Troy Historical Society
Local History and Genealogy Library
Troy-Hayner Cultural Center
301 West Main Street
Troy, OH 45373
(937) 339-0457
http://www.erinet.com/troy/history/
troyhistory.html
Juda M. Moyer, Archivist
Hours: Tue–Sat 10:00–4:00, Tue–Wed
7:00 P.M.–9:00 P.M., Sun 1:30–4:30
Pub. *The Troy Times*, nine times per year
(monthly, October–June)
$7.00 per year membership for
individuals, $12.00 per year
membership for families, $25.00 per
year Sustaining membership, $50.00
per year Patron membership, $100.00
life membership; research fee: LSASE
a must, $5.00–$10.00, depending upon
how much time is needed to complete
the request, and those requiring a lot
of time will be turned over to a
professional researcher

Trumbull County Historical Society
303 Monroe, N.W.
Warren, OH 44483

Tuscarawas County Historical Society
629 Wabash Avenue, N.W.
PO Box 462
New Philadelphia, OH 44663
(216) 364-5577

Twinsburg Historical Society
(8996 Darrow Road—location)
PO Box 7 (mailing address)
Twinsburg, OH 44087
(216) 425-2743
Lea M. Bissell, Secretary
Hours: last Sun (Apr–Dec) 2:00–5:00,
and special scheduled tours and open
house dates
Pub. *Twinsburg Historical Society
Newsletter*, monthly
$6.00 per year membership for
individuals, $12.00 per year
membership for families, $15.00 per
year Contributing membership;
$35.00 per year membership for
businesses or professionals, $100.00
life membership; search fees: cost
of copies made

Union County Historical Society
PO Box 303
Marysville, OH 43040

Utica Historical Society
Herv-Utica Library
15 North Main Street
Utica, OH 43080

Van Wert County Historical Society
602 North Washington Street
PO Box 621
Van Wert, OH 45891-0621
(419) 238-5297
Helen L. Prill, Secretary
Hours: Sun 2:00–4:30, and tours on
request
Pub. *Historical Happenings*, quarterly
(Van Wert County artifacts)
$10.00 per year membership for
individuals, $30.00 per year Patron
membership, $100.00 per year
Corporate membership; $200.00 life
membership; search fees: $14.00 per
hour plus copying costs

**The Village Historical Society, Inc.
of Harrison, Ohio**
(10580 Marvin Road, Harrison
Township—location)
c/o 6590 Kilby Road (mailing address)
Harrison, OH 45030-8914
E. B. Woelfel, Chr. Restoration, Trustee
Hours: third Sun (May–Oct) 1:30–4:00
("names" quilt of area, genealogies,
restored home of Othniel Looker, fifth
governor of Ohio, Looker information)
$7.50 per year membership for
individuals, $10.00 per year
membership for couples

**The Vinton County Historical &
Genealogical Society, Inc., Chapter
OGS**
(20 West Railroad Street—location)
PO Box 306 (mailing address)
Hamden, OH 45634-0306
(614) 384-6305 (days); (614) 384-2467
(nights)
Lawrence McWhorter, President
Hours: by appointment
Pub. *Vinton County Heritage*, quarterly
$10.00 per year membership for
individuals or families

Warren County Historical Society
105 South Broadway
PO Box 223
Lebanon, OH 45036-0223
(513) 932-1817
http://www2.eos.net/edsale/cities/
lebanon/warrencomuseum.html
Mary Payne, Director
Hours: Tue–Sat 9:00–4:00, Sun noon–
4:00
Pub. *Historicalog*, quarterly with updates
(Warren County genealogy, Shaker,
Quaker, *Western Star* on microfilm)
$20.00 per year membership for
individuals, $30.00 per year
membership for families

**Historical Society of Warren
Township**
211 Main Street
Tiltonsville, OH 43963
Robert Richardson

**Washington County Historical
Society Library**
417 Second Street—Rear
Marietta, OH 45750
(614) 373-1788
Fran Kigans, Director
Hours: Mon–Fri 10:00–4:00,
weekends and evenings by
appointment
Pub. *Tallow Light*, quarterly
(Washington County quadrennial
enumerations from 1807–1911; over
10,000 court records between 1789
and 1804)
$20.00 per year membership

Waterville Historical Society
10243 Rue de Lac Road
Whitehouse, OH 43571-9522
Sara C. Holliker

Wayne County Historical Society
546 East Bowman Street
Wooster, OH 44691-3110
(330) 264-8856
Patricia Crook, Executive Secretary;
Bonnie Knox, Co-editor of *Ancestors*
Hours: Tue–Sun 2:00–4:30 (except
holidays)
Pub. *Wayne County Historical Society
Quarterly Newsletter*
$13.00 per year membership ($3.00
per year for Genealogical Section,
$10.00 per year for Historical
Society)

Wellsville Historical Society
River Museum, 1003 Riverside
PO Box 13
Wellsville, OH 43968
(330) 532-1018; (330) 532-1176
(Genealogist)
Mary Clark, Genealogist
Hours: Museum: Sun (Jun–Sept) 1:00–
5:00
(research in Columbiana and Jefferson
counties)
$5.00 per year membership; search fees:
$1.00 per page

**West Augusta Historical and
Genealogical Society**
1510 Prairie Drive
Belpre, OH 45714
Pub. *West Augusta Historical and
Genealogical Society Newsletter*

**Western Columbiana County
Historical Society**
(4355 Homeworth Road—location)
3530 Bandy Road (mailing address)
Homeworth, OH 44634
(330) 525-7804 (Treasurer)
Rosanna J. McGee, Treasurer
Pub. *Middle Sandy Flintstone*, quarterly
$6.00 per year membership

Western Lake Erie Historical Society

(2319 Torrey Hill Drive, Toledo, OH 43606—location)
PO Box 5311 (mailing address)
Toledo, OH 43611-0311
(419) 473-9534
Harry Archer, Historian
Hours: by appointment
Pub. *Marine History Lines*, approximately quarterly
$15.00, $25.00, $50.00, $500.00 per year membership; search fees negotiable

The Western Reserve Historical Society Library

10825 East Boulevard
Cleveland, OH 44106-1777
(216) 721-5722; (216) 721-5702 FAX
http://www.wrhs.org/
Kermit J. Pike, Library Director
Hours: Tue & Thur–Sat 9:00–5:00, Wed 9:00–9:00
Pub. *The Western Reserve Historical Society Genealogical Committee Bulletin*, quarterly, $5.00 per year subscription
(235,000 books, 25,000 volumes of newspapers, 30,500 rolls of microfilm, 1,000,000 prints and photographs, and more than 3,000 collections of manuscripts and archives which comprise more than six million items from New England to Georgia and west to the Mississippi River; also regional African American and ethnic archives, Ohio Labor history and urban archives; member of the Ohio Network of American History Research Centers, the designated repository for local government records and historical manuscript materials from Ashtabula, Cuyahoga, Geauga, Lake, Lorain and Medina counties)
$4.00 per year membership; admission: $6.00 for adults, $5.00 for senior citizens, $6.00 for three-month student pass, $4.00 for children (ages 6–12), members free; search service: $30.00 per hour (one-half hour minimum), includes up to ten photocopies, $10.00 for each additional ten photocopies, plus postage and handling

Whitehouse Historical Society

PO Box 2571
Whitehouse, OH 43571

Williams County Historical Society

(Williams County Fairgrounds, State Route 107—location)
PO Box 415 (mailing address)
Montpelier, OH 43543
(419) 485-8200
Carol Eschhofen, Director of Education and Development
Hours: second & fourth Sun (May–Oct) 2:00–4:00

Pub. *Northwest Historian*, quarterly
$7.50 per year membership for individuals, $10.00 per year membership for families, $100.00 life membership for individuals, $150.00 per year life membership for couples

Willoughby Historical Society

Willoughby-Eastlake Public Library
The Collection Room
30 Public Square
Willoughby, Ohio 44094
(440) 942-3200
E-mail: webmaster@wepl.lib.oh.us
http://www.wepl.lib.oh.us/
Hours: fourth Tue 6:00 P.M.–8:00 P.M., second Wed 1:00–3:00
(manuscripts, scrapbooks, maps, roster of Ohio soldiers, history books, pioneer history, photographs, school histories, directories, diaries, school annuals and microfilm of Willoughby newspapers from 1879)
$5.00 per year membership

Wood County Historical Society

Wood County Historical Museum
13660 County Home Road
Bowling Green, OH 43402
(419) 352-0967
Sandra Fouty, Director; Andrew S. Kalmar, President
Hours: Tue–Fri 9:30–4:30, Sat–Sun 1:00–4:00
Pub. *The Black Swamp Chanticleer*, bimonthly
$7.50 per year membership for individuals, $10.00 per year membership for families, $20.00 per year membership for businesses, $25.00 per year Sustaining membership, $100.00 life membership for individuals, $150.00 life membership for families

Woodville Historical Society

107 East Main Street
Woodville, OH 43469
Kermit Hoesman, President
Hours: Museum: Wed–Fri (except Jan–Feb) 2:00–4:00
$2.00 per year membership for individuals, $3.00 per year membership for families

Worthington Historical Society Library

50 West New England Avenue
PO Box 355
Worthington, OH 43085
(614) 885-1247
Lillian Skeele, Librarian
Hours: Wed 10:00–3:00, and by appointment
Pub. *The Intelligencer*, ten times per year
(Worthington history, art history, lace, interior design)
$7.00 per year membership

Wyandot County Historical Society

(130 South Seventh Street—location)
PO Box 372 (mailing address)
Upper Sandusky, OH 43351
(419) 294-3857
David Barth, Treasurer
Hours: Thur–Sun (May 1–Oct 31) 1:00–4:30
Pub. *News Letter*, five times per year
$10.00 per year membership

Yellow Springs Historical Society

405 Corry Street
PO Box 501
Yellow Springs, OH 45387
(937) 767-7375

LDS Family History Centers

Akron
(see Tallmadge)

Cleveland
(see Kirtland)

Columbus
(see Reynoldsburg)

Dayton
(see Fairborn)

Fairborn
(513) 878-9551

Kirtland
(216) 256-8808

Perrysburg
(419) 872-9491

Reynoldsburg
(614) 866-7686

Tallmadge
(216) 630-3365

Toledo
(see Perrysburg)

Genealogical Societies

State Genealogical Society

The Ohio Genealogical Society (OGS)
Library
713 South Main Street
PO Box 2625
Mansfield, OH 44907-1644
(419) 756-7294; (419) 756-8681 FAX
E-mail: ags@ogs.org
http://www.ogs.org
Thomas Stephen Neel, Office Manager

Hours: Tue–Sat 9:00–5:00; closed for holidays and OGS annual conference in April
Pub. *The Report*, quarterly; *The Ohio Genealogical Society Newsletter*, monthly; *Ohio Records and Pioneer Families*, quarterly, $18.00 per year subscription; *Ohio Civil War Genealogy Journal*, quarterly, $18.00 per year subscription
(sponsors First Families of Ohio, a lineage society for members with pre-Dec 31, 1821 Ohio ancestors; The Society of Civil War Families of Ohio, a lineage society for members with Ohio ancestors who served in the Civil War)
$27.00 per year membership for individuals, $32.00 per year joint membership (includes *The Report* and *The Ohio Genealogical Society Newsletter*)

OGS Chapters

Allen County Chapter OGS
Allen County Historical Society
Elizabeth M. MacDonell Memorial Library
620 West Market Street
Lima, OH 45801-4665
Judith S. Hauenstein, Newsletter Editor
Hours: Library: Tue–Sat 1:00–5:00
Pub. *The Newsletter*, bimonthly
$10.00 per year membership for individuals

Alliance Genealogical Society Chapter OGS
The Alliance Genealogy Society (TAGS)
PO Box 3630
Alliance, OH 44601-7630
Carolyn Miller, President; Alice Bidlack, Secretary
Hours: Alliance Rodman Public Library: Mon–Thur 9:00–9:00, Fri–Sat 9:00–5:30
Pub. *TAGS—The Alliance Genealogy Society*, ten times per year (monthly, except July and December)
$10.00 per year membership for individuals

Ashland County Chapter OGS
Ashland Public Library
(117 West Main Street, Geneva, OH 44041—location)
PO Box 681 (mailing address)
Ashland, OH 44805-0681
http://www.ashtabulagen.org
Rita Kopp, Librarian
Hours: Mon–Thur 9:00–9:00, Fri–Sat 9:00–5:00; Library research help: first Tue 7:00–9:00, second Thur 1:00–3:00, third Sat 10:00–noon; meetings third Tue (Mar–Nov) 6:30–8:45

Pub. *Pastfinder*, quarterly
(specializes in Ashland County)
$7.00 per year membership

Athens County Chapter OGS
Athens County Historical Society and Museum
65 North Court Street
Athens, OH 45701-2506
(614) 592-2280
Joanne D. Prisley, Director ACHS&M
Hours: Mon–Fri 1:00–4:00, and by appointment
Pub. *The Bulletin*, bimonthly
$10.00 per year membership; search fee: $10.00 per hour plus copies

Auglaize County Genealogical Society Chapter OGS
(County Library, Wapakoneta, OH—location)
PO Box 2021 (mailing address)
Wapakoneta, OH 45895-0521
Richard Bowersock, President
Hours: Mon–Fri 10:00–8:00, Sat (winter) 10:00–5:30
Pub. *Fallen Timbers—Genealogical Newsletter*, quarterly
$10.00 per year membership

Belmont County Chapter OGS
125 East Main Street
PO Box 285
Barnesville, OH 43713-0285
Betsy Hartley, President
Hours: Barnesville Hutton Memorial Library: summer: Mon–Wed 10:00–6:00, Thur & Sat 10:00–5:00, Fri 10:00–8:00; winter: Mon–Wed & Fri 10:00–8:00, Thur & Sat 10:00–5:00
Pub. *Belmont County Genealogy News*, quarterly, $3.00 per year subscription
$5.00 per year membership for individuals, $7.00 per year joint membership

Brown County Chapter OGS
(Corner of Apple and Cherry Street, Old County Jail—location)
PO Box 83 (mailing address)
Georgetown, OH 45121-0083
(937) 444-3521
Dorothy Helton, Corresponding Secretary
Hours: Thur–Sat 12:00–5:00
Pub. *On the Trail*, quarterly
$7.00 per year membership for individuals

Butler County Chapter OGS
(Middletown Public Library—location)
PO Box 2011 (mailing address)
Middletown, OH 45044-2011
(440) 422-1490
Ellen Essig, Corresponding Secretary
Hours: meetings: second Sat
Pub. *Pathways*, quarterly
$10.00 per year membership for individuals, $12.00 per year joint membership

Carroll County Chapter' OGS
59 Third Street, N.E.
Carrollton, OH 44615-1205
(330) 627-2094
Lois Hemming, Librarian
Hours: 9:00–5:00, drop-ins welcome, appointments accepted
Pub. *Carroll Cousins*, six times per year
$7.00 per year membership for individuals, $10.00 per year membership; no charge for reasonable amount of research, except cost of copies and postage, $5.00 per hour for most researchers to do more extensive search

Champaign County Genealogical Society Chapter OGS
PO Box 680
Urbana, OH 43078-0680
(937) 652-3673
Pat Stickley, Corresponding Secretary
Pub. *Champaign County Genealogical Society Newsletter*, quarterly
$8.00 per year membership for individuals, $10.00 per year membership for families, $100.00 life membership for individuals, $150.00 life membership for families; free queries; research in library and courthouse: $5.00 per hour plus copies

Clark County Genealogical Society Chapter OGS
City Place Apartments
102 East Main Street, Suite 204
Springfield, OH 45501-1412
Susanne Fike, President
Hours: Tue & Thur 1:00–4:00
Pub. *Clark County Kin*, quarterly
(specializes in Clark County and Ohio)
$7.00 per year membership for individuals, $8.50 per year membership for families; search fees: $5.00 for members, $7.00 for non-members

Clermont County Genealogical Society Chapter OGS
Clermont County Public Library
Doris Wood Branch
Genealogy Section
180 South Third Street
PO Box 394
Batavia, OH 45103-0394
(513) 732-2128 (Library); (513) 723-3423 (Society voice mail)
Debra Geesner, President
Hours: Mon–Thur 9:00–9:00, Fri–Sat 9:00–5:30; meetings: first Thur 7:30
Pub. *Clermont County Genealogical Society Newsletter*, quarterly
(Clermont County newspapers on microfilm)
$10.00 per year membership for families; $200.00 life membership

Clinton County Genealogical Society, Chapter OGS
149 East Locust Street
PO Box 529
Wilmington, OH 45177-0529
(937) 382-4684
http://www.postcom.com/ccgshs
Maxine Miller, Genealogist and
Volunteer Coordinator
Hours: Mar–Dec: Wed–Sat 1:00–4:30;
Jan–Feb: Thur & Sat 1:00–4:30;
meetings at Wilmington United
Methodist Church education center, 74
E. Locust St., Wilmington, Ohio:
fourth Mon (except Dec) 7:30
Pub. *Clinton Chronicle*, quarterly
$8.00 per year membership for
individuals, $10.00 per year
membership for families

Columbiana County Chapter, OGS
PO Box 861
Salem, OH 44460-0861
(330) 332-5263 (Mr. Lewis)
E-mail: clark13@ibm.net
http://www.rootsweb.com/~ohcccogs
Scott Lewis
Hours: Mon–Thur 10:00–9:00, Fri–Sat
10:00–5:00
Pub. *Columbiana County Connection*,
monthly
$10.00 per year membership for
individuals, $12.00 per year
membership for families

Coshocton County Chapter OGS
(Coshocton Public Library—location)
PO Box 128 (mailing address)
Coshocton, OH 43812-0117
(614) 622-4706
http://www.cu.soltec.com/~photo/
coshocton.html
Glenn Kinkade, Editor
Hours: Tue 9:30–11:30
Pub. *The Kinsman Courier*, quarterly
$10.00 per year membership for
individuals, $12.00 per year
membership for two people at same
address

Crawford County Chapter OGS, Inc.
PO Box 92
Galion, OH 44820
(419) 562-5420
Winnie Kleinknecht, Treasurer
Pub. *Tracking in Crawford County, Ohio*,
eight times per year
$6.00 per year membership for
individuals, $8.00 per year joint
membership, $12.00 per year
Sustaining membership

East Cuyahoga Chapter OGS
PO Box 24182
Lyndhurst, OH 44124-0182
Regis Campbell, President

Pub. *Speaking Relatively*, quarterly
$15.00 per year membership for
individuals, $20.00 per year
membership for families

Greater Cleveland Chapter OGS (Cuyahoga County)
PO Box 40254
Cleveland, OH 44140-0254
Carolyn Corcoran, President
Pub. *The Certified Copy*, quarterly
$15.00 per year membership

Parma Cuyahoga Chapter OGS
PO Box 29509
Parma, OH 44129-0509
Pub. *Parma-Cuyahoga Genealogical
Society Newsletter*, three times per
year
$15.00 per year membership (beginning
in June)

Southwest Cuyahoga Chapter OGS
19239 Knowlton Parkway, #102
Strongsville, OH 44136-9021
Grace A. Williams, Query Editor
Pub. *S.W. Cuyahoga Chapter*, three times
per year
$8.00 per year membership for
individuals, $10.00 per year
membership for families

Cuyahoga Valley Chapter OGS
PO Box 41414
Brecksville, OH 44141-0414
Hours: by appointment (mail requests
only)
Pub. *Footsteps to the Past*, quarterly
(emphasis on Brecksville and
Independence area)
$10.00 per year membership for
individuals or families

Cuyahoga West Chapter OGS
PO Box 26196
Fairview Park, OH 44126-0196
Jeanne B. Workman, President
Pub. *Tracer*, quarterly
$5.00 per year membership

Darke County Genealogical Society Chapter OGS
PO Box 908
Greenville, OH 45331-0908
Doris Aultman, Treasurer
Pub. *The Kindling*, quarterly
$9.00 per year membership

Defiance County Chapter OGS
PO Box 7006
Defiance, OH 43512-7006
(419) 782-1456 (Library)
Mrs. Pat Little, Department Head,
Ohioana Room, Defiance Public
Library
Hours: Defiance Public Library, Ohioana
Room: Mon–Fri 9:00–5:00,
"evenings—on your own to 8:00 P.M.";
Library: Mon–Thur 9:00–8:00, Fri–Sat
9:00–5:30 (summer: Sat 9:00–12:00)

Pub. *Yesteryears Trails*, quarterly
$7.00 per year membership for
individuals

Delaware County Genealogical Society, Inc., Chapter OGS
(157 East William—location)
PO Box 1126 (mailing address)
Delaware, OH 43015-8126
(614) 369-3831
E-mail: dchsdcgs@midohio.net
http://www.midohio.net/dchsdcgs
David Harris, President
Hours: Wed & Sun 2:00–4:00, Thur
9:30–4:30, Sat (Apr–Oct) 2:00–
4:00
Pub. *Delaware Genealogist's*, quarterly
$10.00 per year membership for
individuals, $12.00 per year
membership for families

Erie County Chapter OGS
PO Box 1301
Sandusky, OH 44871-1301
Elizabeth N. Proudfoot, President
Pub. *Erie County Connection*, six times
per year (March, April, May,
September, October, November)
$5.00 per year membership

Fairfield County Chapter OGS
PO Box 1470
Lancaster, OH 43130-0570
http://www.greenapple.com/~ksmith/
Pub. *Fairfield Trace*, quarterly
$7.00 per year membership

Fayette County Genealogical Society Chapter OGS
PO Box 342
Washington Court House, OH 43160-
0342
(614) 335-2540 (Library); (614) 335-
6060 (President); (614) 636-9703 (Ms.
Moore)
Bettie Kerr Gray, President; Helen R.
Moore
Hours: meetings at Carnegie Library,
Genealogical Room or Meeting Room
Pub. *The Fayette Connection*, quarterly
$10.00 per year membership for
individuals or families; search fees:
$5.00 and $10.00

Franklin County Chapter OGS
Franklin County Genealogical Society
PO Box 2406
Columbus, OH 43216-2406
(614) 469-1300
Hours: Mon, Wed & Fri 10:00–3:00, Sun
1:00–5:00
Pub. *The Franklintonian*, ten times per
year
$14.00 per year membership

Fulton County Chapter OGS
PO Box 337
Swanton, OH 43558
E-mail: gbroglin@glasscity.net
Jana Broglin, President

Pub. *Fulton Footprints*, quarterly
(collection deposited with Swanton
Public Library)
$12.00 per year membership

Gallia County Chapter OGS
Gallia County Historical/Genealogical
Society
430 Second Avenue
PO Box 295
Gallipolis, OH 45631-0295
(614) 446-7200
Henrietta Evans, Corresponding
Secretary
Hours: Tue–Fri 10:00–4:00, Sat 10:00–
1:00
Pub. *Gallia County Historical/
Genealogical Society Newsletter*,
quarterly
(First Families of Gallia County files;
Revolutionary Soldiers Who Lived in
Gallia County files)
$15.00 per year membership

Greene County Chapter, OGS
(Greene County Room, Greene County
District Library—location)
PO Box 706 (mailing address)
Xenia, OH 45385-0706
(937) 376-2995
http://www.dsenter.com/ohio/greene/
chapter.htm
Helen Steele Lehman, Corresponding
Secretary
Hours: Library: Mon–Thur 9:00–9:00,
Fri–Sat 9:00–6:00, Sun (during school
year) 1:00–5:00
Pub. *Leaves of Greene*, bimonthly
$10.00 per year membership for
individuals, $13.00 per year
membership for two members at same
address

Guernsey County Genealogical Society Chapter OGS
(8583 Georgetown Road—location)
PO Box 661 (mailing address)
Cambridge, OH 43725-0661
(614) 432-9249
Kurt Tostenson, President
Hours: Tue & Thur 1:00–4:00
Pub. *Guernsey Roots and Branches*,
quarterly
(Guernsey County information)
$10.00 per year membership for
individuals, $12.00 per year
membership for couples; copies 20¢
each from paper, 25¢ each from
microfilm

Hamilton County Chapter OGS
PO Box 15851
Cincinnati, OH 45215-0851
(513) 956-7078
http://members.aol.com/ogshc
Kenny R. Burck, President
Pub. *The Tracer*, quarterly; *Gazette*,
quarterly
$12.00 per year membership

Hancock County Chapter OGS
PO Box 672
Findlay, OH 45840-0672
(419) 422-1737 (Reference Department)
http://www.bright.net/ hanogs/
Margaret Kelley, Corresponding
Secretary
Hours: winter: Mon–Thur 9:30–8:30,
Fri–Sat 9:30–5:00; summer: Mon–Sat
9:30–5:00
Pub. *Hancock Heritage*, quarterly
$10.00 per year membership for
individuals or couples

Hardin County Genealogical Society Chapter OGS
PO Box 520
Kenton, OH 43326-0520
(419) 673-1335
E-mail: chuck@kenton.com
Charles R. Kelley, President
Pub. *Track and Trace*, quarterly
$7.50 per year membership for
individuals; $10.00 per year
membership for couples; enclose
SASE and cost of copies with queries

Harrison County Genealogical Society Chapter OGS
First Families of Harrison County
Baker Institute for Local Studies
168 East Market Street
Cadiz, OH 43907
(614) 942-3900; (614) 942-3641
(President); (614) 922-0240 (Ms.
Fergeson); (614) 942-3214
(Membership)
Dorothea L. Greer, President; Bernice
Fergeson; Eleanor Birney,
Membership; Shirley Craker,
Chairperson, First Families of
Harrison County
Hours: Tue & Thur 11:00–4:00, and by
appointment
Pub. *Our Harrison Heritage*, quarterly
(winter, spring, summer, fall)
(members of First Families of Harrison
County must have an ancestor who
was in Harrison County by Dec 31,
1830)
$5.00 per year membership for
individuals, $7.00 per year joint
membership, $100.00 life membership
for individuals, $150.00 joint life
membership

Henry County Genealogical Society
PO Box 231
Deshler, OH 43516
Phyllis LaRue, Corresponding Secretary
Hours: meetings at Edwin Wood
Memorial Library: third Mon (except
Dec) 7:00
Pub. *Henry County Genealogical Society*,
bimonthly
$7.00 per year membership for
individuals, $9.00 per year
membership for two persons at same
address

Hocking County Chapter OGS
(Logan-Hocking Public Library, East
Main Street—location)
PO Box 115 (mailing address)
Rockbridge, OH 43149-0115
(614) 385-6512 (Treasurer)
Robert E. Redd, Treasurer and
Corresponding Secretary
Hours: Library: Mon–Thur 9:00–7:00,
Fri–Sat 9:00–5:00, Sun 1:00–5:00
Pub. *The Hocking Sentinel*, quarterly
$10.00 per year membership for
individuals (calendar year), $12.00 per
year membership for couples; $75.00
life membership for individuals,
$100.00 life membership for couples

Holmes County Chapter OGS
(Agriculture Hall, Courthouse—location)
PO Box 136 (mailing address)
Millersburg, OH 44654-0136
Dená Crider, President
Hours: Presbyterian Church, Millersburg,
OH: meetings fourth Thur 7:30
Pub. *Holmes County Heirs*, bimonthly
(probate and circuit court records, 1824–
1900)
$10.00 per year membership for
individuals, $12.00 per year joint
membership

Hudson Chapter OGS
Hudson Genealogical Study Group
The Hudson Library and Historical
Society
22 Aurora Street, #G
Hudson, OH 44236
(330) 653-6658
James F. Caccamo, Archivist
Pub. *The Hudson Green*, quarterly
(March, June, September and
December)
$7.50 per year membership for
individuals (beginning in March),
$10.00 per year membership for
couples

Huron County Chapter OGS
(5/3 Bank, Executive Drive—location)
PO Box 923 (mailing address)
Norwalk, OH 44857-0923
http://www.accnorwalk.com/~jkelble
Nora Downing, Corresponding Secretary
Hours: fourth Mon (except Dec) 7:30
Pub. *The Kinologist*, four times per year
$10.00 per year membership for
individuals, $12.00 per year
membership for couples

Jackson County Chapter OGS
PO Box 807
Jackson, OH 45640-0807
Ruth Hayth, President
Pub. *Poplar Row*, quarterly
$8.00 per year membership

Jefferson County Chapter OGS
PO Box 4712
Steubenville, OH 43952-8712

(614) 264-0410
Bridgette Osz, President
Pub. *Jefferson County Lines*, quarterly
$8.00 per year membership for
individuals, $10.00 per year
membership for families

Knox County Chapter OGS

PO Box 1098
Mount Vernon, OH 43050-1098
(614) 392-7716
Hours: Public Library of Mount Vernon
and Knox County: Mon–Fri 10:00–
9:00, Sat 9:00–5:00
Pub. *Tree Climbers*, quarterly
$6.00 per year membership

Lake County Chapter OGS

Morley Public Library
184 Phelps Street
Painesville, OH 44077-3927
(440) 352-3383
Hours: Library: Mon–Thur 9:00–9:00,
Fri 9:00–6:00, Sat 9:00–5:00, Sun
(mid-Oct to Apr) 1:00–5:00
Pub. *Lake Lines*, quarterly
(specializes in Lake County)
$5.00 per year membership for
individuals, $7.00 per year
membership for couples

Lawrence County Genealogical Society, Chapter OGS

PO Box 945
Ironton, OH 45638-0955
(614) 532-1124
E-mail: Historical@wwd.net (Lawrence
Register)
http://www.wwd.net/user/historical/
(Lawrence Register)
Sherri Pettit, President
Hours: Library: Mon–Thur 9:30–8:30,
Fri–Sat 9:00–5:30; Phyllis Hamner
Room for Local History and
Genealogy: Mon & Wed 9:30–12:00 &
1:00–5:30, Tue & Thur 12:00–4:30 &
5:30–8:30, Fri–Sat 9:00–12:00 &
1:00–5:30
Pub. *Lawco Lore*, quarterly; *The
Lawrence Register—Southern Ohio's
Genealogical and Historical Website,
Lawrence County*, online magazine
$7.00 per year membership for
individuals, $10.00 per year
membership for families

Licking County Genealogical Society Chapter OGS

743 East Main Street
PO Box 4037
Newark, OH 43058-4037
(614) 345-3571; (614) 344-6777
(Librarian's home)
Betty Rose, Head Librarian
Hours: Tue–Thur & Sat 1:00–4:00, Wed
(Mar–Nov) 6:30 P.M.–9:00 P.M.
Pub. *Licking Lantern*, quarterly (plus
index issue)

$12.00 per year membership for
individuals, $14.00 per year joint
membership

Logan County Genealogical Society, Chapter OGS

521 East Columbus Avenue
PO Box 36
Bellefontaine, OH 43311-0036
(937) 592-6191 (President of Society, no
phone on premises)
Edith Eads
Hours: May–Oct: Wed & Fri 1:00–5:00,
Sun 2:00–5:00; Nov–Apr: Fri 1:00–
4:00
Pub. *Branches and Twigs*, quarterly
$12.00 per year membership; search fee:
$7.00 per hour plus copies and
postage

Lorain County Chapter OGS

PO Box 865
Elyria, OH 44036-0865
(216) 366-8121 (President); (216) 322-
3341 (Library)
Dale C. Kellogg, President
Hours: Lorain County Historical Society,
Hicks Memorial Library: Mon–Fri
8:30–4:30, Sun 1:00–4:00
Pub. *Lorain County Researcher*,
quarterly
(specializes in genealogy and history of
Lorain and neighboring counties in the
Western Reserve)
$5.00 per year membership for
individuals, $8.00 per year
membership for families

Lucas County Chapter OGS

Toledo-Lucas County Public Library
Local History and Genealogy
Department
325 North Michigan Street
Toledo, OH 43624-1614
http://www.utoledo.edu/ gried/lcogs.htm
Hours: Library: Mon–Thur 9:00–9:00,
Fri–Sat 9:00–5:30
Pub. *Fort Industry Reflections*, quarterly
(Lucas County, Ohio, and state of Ohio
genealogy)
$8.00 per year membership for
individuals, $12.00 per year
membership for families

Madison County Chapter OGS

PO Box 102
London, OH 43140-0102
Pub. *Madison County Chapter OGS
Newsletter*
$7.00 per year membership

Mahoning County Chapter OGS

PO Box 9333
Boardman, OH 44513-9333
Judy J. Bishara, Treasurer
Pub. *Mahoning Meanderings*, nine times
per year
$13.00 per year membership

Marion Area Genealogical Society Chapter OGS

(169 East Church Street)
PO Box 844 (mailing address)
Marion, OH 43301-0844
http://www.genealogy.org/~smoore/
marion/
Elsie Schnitzler, President
Hours: meetings: first Mon (Apr–Jun &
Sept–Oct) 7:30, first Sat (Nov–Mar)
1:00
Pub. *Marion Memories*, quarterly
(February, May, August, November)
$8.00 per year membership for
individuals, $10.00 per year
membership for families at same
address; free queries; Corresponding
Secretary will do limited research at
the Marion Public Library, which
charges 15¢ per copy, several
members will do more in-depth
research for a fee

Medina County Genealogical Society Chapter OGS

PO Box 804
Medina, OH 44256-0804
Pub. *Medina County Story*, quarterly
$10.00 per year membership

Meigs County Chapter OGS

PO Box 346
Pomeroy, OH 45769-0346
Pub. *The Megaphone*, quarterly
$6.00 per year membership

Mercer County Chapter OGS

PO Box 437
Celina, OH 45822-0437
Pub. *Mercer County Monitor*, quarterly
$8.00 per year membership

Miami County Historical and Genealogical Society, Chapter OGS

PO Box 305
Troy, OH 45373-0305
Virginia L. Brown, Corresponding
Secretary
Pub. *Miami Meanderings*, quarterly
$10.00 per year membership for
individuals, $12.00 per year
membership for families; research fees
set by individuals

Miami Valley Chapter OGS

PO Box 1364
Dayton, OH 45401-1364
(513) 890-6883
Mary Ellen Cassel Case, President
Pub. *Miami Valley Genealogical Society
Bulletin*, quarterly, $9.00 per year
subscription; *Genealogical Aids
Bulletin*, quarterly, $9.00 per year
subscription

Monroe County Ohio Chapter OGS

PO Box 641
Woodsfield, OH 43793-0641
E-mail: neiswong@1st.net

Shirley Neiswonger, Corresponding
  Secretary
Pub. *The Navigator*, quarterly (January,
  April, July, October)
$7.00 per year membership for
  individuals, $10.00 per year
  membership for families

Montgomery County Genealogical Society, Chapter OGS
PO Box 1584
Dayton, OH 45401-1584
(937) 274-3502; (937) 236-4617
  (President)
http://www.dayton.lib.oh.us/~ads_elli/
  newcom2.htm#TOC
Donna Tusty, Corresponding Secretary
Hours: meetings at Dayton and
  Montgomery County Public Library:
  second Sat 1:30–4:00
Pub. *Family Tree*, monthly
$12.00 per year membership for
  individuals, $15.00 per year
  membership for families, $25.00 per
  year Sustaining membership

Morgan County Chapter OGS
PO Box 418
McConnelsville, OH 43756-0418
Verna Trayer, Corresponding Secretary
Hours: Kate Love Simpson Library:
  Mon–Thur 10:00–8:00, Fri–Sat 10:00–
  5:00
Pub. *Morgan Link*, quarterly
$8.00 per year membership for
  individuals (calendar year), $10.00 per
  year membership for families; free
  queries for members, $1.00 each for
  non-members; $10.00 donation for
  limited research for non-members, no
  charge for members

Morrow County Genealogical Society Chapter OGS
PO Box 401
Mount Gilead, OH 43338-0401
E-mail: patron@bright.net;
  b.j.gameier@juno.com
http://www.rootsweb.com/~ohmorrow
Betty Meier
Pub. *The Monument*, quarterly
$5.00 per year membership

Muskingum County Genealogical Society, Chapter OGS
PO Box 3066
Zanesville, OH 43702-3066
Trudi Tipton, Corresponding Secretary;
  Doug Kress, President
Hours: Muskingum County
  |Genealogical Library: Mon–Thur
  9:00–9:00, Fri 9:00–5:00, Sat
  11:00–5:00, Sun (winter only) 1:00–
  5:00
Pub. *The Muskingum*, ten times per year
$10.00 per year membership

Noble County Chapter OGS
(Caldwell Public Library, Genealogy
  Room—location)
PO Box 174 (mailing address)
Caldwell, OH 43724-0174
(614) 732-2093 (Secretary)
Susan K. Radcliff, Secretary
Hours: Caldwell Public Library: Mon–
  Wed 9:00–8:00, Thur–Fri 9:00–5:00,
  Sat 9:00–2:00; meetings at Senior
  Citizens Building, Cumberland Street,
  one block off Square: fourth Sun 1:30
  (except Dec)
Pub. *Noble County Newsletter*, quarterly
$8.00 per year membership for
  individuals, $10.00 per year
  membership for couples; copies 10¢
  per page

Ottawa County Chapter OGS
PO Box 193
Port Clinton, OH 43452-0193
(419) 734-7396
Martha Grindstaff, Editor
Hours: meetings: third Tue 7:30
Pub. *Marshland to Heartland*, quarterly,
  $2.00 per issue
(Ottawa County records of genealogical
  interest)
$8.00 per year membership for
  individuals, $10.00 per year
  membership for families

Paulding County Genealogical Society Chapter OGS
Paulding County Carnegie Library
205 South Main Street
Paulding, OH 45879-1492
(419) 399-2032 (library); (419) 399-4663
  (evening)
Marilyn J. Smith, Corresponding
  Secretary
Hours: Library: Mon–Thur 9:00–8:00,
  Fri 9:00–5:30, Sat (Sept–May) 9:00–
  3:00, Sat (Jun–Aug) 9:00–noon
Pub. *Paulding Pathways*, quarterly
$10.00 per year membership for
  households; research (in library and at
  courthouse) for cost of copies: 10¢ per
  page from paper originals, 15¢ per
  page from microform originals

Perry County Chapter OGS
PO Box 275
Junction City, OH 43748-0275
(614) 987-7646 (Library)
Evelyn Angle Wolfe, District Manager at
  Junction City Branch Library; Sue
  Saylor, Chapter Librarian and
  Corresponding Secretary
Hours: Junction City Branch Library:
  Mon & Wed 10:00–7:00, Fri 10:00–
  6:00, Sat 9:00–1:00; Perry County
  Chapter OGS Collection at New
  Lexington Library: Mon–Thur 9:00–
  8:00, Fri–Sat 9:00–6:00
Pub. *Perry County Heirlines*, quarterly
(cemetery, marriage, death and census
  publications)

$10.00 per year membership for
  individuals, $13.00 per year joint
  membership; research fee: $10.00 per
  surname, brief inquiries answered free
  by a few volunteers

Pickaway County Historical Society, Chapter OGS
Genealogical Library
(304 South Court Street—location)
PO Box 85 (mailing address)
Circleville, OH 43113
(614) 474-9144
Darlene Weaver, Library Director
Hours: Tue–Fri 1:00–4:00
Pub. *Pickaway Quarterly*
(Pickaway County obituaries 1826–1996)
$16.00 per year membership; research:
  $8.00 per surname

Pike County Chapter OGS
PO Box 224
Waverly, OH 45690-0224
Pub. *Pike Speaks*, quarterly
$4.00 per year membership

Portage County Chapter OGS
PO Box 821
Ravenna, OH 44266
Pub. *Portage Path to Genealogy*, six
  times per year (January, March, May,
  September, October, November)
$6.00 per year membership for
  individuals, $8.00 per year
  membership for two at same address

Preble County Chapter OGS
Preble County District Library
Eaton Branch
301 North Barron Street
Eaton, OH 45320-1705
(937) 456-4331
Susan H. Kendall, Library Director/
  Newsletter Editor
Hours: Mon–Fri 9:00–8:00, Sat 9:00–
  5:00, Sun 1:00–5:00
Pub. *Preble's Pride* (emphasis on
  southwest Ohio), quarterly
$9.00 per year membership for
  individuals, $11.00 per year
  membership for households

Putnam County Chapter OGS
Putnam County Genealogical Society
PO Box 403
Ottawa, OH 45875-0403
(419) 523-3747
Linda Hermiller, Corresponding
  Secretary
Hours: Heritage Room, Putnam County
  District Library: Mon–Thur 9:00–8:00,
  Fri–Sat (winter) 9:00–5:00
Pub. *Putnam Pastfinder*, quarterly
  (February, May, August, November,
  and an index in December)
(cemetery books)
$8.00 per year membership for
  individuals, $10.00 per year joint
  membership, $100.00 life membership

Richland County Chapter OGS
PO Box 3823
Mansfield, OH 44907-0823
http://www.rootsweb.com/~ohrichgs
Pub. *The Pastfinder*, quarterly
$5.00 per year membership

Richland County-Shelby City Genealogical Society, Chapter OGS
PO Box 766
Shelby, OH 44875-0766
Ruby Bonecutter, Newsletter Editor
Hours: Sutter-Roush Room, Rear 23 East
   Main Street: first Thur (except Jul &
   Aug) 7:00
Pub. *Shelby Spirits*, ten times per year
$10.00 per year membership for
   individuals (beginning September 1),
   $12.00 per year joint membership

Ross County Chapter OGS
(444 Douglas Avenue—location)
PO Box 6352 (mailing address)
Chillicothe, OH 45601-6352
(614) 773-2715
Caroline Whitten, President; Grace Baer,
   Librarian
Hours: Mon, Wed & Fri 1:00–4:00, Thur
   6:00–9:00, Sat 9:00–noon
Pub. *Ross County Genealogical Society
   Newsletter*, quarterly
$12.00 per year membership for
   individuals or joint membership;
   $10.00 donation for search of indexes
   of material in library

Sandusky County Kin-Hunters Organization, Chapter OGS
(Sandusky Township House—location)
1337 Hayes Avenue (mailing address)
Fremont, OH 43420-2796
Dave Golden, President
Pub. *Kith 'n Kin*, bimonthly
$10.00 per year membership for
   individuals, $12.00 per year
   membership for two persons in same
   household, $3.00 per year membership
   for youths

Scioto County Chapter OGS
PO Box 812
Portsmouth, OH 45662-0812
(614) 259-4649
E-mail: mmeadows@bright.net
http://www.geocities.com/vienna/1943/
   sccogs.html
Mary Meadows Crabtree, Corresponding
   Secretary
Hours: Portsmouth Public Library: Mon–
   Fri 9:00–8:00, Sat 9:00–5:30, Sun
   1:00–5:00
Pub. *Scioto County Chapter Ohio
   Genealogical Society*, bimonthly
$10.00 per year membership; research
   $10.50 per hour (two hour retainer)

Seneca County Genealogical Society Chapter OGS
PO Box 157
Tiffin, OH 44883-0157

Ruth Brill, Co-editor
Hours: Mon–Thur 10:00–9:00, Fri–Sat
   10:00–5:00
Pub. *Seneca Searchers*, bimonthly
(specializes in Seneca County, Ohio,
   genealogy)
$10.00 per year membership for
   individuals, $12.00 per year
   membership for families in the U.S. or
   for foreign individuals

Southern Ohio Chapter OGS
Southern Ohio Genealogical Society
PO Box 414
Hillsboro, OH 45133
Pub. *Roots & Shoots*, quarterly
$9.00 per year membership

Stark County Chapter OGS
(Canton, OH—location)
7300 Woodcrest, N.E. (mailing address)
North Canton, OH 44721-1949
(330) 494-9574
Clifford T. Wig, Corresponding Secretary
Hours: Stark County District Library:
   second Thur 7:30–9:00
Pub. *Tree Climber*, monthly
(books on Stark County, Ohio)
$10.00 per year membership

Summit County Chapter OGS
PO Box 2232
Akron, OH 44309-2232
(330) 699-4511
Marilyn Kirn Kovatch, Editor
Pub. *The Highpoint*, ten times per year
("Primarily Summit County genealogical
   material")
$7.00 per year membership for
   individuals, $8.00 per year
   membership for families; free queries

Trumbull County Chapter OGS
PO Box 309
Warren, OH 44482-0309
Pub. *Ancestry Trails*, monthly
$10.00 per year membership for
   individuals, $12.00 per year joint
   membership

Tuscarawas County Chapter OGS
Tuscarawas County Genealogical
   Society, Inc.
(Bonifay Building, 310 Grant Street,
   Dennison—location)
PO Box 141 (mailing address)
New Philadelphia, OH 44663-0141
(614) 269-2602
Keith A. Schaar, President
Hours: May–Aug: Tue–Sat 11:00–3:00;
   Sept–Apr: Tue, Thur & Sat 11:00–3:00
Pub. *Tuscarawas County Pioneer
   Footprints*, quarterly (February, May,
   August, November)
(Tuscarawas County and surrounding
   counties; Moravian history and
   ancestry)
$10.00 per year membership for
   individuals, $12.00 per year
   membership for couples, $150.00 life

membership for individuals, $200.00
life membership for couples, $2.00 per
day library charge for non-members
over 18

Union County Chapter OGS
(Marysville Public Library, 231 South
   Court Street—location)
PO Box 438 (mailing address)
Marysville, OH 43040-0438
(937) 642-4694; (937) 642-6147
   (Secretary)
Dorothy McKitrick, Corresponding
   Secretary; Mary Seslar, Secretary
Hours: meetings third Tue (except Dec)
   7:00
Pub. *Union Echoes*, bimonthly
$8.00 per year membership for
   individuals, $10.00 per year
   membership for families at same
   address; unlimited queries free for
   members, one free query for non-
   members; research limited to Union
   County only: $10.00 deposit

Van Wert County Chapter OGS
PO Box 485
Van Wert, OH 45891-0485
Helen L. Prill, Trustee
Pub. *Van Wert County Connection*,
   quarterly (January, April, July,
   October)
$8.00 per year membership

The Vinton County Historical & Genealogical Society, Inc., Chapter OGS
(20 West Railroad Street—location)
PO Box 306 (mailing address)
Hamden, OH 45634-0306
(614) 384-6305 (days); (614) 384-2467
   (nights)
Lawrence McWhorter, President
Hours: by appointment
Pub. *Vinton County Heritage*, quarterly
$10.00 per year membership for
   individuals or families

Warren County Genealogical Society and Research Library, Chapter OGS
300 East Silver Street
Lebanon, OH 45036-1800
(513) 933-1144
Chester Dunn, President
Hours: Mon & Thur–Fri 9:00–4:00
Pub. *Heir-Lines*, quarterly, $3.00 per
   issue
$10.00 per year membership, $15.00 per
   year membership for couples; three
   free queries for members, $3.00 per
   query for non-members

Washington County Chapter OGS
PO Box 2174
Marietta, OH 45750-2174
(614) 373-1641
Sharon Cory Gardner, Newsletter Editor

Hours: Washington County Public
Library: Mon–Thur 9:00–8:30, Fri–Sat
9:00–5:00
Pub. *Washington*, quarterly
$8.00 per year membership

Wayne County Genealogical Society, Chapter OGS

PO Box 856
Wooster, OH 44691
Mary Lou Frost, President
Hours: meetings at Wayne County Public
Library: first Sat (except Jul) 2:00
Pub. *Ancestors*, quarterly (spring,
summer, fall, winter)
$10.00 per year membership for
individuals (includes quarterly and
search fees), $15.00 per year
membership for families, $5.00 per
year membership for families, $100.00
life membership for individuals

Williams County Chapter OGS

PO Box 293
Bryan, OH 43506-0293
(419) 636-4151
Alice Shaffer, President
Hours: Community Room, East End
Pool, East High Street, Bryan, OH:
second Mon 7:30 P.M.
Pub. *Ohio's Last Frontier*, eleven times
per year (monthly, except single issue
for July–August)
("The society maintains a surname file in
addition to pedigree charts submitted
by WCGS members; this file is
maintained at the Bryan Public
Library; has set up a First Families of
Williams County, open to WCGS
members who can provide
documentation proving a direct line
ancestor residing in what was known
as Williams County, Ohio, as of
1860.")
$10.00 per year membership for
individuals, $11.00 per year joint
membership, $12.00 per year
membership for families

Wood County Chapter OGS

Wood County Genealogical Society
(Local and Family History Center, Old
Jail, Courthouse Square—location)
PO Box 722 (mailing address)
Bowling Green, OH 43402-0722
Lolita Guthrie, Editor
Hours: Mon–Fri 9:00–noon
Pub. *Newsletter of Wood County
Genealogical Society*, bimonthly, back
issues $5.00 per year plus $2.50
postage and handling
$10.00 per year membership for
individuals, $122.00 per year
membership for couples

Wyandot Tracers: Wyandot County Chapter OGS

PO Box 414
Upper Sandusky, OH 43351-0414
Sue Culver, President
Hours: Upper Sandusky Community
Library: Mon–Fri 9:00–9:00, Sat
9:00–1:00
Pub. *Newsletter*, bimonthly
$8.00 per year membership (calendar
year)

Out-of-State OGS Chapters

Arizona Chapter (OGS)

PO Box 677
Gilbert, AZ 85234-0677

Southern California Chapter (OGS)

PO Box 5057
Los Alamitos, CA 90721-5057
Bonnie Morris, President
Pub. *Buckeye Californian*, quarterly (or
more often)
(Los Angeles, Ventura, San Diego and
Orange counties)
$9.00 per year membership for
individuals, $12.00 per year joint
membership

Colorado Chapter (OGS)

PO Box 1106
Longmont, CO 80502-1106

Madison County Florida Genealogical Society

Florida Chapter of the Ohio Genealogical
Society, Inc.
RR 3, Box 1720
Madison, FL 32340-9531
(904) 929-2846; (904) 929-2970 FAX
E-mail: espear@worldnet.att.net
Elmer C. Spear, Editor
Hours: by appointment
Pub. *The Quest*, bimonthly (January,
March, May, July, September,
November)
(library of 3,948 books and 2,429 rolls of
film, including 2,459 books and 2,072
films dealing with Ohio, plus 119
books and 345 films dealing with
Florida and 132 books and 92 films
dealing with Georgia; Madison County
federal census and Soundex, local
newspaper from 1901, and State of
Florida pension index for all CSA
soldiers)
$10.00 per year membership for
individuals, $15.00 per year
membership for families, $150.00 life
membership for individuals, $200.00
life membership for families; no
search services; copies: 20¢ per page
from paper originals, 25¢ per page
from microfilm originals

National Capital Buckeye Chapter (OGS)

PO Box 105
Bladensburg, MD 20710-0105

Regional Genealogical Societies

The Adams County Genealogical Society

Adams County Heritage Center
State Route 247 North
PO Box 231
West Union, OH 45693
(937) 544-8522
Jean Tolle, President; Betty Lathrop,
Secretary
Hours: Thur & Sat noon–4:00
Pub. *Our Heritage*, quarterly
$6.00 per year membership

Alexander Local Genealogical and Historical Society

Rt. 5, Box 157
Athens, OH 45701
M. L. Bowman

Ashtabula County Genealogical Society, Inc.

Geneva Public Library
860 Sherman Street
Geneva, OH 44041-9101
(440) 466-4521, ext. 13 (Library)
Hours: Mon 10:30–noon & 12:30–8:00,
Tue–Wed 10:30–8:00, Thur 10:30–
5:00, Fri 11:00–4:00, Sat (except
summer) 10:30–4:00
Ancestor Hunt, quarterly (February, May,
August, November)

Cumberland Trail Genealogical Society

(Saint Clairsville Public Library, across
the street from the Belmont County
Courthouse on Main Street, U.S.
Route 40—collection location)
PO Box 576 (mailing address)
Saint Clairsville, OH 43950
(614) 695-2062 (Library); (614) 676-
4132 (Rick Sowinski); (614) 695-1355
(Kim Conley)
Rick Sowinski and Kim Conley, Co-
Presidents
Hours: meetings: second Mon 6:30
Pub. *Trail Blazer*
(primarily interested in Belmont County,
but also the surrounding counties of
Monroe, Noble, Guernsey, Harrison
and Jefferson; county histories, family
genealogies, local census, local
newspapers, Ohio Civil War Veterans,
cemetery records, obituary file,
surname file, etc.)
$10.00 per year membership for
individuals (calendar year), $15.00 per
year membership for families, $100.00
life membership

Fostoria Lineage Research Society
Kaubesch Library
205 Perry Street
Fostoria, OH 44830
Jan Herbert, Vice President
$5.00 per year membership; will answer
queries for cost of postage and
photocopies

Friends of the Library Genealogical Research Group
(Clark County Public Library, 201 South
Fountain Avenue—location)
PO Box 1080 (mailing address)
Springfield, OH 45501-1080
(937) 323-8616
Janet McCrosky, Secretary-Treasurer
Hours: Mon–Fri 9:00–9:00, Sat 9:00–
6:00, Sun 1:00–5:00
$3.00 per year membership

Geauga County Genealogical Society
Anderson Allyn Room for Genealogical
Research
Chardon Library
110 East Park Street
Chardon, OH 44024-1213
(440) 285-7601
Jeannette Grosvenor, Editor
Hours: Library: Mon–Thur 9:00–9:00,
Fri–Sat 9:00–5:00, Sun (during school
year) 1:00–5:00
Pub. *Raconteur*, five times per year
(January, March, May, September,
November)
(specializes in Geauga County)
$7.50 per year membership

Johnstown Genealogy Society
PO Box 345
Johnstown, OH 43031

KYOWVA Genealogical Society
(see West Virginia)

Meigs County Pioneer and Historical Society, Inc.
Meigs County Museum
(144 Butternut Avenue—location)
PO Box 145 (mailing address)
Pomeroy, OH 45769
(614) 992-3810
Margaret Parker, President
Hours: Tue–Sat 1:00–4:30
Pub. *Meigs County Historian*, quarterly
$7.50 per year membership, museum
$1.00 donation

Miami Valley Council on Genealogy and History
4290 Honeybrook Avenue
Dayton, OH 45415
(937) 290-2811
Hours: Wright State University, Special
Collections and Archives: Mon–Fri
8:30–5:00, Tue & Wed (academic
quarter only) 7:00 P.M.–10:00 P.M.,
Sun (academic quarter only) 2:00–
5:00

Pub. *The History Tree*, quarterly
$10.00 per year membership

Pioneer and Historical Society of Muskingum County
304 Woodlawn Avenue
PO Box 2201
Zanesville, OH 43701
Wendell Litt, Director
Pub. *Quarterly*
$7.50 per year membership

Northwest Territory Genealogical Society
(see Indiana)

Shelby County Genealogical Society
17755 State Route 47
Sidney, OH 45365-9242
(937) 492-0071 (Editor)
Betty Bevans, Editor
Pub. *Shelbyana*, quarterly (January,
April, July, October)
(specializes in Shelby County, Ohio)
$10.00 per year membership (1 or 2
people at same address)

South Central Ohio Genealogical Society
PO Box 6352
Chillicothe, OH 45601

Southwest Butler County Genealogical Society
c/o Soldiers, Sailors and Pioneers
Monument
3 South Monument Avenue
Hamilton, OH 45011

Toledo Area Genealogical Society
PO Box 352258
Toledo, OH 43635-2258
http://wwwatoledo.edu/drostet/tags/
Jeanne Reisler, President
Pub. *Newsletter—Northwestern Ohio
Genealogical Society Newsletter*,
quarterly
$8.00 per year membership for
individuals, $4.00 per year
membership for each additional family
member

Tri-State Genealogical Society
Carnegie Public Library
219 East Fourth Street
East Liverpool, OH 43920
(330) 385-2048 (Library)
Hours: Library: Mon–Fri 10:00–8:00, Sat
9:00–5:00
Pub. *TSGS Quarterly Newsletter*
(Ohio, Pennsylvania and West Virginia)
$7.00 per year membership (calendar
year), $10.00 per year membership for
families

Wayne County, Indiana, Genealogical Society
(see Indiana)

Wellington Genealogical Workshop
515 West Herrick Avenue
Wellington, OH 44090
A. E. Glendening

West Augusta Historical and Genealogical Society
1510 Prairie Drive
Belpre, OH 45714
Pub. *West Augusta Historical and
Genealogical Society Newsletter*

Independent Publications and Miscellany

Canal Society of Ohio
Summit County Historical Society
550 Copley Road
Akron, OH 44320
Pub. *Towpaths*, quarterly, $10.00 per
year library subscription
$18.00 per year membership for
individuals, $20.00 per year
membership for families or non-profit
corporations, $10.00 per year
membership for students, $30.00 per
year Contributing membership or
membership for for-profit
corporations, $50.00 per year Patron
membership

Central Ohio Alliance of Historical Societies
1742 Franklin Avenue
Columbus, OH 43205
(614) 253-4459

Council of Historic Institutions and Preservation Societies (CHIPS) (Summit and Portage Counties)
The Hudson Library and Historical
Society
22 Aurora Street
Hudson, OH 44236
(330) 653-6658
James F. Caccamo, Director

Electronic Oberlin Group Website
http://ocaxp1.cc.oberlin.edu/~EOG/
(pictures and short biographies of people
in Oberlin's history; images of
buildings and landmarks in Oberlin,
past and present; short histories of
local organizations, including
churches; records from Oberlin's past,
including census data; links to other
web sites relevant to Oberlin; Oberlin
History Timeline through 1900)

French Ancestors
2923 Tara Trail
Beavercreek, OH 45434-6252
(937) 429-2979
Marianne R. Doyle
Pub. *French Ancestors*, bimonthly, $8.00
per year subscription

("This is a small newsletter which deals with the French ancestors of families who settled in western Ohio in the mid-1800s, includes extracts from original French records and cultural, historical, and genealogical information of general interest.")

Genealogical Research and Consultation

PO Box 119
Washington Court House, OH 43160-0119
(614) 335-0266; (614) 333-3530 FAX
Ms. Sandy Fackler, Editor and Publisher
Pub. *The Fayette County Journal of Genealogy and History*, quarterly, $20.00 per year subscription

Governor's Office of Veterans' Affairs

65 South Front Street, Suite 426
Columbus, OH 43215
(614) 728-0155
Frank Mechem, Administrative Assistant
Hours: 8:00–4:30
(maintains wartime discharge papers and form DD-214; Civil War records, etc.)

Historic New Richmond

(125 George Street—location)
PO Box 2 (mailing address)
New Richmond, OH 45147
(513) 553-9770
Hazel Davis, Curator
Hours: Sun 1:00–5:00, and by appointment

Historic Perrysburg, Inc.

420 East Front Street
PO Box 703
Perrysburg, OH 43551
(419) 874-2815

Historic Preservation Guild of Hancock County

315 East Crawford
PO Box 621
Findlay, OH 45840
Rev. James H. Nye, President and Curator
Hours: second & fourth Sat & Sun: 1:00–4:00
Pub. *Patchworks of History*
(owns and operates the 1840 DeWald-Funk House Museum)
$10.00 per year membership for individuals, $15.00 per year membership for couples; museum admission: $3.00 for adults, $1.50 for children under 12

Hunting for Bears Genealogical and Historical Society

(see Alabama)

Main Street Preservation Society

PO Box 101
Grafton, OH 44044
(440) 926-3488

Miami County Genealogical Researchers Homepage

http://www.TDN-NET.com/genealogy/

Muskingum County Footprints

2740 Adamsville Road
Zanesville, OH 43701
(614) 453-8231
Hilda E. Yinger, Co-Author
Pub. *Muskingum County Footprints* (Muskingum County records and miscellaneous information, church, school and newspaper extracts), semiannually, costs vary with size of publication

OhGenWeb

Part of U.S. GenWeb Project
E-mail: oh@usgenweb.com
http://www.rootsweb.com/~ohgenweb
(links to other Ohio resources)

Ohioana Library Association

65 South Front Street, Room #1105
Columbus, OH 43266-0334
(614) 728-6974
E-mail: ohioana@winslo.ohio.gov
Barbara Meister, Librarian
Hours: Mon–Fri 8:30–4:30
Pub. *Ohioana Quarterly* (not genealogical, contains reviews of books written by Ohioans or about Ohio), quarterly (March, June, September, December), $20.00 per year subscription
(archive for works by and about Ohio/Ohioans, with biographies of over 10,000 Ohio writers, also music, William Dean Howells, and family histories)

Ridgewood Preservation, Inc.

256 21st Street, N.W.
Canton, OH 44709
(330) 454-8471

Tiffin Historic Trust

172 Jefferson Street
PO Box 333
Tiffin, OH 44883
(419) 447-4789
Mary Lewis, Treasurer
(local preservation)

Van Wert and Surrounding Counties, Ohio

19133 Plum Street
Venedocia, OH 45894
(419) 667-3151
Lois Bassett, Editor and Owner
Pub. *Van Wert and Surrounding Counties, Ohio* (early county records of genealogical interest, every-name index), annually, $14.50 per year issue

OKLAHOMA

Archives and Libraries with Holdings in Genealogy

State Archives and Library

Office of Archives and Records (Oklahoma)

The Oklahoma Department of Libraries
200 N.E. 18th Street
Oklahoma City, OK 73105-3298
(405) 521-2502 (Department of Libraries); (405) 521-2502 (Archives and Records); (405) 525-7804 FAX; (800) 522-8116
E-mail: tkremm@oltn.odl.state.ok.us
http://www.state.ok.us/~odl/oar/arrccom.htm
Gary Harrington, Head, Archives Division
Hours: Mon–Fri 8:00–5:00

State Historical Society

Oklahoma Historical Society

Library Resources Division
Archives and Manuscripts Division
Wiley Post Historical Building
2100 North Lincoln Boulevard
Oklahoma City, OK 73105-4997
(405) 521-2491; (405) 521-2492 FAX
http://www.keytech.com/~frizzel/ohspage.html
Edward Connie Shoemaker, Director, Library Resources Division
Hours: Library Resources Division: Mon 9:00–8:00, Tue–Sat 9:00–5:00; Archives and Manuscripts Division: Mon 9:00–5:00, Sat 9:00–noon & 1:00–5:00
Pub. *Mistletoe Leaves*, monthly; *The Chronicles of Oklahoma*, quarterly
(family histories, Oklahoma history—including local and county histories; Native Americans of Oklahoma)
$20.00 per year membership for individuals, $30.00 per year membership for families, $15.00 per year membership for students and retirees aged 65 and older, $30.00 per year membership for institutions, $75.00 per year Supporting membership, $400.00 life membership, $1,000.00 Benefactor membership; research: $15.00 for all out-of-state letters, plus photocopies and shipping (to be invoiced)

City, County and Regional Archives and Libraries

Alva Public Library
504 Seventh Street
PO Box 234
Alva, OK 73717
(405) 327-1833
Merle Jean Klick-Murrow
Hours: Mon 10:00–9:00, Tue–Sat 10:00–5:00

American Heritage Library
102 South Third
Davis, OK 73030

Ardmore Public Library
320 E Street, N.W.
Ardmore, OK 73401
(405) 223-8290; (405) 223-2033 FAX
Hours: Mon–Thur 10:00–8:30, Fri–Sat 10:00–4:00
(home of Mac McGalliard Historical Collection of local history)

Ataloa Lodge Museum
(On the campus of Bacone College— location)
2299 Old Bacone Road (mailing address)
Muskogee, OK 74403
(918) 683-4581, ext. 283; (918) 687-5913 FAX
Thomas R. McKinney, Museum Director
Hours: Mon–Fri 10:00–4:00
(Dawes Commission papers)

Atoka County Library
205 East First
Atoka, OK 74525

Bartlesville Public Library and History Museum
600 South Johnstone
Bartlesville, OK 74003
(918) 337-5353; (918) 337-5338 FAX
http://netra.bartlesville.lib.ok.us:8080/
Joan Singleton, Public Services Librarian
Hours: Mon–Thur 9:00–9:00, Fri–Sat 9:00–5:30
(Cherokee and Delaware Rolls, local newspaper from 1895, Indiana Territory and Oklahoma Territory census)

Caddo Indian Territory Museum and Library Society
PO Box 65
Caddo, OK 74729-0065
(580) 367-2580
Mrs. T. M. Markham, Curator

Carnegie Library
Archives Room
215 East Wade
El Reno, OK 73036
Hours: Mon–Fri 9:00–5:00, Sat 9:00–1:00

Carnegie Library
221 West Broadway
Elk City, OK 73644

Center for Great Plains Studies
(see Kansas)

Center for Great Plains Study
(see Nebraska)

Chandler-Watts Library
History-Genealogy Department
321 North Oak
PO Box 696
Stratford, OK 74872
Hours: 9:00–6:00, Tue 9:00–8:00

Cherokee City-County Public Library
602 South Grand Avenue
Cherokee, OK 73728
(405) 596-2366
Mary Berry
Hours: Mon–Fri 1:00–6:00, Sat 9:00–12:00

Cherokee Strip Museum of Alva
901 14th Street
Alva, OK 73717
(405) 327-2030

Chickasha Public Library
527 Iowa Avenue (Sixth and Iowa)
Chickasha, OK 73018

Coal County Historical and Mining Museum, Inc.
212 South Broadway Street
Coalgate, OK 74538-2612
(genealogical services)

Cushing Public Library
215 North Steele
PO Box 551
Cushing, OK 74203

Oklahoma State D.A.R. Library
c/o Oklahoma Historical Society
Library Resources Division
Wiley Post Historical Building
2100 North Lincoln Boulevard
Oklahoma City, OK 73105-4997
(405) 521-2491 (Oklahoma Historical Society)
Hours: Library Resources Division: Mon 9:00–8:00, Tue–Sat 9:00–5:00

Public Library of Enid and Garfield County
(120 West Maine, Enid, OK 73701— location)
PO Box 8002 (mailing address)
Enid, OK 73702-8002
(405) 234-6313; (405) 233-2948 FAX
http://www.enid.org/library.htm
Glenda B. Lamb, Director
Hours: Mon–Thur 9:00–9:00, Fri–Sat 9:00–6:00, Sun 1:00–6:00

Fort Sill Museum
Department of Army
437 Quanah Road
Fort Sill, OK 73503-5100
(405) 442-5123
Towana D. Spivey, Director/Chief Curator
Hours: 7:30–4:30
Pub. *Fort Sill Museum*
(specializes in Native Americans and frontier military)
free

Gateway to the Panhandle
PO Box 27
Gate, OK 73844
(405) 934-3133
Florence Whisenhurt, Curator
Hours: Mon–Sat 1:00–6:00

Thomas Gilcrease Institute of American History and Art
1400 Gilcrease Museum Road
Tulsa, OK 74127-2100
(918) 596-2700 phone and FAX
Sarah Erwin, Curator of Archival Collections
Hours: Tue–Sat 9:00–5:00, Sun & federal holidays 11:00–5:00
Pub. *Gilcrease Journal*, two times per year
(historical archives, documents and maps)
$30.00 per year out-of-state membership

Grove (Oklahoma) Public Library
206 South Elk Street
Grove, OK 74344
(918) 786-2945; (918) 786-5233 FAX
Marcia Austin, Librarian
Hours: Mon, Wed & Fri 8:30–5:00, Tue & Thur 8:30–9:00, Sat 8:00–noon
(Delaware and adjoining counties, Cherokee records, all Oklahoma censuses, Soundex for 1900 Indian Territory and Oklahoma Territory, excellent general collection)

Henryetta Public Library
518 West Main
Henryetta, OK 74437
(918) 652-7377; (918) 652-2797 FAX
Ruby Wesson, Library Director
Hours: Mon–Fri 10:00–6:00, Sat 10:00–1:00
(Westlawn Cemetery index; obituary index, 1913-1941, taken from the *Henryetta Daily Free-Lance*)
$1.00 per page copied from microfilm by correspondence, other limited searches on a case-by-case basis

Idabel Public Library
PO Box 778
Idabel, OK 74745
Hours: 9:00–6:00

Lawton Public Library
Family History Research Room
110 S.W. Fourth Street
Lawton, OK 73501
(405) 581-3450; (405) 248-0243 FAX
Marion F. Donaldson, Library Director;
    Paul Follett, Genealogy Librarian
Hours: Mon–Thur 10:00–9:00, Fri
    10:00–6:00, Sat 10:00–5:00, Sun
    (Sept–May) 1:00–5:00
(emphasis on Oklahoma, the south, and
    Native Americans—houses the Kowa,
    Comanche, and Apache (KCA)
    Research Collection; has little on other
    tribes)

McAlester Public Library
401 North Second Street
McAlester, OK 74501
(918) 426-0930
Evelyn McWaters, Librarian
Hours: Mon–Tue & Thur 9:00–8:00,
    Wed & Fri 9:00–5:00, Sat 9:00–1:00

Metropolitan Library System
Downtown Library
131 Dean A. McGee Avenue
Oklahoma City, OK 73102
(405) 231-8650; (405) 232-5493 FAX;
    telnet://mars.mls.lib.ok.us
Kay Bauman, Library Manager
Hours: Mon & Wed–Thur 9:00–6:00,
    Tue 9:00–9:00, Fri & Sat 9:00–5:00
(limited genealogical use, *Daily
    Oklahoman* on microfilm but no
    index)
copies: 25¢ per page plus postage

Miami Public Library
Miami, OK 74354
(918) 542-3064; (918) 542-9363 FAX
Joyce Wallen, Director
Hours: Mon & Wed–Thur 9:00–8:00,
    Tue & Fri–Sat 9:00–5:00, Sun 1:00–
    5:00

Muldrow Public Library
City Hall Building
Main Street
Muldrow, OK 74948

Museum of the Great Plains
601 Ferris
PO Box 68
Lawton, OK 73502
(405) 581-3460; (405) 581-3458 FAX
Steve Wilson, Director (History)
Hours: Mon–Fri 8:00–5:00
Pub. *Great Plains Journal*, annually;
    *Museum of the Great Plains
    Newsletter*, $15.00 per year
    subscription
(specializes in ten-state Great Plains
    region: Colorado, Kansas, Montana,
    North Dakota, Nebraska, New Mexico,
    Oklahoma, South Dakota, Texas, and
    Wyoming)
$30.00 per year membership

Museum of the Western Prairie
1100 North Hightower
PO Box 574
Altus, OK 73521
(405) 482-1044

Muskogee Public Library
801 West Okmulgee
Muskogee, OK 74401
Hours: Mon–Thur 9:00–9:00, Fri 9:00–
    6:00, Sat 9:00–4:00

Norman Public Library
225 North Webster
Norman, OK 73070
Hours: Tue–Thur 1:00–5:00, Sat 9:00–
    3:00

Oklahoma State University
OSU Library, Special Collections
Stillwater, OK 74078
(405) 744-6311
E-mail: www-master@www.okstate.edu;
    hmlloyd@okway.okstate.edu (Special
    Collections)
http://www.library.okstate.edu/dept/scua/
    scuahp.htm
Heather Lloyd

Oklahoma Territorial Museum
406 East Oklahoma Avenue
Guthrie, OK 73044
(405) 282-1889
Wayne A. Ward, Museum Supervisor
(genealogical services)

**Old Greer County Museum and Hall
of Fame, Inc.**
222 West Jefferson
Mangum, OK 73554
(405) 782-2851
Shirley Stark, Co-Curator
Hours: Tue–Fri 9:00–12:00
(genealogical services)
$25.00 per year membership; donation
    accepted for searches

Perry Carnegie Library
302 North Seventh Street
Perry, OK 73077
(405) 336-4721
Karen Bigbee, Head Librarian
Hours: Mon 1:00–6:00, Tue–Fri 9:00–
    6:00, Sat 9:00–12:00

Pioneer Museum and Art Center
2009 Williams Avenue
Woodward, OK 73801
(405) 256-6139
Kathy Smith, Assistant Curator; Joyce
    Read, Tourism
Hours: 10:00–5:00
(family history books 1915–1994, 1910
    plat book)

Pioneer Woman Museum
3320 North 14th
Ponca City, OK 74601
(405) 765-6108

Jan Prough, Manager
Hours: call for hours
(specializes in Oklahoma, 101 Ranch, E.
    W. Marland, Cherokee Outlet Run)
copies 20¢ per page

Ponca City Library
Genealogy Department
515 East Grand Avenue
Ponca City, OK 74601
(405) 767-0345; (405) 767-0377 FAX
Loyd M. Bishop, Genealogy Librarian
Hours: Mon–Thur 9:00–9:00, Fri 9:00–
    6:00, Sat 9:00–5:00, Sun (winter)
    2:00–5:00

Rudisill North Regional Library
Tulsa City-County Library System
1520 North Hartford
Tulsa, OK 74106
(918) 596-7280
Kathy Huber, Genealogy Librarian
Hours: Mon–Thur 9:00–9:00, Fri–Sat
    9:00–5:00, Sun (Oct–Apr) 1:00–5:00
(emphasis on five civilized tribes, eastern
    and southern states)

Sapulpa Public Library
27 West Dewey
Sapulpa, OK 74066
(918) 224-5624; (918) 224-3546 FAX
E-mail: spl27@juno.com
Mary A. Sage, Director
Hours: Mon–Tue & Thur 9:00–8:00,
    Wed 9:00–6:00, Fri 9:00–5:00, Sat
    9:00–1:00
copies: 25¢ each plus SASE

Stephens County Historical Museum
PO Box 1294
Duncan, OK 73534
(405) 252-0717
Don Stevens, Director
(genealogical services)

Stillwater Public Library
Stillwater, OK 74074
(405) 372-3633
Hours: Mon–Thur 9:00–9:00, Fri–Sat
    9:00–6:00, Sun 1:00–5:00

The Talbot Library and Museum
406 South Colcord Avenue
PO Box 349
Colcord, OK 74338-0349
(918) 326-4532
Virgil Talbot, Librarian and Curator
Hours: Tue–Sat 9:00–5:00, Sun &
    holidays 1:00–5:00, closed Christmas
Pub. *T.L.& M. Genealogy*, bimonthly,
    $5.00 per year subscription
("We have a rapidly growing Genealogy,
    Area & Indian History Section; we are
    constantly building Cherokee
    genealogy and history material;
    generally cover northeast Oklahoma,
    northwest Arkansas.")
no admission fee or membership fee

Stanley Tubbs Memorial Library
101 East Cherokee
Sallisaw, OK 74955

University of Oklahoma
Western History Collections
630 Parrington Oval, Room 452
Norman, OK 73069
(405) 325-3641
Bradford Koplowitz, Assistant Curator
Hours: Mon–Fri 8:00–5:00, Sat 8:00–
12:00 (during school year)

University of Tulsa
McFarlin Library
2933 East Sixth Street
Tulsa, OK 74104-3123
(918) 631-2880; (918) 631-3791 FAX
E-mail: lib_ssk@centum.utulsa.edu
http://www.utulsa.edu
(Cherokee, Choctaw and Creek
manuscripts, Oklahoma history and
special collections)

Vinita Public Library
Maurice Haynes Memorial Building
215 West Illinois
Vinita, OK 74301
(918) 256-2115
Hours: Mon & Thur 10:00–8:00, Tue–
Wed & Fri 12:00–6:00, Sat 10:00–4:00

Waynoka Public Library
113 East Cecil
Waynoka, OK 73860
(405) 824-6181
Mae Converse, Librarian
Hours: Mon–Fri 10:00–noon & 1:00–
5:30
("complete microfilm copies of Waynoka
newspapers from the 1890s, also area
towns' newspapers: Quinlan, Alva,
Avard, Dacoma, Freedom, and
others")

Woodward Public Library
Genealogy Department
1508 Main Avenue
Woodward, OK 73801
Hours: Mon–Sat

Historical Societies— Local and Regional

Adair County History Commission
Rt. 1, Box 1955
Stilwell, OK 74960
(918) 696-2749
Mack Starr, Treasurer
Hours: daily 8:00–10:00
(specializes in history of Adair County,
Cherokee history, genealogy;
publication sold out)

**Alfalfa County Historical Society
Museum**
(119 West Main—location)
PO Box 201 (mailing address)
Cherokee, OK 73728
(405) 596-2513
Nancy Harmon, President
Hours: Tue & Thur–Fri 10:00–5:00
Pub. *Alfalfa County Historical Society
Newsletter*, quarterly
$10.00 per year membership for
individuals

Apache Historical Society
(100 West Evans—location)
PO Box 101 (mailing address)
Apache, OK 73006
(405) 588-3392
Mary Joyce Swanda, Secretary-Treasurer
Hours: Mon–Fri 1:00–5:00
(very little research material)
$5.00 per year membership for families

Arbuckle Historical Society
201 South Tenth Street
Davis, OK 73030
(405) 369-3721

**Arkansas River Historical Society
Museum**
5350 Cimarron Road
Catoosa, OK 74015
(918) 266-2291; (918) 266-7678 FAX
E-mail: museum@tulsaport.com
http://www.tulsaweb.com/port/
Allan Avery, Curator
Hours: Mon–Fri 8:00–4:30
Pub. *Reflections*, two times per year, free
on request
(covers Oklahoma, Arkansas, Kansas and
Colorado region)

Atoka County Historical Society
(Confederate Memorial Museum,
Highway 69 North—location)
PO Box 245 (mailing address)
Atoka, OK 74525
(405) 889-7192
Gwen Walker, Site Manager
Hours: Mon–Sat 9:00–4:00
Pub. *Confederate Memorial Museum
Newsletter*, quarterly
$5.00 per year membership for
individuals, $10.00 per year
membership for families; search fee:
$20.00, includes search of local
funeral home records, our cemetery
inventory, marriage records and
newspaper files for obituaries if a
death date is supplied and copies if
appropriate

**Beaver County Historical Society,
Inc.**
Beaver County Fairgrounds
PO Box 457
Beaver, OK 73932
(405) 625-4439
Jean Long, Curator

Hours: Wed–Sat 1:30–5:30, Sun 1:30–
4:30
$10.00 per year membership

**Beaver River Genealogical and
Historical Society**
Rt. 1, Box 79
Hooker, OK 73945
(405) 652-2716; (405) 652-2766 FAX
E-mail: tyler@brightok.net
Dallas Mayer, Founder
Hours: Mon–Sun 9:00–10:00
Pub. *Beaver River News*, bimonthly
$10.00 per year membership for
individuals, $15.00 per year
membership for families; research fee:
$5.00 plus copy cost

**Bryan County Heritage Association,
Inc.**
Corner of Main and McKinley Streets
PO Box 153
Calera, OK 74730
(405) 434-5848
Wanda Shelton, Treasurer
Hours: Mon–Fri 10:00–4:00
Pub. *Bryan County Heritage Quarterly*
(May, August, November, February)
$12.50 per year membership

Canadian County Historical Society
600 West Wade
El Reno, OK 73036
(405) 262-5121
Pub. *Canadian County Historical
Society*, monthly
$10.00 per year membership

Canadian Rivers Historical Society
R.P. 1, Box 135
Geary, OK 73040

**Historical and Genealogical Society
of Carter County**
PO Box 1326
Ardmore, OK 73402

Cherokee Strip Museum
2617 West Fir
Perry, OK 73077
(405) 336-2405
Kaye Bond, Curator
Hours: Tue–Fri 9:00–5:00, Sat 10:00–
4:00

**Choctaw Historical Society/Choctaw
Caboose Museum**
(Corner of N.E. 23rd and Henney
Road—location)
2701 North Triple XXX Road (mailing
address)
Choctaw, OK 73020-8402
(405) 390-2771
Grady A. O'Connor, Custodian of
Museum
Hours: Memorial Day–Labor Day: Sat
10:00–4:00, Sun 2:00–5:00, and by
appointment

Cleveland County Historical Society
Norman and Cleveland County Historical
    Museum
Genealogist Library
1500 North Flood, #132
Norman, OK 73069
(405) 321-0156
Hours: Wed (winter) 10:00–noon, Wed
    (summer) 1:00–5:00, Sat 10:00–5:00
Pub. *The Round Tower Newsletter*,
    quarterly

**Coal County Historical and
Genealogical Society**
PO Box 436
Coalgate, OK 74538
(405) 428-3237
Doris Breger, President
Hours: Tue & Thur–Fri 4:00–6:30;
    meetings second Mon 7:00 P.M.
Pub. *Coal County News Letter*,
    bimonthly
$10.00 per year membership

Cotton County Historical Society
Walters Museum
116 North Broadway
Walters, OK 73572
(405) 875-3335
Byrleta Holt, President

**Delaware County (Oklahoma)
Historical Society**
(538 Krause Street—museum location)
PO Box 567 (mailing address)
Jay, OK 74346
(918) 253-4345
Wynona S. Nelson, Curator
Hours: Mon, Wed & Fri 1:00–4:00
Pub. *Heritage of the Hills*, two times per
    year (spring and fall)
$15.00 per year

Dewey County Historical Society
Rt. 1, Box 53
Camargo, OK 73835
(405) 328-5623

**Drumright Community Historical
Society, Inc.**
RR 1, Box 214
Drumright, OK 74030-9727
Elizabeth Ann Bozworth

**Eastern Oklahoma Historical
Society**
Robert S. Kerr Museum
Rt. 1, Box 111
Poteau, OK 74953
(918) 647-8221, ext. 116
Carol A. Spindle, Director
Hours: Tue–Sun 1:00–4:00, and by
    appointment
(covers seven counties; "Senator Robert
    S. Kerr memorabilia, Viking
    runestones, Cherokee and Choctaw
    Indians, pioneers")
donations encouraged

Edmond Historical Society
431 South Boulevard
Edmond, OK 73034
(405) 340-0078; (405) 340-2771 FAX
Newton Weiss, President; Brenda Peck
    Green, Museum Director
Hours: Tue–Fri 10:00–4:00, Sat 1:00–
    4:00
Pub. *The Society Report*, quarterly
    (genealogy computer center)
$25.00 per year membership for
    individuals, $40.00 per year
    membership for families, $10.00 per
    year membership for senior citizens or
    students

The Ellis County Historical Society
Arnett, OK 73832
(405) 885-7287 (President); (405) 885-
    7705 (evenings)
Linda Fox, President
Pub. *Key Finder*, quarterly (each season),
    $3.00 per issue
$15.00 per year membership; fifty-word
    queries free to members, $2.00 for
    non-members

Fairfax Area Historical Society
332 South Fourth
Fairfax, OK 74637
(918) 642-3834
Mary L. Clement, Treasurer

**Fort Gibson Genealogical and
Historical Society**
PO Box 416
Fort Gibson, OK 74434
Pub. *Newsletter of the Fort Gibson
    Genealogical and Historical Society*,
    quarterly
$5.00 per year membership

45th Infantry Division Museum
2145 N.E. 36th Street
Oklahoma City, OK 73111
(405) 424-5313
Hours: Tue–Fri 9:00–5:00, Sat 10:00–
    5:00, Sun 1:00–5:00

Garfield County Historical Society
Public Library of Enid and Garfield
    County
(120 West Maine, Enid, OK 73701—
    location)
PO Box 8002 (mailing address)
Enid, OK 73702-8002
(405) 234-6313 (Library); (405) 233-
    2948 FAX (Library)
http://www.enid.org/library.htm
Glenda B. Lamb, Director
Hours: Library: Mon–Thur 9:00–9:00,
    Fri–Sat 9:00–6:00, Sun 1:00–6:00

**Goingsnake District Heritage
Association**
Westville John Henderson Library
PO Box 180
Westville, OK 74965

(918) 326-4532 (Editor at The Talbot
    Library and Museum)
Virgil Talbot, Editor and Historian
Pub. *The Goingsnake Messenger*,
    quarterly, $4.25 per issue
$10.00 per year regular membership,
    $15.00 per year Contributing
    membership

Grady County Historical Society
PO Box 495
Chickasha, OK 73023
(405) 224-0442
Mavis Miller Clark, President
Hours: Sat & third Sun 2:00–4:00, and
    by appointment
$7.50 per year membership for
    individuals

**Grant County Historical Society and
Museum**
PO Box 31
Medford, OK 73759-0031
(405) 395-2888
Hours: Wed 2:00–5:00
$5.00 per year membership; $5.00 for
    research

**Greer County Genealogical and
Historical Society**
204 West Lincoln
Mangum, OK 73554
(405) 782-3185; (405) 782-2477
Hettie Day, Member; Mary Beth Jones,
    President
Hours: Library: Mon–Fri 10:00–noon &
    1:00–5:00, Sat 9:00–noon
Pub. *Greer Frontier*, semiannually
$10.00 per year membership; search fee:
    $10.00 for census or newspapers

**Indian Territory Genealogical and
Historical Society**
c/o University Archives
Northeastern Oklahoma State University
Tahlequah, OK 74464

**Johnston County Genealogical and
Historical Society**
308 East 21st Street
Tishomingo, OK 73460
(405) 371-3351

**Konawa Genealogical and Historical
Society of Seminole County,
Oklahoma**
(Kennedy Library, at Konawa Public
    Schools, 700 West South Street—
    location)
Rt. 1, Box 3 (mailing address)
Konawa, OK 74849
(405) 925-3662
E-mail: nealje@konawa.k12.ok.us
June Neal, Secretary; Anita Ranells,
    Secretary
Hours: Mon–Fri (during school year)
    8:00–3:30, Mon–Tue (summer) 8:00–
    3:30, Thur 6:00–8:00
Pub. *String of Beads*, quarterly

("Working on Seminole County abstracting cemeteries, marriages, school districts, etc.; trying to preserve Seminole County records")

$10.00 per year membership (beginning in July), $5.00 per year membership for senior citizens; search free to members, fee according to work needed for non-members

Lincoln County Historical Society

Museum of Pioneer History
717–719 Manvel on Route 66
Chandler, OK 74834
(405) 258-2425
Jeanette Haley, Curator
Hours: Mon–Sat 9:30–4:00
Pub. *Lincoln County Historical Society Newsletter*, quarterly
(cemetery records of Lincoln County, census, newspapers on microfilm, family and town history)
$10.00 per year membership for individuals, $25.00 per year membership for families; donations accepted for research

Logan County Historical Society

107 East Oklahoma Avenue
PO Box 1280
Guthrie, OK 73044
(405) 282-3706

Love County Historical Society, Inc.

101 S.W. Front
PO Box 134
Marietta, OK 73448
(405) 276-5888; (405) 276-3477
Laquitta Ladner
Hours: summer: Thur–Fri 1:00–4:00
Pub. *LCHS Newsletter*, quarterly
$5.00 per year membership

Mayes County Historical Society, Inc.

Coo-Y-Yah County Museum
Eighth Street and South 69 Highway
PO Box 969
Pryor, OK 74362
(918) 825-2222
Mrs. William M. Thomas, President
Hours: Tue–Wed & Sat–Sun 1:00–4:00
Pub. *NewsLetter*, quarterly, free

McClain County Historical and Genealogical Society

203 Washington Street
Purcell, OK 73080
(405) 527-5894
Joyce A. Rex, Curator and County Historian
Hours: McClain County Museum: Mon–Fri 12:00–4:00, and by reservation (five days in advance)
Pub. *McClain County, Oklahoma Historical and Genealogical Society Quarterly* (February, May, August, November)

(Old Pontotoc County, Chickasaw Nation, Indian Territory; obituary abstraction in progress, microfilm of county records and family histories)

$5.00 per year Active Working membership (calendar year), $10.00 per year Sustaining membership, $50.00 life membership

Newkirk Community Historical Society

(101 South Maple Street—location)
500 West Eighth (mailing address)
Newkirk, OK 74647
(405) 362-3330
Karen Dye, Project Director
Hours: Sun 2:00–4:00
$4.00 per year membership, $10.00 per year Sustaining membership

No Man's Land Historical Society and Museum

207 West Sewell Street
PO Box 278
Goodwell, OK 73939
(405) 349-2670
Dr. Kenneth R. Turner, Director
Hours: Tue–Sat 9:00–noon & 1:00–5:00
Pub. *Vox Nemenis*, quarterly
("Area newspapers, archives, some civil records, photographs related to Oklahoma Panhandle.")
$15.00 per year membership for individuals, $25.00 per year membership for families, $100.00 life membership

Nowata County Historical Society

121 South Pine Street
Nowata, OK 74048
(918) 272-1191
Maudie Randall, Curator
Pub. *NCHS Newsletter*

Oklahoma County Historical Society

Museum of the Unassigned Lands
4300 North Sewell
Oklahoma City, OK 73118
(405) 521-1889
Margaret R. Woods, Curator
Hours: Mon, Wed & Fri 10:00–3:00, Tue & Thur by appointment for groups
Pub. *Oklahoma County Historical Society Newsletter*, quarterly
("The Museum of the Unassigned Lands tells the story of the Oklahoma land run of 1889.")
$10.00 per year membership, $100.00 life membership

Oklahoma Heritage Association

201 N.W. 14th Street
Oklahoma City, OK 73103
(405) 235-4458
Paul Lambert, Ph.D., Executive Director
Pub. *Oklahoma Heritage News*

Osage County Historical Society

700 North Lynn Avenue
Pawhuska, OK 74056

(918) 287-9924
Betty W. Smith, Director
Hours: Mon–Fri 9:00–5:00

Pawnee County Historical Society

605 Fifth Street
PO Box 472
Pawnee, OK 74058
(918) 762-3881
Dana Hicks, President
Hours: Wed 10:00–4:00, and by appointment

Pioneer Historical Society

1127 South Seventh Street
Ponca City, OK 74601-6712

Pittsburg County Genealogical and Historical Society

113 East Carl Albert Parkway
McAlester, OK 74501
(918) 426-0388
Thurman Shuller, President; Joan Shuller, Librarian
Hours: Mon–Fri 9:00–3:00
Pub. *Tobucksy News*, three times per year, $3.50 per issue
(also Indian genealogical resource)
$15.00 per year membership for individuals or families

Plains Indians and Pioneers Historical Foundation

Plains Indians and Pioneers Museum
2009 Williams Avenue
Woodward, OK 73801
(405) 256-6136
Frankie A. Herzer, Director
(Southern Cheyenne and Arapaho Indians and European settlers)

Pontotoc County Historical and Genealogical Society

Mattie Logsdon Memorial Library
221 West 16th Street
Ada, OK 74820
Arlene Treas, President
Hours: Mon–Wed 12:30–4:00, Mon 6:30–8:30
Pub. *Pontotoc County Quarterly*
$15.00 per year membership; admission: $.50 per day for members, $2.00 per day for non-members

Historical Society of Pottawatomie County

1301 East Farrall
Shawnee, OK 74801
(405) 273-5062

Pushmatah County Historical Society

125 West Main Street
PO Box 285
Antlers, OK 74523
(405) 587-2304 (President)
Myrtle Edmond, President
Hours: Tue 9:00–noon

$10.00 per year membership for individuals, $15.00 per year membership for families; $100.00 life membership; search fees: $5.00 donation to research library

Red River Valley Historical Association
Southeastern Oklahoma State University
Durant, OK 74701
(405) 924-0121, ext. 203

Sapulpa Historical Society, Inc.
100 East Lee Street
PO Box 278
Sapulpa, OK 74067
(918) 224-4871
Ken Blackburn, President
Hours: Mon–Thur 10:00–3:00

Southwestern Oklahoma Historical Society
PO Box 3693
Lawton, OK 73502
Pub. *Prairie Lore*, semiannually
$5.00 per year membership

Tillman County Historical and Educational Society
201 North Ninth Street
PO Box 833
Frederick, OK 73542
(405) 335-5844; (405) 335-2805 (President)
Frances Goodknight, President
Hours: Sat–Sun 2:00–4:00, and by appointment
Pub. *TCHES Newsletter*, annually
$5.00 per year membership for individuals, $10.00 per year membership for households, $15.00 per year membership for businesses or organizations; no search services

Tonkawa Historical Society
PO Box 27
Tonkawa, OK 74653
(405) 628-2702

Top of Oklahoma Historical Society
303 South Main
Blackwell, OK 74631
(405) 363-0209
Ocie Anderson, Director

Tulsa County Historical Society
2501 West Newton
PO Box 27303
Tulsa, OK 74149
(918) 585-5520
Robert Powers, Curator

Washington County Historical Society, Inc.
PO Box 255
Bartlesville, OK 74003
(918) 333-0073

Washita County Historical Society
105 East First Street
PO Box 153
Cordell, OK 73632
(405) 343-2554

Waynoka Historical Society
Waynoka and Cleveland
PO Box 193
Waynoka, OK 73860
(405) 824-5871
Rex Olson, President
Hours: weekends (Easter through Labor Day) 2:00–4:00, and by appointment
$10.00 per year membership

Western Trail Historical and Genealogical Society
Museum of the Western Prairie
1100 North Hightower
PO Box 574
Altus, OK 73521
(405) 482-1044

Western Trails Museum
2229 Gray Freeway
Clinton, OK 73601
(405) 323-1020

Wynnewood Historical Society
Rt. 1, Box 189
Wynnewood, OK 73098

LDS Family History Centers

Norman
(405) 364-8337

Oklahoma City
(405) 721-8455

Tulsa
(918) 437-5690

Genealogical Societies

State Genealogical Societies

Genealogical Institute of Oklahoma
3813 Cashion Place
Oklahoma City, OK 73112
Pub. *Dusty Trails*, quarterly

Federation of Oklahoma Genealogical Societies (FOGS)
PO Box 26151
Oklahoma City, OK 73126
Pub. *Newsletter*, quarterly; *Directory of Oklahoma Sources*, annually

Oklahoma Genealogical Society
PO Box 12986
Oklahoma City, OK 73157-2986
http://www.fgs.org/~fgs/soc0379.htm
Pub. *Oklahoma Genealogical Society Quarterly*
(specializes in Oklahoma and Indian Territory)
$15.00 per year membership for individuals, $18.00 per year membership for families

Regional Genealogical Societies

Atoka County Genealogical Society
PO Box 245
Atoka, OK 74525

Bartlesville Genealogical Society
Bartlesville Public Library and History Museum
600 S.E. Johnstone
Bartlesville, OK 74003
(918) 337-5353; (918) 337-05336 FAX
http://netra.bartlesville.lib.ok.us:80801
Joan Singleton, Public Services Librarian
Hours: Library: Mon–Thur 9:00–9:00, Fri–Sat 9:00–5:30
Pub. *Bartlesville Genealogical Society Newsletter*, monthly
$9.00 per year membership

Beaver River Genealogical and Historical Society
Rt. 1, Box 79
Hooker, OK 73945
(405) 652-2716
Dallas Mayer, Founder
Pub. *Beaver River News*, bimonthly
$10.00 per year membership, $15.00 per year membership for families (husband and wife); research fee: $5.00 plus copy cost

Bristow Genealogical Society
418 East Second
Bristow, OK 74010
(918) 367-6633
Mrs. Mack Morton, Executive Officer
Hours: volunteer
(Creek County)
$10.00 per year membership

Broken Arrow Genealogical Society
(The Main Place, 1800 South Main Street—location)
PO Box 1244 (mailing address)
Broken Arrow, OK 74013-1244
(918) 455-8619
Marmie Apsley, Librarian
Hours: Tue noon–4:00, Thur 9:00–1:00, Sat 10:00–2:00
Pub. *The Green Country Quarterly*
$10.00 per year membership for individuals, $12.00 per year membership for families

Canadian County Genealogical Society
PO Box 866
El Reno, OK 73036
(405) 262-2409; (405) 262-1551
http://www.rootsweb.com/~okcanadi/
okcanad.htm
Joann Nitzel, President
Hours: Archives Room, Carnegie
Library: Mon–Fri 9:00–5:00, Sat
9:00–1:00
(information on Fort Reno and Fort Reno
Cemetery; over 400 microfilm rolls of
county newspapers, probate records
and marriages, also census 1890–1920,
county history book and county family
history book)
$10.00 per year membership; research in
Canadian County: $6.00 per hour plus
cost of copies and postage

Historical and Genealogical Society of Carter County
PO Box 1326
Ardmore, OK 73402

Cleveland County Genealogical Society/Library
(Park Plaza II Building, 1005 North
Flood, Suite 136, Norman, OK
73069—location)
PO Box 6176 (mailing address)
Norman, OK 73070
(405) 329-9180
Olier Valliere, Library Director; Alan
Montgomery, President
Hours: Tue, Thur & Sat 1:00–5:00,
closed football Saturdays
Pub. *Cleveland County Genealogical
Society Newsletter*, quarterly
$15.00 per year membership for
individuals, $18.00 per year
membership for husband and wife

Coal County Historical and Genealogical Society
PO Box 436
Coalgate, OK 74538
(405) 428-3237
Doris Breger, President
Hours: Tue & Thur–Fri 4:00–6:30;
meetings second Mon 7:00 P.M.
Pub. *Coal County News Letter*,
bimonthly
$10.00 per year membership

Craig County Oklahoma Genealogical Society
(Vinita Public Library, 215 West
Illinois—location)
PO Box 484 (mailing address)
Vinita, OK 74301
(918) 256-2115 (no research); (918) 256-
2309 FAX
Connie Schofield, President
Hours: Mon & Thur noon–8:00, Tue–
Wed & Fri noon–6:00, Sat noon–
4:00

Pub. *Craig County Genealogical Society
Newsletter*, two times per year
(specializes in Cherokee Indians and
Cherokee Nation records and local
history)
$3.00 per year membership; research:
$5.00 plus SASE for one hour, $7.50
per hour thereafter

Cushing Genealogical Society
PO Box 551
Cushing, OK 74023

Delaware County Genealogical Society
c/o Grove Public Library
206 South Elk Street
Grove, OK 74344

Fairfax Genealogical Society
432 South Fifth Street
Fairfax, OK 74637

Family Finders Genealogy Club
PO Box 738
Nowata, OK 74048

Fort Gibson Genealogical and Historical Society
PO Box 416
Fort Gibson, OK 74434
Pub. *Newsletter of the Fort Gibson
Genealogical and Historical Society*,
quarterly
$5.00 per year membership

Frontier Researchers Genealogical Society
(see Arkansas)

Garfield County Genealogical Society
PO Box 1106
Enid, OK 73702-1106
Teresa Yoho Ballard, Editor
Pub. *Roots and Branches*, quarterly
$15.00 per year membership for
households, $1.00 per year
membership for students

Grady County Genealogical Society
PO Box 767
Chickasha, OK 73023-0767
(405) 224-7482
Jean Moore, Treasurer; Janell Looney,
Editor
Hours: 9:00–5:30, Mon & Thur 9:00–
8:00
Pub. *Grady County Genealogical Society
Newsletter*, quarterly (spring, summer,
fall, winter)
$12.00 per year membership

Greer County Genealogical and Historical Society
204 West Lincoln
Mangum, OK 73554
(405) 782-3185; (405) 782-2477
Hettie Day, Member; Mary Beth Jones,
President

Hours: Library: Mon–Fri 10:00–noon &
1:00–5:00, Sat 9:00–noon
Pub. *Greer Frontier*, semiannually
$10.00 per year membership; search fee:
$10.00 for census or newspapers

Haskell County Genealogy Society
408 N.E. Sixth Street
Stigler, OK 74462

Indian Territory Genealogical Society
Tahlequah, OK 74465
Mr. Lee, Registrar of Cherokee Nations

Johnston County Genealogical and Historical Society
308 East 21st Street
Tishomingo, OK 73460
(405) 371-3351

Konawa Genealogical and Historical Society of Seminole County, Oklahoma
(Kennedy Library, at Konawa Public
Schools, 700 West South Street—
location)
Rt. 1, Box 3 (mailing address)
Konawa, OK 74849
(405) 925-3662
E-mail: nealje@konawa.k12.ok.us
June Neal, Secretary; Anita Ranells,
Secretary
Hours: Mon–Fri (during school year)
8:00–3:30, Mon–Tue (summer) 8:00–
3:30, Thur 6:00–8:00
Pub. *String of Beads*, quarterly
("Working on Seminole County
abstracting cemeteries, marriages,
school districts, etc.; trying to preserve
Seminole County records")
$10.00 per year membership (beginning
in July), $5.00 per year membership
for senior citizens; search free to
members, fee according to work
needed for non-members

LeFlore County Genealogist
Rt. 2, Box 55
PO Box 21
Wister, OK 74966
(918) 655-3126
Gloryann Hankins Young
(eastern Oklahoma and western Arkansas
research books)
catalog for SASE

Liberal Area Genealogical Society
(see Kansas)

Logan County Genealogical Society
c/o Oklahoma Territorial Museum
406 East Oklahoma Avenue
PO Box 1419
Guthrie, OK 73044
(405) 282-2200
Merle Smith, President
Hours: "not attended, hours same as
Museum if member"

Pub. *Logan County Genealogical Society (Quarterly)*
$9.00 per year out-of-town membership, $15.00 per year membership for families

Major County Genealogical Society
621 N. Main
Okeene, OK 73763
Ruth Keeton

Mayes County Genealogical Society
PO Box 924
Chouteau, OK 74337
Pub. *M.C.G.S. Newsletter*, quarterly
$10.00 per year membership

McClain County Historical and Genealogical Society
203 Washington Street
Purcell, OK 73080
(405) 527-5894
Joyce A. Rex, Curator and County Historian
Hours: McClain County Museum: Mon–Fri 12:00–4:00, and by reservation (five days in advance)
Pub. *McClain County, Oklahoma Historical and Genealogical Society Quarterly* (February, May, August, November)
(Old Pontotoc County, Chickasaw Nation, Indian Territory; obituary abstraction in progress, microfilm of county records and family histories)
$5.00 per year Active Working membership (calendar year), $10.00 per year Sustaining membership, $50.00 life membership

McCurtain County Genealogy Society
PO Box 1832
Idabel, OK 74745
(405) 286-6406
Hours: Idabel Public Library: 9:00–6:00
Pub. *Intikba*, quarterly
$10.00 per year membership

The McIntosh County Lake Eufaula Area Genealogical Society
PO Box 1035
Eufaula, OK 74432
Loy Sunday, President
Pub. *McIntosh County Lake Eufaula Area Genealogical Society Newsletter*, quarterly

Muldrow Genealogical Society
(Muldrow Public Library—location)
PO Box 1253 (mailing address)
Muldrow, OK 74948
Donald Stewart, President
Pub. *Newsletter*, quarterly (March, June, September, December)
$5.00 per year membership for individuals, $7.50 per year membership for couples

Muskogee County Genealogical Society
Muskogee Public Library
801 West Okmulgee
Muskogee, OK 74401
(918) 682-6657
Cleo Shamblin, Vice President
Hours: Library: Mon–Thur 9:00–9:00, Fri 9:00–6:00, Sat 9:00–4:00
Pub. *Muskogee County Genealogical Society Quarterly*, $8.00 per year subscription
$10.00 per year membership

Noble County Genealogy Society
1409 Country Club Drive
Perry, OK 73077
Dr. Charles Martin

Northwest Oklahoma Genealogical Society
(Woodward Public Library, 1508 Main Avenue, Woodward, OK 73801—location)
PO Box 834 (mailing address)
Woodward, OK 73801-0834
(405) 256-8916
Christy Siemsen
Hours: Library: Mon–Sat
Pub. *Key Finder*, quarterly
(emphasis on Woodward, Harper, Ellis and Dewey counties)
$15.00 per year membership

Okmulgee County Genealogical Society
PO Box 805
Okmulgee, OK 74447
Johnny Johnson, President
Pub. *Newsletter*, semiannually
$8.00 per year membership (beginning in September)

Osage County Genealogical Society
301 East Sixth Street
Pawhuska, OK 74056
Juanita Neighbors, Secretary-Treasurer
Hours: Mon–Fri 8:00–6:00, Sat 8:00–4:00
(Osage Indian research, Osage County research)
$7.00 per year membership

Ottawa County Genealogical Society
PO Box 1383
Miami, OK 74354
Hours: meetings third Mon 7:00 in the Nine Tribes Towers Dining Room
Pub. *Smoke Signals*, quarterly
(specializes in Oklahoma and American Indian genealogy)
$7.00 per year membership; search fee: $15.00 basic plus $4.00 per hour

Payne County Genealogical Society
PO Box 2708
Stillwater, OK 74076
(405) 372-3633 (Library)

Hours: Stillwater Public Library: Mon–Thur 9:00–9:00, Fri–Sat 9:00–6:00, Sun 1:00–5:00
Pub. *Payne County Genealogical Society Quarterly*, three times per year
$10.00 per year membership; research: $10.00 per hour

Pioneer Genealogical Society
515 East Grand
PO Box 1965
Ponca City, OK 74602-1965
http://www.brigadoon.com/~nipperb/pgs/piogenhp.htm
Pat Martin, Corresponding Secretary
Pub. *Pioneer Genealogical Society Newsletter*, quarterly, $5.00 per year subscription
(Cherokee Strip Land Run, computer users' group)
$8.00 per year membership, $75.00 life membership

Pittsburg County Genealogical and Historical Society
113 East Carl Albert Parkway
McAlester, OK 74501
(918) 426-0388
Thurman Shuller, President; Joan Shuller, Librarian
Hours: Mon–Fri 9:00–3:00
Pub. *Tobucksy News*, three times per year, $3.50 per issue
(also Indian genealogical resource)
$15.00 per year membership for individuals or families

Pocahontas Trails Genealogical Society
Oklahoma Regional Chapter
Rt. 1, Box 93
Mangum, OK 73554
(405) 679-3865
Susan Bradford, Chairman
("Collecting information on Pocahontas descendants in Oklahoma; chapter currently inactive.")
search fee: $5.00 plus SASE

Pontotoc County Historical and Genealogical Society
Mattie Logsdon Memorial Library
221 West 16th Street
Ada, OK 74820
Arlene Treas, President
Hours: Mon–Wed 12:30–4:00, Mon 6:30–8:30
Pub. *Pontotoc County Quarterly*
$15.00 per year membership; admission: $.50 per day for members, $2.00 per day for non-members

Poteau Valley Genealogical Society
(Buckley Public Library, 408 Dewey—research library location)
PO Box 1031 (mailing address)
Poteau, OK 74953
Arlene LeMaster, President
Hours: Research Library: Mon–Fri 9:00–6:00, Sat 9:00–3:00

Pub. *The LeFlore County Heritage*, four times per year

(publishes books of LeFlore County genealogical and historical information)

$10.00 per year membership; search fee: $5.00 per hour, free queries for members

Pottawatomie County Genealogy Club

(241 Masonic Building, Ninth and Bell, Shawnee, OK 74801—location)

PO Box 3256

Shawnee, OK 74802

(405) 273-5695

Laquita Hackett, President

Hours: Wed–Fri 10:00–1:00

Pub. *Pottawatomie County Genealogy Club Newsletter*, quarterly

(index of marriages and deeds, cemetery books, probate records)

$15.00 per year membership

Sequoyah Genealogical Society

PO Box 1112

Sallisaw, OK 74955

Southwest Oklahoma Genealogical Society

PO Box 148

Lawton, OK 73502-0148

http://www.sirinet.net/~lgarris/swogs

Aulena Scearce Gibson, Corresponding Secretary

Hours: Lawton Public Library, Family History Research Room: Mon–Thur 10:00–9:00, Fri 10:00–6:00, Sat 10:00–5:00, Sun (Sept–May) 1:00–5:00

Pub. *Tree Tracers*, quarterly

$15.00 per year membership for individuals, $18.00 per year membership for families

Stephens County Genealogical Society

Stephens County Genealogical Research Library

301 North Eighth

Duncan, OK 73533

Stratford Roots

c/o Chandler-Watts Library

History-Genealogy Department

321 North Oak

PO Box 696

Stratford, OK 74872

(405) 759-2684

Lorene Donehew, Corresponding Secretary

Hours: Library: 9:00–6:00, Tue 9:00–8:00

Pub. *Stratford Oklahoma Roots*, quarterly

(includes area within 10- to 12-mile radius around Stratford, in Garvin, Ponotoc and McClain counties, including Old McGee Indian Territory)

$10.00 per year membership

Tecumseh Genealogy Club

718 West Washington Street

Tecumseh, OK 74873

TX-OK Panhandle Genealogical Society

(see Texas)

Three Forks Genealogical Society

102 South State Street

Wagoner, OK 74467

(918) 485-2370

Mabel Flippin

Hours: Mon 9:00–3:00, and by appointment

Pub. *Three Forks Genealogical Society Bulletin*, quarterly

$10.00 per year membership

Tulsa Genealogical Society

PO Box 585

Tulsa, OK 74101-0585

Janice Meredith, President

Hours: Rudisill North Regional Library: Mon–Thur 9:00–9:00, Fri–Sat 9:00–5:00, Sun (Oct–Apr) 1:00–5:00

Pub. *Tulsa Annals*, three times per year

$15.00 per year membership

Western Plains-Weatherford Genealogy Society

(219 East Franklin—location)

PO Box 1672 (mailing address)

Weatherford, OK 73096

Jo Crowdis

Hours: Library: Mon–Fri 10:00–7:00, Sat 10:00–1:00

Pub. *Western Plainsman*, three times per year

$12.00 per year membership for individuals, $15.00 per year for families

Western Trail Historical and Genealogical Society

Museum of the Western Prairie

1100 North Hightower

PO Box 574

Altus, OK 73521

(405) 482-1044

Western Trails Genealogical Society

(Jackson County, Oklahoma, Southern Prairie Library, Altus, TX—location)

PO Box 70 (mailing address)

Altus, OK 73522

(405) 266-3358

Jodean McGuffin Martin, Librarian

Pub. *Western Trail Newsletter*, quarterly

("We are a depository for old Greer County, Texas, from 1880–1907; at statehood we became Greer, Harmon, Beckham, and Jackson counties, Oklahoma.")

$10.00 per year membership; $25.00 per family name (three hours)

Woods County Genealogists

Alva Public Library

504 Seventh Street

PO Box 234

Alva, OK 73717

Norma Rauh, Corresponding Secretary

Pub. *Woods County Genealogists Journal*, quarterly (mailed semiannually)

$12.50 per year membership

Independent Publications and Miscellany

Blaine County People and Place History, Inc.

PO Box 30

Watonga, OK 73772

(405) 623-4922

Center for Southwest Research

(see New Mexico)

Elk River Current

(see Missouri)

Mountain Press

(see Tennessee)

OkGenWeb

Part of U.S. GenWeb Project

E-mail: ok@usgenweb.com

http://www.rootsweb.com/~okgenweb/okindex.htm; http://www.rootsweb.com/~itgenweb/ (Indian Territory)

(links to other Oklahoma resources)

Oklahoma Military Department

3501 Military Circle

Oklahoma City, OK 73111-4398

(405) 425-8000

Col. William Francis, PIO

Hours: Mon–Fri 7:00–4:30

Oklahoma Union Grave Project

1008 N.W. 14th Place

Moore, OK 73160-1614

Dale Talkington

Oklahoma Yesterday Publications

8745 East Ninth Street

Tulsa, OK 74112

Dorothy J. Mauldin, Editor

Pub. *Oklahoma Yesterday*, quarterly

Sons and Daughters of the Cherokee Strip Pioneers
PO Box 465
Enid, OK 73701
Pub. *Journal of the Cherokee Strip*,
  annually, $5.00 per issue
$5.00 per year membership

Southwest Field Office-National Trust for Historic Preservation
(see Texas)

University of Arizona Press
Journal of the Southwest
(see Arizona)

OREGON

Archives and Libraries with Holdings in Genealogy

State Archives and Library

Archives Division
Secretary of State
800 Summer Street, N.E.
Salem, OR 97310
(503) 373-0701; (503) 373-0953 FAX
E-mail: reference.archives@state.or.us
http://arcweb.sos.state.or.us
Roy C. Turnbaugh, State Archivist;
  Layne Sawyer, Supervising Reference
  Archivist
Hours: Mon–Fri 8:00–5:00

Oregon State Library
State Library Building
Winter and Court Streets, N.E.
Salem, OR 97310
(503) 378-4277; (503) 588-7119 FAX
E-mail:
  merrialyce.k.blanchard@state.or.us
http://www.osl.state.or.us/oslhome.html
Craig Smith, Reference Supervisor
Hours: Mon–Fri 10:00–5:00

State Historical Society

Oregon Historical Society
Oregon Historical Records Advisory
  Board
1200 S.W. Park Avenue
Portland, OR 97205
(503) 222-1741; (503) 306-5240
  (Reference Department)
John Mead, Director of Reference and
  Research
Hours: Wed–Sat 11:30–5:00
Pub. *Oregon History Magazine*,
  quarterly; *Oregon Historical Quarterly*
("photograph collection with
  reproduction services")
$40.00 per year membership for
  individuals, $60.00 per year
  membership for families, $35.00 per
  year membership for senior citizen
  individuals, $55.00 per year
  membership for two senior citizens;
  $25.00 per year membership for
  students, $30.00–50.00 per year
  affiliate membership; complex
  admission: free to members, $6.00 for
  non-members, $3.00 for teachers or
  students, senior citizens free on Thur,
  children under 10 not admitted to
  library; research: $35.00 per hour,
  $20.00 minimum for ½ hour,
  photocopies 20¢ per page from paper

originals ($1.00 minimum), $1.00 each
from microform originals (non-
commercial use) plus $1.00 surcharge
for each multiple of 10, $3.00 postage

City, County and Regional Archives and Libraries

Albany Public Library
1390 Waverly Drive, S.E.
Albany, OR 97321-6945
(541) 917-7581; (541) 917-7586 FAX
Kimberly Kuhn, Library Assistant II
Hours: Mon 10:00–8:00, Tue–Fri 10:00–
  6:00, Sat 10:00–5:00, Sun 1:00–5:00
("Albany, Linn County, and Oregon
  archives; Oregon history collection,
  genealogy library")
"ready reference" searches free, in-depth
  searches $7.50 per hour

Astoria Public Library
450 Tenth Street
Astoria, OR 97103
(503) 325-7323
Judy Dugan, Library Director
Hours: Mon–Thur 10:00–8:00, Fri–Sat
  10:00–6:00, Sun (except summer)
  2:00–5:00
(local newspaper index card file, 1873–
  1957, plus some recent years)

Lavola Bakken Memorial Library
Douglas County Museum of History and
  Natural Histoy
(123 Museum Drive—location)
PO Box 1550 (mailing address)
Roseburg, OR 97470
(541) 957-7007; (541) 440-4506 FAX
E-mail: museum@rosenet.net
Fred R. Reenstjerna, Research Librarian
Hours: Library: Mon–Fri noon–4:30
(22,000 photos, 1,000 books and 300+
  manuscripts, 5,000 documentary
  artifacts; collection documenting
  Douglas County history and natural
  history)
no charge for brief inquiries, extensive
  research at $25.00 per hour (one-hour
  minimum), plus cost of copies;
  museum admission: $3.50 per person

Mary Jane Brookfield Library
PO Box 34
Brookings, OR 97415

Corvallis-Benton County Public Library
Reference
645 N.W. Monroe Avenue
Corvallis, OR 97330
(541) 757-6793; (541) 757-6726 FAX
http://www.ci.corvallis.or.us/library
Hours: Mon–Fri 9:00–9:00, Sat 9:00–
  6:00, Sun noon–6:00
(Oregon and Benton County history,
  Oregon census microfilm, Corvallis
  newspaper on microfilm)

Dallas Public Library
950 Main Street
Dallas, OR 97338-2802

Eastern Oregon State College
Walter M. Pierce Library
Eighth and K
La Grande, OR 97850
(541) 963-1540
Douglas Oleson, Director
Hours: Mon–Thur 7:30–11:00, Fri 7:30–
4:30, Sat 1:00–5:00, Sun 5:00–11:00;
vacation periods: Mon–Fri 7:30–4:30

City Library, Eugene
100 West 13th Avenue
Eugene, OR 97401

Grant County Historical Museum
(101 South Canyon City Boulevard,
Highway 395—location)
PO Box 464 (mailing address)
Canyon City, OR 97820
(541) 575-0362; (541) 575-0666 (Co-
chairman); (541) 575-1578 (Mr.
Round)
Grace K. Williams, Co-chairman; Louis
Round
Hours: 1 Jun–30 Sept: Mon–Sat 9:00–
4:30, Sun 1:00–5:00
(pictures and records of families and
people in Grant County)

Harney County Historical Museum
18 West D Street
Burns, OR 97720
(541) 573-2636
Pub. *HCHS Newsletter*

Hood River County Museum
Port Marine Park
PO Box 781
Hood River, OR 97031
(541) 386-6772
Earlene A. Hinrich, Secretary
Hours: Wed–Sun (Apr–Oct) 10:00–4:00
(historical and biographical resources)

Klamath County Library
126 South Third Street
Klamath Falls, OR 97601
(541) 882-8894
Helen Morehouse, Branch Coordinator
Hours: winter: Tue 11:30–8:00, Wed–Sat
9:30–6:00; summer: Mon 11:30–8:00,
Tue–Fri 9:30–6:00

Public Library, La Grande
1006 Penn Avenue
La Grande, OR 97850
(541) 962-1339
Jo Cowling, Director
Hours: Mon–Fri 10:00–6:00

**Linn County Historical Museum and
Moyer House**
101 Park Avenue
PO Box 607
Brownsville, OR 97327
(541) 466-3390

Charlene Scott, Museum Manager;
Richard R. Milligan, Historian
Hours: Mon–Sat 11:00–4:00, Sun 1:00–
5:00
Pub. *Friends Newsletter*, semiannually,
$15.00 per year subscription

McMinnville Public Library
225 North Adams
McMinnville, OR 97128
(503) 472-5247; (503) 472-1429 FAX
E-mail: blevinm@ci.mcminnville.or.us
Marcia Blevins, Reference Supervisor
Hours: Tue–Thur 9:00–9:00, Fri–Sat
9:00–5:00, Sun (Sept–May) 1:00–5:00

Multnomah County Public Library
801 S.W. Tenth Avenue
Portland, OR 97205
(503) 248-5123
http://www.multnomah.lib.or.us
Joan Zornman
Hours: Mon–Thur 10:00–8:00, Fri–Sat
10:00–5:30, Sun 1:00–5:00

**Multnomah County School District
No. 1**
Portland Public Schools
Records Management Office
Child Services Center
531 S.E. 14th Avenue
Portland, OR 97214-2485
(503) 916-5840, ext. 273; (503) 916-
2727 FAX (attention: Records
Management)
Hours: Mon–Fri 8:00–5:00
(public school records from 1856)
no search or copy fee for most records,
no patron direct access to records

Oregon City Public Library
362 Warner Milne Road
Oregon City, OR 97045
(503) 657-8269
Steve Rauch, Reference Librarian
Hours: Mon–Thur 10:00–9:00, Fri–Sat
10:00–5:00, Sun (Oct–May) 1:00–5:00
(Oregon history, Oregon indexes, local
newspapers)
no research or genealogical librarians on
location

Oregon Institute of Technology
3201 Campus Drive
Klamath Falls, OR 97601
Pub. *Shaw Historical Library Journal*,
semiannually, $18.00 per year
subscription

Oregon Museum Park
Lane County Museum
740 West 13th Avenue
Eugene, OR 97402
(541) 687-4239

Oregon State University
Archives
94 Kerr Administration Building
Corvallis, OR 97331-2103
(541) 737-2165; (541) 737-2400

E-mail: archives@ccmail.orst.edu
(Archives); krishnar@ucs.orst.edu
(Special Collections)
http://www.orst.edu/Dept/archives
(Archives); http://www.orst.edu/Dept/
Special_Collections/ (Special
Collections)

**Pacific University Archives and
Museum**
Pacific University
2043 College Way
Forest Grove, OR 97116
(503) 359-2117; (503) 359-2236 FAX
E-mail: readrt@pacificu.edu
Richard T. Read, University Archivist/
Museum Curator
Hours: Archives: Mon–Fri 9:00–5:00;
Museum: Tue–Fri 1:00–4:30
(university publications from 1863,
papers and manuscripts,
Congregational Church publications
and documents to about 1925,
historical monographs, "Pacificana
Collection" and photographs)

**City of Portland Stanley Parr
Archives and Records Center**
9360 North Columbia Boulevard
Portland, OR 97203
(503) 823-4631
Josephine Dwyer, Records Management
Officer; Marcus Robbins, Archivist
Hours: 8:00–5:00

Siuslaw Pioneer Museum
PO Box 2637
Florence, OR 97439
(541) 997-3037

Siuslaw Public Library
PO Box A
Florence, OR 97439

Spokane Public Library
(see Washington)

Springfield Public Library
225 Fifth Street
Springfield, OR 97477
(541) 726-3766; (541) 726-3747 FAX
Jenny Peterson, Reference Librarian
Hours: Mon–Tue 10:00–8:00, Wed–Thur
10:00–5:00, Fri–Sat 12:00–5:00

Tillamook County Pioneer Museum
Research Library
2106 Second Street
Tillamook, OR 97141
(503) 842-4553; (503) 842-4553 FAX
M. Wayne Jensen, Jr., Director
Hours: Mon–Sat 8:00–5:00 (Oct–Mar
15: closed Mon), Sun 12:00–5:00
(Tillamook County cemetery records,
pioneer records)

Toledo Public Library
173 N.W. Seventh Street
Toledo, OR 97391
(541) 336-3132

Hours: Mon–Fri 1:00–9:00, Sat 10:00–
5:00, Sun 1:00–5:00
(has *Lincoln County Leader* newspaper;
"no searching, limited staff")

University of Oregon
Knight Library, Special Collections
Eugene, OR 97403-1299
(541) 346-3068; (541) 346-1818
(Reference)
E-mail: bmctigue@oregon.uoregon.edu
http://libweb.uoregon.edu/
Fraser Cocks, Curator, Special
Collections
Hours: Mon–Fri 8:30–4:30
(emphasis on Oregon history)

University of Washington Libraries
(see Washington)

Wallowa County Museum
Main Street
Joseph, OR 97846
(541) 432-1794
Callol Coppin, Director; Grace Bartlett,
Curator
Hours: end of May to end of Sept:
10:00–5:00

Historical Societies— Local and Regional

ALSI Historical and Genealogical Society, Inc.
(320 Grant—location)
PO Box 822 (mailing address)
Waldport, OR 97394
(541) 563-7092
Hours: Sat–Sun 10:00–4:00
$3.00 per year membership for
individuals

The Aurora Colony Historical Society
15008 Second Street
Aurora, OR 97002
(503) 678-5754
Daniel E. McElhinny, Executive Director
Hours: Feb–Dec: Tue–Sat 10:00–4:00,
Sun noon–4:00
Pub. *ACHS Newsletter*

Bandon Historical Society/Coquille River Museum
(270 Fillmore Street, Highway 101 and
Fillmore—location)
PO Box 737 (mailing address)
Bandon, OR 97411
(541) 347-2164
Judith Knox, Assistant Curator
Hours: Mon–Sat 10:00–4:00, Sun (spring
& summer) noon–3:00
("not set up for research at present")
$15.00 per year membership for
individuals, $25.00 per year
membership for families, $150.00 life
membership

Benton County Historical Society and Museum
1101 Main Street
PO Box 47
Philomath, OR 97370-0047
(541) 929-6230
William Lewis, Director
Hours: Tue 12:30–3:00
Pub. *The Society Record*

Boston Mill Society
222 First Avenue, West
Albany, OR 97321
(541) 928-5008
("to interpret the agricultural,
commercial, industrial and social life
of Oregon's Willamette Valley")

Clackamas County Historical Society
211 Tumwater Drive
PO Box 294
Oregon City, OR 97045
(503) 655-5574
Joan Deroko, Administrative Assistant
Hours: Mon–Fri 10:00–4:00, Sat–Sun
1:00–5:00
Pub. *Clackamas County History Notes*,
monthly

Clatsop County Historical Society
1618 Exchange Street
Astoria, OR 97103
(503) 325-2203 phone and FAX
Jeffrey H. Smith, Executive Director
Hours: Office: 9:00–4:00; Museum:
(Oct–May) 11:00–4:00, (May–Oct)
10:00–5:00
Pub. *CUMTUX, Clatsop County
Historical Society Quarterly*; *Clatsop
County Historical Society Newsletter*,
monthly
(county, regional, and state history)
$25.00 per year membership for
individuals, $50.00 per year
membership for families, $15.00 per
year membership for students

Columbia County Historical Society
Columbia County Historical Museum
Old County Courthouse
Saint Helens, OR 97051
(503) 397-3868
Mrs. Billie S. Ivey, Curator
Hours: Thur (summer) & Fri–Sun noon–
4:00
Pub. *Columbia County Histories*, $3.00
each or set of 24 for $60.00
(marriages 1850–1900, cemetery records
from 1850, of the entire county)

Coos County Historical Society Museum
1220 Sherman Avenue
North Bend, OR 97459
(541) 756-6320
Ann Koppy, Director
Hours: Tue–Sat 10:00–4:00

Pub. *Newsletter*, three times per year
$10.00 per year membership

Crook County Historical Society
A. R. Bowman Museum
246 North Main Street
Prineville, OR 97754
(541) 447-3715
Gordon Gillespie, Director
Hours: Museum: Mar–Dec: Mon–Sat
10:00–5:00
Pub. *Crook County Historical Society
Newsletter*, quarterly
$10.00 per year membership for
individuals, $15.00 per year
membership for families; free
admission

Curry County Historical Society
Curry County Museum
29410 Ellensburg
Gold Beach, OR 97444
(541) 247-6113
Mildred Walker, Curator; Walt
Schroeder, President
Hours: May 30-Sept 30: Tue–Sat noon–
4:00; Oct 1-May 29: Sat noon–4:00
Pub. *Curry County Echoes*, monthly
(Curry history, genealogy)
$10.00 per year membership, $125.00
life membership (under 55 years of
age), $100.00 life membership (over
55 years of age)

Deschutes County Historical Society, Genealogical Committee
(Idaho and Wall Street—location)
PO Box 5252 (mailing address)
Bend, OR 97708
(541) 389-1813
Roland Anderson, Manager
Hours: Tue–Sat 10:00–4:30
Pub. *Newsletter*, monthly
(specializes in central Oregon history,
Deschutes and Crook counties)
$10.00 per year membership for
individuals, $15.00 per year
membership for couples

Deschutes Pioneers Association
2861 N.W. Polarstar Avenue
Bend, OR 97701-8664
(541) 382-3456
Barbara Buxton, Membership Chair
Pub. *Deschutes Pioneers' Gazette*,
annually
$3.00 per year membership

Gilliam County Historical Society Museum Complex
(Highway 19, adjacent to Burns Park and
the fairgrounds—location)
PO Box 377 (mailing address)
Condon, OR 97823
(541) 384-4233
June Mikkalo, President
Hours: 1 May–31 Oct: Wed–Sun 1:00–
5:00

$7.50 per year membership for individuals, $10.00 per year membership for families; admission: $2.50 suggested donation for adults

Gresham Historical Society
PO Box 65
Gresham, OR 97030
(503) 665-5579

Harney County Historical Society
PO Box 388
Burns, OR 97720
Pub. *Harney Historical Highlights*, ten times per year

Jewish Historical Society of Oregon
Mittleman Jewish Community Center
6651 S.W. Capitol Highway
Portland, OR 97219
(503) 246-9844
Lora R. Meyer, President

Josephine County Historical Society
508 S.W. Fifth Street
Grants Pass, OR 97526
(541) 479-7827
Rose M. Scott, Executive Director
Hours: Tue–Fri 1:00–4:00
Pub. *The Oldtimer Newsletter*, quarterly (specializes in southern Oregon)
$15.00 per year membership for individuals, $25.00 per year membership for families, $55.00 per year membership for corporations

Junction City Historical Society
655 Holly Street
Junction City, OR 97448

Lake County Historical Society
PO Box 48
Lakeview, OR 97630
Edward A. Henry, President
Hours: meetings at the Lake County Courthouse: third Wed
Pub. *Lake County*
$15.00 per year membership for individuals or families

Lane County Historical Society
PO Box 11532
Eugene, OR 97440-3732
Pub. *Lane County Historian*, three times per year, no subscriptions; *Lane County Historical Society Newsletter*, five times per year, no subscriptions
$10.00 per year membership (calendar year)

Lincoln County Historical Society
Burrows House Museum
545 S.W. Ninth
Newport, OR 97365
(503) 265-7509
Loretta Harrison, Executive Director
Hours: summer: Tue–Sun 10:00–5:00; winter: Tue–Sun 11:00–4:00
Pub. *The Quarterly*

("maritime history focus, central Oregon coast")
$10.00 per year membership for individuals, $25.00 per year membership for families

Linn County Historical Society
1132 30th Place, S.W.
Albany, OR 97321
(503) 926-4680
Glenn Harrison, Newsletter Editor
Pub. *Linn County Historical Society Newsletter*, quarterly
$5.00 per year membership

Malheur County Historical Society
1186 S.W. Sixth Avenue
Ontario, OR 97914-3310
(503) 889-5073
Hugh R. Lackey, Treasurer
Hours: meetings second Thur
Pub. *Malheur County Review*, bimonthly
$8.00 per year membership for individuals, $10.00 per year membership for families

Marion County Historical Society
(on N.W. corner, Mission Mill Village—location)
260 12th Street, S.E. (mailing address)
Salem, OR 97301
(503) 364-2128; (503) 391-5356 FAX
E-mail: mchs@open.org
Kyle Jansson, Executive Director
Hours: Mon–Sat 9:30–4:30
Pub. *Historic Marion*, quarterly; *Marion County History*, intermittently
(a non-profit, educational society with museum, research library and archives for the preservation of Marion County history)
$20.00 per year membership (includes only quarterly); general admission: $1.00, 50¢ for senior citizens and children

Morrow County Historical Society
Main Street
Heppner, OR 97856
Ruth McCabe, Secretary

Oakland Museum Historical Society
4999 Nonpareil Road
Sutherlin, OR 97479-9709

Oregon Lewis & Clark Heritage Foundation
(Oregon Historical Society, 1230 S.W. Park Avenue, Portland, OR 97205—location)
511 East Bridge Street (mailing address)
Vernonia, OR 97064
(503) 429-3713

Pacific Northwest Historians Guild
(see Washington)

Polk County Historical Society
(187 S.W. Court Street, Dallas, OR 97338—museum location
5705 Salem-Dallas Highway—society location)
PO Box 67 (mailing address)
Monmouth, OR 97361
(503) 371-8586 (Tue A.M.); (503) 371-3831 (Archivist); (503) 623-6251 (Polk County Museum)
Thomas D. Pomeroy, Archivist; Georgia Wildfang, President
Hours: Tue 9:00–noon & (1 Jun–1 Sept) noon–4:00; Museum: Mon, Wed & Sat 1:00–4:00
Pub. *The Polk Poker*, quarterly
(depository for Polk County Genealogical Society)
$7.50 per year membership for individuals, $10.00 per year membership for families, $15.00 per year membership for businesses, $30.00 per year Supporting membership, $100.00 life membership; research: $10.00 per hour plus copying costs

Scotts Mills Area Historical Society
Second and Grandview
PO Box 80
Scotts Mills, OR 97375

Seaside Museum and Historical Society
570 Necanicum Drive
PO Box 1024
Seaside, OR 97138-1024
(503) 738-7065; (503) 738-8438 (President's home)
Phyllis Hamlin, Office Manager
Hours: Office: 9:00–1:00; Museum: Mon–Sun 10:30–4:30
Pub. *Making History Together*, quarterly
(collecting and interpreting materials illustrative of the history of Seaside and the surrounding area)
$10.00 per year membership for individuals, $15.00 per year membership for couples, $18.75 per year membership for families, $4.50 per year membership for students (ages 6–18 years); search fees: free to members, except 10¢ per copy; museum admission: $2.00 for adults, $1.50 for senior citizens (ages 62+), $10.00 for youth (ages 13–18), children (under 12) free when accompanied by an adult

Sherman County Historical Society
(200 Dewey Street—location)
PO Box 173 (mailing address)
Moro, OR 97039
(541) 565-3232
Joe Weber, President
Hours: Museum: May–Oct 1:00–5:00
Pub. *Sherman County: For the Record*, semiannually, $5.00 per issue

(publishes historical anthology)
$17.50 per year membership for individuals

Southern Oregon Historical Society
Research Library
106 North Central Avenue
Medford, OR 97501
(541) 773-6536; (541) 776-7994 FAX
Carol Harbison, Library Manager
Hours: Tue–Sat 1:00–5:00
Pub. *Southern Oregon Heritage*, quarterly, $29.00 per year subscription from $15.00 per year membership; research library search fee: first half-hour free, $10.00 per half-hour thereafter, plus $5.00 user fee

Tillamook County Historical Society Genealogy Study Group
PO Box 123
Tillamook, OR 97141

Troutdale Historical Society
(Harlow House Museum, 726 East Historic Columbia River Highway—location)
104 S.E. Kibling (mailing address)
Troutdale, OR 97060
(503) 661-2164
Ellen Brothers, Director
Hours: Jun–Oct: Wed–Thur & Fri–Sat 10:00–4:00, Sun 1:00–4:00; Nov–May: Sat–Sun 1:00–4:00
Pub. *Bygone Times*, monthly
(no genealogical records, no genealogical research)
$8.00 per year membership for individuals, $12.00 per year membership for couples, $20.00 per year membership for families, $50.00 per year Directors Club membership for individuals, $75.00 per year Directors Club membership for couples

Umatilla County Historical Society
(108 S.W. Frazer—location)
PO Box 253 (mailing address)
Pendleton, OR 97801
(541) 276-0012; (541) 276-7989
Julie Reese, Executive Director
Hours: Tue–Sat 10:00–4:00
Pub. *Pioneer Trails*, three times per year
$15.00 per year membership for individuals

Washington County Historical Society
17677 N.W. Springville Road
Portland, OR 97229
(503) 645-5353
Joan H. Smith, Executive Director
Hours: Mon–Sat 10:00–4:30
Pub. *The Express*, quarterly
$20.00 per year membership for individuals

Yamhill County Historical Society
(Corner of Sixth and Market Streets—location)
PO Box 484 (mailing address)
Lafayette, OR 97127
(503) 472-7328 (President)
E-mail: jwhite@orednet.org
Shirley Venhaus, President
Hours: Sept 1–May 31: Sat–Sun 1:00–4:00; Jun 1–Aug 31: Wed–Sun 1:00–4:00
Pub. *The Westside*, 9 times per year (monthly, Sept–May)
$7.50 per year membership for individuals, $15.00 per year membership for families (spouse and minor children); $100.00 life membership

LDS Family History Centers

Beaverton
(503) 644-7782

Bend
(503) 382-9947

Eugene
(503) 343-3741

Gresham
(503) 665-1524

Hillsboro
(503) 640-4658

La Grande
(503) 963-5003

Lake Oswego
(503) 638-1410

Medford
(503) 773-3363

North Bend
(503) 756-3575

Portland
(503) 235-9090; (503) 238-1671

Salem
(503) 363-0374

Genealogical Societies

State Genealogical Societies

Genealogical Forum of Oregon, Inc.
Headquarters and Library
2130 S.W. Fifth Avenue, Suite 220
Portland, OR 97201-4934
(503) 227-2398
http://www.rootsweb.com/~genepool/forum.htm
Mary Lou Stroup, Library Director; Eileen Chamberlin, President
Hours: Mon–Wed & Fri–Sat 9:30–3:00, Tue 5:00–8:00, Thur 9:30–8:00
Pub. *Bulletin—Genealogical Forum of Oregon*, quarterly (September, December, March, June); *The Forum Insider Newsletter*, eight times per year; *Genealogical Forum of Oregon, Inc.* (membership directory), annually
$21.00 per year membership

Genealogical Heritage Council of Oregon
PO Box 628
Ashland, OR 97520-0021

Oregon Genealogical Society
(223 North A Street, Springfield, OR—library location)
PO Box 10306 (mailing address)
Eugene, OR 97440-2306
(541) 746-7924
Hours: Mon 10:00–2:00, Wed & Fri 10:00–6:00, Sat (except fourth Sat) 10:00–4:00, Sun noon–4:00
Pub. *The Quarterly* (January, April, July, October), $3.00 per issue; *Oregon Genealogical Society Newsletter*, bimonthly
(Oregon history and research; issued Oregon Pioneer Certificates)
$22.00 per year membership for individuals (calendar year), $25.00 per year membership for households, $500.00 life membership

Regional Genealogical Societies

ALSI Historical and Genealogical Society, Inc.
(320 Grant—location)
PO Box 822 (mailing address)
Waldport, OR 97394
(541) 563-7092
Hours: Sat–Sun 10:00–4:00
$3.00 per year membership for individuals

Baker County Genealogy Club
c/o Baker County Public Library
2400 Resort Street
Baker City, OR 97814

Bend Genealogical Society
PO Box 8254
Bend, Oregon 97708
Adele Loudermilk
$10.00 per year membership

Benton County Genealogical Society
PO Box 1511
Corvallis, OR 97330
(541) 757-2316
http://www.rootsweb.com/~orbentgs
Gene Kelsey, President

Hours: Benton County Historical Society and Museum Annex: Tue 12:30–3:00; meetings: second Sat (Sept–Jun) 10:00–3:00
Pub. *Newsletter*, monthly
(library covers all fields of genealogy)
$10.00 per year membership for individuals, $15.00 per year membership for families; first time library use free to non-members

Blue Mountain Genealogical Society
PO Box 1801
Pendleton, OR 97801
E-mail: rose@oregontrail.net; bopp@oregontrail.net
Rosemary Farley, Researcher; Karen Bopp, President
(Umatilla County cemetery records)
$7.50 per year membership for individuals, $10.00 per year membership for families; research: $7.50 per hour

Clackamas County Family History Society
211 Tumwater Drive
PO Box 995
Oregon City, OR 97045-2900
(503) 657-4325
Sandy McGuire, President
Hours: Tue–Wed 10:00–4:00, first & third Sat 1:00–5:00; meetings at West Linn Public Library, 1595 Burns Street, West Linn, OR: fourth Mon 7:00
Pub. *Clackamas Legacy*, quarterly; *Newsletter*, quarterly
(library, located in the building of the Clackamas County Historical Society, includes census 1842–1900, 1910 Soundex, cemetery records, donation land claims, family histories, first jail book, Grand Army of the Republic members pedigree charts, marriage records 1848–1925, probate from 1854, provisional land claim records, taxes from 1865)
$12.00 per year membership for individuals (calendar year), $15.00 per year membership for families

Clatsop County Genealogical Society
Astoria Public Library
450 Tenth Street
Astoria, OR 97103
E-mail: pmurray@orednet.org
Patti Murray, President
Pub. *The Forebears*, quarterly
$12.00 per year membership

Columbia Gorge Genealogical Society
The Dalles-Wasco County Public Library
722 Court Street
The Dalles, OR 97058
Larry Kuttner, President
Pub. *Tales and Trails—Newsletter*, monthly (September–June)

$7.50 per year membership for individuals, $10.00 per year membership for families

Coos Bay Genealogical Forum
PO Box 1067
North Bend, OR 97459
Hours: *Coos Genealogical Bulletin*, semiannually (mailed once a year— Spring), $1.00 per year subscription

Cottage Grove Genealogical Society
207 North H Street
PO Box 388
Cottage Grove, OR 97424
Gene Savage, Librarian; Joanne Skelton, Editor; Frances Quinn, President
Hours: Wed–Sat 1:00–4:00
Pub. *Trees from the Grove*, quarterly (February, May, August, November)
("We have over 3,000 volumes in our library and a fast-growing film and fiche collection that covers entire U.S. and a fairly well known vertical file; special collection: Cottage Grove, Oregon, area.")
$10.00 per year membership

Crook County Genealogical Society
A. R. Bowman Museum
246 North Main Street
Prineville, OR 97754
(541) 447-3715 (days)
E-mail: jkaney@bendnet.com
Vivian Zimmerlee, Librarian
Hours: Tue–Fri 10:00–5:00, Sat 11:00– 4:00, Sun (Memorial Day–Labor Day) 11:00–4:00, closed January
Pub. *Crook County Genealogical Society Newsletter*, quarterly
(Crook County census, courthouse and cemetery records, all the Crook County newspaper from 1887)
$10.00 per year membership for individuals, $15.00 per year membership for couples, $5.00 per year membership for students; no charge for search, free queries for members

Deschutes County Historical Society, Genealogical Committee
(Idaho and Wall Street—location)
PO Box 5252 (mailing address)
Bend, OR 97708
(541) 389-1813
Roland Anderson, Manager
Hours: Tue–Sat 10:00–4:30
Pub. *Newsletter*, monthly
(specializes in central Oregon history, Deschutes and Crook counties)
$10.00 per year membership for individuals, $15.00 per year membership for couples

Digger O'Dells Restaurant Genealogical Society
2211 Spring Street
Medford, OR 97504-6377
Susan Geear

Genealogical Society of Douglas County
Douglas County Courthouse, Room 111
PO Box 579
Roseburg, OR 97470
(541) 440-6178; (541) 673-6940 (Librarian)
Eileen Talburt, Librarian
Hours: Tue–Fri 1:00–4:00
Pub. *Douglas County Pioneer*, quarterly
$10.00 per year membership

Emerald Empire Genealogical Workshop
2540 Barnett Street
Bremerton, WA 98310-5202
Lorraine Cowles Sencevicky

End of the Trail Researchers (EOTR)
145 24th Avenue, S.E.
Salem, OR 97301
Chapter: **Central Oregon Chapter**, c/o Clark, 6060 Coyote, Redmond, OR 97465

Grant County Genealogical Society
PO Box 418
Canyon City, OR 97820
(541) 575-0545 (President)
Betty Elliott, President
Pub. *Grant County Genealogical Society Newsletter*, quarterly
$10.00 per year membership for individuals, $12.50 per year membership for households

Grants Pass Genealogical Society
PO Box 1834
Grants Pass, OR 97526

Harney County Genealogy Society
c/o 426 East Jefferson
Burns, OR 97720

Juniper Branch of the Family Finders, Inc.
PO Box 652
Madras, OR 97741
(541) 475-6918
Dorothy Burgess, Past President
Hours: business meetings: second Tue 7:30, research: fourth Tue 2:00–8:00
Pub. *Newsletter*, eight times per year (monthly, January to May and September to November)
$10.00 per year membership for individuals, $12.50 per year membership for families, $7.50 per year membership for senior citizens; search fee: $10.00 per hour plus copy and postage costs

Klamath Basin Genealogical Society
PO Box 366
Klamath Falls, OR 97601
George Norman, President
Hours: meetings at Klamath County Library
$10.00 per year membership

La Pine Genealogical Society
(La Pine Branch Deschutes County
    Library—location)
PO Box 1081 (mailing address)
La Pine, OR 97739
$5.00 per year membership

Lebanon Genealogical Society
Lebanon Public Library
626 Second Street
Lebanon, OR 97355
Jane Hutchings, Secretary
Hours: Library: Mon–Thur 10:00–8:00,
    Fri–Sat 10:00–4:00; meetings at
    library: first Fri 7:00
(specializes in Oregon, Linn County,
    Lebanon)
$5.00 per year membership; search fee:
    donation plus cost of copies and
    postage

Linn Genealogical Society
Albany Public Library
1390 Waverly Drive, S.E.
Albany, OR 97321-6945
(541) 967-4304
Edward House
Hours: Tue–Fri 10:00–9:00, Sat 10:00–
    6:00

Madras Genealogical Society
671 Southwest Fairgrounds
Madras, OR 97741
Pauline Chain

Milton-Freewater Genealogical Club
127 S.E. Sixth Street
Milton-Freewater, OR 97862
Carmen Buff

Mount Hood Genealogical Forum
950 South End Road
PO Box 744
Oregon City, OR 97045
(503) 656-6021
Theoda Burns, Librarian
Hours: Tue 10:00–8:00
$8.00 per year membership

Pocahontas Trails Genealogical Society
Oregon Regional Chapter
406 Casa De Loma
Sutherlin, OR 97479

Polk County Genealogical Society
(Polk County Museum, 187 S.W. Court
    Street—records location)
535 S.E. Ash Street (mailing address)
Dallas, OR 97338
(503) 623-3467
Katherine Johnson, Secretary and
    Treasurer
Hours: Mon, Wed & Sat 1:00–4:00, and
    by appointment; meetings at museum:
    first Thur 7:30
no membership dues; search fee: copy
    costs plus SASE

Port Orford Genealogical Society
Port Orford Public Library
555 West 20th Street
Port Orford, OR 97465

Rogue Valley Genealogical Society, Inc.
133 South Central
Medford, OR 97501-7221
(541) 770-5848
http://www.grrtech.com/rvgs
Emillee Brazill, Library Director
Hours: Mon & Thur–Sat 1:00–4:30, Wed
    9:30–4:30
Pub. *Rogue Digger*, quarterly
(largest genealogical library in southern
    Oregon, with over 3,000 volumes)
$20.00 per year membership for
    individuals (calendar year), $10.00 per
    year membership for each additional
    individual in a household; library use:
    free to members, $3.00 per day for
    non-members

Siuslaw Genealogical Society
PO Box 1540
Florence, OR 97439
Eleanor Duree, President
Hours: meetings at Siuslaw Public
    Library: third Wed (Sept–Jun)
Pub. *GEN-TREE*, quarterly (September,
    December, March, June)
$12.00 per year membership for
    individuals, $18.00 per year
    membership for families

Sweet Home Genealogical Society
Sweet Home Library
13th and Kalmia Streets
Sweet Home, OR 97386
(541) 367-5007
Rosella Burns, President
Hours: Library: Mon–Tue & Thur 11:00–
    8:00, Fri–Sat 11:00–5:00
Pub. *Distant Trails*, quarterly (December,
    March, June, September)
(Collection, housed in the city library,
    includes death, marriage and divorce
    indexes, Oregon donation land claims,
    census records.)
$5.00 per year membership for
    individuals, $7.50 per year
    membership for families

Tillamook County Historical Society Genealogy Study Group
PO Box 123
Tillamook, OR 97141

Willamette Valley Genealogical Society
Oregon State Library
Genealogy Room
PO Box 2083
Salem, OR 97308
Hours: Mon–Fri 10:00–4:00; meetings at
    library: second Sat 10:00–4:00

Pub. *Willamette Valley Genealogical
    Society Newsletter*, monthly; *Beaver
    Briefs*, quarterly
(Marion County, Oregon and Oregon
    research)
$15.00 per year membership for
    individuals (calendar year), $20.00 per
    year membership for couples

Woodburn Genealogical Club
1015 McKinley
Woodburn, OR 97071
Lynn Faulk
("Work in conjunction with Woodlawn
    Public Library; sponsor continual field
    trips; on-going class; we do help with
    queries on local research when we
    can.")
$10.00 per year membership

Yamhill County Genealogical Society
(McMinnville Public Library, 225 North
    Adams Street—location)
PO Box 568 (mailing address)
McMinnville, OR 97128
Barbara Koch, Editor
Hours: Library: Mon–Thur 10:00–9:00,
    Fri–Sat 10:00–6:00 (volunteers
    available most Weds 1:30–3:30);
    meetings first Sat 9:30–12:30
Pub. *Timber Trails*, quarterly (January,
    April, July, October)
(specializes in family reunions, family
    newsletters, queries; Yamhill County
    marriages, deaths, cemetery records)
$15.00 per year membership (beginning
    1 June)

Yaquina Genealogical Society
c/o Toledo Public Library
173 N.W. Seventh Street
Toledo, OR 97391
(541) 336-3132
Hours: Mon–Fri 10:00–9:00, Sat 10:00–
    5:00, Sun 1:00–5:00
Pub. *The Searchlight*, quarterly, $5.00
    per year subscription

Independent Publications and Miscellany

Family Publications
5628 60th Drive, N.E.
Marysville, WA 98270-9509
E-mail: cxwp57a@prodigy.com
Rose Caudle Terry, Publisher
Pub. *Oregon Trail Sources, Queries &
    Reviews*, two to four times per year,
    $8.95 per volume subscription, plus
    $1.50 postage per order

The Heritage
35145 Balboa Place, S.E.
Albany, OR 97321
Richard R. Milligan, Co-publisher
Pub. *The Heritage*, monthly, $12.00 per
    year subscription

Historic Preservation League of Oregon
PO Box 40053
Portland, OR 97240

Kindred Keepsakes
PO Box 41552
Eugene, OR 97404-0369
E-mail: jrabun@ix.netcom.com
http://www.rootsweb.com/ genepool/
    oregon.htm

Northwest Pioneer
(see Washington)

Oregon-California Trails Association
(see Miscellaneous)

Oregon Geographic Names Board
1230 S.W. Park Avenue
Portland, OR 97205
(503) 222-1741
Tom McAllister, Chair

Oregon Historic Cemeteries Association
PO Box 802
Boring, OR 97009
(503) 658-4522
Hours: annual meeting: second Sat Mar;
    other meetings in Jul & Nov
Pub. *Newsletter*
(long-term goal to create an all-name
    database of Oregon burials)
$15.00 per year membership

Oregon/Washington Queries
419 West Third
Box 117
Everson, WA 98247
Pub. *Oregon/Washington Queries*

OrGenWeb
Part of U.S. GenWeb Project
E-mail: or@usgenweb.com
http://www.rootsweb.com/~orgenweb
(links to other Oregon resources)

University of California Press
Pacific Historical Review
(see California)

PENNSYLVANIA

Archives and Libraries with Holdings in Genealogy

State Archives and Library

Pennsylvania State Archives
Reference Section
Third and Forster Streets
PO Box 1026
Harrisburg, PA 17108-1026
(717) 783-3281
http://www.state.pa.us/PA_Exec/
    Historical_Museum/DAM/genie1.htm
Hours: Tue–Fri 9:00–4:00, Sat
    (microfilm only) 9:00–noon & 1:00–
    4:00, audio and video collections by
    appointment only
(collection features military records,
    immigration and naturalization
    records, vital statistics, prison records,
    census and land records, etc., plus
    special collections of maps and
    photographs)
search fee: $10.00 per name per item in
    indexed records only, including
    copying up to 10 pages

State Library of Pennsylvania
Forum Building
Walnut Street and Commonwealth
    Avenue
PO Box 1601
Harrisburg, PA 17105-1601
(717) 783-5950 (Information)
http://www.cas.psu.edu/docs/pde/
    libstate.html
Susan Payne, Assistant Director
Hours: Mon & Wed–Sat 9:30–4:30, Tue
    9:30–8:30
(Pennsylvania local history and
    genealogy collection is "available on
    self-service basis; there is no staff
    assigned, and no service by mail from
    the collection.")

State Historical Societies

Heritage Society of Pennsylvania
PO Box 146
Laughlintown, PA 15655

The Pennsylvania Federation of Museums and Historical Organizations
(Third and Forster Streets, Harrisburg,
    PA 17120—location)
PO Box 1026 (mailing address)
Harrisburg, PA 17108-1026
(717) 787-3253; (717) 787-4822 FAX
E-mail: jcutler@llpptn.pall.org;
    museumpa@llpptn.org
Jean H. Cutler, Executive Director

Hours: 8:30–4:30
Pub. *Tapestry*, quarterly; *Directory of
    Museums and Historical
    Organizations in Pennsylvania*, $5.95
(a professional association of
    Pennsylvania museums and historical
    organizations; not a genealogical
    society)
$30.00 per year membership for
    individuals, institutional membership
    varies

Pennsylvania Heritage Society
Third and North Streets
PO Box 11466
Harrisburg, PA 17108-1466
(717) 787-2407; (717) 783-9924 FAX
Marcia B. Gobrecht, Executive Secretary
Hours: 10:00–4:30
Pub. *Pennsylvania Heritage Quarterly
    Newsletter*; *Pennsylvania Heritage
    Magazine*, quarterly, $20.00 per year
    subscription
(a non-profit support organization of the
    Pennsylvania Historical and Museum
    Commission)
$35.00/$50.00/$75.00/$100.00 per year
    full membership

Pennsylvania Historical and Museum Commission
Third and North Streets
PO Box 1026
Harrisburg, PA 17108-1026
(717) 787-3362
http://www.state.pa.us/PA_Exec/
    Historical_Museum/orgtext.htm#bhsm
Brent D. Glass, Ph.D., Executive
    Director
Pub. *Pennsylvania Heritage*, quarterly,
    $15.00 per year subscription, $5.00 per
    issue

The Pennsylvania Historical Association
Penn State—Harrisburg
Swatara Building
777 West Harrisburg Pike
Middletown, PA 17057-4898
(717) 774-4829
LeRoy W. Toddes, Business Secretary
Hours: Wed 9:30–noon
Pub. *Pennsylvania History: A Journal of
    Mid-Atlantic Studies* (not
    genealogical), quarterly
$25.00 per year membership for
    individuals, $15.00 per year
    membership for students, $30.00 per
    year membership for institutions

Historical Society of Pennsylvania
1300 Locust Street
Philadelphia, PA 19107-5699
(215) 732-6200; (215) 732-2680 FAX
E-mail: hsppr@aol.com
http://www.libertynet.org/~pahist
Susan Stitt, President; Lee Arnold,
    Library Director; Linda Stanley,
    Curator of Manuscripts; Laura

Beardsley, Research Services Librarian; Dan Rolph, Reference Librarian

Hours: Library and Galleries: Tue & Thur–Sat 10:00–5:00, Wed 1:00–9:00

Pub. *The Pennsylvania Magazine of History and Biography*, quarterly; *The Pennsylvania Correspondent*

(genealogical library for eastern United States)

$35.00 per year membership for individuals, $65.00 per year membership for households, $25.00 per year membership for students, $125.00 per year Patron membership, $250.00 per year Contributor membership, $500.00 per year Connoisseurs' Circle membership, $1,000 per year Benefactor membership; research: $30.00 for members, $35.00 for non-members

City, County and Regional Archives and Libraries

Aaronsburg Historical Museum Association

(116 West Plum Street—location)
PO Box 80 (mailing address)
Aaronsburg, PA 16820
(814) 349-8276
Bruce Teeple, Curator
Hours: Wed 7:00 P.M.–9:00 P.M., Sat 1:00–4:00, and by appointment
$5.00 per year membership for families; no search fees, but would appreciate copies of work

Allegany College of Maryland Library

Appalachian Collection
(see Maryland)

Community Library of Allegheny Valley

315 East Sixth Avenue
Tarentum, PA 15084
Hours: Tue–Fri 10:00–8:00, Sat 10:00–4:00

Allentown Public Library

1210 West Hamilton Street
Allentown, PA 18102-4371
(610) 820-2400

Altoona Area Public Library

The Pennsylvania Room
1600 Fifth Avenue
Altoona, PA 16602-3693
(814) 946-0417
E-mail: altpublib@hslc.org
Sonia L. Keiper, Reference Librarian
Hours: winter: Mon–Tue & Thur 8:30–9:00, Wed & Fri 8:30–5:00, Sat 9:00–5:00, Sun 1:00–4:00; summer: hours vary

(primarily Blair County; Altoona and Blair County histories, obituary index from 1967)

$1.00 per page for mailed photocopies; staff cannot do genealogy searches

Atwater Kent Museum

15 South Seventh Street
Philadelphia, PA 19106
(215) 922-3031

Benson Memorial Library

213 North Franklin Street
Titusville, PA 16354

Bloomsburg Public Library

225 Market Street
Bloomsburg, PA 17815
(717) 784-0883
Hours: Mon–Fri 9:00–8:00, Sat 9:00–1:00

Eva K. Bowlby Public Library

311 North West Street
Waynesburg, PA 15370
(724) 627-9776
Hours: Mon–Fri 1:00–4:00, Sat 10:00–4:00

James V. Brown Library

19 East Fourth Street
Williamsport, PA 17701
(717) 326-0536, ext. 24 or ext. 13
E-mail: rfisher@jvbrown.edu
http://www.jvbrown.edu
Rhonda Fisher, Reference Librarian
Hours: Mon–Thur 9:00–9:00, Fri 9:00–6:00, Sat 9:00–5:00, Sun 1:00–5:00
(Lycoming County history and genealogy; does not answer genealogical questions by phone or FAX)
search fee: $10.00 plus copies and postage for out-of-state inquiries

Buhl-Henderson Community Library

11 North Sharpsville Avenue
Sharon, PA 16146
(724) 981-4360
Loretta DeSantis
Hours: Tue–Thur 10:00–8:00, Fri–Sat 10:00–5:00

Cambria County Library System

248 Main Street
Johnstown, PA 15901
(814) 536-5131; (814) 535-4140
Louis Pocchiari, Reference Librarian
Hours: winter: Mon–Thur 9:00–9:00, Fri–Sat 9:00–5:00, (closed Sat from Memorial Day weekend through Labor Day weekend)
(index to the obituaries from the *Johnstown Tribune Democrat* 1853–1939; local history on the Johnstown floods)

Carnegie Free Library

Resource and Research Center for Beaver County and Local History
1301 Seventh Avenue
Beaver Falls, PA 15010
(724) 846-4340, ext. 5
William E. Irion, Director
Hours: Mon 5:00–8:00, Tue–Thur 11:00–5:00, Fri 11:00–3:00
Pub. *Milestones*, quarterly, $5.00 per year subscription

The Carnegie Library of Pittsburgh

Pennsylvania Department
4400 Forbes Avenue
Pittsburgh, PA 15213-4080
(412) 622-3154
E-mail: padept@alphaclp.clpgh.org
http://alphaclp.clpgh.org/CLP
Marilyn Holt, Department Head
Hours: Mon–Thur 9:00–9:00, Fri–Sat 9:00–5:30, Sun (Oct–May) 1:00–5:00

Centre County Library and Historical Museum

203 North Allegheny Street
Bellefonte, PA 16823
(814) 355-1516
Gladys C. Murray, Archivist/Genealogist
Hours: Mon–Fri 9:00–5:00, Sat 9:00–12:00 & 1:00–5:00
(Pennsylvania history and genealogy: Spangler genealogical papers, J. Marvin Lee genealogical collection, newspapers, census, county histories, 480 family histories, general reference sources and indexes)
limited research to answer one or two specific questions, copy fees and postage

Chester County Archives and Records Service

Government Services Center, Suite 080
601 Westtown Road
West Chester, PA 19382-4527
(610) 344-6760
Jeffrey D. Rollison, Director of Archives
Hours: Mon–Fri 9:00–4:00

Coyle Free Library

102 North Main Street
Chambersburg, PA 17201
(717) 263-1054; (717) 263-2248 FAX
Paula Schechter, Reference Librarian
Hours: summer: Mon–Thur 9:00–8:30, Fri 9:00–5:00, Sat (Jun–Aug) 9:00–noon
(Franklin County local hsitory and genealogy)
copies at 15¢ per page plus postage

Dayton and Montgomery County Public Library

(see Ohio)

Easton Area Public Library

515 Church Street
Easton, PA 18042

(215) 258-2917, ext. 115
Barbara Bailey Bauer, Curator of Special
  Collections; Sharon Gothard, Library
  Assistant
Hours: History Room: Mon–Fri 10:00–
  noon & 1:00–4:00, Wed (summer)
  5:00–9:00, Sat (school year) 9:00–
  noon & 1:00–5:00
(more than 10,000 volumes of local and
  family history, abstracts of
  Northampton County wills 1752–1840
  and every-name index, union index to
  local religious records, newspaper
  abstracts of marriages and deaths
  1799–1902, scattered obituary index
  from 1909, Northampton County
  cemetery project, newspaper item file
  from 1799, family history files,
  historical vertical files, picture file)
queries should be accompanied by
  SASE, donation appreciated; copying
  costs: 20¢ per page, 25¢ each from
  microfilm, plus postage: $.90 for up to
  five pages, $1.50 for up to maximum
  of 10 pages

Erie County Library System
160 East Front Street
Erie, PA 16507
(814) 451-6900; (814) 451-6907 FAX
http://www.ecls.lib.pa.us/
Cindy Kerchoff, Head of Reference
Hours: Mon–Tue 9:00–9:00, Wed–Fri
  9:00–8:00, Sat 9:00–5:00

Everett Free Library
137 East Main Street
Everett, PA 15537
(814) 652-5922; (814) 652-5425
E-mail: evt@twd.net
Diana L. Megdad, Librarian
Hours: Mon–Tue & Thur 1:00–8:00,
  Wed 1:00–5:00, Fri 10:00–8:00, Sat
  10:00–3:00
(census, *Bedford County Press* on
  microfilm from 1868–1892 and 1894–
  1982, except 1905, 1918, 1928, 1930)

Ford City Public Library
1136 Fourth Avenue
Ford City, PA 16226
(724) 763-3591
Joanne Germy, Library Director
Hours: Mon–Fri 1:00–8:00
$12.00 per year membership

Franklin and Marshall College
Shadek-Fackenthal Library
Archives and Special Collection Division
College Avenue and James Street
PO Box 3003
Lancaster, PA 17604-3003
(717) 291-4225
Ann Kenne, College Archivist and
  Special Collections Librarian
Hours: Mon–Fri 9:00–noon & 1:00–5:00
("Not interested in the genealogical
  aspect," collection includes
  information about people who were
  associated with college from 1787;

"Archives no longer has microfilm of
  church and pastoral records of the
  Evangelical and Reformed Churches.")

Franklin Public Library
Pennsylvania Room
421 12th Street
Franklin, PA 16323
(814) 432-8998
Sylvia M. Coast
Hours: Library: Mon–Sat; Pennsylvania
  Room: Mon–Tue & Fri 10:00–5:00
(emphasis on Venango County, not
  Franklin County)
donation

Gilman Museum
East Durham Street
PO Box M
Hellertown, PA 18055
(610) 838-8767
Robert Gilman, Jr., Co-owner

Amelia S. Givin Free Library
114 North Baltimore Avenue
Mount Holly Springs, PA 17065-1201
(717) 486-3688

Green Free Library
134 Main Street
Wellsboro, PA 16901
(717) 724-4876
Cassandra Grant
Hours: Mon–Fri 12:00–8:00, Sat 10:00–
  4:00
(local history)

Greensburg Hempfield Area Library
237 South Pennsylvania Avenue
Greensburg, PA 15601

Haverford College
Magill Library
370 Lancaster Avenue
Haverford, PA 19041-1392
(610) 896-1274
E-mail: elapsans@haverford.edu
http://www.haverford.edu/library/sc/
  sc.html (Special Collections)

Historic Yellow Springs, Inc.
Art School Road
PO Box 62
Chester Springs, PA 19425
(610) 827-7414; (610) 827-1336 FAX
Sandra S. Momyer, Executive Director
Hours: Mon–Fri 9:00–4:00
(historical site with a historic archives
  and library "to enhance our heritage
  and provide a center for research")
membership fee

Jenkintown Library
York and Vista Roads
Jenkintown, PA 19046

**Lackawanna County Library
System**
Vine & Washington Streets
Scranton, PA 18510

Lancaster County Library
125 North Duke Street
Lancaster, PA 17602
(717) 394-2651; (717) 394-3083 FAX
E-mail: lanpublib@shrsys.hslc.org
Gerald Bruce, Reference Librarian
Hours: Mon–Thur 9:00–9:00, Fri–Sat
  9:00–5:30 (no staff available to do
  research)
photocopies 25¢ or 32¢

Lebanon Community Library
125 North Seventh Street
Lebanon, PA 17042
(717) 273-7624
Jayne Tremaine, Director
Hours: Mon–Thur 9:00–8:00, Fri–Sat
  9:00–5:00

**Martinsburg Community Library—
Liebegott Collection**
201 South Walnut Street
Martinsburg, PA 16662
(814) 793-3335
Joyce A. Paden, Head Librarian
Hours: Mon–Sat 1:00–4:30, Mon–Thur
  6:30–8:30, Sun 2:00–4:30 (summer
  hours may vary)
(collection of family histories)

McKeesport Heritage Center
1832 Arboretum Drive
McKeesport, PA 15132
(412) 678-1832

Meadowcroft Foundation
Meadowcroft Village
Rt. 2
Avella, PA 15312
(724) 587-3412

Mechanicsburg Museum Association
(3 West Allen Street—location)
PO Box 182 (mailing address)
Mechanicsburg, PA 17055
(717) 697-6088
Fern Oram, Acquisitions
Hours: Tue–Thur 9:00–noon

Menno Simons Historical Library
(see Virginia)

**Mennonite Historians of Eastern
Pennsylvania**
565 Yoder Road, Box 82
Harleysville, PA 19438
(215) 256-3020
Joel D. Alderfer, Librarian
Hours: Tue–Fri 10:00–4:00, Thur
  7:00 P.M.–10:00 P.M.
Pub. *Mennonite Historians of Eastern
  Pennsylvania (MHEP) Newsletter*,
  bimonthly
(local Mennonite history, Pennsylvania-
  German studies, genealogy and local
  history of Bucks and Montgomery
  counties, Pennsylvania)
$20.00 per year membership for
  individuals (includes 10% discount on
  book sales and on research fees)

Monroe County Public Library, Inc.

a.k.a. Eastern Monroe Public Library
1002 North Ninth Street
Stroudsburg, PA 18360
(717) 421-0800; (717) 424-1546 FAX
E-mail: monroepl@epix.net
Barbara Reiser, Adult Services Librarian
Hours: Mon–Thur 9:00–9:00, Fri 9:00–
6:00, Sat 9:00–5:00

Montgomery County-Norristown Public Library

1001 Powell Street
Norristown, PA 19401
(215) 278-5100
Loretta Righter, Head, Reference
Department
Hours: winter: Mon–Wed 9:00–9:00,
Thur 9:00–6:00, Fri–Sat 9:00–5:00,
Sun 1:00–5:00; summer: Mon–Wed
9:00–8:00, Thur 9:00–6:00, Fri 9:00–
5:00

Mount Lebanon Public Library

(address withheld upon request)

Myerstown Community Library

PO Box 242
199 North College Street
Myerstown, PA 17067-0246
(717) 866-2800; (717) 866-5898 FAX
Linda Manwiller, Librarian
Hours: Mon & Wed–Thur noon–8:00,
Tue noon–6:00, Fri 10:00–6:00, Sat
9:30–noon

New Castle Public Library

207 East North Street
New Castle, PA 16101
(724) 658-6659, ext. 23; (724) 658-9012
FAX
Betty Pallerino, Periodicals/Genealogy;
Chris Fabian; Kate Minteer
Hours: winter: Mon–Thur 8:30–8:30,
Fri–Sat 8:30–5:30; summer: Mon &
Thur 8:30–8:00, Tue–Wed & Fri 8:30–
5:30, Sat 9:00–1:00
(Pennsylvania county histories, census
1790-1920, Soundex, DAR repository,
DAC collection, marriage/obituary
index for New Castle News 1849 to
date)

Northland Public Library

300 Cumberland Road
Pittsburgh, PA 15237-5455

Ohoopee Regional Library

(see Georgia)

Oil City Library

2 Central Avenue
PO Box 811
Oil City, PA 16301
(814) 677-4057
Heritage Room Staff
Hours: Tue & Sat 1:00–5:00

Old Mill Village Museum Association, Inc.

(Pennsylvania Route 848, Harford Road,
1 mile south of New Milford—
location)
PO Box 434 (mailing address)
New Milford, PA 18834
(717) 465-9508
Col. Daw Lee, Vice President
Hours: summer: noon–6:00
Pub. *Museum-Archives-Historical
Library*, bimonthly
(history and genealogy, 1620–1890)
$15.00 per year membership for
individuals, $25.00 per year
membership for families

Osterhout Free Public Library

71 South Franklin Street
Wilkes-Barre, PA 18701
(717) 823-0156, ext. 11
Dianne Suffren
Hours: Sept–Jun: Mon–Thur 9:00–9:00,
Fri 9:00–6:00, Sat 9:00–5:00; Jun–
Sept: Mon & Thur 9:00–9:00, Tue–
Wed 9:00–6:00, Fri 9:00–5:00
(some local history books)
copies 10¢ each, 25¢ each from
microfilm

Pennsylvania State University

University Library
University Park, PA 16802

Philadelphia Area Consortium of Special Collections Libraries (PACSCL)

Van Pelt-Dietrich Library Center
3420 Walnut Street, Room 240
Philadelphia, PA 19104-6206
(215) 985-1445; (215) 985-1446 FAX
E-mail: lblancha@pobox.upenn.edu
http://www.libertynet.org:80/ pacscl/

The Athenaeum of Philadelphia

219 South Sixth Street
Philadelphia, PA 19106-3794
(215) 925-2688; (215) 925-3755 FAX
E-mail: athena@libertynet.org
http://www.libertynet.org/~athena/
Roger W. Moss, Ph.D., Executive
Director
Hours: Mon–Fri 9:00–5:00 by
appointment only
(research library specializing in
American architecture and interior
decoration, 1790–1945, also
biographies of architects; extensive
holdings of rare books, drawings,
manuscripts)
no research for hire available

City of Philadelphia

Department of Records
Philadelphia, PA 19107-3209
(215) 686-2263
David Miller, Editor
Hours: 8:15–4:45
Pub. *The Philadelphia Record*,
biannually, free

(records management, archival and
general information)

Free Library of Philadelphia

1901 Vine Street
Philadelphia, PA 19103
(215) 686-5396
http://www.library.phila.gov/central/ssh/
waltgen/geneal/1.htm
Walter D. Stock, Library Supervisor I
Hours: Mon–Wed 9:00–9:00, Thur–Fri
9:00–6:00, Sat 9:00–5:00, Sun (during
school year) 1:00–5:00

The Library Company of Philadelphia

1314 Locust Street
Philadelphia, PA 19107
(215) 546-3181
John C. Van Horne, Ph.D., Librarian

Pittsburgh History and Landmarks Foundation

James D. Van Trump Library
1 Station Square, Suite 450
Pittsburgh, PA 15219-1134
(412) 471-5808; (412) 471-1633 FAX
Albert M. Tannler, Historical Collections
Director
Hours: Mon–Fri 9:00–5:00 by
appointment only
(houses books, manuscripts, periodicals,
historic site survey data, photographs
and other visual documentation, maps
and plat books, renderings and
blueprints, and other materials
pertaining to architecture and
preservation; not genealogical)

Pottsville Free Public Library

16 North Third Street
Pottsville, PA 17901
(717) 622-8880; (717) 622-2157
http://www.pottsville.com/library/
John Walker, Head Reference Librarian
Hours: Mon–Thur 8:30–8:30, Fri–Sat
8:30–5:00
(Schuylkill County with particular
emphasis on county seat, Pottsville;
Molly Maguires)

Priestly-Forsythe Library

(address withheld upon request)

Memorial Library of Radnor Township

114 West Wayne Avenue
Wayne, PA 19087
(215) 687-1124
Hours: winter: Mon–Fri 9:00–9:00, Sat
9:00–5:00, Sun 2:00–5:00; summer:
Mon–Fri 9:00–9:00

Reading Public Library

100 South Fifth Street
Reading, PA 19602
(215) 478-6355
Donna Geib, Head of Reference
Hours: Mon–Wed 8:15–9:00, Thur–Fri
8:15–5:30, Sat (closed in summer)

8:45–5:00; Local History Room: by appointment with volunteer staff

Pub. *Bookends* (not genealogical), bimonthly

(Pennsylvania-German culture; "We don't have enough staff to undertake open searches.")

$8.00 per year membership in Friends of the Reading-Berks Public Library; letters: $2.00 plus cost of photocopies at 10¢ each

Reading Public Museum and Art Gallery
500 Museum Road
Reading, PA 19611
(215) 371-5850

The Rosenbach Museum and Library
2010 DeLancey Place
Philadelphia, PA 19103
(215) 732-1600
Ellen S. Dunlap, Director

Annie Halenbake Ross Library
Pennsylvania Room
232 West Main Street
Lock Haven, PA 17745
(717) 748-3321
Audrey Miller-Bongar
Hours: Mon & Thur 9:00–8:00, Tue–Wed & Fri–Sat 9:00–5:00

Rough and Tumble Engineers Historical Association, Inc.
(U.S. Route 30, halfway between Coatesville and Lancaster, PA—location)
PO Box 9 (mailing address)
Kinzers, PA 17535
(717) 442-4249
Dale Young, President
Hours: Memorial Day–Labor Day: Fri–Sat 10:00–3:00
Pub. *The Whistle*, quarterly
$15.00 per year membership for individuals (calendar year), $20.00 per year membership for families (parents and children under 16 years), $150.00 Sustaining-Lifetime membership

Christian C. Sanderson Museum
(Route 100, north of Rt. 1—location)
PO Box 153 (mailing address)
Chadds Ford, PA 19317
(610) 388-6545
T. R. Thompson
(very little genealogical information)

Saxton Community Library
(Front Street—location)
PO Box 34 (mailing address)
Saxton, PA 16678
(814) 635-3533
Linda Barton, Librarian
Hours: Mon & Wed 1:00–8:00, Tue & Thur 5:00–8:00, Sat 10:00–4:00

Schwenkfelder Library, Inc.
1 Seminary Street
Pennsburg, PA 18073-1804
(215) 679-3103
Dennis K. Moyer, Director
Hours: Mon–Fri 9:00–4:00
(radical reformation, Schwenkfelders, local history, and Pennsylvania German culture; "Library is known for genealogy research of the area.")

Sewickley Public Library
500 Thorn Street
Sewickley, PA 15143
(412) 741-6920; (412) 741-6099
http://www.clpgh.org/ein/sewickley/
Lynne Schneider, Public Services Librarian
Hours: winter: Mon–Fri 9:30–9:00, Sat 9:00–5:00, Sun 1:00–5:00; summer: Mon–Fri 9:30–8:00, Sat 9:30–5:00

Swigart Museum
PO Box 214, Museum Park
Huntingdon, PA 16652
(814) 643-0885

Bayard Taylor Memorial Library
216 East State Street
Kennett Square, PA 19348
(215) 444-2988

Temple University
Paley Library
13th Street and Berks Mall
Philadelphia, PA 19122
(215) 204-8230; (215) 204-5201 FAX
E-mail: whitetm@astro.ocis.temple.edu
http://www.temple.edu/

Union City Area Historical Museum
PO Box 321
Union City, PA 16438
(814) 438-7573
Thomas Schiewe, President

University of Pennsylvania Van Pelt-Dietrich Library
3420 Walnut Street
Philadelphia, PA 19104-6206
(215) 898-7555; (215) 898-7556 (Reference Department)
Hours: various

University of Pittsburgh
Archives Service Center
363 Hillman Library
Pittsburgh, PA 15260
(412) 648-7977
E-mail: rcc13@vms.cis.pitt.edu
Dr. Ruth C. Carter, Head, Archives Service Center
Hours: Mon–Fri 9:00–5:00
("multi sources for genealogy and family history research")

University of Pittsburgh Library System
(Darlington Memorial Library, 601 Cathedral of Learning—location)
363 Hillman Library (mailing address)
Pittsburgh, PA 15260
(412) 624-4491
Charles E. Aston, Jr., Head, Special Collections Department
Hours: Mon–Fri 1:00–5:00

Upper Darby Free Public Library
76 South State Road
Upper Darby, PA 19082
(610) 789-5319
Thomas Roy Smith, Sellers Archivist
Hours: Special Collections-Local History Section: Mon–Tue 10:00–4:00
(Darby Watershed historical background, 1200 Upper Darby Township photographs 1840–1940; Upper Darby Township is situated at the interior limits of the state's first permanent European settlement)

Warren Public Library
205 Market Street
Warren, PA 16365
(814) 723-4650; (814) 723-4521 FAX
E-mail: wla@penn.com
http://users.penn.com/ wla
Patricia Hutchison, Head of Reference
Hours: Mon–Fri 9:30–9:00, Sat 9:00–5:00, Sat (summer) 9:00–1:00
(emphasis on Warren County and petroleum history)

Citizens Library, Washington
Special Reference Room
55 South College Street
Washington, PA 15301
(724) 222-2400
Hours: Mon–Fri 10:00–9:00, Sat 10:00–5:00, Sun 2:00–5:00; summer: Mon–Thur 10:00–9:00, Fri 10:00–6:00, Sat 10:00–5:00

Mary H. Weir Public Library
(see West Virginia)

West Overton Museums
West Overton Village
Scottdale, PA 15683-1168
(724) 887-7910
Rodney A. Sturtz, Executive Director
Hours: Museum: 15 May–31 Oct: Tue–Sat 10:00–4:00; Archives: Mon–Fri 10:00–4:00
Pub. *The Village Progress*, bimonthly
(archival resources available focusing on Overholt family, West Overton Village, and limited local history)
$10.00 per year membership for individuals, $25.00 per year membership for families, $5.00 per year membership for students, $100.00 per year Patron membership

Whitehall Township Public Library

3700 Mechanicsville Road
Whitehall, PA 18052
(215) 432-4339
Hours: Labor Day to Memorial Day:
   Mon–Thur 10:00–9:00, Fri 10:00–
   6:00; Memorial Day to Labor Day:
   Mon–Thur 10:00–8:00, Fri 10:00–
   6:00
(emphasis on Whitehall local history)

Historical Societies— Local and Regional

Adams County Historical Society

(111 West Confederate Avenue—
   location)
PO Box 4325 (mailing address)
Gettysburg, PA 17325
(717) 334-4723
Charles H. Glatfelter, Director
Hours: Wed & Sat 9:00–5:00
Pub. *Adams County History*, annually;
   ACHS Newsletter, nine times per year
$25.00 per year membership for
   individuals (calendar year), $35.00
   per year membership for families;
   research and copying fee: $25.00 per
   hour, minimum $25.00

Allegheny Foothills Historical Society

Boyce Park Administration Building
675 Old Frankstown Road
Pittsburgh, PA 15239
(412) 327-0338 (Boyce Park Business
   Office)
Hours: Sun (Jun–Sept) 1:00–4:00
no genealogical research at this time

Allegheny-Kiski Valley Historical Society, Inc.

224 East Seventh Avenue
Tarentum, PA 15084-1513
(724) 224-7666
(no genealogy department)

Apollo Area Historical Society

219 North Penn
Apollo, PA 15613
(724) 478-4214

Armstrong County Historical Society

Lankerd Thomas Genealogical Library
300 North McKean Street
PO Box 735
Kittanning, PA 16201
(724) 548-5707
Connie Mateer, Research
Hours: Tue–Thur noon–4:00, and by
   appointment
Pub. *Newsletter*, quarterly
(Armstrong County records)
$8.00 per year membership

Avonmore Area Historical Society

209 Fifth Street
Avonmore, PA 15618
(724) 697-4963
Charles Sharek, President
Pub. *AAHS Newsletter*

Beaver Falls Historical Society and Museum

Carnegie Free Library
Resource and Research Center for
   Beaver County and Local History
1301 Seventh Avenue
Beaver Falls, PA 15010
(724) 843-6930
Hours: Resource and Research Center:
   Mon 5:00–8:00, Tue–Thur 11:00–5:00,
   Fri 11:00–3:00
Pub. *The "Beaver Countian,"* quarterly
donations accepted

Bedford County Heritage Commission, Inc.

137 East Pitt Street
PO Box 1771
Bedford, PA 15522
(814) 623-1771

Bedford County Historical Commission

242 East John Street
Bedford, PA 15522

Pioneer Historical Society of Bedford County

Pioneer Library
242 East John Street
Bedford, PA 15522
(814) 623-2011
William Clark, President; Kay Williams,
   Librarian
Hours: Mon–Fri 9:00–4:00, first Tue &
   Thur 7:30–9:30, Sat 9:00–12:00
Pub. *The Pioneer*, quarterly
(history and genealogy)
$15.00 per year membership for
   individuals, $20.00 per year
   membership for families or couples,
   $35.00 per year Patron membership;
   $150.00 life membership for
   individuals, $225.00 life membership
   for couples

Bell Township Historic Preservation Society

Saint James Church Road
PO Box 286
Salina, PA 15680
(724) 349-3825
A. William Wolford, President
Pub. *Meetinghouse News*

Historical Society of Berks County

940 Centre Avenue
Reading, PA 19605
(610) 375-4375
Barbara Gill, Director of Library and
   Archives
Hours: Tue–Sat 9:00–4:00
Pub. *Historical Society Review*, quarterly
(Pennsylvania-German materials)
$25.00 per year membership for
   individuals, $30.00 per year
   membership for families

Berwick Historical Society

102 East Second Street
Berwick, PA 18603
(717) 759-8020

Blair County Historical Society

(Baker Mansion Museum, 3500 Baker
   Boulevard—location, visitor's
   entrance at 3415 Oak Lane, rear of
   building)
PO Box 1083 (mailing address)
Altoona, PA 16603
(814) 942-3916
Timothy C. Van Scoyoc, Curator
Hours: summer: Tue–Sun 1:00–4:30;
   winter: Tue & Fri 9:30–4:30
Pub. *The Mansion*, quarterly
(Blair County newspapers, marriage
   records, some Civil War histories)
$12.00 per year membership; $3.00
   library admission for non-members;
   surname search fee: $10.00

Boyd County Historical Society

(see Kentucky)

Bradford County Historical Society

21 Main Street
Towanda, PA 18848
(717) 265-2240
Henry G. Farley, President
Hours: Thur–Sat 10:00–4:00
Pub. *The Settler*, quarterly
(sells county histories)
$20.00 per year membership; search fee:
   $20.00 per surname

Brownsville Historical Society

PO Box 24
Brownsville, PA 15417

Bucks County Historical Society

Spruance Library
84 South Pine Street
Doylestown, PA 18901
(215) 345-0210
Betsy Smith, Librarian
Hours: Tue 1:00–9:00, Wed–Sat 10:00–
   5:00
Pub. *Penny Lots*, ten times per year
$30.00 per year membership

Butler County Historical Society

(National City Bank Building, 106 North
   Main Street, Seventh Floor—location)
PO Box 414 (mailing address)
Butler, PA 16001
(724) 283-8116
Hours: Office: Mon–Fri 9:00–1:00
   (closed government holidays)
Pub. *Butler County Historian*, bimonthly
(Butler County history)
$15.00 per year membership for
   individuals; search fee $15.00 plus
   copies and postage

Cambria County Historical Society
615 North Center Street
Ebensburg, PA 15931-1122
(814) 472-6674
Leslie Conrad, Curator
Hours: Mon–Fri 10:30–4:30, Sat 9:00–1:00
Pub. *The Cambria County Heritage*, quarterly
$10.00 per year membership for individuals, $15.00 for families

Cameron County Historical Society, Inc.
102 West Fourth Street
Emporium, PA 15834
Sandra R. Hornung, Genealogist
Hours: anytime by appointment
(Cameron County, Pennsylvania, only)
search fee: $25.00 per family name

Carbondale Historical Society and Museum, Inc.
(Carbondale City Hall and Courthouse—location)
PO Box 151 (mailing address)
Carbondale, PA 18407
(717) 282-0385
S. Robert Powell, President
Hours: Mon–Fri 9:00–1:00
Pub. *Newsletter*, quarterly
(emphasis on Carbondale, anthracite mining and the Delaware and Hudson Railroad)
$25.00 per year membership

Carnegie Historical Society
140 East Mall Plaza
Carnegie, PA 15106
(412) 276-7447

Centre County Historical Society
Centre Furnace Mansion
1001 East College Avenue
State College, PA 16801
(814) 234-4779
Jacqueline J. Melander, President
Hours: Mon, Wed, Fri & Sun 1:00–4:00
Pub. *Centre County Heritage*
(not the county's source for most genealogical records)

Chadds Ford Historical Society
(Route 100, ¼ mile north of Route 1—location)
PO Box 27 (mailing address)
Chadds Ford, PA 19317
(610) 388-7376; (610) 388-7480 FAX
Elizabeth Y. Rump, Administrator
Hours: Mon, Wed & Fri 9:00–2:00, and by appointment
Pub. *Chadds Ford Historical Society Newsletter*, quarterly
(research library contains primarily references for the Chadds Ford area, limited collection of genealogy of local families)
$20.00 per year membership for individuals, $30.00 per year membership for families, $50.00 per year Contributing membership, $100.00–$499.00 per year Patron membership, $500.00+ per year Corporate membership

Chester County Historical Society
225 North High Street
West Chester, PA 19380-2691
(610) 692-4800; (610) 692-4357
Roland H. Woodward, Executive Director
Hours: Tue & Thur–Sat 10:00–4:00, Wed 1:00–8:00
Pub. *Chester County Historical Society Newsletter*, quarterly
$30.00 per year membership for individuals, $40.00 per year membership for families, $25.00 per year membership for senior citizens, $100.00 per year Contributor membership, $250.00 per year Patron membership, $500.00 per year Associate membership, $1,000.00 per year Benefactor membership; research: $20.00 per name

Chestnut Hill Historical Society
8708 Germantown Avenue
Philadelphia, PA 19118
(215) 247-0417

Clarion County Historical Society
Sutton-Ditz House Museum and Library
18 Grant Street
Clarion, PA 16214-1015
(814) 226-4450 phone and FAX
Lindsley A. Dunn, Director-Curator
Hours: Museum: Tue–Sat 10:00–4:00; Library: Tue–Fri 10:00–4:00, and by appointment
Pub. *The Iron County Chronicle*, quarterly
(genealogy and local history of western Pennsylvania counties)
$10.00 per year membership for individuals, $18.00 per year membership for families, $35.00 per year Sustaining membership, $50.00 per year Patron or Business membership, $200.00 life membership; search fee: $15.00

Clearfield County Historical Society
104 East Pine Street
Clearfield, PA 16830
(814) 765-6125

Clinton County Historical Society
Heisey Museum
362 East Water Street
Lock Haven, PA 17745
David Winton, Executive Director
Hours: Tue–Fri 10:00–4:00
Pub. *Newsletter*, quarterly
$10.00 per year membership

The Historical Society of the Cocalico Valley
249 West Main Street
PO Box 193
Ephrata, PA 17522
(717) 733-1616
Cynthia Marquet, Librarian
Hours: Mon & Wed–Thur 9:30–6:00, Sat 8:30–5:00
Pub. *Journal of the Historical Society of the Cocalico Valley*, annually
(emphasis on northern Lancaster County)
$15.00 per year membership for individuals, $25.00 per year membership for families; $25.00 flat mail research fee

Colonial Philadelphia Historical Association
The Independence Hall Association
Carpenter's Hall
320 Chestnut Street
Philadelphia, PA 19106
(215) 925-7887

Columbia County Historical Society
(410 Main Street—location)
PO Box 197 (mailing address)
Orangeville, PA 17859-0197
(717) 683-6011
Bonnie Farver, Executive Director
Hours: Thur–Sat 11:00–4:00
Pub. *Columbia County Historical Society Newsletter*, quarterly
$12.00 per year membership for individuals, $15.00 per year membership for husband and wife

Connellsville Area Historical Society
275 South Pittsburgh Street
Connellsville, PA 15425-3580
(724) 628-5640
Barbara Lowry, Secretary
Hours: Mon–Fri 10:00–3:00
Pub. *Connellsville Area Historical Society Newsletter*, quarterly
(census records, local newspapers, obituaries, printed histories)
$6.00 per year membership; research: $5.00 per research unit

Conshokocken Historical Society
Fifth Avenue and Harry Street
Conshokocken, PA 19428

Corry Area Historical Society
935 Mead Avenue
PO Box 107
Corry, PA 16407-1247
(814) 664-4749

Crawford County Historical Society
848 North Main Street
Meadville, PA 16335

Crescent-Shousetown Area Historical Association
PO Box 253
Glenwillard, PA 15046

Cressona Historical Society
RD 5
Pottsville, PA 17901
(717) 385-1144

Cumberland County Historical Society and The Hamilton Library Association

21 North Pitt Street
PO Box 626
Carlisle, PA 17013-0626
(717) 249-7610; (717) 258-9332 FAX
Linda F. Witmer, Executive Director; Christa Bassett, Librarian
Hours: Mon 7:00 P.M.–9:00 P.M., Tue–Fri 10:00–4:00, Sat 10:00–1:00
Pub. *Cumberland County History*, semiannually; *Newsletter*, quarterly
$30.00 per year membership for individuals, $35.00 per year membership for families; search fee: $30.00

The Historical Society of Dauphin County

John Harris/Simon Cameron Mansion
219 South Front Street
Harrisburg, PA 17104
(717) 233-3462; (717) 233-6059 FAX
Warren W. Wirebach, Librarian
Hours: Alexander Family History Library: Mon–Thur 1:00–4:00; Photograph and Manuscript Archives: by appointment
Pub. *Oracle* (not genealogical, "merely an events schedule"), quarterly
(Dauphin county family history)
$25.00 per year membership for individuals, $50.00 per year Heritage Circle membership, $10.00 per year Cameron Circle membership, $250.00 per year John Harris Circle membership, $500.00 per year Penn Family Circle membership, $1,000 per year Susquehanna Circle membership; search fees vary

The Delaware County Historical Society

(Room 208 of the DCCC Malin Road Center—location)
85 North Malin Road (mailing address)
Broomall, PA 19008-1928
(610) 359-1148
Christine Templin, Administrator
Hours: Mon & Wed–Thur 9:00–3:00, Tue 1:00–8:00
Pub. *The Bulletin*, quarterly
(Chester F. Baker Notebooks, Dr. Anna Broomall Collection, books, periodicals, county newspapers, atlases, census, genealogies, directories, photographs, church and cemetery records, vital records, etc.)
$20.00 per year membership for individuals (beginning 1 September), $35.00 per year membership for families, $5.00 per year membership for students, $50.00 per year Sponsor membership; research: $12.00 per hour for members, $15.00 per hour for non-members; admission $3.00 for non-members

Depreciation Lands Association

Depreciation Lands Museum
(Hampton Historical Commission, 4743 South Pioneer Road, Hampton, PA—location)
PO Box 174 (mailing address)
Allison Park, PA 15101
(412) 486-0563 (Office); (412) 486-2187 (Home)
Elizabeth M. Hunter, Chairman, Hampton Historical Commission
Hours: Sun 1:00–4:00
Pub. *The Newydd*, quarterly
(genealogical services)
$10.00 per year membership for individuals, $20.00 per year membership for families

Donora Historical Society

510 Meldon Avenue
Donora, PA 15033-1333
(724) 379-7014; (412) 379-8809 FAX
E-mail: shawley@westol.com
http://www.westol.com/~shawley/dhs

Downington Historical Commission

Borough of Downington
4 West Lancaster Avenue
Downingtown, PA 19335
(215) 269-0344

Downingtown Historical Society

PO Box 9
Downingtown, PA 19335
(215) 269-6009
Leonard Sideman, President

Elizabeth Township Historical Society

5811 Smithfield Street
Boston, PA 15135
(412) 754-2030
E-mail: eths@sgi.net
Ellen J. Ballas, Genealogical Department
Hours: Tue–Wed 9:30–3:30, Thur 9:30–1:00, Fri 7:00 P.M.–10:00 P.M.
Pub. *Newsletter*, bimonthly
(reference library-museum, offices; genealogical data)
$10.00 per year membership; search fee: $5.00 per hour plus postage and copies at 25¢ each

Elk County Historical Society

109 Center Street
PO Box 361
Ridgway, PA 15853
(814) 776-1032
Iva A. Fay, Archivist
Hours: Tue–Thur 1:30–4:00, and by appointment
Pub. *The Elk Horn*, three times per year at irregular intervals, $8.00 per year subscription
$5.00 per year membership; search fees charged by genealogist, who is away January through March, and vary with amount of time or money spent

Erie County Historical Society

417 State Street
Erie, PA 16501
(814) 454-1813
Annita Andrick, Librarian and Archivist
Hours: Tue–Sat 9:00–5:00
Pub. *Journal of Erie Studies*, two times per year
(history of northwestern Pennsylvania, particularly Erie County)
$20.00 per year membership for individuals, $35.00 per year membership for families; all genealogy requests are referred to Erie Society for Genealogical Research

Fallowfield Historical Society

(Ercildoun, Chester County, PA—location)
Rt. 3, Box 209 (mailing address)
Coatesville, PA 19320
(215) 383-1591
Margaret S. Young, President
Hours: fourth Mon (except Jun–Aug & Dec)
$2.00 per year membership

Forest County Historical Society

PO Box 546
Tionesta, PA 16353

Fort Le Boeuf Historical Society

31 High Street
Waterford, PA 16441
(814) 796-6654

Fort Loudon Historical Society

PO Box 181
Fort Loudon, PA 17224
(717) 369-3473

Fort Shirley Heritage Association

RD 1
Shirleysburg, PA 17260
Barbara McMath

Fort Vance Historical Society

2 Kerr Street
Burgettstown, PA 15021

Historical Society of Fort Washington

473 Bethlehem Pike
Fort Washington, PA 19034
Hours: Wed 2:00–4:00, first & third Sun 2:00–4:00 (closed Jul–Aug)
Pub. *The Bulletin*, ten times per year (monthly September to June)
$15.00 per year membership for individuals, $25.00 per year membership for couples, $5.00 per year membership for students, $50.00 per year membership for businesses, $150.00 per year Sponsor membership, $150.00 life membership for individuals, $250.00 life membership for couples; no fees for search, donations welcome

Friendship Hill Association
PO Box 24
New Geneva, PA 15467
(724) 725-9190
Guy Clegg, President
Pub. *Echoes*

Fulton County Historical Society, Inc.
110 Lincoln Way, East
PO Box 115
McConnellsburg, PA 17233
(717) 485-3207 (Secretary); (717) 485-3134 (Librarian)
Glenn Cordell, Secretary; Hazel Harr, Librarian
Hours: Thur 1:00–4:00 & 7:00–9:00
Pub. *Local History or Genealogical Resource Booklet*, annually, $4.00 per issue
$5.00 per year membership

Germantown Historical Society
5501 Germantown Avenue
Philadelphia, PA 19144
(215) 844-0514

Goschenhoppen Historians, Inc.
(116–118 Gravel Pike—location)
PO Box 476 (mailing address)
Green Lane, PA 18054
(215) 234-8953
"Abe" Roan, First Vice President
Hours: Museum: Sun (Apr–Nov) 1:30–4:00; Library: by appointment
(Pennsylvania-German history and folk culture, local and regional history of Goschenhoppen Folk Region)

Gratz Historical Society
(Market Street—location)
PO Box 507 (mailing address)
Gratz, PA 17030
(717) 365-3342
Lois E. Schoffstall, Director
Hours: Wed 10:00–5:00
Pub. *Die Tseiding*, quarterly, not available by subscription
(information on Dauphin, Schuylkill and Northumberland counties)
$7.00 per year membership; library use: $2.00 per day

Great Arrow Historical Association
968 Chapel Road
Monaca, PA 15061
(724) 744-8129

Greater Hazelton Historical Society
55 North Wyoming Street
Hazelton, PA 18201
(717) 455-8576

The Historical Society of Green Tree
10 West Manilla Avenue
Pittsburgh, PA 15220
(412) 921-2319
Marilyn Albitz, President
Hours: Tue 9:00–noon and 7:00–9:00, and by appointment

Pub. *Green Tree Lore*, quarterly
(Green Tree area history, southwest Allegheny County census)
$10.00 per year membership

Greene County Historical Society
Rt. 2
PO Box 127
Waynesburg, PA 15370
(724) 627-3204
Elizabeth Glass, Director
$5.00 per year membership

Greenville Area Historical Society
946 College Avenue
PO Box 25
Greenville, PA 16125
(724) 588-5736
Gwinn Linegar

Hanover Area Historical Society
105 High Street
PO Box 305
Hanover, PA 17331
(717) 632-3207; (717) 632-5199 FAX
Carolyn S. Stauffer, Executive Director
Hours: Mon–Fri 9:00–2:00
Pub. *HAHS News*, bimonthly
$15.00 per year membership for individuals, $25.00 per year membership for couples, $30.00 per year membership for families; search fee: $10.00

Haverford Township Historical Society
Karokung Drive, Powder Mill Valley Park
PO Box 825
Havertown, PA 19083
(610) 446-7988
Carolyn Joseph, President
Hours: Tue 10:00–noon, first weekend May–Oct, weekends in Dec, and by appointment

Hay Creek Valley Historical Association
(Joanna Furnace—location)
PO Box 36 (mailing address)
Geigertown, PA 19523
(610) 286-0388
Mark Zerr, President
Pub. *The Journal*, quarterly
("We are a nonprofit group working with volunteer time and labor to restore historic Joanna Furnace, an early American iron-making community.")
$3.00 per year membership for individuals, $5.00 per year membership for families

Historic Langhorne Association
160 West Maple Avenue
Langhorne, PA 19047
(215) 757-1888
Romaine Boyer Macht, President
Hours: Wed noon–1:00
Pub. *HLA Newsletter*, monthly
(research library)

$15.00 per year membership for individuals, $20.00 per year membership for families, $50.00 per year Patron membership, $100.00 per year Century membership, $250.00 per year Historic membership, $500.00 per year Thelma Worthington Associated membership, $1,000.00 Anna Mary Williamson life membership

Homestead Pennsylvania Historical Society
1110 Silvan Avenue
Homestead, PA 15120

Hulmeville Historical Society, Inc.
(114 Trenton Avenue—location)
PO Box 7002 (mailing address)
Penndel, PA 19047
E-mail: dhaefner@erols.com
Donald L. Haefner, Archivist
Pub. *Town Crier*, four times per year, free

The Hummelstown Area Historical Society
North Rosanna Street and North Alley
PO Box 252
Hummelstown, PA 17036
(717) 566-8447
Joseph M. Brightbill, President
Hours: winter: third Sun 2:00–4:00, and by appointment; summer: Sun 2:00–4:00
Pub. *Newsletter*, quarterly
(emphasis on central Pennsylvania [Hummelstown area], family genealogies and cemetery records)
$5.00 per year active membership for individuals, $2.50 per year membership for students

Huntingdon County Historical Society
106 Fourth Street
PO Box 305
Huntingdon, PA 16652
(814) 643-5449
Joanne Dolnikowski, Genealogist
Hours: mid-Mar to mid-Nov: Tue–Wed 9:00–4:00; 1 Jan–15 Mar: Wed only and by special advance appointment
Pub. *Newsletter* (not genealogical), four to five times per year, no regular schedule
$10.00 per year membership for individuals

Historical and Genealogical Society of Indiana County
200 South Sixth Street
Indiana, PA 15701-2999
(724) 463-9600; (724) 463-9899 FAX
Alice K. Lackner, Executive Director
Hours: Mon–Fri 9:00–4:00, Sat 10:00–3:00
Pub. *Clark House Newsletter*, monthly; *Indiana County Heritage*, irregularly,

free with membership or $4.95 per issue; *Clark House Quarterly*, free with membership or $1.00 per issue
$15.00 per year membership for individuals, $20.00 per year membership for families; $3.00 per day non-member library use fee

Indiana University of Pennsylvania
IUP Library
Special Collections
Indiana, PA 15705-1096
(724) 357-3039
Dr. Larry Krorh, Director of Libraries
Hours: Mon–Fri 9:00–4:30

Jacobsburg Historical Society
PO Box 345
Nazareth, PA 18064
(610) 759-9029
A. James Shedlauskas, President
Pub. *Jacobsburg Record*, bimonthly
$7.50 per year membership

Jefferson County Historical and Genealogical Society
(232 Jefferson Street, across from police station, behind courthouse—location)
PO Box 51 (mailing address)
Brookville, PA 15825
(814) 849-0077
Bruce McMurray, Secretary; Carole Briggs, Curator
Hours: Tue–Sun 2:00–5:00 (winter hours may vary, closed major holidays)
Pub. *The Jeffersonian*, quarterly
(library contains all authoritative histories of Jefferson County, directories, genealogical reference volumes, newspaper collection, periodicals; archives contains surname, topical and ephemera files, family genealogies, manuscripts [Bibles, diaries, scrapbooks, account books, personal and family papers, etc.], maps, photographs, census microfilms, plus records from civic, fraternal and professional organizations, churches and cemeteries, schools, business and industry)
$10.00 per year membership for individuals, $15.00 per year membership for families, $150.00 life membership; research: $15.00 per hour

Jefferson County Historical Society
100 Franklin Avenue, #B
Brookville, PA 15825-1166
Mr. Altman

Jersey Shore Historical Society
200 South Main Street
Jersey Shore, PA 17740
(717) 398-1973

Juniata County Historical Society
498 Jefferson Street, Suite B
Mifflintown, PA 17059
(717) 436-5152

Kittochtinny Historical Society, Inc.
"The Old Jail"
175 East King Street
PO Box 733
Chambersburg, PA 17201
(717) 264-1667
Lillian Colletta, President
Hours: Library: winter (29 Nov–30 Apr): Tue 5:00–8:00, Wed–Thur 12:00–4:00; summer (1 May–30 Aug): Tue 5:00–8:00, Wed–Sat 9:30–4:00; fall (1 Sept–28 Nov) Tue 5:00–8:00, Thur–Sat 9:30–4:00; Museum: Apr–Dec: Thur–Sat 9:30–4:00
Pub. *Newsletter*, eight times per year (monthly, April–December)
(publishes Franklin County research materials; library is a historical/genealogical resource center)
$15.00 per year membership for individuals, $25.00 per year membership for couples, $5.00 per year junior membership (under 18), $35.00 per year Patron membership, $50.00 per year Contributing membership, $100.00 per year Corporate/Business membership, $250.00 life membership; research: 20¢ per page for copies

Kutztown Area Historical Society
Normal Avenue and Whiteoak Street
PO Box 307
Kutztown, PA 19530
(215) 683-7697
Ms. P. Allison duPont, President
Hours: first Sun 2:00–4:00, and by appointment; monthly programs third Tue
Pub. *Along the Saucony*, quarterly; *Newsletter*, monthly
(library specializing in local history; no genealogical records)
$15.00 per year membership

The Lackawanna Historical Society
The Catlin House
232 Monroe Avenue
Scranton, PA 18510
(717) 344-3841
Maryellen Calemmo, Executive Director; Mary Ann Moran, Researcher
Hours: Tue–Fri 10:00–5:00, Sat noon–3:00
Pub. *Lackawanna Historical Society Journal* (emphasis on scholarly articles, no queries), quarterly
(collection pertaining to the history of Lackawanna County and northeastern Pennsylvania from the 1700s: books, photographs, manuscripts, etc.)
$22.00 per year membership for individuals, $30.00 per year membership for families (of four), $10.00 per year membership for students, $75.00 per year Contributing membership, $150.00 per year

Sustaining membership; research fee: $5.00 for members, $10.00 for non-members

Lakemont Historical Park Museum, Inc.
411 Fourth Street, Lakemont
Altoona, PA 16602
(814) 943-1761; (814) 943-7449
Robert Leidy

Lancaster County Historical Society
Willson Memorial Building
230 North President Avenue
Lancaster, PA 17603-3125
(717) 392-4633; (717) 293-2739 FAX
http://lanclio.org
Mary Virginia Shelley, Librarian; Thomas Ryan, Director
Hours: Tue–Wed & Fri–Sat 9:30–4:30, Thur 9:30–9:30
Pub. *Journal of the Lancaster County Historical Society*, quarterly; *Lancaster County Historical Society Newsletter*, semiannually
(genealogical and historical research library; archives of Lancaster County Historical Society, Jasper Yeates Colonial Law Library)
$30.00 per year membership for individuals, $40.00 per year membership for families

Latrobe Area Historical Society
1501 Ligonier Street
PO Box 266
Latrobe, PA 15650
(724) 539-8889
Kit Snyder, Treasurer
Hours: Tue 9:00–noon, Fri 9:00–3:00
small fee charged

Lawrence County Historical Society
408 North Jefferson Street
PO Box 1745
New Castle, PA 16103
(724) 658-4022
Beverly Zona
Hours: Mon–Fri 9:00–5:00
donation

Lebanon County Historical Society
Hauck Memorial Library
924 Cumberland Street
Lebanon, PA 17042
(717) 272-1473
Christine L. Mason, Librarian/Assistant Coordinator
Hours: Mon–Fri & Sun 1:00–4:30, Mon 7:00–9:00
Pub. *Seeds of History*, bimonthly
(Lebanon County genealogy; Coleman Collection; Bethlehem Steel Collection)
$20.00 per year membership for individuals; research: $10.00 per hour, copies: 40¢ per page

Lehigh County Historical Society

Old Courthouse, Hamilton at Fifth
PO Box 1548
Allentown, PA 18105
(610) 435-4664; (610) 435-9812
http://www/geocities.com/Heartland/
plains/3955/LCHS.htm
Carol Herrity, Assistant Librarian
Hours: Mon–Sat 10:00–4:00
Pub. *Proceedings*, biannually (even
years); *Town Crier*, four times per year
(a large collection of church records of
Lehigh and surrounding counties;
census; published genealogies; city
and county directories)
$25.00 per year membership for
individuals, $35.00 per year
membership for families; research:
$15.00 per hour plus $5.00 postage
and handling and copy costs at 25¢
each; $4.00 per day admission for non-
members

Ligonier Valley Historical Society

(Route 30, East Laughlintown—location)
PO Box 167 (mailing address)
Laughlintown, PA 15655-0167
(724) 238-6818
Hours: Tue–Fri 10:00–4:00
Pub. *Newsletter*, quarterly
(Ligonier Valley history; limited library
of photos, letters; other documents,
which have not been indexed or
copied, are not available for public
research)
$15.00 per year membership for
individuals, $25.00 per year
membership for households, $5.00 per
year membership for students; free
access to library

Linesville Historical Society

Erie Street
RD 2
Linesville, PA 16424
(814) 683-4035

Lititz Historical Foundation, Inc.

(137–139 East Main Street—location)
PO Box 65 (mailing address)
Lititz, PA 17543
(717) 627-4636
Charles Steffy
Hours: May–Oct: Mon–Sat 10:00–4:00;
Nov–Dec: limited hours
Pub. *Historic Journal*, four times per
year
$10.00 per year membership for
individuals, $15.00 per year
membership for husband and wife,
$20.00 per year membership for
families

Little Beaver Historical Society, Inc.

PO Box 304
Darlington, PA 16115
(724) 843-5688

Lower Merion Historical Society, Inc.

(Ashbridge House, Rosemont, PA—
location)
PO Box 51 (mailing address)
Ardmore, PA 19003-0051
(215) 525-5831
Hours: Thur 1:00–4:00 (except holidays)
Pub. *Newsletter*, quarterly
(library and museum, emphasizing lower
Merion Township)

Lycoming County Historical Society and Museum

858 West Fourth Street
Williamsport, PA 17701-5824
(717) 326-3326; (717) 326-3689 FAX
Sandra B. Rife, Director
Hours: Museum: Tue–Fri 9:30–4:00, Sat
11:00–4:00, Sun (May–Oct) 1:00–
4:00; Library: Tue–Thur noon–4:00,
and by appointment
Pub. *Society News*, bimonthly; *Lycoming
County Historical Society Journal*,
quarterly
(Lycoming County local history and
genealogy)
$25.00 per year membership for
individuals; research: $15.00 per hour

Mahonoy Valley Historical Society

312 Hobart Street
Gordon, PA 17936
(717) 875-3347
Virginia Yarnell

Marple Newtown Historical Society

PO Box 755
Broomall, PA 19008
(610) 353-4967
E-mail: mnhistsoc@juno.com
A. Richard Paul, President
Pub. $5.00 per year membership

Masontown Historical Society

PO Box 769
Masontown, PA 15461

Mauch Chunk Historical Society

14 West Broadway
Jim Thorpe, PA 18229
(717) 325-4439
(Carbon County)

McKean County Historical Society

Courthouse
Main Street
PO Box 202
Smethport, PA 16749
(814) 887-5142; (814) 887-5571
(Courthouse)
George E. Berkwater, President
Hours: Tue & Thur 1:00–4:00; summer:
Tue–Fri 1:00–4:00
Pub. *Newsletter*, quarterly
(genealogical services)
$5.00 per year membership, $25.00 life
membership

Mercer County Historical Society

119 South Pitt Street
Mercer, PA 16137
(417) 662-3490
http://www.mchs.pathway.net
Robert B. Fuhrman, Executive Director
Hours: Tue–Fri 10:00–4:30, Sat 10:00–
3:00
Pub. *Mercer County Heritage*, quarterly
$15.00 per year membership for
individuals, $15.00 per year
membership for families, $6.00 per
year membership for senior citizens
or students; research: $10.00 initial
fee

Middletown Historical Association

2651 Langhorne Yardley Road
Langhorne, PA 19047
(215) 968-5119

Mifflin County Historical Society

(1 West Market Street, Suite 1,
Lewistown, PA 17044-2128—research
library location)
17 North Main Street (museum location
and mailing address)
Lewistown, PA 17044
(717) 242-1022
Karen L. Aurand, Library Secretary
Hours: Tue 10:00–8:30, Wed 10:00–4:00
Pub. *Mifflin County Historical News*,
quarterly
$10.00 per year membership for
individuals, $15.00 per year
membership for families

Mill Creek Valley Historical Association

Baker-Dungan Museum
Pennsylvania State University
(Beaver Campus, Monaca, PA 15061—
location)
1334 Midland Beaver Road (mailing
address)
Industry, PA 15052
(724) 643-8969
Clude Piquet

The Millbrook Society/Amy B. Yerkes Museum

(32 North York Road, second floor—
location)
PO Box 506 (mailing address)
Hatboro, PA 19040
(215) 957-1877
E-mail: milbrook@voicenet.com
David T. Shannon, Jr., Executive
Director
Hours: Tue 7:00–9:00, and by
appointment
Pub. *Grist: The Millbrook Society
Journal*, four times per day
(historical archives for the Hatboro-
Horsham area)
$15.00 per year membership for
individuals, $20.00 per year
membership for families

Historical Society of Millersburg and Upper Paxton Township
(330 Center Street—location)
PO Box 171 (mailing address)
Millersburg, PA 17061
(717) 692-4084; (717) 692-4933
Harry S. Mayhew, Genealogy Committee Chairman
Hours: Tue–Fri 9:00–11:00, and by appointment
Pub. *The Herald*, quarterly
$7.00 per year membership

Monongahela Area Historical Society
717 West Main Street
PO Box 152
Monongahela, PA 15063
(724) 258-7148

Monroe County Historical Association
(900 Main Street—location)
537 Ann Street (mailing address)
Stroudsburg, PA 18360
(717) 421-7703; (717) 421-9199 FAX
Janet Mishkin, Executive Director
Hours: Tue–Fri 10:00–4:00; Sun 1:00–4:00
Pub. *The Fanlight*, quarterly
(Monroe County genealogy and local history)
$20.00 per year membership for individuals, $30.00 per year membership for families; research: $10.00 per hour

Monroeville Historical Society
2700 Monroeville Boulevard
Monroeville, PA 15146
(412) 372-9133

The Historical Society of Montgomery County
1654 DeKalb Street
Norristown, PA 19401
(215) 272-0297
Mrs. William H. Smith, Director and Librarian
Hours: Mon & Wed–Fri 10:00–4:00, Tue 1:00–9:00
Pub. *The Historical Society of Montgomery County Bulletin*, semiannually
$20.00 per year membership for individuals, $25.00 per year membership for couples

Montour County Historical Society
1 Bloom Street
PO Box 8
Danville, PA 17821

Mount Union Historical Society
27 East Market Street
PO Box 1976
Mount Union, PA 17066
(814) 542-2974

Muncy Historical Society and Museum of History
(44 North Main Street—location)
PO Box 11 (mailing address)
Muncy, PA 17756
(717) 546-3431
Pub. *Now and Then*, three times per year
$10.00 per year membership

New Berlin Heritage Association
Market and Vine Street
New Berlin, PA 17855
(717) 966-0065

New Hope Historical Society
(Main and Ferry Streets—location)
PO Box 41 (mailing address)
New Hope, PA 18938-0041
(215) 862-5652 (A.M.); (215) 794-8932 (information/appointment)
Faith W. Crown, Archivist
Hours: tours: end of Apr–beginning of Dec: Fri–Sun 1:00–5:00
Pub. *Newsletter*, irregularly (usually three to four times per year)
(some genealogies, local periodicals, New Hope Impressionist School; Parry family)
inquiries for donation

Newcomen Society of the United States
412 Newcomen Road
Exton, PA 19341
(215) 363-6600

Newtown Historic Association, Inc.
PO Box 303
Newtown, PA 18940
(215) 968-4004
David Callahan, President; Mary T. Kester, Librarian
Hours: Tue 9:00–3:00, Thur 7:00 P.M.–9:00 P.M.
(local history library, genealogy and property searches)
$10.00 per year membership for individuals, $15.00 per year membership for families

Newville Historical Society
69 South High Street
Newville, PA 17241
(717) 776-6210
E-mail: jbrehm@epix.net
Joan L. Brehm, Librarian
Hours: Mon–Fri 9:30 A.M.–11:30 A.M., Fri 6:30 P.M.–8:30 P.M., and by appointment
(local history)
$10.00 per year membership for individuals, $20.00 per year membership for families, $100.00 life membership; no search fees; copies: 10¢ per page plus postage

North-Central Pennsylvania Historical Association
311 North Front Street
Milton, PA 17847
(717) 742-9323

Northampton County Historical and Genealogical Society
Mary Illick Memorial Library
107 South Fourth Street
Easton, PA 18042
(610) 253-1222
Paul A. Goudy, Executive Director
Hours: Thur & Fri 1:00–4:00
Pub. *Northampton Notes* (no queries), quarterly
(3,000 family files, 5,000 books, 500 maps, 2,000 photos of places, 120,000 photos of people)
$25.00 per year membership; research: $25.00 for the first hour

Northumberland County Historical Society
The Hunter House
1150 North Front Street
Sunbury, PA 17801
(717) 286-4083
Jane D. Richardson, Director
Hours: Charlotte Darrah Walter Genealogical and Historical Library: Mon, Wed, Fri & first Sat 1:00–4:00; Museum: Mon, Wed & Fri–Sat 1:00–4:00
Pub. *Proceedings*, irregularly, $10.00 per issue for members, $12.00 per issue for non-members
(surname files, published family histories, vital records, cemetery records, church records, tax records, Orphans Court docket, W.P.A. files for a five-county area, city directories, nineteenth century newspapers and personnel rosters from the French and Indian War, Revolutionary War and Civil War)
$12.00 per year membership for individuals, $20.00 per year membership for families; library admission: $3.00 per day for non-members; search fee: $10.00 for one name only, photocopies: 25¢ each

Octarara Area Historical Society
440 Strasburg Avenue
Parkesburg, PA 19365
(610) 857-3830

Oil City Heritage Society
PO Box 962, Oil Creek Station
Oil City, PA 16301

Old York Road Historical Society
Jenkintown Library
Old York and Vista Roads
Jenkintown, PA 19046-2303
(215) 886-8590
Hours: Mon 7:00–9:00, Tue 11:00–2:00, and by appointment
Pub. *Old York Road Historical Society Bulletin*, annually, $10.00 per year subscription
$15.00 per year membership for individuals, $25.00 per year membership for families; no search fees at present

Oswayo Valley Historical Society
PO Box 639
Shinglehouse, PA 16748
(814) 697-6964

Pennsylvania Folklife Society
Ursinus College
PO Box 92
Collegeville, PA 19426
(215) 489-4111, ext. 2388; (610) 489-9509
Nancy K. Gaugler, Managing Editor
Hours: 9:00–5:00
Pub. *Pennsylvania Folklife*, three times per year (autumn, winter, spring)
$15.00 per year membership

Historical Society of Perry County
Headquarters and Museum
PO Box 81
Newport, PA 17074
(717) 567-3079
Resta Tressler, President
Hours: Museum, Blue Ball Tavern, Little Buffalo State Park, Newport, PA: Sun (Memorial Day–Labor Day) 2:00–4:30, and by appointment
(no genealogical research services provided by staff)
$7.50 per year membership for individuals, $15.00 per year membership for families, $100.00 life membership

The Perry Historians
(Rt. 34 between Newport and New Bloomfield—location)
PO Box 73 (mailing address)
Newport, PA 17074
Fae Cupp
Hours: Wed 3:00–9:00, daytime hours posted in Mar each year
Pub. *The Perry Review*, annually; *The Airy Review*, bimonthly
$20.00 per year membership for individuals, $25.00 per year membership for couples, $15.00 per year membership for senior citizens, $17.00 per year membership for senior citizen couples, $35.00 per year Contributing membership for individuals, $45.00 per year Contributing membership for couples, $225.00 per year life membership for individuals, $325.00 life membership for couples, $150.00 life membership for senior citizens, $200.00 life membership for senior citizen couples

Perryopolis Area Historical Society, Inc.
PO Box 303
Perryopolis, PA 15473

Peters Creek Historical Society
Wright House
Finleyville, PA 15332
(412) 384-5991

Pike County Historical Society
c/o Milford Community House
PO Box 915
Milford, PA 18337
(717) 296-8126

Pine Grove Historical Society
240 South Tultehocken Street
Pine Grove, PA 17963
(717) 345-6559

Plymouth Meeting Historical Society
2130 Sierra Road
PO Box 167
Plymouth Meeting, PA 19462
(215) 828-8111
Suzanne Marinell, Administrative Assistant
Hours: Tue & Fri 10:00–4:00
Pub. *PMHS Newsletter*
$10.00 per year membership for individuals; search fee: $10.00 per hour

Potter County Historical Society
308 North Main Street
PO Box 605
Coudersport, PA 16915
Robert K. Currin, President
Hours: Mon & Fri 1:00–4:00
Pub. *Potter County Historical Society Quarterly Bulletin*, $5.00 per year subscription
(county history)

Pottstown Historical Society
PO Box 120
Pottstown, PA 19464
(610) 323-8500
George Wausnock

Punxsutawney Area Historical and Genealogical Society, Inc.
401 West Mahoning Street
PO Box 286
Punxsutawney, PA 15767
(814) 938-2555; (814) 938-4434 (Genealogy Chairman)
Vivian Waite, Genealogy Chairman
Hours: Tue 10:00–4:00, Fri–Sun (1 Jun–31 Aug) 2:00–4:00
Pub. *Histo-Report*, irregularly
$5.00 per year membership; $10.00 search fee, copies: 25¢ each for non-members, 10¢ each for members

Quakertown Historical Society, Inc.
(126 North Main Street—location)
PO Box 846 (mailing address)
Quakertown, PA 18951
(215) 536-3298
Glenn Bosworth, President
Hours: by appointment
$10.00 per year membership

Radnor Historical Society
Finley House
113 West Beechtree Lane
Wayne, PA 19087
(215) 688-2668

Pub. *Radnor Historical Society Bulletin*, annually
$3.00 per year membership

Red Lion Area Historical Society
PO Box 94
Red Lion, PA 17356
(717) 244-2501
Bruce F. Knisley, President
Pub. *Newsletter*, monthly
(baptismal and marriage records by parish to 1920; "Information provided through the mail, no visits by the public.")
$20.00 per hour for research

John Timon Reily Historical Society (Conewago Valley)
410 Irishtown Road
Hanover, PA 17331

Richmond Little Red School House Association
(Dutch Ridge Road, Beaver, PA 15009—location)
Rt. 1 (mailing address)
Fombell, PA 16123
(412) 412-7073

Ross Township Historical Society
102 Evergreen Hamlet
Pittsburgh, PA 15209
(412) 821-8888

Roxborough-Manayunk-Wissahickon Historical Society
3612 Earlham Street
Philadelphia, PA 19129
(215) 438-1368

Historical Society of Saint Mary's and Benzinger Township
Genealogy Department
319 Erie Avenue, Room 13
PO Box 584
Saint Mary's, PA 15857
(814) 834-6525

Saltsburg Area Branch Historical Society, Inc.
PO Box 12
Saltsburg, PA 15681
(724) 639-3692
Rebecca B. Hadden, President

The Historical Society of Schuylkill County
14 North Third Street
Pottsville, PA 17901
(717) 622-7540
John Joy, Curator
Hours: Tue–Sat 10:00–noon & 1:00–4:00
$20.00 per year membership; search fees: $20.00 per hour

Sewickley Valley Historical Society
200 Broad Street
Sewickley, PA 15143
(412) 741-5315; (412) 741-3458 (Archivist)

Betty G. Y. Shields, Executive Director
Hours: Tue–Fri 10:00–2:00, and by
appointment
Pub. *Signals*, eight to ten times per year
(extensive collection of obituary notices)
$20.00 per year membership

Shippensburg Historical Society
(52 West King Street—location)
PO Box 539 (mailing address)
Shippensburg, PA 17257
(717) 532-6727
Myrtle Yohe, Genealogy Chairman
Hours: Wed 1:00–4:00, Sat 1:00–4:00
$10.00 per year membership

Skippack Historical Society
PO Box 389
Eagleville, PA 19408
(215) 539-6224
G. Keith Funk, President
Hours: 8:00–5:00

Slippery Rock Heritage Association, Inc.
PO Box 511
Slippery Rock, PA 16057
(724) 794-3140
Pub. *Slippery Rock Heritage Association, Inc., Newsletter*, quarterly
$3.00 per year membership (beginning in November)

Snyder County Historical Society
30 East Market Street
PO Box 276
Middleburg, PA 17842
(717) 837-6191; (717) 837-4282 FAX
Lee E. Knepp, Secretary
Hours: Tue & Fri 10:00–3:00
Pub. *Annual Bulletin*
(local history and genealogy)
$10.00 per year membership

Solebury Township Historical Society
PO Box 223
Solebury, PA 18963
(215) 297-8771

Historical and Genealogical Society of Somerset County, Inc.
10649 Somerset Pike
Somerset, PA 15501
(814) 445-6077; (814) 443-6621 FAX
Barbara Black, Curator/Librarian
Hours: Wed–Sat 9:00–5:00, Sun noon–5:00
Pub. *The Laurel Messenger*, quarterly
(February, May, August, November)
$20.00 per year membership for
individuals, $30.00 per year
membership for families, $5.00 per
year membership for students (age 18
or under), $50.00 per year Sustaining
membership, $1,000.00 life
membership; search for one name:
$20.00 for the first hour and $15.00
for each additional hour for non-
members, $15.00 for the first hour and

$10.00 for each additional hour for
members; specific copy requests:
$2.00 each, plus postage and copy fee
of 25¢ per page from paper originals
or 50¢ each from microfilm originals

Springs Historical Society/Casselman Valley
PO Box 62
Springs, PA 15562
(814) 662-2625
Eileen Mort, Curator
Hours: Museum: Wed–Sat (24 May to
mid-Oct) 1:00–5:00
Pub. *Chronicle*, annually
$10.00 per year membership; non-
member museum admission: $1.50 for
adults, 50¢ for children

State Belt Historical Society
PO Box 58
Mount Bethel, PA 18343
(717) 897-6521
Diane Temples, President
(State Belt region of Northampton
County)

Strongstown Historical Society
(Route 422, Strongstown, PA 15956—
location)
PO Box 75 (mailing address)
Strongstown, PA 15957
(814) 749-0722

Sullivan County Historical Society and Museum
Courthouse Square
LaPorte, PA 18626
(717) 924-3549
Louise Woodhead, President
Hours: Jun–Sept: Wed & Sat

Susquehanna County Historical Society
2 Monument Square
Montrose, PA 18801
(717) 278-1881; (717) 278-9336 FAX
Elizabeth A. Smith, Curator; Linda
Smith, Assistant Curator
Hours: May–Sept: Mon–Fri 9:00–5:00;
Oct–Apr: Mon & Thur–Fri 9:00–5:00,
Tue–Wed noon–5:00
Pub. *Susquehanna County Historical
Society Newsletter*, biannually
$15.00 per year membership for
individuals, $20.00 per year dual
membership; reference room fee:
$2.00 for non-members; research:
$30.00 plus postage and copying costs

Susquehanna Depot Historical Society
PO Box 161
Susquehanna, PA 18847

Tamaqua Historical Society
118 West Broad Street
Tamaqua, PA 18252
(717) 668-5722

Tioga County Historical Society
120 Main Street
PO Box 724
Wellsboro, PA 16901
(717) 724-6116
Scott P. Gitchell, Director
Hours: Mon–Fri noon–4:00
Pub. *Tioga County Historical Society
Newsletter*, quarterly
(history of Tioga County, general and
family)
$10.00 per year membership for
individuals, $15.00 per year
membership for families, $25.00 per
year Sustaining membership, $200.00
life membership

Titusville Historical Society
Benson Memorial Library
213 North Franklin Street
Titusville, PA 16354

Tulpehocken Settlement Historical Society
116 North Front Street
PO Box 53
Womelsdorf, PA 19567
(215) 589-2527
Earl W. Ibach, Director
Hours: Apr–Oct: Mon–Tue & Thur–Sun
1:00–4:00; Nov–Mar: Mon–Tue,
Thur–Fri & Sun 1:00–4:00
Pub. *Tulpehocken Tattler*, quarterly,
$2.00 per issue; *Die Shilgrut fun der
Tulpehock*, annually
(genealogical library and rotating
historical exhibits in museum)
$15.00 per year membership, $200.00
life membership

Tuscarora Township Historical Society
Bradford County
RD 2, Box 105-C
Laceyville, PA 18623
(717) 869-2184
Hedy Chaffee, Presiding Director
Hours: Mon 9:00–5:00, and anytime
upon request
Pub. *Once Upon a Time*, monthly
(genealogy and local history of
Susquehanna, Bradford and Wyoming
counties)
$15.00 per year membership; research:
$10.00 per hour

Tyrone Area Historical Society
5 Oak Hill Lane
PO Box 81
Tyrone, PA 16686
(814) 684-3248
Suzanne Sickler Ohl
Hours: by appointment
Pub. *Society Newsletter*, three times per
year; *Annual Report*
(Tyrone area history: people, places,
events)
$10.00 per year membership

Union County Historical Society

Union County Courthouse
102 South Second Street
Lewisburg, PA 17837
(717) 524-8666
Robert Linke, President
Hours: Mon–Fri 8:30–noon & 1:00–4:30
Pub. *Union County Heritage*, biannually
(in even numbered years), $8.00 per
issue
$20.00 per year membership for
individuals (includes *Heritage*),
$30.00 per year membership for
families, $50.00 per year Contributor
membership, $100.00 per year Patron
membership, $150.00 per year
Sponsor membership, $300.00 life
membership

Uniontown Area Historical Society

PO Box 193
Uniontown, PA 15401
(724) 439-8571

The Valley Forge Historical Society

PO Box 122
Valley Forge, PA 19481-0122
(610) 783-0535; (610) 783-0448 FAX
E-mail: vfhs@ix.netcom.com
http://www.libertynet.org/lha/valleyforge
Ms. Stacey A. Swigart, Curator
Hours: Mon–Sat 9:30–4:30, Sun 1:00–
4:30 (call for winter hours)
(no genealogical resources; information
pertains to history of Valley Forge and
the collection of artifacts)
$20.00 per year membership for
individuals, $30.00 per year
membership for families, $50.00 per
year Supporting membership

Venango County Historical Society

301 South Park Street
PO Box 101
Franklin, PA 16323
(814) 437-2275
Rainy Linn, President
Hours: Jan–Apr: Sat 10:00–2:00; May–
Dec: Tue–Thur & Sat 10:00–2:00 (call
before out-of-town visit)
Pub. *The Venango Intelligencer*,
quarterly
$10.00 per year membership for
individuals, $15.00 per year
membership for families

Warren County Historical Society

(210 Fourth Avenue—office location)
PO Box 427 (mailing address)
Warren, PA 16365
(814) 723-1795
Hours: Mon–Fri 8:30–4:30, Sat 9:00–
noon
Pub. *Stepping Stones* (not genealogical),
three times per year
$20.00 per year membership for
individuals, $35.00 per year
membership for families at one
address, $10.00 per year membership
for students (under 18 years), $15.00

per year membership for senior
citizens (65 and older), $25.00 per
year membership for senior citizen
families, $75.00 per year Contributing
family membership, $100.00 Patron
family membership, $50.00 per year
membership for non-profit
organizations, $500.00 life
membership; search: $7.50 per hour,
$25.00 minimum

Warrior Run Fort Freeland Heritage Society

PO Box 26
Turbotville, PA 17772
(717) 538-1417

Washington County Historical Society

LeMoyne House
49 East Maiden Street
Washington, PA 15301
(724) 225-6740
Melissa Metz, Administrative Assistant
Hours: Tue–Fri 11:00–4:00
Pub. *Focus*, bimonthly
(history of Washington County, also
regimental histories from Washington
County regiments)
$15.00 per year membership for
individuals, $25.00 per year
membership for couples; research:
$15.00 per hour, discounted to
members

Wattsburg Area Historical Society

Main Street
PO Box 240
Wattsburg, PA 16442-0240
(814) 739-2952
Thomas Coatoam, Secretary
Hours: by appointment
Pub. *Wattsburgh Occasional*, quarterly
(Wattsburg Borough and Amity,
Venango, Union townships)
$5.00 per year membership

Wayne County Historical Society

810 Main Street
PO Box 446
Honesdale, PA 18431
(717) 253-3240
Gloria McCullough, Research Librarian
Hours: Museum: Jan–Feb: Sat 10:00–
4:00; Mar–May: Wed–Fri 1:00–4:00,
Sat 10:00–4:00; Jun–Sept: Mon &
Wed–Sat 10:00–4:00, Sun (except first
three Sun in Jun & first Sun in Jul)
noon–5:00; Oct–Dec: Mon & Wed–Fri
1:00–4:00, Sat 10:00–4:00, first &
second Sun in Oct noon–5:00; Library:
same as museum, except closed Sun
Pub. *Wayne County Historical Society
Newsletter*, four times per year
(Wayne County history and genealogy)
$15.00 per year membership for
individuals, $20.00 per year
membership for families, $200.00 life
membership; research fee: $30.00 for
initial two-hour search, $15.00 for

each additional hour; copies: $3.00
minimum; research library use free for
members, $3.00 for non-members

Waynesboro Historical Society

138 West Main Street
Waynesboro, PA 17268
(717) 762-1747
Todd A. Dorsett, President
Hours: Wed 1:00–9:00, Thur & Sat
10:00–4:00, Fri 10:00–1:00
Pub. *Antietam Ancestors*, annually,
$22.50 per year subscription
$20.00 per year membership for
individuals, $35.00 per year
membership for families, $50.00 per
year Supporting membership, $100.00
per year Sustaining or Business
membership, $500.00 life
membership; donation for research

Historical Society of Western Pennsylvania

1212 Smallman Street
Pittsburgh, PA 15222-4208
(412) 454-6364 (Reference desk)
Sharon Watson-Mauro, Librarian
Hours: Tue–Sat 9:30–4:30
Pub. *Jots from the Point*, nine times per
year; *Pittsburgh History*, quarterly
$25.00 per year membership

Westmoreland County Historical Society

951 Old Salem Road
Greensburg, PA 15601
(724) 836-1800
Hours: Tue–Fri 10:00–5:00, Sat 10:00–
1:00
Pub. *The Westmoreland Chronicle*,
monthly; *Westmoreland History*,
quarterly
$15.00 per year membership for
individuals, $25.00 per year
membership for families; volunteer
genealogist answers genealogy
correspondence

Wilkinsburg Historical Society

Wilkinsburg Public Library
605 Ross Avenue
Pittsburgh, PA 15221
(412) 244-2940

Wissahickon Valley Historic Society

(1400 Blue Bell Road—location)
PO Box 2 (mailing address)
Blue Bell, PA 19422
(215) 646-6541

Wyoming County Historical Society

(Corner of Bridge and Harrison Streets—
location)
PO Box 309 (mailing address)
Tunkhannock, PA 18657-0309
(717) 836-5303
Paula Radwanski, Secretary
Hours: Oct 15–Apr 15: Wed 10:00–4:00;
Apr 15–Oct 15: Tue, Wed & Sat
10:00–4:00

Pub. *Lest We Forget—Wyoming County Pioneers*, semiannually (February and September)

(genealogical library and museum; "The collection includes numerous books on New England ancestry, newspapers dating back to 1796 and census records for Wyoming and surrounding counties; also on file are records for over 90 area cemeteries as well as various other information about local history.")

$12.00 per year membership for individuals, $18.00 per year membership for families, $30.00 per year Supporting membership, $125.00 life membership; research fee: $20.00 initial research plus copies; queries: 15¢ per word (first 30 words free to members)

Wyoming Historical and Geological Society

Bishop Memorial Library
49 South Franklin Street
Wilkes-Barre, PA 18701
(717) 823-6244 (Library); (717) 822-1727 (Museum); (717) 823-9011 FAX
http://www.whgs.org
Jesse Teitelbaum, Librarian/Archivist
Hours: Library: Tue–Fri 12:00–4:00, Sat 10:00–4:00; Museum, 69 South Franklin Street (behind the Osterhout Free Library): Tue–Fri 12:00–4:00, Sat 10:00–4:00
Pub. *Forecast*, quarterly
$25.00 per year membership for individuals, $40.00 per year membership for families; in-house research fee: $2.00 for non-members

Yardley Historical Association, Inc.

46 West Afton Avenue
PO Box 212
Yardley, PA 19067
(215) 493-9883

The Historical Society of York County

250 East Market Street
York, PA 17403
(717) 848-1587
June Lloyd, Librarian
Hours: Mon–Sat 9:00–5:00
(local history and genealogy)

Zelienople Historical Society

243 South Main Street
PO Box 45
Zelienople, PA 16063-0045
(724) 452-9457
Joyce M. Bessor, Administrator
Hours: Mon–Fri 9:00–noon & 1:00–4:00
Pub. *Zelienople Historical Society Newsletter*, quarterly
(concentration on southwest Butler County and northwest Beaver County

families, history of local area; specialty: Passavant and Buhl and Ziegler/Zeigler family histories)
$15.00 per year membership for individuals, $25.00 per year membership for husband and wife, $2.00 per year membership for students, $100.00 life membership for individuals, $150.00 life membership for husband and wife; research: $5.00 per hour (maximum $25.00 per day), search fees vary, based on complexity

---

LDS Family History Centers

Broomall
(610) 356-8507

Philadelphia
(see Broomall)

Pittsburgh
(412) 921-2115

Reading
(610) 929-0235

York
(717) 854-9331

Genealogical Societies

State Genealogical Society

The Genealogical Society of Pennsylvania

1305 Locust Street, Third Floor
Philadelphia, PA 19107-5405
(215) 545-0391; (215) 545-0936 FAX
http://libertynet.org/~gencap/gsp.html
Jane Adams Clarke, Executive Director
Hours: Office: Mon–Fri 9:00–5:00; Library: Mon & Wed 1:00–4:00, and by appointment
Pub. *The Pennsylvania Genealogical Magazine*, semiannually, $15.00 per year subscription; *Penn in Hand*, quarterly
$35.00 per year membership for individuals, $65.00 per year membership for families, $125.00 Patron membership, $500.00 life membership, $5,000 per year Benefactor membership; search fee: $20.00 per hour; members have access twelve times per year to the Historical Society of Pennsylvania collection, which includes collections donated by the Genealogical Society of Pennsylvania

Regional Genealogical Societies

Beaver County Genealogical Society

Resource and Research Center for Beaver County and Local History
c/o Nancy Y. Lindemann
3225 Dutch Ridge Road
Beaver, PA 15009
E-mail: mruckert@lg.com
W. Martin Ruckert, President; William E. Irion, Resource and Research Center Director
Hours: Resource and Research Center: Mon 5:00–8:00, Tue–Thur 11:00–5:00, Fri 11:00–3:00
Pub. *Gleanings*, quarterly
$10.00 per year membership for households, $15.00 per year foreign membership (beginning in July)

Berks County Genealogical Society

15197 Kutztown Road
Kutztown, PA 19530
(610) 683-9420
Sylvia Graybill, Corresponding Secretary
Hours: Albright College Library: open to members only
Pub. *Journal*, quarterly; *Branches of Berks*, eight times per year
(Berks County and bordering counties)
$15.00 per year membership for individuals, $20.00 per year membership for families

Blair County Genealogical Society, Inc.

(2012 Twelfth Avenue—location)
PO Box 855 (mailing address)
Altoona, PA 16603
(814) 942-3681 (Library)
Helen Danemark, Librarian; Jennie Amrhein, Corresponding Secretary
Hours: Mon 6:30 P.M.–9:30 P.M., Wed 10:00–3:30 & 6:30–9:30, Thur 10:00–3:30
Pub. *Blair County Genealogical Society Newsletter*, quarterly
$15.00 per year membership for individuals (beginning in January), $7.50 per year Associate membership (for each additional relative who lives in the same household with a regular member); free access to library

Bradford County Genealogical Society

21 Main Street
Towanda, PA 18848

Bucks County Genealogical Society

(German Baptist Brethren Meeting House, Ferry Road, New Britain Township—location)
PO Box 1092 (mailing address)
Doylestown, PA 18901
(215) 230-9410

Audrey J. Wolfinger, President
Hours: Wed–Fri 1:00–5:00
Pub. *Bucks County Genealogical Society Newsletter*, quarterly
(sponsors an annual two-day conference)
$15.00 per year membership for individuals (beginning July), $20.00 per year membership for families; research fee: $5.00

Cameron County Genealogical Society

102 West Fourth Street
Emporium, PA 15834
(814) 486-2162

Capital Area Genealogical Society

PO Box 4502
Harrisburg, PA 17111-0502
(717) 5435-2622
Robert Viguers, Jr.
Hours: second Sun 2:00–2:30
Pub. *Keystone Seekers*, quarterly
(Dauphin and Cumberland counties; capital area cemeteries; no library or research facility)
$13.00 per year membership for individuals, $15.00 per year membership for families

Central Pennsylvania Genealogical Pioneers

120 Catawissa Avenue
Sunbury, PA 17801
Mrs. Strive

Central Susquehanna Valley Genealogy Society

PO Box 197
Orangeville, PA 17859-0197
Hours: meetings: second Wed (Mar–Nov)
(Columbia and surrounding counties; genealogies, church and cemetery records)
$10.00 per year membership (includes *Columbia County Historical Society Newsletter*)

Centre County Genealogical Society

PO Box 1135
State College, PA 16804
(814) 238-4060
Elizabeth Dutton, Corresponding Secretary
Pub. *C.C.G.S. Newsletter*, six times per year
(limited to Centre County)
$10.00 per year membership

Cornerstone Genealogical Society

(311 North West Street—location)
PO Box 547 (mailing address)
Waynesburg, PA 15370
(724) 627-5653
Laurine Williams, President
Hours: Eva K. Bowlby Public Library: Mon–Fri 1:00–4:00, Sat 10:00–3:30
Pub. *Cornerstone Clues*, quarterly

$15.00/$20.00/$50.00 per year membership

Crawford County Genealogical Society

848 North Main Street
Meadville, PA 16335
Annette Lynch, Corresponding Secretary
Pub. *Crawford County Genealogy*, semiannually
(inquiries welcome)
$15.00 per year membership

Elk County Genealogical Society

RR 2, Box 64
Johnsonburg, PA 15845

Erie Society for Genealogical Research

PO Box 1403
Erie, PA 16512-1403
(814) 454-1813 (Erie County Historical Society)
Hours: Tue–Sat 9:00–4:00
Pub. *Keystone Kuzzins*, quarterly
$12.00 per year membership; mail requests for research accepted

Historical and Genealogical Society of Indiana County

200 South Sixth Street
Indiana, PA 15701-2999
(724) 463-9600; (724) 463-9899 FAX
Alice K. Lackner, Executive Director
Hours: Mon–Fri 9:00–4:00, Sat 10:00–3:00
Pub. *Clark House Newsletter*, monthly; *Indiana County Heritage*, irregularly, free with membership or $4.95 per issue; *Clark House Quarterly*, free with membership or $1.00 per issue
$15.00 per year membership for individuals, $20.00 per year membership for families; $3.00 per day non-member library use fee

Jefferson County Historical and Genealogical Society

(232 Jefferson Street, across from police station, behind courthouse—location)
PO Box 51 (mailing address)
Brookville, PA 15825
(814) 849-0077
Bruce McMurray, Secretary; Carole Briggs, Curator
Hours: Tue–Sun 2:00–5:00 (winter hours may vary, closed major holidays)
Pub. *The Jeffersonian*, quarterly
(library contains all authoritative histories of Jefferson County, directories, genealogical reference volumes, newspaper collection, periodicals; archives contains surname, topical and ephemera files, family genealogies, manuscripts (Bibles, diaries, scrapbooks, account books, personal and family papers, etc.), maps, photographs, census microfilms, plus records from civic, fraternal and

professional organizations, churches and cemeteries, schools, business and industry)
$10.00 per year membership for individuals, $15.00 per year membership for families, $150.00 life membership; research: $15.00 per hour

Johnstown Genealogical Society

26 Paint Street
Windber, PA 15963

Lycoming County Genealogical Society

(Lycoming County Historical Museum, 858 West Fourth Street—location)
PO Box 3625 (mailing address)
Williamsport, PA 17701
Robin Leidhecker, President
Hours: Tue–Thur 1:00–4:00 by appointment only
Pub. *Lycoming Lineage*, bimonthly
(county-wide tax records 1850–1950, family files, church and cemetery records)
$10.00 per year membership; search fee: $12.00 per hour

McKean County Genealogical Society

PO Box 207A
Derrick City, PA 16727

Mercer County Genealogical Society

PO Box 812
Sharon, PA 16146-0812
(724) 346-5117
E-mail: lorgen@infonline.net
Loretta Barker De Santis, Librarian
Hours: Tue 10:00–4:00
Pub. *Past Times*, eight times per year, $10.00 per year subscription; *Mercer County Genealogical Society Newsletter*
(emphasis on Mercer and adjoining counties; cemetery books, history books, vertical files, census)

Montgomery Area Genealogical Society

Montgomery Public Library
1 South Main Street
Montgomery, PA 17751
(717) 547-6212

Montgomery County Genealogical Club

The Historical Society of Montgomery County
1654 DeKalb Street
Norristown, PA 19401
(215) 272-0297
Mrs. William H. Smith, Historical Society Director and Librarian
Hours: Historical Society: Mon & Wed–Fri 10:00–4:00, Tue 1:00–9:00
Pub. *The Historical Society of Montgomery County Bulletin*, semiannually

$20.00 per year membership for individuals, $25.00 per year membership for couples

North Hills Genealogists
c/o Northland Public Library
300 Cumberland Road
Pittsburgh, PA 15237-5455
(412) 931-5406
Pub. *The Newsletter*, ten times per year (monthly, except July and December)
(publishes cemetery listings by township)
no research, queries free in newsletter

Northampton County Historical and Genealogical Society
Mary Illick Memorial Library
107 South Fourth Street
Easton, PA 18042
(610) 253-1222
Paul A. Goudy, Executive Director
Hours: Thur & Fri 1:00–4:00
Pub. *Northampton Notes* (no queries), quarterly
(3,000 family files, 5,000 books, 500 maps, 2,000 photos of places, 120,000 photos of people)
$25.00 per year membership; research: $25.00 for the first hour

Northeast Pennsylvania Genealogical Society
Wilkes-Barre, PA
E-mail: tamlamb@postoffice.ptd.net
http://home.ptd.net/~tamlamb/gene.htm
John and Tammy Lamb

Genealogical Research Society of Northeastern Pennsylvania, Inc. (GRSNP)
PO Box 1
Olyphant PA 18447-0001
(717) 383-7661; (717) 383-7466 FAX
E-mail: searcher@microserve.net; genealogy@usnetway.com
http://www.clark.net/pub/mjloyd/grsnp/grsnp.html
Joseph J. Bryer, Research Coordinator
Hours: meetings: at the Lackawanna County Housing Authority Community Room, 201 West Grant Street, Olyphant: third Wed 7:00
Pub. *The Searcher*, quarterly
(Lackawanna, Luzerne, Wayne, Pike, Monroe and Susquehanna counties)
$15.00 per year membership, $200.00 life membership; research: $20.00 per hour, one-hour minimum, includes photocopying and postage up to $1.00

Old York Road Genealogical Society
1030 Old York Road
Abington, PA 19001
(215) 887-7683
E-mail: kenhayes@worldnet.att.net
Kenneth F. Hayes, President
Hours: second Tue 7:00
Pub. *Old York Road Genealogical Society Quarterly Newsletter*

(emphasis on education for local family genealogists)
$10.00 per year Sustaining membership for individuals, $12.00 per year Sustaining membership for families

Palm Beach County Genealogical Society, Inc.
(see Florida)

Punxsutawney Area Historical and Genealogical Society, Inc.
401 West Mahoning Street
PO Box 286
Punxsutawney, PA 15767
(814) 938-2555; (814) 938-4434 (Genealogy Chairman)
Vivian Waite, Genealogy Chairman
Hours: Tue 10:00–4:00, Fri–Sun (1 Jun–31 Aug) 2:00–4:00
Pub. *Histo-Report*, irregularly
$5.00 per year membership; $10.00 search fee, copies: 25¢ each for non-members, 10¢ each for members

Historical and Genealogical Society of Somerset County, Inc.
10649 Somerset Pike
Somerset, PA 15501
(814) 445-6077; (814) 443-6621 FAX
Barbara Black, Curator/Librarian
Hours: Wed–Sat 9:00–5:00, Sun noon–5:00
Pub. *The Laurel Messenger*, quarterly (February, May, August, November)
$20.00 per year membership for individuals, $30.00 per year membership for families, $5.00 per year membership for students (age 18 or under), $50.00 per year Sustaining membership, $1,000.00 life membership; search for one name: $20.00 for the first hour and $15.00 for each additional hour for non-members, $15.00 for the first hour and $10.00 for each additional hour for members; specific copy requests: $2.00 each, plus postage and copy fee of 25¢ per page from paper originals or 50¢ each from microfilm originals

South Central Pennsylvania Genealogical Society, Inc.
PO Box 1824
York, PA 17405-1824
(717) 843-6169 (Director)
Mrs. Pat Gross, Director of Operations
Hours: meetings: first Sun (Sept–Jun) 2:15
Pub. *Our Name's the Game*, eleven times per year (monthly, except July/August combined issue)
(emphasis on York and Adams counties; maintains file of surnames being researched by members)
$15.00 per year membership for individuals, $18.00 per year

membership for families, $500.00 life membership; free queries to members; research: $10.00 donation from members, $20.00 fee from non-members

Genealogical Society of Southwestern Pennsylvania
(Citizens Library, Special Reference Room—collection location)
PO Box 894 (mailing address)
Washington, PA 15301-0984
Mary B. Chadwick, President
Hours: Library: Mon–Fri 10:00–9:00, Sat 10:00–5:00, Sun 2:00–5:00; summer: Mon–Thur 10:00–9:00, Fri 10:00–6:00, Sat 10:00–5:00
Pub. *Keyhole*, quarterly (southwestern Pennsylvania)
$10.00 per year membership if paid by 15 Jan, $12.00 thereafter, $14.00 per year foreign membership

Tarentum Genealogical Society
Community Library of Allegheny Valley
315 East Sixth Avenue
Tarentum, PA 15084
(724) 226-0770
Hours: Library: Tue–Fri 10:00–8:00, Sat 10:00–4:00; meetings: third Thur
Pub. *Newsletter*, quarterly
(records pertaining to Allegheny, Armstrong, Butler, and Westmoreland counties)
$10.00 per year membership (beginning in May)

Tri-State Genealogical Society
(see Ohio)

Twin Tier Genealogical Society, Inc. (Bradford and Tioga counties, PA)
(see New York)

Venango County Genealogical Club
Oil City Library
Heritage Room
2 Central Avenue
PO Box 811
Oil City, PA 16301
(814) 678-3077
Hours: Heritage Room: Tue & Sat 1:00–5:00
Pub. *V.C.G.C. Newsletter*, quarterly
(Venango County and northwest Pennsylvania genealogy and history)
$10.00 per year membership

Warren County Genealogical Society
50 Second Street
Youngsville, PA 16371
(814) 563-9696
Virginia Roberts

Western Pennsylvania Genealogical Society
4400 Forbes Avenue
Pittsburgh, PA 15213-4080
(412) 687-6811

Hours: The Carnegie Library of
Pittsburgh: Mon–Thur 9:00–9:00, Fri–
Sat 9:00–5:30, Sun (Oct–May) 1:00–
5:00
Pub. *The Quarterly*; *JOTS*, ten times per
year
(sponsors Computer, English-Welsh,
German, Irish, New England and
Scottish interest groups)
$20.00 per year membership for
individuals (beginning 1 July); $26.00
per year joint membership (two
members at one address); two free
queries per quarter

**Windber-Johnstown Area
Genealogical Society**
1401 Graham Avenue
Windber, PA 15963
(814) 467-4950

Independent Publications and Miscellany

Appalachian Roots
(see West Virginia)

**Armstrong-Kittaning Trail Society
of Pennsylvania**
514 Penn Street
Hollidaysburg, PA 16648
(814) 695-0777
Sylva L. Emerson, Secretary-Treasurer
(Huntingdon, Blair, Cambria, Indiana
and Armstrong counties)

Bradford Landmark Society
45 East Corydon Avenue
Bradford, PA 16701
(814) 362-3906
Sally Costik, Curator
Hours: Mon, Wed & Fri 11:00–2:00

Canal Museum
Hugh Moore Park
200 South Delaware Drive
PO Box 877
Easton, PA 18044
(215) 258-7155

Family Line Publications
(see Maryland)

Fayette Families
204 Tapaingo Road, S.E.
Vienna, VA 22180-5974
Victoria Hook, Editor
Pub. *Fayette Families*, quarterly
(January, April, July, October), $15.00
per year subscription
(members have ancestors who once
resided in Fayette County,
Pennsylvania)

$15.00 per year membership in the U.S.
and Canada, $20.00 per year
membership overseas

**French and Pickering Creek
Conservation Trust, Inc.**
Rt. 2, Box 360
Pottstown, PA 19464
(215) 469-0150

**Genealogical Computing Association
of Pennsylvania (GENCAP)**
51 Hillcrest Road
Barto, PA 19504
http://libertynet.org/~gencap/

Historic Schaefferstown, Inc.
Thomas R. Brendle Memorial Library
and Museum
PO Box 307
Schaefferstown, PA 17088
(717) 949-2626
John T. Hickernell, Committee Chairman
Hours: weekends (Jun–Oct) 12:00–4:00

Historical Center
PO Box 81
Richfield, PA 17086
(717) 694-3211; (717) 694-3543
Noah L. Zimmerman; J. Lloyd Gingrich
Hours: Tue 7:00 P.M.–9:00 P.M., Sat
9:00–4:30
Pub. *Historical Center Echoes*, quarterly
$15.00 per year membership (includes
Echoes) or $20.00 per year
membership (includes *Pennsylvania
Mennonite Heritage*, published by
Lancaster Mennonite Historical
Society, and *Echoes*)

Hoenstine Rental Library
414 Montgomery Street
Hollidaysburg, PA 16648
(814) 695-0632; (814) 696-7310
Barbara Ann Hoenstine
Hours: Mon–Fri 9:00–12:00 & 1:00–
4:00
(sales of new and used books on
Pennsylvania history and genealogy;
collection of over 4,000 books for
rent)

Lancaster County Connections
PO Box 207
Hershey, PA 17033-0207
(717) 533-5662
E-mail: lcc@redrose.net
http://www.redrose/lcc
Gary T. Hawbaker, Owner/Editor
Pub. *Lancaster County Connections*,
quarterly, $17.50 per year subscription

Lancaster County Heritage
PO Box 7773
Lancaster, PA 17604-7773
Peggy Sheets Manning, C.G., Editor
Pub. *Lancaster County Heritage*,
quarterly, $15.00 per year subscription

PaGenWeb
Part of U.S. GenWeb Project
E-mail: pa@usgenweb.com
http://www.libertynet.org/~gencap/
pacounties.html
(links to other Pennsylvania resources)

**Pennsylvania Dutch Folk Culture
Society**
Baver Memorial Library
Folklife Museum
Main and Willow Streets
Lenhartsville, PA 19534
(215) 562-4803
Florence Bauer, President
Hours: Apr–May & Sept–Oct: Sat 10:00–
4:00, Sun 1:00–4:00; summer: Mon–
Sun 10:00–5:00
Pub. *Pennsylvania Dutch News and
Views*, semiannually
(Berks and neighboring counties;
Pennsylvania German folklife and
genealogy library)
$10.00 per year membership for
individuals, $12.00 for couples

**Southwest Pennsylvania
Genealogical Services**
PO Box 253
Laughlintown, PA 15655
(724) 238-3176
William L. Iscrupe, Editor/Publisher
Pub. *Saint Clair's Bedford: The History
and Genealogy of Bedford County, PA*,
quarterly, $14.00 per year
subscription; *Pennsylvania
Genealogist and Historian*, quarterly,
$16.00 per year subscription; *La
Fayette: The History and Genealogy
of Fayette County, PA*, quarterly,
$17.00 per year subscription; *Old
Westmoreland: The History and
Genealogy of Westmoreland County,
PA*, quarterly, $17.00 per year
subscription; *Somerset Past: The
History and Genealogy of Somerset
County, PA*, quarterly, $14.00 per year
subscription

Susquehanna Magazine
Rt. 1, Box 75A
Marietta, PA 17547-9983
Pub. *Susquehanna Magazine*, $15.00 per
year subscription

Warrior Trail Association, Inc.
Rt. 1, Box 35
Spraggs, PA 15362
Lucille Phillips

RHODE ISLAND

Archives and Libraries with Holdings in Genealogy

State Archives and Library

Rhode Island State Archives
337 Westminster Street
Providence, RI 02903
(401) 277-2353
http://archives.state.ri.us/
Hours: Mon–Sat 8:30–4:30
(state government records)
limited research performed by Archives staff, but written requests can contain no more than two names per request; charge for photocopies

Rhode Island State Library
Office of the Secretary of State
337 Westminster Street
Providence, RI 02903
(401) 277-2353
Gwenn Stearn, Archivist
Hours: Mon–Sat 8:30–4:30

Rhode Island Department of Library Services
300 Richmond Street
Providence, RI 02903-4222
(401) 277-2726; (401) 277-4195 FAX
http://www.dsls.state.ri.us/
(directory of Rhode Island libraries)

State Historical Society

Rhode Island Historical Society
(121 Hope Street at the corner of Power—Library location)
110 Benevolent Street (mailing address)
Providence, RI 02906
(401) 331-8575; (401) 751-7930
Reference Librarian
Hours: Tue–Sat 9:00–5:00, Sun noon–4:00
Pub. *Rhode Island History*, quarterly, back issues $5.00 each
(copies of statewide marriage and death indexes, 1853–1900)

City, County and Regional Archives and Libraries

The John Nicholas Brown Center for the Study of American Civilization
(357 Benefit Street—location)
PO Box 1880, Brown University (mailing address)
Providence, RI 02903
(401) 272-0357; (401) 272-1930 FAX

Joyce M. Botelho, Director; Denise Bastien, Assistant Director
Hours: Mon–Fri 9:00–5:00; Memorial Day–Labor Day: Mon–Fri 8:00–4:00; research by appointment only
("Our archival collections focus on the Brown family of Providence, Rhode Island.")

Brown University
The John Hay Library
20 Prospect Street
PO Box A
Providence, RI 02912
(401) 863-2146; (401) 863-2093
E-mail: rock@brown.edu (Reference)
http://www.brown.edu/facilities/University_Library/general/libraries/hay.html
Jean Rainwater, Coordinator of Reader Services
Hours: Mon–Fri 9:00–5:00
Pub. *Books at Brown*, annually, $10.00 per issue
("We do not collect with genealogy in mind or offer services geared to the needs of genealogists.")

Connecticut Valley Historical Museum
(see Massachusetts)

East Greenwich Free Library
82 Peirce Street
East Greenwich, RI 02818
(401) 884-9510
http://www.ultranet.com/~egrlib/
Robert Balliot, Information Services Librarian
Hours: Mon–Thur 10:00–8:00, Fri–Sat 10:00–4:00
(extensive Rhode Island genealogy and history sources)

Langworthy Public Library
Historical Archives
24 Spring Street
Hope Valley, RI 02832
(401) 539-2851
Lynn Thompson, Director
Hours: Library: Mon–Tue & Thur 6:00–9:00, Wed 10:00–5:00, Fri 2:00–5:00, Mon (winter) 2:00–5:00, Sat (winter) 10:00–5:00, Sat (summer) 9:00–noon; Archives: Wed 1:00–3:00, and by appointment
(local genealogical collections)

The Providence Athenaeum
251 Benefit Street
Providence, RI 02903
(401) 421-6970; (401) 421-2860 FAX
Lee Tererow, Assistant Director
Hours: Mon–Fri 8:30–5:30, staff assistance by appointment
$135.00 per year membership; no admission charge for non-members

Providence City Archives
Providence City Hall
25 Dorrance Street
Providence, RI 02903
(401) 421-7740, ext. 314 or 315
Carole B. Pace
Hours: 8:30–4:30 by appointment
(municipal documents 1636–1900)

Providence Public Library
225 Washington Street
Providence, RI 02903
(401) 455-8000
Hours: Mon 1:00–5:00, Tue & Thur 9:30–6:00, Fri–Sat 9:30–5:30

South County Museum, Inc.
Quaker Lane, Rt. 2
Newport, RI 02852
(401) 295-0498

University of Rhode Island Library
15 Lippitt Road
Kingston, RI 02881
(401) 874-2594; (401) 874-4608 FAX
http://www.library.uri.edu/Web_Files/Library_Services/Special Collections.html#TOP (Special Collections)
David C. Maslyn, Head, Special Collections
Hours: Mon–Fri 9:00–4:00

Warwick Public Library
600 Sandy Lane
Warwick, RI 02886
(401) 739-5440
Hours: Mon–Thur 9:00–9:00, Fri–Sat 9:00–5:00, Sun (Sept–May) 1:00–5:00

Westerly Public Library
Broad Street
PO Box 356
Westerly, RI 02891
(401) 596-2878; (401) 596-2877
Margaret Victoria, Head of Reference; J. Michael Barber, Reference Assistant
Hours: Mon–Wed 8:00 A.M.–9:00 P.M., Thur–Fri 8:00–5:00, Sat (except summer) 8:00–3:00

Historical Societies—Local and Regional

Barrington Preservation Society
281 Country Road
PO Box 178
Barrington, RI 02806
Jean Robertson, President
(genealogical services)

Blackstone Valley Historical Society
1873 Old Louisquisset Pike
Lincoln, RI 02865
(401) 725-BVHS
Hours: third Sun (Sept–Jun) 1:30, and by appointment

Pub. *The Landmark*, ten times per year
(monthly, September to June)
$15.00 per year membership for
individuals, $25.00 per year
membership for couples

Block Island Historical Society
Corner of Old Town Road and Ocean
Avenue
PO Box 79
Block Island, RI 02807
(401) 466-2481 (Jul–Aug); (401) 466-
5009 (all year, off season)
Robert B. Willis, Treasurer and
Genealogist
Hours: Jul–Aug: daily 10:00–4:00; Jun &
Sept–Oct: weekends
$10.00 per year membership for
individuals, $1.00 per year junior
membership (to age 16), $200.00 life
membership; search fee: discretionary
donation

Bristol Historical and Preservation Society
48 Court Street
Bristol, RI 02809
(401) 253-5705; (401) 253-8825

Burrillville Historical and Preservation Society
PO Box 93
Pascoag, RI 02859
(401) 569-5451

Coventry Historical Society
Route 117
PO Box 401
Coventry, RI 02816
Lillian Thurston, President
Hours: fourth Thur: 7:00 P.M.–9:00 P.M.
$5.00 per year membership

Cranston Historical Society
Governor Sprague Mansion
1351 Cranston Street
Cranston, RI 02920
(401) 944-9226

Glocester Heritage Society
(1181 Main Street—location)
PO Box 269 (mailing address)
Chepachet, RI 02814
(401) 568-1866
Joanne S. Anderton, Archivist
Hours: Sat 11:00–3:00, and by
appointment
$15.00 per year membership for
individuals, $25.00 per year
membership for families, $10.00 per
year membership for students and
senior citizens

Heritage Foundation of Rhode Island
Rhode Island Hospital Trust National
Bank
1 Hospital Trust Plaza
Providence, RI 02903
(401) 278-8353

Hopkinton Historical Association
Town House Road
Hopkinton, RI 02833

Jamestown Historical Society
(92 Narragansett Avenue—location)
PO Box 156 (mailing address)
Jamestown, RI 02835
(401) 423-0784
Mary Miner, Archivist
Hours: Museum: late Jun–Aug: Tue–Sat
1:00–4:00
$10.00 per year membership for
individuals, $15.00 per year
membership for families

Little Compton Historical Society
(548 West Main Road—location)
PO Box 577 (mailing address)
Little Compton, RI 02837
(401) 635-4035
Sheila Mackintosh, President
Hours: Mid-Jun to mid-Sept: Mon &
Thur–Sun 2:00–5:00

Main Street Association of Wickford
68 Main Street
Wickford, RI 02852
(401) 294-6479

Massasoit Historical Association
PO Box 203
Warren, RI 02885

Middletown Historical Society, Inc.
(Corner Prospect and Paradise Avenues,
Middletown, RI 02840—location)
PO Box 4196 (mailing address)
Middletown, RI 02842
(401) 849-1870
Stanley Grossman, President
Pub. *MHS Newsletter*, quarterly
(New England heritage)

The New England Historic Genealogical Society
(see Massachusetts)

Preservation Society of Newport County
PO Box 510
Newport, RI 02840
Pub. *Newport Gazette*, quarterly;
*Preservation Society of Newport
County Annual Report*

Newport Historical Society
82 Touro Street
Newport, RI 02840
(401) 846-0813; (401) 846-1853
Bertram Lippincott,III, C.G., Librarian
Hours: Tue–Fri 9:30–4:30, Sat 9:30–
noon
Pub. *Newport History*, quarterly;
Newport Historical Society Newsletter
(second largest genealogical collection in
Rhode Island)
$30.00 per year membership for
individuals

North Smithfield Heritage Association
PO Box 413
Slatersville, RI 02876

Pettaquamscatt Historical Society
2636 Kingstown Road
Kingston, RI 02881
(401) 783-1328
Cecilia A. Boggs, Executive Director
Hours: Tue, Thur & Sat (May–Oct)
1:00–4:00
Pub. *The Reporter*, quarterly
(history of Washington county)
$10.00 per year membership

Scituate Preservation Society, Inc.
706 Hartford Pike
PO Box 551
North Scituate, RI 02857
(401) 647-5010
Fred T. Faria, President
(genealogical services)
no costs

Tiverton Historical Society
3908 Main Road
Tiverton, RI 02878
(401) 624-8881
John L. Berg, President
Pub. *Patchwork History of Tiverton*

The Warwick Historical Society
25 Roger Williams Circle
Warren, RI 02888
(401) 737-8160; (401) 467-7647
(Wednesdays)
Mildred Longo, Librarian
Hours: Wed 9:00–1:00
(history and genealogy research center
for Warwick only)
$10.00 per year membership for
individuals

Westerly Historical Society
PO Box 91
Westerly, RI 02891
(401) 377-2602
Dwight Brown, First Vice President
$5.00–$25.00 per year membership;
search fees: $5.00 for first half-hour,
$10.00 for each additional hour

Western Rhode Island Civic Historical Society
1 Station Street
Coventry, RI 02816
(401) 397-5135
Paula Rossi, Curator
Hours: Jun–Sept: Sat 1:00–4:00

Woonsocket Historical and Preservation Society
563 South Main Street
Woonsocket, RI 02895
(401) 769-9846
Phyllis H. Thomas, President
Hours: Tue 11:00–3:00, Sat noon–4:00

LDS Family History Centers

Providence
(see Warwick)

Warwick
(401) 463-8150

Genealogical Societies

State Genealogical Society

Rhode Island Genealogical Society
49 Farm Street
Dover, MA 02030
Robert Carter Arnold
Pub. *Rhode Island Roots*, quarterly
(March, June, September, December)
$10.00 per year membership

Regional Genealogical Societies

American-Canadian Genealogical Society
(see New Hampshire)

Minnesota Genealogical Society, Yankee Branch
(see Massachusetts)

The New England Historic Genealogical Society
(see Massachusetts)

Independent Publications and Miscellany

Company of the Gloucester Light Infantry
(Dorr Drive, Chepachet, RI 02814—
location)
212 Farnum Pike
Smithfield, RI 02917
(401) 568-0034
Ens. Sheri L. Vieira, R.I.M., Secretary
(Rhode Island Historical Commands
Member; "We are an original charter
group, 1774 Rhode Island Militia.")

Foster Preservation Society
PO Box 51
Foster, RI 02825

The League of Rhode Island Historical Societies
39 Forsythia Lane
Cranston, RI 02920
(401) 942-3015
Robert Drew, President

The New England Quarterly
(see Massachusetts)

Society for the Preservation of New England Antiquities—Archives
(see Massachusetts)

Providence Preservation Society
24 Meeting Street
Providence, RI 02903
(401) 831-7440

Rhode Island Families Association
PO Box 1414
Ashburn, VA 20146-1414
E-mail: rigr@pop.erols.com
http://www.erols.com/rigr
Nellie Beaman,Editor
Pub. *Rhode Island Genealogical
Register*, annually
(index to all the wills in Rhode Island
from 1636–1850)
$35.00 per year membership for
individuals (libraries and societies
inquire)

RIGenWeb
Part of U.S. GenWeb Project
E-mail: ri@usgenweb.com
http://www.rootsweb.com/~rigenweb
(links to other Rhode Island resources)

SOUTH CAROLINA

Archives and Libraries with Holdings in Genealogy

State Archives and Library

South Carolina Department of Archives and History
1430 Senate Street
PO Box 11669
Columbia, SC 29211-1669
(803) 734-8577; (803) 734-8596
E-mail: sox@history.scdah.sc.edu
http://www.scdah.sc.edu/homepage.htm
Alexia J. Helsley, Director, Public
Programs
Hours: Tue–Fri 9:00–9:00, Sat 9:00–
6:00, Sun 1:00–6:00
Pub. *South Carolina State Gazette*,
semiannually

South Carolina State Library
1500 Senate Street
PO Box 11469
Columbia, SC 29211-1469
(803) 734-8666; (803) 734-8676 FAX;
(803) 734-7298 TTD
E-mail: reference@leo.scsl.state.sc.us
http://www.state.sc.us/scsl/
Anne M. Schneider, Director of Reader
Services
Hours: Mon–Fri 8:15-5:30, Sat 9:00–
1:00
(materials relating to South Carolina
History, not a genealogy library)

State Historical Societies

South Carolina Historical Society
Fireproof Building, 100 Meeting Street
Charleston, SC 29401-2299
(843) 723-3225; (843) 723-8584 FAX
http://www.historic.com/schs/index.html
C. Patton Hash, Research Consultant;
Stephen Hoffius, Director of
Publications
Hours: Tue–Fri 9:00–4:00, Sat 9:00–2:00
(call in advance in case of schedule
change)
Pub. *South Carolina Historical
Magazine*, quarterly; *Carologue*,
quarterly
("Historical Society maintains the most
extensive private collection of South
Carolina genealogical material; also
material on other states.")
$50.00 per year membership for
individuals or couples, $25.00 per year
membership for students; library use
fee: $5.00 per day for non-members;
research from Research Consultant:

$10.00 for search of *The South Carolina Historical and Genealogical Magazine*, index of wills transcribed by the W.P.A., W.P.A. cemetery index, and *Abstracts of Deeds to 1774*, $5.00 for search of the society's vertical file or of census indices from 1790 through 1870 (not the censuses themselves), $15.00 for search of deeds of the Charleston County Register of Mesne Conveyance, $10.00 for search of relevant county publications, $75.00 for up to four hours of unrestricted search of all materials

South Carolina Historical Association

Francis Marion College
Florence, SC 29501
Pub. *South Carolina Historical Association Proceedings*, annually

Confederation of South Carolina Local Historical Societies

1430 Senate Street
Columbia, SC 29201
(803) 734-8577
Sarah C. Spruill, President

City, County and Regional Archives and Libraries

Abbeville-Greenwood Regional Library

Greenwood County Library
North Main Street
Greenwood, SC 29646
(803) 223-4515
Hours: Mon–Tue & Thur 9:00–9:00, Wed & Fri 9:00–5:30, Sat 10:00–5:00, Sun 2:00–5:00
(houses collection of the Old Ninety Six District Chapter [SCGS] and the DAR, but has no staff to handle correspondence)

Aiken County Historical Museum

433 Newberry Street, S.W.
Aiken, SC 29801
(803) 642-2015
Nana Farris, Museum Director
Pub. *MuseNews*
(research facility)

Anderson County Museum

PO Box 8002
Anderson, SC 29622
(864) 260-4737
Donna Roper, Curator
Hours: to be established

Beaufort County Library

South Carolina Room
311 Scott Street
Beaufort, SC 29902

Col. William Bratton Chapter, S.A.R.

PO Box 440
Rock Hill, SC 29732
(803) 324-5300
John A. Gill, President
Hours: 9:00–5:00
(genealogical services)

Calhoun County Museum

Archives Library
303 Butler Street
Saint Matthews, SC 29135
(803) 874-3964
Debbie Roland, Director
Hours: 9:00–4:00 by appointment only

Camden Archives and Museum

1314 Broad Street
Camden, SC 29020-3535
(803) 425-6050
Agnes B. Corbett, Director
Hours: Mon–Fri 8:00–5:00, first Sun 1:00–5:00
("Museum with local artifacts and research library operated by City of Camden; general history and genealogy, SCDAR Library located here.")
free in-house research, $10.00 per hour for requests by mail (subject to change)

Charleston County Library

Reference Department
68 Calhoun Street
Charleston, SC 29401
(843) 723-1645
http://www.ccpl.org/opener.html
Hours: Mon–Thur 9:30–9:00, Fri–Sat 9:30–6:00, Sun 2:00–5:00
(Charleston and the Low Country)

Charleston Library Society

164 King Street
Charleston, SC 29401
(843) 723-9912
Patricia Glass Bennett, Assistant Librarian
Hours: Mon–Fri 9:30–5:30, Sat 9:30–2:00
(a full-service library and archives—limited genealogical materials are available: early South Carolina newspapers, census, city directories of Charleston from 1782)
$35.00 per year subscription fee, $3.00 per day in-person research fee

Cherokee County Public Library

300 East Rutledge Avenue
Gaffney, SC 29340
(864) 487-2711; (864) 487-2752 FAX
Anne Moseley, Director
Hours: Mon–Tue 10:00–8:00, Wed–Fri 10:00–6:00, Sat 10:00–4:00
(small library of genealogical books, microfilms of newspapersand Draper Papers)

The Citadel Archives and Museum

The Citadel, 171 Moultrie Street
Charleston, SC 29409
(843) 953-6846
Jane Yates, Director
Hours: Archives: Mon–Fri 8:30–5:00 by appointment; Museum Mon–Fri & Sun 2:00–5:00, Sat 12:00–5:00, closed for college, religious, and national holidays
(specializes in The Citadel, history of The Military College of South Carolina)

Columbia Museum

1112 Bull Street
Columbia, SC 29201
(803) 799-2810

Darlington County Library

204 North Main Street
Darlington, SC 29532
(843) 398-4940; (843) 398-4942 FAX
Sue Rainey, Director
Hours: Mon & Wed 9:00–9:00, Tue & Thur–Fri 9:00–6:00, Sat 10:00–2:00, Sun 2:00–5:00

Fairfield County Museum

Fairfield Genealogy Room
231 South Congress Street
PO Box 6
Winnsboro, SC 29180
(803) 635-9811
Mrs. Marion E. Stevenson
Hours: Wed 10:30–4:30

The Florence Museum

558 Spruce Street
Florence, SC 29501
(843) 662-3351
Dana Parker, Executive Director
Hours: Tue–Sat 10:00–5:00, Sun 2:00–5:00

Fort Jackson Museum

Fort Jackson, SC 29207
(803) 751-7419

The Genealogical and Historical Research Center

PO Box 2543
Sumter, SC 29151-2543
(803) 773-9144
Katherine Richardson, Museum Archivist
Hours: Tue–Sat 10:00–1:00 & 2:00–5:00
(specializing in Old Sumter District area history and genealogy)
$5.00 per day research fee for individuals who are not members of Sumter County Genealogical Society

Greenville County Library

Stow South Carolina Historical Collection
300 College Street
Greenville, SC 29601
(864) 242-5000, ext. 269
Joyce Borders, Head, Local Information and History Section

Hours: Mon–Fri 9:00–9:00, Sat 9:00–
6:00, Sun 2:00–6:00
(emphasis on South Carolina and
southeastern U.S.)

Gulluh Gyap
1243 Sunset Drive
Charleston, SC 29407
(843) 556-4701

Kershaw County Library
1304 Broad Street
Camden, SC 29020
(803) 425-1508; (803) 425-7180 FAX
Hours: Mon–Thur 9:00–9:00, Fri 9:00–
6:00, Sat 9:00–1:00, Sun 2:00–5:00

Lancaster County Library
313 South White Street
Lancaster, SC 29720
(803) 285-1502; (803) 285-6004 FAX
Richard A. Band, Library Director
Hours: Mon–Thur 9:00–8:00, Fri 9:00–
5:30, Sat 9:00–5:00

Laurens County Library
1017 West Main Street
Laurens, SC 29360
(864) 984-0596; (864) 984-0598 FAX
Elaine Martin
Hours: Mon & Thur 9:00–9:00, Tue–
Wed 9:00–6:00, Fri 9:00–5:00, Sat
9:00–1:00

Marion County Library
101 East Court Street
Marion, SC 29571
(843) 423-8300
Hours: Mon & Wed 9:30–8:30, Tue &
Thur 9:30–6:00, Fri 9:30–5:30, Sat
9:30–1:00

Marion County Museum
101 Willcox Avenue
PO Box 220
Marion, SC 29571
(843) 423-8299
W. Thomas Lett, Director
Hours: Tue–Fri 9:00–noon & 1:00–5:00

Newberry-Saluda Regional Library
1300 Friend Street
Newberry, SC 29108
(803) 276-0854; (803) 276-7476 FAX
Tucker Neel Taylor, Library Director
Hours: Mon–Fri 9:00–6:00, Sat 9:00–
4:00

Oconee County Library
501 West South Broad Street
Walhalla, SC 29691
(803) 638-4133
Hours: Mon–Tue 9:00–9:00, Wed–Fri
9:00–6:00, Sat 9:00–1:00

Ohoopee Regional Library
(see Georgia)

Orangeburg County Library
510 Louis Street, N.E.
PO Box 1367
Orangeburg, SC 29115
(803) 531-4636

Capers B. Bull, Jr.
Hours: Mon–Tue 10:00–9:00, Wed–Fri
10:00–6:00, Sat 9:00–5:00

**Pendleton District Historical,
Recreational and Tourism
Commission**
125 East Queen Street
PO Box 565
Pendleton, SC 29670
(864) 646-3782; (864) 646-2506 FAX
E-mail: pendtour@innova.net
Donna Roper, Assistant Director
Hours: Mon–Fri 9:00–4:30
Pub. *Friends of the Pendleton District
Commission Newsletter*, three times
per year
("We are a three-county government
agency; our work includes
maintaining a local history/genealogy
archives and support library, as
well as tourism promotion, festivals,
etc.")
$25.00–$250.00 per year membership

Pickens County Library
110 West First Avenue
Easley, SC 29640
(864) 859-9679
Kay Pettit
Hours: Mon–Thur 9:00–9:00, Fri 9:00–
6:00, Sat 9:00–4:00, Sun 2:30–5:30

Rice Museum
Front and Screven Streets
PO Box 902
Georgetown, SC 29440
(843) 546-7423

Richland County Public Library
1431 Assembly Street, #8
Columbia, SC 29201-3101

South Carolina State Museum
South Carolina Museum Commission
301 Gervais Street
Columbia, SC 29201
(803) 737-4921
Overton G. Ganong, Director

**Spartanburg County Public
Libraries**
Chesnee Branch Library
716 South Alabama Street
Chesnee, SC 29323
(864) 461-2423
Mary Mills, Genealogical Advisor; Lynn
Goen, Staff Genealogist; Mike Seagle,
Head Librarian
Hours: Mon, Wed & Fri 12:00–6:00,
Tue & Thur 10:00–8:00, Sat 10:00–
4:00
(the bulk of the genealogical collection
has been moved to Spartanburg
County, Public Libraries, Spartanburg,
except for vertical files of families and
some abstracts)

**Spartanburg County Public
Libraries**
151 South Church Street
Spartanburg, SC 29306-3241
(864) 596-3508
Martha Dickens, Local History/
Genealogy Librarian
Hours: Mon–Fri 9:00–9:00, Sat 9:00–
6:00, Sun 1:30–6:00
(specializes in South Carolina; recently
acquired Mary Mills collection from
Chesnee Branch Library)

Troy Public Library
(see Alabama)

University of South Carolina
University South Caroliniana Society
The South Caroliniana Library
Columbia, SC 29208
(803) 777-3131; (803) 777-3132; (803)
777-5183 (Manuscripts)
E-mail: rcopp@tcl.sc.edu
http://www.sc.edu/library/socar/
Roberta V. H. Copp, Head, Book
Division
Hours: Library: Mon, Wed & Fri 8:30–
5:00, Tue & Thur 8:30–8:00, Sat 9:00–
5:00; schedule varies during
intersession periods; Manuscripts:
Mon–Fri 8:30–5:00, Sat 9:00–1:00
photocopying: 35¢ per page in house,
50¢ per page plus $5.00 postage and
handling by mail

York County Library
Local History Collection
138 East Black Street
PO Box 10032
Rock Hill, SC 29731
(803) 324-3055
Mary Mallaney
Hours: Mon–Thur 9:00–9:00, Fri–Sat
9:00–6:00
search fees: $10.00 per hour, photocopies
25¢ per page, 50¢ per copy from
microfilm ("will not do detailed
lineage requests, only search for
specific questions; contact before
sending money").

Historical Societies—
Local and Regional

Abbeville County Historical Society
202 Church Street
Abbeville, SC 29620
(864) 459-2466

**Abbeville District Historical
Association**
PO Box 578
McCormick, SC 29835
(864) 465-2347

Abbeville Historic Preservation Commission
313 Greenville
Abbeville, SC 29620
(864) 459-4297

Aiken County Historical Commission
433 Newberry Street, S.W.
Aiken, SC 29801
(803) 649-4658

Aiken County Historical Society
PO Box 1775
Aiken, SC 29802
(803) 649-9653
Edward Cushman, President
Pub. *Journal of the ACHS*

Allendale County Historical Society
University of South Carolina,
  Salkehatchie
Allendale, SC 29810
(803) 584-3446

Anderson County Historical Society
PO Drawer 785
Anderson, SC 29622
(864) 646-3782 (information)
Donna Roper, Curator
Pub. *New Highland Sentinel*,
  semiannually (April and October)
$6.00 per year membership for
  individuals, $10.00 per year
  membership for couples

Bamberg County Historical and Genealogical Society
604 East Railroad Avenue
Bamberg, SC 29003
(803) 245-2901

Barnwell County Historical Society
Rt. 2, Box 166
Blackville, SC 29817
Mrs. D. Ross

Beaufort County Historical Society
PO Box 55
Beaufort, SC 29901-0055

Berkeley County Historical Society
Berkeley County Historic Preservation
  Commission
1706 Ranger Drive
Cross, SC 29436

The Bluffton Historical Preservation Society, Inc.
PO Box 742
Bluffton, SC 29910
(803) 757-3650 (Mrs. Caldwell); (803)
  757-6604 FAX
Mrs. Arthur B. Elliott, Secretary; Mrs.
  B. M. Caldwell
Pub. *Newsletter*, annually
$10.00 per year membership for
  individuals, $15.00 per year
  membership for families, $100.00 life
  membership

Calhoun County Historical Society
Calhoun County Museum/Cultural
  Center
(303 Butler Street, Saint Matthews—
  location)
PO Box 367 (mailing address)
Cameron, SC 29030
Debbie U. Roland, Director
Hours: by appointment only
Pub. *Calhoun County Historical Society
  Monthly*

Charleston City Archives and Records
701 East Bay Street
Charleston, SC 29402
(843) 724-7301; (843) 720-3897 FAX
Jane Boyd, Archivist
Hours: Mon–Fri 8:30–5:00
("Primarily a records storage facility/
  warehouse for modern municipal
  records; there are no records stored
  here which would be of much
  assistance to researchers.")

Cherokee Historic and Preservation Society, Inc.
Winnie Davis Hall of History
Limestone College
PO Box 998
Gaffney, SC 29340
(864) 489-4172

Cherokee Historical Society
PO Box 998
Gaffney, SC 29340
Sarah Blanton

Chester County Historical Society Museum
McAlily Street
Chester, SC 29706
Gary Roberts, Museum Director
Pub. *CCHSM Quarterly Newsletter*

Chesterfield Historical Society
209 Green Street
Cheraw, SC 29520
Mrs. J. H. Wannamaker

Clarendon County Historical Society
3509 Lake Avenue, Apartment 1213
Columbia, SC 29206-5185
Mrs. W. H. Threatt

Coker College
Pee Dee Heritage Center
(address withheld upon request)

Darlington County Historical Commission
204 Hewitt Street
Darlington, SC 29532
(843) 398-4710
Horace F. Rudisill, Director; Doris G.
  Gandy, Assistant Director
Hours: Mon–Fri 8:30–5:00
Darlington County records prior to 1900,
  courthouse records, newspapers,
  family name records)

Darlington County Historical Society
200 Woodland Drive
Darlington, SC 29532
Mrs. Blanding Clarkson

Dillon County Historical Society
PO Box 187
Lake View, SC 29563
(843) 759-2773

Edgefield County Historical Society
320 Norris Street
PO Box 174
Edgefield, SC 29824
(803) 637-5306
Joanne T. Rainsford, President
Hours: Mon–Fri 9:00–5:00; tours by
  appointment
$2.00 donation

Fairfield County Historical Commission
Fairfield County Museum
231 South Congress Street
Winnsboro, SC 29180
(803) 635-9811

Florence Heritage Foundation, Inc.
(1159 Brunwood, Florence, SC 29501—
  location)
PO Box 1909 (mailing address)
Florence, SC 29503
(843) 662-3258

Georgetown County Historical Commission
PO Box 902
Georgetown, SC 29440
(843) 546-7423

Georgetown County Historical Society
719 Prince Street
Georgetown, SC 29440
Leta Stearns

Greenville County Historical Society
201 Crescent Avenue
Greenville, SC 29602
Nancy Hassold
Pub. *Greenville County Historical
  Society Proceedings and Papers*,
  irregularly

Greenwood County Historical Society
Abbeville-Greenwood Regional Library
Greenwood County Library
North Main Street
Greenwood, SC 29646
Hours: Library: Mon–Tue & Thur 9:00–
  9:00, Wed & Fri 9:00–5:30, Sat 10:00–
  5:00, Sun 2:00–5:00

Hampton County Historical Society
79 Second Street East
Estill, SC 29918
Mrs. S. G. Solomons

Hilton Head Island Historical Society
PO Box 5492
Hilton Head Island, SC 29938-5492
Thomas McCammon

Historic Camden Revolutionary War Site
222 Broad Street
PO Box 710
Camden, SC 29020-0710
(803) 432-9841; (803) 432-3815 FAX
Joanna B. Craig, Director
Hours: Museum shop: Mon 10:00–5:00;
   Guided tours: Tue–Sat 10:00–5:00;
   Self-guided tour: Sun 1:00–5:00
Pub. *Historic Camden Newsletter*,
   annually
(a museum offering help with
   genealogical research)
$25.00 per year membership for
   individuals, $35.00 per year
   membership for families, $15.00 per
   year membership for students and
   senior citizens, $50.00 per year
   Contributing membership, $100.00 per
   year Sustaining membership, $250.00
   per year Leadership membership,
   $500.00 per year Fellow membership,
   $1,000.00 per year Patron
   membership, $2,500.00 Angel
   membership, $5,000.00 per year
   Mentor membership

Horry County Historic Preservation Commission
706 15th Avenue, South
North Myrtle Beach, SC 29582
(843) 272-6303

Jasper County Historical Society
PO Box 1267
Ridgeland, SC 29936
(843) 726-8126
Zenie Ingram

Kershaw County Historical Society
Bonds Conway House
811 South Fair Street
PO Box 501
Camden, SC 29020
(803) 425-1123
Kathleen P. Stahl, Executive Secretary
Hours: Thur 1:00–5:00
Pub. *Update—Newsletter of the Kershaw
   County Historical Society*, quarterly
("We publish books on county history;
   we do not do genealogical research.")
$20.00 per year membership for
   individuals, $30.00 per year member-
   ship for families, $15.00 per year
   membership for senior citizens, $35.00
   per year membership for businesses

Lancaster County Society for Historical Preservation
PO Box 1132
Lancaster, SC 29721
(803) 285-9455

D. Lindsay Pettus, President
Pub. *Newsletter*, quarterly
$20.00 per year membership

Laurens County Historical Society
Rt. 2, Box 675
Laurens, SC 29360
Mrs. Fred Irwin

Lexington County Historical Society
231 Devin Drive
Lexington, SC 29070
Laura S. McMahan, President

Lynches River Historical Society
College Street
PO Box 26
Bethune, SC 29009

Marion County Historical Society
PO Box 188
Marion, SC 29571
(843) 464-8685 (President)
Reginald McDaniel, President
Pub. *Newsletter*, irregularly
$5.00 per year membership for
   individuals

Marlborough Historical Society Archives
121 South Marlboro Street
Bennettsville, SC 29512
(843) 479-5624
Susan Turpin, Director
Hours: by appointment only
Pub. *Marlborough Historical Society
   Newsletter*, quarterly
(history of Marlboro County and Pee
   Dee area)
$10.00 per year membership for
   individuals, $15.00 per year
   membership for couples, $20.00 per
   year membership for families; search
   fees vary

McCormick County Historical Commission
PO Box 578
McCormick, SC 29835
(864) 465-2347

McCormick County Historical Society
PO Box 230
Mount Carmel, SC 29840
(864) 391-2131
Wes McAllister
Hours: 8:00–5:00
("We are an educational type organization
   meeting semiannually, fall and spring)

Newberry County Historical Society
PO Box 393
Newberry, SC 29108
Mrs. Sudie Crump Wicker

North Augusta Historical Society
107 West Pine Grove Avenue
North Augusta, SC 29841
(803) 279-2951
Lark W. Jones, President

Orangeburg County Historical Commission
Courthouse
PO Box 219
Orangeburg, SC 29115
(803) 534-5176

The Orangeburg County Historical Society, Inc.
Bull and Middleton Streets
PO Box 1881
Orangeburg, SC 29116-1881
Alfred S. Gramling, Director, A. S.
   Salley Archives
Hours: by appointment only
Pub. *OCHS, Inc. Newsletter*, two or three
   times per year as needed

Orangeburg Historical and Genealogical Society, Inc.
467 Palmetto Parkway, N.E.
Orangeburg, SC 29115
(803) 536-1305
Lawrence C. Bryant, Ph.D., President
Pub. *Orangeburg Historical and
   Genealogical Record*

Pickens County Historical Society
104 North Lewis Street
PO Box 775
Pickens, SC 29671
(864) 878-7847
Anne Poulos, President
Pub. *Pickens County Historical Museum*

Piedmont Historical Society
PO Box 8096
Spartanburg, SC 29305
Faye Berry, Co-editor
Pub. *Upper South Carolina Genealogy
   and History*, quarterly
(history and genealogy for upstate South
   Carolina)
$20.00 per year membership

Saluda County Historical Society
Law Range
PO Box 22
Saluda, SC 29138
(864) 445-8550
Mary B. Parkman, President
Pub. *SCHS Newsletter*

Southern Studies Institute
(see Louisiana)

Spartanburg County Historical Association
(501 Otis Boulevard in Regional
   Museum—location)
PO Box 887 (mailing address)
Spartanburg, SC 29304-0887
(864) 596-3501 phone and FAX
Carolyn Creal, Curator
Hours: Mon–Fri 9:00–5:00
Pub. *The Drover' Post*, quarterly
$15.00 per year membership for
   individuals, $25.00 per year
   membership for families, $5.00 per
   year membership for students

The Summerville Preservation Society
(201 West Caroline Avenue—location)
PO Box 511 (mailing address)
Summerville, SC 29484
(843) 873-1006
Heyward G. Hutson, President
Hours: no regular hours

Sumter County Historical Commission
(Sumter County Cultural Center, 155 Haynsworth Street, Room 142, Patriot Hall—location)
PO Box 306 (mailing address)
Sumter, SC 29151-0306
(803) 436-2257
James M. Eaves, Corresponding Secretary and Archivist
Hours: Wed & Thur 1:00–4:00
(historical preservation, publications of a historical orientation, erecting of historical markers, and research into items of interest to Sumter County, including genealogical studies: special project: Afro-American Sumter County, South Carolina genealogies)
queries answered at no cost, except for copying, if found in archives

Three Rivers Historical Society
Main Street
PO Box 811
Hemingway, SC 29554
(843) 558-2355
Nell G. Morris, Registrar and Publications Chairman
Hours: usually 9:00–5:00, call for appointment
Pub. *The Three Rivers Chronicle*, quarterly
$12.00 per year membership

Union County Historical Foundation
(Corner East Main and South Church Streets—location)
PO Drawer 220 (mailing address)
Union, SC 29379
(864) 427-3134
Thomas E. Bishop, Curator
Hours: by appointment, except summer and Nov–Dec; Museum: first Sat & Sun (Feb–Nov) 3:00–5:00, and by appointment; meetings: fourth Tue (Feb, May, Aug, Nov)
Pub. *Historical Newsletter*, semiannually from $5.00 per year membership

Williamsburg County Historical Society
124 South Academy Street
PO Box 24
Kingstree, SC 29556
(843) 354-7124
Samuel McIntosh

York County Historical Society
PO Box 3061
Rock Hill, SC 29730
Dr. Lucille Delano

LDS Family History Centers

Charleston
(803) 766-6017

Columbia
(803) 782-7141

Genealogical Societies

State Genealogical Society

South Carolina Genealogical Society (SCGS)
PO Box 16236
Greenville, SC 29606
Pub. *The Carolina Herald*, semiannually; *South Carolina Genealogical Newsletter*, quarterly

SCGS Chapters

Anderson County Chapter (SCGS)
PO Box 5743
Anderson, SC 29623

Catawba-Wateree Chapter (SCGS)
Camden Archives and Museum
1314 Broad Street
Camden, SC 29020
Shelby B. Pittman, Editor
Pub. *Catawba-Wateree Messenger*, monthly
(covering Kershaw and Lancaster counties, South Carolina)
$15.00 per year membership

Charleston Chapter (SCGS)
PO Box 20266
Charleston, SC 29413-0266
Doris O'Brien, Secretary; Jack Garves, Membership
Pub. *Low Country Courier*, ten times per year
$12.00 per year membership for individuals, $18.00 per year membership for families, $8.00 per year Associate membership; queries accepted

Columbia Chapter (SCGS)
PO Box 11353
Columbia, SC 29211
Sylvia Castles, Archivist

Hours: by appointment
Pub. *The Columbia Journal*, irregularly
$12.00 per year membership for individuals, $16.00 per year membership for families, $7.00 Associate membership

Dutch Fork Chapter (SCGS)
PO Box 481
Chapin, SC 29036
(803) 279-0322
E-mail: lujon@worldnet.att.net
John C. Eargle, President
Hours: meetings: third Wed 10:00 A.M.–11:00 A.M.
Pub. *Dutch Fork Digest*, quarterly
(dedicated to research of families with origins in the Dutch Fork section of South Carolina; family name queries, family histories)
$20.00 per year membership for individuals, $25.00 per year membership for families

Fairfield Chapter (SCGS)
PO Box 696
Winnsboro, SC 29180

Georgetown Chapter (SCGS)
PO Box 712
Georgetown, SC 29442-0712

Greenville Chapter (SCGS)
PO Box 16236
Greenville, SC 29606
Pub. *Greenville Chapter Newsletter-South Carolina Genealogical Society*, monthly

Hilton Head Island Chapter (SCGS)
Hilton Head Island Genealogical Society
PO Box 5492
Hilton Head, SC 29938-5492
(includes north central upstate area: Chester, York, Lancaster, Union and Fairfield counties)

Laurens County Chapter (SCGS)
PO Box 1217
Laurens, SC 29360-1217

Lexington Chapter SCGS
Lexington County Genealogical Association
PO Box 1442
Lexington, SC 29072
Pub. *Lexington Genealogical Exchange*, quarterly, $5.00 per issue
$20.00 per year membership

Old Darlington District Chapter (SCGS)
201 Green Street
Hartsville, SC 29550
(843) 332-1071
John L. Andrews, Jr., President
Pub. *Old Darlington District Flag*, quarterly
$15.00 per year membership

Old Edgefield District Chapter (SCGS)

Old Edgefield District Archives
  Genealogical Society
104 Courthouse Square
PO Box 546
Edgefield, SC 29824-0546
(803) 637-5652
Laurie Robinson, Director; Carol Bryan,
  Editor
Hours: Mon–Fri 9:00–4:00
Pub. *The Quill*, bimonthly
$25.00 per year membership

Old Newberry District Chapter (SCGS)

PO Box 154
Newberry, SC 29108-0154
(803) 276-4097
E-mail: desease@netside.com
David E. Sease, Treasurer
Hours: monthly meeting
Pub. *Old Newberry District Quarterly*
$20.00 per year membership for
  individuals, $25.00 per year
  membership for families of two
  persons at the same address

Old Ninety Six District Chapter (SCGS)

PO Box 3468
Greenwood, SC 29648
(864) 223-7374 phone and FAX
Henrietta R. Morton, Editor
Hours: Abbeville-Greenwood Regional
  Library: Mon–Tue & Thur 9:00–9:00,
  Wed & Fri 9:00–5:30, Sat 10:00–5:00,
  Sun 2:00–5:00; meetings third Sun
  except Jul–Aug & Dec
Pub. *Genealogical Roots and Branches
  (GRAB)*, quarterly, free newsletter
  exchange
(western South Carolina: Old Abbeville
  District, Old 96 District)
$14.00 per year membership for
  individuals, $21.00 per year
  membership for families, $10.00 per
  year Associate membership
  (individuals who are already members
  of one of the twenty chapters of
  SCGS)

Old Pendleton District Chapter (SCGS)

247 Cross Hill Road
Easley, SC 29640-8857
(864) 859-2392
E-mail: lgcheek@aol.com
Linda Gale Smith Cheek, Editor
Pub. *Old Pendleton District Chapter
  Newsletter*, nine times per year
  (monthly, except July, August and
  December) (contains information on
  Pickens, Anderson and Oconee
  counties, South Carolina, formerly Old
  Pendleton District and Pickens
  District)

$20.00 per year membership for
  individuals, $25.00 per year
  membership for families

Old Saint Bartholomew Chapter (SCGS)

125 Wade Hampton
Walterboro, SC 29488

Pee Dee Chapter (SCGS)

400 North Main Street
PO Box 1428
Marion, SC 29571
Dorothy D. McIntyre, Treasurer
Hours: Tue 2:00–5:00
Pub. *Pee Dee Queue*, bimonthly
$15.00 per year membership for
  individuals, $17.00 per year
  membership for families

Pinckney District Chapter (SCGS)

(385 South Spring Street, Spartanburg,
  SC 29301—location)
PO Box 5281 (mailing address)
Spartanburg, SC 29304
Mike Becknell, President
Pub. *Bulletin*, quarterly (March, June,
  September, December)
(emphasis on Spartanburg, Cherokee and
  Union counties)
$13.00 per year membership for
  individuals, $19.00 per year
  membership for two persons (one
  mailing), $9.00 per year Associate
  membership (member of another
  chapter of SCGS)

Sumter County Genealogical Society

(Old Carnegie Library Building, Liberty
  Street, Sumter, SC 29150—location)
PO Box 2543 (mailing address)
Sumter, SC 29151-2543
(803) 773-9144
Dorothy Kinney Reynolds, President
Hours: Tue–Sat 10:00–1:00 & 2:00–5:00
Pub. *The Sumter Black River Watchman*,
  nine times per year (monthly, except
  June–August)
(has U.D.C. applications and the Janie
  Revill files)
$15.00 per year membership for
  individuals (includes membership in
  and publications of South Carolina
  Genealogical Society), $22.00 per year
  membership for families, $10.00 per
  year Associate membership (members
  of another chapter of SCGS)

Regional Genealogical Societies

Aiken-Barnwell Genealogical Society

PO Box 415
Aiken, SC 29801-0415
(803) 648-3898
William S. Young, President

Hours: Mon, Wed & Fri 10:00–5:00,
  Tue & Thur 12:00–9:00, Sat 9:00–
  1:00
Pub. *Newsletter*, quarterly; *Journal*,
  semiannually
$13.00 per year membership

Carolinas Genealogical Society (Upper-Central South Carolina)

(see North Carolina)

Chester District Genealogical Society

PO Box 336
Richburg, SC 29729-0336
Jean Nichols, Editor
Hours: by appointment
Pub. *The Bulletin*, quarterly
(serves the upper central part of South
  Carolina: Chester, Lancaster, York,
  Fairfield, and Union counties; has
  surname book listing members
  and up to ten surnames they're
  searching)
$16.00 per year membership for
  individuals

Huxford Genealogical Society, Inc.

(see Georgia)

Orangeburg Historical and Genealogical Society, Inc.

467 Palmetto Parkway, N.E.
Orangeburg, SC 29115
(803) 536-1305
Lawrence C. Bryant, Ph.D., President
Pub. *Orangeburg Historical and
  Genealogical Record*

Independent Publications and Miscellany

Appalachian Roots

(see West Virginia)

Genealogical Institute

(see Virginia)

Genealogy Books and Consultation

(see Texas)

Hunting for Bears Genealogical and Historical Society

(see Alabama)

Mountain Press

(see Tennessee)

SCGenWeb

Part of U.S. GenWeb Project
E-mail: sc@usgenweb.com
http://www.geocities.com/Heartland/
  Hills/3837/
(links to other South Carolina resources)

The South Carolina Magazine of
Ancestral Research (SCMAR)
PO Box 21766
Columbia, SC 29221
(803) 772-6919
Brent H. Holcomb, Editor
Pub. *The South Carolina Magazine of*
Ancestral Research, quarterly, $27.50
per year subscription

Southern Genealogist's Exchange
Society
(see Florida)

SOUTH DAKOTA

Archives and Libraries with Holdings in Genealogy

State Archives and Library

South Dakota State Archives
Cultural Heritage Center
900 Governors Drive
Pierre, SD 57501-2217
(605) 773-3804; (605) 773-6041 FAX
E-mail: archref@chc.state.sd.us
http://www.state.sd.us/state/executive/
deca/cultural/archives.htm
Richard L. Popp, State Archivist
Hours: Mon–Fri 9:00–4:30, except legal
holidays

South Dakota State Library
Memorial Building Branch
800 Governors Drive
Pierre, SD 57501-2294
(605) 773-3131; (605) 773-4369; (800)
423-6665; (605) 773-4950 FAX
E-mail: refrequest@stlib.state.sd.us
http://www.state.sd.us/state/executive/
deca/ST_LIB/st_lib.htm
Dayton W. Canaday, History; Laura
Glum, Genealogy
Hours: Mon–Fri 8:00–5:00

State Historical Society

South Dakota State Historical
Society
South Dakota State Archives
Cultural Heritage Center
900 Governors Drive
Pierre, SD 57501-2217
(605) 773-3804 (Archives); (605) 773-
6041 FAX (Archives)
E-mail: archref@chc.state.sd.us
http://www.state.sd.us/state/executive/
deca/cultural/archives.htm
Richard L. Popp, State Archivist
Hours: Archives: Mon–Fri 9:00–4:30,
except legal holidays
Pub. *South Dakota History*, quarterly;
History Notes, biannually
$30.00 per year membership

City, County and Regional Archives and Libraries

Adams Museum
54 Sherman
PO Box 252
Deadwood, SD 57732
(605) 578-1714
Carolee Smith-Rogers, Curator

Hours: Oct 1–Apr 30: Tue–Sat 10:00–
4:00, Sun noon–4:00; May 1–Sept 30:
Mon–Sat 9:00–6:00, Sun 9:00–5:00
(museum archives)
search fee: $50.00 per hour

Augustana College
The Center for Western Studies
28th and Summit Streets
PO Box 727
Sioux Falls, SD 57197
(605) 336-4007
Don L. Hofsommer, Ph.D., Executive
Director

Belle Fourche Public Library
905 Fifth Avenue
Belle Fourche, SD 57717-1702
(605) 892-4407
Pat Engebretson, Librarian
Hours: Mon–Thur 10:00–7:00, Fri–Sat
10:00–5:00

Black Hills Mining Museum
(323 West Main—location)
PO Box 694 (mailing address)
Lead, SD 57754
(605) 584-1605
Donald D. Toms, Curator
Hours: May–Oct: Mon–Sun 9:00–5:00
Pub. *BHMM Newsletter*
("Black Hills mining history, Lead
historical and genealogical
information)
$5.00 per year membership

Brookings Public Library
515 Third Street
Brookings, SD 57006
(605) 692-9407; (605) 692-9386
E-mail: elandau@sdln.net
www.brookings.com/library/
Elvita Landau, Director
Hours: Mon–Thur 10:00–9:00, Fri
10:00–5:00, Sat 9:00–5:00, Sun
(except Aug) 2:00–5:00

Leland D. Case Library for Western
Historical Studies
E. Y. Berry Library Learning Center
Black Hills State University
University Station, Box 9548
Spearfish, SD 57799
(605) 642-6361
Colleen Kirby, Special Collections
Librarian
Hours: Mon–Fri (when school is in
session) 8:00–noon & 2:00–5:00

Center for Great Plains Studies
(see Kansas)

Center for Great Plains Study
(see Nebraska)

Dacotah Prairie Museum
21 South Main Street
PO Box 395
Aberdeen, SD 57402-0395
(605) 622-7117

Sue Gates, Director
Hours: Office: Mon–Fri 8:00–5:00;
  Galleries: Tue–Fri 9:00–5:00, Sat–Sun
  1:00–4:00
Pub. *Dacotah Prairie Times*, quarterly
(Brown County, SD, history, oral history
  tapes, family history files, newspapers,
  city directories)
$25.00 per year membership; search:
  $5.00 per hour plus copies at 15¢ per
  page

Deadwood Public Library
435 Williams Street
Deadwood, SD 57732-1113
(605) 578-2821; (605) 578-2170 FAX
E-mail: tdavis@sdln.net
Terri Davis, Director
Hours: Mon–Wed 10:00–8:00, Thur–Sat
  noon–4:00
(primarily Deadwood family
  information, limited information for
  remainder of Lawrence County, index
  to newspapers from 1876)
archival search fee: $5.00 minimum, plus
  photocopies at 20¢ per page and
  postage

**Eureka Pioneer Museum of
McPherson County, Inc.**
(Highway #10—location)
1210 North Lake Drive (mailing address)
Eureka, SD 57437
(605) 284-2711; (605) 284-2987 (Home)
Edmund Opp, Curator
Hours: Wed–Fri 9:00–5:00, Sat–Sun
  2:00–5:00
Pub. *Eureka Pioneer Museum of
  McPherson County, Inc.*, as needed,
  free subscription
$5.00 per year membership for
  individuals, $30.00 per year
  membership for businesses; free
  admission

**Friends of the Middle Border
Museum of American Indian and
Pioneer Life**
(1311 South Duff Street—location)
PO Box 1071 (mailing address)
Mitchell, SD 57301
(605) 996-2122; (605) 996-0323 FAX
Chris Hanson Executive Director
Hours: Jun–Aug: Mon–Sat 8:00–6:00;
  May & Sept: Mon–Fri 9:00–5:00, Sat–
  Sun 1:00–5:00; Oct–Apr: by
  appointment
Pub. *Middle Border Bulletin*, quarterly
$15.00 per year membership for
  individuals, $30.00 per year
  membership for families, $50.00 per
  year membership for businesses and
  organizations

**High Plains Heritage Center
Museum**
825 Heritage Drive
PO Box 542
Spearfish, SD 57783

(605) 642-9378
Leo E. Giacometto, Executive Director
Hours: Mon–Sun 9:00–5:00
$200.00 life membership

Klein Foundation, Inc.
1820 West Grand Crossing
Mobridge, SD 57601
(605) 845-7243
Diane Kindt, Director
Hours: Mon & Wed–Fri 9:00–noon &
  1:00–5:00, Sat–Sun 1:00–5:00
(collection of pioneer and Native
  American artifacts from the Dakota
  Plains)

Mitchell Public Library
221 North Duff Street
Mitchell, SD 57301-2596
(605) 996-6693
Sandra Spanos, Assistant Librarian
Hours: winter: Mon–Thur 10:00–
  8:00, Fri–Sat 10:00–6:00, Sun
  2:00–5:00; summer: Mon–Sat
  10:00–6:00
(genealogical material available through
  Online Computer Library Center
  [OCLC] member libraries)

Alexander Mitchell Public Library
519 South Kline Street
Aberdeen, SD 57401-2596
(605) 626-7097
Shirley Arment, Reference and
  Genealogy Librarian
Hours: Mon–Thur 9:00–9:00, Fri 9:00–
  6:00, Sat 1:00–5:00, Sun (Sept–Jun)
  1:00–5:00

Museum of the Great Plains
(see Oklahoma)

W. H. Over State Museum
South Dakota State Historical Society,
  USD
414 East Clark Street
Vermillion, SD 57069
(605) 677-5228
Julia Vidicka, Museum Director

Prayer Rock Museum
Main Street
Britton, SD 57430

Rapid City Public Library
610 Quincy Street
Rapid City, SD 57701
(605) 394-4171
Eka M. Parkison
Hours: Mon–Thur 9:00–9:00, Fri–Sat
  9:00–5:30, Sun (Sept–May) 1:00–
  5:00

Robinson State Museum
Association of South Dakota Museums
(Memorial Building, 500 East Capitol,
  Pierre, SD 57102—location)
200 West Sixth Street (mailing address)
Sioux Falls, SD 57102
(605) 773-3797

Siouxland Libraries
201 North Main Avenue
Sioux Falls, SD 57104
(605) 367-7082
Doug Murdock, Reference Department
  Head
Hours: Mon–Thur 9:30–9:00, Fri 9:30–
  6:00, Sat 9:30–5:00, Sun (Sept–May)
  1:00–4:00

Smith-Zimmermann State Museum
Dakota State College
Madison, SD 57042·
(605) 256-5308; (605) 256-5643 FAX
E-mail: brashiec@columbia.dsu.edu
Dr. Clyde Brashier
Hours: Thur–Sun 1:00–4:30, and by
  appointment
Pub. *Heritage Herald*, quarterly
$5.00 per year membership

State Fair Pioneer Museum
(State Fairgrounds—location)
479 Montana, S.W. (mailing address)
Huron, SD 57350

University of South Dakota Library
Vermillion, SD 57069

Verendrye Museum
PO Box 643
Fort Pierre, SD 57532

Vermillion Public Library
18 Church Street
Vermillion, SD 57069
(605) 624-2741
Jane Larson, Director
Hours: Mon–Thur 10:00–9:00, Fri
  10:00–6:00, Sat–Sun 10:00–5:00
(summer closed Sun)

Historical Societies—
Local and Regional

Bowdle Historical Society
North of Main Street
Bowdle, SD 57428
Erma Maier, President

Brule County Historical Society
Rt. 1, Box 175
Pukwana, SD 57370
(605) 894-4337

Butte County Historical Society, Inc.
PO Box 2
Newell, SD 57760
(605) 456-2938
Tim Velder, President
$3.00 per year membership

**Charles Mix County Historical
Society**
Wagner, SD 57380
(605) 384-5642

Clark County Historical Society
(Beauvais Heritage Museum, HiWay 212
   and Dakota Street—location)
100 South Cloud
Clark, SD 57225
Ailene Luckhurst, President
Hours: by appointment; Heritage Day:
   second Sun after the second Sat in Jun
Pub. *Newsletter*, annually
$3.00 per year membership for
   individuals, $5.00 per year
   membership for families, $25.00 per
   year membership for businesses

**Codington County Historical
Society, Inc.**
27 First Avenue, S.E.
Watertown, SD 57201
(605) 886-7335
Joanita Kant Monteith, Executive
   Director
Hours: Tue–Sat 1:00–5:00, mornings by
   appointment
Pub. *CCHS Newsletter*, bimonthly
   (Codington County history)
$10.00 per year membership for
   individuals

Custer County Historical Society
PO Box 826
Custer, SD 57730

Deuel County Historical Society, Inc.
Clear Lake, SD 57226
(605) 874-2397

Douglas County Historical Society
(Courthouse Grounds—location)
PO Box 638 (mailing address)
Armour, SD 57313
(605) 724-2129
Sharon Wiese, President
Hours: by appointment
(family histories on file)
search fee: SASE

Dunham Historical Society
(107 West Main, Jerauld County Pioneer
   Museum, Dean Annex—location)
Rt. 2, Box 215 (mailing address)
Wessington Springs, SD 57382-9006
(605) 539-1852
Roberta Unruh, Curator
Hours: Thur–Fri 10:00–noon & 1:30–
   4:30, and by appointment
("We are developing genealogy and
   history files for former and present
   residents, organizations, clubs,
   schools, business, military, city and
   county history, agriculture, etc.")

Fall River County Historical Society
Rt. 1, Box 180
Hot Springs, SD 57747
(605) 745-4725
Mabel M. Gillis, President
Hours: first Mon in Jun–after Labor Day:
   9:00–5:00
free to public, donations accepted

Faulk County Historical Society
PO Box 584
Faulkton, SD 57438
(605) 598-4285
Bonnie Wuger, President; Beverly
   Brewer, Secretary
Hours: Pickler Mansion Museum: 1
   May–Labor Day: daily 1:00–5:00
$5.00 per year membership

Gary Historical Association
Gary, SD 57237
(605) 272-5553; (605) 272-5267

Grant County Historical Society
Third Avenue and Third Street
Milbank, SD 57252
Alfred Pay, President
Pub. *GCHS Newsletter*

**Gregory County Historical Society,
Inc.**
PO Box 376
Burke, SD 57523
(605) 775-2641

Heartland Historical Society, Inc.
622 Utah, S.E.
Huron, SD 57350
(605) 352-4623
Ivan L. Loesch, President
Pub. *Heartland Highlights*

Hurley Historical Society
PO Box 302
Hurley, SD 57036
(605) 238-5725

**Hyde County Historical and
Genealogical Society**
Star Route C, Box 41
Holabird, SD 57540
(605) 852-2543
Birgit Hinkle
Hours: summer months

James Valley Historical Society
(South Dakota State Fairgrounds—
   location)
PO Box 607 (mailing address)
Huron, SD 57350
(605) 352-8122
Louella Barrows, President
Hours: Fair week: 9:00–7:00; and by
   appointment

Keystone Area Historical Society
PO Box 658
Keystone, SD 57751
(605) 666-4667

Lennox Area Historical Society
Main Street
PO Box 337
Lennox, SD 57039
(605) 647-2287

**McCook County Museum and
Historical Society**
(120 West Norton—location)
PO Box 176 (mailing address)
Salem, SD 57058
(605) 425-3181
Lois Melton, President
Hours: Apr–Nov: Mon 1:30–5:00

Mellette County Historical Society
(Corner Main and State Street—location)
PO Box 282 (mailing address)
White River, SD 57579
(605) 259-3429
James Vos, President
Hours: May–Sept: 9:30–4:30

Menno Historical Society
Menno Heritage Museum
150 Poplar
Menno, SD 57045
(605) 387-2867
Dorothy Harnisch, President

**Minnehaha County Historical
Society**
Old Courthouse Museum
200 West Sixth Street
Sioux Falls, SD 57102
William Webster
Hours: Siouxland Heritage Museum:
   Wed 1:00–5:00
Pub. *Newsletter*, nine times per year
   (monthly, September–May)
$10.00 per year membership for
   individuals, $15.00 per year
   membership for families, $3.50 per
   year membership for senior citizens

**Crooks Council of the Minnehaha
County Historical Society**
Rt. 11, Box 339
Crooks, SD 57020
(605) 543-5232

MonDak Historical and Arts Society
(see Montana)

Moody County Historical Society
East Park Road
Flandreau, SD 57028
(605) 997-2198

Oelrichs Historical Society
PO Box 104
Oelrichs, SD 57763
(605) 535-6375
Violet S. Biever, President

**Old Stanley County Historical
Society**
PO Box 698
Fort Pierre, SD 57532
(605) 223-2757

**Oldham Library and Historical
Association**
PO Box 243
Oldham, SD 57051
(605) 482-8178; (605) 482-8158

Shirley Gruenhagen, President; JoAnn
  Nelson, Librarian
Hours: Museum: Sun in the summer;
  Library: limited hours

Perkins County Historical Society
HCR-69
PO Box 417C
Bison, SD 57620
(605) 244-5416
Dorothy Haugen, Secretary

**Potter County Historical
Association**
PO Box 1
Gettysburg, SD 57442
(605) 765-5691

Prairie Historical Society, Inc.
(Prairie Village, two miles west of
  Madison on Highway 34—location)
PO Box 256 (mailing address)
Madison, SD 57042
(800) 693-3644
Karen Becker, Village Manager; Sue
  Janssen, Administrator
Hours: 1 May–1 Oct: 9:00–6:00

Scotland Historical Society
331 Fourth Street
Scotland, SD 57059
(605) 583-2978
Viola L. Bauder, President
Hours: Memorial Day–Labor Day: Sun
  1:30–5:00

Spink County Historical Society
(Redfield, SD—location)
Frankfort, SD 57440 (mailing address)
(605) 472-0758

Springfield Historical Society
PO Box 333
Springfield, SD 57062
(605) 369-2498

**Timber Lake and Area Historical
Society**
(Cheyenne River Sioux Reservation—
  location)
PO Box 181 (mailing address)
Timber Lake, SD 57656
(605) 865-3546
Jim Nelson, Board Member
Hours: Mon–Tue 9:00–5:00
Pub. *Timber Lake and Area Historical
  Society Newsletter*, quarterly
("Reservation and homesteading history
  of northwestern South Dakota;
  museum and photo archives")
$10.00 per year membership

Tripp County Historical Society
801 West Fifth Street
Winner, SD 57580-1416

Wakonda Historical Society
Wakonda, SD 57073
(605) 267-2847
Dolores Haver, President

**Yankton County Historical Society,
Inc.**
Dakota Territorial Museum
Westside Park, 610 Summit
PO Box 1033
Yankton, SD 57078
(605) 665-3898
Mary E. Rasmussen, President
Pub. *Museum Chronicle*, semiannually

LDS Family History Centers

Rapid City
(605) 343-8656

Rosebud
(605) 747-2128

Sioux Falls
(605) 361-1070

Genealogical Societies

State Genealogical Society

South Dakota Genealogical Society
PO Box 1101
Pierre, SD 57501
Pub. *SDGS Quarterly*, quarterly, $15.00
  per year subscription; *South Dakota
  Genealogical Society Newsletter*

Regional Genealogical Societies

Aberdeen Area Genealogical Society
PO Box 493
Aberdeen, SD 57401-0493
Bud Schaffer, President
Hours: meetings second Sat 2:00
Pub. *The Tree Climber*, quarterly
$12.00 per year membership for
  individuals, $15.00 per year
  membership for families, $15.00 per
  year membership for libraries or
  societies; research: $2.00 per name

Black Hills Genealogy Club
PO Box 372
Rapid City, SD 57701
Pub. *Dakota Territory*, quarterly

Brookings Area Genealogical Society
524 Fourth Street
Brookings, SD 57006
Pub. *Brookings Area Genealogical
  Society*, bimonthly
$6.00 per year membership

**Hyde County Historical and
Genealogical Society**
(113 Iowa South—location)
PO Box 392 (mailing address)
Highmore, SD 57345
(605) 852-2251; (605) 852-2376 (Work)
Ms. Skyla L. Ratzlaff, President
Hours: by appointment
Pub. *Tumbleweeds*, quarterly, $1.00 per
  issue
$3.00 per year membership for
  individuals, $5.00 per year
  membership for couples or families

Lake County Genealogical Society
Dakota State College
Karl Mundt Library
Madison, SD 57042

Lyman-Brule Genealogical Society
PO Box 555
Chamberlain, SD 57325
(605) 734-5862; (605) 473-5391
Gay Murphy, President; Marlys
  Swanson, Secretary
Hours: daytime or evening
$12.00 per year membership

Mitchell Area Genealogical Society
c/o Mitchell Public Library
221 North Duff Street
Mitchell, SD 57301
(605) 996-6321 (Chairperson)
Marilyn Roth, Chairperson
Hours: Library: winter: Mon–Thur
  10:00–8:00, Fri–Sat 10:00–6:00, Sun
  2:00–5:00; summer: Mon–Sat 10:00–
  6:00
$5.00 per year membership

**Pierre-Fort Pierre Genealogical
Society**
PO Box 925
Pierre, SD 57501
(605) 223-9773
Tina Manning, President
Hours: Mon–Fri 9:00–9:00, Sat–Sun
  1:00–5:00
Pub. *Pierre-Fort Pierre Genealogical
  Society Newsletter*, quarterly
$10.00 per year membership

**Rapid City Society for Genealogical
Research**
PO Box 1495
Rapid City, SD 57709
E-mail: ghost@anetis.net
Jim Miller, President
Hours: Rapid City Public Library: Mon–
  Thur 9:00–9:00, Fri–Sat 9:00–5:30
Pub. *Black Hills Nuggets*, four times per
  year
$15.00 per year membership for families

Sioux Valley Genealogical Society
(Siouxland Heritage Old Courthouse
  Museum—library location)
200 West Sixth Street (mailing address)
Sioux Falls, SD 57104-6001
(605) 367-4210 (Museum)

Jeannette Allard-Fiskum, Library
Committee
Hours: Mon–Sat 1:00–5:00
Pub. *The Pioneer Pathfinder*, quarterly
(Pioneer Certificates are available to the
descendants of those who lived in
Dakota Territory prior to statehood on
2 November 1889.)
$12.00 per year membership for
individuals, $18.00 per year
membership for families (2 votes, 1
quarterly), $25.00 per year foreign or
Contributing membership

Tri-State Genealogical Society
c/o Belle Fourche Public Library
905 Fifth Avenue
Belle Fourche, SD 57717-1702
(605) 892-4407 (Library)
Pat Engebretson, President
Hours: Library: Mon–Thur 10:00–7:00,
Fri–Sat 10:00–5:00
Pub. *Wymon Dak Messenger*, quarterly
(emphasis on western South Dakota)
$5.00 per year membership

**Watertown Area Genealogical
Society**
611 N.E. "B" Avenue
Watertown, SD 57201
(605) 882-6220

**Winner, South Dakota, Family Tree
Society**
Rt. 3, Box 29
Colome, SD 57528
Helen Turnquist, Secretary

Independent Publications and Miscellany

Brown County Territorial Pioneers
4202 N.W. 24th Avenue
Aberdeen, SD 57401
(605) 225-6643

Homestead Records
E-mail: gkrell@aol.com
http://members.aol.com/gkrell/
homestead/home.html
Gary E. Krell
(information on homestead and other
land patent records for South Dakota)

**Charles Mix Historical Restoration
Society**
Geddes Historic District
PO Box 97
Geddes, SD 57342
(605) 337-2501
Ron Dufek, Secretary
Hours: May–Sept: 7:00–7:00
no charge

**Pioneer Club of Western South
Dakota**
HCR 61, Box 3
Midland, SD 57552
(605) 843-2150
Elaine Koehler, President
(genealogical services)

SDGenWeb
Part of U.S. GenWeb Project
E-mail: sd@usgenweb.com
http://www.rootsweb.com/~sdgenweb
(links to other South Dakota resources)

**Westerners International, Dakotah
Corral**
1905 South Sixth Avenue
Sioux Falls, SD 57105
(605) 332-4188

TENNESSEE

Archives and Libraries with Holdings in Genealogy

State Archives and Library

**Tennessee State Library and
Archives**
State Library and Archives Building
403 Seventh Avenue, North
Nashville, TN 37243-0312
(615) 741-2764; (615) 741-6471 FAX
E-mail: referenc@mail.state.tn.us
http://www.state.tn.us/sos/statelib/
tslahome.htm
Charles Sherrill, Director, Public
Services
Hours: Mon–Sat 8:00–6:00

State Historical Societies

Tennessee Historical Commission
Department of Environment and
Conservation
2941 Lebanon Road
Nashville, TN 37243-0440
(615) 532-1550; (615) 532-1549 FAX
Herbert L. Harper, Executive Director
Hours: Mon–Fri 8:00–4:30
Pub. *The Courier* (not genealogical,
deals with preservation of historic
buildings), three times per year, free;
The Tennessee Conservationist, $10.00
per year subscription

Tennessee Historical Society
Ground Floor
War Memorial Building
300 Capital Boulevard
Nashville, TN 37243-0084
(615) 741-8934
Pub. *The Tennessee Historical Quarterly*,
$25.00 per year subscription; *News in
Tennessee History*
research $25.00 and up

County Historians

Anderson County Historian
Offutt Road
Clinton, TN 37716
Sue Harris

Bedford County Historian
912 Shelbyview Drive
Shelbyville, TN 37160
Tim and Helen Marsh

Benton County Historian
Benton County Library
122 West Walnut Street
Camden, TN 38320
Virginia L. Whitworth

Bledsoe County Historian
Route One
Pikeville, TN 37367
Elizabeth Robnett

Blount County Historian
1308 Brannon Drive
Maryville, TN 37801
Inez Burns

Bradley County Historian
3765 Hillsdale Drive, N.E.
Cleveland, TN 37312
Dr. Bill Snell

Cannon County Historian
Courthouse Square
Woodbury, TN 37190
Harold Patrick

Carroll County Historian
166 North Main Street
McKenzie, TN 37201
Mary Ruth Devault

Cheatham County Historian
106 Smith Street
Ashland City, TN 37015
James B. Hallums

Chester County Historian
282 Old Finger Road
Henderson, TN 38340
Mr. Bobby Barnes

Claiborne County Historian
Post Office Box 6
Tazewell, TN 38340
John J. Kivette

Clay County Historian
Celina, TN 38551
Mrs. W. B. Upton

Cocke County Historian
532 Fourth Street
Newport, TN 37821
Edward R. Walker, III

Coffee County Historian
7614 Maple Springs Road
Manchester, TN 37355
Mr. Jess Lewis

Crockett County Historian
Route One
Humboldt, TN 38343
Mrs. Charles C. James

Cumberland County Historian
306 North Main Street
Crossville, TN 38555
Donald Brookhart

Davidson County Historian
4204 Hood Avenue
Nashville, TN 37215
John L. Connelly

Decatur County Historian
59 East 4th Street
Parsons, TN 38363
A. W. Primm

Dekalb County Historian
Route One, Box 5
Smithville, TN 37166
Thomas G. Webb

Dickson County Historian
206 Bellwood Circle
Dickson, TN 37055
George Jackson

Dyer County Historian
360 Greenway St. Apt. #1
Dyersburg, TN 38024-2459
Wallace Milan

Fayette County Historian
Post Office Box 127
Moscow, TN 38057
Mrs. J. R. Morton

Fentress County Historian
Route 2, Box 150
Jamestown, TN 38556
Lorraine Cargile

Franklin County Historian
Route 2
Belvidere, TN 37306
Howard M. Hannah

Gibson County Historian
Route 1, Box 266
Trenton, TN 38382
Fred Culp

Giles County Historian
307 Longmeadow Circle
Pulaski, TN 38478
Pauline Cross

Grainger County Historian
Route 3
Rutledge, TN 37861
John M. Clark

Greene County Historian
105 Monument Avenue
Greeneville, TN 37743
Harry Roberts

Grundy County Historian
Beersheba Springs, TN 37305
Margaret Coppinger

Hamblen County Historian
1960 Silver City Road
Russellville, TN 37860
Mrs. Berwin Haun

Hamilton County Historian
Chattanooga News-Free Press
400 East 11th Street
Chattanooga, TN 37403
John Wilson

Hancock County Historian
Post Office Box 277
Sneedville, TN 37869
Scott Collins

Hardeman County Historian
618 Clifft Street
Bolivar, TN 38008
Faye Tennyson Davidson

Hardin County Historian
Route 7, Box 65A
Savannah, TN 38372
Mary Hitchcock

Hawkins County Historian
426 West Main
Rogersville, TN 37857
Henry R. Price

Haywood County Historian
(Haywood County Historical Committee)
P.O. Box 207
Brownsville, TN 38012
Mr. Lynn Shaw

Henderson County Historian
Route One
Reagan, TN 38368
Randy Hart

Henry County Historian
511 North Poplar
Paris, TN 38242
Mary Ashley Morris

Hickman County Historian
Route 1, Box 64
Nunnelly, TN 37061
Edward Dotson

Houston County Historian
Rt. 1, Box 135
Erin, TN 37061
Nina Finley

Humphreys County Historian
Route One
Waverly, TN 37185
Mrs. Bill Anderson

Jackson County Historian
Post Office Box 342
Gainesboro, TN 38562
Ms. Moldon Tayse

Jefferson County Historian
1428 Russell Avenue
Jefferson City, TN 37760
Dr. E. P. Muncy

Johnson County Historian
508 Hospital Road
Mountain City, TN 37683
Thomas W. Gentry

Knox County Historian
1216 Weisgarber Road
Knoxville, TN 37919
Mrs. Park Niceley

Lake County Historian
303 Lake Street
Ridgely, TN 38080
Abigail Hyde

Lauderdale County Historian
Post Office Box 289
Ripley, TN 38063
Mr. Terry Ford

Lawrence County Historian
218 N. Military Avenue
Suite B-1
Lawrenceburg, TN 38464
Kathy Niedergeses

Lewis County Historian
205 West Main Street
Hohenwald, TN 38462
Marjorie B. Graves

Lincoln County Historian
Winchester Highway
Fayetteville, TN 37334
Sarah Byrd Posey

Loudon County Historian
309 Elkmont Road
Knoxville, TN 37922
Joe Spence

Macon County Historian
Route 4, Box 53
Lafayette, TN 37083
Harold Blankenship

Madison County Historian
1723 North Highland
Jackson, TN 38301
Harbert Alexander

Marion County Historian
618 Holly Avenue
South Pittsburg, TN 37380
Patsy Beene

Marshall County Historian
310 Farmington Road
Lewisburg, TN 37091
Charlene Nicholas

Maury County Historian
609 W. 7th Street
Columbia, TN 33401
Bob Duncan

McMinn County Historian
Route One
Riceville, TN 37370
Bill Akins

McNairy County Historian
Post Office Box 317
Adamsville, TN 38310
Bill Wagoner

Meigs County Historian
River Road
Decatur, TN 37322
Shirley Jennings

Monroe County Historian
508 West North Street
Sweetwater, TN 37874
Walter Lumsden, Jr.

Montgomery County Historian
Post Office Box 3533
Clarksville, TN 37043
Eleanor Williams

Moore County Historian
Route 3, Box 3164
Tullahoma, TN 37388
Joyce Neal

Morgan County Historian
Post Office Box 336
Wartburg, TN 37887
Donald Todd

Obion County Historian
Post Office Box 336
Union City, TN 38281-0336
Mr. Rebel C. Forrester

Perry County Historian
Box 105
Linden, TN 37096
Gus A. Steele

Pickett County Historian
Route 1, Box 160
Byrdstown, TN 38549
Richard W. Pierce

Polk County Historian
Route 1, Box 548
Benton, TN 37307
Ms. Marian Presswood

Putnam County Historian
1009 West Cemetery Road
Cookeville, TN 38501
Ms. Pat Franklin

Rhea County Historian
3433 Knollwood Hills Drive
Chattanooga, TN 37415
Betty Broyles

Roane County Historian
P.O. Box 493
Kingston, TN 37763
Robert L. Bailey

Robertson County Historian
3512 Pleasant Grove Road
White House, TN 37188
Yolanda Reid

Rutherford County Historian
7931 West Jefferson Pike
Smyrna, TN 37167
Ernest K. Johns

Scott County Historian
Huntsville, TN 37756
Irene Baker

Sequatchie County Historian
Route 1, Box 3
Dunlap, TN 37327
Henry Camp

Sevier County Historian
220 Dollywood Lane
Pigeon Forge, TN 37863
Beulah D. Linn

Shelby County Historian
Post Office Box 241813
Memphis, TN 38124-1813
Edward F. Williams, III

Smith County Historian
1117 Main Street
Carthage, TN 37030
Sue W. Maggort

Stewart County Historian
607 Jackson Avenue
Carthage, TN 37030
Nelda Saunders

Sullivan County Historian
320 Highridge Road
Kingsport, TN 37660
Dr. Elery A. Lay

Sumner County Historian
332 East Main Stret
Gallatin, TN 37066
John Garrott

Tipton County Historian
1505 Evergreen
Covington, TN 38019
Russell Bailey

Trousdale County Historian
165 Averitt Ferry Lane
Lebanon, TN 37087
Walter L. Buckingham

Unicoi County Historian
453 Ash Street
Erwin, TN 37650
Walter B. Garland

Union County Historian
Union County Historian
3212 Curtis Lane
Knoxville, TN 37918-4003
Bonnie Heiskell Peters

Van Buren County Historian
HC69 Box 688
Spencer, TN 38585
Agnes C. Jones

Warren County Historian
Post Office Box 563
McMinnville, TN 37110
James A. Dillon, Jr.

Washington County Historian
2020 Sherwood Drive
Apt. 304
Johnson City, TN 37601
Ruth Broyles

Wayne County Historian
Route 2, Box 308
Waynesboro, TN 38485
June Scott

Weakley County Historian
204 Poplar Street
Martin, TN 38238-3120
Virginia C. Vaughan

White County Historian
Post Office Box 15
Doyle, TN 38559
Mary West Holland

Williamson County Historian
1135 Lewisburg Pike
Franklin, TN 37064
Joe Bowman

Wilson County Historian
Post Office Box 309
Lebanon, TN 37088
William "Vincent" Simms

City, County and Regional Archives and Libraries

Archives of Appalachia
Sherrod Library
East Tennessee State University
PO Box 70,665, ETSU
Johnson City, TN 37614
(423) 929-4338
Hours: Mon–Fri 8:00–4:30
Pub. *Archives of Appalachia Newsletter*,
  semiannually, free

Birmingham Public Library
(see Alabama)

Bledsoe County Public Library
Pikeville, TN 37367
Carolyne Knight

Blount County Public Library
301 McGhee Street
Maryville, TN 37801
(423) 982-0981
Hours: Mon–Thur 9:00–8:00, Fri 9:00–
  5:30, Sat 9:00–5:30, Sun 1:00–5:00
(emphasis on Blount County and
  surrounding area)
search fees: $10.00 minimum

Calumet Center
1101 Kermit Drive
Nashville, TN 37217
(615) 361-8700

Carroll County Library
159 East Main Street
Huntingdon, TN 38344
(901) 986-1919
Karen Pierce, Director
Hours: Mon–Sat 9:00–4:00
(a small genealogy room)

Chattanooga-Hamilton County Bicentennial Library
Local History and Genealogy
  Department
1001 Broad Street
Chattanooga, TN 37402
(423) 757-5317
Clara W. Swann, Head, Local History
  and Genealogy
Hours: Mon–Thur 9:00–9:00, Fri–Sat
  9:00–6:00, Sun (Sunday after Labor

Day through Sunday before Memorial
  Day) 2:00–6:00
(southeast U.S. genealogy, local and state
  history)

Clarksville-Montgomery County Historical Museum
(200 South Second Street, Clarksville,
  TN 37040—location)
PO Box 383 (mailing address)
Clarksville, TN 37041
(615) 648-5780
Jill Hosmer, Registrar
Hours: Museum: Mon–Fri 8:00–5:00;
  Archives: by appointment only
(local archives)
no admission fee, reproduction fees
  vary

Clarksville-Montgomery County Public Library
350 Pageant Lane, #501
Clarksville, TN 37040
(615) 648-8824; (615) 648-8831 FAX
Tim Pulley, Reference Assistant
Hours: Mon, Wed & Fri–Sat 9:00–6:00,
  Tue & Thur 9:00–8:00
search fees vary with information
  requested

Cleveland Public Library-History Branch
833 North Ocoee Street
Cleveland, TN 37311
(423) 479-8367 phone and FAX
http://www.usit.net/tngenweb/
  bradley.htm
Barbara Fagen, CRGS, History Branch
  Manager
Hours: Mon & Fri–Sat 9:00–2:00, Tue &
  Wed 9:00–noon & 1:00–5:00, Thur
  1:00–5:00 & 6:00–9:00
(emphasis on Bradley County and
  surrounding areas, local family
  history)

Clinton Public Library
118 South Hicks Street
Clinton, TN 37716

Coffee County Lannom Memorial Library
312 North Collins
Tullahoma, TN 37388
(931) 455-2460
Leah Bumbalough, Library Director
Hours: Mon–Tue & Thur 9:00–9:00,
  Wed & Fri 9:00–5:00, Sat 9:00–4:00

Cumberland Science Museum
800 Fort Negley Boulevard
Nashville, TN 37203
(615) 862-5160
Gina Jones, Marketing Manager
Pub. *Museum*, monthly
$6.00 admission for adults, $4.50
  admission for children (ages 3–12) or
  senior citizens (ages 65 and up)

Cumberland University
Stockton Archives
Lebanon, TN 37087
(615) 444-2762

Davidson County/Metropolitan Government Archives
The Public Library of Nashville and
  Davidson County
113 Elm Hill Pike
Nashville, TN 37210
(615) 862-5880
E-mail: archives@waldo.nashv.lib.tn.us
C. Kenneth Fieth, Director
Hours: Mon–Fri 8:00–4:30
(Nashville/Davidson County archives,
  congressional papers also)

Deer Lodge Abner Ross Memorial Center
(Harker Street—location)
PO Box 127 (mailing address)
Deer Lodge, TN 37726-0127
(423) 965-3472
Susie Kries, Publisher
(publishes Morgan County cemetery
  records)

Fort Loudoun Regional Library Center
718 George Street, N.W.
Athens, TN 37303
(423) 745-5194
Marie D. Middleton, Regional Director

Giles County Public Library
122 South Second Street
Pulaski, TN 38478
(931) 363-2720 (ask for Genealogy
  Room)
Hours: Giles County Public Library:
  Mon–Tue 10:00–8:00, Wed & Fri
  10:00–5:00, Sat 10:00–4:00, Sun
  2:00–4:00

Hacksma House Genealogy Library
(see Washington)

Jackson-Madison County Library
433 East Lafayette
Jackson, TN 38301
(901) 423-0225
http://erc.jscc.cc.tn.us/jfn/libjmc
Jack Darrel Wood, Tennessee Room
Hours: Mon, Wed & Fri–Sat 9:30–5:30,
  Tue & Thur 9:30–9:00, Sun 1:30–4:30
limited searches only, minimum $3.00
  (includes four photocopy pages) plus
  copy charges of 25¢ per page for each
  additional page

Johnson City Public Library
103 South Roan Street
Johnson City, TN 37601-5721
(423) 434-4450
Linda Blanton, Technical Services
  Librarian; John Hart, Adult Reference
  Librarian
Hours: Mon–Thur 9:00–8:00, Fri 9:00–
  6:00, Sat (winter) 10:00–6:00, Sat

(summer) 10:00–3:00, Sun (winter)
1:00–5:00
(emphasis on Upper East Tennessee,
southwest Virginia and western North
Carolina)

Jonesborough-Washington County History Museum

Jonesborough Civic Trust
Boone Street
PO Box 375
Jonesborough, TN 37659
(423) 753-5961 (Visitors Center); (423)
753-9775 (Museum)
Cindy Lucas, Interim Director
Hours: Mon–Fri 8:00–5:00, Sat–Sun
10:00–5:00
research fee differs according to
information desired

Kingsport Public Library

J. Fred Johnson Memorial Library
400 Broad Steet
Kingsport, TN 37660
(423) 224-2539
Helen F. Hamilton, Library Assistant
Hours: Mon–Thur 9:00–8:45, Fri–Sat
9:00–5:15, Sun 2:00–5:15;
(Tennessee history and local history and
genealogy)

Kingston Public Library

1001 Bradford Way, #3
Kingston, TN 37763
(423) 376-9905
Susan Ladd, Librarian
Hours: Mon & Thur 10:00–7:30, Tue–
Wed & Fri 10:00–5:30, Sat 10:00–2:00

Knox County Archives

(East Tennessee Historical Center, 314
West Clinch Avenue, Knoxville, TN
37902-2203—location)
500 West Church Avenue (mailing
address)
Knoxville, TN 37902-2505
(423) 544-5741; (423) 544-5739
Archives; (423) 544-5744 Calvin M.
McClung Historical Collection
Doris R. Martinson, Archivist and Head
of Knox County Archives
Hours: Archives: Mon–Fri 9:00–5:30;
Calvin M. McClung Historical
Collection: Mon–Tue 9:00–8:30, Wed–
Fri 9:00–5:30, Sun 1:00–5:00
(Knox County governmental records:
"wills, estates, deeds, court records,
marriages, school records, tax
records")

Lenoir Museum

Norris Dam State Park
Highway 441
PO Box 53
Norris, TN 37828
(423) 494-9688; (423) 494-0488

Linden Public Library

Rt. 10, Box 3A
Linden, TN 37096

Macon County Public Library

294 Chaffin Road
Lafayette, TN 37083
Hours: Mon–Fri 8:00–4:45, Sat 8:00–
1:45

Magness Memorial Library

118 West Main Street
McMinnville, TN 37110
(423) 473-2428; (423) 473-6778 FAX
Susan E. Curtis, Director; Brad Walker,
Staff Genealogist
Hours: Mon 8:00–8:00, Tue 9:00–8:00,
Wed & Fri 9:00–5:00, Sat 8:00–2:00

Calvin M. McClung Historical Collection

Knox County Public Library System
(East Tennessee Historical Center, 314
West Clinch Avenue, Knoxville, TN
37902-2203—location)
500 West Church Avenue (mailing
address)
Knoxville, TN 37902-2505
(423) 544-5744
J. Stephen Cotham, Head
Hours: Mon–Tue 9:00–8:30, Wed–Fri
9:00–5:30, Sun 1:00–5:00
(Specializes in East Tennessee;
"Holdings include books, maps,
manuscripts, newspapers, photographs,
clippings files, architectural plans and
drawings, microfilm.")

McWherter Library

Special Collections/Mississippi Valley
Collection
Campus Box 52-6500
Memphis State University
Memphis, TN 38152
(901) 678-2210; (901) 678-8218
http://www.lib.memphis.edu
Ed Frank, Curator
Hours: Mon–Fri 8:00–4:30, Sun 1:00–
5:00 during semesters
(Tennessee and mid-south materials;
"Genealogy collection supports our
historical materials, genealogy is not
the main focus of the collection.")

The Memphis and Shelby County Archives

A Division of the Memphis and Shelby
County Public Library and
Information Center
33 South Front Street
Memphis, TN 38103
Dr. Barbara Flanary, Archivist
(houses government records, including
marriage, death, probate and estate
documents)

Memphis and Shelby County Public Library and Information Center

1850 Peabody Avenue
Memphis, TN 38104
(901) 526-1713
Dr. Barbara Flanary, Archivist
Hours: Mon–Fri 10:00–5:00

reference service: $15.00 minimum
for up to one half hour service,
payable in advance, $15.00 for each
additional half hour, $15.00 additional
for same-day or next-day service;
photocopies: 20¢ per page, $4.00
minimum handling for 1–5 copies,
$15.00 per hour additional charge for
more than 5 copies (not applicable to
libraries)

Memphis State University Library

Mississippi Valley Collection
Memphis, TN 38104

Middle Tennessee State University

Center for Historic Preservation
PO Box 80
Murfreesboro, TN 37132
(615) 898-2947
James K. Huhta, Ph.D., Director
(not genealogical)

Middle Tennessee State University

Todd Library
Murfreesboro, TN 37132
(615) 898-2549
E-mail: kmiddlet@frank.mtsu.edu
http://frank.mtsu.edu/~kmiddlet/history/
women.html

Morgan County Library

Wartburg, TN 37887

Morristown-Hamblen Library

Meta Turley Goodson Historical Room
417 West Main Street
Morristown, TN 37814
(423) 586-6410
Ann C. Steffen, Library Director
Hours: Mon, Wed & Fri–Sat 9:30–5:30,
Tue & Thur 9:30–8:00
(more than 1,500 books as well as
microfilm copies of census records
and the local newspapers)
limited research and information on fees:
Sandra Menders, 5642 Long Creek
Road, Morristown, TN 37813

Mount Juliet-Wilson County Library

Madelon Wright Smith Memorial
Archives
2765 North Mount Juliet Road
PO Box 319
Mount Juliet, TN 37122
(615) 758-7051; (615) 754-2439 FAX
Cyndie Todd, Genealogist
Hours: Mon–Tue & Thur 9:00–8:00,
Wed & Fri–Sat 9:00–5:00;
genealogist on site Mon, Wed & Sat
9:00–noon

Museum of Appalachia

PO Box 359
Norris, TN 37828
John Rice Irwin

The Public Library of Nashville and Davidson County
The Ben West Library
Nashville Room
225 Polk Avenue
Nashville, TN 37203
(615) 862-5783
Mary Glenn Hearne, Nashville Room
    Manager
Hours: Mon–Sat 9:00–5:00, Sun (Oct–
    May) 2:00–5:00
(emphasis on middle Tennessee history
    and genealogy)

Oak Ridge Public Library
Civic Center
Oak Ridge, TN 37830
(423) 482-8455; (423) 482-8459
E-mail: mlux@ci.oak-ridge.tn.us
Martha W. Lux, Head of Reference
Hours: Mon–Thur 10:00–9:00, Fri
    10:00–6:00, Sat 9:00–6:00, Sun 2:00–
    6:00

Ohoopee Regional Library
(see Georgia)

Old Jail Museum
400 First Avenue, N.E.
Waynesboro, TN 37398
(931) 967-0524

Buford Pusser Home and Museum
342 Pusser Street
PO Box 301
Adamsville, TN 38310
(901) 632-1401
Janese Newell, Hostess
Hours: 1 May–31 Oct: 9:00–5:00; 1
    Nov–Apr 30: 10:00–4:00

Carroll Reece Museum
East Tennessee State University
PO Box 70660, ETSU
Johnson City, TN 37614-0660
(423) 929-4392
Helen Roseberry, Director
Hours: Museum: Mon–Sat 9:00–4:00,
    Sun 1:00–4:00; Office: Mon–Fri
Pub. *Newsletter*, three times per year
("We are a collecting and exhibiting
    museum.")
$10.00 per year membership for
    individuals, $15.00 per year
    membership for families, $1.00 per
    year membership for students, $25.00
    per year Supporting membership

Rhea Library
400 West Washington Street
Paris, TN 38242

Robertson County Archives
600 South Locust Street
Springfield, TN 37172
(615) 382-2316
Yolanda Reid, County Historian
Hours: Mon–Fri 8:00–4:00
search fee: $5.00 plus copy costs for one
    surname, one type of record, for a ten-
    year time period

Sevier County Library
321 Court Avenue
Sevierville, TN 37862
(423) 453-3532; (423) 453-3532 FAX
Reese Ripatti, Library Director
Hours: Mon & Thur 10:30–8:00, Tue–
    Wed & Fri 10:30–6:00, Sat 10:30–
    4:00

Springfield Public Library
405 White Street
Springfield, TN 37172
(615) 384-5123; (615) 384-0106 FAX
Hours: Mon, Wed & Fri–Sat 9:00–5:00,
    Tue & Thur 9:00–8:00, Sun 2:30–
    5:00

H. B. Stamps Memorial Library
407 East Main Street
Rogersville, TN 37857
(615) 272-8710
Kathy Campbell, Director
Hours: Mon, Wed & Fri 9:30–5:00, Tue
    & Thur 9:30–8:00, Sat (Sept–May)
    9:30–5:00

Sullivan County Library
(1655 State Route 37—location)
PO Box 510 (mailing address)
Blountville, TN 37617
(423) 279-2714
E-mail: kayscl@preferred.com
Kay P. Hamrick, Director
Hours: Mon, Wed & Fri–Sat 9:00–5:00,
    Tue & Thur 9:00–6:30
(specializes in eastern Tennessee,
    northwestern North Carolina, and
    southwestern Virginia)

Sumner County Archives
155 East Main Street
Gallatin, TN 37066
(615) 452-0037
Dr. James Thomas, Director
Hours: Mon–Fri 8:00–4:30, occasional
    Sat by appointment
(library collection and court records,
    middle Tennessee genealogy with
    emphasis on Sumner County)
search fee: $5.00 plus SASE

The University of Tennessee
The Frank H. McClung Museum
1327 Circle Park Drive
Knoxville, TN 37996-3200
(423) 974-2144; (423) 974-3827 FAX
E-mail: jchapman@utk.edu
http://mcclungmuseum.utk.edu
Jefferson Chapman, Ph.D., Director
Hours: Mon–Fri 9:00–5:00, Sat 10:00–
    3:00, Sun 1:00–5:00
(local history collection, library,
    photographic resources; no
    genealogical data)

University of the South Archives
Jessie Ball DuPont Library
Sewanee, TN 37375-4005
(931) 598-1387

Washington County-Jonesborough Library
200 Sabin Drive
Jonesborough, TN 37659
(423) 753-1800; (423) 753-1802
Debra B. Mattingly, Director
Hours: Mon & Thur 9:00–8:00, Tue–
    Wed & Fri 9:00–6:00, Sat 9:00–2:00
(emphasis on east Tennessee and
    Washington County)
photocopies 15¢ per page, searching
    done as volunteers have the time

Williamson County Public Library
(Genealogy Library, Old Post Office,
    Five Points—location)
611 West Main (mailing address)
Franklin, TN 37064
(615) 794-3156
Kathy Ossi, Genealogy Reference
    Assistant
Hours: Tue–Sat 8:30–5:30
(houses the Edythe Rucker Whitley
    Collection)
SASE with inquiries

Wynnewood
Rt. 1, Box 5
Castilian Springs, TN 37031
(615) 452-5463

Historical Societies— Local and Regional

Association for the Preservation of Tennessee Antiquities (APTA)
Belle Meade Mansion, 110 Leake
    Avenue
Nashville, TN 37205
(615) 352-8247
Cherrie H. Hall, Executive Director
Hours: Mon–Thur
Pub. *Intercom*, biannually
Chapters: **Arlington Chapter**: Eileen
    Hinders, President, PO Box 443,
    Arlington, TN 38002, (901) 867-8825;
    Bedford County Chapter: Mariana
    B. White, President, 528 Charlie
    Russell Road, Shelbyville, TN 37160,
    (615) 684-1446; **The Carter House
    Chapter**: Eugene McNeil, President,
    122 Trace End, Franklin, TN 37064,
    (615) 373-8121 (Home), (615) 742-
    6719 (Work); **Donelson-Hermitage
    Chapter**: William Howell, President,
    1007 Stonewall Drive, Nashville, TN
    37220, (615) 269-4532 (Home), (615)
    356-0056 (Work); **Fort Blount
    Chapter**: Mr. Ronny West, President,
    307 Hull Street, Gainesboro, TN
    38562, (615) 268-9927 (Home), (615)
    268-2161; **Hamblen County
    Chapter**: Cindy Moses, President, PO
    Box 524, Morristown, TN 37815,
    (615) 581-1675 (Home), (615) 586-

6653 (Work); **Hardeman County Chapter**: Peggy Weaver, President, 600 Heritage Plantation Way, Hickory Valley, TN 38042, (901) 764-6612; **Hawkins County Chapter**: Marian Slaughter, President, 515 West Broadway, Rogersville, TN 37857, (615) 272-7436; **Jefferson County Chapter**: Mr. Chris McDowell, President, 1280 North Chucky Pike, Jefferson City, TN 37760, (615) 475-7643; **Knoxville Chapter**: Virginia Niceley, President, 1216 Weisgarber Road, Knoxville, TN 37909, (615) 588-3342; **Maury County Chapter**: Sarah Johnson, President, PO Box 894, Columbia, TN 38402; **Memphis Chapter**: Robert Myers, President, 1780 Galloway, Memphis, TN 38112, (901) 278-4004; **Nashville Chapter**: Mrs. Pat Madden, 7401 Huntwick Trail, Nashville, TN 37221, (615) 646-6528; **Rutherford County Chapter**: Edward DeBoer, President, 526 Crosswood Court, Murfreesboro, TN 37130, (615) 895-4286 (Home), (615) 893-0022 (Work); **Sumner County Chapter**: Jaunita Gourley, President, 1011 Durham Drive, Gallatin, TN 37066, (615) 452-3973
$10.00 per year membership-at-large

Bedford County Historical Society
250 Riverbend Road
Shelbyville, TN 37160
(931) 684-4428
Mrs. R. B. McLean, Secretary
Pub. *Bedford County Historical Quarterly* (March, June, September, December), $3.25 per issue
$12.50 per year membership; no research service available

Blount County Genealogical and Historical Society
Blount County Public Library
(301 McGhee Street—location)
PO Box 4986 (mailing address)
Maryville, TN 37802-4986
(423) 982-0981 (Library)
Jane Kizer Thomas, President
Hours: Mon–Thur 9:00–8:00, Fri 9:00–5:30, Sat 9:00–5:30, Sun 1:00–5:00
Pub. *The Blount Journal*, semiannually (spring and fall)
$10.00 per year membership; queries free for members only; search fees: $5.00 minimum

Bradley County Historical Society
Lee College
Cleveland, TN 37311
(423) 479-8367
Dr. William Snell
Hours: Cleveland Public Library—History Branch: Tue–Wed 9:00–noon & 1:00–4:00, Thur 1:00–5:00 & 6:00–9:00, Fri–Sat 9:00–2:00

(emphasis on Bradley County and surrounding areas, local family history)

Brentwood Historical and Genealogical Society
Middle Tennessee Society of Professional Genealogists
PO Box 21
Brentwood, TN 37024-0021
(615) 794-7137
Richard Carlton Fulcher, Chairperson
Hours: Mon–Fri 9:00–4:00
Pub. *Tennessee Genealogical Review Quarterly*, $25.00 per year subscription
("Maintain computerized bibliography of original and secondary sources for each county and state available from leading archives and record repositories.")
quotations offered on specific research needs

Bristol Historical Association, Inc.
PO Box 204
Bristol, TN 37621

Campbell County Historical Society & Historic Wedding Chapel
101 South Sixth Street
LaFollette, TN 37766
(423) 566-2127
Trulene H. Nash, Vice President, Publications
Pub. *The Campbell Countian*, quarterly
$10.00 per year membership

Caney Fork River Historical Association, Inc.
Luttrell Avenue
PO Box 153
Smithville, TN 37166
(615) 597-4646

Carroll County Historical Society
Gordon Browning Museum and Genealogical Library
640 North Main Street
McKenzie, TN 38201
(901) 352-3510; (901) 352-3456 FAX
Patricia J. Clark, Curator/Librarian
Hours: Mon–Tue & Thur–Fri 9:00–5:00, Sat 9:00–3:00
(general research for Carroll and adjacent counties)
$5.00 per year membership; search fees: 20¢ per copy plus postage and donation

Chattanooga Area Historical Association
Chattanooga, TN 37402
Pub. *Chattanews*

Claiborne County Historical Society
PO Box 32
Tazewell, TN 37879
(423) 626-7261
Brenda Burchfield, Treasurer

Pub. *Reflections*, quarterly, $5.00 per issue
$10.00 per year membership for individuals, $12.50 per year membership for families, $1.00 per year membership for students

Coffee County Historical Society, Inc.
304 South Irwin Street
PO Box 524
Manchester, TN 37355
(423) 728-0764
Grady L. York, President
Pub. *Coffee County Historical Quarterly*

Sam Davis Memorial Association
Sam Davis Road
Smyrna, TN 37167
(615) 459-2341

East Tennessee Historical Society
(600 Market Street—location)
PO Box 1629 (miling address)
Knoxville, TN 37901
(423) 544-5732; (423) 544-4319 FAX
Kent Whitworth, Executive Director; Cherel Henderson, Associate Director
Hours: Calvin McClung Historical Collection: Mon–Tue 9:00–8:30, Wed–Fri 9:00–5:30, Sun 1:00–5:00; Office: Mon–Fri 9:00–5:00; Museum: Tue–Sat 10:00–4:00, Sun 1:00–5:00
Pub. *Journal of East Tennessee History*, annually; *Tennessee Ancestors*, three times per year; *Newsline*, quarterly
Chapters: **Greene County Chapter**: PO Box 1202, Greenville, TN 37743; **Monroe County Chapter**: c/o Joe Benthall, Rt. 4, Ball Play Road, Madisonville, TN 37854
Affiliates: **First Families of Tennessee**, c/o East Tennessee Historical Society; **The East Tennessee Society for the Preservation of Friends (Quaker) History**, c/o Scott Knight, Secretary, 2429 Brook Road, Greenback, TN 37742; **Grainger County Historical Society**, c/o Louisa Hodge, President, PO Box 215, Rutledge, TN 37861; **The Overmountain Victory Trail Association, Inc.**, Sycamore Shoals State Park, 1651 West Elk Avenue, Elizabethton, TN 37643 ($8.00 per year membership for individuals, $10.00 per year membership for families)
$35.00 per year membership for individuals, $45.00 per year membership for families, $20.00 per year membership for students, $25.00 per year membership for non-profit institutional membership

Fayette County Historical Society
PO Box 304
Somerville, TN 38068
Anne H. Thompson, President
Pub. *The Fayette County Historical Society Bulletin*

Fentress County Historical Society
PO Box 178
Jamestown, TN 38556
(931) 879-7512
Christene Barton, Librarian
Hours: Mon–Tue & Thur–Sat 9:00–11:00
& 12:00–5:00
Pub. *Fentress County (TN) Historical
Society Newsletter*, quarterly, $5.00
per year subscription
$8.00 per year membership

Franklin County Historical Society
PO Box 130
Winchester, TN 37398-0130
(931) 962-1476
Travis Hitt, President
Hours: 11:30–4:30
Pub. *Franklin County Historical Review*,
annually; *Historical Tidings*, quarterly
$25.00 per year membership for families
or households, $30.00 per year
Contributing membership, $200.00 life
membership

Giles County Historical Society
(122 South Second Street—location)
PO Box 693 (mailing address)
Pulaski, TN 38478
(931) 363-2720 (ask for Genealogy
Room)
George Newman, President
Hours: Giles County Public Library:
Mon–Tue 10:00–8:00, Wed & Fri
10:00–5:00, Sat 10:00–4:00, Sun
2:00–4:00
Pub. *Giles County Historical Society
Bulletin*, quarterly
$8.00 per year membership (beginning in
January)

Greene County Heritage Trust
PO Box 1630
Greenville, TN 37744
(931) 638-6303

**Hancock County Historical and
Genealogical Society**
PO Box 277
Sneedville, TN 37869
Hours: various
Pub. *Our Mountain Heritage*, quarterly
$5.00 per year membership for
individuals the first year, $10.00 per
year membership for individuals
thereafter, $7.50 per year membership
for families for the first year, $10.00
per year membership for families
thereafter, $100.00 life membership

Hardin County Historical Society
PO Box 1012
Savannah, TN 38372
(901) 925-3106
Henry Williams, Treasurer
Hours: Mon–Fri 8:00–4:00
Pub. *Hardin County Historical Quarterly*
$12.00 per year membership; free
queries

**Hawkins County Genealogical and
Historical Society**
PO Box 429
Rogersville, TN 37857
Pub. *Distant Crossroads*, quarterly
$10.00 per year membership

**Henderson County Historical
Society**
PO Box 128
Wildersville, TN 38388

**The Heritage Foundation of
Franklin and Williamson County**
(510 Fifth Avenue—location)
PO Box 723 (mailing address)
Franklin, TN 37065-0723
(615) 591-8500; (615) 591-8502 FAX
Mary Pearce, Executive Director
Hours: 9:00–4:00
Pub. *The Sentinel*, quarterly
$35.00 per year membership

Highland Rim Historical Society
PO Box 411
Portland, TN 37148
(615) 325-6029
Vivian Russell, President

**Humphreys County Historical
Society**
105 Carroll Avenue
Waverly, TN 37185
John H. Whitfield, President

Jefferson County Historical Society
PO Box 325
Dandridge, TN 37725

Lawrence County Historical Society
PO Box 431
Lawrenceburg, TN 38464

Lincoln County Historical Society
202 East Washington Street
Fayetteville, TN 37334
Pub. *The Volunteer*
$7.50 per year membership

**Love Historical and Genealogical
Association**
River Oaks Road
Brentwood, TN 37027

Macon County Historical Society
PO Box 231
Lafayette, TN 37083
(615) 666-6030
Randy G. East, President
Pub. *Macon County Historical Society
Newsletter*, quarterly
(Macon County and surrounding area
history and genealogy)
$12.50 per year membership; queries

Marshall County Historical Society
224 Third Avenue, North
Lewisburg, TN 37091
(931) 359-2383
Mrs. Knox Bigham, Secretary

Pub. *Quarterly*
$10.00 per year membership

Maury County Historical Society
PO Box 147
Columbia, TN 38401
Hours: Columbia Public Library: Mon–
Fri 9:00–5:00
Pub. *Historic Maury*, quarterly;
Newsletter, monthly
$10.00 per year membership

**Historical Commission of
Metropolitan Nashville-Davidson
County**
701 Broadway, B-20
Nashville, TN 37203
(615) 259-5027

**Montgomery County Historical
Society**
1650 Simpson Drive
Clarksville, TN 37043
(931) 647-6817

**Morgan County Genealogical and
Historical Society**
(Morgan County Library—location)
PO Box 684 (mailing address)
Wartburg, TN 37887
(423) 346-3137
Sammy Ruth McPeters, President
Hours: Mon–Fri noon–6:00, Sat 10:00–
1:00
Pub. *The Morgan County Messenger*,
quarterly (spring, summer, fall, winter)
$15.00 per year membership; research
fees: $4.00 plus $1.00 per page copied
of courthouse records

**Morristown-Hamblen Historical and
Bicentennial Commission**
Rose Center
432 West Second Street, North
PO Box 1976
Morristown, TN 37814
(423) 581-4330

**Mount Juliet-West Wilson County
Historical Society**
(Mount Juliet Senior Center—location)
PO Box 337
Mount Juliet, TN 37122
(615) 754-2418
E-mail: dgferrell@aol.com
Donna Graves Ferrell, President
Hours: Mount Juliet Senior Center:
meeting second Sun 2:00
Pub. *The Chronicle*, quarterly
(collects family histories of Mount Juliet-
West Wilson people; archives housed
in the Mount Juliet Public Library)
$10.00 per year membership for
individuals, $15.00 per year
membership for couples in the same
household; queries accepted

Obion County Historical Society
PO Box 241
Union City, TN 38281

(901) 885-2322 (Secretary)
Martha Clendenin, Corresponding
Secretary
Hours: various
Pub. *Obion Origins*, quarterly
$10.00 per year membership; research
Obion County records: $5.00 per hour
plus cost of copies and postage

**Old James County Historical
Society**
PO Box 203
Ooltewah, TN 37363
(423) 238-4825
Nancylene Monroe, Book Sales Manager
Hours: by appointment
("County officers, post offices, schools,
marriage records, service records
collected by members")

**Pellissippi Genealogical and
Historical Society**
Clinton Public Library
118 South Hicks Street
Clinton, TN 37716
(423) 457-5400, ext. 379
Mary S. Harris, County Historian at the
Courthouse
Hours: Courthouse, 100 South Main,
Room 204 Vault, Clinton, TN 37716:
Mon–Fri: 8:30–4:30
Pub. *The Pellissippian*, quarterly
(emphasis on Anderson County)
$16.00 per year membership

Perry County Historical Society
Linden Public Library
Rt. 10, Box 3A
Linden, TN 37096
(931) 593-3373 (Editor)
http://www.tngenweb.usit.com/perry
Mary Bowen, Editor
Hours: Mon–Tue & Thur–Fri 9:00–5:00,
Sat 9:00–noon
Pub. *Perry County Historical Society
Quarterly*
$5.00 per year membership; free answer
to queries regarding Perry County
genealogy

**Pleasant Hill Historical Society of
the Cumberlands, Inc.**
Main Street
PO Box 264
Pleasant Hill, TN 38578
(931) 277-3193

**Polk County Historical and
Genealogical Society**
PO Box 636
Benton, TN 37307
E-mail: presswood@wingnet.net
http//www.tngenweb.usit.com/polk
Marian Bailey Presswood, President and
Polk County Historian
Pub. *Polk County Historical &
Genealogical Quarterly & Newsletter*
$10.00 per year membership

Rhea County Historical Society
PO Box 31
Dayton, TN 37321

**Roane County Heritage
Commission, Inc.**
119 Court Street
PO Box 738
Kingston, TN 37763
(615) 376-9211
Oscar C. Rogers, Director of Heritage
Square
Hours: Tue–Fri 9:00–4:00
Pub. *Heritage Newsletter*, quarterly
$25.00 per year membership for
individuals

Robertson County Historical Society
509 West Court Square
Springfield, TN 37172
(615) 382-7173
Maxine Elliott, President
Hours: Fri 10:00–4:00, and by
appointment; meets first Mon
$10.00 per year membership

Rocky Mount Historical Association
Rocky Mount Museum, A Living History
Site
200 Hyder Hill Road
Piney Flats, TN 37686-4630
(423) 538-7396; (888) 538-1791; (423)
538-5983 FAX
Norman O. Burns, III, Executive
Director
Hours: Mon–Sat 10:00–5:00, Sun 2:00–
6:00 (closed Thanksgiving, Dec 21–
Jan 5, and weekends in Jan & Feb)
Pub. *Rocky Mount Gazette*, bimonthly
(tours and educational programs and
special events throughout the year)
$25.00 per year membership for
individuals, $35.00 per year
membership for families, $50.00 per
year Contributing membership

**Rutherford County Historical
Society, Inc.**
PO Box 906
Murfreesboro, TN 37133-0906
Pub. *Frow Chips*, eleven times per year;
*Rutherford County Historical Society
Publications*, semiannually
$10.00 per year membership

Scott County Historical Society
PO Box 7
Huntsville, TN 37756
Irene Baker, President
Pub. *SCHS Newsletter*, quarterly

Smoky Mountain Historical Society
(167 East Bruce Street—location)
PO Box 5078 (mailing address)
Sevierville, TN 37864
E-mail: smhsquery@smokykin.com
Roy Glenn Cardwell
Hours: meetings: Jan, Mar, May, Jul,
Sept, Nov

Pub. *The Smoky Mountain Historical
Society Journal*, quarterly (spring,
summer, fall, winter), $4.00 per issue
(Tennessee regional and local history)
$10.00 per year membership (calendar
year)

Southern Studies Institute
(see Louisiana)

Sullivan County Historical Society
PO Box 60
Blountville, TN 37617
Elizabeth Hockman, Corresponding
Secretary

Sumner County Historical Society
PO Box 1871
Gallatin, TN 37066
(615) 452-2701 (Secretary)
Shirley Wilson, President

**Tipton-Haynes Historical
Association**
PO Box 225
Johnson City, TN 37605-0225

Unicoi County Historical Society
c/o Hilda Padgett
405 Ohio Avenue
Erwin, TN 37650
James Stevens, President
Hours: Erwin Utilities Building: fourth
Mon
$5.00 per year membership; non-
members may use the society's library

**Union County Historical Society,
Inc.**
PO Box 95
Maynardville, TN 37807
(423) 687-2137
William G. Tharpe, President
Hours: Roy Acuff Union Museum and
Library, Maynardville: Mon–Tue
10:00–4:00, Sun 1:00–5:00
Pub. *Pathways: History and
Genealogical Journal*, quarterly, $4.00
per issue (for back issues)
$12.00 per year membership for
individuals, $17.00 per year
membership for families or out-of-
state membership, $100.00 life
membership

Van Buren County Historical Society
c/o Courthouse
PO Box 857
Spencer, TN 38585
(931) 946-7607
Oliver A. Bayless, Treasurer
Hours: Mon, Wed & Fri 9:00–11:00
Pub. *Van Buren County Historical
Journal*, annually, $12.00 per issue
postpaid; *Van Buren County Historical
Society Newsletter*, quarterly
(census, marriages, cemetery and other
records available)
$12.50 per year membership

Washington County Historical Association
2007 Sherwood Drive, #D
Johnson City, TN 37601-3236
Ray Stahl

Wayne County Historical Society
PO Box 866
Waynesboro, TN 38485
Pub. *Wayne County Historian*, quarterly
$5.00 per year membership for
    individuals, $10.00 per year
    membership

West Tennessee Historical Society
PO Box 111046
Memphis, TN 38111
(901) 372-7495
Douglas W. Cupples, Ph.D., President
Pub. *West Tennessee Historical Society
    Papers*, annually
$15.00 per year membership

Williamson County Historical Society
PO Box 72
Franklin, TN 37064
Pub. *Williamson County Historical
    Society Journal*, irregularly
$10.00 per year membership

The Wise County Historical Society
The Appalachian Quarterly
(see Virginia)

LDS Family History Centers

Chattanooga
(423) 892-7632

Cordova
(901) 754-2545

Knoxville
(423) 693-8252

Madison
(615) 859-6926

Memphis
(see Cordova)

Nashville
(see Madison)

Genealogical Societies

State Genealogical Society

The Tennessee Genealogical Society
(9114 Davies Plantation Road—library
    location)
PO Box 247 (mailing address)
Brunswick, TN 38014-0247

Nelson Dickey
Hours: Tue & Thur 10:00–2:00
Pub. *The Tennessee Genealogical
    Magazine, "Ansearchin'" News*,
    quarterly (March, June, September,
    December), $20.00 per year
    subscription
(emphasis on the state of Tennessee)
one fifty-word query per year free to
    subscribers

Regional Genealogical Societies

Blount County Genealogical and Historical Society
Blount County Public Library
(301 McGhee Street—location)
PO Box 4986 (mailing address)
Maryville, TN 37802-4986
(423) 982-0981 (Library)
Jane Kizer Thomas, President
Hours: Mon–Thur 9:00–8:00, Fri 9:00–
    5:30, Sat 9:00–5:30, Sun 1:00–5:00
Pub. *The Blount Journal*, semiannually
    (spring and fall)
$10.00 per year membership; queries
    free for members only; search fees:
    $5.00 minimum

Brentwood Historical and Genealogical Society
Middle Tennessee Society of
    Professional Genealogists
PO Box 21
Brentwood, TN 37024-0021
(615) 794-7137
Richard Carlton Fulcher, Chairperson
Hours: Mon–Fri 9:00–4:00
Pub. *Tennessee Genealogical Review
    Quarterly*, $25.00 per year
    subscription
("Maintain computerized bibliography of
    original and secondary sources for
    each county and state available from
    leading archives and record
    repositories.")
quotations offered on specific research
    needs

Delta Genealogical Society (southeast Tennessee)
(see Georgia)

Greene County Genealogical Society
(Tennessee Room, Greeneville Public
    Library—location)
PO Box 1903 (mailing address)
Greeneville, TN 37744
Jan Maddux, Vice President; Wesley
    Lott, Vice President
Hours: meetings: first Thur 7:00 P.M.
Pub. *The Greene County Pioneer*,
    semiannually (May and November)
(upper east Tennessee)
$15.00 per year membership

Hamblen County Genealogical Society
(Morristown-Hamblen Library, 417 West
    Main Street, Morristown, TN 37814—
    location)
PO Box 1213 (mailing address)
Morristown, TN 37816-1213
(423) 586-6410
Mrs. Billie H. Inman, President
Hours: Morristown-Hamblen Library,
    Meta Turley Goodson Historical
    Room: Mon, Wed & Fri–Sat 9:30–
    5:30, Tue & Thur 9:30–8:00
Pub. *Hamblen Heritage*, quarterly
(specializes in Hamblen County, formed
    1870 from Jefferson, Grainger and part
    of Hawkins counties)
$10.00 per year membership (beginning
    in January); members try to answer all
    letters accompanied by SASE; free
    queries and surname listings

Hancock County Historical and Genealogical Society
PO Box 277
Sneedville, TN 37869
Hours: various
Pub. *Our Mountain Heritage*, quarterly
$5.00 per year membership for
    individuals the first year, $10.00 per
    year membership for individuals
    thereafter, $7.50 per year membership
    for families for the first year, $10.00
    per year membership for families
    thereafter, $100.00 life membership

Hawkins County Genealogical and Historical Society
PO Box 429
Rogersville, TN 37857
Pub. *Distant Crossroads*, quarterly
$10.00 per year membership

Holston Territory Genealogical Society
(see Virginia)

Jefferson County Genealogical Society
PO Box 267
Jefferson City, TN 37760
(931) 397-9050
Janet McLain
Hours: meeting third Mon
Pub. *Jefferson County Genealogical
    Society Journal*, quarterly
$10.00 per year membership; free
    queries for members

Jonesborough Genealogical Society
200 Sabin Drive
Jonesborough, TN 37659
(423) 753-5000 (Washington County-
    Jonesborough Library)
Anne Shaw, Library Services
Hours: Mon & Fri 9:00–8:00, Tue–Thur
    9:00–6:00, Sat 9:00–2:00

Pub. *The Jonesborough Record*, quarterly
$15.00 per year subscription or membership; limited search: 25¢ per copy plus postage and mailing costs

Lincoln County Genealogical Society

1508 West Washington Street
Fayetteville, TN 37334
(931) 433-5991
Mabel Abbott Tucker, Founder and Treasurer
Hours: Sat–Sun 1:00–5:00
$10.00 per year membership, $13.00 per year membership plus independently published periodical, *Lincoln County Tennessee Pioneers*, semiannually (January and July); "search is free for members in our library"; queries free to members or subscribers

Love Historical and Genealogical Association

River Oaks Road
Brentwood, TN 37027

Mid-West Tennessee Genealogical Society

PO Box 3343
Jackson, TN 38303-0343
Pub. *Family Findings*, quarterly
$15.00 per year membership

Middle Tennessee Genealogical Society

PO Box 190625
Nashville, TN 37219-0625
(615) 297-3085
Pub. *The Middle Tennessee Journal of Genealogy and History*, quarterly (includes Bedford, Cannon, Cheatham, Clay, Coffee, Davidson, DeKalb, Dickson, Fentress, Franklin, Giles, Grundy, Hickman, Houston, Humphreys, Jackson, Lawrence, Lewis, Lincoln, Macon, Marshall, Maury, Montgomery, Moore, Overton, Perry, Pickett, Putnam, Robertson, Rutherford, Sequatchie, Smith, Stewart, Sumner, Trousdale, Van Buren, Warren, Wayne, White, Williams and Wilson counties)
$18.00 per year membership for individuals, $21.00 per year membership if paid mid-year; no search services but a list of professional researchers is available

Morgan County Genealogical and Historical Society

(Morgan County Library—location)
PO Box 684 (mailing address)
Wartburg, TN 37887
(423) 346-3137
Sammy Ruth McPeters, President
Hours: Mon–Fri noon–6:00, Sat 10:00–1:00
Pub. *The Morgan County Messenger*, quarterly (spring, summer, fall, winter)

$15.00 per year membership; research fees: $4.00 plus $1.00 per page copied of courthouse records

Pellissippi Genealogical and Historical Society

Clinton Public Library
118 South Hicks Street
Clinton, TN 37716
(423) 457-5400, ext. 379
Mary S. Harris, County Historian at the Courthouse
Hours: Courthouse, 100 South Main, Room 204 Vault, Clinton, TN 37716: Mon–Fri: 8:30–4:30
Pub. *The Pellissippian*, quarterly (emphasis on Anderson County)
$16.00 per year membership

Polk County Historical and Genealogical Society

PO Box 636
Benton, TN 37307
E-mail: presswood@wingnet.net
http//www.tngenweb.usit.com/polk
Marian Bailey Presswood, President and Polk County Historian
Pub. *Polk County Historical & Genealogical Quarterly & Newsletter*
$10.00 per year membership

Roane County Genealogical Society

(Kingston Public Library, 1001 Bradford Way, #3, Kingston, TN 37763—location)
PO Box 297 (mailing address)
Kingston, TN 37763-0297
Marjory M. Watts, Corresponding Secretary
Hours: Library: Mon & Thur 10:00–7:30, Tue–Wed & Fri 10:00–5:30, Sat 10:00–2:00
Pub. *Roane Ramblings*, quarterly (John M. McMurray Collection includes "printed materials, vertical family files, Researcher's Crossfile, every record available on microfilm for Roane and adjacent counties.")
$15.00 per year membership; research of indexed materials: $4.00 per hour plus postage and copying

Signal Mountain Genealogical Society

103 Florida Avenue
Signal Mountain, TN 37373
James L. Douthat, President
Pub. *Genealogical Signals*, monthly
$5.00 per year membership

Sullivan County Genealogy Club

(Sullivan County Library, 1655 State Route 37—location)
PO Box 568 (mailing address)
Blountville, TN 37617
(423) 279-2714 (Library)
http://www.usit.net/tngenweb/sullivan/sullclub.htm
Kay P. Hamrick, Library Director

Hours: Library: Mon, Wed & Fri–Sat 9:00–5:00, Tue & Thur 9:00–6:30; meeting: third Thur 7:00
$15.00 per year membership for individuals, $20.00 per year membership for families

Upper Cumberland Genealogical Association

Putnam County Library
48 East Broad Street
PO Box 575
Cookeville, TN 38503-0575
Maurine Patton, Treasurer
Pub. *The Upper Cumberland Researcher*, quarterly
$10.00 per year membership; queries free to members

Warren County Genealogical Association, Inc.

(Wm. H. & Edgar Magness Community House and Library, 118 West Main Street—location)
PO Box 411 (mailing address)
McMinnville, TN 37110-0411
(423) 473-2428; (931) 657-2813 (Editor)
Fred L. Clark, Bulletin Editor/Board of Directors
Hours: Mon 8:30–9:30, Tue–Wed & Fri–Sat 10:00–4:30
Pub. *Warren County Tennessee Genealogical Bulletin*, quarterly
$10.00 per year membership

Watauga Association of Genealogists—Upper East Tennessee

PO Box 117
Johnson City, TN 37605-0117
(423) 753-3116 (Secretary)
Mary Sue Going, Corresponding Secretary
Hours: Johnson City Public Library: monthly meeting
Pub. *Watauga Association of Genealogists Bulletin*, semiannually (May and October)
$12.00 per year subscription or membership; no research services, but referrals provided

Weakley County Genealogical Society

PO Box 894
Martin, TN 38237
Pansy N. Baker, President
Pub. *Forget Me Not*, quarterly
$7.50 per year membership

Independent Publications and Miscellany

Appalachian Roots
(see West Virginia)

Bailey Publishing and Research Associates
(630 Old Poplar Springs Road—
location)
PO Box 493 (mailing address)
Kingston, TN 37763
E-mail: bphs52a@prodigy.com
Robert L. Bailey, Owner
Pub. *Roane Roots*, quarterly, $12.00 per
year subscription for individuals or
families, $6.00 per year subscription
for students, $20.00 per year
subscription for institutions
(publishes books on Roane and Morgan
counties, Tennessee and performs
genealogical research for all east
Tennessee counties)
research: $13.00 per hour (includes up to
10 photocopies), single document
retrieval: $5.00 (includes one
photocopy), 25¢ per page for each
additional photocopy

Beech Grove Confederate Cemetery
206 Greenfield Avenue
Tullahoma, TN 37388
Carl Monin

Blount County Heritage Trust
PO Box 4093
Maryville, TN 37802

Blount County Historic Trust, Inc.
PO Box 161
Maryville, TN 37803-0161

Byron Sistler and Associates, Inc.
1712 Natchez Trace
PO Box 120934
Nashville, TN 37212
(615) 297-3085; (615) 298-2807 FAX;
(800) 578-9475 (orders only)
Hours: including nights and weekends
(emphasis on Tennessee censuses,
marriages, church records; dealer in
Tennessee, North Carolina, Kentucky
and Virginia genealogical books)

Center for Southern Folklore
1216 Peabody Avenue
PO Box 40105
Memphis, TN 38174
(901) 726-4205

Certified Genealogist
2400 Lysle Lane
Norwood, OH 45212-1222
Sandra Evans Smith, C.G.
(author specializing in genealogical and
historical books and articles on
Kentucky and East Tennessee)

Duck's Old Time Journal
3351 Oak Ridge Road
Palmyra, TN 37142
(423) 326-5389
Don "Duck" Davidson
Hours: 6:00–8:00
Pub. *Duck's Old Time Journal*, monthly,
$6.00 per year subscription; *Yearbook*
(with index), annually

("Old time news of happenings 'South of
the River' Montgomery County,
Tennessee, includes some family
history, but mostly weddings, school,
church, accidents, murders, etc.,
everything at least fifty years old.")
research available

East Tennessee Heritage Foundation, Inc.
1345 Oak Ridge Turnpike #318
Oak Ridge, TN 37830
(423) 691-4031
Paula Gammell, Editor
Pub. *East Tennessee Roots Genealogical/
Historical Quarterly*, $30.00 per year
subscription

Genealogical Institute
(see Virginia)

Genealogy Books and Consultation
(see Texas)

Genealogy Friends: Partyline
PO Box 863
Hendersonville, TN 37077
(615) 824-2317
Nancy P. Goodman, Editor and Publisher
Pub. *Genealogy Friends: Partyline*
(emphasis on Middle Tennessee),
bimonthly, $10.00 per year
subscription, $1.00 plus SASE for
sample copy

Historic Rugby, Inc.
Rugby Restoration Association
(Highway 52—location)
PO Box 8 (mailing address)
Rugby, TN 37733
(423) 628-2441
Hours: Office: Mon–Fri 9:00–5:00
Pub. *Rugbeian*, quarterly, $15.00 per
year subscription

Hunting for Bears Genealogical and Historical Society
(see Alabama)

Lovelady Publications
280 Maple Street
Erin, TN 37061
(931) 289-3751
Charles Lovelady, Publisher, Joyce
Lovelady, Editor
Hours: 12:00–9:00
Pub. *Hornberger Journal* (includes
Stewart, Houston, Humphries,
Dickson, Montgomery, Robertson,
Hickman counties and the old
Tennessee County; history, genealogy
articles, queries for Tennessee and
adjoining states), bimonthly, $17.00
per year subscription

The Mountain Empire Genealogical Quarterly
(see Virginia)

Mountain Press
4503 Anderson Pike
PO Box 400
Signal Mountain, TN 37377-0400
(423) 886-6369 (Office); (423) 886-5312
FAX
James L. Douthat, Owner
Hours: daily 9:00–5:00
Pub. *Southern Genealogical Index*
(seventeen southern states: Alabama,
Arkansas, Florida, Georgia, Kansas,
Kentucky, Louisiana, Maryland,
Mississippi, Missouri, North Carolina,
Oklahoma, South Carolina, Tennessee,
Texas, Virginia, West Virginia),
annually, $10.00 per issue;
Appalachian Families (migration of
families through the Appalachian
region of the mid-Atlantic states),
quarterly, $15.00 per year
subscription; *TN Genealogy & History*,
three times per year, $20.00 per year
subscription

Name Game Enterprises
PO Box 8754
Spokane, WA 99203-0754
Mrs. E. Dale Hastin Smith
Pub. *Tennessee and Kentucky Queries*,
$5.75 plus $2.00 postage per issue
(Washington residents add 7.9% tax)

Reppert Publications
Antique and Collectible News
(see Illinois)

Restore Our County, Inc.
PO Box 325
Dandridge, TN 37725
(931) 397-9392; (615) 397-2373

Rowan County Register
(see North Carolina)

Serviceberry Press
A Subsidiary of New South Architectural
Press
5632 Meadowcrest Lane
Nashville, TN 37209
(615) 356-3136
E-mail: ilene.jones-
cornwell@nashville.com
Ilene Jones-Cornwell, General Editor
(devoted to genealogy and southern/local
history)

Simmons Historical Publications
(see Kentucky)

Southern Genealogist's Exchange Society
(see Florida)

Tennessee Association of Museums
4 Music Square, East
Nashville, TN 37203
(615) 256-1639

*Tennessee Genealogy and History
News*
Rt. 3, Box 65
Chandler, OK 74834-8504
R. D. Bradshaw, Editor
Pub. *Tennessee Genealogy and History
  News*

Tennessee Valley Authority
400 West Summit Hill Drive
Knoxville, TN 37902
(423) 632-3466

TnGenWeb
Part of U.S. GenWeb Project
E-mail: tn@usgenweb.com
http://www.tngenweb.usit.com/
(links to other Tennessee resources)

**Mary Walker Historical and
Educational Foundation**
3031 Wilcox Boulevard
Chattanooga, TN 37411
(423) 622-3217

TEXAS

Archives and Libraries with Holdings in Genealogy

State Archives and Library

**Texas State Library and Archives
Commission**
(1201 Brazos Street, Austin, TX 78701—
  location)
Capitol Station, Box 12927 (mailing
  address)
Austin, TX 78711
(512) 463-5463 (Genealogy); (512) 463-
  5455 (Information Services Division,
  Reference Collection); (512) 463-5480
  (State Archives Division, Network of
  Statewide Depositories—RHRD);
  (512) 463-5436 FAX
E-mail: geninfo@tsl.state.tx.us
  (Genealogy); archinfo@tsl.state.tx.us
  (Archives)
http://www.tsl.state.tx.us
Wendy Clark, Genealogy Supervisor
Hours: Genealogy: Tue–Sat 8:00–5:00;
  Archives and Reference Documents:
  Mon–Fri 8:00–5:00

Texas General Land Office
Archives and Records Division
1700 North Congress
Austin, TX 78701-1495
(512) 463-5277
E-mail: tgloarc@glo.state.tx.us
http://www.glo.state.tx.us/

Texas Historical Commission
(1511 Colorado, Austin, TX 78701—
  location)
PO Box 12276
Austin, TX 78711-2276
(512) 463-6100; (512) 475-4872 FAX
E-mail: thc@nueces.thc.state.tx.us
Curtis Tunnell, Executive Director and
  State Historic Preservation Officer
(not genealogical: site preservation)

State Historical Society

Texas State Historical Association
2.306 SRH, University Station
Austin, TX 78712
(512) 471-1525
Ron Tyler, Ph.D., Director
Hours: Mon–Fri 8:00–5:00
Pub. *Texas Historian*, quarterly, $7.00
  per year subscription; *Riding Line*,
  quarterly; *Southwestern Historical
  Quarterly*
(no reference departments, no
  genealogical searches)
$35.00 per year membership

City, County and Regional Archives and Libraries

Abilene Public Library
202 Cedar Street
Abilene, TX 79601
(915) 677-2474, ext. 115
Susan Tipton, Genealogy Department
Hours: Mon–Tue & Thur 9:00–9:00,
  Wed & Fri–Sat 9:00–6:00

Amarillo Public Library
413 East Fourth Street
PO Box 2171
Amarillo, TX 79189-2171
(806) 378-3054
Mary Kay Snell, Director of Library and
  Information Services
Hours: Mon–Thur 9:00–9:00, Fri–Sat
  9:00–6:00, Sun 2:00–6:00
(genealogical collection with strength in
  the southern states)

American Cotton Museum
(600 East Interstate 30—location)
PO Box 347 (mailing address)
Greenville, TX 75403
(903) 454-1990
Carol Taylor, Executive Director
Hours: Tue–Sat 10:00–5:30, Sun 1:00–
  5:00
Pub. *The History Hunter*, quarterly
(Hunt County, northeast Texas, cotton
  production)
$10.00–$100.00 per year membership;
  search fee: $5.00 per hour

Angelo State University
Porter Henderson Library
2601 West Avenue N
PO Box 11014, ASU Station
San Angelo, TX 76909
Hours: Mon–Fri 1:00–5:00

Aransas County Library
701 East Mimosa
Rockport, TX 78382
Mary Ragsdale, Librarian
Hours: Mon–Fri 9:00–6:00, Sat 10:00–
  2:00
volunteers do research

Archer County Museum
(201 North Sycamore—location)
PO Box 102 (mailing address)
Archer City, TX 76351
(940) 423-6426
Jack Loftin, Chairman
Hours: Sat 9:00–5:00, Sun 1:00–5:00
(complete grave census of 70,000 in the
  70 mile by 80 mile north Texas area,
  Archer, Clay, Jack and Young
  counties)

Arlington Public Library
101 East Abram Street
Arlington, TX 76010
(817) 459-6900
Hours: Mon–Thur 9:00–9:00, Fri–Sat
  9:00–6:00

Austin Public Library
Austin History Center
810 Guadalupe
PO Box 2287
Austin, TX 78768-2287
(512) 499-7480
E-mail: aplmail@library.ci.austin.tx.us
http://www.ci.austin.tx.us/library/
Biruta Celmins Kearl, Administrator
Hours: Mon–Thur 9:00–9:00, Fri–Sat
  9:00–6:00, Sun 12:00–6:00
(Travis County, Texas)

Austin Public Library
Austin Records Center
211 East Alpine
Austin, TX 78768
http://www.ci.austin.tx.us/library/
  lbahc.htm

Stephen F. Austin State University
The Center for East Texas Studies
Ferguson Building 340
PO Box 6134, Stephen F. Austin Station
Nacogdoches, TX 75962
(409) 468-1392; (409) 468-2190 FAX
E-mail: CETS@sfasu.edu
http://www.sfasu.edu/

Stephen F. Austin State University
Steen Library
East Texas Research Center
PO Box 13055, Stephen F. Austin Station
Nacogdoches, TX 75962-3055
(409) 468-4100
E-mail: lnicklas@sfalib.sfasu.edu
http://libweb.sfasu.edu/etrc/etrcbro.htm
Linda Cheves Nicklas, Director
Hours: Mon–Fri 8:00–5:00, Sat 10:00–
  6:00

Stephen F. Austin State University
Texas Folklore Society
108 Rusk Building
PO Box 13007, Stephen F. Austin Station
Nacogdoches, TX 75962-3007
(409) 468-4407; (409) 468-1028 FAX
E-mail: fabernethy@sfasu.edu
http://jacobi.sfasu.edu/tfs
F. E. Abernethy, Secretary-Editor
Hours: Mon–Fri 8:00–5:00
Pub. *Publications of the Texas Folklore
  Society*, annually
$15.00 per year membership for
  individuals, $20.00 per year
  membership for families, $30.00 per
  year Patron membership, $50.00 per
  year *Paisano Grande* membership

Bay City Public Library
1100 Seventh Street
Bay City, TX 77414
(409) 245-6931
Rosanne Burgess, Director
Hours: Mon–Thur 9:00–8:00, Fri 11:00–
  6:00, Sat 9:00–6:00

Baylor County Historical Museum
(200 West McLain Street—location)
Rt. 2, Box 48 (mailing address)
Seymour, TX 76380

Belton City Library
301 East First Avenue
Belton, TX 76513
(254) 933-5830
E-mail: blibrary@vvm.com
http://www.cityofbelton.org
Lena Armstrong, Director
Hours: Mon–Fri noon–5:00, Sat 9:00–
  1:00
(Belton and Bell County history and
  genealogy)
no search service, will supply names of
  professional researchers

Bigfoot Wallace Museum
Big Foot, TX 78005

Bonham Public Library
City Hall
Bonham, TX 75418

Brazoria County Historical Museum
100 East Cedar
Angleton, TX 77515
(409) 849-5711, ext. 1208
E-mail: handy@bchm.org
http://www.bchm.org
Jamie Murray, Information Resources
  Coordinator
Hours: Tue–Fri 9:00–5:00, Sat 9:00–3:00
Pub. *The Window Pane*, quarterly
("Old 300" genealogy database; Brazoria
  County family biography file; oral
  history audio tape collection)
$25.00 per year membership

Herman Brown Free Library
Burnet County Library System
J. Frank Dobie Room
100 East Washington Street
Burnet, TX 78611
Hours: Mon–Fri 10:00–6:00

Bryan Public Library
201 East 26th Street
Bryan, TX 77803
(409) 779-1736 (Reference)
Nancy McCraw Ross, Senior Reference
  Librarian
Hours: Mon–Tue & Thur 9:00–9:00,
  Wed & Fri–Sat 9:00–5:00
(genealogical and local history
  collections with emphasis on Brazos
  County history)

C. W. M. Memorial Library
121 South Prairieville Street
Athens, TX 75751
Hours: Mon–Fri 10:00–6:00, Sat 9:00–
  1:00

Cactus Park and Museum
PO Drawer F
George West, TX 78022
(512) 449-1556

Cameron Public Library
304 East Third Street
Cameron, TX 76520
(254) 697-2401
Kay King, Director
Hours: Mon 12:00–7:00, Tue–Fri 9:00–
  5:00

Carnegie History Center
125 South College Avenue
Tyler, TX 75702
(972) 593-7989
Geoffrey Willbanks, Executive Director

Center for Great Plains Studies
(see Kansas)

Center for Great Plains Study
(see Nebraska)

Chambers County Library
PO Box 520
202 Cummings Street
Anahuac, TX 77514
(409) 267-8261
Ann Weaver
Hours: Mon–Tue 8:00–6:00, Wed–Fri
  8:00–5:00, Sat 9:00–1:00

Childress Heritage Museum
210 Third Street, N.W.
Childress, TX 79201
(940) 937-2261
Jenny Lou Taylor, Executive Director
Hours: Mon–Fri 9:00–5:00
(Childress County exhibits and history)

Colorado City Historical Museum
183 West Third Street
Colorado City, CO 79512
(915) 728-8285

**Comanche County Historical
Museum**
100 Moorman Drive
PO Box 22
Comanche, TX 76442
Fain McDaniel, President
Hours: Sat–Sun 2:00–4:00
(collection of artifacts and memorabilia)

Corpus Christi Public Library
Local History/Genealogy Department
805 Comanche
Corpus Christi, TX 78401
(512) 880-7030
http://www.ci.corpus-christi.tx.us
Margaret Rose, Librarian
Hours: Mon–Thur 9:00–9:00, Fri–Sat
  9:00–6:00, Sun 2:00–6:00

Corsicana Public Library
Genealogy Room
100 North 12th Street
Corsicana, TX 75110
(903) 872-3071
Greg Hill, Library Director
Hours: Mon–Tue 10:00–8:00, Wed–Fri
  10:00–6:00, Sat 10:00–4:00
volunteer research only

Coryell County Museum Foundation, Inc.
110 Eighth Street
PO Box 24
Gatesville, TX 76528
(254) 865-5421
Helen Swift, Board Chairperson
Hours: Fri–Sat 9:00–5:00, Sun 1:00–5:00

Cowboy Country Museum
113 Wetherbee
PO Box 1206
Stamford, TX 79553
(915) 773-2411

John H. Wootters Crockett Public Library
708 East Goliad
PO Box 1226
Crockett, TX 75835
(409) 544-3089
Marsha Edmiston, Director
Hours: Tue 9:00–8:00, Wed 9:00–5:00, Thur 9:00–1:00
Pub. *Newsletter*, monthly
search fee: donation plus $1.00 per page for copies

Crosby County Pioneer Memorial
101 West Main
Crosbyton, TX 79322
(806) 675-2331
Verna Anne Wheeler, Executive Director
Hours: Tue–Sat 9:00–noon & 1:00–5:00
("Material available that relates to Crosby County: histories and obituaries.")

Dallas Public Library
Genealogy Section
1515 Young Street
Dallas, TX 75201
(214) 670-1433; (214) 670-1434
Lloyd DeWitt Bockstruck, F.N.G.S., Supervisor, Genealogy Section
Hours: Mon–Thur 9:00–9:00, Fri–Sat 9:00–5:00, Sun 1:00–5:00

Dallas Public Library
Texas-Dallas History and Archives Division
1515 Young Street
Dallas, TX 75201
(214) 670-1435
http://205.165.160.15/home.htm
Marvin H. Stone, Division Manager
Hours: Mon–Thur 9:00–9:00, Fri–Sat 9:00–5:00, Sun 1:00–5:00
(specializes in historic photographs, maps, newspapers, JFK assassination collection)

The Daughters of the Republic of Texas Library
(300 Alamo Plaza at Crockett Street—location)
PO Box 1401 (mailing address)
San Antonio, TX 78295-1401
(210) 225-1071; (512) 225-8155
E-mail: drtl@salsa.net

http://www.drtl.org/
Cathy Herpich, Director
Hours: Mon–Sat 9:00–5:00
(Texas history and early Texas genealogy)

Deaf Smith County Museum
400 Sampson
PO Box 1007
Hereford, TX 79045
(806) 364-4338
Donna Brockman, Executive Director
Hours: Mon–Sat 10:00–5:00
Pub. *Deaf Smith County Historical Society Newsletter* (not genealogical), three times per year

Deer Park Independent School District Historical Museum
204 Ivy
Deer Park, TX 77536
(281) 479-2831

Denton Public Library
502 Oakland
Denton, TX 76201
(940) 349-8569; (940) 349-8260 FAX
Linda Touraine, Library Services Manager
Hours: Mon, Wed & Fri–Sat 9:00–6:00, Tue & Thur 9:00–9:00
limited research, charges for photocopies and postage

Denver City Museum
(505 North Avenue C—location)
PO Box 1530 (mailing address)
Denver City, TX 79323
(806) 592-2897
Carl Johnson, President
Hours: Tue–Thur 1:00–4:00, and by appointment
$10.00 per year membership for individuals, $15.00 per year membership for families, $100.00 life membership

DeWitt County Historical Museum
PO Box 745
Cuero, TX 77954
(512) 275-6322
Mrs. A. W. Schaffner, Curator

Ector County Library
321 West Fifth Street
Odessa, TX 79761
(915) 332-0633
Doris Baker, Head, Southwest History/ Genealogy Department
Hours: Genealogy Department: Mon–Thur 9:30–8:30, Fri–Sat 9:30–6:00, Sat 9:00–noon & 1:00–6:00

El Campo Museum of Art, History and Natural Science
2350 North Mechanic
PO Box 23
El Campo, TX 77437-0023
(409) 541-5092
Denise Prochazka, Curator

El Paso Main Public Library
501 North Oregon Street
El Paso, TX 79901
(915) 543-5474 (Government Documents/Genealogy); (915) 543-5440 (Southwest Collection)
Hours: Mon–Thur 8:30–9:00, Fri–Sat 8:30–5:30

El Paso Museum of History
12901 Gateway West
El Paso, TX 79927
(915) 858-1928
Barbara J. Ardus, Curator

El Progreso Memorial Library
129 West Nopal Street
Uvalde, TX 78801
(830) 278-2017 phone and FAX
E-mail: elpro@admin.hilconet.com
Susan Anderson, Director
Hours: Mon–Wed & Fri 9:00–6:00, Thur 9:00–8:00, Sat 9:00–1:00

Ellis County Museum, Inc.
201 South College Street
PO Box 706
Waxahachie, TX 75165
(972) 937-9283

Euless Public Library
Genealogy Room
201 North Ector Drive
Euless, TX 76039
(817) 685-1483
Hours: Mon–Tue & Thur 10:00–9:00, Wed 10:00–6:00, Fri–Sat 10:00–5:00, Sun 1:00-5:00

Fannin County Museum of History
1 Main Street
Bonham, TX 75418
(903) 583-8042
Tom Scott, President/Director
Hours: Tue–Thur 10:00–4:00
(some basic area history available, but all genealogical material has been donated to Bonham Public Library)
$20.00–$500.00 per year membership

Fayette Heritage Museum and Archives
855 South Jefferson
La Grange, TX 78945
(409) 968-6418; (409) 968-5357 FAX
E-mail: library@fais.net
Margaret Huenefeld, Curator/Archivist
Hours: Tue 10:00–6:30, Wed–Fri 10:00–5:00, Sat 10:00–1:00, Sun 1:00–5:00
(Fayette County, Texas)

Floyd County Historical Museum
105 East Missouri Street
PO Box 304
Floydada, TX 79235-0304
(806) 983-2415
Nancy Marble
Hours: Mon–Fri 1:00–5:00
Pub. *MuseBriefs*, annually

(genealogical library specializing in local history and genealogy)
no cost; no fee for research inquiries

Foard County Museum/McAdams Ranch
PO Box 609
Crowell, TX 79227
(940) 655-3395

Fort Belknap Archives (Young County)
Rt. 1, Box 27
Newcastle, TX 76372
B. A. Ledbetter, Archivist
Hours: Sat–Sun 9:00–5:00
$5.00 per year membership

Fort Bend Museum Association
(500 Houston Street, Richmond, TX 77469—location)
PO Drawer 460 (mailing address)
Richmond, TX 77406
(281) 342-6478
http://www.georgeranch.org
Michael Rugeley Moore, Executive Director
Hours: Tue–Fri 10:00–5:00, Sat–Sun 1:00–5:00, research in archives by appointment only
(emphasis on Austin's Colony, 1820–1836, and local history)

Fort Concho National Historic Landmark
630 South Oakes
San Angelo, TX 76903
(915) 657-4441
John Neilson, Historian/Archivist
Hours: by appointment
Pub. *Fort Concho Guidon*, quarterly
(Indian Wars military history 1866–1891, west Texas history 1866–1920, local history, Texas history)
$25.00 per year membership

Fort Stockton Historical Society
Riggs Museum
301 South Main
Fort Stockton, TX 79735
(915) 336-2167
ViCindy Riggs, Director/Curator
Hours: Mon–Sat 10:00–5:00, Sun 1:30–5:00, Sun (summer) 1:30–8:00
Pub. *Fort Stockton Historical Society Newsletter*, quarterly

Fort Worth Museum of Science and History
1501 Montgomery
Fort Worth, TX 76107
(817) 732-1631
T. Lindsay Baker, Curator of History; Karen Turner, Manager of Volunteer Services and Public Relations

Fort Worth Public Library
Genealogy and Local History Department
300 Taylor Street
Fort Worth, TX 76102-7309

(817) 871-7701; (817) 871-7740 (Genealogy)
E-mail: wmaster@amon.pub-lib.ci.fort-worth.tx.us
http://198.215.16.7:443/fortworth/Fwpl/index.htm
Linda Bostic, Social Science Unit Manager
Hours: Mon–Thur 9:00–9:00, Fri 9:00–6:00, Sat 10:00–6:00
(Tarrant County and Northwest Texas; Huguenots; Scotch-Irish; ante-bellum Southern plantation records; cowboy oral histories)

Frankston Depot Library and Museum, Inc.
Town Square, South
PO Box 639
Frankston, TX 75763
(903) 876-4463; (903) 876-3226 FAX
Patricia Montrose, Library Director
Hours: Tue & Sat 9:00–5:00, Thur noon–7:00
out-of-county user fee: $15.00 per year

Freestone County Historical Museum
302 East Main Street
PO Box 524
Fairfield, TX 75840
(903) 389-3738

Frontier Times Museum
506 13th Street
PO Box 1918
Bandera, TX 78003-1918
(830) 796-3864
Pat D'Spain, President
Hours: Mon–Sat 10:00–4:30, Sun 1:00–4:00

Galveston County Historical Museum
2219 Market Street
Galveston, TX 77550
(409) 766-2340; (409) 766-1560 FAX
Alice Wygant, Director
Hours: Mon–Sat 10:00–4:00, Sun noon–4:00

George Memorial Library
Fort Bend County Libraries
1001 Golfview Drive
Richmond, TX 77469-5141
(281) 342-4455; (281) 341-2608
http://www.fortbend.lib.tx.us/gm.html
W. M. Von Maszewski, Department Manager
Hours: Mon–Thur 9:00–9:00, Fri–Sat 9:00–5:00, Sun (except summer) 1:00–5:00
("genealogical materials pertain primarily to the southeastern U.S.; Civil War [Confederacy] microfilm collection")

Grand Prairie Memorial Library
901 Conover
Grand Prairie, TX 75051

(972) 264-9523; (972) 264-3823 FAX
Hours: varies

Grand Saline Public Library
201 East Pacific Avenue
Grand Saline, TX 75140
(903) 962-5516

Grapevine Public Library
1201 South Main
Grapevine, TX 76051
(817) 481-0336
Mrs. Jerre Williams, Reference Librarian
Hours: Mon–Tue & Thur 10:00–8:00, Wed & Fri 10:00–6:00, Sat 10:00–5:00

Gregg County Historical Museum
(214 North Fredonia Street, Longview, TX 75601—location)
PO Box 3342 (mailing address)
Longview, TX 75606
(903) 753-5840
Ellie Caston, Ph.D., Museum Director
Hours: Tue–Sat 10:00–4:00
Pub. *Museumemo*, semiannually (spring and fall)
("We provide information about our local history, but offer very little genealogical information.")
from $25.00 to $1,000 per year membership

Hacksma House Genealogy Library
(see Washington)

Z. I. Hale Museum
242 West Dole Street
PO Box 42
Winters, TX 79567

Nita Stewart Haley Memorial Library and History Center
1805 West Indiana
Midland, TX 79701
(915) 682-5785
Robin L. McWilliams, Curator

Harlingen Public Library
410 76 Drive
Harlingen, TX 78550
(956) 430-6650
Dorothy McBride, Genealogical Society Representative
Hours: Mon–Thur 10:00–9:00, Fri 1:00–5:00

Gladys L. Harrington Public Library
1501 18th Street
Plano, TX 75074
(972) 461-7175; (972) 461-7292
http://www.ci.plano.tx.us/library/genealgy.htm
Anne Womack, Library Manager
Hours: Mon–Thur 10:00–9:00, Fri–Sat 10:00–6:00, Sun 1:00–5:00

Harrison County Historical Museum
Peter Whetstone Square
Marshall, TX 75670
(903) 938-2680

Mildred Hooper, Office Manager
Hours: Mon–Sat 10:00–5:00, Sun 1:30–
5:00
Pub. *Harrison County Historical
Museum Monthly Newsletter*
$25.00 per year membership for
individuals (beginning in September),
$35.00 per year membership for
families, $50.00 per year Sustaining
membership, $100.00 per year Patron
membership, $350.00 life membership

W. Walworth Harrison Public Library

Genealogy Room
3716 Lee Street
Greenville, TX 75401
(903) 457-2992
Gail Slater, Genealogy/Local History
Librarian
Hours: Mon–Sat 9:30–4:30, Sun (winter)
1:30–5:30
(specializes in Texas, southern states, and
Hunt County, Texas)
will answer minimal research questions
if accompanied by SASE, no in-depth
research

Heritage House Museum of Orange County, Inc.

905 West Division Street
Orange, TX 77630
(409) 886-5385
Carolyn Rose, Administrator
Pub. *Nostalgia News*

Hickman Library and Museum

609 Main Street
PO Box 66
Big Lake, TX 76932
(915) 884-2793

Hidalgo County Historical Museum

121 East McIntyre
Edinburg, TX 78539
(956) 383-6911; (956) 381-8518 FAX
David J. Mycue, Curator of Archives and
Collections
Hours: Museum archives and library:
Tue–Fri 9:00–5:00
Pub. *Rio Grande Heritage* (a
photohistory book, not genealogical)
("Archives and photo files specialize in
Mexican-American families in the
lower Rio Grande Valley, 1750 to the
present.")
research: $12.00 per hour, photocopies
10¢ each

Hood County Library

222 North Travis
Granbury, TX 76048
(817) 573-3569
Jeanell Morris, Librarian
Hours: Mon 10:00–7:00, Tue 10:00–
9:00, Wed–Sat 10:00–6:00

Houston County Visitors Center/ Museum, Inc.

(303 South First Street—location)
PO Box 449 (mailing address)
Crockett, TX 75835
(409) 544-9520
Mary A. Lowe, President
Hours: Wed 2:00–4:00, and by
appointment
("diaries, photos, Houston County
history segments, exhibits")
$10.00 per year membership

Clayton Library, Center for Genealogical Research

a unit of the Houston Public Library
5300 Caroline
Houston, TX 77004-6896
(713) 284-1999
http://sparc.hpl.lib.tx.us/hpl/clayton.html
Margaret J. Harris, Manager
Hours: Mon–Wed 9:00–9:00, Thur–Sat
9:00–5:00
(a nationwide genealogical collection
with some foreign materials; complete
collection of federal census through
1920 and Soundex through 1910, plus
indexes to federal military service and
pensions through Spanish American
War; county, state and federal records,
passenger lists, lineage material from
many patriotic societies, family
histories, vertical files, periodicals,
maps, finding aids)

Sam Houston Regional Library and Research Center (Southeast Texas)

FM RD 1011
PO Box 310
Liberty, TX 77575-0310
(409) 336-8821
http://link.tsl.state.tx.us
Robert L. Schaadt, Director-Archivist
Hours: Mon–Fri 8:00–5:00, Sat 9:00–
4:00
(part of the Archives and Information
Services Division of the Texas State
Library, serves as the Regional
Historical Resource Depository for
Southeast Texas: Chambers, Hardin,
Jasper, Jefferson, Liberty, Newton,
Orange, Polk, San Jacinto and Tyler
counties)

Huntsville Public Library

1216 14th Street
Huntsville, TX 77340
(409) 291-5472
E-mail: jhunter@hals.lib.tx.us
Judy Hunter, Librarian
Hours: Mon–Thur 9:00–7:00, Fri–Sat
10:00–5:00
(Texara Collection, family Bible records,
Civil War and World War II
collections)

Hutchinson County Historical Museum

618 North Main
Borger, TX 79007
(806) 273-0130
Ed Benz, Director
Hours: Mon–Fri 9:00–5:00, Sat 11:00–
4:30, Sun (Labor Day–Memorial Day)
2:00–5:00
Pub. *Quarterly Newsletter*, free
(county families up to 1979, limited
research resources)

Jacksonville Public Library

502 South Jackson
Jacksonville, TX 75766

Key Genealogical Library

2200 North Yarbrough Drive, #B-281
El Paso, TX 79925-6333
Hours: Tue–Wed 10:00–4:00, Sat 10:00–
2:00, Tue 6:00 P.M.–9:00 P.M.

Kurth Memorial Library

Ora McMullen Room, Genealogy, Local
and State History
101 North Cotton Square
Lufkin, TX 75904-2997
(409) 634-7617; (409) 639-2487 FAX
John W. Wilkins, Head
Hours: Tue–Wed 1:00–6:00, Thur 1:00–
8:00, Fri 1:00–5:30, Sat 9:00–1:00

Lamar University

(Highway 69 at University Drive—
location)
PO Box 1007 (mailing address)
Beaumont, TX 77710
(409) 835-0823; (409) 838-9107 FAX
Christy Marino, Curator
Hours: Tue–Sun 1:00–5:00
costs vary

Lamesa-Dawson County Museum

(South Second Street and Avenue M—
location)
404 21st Place (mailing address)
Lamesa, TX 79331

The Laredo Children's Museum

West End, Washington Street
Laredo, TX 78040
(210) 721-5321
Irma Peña, Executive Director
Hours: Office: Mon–Fri 8:00–5:00;
Museum: Thur–Sat 10:00–5:00, Sun
1:00–5:00
$35.00 per year membership for families;
admission: adults $2.00, children $1.00

Laredo Public Library

Bruni Plaza
Laredo, TX 78040
(210) 722-2435
Sandra L. Chamberlain, Librarian
Hours: Tue–Thur 9:00–9:00, Fri–Sat
9:00–6:00

Layland Museum
201 North Caddo
Cleburne, TX 76031
(817) 645-0940; (817) 641-3321, ext. 375
Julie P. Baker, Curator
(research libraries on local history, Native Americans, and the Civil War)

Longview Public Library
222 West Cotton
Longview, TX 75601
(903) 237-1350
Pauline Cox
Hours: Mon, Wed–Fri 9:00–12:00 & 1:00–6:00

Lubbock City-County Library
1306 Ninth Street
Lubbock, TX 79401
(806) 767-2836; (806) 767-2830 FAX
Jane Clausen, Public Services Director
Hours: Mon–Thur 9:00–9:00, Fri–Sat 9:00–6:00, Sun 1:00–5:00
(has genealogy department)

Luling Public Library
215 South Pecan Avenue
Luling, TX 78648

Martin County Historical Museum
207 Broadway
PO Box 929
Stanton, TX 79782
(915) 756-2722
Hours: Tue–Sat 9:00–4:00

Matagorda County Museum
2100 Avenue F
Bay City, TX 77414
(409) 245-7502
Mary Belle Ingram, Archives Chair
Hours: Tue–Fri 10:00–4:00, Sat–Sun 1:00–4:00
(Matagorda County history and genealogy; "We have an early newspaper collection of Matagorda County.")

Medallion Home/Pioneer Park Association
c/o Chamber of Commerce, School Street
PO Box 662
Kermit, TX 79745
(915) 586-2507
Hours: first Sun 3:00–5:00

Mendoza Trail Museum
PO Box 782
McCamey, TX 79752-0782
(915) 652-3192
Sandra Vickers, Curator

Mesquite Public Library
300 Grubb Drive
Mesquite, TX 75149
(972) 216-6229
Marjorie Bays
Hours: Mon–Thur 9:00–9:00, Fri–Sat 9:00–6:00

Midland County Historical Museum
301 West Missouri
Midland, TX 79701
(915) 688-8947
Nancy R. McKinley, Director
Hours: Mon–Wed & Fri–Sat 2:00–5:00
(archival material)

Midland County Public Library
The John and Rosalind Redfern Genealogical Research Center
301 West Missouri
PO Box 1191
Midland, TX 79702
(915) 683-2708
Sandra De Fore Wegner, County Librarian
Hours: Sept–May: Mon–Thur 9:00–9:00, Fri–Sat 9:00–6:00; Jun–Aug: Mon 9:00–9:00, Tue–Sat 9:00–6:00

Montgomery County Memorial Library
Central Library
104 I 45 North
Conroe, TX 77301
(409) 788-8363; (409) 788-8324 FAX
Barbara Hawkins Franz, Genealogy Librarian
Hours: Mon & Fri–Sat 9:00–5:00, Tue–Thur 9:00–9:00
(Texas and the southern states, including Arkansas, Missouri and Oklahoma)

Moody Museum
114 West Ninth Street
PO Box 765
Taylor, TX 76574

Moore Memorial Public Library
1701 Ninth Avenue, North
Texas City, TX 77590
Hours: Mon–Wed 9:00–9:00, Thur–Fri 9:00–6:00, Sat 10:00–4:00

Morton Museum of Cooke County
210 South Dixon
Gainesville, TX 76240
(940) 668-8900
Shana Powell, Curator
Pub. *Heritage Highlights*

Mount Pleasant Municipal Library
213 North Madison
Mount Pleasant, TX 75455
(903) 575-4180
Hours: Mon 1:00–6:00, Tue–Fri 9:00–6:00, Sat 9:00–1:00
no research by staff, but will put patrons in touch with a freelance researcher

Museum and Archives of the Big Bend
PO Box C-210
Alpine, TX 79832
(915) 837-8143
Hours: Tue–Sat 9:00–5:00, Sun 1:00–5:00

Museum for East Texas Culture
400 Micheaux Avenue
Palestine, TX 75801-3628
(903) 723-1914
Drew Franklin, Director

The Museum of East Texas
503 North Second Street
Lufkin, TX 75901
(409) 639-4434
Mark A. Tullos, Jr., Executive Director

Museum of the Great Plains
(see Oklahoma)

Nicholson Memorial Library
625 Austin
Garland, TX 75040
(972) 205-2503; (972) 205-2523 FAX
Terry Tule, Genealogical Librarian
Hours: Mon–Thur 10:00–9:00, Fri–Sat 10:00–6:00
Pub. *Garland Genealogical Society Newsletter*, monthly
$15.00 per year membership

Old Rock House
Highway 84
PO Box 335
Santa Anna, TX 76878
(915) 348-3283

Old Spanish Missions Historical Research Collection and Texana Collection
411 S.W. 24th Street
San Antonio, TX 78207-4600
(210) 434-6711, ext. 321
E-mail: marlv@lake.ollusa.edu
http://www.ollusa.edu/collections.htm
Vicky Marlette, Special Collections Librarian
Hours: Mon–Fri by appointment

Palacios Area Historical Association
401 Commerce
PO Box 11
Palacios, TX 77465
(512) 972-2270
Colleen Claybourn, Chair
Hours: Museum: Thur–Sun 1:00–4:00, and by appointment
Pub. *Newsletter*, quarterly
("We have begun genealogy files at the museum: clippings, photos, letters, etc.")
$5.00 per year membership

Panhandle-Plains Historical Museum
2401 Fourth Avenue
PO Box 967, WTAMU
Canyon, TX 79015
(806) 656-2261; (806) 656-2250 FAX
E-mail: llambert@wtpphmfs.wtamu.edu
http://www.wtamu.edu/museum/home.html
Lisa S. Lambert, Archivist
Hours: Mon–Fri 9:00–12:00 & 1:00–5:00

Paris Junior College
A. M. and Welma Aikin, Jr., Regional
   Archives
2400 Clarksville Street
Paris, TX 75460-6298
(903) 784-9411
Daisy Harvill, Director
(northeast Texas)

Paris Public Library
326 South Main Street
Paris, TX 75460
(903) 785-8531
(has city directories from 1940)

Lucy Hill Patterson Memorial Library
201 Ackerman Street
Rockdale, TX 76567
(512) 446-3410
Melanie Todd, Head Librarian
Hours: Tue–Wed & Fri 10:00–5:00, Thur
   1:00–8:00, Sat 10:00–2:00

Perry Memorial Library
Fifth and Ash
Perryton, TX 79070
(806) 435-5801
Hours: Mon 10:00–8:00, Tue–Fri 10:00–
   5:30, Sat 10:00–1:00

Pilot Point Community Library
PO Box 969
Pilot Point, TX 76258

Pioneer City/County Museum
610 East Third
Sweetwater, TX 79556
(915) 235-8547
H. E. Pepper, Manager
(manuscript collection)

Pioneer Town
333 Wayside Drive
Wimberley, TX 78676
(512) 847-2517

Pioneer, Trail Driver and Former Texas Rangers Association, Inc.
3805 Broadway
San Antonio, TX 78209
(210) 822-9011
Pat Halpin, Secretary-Treasurer
Hours: Tue–Sun (May 1–Sept 1) 10:00–
   5:00, Wed–Sun (Sept 1–May 1) 11:00–
   4:00
(Texas history)

Port Arthur Public Library
3601 Cultural Center Drive
Port Arthur, TX 77642
(409) 985-8838; (409) 985-5969 FAX
Jill Stockinger, Chief Librarian and
   Reference Department Head
Hours: Mon–Thur 10:00–9:00, Fri
   10:00–6:00, Sat 10:00–5:00, Sunday
   (except summer) 2:00–5:00

Quitman Public Library
202 East Goode Street
PO Box 77
Quitman, TX 75783
(903) 763-4191
Dorothy Demontigny, Library Director
Hours: Mon & Thur 9:00–9:00, Tue &
   Fri 9:00–5:00

Ralls Historical Museum
801 Main Street
PO Box 384
Ralls, TX 79357
(806) 253-2425
Pauline Watkins, Executive Director

Rankin Museum
Fifth and Main Streets
PO Box 82
Rankin, TX 79778
(915) 693-2371
Helen Hurst
Hours: Thur–Sat afternoons
(archives focus on Upton County;
   obituaries, newspapers)

Red River Historical Museum of Sherman
301 South Walnut
Sherman, TX 75090
(903) 893-7623
E-mail: rrhms@texoma.net
Kelli L. Pickard, Director
Hours: Tue–Fri 10:00–noon & 1:00–
   4:30, Sat 2:00–5:00
Pub. *Red River Historical Museum
   Sentinel*, bimonthly
("We have limited information on
   specific families of the county; we
   mostly have general history of the
   area.")
$25.00 per year membership for
   individuals, $45.00 per year
   membership for families, $5.00 per
   year membership for students, $10.00
   per year membership for senior
   citizens; search fees: $10.00 per hour
   plus copy costs

Red River Valley Museum
4600 College Drive, West
PO Box 2004
Vernon, TX 76384
(940) 553-1848
Ann G. Huskinson, Executive Director

Rice University
Woodson Research Center
Fondren Library
6100 South Main Street
PO Box 1892
Houston, TX 77251-1892
(713) 527-8101, ext. 2586; (713) 285-
   5207 FAX
E-mail: boothe@rice.edu; jsh@rice.edu
   (*Journal*)
Pub. *Journal of Southern History*

Rio Grande Valley Museum
Boxwood at Raintree
Harlingen, TX 78550
(210) 430-8500; (210) 430-8502 FAX
E-mail: rgvmuse@hiline.net
http://www.hiline.net/rgvmuse/
Linn R. S. Keller, Museum Director
Hours: Wed–Sat 10:00–4:00, Sun 1:00–
   4:00

River Valley Pioneer Museum
118 North Second
PO Box 1201
Canadian, TX 79014
(806) 323-6548
Pam Spencer, Museum Director

Riviera Historical Museum
Seventh and North Boulevard
Riviera, TX 78379
(512) 296-3676

Rosenberg Library
2310 Sealy Avenue
Galveston, TX 77550
(409) 763-8854; (409) 763-0275 FAX
Casey Edward Greene, Head of Special
   Collections
Hours: Tue–Sat 9:00–5:00

Round Rock Public Library
211 East Main
Round Rock, TX 78680
(houses collection of the Williamson
   County Genealogical Society)

San Antonio Public Library
Texana/Genealogy Department
600 Soledad
San Antonio, TX 78205
(210) 207-2500; (210) 207-2558 FAX
E-mail: jmyler@xl.ci.sat.tx.us
http://www.ci.sat.tx.us/sapl/html/
   genealogy.html
Jo Myler, Librarian III
Hours: Mon–Thur 9:00–9:00, Fri–Sat
   9:00–5:00, Sun 11:00–5:00
Pub. *The Explorer*, quarterly
(San Antonio and Texas; U.S.; Mexico)

San Augustine Public Library
413 East Columbia Street
San Augustine, TX 75972
(409) 275-5367
Mrs. Pat Snider, Director
Hours: Mon–Fri 9:00–5:00, Sat 9:00–
   2:00
(local history and genealogy; "carefully
   compiled cataloging of cemeteries of
   San Augustine County.")

San Jacinto Museum of History Association
3800 Park Road, 1836
La Porte, TX 77571
(281) 479-2421

Schleicher County Public Library
201 South Main
PO Box 611
Eldorado, TX 76936

E-mail: sepl@wcc.net
Jeri Whitten
Hours: 10:00–5:00

Scurry County Library
1916 23rd Street
Snyder, TX 79549
(915) 573-5572
Noreen E. Taylor, Librarian
Hours: Mon, Wed & Fri–Sat 10:00–6:00,
Tue & Thur 10:00–9:00

Seguin/Guadalupe County Public Library
707 East College Street
Seguin, TX 78155
Hours: Mon–Thur 10:00–9:00, Fri–Sat
9:00–5:00

Sherman Public Library
Local History and Genealogy
Department
421 North Travis
Sherman, TX 75090
(903) 892-7240
Jacqueline Banfield, Assistant Library
Director
Hours: Mon, Wed & Fri 9:00–6:00, Tue
& Thur 9:00–9:00, Sat 9:00–5:00

Singletary Memorial Library
Sixth Street
Rusk, TX 75785

Slaton Museum Association
155 North Eighth
PO Box 555
Slaton, TX 79364
Almarine Childers, President
Hours: Tue–Fri 1:00–5:00
$10.00 per year membership for
individuals, $15.00 per year
membership for families; free
admission

South Plains Museum Association
608 Avenue H
PO Box 1304
Levelland, TX 79336
(806) 894-7547

Genealogical Research Center and Library of Southeast Texas
Rt. 1, Box 405
Kountze, TX 77625
Pub. *International Genealogical
Exchange*, monthly, $12.00 per year
subscription

Southern Methodist University
DeGloyer Library of Special Collections
Dallas, TX 75275
(214) 768-2012; (214) 768-1565 FAX
E-mail: dfarmer@mail.smu.edu
http://www.smu.edu/~cul/degolyer/
index.html

Southmost College
Arnulfo L. Oliveira Memorial Library
Hunter Room
83 Fort Brown
Brownsville, TX 78520
(956) 544-8221
Yolanda Gonzalez
Hours: Mon–Thur 7:30–10:00, Fri 7:30–
5:00, Sat 10:30–4:00, Sun 2:00–9:00

Southwestern University
A. Frank Smith, Jr., Library Center
Special Collections Department
PO Box 770
Georgetown, TX 78627-0770
(512) 863-1568
E-mail: stallark@southwestern.edu
http://www.southwestern.edu/library/
special-collections.html

Star of the Republic Museum
Washington-on-the-Brazos State
Historical Park
PO Box 317
Washington, TX 77880
(409) 878-2461
Houston McGaugh, Director
Hours: daily 10:00–5:00

Sterling Municipal Library
Mary Elizabeth Wilbanks Avenue
Baytown, TX 77520
Hours: Mon–Thur 10:00–9:00, Fri–Sat
10:00–6:00

Swenson Memorial Museum Research Library
116 West Walker
PO Box 350
Breckenridge, TX 76424
(254) 559-8471
Freda Mitchell, Museum Director
Hours: Tue–Sat 10:00–noon & 1:00–5:00
search fee: $5.00 plus copy expenses

Temple Public Library
101 North Main Street
Temple, TX 76501
(254) 770-5702
Beverly Snow, Reference Librarian
Hours: Mon, Wed & Fri 10:00–6:00, Tue
& Thur 10:00–9:00, Sat 10:00–5:00

Texarkana Museums System
(219 Sate Line Avenue, Texarkana, TX
75501—location)
PO Box 2343 (mailing address)
Texarkana, TX 75504
(903) 793-4831; (903) 793-7108 FAX
Jamie Simmons, Curator
Hours: by appointment
Pub. *Artifacts*, quarterly
(Texas and Arkansas regional history)

Texarkana Public Library
600 West Third
Texarkana, TX 75501
(903) 794-2149
Hours: Mon–Wed 9:00–9:00, Thur–Sat
9:00–6:00

Texas A & I University
South Texas Archives
821 West Santa Gertrudis Avenue
Kingsville, TX 78363
(512) 595-2819
Toni Nagel, Archivist

Texas A & M University—Corpus Christi
University Library
6300 Ocean Drive
Corpus Christi, TX 78412
(512) 994-2301
Dr. Thomas H. Kreneck, Special
Collections Librarian/Archivist
Hours: Mon–Fri 8:00–5:00
(special emphasis on history of south
Texas and northern Mexico)

Texas Seaport Museum
(Pier 21—location)
2016 Strand (mailing address)
Galveston, TX 77550-1631
(409) 763-1877; (409) 763-3037 FAX
E-mail: tsm@phoenix.net
http://www.phoenix.net/~tsm
Kurt Voss, Director
Hours: daily 10:00–5:00
(includes immigration database, mostly
Germans and Eastern Europeans,
entering through the Port of Galveston
1840–1950)
$5.00 admission for adults, includes use
of immigration database; mail-in
search: $10.00 per person

Texas State Museum of History
1616 West Abram Street
Arlington, TX 76013
(817) 460-4001; (817) 460-4017 FAX
Dr. R. Peter Mooz, Executive Director
Hours: Wed–Fri 10:00–4:00, Sat–Sun
1:30–4:30
Pub. *TSMH Universe and Fielder World*,
quarterly
from $35.00 per year membership for
individuals; admission charge for non-
members

Texas Women's University
Blagg-Huey Library
Denton, TX 76204
(940) 898-3708; (940) 898-3808 FAX
E-mail: s_hepner@twu.edu
http://www.twu.edu/

Toa Mo Ga Memorial Museum
PO Box 455
Plains, TX 79355
(806) 456-4823

Tyler Public Library
Genealogy/Local History Room
201 South College Avenue
Tyler, TX 75702
(903) 531-1316
Penny Reynolds, Senior Librarian
Hours: Mon–Wed 10:00–8:00, Thur–Sat
10:00–5:00, Sun 1:00–5:00
(emphasis on Tyler and Smith County)

Unger Memorial Library
825 Austin Street
Plainview, TX 79072
Hours: six days per week (summer five
days per week)

University of North Texas Archives
PO Box 5188, NT Station
Denton, TX 76203
(940) 565-2766
Richard L. Himmel, Archives Librarian
(emphasis on north central Texas)

University of Southern Alabama
Gulf Coast Historical Review
(see Alabama)

University of Texas at Arlington
Special Collections
University Library
PO Box 19497
Arlington, TX 76019-0497
(817) 272-3393; (817) 272-3360 FAX
http://www.uta.edu/library/SpCo/
special_collections.html
Dr. Gerald D. Saxon, Assistant Director
for Special Collections
Hours: Mon–Fri 8:00–5:00, Sat 10:00–
5:00
Pub. *The Compass Rose*, semiannually,
free

The University of Texas at Austin
Eugene C. Barker Texas History Center
The Center for American History
Sid Richardson Hall 2.101
Austin, TX 78712
(512) 495-4515; (512) 495-4542 FAX
http://www.lib.utexas.edu/Libs/CAH/
cah.html
Dr. Don E. Carleton, Director; Reference
Librarian
Hours: Mon–Sat 9:00–5:00
Pub. *Center for American History
Newsletter*, irregularly
(a national collection with emphasis on
Texas, southern and southwestern
U.S., and the Rocky Mountain west)
charges for photocopying and
photographs and other duplication of
materials

The University of Texas at Austin
Mirabeau B. Lamar Library
Austin, TX 78712

The University of Texas at Austin
Winedale Historical Center
PO Box 11 (FM 2714)
Round Top, TX 78954
(409) 278-3530
Gloria Jaster, Administrator
Hours: weekdays 9:00–5:00
Pub. *The Ouid Nuch*, quarterly

University of Texas at San Antonio
Institute of Texan Cultures
801 South Bowie Street
San Antonio, TX 78205-3296
(210) 458-2228; (800) 776-7651; (210)
458-2218

E-mail: lcatalin@itcpost1.utsa.edu
http://www.utsa.edu/itc/libsvc1.htm

University of Texas at San Antonio
Library, Special Collections Department
6900 North Loop 1604 West
San Antonio, TX 78249-0651
(210) 458-5505; (210) 458-4571
E-mail: dguerra@lonestar.utsa.edu
http://www.lib.utsa.edu/
Special_Collections/lib.

The University of Texas-Pan American Library
Special Collections/Rio Grande Valley
Historical Collection
1201 West University Drive
Edinburg, TX 78539-2999
(210) 381-2726
E-mail: ggause@panam.edu
http://www.lib.panam.edu
George R. Gause, Jr., Special Collections
Librarian
Hours: Mon–Thur 8:00–6:00, Fri 8:00–
5:00, first Sat 10:00–6:00
(comprehensive coverage of
geographical area from Laredo to
Corpus Christi to Brownsville, Texas,
and the Mexican states of Tamaulipas,
Nuevo Leon, and Coahuila, Mexico)

Valley Mills History Museum
Fifth Street and Avenue E
PO Box 168
Valley Mills, TX 76689
(254) 932-5277

Waco-McLennan County Library System
1717 Austin Avenue
Waco, TX 76701
(254) 750-5945 (Genealogy Librarian);
(254) 750-5954 (Volunteer Desk);
(254) 750-5946 (Library); (254) 750-
5940 FAX (Library)
Terri Hugo, Librarian, Special
Collections
Hours: Mon–Thur 10:00–9:00, Fri–Sat
10:00–6:00, Sun 1:00–5:00
(specializes in Texas and genealogy)

Waller County Historical Museum
4026 Fifth Street
PO Box 235
Brookshire, TX 77423
(281) 934-2826

Wayland Baptist University
Hale County Historical Commission
Museum of the Llano Estacado
1900 West Seventh Street
Plainview, TX 79072
(806) 296-5521
Eddie Guffee, Museum Director

Weatherford Public Library
1214 Charles Street
Weatherford, TX 76086
(817) 594-2767
Evlyn Broumley, Librarian

Hours: Mon, Wed & Fri–Sat 10:00–6:00,
Tue & Thur 1:00–9:00

Weslaco Library
525 South Kansas Avenue
Weslaco, TX 78596
(956) 968-4533
Michael Fisher, Acting Director
Hours: Mon–Tue & Thur–Fri 9:30–6:00,
Wed 1:00–7:00

West of the Pecos Museum
First and Cedar Streets at Highway 285
PO Box 1784
Pecos, TX 79772
(915) 445-5076

Western Texas College
Learning Resource Center
Snyder, TX 79549

Western Texas College
Scurry County Museum
6200 College Avenue
Snyder, TX 79549-6105

Wharton County Historical Museum
(3615 North Richmond Road—location)
PO Box 349 (mailing address)
Wharton, TX 77488
(409) 532-2600
Sylvia B. Ellis, Executive Director
Hours: Tue–Fri 9:30–noon & 1:00–4:30,
Sat 1:00–4:00
(genealogical services)
$25.00 per year Associate membership,
$50.00 per year Friend membership,
$100.00 per year Supporter
membership, $250.00 per year Patron
membership, $500.00 per year
Sponsor membership, $1,000.00 per
year Benefactor membership

Whitesboro Public Library
308 West Main Street
Whitesboro, TX 76273
(903) 564-5432
Priscella Thetford, Library Director
Hours: Mon–Fri 9:00–5:30

Wichita County Archives
600 Scott Street, Room 305
Wichita Falls, TX 76301
(940) 766-8137
Lita Watson, Archivist
Hours: Tue–Wed 9:00–11:30 & 1:00–
4:00
(Wichita County history: people,
businesses, events)
charges for copying and postage

Wichita Falls Museum and Art Center
2 Eureka Circle
Wichita Falls, TX 76308
(940) 696-5358
Carole Bonaman, Executive Director
Hours: Tue–Sat 10:00–5:00

Witte Museum
San Antonio Museum Association
3801 Broadway
PO Box 2601
San Antonio, TX 78209
(210) 226-5544

Edwin Wolters Museum
(306 South Avenue I—location)
Rt. 1, Box 16 (mailing address)
Shiner, TX 77984
(512) 594-3566
Bernard J. Siegel, Jr., Curator
Hours: Mon–Fri 8:00–5:00, second &
    fourth Sun 2:00–5:00

Yoakum Heritage Museum
312 Simpson
PO Box 2
Yoakum, TX 77995
(512) 293-7022
Dennis Rowan, Executive Director
Hours: Mon–Sat 1:00–5:00, Sun 3:00–
    5:00
Pub. *The Newsletter*, annually

Historical Societies—
Local and Regional

Atascosito Historical Society
(Liberty County)
PO Box 4003
Liberty, TX 77575-4003
Charles W. Fisher, Jr., President
(acts as Friends of the Sam Houston
    Regional Library and Research
    Center)
$5.00 per year membership

Austin County Historical
Commission
206 South Masonic Street
Bellville, TX 77418

Heritage Society of Austin, Inc.
(Driskill Hotel, Austin, TX 78701—
    location)
PO Box 2113 (mailing address)
Austin, TX 78768
(512) 474-5198

Bandera County Historical
Commission
Rt. 2, Box 6408
Pipe Creek, TX 78063
(830) 796-3718; (830) 535-4269
Carolyn B. Edwards, County Chair

Beaumont Heritage Society
(Jefferson County)
2985 French Road
Beaumont, TX 77706
(409) 898-0348
Becki Stedman
Hours: Tue–Sat 10:00–1:00, Sun 1:00–
    4:00
Pub. *We're Making History*, quarterly

Bell County Historical Commission
PO Box 235
Belton, TX 76513
(254) 938-2426
Haroldene Early, Chairperson

Bellville Historical Society (Austin
County)
PO Box 67
Bellville, TX 77418

Bexar County Historical
Commission
233 North Pecos La Trinidad, Suite 420
San Antonio, TX 78207
(210) 270-6581; (210) 270-6713 FAX
Virginia S. Nicholas, Chair
(considers requests for historical
    markers)

Big Thicket Association
FM-770
PO Box 198
Saratoga, TX 77585
(409) 274-5000

Boerne Area Historical Preservation
Society (Kendall County)
402 Blanco Street
PO Box 178
Boerne, TX 78006
(830) 249-2030
Betty Thomas, President
Hours: Boerne Public Library

Borden County Historical
Commission
PO Box 23
Gail, TX 79738

Bosque County Historical
Commission
PO Box 534
Meridian, TX 76665
(254) 435-6182
Elizabeth Torrence, Chair
Hours: Mon–Tue & Thur 10:00–4:00

Bosque Valley Heritage Society
PO Box 168
Valley Mills, TX 76689

Historical Commission
PO Box 1791
Brackettville, TX 78832

Brewster County Historical
Commission
PO Box 1620
Alpine, TX 79831

Brooks County Historical
Commission
604 West Blucher
Falfurrias, TX 78355
Florence Schuetz

Brown County Historical Society
(109 Azalea Drive, Brownwood, TX
    76801—location)
PO Box 146 (mailing address)
Brownwood, TX 76804-0146
(915) 646-8208
Pauline G. Hochhalter, Treasurer
(publishes historical books on Brown
    County)
$4.00 per year membership for
    individuals, $6.00 per year
    membership for couples

Brownsville Historical Association
Stillman House Museum
(1305 East Washington Street—location)
PO Box 846 (mailing address)
Brownsville, TX 78520
(956) 542-3929; (956) 541-5560
Rita Krausse, Acting Executive Director
Hours: Museum: Mon–Fri 10:00–noon &
    2:00–5:00, Sun 3:00–5:00
Pub. *BHA Newsletter*, bimonthly
(Pierce Collection contains birth,
    marriage and death records for
    Mexican towns of Matamoros,
    Reynosa, Mier and Camargo, 1800–
    1900)
$12.00 per year membership for
    individuals, $18.00 per year
    membership for couples

Burnet County Heritage Society
(Fort Croghan Grounds and Museum,
    703 Buchanan Drive, Highway 29
    West—location)
PO Box 74 (mailing address)
Burnet, TX 78611
(512) 756-8281
Thur–Sat 10:00–4:00
$5.00 per year membership

Genealogical and Historical Society
of Caldwell County
Luling Public Library
215 South Pecan Avenue
Luling, TX 78648
Mary Wanda Harp, Ph.D., Editor
Pub. *Plum Creek Almanac*, semiannually
    (May and November), $8.00 per issue
$15.00 per year membership for
    individuals, $18.00 per year
    membership for couples

Calhoun County Historical
Commission
202 South Ann Street
PO Box 988
Port Lavaca, TX 77979
(512) 553-6342; (512) 553-4689
    (Museum); (512) 553-7070 FAX
George Fred Rhodes, Chairman and
    Curator
Hours: Mon–Fri 9:00–5:00; Calhoun
    County Museum, 301 South Ann
    Street, Port Lavaca, TX 77979: Tue–
    Fri 1:30–4:30, Sat 10:00–2:00
free admission to museum

Carson County Historical Commission
PO Box 310
Panhandle, TX 79068
(806) 537-5237
Mrs. J. B. McCray, Chairman

Carson County Historical Survey Committee
Carson County Square House Museum
Fifth and Elsie Streets
PO Box 276
Panhandle, TX 79068-0276
(806) 537-3118 (Committee); (806) 537-3524 (Museum)
Don L. Markham, Museum Director

Carza County Historical Museum
111 North Avenue, North
Post, TX 79356
(806) 495-2782
Maxine Earl, Secretary
Hours: 10:00–noon & 1:00–3:00
("C.W. Post, cereal king, planned our town 1907.")

Chambers County Heritage Society
PO Box 870
Mont Belvieu, TX 77580
(281) 576-2594
Harry Daves, President
(Chambers County history and genealogy)
$5.00 per year membership

Cherokee County Historical Commission
(Wells Fargo Bank Building, Suite 300—location)
PO Box 1128 (mailing address)
Jacksonville, TX 75766
(903) 586-4057
John Allen Templeton, Chairman
Hours: Mon, Wed & Fri 10:00–noon & 2:00–4:00
(a unit of the Texas Historical Commission, not involved in genealogy)

Coke County Historical Commission
PO Box 52
Robert Lee, TX 76945
(915) 453-2641
Fran Lomas, Commission Chairman

Collin County Historical Commission
Court House
McKinney, TX 75069
Herb Yoehle, Chairman

Collin County Historical Society, Inc.
Old Post Office Museum
Chestnut at Virginia Streets
McKinney, TX 75069
(972) 542-9457; (972) 377-2949
Elisabeth R. Pink, Director
Hours: Tue (May–Sept) 1:00–5:00, first Sat

Collingsworth County Historical Commission
1307 Bowie
PO Box 169
Wellington, TX 79095
(806) 447-5496

Comfort Heritage Foundation, Inc.
(Comfort Public Library, High and Seventh Street—archives location)
PO Box 433 (mailing address)
Comfort, TX 78013
(830) 995-2398; (830) 995-5018 (Archivist)
Don Breithaupt, Archivist
Hours: Tue–Fri noon–6:00 by appointment only, Sat 10:00–2:00 by appointment only
(historic photographs, documents, etc.; just beginning a genealogy department)
$5.00 per year membership for individuals

Cooke County Heritage Society
(210 South Dixon—location)
PO Box 150 (mailing address)
Gainesville, TX 76241
(940) 668-8900
Shana Powell, Curator
Hours: Tue–Fri 10:00–5:00

Crockett County Historical, Scientific and Museum Society
(404 Eleventh Street—location)
PO Box 1444 (mailing address)
Ozona, TX 76943
(915) 392-2837
Geniece Childress, Director of Museum
Hours: Mon–Fri 9:00–5:00, some Sat 10:00–4:00
search fee varies

Cypress Basin Genealogical and Historical Society (Titus County)
PO Box 403
Mount Pleasant, TX 75455
Billy F. Walker, President
Hours: meetings second Thur
Pub. *Cypress Basin Genealogical and Historical Society Reporter*, three times per year
$10.00 per year membership for individuals, $12.00 per year membership for families

Dallam-Hartley Counties Historical Association, Inc.
Dallam-Hartley Counties XIT Museum
108 East Fifth Street
PO Box 710
Dalhart, TX 79022
(806) 249-5390
Dessie M. Hanburg, Director
Hours: Mon–Sat 9:00–5:00

Dallas County Historical Commission
634 Records Building
Dallas, TX 75202-3504
(972) 653-6714
Hours: 8:00–4:30
Pub. *County Chronicle*, bimonthly

Dallas Historical Society
1717 Gano Street
Dallas, TX 75215
E-mail: dhs@startext.net
http://www.arlington.net/interact/library.htm
Pub. *The Register*

Denison Historical Society
530 West Hanna Street
Denison, TX 75020
(903) 465-1075

Denison Library Historical and Genealogical Society
(300 West Gandy, Denison, TX 75020—location)
Rt. 1, Box 237C (mailing address)
Denison, TX 75021
(903) 465-9447
Vicki E. Hempkins, President
Hours: Sun–Sat 9:00–5:00
(film and books available)

Denton County Historical Commission
Courthouse-on-the-Square Museum, Inc.
(First Floor, Historic 1896 Restored Courthouse on the Square, 110 West Hickory, Denton, TX 76201—location)
PO Box 2800 (mailing address)
Denton, TX 76202
(800) 346-3189; (940) 565-8697; (940) 565-8693 FAX
Norma Lynn Gamble, Museum Director
Hours: Research facilities and Office: Mon–Fri 8:00–5:00; Exhibit Rooms: Tue–Sat 10:30–4:30
(early newspapers on microfilm, *Pilot Point Post Signal* pre-1925; extensive photograph collection from the 1800s through the 1950s; family histories; cemetery surveys for Denton County)

Historical Society of Denton County
PO Box 50503
Denton, TX 76206-0503
(940) 387-0995
E-mail: Mcochran@iglobal.net
http://www.iglobal.net/mayhouse/hsdc.html
Mike Cochran, Chairman

Dimmit County Historical Society
Faren Road
Carrizo Springs, TX 78834
Mr. Bradshaw

Dumas Genealogical and Historical Society
127 Oak Avenue
Dumas, TX 79029

Duncanville Historical Commission, Inc.
100 East Center
PO Box 280
Duncanville, TX 75116
(972) 296-1401

East End Historical Association (Galveston County)
PO Box 2424
Galveston, TX 77550

East Texas Historical Association
PO Box 6223, Stephen F. Austin Station
Nacogdoches, TX 75962
(409) 468-2407; (409) 468-2190 FAX
Archie P. McDonald, Ph.D., Executive
  Director and Editor
Pub. *East Texas Historical Journal*, two
  times per year (spring and fall)
$25.00 per year membership for
  individuals, $12.00 per year
  membership for students, $25.00 per
  year membership for libraries

El Paso County Historical Commission
PO Box 701
El Paso, TX 79945-9998
(915) 581-1111 (Chairperson's work);
  (915) 751-3631 (Chairperson's home)
Prestene M. Dehrkoop, Chairperson
Hours: meetings second Mon

El Paso County Historical Society
(207 Maricopa Drive—location)
PO Box 28 (mailing address)
El Paso, TX 79940
Lillian Collingwood, Editor
Pub. *Password*, quarterly
(emphasis on west Texas, New Mexico,
  northern Mexico and eastern Arizona)
$25.00 per year membership

Ennis Heritage Society
PO Box 189
Ennis, TX 75120
Louise McCall, President
Pub. *EHS Newsletter*

Donna Hooks Fletcher Historical Museum
331 South Main Street
Donna, TX 78537
(956) 464-3285

Forney Heritage Society (Kaufman County)
98 FM 2757
PO Box 1292
Forney, TX 75126
(972) 552-3681
Linda F. Harwell, President
Pub. *The Timekeeper*, quarterly

$7.50 per year membership for
  individuals, $10.00 per year
  membership for families or businesses

Fort Clark Historical Society (Kinney County)
PO Box 1061
Brackettville, TX 78832
(830) 563-2709 (Curator)
Hours: Sat–Sun 1:00–4:00, and by
  appointment
(emphasis on U.S. Cavalry, southwestern
  Texas frontier)

Galveston Historical Foundation
2016 Strand
Galveston, TX 77550
(409) 765-7834
Peter Brink, Executive Director
Pub. *Membership Update*

Gillespie County Historical Society
312 West San Antonio Street
Fredericksburg, TX 78624
(830) 997-2835
E-mail: gchs@ktc.com
Paul Camfield, Museum Director
Hours: Mon–Sat 10:00–5:00, Sun 1:00–
  5:00
Pub. *GCHS De Trompetour*, quarterly
(no in-depth genealogical archive,
  holdings are more general in nature)

Grand Prairie Historical Commission
PO Box 534045
Grand Prairie, TX 75051
(972) 264-9536

Grayson County Historical Commission
Room 5, Grayson County Courthouse
Sherman, TX 75090
Clyde L. Hall, Ph.D., Chairman

Gregg County Historical Commission
417 Mobberly Avenue
Longview, TX 75602
(903) 753-5337
Norman W. Black, D.D.S., Chairman

Gregg County Historical Society
PO Box 542
Longview, TX 75606

Grimes County Heritage Association
1215 East Washington Avenue
PO Box 546
Navasota, TX 77868

Grimes County Historical Commission
Rt. 2, Box 3494
Navasota, TX 77868
(409) 894-2520

Hansford County Historical Commission
Stationmaster's House Museum
30 South Townsend
Spearman, TX 79081
(806) 659-3008; (806) 659-2692
Sylvia M. Robertson, Chairman

Harris County Heritage Society
1100 Bagby
Houston, TX 77002
(713) 655-1912
Jane N. Cable, Director
Pub. *Panorama*

Hays County Historical and Genealogical Society
PO Box 1837
San Marcos, TX 78666

Hemphill County Historical and Genealogical Society
Rt. 2
Canadian, TX 79014
Mr. and Mrs. John Ramp

Henderson County Historical Commission
(Old Henderson Jail, 201 East Larkin
  Street—location)
PO Box 1412 (mailing address)
Athens, TX 75751
(903) 677-7269
Frank E. LaRue, Jr., Commission
  Chairman; Jewel Lambright; Vesta
  Hall
Hours: Office: Mon–Tue 8:00–5:00, Fri
  8:00–2:00
(genealogical records and county records
  of Henderson County only; handles
  referrals of genealogical research from
  the Henderson County Clerk's Office)

Henderson County Historical Society
PO Box 943
Athens, TX 75751
(903) 677-7269

Heritage Farmstead Association (Collin County)
1900 West 15th Street
Plano, TX 75075
(972) 424-7874
Hours: by appointment
Pub. *Newsletter*, quarterly

Hidalgo County Historical Commission
313 Vermont Street
McAllen, TX 78501
(956) 687-4736

Hidalgo County Historical Society
PO Box 81
Edinburg, TX 78540-0081

Hillsboro Heritage League (Hill County)
PO Box 2
Hillsboro, TX 76645

Historic Waco Foundation
407 Columbus Avenue
Waco, TX 76701

Houston County Historical Commission
Courthouse, First Floor
629 North Fourth
Crockett, TX 75835
(409) 544-3255, ext. 238; (409) 544-8053 FAX
Eliza H. Bishop, Researcher
Hours: Mon–Fri 10:00–4:00
$10.00 per year membership

Ingleside-On-The-Bay Historical Society/Museum
(475 Starlight at the corner of Ebony at IOB City Hall Building—location)
PO Box 553
Ingleside, TX 78362-0553
(512) 776-2658
Chris Mircovich, Vice President
Hours: Mon–Fri 10:00–1:00, Sun 2:00–5:00
(cemetery records for Nueces, San Patricio, Refugio, Beem, Live Oak, Aransas and Goliad counties)
$10.00 per year membership, $100.00 per year membership for businesses, $500.00+ per year Humanitarian membership

Jefferson County Historical Commission
(1149 Pearl Street, Beaumont, TX 77701—location)
PO Box 4025 (mailing address)
Beaumont, TX 77704
(409) 835-8701
Susan C. Arceneaux, Coordinator
Hours: Mon–Thur 8:00–3:00
Pub. *Jefferson County History News*, four times per year (not necessarily quarterly)
(Jefferson County history and general Texas history)
membership is by appointment, but anyone may be on our mailing list

Jefferson Historical Society and Museum
223 Austin Street
Jefferson, TX 75657
Mrs. E. P. Starie

Jollyville-Pond Springs Historical Association
7203 South Ute Terrace
Austin, TX 78729
(512) 258-5688
(specializes in the history of the Republic of Texas, 1821–1846)

Joshua Historical Society
402 South Main
PO Box 256
Joshua, TX 76058

Karnes County Historical Society
Karnes County Museum at Old Helena
(Highway 81, Courthouse Square—location)
PO Box 162 (mailing address)
Karnes City, TX 78118
(830) 780-3210
Letha McClure, Manager/Curator
Hours: Tue–Sat 9:00–5:00
Pub. *Yearly Newsletter*, annually (October)
$3.00 per year membership for individuals, $15.00 per year membership for families, $10.00 per year Supporting membership

Kent County Genealogical and Historical Society
PO Box 6
Jayton, TX 79528

Knox County Historical Commission
Courthouse Square
PO Box 77
Benjamin, TX 79505
(940) 454-2191 (County Judge)
Mary Jane Young
Hours: Mon–Fri 8:00–5:00
(family history file, county cemetery survey; books on Gilliland, Munday, Rhineland and Truscott communities)
research: $5.00

Lake Cities Historical Society
PO Box 1222
Lake Dallas, TX 75065

Lake Jackson Historical Association (Brazoria County)
122 South Parking Place
PO Box 242
Lake Jackson, TX 77566
(409) 297-2850

Leon County Historical Commission
417 Post Street
PO Box 141
Centerville, TX 75855
(903) 545-2283
Ruby Johnson, Chairman (History-Genealogy)

Liberty County Historical Commission
(1710 Sam Houston—library location)
PO Box 334 (mailing address)
Hardin, TX 77561
(409) 298-9202
Kevin R. Ladd, Chairman
no search fees

Lipscomb County Historical Commission
Lipscomb, TX 79056
(806) 862-4131
Marki Loughlin, President
Pub. *Lipscomb Heritage Quarterly*

Lubbock Heritage Society
PO Box 5443
Lubbock, TX 79417

Mason County Historical Society
Mason County Historical Museum
303 Moody
PO Box 303
Mason, TX 76856
Mrs. Hilton Moneyhon, Museum Director

Mesquite Historical and Genealogical Society
300 Grubb Drive
PO Box 850165
Mesquite, TX 75185-0165
(972) 216-6229
Marjorie Bays, Librarian
Hours: Mon–Tue & Thur 9:00–9:00, Wed & Fri–Sat 9:00–6:00
Pub. *The Mesquite Tree*, quarterly; *Mesquite Historical and Genealogical Society Newsletter*, monthly
$12.00 per year membership

Midland County Historical Society
Midland County Historical Commission
2102 Community Lane
Midland, TX 79701
Nancy R. McKinley, President and Chair of Commission
Hours: monthly meetings
Pub. *The Staked Plains*, quarterly
$10.00+ per year membership; search: $20.00 per hour

Mineral Wells Heritage Association
(201 N.W. Fifth Avenue—location)
400 N.W. Seventh Street (mailing address)
Mineral Wells, TX 76067
Effie Birdwell, Museum Curator
Hours: by appointment
("We are a preservation group of the history of our city.")
$10.00 per year membership

Mission Trail—Los Pueblos Association
453 West Burt
El Paso, TX 79927
(915) 859-6956

Monte Vista Historical Association
PO Box 12386
San Antonio, TX 78212
(512) 735-5533

Montgomery County Genealogical and Historical Society, Inc.
PO Box 867
Conroe, TX 77305-0867
(409) 788-8363
http://mcia.com/gsociety.htm
Melvin Westmoreland, President
Hours: Montgomery County Library, Conroe, TX: Mon & Fri 10:00–5:00, Tue–Thur 10:00–8:00, Sat 9:00–5:00; Office: Mon & Wed 10:00–3:00
Pub. *The Herald*, quarterly
$18.00 per year membership

Nederland Historical Society
1903 Atlanta
Nederland, TX 77627
Wanda Weatherford, President

New Braunfels Conservation Society
PO Box 310933
New Braunfels, TX 78130-0933
(830) 625-5593

Newton County, Texas, Historical Commission
(½ block east of Courthouse—location)
PO Box 1383 (mailing address)
Newton, TX 75966
(409) 379-2109
http://www.jas.net/~newton/links.htm
Pauline Hines; Bonnie Smith, Chairperson
Hours: Mon–Fri 9:00–5:00
("Historical Newsletter," a weekly column in *Newton County News*)

North Fort Worth Historical Society
131 East Exchange, Suite 110
Fort Worth, TX 76106
(817) 625-5082; (817) 625-5083 FAX
Sue McCafferty, President
Hours: Museum, Suite 113: Mon–Fri 10:00–5:00, Sun 12:30–4:30; Office, Suite 110: Mon–Fri 10:00–5:00
(operates the Stockyards Museum)

Old Mageetie Association
700 Alan Bean
PO Box 189
Wheeler, TX 79096
(806) 826-3289

Old Mobeetie Association of Mobeetie Jail Museum
Old Town
Mobeetie, TX 79061
(806) 845-3401
Dale Corcoran, President
(Early Panhandle family histories and museum; archives also includes records of Czech Poban community)
$5.00 per year membership

Orange County Historical Commission
1301 Park Avenue
Orange, TX 77630
(409) 886-1312; (409) 886-0450 FAX
Howard C. Williams, M.D., Chairman
(large collection of Orange County photos and historical material)

Orange County Historical Society
PO Box 1345
Orange, TX 77630-1345
(409) 883-2925
Juanita Toronjo, Treasurer
Pub. *Las Sabinas*, quarterly, $6.00 per issue
$20.00 per year membership for families, $15.00 per year membership for senior citizens

Palo Pinto County Historical Association
(two blocks south Highway 180, N.E. Courthouse corner—location)
PO Box 91 (mailing address)
Palo Pinto, TX 76484
(940) 659-2755
Jean Price, Secretary
Hours: Jun–Aug: Sat–Sun 2:00–4:00, tours by appointment only; meetings in County 4-H Building
$5.00 per year membership

Panhandle-Plains Historical Society (Randall County)
Panhandle-Plains Historical Museum
2401 Fourth Avenue
PO Box 967, W. T. Station
Canyon, TX 79016
(806) 656-2261
Claire R. Kuehn, Archivist
Hours: Museum: Mon–Fri 9:00–12:00 & 1:00–5:00
Pub. *Panhandle-Plains Historical Review* (northwest Texas), annually (February), $10.00 per year subscription
$20.00 per year membership

Panola County Heritage Foundation
100 East Sabine
Carthage, TX 75633
(903) 693-8689
Helen Williamson, President
Pub. *Heritage Gazette*

Permian Historical Society
University of Texas of the Permian Basin
4901 West University
Odessa, TX 79762-0001
(915) 552-2381
Bobbie Jean Klepper, Archivist
Hours: Mon, Wed & Fri 8:00–noon & 1:00–5:00, Thur 8:00–noon & 1:00–10:00, shortened hours between semesters, closed weekends and all university holidays
Pub. *Permian Historical Annual*
(Permian Basin includes Andrews, Crane, Crockett, Culberson, Ector, Gaines, Glasscock, Howard, Loving, Martin, Midland, Mitchell, Pecos, Reagan, Reeves, Upton, Ward, and Winker counties, Texas, and Lea County, New Mexico; archival collection, housed in the UTPB library, contains "records, documents, photographs, biographical data and other historical material and books to benefit the student researcher, scholar, genealogist, and history buff.")
$10.00 per year membership for individuals, $20.00 per year membership for families, $15.00 per year membership for museums, libraries or historical groups, $35.00 per year membership for businesses, $200.00 life membership

Peters Colony Historical Society
PO Box 110846
Carrollton, TX 75011
John England, President
Pub. *Elm Fork Echoes*, semiannually, $6.36 per issue postpaid, including tax
(specializes in northwest quadrant of Dallas County, Texas)

Polk County Heritage Society
207 North Beaty
Livingston, TX 77351
(409) 327-5945

Presidio La Bahia
U.S. Highway 183 and 77-A
PO Box 57
Goliad, TX 77963
(512) 645-3752

Randall County Historical Commission
503 A Harrell Lane
Canyon, TX 79015
(806) 656-2261
Claire R. Kuehn, Chairman

Refugio County Historical Society
Refugio County Museum
102 West Street
Refugio, TX 78377
(512) 526-4943
Maxine Reilly, Director
Hours: Tue–Fri 9:00–5:00, Sat 1:00–5:00
$10.00 per year membership for individuals

Roberts County Historical Commission
Roberts County Museum
(Highway 60—location)
PO Box 306 (mailing address)
Miami, TX 79059
(806) 868-3291
Hours: Tue–Fri 10:00–5:00, Sun 2:00–5:00
(specialty: "THS-TAM-NWTMA")

Roscoe Historical Society
PO Box 421
Roscoe, TX 79545
Billy Joe Jay

Rusk County Historical Association
Howard-Dickinson House
501 South Main
Henderson, TX 75652
(903) 657-6925
Judy McMillian, President
(genealogical services)

Rusk County Historical Foundation
(514 North High Street—location)
PO Box 1773 (mailing address)
Henderson, TX 75652
(903) 657-2261
Virginia Knapp, President
Hours: Mon–Fri 1:00–5:00
(emphasis on Texas, Georgia and other states)
no fee

Salado Historical Society (Bell County)
PO Box 251
Salado, TX 76571
Patricia L. Barton, President
(not a genealogical group)

San Angelo Genealogical and Historical Society, Inc.
(Church of Christ Fellowship Hall, 902 North Main Street—location)
PO Box 3453 (mailing address)
San Angelo, TX 76902-3453
(915) 949-3223
http://www.rootsweb.com/saghs
Betty Varner, Researcher
Hours: meetings first Tue (Sept–May) 7:30
Pub. *Stalkin' Kin*, quarterly (August, November, February and May)
(Coke, Concho, Crockett, Glasscock, Irion, Kimble, Menard, Reagan, Runnels, Schleicher, Sterling, Sutton, and Tom Green counties; Bible records, members' ancestor charts, court records, cemeteries, etc.)
$15.00 per year membership for individuals, $18.00 per year membership for families (beginning August 1, add $2.50 after 1 August); free queries to members first and to others as space allows

San Antonio Conservation Society
107 King William Street
San Antonio, TX 78204-1399
(210) 224-6163; (210) 224-6163 FAX
E-mail: conserve@saconservation.org
Bruce MacDougal, Executive Director

San Antonio Genealogical and Historical Society
(401 Isom Road, Suite 550, San Antonio, TX 78216—location)
PO Box 17461 (mailing address)
San Antonio, TX 78217-0461
(210) 342-5242
Rita Woodward, President
Hours: Mon & Sat 10:00–4:00, Wed 10:00–9:00, Sun 1:00–5:00; meetings third Sat (Jan–May & Sept–Oct)
Pub. *Our Heritage*, quarterly (fall, winter, spring, summer), $25.00 per year subscription for libraries and societies; *Newsletter*
$35.00 per year full membership for individuals (beginning in July), $20.00 per year full membership for spouses

San Jacinto County Historical Commission and Heritage Society
PO Box 505
Coldspring, TX 77331
(409) 653-2009

The Heritage Association of San Marcos, Inc.
(308 East Hopkins Street—location)
20 Timbercrest Street (mailing address)
San Marcos, TX 78666-3018

(512) 392-9997; (512) 393-3735 FAX
E-mail: frances76@centuryinter.net
http://www.centuryinter.net/smheritage
Frances E. Stovall, Coordinator Heritage Tourism
Pub. *Heritage Highlites*, quarterly
(maintains a house museum)
$25.00 per year membership

Santa Fe Area Historical Foundation, Inc.
11225 Texas Highway 6
PO Box 275
Santa Fe, TX 77517
(409) 925-3009
Hours: third Sun 2:00–5:00, special events, and by appointment
("The Depot Museum of the Towns Along the Santa Fe; extensive pictorial files of West Galveston County, 1890–ca 1950")

Schleicher County Historical Society
PO Box 473
Eldorado, TX 76936

Sherman County Historical Society
17 North Main
PO Box 1248
Stratford, TX 79804

Smith County Historical Society, Inc.
Carnegie History Center
125 South College Avenue
Tyler, TX 75702
(903) 592-5993
Jack Pollard, President
Hours: Wed & first Sat 1:00–4:30
Pub. *Chronicles of Smith County, Texas*, semiannually
$15.00 per year membership or subscription

Somervell County Historical Society
Somervell County Museum
Corner Vernon and Elm
PO Box 669
Glen Rose, TX 76043
(254) 897-2739; (254) 897-4529; (254) 897-3675 (Museum)
Jeanne P. Mack, Museum Director

Sophienburg Museum and Archives
401 West Coll Street
New Braunfels, TX 78130
(830) 629-1572
http:/www.new-braunfels.com/sophieburg
Michelle Oatman
Hours: Archives: Mon–Fri 10:00–4:00, Museum: Mon–Sat 10:00–5:00, Sun 1:00–5:00
(holds collection of the Comal County Genealogy Society)
library use: $2.50 per day; research by mail: $10.00 per hour

Southeast Texas Genealogical and Historical Society
Tyrrell Historical Library
Beaumont Public Library System
695 Pearl Street
PO Box 3827
Beaumont, TX 77704
(409) 833-2759; (409) 833-5828 FAX
David E. Montgomery, Library Manager
Hours: Library: Tue–Sat 8:30–5:30
Pub. *Tyrrell Historical Library Association Newsletter*, various; *Southeast Texas Genealogical and Historical Society—Yellowed Pages*, quarterly, $14.00 per year subscription
$15.00 per year membership for individuals, $25.00 per year membership for families

Southern Studies Institute
(see Louisiana)

Starr County Historical Society
601 East Main
Rio Grande City, TX 78582
(956) 487-4839
Dr. Bruno M. Trevino
Hours: 8:00–6:00

State Association of Texas Pioneers
(3805 Broadway—location)
137 West Mafield (mailing address)
San Antonio, TX 78221
(210) 822-9011

Stephens County Historical Association
201 North Harding
Breckenridge, TX 76024

The Sugar Land Heritage Society
302 Oyster Creek
Sugar Land, TX 77478
(281) 494-3485
Mrs. Walter S. McMeans, President
(emphasis on Sugar Land and Fort Bend County)
$3.00 per year membership

Tarrant County Historical Commission
100 East Weatherford Street
Fort Worth, TX 76196
(817) 884-3271
Hours: Tue 10:00–3:00, and by appointment

Tarrant County Historical Society
3724 Cresthaven Terrace
Fort Worth, TX 76107
(817) 625-1881

Taylor Heritage Society (Williamson County)
PO Box 385
Taylor, TX 76574

Terrell County Historical Commission
PO Box 7
Sanderson, TX 79848

(915) 345-2648 (President); (915) 345-2285 (Corresponding Secretary); (915) 345-2177 (Staff Person)
Patty Phillips, President; Margaret Farley, corresponding Secretary; Carolyn Hutto, Staff Person
Hours: Mon–Fri 1:00–5:00, Sat–Sun 3:00–5:00

Texas City Heritage Association
PO Box 2091
Texas City, TX 77590
(713) 948-3411

Texas Gulf Coast Historical Association
Department of History
University of Houston
Houston, TX 77004
(713) 749-4680

Texas Gulf Historical Society
Goodhue Building
PO Box 1621
Beaumont, TX 77704
(409) 833-0817
W. S. Shepherd, Secretary and Treasurer
Pub. *Texas Gulf Historical and Biographical Record*, annually (December), $10.00 per issue
$15.00 per year membership for individuals, $10.00 per year membership for libraries

Texas Old Missions and Forts Association
7617 Woodthrush Drive
Dallas, TX 75230-4860

Tom Green County Historical Preservation League
PO Box 1625
San Angelo, TX 76902

Tom Green County Historical Society
(2401 Colorado, San Angelo, TX 76901—location)
PO Box 2656 (mailing address)
San Angelo, TX 76902
(915) 949-2920
Ross McSwain, President
Hours: meetings: third Mon (Jan–Oct)
$10.00 per year membership for individuals, $15.00 per year membership for couples

Trinity County Historical Commission
PO Box 386
Trinity, TX 75862

Truscott Historical Preservation Association
Truscott, TX 79260
(940) 474-3339
Margaret Daniel, Chairman
Pub. *Between the Wichitas*

Tyler County Heritage Society/ Whitmeyer Genealogy Library
Heritage Village Museum
Highway 190 West
PO Box 888
Woodville, TX 75979
(409) 283-2272; (409) 283-2194 FAX
Carol Phillips, Chairman
Hours: Tue, Thur & Sat 10:00–2:00
Pub. *Sketches of Tyler County*, once every ten years
$15.00 per year membership for individuals

Uvalde County Historical Commission
141 Bluebonnet, South
Uvalde, TX 78801
(830) 278-2193

Van Alstyne Historical Society Museum
(216 East Jefferson—location)
PO Box 1552 (mailing address)
Van Alstyne, TX 75495-1552
(903) 482-5877
Ruth-Lee Cason, Secretary
Hours: May–Sept: Tue & Thur 2:00–4:00, Sat noon–2:00, and by appointment
$3.00 per two-year membership for individuals, $5.00 per two-year membership for couples, $10.00 per year Sustaining membership for individuals or couples, $25.00 per year Sponsor membership for individuals or couples, $50.00 per year Memorial membership for individuals or couples, $100.00 life membership for individuals or couples

Victoria County Historical Commission
210 East Forrest
Victoria, TX 77901
(512) 575-5210
Charles Spurliz, Chairman

Waller County Historical Commission
PO Box 1099
Waller, TX 77484
(409) 826-3617 (Chairman)
Richard L. Senasac, Chairman
(operates museum and has an extensive list of publications, many of which would be of genealogical interest)

Waller County Historical Society, Inc.
PO Box 1099
Waller, TX 77484
(409) 826-3617 (President)
Richard L. Senasac, President
(no museum or publishing program, concentrates on research and restoration)

Wallisville Heritage Park (Chambers County)
(Exit 807 on Interstate 10 East, Wallisville exit—location)
PO Box 16 (mailing address)
Wallisville, TX 77597-0016
(409) 389-2252; (409) 389-2466 FAX
Kevin R. Ladd, Director
Hours: Mon–Sat 8:00–5:00
Pub. *The Age*, monthly
(genealogy library and local history research center with extensive genealogical files on Chambers County and southeast Texas families)
$20.00 per year membership; search: cost of photocopies

Webb County Heritage Foundation
(500 Flores Avenue—location)
PO Box 446 (mailing address)
Laredo, TX 78042-0446
(210) 727-0977
Margarita Araiza, Interim Director
Hours: 8:30–5:00
Pub. *The Heritage Register*, quarterly
$25.00 per year membership

West Texas Historical Association
Hardin-Simmons University
PO Box 16172
Abilene, TX 79698
(915) 677-8351
Dr. B. W. Aston, Executive Director
Hours: Mon–Fri 8:00–5:00
Pub. *WTHA Year Book*, annually (November)
$15.00 per year membership

White Settlement Historical Society
214 Meadow Park Road
White Settlement, TX 76108
(817) 246-4971

Whiteface Historical Society
PO Box 65
Whiteface, TX 79379
(806) 287-1132

Wichita County Heritage Society
900 Bluff
Wichita Falls, TX 76301
(940) 723-0623

Wise County Historical Society, Inc.
(Wise County Heritage Museum, 1602 South Trinity—location)
PO Box 427 (mailing address)
Decatur, TX 76234
(940) 627-5586; (940) 627-3732
Rosalie Gregg, Executive Director
Hours: Mon–Sat 9:00–4:00, Sun 1:30–5:00
Pub. *Wise County Historical Commission and Wise County Historical Society Newsletter*, eleven times per year (monthly except August)
(collection of research material: census records, newspapers, county histories, birth, marriage and death records, books on Lost Battalion)

$5.00 per year membership for individuals, $7.50 per year membership for couples; free admission for members; search: $1.00 for first hour, 50¢ for each additional hour, copies 25¢ each

Yoakum County Historical Commission
PO Box 960
Plains, TX 79355

Yorktown Historical Society (De Witt County)
Yorktown Historical Museum
(Main and Eckhardt Streets—location)
Rt. 2, Box 123-C-1 (mailing address)
Yorktown, TX 78164
(512) 564-2174 (President)
Mrs. Kurt Hartmann, President
Hours: Thur & Sun 2:30–4:30
(artifacts, books, antiques, etc., depicting local history; published book, *Yorktown, Its History, 1848–1989*)

Zapata County Historical Commission
La Paz Museum
A. L. Benavides Elementary School
PO Box 219
San Ygnacio, TX 78067
(512) 765-5611

LDS Family History Centers

Abilene
(915) 673-8836

Amarillo
(806) 352-2409

Austin
(512) 837-3626

Corpus Christi
(512) 993-2970

Dallas
(see Denton, Duncanville or Plano)

Denton
(817) 387-3065

Duncanville
(214) 709-0066

El Paso
(915) 581-8849; (915) 565-9711

Fort Worth
(817) 284-4472; (817) 292-8393

Friendswood
(713) 996-9346

Houston
(713) 785-2105; (713) 488-4406

Lubbock
(806) 792-5040

Mcallen
(210) 682-1061

Midland
(915) 697-6755

Pasadena
(713) 487-3623

Plano
(214) 867-6479

Port Arthur
(409) 727-3548

San Antonio
(210) 736-2940

Spring
(713) 251-5931

Sugar Land
(713) 240-1524

Tyler
(903) 509-8322

Genealogical Societies

State Genealogical Society

Texas State Genealogical Society (TSGS)
2507 Tannehill Drive
Houston, TX 77008-3052
(713) 864-6862
Pub. *Stirpes*, quarterly; *Texas State Genealogical Society Newsletter*
$18.00 per year membership

Regional Genealogical Societies

Amarillo Genealogical Society
Amarillo Public Library
413 East Fourth Street
PO Box 2171
Amarillo, TX 79189-2171
(806) 378-3054 (Library)
Hours: Library: Mon–Thur 9:00–9:00, Fri–Sat 9:00–6:00, Sun 2:00–6:00
Pub. *Amarillo Genealogical Society Newsletter*, irregularly; *The Reflector*, quarterly
$10.00 per year membership

Ancestor Club
PO Box 228
Winnie, TX 77665-0228
Mr. Silva

Anderson County Genealogical Society
PO Box 2045
Palestine, TX 75801

Angelina County Genealogical Society
PO Box 150631
Lufkin, TX 75915-0631
Delbert Richardson, President
Pub. *Echoes Through the Pines*
$7.50 per year membership

Ark-La-Tex Genealogical Association, Inc.
(see Arkansas)

Arlington Genealogical Society (Tarrant County)
Arlington Public Library
101 East Abram Street
Arlington, TX 76010-1183
(817) 459-6900 (Library)
E-mail: maconrad@flash.net
Mary Ann Conrad, President
Hours: Library: Mon–Thur 9:00–9:00, Fri–Sat 9:00–6:00
Pub. *Newsletter*, monthly
$10.00 per year membership for individuals (beginning in September), $15.00 per year membership for families

Athens Genealogical Organization
c/o C. W. M. Memorial Library
121 South Prairieville Street
Athens, TX 75751
(903) 675-2694
Mary Lee Barnes, Editor
Hours: Library: Mon–Fri 10:00–6:00, Sat 9:00–1:00
Pub. *Texas AGO*, two times per year (Henderson County, Texas, records)
$10.00 per year membership for individuals, $12.00 per year out-of-town membership for individuals; research fee: $10.00 per hour

Austin Genealogical Society
PO Box 1507
Austin, TX 78767-1507
Hours: meetings fourth Tue (Jan–Jul & Sept–Oct) & third Tue (Nov) 7:30 at Covenant Presbyterian Church, 3003 Northland Drive, Austin, TX 78731
Pub. *Austin Genealogical Society Quarterly*; *Austin Genealogical Society Newsletter*, irregularly
$16.00 per year membership for individuals, $18.00 per year membership for families

Baytown Genealogical Society
PO Box 2486
Baytown, TX 77522
(281) 479-3244
Victoria L. Klehn, President
Hours: Sterling Municipal Library: Mon–Thur 10:00–9:00, Fri–Sat 10:00–6:00
Pub. *Baytown Genealogical Society Newsletter*, monthly
$10.00 per year membership

Genealogical Society of the Big Spring
(Howard County Library, Fourth and
  Scurry Streets—location)
810 East 12th (mailing address)
Big Spring, TX 79720
(915) 267-7236 (President)
R. W. Reagan, President
Pub. *Signal Peak*, monthly

Big Thicket Genealogical Club
PO Box 1260
Kountze, TX 77625

Brazos Genealogical Association
PO Box 5493
Bryan, TX 77805-5493
Pub. *Brazos Genealogical Advertiser*,
  quarterly
$14.00 per year membership

Brazosport Genealogical Society
Brazosport College Library
PO Box 813
Lake Jackson, TX 77566
http://www.brazosport.cc.tx.us/~gensoc
Dr. Don Pugh, President
(some publication of local records)
$12.00 per year membership for
  individuals, $15.00 per year
  membership for families

Burkburnett Genealogical Society
Burkburnett Library
215 East Fourth Street
Burkburnett, TX 76354-3446
(940) 569-2991
G. Thomas Fairclough, Librarian
Hours: Tue–Fri 11:30–6:00, Sat 10:00–
  2:00

Burnet County Genealogical Society
c/o Herman Brown Free Library
Burnet County Library System
J. Frank Dobie Room
100 East Washington Street
Burnet, TX 78611
Edna Hood Cheatham, Editor
Hours: Library: Mon–Fri 10:00–6:00;
  meetings: third Thur 10:15
Pub. *Burnet County Genealogical
  Society Newsletter*, quarterly
$8.00 per year membership (calendar
  year)

**Genealogical and Historical Society
of Caldwell County**
Luling Public Library
215 South Pecan Avenue
Luling, TX 78648
Mary Wanda Harp, Ph.D., Editor
Pub. *Plum Creek Almanac*, semiannually
  (May and November), $8.00 per issue
$15.00 per year membership for
  individuals, $18.00 per year
  membership for couples

**Calhoun County Genealogical
Society**
PO Box 299
Port Lavaca, TX 77979-0299

(512) 552-2588
Pub. *Karankawa Kountry*, semiannually
$10.00 per year membership

Camp County Genealogical Society
(102 Quitman Street, Garrett/Shelby
  Building—location)
PO Box 1083 (mailing address)
Pittsburg, TX 75686
(903) 856-2062
Glenda Kinard, President
Hours: meetings: fourth Tue 7:00 P.M.
Pub. *Rear View Notes*, quarterly
$12.00 per year membership for
  individuals, $15.00 per year
  membership for families; free queries
  in periodical

Cass County Genealogical Society
PO Box 880
Atlanta, TX 75551-0880
(903) 796-2107
http://www.rootsweb.com/~txcass/
Patsy R. Livingston, President
Hours: Mon–Fri 10:00–5:30, Sat 10:00–
  2:00
Pub. *Cass County Connections*, four
  times per year (March, June, October,
  December)
(county cemetery books, county records)
$12.00 per year membership

Central Texas Genealogical Society
Waco-McLennan County Library System
1717 Austin Avenue
Waco, TX 76701
(254) 750-5945 (Genealogy Librarian);
  (254) 750-5954 (Volunteer Desk);
  (254) 750-5946 (Library); (254) 750-
  5940 FAX (Library)
E-mail: wayne@eramp.net
http://aisi.net/GenWeb/McLennanCo/
  (home page for seven counties:
  Bosque, Coryell, Falls, Freestone, Hill,
  Limestone and McLennan)
Terri Hugo, Librarian, Special
  Collections; Wayne Stinson,
  Webmaster
Hours: Library: Mon–Thur 10:00–9:00,
  Fri–Sat 10:00–6:00, Sun 1:00–5:00;
  meetings: fourth Mon 7:00 P.M.
Pub. *Heart of Texas Records*, four times
  per year (April, June, September,
  January)
$12.50 per year membership for
  individuals, $2.50 per year
  membership for each additional
  household member, $25.00 per year
  Fellows membership, $100.00 per year
  Patrons membership

**Chaparral Genealogical Society and
Library**
(310 North Live Oak, Tomball, TX
  77375—location)
PO Box 606 (mailing address)
Tomball, TX 77377
(281) 255-9081
Janis Duhe, Trustee
Hours: Mon–Wed & Sat 10:00–3:00

**Cherokee County Genealogical
Society**
PO Box 1332
Jacksonville, TX 75766
(903) 586-9067 (Editor); (903) 586-8750
  (President)
E-mail: gordonbe@e-tex.com
IdaLee D. Edmiston; W. Harold Acker,
  Sr., President
Pub. *Tree Talk*, quarterly
(publishes genealogical or historical
  material from Cherokee County)
$12.00 per year membership (beginning
  in September); limited research may
  be available for a nominal fee

Childress Genealogical Society
Childress Public Library
117 Avenue B, N.E.
Childress, TX 79201

Clayton Library Friends
PO Box 271078
Houston, TX 77277-1078
Pub. *CLF Newsletter*, quarterly
$10.00 per year membership for
  individuals, $15.00 per year
  membership for couples

Coastal Bend Genealogical Society
PO Box 6881
Corpus Christi, TX 78466
Hours: Corpus Christi Public Library
Pub. *Reflections*, quarterly
$15.00 per year membership

Collin County Genealogical Society
PO Box 865052
Plano, TX 75086-5052
(972) 596-3567
http://www.staubase21.com/
  PSGenealogy/
Aurora Chancy, Editor
Hours: Gladys L. Harrington Public
  Library: Mon–Thur 10:00–9:00, Fri–
  Sat 10:00–6:00, Sun 1:00–5:00;
  meetings: second Wed (Aug–May)
  7:30; Collin County Genealogical
  Society Computer User's Group
  meetings: fourth Wed 7:30
Pub. *Collin Chronicles*, quarterly; *Collin
  County Genealogical Society
  Newsletter*, bimonthly
$18.00 per year membership for
  individuals (beginning 1 June), $10.00
  per year membership for each
  additional family member

Comal County Genealogy Society
(Sophienburg Museum and Archives,
  Research Room—location)
PO Box 310583
New Braunfels, TX 78130-0583
(830) 629-1572 (Sophienburg Museum
  and Archives)
Ethel Canion, President
Hours: Archives: Mon–Fri 10:00–4:00
Pub. *Family Footsteps*, three times per
  year (March, July, November)

(German/Texas research Comal County and other German settlements in Texas)

$15.00 per year membership for individuals, $20.00 per year membership for families; search fee: $5.00 minimum

Coryell County Genealogical Society
Gatesville Public Library
811 Main Street
Gatesville, TX 76528
(254) 865-5367 (Library)
Faye McCracken
Hours: Mon, Wed & Fri 9:00–5:00, Tue & Thur noon–8:00, Sat 9:00–3:30
Pub. *Coryell Kin*, quarterly
$12.50 per year membership

Cottle County Genealogical Society
PO Box 1005
Paducah, TX 79248

Cross Timbers Genealogical Society, Inc.
PO Box 197
Gainesville, TX 76240
Wanda Fleitman, President
Hours: meetings first Mon at Cooke County Library
Pub. *Cross Timbers' Post*, quarterly (March, June, September, December)
$10.00 per year membership for individuals; free queries

Cross Timbers Genealogical Society
PO Box 197
Gainesville, TX 76241
Wanda Fleitman, President
Hours: meetings: first Mon (Feb–Jun, Aug & Oct–Dec), first Tue (Sept)
Pub. *Cross Timbers Post*, quarterly (March, June, September, December)
(Cooke County, Texas, and some surrounding counties)
$10.00 per year membership for individuals, $12.00 per year membership for couples

Cypress Basin Genealogical and Historical Society (Titus County)
PO Box 403
Mount Pleasant, TX 75455
Billy F. Walker, President
Hours: meetings second Thur
Pub. *Cypress Basin Genealogical and Historical Society Reporter*, three times per year
$10.00 per year membership for individuals, $12.00 per year membership for families

Dallas County East Genealogical Society
7637 Mary Dan Drive
Dallas, TX 75217-4603
Pub. *Texas Kin*, three times per year
$10.00 per year membership

Dallas Genealogical Society
PO Box 12648
Dallas, TX 75225-0648
(214) 670-7932 phone & FAX
E-mail: don.raney@chrysalis.org
http://www.chrysalis.org/dgs/
Hours: meetings in the auditorium of the J. Erik Jonsson Library, 1515 Young Street
Pub. *The Dallas Quarterly*; *Dallas Genealogical Society Newsletter*, bimonthly
(sponsors African American Network Group, Latin-American Interest Group, Computer Interest Group and Professional Interest Group)
$18.00 per year membership

Deaf Smith County Genealogical Society
Deaf Smith County Library
211 East Fourth Street
Hereford, TX 79045

Denison Library Historical and Genealogical Society
300 West Gandy
Denison, TX 75020
(903) 465-9447
Vicki Hempkins, President
Hours: monthly meetings

Denton County Genealogical Society
PO Box 424707
Denton, TX 76204
Miss Hollace Hervey, Columnist
Hours: Denton Public Library
research: $20.00 for two hours

Donley County Genealogical Society
PO Box 116
Clarendon, TX 79226

Dumas Genealogical and Historical Society
127 Oak Avenue
Dumas, TX 79029

East Bell County Genealogical Society
3219 Meadow Oaks Drive
Temple, TX 76502-1752
(254) 778-2073 (President)
Wanda Donaldson, President
Hours: meetings at Temple Public Library: third Mon
(Texas State Genealogical Society, Partner Society Member)
$12.00 per year membership for individuals, $15.00 per year membership for families

East Texas Genealogical Society
PO Box 6967
Tyler, TX 75711
(903) 561-3830
Jack Russell, President; Fred A. Brock, Corresponding Secretary
Hours: 8:00–5:00

Pub. *East Texas Family Records* (*EFTR*), quarterly; *Newsletter: The Bulletin*, monthly
(publishes books on East Texas family records)
$12.00 per year membership for individuals, $14.00 per year membership for families, $5.00 per year membership for students under 18; free queries to members and non-members

El Paso Genealogical Society
El Paso Main Public Library
501 North Oregon Street
El Paso, TX 79901
(915) 543-5474 (Government Documents/Genealogy); (915) 543-5440 (Southwest Collection)
Hours: Library: Mon–Thur 9:00–8:00, Fri–Sat 9:00–5:30, Sun 1:00–5:00
Pub. *Rio Grande Researcher*, quarterly (emphasis on southwest genealogy)
$12.00 per year membership

Ellis County Genealogical Society
PO Box 479
Waxahachie, TX 75168-0479
Robert Harding, President; Dan Barker, Editor
Pub. *Searchers and Researchers*, quarterly (March, June, September, December), $3.00 per issue
$12.00 per year membership

Fannin County Genealogical Society
605 Agnew
Bonham, TX 75418
Pub. *Fannin County Genealogical Quarterly*

Fort Belknap Genealogical Association
Murray Route
Graham, TX 76046
Barbara Ledbetter
Pub. *Fort Belknap Genealogical Association Bulletin*, semiannually

Fort Bend County Genealogical Society
PO Box 274
Richmond, TX 77469
(281) 341-2608
http://www.intertexd.net/fbclib/lib.html
W. M. Von-Maszewski, President
Hours: meetings at George Memorial Library: second Mon (Sept–Jun) 7:00
Pub. *Around the Bend*, quarterly
$15.00 per year membership for individuals

Fort Brown Genealogical Society
608 East Adams
Brownsville, TX 78520
(956) 542-4824

Fort Worth Genealogical Society
PO Box 9767
Fort Worth, TX 76147-0767

E-mail: joegrant@flash.net
http://www.chrysalis.org/business/fwgen/
  default.htm
Barbara Knox, Editor
Pub. *Footprints*, quarterly
("Source material-Tarrant County and
  surrounding counties, including Bible
  records, court records, misc.
  genealogical materials"; sponsors
  Computer Users Group)
$18.00 per year membership for
  individuals, $20.00 per year
  membership for families, $25.00 per
  year Sustaining membership, $250.00
  Contributing membership; free queries
  with Texas connection

**Freestone County Genealogical
Society**
(East side of Square—location)
PO Box 14 (mailing address)
Fairfield, TX 75840
(903) 389-2292
Lena Bonner, Vice President
Hours: by appointment
Pub. *Freestone Frontiers*, quarterly
  (February, May, August, November),
  $3.50 per issue (for back issues)
$12.50 per year membership

Garland Genealogical Society
PO Box 461882
Garland, TX 75046
http://www.geocities.com/TheTropics/
  1926/society.html
Jimmie DeFord, President
Hours: meetings in the North Room of
  the Nicholson Memorial Library: third
  Tue (Sept–May) 2:30 or 6:30
Pub. *Garland Genealogical Society
  Quarterly*; *GGS Newsletter*
$15.00 per year membership (beginning
  1 June)

German-Texan Heritage Society
507 East Tenth Street
PO Box 684171
Austin, TX 78768-4171
(512) 482-0927
Teresa Chavez, Director; Theresa G.
  Gold, Genealogy Editor
Hours: Mon–Fri 8:00–4:30
Pub. *Journal*, three times per year;
  Newsletter, three times per year
("Preservation of German heritage in
  Texas; German-Texan family histories;
  we are in the process of building a
  library for historians and
  genealogists.")
$10.00 per year membership (calendar
  year), $16.00 per year foreign
  membership; search fees: free form
  members, $10.00 for non-members

Gilmer Genealogical Society
West Pine Street
Gilmer, TX 75644

Grand Prairie Genealogical Society
PO Box 532026
Grand Prairie, TX 75053-2026

Grapevine Name-Droppers
Grapevine Public Library
1201 South Main
Grapevine, TX 76051
(817) 481-0339 (Reference Librarian);
  (817) 267-1645 (Coordinator); (817)
  481-0424 FAX
Bruce Bumbalough, Reference Librarian;
  Frances P. Malcolm, Coordinator
Hours: Library: second Monday 10:00–
  12:30

**Grayson County Genealogical
Society**
Sherman Public Library
Local History and Genealogy
  Department
421 North Travis
Sherman, TX 75090
(903) 892-7240
Jacqueline Banfield, Assistant Library
  Director
Hours: Mon, Wed & Fri 9:00–6:00, Tue
  & Thur 9:00–9:00, Sat 9:00–5:00
Pub. *Bulletin*, irregularly
$10.00 per year membership for
  individuals, $12.00 per year
  membership for couples

**Gregg County (TX) Genealogical
Society**
(Longview Public Library, 222 West
  Cotton, Longview, TX 75601—
  location)
PO Box 2985 (mailing address)
Longview, TX 75606-2985
(903) 237-1350
http://www.chrysalis.org/DallasGen.So/
  gcgs.htm
Hours: Library: Mon, Wed & Thur–Fri
  9:00–12:00 & 1:00–6:00
Pub. *Gregg County Genealogy Society*,
  monthly
$15.00 per year membership for
  individuals, $18.00 per year
  membership for families

**Guadalupe County Genealogical
Society**
Seguin/Guadalupe County Public Library
707 East College Street
Seguin, TX 78155
(830) 379-1531; (830) 488-2337
  (Treasurer)
Al Hagedorn, Treasurer
Hours: Library: Mon–Thur 10:00–9:00,
  Fri–Sat 9:00–5:00
Pub. *Journal*, quarterly (February, May,
  August, November)
$15.00 per year membership for
  individuals, $18.00 per year
  membership for families, $50.00 per
  year Sponsor membership, $100.00
  per year Patron membership

**Hamilton County Genealogy Society
and Central Texas Research Center**
209 West Henry
Hamilton, TX 76531
(800) 460-2847; (254) 386-4566
E-mail: hcgs@htcomp.net;
  carlian@why.net
http://207.17.189.3:80/hcgs
Carlian Massingaill Pittman, President;
  Nancy Hengst, Secretary/Treasurer
Hours: Mon–Sat 9:00–5:00; meetings:
  fourth Thur 7:00
Pub. *Family Circle Journal*, three times
  per year (April, August, December)
$15.00 per year membership for
  individuals, $20.00 per year
  membership for couples, $5.00 per
  year junior membership

Harris County Genealogical Society
PO Box 391
Pasadena, TX 77501
Pub. *Living Tree News*, quarterly
$11.50 per year membership

**Hays County Historical and
Genealogical Society**
PO Box 1837
San Marcos, TX 78666

Heart of Texas Genealogical Society
PO Box 133
Rochelle, TX 76872

**Hemphill County Historical and
Genealogical Society**
Rt. 2
Canadian, TX 79014
Mr. and Mrs. John Ramp

Hi-Plains Genealogical Society
c/o Unger Memorial Library
825 Austin Street
Plainview, TX 79072
(806) 296-1148
Ruth Gooch or Joy Denton, Volunteers
Hours: Library: six days per week
  (summer five days per week)
(marriage records to 1941, burials for
  Hale County from the late 1800s to the
  present)
$10.00 per year membership for
  individuals, $12.50 per year
  membership for couples

Hill Country Genealogical Society
HC 07, Box 52
Llano, TX 78643
Evelyn Wade
Pub. *Hill Country Genealogical Society
  Quarterly*
$7.00 per year membership

Hill County Genealogical Society
PO Box 636
Hillsboro, TX 76645-0636
(254) 694-5483
Peggy Fox, President; Wilna Sawyer,
  Editor
Hours: Mon–Fri 9:00–5:00, Thurs 9:00–
  8:30

Pub. *Hill County Crossroads*, quarterly, $2.50 per issue
$10.00 per year membership

Hood County Genealogical Society
Restored Granbury Depot, 109 Ewell Street
PO Box 1623
Granbury, TX 76048-8623
(817) 573-2557 (Depot); (817) 573-9246 (Chairman); (817) 573-4432 (Editor)
E-mail: granbury@emcee.com (queries)
http://genealogy.emcee.com:80/granbury/welcome.html
Syvilla Lemons, Chairman of the Depot Preservation Committee; Roy E. Malone, Editor
Hours: Tue & Thur noon–4:00, Sat 10:00–3:00
Pub. *Hood County Genealogical Society Newsletter*, quarterly (May, August, November, February)
$10.00 per year membership for individuals, $12.00 per year membership for couples; indepth research: $5.00 per hour

Hopkins County Genealogical Society
312 North Davis Street
PO Box 624
Sulphur Springs, TX 75483-0624
(903) 885-8523
Danna E. Elliott, President
Hours: Research Center: Mon–Fri 9:00–5:00, Sat 9:00–12:00
Pub. *Hopkins County Heritage*, quarterly
$12.00 per year membership

Houston Genealogical Forum
PO Box 271466
Houston, TX 77277-1466
(713) 827-4440 (message line)
Pat Metcalfe, Librarian
Hours: meetings: first Sat (Sept–May) 10:00 A.M.-11:00 A.M.
Pub. *The Bulletin*, nine times per year (monthly, September–May); *The Genealogical Record*, quarterly (March, June, September, December)
$18.00 per year membership for individuals, $25.00 per year membership for two in the same household, $10.00 additional for membership outside the U.S.

The Humble Area Genealogical Society
PO Box 2723
Humble, TX 77347-2723
(281) 358-3062
D. E. MacGregory, President
Hours: meetings: second Mon (Sept–May) 7:15; collection housed at Kingwood College, Kingwood, TX 77339
Pub. *The Humble Genealogist*, quarterly
$10.00 per year membership for individuals, $12.00 per year membership for families

The Hunt County Genealogical Society
PO Box 398
Greenville, TX 75403-0398
(903) 886-8690 (after 4:00 P.M.)
Dorothy Wood Moore, Corresponding Secretary
(publishes books of marriage records, funeral home records, school records, etc.)
$7.50 per year membership for individuals, $10.00 per year membership for families; brief responses to research questions will be answered and more detailed research for $7.50 per hour plus costs

Hutchinson County Genealogical Society
Hutchinson County Library
625 Weatherly Street
Borger, TX 79007
(806) 273-0126; (806) 273-0128 FAX
Hours: Mon–Tue & Thur 10:00–8:00, Wed & Fri 10:00–6:00, Sat 1:00–5:00

Johnson County Genealogical Society
PO Box 1256
Cleburne, TX 76031-1256
http://www.htcomp.net/jcgs/soc/soc.htm
Vivian Morris, President
Hours: meetings second Thur at Cleburne Civic Center, 1501 West Henderson, Room 100, Cleburne
Pub. *Finders Keepers*, quarterly (spring, summer, winter, fall)
$15.00 per year membership for individuals, $20.00 per year membership for families

Kaufman County Genealogical Society
PO Box 337
Terrell, TX 75160-0337
Barbara Sloan, President
Hours: Terrell Public Library: Mon–Tue 10:00–8:00, Wed–Thur 10:00–6:00, Fri 12:00–5:00, Sat 10:00–4:00
Pub. *Kaufman Kounty Konnections*, quarterly (March, June, September, December)
(specializes in genealogy, family history, cemeteries, and census records of the area, obituaries from county newspapers, microfilmed church records)
$15.00 per year membership for individuals or families; limited free research for members only

Genealogical Society of Kendall County
PO Box 623
Boerne, TX 78006
Hours: Boerne Public Library
Pub. *Keys to the Past*, quarterly
(some local family histories, but expanded collection covers a great

deal of the rest of the U.S. in different time periods, and some foreign material)
$15.00 per year membership, $25.00 per year membership for husband and wife

Kent County Genealogical and Historical Society
PO Box 6
Jayton, TX 79528

Genealogical Society of Kerrville
c/o Butt-Holdsworth Memorial Library
505 Water Street
Kerrville, TX 78028
(830) 257-8422 (Library); (830) 792-5552 FAX
http://www.ktc.net/kgs/
Judith A. Trolinger, Volunteer KGS Librarian
Hours: Mon–Sat 1:00–4:00 volunteer on duty
Pub. *Kerr Trails*, quarterly
(library collection of several thousand volumes, strong on local area)
$10.00 per year membership

Lamar County Genealogical Society
2400 Clarksville Street
Paris Junior College Box 187
Paris, TX 75460
(903) 782-0448
http://gen.1starnet.com
Hours: Mon–Thur noon–4:00
Pub. *Lamar County History and Genealogy*, annually
$15.00 per year membership for individuals (beginning in April), $25.00 per year I Care membership, $50.00 per year Cornerstone membership

Lamesa Area Genealogical Society
(511 North Third Street—location)
PO Box 1264 (mailing address)
Lamesa, TX 79331
Nina West, Corresponding Secretary
Hours: Mon–Fri 9:30–5:30
Pub. *Lamesa Area Genealogical Society Bulletin*, semiannually; *Threads of Life*, semiannually
(genealogical and local source material)
$5.00 per year membership

Lee County Genealogical Society
Rt. 1, Box 8-D
Ledbetter, TX 78946
Jan Conn

Leon County Genealogical Society
Old Courthouse
PO Box 400
Centerville, TX 75833
Fae Boutotte, Corresponding Secretary
Hours: Mon–Fri 1:00–4:00
Pub. *Leon Hunters Dispatch (Quarterly)*, quarterly
$15.00 per year membership for individuals

Liberal Area Genealogical Society
(see Kansas)

Llano Estacado Genealogical Society
1313 West Ninth Street
Littlefield, TX 79339

Los Bexarenos Genealogical Society
PO Box 1935
San Antonio, TX 78297
(210) 822-1526
Gloria Cadena, Editor
Pub. *Los Bexarenos Genealogical Register*, quarterly (March, June, September, December)
$20.00 per year for individuals and families, $15.00 per year membership for institutions or libraries

Madison County Genealogical Society
PO Box 26
Madisonville, TX 77864

Matagorda County Genealogical Society
(1100 Seventh Street, Bay City, TX 77414—location)
PO Box 264 (mailing address)
Bay City, TX 77404-0264
(409) 245-6931 (Library)
Carol Sue Gibbs
Hours: Bay City Public Library: Mon–Thur 9:00–8:00, Fri 11:00–6:00, Sat 9:00–6:00
Pub. *Oak Leaves*, semiannually, $10.00 per issue
$15.00 per year membership

McAllen Genealogical Society
McAllen Memorial Library
601 North Main Street
PO Box 4714
McAllen, TX 78502
(956) 686-5669 (Librarian's home)
Janette Josserand, Genealogical Librarian
Hours: Mon–Wed 9:00–9:00, Thur–Fri 9:00–5:00, Sat–Sun 1:00–5:00
Pub. *Palm Breezes Newsletter*, quarterly
(complete *New England Historical and Genealogical Register*, *The America Genealogist*, *Arkansas Family Historian*, *Connecticut Nutmegger*, *The Georgia Genealogical Magazine*, *Hawkeye Heritage* (Iowa), *"Ansearchin'" News* (Tennessee), *The Virginia Genealogist*, *Confederate Veteran*, *Periodical Source Index* (PERSI); 4,500 volumes in an all-around collection, except the West)
$15.00 per year membership for individuals, $18.00 per year membership with spouse

Mesquite Historical and Genealogical Society
Mesquite Public Library
300 Grubb Drive
PO Box 850165
Mesquite, TX 75185-0165
(972) 216-6229
http://members.aol.com/dstuart101/mesquite/page1.htm
Marjorie Bays, Librarian
Hours: Mon–Tue & Thur 9:00–9:00, Wed & Fri–Sat 9:00–6:00; meetings: second Thur (Oct–Jun) 7:00 P.M.–9:00 P.M.
Pub. *The Mesquite Tree*, quarterly (March, June, September, December); *Mesquite Historical and Genealogical Society Newsletter*, monthly
$15.00 per year membership; queries to Deborah Stuart, Editor, E-mail: DStuart101@aol.com; research register: $3.00

Mid-Cities Genealogical Society
PO Box 407
Bedford, TX 76095-0407
(817) 283-3422
Sherlene Rogers Baab, Editor
Hours: Euless Public Library, Genealogy Room: Mon–Tue & Thur 10:00–9:00, Wed 10:00–6:00, Fri–Sat 10:00–5:00, Sun 1:00–5:00; meetings at Pipeline Road Church of Christ, 824 West Pipeline Road, Hurst, TX: first Thur 7:00
Pub. *A Tale of Mid-Cities*, quarterly (fall, winter, spring and summer); *Mid-Cities Genealogical Society Newsletter*, bimonthly
$15.00 per year membership for individuals, $20.00 per year membership for couples

Midland Genealogical Society
Midland County Public Library
The John and Rosalind Redfern Genealogical Research Center
301 West Missouri
Midland, TX 79701
(915) 688-8991; (915) 688-8996 FAX
E-mail: mcpl@apex2000.net
Sandra De Fore Wegner, County Librarian
Hours: Library: Sept–May: Mon–Thur 9:00–9:00, Fri–Sat 9:00–6:00; Jun–Aug: Mon 9:00–9:00, Tue–Sat 9:00–6:00
Pub. *Midland Genealogical Newsletter*; *The Thorny Trail*, biannually, $12.00 per year subscription
(microfilm copies of all Midland unprotected birth and death records)

Milam County Genealogical Society
Lucy Hill Patterson Memorial Library
201 Ackerman Street
Rockdale, TX 76567
(512) 446-3410
http://www.aisi.net/GenWeb/MilamCo/mcgs.htm
Melanie Todd, Head Librarian
Hours: Library: Tue–Wed & Fri 10:00–5:00, Thur 1:00–8:00, Sat 10:00–2:00; meetings at the NBC Bank Community Room across the street from the Library, at the corner of Ackerman and Cameron Streets, Rockdale, TX: first Thur 7:00
Pub. *The Legacy*, monthly
$15.00 per year membership for individuals (calendar year), $20.00 per year membership, $25.00 or more per year Supporting membership

Montgomery County Genealogical and Historical Society, Inc.
PO Box 867
Conroe, TX 77305-0867
(409) 788-8363
http://mcia.com/gsociety.htm
Melvin Westmoreland, President
Hours: Montgomery County Library, Conroe, TX: Mon & Fri 10:00–5:00, Tue–Thur 10:00–8:00, Sat 9:00–5:00; Office: Mon & Wed 10:00–3:00
Pub. *The Herald*, quarterly
$18.00 per year membership

Nacogdoches Genealogical Society
(First United Methodist Church—location)
PO Box 4634, Stephen F. Austin Station (mailing address)
Nacogdoches, TX 75962
(409) 564-5544
Mary Hearn, Treasurer
Hours: Steen Library, Special Collections Department: 10:00–5:00
Pub. *Yesterday*, annually
$15.00 per year membership (beginning in November)

Navarro County Genealogical Society
(Corsicana Public Library, Genealogy Room, 100 North 12th Street, Corsicana, TX 75110—location)
PO Box 2278 (mailing address)
Corsicana, TX 75151-2278
(903) 654-4846; (903) 654-4810; (903) 654-4812
David Franklin, President; Verna Bonner, Vice President
Hours: Corsicana Public Library, Genealogy Department: Mon–Tue 10:00–8:00, Wed–Fri 10:00–6:00, Sat 10:00–4:00
Pub. *Navarro Leaves and Branches*, quarterly
$10.00 per year membership for individuals, $15.00 per year membership for families or Sustaining membership; volunteer research only

New Boston Genealogical Society
PO Box 104
New Boston, TX 75570
(903) 628-3467
Edith Terrell
Pub. *The New Bostonian*, quarterly
$10.00 per year membership (beginning in May)

New Boston Public Library
127 North Ellis
New Boston, TX 75570-2905
(903) 628-5414
Julie Woodrow, Librarian
Hours: Mon 10:00–6:30, Tue 10:00–
8:00, Wed–Fri 10:00–5:00, Sat 9:00–
1:00

North Collin County Genealogical Society
E-mail: kcole@waymark.net
http://www.psyberlink.net/ kcole/
nccgs.htm
Kenneth Cole, Webmaster
Hours: meetings in the Dulaney Room of
the McKinney Memorial Library: on
the first Sat 10:15 A.M.

North Texas Genealogical Association
PO Box 4602
Wichita Falls, TX 76308
(940) 692-7089
http://www.wf.net/~fmaier/
Peggy Maier, Library Chairman
Hours: Kemp Public Library, Genealogy
Room: Mon–Fri 10:00–8:00, Sat
10:00–5:00
Pub. *North Texas Trail Tracers*, quarterly
$10.00 per year membership

Parker County Genealogical Society
Weatherford Public Library
1214 Charles Street
Weatherford, TX 76086
(817) 594-2767
Evlyn Broumley, Librarian
Hours: Mon, Wed & Fri–Sat 10:00–6:00,
Tue & Thur 1:00–9:00
Pub. *Trails West*, quarterly
$10.00 per year membership for
individuals, $12.50 per year
membership for families

Pecan Valley Genealogical Society (Brown County)
Brownwood Public Library
600 Carnegie Boulevard
Brownwood, TX 76801

Permian Basin Genealogical Society
Ector County Library
321 West Fifth Street
Odessa, TX 79761
(915) 332-0633
Doris Baker, Head, Southwest History/
Genealogy Department
Hours: Genealogy Department: Mon–
Thur 9:30–8:30, Fri–Sat 9:30–6:00,
Sat 9:00–noon & 1:00–6:00
Pub. *Treeshaker*, semiannually; *Permian
Basin Genealogical Society
Newsletter*, monthly
$15.00 per year membership for
individuals, $20.00 per year
membership for couples

Piney Woods Pioneer Genealogical Society
Genealogical Research Center and
Library of Southeast Texas
Rt. 1, Box 405
Kountze, TX 77625

Porciones Genealogical Society
PO Box 392
Edinburg, TX 78540-0392
Pub. *Porciones Genealogical Society
Journal*, semiannually

Randolph Area Genealogical Society
PO Box 2134
Universal City, TX 78148
(210) 659-7881 (President)
Hours: meetings third Wed (Jan–Nov)
7:00
Pub. Trudy Messick, Secretary/Treasurer
("Society family names in search;
presently performing cemetery
research with published indexes soon
to be printed of Guadalupe County,
Texas.")
$12.00 per year membership for
individuals, $15.00 per year
membership for couples

Red River County Texas Genealogical Society
(Red River County Public Library,
Locust Street—location)
PO Box 516 (mailing address)
Clarksville, TX 75426
(903) 427-3991 (Library); (903) 784-
4975 (President)
Zoe Farmer, President
Hours: meetings second Mon 7:30
Pub. *Red River County Texas
Genealogical Society Newsletter*,
quarterly
$10.00 per year membership for
individuals, $12.50 per year
membership for families, $4.00 per
year membership for students

Rockwall County Genealogical Society
PO Box 471
Rockwall, TX 75087
(972) 771-9018
E-mail: pat5@airmail.net; prash@gte.net
(Research Requests)
http://www.geocities.com/Heartland/
Ranch/7757
Pat Dollinger, President
Hours: meetings at the Government
Center, 1101 Ridge Road, Rockwall:
third Tue 7:30
Pub. *RockwallCoGenSoc Quarterly*
$15.00 per year membership for
individuals (beginning 1 June), $18.00
per year membership for families

Rusk County Genealogical Society
PO Box 1314
Henderson, TX 75653-1314

San Angelo Genealogical and Historical Society, Inc.
(Church of Christ Fellowship Hall, 902
North Main Street—location)
PO Box 3453 (mailing address)
San Angelo, TX 76902-3453
(915) 949-3223
http://www.rootsweb.com/saghs
Betty Varner, Researcher
Hours: meetings first Tue (Sept–May)
7:30
Pub. *Stalkin' Kin*, quarterly (August,
November, February and May)
(Coke, Concho, Crockett, Glasscock,
Irion, Kimble, Menard, Reagan,
Runnels, Schleicher, Sterling, Sutton,
and Tom Green counties; Bible
records, members' ancestor charts,
court records, cemeteries, etc.)
$15.00 per year membership for
individuals, $18.00 per year
membership for families (beginning
August 1, add $2.50 after 1 August);
free queries to members first and to
others as space allows

San Antonio Genealogical and Historical Society
(401 Isom Road, Suite 550, San Antonio,
TX 78216—location)
PO Box 17461 (mailing address)
San Antonio, TX 78217-0461
(210) 342-5242
Rita Woodward, President
Hours: Mon & Sat 10:00–4:00, Wed
10:00–9:00, Sun 1:00–5:00; meetings
third Sat (Jan–May & Sept–Oct)
Pub. *Our Heritage*, quarterly (fall,
winter, spring, summer), $25.00 per
year subscription for libraries and
societies; *Newsletter*
$35.00 per year full membership for
individuals (beginning in July), $20.00
per year full membership for spouses

San Marcos/Hays County Genealogy Society
PO Box 503
San Marcos, TX 78667
(512) 353-5823
Pat Young, President
$12.00 per year membership

Scurry County Genealogical Society
(Scurry County Library, 1916 23rd
Street, Snyder, TX 79549—location)
PO Box 195 (mailing address)
Snyder, TX 79550
Hours: Library: Mon, Wed & Fri–Sat
10:00–6:00, Tue & Thur 10:00–9:00
Pub. *White Buffalo Tales*, semiannually
(April and October)
(courthouse records)
$12.50 per year membership

Scurry County Museum Genealogical Group
6200 College Avenue
Snyder, TX 79549-6105

South Plains Genealogical Society

PO Box 6607
Lubbock, TX 79493-6607
(806) 747-1319
Yvonne S. Perkins, President
Hours: Mahon Public Library: Mon–
Thur 9:00–9:00, Fri–Sat 9:00–6:00,
Sun 1:00–5:00
Pub. *SPGS Newsletter*, monthly, $7.50
per year subscription
$10.00 per year membership for
individuals, $15.00 per year
membership for couples; quick
research fee: $10.00

South Texas Genealogical Society, Inc.

(Bee County Public Library—location)
PO Box 754 (mailing address)
Beeville, TX 78104-0754
(512) 358-8757
Kay Mix, Corresponding Secretary
Hours: meetings third Tue 7:00
Pub. *South Texas Genealogical Society,
Inc., Quarterly*, $10.00 per year
subscription
(Bee, Live Oak, Goliad, Refugio, Karnes
and San Patricio counties)
$15.00 per year membership for member
and spouse

Southeast Texas Genealogical and Historical Society

Tyrrell Historical Library
Beaumont Public Library System
695 Pearl Street
PO Box 3827
Beaumont, TX 77704
(409) 833-2759; (409) 833-5828 FAX
David E. Montgomery, Library Manager
Hours: Library: Tue–Sat 8:30–5:30
Pub. *Tyrrell Historical Library
Association Newsletter*, various;
*Southeast Texas Genealogical and
Historical Society—Yellowed Pages*,
quarterly, $14.00 per year subscription
$15.00 per year membership for
individuals, $25.00 per year
membership for families

Southwest Genealogical Society

San Antonio College Library
1300 San Pedro Avenue
San Antonio, TX 78212

Southwest Texas Genealogical Society

PO Box 295
Uvalde, TX 78802
Scottie Molloy, Editor/Publisher
Hours: El Progreso Memorial Library:
Mon–Wed & Fri 9:00–6:00, Thur
9:00–8:00, Sat 9:00–1:00
Pub. *Branches and Acorns*, quarterly,
$10.00 per year subscription
(Dimmit, Edwards, Frio, Kinney,
Medina, Real, Uvalde and Zavala
counties)
$15.00 per year membership

Stephens County Genealogical Society

Swenson Memorial Museum Research
Library
116 West Walker
PO Box 350
Breckenridge, TX 76424
(254) 559-8471
Freda Mitchell, Corresponding Secretary
Hours: Library: Tue–Sat 10:00–noon &
1:00–5:00

Texarkana U.S.A. Genealogy Society

PO Box 2323
Texarkana, TX 75504-2323
Pub. *Texarkana U.S.A. Quarterly*
$10.00 per year membership for
individuals, $12.50 per year
membership for families

Texas City Ancestry Searchers

(Moore Memorial Library, 1701 Ninth
Avenue, North, Texas City, TX
77590—location)
PO Box 3301 (mailing address)
Texas City, TX 77592-3301
(409) 935-5343
Zora A. Evans, Editor and Newspaper
Column Chairman
Hours: 8:00–4:00 or evenings
Pub. *Through the Spyglass*, quarterly,
$12.00 per year subscription
(local history, copies of local records)
$7.00 per year membership

TX-OK Panhandle Genealogical Society

c/o Perry Memorial Library
Fifth and Ash
Perryton, TX 79070
(806) 435-5801 (Library)
Hours: Mon 10:00–8:00, Tue–Fri 10:00–
5:30, Sat 10:00–1:00
Pub. *The TX-OK Panhandler*, quarterly
$10.00 per year membership (beginning
in March)

Texas Research Ramblers

740 Garden Acres
Bryan, TX 77802-4005
(409) 846-8278
Mary Collie Cooper, President
Pub. *Newsletter*

Timpson Area Genealogical and Heritage Society

PO Box 726
Timpson, TX 75975
(409) 254-3344 (President); (409) 254-
2374 (Archivist); (409) 254-2444 (Ms.
Shepherd)
Sandra Brownlow, President; Esther
Marie Harvey, Archivist; Beth
Shepherd
Hours: meetings at Timpson High School
Library: fourth Wed (Jan–Oct) 3:00
Pub. *Tap Root*, quarterly

Tip-O-Texas Genealogical Society

Harlingen Public Library
410 76 Drive
Harlingen, TX 78550
(956) 430-6650 (Library); (956) 423-
1941 (President)
Carolyn McCarley, President
Hours: Library: Mon–Thur 10:00–9:00,
Fri 1:00–5:00
Pub. *The Tips*, quarterly
(volumes in every category of research,
planned to complement the McAllen
and Brownsville, Texas, genealogical
collections and includes local material
as well)
$15.00 per year membership, $100.00
life membership

Tri-County Genealogical Society and Library

(Corner of Connett and Thomas Streets
in the historic First Presbyterian
Church—location)
PO Box 107 (mailing address)
Leonard, TX 75452-0107
(903) 587-2246
Louise Karr, President
Hours: Library: by appointment; meeting
first Tue 7:00
Pub. *Tri-County Newsletter*, quarterly
("Our area of interest has grown from the
original three counties of Collin,
Fannin, and Hunt, to include all of the
north Texas area.")
$15.00 per year membership for
individuals, $5.00 per year
membership for each additional family
member

Upton County Genealogical Society

PO Box 6
Rankin, TX 79778

Van Zandt County Genealogical Society

(Van Zandt County Courthouse Annex
Building, Corner of Highway 19 and
Terrell Street—location)
PO Box 716 (mailing address)
Canton, TX 75103-0716
(903) 567-5012
Sibyl Creasey, President
Hours: Mon–Fri 9:00–4:00, Sat 9:00–
1:00
Pub. *Our Heritage*, quarterly (February,
May, August, November)
$10.00 per year membership for
individuals, $12.00 per year
membership for families; free queries;
limited amount of research can be
done by members

Victoria County Genealogical Society

Victoria Public Library
302 North Main Street
Victoria, TX 77901

Pub. *Victoria—Crossroads of South Texas*, quarterly
$15.00 per year membership

Walker County Genealogical Society
Rt. 1, Box 96
Oakhurst, TX 77359
Ynette Boyce

Ward County Genealogical Society
400 East Fourth Street
Monahans, TX 79756
(915) 943-6312
Nancy Tucker Jordan, Librarian
Hours: Mon–Fri 10:00–5:15
Pub. *Ward County Heritage*, semiannually (April and October)
(local newspaper on microfilm, 1931 to date; poll tax transcribed, 1913–1961; funeral homes records and cemetery lists)
$15.00 per year membership; search: $5.00 per hour plus copies at 10¢ per page

West Bell Genealogical Society
PO Box 851
Killeen, TX 76540
(254) 699-2143
Warren Cantrell, President
Hours: meetings at City Library: first Thur
Pub. *Bell County Genealogist*, quarterly
$12.00 per year membership

West Texas Genealogical Society
PO Box 2307
Abilene, TX 79604
Hours: Abilene Public Library: Mon–Tue & Thur 9:00–9:00, Wed & Fri–Sat 9:00–6:00
Pub. *West Texas Genealogical Society Bulletin*, quarterly
$10.00 per year membership for individuals, $12.00 per year membership for families

Western Trails Genealogical Society
(see Oklahoma)

Williamson County Genealogical Society
PO Box 585
Round Rock, TX 78680-0585
http://www.flash.net/~hmwalden/wcgs.htm
Hours: meetings at the Georgetown Public Library, 800 Martin Luther King, Georgetown, TX: second Tue (Jan–Jun, Sept–Nov) 7:30
Pub. *The Chisholm Trail*, quarterly, $4.00 each
(sponsors annual seminar; issues a Pioneer Families of Williamson County certificate to descendants of any person living in Williamson County before the end of 1880; collection housed at Round Rock Public Library)

$15.00 per year membership for individuals (beginning 1 May), $18.00 per year membership for families, $250.00 life membership

Genealogical Society of Winters High School
PO Box 125
Winters, TX 79567

Wood County Genealogical Society
PO Box 832
Quitman, TX 75783
(903) 763-4191 (Library)
Mrs. Howard W. Dougherty, Corresponding Secretary
Hours: Quitman Public Library: Mon & Thur 9:00–9:00, Tue & Fri 9:00–5:00
Pub. *Wood County Genealogical Society Newsletter*, quarterly
$10.00 per year membership for individuals, $15.00 per year membership for families

---

Independent Publications and Miscellany

Bell County Homepage
http:www.rootsweb.com/ txbell/
Kay Bradley

Center for Southwest Research
(see New Mexico)

Collie-Cooper Enterprises
740 Garden Acres
Bryan, TX 77802-4005
(409) 846-8278
Mary Collie Cooper
(book publications on Brazon, Madison and Robertson counties)
no periodical

Family History Research Foundation
1300 Dominik Drive
College Station, TX 77840-3618

Genealogical Institute
(see Virginia)

The Genealogical Institute of Texas
PO Box 832856
Richardson, TX 75083-2856
(972) 341-0212
Mary Reid Warner, Founding Director
("Military paper trail, Texas research, land platting; week-long intensive courses from beginners, advanced, problem solving and analyzing")
tuition: $250.00–$275.00 ($100.00 deposit)

Genealogy Books and Consultation
1217 Oakdale
Houston, TX 77004
(713) 522-7444
Norma Chudleigh, Ph.D., A.G., Owner

Hours: Mon–Wed & Fri 1:00–5:00, Sat 10:00–5:00
(specializes in The South)

Gowen Research Foundation (GRF)
5708 Gary Avenue
Lubbock, TX 79413
E-mail: gowen@llano.net
http://www.llano.net/gowen
Arlee Gowen, President
Hours: 9:00–5:00
$15.00 per year membership

Historical Projects Houston County, Texas, Inc.
629 North Fourth Street
Crockett, TX 75835
(409) 544-3269
Eliza H. Bishop, Director
Hours: 24-hours per day
(specializes in Houston County; "supports and guides Houston County historical work.")
$10.00 per year membership

Hunting for Bears Genealogical and Historical Society
(see Alabama)

The Institute of Genealogical Studies
PO Box 25556
Dallas, TX 75225-5556
(972) 341-5116 (evenings); (972) 341-3963 FAX
(along with the Dallas Genealogical Society, sponsors a week-long seminar offering eight levels of courses in American Genealogy)

Lone Star Junction
http://www.lsjunction.com/index.htm

Milam County Homepage
http://www.aisi.net/GenWeb/MilamCo/
Brad Thomas

Mountain Press
(see Tennessee)

Our Family Times
PO Box 387
Port Neches, TX 77651
Pub. *Our Family Times*, quarterly, $15.00 per year subscription

Robertson County Homepage
http://www.geocities.com/Heartland/Plains/3451
Shari Simonds

Society of Southwest Archivists
Texas Tech University
PO Box 4090
Lubbock, TX 79409

Southwest Field Office-National Trust for Historic Preservation
500 Main Street, Suite 1036
Fort Worth, TX 76102
(817) 332-4398; (817) 332-4512 FAX
Hours: Mon–Fri 9:00–5:00

Pub. *Preservation Magazine*, bimonthly
(New Mexico, Texas, Oklahoma)

Taproot Publishers
PO Box 15153
Dallas, TX 75201
Pub. *Genealogical Query Index*,
   quarterly, $24.00 per year subscription

Tarrant County Homepage
auntjean@ProMail.com
http://www.rootsweb.com/ txtarran/
Jean Jones

Tejas Publications and Research
2507 Tannehill Drive
Houston, TX 77008-3052
(713) 864-6862; (713) 864-3540 FAX
Trevia Wooster Beverly, Editor/
   Researcher/Instructor
Pub. *The Tejas Gazette*, quarterly, $20.00
   per year subscription
search fees vary

Texas Ancestry Researchers
1009 Eric Avenue
Arlington, TX 76012-3205
(817) 265-0044
Gayle W. Hanson
(specializes in Texas African-American
   research, publishes record abstracts)

Texas Oral History Association
Carroll Library, Baylor University
PO Box 97271
Waco, TX 76798-7271
(254) 755-3437; (254) 755-1571 FAX
E-mail: lois_myers@baylor.edu
Lois E. Myers, Secretary-Treasurer
Pub. *TOHA Newsletter*, three to four
   times per year; *The Sound Historian*,
   annually, $5.00 per issue
$8.50 per year membership for
   individuals, $25.00 per year
   institutional membership

Texas State Cemetery
901 Novasota Street
PO Box 13047
Austin, TX 78711-3047
(512) 463-0605; (512) 463-3311
E-mail: statecemetery@gsc.state.tx.us
http://sparky.gsc.state.tx.us/
   statecemetery/

TxGenWeb
Part of U.S. GenWeb Project
E-mail: tx@usgenweb.com
http://www.rootsweb.com/ txgenweb
(links to other Texas resources)

University of Arizona Press
Journal of the Southwest
(see Arizona)

Williamson County Homepage
http://www.flash.net/ hmwalden/
   willcoun.htm
Harry Walden
free queries

UTAH

Archives and Libraries with Holdings in Genealogy

State Archives and Library

State Archives and Record Services
Archives Building
State Capitol
Salt Lake City, UT 84114-1021
(801) 538-3013; (801) 538-3354 FAX
E-mail: research@state.ut.us
http://www.archives.state.ut.us
Jeffery O. Johnson, State Archivist
Hours: Mon–Fri 8:00–5:00

Utah State Library
2150 South 300 West
Salt Lake City, UT 84115
(801) 466-5888
E-mail: dslater@inter.state.lib.us
http://www.state.lib.ut.us/
Chip Ward, Librarian
Hours: Mon–Fri 8:00–5:00
Pub. *Directions for Utah Libraries*,
   monthly

State Historical Societies

Utah State Historical Society
300 Rio Grande
Salt Lake City, UT 84101-1182
(801) 533-3500; (801) 533-3504 FAX
E-mail: cehistry.uhic@email.state.ut.us
http://www.ce.ex.state.us/history/
   welcome.htm state history
Alan Barnett
Hours: Mon–Fri 10:00–5:00, Sat 10:00–
   2:00
Pub. *Utah Historical Quarterly*, $20.00
   per year subscription; *Beehive History*,
   annually; *Utah State Historical Society
   Newsletter*, bimonthly
(50,000 volumes plus manuscripts,
   photographs, microform, maps and
   architectural drawings)
$20.00 per year membership for
   individuals, $15.00 per year
   membership for students and senior
   citizens (65+)

Association of Utah Historians
1845 South 1800 East
Salt Lake City, UT 84108
(801) 533-7037
Craig Fuller, Executive Secretary

City, County and Regional Archives and Libraries

Brigham Carnegie Library
26 East Forest
Brigham City, UT 84302

Brigham Young University
Harold B. Lee Library
Provo, UT 84602
(801) 378-6200; (801) 378-6091
Diane Parkinson
Hours: Mon–Fri 7:00 A.M.–midnight, Sat
   8:00 A.M.–midnight

Cedar City Public Library
Cedar City, UT 84720

**Daughters of Utah Pioneers Relic
Hall**
(420 Clay Street—location)
Old Mill Road (mailing address)
Montpelier, ID 83254
(208) 847-1069

**Fairview Museum of History and
Art**
(85 North 100 East—location)
PO Box 157 (mailing address)
Fairview, UT 84629
(435) 427-9216
Betty N. Jorgensen, President
Hours: 10:00–6:00

**Family History Library of The
Church of Jesus Christ of Latter-day
Saints**
Genealogical Society of Utah
35 North West Temple
Salt Lake City, UT 84150
(801) 240-2331; (801) 240-5551
http://www.lds.org/
   Welcome_to_FamHist/
   Welcome_to_FamHist.html
Jimmy B. Parker, Manager
Hours: Mon 7:30 A.M.–6:00 P.M., Tue–
   Sat 7:30 A.M.–10:00 P.M.
(The Genealogical Society of Utah is the
   acquisitions arm of the Family History
   Library. Membership is limited to
   employees of the Church's
   corporation. No individual research
   services are provided by the Society.
   At the present time Church policy is
   opposed to commercial publication of
   the names and mailing addresses of
   the various branch libraries [Family
   History Centers] throughout the world,
   but has released the phone numbers of
   selected centers, which are included
   here in the state-by-state listings. A
   partial list of centers is available upon
   request from the Family History
   Library. The location of the nearest
   library, where microfilm copies of the
   Family History Library's holdings can
   be viewed, may be obtained by
   phoning local LDS church
   representatives, usually listed in the
   yellow pages of the phone book.
   Accredits professional genealogists.)

Fort Lewis College
(see Colorado)

Hyrum City Museum
(3 South Center—location)
42 West Third South (mailing address)
Hyrum, UT 84319
(435) 245-6850

Manti City Library
Manti, UT 84642

Moab Museum
118 East Center Street
Moab, UT 84532
(435) 259-7430

Mountain West Center for Regional Studies
University Hill
Logan, UT 84322-0735
(435) 750-3630
F. Ross Peterson, Ph.D., Director

Salt Lake City Public Library
209 East 500 South
Salt Lake City, UT 84111
(801) 363-5733
Michael R. Mabe, Serials Librarian
Hours: Mon–Thur 9:00–9:00, Fri–Sat
    9:00–6:00

Southern Utah State College Library
Special Collections
351 West Center Street
Cedar City, UT 84720
(435) 586-7945
Jackie F. Robinson
Hours: Mon–Fri 8:00–5:00

Public Library, Springville
50 South Main
Springville, UT 84663
(801) 489-2720
Lynette Catherall, Director
Hours: Mon–Thur 10:00–9:00, Fri
    10:00–6:00, Sat 10:00–4:00

Uintah County Library
Regional History Center
155 East Main Street
Vernal, Utah 84078
(435) 789-0091
Doris Burton
Hours: Mon 8:00–noon, Tue–Thur 2:00–
    8:00, Fri–Sat 2:00–6:00
Pub. *Outlas Trail History Journal*, two
    times per year
$15.00 per year membership; search fee:
    $5.00 per hour

University of Utah Marriott Library
Special Collections
Salt Lake City, UT 84112
(801) 581-8864 (Manuscripts); (801)
    581-8863 (Western Americana)
E-mail:
    gthompso@alexandria.lib.utah.edu
http://www.lib.utah.edu/spc/spc.html
Dr. Gregory Thompson, Curator; Nancy
    Young, Head, Manuscripts; Walter
    Jones, Head, Western Americana
(manuscripts, books, periodicals, etc., on
    Utah, the Mormons and the West)

Utah State University Library
Logan, UT 84321
Pub. *Western Historical Quarterly*

Weber County Library
Nonfiction Department
Special Collection Room
2464 Jefferson
Ogden, UT 84401
(801) 627-6920
Hours: Mon–Thur 10:00–9:00, Fri–Sat
    10:00–6:00
(emphasis on Utah history, Mormonism,
    railroad history)

Western Mining and Railroad Museum
296 South Main
Helper, UT 84526
(435) 472-3009
Lori Perez, Archivist
Hours: Museum: winter: noon–5:00,
    summer: 10:00–6:00; Archives: by
    appointment
(local history, Coal Camps, railroad
    stops, pioneer history, etc.)

Historical Societies— Local and Regional

Alta Historical Society
PO Box 8016
Alta, UT 84092
(801) 742-3522
Hours: by appointment
("Very informal collection of Alta
    memorabilia")

Brigham Young University
Charles Redd Center for Western Studies
Provo, UT 84602
(801) 378-4048
Thomas G. Alexander, Ph.D., Director

Cache Valley Historical Society
290 West Center Street
Logan, UT 84321

Carbon County Historical Society
198 North 400 West
Price, UT 84501
(435) 637-6126
Ileen Gibbons, President
Pub. *Carbon County Journal*, annually
$6.00 per year membership

Centerville Historical Society
511 East 400 South
Centerville, UT 84014
(801) 295-2742

Daggett County Historical Society
PO Box 428
Dutch John, UT 84023

International Society, Daughters of Utah Pioneers
300 North Main Street
Salt Lake City, UT 84103-1699
(801) 538-1050
Louise C. Green, President
Hours: Museum: Mon–Sat 9:00–5:00
Pub. *Yearly Historical Book*, annually

Rhoades Valley Camp, Daughters of Utah Pioneers
PO Box 311
Kamas, UT 84036

South Box Elder, Daughters of Utah Pioneers
566 North First Street East
Brigham City, UT 84302
(435) 723-3819

Draper Historical Society
12441 South 900 East
Draper, UT 84020

Emery County Historical Society
PO Box 862
Castle Dale, UT 84513
(435) 381-2428

Emery County Museum
PO Box 357
Castle Dale, UT 84513
(435) 748-2444

Historic Willard Society
156 North 200 West
Willard, UT 84340

Iron County Historical Society
c/o Southern Utah State College Library
Special Collections
351 West Center Street
Cedar City, UT 84720
York Jones, President
Hours: Library: Mon–Fri 8:00–5:00

Old Court House Museum
190 East Center Street
Beaver, UT 84713

Park City Historical Society
PO Box 668
Park City, UT 84060

National Society, Sons of Utah Pioneers
3301 East 2820 South
Salt Lake City, UT 84109
(801) 484-4441; (801) 328-8200
    (*Pioneer*); (801) 328-8249 FAX
    (*Pioneer*)
E-mail: editor@uvol.com
http://uvol.com/sup/
Florence C. Youngberg, Director; Martin
    Lewis, Vice President Sales and
    Marketing
Hours: Tue 9:00–4:00, Wed & Thur
    9:00–9:00

Pub. *Pioneer*, bimonthly, $2.95 per issue
from 180 North Wright Brothers
Drive, Building 6, Salt Lake City, UT
84116
$12.50 per year membership

Utah Heritage Foundation
355 Quince Street
Salt Lake City, UT 84103
(801) 533-0858

LDS Family History Centers

American Fork
(801) 763-2093

Brigham City
(801) 723-5995

Cedar City
(801) 586-2296

Kaysville
(801) 543-2869

Lehi
(801) 768-3054

Logan
(801) 755-5594

Ogden
(801) 626-1132

Orem
(801) 222-0529

Price
(801) 637-2071

Provo
(801) 378-6200

Richfield
(801) 896-8057

Saint George
(801) 673-4591

Salt Lake City
(801) 240-2331

Spanish Fork
(801) 798-5535

Tooele
(801) 882-7514

Vernal
(801) 789-3618

Genealogical Societies

State Genealogical Societies

Utah Genealogical Association
PO Box 1144
Salt Lake City, UT 84110-1144
(888) INFO UGA (463-6842)
E-mail: perkes@mail.utah.uswest.net
http://www.infouga.org/
Kory Meyerink, President
Pub. *UGA Newsletter*, quarterly (March,
June, September, January); *Utah
Genealogical Journal* (treats Utah,
U.S., and International genealogical
and local history topics), quarterly
(March, June, September, January),
$5.00 postpaid per issue
Chapters: **Computer Chapter**, Randall
Hamilton, President, 1552 North 1725
West, Layton, UT 84041, (801) 544-
0821; **Irish Chapter**, Josie Bullock,
President, 1590 Treeview Drive, Salt
Lake City, UT 84124, (801) 227-9057;
Great Salt Lake Chapter, Vaughn
Simon, President, PO Box 11193, Salt
Lake City, UT 84147, (801) 596-9881;
Northern Idaho Chapter, Ellie
Grover, President, PO Box 685,
Bonners Ferry, ID 83805, (208) 267-
7939; **Utah Valley Chapter**, John
Whitaker, President; **Morgan Valley
Chapter**, Holly Hansen, President,
1950 North 6900 East, Croydon, UT
84018-9707, (801) 829-3295; **Tooele
Chapter**, John Peck, President, 206
East Vine Street, Tooele, UT 84074,
(435) 882-3648
$25.00 per year membership for
individuals, $5.00 additional per year
spouse membership, $5.00 additional
for postage outside the U.S.

Genealogical Society of Utah
(see Family History Library of The
Church of Jesus Christ of Latter-day
Saints, under City, County and
Regional Archives and Libraries)

Independent Publications and Miscellany

**Conference of Intermountain
Archives**
The Church of Jesus Christ of Latter-day
Saints
50 East North Temple
Salt Lake City, UT 84150
(801) 240-3644
Wayne Harper, Secretary

Mormon Pioneer Trail Home Page
E-mail: dbylund@mail.unmc.edu
http://www.omahafreenet.org/ofn/trails

Temple Area Genealogical Library
Manti, UT 84642

Tracing Mormon Pioneers
http://www.vii.com/ nelsonb/pioneer.htm
(emigration card index, handcart
companies, Mormon emigrant ships,
pioneer companies, etc.)

UtGenWeb
Part of U.S. GenWeb Project
E-mail: ut@usgenweb.com
http://www.lofthouse.com/USA/Utah/
(links to other Utah resources)

VERMONT

Archives and Libraries with Holdings in Genealogy

State Archives and Library

Public Records Division
General Services Department
(U.S. Route 2, Middlesex—location)
PO Drawer 33 (mailing address)
Montpelier, VT 05633-7601
(802) 828-3700; (802) 828-3710 FAX
A. John Yacauum, Director Public
Records/General Services
Hours: Mon–Fri 8:00–4:00

Secretary of State
State Papers
(26 Terrace Street, Redstone Building—
location)
109 State Street (mailing address)
Montpelier, VT 05609
(802) 828-2363
(biographical material in the archives
may be of genealogical interest)

Vermont State Archives
(Office of the Secretary of State, 26
Terrace Street, Redstone Building—
location)
109 State Street (mailing address)
Montpelier, VT 05609-0601
(802) 828-2308; (802) 828-5171 FAX
E-mail: kwhite@sec.state.vt.us
http://www.sec.state.vt.us/archives/
archives.htm
Kathy White, Staff Assistant
Hours: Mon–Fri 7:45-4:30
(governor's records, election records,
legislative records, surveyors general
records, Manuscript Vermont State
Papers, municipal charters and charter
amendments, deeds and leases,
Stevens Collection and miscellaneous
records)
copies: 4¢ per page

Vermont Department of Libraries
Reference and Law Services
109 State Street
Montpelier, VT 05609-0601
(802) 828-3268
http://dol.state.vt.us
Marjorie D. Zunder, Head
Hours: Mon–Fri 7:45-4:30

State Historical Society

Vermont Historical Society
Pavilion Office Building
109 State Street
Montpelier, VT 05609-0901
(802) 828-2291; (802) 828-3638 FAX
E-mail: Vhs@vhs.state.vt.us

http://www.cit.state.vt.us:80/vhs/
Paul A. Carnahan, Librarian
Hours: Tue–Fri 9:00–4:00
Pub. *Vermont History*, irregularly
$30.00 per year regular membership

City, County and Regional Archives and Libraries

Bennington Museum
West Main Street
Bennington, VT 05201
(802) 447-1571; (802) 442-8305 FAX
Tyler Resch, Librarian
Hours: Museum: Mon–Sun 9:00–5:00;
Library: Nov–May: Mon, Thur & Sat
11:00–5:00; Jun–Oct: Mon–Sat 11:00–
5:00
(family and local history: Vermont, New
England, New York)
photocopies: 10¢ per image

The Berkshire Athenaeum
(see Massachusetts)

Billings Farm and Museum
River Road
PO Box 489
Woodstock, VT 05091-0489
(802) 457-2355; (802) 457-4663 FAX
David A. Donath, Director; Esther
Munroe Swift, Librarian/Archivist
Hours: Museum: daily (May 1–Oct 31)
10:00–5:00
(history and 19th-century agricultural
history)

Bixby Memorial Free Library
285 Main Street
Vergennes, VT 05491
(802) 877-2211
http://www.vetc.vsc.edu/vuhs/bixby/
Lois Noonan, Librarian
Hours: Mon & Fri, 12:30–8:00, Tue &
Thur 12:30–5:00, Wed, 10:00–5:00
(collection of Vermontiana in the Lois
Noonan Vermont Room)

Brooks Memorial Library
224 Main Street
Brattleboro, VT 05301
(802) 254-5290; (802) 257-2309 FAX
E-mail: Brattlib@brooks.lib.vt.us;
Jerry@brooks.lib.vt.us
http://www.state.vt.us/libraries/b733/
brookslibrary
Jerry Carbone, Library Director
Hours: Mon–Wed 9:00–9:00, Thur–Fri
9:00–6:00, Sat (Labor Day–Memorial
Day) 9:00–5:00, Sat (summer) 9:00–
12:00
(collection includes Brattleboro and
Windham County)

Connecticut Valley Historical Museum
(see Massachusetts)

Craftsbury Public Library
PO Box 74
Craftsbury Common, VT 05827
(802) 586-9683
Linda Wells, Librarian

Discovery Museum
51 Park Street
Essex Junction, VT 05452
(802) 878-8687
Lynnette Donahue, President Board of
Directors
Hours: Sept–Jun: Tue–Wed 11:00–4:00,
Thur–Sat 10:00–5:00, Sun 1:00–5:00;
Jul–Aug: Tue–Sat 10:00–5:00, Sun
1:00–5:00
(children's museum)

Fletcher Free Library
235 College Street
Burlington, VT 05401
(802) 863-3403 (Library); (802) 865-
7217 (Reference Desk)
Anita Danigelis, Reference Librarian
Hours: Library: Mon–Tue & Thur–Fri
8:30–6:00, Wed 8:30 A.M.–9:00 P.M.,
Sat 9:00–5:30, Sun (Sept–May) 2:00–
5:00; Reference Service: Mon–Tue &
Thur–Fri 10:00–5:00, Wed 10:00–
9:00, Sat 10:00–1:00 & 2:00–5:00
fees for obituary searches and for faxing
materials

Goodrich Memorial Library
70 Main Street
Newport, VT 05855
(802) 334-7902
http://www.state.vt.us/libraries/n47
Louise Kennison, Librarian
Hours: Mon–Fri 9:30–5:00, Sat 9:30–
3:00

Haskell Free Library and Opera House
(Caswell Avenue—location)
PO Box 337 (mailing address)
Derby Line, VT 05830
Kim Prangley, Librarian
Hours: Tue–Wed 10:00–5:00, Thur 1:00–
8:00, Fri–Sat 1:00–5:00

Hitchcock Memorial Library and Museum
(Route 100—location)
PO Box 148 (mailing address)
Westfield, VT 05847
(802) 744-6621
Jeanne Beaulieu, Librarian
Hours: Thurs 1:00–4:00 & 7:00–8:00,
and by appointment in the summer

Rockingham Free Public Library
65 Westminster Street
Bellows Falls, VT 05101
(802) 463-4270
E-mail: rockingham@dol.state.vt.us
Becky Hollis, Librarian
Hours: Mon & Thur 1:00–8:00, Tue
9:00–8:00, Wed (except summer)

1:00–8:00, Fri 9:00–5:00, Sat 9:00–
noon
$15.00 non-resident's fee

Rokeby Museum
(Route 7—location)
RD 1, Box 1540
Ferrisburg, VT 05456
(802) 877-3406
Jane Williamson, Director
Hours: Tue–Fri 9:00–5:00
Pub. *Messenger*, quarterly
(Quakerism, abolition, agricultural
history, and Robinson family)
$15.00 per year membership for
individuals, $25.00 per year
membership for families, $10.00 per
year membership for students or senior
citizens

Russell Vermontiana Collection
Martha Canfield Library
Main Street
Arlington, VT 05250
(802) 375-6307
David and Mary Lou Thomas, Directors
Hours: Tue 9:00–5:00, and by
appointment

Rutland Free Library
10 Court Street
Rutland, VT 05701-4058
(802) 773-1860; (802) 773-1861
Hours: Mon–Wed 9:00–9:00, Thur–Fri
9:00–5:30, Sat 9:00–5:00

Sheldon Museum
1 Park Street
Middlebury, VT 05753
(802) 388-2117
E-mail:
sheldon_mus@myriad.middlebury.edu
Nancy Rucker
Hours: Tue–Fri 1:00–5:00
Pub. *Sheldon Museum News & Notes*,
quarterly
from $20.00 per year membership

Shores Memorial Museum
(Center Street—location)
PO Box 35 (mailing address)
Lyndon Center, VT 05850
(802) 626-5742; (802) 626-8574
(Curator)
Ruth McCarty, Curator
Hours: Sat–Sun (Memorial Day–Labor
Day) 2:00–4:00, and by appointment

John Woodruff Simpson Library
(East Craftsbury, VT—location)
RR 1, Box 1035 (mailing address)
Craftsbury Common, VT 05826
(802) 586-9692
Sherry Urie, Librarian
Hours: Wed & Sat 9:00–noon, 2:00–5:00
& 7:00–9:30, Sun after Sunday school

Springfield Town Library
43 Main Street
Springfield, VT 05156
(802) 885-3108

Russell Moore, Director
Hours: Tue–Thur 10:00–8:00, Fri 10:00–
5:00, Sat 10:00–3:00
(Vermont genealogies, family and town
histories, with emphasis on Springfield
and Windsor County, some New
Hampshire and Massachusetts records)
$25.00 per year fee for non-resident
borrowers; in-house use of materials at
no charge

University of Vermont
Special Collections, Bailey/Howe
Memorial Library
Burlington, VT 05405
(802) 656-2138; (802) 656-4038 FAX
E-mail: edow@zoo.uvm.edu
http://moose.uvm.edu/
Reference Specialist
Hours: Mon–Thur 10:00–9:00, Fri
10:00–5:00, Sat 10:00–1:00, Sun
1:00–4:00; call for intersession hours
(Vermont history; "Our primary clientele
is the University of Vermont academic
community and researchers of
Vermont history.")
charge for photocopying and other
reproductions

University of Vermont Library
Wilbur Collection of Vermontiana
Burlington, VT 05405-0036
(802) 656-2631
J. Kevin Graffagnino, Curator
Pub. *Liber*

Alice Ward Library
(Village Green—location)
PO Box 134 (mailing address)
Canaan, VT 05903
(802) 266-7135; (802) 266-7766
Joan Cowan, Curator; Gloria Bunnell,
Librarian
Hours: Library: Tue & Fri 1:00–4:00;
Museum: by appointment
(a local heritage museum on the second
floor of the library, developed by the
Canaan Historical Society)

Norman Williams Public Library
10 South Park Street
Woodstock, VT 05091
(802) 457-2295
Katherine Ludwig, Librarian
Hours: Mon–Fri 10:00–5:00, Tue–Wed
7:00 A.M.–9:00 P.M., Sat 10:00–4:00

Historical Societies— Local and Regional

Addison Town Historical Society
RD 1, Box 1348
Vergennes, VT 05491
(802) 759-2406
Thomas Johnson, President

Aldrich Public Library
Barre Museum
9 Washington Street, Second Floor
PO Box 453
Barre, VT 05641
(802) 479-0450
Susan L. Teale, Librarian; Marjorie
Strong, Museum Curator
Hours: Museum: Mon & Fri noon–5:00,
Thur 10:00–5:00, Sat 10:00–4:00; Sat
(summer) 9:00–noon, and by
appointment

Barnard Historical Society Museum
Charles Danforth Public Library
Barnard, VT 05031
(802) 234-9183
Eleanor Tatro
Hours: Fri 2:00–4:00, Sat 10:00–noon,
and by appointment

Barnet Historical Society
RR 1, Box 241
Barnet, VT 05821
(802) 633-2563 (Treasurer); (603) 726-
2267 (President)
Florence E. Grahek, Treasurer; Lorna
Grady, President
Hours: summer, by appointment only
(maintains 1791 Goodwillie House,
artifacts, pictures, products of local
industry)
$5.00 per year membership

The Bellows Falls Historical Society
(Adams Grist Mill Museum, Mill
Street—location)
7 Atkinson Street (mailing address)
Bellows Falls, VT 05101
(802) 463-3374 (President); (802) 463-
3092 (Secretary)
E-mail: facades@sover.net (President);
ourtown@sover.net (Secretary)
Dennis Ladd, President; Cathy
Bergmann, Secretary
Hours: Jul & Aug: Sat & Sun: 1:00–4:00,
and by appointment

Berlin Historical Society, Inc.
RR 4, Box 2210
Montpelier, VT 05602
(802) 223-1203
Norbert Rhinerson, President

Bethel Historical Society, Inc.
Bethel Historical Society Museum
Church Street
Bethel, VT 05032
(802) 234-9413
Clara Abbott and Richard Edmunds,
Curators
Hours: Jul & Aug: Sun 2:00–5:00

Black River Historical Society
(14 High Street—location)
PO Box 73 (mailing address)
Ludlow, VT 05149
(802) 228-5050
Georgia L. Brehm, Museum Director
Hours: Tue–Sat noon–4:00

(published local history)
$10.00 per year membership for individuals, $15.00 per year membership for families, $100.00 life membership

Bradford Historical Society

(Bradford Academy—location)
PO Box 301 (mailing address)
Bradford, VT 05033
(802) 222-9026; (802) 222-4727 (Town Hall)
Phyllis Lavelle, Curator
Hours: May–Sept: Tue 10:00–1:00
(Bradford history)

Braintree Historical Society

Rt. 2, Peth Road
Randolph, VT 05060
(802) 728-5272
Phyllis Hawley, Secretary
Hours: by appointment
Pub. *Braintree Historical Society Newsletter*, annually
$2.00 per year membership for individuals, $5.00 per year Supporting membership, $10.00 per year Contributing membership, $50.00 life membership

Brattleboro Historical Society

(230 Main Street, Brattleboro, VT 05301—location)
PO Box 6392 (mailing address)
Brattleboro, VT 05302
(802) 254-5037
Gerry Gatz, President
Hours: Thur 1:00–4:00
Pub. *Newsletter—Brattleboro Historical Society*, semiannually
(Brattleboro history)
$5.00–$100.00 per year membership

Bridport Historical Society Museum

(Route 22-A—location)
RR 1, Box 656 (mailing address)
Bridport, VT 05734
(802) 758-2654
Margaret Sunderland, Curator
Hours: Father's Day, and by appointment

Bristol Historical Society Museum

Howden Hall Community Center
Main Street
Bristol, VT 05443
(802) 453-6029
Evelyn Dike, President
Hours: summer: Mon–Sun 10:00–4:00; Mar–Oct: Thur 7:30–9:30, and by appointment

Cabot Historical Society, Inc.

(Main Street, Cabot, VT 05647—location)
R.F.D., Lower Cabot (mailing address)
Marshfield, VT 05658
(802) 563-2558
Leonard Spencer, President
Hours: 4 Jul, Old Home Week, Fall Foliage Festival, and by appointment

Canaan Historical Society

PO Box 371
Canaan, VT 05903
(802) 266-8845
Virginia Carr, President
Hours: by appointment

Castleton Historical Society Museum

(Main Street—location)
PO Box 219
Castleton, VT 05735
(802) 468-5523
Mary Williamson
summer and fall: Sun 1:00–4:00

Cavendish Historical Society

(Main Street—location)
PO Box 110 (mailing address)
Cavendish, VT 05142
(802) 484-7498
E-mail: Linda.M.Welch@Dartmouth.edu
http://www.web-home.com/vt-genealogy/cavendish.htm
Mr. Carmine Guica, Genealogist and Historian
Hours: Jun–Oct: Sun 2:00–4:00, and by appointment
$5.00 per year membership

Charleston Historical Society Museum

RR 1, Box 710
West Charleston, VT 05872
(802) 895-4329
Colleen Comeau, President
Hours: 25 Jun–27 Aug: Wed 2:00–4:00

Chelsea Historical Society, Inc.

(Main Street—location)
PO Box 206 (mailing address)
Chelsea, VT 05038
W. S. Gilman, Vice President

Chester Historical Society

Main Street
Chester, VT 05143
(802) 875-3767; (802) 875-2497
Pat Ballou
Hours: Sat–Sun 2:00–5:00, and by appointment

Chittenden County Historical Society

PO Box 1576
Burlington, VT 05402-1576
Pub. *Chittenden County Historical Society Bulletin*, quarterly

Concord Historical Society Museum

(Concord Town Hall, Concord, VT—location)
HCR 60, Box 40 (mailing address)
North Concord, VT 05858
(802) 695-2288
Bernice Payeur, President
Hours: last weekend in Sept, and by appointment

Crystal Lake Falls Historical Association

(The Pierce House, Water Street—location)
PO Box 253 (mailing address)
Barton, VT 05822
(802) 525-6251; (802) 525-3583
Avis Harper; Robin Tenny
Hours: Mid-Jun to mid-Sept: Tue & Thur 2:00–4:00, and by appointment

Danville Historical Archives

(Pope Memorial Library, The Green—location)
PO Box 260 (mailing address)
Danville, VT 05828
(802) 684-2256
Jean Ashley, Librarian
Hours: Mon & Wed 9:00–7:00, Fri 9:00–6:00, Sat 9:00–noon

Derby Historical Society

(Main Street—location)
PO Box 357 (mailing address)
Derby, VT 05829
(802) 766-5324
Bill Gardyne, President
Hours: by appointment

Dorset Historical Society

(Main Street—location)
PO Box 52 (mailing address)
Dorset, VT 05251
(802) 867-0331
Patricia Carmichael, President
Hours: winter: Fri–Sat 10:00–noon; summer: Fri 10:00–noon, Sat 10:00–2:00
$7.00 per year membership for individuals, $25.00 per year membership for families

Enosburgh Historical Society

(Over Town Offices, Main Street—location)
PO Box 98
Enosburgh Falls, VT 05450
(802) 933-2102; (802) 933-4708
John Whiting, President; Janice Geraw, Secretary
Hours: Jun–Aug: Sat 1:00–4:00, and by appointment

Fairfax Historical Society

(1181 Main Street, Route 104—location)
PO Box 145 (mailing address)
Fairfax, VT 05454
(802) 849-6638 (President)
E-mail: mcain@together.net
Michael R. Cain, President
Hours: weekends during the summer, and by appointment
$2.00 per year membership for individuals

Fairfield Historical Society

c/o Fairfield Town Clerk
Fairfield, VT 05455

(802) 827-6160; (802) 827-3261
Julie Wolcott, President; Patty Esden,
  Vice President

Fairlee Historical Society
Fairlee Town Hall
PO Box 95
Fairlee, VT 05045
(802) 333-9729; (802) 333-4363
Hester Gardner, Curator
Hours: as needed
(local genealogical research)
$2.00 per year membership

Farrar-Mansur House Museum
(On The Green—location)
PO Box 247 (mailing address)
Weston, VT 05161
(802) 824-6781
Hours: Museum: May–Oct
Pub. *Times of Weston*
(provides genealogical services)

Ferrisburg Historical Society
Rt. 1, Box 2870
North Ferrisburg, VT 05473
(802) 425-3380
Silas Towler, President
Pub. *Ferrisburg Memoirs*

Georgia Historical Society
(Route 7, Georgia Center, VT—location)
RD 3 (mailing address)
Saint Albans, VT 05478
(802) 524-3318
Edmund Wilcox
Hours: 4 Jul–Labor Day: Mon, Wed &
  Sat 2:00–4:00

Glover Historical Society
Municipal Building, Second Floor
Glover, VT 05839
(802) 525-6227 (Town Clerk)
Wayne H. Alexander, President
Hours: Jun–Aug: Wed P.M., and by
  appointment

Grafton Historical Society, Inc.
Main Street
Grafton, VT 05146
(802) 843-2489
http://www.sover.net/~grafton/guide.html
Rosalys B. Wilson
Hours: weekends (May 30–Oct 12)
(published history of Grafton)
$5.00 per year membership; search fee:
  $25.00 per hour

Greensboro Historical Society
(Main Street—location)
PO Box 151
Greensboro, VT 05841
(802) 472-3381; (802) 533-2609 (Mr.
  Hill)
Barbara Woodward, President; Pat
  Haslem, Genealogy Expert
Hours: Tue–Thur 10:00–2:00, Sat (Jul–
  Aug) 9:00–11:00
Pub. *Hazen Road Dispatch*, annually,
  $4.50 postpaid per issue
$10.00 per year membership

Groton Historical Society
(Rt. 302, Main Street—location)
PO Box 89 (mailing address)
Groton, VT 05046
(802) 584-3417
Richard Brooks, President
Hours: Sun (Jul–Aug) 2:00–5:00, all day
  on Fall Foliage Day

Guilford Historical Society
RR 3, Box 255
Brattleboro, VT 05301
(802) 257-7306
Fred Humphrey, President
Hours: Jul–Aug: Sun afternoons, and by
  appointment
Pub. *The Guilford Slate*, three to four
  times per year
$5.00 per year membership for
  individuals, $10.00 per year
  membership for families, $100.00 life
  membership

Halifax Historical Society Museum
(West Halifax, VT—location)
RR 4, Box 531 (mailing address)
Brattleboro, VT 05301
(802) 368-7490
Susan Rusten and Edith Bickle, Curators
Hours: open periodically throughout the
  summer and by request

Hartford Historical Society
(15 Bridge Street—location)
PO Box 547 (mailing address)
Hartford, VT 05047
(802) 295-9353; (802) 295-6382 FAX
Pat Stark; Priscilla Gadzinski
Hours: by appointment

Hartland Historical Society
Hartland, VT 05048
(802) 436-2444 (Town Clerk)
Lee Motschman, President
Hours: Mon 2:00–4:00; meetings: second
  Wed
Pub. *Newsletter of Hartland Historical
  Society*, semiannually
$5.00 per year membership; genealogical
  research for donation

The Highgate Historical Society
PO Box 71
Highgate Center, VT 05459
Evangeline A. Malaney, Secretary

Holland Historical Society, Inc.
RD 1, Box 37
Holland, VT 05830
(802) 895-4440
Isabel McInnis, President
Hours: by appointment

Island Pond Historical Society, Inc.
(Canadian National Railway Station—
  location)
PO Box 408 (mailing address)
Island Pond, VT 05846
(802) 482-3923
C. F. Biron, President
Hours: by appointment

Isle La Motte Historical Society
Isle La Motte, VT 05463
(802) 928-3422
Howard or Harriot Schwenker
Hours: Jul–Aug: Sat 1:00–4:00

Jericho Historical Society
(Old Mill, Rt. 15—location)
PO Box 35 (mailing address)
Jericho, VT 05465
(802) 899-3225
Ray Miglionico, Archivist
Hours: Mon 2:30–4:00, Thur 6:30–7:30
Pub. *The Jericho Reporter*, quarterly
(local history)

Lincoln Historical Society
(Quaker Street—location)
c/o Town Clerk (mailing address)
Lincoln, VT 05443
(802) 453-3628 phone & FAX
Steve Harris, President
Hours: Memorial Day–12 Oct: Sun
  noon–4:00, and by appointment

Londonderry Historical Society
(Custer Sharp House, Middletown
  Road—location)
PO Box 398 (mailing address)
Londonderry, VT 05148
(802) 824-4406
Robert McCabe, M.D., President;
  Kathleen Wright, Corresponding
  Secretary
Hours: summer: Sat 10:00–2:00
$15.00 per year membership for
  individuals, $15.00 per year
  membership for families, $100.00 life
  membership

**Town of Lunenburg Historical
Society**
Rt. 1, Box 29A
Lunenburg, VT 05906
(802) 892-5317
Evan Hammond, President; Judith C.
  Young, Secretary
Pub. *Echoes*, occasionally
$3.00 per year membership for
  individuals, $5.00 per year
  membership for families

Lyndon Historical Society
PO Box 85
Lyndon Center, VT 05850
(802) 626-8746
E-mail: boerad@sover.net
http://www.sover.net/ boerad/historical
Virginia C. Downs, Co-Editor and Co-
  President
Hours: meetings at the Cobleigh Library,
  Lyndonville at least four times a year
Pub. *Lyndon Legacy*, quarterly
$5.00 per year membership

Manchester Historical Society
(Mark Skinner Library—museum
  location)
PO Box 363 (mailing address)
Manchester, VT 05254

(802) 362-3747
Mary Bort, Curator
Hours: by appointment; monthly
  meetings
(local history and genealogy)

Historical Society of Marlboro
PO Box 131
Marlboro, VT 05344
(802) 254-9152
L. Bourne, President; Tom Huenik,
  Secretary
Hours: Jul–Aug: Sat 2:00–5:00

Middlesex Historical Society
RR 3, Box 3395
Middlesex, VT 05602
(802) 223-2201
Patricia Wiley, President

Middletown Springs Historical Society, Inc.
(The Green—location)
PO Box 1001 (mailing address)
Middletown Springs, VT 05757
(802) 235-2144
Jim Geddes, President
Hours: Sun (30 May–30 Oct) 2:00–4:00
Pub. *Middletown Springs Historical
  Society Newsletter*, three to four times
  per year
$5.00 per year membership for
  individuals, $8.00 per year
  membership for families; search fee:
  donation

Milton Historical Society
(Main Street—location)
PO Box 2 (mailing address)
Milton, VT 05468
(802) 893-2267 (Ms. Brown); (802) 893-
  2340 (Curator)
Gwen Brown; Jane FitzGerald, Curator

Missisquoi Valley Historical Society
(Main Street—location)
PO Box 237 (mailing address)
North Troy, VT 05859
(802) 988-2677
Maurice Phillips, President
Hours: Jun–Aug: Sat–Sun 2:00–5:00

Montgomery Historical Society Museum
(Montgomery Village—location)
PO Box 47 (mailing address)
Montgomery, VT 05470
(802) 326-4404
Sally Newton, Secretary
Hours: Sat (Jul–Aug) noon–3:00, and by
  appointment

Montpelier Heritage Group, Inc.
PO Box 671
Montpelier, VT 05601-0671
Pub. *Montpelier Heritage Group
  Newsletter*, quarterly
(historical society and historic
  preservation group)

$10.00 per year membership for
  individuals, $5.00 per year
  membership for senior citizens, $25.00
  per year membership for businesses

Morristown Historical Society
(Noyes House Museum, Main Street—
  location)
PO Box 1299 (mailing address)
Morrisville, VT 05661-1299
(802) 888-7617; (802) 888-5605
Dawn K. Andrews, President
Hours: Jul–Aug: Wed–Sat 1:00–4:00
Pub. *Morristown Two Times*

The New England Historic Genealogical Society
(see Massachusetts)

Northfield Historical Society
(South Main Street—location)
PO Box 88 (mailing address)
Northfield, VT 05663
(802) 485-8081
Alan H. Weiss, President
Pub. *Dog River Crier*, three times per
  year
$5.00–$25.00 per year membership

Norwich Historical Society
37 Church Street
PO Box 284
Norwich, VT 05055
(802) 649-0124; (802) 649-2711
Fran Niles, Treasurer
Hours: Wed 2:30–4:30, and by
  appointment
Pub. *Museum Muse*, quarterly
$10.00 per year membership for
  individuals, $35.00 per year Sustaining
  membership, $100.00 life membership

Orleans County Historical Society, Inc.
Old Stone House Museum
Brownington Village
RR 1, Box 500
Orleans, VT 05860
(802) 754-2022
E-mail: osh@together.net;
  1hdtp@sover.net
http://homepages.together.net/~osh/
Tracy N. Martin, Museum Director
Hours: Museum: Jul & Aug: Mon–Sun
  11:00–5:00; 15 May–30 Jun & 1 Sept–
  15 Oct: Mon–Tue & Fri–Sun: 11:00–
  5:00; Archives: by appointment only
Pub. *The Old Stone House Museum
  Bulletin*, three times per year, $10.00
  per year subscription, free on request
  to non-profit institutions
(Orleans County, Vermont)
admission: $5.00 general admission,
  $4.00 for Orleans County residents,
  $2.00 for students under 12

Pawlett Historical Society
Pawlet, VT 05761

Peacham Historical Association
Church Street
Peacham, VT 05862
(802) 592-3571
Lorna Quimby, Curator and President
Hours: by appointment
Pub. *Peacham Patriot*, irregularly
$5.00 per year membership for
  individuals; $5.00 per hour search fee

Pittsfield Historical Society
(Town Hall—location)
PO Box 808 (mailing address)
Pittsfield, VT 05762
(802) 746-8147
E-mail: afifield@aol.com
L. Fifield, Secretary/Treasurer
Hours: Apr–Nov: 1:00–3:00, and by
  appointment

Pittsford Historical Society
(Eaton Hall, Route 7—location)
PO Box 423 (mailing address)
Pittsford, VT 05763
(802) 483-6623
Jean Davies, Curator
Hours: Tue (Mar–Nov) 9:00–4:00, Sat
  (Jul–Aug) 9:00–4:00

Poultney Historical Society
RFD 1, Box 177
Poultney, VT 05764
(802) 287-5268
Ruth Czar, President
Hours: Sun (Jun–Aug) 1:00–5:00, and by
  appointment

Putney Historical Society
(Main Street, Town Hall—location)
PO Box 233 (mailing address)
Putney, VT 05346
(802) 387-5862
Laura Heller
Hours: Wed 2:00–4:00, and by
  appointment

Randolph Historical Society, Inc.
(Salisbury Street, Randolph—location)
PO Box 15 (mailing address)
Randolph Center, VT 05061
(802) 728-5398
Wes Herwig, Curator
Hours: by appointment
fee for research

Reading Historical Society Museum
Reading, VT 05062
(802) 484-7271
Walter Mendoza
Hours: Thur (mid-Jun to mid-Sept) 2:00–
  4:00

Readsboro Historical Society
(Route 100 across from the Post
  Office—location)
RR 1, Box 277 (mailing address)
Readsboro, VT 05350
(802) 423-5394
Mrs. Melvin H. Coe, President
Hours: by appointment

$3.00 per year membership for individuals, $5.00 per year membership for families

Rochester Historical Society
Rochester, VT 05767
(802) 767-4453
Charles Woolley, President
Hours: Memorial Day to mid-Oct: Tue 1:00–7:00, Thur 1:00–5:00, Sat 9:00–1:00

Rockingham Meeting House Association
(Rockingham, VT—location)
29 Oak Hill Terrace (mailing address)
Bellows Falls, VT 05101
(802) 463-3941
John A. Leppman, President
Hours: Jul–Aug: daily 10:00–5:00

Royalton Historical Society
RR 1, Box 89D
Royalton, VT 05068
(802) 763-8567
jdumville@gate.dca.state.vt.us
John P. Dumville, President
Hours: by appointment
(small local historical society with collections focused on town)
$5.00 per year membership

Rutland Historical Society
Nickwackett Fire Station
96 Center Street
Rutland, VT 05701-4023
(802) 775-2006; (820) 775-2761 (President)
Don Bordeau, President
Hours: Mon 6:00 P.M.–9:00 P.M., Sat 1:00–4:00, and by appointment
Pub. *Rutland Historical Society Quarterly*; *News from Nickwackett*, quarterly
(a volunteer, non-profit organization, not a major resource for genealogy; specializing in Rutland City, Rutland Town, West Rutland and Proctor history)
$10.00 per calendar year membership for individuals, $8.00 per year membership for students (18 and under) or senior citizens (62 or over), $20.00 per year Contributing membership, $50.00 per year Sponsor membership, $200.00 life or Memorial membership

Saint Albans Historical Society
Saint Albans Historical Museum
(Corner of Bishop and Church Street—location)
PO Box 722 (mailing address)
Saint Albans, VT 05478
(802) 527-7933
Donald J. Miner, Director
Hours: Jun–Sept: Mon–Sat 1:00–4:00
Pub. *St. Albans Historical Society Newsletter*, three times per year

(a historical museum specializing in local history)
$15.00 per year membership; no genealogical search services

Saxtons River Historical Society Museum
PO Box 18
Saxtons River, VT 05154
(802) 869-2657; (802) 869-2328
John Lucy; Lawrence O'Connor
Hours: Jun–Aug & foliage season: Sat & Sun 2:00–4:30, and by appointment

Shaftsbury Historical Society
(Route 7-A, Center Shaftsbury, VT—location)
PO Box 401 (mailing address)
Shaftsbury, VT 05262
(802) 447-7488
Robert J. Williams, Curator
Hours: Tue–Sun (15 Jun–15 Oct) 2:00–4:00
$5.00 per year membership for individuals, $10.00 per year membership for families, $2.00 per year membership for students, $25.00 per year Corporate or Sustaining membership, $100.00 life or Patron membership or memoriam; no search fee

Shelburne Historical Society
Rt. 7
Shelburne, VT 05482
(802) 985-2682
Helen Ranks Gadhue, President
(local history)

Shoreham Historical Society
Route 22-A
Shoreham, VT 05770
(802) 897-2600
Sue MacIntire, Curator
Hours: year-round by appointment

Shrewsbury Historical Society, Inc.
(Town of Shrewsbury in Village of Cuttingsville)
Cuttingsville, VT 05738
(802) 492-3410 (Shrewsbury Library); (802) 492-3378 (Curator)
Anne F. Spencer, Curator
Hours: Sat (summer) noon–2:00, and by appointment
(Shrewsbury history: account books, diaries, business records, school records, town reports, photographs; Shrewsbury genealogies, etc.)
$7.00 per year membership for individuals, $10.00 per year membership for families, $25.00 per year Contributing membership, $100.00 life membership, $5.00 per year non-voting Friend

Springfield Art and Historical Society
(9 Elm Street—location)
PO Box 313 (mailing address)
Springfield, VT 05156
Fred Richardson, Treasurer and Researcher
Hours: Tue–Fri 10:00–4:00, Sat 1:00–4:00
Pub. *News & Reviews*, quarterly
(Springfield history from 1750)
$15.00 per year membership for individuals, $25.00 per year membership for families; donation or exchange asked for research

Stannard Historical Society
Rt. 1
Greensboro Bend, VT 05842
(802) 533-2561
Ann Lawless, Chairperson
(no genealogical material, maintains church building)

Stowe Historical Society
Akeley Memorial Building, Town Hall
Main Street
Stowe, VT 05672
(802) 253-6133
Edwin F. Lang, Jr., M.D., President
Hours: by appointment

Strafford Historical Society
PO Box 67
Strafford, VT 05072-0067
Gwenda Smith, Historian-Curator
Hours: by appointment only
("information on Strafford families ONLY")
search fees negotiable

Thetford Historical Society
(Bicentennial Building, Academy Road—location)
PO Box 33 (mailing address)
Thetford, VT 05074
(802) 785-2068
Charles Latham, Librarian
Hours: Mon & Thur 2:00–4:00, Tue 10:00–noon
Pub. *Newsletter*, irregularly
(genealogical files on Thetford families)
membership for donation; no search service available

Tinmouth Historical Society, Inc.
Rt. 1, Box 551 (corner TH2 and Route 140)
Tinmouth, VT 05773
(802) 446-2498 phone and FAX
Gail Fallar, President and Town Clerk
Hours: Mon & Thur 8:00–noon & 1:00–4:00
(very small)

Twinfield Historical Society
Rt. 2, Box 290
Plainfield, VT 05667
(802) 454-8419

Vernon Historians, Inc.
(Route 142 and Pond Road—location)
RR 1, Box 196, Pond Road (mailing address)
Vernon, VT 05354
(802) 254-8015
Robert Johnson, President
Hours: Sun (early Jun–late Aug) 2:00–4:00, closed 4 Jul weekend

Walden Historical Committee
PO Box 54
West Danville, VT 05873
(802) 563-2472
Elizabeth P. Hatch, Chairman
Pub. *Walden 200*, two times per year (spring and fall), $6.00 postpaid per year
(Walden folk history)
genealogical research available

Wallingford Historical Society
(Second Floor of the Town Hall—museum location)
PO Box 327 (mailing address)
Wallingford, VT 05773
(802) 446-2336
Joyce Barbieri

Waterbury Historical Society Museum
28 North Main Street
Waterbury, VT 05676
(802) 244-7036
Lois Sabin
Hours: Mon–Wed 1:00–8:00, Fri 10:00–5:00, Sat 10:00–3:00

Weathersfield Historical Society Museum
(The Reverend Dan Foster House, Center Road, Weathersfield, VT—location)
Perkinsville, VT 05151 (mailing address)
(802) 263-5230; (802) 263-5361; (802) 263-9462; (802) 263-9263 FAX
Edith Hunter
Hours: Late Jun–early Oct: Mon & Thur–Sun 2:00–5:00, and by appointment

Wells Historical Society
RR 1, Box 37
Wells, VT 05774
(802) 645-0435
Barbara J. Goodspeed, President

West Windsor Historical Society
(Route 44, Brownsville, VT—location)
PO Box 12 (mailing address)
West Windsor, VT 05037
(802) 484-7474
Mary B. Fenn, Chairman of Historic Records Committee
Hours: Thur 9:00 A.M.–11:00 A.M., and by appointment
Pub. *West Windsor Historical Society Newsletter*, quarterly
$5.00 per year membership for individuals, $10.00 per year membership for husband and wife,
$2.00 per year membership for students (age 17 and under)

Westminster Historical Society
(Town Hall, Route 5, Westminster, VT—location)
Rt. 3, Box 634 (mailing address)
Putney, VT 05346
(802) 387-5778
Patricia Haas, President
Hours: Sun (summer) 2:00–4:00
("will look up information for people in our and the town records on request")

Whitingham Historical Society
(Whitingham, VT—location)
PO Box 125 (mailing address)
Jacksonville, VT 05342
Stella Stevens, President
Hours: Sun 2:00–4:00

Williston Historical Society
PO Box 995
Williston, VT 05495
Brad Witham, President
Pub. *Williston Historical Society Bulleton*, quarterly
from $4.00 per year membership for individuals, $50.00 life membership

Historical Society of Windham County
(Rt. 30—location)
PO Box 246 (mailing address)
Newfane, VT 05345
(802) 365-4148
Joan Marr, Curator
Hours: Late May through mid-October: Wed–Sun 2:00–5:00
Pub. *News & Views*, three times per year (county history and genealogy)
$7.00 per year membership for individuals, $10.00 per year membership for families, $25.00 per year Contributing membership; copies: 25¢ each

Woodstock Historical Society, Inc.
26 Elm Street
Woodstock, VT 05091
(802) 457-1822
Marie McAndrew-Taylor, Archivist
Hours: Mon–Fri 10:00–5:00 by appointment
(emphasis on central Windsor County, special publications on specific topics)
photocopying fees and shipping and handling fees

LDS Family History Centers

Berlin
(802) 229-0482

Burlington
(see Berlin)

Montpelier
(see Berlin)

Genealogical Societies

State Genealogical Society

Genealogical Society of Vermont
PO Box 1553
Saint Albans, VT 05478
Hours: by appointment
Pub. *Branches & Twigs*, quarterly
$20.00 per year membership for individuals in the U.S., $25.00 per year in membership for individuals in Canada and Mexico, $30.00 per year membership for individuals overseas (beginning in October)

Regional Genealogical Societies

American-Canadian Genealogical Society
(see New Hampshire)

Minnesota Genealogical Society, Yankee Branch
(see Massachusetts)

The New England Historic Genealogical Society
(see Massachusetts)

Independent Publications and Miscellany

Claudette's
3962 Xenwood Avenue South
Saint Louis Park, MN 55416-2842
Claudette Atwood Maerz
Pub. *Across the Border* (includes northern Vermont counties of Essex, Lamoille, Chittenden, Caledonia, Grand Isle, Franklin, Washington and Orleans, and Quebec's eastern townships), quarterly, $14.00 per year subscription in the U.S., $16.00 per year subscription in Canada

The New England Quarterly
(see Massachusetts)

Society for the Preservation of New England Antiquities—Archives
(see Massachusetts)

Vermont Old Cemetery Association
PO Box 132
Townshend, VT 05353
(802) 365-7937
Charles Marchant, Secretary
Pub. *VOCA Newsletter*, quarterly, $5.00

per year subscription, $20.00 for five years

VtGenWeb
Part of U.S. GenWeb Project
E-mail: vt@usgenweb.com
http://homepages.together.net/~cmfelone/
  vtgenweb.htm
(links to other Vermont resources)

VIRGINIA

Archives and Libraries with Holdings in Genealogy

State Archives and Library

Virginia State Library and Archives
800 East Broad Street
Richmond, VA 23219-1905
(804) 692-3777 (Library Reference);
  (804) 692-3888 (Archives Reference);
  (804) 692-3556 FAX
E-mail: wwweb@leo.vsla.edu
http://leo.vsla.edu/lva.html
Conley L. Edwards, State Archivist;
  Catherine Mishler, Head of Library
  Reference
Hours: Mon–Sat 9:00–5:00 (except legal
  holidays)
Pub. *Virginia Cavalcade*, quarterly, $6.00
out-of-state correspondent search fee:
  $10.00

State Historical Society

Virginia Historical Society
(428 North Boulevard, Richmond, VA
  23220—location)
PO Box 7311 (mailing address)
Richmond, VA 23211-0311
(804) 342-9677
http://www.vahistorical.org
Frances S. Pollard, Senior Librarian
Hours: Mon–Sat 10:00–5:00
Pub. *Virginia Magazine of History and
  Biography*, quarterly
(magazine does not publish genealogical
  material)
$35.00 per year membership for
  individuals

City, County and Regional Archives and Libraries

**City of Alexandria Archives and
Records Center**
(801 South Payne Street—location)
Box 178, City Hall (mailing address)
Alexandria, VA 22313
(703) 519-3326
Tod Chernikoff, Records Administrator
  and Archivist
Hours: Mon–Fri 8:00–4:00
(Records of the City of Alexandria, 1920
  to the present; local government
  archives only)
copying fee

Alexandria Public Library
Lloyd House Branch
220 North Washington Street
Alexandria, VA 22314

(703) 838-4577; (703) 706-3912 FAX
http://www.alexandria.lib.va.us/
  lloyd.html
Joyce A. McMullin, Branch Librarian
Hours: Mon–Sat 9:00–5:00
Pub. *The Doorway*, quarterly, free

Amherst County Historical Museum
154 South Main Steet
PO Box 741
Amherst, VA 24521
(804) 946-9068
E-mail: achmuseum@aol.com
http://members.aol.com/achmuseum/
  achmhis.htm
Michael N. Morell, County Museums
  Coordinator
Hours: Tue–Sat 9:00–4:30
Pub. *Muse*, quarterly
(general county history and genealogy)
$15.00 per year museum membership for
  individuals, $10.00 per year museum
  membership for senior citizens, $5.00
  per year membership for students;
  genealogy search fee: $15.00 for one
  name, $25.00 for three names

Arlington County Public Library
Virginia Room
1015 North Quincy Street
Arlington, VA 22201
(703) 358-5966
Sara Collins
Hours: Mon–Tue, Thur & Sat 10:00–
  5:00, Wed 1:00–9:00
("Historical, genealogical, and current
  information about Virginia and
  Arlington County")

Augusta County Library
PO Box 660-C
Fishersville, VA 22939
(540) 949-6354; (540) 885-3961
Barbara Olsen, Reference Librarian
Hours: Mon–Thur 9:00–9:00, Fri–Sat
  9:00–5:00

Thomas Balch Library
208 West Market Street
Leesburg, VA 22075
(703) 779-1328; (703) 779-6993
E-mail: janetbl@erols.com
Jane Sullivan, Branch Manager
Hours: Mon 10:00–5:00, Tue 10:00–
  8:00, Wed 2:00–8:00, Thur–Fri 11:00–
  5:00, Sat 11:00–4:00
(Loudoun County collection:
  genealogies, family files, obituaries,
  marriage records, census, wills, deeds,
  newspapers, tax rolls, cemetery
  records, etc.)

Bassett Branch Library
Genealogy Room
3964 Fairystone Park Highway
Bassett, Virginia 24055
(540) 629-9191; (540) 629-9840 FAX
E-mail: pross@leo.vsla.edu
Patricia C. Ross, Head of Genealogy
  Services

Hours: Mon, Wed & Thur 10:00–5:30, Tue noon–8:00, Fri–Sat 10:00–2:00 (Henry County and the surrounding area)

Blue Ridge Regional Library
310 East Church Street
Martinsville, VA 24112

Bridgewater College
Alexander Mack Memorial Library
East College Street
Bridgewater, VA 22812
(520) 828-5410
E-mail: rgreenaw@bridgewater.edu
Ruth Greenawalt, Library Director
Hours: Mon–Fri 8:00–5:00

Bristol Public Library
701 Goode Street
Bristol, VA 24201
(540) 669-9444; (540) 669-5593 FAX
Susan Whitt, Assistant Director
Hours: Mon–Thur 9:00–8:00, Fri–Sat 9:00–5:00
(Bristol, Virginia and Tennessee history, area family files, area cemetery records)
search fee: $25.00 per hour for searches over 30 minutes, plus 25¢ per page for copies

Buchanan County Public Library
(Poe Town Road—location)
Rt. 2, Box 3 (mailing address)
Grundy, VA 24614
(540) 935-6581
E-mail: phatfiel@leo.usla.edu
Pat Hatfield, Director
Hours: Mon 1:00–8:00, Tue–Wed & Fri–Sat 8:30–5:00, Thur 8:30–8:00
(southwest Virginia history and genealogy, also collects eastern Kentucky and some western North Carolina records)

Campbell County Public Library
Main Street
PO Box 310
Rustburg, VA 24588
(804) 332-5161, ext. 127
Connie D. Curtis, Director
Hours: Mon, Wed & Fri–Sat 9:00–5:30, Tue & Thur 9:00–9:00

Central Rappahannock Regional Library
1201 Caroline Street
Fredericksburg, VA 22401
(540) 372-1144
Barbara P. Willis
Hours: Mon–Thur 9:00–9:00, Fri–Sat 9:00–5:30

Chesterfield County Library
9501 Lori Road
PO Box 297
Chesterfield, VA 23832
(804) 784-1603
Barbara A. Lattimer, Librarian
Hours: Mon–Thur 10:00–9:00, Fri–Sat 10:00–5:30

College of William and Mary
Omohundro Institute of Early American History and Culture
Earl Gregg Swem Library Building
PO Box 8781
Williamsburg, VA 23187-8781
(757) 221-1126 (*Quarterly*); (757) 221-3508 (Reference and Information Department, Swem Library); (757) 221-1110 (Omohundro Institute); (757) 221-1047 FAX (Omohundro Institute)
E-mail: pvhigg@facstaff.wm.edu; ieahc1@facstaff.wm.edu (Omohundro Institute)
Pat Higgs, Office Manager; Beverly Smith, Secretary to the Director
Hours: Mon–Fri 8:30–5:30
Pub. *The William and Mary Quarterly: A Magazine of Early American History and Culture*, 3rd series (emphasis is no longer on Virginia history or genealogy), quarterly, $30.00 per year subscription, $4.00 surcharge for foreign address, $15.00 per year subscription for students; *Uncommon Sense*, two times per year, not available by subscription
(not a historical society but maintains a small library and is devoted to the publication of scholarly articles and books in the field of early American studies from discovery to approximately 1815)
$50.00 per year Associate membership for individuals, $25.00 per year Associate membership for students.

Culpeper County Library
105 East Mason Street
Culpeper, VA 22701
(540) 825-8691
Susan J. Keller, Director
Hours: Mon–Thur 10:00–9:00, Fri–Sat 10:00–5:00, Sun 1:30–5:00; Memorial Day to Labor Day: Mon–Thur 10:00–8:00, Fri 10:00–5:00, Sat 10:00–3:00

The Danville Public Library
511 Patton Street
Danville, VA 24541
(804) 799-5195
Denise Johnson, Head Administration
Hours: Mon & Thur 9:00–9:00, Tue–Wed & Fri 9:00–5:00, Sat 9:00–1:00

Fairfax County Public Library
Fairfax City Regional Library
Virginia Room
3915 Chain Bridge Road
Fairfax, VA 22030
(703) 246-2123; (703) 385-1911 FAX
http://s70itw01.dit.co.fairfax.va.us/library/va_room/htm
Suzanne Sheldon Levy, Virginia Room Librarian
Hours: Mon–Thur 10:00–9:00, Fri 10:00–6:00, Sat 10:00–5:00, Sun 12:00–6:00

("We have a good basic genealogical/local history collection.")
photocopies: 15¢ each

Franklin County Public Library
120 East Court Street
Rocky Mount, VA 24151
(540) 483-3098; (540) 483-1568 FAX
Dorothy Hodges, Technical Services Librarian
Hours: Mon–Tue & Thur 8:30–8:00, Wed & Fri–Sat 8:30–5:00
(genealogy materials are non-circulating; "Due to limited staff, extensive searches are not available; lists of amateur genealogists available for specific searches.")
copies 10¢ per page, up to 10 pages, plus postage

Fredericksburg Regional Genealogical Society
c/o Fredericksburg Methodist Church
308 Hanover Street
Fredericksburg, VA 22404
(540) 373-7114

Hacksma House Genealogy Library
(see Washington)

Hampton Center for the Arts and Humanities
Hampton Recreation Department
22 Wine Street
Hampton, VA 23669

Hampton Public Library
4207 Victoria Boulevard
Hampton, VA 23669-3596
(757) 727-1314
Elizabeth A. Wilson, Senior Library Assistant
Hours: Mon–Thur 9:00–9:00, Fri–Sat 9:00–5:00, Sun 1:00–5:00
(a special collection of materials on Virginia history and genealogy, focusing primarily on the local area; housing over 7,000 titles, which include published materials, microform, maps, vertical files, and photos)

Handley Regional Library
Archives Room
(Corner of Braddock and Piccadilly Streets—location)
PO Box 58 (mailing address)
Winchester, VA 22604
(540) 662-9041; (540) 722-4769 FAX
E-mail: handley@shentel.net
http://www.shentel.net/handley-library/index.html
Hours: Tue–Wed 1:00–9:00, Thur–Sat 10:00–5:00
(manuscripts, maps, photographs, published books and ephemera; "Our collection focus is the lower Shenandoah Valley; the Archives is jointly operated by The Handley Library and the Winchester-Frederick County Historical Society.")

Historic Crab Orchard Museum and Pioneer Park, Inc.
(Route 19-460—location)
Rt. 1, Box 194 (mailing address)
Tazewell, VA 24651
(540) 988-6755; (540) 988-9400
E-mail: histcrab@netscope.net
Ross Weeks, Jr., Director
Hours: Mon–Sat 9:00–5:00, Sun (May–Sept) 2:00–5:00
Pub. *Pisgah Pathfinder*, quarterly
$25.00 per year membership for individuals, $35.00 per year membership for families; searches not done by staff

Information Center
400 East Washington Street
PO Box 2107
Petersburg, VA 23803
(804) 861-8080

Jones Memorial Library
2311 Memorial Avenue
Lynchburg, VA 24501
(804) 846-0501
Edward Gibson, Librarian
Hours: Tue & Thur 1:00–9:00, Wed & Fri 1:00–5:00, Sat 9:00–5:00
Pub. *JML Notes*, semiannually
(Virginia genealogy, Lynchburg-area history)
interlibrary loans and OCLC $10.00 each, copies by mail $5.00, in-house copies 25¢ each

The Charles Pinckney Jones Memorial Library, Inc.
406 West Riverside Street
Covington, VA 24426
(540) 962-3321; (540) 962-8447 FAX
Thurman Pugh, Director; Diana Hawkins, Assistant Director
Hours: Mon, Wed & Fri 9:30–5:30, Tue & Thur 9:30–8:30, Sat (school year) 9:30–5:30, Sat (summer) 9:30–12:30
(genealogy and local history collection including Alleghany County, City of Covington, Clifton Forge, and some other Virginia counties' history)

Kirn Memorial Library
Sargeant Memorial Room
Norfolk Public Library
301 East City Hall Avenue
Norfolk, VA 23510
(757) 664-7323, ext 3736; (757) 664-7321 FAX
http://www.whro.org/cl/npl
Peggy A. Haile, Librarian
Hours: Mon & Sat 10:00–5:00, Tue, Thur & Sun 1:00–5:00, Wed 1:00–9:00
(collects and maintains a historical collection of Norfolkiana, Virginiana and genealogy, now more than 16,000 books, 3,700 microforms and 20,000 photographs)
no search fee, charges for photocopying and mailing only

Loudoun Museum, Inc.
14-16 Loudoun Street, S.W.
Leesburg, VA 20175
(703) 777-7427; (703) 777-8331 FAX
Tracy Gillespie, Executive Director
Hours: Feb–Dec: Mon–Sat 10:00–5:00, Sun 1:00–5:00
Pub. *The Loudoun Museum Heritage Review*, quarterly
(history museum for Loudoun County and Leesburg; a good historical resource with limited genealogical information)
$15.00 per year membership for individuals, $20.00 per year membership for families, $10.00 per year membership for senior citizens, $100.00 per year Patron membership

The Lyceum—Alexandria's History Museum
George Washington Bicentennial Center
201 South Washington Street
Alexandria, VA 22314
(703) 838-4994; (703) 838-4997 FAX
E-mail: thelyceum@compuserve.com
http://www.virginia.org
James C. Mackay, Director
Hours: Mon–Sat 10:00–5:00, Sun 1:00–5:00
Pub. *The Alexandria Observer*, quarterly
(includes Virginia history and local history)

Lynchburg Museum System
(901 Court Street, Lynchburg, VA 24504—location)
PO Box 60 (mailing address)
Lynchburg, VA 24505
(804) 847-1459
Adam E. Scher, Curator of Collections
Hours: Mon–Fri 8:00–4:30
Pub. *Signpost*, quarterly, free to volunteers and donors
(manuscript and photographic collections related to Lynchburg, Virginia; Museum System operates Lynchburg Museum, Point of Honor and the Miller-Claytor House)

James Madison University
Carrier Library
Special Collection Department
Harrisonburg, VA 22807
(540) 568-3612; (540) 568-3405
E-mail: bolgiace@jmu.edu
http://www.jmu.edu/libliaison/sc/aboutsc.htm
(central Shenandoah Valley: Page, Rockingham, Shenandoah and Augusta counties; little genealogical data)

Mariner's Museum
100 Museum Drive
Newport News, VA 23606-3759
(757) 596-2222; (800) 581-7245
E-mail: tmmlib@infi.net
http://www.mariner.org/library.html

George Mason University
Special Collections Department
Fenwick Library
Fairfax, VA 22030-4444
(703) 993-2220; (703) 993-2200 FAX
E-mail: speccoll@osfl.gmu.edu
http://www.gmu.edu/library/specialcollections/

Jeff Matthews Memorial Museum
606 West Stuart Drive
Galax, VA 24333

Menno Simons Historical Library
Eastern Mennonite University
Harrisonburg, VA 22802
(540) 432-4178; (540) 432-4977 FAX
E-mail: bowmanlb@emu.edu
Lois B. Bowman, Associate Director
Hours: during regular school sessions: Mon–Fri 8:00–5:00, Sat 10:00–1:00; summer: Mon–Fri 8:00–noon & 1:00–5:00
(including Anabaptist, Mennonite, Amish and local Virginia materials; Mennonite and local Germanic genealogy; local Lutheran and Reformed Church records; material on Pennsylvania, Maryland, West Virginia and Ohio)
donations accepted

Montgomery-Floyd Regional Library
125 Sheltman Street
Christiansburg, VA 24073
(540) 382-6965
Ida Comparin, Interim Director
Hours: Mon–Thur 10:30–8:30, Sat 10:30–5:30, Sun 2:00–5:30

Museum in Memory of Virginia E. Randolph
2200 Mountain Road
Glen Allen, VA 23060
(804) 262-3363

Museum of American Frontier Culture
(1250 Richmond Road, Staunton, VA 24401—location)
PO Box 810 (mailing address)
Staunton, VA 24402-0810
(540) 332-7850; (540) 332-9989 FAX
E-mail: klbrown@leo.vsla.edu
Katharine L. Brown, Ph.D., Director of Research and Collections
Hours: Museum: Mon–Sun 9:00–5:00; Library: Mon–Fri 10:00–4:00 by appointment only
Pub. *Newsletter*, quarterly
(library and research center; 17th & 18th century English, Irish, Scotch-Irish, German, Valley of Virginia)
$35.00 per year membership (includes museum admission and ship discount); staff cannot undertake searches

Newport News Public Library System
Martha Woodroof Hiden Virginiana
    Room
Main Street Library
1100 Main Street
Newport News, VA 23601-4105
(757) 591-4858
Margaret Moseley, Library Technician
Hours: Mon–Thur 9:00–9:00, Fri–Sat
    9:00–6:00, Sun (Sept–May) 1:00–5:00
(includes Old Dominion Land Company
    records: company developed city of
    Newport News—497 deeds and
    abstracts, 775 maps and company
    records, 1829–1948)
queries: $1.00 mailing fee, 15¢ per page
    for copies

Ohoopee Regional Library
(see Georgia)

Old Dominion University
Special Collections Department
Library
Norfolk, VA 23529
(757) 683-4178
E-mail: userid@shakespeare.lib.odu.edu
http://www.odu.edu/special.collections/

Page Public Library
PO Box 734
Luray, VA 22835
(540) 743-6867
Mon, Wed & Fri–Sat 10:00–5:00, Tue
    10:00–6:00, Thur 10:00–9:00
Hours: Debby J. Owens, Secretary/
    Treasurer
Pub. *The Genealogical Society of Page
    County Quarterly Newsletter*
(preserves Page County's past for
    genealogical researchers)
$10.00 per year membership; free
    queries to members

Pamunkey Regional Library
PO Box 119
Hanover, VA 23069
(804) 537-6210
Hours: Mon–Wed 9:00–9:00, Tue & Fri
    9:00–6:00, Sat 9:00–2:00

Pearisburg Public Library
209 Fort Branch Road
Pearisburg, VA 24134
(540) 921-2556; (540) 921-1708 FAX
E-mail: sroberts@leo.vsla.edu
Sandra V. Robertson, Librarian
Hours: Mon 12:00–8:00, Tue 12:00–
    5:00, Wed & Fri 9:00–5:00, Thur
    9:00–8:00, Sat 9:00–1:00

The Petersburg Museums
15 West Bank Street
Petersburg, VA 23803
(804) 733-2404
Suzanne Savery, Director
Hours: Trapezium House: Mon–Sun
    (1 Apr–31 Oct) 10:00–5:00; Farmer's
    Bank: Fri–Mon (1 Apr–31 Oct) 10:00–

5:00; Seige Museum, Centre Hill
    Mansion, Visitor's Center, Blandford
    Church: Mon–Sun 10:00–5:00

Petersburg Public Library
William R. McKenney Building
Reference Department
137 South Sycamore Street
Petersburg, VA 23803
(804) 733-2387
Pat Ward, Public Services Librarian
Hours: Mon & Wed 9:00–9:00, Tue &
    Thur–Sat 9:00–5:30
(Civil War and Virginia interest)

The Portsmouth Museums
420 High Street
Portsmouth, VA 23704
(804) 393-8983

Portsmouth Public Library
601 Court Street
Portsmouth, VA 23704
(757) 393-8501; (757) 393-5107 FAX
Mary E. Goodman, Manager Main
    Library
Hours: Mon–Fri 9:00–9:00, Sat 9:00–
    5:00
(includes records of Norfolk County, of
    which Portsmouth was the county seat
    until 1858 when it became an
    independent city)

Prince William Public Library System
RELIC (Ruth Emmons Lloyd
    Information Center): Virginiana
    Collection
Bull Run Regional Library
8051 Ashton Avenue
Manassas, VA 20109-2892
(703) 792-4540; (703) 792-4520
http://www.co.prince-william.va.us/
    library/services/relic/relic.htm
Donald L. Wilson, Virginiana Librarian
Hours: Mon–Thur 10:00–9:00, Fri–Sat
    10:00–5:00, Sun (mid-Sept to mid-
    Jun) noon–5:00

Radford Public Library
30 First Street
Radford, VA 24141
(540) 731-3621
Ann Fisher, Library Director
Hours: Mon–Wed 10:00–8:30, Thur–Fri
    10:00–5:30, Sat 10:00–4:30, Sun
    (winter) 2:00–5:00
(mostly southwestern Virginia material;
    Internet access available for public
    use)

Walter Cecil Rawls Library and Museum
22511 Main Street
PO Box 310
Courtland, VA 23837
(757) 653-2821
Beverly Worsham, Assistant Director
Hours: Mon & Wed–Thur 9:00–8:30,
    Tue & Fri 9:00–5:00, Sat 9:00–3:00

Richmond Public Library
101 East Main Street
Richmond, VA 23219
(804) 780-4672
Ellen Parnell, Senior Librarian,
    Literature and History Department
Hours: Sept–May: Mon–Thur 9:00–9:00,
    Fri 9:00–6:00, Sat 9:00–5:00; Jun–
    Aug: Mon–Thur 9:00–9:00, Fri 9:00–
    6:00, Sat 9:00–1:00
("does not acquire genealogical
    material"; has Richmond city
    directories 1819 to the present)

Roanoke City Public Library
Virginia Room
706 South Jefferson Street
Roanoke, VA 24016
(540) 981-2073
Alice Carol Tuckwiller
Hours: Mon–Sat 9:00–5:00

Rockingham Public Library
45 Newman Avenue
Harrisonburg, VA 22801
(540) 434-4475; (540) 434-4382 FAX
Nicki M. Lynch, Library Director
Hours: Mon & Fri 9:00–6:00, Tue–Thur
    9:00–9:00, Sat 9:00–5:00

Samuels Public Library
538 Villa Avenue
Front Royal, VA 22630
(540) 635-3153
Hours: Mon–Wed 10:00–8:00, Thur–Sat
    10:00–5:00
copies 20¢ per page

Shenandoah County Library
300 Stoney Creek Boulevard
Edinburg, VA 22824
(540) 984-8200; (540) 984-8207 FAX
David L. Sternberg, Director of the
    Library
Hours: Mon, Wed & Fri 10:00–6:00, Tue
    & Thur 10:00–9:00, Sat 11:00–5:00

Southside Regional Library
PO Box 10
Boydton, VA 23917

Anne Spencer Memorial Foundation
(1313 Pierce Street—location)
1306 Pierce Street (mailing address)
Lynchburg, VA 24501
(804) 845-1313

Sullivan County Library
(see Tennessee)

Tazewell County Public Library
Genealogy Department
310 East Main Street
PO Box 929
Tazewell, VA 24651
(540) 988-2541; (540) 988-5980
Nora W. Lockett, Reference Librarian
Hours: Mon–Wed & Fri–Sat 9:00–5:30,
    Thur 9:00–8:30, Sun 2:00–6:00
copies: first ten pages free, 10¢ per page
    for each additional page, plus postage

Troy Public Library
(see Alabama)

University of Virginia
Special Collections Department
Alderman Library
Charlottesville, VA 22903-2498
(804) 924-3021 (Reference Department);
    (804) 924-3243
E-mail: mssbks@virginia.edu
http://www.virginia.edu/speccol/
Hours: various; call (804) 924-7911

University of Virginia
Mary Washington College
Simpson Library
1801 College Avenue
Fredericksburg, VA 22401-4664
(540) 654-1125; (540) 654-1147
http://library.mwc.edu

Valentine Museum
Reference Services
1015 East Clay Street
Richmond, VA 23219
(804) 649-0711
Hours: Reference Services: Wed & Fri
    9:00–noon & 1:00–4:00
Pub. *VM News*

Virginia Beach Central Library
Local History Genealogy Collection
4100 Virginia Beach Boulevard
Virginia Beach, VA 23452
(757) 431-3071; (757) 431-3018 FAX
Carolyn L. Barkley, Central Librarian
Hours: Mon–Thur 10:00–9:00, Fri–Sat
    10:00–5:00, Sun (Oct–May) 1:00–5:00

Virginia Commonwealth University
James Branch Cabell Library
Special Collections Department
901 Park Avenue
PO Box 842033
Richmond, VA 23284-2033
(804) 828-1108; (804) 828-0151 FAX
E-mail: bpittman@gems.vcu.edu
http://exlibris.uls.vcu.edu/library/jbc/
    speccoll/speccoll.html

Virginia Commonwealth University
Tompkins-McCaw Library
509 North 12th Street
PO Box 980582
Richmond, VA 23298-0582
(804) 828-9898; (804) 828-6089 FAX
E-mail: jkoste@gems.vcu.edu
http://exlibris.uls.vcu.edu/library/tml/
    speccoll/hmpge.html

Virginia Living Museum
524 J. Clyde Morris Boulevard
Newport News, VA 23601-1999
Robert P. Sullivan

Virginia Military Institute
VMI Archives
Preston Library
Lexington, VA 24450
(540) 464-7566; (540) 464-7279
E-mail: jacobdb@vax.vmi.edu
http://www.vmi.edu/~archtml/index.html

Virginia Polytechnic Institute and State University
University Libraries
Virginia Tech
Blacksburg, VA 24062-9001
(540) 231-6308; (540) 231-9263
E-mail: gailmac@vt.edu
http://www.lib.vt.edu/
(Appalachian history, Civil War, maps,
    oral history, photographs, special
    collections)

Virginia War Museum
9285 Warwick Boulevard
Newport News, VA 23607
(757) 247-8523; (757) 247-8627
John V. Quarstein, Director and
    Administrator of Museums and
    Historical Services
Hours: Mon–Sat 9:00–5:00, Sun 1:00–
    5:00
Pub. *The Correspondent*, quarterly
(maintains the 1899 Newsome House,
    1820 Young's Mill, 5 April 1862 Lee
    Mill's Battlefield, 1810 Warwick
    Court House, c. 1850 Lee Hall
    Mansion, c. 1760 Endview Plantation)
$20.00 per year membership for
    individuals, $25.00 per year
    membership for families, $10.00 per
    year membership for students; $2.00
    entrance fee for adults, $10.00
    admission for children 7–15, senior
    citizens or active military

Washington and Lee University
James G. Leyburn Library
Special Collections
Lexington, VA 24450
(540) 463-8663
C. Vaughan Stanley, Special Collections
    Librarian
Hours: Mon–Fri 9:00–5:00, when
    university is in session; summer:
    Mon–Fri various, please call
(specializing in Rockbridge County,
    Virginia, genealogy)
photocopies: 15¢ per page plus $2.00
    service charge

Washington County Public Library
Oak Hill and Valley Streets
Abingdon, VA 24210
(540) 676-6222
Emily Umbarger, Reference Librarian
Hours: Mon–Thur 9:00–9:00, Fri–Sat
    9:00–5:00, Sun (during school year)
    2:00–5:00
(emphasis on history rather than
    genealogy; Virginia material in
    general, southwest Virginia in
    particular)
no fees except small fees for copying

Mary Ball Washington Museum
(8346 Mary Ball Road—location)
PO Box 97 (mailing address)
Lancaster, VA 22503-0097

(804) 462-7280; (804) 462-6107
Christine C. Townley, Executive Director
Hours: Tue by appointment, Wed–Fri
    10:00–5:00, Sat 10:00–3:00
Pub. *Mary Ball Washington Museum
    Journal*, quarterly; *Post Rider
    Quarterly* (in planning)
(genealogical research center, Virginia
    history research library; various
    genealogical research services,
    workshops, classes, seminars and
    group research trips)

Waynesboro Public Library
600 South Wayne Avenue
Waynesboro, VA 22980
(540) 949-6173
Dorothy Anne Reinbold, Library
    Director
Hours: Mon–Fri 9:00–9:00, Sat 9:00–
    5:00

Wytheville Community College Library
1000 East Main Street
Wytheville, VA 24382
(540) 223-4742
E-mail: wcrobea@wc.cc.va.us
Anna Ray Roberts, Coordinator of
    Library Services
Hours: Mon–Fri 8:00–5:00
(southwest Virginia local history and
    genealogy)

York County Public Library
8500 George Washington Highway
Yorktown, VA 23692
(757) 890-3377
Mrs. Dudley, Library Director
Hours: Mon–Thur 10:00–9:00, Fri
    10:00–6:00, Sat 10:00–5:00, Sun
    1:00–5:00

Historical Societies—Local and Regional

Albemarle County Historical Society
The McIntire Building
200 Second Street, N.E.
Charlottesville, VA 22902
(804) 296-1492 (Executive Director);
    (804) 296-7294 (Librarian); (804) 296-
    4576 FAX
http://monticello.avenue.gen.va.us/
    community/agencies/achs
Lynne C. Ely, Executive Director;
    Margaret M. O'Bryant, Librarian
Hours: Charlottesville-Albemarle
    Historical Collection: Mon–Fri 9:00–
    5:00, Sat 10:00–1:00
Pub. *Magazine of Albemarle County
    History*, annually; *Bulletin of the
    Albemarle County Historical Society*,
    quarterly
$25.00 per year regular membership

Alexandria Historical Society, Inc.
The Lyceum
George Washington Bicentennial Center
201 South Washington Street
Alexandria, VA 22314
(703) 548-1776 (Society); (703) 838-4994 (Lyceum)
Lynn Rozental, Lyceum Director
Hours: Lyceum: Mon–Sat 10:00–5:00, Sun 1:00–5:00

Amelia Historical Commission
PO Box 113
Amelia, VA 23002

Amelia Historical Society
Church Street
Amelia, VA 23002

Arlington Historical Society, Inc.
(1805 South Arlington Ridge Road, Arlington, VA 22202—location)
PO Box 402 (mailing address)
Arlington, VA 22210
(703) 892-4204
Dr. Harold Handerson
Hours: Fri–Sat 11:00–3:00, Sun 2:00–5:00
Pub. *Arlington Historical Magazine*, annually, $9.50 per year subscription

Augusta County Historical Society
PO Box 686
Staunton, VA 24402-0686
(540) 886-1479 (Editor)
Katherine G. Bushman, Editor
Pub. *Augusta Historical Bulletin*, semiannually (May and November)
$10.00 per year membership for individuals; search fee: $8.00 per hour plus cost of copies and postage over 32¢

Bath County Historical Society, Inc.
PO Box 212
Warm Springs, VA 24484
(540) 839-2543
E-mail: cmetheny@leo.vsla.edu
Connie Metheny, Secretary
Hours: Mon–Fri 8:30–4:30
Pub. *Bath County Heritage*, annually; *Newsletter*, quarterly
$15.00 per year membership for individuals, $20.00 per year membership for families

Bedford City/County Museum
201 East Main Street
Bedford, VA 24523
(540) 586-4520
Ellen A. Wandrei, Managing Director
Hours: Mon–Sat
Pub. *Museum Newsletter*, quarterly, $5.00 donation for subscription
(small genealogical library and research room)
$1.00 admission to museum and/or research library

Bedford Historical Society, Inc.
(149 West Main Street—location)
PO Box 602 (mailing address)
Bedford, VA 24523
(540) 586-8188
Clara S. Lambeth, Executive Secretary

Boyd County Historical Society
(see Kentucky)

Brunswick County Historical Society, Inc.
PO Box 554
Lawrenceville, VA 23868
(804) 848-2795

Campbell County Historical Society
PO Box 560
Rustburg, VA 24588

Carroll County Historical Society
PO Box 937
Hillsville, VA 24343
(540) 728-2125 Secretary (daytime)
Shelby Inscore Puckett, Editor
Hours: Mon–Fri 8:00–3:30
Pub. *Carroll County Chronicles*, quarterly
$12.00 per year membership

Chesterfield Historical Society of Virginia
(10011 Iron Bridge Road—location)
PO Box 40 (mailing address)
Chesterfield, VA 23832
(804) 748-1026
Nancy Carter Crump, Executive Director
Hours: Mon–Fri 10:00–4:00
Pub. *The Messenger*, quarterly; *The Journal of the Chesterfield Historical Society*, annually
$12.00 per year membership for individuals, reduced rates for couples, families and students

Claiborne County Historical Society
Rt. 1, Box 589
Jonesville, VA 24263
Mary E. Parkey, President

Clarke County Historical Association
North Church Street
Old Courthouse Wing, First Floor
PO Box 306
Berryville, VA 22611
(540) 955-2600
Sally Trumbower, President; Mary T. Morris, Archivist
Hours: Thur–Sat 10:00–3:30
Pub. *Clarke County Proceedings*, annually
$10.00 per year membership for individuals, $15.00 per year membership for families

Craig County Historical Society
223 Main Street
PO Box 206
New Castle, VA 24127-0206
(540) 864-5220

L. Clayton Abbott, Chairman
Hours: mornings only
Pub. *Our Proud Heritage*, semiannually
$3.00 per year membership for individuals, $6.00 per year membership for families

Culpeper Historical Society, Inc.
PO Box 785
Culpeper, VA 22701

Cumberland County Historical Society
PO Box 188
Cumberland, VA 23040-0188
(804) 492-4533
Sue C. Seawell, Secretary
Pub. *Cumberland County, Virginia, Historical Bulletin*, annually (October), $6.50 per year subscription
$10.00 per year membership

Eastern Shore of Virginia Historical Society
(Kerr Place, 69 Market Street—location)
PO Box 193 (mailing address)
Onancock, VA 23417
(804) 787-8012
John H. Verrill, Executive Director; Lacy Dick, Archivist
Hours: Library: Wed 1:00–4:00; Museum: Tue–Sat 10:00–4:00
(library with many local sources)
$3.00 admission

Historical Society of Fairfax County, VA
PO Box 415
Fairfax, VA 22030
(703) 246-2123
Susan Leigh, Secretary; Suzanne Sheldon Levy, Virginia Room Librarian
Hours: Fairfax City Regional Library, Virginia Room: Mon–Thur 9:00–9:00, Fri 9:00–6:00, Sat 9:00–5:00, Sun 12:00–8:00
Pub. *Historical Society of Fairfax County, VA Yearbook*, biannually, $7.50 per issue
$15.00 per year membership for individuals, $20.00 per year membership for families, $7.50 per year membership for students, $25.00 Contributing membership, $50.00 per year Sustaining membership, $250.00 life membership

Falls Church Historical Commission
City Clerk
300 Park Avenue
Falls Church, VA 22046
(703) 241-5014
Hours: 8:00–5:00
("We are just beginning to inventory births, marriages, burials, wills.")

The Fauquier Heritage Society for Local History and Genealogy, Inc.
(8266 East Main Street—location)
PO Box 548 (mailing address)
Marshall, VA 20116
(540) 364-3440
Robert L. Sinclair, President
Hours: Tue–Thur: 10:00–4:00, other days by appointment
Pub. *The Fauquier Heritage Society News*, quarterly
(Virginia local history and genealogy; houses entire collection of John K. Gott, local author and historian, who is on site on Wednesdays; plus other publications, family histories and genealogies)
$10.00 per year membership for individuals, $15.00 per year membership for families, $25.00 per year Sustaining membership, $100.00 Charter or life membership; queries answered by mail or published in newsletter

Fauquier Historical Society, Inc.
The Old Jail Museum
(Court House Square and Ashby Street—location)
PO Box 675 (mailing address)
Warrenton, VA 22188
(540) 347-5525 (Museum); (540) 347-0607 (Museum Director)
Jackie Lee, Museum Director
Hours: Museum: Tue–Sun 10:00–4:00
Pub. *Fauquier Historical Society News & Notes*, biannually
(Virginia local and regional history and genealogy, especially history of Warrenton and Fauquier counties: names, places, events; museum exhibits covering pre-Revolutionary to twentieth century; resource material for county sites)
$10.00 per year membership for individuals, $15.00 per year membership for families or Contributing membership, $3.00 per year membership for students, $25.00 per year membership for businesses, from $25.00 per year Sustaining membership; search fees by genealogist, Phyllis Scott, (703) 364-1992

Flowerdew Hundred Foundation
1617 Flowerdew Hundred Road
Hopewell, VA 23860
Becky Ritter

Fluvanna County Historical Society
Old Stone Jail Museum
PO Box 132
Palmyra, VA 22963
(804) 842-3557
Josephine Snead, President
Hours: May–Sept: Sat & Sun afternoons

Pub. *Fluvanna County Historical Society Bulletin*, semiannually
$10.00 per year membership

Franklin County Historical Society
PO Box 86
Rocky Mount, VA 24151

Giles County Historical Society
208 North Main Street
PO Box 404
Pearisburg, VA 24134
(540) 921-1050 (Thur only)
Ruth Blevins, Research Chairman
Hours: Thur 10:00–3:00
Pub. *Newsletter*, quarterly
$10.00 per year membership; research by donation fees

Gloucester Historical Commission
PO Box 1176
Gloucester, VA 23061

Goochland County Historical Society
(2875 River Road West—location)
PO Box 602 (mailing address)
Goochland, VA 23063
(804) 556-3966
Hours: Apr through Oct: Wed–Fri 10:00–3:00, and some Sat 10:00–2:00 by appointment; winter: by appointment only
Pub. *Goochland County Historical Society Magazine*, annually, $10.00 per issue; *Goochland County Historical Society Newsletter*, three times per year
(includes research library with central Virginia and James River records)
research: $15.00 and $30.00 contributions

Grayson County Historical Society, Inc.
PO Box 529
Independence, VA 24348
Pub. *Glimpses of Grayson*
$5.00 per year membership

Great Falls Historical Society
PO Box 56
Great Falls, VA 22066
(703) 759-5803
Susan Cochran, President
Pub. *Reflections*, biennially, costs vary

Greene County Historical Society
PO Box 185
Stanardsville, VA 22973
Pub. *Greene County Magazine*, annually
$5.00 per year membership

Hanover County Historical Society, Inc.
(Old Jail-Hanover County Courthouse, Route 301—location)
PO Box 91 (mailing address)
Hanover, VA 23069
(804) 537-6262 (Office); (804) 746-2377 (President)

Anne Geddy Cross, President
Pub. *Hanover County Historical Society Bulletin*, semiannually (June and November); *Highlights*, about three times per year
$10.00 per year membership for individuals (by calendar year), $15.00 per year membership for couples, $100.00 life membership for individuals; research services not available

Harrisonburg-Rockingham Historical Society
(382 High Street—location)
PO Box 716 (mailing address)
Dayton, VA 22821
(540) 879-2616 phone and FAX
Faye A. Witters, Administrator
Hours: Mon & Wed–Sat 10:00–4:00
Pub. *Harrisonburg-Rockingham Historical Society Newsletter*, quarterly; *Rockingham Recorder*, irregularly
(genealogical library which also holds history and Civil War information related primarily to Rockingham County; a bookstore which carries a wide range of genealogical books)
$25.00 per year membership for individuals; library fee: $5.00 per person for non members

Historic Alexandria Foundation
220 South Fayette Street
Alexandria, VA 22314
(202) 548-2267

Historic Dumfries Virginia, Inc.
Weems-Botts Museum
(300 Duke Street, corner of Duke and Cameron Streets—location)
PO Box 26 (mailing address)
Dumfries, VA 22026
(703) 221-3346; (703) 221-3544 FAX
http:/mbti.gmu.edu/~cgrymes/dumfries/index.html
Jeanne Hochmuth, Curator
Pub. *Historic Dumfries, Virginia, Inc. Newsletter*, bimonthly
(includes books, periodicals, articles, etc., concerning the heritage of the people and places of historic Dumfries; issues certificates of ancestry to descendants of pioneers who came to Dumfries or the surrounding area by 1850)
$10.00 per year membership for individuals, $20.00 per year membership for families, $5.00 per year membership for senior citizens, $100.00 life membership; $15.00 for Pioneers of Dumfries, Virginia, Certificate of Ancestry; $5.00 per hour research fee in the museum's files, $10.00 per hour otherwise, 25¢ per page for copies, $3.00 postage and handling; $3.00 admission for adults, $2.00 admission for senior citizens, $1.50 admission for children over 6

King and Queen Historical Society

(King and Queen Court House—
location)
Rt. 1, Box 18 (mailing address)
Walkerton, VA 23177
(804) 769-3959
John F. Jones, Treasurer
Pub. *Bulletin of King and Queen
Historical Society*, semiannually
(January and July), $1.00 plus mailing
per issue
("In our archives we have a few early
records given by individuals; most of
county's records burned by Yankees
1863.")
$6.00 per year membership for
individuals (beginning in July), $10.00
per year membership for couples

King George County Historical Society

PO Box 424
King George, VA 22485

Louisa County Historical Society

(Museum in the old jail adjacent to the
Louisa County Courthouse—location)
Louisa, VA 23117 (mailing address)
Hours: Sat–Sun 2:00–4:00
Pub. *Louisa County Historical
Magazine*, semiannually; *Louisa
County Historical Society Newsletter*
(archives not yet open to researchers,
hence no genealogical services)
$15.00 per year membership

Lynchburg Historical Foundation, Inc.

(325 12th Street, Lynchburg, VA
24504—location)
PO Box 248 (mailing address)
Lynchburg, VA 24505
(804) 528-5353
Nancy Jamerson Weiland, Office
Manager
Hours: Tue–Thur 8:30 A.M.–12:30 P.M.
Pub. *Lynch's Ferry Magazine*,
semiannually, $4.18 per year
subscription; *View From the Terrace*,
quarterly, free
$20.00 per year membership

Mathews County Historical Society, Inc.

PO Box 855
Mathews, VA 23109

New River Historical Society

Wilderness Road Regional Museum
(State Route #611—location)
PO Box 373 (mailing address)
Newbern, VA 24126
(540) 674-4835; (540) 674-1266 FAX
Elinor Morgan
Hours: Tue–Sat 10:30–4:30; Museum:
Tue–Sat 10:30–4:30, Sun 1:30–4:30
Pub. *NRHS Journal*, annually, $2.50 per
issue for non-members; *Benchmarks*,
quarterly

(local history of Floyd, Giles,
Montgomery and Pulaski counties, and
the city of Radford)
$10.00 per year membership; museum
admission: $7.00 for adults, $1.00 for
children 6–12

Norfolk County Historical Society of Chesapeake, VA

Chesapeake Public Library
Wallace Memorial Room
298 Cedar Road
Chesapeake, VA 23320
(757) 382-6591
Joe Law, President
Hours: Mon–Thur 9:00–9:00, Fri–Sat
9:00–5:00, Sun 1:00–5:00
("Neither the library nor the historical
society do genealogical research for
patrons; list of researchers for hire
available on request.")
$7.50 per year membership

Northern Neck of Virginia Historical Society

Westmoreland County
PO Box 716
Montross, VA 22520
Mrs. George Mason, III, Executive
Secretary
Pub. *Northern Neck of Virginia
Historical Magazine*, annually
(maintains Research Library, Montross
Museum, Second Floor)
$14.00 per year membership

Nottoway County Historical Association

503 Seventh Street
Blackstone, VA 23824
(804) 292-3381
W. C. Crawley

Orange County Historical Society, Inc.

130 Caroline Street
Orange, VA 22960
(540) 672-5366
http://home.rica.net/tel26/orange/
orange.htm
Kenneth M. Clark, Administrator
Hours: Mon–Fri 1:00–5:00
Pub. *Orange County Historical Society
Newsletter*, bimonthly
("The Society's library contains more
than 2,000 volumes, and there are over
1,000 files with information on local
families, historic buildings and sites,
plus a map collection. Information is
available not only on Orange County,
but also on our neighboring counties,
such as Madison, Culpeper and
Greene; there is also data on the early
settlement of the Virginia Piedmont,
historic homes, Civil War history, and
many other fields of interest.")
$12.50 per year membership (beginning
in January), $50.00 per year

Sustaining membership, $100.00–
$300.00 per year Patron membership,
$300.00 life membership

Patrick County Historical Society, Inc.

PO Box 1045
Stuart, VA 24171
(540) 694-2840
Barbara C. Baughan, Museum
Genealogist
Hours: Tue–Sat 10:00–2:00
(local family files and others related to
this area of Virginia, deed index,
cemeteries, etc.)
$10.00 per year membership; search in
society holdings for postage and copy
costs only

Pittsylvania Historical Society

PO Box 1206
Chatham, VA 24531
(804) 432-5031
Preston B. Moses, President
Hours: various
Pub. *The Packet*, quarterly (February
May, August, November)
("Pittsylvania-Virginia genealogical-
historical events, etc.")
$10.00 per year membership for
individuals, $15.00 per year
membership for couples

Portsmouth Historical Association

221 North Street
Portsmouth, VA 23704
(804) 393-0241
Alice C. Hanes, President

Princess Anne County-Virginia Beach Historical Society

2040 Potters Road
Virginia Beach, VA 23454
J. Davis Reed, III, President
Pub. *PAC Newsletter*

Roanoke Valley Historical Society

(1 Market Square, Center-in-the-Square,
Roanoke, VA 24011—location)
PO Box 1904 (mailing address)
Roanoke, VA 24008
(540) 342-5770; (540) 224-1238 FAX
Clare White, Librarian
Hours: weekdays 10:00–5:00, Sun 1:00–
5:00
Pub. *Newsletter*, monthly; *Journal*,
annually

Rockbridge Historical Society

(101 East Washington Street—location)
PO Box 514 (mailing address)
Lexington, VA 24450
(540) 464-1058; (540) 463-8663
(Washington and Lee University
Library Special Collections
Department)
Alice Williams, Curator
Hours: Campbell House: summer: Tue–
Fri 10:00–3:00, Sat 10:00–1:00;
winter: Tue–Sat 10:00–1:00

Pub. *News Notes*; *Proceedings of the Rockbridge Historical Society*
$7.50 per year membership (includes *News Notes*)

Seneca Road Historical Society
625 Seneca Road
PO Box 32
Great Falls, VA 22066

Shenandoah County Historical Society
c/o Shenandoah County Library
300 Stoney Creek Boulevard
Edinburg, VA 22824
(540) 984-8200; (540) 984-8207 FAX
David L. Steinberg, Director of the Library
Hours: Library: Mon–Tue & Thur 10:00–8:00, Wed & Fri 10:00–6:00, Sat 10:00–4:00
Pub. *Shenando News* (emphasis on Shenandoah County and Valley of Virginia), quarterly
$10.00 per year membership for individuals, $15.00 per year membership for couples

Smyth County Historical and Museum Society, Inc.
(Stadium Road—location)
PO Box 788 (mailing address)
Marion, VA 24354-0788
(540) 783-2745 (Curator)
Mrs. H. B. Eller, Curator
Hours: Sun (1 June to 1 Sept) 2:00–5:00, special openings for students from grade and high schools
$5.00 per year membership

Southern Studies Institute
(see Louisiana)

The Historical Society of Southwest Virginia
PO Box 3877
Wise, VA 24293
Rhonda Robertson, Secretary
Pub. *Historical Sketches of Southwest Virginia*, annually
$7.00 per year membership for individuals, $10.00 per year membership for families

Spotsylvania Historical Association, Inc.
PO Box 64
Spotsylvania, VA 22553
(540) 582-5672

Staunton River Historical Society
Willie Hodges Booth Museum
Main Street
PO Box 270
Brookneal, VA 24528

Suffolk-Nansemond Historical Society
PO Box 1255
Suffolk, VA 23439-1255
(757) 562-4403

Mrs. Carl R. Saunders, Chair, Genealogy Committee

Tazewell County Historical Society, Inc.
100 Fincastle Turnpike
PO Box 916
Tazewell, VA 24651-0916
(540) 988-4069; (540) 988-3581 (Mrs. Surface)
Patricia W. Surface
Hours: Wed 11:00–1:00, and by appointment; meetings first Sun 2:30
Pub. *Tazewell County Historical Society Newsletter*, quarterly (March, June, September, December)
(five published volumes of photo albums, mostly before 1925)
$12.00 per year membership, $125.00 life membership

Warren Heritage Society
101 Chester Street
Front Royal, VA 22630
(540) 636-1446
Ben Weddle, President
Hours: Mon–Fri 10:00–4:00
Pub. *WHS Newsletter*, quarterly
$15.00 per year membership for individuals, $25.00 per year membership for families

Historic Society of Washington County, Virginia, Inc.
Old Courthouse
East Main Street
PO Box 484
Abingdon, VA 24212-0484
(540) 628-2813 (President); (540) 628-4052 (Librarian)
L. C. Angle, Jr., President; Nancy Leasure, Librarian
Hours: Mon–Fri 10:00–4:00
Pub. *News Letter*, five times per year; *The Historical Society of Washington County Virginia Bulletin*, annually
(computer database with over 240,000 entries)
$15.00 per year membership for individuals, $20.00 per year membership for families; free search, copies 20¢ each plus postage, send SASE for information

Waterford Foundation, Inc.
PO Box 142
Waterford, VA 20197
(540) 882-3018; (540) 882-3921 FAX
Martha Baine, Archivist; Bronwen Souders, Genealogical Researcher and Historian
Hours: by appointment
(Waterford families and history, especially history and genealogies of the black families in Waterford)
$35.00 per year foundation membership, from $50.00 Friends of Waterford membership

Williamsburg Area Historical Society
285 Neck-O-Land Road
Williamsburg, VA 23185
(757) 229-2158
Ed Belvin, Former Vice President
(presently inactive but still answers inquiries; deals only with local history from 1800, not genealogy)

Winchester-Frederick County Historical Society
1340 South Pleasant Valley Road
Winchester, VA 22601-4447
(540) 662-6550; (540) 662-6991 FAX
E-mail: wfchs@shentel.net
Cissy Shull, Executive Director
Hours: Mon–Fri 9:00–5:00
Pub. *Winchester-Frederick County Historical Society Journal*; *Newsletter*, quarterly
$15.00 per year membership for individuals, $25.00 per year membership for couples, $100.00 per year Patron membership, $350.00 life membership for individuals, $500.00 per year life membership for couples

The Wise County Historical Society
(Wise County Courthouse, Main Street—archives and office location)
PO Box 368 (mailing address)
Wise, VA 24293
(540) 328-6451
Rhonda Robertson, Secretary
Hours: 9:00–4:30 by appointment (office manned by volunteers)
Pub. *The Appalachian Quarterly* (March, June, September, December), $10.00 per year subscription
(quarterly covers the southern Appalachians: Kentucky, Tennessee, North Carolina, Virginia and West Virginia)
$10.00 per year membership for individuals, $15.00 per year membership for families; queries answered if accompanied by SASE

Wythe County Historical Society
(Rock House Museum, Monroe and Tazewell—location)
205 Tazewell Street (mailing address)
Wytheville, VA 24382-2313
(540) 228-3841
Pub. *Wythe County Historical Review*, quarterly
$15.00 per year membership

LDS Family History Centers

Arlington
(see Falls Church or Oakton)

Chesapeake
(see Virginia Beach)

Falls Church
(703) 256-5518

Newport News
(see Virginia Beach)

Norfolk
(see Virginia Beach)

Oakton
(703) 281-1836

Richmond
(804) 288-8134

Roanoke
(see Salem)

Salem
(540) 562-2052

Virginia Beach
(757) 467-3302

Genealogical Societies

State Genealogical Societies

Genealogical Research Institute of Virginia
PO Box 29178
Richmond, VA 23242-0178
Jean B. Robinson, President
Pub. *G.R.I. News 'N Notes*, quarterly
(September, December, March, June)
$10.00 per year subscription
$10.00 per year membership for
individuals, $15.00 per year
membership for couples (beginning in
July); no research is done

Virginia Genealogical Society
5001 West Broad Street, Suite 115
Richmond, VA 23230-3023
(804) 285-8954; (804) 285-0394 FAX
http://www.fgs.org/~fgs/soc0197.htm
Emily Rusk, Executive Director
Pub. *Magazine of Virginia Genealogy*,
quarterly; *The Virginia Genealogical
Society Newsletter*, bimonthly
(February, April, June, August,
October, December)
$23.00 per year membership for
individuals and institutions/
associations $25.00 per year
membership for families

Regional Genealogical Societies

**Central Virginia Genealogical
Association, Inc. (CVGA)**
PO Box 5583
Charlottesville, VA 22905-5583
Marilyn Koleszar, President

Pub. *Central Virginia Heritage*, quarterly
(includes present-day Albemarle,
Amherst, Appomattox, Augusta,
Bedford, Buckingham, Campbell,
Culpeper, Cumberland, Fluvanna,
Greene, Goochland, Louisa, Madison,
Nelson, Orange, Page, Rockbridge,
Rockingham and Shenandoah
counties)
$12.50 per year membership for
individuals (beginning in January),
$15.00 per year membership for
couples

Fairfax Genealogical Society
PO Box 2290
Merrifield, VA 22116-2290
(703) 536-6205; (888) 828-4121
Hours: Fairfax City Regional Library,
Virginia Room: Mon–Thur 9:00–9:00,
Fri 9:00–6:00, Sat 9:00–5:00, Sun
12:00–8:00
Pub. *Newsletter*, five times per year
(September to May)
(published five volumes of Fairfax
County gravestones)
$10.00 per year membership for
individuals, $15.00 per year
membership for families; list of local
researchers available

**Harrisonburg-Rockingham
Genealogical Society**
Rt. 1, Box 489
Mount Crawford, VA 22841-9522
Elizabeth Keagy, Past Secretary
(society currently inactive, but the past
secretary will answer queries with
SASE and will do some research for a
fee)

**Holston Territory Genealogical
Society**
PO Box 433
Bristol, VA 24203-0433
(423) 968-4815
Mrs. Vandy Mauk, Corresponding
Secretary
Pub. *The Holston Pastfinder*, quarterly
(September, December, March, June)
(emphasis on southwest Virginia and
northeast Tennessee genealogy and
history)
$18.00 per year membership for
individuals, $20.00 per year
membership for couples

Loudoun Genealogy Society
PO Box 254
Leesburg, VA 20178
(703) 779-1328 (Thomas Balch Library)
E-mail:ktitus@mindspring.com
Karen Titus, President
Hours: meeting first Wed 7:00
Pub. *Loudoun: The 1757 Legacy*,
quarterly
$10.00 per year membership

**Lower Delmarva Genealogical
Society**
(see Maryland)

**The Memorial Foundation of the
Germanna Colonies in Virginia, Inc.**
PO Box 693
Culpeper, VA 22701-0693
(540) 825-1496; (540) 825-6572 FAX
E-mail: germanna@summit.net
http://www.summit.net/germanna/
Rose Marie Martin, Office Administrator
Hours: Germanna Community College
Library: Mon–Fri 9:00–5:00
Pub. *Germanna*, quarterly; *The
Germanna Record*, occasionally
(extensive collection of genealogy,
history and biography pertaining to the
pioneer settlers composing the
Germanna Colonies in Virginia, 1714
and 1717, later arrivals and their
descendants, including the following
families: Aker, Albright, Amberger,
Amburger, Ashby, Aylor, Bach, Back,
Baker, Ballenger, Barber, Barler,
Barlow, Baumgardner, Beer, Bender,
Benneger, Beyerback, Blankenbaker,
Boehm, Broyles, Brumbach,
Brumback, Bungard, Burdyne, Bush,
Button, Camper, Carpenter, Castler,
Chelf, Christler, Christopher, Clore,
Cobbler, Coller, Cook, Coon, Coons,
Corber, Cornwell, Crecelieus, Crees,
Crest, Crible, Crigler, Crim, Crumber,
Cuntz, Darnall, Deal, Deer, Delf,
Delph, Diehl, Duncan, Everhart,
Farrow, Fick, Finder, Finks, Fishbach,
Fishback, Fisher, Fite, Flender,
Fleshman, Folg, Frank, Fray,
Friesenhagen, Gansler, Garr, Graham,
Haeger, Hager, Hanback, Harnsberger,
Heide, Heite, Herndon, Hirsh, Hitt,
Hoffman, Holt, Holtzclaw, Hoop,
House, Huettenhen, Huffman, Jacoby,
Kabler, Kaifer, Kaiffer, Kaines,
Kemper, Kerchler, Kerker, Kines,
Klug, Kneisler, Koontz, Kooper,
Kriebel, Kuenzle, Kyner, Lang,
Langenbuehl, Latham, Leach,
Leatherer, Leathers, Lederer, Lehman,
Lipp, Long, Lotspeich, Lyons,
Manspeil, Martin, Mauck, McClure,
Michael, Miller, Motz, Moyer, Nay,
Newby, Noeh, Nunnamaker, Oehler,
Oehlschutt, Ohlschlagel, Patt, Paulitz,
Peck, Prosie, Racer, Railsback,
Reading, Rector, Rinehart, Riner,
Rodeheaver, Rouse, Russell, Schut,
Shafer, Sheible, Sheibley, Sheibly,
Sinclair, Slaughter, Slucter, Smith,
Snyder, Sohlbach, Souther, Spillman,
Spilman, Staehr, Stature, Stigler,
Stinesyfer, Stoever, Stoltz,
Stonecipher, Stover, Stuell, Swindell,
Tanner, Tapp, Teter, Thomas, Troller,
Tullser, Urbach, Utterback, Utz,
VanMeter, Vaught, Vogt, Walke,
Walker, Wayland, Wayman, Weaver,

Weingart, Whitescarver, Wieland, Wiley, Wilhoit, Willer, Willheit, Yager, Yeager, Young, Yowell, Ziegler, Zimmerman, Zollicoffer)
$10.00 per year membership for individuals, $15.00 per year membership for families, $150.00 life membership

Mount Vernon Genealogical Society

Hollin Hall Senior Center
1500 Shenandoah Road
Alexandria, VA 22308
E-mail: mdcb77a@prodigy.com
Ed Schott, Coordinator
Hours: Library: Tuesday 10:00–2:00; meetings: second Wed 1:00
Pub. *Mt. Vernon Genealogical Society Newsletter*, monthly
$10.00 per year membership for individuals, $12.00 per year membership for couples/families

Genealogical Society of Page County, Virginia

Page Public Library
100 Zerkel Street
Luray, VA 22835

Palm Beach County Genealogical Society, Inc.

(see Florida)

Portsmouth Genealogical Society

Portsmouth Public Library
(601 Court Street, Portsmouth, VA 23704—location)
3908 Turnpike Road (mailing address)
Portsmouth, VA 23701
(757) 393-1205; (757) 393-8501 (Library)
Bettie Jo Matthews, President
Hours: Library: Mon–Fri 9:00–9:00, Sat 9:00–5:00; meeting: fourth Sat 2:00
Pub. *Portsmouth Genealogical Society Newsletter*, quarterly
(extensive information on Norfolk County, including every tombstone in the area, births, deaths, obituaries)
$12.00 per year membership; research: $7.50 per hour, five-hour minimum

Prince William County Genealogical Society

PO Box 2019
Manassas, VA 22110-0812
(703) 754-2234
Sallie C. Pusey, Registrar
Pub. *Kindred Spirits (The Newsletter of the Prince William County Genealogical Society)*, monthly
$10.00 per year membership for individuals, $12.00 per year membership for families

Southwestern Virginia Genealogical Society, Inc.

PO Box 12485
Roanoke, VA 24026-2485

Pub. *Virginia Appalachian Notes (VAN)*, quarterly (February, May, August, November)
(includes southwestern Virginia and Roanoke Valley)
$20.00 per year membership for individuals and families, $15.00 per year membership for organizations and libraries (beginning in January), $10.00 additional for membership outside the U.S

The Hugh S. Watson, Jr., Genealogical Society of Tidewater Virginia

(d.b.a. Tidewater Genealogical Society)
PO Box 7650
Hampton, VA 23669
(757) 220-0618 (President)
William B. Hankins, Jr., President
Pub. *Virginia Tidewater Genealogy*, quarterly
("No capability for individual research but will answer queries with SASE.")
$15.00 per year membership

Virginia Beach Genealogical Society

PO Box 62901
Virginia Beach, VA 23466-2901
(757) 340-0770 (President)
http://www.infirnet/~cwt/vbas.html
R. W. Kirby, President
Hours: Virginia Beach Central Library: Mon–Thur 10:00–9:00, Fri–Sat 10:00–5:00, Sun (Oct–May) 1:00–5:00
Pub. *VBGS Newsletter*, quarterly (February, May, August, November)
$10.00 per year membership for individuals, $15.00 per year membership for families living at the same address; queries for non-members: $1.00 each

VA-NC-Piedmont Genealogical Society

(The Danville Public Library, 511 Patton Street, Second Floor—library and office location)
PO Box 2272 (mailing address)
Danville, VA 24541-0272
(804) 799-5195
E-mail: vancsoc@juno.com
Marilyn Halstead, Corresponding Secretary
Hours: Search Room: Tue 2:00–5:00, Thur 6:00–9:00 (first Thur 3:00–6:00), Fri 10:00–5:00, Sat 10:00–1:00
Pub. *Piedmont Lineages*, quarterly, $5.00 per issue
$15.00 per year membership; queries free to members, $1.00 for first 50 words and $2.00 for anything over 50 words to non-members

Independent Publications and Miscellany

Appalachian Roots

(see West Virginia)

Beyond Germanna

PO Box 120
Chadds Ford, PA 19317
(610) 388-1305
E-mail: johblank@pipeline.com
http://www.wp.com/germanna; http://www.concentric.net/nsgtgeorg/germhist.shtml
John Blankenbaker, Publisher
Hours: varies
Pub. *Beyond Germanna, A Newsletter for Virginia Piedmont Germans*, six times per year, $12.00 per year subscription
(specializes in early 18th century, interested in settlers' origins, history, genealogies, associated families, and dispersion to other areas; "The word 'Germanna' refers to the location in Virginia where Lt. Gov. Alexander Spotswood settled a small group of Germans in 1714; today Germanna is located in Orange County in a horseshoe bend of the Rapidan River where Virginia State Highway 3 crosses the Rapidan.")

Blue Ridge Institute

State Route 40
Ferrum, VA 24088
(540) 365-4415
J. Roderick Moore, Director
Pub. *BRI Records*

The Colonial Williamsburg Foundation

Foundation Library
415 North Boundary Street
PO Box 1776
Williamsburg, VA 23187-1776
(757) 220-7423 (Reference Desk)
Elizabeth Ackert, Public and Information Services Librarian
Hours: Reference: Mon–Fri 10:00–5:00
Pub. *Colonial Williamsburg*, quarterly, $35.00 per year subscription
(Williamsburg, Virginia—18th-century; "Our focus is Williamsburg residents.")

Cox/Phillips

PO Box 186
Southmont, NC 27351
(910) 798-2401
Elza B. Cox, Editor
Pub. *Cox/Phillips Newsletter*, quarterly, $10.00 per year subscription
(emphasis on southwest Virginia)

Fairfax County Publications Center

12000 Government Center Parkway, Suite 156
Fairfax, VA 22035
(703) 324-2974

(distributes books published by the Fairfax County Office of Comprehensive Planning, by the Fairfax County History Commission, and by other county governmental organizations)

Family Line Publications
(see Maryland)

Family Tree Exchange
Rt. 1, Box 330
Fulks Run, VA 22830
Jackie Puffenberger,Editor
Pub. *Family Tree Exchange* (Pendleton County, West Virginia, and Rockingham County, Virginia), irregularly

Genealogical Institute
Family History World
(875 North 300 East, Tremonton, UT—location)
PO Box 22045 (mailing address)
Salt Lake City, UT 84122
(801) 250-6717 phone and FAX; (801) 245-0256; (801) 829-4030
E-mail: eakle@xmission.com
Arlene H. Eakle; JoAnn Jackson, Office Manager
Hours: Mon–Fri 9:00–5:00
Pub. *Research News*, occasionally, $3.00 per issue plus postage and handling; *Immigration Digest* (English and Southern research), occasionally, $13.50 per issue plus postage and handling

Genealogy Books and Consultation
(see Texas)

Historic Fincastle, Inc.
East Murray Street
PO Box 19
Fincastle, VA 24090
(540) 473-2022
Mrs. Harry Kessler, Chairman, Archives
Hours: by appointment only
(Fincastle Rifles, Civil War Unit, G. N. Fulton-Potter, Lewis and Clark, cemetery records before 1900, Fincastle and Botetourt counties history; "We offer limited genealogy research.")
$5.00 per year membership

Historic Occoquan, Inc.
413 Mill Street
PO Box 65
Occoquan, VA 22125
(703) 491-7525

Historic Vienna, Inc.
PO Box 53
Vienna, VA 22180
(703) 938-5187

Hunting for Bears Genealogical and Historical Society
(see Alabama)

Lineage Search Associates
6419 Colts Neck Road
Mechanicsville, VA 23111-4233
(804) 730-7414 phone and FAX; (800) 728-1935
E-mail: michael-pollock1@juno.com
Michael E. Pollock, President
Hours: Mon–Sat 8:00 A.M.–10:00 P.M.
Pub. *Frederick Findings*, quarterly, $25.00 per year ($47.50 for two years) subscription for individuals, $22.50 per year ($40.00 for two years) subscription for libraries
(the Shenandoah Valley and eastern panhandle of West Virginia: Clarke, Frederick, Page, Shenandoah and Warren counties, Virginia, and Berkeley, Grant, Hampshire, Hardy, Jefferson, Mineral and Morgan counties, West Virginia)
three free queries per issue to members, $8.00 for non-subscriber queries, includes issue in which the query appears

Lineages, Inc.
Department A-F
PO Box 417
Salt Lake City, UT 84110
(800) 338-5114
Johni Cerny, President
Pub. *Before Germanna* (monograph series), $10.00 per issue

The Mountain Empire Genealogical Quarterly
PO Box 628
Pound, VA 24279
(540) 796-5233
Joan S. Vanover, Executive Secretary
Pub. *The Mountain Empire Genealogical Quarterly* (Kentucky, North Carolina, Tennessee, Virginia and West Virginia), quarterly, $20.00 per year subscription

Mountain Press
(see Tennessee)

Northern Virginia Association of Historians
George Mason University, History Department
Fairfax, VA 22030
(703) 323-2242

Northern Virginia Genealogy
39475 Tollhouse Road
Lovettsville, VA 20180-9703
(540) 822-5292
E-mail: willowbend@mediasoft.net
Craig R. Scott, Editor
Pub. *Northern Virginia Genealogy*, quarterly (January, April, July, October), $22.00 per year subscription
(includes records relating to Alexandria City and the counties of Arlington, Fairfax, Fauquier, Loudoun, and Prince William)
free queries to subscribers

Simmons Historical Publications
(see Kentucky)

Southern Genealogist's Exchange Society
(see Florida)

The Southside Virginian
(2236 Cedar Crest Road—location)
PO Box 3684 (mailing address)
Richmond, VA 23235
(804) 272-4875
Kathryn Hooper, Managing Editor
Pub. *The Southside Virginian: A Journal of Genealogy and History*, quarterly (January, April, July, October)
$20.00 per year membership

Southwest Virginia Ancestors Quarterly
Rt. 2, Box 307
Clintwood, VA 24228
(540) 926-6837
Betty R. Mullins, Editor
Hours: Mon–Fri 8:00–5:00
Pub. *Southwest Virginia Ancestors Quarterly* (spring, summer, fall, winter)
$20.00 per year membership

Southwest Virginian
1046 Spruce Street
Norton, VA 24273
Rhonda S. Roberson,Editor
Pub. *Southwest Virginian, Journal of Genealogy and History Covering Virginia This Side of the Blue Ridge*, bimonthly, $14.00 per year subscription

Surname Searchers Quarterly
1231 Quicksburg Road
Quicksburg, VA 22847
Pub. *Surname Searchers Quarterly*

Tidewater Virginia Families
316 Littletown Quarter
Williamsburg, VA 23185-5519
(757) 220-4888; (757) 220-0975 FAX
Virginia Lee Hutcheson Davis, Publisher/Editor
Hours: 9:00–5:00 & 7:00–8:00
Pub. *Tidewater Virginia Families: A Magazine of History and Genealogy* (Tidewater history and genealogy, including Caroline, Charles City, Elizabeth City, Essex, Gloucester, Hanover, Henrico, James City, King and Queen, King George, King William, Lancaster, Mathews, Middlesex, New Kent, Richmond, Northumberland, Warwick, Westmoreland, and York counties; "unpublished county, church, Bible records, and family histories"), quarterly (February/March, May/June, August/September, November/December), $20.00 per year subscription; $25.00 per year foreign subscription

Topp of the Line
1304 West Cliffwood Court
Spokane, WA 99218-2917
(509) 467-2299
E-mail: toppline@cet.com
Bette Butcher Topp
Pub. *Virginia/West Virginia Queries*,
  irregularly, $7.75 postpaid, standing
  order option

VaGenWeb
Part of U.S. GenWeb Project
E-mail: va@usgenweb.com
http://www.rootsweb.com/ vagenweb
(links to other Virginia resources)

The Virginia Genealogist
PO Box 5860
Falmouth, VA 22403-5860
John Frederick Dorman,Editor
Pub. *The Virginia Genealogist*, quarterly,
  $25.00 per year subscription
(includes Virginia and West Virginia)

Virginia Genealogy and History News
Rt. 3, Box 65
Chandler, OK 74834-8504
R. D. Bradshaw,Editor
Pub. *Virginia Genealogy and History
  News*

Virginia Military Institute
Virginia History and Museums
  Federation
Jackson Memorial Hall
Lexington, VA 24450
(703) 463-6232

Virginia Settlers
653 Pershing Drive
Walnut Creek, CA 94596
(510) 938-9248
A. Maxim Coppage, F.S.A. Scot, Editor
Pub. *Virginia Settlers*, quarterly, $12.50
  per year subscription
(families to and from "Old" Virginia and
  Kentucky, Maryland and North
  Carolina)

Virtual Library of Virginia
E-mail: gailmac@vt.edu
http://scholar2.lib.vt.edu/spec/viva/
  viv.htm

WASHINGTON

Archives and Libraries with Holdings in Genealogy

State Archives and Library

Washington State Archives, Main Office
Division of Archives and Records
  Management
Office of the Secretary of State
Washington State Archives and Records
  Center Building
1120 Washington Street, S.E. (EA-11)
Olympia, WA 98504
(360) 586-1492
David Hastings, Chief, Archival Services
  Section
Hours: Mon–Fri 8:00–12:00 & 1:00–
  4:30

Washington State Archives, Central Regional Branch
Bledsoe-Washington Archives Building
Central Washington University-MS 7547
Ellensburg, WA 98926-7547
(509) 963-2136; (509) 963-1753 FAX
Hours: Mon–Fri 8:30–4:30
(Benton, Chelan, Douglas, Franklin,
  Grant, Kittitas, Klickitat, Okanogan,
  and Yakima counties)

Washington State Archives, Eastern Regional Branch
Eastern Washington University, MS-84
TAW 211
Cheney, WA 99004-2423
(509) 359-6900; (509) 359-2476 FAX
Richard Hobbs
Hours: 8:00–5:00; research: 9:00–noon
  & 1:00–4:00
(Adams, Asotin, Columbia, Ferry,
  Garfield, Lincoln, Pend Oreille,
  Spokane, Stevens, Walla Walla, and
  Whitman counties; records of local
  government agencies and state
  agencies with local offices)
free admission; search fees: $25.00 per
  hour, $10.00 minimum

Washington State Archives, Northwest Region
State Archives Building
Western Washington University
Bellingham, WA 98225-9123
(360) 650-3125
James D. Moore, Regional Archivist;
  Susan B. Fahey, Regional Archivist
Hours: Mon–Fri 8:30–noon & 1:30–
  4:30; on-site research by appointment
  only
(Clallam, Island, Jefferson, San Juan,
  Skagit, Snohomis, and Whatcom

---

counties; original records of county,
city government, local schools)

Washington State Archives, Puget Sound Branch
3 Sunset Activity Center
Seattle, WA 98168
(206) 764-4276
(King, Kitsap, and Pierce counties)

Washington State Archives, Southwest Regional Branch
1120 Washington Street, S.E.
Olympia, WA 98504
(360) 459-6363; (360) 753-1684
(Clark, Cowlitz, Grays Harbor, Lewis,
  Mason, Pacific, Skamania, Thurston,
  and Wahkiakum counties)

Washington State Library
Washington/Northwest Collection
PO Box 2475
Olympia, WA 98504-2475
(360) 753-4024
http://www.wa.gov/wsl
Gayle Palmer, Senior Librarian
Hours: Mon–Fri 10:00–5:00
(participates in inter-library loan service;
  genealogical holdings relate to
  Washington state only)

State Historical Societies

Washington State Historical Society
Heritage Resource Center
211 West 21st Avenue
Olympia, WA 98501
(360) 586-0219
E-mail: jpeterson@wshs.wa.gov
http://www.wshs.org/
Jean Peterson, Editor
Pub. *Washington Heritage Bulletin*,
  quarterly
$10.00 per year membership

Washington State Historical Society
Special Collections Division
315 North Stadium Way
Tacoma, WA 98403
(253) 798-5914
http://www.kcts.org/columbia/
  aboutwsh.htm
E. K. C. Nolan, Curator
Hours: Tue–Thur 12:30–4:30, by
  appointment only
Pub. *Columbia: Magazine of Northwest
  History*, quarterly
("We do not gather genealogical
  materials, nor do we do genealogical
  research; we have transferred most of
  our genealogical material to the
  Tacoma Public Library, which does
  specialize in genealogy; we don't
  maintain death indexes, obituary
  collections, photographs, ephemera,
  etc.")
$32.00 per year membership for
  individuals

City, County and Regional Archives and Libraries

Adam East Museum and Art Center
122 West Third
PO Box 1579
Moses Lake, WA 98837
(509) 766-9395
Chris Fiala Erlich, Director
Hours: Tue–Sat: noon-5:00
Pub. *Membership Letter—MAC Happenings*, quarterly
("Historical and archives, scholastic or public; have started an education program and local history project")
$15.00 per year Booster membership for individuals, $10.00 per year membership for families, $50.00 per year Sponsor membership, $100.00 per year Patron membership, $500.00 per year Benefactor membership

Auburn Public Library
808 Ninth Street S.E.
Auburn, WA 98002
Hours: Mon–Thur 10:00–9:00, Fri 10:00–6:00, Sat 10:00–5:00

Bellingham Public Library
Research Desk
210 Central Street
PO Box 1197
Bellingham, WA 98225
(360) 676-6860
Hours: Mon–Thur 10:00–9:00, Fri–Sat 10:00–6:00, Sun (Sept–May) 12:00–5:00; volunteer research help: Wed 10:00–2:00
(genealogy collection of about 1,200 titles, broad coverage; collection of journals from about 140 genealogical societies, many dating 1975–1995)

Bellvue Regional Library
1111 110 Avenue, N.E.
Bellevue, WA 98004
(425) 450-1760
http://www.kcls.org
Hours: Mon–Thur 10:00–9:00, Fri 10:00–6:00, Sat 10:00–5:00, Sun 1:00–9:00

Bleyhl Community Library
311 Division Street
Grandview, WA 98930
(509) 882-9217
Linda Dunham, Librarian
Hours: Mon–Thur 1:30–9:00, Tue & Thur 10:00–noon, Fri–Sat 1:30–5:30
("Grandview history; some early birth, marriage and death records for Yakima County 1869–1903; Grandview cemetery records to 1972; many high school annuals 1913 to the present; Grandview history [some photos] chronological, not indexed")
search fees: postage and photocopies at 50¢ per page

Burlington Public Library
900 East Fairhaven Street
Burlington, WA 98233
(206) 755-0760
E-mail: burlpl@sos.net
M. Darlene Maloy, Library Director
Hours: Mon–Thur 11:00–8:00, Fri–Sat 11:00–5:00

Colville Public Library
195 South Oak
Colville, WA 99114
Hours: Tue–Fri 11:00–6:00

Cowlitz County Historical Museum
405 Allen Street
Kelso, WA 98626
(360) 577-3119
David W. Freece, Museum Director
Hours: Mon–Sat 9:00–5:00 by appointment
Pub. *Cowlitz Historical Quarterly* (emphasis on Cowlitz County and southwest Washington), $15.00 per year subscription

Du Pont Historical Museum
(207 Brandywine Avenue—location)
PO Box 173 (mailing address)
Du Pont, WA 98327-0173
(253) 964-8895

Ellensburg Public Library
209 North Ruby Street
Ellensburg, WA 98926-3338
(509) 962-7250; (509) 962-7295 FAX
Celeste Kline, Library Director
Hours: Mon–Fri 10:00–8:30, Sat 10:00–5:00, Sun 1:00–5:00
("local history collection of books, archival local club materials, extensive local history photographs, oral history audio-cassette collection; pamphlets, newspapers on microfilm")

Everett Public Library
2702 Hoyt Avenue
Everett, WA 98201

The Fiske Genealogical Foundation
1644 43rd Avenue East
Seattle, WA 98112-3222
(206) 328-2716
Mary C. Stevenson, Librarian
Pub. *Newsletter*, quarterly
(over 7,500 volumes concentrating on the thirteen original states plus Tennessee, Kentucky, Ohio and Indiana; also a uniquecollection of card files)
library admission: $5.00 per day or $40.00 per year for individuals, $2.50 per day or $20.00 per year for students

Fort Vancouver Regional Library
1007 East Mill Plain Boulevard
Vancouver, WA 98663
(360) 695-1566
http://www.furl.org

Hours: Mon–Thur 10:00–9:00, Fri–Sat 10:00–6:00, Sun 1:00–9:00
(Clark County history)

Gonzaga University
Special Collections Department
Foley Center Library
Spokane, WA 99258
(509) 328-4220, ext. 3814; (509) 324-5904 FAX
E-mail: edwards@foley.gonzaga.edu
http://www.gonzaga.edu/foley/speccoll.html
(Jesuit Oregon Province Archives)

Hacksma House Genealogy Library
1815 Grant Road
East Wenatchee, WA 98802
(509) 884-7662
Nellie Bruton Hacksma
Hours: by appointment only
(primarily Eastern and Southern emphasis: Alabama, Arkansas, Georgia, Illinois, Indiana, Iowa, Kentucky, Mississippi, Missouri, North Carolina, Tennessee, Texas, and Virginia)

Highline Community College
PO Box 98000
Des Moines, WA 98198
(206) 878-3710, ext. 230
Nancy Lennstrom, Librarian
Hours: Mon–Thur 7:45 A.M.–9:30 P.M., Fri 7:45-4:45, Sat 12:00–4:00 (except summer)

Kittitas County Museum
114 East Third Avenue
PO Box 265
Ellensburg, WA 98926
(509) 925-3778

Klondike Gold Rush National Historical Park—Seattle Unit
117 South Main Street
Seattle, WA 98104
(206) 553-7220; (206) 553-0614 FAX
Willie Russell, Superintendent
Hours: 9:00–5:00
(research library; Klondike Gold Rush 1896–98, emphasis on Seattle)

Longmire Museum
General Delivery
Longmire, WA 98397
(360) 569-2211

Makah Cultural and Research Center
PO Box 160
Neah Bay, WA 98357

Marymoor Museum
6046 West Lake Sammamish Parkway
PO Box 162
Redmond, WA 98073-0162
(425) 885-3684
Kimberly Haas, Director
Hours: Tue–Thur 11:00–4:00, Sun 1:00–5:00

Pub. *Marymoor Musings*, quarterly
$15.00 per year membership for
   individuals, $25.00 per year
   membership for families, $10.00 per
   year membership for senior citizens

Mid Columbia Library
405 South Dayton
Kennewick, WA 99336
(509) 586-3156; (509) 586-8887 FAX
Thomas Moak, Senior Librarian
Hours: Mon–Wed 9:00–9:00, Thur–Sat
   9:00–5:00

Museum and Arts Center
175 West Cedar Street
Sequim, WA 98382-3318
(360) 683-8110; (360) 683-8364 FAX
Margaret De Witt, Director
Hours: Mon–Sun 9:00–4:00
Pub. *Peninsula Arts and History Review*,
   two times per year
$15.00 per year membership for
   individuals, $30.00 per year
   membership for families

Neill Public Library
North 210 Grand Avenue
Pullman, WA 99163

North Central Washington Museum
127 South Mission
Wenatchee, WA 98801
(509) 664-5989
Mary L. Thomsen, Editor; Mark Behler,
   Archivist
Hours: Mon–Fri 8:00–5:00
Pub. *The Confluence*, quarterly, $2.00
   per issue
("We do have an archival library with
   extensive holdings; in addition, we
   house the Genealogical Society of
   North Central Washington's library;
   they are an affiliate organization.")

Old Molson and Schoolhouse Museums
(Main Street, Molson, WA—location)
915 Nine Mile-Molson Road (mailing
   address)
Oroville, WA 98844
(509) 485-3292 phone and FAX
Mary Louise Loe, Museum Director
Hours: Old Molson: Apr–Nov: daylight
   hours; Schoolhouse Museum:
   Memorial Day weekend–Labor Day:
   10:00–5:00
(Okanogan Highlands history and
   artifacts from the early 1900s)

Olympia Timberland Library
Eighth and Franklin Streets
Olympia, WA 98501
(360) 352-0595
Hours: Mon–Thur 10:00–9:00, Fri–Sat
   10:00–5:00, Sun (Oct–May) 1:00–5:00

Othello Community Museum
Third and Lurch
PO Box 121
Othello, WA 99344
(509) 488-2268

Richland Public Library
955 Northgate Drive
Richland, WA 99352
(509) 943-7457
Ms. Judy McMakin, Reference Librarian
Hours: summer: Mon–Thur 10:30–9:00,
   Fri–Sat 10:30–5:30; Sept–May: Mon–
   Fri 10:30–9:00, Sat 10:30–5:30, Sun
   1:00–5:00

Scouting Trail Museum
156th Street, S.E., and Des Moines Way
Seattle, WA 98146
(206) 767-6467

Seattle Municipal Archives
600 Fourth Avenue, Room 104
Seattle, WA 98104
(206) 684-8353; (206) 386-9025
E-mail: scott.cline@ci.seattle.wa.us
http://www.pan.ci.seattle.wa.us/seattle/
   leg/clerk/archhome.htm

Seattle Public Library
Genealogy Section, Humanities
   Department
1000 Fourth Avenue
Seattle, WA 98104
(206) 386-4629 (Genealogy); (206) 386-
   4625 (Humanities)
E-mail: infospl@spl.lib.wa.us
http://www.spl.lib.wa.us/collec/geneal/
   genpage.html
Darlene E. Hamilton, Humanities
   Librarian-Genealogy
Hours: Mon–Thur 9:00–9:00, Fri–Sat
   9:00–6:00
(Genealogy Collection covers U.S., with
   some regions stronger than others;
   library also has a separate Northwest
   History Collection)

Library and Historical Museum (Shaw Island)
Blind Bay Road
Shaw Island, WA 98286
Frances Hilen, Curator

Shoreline Historical Museum
749 North 175th Street
PO Box 7171
Seattle, WA 98133
(206) 542-7111
Victoria Stiles, Director
Hours: Tue–Sat 10:00–4:00
Pub. *Shoreline Historical Museum
   Newsletter*, quarterly
$10.00 per year membership for
   individuals, $25.00 per year
   membership for families, $5.00 per
   year membership for senior citizens or
   students, $50.00 per year membership
   for businesses, $1,000.00 life
   membership

Sidney Museum and Arts Association
202 Sidney Avenue
Port Orchard, WA 98366
(360) 876-3693

Spokane Public Library
West 906 Main Avenue
PO Box 1826
Spokane, WA 99210-1826
Hours: Mon–Tue & Thur–Fri 9:00–9:00,
   Wed 1:00–6:00, Sat (except late Jun–
   Sept) 9:00–6:00
(two different collections, one for
   genealogy and one on the Pacific
   Northwest)

Steilacoom Historical Museum Association
122 Main Street
PO Box 88016
Steilacoom, WA 98388
(253) 584-4133
Hours: Nov–Dec & Feb: Fri–Sun 1:00–
   4:00; Mar–Oct: Tue–Sun 1:00–4:00
Pub. *Steilacoom Historical Museum
   Quarterly*
(some local genealogy materials)
$20.00 per year membership for
   individuals, $30.00 per year
   membership for families, $15.00 per
   year membership for senior citizens,
   $25.00 per year membership for senior
   citizen families; free admission

Suquamish Museum
15838 Sandy Hook Road, N.E.
PO Box 498
Suquamish, WA 98392
(360) 598-3311
Leonard Forsman, Museum Director

Tacoma Public Library
1102 Tacoma Avenue South
Tacoma, WA 98402
(253) 591-5622
http://www.tpl.lib.wa.us/
Gary Fuller Reese, Managing Librarian
Hours: Mon–Thur 9:00–9:00, Fri–Sat
   9:00–6:00

Toppenish Museum
1 South Elm
Toppenish, WA 98948
(509) 865-4510
Hours: Tue–Sat 1:30–4:30, and by
   appointment

University of Washington Libraries
Special Collections and Preservation
   Division
Allen Library
Box 352900
Seattle, WA 98195-2900
(206) 543-1929
E-mail: crick@u.washington.edu
http://www.washington.edu/
Carla Rickerson, Pacific Northwest
   Librarian

Hours: Mon–Fri 10:00–5:00, Sat 9:00–
5:00 (hours vary between quarters
when school is not in session)
(emphasis on local history rather than
genealogy, particularly Pacific
Northwest history)

Walla Walla Public Library

238 East Alder
Walla Walla, WA 99362
(509) 527-4550
Stephen C. Towery
Hours: Mon–Thur 10:00–9:00, Fri–Sat
10:00–5:00

Washington State University

Holland Library
Pullman, WA 99164-5610
Hours: 8:00–11:45
("no genealogy collection, just research
materials")

Western Frontier Museum

2301 23rd Avenue, S.E.
Puyallup, WA 98372
(253) 845-4402

Whitman County Library System

South 102 Main Street
Colfax, WA 99111
(509) 397-4366; (509) 397-6156 FAX
Steve Kenworthy, Director; Kristie
Kirkpatrick, Director of Public
Services
Hours: Mon–Thur 9:00–8:00, Fri 9:00–
6:00, Sat 9:00–5:00

Wilson Library

Western Washington University
Bellingham, WA 98225
(360) 650-3193
Virginia Beck, Special Collections
Manager
Hours: Mon–Fri 8:00–5:00
("We have biographical information for
some faculty and area residents.")

Women's Heritage Center

5226 17th, N.E.
Seattle, WA 98105
(206) 784-6569
Lela Hilton, President

Historical Societies—
Local and Regional

Adams County Historical Society Museum

Phillips Building
Lind, WA 99341
(509) 677-3219

Anderson Island Historical Society

9306 Otso Point Road
Anderson Island, WA 98303
(206) 884-2135
Ray Walberg, President

Hours: Memorial Day weekend to Labor
Day weekend: 12:00–4:00

Asotin County Historical Society

(215 Filmore Street—location)
PO Box 367 (mailing address)
Asotin, WA 99402-0367
(509) 243-4659
Ruth L. Harris, Attendant
Hours: Tue–Sat 1:00–5:00
Pub. *Membership Memos*, two times per
year

Benton County Museum and Historical Society, Inc.

Seventh Street and Paterson Road
PO Box 591
Prosser, WA 99350
(509) 786-3842

Black Diamond Historical Society

32627 Railroad and Baker Streets
PO Box 232
Black Diamond, WA 98010
(360) 886-2142; (360) 886-1168
Robert Eaton, President
Hours: Sat–Sun 12:00–3:00, Thur 9:00–
4:00
Pub. *Newsletter*, quarterly
$5.00 per year membership

Chehalis Valley Historical Society

(703 West Pioneer, Montesano, WA
98563—location)
268 Oak Meadows Lane (mailing
address)
Oakville, WA 98568
(360) 273-8044 (Librarian); (360) 249-
5800 (Museum answering machine)
Mrs. Kelle A. Davis, Genealogical
Librarian
Hours: Museum: Sat–Sun 1:00–4:00
Pub. *The Chehalis Valley Historian*,
quarterly
("Chehalis [pre-1913] and Grays Harbor
County [after 1913] information from
Montesano to eastern county line:
towns of Elma, Malone, Porter,
Oakville and Montesano; this is not
connected with the Town of Chehalis,
Washington, nor the county (Lewis) it
is located in; our county's name was
changed from Chehalis County to
Grays Harbor County in 1913.")
$10.00 per year membership for
individuals, $8.00 per year
membership for students and senior
citizens

Chelan County Historical Society

600 Cottage Avenue
PO Box 22
Cashmere, WA 98815
(509) 782-3230
Jim Wilson, President; Geri Inabnit,
Museum Coordinator
Hours: Mon–Sat 10:00–4:30, Sun 1:00–
4:30
$10.00 per year membership for
individuals, $25.00 per year

---

membership for families, $25.00 per
year junior or senior membership

Clallam County Historical Society

Clallam County Museum
223 East Fourth Street
Port Angeles, WA 98362-3098
(360) 417-2364
Kathy Monds, Museum Manager
Hours: Sept–May: Mon–Fri 10:00–4:00;
Jun–Aug: Mon–Sat 10:00–4:00
(Clallam County history)
$15.00 per year membership

Cle Elum Historical Society

(Carpenter House Museum, 320 West
Third—location)
413 East Second Street (mailing address)
Cle Elum, WA 98922-1205
(509) 674-2268; (509) 674-5702
Cecelie Maybo, President
Hours: May 15–Sept 15
("We do not have much written history at
this time."; also Telephone Museum,
221 East First, PO Box 11, Cle Elum,
WA 98922)

Columbia County Genealogical and Historical Society

Rt. 1, Box 43
Dayton, WA 99328

Duvall Historical Society

PO Box 385
Duvall, WA 98019
Don Williams, President
Pub. *Wagon Wheel Newsletter*, ten times
per year (monthly, September–June),
$5.00 per year subscription
$5.00 per year membership, $2.00 per
year membership for senior citizens

East Benton County Historical Society

(205 Keewaydin Drive—location)
PO Box 6964 (mailing address)
Kennewick, WA 99336
(509) 582-7704
Vickie Bergum, Director
Hours: Tue–Sat 12:00–4:00
Pub. *The Courier*, quarterly
(large local listing of alphabetized
obituaries, research with reference
materials and files which may be used
on site)
$15.00 per year membership

Eastern Lewis County Historical Society

Old Settlers Museum
Gust Backstrom Park
PO Box 777
Morton, WA 98356
(360) 496-5602 (Treasurer); (360) 496-
3348 (President)
Alma Chamberlain, President
Hours: Fri–Sun (Jun–Aug) 1:00–4:00,
and alternated with 5:00–8:00

Eastern Washington State Historical Society

West 2316 First Avenue
Spokane, WA 99204-1006
(509) 456-3931; (509) 456-7690 FAX
Karen DeSeve, Curator of Special
  Collections
Hours: Tue–Thur 1:30–4:30
Pub. *Museum Notes*, quarterly

Eatonville Historical Society

42310 Lynch Creek Road
Eatonville, WA 98328
(360) 832-6096

Edmonds South Snohomish County Historical Society and Museum

118 Fifth Avenue, North
PO Box 52
Edmonds, WA 98020
(425) 774-0900
Joni Sein, Museum Director
Hours: Tue, Thur & Sat–Sun 1:00–4:00
Pub. *Museum Light*, quarterly
(local history of Edmonds and South
  Snohomish County)
$15.00 per year membership for
  individuals, $25.00 per year
  membership for families, $50.00 per
  year membership for businesses,
  $100.00 per year Sustaining
  membership, $300.00 per year
  Benefactor membership

Fort Vancouver Historical Society of Clark County, Inc.

(Clark County Historical Museum, 1511
  Main Street—location)
PO Box 1834 (mailing address)
Vancouver, WA 98668
(360) 695-4681 (Museum)
Gus Norwood, Museum Director; Vernon
  Peterson, President
Hours: Tue–Sat 1:00–5:00
Pub. *Clark County History*, annually
$6.50 per year membership

Fox Island Historical Society

PO Box 242
Fox Island, WA 98333-0242
(206) 549-2461

Franklin County Historical Society and Museum

305 North Fourth Street
Pasco, WA 99301
(509) 547-3714; (509) 545-2168
Jacque Sonderman, Administrator
Hours: Tue–Fri 1:00–5:00, Sat 10:00–
  5:00
Pub. *The Franklin Flyer*, quarterly, $2.25
  per issue; *Newsletter*
$15.00 per year membership; admission:
  $10.00 for non-members

Gig Harbor Peninsula Historical Society

3510 Rosedale Street
PO Box 744
Gig Harbor, WA 98335

Chris Fiala Erlich, M.A.
Hours: Office: Mon & Wed 9:00–12:00;
  Museum: Wed–Sat 1:00–4:00
Pub. untitled membership newsletter,
  quarterly
$15.00 per year membership for
  individuals, $25.00 per year
  membership for families, $5.00 per
  year membership for students, $50.00
  per year Donor membership, $100.00
  per year Supporter membership

Granite Falls Historical Society

Corner Wabash and Indiana Street
PO Box 135
Granite Falls, WA 98252
(360) 691-7640

Greater Des Moines-Zenith Historical Association and Museum

728 225th South
PO Box 98055
Des Moines, WA 98198
(206) 878-7552
Melanie Draper, Curator
Pub. *Timber, Tides and Tales*

Greater Woodinville Historical Society

PO Box 216
Woodinville, WA 98926
(425) 483-2811

Ilwaco Heritage Foundation Research Library

(117 S.E. Lake Street—location)
PO Box 153 (mailing address)
Ilwaco, WA 98624
(360) 665-3446
Theresa Potter
Hours: Mon–Sat 10:00–4:00, Sunday
  (summer) 10:00–4:00

Index Historical Society-Pickett Museum

505 Avenue A
PO Box 107
Index, WA 98256
(360) 793-1534
Louise Lindgren, Director
Hours: Sun (Memorial Day weekend–
  Labor Day weekend) 12:00–3:00
Pub. *Newsletter*, quarterly
(names from town records, extensive
  photo collection; mining, logging and
  quarry history, local floods, and
  general history of the Index area)
$10.00 per year membership for
  individuals, $15.00 per year
  membership for families; free museum

Island County Historical Society

908 N.W. Alexander Street
PO Box 305
Coupeville, WA 98239
(360) 678-3310
Sandra Plush, Museum Manager
Hours: winter: Mon & Fri–Sun 11:00–
  4:00; summer: Mon–Sun 10:00–5:00
Pub. *Island Heritage*, quarterly

Issaquah Historical Society

165 S.E. Andrews Street
PO Box 695
Issaquah, WA 98027
(425) 392-3500
Greg Spranger, Chairman
Hours: noon-4:00, Sat 10:30–2:30, and
  by appointment
Pub. *Newsletter*, quarterly

Jefferson County Historical Society and Museum

210 Madison
Port Townsend, WA 98368
(360) 385-1003
E-mail: jchsmuseum@olympus.net
Dr. Nicki Clark, Director
Hours: Mon–Sat 11:00–4:00, Sun 1:00–
  4:00
Pub. *JCHS Newsletter*, quarterly
(Jefferson County history)
$15.00 per year membership for
  individuals, $20.00 per year
  membership for families, $7.50 per
  year membership for senior citizens,
  $30.00 per year Patron membership,
  $50.00 per year Sponsor membership,
  $200.00 per year Sustaining
  membership, $1,000.00 life
  membership; research: $10.00 per hour

Association of King County Historical Organization

PO Box 3257
Seattle, WA 98114
Dick Wagner, President
Hours: meetings: last Tue (except Jul &
  Dec)
Pub. *AKCHO Member Roster*, biannually
  (even years)
$10.00 per year membership for
  individuals, $25.00 per year
  membership for organizations

Kitsap County Historical Society

PO Box 903
Bremerton, WA 98337-0206
Suzanne T. Anest, Museum Director
Hours: Tue–Sat 10:00–5:00
(Kitsap County history)

Lake Chelan Historical Society

204 East Woodin Avenue
PO Box 1948
Chelan, WA 98816
(509) 682-5644
David H. Davis, President
Hours: Mon–Sun (Jun–Sept) 1:00–4:00,
  and by appointment
Pub. *Lake Chelan History Notes*,
  irregularly
$5.00 per year membership

Lewis County Historical Society

Lewis County Historical Museum
Genealogical Committee
599 N.W. Front Street
Chehalis, WA 98532
(360) 748-0831
Brenda A. O'Connor, Museum Director

Hours: Tue–Sat 9:00–5:00, Sun 1:00–5:00
Pub. *Lewis County Log*, quarterly ("approximately 30,000 obituary files 1966 through 1993, many earlier, but not consecutive; photograph file, 12,000 catalogued, varied subjects; local history files and family files")
$15.00 per year membership, $10.00 per year membership for senior citizens and students

Lincoln County Historical Society
Park and Sixth Street
PO Box 585
Davenport, WA 99122
(509) 725-6711; (509) 726-0561 (Treasurer)
Verna Johns, Treasurer
Hours: Museum: daily (May–Sept) 9:00–5:00
Pub. *Lincoln County Historical Society Newsletter*, semiannually
$10.00 per year membership

Lopez Island Historical Society and Museum
PO Box 163
Lopez Island, WA 98261
(360) 468-2049; (360) 468-3447 (Curator's home)
Nancy McCoy, Curator
Hours: Jul–Aug: Wed–Sun noon–4:00; May–Jun & Sept: Fri–Sun noon–4:00
$5.00 per year membership for individuals

Maple Valley Historical Society
23015 S.E. 216th Way
PO Box 123
Maple Valley, WA 98038
(425) 432-3470
Dan Nicholas, President
Hours: Museum: first & third Sat 11:00–3:00
Pub. *Maple Valley Bugle*, quarterly
$10.00 per year membership for individuals; small local history booklet, annually

Mason County Historical Society Museum
(427 Railroad Avenue—location)
PO Box 1366 (mailing address)
Shelton, WA 98584
(360) 426-1020
Michael Fredson, President; Billie L. Howard, Museum Director
Hours: Tue–Fri noon–5:00, Sat noon–4:00
Pub. *Mason County Historical Society Newsletter*, ten times per year (monthly, March–December)
$12.00 per year membership for individuals, $15.00 per year membership for families, $100.00 life membership

Newcastle Historical Society
14553 S.E. 55th Street
Bellevue, WA 98006
(425) 746-2482

Okanogan County Historical Society and Museum
(1410 Second, North—location)
PO Box 1129 (mailing address)
Okanogan, WA 98840
(509) 422-4272; (509) 422-1355 FAX
Marilynn Moses, Coordinator; Donald Case, Director
Hours: Museum: May–Sept: 11:00–4:00; Research Center: 8:00–noon
Pub. *The Okanogan County Heritage*, quarterly
(Research Center houses library, photo collections, historical documents, interviews, maps, etc.)
$15.00 per year membership for individuals, $300.00 life membership

Pacific County Historical Society and Museum Foundation
(1008 West Robert Bush Drive, South Bend, WA 98588—location)
PO Box P (mailing address)
South Bend, WA 98586
(360) 875-5224
Bruce Weilepp, Museum Director
Hours: Mon–Sun 11:00–4:00
Pub. *The Sou'wester*, quarterly
(Washington history, local history; proper name index to local newspapers)
$20.00 per year membership

Pacific Northwest Historians Guild
PO Box 45687
Seattle, WA 98145-0687
Richard Engeman, President
Pub. *Northwest Historian*, bimonthly
(Washington, Oregon and Idaho region)
$15.00 per year membership

Pend Oreille County Historical Society
402 South Washington Avenue
PO Box 1409
Newport, WA 99156
(509) 447-5388; (509) 447-2770 (President)
Evelyn Reed, President
Hours: Mid-May to end of September: Mon–Sun 10:00–4:00, and the rest of the year by appointment; Research library: by appointment
Pub. *The Big Smoke* (stories written by former or present residents), annually, $7.00 per issue
(some family histories and area histories, large photo collection and local weekly back to 1900)
$5.00 per year membership (does not include periodical); donations accepted

Polson Park and Museum Historical Society
PO Box 432
Hoquiam, WA 98550
(360) 533-5862
Toni Gwin, Curator-Manager

Puget Sound Maritime Historical Society
Museum of History and Industry
2700 24th Avenue, East
Seattle, WA 98112
(206) 524-5013
Robert McNeil, President

Renton Historical Society and Museum
235 Mill Avenue, South
Renton, WA 98055
(425) 255-2330
Stanley D. Greene, President
Pub. *Renton Historical Society and Museum Newsletter*, quarterly
$6.00 per year membership

Roslyn Historical Museum Society
PO Box 281
Roslyn, WA 98941
(509) 649-2776 (Curator)
Mary Andler, Curator
Hours: 1:00–4:00, and by appointment

San Juan Historical Society
405 Price Street
PO Box 441
Friday Harbor, WA 98250
(360) 378-3949
Jennifer Fleming, Director
Hours: Apr–Sept: Wed–Sat 1:00–4:00; Oct–Mar: Tue & Thur 10:00–2:00
Pub. *SJHS Newsletter*, quarterly
$10.00 per year membership for individuals, $25.00 per year membership for families, $5.00 per year membership for senior citizens, $7.50 per year membership for senior citizen couples

Historical Society of Seattle and King County
(d.b.a. Museum of History and Industry)
(address withheld upon request)
$15.00 per year membership

Skagit County Historical Society
Skagit County Historical Museum
501 South Fourth Street
PO Box 818
La Conner, WA 98257
(360) 466-3365
James G. Barmore, Museum Director
Hours: Public: Tue–Sun 11:00–5:00
Pub. *Skagit County Historical Society Quarterly Newsletter*
$15.00 per year membership for individuals, $25.00 per year membership for families, $10.00 per year membership for senior citizens (65 and over) or students (full time, under 21), $50.00 per year Patron

membership, $50.00 per year membership for organizations, $250.00+ Benefactor membership

Skamania County Historical Society
PO Box 396
Stevenson, WA 98648
(509) 427-5141, ext. 235
Sharon Tiffany, Director
Pub. *Skamania County Heritage*, quarterly
$7.00 per year membership

Snohomish County Museum and Historical Association
(Legion Park—location)
2602 Rainier Street (mailing address)
Everett, WA 98201

Snohomish Historical Society
(118 Avenue B—location)
PO Box 174 (mailing address)
Snohomish, WA 98290
(360) 568-5235
Laura Cameron-Behee, Archivist
(maintains Blackman Museum and Old Snohomish Village)

Snoqualmie Valley Historical Society and Museum
320 South North Bend Boulevard
PO Box 179
North Bend, WA 98045
(425) 888-2053
Mary Ferrell, Curator

South Thurston County Historical Society
(Tenino Depot Museum, Park Street—location)
PO Box 339 (mailing address)
Tenino, WA 98589
(360) 264-4321; (360) 264-4637
Jean Montgomery, President
Hours: 18 Apr–15 Oct: Fri–Sun noon–4:00
$5.00 per year membership; search fees vary, including cost for copies

Southeastern Lincoln County Historical Society
General Delivery
Sprague, WA 99032

Southwest Seattle Historical Society
c/o South Seattle Community College
6000 16th Avenue, S.W.
Seattle, WA 98106
(206) 764-5357; (206) 764-5371
Hours: Mon–Fri 8:00–4:30
Pub. *Footprints*, quarterly
(history/artifacts of West Seattle and White Center)
$10.00 per year membership for individuals

Stevens County Historical Society, Inc.
700 North Wynne Street
PO Box 25
Colville, WA 99114

(509) 684-5968
William E. Winn, Jr., Curator/Administrator
Pub. *In-Review*
$10.00 per year membership

Sumner Historical Society
Sumner Ryan House Museum
1228 Main Street
PO Box 517
Sumner, WA 98390
(253) 863-8936
Dorothy Peterkin, Curator
Hours: Apr–Oct & Dec: Wed & Sat–Sun 1:00–4:00, and by appointment
Pub. *Quarterly Newsletter*
("research of pioneer family history and early history of the area")
$7.50 per year membership, $100.00 life membership; donations accepted

Sunnyside Museum and Historical Association
Fourth and Grant Street
PO Box 782
Sunnyside, WA 98944
(509) 837-6010

Tacoma Historical Society
PO Box 1865
Tacoma, WA 98401
Pub. *City of Destiny Newsletter*
$15.00 per year membership

Tumwater Historical Association
PO Box 4315
Olympia, WA 98501-0315

Vashon Maury Island Heritage Association
PO Box 723
Vashon, WA 98070
(206) 567-4663

Waitsburg Historical Society
Fourth and Main Street
PO Box 442
Waitsburg, WA 99361
(509) 337-6582

Walla Walla Valley Pioneer and Historical Society
Fort Walla Walla Museum Complex
Myra Road
Walla Walla, WA 99362
(509) 525-6966 (Museum); (509) 525-7703 (Society)
C. William Burk, Museum Director

Whatcom County Historical Society
PO Box 2116
Bellingham, WA 98227
(360) 676-0582
Neill D. Mullen, Sales
Pub. *Newsletter*, five to six times per year, not available by subscription
$10.00 per year membership

White River Valley Museum
918 H Street, S.E.
Auburn, WA 98002

(253) 939-2783 (information); (253) 939-4523 (staff); (253) 931-5105 FAX
Patricia Cosgrove, Museum Director
Hours: Museum: Thur–Sun 1:30–4:30, and by appointment
Pub. *Newsletter*, quarterly
(reference library with collection of area newspapers, photographs, documents and school annuals)
$15.00 per year membership for individuals, $25.00 per year membership for families, $10.00 per year senior membership, $3.00 per year junior membership, $50.00 per year Club membership, $100.00 per year Corporate membership, $250.00 per year Benefactor membership, $500.00 per year Corporate Benefactor membership

Whitman County Historical Society
PO Box 67
Colfax, WA 99111
(509) 332-5752; (509) 332-1029
Larry R. Stark, Editor
Hours: Wed morning
Pub. *Bunchgrass Historian*, quarterly
$10.00 per year membership

Yakima Valley Museum and Historical Association
2105 Tieton Drive
Yakima, WA 98902
(509) 248-0747
Versa C. K'ang, Director
Pub. *Museum Musette*

LDS Family History Centers

Auburn
(206) 735-2009

Bellevue
(206) 454-2690

Bellingham
(360) 738-1849

Bremerton
(206) 479-9370

Federal Way
(206) 874-3803

Mountlake Terrace
(206) 776-6678

Olympia
(360) 705-4176

Richland
(509) 946-6637

Seattle
(206) 522-1233

Spokane
(509) 926-0551

Tacoma
(206) 564-1103

Vancouver
(360) 896-5567

Yakima
(509) 452-3626

Genealogical Societies

State Genealogical Society

Washington State Genealogical Society
PO Box 1422
Olympia, WA 98507-1422
(360) 352-0595
http://www.thurston.com/~rmccoy/
wsgshome.htm
Roger H. Newman, Corresponding
Secretary
Pub. *Washington State Genealogical
Society Newsletter*, bimonthly
$10.00 per year membership for
individuals or societies

Regional Genealogical Societies

Chelan Valley Genealogical Society
PO Box Y
Chelan, WA 98816
(509) 682-5131 (Library)
Hours: Chelan City (Public) Library:
Mon–Sat
Pub. *The Apple Orchard*, bimonthly
("We are collecting Chelan County
records")
$10.00 per year membership for
individuals, $12.50 per year
membership for families; researchers
available, send SASE for fees

Clallam County Genealogical Society
Clallam County Museum
223 East Fourth Street
Port Angeles, WA 98362-3098
(360) 417-1284
Virginia Fitzpatrick, President
Hours: Mon–Fri 10:00–4:00, Sat (Jul–
Aug) 10:00–4:00
Pub. *CCGS Bulletin*, quarterly
(general genealogical research,
specializing in Clallam County)
$20.00 per year membership for
individuals (includes membership in
Clallam County Historical Society),
$30.00 per year dual membership;
research: $5.00 per hour plus copies,
$5.00 minimum

Clark County Genealogical Society
(Clark County Historical Museum, 1511
Main Street—location)
PO Box 2728 (mailing address)
Vancouver, WA 98668-2728
(360) 695-4681 (Museum); (206) 574-
2909 (President)
E-mail: germann@worldacces.com
http://www.worldaccess.com/
NonProfitOrganizations/ccgs/
Jane Germann, President
Hours: Tue–Sat 1:00–5:00
Pub. *"Trail Breakers"—Clark County
Genealogical Society*, quarterly;
Newsletter
$15.00 per year membership for
individuals, $20.00 per year joint
membership, $300.00 life membership

Columbia County Genealogical and Historical Society
Rt. 1, Box 43
Dayton, WA 99328

Douglas County Genealogical Society
PO Box 580
Waterville, WA 98858

Eastern Washington Genealogical Society
PO Box 1826
Spokane, WA 99210-1826
(509) 838-4226
http://www.onlinepub.net/ewgs
Doris Woodward, Editor
Pub. *The Bulletin*, quarterly
$20.00 per year membership

Eastern Washington Genealogical Society
Metis Genealogical Society Chapter
North 6206 Washington
Spokane, WA 99208
Pub. *Newsletter of Genealogical
Research of the North American
Indian*, quarterly
$3.50 per year membership

Eastside Genealogical Society
PO Box 374
Bellevue, WA 98024
(425) 885-2012 (President)
Connie Balazic, President
Hours: Bellevue, Washington, Public
Library: Mon–Thur 10:00–9:00, Fri
10:00–6:00, Sat 10:00–5:00, Sun
1:00–5:00
Pub. *The Bulletin Board*, eleven times
per year
$10.00 per year membership for
individuals, $15.00 per year dual
membership, $8.00 per year
membership for seniors or students,
$12.00 per year dual membership for
seniors

Grant County Genealogical Society
Ephrata Public Library
45 Alder Street, N.W.
Ephrata, WA 98823-1663
Alvena Johnson, President
Hours: Mon–Thur 10:00–8:00, Fri
10:00–4:00, Sat 11:00–4:00
Pub. *Big Bend Register*, quarterly
$10.00 per year membership; research
fee: by donation

Grays Harbor Genealogy Club
PO Box 867
Cosmopolis, WA 98537-0867
(360) 249-4632
Jack Willis, President
Pub. *Grays Harbor Genealogical Society
News*, monthly
$12.00 per year membership; research
fees vary

Jefferson County Genealogical Society
210 Madison
Port Townsend, WA 98368
(360) 385-1003
Joan Buhler, Corresponding Secretary
Hours: Mon–Sat 11:00–4:00, Sun 1:00–
4:00
Pub. *Jefferson County Genealogical
Society Newsletter*, quarterly
$10.00 per year membership (calendar
year)

Kittitas County Genealogical Society
(413 North Main, Suite D—location)
PO Box 1342 (mailing address)
Ellensburg, WA 98926
(509) 925-5951
Margorie E. Boles, Librarian; Virginia C.
Hanks, Librarian
Hours: Mon–Fri 10:00–4:00
Pub. *Kittitas County Kin Folk*, quarterly
$10.00 per year membership

Lewis County Historical Society
Lewis County Historical Museum
Genealogical Committee
599 N.W. Front Street
Chehalis, WA 98532
(360) 748-0831
Brenda A. O'Connor, Museum Director
Hours: Tue–Sat 9:00–5:00, Sun 1:00–
5:00
Pub. *Lewis County Log*, quarterly
("approximately 30,000 obituary files
1966 through 1993, many earlier, but
not consecutive; photograph file,
12,000 catalogued, varied subjects;
local history files and family files")
$15.00 per year membership, $10.00 per
year membership for senior citizens
and students

Lower Columbia Genealogical Society
(Longview Public Library—location)
PO Box 472 (mailing address)
Longview, WA 98632-7306

(360) 423-1388 (President's home)
Pat Crimmel, President
Hours: Library: Mon noon–9:00, Tue–Thur 10:00–9:00, Fri 10:00–5:00
Pub. *The Key*, quarterly
$10.00 per year membership for individuals, $15.00 per year membership for couples; research: $5.00 per hour, one-hour minimum, plus SASE and copies at 50¢ per page

Northeast Washington Genealogical Society
c/o Colville Public Library
195 South Oak
Colville, WA 99114
(509) 935-6336
Doris Winskie, President
Hours: Library: Tue–Fri 11:00–6:00
Pub. *Pioneer Branches*, quarterly
$12.00 per year membership for individuals, $15.00 per year membership for couples

Okanogan County Genealogical Society
(Okanogan County Historical and Genealogical Research Center, 1410 Second, North, Okanogan, WA 98840—location)
263 Old Riverside Highway (mailing address)
Okanogan, WA 98841
(509) 826-1686
E-mail: lolag@televar.com
Lola Power, Librarian
Hours: Mon–Fri 9:00–noon, afternoons by appointment
$15.00 per year membership for individuals, $20.00 per year membership for families; search fees: variable

Olympia Genealogical Society
PO Box 1313
Olympia, WA 98507
Roger H. Newman, Research Chairman
Pub. *Olympia Genealogical Society Quarterly*
(Thurston County, Washington, records)
$15.00 per year membership; research fee: send SASE

Pacific County Genealogical Society
PO Box 843
Ocean Park, WA 98640
(360) 665-6293
Joy G. Taylor, Editor
Hours: daytime
Pub. *Clan Digger*, monthly
(emphasis on southwest Washington genealogy)
$10.00 per year membership for individuals, $12.50 per year membership for families

Puget Sound Genealogical Society
1026 Sidney Avenue, Suite 110
Port Orchard, WA 98366-4298

http://www.rootsweb.com/~wapsgs/homepage.htm
Bill Richardson, President
Hours: fourth Tue (Mar–Oct) 7:00, (Nov–Dec) 1:00
Pub. *Family Backtracking*, quarterly
$12.00 per year membership for individuals, $15.00 per year membership for families; queries as space allows

Seattle Genealogical Society
8511 15th Avenue, N.E.
PO Box 1708
Seattle, WA 98111
(206) 522-8658
Sarah Little
Hours: Mon 6:30–9:00, Tue–Sat 10:00–3:00
Pub. *Seattle Genealogical Society Newsletter*, monthly; *Seattle Genealogical Society Bulletin*, quarterly
(specializes in Washington and Scandinavia)
$20.00 per year membership for individuals, $25.00 per year dual membership; search fee: $8.00

Skagit Valley Genealogical Society
PO Box 715
Conway, WA 98238-0715
E-mail: hrasar@ncia.com
Hazel Rasar, President
Hours: meetings at Mount Vernon Presbyterian Church, 1511 East Broadway: fourth Tue 7:00
Pub. *Skagit Valley Genealogical Society Newsletter*, quarterly
(publishes local death records)
search for $10.00 donation

Sno-Isle Genealogical Society
(Martha Lake Community Club, Alderwood Manor, WA—location)
PO Box 63 (mailing address)
Edmonds, WA 98020
(425) 776-1938
Judith Thompson, President
Hours: meetings first Wed 7:30
Pub. *The Sounder*, quarterly
$15.00 per year membership, $22.50 per year membership for families; queries free to members

South King County Genealogical Society
(Auburn Public Library, 808 Ninth Street S.E., Auburn, WA 98002—collection location)
PO Box 3174 (mailing address)
Kent, WA 98032-0203
Susan Coles, President
Hours: Library: Mon–Thur 10:00–9:00, Fri 10:00–6:00, Sat 10:00–5:00
Pub. *The So King Newsletter*, bimonthly
$10.00 per year membership

Steilacoom Genealogy Organization
c/o Steilacoom Historical Museum Association
122 Main Street
PO Box 88016
Steilacoom, WA 98388
(253) 588-2585
Cy Happy

Stillaguamish Valley Genealogical Society and Library
(Library, 20325 71st Avenue, Suite B—location)
PO Box 34 (mailing address)
Arlington, WA 98223
(360) 435-4838 (Library)
Darrel Trudeau, Jr., President
Hours: Tue 12:00–4:00, Wed 6:00–9:00, Thur 10:00–4:00
Pub. *Stillaguamish Star*, bimonthly
(Civil War collection, including War of the Rebellion series)
$12.00 per year membership for individuals, $15.00 per year membership for families, $10.00 per year membership for societies or libraries

Tacoma/Pierce County Genealogical Society
PO Box 1952
Tacoma, WA 98401
(253) 572-6650 (President)
Maxine Carpenter, President
Hours: Tacoma Public Library: Mon–Thur 9:00–9:00, Fri–Sat 9:00–6:00
Pub. *The Researcher*, quarterly
$14.00 per year membership for individuals, $15.00 per year dual membership

Tonasket Genealogical Society
PO Box 84
Tonasket, WA 98855
(509) 826-0837; (509) 486-4677; (509) 476-2187
Noma Wyllson, President
Hours: by appointment
(Okanogan County)
$10.00 per year membership

Tri-City Genealogical Society
PO Box 1410
Richland, WA 99352-1410
(509) 783-4262 (Editor's home)
Leona W. George, Editor
Hours: daytime
Pub. *Tri-City Genealogical Society Bulletin*, semiannually (May and November)
(northwest genealogy)
$10.00 per year membership

Walla Walla Valley Genealogical Society
PO Box 115
Walla Walla, WA 99362
E-mail: gengwen@televar.com
Gwen Wall, President

Pub. *Blue Mountain Heritage*, quarterly
$10.00 per year membership for
individuals or families

**Wenatchee Area Genealogical
Society**
(133 South Mission—location)
PO Box 5280 (mailing address)
Wenatchee, WA 98807-5280
(509) 664-3346
Joanne M. Calhoun, President
Hours: North Central Washington
Museum Annex Building: Tue–Thur &
Sat 1:00–4:00
Pub. *Appleland Bulletin*, quarterly
("Records for North Central Washington,
including Chelan and Douglas
counties")
$15.00 per year membership for
individuals, $17.00 per year
membership for two persons at the
same address

Whatcom Genealogical Society
PO Box 1493
Bellingham, WA 98227-1493
(360) 734-9835
Robert G. Witherspoon, President
Hours: meetings at Bellingham Public
Library: second Mon (Sept–Jun) 7:00
Pub. *The Bulletin*, quarterly
(emphasis on northwestern Washington
genealogy, Whatcom, San Juan and
Skagit counties)
$12.00 per year membership for
individuals (calendar year), $18.00 per
year membership for families;
research: $7.50 per hour for local
records; free queries for non-members

**Whitman County Genealogical
Society**
(WCGS Library, Gladish Building, 115
West Main—location)
PO Box 393 (mailing address)
Pullman, WA 99163-0393
(509) 332-2386 (Editor)
http://www.wsu.edu:8080/~mbsimon/
wcgs/index.html
Judy Standar McMurray, Editor
Hours: Neill Public Library: Wed 8:30
A.M.–11:00 A.M., and by appointment
Pub. *Whitman County Genealogical
Society News Letter*, ten times per year
$12.00 per year membership

**Willapa Harbor Genealogical
Society**
Raymond Public Library
507 Duryea Street
Raymond, WA 98577

Yakima Valley Genealogical Society
(basement of First Christian Church,
Third and B Streets—location)
PO Box 445 (mailing address)
Yakima, WA 98907-0445
(509) 248-1328
Ellen Brzoska, Librarian

Hours: Mon–Fri 10:00–4:00, Sat (Oct–
May) 10:00–4:00
Pub. *Yakima Valley Genealogical Society
Bulletin*, quarterly
(Washington area and nationwide
bibliographies, indexes and society
bulletins; obituary index kept to date
of Yakima County deaths, coordinates
cemeteries, sexton's records and
mortuary records)
$15.00 per year membership for
individuals, $16.00 per year
membership for families

Independent Publications and Miscellany

Northwest Pioneer
East 13124 Nixon
Spokane, WA 99216
Joanne M. Elliott
Pub. *Northwest Pioneer (Oregon,
Washington, Idaho, and Montana)*,
$6.00 per volume

Oregon/Washington Queries
(see Oregon)

University of California Press
Pacific Historical Review
(see California)

WaGenWeb
Part of U.S. GenWeb Project
E-mail: wa@usgenweb.com
http://www.rootsweb.com/~wagenweb
(links to other Washington resources)

WEST VIRGINIA

Archives and Libraries with Holdings in Genealogy

State Archives and Library

Archives and History Section
West Virginia Division of Culture and
History
The Cultural Center
Capitol Complex, 1900 Kanawha
Boulevard, East
Charleston, WV 25305-0300
(304) 558-0230
http://www.wvlc.wvnet.edu/history/
wvsamenu.html
Fredrick H. Armstrong, Director,
Archives and History
Hours: Office: 8:30–5:00; Library: Mon–
Fri 11:00–6:00, Sat 1:00–5:00
Pub. *West Virginia History*, annually,
$12.00 per issue; *Goldenseal*,
quarterly, $15.00 per year subscription

State Historical Society

West Virginia Historical Society
West Virginia Division of Culture and
History
The Cultural Center
Capitol Complex, 1900 Kanawha
Boulevard, East
Charleston, WV 25305-0300
(304) 348-2277; (304) 348-0230
Rodney A. Pyles, Director
Hours: Mon–Thur 9:00–9:00, Fri 9:00–
5:00, Sat 1:00–5:00
Pub. *West Virginia Historical Society
Newsletter*
$15.00 per year membership

City, County and Regional Archives and Libraries

Alderson-Broaddus College
Pickett Library
College Hill
Philippi, WV 26416
(304) 457-1700, ext. 306
Edward Gibson, Head Librarian

**Allegany College of Maryland
Library**
Appalachian Collection
(see Maryland)

Americana Museum
401 Aurora Avenue
Terra Alta, WV 26764
(304) 789-2361; (304) 789-2418 FAX
Ruth E. Teets, Owner

Hours: summer: by appointment only
admission $2.00 for adults, $1.00 for
children

Cabell County Public Library
Huntington Public Library
455 Ninth Street Plaza
Huntington, WV 25701
(304) 523-9451
Sarah Gibbs, Head of Reference
Hours: Mon–Wed 9:00–9:00, Thur–Sat
9:00–5:00; summer hours vary

Clarksburg-Harrison Public Library
West Virginia Collection
404 West Pike Street
Clarksburg, WV 26301
(304) 624-6512, ext. 21
Ernest Kalay, Curator, Main Library;
John Nesbitt, Curator, West Virginia
Room
Hours: West Virginia Room: Mon–Fri
9:00–noon & 1:00–5:00, Sat 9:00–
noon

Hampshire County Public Library
153 West Main Street
Romney, WV 26757
(304) 822-3185; (304) 822-3955 FAX
E-mail: riffle_b@wvlc.wvnet.edu
Brenda Riffle, Librarian
Hours: Mon & Fri 10:00–8:00, Tue–Thur
10:00–6:00, Sat 10:00–4:00
copies 50¢ plus SASE; will do limited
research

Hardy County Public Library
102 North Main Street
Moorefield, WV 26836
(304) 538-6560
Marjorie Zirk, Librarian
Hours: Mon–Sat 9:00–4:30
(census & newspapers on microfilm,
family histories, maps, books)
20¢ per page for copying, plus state tax

Jackson County Public Library
208 North Church Street
Ripley, WV 25271
(304) 372-5343; (304) 372-5344 FAX
E-mail: pauleyl@wvlc.wvnet.edu;
rauhed@wvlc.wvnet.edu
http://www.wvlc.wvnet.edu/juackson/
libl.html
Lynn Pauley, Circulation/ILL, Ed Rauh,
Director;
Hours: Mon & Fri 10:00–5:00, Tue–Thur
10:00–8:00, Sat 10:00–3:00; last week
in May through first week in
September: Mon–Wed & Fri 10:00–
5:00, Thur 10:00–8:00, Sat 10:00–3:00
search requests are handed over to a
volunteer and can take some time to
be answered

Kanawha County Public Library
123 Capitol Street
Charleston, WV 25301
(304) 343-4646; (304) 348-6530
http://kanawha.lib.wv.us/

Susan H. Harper
Hours: Mon–Fri 9:00–9:00, Sat 9:00–
5:00, Sun (Sept–Apr) 1:00–5:00
(West Virginia local history only, no
genealogy)

Marshall University
James E. Morrow Library
Special Collections Department
Huntington, WV 25755
(304) 696-2343; (304) 696-5858 FAX
E-mail: speccoll@marshall.edu
http://www.marshall.edu/
Lisle G. Brown
Hours: university sessions: Mon–Wed
8:00–10:00, Thur–Fri 8:00–4:30, Sun
1:30–9:30
(local history and genealogy)

Martinsburg-Berkeley County Public Library
101 West King Street
Public Square
Martinsburg, WV 25401
(304) 267-8933; (304) 267-9720 FAX
Keith E. Hammersla, Reference
Librarian
Hours: Mon–Fri 9:00–9:00, Sat 9:00–
5:00, Sun 1:00–5:00

Menno Simons Historical Library
(see Virginia)

Morgantown Public Library
373 Spruce Street
Morgantown, WV 26505
(304) 291-7425
Donna Rae Houatter, Reference
Specialist
Hours: Mon–Thur 9:00–8:00, Fri–Sat
9:00–5:00
(a small collection specializing in West
Virginia history and Monongalia
County genealogy; "Invites completed
searches (genealogical) pertinent to the
northern West Virginia or southwestern
Pennsylvania area.")
$10.00 per search (includes staff time,
postage, and up to ten pages of
photocopying)

Old Charles Town Library
200 East Washington Street
Charles Town, WV 25414
(304) 725-2208
Anne Post Proudman, Librarian
Hours: Mon–Tue & Thur 9:00–9:00,
Wed & Fri 9:00–6:00, Sat 9:00–1:00
(emphasis on Shenandoah Valley
genealogy, West Virginia history and
Civil War history)

Parkersburg and Wood County Public Library
3100 Emerson Avenue
Parkersburg, WV 26104
(304) 420-2587; (304) 420-4589 FAX
Lindsay Roseberry, Reference Librarian

Hours: Mon–Thur 9:00–9:00, Fri–Sat
9:00–5:00, Sun (Labor Day–Memorial
Day) 1:00–5:00
(local and statewide collection; "One of
the best genealogical libraries in
northern West Virginia.")
$1.00 for research, 10¢ per copy plus
postage or SASE

Philippi Public Library
102 South Main Street
Philippi, WV 26416
Mary Ellen Weekley, Library Director
Hours: Mon–Fri 9:00–8:00, Sat 10:00–
1:00

General Adam Stephen Memorial Association, Inc.
309 East John Street
PO Box 1496
Martinsburg, WV 25402-1496
(304) 267-4434

Sunrise Museums
746 Myrtle Road
Charleston, WV 25314
(304) 344-8035

Mary H. Weir Public Library
3442 Main Street
Weirton, WV 26062-4590
(304) 797-8510
http://weirton.lib.wv.us
Lois Aleta Fundis, Reference Librarian
Hours: winter: Mon–Thur 10:00–8:00,
Fri–Sat 10:00–5:00, Sun 1:00–5:00;
summer: Mon–Thur 10:00–6:00, Fri–
Sat 10:00–5:00
(emphasis on Weirton, along with
Hancock and Brooke counties and
adjacent areas in Pennsylvania and
Ohio; census microfilm for Hancock
and Brooke counties, microfilm of
newspapers)
searches by mail will be charged cost of
postage, photocopies and WV sales
tax; will also send list of local
genealogists and genealogy
organizations

Historical Societies— Local and Regional

Barbour County Historical Society
Main and Depot
Philippi, WV 26416
(304) 457-4846; (304) 457-3349
(appointments)
Virginia Smith, President
Hours: May 1–Nov 1: 11:00–4:00;
winter: by appointment only
Pub. *Barbour County Historical Society
Letter*, quarterly
(specialty: Civil War information—first
land battle, 3 June 1861, and other
information)

$5.00 per year membership, c/o Eliz. Ramsey, 225 Garnett Street, Philippi, WV 26416

The Berkeley County Historical Society
(The Belle Boyd House, 126 East Race Street—location)
PO Box 1624 (mailing address)
Martinsburg, WV 25401
(304) 267-4713
Don C. Wood, President
Hours: Archives Division: Wed–Thur 9:00–4:00, Wed 6:30 P.M.–9:00 P.M.; Headquarters, The Belle Boyd House: Mon–Sat 10:00–4:00, closed Christmas through New Year's Day
Pub. *The Berkeley Journal*, annually, $7.50 postpaid per issue; *Berkeley County Historical Society Newsletter*, quarterly
(national register and landmarks on Berkeley County, genealogy files on Berkeley, Jefferson and Morgan counties, also wills, deeds, birth, death and marriage records)
$20.00 per year membership for individuals (includes both publications), $15.00 per year membership for senior citizens (aged 62 and over), $400.00 life membership; no entrance fee

The Braxton Historical Society
226 Birch Street
Gassaway, WV 26624
(304) 364-5552
Helen L. Traugh, President
Hours: three meetings per year
Pub. *Journal of the Braxton Historical Society*, quarterly (March, June, September, December)
$3.00 per year membership

Brooke County Genealogical-Historical Society
1200 Pleasant Avenue
Wellsburg, WV 26070
Nancy Caldwell

Calhoun County Historical and Genealogical Society
(Board of Education Plaza, High Street—location)
PO Box 242 (mailing address)
Grantsville, WV 26147
(304) 354-7614
Mary Ann Barrows, Secretary
Pub. *Lines and Links*, three times per year
$5.00 per year membership

Doddridge County Historical Society
201 Grand Avenue
West Union, WV 26456

Fayette County Historical Society
PO Box 463
Ansted, WV 25812-0463
(304) 469-9505

Gilmer County Historical Society
214 Walnut Street
Glenville, WV 26351
(304) 462-5620
Glenna Queen, Secretary
Hours: Mon–Fri 9:00–5:00, Sat 10:00–1:00
Pub. *Gilmer County Historical Society Newsletter*, quarterly (April, July, October, January)
$10.00 per year membership; queries to Kyle Emerson, 82 Grand Teton Drive, Saint Peters, MO 63376, E-mail: kemerson@mail.win.org

Grant County Genealogical-Historical Society
Lahmansville, WV 26731
Gail Snyder

Grant County Historical Society, Inc.
PO Box 665
Petersburg, WV 26847
(304) 257-1444

Greenbrier Historical Society
101 Church Street
PO Box 884
Lewisburg, WV 24901
(304) 645-3398
Frances Swope, Archivist
Hours: Thur & Sat 1:00–4:00
Pub. *Journal*, annually, $16.50 per issue for in-state non-members, $16.25 per issue for out-of-state non-members; *Appalachian Springs*, quarterly, $2.50 per issue for in-state non-members, $2.25 per issue for out-of-state non-members
(history, persons, places, events pertaining to the Greenbrier Valley area of West Virginia)
$15.00 per year membership

Hampshire County Historical Society
170 East Birch Lane
Romney, WV 26757
(no research by staff personnel)

Hancock County Historical Society of West Virginia, Inc.
Swaney Library
New Cumberland, WV 26047
(304) 748-4829

Harpers Ferry Historical Association and Bookshop
Harpers Ferry National Historic Park
Shenandoah Street
PO Box 197
Harpers Ferry, WV 25425
(304) 535-6881

Harrison County Historical Society
(123 West Main Street, Clarksburg, WV 26301—location)
PO Box 2074 (mailing address)
Clarksburg, WV 26302-2074

(304) 842-3073
Madge McDaniel, Treasurer
Hours: Fri (May–Sept) 2:00–4:00
Pub. *Harrison County Historical Society Newsletter*, semiannually
$5.00 per year membership for individuals, $7.50 per year membership for families

Hatfield-McCoy Historical Society (Ky.-W.Va.)
(see Kentucky)

Historical Society of Helvetia
General Delivery
Helvetia, WV 26224

Historic Shepherdstown Commission
Historic Shepherdstown Museum
(129 East German Street, Entler Hotel, Room 200—location)
PO Box 1786 (mailing address)
Shepherdstown, WV 25443
(304) 876-0910
Cynthia S. Cook, Administrator; James C. Holland, President
Hours: various, by appointment only to use archival materials
Pub. *Newsletter*, quarterly
$10.00 per year membership for individuals or families, $25.00 per year Sustaining membership, $50.00 per year Sponsor membership, $100.00 per year Patron membership, $250.00 per year Benefactor membership

Jackson County Historical Society
(City Building or Library—location)
PO Box 22 (mailing address)
Ripley, WV 25271
(304) 372-2541 (Treasurer)
Vera S. Crum, Treasurer
Pub. *Jackson County History*, quarterly (January, April, July, October), $10.00 per year subscription
$14.00 per year membership with periodical, $4.00 per year membership without periodical

Jefferson County Historical Society
PO Box 485
Charles Town, WV 25414
Dr. John E. Stealey, III, President
Pub. *Magazine of the Jefferson County Historical Society*, annually
$5.00 per year membership

Mason City Historical Society
(6 Brown Street—location)
5 Pomeroy Street (mailing address)
Mason, WV 25260
(304) 773-5557

Mason County Genealogical-Historical Society
Henderson, WV 25106
Barbara McKinley

Mercer County Historical Society, Inc.

PO Box 5012
Princeton, WV 24740-5012
(304) 425-4990
E-mail: commander@inetone.net
Glenn Belcher, President
Hours: daily 10:00–2:00
Pub. *Mercer Dateline*, monthly
$10.00 per year membership for individuals, $15.00 per year membership for families (children under 18), $100.00 life membership

Mineral County Genealogical-Historical Society

107 Orchard Street
Keyser, WV 26726
Rev. W. W. Harvey

Mingo County Historical Society

PO Box 2581
Williamson, WV 25661
(606) 237-4646
Oscar Atkins
Hours: meeting at Williamson Public Library

Monongalia County Historical Society

PO Box 127
Morgantown, WV 26505
Joseph Costello, President
Pub. *Monongalia Chronicle*

Monroe County Historical Society

PO Box 465
Union, WV 24983
Jay Banks, Corresponding Secretary
Hours: Museum: Mon–Sat 10:00–4:00, Sun 1:00–4:00 (May 30 to mid-Oct)
Pub. *Monroe County Historical Society Newsletter*, quarterly (March, June, September, December)
$10.00 per year membership

Morgan County Historical and Genealogical Society

(Morgan County Public Library—location)
PO Box 52 (mailing address)
Berkeley Springs, WV 25411
Leonard Davis, President
Pub. *Morgan County Historical and Genealogical Society Newsletter*, quarterly
$5.00 per year membership for individuals, $7.50 per year membership for husband and wife

Pendleton County Genealogical-Historical Society

Upper Tract, WV 26886
Donna Kimble

Pendleton County Historical Society, Inc.

Main Street
PO Box 383
Franklin, WV 26807

(304) 358-7366
Richard Ruddle, Jr., President
$3.00 per year membership

Pleasants County Historical Society

PO Box 335
Saint Marys, WV 26170
(304) 684-7621
Walter S. Carpenter, President
Hours: by appointment; meetings: third Thur 7:30
(Pleasants County and West Virginia history)
$3.00 per year membership

Pocahontas County Historical Society, Inc.

810 Second Avenue
Marlinton, WV 24954
William P. McNeel, Historian
Pub. *Pocahontas County Newsletter*, annually

Preston County Historical Society

300 West State Street
Terra Alta, WV 26764
(304) 329-1468

Randolph County Historical Society

PO Box 1164
Elkins, WV 26241
(304) 636-0841
Randolph Allan, President; Madeline Crickard, Librarian
Pub. *Magazine of History and Biography*

Ritchie County Historical Society

200 South Church Street
Harrisville, WV 26362
(304) 643-2738
David M. Scott, President
Hours: Old Stone House Museum, Pennsboro, WV: Wed (Jun–Aug) noon–3:00, and by appointment
Pub. *Ritchie County Historical Society Newsletter*, quarterly
$3.00 per year membership

Saint Albans Historical Society

(2745 Lincoln Avenue—location)
919 Lee Street (mailing address)
Saint Albans, WV 25177
(304) 727-5972
Jack Cook, President
Pub. *Coalsmouth Journal*
$7.00 per year membership

Summers County Historical Society

PO Box 295
Hinton, WV 25951-0295

Taylor County Historical and Genealogical Society, Inc.

(Taylor County Library—location)
PO Box 522 (mailing address)
Grafton, WV 26354
(304) 265-5015 (Library)
Tom Dadisman
Hours: Library: Wed 9:15–noon (only)
Pub. *Taylor County in Profile*, quarterly, $3.00 per issue

(over 1,000 books and papers; assorted genealogical and historical subjects of Taylor County, West Virginia, wills, deeds, obits, pedigrees, etc.)
$12.00 per year membership; queries free to members, $5.00 each for non-members; research fees by arrangement

Tucker County Historical Society, Inc.

(Town Building—location)
PO Box 13 (mailing address)
Hambleton, WV 26269
(304) 478-2916
William Bilby, President
Hours: Memorial Day weekend & Sun (summer) 2:00–4:00
Pub. *News Letter*, annually
(history of Tucker County)
$10.00 per year membership; search fees: $10.00

Tyler County Heritage and Historical Society

PO Box 317
Middlebourne, WV 26149
(304) 758-4288
E. G. Moore
Pub. *Heritage Windows*, quarterly
$9.00 per year membership

Upper Vandalia Historical Society

PO Box 517
Poca, WV 25159
Mrs. Robert Williamson
Pub. *Vandalia Journal*, quarterly
$10.00 per year membership

The Upshur County Historical Society

PO Box 2082
Buckhannon, WV 26201
http://www.msys.net/uchs
Noel W. Tenney, Ph.D., Director of Special Projects
Hours: The Upshur County Public Library Document Repository: Tue 6:00–8:00; Museum: Sun (Jun–Sept) 1:00–4:00
Pub. *UCHS Newsletter*, occasionally
$10.00 per year membership for individuals

West Augusta Historical and Genealogical Society

PO Box 266
Mannington, WV 26582
Janet Cunningham
Pub. *Newsletter, West Augusta Historical and Genealogical Society*, bimonthly
$4.00 per year membership

West Virginia and Regional History Association

West Virginia and Regional History
  Collection
West Virginia University Libraries
Colson Hall, West Virginia University
PO Box 6464
Morgantown, WV 26506-6464
(304) 293-3536
http://www.wvu.edu/ (Library)
Dr. John A. Cuthbert, Editor
Hours: Mon–Fri 8:45–4:45, Sat 9:00–
  4:00, times vary during university
  vacations
Pub. *West Virginia and Regional History
  Collection Newsletter*, three times per
  year
(West Virginia and central Appalachia)
$10.00 per year membership; copying
  fee for non-residents: $10.00 for up to
  50 copies

Wheeling Area Historical Society

PO Box 283
Wheeling, WV 26003
(304) 277-2241
Margaret A. Brennen, President
Pub. *Upper Ohio Valley Historical
  Review*, irregularly

The Wise County Historical Society

The Appalachian Quarterly
(see Virginia)

LDS Family History Centers

Charleston
(304) 984-9333

Huntington
(304) 736-0250

Genealogical Societies

State Genealogical Society

West Virginia Genealogical Society, Inc., and Library

(5238 Elk River Road, North, Rt. 119,
  three miles north of Elkview—
  location)
PO Box 249 (mailing address)
Elkview, WV 25071
(304) 965-1179
Hours: Mon & Wed 10:00–7:00, Sat
  10:00–2:00
Pub. *L.O.G.* (Ledger of Genealogy),
  quarterly
("genealogical data, library volunteer
  eager to help, correspondence and
  library committee to answer short

questions—over 700 volumes to date,
  40 out-of-state journals")
$15.00 per year membership; queries
  $3.00 for non-members; search fee:
  postage and copying fee, donations
  accepted but not necessary

Regional Genealogical Societies

Allegheny Regional Family History Society

PO Box 1804
Elkins, WV 26241
(304) 636-1650
http://www.swcp.com/~dhickman/
  arfhs.html
Madeline Crickard, Librarian
Hours: Wed 1:00–4:00, Sat 10:00–2:00;
  meetings at Randolph County
  Hsitorical Society Museum: first Tue
  7:00
Pub. *Allegheny Regional Journal*,
  quarterly
$20.00 per year membership; search:
  $25.00 for the first five hours

Boone County Genealogical Society

PO Box 306
Madison, WV 25130
Lenore Ferrell, Publication Editor
Hours: Boone-Madison Public Library:
  9:00–5:00
Pub. *Boone Genealogical Quarterly*;
  *Kith and Kin of Boone County, West
  Virginia*, annually, $13.00 per issue
(Boone County, West Virginia, history)
$6.00 per year membership (includes
  only quarterly)

Brooke County Genealogical-Historical Society

1200 Pleasant Avenue
Wellsburg, WV 26070
Nancy Caldwell

Calhoun County Historical and Genealogical Society

(Board of Education Plaza, High
  Street—location)
PO Box 242 (mailing address)
Grantsville, WV 26147
(304) 354-7614
Mary Ann Barrows, Secretary
Pub. *Lines and Links*, three times per
  year
$5.00 per year membership

Genealogical Society: Fayette and Raleigh Counties, Inc.

PO Box 68
Oak Hill, WV 25901-0068
Leon Neal, President
Pub. *Newsnotes*, quarterly
$8.00 per year membership

Grant County Genealogical-Historical Society

Lahmansville, WV 26731
Gail Snyder

Harrison County Genealogical Society

PO Box 387
Clarksburg, WV 26301
Pub. *Harrison County Genealogical
  Society Newsletter*, quarterly
$10.00 donation per year membership;
  free queries for members

KYOWVA Genealogical Society

(232 Main Street, Huntington, WV
  25702—library location)
PO Box 1254 (mailing address)
Huntington, WV 25714-1254
(304) 525-1367; (304) 525-4367
Ernestine Hippert, President; Sheri Pettit
Hours: Mon 6:00 P.M.–9:00 P.M., Wed
  10:00–3:00, Sat 10:00–4:00
Pub. *KYOWVA Genealogical Society*,
  quarterly
(workshops, book fairs, computer
  groups, research help, library
  assistance, books of the area for sale)
$12.00 per year membership for
  individuals, $15.00 per year
  membership for families

Kanawha Valley Genealogical Society, Inc.

(Nitro Community Center, Nitro, WV
  25143—location)
PO Box 8555 (mailing address)
South Charleston, WV 25303
Donald E. Peterson, President
Hours: first & third Wed 10:00–4:00, Tue
  preceding first and third Wed 6:00
  P.M.–9:00 P.M.
Pub. *The Journal*, quarterly
(computer programs and CD-ROM disks
  available; computer interest group
  active)
$15.00 per year membership

Lincoln County Genealogical Society

7999 Lynn Avenue
Hamlin, WV 25523
(304) 524-7326
Carolyn Egnor, Secretary
Pub. *Lincoln Lineage*, quarterly
$6.00 per year membership

Logan County Genealogical Society

(Southern West Virginia Community
  College Library—location)
PO Box 1959 (mailing address)
Logan, WV 25601
Hester Hodges, Treasurer
Hours: The Southern Library: meetings
  on the last Mon (except Dec & Aug)
  7:00 P.M., last Sat (Aug)
Pub. *Logan County Ancestree*, quarterly
$10.00 per year membership for
  individuals, $15.00 per year
  membership for families

Marion County Genealogy Club
Marion County Library
321 Monroe Street
Fairmont, WV 26554
(304) 287-2411
Hours: Library: Mon–Fri 9:00–6:00, Sat
9:00–4:00; Genealogy Department:
Mon–Fri 10:00–2:00
Pub. *Genealogy Gleanings*, quarterly
(March, June, September, December)
$7.00 per year membership

**Mason County Genealogical—
Historical Society**
Henderson, WV 25106
Barbara McKinley

**Mineral County Genealogical—
Historical Society**
107 Orchard Street
Keyser, WV 26726
Rev. W. W. Harvey

Mingo County Genealogical Society
PO Box 2581
Williamson, WV 25661
(606) 237-4646
Oscar Atkins
Pub. *Mingo Heritage*, biannually
$8.00 per year membership

**Morgan County Historical and
Genealogical Society**
(Morgan County Public Library—
location)
PO Box 52 (mailing address)
Berkeley Springs, WV 25411
Leonard Davis, President
Pub. *Morgan County Historical and
Genealogical Society Newsletter*,
quarterly
$5.00 per year membership for
individuals, $7.50 per year
membership for husband and wife

**Pendleton County Genealogical-
Historical Society**
Upper Tract, WV 26886
Donna Kimble

**Taylor County Historical and
Genealogical Society, Inc.**
PO Box 522
Grafton, WV 26354
(304) 265-5015 (Library)
Darlene Ford, President
Hours: Library: Wed 10:00–noon
Pub. *Taylor County in Profile*, quarterly,
$1.50 per issue
("assorted genealogical and historical
subjects of Taylor County, West
Virginia, wills, deeds, obits, etc.")
$8.00 per year membership; queries
$5.00 each

Tri-State Genealogical Society
(see Ohio)

**Tug Valley Genealogical Society
(Ky.—W.Va.)**
(see Kentucky)

**West Augusta Historical and
Genealogical Society**
PO Box 266
Mannington, WV 26582
Janet Cunningham
Pub. *Newsletter, West Augusta Historical
and Genealogical Society*, bimonthly
$4.00 per year membership

**Wetzel County Genealogical Society,
Inc.**
PO Box 464
New Martinsville, WV 26155-0464
Carol Hassig, President
Hours: New Martinsville Public Library:
Mon–Wed & Fri–Sat 10:00–5:00
Pub. *W.C.G.S. Newsletter*, quarterly
(Wetzel County, West Virginia, and
surrounding areas)
$7.00 per year

Wheeling Area Genealogical Society
36 Rockledge Road
Wheeling, WV 26003
(304) 242-1648

Independent Publications and Miscellany

Appalachian Roots
PO Box 165
Davisville, WV 26142
E-mail: mjbrown@eurekanet.com
Mary Jo Brown, Editor and Publisher
Pub. *Appalachian Roots*, monthly,
$18.00 per year subscription
(includes entire Appalachian Mountain
area of the following states: Kentucky,
Maryland, North Carolina,
Pennsylvania, South Carolina,
Tennessee, Virginia, West Virginia)
free queries

Doddridge County Publications
11965 Cameo Place
Granada Hills, CA 91344
(publishes books on Doddridge County)

***Families of Wyoming County, West
Virginia***
PO Box 1035
North Highlands, CA 95660-1035
(916) 991-4165
Sally Williams, Editor
Pub. *Families of Wyoming County, West
Virginia*, quarterly, $15.00 per year
subscription

Family Tree Exchange
(see Virginia)

Genealogical Institute
(see Virginia)

**Hacker's Creek Pioneer
Descendants, Inc.**
(Jackson's Mill Road, about two miles
from Route 19—location)
Rt. 1, Box 238 (mailing address)
Jane Lew, WV 26378
(304) 269-7091; (304) 269-4430 FAX
E-mail: hcpd.lewisco@
westvierginia.com
Joy Gilchrist, Executive Director
Hours: Library: Mon & Thur 10:00–
8:00, Tue–Wed & Fri 10:00–3:00, Sat
10:00–2:00
Pub. *Up the Creek*, quarterly
(includes central West Virginia, with
special emphasis on Lewis, Harrison,
Upshur, Gilmer, Barbour, Randolph,
Doddridge and Braxton counties)
$25.00 per year membership (beginning
October 1)

Lineage Search Associates
Frederick Findings
(see Virginia)

***The Mountain Empire Genealogical
Quarterly***
(see Virginia)

Mountain Press
(see Tennessee)

***Stories About Gilbert, West Virginia,
and Surrounding Communities***
Rt. 4, Box 7-C (Needmore Road)
Cameron, NC 28326-8904
(910) 245-7461 FAX
E-mail: gilbert@pinehurst.net
http://home.pinehurst.net/gilbert
Col. Darrell G. Brumfield (Ret)

Topp of the Line
Virginia/West Virginia Queries
(see Virginia)

Tri-County Researcher
PO Box 196
Proctor, WV 26055-0196
(304) 455-3203
Linda Goddard Stout, Editor
Pub. *Tri-County Researcher*, quarterly,
$15.00 per year subscription
(Marshall, Tyler and Wetzel counties)
queries free for subscribers, $2.00 each
for non-subscribers

The Virginia Genealogist
(see Virginia)

West Virginia Hillbilly
PO Box 430
Richwood, WV 26261
(304) 846-2666; (304) 846-4972 FAX
Sandy McCauley, Owner-Publisher
Hours: Mon–Fri 8:00–5:00
Pub. *West Virginia Hillbilly*, biweekly,
$30.00 per year subscription
(history-education)

WVGenWeb
Part of U.S. GenWeb Project
E-mail: wv@usgenweb.com
http://www.rootsweb.com/ wvgenweb
(links to other West Virginia resources)

WISCONSIN

Archives and Libraries with Holdings in Genealogy

State Archives and Libraries

The State Historical Society of Wisconsin
816 State Street
Madison, WI 53706-1488
(608) 264-6535 (Reference Librarian);
    (608) 264-6460 (Reference Archivist)
http://www.wisc.edu/shs-library/; http://www.wisc.edu/shs-archives
James L. Hansen, Reference Librarian
Hours: when University of Wisconsin is in session: Mon–Thur 8:00–9:00, Fri–Sat 8:00–5:00; when university is not in session: Mon–Sat 8:00–5:00; Archives: Mon–Fri 8:00–5:00, Sat 9:00–4:00
Pub. *Wisconsin Magazine of History*, quarterly; *Columns—Newsletter of the State Historical Society of Wisconsin*, bimonthly
(library has a strong collection with emphasis on North American genealogy; archives serves as Area Research Center for Columbia, Dane and Sauk counties)
$27.50 per year membership for individuals, $32.50 per year membership for families, $22.50 per year membership for individual senior citizens, $27.50 per year membership for senior citizen families, $30.00 per year membership for institutions

Area Research Centers

Northland College
Dexter Library
1411 Ellis Avenue
Ashland, WI 54806
(715) 682-1311
Dr. J. Paul O'Keefe
Hours: Mon 1:00–3:00, Tue 11:30–2:00 & 3:30–10:00, Wed 1:00–3:00 & 5:30–9:00, Thur noon–2:00 & 4:00–10:00, Fri 9:00–11:00
(Area Research Center for Ashland, Bayfield, and Iron counties)

Superior Area Research Center
Superior Public Library
1530 Tower Avenue
Superior, WI 54880
(715) 394-8860
Barry Singer, Archives Director
Hours: Mon & Fri 9:00–noon & 1:00–5:00, Tue–Thur 1:00–5:00
(Area Research Center for Douglas County)

University of Wisconsin—Eau Claire
McIntyre Library, Special Collections
Eau Claire, WI 54702-4004
(715) 836-2739; (715) 836-2949 FAX
E-mail: library.archives@uwec.edu
http://www.uwec.edu/admin/library/speccol.html
Lawrence D. Lynch, University Archivist
Hours: Mon–Fri 8:00–5:00
(emphasis on Chippewa Valley history and genealogy; university archives; Area Research Center for Buffalo, Chippewa, Clark, Eau Claire, Pepin, Price, Rusk, Sawyer, and Taylor counties with manuscripts and public records)

University of Wisconsin—Green Bay
Cofrin Library
Special Collections/Area Research Center
Seventh Floor, Library Learning Center
2420 Nicolet Drive
Green Bay, WI 54311-7001
(920) 465-2539
Debra L. Anderson, Special Collections Librarian
Hours: Mon–Fri 12:30–4:30, Wed 4:30–9:00
(Area Research Center for Brown, Calumet, Door, Florence, Kewaunee, Manitowoc, Marinette, Menominee, Oconto, Outagamie, and Shawano counties)

University of Wisconsin—La Crosse
Eugene W. Murphy Library
1631 Pine Street
La Crosse, WI 54601
(608) 785-8511
Edwin L. Hill, Special Collections Librarian
Hours: Mon–Fri 10:00–12:00 & 1:00–5:00
(Area Research Center for Jackson, La Crosse, Monroe, Trempealeau, and Vernon counties)

Milwaukee Urban Archives/Area Research Center
University of Wisconsin—Milwaukee
Golda Meir Library
Room 250
2311 East Hartford Avenue
PO Box 604
Milwaukee, WI 53201-0604
(414) 229-5402; (414) 229-4046 (offsite access to online catalog); (414) 229-3605 FAX
E-mail: archives@gml.lib.uwm.edu
http://www.uwm.edu/library/arch
Mark A. Vargas, Academic Archivist
Hours: spring and fall semesters: Mon–Tue & Fri 8:00–4:30; Wed–Thur 8:00–8:00; summer and other times: Mon–Fri 8:00–4:30
(Area Research Center for Milwaukee, Ozaukee, Sheboygan, Washington, and Waukesha counties; bibliographic data

is available through the Golda Meir Library's NLS online catalog system, OCLC or WISCAT)

specific research: $7.50 per one-page record, $5.00 for 2–20 additional pages, 25¢ for each additional page, $7.50 per tax roll searched; general research: $25.00 minimum (up to one hour), $12.50 per half-hour, $4.00 for 2–20 additional pages, 25¢ for eachadditional page

University of Wisconsin—Oshkosh
Area Research Center, Forrest R. Polk Library
Oshkosh, WI 54901
(920) 424-3347; (920) 424-2175 FAX
http://www.uwosh.edu/departments/llr/depts/docs/gov/html
Gerald J. Krueger, Documents Librarian
Hours: Mon–Fri 9:00–noon & 1:00–4:00
(Area Research Center for Dodge, Fond du Lac, Green Lake, Marquette, and Winnebago counties; marriages, births and deaths, pre-1907 cannot be photocopied)

University of Wisconsin—Parkside
Parkside Library
(D2 Level of the Library—location)
900 Wood Road, PO Box 2000 (mailing address)
Kenosha, WI 53141-2000
(414) 595-2411
Ellen J. Pedraza, Archivist/Librarian
Hours: Mon–Tue & Thur–Fri 8:00–12:00, Wed 5:00–9:00
(emphasis on local history and genealogy; Area Research Center for Kenosha and Racine counties)

The University of Wisconsin—Platteville
SW Wisconsin Room—Elton S. Karrmann Library
1 University Plaza
Platteville, WI 53818-3099
(608) 342-1719; (608) 342-1645 FAX
E-mail: freymiller@uwplatt.edu
Mary J. Freymiller, Curator
Hours: SW Wisconsin Room, when school is in session: Mon–Fri 1:00–5:00 (closes at 4:00 on Fri during summer session), Tue & Thur 5:00–9:00
(Area Research Center for Crawford, Grant, Green, Iowa, Lafayette, and Richland counties; collection emphasis on southwest Wisconsin and upper Mississippi, including Jo Daviess County, Illinois, and Dubuque; lead-zinc mining district of southwest Wisconsin, northeast Iowa and northwest Illinois)

University of Wisconsin—River Falls
Chalmer Davee Library
410 South Third Street
River Falls, WI 54022
(715) 425-3567

http://www.uwrf.edu
Hours: Mon & Thur 8:00–4:30 & 7:00 P.M.–9:00 P.M., Tue, Wed & Fri 8:00–4:30, Sat 1:00–4:00, Sun 7:00 P.M.–9:00 P.M.; summer and university holidays: Mon–Fri 8:00–4:30
(Area Research Center for Burnett, Pierce, Polk, Saint Croix, and Washburn counties)

University of Wisconsin—Stevens Point
Learning Resources Center
Stevens Point, WI 54481
(715) 346-2586
Bill Paul, University Archivist
Hours: Mon–Fri 8:00–12:00 & 1:00–4:30
(Area Research Center for Adams, Forest, Juneau, Langlade, Lincoln, Marathon, Oneida, Portage, Vilas, Waupaca, Waushara, and Wood counties)

University of Wisconsin—Stout
Robert L. Pierce Library
Menomonie, WI 54751-0790
(715) 232-2300
Gayle Martinson, University and Area Archivist
Hours: Mon–Fri 8:00–5:00, Mon–Wed 7:00–9:00, Sat 12:00–3:00 (hours vary during university recesses, please call)
(Area Research Center for Barron and Dunn counties)

University of Wisconsin—Whitewater
(2210 Harold Anderson Library, 800 West Main Street—location)
PO Box 900 (mailing address)
Whitewater, WI 53190
(414) 472-5520; (414) 472-5727
E-mail: westonk@uwwvax.uww.edu
Karen Weston, Area Research Center Curator
Hours: Mon–Fri noon–4:00
(Area Research Center for Jefferson, Rock, and Walworth counties)
photocopies: 10¢ each

Wisconsin Department of Public Instruction
Division of Library Services
Bureau for Interlibrary Loan and Resource Sharing
2109 South Stoughton Road
Madison, WI 53716
(608) 221-6160
Hours: Mon–Fri 7:45–4:30

State Historical Societies

The State Historical Society of Wisconsin
816 State Street
Madison, WI 53706-1488
(608) 264-6535 (Reference Librarian);
(608) 264-6460 (Reference Archivist)

http://www.wisc.edu/shs-library/; http://www.wisc.edu/shs-archives
James L. Hansen, Reference Librarian
Hours: when University of Wisconsin is in session: Mon–Thur 8:00–9:00, Fri–Sat 8:00–5:00; when university is not in session: Mon–Sat 8:00–5:00; Archives: Mon–Fri 8:00–5:00, Sat 9:00–4:00
Pub. *Wisconsin Magazine of History*, quarterly; *Columns—Newsletter of the State Historical Society of Wisconsin*, bimonthly
(library has a strong collection with emphasis on North American genealogy; archives serves as Area Research Center for Columbia, Dane and Sauk counties)
$27.50 per year membership for individuals, $32.50 per year membership for families, $22.50 per year membership for individual senior citizens, $27.50 per year membership for senior citizen families, $30.00 per year membership for institutions

Wisconsin Council for Local History
816 State Street
Madison, WI 53706
(608) 262-2316

City, County and Regional Archives and Libraries

Appleton Public Library
225 North Oneida Street
Appleton, WI 54911-4780
(920) 832-1695; (920) 832-6182 FAX
http://www.apl.org
Cecilia Wiltzius, Community Services
Hours: Mon–Thur 9:00–9:00, Fri 9:00–6:00, Sat 9:00–5:00

Aram Public Library
404 East Walworth Avenue
Delavan, WI 53115
(414) 728-3719

Beaver Dam Community Library
311 North Spring Street
Beaver Dam, WI 53916
(920) 887-4631; (920) 887-4633 FAX
E-mail: bdlib@peoples.net
Mark Arend, Assistant Librarian
Hours: Mon–Fri 9:00–8:30, Sat 9:00–5:00
copies: 15¢ each from paper originals, 25¢ each from microfilm originals

Beloit Public Library
409 Pleasant Street
Beloit, WI 53511
(608) 364-2905
Hours: Mon–Thur 9:30–8:45, Fri–Sat 9:30–5:15

Brown County Library

Local History and Genealogy
   Department
515 Pine Street
Green Bay, WI 54301
(920) 448-4394
Mary Jane Herber
Hours: winter: Mon–Sat 1:00–5:00, Wed
   6:00–9:00; summer: Mon–Fri 1:00–
   5:00, Wed 6:00–8:00
25¢ per page for photocopies ($3.00
   minimum)

Chalet of the Golden Fleece

618 Second Street
New Glarus, WI 53574
(608) 527-2614

Chippewa Falls Public Library

105 West Central Street
Chippewa Falls, WI 54729-2397
(715) 723-1146; (715) 720-6922 FAX
Jan Adams, Reference Librarian
Hours: winter: Mon–Thur 9:00–8:00, Fri
   9:00–6:00, Sat 10:00–5:00, Sun 1:00–
   5:00; summer: Mon & Thur 9:00–
   8:00, Tue–Wed & Fri 9:00–6:00, Sat
   10:00–1:00

Chippewa Valley Museum

Carsons Park Drive
PO Box 1204
Eau Claire, WI 54702
(715) 834-7871
Susan McLeod, Executive Director
Hours: Tue–Sun 1:00–5:00

Darlington Public Library

525 Main Street
Darlington, WI 53530
(608) 776-4171 (phone and FAX)
Marion Howard, Head Librarian
Hours: Mon & Wed–Thur 1:30–8:30,
   Tue 1:30–5:30, Fri 10:00–5:00, Sat
   1:00–5:00
(Lafayette County historical and
   genealogical research materials)

Door County Library

Door County History Room
107 South Fourth Avenue
Sturgeon Bay, WI 54235
(920) 743-6578
Nancy Emery, Adult Services Librarian
Hours: Mon–Thur 9:00–9:00, Fri 9:00–
   6:00, Sat 9:00–5:00

Door County Museum

PO Box 670
Sturgeon Bay, WI 54235

Fond du Lac Public Library

32 Sheboygan Street
Fond du Lac, WI 54935
(920) 929-7086; (920) 929-7082
Kay Conrad, Reference Librarian
Hours: winter: Mon–Thur 9:00–9:00, Fri
   9:00–6:00, Sat 9:00–5:00, Sun 1:00–
   4:00; summer: Mon & Wed 9:00–9:00,
   Tue & Thur–Fri 9:00–6:00, Sat 9:00–
   12:00

Fox Lake Historical Museum, Inc.

(211 Cordelia Street—location)
W9369 County Trunk C (mailing
   address)
Fox Lake, WI 53933
(920) 929-2376
Norma R. Heuer, Curator
Hours: Memorial Day through first week
   in Oct: first & third Sun 1:00–4:00,
   and by appointment
Pub. *Newsletter*, annually
(local history and large collection of
   Indian artifacts)
$3.00 per year membership for
   individuals and senior citizens, $5.00
   per year membership for families,
   $25.00 per year membership for
   industries and businesses

Hartford Public Library

115 North Main
Hartford, WI 53027
(414) 673-8240
Shirley Hess
Hours: Hartford History Room: first &
   third Thur (Jan–Nov) 9:00–8:00, first
   & third Thur (Dec) 9:00–3:00,
   remaining Thur 9:00–3:00 by
   appointment

Hedberg Public Library

Reference Department
316 South Main Street
Janesville, WI 53545-3971
(608) 758-6581 (Reference Department);
   (608) 758-6615 FAX
http://rals.lib.wi.us
Hours: Mon–Fri 9:00–9:00, Sat 9:00–
   5:30, Sun (Sept–May) 9:00–1:00
(primarily Janesville, some Rock County
   records)
search fees, limited genealogy requests
   by mail only: SASE plus photocopies
   at 15¢ per page from paper original or
   20¢ per page from microform original

Hoard Historical Museum

407 Merchants Avenue
Fort Atkinson, WI 53538
(920) 563-7769
Mike Erickson, Director
Hours: winter: Tue–Sat 9:30–3:30, first
   Sun 1:00–5:00; summer: Tue–Sat
   9:30–4:30, Sun 1:00–5:00
(cemetery records of Jefferson County,
   local family records, platt maps,
   church and school records, local
   business records)

Kenosha Public Library

Reference Department
7979 38th Avenue
Kenosha, WI 53142
Linda Pulera, Branch Head

Kenosha Public Library

Reference Department
Gilbert M. Simmons Library
711 59th Place
Kenosha, WI 53140

(414) 942-3700
E-mail: tblaschk@kenosha.lib.wi.us
Tracy Blaschka, Head of Reference and
   Electronic Services
Hours: Mon–Thur 9:00–8:00, Fri 9:00–
   6:00, Sat 9:00–5:00
Pub. *Genealogy: Resources and Services,
   Kenosha Public Library*, irregularly,
   $5.00 postpaid per issue
photocopy and postage charges

La Crosse Public Library

Department of Archives and Local
   History
800 Main Street
La Crosse, WI 54601-4122
(608) 789-7136; (608) 789-7106 FAX
Anita Taylor Doering, Archivist
Hours: Mon–Thur noon-9:00, Fri–Sat
   9:00–5:00, Sun 1:00–5:00
(depository of the La Crosse Area
   Genealogical Society materials; also
   federal and state census for Wisconsin
   area newspapers, city directories, etc.)
in-depth research by staff: $8.00 per half-
   hour, plus SASE

Lower Wisconsin River Genealogical and Historical Research Center

PO Box 202
Wauzeka, WI 53826-0202
(608) 326-2739; (608) 875-5806 (Editor)
Carol Higgins, Secretary-Treasurer
Pub. *Looking for Yesterday*, quarterly
(Crawford, northern Grant, southern
   Richland, and northwestern Iowa
   counties, Wisconsin)
$5.00 per year membership for
   individuals, $7.00 per year
   membership for families

McMillan Memorial Library

490 East Grand Avenue
Wisconsin Rapids, WI 54494
(715) 423-1040
Hours: Mon–Thur 9:00–9:00, Fri 9:00–
   6:00, Sat 9:00–5:00, Sun 1:00–5:00;
   hours vary during summer
(emphasis on Wood County)

Madison Public Library

201 West Mifflin Street
Madison, WI 53703
(608) 266-6350
Hours: Mon–Wed 8:30–9:00, Thur–Fri
   8:30–5:30, Sat 9:00–5:30

Manitowoc Public Library

808 Hamilton Street
Manitowoc, WI 54220
(920) 683-4862; (920) 683-4873 FAX
Joyce Peterson, Librarian
Hours: school year: Mon–Thur 9:00–
   9:00, Fri 9:00–6:00, Sat 9:00–5:00,
   Sun 12:00–4:00; summer: Mon–Thur
   9:00–7:00, Fri 9:00–6:00, Sat 9:00–
   1:00
(Manitowoc newspaper articles and
   obituaries, church records, published

local histories, and photograph collection)
limited research in the library's collection: $15.00 per hour, $15.00 deposit

Joseph Mann Library
1516 16th Street
Two Rivers, WI 54241
(920) 793-5585
Ken Hall, Director
Hours: Mon–Thur 9:00–8:00, Fri–Sat 9:00–5:00, Fri–Sat (summer) 9:00–3:00

Marathon County Public Library
300 North First Street
Wausau, WI 54401
(715) 847-5400
Mike O'Connor, Head, Adult Services Division
Hours: Mon–Thur 9:30–8:30, Fri–Sat 9:30–5:00, Sun (Sept–May) 1:00–5:00

Mead Public Library
Information Services
710 North Eighth Street
Sheboygan, WI 53081
(920) 459-3400; (920) 459-4336 FAX
Susan Mathews, Coordinator of Information Services
Hours: Sept.-May: Mon–Thur 9:00–9:00, Fri–Sat 9:00–5:00; Oct–Apr: Sun 1:00–5:00; summer: Mon & Wed 9:00–9:00, Tue & Thur–Fri 9:00–5:00, Sat 9:00–1:00

Milwaukee Public Library
814 West Wisconsin Avenue
Milwaukee, WI 53233-2389
(414) 286-3000
Virginia Schwartz, Coordinator of Humanities
Hours: Mon–Thur 9:00–8:30, Fri–Sat 9:00–5:30
(collection of city directories as far back as 1847)

Minocqua Museum
416 Chicago Avenue
PO Box 1007
Minocqua, WI 54548
(715) 356-7666
Dan Scrobell, President, Board of Directors

Monroe County Local History Room
(200 West Main Street—location)
PO Box 419 (mailing address)
Sparta, WI 54656
(608) 269-8680; (608) 269-8921 FAX
Audrey Johnson, County Historian
Hours: Mon–Fri 9:00–4:30

Neenah Public Library
240 East Wisconsin Avenue
PO Box 569
Neenah, WI 54957-0569
(920) 751-4720
http://www.focol.org/~npl

Hours: school year: Mon–Thur 9:00–9:00, Fri 9:00–6:00, Sat 9:00–5:00, Sun 1:00–5:00; summer: Mon–Thur 9:00–8:00, Fri 9:00–6:00, Sat 9:00–1:00

Neville Public Museum
210 Museum Place
Green Bay, WI 54303
(920) 448-4460
Ann L. Koski, Director
Hours: Archives and Library by appointment
(local history collection)
research fee: $25.00 per hour

Oshkosh Public Library
106 Washington Avenue
Oshkosh, WI 54901-4985
(920) 236-5226
Hours: Sept–May: Mon–Fri 9:00–9:00, Sat 9:00–5:00, Sun 1:00–5:00; Jun–Aug: Mon–Fri 9:00–9:00, Sat 9:00–1:00

Oshkosh Public Museum
1331 Algoma Boulevard
Oshkosh, WI 54901
(920) 236-5150
Bradley G. Larson, Director

Peshtigo Fire Museum
(400 Oconto Avenue—location)
North 1997 Hale Road (mailing address)
Peshtigo, WI 54157
(715) 582-3244
Robert Couvillion, President
Hours: 30 May–8 Oct: Mon–Sun 9:00–5:00
Pub. *Peshtigo Fire Museum*

Plymouth Public Library
130 Division Street
Plymouth, WI 53073

Portage County Library
1001 Main Street
Stevens Point, WI 54481
(715) 346-1548

Racine Public Library
Reference and Local History Librarian
75 Seventh Street
Racine, WI 53403
(414) 636-9217; (414) 636-9260 FAX
Hours: Mon–Thur 9:00–9:00, Fri–Sat 9:00–5:30, Sat (Jun–Aug) 9:00–1:00, Sun (Oct–Apr) 2:00–5:00
(Racine and Racine County history)
research: $16.00 per hour

Rhinelander District Library
106 North Stevens Street
Rhinelander, WI 54501

Maude Shunk Public Library
W156 N8446 Pilgrim Road
Menomonee Falls, WI 53051
(414) 255-8390; (414) 255-8408 FAX
Anne Reid, Adult Services Librarian
Hours: Mon–Fri 9:00–9:00, Sat 9:00–5:00

Spillman Library
Village of North Fond du Lac Public Library
719 Wisconsin Avenue
North Fond du Lac, WI 54937

Superior Public Library
1530 Tower Avenue
Superior, WI 54880
(715) 394-8860
Barry Singer, Archives Director
Hours: Mon & Fri 9:00–noon & 1:00–5:00, Tue–Thur 1:00–5:00
(Area Research Center for Douglas County)

University of Wisconsin—Superior
Jim Dan Hill Library
(19th and Weeks Avenue—location)
1800 Grand (mailing address)
Superior, WI 54880
(715) 394-8512; (715) 394-8462 FAX
http://www.uwsuper.edu
Ella Cross, Reference and Government Documents Librarian
Hours: Mon–Fri 8:00–4:30 by appointment
(University of Superior history and archives)

University of Wisconsin—Wausau
University of Wisconsin Center—Marathon County
518 South Seventh Avenue
Wausau, WI 54401
(715) 845-9602
George Newtown, Ph.D., Dean

Vaughn Library
Second and Vaughn Avenues
Ashland, WI 54806

Vernon County Historical Museum
410 South Center Street
PO Box 444
Viroqua, WI 54665
(608) 637-7396
Judy Gates, Curator
Hours: May 15–Sept 15: Tue–Sun 1:00–5:00 by appointment
Pub. *Newsletter*, quarterly
(local genealogy; local history of Vernon County)
$5.00 per year membership for individuals, $10.00 per year membership for families, $100.00 life membership

Waterloo Public Memorial Library
117 East Madison Street
Waterloo, WI 53594
(414) 478-3344
Joel Zibell, Librarian

Waukesha County Museum
Research Center
101 West Main Street
Waukesha, WI 53186
(414) 548-7186
Terry Becker, Librarian

Hours: Tue–Sat 9:00–4:30 (except
  holiday weekends)
(Waukesha County family and local
  history)
$2.50 per day on-site user fee; research
  by mail: $5.00 per year

Waukesha Public Library
321 Wisconsin Avenue
Waukesha, WI 53186
(414) 524-3682
Shirley Chilson, Head of Information
  Services
Hours: Mon–Fri 9:00–9:00, Sat 9:00–
  6:00, Sat (summer) 9:00–1:00, Sun
  (Oct–Apr) 1:00–4:00

Historical Societies— Local and Regional

Ashland County Historical Society
PO Box 906
Ashland, WI 54806-0906

Badger Historical Society
PO Box 186
Shullsburg, WI 53586
(608) 965-3474

Barron County Historical Society
1531 14th Street
Barron, WI 54812
(715) 537-5248
Harold Kringle, President

Bay View Historical Society
PO Box 07614
Milwaukee, WI 53207
(414) 769-0110
Eric Western, President
Pub. *Bay View Historian*

Bayfield County Historical Society
Bayfield County Courthouse
Washburn, WI 54891
(715) 373-5345
Ruth Harnois, Secretary
Hours: by appointment
Pub. *Historical Happenings*, two or three
  times per year
("Bayfield County Historical Society has
  five sub-chapters, but inquiries could
  be directed to proper organization.")
$3.00 per year membership for
  individuals, $5.00 per year
  membership for families; search fee:
  $5.00 minimum

Beloit Historical Society
845 Hackett Street
Beloit, WI 53511
(608) 365-7835; (608) 365-5999 FAX
Paul K. Kerr; Loretta Hatch
Hours: Mon–Fri 8:30–4:00
Pub. *Confluence*, quarterly
$15.00 per year membership for
  individuals, $20.00 per year
  membership for families

Berlin Historical Society
111 South Adams Avenue
PO Box 21
Berlin, WI 54923
(920) 361-4343; (920) 361-0807
  (President's home)
John Wahlers, President
Hours: by appointment
(local history)
$4.00 per year membership

**Historic Blooming Grove Historical
Society**
1000 Nichols Road
Monona, WI 53716
(608) 222-6127

Brown County Historical Society
(1008 South Monroe Avenue, Green Bay,
  WI 54301—location)
PO Box 1411 (mailing address)
Green Bay, WI 54305-1411
(920) 435-4922
Jeanne Jankowski, Executive Director
Hours: Mon–Fri 9:00–noon
Pub. *Voyageur Magazine*, semiannually,
  $5.00 per issue; *Society Newsletter*,
  five times per year
$20.00 per year membership

Brown Deer Historical Society, Inc.
4800 West Green Brook Drive
Brown Deer, WI 53223
(414) 354-4116
Dorothy Kittleson, President
Hours: open houses at 1884 Schoolhouse
  Museum, 1884 Brown Deer School:
  17 May, 4 Jul, 9 Aug
Pub. *Quarterly* (January, April, June,
  October)
$15.00 per year professional or business
  membership

Burlington Historical Society
232 North Perkins Boulevard
Burlington, WI 53105
(414) 767-2884
Forrest Hoganson
Hours: Sun 1:00–4:00

**The Burnett County Historical
Society**
(100 East Johnson Street—location)
PO Box 153 (mailing address)
Danbury, WI 54830-0159
(715) 349-2219
Edgar S. Oerichbauer, Executive
  Director
Hours: by appointment

Clark County Historical Society, Inc.
Rt. 2
Loyal, WI 54446
(715) 255-8968

Clintonville Area Historical Society
(32 11th Street—location)
38 South Main Street (mailing address)
Clintonville, WI 54929
Richard K. Beggs, President

Hours: Memorial Day–Labor Day: Sun
  & holidays 1:00–4:00
(minimal capability for genealogist's
  type work)
$5.00 per year membership

Columbia County Historical Society
(112 Main Street, Pardeeville, WI
  53954—location)
Rt. 1, W 3988 Highway 33 (mailing
  address)
Cambria, WI 53923
(920) 348-5516
Jean Jerred, President
Hours: Tue–Sat (Jun–Aug) 1:00–4:00
$3.00 per year membership

Crawford County Historical Society
505 South State Street
Prairie Du Chien, WI 53821
(608) 326-6330

**Cross Plains-Berry Historical
Society**
2305 Church Street
Cross Plains, WI 53528
(608) 798-2509

Cudahy Historical Society
PO Box 332
Cudahy, WI 53110

Dane County Historical Society
PO Box 5003
Madison, WI 53705
Michael Boure, President; Donna
  Hartshorne, Archivist
Hours: by appointment
Pub. *DCHS Newsletter*, quarterly
$8.00 per year membership for
  individuals, $15.00 per year
  membership for families

Dartford Historical Society
501 Mill Street
PO Box 332
Green Lake, WI 54941
(920) 294-6194
Lawrence Behlen, President
Hours: Fri 10:00–4:00, Sat–Sun 1:00–
  4:00 (additional hours spring, summer
  and fall)
Pub. *Dartford News*, six times per year
(local history archives)
$10.00 per year membership

De Pere Historical Society
White Pillars Museum
403 North Broadway
De Pere, WI 54115
(920) 336-3877
Laurel Towns, Curator
Hours: Wed–Sun 1:00–5:00
Pub. *Pillars*, quarterly
(De Pere, Wisconsin history)
$10.00–$24.00 Brick membership,
  $25.00–$49.00 Arch membership,
  $50.00–$99.00 Pillar membership,
  $100.00–$249.00 Portal membership,

$250.00 or more Cornerstone membership; search fee: $4.00 per hour

DeForest Area Historical Society
119 East Elm Street
PO Box 124
DeForest, WI 53532
(608) 846-5519 (President)
John Englesby, President
Hours: second Sun (Jun–Dec) 1:00–4:00
Pub. *News and Notes*, semiannually (spring and fall)
(history of DeForest area)
$10.00 per year membership

Dells County Historical Society
737 Broadway
PO Box 177
Wisconsin Dells, WI 53965
(608) 254-8321
Bud Gussel, President
Hours: 1:00–2:00
(published book, *Others Before You*)
$5.00 per year membership

Dodge County Historical Society, Inc.
105 Park Avenue
Beaver Dam, WI 53916
(920) 887-1266
Joanne L. Wells, Museum Director
Hours: Tue 10:00–1:00, Wed–Sat 2:00–5:00

Door County Historical Society
18 North Fourth Avenue
Sturgeon Bay, WI 54235
(920) 743-5809

Douglas County Historical Society
906 East Second Street
Superior, WI 54880
(715) 394-5712; (715) 394-2043 FAX
Rachael E. Martin, Executive Director
Hours: daily 9:00–5:00

Drummond Historical Society
Drummond, WI 54832

Dunn County Historical Society
1020 Ninth Street
PO Box 437
Menomonie, WI 54751
(715) 643-2043; (715) 235-3862

East Troy Area Historical Society
PO Box 722
East Troy, WI 53120
(414) 642-5936 (days); (414) 642-5281 (nights)
Alfred Gruling, President
Pub. *Walk Around the Square*

Elmbrook Historical Society
(1050 Legion Drive—location)
845 Morningside Lane (mailing address)
Elm Grove, WI 53122
(414) 782-7818

Evansville Grove Society
Evansville, WI 53536

Fond du Lac County Historical Society
Adams House Resource Center
PO Box 1284
Fond du Lac, WI 54936-1284
(920) 922-1166; (920) 922-9099 FAX
E-mail: mbetz@tcccom.net
John J. Ebert, Director
Hours: winter: Thur & Sat 10:00–4:00, summer: Mon–Fri 9:00–noon
Pub. *Fond du Lac County Historical Society Newsletter*, quarterly
$7.00 per year membership for individuals, $15.00 per year membership for families, $50.00 per year membership for businesses; resource center admission: $3.00 per day for non-members

Genesee Heritage Society
PO Box 52
Genesee Depot, WI 53127
(414) 968-3166

Germantown Historical Society, Inc.
PO Box 31
Germantown, WI 53022
(414) 251-6378
Irene M. Blau, President
Pub. *Newsletter*

Grant County Historical Society
129 East Maple Street
Lancaster, WI 53813
(608) 723-4925 (Museum)
Albert D. Weber, Director Cunningham
Hours: various
Pub. *Here & There in Grant County*, four times per year, $1.50 per issue

Green County Historical Society, Inc.
(1617 Ninth Street—museum location)
2109 20th Avenue (mailing address)
Monroe, WI 53566
(608) 325-2609
http://www.fgs.org/~fgs/soc0203.htm
Mrs. John M. Irvin, Treasurer and Museum Chairman
Hours: Sat–Sun (Jun to mid-Sept) 2:00–5:00
(local history museum, no research facility, no staff to do research, does not operate a library)
$5.00 per year membership; $1.00 museum admission

Greendale Historical Society
6500 Northway
Greendale, WI 53129
(414) 421-1300

Greenfield Historical Society
56th Street and Layton Avenue
Greenfield, WI 53220
(414) 543-3324

Hales Corners Historical Society
5885 South 116th Street
Hales Corners, WI 53130

(414) 529-6150 (Hales Corners Library, inquiries will be forwarded to the Historical Society)
Ruth Johnston, President
(history of Hales Corners and southwestern Milwaukee County)

Hawks Inn Historical Society, Inc.
426 Wells Street
PO Box 104
Delafield, WI 53018
(414) 646-8540
Margaret E. Zerwekh, Chairman, History and Genealogy
Hours: May 1–Oct 31 (last Sun in Oct) 1:00–4:00, and by appointment (hours change for special events)
Pub. *Hawks Inn Newsletter* [sic, no apostrophe], bimonthly
(emphasis on Wisconsin history and stage coach inn restoration; "early settlement and pioneers Delafield area; Hawks family, Cushing family, Delafield family, among others")
$15.00 per year membership

High Cliff Historical Society
PO Box 1
Sherwood, WI 54169
(920) 989-1954

Hillsboro Area Historical Society, Inc.
532 Water Avenue
PO Box 9
Hillsboro, WI 54634
(608) 489-3322
Don Schiefelbein

Horicon Historical Society
322 Winter Street
PO Box 65
Horicon, WI 53032
Margaret Bartelt, Secretary

Hustisford Historical Society
(134 North Ridge Street—location
PO Box 12 (mailing address)
Hustisford, WI 53034
(920) 349-3501
Mary Zastrow, Treasurer
Hours: Jun–Sept: second & fourth Sun 1:00–3:00, and by appointment
Pub. *Hustisford Historical Society*
$5.00 per year membership

Iola Historical Society
300 North Main
Iola, WI 54945
(715) 445-3184

Iowa County Historical Society
PO Box 38
Dodgeville, WI 53533

Iron County Historical Society
303 Iron Street
PO Box 4
Hurley, WI 54534
(715) 561-2244
W. Hoepner, President

Hours: Mon, Wed & Fri–Sat 10:00–2:00
$1.00 per hour to use microfilm reader,
$1.00 per year Iron County
newspapers

Jackson County Historical Society

(13 South First Street—location)
223 North Fourth Street (mailing
address)
Black River Falls, WI 54615
(715) 284-4659

Jackson Historical Society

2860 Division Road
Jackson, WI 53037
(414) 677-2464
Ray Dausman, President
Hours: occasionally by appointment
(history of town and village of Jackson,
Washington County)

Jefferson Historical Society

(333 East Ogden Street—location)
1035 West Racine Road (mailing
address)
Jefferson, WI 53549
(920) 674-5306

Jump River Valley Historical Society

PO Box
Catawba, WI 54515
(715) 474-3408
Donna Krich

Juneau County Historical Society

211 North Union Street
PO Box 321
Mauston, WI 53948
Nancy McCullick, President
Hours: Memorial Day weekend–Labor
Day weekend: Sat–Sun 1:00–4:00;
Christmas open house: Nov 29–30 &
Dec 6–7 1:00–8:00, and by
appointment
Pub. *Juneau County Historical Society
Quarterly Bulletin*
$3.00 per year membership, $2.00 per
year membership for students, $100.00
life membership

Kenosha County Historical Society Museum Library

6300 Third Avenue
Kenosha, WI 53143
(414) 654-5770
Beverly McCumber, Archivist
Hours: Wed–Fri 2:00–4:30
Pub. *Southport Newsletter*, quarterly
$15.00 per year membership for
individuals, $25.00 per year
membership for families, $10.00 per
year membership for students and
senior citizens

Kewaskum Historical Society, Inc.

1202 Park View Drive
Kewaskum, WI 53040

Kewaunee County Historical Society

Kewaunee County Historical Museum
(Court House Square, 613 Dodge Street,
Kewaunee, WI 54216—location)
N9307 Abitz Lane (mailing address)
Luxemburg, WI 54217
(920) 866-2719
E-mail: gabitz@netnet.net
Gerald V. Abitz, President
Hours: Mon–Sun (Memorial Day
weekend–Labor Day) 10:30–4:30, and
by appointment
Pub. *KCHS Newsletter*, semiannually
(spring and fall)
(Kewaunee County history, artifacts, and
genealogy)
museum admission: $2.00

Kiel Historical Society

325 Indian Hill Road
Kiel, WI 53042

Knox Creek Historical Society

N4233 West Knox Road
Brantwood, WI 54513
(715) 564-2525
Marcella Braski

La Crosse County Historical Society

112 South Ninth Street
PO Box 1272
La Crosse, WI 54602
(608) 782-1980
Brenda R. Jordan, Administrative
Curator
Hours: Mon–Fri 10:00–5:00
Pub. *Past, Present and Future*,
bimonthly
(western Wisconsin, upper Mississippi
River valley)
$25.00 per year membership

Lafayette County Historical Society

Darlington Public Library
525 Main Street
Darlington, WI 53530
(608) 776-4171 (Library phone and
FAX)
Marion Howard, Head Librarian
Hours: Library: Mon & Wed–Thur 1:30–
8:30, Tue 1:30–5:30, Fri 10:00–5:00,
Sat 1:00–5:00; Historical Library
Room: Tue 2:00–4:00
Pub. *Looking Backwards*, quarterly
$7.00 per year membership for
individuals

Langlade County Historical Society

PO Box 219
Antigo, WI 54409
(715) 623-3631
Edward Morrissey, President
Hours: May 1–Sept 30: Tue, Thur & Sun
1:00–4:00
$2.00 per year membership for
individuals, $50.00 life membership

The Lemery Heritage Society

222 West Gorham
Madison, WI 53703
(608) 258-8967

Lincoln County Historical Society

1204 Sixth Street
Merrill, WI 54452

Linden Historical Society

General Delivery
Linden, WI 53533
C. D. Caygill

Manitowoc County Historical Society

PO Box 574
Manitowoc, WI 54221-0574
(920) 684-4445
Robert P. Fay, Executive Director
Hours: Mon–Fri 9:00–4:00
Pub. *Pinecrest Spirit Newsletter*,
quarterly; *Manitowoc County
Historical Society Monographs*,
annually
$15.00 per year membership for
individuals

Marathon County Historical Society

Marathon County Historical Museum
410 McIndoe Street
Wausau, WI 54403
(715) 848-6143; (715) 848-0378 Library;
(715) 848-0576 FAX
Mary Jane Hettinga, Librarian/Archivist
Hours: Tue–Thur 9:00–3:30
(logging, native American, regional and
local history)

Marinette County Historical Society

Marinette Historical Museum
(Highway 41 Stephenson Island,
Marinette, WI—location)
PO Box 262 (mailing address)
Marinette, WI 54143
(715) 732-0831
Walter Stepniak, Curator
Hours: 10:00–4:30
Pub. *The Historian*, quarterly
$10.00 per year membership for
individuals, $12.00 per year
membership for husband and wife,
$15.00 per year membership for
families, $30.00 per year Sustaining
membership, $125.00 life membership
for individuals, $175.00 life
membership for husband and wife

Marquette County Historical Society

(125 Lawrence Street—location)
PO Box 172 (mailing address)
Westfield, WI 53964
Fran Sprain, Curator
Hours: end of May–first week of
September: Wed & Sat 1:00–4:00
Pub. *Imprints on the Sands of Marquette
County*, three or four times per year
(growing file of genealogies)
$10.00 per year membership; minimal
searches

Mayville Historical Society, Inc.
(Corner of North German and Bridge
Streets—location)
PO Box 82 (mailing address)
Mayville, WI 53050
(414) 387-5530
James A. Schinderle, President
Hours: second & fourth Sun (May–Oct)
1:30–4:30
does no genealogical research of any
kind

**Mazomanie Historical Society—
Research Center**
Mazomanie Depot Library
104 North John Street
Mazomanie, WI 53560
(608) 795-2216
Jeanne Mahony, Research Historian;
Virgil Matz, Research Historian (1203
Mill Street, Black Earth, WI 53515)
Hours: Library: Mon, Wed & Fri 2:00–
8:00, Tue, Thur & Sat 9:00–noon
(Mazomanie records and newspapers,
etc; limited Black Earth records from
Black Earth location)
no charge for searching records

McFarland Historical Society
5814 Main Street
PO Box 62
McFarland, WI 53558
(608) 838-4185

Mellen Area Historical Society
(City Hall, corner of Main and Bennett
Streets—location)
PO Box 522 (mailing address)
Mellen, WI 54546
Vyola Turney, President
Hours: Mon–Fri 9:00–12:00
$8.00 per year membership for
individuals, $10.00 per year
membership for families, $100.00 life
membership

Menomonee Falls Historical Society
Old Falls Village
N96 W 15791 County Line Road
Menomonee Falls, WI 53051
(414) 255-8346
Carol Prestin, President

Merrill Historical Society
Merrill Historical Museum
804 East Third Street
Merrill, WI 54452
(715) 536-5652
Jeanne Chrudimsky, Administrative
Assistant
Hours: 1:00–4:00
Pub. *Northwoods Historian*, bimonthly
$10.00 per year membership for
individuals, $15.00 per year
membership for families; research
requests referred to a qualified
individual who charges a per-hour fee

Middleton Historical Society
7426 Hubbard Avenue
Middleton, WI 53562
(608) 831-6949

Milton Historical Society
(742 East Madison—winter office
location
18 South Janesville—summer office
location)
PO Box 245 (mailing address)
Milton, WI 53563
(608) 868-7772
E-mail: miltonhouse@inwave.com
http://www.inwave.com/milton/
miltonhouse
Judy Scheehle, Director
Hours: Museum: Mon–Fri (Memorial
Day–Labor Day) 10:00–4:00; research
by appointment
Pub. *The Herald*, quarterly
research by staff: $10.00 per hour,
$10.00 minimum deposit, copies: 25¢
each

**Milwaukee County Historical
Society**
910 North Old World Third Street
Milwaukee, WI 53203
(414) 273-8288
Judith A. Simonsen, Curator of Research
Collections
Hours: Mon–Fri 9:30–12:00 & 1:00–
4:30, Sat 10:00–12:00 & 1:00–4:30
(call ahead to verify Saturday hours)
Pub. *Magazine*, quarterly; *Newsletter*,
monthly
("Naturalization papers, court cases,
coroner's inquests, biographical
indexes, census, city directories, maps,
photographs")
$20.00 per year membership for
individuals, $12.00 per year
membership for senior citizens and
students, $25.00 per year membership
for families; $6.00 general research fee

Mineral Point Historical Society
Davis Street
Mineral Point, WI 53565

**Mount Horeb Area Historical
Society**
(138 East Main Street—location)
408 Lake Street (mailing address)
Mount Horeb, WI 53572

Muskego Historical Society
(Old Town Hall, W180-S7732 Pioneer
Drive—location)
PO Box 137 (mailing address)
Muskego, WI 53150
(414) 679-5667
Ron Peters, President
Pub. *MHS Newsletter*

Neenah Historical Society
PO Box 343
Neenah, WI 54956

Mrs. Nathan Wauda, President
$8.00 per year membership for
individuals

Neosho Historical Society
PO Box 105
Neosho, WI 53059
(920) 625-3632
Michael A. Weynand, President
Hours: second & fourth Sun (Apr–Oct)
1:00–4:00, and by appointment
Pub. *Neosho Museum Researcher*,
quarterly
("developing an excellent regional
county research library")

New Berlin Historical Society
(19765 West National Avenue, New
Berlin, WI 53146—location)
5575 South Maberry Lane (mailing
address)
New Berlin, WI 53151
(414) 679-1783
Jackie Hermann, President
Hours: by appointment, and three special
open houses (various dates)
Pub. *New Berlin Almanack*, irregularly
$5.00 per year membership for
individuals, $7.00 per year
membership for families, $3.00 per
year membership for senior citizens,
$35.00 life membership

New Glarus Historical Society
Swiss Historical Village
612 Seventh Avenue
PO Box 745
New Glarus, WI 53574-0745
(608) 527-2305

New Holstein Historical Society
2025 Randolph Avenue
PO Box 144
New Holstein, WI 53061
(920) 898-5358
Michael Cramer, President
Hours: Sun (Memorial Day–Labor Day)
1:00–4:00, and by appointment
Pub. *New Holstein Historical Society
Annual Newsletter*
$3.00 per year membership for
individuals, $100.00 life membership

**North Wood County Historical
Society, Inc.**
212 West Third Street
PO Box 142
Marshfield, WI 54449
(715) 387-3322
Kathie Haynes, Coordinator
Hours: Mon–Thur 1:00–4:00, Sun 1:30–
4:00
$5.00 per year membership for
individuals, $10.00 per year
membership for families, $25.00 per
year Sustaining membership, $50.00
per year membership for businesses,
$200.00 life membership; search fee:
donation

Northland Historical Society

PO Box 325
Lake Tomahawk, WI 54539
(715) 277-2788

Oak Creek Historical Society

(3201 East Forest Hill Avenue—location)
9472 South 27th Street (mailing address)
Oak Creek, WI 53154

The Oconomowoc Historical Society

(103 West Jefferson Street—museum
   location)
PO Box 969 (mailing address)
Oconomowoc, WI 53066
(414) 569-0740
Kathi Klann, Administrator; Frank
   Anderson, President
Hours: Jun–Sept: Thur–Fri 10:00–1:00,
   Sat–Sun 2:00–5:00
Pub. *Coo-No-Mo-Wauk*, quarterly
$10.00 per year membership

Oconto County Historical Society

917 Park Avenue
Oconto, WI 54153
(920) 834-6206
Diane Nichols, President
Hours: 1 Jun–Labor Day: noon-4:00
Pub. *News from the Northwoods*,
   quarterly
$10.00 per year membership for
   individuals

Omro Area Historical Society

(114 Main Street—location)
PO Box 133 (mailing address)
Omro, WI 54963
Gordon Moran, Secretary-Treasurer
$3.00 per year membership for
   individuals, $5.00 per year
   membership for families

Outagamie County Historical Society, Inc.

330 East College Avenue
Appleton, WI 54911
(920) 735-9370
Matthew Carpenter, Curator of
   Collections
Hours: Mon (Jun–Aug) 10:00–5:00,
   Tue–Sat 10:00–5:00, Sun 12:00–5:00
Pub. *History Today*, bimonthly
("history of lower Fox River Valley;
   Charles A. Grignon family")
$15.00 per year membership for
   individuals, $30.00 per year
   membership for families, $7.00 per
   year membership for seniorcitizens,
   $125.00+ per year Corporate
   membership

Ozaukee County Historical Society Archives

(West 63 North 643 Washington
   Avenue—location)
PO Box 206 (mailing address)
Cedarburg, WI 53012
(414) 377-4510 (Office); (414) 242-6788
   (Home)

Alice Wendt, Librarian
Hours: Tue 9:00–3:00
Pub. *Newsletter*, quarterly
$10.00 per year membership; search fee
   or user fee: $2.00

Palmyra Historical Society

(226 West Main Street—location)
PO Box 265 (mailing address)
Palmyra, WI 53156
Hours: various
Pub. *NewsLetter*, quarterly
$10.00 per year membership

Pierce County Historical Association

414 West Main
Ellsworth, WI 54011
(715) 273-6611
Reta Sanford, Archivist
Hours: weekday afternoons
Pub. *Pierce County's Heritage*,
   irregularly
$8.00 per year membership for
   individuals, $5.00 per year
   membership for students and senior
   citizens

Polk County Historical Society

Balsam Lake, WI 54810
(715) 485-3136

Portage County Historical Society

PO Box 672
Stevens Point, WI 54481
(715) 344-7607
Tim Siebert, President
Pub. *Portage County Historical Society
   Newsletter*, semiannually
$15.00 per year membership; search:
   $5.00 per hour plus costs

Poynette Area Historical Society

(114 North Main Street—location)
PO Box 162 (mailing address)
Poynette, WI 53955
(608) 635-2600; (608) 635-2970
Betty Hutchinson, Vice President;
   Evadne Hahn, President
$5.00 per year membership

Price County Historical Society

Old Town Hall Museum
W7213 Pine
Fifield, WI 54524
(715) 762-4571 (Curator)
Patricia Schroeder, Curator
Hours: Jun–Labor Day: Fri & Sun 1:00–
   5:00, and by appointment
Pub. *Price County Historical Society
   Newsletter*, three to four times per year
$5.00 per year membership for
   individuals, $7.00 per year
   membership for families, $10.00 per
   year Contributing membership, $15.00
   per year Sustaining membership,
   $150.00 life membership; search fee:
   $5.00 for one name, reasonable date,
   in courthouse or newspaper

Princeton Historical Society, Inc.

632 West Water Street
Princeton, WI 54968
(920) 295-4949
Donald C. Gray, President
Hours: by appointment only

Racine County Historical Society and Museum, Inc.

Archives
701 South Main Street
Racine, WI 53403
(414) 636-3926; (414) 636-3940 FAX
Hours: Archives: Tue & Sat 1:00–4:00;
   Museum: Tue–Fri 9:00–5:00, Sat–Sun
   1:00–5:00
Pub. *Focus*, quarterly
(both historical and genealogical; local
   industrial and cultural history)
$20.00 per year membership; research:
   $10.00 per hour minimum, $25.00 per
   hour for rush processing, 25¢ per
   photocopy, plus LSASE

Reedsburg Area Historical Society, Inc.

(3 miles east of Reedsburg on Highway
   33—location)
PO Box 405 (mailing address)
Reedsburg, WI 53959
(608) 727-2922 (President); (608) 524-
   2545 (Mr. Steinweg)
Lavern Kruse, President; Conrad
   Steinweg
Hours: Sat–Sun (Memorial Day weekend
   through Sept) 1:00–4:00
Pub. *Newsletter*, annually
("In the library we have collections of
   various books and scrapbooks.")
$3.00 per year membership for
   individuals, $7.00 per year
   membership for families, $15.00 per
   year membership for businesses,
   $100.00 life membership

Ripon Historical Society

PO Box 274
Ripon, WI 54971-0274
(920) 748-5354

Rock County Historical Society

10 South High Street
PO Box 8096
Janesville, WI 53545
(608) 756-3036
Maurice J. Montgomery, Curator/
   Archivist
Hours: Mon–Fri 9:00–4:00 by
   appointment
Pub. *Rock County Recorder*, quarterly
(Rock County history and genealogy;
   Wisconsin history)
$25.00 per year membership for
   individuals, $45.00 per year
   membership for households, $100.00
   per year Patron membership, $250.00
   per year Benefactor membership,
   $500.00 Corporate membership,
   $1,000.00 life membership

Rusk County Historical Society
(Rusk County Fairgrounds—location)
W7891 Old 8 (mailing address)
Ladysmith, WI 54848
(715) 532-6450
Betty Silvernale, Curator

Saint Croix County Historical Society
Octagon House, 1004 Third Street
Hudson, WI 54016
(715) 386-2654
Dorothy Wilson, President
Hours: Tue–Sat 10:00–11:30 & 2:00–4:30, Sun 2:00–4:30
Pub. *The Bulletin*, semiannually
$5.00 per year membership for individuals, $10.00 per year membership for families

Sauk County Historical Society and Museum
(431 Fourth Avenue—location)
PO Box 651 (mailing address)
Baraboo, WI 53913
(608) 356-1001
Kathy Waddell, Curator; Mona Larsen, President
Hours: Tue–Sun (May–Sept) 2:00–5:00, and by appointment
Pub. *Sauk Trails*, quarterly
(Sauk County history and genealogy)
$8.00 per year membership for individuals, $10.00 per year membership for couples; museum admission: members free, $2.00 for non-members; search fees: cost of copying and postage, accepts donations

Sauk-Prairie Historical Society, Inc.
PO Box 104
Sauk City, WI 53583
(608) 643-3000

Sawyer County Historical Society, Inc.
(Route 6, County Trunk "B"—location)
PO Box 384 (mailing address)
Hayward, WI 54843
(715) 634-3075 (evenings)
Andrea Wittwer, President
Hours: to be determined

Seymour Community Historical Society
PO Box 305
Seymour, WI 54165
(920) 833-2063

Shawano County Historical Society
(524 North Franklin—location)
1003 South Main Street (mailing address)
Shawano, WI 54166
(715) 524-4744
Mrs. William Bayer, President
Hours: Jun–Aug: Wed & Sat–Sun 1:30–4:00

$2.00 per year Active membership, $5.00 per year Sustaining membership, $25.00 life membership

Sheboygan County Historical Research Center, Inc.
518 Water Street
Sheboygan Falls, WI 53085
(920) 467-3106; (920) 467-4667
Rose M. Rumpff, Executive Director; Janice Hildebrand, Librarian
Hours: Tue–Sat 9:00–4:00
Pub. *Quarterly*
(Sheboygan County history and genealogy)
$10.00 per year membership

South Milwaukee Historical Society
(717 Milwaukee Avenue—location)
3516 18th Avenue (mailing address)
South Milwaukee, WI 53172
Dean Marlowe, Jr., President
Hours: summer: Sun
Pub. *Newsletter*, quarterly
$6.00 per year membership for families

South Wood County Historical Corporation
540 Third Street
Wisconsin Rapids, WI 54494
(715) 423-1580
Dave Engel, Director
Pub. *River City Memoirs*

Stanley Area Historical Society
(Corner of Helgerson and Church Street—location)
403 Franklin Street (mailing address)
Stanley, WI 54768
(715) 644-5492 (ask for Betty)
David Jankoski, President
Hours: Sat–Sun (Jun–Sept) 1:00–4:00
Pub. *Stanley Historical Society Newsletter*, semiannually (May and November)
("family information, photos, vital information")
$5.00 per year membership for individuals; research for donation

Stockbridge Historical Society
PO Box 315
Stockbridge, WI 53088

Sun Prairie Historical Library and Museum, Inc.
(115 East Main Street—location)
240 Jones Street (mailing address)
Sun Prairie, WI 53590

Taylor County Historical Society, Inc.
(W845 Broadway—location)
224 South Second Street (mailing address)
Medford, WI 54451
(715) 747-3808
Elaine Mnavik, Curator
Hours: Museum: Thur–Fri 9:00–4:00, except holidays

Pub. *Log Cabin News*, five times per year (prior to membership meetings)
$5.00 per year membership, $75.00 life membership

Three Lakes Historical Society Museum
1798 Huron Street
PO Box 250
Three Lakes, WI 54562
(715) 546-3529; (715) 546-2295
Walt Goldsworthy, Administrator
Hours: May–Sept: 10:00–4:00
Pub. *Echo*
(general and family histories, many pictures, maps, etc.)

Trempealeau County Historical Society
(Whitehall, WI—location)
Bank of Galesville (mailing address)
Galesville, WI 54630
(715) 985-3310
E-mail: agrajag@juno.com
Nancy Bergman, Board Member
$5.00 per year membership for individuals; research: $6.00 per hour

Two Rivers Historical Society, Inc.
Historic Washington House
1622 Jefferson Street
Two Rivers, WI 54241
(920) 793-2490
Walter L. Vogl, President
Hours: Mon–Sun 9:00 A.M.–9:00 P.M.
Pub. *Two Rivers Historical Society Newsletter*, quarterly
$5.00 per year membership

Historical Society of the Upper Baraboo Valley
(Valton, WI—location)
E 940 Painted Forest Drive
Wonewoc, WI 53968
(608) 983-2854
Lorene Simons, President

Vernon County Historical Society
341 Terrace Avenue
Viroqua, WI 54665
(608) 637-7185

Walworth County Historical Society
9 East Rockwell Street
PO Box 273
Elkhorn, WI 53121
(414) 723-4248
Walter Dunn, President
Hours: Wed–Sun 1:00–5:00
(Walworth County history)
$15.00 per year membership; search fees vary

Washburn County Historical Society and Museum
Shell Lake, WI 54871
(715) 468-2982; (715) 468-7615
Lucille Miller, Historical Museum Secretary

Washington County Historical Society, Inc.

Old Courthouse Square Museum
340 South Fifth Avenue
West Bend, WI 53095
(414) 335-4678
Mary Ann Parlow, Museum
   Administrator
Hours: Tours and gift shop: Tue–Thur
   10:00–4:00, Sun 1:00–4:00; research:
   by appointment
Pub. *The Court Reporter*, quarterly;
   exhibit catalogs
(information on Washington County
   dating back to 1840; Old Jailhouse at
   340 South Fifth Avenue, open in 1998
   or 1999)
$8.00 per year membership for
   individuals, $12.00 per year
   membership for families

Waterloo Area Historical Society

South Monroe and East Polk Streets
PO Box 52
Waterloo, WI 53594
(920) 478-2328
Elaine Gorder, Secretary
Hours: Sun (Memorial Day to Mid-
   September) 1:30–4:00, and
   byappointment
Pub. *Timescape*, monthly
$7.00 per year membership for
   individuals, $10.00 per year
   membership for families

Watertown Historical Society

919 Charles Street
Watertown, WI 53094
(920) 261-2796
Bill Jannke, III, Historian/Archivist
Hours: Memorial Day–Labor Day:
   10:00–4:00; after Labor Day–before
   Memorial Day: 11:00–3:00
Pub. *The Historical Review*, quarterly
$8.00 per year membership for
   individuals, $12.00 per year
   membership for couples, $20.00 per
   year membership for families, $30.00
   per year Patron membership, $50.00
   per year Benefactor membership;
   search fee: $20.00 initial search

Waukesha County Historical Society

(Waukesha County Museum, Research
   Center, 101 West Main Street,
   Waukesha, WI 53186—location)
PO Box 833 (mailing address)
Waukesha, WI 53187-0833
(414) 521-2859
Susan K. Baker, Executive Director
Hours: Tue–Sat 10:30–4:30
Pub. *WCHS News*, quarterly; *Landmark*,
   quarterly
$17.00 per year membership

Waupaca County Historical Society

823 Depot Street
Manawa, WI 54949
(920) 596-3467

Waupun Historical Society

(Waupun Heritage Museum, 22 South
   Madison—location)
400 Grove Street (mailing address)
Waupun, WI 53963
(608) 324-5738
Eugene Buchholz, President
Hours: first & third Sun 1:00–4:00, and
   by appointment

Waushara County Historical Society, Inc.

221 Sault Sainte Marie Street
Wautoma, WI 54982
(920) 787-7584
Ardis Spuhler, President
Hours: Jun–Sept: Wed & Sat 1:00–4:00,
   and by appointment
Pub. *Newsletter*, one or two per year
$2.00 per year membership

Wauwatosa Historical Society

Kneeland-Walker House and Gardens
7406 Hillcrest Drive
Wauwatosa, WI 53213-2226
(414) 774-8672
http://www.icomplete.com/
   tosahistoricalsoc
Kathleen Ehley, President
Hours: Mon–Thur 9:00–1:00 (call to
   confirm)
Pub. *Historic Wauwatosa*, bimonthly
(19th century school house program for
   children, adult education programs,
   special events)
$15.00 per year membership for
   individuals, $25.00 per year
   membership for households, $10.00
   per year membership for senior
   citizens, $15.00 per year membership
   for senior citizen households, $75.00
   per year Firefly Art Fair Patron
   membership, $15.00 per year Silver
   Star Patron membership, $500.00 per
   year Gold Star Patron membership,
   $1,000.00 per year Platinum Star
   Patron membership

West Allis Historical Society

8405 West National Avenue
West Allis, WI 53227
(414) 541-6970
John R. Clow, Jr., President
Hours: Museum: Tue 7:00 P.M.–9:00
   P.M., Sun 2:00–4:00
Pub. *Buzz*, bimonthly
$8.00 per year membership per year

West Milwaukee Historical Society

4826 West Beloit Road
West Milwaukee, WI 53214
(414) 384-3522

West Salem Historical Society

360 North Leonard
West Salem, WI 54669
(608) 786-1399 (Memorial Day–Labor
   Day); (608) 786-1675 (President)
Errol Kindschy, President
Hours: 10:00–4:30

("West Salem area; only getting started
   in this field; have old scrapbooks,
   books, information on families of
   area")

Western Bayfield County Historical Society

Rt. 1, Box 34
Iron River, WI 54847
(715) 372-4359
Robert North

Wild Rose Historical Society

Main Street
Wild Rose, WI 54984
(920) 622-3555
Rodney Radloff
Hours: 15 Jun–1 Sept

Winneconne Historical Society, Inc.

611 West Main Street
Winneconne, WI 54986
(920) 582-4132
Loren J. Driscoll, President

Wittenberg Area Historical Society

(Vinal and Home Streets—location)
PO Box 242 (mailing address)
Wittenberg, WI 54499-0242
(715) 253-2581
Wilmarth A. Thayer, Secretary-Treasurer
Hours: Sun (Memorial Day–Labor Day)
   P.M., and by appointment
("Hope this winter to establish early
   1900s law office and archives of early
   printed matter of the local village
   government")
$5.00 per year membership

LDS Family History Centers

Appleton
(414) 733-5358

Hales Corners
(414) 425-4182

Madison
(608) 238-4844

Milwaukee
(see Hales Corners)

Genealogical Societies

State Genealogical Societies

Wisconsin Genealogical Council, Inc.

109 Summer Street
Schofield, WI 54476-1282
Pat Kell, Newsletter Editor
Pub. *WGC Newsletter*, quarterly

$7.00 per year membership for individuals, $15.00 per year membership for organizations

Wisconsin State Genealogical Society, Inc. (WSGS)

(2109 20th Avenue, Monroe, WI 53566—location)
PO Box 5106 (mailing address)
Madison, WI 53705-0106
Mrs. John M. Irvin, Treasurer; Mrs. Gilbert Emmert, President
Pub. *WSGS Newsletter*, quarterly (June, September, January, April)
(Wisconsin source material)
$14.00 per year membership for individuals or institutions, $15.00 per year membership for families (two persons at same address)

WSGS Chapters

La Crosse Area Genealogical Society Chapter (WSGS)

PO Box 1782
La Crosse, WI 54602-1782
(608) 788-1738
Pub. *La Crosse Area Genealogical Society Quarterly*
$3.00 per year membership, $14.00 per year membership (includes membership in WSGS)

South Central Chapter (WSGS)

4817 Hillview Terrace
Madison, WI 53711-1236
Les Floeter, Treasurer
(serves Columbia, Dane, Dodge, Green, Jefferson and Rock counties)
$4.50 per year membership for individuals, $5.00 per year membership for families

Regional Genealogical Societies

Ashland-Bayfield Counties Tree Climbers

Rt. 1, Box 139
Mason, WI 54856
(715) 765-4597
Carol Jones Wilson
(Ashland and Bayfield County research and area surname connections)
organization not formally in existence but still holding meetings; search fees: $10.00 per hour

Bay Area Genealogical Society, Inc.

PO Box 283
Green Bay, WI 54305-0283
(920) 494-9286
Myra Michaletz, Editor
Pub. *Gems of Genealogy*, six times per year
(all Brown County cemeteries, some adjacent counties)

$10.00 per year membership; search fees vary

Chippewa County Genealogical Society

1427 Hilltop Boulevard
Chippewa Falls, WI 54729-1920
Anne Adams Keller; Betty Plombon, President
Hours: Tue 9:00–4:00; meetings at 123 Allen Street
Pub. *Chippewa County (Wisconsin) Newsletter*, five times per year
(all county records; county-wide cemetery index; a highly praised library of research materials)
$7.00 per year membership for individuals

Coon Valley Family Research Society at Norskedalen

Norskedalen
PO Box 225
Coon Valley, WI 54623
(608) 452-3424
James Nestingen, Director
Hours: Mon–Sun 12:00–4:00
(small library; "Norwegian emigration to Coon Valley, Wisconsin")

Dodge/Jefferson Counties Genealogical Society

PO Box 91
Watertown, WI 53094-0091
(920) 261-0943
Elaine Smith
Hours: meetings at Heritage Hall, 504 South Fourth Street, Watertown: second Mon 7:15; Library: Tue 9:00–noon, Thur (except last Thur) 1:00–4:00, last Thur 6:00–9:00
Pub. *Out on a Limb*, four times per year (February, May, August, November)
(holdings housed at Heritage Hall include area church and cemetery records, obituaries and marriages from area newspapers, directories, family histories, county histories, census, passenger lists, vital records, surname card index, etc.)
$8.00 per year membership for individuals, $10.00 per year membership for families; free queries for members; admission: $2.00 per day for non-members

Dubuque County-Key City Genealogical Society Chapter (IGS)

(see Iowa)

Genealogical Research Society of Eau Claire

Chippewa Valley Museum
Carsons Park Drive
PO Box 1204
Eau Claire, WI 54702
Hours: Museum: Tue–Sun 1:00–5:00
(Eau Claire County)

Fond du Lac County Genealogical Society

Spillman Library
PO Box 1264
Fond du Lac, WI 54936
(920) 929-3771; (920) 923-0414 (Ms. Hoffman)
Elaine Hoffman
Hours: Mon & Thur 12:00–8:00, Tue 12:00–5:00, Wed & Fri 10:00–5:00, Sat (Labor Day–Memorial Day) 10:00–1:00
Pub. *Newsletter*, semiannually
$8.00 per year membership for individuals or families

Fox Valley Genealogical Society

425 West Park Ridge Avenue
PO Box 1592
Appleton, WI 54913-1592
(920) 733-5358
Mr. Jerry T. Long, Query Editor
Hours: Wed 10:00–9:00, Fri–Sat 9:00–4:00
Pub. *Genealogical Gems*, quarterly
(northeast Wisconsin: Outagamie, Calumet, and Waupaca counties)
$8.00 per year membership for individuals, $12.00 per year membership for families; search: SASE

Grant County Genealogical Society

PO Box 281
Dickeyville, WI 53808-0281
(608) 568-3124; (608) 568-3753 FAX
E-mail: reese@mwci.net
Karen Reese, President
Pub. *Grant County Heritage*, quarterly
$5.00 per year membership; cemetery surname search: $3.00

Hartford Area Genealogy Society

c/o Hartford Public Library
115 North Main
Hartford, WI 53027
(414) 673-8240 (Library)
Shirley Hess
Hours: meetings in the Hartford Library, Hartford History Room: Jan–Apr & Jun–Nov 1:30

Heart O' Wisconsin Genealogical Society

McMillan Memorial Library
490 East Grand Avenue
Wisconsin Rapids, WI 54494
(715) 423-1040 (Library)
Hours: Library: Mon–Thur 9:00–9:00, Fri 9:00–6:00, Sat 9:00–5:00, Sun 1:00–5:00; hours vary during summer
Pub. *Heart O' Wisconsin Genealogical Society Newsletter*, quarterly
(emphasis on Wood County; local cemetery and newspaper indexes)
$7.00 per year membership

Hillsboro Area Genealogical Society

Albert Field Memorial Park
Hillsboro, WI 54634

Kenosha County Genealogy Society
4902 52nd Street
Kenosha, WI 53144
(414) 652-2410
Lois Roepke Stein, Founding Member and Past President
Pub. *Southport Echo*, bimonthly
$8.00 per year membership for individuals (beginning in February), $9.00 per year membership for families; free queries in newsletter; search fees: donation

Lafayette County Genealogical Society
PO Box 443
Shullsburg, WI 53586
Pub. *Ancestral Diggins of Lafayette County*, quarterly
$7.00 per year membership for individuals, $10.00 per year membership for families or foreign membership

Manitowoc County Genealogical Society
PO Box 1745
Manitowoc, WI 54221-1745
(920) 682-1046
Catherine Coppens
Pub. *Family Vines*, quarterly (April, July, October, January)
$5.00 per year (beginning in October)

Marathon County Genealogical Society
PO Box 1512
Wausau, WI 54402-1512
Mr. Jerry Viste
Pub. *Pinery Pedigree*, bimonthly
$10.00 per year membership for individuals, $15.00 per year membership for families

Marshfield Area Genealogy Group
PO Box 337
Marshfield, WI 54449
Sherrie Framness, President
Hours: by appointment
Pub. *Kith and Kin*, bimonthly
(eastern Clark County, western Marathon County and northern Wood County)
$12.00 per year membership for individuals, $15.00 per year membership for families

Milwaukee County Genealogical Society, Inc.
PO Box 27326
Milwaukee, WI 53227-0326
Betty Jane Larson, Treasurer
Pub. *M.C.G.S. Reporter*, quarterly
$8.00 per year membership for individuals, $10.00 per year membership for families, $18.00 per year foreign membership

Monroe, Juneau, Jackson County, Wisconsin, Genealogy Workshop, Inc.
723 Packard Street
Tomah, WI 54660
(608) 372-5810
Marie Drescher, Treasurer
Pub. *MJJCGW Newsletter*, quarterly
(tri-county genealogical society)
$7.00 per year membership for individuals, $9.00 per year membership for families

Northern Wisconsin Genealogists
(Corner of Zingler and Evergreen—location)
1188 East Ridlington Avenue (mailing address)
Shawano, WI 54116-3724
(715) 526-2946
Kathleen Z. Hoffman
Hours: Tue–Thur & Sat 9:00–4:00
$5.00 per year membership

Northwest Territory Genealogical Society
(see Indiana)

Northwoods Genealogical Society
(see Oneida County Genealogical Society)

Oconomowoc Genealogical Club of Waukesha County
733 East Sherman Avenue
Oconomowoc, WI 53066
(414) 567-3197
Mrs. R. L. Palmer, President
Hours: 10:00–9:00

Oneida County Genealogical Society
Northwoods Genealogical Society
Rhinelander District Library
106 North Stevens Street
Rhinelander, WI 54501

Price County Genealogical Club
W6298 County Road D
Phillips, WI 54555
(715) 339-3667
Linda Loula

Rock County Genealogical Society, Inc.
(Rock County Historical Society, 10 South High Street, Second Floor, Janesville, WI 53545—library location)
PO Box 711 (mailing address)
Janesville, WI 53547-0711
(608) 756-4509 (Library); (608) 752-2688 (Information)
Hours: Tue–Thur 9:00–3:00, appointment helpful
Pub. *The Rock County Genealogical Society, Inc. Member News*, five times per year (September, November, January, March and May)
$8.00 per year membership for individuals, $10.00 per year

membership for families or for individuals in Canada, $5.00 per year membership for students, $150.00 life membership; queries free for members, $1.00 for non-members

Saint Croix Valley Genealogical Society
Attention Chairman
PO Box 396
River Falls, WI 54022
Pub. *Pipost*, quarterly
$8.00 per year membership

Sheboygan County Genealogical Society
518 Water Street
Sheboygan Falls, WI 53085
(920) 467-4667
Wayne G. Koene, President
Hours: Tue–Sat 9:00–4:00
Pub. *Sheboygan County Genealogist*, quarterly
(family histories of Sheboygan County families)
$7.00 per year membership for individuals, $10.00 per year membership for families

Stevens Point Area Genealogical Society
Portage County Library
1001 Main Street
Stevens Point, WI 54481
(715) 346-1548
Ruth Steffen, President
Hours: Library: Mon–Fri 9:30–9:00, Sat 9:30–5:00, reduced summer hours
Pub. *Pedigree Pointers*, quarterly
(serves Portage County)
$10.00 per year membership for individuals, $12.00 per year membership for families

Twin Ports Genealogical Society
(see Minnesota)

Walworth County Genealogical Society
PO Box 159
Delavan, WI 53115-0159
(414) 728-3719 (Treasurer)
John Stevenson, Treasurer
Hours: meetings at United Methodist Church, 213 South Second Street, Delavan, WI 53115: first Tue 7:00; Library in basement of the Aram Public Library: Tue 10:00–2:00, second Sat 11:00–2:00
Pub. *Walworth County Genealogical Society Newsletter*, bimonthly
$10.00 per year membership for individuals (beginning 1 September), $12.50 per year membership for families

Washburn County Genealogical Society

(102 West Second Avenue—location)
PO Box 366 (mailing address)
Shell Lake, WI 54871
(715) 468-2982
Bonnie Brandt, President
Hours: Memorial Day–Labor Day: Wed–
Sat 10:00–4:00
Pub. *Roots in Washburn County*,
quarterly
$7.00 per year membership; search fees
vary

Waukesha County Genealogical Society

PO Box 1541
Waukesha, WI 53187-1541
Pub. *WCGS Newsletter*, three times per
year
("Waukesha County only; we are private
citizens who work on our own family
trees; we have no office and no
government funding; send an SASE if
you want a reply.")
$10.00 per year membership for
individuals or couples; SASE for list
of researchers who require minimum
of three hours with payment in
advance for research in Waukesha
County and Milwaukee only

White Pine Genealogical Society

PO Box 512
Marinette, WI 54143

Winnebagoland Genealogical Society

Oshkosh Public Library
106 Washington Avenue
Oshkosh, WI 54901-4985
(920) 236-5226 (Library)
Hours: Library: Sept–May: Mon–Fri
9:00–9:00, Sat 9:00–5:00, Sun 1:00–
5:00; Jun–Aug: Mon–Fri 9:00–9:00,
Sat 9:00–1:00
Pub. *Winnebagoland Roots*, quarterly
$7.00 per year membership

Independent Publications and Miscellany

WiGenWeb

Part of U.S. GenWeb Project
E-mail: wi@usgenweb.com
http://www.rootsweb.com/~wigenweb
(links to other Wisconsin resources)

Wisconsin State Old Cemetery Society

(6100 West Mequon Road, Mequon, WI
53092—location)
1562 North 119th Street (mailing
address)
Milwaukee, WI 53226-3242
(414) 771-7781; (414) 242-3290
(President)

William Krause, Archivist; Beverly
Silldorff, President
Hours: by appointment with president
Pub. *Inscriptions: Newsletter of the
Wisconsin State Old Cemetery Society*,
four or five times per year
("cemetery stone inscriptions" and
preservation interests)
$8.00 per year membership for
individuals in the U.S., $10.00 per
year (U.S. funds) membership in
Canada, $20.00 per year Contributing
membership

WYOMING

Archives and Libraries with Holdings in Genealogy

State Archives and Library

Wyoming State Archives—Research Division

Barrett State Office Building
2301 Central Avenue
Cheyenne, WY 82002
(307) 777-7826
Rick Ewig, Historic Program Supervisor
Hours: Mon–Fri 8:00–5:00
Pub. *Annals of Wyoming*, quarterly;
Wyoming History News, bimonthly
$9.00 per year membership for
individuals, $12.00 per year joint
membership, $20.00 per year
membership for institutions

Wyoming State Archives

Archives, Records Management, and
Micrographics Services
Barrett State Office Building, Third
Floor
2301 Central Avenue
Cheyenne, WY 82002
(307) 777-7826; (307) 777-7044 FAX
Cindy Brown, Carl Hallberg, Ann
Nelson, Jean Brainerd and LaVaughn
Bresnahan, Sr., Senior Historians
Hours: Mon–Fri 8:00–5:00
(Collection includes city records—
municipal court, city commissioner's
minutes; county records—assessment
rolls, land records, marriages, military
discharge, naturalizations, probate,
civil and criminal cases, school
census; U.S. census; early Poll books;
city directories; biographical files,
Wyoming newspaper collection, death
certificates [50-year restriction]; etc.)
50¢ per page copied, $3.00 certification
fee, $5.00 exemplification fee (if
needed)

Wyoming State Library

Supreme Court Building
2301 Capitol Avenue
Cheyenne, WY 82002-0060
(307) 777-7281; (307) 777-6289 FAX
http://www.wsl.state.wy.us/
Hours: Mon–Fri 8:00–5:00
(no longer houses Wyoming State
Genealogy Collection; see Laramie
County Library System)

State Historical Society

Wyoming State Historical Society

1740 H184 Dell Range Boulevard
Cheyenne, WY 82002
(307) 635-4881

Judy West, Membership Coordinator
Pub. *Annals of Wyoming: The Wyoming History Journal*, quarterly
(no archives or other collection)
$20.00 per year membership for individuals

City, County and Regional Archives and Libraries

Casper College
Goodstein Foundation Library
Special Collections Department
Casper, WY 82601
(307) 268-2680; (307) 268-2682 FAX
E-mail: cspcbibman@wyld.state.wy.us
http://www.cc.whecn.edu/library/sc.htm

Fremont County Pioneer Museum
630 Lincoln Street
Lander, WY 82520
(307) 332-4137; (307) 332-6498 FAX
Todd Guenther, Director
Hours: 48 hours per week
Pub. *Wind River Mountaineer*, quarterly, $16.00 per year subscription
(Fremont County and Lander area history; biographies with family history)
10¢ per page copy charge

Goshen County Public Library
2001 East A Street
Torrington, WY 82240

Hot Springs County Museum and Cultural Center
700 Broadway
Thermopolis, WY 82443
(307) 864-5183
Linda J. Zierke, Director
Hours: Tue–Sat 8:00–5:00
charged for photocopies and reprints of photos only

Johnson County Library
171 North Adams
Buffalo, WY 82834
(307) 684-5546; (307) 684-7888 FAX
E-mail: njenning@will.state.wy.us
Nancy L. Jennings, Genealogy and Local History
Hours: Mon–Thur 10:00–8:00, Fri–Sat 10:00–5:00
(specializes in homesteaders, Indian wars, Bozeman Trail, forts, oral histories, cattle war, all on local level, and area genealogy)

Laramie County Library System
Genealogy Collection
2800 Central Avenue
Cheyenne, WY 82001
(307) 634-3561, ext. 44; (307) 634-2082 FAX
E-mail: larmgen_ill@wyld.state.wy.us
Rick Morgan, Genealogy Specialist; Lucie Osborn, Director

Hours: Mon–Thur 10:00–9:00, Fri–Sat 10:00–6:00, Sun (Sept–May) 1:00–5:00
(western history; houses Wyoming State Genealogy Collection and other local historical and genealogical collections)

Museum of the Great Plains
(see Oklahoma)

Park County Library
1057 Sheridan Avenue
Cody, WY 82414
(307) 587-6205
E-mail: mrobinson@will.state.wy.us
Mary Robinson
Hours: Mon & Thur noon–5:30 & 7:00–9:00, Tue–Wed & Fri 10:00–5:30, Sat 10:00–1:00

Platte County Library
904 Ninth Street
Wheatland, WY 82201
(307) 322-2689
Patty Myers, Director

Riverton Branch Library
1330 West Park Avenue
Riverton, WY 82501
Hours: Mon–Tue & Thur 12:00–9:00, Wed 9:00–9:00, Fri 9:00–1:00

Rockpile Museum
PO Box 455
Gillette, WY 82716
(307) 682-3248

Teton County Historical Research Center
c/o County Clerk's Office
(105 Mercill Avenue—location)
PO Box 1727 (mailing address)
Jackson, WY 83001-1727

Trail End State Historic Site
400 Clarendon Avenue
Sheridan, WY 82801
(307) 674-4589; (307) 672-1729 FAX
E-mail: cgeorg@missc.state.wy.us
http://wave.sheridan.wy.us/trailend.index/html
Cynde Georgen, Site Superintendent
Hours: Jun–Aug: 9:00–6:00; spring/fall: 1:00–4:00; closed 15 Dec–31 Mar

Uinta County Library
Reference Services
701 Main Street
Evanston, WY 82930
(307) 789-1328; (307) 789-0148 FAX
Hours: Mon–Fri 9:00–5:00
(local cemetery listings, local newspapers on microfilm)

University of Wyoming
(American Heritage Center, Centennial Complex, 13th and Ivinson—location)
PO Box 3924 (mailing address)
Laramie, WY 82071-3924
(307) 766-4114; (307) 766-5511 FAX
E-mail: AHCRef@UWyo.edu

http://www.uwyo.edu/ahc/geninfo.htm
Rick Ewig, Assistant Director; Lori Olson, Reference Archivist
Hours: winter: Mon–Fri 8:00–5:00, Sat 11:00–5:00; summer: Mon–Fri 7:30–4:30, Sat 11:00–5:00
Pub. *Heritage Highlights*, biannually no charge

Wyoming Pioneer Memorial Museum
Wyoming State Fair Grounds
Drawer 10
Douglas, WY 82633
(307) 358-9288; (307) 358-6030 FAX
Arlene Ekland-Earnst, Curator
Hours: summer: Mon–Fri 8:00–5:00, Sat 1:00–5:00; winter: by appointment

Historical Societies— Local and Regional

Albany County Historical Society
1409 Downey Street
Laramie, WY 82070
(307) 742-5988

Centennial Valley Historical Association
(Highway 130, west of Laramie—location)
PO Box 130 (mailing address)
Centennial, WY 82055-0130
(307) 742-7158
Jane H. Houston, Secretary
Hours: Nici Self Museum: 14 Jun through Labor Day: 1:00–5:00
("Area collections include ranching, lumbering, railroading and history of area.")
$5.00 per year membership for individuals, $10.00 per year membership for families, $50.00 life membership

Fort Bridger Historical Association, Inc.
Fort Bridger State Historic Site
PO Box 112
Fort Bridger, WY 82933
(307) 782-3842
Karla Behunin, Administrative Assistant
Hours: Mon–Fri 8:30–5:00
$9.00 per year membership for individuals, $12.00 per year membership for families

Fort Laramie Historical Association
(3 miles southwest of the Town of Fort Laramie on Highway 160—location)
HC 72, Box 389 (mailing address)
Fort Laramie, WY 82212
(307) 837-2662; (800) 321-5456
Pat Fullmer, Business Manager

Hours: Mon–Sun 8:00–4:30 (except Christmas, Thanksgiving and New Year)
Pub. *Mail Order Catalog*, annually ("We have one of the best western book stores to choose titles from including westward expansion, overland migration, Native Americans, western military history, and Fort Laramie specific.")
$10.00 per year membership, $100.00 life membership

Fort Phil Kearney/Bozeman Trail Association

PO Box 5013
Sheridan, WY 82801
Patty Myers, Secretary
Pub. *Lookout*, three times per year (November, March, July)
("Historic sites at Fort Phil Kearney and along the Bozeman Trail; focus on Indian Wars related history, 1864–1868.")
$10.00 per year membership for individuals, $25.00 per year membership for families, $200.00 life membership

Jackson Hole Museum and Teton County Historical Society

(105 Mercill Avenue—location)
PO Box 1256 (mailing address)
Jackson, WY 83001
(307) 733-9605
Larry Kummer, Director
Hours: Mon–Fri 9:00–5:00
Pub. *Quarterly Newsletter*
(historical research library and museum collection includes Teton County, Wyoming, archives, photos, oral histories; minimal genealogical records but some biographical records)

Niobara County Historical Society

Stagecoach Museum
322 South Main
PO Box 367
Lusk, WY 82225
(307) 334-3444
Hours: Museum: Sept–May: Mon–Wed 1:00–5:00; Jun: Mon–Fri 1:00–5:00; Jul–Aug: Tue–Sat 1:00–8:00, Sun 1:00–4:00
$5.00 per year membership for individuals; research at Museum: $5.00 per hour

Park County Historical Society Archives

1002 Sheridan Avenue
Cody, WY 82414
(307) 527-8530
Jeanie Cook
Hours: Mon–Fri 9:00–noon & 1:00–4:00
(a small local history archive center; Park County and Big Horn Basin)
$3.50 per year membership for individuals, $5.00 per year joint membership

Saratoga Historical and Cultural Association

Saratoga Museum
104 Constitution Avenue
PO Box 1131
Saratoga, WY 82331
(307) 326-5511
Pat Bensen, Museum Director
Hours: Memorial Day weekend–Labor Day: daily 1:00–5:00
$10.00 per year membership for individuals, $15.00 per year membership for families, free Golden Age membership (over 70 years old), $50.00 per year membership for businesses, $100.00 per year Patron membership

Star Valley Historical Society

PO Box 921
Afton, WY 83110

Sublette County Historical Society, Inc.

Museum of the Mountain Man
700 East Hennick
PO Box 909
Pinedale, WY 82941
(307) 367-4101; (307) 367-6768 FAX
Laurie M. Latta, Executive Director
Hours: May 1–Oct 1: Mon–Sun 10:00–6:00; winter: by appointment
Pub. *Beaver Plew*, three times per year, not available by subscription
(mountain men, local history, western settlement)
$25.00 per year membership for individuals, $40.00 per year membership for families, $50.00 per year Contributing membership, $100.00 per year Patron membership or membership for businesses, $500.00 per year Benefactor membership, $1,000.00 per year Sustaining membership

Sweetwater County Historical Museum

80 West Flaming Gorge Way
Green River, WY 82935
(307) 872-6435; (307) 872-6469 FAX
Ruth Lauritzen, Director
Hours: Mon–Fri 9:00–5:00, Sat (Jul–Aug) 1:00–5:00
minimal copy fees, extensive research projects cannot be undertaken

Washakie County Historical Society

PO Box 292
Worland, WY 82401
Bonnie Tuttle

Weston County Historical Society

Anna Miller Museum
401 Delaware
PO Box 698
Newcastle, WY 82701
(307) 746-4188
E-mail: annamm@mail1.trib.com.
Angelil Cregger, Director

Hours: Mon–Fri 9:00–5:00
("*Newcastle Newsletter Journal* 1890–1949, court dockets, Cambria records, photo archives")

LDS Family History Centers

Casper

(307) 234-3326

Evanston

(307) 789-2648

Genealogical Societies

Regional Genealogical Societies

Casper Amateur Genealogists

Casper College
Administration Building, Room 298
125 College Drive
Casper, WY 82601
Pam Martin, Genealogy Teacher
forwards queries to the Natrona County Genealogical Society

Cheyenne Genealogical Society

Laramie County Library System
Genealogy Collection
2800 Central Avenue
Cheyenne, WY 82001
(307) 634-3561, ext. 44 (Library)
Sharon Lass Field, Book Chairman
Hours: Library: Mon–Thur 10:00–9:00, Fri–Sat 10:00–6:00, Sun (Sept–May) 1:00–5:00
(over 10,000 volumes covering the U.S. and some foreign countries)
search for specific data: ½ hour research for SASE

Fremont County Genealogical Society

Riverton Branch Library
1330 West Park Avenue
Riverton, WY 82501
(307) 856-5310
Marlys Bias, Editor
Hours: Library: Mon–Tue & Thur 12:00–9:00, Wed 9:00–9:00, Fri 9:00–1:00
Pub. *Nostalgia News*, quarterly
$10.00 per year or $3.00 per copy

Laramie Peekers Genealogy Society of Platte County, Wyoming

1108 21st Street
Wheatland, WY 82201
Cindy Anderson

Natrona County Genealogical Society
PO Box 9244
Casper, WY 82609
(307) 265-0206
Pam Martin, President
$3.50 per year membership

Park County Genealogy Society
PO Box 3056
Cody, WY 82414

Powell Valley Genealogical Club
830 North Day
PO Box 184
Powell, WY 82435

Sheridan Genealogical Society, Inc.
Wyoming Room
Sheridan County Library
335 West Alger Street
PO Box 6503
Sheridan, WY 82801
(307) 674-8585
Hours: Mon & Wed–Fri 9:00–noon &
    1:00–4:00, Tue noon-4:00 & 5:00–
    8:00
Pub. *Dusty Trails Newsletter*, quarterly
(county obituary, marriage,
    naturalization, homestead records)
$8.00 per year membership; queries
    $1.00

Sublette County Genealogy Society
PO Box 1186
Pinedale, WY 82941

Independent Publications and Miscellany

El'n Al Enterprises
PO Box 62
Kaycee, WY 82639-0062
E-mail: ASVD@worldnet.att.net
http://www.buffalo.com/JohnsonCounty/
    jchist/jchistmn.htm#mainmenu
(history of Johnson County)

WyGenWeb
Part of U.S. GenWeb Project
E-mail: wy@usgenweb.com
http://www.rootsweb.com/~wygenweb
(links to other Wyoming resources)

Part 2A. American Trust Territories

AMERICAN SAMOA

Archives and Libraries with Holdings in Genealogy

Territorial Archives

Office of Archives and Records Management (American Samoa)
Department of Administrative Services
American Samoa Government
Pago Pago, AS 96799
(684) 633-1609 (Fagatogo Archive);
   (684) 633-1290 (Fagatogo Archive);
   (684) 633-1010 FAX (Fagatogo
   Archive); (684) 699-5148 (Tafuna
   Record Center)
James B. Himphill, Territorial Archivist
Hours: The Fagatogo Archives and
   Tafuna Records Center: Mon–Fri
   7:30–4:00
Pub. *LeOfisa O Teugatusi Taua Ma
   Fa'amaumauga*, two times per year,
   free
(U.S. Naval Station records 1900–1951;
   Department of Interior records 1951–
   1977; and American Samoa
   government records from 1977;
   microfilm collections start from the
   1840s)
research and certifications: $5.00

GUAM

Archives and Libraries with Holdings in Genealogy

City, County and Regional Archives and Libraries

Micronesian Area Research Center
University of Guam
303 University Drive
UOG Station
Mangilao, GU 96923
(671) 735-2160; (671) 734-7403 FAX
Hours: Mon–Fri 9:00–5:00
contact librarian for fees

MARIANA ISLANDS

Independent Publications and Miscellany

Commonwealth Council for Arts and Culture
(Capitol Hill, Saipan—location)
PO Box 553 CHRB
Saipan, MP 96950
(670) 322-9982; (670) 322-9983; (670)
   322-9028 FAX
Genevieve S. Cabrera, Executive
   Director
Hours: Mon–Fri 7:30–4:30
Pub. *Fina'tinas Marianas*, annually, free
   public service publication

PANAMA CANAL ZONE

Archives and Libraries with Holdings in Genealogy

Panama Canal Zone Commission
Washington, DC

PUERTO RICO

Archives and Libraries with Holdings in Genealogy

City, County and Regional Archives and Libraries

Conservation Trust of Puerto Rico
PO Box 4747
San Juan, PR 00905
(787) 722-5834

Genealogical Societies

Regional Genealogical Societies

Hispanic Genealogical Society of New York
Murray Hill Station, PO Box 818
New York, NY 10156-0602
(212) 532-3662
E-mail: HGSNY@aol.com
http://www.webcom.com/hgsny
Charles Fourquet-Batiz, Vice President
   and Co-Founder
Pub. *Nuestra Herencia*
(helping Hispanics/Latinos to find their
   family origins, specializing in Puerto
   Rican genealogy)
free membership

Puerto Rican/Hispanic Genealogical Society
25 Ralph Avenue
Brentwood, NY 11717-2424
(516) 834-2511
E-mail: latinoblu@aol.com
http://www.linkdirect.com/hispsoc/
   hispanic_links.htm
(list of Hispanic genealogical resources
   by country)

VIRGIN ISLANDS

Archives and Libraries
with Holdings
in Genealogy

Territorial Archives and Library

**Virgin Islands Department of
Conservation and Cultural Affairs**
Enid M. Baa Library and Archives
Division of Libraries, Museums and
  Archeological Services
(20 Dronningens Gade, Saint Thomas,
  VI 08802—location)
PO Box 390 (mailing address)
Charlotte Amalie
Saint Thomas, VI 00801
(340) 774-0630
June A. V. Lindqvist, Librarian, Von
  Scholten Collection
Hours: Mon–Fri 9:00–5:00, Sat 9:00–
  3:00

Saint Croix Landmarks Society
Centerline Road
Frederiksted, VI 00840
(340) 772-0593
Barbara Hagan-Smith, Executive
  Director
Pub. *Postkassen*
(genealogical services)

Part 3. Ethnic and Religious Organizations and Research Centers

ETHNIC ARCHIVES, LIBRARIES AND SOCIETIES

General

American Society for Ethnohistory
Duke University Press
6697 College Station
Durham, NC 27708
Pub. *Ethnohistory*

The Augustan Society, Inc.
PO Box P
Torrance, CA 90508-0210
(310) 326-8603; (310) 326-4446 FAX
Sir Rodney Hartwell, KtB(Y), Director
Hours: Tue–Sat 8:00–4:00
Pub. *The Augustan* (heraldry, chivalry, ancient and medieval history, European research, royal and noble genealogy, colonial U.S., ancient Egypt, etc.), quarterly; *Journal of Royal and Noble Genealogy*, irregularly; *Heraldry*, irregularly; *Chivalry*, irregularly

Balch Institute for Ethnic Studies
Center for Immigration Research
18 South Seventh Street
Philadelphia, PA 19106
(215) 925-8090
E-mail: balchlib@hslc.org
http://www.libertynet.org:80/~balch/
Dr. John Tenhula
Hours: Mon–Sat 9:00–5:00
Pub. *New Dimensions*

Center for Ethnic Studies
Kent State University
University Library
Room 318
Kent, OH 44242
Lubomyr R. Wynar, Editor
Pub. *Ethnic Forum*

Ethnic Research Archives
229 Montclair Avenue
Newark, NJ 07104
(973) 482-2297
Dr. Charles Allan Baretski, Executive Director and Archivist
(not open to the public)

Immigration History Society
Immigration History Research Center (IHRC)
University of Minnesota
826 Berry Street
Minneapolis, MN 55114
(612) 627-4208; (612) 627-4190 FAX
E-mail: ihrc@gold.tc.umn.edu
http://www.umn.edu/ihrc/

Pub. *Journal of American Ethnic History*, semiannually (Ronald H. Bayor, Editor); *The Immigration History Newsletter*, semiannually (M. Mark Stolarik, Editor, The Balch Institute for Ethnic Studies, 18 South Seventh Street, Philadelphia, PA 19106)
$17.00 per year membership (includes both publications)

Institute of Texan Cultures
801 South Bowie Street
San Antonio, TX 78205-3296
(210) 226-7651

International Museum of Cultures
7500 West Camp Wisdom Road
Dallas, TX 75236
(972) 298-9446

Maryland Ethnic Heritage Commission
Department of Housing and Community Development
100 Community Place
Crownsville, MD 21032-2025
Pub. *Tapestry*; *Directory of Ethnic Organizations, Associations, Clubs and Societies*

National Association for Ethnic Studies, Inc.
Department of English
Arizona State University
Box 870302
Tempe, AZ 85287-0302
(602) 965-2197
Susan L. Rockwell, Director
Pub. *Ethnic Studies Review*, three times per year; *Explorations in Sights and Sounds*, annually; *The Ethnic Reporter*, semiannually
$45.00 per year membership for individuals or libraries

New York State Association of European Historians
27 Maple Avenue
Highland, NY 12528
(914) 691-8062

Ethnic Heritage Council of the Pacific Northwest
305 Harrison Street, Suite 322
Seattle, WA 98109-4645
(206) 443-1410
Jennifer Kulik, Director
Hours: 9:30–5:30
Pub. *Calendar: Monthly Guide to Northwest Ethnic Events*, $15.00 per year subscription; *Contact: Directory of Ethnic Organizations in Washington*, biannually, $12.00 per issue; *Fortelling*, quarterly

$30.00 per year membership for individuals, $45.00 per year membership for organizations

The University of Texas at El Paso
Centennial Museum
Wiggins and University
El Paso, TX 79968-0533
(915) 747-5565
Pat Mora, Director
(collections in ethnology)

Utah Genealogical Association
PO Box 1144
Salt Lake City, UT 84110-1144
(888) INFO UGA (463-6842)
Kory Meyerink, President
Pub. *UGA Newsletter*, quarterly (March, June, September, January); *Utah Genealogical Journal* (treats Utah, U.S., and International genealogical and local history topics), quarterly (March, June, September, January), $5.00 postpaid per issue
Chapters: **Computer Chapter**, Randall Hamilton, President, 1552 North 1725 West, Layton, UT 84041, (801) 544-0821; **Irish Chapter**, Josie Bullock, President, 1590 Treeview Drive, Salt Lake City, UT 84124, (801) 227-9057; **Great Salt Lake Chapter**, Vaughn Simon, President, PO Box 11193, Salt Lake City, UT 84147, (801) 596-9881; **Northern Idaho Chapter**, Ellie Grover, President, PO Box 685, Bonners Ferry, ID 83805, (208) 267-7939; **Utah Valley Chapter**, John Whitaker, President; **Morgan Valley Chapter**, Holly Hansen, President, 1950 North 6900 East, Croydon, UT 84018-9707, (801) 829-3295; **Tooele Chapter**, John Peck, President, 206 East Vine Street, Tooele, UT 84074, (435) 882-3648
$25.00 per year membership for individuals, $5.00 additional per year spouse membership, $5.00 additional for postage outside the U.S.

Acadian

(see French)

African-American

African American Cultural Alliance
PO Box 22173
Nashville, TN 37202
(615) 299-0412
Kwame Lillard, President
Hours: Office: 4:00–8:00
("We perform historical events, African American Civil War tributes.")

African-American Cultural Center

350 Masten Avenue
Buffalo, NY 14209
(716) 884-2013; (716) 885-2590 FAX
Agnes M. Bain, Executive Director;
   Alicia Banner, Assistant Director
Hours: Mon–Fri 10:00–9:00, Sat 10:00–
   6:00
$5.00 per year membership

African American Cultural Heritage Center and Museum

3434 South R.L. Thornton Freeway
Dallas, TX 75224
(972) 375-7530

African-American Genealogical Society of Central Illinois

314 North Main
Decatur, IL 62523
(217) 429-7458

African-American Genealogical Society of Cleveland, Ohio

PO Box 200382
Cleveland, OH 44120-9998

African American Museum

1765 Crawford Road
Cleveland, OH 44106
(216) 791-1700
Linda Cross, Executive Director
Hours: Mon–Tue & Thur–Fri 10:00–
   5:00, Sat–Sun 11:00–3:00
$20.00 per year membership for
   individuals (includes free general
   admission), $30.00 per year
   membership for families (immediate
   household), $10.00 per year
   membership for students or senior
   citizens

African American Museum and Library at Oakland

5606 San Pablo Avenue
Oakland, CA 94608
(510) 597-5053; (510) 597-5030
E. Hope Hayes, Administrative Director
Hours: Tue 11:30–7:00, Wed–Thur & Sat
   10:00–5:30, Fri noon–5:30
Pub. *From the Archives*, quarterly
   (specializes in African Americans in
   California)
$20.00 per year Sustaining membership,
   $50.00 per year membership for
   churches or non-profit organizations,
   $200.00 per year membership for
   corporations or business/professional
   organizations, $500.00 life
   membership

Africana Studies Research Center Library

310 Triphammer Road
Ithaca, NY 14850
(607) 256-5229
James E. Turner, Director

Center for Afroamerican and African Studies

(200 West Hall—location)
550 East University Street
University of Michigan
Ann Arbor, MI 48109
(734) 764-5518 (Main Office); (734)
   764-5518 (Library); (734) 763-0543
   FAX
Prof. Sharon F. Patton, Director of
   Center; Elizabeth James, Librarian
Hours: Mon–Thur 10:00–5:00, Sun
   1:00–5:00
(reference/resource center with print and
   non-print materials, limited resources
   on genealogy)

Afro-American Communities Project

Constitution Avenue between 12th and
   14th Streets
Room C-340, National Museum of
   American History
Smithsonian Institution
Washington, DC 20560
(202) 357-3182
James O. Horton, Ph.D., Director

Afro-American Cultural and Historical Society

8716 Harkness Road
Cleveland, OH 44106
(216) 795-3121
Icabod Flewellen, Curator and Historian
Hours: by special permission

Afro-American Heritage Association

PO Box 451
Rome, NY 13440
(315) 337-5018
Mrs. Jessie Thorpe, Librarian/Museum
   Chairperson

Afro-American Historical and Cultural Museum

67 West Sharpnack Street
Philadelphia, PA 19119-2722
Nannette A. Clark, Executive Director
Hours: Tue–Sat 10:00–5:00, Sun noon–
   6:00
Pub. *Insight—Quarterly Newsletter*
   (African American history and art of
   Philadelphia, Delaware valley, and
   Pennsylvania, national and
   internationally focused exhibition
   occasionally)

Afro-American Historical and Genealogical Society (AAHGS)

PO Box 73086
Washington, DC 20056-3086
$25.00 per year membership for
   individuals, $30.00 per year
   membership for families, $35.00 per
   year membership for organizations,
   $1,000.00 life membership

Afro-American Historical and Genealogical Society

Chicago Chapter
Patricia Liddell Researchers
PO Box 198321
Chicago, IL 60619
Pub. *AAHGS News*, irregularly; *Afro-
   American Historical and Genealogical
   Journal*, quarterly, $25.00 per year
   subscription for individuals, $30.00
   per year subscription for families,
   $35.00 per year subscription for
   organizations

Afro-American Historical and Genealogical Society

Prince George's County Maryland
   Chapter
PO Box 44772
Fort Washington, MD 20744-9998
(301) 292-2751
Carolyn Corpening Collins Rowe,
   President
Hours: meetings at Saint Ignatius
   Catholic Church, 2315 Brinkley Road,
   Oxon Hill, MD 20745
$10.00 per year membership for
   individuals, $15.00 per year
   membership for families (membership
   in the national organization is a
   prerequisite for membership in the
   local chapter)

Afro-American Historical Association of the Niagara Frontier

PO Box 1663
Buffalo, NY 14216
(716) 883-4418
Monroe Fordham, President
Pub. *Afro-Americans in New York Life
   and History: An Inter-disciplinary
   Journal*, semiannually

Afro-Gen

PO Box 17684
Nashville, TN 37217
(615) 399-7064
Dr. Tammie M. Young, Director
(Black family genealogy/history;
   school's history)

Alexandria Black History Resource Center

638 North Alfred Street
Alexandria, VA 22314
(703) 838-4356, (703) 706-3999 FAX
Audrey Davis, Assistant Director
Hours: Tue–Sat 10:00–4:00

The Amistad Research Center

Tilton Memorial Hall, Tulane University
6823 Saint Charles Avenue
New Orleans, LA 70118-5698
(504) 865-5535; (504) 862-3222; (504)
   865-5580 FAX
E-mail: amistad@tulane.edu;
   ddevore@tulane.edu
http://www.arc.tulane.edu
Donald DeVore, Executive Director

Hours: Mon–Sat 9:00–4:30
Pub. *Amistad Reports*, quarterly
(African-Americans, Native Americans,
Hispanics, Asian-Americans; houses
American Home Missionary Society
Collection; "Genealogical reference
books only.")

The Association for the Study of Afro-American Life and History, Inc.

1407 14th Street, N.W.
Washington, DC 20005-3705
(202) 667-2822; (202) 387-9802 FAX
E-mail: asalh@earthlink.net
Irena T. Webster, Executive Director
Hours: Mon–Fri 9:00–5:00
Pub. *Negro History Bulletin*, quarterly,
$30.00 per year subscription; *Journal
of Negro History*, quarterly, $25.00 per
year subscription for individuals,
$30.00 per year subscription for
institutions
$40.00 per year general membership

Association for the Study of Afro-American Life and History

Savannah-Yamacraw Branch
King-Tisdell Cottage Foundation, Inc.
514 East Huntingdon Street
Savannah, GA 31402
(912) 234-8000
W. W. Law

Avery Research Center for African American History and Culture

125 Bull Street
Charleston, SC 29424
(843) 727-2007
Dr. W. Marvin Dulaney, Director
Hours: Mon–Sat noon–5:00
(African-American history and culture in
South Carolina, verylittle material on
genealogy)

York W. Bailey Museum

PO Box 126
Saint Helena Island, SC 29920
(843) 838-2432 Main Office; (843) 838-
2235
Agnes C. Sherman, Director; Vanessa
Thaxton, Coordinator, History and
Cultural Affairs
Hours: Mon–Fri 9:00–5:00, weekends
by appointment for groups of ten or
more
in process of developing membership

Beck Cultural Exchange Center, Inc.

1927 Dandridge Avenue
Knoxville, TN 37915
(423) 524-8461
Robert J. Booker, Executive Director
Hours: Tue–Sat 10:00–6:00
(local Black history, photographs,
biographies, books of oral histories)
free admission to galleries

Bethune Museum and Archives, Inc.

National Historic Site
1318 Vermont Avenue, N.W.
Washington, DC 20005
(202) 332-9201
Bettye Collien-Thomas, Ph.D., Executive
Director
Pub. *Legacy*
(Afro-American women's history)

Black Archives of Mid-America

2033 Vine
Kansas City, MO 64108
(816) 483-1300

Black Catholic History Project

Office of Black Catholics
Archdiocese of Washington (District of
Columbia)
5001 Eastern Avenue
PO Box 29260
Washington, DC 20017-0260
(301) 853-4579; (301) 853-7671 FAX
Jacqueline E. Wilson, Executive Director
Hours: 9:00–5:00
Pub. *Newsletter: To Give Light*,
bimonthly
(Black Catholics, African-Americans,
racism, Archdiocese of Washington
[Prince George's, Montgomery, St.
Mary's, Charles and Calvert counties,
Maryland, and Washington, DC]; some
Baltimore and national information)

Black Heritage Council

725 Monroe Street
Montgomery, AL 36106
(334) 261-3184
Shirley D. Qualls, Council Liaison

Black Heritage Society of Washington State, Inc.

PO Box 22565
Seattle, WA 98122
(206) 325-8205; (206) 723-0334

Black Resources Information Coordinating Services

614 Howard Avenue
Suite 125-9
Tallahassee, FL 32301
(904) 576-7522
Emily A. Copeland, President

Blockson Afro-American Collection

Temple University
Sullivan Hall, First Floor
12th Street and Berks Mall
Philadelphia, PA 19122
(215) 204-6632; (215) 204-5197
E-mail:
aberhanu@thunder.ocis.temple.edu
http://www.temple.edu/blockson/

The Ollie L. Brown Afro-American Heritage Collection

Alabama State University
Montgomery, AL 36101
(334) 262-3581
Marcia Martin

Chattanooga African-American Heritage Museum

(200 East Martin L. King Boulevard—
location)
PO Box 11493 (mailing address)
Chattanooga, TN 37416
(423) 266-8658; (423) 267-1076 FAX
Vilma Scruggs Fields, Director
Hours: Mon–Fri 10:00–5:00, Sat noon–
4:00
Pub. *The Heritage*, quarterly
$1.00 admission for adults, 50¢
admission for children under 12

Compton Public Library

240 West Compton Boulevard
Compton, CA 90220
(310) 637-0202; (310) 537-1141 FAX
Sharon M. Johnson, Community Library
Manager
Hours: Tue–Thur 10:00–8:00, Fri 10:00–
6:00, Sat 10:00–5:00
("Our library is no longer the site of the
Black Resource Center,a.k.a. Afro-
American Resource Center. We still
carry a substantial amount of Black
titles, however they are general
interest and not necessarily for
scholarly research.")

Connecticut Afro-American Historical Society, Inc.

444 Orchard Street
New Haven, CT 06511
(203) 776-4907
Edna B. Carnegie, Secretary of the Board
Hours: Mon 11:00–1:00, and by
appointment

Digging It Up African-American Research and Consulting Firm

70 Fairlie Street, Suite 330
Atlanta, GA 30303
(404) 688-6509
Herman "Skip" Mason, Jr., President
Hours: 9:00–5:30
(professional research, speakers bureau,
photo archives, tours, appraisals of
Black memorabilia)
hourly fees and package fee

The DuSable Museum of African American History, Inc.

(57th East Cottage Grove Avenue—
location)
740 East 56th Place (mailing address)
Chicago, IL 60637-1495
(773) 947-0600; (773) 947-0677 FAX
Gwendolyn Keità Robinson, Ph.D.,
Executive Director
Hours: Museum: Spring–fall: Mon–Wed
& Fri–Sat 10:00–5:00, Thur 10:00–
6:00, Sun noon–5:00, winter: Mon–Sat
10:00–4:00, Sun noon–4:00; Museum
Archives: Mon–Fri 9:00–5:00, Sat–
Sun noon–5:00
$25.00 per year membership

First African Baptist Church Museum
Franklin Square
23 Montgomery Street
Savannah, GA 31401
Thurmond Tillman

Florida A & M University
Black Archives
Research Center and Museum
Tallahassee, FL 32307
(904) 599-3020
James N. Eaton, Archivist/Curator

The Hollis Burke Frissell Library
Tuskegee Institute
Tuskegee, AL 36088
(334) 727-8888
Daniel T. Williams, Archivist
Hours: Mon–Thur 8:00–10:00 P.M., Fri 8:00–4:30

Great Plains Black Museum Archives and Int. Center
2213 Lake Street
Omaha, NE 68110
(402) 345-2212; (402) 345-6817
Bertha Calloway, Director

Harrison Museum of African American Culture
523 Harrison Avenue, N.W., Ground Floor
Roanoke, VA 24016
(540) 345-4818; (540) 345-4831 FAX
Melody S. Stovall, Executive Director
Hours: Mon–Fri 10:00–5:00, Sat–Sun 1:00–5:00
Pub. *Brochure*, biannually; *Annual Report*
(local archives, museum store)

Collis P. Huntington Memorial Library
University Archives
Hampton University
Hampton, VA 23668
(757) 727-5374
Jeanne Zeidler, Director; Donzella Maupin, Archives Assistant
Hours: Archives: Mon–Fri 8:00–5:00
(African and Native American)

Indiana Historical Society
Indiana State Library and Historical Building
315 West Ohio Street
PO Box 88255
Indianapolis, IN 46202
(317) 232-1879
Wilma Gibbs, Program Archivist
Hours: Mon–Fri 8:00–4:30, Sat (Sept–May) 8:30–4:00
Pub. *Black History News and Notes*, quarterly
$20.00 per year membership

Leavenworth Afro-American Historical Society
PO Box 3151
Fort Leavenworth, KS 66027
(913) 651-4584

Maryland Commission on Afro-American History and Culture
Banneker-Douglass Museum of Afro-American Life and History
84 Franklin Street
Annapolis, MD 21401
(410) 269-2893
Steven C. Newsome, Executive Director

Middle Tennessee Conference
Afro-American Scholars
1721 14th Avenue, South
Nashville, TN 37212
(615) 297-3416

Moorland-Spingarn Research Center
Howard University
500 Howard Place, N.W.
Washington, DC 20059
(202) 806-7239
Dr. Thomas C. Battle, Director
Hours: Mon–Thur 9:00–4:45, Fri 9:00–4:30
(African and African-American)
fee schedule for photoduplication services

Museum of Afro-American History
9 Wyoming Street
Dorchester, MA 02121

National Afro-American Museum and Cultural Center
1985 Velma Avenue
Columbus, OH 43211
(614) 466-1500

The New York Public Library, Schomburg Center for Research in Black Culture
515 Malcolm X Boulevard
New York, NY 10037-1801
(212) 491-2200
Howard Dodson, Director
Hours: Jun–Sept: Mon & Wed 12:00–8:00, Tue & Thur–Fri 10:00–6:00; Oct–May: Mon–Wed 12:00–8:00, Thur–Sat 10:00–6:00 (Archives closes at 5:00, art collection by appointment only)
Pub. *Journal of the Schomburg Center*, quarterly, $35.00 per year for subscription and notices of events
("Librarians at the Center are *not* genealogists and have only a rudimentary knowledge of genealogy; our specialty is Black history.")

Parting Ways—The Museum of Afro-American Ethnohistory, Inc.
(130 Court Street, Plymouth, MA—location)
PO Box 541 (mailing address)
Marion, MA 02738
(508) 746-6028

Pendleton Foundation for Black History and Culture
(address withheld upon request)

Plantation Society in the Americas
University of New Orleans/University of South Florida
Department of History
University of New Orleans
New Orleans, LA 70148-2550
(504) 280-6886; (504) 286-5505 FAX
Professor Edward Lazzerini
Hours: daily
Pub. *Plantation Society in the Americas*, two or three times per year, three issues per volume
(West Indies, plantations, families, Creole studies, Southern U.S., Caribbean, Mississippi Valley, Afro-American)
$25.00 per year membership to individuals in the U.S., $50.00 per year membership for institutions

Mattye Reed African Heritage Center
2711 McConnell Road
Greensboro, NC 27401

Rhode Island Black Heritage Society
1 Hilton Street
Providence, RI 02905
(401) 751-3490

Saint Joseph's Historic Foundation, Inc.
804 Old Fayetteville Street
Durham, NC 27702
(919) 683-1709
Walter J. Norflett, Executive Director
(African American culture and history)

Staten Island Institute of Arts and Sciences
75 Stuyvesant Place
Staten Island, NY 10301
Patricia Gordon Michael, Executive Director
Pub. *Proceedings of the SIIAS*
(history of the Black community)

Taps Quarterly
13509 Pendleton Street
Oxon Hill, MD 20022
Shannon B. Murphy
Pub. *Taps Quarterly*

Tarrant County Black Historical and Genealogical Society, Inc.
1020 East Humbolt Street
Fort Worth, TX 76104
(817) 332-6049; (817) 926-6390

Lenora Rolla, Executive Director; Gayle
W. Hanson, Editor
Hours: Mon–Fri 11:00–5:00
Pub. *Tarrant County Black Historical
and Genealogical Society Newsletter*,
bimonthly, $6.00 per year subscription
(Blacks of the southwest; early Black
settlers of Tarrant County, Texas,
especially the Fort Worth area)
$12.00 per year membership for
individuals, $25.00 per year
membership for organizations, $6.00
per year Jr. Historian membership

Texas Ancestry Researchers
1009 Eric Avenue
Arlington, TX 76012-3205
(817) 265-0044
Gayle W. Hanson
(specializes in Texas African-American
research, publishes record abstracts)

**Fred Hart Williams Genealogical
Society**
Detroit Public Library
Burton Historical Collection
5201 Woodward Avenue
Detroit, MI 48202
(313) 833-1480 (Library); (313) 438-
3233
Roy L. Roulhac, President
Hours: Library: Tue & Thur–Sat 9:30–
5:30, Wed 1:00–9:00
Pub. *Quarterly Newsletter*

**Miriam B. Wilson Foundation/Old
Slave Mart Museum and Library**
(6 Chalmers Street, Charleston, SC
29401—location)
PO Box 446 (mailing address)
Sullivans Island, SC 29482
(843) 883-3797

Albanian

(see also Eastern European, Italian)

Albanian Research List
144 Marine Street, Apartment 1
Saint Augustine, FL 32084-5027
E-mail: jtobia@aug.com
http://feefhs.org/al/alrl.html; http://
dcn.davis.ca.us/~feefhs/al/alrl.html
Joseph A. Tobia

American Indian

(see Native American)

Arab

(see Religious Archives and
Organizations, Islamic)

Armenian

(see also Religious Archives and
Organizations, Armenian)

Armenian Educational Council, Inc.
1330 Massachusetts Avenue, N.W.,
Apartment 405
Washington, DC 20005-4172
(academic studies; Armenian
architecture, photographic-documented
archival collection in microfiche)

Armenian Genealogical Society
(410 East Sumac Avenue, Provo, UT
84601—location)
PO Box 1383
Provo, UT 84603-1383
E-mail: gfa@itsnet.com;
Megerian@fhs.byu.edu
http://feefhs.org/am/frg/amgs.html;
http://dcn.davis.ca.us/~feefhs/am/
frg-amgs.html
Nephi K. Kezerian, M.D., Founding/Past
President; Audrey Megerian, President
Pub. *Armenian Records*
(filmed records from Australia, Austria,
Bangladesh, Burma, Cyprus, Egypt,
England, Greece, Hungary, India,
Indonesia, Israel, Italy, Jordan,
Lebanon, The Netherlands, Poland,
Singapore, Switzerland, Turkey,
U.S.A., the former U.S.S.R., and
Yugoslavia)

**Armenian General Benevolent
Union**
Alex Manoogian School Library
22001 Northwestern Highway
Southfield, MI 48075
(313) 569-2988
Linda Houhanisin, Media Specialist

**Armenian Library and Museum of
America (ALMA)**
65 Main Street
Watertown, MA 02172
(781) 926-2562; (781) 926-0175 FAX
Gary Lind-Sinanian, Curator
Hours: Mon & Sun 1:00–5:00, Tue 1:00–
5:00 & 7:00–9:00
Pub. *Armenian Library and Museum of
America Newsletter*, three times per
year; *Alma Matters*, quarterly
(14,000 volumes in library, but very
limited genealogical materials)
$35.00 per year membership for
individuals, $50.00 per year
membership for families, $100.00 per
year Supporting membership

**National Association for Armenian
Studies and Research, Inc. (NAASR)**
6 Divinity Avenue
Cambridge, MA 02138
Pub. *Report*, quarterly; *Bulletin for
Advancement of Armenian Studies*,
semiannually

University of Michigan-Dearborn
Armenian Research Center
4901 Evergreen Road
Dearborn, MI 48128-1491
E-mail: gottenbr@umich.edu

http://www.umd.umich.edu/dept/
armenian/

Asian

The Amistad Research Center
(see African-American)

The Asia Society
725 Park Avenue
New York, NY 10021
(212) 288-6400

Association for Asian Studies
1 Lane Hall
University of Michigan
Ann Arbor, MI 48109-1290
(734) 665-2490
Carol M. Hansen, Administrative
Associate
Hours: 9:00–5:00
Pub. *Journal of Asian Studies*, quarterly;
Journal of Asian Business, quarterly;
Newsletter, five times per year
(not primarily a resource for genealogical
information)

China Institute in America
125 East 65th Street
New York, NY 10021
(212) 744-8181
F. Richard Hsu, President

**Chinese American Cultural
Association**
1768 Sweetwood Drive
Daly City, CA 94015-2011
Nissi S. Wang

**Chinese American Librarians
Association (CALA)**
American Museum of Natural History
Central Park West at 79th Street
New York, NY 10024-5192
(212) 769-5413
http://www.lib.siu.edu/swen/cala/
calachap.htm (chapters)

**Chinese Culture Center of San
Francisco**
750 Kearny Street, Third Floor
San Francisco, CA 94108
(415) 986-1822; (415) 986-2825 FAX
http://www.c-c-c.org
Manni Liu, Curator
Hours: Tue–Sun 10:00–4:00
Pub. *Chinese Culture Center Newsletter*,
quarterly
(rotating art exhibitions, classes, lectures,
genealogy research program)
$25.00 per year membership

**Chinese Historical Society of
America (CHSA)**
965 Clay Street
San Francisco, CA 94111
(415) 391-1188
http://www.sirius.com/~edwong/CHSA/
chsa_pl.html

Jasmin Tuan, Executive Director
Hours: Mon–Fri 10:00–2:00
Pub. *The Bulletin*, monthly; *Chinese America: History and Perspectives*, annually, $17.50 per issue postpaid, plus 8.5% sales tax
(Chinese in America, including Central and South America, as well as North America; museum has artifacts as well as photographs)
$45.00 per year membership for individuals, $25.00 per year membership for senior citizens (age 60 or more), $60.00 per year membership for institutions or groups, $1,500.00 life membership for individuals

Chinese Historical Society of Southern California
PO Box 862647
Los Angeles, CA 90086-2647
E-mail: chssc@chssc.org
http://www.chssc.org/

Council on East Asian Libraries
c/o East Asian Library
1100 East 57th Strteet
Chicago, IL 60637-1502
(773) 702-8436; (773) 702-6623 FAX
E-mail: felsing@oregon.uoregon.edu
http://darkwing.uoregon.edu/~felsing/ceal/welcome.html

Gardena Library
Los Angeles County Public Library
1731 West Gardena Boulevard
Gardena, CA 90247
(213) 323-6363
Marjorie Delida, Senior Librarian
(Japanese-American)

Hawaii Chinese History Center
111 North King Street, Room 410
Honolulu, HI 96817
(808) 521-5948
Roger K. S. Liu, President
Hours: Mon, Wed & Fri 10:00–noon
Pub. *HCHC Newsletter*, quarterly, $10.00 per year subscription

Japanese American History Archives
1840 Sutter Street
San Francisco, CA 94115
(415) 776-0661
http://www.e-media.com/fillmore/museum/jt/jaha/jaha.html
(photo archives)

The Morikami Museum and Japanese Gardens
4000 Morikami Park Road
Delray Beach, FL 33446
(561) 495-0233; (561) 499-2557 FAX
Larry Rosensweig, Director
Hours: Tue–Sun 10:00–5:00
Pub. *The Morikami Newsletter/Calendar*, quarterly
(Japanese colony, Yawato, FL)
$35.00 per year membership

New York Public Library
Oriental Division, Room 219
Fifth Avenue and 42nd Street
New York, NY 10018
(212) 930-0716

Pacific Asia Museum
46 North Los Robles Avenue
Pasadena, CA 91101
(626) 449-2742; (626) 449-2754 FAX
E-mail: pacasiam@aol.com
Paulitte Pang, Communications Coordinator
Hours: Wed–Sun 10:00–5:00
Pub. *Pacific Asia Museum Newsletter*, bimonthly
(Asian and Pacific Islands art and culture)
$37.00 per year membership

University of Washington Libraries
Manuscripts and University Archives
Box 352900
Seattle, WA 98195-2900
(206) 543-1879
Hours: Mon–Fri 9:00–5:00 (during academic quarters)
(emphasis on ethnic Jewish, ethnic Japanese-American, and ethnic Scandinavian-American; not staffed to provide genealogical research but can suggest professional help)

Wing Luke Asian Museum
407 Seventh Avenue, South
Seattle, WA 98104
(206) 623-5124 (Education Express); (206) 623-5190
Peter Moy, President, Board of Trustees; Ron Chew, Director, Museum; Charlene Mano, Education Coordinator
Hours: Museum: Tue–Fri 11:00–4:30, Sat–Sun 12:00–4:00
Pub. *Newsletter*, quarterly
(specializes in Asian Americans)
$30.00 per year membership for individuals, $20.00 per year membership for senior citizens, $50.00 per year membership for families

Assyrian

(see Religious Archives and Organizations, Islamic)

Australian

Western Australia Genealogical Society, Inc.
PO Box 4327
Davis, California 95617-4327
E-mail: feefhs@feefhs.org
http://feefhs.org/msc/frg/wags.html
John D. Movius, Alternate U.S. FEEFHS Representative
Pub. *Quarterly Western Ancestor Newsletter*

$12.00 initiation fee, $36.00 per year membership for individuals (beginning 1 April), $48.00 per year membership for families

Austrian

(see also Banat, Eastern European, Galician, Hungarian and Slovenian)

American Committee to Promote Studies of the History of the Habsburg Monarchy
c/o Department of History
Louisiana State University
Baton Rouge, LA 70803
(504) 388-4471
Karl A. Roider, Jr., Ph.D., Executive Secretary
Pub. *Newsletter for Habsburg and Austrian History*

Baltic

(see Eastern European, Estonian and Lithuanian)

Banat

Banat Genealogy Mailing List
PO Box 262
Lapeer, Michigan 48446-0262
E-mail: cjl@mail.tir.com; madler@sierra.net
http://feefhs.org/banat/frgbanat.html
Chris J. Lamesfield, Moderator; Bob Madler, President
(devoted primarily to the German settlers in the Banat area, which comprised the Hungarian counties of Torontal, Temes and Krasso-Szereny, which lie north of the Danube, east of the Tisza/Tisa and south of the Maros Rivers, formerly part of the Austrian Empire and now divided among Romania, Yugoslavia and Hungary; also research interests in the neighboring area of Batschka, formerly the Hungarian county of Bacs-Bodrog, which was between the Tisza/Tisa and Danube Rivers)

Liebling Village Association
http://feefhs.org/banat/bua/lva/frg-lva.html
Lou (Ludwig Peter) Arnold
(Liebling, founded in 1786, is a village that was a part of the former Banat of the Hungarian Empire, now within Romania, located about 20 kilometers south of Temosara)

Zichydorf Village Association
E-mail: schwartc@meena.cc.uregina.ca
http://feefhs.org/zva/frg-zva.html
Glenn Schwartz, ZVA Coordinator
Pub. *ZVA Newsletter*

Bangladesh

(see Asian)

Basque

(see Spanish)

Belarusian

Zhurtavannie Bialaruskaj Shliachty
(Association of the Belarusian Nobility)
http://feefhs.org/by/frg-zbs.html
Pub. *Hodnasc* (*Dignity*), irregularly;
Klejnot, at least three times per year
membership restricted to individuals of
noble descent

Belgian

The Belgian Researchers, Inc.
Belgian American Heritage Association
(BAHA)
62073 Fruitdale Lane
La Grande, OR 97850-5312
(541) 963-6697
Pierre L. Inghels, President
Pub. *Belgian Laces*, quarterly
("specializes in history-genealogy-
heraldry, doing research for Belgians
in the states and for Belgian-
Americans in Belgium")
$12.00 per year membership in the U.S.
and Canada, $14.00 per year
membership (U.S. funds) outside the
U.S. and Canada

**Center for Belgian Culture of
Western Illinois**
712 18th Avenue
Moline, IL 61265
(309) 762-0167
Joan Loete, Librarian/Genealogist
Hours: Wed & Saturday afternoons, and
by appointment
Pub. *Newsletter*, monthly
$15.00 per year membership for
individuals, $20.00 per year
membership for families

**Genealogical Society of Flemish-
Americans**
18740 Thirteen Mile Road
Roseville, MI 48066
(313) 776-9579 (Secretary)
Margaret Roets, Corresponding Secretary
Hours: Library: 10:00–2:30, and by
appointment; meetings: Sept–Jun:
second & fourth Sat
Pub. *Flemish-American Heritage*,
semiannually (February and August);
*Genealogical Society of Flemish-
Americans Newsletter*, semiannually
$10.00 per year membership for families
in the U.S. and Canada, $12.00 per
year membership in Europe (U.S.
funds)

**Rock Island County Historical
Society**
Rock Island County Historical Research
Library
822 11th Avenue
PO Box 632
Moline, IL 61266-0632
(309) 764-8590
Lloyd Efflandt, President; N. Lucille
Sampson, Archivist
Hours: Mon & Thur–Sat 9:00–5:00, Sun
(last Sun in May through first Sun in
Dec) 1:30–4:30, closed Christmas and
New Year's weeks
Pub. *Rock Island County Historical
Society Newsletter*, semiannually
("John H. Hauberg Collection, Belgian
Book Collection, oral tapes,
photographs, family collections, books
and manuscripts that fit our purpose:
to collect, preserve and disseminate
Rock Island County history.")
$15.00 per year membership for
individuals; $10.00 per hour research
plus photocopying

**University of Wisconsin—
Green Bay**
Cofrin Library
Special Collections/Area Research
Center
2420 Nicolet Drive
Green Bay, WI 54311-7001
(920) 465-2539
E-mail: speccoll@gbms01.uwgb.edu
Debra L. Anderson, Special Collections
and Area Research Center Coordinator
Hours: Mon–Tue & Thur–Fri 12:30–
4:30, Wed 12:30–5:00 & 6:00–9:00
(Area Research Center for Brown,
Calumet, Door, Florence, Kewaunee,
Manitowoc, Marinette, Menominee,
Oconto, Outagamie, and Shawano
counties; holdings include original
records for the listed counties;
document types include citizenship,
probate, vital records, land records,
censuses and maps)

Bohemian

(see Czech and German)

BosNet
E-mail: albert@infobahnos.com
http://www.bosnet.org/
(Bosnian Ingathering Manuscript
Program)

Bosnian

(see Eastern European)

British

(see also English, Irish, Scottish and
Welsh)

**British Interest Group of Wisconsin
and Illinois (BIGWILL)**
PO Box 192
Richmond, IL 60071-0192
(708) 823-4282 (President); (608) 756-
3759 (Secretary)
Paul Milner, President and Newsletter
Editor; Peggy Rockwell Gleich,
Secretary
Hours: Grace Lutheran Church, 6000
Broadway Street, Richmond, IL: third
Saturday of every other month
(January, March, May, July,
September, November)
Pub. *BIGWILL Newsletter*, six times per
year
$15.00 per year membership for
individuals

**British Isles Family History Society-
USA**
(10741 Santa Monica Boulevard, West
Los Angeles, CA 90025—library
location)
2531 Sawtelle Boulevard, #134 (mailing
address)
Los Angeles, CA 90064-3163
(310) 398-3924
Annie Lloyd, Editor
Hours: Mon & Fri–Sat 9:00–5:00, Tue–
Wed & Thur 9:00–9:00; special British
Isles research help: Wed 10:00–8:00;
meetings: second Wed (except Aug &
Dec) 7:00; classes on British and Irish
genealogical subjects: second Wed
(except Aug & Dec) 3:00
Pub. *Newsletter*, bimonthly; *British Isles
Family History Society-USA, Journal*,
quarterly (spring, summer, fall and
winter); *Y Ddraig Goch* (The Red
Dragon); quarterly
$20.00 per year membership for
individuals, $25.00 per year
membership for families, $200.00 life
membership for individuals, $250.00
life membership for families, an
additional $5.00 to join the Irish and
the Welsh Interest Groups to cover
cost ofnewsletters

Bukovinian

Bukovina Society of the Americas
PO Box 81
Ellis, KS 67637-0081
E-mail: owindholz@dailynews.net;
LJensen@aol.com
http://members.aol.com/LJensen/
bukovina.html; http://feefhs.org/
bukovina/bukovina.html
Oren Windholz, President; Larry R.
Jensen, Webmaster
Pub. *Bukovina Society of the Americas
Newsletter*, quarterly
(Bukovina: From 1775 to 1918, the
easternmost crown land of the
Austrian Empire; now divided

between Romania and Ukraine;
Bukowina or Buchenland in German,
Bukowina in Polish, Bucovina in
Romanian, and Bukovyna in
Ukrainian)
$10.00 per year membership, $150.00
life membership

Bulgarian

(see also Eastern European)

Bulgaria National Front
PO Box 59240
Chicago, IL 60659

Byelorussian

(see Eastern European and Russian)

Canadian

(see also French)

Association Canado-Américaine
PO Box 989
Manchester, NH 03105-0989
(800) 222-8577
http://www.acafraternal.org/~aca/

Heritage North
PO Box 205
Colton, NY 13625
Dennis E. Eickhoff, Director
(publishes records of northern New York
State, Ontario and Quebec)

**The New England Historic
Genealogical Society**
(see Massachusetts)

**Northern New York American-
Canadian Genealogical Society**
(Community Center, Old High School
Building, Main Street, Keeseville,
NY—location)
PO Box 1256 (mailing address)
Plattsburg, NY 12901-1256
(518) 846-7707
Richard Ward, President
Hours: Community Center: May–Oct:
Wed 1:00–7:00, Sat 10:00–4:00, and
by appointment with two-weeks notice
Pub. *Lifelines*, two times per year
(southern Quebec, Northern New York,
and Northern Vermont)
$20.00 per year membership for
individuals ($25.00 outside the U.S.),
$25.00 per year membership for
families, libraries or institutions
($30.00 outside the U.S.), $7.50 per
year membership for students ($10.00
outside the U.S.)

Carpatho-Rusin

(see Slovak)

Celtic

(see Irish, Scottish and Welsh)

Chicano

(see Spanish)

Chinese

(see Asian)

Cornish

(see also English)

Cornish-American Heritage Society
(29 Ninth Ave., Terrasse-Vaudreuil,
Quebec J7V 3L5 Canada—location)
2405 North Brookfield Road (mailing
address)
Brookfield, WI 53045
(414) 453-8719
Jean Jolliffe, Vice President; Rosalie
Armstrong, President
Pub. *Tam Kernewek*, quarterly
(Cornish genealogy)
$10.00 per year membership

Creole

(see also French and Spanish)

**Creole-American Genealogical
Society, Inc.**
PO Box 3215, Church Street Station
New York, NY 10008
Carmen Uter, Director
(persons descended from the French-
German settlers of Louisiana, and the
Spanish, and the Portuguese of
American colonies, including New
England; publishes a brochure, $2.55
plus SASE)
$150.00 life membership

Croatian

(see also Eastern European and
Hungarian)

**American Society for Croatian
Migration**
1062 East 62nd Street
Cleveland, OH 44103
(216) 431-2770
Joseph Bosilievic, President

**The Association for Croatian Studies
(ACS)**
Department of History
John Carroll University
Cleveland, OH 44118
(216) 397-4758
George J. Prpic

Croatia Genealogy Home Page
PO Box 4327
Davis, CA 95617-4327
E-mail: feefhs@feefhs.org
http://dcn.davis.ca.us/~feefhs/cro/frg-
hr.html

Croatian Ethnic Institute, Inc.
4851 South Drexel Boulevard
Chicago, IL 60615
(773) 373-2248
Ljubo Krasic, Secretary-Treasurer
Pub. *Hisak-Cisac Newsletter*, bimonthly

Croatian Fraternal Union
100 Delaney Street
Pittsburgh, PA 15235
(412) 351-3909
Pub. *Zajednicar*, weekly
$45.00 per year Associate membership

**Croatian Genealogical and Heraldic
Society**
2527 San Carlos Avenue
San Carlos, CA 94070-1747
(650) 592-1190
E-mail: croatians@aol.com
http://feefhs/cro/frg-cghs.html
Adam S. Eterovich, Founder
Hours: by appointment
Pub. *Croatian-American Academic
Association and Croatian
Genealogical Society Quarterly
Bulletin*
research: $25.00 (one-time fee)

Croatian Information Service
PO Box 660546
Arcadia, CA 91006

Croatian National Association
1608 South Fremont
Alhambra, CA 91803

Croatian National Congress
10 Ackerman Drive
Saddle River, NJ 07458

Cuban

(see also Spanish)

Circulo Guinerode Los Angeles
434 South Alvarado Street
Los Angeles, CA 90057
(213) 483-9126
Efren Besanilla, President
(Cuban)

Cuban Genealogical Resources
E-mail: ee@acm.org
http://ourworld.compuserve.com/
homepages/ee/

Cuban Genealogical Society
(2552 Tamara Drive—location)
PO Box 2650 (mailing address)
Salt Lake City, UT 84110-2650
(801) 968-7312
Mayra F. Sanchez-Johnson, President
Pub. *Revista*, quarterly
$18.00 per year membership (calendar
year)

University of Miami
Archives and Special Collections
  Department
Richter Library
Coral Gables, FL 33124
(305) 284-3247; (305) 665-7352 FAX
E-mail: wbrown@miami.ir.miami.edu
http://www.miami.edu/archives/
  intro.html
(also Cuban collection)

Czech

(see also Eastern European, Slovak, and
  Polish)

Archives of the Czechs and Slovaks Abroad
The University of Chicago Library
c/o June Pachuta Farris, Curator
1100 East 57th Street
Chicago, IL 60637-1502
(773) 753-2856 (Dr. Hruban)
http://www.lib.uchicago.edu:80/libinfo/
  sourcesbysubject/slavic/acasa.html
Dr. Zdenek Hruban, Contact Person
Hours: by appointment only
(primarily a research collection, not
  organized for genealogical searching;
  specializes in Czechs, Slovaks and
  Moravians, general and local history
  of Czech and Slovak emigration)

California Czech and Slovak Club
PO Box 20542
Castro Valley, CA 94546-8542
(510) 581-9986; (510) 581-0213 FAX
http://www.rahul.net/njs/ccsc/index.html
Ilonka Martinka-Torres, President
Pub. *Noviny* (*News*), four times per year
  (March, June, September, December)
(maps, dictionaries, novelty items,
  books; translation services available;
  Czech, Slovak, Moravian, Ruthenian,
  and Silesian history, language, culture,
  heritage and customs; Czech and
  Slovak genealogy, heritage, culture
  and customs)
$15.00 per year membership for
  individuals, $20.00 per year
  membership for families

Czech and Slovak American Genealogy Society of Illinois
PO Box 313
Sugar Grove, IL 60554-0313
E-mail: Jzel@aol.com
http://members.aol.com/chrismik/
  csagsi.htm
Joe Hartzel, President; Paul S. Valasek,
  D.D.S., Editor
Pub. *Koreny* (*Roots*), quarterly
(interested in Bohemia, Slovakia,
  Moravia, Silesia, Ruthenia, etc.)
$15.00 per year membership for
  individuals or institutions (beginning 1
  September), $20.00 per year
  membership for families

The Czech, Bohemian, and Moravian Genealogical Research Page
E-mail: Czeching@iarelative.com
http://iarelative.com/czech/

Czech Cultural Club
(13th and Martha Streets—location)
2234 South 13th Street (mailing address)
Omaha, NE 68103
Lorraine Duggin, Secretary
Pub. *Sokol Omaha News*, about ten times
  per year
$10.00 per year membership

Czech Heritage Preservation Society, Inc.
PO Box 3
Tabor, SD 57063
(605) 589-3494
Vlasta Miller, Secretary
Pub. *CHPS Annual Newsletter*, annually
  (October)
$3.00 per year membership

Czech Heritage Society of Texas
4810 Spellman
Houston, TX 77035
(713) 726-0282
Anna Kprec, State President
Pub. *Český Hlas*, quarterly
(specializes in history of Czechs in
  Texas, and genealogy)
$8.00 per year membership

Czechoslovak Community Festival
700 Cypress
Marshfield, WI 54449
Toni Birmingham

Czechoslovak Genealogical Society International
(1650 Carroll Avenue, Saint Paul, MN
  55104—location)
PO Box 16225 (mailing address)
Saint Paul, MN 55116-0225
(612) 645-4585
http://members.aol.com/cgsi
Mark Vasko-Bigaouette
Pub. *Nase Rodina (Our Family)
  Quarterly Publication*, quarterly;
  Rocenka, bi-yearly (every other year)
(Bohemian, German, Hungarian, Jewish,
  Moravian, Russian, Ruthenian, Slovak,
  Silesian ancestry)
$20.00 per year membership for
  individuals, $30.00 per year
  membership for families, $40.00 per
  year Sponsor membership, $100.00
  per year Corporate membership,
  additional $8.00 for foreign
  membership

National Czech and Slovak Museum and Library
30 16th Avenue S.W.
Cedar Rapids, IA 52404-5904

Oklahoma Czechs, Inc.
(Fifth and Cedar, Yukon, OK 73099—
  location)
PO Box 850211 (mailing address)
Yukon, OK 73085
(405) 354-7573
Al Zajic, President
Hours: meetings: last Mon 7:30

Old Homestead Publishing Company
PO Box 45
Hallettsville, TX 77964
Doug Kubicek, Editor
Pub. *Nase Dejiny, The Magazine of
  Czech Genealogy*, bimonthly

Old Mobeetie Association of Mobeetie Jail Museum
Old Town
Mobeetie, TX 79061
(806) 845-3401
Dale Corcoran, President
(Early Panhandle family histories and
  museum; archives also includes
  records of Czech Poban community)
$5.00 per year membership

Society for the History of Czechoslovak Jews, Inc.
87-08 Santiago Street
Holliswood, NY 11423
(718) 468-6844
Lewis Weiner and Gertrude Hirschler,
  Editors
Pub. *Review of the Society for the
  History of Czechoslovak Jews*,
  annually, $9.00 per issue for non-
  members, $8.00 per issue for members
$15.00 per year regular membership
  (does not include periodical), $30.00
  per year Contributing membership,
  $50.00 per year Member-friend
  membership, $100.00 per year
  Member-patron membership

Sokol Detroit
23600 West Warren Avenue
Dearborn Heights, MI 48127
(313) 278-2558
Mr. G. Durkin
Pub. *Sokol Detroit News*, monthly, $5.00
  per year subscription

Wilber Czech Museum
102 West Third Street
PO Box 253
Wilber, NE 68465
(402) 821-2183

Danish

(see also Swedish and Norwegian)

C. A. Dana—Life Library
(address withheld upon request)
(resource for the United Evangelical
  Lutheran Church and the Danish
  immigrant archive; not a genealogical

resource for the general public and does not encourage unsolicited requests)

Danish American Fellowship
4200 Cedar Avenue, South
Minneapolis, MN 55407
(612) 729-3800

Danish American Heritage Society
29681 Dane Lane
Junction City, OR 97448
(541) 998-8562
Gerald Rasmussen, President
Pub. *The Bridge*, semiannually; *Newsletter*, semiannually
("The DAHS is a historical association interested in recording the contributions of Danish immigrants to American culture and society.")
$20.00 per year membership to George M. Norman, Treasurer, 132 North 132nd #301, Seattle, WA 98133

Danish Emigration Archives
E-mail: emiarch@vip.cybercity.dk
http://www.cybercity.dk/users/ccc13656

The Danish Immigrant Museum
(2212 Washington Street, on the west edge of Elk Horn—location)
PO Box 470 (mailing address)
Elk Horn, IA 51531
(712) 764-7001
Richard Burns, Executive Director; Barbara Lund-Jones, Curator
Hours: Mon–Fri 9:00–5:00, Sat–Sun 12:00–4:00
Pub. *America Letter* (not genealogical, except for an article from the Family History and Genealogy Center), quarterly
$25.00 per year full membership

University of Washington Libraries
Manuscripts and University Archives
Box 352900
Seattle, WA 98195-2900
(206) 543-1879
Hours: Mon–Fri 9:00–5:00 (during academic quarters)
(emphasis on ethnic Jewish, ethnic Japanese-American, and ethnic Scandinavian-American; not staffed to provide genealogial research but can suggest professional help)

Dutch
(see also Belgian)

Dutch Family Heritage Society
2463 Ledgewood Drive
West Jordan, UT 84084
(801) 967-8400; (801) 963-4604 FAX
Mary Lynn Spijkerman Parker, President and Editor
Pub. *Dutch Family Heritage Society Quarterly*
(specializes in Dutch in America, Dutch culture, and genealogical research in

America and The Netherlands, includes book reviews, immigrant databases)
$20.00 per year membership

The Dutch Settlers Society of Albany
RD 2, Box 313
Altamont, NY 12009
Joan Burns, President
Pub. *Yearbook of the Dutch Settlers Society of Albany*, every two to three years
$25.00 regular or Associate membership the first year, $12.00 per year thereafter

The Frisian Roundtable
2885 Roosevelt Avenue
Bronx, NY 10465
Roy C. Ketlsen, Editor
Pub. *The Frisian Roundtable*

Greater Sioux County Genealogical Society Chapter (IGS)
Sioux Center Public Library
327 First Avenue, N.E.
Sioux Center, IA 51250
Jennie Den Besten, President; Wilma J. Vande Berg, Corresponding Secretary
Hours: meetings in the Robert Frost Room (lower level) of the library: fourth Monday (except May & Dec) 7:30
(Lyon, Sioux and O'Brien counties and Dutch genealogy)
$5.00 per year membership for individuals, $6.00 per year membership for couples; search fee: donation

Heritage Hall-Calvin College and Calvin Theological Seminary Archives
3207 Burton Street, S.E.
Grand Rapids, MI 49546
(616) 957-6313
W. Blankespoor, MLS
Hours: Mon–Fri 8:30–4:30
Pub. *Origins—Historical Magazine of the Archives*, semiannually, $10.00 per year subscription
(obituaries, anniversary announcements in *Banner* and *De Wachter* from 1868, shipping records 1835–1880)

Herrick Public Library
300 River Avenue
Holland, MI 49423
Hours: winter: Mon–Thur 9:00–9:00, Fri–Sat 9:00–6:00, Sun 2:00–5:00; summer: Mon–Thur 9:00–9:00, Fri 9:00–6:00, Sat 9:00–1:00
(specializes in Dutch genealogy, Holland, Michigan, genealogy)

Hillsboro Historical Society and Museum
501 South Ash Street
Hillsboro, KS 67063
(316) 947-3775

David F. Wiebe, Director
Hours: Mar–Dec: daily
(Dutch/German research center)

The Holland Page
http://ourworld.compuserve.com/homepages/paulvanv/homepage.htm

Holland Society of New York Library
122 East 58th Street
New York, NY 10022-1939
(212) 758-1875
Delia Nelson, Genealogist for Library; Dr. David Voorhees, Historian and Editor
Hours: Fri 11:00–4:00 (closed Aug)
Pub. *de Halve Maen (Half Moon)*, quarterly, $28.50 postpaid per year subscription

The Joint Archives of Holland
History Research Center
Hope College
PO Box 9000
Holland, MI 49422-9000
(616) 395-7798; (616) 395-7197
E-mail: archives@hope.edu
Larry J. Wagenaar, Director
Hours: Mon–Fri 9:00–5:00 (call for holiday hours)
(houses "the collections of The Holland Historical Trust (Holland Museum) Hope College and Western Theological Seminary")
Pub. *The Joint Archives Quarterly*

Mennonite Historical Library
Goshen College
Goshen, IN 46526
(219) 535-7418; (219) 535-7438 FAX
E-mail: anetss@goshen.edu
John D. Roth, Director
Hours: Mon–Fri 8:00–5:00, Sat 9:00–1:00
Pub. *Mennonite Quarterly Review* (a scholarly historical publication), $24.00 per year subscription
(strong in genealogy of Amish and Mennonite families from Switzerland, Germany, The Netherlands, West Prussia and Russia, U.S., European and Canadian records)
$30.00 per year membership in Mennonite Historical Society includes periodical

Northwestern College
Dutch Heritage Room
Orange City, IA 51041
(712) 737-4821
Nella Kennedy, Curator
Hours: Mon–Thur 8:00–midnight, Fri 7:30 A.M.–10:00 P.M., Sat 8:30 A.M.–10:00 P.M., Sun 8:30 P.M.–midnight (closes at 4:30 weekdays and closed Sat & Sun during school holidays)

Historical Society Reformed Church of America

Gardner A. Sage Library
21 Seminary Place
New Brunswick, NJ 08901
(732) 246-1779 (Archives)
Russell L. Gasero, Editor
Hours: by appointment only
Pub. *Dutch American Genealogist*,
quarterly, $15.00 per year subscription

Van Harlingen Historical Society of Montgomery

(Blaidenburg Road—location)
PO Box 23 (mailing address)
Belle Mead, NJ 08502
(908) 359-3498
Jessie Havens, President; Ursula
Brecknell, Historian, Editor, Librarian,
Trustee
Hours: by appointment
Pub. *The Van Harlingen Historian*, three
times per year
(Dutch heritage, Somerset County area)
$10.00 per year membership for
individuals, $15.00 per year
membership for families; simple
questions: no charge

Eastern European

(see also Balkan and Russian)

Federation of Eastern European Family History Societies (FEEFHS)

PO Box 4327
Davis, CA 95617-4327
(530) 753-3206
http://feefhs.org; http://dcn.davis.ca.us/
~feefhs/
John D. Movius, Second Vice President
Pub. *FEEFHS Newsletter*, quarterly
(January, April, July, October), $10.00
per year subscription (does not include
query privileges); *FEEFHS
Addressbook & Resource Guide*,
biannually, $4.00 postpaid (available
in hard copy or on diskette in DOS
6.2)
(embraces the political boundaries of
Albania, Austria [including Italy's
Friuli and Tyrol], Belarus, Bosnia and
Herzegovina, Bulgaria, Croatia, former
Czechoslovakia [Czech and Slovak
republics], Estonia, Germany [all, but
emphasizing former East Germany],
Greece, Hungary, Latvia, Lithuania,
Macedonia, Moldova, Poland,
Romania, Russia [including Siberia],
Slovenia, Ukraine, Yugoslavia [both
Serbia and Montenegro], and virtually
all of the areas settled or once
controlled by Germany [except
Alsace-Lorraine], including East and
West Prussia, the Baltic states, Polish
Pomerania, Posen and Silesia, Galacia,
the Banat, Rusin, Volhynia and all
German-Russian colonies; maintains
Internet lists of professional

genealogists, translators, authors and
lecturers)
$15.00 per year membership for
individuals or organizations in the
U.S. and Canada, $20.00 per year
membership for individuals or
organizations outside the U.S. and
Canada, $250.00 life membership for
individuals; free queries for members

New York Public Library

Slavic and Baltic Division, Room 216-7
Fifth Avenue and 42nd Street
New York, NY 10018
(212) 930-0714; (212) 930-0940 FAX
E-mail: slavicref@nypl.org

Egyptian

(see also Religious Archives and
Organizations, Islamic)

American Coptic Association

PO Box 9119
Jersey City, NJ 07304

English

(see also British, Cornish and Irish)

British Heritage
PO Box 8200
Harrisburg, PA 17105-8200
Pub. *British Heritage*, bimonthly, $19.95
per year subscription

Genealogical Institute

Family History World
(875 North 300 East, Tremonton, UT—
location)
PO Box 22045 (mailing address)
Salt Lake City, UT 84122
(801) 250-6717 phone & FAX; (435)
245-0256; (801) 829-4030
E-mail: eakle@xmission.com
Arlene H. Eakle; JoAnn Jackson, Office
Manager
Hours: Mon–Fri 9:00–5:00
Pub. *Research News*, occasionally, $3.00
per issue plus postage and handling;
Immigration Digest (English and
Southern research), occasionally,
$13.50 per issue plus postage and
handling

International Society for British Genealogy and Family History

PO Box 3115
Salt Lake City, UT 84110-3115
Hazel M. Tibbitts, Corresponding
Secretary
Pub. *International Society for British
Genealogy and Family History
Newsletter*, quarterly
$15.00 per year membership

International Society of Shropshire

Rt. 2, Box 298A
Staunton, VA 24401

Pub. *International Society of Shropshire
Newsletter*, quarterly
$6.00 per year membership

Krans-Buckland Family Association, Inc.

PO Box 1025
North Highlands, CA 95660-1025
(916) 332-4359; (916) 331-4349 (to
leave a message)
Joyce Buckland, Editor/President
Hours: by appointment only
Pub. *The English Researcher*, quarterly
(February, May, August and
November), $10.00 per calendar year
subscription (for those researching in
England)

The Watkinson Library

Trinity College
300 Summit Street
Hartford, CT 06106
(860) 297-2268
Alesandra M. Schmidt, Associate Curator
Hours: When college is in session: Mon–
Fri 9:30–4:30, call for Sat & summer
hours
(British history, topography, genealogy,
and heraldry)
no research services available

Western Pennsylvania Genealogical Society

4400 Forbes Avenue
Pittsburgh, PA 15213-4080
(412) 687-6811
Hours: The Carnegie Library of
Pittsburgh: Mon–Thur 9:00–9:00, Fri–
Sat 9:00–5:30, Sun (Oct–May) 1:00–
5:00
Pub. *The Quarterly*; *JOTS*, ten times per
year
(sponsors Computer, English-Welsh,
German, Irish, New England and
Scottish interest groups)
$20.00 per year membership for
individuals (beginning 1 July); $26.00
per year joint membership (two
members at one address); two free
queries per quarter

Eskimo

(see Native American)

Estonian

(see also Eastern European)

Estonian American National Council

Estonian House
243 East 34th Street
New York, NY 10016
(212) 684-0336
Jaan Ulesoo, President

Estonian Educational Society of Detroit

PO Box 344
Trenton, MI 48183

(734) 676-8783
Thomas Ruben, President

European

(see also Balkan, Eastern European, and German)

Immigration History Research Center
University of Minnesota
826 Berry Street
Saint Paul, MN 55114
(612) 627-4208; (612) 627-4190 FAX
E-mail: ihrc@gold.tc.umn.edu
http://www.umn.edu/ihrc
Judith Rosenblatt, Public Relations
Hours: Mon–Fri 8:30–4:30
Pub. *Spectrum*, irregularly, $8.50 per issue; *IHRC News*, three times per year, free upon request
(resources focus on immigration from and ethnic groups originating in eastern, central, and southern Europe; fraternal society and church records, newspapers and serials, but no ship manifests or naturalization records, concentration on second wave [turn of the century] immigrants, including from the Near East)
$15.00 per year membership in Friends of the IHRC, $25.00 per year membership for families, $10.00 per year membership for senior citizens or students, $25.00 or more per year membership for organizations, depending on the organization's membership; special search fee: $15.00 per hour (beyond a few minutes)

Filipino

Filipino American Historical Society of Chicago
5462 South Dorchester Avenue
Chicago, IL 60615-5309
(773) 752-2156; (773) 955-3635 FAX

Finnish

(see also Norwegian and Swedish)

Family Sleuths
PO Box 526163
Salt Lake City, UT 84152-6163
(801) 467-4201 phone & FAX
E-mail: sleuths@sisna.com
http://feefhs.org/fi/frg-fs.html
Timothy Laitila Vincent, A.G.
(links to other sites; Finnish, Swedish, Norwegian)

Finland Historical Society
PO Box 583
Finland, MN 55603
(218) 353-7393
Dave Geist
(specializes in Finnish immigrants)

Finn Creek Museum
Minnesota Finnish-American Historical Society, Chapter 38
(four miles south of New York Mills on County Road #135—location)
PO Box 134 (mailing address)
New York Mills, MN 56567
(218) 385-2200 (Chairperson); (218) 385-2233 (Museum)
Reuben Anderson, Chairperson
Hours: Memorial Day through Labor Day: noon–5:00, and by appointment
(preserving Finnish heritage)

Finnish American Heritage Society of Maine
PO Box 249
West Paris, ME 04289
(207) 674-3094
Barbara Payne, Treasurer
Hours: Sept–Jun: third Sun
Pub. *The Maine Finn*, quarterly, $3.00 per year subscription
$5.00 per year membership, restricted to persons of Finnish descent, and their spouses

Finnish-American Historical Archives
Suomi College
601 Quincy Street
Hancock, MI 49930
(906) 487-7273; (906) 487-7347
E. Olaf Rankinen, Archivist; Lorraine Richards, Archives Assistant
Hours: Mon–Fri 9:00–4:00
$30.00 per year membership, $750 life membership; search fees lower

Finnish American Historical Society of Michigan, Inc.
19885 Melrose
Southfield, MI 48075
(313) 354-1994
Felix V. Jackonen, President

Finnish-American Historical Society of the West
PO Box 5522
Portland, OR 97228-5522
(503) 654-0448
E-mail: finamhsw@teleport.com
http://www.teleport.com/~finamhsw
Gene A. Knapp, Editor/State Corp Agent
Hours: Mon–Fri 10:00–5:00
Pub. *Finnam Newsletter* (not genealogical), quarterly
(not able to respond to genealogical requests; documents immigrant culture using manuscripts, oral histories, photographs and maps)
$10.00 per year membership for individuals (calendar year), $15.00 per year membership for families

Finnish American League for Democracy
147 Elm Street
Fitchburg, MA 01420

Finnish Genealogy Group
2119 21st Avenue South
Minneapolis, MN 55404
(612) 333-6028
http://feefhs.org/misc/frgfinmn.html
Marian Eliason, Secretary
Hours: The Minnesota Genealogical Society Library: Wed–Thur & Sat 10:00–4:00, Tue & Thur 6:30–9:30; meetings at The Immigration History Research Center, University of Minnesota, 826 Berry Street, Saint Paul, MN: Sept–Nov & Jan–Apr: Sat A.M.
Pub. *Newsletter*
$10.00 per year membership for families

Finnish Pioneer Crafts Guild
Superior Restorations, Inc.
PO Box 31
Greenbush, WI 53026
(920) 526-3433

Fitchburg State College Library
Highland Avenue
Fitchburg, MA 01420
(978) 343-6417
William T. Casey, Head Librarian

Minnesota Finnish-American Historical Society
Chapter 38
Rt. 3, Box 312
Sebeka, MN 56477
Fred Siirila, President
$7.00 per year membership for individuals, $8.00 per year membership for families

Minnesota Historical Society
345 Kellogg Boulevard, West
Saint Paul, MN 55102-1906
(612) 296-2143; (612) 297-7436 FAX
http://www.mnhs.org
Denise Carlson, Head of Reference
Hours: Mon–Wed & Fri–Sat 9:00–5:00, Thur 9:00–9:00
Pub. *Minnesota History*, quarterly, $10.00 per year subscription; *Roots*, quarterly, $5.00 per year subscription

Pasadena Historical Museum and Finnish Folk Art Exhibit
Pasadena Historical Society Research Library
470 West Walnut Street
Pasadena, CA 91103
(626) 795-3002
Tim Gregory, Archivist
Hours: Thur–Sun 1:00–4:00

Sampo Publishing, Inc.
PO Box 120804
New Brighton, MN 55112
(612) 636-6348
Mike Karni, Editor and Publisher
Hours: Mon–Fri 9:00–5:00
Pub. *Finnish Americana*, annually, $6.00 per issue, plus $1.00 postage and handling

("Finnish immigration to North America, its history and culture")

Sisu Heritage, Inc.
Rt. 1, Box 127
Embarrass, MN 55732
(218) 984-3012
Marilin Bjornrud, President
(local Finnish heritage)

Suomi Conference of the Lutheran Church in America
516 Villa Verde
Rio Rancho, NM 87124
(505) 898-6673
E. Olaf Rankinen, Archivist

Flemish

(see Belgian)

French

(see also Canadian, Creole, Irish, and Lineage, Hereditary and Patriotic Societies—Huguenot, Part 4)

The Acadian Cultural Exchange of Northern Maine
Rt. 2, Box 99
Madawaska, ME 04756
(207) 738-4272
Géraldine Pelletier Chassé, Chairman
Hours: 8:00–5:00
(covers The Saint John Valley, formerly known as the Madawaska Territory, home of a people divided by an international boundary: Allagash, Daigle, Eagle Lake, Fort Kent, Frenchville, Grand Isle, Hamlin, Keegan, Lille, Madawaska, Saint David, Saint Francis, Saint John, Sainte Agathe, Sinclair, Soldier Pond, Van Buren and Wallagrass)

Acadian Cultural Society
PO Box 2304
Fitchburg, MA 01420
(978) 342-7173
Lillian G. Leger, Librarian
Hours: by appointment
Pub. *Le Reveil Acadien: The Acadian Awakening*, quarterly
(cultural issues of French-speaking Canadians who migrated as far south as Louisiana)
$20.00 per year membership (U.S.), $25.00 (American) per year membership (outside the U.S.)

Acadian Genealogy Exchange
863 Wayman Branch Road
Covington, KY 41015
(606) 356-9825 (voice and FAX)
Janet Jehn, Editor
Hours: by appointment
Pub. *Acadian Genealogy Exchange*, quarterly, $15.00 per year subscription, including annual every-name index in

October issue, $17.00 per year subscription outside U.S
(French-Canadian, Acadian and Cajun genealogy and history)

Acadian Heritage Society
159 East Andover Road
Rumford, ME 04276
(207) 364-8651
Marie Thérèse Martin, President
Hours: seasonal
(Acadian genealogy)

Acadian House Publishing
PO Box 52247
Lafayette, LA 70505
(318) 235-7919; (318) 235-8851; (318) 235-9925 FAX
Trent Angers, Publisher
Hours: Mon–Fri 8:00–5:00
Pub. *Acadiana Profile, the Magazine of the Cajun Country*, bimonthly, $17.00 per six-issue subscription, $33.00 pertwelve-issue subscription, $49.00 per eighteen-issue subscription, $65.00 per twenty-four issue subscription
(south Louisiana, "Cajun Country")
free catalog available on request

Les Acadiens Du Texas
La Maison Beausoleil
(Port Neches, TX—location)
2015 Kingsley (mailing address)
Beaumont, TX 77705
(409) 832-6733
Clyde Vincent, President

American-Canadian Genealogical Society
(4 South Elm Street—location)
PO Box 6478 (mailing address)
Manchester, NH 03108-6478
(603) 622-1554; (603) 626-9812 FAX
E-mail: 102475.2260@compuserve.com; AMPerrault@aol.com (Editor)
http://ourworld.compuserve.com/homepages/acgs/
Anne-Marie Perrault, President
Hours: Wed & Fri 10:00–9:00, Sat 9:00–4:00, and by appointment
Pub. *American-Canadian Genealogist*, quarterly
(an international organization; primarily French-Canadian and Franco-American resources, vital records from all New England and New York)
Chapter: **Father Leo Begin Chapter**, American-Canadian Genealogical Society, PO Box 2125, Lewiston, ME 04240
$25.00 per year membership for individuals, $12.50 for each additional person in the same household, $375.00 life membership, $30.00 per year institutional or foreign membership

American-French Genealogical Society
(First Universalist Church, 78 Earle Street, Woonsocket, RI 02895—location)
PO Box 2113 (mailing address)
Pawtucket, RI 02861-2113
(401) 765-6141 phone and FAX
E-mail: afgs@ids.net
Roger Beaudry, President
Hours: Tue noon–10:00 P.M., first Sat 10:00–4:00
Pub. *Je Me Souviens*, semiannually (fall and spring)
(French/Canadian descent; large collection of books, 3,600 rolls of microfilm originally from the Drouin Institute in Montreal, and microfiche)
$30.00 per year membership for individuals, $10.00 per year membership for each additional family member

Jacqúes Timothé Boucher de Montbrun Heritage Society
2156 Valley View Road
Joelton, TN 37080
(502) 895-5682 (President)
T. Weldon DeMunbrun, President
Pub. *Le Journal*, quarterly
(French colonial history and family genealogy; specific interest in the French colonial history of the Greater Mississippi Valley, computer data on 6000 de Montbruns)
$15.00 per year membership

Bourbonnais Grove Historical Society
(Stratford Drive at Illinois Route 102—location)
PO Box 311 (mailing address)
Bourbonnais, IL 60914-0311
(815) 933-2308; (815) 933-6452
James V. Johnson
Hours: first & third Sun 1:00–4:00 by appointment
(French-Canadian heritage, county pioneer history)

La Société de Cajuns
121 West 111 Street
Cutoff, LA 70345
Audrey Hubert

La Société Canadienne-Française du Minnesota
PO Box 10913
Minneapolis, MN 55458
Mark Labine, President

Le Cercle de La Fleur de Lis
PO Box 2756
Gary, IN 46403
(219) 938-7403; (219) 882-2655

Claudette's
3962 Xenwood Avenue South
Saint Louis Park, MN 55416-2842
Claudette Atwood Maerz

Pub. *Across the Border* (includes northern Vermont counties of Essex, Lamoille, Chittenden, Caledonia, Grand Isle, Franklin, Washington and Orleans, and Quebec's eastern townships), quarterly, $14.00 per year subscription in the U.S., $16.00 per year subscription in Canada

Cloud County Genealogical Society

(Frank Carlson Library, 702 Broadway—location)
PO Box 202 (mailing address)
Concordia, KS 66901
(785) 243-4618
Jeanne M. Chubbuck, Archivist and Researcher
Hours: Library: Mon–Thur 9:00–9:00, Fri–Sat 9:00–5:00
Pub. *Cloud County (KS) Genealogical Society Newsletter*, quarterly
(Cloud County and French-Canadian settlements in eastern Cloud County)
$5.00 per year membership for individuals, $6.00 per year membership for families; research: $5.00 per hour plus costs

Le Comité des Archives de la Louisiane

PO Box 44370, Capitol Station
Baton Rouge, LA 70804
(504) 355-9906; (504) 387-4264 (President)
E-mail: judy.riffel@cajunelectric.com
Judy Riffel, Treasurer and Editor
Pub. *Le Raconteur*, three times per year, $15.00 per year (plus $3.00 after March 1) subscription

Comité Louisiane Française

2717 Massachusetts Avenue
Metairie, LA 70003
(504) 469-2555

Commission des Avoyelles, Inc.

PO Box 26
Hamburg, LA 71339
(318) 964-2675

La Société Historique Franco-Américaine

PO Box F
Woonsocket, RI 02895-0989
(401) 769-0520

Franco-American Genealogical Society of York County

(McArthur Library—location)
PO Box 472
Biddeford, ME 04005
(207) 284-4167 (Secretary)
Camille L. Bolduc, Secretary
Pub. *Maine's Franco-American Heritage*, annually (October)
$15.00 per year membership (beginning 1 September); queries free to members

Le Centre D'Heritage Franco American

81 Ash Street
Lewiston, ME 04240
(207) 783-9248
Lucille Dulee

French Ancestors

2923 Tara Trail
Beavercreek, OH 45434-6252
(937) 429-2979
E-mail: doylemr@aol.com
Marianne R. Doyle
Pub. *French Ancestors*, bimonthly, $8.00 per year subscription
("This is a small newsletter which deals with the French ancestors of families who settled in western Ohio in the mid-1800s, includes extracts from original French records and cultural, historical, and genealogical information of general interest.")

French Azilum, Inc.

Rt. 2, Box 266
Towanda, PA 18848
(717) 265-3376
Pat Zalinski, Site Manager
Hours: 1 May–15 Oct: 11:00–4:30 (last tour 4:00)
(site of colony for refugees from the French Revolution and from the Haitian Revolution)
admission: $4.50, $4.00 for senior citizens, $3.00 for students

French-Canadian Genealogical Society of Connecticut, Inc.

53 Tolland Green
PO Box 45
Tolland, CT 06084
(860) 872-2597
Mary Ann LeGrow, Library Director
Hours: Mon & Wed 4:00–8:00, Sat 9:00–4:00, Sun 1:00–4:00
Pub. *Connecticut Maple Leaf*, quarterly
$20.00 per year membership for individuals, $22.50 per year membership for families; visitors fee: $5.00

French Canadian Genealogists of Wisconsin

4624 West Tesch Avenue
Greenfield, WI 53220
(414) 541-8820
Patricia Geyh, Editor
Hours: by appointment
Pub. *French Canadian/Acadian Genealogists of Wisconsin Quarterly*
$7.00 per year membership for individuals, $10.00 per year membership for families receiving only one publication

French-Canadian Heritage Society of Michigan

Detroit Chapter
1056 Balfour Road
Grosse Pointe, MI 48230
Jerry Ricard

French-Canadian Heritage Society of Michigan

PO Box 10028
Lansing, MI 48901-0028
(517) 372-9707
Kathleen Kapalla, Corresponding Secretary
Pub. *Michigan's Habitant Heritage*, quarterly (January, April, July, October)
$15.00 per year U.S. membership (calendar year), $18.00 (U.S. funds) per year Canadian membership; send SASE for list of search fees

French Institute/Alliance Française

Library
22 East 60th Street
New York, NY 10022-1077
(212) 355-6100
E-mail: frinst1@metgate.metro.org
http://www.fiaf/org
Katharine Branning, Library Director
Hours: Mon 4:00–8:00, Tue noon–8:00, Wed–Thur 1:00–8:00, Fri 11:00–3:00, Sat 10:00–1:30
will provide brief information and referrals, but will not undertake detailed genealogical research

The French Library and Cultural Center

53 Marlborough Street
Boston, MA 02116
(617) 266-4351
E-mail: library@frenchlib.org
Jane M. Stahl, Librarian
Hours: Library: Labor Day through Jul: Tue–Thur 10:00–8:00, Fri–Sat 10:00–5:00
Pub. *Bibliophile*, five times per year
(French and Francophone studies, no genealogical material)
from $25.00 per year membership

French Settlement Historical Society

General Delivery
French Settlement, LA 70733
Pub. *French Settlement Historical Register*, annually

Heritage North

PO Box 205
Colton, NY 13625
Dennis E. Eickhoff, Director
(publishes records of northern New York State, Ontario and Quebec)

Center for Icarian Studies

Western Illinois University Library
1 University Circle
Macomb, IL 61455-1391
(309) 298-1575; (309) 298-2767

Pub. *Newsletter* (utopian groups, established by mostly French-born immigrants, near Dallas, Texas, Nauvoo, Illinois, Corning,Iowa, Saint Louis, Missouri, and San Francisco, California)

Institut Canado-Américain
52 Concord Street
Manchester, NH 03101
(603) 625-8577
Sr. Alice Aubé, Librarian in Charge
Pub. *Le Canado-Américain*

Mallet Library
Union Saint-Jean-Baptiste, A Division of Catholic Family Life Insurance
(68 Cumberland Street—location)
PO Box F (mailing address)
Woonsocket, RI 02895-0989
(800) 225-8752, ext. 143; (401) 766-3014 FAX
Dr. Charles Emile, Librarian
Hours: Wed 9:00–noon, Thur–Fri 9:00–3:00
(Franco-American history, genealogy, parish records, out-of-circulation French newspapers, photographs)

Mississippi Valley French Research
PO Box 502
Cambria, IL 62915-0502
(618) 985-6857
Eugene Beckett, Genealogist
Hours: after 5:30 P.M.
Pub. *Hello Cousins*, monthly, $22.00 per year subscription
(Includes Missouri and Illinois, "as most Mississippi Valley French were in these states.")

Northern New York American-Canadian Genealogical Society
(Community Center, Old High School Building, Main Street, Keeseville, NY—location)
PO Box 1256 (mailing address)
Plattsburg, NY 12901-1256
(518) 846-7707
Richard Ward, President
Hours: Community Center: May–Oct: Wed 1:00–7:00, Sat 10:00–4:00, and by appointment with two-weeks notice
Pub. *Lifelines*, two times per year
(southern Quebec, Northern New York, and Northern Vermont)
$20.00 per year membership for individuals ($25.00 outside the U.S.), $25.00 per year membership for families, libraries or institutions ($30.00 outside the U.S.), $7.50 per year membership for students ($10.00 outside the U.S.)

Northwest Territory, Canadian and French Heritage Center
Minnesota Genealogical Society, Northwest Territory, Canadian and French Branch
(1650 Carroll Avenue, Saint Paul, MN 55104—location)
PO Box 29397 (mailing address)
Brooklyn Center, MN 55443
Al Dahlquist, Vice President Publications
Pub. *Cousins et Cousines*, quarterly

Saint Lawrence Valley Genealogical Society
PO Box 341
Colton, NY 13625-0341
Dennis E. Eickhoff, Editor
Hours: Tue–Sat 2:00–5:00
Pub. *SLVGS News*, bimonthly
(northern New York State, Ontario and Quebec)
$7.00 per year membership

1699 Historical Committee
PO Box 713
Ocean Springs, MS 39564
(228) 875-0664
(first French Colony)

TCI Genealogical Resources
(see Spanish)

Museum of Waldensian Heritage
Rodoret Street
Valdese, NC 28690
(704) 874-2531
(Waldenses, French Christian followers of Pierre Waldo)

French-Canadian

(see French)

Galician

Along the Galician Grapevine
PO Box 194
Butterfield, MN 56120-0194
(507) 956-5815
E-mail: Mikeaf@mnic.net
http://feefhs.org/gal/aga/frg-aga.htm
Glen Linscheid, Editor
Hours: 8:00 A.M.–10:00 P.M.
Pub. *Along the Galician Grapevine*, annually (December), no subscriptions available, examination copy for LSASE
(lists births, deaths, marriages, and family reunions for the dispersed descendants of the 1880s Mennonite emigrants to North America from the Austrian Crownland of Galicia, at times referred to as Kleinpolen in the German; 17,000-entry database on the surnames Bachmann, Bergthold, Brubacher, Ewy, Forrer Hubin, Jotter, Kintzi, Klein, Linscheid, Merk, Miller, Rupp, Schmidt and Stauffer)

German

(see also Banat, Czech, Eastern European, Galician, Jewish, Polish, and Swiss)

American Historical Society of Germans from Russia, Ventura Chapter
13065 Westport Street
Moorpark, CA 93021
(310) 454-5749
E-mail: hmehrman@jovanet.com
http://feefhs.org/frgahrue.html
Carolyn Wheeler, President
Pub. *AHSGR Ventura Chapter Newsletter*
(includes Ventura and Santa Barbara counties, and parts of Los Angeles County)
$6.00 per year chapter membership, in addition to membership in the parent organization

American Historical Society of Germans from Russia, Southern California Chapter
15619 Ogram Avenue
Gardena, CA 90249-4445
(310) 675-2745
E-mail: whbonner@aol.com; gcra31@aol.com (Library)
http://feefhs.org/frgahssc.html
Wayne H. Bonner, President
Pub. *AHSGR Southern California Chapter Newsletter*, quarterly
(includes Los Angeles, San Diego, Riverside, San Bernardino and Orange counties)
$5.00 per year chapter membership, in addition to membership in the parent organization

American Historical Society of Germans from Russia
631 D Street
Lincoln, NE 68502-1199
(402) 474-3363; (402) 474-7229
E-mail: ahsgr@aol.com
JoAnn Kuhr, Research Director
Hours: Mon–Fri 9:00–4:00, Sat 9:00–1:00
Pub. *Clues*, quarterly; *Journal*, quarterly; *Newsletter*, quarterly
$40.00 per year membership; $4.50 for individual copies plus $2.50 postage and handling for the first item, $.75 for each additional item

American/Schleswig-Holstein Heritage Society
PO Box 313
Davenport, IA 52805-0313
(319) 324-7326 (phone and FAX)
Scharlott Goetsch Blevins, Genealogy Director and Librarian
Hours: by appointment only
Pub. *American/Schleswig-Holstein Heritage Society Newsletter*, bimonthly

$12.00 per year U.S. membership,
$18.00 foreign membership

Anglo-German Family History Society

13 - 27th Avenue, S.E.
Minneapolis, Minnesota 55414-3101
(612) 338-2001
E-mail: 100535.2632@compuserve.com
http://feefhs.org/uk/frgagfhs.html
Edward R. Brandt, A.G., Alternate U.S.
  FEEFHS Representative
Pub. *Mitteilungsblatt*, quarterly (in
  English)
£5.00 initiation fee, £8.50 per year
  membership for individuals in the
  U.K. (from 1 August), £9.00 per year
  membership for individuals in Europe,
  £11.00 per year membership for
  individuals in the rest of the world;
  free queries to members

Association of German Nobility in North America

3571 East Eighth Street
Los Angeles, CA 90023

Beyond Germanna

PO Box 120
Chadds Ford, PA 19317
(610) 388-1305
E-mail: johblank@pipeline.com
http://www.wp.com/germanna; http://
  www.concentric.net/nsgtgeorg/
  germhist.shtml
John Blankenbaker, Publisher
Hours: varies
Pub. *Beyond Germanna, A Newsletter for
  Virginia Piedmont Germans*, six times
  per year, $12.00 per year subscription
(specializes in early 18th century,
  interested in settlers' origins, history,
  genealogies, associated families, and
  dispersion to other areas; "The word
  'Germanna' refers to the location in
  Virginia where Lt. Gov. Alexander
  Spotswood settled a small group of
  Germans in 1714; today Germanna is
  located in Orange County in a
  horseshoe bend of the Rapidan River
  where Virginia State Highway 3
  crosses the Rapidan.")

Broad Bay Family History Projects

(Waldoboro, ME 04572-0010—location)
6094 South Glen Oaks Drive (mailing
  address)
Murray, UT 84107
W. W. "Will" Whitaker, Editor
Pub. *Old Broad Bay Bund und Blatt*
(includes the 100+ families which
  established a German colony in Broad
  Bay (Waldoboro, Maine) in 1740–
  1753)

Bush-Meeting Dutch

Illinois College
Jacksonville, IL 62650
(217) 245-3460

Dr. David Koss, Professor of Religion,
  Editor
Pub. *The Bush-Meeting Dutch: A
  Quarterly Newsletter of Local History
  and Genealogy of the Former
  Evangelical United Brethren Church,
  Its Predecessors, and Sister Churches*,
  quarterly, $5.00 per year subscription
(German-American churches)
$2.00 per obituary search

Comal County Genealogy Society

(Sophienburg Museum and Archives,
  Research Room—location)
PO Box 310583
New Braunfels, TX 78130-0583
(830) 629-1572 (Sophienburg Museum
  and Archives)
Ethel Canion, President
Hours: Archives: Mon–Fri 10:00–4:00
Pub. *Family Footsteps*, three times per
  year (March, July, November)
(German/Texas research Comal County
  and other German settlements in
  Texas)
$15.00 per year membership for
  individuals, $20.00 per year
  membership for families; search fee:
  $5.00 minimum

Die Pommerschen Leute

1260 Westhaven Drive
Oshkosh, WI 54904-8142
(920) 235-7398
E-mail: myrondpl@vbe.com
http://feefhs.org/dpl/frg-dpl.html
Myron E. Gruenwald, Publisher
Pub. *Die Pommerschen Leute*
  (Pomeranians 1839–1899), quarterly,
  $10.00 per year subscription

The Emsland Society

4325 Saint Lawrence Avenue
Cincinnati, OH 45205-1539
(513) 921-0629
http://geocities.com/heartland/4018
Albert Olthaus, President
(covers Landkreis Emsland in the former
  Prussian province of Hannover,
  including the towns of Andervenne,
  Bawinkle, Beesten, Bockhorst, Börger,
  Breddenberg, Dersum, Dörpen,
  Dohren, Emsbüren, Esterwegen,
  Freren-Stadt, Fresenburg, Geeste,
  Gersten, Groß Berßen, Handrup,
  Haren Stadt, Haselünne-Stadt, Heede,
  Herzlake, Hilkenbrook, Hüven, Klein
  Berßen, Kluse, Lähden, Lahn, Langen,
  Lathen, Lehe, Lengenreich, Lingen
  (Ems)-Stadt, Lorup, Lünne, Meppen-
  Stadt, Messingen, Neubörger, Neulehe,
  Neiderlangen, Oberlangen, Papenburg-
  Stadt, Rastdorf, Renkenberge, Rhede,
  Salzbergen, Schapen, Sögel,
  Spahnharrenstätte, Spelle, Stavern,
  Surwold, Sustrum, Thuine, Twist,
  Vrees, Walchum, Werlte, Werpeloh,
  Wettrup, and Wippingen; northwest
  German genealogy and history)

free exchange of information

Frankenmuth Historical Association

613 South Main
Frankenmuth, MI 48734
(517) 652-9701; (517) 652-9390 FAX
Mary Nuechterlein, Collections Manager
Hours: Mon–Fri 9:00–5:00, and some
  weekends by appointment
Pub. *FHA Newsletter*, quarterly
("Library covers only descendants of
  communities of Frankenmuth,
  Frankentrost, Frankenlust and
  Richville/Frankenhilf.")
$15.00 per year membership for
  individuals, $25.00 per year
  membership for families, $10.00 per
  year membership for students or senior
  citizens, $75.00 Sustaining
  membership, $500.00 life
  membership; search fee: $10.00 per
  hour

The Georgia Salzburger Society

2889 Ebenezer Road
Rincon, GA 31326-3716
(912) 754-7001
Frank L. Perry, Jr., President
Hours: 12 March and Labor Day
Pub. *The Georgia Salzburger Society
  Newsletter* (perpetuates the memory of
  Lutherans who emigrated from
  Salzburg and Germany from 1734–
  1752 to the Colony of Georgia, and
  updates the genealogy of their
  descendants; settled by General
  Edward Oglethorpe thirty miles north
  of Savannah on the Savannah River as
  a buffer with the Uchee Indians)

German-American Family Society of Akron, Inc.

3871 Ranfield Road
Brimfield, OH 44240
(330) 678-8229
Pub. *Newsletter (Rundschreiben)*,
  irregularly
(no genealogy functions, only a social/
  cultural organization)

German-American Genealogical Association Europe

HQ USAREUR
CMR 420, Box 502
APO, AE 09063
011-49-6227-51942; 011-49-6227-54008
  FAX
Lu Hays Whitworth, President
Pub. *Family Finder Newsletter*

German-American Genealogical Club

86th CSG/RSSRR, Box 24
APO New York, NY 09012
Terryl M. Allen, President

German American Heritage Association of Oklahoma (GAHA)

Modern Language Department
Oklahoma City University
2501 North Blackwelder
Oklahoma City, OK 73106
Christiane Faris, President
$10.00 per year membership

The German-American Heritage Institute

7824 West Madison
Forest Park, IL 60130-1485
(708) 366-0017
Gary Neusbieser

German-Bohemian Heritage Society

(800 West Idaho Avenue, Saint Paul, MN
55117—location)
PO Box 822 (mailing address)
New Ulm, MN 56073-0822
(612) 488-0405
E-mail: rpaulgb@pioneerplanet.infi.net;
LALGHBS@newulmtel.net
http://feefhs.org/ger/gbhal/frg-gbhs.html
Robert J. Paulson, Founder

German Genealogical Digest

(245 North Vine Street, Suite 106, Salt
Lake City, UT 84103—location)
PO Box 112054 (mailing address)
Salt Lake City, UT 84147
http://feefhs.org/pub/frg-ggdp.html
Laraine Ferguson, Editor; Gay Kowallis,
Editor
Pub. *German Genealogical Digest*,
quarterly, $25.00 per year subscription
or $8.00 per issue in the U.S., $28.00
per year subscription in Canada,
$36.00 per year subscription or $10.00
per issue elsewhere
list of published articles for SASE

German Genealogical Index

PO Box 582155
Minneapolis, MN 55458-2155

German Genealogical Society of America (GGSA)

(2125 Wright Avenue, Suite C-9, La
Verne, CA 91750—location)
PO Box 291818 (mailing address)
Los Angeles, CA 90029
(909) 593-0509
Ken Michel, Research Director; William
Toeppe, Librarian
Hours: Wed & Sat 1:00–5:00, and by
appointment
Pub. *Newsletter*, ten times per year
("CD-ROM lists; international phone
books, current from German-speaking
nations")
$20.00 per year membership for
individuals, $8.00 per year Associate
membership (residing at same address
as member), $30.00 foreign
membership (U.S. funds), $30.00
Contributing membership, $50.00

Supporting membership; library use:
$3.00 per day for non-members;
research fees: $16.00 per hour

German Genealogy Group

5 Eden Drive
Smithtown, NY 11787
(516) 979-6241
E-mail: hschrade@suffolk.lib.ny.us
Hans W. Schrader, President
Pub. *Newsletter*, ten times per year
(lending library, translation service,
GEDCOM indexes, proposed
mentoring service)
$15.00 per year membership for families

German Interest Group (GIG)

(Wisconsin Power and Light Company,
3730 Kennedy Road—location)
PO Box 2185 (mailing address)
Janesville, WI 53547-2185
Pub. *German Interest Group Newsletter*,
quarterly
$7.50 per year membership for
individuals, $10.00 per year
membership for families of two;
$12.50 European or Canadian
membership (U.S. funds)

German Interest Group (Chicago)

Chicago Genealogical Society
16828 Willow Lane Drive
Tinsley Park, IL 60477
Ron Otto

German Research Association

PO Box 711600
San Diego, CA 92171-1600
http://www.feefhs.org/gra/frg-gra.html
Hours: 8:00–5:00
Pub. *The German Connection*, quarterly
$18.00 per year membership for
individuals in the U.S., $5.00 per year
membership for each additional family
member at the same address, $24.00
per year foreign membership

German Society of Pennsylvania

611 Spring Garden Street
Philadelphia, PA 19123
(215) 627-2332
E-mail: germanscty@aol.com
http://www.german-society.org
Ms. Jackie Schmenger, Business
Manager
Hours: Library: Tue, Thur & Sun 10:00–
4:00 (archives are in storage at
present)
Pub. *Die neue Pennsylvanische
Staatsbote*, monthly (except summer)
$40.00 per year membership

German-Swiss Newsletter

PO Box 13548
Saint Louis, MO 63138
Maryann Schicker
Pub. *German-Swiss Newsletter
(Dietwiler-Fechter-Schicker-Hahn-
Eck-Schmitz-Kuhlman-Rower-Redre)*

German-Texan Heritage Society

507 East Tenth Street
PO Box 684171
Austin, TX 78768-4171
(512) 482-0927
Teresa Chavez, Director; Theresa G.
Gold, Genealogy Editor
Hours: Mon–Fri 8:00–4:30
Pub. *Journal*, three times per year;
Newsletter, three times per year
("Preservation of German heritage in
Texas; German-Texan family histories;
we are in the process of building a
library for historians and
genealogists.")
$10.00 per year membership (calendar
year), $16.00 per year foreign
membership; search fees: free for
members, $10.00 for non-members

Germanic Genealogy Society

Minnesota Genealogical Society, German
Branch
(Buenger Memorial Library, Concordia
College, 275 North Syndicate Street,
Saint Paul, MN 55104-5494—library
location)
PO Box 16312 (mailing address)
Saint Paul, MN 55116-0312
(612) 777-6463; (612) 641-8240 (for
Library hours)
Michael Haase, President
Pub. *G.G.S. Newsletter*, four or five
times per year (prior to meetings in
February, May, September and
November)
$5.00 per year membership; $2.00 per
surname or specific question for
members, $7.00 for non-members
(making them members)

Germans from Russia Heritage Society

1008 East Central Avenue
Bismarck, ND 58501-1936
(701) 223-6167
E-mail: grhs@btigate.com
http://www.teleport.com/nonprofit/grhs/
Rachel Schmidt, Office Manager
Hours: Mon–Fri 9:30–5:00
Pub. *Heritage Review*, quarterly
("The GRHS Library contains family
histories, local histories, obituaries,
pedigree charts, and passenger lists as
well as other reference materials.")
Chapters: **British Columbia**, Pat Hagel,
President, 2400 25th Street, Vernon,
British Columbia V1T 4P5, Canada,
(604) 542-2110; **First California
Chapter**, c/o Tom Hoffman, 5070
Ducos Place, San Diego, CA 92124,
(619) 277-9721; **Northern California**,
Don Merton Schell, President, 6304
39th Avenue, Sacramento, CA 95824-
1912, (916) 456-5035, *Northern
California GRHS Chapter Newsletter*,
quarterly; **Puget Sound**, Bob Schuh,
Past President, 724 S.W. Hayter Street,

Dallas, OR 97338-1845, (503) 623-5529, E-mail: rpschuh@teleport.com, *Puget Sound Chapter Newsletter*, quarterly
$25.00 per year membership; search fee: $10.00 per hour

Glückstal Colonies Research Association
611 Esplanade
Redondo Beach, CA 90277-4130
(310) 540-1872
E-mail: gcra31@aol.com
http://feefhs.org/FRGGRA/gcra.html
Margaret Freeman, Executive Director
Hours: by appointment
Pub. *GRCA Newsletter*, semiannually (specializes in inhabitants of the Glückstal colonies in South Russia; "goal: list all of inhabitants of the colony group from founding, 1803–1809, to demise during World War II")
$15.00 per year membership

Goschenhoppen Historians, Inc.
(116–118 Gravel Pike—location)
PO Box 476 (mailing address)
Green Lane, PA 18054
(215) 234-8953
"Abe" Roan, First Vice President
Hours: Museum: Sun (Apr–Nov) 1:30–4:00; Library: by appointment
(Pennsylvania-German history and folk culture, local and regional history of Goschenhoppen Folk Region)

The Gottscheer Research and Genealogy Association (GRGA)
174 South Hoover Avenue
Louisville, CO 80027-2130
(303) 665-2986
E-mail: anthro@privatei.com
http://www.geocities.com/~gottschee
Elizabeth A. Nick, Ed.D., Editor
Hours: 8:00–5:00
Pub. *The Gottschee Tree* (includes history and genealogy of the Gottscheers, an ethnic German group, and their descendants in the United States and Canada; residents of Gottschee, now known as Kočvje, formerly part of the Austrian-Hungarian Empire, now in Slovenia, Yugoslavia), quarterly
$20.00 per year membership

Harmonie Associates, Inc.
Old Economy Village
14th and Church Streets
Ambridge, PA 15003
(724) 266-1803
Raymond V. Shepherd, Jr., Director
(Harmonists, a German, Christian communal society, 1785–1905)

The Sidney Heitman Germans from Russia Collection
Colorado State University
University Archives, Morgan Library
Fort Collins, CO 80523-1019

(970) 491-1844; (970) 491-1195 FAX
E-mail: pvandeve@manta.colostate.edu.; JNewman@vines.colostate.edu
Patricia Van Deventer, Library Technician II, University Archives Staff Supervisor; John Newman, Archivist, Special Collections Department, Colorado State University Libraries

Hillsboro Historical Society and Museum
501 South Ash Street
Hillsboro, KS 67063
(316) 947-3775
David F. Wiebe, Director
Hours: Mar–Dec: daily
(Dutch/German research center)

Historic Bethel German Colony
PO Box 127
Bethel, MO 63434
(660) 284-6200
Elizabeth Fakazis, Executive Director
("Bethel was established as a communal colony in the mid-1800s; many of the original structures, and descendants of the founders, are still here.")

Historic Harmony/Harmony Museum
218 Mercer Street
PO Box 524
Harmony, PA 16037
(724) 452-7341
Kathy Luck, Administrator
Hours: Tue–Fri & Sun 1:00–4:00
Pub. *Newsletter*, monthly
(emphasis on Germans, Harmony Society, Mennonites; "Harmony wasfirst home (1804–1814) of communal Harmony Society of German immigrants, subsequently was a Mennonite community for much of the 19th century.")
$15.00 per year membership for individuals, $20.00 per year membership for families, $10.00 per year membership for senior citizens, $15.00 per year membership for senior citizen families, $3.00 per year membership for students, $30.00 per year institutional membership, $75.00 per year Sustaining membership, $200.00 life membership for individuals, $250.00 life membership for families; charges fees for research by non-members or conducted for anyone, and for photocopies

Immigrant Genealogical Society
Immigrant Library
1310-B West Magnolia Boulevard
PO Box 7369
Burbank, CA 91510-7369
(818) 848-3122
http://feefhs.org/igs/frqigs.html
Marilyn Deatherage, Corresponding Secretary

Hours: Wed & Sun noon–5:00, Sat 10:00–5:00; meetings first Fri 7:30
Pub. *German American Genealogy*, semiannually; *Immigrant Genealogical Society Newsletter*, monthly (especially German and Swiss)
$20.00 per year membership for individuals, $25.00 per year membership for families at the same address, additional $10.00 per year for first class mail delivery, additional $15.00 for airmail delivery overseas; library admission free to members, $2.00 per visit to non-members

Indiana German Heritage Society
401 East Michigan Avenue
Indianapolis, IN 46204
(317) 464-9004
Ernestine Dillon, President
Hours: none at present, but will establish soon
Pub. *The Indiana German Heritage Society Newsletter*, quarterly
$12.00 per year membership for individuals, $20.00 per year membership for families

Jensen Publications
PO Box 441
Pleasant Grove, UT 84062-0441
http://feefhs.org/frg-jp.html
Larry R. Jensen, Author, Self-Publisher and Lecturer
(publishes books on German research)

Landsmannschaft der Bessarabiendeutschen
Heimatmuseum der Deutschen aus Bessarabien
c/o North Dakota State University Libraries
PO Box 5599
Fargo, ND 58105-5599
(701) 231-8416
E-mail: mmmiller@badlands.nodak.edu
http://feefhs.org/frghdblb.html
Michael M. Miller, Germans from Russia Bibliographer
Pub. *Mitteilungsblat*, monthly

Landsmannschaft der Deutschen aus Russland
c/o North Dakota State University Libraries
PO Box 5599
Fargo, ND 58105-5599
(701) 231-8416
E-mail: mmmiller@badlands.nodak.edu
http://feefhs.org/frgland.html
Michael M. Miller, Germans from Russia Bibliographer
Pub. *Volk auf dem Weg*, monthly, 54.00 DM per year subscription
(Black Sea Germans, Crimean Germans, Caucasus Germans, Mennonite Germans, Volga Germans)

Lineages, Inc.
Department A-F
PO Box 417
Salt Lake City, UT 84110
(800) 338-5114
Johni Cerny, President
Pub. *Before Germanna* (monograph series), $10.00 per issue

Links Genealogy Publications
8125 Arroyo Vista Drive
Sacramento, CA 95823-5935
(916) 428-2245; (916) 628-3381
E-mail: ijones@ns.net
Iris Carter Jones, Owner
Hours: Mon–Fri 8:00–5:00
Pub. *Krefeld Immigrants and Their Descendants* (for descendants of the 1683 immigrants who settled Germantown in Philadelphia: Aret/Arent(s), Bebber/van Bebber, Bleikers/Blijkers, van Bom/Bon/Bun(n), Bucholtz, DeHaven/in den Hoffe(e), Dewees(e)/DeWeese, Do(o)rs/Daurss/Dohrs, Frey(s), Hendricks, Keurlis/Kurlis, Klinken, Klosterman, Kuster/Custer/Custard, Kunders/Donard/Cunard/Conrad, Lensen, Linderman, Levering, Lucken/Luken/Luyken(s), Neusz/Nice, op de Trap(p), op den Graeff/up de Graeff/Updegrove, Plejtes/Peters, Pastaorius, Rittenhouse/Rittenhuysen, Scherkes, Schumacher/Shoemaker, Seimen/Siemes, Sellen/Cellen/Zellen, Sellers/Cellers, Sivert, Streepers/Streypers, Telnes, Theison/Teison/Tyson, Tennis/Tunes/Tunis/Tunnis, van Aaken, Wil(l)ems/Williams, and allied names of Beal, Cassell/Kassel(l), Copeland, Delaplaine, Duplovys, Garret/Jarrett, Hirst, Jansen/Johnson/Johnston, Jones/Johns, Kyser/Kiser, Loers, Papen, Penn, Pockhoy, Potts, Rutter, Supplees/Souples, Thatcher, Umstead/Umstat(t)d, Wisee, etc.), $14.00 per year subscription (subscribers receive free queries, surname registration, family charts computerized)

The Memorial Foundation of the Germanna Colonies in Virginia, Inc.
PO Box 693
Culpeper, VA 22701-0693
(540) 825-1496; (540) 825-6572 FAX
E-mail: germanna@summit.net
http://www.summit.net/germanna/
Rose Marie Martin, Office Administrator
Hours: Germanna Community College Library: Mon–Fri 9:00–5:00
Pub. *Germanna*, quarterly; *The Germanna Record*, occasionally
(extensive collection of genealogy, history and biography pertaining to the pioneer settlers composing the Germanna Colonies in Virginia, 1714 and 1717, later arrivals and their descendants, including the following

families: Aker, Albright, Amberger, Amburger, Ashby, Aylor, Bach, Back, Baker, Ballenger, Barber, Barler, Barlow, Baumgardner, Beer, Bender, Benneger, Beyerback, Blankenbaker, Boehm, Broyles, Brumbach, Brumback, Bungard, Burdyne, Bush, Button, Camper, Carpenter, Castler, Chelf, Christler, Christopher, Clore, Cobbler, Coller, Cook, Coon, Coons, Corber, Cornwell, Crecelieus, Crees, Crest, Crible, Crigler, Crim, Crumber, Cuntz, Darnall, Deal, Deer, Delf, Delph, Diehl, Duncan, Everhart, Farrow, Fick, Finder, Finks, Fishbach, Fishback, Fisher, Fite, Flender, Fleshman, Folg, Frank, Fray, Friesenhagen, Gansler, Garr, Graham, Haeger, Hager, Hanback, Harnsberger, Heide, Heite, Herndon, Hirsh, Hitt, Hoffman, Holt, Holtzclaw, Hoop, House, Huettenhen, Huffman, Jacoby, Kabler, Kaifer, Kaiffer, Kaines, Kemper, Kerchler, Kerker, Kines, Klug, Kneisler, Koontz, Kooper, Kriebel, Kuenzle, Kyner, Lang, Langenbuehl, Latham, Leach, Leatherer, Leathers, Lederer, Lehman, Lipp, Long, Lotspeich, Lyons, Manspeil, Martin, Mauck, McClure, Michael, Miller, Motz, Moyer, Nay, Newby, Noeh, Nunnamaker, Oehler, Oehlschutt, Ohlschlagel, Patt, Paulitz, Peck, Prosie, Racer, Railsback, Rector, Reading, Rinehart, Riner, Rodeheaver, Rouse, Russell, Schut, Shafer, Sheible, Sheibley, Sheibly, Sinclair, Slaughter, Slucter, Smith, Snyder, Sohlbach, Souther, Spillman, Spilman, Staehr, Stature, Stigler, Stinesyfer, Stoever, Stoltz, Stonecipher, Stover, Stuell, Swindell, Tanner, Tapp, Teter, Thomas, Troller, Tullser, Urbach, Utterback, Utz, VanMeter, Vaught, Vogt, Walke, Walker, Wayland, Wayman, Weaver, Weingart, Whitescarver, Wieland, Wiley, Wilhoit, Willer, Willheit, Yager, Yeager, Young, Yowell, Ziegler, Zimmerman, Zollicoffer)
$10.00 per year membership for individuals, $15.00 per year membership for families, $150.00 life membership

Mennonite Historians of Eastern Pennsylvania
565 Yoder Road, Box 82
Harleysville, PA 19438
(215) 256-3020
Joel D. Alderfer, Librarian
Hours: Tue–Fri 10:00–4:00, Thur 7:00 P.M.–10:00 P.M.
Pub. *Mennonite Historians of Eastern Pennsylvania (MHEP) Newsletter*, bimonthly
(local Mennonite history, Pennsylvania-German studies, genealogy and local history of Bucks and Montgomery counties, Pennsylvania)

$20.00 per year membership for individuals (includes 10% discount on book sales and on research fees)

The Mid-Atlantic Germanic Society
PO Box 2642
Kensington, MD 20895
Pub. *Der Kurier*, quarterly
$10.00 per year membership

North Dakota State University
Germans from Russia Heritage Collection
(North Dakota Institute for Regional Studies—location)
North Dakota State University Libraries
PO Box 5599 (mailing address)
Fargo, ND 58105-5599
(701) 237-8914; (701) 231-8416 (to confirm library hours); (701) 293-5564 (Bibliographer); (701) 231-7138 FAX
E-mail: mmmiller@badlands.nodak.edu
http://www.lib.ndsu.nodak.edu/gerrus/
Professor Michael M. Miller, Bibliographer
Hours: Mon–Fri (academic year) 8:00–5:00; Mon–Fri (summer) 7:30–5:00
(emphasis on Black Sea and Bessarabian German villages, south Russia, Ukraine and Moldova)

Orangeburg German-Swiss Genealogical Society
3415 Pine Belt Road
Columbia, SC 29204
(843) 577-5898
Louis U. Ulmer
Pub. *Orangeburg German-Swiss Newsletter*, bimonthly
$10.00 per year membership, c/o Bill R. Linder, 6129 Leesburg Pike, No. 820, Falls Church, VA 22041

Ostfriesen Ancestral Research Association
143 Virginia Avenue
Bethalto, IL 62010
Rev. Kenneth DeWall

Ostfriesian Genealogical Society
(address withheld upon request)
Pub. *Ostfriesen Genealogical Society Newsletter*, monthly
(covers Illinois, Iowa, South Dakota and Minnesota)
$25.00 per year membership (calendar year)

Palatines to America
(Saylor-Ackerman Hall—location)
Capital University, Box 101AB (mailing address)
Columbus, OH 43209-2394
(614) 236-8281 phone and FAX
E-mail: pal-am@juno.com
http://genealogy.org/~palam/
Sophia Jean Hall, Membership Registrar
Hours: Office: 8:30–12:30 P.M.; Library: Wed 12:30–4:00, first Sat 10:00–2:00, third Fri 9:00–4:00, and by

appointment; annual convention: third Fri & Saturday in Jun
Pub. *Palatine Patter*; *The Palatine Immigrant*, quarterly
("A national genealogical society of those seeking the origin of their German-speaking ancestors")
$20.00 per year membership for individuals (beginning in October, includes membership in one state chapter, $5.00 per year membership in each additional chapter), $22.00 per year membership for families, $30.00 (U.S.) per year membership for individuals in Canada or Mexico, $40.00 (U.S.) per year membership for individuals in Europe, $50.00 per year Contributing membership, $500.00 life membership; research and queries for members only, library open to all

Palatines to America, Colorado Chapter
7079 South Marshall Street
Littleton, CO 80123-4607
(303) 979-5968
Pub. *CO-PAL-AM*
$20.00 per year membership in national society includes membership in one state chapter

Palatines to America, Illinois Chapter
PO Box 3448
Quincy, IL 62305-3448
(708) 599-7818
Nadine Blocker, Chapter President
Pub. *Illinois Chapter Newsletter*, quarterly
$20.00 per year membership in national society includes membership in one state chapter

Palatines to America, Indiana Chapter
1801 North Duane Road
Muncie, IN 47304-2649
(765) 284-1841
E-mail: krohler@ecicnet.org\ancestors
Beth Ann Kroehler, President
Pub. *Indiana Chapter Newsletter*, quarterly
$20.00 per year membership in national society includes membership in one state chapter

Palatines to America, New York Chapter
PO Box 14
Alcove, NY 12077
(518) 756-9002
Pub. *Yorker Palatine*
$20.00 per year membership in national society includes membership in one state chapter

Palatines to America, Ohio Chapter
Capital University, Box 101
Columbus, OH 43209-2394
(330) 828-2019

Pub. *Ohio Palatine Heritage*, quarterly
$20.00 per year membership in national society includes membership in one state chapter

Palatines to America, Pennsylvania Chapter
PO Box 280
Strasburg, PA 17579-0280
(717) 244-7358
Lois C. Byrem, Membership Registrar
Pub. *Penn Pal*, quarterly
$20.00 per year membership in national society includes membership in one state chapter

Palatines to America, Virginia Chapter
3249 Cambridge Court
Fairfax, VA 22030-1942
(703) 591-3656
E-mail: toedick@aol.com
Monika E. Edick, President
Pub. *That Wagon Road*, quarterly
$20.00 per year membership in national society includes membership in one state chapter

Palatines to America, West Virginia Chapter
572 Plymouth Avenue
Morgantown, WV 26505-2142
(304) 599-1672
Antialee M. Garletts, President
Pub. *Pal-Am Mountaineer*, three or four times per year
$20.00 per year membership in national society includes membership in one state chapter

Pennsylvania Dutch Folk Culture Society
Baver Memorial Library
Folklife Museum
Main and Willow Streets
Lenhartsville, PA 19534
(215) 562-4803
Florence Bauer, President
Hours: Apr–May & Sept–Oct: Sat 10:00–4:00, Sun 1:00–4:00; summer: Mon–Sun 10:00–5:00
Pub. *Pennsylvania Dutch News and Views*, semiannually
(Berks and neighboring counties; Pennsylvania German folklife and genealogy library)
$10.00 per year membership for individuals, $12.00 for couples

The Pennsylvania German Research Society
Rt. 1, Box 478
Sugarloaf, PA 18249
(717) 788-5133
Carolyn Boyer-Dryfoos, President
Pub. *Der Überblick*, quarterly
(Pennsylvania-Germanic research, German emigrant searches; annual

genealogical research tour to Germany, Austria, and Switzerland)
$20.00 per year membership

The Pennsylvania German Society
PO Box 397
Birdsboro, PA 19508
(215) 582-1441
Robert M. Kline, President
Pub. *Proceedings*, annually; *Der Reggeboge* (*The Rainbow*), semiannually
$50.00 per year Patron membership, $60.00 per year Benefactor membership; $100.00 per year Sustaining membership; $5.00 per year membership for institutions and libraries; $1,000.00 life membership.

Pommerscher Verein—Central Wisconsin
PO Box 358
Wausau, WI 54402-0358
E-mail: Zamzow@dwave
Donald D. Zamzow
Pub. *Newsletter*, quarterly

Pommerscher Verein-Freistadt
(Lindenwood School, 12351 North Granville Road, Mequon, WI—location)
PO Box 204 (mailing address)
Germantown, WI 53022-0204
(414) 353-8949
E-mail: pommern@execpc.com
http://www.execpc.com/~pommern
Norman Schroeder, Chairman Computer and Website Committee
Hours: second Thur 10:00–4:00, second Fri 7:00 P.M.–10:00 P.M.
Pub. *Rundschreiben-Pom. Ver. Freistadt*, quarterly
(Pommeranian history and genealogy, books, maps, also studies and collects items on customs and trachts or period dress)
$15.00 per year membership for individuals, $20.00 per year membership for families, $10.00 per year Associate membership

Sacramento German Genealogy Society
PO Box 660061
Sacramento, CA 95866-0061
(530) 753-3206; (916) 421-8032 FAX
E-mail: sacgermgs1@aol.com
http://feefhs.org/sggs/frg-sggs.html
Victor Boisserée, President
Hours: meetings at Northminster Presbyterian Church, 3235 Pope Avenue (near Watt Avenue, south of I-80), Sacramento: fourth Tue (Jan–Oct) 1:00
Pub. *Der Blumenbaum*, quarterly (January, April, July, October)
$15.00 per year membership for individuals, $20.00 per year membership for couples

Johannes Schwalm Historical Association, Inc.
PO Box 99
Pennsauken, NJ 08110
(609) 663-8292
R. C. Barth, Executive Director
Hours: Gratz Historical Society, Gratz, PA: Wed P.M. only
Pub. *Journal of the Johannes Schwalm Historical Association, Inc.*, annually
(descendants of Hessian soldiers)
$20.00 per year membership

Society for German American Studies
German Department
Saint Olaf College
Northfield, MN 55057-1098
(507) 645-8562 (*Newsletter* Editor);
   (913) 864-4803 (*Yearbook* Editor)
(507) 646-3732 FAX
E-mail: rippley@stolaf.edu
http://feefhs.org/frg-sgas.html
Professor LaVern Rippley, Newsletter Editor
Pub. *Society for German-American Studies Newsletter*, quarterly;
Yearbook of German-American Studies, annually, $20.00 per issue, c/o William Keel, German Department, University of Kansas, 2080 Wescoe Hall, Lawrence, KS 66045
$20.00 per year membership

Society for the History of Germans in Maryland
107 East Chase Street
PO Box 22585
Baltimore, MD 21203
(410) 685-0450
Gerard Wm. Wittstadt, President
Pub. *The Report: A Journal of German-American History*, every year or two
("The Society does not provide a genealogy service, nor does it maintain a research library.")
$15.00 per year membership

Texas Seaport Museum
(Pier 21—location)
2016 Strand (mailing address)
Galveston, TX 77550
(831) 763-1877; (831) 763-3037 FAX
E-mail: tsm@phoenix.net
http://www.phoenix.net/~tsm
Kurt Voss, Director
Hours: daily 10:00–5:00
(includes immigration database, mostly Germans and Eastern Europeans, entering through the Port of Galveston 1840–1950)
$5.00 admission for adults, includes use of immigration database; mail-in search: $10.00 per person

Texas Wendish Heritage Society
Texas Wendish Heritage Museum
Rt. 2, Box 155
Giddings, TX 78942

(409) 366-2441
Barbara P. Hielscher, Museum Director; Georgie B. Boyce, President
Hours: Mon–Fri & Sun 1:00–5:00, Sat (Easter–Labor Day) 1:00–5:00
$12.50 per year membership for individuals, $7.50 per year membership for students

Transylvania Saxon Genealogy and Heritage Society, Inc.
PO Box 3319
Youngstown, OH 44513-3319
(330) 783-1947
E-mail: pkreutzerj@aol.com;
   bn656@yfn.ysu.edu
http://www.feefhs.org/ah/hu/
   frgtsghs.html
Pau Kreutzer, Jr., Executive Director
Pub. *Transylvania Saxon Tapestry*, quarterly
(area is variously named Transilvania, Ardeal, Siebenbürgen or Siebenbuergen, and Erdély)
$15.00 per year membership for individuals, $250.00 life membership

Tulpehocken Settlement Historical Society
116 North Front Street
PO Box 53
Womelsdorf, PA 19567
(215) 589-2527
Earl W. Ibach, Director
Hours: Apr–Oct: Mon–Tue & Thur–Sun 1:00–4:00; Nov–Apr: Mon–Tue, Thur–Fri & Sun 1:00–4:00
Pub. *Tulpehocken Tattler*, quarterly, $2.00 per issue; *Die Shilgrut fun der Tulpehock*, annually
(genealogical library and rotating historical exhibits in museum)
$15.00 per year membership, $200.00 life membership

University of Cincinnati
University Libraries
Archives and Rare Books Department
German-Americana Collection
PO Box 210113
Cincinnati, OH 45221-0113
(513) 556-1955; (513) 556-2113 FAX
E-mail: don.tolzmann@uc.edu
Dr. Don Heinrich Tolzmann, Curator
Hours: Mon, Wed & Fri 8:00–noon

The University of Texas at Austin
Winedale Historical Center
PO Box 11 (FM 2714)
Round Top, TX 78954
(409) 278-3530
Gloria Jaster, Administrator
Hours: weekdays 9:00–5:00
Pub. *The Ouid Nuch*, quarterly

Wandering Volhynian Group
PO Box 97
Ossian, IA 52161-0097
(319) 532-9265
E-mail: irmgard@polaristel.net

Irmgard Hein Ellingson, U.S. Circulation
Pub. *Wandering Volhynians: A Magazine for the Descendants of Germans from Volhynia and Poland*, quarterly, $15.00 per year subscription
(from Poland, Volhynia and Ukraine)
search not done unless arrangements made with Mr. Wuschke, 3492 West 39th Avenue, Vancouver, British Columbia V6N 3A2, Canada, fees beginning at $10.00; member queries free

Weld Library District
Lincoln Park Branch
919 Seventh Street
Greeley, CO 80631
(970) 350-9210 (Circulation); (970) 350-9212 (Reference); (970)350-9215 FAX
Margaret Langley, Reference Librarian
Hours: Mon–Thur 9:00–8:00, Fri–Sat 10:00–5:00, Sun (Sept–May) 1:00–5:00
(collection of materials on the German Russians)

Western Pennsylvania Genealogical Society
4400 Forbes Avenue
Pittsburgh, PA 15213-4080
(412) 687-6811
Hours: The Carnegie Library of Pittsburgh: Mon–Thur 9:00–9:00, Fri–Sat 9:00–5:30, Sun (Oct–May) 1:00–5:00
Pub. *The Quarterly*; *JOTS*, ten times per year
(sponsors Computer, English-Welsh, German, Irish, New England and Scottish interest groups)
$20.00 per year membership for individuals (beginning 1 July); $26.00 per year joint membership (two members at one address); two free queries per quarter

Greek

(see also Eastern European)

Chian Federation
44-01 Broadway
New York, NY 11103

Evrytanian Association
121 Greenwich Road
Charlotte, NC 28211
(704) 366-6571
Olga Kleto
Pub. *Velouchi Bulletin*, quarterly
("founded as a philanthropic organization in 1944 by Evrytanians (from the state of Evrytania, central Greece) emigrating to the U.S.")

Greek Family Heritage Committee
75-21 177th Street
Flushing, NY 11366
(718) 591-9342
E-mail: alonakia@worldnet.att.net

Antonia Mattheou, Archivist Historian
Hours: Mon–Sat noon–9:00
(Greek genealogy; published how-to book)
no genealogical research services offered

Hellenic Museum and Cultural Center
168 North Michigan Avenue, Fourth Floor
Chicago, IL 60601-7509
(312) 726-1234; (312) 726-8539 FAX
Themi Vasils
Hours: Wed–Fri 11:00–3:00
(Greek immigrant experience)

Saint Photios Greek Orthodox National Shrine
41 Saint George Street
PO Box AF
Saint Augustine, FL 32085
(904) 829-8205
(New Smyrna Colony of Greeks in America)

Guatemalan
(see Spanish)

Hispanic
(see Spanish)

Hungarian
(see also Banat, Czech, Eastern European, Polish, and Slovenian)

American Hungarian Federation
1450 Grace Avenue
Cleveland, OH 44107

American Hungarian Library and Historical Society
215 East 82nd Street
New York, NY 10028
(212) 744-5298
Dr. Leslie E. Acsay
Pub. *Hungarian Digest*, quarterly

Hungarian/American Friendship Society
2701 Corabel Lane, Apartment 34
Sacramento, CA 95821-5233
(916) 489-9599; (916) 489-9599 FAX
E-mail: doug@dholmes.com
http://www.dholmes.com/hafs.html
Douglas P. Holmes, Director
Hours: by appointment only
Pub. *Régi Magyarország "Old Hungary"*
(the newsletter of the Sacramentói Magyar/Amerikai Barati Társaság (Hungarian/American Friendship Society of Sacramento), quarterly, $3.00 per issue
(covers modern Hungary, Slovakia, and parts of Romania—Transylvania "Erdély" and the Banat; part of far-western Ukraine; and parts of Croatia, Slovenia and Serbia; books and maps

of Hungary, Slovakia, Ukraine, Transylvania, Banat)
$10.00 per year membership (includes free advice during research); Hungarian, German, Romanian and Slovak translation services for members only

Hungarian Genealogy Newsletter
PO Box 13548
Saint Louis, MO 63138
Maryann Schicker
Pub. *Hungarian Genealogy Newsletter* (primarily Baldman, Friez, Horvath, Siklost, Staub, Tinya, Toth and Weisz families)

Hungarian Genealogy Society
415 Bridgeview Drive
Perrysburg, OH 43551-1958
Pub. *Newsletter*, quarterly

Hungarian Heritage Center
300 Somerset Street
New Brunswick, NJ 08903
(201) 846-5777

Hungarian-Jewish Special Interest Group
PO Box 34152
Cleveland, OH 44134-0852
(216) 661-3970; (216) 291-0824 FAX
E-mail: lmagyar@en.com
http://feefhs.org/jsig/frg-hsig.html
Louis Schonfeld, Editor
Hours: by appointment only
Pub. *Magar Zsido*, two times per year
$10.00 per year membership

Hungarian Research Library, Kossuth Foundation
Butler University
Indianapolis, IN 46208
(317) 283-9225
Dr. Janos Horvath, President
Hours: by special permission

Dr. Andrew T. Udvardy Reference Library
66 Plum Street
New Brunswick, NJ 08902

University of Chicago Library
Louis Szathmary Family Collection
1100 East 57th Street
Chicago, IL 60637
(773) 702-0691
Barbara Van Deventer, Assistant Director for Collection
Hours: development items from the collection that are not cataloged may be paged from special collections Mon–Fri 9:00–5:00
(A large collection of books and serials in broad subjects, not primarily genealogy-related; "The Hungarian works have not been cataloged, but brief records for over 2,000 of them are in our online catalog.")

Icarian
(see French)

Icelandic
(see Swedish)

Indian
(see Asian or Native American)

Irish
(see also British, English and Scottish)

All-Ireland Heritage, Inc.
PO Box 7
Dunn Loring, VA 22027
(703) 560-4496
Donna Reid Hotaling, President
Pub. *All-Ireland Heritage*, quarterly, $24.00 per year subscription

American Committee for Irish Studies
Department of English
University of Wisconsin
Milwaukee, WI 53201
(414) 963-4508
John R. Moore, President

American Irish Historical Society (AIHS)
Library
991 Fifth Avenue
New York, NY 10028
(212) 288-2263; (212) 628-7927
http://www.aihs.org
Paul Ruppert, Director
Hours: Mon–Fri 10:30–5:30
Pub. *Recorder*, semiannually, $22.50 per year subscription
("Our library has only a very small and selective genealogical collection; we do not undertake genealogical research on behalf of interested parties.")
$100.00 per year Sustaining membership, $50.00 per year Junior or Senior membership, $25.00 per year Student membership

Ancient Order of Hibernians
McKeesport Heritage Center
180 West Schwab Avenue
Munhall, PA 15120
Timothy Cox

Belgrave Publications
(distributed by Irish Books and Media, Inc.)
1433 Franklin Avenue, East
Minneapolis, MN 55404-2135
(612) 871-3505; (612) 871-3358
E-mail: irishbook@aol.com
Ethna McKiernan, President
Hours: Mon–Fri 8:30–5:00
Pub. *Irish Roots*, quarterly, $18.00 per year subscription

County Galway Chronicles
PO Box 535
Farmington, MI 48332
Andrew J. Morris
Pub. *County Mayo Chronicles*, quarterly,
$14.00 per year subscription

Irish America Magazine
PO Box 200
Congers, NY 10920-9929
Pub. *Irish America Magazine*, bimonthly,
$19.95 per year subscription
(includes "Irish Roots," genealogy
column)

Irish American Cultural Association
10415 South Western Avenue
Chicago, IL 60643

The Irish American Cultural Institute (IACI)
University of Saint Thomas
2115 Summit Avenue
Mail #5026
Saint Paul, MN 55105-1096
(612) 962-6040
Pub. *Journal of Irish Studies, Éire-Ireland*, quarterly, $35.00 per year
subscription

Irish American Heritage Center
4626 North Knox Avenue
Chicago, IL 60630-4030
(773) 282-7035; (773) 282-7045; (773)
282-0380 FAX
Frank Kilker
Hours: Office: Mon–Fri 9:00–5:00, Sat
9:00–2:00; Museum: Wed–Sat by
appointment
(culture and community life)

TIARA (The Irish Ancestral Research Association)
PO Box 619
Sudbury, MA 01776-0619
(978) 894-0062
E-mail: ahern@world.std.com
http://world.std.com/~ahern/TIARA.html
Hours: meetings in Lecture Room 307,
Higgins Hall, Boston College,
Commonwealth Avenue, Chestnut
Hill, MA: second Fri (Sept–Jun) 7:30
Pub. *TIARA*, quarterly; *Meeting Notice*,
monthly
(Irish, Irish-American, Irish-Canadian;
publishes *Helpful Suggestions for Irish
Research*, $6.00 postpaid)
$10.00 per year membership for
individuals, $15.00 per year
membership for families, $2.00
additional for membership in Canada,
$10.00 additional for membership
elsewhere

The Irish Family History Forum, Inc.
PO Box 67
Plainview, NY 11803-0067
E-mail: mornan@nais.com

Maureen Winkski, Corresponding
Secretary
Pub. *News Letter of the Irish Family
History Forum, Inc.*, ten times per year
(monthly, September–June)
(metropolitan New York area and U.S.;
member surname search list)
$15.00 per year membership for
individuals, $25.00 per year
membership for families, $50.00 per
year Corporate membership

The Irish Family Names Society
PO Box 2095
La Mesa, CA 91943-2095
(619) 466-8739
William P. Durning, Director
Hours: Mon–Fri 8:00–noon
(publishes books only: Irish and Scotch-
Irish)

The Irish Genealogical Foundation
PO Box 7575
Kansas City, MO 64116
(816) 454-2410 phone and FAX
E-mail: Irelande@compuserve.com
http://www.irishroots.com (free
newsletter on home page)
Michael C. O'Laughlin, Proprietor and
Editor
Pub. *Journal of Irish Families*, monthly;
quarterly E-mail newsletter available
free on home page
(1,000 volume lending library for Irish
research; database of 62,000 surname
listings; publisher of Irish family
works in America; seller of new and
used books of Irish interest)
$54.00 per year membership (includes
six issues of journal per year), $104.00
per year gold membership (includes
twelve issues of journal per year); free
catalog on request

Irish Genealogical Society, International
(Minnesota Genealogical Society
Library, 5768 Olson Memorial
Highway, Golden Valley, MN 55422—
location)
PO Box 16585 (mailing address)
Saint Paul, MN 55116-0585
(612) 595-9347 (Library); (612) 633-
5192 (President)
E-mail: raymarsh@minn.net
http://www.rootsweb.com/~irish/
index.html
Florence Baskfield Myslajek, President
Hours: Library: Wed–Thur & Sat 9:00–
3:00, Tue & Thur 6:30–9:30; Irish
Days: second Sat
Pub. *The Septs*, quarterly (January, April,
July, October)
(Irish and Ireland, including the Scots-
Irish)
$15.00 per year membership for
individuals in the U.S., $20.00 per
year membership outside the U.S.; free
research advice to members

Irish Genealogical Society of Wisconsin
2476 Lefeber Avenue
Wauwatosa, WI 53213-1220
Hours: meetings at The Shorewood
Library Community Center, 2030 East
Shorewood Boulevard, Shorewood,
WI: usually on a Mon 7:00
Pub. *The Irish Genealogical Quarterly*
(Irish family research, Irish-American
and Irish history)
$10.00 per year membership for
individuals (beginning 1 March),
$11.00 per year membership for
families

Irish Heritage Foundation
2123 Market Street
San Francisco, CA 94114

Irish Interest Group (GFO)
801 S.W. Tenth Avenue
Portland, OR 97205
Jo Alice Wright

Southern Illinois University
Morris Library Special Collections
(SIU-C)
Carbondale, IL 62901
(618) 458-3516; (618) 453-3451; (618)
453-6851 (American Conference for
Irish Studies)
E-mail: dkoch@lib.siu.edu
http://www.lib.siu.edu/
David V. Koch, Curator, Special
Collections
Hours: Mon–Fri 8:30–4:30
Pub. *I Carbs*

University of Saint Thomas
Department of Special Collections
O'Shaughnessy-Frey Library
2115 Summit Avenue
PO Box 5004
Saint Paul, MN 55105-1096
(612) 962-5467
E-mail: jbdavenport@stthomas.edu
http://www.lib.stthomas.edu/
Dr. John Davenport, Head of Special
Collections
Hours: Mon–Fri 1:00–4:30, third Sat
10:00–noon & 1:00–5:00, and by
appointment
Pub. *Varia*, one or two times per year
(Luxembourg; Celtic nations: Ireland,
Scotland, Wales; Isle of Man,
Cornwall, and Brittany)
photocopies: 10¢ per page

Utah Genealogical Association
PO Box 1144
Salt Lake City, UT 84110-1144
(888) INFO UGA (463-6842)
Kory Meyerink, President
Pub. *UGA Newsletter*, quarterly (March,
June, September, January); *Utah
Genealogical Journal* (treats Utah,
U.S., and International genealogical
and local history topics), quarterly

(March, June, September, January),
$5.00 postpaid per issue
Chapters: **Computer Chapter**, Randall
Hamilton, President, 1552 North 1725
West, Layton, UT 84041, (801) 544-
0821; **Irish Chapter**, Josie Bullock,
President, 1590 Treeview Drive, Salt
Lake City, UT 84124, (801) 227-9057;
Great Salt Lake Chapter, Vaughn
Simon, President, PO Box 11193, Salt
Lake City, UT 84147, (801) 596-9881;
Northern Idaho Chapter, Ellie
Grover, President, PO Box 685,
Bonners Ferry, ID 83805, (208) 267-
7939; **Utah Valley Chapter**, John
Whitaker, President; **Morgan Valley
Chapter**, Holly Hansen, President,
1950 North 6900 East, Croydon, UT
84018-9707, (801) 829-3295; **Tooele
Chapter**, John Peck, President, 206
East Vine Street, Tooele, UT 84074,
(435) 882-3648
$25.00 per year membership for
individuals, $5.00 additional per year
spouse membership, $5.00 additional
for postage outside the U.S.

Western Pennsylvania Genealogical Society

4400 Forbes Avenue
Pittsburgh, PA 15213-4080
(412) 687-6811
Hours: The Carnegie Library of
Pittsburgh: Mon–Thur 9:00–9:00, Fri–
Sat 9:00–5:30, Sun (Oct–May) 1:00–
5:00
Pub. *The Quarterly*; *JOTS*, ten times per
year
(sponsors Computer, English-Welsh,
German, Irish, New England and
Scottish interest groups)
$20.00 per year membership for
individuals (beginning 1 July); $26.00
per year joint membership (two
members at one address); two free
queries per quarter

Italian

(see also Eastern European)

American Italian Heritage Association

Upstate Italian Cultural Center and
Museum
(668 Catherine Street, Utica, NY
13501—museum location)
PO Box 419 (mailing address)
Morrisville, NY 13408
(315) 735-0336 (Museum); (315) 684-
6056 (Office); (315) 735-0960
(Cultural Center); (315) 684-9502
(President, after 4:30 P.M.)
Prof. Philip J. Di Novo, President/
Director
Hours: Sat–Sun 1:00–4:30, and by
appointment
Pub. *American Italian Heritage
Association Newsletter*, bimonthly

(Italian culture, history, heritage, and
Italian American news in *Newsletter*;
library has a genealogy section)
$12.00 per year membership for
individuals, $14.00 per year
membership for couples, $18.00 per
year membership for families, $8.00
per year membership for religious and
for students under 24; no genealogical
research services

American-Italian Historical Association

209 Flagg Place
Staten Island, NY 10304
(718) 667-6628
Anthony J. Tamburri, Editor
Pub. *Newsletter*, quarterly, $10.00 per
year subscription
(Italian and Italian/American Culture)
Chapters: **AIHA/CNJ Central New
Jersey**, c/o Robert Marchisotto,
President; **AIHA/Central New York**,
29 Roxbury Place, Glen Rock, NJ
07452; **AIHA/DETROIT**, c/o Vittore
Re, President; **AIHA/IWI Illinois-
Wisconsin-Indiana**, c/o Fred L.
Gardaphe, President, Columbia
College, Chicago, IL 60611; **AIHA
LIRC Long Island, New York**, c/o
Teresa Cerasuola, President; **AIHA/
MNY Metropolitan New York City**,
c/o Emelise Aleandri, President;
**AIHA/SdN Stella del Nord,
Minnesota**, c/o Jeff Rossi, President;
**AIHA/WRC Western Regional
Chapter**, c/o Gloria Eive, President
$35.00 per year membership

American-Italian Renaissance Foundation

537 South Peters Street
New Orleans, LA 70130
(504) 522-7294

The John D. Calandra Italian American Institute

The City University of New York
Graduate Center
25 West 43rd Street
New York, NY 10036
(212) 642-2094; (212) 642-2030 FAX
Dr. Joseph V. Scelsa; Maria Fosco
Pub. *Quarterly*, free

Enrico Fermi Cultural Center

610 East 186th Street
Bronx, NY 10458
(212) 933-6410

Genealogical and Heraldic Institute of America

American Italian Congress
111 Columbia Heights
Brooklyn, NY 11201

Italian American Cultural Society

28111 Imperial
Warren, MI 48063

Italian Cultural Center

1621 North 39th Avenue
Stone Park, IL 60165-1105
(708) 345-3842
Hours: Mon–Fri 10:00–5:00

Italian Cultural Society

PO Box 189427
Sacramento, CA 95818
(916) 482-5900 or ITALY-00; (916) 482-
5909 or ITALY-09 FAX
Pub. *Altre Voci*, five times per year
$20.00 per year membership

Italian Genealogical Society

74 Lafayette Avenue
Buffalo, NY 14213
(716) 883-4547
Terry Fiorella

Italo-Albanian Home Page

E-mail: Stradiotti@aol.com
http://members.aol.com/itaalbi/web/
arberesh/htm
John D. Cusimano
(descendants of Western Balkan people
who migrated to Italy in the Fifteenth
and Sixteenth Centuries because of the
Ottoman Turkish invasions of their
ancestral homelands)

Order of Italian Sons and Daughters of America

351 Fairview Drive
Weirton, WV 26062
(304) 797-7680

Order of Sons of Italy in America

Garibaldi-Meucci Museum
420 Tompkins Avenue
Staten Island, NY 10305
(718) 442-1608
Patricia Whitehouse, Education
Consultant
Hours: Tue–Sun 1:00–5:00
(library and research facility)

Order of the Sons of Italy

219 E Street, N.E.
Washington, DC 20002

POINT/POINTers (Pursuing Our Italian Names Together)

PO Box 2977
Palos Verdes, CA 90274
Thomas E. Militello, M.D., Founder
Pub. *POINTers*, quarterly; *Directory*
(lists all surnames in the POINT
surname database), annually
(database includes 20,000 surnames from
3,500 members)
$40.00 per year membership
(submissions to database are free)

Society for Italian American History

Boston College
Chestnut Hill
Boston, MA 02167

Japanese

(see Asian)

Jewish

American Federation of Polish Jews

342 Madison Avenue, Suite 717
New York, NY 10173
(212) 687-9141
Esther Brumberg, Research Coordinator
Hours: by appointment
Pub. *Newsletter*, irregularly

American Jewish Archives

Hebrew Union College
3101 Clifton Avenue
Cincinnati, OH 45220-2488
(513) 221-1875, ext. 403; (513) 221-7812
http://home.fuse.net/aja/
Kevin Proffitt, Archivist
Hours: Mon–Fri 8:30–5:00
Pub. *American Jewish Archives*,
  semiannually
no admission fee, but donations
  requested

American Jewish Historical Society

2 Thornton Road
Waltham, MA 02154
(781) 891-8110; (781) 899-9208
E-mail: ajhs@ajhs.org
http://www.ajhs.org
Hours: Mon–Fri 8:30–5:00; Reading
  Room: Mon–Fri 9:00–4:30 by
  appointment
Pub. *American Jewish History*, quarterly;
  Heritage, semiannually
from $50.00 per year membership;
  research and photocopying fees

Archives of the Jewish Federation of Nashville and Middle Tennessee

801 Percy Warner Boulevard
Nashville, TN 37205
(615) 356-3242, ext. 255; (615) 352-0056 FAX
Lee Haas, Director of Libraries and
  Archives
Hours: Mon–Fri 8:30–5:00

Arizona Jewish Historical Society

4710 North 16th Street, Suite 201
Phoenix, AZ 85013
(602) 241-7870; (602) 264-9773 FAX
E-mail: azjhs@aol.com
Mrs. Beryl Morton, Archivist
Hours: Mon–Fri 9:00–1:00
Pub. *Heritage*, semiannually
("Genealogy is not our primary mission;
  it is a committee.")
$25.00–$500.00 per year membership

Arizona Jewish Historical Society—Historical Committee

720 West Edgewood Avenue
Mesa, AZ 85210

Arizona Jewish Historical Society of Southern Arizona, Inc.

Committee on Genealogy
4181 East Pontatoc Canyon Drive
Tucson, AZ 85718
(520) 299-4486
E-mail: huhk72a@prodigy.com
Alfred E. Lipsey, Chair
Hours: 8:00–5:00
Pub. *The Chronicle*, three times per year
$25.00 per year membership

Association of Jewish Genealogical Societies

PO Box 50245
Palo Alto, CA 94303
Bob Weiss

Avotaynu, Inc.

155 North Washington Avenue
Bergenfield, NJ 07621
(201) 387-7200; (201) 387-2855 FAX
E-mail: garymokotoff@avotaynu.com
http://www.avotaynu.com
Gary Mokotoff, Publisher
Hours: 9:00–5:00
Pub. *Avotaynu, The International Review
  of Jewish Genealogy*, quarterly, $29.00
  per year subscription in the U.S. or
  Canada, $56.00 for two years, $82.00
  for three years, add $8.00 for each
  year's subscription outside the U.S. or
  Canada
(Jewish and central and eastern
  European)

Leo Baeck Institute

129 East 73rd Street
New York, NY 10021
(212) 744-6400; (212) 988-1305
E-mail: frank@lbi.com
http://www.jewishgen.org
Dr. Diane Spielmann and Dr. Frank
  Mecklenburg, Archivists; Robert A.
  Jacobs, Executive Director
Hours: Mon–Thur 9:00–5:00, Fri 9:00–3:00
Pub. *LBI News*, semiannually; *LBI
  Yearbook*, annually; *Bulletin des LBI*
  (in German), quarterly
(especially deals with history and culture
  of German-speaking Jewry since the
  17th century)
minimum $50.00 per year membership

B'nai B'rith Klutznick National Jewish Museum

1640 Rhode Island Avenue, N.W.
Washington, DC 20036
(202) 857-6583; (202) 857-6609
E-mail: krutt@bnaibrith.org
Ori Z. Soltes, Director
Hours: Mon–Fri & Sun 10:00–5:00
Pub. *Museum Newsletter*, semiannually;
  exhibit catalogues
(holdings also include archaeology and
  contemporary art, not only ritual and
  folk art)
from $36.00 per year membership

Chicago Jewish Historical Society

Spertus Museum of Judaica
618 South Michigan Avenue
Chicago, IL 60605
(312) 663-5634 (answering machine)
Walter Roth, President; Clare Greenberg,
  Secretary
Pub. *Chicago Jewish History*, quarterly,
  $1.50 postpaid per issue
("The Society seeks out, collects and
  preserves appropriate written, spoken
  and photographic records; publishes
  historical information; holds public
  meetings at which various aspects of
  Chicago Jewish history are treated;
  mounts appropriate exhibits; and
  offers tours of Jewish historical sites.")
$25.00 per year membership for
  individuals or synagogues and
  organizations, $35.00 per year
  membership for families, $10.00 per
  year membership for students, $15.00
  per year membership for senior
  citizens, $50.00 per year Patron
  membership, $100.00 per year
  Sponsor membership, $1,000.00 life
  membership

Columbus Jewish Historical Society

1175 College Avenue
Columbus, OH 43209
(614) 237-7686
Barbara R. Schehr, Executive Director
Hours: Mon–Thur 9:00–3:00
Pub. *Reflections*, three times per year
$25.00 per year membership for
  individuals, $35.00 per year
  membership for families, $50.00 per
  year membership for organizations,
  $75.00 per year Patron membership,
  $125.00 per year Sustaining
  membership

Computer Center for Jewish Genealogy

654 Westfield Avenue
Elizabeth, NJ 07208
(908) 353-5575; (908) 353-6080 FAX
Dr. Neil Rosenstein
Hours: by appointment
(Jewish and rabbinical genealogy;
  Chassidic dynasties)

Congregation Beth Ahabah Museum and Archives Trust

1109 West Franklin Street
Richmond, VA 23220
(804) 353-2668
Cynthia N. Krumbein, Director/Archivist
Hours: Mon & Sun 10:00–3:00, Tue–
  Wed 10:00–4:00, Thur 10:00–2:00
Pub. *Generations*, three times per year
$25.00 per year membership; search fee:
  $25.00 minimum; $2.00 per person
  suggested donation for museum visit

Congregation Bina

600 West End Avenue, Apartment 1-C
New York, NY 10024-1643

(212) 873-4261
Samuel M. Daniel, Editor
Hours: 9:00–5:00
Pub. *Kol Bina*, occasionally, free
(concerning the Jews of India in the
U.S.)

Congregation Mickve Israel
20 East Gordon Street
Savannah, GA 31401
Saul Rubin

**Czechoslovak Genealogical Society
International**
(1650 Carroll Avenue, Saint Paul, MN
55104—location)
PO Box 16225 (mailing address)
Saint Paul, MN 55116-0225
(612) 645-4585
http://members.aol.com/cgsi
Mark Vasko-Bigaouette
Pub. *Nase Rodina (Our Family)
Quarterly Publication*; *Rocenka*, bi-
yearly (every other year)
(Bohemian, German, Hungarian, Jewish,
Moravian, Russian, Ruthenian, Slovak,
Silesian ancestry)
$20.00 per year membership for
individuals, $30.00 per year
membership for families, $40.00 per
year Sponsor membership,$100.00 per
year Corporate membership, additional
$8.00 for foreign membership

Dallas Jewish Historical Society
Genealogy Division
7900 Northaven Road
Dallas, TX 75230
(972) 739-2737, ext. 261
Elias Baron, Director; Ana Vogel,
Assistant Director
Hours: Mon–Tue & Thur 10:00–3:00,
Sun noon–5:00
Pub. *Journal of Dallas Jewish Historical
Society*, quarterly
(dealing specifically with Dallas Jewish
history and genealogy, although has
some U.S. and foreign historical and
genealogical publications and
newsletters on site)
$25.00 per year membership for families,
$50.00 per year Supporting
membership, $100.00 per year
Sponsor membership

El Paso Jewish Historical Society
Temple Mount Sinai
4408 North Stanton
El Paso, TX 79902
(915) 532-5959

**Genealogy and Family History
Committee of the New Mexico
Jewish Historical Society**
1428 Miracerros Loop, South
Santa Fe, NM 87501-4024
(505) 988-5751
E-mail: sgitomer@aol.com
Steven J. Gitomer

Pub. *Newsletter*, quarterly
$24.00 per year membership

**The Genealogy Council of the
Jewish Museum of Maryland**
3200 Pinkney Road
Baltimore, MD 21215
Elizabeth Carus

Gesher Galicia
549 Cypress Lane
Severna Park, MD 21146
(410) 315-8188 FAX
E-mail: rpollero@umd5.umd.edu;
ggalicia@jewishgen.org
http://feefhs.org/jsig/frg-gsig.html
Shelley Kellerman Pollero, Coordinator/
Membership Chairman
Pub. *The Galitzianer*, quarterly
(a membership organization for those
interested in researching their *Jewish*
roots in the former Austrian province
of Galicia, now part of southern
Poland and part of western Ukraine)
$20.00 per year membership in the U.S.
and Canada, $27.00 per year
membership elsewhere

**Hungarian-Jewish Special Interest
Group**
PO Box 34152
Cleveland, OH 44134-0852
(216) 661-3970; (216) 291-0824 FAX
E-mail: lmagyar@en.com
http://feefhs.org/jsig/frg-hsig.html
Louis Schonfeld, Editor
Hours: by appointment only
Pub. *Magar Zsido*, two times per year
$10.00 per year membership

Illiana Jewish Genealogical Society
404 Douglas Street
Park Forest, IL 60466
(708) 748-5962
Henry Landauer, President
Pub. *Illiana Jewish Genealogical Society*,
quarterly
$20.00 per year membership

Indiana Jewish Historical Society
124 West Wayne Street, #216
Fort Wayne, IN 46804
(219) 422-3862 phone and FAX
Eileen Baitcher, Executive Director
Hours: Mon–Fri 10:00–2:00
Pub. *Indiana Jewish Historical Society
Newsletter*, quarterly; *Indiana Jewish
History*, annually
$25.00 per year active membership,
$10.00 per year membership for
students, $50.00 per year membership
for organizations or Sustaining
membership, $125.00 per year Patron
membership

The Jewish Family Name File
c/o *The National Jewish Post and
Opinion*
238 South Meridian Street, Room 502
Indianapolis, IN 46225-1024

David L. Gold
(mail inquiries only, no telephone or
personal inquiries)
75¢ plus SASE for information on
services and other publications

Jewish Genealogical Society, Inc.
PO Box 6398
New York, NY 10128
(212) 330-8257
Estelle M. Guzik, President
Hours: monthly meetings: Sept–Jun
Pub. *Dorot*, quarterly
$25.00 per year membership in New
York area, $20.00 per year
membership if more than 100 miles
from New York

**Jewish Genealogical Society, Los
Angeles**
PO Box 55443
Sherman Oaks, CA 91413-5544
(818) 991-5864
E-mail: tedgostin@juno.com
http://www.jewishgen.org/jgsla
Ted Gostin, President
Hours: meetings: third Mon (except Jul)
Pub. *Roots-Key*, quarterly
$20.00 per year membership for
individuals, $35.00 per year
membership for families

**Jewish Genealogical Society of
Arizona**
720 West Edgewood Avenue
Mesa, AZ 85210
(602) 969-1201
Carlton Brooks

**Jewish Genealogical Society of
Connecticut, Inc.**
17 Salem Walk
Milford, CT 06430
(203) 874-4572
Howard Siegel
Hours: Kol Havarim, Glastonbury
Congregation, or Shalom, Orange
Congregation: third Sun 1:30
Pub. *Quest*, quarterly
$24.00 per year membership for
individuals, $36.00 per year
membership for married couples

**Jewish Genealogical Society of
Dayton**
PO Box 338
Dayton, OH 45406
(937) 277-3995
Dr. Leonard Spialter, President
Pub. *HA-GESHER (The Bridge)*,
monthly
(computerized database on past and
current Jewish community of Dayton)
$15.00 per year membership

**Jewish Genealogical Society of
Georgia**
2700 Claridge Court
Atlanta, GA 30360
(770) 458-6664

Gary Palgon, President
Pub. *Yichus Y'all*, quarterly
$25.00 per year membership

Jewish Genealogical Society of Greater Boston
PO Box 610366
Newton Highlands, MA 02161-0004
(781) 283-8003
http://www.jewishgen.org/boston/
jgsgb.html
Fred Davis, President
Pub. *Mass-Pocha*, quarterly, $12.00 per
year subscription
$20.00 per year membership for
individuals, $25.00 per year
membership for families, $35.00 per
year Contributory membership, $50.00
per year membership for organizations
or Sustaining membership

Jewish Genealogical Society of (Greater) Broward County
PO Box 17251
Fort Lauderdale, FL 33318
(954) 472-5455
Bernard I. Kouchel, President
Hours: monthly meetings: Sept–Jun
Pub. *Family Gatherings*, monthly

Jewish Genealogical Society of Greater Buffalo
174 Peppertree Drive, #7
Amherst, NY 14228
(716) 691-4828
Muriel Selling

Jewish Genealogical Society of Greater Miami
18441 N.E. 20th Court
North Miami Beach, FL 33179
(305) 932-1725
Anita R. Drexler, Historian/Librarian
Hours: monthly Sun morning

Jewish Genealogical Society of Greater Orlando
PO Box 941332
Maitland, FL 32794
(407) 862-0043
Jay Schleichkorn, President
Hours: second Tues (except Jul–Aug)
Pub. *Etz Chaim* (*Tree of Life*), quarterly,
$5.00 per copy
$25.00 per year membership

Jewish Genealogical Society of Greater Washington
PO Box 31122
Bethesda, MD 20824-1122
Faith Nachman Klein, President
Hours: most Sundays 10:00–12:00
Pub. *Mishpacha*, quarterly, $10.00 per
year subscription
$20.00 per year membership for
individuals, $30.00 per year
membership for families

Jewish Genealogical Society of Illinois
(North Shore Congregation Israel, 1185
North Sheridan Road, Glencoe, IL
60022—library location)
PO Box 515 (mailing address)
Northbrook, IL 60065-0515
(708) 679-1995; (708) 835-0724
(Library); (708) 679-3268 FAX
http://feefhs.org/frgigsil.html
Belle Holman, President
Hours: Mon & Sun by appointment and
1:00 before meetings; meetings: third
or fourth Sun 2:00–4:00
Pub. *Search, International Quarterly for
Researchers of Jewish Genealogy*,
quarterly; *Morasha/Heritage*, monthly
$21.00 per year membership in the U.S.,
$23.00 per year membership in
Canada, $29.00 per year membership
elsewhere; Hebrew, Yiddish, German
and Polish translation services for
members

Jewish Genealogical Society of Louisville
Israel T. Naamani Library
3600 Dutchmans Lane
Louisville, KY 40205
(502) 459-0798
Milton Z. Russman, Special Librarian
Hours: Mon & Wed 9:00–5:00, Tue
9:00–7:00, Thur 9:00–6:00, Fri 1:00–
3:00, Sun 1:00–5:00
Pub. *Toledoth—These Are the
Generations*, free

Jewish Genealogical Society of Michigan
4275 Strathdale Lane
West Bloomfield, MI 48323
(313) 851-1123
Pam Gordon
Pub. *Generations*, irregularly, $15.00 per
year subscription

Jewish Genealogical Society of North Jersey
(YM-YWHA of North Jersey, 1 Pike
Road, Wayne, NJ 07470—location)
1 Bedford Road (mailing address)
Pompton Lakes, NJ 07442
(973) 839-4095; (973) 595-0100
Ms. Evan Stollbach
Hours: third Thur 7:30 P.M.
Pub. *Yichus*
$20.00 per year membership

Jewish Genealogical Society of Oregon
(Mittleman Jewish Community Center,
6651 S.W. Capitol Highway, Portland,
OR 97219—location)
5437 S.W. Wichita Street (mailing
address)
Tualatin, OR 97062
(503) 692-6515
Lorraine Greyson, President

Hours: meetings: bimonthly (Sept–May)
Pub. *Shalshelet*, quarterly
$15.00 per year membership for
individuals, $25.00 per year
membership for families

Jewish Genealogical Society of Philadelphia
332 Harrison Avenue
Elkins Park, PA 19027
(215) 635-3263
Jon E. Stein, President; Harry D. Boonin,
Editor
Hours: open during meetings at National
Museum of American Jewish History,
55 North Fifth Street, Independence
Mall East, Philadelphia: second Mon
(except Jan, Feb, Jul, Aug) 7:45 P.M.
Pub. *Chronicles*, quarterly; *Bulletin*,
eight times per year (not included in
non-resident membership)
(lending library for members; computer
database of surnames and towns being
searched by members; annual seminar
and special interest groups)
$20.00 per year membership for
individuals, $30.00 per year
membership for families (two family
members in same household), $50.00
per year Sponsor membership, $12.00
per year membership for non-residents
(over 100 miles from Philadelphia),
$15.00 per year membership for
overseas membership (includes airmail
delivery of *Chronicles*); queries: $6.00
for first 25 words, 25¢ for each
additional word, free name, address
and phone number

Jewish Genealogical Society of Pittsburgh
2131 Fifth Avenue
Pittsburgh, PA 15219
(412) 471-0772; (412) 471-1004 FAX
Julian Falk, Chairman
Pub. *Z'chor/Remember*, semiannually,
$2.50 per issue for non-members
$20.00 per year membership for
individuals or families

Jewish Genealogical Society of Rochester
265 Viennawood Drive
Rochester, NY 14618
(716) 271-2118, (716) 477-5789 FAX
E-mail: bkahn@servtech.com
http://www.memo.com/jcc/jgsr
Bruce Kahn, President

Jewish Genealogical Society of Sacramento
2351 Wyda Way
Sacramento, CA 95825-1160
(916) 485-7258
Judith Persin
Hours: meetings: third Mon (Sept–Jul)

Jewish Genealogical Society of Salt Lake City

3510 Fleetwood Drive
Salt Lake City, UT 84109
Thomas W. Noy

Jewish Genealogical Society of San Diego

(Jewish Community Center-La Jolla—location)
255 South Rios Avenue (mailing address)
Solana Beach, CA 92075
(619) 481-8511
Carol Davidson Baird, President
Hours: meetings: second Sun (Sept–Nov & Jan–Jun)
Pub. *Discovery*, quarterly, $3.00 per issue in the U.S., $4.00 per issue outside the U.S.
$22.00 per year membership for individuals, $15.00 per year out-of-town membership, $18.00 per year foreign membership

Jewish Genealogical Society of South Palm Beach

2247 N.W. 62nd Drive
Boca Raton, FL 33496
Mona Morris

Jewish Genealogical Society of Southern Florida

1501 Cayman Way, Apartment 2
Wynmoor Village
Coconut Creek, FL 33066
Herbert Unger
Pub. *Tayerer Landsman*, annually

Jewish Genealogical Society of Southern Nevada

PO Box 29342
Las Vegas, NV 89126
(702) 871-9773
E-mail: carmont7@juno.com
Carole Montello, Founder
Hours: meetings: first Mon 7:00
$20.00 per year membership

Jewish Genealogical Society of Tidewater Virginia

Jewish Community Center
7300 Newport Avenue
Norfolk, VA 23505
(757) 489-1371
Hours: meetings: fourth Sun (Sept–Jun)

Jewish Genealogical Society of Washington

14222 N.E. First Lane
Bellevue, WA 98007
(425) 562-0533
Jerome Becker

Jewish Genealogy Society of Cleveland, Inc.

996 Eastlawn Drive
Highland Heights, OH 44143-3126
(440) 449-2326; (216) 621-7560 FAX
E-mail: abr2326@aol.com
Arlene Blank Rich, President

Hours: Volunteer Group: 9:00–9:00
Pub. *The Cleveland Kol*, quarterly, $6.50 per issue
("We strongly emphasize networking and help out-of-towners locate their family roots.")
$25.00 per year membership for individuals, $35.00 per year membership for families, $60.00 per year Sustaining membership, $120.00 per year Endorsing membership, $240.00 per year Patron membership, $350.00 per year Donor membership

Jewish Genealogy Society of Long Island, Inc.

37 Westcliff Drive
Dix Hills, NY 11746
(516) 549-9532
E-mail: resteinig@suffolk.lib.ny.us
Renée Steinig, President
Hours: Library housed at the Plainview-Old Bethpage Public Library, 999 Old Country Road, Plainview, NY 11803: Mon–Fri 9:00–9:00, Sat 9:30–5:30, Sun 1:00–9:00; meetings: fourth Sun (Sept–Jun)
Pub. *Lineage*, quarterly
$20.00 per year membership, $12.00 out-of-town

Jewish Genealogy Society of Orange County

2370-1D Via Mariposa, West
Laguna Hills, CA 92653-2150
(949) 855-4692
E-mail: dkohanski@net-star.net
Dorothy Kohanski, Membership
Hours: meetings: second Sun 2:00–4:00
Pub. *Shorashim*, three times per year, $8.00 per year subscription
$18.00 per year membership for individuals, $25.00 per year membership for couples

Jewish Genealogy Society of Raleigh

8701 Sleepy Creek Drive
Raleigh, NC 27612
Chava Katibian
$20.00 per year membership

Jewish Historical Society of Central Jersey

228 Livingston Avenue
New Brunswick, NJ 08901
(732) 249-4894
http://jewishgen.org/JHSCJ
Dr. Edith Neimark, President
Hours: Mon–Wed 9:00–2:00, Thur noon–2:00
Pub. *JHSCJ Newsletter*, four to five times per year
("Professional archivist on staff; archival holdings now exceed 130 linear feet, reference library over 450 volumes; affiliated with the Jewish Genealogical Society of America.")
$25.00 per year membership for families, $50.00 per year Patron membership or

membership for organizations, $250.00 life membership

Jewish Historical Society of Greater Hartford

Simons Family Suite
335 Bloomfield Avenue
West Hartford, CT 06117-1542
(860) 236-4571, ext. 341; (860) 233-0802 FAX
Marsha Lotstein, Director
Hours: by appointment
Pub. *Connecticut Jewish History*, irregularly, $13.00 postpaid per volume to non-members, $6.00 postpaid per volume for members
(library and archival material relating to greater Hartford)
$25.00 per year membership

Jewish Historical Society of Greater New Haven, Inc.

SCSU - Wintergreen Building
501 Crescent Street
New Haven, CT 06515-1355
(203) 392-6125
Marian Ottaviano, Administrator
Hours: Mon–Fri 8:30–12:30
Pub. *Jews in New Haven*, approximately every two years
("Our holdings consist of archival information and memorabilia documenting the history of the Jewish community of the New Haven area.")
$15.00 per year membership for individuals, $25.00 per year membership for families, $200.00 life membership; search fee: $20.00 for the first hour, $9.00 for each additional half-hour

Jewish Historical Society of Greater Stamford

1035 Newfield Avenue
PO Box 3326
Stamford, CT 06905
(203) 321-1373, ext. 150; (203) 322-6081 FAX
Irwin J. Miller, Historian
Hours: archives open by appointment only
Pub. *Heritage*, two times per year
(Colonial Jewish families in Connecticut; Greater Stamford includes Greenwich, New Canaan, Darien and Pound Ridge)
$15.00 per year membership for individuals, $25.00 per year membership for households; no search fee

Jewish Historical Society of Memphis

163 Beale Street
Memphis, TN 38103
(901) 682-3023
Harriet W. Stern, President
Pub. *JHSM Newsletter*

Jewish Historical Society of Michigan

(163 Madison Avenue, Detroit, MI 48226—location)
24680 Rensselaer (mailing address)
Oak Park, MI 48237
Pub. *Michigan Jewish History*, irregularly
$15.00 per year membership

Jewish Historical Society of Michigan, Genealogical Branch

Jewish Genealogical Society of Detroit
3345 Buckingham Trail
West Bloomfield, MI 48033
Janice Goldstein

The Jewish Historical Society of North Jersey

PO Box 708
West Paterson, NJ 07424-0708
(973) 785-9119
Jerry Nathans, President
Pub. *Newsletter*, semiannually
(local Jewish history; "We do not have personnel or facilities to allow access to our collection.")
$10.00 per year membership

Jewish Historical Society of the Upper Midwest

Hamline University
1536 Hewitt Avenue
Saint Paul, MN 55104
(612) 641-2407; (612) 641-2956 FAX (to Jewish Historical Society)
E-mail: jhsum@piper.hamline.edu
Linda Schloff, Ph.D., Director
Hours: Mon & Wed 9:00–5:00, Thur 9:00–12:00
Pub. *The Legend*, three to four times per year
$25.00 per year membership for individuals, $35.00 per year membership for families, $15.00 per year membership for senior citizens; search fees: first 15 minutes free, will offer list of searchers for hire

Jewish Museum of Maryland

15 Lloyd Street
Baltimore, MD 21202
(410) 732-6400; (410) 732-6451 FAX
http://www.jshm.org
Virginia R. North, Archivist
Hours: Library and Archives: Mon–Fri 9:30–4:30 by appointment with Archivist; Museum and tours: Tue–Thur & Sun noon–4:00
Pub. *Generations*, annually, $4.00 per issue; *Historical Happenings*, semiannually
(Archives of some synagogues, histories, midwife records, rabbi marriage records, personal papers of some outstanding Jewish leaders of Baltimore; "Genealogies of Maryland Jewish families are indexed and actively sought.")

$25.00 per year membership for individuals, $40.00 per year membership families, $60.00 per year Sponsor membership, $120.00 Patron membership; research fee: $12.00 per surname within facility, $20.00 per surname outside

Jewish Theological Seminary of America

Library, Archives and Rare Book Room
3080 Broadway
New York, NY 10027
(212) 678-8080
Hours: Mon–Fri 8:30–5:00

K.A.M. Isaiah Israel Congregation

Morton B. Weiss Museum of Judaica
1100 Hyde Park Boulevard
Chicago, IL 60615-2899
(773) 924-1234; (773) 924-1238 FAX
Vicki Goldwyn, Administrator; Rabbi Arnold Jacob Wolf
Hours: Mon–Thur 8:30–5:00, Fri 8:30–4:00
(research library)

Kielce-Radom Special Interest Group

PO Box 520583
Longwood, FL 32752
(407) 788-3898; (407) 831-0507 FAX
E-mail: genes@iag.net
http://www1.jewishgen/krsig
Gene Starn, Coordinator
Pub. *Kielce-Radom SIG Journal*, quarterly, $5.00 per copy
(extracts of vital Jewish records from Polish archives or microfilm of the Family History Library for people tracing Jewish roots in Kielce and Radom provinces of Poland as they existed during the Kingdom of Poland)
$24.00 per year membership in the U.S. and Canada, $30.00 per year membership elsewhere

Latvian Jewish Genealogy Special Interest Group

PO Box 3581
Granada Hills, CA 91394-3581
E-mail: werle@pacificnet.net
http://www1.jewishgen.org/latvia
Marion Werle, Vice-President
Pub. *Latvia SIG*, quarterly
$20.00 per year membership in the U.S. and Canada, $30.00 per year membership elsewhere

A Living Memorial to the Holocaust-Museum of Jewish Heritage

342 Madison Avenue, Suite 706
New York, NY 10173
(212) 687-9141
Esther Brumberg, Research Coordinator
Hours: by appointment
Pub. *Newsletter*, quarterly
(not genealogical)

National Museum of American Jewish History

55 North Fifth Street, Independence Mall East
Philadelphia, PA 19106
(215) 923-3811
Sallie M. Gross, Associate Director

National Museum of American Jewish Military History

1811 R Street, N.W.
Washington, DC 20009
(202) 265-6280; (202) 462-3192 FAX
E-mail: jwv@erols.com
http://www.penfed.org/jwv/home.htm
Larry J. Richardson, Administrator
Hours: Mon–Fri 9:00–5:00; Museum: Sun 1:00–5:00
Pub. *Museum News*, quarterly
(Jewish military; museum, archives, library)
$18.00 per year membership

Nebraska Jewish Historical Society

333 South 132nd Street
Omaha, NE 68154
(402) 334-6442; (402) 334-6441
Barbara Morrison-Bresler, Archivist/ Historian
Hours: Mon–Thur 9:00–5:30, Fri 9:30–4:00
("We do not specialize in genealogy but have some limited genealogical information in our files.")
$15.00 per year membership for individuals, $25.00 per year membership for families, $30.00 per year membership for organizations, $50.00 per year Sponsor Organization membership, $100.00 per year Patron membership, $250.00 per year Business membership, $500.00 life membership

New York Public Library

Jewish Division, Room 84
Fifth Avenue and 42nd Street
New York, NY 10018
(212) 930-0601

North Shore Jewish Historical Society

31 Exchange Street, Suite 27
Lynn, MA 01901
(781) 593-2386
Dr. Richard A. Winer, President
Hours: Mon 11:00–3:00, and by appointment
Pub. *Newsletter*, semiannually (Oct & May)
("We are a historical society, and because of limited human resources do not get involved in genealogy.")

Peninsula Jewish Historical Society

2700 Spring Road
Newport News, VA 23606
(804) 930-1422; (804) 435-0737 (President)

Sue Anne Bangel, President
("Small collection of photographs and memorabilia with oral history tapes and transcripts of 100, telling the story of Peninsula Jewry.")
$15.00 per year membership for individuals, $25.00 per year membership for families, $50.00 per year Benefactor membership, $100.00 per year Century membership

Philadelphia Jewish Archives Center at the Balch Institute
The Balch Institute for Ethnic Studies
Center for Immigration Research
18 South Seventh Street
Philadelphia, PA 19106
(215) 925-8090, ext. 228
Lily G. Schwartz, Archivist
Hours: Mon–Fri 9:00–5:00 (closed Jewish holidays)
Pub. *Philadelphia Jewish Archives Center News*, semiannually
(The greater Philadelphia Jewish community)
fee scale for staff search of records

Sylvia Plotkin Judaica Museum
10460 North 56th Street
Scottsdale, AZ 85253
Pamela Levin, Director
Hours: Tue–Thur 10:00–3:00, Sun 12:00–3:00
admission: $2.00; Friends Membership program

Rhode Island Jewish Historical Association
130 Sessions Street
Providence, RI 02906
(401) 728-5067
Eleanor F. Horvitz, Librarian/Archivist
Hours: Mon–Fri 9:00–1:30
Pub. *Rhode Island Jewish Historical Association Newsletter*, quarterly; *Rhode Island Jewish Historical Notes*, annually, $20.00 per issue for non-members
(city directories, archives on individual Jewish families and organizations to which they belonged, synagogue and cemetery records)
$25.00 per year membership for individuals, $30.00 per year membership for families, $20.00 per year membership for libraries; no standard fee for research, copying on acid-free paper: 25¢ per sheet

Rocky Mountain Jewish Historical Society and Beck Archives
Penrose Library
University of Denver
2199 South University Boulevard
Denver, CO 80208
(303) 871-3020
Jeanne Abrams, Ph.D., Executive Director
Hours: by appointment

Pub. *Rocky Mountain Jewish Historical Notes*, irregularly
(collection includes records of the National Jewish Hospital and the Jewish Consumptives Relief Society (JCRS))
$30.00 per year membership for individuals

Romanian Jewish Genealogical Special Interest Group
10571 Colorado Blvd, J-102
Thornton, CO 80233-3969
(303) 451-6080 (Publisher)
E-mail: samelpern@aol.com; zakai@aol.com
http://www.memo.com/jgsr/database/rsff.cgi
Sam Elpern, Publisher; Marlene Zakai, Editor
Pub. *ROM-SIG NEWS*, quarterly; *Romanian Jewish Family Finder*, annually (also available on the Internet)
(exchanging information about their genealogical research for Jewish ancestors from Romania—past and present boundaries, including Bessarabia and Bukovina; searchers for non-Jewish ancestors are welcome to join, but emphasis is on finding old censuses, vital statistics, synagogue, school, and burial society records specifically identified as Jewish)
$20.00 per year membership; translation of Romanian, Hebrew and/or Yiddish texts for members only

"Roots and Branches"
136 Sandpiper Key
Secaucus, NJ 07094
(201) 866-4075; (201) 864-9222 FAX
Miriam Weiner, C.G.
(syndicated column in Jewish newspapers throughout the U.S.: *Jewish Star*, Birmingham, AL; *Phoenix Jewish News*, Phoenix, AZ; *Arizona Post*, Tucson, AZ; *Jewish Federation News*, Long Beach, CA; *Jewish Calendar*, Los Angeles, CA; *Jewish Journal*, Los Angeles, CA; *Israel Today*, Los Angeles, CA; *Shofar*, Sacramento, CA; *San Diego Jewish Times*, San Diego, CA; *Northern California Jewish Bulletin*, San Francisco, CA; *Jewish Community News*, San Jose, CA; *Jewish Leader*, New London, CT; *Jewish Voice*, Wilmington, DE; *Washington Jewish Week*, Washington, DC; *Federation News and Views*, Daytona Beach, FL; *L'Chaim*, Fort Myers, FL; *Jewish Advocate*, Hollywood, FL; *The Kehillah*, Jacksonville, FL; *Miami Jewish Tribune*, Miami, FL; *Heritage Florida Jewish News*, Orlando, FL; *The Chronicle*, Sarasota, FL; *Jewish Press*, Tampa, FL; *Palm Beach Jewish World*, West Palm Beach, FL; *Atlanta*

Jewish Times, Atlanta, GA; *Jewish Augustan*, Augusta, GA; *Des Moines Jewish Press*, Des Moines, IA; *Jewish Federation Newsletter*, Sioux City, IA; *Southern Illinois Jewish News*, Belleville, IL; *Jewish Community Journal*, Champaign, IL; *JUF News*, Chicago, IL; *Illiana News*, Highland, IN; *Kansas City Jewish Chronicle*, Kansas City, KS; *Kol Shalom*, Wichita, KS; *Community*, Louisville, KY; *News and Notes*, Baton Rouge, LA; *Jewish Civic Press*, New Orleans, LA; *Hayom*, Portland, ME; *Baltimore Jewish Times*, Baltimore, MD; *Jewish Advocate*, Boston, MA; *Jewish Messenger*, North Dartmouth, MA; *Journal of the North Shore*, Salem, MA; *The Shofar*, Springfield, MA; *The Jewish News*, Detroit, MI; *Jewish Reporter*, Flint, MI; *Jewish Fellowship News*, Duluth, MN; *American Jewish World*, Minneapolis, MN; *Saint Louis Jewish Light*, Saint Louis, MO; *Jewish Press*, Omaha, NE; *Jewish Reporter*, Las Vegas, NV; *Jewish Community Reporter*, Manchester, NH; *Jewish Record*, Atlantic City, NJ; *The Speaker*, Bridgewater, NJ; *Jewish Community Voice*, Cherry Hill, NJ; *Jewish Community News*, Clifton, NJ; *Jewish Voice*, Deal Park, NJ; *Jewish News*, East Orange, NJ; *Jewish Star*, Edison, NJ; *Jewish Standard*, Hackensack, NJ; *Federation Journal*, Lakewood, NJ; *Jewish Horizon*, Scotch Plains, NJ; *Jewish Star*, Sullivan County, NJ; *Jewish Chronicle*, Vineland, NJ; *The Link*, Albuquerque, NM; *Albany Jewish World*, Albany, NY; *The Reporter*, Binghamton, NY; *Buffalo Jewish Review*, Buffalo, NY; *Jewish Week*, New York, NY; *Jewish Ledger*, Rochester, NY; *Jewish Observer*, Syracuse, NY; *Jewish Community News*, Utica, NY; *Charlotte Jewish News*, Charlotte, NC; *American Israelite*, Cincinnati, OH; *Cleveland Jewish News*, Cleveland, OH; *Ohio Jewish Chronicle*, Columbus, OH; *Jewish Journal*, Youngstown, OH; *Tulsa Jewish Review*, Tulsa, OK; *Jewish Review*, Portland, OR; *HaKol*, Allentown, PA; *Jewish Exponent*, Philadelphia, PA; *Jewish Times*, Philadelphia, PA; *Jewish Chronicle*, Pittsburgh, PA; *The Shalom*, Reading, PA; *Federation Voice*, Providence, RI; *Charleston Jewish Journal*, Charleston, SC; *Jewish News*, Columbia, SC; *Shofar*, Chattanooga, TN; *Hebrew Watchman*, Memphis, TN; *Observer*, Nashville, TN; *Jewish Herald-Voice*, Houston, TX; *Jewish Journal*, San Antonio, TX; *Renewal*, Norfolk, VA; *Reflector*, Richmond, VA; *Jewish Transcript*, Seattle, WA;

Wisconsin Jewish Chronicle,
Milwaukee, WI)

Routes to Roots
136 Sandpiper Key
Secaucus, NJ 07094-2210
(201) 866-4075; (201) 864-9222 FAX
E-mail: Routestoroots@worldnet.att.net
http://www.routestoroots.com; http://
www.rtrfoundation.org
Miriam Weiner, C.G., President
Pub. *Routes to Roots*

**Russian-Baltic Information
Center—Blitz**
907 Mission Avenue
San Rafael, CA 94901
(415) 453-3579; (415) 453-0343 FAX
E-mail: enute@igc.apc.org
http://feefhs.org/blitz/frgblitz.html
W. Edward Nute, Coordinator
Hours: Mon–Fri 8:00–5:00
(search of the records of Russian
Archives, publishes historic and
archival reference books; Russian
Empire, Russian, Jewish, German,
Baltic, Ukranian)
$50.00 for preliminary search

**San Francisco Bay Area Jewish
Genealogical Society**
PO Box 471616
San Francisco, CA 94147-1616
(415) 921-6761
E-mail: dlkurtz@ix.netcom.com
http://www.jewishgen.org/sfbajgs
Dana L. Kurtz, President and Editor
Hours: meetings: third Sun (odd-
numbered months in San Francisco)
1:00, third Mon (even-numbered
months in Palo Alto) 7:30
Pub. *Zichron Note: San Francisco Bay
Area Jewish Genealogical Society
Newsletter*, quarterly, $5.00 per issue
$20.00 per year membership

Society of Czechoslovakian Jews
87 Santiago Street
Holliswood, NY 11423

Southern Jewish Historical Society
History Department
Valdosta State College
PO Box 179
Valdosta, GA 31698
(912) 333-5947

Suwalk-Lomza Interest Group
3701 Connecticut Avenue, N.W.,
Apartment #228
Washington, DC 20008-4556
http://feefhs.org/jsig/frgslsig.html
Marlene Silverman, Ph.D., Chairman and
Editor
Pub. *Landsman*, quarterly
(for Jewish genealogy; focus on the
former Polish provinces of Suwalki
and Lomza as constituted in 1866–
1914, today's southern Lithuania and
northeastern Poland)

$22.00 per year membership in the U.S.,
Canada and Mexico, $28.00 per year
membership elsewhere (airmail
delivery), $40.00 per year Patron
membership

Temple Israel Library
Longwood Avenue and Plymouth Street
Boston, MA 02215
(617) 566-3960
Ann Abrams, Librarian
Hours: Sept–May: Mon 3:00–9:00, Tue
1:00–6:00, Wed 11:00–3:00, Thur
9:00–6:00, Sun 9:00–1:00; Jun–Aug:
Mon–Thur 9:00–5:00

U.S. Holocaust Museum
100 Raoul Wallenberg Place, S.W.
Washington, DC 20024-2150
(202) 488-0400; (202) 488-2690 FAX;
(202) 828-9583 (Registry)
Radu Ioanid, Ben and Vladka Meed
National Registry of Jewish Holocaust
Survivors

University of Judaism
Department of Jewish History
Los Angeles, CA 90077
Joel Rembaum, Chair

University of Washington Libraries
Manuscripts and University Archives
Box 352900
Seattle, WA 98195-2900
(206) 543-1879
Hours: Mon–Fri 9:00–5:00 (during
academic quarters)
(emphasis on ethnic Jewish, ethnic
Japanese-American, and ethnic
Scandinavian-American; not staffed to
provide genealogical research but can
suggest professional help)

Western Jewish History Center
Judah L. Magnes Museum
2911 Russell Street
Berkeley, CA 94705
(510) 549-6932; (510) 549-6956
Ruth Kelson Rafael, Head Archivist
Hours: Mon–Thur 10:00–4:00 by
appointment
(primarily northern California, but also
includes material from thirteen
western states)
no fee for on-premise research help; off-
premise researchers pay $15.00 per
hour if non-commercial, $25.00 if
commercial; the first $1/2$ hour of
research is free

**Western States Jewish History
Association**
3111 Kelton
Los Angeles, CA 90034
(310) 475-1415
Rabbi William Kramer
Pub. *Western States Jewish History*,
quarterly, $25.00 per year subscription
from Subscription Office, 22711 Cass
Avenue, Woodland Hills, CA 91364

**Wisconsin Jewish Genealogical
Society**
9280 North Fairway Drive
Milwaukee, WI 53217
(414) 351-2190
E-mail: deshur@execpc.com
Penny Deshur; Manning Bookstaff,
Editor
Pub. *Family Finding*, quarterly
$20.00 per year membership

**World Jewish Genealogy
Organization/Yochson Institute**
PO Box 190420
Brooklyn, NY 11219-0009
(718) 435-4400; (718) 633-7050 FAX
Rabbi N. Halberstam
Hours: by appointment only
(computer database of names, not on-
line; published 640 volume *Avoth
Ubinim* and encyclopedia of Jewish
genealogy, also available on CD in
Hebrew and English)
catalog available on request

YIVO Institute for Jewish Research
555 West 57th Street, Suite 1100
New York, NY 10019-2925
Pub. *YIVO Annual*, annually; *News of the
YIVO*, semiannually
(Eastern European Jewish history and
culture; Yiddish language and
literature; Jewish immigration to the
U.S.; anti-Semitism; holocaust)
$50.00 per year membership

Kashubian

(see Polish)

Korean

(see Asian)

Latin American

(see Spanish)

Latvian

(see also Eastern European and Jewish)

American Latvian Association
(400 Hurley Avenue, Rockville, MD
20850—location)
PO Box 4578 (mailing address)
Rockville, MD 20849-4578
(301) 340-1914
Anita Terauds, Secretary General
Hours: 9:00–5:00
Pub. *Latvian Dimensions*, quarterly
$25.00 per year membership, $40.00
membership for two years

Latvia Research List
Rt. 2, Box 1619A
McAllen, TX 78504-9802
E-mail: price@mcal.vt.com or
texprice97@aol.com

http://feefhs.org/baltic/lv/lvrl.html
Bonnie Price

Latvian Society of Iowa
(1372 East 12th, Des Moines, IA
    50316—location)
2653 Grandview Avenue (mailing
    address)
Des Moines, IA 50317
(515) 262-7707
Imants Kalnins, President

Lebanese

Lebanese Information and Research
1925 Eye Street
Washington, DC 20066

Lithuanian

(see also Eastern European, and Polish)

**American Lithuanian Roman
Catholic Women**
8 Hartford Road
Worcester, MA 01606

Baltech Publishing
PO Box 225
Lemont, IL 60439-0225
(630) 257-7547 FAX; (630) 257-7547
    FAX
Val Ramonis, Editor in Chief
Pub. *Lithuanian Heritage Magazine*,
    bimonthly, $29.95 per year
    subscription (includes column, "Our
    Lithuanian Roots")

**The Balzekas Museum of Lithuanian
Culture**
Immigration History and Genealogy
    Department
6500 South Pulaski Road
Chicago, IL 60629-5136
(773) 582-6500
http://dcn.davis.ca.us/~feefhs/frg-
    lags.html
Mrs. Jessie Daraska, Director
Hours: Reference Library: by
    appointment; Museum: Mon–Sun
    10:00–4:00 ($3.00 admission for non-
    members)
Pub. *Genealogija: The Lithuanian-
    American Genealogy Newsletter*,
    quarterly, $10.00 donation for
    subscription

How To Find Lithuanian Relatives
http://www.geocities.com/Colosseum/
    3701/findrel.htm
Antanas Marcelionis
(online help)

How to Find Relatives in Lithuania
Lithuanian Folk Culture Centre
http://www.ktl.mii.lt/heritage/lfcc/
    howfind.html
Paulius Jurkus
(links to other sources)

Institute of Lithuanian Studies, Inc.
4082 Ruxton Lane
Columbus, OH 43220
(614) 451-0576

Lithuanian American Committee
2370 Canterbury Road
University Heights, OH 44118

Lithuanian Research List
E-mail:Teganator@aol.com
http://feefhs.org/baltic/lt/ltrl.html
Tegan Gillette

World Lithuanian Archives
5620 South Claremont Avenue
Chicago, IL 60636
(773) 434-4545
(archives primarily of societies, etc.; no
    interest in genealogy, refers queries to
    The Balzekas Museum of Lithuanian
    Culture)

Luxembourgian

(see Belgian and Irish)

Macedonian

(see Eastern European)

Mexican

(see also Spanish)

**The University of Texas-Pan
American Library**
Special Collections/Rio Grande Valley
    Historical Collection
1201 West University Drive
Edinburg, TX 78539-2999
(956) 381-2726
E-mail: ggause@panam.edu
http://www.lib.panam.edu
George R. Gause, Jr., Special Collections
    Librarian
Hours: Mon–Thur 8:00–6:00, Fri 8:00–
    5:00, first Sat 10:00–6:00
(comprehensive coverage of
    geographical area from Laredo to
    Corpus Christi to Brownsville, Texas,
    and the Mexican states of Tamaulipas,
    Nuevo Leon, and Coahuila, Mexico)

Moldavian

(see Eastern European)

Montenegrin

(see Eastern European)

Moravian

(see Czech, above, and Religious
Archives and Organizations—Moravian)

Native American

Adair County History Commission
Rt. 1, Box 1955
Stilwell, OK 74960
(918) 696-2749
Mack Starr, Treasurer
Hours: daily 8:00–10:00
(specializes in history of Adair County,
    Cherokee history, genealogy;
    publication sold out)

**The Lydia Adams Native American
Ancestry Hunting Reading Room
and Cultural Center**
3308 Acapulco Drive
Riverview, FL 33569
(813) 653-0015
E-mail: laurie.duffy@pchelp.com
Laurie Beth Duffy, Publisher/Executive
    Editor
Pub. *Native American Ancestry Hunting
    to Help Unrecognized Native
    Americans Find and Build Upon Their
    Heritage & Reunite Present Day
    Relatives*, monthly, $39.00 per year
    subscription, $3.95 for sample
(free database referrals from Native
    American Ancestor Roster,
    information is printed in "Who's
    Looking for Whom in Native
    American Ancestry," no cost for
    registration)

Alabama-Quassarte Tribal Town
PO Box 537
Henryetta, OK 74437
(918) 652-8708 phone & FAX (call
    before faxing)

Alaska Indian Arts, Inc.
Building 13, Fort Seward Drive
PO Box 271
Haines, AK 99827
(907) 766-2160
(not primarily genealogical)

Am-Toola Publications
East 4516 Sixth Avenue
Spokane, WA 99212
Pub. *American Indian Family Lines*,
    $20.00 per year subscription, $7.00 per
    issue

**American Indian Culture Research
Center**
Blue Cloud Abbey, Box 98
Marvin, SD 57251
(605) 432-5528
Rev. Stanislaus Maudlin, O.S.B.,
    Director
Hours: 8:00–4:30

American Indian Studies Center
3220 Campbell Hall, Box 951548
UCLA
Los Angeles, CA 90095-1548
(310) 825-7315
E-mail: aisc@ucla.edu

http://www.sscnet.ucla.edu/indian/
Pamela Grieman, Managing Editor
Hours: Mon–Fri 8:00–5:00
Pub. *American Indian Culture and Research Journal*, quarterly, $7.00 per issue
$25.00 per year membership for individuals, $35.00 per year membership for institutions, additional $10.00 per year foreign membership

The Amerind Foundation, Inc.
Triangle T. Road
PO Box 248
Dragoon, AZ 85609
(520) 586-3666
Anne I. Woosley, Ph.D., Director
(research library)

The Amistad Research Center
(see African-American)

Anchorage Museum of History and Art
121 West Seventh Avenue
Anchorage, AK 99501
(907) 343-6189 (Archives); (907) 343-6149 FAX
http://www.ci.anchorage.ak.us
M. Diane Brenner, Museum Archivist
Hours: Mon–Fri 10:00–noon, afternoons by chance or appointment
("The museum does not specialize in genealogy. The only holdings that may relate are historical photographs. We are not equipped to do genealogical research for others but can respond to specific questions. The museum holds all the material of the Cook Inlet Historical Society.")

Branch of Tribal Operations
Bureau of Indian Affairs
101 North Fifth Street
Muskogee, OK 74401-6206
(918) 687-2313
Dennis Springwater, Tribal Operations Officer
Hours: 7:45-4:30
(verifying and researching roll numbers for the Five Civilized Tribes of northeastern Oklahoma: Cherokee, Choctaw, Creek, Chickasaw, and Seminole; tribes do their own ancestral research)

Brenorsome Historical Society
PO Box 232
Tokio, ND 58379
(701) 294-3351
Louis Garcia, President
(Spirit Lake Dakota Nation, formerly Devils Lake Sioux Tribe; genealogy, history, customs, traditions; also local county history, etc.)

Bridgeton Free Public Library
George J. Woodruff Collection of Indian Artifacts
150 East Commerce Street
Bridgeton, NJ 08302

(609) 451-2620
Patricia W. McCulley, Director
Hours: Mon–Thur 9:00–9:00, Fri 9:00–5:00, Sat (Sept–May) 10:00–4:00, Sat (Jun–Aug) 9:00–1:00

Buechel Memorial Lakota Museum
(address withheld upon request)

Caddo Indian Territory Museum and Library Society
PO Box 65
Caddo, OK 74729-0065
(580) 367-2580
Mrs. T. M. Markham, Curator

Cherokee Blood Newsletter
RR 3, Box 243
Decatur, TN 37322-9100
Shirley Hoskins, Editor
Pub. *Cwy Ye, Cherokee Blood Newsletter*, quarterly; *Cherokee Blood Quarterly*, $20.00 per year subscription

Cherokee Heritage and Museum Association
Rt. 7, Box 297
Cherokee, CA 95965
(530) 533-1849

Cherokee Historical Association
PO Box 398
Cherokee, NC 28719
(704) 497-2111; (704) 497-6987
Barry Hipps, General Manager; Margie Douthit, Marketing Director
("The Cherokee Historical Association has no access to any tribal enrollment or other records, as its function on the Cherokee Reservation is to produce the outdoor drama, "Unto These Hills", and present other attractions such as Oconaluftee Indian Village, with a goal to preserve and perpetuate the history and tradition of the Cherokee Indian.")

Cherokee Indian Descendants Genealogical, Cultural and Research Organization
1300 North Hatchery Road
Morgan, UT 84050
(801) 829-6758
Lanora M. Grondel

Museum of Cherokee Indian
PO Box 1599
Cherokee, NC 28719
(704) 497-3481
Joan Greene, Archivist
Hours: Tue–Thur 9:00–3:30
Pub. *Journal of Cherokee Studies*, annually, $5.00 per issue

Cherokee Nation of Oklahoma
PO Box 948
Tahlequah, OK 74465
(918) 456-6485
(northeastern Oklahoma counties of Adair, Cherokee, Craig, Delaware,

Mayes, McIntosh [part], Nowata, Ottawa [part], Rogers, Sequoyah, Tulsa [part], Wagoner, Muskogee [part], and Washington)

Cherokee National Historical Society, Inc.
Cherokee Heritage Center
PO Box 515
Tahlequah, OK 74465-0515
(918) 456-6007; (918) 456-6165 FAX
http://www.powersource.com/powersource/heritage/center.html
Charles 'Chief' Boyd, President; Mac R. Harris, Executive Director
Hours: Mon–Sat 10:00–5:00, Sun noon–5:00
Pub. *The Columns*, quarterly

Cheyenne and Arapaho Tribal Museum and Archives
Rt. 1, Box 138
Watonga, OK 73772
(580) 886-3479
George F. Sutton, Director

The Chickasaw Nation Headquarters
(Chickasaw Cultural Center, 520 East Arlington at Mississippi—location)
PO Box 1548 (mailing address)
Ada, OK 74820
(580) 436-2603, ext. 303; (580) 436-7226 FAX
E-mail: cnation@chickasaw.com
Glenda A. Galvan, Library/Curator
Hours: Mon–Fri 9:00–5:00
Pub. *Chickasaw Times*, monthly, free; *Journal of Chickasaw History*, $15.00 per year subscription
(Chickasaw history, genealogy, biographies)

Choctaw Nation of Oklahoma
PO Drawer 1210
Durant, OK 74701
(580) 924-1150

Collier County Museum
Collier County Government Center
3301 Tamiami Trail East
Naples, FL 34112
(941) 774-8476; (941) 774-8580 FAX
Carrie Lee Welch, Curator of Collections
Hours: Museum: Mon–Fri 9:00–5:00; Library: by appointment only
(documents from the pioneer era and Seminole Indian culture)

Colorado River Indian Tribes Museum/Library
Rt. 1, Box 23-B
Parker, AZ 85344
(520) 669-9211
Mike Flores, Librarian

Comanche Tribe of Oklahoma
Enrollment Office
PO Box 908
Lawton, OK 73502

(580) 492-3775; (580) 492-4981 FAX
Zenia Anderson, Enrollment Director
Hours: 8:00–5:00

Commission on Indian Affairs
Department of Housing and Community
Development
100 Community Place
Crownsville, MD 21032-2025

Community Memorial Museum of Sutter County
(1333 Butte House Road, Yuba City, CA
95993—location)
PO Box 1555 (mailing address)
Yuba City, CA 95992
(530) 822-7141; (530) 822-7291 FAX
Julie Stark, Director/Curator
Hours: Tue–Fri 9:00–5:00, Sat–Sun
noon–4:00
Pub. *Muse News, Sutter County
Historical Society Bulletin*, quarterly
(collection includes Maidu Indian
artifacts)
$15.00 per year membership for
individuals, $30.00 per year
membership for families

Craig County Oklahoma Genealogical Society
(Vinita Public Library, 215 West
Illinois—location)
PO Box 484 (mailing address)
Vinita, OK 74301
(918) 256-2115 (no research); (918) 256-
2309 FAX
Connie Schofield, President
Hours: Mon & Thur noon–8:00, Tue–
Wed & Fri noon–6:00, Sat noon–4:00
Pub. *Craig County Genealogical Society
Newsletter*, two times per year
(specializes in Cherokee Indians and
Cherokee Nation records and local
history)
$3.00 per year membership; research:
$5.00 plus SASE for one hour, $7.50
per hour thereafter

Custer Battlefield Historical and Museum Association
Custer Battlefield National Monument
PO Box 36
Crow Agency, MT 59022
(406) 638-2382

Dacotah Prairie Museum
21 South Main Street
PO Box 395
Aberdeen, SD 57402-0395
(605) 622-7117
Sue Gates, Director
Hours: Office: Mon–Fri 8:00–5:00;
Galleries: Tue–Fri 9:00–5:00, Sat–Sun
1:00–4:00
Pub. *Dacotah Prairie Times*, quarterly
(Brown County, SD, history, oral history
tapes, family history files, newspapers,
city directories)

$25.00 per year membership; search:
$5.00 per hour plus copies at 15¢ per
page

Eastern Band of Cherokee Office Headquarters
Cherokee Enrollment Office
(Highway 441N, approximately ³⁄₄ mile
from town—location)
PO Box 455 (mailing address)
Cherokee, NC 28719
(704) 497-4072; (704) 497-2952 FAX
Hours: 8:00–4:30
(tribal rolls, 1835–1924, begin with those
who were living on the reserved land
established in western North Carolina,
cover areas of North Carolina,
Georgia, Tennessee, Alabama.)
search fee: $100.00 (allow 10–12 weeks)

Eastern Shawnee Tribe of Oklahoma
PO Box 350
Seneca, MO 64865
(417) 666-2435; (918) 666-3325 FAX

Eastern Washington Genealogical Society
Metis Genealogical Society Chapter
North 6206 Washington
Spokane, WA 99208
Pub. *Newsletter of Genealogical
Research of the North American
Indian*, quarterly
$3.50 per year membership

Five Civilized Tribes Museum
Agency Hill, Honor Heights Drive
Muskogee, OK 74401
(918) 683-1701
(Cherokee, Choctaw, Creek, Chickasaw
and Seminole)

Forsyth County Heritage Foundation
County Government Building
PO Box 762
Cummings, GA 30130
(770) 887-1626
Don L. Shadburn, County Historian and
Director
Hours: by appointment only
(historical/genealogical materials on
pioneer families and Cherokee mixed-
blood families of Forsyth County)

Fort Lewis College
Center of Southwest Studies
1000 Rim Drive
Durango, CO 81301-3999
(970) 247-7456
E-mail: ellison_t@flc.colorado.edu
Richard N. Ellis, Ph.D., Archivist/
Assistant Professor
Hours: Mon–Thur 11:00–8:00, Fri
11:00–4:00, Sun 3:00–7:00 (more
limited hours during academic breaks,
May–Aug)
("Collection strengths include
ethnographic and historic records and
artifacts relating to Native Americans

(especially their U.S. government
relations) and other peoples of the
southwest; local and regional historic
newspapers, U.S. census records for
the Four Corners States, census
records for Indians of North America,
and records of businesses and
organizations of southwest Colorado;
center's holdings include over 13,000
volumes of published research
material concerning the southwest,
over 1,200 linear shelf feet of
manuscripts and unbound printed
materials, over 5,000 rolls of historic
microfilm, and more than 15,000
historic photos; we require a
weekday's advance notice for retrieval
of microfilm materials")

Fort Ticonderoga
Thompson-Pell Research Center
PO Box 390
Ticonderoga, NY 12883
(518) 585-2821
Nicholas Westbrook, Director; Bruce M.
Moseley, Curator
Hours: weekdays by appointment only
Pub. *Bulletin of the Fort Ticonderoga
Museum*, annually, $10.00 per issue
(Colonial history, military and Native
American; topical finding aids to the
collection are available)
from $20.00 per year membership in
Friends

Fox Lake Historical Museum, Inc.
(211 Cordelia Street—location)
W9369 County Trunk C (mailing
address)
Fox Lake, WI 53933
(920) 929-2376
Norma R. Heuer, Curator
Hours: Memorial Day through first week
in Oct: first & third Sun 1:00–4:00,
and by appointment
Pub. *Newsletter*, annually
(local history and large collection of
Indian artifacts)
$3.00 per year membership for
individuals and senior citizens, $5.00
per year membership for families,
$25.00 per year membership for
industries and businesses

Samuel K. Fox Museum
PO Box 273
Dillingham, AK 99576
(907) 842-2322
Lynn Fox, Museum Director
Hours: Mon–Thur 12:00–5:00, Sat
12:00–4:00
(not primarily genealogical, emphasis on
art, especially Yupik Eskimo)

Fulton County Historical Society, Inc.
(4 miles north of Rochester on U.S. 31—
location)
37 East 375 North (mailing address)
Rochester, IN 46975

(219) 223-4436
Shirley Ogle Willard, President and
   Museum Director
Hours: Mon–Sat 9:00–5:00
Pub. *Fulton County Folk Finder*,
   semiannually, $6.00 per year
   subscription; *Fulton County Images*,
   biannually, $15.00 per issue
   subscription; *Fulton County Historical
   Society Newsletter-scrapbook*,
   semiannually
(specializes in Potawatomi Indians)
$15.00 per year membership (includes
   Newsletter only)

Genealogical Institute

Family History World
(875 North 300 East, Tremonton, UT—
   location)
PO Box 22045 (mailing address)
Salt Lake City, UT 84122
(801) 250-6717 phone and FAX; (435)
   245-0256; (801) 829-4030
E-mail: eakle@xmission.com
Arlene H. Eakle; JoAnn Jackson, Office
   Manager
Hours: Mon–Fri 9:00–5:00
Pub. *Research News*, occasionally, $3.00
   per issue plus postage and handling;
   Immigration Digest (English and
   Southern research), occasionally,
   $13.50 per issue plus postage and
   handling

The Grand Village of the Natchez Indians

400 Jefferson Davis Boulevard
Natchez, MS 39120
(601) 446-6502
Jim Barnett, Director

Ned A. Hatathli Museum

Navajo Community College
Tsaile, AZ 86556
(520) 724-3311, ext. 206
Harry Walters
Hours: Mon–Fri 8:00–5:00

Hauberg Indian Museum

Black Hawk State Park
1510 46th Avenue
Rock Island, IL 61201
(309) 788-9536

Hoonah Indian Association

PO Box 144
Hoonah, AK 99829
(907) 945-3600
Wanda Culp, Tribal Administrator

Huntington Free Library and Reading Room

(Serves as the library for the National
   Museum of the American Indian)
9 Westchester Square
Bronx, NY 10461
(718) 829-7770; (718) 829-4875
E-mail: hflib1@metgate.metro.org
Mary B. Davis, Librarian

Hours: Mon–Fri 10:00–4:30, by
   appointment

Collis P. Huntington Memorial Library

(see African-American)

Indian and Colonial Research Center

The Eva Butler Library
Main Street, Route 27
PO Box 525
Old Mystic, CT 06372
(860) 536-9771
Kathleen Greenhalgh, Librarian
Hours: Apr–Nov: Tue, Thur & Sat 2:00–
   4:00
Pub. *ICRC Newsletter*, quarterly
$10.00 per year membership for
   individuals, $15.00 per year
   membership for families, $25.00 per
   year Contributing membership or
   membership for organizations or clubs,
   $50.00 per year Sustaining
   membership, $100.00 per year Patron
   membership, $250.00 life
   membership; free admission, in-house
   genealogy research for $10.00 per
   surname plus 25¢ per copy

Indian City U.S.A., Inc.

(2 miles southeast on Highway #8—
   location)
PO Box 695 (mailing address)
Anadarko, OK 73005
(405) 247-5661
George F. Moran, Manager
Hours: Sept 4-May 20: 9:00–5:00;
   1 Jun–3 Sept: 9:00–6:00

Indian Museum of the Carolinas, Inc.

607 Turnpike Road
Laurinburg, NC 28352
(919) 276-5880
Margaret Houston, Ph.D., Director

Indian Pueblo Cultural Center, Inc.

2401 12th Street, N.W.
Albuquerque, NM 87102
(505) 843-7270
Pat Reck, Museum Curator
Hours: Museum: daily 9:00–5:00

Indian Temple Mound Museum

(139 Miracle Strip Parkway, Fort Walton
   Beach, FL 32548—location)
PO Box 4009 (mailing address)
Fort Walton Beach, FL 32549
(904) 243-6521
Steven Tuthill, Curator

Indian Territory Genealogical Society

Tahlequah, OK 74465
Mr. Lee, Registrar of Cherokee Nations

Indian Village Association

2177 Burns
Detroit, MI 48214
(313) 821-9165

The Institute for American Indian Studies

38 Curtis Road
PO Box 1260
Washington, CT 06783
(860) 868-0518; (860) 868-1649 FAX
Alberto C. Meloni, Executive Director
Hours: Mon–Sat 10:00–5:00, Sun noon–
   5:00
Pub. *NETOP*, four times per year

Institute of American Indian Arts Museum

(108 Cathedral Place, Santa Fe, NM
   87501—location)
PO Box 20007 (mailing address)
Santa Fe, NM 87504
(505) 988-6281
Paul D. Gonzales, Museum Director
Hours: Office: Mon–Fri 8:00–5:00;
   Museum: Mon–Fri 10:00–5:00

Iroquois Indian Museum

(Caverns Road—location)
PO Box 7 (mailing address)
Howes Cave, NY 12092-0007
(518) 296-8949; (518) 296-8955 FAX
E-mail: iroquois@telenet.net
Sylvia Van Houten, Genealogist
Hours: Museum (1 Apr–31 Dec): spring
   & fall: Tue–Sat 10:00–5:00, Sun
   noon–5:00; summer: Mon–Sat 10:00–
   6:00, Sun noon–6:00; Library: by
   appointment only
Pub. *Museum Notes*, quarterly
(specializes in the Iroquois—Mohawk,
   Oneida, Onondaga, Cayuga, Seneca,
   Tuscarora)

Public Library, Kansas City

625 Minnesota
Kansas City, KS 66101-2872
(913) 551-3280
Eleanor Fox, Reference Librarian
Hours: Mon–Fri 3:00–5:00, and by
   appointment
("A part of the William E. Connelley
   manuscript collection that pertains to
   the Wyandotte Indians and early local
   history.")

Kialegee Tribal Town

PO Box 332
Wetumka, OK 74883
(405) 452-3413

Koshare Indian Museum, Inc.

115 West 18th Street
PO Box 580
La Junta, CO 81050-0580
(719) 384-4411
Michael J. Menard, Museum Director
Hours: summer: 10:00–5:00; winter Tue–
   Sun 12:30–4:30
Pub. *Koshare News*, semiannually
copy costs

Lawton Public Library

Family History Research Room
110 S.W. Fourth Street
Lawton, OK 73501
(580) 581-3450; (580) 248-0243 FAX
Marion F. Donaldson, Library Director;
Paul Follett, Genealogy Librarian
Hours: Mon–Thur 10:00–9:00, Fri
10:00–6:00, Sat 10:00–5:00, Sun
(Sept–May) 1:00–5:00
(emphasis on Oklahoma, the south, and
Native Americans—houses the Kowa,
Comanche, and Apache (KCA)
Research Collection)

Layland Museum

201 North Caddo
Cleburne, TX 76031
(817) 641-3321, ext. 375
Mildred Padon, Curator
(research libraries on local history,
Native Americans, and the Civil War)

Legacy Plus

516 North 38th Street
Mesa, AZ 85205
(602) 832-1467
Donna Williams, Editor and President
Hours: second Mon (except Jun–Aug &
Dec) 6:30–9:00 P.M.
Pub. *Cherokee Family Researcher*
(Cherokee research tips and queries
from around the country, reproductions
of old Cherokee records),
semiannually, $7.95 per year
subscription
$10.00 per year membership

William Pryor Letchworth Museum

Letchworth State Park
Castile, NY 14427
(716) 493-3617; (716) 493-5272 FAX
Brian Scriven, Historic Site Manager
Hours: daily (mid-May through Oct)
10:00–5:00
(archives and private library of W. P.
Letchworth with Native American
material)

Luna County Historical Society, Inc.

Deming Luna Mimbres Museum
301 South Silver Avenue
Deming, NM 88030
(505) 546-2382
Dolly Shannon, Archivist
Hours: Museum: daily 9:00–5:00;
Archives: by appointment
("We operate chiefly as a museum,
specializing in southern New Mexico
and the Mimbres Indians; genealogy
search as time permits.")
$3.00 per year membership; research fee:
donation

Marquette Mission Park and Museum of Ojibwa Culture

500–566 North State Street
Saint Ignace, MI 49781
(906) 643-9161 (Museum and Director's
Office)

Molly M. Perry, Museum Director
Hours: Memorial Day weekend to late
Jun: Mon–Sun 11:00–5:00, late Jun–
Labor Day: Mon–Sun 10:00–8:00, Sun
noon–8:00; Labor Day–early Oct:
Mon–Sun 11:00–6:00
Pub. *The Bridge: Bridging Culture and
History*, about three times per year
("We do not have genealogical
information in our collections, but one
of our staff members provides her
services on a free-lance basis,
especially for Native American
genealogy.")
$2.00 museum admission for adults

Mashpee Historical Commission

(13 Great Neck Road, North—location)
Mashpee Town Hall, 16 Great Neck
Road, North (mailing address)
Mashpee, MA 02649
(508) 539-1438
Joanne M. Ferragamo, Chairperson
Hours: Mon, Thur & first Sat 9:00–1:00,
and by appointment
(town history, Wampanoag history,
Native Americans of the northeast)
free admission; research: donation plus
copy costs

Mashpee Wampanoag Indian Tribal Council, Inc.

Route 130
PO Box 1048
Mashpee, MA 02649
(508) 477-0208
John Peters, Jr., Director

Mesa Southwest Museum

53 North Macdonald
Mesa, AZ 85201-7325
(602) 644-2169
Tray C. Mead, Museum Administrator
(features native cultures)

Miami Tribe of Oklahoma

PO Box 1326
Miami, OK 74355
(918) 542-1445; (918) 542-7260 FAX

Mid-America All Indian Center Museum

650 North Seneca
Wichita, KS 67203
(316) 262-5221
Carl Ponce, Museum Director
Pub. *M.A.A.I.C. Newsletter*, monthly;
Museum Notes, quarterly

Modoc Tribe of Oklahoma

515 G Southeast
Miami, OK 74354-8224
(918) 542-1190; (918) 542-5415 FAX

Muscogee (Creek) Nation

PO Box 580
Okmulgee, OK 74447
(918) 756-2911

Museum of Evangel College of Arts and Sciences

1111 North Glenstone
Springfield, MO 65802
(417) 865-2811
J. C. Holsinger, Ph.D., Director
Hours: when college is open
(Ozark Indian artifacts and pioneer
materials; also Eskimo and Near
Eastern objects)
free

Museum of Native American Cultures

West 2316 First Avenue
Spokane, WA 99204-1006

Museum of the Cherokee Strip

507 South Fourth Street
Enid, OK 73701-5835
(580) 237-1907
Glen McIntyre, Site Attendant
Hours: Tue–Fri 9:00–5:00, Sat 2:00–5:00
(Cherokee and Cheyenne)

NANA Museum of the Arctic

Corner Second and Third Streets
PO Box 49
Kotzebue, AK 99752
(907) 442-3304
Kari Westlund, Program Consultant
(not primarily genealogical, emphasis on
Inupiat Eskimo culture)

Nanticoke Indian Association, Inc.

(Route 24, 7 miles east of Millsboro—
location)
Rt. 4, Box 107-A (mailing address)
Millsboro, DE 19966
(302) 945-3400 (Tribal Office); (302)
945-7022 (Museum)
Odette Wright, Curator
Hours: Museum: winter: Tue–Thur 9:00–
4:00, Sat noon–4:00; summer: Tue–
Thur 9:00–4:00, Sat 10:00–4:00, Sun
noon–4:00
admission: $1.00 for adults, 50¢ for
children

National Museum of the American Indian

George Gustav Heye Center
1 Bowling Green
New York, NY 10004
(212) 668-6624 (recorded message)
Hours: Museum: Tue–Sat 10:00–5:00,
Sun 1:00–5:00; Archives: by
appointment
Pub. *Native Peoples*; *Smithsonian
Runner*
(the archives contains the primary
documentation of the museum; the
photography archives contains
approximately 100,000 images; the
resource center makes available to the
public a variety of information
concerning the native peoples of the
Americas)
$20.00 per year charter membership
(*Native Peoples* only), $35.00 or more

per year membership (includes both periodicals); $5.00 admission for adults, $2.00 admission for students and senior citizens, free admission for members

Native American Heritage Commission
Office of the Governor
915 Capitol Mall, Room 364
Sacramento, CA 95814
(916) 653-4082
Larry Myers, Executive Secretary

Native American Resource Center
University of North Carolina at Pembroke
PO Box 1510
Pembroke, NC 28372-1510
(910) 521-6282
Stanley Knick, Ph.D., Director/Curator
Hours: Mon–Fri 8:00–5:00
Pub. *Spirit*, quarterly

Newberry Library
60 West Walton Street
Chicago, IL 60610-3305
(312) 943-9090; (312) 255-3506 (Reference); (312) 255-3512 (Genealogy)
http://www.newberry.org/
David T. Thackery, Curator of Local and Family History
Hours: Tue–Thur 10:00–6:00, Fri–Sat 9:00–5:00
Pub. *Newberry Newsletter*, quarterly; *Origins: A Newsletter of the Local & Family History Section and the Family & Community Center at the Newberry Library*, quarterly
("North American local and family history; non-genealogical areas of strength include history of cartography and history of Native Americans.")

Nez Perce National Historical Park
(U.S. Highway 95 South, ¹/₂ mile south of Highway 12 Junction—location)
Rt. 1, Box 100 (mailing address)
Spalding, ID 83540
(208) 843-2261; (208) 843-2201 FAX
Franklin C. Walker, Superintendent
Hours: Mon–Fri 8:00–4:30
(specializes in history of Nez Perce Indians; does not have genealogical records)

Old Northwest Historical Society
c/o Victoria Retirement Center
1500 Sherman Avenue
Cincinnati, OH 45212
E-mail: rrowan@fuse.net
Hours: meetings: second Sun 2:30
Pub. *The Old Northwest Historical Society "Trading Post"*
(The Tecumseh Club is a support organization to benefit the Loyal Shawnee Tribe of Oklahoma)

Oneida Tribe of Indians of Wisconsin
Norbert Hill Center, South Building
7210 Seminary Road
PO Box 365
Oneida, WI 54155
(920) 869-2130 (Records Management System); (920) 869-2194 FAX
Charlene E. Cornelius, Records Manager/Archivist
Hours: Mon–Fri 8:00–4:30
Pub. *Kalihwisaks* (local tribal news), monthly, $24.00 per year subscription
(genealogy for tribal enrolled members only)
fee: $15.00 (provided by enrollment office)

Oregon Province Archives of the Society of Jesus
Gonzaga University
Spokane, WA 99258
(509) 328-4220, ext. 3144
Fr. Neill R. Meany, S.J., Archivist
Hours: 9:00–4:30
(northwest U.S. and Alaska)

Osage Nation of Oklahoma
PO Box 53
Pawhuska, OK 74056
(918) 287-1259 FAX

Ottawa County Genealogical Society
PO Box 1383
Miami, OK 74354
Hours: meetings at the Nine Tribes Towers Dining Room: third Mon 7:00
Pub. *Smoke Signals*, quarterly
(specializes in Oklahoma and American Indian genealogy)
$7.00 per year membership; search fee: $15.00 basic plus $4.00 per hour

Ottawa Tribe of Oklahoma
PO Box 110
Miami, OK 74355
(918) 540-1536; (918) 542-3214 FAX

Owasco Stockaded Indian Village
Cayuga Museum of History and Art (Emerson Park—location)
203 Genesee Street (mailing address)
Auburn, NY 13021
(315) 253-8051
Professor Long and Ms. Logan

Peoria Tribe of Indians of Oklahoma
PO Box 1527
Miami, OK 74354
(918) 540-2535; (918) 540-2538 FAX

Plains Indians and Pioneers Historical Foundation
Plains Indians and Pioneers Museum
2009 Williams Avenue
Woodward, OK 73801
(580) 256-6136
Frankie A. Herzer, Director
(Southern Cheyenne and Arapaho Indians and European settlers)

Ponca City Cultural Center and Indian Museum
1000 East Grand
Ponca City, OK 74601
(408) 762-6123
Delia F. Castor, Curator

Quapaw Tribal Business Committee
PO Box 765
Quapaw, OK 74363
(918) 542-1853; (918) 542-4694 FAX

Quechan Indian Museum
Fort Yuma Indian Hill
PO Box 1899
Yuma, AZ 85366
(760) 572-0661
Pauline Jose, Manager
Hours: Mon–Fri 8:00–5:00, Sat 10:00–4:00
("Museum also has military and Spanish era history.")

Red Clay State Historic Park
1140 Red Clay Park Road, S.W.
Cleveland, TN 37311
(423) 478-0339
Lois I. Osborne, Park Manager
Hours: Visitors' Center and Library: March 1–Nov 30: Mon–Sat 8:00–4:30 Sun 1:00–4:30; Dec 1–Dec 21 & Jan 2–Feb 29: Mon–Fri 8:00–4:15, Sat–Sun 1:00–4:15
("Native American and Cherokee holdings in our library but all genealogical works are Cherokee.")
copies 10¢ each

Rudisill North Regional Library
Tulsa City-County Library System
1520 North Hartford
Tulsa, OK 74106
(918) 596-7280
Kathy Huber, Genealogy Librarian
Hours: Mon–Thur 9:00–9:00, Fri–Sat 9:00–5:00, Sun (Oct–Apr) 1:00–5:00
(emphasis on five civilized tribes, eastern and southern states)

San Gabriel Historical Association
546 West Broadway
San Gabriel, CA 91776
(626) 308-3223
Hours: Museum: Wed & Sat–Sun 1:00–4:00
Pub. *San Gabriel Historical News*, five times per year (January, March, May, September, November)
(local history, Gabrielino Indians, California missions, etc.)
$5.00 per year membership for individuals, $10.00 per year membership for families, $35.00 per year membership for businesses

Schiele Museum
Southeastern Native American Studies Program
1500 East Garrison Boulevard
Gastonia, NC 28054

(704) 866-6900
Steven M. Watts, Program Director

Schingoethe Center for Native American Cultures
(Dunham Hall, corner of Marseillaise
    and Randolph—location)
347 South Gladstone (mailing address)
Aurora, IL 60506-4892
(630) 844-4892; (630) 844-5512; (630)
    844-7830 FAX
Dr. Michael J. Riley, Director
Hours: Mon–Tue & Thur–Fri 10:00–
    4:30, Sun 1:00–4:00

Seminole Nation Historical Society
524 South Wewoka
PO Box 1532
Wewoka, OK 74884
(405) 257-5580
Hours: Tue–Sun 1:00–5:00

Seminole Nation of Oklahoma
PO Box 1498
Wewoka, OK 74884
(405) 257-5017 FAX

Seminole Tribe of Florida
Library
E-mail: semtribe@gate.net
http://www.gate.net/~semtribe/library/
    library.html

Seneca-Cayuga Tribe of Oklahoma
PO Box 1283
Miami, OK 74355
(918) 542-6609; (918) 542-3684 FAX

Seneca-Iroquois National Museum
794-814 Broad Street
PO Box 442
Salmanca, NY 14779
(716) 945-1738; (716) 945-1760 FAX
Judith Greene, Director
Hours: 1 Apr–30 Sept: Mon–Sun 9:00–
    5:00; Oct–Mar: Mon–Fri 9:00–5:00
no genealogical research, refers inquiries
    to Seneca Nation of Indians, Clerk's
    Office

Seneca Nation of Indians
Tribal Clerk's Office
1490 Route 438
Irving, NY 14081
(716) 532-4900
Hours: Mon–Fri 8:00–4:30
(tribal enrollment records for Seneca
    Nation of the Iroquois Confederacy
    only)
$50.00 fee

Shawnee Mission Indian Historical Society
4833 Black Swan
Shawnee Mission, KS 66202
(913) 631-9990

Sheldon Jackson Museum, Division of Alaska State Museums
104 College Drive
Sitka, AK 99835

(907) 747-8981; (907) 747-3004 FAX
Peter L. Corey, Curator of Collections
Hours: winter: Mon–Fri 8:00–5:00, Sat
    9:00–4:00; summer (approximately
    May 15–Sept 15): Mon–Sun 8:00–
    5:00
(Tingit, Haida, Tsimshian, Aleut,
    Athabaskan and Eskimo ethnographic
    materials; no archives other than what
    applies to the history of the institution
    and collections, no genealogical
    records)

Sheldon Museum and Cultural Center
(11 Main Street, just above boat
    harbor—location)
PO Box 269 (mailing address)
Haines, AK 99827
(907) 766-2366; (907) 766-2368 FAX
E-mail: sheldmus@seaknet.alaska.edu
Cynthia Jones, Director/Curator
Hours: winter: Mon, Wed & Sun 1:00–
    4:00, Tue & Thur–Fri 3:00–5:00;
    summer: daily 1:00–5:00
(pioneer history, Tingit Indian art and
    culture)
museum admission: $3.00; photocopies
    25¢ per page

Siouxland Heritage Old Courthouse Museum
c/o Sioux Valley Genealogical Society
200 West Sixth Street (mailing address)
Sioux Falls, SD 57104-6001
(605) 367-4210
Jeannette Allard-Fiskum, Library
    Committee
Hours: Wed 1:00–5:00

Six Nations Indian Museum
HCR 1, Box 10
Onchiota, NY 12989
(518) 891-2299
John Fadden, Curator
Hours: Jul–Aug: Tue–Sun 10:00–6:00,
    and by appointment to groups from
    mid-May through 30 Jun & Sept
(particularly the Haudenosaunee;
    informational charts on Six Iroquois
    Nations Confederacy: Cayuga,
    Mohawk, Oneida, Onondaga, Seneca
    and Tuscarora)
admission charge

Society for American Indian Studies and Research
PO Box 443
Hurst, TX 76053
(817) 281-3784
William L. Turnbull, Director
Pub. *American Indian Quarterly: A
    Journal of Anthropology, History, and
    Literature*, quarterly

Southern Ute Indian Cultural Center
Highway 172
PO Box 737
Ignacio, CO 81137
(970) 563-4531

Helen Hoskins, Director
Pub. *Ute Legacy*

Stockbridge-Munsee Historical Library/Museum
Rt. 1
Bowler, WI 54416
(715) 793-4270
Bernice Miller, Research Historian
Hours: Mon–Fri 8:00–4:30, Sat by
    appointment

Teysen's Woodland Indian Museum
416 South Huron Avenue
PO Box 399
Mackinaw City, MI 49701
(616) 436-7011

Thlopthlocco Tribal Town
PO Box 706
Okemah, OK 74859
(918) 623-2620; (918) 623-0419 FAX
    (call before faxing)

Three Affiliated Tribes Museum
(Hiway 23, 4 miles west of New Town—
    location)
PO Box 147 (mailing address)
Newtown, ND 58763
(701) 627-4477
Marilyn Hudson, Administrator
Hours: daily 10:00–6:00

United Keetoowah Band of Cherokee Indians
PO Box 746
Tahlequah, OK 74465-0746
(918) 456-9601 FAX

University of Nebraska Press
PO Box 880484
Lincoln, NE 68588
Kirt Card
Pub. *American Indian Quarterly*, $40.00
    per year subscription

University of Nevada, Reno
Special Collections Department
University Library/322
Reno, NV 89557-0044
(702) 784-6538
http://www.unr.edu/~specoll/index.html
Hours: Mon–Fri 8:00–5:00, Sat (Sept to
    mid-Dec & Feb to mid-May) 1:00–
    5:00
("Nevada and the Great Basin history,
    includes books, photos, maps and
    manuscripts; Great Basin Indians and
    women in the trans-Mississippi West")

University of Oklahoma
Western History Collections
630 Parrington Oval, Room 452
Norman, OK 73069
(405) 325-3641
Bradford Koplowitz, Assistant Curator
Hours: Mon–Fri 8:00–5:00, Sat 8:00–
    12:00 (during school year)

University of Tulsa

McFarlin Library
2933 East Sixth Street
Tulsa, OK 74104-3123
(918) 631-2880; (918) 631-3791 FAX
E-mail: lib_ssk@centum.utulsa.edu
http://www.utulsa.edu
(Cherokee, Choctaw and Creek
    manuscripts, Oklahoma history and
    special collections)

John Vaughan Library/Learning Resources Center

Special Collections Department
Northeastern Oklahoma State University
Tahlequah, OK 74464
(918) 456-5511
Helen Wheat, Special Collections
    Librarian

West Florida Regional Library System

200 West Gregory Street
Pensacola, FL 32501-4878
(904) 435-1763
http://www.rootsweb.com.1~f/lscamb/
    index.htm
Dolly Pollard, Librarian
Hours: Tue–Thur 9:00–8:00, Fri–Sat
    9:00–5:00
(northwest Florida and Native American
    genealogy, mainly Creek and
    Cherokee tribes)
no extensive research service

Wheelwright Museum of the American Indian

(704 Camino Lejo, Santa Fe, NM
    87501—location)
PO Box 5153 (mailing address)
Santa Fe, NM 87502
(505) 982-4636; (800) 607-4636; (505)
    989-7386 FAX
Yvonne Bond, Public Relations
Hours: Mon–Sat 10:00–5:00, Sun 1:00–
    5:00
Pub. *The Messenger*, annually;
    Wheelwright News Calendar,
    bimonthly
(library and archives emphasis on Navajo
    tribe)
$25.00 per year membership for
    individuals, $35.00 per year
    membership for families

Wyandotte of Oklahoma

PO Box 250
Wyandotte, OK 74370
(918) 678-2297; (918) 678-2944 FAX

Yakima National Museum

Highway 97
PO Box 151
Toppenish, WA 98948
(509) 865-2800

Norse

(see Norwegian, Swedish and Scottish)

Norwegian

(see also Finnish and Swedish)

Coon Valley Family Research Society at Norskedalen

Norskedalen
PO Box 225
Coon Valley, WI 54623
(608) 452-3424
James Nestingen, Director
Hours: Mon–Sun 12:00–4:00
(small library; "Norwegian emigration to
    Coon Valley, Wisconsin")

Little Norway, Inc.

3576 Highway JG-N
Blue Mounds, WI 53517
(608) 437-8211

Norwegian-American Historical Association

Rolvaag Memorial Library
Saint Olaf College
1510 Saint Olaf Avenue
Northfield, MN 55057-1097
(507) 646-3221; (507) 646-3734
E-mail: naha@stolaf.edu
http://www.stolaf.edu/stolaf/other/naha/
    naha.html
Ruth Hanold Crane, Assistant Secretary
Hours: Archives: Mon–Fri 8:00–noon &
    1:00–4:00
(Houses manuscripts, diaries, periodicals,
    newspapers, family histories,
    organizational records, etc.; main
    emphasis is the history of Norwegian
    emigration, settlement and
    development of Norwegian America;
    has several genealogical resources, but
    genealogy is not primary work;
    publishes about one historical title per
    year)
$25.00 per year Associate membership,
    $35.00 per year Sustaining
    membership, $50.00 per year Patron
    membership, $250.00 life membership
    for individuals or twenty-five year
    membership for institutions; research:
    $20.00 for non-members

Norwegian Genealogical Group

1046 19th Avenue, S.E.
Minneapolis, MN 55414
Susan Lee

Sons of Norway, Supreme Lodge

1455 West Lake Street, Second Floor
Minneapolis, MN 55408
(612) 827-3611; (800) 945-8851
Hildegarde Strom, Communications
    Coordinator
Hours: 8:00–4:30
Pub. *Viking* (monthly query column,
    "The Lost Branch," printed every third
    month), monthly, $20.00 per year
    subscription
$28.00 per year membership

University of North Dakota

Elwyn B. Robinson Department of
    Special Collections
Chester Fritz Library
PO Box 9000
Grand Forks, ND 58202-9000
(701) 777-4625 (Special Collections);
    (701) 777-3319 FAX
E-mail: slater@plains.nodak.edu
http://www.und.nodak.edu/dept/library/
    Collections/spk.html
Sandra J. Slater
Hours: Mon–Thur 8:00–5:00, Fri 8:00–
    4:30, Wed 8:00–9:00
Pub. *Guide to Norwegian Bygdeboker*,
    annually; *Guide to Family History
    Resources*, annually
(specializes in Norwegian ancestry, "825
    vols. bygde boker")
research: $10.00 per hour plus 20¢ per
    page for photocopies

Valdres Samband Lag

1522 North Greenwood Court North
Eagan, MN 55122
E-mail: bettylou@spacestar.net
Betty Rockswold, Genealogist
Pub. *Budstikken*, semiannually (May and
    December)
(Norwegian (Valdres) culture and
    genealogy, concerning the Valdres part
    of Norway)
$8.00 per year membership, $10.00 per
    year membership overseas

Vesterheim Genealogical Center and Naeseth Library

415 West Main Street
Madison, WI 53703
(608) 255-2224; (608) 255-6842 FAX
E-mail: vesterheim@juno.com
Blane Hedberg, Director
Hours: Tue–Fri 1:00–5:00 by
    appointment only
Pub. *Norwegian Tracks*, quarterly
(the genealogical division of the
    Norwegian-American Museum)
$35.00 per year museum and center
    membership

Carl B. Ylvisaker Library

Concordia College
Moorhead, MN 56562
(218) 299-4640; (218) 299-4253 FAX
Hours: School year: Mon–Thur 7:45–
    midnight, Fri 7:45-5:00, Sat 10:00–
    10:00, Sun noon–midnight; summer:
    Mon–Fri 8:00–4:30 (school vacations
    may vary), call ahead for appointment
(emphasis on Norway and Sweden)

Palatine

(see Galician and German)

Polish

(see also Eastern European)

Alliance of Poles of America

6966 Broadway Avenue
Cleveland, OH 44105
(216) 883-3131
Ewa Trzeciak, Librarian; Barbara
   VonBenken, Recording Secretary of
   Alliance and Chair of Library
   Committee
Hours: Wed evening, Sun afternoon
Pub. *Alliancer (Zwiazkowiec)*, monthly

The Central Archives of Polonia

The Orchard Lake Schools
3535 Indian Trail
Orchard Lake, MI 48324
(248) 683-0412; (248) 683-0409
Mrs. Carol Pettey Baerman, Vice
   Director
Hours: Mon–Thur 9:00–noon & 1:00–
   4:00 (appointment suggested)
("We do not do research for individuals;
   our reading room is open to the
   public.")

Freistadt Historical Society

Trinity Lutheran Church
10729 West Freistadt Road
Mequon, WI 53092
(414) 242-0653
Leroy Boehlke, Vice President
Hours: by appointment
(Lutheran and Pomeranian genealogy)

Kashubian Association of North America

2041 Orkla Drive
Minneapolis, MN 55427
(612) 545-7107
E-mail: bkrbechek@worldnet.att.net
http://feefhs.org/kana/frg-kana.html
Blanche Krbechek, Founding President
Pub. *Przyjaciel ludu Kaszubskiego*
   (Friend of the Kashubian
People), quarterly (spring, summer, fall
   and winter)
(Kaszuby includes Gdansk [Danzig] and
   an egg-shaped region north, south and
   west of Gdansk, covering part of the
   present-day Polish provinces of
   Bydgoszcz, Gdansk and Slupsk)
$15.00 per year membership; free
   queries for members

American Federation of Polish Jews

342 Madison Avenue, Suite 717
New York, NY 10173
(212) 687-9141
Esther Brumberg, Research Coordinator
Hours: by appointment
Pub. *Newsletter*, irregularly

Józef Piłsudski Institute of America

180 Second Avenue
New York, NY 10003-5778
(212) 505-9077; (212) 505-9052 FAX
Mr. Andrzez Beck, President
Hours: 10:00–5:00
Pub. *Niepodleglosc (Independence)*,
   annually, $15.00 plus postage per
   issue; *Bulletin*, annually

(history of modern Poland from 1863)
membership includes only *Bulletin*

Polish American Historical Association

The Polish Museum of America Library
984 North Milwaukee Avenue
Chicago, IL 60622-4101
(773) 229-1493
M. B. Biskupski, Ph.D., President
Hours: Library: 10:00–4:00
Pub. *Bulletin*, quarterly; *Polish American
   Studies*, semiannually

The Polish Genealogical Society of America, Inc.

The Polish Museum of America Library
984 North Milwaukee Avenue
Chicago, IL 60622-4101
(773) 384-3352
E-mail: pgsamerica@aol.com
http://members.aol.com/pgsamerica
Dr. Paul S. Valasek, President
Hours: Library: 10:00–4:00 (volunteers
   work at different times)
Pub. *PGSA Newsletter*, quarterly;
   Rodziny: PGSA Journal, semiannually
(researching all lands and people who are
   or were under Polish rule and
   sovereignty)
$15.00 per year membership (calendar
   year)

Polish Genealogical Society of California

PO Box 713
Midway City, CA 92655-0713
E-mail: paul.lipinski@acm.org
http://feefhs.org/pol/frgpgsca.html
Paul R. Lipinski, President
Pub. *Bulletin*, quarterly
$20.00 per year membership for
   individuals, $30.00 per year
   membership for families

The Polish Genealogical Society of Greater Cleveland

906 College Avenue
Cleveland, OH 44113
(216) 459-0209
Edward J. Mendyka
Pub. *Our Polish Ancestors*, quarterly
("Genealogical interest generally; Polish
   genealogy specifically.")
$20.00 per year membership

Polish Genealogical Society of Massachusetts

PO Box 381
Northampton, MA 01061-0381
(413) 586-1827 FAX
http://feefhs.org/frgpgsma.html
John F. Skibiski, Jr., President
Hours: three program meetings per year
Pub. *Biuletyn Korzenie (Roots
   Newsletter)*, two times per year
   (March and October)
$10.00 per year membership for
   individuals, $15.00 per year

membership for families, $100.00 life
membership

Polish Genealogical Society of Michigan

Detroit Public Library
Burton Historical Collection
5201 Woodward Avenue
Detroit, MI 48202-4007
(313) 833-1480 (Library); (313) 833-
   1485
http://feefhs.org/pol/frgpgsmi.html
Edmund L. Ura, President
Hours: Library: Tue & Thur–Sat 9:30–
   5:30, Wed 1:00–9:00
Pub. *The Eaglet*, three times per year
$15.00 per year membership for
   individuals, $20.00 per year
   membership for families

Polish Genealogical Society of Minnesota

Minnesota Genealogical Society, Polish
   Branch
(1650 Carroll Avenue, Saint Paul, MN
   55104—location)
PO Box 16069 (mailing address)
Saint Paul, MN 55116-0069
(612) 645-3671
http://feefhs.org/pol/frgpgsmn.html
W. Kornel Kondy, President and Editor
Pub. *Polish Genealogical Society of
   Minnesota Newsletter*, quarterly
$10.00 per year membership

Polish Genealogical Society of New York State (PGSNYS)

299 Barnard Street
Buffalo, NY 14206
(716) 826-9482
http://feefhs.org/pol/frgpgswn.html
Michael Drabik, Founder
Hours: meetings at Villa Maria College,
   Pine Ridge Road, Cheektowaga:
   second Thur (Aug–Jun) 7:00–9:00
   (research hours Jan, Mar, Apr, Jun,
   Sept, Oct)
Pub. *Searchers*, triannually (March, Jul,
   November)
$15.00 per year membership (calendar
   year), exchanged newsletters with
   sister societies

Polish Genealogical Society of Texas

218 Beaver Bend
Houston, TX 77037
(281) 447-2914
Pub. *PGST News*, quarterly
$10.00 per year membership

Polish Genealogical Society of the Northeast

8 Lyle Road
New Britain, CT 06053-2104
(860) 229-8873; (860) 223-5596
E-mail:
   PolishGenSocietyofNE@mailcity.com
http://feefhs.org/pol/frgpgsct.html
Jonathan D. Shea, President/Archivist

Hours: Mon 10:00–2:30, and by appointment (call first for use of most materials, which are stored off-site)
Pub. *Pathways and Passages*, semiannually, $15.00 per year subscription, $27.00 for two-year subscription
professional translators and researchers available on a fee basis: Polish, Russian, German, Latin, Spanish

Polish Genealogical Society of Wisconsin
PO Box 342341
Milwaukee, Wisconsin 53234-2341
(414) 628-3742
http://feefhs.org/pol/frgpgswi.html
Raymond Supercynski, President
Pub. *Korzenie (Roots)*, quarterly
$10.00 per year membership

Polish Historical Commission
Central Council of Polish Organizations
4219 Stanton Avenue
Pittsburgh, PA 15201-2252
(412) 782-2166
Joseph A. Borkowski, Chairman
Hours: University of Pittsburgh, Hillman Library: Mon–Fri 10:00–3:00
Pub. *Polish Day Annual Program*, $2.50 per issue
inquiries must be accompanied by SASE

The Polish Museum of America Library
984 North Milwaukee Avenue
Chicago, IL 60622-4101
(773) 384-3352
Joanna Janowska, Director/Curator of Museum
Hours: Library: 10:00–4:00
(Polish literature and Polonica)
$25.00 per year museum membership, $15.00 per year library fee

Polish National Alliance
6100 North Cicero
Chicago, IL 60646

Polish Nobility Association Foundation
Villa Anneslie
529 Dunkirk Road
Baltimore, MD 21212-2014
(718) 383-0594; (718) 383-0594 FAX (Heraldry)
http://www.pgsa.org/pna.htm
Leonard J. Suligowski, Director of Heraldry
Pub. *White Eagle: Journal of the Polish Nobility Association Foundation*, semiannually
(Polish-Lithuanian)
$15.00 per year membership for individuals, $25.00 per year Associate membership, $35.00 per year Contributing membership, $50.00 per year Supporting membership, $75.00 per year Benefactor membership; search fee: $25.00 per name

Polishville Cemetery and Grotto Association and Esther Johanna Peck Museum
(1345 Tamarack Avenue—location)
1157 Raspberry Avenue (mailing address)
Brighton, IA 52540-8553
(319) 694-3495; (319) 694-3580
William E. Peck, President
Hours: by appointment
Pub. *Newsletter*, usually four times per year
(Polish heritage, operating on a very small scale)

Pomeranian

(see Eastern European and Polish)

Portuguese

(see also Spanish)

The American-Portuguese Genealogical and Historical Society, Inc.
PO Box 644
Taunton, MA 02780-0644
Cecilia M. Rose, Executive Secretary
Pub. *Bulletinboard*, quarterly
$10.00 per year membership

Hawaii Council on Portuguese Heritage
810 North Vineyard Boulevard, Room 7
Honolulu, HI 96817
(808) 845-1616; (808) 841-0066

Portuguese Continental Union of the U.S.A. (P.C.U.U.S.A.)
União Portuguesa Continental Dos E.U.A.
899 Boylston Street
Boston, MA 02115
(617) 536-2916; (617) 536-8301 FAX
E-mail: UPCEVA@aol.com
http://members.aol.com/UPCEVA
Francisco J. Mendonca, Supreme Secretary/CEO
Hours: 9:00–4:30
Pub. *Bulletin*, quarterly, $20.00 per year subscription

Portuguese Genealogical Society of Hawaii (PGSH)
810 North Vineyard Boulevard, Room 11
Honolulu, HI 96817
(808) 841-5044
Doris Naumu, President
Hours: Mon, Wed & Fri–Sat 10:00–3:00
Pub. *A Nossa Herança* (Our Portuguese Heritage), quarterly
(whalers and families before 1878, 20,000 family names of emigrants from Portugal to Hawaii, 1878 to 1913)
$10.00 per year membership for individuals, $12.00 per year membership for families; research by donation

Portuguese Historical and Cultural Society
PO Box 161990
Sacramento, CA 95816
(916) 392-1048
Lionel Holmes, Director and Editor
Hours: meetings: first Tue 7:00 in Saint Elizabeth Church Hall, 12th and S Streets, Sacramento
Pub. *O Progresso*, quarterly (March, June, September, December)
$10.00 per year membership

Sociedade Portuguesa Raintta Santa Isabel (S.P.R.S.I.)
3031 Telegraph Avenue
Oakland, CA 94609
(510) 658-0983; (510) 658-6517 FAX
Silvia Ponte, Business Manager
Hours: 8:00–4:30
Pub. *Buletim*, quarterly
(a benefit fraternal society)
$6.00 per year membership

Prussian

(see Eastern European, German)

Romanian

(see also Banat, Eastern European)

Romania Research List
E-mail: barbara@bc.seflin.org
http://feefhs.org/ro/rorl/rorl.html
Barbara Foosaner

The Romania (Rumania) Homepage
E-mail: SNiculescu@aol.com
http://feefhs.org/ro/frg-ro.html
Susan Niculescu

Romanian American Heritage Center
2540 Grey Tower Road
Jackson, MI 49201-2208
(517) 522-8260; (517) 522-8236 FAX
http://feefhs.org//ro/frg-rahc.html
Eugene S. Raica, President and Editor
Pub. *Information Bulletin*, bimonthly
(has Andrica collection, from discontinued *American Romanian Review*; Romanian/Eastern Orthodox, Byzantine Rite Catholic)

Romanian Folk Art Collection
Iuliu Maniu American Romanian Relief Foundation
55 West 42nd Street
New York, NY 10036

Romanian Jewish Genealogical Special Interest Group
10571 Colorado Blvd, J-102
Thornton, CO 80233-3969
(303) 451-6080 (Publisher)
E-mail: samelpern@aol.com; zakai@aol.com

http://www.memo.com/jgsr/database/
rsff.cgi
Sam Elpern, Publisher; Marlene Zakai,
Editor
Pub. *ROM-SIG NEWS*, quarterly;
Romanian Jewish Family Finder,
annually (also available on the
Internet)
(exchanging information about their
genealogical research for Jewish
ancestors from Romania—past and
present boundaries, including
Bessarabia and Bukovina; searchers
for non-Jewish ancestors are welcome
to join, but emphasis is on finding old
censuses, vital statistics, synagogue,
school, and burial society records
specifically identified as Jewish)
$20.00 per year membership; translation
of Romanian, Hebrew and/or Yiddish
texts for members only

Romanian Library
200 East 38th Street
New York, NY 10016
(212) 687-0181
Emilia Gheorghe, Acting Director
Pub. *Romanian Bulletin*, monthly

Society Farsarotul
593 Clinton Avenue
Bridgeport, CT 06605

United Romanian Society
PO Box 03189
Detroit, MI 48203-3189
Eugene S. Raica, Cultural Activities
Director

Russian

(see also Czech, Eastern European,
German and Slovak)

American Russian History Society
1272 47th Avenue
San Francisco, CA 94107

**Byelorussian Charitable Educational
Fund, Inc.**
1716 N.E. Seventh Terrace
Gainesville, FL 32601

Facts OnLine
812 Vista Drive
Camano Island, WA 98292
(360) 387-8901
Julia Petrakis, Owner
Hours: 9:00–6:00
(maintains an office in Moscow,
providing access to records in Russian
archives)
research: $10.00 per hour, plus $1.00 per
photocopy, plus travel, archive and
shipping fees from Russia

Mennonite Historical Library
Goshen College
Goshen, IN 46526
(219) 535-7418; (219) 535-7438 FAX
E-mail: anetss@goshen.edu

John D. Roth, Director
Hours: Mon–Fri 8:00–5:00, Sat 9:00–
1:00
Pub. *Mennonite Quarterly Review* (a
scholarly historical publication),
$24.00 per year subscription
(strong in genealogy of Amish and
Mennonite families from Switzerland,
Germany, The Netherlands, West
Prussia and Russia, U.S., European
and Canadian records)
$30.00 per year membership in
Mennonite Historical Society includes
periodical

Museum of Russian Culture, Inc.
2450 Sutter Street
San Francisco, CA 94115
(415) 751-1572
Nicholas A. Slobedehikoff, Director

**Russian-American Genealogical
Archival Source (RAGAS)**
(Moscow, Russia—location)
1929 18th Street, N.W.
Washington, DC 20009-1710
E-mail: ragas02@infonet.ee;
rags@dgsys.com (periodical)
http://feefhs.org/ragas/frgragas.html
Vladislav Y. Soshnikov, Historian/
Archivist, Director, RAGAS/Moscow;
Patricia A. Eames, Editor
Pub. *RAGAS Resources*, quarterly
(spring, summer, fall, winter), $15.00
per year subscription from PO Box
236, Glen Echo, MD 20812-0236
(includes pre-revolution, 1917, archival
records in Byelarus, Ukraine, Russia)
$25.00 non-refundable fee for
information, $50.00 deposit for more
involved research

**Russian-Baltic Information
Center—Blitz**
907 Mission Avenue
San Rafael, CA 94901
(415) 453-3579; (415) 453-0343 FAX
E-mail: enute@igc.apc.org
http://feefhs.org/blitz/frgblitz.html
W. Edward Nute, Coordinator
Hours: Mon–Fri 8:00–5:00
(search of the records of Russian
Archives, publishes historic and
archival reference books; Russian
Empire, Russian, Jewish, German,
Baltic, Ukranian)
$50.00 for preliminary search

Russian Heritage Society
PO Box 364
Agoura Hills, CA 91376-0364
(818) 991-0242; (818) 991-6752 FAX
http://feefhs.org/frg-rhs.html
H. Diane Connolly, U. S. Representative

Russian Nobility Association
971 First Avenue
New York, NY 10022
(212) 755-7528
Prince Alexes Scherbatan, President

**Soviet-American Genealogical
Archival Service**
National Archives and Records
Administration
Office of Public Programs
Seventh and Pennsylvania Avenue, N.W.
Washington, DC 20408
Pat Eames, Volunteer Coordinator

Ruthenian

(see Czech)

Scandinavian

(see Danish, Finnish, Norwegian,
Swedish and Scottish)

Scottish

(see also British, English, and Irish)

Argyll Colony Plus
6716 Meadow Haven
Fort Worth, TX 76132
Scott Buie, Editor
Pub. *Argyll Colony Plus* (Highland Scots
of North Carolina), quarterly, $20.00
per year subscription

**Council of Scottish Clan
Associations**
PO Box 27268
Houston, TX 77227

**Council of Scottish Clans and
Associations, Inc.**
PO Box 1110
Moultrie, GA 31776
Robert McWilliam, FSA Scot, President

Gold Country Celtic Society
(Nevada City, CA—location)
13340 Thistle Loop (mailing address)
Penn Valley, CA 95946
(530) 432-9350
Barbara Pixley, Publicity Chairman
Hours: meetings second Wed in Nevada
City
Pub. *Celtic Chronicle*, monthly
("Membership open to Scots, Irish,
Cornish, Welsh, Breton and interested
others")
$15.00 per year membership for
individuals, $20.00 per year
membership for families

The Highlander
Angus J. Ray Associates, Inc.
(6225 Brookside Boulevard, Suite 204—
location)
PO Box 22307 (mailing address)
Barrington, IL 60011
(816) 523-4141; (816) 523-7474 FAX
David K. Ray, Publisher
Hours: Mon–Fri 9:00–5:00
Pub. *The Highlander*, seven times per
year (January, March, April, May, July,
September, November), $17.50 per
year subscription

Institute of Scottish Studies
Old Dominion University
Department of History
College of Arts and Letters
Norfolk, VA 23529-0336
(757) 683-3949; (757) 683-5644 FAX
E-mail: wsr100f@oduvm.cc.odu.edu
William S. Rodner, Ph.D., Editor
Pub. *Scotia: Interdisciplinary Journal of Scottish Studies*, annually, $10.00 per year subscription

Link O Mania Scotland on the Web
E-mail: webmaster@link-on-mania.com
http://link-o-mania.com/scotgen.htm

Minnesota Coalition of Scottish Clans
1940 Inglehart Avenue, #31
Saint Paul, MN 55104
(612) 645-7413
Judith Lynn Finley, Toiseach (President)
("Only clan societies are members, but we are pleased to help inquirers find a clan connection and to help new clan societies become organized; we offer diverse historic and genealogical services through our membership; resource for all clans in Minnesota, especially for Macalester Fair and other Celtic celebrations.")

Minnesota Genealogical Society, Scottish Branch
(1650 Carroll Avenue, Saint Paul, MN 55104—location)
PO Box 16069 (mailing address)
Saint Paul, MN 55116-0069

Ellen Payne Odom Genealogy Library
(204 Fifth Street, S.E., Moultrie, GA 31768—location)
PO Box 1110 (mailing address)
Moultrie, GA 31776-1110
(912) 985-6540; (912) 985-0936 FAX
http://www.teleport.com/~binder/famtree.html (Internet edition)
Beth Gay, FSA SCOT, Public Relations Director and Editor
Hours: Mon–Sat 8:30–5:00
Pub. *The Family Tree: The Ellen Payne Odom Genealogy Library*, bimonthly, no charge (postage contributions appreciated)
(includes Scots Clan archival and genealogical material; "now home to more than ninety Scots Clans")

Pence Publications
911 Moyer
Cheney, WA 99004
(509) 235-8614
Maxine Pence, Editor
Pub. *Scottish Queries*, individually, $6.00 per issue

Ralston Public Library
7900 Park Lane
Ralston, NE 68127

(402) 331-7636; (402) 331-1168 FAX
E-mail: ralstlib@neoramp.com
Jan Gorman, Library Director
Hours: Mon–Thur 10:00–9:00, Fri–Sat 10:00–5:00
(houses the Nebraska Scottish Society's library of over 100 Scottish items and books on Scotland and Scottish history, available on interlibrary loan; very little on the history of Ralston, vertical file folders of clippings, archival documents and artifacts)

Royal Bruce Society
621 Jennings Lane
Battle Creek, MI 49015
Dr. Thomas Allen Bruce, Director
Pub. *The Bruce Journal*, quarterly, $17.50 per year subscription
(Royal and noble Bruce; Scots and Europeans)
$35.00 membership ($15.00 registration plus $20.00 annual dues)

The Saint Andrew's Society
150 Washington Avenue
Albany, NY 12210

The Scotch-Irish Foundation
PO Box 181
Bryn Mawr, PA 19010
(609) 429-5747 (President); (609) 354-0848 FAX; (215) 925-8090 (Custodian of the Records)
Barton E. Harrison, President
Hours: The Balch Institute for Ethnic Studies: Mon–Sat 9:00–5:00
Pub. *Library and Archives Catalogue*, irregularly, $10.00 per issue
(organized by The Scotch-Irish Society of the United States of America to collect material on Ulster Plantation, Scotch-Irish settlements in America, and colonies' influence in building the U.S., also family registrations and related documents; "We do not provide a genealogical service; all of our books, family records are available to the public free of charge at The Balch Institute for Ethnic Studies, Philadelphia.")

The Scotch-Irish Society of the United States of America
PO Box 181
Bryn Mawr, PA 19010
(609) 429-5747 (President); (609) 354-0848 FAX
Barton E. Harrison, President
(no genealogical services; exists for "the preservation of Scotch-Irish history, the keeping alive the esprit de corps of the race, and the promotion of social intercourse and fraternal feeling among its members now and hereafter"; in 1949 established The Scotch-Irish Foundation, whose collection is deposited at The Balch Institute for Ethnic Studies, Philadelphia)

$15.00 application fee, $20.00 per year membership; research: contact Mrs. D. J. Pontarelli, 449 West Montgomery Avenue, Apartment 209, Haverford, PA 19041, (610) 649-4772 or Stewart Yost, 1530 Locust Street, Suite K, Philadelphia, PA 19602, (215) 985-0583

Scott One-Name Study
Clan Scott Society of the Americas
39475 Tollhouse Road
Lovettsville, VA 20180-9703
(540) 822-5292
E-mail: willowbend@mediasof.net
Craig Roberts Scott, C.G.R.S., FSA Scot, Clan Scott Genealogist
Pub. *The Scott Genealogical Quarterly*, $22.00 per year subscription, not included in membership to Clan Scott Society of the Americas
(Scotts worldwide)

Scottish Historic and Research Society of the Delaware Valley, Inc.
102 Saint Paul's Road
Ardmore, PA 19003-2811
(610) 649-4144
Blair C. Stonier, President
Hours: evenings and weekends by appointment
Pub. *The Rampant Lion*, eleven times per year
$15.00 per year membership for individuals, $20.00 per year membership for families

Unicorn Limited, Inc.
PO Box 397
Bruceton Mills, WV 26525
(304) 379-8803; (304) 379-8923 FAX
Pub. *Catalog*, bimonthly, $10.00 per year subscription (genealogy catalog issued every January–March period)
(books and audio cassettes on history, folklore, language, music, genealogy, and related areas of Scottish, Celtic and Norse peoples)

Western Pennsylvania Genealogical Society
4400 Forbes Avenue
Pittsburgh, PA 15213-4080
(412) 687-6811
Hours: The Carnegie Library of Pittsburgh: Mon–Thur 9:00–9:00, Fri–Sat 9:00–5:30, Sun (Oct–May) 1:00–5:00
Pub. *The Quarterly*; *JOTS*, ten times per year
(sponsors Computer, English-Welsh, German, Irish, New England and Scottish interest groups)
$20.00 per year membership for individuals (beginning 1 July); $26.00 per year joint membership (two members at one address); two free queries per quarter

Serbian

(see Croatian, Eastern European, and
Hungarian)

Siberian

(see Eastern European)

Silesian

(see also Czech and Eastern European)

Silesian/Schlesien Research List

1910 East 5685 South
Salt Lake City, UT 84121-1343
E-mail: goldcontac@aol.com
http://feefhs.org/de/sil/silrl/silrl.html
Joseph L. (Joe) Reimann
(attempting to establish a Silesian-
American Genealogy Society)

Slavic

(see also Eastern European)

East Europe Connection

(formerly The Slavic Connection)
1711 Corwin Drive
Silver Spring, MD 20910-1533
(301) 585-0117
http://feefhs.org/frg-eec.html
Lawrence Krupnak

Slavic Research Institute

31910 Road 160
Visalia, CA 93292-9044
(209) 798-1490; (209) 798-1922 FAX
http://feefhs.org/frg-sri.html
Thomas Hrncinik, A.G., President

Soc.Genealogy.Slavic

E-mail: kymlicka@sasknet.sk.ca
http://feefhs.org/socslav/frg-slav.html
Stephen Kymlicka
(newsgroup, help and links to other
resources)

Slovak

(see also Czech, Eastern European, and
Hungarian)

Carpatho-Rusyn Knowledge Base

PO Box 339
Davisburg, MI 48350-0339
(248) 620-0234 FAX
E-mail: ggressa@carpatho-rusyn.org;
76163.1402@compuserve.com
http://www.carpatho-rusyn.org
Gregory A. Gressa, Director; Megan A.
Smolenyak, Assistant Director

Carpatho-Rusyn Research Center

PO Box 131B
Orwell, VT 05760
Pub. *The Carpatho-Rusyn American*,
quarterly, $12.00 per year subscription

The Carpatho-Rusyn Society

125 Westland Drive
Pittsburgh, PA 15217-2538

E-mail: custer@paonline.com
http://www.carpatho-rusyn.org/carpatho/
Richard D. Custer, Editor
Pub. *New Rusyn Times*, six times a year
$20.00 per year membership for
individuals, $10.00 per year
membership for students and retirees

The Eastern Slovakia, Slovak and Carpatho-Rusyn Genealogical Research Page

2233 Keeven Lane
Florissant, MO 63031
(314) 831-9482
E-mail: ancestors@iarelative.com;
Greg@iarelative.com
http://feefhs.org/iar/slovakia.html
Greg Kopchak
(offers tools, resources, and information
to help you search your Slovak or
Carpatho-Rusyn family history and
ancestry; links to other sites)

Jankola Library and Slovak Archives

Danville, PA 17821
(717) 275-3581; (717) 275-5606
Sister M. Martina Tybor, Director and
Archivist
Hours: by arrangement ("We prefer
exploring our reserves for data on a
given topic and forwarding relevant
material preparedon our copier; our
books do not circulate.")

Lemko Association of the United States and Canada

(556 Yonkers Avenue, Yonkers, NY
10704—location)
555 Provinceline Road, PO Box 156
(mailing address)
Allentown, NJ 08501
(609) 758-1115; (609) 758-7301 FAX
Alexander Hezenchak, President
Hours: 9:00–5:00
Pub. *Karpatska Rus*, bi-weekly
(Carpatho-Rusyn)
$20.00 per year membership

National Slovak Society of the U.S.A.

2325 East Carson
Pittsburgh, PA 15203
Pub. *National News (Narodyne Noviny)*,
bimonthly; *N.S.S. Almanac (N.S.S.
Kalendar)*, annually

Osturna Descendants

119 Belvedere Street
Nazareth, PA 18064-2112
(610) 759-2740; (610) 882-8836, FAX
http://feefhs.org/rusyn/frg-od.html
Mike Smolenyak, Co-editor
Pub. *Osturna Descendants*, quarterly,
$8.00 per year subscription
(Osturna was originally the most western
outpost of the Carpathian-Rusyn
ethnic region and is now in the
Republic of Slovakia, on the border
with Poland)

The Rusin Association of Minnesota

1115 Pineview Lane North
Plymouth, Minnesota 55441-4655
(612) 595-9188 (Founder, evenings)
http://feefhs.org/rusyn/frg-ramn.html
Lavrentyj "Larry" Goga, Founder and
Editor
Hours: by appointment only
Pub. *Trembita*, quarterly
$10.00 per year membership

Saint Leo's Genealogy Group

16253 Glendale Avenue
Strongville, Ohio 44136
(216) 391-4977, ext. 208 (days); (440)
572-0139 (evenings)
http://feefhs.org/slovak/frg-slgg.html
Louise K. O'Boyle, Secretary
Hours: meetings at St. Leo's Parish
Community Center, 4940 Broadview
Road, Cleveland: third Wed 7:45
$10.00 per year membership

Slovak and Rusyn Roots

123 Baywood Road
Boulder Creek, CA 95006
(831) 338-2120 FAX
E-mail: hudickj@pab281a.ssd.loral.com;
mtnmann@aol.com;
mtnmann@got.net
http://www.dcn.davis.ca.US/go/feefhs/
socslav/hudick1.html
John A. Hudick
(guide for research in the Slovak and
Czech republics, links to Internet
sources and newsgroups)

Slovak Heritage and Folklore Society International

151 Colebrook Drive,
Rochester, NY 14617-2215
(716) 342-9383 phone & FAX
E-mail: helenezx@aol.com
http://feefhs.org/slovak/frgshfsi.html
Helene Cincebeaux, Director and Editor
Pub. *Slovakia*, quarterly
$10.00 per year membership for
individuals, $15.00 per year Patron
membership

Slovak Institute

2900 East Boulevard
Cleveland, OH 44104
Andrew Pier, Director

Slovak Interest Group

Southern California Genealogical
Society
23301 Sandlewood Street
West Hills, CA 94307
Curtis Barrett

Library and Museum of Slovak Language, History, Literature, and Culture

Slovak Cultural, Educational and
Literary Center
775 West Drahner Road
PO Box 167
Oxford, MI 48371-5315

(313) 628-2872
Sister Gabrielle Woytko, O.P., Librarian-
Curator
Hours: by appointment

Slovak League of the American Heritage Foundation
80 Cartright Street, Apartment 7C
Bridgeport, CT 06604-2026
Catherine Behuncik

The Slovak Museum and Archives
(Jednota Press, Rosedale Avenue and
Jednota Lane—location)
PO Box 750 (mailing address)
Middletown, PA 17057
(717) 944-2403
http://feefhs.org/slovak/frg-sgrc.html
Anna Chladek Sutherland, Curator and
Archivist
Hours: Mon–Fri 8:30–4:00
Pub. *Jednota*, two times per month,
$25.00 per year subscription in the
U.S., $50.00 per year subscription
abroad

Slovak-World Home Page
E-mail: gecovic@fris.sk; pobis@fris.sk
http://www.fris.sk/Slovak-World/

Slovakia—Surname Location Reference Project (SLRP)
PO Box 31831
Cleveland, OH 44131-0831
(216) 642-8954 FAX
E-mail: jhornack@rampant.com
http://www.feefhs.org/frg-slrp.html
Joseph J. Hornack, Founder/Director
(provides query and information
columns, series by county, in English,
to Slovak/American publications;
database of surnames and their origins
in Slovakia, free access to those
contributing additional information)
fee is submission of a pedigree chart
starting from the submitter, who must
have some known roots in Slovakia

Wisconsin Slovak Historical Society
PO Box 164
Cudahy, WI 53110-0164
(414) 681-1692
Laura Thompson, Research Director
Hours: various
Pub. *Wisconsin Slovak*, four times per
year
$10.00 per year membership for
individuals, $15.00 per year
membership for families, $150.00 life
membership for individuals

Slovenian

(see also Croatian, Eastern European,
and Hungarian)

Pokrajinski Arhiv Maribor
Slovenian Regional Archives at Maribor
E-Mail: miro@parmb.pokarh-mb.si
http://www.pokarh-mb.si/pamb.html

Slovene National Benevolent Society
247 West Allegheny Road
Imperial, PA 15126-9786

Slovenian Genealogical Society
International Headquarters
52 Old Farm Road
Camp Hill, PA 17011-2604
(717) 731-8804
E-mail: apeterlin@panetwork.com
http://feefhs.org/frg-sgsi.html
Al Peterlin, President
Pub. *Newsletter*, quarterly
(Slovenia once was the northernmost
republic of Yogoslavia; it was once
part of Austria-Hungary; it is now an
independent country)
Chapters: **Australia**, Joseph and Kate
Hren, President, R.N.B. 3399, "The
Cottage," Coomorra, Victoria, 3461
Australia, E-mail:
jdink@mel.dbce.csiro.au; **California**,
Joann Hanson, President, 8588
Woodpecker Avenue, Fountain Valley,
CA 92708-6239, E-mail:
jhanson143@aol.com; **Canada**, Linda
Tomlin, President, 1383 Maple Bay
Road, RR 5, Duncan, British
Columbia, V9L 4T6, Canada;
Colorado, Cathie Kimmel, President,
837 Swiggler Road, Jefferson, CO
90456-9732; **Florida**; **Kansas**;
Christie R. Supancic Johnson,
President, 2322 Payne Street, Wichita,
KS 67204-5840, E-mail:
sgsks@mindspring.com; **Maryland**,
Ted Chiappelli, President, 207 Drum
Avenue South, Pasadena, MD 21122-
3920, E-mail: chiap@pipeline.com;
Minnesota, Terry Rupar, President,
417 NW 9th Street, Chisholm, MN
55719-1542, (218) 254-5891, E-mail:
trupar@uslink.net; **Missouri**
(temporarily unavailable); **Ohio**, PO
Box 501, Edgewater Branch,
Lakewood, OH; **Oklahoma**, Patrick
Sterbank, President, 4204 Tamarisk
Drive, Oklahoma City, OK 73120-
8114, E-mail: pa-hand@worldnet.att.
net; **Oregon**, Alfred Stoinich,
President, 5755 Guardenia Avenue,
Clovedale, OR 97112-9629, E-mail:
bigal@oregoncoast.com; **Texas**, Mike
Fox, President, 14511 Star Cross Trail,
Helotes, TX 78023-4050, E-mail:
mikefox@ns.NetXpress.com;
Wisconsin, Mary Lou Voelk,
President, Route 1, Box 258A, Iron
River, WI 54847
$10.00 per year membership (calendar
year)

Slovenian Women's Union of America
Slovenian Heritage Museum
431 North Chicago Street
Joliet, IL 60432
(815) 727-1926

Irene Odorizzi, Heritage Director
Hours: Mon–Thur 10:00–2:00
Pub. *Zarja—The Dawn*, nine times per
year, $15.00 per year subscription

Spanish

(see also Creole)

The Amistad Research Center
(see African-American)

Apache Genealogy Society
Sierra Vista Public Library
Maria Bishop Room
PO Box 1084
Sierra Vista, AZ 85636-1084
(520) 458-7770
Bonnie Temple Blackwell, President
(specializes in Tombstone, Arizona and
Cochise County marriages; how to do
Hispanic research)
Pub. *The Genealogist*, quarterly
$5.00 per year membership

Basque Studies Program
(address withheld upon request)

Buber's Basque Page
E-mail: buber@u.washington.edu
http://weber.u.washington.edu/ buber/
basque.html

Centro de Studios Chicanos Research Center
San Diego State University
San Diego, CA 92182
(714) 286-5145
Juan D. Tapia, Coordinator

Chicano Reference Library
590S The Nitery
Stanford University
Stanford, CA 94305
(650) 497-2798
Juanita Villalobos, Director
Hours: Green Library
Pub. *Chicano Reference Library
Bibliography*, annually

Chicano Research Collection
Department of Archives and Manuscripts
Hayden Library
Arizona State University
Tempe, AZ 85287-1006
(602) 965-3145
Christine Marin, Curator
Hours: Mon 11:00–7:00, Tue–Wed 8:00–
7:00, Thur–Fri 8:00–5:00, Sat 1:00–
5:00
(Mexican-American history; Mexican-
Americans in the U.S.)

Chicano Studies Library
University of California
3408 Dwinelle Hall
Berkeley, CA 94720
(415) 642-3859
Oscar Trevino, Serials Librarian

Duke University Press
6697 College Station
Durham, NC 27708
Pub. *Hispanic American Historical Review*

El Paso County Historical Society
(see Texas)

Mel Fisher Maritime Heritage Society
(200 Greene Street, Key West, FL 33040—location)
PO Box 511 (mailing address)
Key West, FL 33041
(305) 294-2633
Dr. Madeleine Burnside, Executive Director
Hours: Mon–Sun 9:00–5:00
Pub. *Astrolabe*, annually; *Navigator*, monthly
(Spanish colonial era)
$20.00 per year membership in the U.S., $30.00 per year foreign membership, $50.00 per year Patron membership

FLSV Genealogy Record
7747 Wildwood Road
Findlay, OH 45840-9538
(419) 424-1199
Alicia Dapore
Hours: 8:00–5:00
Pub. *FLSV Genealogy Record (Fabela/ Lozano/Solis/Villanueva)*, quarterly, $10.00 per year subscription
(Mexican)
free searches

Hidalgo County Historical Museum
121 East McIntyre
Edinburg, TX 78539
(956) 383-6911; (956) 381-8518 FAX
David J. Mycue, Curator of Archives and Collections
Hours: Museum archives and library: Tue–Fri 9:00–5:00
Pub. *Rio Grande Heritage* (a photohistory book, not genealogical)
("Archives and photofiles specialize in Mexican-American families in the lower Rio Grande Valley, 1750 to the present.")
research: $12.00 per hour, photocopies 10¢ each

Genealogical Society of Hispanic America
PO Box 9606
Denver, CO 80209-0606
Shirley H. Clayton, Second Vice President and Membership Chair
Pub. *Nuestras Raices Quarterly Journal*, quarterly; *Nuestras Raices Newsletter* (primarily refers to Colorado and New Mexico), two or three times per year, between quarterlies
$15.00 per year membership for individuals, $20.00 per year membership for families, $12.00 per year membership for senior citizen

individuals, $17.00 per year membership for senior citizen families

Hispanic Genealogical Research Center of New Mexico
1331 Juan Tabo, N.E., Suite P #18
Albuquerque, NM 87112
(505) 836-5438
E-mail: HGRC@HGRC-NM.ORG
http://www.hgrc-nm.org
Ron Miera, President
Hours: meetings at Albuquerque Public Library, Special Collections Library: first Sat 10:00
Pub. *Herencia*, quarterly
$20.00 per year membership for individuals, $25.00 per year membership for couples, $17.00 per year membership for senior citizen individuals, $22.00 per year membership for senior citizen couples

Hispanic Genealogical Society
PO Box 231271
Houston, TX 77223
Pub. *Hispanic Genealogical Journal*, semiannually
$15.00 per year membership

Hispanic Genealogical Society of New York
Murray Hill Station, PO Box 818
New York, NY 10156-0602
(212) 532-3662
E-mail: HGSNY@aol.com
http://www.webcom.com/hgsny
Charles Fourquet-Batiz, Vice President and Co-Founder
Pub. *Nuestra Herencia*
(helping Hispanics/Latinos to find their family origins, specializing in Puerto Rican genealogy)
free membership

Hispanic History and Ancestry Research
9511 Rockpoint Drive
Huntington Beach, CA 92646

Hispanic Institute of Columbia University
(Casa Hispánica, Room 405—location)
612 West 116th Street (mailing address)
New York, NY 10027
(212) 854-5610; (212) 854-5322 FAX
Dr. Elzbieta Szoka, Editor
Hours: Mon–Fri 9:00–5:00
Pub. *Revista Hispánica Moderna*, semiannually (June and December), $25.00 per year subscription for individuals, $40.00 per year subscription for institutions, additional $5.00 per year for delivery foreign countries
("Our archives—very well-known among scholars—have an extensive bibliography and numerous clippings dealing with the literature and culture of the Spanish- and Portuguese-speaking countries; although the

archives have been closed since 1969, they are valuable and are open to all students and members of the Hispanic Institute.")

Hispanic Society of America
613 West 155th Street
New York, NY 10032
(212) 926-2234
Gerald J. MacDonald, Curator, Modern Library
Hours: Museum: Tue–Sat 10:00–4:30; Library: Tue–Fri 1:00–4:15, Sat 10:00–4:15
(Spanish and Portuguese)
membership by election only

Jesuit Historical Institute, American Division
University of Arizona
Arizona State Museum
Building 26
Tucson, AZ 85721
(520) 621-6278; (520) 621-9188 FAX
Charles Polzer, Sr., Curator and Director
Hours: 8:00–5:00
(holdings on Spanish colonial New Spain [Mexico])

Los Bexareños Genealogical Society
PO Box 1935
San Antonio, TX 78297
(210) 822-1526
Dan Gomez, Editor
Pub. *Los Bexareños Genealogical Register*, quarterly (March, June, September, December)
$25.00 per year for individuals and families, $20.00 per year membership for institutions or libraries

Los Californianos, Hispanic Ancestors of Alta California
4530 LaCrosse Avenue
San Diego, CA 92117
(619) 273-2260
Alice Thomson, Membership Chairman
Hours: quarterly meetings at various locations: Sat & Sun
Pub. *Antepasados*, annually; *Noticias*, quarterly
(descendants of Hispanics in Alta California before February 1848)
regular membership subject to approval of Genealogy Committee, spouses also eligible, historians and libraries (corresponding) eligible with approval of board

Los Descendientes del Presidio de Tucson
(1711 North Painted Hills Road, Tucson, AZ 85745-1535—location)
PO Box 50871 (mailing address)
Tucson, AZ 85703
(520) 743-8233
Theresa G. Montaño, President
Hours: 8:00–5:00
Pub. *Newsletter*, quarterly
about $300.00

Los Fundadores, The Founders and Friends of Santa Clara County
(City of Santa Clara Civic Center, 1509 Warburton Avenue, Santa Clara, CA 95050—location)
1053 South White Road (mailing address)
San Jose, CA 95127
(408) 926-1165; (408) 248-ARTS (24-hour message)
Hours: meetings: first Sun
Pub. *Los Fundadores* (California's Spanish/Mexico period, genealogy of early California; articles about the Hispanic progenitors of California; early American pioneers, recognition of Native Americans), quarterly
$11.00 per year membership for individuals, $16.50 per year membership for families or societies; free queries for members

Los Pobladores 200
2830 East 56th Way
Long Beach, CA 90805

Mexican American Cultural Heritage Center
2940 Singleton Boulevard
Dallas, TX 75212
(972) 630-1680

Museum of New Mexico
The Palace of the Governors
113 Lincoln Avenue
PO Box 2087
Santa Fe, NM 87504-2087
(505) 827-6473; (505) 827-6451; (505) 827-6450; (505) 827-6521 FAX
Orlando Romero, History Librarian; Hazel Romero, History Librarian; Thomas A. Livesay, Director of Museum; Thomas E. Chavez, Ph.D., Director of The Palace of the Governors
Hours: Mon–Fri 1:00–5:00
Pub. *El Palacio*, quarterly
(a historical rather than a genealogical resource; no staff to conduct genealogical searches, and refers questions to the Special Collections Branch at the University of New Mexico)

New Mexico Hispanic Cultural Center
1701 Fourth Street, S.W.
PO Box 12317
Albuquerque, NM 87195
(505) 246-2261; (505) 246-2613
(oral history, genealogy, research, etc.)

New Mexico Records Center and Archives
404 Montezuma Street
Santa Fe, NM 87501
(505) 827-7332; (505) 827-7331 FAX
http://www.state.nm.us/
Elaine Olah, State Records Administrator

Hours: Mon–Fri 8:00–5:00
Pub. *Quipu*, irregularly
(Spanish archives of New Mexico, 1621–1821)

Puerto Rican/Hispanic Genealogical Society
25 Ralph Avenue
Brentwood, NY 11717-2424
(516) 834-2511
E-mail: latinoblu@aol.com
http://www.linkdirect.com/hispsoc/hispanic_links.htm
(list of Hispanic genealogical resources by country)

RevMex (Revolutionary Mexican Historical Society)
Sunset Ridge Road
Ozawkie, KS 66070
(785) 945-3800

Saint Augustine Historical Society
271 Charlotte Street
Saint Augustine, FL 32084
(904) 824-2872
Page Edwards, Director
Hours: Mon–Fri 9:00–noon & 1:00–5:00
Pub. *East Florida Gazette*, quarterly; *El Escribano*, annually
(Spanish, Saint Augustine, Saint Johns County, Florida)
$35.00 per year membership for individuals, $10.00 per year membership for students

Santa Barbara Historical Society
136 East De La Guerra Street
PO Box 578
Santa Barbara, CA 93102
(805) 966-1601; (805) 966-1603 FAX
Michael Redmon, Librarian
Hours: Tue–Sat 10:00–5:00, Sun noon–5:00; Gledhill Library: Tue–Fri 10:00–4:00, first Sat 10:00–1:00
Pub. *Noticias*, quarterly; *Santa Barbara Historical Museum Newsletter*, monthly
$40.00 per year membership

Society for Spanish and Portuguese History
Boston College
Chestnut Hill
Boston, MA 02167

Society of Descendants of Colonial Hispanics
Brooks Enterprises
1718 West Robinson Street, #A
Norman, OK 73069-7311
Clifton Brooks, M.D.

Southmost College
Arnulfo L. Oliveira Memorial Library
Hunter Room
83 Fort Brown
Brownsville, TX 78520
(956) 544-8221
Yolanda Gonzalez

Hours: Mon–Thur 7:30–10:00, Fri 7:30–5:00, Sat 10:30–4:00, Sun 2:00–9:00

Spanish American Genealogical Association
PO Box 5407
Corpus Christi, TX 78405

Spanish History Museum Publications and Shields
PO Box 25531
Albuquerque, NM 87125-0531
(505) 864-2919
Elmer Martinez, Publisher
Hours: Mon–Sun 9:00–5:00
Pub. *Heraldic Research Reports*, quarterly
(publishes Spanish Colonial History and miscellaneous titles, produces wall hanging coats of arms; catalog available)

University of Texas at Austin
Benson.Latin American Collection
PO Box P
Austin, TX 78713-8916
(512) 495-4520; (512) 495-4568
E-mail: blac@lib.utexas.edu
http://www.lib.utexas.edu/Libs/Benson/benson.html

Swedish

(see also Finnish and Norwegian)

American Friends of the Swedish Emigrant Institute of Sweden, Inc.
3452 Fourth Street
East Moline, IL 61244
(309) 755-2858
Lennart Setterdahl
("As of now we are only working with direct research 'out in the field.' The result will be handled by Svenska Emigrantinstitutet, Växjö, Sweden. Our office will not answer any inquiries from the public.")

American Swedish Historical Museum
1900 Pattison Avenue
Philadelphia, PA 19145
(215) 389-1776; (215) 389-7701 FAX
E-mail: ashm@libertynet.org
http://www.libertynet.org/~ashm
Ann Barton Brown, Executive Director
Hours: Office: Mon–Fri 8:30–4:00
Pub. *Newsletter*, three times per year
$35.00 per year membership for individuals, $30.00 per year membership for senior citizens or students

The American Swedish Institute
2600 Park Avenue
Minneapolis, MN 55407
(612) 871-4907; (612) 871-4908; (612) 871-8682 FAX
Jan McElfish, Editor/Publicist; Marita Karlisch, Archives and Library

Hours: Tue & Thur–Sat 12:00–4:00, Wed 12:00–8:00, Sun 1:00–5:00; Archives and Library: by appointment only Tue & Thur–Fri 12:00–4:00, Wed 12:00–8:00, third Sat 12:00–4:00
Pub. *ASI Posten*, eleven times per year (monthly)
$33.00 per year membership

Bishop Hill Heritage Association

Bishop Hill Heritage Museum
103 North Bishop Hill Street
PO Box 92
Bishop Hill, IL 61419-0092
(309) 927-3899; (309) 927-3010 FAX
Crystle D. Clark, Museum Director
Hours: Mon–Fri 10:00–4:00
Pub. *Heritage Newsbulletin*, three to four times per year
("Information on Bishop Hill and the Swedish immigrants whofounded it; we have a library and an archives which contains many documents and photographs.")
$25.00–$500.00 membership; search fees vary by time involved

The Delaware Swedish Colonial Society

606 Church Street
Wilmington, DE 19801
Al Ostrand, President
Pub. *Smörgåsnews*
(ethnic and colonial Swedish)
$10.00 per year

Independent Order of Svithiod

5518 West Lawrence Avenue
Chicago, IL 60630
(773) 736-1191
Betty Jane Clausen, Secretary-Treasurer
Hours: 9:00–5:00
Pub. *Svithiod Journal*, monthly
$1.00 per year membership for individuals

Lewes Historical Society

119 West Third
Lewes, DE 19958
(302) 645-7640
Dr. James E. Marvil, President

National Council of the Swedish Cultural Society in America

PO Box 8042
Saint Paul, MN 55108-8042
(612) 645-8578 phone and FAX
L. Christina Sjostedt, National President
Pub. *Swedish Heritage*, quarterly
$5.00 per year membership

New Sweden, Iowa, Descendants

3623 North 37th Street
Arlington, VA 22207-4821
(703) 276-8228; (703) 276-8236 FAX
E-mail: BAnnMunsey@aol.com
Bernice Wilson Munsey
(assisting those beginning to search their own families)

Nordic Heritage Museum

3014 N.W. 67th
Seattle, WA 98117
(206) 789-5707; (206) 789-3271 FAX
Marianne Forssblad, Ph.D., Director
Hours: Tue–Sat 10:00–4:00, Sun 12:00–4:00
Pub. *Nordic News*, bimonthly
(Nordic-Scandinavian: Denmark, Finland, Iceland, Norway, Sweden); genealogical information with largest holdings in Norwegian "Bygdevøker")
$30.00 per year membership for individuals, $50.00 per year membership for families

Old Swedes' Foundation

Holy Trinity (Old Swedes') Church Foundation, Inc.
Hendrickson House Museum and Old Swedes' Church
606 Church Street
Wilmington, DE 19801
(302) 652-5629; (302) 652-8615 FAX
E-mail: oldswedes@aol.com
Jo Thompson, Curator/Business Manager
Hours: Mon, Wed & Fri–Sat 1:00–4:00
Pub. *Old Swedes' Foundation Newsletter*, annually
(genealogy/history; Swedish/Finnish)
$25.00 per year membership for individuals (beginning in June), $45.00 per year membership for families, $15.00 per year membership for senior citizens or students, $100.00 per year Patron membership, $500.00 life membership; search for baptism, marriage or burial of one individual: $10.00 (includes photocopies of the event from printed copies of the church records, but a letter attesting to the information is $5.00 extra), determining if and when members of a certain family were buried in the church yard: $10.00 (includes a photocopy of records, where possible, and a letter attesting to the information), researching records on some of the early Swedish families for a specific name and making photocopies: $10.00 plus 20¢ per page

Scandinavian-American Genealogical Society

Minnesota Genealogical Society, Scandinavian Branch
(1650 Carroll Avenue, Saint Paul, MN 55104—location)
PO Box 16069 (mailing address)
Saint Paul, MN 55116-0069
(612) 645-3671
http://www.mtn.org/mgs/branches
Marie Davis, President
Hours: Library: Wed–Thur & Sat 10:00–4:00, Tue & Thur 6:30–9:30
Pub. *Scandinavian Saga*, two times per year
$5.00 per year membership

Scandinavian Genealogical Society of Oregon

1123 Seventh Street, N.W.
Salem, OR 97304

Scandinavian Queries

Rt. 2, Box 671
Grangeville, ID 83530-9635
(208) 983-0515
Anne Long
Pub. *Scandinavian Queries* (Denmark, Finland, Norway, Sweden, Iceland), irregularly, $6.50 per year subscription (Idaho residents add 5% sales tax)

Seattle Genealogical Society

8511 15th Avenue, N.E.
PO Box 1708
Seattle, WA 98111
(206) 522-8658
Sarah Little
Hours: Mon 6:30–9:00, Tue–Sat 10:00–3:00
Pub. *Seattle Genealogical Society Newsletter*, monthly; *Seattle Genealogical Society Bulletin*, quarterly
(specializes in Washington and Scandinavia)
$20.00 per year membership for individuals, $25.00 per year dual membership; search fee: $8.00

Swedish American Historical Society

North Park College
5125 North Spaulding Avenue
Chicago, IL 60625-4816
(773) 583-5722
E-mail: kanders3@northpark.edu
http://www.northpark.edu/library/swedish-american_history/index.html
Karna Anderson, Office Manager
Hours: 9:00–noon
Pub. *Swedish American Historical Quarterly*
$25.00 per year basic membership

Swedish American Museum

5211 North Clark Street
Chicago, IL 60640-2101
(773) 728-8111; (773) 728-8870 FAX
Kerstin Lane, Executive Director
Hours: Tue–Fri 10:00–4:00, Sat–Sun 10:00–3:00
Pub. *SAMAC News*, quarterly
$25.00 per year membership

Swedish Colonial Society

916 Swanson Street
Philadelphia, PA 19147
(215) 389-1513
Rev. David Rivers, Secretary
Pub. *Swedish Colonial Society Newsletter*, semiannually
("New Sweden period, 1638–1786")
$20.00 per year membership

The Swedish Finn Historical Society

6512 23rd Avenue, N.W.
Seattle, WA 98117-5728

(206) 706-0738; (206) 782-5813 FAX
Bonnie Olson, Secretary
Hours: Mon 9:30–12:30, Thur 9:30–
12:30, and by appointment
Pub. *The Swedish Finn Historical
Society Newsletter*, quarterly
(specializes in Finland's Swedes)
$12.50 per year membership for
individuals, $22.50 per year
membership for families, $10.00 per
year membership for senior citizens
(65+), $50.00 per year Patron
membership, $100.00 per year
Business Sponsor membership;
$500.00 life membership; research:
donation

**Swedish Genealogy Club of the
American Swedish Historical
Museum**
2700 Pattison Avenue
Philadelphia, PA 19145
(215) 389-1776
William Fagerstrom, President
Hours: meetings: third Thur (Jan, Mar,
May, Sept, Nov) 7:00 P.M.–9:00 P.M.
$10.00 per year membership

Swedish Genealogy Pages
E-mail: floyd@algonet.se
http://algonet.se/~floyd/scandgen/

Swedish Historical Society
404 South Third Street
Rockford, IL 61104-2013
(815) 963-5559
Rev. Ragnar Moline, President
Hours: by appointment
Pub. *Swedish Heritage*, annually, $3.00
per year subscription
$8.00 per year membership for
individuals, $15.00 per year
membership for couples

**Swenson Swedish Immigration
Research Center**
Augustana College
639 38th Street
Rock Island, IL 61201-2273
(309) 794-7204; (309) 794-7443 FAX
http://viking.augustana.edu/admin/
swenson/
Jill A. Seaholm, Researcher; Christina
Johansson, Head of Genealogical
Services; Victoria A. Oliver, Head of
Library Services
Hours: Mon–Fri 9:00–4:30 by
appointment (except during holidays
and school vacation)
Pub. *Swenson Center News*, annually;
Swedish American Genealogist,
quarterly, $25.00 per year subscription
in the U.S.(calendar year)
(Augustana Lutheran Church (Swedish),
Evangelical Covenant Church,
Swedish Baptist Conference, Swedish
Methodist Church, Evangelical Free
Church and Swedish Episcopal)
$25.00 per year Associate membership,
$100.00 per year membership for

scholars, $250.00 per year
membership in Swenson Center Circle

**Vasa Order of America National
Archives, Inc.**
109 South Main
PO Box 101
Bishop Hill, IL 61419
(309) 927-3898 phone and FAX
Richard W. Horngren, Archivist
Hours: Apr 1–Dec 20: Mon–Sat 10:00–
3:00, Sun noon–4:00, and other times
by appointment
Pub. *The Vasa Star* (published by VOA
Grand Lodge), six times per year
(specializes in Swedish-American,
Swedish, Scandinavian material, not
primarily a genealogical resource, but
"happy to give basic information on
Swedish genealogy and the Swedish
language, geography, etc.")
$10.00 per year membership for
individuals in the U.S., $15.00 per
year membership for individuals
outside the U.S.; searches generally
free to members, negotiated for others

Swiss

(see also Galician and German)

American Swiss Association
Swiss National Tourist Office
608 Fifth Avenue
New York, NY 10020

Immigrant Genealogical Society
Immigrant Library
1310-B West Magnolia Boulevard
PO Box 7369
Burbank, CA 91510-7369
(818) 848-3122
http://feefhs.org/igs/frqigs.html
Marilyn Deatherage, Corresponding
Secretary
Hours: Wed & Sun noon–5:00, Sat
10:00–5:00; meetings first Fri 7:30
Pub. *German American Genealogy*,
semiannually; *Immigrant Genealogical
Society Newsletter*, monthly
(especially German and Swiss)
$20.00 per year membership for
individuals, $25.00 per year
membership for families at the same
address, additional $10.00 per year for
first class mail delivery, additional
$15.00 for airmail delivery overseas;
library admission free to members,
$2.00 per visit to non-members

New Glarus Historical Society
Swiss Historical Village
612 Seventh Avenue
PO Box 745
New Glarus, WI 53574-0745
(608) 527-2317
Gail Beal, Correspondence Secretary
Hours: May 1–Oct 31: Mon–Fri 9:00–
4:30

Swiss American Historical Society
(Washington, DC—location)
6440 North Bosworth Avenue (mailing
address)
Chicago, IL 60626
(773) 262-8336
Prof. Erdmann Schmocker, President
Pub. *Swiss American Historical Society
Review*, three times per year
(promotes research involving Swiss
immigrants)
$30.00 per year membership for
individuals, $15.00 per year
membership for students, $50.00 per
year membership for institutions,
$350.00 life membership

Swiss Community Historical Society
9255 Lugabell Road
Bluffton, OH 45817
Herman Hilty

Swiss Heritage Society
1200 Swiss Way
Berne, IN 46711
(219) 589-8007 (summer months only)
Gretchen Lehman, Secretary
Hours: Mon–Sat 10:00–4:00
Pub. *Swiss Echoes*, semiannually (spring
and fall), donation
(specializes in Swiss culture)

**Swiss Historical Society of Gruetli,
Tennessee**
(address withheld upon request)

The Swiss Connection
2845 North 72nd Street
Milwaukee, WI 53210
(414) 778-1224; (414) 778-2109 FAX
E-mail: swissmis@interserv.com
Maralyn A. Wellauer, Editor
Hours: Mon–Sat noon–8:00
Pub. *The Swiss Connection*, quarterly,
$12.00 per yearsubscription
(September–June), $20.00 per year
overseas subscription
research: $45.00–$65.00 per hour

Taiwanese

(see Asian)

Ukrainian

(see also Eastern European, German,
Hungarian, and Russian)

Fox Chase Manor
701 Fox Chase Road
Jenkintown, PA 19111

Saint Basil's College
195 Glenbrook Road
Stamford, CT 06902

Ukrainian Fraternal Association
440 Wyoming Avenue
Scranton, PA 18503
(717) 347-5649
Ivan Oleksyn, President

Hours: 8:00–4:30
Pub. *Forum, Ukrainian Review,*
    quarterly, $12.00 per year
    subscription; *Narodna Volya*
    (newspaper), weekly, $10.00 per year
    subscription

Ukrainian Genealogical and Heraldic Society

573 N.E. 102nd Street
Miami Shores, FL 33138

Ukrainian Genealogical and Historical Society of Canada

1530 23rd Avenue
Calgary, Alberta T2M 1V1
Canada
Walter Rusel

The Ukrainian Museum

203 Second Avenue
New York, NY 10003
(212) 228-0110; (212) 228-1947 FAX
Lydia Hajduczok
Hours: Wed–Sun 1:00–5:00

Ukrainian Museum-Archives, Inc.

1202 Kenilworth Avenue
Cleveland, OH 44113
(216) 741-4537

United Ukrainian American Relief Committee

1206 Cootman Avenue
Philadelphia, PA 19111
(215) 728-1630; (215) 728-1631 FAX
Stepan Hawrysz, Executive Director
Hours: Mon–Fri 9:00–4:00

Vietnamese

Vietnam Foundation

6713 Lumsden Street
McLean, VA 22101

Welsh

(see also British, English, Irish and
Scottish)

The Arizona Welsh Society, Sun City Chapter

(Menke's Sun City Meeting Room,
    103rd and Coggins, Sun City—
    location)
12834 Paintbrush Drive (mailing
    address)
Sun City West, AZ 85375-2551
(602) 584-5967
Edie Steving, President
Hours: 1:30–4:00

Bryn Mawr Club of Akron

1860 Second Street, Apartment 663
Cuyahoga Falls, OH 44221
Judith Hedges

Cambrian Benevolent Society of Chicago

106 Oxford Avenue
Clarendon Hills, IL 60514
George Bowen Williams, President

Cambrian Society of Portland

13508 278th Street East
Graham, WA 98338-8757
Richard J. Davies

Celtic Cultural Coalition

One West 69th Street
Kansas City, MO 64113
Ann McFerrin

Celtic Photos and Crafts

10 Hemingway Road
North Haven, CT 06473-3737
(800) IM-WELSH phone & FAX (8:00
    A.M.–9:00 P.M.)
E-mail: celticpandc@mindspring.com
http://www.celticpandc.com/
Earl T. Williams, Jr., B.A.M., Director/
    Owner
Pub. *Catalog,* annually, free
(books, recordings, Welsh learning
    materials, etc.; mail-order Welsh
    imports)

Celtic (Welsh, Irish, Scottish) Society of the Ozarks

2214 East Cherryvale
Springfield, MO 65804-4524
(417) 883-8396
E-mail: jholsing@mail.orion.org
Dr. J. C. Holsinger, Secretary
Hours: quarterly public meetings
Pub. *The Dragon, The Thistle, and The
    Harp,* quarterly
(an interest group that meets for lectures
    and singing of Celtic music; no
    genealogical research)
$5.00 per year membership

Cleveland Welsh Society

4988 Farnhurst Road
Lyndhurst, OH 44124
Alcwyn Isaac

Gomer Welsh Society

Allen County Museum
620 West Market Street
Lima, OH 45801

Green Mountain College

(Griswold Library, Poultney, VT 05764-
    1199—location)
Clover Street, Box 113 (mailing address)
Ocean Park, ME 04063
(802) 287-9313
Charles Schwartz, Curator
Hours: academic year 8:00 A.M.–10:30
    P.M., summer 8:00–4:00 (closed
    weekends)
(Troy Conference United Methodist and
    Welsh ethnic materials; no research in
    this collection is done by on-site
    library staff)

Gulf Coast Saint David's Welsh Society of Sarasota, Florida

1528 Vermeer Drive
Nokomis, FL 34275
(941) 488-5793 (President); (941) 349-
    5558 (Secretary)
Russell Williams, President; Mrs.
    Rhianon Hardy, Corresponding
    Secretary (Welsh-speaking)

Iowa Welsh Society-Cymdeithas Gymreig Iowa

408 East Salem
Indianola, IA 50125
(515) 961-3201
E-mail: hallross@aol.com
Ruth Hall, President
Pub. *Iowa Welsh Society-Cymdeithas
    Gymreig Iowa Newsletter,* usually four
    times per year
$7.50 per year membership (beginning
    March 1); translation services
    available by some members

Minnesota Gymanfa Ganu Association

Rt. 1
Lake Crystal, MN 56055
Wayne Hughes, President

National Welsh-American Foundation

(Sefydliad Cenedlaethol Cymru-
    America)
24 Carverton Road
Trucksville, PA 18708
(717) 696-NWAF; (717) 696-1525; (717)
    696-1808 FAX
Warren E. Watkins, Secretary
Hours: Tue–Fri noon–5:00
Pub. *The Eagle and the Dragon (Yr Eryr
    A'r Ddraig),* quarterly (January, April,
    July, October)
(dedicated to the preservation of Welsh
    culture, also locates books,
    manuscripts, and other printed
    memorabilia of historical value to
    libraries)
$10.00 per year membership for
    individuals, $15.00 per year
    membership for families, $50.00 per
    year membership for organizations or
    Sustaining membership, $100.00 per
    year Contributing membership,
    $250.00 per year Patron membership,
    $150.00 life membership for
    individuals (or 15 times annual dues of
    the selected membership category)

Nebraska Welsh Gymanfa Ganu Association

8310 Elizabeth Drive
Lincoln, NE 68505
Dr. Orvid Owens, President

Nebraska Welsh Society

5446 Locust Street
Lincoln, NE 68516
Morgan Bevan, President

Ninnau Publications, Inc.
11 Post Terrace
Basking Ridge, NJ 07920
(908) 766-6736; (908) 221-0744 FAX
Arturo Roberts, President
Hours: 8:00 A.M.–10:00 P.M.
Pub. *Ninnau—The North American Welsh Newspaper*, monthly, $15.00 per year subscription in the U.S., $18.00 per yearsubscription in Canada, £10.00 per year subscription in Britain
(Welsh news and features of interest to Welsh Americans, including genealogy, English language)

Northwestern Ohio Welsh Society
3837 Pioneer Road
Elida, OH 45807
Alice Davis Bushong

The Owain Glendower Society
2144 Elmwood
Tulsa, OK 74106
Stafford Davis

Pottsville Welsh Society
504 Union Street
Schuylkill Haven, PA 17962
Karen Saylor

Puget Sound Welsh Association
PO Box 19344
Seattle, WA 98109
Jackie Cedarholm, President

Radnor Heritage Society
5767 Hadley Road
Radnor, OH 43066
Mary Anne Thomas, President

Remsen-Steuben Historical Society
Prospect Street
PO Box 284
Remsen, NY 13438
(315) 831-5443
Leonard Wynne, President

Sacramento Cylch Cymraeg
4916 Palm Avenue
Sacramento, CA 95841
(916) 332-4550
Patricia Hillman, President

Saint David's Society
139 South Mill Street
Saint Clair, PA 17970
Ron Davenport

Saint David's Society of Connecticut, Inc.
PO Box 193
North Haven, CT 06473
(203) 239-1410
Earl T. Williams, Jr.
Pub. *Newsletter*, quarterly
$12.00 per year membership for individuals, $15.00 per year membership for families

Saint David's Society of Georgia
3484 River Heights Crossing, S.E.
Marietta, GA 30067-4502
Sally Evans Funderburk

Saint David's Society of Greater Buffalo, N.Y.
552 East River Road
Grand Island, NY 14072
Tom Edwards, President

Saint David's Society of Greater Saint Louis
3563 Lost Meadow Court
Saint Louis, MO 63129
Ida Mae Williams Arnold

Saint David's Society of Minnesota
8004 Lad Parkway
Minneapolis, MN 55443-2813
Ann St. Martin

Saint David's Society of Oshkosh, Wisconsin and Winnebago County, Welsh Settlement
321 East Sullivan Street
Ripon, WI 54971
(920) 748-6237
Mrs. Olwen Morgan Welk, President; Mr. Lee E. Morgan, Vice President; Eleanor Jones, Secretary; Miss Ilah E. Morgan, Treasurer
Hours: annual meetings at Algoma Boulevard United Methodist Church, 1174 Algoma Boulevard, Oshkosh, WI 54901: Sun afternoon near 1 Mar, Saint David's Day
(Welsh heritage and social organization)

Saint David's Society of Pittsburgh
3107 Greenfield Road
Glenshaw, PA 15116
Dave Lewis

Saint David's Society of Rochester and Genesee Region
1523 North Winton Road
Rochester, NY 14609
Don R. Jones, President

Saint David's Society of South Carolina
PO Drawer 150
Florence, SC 29503

Saint David's Society of the Inland Empire
3503 North Calispel
Spokane, WA 99215
Mrs. Robert Valentine

The Saint David's Society of the State of Kansas
(Emporia, KS—location)
PO Box 11 (mailing address)
Lebo, KS 66856-0011
(316) 256-6687
Paula or Buddy, Members
Hours: 24-hours

Saint David's Society of Utica, Inc.
2311 West Highland Avenue
Yorkville, NY 13495
(315) 797-3247
Patricia C. Divers, Membership Chair
$5.00 per year membership, $25.00 life membership

Saint David's Society of Waukesha County
(Waukesha, WI—location)
110 North Fairview Avenue (mailing address)
North Prairie, WI 53153
(414) 392-2717
Alice Whitmore
Hours: annual meetings: first week in March

Saint David's Society of Wyoming Valley
158 Courtdale Avenue
Courtdale, PA 18704
(717) 283-0417
David Martin, Secretary

Saint David's Society of Youngstown
855 Larkridge Avenue
Youngstown, OH 44512
Robert J. Garver

Saint David's Welsh-American Society of Baltimore
1446 Battery Avenue
Baltimore, MD 21230
Eugene Owen, President

Saint David's Welsh-American Society of Washington, D.C.
1420 Madison Court
Hyattsville, MD 20782
Cheryl Mitchell, President

Saint David's Welsh Society of Greater Kansas City
6904 Wildwood Drive
Kansas City, MO 64133
(816) 356-7272
Jack Nesbitt, President
Pub. *The Red Dragon*, bimonthly (specializes in Welsh Culture)
$5.00 per year membership

Saint David's Welsh Society of Nebraska
8310 Elizabeth Drive
Lincoln, NE 68505
(402) 483-7237
Gweneth Colgrove, President; Orvid Owens, Editor
Pub. *Saint David's Welsh Society of Nebraska Newsletter*, two times per year, $4.00 per year subscription

Saint David's Welsh Society of Saint Petersburg and the Suncoast
1020 Lake Auoca Drive
Tarpon Springs, FL 34689
(813) 446-1431

Rhys Moore, President
Hours: Wesleyan Church, Largo, FL:
    third Tue (Oct–May)
$5.00 per year membership

Sons and Daughters of Wales
PO Box 352
Ipswich, SD 57451
Beth Pond, President

The Welsh-American Family History Association (W.A.F.H.A.)
4202 Clark Street
Kansas City, MO 64111
Judith Brougham

Welsh-American Genealogical Society (WAGS)
13 Norton Avenue
Poultney, VT 05764-1011
E-mail: wagsjan@sover.net
Janice B. Edwards, Vice President/
    Secretary
Pub. *Newsletter*, quarterly
$10.00 per year membership for
    individuals

Welsh American Heritage Museum
Cambria Women's Welsh Club of Niles,
    Ohio
1525 Stewart Circle, N.W.
Warren, OH 44484
Irene Brooks

Welsh-American Heritage Museum
412 East Main Street
Oak Hill, OH 45656
(740) 682-7172
Mildred Bangert, Curator
Hours: Mon, Wed & Fri 8:00–12:00, Tue
    & Thur 8:00–5:00, weekends by
    chance
(Family histories, old S.S. books of area;
    "We have a limited genealogy section
    but hope to add to it.")
$5.00 per year membership, $100.00 life
    membership

Welsh American Society of Northern California
119 Bucareli Drive
San Francisco, CA 94132
Edith J. Moody

The Welsh National Gymanfa Ganu Association, Inc.
662 Melwood Drive, N.E.
Warren, OH 44483-4438
(330) 372-5885; (330) 652-1292 (Office
    and FAX)
E-mail: nllwngga@aol.com
http://www.cais.net/web/welsh/
    wngga.htm
Nelson L. Llewellyn, Executive Director
Hours: Mon–Fri 8:00–5:00
Pub. *HWYL*, quarterly
(to preserve, develop and promote our
    Welsh religious and cultural heritage)

$7.00 per year membership for
    individuals, $30.00 life membership
    for individuals, $50.00 life
    membership for Welsh organizations

Welsh Saint David's Society of Spokane
West 624 Providence
Spokane, WA 99205

Welsh Society of Berks County
Rt. 6, Box 53
Sinking Spring, PA 19608
(610) 777-7168
Rush C. Gwyn, President

Welsh Society of Central New Jersey
24 Essex Road
Scotch Plains, NJ 07076
Dr. Phillip Davies

Welsh Society of Central Ohio
PO Box 12023
Columbus, OH 43212

Welsh Society of Detroit
10 Dorothea
Mount Clemens, MI 48043
John O. Morgans

Welsh Society of Greater Cincinnati
6327 Parkman Place
Cincinnati, OH 45213
David Taliesin Richards, Interim
    President

Welsh Society of Greater Harrisburg, Pa.
130 Conodoguinet Avenue
Camp Hill, PA 17011
(717) 761-0639
Betty Lindermann, President
Hours: 9:00–5:00
Pub. *The Dragon Speaks*, monthly
$7.00 per year membership

Welsh Society of New Mexico
513 Barlane N.W.
Albuquerque, NM 87107
Rhianwen Roberts Gerard, President

Western Pennsylvania Genealogical Society
4400 Forbes Avenue
Pittsburgh, PA 15213-4080
(412) 687-6811
Hours: The Carnegie Library of
    Pittsburgh: Mon–Thur 9:00–9:00, Fri–
    Sat 9:00–5:30, Sun (Oct–May) 1:00–
    5:00
Pub. *The Quarterly*; *JOTS*, ten times per
    year
(sponsors Computer, English-Welsh,
    German, Irish, New England and
    Scottish interest groups)
$20.00 per year membership for
    individuals (beginning 1 July); $26.00
    per year joint membership (two
    members at one address); two free
    queries per quarter

Y Drych
PO Box 8089
Saint Paul, MN 55108-0089
(612) 642-1653; (612) 642-0170 FAX
Mary Morris Mergenthal, Owner, Editor,
    and Publisher
Pub. *Y Drych* (*The Mirror*), eleven times
    per year (monthly, except July),
    $20.00 per year U.S. subscription,
    $35.00 for two-year U.S. subscription,
    $30.00 per year Canadian subscription,
    $50.00 for two-year Canadian
    subscription
(includes news of Wales, news of Welsh
    North American people and events,
    Welsh language lessons, Welsh
    recipes, features on Welsh culture and
    history)

Yugoslavian

(see also Banat, Croatian, Eastern
    European, Slavic and Slovenian)

Cultural Society of South Slavs (CSSS)
3510 Xylon Avenue North
New Hope, MN 55427
(612) 544-6433
http://feefhs.org/frg-csss.html
James J. Smrekar
Pub. *Adria*, six times per year
(covers Bosnia, Bulgaria, Croatia,
    Macedonia, Serbia and Slovenia, all
    persons with ancestral links to any
    region in former Yugoslavia)
$20.00 per year membership for
    individuals, $25.00 per year
    membership for families, $10.00 per
    year membership for senior citizens;
    research services for members only,
    including some translation of
    Slovenian and Croation

RELIGIOUS ARCHIVES AND ORGANIZATIONS

Indiana Religious History Association
PO Box 88267
Indianapolis, IN 46208
James J. Divita, Ph.D., President
Pub. *IRHA Newsletter*, quarterly
$10.00 per year membership for individuals, $7.50 per year membership for retirees, $5.00 per year membership for students, $15.00 per year membership for institutions

Advent Christian

Charles B. Phillips Library
Aurora University
Aurora, IL 60506-4892
(630) 844-5438; (630) 844-3848 FAX
Susan L. Craig, Director of the Library

American Lutheran Church

(see Lutheran)

Amish

(see Mennonite)

Anabaptist

(see Hutterite, Mennonite, Moravian, Schwenkfelder)

Anglican

(see Church of England and Episcopal)

Armenian

Armenian Church of North America, Western Diocese
1201 North Vine Street
Hollywood, CA 90038
(213) 466-5265
Archbishop Vatche Hovsepian

Diocese of the Armenian Church of America
630 Second Avenue
New York, NY 10016
(212) 686-0710
Very Reverend Father Krikor Maksoudian
Hours: Mon–Fri 9:00–5:00
Pub. *The Armenian Church (Hagastanyants Yegeghestsi)*, monthly

Baptist

(see also Lutheran)

Alabama Baptist Historical Society
Samford University
American Genealogical Society Depository and Headquarters
Harwell Goodwin Davis Library
Special Collection Department
800 Lakeshore Drive
Birmingham, AL 35229
(205) 870-2749 (Library)
Elizabeth C. Wells, Librarian
Hours: Library: Mon 8:00–9:00, Tue–Fri 8:00–4:30

American Baptist Churches of New Hampshire
89 North State Street
Concord, NH 03301

American Baptist Historical Society
The American Baptist—Samuel Colgate Historical Library
1106 South Goodman Street
Rochester, NY 14620-2532
(716) 473-1740
Dana Martin, Acting Director of the Library
Hours: Mon–Fri 9:00–5:00
Pub. *American Baptist Quarterly*, $21.00 per year subscription
("Persons join Baptist churches as adults. Baptismal records do not include birth dates, birthplaces, or names of parents. Marriage records have been considered the private property of the officiating minister and are not kept with church records. There is normally no place in Baptist church records where birth dates, birthplaces, names of parents or names of other family members can be found. To search for information in Baptist congregational records, the inquirer must identify the name of the congregation, its location, and which of the 50+ different Baptist denominations it is affiliated with before he or she can begin to determine which library might hold such a record—in the unlikely event it has not been destroyed. There is no indexing of church records by member; it is useless to ask for the 'Smith family church records.' The only record of membership in a Baptist church is the record kept by the local church. Whether that record will be preserved when the church is disbanded is the separate decision of each individual congregation.")

Archives of the Mexican Baptist Convention of Texas
8019 Panama Expressway, South
San Antonio, TX 78224
(210) 924-4338

Arkansas Baptist State Convention Collection
Ouachita Baptist University
Riley-Hickingbotham Library
410 Ouachita
PO Box 3742
Arkadelphia, AR 71923
(870) 245-5332
Wendy Richter, Archivist
Hours: Mon–Fri 8:00–4:00

Ethel Taylor Crittenden Collection in Baptist History
Z. Smith Reynolds Library, Room 207
Wake Forest University
PO Box 7777
Winston-Salem, NC 27109
(919) 759-5472
http://www.wfu.edu/library/baptist
John R. Woodard, Director
Hours: Mon–Fri 8:30–5:00

Eastern Baptist Theological Seminary
The Library
6 Lancaster Avenue
Wynnewood, PA 19096
(215) 645-9318
Melody Mazuk, Director
Hours: Mon–Thur 8:30–10:00, Fri 8:30–4:30, Sat 9:00–4:30
$5.00 per photocopy request ("We require ALA form")

Florida Baptist Historical Society
Stetson University
Campus PO Box 8353
Deland, FL 32720-3757
(904) 822-7186
E. Earl Joiner, Th.D., Curator and Secretary-Treasurer
Hours: varies
Pub. *Newsletter*, annually, $2.00 per issue

Franklin College Library
501 East Monroe Street
Franklin, IN 46131-2598
(317) 738-8162; (317) 736-6030 FAX
Mary A. Medlicott, Archivist
Hours: various (call or write to confirm)
("Archives, American Baptist churches of Indiana; Archives, Franklin College; David Demaree Banta Indiana History Collection.")
fee for photocopies mailed to patrons

Free Will Baptist Historical Collection
Moye Library
Mount Olive College
634 Henderson Street
Mount Olive, NC 28365
(919) 658-7168; (919) 658-8934 FAX
E-mail: moyelibrary@horizon.moc.edu
Gary Fenton Barefoot, Librarian
Hours: Mon–Thur 8:00 A.M.–10:00 P.M., Fri 8:00–5:00, Sat 1:00–5:00, Sun 6:00–10:00

(Free Will Baptists, especially in north and southeast North Carolina concentration)
limited searching free, photocopy charges for information supplied

Georgia Baptist History Depository
Special Collections
Mercer University Main Library
1300 Edgewood Avenue
Macon, GA 31207-0001
(912) 752-2968; (912) 752-2111 FAX
Susan G. Broome, special Collections Librarian
Hours: Mon–Fri 9:00–noon & 1:00–5:00

Kentucky Baptist Convention Archives
10701 Shelbyville Road
PO Box 43433
Louisville, KY 40253-0433
(502) 245-4101
Cheryl Doty, Archivist
Hours: Tue–Thur 10:00–2:00
Pub. *Kentucky Baptist Heritage* (not genealogical, Kentucky Baptists and Southern), annually
(nothing in the way of genealogy, archives of the state Baptist organization, not of the churches)
$10.00 per year membership

Linfield College Library
McMinnville, OR 97158

Mississippi Baptist Historical Commission
Special Collections, Mississippi College
Leland Speed Library
PO Box 51
Clinton, MS 39060-0051
(601) 925-3434
Rachel A. Pyron, Special Collections Librarian
Hours: Mon–Fri 8:30–noon & 1:00–4:30 (except college holidays)
(history of Mississippi Baptists)

Missouri Baptist Historical Society
William Jewell College Library
Liberty, MO 64068
(816) 781-7700, ext. 5490 or 5341
Adrian Lamkin, Director
Hours: Mon–Fri 9:00–5:00
Pub. *Journal of Missouri Baptist History*, annually
$5.00 per year membership.

North American Baptist Heritage Commission
1525 South Grange Avenue
Sioux Falls, SD 57105
(605) 335-9071
George A. Dunger, Ph.D., Archivist
Hours: Mon–Fri 1:30–4:30, research by appointment
Pub. *Heritage Horizons*, occasionally
(auxiliary of the North American Baptist Conference; archival-rare books-museum holdings)
research cost: varies

Ottawa University
Myers Library
1001 South Cedar Street
Ottawa, KS 66067-3399
(913) 242-5200, ext. 5444; (913) 242-7429 FAX
Jane Ann Westrum, Library Director
Hours: Mon–Thur 7:45–10:30, Fri 7:45–4:30, Sat noon–5:00, Sun 2:00–10:30; summer hours vary
(university and Baptist history)

Samford University
American Genealogical Society Depository and Headquarters
Harwell Goodwin Davis Library
Special Collection Department
800 Lakeshore Drive
Birmingham, AL 35229
(205) 870-2749
Elizabeth C. Wells, Librarian
Hours: Mon 8:00–9:00, Tue–Fri 8:00–4:30

Seventh Day Baptist Historical Society
3120 Kennedy Road
PO Box 1678
Janesville, WI 53547-1678
(608) 752-5055
Rev. Don A. Sanford, Historian
Pub. *SDBHS Annual Report*, annually

South Carolina Baptist Historical Society
South Carolina Baptist Historical Collection
James B. Duke Library
Furman University
Poinsett Highway
Greenville, SC 29613
(843) 294-2194
J. Glen Clayton, Curator
Hours: Mon–Fri 8:30–4:30, except school holidays, please call before coming
Pub. *Journal of the South Carolina Baptist Historical Society*, annually

Southern Baptist Historical Library and Archives
901 Commerce Street, Suite 400
Nashville, TN 37203-3630
(615) 244-0344
Bill Sumners, Director of Library and Archives
Hours: Mon–Fri 9:00–4:00
Pub. *Baptist History and Heritage* (Baptist historical materials, especially Southern Baptist), quarterly, $10.95 per year subscription

Tennessee Baptist Historical Society
PO Box 347
Brentwood, TN 37027
(615) 373-2255

Texas Baptist Historical Center-Museum
10405 FM 50
Brenham, TX 77833
(831) 836-5117
Paul Sevar, Director
Hours: Wed–Sat 10:00–4:00
free

Texas Baptist Historical Society
Texas Baptist Historical Collection
Southwestern Baptist Theological Seminary
A. Webb Roberts Library
2001 West Seminary Drive
PO Box 22000
Fort Worth, TX 76122-2490
(817) 923-1921, ext. 3330
Dr. Alan J. Lefever, Archivist/Special Collections Librarian
Hours: Mon–Fri 8:00–noon & 1:00–5:00
Pub. *Texas Baptist History*, annually
("We major in historical research, primarily Texas Baptist church history, but do answer some genealogical questions, whenever we can, from our resources.")
$10.00 per year membership; no search fee except cost of materials

Virginia Baptist Historical Society
PO Box 34
University of Richmond
Richmond, VA 23173
(804) 289-8434
Darlene Slater, Research Assistant
Hours: weekdays 9:00–noon & 1:00–4:00 by appointment only
Pub. *Virginia Baptist Register*, annually, $4.50 per year subscription
$10.00 per year membership; research by mail, $22.00 per hour

West Virginia Baptist Historical Society, Inc.
Parchment Valley Conference Center
Rt. 2, Box 304
Ripley, WV 25271
(304) 346-2036
Roscoe C. Keeney, Jr., Archivist
Hours: weekdays by appointment
Pub. *West Virginia Baptist Historical Society News Letter*, semiannually
(depository for West Virginia Baptist history: organizational, churches, clergy, laity and youth; individual files and church files, as well as annual reports, clippings, and library available)
$5.00 per year membership, $100.00 life membership

Brethren

(does not include The United Brethren in Christ, formerly The Church of the United Brethren in Christ [Old Constitution], formerly part of the Church of the United Brethren in

Christ; does not include the former
Evangelical United Brethren Church
[see United Methodist]; see also
Mennonite.)

Archives of the Brethren in Christ Church and Messiah College

Messiah College
Grantham, PA 17027
(717) 691-6048; (717) 691-6042 FAX
E-mail: msider@mcis.messiah.edu
E. Morris Sider, Archivist
Hours: Mon–Fri 8:00–5:00
Pub. *Brethren in Christ History and Life,*
Evangelical Visitor, three times per
year, $10.00 per year subscription
(obituaries, marriages and births from
1885 of people associated with the
Brethren in Christ Church; genealogies
of Brethren in Christ and some
Mennonite families)

The Church of the Brethren General Board

Brethren Historical Library and Archives
1451 Dundee Avenue
Elgin, IL 60120-1694
(847) 742-5100, ext. 294; (847) 742-
6103 FAX
Kenneth M. Shaffer, Jr., Director
Hours: Mon–Fri 9:00–12:00 & 1:00–
4:00
(formerly The German Baptist Brethren;
for Brethren who trace their origins to
Schwarzenau, Germany, in 1708)
genealogical research: $25.00 per hour

Fellowship of Brethren Genealogists

Indiana Section
Timbercrest Home
North Manchester, IN 46962
(219) 982-4732
Keith E. Ross

Fellowship of Brethren Genealogists (Church of the Brethren)

1451 Dundee Avenue
Elgin, IL 60120-1694
(708) 742-5100
Gwendolyn F. Bobb, Executive Director
Hours: Brethren Historical Library and
Archives: Mon–Fri 9:00–12:00 &
1:00–4:00
Pub. *Newsletter, Fellowship of Brethren*
Genealogists, quarterly
("Brethren related to the group founded
1708, Schwarzenau, Germany; there
are many other Brethren groups that
are not in our purview, such as the
United Brethren, about which we often
receive inquiries.")
$10.00 per year membership

Byzantine

(see also Orthodox)

Byzantine Catholic Diocese of Passaic

101 Market Street
Passaic, NJ 07055

Byzantine Catholic Seminary Library

3605 Perrysville Avenue
Pittsburgh, PA 15214
(412) 321-8383
Rev. John S. Custer, S.T.D., Librarian
Hours: by appointment

Byzantine Rite Eparchy of Parma

1900 Carlton Road
Cleveland, OH 44134-3129
Mr. Pataki

Metropolitan Archdiocese of Pittsburgh, Byzantine

Byzantine Catholic World
66 Riverview Avenue
Pittsburgh, PA 15214-2253

Romanian American Heritage Center

2540 Grey Tower Road
Jackson, MI 49201-2208
(517) 522-8260; (517) 522-8236 FAX
http://feefhs.org/ro/frg-rahc.html
Eugene S. Raica, President and Editor
Pub. *Information Bulletin*, bimonthly
(has Andrica collection, from
discontinued *American Romanian*
Review; Romanian/Eastern Orthodox,
Byzantine Rite Catholic)

Catholic

(see Byzantine, Roman Catholic,
Maronite Catholic and Orthodox)

Christian Science

The First Church of Christ, Scientist

Church History, A221
175 Huntington Avenue
Boston, MA 02115
(617) 450-3503
Yvonne C. Fettweis, Manager, Church
History
Hours: 8:00–4:15
(very little vital statistics information)
$30.00 search fees

Church of Christ

Center for Restoration Studies

Brown Library
Abilene Christian University
ACU Station Box 29429
Abilene, TX 79699-9429
(915) 674-3795
Douglas Allen Foster, Ph.D.
Hours: various
("Churches of Christ; Restorationism/
Restitutionism; files on preachers,
churches, missions, etc.")

The Gospel Advocate Archives and Library

The Gospel Advocate Company
1006 Elm Hill Park
Nashville, TN 37210
(615) 254-8781
Hours: by appointment
Pub. *The Gospel Advocate*, monthly,
$14.95 per year subscription
(Restoration Movement/Churches of
Christ)

Church of England

(see Episcopal)

The Church of Jesus Christ of Latter-day Saints

(see Latter-day Saint and Reorganized
Church of Jesus Christ of Latter Day
Saints)

Church of the Brethren

(see Brethren)

Church of the Nazarene

Church of the Nazarene Archives

6401 The Paseo
Kansas City, MO 64131
(816) 333-7000
http://www.nazarene.org/hoo/
archives.html
Stan Ingersol, Ph.D., Denominational
Archivist
Hours: Mon–Fri 8:00–4:30
("Materials on all phases of The Church
of the Nazarene: congregation, district,
international")

Church of the United Brethren in Christ

(see Brethren, United Brethren in Christ
and United Methodist)

Congregational

(see United Church of Christ)

Covenant

Covenant Archives and Historical Library

North Park College
5125 North Spaulding Avenue
Chicago, IL 60625
(773) 244-6224; (773) 267-2362
E-mail: tjohnso1@northpark.edu
Tim Johnson, Archivist
Hours: by appointment

Disciples of Christ

Brite Divinity School Collection
Mary Couts Burnett Library
Texas Christian University
PO Box 298400
Fort Worth, TX 76129
(817) 921-7668; (817) 921-7282 FAX
E-mail: b.olsen@tcu.edu
http://www.library.tcu.edu
Robert A. Olsen, Librarian
(specialty: "Christian Church [Disciples of Christ]")

Disciples of Christ Historical Society
1101 19th Avenue, South
Nashville, TN 37212-2196
(615) 327-1444
May Reed, Assistant to the Director of Library and Archives
Hours: Mon–Fri 8:00–4:30
Pub. *Discipliana*, quarterly
("We are primarily a church archives but have a large amount of congregational information.")
$15.00 per year membership for individuals, $7.50 per year membership for students

Hiram Township Historical Society, Inc.
(Century House Museum, Garfield Road—location)
PO Box 1775 (mailing address)
Hiram, OH 44234
Monica W. Fratus, President
Hours: Hiram College Archives: Mon–Fri 9:00–5:00
Pub. *Newsletter*, quarterly
(specializes in Ohio, Connecticut Western Reserve, Disciples of Christ, Hiram College)
$10.00 per year membership

Eastern Orthodox

(see Orthodox)

Episcopal

Archives of the Diocese of Delaware (Episcopal)
2020 Tatnall Street
Wilmington, DE 19802
(302) 656-5441
Cabell Tennis, Bishop

Archives of the Diocese of West Missouri (Episcopal)
420 West 14th Street
PO Box 413227
Kansas City, MO 64141
(816) 471-6161
Doris M. Anderson, Historiographer

Archives of the Episcopal Diocese of Connecticut
1335 Asylum Avenue
Hartford, CT 06105-2295
(860) 521-8975; (860) 523-1410
E-mail: diocese@tiac.net
The Rev. Dr. Robert G. Carroon, Archivist
Hours: Mon–Fri 8:30–4:30 by appointment
(Episcopal church records from Colonial period to mid-twentieth century)
copies: 25¢ per page

Archives of the Episcopal Diocese of Maine
(address temporarily withheld upon request)

Archives of the Episcopal Diocese of North Carolina
201 Saint Alban's Drive
PO Box 17025
Raleigh, NC 27619
(919) 787-6313
Michelle A. Francis, Archivist

Church Historical Society
Archives of the Episcopal Church, USA
General Convention of the Episcopal Church
606 Ratherview Place
PO Box 2247
Austin, TX 78768-2247
(512) 472-6816
V. Nelle Bellamy, Ph.D., Archivist
Pub. *Anglican and Episcopal History*
(houses records of the Domestic and Foreign Missionary Society)

Episcopal Diocese of California
1055 Taylor Street
San Francisco, CA 94108
Elizabeth Lee Abbott, Archivist
Hours: by appointment

The Diocese of Colorado
1300 Washington
Denver, CO 80203

Diocese of Olympia Archives
Episcopal Church in Western Washington
(1551 Tenth East, Seattle, WA 98102-4298—location)
PO Box 12126 (mailing address)
Seattle, WA 98102-0126
(206) 325-4200; (206) 325-4631 FAX
Diane Wells, Archivist/Records Manager
Hours: Archives: Tue–Thur 9:00–5:00; Office: Mon–Fri 9:00–5:00
(Journals, sacramental records, official records of the diocese; "genealogical requests as time allows")
search fees: by the hour plus costs of copying

Diocese of Vermont
Diocesan Center
5 Rock Point Road
Burlington, VT 05401

Professor R. L. Patterson, Registrar
Hours: 9:30–5:00 (vault is not open to the public)
(archives contain some "parish registers from a few, small churches which are no longer in existence," also "microfilm of old parish registers from active churches around the diocese," copies of which are available through the Family History Library of The Church of Jesus Christ of Latter-day Saints; "with some books of bishops' official acts, etc.")

Episcopal Church, Diocesan Archives
Queen Emma Square
Honolulu, HI 96813
(808) 536-7776
Donald Hart, Episcopal Bishop of Hawaii

Episcopal Diocese of Kentucky
6 Eastover Court
Louisville, KY 40206
(502) 893-2632
Sharon Receveur, Historiographer
Hours: by appointment
(Diocesan records since 1895, office records, diocesan reports, some church records)

Episcopal Diocese of Massachusetts
The Diocesan Library and Archives
138 Tremont Street, Third Floor
Boston, MA 02111
(617) 482-5800, ext. 504; (617) 482-8431 FAX
E-mail: nora.murphy@ecunet.org
Mary Eleanor Murphy, Diocesan Archivist
Hours: winter: Mon–Fri 8:30–4:30; summer: Mon–Fri 8:30–3:30; call for appointment
donation suggested for reference services

Episcopal Diocese of Utah-Resource Center
80 South 300 East
PO Box 3090
Salt Lake City, UT 84110-3090
(801) 322-4131; (801) 322-5096 FAX
Paula C. Madsen, Coordinator
Hours: Mon–Fri 8:30–5:00

Episcopal Diocese of Washington
Washington National Cathedral
Mount Saint Albans
Massachusetts and Wisconsin Avenues, N.W.
Washington, DC 20016-5098
(202) 537-6889
Richard G. Hewlett, Historiographer
(a few twentieth-century parish registers for parishes which are no longer in existence, no staff research services are provided)

Episcopal Diocese of West Virginia
1608 Virginia Street East
Charleston, WV 25311

Saint Anne's Episcopal Church Historical Commission
8 Kirk Street
Lowell, MA 01852
(978) 452-2150
Louise K. Hunt, Chairperson
Hours: Library: Wed 9:00–noon, and by
appointment
search fee $10.00 per hour

Evangelical

(see Lutheran, Protestant, United Church
of Christ and United Methodist)

Evangelical and Reformed

(see United Church of Christ)

Evangelical Covenant

(see Covenant and Lutheran)

Evangelical Lutheran

(see Lutheran)

Evangelical United Brethren

(see United Methodist)

Free Methodist

(see United Methodist)

Free Will Baptist

(see Baptist)

French Protestant

(see Lineage, Hereditary and Patriotic
Societies—Huguenot, Part 4)

Friends

Archives of the New England Yearly Meeting of Friends
Rhode Island Historical Society
121 Hope Street
Providence, RI 02906
(401) 331-8575
Rick Stattler, NEYM Archivist
Hours: Tue–Sat 9:00–5:00, Sun noon–
4:00; appointments required to view
original records
(most records available on microfilm in
the Rhode Island Historical Society
Library)
free admission; research: $25.00 per hour

Baltimore Yearly Meeting of the Religious Society of Friends
Baltimore Monthly Meeting of Friends,
Stony Run
5116 North Charles Street
Baltimore, MD 21210
(410) 435-3773; (410) 435-3779 FAX
Ronald Mattson, Executive Secretary;
Mary Dunlap, Archivist
Hours: 9:00–3:00

National Society, Descendants of Early Quakers
111 Webster Park Avenue
Columbus, OH 43214
Pub. *Plain Language*, semiannually,
$15.00 per year subscription
(genealogy, history, and records of early
Quakers; membership open to men,
women and children who can establish
descent, lineal or collateral, from an
early member of the Society of
Friends throughout the world)
$25.00 non-refundable application fee,
$100.00 life membership, $20.00
junior membership transferrable at age
25 toward life membership

Earlham College
Friends Collection
Lilly Library
West National Road
Richmond, IN 47374
(765) 983-1511
E-mail: tomh@earlham.edu
Thomas D. Hamm, Archivist and Curator
Hours: Mon–Fri 9:00–noon & 1:00–4:00,
some evenings and weekends
(specializes in Friends of Wayne County,
Indiana; Quakers in the midwest, and
Quaker genealogy)

The East Tennessee Society for the Preservation of Friends (Quaker) History
An Affiliate of the East Tennessee
Historical Society
2429 Brook Road
Greenback, TN 37742
Scott Knight, Secretary
$5.00 per year membership for
individuals, $7.00 per year
membership for families, $2.50 per
year membership for students

George Fox College
Quaker Collection
Shambaugh Library
Newberg, OR 97132

Friends General Conference (FGC)
Religious Society of Friends
1216 Arch Street, 2B
Philadelphia, PA 19107
(215) 561-1700
Jennifer Stromsten, Development
Secretary
Pub. *Friends Journal*, twenty times per
year

(does not keep historical records or
archives, but has a bookstore for
people to learn about Quaker history
and heritage)

Friends University Library
Quaker Collection
2100 University Avenue
Wichita, KS 67213-3397
(316) 261-5880
Avis German, Acting Curator
Hours: Mon, Wed & Fri 8:00–4:00

Genealogical Society of Pennsylvania
(see Pennsylvania)

Guilford College
Friends Historical Collection
5800 West Friendly Avenue
Greensboro, NC 27410-4175
(910) 316-2264; (910) 316-2950
Carole M. Treadway, Librarian
Hours: Tue–Fri 9:00–noon & 2:00–5:00
Pub. *The Southern Friend: Journal of the
North Carolina Friends Historical
Society*, semiannually
$15.00 per year membership

Haverford College
Friends Historical Association
Haverford College Library
Haverford, PA 19041-1392
(610) 896-1161; (610) 896-1102 FAX
E-mail: fha@haverford.edu
Ann W. Upton, Office Manager
Pub. *Quaker History*, semiannually
(spring and fall)
(Religious Society of Friends-Quakers)
$15.00 per year membership

Haverford College
The Quaker Collection
Haverford College Library
Haverford, PA 19041-1392
(610) 896-1161; (610) 896-1102 FAX
E-mail: aupton@haverford.edu
http://www.haverford.edu/library/sc
Ann W. Upton, Office Manager
Hours: Mon–Fri 9:00–12:30 & 1:30–
4:30 (holidays & summer till 4:00)
(Religious Society of Friends resources)

Historical Committee of the Yearly Meeting
Rt. 2
Barnesville, OH 43713

Historical Society of Pennsylvania
(see Pennsylvania)

Honey Creek Church Preservation Group
30293 O Avenue
New Providence, IA 50206-8008
(515) 497-5458
Vera Cutler, Historian, Library
Hours: by appointment
(local Iowa history, Quaker records,
genealogy; Honey Creek Friends
Meetinghouse on Registry of National
Historic Places)

Indiana Historical Society
(see Indiana)

Indiana University
Library
Bloomington, IN 47401

Malone College
Quaker Collection
Everett L. Cattell Library
515 25th Street, N.W.
Canton, OH 44709
(330) 471-8317; (330) 454-6977 FAX
Stanford Terhune, Director
Hours: Mon–Thur 8:00 A.M.–11:30 P.M.,
Fri 8:00–10:00, Sat 10:00–10:00, Sun
2:00–10:00
(Ohio Yearly Meeting, Evangelical
Friends Church—Eastern Region)

Maryland State Archives
(see Maryland)

New York Yearly Meeting
Haviland Records Room
Religious Society of Friends
(222 East 16th Street—location)
15 Rutherford Place (mailing address)
New York, NY 10003
(212) 673-6866
Elizabeth H. Moger, Keeper of the
Records
Hours: Wed–Thur 10:00–noon & 1:00–
4:00 by appointment
(minutes and membership records,
constituent meetings; Records Room
collection transferred to Friends
Historical Library, Swarthmore
College, Swarthmore, PA, microfilm
copies available at SUNY Buffalo, the
New York State Library, The New
York Public Library, Rutgers
University, New York Genealogical
and Biographical Society Library, the
Long Island Studies Institute, and
Hofstra University)
research by staff limited to 1 hour
($20.00), referred thereafter to outside
genealogists; $5.00 per visit

Newport Historical Society
(see Rhode Island)

Ohio Historical Society
(see Ohio)

Pendle Hill Library
Pendle Hill
Wallingford, PA 19086

William Penn College
Quaker Collection
Wilcox Library
North Market Street
201 Trueblood Avenue
Oskaloosa, IA 52577
(515) 673-1096
Hours: Mon–Thur 8:00–10:00, Fri 8:00–
5:00, Sat 9:00–5:00, Sun 12:00–10:00

State Library of Pennsylvania
(see Pennsylvania)

Quaker Queries
323 Cedarcrest Court, East
PO Box 779
Napavine, WA 98565-0779
(360) 262-3300
E-mail: rubym@localaccess.com
http://www.localaccess.com/rubym
Ruby Simonson McNeill
Pub. *Quaker Queries*, irregularly, $7.75
postpaid per issue

Quaker Yeomen
1190 N.W. 183rd Avenue
Beaverton, OR 97006
(503) 629-9047
E-mail: psl@aracnet.com
Patti Smith Lamb, Editor and Publisher
Pub. *Quaker Yeomen*, quarterly, $18.00
per year U.S. subscription, $24.00 per
year foreign subscription

Rokeby Museum
(Route 7—location)
RD 1, Box 1540
Ferrisburg, VT 05456
(802) 877-3406
Jane Williamson, Director
Hours: Tue–Fri 9:00–5:00
Pub. *Messenger*, quarterly
(Quakerism, abolition, agricultural
history, and Robinson family)
$15.00 per year for individuals, $25.00
per year for families, $10.00 per year
membership for students or senior
citizens

Swarthmore College
Friends Historical Library of Swarthmore
College
500 College Avenue
Swarthmore, PA 19081-1399
(610) 328-8496; (610) 328-7329 FAX
E-mail: friends@swarthmore.edu
Mary Ellen Chijioke, Curator
Hours: Mon–Fri 8:30–4:30, Sat (when
the college is in session) 9:00–noon
(closed 1 Jan, 4 Jul, Thanksgiving
weekend & Christmas week)
Pub. *Guide to Manuscript Collections*
(Quaker history and genealogy)
SASE with inquiries

University of Illinois
(see Illinois)

Whittier College
Quaker Collection
Wardman Library
Whittier, CA 90608
(562) 907-4247
Hours: 8:00–4:30

**Wrightsboro Quaker Community
Foundation, Inc.**
633 Hemlock Drive
Thomson, GA 30824
(404) 595-5584

German Reformed

(see United Church of Christ)

Greek Orthodox

(see Orthodox)

Harmonist

Harmonie Associates, Inc.
Old Economy Village
14th and Church Streets
Ambridge, PA 15003
(724) 266-1803
Raymond V. Shepherd, Jr., Director
(Harmonists, a German, Christian
communal society, 1785–1905)

**Historic Harmony/Harmony
Museum**
218 Mercer Street
PO Box 524
Harmony, PA 16037
(724) 452-7341
Kathy Luck, Administrator
Hours: Tue–Fri & Sun 1:00–4:00
Pub. *Newsletter*, monthly
(emphasis on Germans, Harmony
Society, Mennonites; "Harmony was
first home (1804–1814) of communal
Harmony Society of German
immigrants, subsequently was a
Mennonite community for much of the
19th century.")
$15.00–$250.00 membership fees

Hoffmanite

(see United Christian Church)

Huguenot

(see Lineage, Hereditary and Patriotic
Societies, Part 4)

Hutterite

Hutterite Genealogy Cross-index
http://feefhs.org/hut/indexhut.html
(Hutterian Brethren, 1755-1879; links to
other sites)

Islamic

**American Institute of Islamic
Studies**
Muslim Bibliographic Center
PO Box 100398
Denver, CO 80250

(303) 936-0108
Charles L. Geddes, Director

Islamic Center of New York
Mosque of New York
1711 Third Avenue
New York, NY 10029
Pub. *Bulletin*, quarterly, contribution
(non-ethnic, non-racial)

Jewish

(see Ethnic Archives, Libraries and
Societies)

Latter-day Saint (Mormon)

(see also Reorganized Church of Jesus
Christ of Latter Day Saints)

Brigham Young University
Hawaii Campus
Joseph F. Smith Library
55-220 Kulanui Street
Laie, HI 96744
(808) 293-3878; (808) 293-3850
(Director); (808) 293-3877 FAX
Rex Frandsen, Director
Hours: Mon–Thur 7:00 A.M.–midnight,
Fri 7:00–6:00, Sat 10:00–9:00
Pub. *Pacific Studies* (emphasis on Pacific
islands and Mormonism),
semiannually
$5.00 per year membership

Early Mormon Research Institute
PO Box 2650
Salt Lake City, UT 84110-2650
Pub. *The Nauvoo Journal*, quarterly,
$18.00 per year subscription

**Family History Library of The
Church of Jesus Christ of Latter-day
Saints**
Genealogical Society of Utah
35 North West Temple
Salt Lake City, UT 84150
(801) 240-2331; (801) 240-5551
http://www.lds.org/
Welcome_to_FamHist/
Welcome_to_FamHist.html
Jimmy B. Parker, Manager
Hours: Mon 7:30 A.M.–6:00 P.M., Tue–
Sat 7:30 A.M.–10:00 P.M.
(The Genealogical Society of Utah is the
acquisitions arm of the Family History
Library. Membership is limited to
employees of the Church's
corporation. No individual research
services are provided by the Society.
At the present time Church policy is
opposed to commercial publication of
the names and mailing addresses of
the various branch libraries [Family
History Centers] throughout the world,
but has released the phone numbers of
selected centers, which are included
below in the state-by-state listings. A
partial list of centers is available upon
request from the Family History
Library. The location of the nearest

library, where microfilm copies of the
Family History Library's holdings can
be viewed, may be obtained by
phoning local LDS church
representatives, usually listed in the
yellow pages of the phone book.
Accredits professional genealogists.)

**Historical Department, Church of
Jesus Christ of Latter-day Saints**
50 East North Temple Street, East Wing
Salt Lake City, UT 84150
(801) 240-2745 (Library—Archives
Division)
Christine Cox, Director, Library Division
Hours: Mon–Fri 8:00–4:30
(*historical*, not genealogical focus; do
not confuse with the Family History
Library)

Mormon Historical Association
PO Box 7010, University Station
Brigham Young University
Provo, UT 84602
Pub. *Journal of Mormon History*,
annually

Pioneer Genealogy Society
PO Box 11488
Salt Lake City, UT 84147
Michel L. Call, President
(specializes in royal ancestry,
Mayflower, New England colonial and
pre-colonial, Mormon pioneer
ancestry)
$2.00 plus SASE for list of colonists
with royal descent and price list for
indexes and other services

Tracing Mormon Pioneers
http://www.vii.com/ nelsonb/pioneer.htm
(emigration card index, handcart
companies, Mormon emigrant ships,
pioneer companies, etc.)

University of Utah Marriott Library
Special Collections
Salt Lake City, UT 84112
(801) 581-8864 (Manuscripts); (801)
581-8863 (Western Americana)
E-mail:
gthompso@alexandria.lib.utah.edu
http://www.lib.utah.edu/spc/spc.html
Dr. Gregory Thompson, Curator; Nancy
Young, Head, Manuscripts; Walter
Jones, Head, Western Americana
(manuscripts, books, periodicals, etc., on
Utah, the Mormons and the West)

Lutheran

(see also Mennonite)

Archives, North Carolina Synod
Evangelical Lutheran Church in America
(ELCA)
1988 Lutheran Synod Drive
Salisbury, NC 28144-5700
(704) 633-4861
Pastor Karl M. Park
Hours: Tue & Thur 9:30–noon, and by
appointment

(Lutheran congregation records, North
Carolina and Tennessee synod records,
all records filed by church categories
rather than family names)
search fee: initially free, detailed at
$15.00 per hour; photocopies 25¢ per
page

**Archives of the Kentucky-Indiana
Synod**
3733 North Meridian Street
Indianapolis, IN 46208

**Archives of the Maryland Synod
Church in America**
7604 York Road
Towson, MD 21204

Concordia Historical Institute
The Lutheran Church—Missouri Synod
801 DeMun Avenue
Saint Louis, MO 63105
(314) 505-7900; (314) 505-7901 FAX
E-mail: chi@trucom.com
http://www.chi.lcms.org/
Rev. Daniel Preus, Director
Hours: Mon–Fri 8:30–4:30
Pub. *Concordia Historical Institute
Quarterly*
(emphasis on Lutheran and German-
American records; "We can help
people determine the best places to
check for church records, family
history, Lutheran related.")
$25.00 per year membership; loan of
materials by mail: $20.00; research:
first half-hour free for members and
non-members, second half-hour free
for members and $10.00 for non-
members, each additional hour $20.00
for members and $30.00 for non-
members; admission free for members
and $10.00 per day for non-members;
photocopies: 15¢ per page for
members and 20¢ for non-members,
up to 149 pages, 30¢ per page
thereafter for members and 40¢ for
non-members

**Evangelical Lutheran Church in
America**
(5400 Milton Parkway, Rosemont, IL—
location)
8765 West Higgins Road (mailing
address)
Chicago, IL 60631-4198
(773) 380-2818
E-mail: archives@elca.org
http://www.elca.org/os/archives/
intro.html
Elisabeth Wittman, Director for Archives
Hours: Mon–Fri 8:30–5:00 (advance
appointment required)
Pub. *ELCA Archives Network News*, two
times per year, available on request
(church formed 1 Jan 1988 by the merger
of the Lutheran Church in America,
the American Lutheran Church and the
Association of Evangelical Lutheran
Churches; specialty in immigration
and ethnic history)

genealogical research: $20.00 per hour, limit two hours

Evangelical Lutheran Synod Historical Society
6 Browns Court
Mankato, MN 56001-6121
(507) 388-5969
Prof. Norman Holte, President and Archivist
Hours: Mon & Wed–Thur 9:00–11:00 A.M.
Pub. *Oak Leaves*, quarterly
$15.00 per year membership

Folke Bernadette Memorial Library
Gustavus Adolphus College
Saint Peter, MN 56082
(507) 933-7572
Hours: 8:00 A.M.–midnight
(includes church records of five earlier conferences of the Lutheran Church, basically those based in Minnesota)

Freistadt Historical Society
Trinity Lutheran Church
10729 West Freistadt Road
Mequon, WI 53092
(414) 242-0653
Leroy Boehlke, Vice President
Hours: by appointment
(Lutheran and Pomeranian genealogy)

The Georgia Salzburger Society
2980 Ebenezer Road
Rincon, GA 31326-3716
(912) 754-7001
Frank L. Perry, Jr., President
Hours: 12 March and Labor Day
Pub. *The Georgia Salzburger Society Newsletter* (perpetuates the memory of Lutherans who emigrated from Salzburg and Germany from 1734–1752 to the Colony of Georgia, and updates the genealogy of their descendants; settled by General Edward Oglethorpe thirty miles north of Savannah on the Savannah River as a buffer with the Uchee Indians)

Indiana District Archives
South Barr Street
Fort Wayne, IN 46802
(Missouri Synod)

Luther College Archives
Preus Library
Decorah, IA 52101
(319) 387-1805
Shan Thomas, Archivist
Hours: Mon–Fri 1:30–5:00, and by appointment
(specializes in Luther College and Norwegian Synod Records)

Lutheran Archives Center at Philadelphia
Krauth Memorial Library
Lutheran Theological Seminary
7301 Germantown Avenue
Philadelphia, PA 19119-1794

(215) 248-6383 (long distance calls cannot be returned); (215) 248-4577 FAX
E-mail: luthlib@ltsp.edu
John E. Peterson, Curator
Hours: by appointment
Pub. *The Reporter* (a non-genealogical newsletter), occasionally, $10.00 donation for subscription
(regional archival unit of the Evangelical Lutheran Church in America (New England, upstate New York, New Jersey, and roughly the eastern third of Pennsylvania—ELCA Region Seven), housing records from defunct congregations or those few congregations which have chosen to deposit them in the center)
search fee: $18.00 for the first hour, $15.00 for each additional hour (extremely limited budget and time for research); access fee: $5.00

Lutheran Church Archives of Metropolitan New York
Wagner College Library
Staten Island, NY 10301
(516) 271-2466

Lutheran Historical Society
(address withheld upon request)
(no archives and no library)

The Lutheran Historical Society of Eastern Pennsylvania
(Krauth Memorial Library, Lutheran Archives Center at Philadelphia— business office location)
7301 Germantown Avenue
Philadelphia, PA 19119-1794
(215) 248-4656; (215) 248-4577 FAX
Dr. David Warfluft, Librarian
Hours: Mon–Fri 9:00–9:00, Sat 9:00–4:00
Pub. *The Periodical*, semiannually (April and October)
(has no records and no staff and can provide no genealogical services, for which contact Lutheran Archives Center at Philadelphia)
$7.50 per year membership for individuals

Lutheran Theological Seminary
A. R. Wentz Library
Gettysburg, PA 17325
Sara Mummert
(some data about Lutheran records in central Pennsylvania; library not open to genealogists; microfilm copies of the records are available through the Family History Library of The Church of Jesus Christ of Latter-day Saints)

Perry County Lutheran Historical Society, Inc.
H.C.R. 61, Box 187
Altenburg, MO 63732
(573) 824-5542
Leonard A. Kuehnert, President

(synod has its roots in the Saxon Immigration to Perry County in 1839; Altenburg has the first Lutheran seminary building [now a museum] west of the Mississippi River)

University of New Orleans
Earl K. Long Library/Louisiana and Special Collections
Lakefront Campus
New Orleans, LA 70148
(504) 280-6543
http://www.uno.edu/welcome.shtml
Florence M. Jumonville, Head of Louisiana and Special Collections
Hours: Louisiana and Special Collections: Mon–Fri 8:00–4:30, Sat (when classes are in session) 10:00–4:00 (some collections available by appointment only)
(specializes in Lutheran records, ethnic groups of New Orleans, preservation groups, Louisiana Supreme Court legal archives, business records, Orleans Parish School Board records, records of civic organizations)

Wartburg Theological Seminary
333 Wartburg Place
Dubuque, IA 52001
Robert C. Wiederaenders, Archivist
(microfilm copies of records of dissolved congregations)

Wisconsin Evangelical Lutheran Synod (WELS) Historical Institute
2929 North Mayfair Road
Milwaukee, WI 53222
(414) 256-3201
Dr. James G. Kiecker
Hours: by appointment
Pub. *Wels Historical Institute Journal*, two times per year

Maronite Catholic

Saint Ephrem Educational Center
1555 South Meridian Road
Youngstown, OH 44511
(330) 792-1532
Helen Catherman, Librarian
Pub. *Saint Ephrem Quarterly*

Mennonite

Along the Galician Grapevine
PO Box 194
Butterfield, MN 56120-0194
(507) 956-5815
E-mail: Mikeaf@mnic.net
http://feefhs.org/gal/aga/frg-aga.htm
Glen Linscheid, Editor
Hours: 8:00 A.M.–10:00 P.M.
Pub. *Along the Galician Grapevine*, annually (December), no subscriptions available, examination copy for LSASE

(lists births, deaths, marriages, and family reunions for the dispersed descendants of the 1880s Mennonite emigrants to North America from the Austrian Crownland of Galicia, at times referred to as Kleinpolen in the German; 17,000-entry database on the surnames Bachmann, Bergthold, Brubacher, Ewy, Forrer Hubin, Jotter, Kintzi, Klein, Linscheid, Merk, Miller, Rupp, Schmidt and Stauffer)

Center for Mennonite Brethren Studies

4824 East Butler
Fresno, CA 93727-5097
(209) 453-2225; (209) 452-1757 FAX
E-mail: kennsrem@fresno.edu
http://www.fresno.edu/cmbs
Kevin Enns-Rempel, Archivist
Hours: Mon–Fri 8:00–noon & 1:00–5:00
Pub. *California Mennonite Historical Society Bulletin*, semiannually
$25.00 per year membership

Center for Mennonite Brethren Studies

Tabor College
400 South Jefferson
Hillsboro, KS 67063
(316) 947-3121, ext. 342; (316) 947-3121, ext. 318
Peggy Goertzen, Director
Hours: Mon–Fri 9:00–noon & 1:30–4:00, and by appointment
Pub. *Newsletter*, annually
("Mennonite Brethren historical records: congregational,conference, photographs, manuscripts, as well as materials on Mennonites in general and Germans from Russia, also strong collection of Marion County, Kansas records.")

Centre For Mennonite Brethren Studies

J. A. Toews Historical Collection
(204) 669-6575, ext. 245; (204) 654-1865 FAX
E-mail:
CmbsArchives@CdnMBConf.ca;
adueck@CdnMBConf.ca (Director)
http://www.cdnmbconf.ca/mb/cmbs.htm
Abe Dueck, Director
Pub. *Mennonite Historian*, quarterly, published jointly with the Mennonite Historical Centre, $8.00 (Canadian) per year subscription in the Canada, $8.00 (U.S.) per year subscription in the U.S.

Germantown Mennonite Historic Trust

6133 Germantown Avenue
Philadelphia, PA 19144
(215) 843-0943; (215) 843-6263
Mr. Galen Horst-Martz, Executive Director

Hours: Tue–Fri 9:00–3:00 by appointment only
Pub. *Friends of Germantown* (primarily relating to those families who had some connection with the Germantown Mennonite congregation), three times per year
$25.00 per year contribution for membership

Historical Committee and Archives of the Mennonite Church

1700 South Main Street
Goshen, IN 46526
(219) 535-7477; (219) 535-7293 FAX
E-mail: ohnes@goshen.edu
http://www.goshen.edu/mcarchives
John E. Sharp, Director; Dennis Stoesz, Archivist
Hours: Mon–Fri 8:00–noon & 1:00–5:00
Pub. *Mennonite Historical Bulletin*, quarterly, $25.00 per year subscription

Illinois Mennonite Historical and Genealogical Society

State Route 16
PO Box 819
Metamora, IL 61548-0819
(309) 367-2551; (815) 796-2918 (President)
Edwin J. Stalter, President
Hours: Apr–Oct: Fri & Sat 10:00–4:00, Sun 1:30–4:30
Pub. *Mennonite Heritage*, quarterly; *Illinois Mennonite Heritage Newsletter*, semiannually
$10.00 per year membership for individuals

Kidron Community Historical Society

Kidron-Sonnenberg Heritage Center
(13153 Emerson Road—location)
PO Box 234
Kidron, OH 44636-0234
(330) 857-9111; (330) 857-1475 (Director)
E-mail: bruce—i-db@juno.com (Director)
http://www.bright.net/~swisstea/
Bruce Detweiler Breckbill, Director
Hours: summer: Tue, Thur & Sat noon–4:00; winter: Thur & Sat noon–4:00
Pub. *Bit o' Vit*, quarterly
(access to over 500,000 names in different databases plus many books, primarily Swiss Mennonite, German/Russian Mennonite, and Amish in origin)
$10.00 per year regular membership for individuals, $15.00 per year regular membership for couples, $35.00 per year membership for organizations; $150.00 life membership for individuals; search fee: $1.00 per page printout plus donation for search time

Lancaster Mennonite Historical Society

2215 Millstream Road
Lancaster, PA 17602-1499
(717) 393-9745
David J. Rempel Smucker, Genealogist; Lloyd Zeager, Librarian
Hours: Tue–Sat 8:30–4:30
Pub. *Pennsylvania Mennonite Heritage* (illustrated journal), quarterly; *Mirror* (newsletter), bimonthly
(Mennonite and Amish information)
$25.00 per year membership

Masthof Press and Bookstore

Rt. 1, Box 20, Mill Road
Morgantown, PA 19543-9701
(610) 286-0258; (610) 286-6860 FAX
E-mail: masthof@ptd.net; mefamhis@ptd.net
Lois Ann Mast, Publisher
Hours: Mon–Sat 9:00–5:00
Pub. *Mennonite Family History* (Mennonite, Anabaptism, Amish and Brethren; genealogy and family history), quarterly, $18.00 per year subscription, $34.00 for two years

Menno Simons Historical Library

Eastern Mennonite College and Seminary
Harrisonburg, VA 22801-2462
(540) 432-4178
Lois B. Bowman, Associate Director
Hours: during regular school sessions: Mon–Fri 10:00–noon & 1:00–5:00, Sat 10:00–1:00; summer: Mon–Fri 10:00–noon & 1:00–5:00
(including Anabaptist, Mennonite and local Virginia materials; Mennonite and local Germanic genealogy; local Lutheran and Reformed Church records; material on Pennsylvania, Maryland,West Virginia and Ohio)
donations accepted

Mennonite Heritage Centre

MHC Library and Archives
(204) 888-6781; (204) 831-5675 FAX
E-mail: lklippen@mbnet.mb.ca; aredek@mbnet.mb.ca
http://www.mbnet.mb.ca/~lklippen/
Lawrence Klippenstein, Director; Alf Redekopp, Archivist
Hours: daily 8:30–5:00
Pub. *Mennonite Historian*, quarterly, published jointly with the Centre for Mennonite Brethren Studies, $8.00 (Canadian) per year subscription in the Canada, $8.00 (U.S.) per year subscription in the U.S.

Mennonite Heritage Museum

200 North Poplar
PO Box 231
Goessel, KS 67053
(316) 367-8200
Kristine Schmucker, Director/Curator

Hours: May–Sept: Tue–Fri 10:00–5:00, Sat–Sun 1:00–5:00; Oct–Dec & Mar–Apr: Tue–Sun 1:00–4:00
Pub. *The Heritage Newsletter*, semiannually
$10.00 per year membership for individuals, $25.00 per year membership for families, $50.00 per year Contributing membership, $250.00 life membership; $2.50 admission for adults

Mennonite Historians of Eastern Pennsylvania
565 Yoder Road, Box 82
Harleysville, PA 19438
(215) 256-3020; (215) 256-3023 FAX
E-mail: mennhist@pond.com
http://www.pond.com/~mennhist
Joel D. Alderfer, Librarian
Hours: Tue–Fri 10:00–5:00, Thur 7:00 P.M.-10:00 P.M.
Pub. *MHEP Newsletter/Bulletin*, quarterly
(local Mennonite history, Pennsylvania-German studies, genealogy and local history of Bucks and Montgomery counties, Pennsylvania)
$25.00 per year membership for individuals (includes 10% discount on book sales and on research fees)

Mennonite Historical Library
Goshen College
Goshen, IN 46526
(219) 535-7418; (219) 535-7438 FAX
E-mail: anetss@goshen.edu
John D. Roth, Director
Hours: Mon–Fri 8:00–5:00, Sat 9:00–1:00
Pub. *Mennonite Quarterly Review* (a scholarly historical publication), $24.00 per year subscription
(strong in genealogy of Amish and Mennonite families from Switzerland, Germany, The Netherlands, West Prussia and Russia, U.S., European and Canadian records)
$30.00 per year membership in Mennonite Historical Society includes periodical

Mennonite Historical Library
Bluffton College
Bluffton, OH 45817-1195
(419) 358-3365
Ann Hilty, Librarian
Hours: Mon–Fri 1:00–5:00 (call before travelling to the library)

Mennonite Historical Society of Iowa
Mennonite Historical Museum
411 Ninth Street
PO Box 576
Kalona, IA 52247
(319) 656-3271
Lester J. Miller, President
Hours: Apr–Oct: 10:00–4:00; Nov: 11:00–3:00

Pub. *Iowa Mennonite Historical Reflections*, quarterly, $3.00 per year subscription

Mennonite Library and Archives
Bethel College
300 East 27th
North Newton, KS 67117-9989
(316) 284-5304
E-mail: mla@bethelks.edu
http://www.bethelks.edu/services/mla/
John D. Thiesen, Archivist
Hours: Mon–Fri 10:00–12:00 & 1:00–5:00
Pub. *Mennonite Life*, quarterly, $18.00 per year subscription, $27.00 for two-year subscription

Molotschna Villager
4254 West Camino Acequila
Phoenix, AZ 85051
(602) 934-7972
http://feefhs.org/men/frg-mv.html
Hildegard Wasnick, Village Coordinator
Pub. *Mennonite German-Russian Newsletter*

Oregon Mennonite Historical and Genealogical Society
675 Elma Avenue, S.E.
Salem, OR 97301

Methodist
(see Lutheran and United Methodist)

Methodist Episcopal
(see United Methodist)

Methodist Protestant
(see United Methodist)

Moravian

Moravian Archives
4 East Bank Street
Winston-Salem, NC 27101
(910) 722-1742
Dr. C. Daniel Crews, Archivist
Hours: weekdays 9:30–12:00 & 1:30–4:30
Pub. *Annotations*, semiannually, distributed to Friends who give to the Archives

The Moravian Archives
41 West Locust Street
Bethlehem, PA 18018
(610) 866-3255
Vernon H. Nelson, Archivist; Albert H. Frank, Assistant Archivist
Hours: Mon–Fri 8:00–noon & 1:00–4:00
fee for staff research or German translation: $20.00 per hour

The Moravian Heritage Society
31910 Road 160
Visalia, CA 93292-9044

(209) 798-1490; (209) 798-1922 FAX
Thomas Hrncinik, A.G., and Helene Cincebeaux, Co-directors
Pub. *Morava Krasna*, quarterly
$10.00 per year membership

Moravian Historical Society
Whitefield House
214 East Center Street
Nazareth, PA 18064
(610) 759-5070 phone & FAX
Susan M. Dreydoppel, Executive Director
Hours: Moravian Historical Museum: Mon–Sun 1:00–4:00, and by appointment
Pub. *Transactions of the Moravian Historical Society*, biennially (Oct of even years); *Moravian Historian*, quarterly
$15.00 per year membership

Moravian Museums and Tours
66 West Church Street
Bethlehem, PA 18018
(610) 867-0173; (610) 694-0960 FAX
Rebecca Hordis, Collections Manager
Hours: Mon–Fri 9:00–5:00
Pub. *Moravian Museum of Bethlehem News*, quarterly

Tuscarawas County Chapter OGS
Tuscarawas County Genealogical Society, Inc.
(Bonifay Building, 310 Grant Street, Dennison—location)
PO Box 141 (mailing address)
New Philadelphia, OH 44663-0141
(740) 269-2602
Keith A. Schaar, President
Hours: May–Aug: Tue–Sat 11:00–3:00; Sept–Apr: Tue, Thur & Sat 11:00–3:00
Pub. *Tuscarawas County Pioneer Footprints*, quarterly (February, May, August, November)
(Tuscarawas County and surrounding counties; Moravian history and ancestry)
$10.00 per year membership for individuals, $12.00 per year membership for couples, $150.00 life membership for individuals, $200.00 life membership for couples, $2.00 per day library charge for non-members over 18

Mormon
(see Latter-day Saint)

Muslim
(see Islamic)

Nazarene
(see Church of the Nazarene)

Orthodox

(see also Byzantine)

**American Carpatho-Russian
Orthodox Diocese**
312 Garfield Street
Johnstown, PA 15906
(814) 536-4207
Msgr. John Yurisin, Diocesan Vicar
Hours: 9:00–5:00
Pub. *The Church Messenger*, biweekly,
$12.00 per year subscription

**Antiochian Orthodox Christian
Archdiocese of North America**
358 Mountain Road
Englewood, NJ 07631
(201) 871-1355
The Very Reverend George S. Corey,
Vicar General
Hours: 9:00–5:30
Pub. *The Word*, ten times per year
(monthly, except July and Aug), $3.00
per issue, $20.00 per year subscription
in the U.S. and Canada, $26.00 per
year foreign subscription

**Byelorussian Autocephalic Orthodox
Church**
3517 West 25th Street
Cleveland, OH 44109
(216) 351-3730
Konstantin Kalosha, Administrator
Pub. *Holas Carkvy*, semiannually

Diocese of Saint Nicholas
2245 West Rice Street
Chicago, IL 60622

Eparchy of Van Nuys
5335 Sepulveda Boulevard
Van Nuys, CA 91411

**Greek Orthodox Archdiocese, North
and South America**
10 East 79th Street
New York, NY 10021
(212) 628-2500
Miss Niki Calle, Archivist
Pub. *Orthodox Observer*, biweekly

**Holy Cross Romanian Orthodox
Church**
950 Maple Street
Hermitage, PA 16146
(724) 346-3151
Rev. Fr. Nathaniel Popp, Pastor

Orthodox Church in America
(6850 Northern Boulevard, Route 25A,
Oyster Bay Cove—location)
PO Box 675 (mailing address)
Syosset, NY 11791
(516) 922-0550
Alexis Liberovsky, Archivist
Hours: Mon–Fri 9:00–5:00 by
appointment
("We have in our repository the records
of the central administration of the

Orthodox Church in America dating
back to 1840, as well as about thirty
collections of personal papers of
various bishops, clergy and other
active churchmen. Also included in
our collection are the records of a few
church related organizations as well as
periodicals, books and video tapes.
However, genealogical material in our
collection is limited since metrical
books (church records, baptisms,
funerals, weddings), with a few
exceptions, are usually kept and
maintained by the local parishes. We
are, however, able to provide
genealogicaldata on our clergy. I
would be able also to refer researchers
to the appropriate parish.")

**Saint Josaphat's Ukrainian Catholic
Seminary**
201 Taylor Street, N.E.
Washington, DC 20017-1097
(202) 529-1177
Msgr. John Bura, Rector
Hours: 9:00–5:00

Saint Mary Protectress
1745 Washington Avenue
Bronx, NY 10457

Ukrainian Catholic Diocese
161 Glenbrook Road
Stamford, CT 06902

**Ukrainian Catholic Eparchy of
Philadelphia**
815 North Franklin Street
Philadelphia, PA 19123

Presbyterian

The Amistad Research Center
Tilton Memorial Hall, Tulane University
6823 Saint Charles Avenue
New Orleans, LA 70118-5698
(504) 865-5535; (504) 862-3222; (504)
865-5580 FAX
E-mail: amistad@tulane.edu;
ddevore@tulane.edu
http://www.arc.tulane.edu
Donald DeVore, Executive Director
Hours: Mon–Sat 9:00–4:30
Pub. *Amistad Reports*, quarterly
(African-Americans, Native Americans,
Hispanics, Asian-Americans; houses
American Home Missionary Society
Collection; "Genealogical reference
books only.")

Columbia Theological Seminary
J. B. Campbell Library
701 Columbia Drive
Decatur, GA 30030
(404) 378-8821
Hours: Mon–Thur 8:30–10:00, Fri 8:30–
6:00, Sat 9:00–5:00
(Southern Presbyterianism; "We have
almost nothing to help with

genealogical research; our collection is
for ministerial training.")

Hanover College
Duggan Library
PO Box 287
Hanover, IN 47243-0287
(812) 866-7164; (812) 866-7172 FAX
Dennis K. Kovener, Assistant Librarian
Hours: Mon–Thur 7:45 A.M.–11:00 P.M.,
Fri 7:45 A.M.–10:00 P.M., Sat 10:00
A.M.–10:00 P.M., Sun 1:00 P.M.–11:00
P.M.
(records of the Presbyterian Church in
Indiana)

**Historical Foundation of the
Cumberland Presbyterian Church
and the Cumberland Presbyterian
Church in America**
1978 Union Avenue
Memphis, TN 38104
(901) 276-8602; (901) 272-3913 FAX
E-mail: skg@cumberland.org
http://www.cumberland.org/center/
hfcpc.htm
Susan Knight Gore, Director
Hours: by appointment
(Cumberland Presbyterian, 1810 to the
present)

**North Carolina Presbyterian
Historical Society**
Trinity Presbyterian Church
PO Box 794
Starksville, MS 39760-0794
(601) 323-9340
James D. MacLeod, Jr.
Pub. *Sketches of North Carolina*

Presbyterian Church Archives
Union Theological Seminary in Virginia
3401 Brook Road
Richmond, VA 23227
(804) 355-0671; (804) 378-4375 FAX
William A. Smith, Assistant Archivist
Hours: Mon–Fri 8:30 A.M.–11:00 P.M.,
Sat 8:30–5:00 (when school is in
session, except closed for
Thanksgiving, Christmas and Easter
vacations); summer: Mon–Fri 8:30–
5:00, Sat 8:30–1:00
(microfilm records of local Presbyterian
churches in Virginia, as of 1985)

**Presbyterian Church (U.S.A.),
Department of History (Montreat)**
318 Georgia Terrace (at Assembly Drive)
PO Box 849
Montreat, NC 28757
(704) 669-7061
William B. Bynum, Assistant Director
for Reference
Hours: Mon–Fri 8:30–4:30, except
holidays
(specializes in Presbyterian Church
records from southern states;
organization formerly known as

Historical Foundation of the Presbyterian and Reformed Churches)
$40.00 per year membership; research: $5.00 per day in person fornonmembers

Presbyterian Historical Society

Reference Services
425 Lombard Street
Philadelphia, PA 19147
(215) 627-1852
Hours: Mon–Fri 8:30–4:30 by appointment (except holidays)
Pub. *American Presbyterians, Journal of Presbyterian History*, quarterly
("The Society cannot do genealogical searches for patrons. We do assist visiting researchers and can refer inquirers to individuals familiar with our records, who search for a fee.")
$15.00 per year membership

Presbytery of Utah

Presbyterian Church
175 West 200 South, #3006
Salt Lake City, UT 84101

San Francisco Theological Seminary

Library
San Anselmo, CA 94960

Protestant

Billy Graham Center

Wheaton College
500 East College Avenue
Wheaton, IL 60187-5593
(630) 752-5910 (The Archives)
Janyce Nasgowitz, Reference Archivist
Hours: Mon–Fri 10:00–6:00, Sat 10:00–2:00
Pub. *Centerline* (general); *Witness* (The Archives); *Resource Notes* (Library)
(Archives focus on the history of Protestant missions and non-denominational evangelism; "Personnel files of missionary organizations.")

Protestant Episcopal

(see also Episcopal)

Dalcho Historical Society of the Protestant Episcopal Church in South Carolina

1020 King Street
PO Box 2127
Charleston, SC 29403
(843) 722-4075

Nevada Historical Society

1650 North Virginia Street
Reno, NV 89503
(702) 688-1190
Lee Mortensen, Librarian
Hours: Tue–Sat noon–4:00
Pub. *Nevada Historical Society Quarterly*

(Nevada and the Great Basin; "we are not a genealogical library, but we do have a lot of local history material.")
$25.00 per year membership

Quaker

(see Friends)

Reformed

(see also Evangelical, Presbyterian and Mennonite)

Calvin College

Christian Reformed Church
3201 Burton, S.E.
Grand Rapids, MI 49506
(616) 957-6000
(Dutch-American settlement in western Michigan, church history)

Historical Society Reformed Church of America

Gardner A. Sage Library
21 Seminary Place
New Brunswick, NJ 08901
(732) 246-1779 (Archives)
Russell L. Gasero, Editor
Hours: by appointment only
Pub. *Dutch American Genealogist*, quarterly, $15.00 per year subscription

Reorganized Church of Jesus Christ of Latter Day Saints

Reorganized Church of Jesus Christ of Latter Day Saints Archives

River and Lexington Streets
PO Box 1059
Independence, MO 64051
(816) 833-1000, ext. 2457
E-mail: bernauer@rlds.org
http://www.rlds.ort
Barbara Bernauer, Assistant Archivist
Hours: Mon–Fri 8:00–5:00, Sat 9:00–1:00
(specializes in RLDS history, RLDS members only)

Roman Catholic

(Roman Catholic church records useful to genealogical searchers of baptisms, marriages, and funerals are generally kept in theparishes or centralized in the chancery office of the appropriate diocese or archdiocese.)

American Catholic Historical Society

PO Box 84
Philadelphia, PA 19105
(215) 925-5752
Hours: Philadelphia Archdiocesan Historical Research Center: Mon–Fri 9:00–4:00

Pub. *American Catholic Historical Society Records*, quarterly

Association of Catholic Diocesan Archivists

15151 San Fernando Mission Boulevard
Mission Hills, CA 91345
(818) 365-1501; (818) 361-3276 FAX
Msgr. Francis J. Weber, President
Hours: Mon–Fri 8:30–4:30
ACDA Bulletin, quarterly, $15.00 per year subscription

Augustine Fathers

Province of Our Mother of Good Counsel
20300 Governors Highway
Olympia Field, IL 60461

Boston College

The John J. Burns Library
140 Commonwealth Avenue
Chestnut Hill, MA 02167
(617) 552-3282 (main number); (617) 552-8297
E-mail: robert.oneill.1@bc.edu
Robert K. O'Neill, Ph.D., Burns Librarian
Hours: Mon–Fri 9:00–5:00
(local Boston history, West African and Caribbean history, the American Catholic Church and Jesuitana)

Catholic Apostolic Administration of Asian Russia

1701 Hall Street
Hays, KS 67601-3199
(785) 625-6577 (school hours); (785) 625-4483 (other hours); (785) 625-3912 FAX
e-mail: tmpbb@fhsuvm.fhsu.edu
http://feefhs.org/fg/frg-lfs.html
Father Blaine Burkey of the Capuchin-Franciscan Order (O.F.M.Cap), Editor
Pub. *a letter from SIBERIA*, irregularly, archives on line
(Siberia and the Russian Far East, and the Roman Catholic Church under the leadership of Bishop Joseph Werth, S.J., which serves several hundred thousand Germans, Poles, Ukrainians, Lithuanians, and other ethnic groups, most of whom were displaced from other parts of the C.I.S. during the Stalinist era)

Catholic Record Society—Diocese of Columbus

197 East Gay Street
Columbus, OH 43215
(614) 241-2571
Donald M. Schlegel, Vice Chairman/ Secretary
Hours: Wed mornings
Pub. *Barquilla de la Santa Maria*, monthly
(Ohio east of a line drawn from Kenton to Portsmouth)
$10.00 per year membership; research by volunteers

The Catholic University of America
Department of Archives, Manuscripts
and Museum Collections
5 Mullen Library
Washington, DC 20064
(202) 319-5065; (202) 319-4735 FAX
Dr. Timothy Meagher, Archivist
Hours: Mon–Fri: 9:00–5:00
(not a repository for records of baptism,
marriage or burial, which are generally
kept in the parishes or centralized in
the chancery offices of the appropriate
diocese or archdiocese; includes
official depository for such
organizations as the National Catholic
Educational Association, the National
Conference of Catholic Charities (now
Catholic Charities USA), the National
Councils of Catholic Women and Men,
and the United States Catholic
Conference & National Conference of
Catholic Bishops, as well as Catholic
University)

**Cushwa Center for the Study of
American Catholicism**
Room 614, Hesburgh Library
University of Notre Dame
Notre Dame, IN 46556
(219) 631-5441; (219) 631-8471 FAX
E-mail: cushwa.1@nd.edu
Barbara Lockwood, Assistant to the
Director
Hours: 8:00–5:00
Pub. *American Catholic Studies
Newsletter*, semiannually (spring and
fall), $12.00 for two-year subscription
(no archives, but passes everything on to
the University of Notre Dame
archives)

**Daughters of Charity Archives—
Albany**
96 Menands Road
Albany, NY 12204-1499
(518) 462-5593
Elaine Wheeler, Provincial Archivist
Hours: Mon–Fri 8:30–4:30, weekends by
appointment
(Roman Catholic records, also history of
care of orphans in manycities, but does
not have children's records; records of
hospitals from 1848)

Diocese of Birmingham
PO Box 12047
Birmingham, AL 35202-2047
Most Rev. David E. Foley, Bishop of
Birmingham

The Archdiocese of Mobile Archives
400 Government Street
PO Box 1966
Mobile, AL 36633
(334) 434-1583
Shirley Zieman, Archival Secretary
Hours: Mon & Wed 9:00–4:00
("Archival records of baptisms,
marriages, and burials begin in 1704

and end in 1860 except for a few
burial records which end in 1880;
there are gaps in the records due to
fires, hurricanes, war and itinerant
missionaries, some of whom kept
sketchy records or no records.")
$7.50 per hour research; $5.00 per copy
of record

Diocese of Anchorage
225 Cordova Street
Anchorage, AK 99501
(907) 258-7898; (907) 279-3885 FAX
Brother Charles McBride, CSC, Archives
Director
Hours: by appointment only
(history of archdiocese since 1966,
Alaska since 1900)

Diocese of Fairbanks
1316 Peger Road
Fairbanks, AK 99709
(907) 474-0753; (907) 474-8009 FAX
Sr. Marilyn Marx, SNJM, Chancellor
Hours: Mon–Fri 8:30–4:30
search fee: $5.00

The Diocese of Phoenix
400 East Monroe
Phoenix, AZ 85004
(602) 257-0030
Hours: Mon–Fri 8:00–4:30

The Archives, Diocese of Tucson
8800 East 22nd Street
Tucson, AZ 85710
(520) 886-5223
Dan Brosnan, Archivist, Historian,
Records Manager, and Museum
Director
Hours: Tue–Thur 8:00–2:00

Diocese of Little Rock
2415 North Tyler Street
PO Box 7239
Little Rock, AR 72217-7239
(501) 664-0340, ext. 366; (501) 664-
9186 FAX
Sister Catherine Markey, Archivist
Hours: by appointment only

The Diocese of Los Angeles
Archival Center
15151 San Fernando Mission Boulevard
Mission Hills, CA 91345
(818) 365-1501; (818) 365-3276 FAX
Kevin Feeney, Adjunct Archivist and
Records Manager
Hours: Mon–Fri 8:30–4:30

The Diocese of Monterey Archives
(690 Figueroa Street—location)
PO Box 2048 (mailing address)
Monterey, CA 93940
(831) 373-4345; (831) 373-1175 FAX
Brother John F. O'Brien, C.F.X.,
Archivist
Hours: Mon–Fri 9:00–3:00
(sacramental registers: baptisms,
confirmations, marriages, deaths for
Old California missions: Carmel

Mission, Carmel; San Antonio
Mission, Jolon; San Juan Bautista
Mission, San Juan Bautista; San
Carlos Cathedral, Monterey; Mission
Soledad, Soledad; San Luis Obispo
Mission, San Luis Obispo; San Miguel
Mission, San Miguel; Santa Cruz
Mission, Santa Cruz)
$20.00 per search

**Roman Catholic Diocese of Oakland
Archives**
3014 Lakeshore Avenue
Oakland, CA 94610-3615
(510) 893-4711; (510) 273-4946 FAX
E-mail: archives@oakdiocese.org
Mary C. Batiza, Archivist
Hours: Tue 8:45-4:45
Pub. *The Catholic Voice* (Diocesan
newspaper), biweekly

Diocese of Orange
990 Temple Terrace
Laguna Beach, CA 92651
(949) 494-9701
Rev. William Krekelberg, Archivist

**Historical Archives of the Diocese of
Sacramento**
(1119 K Street, Sacramento, CA 95812—
location)
PO Box 1706 (mailing address)
Sacramento, CA 95865
(916) 482-6060
Rev. William Breault, S.I., Archivist
Hours: very flexible, ordinarily not open
(yet) to public
("Archives are parish and diocese-
centered, 1850–1930, as continued in
newspapers, baptismal, confirmation,
or registers from the beginning of the
diocese—and earlier; some original
diaries and journals, information on
early priests and bishops—and
histories of the diocese")

The Diocese of San Diego
Mission San Diego de Alcala—Archive-
Library
10818 Mission San Diego Road
San Diego, CA 92108
(619) 283-6338; (619) 490-8200
(Diocesan Archives)
Sister Catherine Louise La Coste, C.S.J.,
Archivist-Librarian
Hours: Tue & Thur 10:00–noon;
Diocesan Archives is not staffed and is
closed to research except by
appointment (PO Box 85728, San
Diego, CA 92186)
Pub. *Newsletter—Mission San Diego
Historical Society Quarterly*
(not only religious, lots of California
history and original documents, also
Spanish, Mexican and American
history, San Diego history from 1769
onward, and lots of Indian history for
California and the California missions)
$10.00 per year membership for
individuals, $15.00 per year

membership for couples, $200.00 life membership; copy costs: 5¢ per page

Diocese of San Francisco
320 Middlefield Road
Menlo Park, CA 94025
(650) 328-6502
Dr. Jeffrey Burns, Archivist
Hours: Mon–Fri 10:00–4:00

Diocese of Santa Rosa
547 B Street
PO Box 1297
Santa Rosa, CA 95402
(707) 545-7610
Msgr. James Pulskamp, Archivist

Diocese of Colorado Springs
29 West Kiowa Street
Colorado Springs, CO 80903
(719) 636-2345; (719) 636-1216
Sister J. Jacobsen, O.S.B., Archivist
Hours: Mon–Fri 1:00–4:00

Archives of the Archdiocese of Denver
200 Josephine Street
Denver, CO 80206-4710
(303) 388-4411; (303) 321-3693 FAX
Rev. E. Hoffman, Vicar General
Hours: Mon–Fri 9:00–2:00

Diocese of Pueblo
Catholic Pastoral Center
1001 North Grand Avenue
Pueblo, CO 81003
(719) 544-9861; (719) 544-5202 FAX
Lorraine Guerin, Archivist
Hours: 8:00–noon & 1:00–5:00
search fee: $7.00 per hour

Diocese of Bridgeport
The Catholic Center
238 Jewett Avenue
Bridgeport, CT 06606-2892
(203) 372-4301
Rev. John Horgan, Archivist

Archives of the Archdiocese of Hartford
134 Farmington Avenue
Hartford, CT 06105
(860) 527-4201; (860) 541-6491; (860) 525-2037 FAX
Theresa McQueeney, S.N.D., Ph.D., Archivist
Hours: Mon–Fri 9:00–noon
("An archives with information relative to the development of the archdiocese: bishops, priests and churches. Sacramental records are in the local parishes, but microfilms are available for some.")
charges for photocopying and loan of microfilms

The Diocese of Norwich
201 Broadway
PO Box 587
Norwich, CT 06360
(860) 887-9294

Rev. Msgr. Thomas R. Bride, V.G.
Hours: 9:00–5:00
Pub. *Four County Catholic*, free

The Diocese of Wilmington Archives
(10 Montchanin Road, Route 100, at Route 52—location)
PO Box 4019 (mailing address)
Greenville, DE 19807
(302) 655-0597 (Tue only)
E-mail: donndevine@aol.com
http://www.magpage.com/~tdoherty/dioceswm.html (for list of film numbers)
Donn Devine, Archivist
Hours: Tue 10:00–3:00, and by appointment (advance reservation for microfilm reader suggested)
(Roman Catholic records of Delmarva Peninsula; holds microfilms of parish records through 1960, which are also available at other local area research libraries and through the Family History Library of The Church of Jesus Christ of Latter-day Saints)

The Archdiocese of Washington (District of Columbia)
5001 Eastern Avenue
PO Box 29260
Washington, DC 20017-0260
(301) 853-3800; (301) 853-3246
Deac. Bernard Bernier, Archivist
Hours: Mon–Fri 8:30–5:30

The Archdiocese of Miami
9401 Biscayne Boulevard
Miami Shores, FL 33138
(305) 757-6241

Archives, Diocese of Orlando
421 East Robinson
PO Box 1800
Orlando, FL 32802
(407) 246-4924; (407) 246-4942 FAX
Jane Quinn, Archivist
Hours: Mon–Fri 9:00–3:00

Diocese of Palm Beach
PO Box 109650
Palm Beach Gardens, FL 33410-9650
(561) 775-9507; (561) 775-9556 FAX
Mary Lou Hughes, Archivist and Records Manager

Diocese of Pensacola-Tallahassee
PO Drawer 17329
Pensacola, FL 32522
(904) 432-1515; (904) 436-6424 FAX

Diocese of Saint Augustine
PO Box 24000
Jacksonville, FL 32241
(904) 262-3200; (904) 262-0698
Rev. Philip Gagan, Archivist
Hours: Mon–Thur 10:00–3:00
(microfilm of the Diocesan records available at the Saint Augustine Historical Society, Saint Augustine, FL)

Diocese of Saint Petersburg
6363 Ninth Avenue, North
Saint Petersburg, FL 33743
(813) 344-1611; (813) 345-2145
Lisa B. Mobley, Archivist
Hours: Mon–Fri 8:30–5:00

The Archdiocese of Atlanta
680 West Peachtree Street, N.W.
Atlanta, GA 30308
(404) 885-7253; (404) 885-7494 FAX
http://www.archatl.com/archatl.htm
Anthony R. Dees, Archivist
Hours: Mon–Thur 8:00–4:00 by appointment only
(very little genealogical material, as the sacramental registers are at the parishes)

Catholic Diocese of Savannah
Catholic Pastoral Center
601 East Liberty Street
Savannah, GA 31401-5196
(912) 238-2320
Sister Mary Faith McKean, RSM, Vice Chancellor
Hours: Mon–Fri 9:00–4:00 by appointment only
Pub. *The Southern Cross Newspaper*, weekly, $15.00 per year subscription

Roman Catholic Church in the State of Hawaii
Diocese of Honolulu
Chancery Office
1184 Bishop Street
Honolulu, HI 96813
(808) 533-1791; (808) 521-8428 FAX
Rev. Msgr. Raymond J. Nishigaya
Hours: 9:00–3:00

The Diocese of Boise
Chancery Office
303 Federal Way
Boise, ID 83705
(208) 342-1311; (208) 342-0224 FAX
James E. Bowen, Chancellor/Archivist
Hours: 9:00–5:00
search fees based on information requested

Diocese of Belleville
(222 South Third Street—location)
220 West Lincoln Street (mailing address)
Belleville, IL 62220
(618) 234-3157; (618) 277-0387 FAX
Sister Mary Kenan Wolff, Archivist
Hours: by appointment only (archives not open to the public)

Archdiocese of Chicago
Archives and Records Center
5150 Northwest Highway
Chicago, IL 60630
(773) 736-5150; (773) 736-0488 FAX
Nancy Sandleback, Assistant Archivist
Hours: by appointment only, genealogical research through the mail

Diocese of Joliet
425 Summit Street
Joliet, IL 60435
(815) 722-6606; (815) 722-6602
Sister Judith Davies, O.S.F., Chancellor
Hours: by appointment only

Diocese of Rockford
1245 North Court Street
Rockford, IL 61103
(815) 962-3709; (815) 968-2824 FAX
Rev. Charles McNamee, Chancellor and
    Archivist
Hours: by appointment only

Diocese of Evansville
Catholic Center
PO Box 4169
Evansville, IN 47724-0169
(812) 424-5536
Judy Neff, Chancellor
Hours: Archives: by appointment; Brute
    Library: Memorial Day to Labor Day:
    12:30–4:00

Archdiocese of Indianapolis
1400 North Meridian Street
PO Box 1410
Indianapolis, IN 46206
(317) 236-1429; (317) 236-1401 FAX
Rev. Jack W. Porter, Ph.D., Archivist
Hours: Mon–Fri 9:30–4:30 by
    appointment only
(Parish histories, priests' biographies,
    etc.; "Sacramental records are kept in
    each individual parish.")

Diocese of Lafayette-in-Indiana
The Bishop's Office
PO Box 260
Lafayette, IN 47902-0260
(765) 742-0275
Rev. Robert Leo Sell, Vicar General and
    Moderator of the Curia
Hours: Mon–Fri 7:30–4:30

Diocese of Davenport
Saint Vincent Center
2706 North Gaines
Davenport, IA 52804
(319) 324-1911; (319) 324-5842
Sister Madeleine Schmidt, Archivist and
    Historian
Hours: Mon–Fri 8:00–3:00 by
    appointment

The Diocese of Des Moines
Chancery
PO Box 1816
Des Moines, IA 50306

The Archives of the Archdiocese of Dubuque
(1229 Mount Loretta Avenue, Dubuque,
    IA 52003—location)
PO Box 479
Dubuque, IA 52004-0479
(319) 556-2580
Rev. Loras C. Otting, Director

Hours: Mon–Fri 8:30–5:00
(original correspondence of Bishop Loras
    and of Bishop Cretin)

The Diocese of Sioux City
(1821 Jackson Street, Sioux City, IA
    51105—location)
PO Box 3379 (mailing address)
Sioux City, IA 51102-3379
(712) 255-7933; (712) 233-7525; (712)
    233-7598 FAX
Sister Kevin Cummings, Archivist and
    Records Manager
Hours: Mon–Fri 9:00–noon & 1:00–5:00
Pub. *The Globe* (not genealogical),
    weekly (50 times per year), $14.00 per
    year subscription
("Basically we have corporate records of
    the diocese, sketchy until 1940s; we
    are not computerized; although we
    have transcripts of extant sacramental
    and burial records from parishes of the
    diocese from approximately 1918, and
    for many of the earlier ones, we have
    many still missing; we can sometimes
    tell which parish should be consulted
    by dates of first resident pastor; for
    social security, the person must make
    the request, or the Social Security
    Office; post 1920 personal information
    released only to the individual or to
    one that person has authorized to
    receive it—authorization proven.")
search fee: $15.00 in the Diocese of
    Sioux City, $16.00 outside the diocese

Diocese of Dodge City
910 Central
PO Box 137
Dodge City, KS 67801
(316) 227-2500; (316) 227-1570 FAX
Timothy Wenzl, Archivist
Hours: Mon–Fri by appointment

The Archdiocese of Kansas City in Kansas
Chancery Office
12615 Parallel Avenue
Kansas City, KS 66107
(913) 721-1570; (913) 721-1577 FAX
Rev. Leo Cooper, Archivist and Assistant
    Chancellor
Hours: Mon–Fri 8:30–noon & 1:00–5:00

Diocese of Salina
103 North Ninth Street
PO Box 980
Salina, KS 67402-0980
(785) 827-8746; (785) 827-6133 FAX
Msgr. James E. Hake, Chancellor and
    Archivist
Hours: by appointment only

The Diocese of Covington
1140 Madison Avenue
PO Box 192
Covington, KY 41017

Diocese of Lexington
1310 Leestown Road
PO Box 12350
Lexington, KY 40508
(606) 253-1993; (606) 254-6284 FAX
Sister Mary K. Seibert, Chancellor
Hours: by appointment only
("Catholic Diocese of Lexington was
    established in 1988 from counties
    formerly part of the Diocese of
    Covington and the Archdiocese of
    Louisville; older records are not
    always available at this office.")

Roman Catholic Archdiocese of Louisville
PO Box 1073
Louisville, KY 40203
(502) 585-3291
The Rev. Robert Dale Cieslik,
    Chancellor-Archivist
Hours: Mon–Fri 8:30–4:30 by
    appointment only
all requests must be made in writing

Roman Catholic Diocese of Owensboro
Catholic Pastoral Center
600 Locust Street
Owensboro, KY 42301-2130
(502) 683-1545, ext. 133; (502) 683-
    6883 FAX
http://www.catholic-chur/archivist.html
Sister Emma Cecilia Busam, O.S.U.,
    Archivist and Records Manager
Hours: Tue–Wed 8:00–4:00, and by
    appointment
Pub. *Western Kentucky Catholic* (not an
    archival publication but diocesan), ten
    times per year (monthly, except July–
    August), $7.00 per year subscription
(seeks to promote understanding of the
    origins, aims and goals of the diocese;
    collects, preserves and makes available
    records of individuals and
    organizations engaged in work which
    reflects that of the Catholic Church in
    the diocese to researchers in pursuit of
    historical and genealogical research)

The Diocese of Alexandria
(4400 Coliseum Boulevard, Alexandria,
    LA 71303—location)
PO Box 7417 (mailing address)
Alexandria, LA 71306
(318) 445-2401; (318) 448-6121
E-mail: dioalex@timetrend.com
Msgr. Joseph Susi, Chancellor/Archivist
Hours: 8:00–4:30
("We only do baptismal searches as we
    do not have all the records for our
    Diocese.")
research: $10.00 for the first hour, $2.00
    for each additional hour, plus $4.00
    per certificate

The Diocese of Baton Rouge

Department of the Archives
1800 South Acadian Thruway
PO Box 2028
Baton Rouge, LA 70821-2028
(504) 387-0561 (for information only);
(504) 336-8789 FAX
John Pastorek, Archivist
Hours: Mon–Fri 9:00–2:00
(repository of the sacramental records of
the Catholic churches within the civil
parishes of Ascension, Assumption,
East Baton Rouge, East Feliciana,
Iberville, Livingston, Pointe Coupee,
Saint Helena, Saint James,
Tangipahoa, West Baton Rouge and
West Feliciana, generally prior to
1900; published fourteen volumes of
sacramental records from the Acadian
records of St. Charles-aux-Mines,
Grand Pré in Acadia [1707–1748] and
St. Francis of Point Coupée [1728–
1769], through the Colonial period
[1770–1803], and up to 1879)
research: $6.00 for the first hour, $5.00
for each additional hour; copies: $7.50
payable in advance

Diocese of Houma-Thibodaux

Historical Research Center
205 Audubon Avenue
Thibodoux, LA 70301
(504) 446-2383; (504) 449-0574 FAX
Msgr. R. Boudreaux, Archivist
Hours: Mon–Tue & Thur 8:00–4:00

The Archdiocese of New Orleans

Archdiocesan Historical Archives
1100 Chartres Street
New Orleans, LA 70116-2596
(504) 529-2651; (504) 529-2001 FAX
Dr. Charles E. Nolan, Archivist
Hours: Mon–Fri 9:00–5:00 by
appointment for historical research (all
genealogical requests handled by mail)
(Comprised eight civil parishes:
Jefferson, Orleans, Plaquemines, Saint
Bernard, Saint Charles, Saint John the
Baptist, Saint Tammany, and
Washington; baptisms, marriages and
funerals records 1718–1806; archives
also houses early records from four
New Orleans cemeteries: Saint Louis,
Saint Patrick, Saint Joseph, and Saint
Roch; has published eleven volumes
of sacramental records, 1718–1815)
$12.00 plus SASE per family history
record requested, plus an additional
$8.00 for a photocopy (if possible) in
addition to the English certificate (no
more than four requests at a time), c/o
Department of Sacramental Registers

Diocese of Shreveport (Louisiana)
Archives

2500 Line Avenue
Shreveport, LA 71104-3043
(318) 222-2006; (318) 222-2080 FAX
E-mail: crivers@dioshpt.org

http://www.dioshpt.org
Christine D. Rivers, Archivist
Hours: Mon–Fri 8:00–4:00 by
appointment only
(in the beginning phase of digitizing
sacramental records 72 years old or
older for Catholic churches in the civil
parishes of Bienville, Bossier, Caddo,
Claiborne, DeSoto, East Carroll,
Jackson, Lincoln, Morehouse,
Ouachita, Red River, Richland,
Sabine, Union, Webster and West
Carroll, the northenmost quarter of the
state; some requests must still be
directed to individual churches)
charge for photocopies

The Chancery of the Diocese of Portland

(510 Ocean Avenue, Portland, ME
04103—location)
PO Box 11559 (mailing address)
Portland, ME 04104-7559
(207) 773-6471; (207) 773-0182 FAX
Sister Therese Pelletier, Archivist
Hours: Tue & Thur 9:00–4:30
(does not hold materials for genealogy at
the chancery)

Archives of the Archdiocese of Baltimore

320 Cathedral Street
Baltimore, MD 21201
(410) 547-5443
Rev. Paul K. Thomas, Archivist
Hours: Mon–Fri 10:00–6:00 by
appointment only
("Original sacramental records of our
Roman Catholic Archdiocese are kept
in each individual parish rather than in
our central archives. Microfilms of
such records of about 75 parishes are
available to the public at the Maryland
State Archives. The records of closed
Catholic parishes are usually available
at the next nearest Catholic church. A
few have been transferred to our
central archives, but, due to their
historical value, they can generally be
viewed only on microfilm at the
Maryland State Archives.")

Archdiocese of Boston

2121 Commonwealth Avenue
Brighton, MA 02135
(617) 254-0100; (617) 783-5642 FAX
Hours: Mon–Fri 10:00–4:30 by
appointment (closed holidays and holy
days)
20¢ per photocopy from paper, 50¢
photocopy from microfilm, $25.00 per
hour for research by staff

Diocese of Fall River

Box 2577 Fall River
Fall River, MA 02722-2577
(508) 675-1311
Msgr. John J. Oliviera, Chancellor and
Archivist

Diocese of Worcester

49 Elm Street
Worcester, MA 01609
(508) 791-7171; (508) 753-7180 FAX
Rev. F. Stephen Pedone, Judicial Vicar
(religious; canon law archives and
library)

The Archdiocese of Detroit

Archives
1234 Washington Boulevard
Detroit, MI 48226
(313) 237-5846; (313) 965-3989 FAX
Roman P. Godzak, Archivist/Records
Manager
Hours: Mon–Fri 8:30–4:30

Diocese of Gaylord (Roman Catholic)

1665 West M-32
Gaylord, MI 49735-8932
(517) 732-5147; (517) 732-1706 FAX
Rev. Gerald F. Micketti, Archivist
Hours: Mon–Fri 8:00–4:30

Diocesan Archives, Diocese of Grand Rapids

660 Burton Street, S.E.
Grand Rapids, MI 49507-3290
(616) 243-0491; (616) 243-4910 FAX
Fr. Dennis W. Morrow, Archivist
Hours: by appointment
$10.00 search fee, $5.00 per record
found

Catholic Diocese of Lansing

Archives
1500 East Saginaw Street, Suite 2
Lansing, MI 48906-5550
(517) 485-9902; (517) 484-8880 FAX
Rev. George C. Michalek, Archivist
Hours: Tue 9:00–4:00
(focuses on the history of Catholicism in
Clinton, Eaton, Genesee, Hillsdale,
Ingham, Jackson, Lenawee,
Livingston, Shiawassee and
Washtenaw counties of south central
Michigan)

The Diocese of Marquette

444 South Fourth Street
PO Box 550
Marquette, MI 49855
(906) 225-1141; (906) 225-0437
Rev. Peter Oberto, Chancellor and
Judicial Vicar; Rev. Howard Brown,
Archivist; Ms. Regis Walling, U.P.
Historical Society
Hours: Mon–Fri 8:00–noon & 1:00–4:00
Pub. *U. P. Catholic Diocesan
Newspaper*, semimonthly, $18.00 per
year subscription

Diocese of Newton

8525 Cole
Warren, MI 48093-5239
(313) 558-0143
Bishop Nicholas Samra, Auxiliary
Bishop, Diocese of Newton (Melkite)

The Diocese of Saginaw
5800 Weiss Street
Saginaw, MI 48603

The Diocese of Duluth
2830 East Fourth Street
Duluth, MN 55812
(218) 724-9111; (218) 724-1056 FAX
Rev. Patrick Moran, Archivist
Hours: daily 8:30–4:30

The Diocese of New Ulm
1400 Sixth North Street
New Ulm, MN 56073
(507) 359-2966
Rev. Dennis Labat, Chancellor

Archives—Diocese of Saint Cloud
214 Third Avenue South
Saint Cloud, MN 56301
(320) 251-2340; (320) 251-0470 FAX
Louise Theisen, Archivist
Hours: daily 8:00–12:00

The Archdiocese of Saint Paul and Minneapolis
226 Summit Avenue
Saint Paul, MN 55102
(612) 291-4429; (612) 290-1629 FAX
Patrick Anzelc, Assistant Archivist
Hours: Mon–Fri 9:00–5:00, researchers
Tue & Wed
(parish records available on microfilm,
small charge for copies)
admission: $8.00 per day; research by
mail: $8.00 per hour

The Diocese of Winona
55 West Sanborn
PO Box 588
Winona, MN 55987
(507) 452-7692; (507) 454-8106
Rev. Edward McGrath, Chancellor
Hours: Mon–Fri 8:00–4:30

Catholic Diocese of Biloxi
120 Reynoir Street
PO Box 1189
Biloxi, MS 39533
(228) 374-0222
Msgr. Andrew Murray, Vicar General
and Chancellor
Hours: 8:30–5:00

Catholic Diocese of Jackson
237 East Amite Street
PO Box 2248
Jackson, MS 39225-2248
(601) 969-1880; (601) 960-8455 FAX
Jo Ann Haien, Archivist
Hours: Tue 1:00–4:00, Wed 10:00–4:00
by appointment
no research by mail, but all sacramental
requests are honored and research
through the archives' microfilm or
referral to the original parish is
facilitated

Diocese of Jefferson City
PO Box 417
Jefferson City, MO 65102

(573) 635-9127; (573) 635-2286 FAX
Sister M. Johanning, Chancellor
Hours: Mon–Fri 8:00–5:00

Diocese of Kansas City/Saint Joseph
300 East 36th Street
PO Box 419037
Kansas City, MO 64141-6037
(816) 756-1850; (816) 756-0878 FAX
Rev. Michael Coleman, Volunteer
Hours: Mon–Fri 9:00–5:00

Archives of the Archdiocese of Saint Louis
(7800 Kenrick Road—location)
4445 Lindell Boulevard (mailing
address)
Saint Louis, MO 63108
(314) 961-4320
Rev. Mr. Martin G. Towey, Archivist
Hours: Mon–Fri 9:00–4:00

Archives of the Diocese of Great Falls-Billings
121 23rd Street South
PO Box 1399
Great Falls, MT 59403
(406) 727-6683; (406) 454-3480 FAX
Rev. Dale McFarlane, Diocesan Archivist
Hours: Mon–Fri 8:00–5:00 preferably by
appointment

The Diocese of Helena
515 North Ewing
PO Box 1729
Helena, MT 59624-1729
(406) 442-5820; 406) 442-5191 FAX
Rev. John W. Robertson, Historian
Archivist
Hours: not open to the public for
genealogical research; submit written
request
("Our genealogical information is
confined to records of baptism and
marriage in western Montana. We
must know approximate date, place
[and parish if at all possible] and
parents' names.")

Diocese of Lincoln
3400 Sheridan Boulevard
Lincoln, NE 68506
(402) 488-0921
Sister Loretta Gosen, Archivist
Hours: Mon–Fri 8:30–4:30

The Archdiocese of Omaha
Chancery Office
100 North 62nd Street
Omaha, NE 68132
(402) 558-3100; (402) 551-4212 FAX
Fr. Michael F. Gutgsell, Chancellor
Hours: Mon–Fri 8:30–5:00

The Diocese of Reno-Las Vegas
(Chancery Office, 515 Court Street—
location)
PO Box 1211 (mailing address)
Reno, NV 89504
(702) 329-9274, ext. 19; (702) 329-6581
FAX

Carmen Goday, Office Manager
Hours: 8:30–noon & 1:00–4:30
(some baptismal records from 1800 to
early 1900s for state of Nevada; most
sacramental records were destroyed
during some of the fires in a couple of
churches in Virginia City and Gold
Hill)
$5.00 per copy for certificates

The Diocese of Manchester
Chancery Office
153 Ash Street
PO Box 310
Manchester, NH 03105

Archdiocese of Newark
Seton Hall University
University Archives
Duffy Hall
South Orange Avenue
South Orange, NJ 07079-2696
(973) 761-9476; (973) 761-9550 FAX
http://www.shu.edu/library/speccoll.html
Msgr. William Noe Field, Archivist and
Records Manager
Hours: Mon–Fri 8:30–5:00

Diocese of Paterson
777 Valley Road
Clifton, NJ 07013
(973) 777-8818; (973) 777-8976 FAX
Rev. Raymond Kupke, Archivist
Hours: by appointment only

Diocese of Trenton
701 Lawrenceville Road
Trenton, NJ 08648
(609) 882-7125; (908) 350-5001
Msgr. Joseph Shenrock, Archivist
Hours: by appointment only

The Diocese of Gallup
(711 South Puerco Drive, Gallup, NM
87301—location)
PO Box 1338 (mailing address)
Gallup, NM 87305
(505) 863-4406
Brother Duane Torisky, Chancellor and
Archivist

The Diocese of Las Cruces
1280 Med Park Drive
Las Cruces, NM 88005
(505) 523-7577; (505) 524-3874
Rev. John Tickle, Archivist; Dolores
Diaz, Librarian
Hours: Mon–Fri 8:00–5:00

The Archdiocese of Santa Fe
213 Cathedral Place
Santa Fe, NM 87501
(505) 983-3811; (505) 982-5619
Marina Ochoa
Hours: by appointment

Roman Catholic Diocese of Albany Archives
40 North Main Avenue
Albany, NY 12203
(518) 453-6633; (518) 453-6793 FAX

Sister M. Berchmanns Mahoney,
Archivist
Hours: Mon–Fri 8:30–4:30

Diocese of Brooklyn
Immaculate Conception Center
7200 Douglaston Parkway
Douglaston, NY 11362
(718) 229-8001, ext. 475; (718) 229-
2658 FAX
Joseph W. Coen, Archivist
Hours: Mon–Wed & Thur–Fri 9:30–4:00
by appointment
(sacramental registers not centralized,
except closed parishes/hospitals; see
*Priests & Parishes of the Diocese of
Brooklyn 1853–1990*, 2 vols., $15.00
each, and *Chronological List of
Churches in the Diocese of Brooklyn*,
Brooklyn Parishes $2.00, Queens
Parishes $2.00)
search fee: $10.00 for one name in one
sacramental register in one parish

The Catholic Center (Buffalo)
795 Main Street
Buffalo, NY 14203
(716) 847-5561
Msgr. Walter Kern, Archivist
Hours: Mon–Fri 9:00–4:00 by
appointment
("We do not have personnel to do
research; many of our sacramental
records also contain confidential
information.")

Archdiocese of New York
(address withheld upon request)
does not do genealogical research and
does not want inquiries relating to
genealogy

Diocese of Ogdensburg
Chancery Office
PO Box 369
Ogdensburg, NY 13669
(315) 292-2920
Rev. Lawrence Cotter, Archivist
Hours: Mon–Fri 9:00–noon & 1:00–4:00

Archives, Diocese of Rochester
1150 Buffalo Road
Rochester, NY 14624
(716) 328-3210
Rev. William Graf, Associate Archivist
Hours: 9:00–4:00 by appointment only
(will direct calls and requests to proper
church for marriage, baptism and
burial records from 1914)

Diocese of Syracuse
(240 East Onondaga Street, Syracuse,
NY 13202-2608—location)
PO Box 511 (mailing address)
Syracuse, NY 13201
(315) 470-1493
Carl H. Roesch, Archivist
Hours: Mon–Tue & Thur–Fri 9:00–noon

Catholic Diocese of Charlotte
(1524 East Morehead Street, Charlotte,
NC 28207—location)
PO Box 36776 (mailing address)
Charlotte, NC 28236
(704) 377-6871; (704) 358-1208 FAX
Johanna Mims, Archivist
Hours: Tue & Thur 9:00–3:00

The Diocese of Raleigh Archives
(300 Cardinal Gibbons Drive—location)
715 Nazareth Street (mailing address)
Raleigh, NC 27606
(919) 821-9709
Bradley K. Blake, Archivist
Hours: Mon, Wed & Fri 8:30–5:00

The Diocese of Bismarck Archives
(520 North Washington Street, Bismarck,
ND 58501—location)
PO Box 1137 (mailing address)
Bismarck, ND 58502-1137
(701) 222-3035
Marge Grosz, Librarian
Hours: Mon–Fri 8:00–5:00

The Diocese of Fargo Archives
1310 Broadway
PO Box 1750
Fargo, ND 58107
(701) 235-6429
Sister M. James Merrick, Archivist

Archdiocese of Cincinnati
Historical Archives of the Chancery
Mount Saint Mary's Seminary
6616 Beechmont Avenue
Cincinnati, OH 45230-5900
(513) 231-0810; (513) 231-3254 FAX
Don H. Buske, Archivist
Hours: Mon–Wed 8:30–4:30
(sacramental records for the nineteen-
county area of southwestern Ohio; all
genealogical research done by mail)
research: $25.00 fee, check or money
order to the Historical Archives of the
chancery, submit full name, type of
record, approximate date (within five
years), exact parish

Archives, Diocese of Cleveland
Chancery Building
1027 Superior Avenue
Cleveland, OH 44114
(216) 696-6525, ext. 345
Christine L. Krosel, Director of Archives
Hours: Mon–Fri 9:00–5:00 by
appointment only
(northern Ohio, eight-county area:
Cuyahoga, Geauga, Lake, Lorain,
Medina, Summit, Ashland and Wayne
counties)
$6.50 per hour for research, rates subject
to change

The Diocese of Columbus
Saint Charles Prep School, Archives
2010 East Broad Street
Columbus, OH 43209
(614) 252-1225

Rev. Thomas Bennett, Archivist
Hours: by appointment only

The Diocese of Steubenville
422 Washington Street
PO Box 969
Steubenville, OH 43952
(740) 282-3631
Linda Nichols, Chancellor
Hours: 9:00–noon & 1:00–4:00
Pub. *Domina* (Diocesan Directory),
biannually (every two years), $7.00
per issue
(specializes in "parishes, institutions,
departments, priests, religious of
diocese.")

The Diocese of Toledo Archives
2544 Parkwood Avenue
Toledo, OH 43610
(419) 255-1890; (419) 244-0471 FAX
Rev. Bruce Farmer, Director
Hours: Wed & Fri
(has some parishes' sacramental books
on microfilm)
no search service unless provided with
name, year, and specific parish church

The Diocese of Youngstown
Chancery Office
144 West Wood Street
Youngstown, OH 44503
(330) 744-8451; (330) 742-6448 FAX
Nancy L. Yuhasz, Chancellor
Hours: Mon–Fri by appointment only

Diocese of Tulsa
(820 South Boulder, Tulsa, OK 74119—
location)
PO Box 2009 (mailing address)
Tulsa, OK 74101
(918) 587-3115; (918) 587-6692 FAX
Rita Burns, Archivist
Hours: Mon–Fri 9:00–5:00

Diocese of Portland
2838 East Burnside Street
Portland, OR 97214-1895
(503) 233-8334
Mary A. Grant, Archivist

Diocese of Erie
Saint Mark's Center
PO Box 10397
Erie, PA 16514
(814) 824-1138
Chris Prehoda, Secretary
Hours: Mon–Fri 9:30–noon & 2:00–4:30
(published two volumes of the history of
the diocese)

Diocese of Greensburg
723 East Pittsburgh Street
Greensburg, PA 15601
(724) 837-0901; (724) 837-0857
Bina Guerrieri, Secretary to the Archives
Hours: Mon–Fri 9:00–5:00

Archives, Roman Catholic Diocese of Harrisburg
(4800 Union Deposit Road—location)
PO Box 2153 (mailing address)
Harrisburg, PA 17105-2153
(717) 657-4804, ext. 214; (717) 657-7673 FAX
Kathleen Signor, Assistant Chancellor for Archives/Archivist
Hours: Mon–Fri 8:30–4:30
Pub. *Catholic Witness*, bimonthly
(sacramental records; parish histories for Catholic Diocese of Harrisburg)
genealogical research: $25.00 per hour

Philadelphia Archdiocesan Historical Research Center
Archives and Historical Collections
1000 East Wynnewood Road
Overbrook, PA 19096-3001
(215) 667-2125
Joseph J. Casino, Archivist
Hours: Mon–Fri 9:00–4:00
(holds baptismal and marriage records prior to 1900 for parishes presently within the Archdiocese of Philadelphia)
genealogical research: $15.00 for first hour, $10.00 for each additional hour

Archives and Record Center (Pittsburgh)
125 North Craig
Pittsburgh, PA 15213
(412) 621-6217; (412) 621-5237 FAX
E-mail: archives@diopitt.org
Kenneth White, Director; Rev. E. McSweeney, Archivist
Hours: Mon–Fri 8:30–4:30
(files of deceased clergy of the Catholic Diocese of Pittsburgh; publishes parish sacramental records, which have been centralized in the archives if over seventy years old)
search: $15.00 for the first hour and $10.00 for each additional hour

Diocese of Scranton
300 Wyoming Avenue
Scranton, PA 18503-1279
(717) 346-8910
Msgr. Neil J. Van Loon, Chancellor
Hours: by appointment only

The Diocese of Providence
(address withheld upon request)
(collects documentation on the acts, the agencies, and the institutions of the diocese, does not collect personal histories or sacramental records, which are kept by individual parishes)

Charleston Diocesan Archives
(114-Rear Broad Street—location)
PO Box 818 (mailing address)
Charleston, SC 29402
(843) 724-8372
Susan L. King, Archivist
Hours: Mon–Fri 9:00–4:30 by appointment

The Diocese of Rapid City
Chancery Office
606 Cathedral Drive
PO Box 678
Rapid City, SD 57709
(605) 343-3541; (605) 348-7985 FAX
Sister Celine Erk, Chancellor and Archivist

The Diocese of Sioux Falls Archives
Catholic Chancery
3100 West 41st Street
Sioux Falls, SD 57105-4294
Hours: Mon–Fri 9:00–5:00

Diocese of Memphis
1325 Jefferson Avenue
Memphis, TN 38104
(901) 722-4700; (901) 722-4769
Mrs. V. Dominioni, Administrative Assistant, Office of the Bishop

Diocese of Nashville
The Catholic Center
2400 21st Avenue, South
Nashville, TN 37212
(615) 383-6393
Ann Krenson, Chancellor
Hours: by appointment only

Catholic Historical Society of the Diocese of Amarillo
(2200 North Spring Street—location)
PO Box 5664 (mailing address)
Amarillo, TX 79117-5644
(806) 381-9866; (806) 383-8452 FAX
Margret Ference, Curator
Hours: Tue & Thur 10:00–2:00, and by appointment
$10.00 per year membership

Catholic Archives of Texas (Diocese of Austin)
(1600 North Congress Avenue, Austin, TX 78701—location)
PO Box 13124, Capitol Station (mailing address)
Austin, TX 78711-3124
(512) 476-6296; (512) 476-3715 FAX
E-mail: cat@onr.com
http://www.onr.com/user/cat
Kinga Perzynska, Archivist
Hours: Mon–Fri 9:00–5:00
(Catholic sacramental records on microfilm to be viewed at the archives)
search: $10.00 per hour plus copies at 25¢ per page from paper originals or 50¢ per page from microfilm originals

Diocese of Beaumont
PO Box 3948
Beaumont, TX 77704-3948
(409) 838-0451; (409) 838-4511
Rev. Bennie Patillo, Chancellor, Vicar-General, and Archivist
Hours: Mon–Fri 8:30–4:30

Diocese of Brownsville
PO Box 2279
Brownsville, TX 78522

(512) 542-2501
Sister Esther Dunegan, Archivist

Diocese of Corpus Christi
(address withheld upon request)

Diocese of Dallas
3725 Blackburn
Dallas, TX 75219
(972) 528-2240; (972) 526-1743
Estelle Metzger, Archivist
Hours: Mon–Wed 9:00–5:00
("We do not profess to do genealogy; on rare occasion we do issue a baptismal certificate; we have to know the name and birth date and the family connection to even consider this type of inquiry; and since some information is really confidential and sacred, we do not participate in this type of exercise.")
search fees: $25.00 for the first hour

Historical Archives, Catholic Diocese of El Paso
499 Saint Matthew's Street
El Paso, TX 79907
(915) 595-5008
Very Rev. Edward Roden-Lucero, Chancellor

Diocese of Fort Worth
800 West Loop, 820 South
Fort Worth, TX 76108
(817) 560-3300; (817) 244-8839 FAX
Carol Watson, Records Manager
Hours: Mon–Fri 8:00–5:00

Archives, Diocese of Galveston-Houston
1700 San Jacinto
PO Box 907
Houston, TX 77001
(713) 659-5461; (713) 759-9151 FAX
Lisa May, Archivist
Hours: Mon–Fri 8:30–noon & 1:00–4:30; research by appointment
(sacramental records after 1920 are closed to research)

Diocese of San Angelo
804 Ford
San Angelo, TX 76905
(915) 651-7500; (915) 651-6688 FAX
Mary Sue Brewer, Secretary to the Bishop and Archivist
Hours: Mon–Fri 9:00–5:00

Archdiocese of San Antonio
2718 West Woodlawn
PO Box 24810
San Antonio, TX 78228-0410
(210) 734-2620
Brother Edward Loch, Archivist
Hours: Mon–Fri 9:00–noon & 1:00–4:00
Pub. *Guide to Catholic Archives at San Antonio*, occasionally
("Sacramental records from 1703 to present (open to the public to 1920); Bishop's and Chancery papers,

Catholic newspaper since 1892, matrimonial investigations 1755–1870 Rio Grande Valley.")

research: $10.00 per hour, $20.00 minimum, plus $1.00 per print from film, $3.00 per hour for individual use of microfilm

Archives, Diocese of Salt Lake City

Pastoral Center
27 C Street
Salt Lake City, UT 84103-2397
(801) 328-8641, ext. 346; (801) 328-9680 FAX
Bernice M. Mooney, Archivist
Hours: Mon–Wed 8:30–noon

Archives of the Roman Catholic Diocese of Burlington

Bishop Brady Center
351 North Avenue
Burlington, VT 05401
(802) 658-6110
William W. Goss, Archivist
Hours: by appointment

Diocese of Arlington

(200 North Glebe Road, Suite 608—location)
80 North Glebe Road (mailing address)
Arlington, VA 22203
(703) 524-2124
Sister Mary Arthur, Archivist

Diocese of Richmond

811 Cathedral Place
Richmond, VA 23220
(804) 359-5661; (804) 358-9159
Hours: by appointment only

Archdiocese of Seattle

The Chancery
910 Marion Street
Seattle, WA 98104
(206) 382-4857
Christine Taylor, Archivist
Hours: Mon–Fri 9:00–5:00 by appointment only
(Roman Catholic sacramental records)
research fee: $5.00

Diocese of Spokane

Catholic Chancery
Po Box 1453
Spokane, WA 99210
(509) 358-7349
Rev. Ted Bradley, Archivist-Records Manager
Hours: Fri 10:00–5:00

The Diocese of Wheeling-Charleston

1300 Bryan Street
PO Box 230
Wheeling, WV 26003
(304) 233-0880
Rev. Robert C. Nash, Archivist

The Diocese of Green Bay

1910 South Webster Avenue
PO Box 23066
Green Bay, WI 54305-3066

(920) 437-7531, ext. 8186; (920) 435-1300 FAX
Sister Ella Kaster, CSJ, Archivist
Hours: Mon–Tue 8:30–4:30 (call for appointment)
("We have microfiche copies of sacramental records for entire diocese—sixteen counties of northeastern Wisconsin; some records begin in 1830s.")
mail request for research: $10.00 per hour donation

The Diocese of La Crosse Archives

3710 East Avenue, South
PO Box 4004
La Crosse, WI 54602-4004
(608) 788-7700; (608) 788-8413
Rev. Michael Gorman, Chancellor/Archivist
Hours: Mon–Fri 8:00–4:30

The Diocese of Madison

15 East Wilson Street
Madison, WI 53703

The Archdiocese of Milwaukee

PO Box 07912
Milwaukee, WI 53207-0912
(414) 769-3407; (414) 769-3408 FAX
E-mail: chanmin@execpc.com
Timothy Cary, Archivist and Records Manager
Hours: by appointment only
(microfilms of pre-1921 sacramental records available from the Family History Library of The Church of Jesus Christ of Latter-day Saints)

The Diocese of Superior

1201 Hughitt Avenue
PO Box 969
Superior, WI 54880
(715) 392-2937; (715) 392-2015 FAX
Rev. James Tobalski, Chancellor and Archivist
Hours: Mon–Fri 8:30–5:00

The Diocese of Cheyenne

PO Box 426
Cheyenne, WY 82003

Diocesan School Archive

Office of Catholic Education
Diocese of Brooklyn
6025 Sixth Avenue
Brooklyn, NY 11220
(718) 492-1800, ext. 18
Susan Hamilton, Registrar

Grace and Holy Trinity Cathedral

415 West 13th Street
PO Box 23218
Kansas City, MO 64141
(816) 474-8260

Indiana Province Archives Center

Congregation of Holy Cross
(Douglas Road between U.S. 33 and Juniper Road—location)
PO Box 568 (mailing address)
Notre Dame, IN 46556
(219) 631-5371
William G. Blum, C.S.C., Archivist
Hours: Mon–Fri 8:30–noon
(archival collection of Indiana Provence of Priests of Holy Cross)
research: $5.00 per hour, photocopies: 25¢ per sheet, photographs: cost of lab

Jesuit Historical Institute, American Division

University of Arizona
Arizona State Museum
Building 26
Tucson, AZ 85721
(520) 621-6278; (520) 621-9188 FAX
Charles Polzer, Sr., Curator and Director
Hours: 8:00–5:00
(holdings on Spanish colonial New Spain [Mexico])

Nazareth Archival Center

PO Box 3000
Nazareth, KY 40048-3000
(502) 348-1500
Hours: 8:30 A.M.–11:30 A.M., and by appointment
(Catholic church in Kentucky since 1812; genealogies of some families of members of SCN congregation)

The Old Bohemia Historical Society, Inc.

(Bohemia Church Road—location)
PO Box 61 (mailing address)
Warwick, MD 21912
(302) 378-5800 (in Delaware)
Rev. Thomas A. Flowers, President and Pastor
Hours: by appointment
(Maryland ecclesiastical history, Catholic Diocese of Wilmingtonhistory, no sacramental records, which have been taken to the The Diocese of Wilmington Archives, Greenville, DE; "Old Bohemia" is the popular name given to the first permanent Catholic site on the Delmarva Peninsula, established in 1704 and has no particular connection to Bohemia in Europe or to those of Czech or Slovak ancestry)
$15.00 per year membership; $40.00 for three years membership

The Saint Paul Mission Historical Society

4225 Mission Avenue, N.E.
PO Box 158
Saint Paul, OR 97137-0158
(503) 633-2501
Joe McKay, President
Hours: by appointment

(Catholic Church records of the Pacific
Northwest)

Seton Hall University
Special Collections Center
Walsh Library
400 South Orange Avenue
South Orange, NJ 07079-2696
(973) 761-9476
http://www.shu.edu/library/catholicrec/
index.html (Newsletter)
Msgr. William Noe Field, Director;
JoAnn Cotz, Associate Director
Hours: Mon–Fri 9:15–4:30 by
appointment only
Pub. *New Jersey Catholic Records
Newsletter*
(New Jersey Roman Catholic history,
sacramental records, 1850–1925)

**The Texas Catholic Historical
Society**
c/o Texas Catholic Conference
1625 Rutherford Lane
Austin, TX 78754-5105
(512) 339-9882; (512) 339-8670
E-mail: jd10@swt.edu
http://www.history.swt.edu/
Catholic_Southwest.htm
Pub. *The Texas Catholic Historical
Society Newsletter*, free; *The Journal
of Texas Catholic History and Culture*,
annually
$15.00 per year membership for
individuals, $20.00 per year Parish
membership

University of Notre Dame Archives
607 Hesburgh Library
Notre Dame, IN 46556
(219) 631-6448; (219) 631-7980 FAX
E-mail: archives.1@nd.edu
http://archives1.archives.nd.edu
Sharon Sumpter, Assistant Archivist
Hours: Mon–Fri 8:00–5:00
("We hold few genealogical records.
Please note that each diocese is
responsible for keeping the records of
the parishes within its borders. Contact
the Chancery Office of each diocese
for their records. We do hold
genealogical records for the local area
here, i.e. South Bend-Niles, Kentucky,
and colonial Louisiana, among
others.")

Ursuline Sisters Archives
Mount Saint Joseph
Maple Mount, KY 42356-9999
(502) 299-4103; (502) 299-4127
http://www.catholic-chur...owensboro/
archivist.html
Sister Emma Cecilia Busam, O.S.U.,
Archivist and Records Manager
Hours: Mon–Fri 8:00–4:00, and by
appointment
Pub. *The Community Newsletter*,
bimonthly, voluntary offering

(archives set up in 1983; files and folders
on Sisters, employees and others, and
a genealogy section in our Research
Room)

Vincentian Studies Institute
1701 West Joseph Street
Perryville, MO 63775
(573) 547-6533
Gerry Hartel, Executive Secretary
(especially Missouri, Louisiana,
Pennsylvania, Illinois, California and
New York, from 1818)

Romanian Orthodox

(see Orthodox)

Russian Orthodox

(see Orthodox)

Salvation Army

**The Salvation Army Southern
Historical Center**
1032 Stewart Avenue, S.W.
Atlanta, GA 30310
(404) 752-7578; (404) 753-4166
John G. Merritt, Director

**The Salvation Army Western
Territorial Museum**
(30840 Hawthorne Boulevard, Rancho
Palos Verdes, CA 90275—location)
2780 Lomita Boulevard (mailing
address)
Torrance, CA 90505
(310) 534-6097; (310) 534-7157 FAX
Frances C. Dingman
Hours: museum temporarily closed, only
historical services
(collection restricted to Salvation Army
officers in the thirteen western states,
cannot help with people who just
attended the army at some time)

Schwenkfelder

Schwenkfelder Library, Inc.
1 Seminary Street
Pennsburg, PA 18073-1804
(215) 679-3103
Dennis K. Moyer, Director
Hours: Mon–Fri 9:00–4:00
(radical reformation, Schwenkfelders,
local history, and Pennsylvania
German culture; "Library is known for
genealogy research of the area.")

Seventh Day Adventist

**General Conference of Seventh Day
Adventists**
12501 Old Columbia Pike
Silver Spring, MD 20904-6600
(301) 680-6000

F. Donald Yost, Director of Archives and
Statistics

Shaker

Shaker Heritage Society
1848 Shaker Meeting House
Albany-Shaker Road
Albany, NY 12211
(518) 456-7890
Ned Pratt, Director
Hours: Mon (1 Nov–21 Dec) 9:30–4:00,
Tue–Sat 9:30–4:00
Pub. *Watervliet Shaker Journal*, quarterly
$20.00 per year membership for
individuals

Shaker Historical Society
16740 South Park Boulevard
Shaker Heights, OH 44120
(216) 921-1201
E-mail: shahist@wviz.org
http://www.cwru.edu/orgs/shakhist/
shaker.htm
Catherine R. Winans, Director
Hours: Tue–Fri & Sun 2:00–5:00
Pub. *The Journal*, quarterly
(Nord Library: Shaker societies; North
Union Shakers; local history)
$20.00 per year membership for
individuals, $30.00 per year
membership for families; students may
borrow books with a $20.00 returnable
deposit

United Society of Shakers
The Shaker Library at Sabbathday Lake
(Route 26, New Gloucester, ME—
location)
Rt. 1, Box 640 (mailing address)
Poland Spring, ME 04274
(207) 926-4597
Anne Gilbert, Librarian/Archivist
Hours: Mon–Fri 8:30–4:30,
appointments preferred
Pub. *The Shaker Quarterly*, $4.00 per
issue, $15.00 per year subscription
(Shakers and other radical Christian
groups; Shaker manuscript collection;
Index Nominum of over 15,000 names
with biographical data; library
collection brochure available on
request)
$15.00 per year membership

Unitarian Universalist

**Unitarian Universalist Association of
Congregations Archives**
25 Beacon Street
Boston, MA 02108
(617) 742-2100
Deborah Weiner, Director of Public
Information
Hours: winter: Mon–Fri 9:00–5:00;
summer: Mon–Fri 9:00–4:00

Unitarian Universalist Historical Society
c/o Unitarian Universalist Association
25 Beacon Street
Boston, MA 02108
Pub. *Proceedings of the UU Historical Society*

United Brethren

(see Brethren, United Brethren in Christ, and United Methodist)

United Brethren in Christ

(see also Brethren and United Methodist)

United Brethren Historical Center
RichLyn Library
Huntington College
Huntington, IN 46750
(219) 359-4064, (219) 358-3698 FAX
E-mail: jmason@huntcol.edu
Jane E. Mason, Archivist
Hours: Mon–Thur 9:00–5:00 by appointment only to insure access
(Archives of Huntington College and the Church of the United Brethren in Christ; does not include the "Liberal" or "New Constitution" branch of the United Brethren in Christ which broke away in 1889 and merged in 1946 with the Evangelical Church to form the Evangelical United Brethren Church; no birth or baptismal records)
$15.00 for genealogical research done by staff; copies: 25¢ per page

United Christian Church

(formerly known as Hoffmanites, the early founders left the United Brethren in Christ and in 1878 officially organized as today's United Christian Church)

United Christian Church Archives
2080 White Oak Street
Lebanon, PA 17042
Elder David W. Heagy, General Conference Secretary
(formerly part of the Church of the United Brethren in Christ)

United Church of Christ

(formed in the 1957 merger of the Congregational Christian Churches and the Evangelical and Reformed Church)

Congregational Christian Historical Society, Inc.
14 Beacon Street
Boston, MA 02108
(617) 523-0470; (617) 523-0491
E-mail: blwhfus@aol.com

Harold F. Worthley, Th.D., Executive Secretary/Archivist
Hours: Mon–Fri 8:30–4:30
Pub. *News from the Congregational Christian Historical Society*, semiannually
(United Church of Christ and Congregational Christian Churches)
$25.00 per year membership for individuals, $50.00 per year membership for institutions

Eden Archives (United Church of Christ)
Eden Theological Seminary
475 East Lockwood Avenue
Saint Louis, MO 63119-3192
(314) 961-3627; (314) 961-5738 FAX
Dr. Lowell H. Zuck, Archivist
Hours: Mon–Thur 8:00–11:30; summer: Tue & Thur
(Evangelical Synod of North America church and pastoral records, especially German Evangelical churches and agencies)
no search service

Evangelical and Reformed Historical Society
Phillip Schaff Library
555 West James Street
Lancaster, PA 17603
(717) 290-8711
Hours: Mon–Thur 9:00–4:00
(includes German Reformed as well as Evangelical and Reformed records in Pennsylvania, most holdings available onmicrofilm from LDS Family History Centers)
$25.00 per year membership; genealogical research fee: $5.00 per day

Hammond Library
Chicago Theological Seminary
5757 University Avenue
Chicago, IL 60637
("Records from Chicagoarea Congregational Churches that closed in the 1930s; no staff to service records, requests handled on a timeavailable basis.")
$3.00 for searches within our parameters

Hawaiian Mission Children's Society Library
553 South King Street
Honolulu, HI 96813
(808) 5310481; (808) 545-2280 FAX
Marilyn L. Reppun, Head Librarian
Hours: Mon–Fri 10:00–4:00
("19th century Hawaiiana; Congregational Church records beginning 1820; unpublished letters, journals, reports of Protestant missionaries to Hawaii, personal as well as business; Hawaiian-language books; Micronesian-language books;

early voyages to Hawaii and the Pacific; early photographs and drawings of Hawaii")
no library admission fees

United Church of Christ Historians
5919 Cullen Drive
Lincoln, NE 68506
Charles Kennedy

United Methodist

(see also Brethren and Lutheran; the United Methodist Church includes the former Methodist Church and the former Evangelical United Brethren Church; the EUB was formed in 1946 by the merger of the majority "Liberal" or "New Constitution" branch of the Church of the United Brethren in Christ, formed in 1889, and the former Evangelical Church; the group of ministers and their followers known as the United Brethren since 1767, added the words "in Christ" to the denomination's name when it was officially organized in 1800, so they would not be confused with the Moravians who also had been known as the "United Brethren" or "Unitas Fratrum" since 1727; in the late 1860s the Hoffmanites left the United Brethren in Christ and in 1878 officially organized themselves as today's United Christian Church; the minority "Radical" or "Old Constitution" United Brethren in Christ have retained their independence since the 1889 scism)

Arkansas Area United Methodist Archives
Olin C. Bailey Library
Hendrix College
1601 Harkrider
Conway, AR 72032-3080
(501) 450-1303; (501) 663-6050 (Little Rock Conference Archivist); (501) 336-9321 (North Arkansas Conference Archivist)
Katy Rice, Little Rock Conference Archivist; Mauzel Beal, North Arkansas Conference Archivist
(Arkansas area Methodist clergy only, SASE required)

Baker University
United Methodist Historical Library
606 Eighth Street
Baldwin City, KS 66006
(785) 594-6451, ext. 380
Harvey Kreutziger
Hours: Mon–Fri 8:00–noon, and by appointment

Barratt's Chapel and Museum

Peninsula Conference, United Methodist
Church
(U.S. Route 113 or State Route 12—
location)
6362 Bay Road (mailing address)
Frederica, DE 19946
(302) 335-5544
E-mail: barratts@aol.com
http://users.aol.col/barratts/home.html
Lynn Hobbs, Curator
Hours: Sat–Sun 1:30–4:30
(the oldest house of worship still extant
in the U.S. built solely for and by a
Methodist Society)

Bridwell Library

(address withheld upon request)

Bush-Meeting Dutch

Illinois College
Jacksonville, IL 62650
(217) 245-3460
Dr. David Koss, Professor of Religion,
Editor
Pub. *The Bush-Meeting Dutch: A
Quarterly Newsletter of Local History
and Genealogy of the Former
Evangelical United Brethren Church,
Its Predecessors, and Sister Churches*,
quarterly, $5.00 per year subscription
(German-American churches)
$2.00 per obituary search

J. B. Cain Archives of Mississippi Methodism

Millsaps-Wilson Library
Millsaps College
Jackson, MS 39210
(601) 974-1077; (601) 974-1082 FAX
E-mail: mcintdw@okra.millsaps.edu
http://www.millsaps.edu/www/library/
cain/index.html
Debra McIntosh, College Archivist
Hours: weekdays 8:30 A.M.–12:30 A.M.
(when the college is in session)
("Methodist church history in
Mississippi; genealogy is not a focus
of this collection.")
research $10.00 per name

California-Nevada United Methodist Archives

Graduate Theological Union
2400 Ridge Road
Berkeley, CA 94709
(650) 952-6219
E-mail: yale@sirius.com
Dr. Stephen E. Yale
Hours: by appointment
Pub. *Newsletter*, semiannually
(second depository at University of the
Pacific)
$5.00 per year membership in Methodist
Historical Society (address withheld,
see below); genealogical research:
$25.00 per hour

Centenary United Methodist Church (Missouri East)

(16th and Pine Streets—location)
55 Plaza Square (mailing address)
Saint Louis, MO 63103
(314) 421-3136
Paula Price, Membership Secretary
Hours: Mon–Fri 9:00–4:00

Commission on Archives and History

35 Highland Avenue
Gardiner, ME 04345
Elizabeth Bachelder, Chairman
(handles historical operations of the New
England Conference (formerly the
Maine Conference, the New
Hampshire Conference, and the
Southern New England Conference) of
the United Methodist Church; the
collection, which pertains primarily
but not exclusively to Methodist
clergy, is currently unavailable, due to
relocation; for New Hampshire
matters, contact Charles W. Kern,
Conference Historian, 4192-09
Northgate Drive, KK9, Kissimmee, FL
34746-6444, (407) 933-0412)

Commission on Archives and History

Western Pennsylvania Conference
United Methodist Church
714 Walnut Street
Mount Pleasant, PA 15666
(724) 547-2288

Archives of DePauw University and Indiana United Methodism

Roy O. West Library
400 South College Avenue
Greencastle, IN 46135
(765) 658-4406; (765) 658-4423
E-mail: wwwilson@depauw.edu
Wesley W. Wilson, Coordinator of
Archives and Special Collections
Hours: Mon–Fri 8:00–5:00, Tue 6:00–
9:30; summer: Mon–Fri 8:00–4:00
Pub. *Newsletter*, annually; *Annual
Report*, free
(includes members of the former Church
of the United Brethren in Christ and
Evangelical Church in Indiana)
fee schedule available upon request

Detroit Conference United Methodist Archives

Shipman Library
Adrian College
111 South Madison
Adrian, MI 49221
(517) 265-5161 (ask for library, then
Methodist Archivist)
Rev. James G. Simmons, Archivist
Hours: usually Mon–Thur 8:00–noon
Pub. *The Historical Messenger*, quarterly
(archives for Detroit Conference
Methodist Episcopal, Methodist
Protestant, Methodist, and United
Methodist churches and clergy)
$4.00 per year membership in The
Friends of the Archives

B. L. Fisher Library

Asbury Theological Seminary
North Lexington Avenue
Wilmore, KY 40390
(606) 858-3581, ext. 235
Sylvia U. Brown, Special Collections
Librarian
Hours: 8:00–12:00 & 1:00–4:30

Florida Conference Archives

(E. T. Roux Library, Florida Southern
College—location)
PO Box 3767 (mailing address)
Lakeland, FL 33802
(941) 688-9276
Nell Thrift, Archivist
Hours: varies
$10.00 donation requested for
genealogical research

General Commission on Archives and History

The United Methodist Church
Drew University Campus
36 Madison Avenue
Madison, NJ 07940
(973) 408-3189; (973) 408-3909 FAX
http://www.gcah.org
Charles Yrigoyen, Jr., Ph.D., Editor
Hours: Mon–Fri 9:00–4:30
Pub. *Methodist History*, quarterly, $15.00
per year subscription; *The Historian's
Digest*
("The center undertakes limited
genealogical research. Our work is
usually limited to obituaries of
ordained clergy, though sometimes we
can find information on missionaries.
The fee is $15.00, non-refundable. We
cannot provide baptismal, death or
marriage data for non-ordained
members of the church, with the
exception of the Northern New Jersey
Conference. It must be noted that
churches are not required to give their
records to a conference archive. We
also undertake limited general research
on subjects pertaining to Methodism.")

Green Mountain College

(Griswold Library, Poultney, VT 05764-
1199—location)
Clover Street, Box 113 (mailing address)
Ocean Park, ME 04063
(802) 287-9313
Charles Schwartz, Curator
Hours: academic year 8:00 A.M.–10:30
P.M., summer 8:00–4:00 (closed
weekends)
(Troy Conference United Methodist and
Welsh ethnic materials; no research in
this collection is done by on-site
library staff)

Historical Library and Archives

Wisconsin United Methodist Conference
Center
750 Windsor Street
PO Box 620
Sun Prairie, WI 53590-0620
(608) 837-7328, ext. 243
Mary Schroeder, Archivist and Historical
Librarian
Hours: Mon–Tue & Thur 8:00–noon
Pub. *Wisconsin Annual Conference
Yearbook and Journal*, annually
research fee requested

The Iliff School of Theology Archives

2201 South University Boulevard
Denver, CO 80210
(303) 744-1287; (303) 777-0164 FAX
Paul Millette, Archivist
Hours: Mon–Fri noon–4:00
(United Methodist Church, Rocky
Mountain Conference, including
church membership and baptism
records)

Illinois Great Rivers Conference

United Methodist Church
Historical Society and Conference
Archives
1211 North Park Street
PO Box 515
Bloomington, IL 61702-0515
(309) 828-5092; (309) 827-4820 FAX
Richard A. Chrisman, Conference
Historian
Pub. *Historical Messenger*, quarterly
search fee: $10.00 per hour plus copy
costs, must send SASE

Archives of the Iowa Conference of the United Methodist Church

Chadwick Library
Iowa Wesleyan College
601 North Main
Mount Pleasant, IA 52641
(319) 385-6321
Esther Wonderlich, Archives Assistant
Hours: Mon–Fri 1:00–3:00 (prefer
written requests)
(Iowa Methodist pastors and Iowa
churches)
$10.00 per name per search

Kansas West Conference Archives of the United Methodist Church

9440 East Boston, Suite 198
Wichita, KS 67207-3600
(316) 684-0266
Leda Bechtel, Archivist
Hours: by appointment
("Emphasis on United Methodist and
predecessor denomination history in
western two-thirds of Kansas, as well
as local churches in that geographic
area, and former clergy.")
research: $8.00 per hour by archivist, no
charge for local church information

Little Rock Conference Depository

Methodist Headquarters Building
1723 Broadway
Little Rock, AR 72204

McKendree College

Lebanon, IL 62254

Memphis Conference United Methodist Archives

Luther L. Gobbel Library
Lambuth University
Lambuth Boulevard
Jackson, TN 38301
(901) 425-3290; (901) 427-3975
Ann R. Phillips, Archivist
Hours: Archives by appointment only
Pub. *Journal of the Memphis Annual
Conference of the United Methodist
Church* (minutes and reports of yearly
meeting), annually, not available by
subscription
(United Methodist religious archives of
extreme West Tennessee and Kentucky
only: obituaries of ministers who died
in the immediate area, no information
on individual church members;
depository of the administrative
business records, not of individual
church records; "We have no paid staff
and can do minimal genealogy
requests on a 'when we have time'
basis, must have SASE.")

Methodist Archives

Houghton Memorial Library
Archives and Special Collections
Huntingdon College
1500 East Fairview Avenue
Montgomery, AL 36106-2148
(334) 833-4413; (334) 263-4465
E-mail: mpickard@huntingdon.edu
Mary Ann Pickard, Archivist
Hours: Mon–Fri 9:00–4:00 by
appointment
(genealogical data limited to Methodist
ministers in Alabama and West
Florida, and college alumni: Methodist
Episcopal Church 1808–1938,
Methodist Protestant Church 1829–
1938, Methodist Episcopal Church,
South 1846–1938, The Methodist
Church 1939–1967, United Methodist
Church from 1968)

Methodist Historical Center

c/o Saint George Church
326 New Street
Philadelphia, PA 19106
(215) 925-7788
Brian McCloskey, Administrator
Hours: 10:00–3:00
(Methodist library and archives for
eastern Pennsylvania Conference—
United Methodist Church only)

Methodist Historical Society

PO Box 127
Madison, NJ 07940
(973) 822-2826

Arthur W. Swartout, Coordinator
Pub. *The Historian's Digest*, quarterly

Methodist Historical Society

(address withheld upon request)

The Methodist Museum

Epworth By The Sea
South Georgia Methodist Conference
Center
PO Box 20407
Saint Simons Island, GA 31522
(912) 638-4050 (Museum)
Mary McCook, Museum Director
Hours: Tue–Sat 9:00–4:00
Pub. *Historical Highlights*, biannually by
the South Georgia Conference
Historical Society
$10.00 per year membership

Minnesota Conference Archives, United Methodist Church

122 West Franklin Avenue, Room 400
Minneapolis, MN 55404
(612) 870-0058, ext. 249; (612) 870-
1260 FAX
E-mail: thelma.boeder@mnumc.org
Thelma Boeder, Archivist
Hours: weekdays only, hours and days
vary

Missouri United Methodist Archives

Central Methodist College Library
Fayette, MO 65248
(660) 248-3391
E-mail: muma@cmc2.cmc.edu
Joy Dodson, Archives Technician
Hours: Mon–Fri 8:00–5:00
research: $5.00 per hour

Historical Center of the Nebraska Conference of the United Methodist Church

(Third Floor, Old Main, Nebraska
Wesleyan University—location)
PO Box 4553 (mailing address)
Lincoln, NE 68504-0553
(402) 465-2175
Erin Nellessen, Curator
Hours: Mon 10:00–12:00, Tue–Fri 9:00–
12:00, and by appointment

North Georgia Methodist Historical Society

1015 Ruckersville Road
Elberton, GA 30635
Rev. Ann Nell Fletcher, Chair
$10.00 per year membership for
individuals, $15.00 per year
membership for families, $5.00 per
year membership for students

Northern Illinois Conference of the United Methodist Church

Garrett-Evangelical Theological
Seminary
2121 Sheridan Road
Evanston, IL 60201
Kevin B. Leonard, Archivist

Hours: by appointment only, written inquiries welcome

(United Methodist and antecedent denominations in approximately the northern third of Illinois: Methodist Church, Methodist Episcopal Church, Evangelical United Brethren, United Brethren in Christ, Evangelical Church, Evangelical Association; also some records of Scandinavian Methodist Churches and organizations from other regions of the United States)

Pacific Northwest Conference Depository
United Methodist Church
Collins Memorial Library
5323 97th Avenue Court West
Tacoma, WA 98416
(253) 627-0700
Rev. Richard A. Seiber, Archivist
Hours: by appointment only

Red Bird Missionary Conference
The United Methodist Church
General Delivery
Roark, KY 40979
(606) 374-6341
Jim W. Morris, Ph.D., Archivist/Secretary

Charles Andrew Rush Library
Birmingham-Southern College
Arkadelphia Road
Birmingham, AL 35254
(205) 226-4740
Hours: Mon–Thur 8:00–midnight, Fri 8:00–5:00, Sat 9:00–5:00, Sun 2:00–12:00

South Carolina United Methodist Church Conference Historical Society
Sandor Teszler Library
Wofford College
North Church Street
Spartanburg, SC 29303-3663
(864) 597-4309
Herbert Hucks, Jr., Curator
Hours: Mon–Fri 9:00–12:00 & 1:30–3:30

Historical Committee, South Dakota Conference
Dakota Wesleyan University
Mitchell, SD 57301

Southeastern Jurisdictional Administrative Council
The United Methodist Church
Commission on Archives and History
The SEJ Heritage Center
PO Box 1165
Lake Junaluska, NC 28745
(704) 452-2881, ext. 781
Mrs. Gerry Reiff, SEJ Director of Archives and History
Hours: Tue–Fri 9:30–4:00; longer hours during summer season

Pub. *SEJ/HS Notes: The Newsletter of the Southeastern Jurisdictional Historical Society, The United Methodist Church*, quarterly, $7.00 per year subscription to Rev. Lawrence Lugar, 334 Grape Arbor Drive, Fayetteville, NC 28301)
(history of Methodism in the southeast and the history of the Lake Junaluska Assembly, but limited genealogical resources, only on United Methodist clergy of the southeast; all local church membership rolls and other records of local churches go to the annual conference depository when no longer needed by the local church)

Southern Illinois Conference of the United Methodist Church
Commission on Archives and History
1919 West Broadway
Mount Vernon, IL 62864
(618) 242-4070; (618) 242-9227 FAX
Rev. Eugene Black, Chairperson
Hours: 9:00–4:00

Southern Methodist University
DeGloyer Library of Special Collections
Dallas, TX 75275
(972) 768-2012; (972) 768-1565 FAX
E-mail: dfarmer@mail.smu.edu
http://www.smu.edu/~cul/degolyer/index.html

Southwestern College
Memorial Library
100 College Street
Winfield, KS 67156

United Methodist Archives—Yellowstone Conference
(Paul M. Adams Memorial Library, Rocky Mountain College, 1511 Poly Drive, Billings, MT 59102—location)
531 Conway (mailing address)
Billings, MT 59105
(406) 248-4401
Rev. Ruth Wight, Archivist; Joyce Jensen, Committee Chair
Hours: by appointment when Adams Library is open
("Yellowstone Conference, particularly Montana portion")
donations accepted

United Methodist Church
Fountain Square
PO Box 505
Contoocock, NH 03229

United Methodist Church, New England Conference, Commission on Archives and History
Historical Society Library
745 Commonwealth Avenue
Boston, MA 02215
(617) 353-1323; (617) 353-3061 FAX
Stephen Pentek, Archives Coordinator
Hours: Mon–Fri 9:00–3:00 (mail inquiries only: Methodist Episcopal,

Methodist or United Methodist Church in New England)

United Methodist Historical Society, Inc.
Lovely Lane Museum
2200 Saint Paul Street
Baltimore, MD 21218
(410) 889-4458
Rev. Edwin Schell, Executive Secretary; Dr. Arthur Thomas, Director of Archives History
Hours: Mon & Fri 10:00–4:00
Pub. *Newsletter 3rd Century Methodism*, three or four times per year
("We are not a genealogical collection; almost all our records may be consulted at the Maryland State Archives.")
$10.00 per year membership for individuals, $20.00 life membership; $10.00 plus SASE for genealogical queries

United Methodist Museum
Epworth By The Sea
PO Box 407
Saint Simons Island, GA 31522
(912) 638-4050
Mary McCook, Director
Hours: Mon 1:00–4:00, Tue–Fri 9:00–12:00 & 1:00–4:00, Sat 9:00–12:00
Pub. *Historical Highlights*, semiannually, $10.00 per year subscription

United Theological Seminary Library
United Methodist Church
1810 Harvard Boulevard
Dayton, OH 45406-4599
(937) 278-5817; (937) 275-5701 FAX
E-mail: library@dnaco
Barry Hamilton, Assistant Librarian
Hours: Mon–Fri (varies with academic terms)
Pub. *Telescope-Messenger*, semiannually, $10.00 per year subscription
(significant holdings relating only to former Evangelical United Brethren Church)

Virginia United Methodist Historical Society
(address withheld upon request)

West Ohio Conference United Methodist Archives Center
Beeghly Library
Ohio Wesleyan University
Delaware, OH 43015
(740) 368-3285
Susan Cohen, Curator
Hours: Mon–Fri 9:00–2:30
(United Methodist, especially Ohio)

West Virginia Conference Methodist Collection
West Virginia Wesleyan College Library
Buckhannon, WV 26201
(304) 473-8456

E-mail: tolliver_t@academ.wvwc.edu
Patricia Prout Tolliver, Researcher
Hours: Mon–Fri 9:00–noon, and by
appointment (please call first, because
the college staff is not able to help
visitors to this collection)
(West Virginia Conference United
Methodist and predecessors; "This is
the depository for the West Virginia
Conference under the Commission on
Archives and History for that
conference.")
no fee required, but donation requested,
copies 10¢ per page

Western North Carolina United Methodist Commission on Archives and History

3400 Shamrock Drive
PO Box 18005
Charlotte, NC 28218-0005
(704) 535-2260, ext. 43
Rev. Gary Ferrell, Archivist; Nancy
Spaine, Assistant Archivist
Hours: Tue–Wed 9:00–4:00 (appointment
requested)
(Western North Carolina Conference of
the United Methodist Church)

World Methodist Council

39 Lakeshore Drive
PO Box 518
Lake Junaluska, NC 28745
(704) 456-9432
Dr. Joe Hale, General Secretary

Andover Harvard Theological Seminary

Library
45 Francis Avenue
Cambridge, MA 02138
(617) 496-1618; (617) 496-4111
E-mail: cwillard@div.harvard.edu
http://divweb.harvard.edu/library/
(manuscript church records)

Universalist

(see Unitarian Universalist)

Waldensian

Museum of Waldensian Heritage
Rodoret Street
Valdese, NC 28690
(704) 874-2531
(Waldenses, French Christian followers
of Pierre Waldo)

Part 4. Special Resources

LINEAGE, HEREDITARY AND PATRIOTIC SOCIETIES

Colonial

Society of Americans of Colonial Descent
PO Box 231
Mill Neck, NY 11765
Roger M. L. Schmitt

Ancient and Honorable Artillery Company of Massachusetts
(4th Floor of Faneuil Hall—location)
Armory, Faneuil Hall (mailing address)
Boston, MA 02109
(617) 227-1638; (617) 227-7221 FAX
Dr. John F. McCaulay, Curator
Hours: Military Museum and Library:
   Mon–Fri 10:00–4:00
(oldest chartered military organization in
   the western hemisphere, and the third
   oldest in the world)

The Order of Descendants of the Ancient and Honorable Artillery Company
Committee on Lineages
253 Tremont Street
Melrose, MA 02176-1835
(781) 662-8034
Dr. Roswell Levi Atwood, Chairman,
   Committee on Lineages
Hours: 9:00–3:00
Pub. *The Ancients*, annually
("male having descent from member of
   The Ancient and Honorable Artillery
   Company 1637–1774, descent from
   minister who preached The Election
   Sermon, General Court member,
   present Company member 'by right of
   descent'.")
$100.00 charter life membership

National Society, Women Descendants of the Ancient and Honorable Artillery Company
1234 South Cumberland Avenue
Park Ridge, IL 60068-5238
(847) 823-0502
Adeline Potter Beier, Honorary President
   National

Society of the Ark and the Dove
c/o Maryland Historical Society
201 West Monument Street
Baltimore, MD 21201
Charles B. Calvert, Governor
Pub. *Chronicles of the Society of the Ark
   and the Dove*, semiannually or as
   needed

National Society, Children of the American Colonists
(see National Society, Daughters of
   American Colonists)

The National Society of the Colonial Dames of America
Dumbarton House
2715 Q Street, N.W.
Washington, DC 20007
(202) 337-2288
Linda H. Mattingly, Administrator
Hours: Mon–Fri 9:00–5:00; Museum:
   Tue–Sat 10:00–1:00

The National Society of the Colonial Dames, Colorado
McAllister House Museum
423 North Cascade Avenue
Colorado Springs, CO 80903
(970) 635-7925

The National Society of the Colonial Dames of America in the State of Connecticut
The Webb-Deane-Stevens Museum
211 Main Street
Wethersfield, CT 06109
(860) 529-0612
Robert A. Guffin, Jr., Director/Curator

The National Society of the Colonial Dames of America, Georgia
329 Abercorn Street
Savannah, GA 31405
Shelby Myrick, Jr.

The National Society of the Colonial Dames of America, Maine
Tate House
(1270 Westbrook Street—location)
4 Walker Street (mailing address)
Portland, ME 04102
(207) 772-2023

The National Society of the Colonial Dames of America in the State of New Jersey
Buris Road
Mount Holly, NJ 08060
(609) 267-1054

The National Society of Colonial Dames of America in the State of New York
Library
215 East 71st Street
New York, NY 10021
(212) 744-3572
Margaret Warner, Executive Secretary
Hours: by appointment

The National Society of the Colonial Dames of America in the State of South Carolina
79 Cumberland Street
Charleston, SC 29401
(843) 722-3767

The National Society of the Colonial Dames of America in Tennessee
Travellers' Rest Historic House Museum
636 Farrell Parkway
Nashville, TN 37220
(615) 832-8197
Mrs. Fletch Coke, Archivist

The National Society of the Colonial Dames of America, Wisconsin
4529 West Bonnie Court
Mequon, WI 53092
(414) 242-4529
Mrs. Samuel E. Greeley, Registrar

National Society, Colonial Dames, XVII Century
1300 New Hampshire Avenue, N.W.
Washington, DC 20036-1595
(202) 293-1700
Sara Downs, Headquarters Secretary
Hours: Mon–Fri 10:00–3:00
Pub. *Review*, three times per year

Georgia Society, Colonial Dames, XVII Century
709 Maple Drive
Griffin, GA 30223
John H. Goddard

South Carolina Society, Colonial Dames, XVII Century
124 Dunbarton Circle
Aiken, SC 29801
(803) 648-8516

Colonial Order of the Acorn
122 East 58th Street
New York, NY 10022-1939

General Society of Colonial Wars
122 East 58th Street
New York, NY 10022-1939

National Society of the Dames of the Court of Honor
2165 Leafmore Drive
Decatur, GA 30033
Harvey Cromwell

National Society of the Dames of the Court of Honor
Oklahoma Society
1111 Ridge Road
Stillwater, OK 74074
Mrs. Pete Pappas, President

National Society, Daughters of American Colonists

National Society, Children of the
American Colonists
2205 Massachusetts Avenue, N.W.
Washington, DC 20008-2813
(202) 667-3076
Mrs. Charles W. Miles, III, Editor
Hours: Tue–Thur 9:00–4:00
Pub. *The Colonial Courier*, three times
per year (spring, fall and winter),
$5.00 per year subscription
invitational membership fees vary by
state; no search fees, contact National
Librarian; queries to be printed in the
magazine, contact National Chairman
of Genealogical Department

Daughters of the American Colonists

Alabama Society
433 West Vista Court
Mobile, AL 36609
(334) 342-6350

Oklahoma Society, National Society, Daughters of American Colonists

11805 Camelot Drive
Oklahoma City, OK 73120-6715
(405) 755-4428
Mrs. Earl J. Hampton, Oklahoma State
Regent

National Society, Daughters of Founders and Patriots of America

National Headquarters
Park Lane Building, Suites 300-05
2025 Eye Street, N.W.
Washington, DC 20006
Stephanie White-Trivas, National
Headquarters Chairperson
Hours: various
Pub. *Newsletter—The Gazette*, three to
four times per year
(requires "an unbroken paternal line of
either the applicant's father or mother,
going back to a founder who arrived in
one of the colonies between May 13,
1607, and May 13, 1687, and further
that in this unbroken line there be an
intermediary patriot ancestor who gave
military or civil service in establishing
American independence in the period
of 1775 to 1784.")

National Society, Daughters of the 17th Century

(address withheld upon request)

Society of Descendants of Colonial Hispanics

Brooks Enterprises
1718 West Robinson Street, #A
Norman, OK 73069-7311
Clifton Brooks, M.D.

Order of Descendants of Colonial Physicians and Chirurgeons

9317 Bent Tree Circle
Wichita, KS 67226
(316) 634-1930

Mrs. Richard C. McGehee, President
General
$100.00 life membership

National Society, Descendants of Early Quakers

(see Religious Archives and
Organizations—Friends)

National Society of Descendants of Lords of Maryland Manors

3721 Alton Place, N.W.
Washington, DC 20016

The Society of Descendants of the Colonial Clergy

255 Madison Street
Dedham, MA 02026
Mrs. Frederick Johnson

Order of the Founders and Patriots of America

15 Pine Street
New York, NY 10005
Pub. *Bulletin*, semiannually
cost set by state societies

The Georgia Salzburger Society

2889 Ebenezer Road
Rincon, GA 31326-3716
(912) 754-7001
Frank L. Perry, Jr., President
Hours: 12 March and Labor Day
Pub. *The Georgia Salzburger Society
Newsletter* (perpetuates the memory of
Lutherans who emigrated from
Salzburg and Germany from 1734–
1752 to the Colony of Georgia, and
updates the genealogy of their
descendants; settled by General
Edward Oglethorpe thirty miles north
of Savannah on the Savannah River as
a buffer with the Uchee Indians)

Holland Society of New York Library

122 East 58th Street
New York, NY 10022-1939
(212) 758-1875
Delia Nelson, Genealogist for Library;
Dr. David Voorhees, Historian and
Editor
Hours: Fri 11:00–4:00 (closed Aug)
Pub. *de Halve Maen (Half Moon)*,
quarterly, $28.50 postpaid per year
subscription

Huguenots

(see Lineage, Hereditary, and Patriotic
Societies—Huguenot)

Jamestowne Society

PO Box 17426
Richmond, VA 23226-7426
(804) 673-6006
Judith N. Hart, Executive Director
Pub. *The Jamestown Society Register of
Qualifying Seventeenth Century
Ancestors*, $10.00
$300.00 life membership

General Society of Mayflower Descendants

National Headquarters
(4 Winslow Street, Plymouth, MA
02360—location)
PO Box 3297 (mailing address)
Plymouth, MA 02361
(508) 746-3188
Caroline Lewis Kardell, Historian
General
Hours: 10:00–3:30
Pub. *The Mayflower Quarterly*, $10.00
per year subscription for non-members

Society of Mayflower Descendants

1825 Catala Road
Birmingham, AL 35216-1746
Mrs. Irvine C. Porter, Corresponding
Secretary

Society of Mayflower Descendants

6208 Staedem Drive
Anchorage, AK 99504
Mrs. Ira E. Walker, Secretary

Society of Mayflower Descendants

1405 West 670 North
Saint George, UT 84770-4644
Mrs. John H. Abraham, Secretary
(Arizona society)

Society of Mayflower Descendants

PO Box 1477
Rogers, AR 72757
(501) 925-1638 (daytime); (501) 925-
3100 (evenings and weekends)
Duane A. Cline, Governor

Society of Mayflower Descendants

405 14th Terrace Level
PO Box 20417
Oakland, CA 94620-0417
(415) 451-9599
Dr. Oliver S. Hayward, Librarian
Hours: Mon 8:00–4:00

Mother Lode Colony of the Society of Mayflower Descendants

3130 Sierra Oaks Drive
Sacramento, CA 95864-5653
(916) 487-7158
Mildred Stanger
Hours: meetings: second Sat (Sept, Nov,
Jan, Mar, May) 12:00
no research locally

The Society of Mayflower Descendants in the State of Connecticut

6 Rogers Drive
Mystic, CT 06355-2951
E-mail: ctsmdh@snet.net
John H. Somers, Historian
Pub. *(Connecticut) Nutmeg Gratings*,
three times per year

Society of Mayflower Descendants in the State of Delaware

111 Norris Road, Alapocas
Wilmington, DE 19803

(302) 655-8066
Mrs. Ellsworth K. Holden, Governor
Pub. *Mayflower Lynes*, semiannually

Society of Mayflower Descendants
9221 West Broward Boulevard, #2411
Plantation, FL 33324
Mrs. George J. Ernst, Secretary

Georgia Society of Mayflower Descendants
359 Whitlock Avenue, S.W.
Marietta, GA 30064
(770) 428-4706
Virginia Hargis, Corresponding Secretary
Pub. *Mayflower News of Georgia*,
semiannually (usually March and
October)

Society of Mayflower Descendants
17 Holua Way
Wahiawa, HI 96786-2715
(808) 621-5277
Mrs. Ramon Maddox, Historian, Editor,
and Administrative Secretary
Pub. *Ka Pupu Nihoniho*, quarterly
$15.00 per year membership

Society of Mayflower Descendants
3860 Elgin Way
Boise, ID 83704
Wilhelmina L. Sackman, Secretary

Society of Mayflower Descendants
703 South Bodin
Hinsdale, IL 60521
Mrs. William van Cleve, Membership
Secretary

Society of Mayflower Descendants
1203 Oakwood Trail
Indianapolis, IN 46260
Mrs. Mack O. Blackburn, Corresponding
Secretary

Iowa Society of Mayflower Descendants
9107 Tanglewood Drive
Des Moines, IA 50322-7422
(515) 252-0929
E-mail: maureenwilson@juno.com
Maureen Wilson, Editor
Pub. *Hawkeye Newsletter*, semiannually
(April and October), $1.00 per issue to
non-members

Society of Mayflower Descendants
516 West Franklin
Liberty, KS 64068
Ernest L. Washburn, Corresponding
Secretary

Louisiana Society of Mayflower Descendants
1582 Henry Clay Avenue
New Orleans, LA 70118
(504) 523-5100 (Secretary's office);
(504) 891-9817 (Secretary's home)
Lydia H. Toso, Secretary
Pub. *Drumbeats*, quarterly

$50.00 application fee, $50.00
membership initiation fee, $38.00 per
year dues

Society of Mayflower Descendants
7 Surrey Lane
Cumberland Foreside, ME 04110
Allison V. Brown, Corresponding
Secretary

Society of Mayflower Descendants in the State of Maryland
5215 Saint Alban's Way
Baltimore, MD 21212-3323
(410) 433-4992
Claire A. Richardson, State Historian
Pub. *The Maryland Mayflower Log*,
irregularly
$25.00 per year membership for
individual Mayflower descendants
only, $250.00 life membership

Massachusetts Society of Mayflower Descendants
376 Boylston Street
Boston, MA 02116-3812
(617) 266-1624; (617) 749-5747 (Editor)
Alicia Crane Williams, Editor
Hours: Mon–Fri 9:00–4:00, open to
members and applicants only
Pub. *The Mayflower Descendant, A
Magazine of Pilgrim Genealogy and
History*, semiannually (c/o 18 Martin's
Cove Road, Hingham, MA 02043;
vols. 1–34 published 1899–1937,
revived in 1985 with vol. 35)
$18.00 per year membership

Society of Mayflower Descendants in the State of Minnesota
1022 Brompton Place
Saint Paul, MN 55118
(612) 457-1022; (612) 871-9191 (Editor)
Donald E. Woods, Historian; John A. S.
Webster, Editor
Hours: noon–5:00
Pub. *Minnesota Pilgrim News*, quarterly,
$3.00 per year subscription

Society of Mayflower Descendants in the State of Mississippi
1540 Kimwood Circle
Jackson, MS 39211-5916
(601) 362-2814; (601) 981-8352
E-mail: bbjonson@teclink.net
Ben B. Johnson, M.D., Deputy Governor
General
Hours: 10:00–4:00
Pub. *Mississippi Mayflower Messenger*,
semiannually (spring and fall)
$15.00 per year membership

The Society of Mayflower Descendants in the State of Missouri
22 Cloverleaf Lane
Saint Louis, MO 63011-4001
(314) 391-1603
E-mail: asimov@mo.net
Matt Cavic, Corresponding Secretary;
Leslie V. Canavan, Governor

Pub. *The Compact*, two to three times
per year
$20.00 per year membership (calendar
year)

Society of Mayflower Descendants
PO Box 366
Manhattan, MT 59741
Mrs. John S. West, Secretary

Society of Mayflower Descendants
8320 North Hazelwood Drive
Lincoln, NE 68510
Florence Clark

Nevada Society of Mayflower Descendants
1839 Deep Creek Drive
Sparks, NV 89434
J. B. Coats, Historian

Society of Mayflower Descendants
1 Oakwood Lane, #6
Goffstown, NH 03045
Edward F. Holden, Editor
Pub. *The Shallop*, semiannually

Society of Mayflower Descendants in the State of New Jersey
142 North Chestnut Street
Westfield, NJ 07090
(908) 233-7410
Mrs. Carl B. Hansen, Secretary
Pub. *New Jersey Newsletter*,
semiannually

New Mexico Society of Mayflower Descendants
6716 McCallum Boulevard
Dallas, TX 75252-5931
Mrs. Charles Runyan, Corresponding
Secretary

Society of Mayflower Descendants in the State of New York
122 East 58th Street
New York, NY 10022-1939
(212) 759-1620
Sondra G. Blewer, Executive Secretary
Hours: Sept–Jun: 9:00–4:30
Pub. *New York Newsletter*, semiannually
$75.00 application fee, $75.00 per year
membership for individuals, $1,000.00
life membership

Society of Mayflower Descendants in the State of North Carolina
219 Woodhaven Road
Greenville, NC 27834-6919
Sylvia Corey, Membership Chairman

Society of Mayflower Descendants
1245 11th Street, North
Fargo, ND 58102
Vivian W. Broberg, Secretary

Society of Mayflower Descendants in Ohio
12145 Thames Place
Cincinnati, OH 45241-6019
(513) 761-6513

Nancy Foster, Corresponding Secretary

Society of Mayflower Descendants in the Commonwealth of Pennsylvania

280 Upper Gulph Road
Wayne, PA 19087-2416
(610) 526-9162 FAX
E-mail: janet_springer@prodigy.com
http://www.libertynet.org/~maflower
Janet Springer, Secretary
Pub. *Pennsylvania Mayflower Quarterly*
$40.00 + $15.00 to join, $20.00 per year
  membership, sliding scale of life
  memberships

Rhode Island Mayflower Descendants

35 Hodsell Street
Cranston, RI 02910
Mrs. Harold P. Williams, Secretary

Society of Mayflower Descendants

843 O'Sullivan Drive
Mount Pleasant, SC 29464
Nancy B. Hill, Corresponding Secretary

Society of Mayflower Descendants in South Dakota

PO Box 638
Armour, SD 57313
(605) 724-2129
Sharon Wiese, Secretary

Society of Mayflower Descendants in Texas

7923 Woodway
Houston, TX 77063
(713) 974-2766
Mrs. Jack L. Vandagriff
Pub. *Quarterly*
$14.00 per year membership; $35.00
  admission fee

Society of Mayflower Descendants, State of Utah

3608 South 2400 East
Salt Lake City, UT 84109
Russell Nichols, Governor; Lynne
  Turner, Secretary

Society of Mayflower Descendants in Washington State

715 North 77th Street
Seattle, WA 98103
(206) 783-7674
Margaret Hyre, Corresponding Secretary
Hours: 9:00–5:00
Pub. *Evergreen Log*, three times per year

Society of Mayflower Descendants

4414 Staunton Avenue
Charleston, WV 25304
Mrs. Charles A. Wood, Secretary

Society of Mayflower Descendants

352 River Drive
Appleton, WI 54915
Mary C. Howden, Secretary

Society of Mayflower Descendants

21 South Vale
Sheridan, WY 82801
Helen H. Benth, Secretary

National Society of New England Women

24 Elizabeth Drive
Bella Vista, AR 72714-2452
Ruth M. Oberhelman, President General
Pub. *The Clipper*, quarterly, $3.00 per
  year subscription

National Society of Old Plymouth Colony Descendants

24 Pilgrim Drive
Winchester, MA 01890-3371
Mrs. Francis Harding Huron, President
  General
$75.00 life membership

Saint Nicholas Society of the City of New York

122 East 58th Street
New York, NY 10022-1939

Sons and Daughters of the Pilgrims, National Society

3917 Heritage Hills Drive, #104
Bloomington, MN 55437-2633
(612) 893-9747 (evenings); (612) 885-
  9776 (days)
E-mail: alf22@juno.com
Arthur Louis Finnell, Registrar General
Pub. *The Pilgrim News-Letter*, two times
  per year

Sons and Daughters of the Pilgrims

Massachusetts Branch
PO Box 164
Stoneham, MA 02180
(781) 438-4165
Wayne E. Higley, Jr., Registrar

Sons and Daughters of the Victims of Colonial Witch Trials

PO Box 164
Stoneham, MA 02180
(781) 438-4165
Wayne E. Higley, Jr., Registrar

National Society Sons of American Colonists

9033 Lyndale Avenue, South, Suite 108
Bloomington, MN 55420-3535
(612) 885-9776
Arthur Louis Finnell, Registrar General
Hours: by appointment
Pub. *The Colonial Son*, one or two times
  per year

National Society Southern Dames of America

414 North Walnut Street
PO Box 43
Florence, AL 35631
Mrs. James A. Koonce

The Welcome Society of Pennsylvania

415 South Croskey Street
Philadelphia, PA 19146
(215) 732-2322
Sara L. March, Secretary
Hours: Mon–Fri 9:00–5:00
(descendants of those who arrived in
  Pennsylvania with William Penn
  between December 1681 and
  December 1682)
$20.00 per year membership, $18.00 per
  year membership for individuals living
  over 100 miles away, $400.00 life
  membership

Society of Mayflower Descendants in the State of Colorado

1069 South Garfield Street
Denver, CO 80209-5007
(303) 759-5989
Virginia Kracaw, Deputy Governor and
  Editor; Helen M. Clark, Secretary
Pub. *The Pilgrim Times*, two times per
  year
$20.00 per year membership for
  individuals, $30.00 initiation fee,
  $300.00 life membership

Revolutionary War

National Society, Children of the American Revolution (D.A.R.)

1776 D Street, N.W.
Washington, DC 20006-5392

Continental Ladies

57 Peirce Street
PO Box 14
East Greenwich, RI 02818
(401) 884-4110

National Society, Daughters of the American Revolution (D.A.R.)

1776 D Street, N.W.
Washington, DC 20006-5392
(202) 879-3229
http://www.dar.org
Eric G. Grundset, Library Director
Hours: Mon–Fri 8:45–4:00, Sun 1:00–
  5:00 (closed Sun before holiday, and
  closed to the public in mid-Apr)
Pub. *Daughters of the American
  Revolution Magazine*, ten times per
  year, $12.00 per year subscription;
  Continental Columns, quarterly
  (reprinted in *DAR Magazine*)
(collection includes "all periods of U.S.
  history and records for the entire
  country")
entrance fee to non-members

Daughters of the American Revolution

General John Sutter Chapter
(916) 488-4856
Margaret Wilson
Hours: meetings third Sat 1:00

Daughters of the American Revolution
Francis Vigo Chapter DAR Genealogical
  Library
3 West Scott Street
Vincennes, IN 47592
(812) 882-2096
Jane Prather Niehaus, Librarian
Hours: Thur 10:00–4:00
(early Knox County, Indiana, genealogy
  and history)
photocopies: 10¢ each

Daughters of the American Revolution
1887 Northcliff Drive
Columbus, OH 43229-5332
http://www.Chesapeake.net/DAR/

Daughters of the Cincinnati
122 East 58th Street
New York, NY 10022-1939
Mrs. Robert G. Shaw, Registrar

Descendants of the Signers of the Declaration of Independence
c/o Historical Society of Pennsylvania
1300 Locust Street
Philadelphia, PA 19107

Society of the Descendants of Washington's Army at Valley Forge
PO Box 915
Valley Forge, PA 19482-0915
(610) 666-5464
Betty Brown Miller, Commander-in-
  Chief
Pub. *The Encampment*, quarterly

Rosalie Daughters of the American Revolution
100 Orleans Street
Natchez, MS 39120
(601) 445-4555

Society of the Cincinnati Library
2118 Massachusetts Avenue, N.W.
Washington, DC 20008
(202) 785-2040
Sandra L. Powers, Library Director;
  Ellen McCallister Clark, Public
  Services Librarian
Hours: Mon–Fri 10:00–4:00
(not a genealogical library, but for
  Revolutionary War research)

The National Society of the Sons of the American Revolution
National Headquarters
1000 South Fourth Street
Louisville, KY 40203
(502) 589-1776
Michael Christian, Librarian; Robert A.
  Lentz, Executive Director
Hours: 9:30–4:30
Pub. *SAR Magazine*, quarterly, $10.00
  for four consecutive issues
  subscription
$12.00 per year membership

Sons of the Revolution
Sons of the Revolution Building
600 South Central Avenue
Glendale, CA 91204
(818) 240-1775
Edwin W. Coles, Library Director
Hours: Wed 12:00–8:00; Thur–Sat
  10:00–4:00

Sons of the Revolution in the State of Michigan
411 Bartlett Street
Lansing, MI 48915
James T. Lyons

Varnum Continentals
6 Main Street
PO Box 14
East Greenwich, RI 02818
(401) 884-4110

War of 1812

National Society, United States Daughters of 1812
1461 Rhode Island Avenue, N.W.
Washington, DC 20005
(202) 745-1812
Hours: by appointment
Pub. *National Society United States
  Daughters of 1812 Newsletter*,
  quarterly

Oklahoma Society, National Society United States Daughters of 1812
9015 East 28th Street
Tulsa, OK 74129-6801
(918) 627-1431
Mrs. George F. Williams, State President

United States Daughters of 1812
Alexander Daugherty Chapter
901 Storey
Midland, TX 79701
(915) 683-2015

Veteran Corps of Artillery, State of New York
Constituting the Military Society of the
  War of 1812
Seventh Regiment Armory
643 Park Avenue
New York, NY 10021
(212) 249-3919
John E. Connelly, III, Major General
Hours: Tue 5:30–10:00
Pub. *Red Book*, biannually

General Society of the War of 1812
PO Box 106
Mendenhall, PA 19357
Dr. Forrest R. Schäeffer
membership fees from state societies;
  search fee: $10.00 per name

Society of the War of 1812 in the State of Ohio
34465 Crew Road
Pomeroy, OH 45769

(740) 992-7874
Keith D. Ashley, Secretary-Treasurer
Pub. *Lake Erie Ledger*, semiannually
$21.00 per year membership

Society of the Descendants of the Alamo
PO Box 4641
Honolulu, HI 96812
Charles Edward Phebus, President
  General
Pub. *Alamo Descendants Newsletter*
membership open to any person twenty-
  one years of age or older who can
  prove their legal, lineal, or collateral
  descent from one of the heroes of the
  Alamo who died in its defense

Mexican War

Aztec Club of 1847
The Military Society of the Mexican War
  1846–1848
9101 MacMahon Drive
Burke, VA 22015
C. Lansdown Hunt
(descendants of participants in the war
  with Mexico)

Descendants of Mexican War Veterans, DMWV
National Office
PO Box 830482
Richardson, TX 75083-0482
E-mail: dmwv@aol.com;
  members.aol.com/dmwv/home.htm
Steven R. Butler, President
Pub. *Mexican War Journal*, quarterly,
  $25.00 per year subscription for non-
  members; *The American Eagle, A
  Newsletter of the Descendants of
  Mexican War Veterans*, quarterly,
  $15.00 per year subscription for non-
  members
$10.00 adult initiation fee, $5.00 junior
  initiation fee, $25.00 per year adult
  membership; no search fees

Civil War

Children of the Confederacy
Memorial Building
328 North Boulevard
Richmond, VA 23220-4057
(804) 355-1636; (804) 353-1396 FAX
E-mail: hqudc@aol.com
Hours: Mon–Fri 9:00–4:30
Pub. *The Courier*, quarterly, $8.00 per
  issue

Children of the Confederacy, Chapter 425
6318 East Ridge Drive
Shreveport, LA 71106
(318) 868-8214

Civil War Descendants Society
Confederate Descendants Society
PO Box 233
Athens, AL 35611

Civil War Plymouth Pilgrims Descendants Society
113 Briarwood Lane
Summerville, SC 29483
(843) 875-9013
E-mail: Qmsgtboots@aol.com
http://members.aol.com/CWPPDS/
   homepage.html
Edward Boots, President
Pub. *Voices From Plymouth*
(membership open to descendants of and
   anyone interested in the Union
   soldiers, dubbed "The Plymouth
   Pilgrims," who participated in the
   Battle of Plymouth, North Carolina, in
   April of 1864: 101st and 103rd
   Pennsylvania, 16th Connecticut, 85th
   New York and Second North Carolina
   regiments; not to be confused with the
   Plymouth Pilgrims of Massachusetts)
$15.00 per year membership, c/o Scott
   Holmes, 4910 Grape Tree Lane,
   Roanoke, VA 24018

Dames of the Loyal Legion of the United States
(see Military Order of the Loyal Legion
   of the United States)

Daughters of the Union, 1861–1865, Inc.
11396 Grand Oak Drive
Grand Blanc, MI 48439
(313) 694-6879
Mrs. Robert Hatten

Daughters of Union Veterans of the Civil War, 1861–1865
National Headquarters, D.U.V.
   Registrar's Office
503 South Walnut Street
Springfield, IL 62704-1932
(217) 544-0616
Anna Kinnison, National Treasurer
Hours: Mon–Fri 9:00–4:00, Sat–Sun by
   appointment
(membership limited to descendants of
   Civil War Union veterans)
visitations free

Daughters of Union Veterans of the Civil War, 1861–1865
4103 Sudley Road
Haymarket, VA 22069
(202) 785-2316
Sallie C. Pusey, Department President
Pub. *General Orders*, semiannually

Daughters of Union Veterans of the Civil War, 1861–1865
Iowa Department
2787 335th Street
Menlo, IA 50164
(515) 524-5110
Sherry Foresman

Daughters of Union Veterans of the Civil War, 1861–1865
Minnesota Department
325 South Maple
LeCenter, MN 56057
(507) 357-4488
Helen Meyer, National President
$10.00 per year membership

Daughters of Union Veterans of the Civil War, 1861–1865
3601 N.W. 19th
Oklahoma City, OK 73107
Mrs. Joe J. Stone, Department President

Daughters of Union Veterans of the Civil War, 1861–1865
425 Evergreen Drive
Hurst, TX 76054-2013
(817) 577-0645
E-mail: rebeltrumpet@worldnet.att.net
Kathy Wells, President Tent #1, Texas
Hours: meetings: fourth Sat 11:00
(a patriotic and historical organization)
$17.25 per year membership

Ladies of the Grand Army of the Republic, Inc.
46 Chassin Avenue
Eggertsville, NY 14226-4203
(716) 833-6308
Evelyn Petch Krantz, National Registrar
Pub. *Bugle Call*, quarterly, $4.00 per
   year subscription
(open to all female blood-relatives, ten
   years of age or older, of honorably
   discharged Union soldiers, sailors and
   marines of the Civil War, and also ex-
   army nurses of that war, 20,000
   records of eligibility on file; oldest of
   the Allied Orders that require direct
   lineage with a Union Civil War
   Veteran)
donations accepted, SASE required

G.A.R. Memorial and Veterans' Military Museum
23 East Downer Place
PO Box 1865
Aurora, IL 60507-1865
(630) 897-7221
Art Stiegleiter, Director
Hours: Mon, Wed & Fri noon–4:00, and
   by appointment
(local history, genealogy, military)

Grand Army of the Republic
Grand Army of the Republic Memorial
   Museum
78 East Washington Street
Chicago, IL 60602
(312) 269-2926
Laura Linard, Curator

Women's Relief Corps National Headquarters
Grand Army of the Republic Museum
629 South Seventh Street
Springfield, IL 62703-1636
(217) 522-4373

Bonita Wiggins
Hours: Wed–Sat 10:00–4:00, and by
   appointment

Hood's Texas Brigade Association
The Harold B. Simpson Confederate
   Research Center
Hill College
Lamar Drive
PO Box 619
Hillsboro, TX 76645
(254) 582-2555
Dr. B. D. Patterson, Director; Peggy Fox,
   Assistant Director
Hours: Mon–Fri 8:00–12:00 & 1:00–
   4:00
Pub. *Newsletter* (not genealogical),
   semiannually
(The Confederacy: Alabama, Arkansas,
   Florida, Georgia, Louisiana,
   Mississippi, North Carolina, South
   Carolina, Tennessee, Texas and
   Virginia; also Kentucky, Maryland and
   Missouri)
$5.00 per year membership

Military Order of the Loyal Legion of the United States
Dames of the Loyal Legion of the United
   States
1805 Pine Street
Philadelphia, PA 19103
(215) 546-2425
William A. Hamann, III, Recorder-in-
   Chief
Hours: Mon–Sat 10:00–4:00
Pub. *Historical Journal Quarterly*
(for descendants of Union officers or
   their siblings)

Military Order of the Stars and Bars
Sons of Confederate Veterans
1307 Concord Road
Smyrna, GA 30080
C. D. Eubanks

Military Order of the Stars and Bars
New Mexico Sons of Confederate
   Veterans
3021 Espanola, N.E.
Albuquerque, NM 87111

Indian Territory Society—Military Order of the Stars and Bars
730 Lakeshore Drive
Stillwater, OK 74075
(405) 743-0103
K. Patrick Sohrwide, Society
   Commander
$30.00 per year membership (open to all
   male descendants of Confederate
   officers and civil officials of the
   Confederate states and Confederate
   government)

Military Order of the Stars and Bars
Sons of Confederate Veterans-Camp
   McIntosh (Tulsa)
PO Box 35851
Tulsa, OK 74153-0851

(918) 252-2890; (918) 492-1054
(Commander)
Carl Fallen, Commander
Hours: meetings at Promonade Meeting
Room: third Thur 6:15
Pub. *Confederate Veteran*, bimonthly
(Oklahoma Confederate Veteran Grave
Location Project: "The Camp is
searching for Confederate Veterans
buried in Oklahoma only; the public is
requested to send any known
information concerning the burial
locations of Confederate Veterans
nationally"; history, genealogy,
southern heritage)
$14.00 per year membership

Military Order of the Stars and Bars

Sons of Confederate Veterans
PO Box 59
Columbia, TN 38402-0059
(800) MY-SOUTH
E-mail: scvihq@edge.net.scv.org
Ronald T. Clemmons, Executive Director
Hours: Mon–Fri 9:00–5:00
Pub. *Confederate Veteran*, bimonthly,
$14.00 per year subscription in the
U.S., $26.00 per year subscription
elsewhere
$19.00 per year membership

Military Order of the Stars and Bars

Sons of Confederate Veterans
West Virginia Division
RR 9, Box 67
Princeton, WV 24740
(304) 487-0829
E-mail: commander@inetone.net
Glenn Belcher, Division Commander
Hours: daily 10:00–5:00
Pub. *Mountain Rebel*, quarterly
$3.00 per year full membership for
individuals

Military Order of the Stars and Bars

Sons of Confederate Veterans
Flat Top Copperheads Camp 1694
PO Box 1846
Princeton, WV 24740
(304) 425-4990
E-mail: commander@inetone.net
Glenn Belcher, Commander
Pub. *Copperhead Courier*, monthly
$34.00 per year Full membership for
individuals, $8.00 per year Associate
membership for individuals

Sons of Confederate Veterans

(see Military Order of the Stars and
Bars)

Oklahoma Division—Sons of Confederate Veterans

3500 Wagonwheel Road
Edmond, OK 73083
(405) 348-7907
E-mail: rebeljag@aol.com
Jeff Massey, Division Commander
Pub. *The Rebel Yell*, monthly, $20.00 per
year subscriptions

$350.00 per year membership (open to
all male descendants of War Between
the States Confederate veterans)

Sons of Union Veterans of the Civil War

411 Bartlett Street
Lansing, MI 48915
James T. Lyons, National Secretary

New Jersey Department, Sons of Union Veterans of the Civil War

67 Pilgrim Pathway
Ocean Grove, NJ 07756
William Freck
(has over 60,000 burial sites of New
Jersey Civil War veterans)

New York Department Sons of Union Veterans of the Civil War

501 Willow Avenue
Ithaca, NY 14850
(607) 272-7314 (Home); (607) 273-1611
(Work)
Danny Wheeler, State Commander and
National History Book Coordinator
(has lists and old books of Sons of Union
Veterans of the Civil War and of the
G.A.R.)

New York Sons of Union Veterans of the Civil War

213 Dixon Drive
Syracuse, NY 13219-2711
(315) 488-4076
Jerome L. Orton, Secretary-Treasurer
Pub. *The Volunteer*, five times per year,
$4.00 per year subscription
(records of the G.A.R., especially Posts
#2, 9, 140, numerous state and
national proceedings, numerous
"Sons" records of New York State;
unit histories, but no in-depth
genealogy; large collection of material
on children of Civil War soldiers still
alive, and some widows)
membership open to direct descendants
or collateral relatives, plus Associate
membership available

Department of Ohio Sons of Union Veterans of the Civil War

2449 Center Avenue
Alliance, OH 44601
(330) 823-6919
Richard L. Greenwalt, Past Commander-
in-Chief, Ohio Department Secretary
Pub. *Lineage Society*
(tracing Ohio Civil War veterans, no in-
depth genealogy)

Sons of Union Veterans of the Civil War

H.E.K. Hall Camp #28
Rt. 1, Box 239
Chelsea, VT 05038
Merlin T. Doyle, Secretary-Treasurer

United Daughters of the Confederacy

Memorial Building
328 North Boulevard
Richmond, VA 23220-4057
(804) 355-1636; (804) 353-1396 FAX
E-mail: hqudc@aol.com
Hours: Mon–Fri 9:00–4:30
Pub. *United Daughters of the
Confederacy*, eleven times per year
(monthly, except June/July combined),
$12.00 per year subscription, includes
queries

United Daughters of the Confederacy

Joseph E. Johnston Chapter #198
261 Anderson Drive
Eufaula, AL 36027-6020
Mrs. Curtis A. Hicks, President

United Daughters of the Confederacy

Alabama Division
403 Sunset Avenue
Albertville, AL 35950
(205) 878-2920

A & I Van Nostrand Woman's Relief Corps #169

(Town of Granger, Allegany County—
location)
5507 County Road 4 (mailing address)
Fillmore, NY 14735
(716) 567-8718
Delores B. Curry, President, Corps #169
Hours: meetings: second Mon 7:00
$2.00 membership

Wisconsin Veterans Museum Research Center

30 West Mifflin Street
Madison, WI 53707
(608) 267-1790; (608) 264-7615 FAX
E-mail: museum@mail.state.wi.us
http://badger.state.wi.us/agencies/dva/
museum/wvmmain.html
Hours: Tue–Fri 9:30–4:30
("Computerized listing of Wisconsin
Civil War soldiers")

The Society of Civil War Families of Ohio

The Ohio Genealogical Society (OGS)
Library
34 Sturges Avenue
PO Box 2625
Mansfield, OH 44906-0625
(419) 522-9077; (419) 522-0224 FAX
http://www.ogs.org
Thomas Stephen Neel, Office Manager;
Elizabeth S. Glasgow, Librarian
Hours: summer (1 Jun–1 Sept): Tue–Sat
9:00–5:00; winter (1 Sept–1 Jun): Tue
& Thur 1:00–5:00, Wed 9:00–1:00,
Fri–Sat 9:00–5:00
Pub. *The Report*, quarterly; *The Ohio
Genealogical Society Newsletter*,
monthly; *Ohio Records and Pioneer*

Families, quarterly, $18.00 per year subscription; *Ohio Civil War Genealogy Journal*, quarterly, $18.00 per year subscription

(sponsors First Families of Ohio, a lineage society for members with pre-Dec 31, 1821 Ohio ancestors; The Society of Civil War Families of Ohio, a lineage society for members with Ohio ancestors who served in the Civil War)

$27.00 per year membership for individuals, $32.00 per year joint membership (includes *The Report* and *The Ohio Genealogical Society Newsletter*)

Indian Wars

Continental Society Sons of Indian Wars
3917 Heritage Hills Drive, #104
Bloomington, MN 55437-2633
(612) 893-9747 (evenings); (612) 885-9776 (days)
Arthur Louis Finnell, Registrar General
Pub. *Peace Pipe*, two times per year

Spanish-American War

National Fort Daughters of '98
Junior Organization of United Spanish War Veterans
7101 Hope Avenue
Cleveland, OH 44102
Mrs. Marion E. Gross, National Adjutant
Hours: Mon–Fri 9:00–5:00
Pub. *Daughters of '98 Bulletin*, quarterly
$2.00 per year membership

Sons of the Spanish-American War Veterans
1560 Sonoma Avenue
Santa Rosa, CA 95405-6644
Jack A. Dempsey, National Secretary
(membership open to sons, grandsons, great-grandsons, nephews, grand nephews, great-grand nephews of veterans of the Spanish-American War; no information on veterans available from Secretary)
$3.00 per year membership

National Auxiliary United Spanish War Veterans
414 East Avenue
North Augusta, SC 29841-3837
(803) 442-9321
Marie C. Cruise, National Secretary-Treasurer
Hours: Mon–Fri 9:00–5:00
Pub. *General Orders*, semiannually; special notices as needed
(primarily interested in Veterans)
$3.00 per year membership, special mailing list $3.00 per year

Miscellaneous Military

Military Order of Foreign Wars of the United States 1894-1994
45 Robert Circle
Cranston, RI 02905
Col. John Skadorowski
("Membership is bestowed upon officers and former officers of the Armed Forces of the United States, and its allies, who meet certain requirements. So too lineal descendants of officers who served in foreign wars of the United States from The War of the Revolution to The Persian Gulf Conflict are welcome to inquire as to eligibility. It is well to keep in mind that membership is by invitation only. Candidates must be sponsored and seconded by men and women on the active membership roster.")

Military Order of the Purple Heart in the United States
5413-B Backlick Road
Springfield, VA 22151
(703) 642-5360
John B. Kirby, Adjutant General
Pub. *Purple Heart Magazine*, bimonthly (for combat wounded veterans), $5.00 per year subscription

Military Order of the Purple Heart in the United States
Ladies Auxiliary
419 Franklin Street
Reading, MA 01867
(781) 944-1844
Nancy C. Klare, National Secretary
Hours: 9:00–6:00
Pub. *Purple Heart Magazine*, bimonthly

Order of Daedalians
Building 1635, Kelly Air Force Base
San Antonio, TX 78241

Regional

Native Daughters of the Golden West
555 Baker Street
San Francisco, CA 94117-1405
(415) 921-2664
Hours: Reference Room: first Tue 10:00–2:00 and by appointment
(includes over 33,000 entries in *Roster of California Pioneers*, people who entered the state or were born in the state prior to 1870)

Grand Parlor, Native Sons of the Golden West
414 Mason Street, Suite 300
San Francisco, CA 94102
(415) 392-1223; (415) 392-1224 FAX
Ronald W. Koepen, Grand Secretary
Hours: 7:00–3:00

Pub. *The Native Son*, six times per year
$15.00 per year membership

Los Fundadores, The Founders and Friends of Santa Clara County
(City of Santa Clara Civic Center, 1509 Warburton Avenue, Santa Clara, CA 95050—location)
1053 South White Road (mailing address)
San Jose, CA 95127
(408) 926-1165; (408) 248-ARTS (24-hour message)
Hours: meetings: first Sun
Pub. *Los Fundadores* (California's Spanish/Mexican period, genealogy of early California; articles about the Hispanic progenitors of California; early American pioneers, recognition of Native Americans), quarterly
$11.00 per year membership for individuals, $16.50 per year membership for families or societies; free queries for members

Los Californianos, Hispanic Ancestors of Alta California
4530 LaCrosse Avenue
San Diego, CA 92117
(619) 273-2260
Alice Thomson, Membership Chairman
Hours: quarterly meetings at various locations: Sat & Sun
Pub. *Antepasados*, annually; *Noticias*, quarterly
(descendants of Hispanics in Alta California before February 1848)
regular membership subject to approval of Genealogy Committee, spouses also eligible, historians and libraries (corresponding) eligible with approval of board

Descendants of the Founders of Ancient Windsor
33 Hillcrest Road
Windsor, CT 06095
(860) 688-6822
Donna H. Siemiatkoski, Editor
Hours: Windsor Historical Society: Tue–Sat (Apr–Nov), Mon–Fri (Dec–Mar) by appointment 10:00–4:00
Pub. *Newsletter: Descendants of the Founders of Ancient Windsor*, quarterly
$5.00 per year membership, plus $15.00 (one time) registration fee

Saybrook Colony Founders Association, Inc.
PO Box 1635
Old Saybrook, CT 06475-1000
(860) 388-2234; (860) 395-3123
Elaine F. Staplins, President
Pub. *Hear-Saye*, quarterly
(genealogical services; social history of Saybrook Colony)
$12.00 per year membership

Society of the Descendants of the Founders of Hartford
PO Box 215
West Hartford, CT 06107
Allen R. Yale, Genealogist
$25.00 initial membership, $10.00 per year thereafter, $150.00 life membership

Society of the Founders of Norwich, Connecticut
348 Washington Street
PO Box 13
Norwich, CT 06360

Daughters of Hawaii
(address withheld upon request)

The Idaho Genealogical Society, Inc.
4620 Overland Road, #204
Boise, ID 83705-2867
(208) 384-0542
Jane Walls Golden, President
Hours: daily with volunteers
Pub. *Idaho Genealogical Society Quarterly*
(sponsors Oregon Trail Project: certificates given to descendants of Oregon Trail pioneers—families who came west 1811–1911; to descendants of pioneers—residing in Idaho on or before 3 July 1890; and to descendants of early settlers—settled in Idaho between 4 July 1890 and December 31, 1900)
$10.00 per year membership for individuals, $12.50 per year membership for couples; $10.00 application fee for Oregon Trail certificate; research $10.00 per hour

Society of Indiana Pioneers
Indiana State Library and Historical Building
315 West Ohio Street
Indianapolis, IN 46202-3299
(317) 233-6588
Colleen Ridlen, Genealogist
Hours: by appointment
Pub. *Yearbook*, annually

Kansas Council of Genealogical Societies, Inc.
PO Box 3858
Topeka, KS 66604-6858
(785) 774-4411 (President)
Ruth Keys Clark, President
Pub. *The Kansas Review*, quarterly
(sponsors Certificate Program and *Forgotten Settlers of Kansas* series: Territorial Certificate for direct descendants of ancestors who lived in Kansas prior to 29 January 1861, Pioneer Certificate for direct descendants of ancestors who lived in Kansas between 29 January 1861 and 31 December 1880, and Early Settler Certificate for direct descendants of ancestors who lived in Kansas between 1 January 1881 and 31 December 1900)
$10.00 per year voting membership (any genealogical or historical organization in Kansas), $10.00 per year affiliate membership (any person or organization with an interest in genealogy)

Native Sons of Kansas City
(4200 West 54th Street, Shawnee Mission, KS 66205—location)
PO Box 1111 (mailing address)
Shawnee Mission, KS 66222
(913) 432-9231

Sons and Daughters of the Soddies
The Sod House Society of America
Sod Town Pioneer Homestead Museum
PO Box 393
Colby, KS 67701

Society of Boonesborough
PO Box 859
Richmond, KY 40476-0859
(606) 623-3471
Joseph F. Ballew, Jr., Registrar and Treasurer
Hours: anytime
Pub. *Boonesborough Post*, semiannually; *Society of Boonesborough Yearbook*, biannually, no subscription available
(descendants of pioneers who lived at Boonesborough between 1775 and 1810)
$10.00 per year membership

Society of Kentucky Pioneers
(address withheld upon request)
Pub. *Kentucky Pioneer Genealogy and Records*

Louisiana Colonials
1911 Octavia Street
New Orleans, LA 70115

Piscataqua Pioneers
210 Lowell Street
Wilmington, MA 01887
William Frost
(descendants of original settlers on the Piscataqua River in Maine and New Hampshire prior to 1776)

The Hereditary Order of the First Families of Massachusetts
The Committee on Admissions
253 Tremont Street
Melrose, MA 02176-1835
(781) 662-8034
Dr. Roswell Levi Atwood, Chairman, Committee on Admissions
Hours: 9:00–3:00
Pub. *Puritan Chronicle*, annually
(descendants of settlers in the Massachusetts Bay Colony before 1650)
$65.00 entrance fee, $20.00 per year membership

National Society of Old Plymouth Colony Descendants
(see Lineage, Hereditary, and Patriotic Societies—Colonial)

The Plymouth Hereditary Society
The Secretary General
253 Tremont Street
Melrose, MA 02176-1835
(781) 662-8034
Dr. Roswell Levi Atwood, Secretary General
Hours: 9:00–3:00
Pub. *Plymouth Annals*, annually
("An applicant must be a member of one of the following: The General Society Sons of the Revolution, The National Society Sons of the American Revolution, The National Society of the Daughters of the American Revolution. There must be proven descent from ancestors who resided in Plymouth Colony previous to the year 1692.")
$100.00 life membership

Sons and Daughters of the First Settlers of Newbury, Massachusetts
76 State Street
PO Box 444
Newburyport, MA 01950
Noreen Pramberg, Executive Secretary/ Editor
Hours: by appointment
Pub. *Descend-O-Gram*, quarterly
$25.00 membership application, $10.00 per year membership for individuals, $5.00 per year junior membership, $250.00 life membership

Descendants of the First Families of Minnesota
3917 Heritage Hills Drive, #104
Bloomington, MN 55437-2633
(612) 893-9747 (evenings); (612) 885-9776 (days)
E-mail: alf22@juno.com
Arthur Louis Finnell, Registrar General
Hours: by appointment

Descendants of the Founders of New Jersey
109 Christopher Street
Montclair, NJ 07042
(973) 744-2926
Dorothy E. Baldwin, Registrar General
Pub. *Founders of New Jersey—Brief Biographies by Descendants*, irregularly

Society of Richmond County (North Carolina) Descendants and Richmond County Historical Collection
PO Box 848
Rockingham, NC 28380
(910) 997-6641
Joe M. McLaurin, President

Pub. *The Richmond County Record*, three times per year
$18.00 per year membership

Pioneer Daughters
Pembina County Chapter
Neche, ND 58265
(701) 886-7619

First Families of Guernsey County
65664 North 77 Drive
Cambridge, OH 43725
Mary Kappes
(membership open to descendants of residents of Guernsey County before 1830)

First Families of Harrison County
Harrison County Genealogical Society, Chapter OGS
Baker Institute for Local Studies
168 East Market Street
Cadiz, OH 43907
(740) 942-3900; (740) 942-3641 (President); (740) 922-0240 (Ms. Fergeson); (740) 942-3214 (Membership)
Dorothea L. Greer, President; Bernice Fergeson; Eleanor Birney, Membership; Shirley Craker, Chairperson, First Families of Harrison County
Hours: Tue & Thur 11:00–4:00, and by appointment
Pub. *Our Harrison Heritage*, quarterly (winter, spring, summer, fall)
(members of First Families of Harrison County must have an ancestor who was in Harrison County by Dec 31, 1830)
$5.00 per year membership for individuals, $7.00 per year joint membership, $100.00 life membership for individuals, $150.00 joint life membership

The First Families of Ohio
The Ohio Genealogical Society (OGS)
Library
34 Sturges Avenue
PO Box 2625
Mansfield, OH 44906-0625
(419) 522-9077; (419) 522-0224 FAX
http://www.ogs.org
Thomas Stephen Neel, Office Manager; Elizabeth S. Glasgow, Librarian
Hours: summer (1 Jun–1 Sept): Tue–Sat 9:00–5:00; winter (1 Sept–1 Jun): Tue & Thur 1:00–5:00, Wed 9:00–1:00, Fri–Sat 9:00–5:00
Pub. *The Report*, quarterly; *The Ohio Genealogical Society Newsletter*, monthly; *Ohio Records and Pioneer Families*, quarterly, $18.00 per year subscription; *Ohio Civil War Genealogy Journal*, quarterly, $18.00 per year subscription
(sponsors First Families of Ohio, a lineage society for members with pre-Dec 31, 1821 Ohio ancestors; The

Society of Civil War Families of Ohio, a lineage society for members with Ohio ancestors who served in the Civil War)
$27.00 per year membership for individuals, $32.00 per year joint membership (includes *The Report* and *The Ohio Genealogical Society Newsletter*)

Williams County Chapter OGS
PO Box 293
Bryan, OH 43506-0293
(419) 636-3959
Ernest K. Gentit, President
Hours: Community Room, East End Pool, East High Street, Bryan, OH: second Mon 7:30 P.M.
Pub. *Ohio's Last Frontier*, eleven times per year (monthly, except single issue for July–August)
("The society maintains a surname file in addition to pedigree charts submitted by WCGS members; this file is maintained at the Bryan Public Library; has set up a First Families of Williams County, open to WCGS members who can provide documentation proving a direct line ancestor residing in what was known as Williams County, Ohio, as of 1860.")
$10.00 per year membership for individuals, $11.00 per year joint membership, $12.00 per year membership for families

1889'er Society
3621 N.W. 43rd Street
Oklahoma City, OK 73112-6359

First Families of the Twin Territories (FFTT)
(a committee of the Oklahoma Genealogical Society)
PO Box 12986
Oklahoma City, OK 73157-2986
$15.00 per year membership for individuals, $18.00 per year membership for families

Sons and Daughters of the Cherokee Strip Pioneers
PO Box 465
Enid, OK 73701
Pub. *Journal of the Cherokee Strip*, annually, $5.00 per issue
$5.00 per year membership

Oregon Genealogical Society
(223 North A Street, Springfield, OR—library location)
PO Box 10306 (mailing address)
Eugene, OR 97440-2306
(541) 746-7924
Hours: Mon 10:00–2:00, Wed & Fri 10:00–6:00, Sat (except fourth Sat) 10:00–4:00, Sun noon–4:00
Pub. *The Quarterly* (January, April, July, October), $3.00 per issue; *Oregon*

Genealogical Society Newsletter, bimonthly
(Oregon history and research; issued Oregon Pioneer Certificates)
$22.00 per year membership for individuals (calendar year), $25.00 per year membership for households, $500.00 life membership

Sons and Daughters of Oregon Pioneers
PO Box 6685
Portland, OR 97228
(503) 222-5014
Frances Caskey, Membership and Former President
Pub. *Newsletter*, occasionally
(membership is open to anyone whose family came to Oregon before 14 Feb 1859)
$10.00 per year membership, plus one-time $10.00 fee for a membership certificate

The Society of First Families of South Carolina, 1670–1700
PO Box 21328
Charleston, SC 29413-1328
(843) 577-4324
William E. Craver, Jr., President
Hours: 9:00–5:00

Sioux Valley Genealogical Society
(Siouxland Heritage Old Courthouse Museum—library location)
200 West Sixth Street (mailing address)
Sioux Falls, SD 57104-6001
(605) 367-4210 (Museum)
Jeannette Allard-Fiskum, Library Committee
Hours: Mon–Sat 1:00–5:00
Pub. *The Pioneer Pathfinder*, quarterly
(Pioneer Certificates are available to the descendants of those who lived in Dakota Territory prior to statehood on 2 November 1889.)
$12.00 per year membership for individuals, $18.00 per year membership for families (2 votes, 1 quarterly), $25.00 per year foreign or Contributing membership

First Families of Tennessee
Affiliate of the East Tennessee Historical Society
(600 Market Street—location)
PO Box 1629 (mailing address)
Knoxville, TN 37901
(423) 544-5732; (423) 544-4319 FAX
Kent Whitworth, Executive Director; Cherel Henderson, Associate Director
Hours: Calvin McClung Historical Collection: Mon–Tue 9:00–8:30, Wed–Fri 9:00–5:30, Sun 1:00–5:00; Office: Mon–Fri 9:00–5:00; Museum: Tue–Sat 10:00–4:00, Sun 1:00–5:00
(descendants of persons living in Tennessee prior to its admission into the union in 1796)

First Families of the State of Franklin
2007 Sherwood Drive, #D
Johnson City, TN 37601-3236
Mrs. Ray Stahl
(descendants of pioneers who lived in the
area that was the state of Franklin in
1788 or before)

Daughters of the Republic of Texas
French Legation Museum
802 San Marcos Street
Austin, TX 78702-2647
(512) 472-8180; (512) 472-9457 FAX
Diane Long, Director
Hours: Tue–Sun 1:00–5:00

The Daughters of the Republic of Texas Library
(300 Alamo Plaza at Crockett Street—
location)
PO Box 1401 (mailing address)
San Antonio, TX 78295-1401
(210) 225-1071; (210) 225-8155
E-mail: drtl@salsa.net
http://www.drtl.org/
Cathy Herpich, Director
Hours: Mon–Sat 9:00–5:00
(Texas history and early Texas
genealogy)

Daughters of the Republic of Texas
Caddel-Smith Chapter
909 South Park
Uvalde, TX 78801
(830) 278-6102
Dr. Jane Knapik, President

San Jacinto Descendants
1718 Searcy
San Antonio, TX 78232
(210) 494-7278
Carl S. Mauthe, President General

International Society, Daughters of Utah Pioneers
300 North Main Street
Salt Lake City, UT 84103-1699
(801) 538-1050
Louise C. Green, President
Hours: Museum: Mon–Sat 9:00–5:00
Pub. *Yearly Historical Book*, annually

Daughters of Utah Pioneers Relic Hall
(420 Clay Street—location)
Old Mill Road (mailing address)
Montpelier, ID 83254
(208) 847-1069

Rhoades Valley Camp, Daughters of Utah Pioneers
PO Box 311
Kamas, UT 84036

South Box Elder, Daughters of Utah Pioneers
566 North First Street East
Brigham City, UT 84302
(435) 723-3819

National Society, Sons of Utah Pioneers
3301 East 2820 South
Salt Lake City, UT 84109
(801) 484-4441; (801) 328-8200
(*Pioneer*); (801) 328-8249 FAX
(*Pioneer*)
E-mail: editor@uvol.com
http://uvol.com/sup/
Florence C. Youngberg, Director; Martin
Lewis, Vice President Sales and
Marketing
Hours: Tue 9:00–4:00, Wed & Thur
9:00–9:00
Pub. *Pioneer*, bimonthly, $2.95 per issue
from 180 North Wright Brothers
Drive, Building 6, Salt Lake City, UT
84116
$12.50 per year membership

Fayette Families
204 Tapaingo Road, S.E.
Vienna, VA 22180-5974
Victoria Hook, Editor
Pub. *Fayette Families*, quarterly
(January, April, July, October), $15.00
per year subscription
(members have ancestors who once
resided in Fayette County,
Pennsylvania)
$15.00 per year membership in the U.S.
and Canada, $20.00 per year
membership overseas

Jamestowne Society
(see Lineage, Hereditary, and Patriotic
Societies—Colonial)

Order of the First Families of Virginia
5055 Seminary Road, #439
Alexandria, VA 22311
Mrs. Charles Seaman, Sr.

Descendants of the French Creek Pioneers
RFD 2, Box 69
French Creek, WV 26218
(304) 924-6374
Virginia Bly Hoover, Secretary
Pub. *The Pioneer*, biannually (August of
even-numbered years)
(responds only to descendants of pioneer
or village present and former
inhabitants; no information furnished
to professional genealogists)
$12.00 per year membership

Royal and Noble

Colonial Order of the Crown
PO Box 27023
Philadelphia, PA 19118

National Society, Daughters of the Barons of Runnymeade
(address withheld upon request)

International Society of the Descendants of Charlemagne
Office of the Governor General
3960 Barcelona Street
PO Box 5259
Titusville, FL 32783
(407) 267-0351; (407) 267-0263 FAX
Rt. Rev. Lowell A. Barker, Governor
General
Hours: by appointment only
Pub. *News Letter*, occasionally
(Royal and noble lineages)
$50.00 life membership; computer search
5¢ per page

Descendants of Edward I
(916) 344-7579
Virgil Obert

Society of Descendants of Knights of the Most Noble Order of the Garter
PO Box 4944
Philadelphia, PA 19119

Descendants of the Illegitimate Sons and Daughters of the Kings of Britain
45 East 200 North
Salt Lake City, UT 84103
(801) 359-2378
Grahame T. Smallwood, Jr., Former
Secretary-Treasurer
Pub. *Annual Roster*, annually

National Society of Magna Carta Dames
PO Box 4222
Philadelphia, PA 19144

Order of the Crown of Charlemagne in the United States of America
PO Box 808
Beech Grove, IN 46107-0808
William Prosser Nottingham, President
General

Plantagenet Society
PO Box 27165
Philadelphia, PA 19118

Sovereign Colonial Society, Americans of Royal Descent
PO Box 27112
Philadelphia, PA 19118

Niadh Nask (The Military Order of the Golden Chain)
PO Box 11084
Tuscaloosa, AL 35486-0025
Dr. David Pittman Johnson
Hours: various
Pub. *The International Journal of the
Niadh Nask*, two times per year,
$25.00 per year subscription
(The Niadh Nask is an order of
knighthood established in Ireland in
the pre-Christian era; The Hereditary
Head is The MacCarthy Mór, Prince of
Desmond and Head of the ancient
Irish Royal House of Munster)

Huguenot

Huguenot Heritage
35 Sutton Place, Suite 6-E
New York, NY 10022-2464
(212) 759-6222
Karen McGarry

The Huguenot Historical Society
PO Box 339
New Paltz, NY 12561-0339
(914) 255-1660; (914) 255-0376 FAX
E-mail:
    huguenothistoricalsociety@worldnet.att.net
Timothy F. Harley, Director
Hours: May 30-Oct 31: Wed–Sat 10:00–
    4:00; Nov–May 30: by appointment
Pub. *The Messenger*, three times per year
(is supported in part by its member
    family associations: The Bevier-Elting
    Family, The Crispell Family, The
    Deyo Family, The Freer-Low Family,
    The Gerow Family, The LeFevre
    Family, the Magny Family, The
    Schoonmaker Family and The
    Terwilliger Family associations)
$15.00 per year membership for
    individuals (includes membership in
    one family association)

Huguenot Memorial Society
Oxford Archives
12 Rexharme Road
Worcester, MA 01606
(508) 752-6994
Mrs. Clovis L. Carpenter
(not open to the public)

**Huguenot Memorial Society of
Oxford**
3 West Street
Oxford, MA 01540
(508) 987-2502
Harlan P. Moore, President

National Huguenot Society
9033 Lyndale Avenue, South, Suite 108
Bloomington, MN 55420-3535
(612) 885-9776
Arthur Louis Finnell, Executive Director
Hours: Mon–Fri 1:00–5:00
Pub. *The Cross of Languedoc*, two times
    per year

The Huguenot Society of America
Library
122 East 58th Street
New York, NY 10022-1939
(212) 755-0592
Mrs. Dorothy F. Kimball, Executive
    Secretary
Hours: Tue–Wed 10:00–4:00

**The Huguenot Society of South
Carolina**
138 Logan Street
Charleston, SC 29401
(843) 723-3235; (843) 853-8476 FAX
E-mail: huguenot@cchat.com
Melissa W. Ballentine, Archivist

Hours: 9:00–2:00
Pub. *Transactions of Huguenot Society of
    South Carolina*, annually, available
    only to members and libraries
$15.00 per year membership

**The Huguenot Society of the
Founders of Manakin in the Colony
of Virginia**
6515 Martin Mill Pike
Knoxville, TN 37920
Rick Ford
Hours: by appointment
Pub. *The Huguenot*, biannually (every
    two years), $10.00 per issue

Miscellaneous

**Descendants of Whaling Masters,
Inc.**
28 Fort Street
Fairhaven, MA 02719
Hours: weekdays 10:00–12:00 & 1:00–
    4:00
$5.00 per year Active membership for
    individuals, $8.00 per yearmembership
    for families, $3.00 per year Associate
    membership (spouse of Active
    member); $100.00 Active life
    membership; $60.00 Associate life
    membership

**Saint Nicholas Society of New York
City**
122 East 58th Street
New York, NY 10022-1939
Pub. *Weathercock*, quarterly

SURNAME REGISTRIES

Ancestors Unlimited
10853 Danube Avenue
Granada Hills, CA 91344

Association of One-Name Studies
2509 Placid Place
Virginia Beach, VA 23456-3743
(757) 468-5829
E-mail: clbarkle@leo.vsla.edu
http://www.mediasoft.net/scottc/aans.htm
Carolyn L. Barkley, Secretary
Pub. *Association of One-Name Studies
    Newsletter*, quarterly; *Directory of
    One-Name Studies and Surname
    Genealogists*, annually
$20.00 membership includes registration
    of up to five variants of one surname,
    additional surnames at $5.00 each

Dead End Surname Exchange
1209 Hill Street
Greensboro, NC 27408
Garland P. Stout

Double Check Research
Box 126
Higgins, TX 79046

The Everton Publishers, Inc.
(3223 South Main Street, Nibley, UT—
    location)
PO Box 368 (mailing address)
Logan, UT 84323-0368
(435) 752-6022; (800) 443-6325; (435)
    752-0425 FAX
Bob Arbon, Manager
Hours: Mon–Fri 8:00–5:00
Pub. *Everton's Genealogical Helper*,
    bimonthly, $4.50 per issue, $24.00 per
    year subscription
(queries, classified advertisements;
    directories of genealogical researchers,
    periodical publications, etc.;
    computerized database of ancestor
    data: Computerized "Roots Cellar";
    computerized Family File;
    computerized Pedigree Library)
Roots Cellar registration: $5.00 for one
    name, $1.00 for each additional name

Family Data Exchange
314 West Center, #134
Bountiful, UT 84010

Family Exchange Service
PO Box 5283
Concord, CA 94520-9998
Shirley Call
free registration; access: $1.50 per
    surname, $2.00 per IGI search, full
    refund if no listings found or, if only
    one or two names are listed, a credit
    for an alternate search

Family Registry™
(see Computer Interest—Ancestral File
    Operations)

Family Services
East 12502 Frideger
Elk, WA 99009
E-mail: 102062,610@compuserve.com
(data available on 3½" disks in
    GEDCOM format, uploaded to
    Compuserve)
free submission and notification of all
    matches of your ancestors when you
    submit to database, free electronic
    catalog; family disk or family group
    sheets: $15.00 per surname ($25.00 for
    common surname in FGS format,
    $2.00 for index)

G-Tree
1021 Market Street
Sainte Genevieve, MO 63670

Genealogical Research Directory
3324 Crail Way
Glendale, CA 91206-1107
(818) 790-2642; (818) 952-3462 FAX
http://www.ozemail.com.au/ grdxxx
Mrs. Jan Jennings, U.S. Agent
Pub. *Genealogical Research Directory*,
    annually, $29.75 postpaid for current
    year
(150,000 surname entries worldwide
    with names and addresses of

worldwide listing of libraries and archives and genealogical societies)

German Genealogical Index
PO Box 10155
Minneapolis, MN 55440

Heritage Genealogical Society
2552 Snow Mountain Drive
Sandy, UT 84092

International Genealogical Directory
International Society for British
    Genealogy and Family History
PO Box 3115
Salt Lake City, UT 84110-3115

The Irish Family Group Sheet Exchange (IFGSX)
PO Box 535
Farmington, MI 48332
Andrew J. Morris
free registration; access: up to 20 sheets
    on one surname (and variants) for
    $4.00 (add $1.00 for postage outside
    the U.S.)
database: 600 surnames

Personalized Computer Service
4032 North Main Street, Suite 803
Dayton, OH 45405
free registration (prefers group sheets or
    full data of each surname: last name,
    first, middle, event, year, city or
    county and state or country); access:
    $1.00 per surname; database: over
    500,000 (surnames continually added);
    established 1979

Ray's Genealogical Services
PO Box 482
McCook, NE 69001
(308) 345-1443
Robert T. Ray
Pub. *Ray Newsletter*, $12.00 per year
    subscription

Researchers Surname Index
6616 Royal Parkway, South
Lockport, NY 14094
Faith G. Haungs
free registration; access: $1.00 per
    surname, plus SASE (full refund if
    nothing found); database: 29,000
    surnames from around the world;
    established 1981

Surname Databank
3227 Travelers Palm Drive
Edgewater, FL 32141
G. & B. Morgan
free registration; access: $1.00 per
    surname

Surname Exchange
152-18 Union Turnpike, #5E
Flushing, NY 11367
Leonard Jacobs
(includes Ackerman, Baker, Brown,
    Carroll, Carson, Cisneros, Clark,
    Cobb, Crane, Donovan, Elliott,

Faucett, Fox, Gallagher, Hoffman,
    Jacobs, James, Kelly, Lang,
    McLaughlin, Martin, Moore, O'Neill,
    Phillips, Peters, Sanders, Schmidt,
    Shepard, Singer, Thompson, Walsh,
    Winter)
registration: $1.00 per surname, $7.00
    for all surnames, free registration for
    researchers; access: $1.00 per
    surname, $7.00 for all surnames

Surname Heritage
3569 Ledyard Way
Aptos, CA 95003

Surname Research
Rt. 1 Box 359
Mounds, OK 74047

United Ancestries
PO Box 2408
Park City, UT 84060-2408

Western Heraldry Organization
General Surname Index
10195 West 17th Place
Lakewood, CO 80215-2805
Florence N. Young, President
free registration; access: $1.00 per
    surname, plus SASE; established 1973

Yates Publishing
Family Group Sheet Exchange
PO Box 67
Stevensville, MT 59870
(406) 777-3797
Bill Yates, Editor
Hours: Mon–Fri 8:30–4:30
(U.S. before 1900)
registration: free with order; access:
    copies of files vary; database: over
    120,000 records (sheets); established
    1981

ADOPTION REGISTRIES, SEARCH GROUPS AND INFORMATION CENTERS

Adopted Child
PO Box 9362
Moscow, ID 83843
(208) 882-1794

Adoptee Awareness
PO Box 23019
Anchorage, KY 40223
(502) 245-2811; (502) 249-7772
Nancy Comstock, Past President
(a self-help volunteer group working in
    Kentucky)

Adoptee-Birthfamily Connection (ABC)
PO Box 22611
Fort Lauderdale, FL 33335-2611
(954) 584-0003; (954) 370-7100 (voice
    mail, 24-hour-a-day national search
    hotline)
Lynn Claire Davis, Co-ordinator and
    Editor
Hours: 4:00 P.M.–10:00 P.M.
Pub. *People Searching News* (*PSN*),
    quarterly, $18.50 for six-issue
    subscription
(serves adoptees and birthfamilies in the
    U.S., especially Florida)

Adoptee/Birthfamily Registry
PO Box 803
Carmichael, CA 95608
(916) 485-4119; (916) 944-7312
Trudy Helmlinger, Ph.D.
Hours: Mon–Fri 8:00–5:00
Pub. *Adoptee/Birthfamily Registry*,
    annually, $25.00 per issue
free listing

Adoptee/Birthparent Connections
8820 Kennedy Lane
San Miguel, CA 93451
E-mail: ccsd62B@prodigy.com;
    72103.2257@compuserve.com
Tina Peddie, Adoption Search Consultant
(includes Brynberg)

Adoptee Identity Doorway
PO Box 361
South Bend, IN 46624
(219) 272-3520

Adoptees Adult Liberation Movement Triad
1725 Atascadero Drive
Columbia, SC 29206
(803) 787-3778; (803) 787-4192
Mildred Szakacsi, Founder
Pub. *Search-Support and Birth Registry*,
    three times per year
(serves South Carolina)
$35.00 per year membership

Adoptees and Birthparents in Search
PO Box 6426B
Greenville, SC 29606

Adoptees and Birthparents in Search (A.B.I.S.)
PO Box 5551
West Columbia, SC 29171
(803) 791-1133
Karen Connor, Director
Hours: Mon–Fri 8:30–4:00
(assistance in searching in South
  Carolina only; adoptee must be at least
  18 years of age, computerized reunion
  registry for adoptees and birth parents)
$25.00 per year membership

Adoptees and Natural Parents Organization
949 Lacon Drive
Newport News, VA 23608
(757) 764-9091 (no calls after 10:00 P.M.
  eastern time)
Billie Quigley, President
(a support group for adoptees,
  birthparents; search assistance limited
  to some areas of Virginia)

Adoptees', Birthparents' Association
2027 Finch Court
Simi Valley, CA 93063-3720

Adoptees Birthrights Committee
PO Box 7213
Metairie, LA 70010

Adoptees Identity Discovery (AID)
PO Box 2159
Sunnyvale, CA 94087
(408) 737-2222
Neil Kelly
(search aid)
$65.00 suggested contribution

Adoptees in Search (AIS)
PO Box 41016
Bethesda, MD 20824
(301) 656-8555; (301) 652-2106 FAX
E-mail: ais20824@aol.com
Joanne W. Small, MSW., Director
Hours: Mon–Fri 9:00–5:00, plus 24-hour
  answering service
Pub. *AIS Newsnotes*, bimonthly
(adoptee/birth relative searches)
$75.00 (tax-deductible) membership plus
  benefits (search registry); search fee:
  hourly rate, with retainer (non-tax-
  deductible)

Adoptees Information Service, Inc.
19 Marion Avenue
Mount Vernon, NY 10552

Adoptees Liberty Movement Association (ALMA)
PO Box 154, Washington Bridge Station
New York, NY 10033
(212) 581-1568
Florence Fisher, President
Pub. *The Alma Searchlight*, quarterly
Chapters: **Alaska**: Northwest Regional
  Office, PO Box 372, Glennallen, AK
  99588; **California**: Emily Carter, PO
  Box 2341, Alameda, CA 94501;

Henrietta Buchanan, PO Box 9425,
Canoga Park, CA 91309-0425; Gary &
Carol McDowell, PO Box 8081,
Sacramento, CA 95818; Bridie Kelly,
PO Box 880335, San Diego, CA
92108; Mary Anna DeParcq, PO Box
1233, Simi Valley, CA 93062; Leila
Higgs, PO Box 271, Vina, CA 96092;
Michigan: Deborah Smith, Michigan
Coordinator, PO Box 1804, Royal
Oak, MI 48068-1804, (313) 542-2930
$55.00 registration fee

Adoptees' Research Association
PO Box 304
Montrose, CA 91020
Kathy Wudel, Founder
(specializes in searches for adoptees and
  natural parents living in Canada,
  Germany and the U.S.; searches are
  conducted for the purpose of a
  reunion)
$125.00 per year for private research

Adoptees Search Connection
1203 Hill Street
Suffield, CT 06078
(860) 668-1042
Nancy Sitterly
(serves western Massachusetts and
  Connecticut)

Adoptee's Search for Knowledge
PO Box 762
East Lansing, MI 48826-0762
(517) 321-7291
Jeanette Abronowitz, Executive Director
Hours: 10:00–3:00
(Adoption searches (siblings, relatives,
  biological parents and others separated
  by adoption); certified confidential
  court intermediary; adoptee must be
  18 years old)
$40.00 per year membership

Adoptees Search Rights
PO Box 8713
Toledo, OH 43623
Nancy Gillen
(helps adoptees born in Lucas County)
$50.00 fee

Adoption Advisory Council, Inc.
2448 Stuart Street
Brooklyn, NY 11229
Dr. Irene Ganelli

Adoption Alliance of Vermont
21 Court Street
Middlebury, VT 05753
(802) 388-7569
C. Tiley
(serves Vermont)

Adoption Alliance of Vermont
17 Hopkins Street
Rutland, VT 05701
(802) 773-7078
Maureen S. Vincent
(serves Vermont and the surrounding
  area)

Adoption and Family Reunion Center
PO Box 239
Moore, SC 29369
(843) 574-0681
Liz White
(serves South Carolina)

Adoption and Family Search
PO Box 61078
Boulder City, NV 89006-1078
(702) 293-6863; (702) 293-0844 FAX
Michael Paris, Consultant
Hours: by appointment

Adoption and Medical Information Registry
New York State Department of Health
Corning Tower
Empire State Plaza
Albany, NY 12237-0023
(518) 474-9600
Peter M. Carucci, Director of Vital
  Records
Hours: 8:30–4:30
("Provides general, non-identifying
  information to adoptees who are 18
  years of age or older and who were
  born and adopted in New York State.
  Also provides current names and
  address upon registration of adoptee
  and biological parents. Files certified
  medical information updates from
  birth parents anytime after the
  adoption, and updates are available
  upon request by adoptee on adoptive
  parents, if adoptee is under eighteen
  years of age.")
$75.00 for adoptees, $20.00 for
  birthparents (waived if currently
  receiving public assistance)

Adoption Answers Support Kinship (AASK)
8 Homestead Drive
South Glastonbury, CT 06073-2804
(860) 657-4005 phone & FAX
Judy Taylor, Director
Hours: 10:00–10:00; meetings: third Sun
  2:00–5:00
("Search assistance is offered on the
  phone.")
$5.00 meeting fee

Adoption Circle of Hawaii
4614 Kilauea Avenue, #431
Honolulu, HI 96816
(808) 737-7969

Adoption Connection
842 Country Stone Drive
Saint Louis, MO 63021

Adoption Connection Exchange
Family and Childrens Services
4623 Falls Road
Baltimore, MD 21209-4900

Adoption Connection, Inc.
O'Shea Building
11 Peabody Square, Number 6

Peabody, MA 01960
(978) 532-1261; (978) 532-0427
Susan Darke
Hours: 9:00–4:00
Pub. *Happenings*, quarterly
(serves New England; reunites adoptees, birthparents and adoptive families)
fees from $50.00 to $400.00

Adoption Connection of Louisiana
PO Box 6921
Metairie, LA 70009
(504) 277-0030; (504) 887-7198
Dianne Sercovich

Adoption Crossroads
PO Box 9025
Schenectady, NY 12309
(518) 377-5936

Adoption Crossroads/Council for Equal Rights in Adoption
356 East 74th Street, Apartment 2
New York, NY 10021-3751
Pub. *Access*, quarterly, $10.00 per year subscription
(265 locations in eight countries)
$20.00 per year membership, $100.00 per year search and help

Adoption Education of Lexington/ Kentucky Reunion Registry
PO Box 13033
Lexington, KY 40583
(606) 873-3753; (606) 272-0422
Susan Monroe; Barbara Stepter
(serves Central Kentucky)

Adoption Identity Movement of Grand Rapids (AIM)
PO Box 9265
Grand Rapids, MI 49509
(616) 531-1380 (24-hour answering service)
Peg Richer, Director
(serves western Michigan; adoption searches)
one-time $30.00 donation for membership

Adoption Information and Direction, Inc. (AID)
PO Box 174
Coon Valley, WI 54623
(608) 452-3146 (8:00 A.M.–10:00 P.M., will return calls collect)
Pat Helgerson, Director, LaCrosse Area
(serves Wisconsin, Iowa and Minnesota; adoption search and support for adoptee, birthparent, adoptive parent, concerned others)
$20.00 per year membership; search fees: depending on services rendered

Adoption Information and Direction, Inc. (AID)
PO Box 875
Green Bay, WI 54305-0875
(920) 497-9720; (920) 336-3005

Maureen Vanden Hogen, Director; Kate Ross, Certified Search Consultant
Hours: meetings first Thur 7:00 at Bosco Hall on Diocesan Grounds, 1825 Riverside Drive
(serves Green Bay, Wisconsin; adoption search)
$25.00 per year membership for individuals, $30.00 per year membership for families

Adoption Information and Direction, Inc. (AID)
PO Box 2043
Oshkosh, WI 54903
(920) 233-6487 (Carroll); (920) 233-2608 (Carol)
Hours: meetings last Thur 7:00 at Presbyterian Church, 110 Church Avenue
(serves Oshkosh, Wisconsin; search and support)

Adoption Information and Direction, Inc. (AID)
2116 Ellis Street
PO Box 516
Stevens Point, WI 54481-0516
(715) 345-1290 (President)
Doug Henderson, State President
Hours: meetings second Mon 7:00 at Evangelical Free Church, 301 Dearborn Avenue
(serves central Wisconsin; adoption search for all sides of triad served)
$25.00 per year membership for individuals, $30.00 per year membership for families

Adoption Information Exchange
PO Box 1917
Matthews, NC 28106-1917
(704) 537-5919; (704) 846-5123
E-mail: mzchrislee@aol.com
http://kinsolving.com
Chris Lee
Hours: 9:00–5:00
(serves North Carolina, Tennessee and Virginia; free North Carolina reunion registry)
search fee varies, "no find, no fee"

Adoption Insight
PO Box 171
Portage, MI 49081
(616) 327-1999 (24-hour answering machine)
Elaine Meints, Director
("We are a search and support group for adult adoptees, birth parents, and separated family members.")

Adoption Network Cleveland
291 East 222
Cleveland, OH 44123-1751
(216) 261-1551 (24-hour voice mail); (216) 261-1164 FAX
E-mail: bln2@po.cwru.edu
http://pages.prodigy.com/adoptreform/ anc.com

Betsie Norris, Executive Director
Hours: Mon–Fri 9:00–5:00, Sat 10:00–2:00
Pub. *Adoption Network News*, bimonthly
("Specializing in Cleveland area searches (adoption); services include support, education and advocacy.")
$30.00 per year membership for individuals, $40.00 per year membership for families, $75.00 per year membership for organizations; search fee: $25.00

Adoption Option
PO Box 429327
Cincinnati, OH 45242
(419) 244-7072; (513) 793-7268
Carole Adlard
(serves southwest Ohio)

Adoption Reality/Adoption Research Services
2180 Clover Street
Simi Valley, CA 93065
(805) 526-2289
Gayle L. Beckstead, ISC

The Adoption Reconnection Directory
PO Box 230643
Encinitas, CA 92023-0643
(760) 753-8288 (home); (760) 753-8073 FAX
E-mail: ccwolfe@worldnet.att.net
http://www.crashers.com/search (Reconnections in Adoption)
Curry Wolfe
Hours: Mon–Fri 10:00–5:00
Pub. *The Adoption Reconnection Directory*, annually (spring), $17.00 postpaid per issue
(adoption search and support groups, searches U.S., Canada and more)

Adoption Records Search Program
Department of Health and Family Services
1 West Wilson Street, Room 465
Box 8916
Madison, WI 53708-8916
(608) 266-7163; (608) 264-9852
http://www.dhfs.state.wi.us
Theodora A. Christensen, MSSW, Adoption Search Specialist, Bureau of Programs and Policies, Division of Children and Family Services
Hours: 8:00–4:30
(prepares closed adoption record in non-identifying fashion, searches for birth parents and updated medical/genetic information, and maintains files for birth parents who are willing to disclose their identities should the adopted person request a search)

Adoption Reform Movement of Michigan
95 North Whitesbridge Road
Belding, MI 48809

(616) 897-5342
Bob Schafer, Co-Director
Hours: 24 hours
Pub. *Newsletter*, irregularly
(adoption reform activist organization,
   legislative reform, support group
   referral)

Adoption Resource Center of Children's Home Society of Washington
3300 N.E. 65th Street
PO Box 15190
Seattle, WA 98133
(206) 524-6020
Hours: Mon–Fri 8:30–5:30
("Provide search services for those
   adopted through CHSW, or for those
   who relinquished their children
   through CHSW; provide information
   and referral for others")
call for information on search fees

Adoption Resource Service, Inc.
1904 North Avenue
Burlington, VT 05401

Adoption Reunion Connection
263 Lemonade Road
Pacolet, SC 29372
(864) 474-3479
Pollie Robinson, Search Consultant and
   Co-Director
(serves South Carolina, offers adoption
   search help)
$35.00 per year membership

Adoption Search and Reconciliation
14320 S.E. 170th Street
Renton, WA 98058
(425) 228-6179

Adoption Search and Support Group of Tallahassee
PO Box 3504
Tallahassee, FL 32315-3504
(904) 893-0004
Judy Young, Leader
Hours: Faith Presbyterian Church: fourth
   Tue 7:00–9:00
$20.00 per year membership fee for
   search assistance

Adoption Search Consultants
8539 Monroe Road, Suite 25
Charlotte, NC 28212-7150
(704) 537-5919

Adoption Search Consultants of Maine (ASC ME)
PO Box 2793
South Portland, ME 04106-2793
(207) 773-3378
Mina Bicknell
(serves Maine)

Adoption Search for Life
303 Brighton Road
Anderson, SC 29621
(803) 224-8020

Adoption Search/Support Network
RR 1, Box 83
East Calais, VT 05650
(802) 456-8850
E-mail: beleaf4u@aol.com
Marge Garfield, Director
Hours: Mon–Fri 9:00–5:00

Adoption Support Group
PO Box 2316
Ketchum, ID 83340
(208) 726-8543

Adoption Triad Midwest
PO Box 37273
Omaha, NE 68137
(402) 895-3706 (6:00 P.M.–8:00 P.M.,
   long distance calls will be returned
   collect)
Nancy Sullivan
(adoption search support)
$25.00 per year membership

Adoption Triad Network, Inc.
PO Box 3932
Lafayette, LA 70502
(318) 984-3682
Johnnie Kocurek, Search Consultant
Hours: various; monthly meeting
(search and support)
$30.00 per year membership

Adoption Triangle
PO Box 384
Park Forest, IL 60466
(219) 365-0574
E-mail: gtrv63a@prodigy.com
Beth Duensing, Independent Search
   Consultant
Hours: Mon–Fri noon–5:00
(search and support group for adoptees,
   birth parents and adoptive parents)
send LSASE for information

The Adoption Triangle of Rockford
318 North Church Street
Rockford, IL 61101
(815) 877-2269
Kathryn Pearce
(serves northern Illinois)

Adoption with Truth
66-C Panoramic Way
Berkeley, CA 94704
Sara Vick

The Adoptive Experience
Rt. 5, Box 22
Osceola, IA 50213
(515) 342-4803
Marianne Lippold
(serves Iowa)

Adoptive Forum
525 South Fourth Street, #3465
Philadelphia, PA 19147-1570
(215) 238-1116 (recorded message with
   hours)
Pub. *Adoption Forum Newsletter*,
   bimonthly, $12.00 per year subscription

(support and search services for
   adoptees, birthparents and adoptive
   parents; serves Pennsylvania, southern
   New Jersey and Delaware)
$40.00 new member fee, $30.00 per year
   membership renewal

Adoptive Parents for Open Records
PO Box 193
Long Valley, NJ 07853
(201) 850-1706

Advocating Legislation for Adoptive Reform Movement (ALARM) Network
9203 S.W. Cree Circle
Tualatin, OR 97062
(503) 692-5794

American Adoption Congress
1000 Connecticut Avenue, N.W., Suite 9
Washington, DC 20036
(202) 483-3399
http://pages.prodigy.com/adoptreform./
   aacorg.htm
Hours: 24 hours
Pub. *The Decree*, quarterly
membership-open fees

Americans for Open Records (AmFOR)
PO Box 401
Palm Desert, CA 92261
Lori Carangelo, President
Hours: (900) LOCATOR, ext. 11 ($2.50
   per minute, must be 18 years of age or
   older and have a touchtone phone)
http://www.genealogymall.com
Pub. *The Open Record*, irregularly,
   depending on available funds
(a non-profit, international, voluntary
   civil liberties network, established to
   promote the inherent right of
   Americans to information about
   themselves without court or agency
   intervention; no fee for search help—
   10,000 families reunited since 1989;
   pro se legal help, referrals and other
   information; civil liberties legal
   advocacy; publishes client case
   histories with permission; publishes
   *The Ultimate Search Book: From the
   Files of Americans For Open Records
   (AmFOR) (how to find anyone, with or
   without a name, in 50 states and 200
   countries*, $69.95)
$5.00 total fee covers Registry,
   computer-matching, materials, postage

Arkansas Adoption Triad
5900 Scenic Drive
Little Rock, AR 72202

B.K.I.D.S.
PO Box 43
Erin, NY 14838
(607) 739-2957

Baccus Genealogical Research
5817 144 Street East
Puyallup, WA 98373-5221
(253) 537-8288
E-mail: janetgb@worldnet.att.net
Janet G. Baccus, Owner
(adoptions, Pierce County, and
Washington state research)

Birthparent Support Network
PO Box 34
Old Bethpage, NY 11804
(516) 931-5925; (516) 931-5537 FAX
Carole Whitehead, Leader
Hours: evenings and weekends
(free support group, search referrals, teen
programs)

**Birthparents Adoptees Adoptive
Parents United in Support (B.U.S.)**
PO Box 299
Victor, NY 14564-0299
(716) 924-0410
Marcia Brady-Cohen, Founder and
Director
Hours: 9:00 A.M.–10:00 P.M.
Pub. *B.U.S. Bulletin*, quarterly
(serves eastern, central, and upstate New
York; adoption, twelve-step self-help
group)
$20.00 per year membership

Birthright of Greater Kansas City
6309 Walnut
Kansas City, MO 64113
(816) 444-7090; (800) 550-4900
Glenda Merten, Director
Hours: Mon–Tue & Thur–Fri 10:00–
2:00, Tue 6:00–8:00, Wed 2:00–8:00
Pub. *Heartbeat*, quarterly
(emotional support and practical
assistance to pregnant women;
international organizaiton based in
Toronto, Ontario)

Bonding by Blood, Unlimited
4710 Cottrell Road
Vassar, MI 48768-9256
(517) 823-8248
Mary Louise Foess, Founder and
President
Hours: Sat–Sun 1:00–5:00
(adoption—sealed record—search help)
$5.00 for initial 1995 Confidential
Intermediary Open Records Law and
other search tips packet

Catholic Community Services
PO Box 61483
Vancouver, WA 98666
Carol Sherrin, M.A., L.P.C.
(serves Washington)

Catholic Social Service
2546 20th Street
Great Bend, KS 67530
(316) 792-1393 phone and FAX
Shirley Lytle, Search Coordinator

Hours: Mon–Fri 9:00–5:00
(adoption, search and reunion; serves
southwest Kansas)

Center for Family Connections
(Cambridge, MA, and New York City—
location)
PO Box 383246
Cambridge, MA 02238-3246
(617) 547-0909; (800) KINNECT; (212)
777-7270 (New York); (617) 497-5952
FAX
E-mail: kinnect@aol.com
Dr. Joyce Maguire Pavao
Hours: Mon–Thur 9:00–7:00, Fri 9:00–
5:00
Pub. *Compact*, three times per year;
ARCtype, annually
(serves New England and the U.S.;
specializing in adoption, foster care,
kinship care)
$50.00 per year membership

**Central Coast Adoption Support
Group**
94 Manchester Place
Goleta, CA 93117
(805) 968-4351
Susan Bott
(serves Southern California)

Children and Families First
2005 Baynard Boulevard
Wilmington, DE 19802
(302) 658-5177; (302) 658-5170 FAX
Sally Decker, Search Coordinator
Hours: Mon–Fri 9:00–5:00
(search only for adoptees and birth
parents who used agency adoption
services)
sliding-scale fees

**Chosen Children/Ohio Coalition for
Adoption Reform**
31 Springbrook Boulevard
Dayton, OH 45405
(937) 274-8017

Circle of Hope
PO Box 127
Somersworth, NH 03878
(603) 692-5917
Karen Amos
Hours: 9:00–5:00
(adoption search and support group,
some missing relatives (i.e. aunt,
father, daughter, etc.); serves New
Hampshire and New England)
$30.00 per year membership; search fees
vary

**Colorado Confidential Intermediary
Service**
PO Box 260460
Lakewood, CO 80226
(303) 237-6919

**Colorado Department of Public
Health and Environment**
4300 Cherry Creek Drive, South
Denver, CO 80222-1530

(303) 692-2188
E-mail: theresa.salazar@state.co.us
Theresa Salazar, Adoption Registry
Coordinator
Hours: Mon–Fri 8:30–4:30, except
holidays
$15.00 registration fee

**Concerned United Birthparents
(CUB)**
National Headquarters
2000 Walker Street
Des Moines, IA 50317
(800) 822-2777 (24-hours); (515) 263-
9541 FAX
E-mail: cub@webnations.com
http://www.webnations.com/cub
Bonnie Bis, President
Pub. *CUB Communicator*, monthly
$50.00 initial year's membership in
support group, $35.00 per year
renewal

**Concerned United Birthparents
(CUB)**
7105 Shoresin Circle
Anchorage, AK 99504
(907) 333-2272

**Concerned United Birthparents
(CUB)**
2041 Willowood Lane
Encinitas, CA 92024
(760) 436-0892
Janet Appleford

**Concerned United Birthparents
(CUB)**
10801 San Paco Circle
Fountain Valley, CA 92708
(714) 962-8866

**Concerned United Birthparents
(CUB)**
1008 West Kensington Road
Los Angeles, CA 90026
Patti Prickett

**Concerned United Birthparents
(CUB)**
10511 104th Avenue
Broomfield, CO 80021
(303) 466-8554
Vickie Ransier

**Concerned United Birthparents
(CUB)-Honolulu**
47-213B Hui Akikiki Place
Kaneohe, HI
(808) 239-5819
Mary Gallano, Independent Search
Consultant, Branch Coordinator
(serves all islands and California)

**Concerned United Birthparents
(CUB)**
130 33rd Avenue, S.W.
Cedar Rapids, IA 52404
(319) 363-6929
Judy Wilkins

Concerned United Birthparents (CUB)
500 Kimberly Lane
Des Moines, IA 50317
(515) 262-2334

Concerned United Birthparents (CUB)
PO Box 22795
Louisville, KY 40252-0795
(505) 589-3320

Concerned United Birthparents (CUB)
14914 Nighthawk Lane
Bowie, MD 20716
(301) 249-8135

Concerned United Birthparents (CUB)
PO Box 380-396, Harvard Square
Cambridge, MA 02238
(617) 328-3005 (9:00 P.M.–9:00 P.M.)
Libbi Campbell, Coordinator
Hours: meetings at Plymouth
    Congregational Church, Edgell Road,
    Framingham Center
Pub. *CUB Communicator*, monthly
(support for birthparents and other
    adoption-affected people; search
    referrals, advocacy and education)
$50.00 initial year's membership, $35.00
    per year membership thereafter

Concerned United Birthparents (CUB)
Twin City Metro-Area Branch
6429 Mendelssohn Lane
Edina, MN 55343-8424
(612) 930-9058
Sandra L. Sperruzzu, Branch Coordinator
Hours: Mon–Fri 9:00–5:00
Pub. *Cub Communicator* (out of CUB
    headquarters), monthly
(searcher for those separated by adoption
    as well as for those looking for heirs
    to finalize estates)
$50.00 for first-year membership, $35.00
    per year membership renewal

Concerned United Birthparents (CUB)
7000 Jackson
Kansas City, MO 64132

Concerned United Birthparents (CUB)
4589 Hopewell Road
Wentzville, MO 63385
(314) 828-5726

Concerned United Birthparents (CUB)
6704 Inglewood
Holland, OH 43528
(419) 865-9604
Lisa Dinges

Cooperative Adoption Consulting
54 Wellington Avenue
San Anselmo, CA 94960
(415) 453-0902 phone and FAX

Ellen Roseman, Director
Hours: Mon–Fri 9:00–5:00
(Serves Japan, Europe and the U.S.;
    helps with searching; special focus on
    bonding/attachment issues; service is
    international, serving both couples and
    singles across the United States and
    abroad—mainly U.S. military families
    in foreign locations; infant open
    adoption placement)

Coping with Adoption
61 County Farm Road
Peru, IN 46970
(765) 472-7425

Department of Children and Family Services
Director's Office, Closed Records
406 East Monroe
Springfield, IL 62701-1498
(217) 785-2509

Department of Children's Services
Post Adoption Services
436 Sixth Avenue
North Nashville, TN 37243-1290
(615) 532-5637
Hours: 8:00–4:30
fee for services

Division of Child and Family Services—Adoption Registry (Search)
711 East Fifth Street
Carson City, NV 89710
(702) 687-5982
Jann Young, Program Assistant II
Hours: 8:00–5:00
(free adoption search services only for
    eligible registrants)

Division of Youth and Family Services, Adoption Unit
Adoption Registry
50 East State Street
CN 717
Trenton, NJ 08625-0717
(609) 292-8816
Gerald R. Gioglio, Adoption Registry
    Coordinator
Hours: 9:00–4:00
(post adoption services, registry for
    DYFS clients—adoptees, birthfamily
    members, and adoptive parents—only)
no charge

Donor's Offspring
PO Box 37
Sarcoxie, MO 64862
(417) 548-3679
Candace Turner
(serves the U.S. and the world for DI/
    Adoptees, the southwest and Missouri)

Families First
1105 West Peachtree Street, N.E.
Atlanta, GA 30305
(404) 853-2800

Family Court, First Circuit
Adoption Records Clerk

(777 Punchbowl Street, Second Floor/
    First Circuit Court—location)
PO Box 3498 (mailing address)
Honolulu, HI 96811-3498
(808) 539-4424 (calls returned collect)
Hours: Mon–Fri 7:45–4:30

Family Ties
4537 Souza Street
Eugene, OR 97402-6122
(541) 461-0752
Helen Gallagher, Independent Search
    Consultant
Hours: 9:00 A.M.–9:00 P.M.
(adoption support group, also helps
    children of divorce, separated families,
    etc.)
$25.00 one-time fee membership; search
    fees negotiable, depending upon
    services, membership not required

Finders Keepers
PO Box 748
Bear, DE 19701-0748
(302) 834-8888
Ginger Farrow
(serves Delaware, Maryland, New Jersey
    and Pennsylvania)

Full Circle
PO Box 1
Lake Forest, CA 92630
(949) 859-1952 (24-hour answering
    machine); (949) 951-1689 (Cindy
    Shacklett); (714) 544-4752 (Carol
    Caramango)
Cindy Shacklett, ISC; Carol Caramango
Hours: various
(post adoption support, search,
    education)
no charge; SASE for meeting
    information and referral outside of
    meeting

Full Circle
203 South German Church Road
Indianapolis, IN 46229
Rhonda Mayhew

Group for Openness in Adoption
518 General George Patton Road
Nashville, TN 37221
(615) 646-8116
Sandra
(support group for adoptee and
    birthparents in search, primarily
    addressing feelings involved when
    searching)

Heritage Searching
4308 San Mateo Street
North Las Vegas, NV 89030-2822
Mary Buckley
("adoption researcher and support to
    people in search")

Independent Search Consultant
20111 Riverside Drive
Santa Ana, CA 92707
(714) 669-8100

Independent Search Consultant (ISC)
1602 Cole Street
Birmingham, MI 48009
Mrs. Chris Spurr, ISC
(serves Michigan)

Independent Search Consultant
512 Wayside
Albert Lea, MN 56007
(507) 377-0517

Independent Search Consultants, Inc.
PO Box 10192
Costa Mesa, CA 92627
(949) 225-9245
E-mail: isc@rmci.net
http://www.rmci.net/isc
Pat Sanders, Executive Director
Pub. *The ISC Searchbook*, annually,
   $10.00 per issue
(referrals to adoption search consultants,
   U.S., Canada and Germany;
   certification of consultants)

Indiana Adoption Coalition
PO Box 1292
Kokomo, IN 46901
(765) 453-4427
Suzy Singleton

Indiana State Board of Health
1330 West Michigan Street, Room 121
PO Box 1964
Indianapolis, IN 46206-1964
(317) 633-0276

International Soundex Reunion Registry (I.S.R.R.)
PO Box 2312
Carson City, NV 89702-2312
(702) 882-7755
Anthony S. Vilardi, Registrar
Hours: Mon–Fri 9:00–4:00
("to serve and promote, through the
   Reunion Registry, the interests of any
   adult persons desiring and seeking a
   reunion with next-of-kin by birth;
   adoption, divorce, foster—any cause
   of separation")
free, but donations accepted

Iowa Reunion Registry
PO Box 8
Blairsburg, IA 50034-0008
Doris Smith
(serves Iowa and surrounding states)
no charge, donations accepted, LSASE
   requested

Jewish Family Services
Birth Parent Support Group
229 Waterman Street
Providence, RI 02906
(401) 331-1244
Hours: 8:30–4:30

Kansas City Adult Adoptees Organization
(Kansas City Public Library, 311 East
12th Street, Kansas City, MO 64106—
   location)
PO Box 11828 (mailing address)
Kansas City, MO 64138-9998
(816) 356-5213; (816) 229-4075
   (President, before 10:00 A.M. or after
   3:00 P.M.)
E-mail: ulqq10a@prodigy.com (long
   distance calls returned collect)
Sandy Hassler, President; Mary Ellen
   Hixson, Contact Person
Hours: meetings third Sat 10:00 A.M.
$35.00 one-time fee

Kentucky Department for Social Services—Adult Adoptees
275 East Main Street
Frankfort, KY 40621
(502) 564-2147
Virginia Nester, Program Specialist
Hours: Mon–Fri 8:00–4:30

Kinsolving Investigations
PO Box 471921
Charlotte, NC 28247-1921
(704) 537-5919; (704) 849-5572 (Voice
   Mail); (704) 846-5123 FAX
E-mail: mzchrislee@aol.com
http://kinsolving.com
Christine Lee, Owner/Private
   Investigator
Hours: 10:00–5:00
Pub. *The Vanguard*, quarterly
(adoption searches)
search fees based on case

L.A.S.S.O. (Lafayette Adoption Search/Support Organization)
5936 Lookout Drive
West Lafayette, IN 47906
(765) 567-4139
Sue Madden, Convener
Hours: Bethany Presbyterian Church,
   3305 Longlois Drive, Lafayette, IN
   47905: second & fourth Thur (except
   Thanksgiving or Maundy Thursday)
   7:30–9:30
(adoptive search and support)
free-will donation

Life Adoption Ministry
1350 Placer Street
Redding, CA 96001-1013
(800) 57 ADOPT
Donna Lessard Pratt
Hours: Mon–Fri 8:30–5:30
Pub. *Prose & Coos Adoption News*,
   bimonthly

Lifeline International
702 Brandywine Boulevard
Wilmington, DE 19809

Lincoln County Department of Social Services
PO Box 130
Lincolnton, NC 28093-0130
(704) 732-0738
Pat Hovis
(serves Lincoln County)

Living in Search of Answers
PO Box 215
Gilsum, NH 03448-0215
(802) 722-3008

Locators Unlimited
PO Box 1218
Nicholasville, KY 40340
(606) 885-6634

Los Angeles County Adoption Search Association
PO Box 1461
Roseville, CA 95678
(916) 784-2711
Vikki Schummer
Hours: Tue–Fri 10:00–4:30
(specializing in California searches)
search fees dependent on service needed

Lutheran Social Services of North Dakota
Post Adoption Coordinator
1325 South 11th Street
PO Box 389
Fargo, ND 58107-0389
(701) 235-7341
Hours: 8:00–5:00
(non-identifying information or
   identifying search)
$75.00 for non-identifying information,
   $300.00 for identifying search
   (including non-identifying
   information)

Madison County Historical Society, Inc.
PO Box 523
Anderson, IN 46015-0523
(765) 641-2442 (Library)
Phyllis Leedom, President
Hours: Library: Mon–Thur 9:00–9:00,
   Fri–Sat 9:00–5:30, Sun 1:00–5:00
Pub. *Searchlight* (for adoptees in search)
$4.00 per year membership

Manhattan Birthparents Group
PO Box 20137
New York, NY 10028-0051
(212) 289-6782
Joyce Bahr
Hours: 10:00–3:00
Pub. *Manhattan Birthparents Newsletter*,
   annually, donation
(serves New York City; "member group
   of the American Adoption Congress,
   working for open adoption records")

Maryland Mutual Consent Voluntary Adoption Registry
Social Services Administration
311 West Saratoga Street
Baltimore, MD 21201
(410) 333-0237; (410) 767-7423
http://www.GL.umbc.edu//~hickman/
   voladorr.htm
Sharon Hackett, Administrator
Hours: 8:30–4:30
$25.00 registration

Maternity Home Reconnection Registry
PO Box 230643
Encinitas, CA 92023-0643
(760) 753-8288 (home); (760) 753-8073 FAX
E-mail: ccwolfe@worldnet.att.net
http://www.crashers.com/search
    (Reconnections in Adoption)
Curry Wolfe
Hours: Mon–Fri 10:00–5:00
(registry for women who resided in a
    maternity home)

Mendo Lake Adoption Triad
620 Walnut Avenue
Ukiah, CA 95482
(707) 468-0648

Michigan Association for Openness in Adoption
PO Box 5117
Traverse City, MI 49684
(616) 275-6221
Mike Spry

Minnesota Department of Human Services
Adoption/Guardianship Section
444 Lafayette Road
Saint Paul, MN 55155-3831
(612) 297-1949
Hours: 8:00–4:30

Minnesota Reunion Registry/Liberal Education for Adoptive Families
23247 Lofton Court North
Scandia, MN 55073-9752
(612) 636-7031; (612) 433-5211

National Adoption Information Clearinghouse
5640 Nicholson Lane, #300
Rockville, MD 20852-2952
(301) 231-6512; (301) 984-8527 FAX
Debra Smith, Director
Hours: 9:00–5:00
Pub. *National Adoption Directory*,
    semiannually, $25.00 prepaid
(has an adoption literature database,
    under 50 abstracts free, modest fees
    for more than 50)

National Adoption Registry
(Division of Yesterday's Children)
828 Davis Street
Evanston, IL 60201
(312) 475-1700

New York Foundling Hospital
Record Information Office
590 Avenue of the Americas
New York, NY 10011
Gloria Rella, Director, Public Relations
(Orphan Trains in the late 1800s)

Oasis, Inc. (Organized Adoption Search Information Services, Inc.)
PO Box 53-0761
Miami Shores, FL 33153

(305) 758-5196
Rachel S. Rivers, Director
Hours: Mon–Fri 9:00–6:00
(specializes in research and reunification,
    serves the U.S. and abroad; maintains
    match-up system by date and place of
    birth: OASIS Birth Registry)
$70.00 per year membership; search help
    in adoption to adults

Operation Identity
13101 Blackstone, N.E.
Albuquerque, NM 87111
(505) 293-3144
Sally File

Oregon Adoptive Rights Association (OARA)
PO Box 882
Portland, OR 97207
(503) 235-3669
Delores Teller, President
Pub. *OARA Newsletter*, quarterly
(adoption and reunion registry; search
    and support)
$40.00 for first year's membership,
    $25.00 per year membership renewal

Orphan Train Heritage Society of America, Inc. (OTHSA)
614 East Emma Avenue, Suite 115
Springdale, AR 72764-4634
(501) 756-2780; (501) 756-0769 FAX
E-mail: mjohnson@jcf.jonesnet.com;
    MEJ102339@aol.com
Mary Ellen Johnson, Editor
Hours: Mon–Fri 8:00–1:00, and by
    appointment
Pub. *Crossroads*, quarterly
(orphan train riders, 1854–1929)
$25.00 per year membership

Orphan Voyage of Arizona
PO Box 8245
Scottsdale, AZ 85252
(602) 990-1890; (602) 990-3445
Alice Syman, Owner/Operator
Hours: Mon–Fri 9:00–5:30
(adoptee/birthparent search)
fees: hourly or by the case (some
    pro-bono)

Orphan Voyage
601 South Birch Street
Harrison, AR 72601-5911
Jean Paton
("I deal only with education on adoption
    and referral to others for search for
    living relatives.")

Orphan Voyage of Florida
13906 Pepperrell Drive
Tampa, FL 33624
(813) 961-1393
Audrey Anderson
computer printouts of nationwide
    telephone listings at $150.00 per
    surname, no longer available

Orphan Voyage
1305 Augustine Court
College Station, TX 77840
(409) 764-7157
E-mail: lsc@ag-eco.tamu.edu
Linda Crenwelge, U.S. Search Assistant
Hours: after 6:00 and on weekends
(serves the U.S., adoption searchers, free
    assistance/referrals for all states)

Orphan Voyage of Houston
5811 Southminster
Houston, TX 77035
(713) 723-1762

Ours by Adoption
1209 Illsley Drive
Fort Wayne, IN 46807
C. and D. Schwartz
Pub. *Open Line*

Overseas Brats
PO Box 29805
San Antonio, TX 78229
(210) 349-1394

Parents and Adoptees Liberty Movement
861 Mitchell's Lane
Middletown, RI 02840
(401) 437-1811

PAST
1210 Taki Drive
Erie, PA 16505

Pittsburgh Adoption Connection
37 Edgecliff Road
Carnegie, PA 15106-1006

Pittsburgh Adoption Lifeline
Altoona Chapter
414 28th Avenue
Altoona, PA 16601

Pittsburgh Adoption Lifeline
PO Box 52
Gibsonia, PA 15044
(724) 443-3370 (anytime)
Jean Vincent, Coordinator
Pub. *Lifeline*, three or four times per year
(adoption search and emotional support)
$15.00 per year membership

Post Adoption Center for Education and Research (P.A.C.E.R.)
PO Box 309
Orinda, CA 94563-0309
Virginia Keeler Wolf

Post Adoption Center Support Group
8600 Wurzbach Road, Suite 1110
San Antonio, TX 78240-4334
(serves San Antonio and surrounding
    area)

Pure, Inc.
PO Box 638
Westminster, CA 92684
(The Surname/Birthdate Index—over
    100,000 listings of birth dates,

birthplaces, surnames, given names, and the originating source of the data, listed in Triadoption Services computerized Database; collection of newsletters; etc.)

Rainbow Families, Inc.
734 Pahumele Place
Kailua, HI 96734

Reunion
PO Box 112
Salinda, CO 81201

Reunions, Ltd.
2611 East 25th Street
Topeka, KS 66605-3237
(785) 267-0827
Bonnie Warren, Founder
(search and support for adoptees and birthparents)

Reunite
PO Box 694
Reynoldsburg, OH 43068
(614) 861-2584
Angela Tampone, President; Kathy Singer, Research Coordinator
(serves Ohio)

Right to Know
PO Box 34334
Bartlett, TN 38134
(901) 386-2197

ROOTS
7110 Westway Circle
Knoxville, TN 37919
(423) 691-7412
Susie Thompson
(serves Eastern Tennessee)

Search Consultant
6475-B East Pacific Coast Highway
Long Beach, CA 90803
(213) 427-0463; (213) 596-2466 FAX
Mary Ann Dunkinson
(serves California)

Search-Finders of California
PO Box 24595
San Jose, CA 95154-4595
(408) 356-6711 (24-hour answering machine)
Dorothy Yturriaga, Director
Pub. *Lost & Found*, quarterly
(serves Northern California)
$50.00 per year membership

Search-Finders of Idaho
PO Box 7941
Boise, ID 83707
(208) 375-9803
Lois Wight, Chairman
(non-profit organizaiton; search and support group)
$35.00 per year

Search for Tomorrow
PO Box 441
New Haven, IN 46774
(219) 749-4392

Hours: Mon, Wed & Fri 8:00–4:00, Tue & Thur 5:00–9:00
(maintains a registry of over 4,000 adoptees, birthmothers, adopted parents and separated siblings)
$35.00 application fee; negotiable fee for search, will share information from registry

Search Line of New York
Rt. 2, Whitaker Road
Fulton, NY 13069

Search Line of Texas, Inc.
1516 Old Orchard
Irving, TX 75061
(972) 445-7005
Pat Palmer
Hours: Mon–Fri 10:00–4:00
(serves Texas)
$200.00 for adoptees, $350.00 for birthparents

Search Triad, Inc.
PO Box 1432
Litchfield Park, AZ 85340
(602) 834-7417 (24-hour message machine)
Karen Tinkham, Search Assistant Coordinator and Corresponding Secretary
(participates in the free International Soundex Reunion Registry)
$45.00 membership for the first year, $30.00 renewal

Seek
2410 Manhattan Street
Michigan City, IN 46360-6050
Faith

Shared Heartbeats
PO Box 12125
Oklahoma City, OK 73157
Sue Scott
Hours: 9:00–5:00
(support group for birthmothers and adoptees, specializing in Oklahoma)

South Coast Adoption Research and Support
PO Box 039
Harbor City, CA 90710
(310) 833-5822
Marilyn Miller, ISC
Hours: 8:00 A.M.–8:00 P.M.
$35.00 per year membership

Sunshine Reunions
1175 Virginia Avenue
Akron, OH 44306-3545
(330) 773-4691
Jean Batis, Founder
Hours: Tue–Sat 10:00–7:00
("Reuniting families separated by adoption, since 1977; individual counseling, search assistance, referrals, resources, speakers, legislation (open

records and open adoption advocates), totally confidential, serves all adoption triad members")
$25.00 life membership; search fees by individual case ("For a birth family member to search, amount seldom exceeds $75.00, but for an adopted person to search, fee may be higher.")

Support for Birthparents
35 Demorest Road
Columbus, OH 43204
(614) 274-4492

T.R.I.A.D.
7155 East Freestone Drive
Tucson, AZ 85730
(520) 790-6320

Tennessee Adoptees in Search
PO Box 8684
Chattanooga, TN 37411

Ties That Bind
PO Box 3119
Milford, CT 06460
(203) 874-2023

Tracers Company of America, Inc.
183 Waverly Avenue
Medford, NY 11763
(516) 654-0091; (212) 558-6550
Robert Eisenberg, President
Hours: 10:00–4:00
(specialty: adoption reunion registry and missing persons)
adoption reunion registry one-time fee $50.00

Tracers, Ltd.
(9141 East 38th Street, Tucson, AZ 85731-1851—location)
PO Box 18511 (mailing address)
Tucson, AZ 85731-8511
(520) 885-5958
E-mail: gari8865@aol.com
Gari-Sue Greene, Owner
Hours: 9:00–5:00

Tri-County Genealogical Society
(21715 Brittany, Eastpointe, MI 48021-2503—location)
15492 MacArthur
Redford Township, MI 48239
(313) 255-7319
Karen Mehlberg
(adoption search)

Triad Research
300 Golden West
Shafter, CA 93263

Truth Seekers in Adoption
PO Box 366
Prospect Heights, IL 60070-0366
(847) 342-8742 (24-hour answering machine)
http://www.wbm.com/truthseekers/adoption

Barbara Gonyo, Reunion Consultant
Hours: meetings at Lutheran General
    Hospital, 1775 Dempster Street, Park
    Ridge, Illinois: last Mon 7:00–10:00
(experienced intermediaries; a support
    group for adoption triad members,
    search referrals worldwide)
meeting fee: $10.00

Truths in Adoption Triad

(First of America Bank, Bridgeport, MI,
    just south of Saginaw—location)
1815 Sunrise Drive (mailing address)
Marilyn K. Phillips, Facilitation
Hours: daily 7:00 P.M.–9:00 P.M.;
    meetings: third Sun 2:30–5:30;
    meetings for birthparents: second Tue
    7:00 P.M.; meetings for adoptees: first
    Mon 7:00 P.M.
(serves Flint, Bay City, Saginaw and
    Midland areas)
$30.00 search packet

TRY Resource/Referral Center and Library for Adoption Issues

Today Reunites Yesterday
214 State Street (and Finn)
PO Box 989
Northampton, MA 01061-0989
(413) 568-3663
http://javanet.com/ try
Ann Henry, LSW Program Director
Hours: by appointment
Pub. *Adoption Newsletter*, quarterly,
    $15.00 per year subscription
(nationwide, adoption issues for TRIAD
    members; largest adoption library in
    Massachusetts)
$30.00 per year membership for
    individuals, $50.00 per year
    membership for groups or agencies;
    $3.00 for library loans to non-
    members, photocopies: 5¢ each

University of Southern Maine

Project Director, Human Services
    Development Institute
Law Building 516
96 Falmouth Street
Portland, ME 04103
(207) 780-4403

Utah Department of Health

Bureau of Vital Records and Health
    Statistics
(288 North 1460 West, Salt Lake City—
    location)
PO Box 142855 (mailing address)
Salt Lake City, UT 84114-2855
(801) 538-6363 (Adoption Clerk)
Barry E. Nangle, Bureau Director
Hours: Mon–Fri 8:00–5:00
(Utah Voluntary Mutual Consent
    Adoption Registry)
$25.00 registration fee; preparation of
    new birth certificate after adoption:
    $40.00

Washington Adoption Rights Movement (WARM)

5950 Sixth Avenue, South, Suite 107
Seattle, WA 98108-3317
(206) 767-9510 (24-hour voice mail
    system); (206) 763-4803 FAX
E-mail: warm@wolfenet.com
Marilyn Dean, Staff; Mickey LeClair,
    Staff
Hours: Office: Mon–Wed by
    appointment
Pub. *Warm Journeys*
(reuniting families, court and non-court
    searches, training ofconfidential
    intermediaries, support groups, search
    registry, legislative lobbying)
$10.00 per year membership; $350.00 for
    court search, $250.00 for non-court
    search; WARM registry: $5.00

Wichita Adult Adoptees

4551 South Osage
Wichita, KS 67217
(316) 522-8772 (Director, 11:00 A.M.–
    9:00 P.M.); (316) 729-7474 (Assistant
    Director, 11:00 A.M.–9:00 P.M.)
http://www2.southwind.net/-1peters/
    waaindex.html
Rochelle Harris, Director; Tanya Sultz,
    Assistant Director
Pub. *News 'n' Views*, bimonthly
(serves Kansas; postadoption search)
$25.00 per year membership; search
    fees: expenses

Yesterday's Children

77 Homer Street
Providence, RI 02903

IMMIGRATION RESEARCH CENTERS

The first Naturalization Act, in 1790, made naturalization possible for any free, white adult with four years of U.S. residency. From then until 1906, any federal, state or local court of record could confer citizenship. At that time, the Immigration and Naturalization Service, established to bring order to the process, began reporting its findings to the judge of the relevant court, who then signed the Court Order. Naturalization of women and children differed in that, before 1952, children under 21 years of age received derivative citizenship and have no separate file. Women, on the other hand, received automatic citizenship by marriage, after one year of residency, and needed no Declaration of Intent.

Many persons were granted citizenship outside the normal process. Blacks became citizens by constitutional amendment in 1868. Indians, who were wards of the state until 1924, became citizens by an Act of Congress. Citizens who were living in territories which were brought into the U.S. as a block, by treaty, were often awarded citizenship *en masse*. The incorporation of Texas in 1845 is a case in point.

The forms used for naturalization documents have also varied. Before 1906 each court had its own form, usually one which required only the foreswearing of allegiance to the head of the state from which the applicant came and the signature of two witnesses. The Immigration and Naturalization Service required forms to include name, age, date and place of birth, occupation, physical description, current and former residences, ports of debarkation and arrival, name of the ship, and date of arrival in the U.S. In 1912 names and birth dates of spouses and children were added. Beginning in 1930, photographs were often included.

The normal naturalization process required two classes of documents. The Declaration of Intent was often filed upon arrival in order to begin establishment of residency without delay. With a copy of this filing in hand, final papers could be obtained from any court after residency requirements had been met. A two-to-seven-year lapse between the Declaration and final papers is common. The final papers consist of four parts: Petition, which carries the most information; Affidavits of witnesses and petitioner; Oath of Allegiance; and Court Orders of admitting, denial, or continuance. Name changes often occurred at this time.

Balch Institute for Ethnic Studies
Center for Immigration Research
18 South Seventh Street
Philadelphia, PA 19106
(215) 925-8090
E-mail: balchlib@hslc.org
http://www.libertynet.org:80/~balch/
Dr. John Tenhula
Hours: Mon–Sat 9:00–5:00
Pub. *New Dimensions*

Center for Migration Studies of New York, Inc.
209 Flagg Place
Staten Island, NY 10304
(212) 351-8800
Olha della Cava, Ph.D., Archivist
Pub. *International Migration Review*, quarterly

Ellis Island Immigration Museum/ Statue of Liberty National Monument
Liberty Island, NY 10004
(212) 363-5804 (Museum); (212) 363-8347 FAX; (212) 363-6307 (Library); (212) 363-6302 FAX (Library)
Jeffrey Dosik and Barry Moreno, Librarians
Hours: Mon–Fri 9:00–5:00
Pub. *Ellis Island and Statue of Liberty Magazine*, annually, free
(history of Ellis Island, Castle Garden, immigration and Statue of Liberty; holdings include books, manuscripts, photographs, clippings; currently no genealogical or immigration records on site)

Genealogical Institute
Family History World
(875 North 300 East, Tremonton, UT—location)
PO Box 22045 (mailing address)
Salt Lake City, UT 84122
(801) 250-6717 phone and FAX; (435) 245-0256; (435) 829-4030
E-mail: eakle@xmission.com
Arlene H. Eakle; JoAnn Jackson, Office Manager
Hours: Mon–Fri 9:00–5:00
Pub. *Research News*, occasionally, $3.00 per issue plus postage and handling; *Immigration Digest* (English and Southern research), occasionally, $13.50 per issue plus postage and handling

Great Migration Study Project
The New England Historic Genealogical Society
101 Newbury Street
Boston, MA 02116-3007
(617) 284-9240; (617) 536-7307 FAX
E-mail: nehgs@nehgs.org
Robert C. Anderson, Editor
Hours: 9:00–5:00
Pub. *Great Migration Newsletter*, bimonthly, $10.00 per year subscription
(immigration to New England, 1620–1643)

Immigrant City Archives, The Historical Society of Lawrence and Its People
6 Essex Street
PO Box 1638
Lawrence, MA 01842
(978) 686-9230
Eartha Dengler, Executive Director
Hours: Mon–Fri 9:00–4:30 by appointment only
(local history, especially ethnic, labor, urban planning, and history of immigrants to New England; large collection of photographs and oral history interviews)
$15.00 per year membership for individuals, $25.00 per year membership for families; $5.00 per year membership for senior citizens; $10.00 per year membership for students

Immigrant Genealogical Society
Immigrant Library
(1310-B West Magnolia Boulevard—location)
PO Box 7369 (mailing address)
Burbank, CA 91510-7369
(818) 848-3122; (818) 716-6300 FAX
http://feefhs.org/igs/frqigs.html
Marilyn Deatherage, Corresponding Secretary
Hours: Wed & Sun noon–5:00, Sat 10:00–5:00; meetings: first Fri 7:30
Pub. *German American Genealogy*, semiannually; *Immigrant Genealogical Society Newsletter*, monthly
(especially German and Swiss)
$20.00 per year membership for individuals, $25.00 per year membership for families at the same address, additional $10.00 per year for first class mail delivery, additional $15.00 for airmail delivery overseas, $50.00 per year Supporting membership, $100.00 per year Sustaining membership; library admission: free to members, $2.00 per visit to non-members

Immigration History Research Center
University of Minnesota
826 Berry Street
Saint Paul, MN 55114
(612) 627-4208; (612) 627-4190 FAX
E-mail: ihrc@gold.tc.umn.edu
http://www.umn.edu/ihrc
Judith Rosenblatt, Public Relations
Hours: Mon–Fri 8:30–4:30
Pub. *Spectrum*, irregularly, $8.50 per issue; *IHRC News*, three times per year, free upon request
(resources focus on immigration from and ethnic groups originating in eastern, central, and southern Europe; fraternal society and church records, newspapers and serials, but no ship manifests or naturalization records, concentration on second wave (turn of the century) immigrants, including from the Near East)
$15.00 per year membership in Friends of the IHRC, $25.00 per year membership for families, $10.00 per year membership for senior citizens or students, $25.00 or more per year membership for organizations, depending on the organization's membership; special search fee: $15.00 per hour (beyond a few minutes)

Immigration History Society
Immigration History Research Center
The Balch Institute for Ethnic Studies
18 South Seventh Street
Philadelphia, PA 19106
M. Mark Stolarik, Editor, *The Immigration History Newsletter*
Pub. *Journal of American Ethnic History*, semiannually (Ronald H. Bayor, Editor); *The Immigration History Newsletter*, semiannually
$17.00 per year membership (includes both publications)

Swenson Swedish Immigration Research Center
Augustana College
639 38th Street
Rock Island, IL 61201-2273
(309) 794-7204; (309) 794-7443 FAX
http://viking.augustana.edu/admin/ swenson/
Jill A. Seaholm, Researcher; Christina Johansson, Head of Genealogical Services; Victoria A. Oliver, Head of Library Services
Hours: Mon–Fri 9:00–4:30 by appointment (except during holidays and school vacation)
Pub. *Swenson Center News*, annually; *Swedish American Genealogist*, quarterly, $25.00 per year subscription in the U.S. (calendar year)
(Augustana Lutheran Church (Swedish), Evangelical Covenant Church, Swedish Baptist Conference, Swedish Methodist Church, Evangelical Free Church and Swedish Episcopal)
$25.00 per year Associate membership, $100.00 per year membership for scholars, $250.00 per year membership in Swenson Center Circle

Texas Seaport Museum
(Pier 21—location)
2016 Strand (mailing address)
Galveston, TX 77550
(831) 763-1877; (831) 763-3037 FAX
E-mail: tsm@phoenix.net
http://www.phoenix.net/ tsm
Kurt Voss, Director
Hours: daily 10:00–5:00
(includes immigration database, mostly Germans and Eastern Europeans, entering through the Port of Galveston 1840–1950)
$5.00 admission for adults, includes use of immigration database; mail-in search: $10.00 per person

COMPUTER INTEREST

America on Line
http://www.aol.com/webchannels/
families/html
(genealogical resources to subscribers
only)

Ancestral File™ Operations
Family History Library
35 North West Temple
Salt Lake City, UT 84150
(801) 240-2585; (801) 240-2466; (801)
240-2584 (for general FamilySearch®
questions)
Jayare Roberts, Specialist, Ancestral
File™ Expansion
Hours: Mon 7:30 A.M.–6:00 P.M., Tue–
Sat 7:30 A.M.–10:00 P.M.
(database not on-line)

A.G.E.S. (Ancestral Genealogical Endexing Schedules, Inc.)
PO Box 2127
Bountiful, UT 84010
Ronald Vern Jackson, Senior Archivist
(958 U.S. and state census volumes,
marriages, land, military, will indexes;
database not on line)
search fee: $5.00 per surname, per year,
per state

Ancestry, Inc.
PO Box 476
Salt Lake City, UT 84110-0476
(800) ANCESTRY (262-3787); (800)
531-1790 (*Genealogical Computing*);
(801) 531-1798 FAX
http://www.ancestry.com
Dean R. Zimmerman, Director of
Marketing and Sales; Dennis
Sampson, Editor, *Genealogical
Computing*
Hours: 8:00–5:00
Pub. *Ancestry* (instructional, international
genealogy, how-to articles, regular
columns), bimonthly, $4.95 per issue
for non-members, $21.00 per year
subscription for non-members, $38.00
two-year subscription for non-
members, $54.00 three-year
subscription for non-members;
Genealogical Computing, quarterly,
$25.00 per year subscription
$24.95 membership in Ancestry
Research Club (includes subscription)

Brother's Keeper
6907 Childsdale Avenue
Rockford, MI 49341
(616) 364-5503; (616) 364-1127
(download by modem); (616) 866-
3345 FAX
http://ourworld.compuserve.com/
homepages/brothers_keeper
John Steed
Brother's Keeper™

Comgenes
PO Box 1581
Silver City, NM 88062
Barbara Holley Rock, Genealogy
Manager
Pub. *Grassroots Catalog*, semiannually
(January and July)
$20.00 per year membership

Commonwealth Network
Online Genealogical Database Index
E-mail: tdoyle@doit.com
http://www.gentree.com
Tim Doyle
(links to all known searchable
genealogical databases searchable
through the Web)

The Genealogy Forum on CompuServe
(5000 Arlington Centre Boulevard,
Columbus, OH 43220—corporate
headquarters location)
PO Box 5273 (mailing address)
Billerica, MA 01822-5273
(800) 848-8199 (Customer Service);
(978) 663-6510 (Forum Manager)
E-mail: roots@compuserve.com;
webmaster@rootscomputing.com
http://www.compuserve.com; http://
www.rootscomputing.com; http://
c.compuserve.com; http://
ourworld.compuserve.com/homepages/
roots/goroots.htm
Richard W. Eastman, Forum Manager;
Martha Reamy, Book Review Editor
Hours: Mon–Sun 24 hours
(worldwide on-line genealogy club, online database of queries, message
capabilities accessed through local
access numbers which connect into the
network)
$9.95 per month

Compute-A-Tree
2238 Cimmaron Pass Road
Fort Wayne, IN 46815
Karen Cavanaugh,Editor
Pub. *Compute-A-Tree*

Computer Rooters
PO Box 161693
Sacramento, CA 95816
(916) 363-8403; (916) 988-1125 (Mr.
Sissell)
Joy Huskey; Alton Sissell
Hours: meetings fourth Wed (odd-
numbered months) 7:30 at SMUD
Auditorium, 6201 S Street,
Sacramento; PAF® Users Group (even-
numbered months; Roots II™ SIG first
Wed
Pub. *Computer Rooters*, quarterly

Cyndi's List of Genealogy Sites
http://www.CyndisList.com

Datatrace Systems
PO Box 1587
Stephenville, TX 76401

(254) 965-6979
James Pylant, Editor
Hours: Mon–Fri 9:00–5:00
Pub. *American Genealogy Magazine*,
quarterly (March, June, September,
December), $22.50 per year
subscription, $43.00 for two-year
subscription, $3.75 sample issue
(Texas residents add 8.25% sales tax)
(Indian records, pension files, Black
Dutch ancestry; also transmitted
electronically on nationwide satellite)

Digital Librarian: A Librarian's Choice of the Best of the Web (Genealogy)
http://www.servtech.com/public/mvail/
genealogy.html

GENDEX
http://www.gendex.com
Gene Stark
(an enterprise devoted to advancing the
progress of family history and
genealogy research on the World Wide
Web)

The Genealogy Home Page
http://www.genhomepage.com
Stephen A. Wood

Genealogy Publishing Service
448 Ruby Mine Road
Franklin, NC 28734
(704) 524-7063
Jane S. Moyer, Co-owner
Hours: 9:00–6:00
SKY Index™ 3.1 (generates an index
from computer text database)

Genealogy Special Interest Group
(Rescue Squad Building, Bartle Avenue,
Scotch Plains, NJ—location)
PO Box 773 (mailing address)
New Providence, NJ 07974
(908) 665-0481
Helen Wolf
Hours: fourth Thur (Sept–Jun) 7:30
Pub. *Amateur Computer Group of N.J.
News* (includes "Genealogy Helpline"
column), ten times per year (monthly,
September–June)
$20.00 per year membership for the
Amateur Computer Group, includes all
special interest groups

Genealogy Toolbox Research Center
http://genealogy.tbox.com
Matthew L. Helm

Kenosha-Lake-Racine County Genealogical Computing User's Group
University of Wisconsin—Parkside
Tallent Hall
Kenosha, WI 53141-2000
(414) 633-2719 (Ms. Hoferitza); (414)
632-4610 (Mr. Ammann)
Michele Hoferitza; Dick Ammann
Hours: meetings third Thur 7:00

("Members use PAF®, Brother's
Keeper™, plus other genealogical and
word processing software, to assist
them in their genealogy activities.")

Minnesota Genealogical Society, Computer Branch
(1650 Carroll Avenue, Saint Paul, MN
55104—location)
PO Box 16069 (mailing address)
Saint Paul, MN 55116-0069

Mission Oaks Genealogy Club
(Mission Oaks Community Center, 4701
Gibbons Drive, Carmichael—location)
PO Box 216 (mailing address)
Carmichael, CA 95609-0216
(916) 482-8531
Elizabeth Kohler
Hours: meetings third Thur 1:00; PAF™
User's Group meetings first Thur
1:00–4:00
Pub. *Mission Oaks Genealogy Club
Newsletter*, quarterly

National Genealogical Society (NGS)
4527 17th Street, North
Arlington, VA 22207-2399
(703) 525-0050; (703) 525-0052 FAX
Jean K. Findeis, Executive Director;
Dereka Smith, Librarian
Hours: Library: Mon & Wed 10:00–9:00,
Fri–Sat 10:00–4:00; Offices: daily
8:30–5:00
Pub. *National Genealogical Society
Quarterly*; *NGS Newsletter*,
bimonthly; *NGS/CIG Digest*,
bimonthly
(NGS Bulletin Board System/BBS)
$35.00 per year membership for
individuals, $10.00 per year
membership for spouse, $30.00 per
year membership for senior citizens

The New England Historic Genealogical Society
101 Newbury Street
Boston, MA 02116-3007
(617) 536-5740; (617) 624-0325 FAX
http://www.nehgs.org
Stephen Kyner, Editor
Pub. *The Computer Genealogist*,
bimonthly, $30.00 per year
subscription for non-members, $20.00
per year subscription for members
(articles and news about the use of
computer hardware and software to
enhance genealogical research)
$50.00 per year membership for
individuals (includes *Register* only),
$70.00 per year membership for
families, $20.00 per year membership
for students, $250.00 per year
Contributing membership, $500.00 per
year Sustaining membership,
$2,000.00 life membership, $5,000 life
Benefactor membership; Enquiry
service: $40.00 per hour for non-
members, $25.00 per hour for
members, $50.00 per hour for

corporate clients (rush and FAX
service additional); copies: 35¢ each,
maximum of 35 copies, plus $5.00
service fee for members, $10.00 for
non-members

Orphan Voyage of Florida
13906 Pepperrell Drive
Tampa, FL 33624
(813) 961-1393
Audrey Anderson
computer printouts of nationwide
telephone listings at $150.00 per
surname, no longer available

PAF® Users Unlimited
2463 Ledgewood Drive
West Jordan, UT 84084
(801) 967-8400; (801) 963-4604 FAX
Vance C. Parker, Editor
Pub. *PAF® Users Unlimited Quarterly*
(Personal Ancestral File computer
software), $15.00 per year subscription

Quinsept User Group Newsletter
102 Broadfield Lane
Spotsylvania, VA 22553
(540) 898-7767
Bob Mitchell,Editor
Pub. *Quinsept User Group Newsletter*
(for users of "Family Roots" computer
software), bimonthly, $18.00 per year
subscription in the U.S., $20.00 per
year subscription in Canada, $24.00
per year subscription overseas

Rand Genealogy Club
E-mail: feedback@rand.org. (for
questions about the server)
http://www.rand.org

Roots Users Group of Portland, Oregon
28750 S.E. Haley Road
Boring, OR 97009-9440
(503) 663-6387
E-mail: ruthmickelson@prodigy.com
Ruth Mickelson, President
Hours: meetings at U.S. Bank, 15900
S.W. 116th Avenue, King City, OR:
third Sat (except Jul and Dec) 9:00–
noon
Pub. *Root Users Group of Portland,
Oregon, Newsletter*, ten times per year
(monthly, except December and July)
(for users of COMMSOFT's ROOTS
III™, ROOTS IV™, ROOTS V™,
Family Gathering, genealogical
software programs)
$15.00 per year membership

RootsWeb
E-mail: Webspinner@rootsweb.com.
http://www.rootsweb.com
(cooperative database, nationwide links
to resources)

RUNGS
2193 Wisconsin
Eugene, OR 97402
Juanite Beagley, Treasurer

Pub. *The Ladder*, quarterly, $12.00 per
year (prorated) subscription

Toolbox Internet Marketing Services, Inc.
E-mail: editor@onlinegenealogy.com
http://www.onlinegenealogy.com
Pub. *Journal of Online Genealogy*
(a free e-zine which focuses on the use
of online resources and techniques in
genealogy and family history)

University of Idaho
University Library
Special Collections
Rayburn Street
Moscow, ID 83844-2351
(208) 885-7951; (208) 885-6817 FAX
E-mail: tabraham@uidaho.edu
http://www.lib.idaho.edu/special-
collections; http://www.uidaho.edu/
special-collections/
Other.Repositories.html (Repositories
of Primary Sources)
Terry Abraham, Head, Special
Collections
Hours: summer: Mon–Fri 8:00–5:00
(Repositories of Primary Sources lists
over 2,500 Web sites, worldwide,
describing holdings of manuscripts,
archives, rare books, historical
photographs, and other primary
sources for the research scholar)

USGenWeb Project
admin@usgenweb.com
http://www.usgenweb.net; http://
www.usgenweb.org
Megan Zurawicz, National Coordinator
(links to every county in the U.S.)

Utah Valley Regional Family History Center
Brigham Young University
4386 Harold B. Lee Library
Provo, UT 84603
(801) 378-6200
Diane R. Parkinson, Director
Hours: Mon–Sat 8:00 A.M.–10:00 P.M.,
2nd & 4th Sun 9:00–7:00.
Pub. *Newsletter*, bimonthly
BYLINE (database not on-line, accessed
through Library Gateway)
(no research by correspondence,
assistance for patrons on site only;
depository library, photo archives,
special collections pertaining to U.S.
western history)

Western Pennsylvania Genealogical Society
4400 Forbes Avenue
Pittsburgh, PA 15213-4080
(412) 687-6811
Hours: The Carnegie Library of
Pittsburgh: Mon–Thur 9:00–9:00, Fri–
Sat 9:00–5:30, Sun (Oct–May) 1:00–
5:00
Pub. *The Quarterly*; *JOTS*, ten times per
year

(sponsors Computer, English-Welsh, German, Irish, New England and Scottish interest groups)

$20.00 per year membership for individuals (beginning 1 July); $26.00 per year joint membership (two members at one address); two free queries per quarter

GENEALOGICAL COMPUTER SOFTWARE

A-Gene
E-mail:Mike.Simpson@btInternet.com
http://www.btinternet.com/ genealogy/ agene.htm
Mike Simpson
A-Gene (Version 2.0.36 for Windows®)

Adventures in Ancestry, Inc.
10714 Hepburn Circle
Culver City, CA 90232-3717
(800) 237-5333; (310) 842-7443 FAX
E-mail: Dan@AIA-AnD.com
http://www.aia-and.com/
Ancestors and Descendants

Ancestral File™ Operations
Family History Library
35 North West Temple
Salt Lake City, UT 84150
(801) 240-2585; (801) 240-2466; (801) 240-2584 (for general FamilySearch® questions)
Jayare Roberts, Specialist, Ancestral File™ Expansion
Hours: Mon 7:30 A.M.–6:00 P.M., Tue–Sat 7:30 A.M.–10:00 P.M.
Personal Ancestral File™

B. K. Times
501 East 63rd N, #12 Sioux
Wichita, KS 67219-1213
Pub. *B. K. Times*
(a newsletter for Brother's Keeper™ software users)

Birthwrite
E-mail: rmcd@interlog.com
http://www.interlog.com/ rmcd/ BirthWrite/
Birthwrite (Version 1.5 for Windows®)

Black Fire Technology
E-mail: info@blackfire.com.au
http://www.blackfire.com.au; http:// www.ozemail.com.au/~pkortge
My Family History (Version 1.02 for Windows®)

Brøderbund Software, Inc.
Banner Blue Division
39500 Stevenson Place, Suite 204
Fremont, CA 94539-3103
(800) 315-0672; (510) 794-6850; (510) 795-4488 FAX
http://www.familytreemaker.com
Family Tree Maker™ (for Windows®); *Biography Maker™* (for DOS)

Brother's Keeper
6907 Childsdale Avenue
Rockford, MI 49341
(616) 364-5503; (616) 364-1127 (download by modem); (616) 866-3345 FAX
E-mail: 75745.1371@compuserve.com
http://ourworld.compuserve.com/ homepages/Brothers_Keeper/
John Steed
Brother's Keeper™ (Version 5.2 for Windows®)

Business Computer of Finland, inc
E-mail: Helpdesk@sytk.fi
http://www.mediabase.fi/suku/ genupgb.htm
Genus Senior (Version 2.13 for Windows®)

Common Sense Software
2068 Trailwood Drive
Cincinnati, OH 45230
(513) 841-7099
Family Tree Print Utility™

Computer Services
1050 East 800 South
Provo, UT 84601
(801) 377-2100
Family Ties™

Cumberland Family Software
385 Idaho Springs Road
Clarksville, TN 37043
(931) 647-4012 (6:00–8:00 P.M.)
E-mail: ira.lund@cf-software.com
http://www.cf-software.com/
Cumberland Family Tree for Windows® (Version 2.21x)

Data Base Systems (DBS)
(295 Mohawk Road, Brownsboro, AL—location)
PO Box 7263 (mailing address)
Huntsville, AL 35807
(205) 518-9957
Paul I. Gulick, Owner
Hours: Mon–Fri 9:00–5:00
The Genealogical Data Base System™ (GDBS™, software to develop, maintain and store genealogy)

The Everton Publishers, Inc.
(3223 South Main Street, Nibley, UT—location)
PO Box 368 (mailing address)
Logan, UT 84323-0368
(435) 752-6022; (800) 443-6325
Valarie N. Chambers
Hours: Mon–Fri 8:00–5:00
My Family Record™ (Version 3.0)

Family Tree
6180 Via Real, S-25
Carpinteria, CA 93013-2863
(805) 684-3366
E-mail: rmmerrill@aol.com; rmmerrill@earthlink.net
Robert M. Merrill, Owner
Hours: Mon–Sat 9:00–1:00
Family Tree, a Genealogists Program™ (Apple IIe enhanced or better, text-based database with GEDCOM™ support)

Family Tree in a Window
PO Box 251752
West Bloomfield, MI 48325
C. A. Hartley
Family Tree in a Window (Version 1.08
for Windows®)

Flying Pigs Software
PO Box 688
Saint George, UT 84771
(435) 628-5713
Generation Gap™

Genius Family Tree
E-mail: genius@gensol.com.au
http://www.gensol.com.au/genius.htm
Peter Resch
Genius Family Tree (Version 1.5 for
Windows®)

The Harbinger Group
6253 BenMore Drive
Fridley, MN 55432
Hyper-Genealogy™

IMSI
1895 Francisco Boulevard East
San Rafael, CA 94901-5506
(415) 257-3000; (415) 257-3565 FAX
E-mail: support@imsisoft.com
http://www.imsisoft.com/familyheritage/
Family Heritage Deluxe (Version 2.0 for
Windows®)

Incline Software
PO Box 17788
Salt Lake City, UT 84117-0788
(800) 825-8864; (801) 278-5886; (801)
273-1535 FAX
E-mail: ancquest@ancquest.com
http://www.ancquest.com
Ancestral Quest (Version 2.0)

JamoDat
E-mail: Jamodat@jamodat.dk
http://www.jamodat.dk
Win-Family (Version 5.01 for
Windows®)

Kindred Konnections, Inc.
PO Box 1882
Orem, UT 84059
(800) 288-6314; (801) 229-7967
E-mail:
feedback@kindredkonnections.com
http://www.kindredkonnections.com
Ron Bremer, President
Kindred Konnections™
(over 12 million name archive, Internet
genealogical research service)

LDB Associates, Inc.
PO Box 20837
Wichita, KS 67208-6837
(316) 683-6200
L. D. Bond, President
Hours: 10:00–4:30
KinWrite™, Kinpublish™

MatterWare
PO Box 2221
Valrico, FL 33495-2221
E-mail: matterware@aol.com
http://members.aol.com/matterware
Family Matters (for Windows®)

MicroFox Company
PO Box 447
Richfield, OH 44286-0447
(216) 659-9489; (216) 659-9489 FAX
E-mail: microfox@compuserve.com
http://ourworld.compuserve.com/
homepages/microfox
EZ-Tree (Version 2.3 for DOS)

Millennia Corporation
PO Box 1800
Duvall, WA 98019
(800) 753-3453; (425) 788-4493 FAX
E-mail: Info@MillenniaCorp.Com
http://www.legacyfamilytree.com
Legacy (Version 2.0 for Windows®)

NickleWare
PO Box 393
Orem, UT 84059
E-mail: 72730.1002@CompuServe.Com
http://ourworld.compuserve.com/
homepages/nickleware/
Parents (Version 4.5 for Windows®)

Palladium Interactive
900 Larkspur Landing Circle, Suite 295
Larkspur, CA 94939
(415) 464-5500; (415) 464-5530
E-mail: UFTHelp@Palladium.net
http://www.uftree.com
Ultimate Family Tree (for Windows
95®)
(As of May 1, 1997, Palladium
Interactive has taken over the ROOTS
product line from COMMSOFT.)

Parsons Technology
1 Parsons Drive
Hiawatha, IA 52233-0100
(319) 395-9626
E-mail: info@parsonstech.com
http://www.parsonstech.com/genealogy/
index.html
Gary D, Genealogy Products Manager
Hours: 9:00–5:00
Family Origins™ (Version 6.0 for
Windows®, formerly AncestraLink™
by FormalSoft)

PRO-GEN
E-mail: mulderij.pro-gen@pi.net
http://www.pi.net/~progen/home.html
PRO-GEN (Version 2.3C for DOS)

Quinsept, Inc.
PO Box 216
Lexington, MA 02173-0003
(781) 862-0404; (800) 637-7668

E-mail: stevevxx@aol.com
http://www.familyroots.com
Steve Vorenberg, President
Hours: 9:00–6:00
Family Roots™

RF Corporation
308 Devon Lane
West Chester, PA 19380
Genealogical Application for dBASE III
+ (c)

S & N Genealogy Supplies
E-mail: 100064.737@compuserve.com;
100570.2221@compuserve.com
http://ourworld.compuserve.com/
homepages/mikeparsons
Mike Parsons
FamilyBase for Windows® (Version
2.10)

Sierra On-Line Inc.
3380 146th Place SE, Suite 300
Bellevue, WA 98007
(800) 757-7707; (425) 649-9800
http://www.sierra.com
Generations (Deluxe Edition for
Windows® 3.1 and Windows 95®)

SKY Software
4675 York Road #1
Manchester, MD 21102
(800) 776-0137; (410) 374-3484 FAX
E-mail: email@sky-software.com
http://www.sky-software.com/about.htm
Kamm or Bette Schreiner, Co-owners
Hours: 10:00–6:00
Pub. *SKY Index™* version 3.1 (for back-
of-book indexing, for Windows®);
SKY Catalog™ version 1.1 (for
cataloging home libraries); *SKY
Filer™* version 1.0 (for keeping track
of data collected, for Windows®);
SKY Address™ (for maintaining
correspondent's list)

SpanSoft
E-mail: SpanSoft@compuserve.com
http://ourworld.compuserve.com/
homepages/SpanSoft
Kith and Kin (Version 3.11 for
Windows®)

Valley Software
PO Box 245
Rescue, CA 95672
(530) 676-8747
The Family Tree Genealogy System

**Visionary Endeavors Software
Development**
PO Box 330439
Atlantic Beach, FL 32233-0439
(904) 247-0062; (904) 247-2762 FAX
E-mail: vesd@southeast.net
http://users.southeast.net/~vesd/
index.html
Family Scrapbook (Version 3.1 for
DOS)

PROFESSIONAL BODIES

American Historical Association
400 A Street, S.E.
Washington, DC 20003
(202) 544-2422
Gretchen Miller, Executive Office
Pub. *American Historical Review*;
   Perspectives
(A membership organization for
   historians)

American Society of Genealogists
PO Box 1515
Derry, NH 03038-1515
Cameron Allen, F.A.S.G., President;
   Roger D. Joslyn, C.G., F.A.S.G.,
   Secretary; Col. Charles M. Hansen,
   U.S.A. (ret.), F.A.S.G., Editor, Gale
   Ion Harris, Ph.D., F.A.S.G., Editor
Pub. *The Genealogist*, semiannually,
   $25.00 per year subscription, $45.00
   for two-year subscription, $65.00 for
   three-year subscription to libraries and
   institutions
(honorary organization; membership by
   election only; to advance genealogical
   research standards and to encourage
   publication of scholarly studies, to
   secure recognition of genealogy as a
   serious subject of research in historical
   and social fields of learning)

Association for the Promotion of Scholarship in Genealogy, Ltd.
255 North Second West
Salt Lake City, UT 84103-4545
(801) 521-4732
Neil D. Thompson, Ph.D., F.A.S.G.,
   Executive Director

Association of Professional Genealogists
PO Box 40393
Denver, CO 80204-0393
(504) 766-3018 (Executive Secretary)
Sharon DeBarotollo, C.G.R.S., Editor;
   James L. Hansen, President; Barbara
   C. Strickland, Executive Secretary
Pub. *Association of Professional
   Genealogists Quarterly* (*APG
   Quarterly*) (March, June, September,
   December)
$35.00 per year membership for
   individuals in the U.S. or Canada,
   $50.00 per year membership for
   families, $45.00 per year membership
   (with airmail delivery)

Board for Certification of Genealogists
PO Box 14291
Washington, DC 20044
Marty Hiatt, CGRS, Executive Director
Pub. *Roster of Persons Certified*,
   biennially, plus updates, $12.00 post
   paid

Council of Genealogy Columnists
158 Lafayette Circle
Ocean Springs, MS 39564
(228) 875-4920
E-mail: cqkb28a@prodigy.com
Regina Hines Ellison, C.G.R.S
("The organization is a professional
   group for journal and newspaper
   columnists.")
Pub. *The Columns*, quarterly
$15.00 per year membership

Family and Regional History Program
Wallace State Community College
   Library
801 Main Street
PO Box 2000
Hanceville, AL 35077-2000
(205) 352-6403 (office); (205) 352-8228
   FAX
Robert Scott Davis, Jr., M.Ed., M.A.,
   Director
Hours: Mon–Thur 7:30 A.M.–8:30 P.M.,
   Fri 7:30–4:00
(Alabama and surrounding states,
   Confederate records; houses collection
   of North Central Alabama
   Genealogical Society; also offers
   college courses and research field trips
   in genealogy)

Family History Library of The Church of Jesus Christ of Latter-day Saints
Genealogical Society of Utah
35 North West Temple
Salt Lake City, UT 84150
(801) 240-2331; (801) 240-5551
Jimmy B. Parker, Manager
Hours: Mon 7:30 A.M.–6:00 P.M., Tue–
   Sat 7:30 A.M.–10:00 P.M.
(The Genealogical Society of Utah is the
   acquisitions arm of the Family History
   Library. Membership is limited to
   employees of the Church's
   corporation. No individual research
   services are provided by the Society.
   At the present time Church policy is
   opposed to commercial publication of
   the names and addresses of the various
   branch libraries (Family History
   Centers) throughout the world. A
   partial list is available upon request
   from the Family History Library. The
   location of the nearest library, where
   microfilm copies of the Family
   History Library's holdings can be
   viewed, may be obtained by phoning
   local LDS church representatives.
   Accredits professional genealogists.)

Federation of Genealogical Societies
FGI Business Office
PO Box 830220
Richardson, TX 75083-0220
(888) FGS-1500; (214) 907-9727 phone
   and FAX; (708) 655-9343 FAX
   (Editorial Office)

E-mail: fgs-office@fgs.org
http://www.fgs.org/~fgs/
David E. Rencher, President; Sandra
   Hargreaves Luebking, Editor
Hours: Mon–Fri
Pub. *FGS Forum*, quarterly, $11.00 per
   year members subscription, $17.00 per
   year non-member subscription
membership for organizations or
   institutions based on the number of
   members in the organization: $25.00
   per year for 0–50 members or
   associate organizations (includes two
   complimentary issues of *FGS Forum*);
   items for inclusion in the *FGS Forum*
   should be sent to the Editorial Office,
   PO Box 271, Western Springs, IL
   60558-0271

Genealogical Research Associates
203 Locust Street, S.W.
PO Box 2253
Vienna, VA 22183
(703) 938-0974
Robert E. Thompson, A.G., Owner
Hours: varies
(offers advanced research courses and
   mini-seminars)
hourly or daily fees for research, plus
   expenses: National Archives, Library
   of Congress, DAR Library, and
   Virginia courthouses and archives, etc.

Genealogical Speaker's Guild
(PO Box 11601, Salt Lake City, UT
   84147—location)
3421 M Street, N.W., Suite 236 (mailing
   address)
Washington, DC 20007
Marsha Hoffman Rising, C.G., C.G.L.,
   President

Houston Area Professional Genealogists
1001 West Loop, North, #144
Houston, TX 77055-7215
(713) 684-4633
Mic Barnette, President

The Institute of Genealogical Studies
PO Box 25556
Dallas, TX 75225-5556
(972) 341-5116 (evenings); (972) 341-
   3963 FAX
(along with the Dallas Genealogical
   Society, sponsors a week-long seminar
   offering eight levels of courses in
   American Genealogy)

The International Genealogy Consumer Organization
4329 South Stafford Way
West Valley City, UT 84119
R. Clayton Brough, President
Pub. *International Genealogy Consumer
   Report*, semiannually (January–June
   and July–December), $8.00 for four-
   issue subscription (two years)

National Institute on Genealogical Research (NIGR)
PO Box 14274
Washington, DC 20044-4274
Lynn C. McMillion, CAILS Director
(an educational institute which holds a
week-long seminar, second week of
July at the National Archives,
enrollment limited to 40)

New England Historical Research Associates
225 South Road
Fremont, NH 03044
(603) 895-4032
Matthew E. Thomas, President
Hours: Mon–Fri 9:00–5:00
(lecturers and researchers of New
England city/town history and
genealogy)

The Ohio Academy of History
1465 Mount Vernon Avenue
Marion, OH 43302-5695
(740) 389-2361
Vladimir Steffel, Ph.D., Secretary-
Treasurer
Hours: 10:00–3:00
Pub. *OAH Newsletter*, three times per
year
$10.00 per year membership

The Organization of American Historians (OAH)
112 North Bryan Street
Bloomington, IN 47408-4199
(812) 855-7311
Arrita A. Jones, Executive Director
Hours: 8:00–5:00
Pub. *Journal of American History*,
quarterly; *OAH Newsletter* (not
genealogical), quarterly; *Magazine of
History*, quarterly, $25.00 per year
subscription
from $30.00–$90.00 per year
membership (depending on member's
income), $40.00 associate (non-
historian) membership, $15.00 per
year membership for students, $120.00
per year membership for institutions

Phi Alpha Theta International Honor Society in History
50 College Drive
Allentown, PA 18104-6186

Professional Business Services
450 Potter Street
Wauseon, OH 43567
(419) 335-6485
Howard V. Fausey
Hours: 8:00–5:00
Pub. *National Directory of Local
Researchers*, annually, $11.00 per
issue, postpaid

The Society of American Archivists
600 South Federal, Suite 504
Chicago, IL 60605
(312) 922-0140; (312) 347-1452 FAX
E-mail: info@archivists.org
Susan E. Fox, Executive Director
Hours: Mon–Fri 8:00–5:00
Pub. *The American Archivist*, two times
per year, $85.00 per year subscription
in the U.S., $100.00 per year
subscription elsewhere
(professional organization)

The Society of American Historians, Inc.
Columbia University
610 Fayerweather
New York, NY 10027
(212) 854-2555
Kenneth T. Jackson, Ph.D., Executive
Secretary

NEWSPAPER COLUMNS

Hundreds of additional columns in
newspapers and magazines may be found
in Anita Cheek Milner's book,
*Newspaper Genealogical Column
Directory.*

Council of Genealogy Columnists
158 Lafayette Circle
Ocean Springs, MS 39564
(228) 875-4920
E-mail: cqkb28a@prodigy.com
Regina Hines Ellison, C.G.R.S
("The organization is a professional
group for journal and newspaper
columnists.")
Pub. *The Columns*, quarterly
$15.00 per year membership

AntiqueWeek
"Genealogy Sources"
Eastern Edition
Mayhill Publications, Inc.
(27 North Jefferson Street—location)
PO Box 90 (mailing address)
Knightstown, IN 46148-9900
(800) 876-5133
Shirley Richardson, Genealogy Editor
Hours: 8:00–4:30
weekly

AntiqueWeek
"Genealogy Week"
Eastern Edition
Mayhill Publications, Inc.
(27 North Jefferson Street—location)
PO Box 90 (mailing address)
Knightstown, IN 46148-9900
(800) 876-5133
Shirley Richardson, Genealogy Editor
Hours: 8:00–4:30
weekly

"Roots and Branches"
136 Sandpiper Key
Secaucus, NJ 07094
(201) 866-4075; (201) 864-9222 FAX
Miriam Weiner, C.G.
(syndicated column in Jewish
newspapers; see "Roots and Branches"
in Ethnic Archives, Libraries and
Societies—Jewish)

*Centreville Press and Marion Times
Standard*
PO Box 73
Centreville, AL 35042
Elia Daws

Cherokee County Herald
"Tracing Southern Families"
Rt. 5, Box 109
Piedmont, AL 36272-8709
(205) 447-2939
Mrs. Frank Ross Stewart, Sr.

Arkansas Democrat Gazette
PO Box 303
Conway, AR 72033
(501) 470-1120 phone and FAX
E-mail: desmond@intellinet.com
http://biz.ipa.net/arkresearch/
Desmond Walls Allen, Editor
(queries related to the Arkansas area, i.e.
    southern Kansas, northeast Oklahoma,
    and Arkansas)
weekly (Sunday)

Northwest Arkansas Times
"Relativity"
PO Box 964
West Fork, AR 72774
(501) 761-3344 FAX
Mary Jo and Gene Godfrey
(queries of 75 words or less,
    announcements of local family
    reunions, genealogical meetings, book
    reviews, local and general topics of
    genealogical interest)

The Record
"Ancestor Ambling"
2328 Oleander
Delano, CA 93215
Ann McDanell

Los Angeles Times Syndicate
"Shaking Your Family Tree"
Times-Mirror Square
Los Angeles, CA 90053
Myra Vanderpool Gormley

Florida Times Union
"Out on a Limb"
1 Riverside Avenue
Jacksonville, FL 32207
LaViece Smallwood

Cotton and Quail Antique Trail
"About Genealogy"
PO Box 326
Monticello, FL 32344
(912) 244-0464
Lillian Newham McRee, Columnist
monthly

Pensacola News Journal
"Southern Roots"
PO Box 12710
Pensacola, FL 32574
(904) 435-8538 (*PNJ*); (904) 432-5291
    (Ms. Palmer)
Janice B. Palmer, Freelance Writer
weekly (Sunday, Life Section); queries
    accepted, announcements of family
    reunions, subjects concerning
    genealogy in the South

"Searching Yesteryear"
Genealogy and Local History
    Department
201 South Coffee Avenue
Douglas, GA 31533
(912) 384-1033 (home)
Winifred Merier Gourley
weekly

The Albany Herald
"Ancestors"
1006 Sixth Avenue
Albany, GA 31701
(912) 435-4032
Mrs. Leonard DeLamar
monthly (third Sunday); queries
    accepted, books reviewed

Atlanta Journal-Constitution
"Genealogy"
(PO Box 4689, Atlanta, GA 30302—
    newspaper's address)
PO Box 901 (mailing address)
Decatur, GA 30031
Kenneth H. Thomas, Jr.
weekly (Sunday), $2.00 per issue
    (column is not in mailed editions)
no queries accepted

The LaGrange Daily News
"History and Your Family"
PO Box 2291
LaGrange, GA 30241
Shirley W. Bowen

The Newnan Times Herald
"Norma's Coweta Chatter"
8031 Highway 54, Rt. 1
Sharpsburg, GA 30277
Norma Gunby

The Thomasville Times-Enterprise
"Genealogy Today"
401 Tuxedo Drive
Thomasville, GA 31792
Annette J. Stewart

The Valdosta Daily Times
"About Genealogy"
201 North Troup Street
Valdosta, GA 31601
(912) 244-0464
Lillian Newham McRee, Columnist
weekly

Idaho Post Register
"Out on a Limb"
333 Northgate Mile
PO Box 1800
Idaho Falls, ID 83403
LaViece Smallwood

The News Gazette
"Illinois Ancestors"
(PO Box 677, Champaign, IL 61824-
    0677—location)
105 Poland Road (mailing address)
Danville, IL 61834-7462
(217) 446-6339
Joan A. Griffis
weekly, Saturday; free queries

Commercial-News
"Illiana Ancestors"
105 Poland Road
Danville, IL 61834-7462
(217) 446-6339
Joan A. Griffis
weekly, Sunday; free queries

Antique and Collectible News
"Ancestoritis"
705 Cathy Lane
Mount Prospect, IL 60056
(708) 398-1884
Carol Sims Rademacher
Hours: 10:00–4:00
monthly

"Genealogical Corner"
Weaver Genealogical Publications
Rt. 3, Box 279
Petersburg, IL 62675
(217) 632-3543
E-mail: jdcweaver@aol.com;
    members@aol.com/jdcweaver/
    index.html
Jeanne Crain Weaver, Publisher-
    Researcher
Hours: Office: 8:00–7:00
(specializing in Menard County, Illinois,
    names)
bimonthly in two area newspapers; free
    queries

STAR Newspapers
"It's All Relative"
6901 West 159 Street
Tinley Park, IL 60477
Linda Swisher
free queries pertaining to south Cook
    County or north Will County, Illinois

The Sunday Herald-Times
"Family Tree Leaves"
1717 East Hunter Avenue
Bloomington, IN 47401
Mona Robinson, Columnist
(southwestern Indiana counties)
weekly; free queries up to 35 words plus
    name and address

The Indianapolis Star
"Indiana Ancestors"
PO Box 145
Indianapolis, IN 46206-0145
(317) 633-9160
Vicktoria Hizer, Columnist
weekly (Sunday), $2.50 per issue

**The National Jewish Post and
Opinion**
"Your Name"
238 South Meridian Street, Room 502
Indianapolis, IN 46225-1024
David L. Gold
(mail inquiries only, no telephone or
    personal inquiries)
weekly

Kokomo Tribune
7 Green Hills Court
Greentown, IN 46936
Judy Lausch

**The Dearborn County Register and
Alsino Sun Recorder**
PO Box 328
Lawrenceburg, IN 47025
Chris McHenry

The Loogootee Tribune
1230 Rowin Road
Indianapolis, IN 46220
Robert Conalty-Webber

The Madison Courier
"Family Trees, Twigs, Chips"
2729 Arbor Avenue
Cincinnati, OH 45209-2206
(513) 351-8639
http://www.seidata.com/~bhoggatt/ruth/
    ingenweb/spiry.html (column archives)
Al and Margaret Spiry, Geneologists and
    Columnists
weekly, Tuesdays in *The Madison
    Courier* and Fridays in *The Weekly
    Herald*, both published at 310 Courier
    Square, Madison, IN 47250, no charge
    for genealogical queries

Martinsville Daily Reporter and
Mooresville Times
"Morgan County Yesterday"
1195 Robb Hill Road
Martinsville, IN 46151
(317) 996-3553
Ms. Dale Drake, Morgan County
    Historian
twice per month; free queries with
    Morgan County connection

Milford Mail-Journal
"Relatively Speaking"
PO Box 214
Warsaw, IN 46581-0214
(219) 267-4271
Doris McManis Camden
(also printed in *The Paper*)
twice per month

The North Vernon Plain Dealer
(528 East O&M Avenue, PO Box 410,
    North Vernon, IN 47265—location)
3345 South County Road 800 East
    (mailing address)
Dupont, IN 47231
(812) 346-3973 (Office); (812) 873-6494
    (Home, Mon–Fri after 6:00 and all day
    weekends); (812) 346-8368
Lilian Hall Carmer
Hours: Office: 8:00–4:00
Pub. *The North Vernon Plain Dealer*,
    weekly, $21.00 per year subscription
    locally
queries accepted free for Jennings and
    surrounding counties

*The Scott County Journal and
Chronicle*
5764 South State Road 203
Lexington, IN 47138-8365
(812) 889-2044 phone and FAX
E-mail: jeannie@hsonline.net
Jeannie Noe Carlisle, Editor
(published in Scottsburg)
every four to eight weeks; free queries
    related to Scott, Washington, Jefferson,
    Clark, Jennings and Jackson counties;

search fee: $10.00 per hour plus
    expenses

The South Bend (Ind) Tribune
"Michiana Roots"
225 West Colfax Avenue
South Bend, IN 46626
(219) 235-6360
E-mail: mroots95@aol.com
Carol H. Collins
(pertaining to northern Indiana, southern
    Michigan)
weekly on Sun; subscription $5.00 per
    month; free queries

Tribune-Star
"Genealogy"
721-25 Wabash Avenue
Terre Haute, IN 47808
(812) 466-4920
Dorothy J. Clark, Professional
    Genealogist and Vigo County
    Historian

Sunday Gazette
"Dear Genie"
PO Box 175
Cedar Rapids, IA 52406

Appalachian News-Express
"Genealogy Notes"
(563 Lower Pompey Road, Shelbiana,
    KY 41562—columnist's location)
PO Box 802 (newspaper mailing
    address)
Pikeville, KY 41501
(606) 432-4904 (Home)
Sharon D. Warrix
weekly (Fridays), $39.00 per year
    subscription in Pike County, $49.00
    per year subscription in Floyd and
    Letcher counties, $65.00 per year
    elsewhere; free queries, also photos
    (include SASE for return)

"The Challenge of Genealogy"
313 Sam Dunham Road
Sulphur, LA 70663
(318) 527-9768
Marie Wise, Columnists
("Runs in thirty-six Louisiana
    newspapers; now in twentieth year.")
weekly

The Times-Picayune
"Louisiana Ancestors"
3800 Howard Avenue
New Orleans, LA 70140
E-mail: bookman@intersurf.com
Damon Veach
("Queries should have a Louisiana
    connection; Louisiana at one time
    covered a large area of the Mississippi
    Valley, and also at one time covered
    much of the South (when it was
    known as Spanish West Florida and
    included southern Mississippi,
    Alabama, and the Florida panhandle."
Also appears in *Sunday Advocate*,
    Baton Rouge)

weekly (Sunday Living section)

Shreveport Journal
"Ancestor Hunting"
PO Box 303
Conway, AR 72033
(501) 470-1120 phone and FAX
E-mail: desmond@intellinet.com
http://biz.ipa.net/arkresearch/
Desmond Walls Allen, Editor
(queries related to northern Louisiana,
    eastern Texas and southern Arkansas)
weekly (Monday)

The Rockland Courier-Gazette
"Your Side of the Family"
19 Trim Street
Camden, ME 04843
(207) 236-4385
Lauralee Clayton
1st and 3rd Tuesdays

"Old Pike Travelers"
PO Box 3103
LaVale, MD 21504

Tri-City Record
"Family Heirlooms"
(PO Box 7—newspaper mailing address/
    location)
PO Box 81 (columnist's mailing address)
Watervliet, MI 49098
Carole Kiernan
(no geographical limitations, free
    queries)

The Sun Herald
"Genealogy"
PO Box 4567
Biloxi, MS 39532
(228) 875-8144 (Office); (228) 875-4920
    (Home, after 5:00)
E-mail: cqkb28a@prodigy.com
Regina Hines, C.G.R.S.
Hours: Office: 7:00–3:00

Advertiser News
"Meet Your Ancestors"
103 North 40th Avenue
Hattiesburg, MS 39401
(601) 583-0336
Dr. Betty Drake
weekly, free newspaper, no charge for
    genealogical/historical queries on
    south Mississippi families, no searches
    done for the public

Clarion Ledger/Jackson Daily News
"Family Trees"
PO Box 387
Louisville, MS 39339
(601) 773-3567
William R. Parkes, Columnist
(Also appears in *Natchez Democrat*,
    Natchez; *Winston County Journal*,
    Louisville, and *Northeast Mississippi
    Daily Journal*, Tupelo)
weekly (usually Sunday), no charge for
    queries

The Mississippi Press
"Branches and Twigs"
1222 Highway 90 East
Ocean Springs, MS 39564
(228) 875-8144 (Office); (228) 875-4920
    (Home, after 5:00)
E-mail: cqkb28a@prodigy.com
Regina Hines, C.G.R.S.
Hours: Office: 7:00–3:00
(Also appears in the *Sun Herald*, Biloxi-
    Gulfport)
weekly

"Family Roots"
5560 Gibson Road
Vicksburg, MS 39180
Lamar Roberts
(appears in six newspapers)

Reynolds County Courier
"Kinfolks Search"
c/o Reynolds County Genealogy and
    Historical Society, Inc.
PO Box 281
Ellington, MO 63638
Lee Sylcox, Treasurer

The Kansas City Times
"Shaking Your Family Tree"
PO Box 64316
Tacoma, WA 98464
Myra Vanderpool Gormley
weekly (Saturday)

Rolla Daily News
"Ancestors Column"
c/o Phelps County Genealogical Society
PO Box 571
Rolla, MO 65402-0571
(573) 265-7401
E-mail: monahale@follanet.org
Mona Hale, Secretary
weekly (Sunday)

West Plains
"Family Tree"
939 Nichols Drive
West Plains, MO 65775
Irene Kimberlin

Pilot Tribune
"Digging for Roots"
2145 Wright Street
Blair, NE 68008
Diane Stier
irregularly; also published in the Blair
    Enterprise

The North Platte Telegraph
"Heritage Lines"
PO Box 474
Anthon, IA 51004-0474
Ruby Coleman
monthly

Herald-American
"Genealogy"
PO Box 4915
Syracuse, NY 13221-4915
Sheila M. Byrnes

(central and upper New York State)
free, biweekly in Sunday newspaper

Asheville Citizen-Times
"Family History"
220 Northwest Avenue
Swannanoa, NC 28778
Joyce Parris
free queries

The Columbus Dispatch
"Find Your Ancestors"
34 South Third Street
Columbus, OH 43216
(614) 457-6703
Joy Wade Moulton, C.G., F.S.G.
semimonthly (2nd Sun: Themes, general
    interest & 4th Sun: answer readers'
    columns), $1.50 per issue

The Hamilton Journal-News
"Genealogy"
312 Ross Avenue
Hamilton, OH 45013
Jim Newton

Murrow Journal
"Woods County Roots"
PO Box 234
Alva, OK 73717
Merle Jean Klick-Murrow

The Lawton Constitution
"Tree Tracers"
3607 Arlington
Lawton, OK 73505-6138
(580) 355-7432; (580) 355-7053 FAX
E-mail: agibson@rli.net
http://www.lawton-constitution.com
Aulena Scearce Gibson, Columnist
(queries relating to southwest Oklahoma
    published free; in cooperation with the
    Southwest Oklahoma Genealogical
    Society, which has volunteers who
    assist out-of-town researchers)
weekly column in daily newspaper

Pond Creek Herald
"Bits and Pieces of Grant County
    History"
PO Box 31
Medford, OK 73759-0031
(580) 395-2888
Nina L. Pond

The Oklahoman
"We The People" and "In Search of
    Family"
PO Box 25125
Oklahoma City, OK 73125-5125
E-mail: sburns@ionet.net
http://www.oklahoman.net/connections/
    familysearch/home.htm/
Sharon King Burns
weekly, Saturday; no charge for queries
    with Oklahoma connections

The Poteau News and Spiro Graphic
"Family Finder"
c/o Poteau Valley Genealogical Society

(Buckley Public Library, 408 Dewey—
    research library location)
PO Box 1031 (mailing address)
Poteau, OK 74953
Arlene LeMaster, President
weekly; free queries

The Spiro Graphic
"Know Your Kin"
Spiro, OK 74959

The Daily News
"Our Keystone Families"
PO Box 43
Rehrersburg, PA 19550
(717) 933-4630
Schuyler C. Brossman
(published in Lebanon, Pennsylvania,
    now in its thirty-first year)
weekly, $22.00 in Pennsylvania, $34.00
    out of state

Press and Journal
"Our Keystone Families"
PO Box 43
Rehrersburg, PA 19550
(717) 933-4630
Schuyler C. Brossman
(published in Middletown, PA)
weekly

Sullivan County News
"Steps to the Past—A Guide to
    Genealogy"
c/o Sullivan County Library
PO Box 510
Blountville, TN 37617

Amarillo (TX) News-Globe
"Kinsearching"
PO Box 6825
Lubbock, TX 79493-6825
Marleta Childs
(column is national in scope; circulation
    includes twenty-eight Texas counties,
    western Oklahoma, northeastern New
    Mexico, and southwestern Kansas)
free

Northeast Texas Chronicle
"Genealogy Corner"
1559 Florence Court
Manteca, CA 95336
Jewel Dixon Johnston
(published in Daingerfield, TX)

The Dallas Morning News
"Family Tree"
PO Box 655237
Dallas, TX 75265
(214) 670-1406
Lloyd DeWitt Bockstruck
weekly (Saturday), (also *Index to 1987
    Family Tree Columns from the Dallas
    Morning News*)

The El Paso Times
"All in Your Family"
PO Box 20
El Paso, TX 79999

(915) 546-6397; (800) 351-6007, ext.
    6397
Mary Margaret Davis, Community News
    Editor
monthly (1st Sunday), free queries

Galveston Daily News
Texas City Ancestry Searchers
(Moore Memorial Library, 1701 Ninth
    Avenue, North, Texas City, TX
    77590—location)
PO Box 3301 (mailing address)
Texas City, TX 77592-3301
(409) 935-5343
Zora A. Evans, Editor and Newspaper
    Column Chairman
Hours: 8:00–4:00 or evenings

The Henderson Daily News
"Footprints"
Rusk County Genealogical Society
PO Box 1314
Henderson, TX 75653-1314
Len Rives

The Houston Chronicle
"Your Family Tree"
1217 Oakdale Street
Houston, TX 77004-5813
(713) 522-7444; (713) 521-1367 FAX
E-mail: barnette@neosoft.com
http://www.neosoft.com/~seahorse/
    genealog.html
Mic Barnette
Hours: Tue–Fri 10:00–6:00, Sat 10:00–
    5:00
(worldwide in scope, no queries
    accepted)
weekly (Saturday)

The Texas Spur
"Family Corner"
PO Box 344
Jayton, TX 79528

The Longview Morning Journal
"East Texas Heritage"
PO Box 1792
Longview, TX 75601
Nancy Ruff

Nacogdoches Daily Sentinel
"Kissin Kuzzins"
1614 Redbud Street
Nacogdoches, TX 75961-2936
(409) 564-3625; (409) 552-8999 FAX
Carolyn Ericson, Editor
weekly, free Texas queries

Newton County News
"Historical Newsletter"
PO Box 1383
Newton, TX 75966
(409) 379-2109
Pauline Hines
weekly

The Pampa News
"Gena on Genealogy"
PO Drawer 2198
Pampa, TX 79066-2198

The Panola Post and Panola Watchman
"Know Your Heritage"
RR 2, Box 138AA
Carthage, TX 75633-9624
Leila B. LaGrone

The Lamar County Echo
"The Family Tree"
PO Box 1078
Paris, TX 75460

The Wise County Messenger
"Wise Ancestry"
PO Box 66
Rhome, TX 76078
Catherine Gonzalez

"Window on San Marcos"
c/o The Heritage Association of San
    Marcos, Inc.
(308 East Hopkins Street—location)
20 Timbercrest Street (mailing address)
San Marcos, TX 78666-3018
(512) 392-9997; (512) 393-3735 FAX
E-mail: frances76@centuryinter.net
http://www.centuryinter.net/smheritage
Frances E. Stovall, Coordinator Heritage
    Tourism

The Seguin Gazette Enterprise
"Family Tree"
208 North Roosevelt Avenue
Nixon, TX 78140-2717
(830) 582-2876
Mary C. Bond
weekly (Wednesday); free queries;
    newspaper subscription from PO Box
    1200, Seguin, TX 78155

The Liberty Gazette
"Tracing Roots"
PO Box 16
Wallisville, TX 77597-0016
(831) 389-2252
Kevin R. Ladd
weekly (Wednesday); queries on Liberty
    or Chambers counties or southeast
    Texas

The Waxahachie Daily Light
PO Box 479
Waxahachie, TX 75165
Donna Lonon

The Weatherford Democrat
"Kissin' Kin"
512 Palo Pinto Street
Weatherford, TX 76086
Evelyn Broumley

The Kenbridge-Victoria Dispatch
4037 Tanglewood Trail
Chesapeake, VA 23325
Mildred W. Steltzner

Times-Mirror
"Loudoun's Legacy"
Loudoun County Genealogy Club
PO Box 254
Leesburg, VA 22075

Mary Fishback, President
biweekly

Spokesman Review
"Heritage Hunting"
West 999 Riverside
Spokane, WA 99210
E-mail: mitzi@arias.net
Donna Potter Phillips
"Pastfinding" column also appears in *Tri-
    City Herald*, Kennewick, and "Family
    History" in *The Columbian*

The Washington News Tribune
"Shaking Your Family Tree"
PO Box 64316
Tacoma, WA 98464
Myra Vanderpool Gormley

Nisqually Valley News
"Routes to Roots"
PO Box 597
Yelm, WA 98597
Janet Nixon Baccus, Genealogist

Morgan Messenger
"Warm Spring Echoes"
6 Rockwell Center
Berkeley Springs, WV 25411
Frederick T. Newbrough

The West Virginia Advocate, Cacapon Bridge
"Genealogical Queries"
4715 North 38th Place
Arlington, VA 22207
Wilmer Kerns, Ph.D.

PUBLISHERS

Many historical and genealogical societies, as well as publishers of independent periodicals, produce original books and reprints. The following list, however, covers only the major book publishers, all of whom furnish catalogs on request. For an exhaustive list of genealogical books and publishers see the current edition of *Genealogical & Local History Books in Print* (*GBIP*), edited by Marian R. Hoffman, published by Genealogical Publishing Company. Some publishers operate outlet stores for their own books and also stock titles by other publishers.

Acadian House Publishing
PO Box 52247
Lafayette, LA 70505
(318) 235-7919; (318) 235-8851; (318) 235-9925 FAX
Trent Angers, Publisher
Hours: Mon–Fri 8:00–5:00
Pub. *Acadiana Profile, the Magazine of the Cajun Country*, bimonthly, $17.00 six-issue subscription, $33.00 per twelve-issue subscription, $49.00 per eighteen-issue subscription, $65.00 per twenty-four issue subscription
(south Louisiana, "Cajun Country")
free catalog available on request

American Heritage Publishing
1500 North Kansas Avenue
Marceline, MO 64658
(660) 376-2301

A.G.E.S. (Ancestral Genealogical Endexing Schedules, Inc.)
PO Box 2127
Bountiful, UT 84010
Ronald Vern Jackson, Senior Archivist
(958 U.S. and state census volumes, marriages, land, military, will indexes; database not on line)
search fee: $5.00 per surname, per year, per state

Ancestry, Inc.
PO Box 990
Orem, UT 84059
(800) ANCESTRY (262-3787); (800) 531-1790 (*Genealogical Computing*); (801) 531-1798 FAX
http://www.ancestry.com
Loretto Dennis Szucs, Executive Editor, *Ancestry;* Dean R. Zimmerman, Director of Marketing and Sales; Dennis Sampson, Editor, *Genealogical Computing*
Hours: 8:00–5:00
Pub. *Ancestry* (instructional, international genealogy, how-to articles, regular columns), bimonthly, $4.95 per issue for non-members, $21.00 per year subscription for non-members, $38.00 two-year subscription for non-

members, $54.00 three-year subscription for non-members; *Genealogical Computing*, quarterly, $25.00 per year subscription
$24.95 membership in Ancestry Research Club (includes subscription)

Barnette's Family Tree Book Company
1217 Oakdale Street
Houston, TX 77004-5813
(713) 522-7444; (713) 521-1367 FAX
E-mail: barnette@neosoft.com
http://www.neosoft.com/~seahorse/genealog.html
Mic Barnette, Proprietor
Hours: Tue–Fri 10:00–6:00, Sat 10:00–5:00
(how-to reference guides, states east of the Mississippi River, Texas, Oklahoma, Arkansas, Louisiana, Native Americans, African Americans)

Betterway Books
1507 Dana Avenue
Cincinnati, OH 45207
(808) 289-0963; (513) 531-2690

Clearfield Company
200 East Eager Street
Baltimore, MD 21202
(410) 625-9004; (800) 296-6687; (410) 752-8492 FAX; (800) 599-9561 FAX
http://www.ClearfieldCompany.com
Roger J. Sherr, President

Closson Press
1935 Sampson Drive
Apollo, PA 15613-9209
(724) 337-4482; (724) 337-9484 FAX
E-mail: rclosson@nb.net
Mary Closson, Correspondent
Hours: 8:00–noon & 1:15–4:00
Pub. *Catalog*, annually, $2.00 per issue or free with book order
(genealogical and historical specialty books and records: Pennsylvania, Ohio, Virginia, West Virginia and European emigration)

Curtis Media Corporation
734 East Pipeline Road
Hurst, TX 76053-6011

Deseret Book Company
PO Box 30178
Salt Lake City, UT 84130-0178
(801) 534-1515; (800) 453-3876; (800) 453-4532 (Deseret Book Direct, Orders); (801) 578-3392 FAX (Deseret Book Direct, Orders)
http://www.deseretbook.com

The Everton Publishers, Inc.
(3223 South Main Street, Nibley, UT—location)
PO Box 368 (mailing address)
Logan, UT 84323-0368
(435) 752-6022; (800) 443-6325; (435) 752-0425 FAX
http://www.everton.com
Bob Arbon, Manager

Hours: Mon–Fri 8:00–5:00
Pub. *Everton's Genealogical Helper*, bimonthly, $4.50 per issue, $24.00 per year subscription
(queries, classified advertisements; directories of genealogical researchers, periodical publications, etc.; computerized database of ancestor data: Computerized "Roots Cellar"; computerized Family File; computerized Pedigree Library)
Roots Cellar registration: $5.00 for one name, $1.00 for each additional name

F & M Enterprises
3058 Carmen Drive
Baton Rouge, LA 70709
(800) 848-2463; (504) 927-0901
Frances X. Westbrook, Owner
Hours: Mon–Fri 9:00–5:00
(southwest Mississippi, and the Mississippi and Florida parishes of Louisiana)

Family Historian Books
404 Tule Lake Road South
Tacoma, WA 98444-1952
(253) 535-0108; (800) 535-0118; (253) 537-8998 FAX
E-mail: jhorn28309@aol.com
http://www.familyhistorianbooks.com
Jeff and Kerstin Horning, Owners
Hours: Mon–Fri 8:00–5:00
(includes Missouri, Cherokee and adoption titles)

Family History Educators
PO Box 510606
Salt Lake City, UT 84151-0606
(801) 359-7391
E-mail: elnichols@compuserve.dom; 102226.1062@compuserve.com
Elizabeth L. Nichols
(instruction in genealogy how-to; genealogy and computers; wholesale and retail mail order)

Family Tree Press
5700 Oaktree Lane North
Plymouth
Minneapolis, MN 55442-1534
(612) 557-7138
http://feefhs.org/pub/frg-ftp.html
Fay Dearden, President

Frontier Press
10 Cadena Drive
Galveston, TX 77554-6329
(831) 740-7988; (800) 772-7559 (order line); (831) 740-0138 FAX
E-mail: kgfrontier@aol.com
http://www.doit.com/frontier
Karen Mauer Green, Owner
(largest genealogical bookstore on the Internet; paper catalog also available)

Gale Research, Inc.
Subsidiary of International Thomson Publishing, Inc.
835 Penobscot Building
Detroit, MI 48226-4094

(800) 347-4253 (in Michigan); (800) 877-GALE (Customer Service)
Karen A. Bratton, Information Coordinator
Hours: Mon–Fri 8:00–5:30
Pub. *Passenger & Immigration Lists Index*, biannually

Genealogical Publishing Company, Inc.
1001 North Calvert Street
Baltimore, MD 21202-3897
(410) 837-8271; (800) 296-6687; (410) 752-8492 FAX; (800) 599-9561 FAX
http://www.genealogical.com
Michael Tepper, Editor-in-Chief
Hours: Mon–Fri 8:30–4:30

Heart of the Lakes Publishing
2989 Lodi Road
PO Box 299
Interlaken, NY 14847-0299
(607) 532-4997; (607) 532-4684 FAX
E-mail: waltsteesy@aol.com
Walt Steesy
Hours: by appointment
(genealogy and local studies)

Heritage Books, Inc.
1540-E Pointer Ridge Place
Bowie, MD 20716
(800) 398-7709 (credit card orders only, Mon–Fri 10:00–4:00); (800) 276-1760 FAX
Laird C. Towle, Editor; Leslie Towle, Marketing Director

Heritage Creations
PO Box 882
Elbe, WA 98330-0882
(253) 770-0551
Leland K. and Patty S. Meitzler, Owners
(books, supplies, CD ROM disks)

Higginson Book Company
148 Washington Street
PO Box 778
Salem, MA 01970
(978) 745-7170; (978) 745-8025 FAX
E-mail: higginsn@cove.com
Hours: Mon–Fri 10:00–7:00, Sat by appointment
Pub. *Family History Catalog*, annually (genealogy); *Source Catalog*, annually (local history); *Historic Map Catalog* (map reprints), $4.00 for the set

Historical Research Associates
PO Box 242
Marshfield Hills, MA 02051
(781) 834-7329
Cynthia Hagar Krusell, Proprietor
(Mayflower lineages—Plymouth, Bristol and Barnstable counties)
$20.00 per hour search fee

Hunterdon House
38 Swan Street
Lambertville, NJ 08530
(609) 397-2523
E-mail: tombwilson@aol.com
Thomas B. Wilson, General Manager

Iberian Publishing Company
548 Cedar Creek Drive
Athens, GA 30605-3408
(706) 546-6740
John Vogt and T. William Kethley, Jr., Editors

Henry Z Jones, Jr.
PO Box 261388
San Diego, CA 92196-1388

Kinship—Sources for Kith and Kin
60 Cedar Heights Road
Rhinebeck, NY 12572
(914) 876-4592; (914) 518-9955
Louise Gay Rogers Till, Editor
Hours: Mon–Sun 9:00–9:00
(publishes New York source records; Palatine transcripts)

Marietta Publishing Company
2115 North Denair Avenue
Turlock, CA 95382
(209) 634-9473
Janet G. Parker, Publisher; J. Carlyle Parker, Editor
Hours: Mon–Sat 8:00 A.M.–9:00 P.M.
(seven titles in print)

Mary and John Clearing House
5602 305th Street, Suite AB
Toledo, OH 43611
(419) 726-4192
Burton W. Spear, President
Hours: 9:00–3:00
(publishes volumes on the English families who came to New England by 1643 from the west country of England, counties of Somerset, Dorset, Devon and Cornwall, approximately annually, fourteen in print)
$1.00 for publication list

Mountain Press
4503 Anderson Pike
PO Box 400
Signal Mountain, TN 37377-0400
(423) 886-6369 (Office); (423) 886-5312 FAX
James L. Douthat, Owner
Hours: daily 9:00–5:00

New England History Press
9 Lakeview Drive
Somersworth, NH 03878-2003

Palmetto Bookworks
PO Box 11551
Columbia, SC 28211
(843) 951-3080; (843) 951-3080 FAX
Gary R. Baker

Picton Press
(120 Union Street—location)
PO Box 250 (mailing address)
Rockport, ME 04856-0250
(207) 236-6565
E-mail: picton@midcoast.com
http://www.midcoast.com/ picton
Stephanie McMahan, Mail Clerk
Hours: Mon–Fri 8:30–5:00
Pub. *Genealogical and Historical Catalog*

Precision Indexing
(593 West 100 North, Bountiful, UT 84010—location)
PO Box 329 (mailing address)
Bountiful, UT 84011-0329
(801) 298-4307; (801) 298-5468 FAX
Richard H. Saldana, Manager
Hours: 7:00 A.M.–6:00 P.M.
("Publisher of census indexes, marriage indexes and other materials in book, microfiche and floppy disk formats; they are a division of American Genealogical Lending Library (AGLL).")

The Reprint Company, Publishers
(611 Perrin Drive, Spartanburg, SC 29307—location)
PO Box 5401 (mailing address)
Spartanburg, SC 29304
(803) 582-0732
Thomas E. Smith, Owner and Publisher
Hours: Mon–Fri 9:00–5:00
(reprint editions of local history and genealogy of the southeast; offers self-publishing services to authors and organizations)

Roadrunner Press
Box 1034
Michigan City, IN 46361-1034
(219) 879-0133; (219) 874-7413 FAX
E-mail: higdon@adsnet.com
http://www.halhigdon.com

Scholarly Resources, Inc.
104 Greenhill Avenue
Wilmington, DE 19805-1897
(302) 654-7713; (800) 772-8937; (302) 654-3871 FAX
E-mail: sales@scholarly.com
Roger Strong, Sales Manager
Hours: 9:00–5:00
(authorized distributor for the National Archives and Records Administration [NARA], also publishes books)

Jonathan Sheppard Books
PO Box 2020, Empire State Plaza Station
Albany, NY 12220
(518) 766-9181 FAX
Meldon J. Wolfgang, Owner
(European and North American map reprints; out-of-print local histories and genealogies; occasionally publishes lists)

Shield's Valley Publishing Company
HC 85, Box 4275
Livingston, MT 59047
(406) 222-2725
E-mail: jdharpor@mcr.net
Hours: Joseph D. Harper, Publisher

Simmons Historical Publications
(see Tennessee)

Southern Historical Press, Inc.
(375 West Broad Street, Greenville, SC 29601—location)
PO Box 1267 (mailing address)
Greenville, SC 29602-1267

(864) 233-2346; (800) 233-0152; (864)
    233-2349 FAX
LaBruce M. S. Lucas
Hours: Mon–Fri 9:00–5:00
(southern source material)

Southwest Pennsylvania Genealogical Services
PO Box 253
Laughlintown, PA 15655
(724) 238-3176
William L. Iscrupe, Editor/Publisher

T.L.C. Genealogy Books and Search Services
PO Box 403369
Miami Beach, FL 33140-1369
(800) 858-8558
E-mail: staff@tlc-gen.com
http://www.tlc-gen.com
Nancy Bradley
(primary record abstracts from Kentucky,
    Maryland, Mississippi, Missouri, New
    Jersey, North Carolina, Ohio,
    Pennsylvania, Virginia, West Virginia
    and Wisconsin; original books, not
    reprints, mostly covering the 1700s)

Texas Ancestry Researchers
1009 Eric Avenue
Arlington, TX 76012-3205
(817) 265-0044
Gayle W. Hanson
(specializes in Texas African-American
    research, publishes record abstracts)

Charles E. Tuttle
26 South Main Street
PO Box 541
Rutland, VT 05701-0541
(802) 773-8930; (802) 773-8229

Virginia Book Company
114 South Church Street
PO Box 431
Berryville, VA 22611
(540) 955-1428
Mrs. L. F. Myers
(Virginiana, Virginia genealogies lists,
    Pocahontas and Patsy Cline)

Ye Olde Genealogie Shoppe
9605 Vandergriff Road
PO Box 39128
Indianapolis, IN 46239-0128
(317) 862-3330; (317) 862-2599 FAX
Ray Gooldy and Pat Gooldy, Co-owners
Hours: Mon–Sat 9:00–3:30
(publishers of genealogy books)

MICROFORM PUBLISHERS

AGLL
(PO Box 40, Orting, WA 98360-0040,
    Editorial Offices location)
PO Box 329 (Subscription Department
    mailing address)
Bountiful, UT 84011-0329
(801) 298-5358 (Subscription
    Department); (801) 298-5446 (Sales);
    (801) 298-1712 (Customer Service);
    (435) 770-0551 (Editorial Offices);
    (800) 760-AGLL (Orders); (801) 298-
    5468 FAX
E-mail: sales@agll.com
http://www.heritagequest.com (Editorial
    Offices); http://www.agll.com (Sales)
Leland K. Meitzler, Executive Editor;
    Steve Williams, Vice President
    Marketing
Hours: Editorial Offices: Mon–Fri 9:00–
    5:00; Sales: 8:00–4:00
Pub. *Heritage Quest* (U.S. and
    international research articles, how-to,
    queries, book reviews), bimonthly,
    $28.00 per year subscription;
    Genealogy Bulletin, $12.00 per year
    subscription
(over 250,000 titles on microfilm and
    microfiche for rent; microfilming of
    books, documents, newspapers;
    microfilm and microfiche duplication
    in both silver and diazo)
$47.50 membership

A.G.E.S. (Ancestral Genealogical Endexing Schedules, Inc.)
PO Box 2127
Bountiful, UT 84010
Ronald Vern Jackson, Senior Archivist
(958 U.S. and state census volumes,
    marriages, land, military, will indexes;
    database not on line)
search fee: $5.00 per surname, per year,
    per state

InfoTech Publications
PO Box 1705
Cottonwood, AZ 86326-1705
Marilyn H. or Everett Moore
Hours: 8:00–5:00
Pub. *Catalog*
(98 titles on Missouri genealogy)

Library Microfilms
Division of Bay Microfilm, Inc.
1115 East Arques Avenue
Sunnyvale, CA 94086
(408) 736-7444; (800) 359-FILM
Jan Hawley, Director
Hours: 8:00–5:00
Pub. *Catalog*

Micro Specialties
19925 Stevens Creek Boulevard
Cupertino, CA 95014
(408) 973-7872
Dennis Lewandowski

Microform Books
4 Mayfair Circle
Oxford, MA 01540-2722
(508) 987-0881
Jay M. Holbrook, Owner
(fiches of old printed records; Mayflower
    Descendant, Massachusetts vital
    records to 1850 for 210 towns)

UMI/Books on Demand
300 North Zeeb Road
Ann Arbor, MI 48106-1346
(800) 521-0600
http://www.umi.com
Karen Kaltz, Product Manager
Hours: 8:00–5:00
Pub. *Books on Demand*
(specializes in out-of-print books,
    genealogy)

ELECTRONIC PUBLISHERS

Accessible Archives, Inc.
697 Sugartown Road
Malvern, PA 19355
(215) 296-7441
John C. Nagy
(publishes items of genealogical importance from major 19th-century newspapers from southeastern Pennsylvania, Delaware, northern Maryland, and southern New Jersey on CD-ROM)

Precision Indexing
(593 West 100 North, Bountiful, UT 84010—location)
PO Box 329 (mailing address)
Bountiful, UT 84011-0329
(801) 298-4307; (801) 298-5468 FAX
Richard H. Saldana, Manager
Hours: 7:00 A.M.–6:00 P.M.
("Publisher of census indexes, marriage indexes and other materials in book, microfiche and floppy disk formats; they are a division of American Genealogical Lending Library [AGLL].")

SELF-PUBLISHING

Following is a list of publishers and printers who are experienced in producing family histories and genealogical reference books. These firms can help an author design an attractive book and may also offer him some limited editorial advice. They print and bind books (or produce microform copies) for an agreed fee. The recent, well-publicized class-action suit against Viking Press has made people more aware of the abuses of "vanity" presses, which promise to promote and distribute a book when, in fact, they do not. Distribution and publicity are usually a self-publisher's own responsibility, unless stated otherwise in the publishing contract.

AGLL
(PO Box 40, Orting, WA 98360-0040, Editorial Offices location)
PO Box 329 (Subscription Department mailing address)
Bountiful, UT 84011-0329
(801) 298-5358 (Subscription Department); (801) 298-5446 (Sales); (801) 298-1712 (Customer Service); (435) 770-0551 (Editorial Offices); (800) 760-AGLL (Orders); (801) 298-5468 FAX
E-mail: sales@agll.com
http://www.heritagequest.com (Editorial Offices); http://www.agll.com (Sales)
Leland K. Meitzler, Executive Editor; Steve Williams, Vice President Marketing
Hours: Editorial Offices: Mon–Fri 9:00–5:00; Sales: 8:00–4:00
Pub. *Heritage Quest* (U.S. and international research articles, how-to, queries, book reviews), bimonthly, $28.00 per year subscription; *Genealogy Bulletin*, $12.00 per year subscription
(over 250,000 titles on microfilm and microfiche for rent; microfilming of books, documents, newspapers; microfilm and microfiche duplication in both silver and diazo)
$47.50 membership

Ancestor Research and Analysis
13727 North Amiss Road
Baton Rouge, LA 70810-5042
(504) 766-0140; (504) 766-3018
Danell Spillman and Barbara Comeaux Strickland, Owners
Hours: Mon–Sat 8:00–5:00
(provides all aspects of genealogical services: research, consultation, publishing, mailing services, word processing for manuscripts, indexing, lecturers, seminar coordinator)

The Anundsen Publishing Company
108 Washington Street
PO Box 230
Decorah, IA 52101
(319) 382-4295
John K. Anundsen, President

The Bookmark
(36 Public Square—location)
PO Box 90 (mailing address)
Knightstown, IN 46148-9900
(765) 345-5133; (800) 876-5133, ext. 170; (800) 695-8153 FAX
Bonnie Manche, Secretary/Clerk
Hours: Mon–Fri 8:00–noon & 12:30–4:30
(publishes atlases and county histories)

Closson Press
1935 Sampson Drive
Apollo, PA 15613-9209
(724) 337-4482; (724) 337-9484 FAX
E-mail: rclosson@nb.net
Mary Closson, Correspondent
Hours: 8:00–noon & 1:15–4:00
Pub. *Catalog*, annually, $2.00 per issue or free with book order
(genealogical and historical specialty books and records: Pennsylvania, Ohio, Virginia, West Virginia and European emigration)

Curtis Media Corporation
530 Bedford Road, Suite 112
Bedford, TX 76022-6554

Dogwood Printing
(Campbell City Shopping Center, Highway 65 and CC—location)
PO Box 716 (mailing address)
Ozark, MO 65721-0716
(417) 581-8585; (800) 862-8382; (417) 581-5858 FAX
Betty R. Braden and Peggy L. Taylor, Owners
Hours: Mon–Fri 8:30–5:00
(specializes in family histories, records, newsletters, quarterlies)

The Everton Publishers, Inc.
(3223 South Main Street, Nibley, UT—location)
PO Box 368 (mailing address)
Logan, UT 84323-0368
(435) 752-6022; (800) 443-6325; (435) 752-0425 FAX
http://www.everton.com
Bob Arbon, Manager
Hours: Mon–Fri 8:00–5:00

F & M Enterprises
3058 Carmen Drive
Baton Rouge, LA 70709
(800) 848-2463; (504) 927-0901
Frances X. Westbrook, Owner
Hours: Mon–Fri 9:00–5:00
(soft-bound, no minimum quantity)

Family History Publishers
845 South Main Street
Bountiful, UT 84010

(801) 295-7490
Jay L. Long, Editor-Publisher

Gateway Press, Inc.
1001 North Calvert Street
Baltimore, MD 21202-3897
(410) 837-8271; (800) 296-6687; (410)
752-8492 FAX; (800) 599-9561 FAX
E-mail: ahughes@genealogical.com
Ann Hughes, Publishing Director
(affiliated with Genealogical Publishing
Company)

Genealogy Publishing Service
448 Ruby Mine Road
Franklin, NC 28734
(704) 524-7063
Jane S. Moyer, Co-owner
Hours: 9:00–6:00

The Gregath Publishing Company
PO Box 505
Wyandotte, OK 74370
(800) 955-5232
Fredrea Gregath Cook
Hours: 9:00–4:30
(specializes in genealogy, folklore,
family history, local history, military
history)

Heart of the Lakes Publishing
2989 Lodi Road
PO Box 299
Interlaken, NY 14847-0299
(607) 532-4997; (607) 532-4684 FAX
E-mail: waltsteesy@aol.com
Walt Steesy
Hours: by appointment
(genealogy and local studies)

Heirloom Publishing Services
PO Box 3011
Lake Placid, FL 33852

Higginson Book Company
148 Washington Street
PO Box 778
Salem, MA 01970
(978) 745-7170; (978) 745-8025 FAX
E-mail: higginsn@cove.com
Hours: Mon–Fri 10:00–7:00, Sat by
appointment

**The New England Historic
Genealogical Society**
101 Newbury Street
Boston, MA 02116-3007
(617) 536-5740, ext. 203
http://www.nehgs.org
D. Brenton Simons, Editor
Hours: Mon–Fri 9:00–5:00

Picton Press
(120 Union Street—location)
PO Box 250 (mailing address)
Rockport, ME 04856-0250
(207) 236-6565
E-mail: picton@midcoast.com
http://www.midcoast.com/ picton
Stephanie McMahan, Mail Clerk
Hours: Mon–Fri 8:30–5:00

Pub. *Genealogical and Historical
Catalog*

The Reprint Company, Publishers
(611 Perrin Drive, Spartanburg, SC
29307—location)
PO Box 5401 (mailing address)
Spartanburg, SC 29304
(803) 582-0732
Thomas E. Smith, Owner and Publisher
Hours: Mon–Fri 9:00–5:00
(reprint editions of local history and
genealogy of the southeast; offers self-
publishing services to authors and
organizations)

Timbercreek, Ltd.
Rt. 1, Box 242
Miami, OK 74354
(918) 542-4148; (800) 955-5232
Fredrea Gregath Cook, President

Wolfe Publishing
PO Box 8036
Fernandina Beach, FL 32035-8036
(904) 277-0555
Betty Wolfe, Owner

Wordsworth Ink
4217 Sheridan Street
Hyattsville, MD 20782
(301) 927-6796
Becky Antoniak

BOOKSELLERS

Alice's Ancestral Nostalgia
PO Box 510092
Salt Lake City, UT 84151
(801) 575-6510
Alice Woods Schiesswohl
$2.00 for catalog

Appleton's Online
8700 Pineville-Matthews Road, Suite
610
Charlotte, NC 28226
(800) 777-3601 (Orders); (704) 341-
2244; (704) 341-0072; (704) 552-1411
BBS
E-mail: catalog.request@appletons.com
http://www.moobasi.com
Hours: Mon–Thur & Sun 10:00–8:00,
Fri–Sat 10:00–10:00
(used books on all subjects, and new
genealogy products)

Automated Research, Inc.
(800) 244-1776

**Barnette's Family Tree Book
Company**
1217 Oakdale Street
Houston, TX 77004-5813
(713) 522-7444; (713) 521-1367 FAX
E-mail: barnette@neosoft.com
http://www.neosoft.com/~seahorse/
genealog.html
Mic Barnette, Proprietor
Hours: Tue–Fri 10:00–6:00, Sat 10:00–
5:00
(how-to reference guides, states east of
the Mississippi River, Texas,
Oklahoma, Arkansas, Louisiana,
Native Americans, African Americans)

The Bookmark
(36 Public Square—location)
PO Box 90 (mailing address)
Knightstown, IN 46148-9900
(765) 345-5133; (800) 876-5133, ext.
170; (800) 695-8153 FAX
Bonnie Manche, Secretary/Clerk
Hours: Mon–Fri 8:00–noon & 12:30–
4:30
(publishes atlases and county histories)

Deseret Book Company
PO Box 30178
Salt Lake City, UT 84130-0178
(801) 534-1515; (800) 453-3876; (800)
453-4532 (Deseret Book Direct,
Orders); (801) 578-3392 FAX (Deseret
Book Direct, Orders)
http://www.deseretbook.com

F & M Enterprises
3058 Carmen Drive
Baton Rouge, LA 70709
(800) 848-2463; (504) 927-0901
Frances X. Westbrook, Owner
Hours: Mon–Fri 9:00–5:00

(southwest Mississippi, and the
Mississippi and Florida parishes of
Louisiana)

Family Tree House
(in the Antique Trove, 232 Vernon Street,
Roseville, CA 95678—location)
PO Box 2262 (mailing address)
Granite Bay, CA 95746
(916) 791-2050; (916) 791-8920 FAX
Gregory B. Bragg, Owner
Hours: Mon–Sun 10:00–6:00
(genealogy and family history how-to
books, computer software, CD-ROMs,
and supplies)
$20.00 per year membership in discount
club (20%)

Fort Laramie Historical Association
(3$^1/_2$ miles southwest of the Town of Fort
Laramie on Highway 160—location)
HC 72, Box 389 (mailing address)
Fort Laramie, WY 82212
(307) 837-2662; (800) 321-5456
Pat Fullmer, Business Manager
Hours: Mon–Sun 8:00–4:30 (except
Christmas, Thanksgiving and New
Year)
Pub. *Mail Order Catalog*, annually
("We have one of the best western book
stores to choose titles from including
westward expansion, overland
migration, Native Americans, western
military history, and Fort Laramie
specific.")
$10.00 per year membership, $100.00
life membership

Frontier Press
10 Cadena Drive
Galveston, TX 77554-6329
(831) 740-7988; (800) 772-7559 (order
line); (831) 740-0138 FAX
E-mail: kgfrontier@aol.com
http://www.doit.com/frontier
Karen Mauer Green, Owner
(largest genealogical bookstore on the
Internet; paper catalog also available)

Genealogy Book Store
1217 Oakdale
Houston, TX 77004
E. Simmons

Genealogy House
3148 Kentucky Avenue, South
Saint Louis Park, MN 55426-3471
(612) 920-6990
Jan Haase, President
Hours: by appointment

Genealogy Unlimited, Inc.
(1060 South 500 East, American Fork,
UT 84003-9723—location)
PO Box 537 (mailing address)
Orem, UT 84059-0537
(800) 666-4363; (801) 763-7132; (801)
763-7185 FAX
E-mail: genun@itsnet.com
http://www.itsnet.com/genun
Carol Mehr Schiffman, President

Hours: Mon–Fri 10:00–4:00
("Genealogical and archival supplies;
importer of European maps and
atlases, free catalog available")
free semiannual mail-order catalog

Hearthstone Bookshop
5735-A Telegraph Road
Alexandria, VA 22303
(703) 960-0086
Stuart and Tammy Nixon, Owners
Hours: Mon–Sat 10:00–5:00, Thur 5:00–
8:00
Pub. *Catalog*, annually, $2.00
(refundable with first order)
("We are devoted entirely to genealogical
books and supplies; we stock more
titles from more publishers than any
other dealer; we also offer
genealogical software, hand-painted
coats of arms, and acid-free
preservation materials for old
photographs and documents.")

Heritage Creations
PO Box 882
Elbe, WA 98330-0882
(253) 770-0551
Leland K. and Patty S. Meitzler, Owners
(books, supplies, CD ROM disks)

Higginson Book Company
148 Washington Street
PO Box 778
Salem, MA 01970
(978) 745-7170; (978) 745-8025 FAX
E-mail: higginsn@cove.com
Hours: Mon–Fri 10:00–7:00, Sat by
appointment
Pub. *Family History Catalog*, annually
(genealogy); *Source Catalog*, annually
(local history); *Historic Map Catalog*
(map reprints), $4.00 for the set

Historic Resources, Inc.
(593 West 100 North, Bountiful, UT
84010—location)
PO Box 329 (mailing address)
Bountiful, UT 84011-0329
(801) 298-5446; (801) 298-5468 FAX
Lorrie M. Gilbert, Manager
Hours: 7:00 A.M.–6:00 P.M.
(genealogical books, microfilm and
microfiche, floppy disk databases,
microfilm and fiche readers; "Historic
Resources is the marketing arm of
Precision Indexing and American
Genealogical Lending Library
(AGLL); they also sell subscriptions to
Heritage Quest.")

History House
PO Box 30093
Raleigh, NC 27622
(919) 755-3952; (919) 781-7240
Mrs. H. A. Smith, Editor
Hours: Mon–Fri 10:00–5:00

The Memorabilia Corner
1312 McKinley Avenue
Norman, OK 73072
(405) 321-8366

The New England Historic Genealogical Society
160 North Washington Street
Boston, MA 02114-2120
(888) 906-3447; (617) 536-5741
E-mail: sales@nehgs.org
http://www.nehgs.org
Lynn Betlock, Sales Manager
Hours: Mon–Fri 9:00–5:00
Catalog, two times per year
(genealogies, histories, reference works,
vital records, software, CD-ROMs,
and preservation supplies)

Origins
4327 Milton Avenue
Janesville, WI 53546-9322
(608) 757-2777
E-mail: herrickd@inwave.com
http://www.angelfire.com/biz/origins1
Wendy Uncapher, Owner; Linda Herrick,
Owner
Hours: Mon–Fri 9:00–5:00, Sat 11:00–
3:00
(genealogy supplies, maps, acid-free
preseervation products)
free catalog upon request

Byron Sistler and Associates, Inc.
1712 Natchez Trace
PO Box 120934
Nashville, TN 37212
(615) 297-3085; (615) 298-2807 FAX;
(800) 578-9475 (orders only)
Hours: including nights and weekends
(emphasis on Tennessee censuses,
marriages, church records; dealer in
Tennessee, North Carolina, Kentucky
and Virginia genealogical books)

Stagecoach Library for Genealogical Research
1840 South Wolcott Court
Denver, CO 80219
(303) 922-8856
Donna J. Porter, Owner
Pub. *Catalog* (mail order rental/sale),
$10.00 per issue

Stevenson's Genealogical Center
230 West 1230 North
Provo, UT 84604
(801) 374-9600
Hours: Mon–Sat 8:00–8:00

Thomsen's Genealogical Center
PO Box 588
Bountiful, UT 84011
(801) 294-5105; (801) 292-7952
(Barbara)
Barbara Ann Orris, Manager
(genealogical supplies, maps and atlases;
Scandinavian)

Virginia Book Company
114 South Church Street
PO Box 431
Berryville, VA 22611
(540) 955-1428
Mrs. L. F. Myers

(Virginiana, Virginia genealogies lists,
    Pocahontas and Patsy Cline)

Willow Bend Books
39475 Tollhouse Road
Lovettsville, VA 20180-9703
(540) 822-5292
E-mail: willowbend@mediasof.net
http://www.mediasoft.net/ScotC
Craig Roberts Scott, C.G.R.S., Proprietor
(Internet bookstore specializing in
    currently in-print books)

Ye Olde Genealogie Shoppe
9605 Vandergriff Road
PO Box 39128
Indianapolis, IN 46239-0128
(317) 862-3330; (317) 862-2599 FAX
Ray Gooldy and Pat Gooldy, Co-owners
Hours: Mon–Sat 9:00–3:30

ANTIQUARIAN BOOK DEALERS

Aceto Bookmen
5721 Antietam Drive
Sarasota FL 34231-4903
(941) 924-9170
Charles Delmar Townsend, Owner
Hours: by appointment
(genealogy and local history)

Americana Books
723 Fifth Avenue, South
Saint Cloud, MN 56301
(American history)

Andover Books
41 Chandler Circle
Andover, MA 01810
(local history)

Book Hawk
236 West East Avenue
Chico, CA 95926
(530) 343-4183

The Bookshelf
43 North Main Street
Ambler, PA 19002
(215) 674-8074 (Mon evening 8:00–
    11:00); (215) 628-2252 (Tues–Sat
    10:00–5:00)

Osee H. Brady, Books
12 Elm Street
Assonet, MA 02702
(508) 644-5073
Althea H. Brady, Owner
Hours: 10:00–5:00 by appointment
(a general stock out-of-print/antiquarian
    shop, with a good selection of New
    England material and limited
    genealogical material)

Vernon and Zona Braun Booksellers
9004 Rosewood Drive
Sacramento, CA 95826
(local history)

Cabin in the Pines Bookshop
Rt. 5, Box 409
Potsdam, NY 13676
(Saint Lawrence and Franklin counties
    history)

A. Eileen Smith Cunningham
(1208 South Fifth Street, also Route
    267—location)
Rt. 2, Box 10 (mailing address)
Carrollton, IL 62016
(217) 942-3868
(genealogy, local history of central-
    western Illinois and the Illinois River
    Valley)

Q. M. Dabney & Co.
11910 Parklawn Drive
Rockville, MD 20852
(301) 881-1470
Michael E. Schnitter, General Manager

Hours: Mon–Fri 9:00–5:30, Sat by
    appointment
Pub. *Catalog*, two or three times per
    year, $3.00 per issue
(old books on American history,
    including some genealogy)

Thomas S. DeLong
RDG Box 336
Sinking Spring, PA 19608
(PA local history)

Fine Books Division
1550 West Mockingbird
Dallas, TX 75235
Pub. *The Americana Catalog*, annually,
    free

**Lawrence Golder Rare Books,
ABAA**
PO Box 144
Collinsville, CT 06022
(860) 693-8631; (860) 693-8110 FAX
Lawrence Golder
Hours: by appointment only
Pub. *Catalog*, annually
(rare general Americana, West, Colonial,
    South, Indians, Canadiana, Arctic,
    world voyages and travels)

Great Bridge Books, Inc.
PO Box 15512
Chesapeake, VA 23328-5512
(VA & NC local history)

Klaus Gruneweld Bookdealer
807 West 87 Terrace
Kansas City, MO 64114
(816) 333-7799
Hours: by appointment
(Kansas, Missouri, and Kansas City local
    history)

Haunted Bookshop
(73 Lincoln Street—location)
PO Box 34 (mailing address)
Paris, ME 04271
(207) 743-6216
Wini Mott, Owner
(Maine town histories and a few books
    on genealogy)

Heinoldt Books
1325 West Central Avenue
Egg Harbor, NJ 08215
(609) 965-2284
Margaret Heinoldt, Owner
Hours: by appointment
(free semiannual catalog of Americana,
    colonial American history, western
    expansion, and local history, especially
    New Jersey, New York and
    Pennsylvania)

Paul Henderson Books
466 Penacook Road
Hopkinton, NH 03229
(603) 746-3396
Joanna Henderson, Owner
Hours: by appointment
(local history and family genealogies)

Peter Hennessey Bookseller
PO Box 393
Peconic, NY 11958
(516) 734-5650; (516) 734-7920
E-mail: hennessey@northfork.net
Peter Hennessey
(complete out-of-print book service)

Higginson Book Company
148 Washington Street
PO Box 778
Salem, MA 01970
(978) 745-7170; (978) 745-8025 FAX
E-mail: higginsn@cove.com
Hours: Mon–Fri 10:00–7:00, Sat by
   appointment
Pub. *Family History Catalog*, annually
   (genealogy); *Source Catalog*, annually
   (local history); *Historic Map Catalog*
   (map reprints), $4.00 for the set

Hoenstine Rental Library
414 Montgomery Street
Hollidaysburg, PA 16648
(814) 695-0632; (814) 696-7310
Barbara Ann Hoenstine
Hours: Mon–Fri 9:00–12:00 & 1:00–
   4:00
(sales of new and used books on
   Pennsylvania history and genealogy;
   collection of over 4,000 books for
   rent)

Dan Jones Research
PO Box 177
Department GA
Salt Lake City, UT 84110-0177
$5.00 plus LSASE for price list of out-
   of-print and hard-to-find family and
   local histories, fee refunded as $10.00
   on first order); genealoical research
   services offered

Light of Parnell Bookshop
3362 Mercersburg Road
Mercersburg, PA 17236-9609
(717) 328-3478
Nathan O. Heckman
Hours: by appointment
(Franklin County local history)

Lindsay's Books, Inc.
106 East Meeting Street
PO Box 1075
Lancaster, SC 29721
(803) 285-9455 (Office); (803) 547-5383
   (Home)
D. Lindsay Pettus, Owner
(historical books, manuscripts, old
   postcards of Lancaster County, South
   Carolina)

**MacDonalds Military Memorabilia
and Maine Mementoes**
PO Box 65
Eustis, ME 04936-0065
(207) 246-5999
Thomas L. MacDonald, Owner
Hours: by appointment only
(free catalog of local history, Civil War

books, paper and photos, published
   every six weeks)
two first-class stamps

Madigan's Books
Rt. 3, Box 128
PO Box 62
Charleston, IL 61920-9339
(217) 345-3657
E-mail: mmadigan@advant.com
http://www.advant.com/madigan
Matt Madigan
Hours: by appointment
Pub. *Catalog*, three to five times per
   year, free
(county, town, family histories, plat
   books, vital records; maintains a book-
   wanted file)

New Englandiana
121 Ben Mont Avenue
PO Box 589
Bennington, VT 05201
(802) 447-1695
Roger D. Harris, Owner
Hours: Mon 8:00–4:30, Tue–Fri by
   chance
(bimonthly used book list, includes
   genealogy)
six issues for $2.00

Nu-tique Shop
Main Street
Newfane, VT 05345
(genealogy and local history)

Otzinachson Bookshop
Rt. 1, Box 30
Allenwood, PA 17810
(PA)

Dick Perier—Books
PO Box 1
Vancouver, WA 98666
(360) 676-2033 (mail order only)
Dick Perier
Hours: 9:00 A.M.–10:00 P.M.
(Washington, Oregon, Idaho and
   Montana state, county and local
   history)

Seven Oak Press
405 South Seventh Street
Saint Charles, IL 60174
(American history)

Tan Bark Books
120 Reist Street
Buffalo, NY 14221-5322
(county and town history)

Tuttle Antiquarian Books, Inc.
28 South Main Street
Rutland, VT 05701
(802) 773-8229
Hours: Mon–Fri 9:00–5:00, Sat 9:00–
   4:00
Pub. *Catalog* (second-hand books;
   genealogy and local history), $7.50 per
   issue

Unicorn Limited, Inc.
PO Box 397
Bruceton Mills, WV 26525
(304) 379-8803; (304) 379-8923 FAX
E-mail: unicorn@access.mountain.net
Dr. W. R. McLeod, President
Pub. *Catalog*, bimonthly, $12.50 per year
   subscription (genealogy catalog issued
   every January–March period)
(history, folklore, children's language,
   bagpipe music, genealogy, and related
   areas of Scottish, Celtic and Norse
   peoples)

Wootens Old and Rare Books
G 3311
Cheyenne Burton, MI 48529
(American history)

The Yankee Book and Art Gallery
10 North Street
Plymouth, MA 02360
(508) 747-2691
E-mail: yankeebk@tiac.net
Charles F. Purro, Owner
Hours: Mon–Sat 11:00–5:00; Sun noon–
   4:00
(Pilgrims and Plymouth history, *The
   Mayflower*)

**George A. Young—Books of Colonial
America**
3611 Janet Road
Wheaton, MD 20906
(301) 946-6490
George A. Young, Owner
(genealogy, history, local history, church
   history)
free search by mail or phone only

Search Services

Booksearch, Inc.
PO Box 16392
Saint Paul, MN 55116-0392
(612) 292-1842; (612) 292-1742 FAX
http://www.booksearch.com
($1.00 fee paid to the bookstore where
   you get the form)

Copy Services

**Photoduplication Service, Library of
Congress**
Washington, DC 20540-5554
(202) 707-5640
Dennis McNew, Head, Public Services
   Section
Hours: Mon–Fri 9:00–4:45
("The Photoduplication Service provides
   access to one of the largest collections
   of genealogical materials, including
   over 35,000 genealogical charts,
   tables, and family trees, and the
   nation's most extensive holdings of
   local and state histories.")

UMI/Books on Demand
300 North Zeeb Road
Ann Arbor, MI 48106-1346
(800) 521-0600
http://www.umi.com
Karen Kaltz, Product Manager
Hours: 8:00–5:00
Pub. *Books on Demand*
(specializes in out-of-print books,
  genealogy)

Periodicals

AntiqueWeek
Mayhill Publications, Inc.
(27 North Jefferson Street—location)
PO Box 90 (mailing address)
Knightstown, IN 46148-9900
(765) 345-5133; (800) 876-5133
Tom Mayhill, Publisher
Pub. *AntiqueWeek*, weekly, Eastern
  Edition $3.70 for eight-week
  subscription, $12.20 for thirty-week
  subscription, $22.70 for sixty-week
  subscription

A. B. Bookman's Weekly
PO Box AB
Clifton, NJ 07015
(973) 772-0020
Pub. *A. B. Bookman's Weekly*

LENDING LIBRARIES

Many of the libraries and societies
listed elsewhere participate in the
Interlibrary Loan program on a selective
basis, depending on the condition of the
books requested. Many more allow only
their members to borrow books by mail.

American Family Records Association (AFRA)
PO Box 15505
Kansas City, MO 64106-0505
(816) 373-6570
Nita Neblock
Hours: Mid-Continent Public Library,
  North Independence Branch,
  Independence, MO: Mon–Thur 9:00–
  9:00, Fri 9:00–6:00, Sat 9:00–5:00
Pub. *Family Records Today, The Journal
  of American Family Records*,
  quarterly; *Interlibrary Loan Catalog*
  (about 3,000 titles in circulating
  collection), $5.00 postpaid
$27.00 per year membership

American Family Records Association (AFRA)
Genealogy Circulation Collection
Alexander Mitchell Public Library
519 South Kline Street
Aberdeen, SD 57401-2596
(605) 626-7097
Shirley Arment, Reference and
  Genealogy Librarian
Hours: Mon–Fri 9:00–6:00
(about 600 titles in circulating collection)

AGLL
(PO Box 40, Orting, WA 98360-0040,
  Editorial Offices location)
PO Box 329 (Subscription Department
  mailing address)
Bountiful, UT 84011-0329
(801) 298-5358 (Subscription
  Department); (801) 298-5446 (Sales);
  (801) 298-1712 (Customer Service);
  (435) 770-0551 (Editorial Offices);
  (800) 760-AGLL (Orders); (801) 298-
  5468 FAX
E-mail: sales@agll.com
http://www.heritagequest.com (Editorial
  Offices); http://www.agll.com (Sales)
Leland K. Meitzler,Executive Editor;
  Steve Williams, Vice President
  Marketing
Hours: Editorial Offices: Mon–Fri 9:00–
  5:00; Sales: 8:00–4:00
Pub. *Heritage Quest* (U.S. and
  international research articles, how-to,
  queries, book reviews), bimonthly,
  $28.00 per year subscription;
  Genealogy Bulletin, $12.00 per year
  subscription
(over 250,000 titles on microfilm and
  microfiche for rent; microfilming of
  books, documents, newspapers;

microfilm and microfiche duplication
  in both silver and diazo)
$47.50 membership

Becker's Bookshelf
1314 Prospect Avenue
Norfolk, NE 68701
Charlene K. Becker, Owner
(sends "new on shelf" lists 3-4 times per
  year)
20% of the value of the book, plus
  postage (special 4th class rate)

Clinton-Essex-Franklin Library System
17 Oak Street
Plattsburgh, NY 12901
(518) 563-5190
Elizabeth Rogers
(Collection available only through Interlibrary Loan [ILL])

The Connecticut Historical Society (CHS)
1 Elizabeth Street at Asylum Avenue
Hartford, CT 06105
(860) 236-5621; (860) 236-2664 FAX
E-mail: cthist@ix.netcom.com
http://www.hartnet.org/chs/main.htm
Judith Ellen Johnson, Reference
  Librarian and Genealogist; David M.
  Kahn, Director
Hours: Library: Tue–Sat 9:00–4:45
Pub. *The Connecticut Historical Society
  Bulletin*, semiannually, $16.00 ($20.00
  foreign) per year subscription to
  members, $20.00 ($25.00 foreign) per
  year subscription to individual non-
  members and to institutions;
  *Connecticut Historical Society Annual
  Report*, annually; *Connecticut
  Historical Society Collections*,
  irregularly; *Notes and News*, three
  times per year; *Loan Catalog* (16,000
  volume Loan Collection available to
  members of The Connecticut
  Historical Society or The Society of
  Mayflower Descendants in the State of
  Connecticut), $7.00 postpaid
  (Connecticut residents add 30¢ tax)
$30.00 per year membership for
  individuals, $45.00 per year
  membership for families, $25.00 per
  year membership for students, senior
  citizens, institutions, and out-of-state
  individuals, $40.00 per year
  membership for senior citizen couples,
  $150.00 per year Sustaining
  membership, $500 per year Standing
  Order membership, $5,000 life
  membership (reduced three-year
  membership rates, membership
  includes *CHS Annual Report* and
  Notes and News, and access to Loan
  Collection); $3.00 per day library and
  museum user's fee for non-members;
  research service for a nominal charge

Sherry Foresman Library
2787 335th Street
Menlo, IA 50164
(515) 524-5110
Sherry Foresman
(30-day book rentals and publications for
sale, $.75 for catalog)

Genealogical Center Library
PO Box 71343
Marietta, GA 30007-1343
Barbara A. Geisert, Director
(over 9,000 books and periodicals, mail
order only)
$25.00 for membership in GUILD,
includes book catalog and book loan
forms; $3.00 per book plus $2.50
handling fee per order of up to five
books

Hoenstine Rental Library
414 Montgomery Street
Hollidaysburg, PA 16648
(814) 695-0632; (814) 696-7310
Barbara Ann Hoenstine
Hours: Mon–Fri 9:00–12:00 & 1:00–
4:00
(sales of new and used books on
Pennsylvania history and genealogy;
collection of over 4,000 books for
rent)

Micro Quix
5615 176th S.W.
Lynwood, WA 98037-2816
free one-year membership

Mid-Continent Public Library
North Independence Branch/Genealogy
and Local History Department
(317 West 24 Highway—location)
15616 East 24 Highway (mailing
address)
Independence, MO 64050
(816) 252-0950
http://www.ge@mcpl.lib.mo.us
Martha L. Henderson, Department Head
Hours: Mon–Thur 9:00–9:00, Fri 9:00–
6:00, Sat 9:00–5:00
(national in scope, includes circulating
collection)

National Archives Microfilm Rental
Program
PO Box 30
Annapolis Junction, MD 20701-0030
(federal population census schedules
1790–1920, American Revolutionary
War service records and pension and
bounty-land warrant application files)

National Genealogical Society (NGS)
4527 17th Street, North
Arlington, VA 22207-2399
(703) 525-0050; (703) 525-0052 FAX
Jean K. Findeis, Executive Director;
Dereka Smith, Librarian
Hours: Library: Mon & Wed 10:00–9:00,
Fri–Sat 10:00–4:00; Offices: daily
8:30–5:00

(members only may borrow books for
use in their own homes)
$35.00 per year membership for
individuals, $10.00 per year
membership for spouse, $30.00 per
year membership for senior citizens

The New England Historic
Genealogical Society
Circulating Library
(101 Newbury Street, Boston, MA
02116-3007—location)
160 North Washington Street, Fourth
Floor (mailing address)
Boston, MA 02114-2120
(888) 906-3447; (617) 624-0325 FAX
http://www.nehgs.org
Timothy G. Salls, Circulation Librarian
Hours: Mon–Fri 9:00–5:00
Circulating Library Catalogs (Vol. I:
Genealogies, Vol. II: Histories and
Research Aids), $10.00 each or $15.00
for the set
(allows only members to borrow family
genealogies, local histories, abstracted
records and reference works, $12.00
for three books for two-week loan,
including USPS shipping in the U.S.,
additional fees for UPS and
international shipping, catalogs and
order forms also on Web site)
$50.00 per year membership for
individuals, $70.00 per year
membership for families, $20.00 per
year membership for students, $250.00
per year Contributing membership,
$500.00 per year Sustaining
membership, $2,000.00 life
membership, $5,000 life Benefactor
membership

Stagecoach Library for Genealogical
Research
1840 South Wolcott Court
Denver, CO 80219
(303) 922-8856
Donna J. Porter, Owner
Pub. *Catalog* (mail order rental/sale),
$10.00 per issue

General

American Association of University
Women
Genealogy Division
6564 DeMuth Circle
Sacramento, CA 95842-2413
(916) 332-9419
Carrol L. Camomile, Chairman
Genealogy Division

American Medical Association
Executive Vice President
515 North State Street
Chicago, IL 60610
(312) 464-5000
http://www.social.com/health/nhic/data/
hr1800/hr1817.html
(database on 350,000 deceased U.S.
physicians, 1878–1969)

Americans for Open Records
(AmFOR)
PO Box 401
Palm Desert, CA 92261
Lori Carangelo, President
http://www.genealogymall.com
Pub. *The Open Record*, irregularly,
depending on available funds
(a non-profit, international, voluntary
civil liberties network, established to
promote the inherent right of
Americans to information about
themselves without court or agency
intervention; no fee for search help—
10,000 families reunited since 1989;
pro se legal help, referrals and other
information; civil liberties legal
advocacy; publishes client case
histories with permission; publishes
*The Ultimate Search Book: From the
Files of Americans For Open Records
(AmFOR) (how to find anyone, with or
without a name, in 50 states and 200
countries*, $69.95)
$5.00 total fee covers Registry,
computer-matching, materials, postage

Anglo-American Genealogical
Society
2686 Claybourne Road
Shaker Heights, OH 44122
Mrs. John Schaltinger

California State Railroad Museum
Library
Big Four Building
111 I Street
Sacramento, CA 95814-2265
(916) 323-8073; (916) 327-5655 FAX
E-mail: csrmlibrary@csrmf.org
Ellen L. Halteman, Librarian
Hours: Tue–Sat 1:00–5:00
(selected railroad employee records for
Southern PacificRailroad, circa 1900
to circa 1930)

Center for Human Genetics

Umbilical Line Project
Municipal Building
PO Box 770
Bar Harbor, ME 04609-0770
(207) 288-3371
E-mail: thr@jax.org
http://feefhs.org/misc/frg-chg.html
Thomas H. Roderick, Ph.D., Project
Director

The Center for Thanatology Research and Education, Inc.

391 Atlantic Avenue
Brooklyn, NY 11217-1701
(718) 858-3026
E-mail: Halporn@NYC.pipeline.com
Hours: Mon–Fri 11:00–5:00, weekends,
by appointment
(gravestone studies of interest to
historians, genealogists and those
devoted to American folk art)

Department of Archives-Manuscripts

University Libraries
Arizona State Library
Box 871006
Tempe, AZ 85287-1006
(602) 965-3145; (602) 965-0776 FAX
E-mail: iacpae@asuvm.inre.asu.edu
http://www.lib.asu.edu/archives/
dampage.htm
Patricia A. Etter, Associate Archivist for
Information Services
Hours: Mon 11:00–7:00, Tue–Wed 8:00–
7:00, Thur–Fri 8:00–5:00, Sat 1:00–
5:00
("The Department of Archives and
Manuscripts at Arizona State
University and the Manuscript Society
have established the Manuscript
Society Information Exchange
Database, which lists collections of
manuscripts, documents, and letters
held by private individuals throughout
the United States. The database
contains a broad range of material,
national and international in scope.
The database can be searched for
documents *by* an individual or *about*
an individual. In addition to name
searches, the database is accessible by
subject. The American Revolution and
the Civil War are heavily
represented.")
$26.50 for each name or subject search,
which includes cost of printout
containing citation and descriptive
information to documents meeting the
search criteria (photocopies of original
documents will be included when
available), $10.00 for a printout
showing names and subjects currently
in the database

Public Library of Des Moines

100 Locust
Des Moines, IA 50309-1791
(515) 283-4152
http://www.pldminfo.org/
M. J. Scott, Research Requests
Hours: Mon–Wed 10:00–9:00, Thur–Fri
10:00–6:00, Sat 10:00–5:00
(Polk County, Des Moines, history, plus
National Bar Association Archives)
research: $90.00 per hour plus 25¢ per
page for photocopies, payable in
advance, $10.00 minimum per request

Genealogical and Heraldic Institute of America

American Italian Congress
111 Columbia Heights
Brooklyn, NY 11201

The Great Lakes Historical Society

480 Main Street
PO Box 435
Vermilion, OH 44089-0435
(440) 967-3467; (440) 967-1519
http://www.inlandseas.org
William A. O'Brien, Executive Director
Hours: 10:00–5:00
Pub. *Inland Seas* (Great Lakes history),
quarterly
$44.00 per year membership

Isle a la Cache Museum

(501 East Romeo Road, Romeoville, IL
60441—location)
Cherry Hill Road and Rt. 52, Rural
Route 4 (mailing address)
Joliet, IL 60433
(815) 886-1467
Jack MacRae, Museum Coordinator
(French and Indian Fur Trade, 17th and
18th century)

Abraham Lincoln Association

2 Williams Street
Providence, RI 02903
(401) 331-2222; (401) 751-5257 FAX
Frank J. Williams, President
Pub. *Journal of the Abraham Lincoln
Association*, semiannually
$25.00 per year membership

Lincoln Group of Boston

27 Forest Trail
East Bridgewater, MA 02333
(508) 697-1387
Professor Thomas R. Turner, President
$20.00 per year membership

Museum Association of the American Frontier

(3 miles east of Chadron, on U.S. 20—
location)
HC 74, Box 18 (mailing address)
Chadron, NE 69337
(308) 432-3843
Charles E. Hanson, Jr., Director
Pub. *Museum of the Fur Trade Quarterly*
("North American fur trade 1500–1900;
emphasis is on objects as well as
people.")
$6.00 per year membership; search fees:
$10.00 per hour

National Frontier Trails Center Archives and Library

318 West Pacific
Independence, MO 64050
(816) 325-7577; (816) 836-7101 FAX
John Mark Lambertson, Director
Mon–Fri 9:00–4:30, Sat–Sun 12:30–4:30
(ninetheenth-century westward overland
migration, especially the Oregon,
California, and Santa Fe trails)

The Old Time Historical Association

9161 N.C. Highway 22
PO Box 220
Climax, NC 27233
(910) 685-4253
James S. Ferree, Jr., President
Hours: by appointment
Pub. *Bulletin Board*, quarterly
(specializes in Frick Steam Engines and
old machinery, worldwide)
$10.00 per year membership

Oregon-California Trails Association

(524 South Osage Street, Independence,
MO 64050—location)
PO Box 1019 (mailing address)
Independence, MO 64051-0519
(816) 252-2276; (816) 836-0989 FAX
E-mail: octahgts@gri.net
Jeanne Miller, Executive Director
Hours: Mon–Fri 9:00–3:00
Pub. *Overland Journal*, quarterly
(the Oregon Trail extended from the
vicinity of Independence, Missouri, to
Fort Vancouver, Washington; the
California Trail branched off the
Oregon Trail, toward Sacramento)
$35.00 per year membership for
individuals, $40.00 per year
membership for families, $60.00 per
year Supporting membership, $100.00
per year Patron membership, $250.00
per year Institutional membership,
$750.00 life membership, $1,000.00
per year Corporate membership

Phillips Library

Peabody Essex Museum of Salem
East India Square
Salem, MA 01970-1682
(978) 745-1876; (978) 744-6776 FAX
Geraldine M. Ayers, Managing Editor;
John Koza, Librarian/Archivist
Hours: Mon–Fri 10:00–5:00
Pub. *American Neptune*, quarterly
(winter, spring, summer, fall), $32.00
per year domestic subscription, $35.00
per year foreign subscription
(maritime history, not limited to
Massachusetts area)

Radcliffe College

Arthur and Elizabeth Schlesinger Library
on the History of Women in America
3 James Street
Cambridge, MA 02138
(617) 495-8647; (617) 496-8340
E-mail: slref@radcliffe.edu
http://www.radcliffe.edu/schles

Wendy Thomas, Public Service Librarian
Hours: Mon–Fri 9:00–5:00
Pub. *Schlesinger Library Newsletter*, two
  times per year
$25.00 per year Active Friend
  membership

Social Security Administration
Department of Health and Human
  Services
Office of Public Inquiries
6401 Security Boulevard
Baltimore, MD 21235
Delmar D. Dowling, Director
(researchers must supply Social Security
  Number or person's full name, date
  and place of birth, and parents' full
  names)
search fee: $7.00 if SSN is known,
  $16.00 if number is unknown

Spanish History Museum Publications and Shields
PO Box 25531
Albuquerque, NM 87125-0531
(505) 864-2919
Elmer Martinez, Publisher
Hours: Mon–Sun 9:00–5:00
Pub. *Heraldic Research Reports*,
  quarterly
(publishes Spanish Colonial History and
  miscellaneous titles, produces wall
  hanging coats of arms; catalog
  available)

Steamship Historical Society of America, Inc.
SSHSA Collection
University of Baltimore
Langsdale Library
1420 Maryland Avenue
Baltimore, MD 21201
(410) 625-3134
E-mail: ahouse@UBmail.UBalt.edu
http://www.ubalt.edu/www//anglib/
  index.html
Henry T. Bishop; Ann House, Librarian
Hours: by appointment only
Pub. *Steamboat Bill*, quarterly
(200,000 photos and 5,000 maritime
  titles; does not have passenger lists)
$25.00 per year membership

Tracers Worldwide Services (TWS)
3214 Reid Drive
Corpus Christi, TX 78404
(512) 854-1892
George Theodore, President
Hours: 9:00–5:00
(database of 95 million households,
  including 45 million people who died
  since 1960)
search fee: living descendants $15.00 per
  100 names, deaths $10.00 per 100
  names

United States Board on Geographic Names
Domestic Geographic Names
United States Department of the Interior

U.S. Geological Survey
523 National Center
Reston, VA 22092
(703) 648-4544
http://www.nmd.usgs.gov/www/gnis
Roger L. Payne, Executive Secretary,
  U.S. Board on Geographic Names
Hours: 8:00–5:00
(free research inquiries)

Products and Services

American Research
PO Box 4043
Salt Lake City, UT 84110-4043
(800) 488-6929
http://www.american-research.com
Rod Stucker, Accredited Genealogist

The Brinkley Press
7345 47th N.E.
Seattle, WA 98115
(206) 524-1910
Allen Norris, President
Hours: 9:00–5:30

Discount Equipment Sales
PO Box 222
Linn, TX 78563
(956) 383-8669
(microfiche readers)

Duplitech
1560 Fir Street, South
PO Box 4154
Salem, OR 97302
(503) 378-0751
Jeff Murray, Owner
(photo restoration; photographic copy
  service)

Family History Company
PO Box 15905
Fort Wayne, IN 46885-5905
(archival-quality forms, research aids)

Genealogy House
3148 Kentucky Avenue, South
Saint Louis Park, MN 55426-3471
(612) 920-6990
Jan Haase, President
Hours: by appointment

Genealogy Unlimited, Inc.
(1060 South 500 East, American Fork,
  UT 84003-9723—location)
PO Box 537 (mailing address)
Orem, UT 84059-0537
(800) 666-4363; (801) 763-7132; (801)
  763-7185 FAX
E-mail: genun@itsnet.com
http://www.itsnet.com/genun
Carol Mehr Schiffman, President
Hours: Mon–Fri 10:00–4:00
("Genealogical and archival supplies;
  importer of European maps and
  atlases, free catalog available")
free semiannual mail-order catalog

The Gold Bug
PO Box 588
Alamo, CA 94507
(925) 838-MAPS
Art Lassagne
(old map reproductions)

The Heritage Project
PO Box 600
Franconia, NH 03580
(603) 823-5848
Sybil C. Carey
(publishes *The Heritage Project*, a
  complete do-it-yourself oral-history
  package, containing a booklet and two
  self-guiding cassettes with tips on
  collecting oral history, including
  sample interview questions and pages
  to record information)
$35.00 per unit

Just Black & White
54 York Street
PO Box 4628
Portland, ME 04112
(207) 761-5861 (in Maine); (800) 827-
  5881
http://www.maine.com/photos
Tracey Mousseau
Hours: Mon–Fri 8:00–5:00
(copies, restoration and enhancements of
  old photos, salt and albumen prints,
  tintypes, daguerreotypes, ambrotypes)

MAPS
PO Box 119
Washington Court House, OH 43160-
  0119
(740) 335-0266; (740) 333-3530 FAX
Ms. Sandy Fackler, Owner
(specializes in maps)
price list for two first-class stamps and
  SAE

Old Photo Copying
3860 Weston Place
Long Beach, CA 90807-3317
(562) 427-8165
E-mail: knatz@bcf.usc.edu
http://feefhs.org/photo/opc/frg-opc.html
John Mulvey
(reproduction, restoration and
  enlargements)

The People's Biographer Workbook
PO Box 3035
Albany, NY 12203
(518) 587-6781
Jackson F. Bullock
(in addition to publishing *The People's
  Biographer Workbook: A Structured
  Biography Writing Guide for the
  Nonprofessional Writer*, specializes in
  general, Christian, and African-
  American editions, the company offers
  word processing from hand-written
  manuscripts, machine transcription of
  audio tape, scanning from type-written
  text, ghost writing, shadow-writing
  [extensive editing of your manuscript],

proofreading, page layout, halftones, printing and binding)

Sampubco

E-mail: dsam@wasatch.com
http://www.wasatch.com/~dsam/ sampubco
W. David Samuelsen
(supplies photocopies of will record including any attached proceedings, not a mere transcription, from selected counties in Alabama, Idaho, Iowa, Kansas, New York, Ohio, Oregon, Pennsylvania and Texas)

Scholarly Resources, Inc.

104 Greenhill Avenue
Wilmington, DE 19805-1897
(302) 654-7713; (800) 772-8937; (302) 654-3871 FAX
Amy Rashap, Marketing Manager
Hours: 9:00–5:00
(authorized distributor for the National Archives and Records Administration (NARA), also publishes books)

Travel Genie Maps

3815 Calhoun Avenue
Ames, IA 50010-4106
(515) 232-1070
E-mail: travgenie@aol.com
http://feefhs.org/pub/tgml/tghfeehs.html
(detailed sectional maps for: Britain, Denmark, Germany, Ireland, Norway, Poland and Sweden)

Military

The American Legion Library

(700 North Pennsylvania, Indianapolis, IN 46204—location)
PO Box 1055 (mailing address)
Indianapolis, IN 46206
(317) 630-1367
E-mail: tal@legion.org
http://www.legion.org
Joseph J. Hovish, Librarian and Curator
Hours: 8:00–4:00
("Almost no information for the genealogist.")

American Society of Military History

1816 South Figueroa Street, Suite 200
Los Angeles, CA 90015
(213) 746-1776

Arizona Military Museum

(52nd Street and McDowell Road— entrance location)
5636 East McDowell Road (mailing address)
Phoenix, AZ 85008-3495
(602) 267-2676
Col. (Ret.) John L. Johnson, Director
Hours: Tue & Thur 9:00–2:00, Sat–Sun 1:00–4:00
Pub. *The Courier*, quarterly
("Wartime casualty data, Arizona only)
$15.00 per year membership

Army Knowledge Network Directorate

Rodler Morris
10 Meade Avenue
Fort Leavenworth, KS 66027-1350
(913) 684-2919; (913) 684-4387 FAX
George Gernert, Director
Hours: daily
(military command documents and images)

Arnold Expedition Historical Society

(Arnold Road, Pittston—location)
RR 4, Box 6895 (mailing address)
Gardiner, ME 04345
(207) 582-7080
Daniel H. Warren, Jr., President
Hours: Weekends in Jul–Aug 10:00–5:00 (subject to change), and by appointment
Pub. *Newsletter*, three to four times per year
(to promote and advance research, preservation and publication projects related to the Arnold Expedition to Quebec in 1775, including biographical and historical records pertaining to the participants)
$10.00 per year membership for individuals, $20.00 per year membership for families, $3.00 per year membership for students, $50.00 per year Contributing membership, $200.00 life membership

Association for Preservation of Civil War Sites

11 Public Square #200
Hagerstown, MD 21740-5510
Pub. *Hallowed Ground*, quarterly
$20.00 per year membership

Atlanta History Center

Library/Archives
3101 Andrews Drive, N.W.
Atlanta, GA 30305
(404) 814-4040
E-mail: webmaster@atlhist.org
http://www.atlhist.org/; http:// www.atlhist.org/html/civilgu.htm (Civil War Manuscript Collections)
Anne Salter, Director of Library/ Archives
Hours: Tue–Fri 9:00–5:00, Sat 10:00– 5:00
Pub. *Atlanta History: A Journal of Georgia and the South*, quarterly
$20.00 per year membership

Battle of Lexington State Historic Site

PO Box 6
North 13th Street
Lexington, MO 64067
(816) 259-4654
Janae Fuller, Administrator
Hours: Mon–Sat 10:00–4:00, Sun (Labor Day–Memorial Day) noon–4:00, Sun (Memorial Day–Labor Day) noon– 5:00, and by appointment

(emphasis on the Battle of Lexington during the Civil War, also family and local history)

Blue & Gray Enterprises

PO Box 28685
Columbus, OH 43228
Pub. *Blue & Gray Magazine*, bimonthly, $19.00 per year subscription
(specializes in Civil War military)

Blue and Gray Memorial Association

(Blue and Gray Museum—location)
Municipal Building (mailing address)
Fitzgerald, GA 31750
(912) 423-5375
Beth M. Davis, Executive Director
Hours: 1 Mar–31 Oct: Mon–Fri 2:00– 5:00
(museum mirrors the history of this former Union veterans' colony in former Confederate territory)
$5.00 per year membership

Eleanor S. Brockenbrough Library

The Museum of the Confederacy
1201 East Clay Street
Richmond, VA 23219-1615
(804) 649-1861, ext. 27/28; (804) 644- 7150 FAX (Museum)
E-mail: library@moc.org
http://www.moc.org/moc-lib.htm
Dr. John M. Coski, Historian
Hours: Mon–Fri 10:00–4:45 by appointment only
Pub. *The Museum of the Confederacy Journal*, annually
(library has no genealogy collection, per se, but has documents of some soldiers, officers, and commands that may be helpful in genealogical research, but does not have Confederate military service/pension records; has Jefferson Davis Collection, Southern Women's History Collection, Confederate Memorial period collections, papers of Confederate units and commands, wartime objects and manuscripts)
$35.00 per year resident membership for individuals (residents of Richmond, Petersburg and the counties of Henrico, Chesterfield, Hanover, Goochland, Charles City, Price George, New Kent, KingWilliam and Dinwiddie), $50.00 per year resident membership for families, $20.00 per year non-resident membership for individuals, $30.00 per year non- resident membership for families, $20.00 per year membership for senior citizens or libraries or non-profit organizations, $75.00 per year Contributing membership, $100.00 per year Sustaining membership; $4.00 admission for non-members; photocopies 25¢ each

California Veterans Museum
PO Box 1200
Yountville, CA 94599-1297
(707) 944-4918 (Workshop); (707) 944-4919 (Museum)
Suzel Ho, Assistant Curator
Hours: Fri–Sun noon–2:00
research: $15.00 suggested donation; museum admission by donation

Cantigny First Division Foundation
The First Division Museum
1 South 151 Winfield Road
Wheaton, IL 60187
(630) 668-5185
John F. Votaw, Director

Center for the Study of the Korean War
208 Main Street
PO Box 456
Independence, MO 64051
E-mail: tems02@rlds.org
Paul M. Edwards, Executive Director
Hours: by appointment
(materials on the Korean War, 1950–1953, and the armistice period)

Champlin Fighter Museum
4636 Fighter Aces Drive
Mesa, AZ 85205
(602) 830-4540
Doug Champlin, President
(WW I through Vietnam)

Civil Engineer Corps—Seabee Museum
Code 22M NCBC
Port Hueneme, CA 93043
(805) 982-5163
Y. H. Ketels, Director

Civil War Museum of Jackson County, Missouri
Lone Jack, MO 64070
(816) 881-4431
Sally Schweick, Site Administrator

Civil War Round Table of Arkansas
PO Box 7281
Little Rock, AR 72217
(501) 225-3996
L. A. Russell, Treasurer
Pub. *CWRTA Newsletter*
(no genealogical information)

The Civil War Round Table of Kansas City
1130 Westport Road
Kansas City, MO 64111
(816) 931-6620
Milton F. Perry, President
Pub. *Border Bugle*

Civil War Soldier System
Federation of Genealogical Societies
PO Box 830220
Richardson, TX 75083-0220
John Peterson, Director; Curt Witcher, National Chairman
$20.00 per year membership for organizations or institutions

Civil War Sons
Sons of Sherman's March to the Sea
1725 Farmer Avenue
Tempe, AZ 85281-6533
(602) 967-5405
Stan Schirmacher, National Director
Pub. "Potpourri Page" in *The National Hobby News*, quarterly, $4.00 per year subscription, c/o PO Box 612, New Philadelphia, OH 44663
(membership in Sons of Sherman's March to the Sea open to all "buffs," not limited to direct descendants)
$3.00 lifetime membership; ancestors' war veterans records information: $1.00

Coast Guard Museum/Northwest
1519 Alaskan Way, South
Seattle, WA 98134
(206) 442-5019

Combined Arms Research Library-Archives
Commandant
ATTN: ATZL-SWS-L (Archives)
Fort Leavenworth, KS 66027-6900
(913) 768-3139
Martha Davis, Director; Ed Burgess, Archives Manager
Hours: Mon–Fri 7:00–5:00
(Fort Leavenworth institutional archives; rare books, special collections)

The Commonwealth of Massachusetts
Military Division History Research and Museum
Massachusetts National Guard Supply Depot, Building 2
143 Speen Street
Natick, MA 01760-2599
(508) 651-5700
James Fahey, Archivist
Hours: Mon–Fri 9:00–4:00

Company of Military Historians
North Main Street
Westbrook, CT 06498
(860) 399-9460

Confederate Historical Institute
PO Box 7388
Little Rock, AR 72217
(501) 225-3996
Hours: Jenny Russel, Chairman
Pub. *Confederate Historical Institute Dispatch*, bimonthly
(Confederate history and battlefield preservation; no genealogical information)
$20.00 per year membership

Confederate Memorial Association, Inc.
The Confederate Embassy
Confederate Memorial Hall
1322 Vermont Avenue, N.W.
Washington, DC 20005
(202) 483-5700
John Edward Hurley, President

Hours: Mon–Fri 10:00–4:00, and by appointment
Pub. *Confederate Embassy News*, quarterly
(museum and library)
$25.00 per year membership for individuals, $50.00 per year Patron membership, $100.00 per year Sustaining membership, $500.00 per year Benefactor membership, $1,000.00 life membership

The Confederate Museum-Museum of Southern History
2740 Farm Road, #359
PO Box 179
Richmond, TX 77406-0179
(281) 342-8787 FAX
Jim Pearson, Director; Joella Morris, President Emeritus
Hours: Tue–Thur 10:00–2:00, Sat–Sun 1:00–4:00
Pub. *Newsletter*, two or three times per year
$35.00 per year membership for individuals, $45.00 per year membership for families, $65.00 per year Contributing membership

Confederate Veteran
(8506 Braesdale, Houston, TX 77071—location)
PO Box 41828 (mailing address)
Houston, TX 77241-1828
(713) 850-5031
James N. Vogler, Jr., Editor-in-Chief
Hours: Mon–Fri 8:00–5:00
Pub. *Confederate Veteran*, bimonthly, $13.00 per year subscription in the U.S., $16.00 per year subscription in Canada, $25.00 per year foreign subscription

Confederated Memorial State Historic Site
Rt. 1, Box 221A
Higginsville, MO 64037
(660) 584-2853
Jill White, Site Administrator
Hours: Mon–Sat 10:00–4:00, Sun noon-5:00
(genealogical services, emphasis on Civil War; "Confederate Chapel and Cemetery files on microfilm, Confederate veterans buried in site cemetery.")
free

Cool Spring Associates/Civil War Society
PO Box 770
Berryville, VA 22611
Pub. *Civil War: Magazine of the Civil War Society*, bimonthly
$24.00 per year membership

Cowles Magazines
6405 Flank Drive
PO Box 8200
Harrisburg, PA 17105-8200

(717) 657-9555
Ed Holm, Editor
Pub. *American History Illustrated*,
  bimonthly, $20.00 per year; *Civil War
  Times Illustrated*, bimonthly, $20.00
  per year subscription

Custer Battlefield Historical Association
PO Box 902
Hardin, MT 59034
(406) 665-2060·
Hours: by appointment
Pub. *The Dispatch*, quarterly
$7.50 per year membership

De Anza Trek Lancer Society
20739 Sunrise Drive
Cupertino, CA 95014
(408) 252-6065
Joseph Adamo, Commander
(emphasis on early California Spanish
  Cavalry)

18th Century Society
Rt. 1, Box 264
New Alexandria, PA 15670
Pub. *F & I War Magazine*, quarterly,
  $10.00 per year

Factor's Walk Historical Commission, Inc.
Factor's Walk Military Museum
PO Box 23057
Savannah, GA 31403
Lindsey Henderson, Jr.

Family Publications
5628 60th Drive, N.E.
Marysville, WA 98270-9509
E-mail: cxwp57a@prodigy.com
Rose Caudle Terry, Publisher
Pub. *Military Sources, Queries &
  Reviews*, two to four times per year,
  $8.95 per volume subscription, plus
  $1.50 postage per order
(information on military records, all
  wars)

1st Cavalry Division Museum
Building 2218, Headquarters Avenue
Fort Hood, TX 76545-5101
(254) 287-3626
Michael P. Bellafaire, Director

Fort Douglas Military Museum
32 Potter Street
Fort Douglas, UT 84110
(801) 588-5188 (voice and FAX)
Jess McCall, Curator
Hours: Tue–Sat 10:00–noon & 1:00–4:00
Pub. *Fort Douglas Vedette and the
  Museum Association Bulletin*,
  quarterly, free while supply lasts
(history of the founding of Fort Douglas,
  of the military in Utah, of the military
  exploration of the Utah Territory, and
  of the early Mormon military
  organizations)

Fort Gibson Military Park
110 East Ash Avenue
PO Box 457
Fort Gibson, OK 74434
(918) 478-2669

Fort Leavenworth Historical Society
Frontier Army Museum
20 Reynolds Avenue
Fort Leavenworth, KS 66027-5072
(913) 684-3191
Stephen J. Allie, Director
Hours: Mon–Fri 9:00–4:00, Sat 10:00–
  4:00, Sun & holidays (except New
  Year's Day, Easter, Thanksgiving,
  Christmas) noon–4:00
(1,500 volumes on the history of Fort
  Leavenworth and the military aspect
  of the western frontier from 1827)

Fort McKavett State Historic Site
PO Box 867
Fort McKavett, TX 76841
(915) 396-2358
David Bischofhausen, Park
  Superintendent

Fort Point and Army Museum Association
Funston Avenue and Lincoln Boulevard
PO Box 29163
Presidio of San Francisco, CA 94129
(415) 921-8193
Milton B. Halsey, Jr., Executive Director
Pub. *Fort Point SALVO* (1776 to the
  present, but primarily Civil War-era)

Fort Polk Military Museum
South Carolina Avenue, Building 917
PO Box 3916
Fort Polk, LA 71459-0916
(318) 531-7905
David S. Bingham, Historian/Curator
Hours: Wed–Fri 10:00–2:00; Sat–Sun
  9:00–4:00

Fort Ticonderoga
Thompson-Pell Research Center
PO Box 390
Ticonderoga, NY 12883
(518) 585-2821
Nicholas Westbrook, Director; Bruce M.
  Moseley, Curator
Hours: weekdays by appointment only
Pub. *Bulletin of the Fort Ticonderoga
  Museum*, annually, $10.00 per issue
(Colonial history, military and Native
  American; topical finding aids to the
  collection are available)
from $20.00 per year membership in
  Friends organization

45th Infantry Division Museum
2145 N.E. 36th Street
Oklahoma City, OK 73111
(405) 424-5313
Hours: Tue–Fri 9:00–5:00, Sat 10:00–
  5:00, Sun 1:00–5:00

Fraser's 78th Highland Regiment
PO Box 214
Topsfield, MA 01983
Walter H. McIntosh
(information regarding Fraser's 78th
  Highland Regiment who fought the
  French at Louisbourg and Quebec in
  1758 and 1760)

Historical Museum at Fort Missoula
Building 322, Fort Missoula
Missoula, MT 59804
(406) 728-3476; (406) 728-5063 FAX
E-mail: ftmslamuseum@marsweb.com
Dr. Robert M. Brown, Director
Hours: Tue–Sun noon–5:00; Memorial
  Day–Labor Day: Mon–Sat 10:00–
  5:00, Sun noon–5:00

Hood's Texas Brigade Association
The Harold B. Simpson Confederate
  Research Center
Hill College
112 Lamar Drive
PO Box 619
Hillsboro, TX 76645
(254) 582-2555
Dr. B. D. Patterson, Director; Peggy Fox,
  Assistant Director
Hours: Mon–Fri 9:00–noon & 1:00–3:00
Pub. *Newsletter* (not genealogical),
  semiannually
(The Confederacy: Alabama, Arkansas,
  Florida, Georgia, Louisiana,
  Mississippi, North Carolina, South
  Carolina, Tennessee, Texas and
  Virginia; also Kentucky, Maryland and
  Missouri)
$5.00 per year membership; admission:
  $3.00, mail research: $15.00

Journals Division
University of North Texas Press
PO Box 13856
Denton, TX 76203
(254) 565-2124
Jane Tanner, Director Journals
Hours: Mon–Fri
Pub. *Military History of the West*
  (Military history west of the
  Mississippi), semiannually
$12.00 per year membership

The Kent State University Press
Journals Department
(307 Lowry Hall, Terrace Drive—
  location)
PO Box 5190 (mailing address)
Kent, OH 44242-0001
(330) 672-7913; (330) 672-3104 FAX
Sandy Clark, Journals Manager
Hours: 7:30–5:00
Pub. *Civil War History* (includes slavery,
  abolition, antebellum and
  reconstruction politics, diplomacy,
  social and cultural developments in
  mid-nineteenth-century America, and
  military history), quarterly (March,
  June, September and December),
  $6.00 per issue or $21.00 per year

subscription for individuals, $39.00 for two-year subscription for individuals, $8.00 per issue or $32.00 per year subscription for institutions, $61.00 for two-year subscription for institutions, add $6.00 per year for foreign surface mail

Kentucky Civil War, Confederate States of America, Orphan Brigade
E-mail: orphans1@mc.net; walden@octagon.tacom.army.mil
http://bl-12.rootsweb.com/~orphanhm/

Kentucky Military History Museum
(Capitol Avenue and Main Street—location)
PO Box 1792 (mailing address)
Frankfort, KY 40602-1792
(502) 564-3265
http://www.state.ky.us/agencies/khs/
Thomas W. Fugate, Museum Curator
Hours: Mon–Sat 9:00–4:00, Sun noon–4:00

Knoxville Civil War Roundtable
PO Box 313
Knoxville, TN 37901

Layland Museum
201 North Caddo
Cleburne, TX 76031
(817) 641-3321, ext. 375
Mildred Padon, Curator
(research libraries on local history, Native Americans, and the Civil War)

Liberty Memorial Museum and Archives
100 West 26th Street
Kansas City, MO 64108
(816) 221-1918; (816) 221-8981 FAX
Lynn M. Ward, Archivist
Hours: Archives: Mon, Wed & Fri 10:00–4:00, by appointment
(materials concerning World War I, including Europe and the home front; American and British unit histories)

Lincoln Memorial Shrine
125 West Vine Street
Redlands, CA 92373
(949) 798-7632
Donald McCue, Curator
Hours: Tue–Sat 1:00–5:00, closed holidays except February 12; Heritage Room: 9:00–noon
Pub. *LMA Newsletter*, approximately quarterly
(not primarily genealogical, but has books, manuscripts, photographs, etc., on Lincoln and the Civil War; research Civil War relatives)
$12.00–$35.00 per year membership

Louisiana Historical Association Confederate Museum
929 Camp Street
New Orleans, LA 70130
(504) 523-4522

Madison County Historical Society, Inc.
PO Box 523
Anderson, IN 46015-0523
(765) 641-2442 (Library)
Phyllis Leedom, President
Hours: Library: Mon–Thur 9:00–9:00, Fri–Sat 9:00–5:30, Sun 1:00–5:00
Pub. *Camp Stilwell* (on the Civil War)
$4.00 per year membership

March Field Museum
(16222 I-215, March Air Force Base, Intersection of I-215 and Van Buren Boulevard—location)
PO Box 6463 (mailing address)
March ARB, CA 92518
(732) 697-6600
Steven P. Clark, Director
Hours: Mon–Sun 10:00–4:00
Pub. *Newsletter*, quarterly
(not genealogical, except concerning people associated with the base or units stationed there; "military aviation history and memorabilia")
$25.00 per year membership, $150–$300.00 life membership, depending on age, $1,000 life memorial membership; admission: $3.00 for adults, $2.00 for senior citizens or military personnel, $1.00 for children

Military Information Enterprises, Inc.
MIE Publishing
PO Box 17118
Spartanburg, SC 29301-0101
Debra A. Knox, Vice President
Hours: Mon–Fri 8:00–5:00
Pub. *How to Locate Anyone Who Is or Has Been in the Military, Armed Forces Locator Directory*, annually, $19.95 per issue
(all military bases in the U.S. and every conceivable place to obtain military records or information)

Military Records and Research Branch
Kentucky Department of Military Affairs
Division of Veterans Affairs
1121 Louisville Road
Frankfort, KY 40601-6169
(502) 564-4883; (502) 564-4437 FAX
C. L. McDaniels, Manager
Hours: 8:30–4:30
no charge

National Temple Hill Association, Inc.
(1042 Route 94—location)
PO Box 315 (mailing address)
Valis Gate, NY 12584
(914) 561-5073
Hours: seasonal and by appointment; Jul–Sept: Sun 2:00–5:00
(The American Revolution; local history)
$15.00 per year membership for individuals, $25.00 per year membership for couples

19th Louisiana Volunteer Infantry
2519 June Street
Baton Rouge, LA 70808
(504) 387-4296

141st Military History Detachment
Washington Army National Guard State Historical Society
Camp Murray
Tacoma, WA 98430
(253) 581-8498
William Woodward, Ph.D., Historian

Order of Confederate Rose
West Virginia Chapter
RR 9, Box 67
Princeton, WV 24740
(304) 487-0829
E-mail: commander@inetone.net
Anna B. Belcher, President
Pub. *Parshandatha Papers*, monthly, $7.00 per year subscription
(for women loving Southern culture and history)
$7.00 per year membership for individuals; search: $10.00

Order of the Indian Wars
PO Box 7401
Little Rock, AR 72217
(501) 225-3996
Jerry L. Russell, National Chairman
Pub. *Dispatch*
(no genealogical information)

Oregon Military Museum
Camp Withycombe
Clackamas, OR 97015-9150
(503) 557-5359; (503) 557-5224 FAX
Maj. (Ret) Stephen C. McGeorge, Director
Hours: Fri–Sat 1:00–4:00, and by appointment

John Pelham Historical Association
7 Carmel Terrace
Hampton, VA 23666
Peggy Vogtsberger
Pub. *Cannoneer*, bimonthly
(emphasis on the War Between the States; Lt.-Col. John Pelham)

Pennsylvania Military Museum
28th Division Shrine
(Business Route 322 and Route 45—location)
PO Box 160A (mailing address)
Boalsburg, PA 16827
(814) 466-6263
William J. Leech, Director
Hours: Tue–Sat 9:00–5:00, Sun noon–5:00

Presidio Lancers
715 Morningside, N.E.
Albuquerque, NM 87110
(505) 268-2896

Rosehill Cemetery Civil War Museum

5800 North Ravenswood Avenue
Chicago, IL 60660
(773) 561-5940
David Wendell
Hours: Mon–Fri 9:00–5:00, Sat–Sun
    9:00–4:00
(Chicago's Civil War history)

2nd Armored Division Museum

418 Battalion Avenue
PO Box 5009
Fort Hood, TX 76546
(254) 287-8812

Society of Civil War Historians

PO Box 7401
Little Rock, AR 72217
(501) 225-3996
Jerry L. Russell, Executive Secretary
Pub. *CWH Newsletter*
(no genealogical information)

Society of World War I Aero Historians

10443 South Memphis Avenue
Whittier, CA 90604

Soldiers' Memorial Military Museum

1315 Chestnut Street
Saint Louis, MO 63103
(314) 622-4550

3rd Cavalry Museum

PO Box 12721
Colorado Springs, CO 80913
Paul D. Martin

U.S. Air Force in Utah Historical Society

Directorate of Material Management
Hill Air Force Base
Ogden, UT 84056
(801) 777-5076

United States Army Military History Institute

22 Ashburn Drive
Carlisle, PA 17013-5008
(717) 245-3611; (717) 245-3205 (Online
    Resources); (717) 245-4370 FAX
    (Online Resources)
E-mail: MHI-HR@CARLISLE-
    EMH2.ARMY.MIL (Historical
    Reference Branch); MHI-
    AR@CARLISLE-EMH2.ARMY.MIL
    (Archives Branch); MHI-
    SC@CARLISLE-EMH2.ARMY.MIL
    (Special Collections Branch);
    STEINKEL@CARLISLE-
    EMH2.ARMY.MIL (Online
    Resources)
http://carlisle-www.army.mil/usamhi/
John Slonaker, Chief, Reference Branch
Hours: Mon–Fri 8:00–4:30 (except
    federal holidays)

(electronic database containing 3,000
    bibliographic references to MHI
    holdings pertaining to specialized
    aspects of military history; army unit
    histories; is compiling a photographic
    collection of those who fought in the
    Civil War)

United States Cavalry Association

(Building 283—location)
PO Box 2325 (mailing address)
Fort Riley, KS 66442
(913) 784-5797
http://see-inc.com/cavalry/
Patricia S. Bright, Executive Director
Hours: Mon–Fri 8:30–4:30
Pub. *The Cavalry Journal*, quarterly
$25.00 per year membership for
    individuals, $40.00 per year
    membership for organizations, $35.00
    per year membership for overseas
    individuals, $50.00 per year Corporate
    membership

Department of Veterans Affairs

National Cemetery System (401B)
810 Vermont Avenue, N.W.
Washington, DC 20420
(202) 535-7832
Alex Havas (402B)
Hours: 7:00–4:30
(for national cemetery burial records
    during and after the Civil War, supply
    full name, dates and places of birth
    and death, state from which entered
    military service, rank and military unit
    in which served on active duty)
no charge

Virginia Country Civil War Society

PO Box 798
Berryville, VA 22611-0798
Pub. *Civil War Society Newsletter*,
    bimonthly

RADIO PROGRAMS

Family History Show

PO Box 116605
Carrollton, TX 75011-6605
(972) 306-8000; (800) 765-1080
http://supertalk.houstonradio.com (for
    information on how to listen to the
    broadcast on the Internet)
Michael Matthews
Hours: broadcast live on KRLD 1080
    AM: Sun 10:00–midnight

Index to Periodicals and Newsletters

General Index*

An asterisk after a page number indicates that the organization responded to the questionnaire.

Galt Historical Society   50
Galva Historical Society/Wiley House Museum   124
Galveston County Historical Museum   485*
Galveston Daily News   673
Galveston Historical Foundation   493
County Galway Chronicles   585
George Gamble Library   303
Gangster Chronicles   16
The Gann Museum of Saline County   33
Garden City Historical Commission   245
Garden City Public Library   174, 334*
Historical Society of Garden County   294
Garden Prairie Genealogical and Historical Society   124
Gardena Library   568
Garfield County Genealogical Society   428
Garfield County Historical Society   295, 425*
Garfield County Museum   287
Garfield Heritage Society   124
Garfield Historical Society   316
Garland County Historical Society   35*
Garland Genealogical Society   501*
Garnavillo Historical Society   164
Garner Public Library   160
Garrard County Historical Society   191
Garrett County Historical Society, Inc.   213
Garrett Historical Society   150
Gary Historical Association   468
Gary Public Library   145
Gasconade County Historical Society   278
Gastineau Genealogical Society   27
Gaston County Historical Society, Inc.   383
Gaston-Lincoln Regional Library   380
Gates County Historical Society   383
Gates Mills Historical Society   404
Gates Public Library   334*
Gateway Press, Inc.   678
Gateway to the Panhandle   422
Gay-Kimball Public Library   303*
Gaylord Fact-Finders Genealogical Society   251*
Geary County Historical Society and Museum   178
Geauga County Genealogical Society   420*
Geauga County Historical Society   404*
Gem County Historical Society   110*
Gem Village Museum   66
GENDEX   664
Genealogical Advisor   71
Genealogical and Heraldic Institute of America   586, 684
The Genealogical and Historical Research Center   460
Genealogical Center Library   11*, 683*
Genealogical Computing Association of Pennsylvania (GENCAP)   456
"Genealogical Corner"   670*
The Genealogical Data Base System   666
Genealogical Forum of Oregon, Inc.   435
Genealogical Heritage Council of Oregon   435*
Genealogical Heritage, Ltd.   16
Genealogical Institute   16*, 528*, 573*, 597*, 663*
Genealogical Institute of Oklahoma   427
The Genealogical Institute of Texas   506*
Genealogical Publishing Company, Inc.   675
Genealogical Queries Magazine   16
Genealogical Questers   138*
Genealogical Research and Consultation   421
Genealogical Research Associates   668*
Genealogical Research Directory   16*, 652*
Genealogical Research Institute of Virginia   526*
Genealogical Roundtable   237
Genealogical Society of North Orange County California (GSNOCC)   59*

Genealogical Speaker's Guild   668
Genealogical Workshop of Mesa, Inc.   31
Genealogy and Family History Committee of the New Mexico Jewish Historical Society   588*
Genealogy Book Store   679
Genealogy Books and Consultation   506
The Genealogy Council of the Jewish Museum of Maryland   588*
Genealogy Digest Magazine   16
Genealogy Friends of The Library   284
Genealogy Friends: Partyline   481
Genealogy Group   251
The Genealogy Home Page   664
Genealogy House   679, 685
Genealogy Publishing Service   664, 678
Genealogy Special Interest Group   664
Genealogy Toolbox Research Center   664
Genealogy Unlimited, Inc.   679*, 685*
Genealogy Unlimited Society, Inc.   104
Genealogy West, Inc.   203
Genee's Exchange   16
General Commission on Archives and History   637*
General Conference of Seventh Day Adventists   635
Generation Gap   667
Generations for Windows   667
Genesee Area Genealogists   376*
Genesee County Historian   350*
Genesee County Museum   334
Genesee Heritage Society   549*
Geneseo City Museum   174
Geneseo Historical Association   124
Geneva Free Library   334
Geneva Historical and Genealogical Society   88, 91
Geneva Historical Society   124
Geneva Historical Society and Museum   351*
Geneva Public Library   395*
Geneva Public Library District   115
Genius Family Tree   667
Genoa Historical Society   295
Gentry County Genealogical Society   284
Gentry County Library   273*
Genus Senior   666
Geographical Center Historical Society   391*
George Memorial Library   485*
Georgetown Chapter (SCGS)   464
Georgetown County Historical Commission   462
Georgetown County Historical Society   462
Georgetown Historical Society   229*
Georgia Association of Historians   105
Georgia Baptist History Depository   616*
Georgia College   95, 95*
Georgia Department of Archives and History   93*
Georgia Department of Human Resources   7
Georgia Division of Public Library Services   93
Georgia Genealogical Society   103*
Georgia Historical Society   93*, 513
Georgia Institute of Technology   95
The Georgia Salzburger Society   105, 578, 622, 642
Georgia Southern College   95
Georgia State Law Library   93
Gering Public Library   292
German-Acadian Coast Historical and Genealogical Society   201, 202
German-American Family Society of Akron, Inc.   578*
German-American Genealogical Association Europe   578*
German-American Genealogical Club   578
German American Heritage Association of Oklahoma (GAHA)   579
The German-American Heritage Institute   579

Grimes County Heritage Association   493
Grimes County Historical Commission   493
Grinnell Historical Museum   161*
Grosse Ile Historical Society   246*
Groton Historical Association   352
Groton Historical Society   513
Groton Public Library   73*
Group for Openness in Adoption   658*
Grout Museum of History and Science   161*
Grove (Oklahoma) Public Library   422*
Groveland Historical Society, Inc.   229
Grundy County Genealogical Society   284*
Grundy County Genealogical Society Chapter (IGS)   169
Grundy County Historian   471
Grundy County Historical Society   125, 164, 279
Grundy County-Jewett Norris Library   273
Klaus Gruneweld Bookdealer   680*
Guadalupe County Genealogical Society   501
Guale Historical Society   100*
Guernsey County District Public Library   395*
Guernsey County Genealogical Society Chapter OGS   415*
Guernsey County Historical Society   405
Guernsey Memorial Library   335*
Guilford College   619
The Guilford County Genealogical Society   386
Guilford Historical Society   513*
Guilford Keeping Society, Inc.   77
Guilford Township Historical Society   150
Gulf Coast Heritage Association, Inc.   88*
Gulf Coast Saint David's Welsh Society of Sarasota, Florida   612
Gulfport-Harrison County Public Library   268
Gulfport Historical Society   88
Gulluh Gyap   461
Gunn Memorial Library and Museum   73*
Gunnison County Pioneer and Historical Society   68*
Guthrie County Genealogical Society Chapter (IGS)   169*
Guthrie County Historical Society   164
Guyton Historical Society   100
Gwinnett Historical Society, Inc.   100*
Gwinnett History Museum   95*

H-California   64
HEFA Kinseekers   59
Hacker's Creek Pioneer Descendants, Inc.   543*
Hackettstown Free Public Library   311*
Hackettstown Historical Society   317*
Hackley Heritage Association, Inc.   246
Hackley Public Library   240
Hacksma House Genealogy Library   530
Haddam Historical Society, Inc.   77*
Haddon Heights Historical Society   317
Haddon Township Historical Society   317
Historical Society of Haddonfield   317
Haddonfield Preservation Society   317
Haddonfield Public Library   311*
Hagerman Valley Historical Society   110
Haggin Museum   42
Hagley Museum and Library   83*
Z. I. Hale Museum   485
Hales Corners Historical Society   549
Nita Stewart Haley Memorial Library and History Center   485
The Half-Shire Historical Society   352
Halifax County Genealogical Society   386
Halifax County Historical Association   383*
Halifax Historical Society Museum   88*, 513
Hall County Historical Society   100
Hall County Library System   95*
Hamblen County Genealogical Society   479

Hamblen County Historian   471
Hamburg Historical Society   352
Hamburg State Park Museum   95
Hamden Historical Society, Inc.   77
Hamilton County Chapter OGS   415*
Hamilton County Genealogy Society and Central Texas Research Center   501*
Hamilton County Historian   150*, 352, 471
Hamilton County Historical Society   125, 150*, 295*
Hamilton County Memorial Building   395
Hamilton Heritage Hunters Chapter (IGS)   169*
Hamilton Historical Society   229
Township of Hamilton Historical Society   317
The Hamilton Journal-News   672
Hamilton Public Library   335
Historical Society of Hamilton Township   317
Hamilton Township Public Library   311
Hamlin Historical Society   352
Hammond Castle Museum, Inc.   220
Hammond Historical Society   150
Hammond Library   636
Hammonton Historical Society   317
Hampden Chapter (M.S.O.G.)   237
Hampden Historical Society   206*
Historical Society of the Town of Hampden, Inc.   229*
Hampshire County Historical Society   540
Hampshire County Public Library   539*
Hampton Antiquarian and Historical Society   77*
Hampton Center for the Arts and Humanities   518
Hampton County Historical Society   462
Hampton Historians, Inc.   306
Hampton Historical Association   306*
Hampton Historical Society   125*
Hampton Public Library   518*
Hanalei Museum   107
Hancock-Chehocton Historical Association   352*
Hancock County Archives   188
Hancock County Chapter OGS   415
Hancock County Foundation for Historic Preservation   100
Hancock County Genealogical Society Chapter (IGS)   169*
Hancock County Historian   150, 471
Hancock County Historical and Genealogical Society   477*, 479*
Hancock County Historical Society   125*, 150*, 191, 269*
Hancock County Historical Society of West Virginia, Inc.   540
Genealogical Society of Hancock County, Kentucky   195*
Hancock Genealogy Committee   309
Hancock Historical Museum   395*
Hancock Historical Society   306
Handley Regional Library   518*
Hanover Area Historical Society   446*
Hanover College   625
Hanover County Historical Society, Inc.   523
Hanover Historical Society   229*, 306*
The Hanover Park Ontarioville Historical Commission   125
Hanover Township Historical Society   317
Hansford County Historical Commission   493
Hanson Historical Society   230
Hapeville Historical Society, Inc.   100
Haralson County Historical Society, Inc.   100
The Harbinger Group   667
Hardeman County Historian   471
Hardin County Genealogical Society Chapter OGS   415*
Hardin County Historian   471
Hardin County Historical and Genealogical Society   125, 138
Hardin County Historical Museums, Inc.   395*
Hardin County Historical Society   164*, 191, 477
Hardin County Library   188
Harding Township Historical Society   317

Kent Memorial Library   73*
Kent State University Libraries   396
The Kent State University Press   688*
Kenton County Historical Society   192*
Kenton County Public Library   188*
Kentucky Baptist Convention Archives   616
Kentucky Cabinet for Economic Development   197*
Kentucky Civil War, Confederate States of America, Orphan
    Brigade   197, 689
Commonwealth of Kentucky Department for Health   7
Kentucky Department for Social Services—Adult
    Adoptees   659*
Kentucky Explorer   197
Kentucky Genealogical Society, Inc.   194
Kentucky Genealogy and History News   197
Kentucky Highlands Museum   188
Kentucky Historical Society Library   187*
Kentucky Military History Museum   188, 689*
Kentucky Oral History Commission   197
Kentucky State Archives   187*
Kentucky State University Archives   188
Kentucky Tree-Search   197*
Keo Mah Genealogical Society Chapter (IGS)   169*
Keokuk County Historical Society   165*
Keokuk Museum Commission   161
Keokuk Public Library   161*
Kern County Genealogical Society   59
Kern County Historical Society   50
Kern County Museum   42*
Kern River Valley Historical Society   50
Genealogical Society of Kerrville   502*
Kershaw County Historical Society   463*
Kershaw County Library   461*
Community Library (Ketchum)   109
Kettering-Moraine Museum and Historical Society   405
Kettlersville Historical Society   405
Kewanee Historical Society, Inc.   126
Kewaskum Historical Society, Inc.   550
Kewaunee County Historical Society   550*
Keweenaw County Historical Society   246*
Key Genealogical Library   486
Key West Art and Historical Society   88
Keya Paha County Historical Society   295
Keyport Historical Society   318*
Keystone Area Historical Society   468
Keystone Genealogical Society   91
Keytesville Public Library   273*
Kialegee Tribal Town   597
Kidron Community Historical Society   405*, 623*
Kids' Genes   17
Kiel Historical Society   550
Kielce-Radom Special Interest Group   591*
Kilgore Memorial Library   292
Kimball Public Library   292
Kimmswick Historical Society   279
Kin Hunters Genealogical Publications and Research   197
Kindred Keepsakes   438
Kindred Konnections, Inc.   667*
King and Queen Historical Society   524
Association of King County Historical Organization   533*
King George County Historical Society   524
Martin Luther King Memorial Library   84
King-Tisdell Cottage Foundation, Inc.   101
Kingdom of Callaway Historical Society   279
Kingdom of the Sun   93
Kingman County Historical Museum   175*
Kings County Historian   354
Kings County Library   42*
Kingsborough Historical Society   354

Kingsbridge Historical Society   354
Kingsley Historical Society   165
Kingsport Public Library   474*
Kingston Improvement and Historical Society, Inc.   306*
Kingston Public Library   474
Kingwood Township Historical Society   318
Kinnelon Historical Commission   318
Kinpublish   667
Kinseeker Publications   254*
Kinseekers Genealogical Society of Lake County   91
Kinship—Sources for Kith and Kin   378, 675
Kinsley Public Library   175
Kinsolving Investigations   659
KinWrite   667
Kirkwood Historical Society   279*
Kirn Memorial Library   519*
Kishwaukee Genealogists   139*
Kishwaukee Valley Heritage Society   126*
Kith and Kin   667
Kitsap County Historical Society   533
Kittitas County Genealogical Society   536*
Kittitas County Museum   530
Kittochtinny Historical Society, Inc.   447*
Kittson County History Center and Museum   260*
Klamath Basin Genealogical Society   436*
Klamath County Library   432
Klamath National Forest   42
Klein Foundation, Inc.   467*
Klondike Gold Rush National Historical Park—Seattle
    Unit   530*
Knickerbocker Historical Society, Inc.   354*
Knott County Historical Society   192
Knox County Archives   474*
Knox County Chapter OGS   416*
Knox County Genealogical Society   139*, 196
Knox County Historian   151, 471
Knox County Historical Commission   494*
Knox County Historical Society   280*
Knox County Public Library Historical Collection   145*
Knox County Records Library   145*
Knox Creek Historical Society   550*
Knox Historical Society   354
Knox Memorial Association   207
Knoxville Civil War Roundtable   689
Kodak Genealogical Club   376
Kodiak Historical Society   27*
Kokomo-Howard County Public Library   145*
Kokomo Tribune   670
Kona Historical Society   108*
Konawa Genealogical and Historical Society of Seminole
    County, Oklahoma   425*, 428*
Koochiching County Historical Society   260
Kootenai County Genealogical Society   111*
Kosciusko-Attala Historical Society   269
Kosciusko County Area Genealogist Researchers   157
Kosciusko County Historian   151
Genealogy Section, Kosciusko County Historical
    Society   151*, 157*
Koshare Indian Museum, Inc.   597
Kotzebue Museum, Inc.   25
Krans-Buckland Family Association, Inc.   573*
KsGenWeb   186
Kurth Memorial Library   486*
Kutztown Area Historical Society   447*
KyGenWeb   198

LDB Associates, Inc.   667
La Crosse Area Genealogical Society Chapter (WSGS)   555
La Crosse County Historical Society   550*

Middletown Historical Society, Inc. 458
Middletown Public Library 146, 397*
Middletown Springs Historical Society, Inc. 514
Middletown Township Historical Society 319*
Middletown Township Public Library 312
Middletown Valley Historical Society 213*
Midland County Historical Museum 487*
Midland County Historical Society 247*, 494*
Midland County Public Library 487
Midland Genealogical Society 252*, 503*
Midland Park Historical Society 319
Midland Park Public Library 312
Midlothian Historical Society 128
Midway Museum, Inc. 96
Midwest Historical and Genealogical Society 180, 184
Mifflin County Historical Society 448
MiGenWeb 255
Milaca Area Historical Society and Museum 261*
Milam County Genealogical Society 503*
Milam County Homepage 506
Milan-Berlin Township Public Library 397*
Milan Historical Association 180
Milan Historical Museum 397*
Miles City Genealogical Society 290
Miles City Public Library 288
Milford Historical Commission 221
Milford Historical Society 77, 83*, 307*
Milford Mail-Journal 671*
Milford Town Library 221
Military Information Enterprises, Inc. 689
Military Library, Jackson Barracks 199
Military Order of Foreign Wars of the United States 1894-1994 648
Military Order of the Loyal Legion of the United States 646
Military Order of the Purple Heart in the United States 648, 648*
Military Order of the Stars and Bars 646, 647*
Indian Territory Society—Military Order of the Stars and Bars 646*
Military Records and Research Branch 198, 689
Mill Creek Valley Historical Association 448
Mill Valley Historical Society 52*
Mill Valley Public Library 43*
Millbrae Historical Society 52*
The Millbrook Society/Amy B. Yerkes Museum 448*
Millbrook Village Society 319
The Millburn-Short Hills Historical Society 319*
Mille Lacs Lake Historical Society 261
Millennia Corporation 667
Phillips S. Miller Branch Library 66
Miller-Cory House Museum 312
Historical Society of Millersburg and Upper Paxton Township 449*
Ralph L. Milliken Museum 43
Million Dollar Museum 327
Mills County Chapter (IGS) 170
Millsaps College Archives 268*
Milltown Historical Society 319
Milton-Freewater Genealogical Club 437
Milton Historical Society 232, 514*, 551*
Township of Milton Historical Society 307
Milton Public Library 221*
Milwaukee County Genealogical Society, Inc. 556*
Milwaukee County Historical Society 551*
Milwaukee Public Library 547*
Milwaukee Urban Archives/Area Research Center 544*
Minatare Public Library 292
Mine Au Breton Historical Society 280*
Mineral County Genealogical-Historical Society 541, 543

Mineral County Museum and Historical Society 289*
Mineral Point Historical Society 551
Mineral Wells Heritage Association 494
Minerva Area Historical Society 408
Minerva Historical Society 356*
Mingo County Genealogical Society 543*
Mingo County Historical Society 541*
Minidoka County Historical Society, Inc. 110
Minisink Valley Historical Society 356*
Minneapolis Public Library and Information Center 256*
Minnehaha County Historical Society 468
Crooks Council of the Minnehaha County Historical Society 468
Minnesota Coalition of Scottish Clans 605
Minnesota Conference Archives, United Methodist Church 638*
Minnesota Department of Health 8*
Minnesota Department of Human Services 660*
Minnesota Finnish-American Historical Society 574*
Minnesota Genealogical Society 264*
Minnesota Genealogical Society, Computer Branch 665
Minnesota Genealogical Society, Douglas County Branch 265
Minnesota Genealogical Society, Scottish Branch 605
Minnesota Genealogical Society, Yankee Branch 237
Minnesota Gymanfa Ganu Association 612
Minnesota Historical Society 255*, 574*
Minnesota Historical Society Research Center 255*
Minnesota Lake Area Historical Society 261
Minnesota Library Association 255
Minnesota Obituaries 267
Minnesota Reunion Registry/Liberal Education for Adoptive Families 660
Minnesota State Archaeologist's Office 255
Minnetonka Historical Society 261*
Minnetrista Cultural Center 146
Minocqua Museum 547
Minot Public Library 390*
Minster Historical Society 408
Mishawaka-Penn Public Library 146
Mission Oaks Genealogy Club 60*, 665*
Mission Trail—Los Pueblos Association 494
Missisquoi Valley Historical Society 514
Mississippi Baptist Historical Commission 616*
Mississippi Coast Historical and Genealogical Society 269*, 271*
Mississippi College 268
Mississippi County Genealogical Society 285*
Mississippi County Historical Society 280*
Mississippi Genealogical Society 271*
Historical and Genealogical Association of Mississippi 267, 271
Mississippi Historical Society 267
Mississippi Junior Historical Society 270
Mississippi Library Commission 267
Mississippi Memories 272*
The Mississippi Press 672*
Mississippi State Department of Health 8*
Mississippi State Historical Museum 268
Mississippi University for Women 268, 268*
Mississippi Valley French Research 142*, 577*
Missoula Public Library 288*
Missouri Alliance for Historical Preservation 280*
Missouri Ancestors 286
Missouri Baptist Historical Society 616
Missouri Department of Health 8*
Missouri Historical Society 280*
Records Management and Archives Service (Missouri) 8
Missouri River Heritage Association 280
Missouri State Archives 272*

Wartburg Theological Seminary   622
Warwick Historical Society   235
The Warwick Historical Society   458
Warwick Public Library   457*
Waseca Area Genealogy Society (WAGS)   266
Waseca County Historical Society Museum   264
Waseca-LeSueur Regional Library   257
Washakie County Historical Society   559
Washburn County Genealogical Society   557*
Washburn County Historical Society and Museum   553
Washington Adoption Rights Movement (WARM)   662*
Washington and Lee University   521
Citizens Library, Washington   442
Washington College   211
Washington County Chapter (IGS)   171*
Washington County Chapter OGS   418
Washington County Free Library   211*
Washington County Genealogical Society   186, 299*
Washington County Historian   155, 372, 472
Washington County Historical Association   479
Washington County Historical Association/Museum   297*
Washington County Historical Society   36*, 167*, 182, 214, 264*, 372*, 435, 452*
Washington County Historical Society, Inc.   155*, 427, 554*
Washington County Historical Society Library   411
Historical Society of Washington County   134
Washington County-Jonesborough Library   475*
Washington County Library System   269
Washington County Museum   20
Washington County Public Library   190*, 399*, 521
Historic Society of Washington County, Virginia, Inc.   525*
The Historical Society of Washington, D.C.   83*
Washington Free Public Library   313
Washington Grove Heritage Committee   214
Washington Historical Society   134, 309
Washington Memorial Library   97*
Mary Ball Washington Museum   521*
Washington National Records Center   2, 83
The Washington News Tribune   673
Washington Parish Library System   200
Washington Public Library   162*, 276
Washington State Archives, Central Regional Branch   529*
Washington State Archives, Eastern Regional Branch   529*
Washington State Archives, Main Office   529
Washington State Archives, Northwest Region   529*
Washington State Archives, Puget Sound Branch   529
Washington State Archives, Southwest Regional Branch   529
Washington State Department of Health   10
Washington State Genealogical Society   536*
Washington State Historical Society   529*
Washington State Library   529*
Washington State University   532
Washington Township Historical Society   56, 324*
Washington-Wilkes Historical Foundation, Inc.   103
Washita County Historical Society   427
Washoe County Historical Society   301
Washtenaw County Historical Society   249*
Washtenaw County History District Commission   249*
Genealogical Society of Washtenaw County, Michigan, Inc.   254*
Wasilla-Knik-Willow Creek Historical Society   27
Watauga Association of Genealogists—Upper East Tennessee   480
Watchung Hills Historical Society   324
Watchung Historical Society   324
Waterborough Historical Society   208
Waterbury Historical Society Museum   516
Waterford Foundation, Inc.   525*
Waterford Historical Museum and Cultural Center   339*

Waterford Historical Society   208
Waterford Historical Society, Inc.   81
Waterloo Area Historical Society   249, 554*
Waterloo Library and Historical Society   373
Waterloo Public Library   162
Waterloo Public Memorial Library   547
Watertown Area Genealogical Society   470*
Watertown Free Public Library   224*
Watertown Historical Society   554*
Watertown Historical Society, Inc.   81
The Historical Society of Watertown   235*
Waterville Historical Society   411
Waterville Public Library   205
Watervliet Historical Society   373
Waterways Journal   287*
Watkins Mill Association   282
The Watkinson Library   573
Watonwan County Historical Society   264*
Wattsburg Area Historical Society   452*
Wauconda Township Historical Society   134
Waukegan Historical Society   134*
Waukesha County Genealogical Society   557*
Waukesha County Historical Society   554*
Waukesha County Museum   547*
Waukesha Public Library   548*
Waupaca County Historical Society   554
Waupun Historical Society   554*
Waushara County Historical Society, Inc.   554*
Wauwatosa Historical Society   554*
Waverly Genealogical and Historical Society   134, 142
The Waxahachie Daily Light   673
Willard V. Way Public Library   399*
Wayland Baptist University   490
Wayland Historical Commission   224
Wayland Historical Society   235
Wayland Public Library   224
Wayland Tree Tracers Genealogy Society   254
The Wayne County Genealogical Organization   271*
Wayne County Genealogical Society Chapter (IGS)   171*
Wayne County Genealogical Society, Chapter OGS   419*
Wayne County Historian   155, 373*, 472
Wayne County Historical Association   385*
Wayne County Historical Museum   155*
Wayne County Historical Society   134, 194, 297, 373, 411, 452*, 479
Wayne County, Indiana, Genealogical Society   158*
Wayne County Public Library   190, 382*, 399*
Wayne Historical Society   249
Wayne Public Library   293*
Wayne Township Historical Commission   324
Waynesboro Historical Society   452*
The Waynesboro Municipal Library   269*
Waynesboro Public Library   521
Waynoka Historical Society   427
Waynoka Public Library   424*
Weakley County Genealogical Society   480
Weakley County Historian   472
Weare Historical Society   309
The Weatherford Democrat   673
Weatherford Public Library   490
Weathersfield Historical Society Museum   516
Weaver Genealogical Publications   143*
Webb City Area Genealogy Society   286*
Webb County Heritage Foundation   497*
Weber County Library   508*
WebLUIS!   84
Webster County Genealogical and Historical Society   194*, 197*
Webster County Genealogical Society Chapter (IGS)   172*

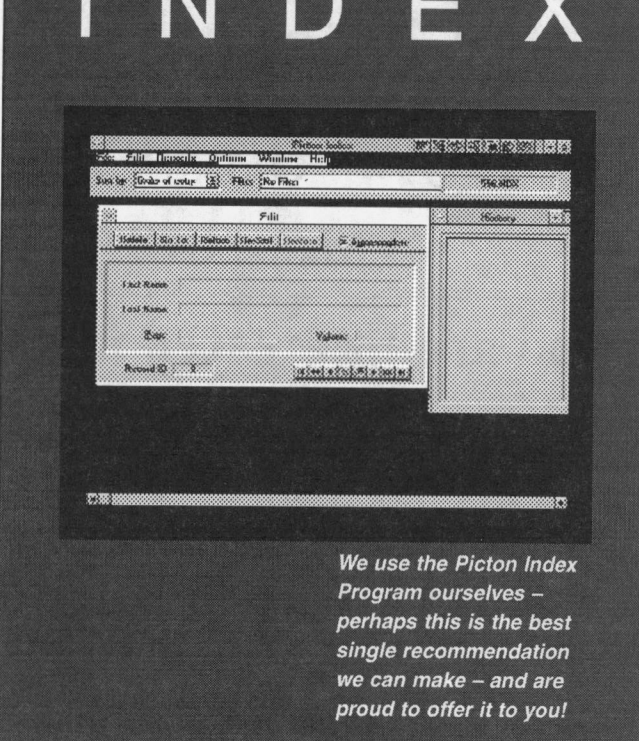

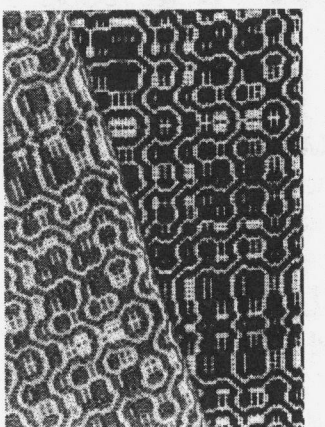

A SPECIAL GIFT
CREATE YOUR OWN FAMILY DOCUMENTARY!

Have you ever wondered what to do with those old family photographs, slides, home movies and video footage collecting dust in the back of the closet? Mary Lou Peterson's **"Gift of Heritage"®,** a video that offers a new challenge for both camcorder enthusiasts and historians, may be just the answer!

Mary Lou was one of five recipients of the **CREATIVE THINKING ASSOCIATION OF AMERICA**™ 1992 National Recognition Awards for her creation, **an instructional video encouraging the preservation of family memories and history on video.**

The concept for "Gift of Heritage" originated with a personal project several years ago, when Mary Lou, a Minneapolis grandmother, marketing product specialist with AT&T, and video novice, decided to commit her family's genealogical tree, history, stories, and old photographs to video. The project mushroomed and soon she was incorporating titles to identify the photographs, and dubbing in background music, sound effects and narration to help tell the story of her family leaving Norway and settling in the Midwest.

The end result was a family documentary that brought the family tree to life! It was shared and appreciated by all current generations of her immediate and extended family at its monumental, 50th reunion. Members of her family told her that they felt they had taken a journey back into the past, where they had met their ancestors face to face and learned about their lives and experiences. Many relatives requested copies of the video to hand down to future generations. What a wonderful gift of their heritage!

Mary Lou had found no resources available to guide her through the development of her family-history video. So she made notes about all the roadblocks she encountered and how she overcame them, and decided to use her own experience to help others who might be interested in recording their family histories on videotape.

This led to the production of "Gift of Heritage," an information-packed instructional video which takes the viewer through the process of beginning the research, planning and organizing materials, combining the family-tree information, photographs, slides, home-movie and video footage, interviewing, and effectively telling the family's story. "Gift of Heritage" also points out that a written script, along with labeled and numbered materials, will help minimize frustration during the actual videotaping process.

In "Gift of Heritage," Mary Lou incorporates several examples from her own family documentary to illustrate a point or suggest a method. Watching "Gift of Heritage" will get viewers' creative juices flowing by convincing them that they can create their own family documentaries. Ideas will start to blossom and viewers will begin to think about what they may want to include, and how they can make the best use of their valuable time by enlisting the aid of other family members who can provide needed information, photos or other contributions.

By using some less-than-perfect footage from her own family-tree video she hopes "Gift of Heritage" will encourage others to use what they have available. Such a video project doesn't have to look like a major motion picture. And while a simple production style won't take a lot of time and money, it will produce a quality video featuring your own family history; a tape that can be proudly handed down to future generations. **What a great way to communicate with your descendants!**

"Gift of Heritage" is not just for videographers and family historians. Mary Lou's goal in having produced "Gift of Heritage" is that, through it, people will find a new hobby -- one that will not only include resources from their immediate families, but also from their extended families.

Mary Lou said, **"In modern times, when families are separated by time and distance, it takes more effort to retain family values and traditions. A sense of belonging -- of connection is what ties the past to the future."**

Members of a **blended family** can enhance their individual sense of belonging through watching this family-tree video because it allows them to recognize and appreciate their own positions in the family structure. According to Mary Lou, "Creating your own family documentary will provide immeasurable pride, curiosity, enlightenment, and entertainment. In addition, recording the story on video is a way to encourage younger family members, already so used to the video medium, to learn about their family history."

Most families have plenty of photos and interesting stories told by older relatives, enabling them to easily put together their own colorful family history on video; a history that links the immediate and extended family to their past and gives them a sense of continuity and tradition.

Families may include video or genealogy hobbyists who are particularly excited about participating in such a project. If no one in the family can do the final video production, this could be handled by a professional video service.

A family gathering is a great place to start the project (and, later, to entertain members with it). At such get-togethers, ask family members to share stories and photographs for the whole family to enjoy before such treasures are lost forever!

The concept of recording our history works not only for families, but for businesses, organizations, religious and ethnic groups, communities and other groups that may want to document their histories, or special events. As an example, ethnic groups could use it to detail their migration, focus on some of their early pioneers, and illustrate the hardships the group has endured and overcome.

"Gift of Heritage" was first introduced in the May 1992 issue of **Camcorder & Computer Video Magazine,** and is now being marketed worldwide.

The cost of "Gift of Heritage"(R) is $29.95 plus $3.00 shipping & handling. (800) All major credit cards are accepted. TO ORDER: Call (800) 774-8511, FAX (800) 335-8511, (612) 727-2705 or send check, money order or credit card information to: Mary Lou Productions P.O. Box 17233, Minneapolis, MN 55417. Minnesota residents add 6.5 percent sales tax, plus any appropriate city tax. For foreign orders send $37.95, which includes shipping and handling. All payments must be in U.S. funds. Videotapes are available in the NTSC system and VHS format only. Taxes, duties and other customs charges are the responsibility of the customer.

For additional information and other products to help document family history call; (800) 224-8511 or visit the web site **http//:www.giftofheritage.com**. To contact Mary Lou Peterson; (612) 726-9432 FAX (612) 727-2705 or **E mail giftofheritage@att.net**.

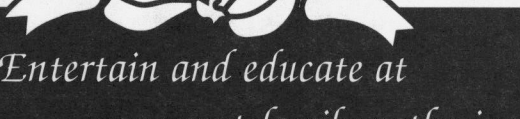

1880 Census of West Virginia

COMPILED BY WILLIAM A. MARSH

The thirteen volume series is a compilation of all the individuals enumerated in the 1880 census for the 54 West Virginia counties and contains over 650,000 listings. The INDEX , Volume 14, covers the entire series and contains 157,432 entries . The INDEX is also an index to the microfilmed census rolls.

These individual volume listings include a code letter designating the enumeration district in the county, along with the page number on which the entry is to be found in the National Archives Microfilm Rolls, the names of each person included in the household, color, sex, age, relationship, occupation, place of birth of each individual, and the birthplace of the father and mother. Cross referencing of non-surname people eliminates the need for a cumbersome index for each county and greatly facilitates its use. The INDEX for the series contains the name of the head of household or non surname member, the volume number, County, code designator for the enumeration district and page number on the microfilmed census rolls.

Sample pages showing how the material is presented are included as attachments to this brochure.

ORDER BLANK

1880 CENSUS OF WEST VIRGINIA

Volume 1 Lewis, Upshur, Taylor, Barbour Counties   792 pages cloth
Volume 2 Randolph, Tucker, Pendleton, Grant, Pocahontas, Hardy
         Webster and Mineral Counties   865 pages cloth
Volume 3 Harrison, Doddridge, Gilmer, Calhoun Counties 740 pages cloth
Volume 4 Braxton, Clay, Nicholas, Fayette, Raleigh, Wyoming
         Counties   776 pages cloth
Volume 5 Ritchie, Wood, Wirt Counties 804 pages cloth
Volume 6 Monongalia, Preston, Marion Counties   846 pages cloth
Volume 7 Pleasant, Tyler, Marshal, Wetzel Counties 767 pages cloth
Volume 8 Roane, Kanawha, Boone Counties   854 pages cloth
Volume 9 Greenbrier, Monroe, Summers, Mercer, McDowell
         Counties   807 pages cloth
Volume10 Jackson, Putnam, Mason Counties   801 pages cloth
Volume11 Cabell, Wayne, Lincoln, Logan Counties   697 pages cloth
Volume12 Ohio, Brooke, Hancock Counties   798 pages cloth
Volume13 Hampshire, Morgan, Berkeley, Jefferson Counties 742 pages cloth
Volume14 INDEX - 1880 Census of West Virginia 1218 pages

Volumes 1-13 $38.50 each postpaid; Volume 14 $78.00 postpaid
(Circle Volumes Desired)

Name..
Address..
City...State.........................Zip Code................

Send check or money order to: William A. Marsh 100 Cynthia St, Rayne, La 70578
Purchase Orders will be honored from libraries, genealogical and historical societies.

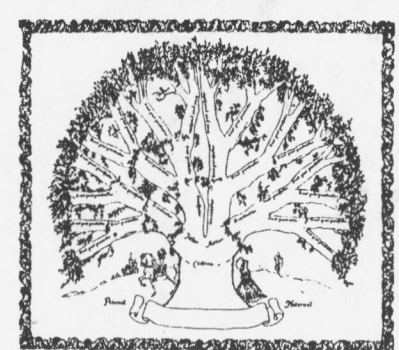

Migrant Birds in the

Neotropics: ECOLOGY, BEHAVIOR, DISTRIBUTION, and CONSERVATION

Edited by
ALLEN KEAST and
EUGENE S. MORTON

A Symposium Held at the
Conservation and Research Center,
National Zoological Park,
Smithsonian Institution,
October 27–29, 1977

Smithsonian Institution Press
Washington, D.C.
1980

Copyright © 1980 Smithsonian Institution
Library of Congress Cataloging in Publication Data
Main entry under title:

Migrant birds in the neotropics.

(Symposia of the National Zoological Park)
Bibliography: p.
1. Birds—Latin America—Congresses. 2. Birds—
Latin America—Migration—Congresses. 3. Birds,
Protection of—Latin America—Congresses. I. Keast,
Allen. II. Morton, Eugene S. III. Series:
Washington, D. C. National Zoological Park. Symposia
of the National Zoological Park.
QL687.A1M53   598.298   80–607031
ISBN 0-87474-660-4
ISBN 0-87474-661-2 pbk.
Second printing, 1982

This volume is dedicated to the memory of Paul Schwartz, whose studies of territoriality in Northern Waterthrushes in Venezuela have stimulated many ornithologists to study migrant birds as integral components of tropical ecosystems.

Contents

Foreword

Thirty years ago and earlier, publications on avian biology in the earth's tropical zones were largely confined to resident species. Interest in temperate zone migrants was rare; mention of such species largely incidental. With the coming of an intensive field of research in theoretical ecology involving spatial arrangements, territory, and competition, a good deal of interest in smaller passerine species, especially migrants, has shifted to speculation on the evolution and life history of such species in the tropics and their dispersal and foraging strategies in different competitive situations with resident congeners.

This interest led us at the Smithsonian to organize a symposium on the avifauna of northern Latin America in 1966, in which one of the major participants was the late Robert H. MacArthur, colleague of many years, whose interest in spatial separation of New World warblers and their evolution, during his graduate work at Yale, had led to his development into one of our foremost theoretical ecologists. The results of this seminar were published in 1970.

Now, nearly 10 years later, we have had a second Smithsonian seminar on the problems of migrant temperate species wintering in the New World tropics. This event, of compelling interest in the field of comparative ecology, has been a source of particular satisfaction to me. The symposium and this volume have combined research of great fascination with a new sense of urgency, including work by Professor John W. Terborgh, a highly appropriate successor to our friend, Professor MacArthur.

As President of the International Council for Bird Preservation, I take especial satisfaction that ecologists of all persuasions are alert to the threat presented to their field of research by the violent and steady degradation of avian habitats. The tropical zones of the world are threatened as never before by the massive assist of technology in the conquest of primary forests. As forests dwindle and disappear from the terrestrial tropics, the relative balance of bird species shifts and crucially changes in the temperate zones as well. The pesticides and herbicides of capital-intensive agriculture complete the destruction of the original flora and fauna, whether resident or, in this case, migratory.

Those of us concerned with conservation fear that we are witnessing an irreversible series of shifts in biotic balance. I pray that the Smithsonian will continue this seminar, in a cyclical series, so that we may document these massive environmental events, if we cannot arrest them. If only an institution had been witness to the degradation and desertification of the Middle East. What a tremendous amount we would have learned if those events, far slower in time, to be sure, could have been documented. Now we know enough to list these current events in the neotropics in detail. Perhaps in a generation the message of this research and scientific reporting will have sunk in. One could wish ecologists of a generation ago had had the intuition and the persuasive power to be able effectively to counsel governments to control careless proliferation of technology and growth of population.

S. Dillon Ripley

Contributors

The most recent addresses of the editors and of the contributors, in alphabetical order, are given below. Their addresses at the time the research results were presented appear at the head of each article.

HUMBERTO ALVAREZ
Departamento de Biología, Universidad del Valle, Apartado Aéreo 2188, Cali, Colombia

JON C. BARLOW
Department of Ornithology, Royal Ontario Museum, 100 Queen's Park, Toronto, Ontario, Canada M5S 2C6

SARA E. BENNETT
Sandy Pond, Richmond, New Hampshire 03470

WILLIAM H. BUSKIRK
Department of Biology, Earlham College, Richmond, Indiana 47374

ROBERT CHIPLEY
The Nature Conservancy, 1800 North Kent, Arlington, Virginia 22209

JEAN-LUC DESGRANGES
Canadian Wildlife Service, 2700 Boulevard Laurier, P.O. Box 10100, Ste. Foy, Quebec, Canada G1V 4H5

JOHN T. EMLEN
Department of Zoology, University of Wisconsin, Madison, Wisconsin 53706

JOHN R. FAABORG
Division of Biological Sciences, University of Missouri-Columbia, Columbia, Missouri 65201

PETER FEINSINGER
Department of Biological Sciences, University of Florida, Gainesville, Florida 32601

JOHN W. FITZPATRICK
Field Museum of Natural History, Roosevelt Rd. at Lake Shore Dr., Chicago, Illinois 60605

STEPHEN FRETWELL
Division of Biology, Kansas State University, Manhattan, Kansas 66502

PETER R. GRANT
Department of Zoology, University of Michigan, Ann Arbor, Michigan 48109

RUSSELL GREENBERG
Museum of Vertebrate Zoology and Department of Zoology, University of California, Berkeley, California 94720

HENRY A. HESPENHEIDE
Department of Biology, University of California, Los Angeles, California 90024

STEPHEN L. HILTY
3401 N. Columbus, Tucson, Arizona 85712

RICHARD L. HUTTO
Department of Zoology, University of Montana, Missoula, Montana 59801

DANIEL H. JANZEN
Department of Biology, University of Pennsylvania, Philadelphia, Pennsylvania 19104

TERRY B. JOHNSON
Department of Ecology and Evolutionary Biology, University of Arizona, Tucson, Arizona 85721

JAMES KARR
Department of Ecology, Ethology, and Evolution, University of Illinois, Champaign, Illinois 61820

ALLEN KEAST
Department of Biology, Queen's University, Kingston, Ontario, Canada K7L 3N6

THOMAS R. KEMP
Department of Biology, University of Toledo, 2801 West Bancroft Street, Toledo, Ohio 43606

Douglass H. Morse
Division of Natural Sciences and Mathematics, Brown University, Providence, Rhode Island 02912

Eugene S. Morton
National Zoological Park, Smithsonian Institution, Washington, D.C. 20008

J. Peter Myers
Museum of Vertebrate Zoology, University of California, Berkeley, California 94720

Jorge E. Orejuela
Departamento de Biología, Universidad del Valle, Apartado Aéreo 2188, Cali, Colombia

David L. Pearson
Department of Biology, Pennsylvania State University, 208 Life Sciences, University Park, Pennsylvania 16802

George V. N. Powell
U.S. Fish and Wildlife Service, Patuxent Wildlife Research Center, Laurel, Maryland 20811

Kerry N. Rabenold
Curriculum in Ecology, University of North Carolina, Chapel Hill, North Carolina 27514

Ralph J. Raitt
Department of Biology, New Mexico State University, Las Cruces, New Mexico 88003

Mario A. Ramos
Instituto de Ecologia Tropical
Xalapa, Veracruz, Mexico

John H. Rappole
Department of Zoology, University of Georgia, Athens, Georgia 30602

Stephen M. Russell
Department of Ecology and Evolutionary Biology, University of Arizona, Tucson, Arizona 85721

Paul Schwartz (deceased)
Ministerio del Ambiente y de los Recursos Naturales Renovables, Estación Biológica de Rancho Grande, Apartado 184, Maracay, Aragua, Venezuela

Neal G. Smith
Smithsonian Tropical Research Institute, APO Miami, 34002 Balboa, Canal Zone

F. Gary Stiles
Escuela de Biología, Universidad de Costa Rica, Ciudad Universitaria "Rodrigo Facio," Costa Rica

John W. Terborgh
Department of Biology, Princeton University, Princeton, New Jersey 08540

Elliot J. Tramer
Department of Biology, University of Toledo, 2801 West Bancroft Street, Toledo, Ohio 43606

Robert B. Waide
Section of Birds, Carnegie Museum, Pittsburgh, Pennsylvania 15213

Dwain W. Warner
Bell Museum of Natural History, University of Minnesota, Minneapolis, Minnesota 55455

Edwin O. Willis
Department of Biology, University of Miami, Coral Gables, Florida 33134

Introduction

The nearctic–neotropical migration system is one of the world's greatest and most complex, birds from the whole length and width of the North American continent being compressed into Middle America and northern South America, a land area a fraction of the breeding area's size. The neotropics are, nevertheless, extremely rich as bird habitat, supporting the world's richest endemic avifauna. These features pose fascinating questions. Where do the different northern migrants winter, what are their spatial utilization patterns in the wintering grounds, how is competition between congeners minimized? Are the adaptations of migrants different in any way from tropical residents; do they exclude each other from certain habitats? What collective devices might be operative to minimize interspecific competition for limited resources?

Many of us who have spent time in the neotropics in winter have asked ourselves these questions. This volume, and its antecedent symposium, came into being thanks to the Smithsonian Institution's National Zoological Park and Friends of the National Zoo who, in October 1977, made funds available to bring together a range of tropical workers at Front Royal, Virginia.

As anyone who has ever organized a symposium knows, there are inevitable gaps (and commonly important gaps) in content. This symposium was no exception. We were however, singularly fortunate to have a dozen or so younger workers who were completing Ph.D. theses on migrant-resident interactions in the neotropics. The book, accordingly, suddenly acquired a highly topical aspect. We tried to find colleagues willing to review such aspects of the migration system as the evolution of migratory and resident races, climatic history in the main overlap zones, and the biology of (admittedly few) migrants within Neotropica. In the interests of making the book relatively complete, the two editors developed syntheses summarizing, or drawing attention to, a series of additional facets of migration systems. A most important facet of the whole story, the future of migrants in a region of the world subject to rapid clearing and biological change was, however, advanced to the preeminent position of the opening chapter. Here, Dr. John W. Terborgh draws on the joint findings of the 40 authors in a synthesis: "The Conservation Status of Neotropical Migrants: Present and Future."

The arrangement followed in the book is for a pair of introductory chapters (Terborgh, Schwartz) to be followed by a series of treatments of specific groups: the shorebirds (that winter in the far south of Neotropica) in associations of austral species (Myers); hawks, where only four species extensively penetrate Neotropica (Smith), and three groups of small insectivores (flycatchers, vireos, and warblers) that together make up the bulk of the northern breeders wintering in Neotropica (Fitzpatrick, Keast, Barlow). A series of regional treatments follow. Here successive authors consider migrant-resident interactions in particular areas: Florida and the Bahamas (Emlen); West Indies (Terborgh and Faaborg); Yucatán Peninsula of Mexico (Waide); Barro Colorado Island, Panama, (Willis); Panamanian forests (Hespenheide); lowlands and highlands of northern Colombia (Russell, Johnson); western Colombian forests (Orejuela, Raitt, Alvarez, and Hilty), and Ecuador, Peru, and Bolivia (Pearson). Resource partitioning between migrant and resident in Mexico is the subject of a chapter by Hutto and comparative foraging ecology (in Costa Rica) of one by Tramer and Kemp. Three studies on specific warbler species follow: Black-throated Green Warbler (Rabenold), Blackburnian Warbler (Chipley), and American Redstart (Bennett), in which the ecology and behavior of these species in breeding and wintering grounds are contrasted. Rappole and Warner review a detailed study on ecological aspects of bird behavior at a specific study site (southern Veracruz, Mexico). Two papers on the comparative ecology of resident and migrant nectar-feeding hummingbirds follow (DesGranges and Grant; Feinsinger). General discussions of the evolutionary implications of habitat relations of migrants and residents by Stiles, and seasonal changes in migrant behavioral ecology (Morton) follow.

Five papers away from the main theme but of particular relevance in the evolutionary context conclude the series. These are the influence of meteorological patterns on trans-Gulf migration patterns (Buskirk); demographic aspects of long-distance migration (Greenberg); population limitation in migrants (Morse); migration relative to the regulation of bird numbers (Fretwell); food abundance (Janzen), and a comparative survey of Old and New World migrants (Karr).

We hope that this volume will answer some of the above questions and, especially, that it will provide the stimulus for much more research in this rich and diversified area of fast-shrinking avian habitat.

We are indebted to the staff of the N.Z.P. Conservation and Research Center at Front Royal for their help during the symposium and to Kathleen A. Lynch for her professional copy editing.

Allen Keast
E. S. Morton

Conservation

JOHN W. TERBORGH
Department of Biology
Princeton University
Princeton, New Jersey 08540

The Conservation Status of Neotropical Migrants: Present and Future

ABSTRACT

There is far more reason to be alarmed about the status of land birds wintering in the neotropics than of water birds. Deforestation is occurring more rapidly than is destruction of water bird habitats.

About half of all land birds breeding in North America go to Mexico, the Bahamas, Cuba, and Hispaniola. Migrants commonly make up 50 percent of bird numbers in these northern areas and lesser percentages as one goes south into southern Middle America. Since many migrants are concentrated in winter, clearing 1 ha of forest in Mexico is probably equivalent to clearing 5–8 ha in northeastern United States.

Many migrant species prefer tropical highlands and these areas are rapidly being preempted for agriculture. Forest habitats are, in general, more important for many migrant species than was previously thought. Continued tropical deforestation will result in major reductions in many species.

Two-thirds of the breeding pairs of birds of many North American forests and woodlands migrate to the neotropics. The annual pilgrimages of this vast avian hoard to and from its tropical retreat are spectacles of such compelling richness and variety that they entice even the most indolent birdwatcher into the field. Yet in spite of our intense preoccupation with their goings and comings, it was not until comparatively recently that we took more than a casual notice of where all the birds go and what they do there.

This symposium, splendidly conceived in its timeliness, presents the first comprehensive information on both these questions, and offers the earliest glimpses of an overview of how more than 150 species sort themselves into their winter homes. My aim here is to draw upon the available information to formulate some broad generalities relating to the present and prospective conservation status of Neotropical migrants.

Before launching into specifics, I will preface my remarks with the qualification that apart from the following paragraphs, they will pertain to land birds only. The fact that only one of the 38 papers given at Front Royal digressed from a staple fare of land birds (Myers' article on shorebirds) suggests that this is where the main focus of interest lies. But more importantly from a conservation standpoint, there is far more reason to be alarmed about the status of land birds. It is the land in the neotropics that is being transformed before our eyes, not so much the water. Shorebirds, ducks, herons, terns, and others tend to scatter widely in the off season and to concentrate opportunistically wherever good feeding sites are discovered. Many live near or in salt water, which, relative to fringing land masses, is a virtually undisturbed environment. Local deterioration due to pesticide run-off or the sluicing of industrial wastes may result in the loss of some feeding areas, or even occasional mass die-offs. But a few widely scattered blots on the shoreline are unlikely to affect the status of whole species populations. It is only when persistent toxic chemicals such as DDT begin to contaminate the seas on a regional or global scale that whole populations become endangered. It is hoped that we are now alert to the threat of global contamination and prepared to take international action to prevent it.

As for the freshwater environments used by grebes, rails, gallinules, some waterfowl, herons, and others, most of these are not currently in serious jeopardy either. Wetlands beyond the limits of North America are largely intact. Drainage, filling, and canalization are in the main conveniences (vices?) of affluent societies. To be sure, there is cause for concern as marshes in Cuba, Colombia, and elsewhere are converted to rice paddies, but as yet the transformation of wetlands has not reached the massive and near universal scale of deforestation. It is the consequences of deforestation that will be our primary concern.

Distribution of Migrants in the Neotropics

Before we consider the effects of habitat destruction per se, it will be helpful to have a general picture of where migrant land birds go. Prior to this symposium, one could have given only a vague account. Now there are some real data (table 1). In terms of absolute numbers, clearly near areas are preferred to far ones. Using the density of resident birds as a gauge against which to calibrate migrant concentrations, the role of distance as a decisive factor in the choice of wintering grounds is obvious. In Mexico and the Bahamas, migrants commonly make up 50 percent or more of the winter populations in a broad spectrum of both natural and disturbed habitats. Progressively more remote destinations in the Caribbean harbor fewer and fewer migrants: Hispaniola—20–40 percent (various habitats); Puerto Rico—10–20 percent; Lesser Antilles, Trinidad and Tobago—1 percent or less. A similar pattern holds along the Central American isthmus and into South America. Decreasing from the high proportions found in Mexico, values of 20–40 percent are reported for Costa Rica and Panama, of 5–15 percent for Colombia, of <1 percent for forested habitats in Venezuela, and presumptively similar values for Ecuador, Peru, and Bolivia.

It seems likely that as much as half of all the land birds that go south of the United States each winter funnel into Mexico, the Bahamas, Cuba, and Hispaniola, which offer a combined area of 2,175,000 km^2 as compared to 16,200,000 km^2 for North America south of the tree line. Rough as these numbers are, they strongly imply that many migratory populations are concentrated severalfold on their wintering grounds. In the case of shorebirds wintering on the Argentine pampas (which may be extreme) the concentration factor can be as much as 10 or more (Myers this volume). The obvious and unsettling implication of this is that the effects of tropical habitat destruction are amplified several times; clearing 1 ha of forest in Mexico is equivalent to expanding urban sprawl by perhaps 5–8 ha in the Northeast. With over half the natural vegetation of Central America and the Greater Antilles already converted to cropland and pasture, and the remainder disappearing at a rate of a few percent a year, we seriously face the prospect that suitable habitat will no longer be available for many migrant species by the end of the century (cf. Food and Agricultural Organization [FAO] estimates in the article by D. H. Morse).

John W. Terborgh

While it may be true that forests are disappearing, it does not follow necessarily that the total amount of usable habitat for migrants is being reduced. Indeed, there is at least one sanguine forecast that opening up of the primary forest may result in a higher carrying capacity for migrants (Monroe 1970). Let us see how the information at hand bears on such predictions.

Habitats Used by Overwintering Migrants

There are two oft-repeated statements about the habitat choice of migrants in the neotropics that lie somewhere between myth and fact. They are that migrants concentrate at middle elevations (1,000–2,000 m; Miller 1963; Willis 1966; Leck 1972; Smith 1975) and in second growth, such as in fragmented woodlands and along edges, more than in primary vegetation (e.g., Slud 1960; Willis 1966; Karr 1976). Results of this symposium provide a basis for evaluating both statements.

Middle Elevation vs Lowlands

The conventional wisdom here appears to be true for some areas and not for others. In west central Mexico, for example, the situation seems quite the reverse. High concentrations of migrants winter in the Pacific lowlands, and declining numbers occur in the interior plateaus and mountains (Hutto this volume). At this latitude (ca 20°N), winter temperatures may be low enough at elevations above 1,500 m to depress insect activity, an interpretation that is in accord with Hutto's data. In southern Mexico (latitude 16–18°), it is probable that larger numbers of migrants occur in the mountains. However, the lowlands at this latitude harbor impressive concentrations (up to >50 percent; Waide et al this volume) so that numbers in the highlands are unlikely to be noticeably higher. In Hispaniola and Jamaica, the only two Carribbean islands with appreciable areas above 1,500 m, the density of migrants appears to be nearly independent of elevation (Terborgh and Faaborg this volume; Lack and Lack 1972).

The initial impressions that migrants prefer highlands came from studies in Panama, Costa Rica, and northern South America. In these regions the generalization does indeed seem to stand up (e.g., Tramer and Kemp; Orejuela et al; Russell; Johnson, all this volume). The reasons for the attraction of mountain habitats at these latitudes is obscure. While a more amenable winter temperature regime may contribute to the preferential concentration of individuals in the northern Mexican lowlands, it is clear that a different explanation will have to be invoked to account for the

pattern at lower latitudes. Migrants abandoned a tract of lowland thorn scrub in Colombia when the vegetation became leafless with the onset of the dry season (Russell this volume). Several sets of measurements agree that insect densities in Panama and Costa Rica reach an annual minimum in the December to March dry season (Janzen 1973; Smythe 1974; Ricklefs 1975; Buskirk and Buskirk 1976). Perhaps the impact of seasonality is reduced at higher elevations, with a consequently better and more reliable supply of harvestable resources. Moreover, Janzen (1973, 1976) has found, both in Costa Rica and in Venezuela, that insect densities are substantially higher in mid-elevation vegetation than in the lowlands or at very high elevation (>2,500 m). This may well be the decisive consideration, because an individual bird's feeding rate will depend, more than on anything else, on the absolute abundance of available prey. Other things being equal, one would expect wintering birds to concentrate in regions offering the greatest abundance of food resources. The number of competitors becomes important only when prey are at low density or are being exploited at greater than the recruitment rate.

There is little consolation to be had in the finding that large numbers of migrants do winter in tropical highlands, for it is the highlands that are preferentially preempted for agricultural use (Monroe 1970; Howell 1970; Terborgh 1977). Very little natural vegetation remains between 1,000 m and 2,000 m in Hispaniola, southern Mexico, the central Andes of Colombia, the pacific slope of Costa Rica, and Panama, for example, and what little remains in other areas is being rapidly reduced. Thus, one prediction that can be made with confidence is that species which use or concentrate in primary forest in the neotropical highlands can be expected to be among the first to come under heavy pressure due to loss of habitat (e.g., Blackburnian Warbler, Black-throated Green Warbler, Cerulean Warbler).

Primary Vegetation vs Disturbed Habitats

Another oft-repeated assertion is that migrants gravitate to disturbed sites such as clearings, second growth, and edges, because such places are presumptively underutilized by resident species (Willis 1966). Some support for this impression is contained in data presented in this volume by Emlen (Bahamas), Hutto (Western Mexico), Pearson (Ecuador, Peru, Boliva), Waide (Southern Yucatan), and Willis (Panama). All these results are concordant in showing greater concentrations of migrants in disturbed or successional vegetation than in nearby undisturbed tracts. (However, in some other regions, migrants seem to be

Table 1. Proportional representation of North American migrants in winter bird populations in the neotropics

Location	Elevation[1]	Vegetation	Method[2]	Number of sites
Middle America				
West Central Mexico	Low	Gallery forest	Strip count	2
" " "	"	Mangrove	" "	3
" " "	"	Plantation	" "	1
" " "	"	Second growth	" "	2
" " "	"	Forest edge	" "	1
" " "	"	Thorn scrub	" "	2
" " "	"	Tropical deciduous forest	" "	2
" " "	Mid	Oak woodland	" "	3
" " "	"	Pine-oak	" "	5
" " "	"	Pine	" "	1
" " "	High	Pine-oak-fir	" "	2
" " "	"	Fir	" "	1
North Yucatán	Low	Disturbed	" "	3
" "	"	Partly disturbed	" "	3
" "	"	Semi-deciduous forest	" "	3
Campeche	"	Old field	Nets	3
"	"	Semi-evergreen forest	"	3
Yucatán Peninsula	"	Semi-evergreen forest	"	2
" "	"	Semi-evergreen forest	Strip count	8
Costa Rica	Mid	Disturbed	? ?	?
" "	"	Cloud forest	?	?
Panama	Low	Moist forest	Nets	1
" (Canal Zone)	"	Late scrub	"	1
" " "	"	Disturbed forest	"	1
Panama (Puercos Island)	Low	Semi-deciduous forest	Nets	1
" (Canal Zone)	"	Moist forest	Strip count	1
" " "	"	Dry forest	" "	1
" (Barro Colorado Island)	"	Moist forest	" "	1
" " "	"	Young moist forest	" "	1
" " "	"	Scrub	" "	1
" " "	"	Grass, trees	" "	1
" " "	"	Lake edge	" "	1
" " "	"	Marsh	" "	1
Carribean Islands				
Bahamas	"	Mature pines	Strip count	?
"	"	Young pines	" "	?
"	"	Old fields	" "	?
"	"	Broadleaf thicket	" "	?
"	"	Marsh	" "	?
"	"	Mangrove flat	" "	?
"	"	Coastal dunes	" "	?
Jamaica	"	Dry limestone forest	" "	?
"	"	Arid limestone scrub	" "	?
"	"	Cut over arid scrub	" "	?
"	"	Cut over limestone forest	" "	?
"	"	Secondary limestone forest	" "	?
"	"	Riverine forest	" "	?
"	"	Gardens, etc.	" "	?
"	Mid	Gardens, etc.	" "	?
"	High	Gardens, etc.	" "	?
"	Low	Mangroves	" "	?
"	"	Evergreen forest	" "	?

Percentage migrants[3]	Reference
68	Hutto[6]
81	"
51	"
62	"
48	"
57	"
19	"
33	"
43	"
32	"
24	"
37	"
34	Tramer 1974
22	" "
26	" "
54	Waide[6]
38	"
53	Waide et al.[6]
29	" " "
20–30	Tramer & Kemp[6]
<5	" " "
5	Karr 1976
4	" "
7	" "
25	Karr 1976
6	Hespenheide[6]
18	"
8	Willis[6]
17	"
100?	"
24	"
17	"
8	"
39	Emlen[6]
28	"
40	"
43	"
47	"
50	"
50	"
31[4]	Lack & Lack 1972
21[4]	" " " "
5[4]	" " " "
42[4]	" " " "
32[4]	" " " "
33[4]	" " " "
13[4]	" " " "
29[4]	" " " "
16[4]	" " " "
49[4]	" " " "
33[4]	" " " "
13[4]	Lack & Lack 1972

equally abundant in various types of primary and secondary vegetation, e.g., Bahamas [Emlen, this volume], Jamaica [Lack and Lack 1972], northern Yucatán [Tramer 1974]). But before we jump to the conclusion that habitat destruction is not a serious threat to migratory populations, let us consider how such findings should be qualified.

First, we should be aware that only minor quantitative differences in the proportions of migrants are involved. In some instances, this could be explained by the presence of relatively fewer residents as well as by increased absolute densities of migrants.

Another, and far more vital consideration, is the identity of the species themselves. It is not surprising that large numbers of Palm Warblers, Yellow Warblers, Orchard Orioles, and Indigo Buntings can be found in settled areas and in early successional growth. But such species are not at present a source of concern. It is the species that shun disturbance that are being threatened by deforestation, and there are a large number of these (table 2). A sizeable fraction of our migrants are intrinsically forest-dwelling species. Those that nest in forest tend to winter in them as well, although on the wintering grounds some of them may be able to make greater opportunistic use of edges and openings than is the case when they are confined to breeding territories.

Finally, it is necessary to take into account the relative areas, and the rates of change in area, of suitable wintering habitat. The weight given to different types of vegetation in the census data reported in this volume is surely biased. Not one observer reported on the birds seen in a fenced cattle pasture, canefield, or rice paddy, yet a large and increasing fraction of the land in tropical America is being occupied by "habitats" such as these. The emphasis on "edge" is certainly exaggerated by the frequency with which roads and paths pass along them, indeed, create them. Unbroken expanses of forest are often inaccessible, lacking trails, and present serious impediments to the ease of bird detection, especially in the canopy. Even if edges and second growth do contain greater concentrations of birds, their combined area in the neotropics as a whole is still a small fraction of that of semimature to mature forest. This means that most individuals are wintering in mature vegetation, as Pearson (this volume) has rightfully emphasized, notwithstanding their somewhat greater dispersion.

Land-Use Trends in Temperate and Tropical America and Their Implications for Migratory Populations

Since the arrival of settlers in North America, all but perhaps 1 percent of the landscape east of the great plains and south of 50° latitude has been logged, and

Table 1. (cont.)

Location	Elevation[1]	Vegetation	Method[2]	Number of sites
Jamaica	Mid	Evergreen forest	Strip count	?
"	High	Evergreen forest	" "	?
"	Low	Riverine forest	" "	1
Hispaniola	"	Moist forest	Nets	1
"	Mid	Moist forest	"	2
"	Low	Limestone forest	"	2
"	"	Arid scrub	"	1
"	"	Open pine forest	Strip count	2
"	Mid	Open pine forest	" "	2
"	High	Open pine forest	" "	1
"	Low	Limestone forest	" "	2
"	"	Secondary scrub	" "	2
"	"	Arid thorn scrub	" "	2
Puerto Rico	"	Limestone scrub	Nets	1
(Mona Island)	"	Limestone scrub	"	1
St. Kitts	"	Montane forest	"	1
" "	"	Shrubby field	"	1
Montserrat	"	Montane forest	"	1
Guadeloupe	"	Montane forest	"	1
"	"	Sclerophyll scrub	"	5
Dominica	"	Montane forest	"	1
Trinidad	Low	Moist forest	"	1
"	"	Semi-deciduous forest	"	1
"	"	Shrubby field	"	1
Tobago	"	Secondary forest	"	1
"	"	Maritime forest	"	1
San Andres	"	Disturbed scrub	"	1
South America				
Northern Colombia	Low	Thorn scrub	Nets	1
" "	"	Mangroves	"	1
" "	"	Disturbed forest	"	1
" "	Mid	Cloud forest	"	1
Southern Colombia	Low	Wet forest	"	1
" "	"	Dry forest	"	1
" "	Mid	Cloud forest	"	1
" "	Low	Wet forest	Strip count	1
" "	"	Dry forest	" "	1
" "	Mid	Cloud forest	" "	1
" "	"	Disturbed oak forest	" "	1
Northern Venezuela	Low	Deciduous forest	Nets	1
" "	Mid	Montane forest	"	1
" "	High	Montane forest	"	1
Ecuador	Low	Moist forest	Strip count	1
"	"	Secondary vegetation	" "	1
Peru	"	Evergreen forest	" "	1
"	"	Secondary vegetation	" "	1
Bolivia	"	Evergreen forest	" "	1
"	"	Secondary vegetation	" "	1

[1] Low 0–1,000 m; Mid 1,000–2,000 m; High >2,000 m.

[2] Included under strip count are many individual variants; most commonly an observer walks slowly along a course, recording all individual birds detected, whether seen or heard.

[3] Percentage of North American migrants in the total of all birds detected.

[4] Lack and Lack recorded the percentage of migrants among passerines only, hence their figures are higher than would be the case if they had included all birds (as nearly all migrants in Jamaica are passerines).

[5] Pearson only provided encounter rates (in birds per hr) for migrants, with no data on residents.

[6] This volume.

Percentage migrants[3]	Reference
17[4]	Lack & Lack 1972
38	Gochfeld 1979
46	Terborgh & Faaborg[6]
22	" " "
31	" " "
3	" " "
29	" " "
40	" " "
28	" " "
16	" " "
25	" " "
3	" " "
14	" " "
7	" " "
1	" " "
4	" " "
0.5	" " "
2	" " "
0.4	" " "
0	" " "
0	" " "
0	" " "
1	" " "
2	" " "
1	" " "
32	Russell & Johnson[6]
(Oct–Nov) 24 (Dec) 0	Russell & Johnson[6]
46	" " "
6	" " "
5	Hilty[6]
0	Orejuela et al.[6]
24	" " "
14	" " "
0	" " "
22	" " "
14	" " "
46	Chipley[6]
2	Terborgh & Faaborg[6]
0	" " "
0	" " "
0.29b/h[5]	Pearson[6]
5.29b/h	"
0.07b/h	"
2.68b/h	"
0.00b/h	"
0.16b/h	"

most of it has been cleared at one time or another. The west has not been ravaged to the same extent because of the low agricultural potential of most naturally forested land in that part of the continent. At no time has the total extent of forest in North America decreased to less than half the original amount. Many eastern states report increasing amounts of forest cover, often exceeding 50 percent of their areas (Aldrich and Robbins 1970). Drastic alterations in the ratio of forested to open land since colonial times have certainly had profound impacts (both positive and negative) on the abundances of many terrestrial species. Many distributions have also changed, although historical documentation is scanty. Taking North America as a whole, the total acreage in forest has decreased by perhaps 30–40 percent since pre-Columbian times. We can expect proportional reductions in the populations of most forest-dwelling birds. Further reductions have probably occurred in some regions due to the fragmentation of forest into discrete woodlots. A growing body of evidence indicates that these insular patches do not provide acceptable habitat for many obligate forest birds (Forman et al 1976; Galli et al 1976; Whitcomb et al 1976; Whitcomb 1977). Species whose population centers lie in the crowded and highly agricultural states of the mid-Atlantic region and Midwest will of course have suffered by greater margins than those that occupy the comparatively undisturbed boreal regions and western mountains.

The wave of agricultural settlement that passed across eastern North America in the nineteenth century did not lead to permanent occupancy because of the availability of even more productive lands farther west. The effects on our forests were partial, transitory, and spread out over more than a century. Such cannot be said of the tropical regions that constitute the winter homes of many forest-dwelling migrants. Settlement of new land is being propelled by rapid population growth, just as it was in nineteenth-century North America, but population densities in many countries are well above current, much less historical, North American levels. Moreover, the best terrain is already under cultivation, and settlement is being pushed by hunger and crowding onto ever more marginal soils and steeper slopes. In my experience, clearing is not selective and confined to the richest hollows as it was, say, in the Appalachians, but instead it advances as a front that consumes the entire landscape, except perhaps for the steepest ridgetops and ravines. Even these are often subject to gradual denudation as the sole remaining sources of firewood in the landscape.

After a few cycles of cropping, cattle or goats are turned onto the land which is periodically burned to keep the weeds in check. I could see this pattern plainly in a recent flight along the Pacific slope of Panama from David to Tocumen. Cattle raising has taken over the whole scene; the land is being used just as intensively as it is in Illinois or Iowa; little or no forest remains, and there is very little that could be called second growth. The Dominican Republic is in much the same state, and Haiti is even worse. Environmental deterioration has not progressed so far in some countries (Guatemala, Nicaragua) but with accelerating population pressure everywhere, it is only a question of time.

The notion that second growth will provide a haven for migratory populations is, I think, largely fallacious. Current land-use practices in tropical America may favor a few species, such as the Yellow Warbler and Indigo Bunting as I suggested above, but most migrants prefer tree crowns or the cool dark recesses of the forest interior. The habitat requirements of the latter categories of species are not met by shrubby pastures or canefields.

Because most migrant species and individuals are essentially forest dwelling birds, it seems clear that the gross carrying capacity of the neotropics is decreasing. This is evident in the FAO statistics quoted by Morse which show that the sum total of primary and secondary forest is declining rapidly as ever greater areas are brought under cultivation or converted to pasture. Even with no acceleration in the rate of deforestation over the 1955–70 averge, the remaining primary forest in Central America will have disappeared completely by the end of the century unless control measures are promptly instituted. This presents a gloomy prospect for migrant and resident species alike.

The likelihood that conditions will stabilize, as they have in North America, with a sizeable portion of the landscape covered by middleaged second growth, seems remote. Under the traditional system of slash-and-burn agriculture, such an equilibrium was possible; indeed it existed in parts of a number of countries. However, the current trend is away from extensive land-use practices and toward more intensive ones. A shifting slash-and-burn economy was possible in low density peasant cultures, or on the frontier. But the frontier era is coming to an end in much of tropical America today, just as it did in North America about a century ago. Central governments are extending their control and services into the remotest villages. Increasingly, land is coming under title, and rural peasants are adapting to a more sedentary way of life for the sake of being close to roads, villages, and schools. These structural transformations in rural society assure ever more intensive exploitation of the landscape.

Table 2. North American migrants wintering in mature tropi[cal] forest[1]

Mississippi Kite	Blue-winged Warbler
Swallow-tailed Kite	Bachman's Warbler
Broad-winged Hawk	Tennessee Warbler
Chuck-will's-widow	Parula Warbler
Whip-poor-will	Magnolia Warbler
Yellow-billed Cuckoo	Cape May Warbler
Black-billed Cuckoo	Townsend's Warbler
Yellow-bellied Sapsucker	Black-throated Green Warbler
Great Crested Flycatcher	Hermit Warbler
Yellow-bellied Flycatcher	Black-throated Blue Warbler
Acadian Flycatcher	Cerulean Warbler
Western Flycatcher	Yellow-throated Warbler[3]
Eastern Wood Pewee	Grace's Warbler[3]
Western Wood Pewee	Blackburnian Warbler
Wood Thrush	Chestnut-sided Warbler
Swainson's Thrush	Bay-breasted Warbler
Gray-cheeked Thrush	Blackpoll Warbler
Veery	Ovenbird
Blue-gray Gnatcatcher	Northern Waterthrush[2]
Solitary Vireo	Louisiana Waterthrush
Yellow-throated Vireo	Kentucky Warbler
Red-eyed Vireo	Hooded Warbler
Philadelphia Vireo	Canada Warbler
Black-and-white Warbler	American Redstart
Prothonotary Warbler[2]	Western Tanager[3]
Swainson's Warbler	Scarlet Tanager
Worm-eating Warbler	Hepatic Tanager[3]
Golden-winged Warbler	

[1] Many of the species listed have broad habitat tolerances and may winter [in] middleaged second growth, such as along borders. Only a relative few sh[ow] strong partiality for undisturbed forest.

[2] Primarily in mangroves.

[3] Primarily in pines.

Other trends reinforce this projection: continued population growth, replacement of labor-intensive farming by capital-intensive agriculture, rising land values, and the existence of inexhaustible export markets for certain commodities, notably timber and beef.

Prospectus

What do these trends presage for the future? Certainly the amount of habitat that is attractive to migrants will diminish, probably drastically. Even generous allotments for parks and reserves will not prevent a very major deterioration of the overall picture. The

John W. Terborgh

best that could be hoped for would be 10–20 percent of the land under some kind of protected status. Because migrant populations are already more crowded on their wintering grounds than in their summer ranges, this amounts to little more than a token solution.

One could anticipate that the landscape of a typical Middle American country by the end of the twentieth century might resemble that of one of our more crowded eastern states. Consider, for example, my own, New Jersey, with a population density of 370 persons per km^2. Virtually all its prime land is under cultivation or engulfed by urban sprawl. Sizeable tracts of forest persist in only two areas of negligible agricultural value. These are the pine barrens and the series of steep rocky ridges transecting the northwestern corner of the state. Elsewhere, the existing forest is highly fragmented into scattered woodlots that show conspicuous signs of pathology with respect to their nesting birdlife (Forman et al 1976; Galli et al 1976). To the extent that it is permissible to project this pattern onto developing countries, we can anticipate that the land will be exploited to the fullest except where rugged topography or infertile soils raise cost/benefit ratios to prohibitive levels. Something akin to natural vegetation will persist longer in the least desirable sectors of the landscape, but eventually the demands for charcoal, firewood, building materials, and ultimately goat range will overtake even the most inhospitable terrain, as indeed they already have in Haiti. This final stage of utter devastation seems to set in when rural population densities reach approximately 150 persons per km.^{2} Some countries (El Salvador, Haiti, Jamaica) have already passed this threshold, while others are only a generation or two away from it. The situation may not be desperate yet, but there is no room for complacency.

Reforestation, as currently practiced in tropical countries, offers little hope of restoring useful habitat to overworked lands. Monocultures of exotic species such as pine, eucalyptus, and teak are notoriously barren of birds. Coffee and cacao plantations provide far more amenable environments. Mixed sylviculture, which at this point in the tropics is more a dream than a reality, would go a good step further.

Another source of relief would be possible if some species could shift the focus of their populations into less-disrupted portions of the tropics. This is a plausible prospect for a few species, such as Swainson's Thrush, Black-and-white Warbler, and Redstart that winter from Mexico well into South America, and which demonstrably possess the ability to live in sympatry with a broad spectrum of potential competitors. The winter ranges of many others, however, are far more limited, and appear frequently to be constrained by the presence of close competitors in adjacent regions (c.f. Fitzpatrick, Keast, Terborgh, and Faaborg, this volume). It is unlikely that many of these would be successful in accomplishing major range shifts.

Conclusion

My own assessment of the situation is that continued deforestation in the near neotropics will result in major reductions in the numbers of many forest-dwelling migrants. We are, in effect, about to play observers in a massive experiment in which there will be dramatic alterations in the relative population sizes of numerous common species. No one can yet say which species will be most affected, or what all the consequences will be.

The most obvious prediction is that in North America permanent residents and temperate migrants will be enabled to expand their populations in substitution for missing tropical migrants. There are already signs that this is taking place in some fragmented eastern woodlands (Whitcomb et al 1976; Whitcomb 1977). We can expect further that the species most versatile at wintering successfully in a wide variety of disturbed habitats will be able to expand into niches left vacant by competitors with more inflexible requirements for mature vegetation. It would be risky to go beyond this level of generality in making more specific predictions. No species, except perhaps for the Bachman's and Kirtland's Warblers, seems under imminent threat of extinction (Terborgh 1973). Indeed, for the foreseeable future, the possibility of outright extinctions seems remote. Some species will surely become rarer, others more abundant. The total biomass of birds breeding in the North American continent will probably change little. What will change is the familiar ambience of our forests in springtime. It just won't sound the way it used to.

Literature Cited

Aldrich, J. W., and C. S. Robbins.
1970. Changing abundance of migratory birds in North America. In: *The Avifauna of Northern Latin America*, eds. H. K. Buechner and J. H. Beuchner, Smithsonian Contrib. Zool. 26:17–25.

Buskirk, R. E., and W. H. Buskirk
1976. Changes in arthropod abundance in a highland Costa Rica forest. Amer. Midland Natur. 95:288–98.

Chipley, R. M.
1976. The impact of wintering migrant wood warblers on resident insectivorous passerines in a subtropical Colombian oak woods. Living Bird 15:119–41.

Forman, R. T. T., A. E. Galli, and C. F. Leck.
1976.   Forest size and avian diversity in New Jersey wood-lots with some land-use implications. Oecologia 26: 1–8.

Galli, A. E., C. F. Leck, and R. T. T. Forman.
1976.   Avian distribution patterns in forest islands of different sizes in central New Jersey. Auk. 93:356–64.

Howell, T. R.
1970.   Avifauna in Nicaragua. In: *The Avifauna of Northern Latin America*, eds. H. K. Buechner and J. H. Buechner, Smithsonian Contrib. Zool. 26:58–61.

Janzen, D. H.
1973.   Sweep samples of tropical foliage insects: effects of seasons, vegetation types, time of day, and insularity. Ecol. 54:687–708.

———
1976.   Changes in the arthropod community along an elevational transect in the Venezuelan Andes. Biotropica 8:193–203.

Karr, J. R.
1976.   On the relative abundance of migrants from the north temperate zone in tropical habitats. Wils. Bull. 88:433–458.

Lack, D. and P. Lack.
1972.   Wintering warblers in Jamaica. Living Bird 11:129–153.

Leck, C. F.
1972.   The impact of some North American migrants at fruiting trees in Panama. Auk 89:842–50.

Miller, A. H.
1963.   Seasonal activity and ecology of the avifauna of an American equatorial cloud forest. Univ. Calif. Publ. Zool. 66:1–78.

Monroe, B. L., Jr.
1970.   Effects of habitat changes on population levels of the avifauna in Honduras. In: *The Avifauna of Northern Latin America*, eds. H. K. Buechner and J. H. Buechner, Smithsonian Contrib. Zool. 26:38–41.

Ricklefs, R. E.
1975.   Seasonal occurrence of night flying insects on Barro Colorado Island. Journ. New York Entomol. Soc. 83:19–32.

Slud, P.
1960.   The birds of Finca "La Selva," Costa Rica: a tropical wet forest locality. Bull. Amer. Mus. Nat. Hist. 121: 53–148.

Smith, N. G.
1975.   "Spshing noise": biological significance of its attraction and non-attraction by birds. Proc. Nat. Acad. Sci. 72:1411–14.

Smythe, N.
1974.   Biological monitoring data-insects. In: *1973 Environmental Monitoring and Baseline Data*, ed. R. W. Rubi-

noff, Smithsonian Inst. Environmental Sci. Prog., Washington, pp. 70–115.

Terborgh, J.
1974.   Preservation of natural diversity: the problem of extinction prone species. Bio Science 24:715–22.

1977.   Bird species diversity on an Andean elevational gradient. Ecol. 58:1007–19.

Tramer, E.
1974.   Proportions of wintering North America birds in disturbed and undisturbed dry tropical habitats. Condor 76:460–64.

Whitcomb, R. F.
1977.   Island biogeography and "habitat islands" of eastern forests I. Introduction. Amer. Birds 31:3–5.

Whitcomb, R. F., J. F. Lynch, P. A. Opler, and C. S. Robbins.
1976.   Island biogeography and conservation: strategy and limitations. Science 193:1030–32.

Willis, E. O.
1966.   The role of migrant birds at swarms of army ants. Living Bird 5:187–231.

John W. Terborgh

PAUL SCHWARTZ
Ministerio del Ambiente y de los Recursos Naturales
    Renovables
Estación Biológica de Rancho Grande
Apartado 184
Maracay, Aragua, Venezuela

Some Considerations on Migratory Birds

ABSTRACT   Migrant species should not be considered "invaders" to the tropics but as species that have tropical niches the same as resident species.

When reading publications relating to the question of the role of migrant birds in tropical ecosystems, and in conversations on this topic, I have been impressed by the apparent belief that such migrants must constitute a rather disturbing force on their wintering grounds. The word impact is used generally, and the migrants are not infrequently referred to as invaders. To some degree this may be a matter of semantics, but it is evident that the implication is in full accord with the basic meaning of the words impact and invader. That implication is not consistent with the true situation.

I make clear that my field work has not been directed specifically to the question at hand. Beginning some 20 years ago, however, I conducted a 6-year study of the Northern Waterthrush (*Seiurus noveboracensis*) on its wintering grounds in northern Venezuela. That study included some work with the American Redstart (*Setophaga ruticilla*) and observations of other migrants from North America. At that time considerations of interspecific competition in regulating animal distributions, now prominent in ecological and speciation research, had barely entered the scene. My investigation was motivated by a desire to determine concretely, using banded birds, if wintering migrants showed intraspecific territoriality and if so whether they returned to occupy the same territories in successive years. Circumstantial evidence from previous observations had suggested that might be the case.

Among the results of that study I found that individual Northern Waterthrushes were commonly present on their winter territories for at least six months and some American Redstarts for at least seven months (Schwartz 1964:172–75). Note that these are residence times of individual birds. The species as a whole is present in northern South America more than eight months. This long period of residence becomes even more significant when we consider that it includes that portion of the year, the dry season, when the food supply for many birds is at a minimum level.

Competition, Resource Levels, and Migrant Niches

At the lower elevations subject to a strong seasonal influence, the depression of resources, at least for insectivorous birds, is readily apparent to the human observer. In riparian or analogous situations, or in montane regions where cloud cover maintains an evergreen vegetation, a depression of such resources is less apparent, but it is necessary only to experience the resurgence of invertebrate life with the return of the rains to realize that there is fluctuation in invertebrate abundance in the annual cycle in the evergreen montane areas.

I shall not discuss the why and how of migration. It is enough for our consideration to think that present patterns of migration and of seasonal climate and resource availability have probably been in effect for thousands of years; and at some time or times in the past the now-migratory species or their ancestral forms may have been resident in tropical areas for even longer periods.

At some times in the past, probably relating to the times of glaciation, the normal processes of evolution have determined which species have survived and the ecological niches they have forged for themselves. The now-migratory species have been subject to selective pressures in the tropics, and in many of the same places, as have the species that are tropical breeding residents. Together with the tropical breeding species, they have been subject also to the effects of climatic cycles that resulted in significant contractions and expansions of wooded areas in the tropics. In that competitive situation, some now-migratory birds won their place, and it seems probable they may have done so at the expense of some tropical breeding residents. Those niches won are still occupied by their winners for almost 70 percent of the year and have been so occupied every year for thousands of years. The competitive situations just mentioned involved not only migratory species vs tropical breeding species but also interspecies interactions among the migratory species themselves (and among the tropical breeding species themselves) which have bearing on the tropical distributions as we find them today.

During the relatively short annual absences of the waterthrush and the redstart I have not seen that their niches are occupied by tropical breeding residents. It should not be inferred from this that these are necessarily marginal niches. They are obviously rewarding niches in communities of dozens of resident breeding species that would almost surely include one to occupy these niches if they had not been won by the migratory species in ecological evolutionary history.

Besides the waterthrush and the redstart, several other migratory species appear to be intraspecifically territorial or competitive in their tropical homes, to judge from circumstantial evidence in casual observation over many years' field work in Venezuela. I have not observed active competition between these species and tropical breeding residents. That some tropical breeding species may sometimes or in some places forage in niches temporarily abandoned by migratory species is not grounds to suppose that they are otherwise being crowded out by migrant "invaders." They may be only exploiting opportunistically a resource area to which they do not have access during the major portion of the time, one that does not really belong to them. It is possible that in some regions seasonal replacement may even have evolved as a fixed

Paul Schwartz

pattern. It is difficult to evaluate this aspect today. Man-wrought changes to natural tropical habitats during the past 100 years (or longer), and especially during the past 15–20 years, have altered conditions to the extent that we are today witnessing a new chapter in ecological evolution.

Of course, not all migratory species (nor all tropical breeding species) are individually territorial in fixed areas during their nonbreeding period. Some, such as the Tennessee Warbler (*Vermivora peregrina*), are partially or largely nectar or fruit eaters. Social behavior and flexible mobility are apparently the most successful strategies for exploiting such resources, which may provide abundant food but are spatially and temporally scattered (Morton 1971; Snow 1971, 1976:72–74). Flocking by some largely insectivorous birds has also, no doubt, its reason for being.

The concepts of impact and invasion are, of course, associated primarily with the time of fall migration, the idea being that, at a time of year when the tropical ecosystem is presumably already saturated with the resident breeders and their offspring of the year, it is invaded by a horde of migrants. The real situation does not conform to that concept.

In those regions subject to seasonal influence, the period of minimum resource availability (the dry season) almost certainly constitutes an important force regulating the density of populations. Even assuming saturation at the minimum resource level, given the low reproduction rate of tropical breeding birds, the population can not expand itself in one season to exploit fully the "normal" resource level; and, anyway, it seems probable that this could be undesirable, as suggested by Willis (1966: 221). The result is that vast portions of habitat apparently appropriate to one or another species are not occupied during the periods of normal abundance (the rainy season). In much of the lower north Tropical Zone, north of the equatorial rain belt, September and October are among the months of greatest rainfall. Insect life, while not at its maximum, is still ample. There are also fruiting and flowering trees. Therefore, at the time of fall migration the tropical ecosystem is in a state of normal abundance and is not saturated by the tropical breeding birds. This, however, is largely irrelevant, for as previously mentioned the tropical breeding species and the migratory species have their respective niches long since established.

The competition during the fall migration is among the migrants, mainly if not entirely at the intraspecific level in recent time. Even this is less than it might seem, for not all the migrants arrive simultaneously; they are spread over a period of two months or more centering around mid-October, so that some migrants of passage have already left a given area before others arrive. And at this time resources are still at normal levels. It is after this time that any separation due to competition occurs. The birds most affected are the offspring of the year. During the previously mentioned Northern Waterthrush study, I could see year after year the effect on November population levels as habitat deteriorated in December and January with the advancing dry season. Bear in mind that those birds over a year old that survive to return to their tropical homes have territories awaiting them that have been proven to hold valuable resources the previous year(s). Besides, the birds have learned something of the hazards and dangers in those territories. Not all losses are attributable directly to insufficient resources; many, maybe most, may be due to inexperience. Under deteriorating conditions, the young birds are continuously more exposed than the old birds to new, unknown conditions.

With regard to the long-running debate as to why birds breeding in northern regions lay more eggs than their tropical breeding counterparts, it has been suggested that an important pressure leading to this may be losses sustained in competition on the tropical wintering grounds. So far as it concerns migratory species I have long believed, and the little evidence available suggests although it cannot prove it, that the most important pressures contributing to evolution to larger clutch size in northern breeders relate directly to the migration process itself. To the obvious hazards deriving from various variable natural phenomena, we may add individual variation in preparation for the migration: individual birds, perhaps influenced by the behavior of their fellows, depart on migratory flights before they are physiologically fully prepared. Also, during the transient period of migration not only the young but also the older individuals are frequently exposed to the inexperience factor in regions where they may descend briefly or through which they may travel during their movements between their tropical homes and their breeding grounds.

Several other topics could be developed under the general theme treated in this paper, but they would do little more than illustrate the many manifestations of the evolutionary process; or would amount mainly to mental exercise, for the fact is that we know little or nothing of the basic material thrown into the process at its beginning. The important point to be made is that during two-thirds of the year, including the periods of least resources for insectivorous birds, the neotropics harbors and has harbored for thousands of years an avifauna that is best treated as a single unit. Some of the species of that avifaunal unit depart for a brief period each year to reproduce. They return to the tropics not as invaders with a disturbing impact but to their long-ago won places.

Literature Cited

Morton, E. S.
1971.   Food and migration habits of the Eastern Kingbird in Panama. Auk 88:925–26.

Schwartz, P.
1964.   The Northern Waterthrush in Venezuela. Living Bird 3:169–184.

Snow, D. W.
1971.   Evolutionary aspects of fruit-eating by birds. Ibis 113:194–202.

Snow, D. W.
1976.   *The Web of Adaptation*. New York: Quadrangle/New York Times.

Willis, E. O.
1966.   The role of migrant birds at swarms of army ants. Living Bird 5:187–231.

Migration of Taxonomic Groups

J. P. MYERS
Museum of Vertebrate Zoology
University of California, Berkeley
Berkeley, California 94720

The Pampas Shorebird Community: Interactions Between Breeding and Nonbreeding Members

ABSTRACT   The shorebird community in coastal Buenos Aires Province, Argentina, includes nonbreeding migrants from North and South America as well as locally nesting species. Data indicate that the nonbreeding birds are numerically dominant through the year, and that they have major effects on the breeding community: 1) local breeders are taxonomically and ecologically distinct from migrants present during the breeding season; 2) those that migrate south from coastal Buenos Aires Province wintering grounds to breed in Patagonia in austral spring are more similar to North American migrants (present during austral spring and summer) than are species which do not leave; 3) the distributions of several potential competitors among South American (breeding) and North American (nonbreeding) species resemble geographic replacement patterns, and 4) aggressive interactions occur repeatedly between North and South American species. High densities of nonbreeding birds may prevent scolopacids from establishing local breeding populations: breeding attempts would be unsuccessful because of behavioral and competitive interactions with "wintering" scolopacids. Patterns in resource use by migrants vs resident shorebirds do not support the generalization that migrants depend on more ephemeral resources than do residents.

Figure 1. Coastal Buenos Aires Province, Argentina, showing the location of the major study site, Estancia Medaland. Inset indicates the position of coastal Buenos Aires Province within South America.

Detailed work to date on migrants within Central and South America in relation to resident avifauna deals almost exclusively with warblers and related passerine groups. This concentrated effort has yielded valuable insights and has generated a set of hypotheses concerning the ways that migrant and resident members of a community coexist (Karr 1976 this volume). But the restricted taxonomic scope needs broadening before we can examine these insights as possible features of migrant-resident interactions in general.

Migrant shorebirds offer a useful system for comparison. We could scarcely ask for a group more taxonomically and ecologically distinct from warblers. But both groups indulge in a wide range of migratory tendencies, from permanent residency to migrations

J. P. Myers

spanning the Northern and Southern Hemispheres. Because of these diverse migratory behaviors, migrants annually descend upon sets of resident species in different areas within the neotropics.

One such place is the coastal zone of Buenos Aires Province, Argentina (figure 1). North American shorebirds invade this region each austral spring just as local birds begin to nest. While few basic ecological data are available for its shorebirds, information which does exist (Dabenne 1920; Wetmore 1927; Olrog 1967; Myers and Myers 1979) offers a tantalizing pattern of clues on the nature and magnitude of interactions within the shorebird community. I will review these patterns here, examining habitat use, representative densities, and seasonal changes in community composition within the area; and then, in a speculative vein, I will consider whether the data suggest important impacts of the North American species on the breeding community.

My approach rests on the assumption that competition plays a fundamental role in generating the observed patterns, despite recent (and merited) criticisms of competition theory (Weins 1977). By all means, the speculative nature of my arguments should be borne in mind. But the fact remains that competition offers a useful, and as yet irreplaceable, paradigm for considering different community patterns. Its limitations do not vitiate its usefulness in an exploratory exercise such as this, so long as they are not ignored.

Coastal Buenos Aires Province: the Shorebird Community

Geographically the coastal zone of Buenos Aires Province sits at the eastern edge of the Argentine Pampas, a vast temperate grassland characterized by low relief, moderate temperatures, and winter and spring rains (Walter 1973). From July 1973 to December 1974 I studied sandpiper spacing patterns in the area between Punta Rasa and Mar del Plata (figure 1). This region abounds in shorebird habitats, and over 30 shorebird species have been observed there (Myers and Myers 1979).

Shorebirds in coastal Buenos Aires use a spectrum of habitats which lie along a gradient extending from littoral sandy beaches to upland grasslands (figure 2). While many species commonly occur in several habitat types, their patterns of habitat use cluster into three overlapping groups: those exclusively littoral, those using wetlands in both tidal and nontidal areas, and those using uplands. Fifteen out of the 26 species in figure 2 restrict themselves to either littoral or inland areas: birds which forage on sandy beaches, for example, tend not to enter the inland grassland-wetland mosaic, while species foraging in grasslands usually do

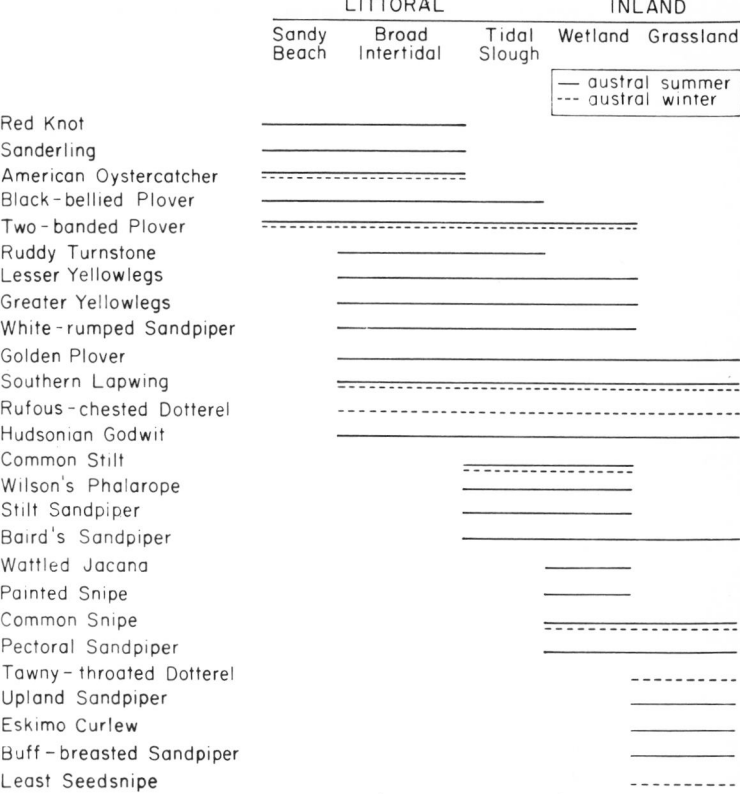

Figure 2.   Habitat use by shorebirds in coastal Buenos Aires Province, Argentina. Habitats are arrayed along a littoral-inland gradient. Solid line represents each species' distribution during austral summer; dashed line during winter.

not stray into littoral areas. The wetland group ranges widely over different habitats, with several members regularly using grasslands, particularly after rains. Although comprised of fewer species (see below), the winter community of austral shorebirds shows the same general pattern along this littoral-inland gradient.

The table does not quite bring out, however, the concentration of shorebird activity in interior habitats during both seasons. Compared to the abundance of wetlands and grasslands, shorebird littoral habitat in coastal Buenos Aires Province is restricted, and as a result, total shorebird numbers are greater in the inland zone. I will return to this point later in considering scolopacid breeding.

Seasonal Changes

The numbers and taxonomic affinities of species using Buenos Aires Province are given for summer and winter seasons in table 1. As shown there, the number of shorebird species present in austral summer far exceeds those present in the winter; migrant sandpipers from North America account for much of the rise.

Table 1. Seasonal representation of shorebird families, coastal Buenos Aires Province, Argentina

Family	Austral summer		Austral winter
	Total	Breeding	Total
Jacanidae	1	1	0
Rostratulidae	1	1	0
Haematopodidae	1	1	1
Recurvirostridae	1	1	1
Charadriidae	4	2	4
Scolopacidae	15	1	1
Thinocoridae	0	0	1
Total	23	7	8

Few scolopacids breed south of 35°N, even though many migrate to the Southern Hemisphere during the boreal winter. Only one scolopacid, the Common Snipe (*Capella gallinago*), remains during austral winter; it is also the only scolopacid to breed locally. Thus, between August and January, the community changes from one dominated by charadriids to one composed largely of scolopacids. This massive replacement must have considerable importance for the competitive environment of other members of the local community. Where charadriids and scolopacids have been compared in north temperate regions, consistent ecological differences emerge at the familial level, both in terms of foraging behavior (Baker and Baker 1973, Pearson and Parker 1973) and the morphology of feeding apparatus (Burton 1974). From winter to summer, the dominant method of feeding in the community of Pampas shorebirds changes from one emphasizing the visual pecking of plovers to the probings of sandpipers.

The magnitude of this switch differs between habitats. Two scolopacid inhabitants of the grasslands in summer are often noted for their plover-like foraging behaviors (Upland Sandpiper, *Bartramia longicauda*, and Buff-breasted Sandpiper, *Tryngites subruficollis*), so that their replacement in winter by South American plovers may make little difference in community feeding style. But seasonal replacements in wetland and littoral habitats will effect radical changes as the summer emphasis on probing disappears abruptly with the onset of northward migration in austral fall.

Densities

North American species pile into coastal Buenos Aires Province in great numbers. Few data describe their densities, but those available suggest that through much of austral spring and summer, North American species dominate the local community. For example, along a 3 km muddy stream transect, I found White-rumped Sandpipers (*Calidris fuscicollis*) in densities of 20 to 30 birds/km for much of the austral summer (Myers and Myers, ms). Only one South American species, the Two-banded Plover (*Charadrius falklandicus*), bred on the stream banks, and during its nesting season its density remained below 3 birds/km. However as nonbreeding plovers began arriving in January its density rose to 15 birds/km, and by late May it reached levels of at least 30 birds/km. By this time White-rumped Sandpipers had left the region in migration. Similarly, in an upland grassland plot North American species were numerically dominant following their arrival in late September. The only breeding species, Southern Lapwings (*Vanellus chilensis*), averaged below 1 bird/ha from September through November. Yet Buff-breasted Sandpipers and American Golden Plovers (*Pluvialis dominica*) reached combined densities of 15 to 25 birds/ha in October and November.

Interactions Among Pampas Shorebirds

The obvious question is whether this accumulation of nonbreeding birds during austral summer affects the breeding community. Several lines of admittedly speculative reasoning indicate that it does. The evidence is of three sorts: marked dissimilarity between North American migrants and locally breeding shorebird species, several cases where the geographic distributions of wintering North American species and breeding South American species resemble allopatric replacement patterns, and consistent aggressive interactions between North and South American shorebirds. And I will argue that the most dramatic effect of nonbreeding waders in South Temperate America has been to prevent all scolopacids (save the Common Snipe) from setting up breeding populations.

Breeding species tend to contrast sharply from the invading North Americans. Four are from taxonomic groups quite distinct from the plovers and sandpipers which arrive from North America: Wattled Jacanas (*Jacana jacana*, Jacanidae), South American Painted Snipe (*Nycticryphes semicollaris*, Rostratulidae), American Oystercatcher (*Haematopus palliatus*, Haematopodidae), and Common Stilt (*Himantopus himantopus*, Recurvirostridae). Species also differ as a result of conspicuous features related to foraging ecology, such as the Common Snipe's feeding behavior and bill, the size difference between Southern Lapwings and the smaller North American plovers, or the crepuscular and nocturnal foraging behaviors of South American

J. P. Myers

Painted Snipe. Or species may differ more subtley, for example in preferred foraging site. In a multivariate study of foraging microhabitat I found the Two-banded Plover uses sites very distinct from any used by North American shorebirds present concurrently in coastal Buenos Aires Province (Myers 1976). Certainly, we expect to find differences between co-occurring species if they are examined with sufficient care (Wiens 1977). In fact it would be surprising to find them the same in all respects. But the point here is that a large number of North American waders spend most of their annual cycle in coastal Buenos Aires Province. Yet none breed there, nor do any similar shorebirds, even though other shorebird species do.

This enigma becomes more apparent upon considering the species which migrate south to breed after spending the austral winter in coastal Buenos Aires Province. Of the eight southern species wintering in the region, those migrating farther south as North American species arrive in austral spring are the ones most likely to face significant competition from the invaders due to size, habitat use, and taxonomy: the Tawny-throated Dotterel (*Oreopholus ruficollis*), the Rufous-chested Dotterel (*Zonibyx modestus*), and the Two-banded Plover (a partially migratory species). Figure 3 shows the winter distributions of several North American species, comparing them with the breeding ranges of the above-mentioned plovers; these maps resemble classic geographic replacements. This is also true for the one breeding scolopacid, the Common Snipe (*Capella gallinago paraguaeiae*, *C. g. magellanica*, and *C. g. andina*), when its range is compared with that of the migrant North American Subspecies, *C. g. delicata*. Lesser Seedsnipe (*Thinocorus rumicivorus*) are a conspicuous exception to this general pattern.

Regular aggressive encounters between North and South American species also suggest competitive interactions. For example, both the Rufous-chested Dotterel and the Two-banded Plover fight repeatedly with White-rumped Sandpipers during late austral summer and early austral spring. This investment of time and energy into aggression is predictable if one assumes that they compete for limited resources (MacArthur 1972). Southern Lapwings provide the most extreme example of aggressive interactions with North American species when they defend a moving territory around their foraging chicks from interspecific intruders, principally North American migrants. Lapwings sporadically chase other species early in their breeding season, but, as hatching nears, the adults attack ferociously. Even after their eggs hatch, adult lapwings may forage closely to other species without aggression. But if the other shorebirds come close to lapwing chicks, the adults chase the other birds

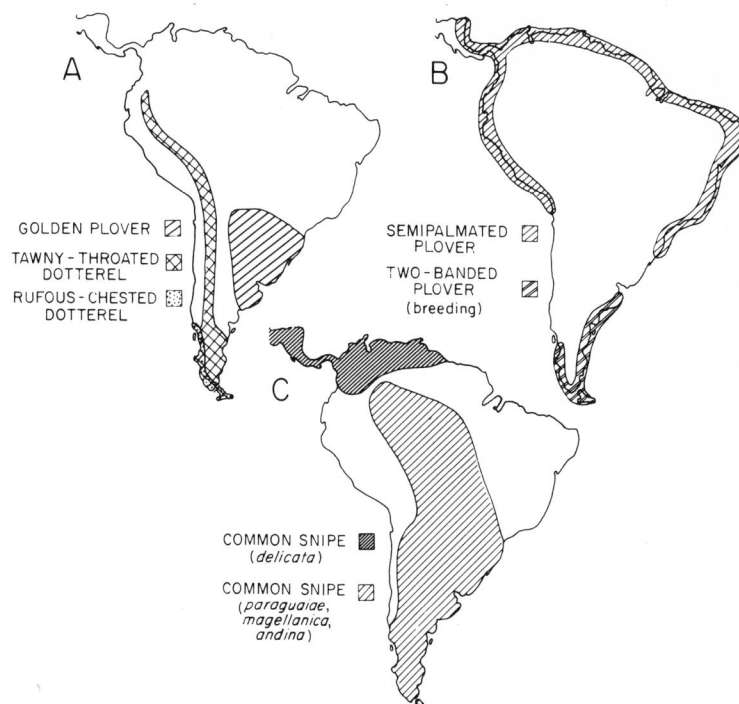

Figure 3. Distributions of shorebird species in South America suggestive of geographic replacements. A. American Golden Plover wintering range compared to Tawny-throated and Rufous-chested Dotterel breeding distributions. Both Dotterel species winter during austral winter in regions used by American Golden Plovers during austral summer. B. Semipalmated Plover winter range during austral summer compared to Two-banded Plover breeding range during same season. Both species use similar microhabitats. Records of Semipalmated Plovers farther south in Chile and Argentina appear to be exceptional occurrences. C. Wintering range of Common Snipe (*Capella gallinago delicata*, the North American subspecies) compared to breeding ranges of South American breeding subspecies (*C.g. paraguaiae*, *C.g. magellanica*, and *C.g. andina*) combined.

away. The contrast in adult behavior—not protecting their own feeding site but chasing others away from their young—is particularly striking in cases when the adults are foraging at some distance from their brood. Under these circumstances, the adults will feed placidly near other species, but, if their chicks are approached, the adults attack ferociously. Two explanations seem possible: adults may be discouraging other shorebirds from the chicks' vicinity to reduce predator attraction, or the behavior may result in lessened competition for food. This latter hypothesis is particularly intriguing because of the lack of aggression toward other shorebirds feeding near the adults. While the lapwing may overlap little with other shorebirds in food choice because of its large size compared to the North American species, this is probably not the case for lapwing chicks.

The Case of the Missing Scolopacids

The almost complete absence of breeding scolopacids is not just a quirk peculiar to Buenos Aires Province, but instead is true for the entire South Temperate Zone (Moreau 1966; Lack 1976). Scolopacid breeding species number rises sharply along a latitudinal gradient north of the equator, particularly above 30°N (figure 4). South of the equator in the New World all breeding scolopacids belong to the genus *Capella*, and there are never more than a few species at a given latitude.

This pattern poses a complex biogeographic problem. Why do not more scolopacids extend their breeding distributions into south temperate areas, and in our case here, to coastal Buenos Aires Province? The issue encompasses a broad set of considerations from both historical zoogeography and ecology, which I suggest can be distilled to two general hypotheses: either that scolopacids cannot reach the Southern Hemisphere, i.e. a problem of dispersal; or that once there, something prevents their establishment. These are difficult ideas to test, but I am willing to speculate here that the latter is more likely, and in fact that the abundance of nonbreeding migrants from the Northern Hemisphere lies at the root of the problem. My argument is as follows.

Scolopacids are a northern group, with much of their diversification understandable in terms of the changing glacial patterns in the Northern Hemisphere (Larson 1957). It could be inferred from this that they simply have not reached the Southern Hemisphere yet. But that is obviously too simple: they arrive each year in hordes during their nonbreeding season, and many individuals remain through austral winter while the bulk of their populations are off breeding in the Arctic. The problem cannot be just the mechanics of getting there.

We might ask, however, whether migration to a winter range can lead to an expansion of breeding distribution. Pitelka (pers. comm.) argues that traditional patterns in migration, breeding, molt, and other physiologically controlled processes pose an insurmountable barrier to the sort of phase change necessary here: to begin breeding in the South Temperate Zone would require a scolopacid to switch its annual cycle 180°, from nesting in May–July to October–December. That would appear highly unlikely for birds just having bred in the north, but it might be more probable for individuals which had not made their northerly migrations that year.

While Pitelka's suggestion deserves full consideration, data suggest that the cycles can be reversed. Moreau (1966) reports a few scattered breeding records for one Old World scolopacid, the Common Sandpiper

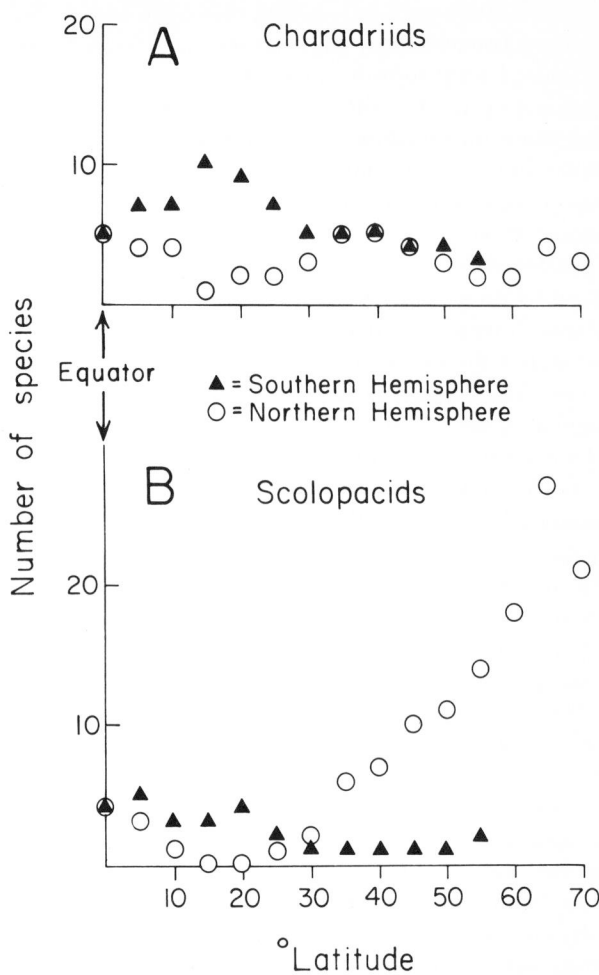

Figure 4. Numbers of breeding shorebird species at different latitudes within the Western Hemisphere. *A. Charadriidae, B. Scolopacidae.*

(*Tringa hypoleucos*) south of the Sahara, even though this species normally breeds in the Northern Hemisphere. Moreau also mentions White Storks (*Ciconia ciconia*), House Martins (*Delichon urbica*), and European Bee-eaters (*Merops apiaster*) as sporadic breeders in their winter ranges. Similar records apparently do not exist for South America. But given the known individual variation in annual cycles (Immelmann 1971; Berthold 1975), the numbers of birds involved in scolopacid migrations, and the length of time over which these migrations have occurred, mistakes in annual cycle must have occurred repeatedly. The problem at hand thus becomes one of identifying factors which preclude these natural experiments in range expansion from succeeding.

This argument does not dismiss the importance of proximate control over physiological processes. Work with Bobolinks (*Dolichonyx oryzivorus*), a North American breeder migrating to temperate South America during the boreal winter, has examined at great length

J. P. Myers

how this species avoids breeding in the Southern Hemisphere (Engels 1962; Hamner and Stocking 1971). Rather, I want to shift our attention toward the evolutionary pressures which place such a strong selective premium on breeding only in the north, that proximate physiological controls exercise such precise, if not immutable, influence over reproductive timing and distribution.

Marked differences exist between breeding habitats used by scolopacids and areas used in coastal Buenos Aires Province, particularly for species using littoral sites. But the extent to which these alone would prevent all scolopacids from breeding is debatable, and probably not enough to account for their absence. That no shorebirds breed in broad intertidal areas is not that surprising, since none in north temperate regions have solved this problem either. Unfledged young would have to move too far too quickly in order to use the food resources normally exploited by shorebirds in these habitats, dominated as they are by tidal changes in water position. Perhaps even more telling is the lack of cover and resultant vulnerability of chicks to predators. If anything, the shiny surface of a mudflat would accentuate the profile of crouching young.

But as I pointed out earlier, many shorebirds in coastal Buenos Aires Province use the inland mosaic of wetlands and grasslands. How habitat characteristics per se might prevent breeding here is much less obvious. Not only do South American waders breed in these habitats, but in North America several shorebirds also reproduce in similar temperate grasslands and wetlands, including two species wintering on the Pampas: Upland Sandpipers breed in grasslands over a wide range of temperate North America, and Wilson's Phalaropes (*Steganopus tricolor*) nest in marshes in northwestern United States not strikingly dissimilar from those they use during the nonbreeding season in Buenos Aires Province. Congeners of the Hudsonian Godwit (*Limosa haemastica*) and of the Eskimo Curlew (*Numenius borealis*) have also succeeded in breeding in North American habitats similar to those used by these two on the Pampas. These observations suggest that habitat differences alone are insufficient to explain the absence of scolopacids.

Instead, it appears that the very presence of high numbers of nonbreeding birds effectively prevents their successful breeding. I will outline the main points of my argument here and then consider them in more detail below. The extent of winter scolopacid habitat in south temperate areas is small relative to the area used during breeding, and this induces very high densities in wintering populations. For a sandpiper to breed during this period would require it to assume large time and energy budget costs, costs compounded

above the levels normally incurred in the breeding season by the density of conspecifics. Yet these same densities generate conditions of very heavy intraspecific competition for food. In fact, evidence suggests that competition during the nonbreeding period may be a limiting factor for shorebird population sizes. Thus, reproductive activities would place large time and energy budget demands on a bird just at a period when its abilities to obtain food were being heavily tried. The combined effects of these two factors—high costs for reproductive behaviors and competition for food—would undermine any attempts at reproduction. Any individual trying to breed under these circumstances, rather than waiting until its return to the normal breeding range, would clearly be selected against.

This speculative argument rests on several considerations. First, the limited availability and dispersion of suitable habitat in shorebird nonbreeding areas induces marked and unavoidable increases in local densities on the wintering ground. Recher (1966) first discussed this with reference to the competitive regime in winter shorebird communities along coastal California. And as Jehl (1975) points out, the effect of limited habitable area for shorebirds is exacerbated in southern South America by the magnitude of difference in land mass available in North and South America at equal latitudes (figure 5). While ideally the comparison should be between a real extent of appropriate habitat in breeding vs winter ranges, total land mass provides a crude index, particularly when the difference is of such strong magnitude. The fact that many arctic species breed along extensive coastal sectors on the Arctic Ocean makes the contrast even starker. For example, the Pectoral Sandpiper (*Calidris melanotos*) breeds in an almost unbroken strip from central Siberia eastward into the Canadian Arctic. Yet the entire species compresses into a small portion of South America during its nonbreeding season (parts of Argentina, Uruguay, and Paraguay), and within that region its habitat is far from continuous. As a result of this sort of compression, shorebirds wintering in South America reach high densities. For example, Golden Plovers maintain densities on an Argentine grassland plot of approximately 10 birds/ha while breeding densities in northern Alaska rarely exceed 0.2 birds/ha (Myers and Myers 1979; Myers and Pitelka unpubl. data). On both these areas, Golden Plovers are defending territories.

Most North American wader species wintering on the Pampas inland habitat mosaic defend nonbreeding territories (Myers and Myers ms); their defended areas are usually one-tenth to one-hundredth the size of those defended by the same species during the breeding season (Myers et al 1979). Certainly the adaptive

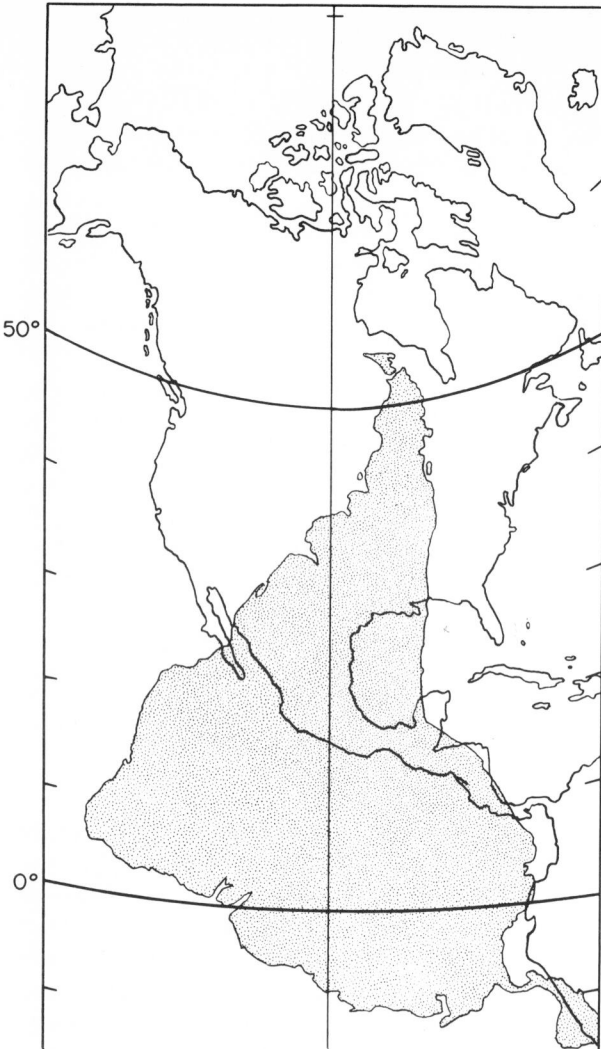

Figure 5.   Equal-area projection of North and South America. South America has been rotated around the equator to illustrate the different amount of land mass available at equivalent latitudes in each hemisphere.

value of these differences is difficult to interpret, especially lacking comparative data on food densities or indisputable evidence on the food-based nature of shorebird breeding territories. Nevertheless, breeding territories are large, limited in supply, and costly to maintain in terms of time and energy required for defense (Holmes 1966; Myers and Pitelka unpubl. data). Similarly, nonbreeding territories require a considerable investment of time for defense (up to 30 percent of time sampled under some circumstances; Myers et al 1979); they are also limited in the sense that territorial individuals are quickly replaced by new birds when removed (based on unpublished experiments with White-rumped Sandpipers in Argentina). If successful reproduction requires exclusive use of an area within the size range of those normally used during the Arctic breeding season, then breeding could

be impossible in coastal Buenos Aires Province simply because a bird would be unable to support the high time and energy budget costs of defense, even given unlimited food.

If resources are limited for wintering shorebirds, as Recher (1966) as well as Baker and Baker (1973) have argued, then it would be unlikely that a bird could achieve any appreciable increase in food intake, making it impossible to obtain the additional energy required for breeding.

Consider the following situation. Each year substantial numbers of several scolopacid species remain during austral winter instead of traveling north to their breeding grounds. Data from other areas suggest that these are probably first-year birds (Elliot et al 1976). It is not surprising that these birds do not breed during austral winter because of seasonally lowered levels in their food supply. But what happens during the subsequent austral spring, when local reproduction gets under way and the bulk of North American shorebird populations return from the Arctic? Given the length of time that these migrations have gone on and the numbers of individuals involved, the natural experiment of trying to breed must have occurred repeatedly, particularly among those first-year birds which remained through austral winter. They are the age class where we can reasonably expect to find the greatest natural variation in reproductive timing—i.e., chance of error—and further, they have not just returned from a reproductive effort in the north. Were such experiments successful, with reproductive success comparable to north temperate breeding areas, scolopacids would quickly become established in the south. They do not because of the high density of competing individuals.

Other factors certainly contribute to the absence of breeding scolopacids. Habitat selection, the improbability of a 180° phase shift in annual cycle, and traditional patterns in migration all reduce the probability of a breeding attempt. In fact by this stage in scolopacid history they may be the most conspicuous and immediate reasons for the low rate of breeding attempts. But these factors have undergone a long selective process and are proximate mechanisms controlling the location and timing of breeding; the density of conspecifics is the chief ultimate selective factor at work. Thus, conspecific density has placed a high premium on precise physiological mechanisms to ensure that the birds go north to breed, and this acts as an insurmountable obstacle for successful reproduction in coastal Buenos Aires Province.

Migrant-Resident Interactions

Finally, we can consider what this community suggests

J. P. Myers

Figure 6. Short-grass Pampas uplands on Estancia Medaland, coastal zone of Buenos Aires Province, Argentina. This habitat is the principal foraging site of several North American shorebirds during austral summer, including the Buff-breasted Sandpiper (*Tryngites subruficollis*) and American Golden Plover (*Pluvialis dominica*). It is also favored nesting habitat for the Southern Lapwing (*Vanellus chilensis*). During austral winter it is used by Tawny-throated Dotterels (*Oreopholus ruficollis*) and Rufous-chested Dotterels (*Zonibyx modestus*).

Figure 8. Mud-banked arroyo in coastal Buenos Aires Province, Argentina. The receding waters generate favored habitat for several North and South American shorebird species, particularly White-rumped Sandpipers (*Calidris fuscicollis*) and the Two-banded Plover (*Charadrius falklandicus*).

Figure 7. Destruction of virgin short-grass uplands for agriculture in coastal Buenos Aires Province, Argentina. Increased planting of corn and other crops in marginal croplands is reducing the area of upland habitat suitable for shorebird foraging.

Figure 9. Southern Lapwing (*Vanellus chilensis*), a common resident shorebird in coastal Buenos Aires Province, Argentina.

Figure 10. Buff-breasted Sandpiper (*Tryngites subruficollis*), a locally abundant North American migrant in coastal Buenos Aires Province, Argentina.

Figure 11. Rufous-chested Dotterel (*Zonibyx modestus*), a common South American migrant shorebird using the coastal zone of Buenos Aires Province, Argentina, during the austral winter.

J. P. Myers

Figure 12 and 13. White-rumped Sandpiper (*Calidris fuscicollis*), an abundant North American migrant shorebird in the coastal zone of Buenos Aires Province, Argentina, during austral spring and summer.

Figure 14. Two-banded Plover (*Charadrius falklandicus*), a common migrant shorebird in coastal Buenos Aires Province, Argentina, during late austral summer, fall, and winter. This species also breeds uncommonly within the region.

about migrant-resident interactions in general. It should be clear that we are not dealing simply with North American migrants vs South American residents; the system is much more complex. During austral summer both migrant and resident species use the region, but the former include South American waders breeding locally (but absent in the austral winter) as well as "wintering" North Americans. Then in austral winter another set of migrants from Patagonian breeding grounds replace the migrants that had been present during summer. As a result, the local shorebird community does not reduce to a simple migrant-resident dichotomy, being instead a complicated amalgam of different migration systems. Its complexities make it difficult to search for any overall generalizations about migrant-resident interactions.

As Karr (1976) points out, studies of nonbreeding North American species in the tropics reached an early consensus that these migrants tended to exploit more ephemeral resources, seasonally superabundant food, or to occur in disturbed habitats and areas of second growth in comparison to residents. Many papers at this symposium question the generality of this analysis, and I suggest that coastal Buenos Aires Province shorebirds also offer it little support. Several Northern Hemisphere waders in coastal Buenos Aires Province do use ephemeral resources. Wetland-inhabiting sandpipers, for example, move between drying ponds as foraging conditions vary, and the time course of drying in these ponds might appear to be too short to allow a complete breeding cycle for locally nesting species. But at least one resident, the Southern Lapwing, moves back and forth between upland grasslands and short-duration ponds; these wetland sites may be preferred foraging areas for adults with chicks (Myers and Myers 1979). Indeed many of the aggressive encounters between adult lapwings and migrant shorebirds described above occur in these sites. Common Stilts and Painted Snipes breed in similar habitat. Further, most migrant species defend long-term territories here. Buff-breasted Sandpipers and Golden Plovers occupy territories through much of austral spring in and around Southern Lapwing breeding territories in the short-grass uplands. The latter species actually begins to move its broods away from the grasslands long before the sandpipers or plovers cease defense. White-rumped Sandpipers as well as other wetland species defend nonbreeding territories for periods up to several months (Myers et al 1979).

Non-territorial White-rumped Sandpipers also return repeatedly to the same foraging area. They do change location more frequently than territorial birds, but they are still strikingly consistent, given the vagility one normally infers for winter flocks of migrant shorebirds (Myers 1976). Similar results emerge from banding studies in California (Connors 1976; Kelly 1979). All these data argue that winter shorebirds depend upon relatively dependable (i.e. nonephemeral) long-term resources, especially when combined with evidence for strong winter philopatry (Connors 1976; Myers 1976; Kelly 1979; Smith and Stiles 1979).

I do not mean to imply that migrant shorebirds do not exploit environmental irregularity. On the contrary, some are very good at it, especially given their vagility compared to breeding birds with reproductive obligations and concomitant site restrictions. But viewing this as some manifestation of a migrant-resident dichotomy is misleading. Within both migrants and residents, there are spectrums of exploitation systems, each adapted to a critical set of species-specific resources. Whatever generalities appear to emerge from neotropic passerine studies may be peculiar to the biology of the migrants involved, on a species-by-species and resource-by-resource basis, and not indicative of a generalized migrant characteristic.

Acknowledgments

My work in Argentina was made possible by the Thomas J. Watson Foundation through a Traveling Fellowship. I thank L. P. Myers for her active involvement in the research and her contributions to data analysis and preparation of manuscripts. Don Juan Arbelaiz and his family, owners of Estancia Medaland, as well as members of their staff, received us with incomparable Pampas hospitality throughout our stay. Maurice Rumboll provided invaluable aid in all matters. The Museo Argentino de Ciencias Naturales, and in particular its Director, Dr. Jose Maria Gallardo, and Curator of Ornithology, Dr. Jorge Navas, greatly facilitated our work in Argentina. F. A. Pitelka, R. S. Greenberg, P. G. Connors, J. V. Remsen, and C. Connors read several versions of this manuscript, helping to clarify my arguments and to control speculative frenzies without necessarily agreeing.

Literature Cited

Baker, M. C., and M. Baker
1973.   Niche relationships among six species of shorebirds on their wintering and breeding ranges. Ecol. Monogr. 43:193–212.

Berthold, P.
1975.   Migration: Control and Metabolic Physiology. In *Avian Biology*, eds. D. S. Farner and J. R. King, Vol. 5, pp. 77–128. New York: Academic Press.

J. P. Myers

Burton, P. J. K.
1974. *Feeding and the Feeding Apparatus in Waders: A Study of Anatomy and Adaptation in the Charadrii.* Brit. Mus. (Nat. Hist.), 150 pp.

Connors, P. G.
1976. Site faithfulness and territoriality in a population of Sanderlings (*Calidris alba*). Paper before Annual Meeting of the Cooper Ornithological Society, Asilomar, Calif., 31 March 1976.

Dabenne, R.
1920. Notas sobre los chorlos de Norte America que inviernan en la Republica Argentina. El Hornero 2:99–128.

Elliot, C. C. H., M. Walther, L. G. Underhill, J. S. Pringle, and W. J. A. Dick
1976. The migration system of the Curlew Sandpiper *Calidris ferruginea* in Africa. Ostrich 47:191–213.

Engels, W. L.
1962. Day-length and termination of photorefractoriness in the annual testicular cycle of a transequatorial migrant *Dolichonyx* (The Bobolink). Biol. Bull. 123:94–104.

Hamner, W. M., and J. Stocking
1971. Why don't Bobolinks breed in Brazil? Ecol. 51:743–751.

Holmes, R. T.
1966. Breeding ecology and annual cycle adaptations of the red-backed sandpiper (*Calidris alpina*) in northern Alaska. Condor 68:3–46.

Immelman, K.
1971. Ecological aspects of Periodic Reproduction. In *Avian biology*, eds. D. S. Farner and J. R. King, vol. 1, pp. 341–89. New York: Academic Press.

Jehl, J. R.
1975. *Pluvianellus socialis*: Biology, ecology, and relationships of an enigmatic Patagonian shorebird. Trans. San Diego Soc. Nat. Hist. 18:25–74.

Karr, J. R.
1976. On the relative abundance of migrants from the North Temperate Zone in tropical habitats. Wils. Bull. 88:433–58.

Kelly, P.
1979. Local movements of winter resident Willets and Marbled Godwits on South San Francisco Bay. In *Shorebirds in the Marine Environments*, ed. F. A. Pitelka. Studies in Avian Biology, No. 2, in press.

Lack, D.
1976. Island biology, In *Studies in Ecology*, eds. D. J. Anderson, P. Greig-Smith, and F. A. Pitelka, vol. 3. Berkeley: Univ. of Calif. Press.

Larson, S.
1957. The suborder Charadrii in arctic and boreal areas during the Tertiary and Pleistocene. Acta Vert. 1:1–81.

MacArthur, R.
1972. *Geographical Ecology: Patterns in the Distribution of Species.* New York: Harper & Row, 269 pp.

Moreau, R. E.
1966. The bird faunas of Africa and its islands. Academic Press, N.Y., viii + 424 pp.

Myers, J. P.
1976. Habitat use and spacing patterns of North American shorebirds wintering in Argentina. Paper before Annual Meeting of the Cooper Ornithological Society, Asilomar, Calif., 31 March 1976.

Myers, J. P., P. G. Connors, and F. A. Pitelka.
1979. Territoriality in non-breeding shorebirds. In *Shorebirds in the Marine Environments*, ed. F.A. Pitelka. Studies in Avian Biology, No. 2, in press.

Myers, J. P. and L. P. Myers
1979. Shorebirds of coastal Buenos Aires Province, Argentina. Ibis 121 (2):186–200.

Olrog, C.C.
1967. Observaciones sobre aves migratorias del Hemisferio Norte. El Hornero 4:292–98.

Pearson, R.G., and Parker, G.A.
1973. Sequential activities in the feeding behavior of some charadriiformes. J. Nat. Hist. 7:573–89.

Pienkowski, M. W.
1976. Recurrence of waders in autumn migration at sites in Morocco. Die. Vögel 28:293–97.

Recher, H. F.
1966. Some aspects of the ecology of migrant shorebirds. Ecol. 47:393–407.

Smith, S. M., and G. Stiles
1979. A banding study of migrant shorebirds in northwestern Costa Rica. In *Shorebirds in the Marine Environments*, ed. F.A. Pitelka. Studies in Avian Biology, No. 2, in press.

Storer, R. W.
1951. The seasonal occurrence of shorebirds on Bay Farm Island, Alameda Co., California. Condor 53:186–93.

Walter, H.
1973. *Vegetation of the Earth in Relation to Climate and the Ecophysiological Conditions.* New York: Springer-Verlag, 237 pp.

Wetmore, A.
1927. Our migrant shorebirds in southern South America. U.S.D.A. Tech. Bull. 26:1–24.

Wiens, J. A.
1977. On competition and variable environments. Amer. Sci. 65:590–97.

NEAL G. SMITH
Smithsonian Tropical Research Institute
Box 2072
Balboa, Canal Zone

Hawk and Vulture Migrations in the Neotropics

ABSTRACT

Nearly all Swainson's and most migratory Broad-winged Hawks pass through Panama during October–November along with Turkey Vultures. Broad-winged hawks spend four months breeding, six months in the tropics and two months on migration. Swainson's Hawk spends four months breeding, four months in South America, and four months on migration. Migrant and resident Turkey Vultures coexist in Panama during November to April.

Thermal soaring is the dominant flight strategy for migration. Heights of 3,600 to 4,000 m are commonly attained, occasionally 6,400 m.

Few aggressive interactions are seen even though large concentrations occur. Migrating Swainson's Hawks and Turkey Vultures were not seen to feed.

Numbers for the three species, censused by photography, were 958,634 in 1972 and 871,286 in 1973. Competition for Broad-winged Hawks that remain in Panama is mainly intraspecific. Use of invertebrate food is characteristic of migratory birds.

Figure 1. This picture was taken with a 1,000-mm lens, and shows 889 Swainson's Hawks and some Turkey Vultures descending from above a tropical storm cloud at approximately 3,600 m over Panama City, 2 November 1974. Their flight speed was guessed to be approximately 60 km/hr.

One of the most spectacular and easily observed movements of birds in the New World, and possibly anywhere, is the passage by the Broad-winged Hawk (*Buteo platypterus*), Swainson's Hawk (*Buteo swainsoni*), and the Turkey Vulture (*Cathartes aura*) through the Isthmus of Panama. This paper documents this seasonal geographic shift between their temperate breeding grounds, and their neotropical and south temperate nonbreeding areas.

Apparently, almost all of the Swainson's and most of the migratory population of the Broad-winged Hawk in existence pass in an aerial river (figure 1) over or within 5 km of Panama City, Republic of Panama, (latitude 9°N) during October and November. One goal of this study was to document this incredible concentration of individuals that occurs on the migration of these normally rather dispersed raptors and to determine how many of them there are.

Neal G. Smith

Here, I will first discuss their geographic distribution and taxonomy. This is followed by a consideration of the actual migration, its timing, the routes followed, and the effects of various meteorological factors. I then treat their social behavior and the question of whether or not they feed during the passage. This is followed by a discussion of my attempts to count or otherwise estimate the numbers involved. Finally, I consider their habitat preferences and habits on the nonbreeding grounds and offer some speculations as to why these birds are such long-distance migrants.

Species of Migrant Hawks and Vultures

Broad-winged Hawk

The range of this small, chunky (490 g ♀♀, 420 g ♂♂, Snyder and Wiley 1976) buteo is shown in figure 2. Five nonmigratory races have been described from the West Indies. It is absent from Jamaica, and there is but one report of it on Hispanola. On Jamaica it is apparently replaced by the very similar *B. ridgwayi* (Brown and Amadon 1968). It is rare on Puerto Rico and said to be common only in western Cuba, and on the southernmost islands (Bond 1961). None of the races are particularly distinctive, suggesting that they are of recent origin (Heintzelman 1975).

Figure 2. The distribution of the Broad-winged Hawk (*Buteo platypterus*). During October–April, most of the nonbreeding individuals in Central America are in immature plumage, while those in adult plumage dominate in South America.

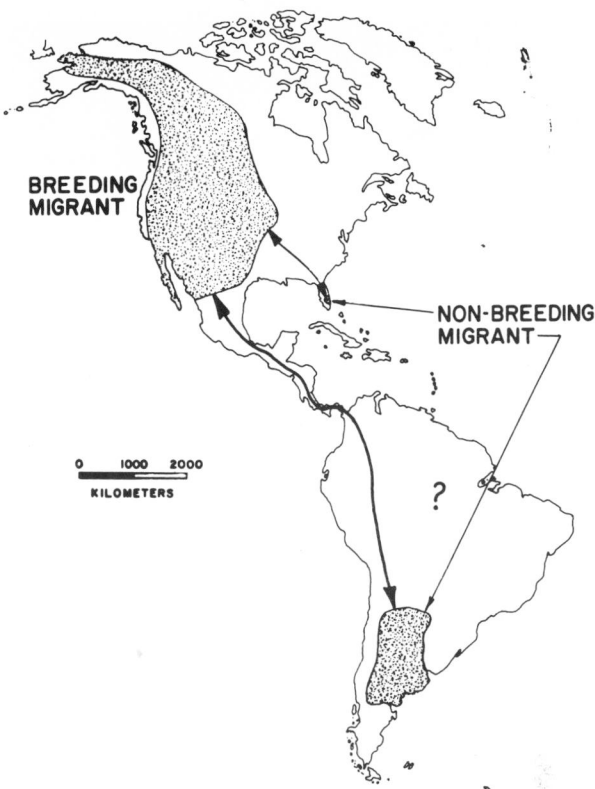

Figure 3. The distribution of the Swainson's Hawk (*Buteo swainsoni*). While the main concentration during the nonbreeding season (November–April) may be in Argentina, scattered individuals are found in Florida, southern Central America, and throughout the savannah areas of South America.

The nominate form, *B. p. platypterus*, is migratory between lower Middle America and amazonian South America, and eastern North America where it breeds. It may also migrate through the northernmost West Indian islands (Recher and Recher 1966; Robertson and Ogden 1968). Broad-winged Hawks reside in the tropics for six months, spend four months in North America reproducing, and two months on migration.

Swainson's Hawk

This is a medium-sized (1,000 g ♀♀, 900 g ♂♂, Snyder and Wiley 1976) raptor of the savannah and prairie regions of North and South America (figure 3). As adults, they are said to be trimorphic in plumage, with light dark, and rufous phases, but intermediates are known between all three phases (Brown and Amadon 1968). This variability makes it difficult to discriminate immatures from adults in the field, a point which makes demographic analysis of migrating individuals almost impossible. The nonbreeding range was thought to be entirely restricted to the savannahs of Argentina, but it is now known that individuals may be found in cleared areas throughout South America, southern Central America, and in the state of Florida in the United States (Brown and Amadon 1968; pers. obs.).

Arrival dates and departure dates for Panama and Argentina (see below) indicate that Swainson's Hawks reside in North America for four months, in South America (at least in Argentina) for four months and spend four months of each year migrating.

Turkey Vulture

This species is the largest of the migratory raptors in the neotropics (1,200–2,000 g). It differs from the other long-distance migrants in that its breeding and non-breeding ranges are continuous. This vulture breeds throughout the New World from southern Canada to Tierra del Fuego. Two races have been described from North America, *C. a. septentrionalis* in the east and *C. a. aura* in the west; the latter is said to be more migratory than the eastern form (Brown and Amadon 1968). The apparently resident race, *C. a. ruficollis*, from Panama southward is easily distinguished from the more northerly forms by the presence of gold bands on the naked red head. This feature is not visible when the individuals are flying overhead. It is not known if *C. a. ruficollis* or its western South American counterpart *C. a. jota* migrate to any extent. Migrant and resident individuals coexist in Panama and in South America during November to April (Wetmore 1965).

The Passage

Timing

Arrival and departure dates from both the nonbreeding and breeding grounds suggest that the average individual of these three species spends between 28 days (Broad-winged Hawk and some Turkey Vultures) and 70 days (most Swainson's) on either the southward or northward movement. The data are best for *Buteo platypterus*. Flocks of Broad-winged Hawk move into Panama from South America around 15 March (Loftin 1963; pers. obs.). Haugh and Cade (1966) report that this species arrives near Lake Ontario during the last 10 days of April, with a peak around April 24. This represents a flight distance from Panama of approximately 6,700 km. Similarly, the southward movement of Broad-winged Hawks peaks in northeastern United States between 9 and 15 September, with an average entry date into northeastern Mexico of about 30 September and a mean arrival date for big flocks over Panama City on 12–14 October.

Of the three species, Turkey Vultures are the first to move north in late February and early March, followed by the Swainson's Hawks, and finally by the

Broad-winged Hawks. There is temporal overlap, and flocks containing two, or all three species, are not infrequent. The passage of the Turkey Vultures is the most drawn out, and I have seen migrating flocks in mid-April. On the return movement, the Broad-winged Hawks are the first to arrive (early to mid-October), followed and overlapped by the Swainson's Hawks (mid-October into early November) and finally the Turkey Vultures (mid-October to early December).

It is not entirely clear just what are the factors that produce this temporal spacing. There is an early peak of Turkey Vultures with the earliest Broad-winged Hawks. I assume that these are vultures from northeastern North America, and that the latter group, by far the larger, are vultures which bred in western North America. A large number of the Turkey Vultures of eastern North America remain in the southeastern section during the north temperate winter (Brown and Amadon 1968). I think that the spacing results from the different distances that the species have to fly before reaching Panama, but it may also reflect different departure times. All three species appear to have roughly the same flight speeds.

Routes, Meteorological Factors, and Speed of Passage

Figures 4 through 6 summarize the autumnal or rainy season migration routes in Central America, South America, and, in more detail, the Republic of Panama. With but few significant deviations, the dry season or spring migration is simply the reverse of the aerial tracks shown for the rainy season.

The autumn of the North Temperate Zone and the rainy season (May to December) of the Central American and northern South American tropics present two somewhat different flying conditions for migrating raptors. In North America, the movement patterns of the raptors are much influenced by wind direction; thermal soaring (see below) is also utilized (Heintzelman 1975) but not to the extent that raptors use it in the tropics. I am not sure what route is employed by the Broad-winged Hawks to cross the Gulf states into southeastern Texas where they enter the lowlands of Mexico. From that point onward, together with the swarm of Swainson's Hawks and Turkey Vultures from the west, they have entered a world of variable light winds, hot air bubbles, and thunderstorms.

Thermal soaring (Cone 1962) now becomes the dominant flight strategy. As the sun rises, the ground becomes differentially heated. Columns of heated air break off from the ground and rise as "hot air bubbles." The migrants seek out such disturbed air and soar up through the thermal area only to break off as

Neal G. Smith

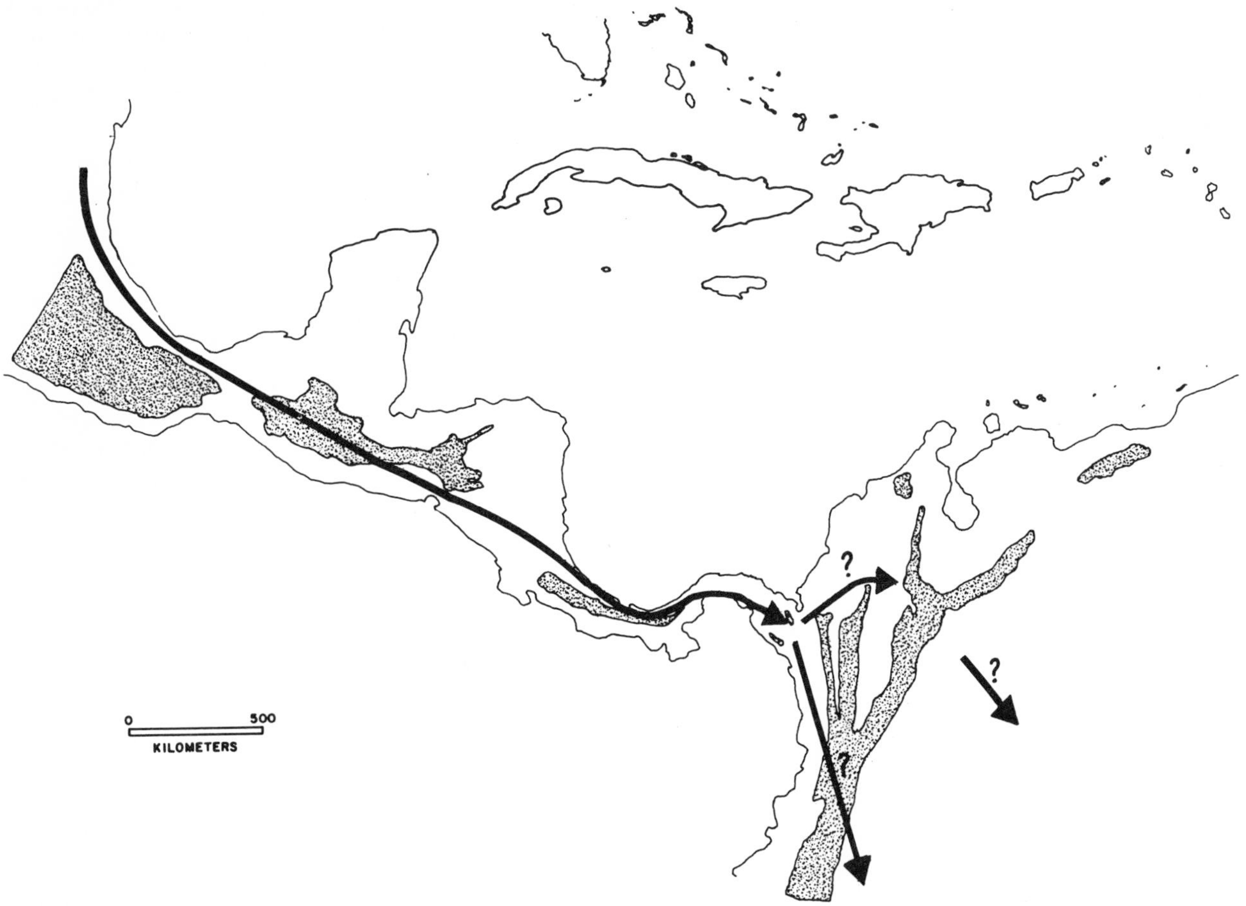

Figure 4.   The autumnal flight path of Swainson's Hawks, Broad-winged Hawks, and Turkey Vultures (*Cathartes aura*) in Central America. This period of October–November is part of the rainy season and is characterized by still air or rather weak southerly winds and the formation of heat thermals. It is not certain where the raptors cross the Andes.

Figure 5.   The autumnal flight path of Broad-winged Hawks into their nonbreeding areas. The main movement is through Central America, but small numbers may leave Florida and cross the 160 km gap to the north coast of Cuba. They may either settle out in the West Indies or cross the 200-km water-gap to the Yucatán Peninsula. Tropical storms may facilitate these over-water flights, but this is still not proven.

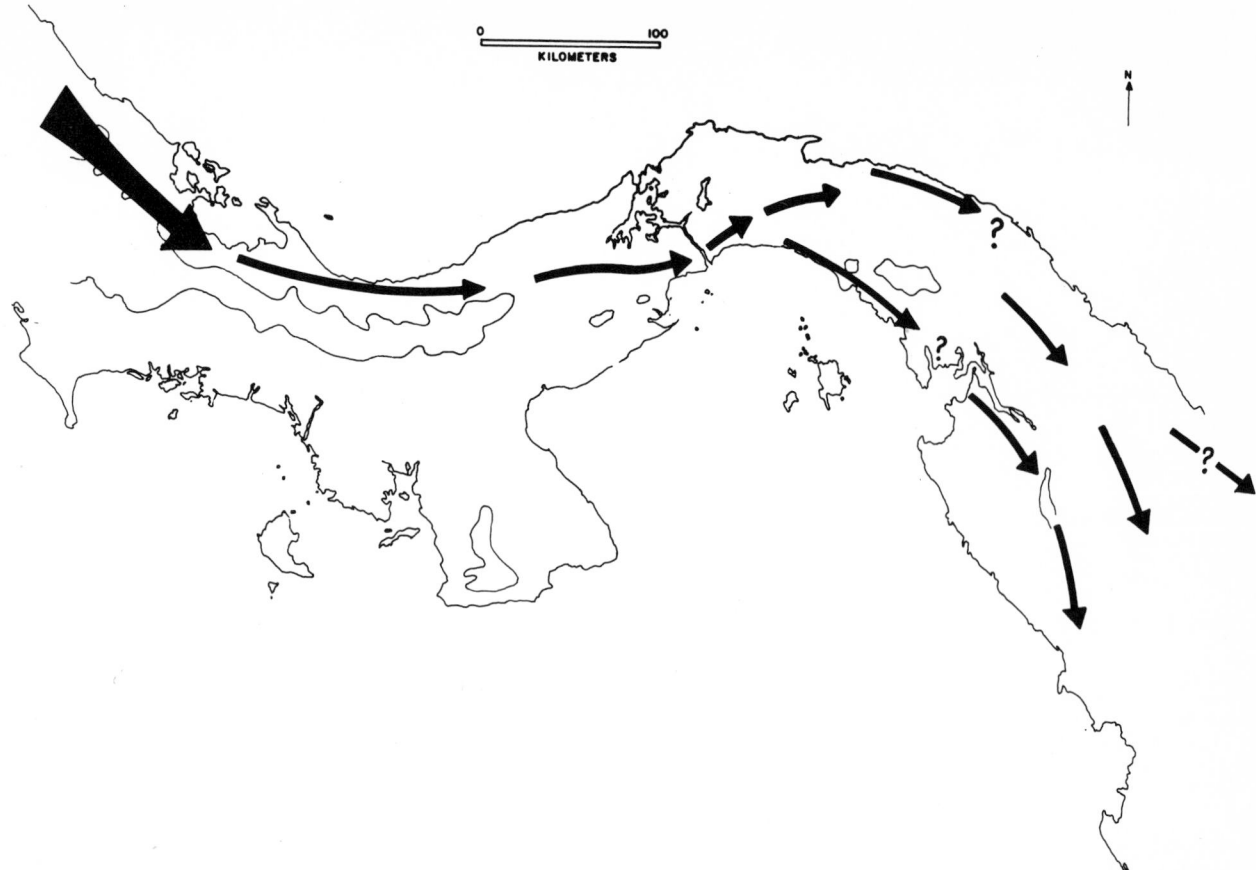

Figure 6. The autumnal or rainy season flight paths of raptors through the narrow Isthmus of Panama. The contour lines represent areas over 1,000-m elevation. The exact entry paths into Colombia are still not known.

the air cools (figure 7). In the early morning over Panama City, this breakup usually occurs between 360 and 700 m above the ground. The raptors then glide downward on an angle of about 10–20° until they intercept the next rising bubble. I judged their flight speed at that time of day to be around 25–35 km/hr. From 1100 hr to around 1500 hr, these thermal bubbles may rise to enormous heights, and the hawks and vultures literally disappear from sight. Reports over several years from pilots from Howard Air Force Base, Canal Zone, indicated that the birds were often attaining altitudes between 3,600 m and 4,000 m above the ground between 1100 and 1330 hr on days of favorable thermal activity. These reports bear on the so called "noon lull" reported by observers in North America (Heintzelman 1975). Briefly, more hawks are seen in the morning and in the afternoon than at midday. It has been suggested that the birds might be coming down to feed at that time, or that midday meteorological conditions might cause the hawks to disperse over a broad front, or that simply they might be flying too high to be seen. Hawks flying at 4,000 m are almost impossible to see without the aid of binoculars, assuming that they are below the cloud cover or against a clear sky. Storm clouds usually begin to build up between 1100 and 1330 hr. Migrating hawks and vultures which are cruising at about 700–800 m usually attempt to avoid local storms by going around them. But when faced with a broad stormfront, the hawks and vultures do not land but rather glide up the face of the advancing storm and go over the top (figure 1). I have received reports from commercial and U.S. air force pilots of large numbers of hawks and vultures gliding over such systems at altitudes in excess of 6,400 m. The raptors are apparently using the convection currents atop such systems to propel themselves along. I do not know how long they remain in this oxygen-poor and cold ($-20°C$) environment.

Small passerines have been recorded flying 6,000 m over the West Indies (Williams et al 1977). Laybourne (1974) reports a collision of a Rüpell's Griffon (*Gyps ruepellii*) with an aircraft at 11,212 m. Tucker (1972) suggests that birds flying at an altitude of 8,000 m must have lower partial pressures of oxygen and carbon dioxide in the gas exchange regions of their lungs than man can tolerate.

Tropical storms have another effect. When heavy

Neal G. Smith

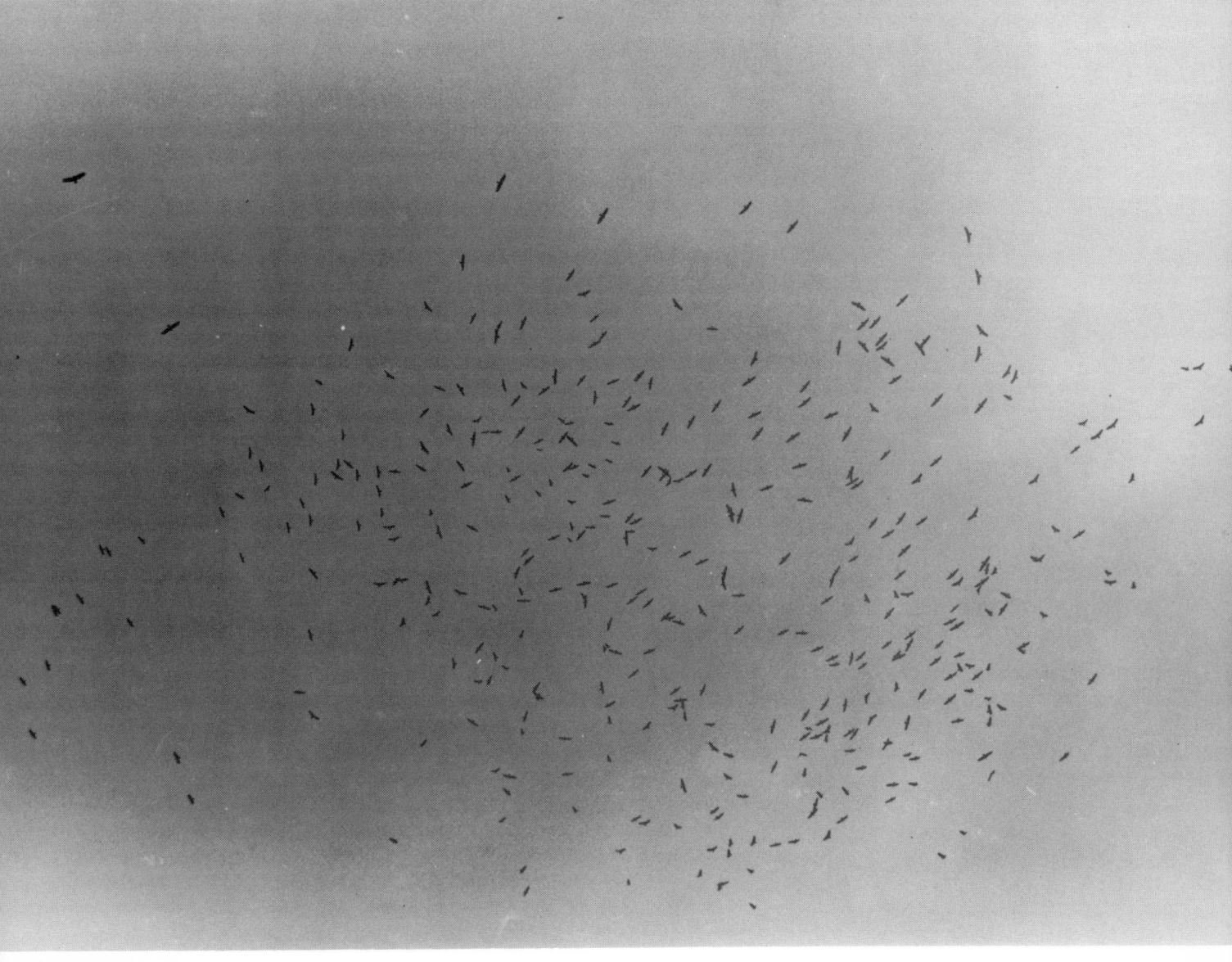

Figure 7. Turkey Vultures and Swainson's Hawks soaring atop a thermal bubble at 400-m elevation over Ancon Hill, Canal Zone, Panama. The birds on the left have broken off in a long shallow dive seeking another thermal area.

rains fall in the morning while hawks and vultures are still on the ground, the birds remain grounded, sometimes for several days (Loftin 1967; pers. obs.). Such delays should be taken into consideration when estimating the speed of passage between the breeding and nonbreeding grounds.

The possible regular utilization of tropical storms by these birds may provide an explanation for another route which may be regularly used by small numbers of Broad-winged Hawks to enter the tropics (figure 5). Robertson and Ogden (1968) reported an observation of thousands of Broad-winged Hawks flying southsouthwest from Key West, Florida, over open water. Observations over several years in Florida suggest that this may be of regular occurrence. Birds which utilize thermals generally avoid open-water crossings (Moreau 1953).

The distance from Florida to the north coast of Cuba is approximately 200 km, and it is about the same distance from the western tip of Cuba to the Yucatán Peninsula. I think that it is very likely that migrant Broad-winged Hawks could utilize tropical

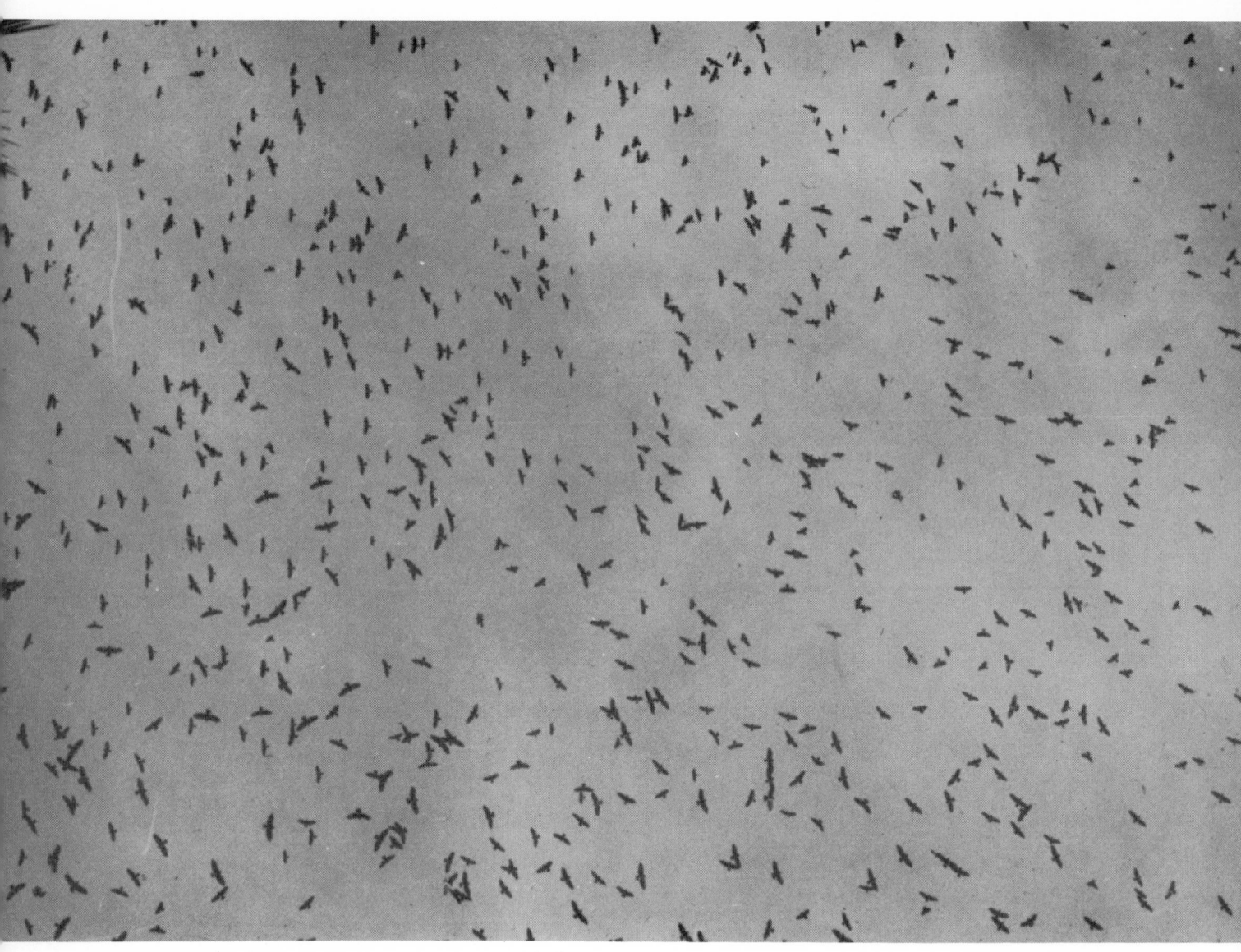

Figure 8. Here are 868 Broad-winged Hawks wheeling upward at 200 m in a weak early morning (0800 hr) thermal bubble over Panama City, Panama, 14 October 1974. This density continued unabated until 1100 hr and it was estimated from photographs that 31,750 individuals must have slept the previous night within 5 km of the city. (105-mm lens)

storms to make these over-water crossings. I wish to emphasize that I know of no reports of Broad-winged Hawks making a landing on the Yucatán Peninsula. Recher and Recher (1966) claim to have observed a dry season or spring movement of the mainland race of *Buteo platypterus* in Puerto Rico. Finally, there is the irony that the first published account of hawk migrations in the New World by Oviedo was of hawks migrating southward from the tip of Cuba (Baughman 1947). The problem remains open.

Conditions in Central America are rather different in the dry season (December to May) as the entire area is dominated by the strong north-northeast trade winds. At that time, the raptors do not pass over Panama City, but rather make a mid-isthmus crossing of the Canal Zone on the windward face of the Continental Divide. Their flight dynamics during the dry season in the tropics are much like those employed during their southward flight in the North American autumn.

Intra- and Interspecific Interactions

Clearly, when predators which are normally highly

Neal G. Smith

dispersed come together in large numbers, one might wonder how individuals behave toward one another, both intra- and interspecifically. On 15 occcasions over the past six years, I have observed large flocks of raptors descend to roost for the night in the wooded areas of the canal Zone. On 13 October 1974, approximately 1,745 Broad-winged Hawks landed over a 15-minute period (1715–1730 hr) on a wooded hillside at Rodman Naval Base on the west bank of the Panama Canal. The hawks did not vocalize nor, once landed, attempt to fly up again. I did not observe more than one individual on any minor branch of a tree, but branches longer than 4 m had several perched hawks. Some trees had more than 35 individuals; some as close as 1 m from their nearest neighbor. This behavior is also typical for both Swainson's Hawks and Turkey Vultures on the intraspecific level.

I returned the following morning at 0600 hr. Several hawks became disturbed by my movements, and flew off several meters only to land again. Between 0735 and 0745 hr, the entire flock took to flight, flapping heavily as they circled their roost area at an altitude of no more than 30–40 m. I observed no interactions between individuals, and no vocalizations were heard. At the same time, other flocks of similar size were seen rising off adjacent hillsides. By 0810 hr, the hawks began to wheel about in weak thermals and began crossing the Panama Canal toward Ancon Hill (207 m) on the east bank (the South American side). I photographed this transcanal flight, and from those pictures I estimated that 18,700 Broad-winged Hawks had crossed between 0815 and 0915 hr (figure 8). This, I would guess, represented the number of Broad-winged Hawks which had slept the night before in an area of approximately 12 km^2.

I have, on several occasions, observed interspecific interactions between Swainson's Hawks and Turkey Vultures. On 18 October 1977, 900 Turkey Vultures and 300–400 Swainson's Hawks began descending along the wooded edge of a road in Fort Clayton Army Base, Canal Zone. The hawks were clearly trying to avoid settling too near any vulture which was already perched. Most of the vultures remained aloft longer (until 1840 hr.) than did the hawks, and, as they settled, they aggressively forced already perched Swainson's Hawks to move to other perches. The vultures which were already settled were not displaced by these late arrivals. At 0730 hr on the next day, the Swainson's Hawks began wheeling up, but the first of the Turkey Vultures did not take off until 0813 hr (figure 9).

Feeding Behavior

The general lore is that the three species of raptors dealt with in this paper do not feed on migration (Brown and Amador 1968). I am uncertain whether or not this is extraordinary.

Most of the evidence is circumstantial, but, in total, supports the fasting hypothesis, at least during the autumn or rainy season passage into the tropics, and for Swainson's, into the South Temperate Zone. I know of but two published accounts of any of the 3 raptors feeding *while on migration*. Slud (1964) observed Swainson's Hawks hunting grasshoppers on the ground in Costa Rica (date unspecified). Littlefield (1973) watched up to 61 Swainson's Hawks feeding over a three-day period on a caterpillar outbreak during early October in Texas.

I have never observed Swainson's Hawks or Turkey Vultures to drop down from the migrating flocks to feed, nor have I ever found feces at roosts where thousands have roosted. Skutch (1971) has made similar observations in Costa Rica. It is somewhat different for Broad-winged Hawks because Panama is part of their nonbreeding range. Thus, it is not unusual to see individuals, usually immatures, hunting at low altitudes while the major mass passes far above. These are almost certainly nonbreeding residents.

I have received reports from country people here in Panama that they have found both Swainson's and Broad-winged Hawks in weak condition on the ground below roosts and that such birds were very thin and unable to fly. C.C. Olrog of the Instituto Miguel Lillo in Tucmán, Argentina, (pers. comm. August 1978) describes the arrival of Swainson's Hawks in Argentina as follows: "They are very tired and it is possible to catch them by hand when they sit down in bushes and small trees; I can't say if they are in a starved state. Anyhow the next day they are soaring around looking for food."

We know very little about the energetic cost of such a long flight. As Tucker (1971) points out, the fuel for flight is primarily fat, but I cannot find any evidence that any of the raptors considered in this paper put on fat prior to the flight. If I am correct about the timing and the speed of passage, the average Broad-winged Hawk fasts for at least 30 days and perhaps double this for a Swainson's Hawk that goes to Argentina. The amount of energy expended by gliding from thermal bubble to thermal bubble or riding the convection currents atop clouds must be very low indeed. As I have previously indicated, the hawks and vultures will not even attempt flight under conditions where thermals or wind is lacking.

Numbers

The narrowest section of the Isthmus of Panama is at the Panama Canal Zone where the oceans are sepa-

Figure 9. This shows a portion of a continuous flow of 7,450 Turkey Vultures which passed over Panama City on 19 October 1977 in approximately two hours. Note the spacing between the birds. (300-mm lens)

rated by only 73 km. But, in the rainy season, the hawks and vultures use only a portion of this, a zone only 5-km wide, bordered on the south by the Pacific Ocean and Panama City and on the north by the Pedro Miguel locks of the Panama Canal. The October–November movement is from the west (Central America) to the east (South America). At any one point in time, there is usually but one aerial flow of raptors crossing the canal, but the vicissitudes of the breezes cause this flow to shift north and south within that zone. Thus, to count all of the raptors, more than one observer is required.

With the exception of a small group (about 300, Brown and Amadon 1968) of Swainson's Hawks which live in Florida during the nonbreeding season (figure 3), all of the Swainson's Hawks pass through this

corridor into South America. A few Broad-winged Hawks remain in the southern United States during the nonbreeding season. Others, mainly immatures, take up nonbreeding residence in Costa Rica and in Panama. But the vast majority, and perhaps most of the adults, pass through this zone and enter South America. This was, then, my rationale for asking the perhaps purely academic question: how many Swainson's and Broad-winged Hawks are there? I have no idea what percentage of the total Turkey Vulture population passes over Panama City, but it must be a sizeable part of the Turkey Vulture population breeding north of Panama. I also hoped to develop a sampling scheme that would permit between-year population comparisons, thus to obtain a grasp of the demographies of these species.

Neal G. Smith

Methods of Census

I censused the hawk and vulture migrations over Panama City during October–November of 1969 through 1974 and again in 1976. Ancon Hill, a 207-m wooded massif on the east bank of the canal overlooking Panama City, was chosen as the main observation point. Because of the updrafts along its sides, Ancon Hill seemed to be the preferred target for transcanal migrants. It was also possible to detect from there, but not to count, if hawks are crossing as far north as the Pedro Miguel locks. I used two 35-mm, motor-driven, cameras with 85-mm and 105-mm lenses, respectively. Because it was difficult to count hawks and vultures as they swirled up in the thermal bubbles, I generally photographed the raptors as they peeled off in a straight line from such a thermal bubble. Care was taken not to overlap the pictures. Counts were made by projecting the negatives with an enlarger onto a white board, ticking off each individual with a pen, and recording the numbers with a hand-counter. I analyzed 4,433 negatives taken over the observation period. I occasionally used a 300-mm lens to examine and document the dynamics of thermal soaring and a 1,000-mm mirror lens to record the very high movements. In 1977, John Fryxell, from the University of British Columbia, continued the censusing and attempted to design a sampling procedure for inter-year comparisons. I will not report on his 1977 results here.

Results

The numbers in table 1 represent counts made from negatives supplemented by visual counts. The figures are conservative, for each year I saw large numbers of hawks and vultures which passed too far to the north of Ancon Hill to be counted. In addition, I was completely blind to those raptors flying above the clouds, and it is almost certain that I missed unknown numbers because of cloud cover. The number of days each year that I was able to spend watching the migration varied greatly, thus making inter-year comparisons difficult. Yet, some trends may be gleaned from the data. Surprisingly, in most years, the Broad-winged Hawk was the most abundant of the three species (figure 10). In four out of six years, I counted more Swainson's Hawks than Turkey Vultures, which might have been predicted. Still, the numbers of Turkey Vultures were very high. If a significant number of Turkey Vultures remained to the north of Panama during the nonbreeding period in North America, and 230,154 individuals flew over Panama City, one wonders just how many of these large scavengers there really are. Total counts were highest in 1972 and 1973, years in which I was able to spend the most time

Table 1. Hawk and vulture migrations over Panama City[1]

Year	Species		
	B. platypterus	*B. swainsoni*	*C. aura*
1970	114,509	175,644	190,017
1971[2]	80,641	77,014	99,612
1972	395,003	344,409	219,222
1973	341,414	299,718	230,154
1974[2]	42,209	54,403	31,114
1976	301,011	207,115	194,646

[1] These figures represent the numbers of Broad-winged Hawks (*B. platypterus*), Swainson's Hawks (*B. swainsoni*) and Turkey Vultures (*C. aura*) counted as they migrated over Panama City, Republic of Panama. The data were from October and November for 6 years.

[2] Incomplete sampling.

observing. The total number of these three species which passed was 958,634 in 1972 and 871,286 in 1973.

I have dwelt on the dynamics of the passage because a very great percentage of the time that the hawks and vultures are in the tropics is spent migrating (50 percent of the time in the case of the Swainson's Hawk). It may now be useful to consider the limited information concerning the life styles of these species while they reside in Central and South America.

Turkey Vulture

This species differs from the other two species in that its breeding and nonbreeding ranges are completely continuous. As already indicated, migrant vultures lack the gold nape of the Central and South American forms and thus can be easily distinguished if they are sitting or flying below eye level. During the months of October to March, there is a noticeable increase in the numbers of Turkey Vultures in Panama, both near towns and in the countryside. In December 1977, I surveyed Turkey Vultures along the Pan American highway from the Costa Rican border to Panama City, a distance of 576 km. I counted 4,892 individuals and was able to see the heads of 1,654 of these. Seven hundred and forty-four (45 percent) of these were migrant vultures. They were not concentrated in any one spot, but were mixed with the locals along the entire stretch. There is nothing known about the seasonal abundance of food for Turkey Vultures. I have never recorded an individual of the northern race here in Panama after 20 April. Of course, migrating flocks are still passing over at that time. Resident Turkey Vultures appear to commence egg laying in February through early April.

Broad-winged Hawk

This is one of the commonest hawks encountered between November and April in the second growth woodlands of Costa Rica and Panama. They are solitary and apparently territorial. Single individuals, presumedly the same birds, may be found in the same place week after week. They are found along the edges of wet woodland and seldom occur within forest. I have examined the stomachs of 15 individuals, all in immature plumage. The stomachs were filled with large grasshoppers, cicadas, frogs, small lizards, and in three cases, with the remains of small snakes. Broad-winged Hawks are sluggish in behavior and generally do not soar very much. They move about their territories in a looping fashion from tree to tree, and peer intently for long periods at the ground below. They often vocalize, and I assume this functions in the establishment of their territories.

In Costa Rica and Panama, there are only two other hawks that have much the same habits and they are the Roadside Hawk (*Buteo magnirostris*) and the Gray Hawk (*Buteo nitidus*). *B. magnirostris* is found in drier, more open country than is *B. platypterus*, and I have never seen them in close proximity to each other. *B. nitidus* does occur in the habitat preferred by *B. platypterus* but is not nearly as abundant. *B. nitidus* soars a great deal and appears to catch its prey (also large insects) from among the branches and seldom from the ground. When Broad-winged Hawks depart from Central America, no other hawk moves into this habitat. I guess, but do not know with certainty, that their nonbreeding territories are considerably smaller than their breeding territories in North America. I conclude that the chief competitor for individual Broad-winged Hawks in the tropics is another Broad-winged Hawk.

Swainson's Hawk

I am unconvinced that Argentina represents the chief residence of this species during the nonbreeding period. Hard data are few, but the numbers reported from Argentina, while considerable, do not approach the numbers that pass through Panama. However, it may well be argued that a survey of the Swainson's Hawks in western North America would also not approach the numbers that pass through Panama. They are too dispersed.

C. C. Olrog (pers. comm. 10 August 1978) provided the most useful information on the species. In a situation that is analogous to the Broad-winged Hawk's in Central America, Olrog reports no records of adult Swainson's Hawks, which is certainly peculiar. The hawks apparently move about the countryside in loose groups of 25, 40, and more, exploiting local outbreaks of locusts. They arrived at the end of November (one month after they have passed Panama) and are still there in early March. Using the species accounts in Wetmore (1926) I find that there are two potential hawk competitors for locusts in Argentina, the caracara, *Milvago chimango* and the falcon, *Cerchneis sparveria*. Both are said to be common, and the caracara occurs in flocks. There would appear to be no other information on the Swainson's Hawk in Argentina.

Concluding Remarks

Most of our concepts concerning the evolution of short- to long-distance migration and the maintenance of a system of widely disjunct living areas comes from the writings of scientists who have resided in the North Temperate Zone (Mayr and Meise 1930; Lincoln 1939; Dorst 1961). Indeed, the jargon of migration studies reflects this historical accident. Birds are said to "winter" in the tropics or to have left for the "wintering grounds" as if the tropics were some sort of limbo in which the migrants remained until they were able to return to their "true homes" with the advent of the north temperate spring.

In the New World, the countless millions of parulids, vireonids, thraupids, icterids, hirundinids, accipitrids, etc., which live seven, eight, or even nine months in the tropics, but which breed in the North Temperate Zone, are designated by students of migration as North American migrants. The use of such a misnomer might be justified for a taxonomist interested in the zoogeographic origins of particular groups of birds, but it would be clearly in error when referring to groups like the tyrannids, thraupids, and icterids which are certainly South American in origin (Mayr 1946). Another justification for the use of this phrase might be that, although many of the groups are South American origin, the present migratory species in these groups are products of the Pleistocene in North America and that they evolved in North America. Mengel's (1964) analysis of parulid speciation is an outstanding example of this reasoning. Granted that the multiple advances and retreats of ice in North America did provide the necessary factors for much speciation (and extinction) there, the effects were not restricted to North America (Haffer 1969). Indeed, the vicissitudes of the Pleistocene in the tropics may have provided the necessary isolation factors to generate many of the present migratory species. It is shaky speculation to

Neal G. Smith

Figure 10. This picture shows 1,206 Broad-winged Hawks gliding at ca 40 km/hr. from a hot air bubble at an altitude of around 330 m over Ancon Hill, on the pacific side of the Panama Canal Zone. This was taken with an 85-mm lens at 1330 hr on 13 October 1977.

equate the present breeding distribution of a species with the area of its origin.

I believe that the real danger of the present system of jargon in discussing migrant birds lies in its tacit denial that these birds are an integral part of the tropical, as well as the temperate, communities. The North American bias (and the paleoarctic one as well) has generated a series of non-real questions such as "what is the impact of the migrants on the tropical birds"? I believe that most of the papers in this volume will affirm that there is no impact other than the species' original integration when the community, or rather when its components, evolved.

Why Fly so Far?

The Broad-winged Hawk, the Swainson's Hawk, and the Turkey Vulture are like all the other migrants. They are neither North American nor tropical, but are simply New World migrants. Some move only a few hundred kilometers, while others, like the Swainson's Hawk may fly more than 10,000 km. There is a complete continuum between these extremes. Raptors migrate to track their food resources. Those which feed primarily on mammals move the least, while those which feed on birds fly much farther. Those raptors which migrate the farthest are those which, from a north temperate point of view, have the most peculiar diets—insects, reptiles, amphibians, and in the case of *Pandion*, fish. Snyder and Wiley (1976) have summarized the diets of all the hawks and owls which breed in North America. Seventy-seven percent of the diet of the Broad-winged Hawk consists of invertebrates and 13 percent of lower vertebrates. Ninety-three percent of the Swainson's Hawk diet is invertebrates. The Mississippi Kite (*Ictinia misisippiensis*) is another long distance migrant which passes through Panama. Its diet is 99.8 percent invertebrates. The trend is clear.

It is less easy to explain why a species like the Broad-winged Hawk does not remain in the tropics. Broad-winged Hawks leave, and Roadside Hawks remain. Both prey on insects, snakes, lizards, and frogs, as do most tropical hawks and falcons. Do migrants like the Broad-winged Hawk occupy suboptimal habitats as the result of competitive interactions with other members of the community? Under the relatively depauperate conditions in the West Indies, the Broad-winged Hawks do not leave but remain to breed. This is an old explanation, and I think it is unsatisfactory. I am impressed that so many migrants possess the characteristics of good colonizing species outlined by Mayr (1965). Among these are the tendencies to be inter- and intraspecifically social and to travel in flocks and the ability to discover new unoccupied habitats. The Swainson's Hawks colonized Florida in 1950; the Broad-winged Hawks are recent colonists to the West Indies. All three species are highly social, at least at certain times of the year. The breeding and nonbreeding ranges of the Swainson's Hawk are separated by thousands of kilometers. Clearly this disjunction did not come about in one step. The intermediate distributions have disappeared. I suspect that man's continued modification of the tropical environment will result in further changes in this bird's distribution. *Buteo swainsoni* has shown itself to be a good tracker of environmental change. I believe that future reasearch on the biology of migrant birds should seek to identify the behavioral and ecological characteristics of migrants which have served as the necessary preadaptations for the evolution of this apparently highly successful habit.

Literature Cited

Baughman, J. L.
1947. A very early notice of hawk migrations. Auk. 64:304.

Bond, J.
1961. *Birds of the West Indies*. Boston: Houghton Mifflin, 256 pp.

Brown, L., and D. Amadon
1968. *Eagles, Hawks, and Falcons of the World*. New York: McGraw-Hill, two vol., 945 pp.

Cone, C. D.
1962. Thermal soaring of birds. Amer. Sci. 50:180–209.

Haffer, J.
1969. Speciation in amazonian forest birds. Science 165(3389):131–37.

Haugh, J. R., and T. J. Cade
1966. The spring hawk migration around the southeastern shore of Lake Ontario. Wils. Bull. 78(1):88–110.

Heintzelman, D. S.
1975. *Autumn Hawk Flights*. New Brunswick, N.J.: Rutgers Univ. Press, 398 pp.

Laybourne, R. C.
1974. Collision between a vulture and an aircraft at an altitude of 37,000 feet. Wils. Bull. 86(4):461–62.

Littlefield, C. D.
1973. Swainson's hawks preying on fall army worms. Southwestern Naturalist 17(4):433.

Loftin, H.
1963. Notes on spring migrants in Panama (Aves). Carib. J. Sci. 3(4):191–95.

1967. Hawks delayed by weather on spring migration through Panama. Florida Nat. 40:29.

Mayr, E.
1946. History of the North American bird fauna. Wils., Bull. 58(1):1–68.

1965. The nature of colonizations in birds. In: *The Genetics of Colonizing Species*, eds. H. G. Baker and G. L. Stebbins, pp. 29–47. New York: Academic Press, 588 pp.

Mayr, E., and W. Meise
1930. Theoretiches zur Geschichte des Vogelzuges Der. Vogelzug (Berlin) 1:149–72.

Mengel, R. M.
1964. The probable history of species formation in some northern wood warblers (Parulidae). Living Bird, 3rd Annual: 9–43.

Moreau, R. E.
1953. Migration in the Mediterranean area. Ibis 95:329–58.

Recher, H. F., and J. T. Recher
1966. A contribution to the knowledge of the avifauna of the Sierra de Luquillo, Puerto Rico. Carib. J. Sci. 6(3–4):151–61.

Neal G. Smith

Robertson, W. B., Jr., and J. C. Ogden
1968.   Florida region. Audubon Field Notes 22:25–31.

Skutch, A. F.
1971.   *A Naturalist in Cost Rica.* Gainesville, Fla.: Univ. of
         Florida Press, 378 pp.

Snyder, N. F. R., and J. W. Wiley
1976.   Sexual Size Dimorphism in Hawks and Owls of
         North America. A.O.U. Ornith. Monogr. 20, 96 pp.

Slud, P.
1964.   The birds of Costa Rica. Bull. Amer. Mus. Nat. Hist.
         128:1–430.

Tucker, V. A.
1971.   Flight energetics in birds. Am. Zoologist 11:115–124.

1972.   Respiration during flight in birds. Respiration Phys-
         iology 14:75–82.

Wetmore, A.
1965.   *The Birds of the Republic of Panama.* Part I. Smithsonian
         Misc. Coll. 150(4617). 483 pp.

Williams, T. C., J. M. Williams, L. C. Ireland, and J. M.
         Teal
1977.   Autumnal bird migration over the western North
         Atlantic Ocean. Amer. Birds 31(3):251–67.

JOHN W. FITZPATRICK
Department of Biology
Princeton University
Princeton, New Jersey 08540

Wintering of North American Tyrant Flycatchers in the Neotropics

ABSTRACT
Twenty-two of 32 flycatcher species winter south of their North American breeding ranges. Only 8 reach South America where no more than 6 are sympatric. Most flycatchers winter in habitat similar to breeding habitat. Food and social habits are discussed.

In some places, migrant species use peripheral habitats, in others, resident species seem peripheral. In Mexico, migrants may prevent the northward spread of more southerly species.

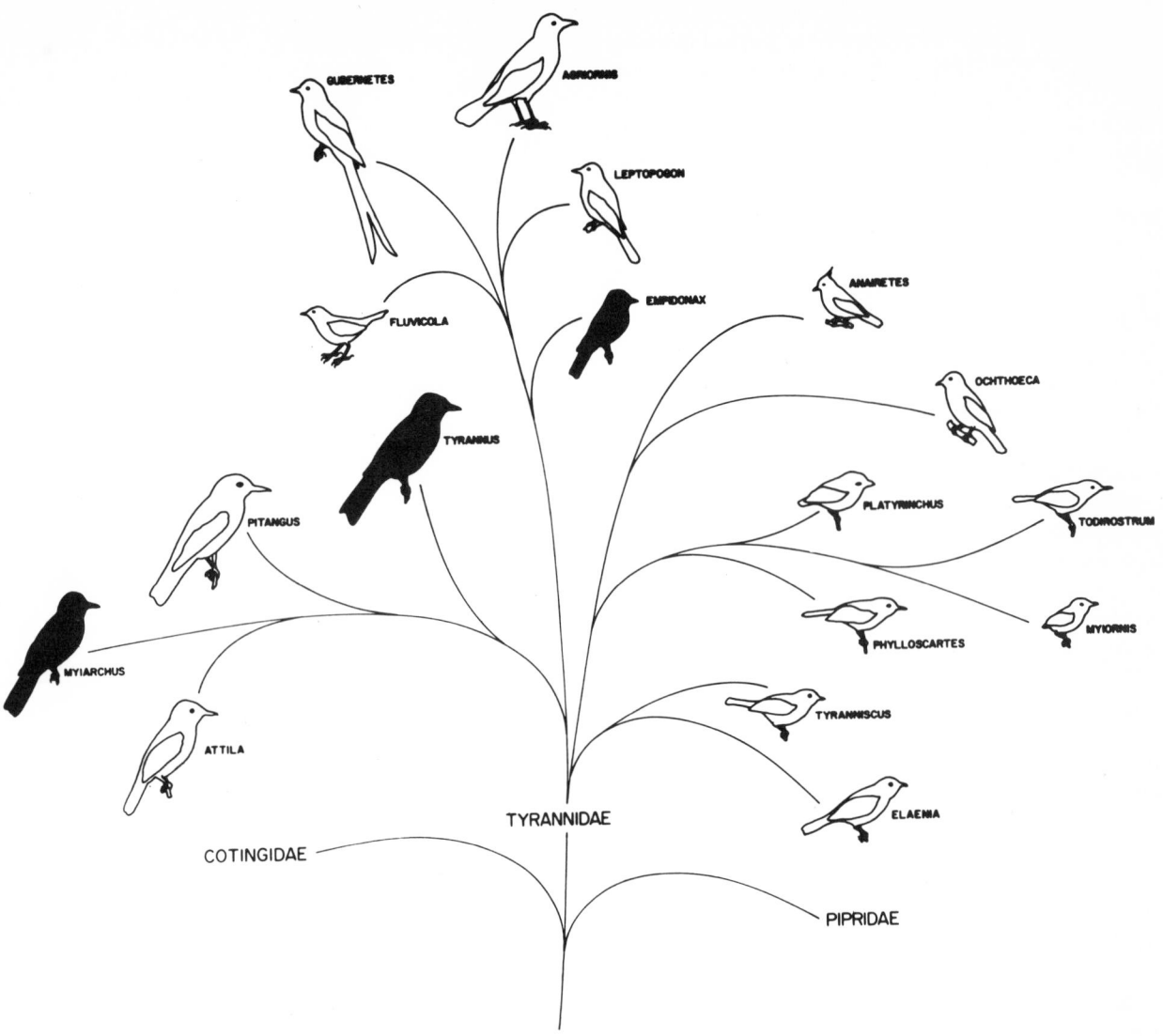

Figure 1. Approximate phylogenetic relationships of the major groups of Tyrant Flycatchers (Tyrannidae), showing representative genera in each group. The three lineages with North American members (blackened figures) are represented, left to right, by *Myiarchus*, *Tyrannus*, and *Empidonax*. Remaining genera (clockwise from lower left): *Attila, Pitangus, Fluvicola, Gubernetes, Agriornis, Ochthoeca, Leptopogon, Anairetes, Platyrinchus, Todirostrum, Myiornis, Phylloscartes, Tyranniscus, Elaenia*. Adapted from M. A. Traylor (MS).

The southward movement of Temperate-Zone breeding Tyrant Flycatchers (family Tyrannidae) presents a unique situation for the ecological study of migration. Each autumn a handful of species move from North America into tropical scrub and forests already teeming with resident species that comprise the most diverse New World bird family (Keast 1972; see figure 1). This paper is an analysis of winter distributions and patterns of habitat use in a group of tyrannids that breed in North America and winter in Central and South America. The objects of this study are, 1) to show how these migrants relate to each other and to permanently resident relatives on a geographic scale

and 2) to indicate some ecological differences between over-wintering migrants in Central versus South America.

I begin with a summary of winter distributions of the North American species, including a breakdown of distributions according to the breeding geography of the species. This is followed by an examination of habitats occupied by species wintering in Central America, using the *Empidonax* complex as an example. The pattern shown by this example, and repeated by other migrant flycatchers, leads to a hypothesis regarding the relative importance of the North American element on its wintering ground in Central Amer-

68

John W. Fitzpatrick

ica. I present next an outline of the ecological positions occupied by tyrannids wintering in western Amazonia, and conclude by contrasting the ecology of South American migrant flycatchers with the apparent situation in Central America.

Species Treated

Thirty-two flycatcher species regularly breed north of the Mexican border (A.O.U. 1957; Robbins et al 1966). Table 1 separates these species into three groups based on their migration habits. Three species are widespread in the tropics, and are non-migratory in their limited breeding range in the United States. An additional 7 tropical species breed in southwestern United States but migrate only from the northern extremities of their range. The remaining 22 species regularly breed north of Mexico and winter wholly or significantly south of their breeding ranges. Species in the first two groups are treated here as residents. The third group forms the set of migrant species discussed in this paper.

Winter Distribution Patterns

Figure 2 is a composite range map showing the densities of wintering flycatchers from northern Mexico south to Argentina. Several features displayed by the figure warrant emphasis. Of the 22 migrant species, only 8 reach South America, and no more than 6 winter sympatrically on that continent. No flycatcher regularly winters in the West Indies, and one species (Gray Kingbird, *Tyrannus dominicensis*) even leaves the Caribbean islands to winter in northern South America. In these respects, the flycatchers differ markedly from the Wood Warblers (Parulidae), which are discussed in great detail elsewhere in this symposium. The bulk of the temperate zone tyrannids move into Central America.

Figure 3 plots the number of wintering species from southern Texas south to Paraguay, and compares their diversity to that of resident flycatchers along the same transect. The figure shows that wintering migrants accumulate in the middle latitudes of Central America, reaching a peak of 13 species in southern Mexico. Because resident diversity increases regularly toward the equator (Cook 1971), temperate zone migrants in Central America coexist with many fewer residents than do those in South America. Furthermore, from southern Mexico southward, the tyrannids reflect the general tendency of migrant land birds to winter in inverse proportions to the number of residents in any given area (c.f. Slud 1976:7). The differing peaks of diversity between migrants and residents shown in figure 3 suggest that the ecological relationships be-

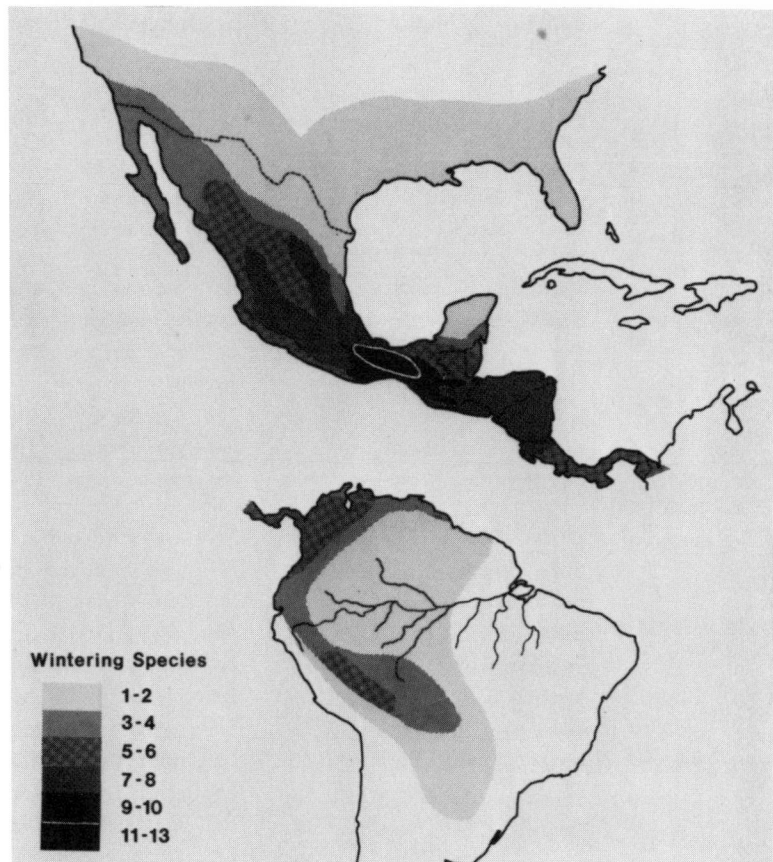

Figure 2. Map of wintering species densities of 22 North American migrant flycatchers in Central and South America.

Wintering Species

1-2
3-4
5-6
7-8
9-10
11-13

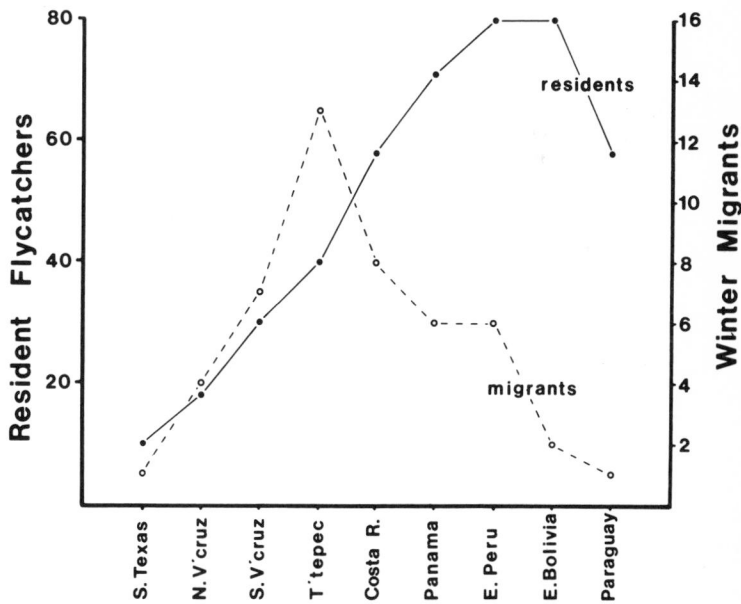

Figure 3. Number of resident (closed circles, solid line) and winter migrant (open circles, dashed line) Tyrant Flycatchers from southern Texas south to northern Paraguay. A peak of 80 resident species occurs in western Amazonia; a maximum of 13 migrant species winter in southern Mexico.

Table 1. Winter distributions of North American Tyrant Flycatchers[1]

Species	Wintering Range
Black Phoebe	Same as breeding range
Couch's Kingbird	Same as breeding range
Great Kiskadee	Same as breeding range
Vermilion Flycatcher	Extreme Southwest United States to South America
Thick-billed Kingbird	Central and Southern Mexico to Guatemala; rare
Wied's Crested Flycatcher	Central Mexico to South America
Olivaceous Flycatcher	Northern Mexico to South America
Coues' Flycatcher	Northern Mexico to Nicaragua
Buff-breasted Flycatcher	Northern Mexico to Honduras
Northern Beardless Tyrannulet	Extreme northern Mexico to Costa Rica
Eastern Phoebe	Southeast United States to southern Mexico (Veracruz, Oaxaca)
Say's Phoebe	Southwest United States to southern Mexico (Chiapas)
Scissor-tailed Flycatcher	Southern Mexico (southern Veracruz, Oaxaca) to Panama
Eastern Kingbird	Southwest Amazonia; rarely to Argentina (Misiones)
Western Kingbird	Southern Mexico (Oaxaca, southern Veracruz) to Nicaragua
Cassin's Kingbird	Extreme southwest United States to Guatemala
Gray Kingbird	South West Indies (rare); Panama to northern Colombia, Guyana
Sulphur-bellied Flycatcher	Southwest Amazonia, Ecuador to Bolivia
Great Crested Flycatcher	Southeast Mexico (Veracruz, Yucatan) to northern Colombia
Ash-throated Flycatcher	Extreme southwest United States to Costa Rica
Eastern Wood Pewee	Panama (?); northwest South America to Bolivia
Western Wood Pewee	Panama, northern Colombia; (uncertain)
Olive-sided Flycatcher	Panama, Andean South America to Bolivia
Yellow-bellied Flycatcher	Northeast Mexico (southern Tamaulipas) to Panama
Willow Flycatcher	Southern Mexico (southern Veracruz, Oaxaca) to northern Colombia
Alder Flycatcher	Northwest Colombia to Paraguay and Argentina (Misiones)
Acadian Flycatcher	Costa Rica to western Colombia and northwest Venezuela
Least Flycatcher	Northern Mexico (Durango, Tamaulipas) to western Panama
Hammond's Flycatcher	Central and southern interior Mexico (Durango to Chiapas)
Dusky Flycatcher	Interior Mexico (Sonora, Chihuahua to Chiapas)
Gray Flycatcher	Extreme southwest United States to southern Mexico (Veracruz, Oaxaca)
Western Flycatcher	Pacific slope of Mexico (Sonora to Oaxaca)

[1] See Appendix 1 for scientific names of species.

tween these groups may differ down the latitudinal gradient. Direct evidence of this difference is presented in the following two sections.

Plotting the winter ranges of eastern versus western breeding species separately (figure 4) provides a revealing comparison. The eastern species build up gradually through Central America, reach a peak in Colombia, and taper off down western Amazonia. Of 10 eastern species, 7 reach South America and 5 winter exclusively there. In contrast, only 2 of 12 western species (Sulphur-bellied Flycatcher *Myiodynastes luteiv-* *entris* and Western Wood Pewee *Contopus sordidulus*) winter in South America, and the remainder funnel into Central America to account for most of the buildup of wintering species in southern Mexico (c.f. figures 2 and 4). The eastern and western flycatcher faunas give the impression of excluding each other gradually across southern Central America. Some ecological correlates of this pattern are discussed in later sections.

Geographic separation seems especially pronounced among complexes of closely related species with similar

John W. Fitzpatrick

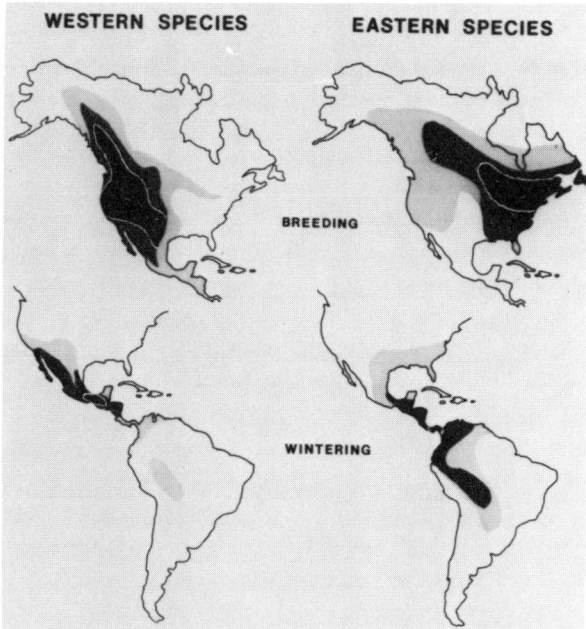

Figure 4. Species densities of 10 eastern and 12 western North American flycatchers on their breeding and wintering grounds. Sparse dots = 1–2 species; dense dots = 3–6 species; black = 7–9 species.

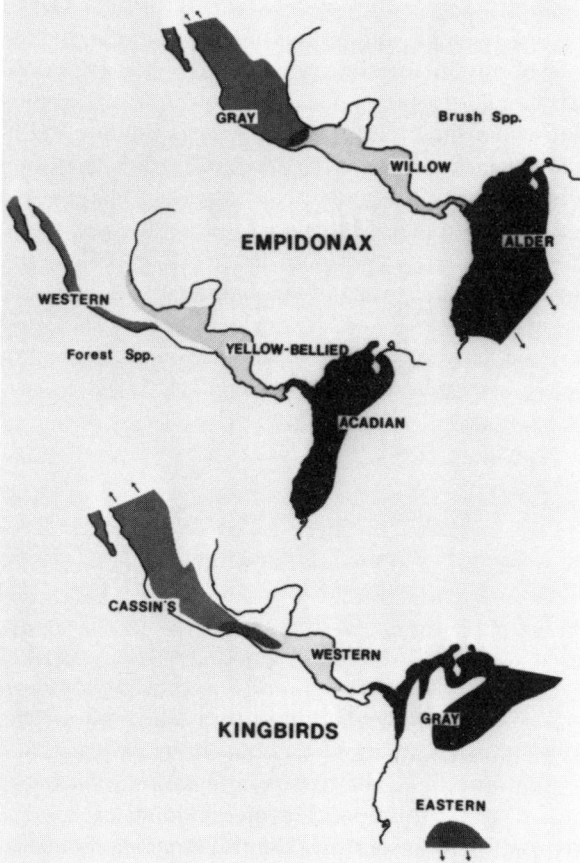

Figure 5. Parapatric winter distributions among three sets of ecologically similar flycatcher species in Central and northern South America. Small arrows indicate distributions that continue beyond the area shown on the maps.

wintering habitats. Figure 5 shows three sets of geographic replacements between species for which wintering habitat data are available (Karr 1976; Monroe 1968; Ridgely 1976; Slud 1964; Willis 1966; various Mexican checklists). These and other examples suggest that, while tyrannid wintering patterns show only slight relationship to the resident community on a gross geographic scale, many wintering species sort out among themselves on a much finer scale. Ecologically dissimilar species show significant geographic overlap on their wintering grounds. This is especially pronounced between members of different genera, but can even occur among close relatives (e.g. Willow and Yellow-bellied Flycatchers *Empidonax brewsteri* and *E. flaviventris* in figure 5). Similar species, with similar winter habitats, often are allopatric. These observations provide a first order indication that competition between close relatives played some role during the development of winter distributions of these species.

Thus, over much of Central America, a wintering tyrannid community should contain only one Kingbird, one *Myiarchus*, one Phoebe, and a few species of ecologically distinct *Empidonax*. If this is true, then the build-up of species in the Isthmus of Tehuantepec (figure 2) may simply reflect a zone of local overlaps between geographically replacing species.

The above generalities emphasize the importance of procuring data on habitat preferences among closely related forms, in order to determine the ecological roles of wintering migrants. Habitat characteristics in two groups of species are examined in detail in the following sections. My choice of groups is intended to illustrate a key difference between the biogeographies of the Central American versus the South American wintering species.

Central American *Empidonax* Flycatcher Habitats

For well over half the year, eight of the nine migrant *Empidonax* considered in this paper reside in Central America, where they join five endemic residents in the genus and three other close relatives, currently placed in adjacent genera. With such an array of migrants and residents, similar both in size and in foraging habits, differences in distribution and habitat use must be paramount in any ecological segregation between them. Examples that support this generalization abound among the temperate zone species on their breeding grounds (Beaver and Baldwin 1975; Hespenheide 1971; Johnson 1963; Johnston 1971). As already shown here, several wintering *Empidonax* species do indeed show distributional separation (figure 5).

Published information on wintering *Empidonax*, though scarce, suggests an interesting pattern of hab-

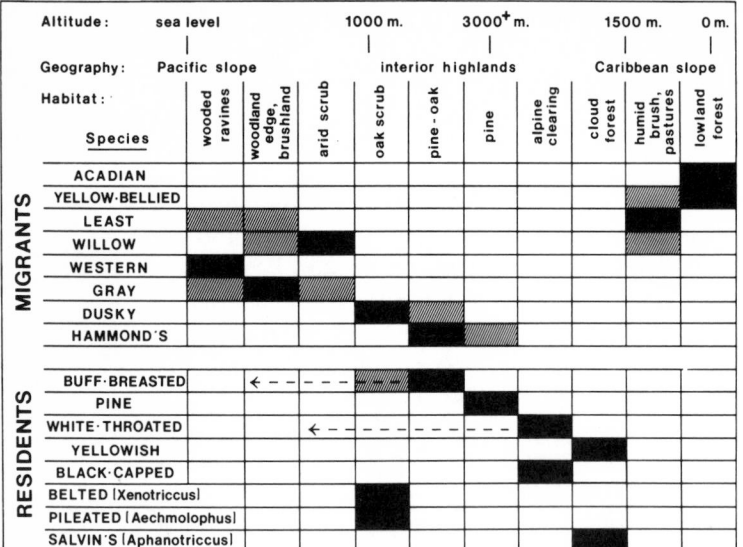

Figure 6. Approximate habitats of resident and winter migrant species of *Empidonax* and relatives in Central America. Left to right corresponds to an eastwest cross-section of Central America. Solid rectangles show preferred habitats, hatched rectangles show habitats in which respective species are less common.

itat use, which is diagrammed in figure 6. Four points illustrated in figure 6 warrant emphasis, as they appear to characterize other groups of flycatchers in Central America as well.

1) Some sharp habitat segregation occurs in the Central American mountains, among residents themselves, between residents and migrants, and even between the migrant species alone. Segregation along the altitudinal gradient, while evident, is probably a byproduct of different habitats characterizing different elevations in this area. Habitat separation also occurs between resident and migrant kingbirds (*Tyrannus*) and in the *Myiarchus* flycatchers.

2) Resident *Empidonax* species are nearly restricted, in the breeding season at least, to upper elevations and habitats. Many of these species, especially the three endemic relatives at the bottom of figure 6, are rare and restricted to local habitat formations. The amount of movement by residents into other habitats during winter remains to be worked out, but it is clear that the migrant fauna predominate in the middle and lower elevations. Resident Kingbirds (Tropical, Couch's, Thick-billed) and certain *Myiarchus* species (Nutting's, Yucatán, Flammulated) also show this re-

striction to peculiar habitats or distributions in Central America.

3) Migrants from eastern North America predominate in the moist Caribbean habitats, while western species are widespread in arid and semi-arid interior highlands and on the Pacific slope. This pattern holds throughout the migrant flycatchers: western species (the kingbirds, Ash-throated and Scissor-tailed Flycatchers, Say's Phoebe) winter widely in the dry interior, while the few eastern species (Great Crested Flycatcher, Eastern Phoebe) occupy the more humid Caribbean habitats.

4) Gross habitat preferences of wintering North American *Empidonax* strongly resemble those on their breeding grounds. Thus, for example, woodland and forest breeders (Western, Yellow-bellied, Acadian) favor forested habitats in Central America, while species that breed in montane pine-oak associations (Hammond's Dusky) winter in similar associations in Mexico. Once again, the pattern is similar for most of the other flycatcher species.

These observations suggest that Central America acts as a simple funnel for migrant western species, which move along the mountain chain between similar, more or less contiguous habitats on their breeding and wintering grounds. These species migrate southward only as far as the dry habitats exist. They stop where forested lowlands begin to predominate, at the end of the funnel. Moreover, the migrant species appear to become a dominant fauna in the middle and lower elevations, occupying habitats that comprise most of Mexico. Their resident relatives occupy restricted areas on mountain slopes (*Contopus* spp., *Empidonax* and relatives), coastal lowlands (*Tyrannus*, certain *Myiarchus*, *Deltarhynchus*), or otherwise restricted habitats (e.g. Black Phoebe).

Migrant Flycatchers in Amazonian Peru

This section briefly summarizes the ecology of some migrant flycatchers that winter in western Amazonia. These observations were made at the Cocha Cashu Biological Station, Manu National Park, Madre de Dios, Peru. I studied migrants at this site from August through December 1976, and returned in May 1977. Other investigators, who were present during the rainy season interim, provided some useful additions to my notes. As my field work centered primarily on the resident flycatcher fauna, my data on migrants are sufficient only to suggest some ecological patterns of interest here.

We recorded only nine North Amerian migrant passerines at Cocha Cashu, of which five were flycatch-

John W. Fitzpatrick

Table 2. Arrival times of 5 migrant flycatchers in south-eastern Peru, 1976

Species	First record	Second record
Eastern Kingbird	26 Sept (20)[1]	30 Sept (120)
Sulphur-bellied Flycatcher	21 Sept (2)	2 Oct (2)
Eastern Wood Pewee[2]	7 Oct (1)	12 Oct (2)
Olive-sided Flycatcher	3 Nov (2)	—
Alder Flycatcher	11 Oct (1)	21 Oct (3)

[1] Numbers in parentheses refer to number of individuals noted on that day.

[2] Eastern Wood Pewee departed in mid-April in 1977.

ers. The others were Barn and Bank Swallows (*Hirundo rustica* and *Riparia riparia*), Swainson's Thrush (*Catharus ustulatus*), and Summer Tanager (*Piranga rubra*). Table 2 lists arrival dates of the five flycatchers, four of which were resident from October at least through December. Unfortunately, departure date could be ascertained only for the Eastern Wood Pewee.

Habitat records for the four common flycatchers are summarized in figure 7. Condensing some 40 habitat subdivisions into 13 categories, I ordered them in figure 7 along a gradient from fully exposed, open edges on one end to deep forest interior on the other. Fifty resident flycatchers have been recorded at this site (excluding nine migrants from southern South America), and figure 7 also shows the number of these that were recorded in each habitat category.

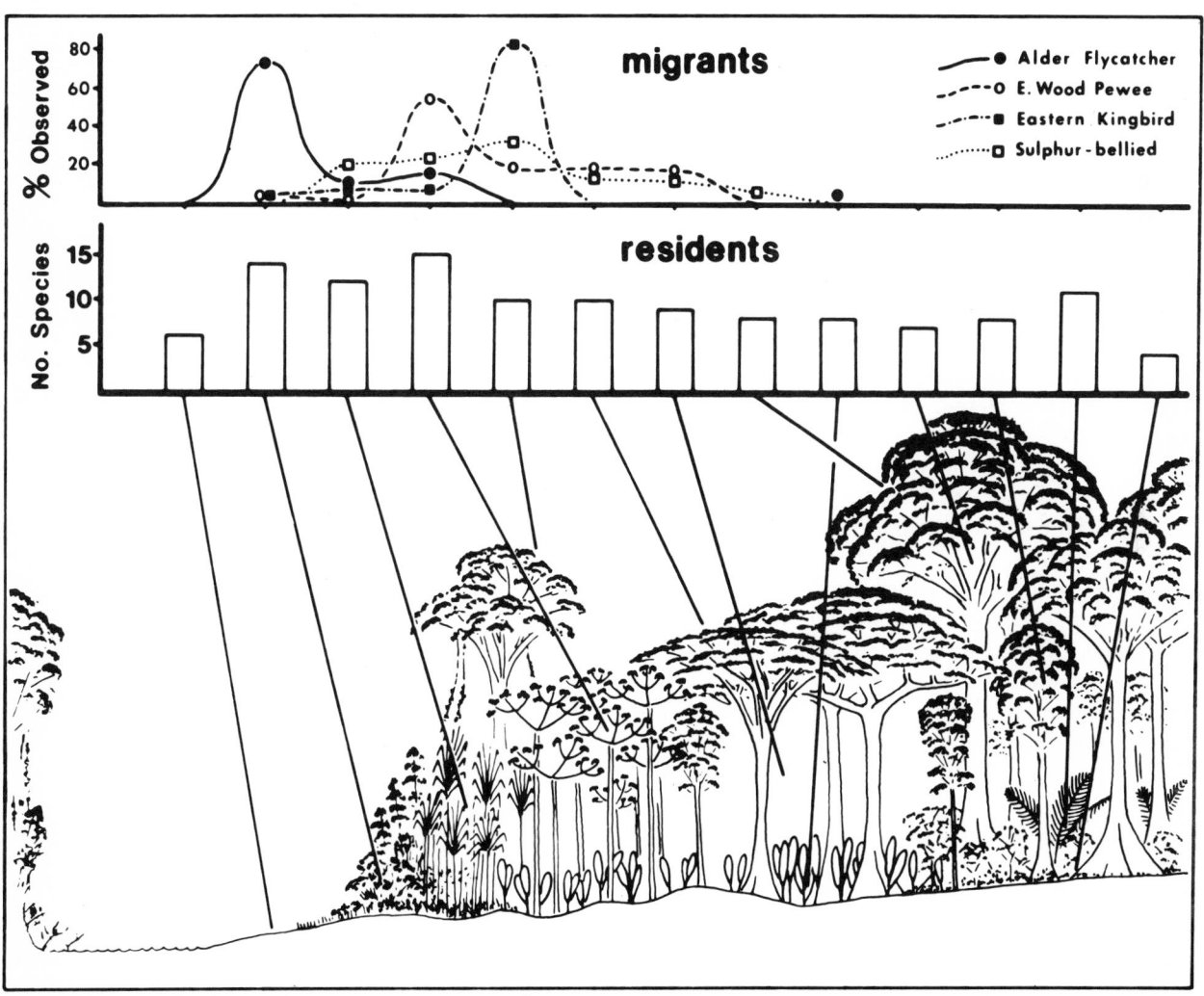

Figure 7. Schematic cross-section of Amazonian river bottom habitats. 13 habitat categories are arranged left to right from river edge to rain forest interior, in order of increasing distance from forest edge. Histogram shows number of resident flycatcher species (50 total) found in each habitat type. Distributions of habitat records for 4 common North American migrant flycatchers are shown on upper axes.

While tyrannids are most numerous in canopy and edge situations (unpubl. data), figure 6 shows that resident species can be found in every habitat at Cocha Cashu. However, the migrant species clearly concentrate at the open end of this habitat spectrum, preferentially occupying vegetation zones that comprise less than 10 percent of the area in our study tract. I have no records of migrants inside any of several types of tall forest. The four common migrants differ greatly in their morphology and feeding habits, hence it is no surprise that each shows a unique distribution of habitat preferences (figure 7).

As no account of the wintering ecology of these migrants is currently available, I present here a summary of my observations for each species, indicating, where possible, its relationship with resident flycatchers in the area.

Alder Flycatcher

I refer all sight records of this form to *Empidonax alnorum* following Gorski (1969, 1971). The species becomes common in its restricted habitat, the brushy new growth of an early successional vegetation along freshly deposited sand beaches. It occurs in smaller numbers in dense brush lining the shores of an oxbow lake. Its foraging behavior, as on its breeding ground, consists of short sally-gleans against leaves, well inside dense vegetation. Aerial hawking is rare, and new perches are almost invariably chosen after each sally.

Three closely related species sporadically use this habitat, but all are uncommon to rare in the study tract: Euler's Flycatcher (*Empidonax euleri*) favors swampy forest understory; Fuscous Flycatcher (*Cnemotriccus fuscatus*) is rare, and nearly restricted to canebrakes; Bran-colored Flycatcher (*Myiophobus fasciatus*) is also rare, and occupies open brushy edges of marshes and wide river cuts. The Alder Flycatcher, for half the year, becomes the most common tyrannid in a transient habitat that is virtually free of resident relatives. Many other, more distantly related flycatchers use this habitat, including a few species that are restricted to it, but I saw no interactions between any of them and the Alder.

Eastern Wood Pewee

Contopus cinereus first appeared in the seasonally flooded, mid-successional *Cecropia* and young *Ficus* stands bordering river edges, where it rapidly became common. Toward the end of migration period (early November), individuals appeared in forest openings along lakeshores and a few sang sporadically from treefall openings. In the mattoral zone individuals occupied small, contiguous territories along a strip of open *Cecropia* canopy parallel to the river. In this area, numerous individuals could be heard calling during all daylight hours. Singing pewees were spaced at roughly 200-m intervals in this favored habitat. Many could be found foraging at the same location, even using the same exposed perches, for the duration of the study period.

I recorded 160 sallies by Eastern Wood Pewees, of which 138 (86 percent) were aerial hawks, and 133 (83 percent) were followed by a return to the same perch. Only one other small tyrannid at Cocha Cashu, the Vermilion Flycatcher, uses this foraging method. Its behavior and habitat preferences are extremely similar to those of Eastern Wood Pewees. However, the Vermilion Flycatcher also is a migrant in southeastern Peru, leaving the region in early September to breed in eastern Bolivia and Argentina. It returns to western Amazonia early in May, three to four weeks after the departure of pewees. Thus, the periods of residence for this pair of ecologically similar migrants at Cocha Cashu are non-overlapping, permitting Eastern Wood Pewees to occupy an ecologically unique position on their wintering ground in Amazonia.

Olive-sided Flycatcher

I found two *Nuttallornis borealis*, probably wandering individuals, perched several meters apart on the bare tips of a 40 m leafless tree along the lakeshore. One bird was chased briefly by a Tropical Kingbird, and the pair departed together after about 15 minutes. This constitutes our only record for the species at Cocha Cashu. Olive-sides normally winter in the Andes in Peru (Meyer de Schauensee 1966).

Sulphur-bellied Flycatcher

Myiodynastes luteiventris becomes fairly common in all types of river edge forest, apparently preferring subcanopy perches in older *Cecropia* stands and adjacent, mature *Ficus* zones. Its habitat preferences precisely match those of the extremely similar Streaked Flycatcher (*M. maculatus*), which it far outnumbers during the latter's breeding season. The Sulphur-bellied is predominantly insectivorous on its breeding grounds (Ligon 1971), as is Streaked at Cocha Cashu (unpubl. data). However, nearly all my records of Sulphur-bellied at Cocha Cashu (n = 50) are of small groups of two to five birds feeding on fruiting vines and trees.

I saw no encounters between Streaked and Sulphur-bellied Flycatchers. The relative scarcity of the resident compared to the abundance of migrant Sulphur-bellies during the late November fruiting peak suggests that opportunities for such an interaction would be rare. Furthermore, Streaked Flycatchers tended to forage from solitary vines when eating fruit, while Sul-

John W. Fitzpatrick

phur-bellies concentrated at large mistletoe clusters, on heavily laden vines of several species, and on fruiting trees (Moraceae, Anonaceae, Lauraceae). A lone Sulphur-bellied was chased once by a Social Flycatcher (*Myiozetetes similis*).

Eastern Kingbird

Migrant kingbirds (*Tyrannus tyrannus*) arrived in small groups, but by mid-October could be seen daily passing overhead in flocks of 25–250 birds. With no exceptions in 41 separate encounters, foraging flocks were found only on fruiting trees. Scattered individuals sallied sporadically for aerial prey, but most birds were consuming immense quantities of fruit. Eastern Kingbirds favored river-edge and lake-edge canopies and seemed to concentrate on a relatively few tree species common in these habitats (Anonaceae and Lauraceae).

Tropical Kingbirds (*T. melancholicus*) are common residents along river and lake margins in western Amazonia. Their annual diet contains only about 2 percent fruit at Cocha Cashu. While this percentage is slightly higher during the fruiting season, their diet remains predominantly insectivorous year round. Figure 8 shows the results of a perch height census of kingbirds along the Manu River in December. The differences in perch height preferences reflect the tendency for Tropicals to perch on exposed snags, often low over the water, for aerial insect hawking. Easterns perched exclusively near the tops of river-edge fruiting trees.

Eastern Kingbirds may be nomadic in western Amazonia. Flocks broke up and coalesced with no obvious pattern and often departed from the study site by flying several kilometers downriver before disappearing. Winter flocking in this species is widely reported, and may be an adaptation associated with the species' reliance upon locally superabundant fruit supplies on its winter range (Horn 1968; Leck 1972; Morton 1971).

An additional advantage to winter flocking is suggested by the species' interactions with resident flycatchers. Eight large-bodied Tyrannine species occur in western Amazonia, on the wintering grounds of the Eastern Kingbird. All of these rely to some extent on fruit, and the diets of several of them contain over 50 percent fruit items (unpubl. data). At Cocha Cashu, four of these species (Great Kiskadee, Social and Gray-capped Flycatchers, and Tropical Kingbird) persistently chased Eastern Kingbirds at fruiting trees. Chases by Social Flycatchers and Tropical Kingbirds were especially intense, and individual Eastern Kingbirds often were driven from the tree altogether. However, the latter species invariably outnumbered all

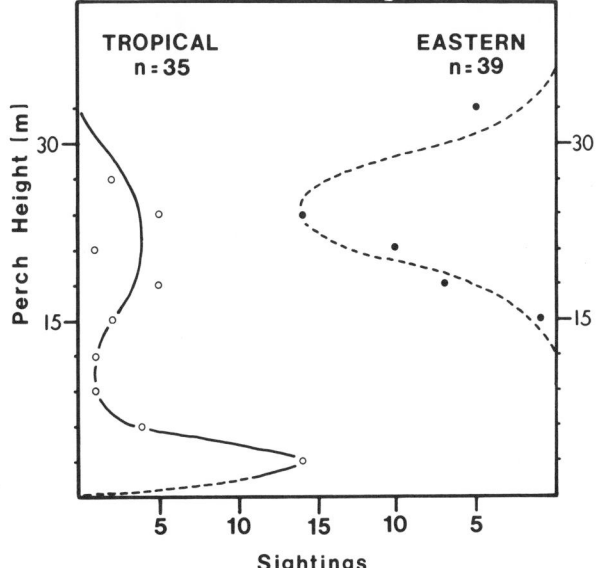

Figure 8.   Perch heights of resident Tropical Kingbirds and migrant Eastern Kingbirds along a Peruvian river edge in southwestern Amazonia in December 1976.

resident flycatchers present on the tree, sometimes by a whole order of magnitude. While subordinate at the individual level, Eastern Kingbirds simply avoided attacks by fleeing, and returned when the resident turned to chase another individual. Lone Eastern Kingbirds would easily be driven out of a fruiting tree, but by traveling in a flock each individual is merely harassed occasionally by the dominant residents. The phenomenon resembles that described by Orians (1961) between Tricolored and Redwing Blackbirds (*Agelaius tricolor, A. phoeniceus*).

Discussion and Conclusion

Karr (1976: 456) concludes his review of temperate zone migrants in the tropics by suggesting that "... migrant birds are keyed to the exploitation of superabundant and/or sporadically available resources in their tropical wintering area. These resources are often most easily exploited in disturbed, transitory, or isolated patches of habitat." This conclusion, which is supported by other studies (Willis 1966; Leck 1972; Tramer 1974b), summarizes widespread notions regarding the role of migrants in the tropics.

My data for South American flycatchers support Karr's conclusion. As figure 7 shows, migrants in western Amazonia occupy early successional habitats, some of which are exceedingly transitory. New growth along Amazonian lakes and rivers either washes away with rainy season floods, or is rapidly superceded by more permanent vegetation formations (Terborgh and

D. Atkin unpubl. data). The smaller migrants occupy territories in habitats largely spurned by their resident relatives. The large-bodied species appear almost nomadic in their use of fruit during its local, seasonal superabundance.

Data on migrant flycatchers elsewhere in South America and in Panama also support Karr's generalization. Many of the larger-bodied species occur commonly at fruit trees (Morton 1971; Leck 1972; pers. comm., O'Neill pers. comm., Fitzpatrick unpubl. data). Willis (1966) reports Sulphur-bellied Flycatchers commonly inhabiting river edge vegetation in eastern Ecuador. Acadian flycatchers, while occurring inside forest, are subordinate but regular army ant followers (Willis 1966). Willis also found Great-crested Flycatchers over army ants in Colombia. Gorski (1971) found Alder Flycatchers several places in northern Peru using brushy growth similar to that used at Cocha Cashu. Munves (1975) reports that Eastern Wood Pewees were common in a middle elevation forest clearing in Colombia, and I have found the Olive-sided Flycatcher foraging over tidal scrub and mangrove flats in northern Venezuela.

Considering these observations, and recalling the winter distributions shown in figure 5, it appears that tyrannids breeding in the moist habitats of eastern North America migrate to the humid tropics, where they fill in at the periphery of the vast resident community that occupies these regions year round.

In contrast, it appears that in Central America, a block of *resident* species actually represents the ecologically peripheral fauna, occupying isolated distributions and variously restricted habitats compared to those occupied by their northern counterparts. Moving southward in the autumn, the western North American species constitute a dominant element in the Central American extension of their mountain chain. They stop, and even concentrate at the southern top of their dry mountain habitats.

This interpretation suggests that a partial ecological vacuum is left when Central American wintering species migrate northward. The key tests of this hypothesis await careful field studies of tyrannid wintering habitats in Central America. Quantitative data in support of my generalizations from figure 5 are unavailable at this time. However, one simple test can be made by comparing the breeding fauna of the Central American scrub with that of adjacent scrub in northern South America. If the North American element does leave a vacuum by departing from the Central American interior, the resident fauna in that area might be expected to be deficient compared with similar habitats in coastal Colombia and Venezuela. Furthermore, the difference should be greatest between the small-

Table 3. Breeding tyrannid faunas of semi-arid scrub in Mexico and Northern Venezuela[1]

Foraging mode	Number of species		Number of genera	
	Mexico	Venezuela	Mexico	Venezuela
Ground and near-ground sally	1	1	1	1
Large-bodied omnivore	3	5	3	4
Medium-bodied omnivore	1	3	1	2
Small-bodied leaf-gleaner	6	12	4	10
Small-bodied perch-gleaner	4	5	4	4
Total	15	26	13	21

[1] Venezuelan data from unpublished field studies in Aragua, Falcón, Zulia states, 1975–77. Mexican data from Peterson and Chalif (1973).

bodied, leaf-gleaning components of the respective faunas, as this group comprises the bulk of the North American migrants. The data shown in table 3 uphold both these predictions.

Whether the differing generic diversities between Mexico and Venezuelan scrub permit the dominance of migrants in interior Mexico, or whether they are caused by that dominance, remains debatable. It is tempting to speculate, however, that the reduced breeding fauna in Mexico may not be a purely historical accident. Rather, it may be reflecting the short-term northward movement of a major subset of the Central American avifauna during the breeding season. Tramer (1974a) shows that the latitudinal gradient in bird species diversity is skewed and irregular during the temperate breeding season, but is a smoothly inclining curve during the temperate winter. This important observation suggests that climatically determined limits to flycatcher species diversity in Mexico are reached during the nonbreeding season, and that the presence of so many migrants for over half the year in that area has prohibited the northward spread of more southerly genera and species.

It is revealing to note that many of the so-called resident species even in Mexico actually move somewhat during the winter. Thus, it may be accurate to consider the flycatchers of western North America and of most of Central America as representing a single montane fauna, in which a continuum of migration habits exists. At one end lie species that do not migrate

John W. Fitzpatrick

Appendix. Flycatcher species mentioned

Common name	Scientific name
Black Phoebe	*Sayornis nigricans*
Eastern Phoebe	*Sayornis phoebe*
Say's Phoebe	*Sayornis saya*
Vermilion Flycatcher	*Pyrocephalus rubinus*
Scissor-tailed Flycatcher	*Tyrannus (Muscivora) forficatus*
Eastern Kingbird	*Tyrannus tyrannus*
Gray Kingbird	*Tyrannus dominicensis*
Thick-billed Kingbird	*Tyrannus crassirostris*
Western Kingbird	*Tyrannus verticalis*
Cassin's Kingbird	*Tyrannus vociferans*
Tropical Kingbird	*Tyrannus melancholicus*
Couch's Kingbird	*Tyrannus couchii*
Streaked Flycatcher	*Myiodynastes maculatus*
Sulphur-bellied Flycatcher	*Myiodynastes luteiventris*
Social Flycatcher	*Myiozetetes similis*
Gray-capped Flycatcher	*Myiozetetes granadensis*
Great Kiskadee	*Pitangus sulphuratus*
Ash-throated Flycatcher	*Myiarchus cinerascens*
Great Crested Flycatcher	*Myiarchus crinitus*
Wied's Crested Flycatcher	*Myiarchus tyrannulus*
Olivaceous Flycatcher	*Myiarchus tuberculifer*
Nutting's Flycatcher	*Myiarchus nuttingi*
Yucatan Flycatcher	*Myiarchus yucatensis*
Flammulated Flycatcher	*Deltarhynchus flammulatus*
Olive-sided Flycatcher	*Contopus (Nuttalornis) borealis*
Coues' Flycatcher	*Contopus pertinax*
Eastern Wood Pewee	*Contopus virens*
Western Wood Pewee	*Contopus sordidulus*
Yellow-bellied Flycatcher	*Empidonax flaviventris*
Acadian Flycatcher	*Empidonax virescens*
Willow Flycatcher	*Empidonax traillii*
Alder Flycatcher	*Empidonax alnorum*
White-throated Flycatcher	*Empidonax albigularis*
Least Flycatcher	*Empidonax minimus*
Hammond's Flycatcher	*Empidonax hammondii*
Dusky Flycatcher	*Empidonax oberholseri*
Gray Flycatcher	*Empidonax wrightii*
Pine Flycatcher	*Empidonax affinis*
Western Flycatcher	*Empidonax difficilis*
Yellowish Flycatcher	*Empidonax flavescens*
Buff-breasted Flycatcher	*Empidonax fulvifrons*
Euler's Flycatcher	*Empidonax euleri*
Black-capped Flycatcher	*Empidonax atriceps*
Pileated Flycatcher	*Aechmolophus mexicanus*
Belted Flycatcher	*Xenotriccus callizonus*
Salvin's Flycatcher	*Aphanotriccus capitalis*
Fuscous Flycatcher	*Cnemotriccus fuscatus*
Bran-colored Flycatcher	*Myiophobus fasciatus*
Northern Beardless Tyrannulet	*Camptostoma imberbe*

at all (table 1), followed by those that descend to lower elevations or move slightly southward during winter. At the other end are the few species that leave the mountain chain entirely to join the eastern North American species in Panama and South America (Western Wood Pewee, Sulphur-bellied Flycatcher). Near this end of the continuum lie the bulk of the western species considered in this paper. This truly mobile fauna comprise, during most of the year, an integral part of the Central American bird community, but it leaves that area entirely for a few months each year to breed farther north, in the rich but ephemeral springtime of the temperate latitudes.

Acknowledgments

I am grateful to the Ministerio de Agricultura and the Dirección General Forestal y Fauna of Peru for their continued cooperation in permitting my field work in the Manu National Park. David Willard provided long hours of assistance with mist-nets in Peru. Richard Oehlenschlager and Steven Hilty sent me useful information on certain Central American flycatchers. Conversations with John W. Terborgh, Henry Horn, and J. Peter Myers were helpful, and Debra Moskovits assisted me in every stage of preparing this paper. I thank these colleagues for their help. Field work in South America was supported by grants from the National Science Foundation and the Chapman Memorial Fund, and by funds from the Biology Department of Princeton University.

Literature Cited

American Ornithologists' Union
1957. *Check-list of North American Birds.* Fifth Edition. Baltimore, Md.: A.O.U., 691 pp.

Beaver, D. L., and P. H. Baldwin
1975. Ecological overlap and the problem of competition and sympatry in the Western and Hammond's Flycatchers. Condor 77:1–14.

Cook, R. E.
1969. Variation in species density of North American birds. Syst. Zool. 18:63–84.

Gorski, L. J.
1969. Traill's Flycatchers of the 'fitz-bew' songform wintering in Panama. Auk 86:745–47.

1971. Traill's Flycatchers of the 'fee-bee-o' songform wintering in Peru. Auk 88:429–31.

Hespenheide, H. A.
1971. Flycatcher habitat selection in the eastern deciduous forest. Auk 88:61–74.

Horn, H. S.
1968. The adaptive significance of colonial nesting in the Brewer's Blackbird (*Euphagus cyanocephalus*). Ecol. 49: 682–94.

Johnson, N. K.
1963. Biosystematics of sibling species of flycatchers in the *Empidonax hammondii-oberholseri-wrightii* complex. Univ. Calif. Publ. Zool. 66:79–238.

Johnston, D. W.
1971. Niche relationships among some deciduous forest flycatchers. Auk 88:796–804.

Karr, J. R.
1976. On the relative abundance of migrants from the North Temperate Zone in tropical habitats. Wils. Bull. 88:433–58.

Keast, A.
1972. Ecological opportunities and dominant families, as illustrated by the Neotropical Tyrannidae (Aves). Evol. Biol. 5:229–77.

Leck, C. F.
1972. The impact of some North American migrants at fruiting trees in Panama. Auk 89:842–50.

Ligon, J. D.
1971. Notes of the breeding of the Sulphur-bellied Flycatcher in Arizona. Condor 73:250–52.

Meyer de Schauensee, R.
1966. *The Species of Birds of South America with Their Distribution.* Narberth, Pa.: Livingston, 577 pp.

Monroe, B. L., Jr.
1968. A distributional survey of the birds of Honduras. A.O.U. Ornith. Monogr. 7:1–458.

Morton, E. S.
1971. Food and migration habits of the Eastern Kingbird in Panama. Auk 88:925–26.

Munves, J.
1975. Birds of a highland clearing in Cundinimarca, Colombia. Auk 92:307–21.

Orians, G. H.
1961. The ecology of blackbird (*Agelaius*) social systems. Ecol. Monogr. 31:285–312.

Peterson, R. T., and E. L. Chalif
1973. A field guide to Mexican birds. Boston: Houghton Mifflin, 298 pp.

Ridgely, R. S., and J. A. Gwynne, Jr.
1976. A Guide to the Birds of Panama. Princeton, N.J.: Princeton Univ. Press, 394 pp.

Robbins, C. S., Bruun, B., and H. S. Zim
1966. Birds of North America. New York: Golden Press.

Slud, P.
1964. The birds of Costa Rica: distribution and ecology. Bull. Am. Mus. Nat. Hist. 128:1–430.

1976. Geographic and climatic relationships of avifaunas with special reference to comparative distribution in the Neotropics. Smithsonian Contr. Zool. 212.

Tramer, E. J.
1974a. On latitudinal gradients in avian diversity. Condor 76:123–30.
1974b. Proportions of wintering North American birds in disturbed and undisturbed dry tropical habitats. Condor 76:460–64.

Traylor, M. A.
In press. A classification of the flycatchers (Tyrannidae). Bull. Mus. Comp. Zool.

Willis, E. O.
1966. The role of migrant birds at swarms of army ants. Living Bird 5:187–31.

John W. Fitzpatrick

JON C. BARLOW
Department of Ornithology
Royal Ontario Museum
100 Queen's Park
Toronto, Ontario,
Canada M5S 2C6

Patterns of Ecological Interactions Among Migrant and Resident Vireos on the Wintering Grounds

ABSTRACT Basic adaptive patterns minimize interspecific competition among migrant and resident vireos. Eleven of the 43 vireo species breed in North America. Competition is reduced by foraging differently and in different strata, habitat differences, and spatial separation.

Winter ranges and habitats are described and a history of vireo distribution and migration patterns is suggested.

In spring vireos (family Vireonidae) are among the most conspicuous of North American migratory passerines. However, compared to wood warblers (Parulidae, 49 species) and tyrant flycatchers (Tyrannidae, 22 species) with only 11 kinds breeding north of Mexico (Gruson 1976) vireos are relatively species poor. From Canada to Argentina, no more than 7 species of vireos breed at any locale (after Slud 1976). In contrast, as many as 50 species of flycatchers may occur in the tropics at a given site. In spite of low species diversity, numbers of individuals of some taxa—notably Red-eyed (*V. olivaceus*), western Solitary (*V. solitarius plumbeus*) and White-eyed (*V. griseus*) vireos—may be very abundant and thus constitute a major source of competition for other migratory and resident insectivorous birds for resources available in winter in Latin America.

Vireos, which are morphologically and behaviorally quite similar (Hamilton 1958, 1962; Barlow and James 1975), are generally broadly sympatric in the breeding season in North America, but demonstrate rather precise ecological spatial separation, usually based on use of different habitats. Habitat co-occupancy, which occurs less frequently among summering species, is facilitated by foraging in different strata (Red-eyed and White-eyed vireos, Williamson 1971) and by in-

Table 1. Morphological, foraging and migratory factors promoting minimization of interspecific competition in North American vireos[1]

| | X̄ wt. (n = 10) | Morphology | | | | | | | | | Foraging Tactic | | | | |
| | | Wing | | Eye | | | Beak <7.5 mm | | Beak >7.5 mm | | Strata | | Dominant site | | |
		Bars	Plain	Iris color	Ring	Stripe	Thick	Thin	Thick	Thin	Above 4 m	Below 4 m	Peripheral foliage	Throughout foliage	Central bark
Subgenus *Lanivireo*															
Hutton's Vireo *Vireo huttoni* ssp.	12.0 g	+	—	Very dk brown	+	—	+	—	—	—	+	—	—	+	—
Gray Vireo *V. vicinior*	12.3 g	+	—	Very dk brown	+	—	+	—	—	—	—	+	—	+	—
Solitary Vireo *V. solitarius*	16.5 g	+	—	Very dk brown	+	—	—	—	+	—	+	—	—	—	+
Yellow-throated Vireo *V. flavifrons*	16.8 g	+	—	Very dk brown	+	—	—	—	+	—	+	—	—	—	+
Subgenus *Vireo*															
White-eyed Vireo *V. griseus* ssp.	11.5 g	+	—	White	+	—	+	—	—	—	—	+	—	+	—
Bell's Vireo *V. bellii* ssp.	9.5 g	+	—	Brown	+	—	+	—	—	—	—	+	—	+	—
Black-capped Vireo *V. atricapillus*	9.5 g	+	—	Brownish red	+	—	—	+	—	—	—	+	—	+	—
Subgenus *Vireosylva*															
Warbling Vireo *V. gilvus*	12.8 g	—	+	Dark brown	—	+	—	—	—	+	+	—	+	—	—
Philadelphia Vireo *V. philadelphicus*	10.8 g	—	+	Dark brown	—	+	—	+	—	—	+	—	+	—	—
Red-eyed Vireo *V. olivaceus*	16.8 g	—	+	Red	—	+	—	—	—	+	+	—	+	—	—
Black-whiskered Vireo *V. altiloquus* ssp.	16.7 g	—	+	Reddish brown	—	+	—	—	+	—	+	—	—	+	—

[1] Data are from Barlow (unpubl.), James (1973), Hamilton (1958, 1962), Marshall (1957), Orenstein and Barlow (unpubl.).

[2] (S = summer, W = winter, + = characteristic present for that species).

Jon C. Barlow

terspecific territoriality based on similarity of song (Red-eyed and Philadelphia vireos, Barlow and Power 1970; Rice 1978 a, b, c; Gray [*V. vicinior*] and Solitary [*V. solitarius*] vireos, Barlow et al 1970).

Until now there has been no assessment of interactions among migrant and sedentary populations of vireos that winter together in the tropics. In this paper by considering separately the relationship of breeding and wintering grounds of the North American species and by comparing ecological and behavioral mechanisms, I attempt to demonstrate basic adaptive patterns that minimize interspecific competition both among migrant vireos and between them and resident species of this family in the tropics. In addition, possible influence of migrant vireos on the breeding schedule of some resident species is examined.

Species Analyzed

Eleven (table 1) of the 43 described species of vireos occur in North America in summer from the Mexican border to 64°N latitude in the Northwest Territories (*A.O.U. Check-List* 1957; Godfrey 1967). They comprise an array of species from permanent resident to long distance migrant (table 1). These vireos belong to

Range			*Habitat*										
Permanent resident	*Migratory pattern*		*Scrub*		*Mixed parkland-ecotonal*			*Deciduous forest*		*Mixed forest*		*Coniferous forest*	
	Contiguous	Disjunct	Xeric	Mesic	Montane	Intermontane	Lowland	Xeric	Mesic	Xeric	Mesic	Xeric	Mesic
+	—	—	—	—	S, W	—	—	S, W	—	S, W	—	S, W	S, W
—	+	—	S, W	—	—	—	—	—	—	S	—	S	—
—	+	—	—	—	S	S, W	W	W	W	S, W	S, W	S, W	S
—	—	+	—	—	—	W	S, W	—	S, W	—	S	—	—
—	+	—	—	S, W	—	—	S, W	—	—	—	—	—	—
—	+	—	S, W	S, W	—	—	—	—	—	—	—	—	—
—	—	+	S, W	—	—	—	—	—	—	—	—	—	—
—	+	—	—	—	S, W	S, W	S	S, W	S, W	S, W	S, W	—	—
—	—	+	—	S	W	W	S, W	—	S, W	—	—	—	—
—	—	+	—	—	—	—	S, W	S	S, W	S	S	—	—
—	—	+	—	—	—	—	S, W	—	S, W	—	—	—	—

three subgenera characterized by differences in bill shape and plumage markings. Each subgenus is also distinguished by specific vocalizations (Barlow and James 1975), habitat use (Barlow and James 1975; Barlow and Rice 1977; James 1973), and differential participation by the sexes in stages of the nesting cycle (Barlow and Rice 1977).

Breeding Ranges

Although it is not my purpose to discuss breeding ranges of North American migratory vireos in detail, they are important to understanding how the evolutionary history of each species may have responded ecologically to interspecific competition. *Vireo huttoni* is a permanent resident in pine-oak belts from southwestern British Columbia to western Guatemala, but is of importance to the present study because it overlaps in winter with *V. vicinior, V. atricapillus, V. solitarius, V. flavifrons, V. griseus, V. gilvus* and *V. philadelphicus* and therefore may influence those species in some biological way or may, in turn, be influenced by them. However, our primary concern is with the migrants of which there are species in each subgenus that have breeding and wintering grounds that are either contiguous or disjunct (table 1). In summer the North American populations of *V. solitarius, V. griseus,* and the Warbling Vireo (*V. gilvus*) form a breeding continuum with sedentary populations in north central Mexico and, in the case of *V. gilvus,* south into South America through the morphologically distinctive but, nonetheless conspecific, *V. "leucophrys."*

Comparison of the ranges (figures 1–9, 11) shows varying degrees of sympatry among the species ranging from complete overlap of ecologically similar and subgenerically related *V. olivaceus* (figure 9) and *V. philadelphicus* (figure 7), and *V. bellii* (figure 3) and *V. atricapillus* (figure 1) to the broadly sympatric species that are separated by foraging differences and belong to different subgenera. Examples are *V. olivaceus* (figure 9) and *V. flavifrons* (figure 6) in southeastern Canada and the eastern United States and *V. olivaceus* (figure 9) and *V. solitarius* (figure 5) across Canada. Scrub-foraging *V. griseus* (figure 2) and *V. bellii* (figure 3) are ecologically similar and closely related species replacing each other in the eastern and western United States, but overlapping extensively in the eastern

Great Plains and at the western edge of the eastern deciduous forest. *V. gilvus* (figure 7) is so widespread in North America that its range overlaps with that of every other North American vireo except *V. altiloquus* (figure 11) which is confined on the continent to peninsular Florida. The distribution of *V. vicinior* is encompassed by that of the western solitary, *V. s. plumbeus;* usually these two species are separated by habitat and elevation differences with *V. solitarius* prefering pine forest or riparian cottonwood (*Populus*) woodland above 1,150 m. However, habitat co-occupancy by these two species in dwarf coniferous woodland at 1,200 m has been reported (Barlow et al 1970).

Ecological Isolating Mechanisms

Detailed ecological studies (Barlow 1962; Graber 1961; James 1973, 1976; Rice 1974; Williamson 1971) have elucidated behavioral and spatial tactics employed by North American vireos on the breeding grounds whereas information on ecology (critical to the present analysis) from the wintering grounds is largely anecdotal. However, foraging tactics and habitat preferences identified in studies of breeding birds have been noted in wintering birds (Slud 1964; Barlow and James unpubl. data).

Vireos can be readily divided into scrub foraging and arboreal foraging species in summer (table 1). Hamilton (1962) postulated that vireos are separated ecologically by habitat preferences or by use of different strata. For example, the three scrub foraging species, *V. griseus* (figure 2), *V. atricapillus* (figure 1) and *V. bellii* (figure 3), all overlap geographically with *V. olivaceus* (figure 9), *V. gilvus* (figure 7), and *V. flavifrons* (figure 6). Both the scrub and arboreal foragers are basically foliage and twig gleaners. But *V. olivaceus* and *V. gilvus* are larger birds and forage higher in the canopy.

Table 1 shows differences in weight (an index of size) and bill dimensions in the 11 North American species. Scrub foraging species generally are smaller by at least 3 g and have smaller beaks than most arboreal vireos (table 1). Species of similar size and foraging tactics are almost certainly spatially separated either by differences in habitat preference or by a combination of elevational and habitat differences. For example, *V. olivaceus* and *V. gilvus* differ along a

Figure 1.   Breeding and wintering ranges of the Black-capped Vireo (*Vireo atricapillus*). Distributional data upon which this and succeeding maps are based, as appropriate, are from: A.O.U. Check-list (1957), Bailey and Neidroch (1967), Bond (1974), Bull (1974), Burleigh (1958), Dickey and van Rossem (1938), Godfrey (1966), Green and Janssen (1975), Grinnel and Miller (1944), Gromme (1963), Hayward (1976), Howell (1932), Imhof (1976), Johnson (1972, 1973, 1974a, b), Land (1970), Lowery (1974), Meyer de Schauensee (1970), Meyer de Schauensee and Phelps (1978), Miller et al (1957), Monroe (1968), Oberholser (1974), Paynter (1955), Peterson and Chalif (1973), Pettingill and Whitney (1965), Phillips et al (1964), Ridgely (1976), Russell (1964), Stewart (1975), Sutton (1967), and van Rossem (1945).

Jon C. Barlow

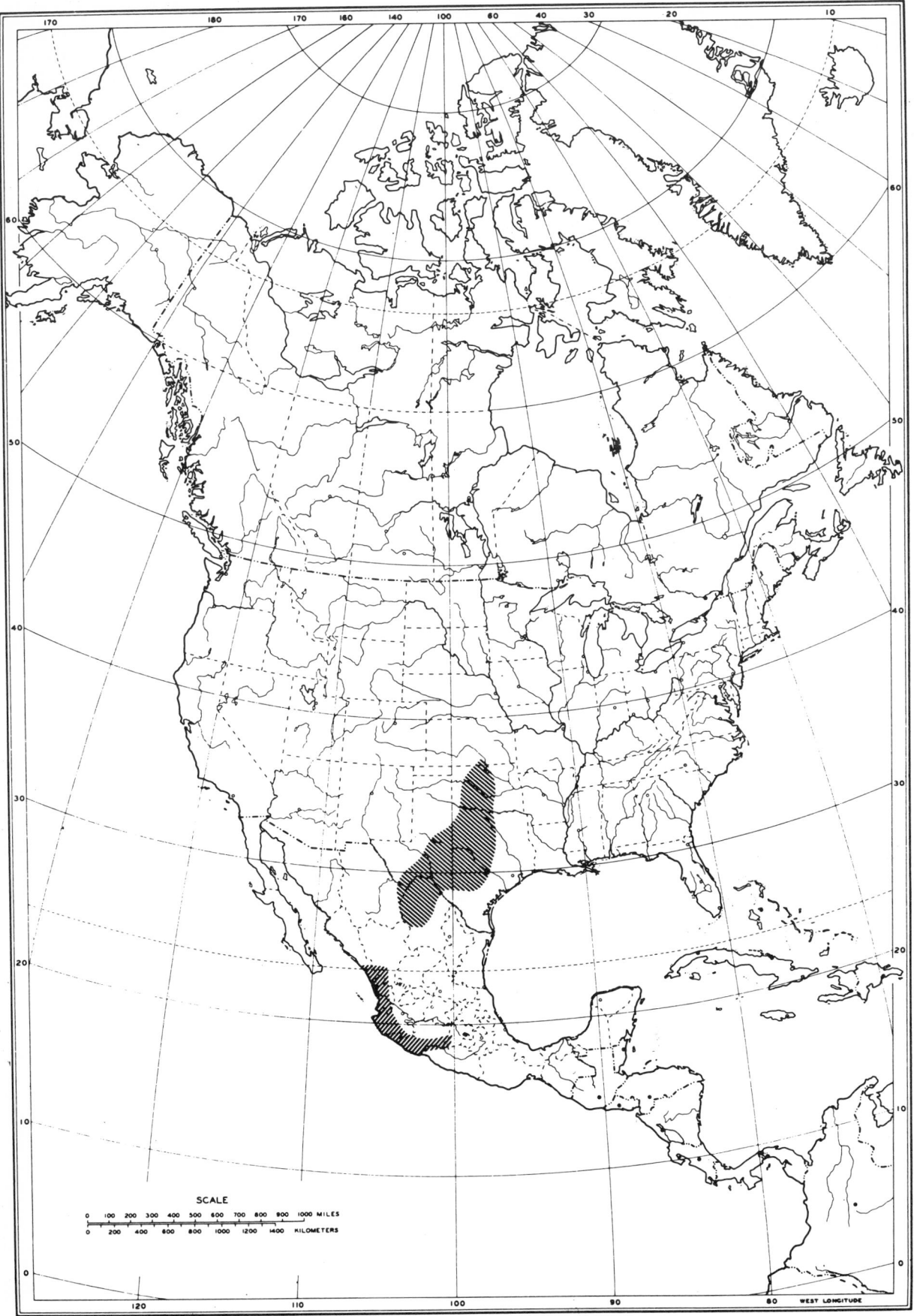

SCALE

0   100 200 300 400 500 600 700 800 900 1000 MILES

0   200 400 600 800 1000 1200 1400 KILOMETERS

Vireos in Neotropica   83

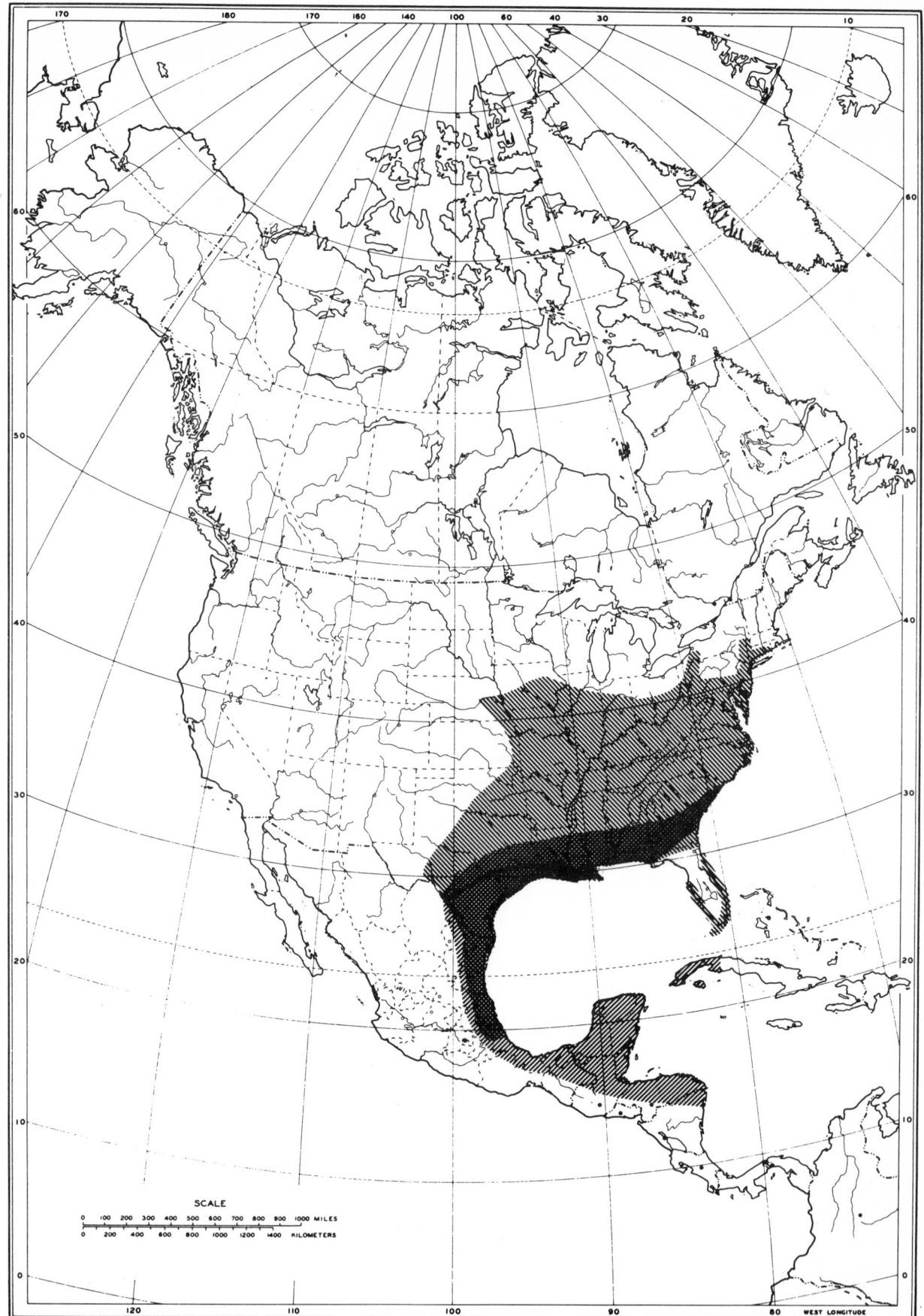

Figure 2.   Breeding and wintering ranges of the migratory White-eyed Vireos (*V. griseus* ssp.). Note areas of overlap in the southern United States and the Gulf coast of Mexico.

Jon C. Barlow

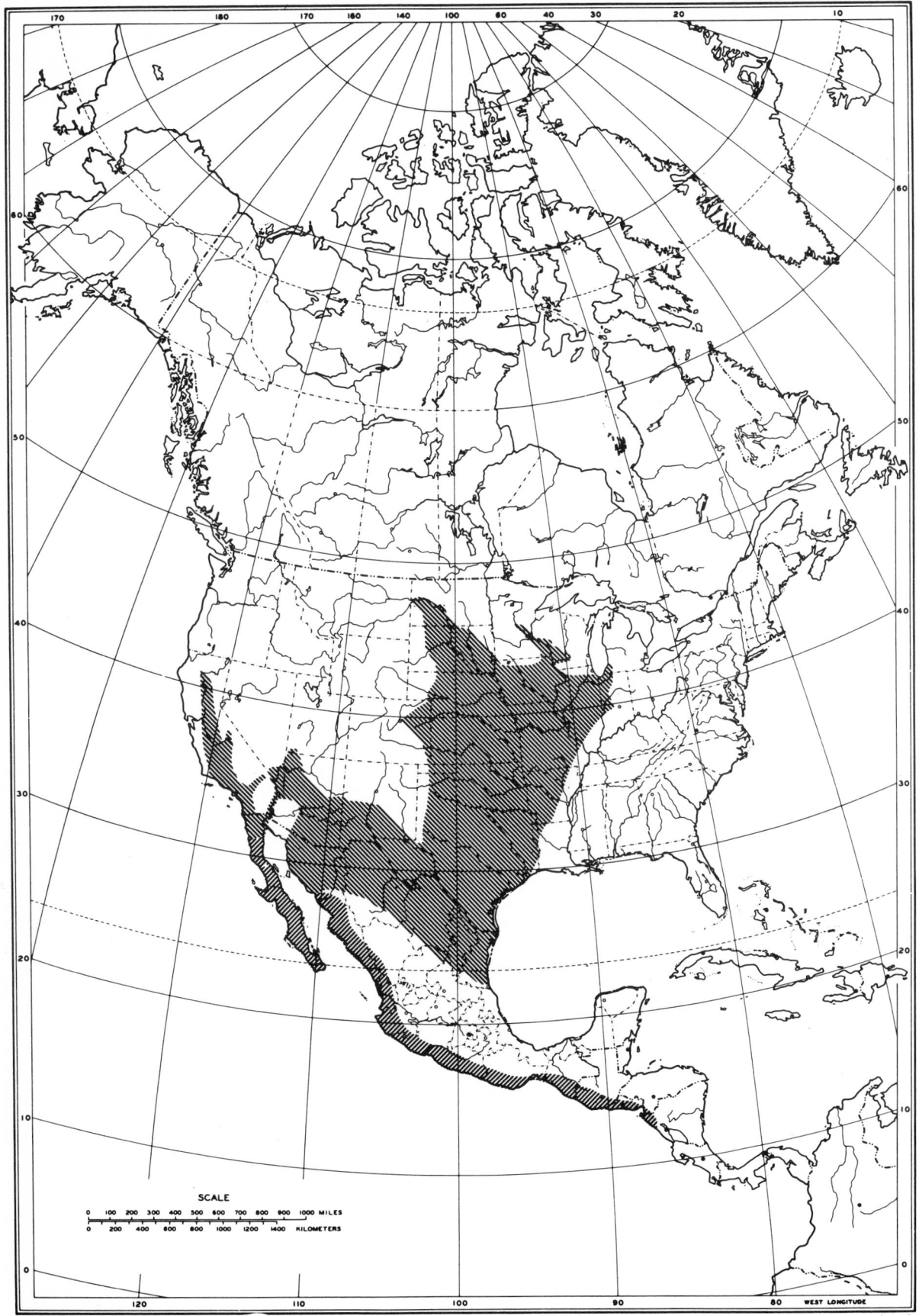

Figure 3.   Breeding and wintering ranges of Bell's Vireo (*V. bellii* ssp.).

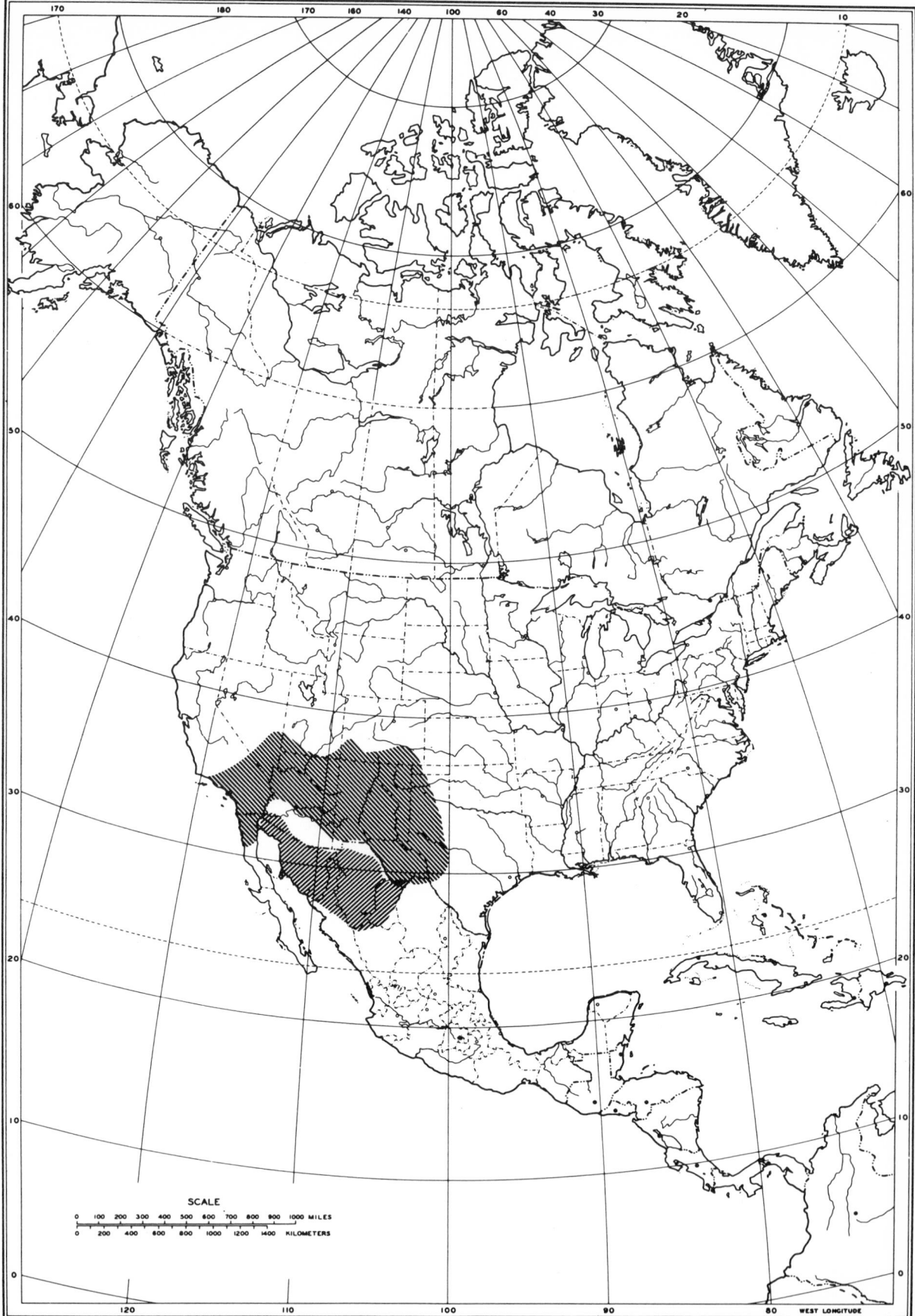

Figure 4.   Breeding and wintering ranges of the Gray Vireo (*V. vicinior*). Note overlapping ranges in the Big Bend, Texas.

Jon C. Barlow

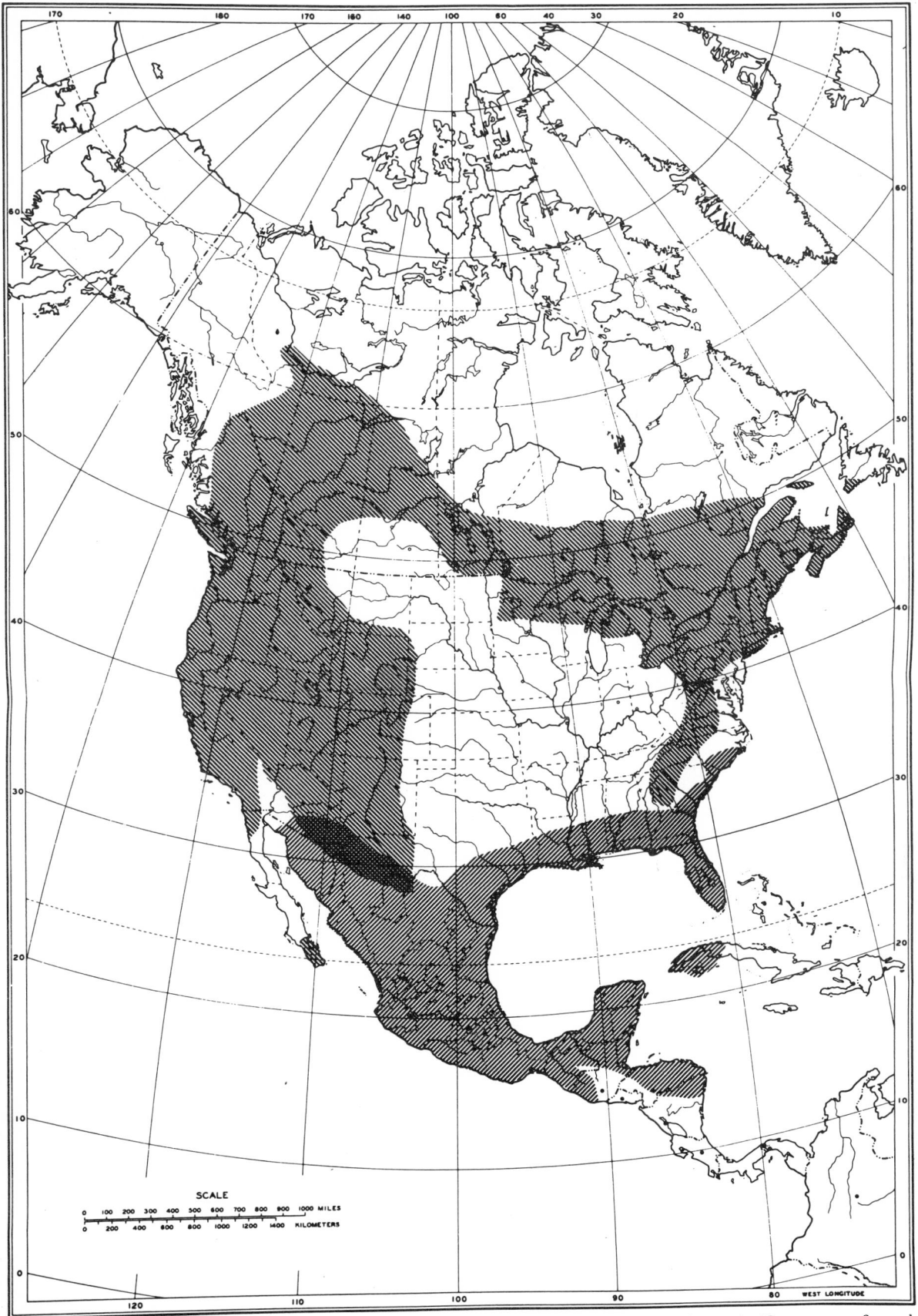

Figure 5. Breeding and wintering ranges of the migratory Solitary Vireos (*V. solitarius* ssp.). Note areas of overlap in southwestern United States and northwestern Mexico.

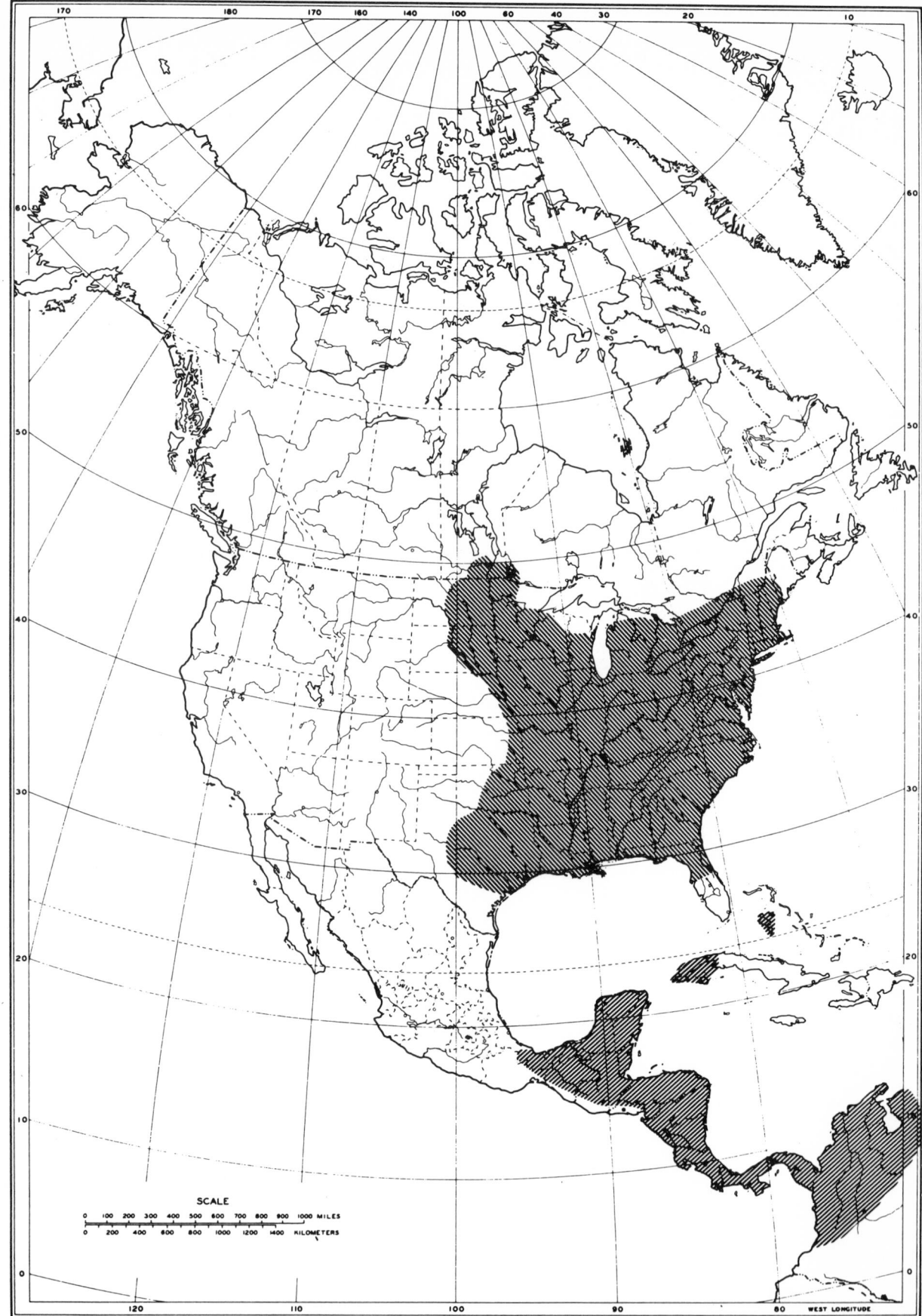

Figure 6.   Breeding and wintering ranges of the Yellow-throated Vireo (*V. flavifrons*).

Jon C. Barlow

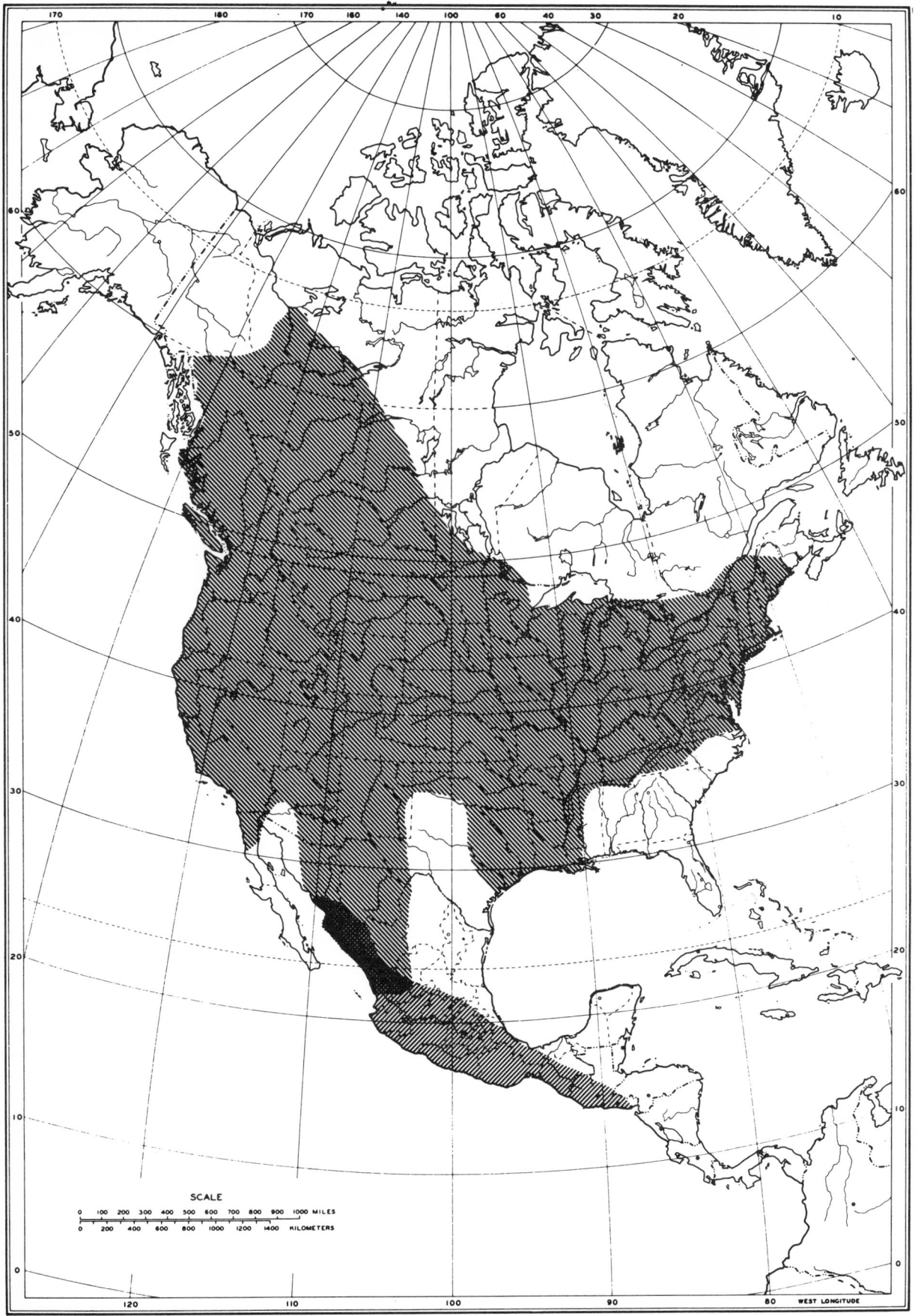

Figure 7. Breeding and wintering ranges of the migratory Warbling Vireos (*V. gilvus* ssp.). Note area of overlap in western Mexico.

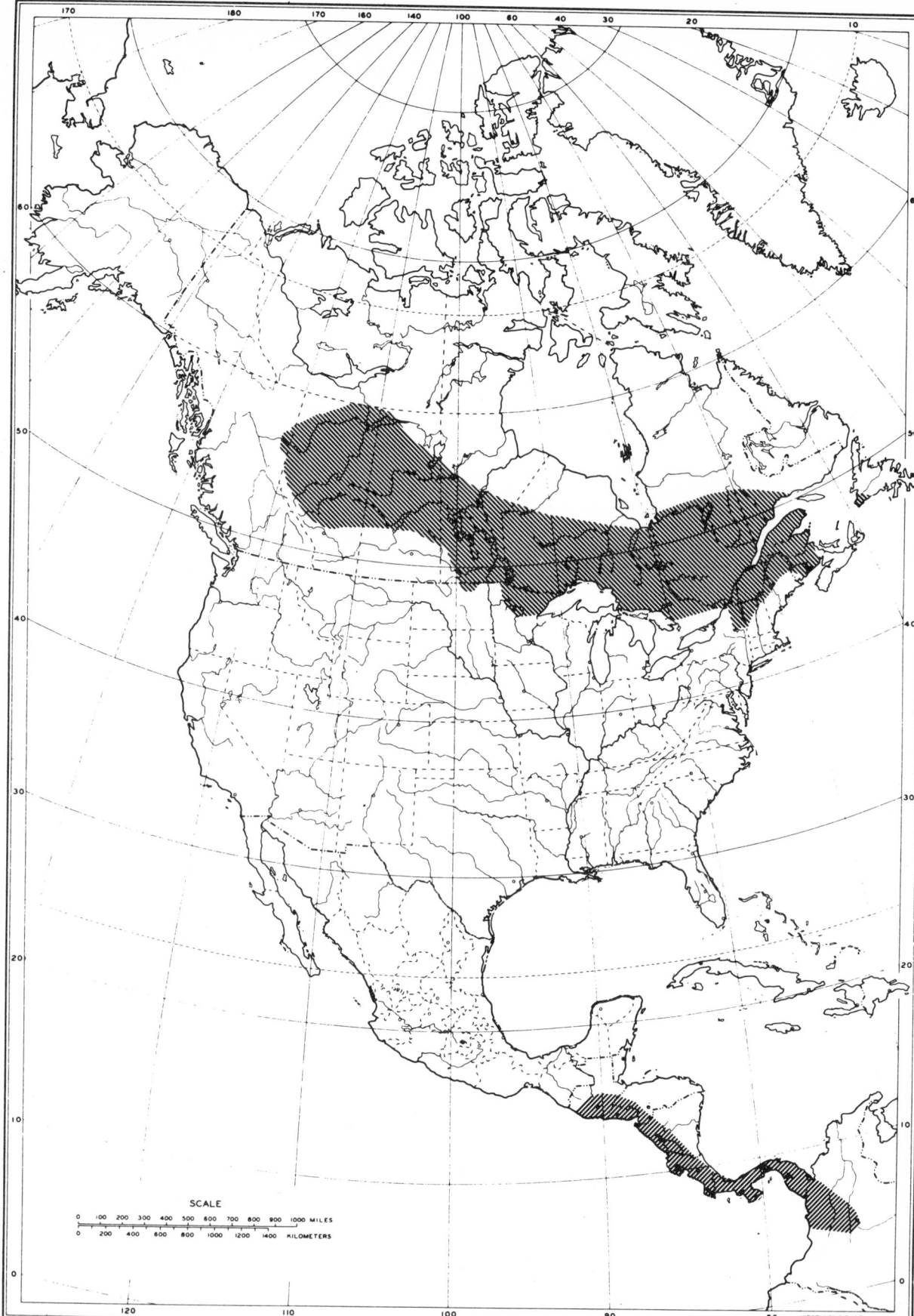

Figure 8. Breeding and wintering ranges of the Philadelphia Vireo (*V. philadelphicus*).

Jon C. Barlow

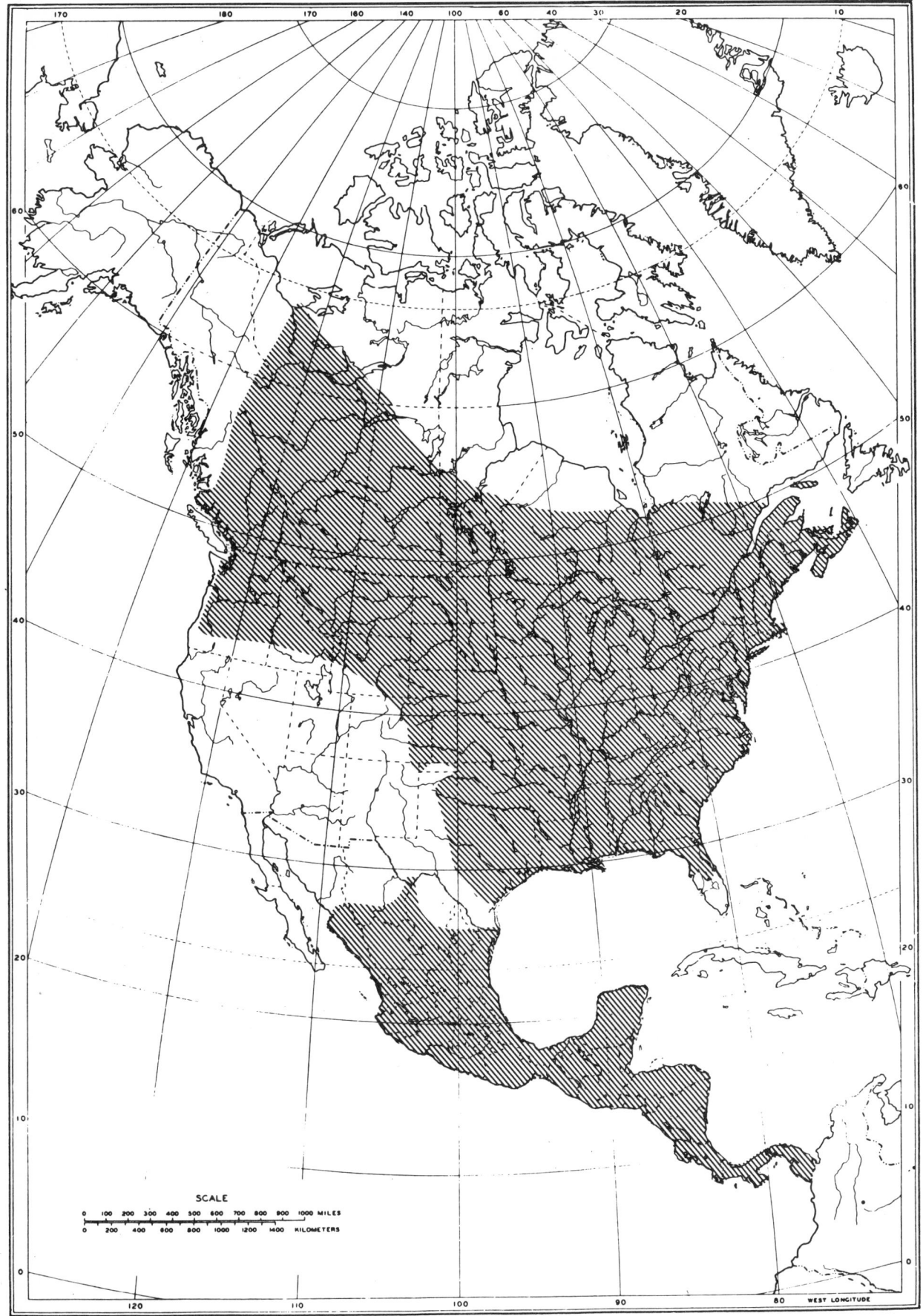

Figure 9. Breeding range of 2 disjunct migrant populations of the Red-eyed Vireo (*V. olivaceus*). *V. o. olivaceus* breeds in the United States and Canada and the "Yellow-green" Vireo (*V. "flavoviridis"*) breeds in Mexico and Central America.

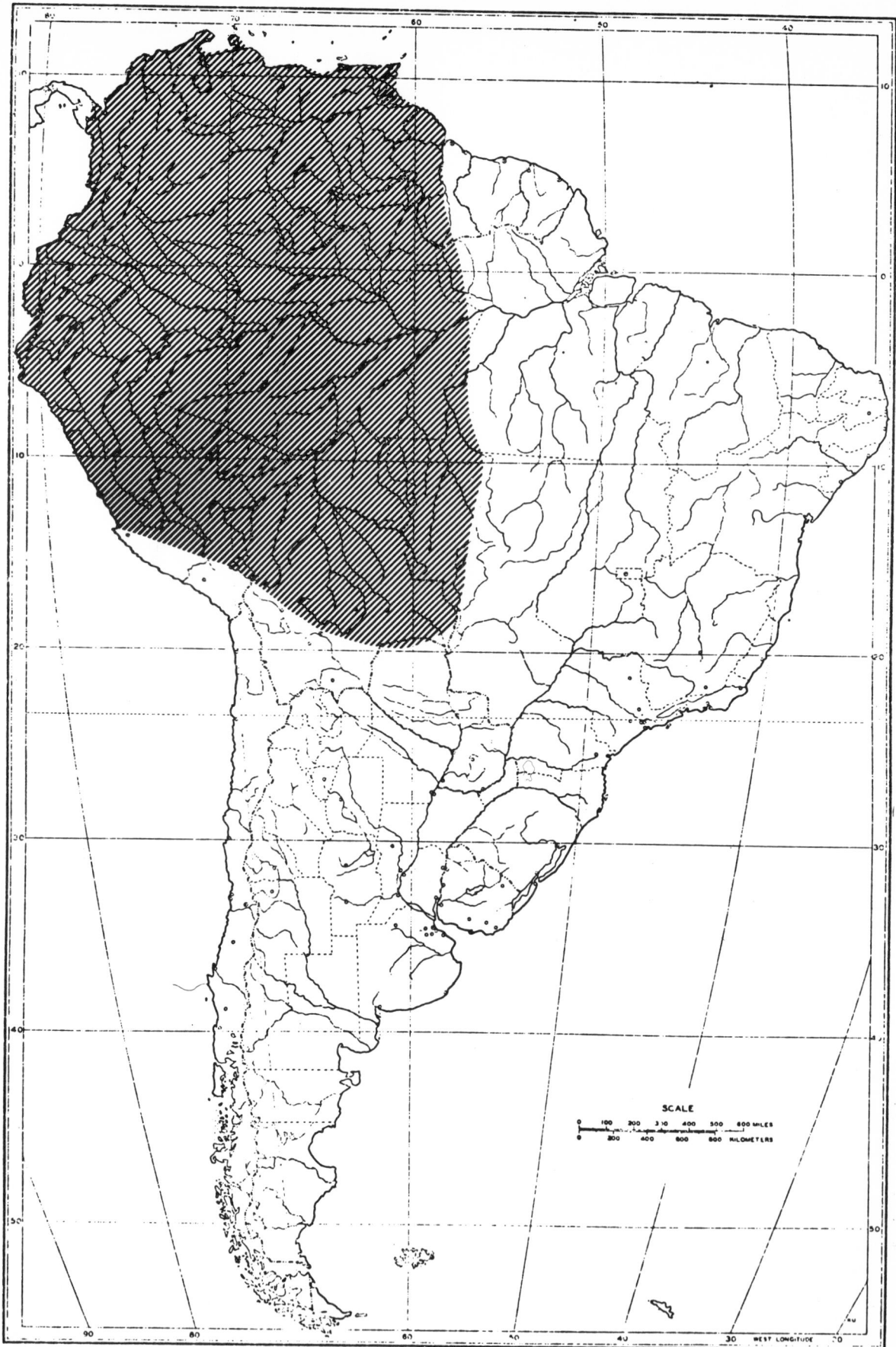

Figure 10. Winter range of Red-eyed Vireos (*V. olivaceus* ssp.).

Jon C. Barlow

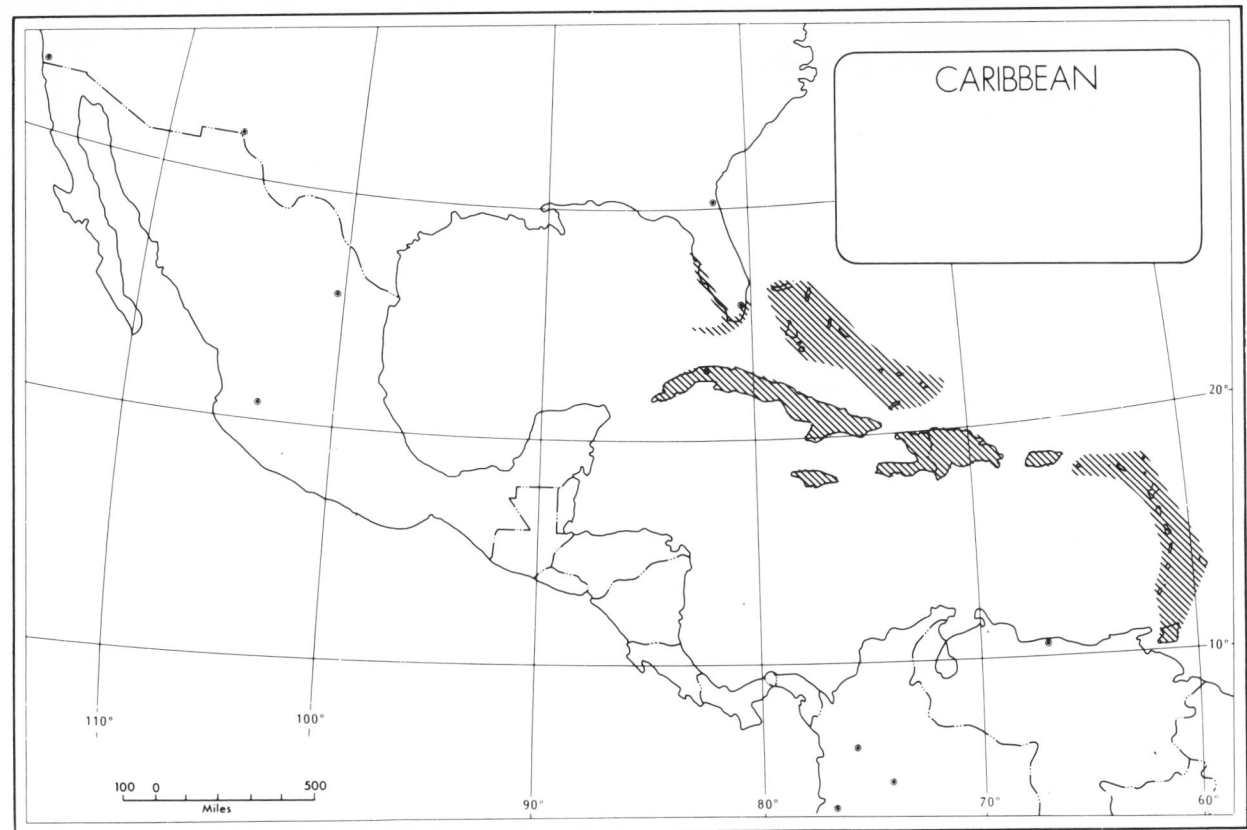

Figure 11. Breeding ranges of the Black-whiskered Vireo (*V. altiloquus* ssp.). Lesser Antillean birds (*V. a. barbadensis*) are sedentary.

horizontal habitat gradient with *V. gilvus* occurring mainly in more open broad-leaved parkland and *V. olivaceus* in heavier deciduous and mixed deciduous forests (see also James 1976). *V. solitarius* and *V. flavifrons* forage more on centrally located large branches in trees and away from the peripheral twigs and foliage favored by *V. olivaceus* and *V. gilvus* (James 1976). In addition, Williamson (1971) found that *V. olivaceus* and *V. flavifrons* foraged at different average heights in the canopy (7.83 m vs 11.3 m); further facilitating separation. These latter species also employ different foraging tactics with 99 percent foliage gleaning in *V. olivaceus* compared to 16 percent foliage gleaning in *V. flavifrons* which takes 84 percent of its prey from bark (James 1976). The way in which the beak is used in foraging is also thought to differ. Jaw musculature of *V. olivaceus* is long-fibered facilitating finely tuned plucking of small, often soft-bodied insects, whereas, that of *V. flavifrons* is short-fibered for picking harder-bodied arthropods from stable surfaces and subsequently crushing them (Orenstein and Barlow unpubl. data).

The ecological relationship between *V. olivaceus* and *V. philadelphicus* on the breeding grounds is based on interspecific territoriality maintained by vocal similarity (Barlow and Power 1970; Barlow and Rice 1977; Rice a, b, c). These two species differ by about 6 g in weight (table 1) and the smaller *V. philadelphicus* has a yellow belly in contrast to the white one of *V. olivaceus*. *V. philadelphicus* has a beak 7 mm in length in contrast to that of *V. olivaceus* at 9.6 mm but in spite of these several differences Rice (1978c) showed that there were no differences between the two species in average foraging height (9.2 m), use of tree species or, so far as is known, preferred prey.

V. atricapillus and *V. bellii* are closely related forms that show both habitat separation and co-occupancy in sympatry. The presence of its black cap and the "lilting-tinkling" quality of the song of *V. atricapillus* serve to reproductively isolate this species from *V. bellii*, a bird of duller appearance having a harsh song. Where the species are sympatric in the mixed oak (*Quercus* sp.), mesquite (*Prosopis* sp.), Juniper (*Juniperus*), Osage orange (*M. pomifera*), dominated thickets

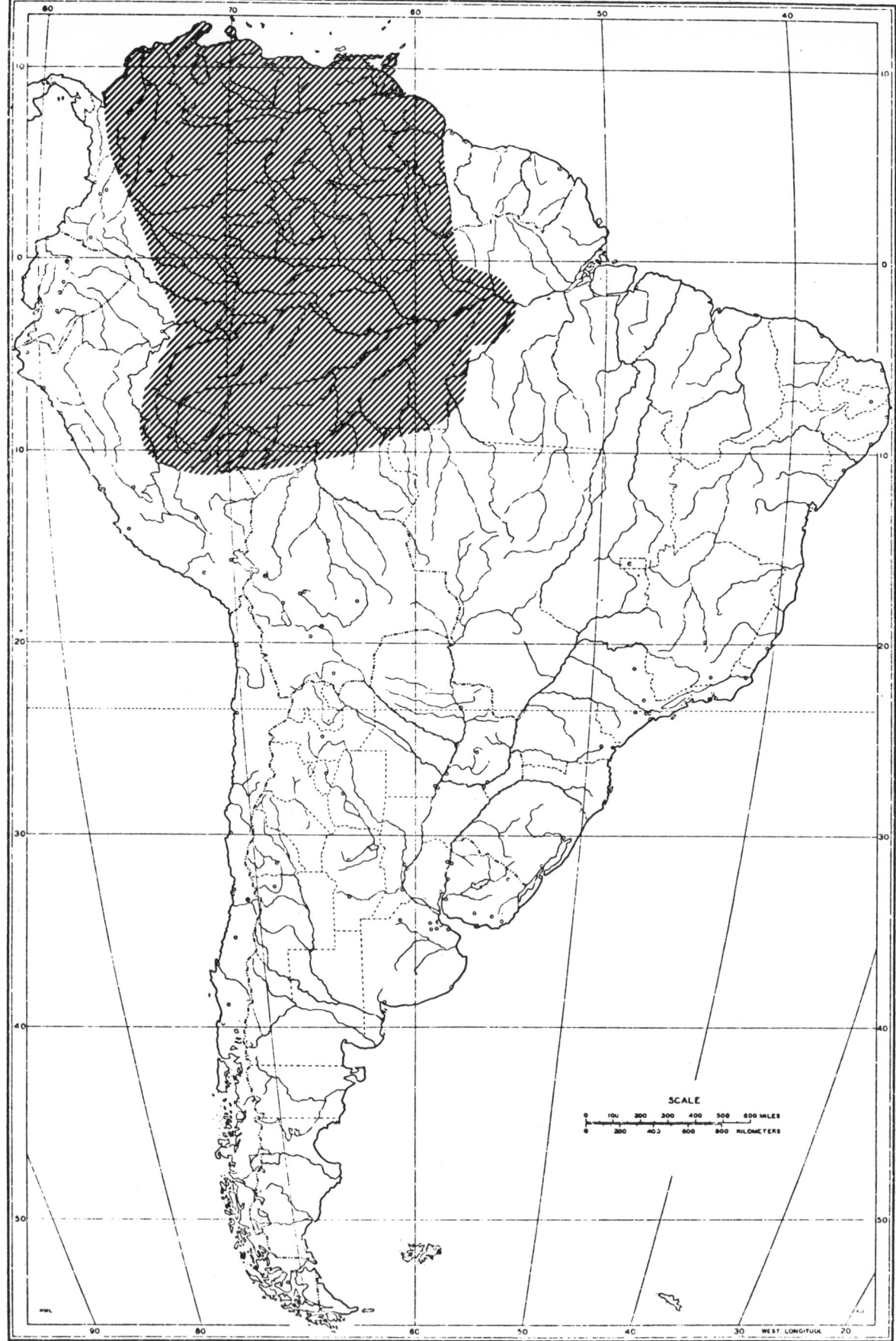

Figure 12. Winter range of migratory Black-whiskered Vireos (*V. a. altiloquus, V. a. barbatulus*).

Jon C. Barlow

the only other common, similar insectivores are Bewick's Wren (*Thryomanes bewickii*), Golden-cheeked (*Dendroica chrysoparia*) and Yellow (*D. petechia*) warblers. Over-exploitation of the lush resource base in the above habitat is unlikely.

Studies by Chapin (1925) and my own inspection of stomach contents (Barlow unpubl. data) indicate that arthropods, especially soft-bodied lepidopterous larvae, predominate in the diets of *Vireosylva*, *Vireo* (subgenus) and *V. huttoni*, but the large-billed species of *Lanivireo* show a higher use of harder-bodied Coleoptera and Orthoptera. Fruit comprised less than 15 percent of stomach contents in both subgenera in the main breeding period between mid-May and mid-July. Exploitation of protein and energy rich animal material coincides with expected maximizing of short-term but extremely rich resources characterizing the northern summer.

In summary then migrant vireos on their breeding grounds minimize interspecific competition by foraging in different strata, by occupying different habitats, and by foraging differently. Further, similar sized, closely related species may be spatially separated by range/or elevation.

Winter Ranges

Figures 1–8, 10, and 12 show the distribution in winter of the 10 migratory forms. Several specific interactions are discussed beyond.

Black-capped Vireo

V. atricapillus (figure 1) has a totally disjunct winter range centered on the central part of the west coast of Mexico. This range is nearly encompassed by that of *V. bellii* (figure 3) although the compatible general behavior between these species on the breeding grounds and the relatively small wintering populations (mostly separated by different elevational preferences) probably means that little competition between them occurs. In winter, *V. atricapillus* is totally, or in part, sympatric with 7 other vireos besides *V. bellii*. Interspecific competition among these taxa may be expected to be minimized by various combinations of differences listed in table 1. Other than the closely related *V. bellii*, the most serious competition might be expected from the Dwarf Vireo (*V. nelsoni*) because of its equal size and similar habitat preference. Also, comparisons of vocalization show that *V. nelsoni* and *V. atricapillus* have songs identical in syllable structure, timing and frequency (Barlow unpubl. data). In spite of the presence of a black crown in *V. atricapillus* and its absence in *V. nelsoni*, they are, in fact, conspecific and bear essentially the same relationship to each

other as do *V. gilvus* and *V. "leucophrys."* Therefore, close resemblance in foraging and general behavior are thought to facilitate habitat co-occupancy in winter between these two taxa. *V. atricapillus* is not a common species (Barlow 1977) and it is doubtful that its small numbers exert any special competitive pressure on any of the species with which it winters. However, it may have some influence on the timing of breeding in *V. "nelsoni"* which, based on the late June egg dates published by Power (1966), probably does not begin until after the departure of *V. atricapillus* in late April. Finally, the altitudinal separation between wintering *V. nelsoni* (1,500 m) and *V. atricapillus*, which is rarely found above 1,000 m in winter (Edwards 1972), may alone suffice to preclude much competitive interaction. See table 2 for further details of factors thought to reduce competition with species having overlapping ranges in winter.

White-eyed Vireo

The polytypic *V. griseus* (figure 2) is represented by three sedentary races, *V. g. maynardi* of coastal peninsular Florida, *V. g. micrus* of extreme southern Texas to southern Tamaulipas and the little known *V. g. perquisitor* of northern Veracruz. The two northern migratory races (*V. g. noveboracensis*, *V. g. griseus*) winter with the two western permanent residents south to northeastern Nicaragua. There are also small wintering populations comprising a mixture of both northern races in western Cuba and the Isle of Pines.

The Gulf coast and circum-Caribbean winter distribution of *V. griseus* completely separates it from the scrub foraging *V. bellii*, *V. atricapillus* and *V. nelsoni* of western Mexico. These are the taxa that would most likely compete for similar resources. *V. griseus* is broadly sympatric in winter with 15 species of vireos, four of which are North American migrants (table 2). Differences in overall size, bill color and pattern, and foraging site in combination with only partial overlap in preferred habitat and altitudinal distribution minimize competition with almost all these species (table 2). *V. griseus* encounters the closely related *V. gundlachii* on Cuba, *V. bairdi* on Cozumel Island, *V. pallens* along coastal Yucatan and narrowly in western Veracruz, and possibly the closely related but distinctively marked, *V. brevipennis* of the upland interior of central eastern Mexico. Greater reliance on fruit (up to 30 percent of its diet, Chapin 1925) by *V. griseus* at this season must diminish pressure on resources shared with other vireos. Stomachs of *V. bairdi*, I took in late November, contained only arthropod remains whereas the one *V. griseus* examined had eaten some fruit. *V. bairdi* sings frequently in late autumn and pairs seem

Table 2. Factors reducing intra- and interspecific competition[1] between wintering species of the subgenus *Vireo* (*V. atricapillus* [A], *V. bellii* [B], *V. griseus* [G]) and resident tropical species

Species	Elevation A	G	B	Habitat A	G	B	Foraging site A	G	B	Fruit eating A	G	B	Forms large flocks A	G	B	Overall size A	G	B	Bill size A	G	B	Color and/or pattern A	G	B
V. magister		0			0			—			0			+			—			—			—	
V. hypochryseus	0	0		0	0		—	—		0	0		0	+		—			—			—		
V. philadelphicus		0	0		0	0		—	—		0	0		+	+		0	—		—	0		0	0
V. gilvus	0	0	0	0	0	0	—	—	—	0	0	0	0	0	0	—	0	—	—	0	—	—	0	0
V. solitarius	0	0	0	0	0	0	—	—	—	0	0	0	+	+	+	—	—	—	—	—	—	—	—	—
V. leucophrys					—			—						0			—			—			—	
V. flavifrons		0	0		0	0		—	—		0	0		+	+		—	—		—	—		0	—
V. vicinior		+			0			0						0			+			—			—	
V. huttoni	0	0	—	0	—	—	0	0	0	0	0	0	0	+	0	—	+	0	—	0	0	—	—	—
V. brevipennis	0	0	0	0	0	0	+	+	0	0	0	0	+	+	+	0	+	—	—	+	0	—	—	—
V. gundlachii		+			+			+			0			+			+			+			0	
V. bairdi		+			+			+			0			+			+			0			—	
V. pallens	0	0	+	0	0	0	+	+	—	0	0	0	+	+	+	0	+	0	0	+	0	—	0	0
V. bellii	0			0			+			0			+			+			+			—		
V. atricapillus					0			—						0			+			+			—	
V. nelsoni	0	0		0	0			+	—	0	0		+	+	+	+	+			0	+		—	0
H. decurtatus		0	—		0	—		0	0		0	0		—	+		—	0		—	0		—	—
H. ochraceiceps		0	—		0	—		0	0		0	0		—	+		—	0		—	0		—	—
C. gujanensis		0	0		0	0		0	—		0	0		+	+		—	—		—	—		—	—
Vl. pulchellus		0	0		0	0		—	—		0	0		+	+		—	—		—	—		—	—
Vl. melitophrys		—	—		—	—		—	—		0	0		+	+		—	—		—	—		—	—

[1] (+ = the same as migrants; 0 = overlaps with migrants; — = differs from migrants; blank space = no overlap in range).

restricted to areas 1–2 ha in size suggesting that year round territories are maintained. I saw single *V. griseus* in mixed flocks of migrant warblers, and Stripe-headed (*Spindalis zena*) and Rose-throated (*Piranga roseogularis*) tanagers. Over-exploitation of resources within a *V. bairdi* territory is probably minimal because of the short time that wandering, mixed flocks spend in any one territory. In this situation, *V. bairdi* or any winter-territorial species would have the advantage over wandering birds in finding local food concentrations through repeated touring and searching of a circumscribed area.

Thus slight differences in diet, a tendency to rove, and similarity in general behavior probably facilitate compatibility between *V. griseus* and resident *V. bairdi*. The same relationship, ameliorating interspecific territoriality, is assumed for contacts with *V. gundlachii*. Habitat differences and large altitudinal differences between *V. griseus* (0–1,300 m) and *V. brevipennis* (highland oak scrub: 1,000–1,400 m) and *V. pallens* (mangroves-coastal scrub: 0–300 m) also probably diminish competition. Breeding seasons in sedentary populations of *V. g. griseus* as well as those of *V. bairdi* begin after the departure of northern *V. griseus* (Barlow unpubl. data).

Bell's Vireo

V. bellii pusillus (figure 3) is the only thicket foraging vireo wintering in Baja California and is separated by preference for desert scrub, differing elevation, and differing foraging tactics from the montane pine-oak woodland residents, *V. huttoni incognitus* and *V. solitarius luscanus*. *V. bellii* comprises three other subspecies that winter along the west coast of Mexico contiguous in southern Sonora with the summer breeding range.

Jon C. Barlow

Although these races overlap in winter, they are distributed more or less linearly then, with the eastern *V. b. bellii* wintering to northwestern Nicaragua, and *V. b. medius* of west Texas occurring from Michoacan north throughout the range of *V. b. arizonae* which is found in Arizona in summer.

V. bellii is at least partially sympatric in winter with 17 other species of which four are North American migrants (table 2). Four species of scrub vireos are encountered, but competitive pressures with two of them, *V. atricapillus* and *V. nelsoni*, have probably been resolved in the behavioral manner suggested previously. *V. bellii* and *V. pallens* are similar in size and appearance, foraging technique, and habitat preference, but the voice differs, and *V. pallens* sings in winter. Possible factors which reduce competition with the disjunct races, *V. p. palustra* of coastal Sinaloa and *V. p. ochraceus* of the Pacific coasts of Chiapas, Guatemala and El Salvador are complex. Their winter territoriality, much as with *V. bairdi* and *V. griseus* on Cozumel Island, their preference for mangroves, and their restricted altitudinal distribution (sea level to 250 m, Land 1970), are all factors that could diminish competition with *V. bellii* which, in turn, prefers scrub at elevations up to 1,350 m. Differing habitat, overall size, or foraging tactics would minimize competition with all other species except *V. brevipennis* where slight distributional overlap occurs in west central Mexico above 1,275 m, and with *V. vicinior* with which *V. bellii* is sympatric in southern Sonora (see below). Preference for oak scrub and winter territoriality by *V. brevipennis* undoubtedly serve to further reduce interaction stemming from this already marginal contact.

Breeding schedules of *V. pallens*, *V. nelsoni* and *V. brevipennis* (Barlow unpubl. data) are initiated after *V. bellii* departs (between late February and late March); thus, a tie may exist between reduced pressure on local resources and the timing of these events.

Gray Vireo

V. vicinior (figure 4) winters below 990 m (Barlow and Wauer 1971) in a restricted area located almost totally in northestern Mexico in a thermal zone that provides a continuous supply of hard-bodied arthropods, especially Orthoptera and Coleoptera. Only a short migration by *V. vicinior* is required to insure that it reaches such a climatically favorable wintering area. Habitat co-occupancy is known in summer with *V. atricapillus* (Barlow 1967), *V. bellii* and *V. solitarius* (Barlow et al 1970), as is occasional parapatry with *V. gilvus* and *V. huttoni* (Barlow unpubl. data). In winter, there is overlap in range with the latter four of the above species (table 3) but *V. vicinior* is restricted to xerophytic broad-leaved scrub in deserts so that contacts with the

latter three species are minimal. Thus, though *V. vicinior* has seven of the eight factors designated to reduce competition in common with *V. solitarius*, in fact foraging site differences prevent winter competition (table 3). *V. vicinior* and *V. bellii* occasionally occur together, but reliance of *V. bellii* on small (4 mm) prey and preference for more mesic scrub associations precludes competitive pressure. Intraspecific competition probably occurs in *V. vicinior* since winter territoriality is strongly maintained by song, and pairs seemingly remain in circumscribed areas. Only *V. bellii* breeds in summer in the main part of the winter range of *V. vicinior* and it is possible that its departure northward in late April may retard breeding in *V. bellii* until that time (no supporting data are available).

Solitary Vireo

V. solitarius is a polytypic species showing some overlap in breeding and wintering grounds in northwestern Mexico (figure 5). In the eastern United States, the southern limits of breeding and northern limits of wintering are only narrowly separated. Western races (*V. s. plumbeus* and *V. s. cassinii*) greatly overlap with sedentary races (*V. s. repetens* and *V. s. montanus*) in southern Mexico and Central America respectively. *V. solitarius* winters mostly north of *V. flavifrons* maintaining essentially the same latitudinal relationship on the wintering grounds as in the breeding season. In the zone of winter sympatry from the Yucatan peninsula south to El Salvador and Nicaragua, *V. flavifrons* concentrates at lower elevations (sea level to 1,500 m) whereas *V. solitarius*, although occasionally found down to sea level, occurs mainly above 1,200 m and up to 2,750 m (Land 1970). South of the range of *V. solitarius*, *V. flavifrons* occurs higher in the mountains in Costa Rica (Hamilton 1958; Slud 1964), Panama (Ridgley 1976), and Venezuela (Meyer de Schauensee and Phelps 1978). These two similarly foraging species are essentially ecological replacements of each other in coniferous and broad-leaved deciduous habitats, respectively.

In addition to *V. flavifrons*, *V. solitarius* winters sparingly to extensively within parts of the ranges of 21 other species (table 3). Interspecific competition is minimized between scrub-foraging species and *V. solitarius* by combinations of altitudinal, habitat, and stratal differences. Preference for foraging in conifers and more centrally in large trees again dissipates competitive pressure with the species of (the subgenus) *Vireosylva*. Preference for marginal habitats, winter territoriality, and winter elevational distribution reduces most competitive interactions between *V. solitarius* and permanent residents.

At 2,400 m in Morelo, I have seen mixed flocks in

Table 3. Factors reducing intra- and interspecific competition[1] between wintering species of the subgenus *Lanivireo* (*V.vicini*‖ [V], *V. solitarius* [S], *V. flavifrons* [F]) and resident tropical species

Species	Elevation			Habitat			Foraging site			Fruit eating			Forms large flocks			Overall size			Bill size			Color and/or pattern		
	V	S	F	V	S	F	V	S	F	V	S	F	V	S	F	V	S	F	V	S	F	V	S	F
V. olivaceus		0			0			—			0			—			0			—			—	
V. altiloquus		0			0			—			0			—			0			—			—	
V. magister		0	+		0	0		—	—		0	0		+	+		0	0		0	—		0	
V. hypochryseus		0			0			—			0			+			0			0			—	
V. philadelphicus		0	0		0	0		—	—		0	0		+	+		—	—		—	—		—	0
V. gilvus ssp.	0	0	0	—	0	0	0	—	—	0	0	0	0	+	+	0	—	—	0	—	—	—	—	0
V. solitarius	0	0	0	0	0	0	—	+	0	0	+	0	+	+	+	—	0	0	—	0	0	0	0	—
V. flavifrons		0			0			+			0			+			0			0			—	
V. carmioli		0			0			0			0			+			—			—				0
V. vicinior		0			0			—			0			—		+				—		0		
V. huttoni	—	0	0	0	0	0	0	—	—	0	0	0	0	0	—	0	—	—	—	—	—	—	0	—
V. brevipennis		0			0			—			0		0				—			—			—	
V. griseus		0	0		0	0		—	—		0	0		+	+		—	—		—	—		—	0
V. crassirostris		+			0			—			0			+			—			—				0
V. gundlachii		0	0		0	0		—	—		0	0		+	+		—	—		0	—		—	0
V. bairdi		0	+		0	+		—	—		0	0		+	+		—	—		0	—		—	0
V. pallens		0	0		0	0		—	—		0	0		+	+		—	—		—	—		—	0
V. bellii	+	0	0	0	0	0	0	—	—	0	0	0	+	+	+	—	—	—	—	—	—	—	—	—
V. atricapillus		0			0			—			0			+			—			—			—	
V. nelsoni		0			0			—			0			+			—			—			—	
H. decurtatus		0	0		0	0		—	—		0	0		—	—		—	—		—	—		—	—
H. ochraceiceps		0	0		0	0		—	—		0	0		—	—		—	—		—	—		—	—
H. flavipes		0			0			—			0			—			—			—				0
H. aurantiifrons		0			0			—			0			—			—			—				0
C. gujanensis		0	0		0	0		0	0		0	0		+	+		—	—		—	—		—	—
Vl. pulchellus		0	0		0	0		0	0		0	0		+	+		—	—		—	—		—	—
Vl. leucotis		0			0			0			0			+			—			—			—	
Vl. melitophrys		0	—		—	0		0	+		0	0		+	+		—	—		—	—		—	—

[1] (+ = the same as migrants; 0 = overlaps with migrants; — = differs from migrants; blank space = no overlap in range).

winter of *V. s. cassinii*, *V. s. plumbeus* or *V. s. repetens*, Chestnut-sided Shrike-Vireos (*Vireolanius melitophrys*), *V. huttoni*, dendrocolaptids, Hepatic Tanagers, (*Piranga rubra*), Stripe-backed Tanagers (*P. bidentata*) and Black-backed Orioles (*Icterus abeillei*). This suggests that cooperative searching as well as winter territoriality are both employed by *V. solitarius* as winter resource exploitation strategies.

Migrant *V. solitarius* intermingles extensively with its own sedentary races in winter. Nesting in *V. s. repetens* in Oaxaca occurs from mid-May well into summer beginning only after the departure of the migratory races Barlow unpubl. data). Thus, the breeding cycle of *V. s. repetens* and other races may be adjusted in part to avoid the increased pressure on local resources by northern conspecifics.

V. solitarius along with the next species (*V. flavifrons*) are known to take up to 25 percent fruit in winter (Chapin 1925). Greater reliance on fruit at this seaon would also reduce competition with more strictly insectivorous local residents.

Jon C. Barlow

Yellow-throated Vireo

By encompassing parts of the Bahamas and western Cuba and extending into northwestern Venezuela, *V. flavifrons* (figure 6) is sympatric in winter with 23 other kinds of vireos, more than any other North American migrant vireo. In summer it has a higher mean foraging height (9.26 m—southern Ontario, James 1976; 15.1 m—Maryland, Williamson 1971) than the other arboreal species, *V. gilvus* (7.74 m—southern Ontario, James 1976) and *V. olivaceus* (7.83 m—southern Ontario, James 1974; 11.3 m—Maryland, Williamson 1971), with which it is most frequently associated. In winter this species forages higher (7 m, Barlow unpubl. data) than scrub-foraging species but lower than in summer (Williamson 1971) and occurs in a wide variety of habitats especially in second growth and forest edge (Land 1970; Slud 1964). It usually is solitary; Slud (1964) observed that individual birds paid little attention to one another upon chance encounters. He heard the species sing only occasionally until after January. I found this species vocal and apparently on winter territory on Cozumel Island in November 1973. It joins flocks of tanagers, migrant warblers and greenlets (*Hylophilus*) but rarely associates with other *V. flavifrons*.

Table 3 summarizes factors diminishing interspecific competition between *V. flavifrons* and the 23 other species with which it overlaps in winter. In the absence of *V. solitarius*, *V. flavifrons* is found widely from sea level up to 1,500 m in a variety of habitats. Its adaptability, generally low numbers, and solitary behavior are critical to reducing impact on resident forms. In the South American part of its range, the Shrike-Vireos (*Vireolanius*) resemble this species in foraging tactics and foraging height, but the vireolaniids are confined to tall forest or second growth and are about a third larger in body size than *V. flavifrons*. Even though only locally common in summer and not especially abundant in winter, *V. flavifrons* seems to be the most frequently seen species on the wintering grounds (Meyer de Schauensee and Phelps 1978; Paynter 1955; Slud 1960, 1967; Ridgely 1976), usually in patchy habitat. The 10 resident species encountered show more precise habitat selection than *V. flavifrons* whereas the migrant vireo most extensively overlapped, *V. philadelphicus*, is a third smaller in size (table 1), takes smaller prey (Barlow unpubl. data), and forages more peripherally (Rice 1974). It is worthy of note that *V. flavifrons* and *V. solitarius* occur together in small numbers in Cuba where the more precise broad-leaved deciduous and coniferous woodland habitat preferences of the breeding season may be maintained. Occurrence of both *Lanivireo* species may be facilitated by the absence in winter of the similar sized *V. altiloquus*

barbatulus which is a foraging generalist. The possible importance of avoiding vireosylvids may be further demonstrated in winter by the tendency of *V. flavifrons* to occur at higher elevations than *V. altiloquus* in Venezuela (800–1,800 m vs 0–1,000 m, respectively, Meyer de Schauensee and Phelps 1978) and generally higher and north of the main mass of wintering *V. olivaceus*. *V. flavifrons* is probably too thinly distributed to alone influence breeding schedules of resident species but, in concert with other migrants, some depression of early season breeding may be experienced by congeners.

Warbling Vireo

The winter range of *V. gilvus* is disproportionately small when compared to the breeding distribution (figure 8). This reflects the short migration distances of many of the southern breeding populations and suggests a substantial and concentrated wintering population. An extensive zone of overlap between longer distance migrants (*V. g. swansoni* and *V. g. gilvus*) and these southern breeding populations occurs in western Mexico. Inspection of the complete range suggests that *V. gilvus* is essentially a highland vireosylvid but that it has spread into lowlands for breeding north of the Mexican border. This species encompasses the ranges of 20 other species in winter, 7 of which are migrants. The tactic of foraging in the canopy in broad-leaved open woodland separates this species spatially from virtually all other highland vireos (table 4). They take some fruit which benefits local insectivorous species by reducing impingement on arthropod prey. Identical foraging and general behavior expedite mixing with local races of *V. gilvus*. Possible competition with *V. philadelphicus* is minimized by the spotty marginal occurrence of the latter in the range of *V. gilvus* in concert with the preference of the former species for smaller trees. Members of the *V. olivaceus* superspecies complex vacate North and Central America completely in winter; thus, competition is obviated between the 2 species groups of *Vireosylva*.

High numbers of overwintering *V. gilvus* may, in part, suppress early breeding in resident populations. In Oaxaca in early May 1971, I found *V. g. connectens* just beginning breeding activities. No northern birds were encountered at this time. Resident vireos of lowland areas would rarely meet *V. gilvus* so that elevation plays a major role in obviating competition between them and *V. gilvus* (table 3).

Throughout its range, *V. huttoni* often occurs with *V. gilvus* and, in California, niche characteristics of the two species resemble each other closely (Hespenheide 1976). In winter when greater numbers of *V. gilvus* occur in highland Mexico, I thought sympatric *V.*

Table 4. Factors reducing intra- and interspecific competition between wintering species of the subgenus *Vireosylva* (*V. philadelphicus* [P], *V. gilvus* ssp. [G], *V. olivaceus* ssp. [O], *V. altiloquus* [A],) and resident tropical species

Species	Elevation				Habitat				Foraging site				Fruit eating				Forms large flocks				Overall size			
	P	G	O	A	P	G	O	A	P	G	O	A	P	G	O	A	P	G	O	A	P	G	O	A
V. olivaceus ssp.	−		+	+	0		0	0	+		+	+	0		0	+	−		+	+	−	0	+	+
V. altiloquus ssp.	0		+	+	0		0	+	+		+	+	0		+	+	−		+	+	−		+	+
V. magister	0				0				0				0				−				−			
V. hypochryseus		0			0					+				0				+			0			
V. philadelphicus	+	0	−	0	+	0	0	0	+	0	0	+	+	0	−	−	+	+	−	−	+	0	−	−
V. gilvus ssp.[2]	0	0	−	0	0	0	0	0	0	+	0	+	+	0	−	−	+	+	0	0	0	+	−	−
V. solitarius ssp.	0	0			0	0			−	−			0	0			0	+			−	−		
V. flavifrons	0	0	0	0	0	0	0		−	−	−	−	0	0	0	0	+	+	−	−	−	−	+	+
V. carmioli	0	0			0	0			0	0			0	0			0	0			+	+		
V. vicinior		0			−				−					0				+			−			
V. huttoni	0	0			0	0			0	0			+	+			0	0			0	+		
V. brevipennis	0	0			0	0			−					0				+			0	+		
V. griseus	0	0			0	0			−	−			0	0			0	+			0			
V. pallens	0	−			0		−		−	−			0	0			0	+			0	−		
V. bellii	0	0			0	0			−	−			0	0			0	+			−	−		
V. atricapillus	0	0			0				−					0				+			−	−		
V. nelsoni	0	0			0				−					0				+			−	−		
V. nanus			0				0				−				0				−					−
V. latimeri			0				0				−				0				−					−
H. decurtatus	0	0			0	−			0	0	0		0	0			0	−			−			
H. ochraceiceps	0	0	0	0	−	−	0	0	−	−	−	−	0	0	0	0	−	−	0	0	−	−	−	−
H. flavipes	0	0	0	0	0		0	0	−		−	−	0		−	0	0		0	0	−			
H. aurantiifrons	0	0	0	0	0		0	0	0		0	−	0		−	0	0		0	0	−			
H. sclateri			0	0			0	0			−	0			−	0			−	0				
H. semibrunneus			0	0			0	0			0	0			−	0			0	+				
H. hypoxanthus			0	0			0	0			0	0			−	0			0	0				
H. muscicapinus			0	0			0	0			0	0			−	0			−	0				
H. pectoralis			0	0			+	0			0	0			−	0			0	0				
H. semicinereus			0	0			0	0			0	0			−	0			−	0				
H. brunneiceps			0	0			0	0			0	0			−	0			−	0				
H. thoracicus			0	0			+	0			+	+			−	0			−	0				
H. poicilotis			+				0				0				−	0			−				−	
C. gujanensis		0	0	0	0	0	0	0	−	−	0	0	0	0	0	0	+	+	−	−	−	−	−	−
C. nigrirostris		−				0				0				0	0			−				−		
Vl. pulchellus	0	0	0	0	0	−	0	0	−	−	0	0	0	0	0	0	+	+	−	−	−	−	−	−
Vl. leucotis		0	0			0	0			0	0			0	0	0			−	−			−	−
Vl. melitophrys	0	0	0		−	0			−	−			0	0	0		+	+			−	−		

[1] (+ = the same as migrants; 0 = overlaps with migrants; − = differs from migrants; blank space = no overlap in range).

[2] Includes *V. leucuphrys*

Jon C. Barlow

Bill size				Color and/or pattern			
P	G	O	A	P	G	O	A
−	−	0	−	−	−	+	0
−	−	−	0	−	−	0	+
−				−			
−	−				−		
+	−	−	−	+	0	−	−
0	0	−	−	0	0	−	−
−	+				−		
−	−	−	−		−	−	
+	−				−	−	
	−				−		
0	0				−	−	
	−				−		
−	−				−	−	
−	−				0	0	
	−				−	−	
	−					−	
		−					−
		−					−
−	−				−	−	
−	−	−	−		−	−	
−		−	−	0		−	−
−		−	−	0		−	−
		−	−			−	−
		−	−			−	−
		−	−			−	−
		−	−			−	−
		−	−			−	−
		−	−			−	−
		−				−	−
−	−	−	−	−	−	−	−
	−				−	−	A
−	−	−	−	−	−	−	−
−	−				−	−	
−	−			−	−		

huttoni favored conifers whereas *V. gilvus* preferred broad-leaved trees.

Philadelphia Vireo

In winter the bulk of migrant *V. philadelphicus* occurs from Guatemala to extreme northwestern Colombia (figure 8) greatly interposed between the ranges of the other larger vireosylvid species suggesting that past interspecific competition with these taxa may have influenced the present distribution of *V. philadelphicus*. (*V. philadelphicus* is regarded as a very rare winter resident in southern Mexico [Edwards 1972] but Monroe [1968] believes that it is more common in Honduras than the few scattered records suggest. For this species only, I have shown the main range and omitted the problematic marginal records.) Apparently no more than two vireosylvids can be readily accommodated in Central America in winter even though *V. "leucophrys"* is largely separated from the widely distributed *V. philadelphicus* by elevation and habitat preference.

V. philadelphicus encounters 20 other vireos in Central America and Colombia (table 4). As indicated earlier, *V. philadelphicus* and *V. flavifrons* overlap extensively in winter but size differences and foraging tactics separate these birds. The variety of open and second growth habitats frequented by *V. philadelphicus*, in concert with its small size, and solitary-to small-group foraging behavior facilitate its ecological and behavioral accommodation in a variety of mixed flocks or in the home ranges of resident vireos which it usually meets only in ecotonal situations.

Red-eyed and Black-whiskered Vireos

It is more convenient to discuss the winter distributions of *V. olivaceus* (figure 10) and *V. altiloquus* (figure 12) together because they represent a breeding and migratory continuum, when North America north of Mexico and the West Indies are considered, but one that comprises distinctively marked regional taxa. This group shows transitional stages in the presumed evolution of migration from sedentary to partially migratory, to short- and then long-distance migratory populations, as outlined by Cox (1968).

V. olivaceus is at least in part sympatric with 21 other species of vireos including several of its own distinctively marked neotropical races and migrant populations of the *V. o. "flavoviridis"* subspecies group from Mexico and Central America (table 4). *V. altiloquus* also occurs with 20 of the same species on the wintering grounds that are encountered by *V. olivaceus* (table 4). The 2 North American migrants, *V. flavifrons* and *V. philadelphicus*, are confined to the northwest of South

America and are found mainly at higher elevations than either member of the *V. olivaceus* superspecies complex. The 12 species of greenlets (*Hylophilus*) encountered are generally only three-fifths the size (9 g vs 16.8 g) of either vireosylvid and are either lowland rain forest forms (*H. thoracicus*) or scrub dwellers (*H. flavipes*). In the latter case, they bear the same stratal relationship to *V. olivaceus* in the neotropics that *V. griseus* does in temperate North America.

V. philadelphicus and *V. gilvus* are largely insectivorous in winter, but take some fruit at that time (Chapin 1925). Red-eyed and "Yellow-green" vireos are apparently nearly completely frugivorous in winter (Morton 1977). Foraging position and techniques of *V. altiloquus* closely resemble those of *V. olivaceus* except that foraging amplitude of the former is greater, possibly because it does not occur with other vireosylvids. On the breeding grounds, the diet consists of about 50 percent fruit (Johnston 1975) and approaches 100 percent on the wintering grounds.

V. olivaceus and *V. altiloquus* are broadly sympatric in northern Amazonia in winter, and their numbers are super-imposed on a polytypic South American Red-eyed Vireo. Competition may be minimized by these similar taxa in part by bill-size differences ($\bar{X}$ = 11.9 mm, N = 10 for *V. a. altiloquus* vs $\bar{X}$ = 9.6 mm, N = 10 for northern *V.* "*olivaceus*" [Barlow unpubl. data]). South of the equator, these migrant vireos, as fruit eaters, would not be competing with territorial breeding red-eyes for the arthropods which they eat at this season. North of the equator, where resident red-eyes winter, size differences would again figure prominently in minimizing competition.

In review then, tropical members of the Red-eyed Vireo superspecies complex are frugivorous as well as insectivorous on the breeding grounds (*V. altiloquus*, Lack 1976; *V. magister caymanensis*, Johnston 1975; *V. o. flavoviridis*, Morton 1977). Migration in the latter form seems tied with the local depletion of fruit abundance, at least in Panama in winter (Morton 1977). Morton further speculates that the Red-eyed Vireo, highly insectivorous in the breeding season, becomes progressively more frugivorous with the waning of summer and in migration and, presumably in winter, ventures to the western Amazon to a winter ground favoring greater fruit abundance at that season. This strategy presumably also obtains for the migratory populations of *V. altiloquus*, such as *V. a. altiloquus* and *V. a. barbatulus*. Unlike *V. o. flavoviridis*, replaced distributionally by *V. philadelphicus* in winter, these insular Black-whiskered Vireos are not replaced in winter by other vireosylvids. Some fruit is available year round in Jamaica where *V. a. altiloquus* breeds. The 26 other fruit-eating species of birds there continue to eat fruit

throughout the autumn and winter (Lack 1976). Eighteen species of warblers winter regularly in Jamaica (another 14 occur irregularly and in small numbers) and at least 3 of them feed noticeably on fruit: the Cape May Warbler (*Dendroica tigrina*), 14 percent; the Black-throated Green Warbler (*D. virens*), 5 percent, and the Parula Warbler (*Parula americana*), 6 percent. It is possible that *V. a. altiloquus* has been excluded from Jamaica in winter by the synergistic effects of the combined niches of the sedentary Jamaican White-eyed (*V. modestus*) and Blue Mountain (*V. osburni*) vireos and the migrant warblers. In any event, it is interesting to note that in the Lesser Antilles where wintering warblers drop off sharply (under 10 species) and scrub foraging vireos are absent, the local race of the Black-whiskered Vireo (*V. a. barbadensis*) is a permanent resident.

Even though separated by diet and by distinctive flocking habits, the enormous numbers of northern *V. olivaceus* augmented by the smaller population of *V. altiloquus* may influence timing of breeding in local populations of *V. olivaceus*. In central Venezuela near Updata in the state of Bolivar, the local race of red-eye, *V. o. vividior*, was just beginning breeding activities in mid-May; by that date no North American migrants were to be found (Barlow unpubl. data).

A Speculative History of Current Distribution and Migration Patterns of Vireos

Vireos are thought to have originated in Middle America, probably toward the end of the Tertiary (Mayr 1946). From there some large proto-vireo, perhaps not unlike present-day Shrike-Vireos (*Vireolanius*) followed broad-leaved rain forests south into northern South America. Divergence early in the evolution of the family is suggested for "*Vireo-lanius*" because of its simple whistled monosyllabic song (Barlow and James 1975) that structurally resembles certain protracted monosyllabic rallying calls of some vireosylvids and lanivireos, taxa with rather complex primary songs. Early Peppershrikes, proto-*Cyclarhis*, may have evolved somewhat later as more complex song was perfected in the family. Other aspects of its projected history will be discussed beyond. Greenlets, proto-*Hylophilus* probably also reached South America over some late Tertiary land bridge between the continental masses. The dearth of small oscine insectivores and the plethora of niches there would have facilitated the minor radiation of arboreal and scrub-foraging forms extant today and subsequent widening of the water gap may have enhanced speciation (through isolation) by the interposition of the ecological and geographic barriers in South America suggested by Haffer (1974).

Jon C. Barlow

The great physical and ecological diversity of Middle America made available a wide variety of niches for small insectivores. These niches contributed to the emergence of stratally separated arboreal and thicket foliage-gleaning forms corresponding to proto-*Vireosylva* and proto-*Vireo*. In addition, an arboreal proto-*Lanivireo* lineage foraging on larger branches may have arisen at this time. Presumably, other opportunities for invasions of South America arose at which time, in the face of intra-group competition, one segment of proto-*Vireosylva* moved into South America, leaving another population in the highlands of Middle America. Perhaps proto-*Cyclarhis* entered South America at this time as well. As the Tertiary drew to a close the Central American protos -*Vireo*, -*Lanivireo* and -*Vireosylva* underwent successive fragmentations as populations of the three taxa with their characteristic foraging tactics, presumably already well under development, became isolated in wet and dry coastal and upland areas. This resulted in a proliferation of species within each of the subgenera. Middle American *Vireosylva* may have divided early, yielding proto-*V. hypochryseus*, proto-*V. philadelphicus* and proto-*V. gilvus*. Somewhat later primitive proto-*V. griseus* moved into the West Indies from Middle America, penetrating eastward to Puerto Rico. On Jamaica a remnant population of an earlier vireonoid invasion was encountered, represented today by the extremely primitive and uncommon *V. osburni*. This species has a simple monosyllabic, trill-like song, structurally resembling rattle calls of *Lanivireo* and the primitive songs of *Vireolanius*. It also has obscure eye-rings and wing-bars and shows no site-specific foraging behavior (Barlow unpubl. data).

Whatever the early steps of evolution may have been, secondary centers of diversification were established in South America and Middle America in the lowlands and highlands from which certain populations later moved as intraspecific pressure began generally to be replaced by developing interspecific competition. Amelioration of harsh arctic climates in interglacial intervals in the Pleistocene of North America resulted in the dramatic expansion of vast resource-rich northern forests.

The speciation process yielding the present array of wood warblers (Parulidae) may have already been well underway in North America when proto-*V. gilvus*, following broad-leaved enclaves in the highland pine forests, reached there. Subsequent waves of early representatives of the *V. olivaceus* sub-species complex may have now emerged from South America, spreading northward into the Caribbean through the Lesser Antilles and from the Middle American mainland, leaving respectively sedentary coastal and Cayman Island populations of proto-*V. magister* and sedentary/migratory populations of *V. altiloquus*. In the latter species, perhaps the necessity to return to the South American mainland from summering in western Caribbean and Bahaman breeding areas was related, as previously suggested, to the permanent competitive presence of members of *V. griseus* superspecies. Continued expansion of proto-*V. olivaceus* from South America may have promoted the roughly concurrent arrival of representatives of all three subgenera in North America. Presence of an already established radiation of warblers and the lateness of the arrival of vireos diminished opportunities for both geographic and niche diversification in that family. However, it seems likely that *V. flavifrons* evolved from *V. solitarius* in a Pleistocene deciduous forest refugium in the manner hypothesized by Hamilton (1958).

The movement of the distinctively marked *V. o. flavoviridis* segment of the *V. olivaceus* complex into Middle America may have been instrumental in producing a northward movement of proto-*V. philadelphicus* which subsequently, through the vocal-similarity mechanism previously described (Rice 1978 a, b, c), was able to coexist with northern populations of *V. olivaceus* but generally north of the summer range of the establishing *V. gilvus* with whom ecological isolation was more critical in view of the similarities in size and general behavior.

Mengel (1964) has suggested that evolving wood warbler taxa gained access to coniferous forest by moving into it through broad-leaved enclaves and subsequently coadapting to conifer use. Then warblers followed conifers northward with glacial recession. It does not seem likely that conifer played a major role in species diversification or the establishment of primordial migration patterns in vireos because all contemporary eastern species are either strictly oriented toward broad-leaved deciduous vegetation or make only partial use of conifers.

Cox (1968) presents models showing stages in the development of migratory patterns in species with breeding and wintering areas totally coinciding, overlapping, contiguous, or disjunct. He proposed that intraspecific and then interspecific competition was instrumental in the development of migratory patterns that fostered spatial isolation in summer and winter in species foraging in the same way for a common resource. The spectrum of patterns in vireos—from permanent residence as in *V. huttoni* to the long distance migration of *V. olivaceus*—implies the operation of a year round strategy of spatial avoidance, mediated by emerging interspecific competition, in North American vireos that could easily have developed according to the scenario I have just suggested.

In summary and from a slightly different perspective, vireos are generally species poor throughout their range, especially in the northern forests, where warblers have demonstrated a major radiation and proliferation of species (Mengel 1964). Vireos of the subgenus *Vireo* (the scrub-foraging species) are competitively excluded from the scrubby habitats of the boreal forest by the plethora of warblers in the north and the combined diversity of suboscines, scrub *Hylophilus*, tanagers and other insectivorous species in the neotropics. The scrub vireo radiation conversely has developed in the lowlands and highlands of south central Mexico which are relatively suboscine and warbler poor. Similarly it seems likely that radiation of suboscines in South America has limited ingress and speciation of the genus *Vireo* on that continent, my hypothesized scenario not withstanding. Those vireos which reached North America have maximized the seasonally abundantly available arthropod fauna, filling the broad niche between the small insectivorous thicket/arboreal foraging parulids and the small insectivorous tyrannids and thrushes.

Review of Evolutionary, Migratory, and Isolating Factors

The history of vireo radiation is one mediated by resolving use of a common resource base through some form of spatial separation. Winter supplementing of an insectivorous diet with partial frugivory or total reliance on the latter serves to reduce competitive pressure on vireos resident in the tropics. Willis (1966), Karr (1976), and others have noted that generalized distribution of over-wintering migrants, including vireos, in patchy second growth and disturbed habitats in Latin America. This broad winter habitat preference tends to further diminish the impact by migrants on native birds which occur in reduced species diversity and numbers in such marginal habitats. Even though an array of ecological, behavioral, and temporal mechanisms have evolved that minimize the impact of migratory vireos on confamilial taxa, it seems likely the timing of breeding has been adjusted to a schedule postdating the northward departure of migratory forms as suggested by Miller (1963), especially in *V. bellii*, *V. atricapillus*, *V. griseus*, *V. solitarius*, *V. gilvus*, and members of the *V. olivaceus* super-species complex. Thus, the greatest benefits of local resources may be realized by the permanent residents because they are simply the tropical component of elastic breeding populations—the northern parts of which spend a few months annually in North America exploiting superabundant resources.

Considerations of Conservation

Critical to the survival of migrant vireos is the main-tenance of substantial tracts of forest or scrub on both the breeding and wintering grounds of these species. I have previously suggested that habitat attrition represents the greatest single threat to the continued well-being of vireo populations in the Chihuahuan Desert (Barlow 1977). Attrition or alteration of habitats currently jeopardize some West Indian populations of *V. altiloquus* and in North America especially the status of *V. atricapillus*, because of its restricted summer and winter ranges in agricultural regions of Texas and western Mexico. The restricted range of *V. carmioli* continues to shrink as highland Costa Rican and Panamanian forests are cut (Skutch 1967). Excessive and continual use of biocides in Latin America comprises an ominous threat to sensitive small insectivorous species. Thus certain rare forms as *V. brevipennis* and *V. nelsoni* of the central Mexican highlands, which have small ranges in regions of heavy primary land use, are surely in jeopardy. These species are so poorly known and infrequently seen that some minimum population size threshold could be breached, causing a rapid and unsuspected decline. The other migrant vireos seem relatively secure at present because they do not now breed in the primary areas of habitat attrition. However, continued vigilance must be maintained against any major inroads on the remaining scrublands and forests of coastal and southern Mexico, Middle America, the vast forests of Colombia and the Amazon Basin if the seven species variously wintering there are to maintain healthy populations at that season.

Acknowledgments

I am most grateful for the extensive help in preparing this manuscript provided by Margaret May and Trudy Rising. Additional typing was kindly provided by Ann Crabtree, Nancy Flood, Sue Merson, Franca Leeson, and Dot Richardson. Diana Gordon is thanked for preparing the maps. Janet Hinshaw, Wilson Ornithological Society Library, University of Michigan, Ann Arbor, assisted in the literature search. Financial support for studies of vireos is from a grant from the National Research Council of Canada.

Jon C. Barlow

Appendix 1. Common names of tropical resident vireos mentioned in text and tables 2–4

Common name	Scientific name
Cyclarhinae (Peppershrikes)	
Rufous-browed Peppershrike	*Cyclarhis gujanensis*
Black-billed Peppershrike	*Cyclarhis nigrirostris*
Vireolaniinae (Shrike-Vireos)	
Chestnut-sided Shrike-Vireo	*Vireolanius melitophrys*
Green Shrike-Vireo	*Vireolanius pulchellus*
Slaty-capped Shrike-Vireo	*Vireolanius leucotis*
Vireoninae (vireos, greenlets)	
Slaty Vireo	*Vireo brevipennis*
Dwarf Vireo	*Vireo nelsoni*
Mangrove Vireo	*Vireo pallens*
Cozumel Vireo	*Vireo bairdi*
Cuban Vireo	*Vireo gundlachii*
Thick-billed Vireo	*Vireo crassirostris*
Jamaican White-eyed Vireo	*Vireo modestus*
Flat-billed Vireo	*Vireo nanus*
Puerto Rican Vireo	*Vireo latimeri*
Yellow-winged Vireo	*Vireo carmioli*
Blue Mountain Vireo	*Vireo osburni*
Golden Vireo	*Vireo hypochryseus*
Yucatan Vireo	*Vireo magister*
Golden-fronted Greenlet	*Hylophilus aurantiifrons*
Brown-headed Greenlet	*Hylophilus brunneiceps*
Gray-headed Greenlet	*Hylophilus decurtatus*
Scrub Greenlet	*Hylophilus flavipes*
Dusky-capped Greenlet	*Hylophilus hypoxanthus*
Buff-chested Greenlet	*Hylophilus muscicapinus*
Tawny-crowned Greenlet	*Hylophilus ochraceiceps*
Ashy-headed Greenlet	*Hylophilus pectoralis*
Rufous-crowned Greenlet	*Hylophilus poicilotis*
Tepui Greenlet	*Hylophilus sclateri*
Rufous-naped Greenlet	*Hylophilus semibrunneus*
Gray-chested Greenlet	*Hylophilus semicinereus*
Lemon-chested Greenlet	*Hylophilus thoracicus*

Literature Cited

American Ornithologists' Union
1957. Check-list of North American birds. Ed. 5. Baltimore, Md.: A.O.U., 691pp.

Bailey, A. M., and R. J. Neidroch
1967. Pictorial checklist of Colorado birds. Denver Museum of Natural History.

Barlow, J. C.
1962. Natural history of the Bell Vireo, *Vireo bellii* Audubon. Univ. Kans. Publs., Mus. Nat. Hist. 12(5):241–296.
1967. Nesting of the Black-capped Vireo in the Chisos Mountains, Texas. Condor 69:605–08.
1978. Effects of habitat attrition on vireo distribution and population density in the northern Chichuahuan Desert. In *Trans. Symp. Biol. Resources of the Chihuahuan Desert Region—United States and Mexico*, eds., R. H. Wauer and D. H. Riskind, pp. 591–96. U.S.D.I. Natl. Park Service Trans. and Proc. Series, No. 3.

Barlow, J. C., James, R. D., and N. Williams
1970. Habitat co-occupancy among some vireos of the subgenus *Vireo* (Aves: Vireonidae). Can. J. Zool. 48:395–98.

Barlow, J. C., and R. D. James
1975. Aspects of the biology of the Chestnut-sided Shrike-vireo. Wils. Bull. 87:320–34.

Barlow, J. C., and D. M. Power
1970. An analysis of character variation in red-eyed and Philadelphia vireos (Aves: Vireonidae) in Canada. Can. J. Zool. 48:673–94.

Barlow, J. C., and J. C. Rice
1977. Aspects of the comparative behaviour of red-eyed and Philadelphia vireos. Can. J. Zool. 55:528–41.

Barlow, J. C., and R. H. Wauer
1970. The Gray Vireo (*Vireo vicinior*; Aves: Vireonidae) wintering in the Big Bend region, west Texas. Can. J. Zool. 49:953–55.

Bond, J.
1974. *Birds of the West Indies*. 4th ed. London: Collins.

Bull, J. L.
1974. *Birds of New York State*. Garden City, N.Y.: Doubleday.

Burleigh, T. D.
1958. *Georgia Birds*. Norman Okla.: Univ. of Oklahoma Press.

Chapin, E. A.
1925. Food habits of vireos: a family of insectivorous birds. U. S. Dept. Agric., Bull 1355.

Cox, G. W.
1968. The role of competition in the evolution of migration. Evol. 22:180–92.

Dickey, D. R., and A. J. van Rossem
1938. The birds of El Salvador. Field Mus. Nat. Hist., Zool. Ser., vol. 23.

Edwards, E. P.
1972. *A Field Guide to the Birds of Mexico*. Sweet Briar, Va.: Ernest P. Edwards.

Eisenmann, E.

1962. Notes on some neotropical vireos in Panama. Condor 6:505–08.

Godfrey, W. E.

1966. The birds of Canada. Nat. Mus. Canada Bull 203.

Graber, J. W.

1961. Distribution, habitat requirements and life history of the Black-capped Vireo (*Vireo atricapillus*). Ecol. Monogr. 31:316–36.

Green, J. C., and R. B. Janssen.

1975. *Minnesota Birds—Where, When, and How Many.* Minneapolis, Minn.: Univ. of Minnesota Press.

Grinnel, J., and A. H. Miller

1944. The distribution of the birds of California. Pacific Coast Avifauna 27.

Gromme, O. J.

1963. *Birds of Wisconsin.* Madison, Wis.: Univ. of Wisconsin Press.

Gruson, E. S.

1976. *Checklist of the World's Birds.* New York: Quandrangle New York Times.

Haffer, J.

1974. Avian speciation in tropical South America with a systematic survey of the toucans (Ramphastidae) and jacamars (Galbulidae) Publ. Nuttall Ornithol. Club 14.

Hamilton, T. H.

1958. Adaptive variation in the genus *Vireo*. Wils. Bull., 70: 307–46.

1962. Species relationships and adaptations for sympatry in the avian genus *Vireo*. Condor 64:40–68.

Hayward, C. L.

1976. *Birds of Utah.* Provo, Utah: Brigham Young Univ. Press.

Hespenheide, H. A.

1976. Prey characteristics and predator niche width. In *Ecology and Evolution of Communities*, eds. M. L. Cody and J. M. Diamond. pp. 158–80. Cambridge Mass.: Belknap Press of Harvard Univ. Press.

Howell, A. H.

1932. *Florida State Bird Life.* Tallahassee, Fla.: Univ. of Florida Press.

Imhof, T. A.

1976. *Alabama Birds.* 2nd ed. University, Ala.: Univ. of Alabama Press.

James, R. D.

1973. Ethological and ecological relationships of the Yellow-throated and Solitary vireos (Aves: Vireonidae) in Ontario. Ph. D. diss., University of Toronto, Canada.

1976. Foraging behaviour and habitat selection of three species of vireos in southern Ontario. Wils. Bull. 88: 62–75.

Johnson, D. W.

1975. Ecological analysis of the Cayman Island avifauna. Bull. Fla. State Mus., Biol. Sci. 19(5):235–300.

Johnson, N. K.

1972. Breeding distribution and habitat preference of the Gray Vireo in Nevada. California Birds 36:72–78.

1973. The distribution of boreal avifaunas in southeastern Nevada. Occ. Pap. Biol. Soc. Nev. 36:1–14.

1974a. Interior bird species expand breeding ranges into southern California. Western Birds 2:45–56.

1974b. Montane avifaunas of southern Nevada: historical change in species composition. Condor 76:334–37.

Karr, J. R.

1976. On the relative abundance of migrants from the north temperate zone in tropical habitats. Wils. Bull. 88:433–58.

Lack, D.

1976. *Island Biology Illustrated by the Land Birds of Jamaica.* Studies in ecology. Vol. 3. Berkeley, Calif.: University of California Press.

Land, H. C.

1970. *Birds of Guatemala.* Wynnewood, Pa.: Livingston.

Lowery, G. H., Jr.

1974. *Louisiana Birds.* Baton Rouge: Louisiana State Univ. Press.

Marshall, J. T.

1957. Birds of pine-oak woodland in southern Arizona and adjacent Mexico. Pacific Coast Avifauna 32.

Mayr, E.

1946. History of the North American bird fauna. Wils. Bull. 58:3–41.

Mengel, R. M.

1964. The probable history of species formation in some northern wood warblers (Parulidae). Living Bird 3: 9–43.

Meyer de Schauensee, R.

1970. *A Guide to the Birds of South America.* Wynnewood, Pa.: Livingston Publ. Co.

Meyer de Schauensee, R., and W. H. Phelps

1978. *A Guide to the Birds of Venezuela.* Princeton, N. J.: Princeton Univ. Press.

Miller, A. H.

1963. Seasonal activity and ecology of the avifauna in an American equatorial cloud forest. Univ. Calif. Publ. Zool. 66:1–78.

Miller, A. H., H. Friedmann, L. Griscom, and R. T. Moore

1957. *Distributional Check-list of the Birds of Mexico.* Pt. 2 Pacific Coast Avifauna 33.

Monroe, B. L., Jr.

1968. A distributional survey of the birds of Honduras. A.O.U. Ornith. Monogr. 7.

Jon C. Barlow

Morton, E. S.
1977. Intratropical migration in the Yellow-green Vireo and Piratic Flycatcher. Auk 94:97–106.

Oberholser, H. C.
1974. *The Bird Life of Texas*, ed. E. B. Kincaid, Jr. Two vols. Austin, Tex.: Univ. of Texas Press.

Paynter, R. A., Jr.
1955. The ornithogeography of the Yucatan Peninsula. Peabody Mus. Nat. Hist. Bull. 9.

Peterson, R. T., and E. L. Chalif
1973. *A Field Guide to Mexican Birds*. Boston, Mass.: Houghton Mifflin.

Pettingill, O. S., and N. R. Whitney
1965. Birds of the Black Hills. Ithaca, N.Y.: Laboratory of Ornithology at Cornell Univ.

Phillips, A. R., J. T. Marshall and G. Monson
1964. *The Birds of Arizona*. Tucson, Ariz.: Univ. of Arizona Press.

Power, D. M.
1966. Parasitism of the Dwarf Vireo (*Vireo nanus*) by cowbirds. Auk 83:476–77.

Rice, J. C.
1974. Social and competitive interactions between two species of vireos (Aves: Vireonidae). Ph. D. diss., University of Toronto, Canada.

1978a. Behavioral interactions of interspecifically territorial vireos. I. Song discrimination and natural interactions. Animal Behavior 2:527–49.

1978b. Behavioral interactions of interspecifically territorial vireos. II. Seasonal variation in response intensity. Animal Behavior 2:550–61.

1978c. Ecological relationships of two interspecifically territorial vireos. Ecol. 59:526–538.

Ridgely, R. S.
1976. A guide to the birds of Panama. Princeton, N.J.: Princeton Univ. Press.

Russell, S. M.
1964. A distributional study of the birds of British Honduras. A. O. U. Ornith. Monogr. 1.

Skutch, A. F.
1967. Life histories of Central American highland birds. Publ. Nuttall Ornith. Club 7.

Slud, P. R.
1960. The birds of Finca "La Selva," Costa Rica: a tropical wet forest locality. Bull. Amer. Mus. Nat. Hist., 121: 49–148.

1964. The birds of Costa Rica: distribution and ecology. Bull. Amer. Nat. Hist., vol. 128.

1976. Geographic and climatic relationships of avifaunas with special reference to comparative distribution in the neotropics. Smithsonian Contr. Zool. 212.

Stewart, R. E.
1975. *Breeding Birds of North Dakota*. Fargo, N.D.: North Dakota State Univ.

Sutton, G. M.
1967. *Oklahoma Birds*. Norman, Okla.: Univ. of Oklahoma Press.

Van Rossem, A. J.
1945. A distributional survey of the birds of Sonora, Mexico, Occ. Pap. Mus. Zool., La. St. Univ., No. 21.

Willis, E. O.
1966. The role of migrant birds at swarms of army ants. Living Bird 5:187–231.

Williamson, P.
1971. Feeding ecology of the Red-eyed Vireo (*Vireo olivaceus*) and associated foliage-gleaning birds. Ecol. Monogr. 41:129–52.

ALLEN KEAST
Department of Biology
Queen's University
Kingston, Ontario
Canada K7L 3N6

Spatial Relationships Between Migratory Parulid Warblers and Their Ecological Counterparts in the Neotropics

ABSTRACT   Consideration of the spatial relationships of the migratory and resident parulids in winter shows that: 1) geographic and habitat separation of congeneric species amongst the migrants is marked; 2) a significant segment of migrants winter at the southern limits of the nearctic region, i.e. do not "compete" with resident neotropical birds, and there is a marked north-south attenuation in numbers of species and absolute numbers of migrants southward through central America and into South America; 3) this attenuation matches a progressive increase in numbers of small foliage-gleaning tyrannids, greenlets, etc., the ecological counterparts of the parulids in Neotropica proper. This also applies to formicariids and furnariids, but these larger-bodied (and especially larger-billed) birds mainly occupy different feeding zones from the parulids; 4) where migratory and resident species of parulids co-occur they tend to differ either in feeding zone or habitat. There are, however, foliage gleaners and low-shrub dwellers among both in the highland areas of central and northern South America; 5) spatial and ecological separation patterns between migrant and resident warblers, and between the various species of migrants, are sufficiently clear-cut to indicate a long period of coevolution. In this respect, it can be noted that the migratory warblers spend six to seven months of the year in their wintering grounds.

By far the largest number of nearctic breeding species wintering in the neotropics are wood-warblers (Parulidae, figure 1). No fewer than 47 species in 13 genera leave Canada and the United States to winter in Mexico, Central America, and northern South America. Much of this migration is spectacular, involving flights of thousands of kilometers: only in those endemic to southern Nearctica are the distances traveled limited. A feature is that migrants from the whole of Nearctica funnel into a wintering area of half the size, or less (figure 2). How do they do it? What are the spatial and ecological interrelationships of the nearctic breeders in their wintering grounds? How do they interrelate with the neotropical resident Parulidae and with the smaller tyrannidae that are their ecological counterparts in most of South America (Keast 1972)? Because of the numbers of species involved, the complexity of the problem is obviously greater in the parulids than in any of the other northern migrants.

Some of the ecological mechanisms that might permit the coexistence of large numbers of small insectivorous bird species in Neotropica are: 1) geographic (allopatric) separation; 2) altitudinal separation; 3) habitat separation; 4) feeding in different vertical zones, i.e. at different levels in the forest; 5) maintenance of low populations in any one place, i.e. being so "diluted" as to have only negligible effect, and 6) by lessening the impact in other ways.

For example, there might be a tendency to occupy marginal habitats, as Willis (1968) has recorded for Barro Colorado Island, or habitats that are only available seasonally—see Blondel (1969) with respect to the Mediterranean macchia. The migrants could be present only when the residents are not breeding, thus avoiding the time of greatest demand on the habitat. Most writers have stressed that migrants are indeed absent during the southern breeding season and hence have little influence on it (Skutch 1950; Moreau 1952;

Figure 1. Migratory warblers illustrating divergence in morphology and behavior to afford diverse food exploitation strategies. Top, bark clinging Black-and-white Warbler; clockwise from top: Tennessee Warbler, nectar and insects; Black-throated Gray Warbler, foliage gleaning; bottom, Northern Waterthrush, terrestrial; Yellow-throated Warbler, probing foliage; American Redstart, aerial flycatching.

Allen Keast

Leck 1972; Howell 1972; Chipley 1976). However, Miller (1963) has suggested that in the highland forests of southern Colombia migrants may outcompete residents to the extent of limiting their breeding between October and February. Finally, the impact of migrants could be lessened by some being nomadic in their wintering grounds, moving from place to place according to abundance of food. In Central America, the Yellow-rumped Warbler, (*Dendroica coronata*) follows such a routine (see Russell 1964; Slud 1964). Possibly other species that also consume berries in winter, such as the Cape May (*Dendroica tigrina*), Tennessee (*Vermivora peregrina*) and the Tropical Parula Warbler (*Parula pitiayumi*)—see Karr (1976) and ffrench (1977)—are locally nomadic. Deterioration in habitat during the course of the season forces some migrants to move about (Schwartz 1964; Hespenheide, Morton, both this volume).

A final way in which partial ecological separation of migrant and migrant, and migrant and resident, could be achieved would be by morphological (body size and bill length) differences that channel them towards different resources.

The present review concentrates on the first five of these possibilities, which are the most important. Some attention is also given to body morphology.

Methods

Field work directed at an analysis of habitat separation and zonal feeding in migrant and resident was carried out at 2 major areas, in northern and southern Central America, Veracruz, Mexico (Jalapa region), and Panama (Chiriqui Highlands, Canal Zone, and Barro Colorado Island), and a series of lesser sites. The Veracruz work was carried out from 26 December 1973 to 12 January 1974; the Panama studies in 18–27 February 1975 and 3–10 March 1976. The supplementary study areas were: Trinidad (22 December 1970–5 January 1971); Anchicayá and San Lorenzo, southwestern Colombia (12–24 February 1971); Santa Marta region, Colombia (26 February–3 March 1973); and Belize (19–26 February 1976).

In the more open habitats abundances were determined by the strip count method (Emlen 1971), the observer working along trails and allowing a count strip width of 10 m in thicker areas, and 20 m in open woodland. Counts were made during the morning and afternoon feeding periods. In Veracruz and Chiriqui the transects consisted of 20 300-m-long ones. At the other sites, 2 200-m ones were made.

To quantify zonal feeding, the forest was divided into eight vertical zones (outer foliage, twigs, outer branches, inner branches and trunk, saplings, low shrubs, ground, and air), and the proportion of feeding

Figure 2. Breeding and wintering areas of the migratory parulids contrasted. The former considerably exceeds the latter.

carried out by each species in each zone determined. The criterion was number of feeding actions (pecks) over a time period. Bias was minimized by limiting observations per individual to 20 sec, and remaining only 4 min at any one place, or time. Counts were repeated over several days. Aerial feeding, infrequent, involving a higher energy outlay, but frequently producing a prey item of larger size, cannot really be energetically equated with arboreal feeding. It has, nevertheless, to be incorporated into the scheme. Problems also apply in relating berry feeding to insect feeding.

Data on winter distributions is drawn from regional works, colleagues, and the field observations. The works consulted include: Mexico—Blake (1953), Peterson and Chalif (1973), Loetscher (1955), Martin et al (1954), Wetmore (1943), Davis (1972); Guatemala—Land (1970), Smythe (1966), Griscom (1932); Nicaragua—Howell (1972); Honduras—Monroe (1968); Belize—Russell (1964); El Salvador—Dickey

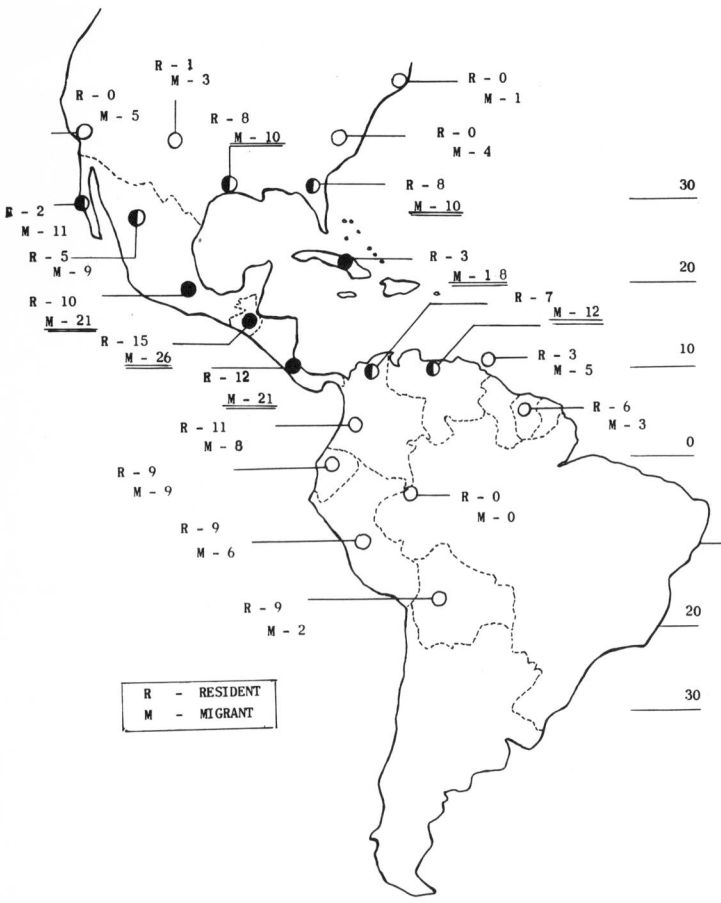

Figure 3.   Relative numbers of species of resident and migratory parulids for a series of areas in southern United States, Central America, and northern South America. A black dot means 18 or more species of wintering migrants, a white circle 8 wintering migrants or less, and a half-white-half-black circle 9 to 17.

and van Rossen (1938); Costa Rica—Skutch (1967), and Slud (1964); Panama—Eisenmann (1952, 1957), Ridgely (1976); Colombia—Todd and Carricker (1922); Miller (1963), de Schauensee (1964); West Indies—Bond (1960); Trinidad—Herklots (1969), ffrench (1977); Surinam—Haverschmidt (1968); Venezuela—de Schauensee and Phelps (1978).

These works are also drawn upon for additional data on winter habitat and, in a few cases, feeding habits.

Winter Ranges of Migratory Parulids Relative to Resident Parulids and Other Small Insect Eaters

The numbers of species of migratory, relative to resi-

dent, parulids present in a series of different localities in winter from the southern United States to northern South America, is shown in figure 3. A black dot indicates 18 or more wintering species; a white circle, 9 or fewer.

Central America, characterized by high physiographic and vegetation diversity, proves to be the major wintering area. There is a marked drop-off in numbers of species to the north (10 on the Gulf coast of the United States), and south (9 in Ecuador, 6 in Peru, 2 in Bolivia). Although up to 18 occur in Cuba, the West Indies are a major wintering area for many fewer species (Terborgh and Faaborg, this volume).

Resident parulids are also most diversified in Central America, 12–15 occurring. There is here, however, less tapering off to the south, Peru and Bolivia still having 9 species. There are resident Mexican highland genera and highland endemic species in southern Nearctica. From Chiapas south, however, they belong mostly to the 2 neotropical genera *Myioborus* and *Basileuterus*.

The numbers of species of migratory parulids, resident parulids, small resident tyrannid flycatchers, sylviids and parids, for a series of sites from the southern United States to Peru are shown graphically in figure 4. Lowland and highland localities are separated, hence species numbers are smaller than in figure 3. Of the lowland localities, Guatemala and Honduras have the most species (about 18), Veracruz about 7, and Panama 12. The numbers drop to 6 in the lowland rain forests of Anchicayá in the Western Andes of southern Colombia. There are about 8 species in the Veracruz highlands, 10 in Honduras, 8–9 in the Chiriqui region, and 4 in the Santa Maria Mountains (subtropical zone).

Resident parulids are represented by 7 species in the lowlands of Guatemala and Honduras, and by 5 in the South American localities. The low figure of 2 for Panama (Morton, pers. comm.) is probably because only the rain forest habitat is represented. In the highlands there are 9 species in central America, and 6–7 in the Andes of Ecuador and Peru.

The numbers of species of "small-bodied" tyrannids are also shown. These, the "ecological counterparts" of the parulids farther south (Keast 1972) are largely unrepresented in Honduras. In Panama there are about 18 species in the lowlands and 7–8 in the highlands. In Ecuador the figures are 26 and 22. (The low count for Anchicayá is because this is a restricted lowland rainforest locality.) A correlation between the north-south drop-off in numbers of wintering parulid species and increase in numbers of small resident tyrannids is obvious. Greenlets (*Hylophilus*, Vireonidae), the most warbler-like of the vireos, have 2 species in the lowland forests of Panama but are absent from the highlands. Their foraging habits resemble those of some warblers although they hang upside down chickadee-like from the outer foliage (Morton, pers. comm.). Eisenmann (1962) discusses habitat separation in Panamanian greenlets.

In the more northern parts of their wintering range the migratory parulids co-occur with a nearctic parid, the Mexican Chickadee (*Parus sclateri*), and a couple of sylviids, the migratory Ruby-crowned Kinglet (*Regulus calendula*), and the Blue-gray Gnatcatcher (*Polioptila caerulea*). In Veracruz the first two are common, the gnatcatcher uncommon. Farther south only resident gnatcatchers are present and these nearctic groups make no impact.

Allopatric Separation of the Migratory Parulid Warblers in Their Wintering Grounds

Geographic Separation

The winter ranges of eight species of the genus *Dendroica*, nine species of *Vermivora*, four of *Oporornis*, and the Black-and-white Warbler (*Mniotilta varia*), are shown in figure 5. The data are drawn from the regional works listed, the American Ornithologists' Union Check-list (1957), and other sources.

A striking level of allopatric separation of species within these genera is apparent. In *Dendroica*, the Cape May Warbler and Black-throated Blue Warbler (*Dendroica caerulescens*) winter mainly in the West Indies, the Chestnut-sided (*Dendroica pensylvanica*) in the lowlands of Panama and southern Central America, Magnolia (*D. magnolia*) in southern Mexico and northern Central America, Kirtland's (*D. kirtlandii*), so far as known in the Bahamas, the Black-throated Green (*D. virens*) in the highlands of Mexico south to Panama, whereas the Blackpoll (*D. striata*) and Blackburnian (*D. fusca*) Warblers winter in South America, the latter exclusively in the highlands. Within *Vermivora* the Nashville (*V. ruficapilla*) winters largely in southern Mexico, with the Tennessee (*V. peregrina*) replacing it in the rest of Central America and northern South America. The Orange-crowned (*V. celata*) is northern. The Colima (*V. crissalis*), Lucy's (*V. luciae*), and the Virginia (*V. virginiae*) Warblers remain in Mexico. Backman's Warbler (*V. bachmanii*) winters in the West Indies, with the Blue-winged and Golden-winged Warblers (*V. pinus* and *V. chrysoptera*) largely replacing each other in northern and southern Central America.

Within *Oporornis* MacGillivray's (*O. tolmiei*), the Kentucky (*O. formosus*), Mourning (*O. philadelphia*), and Connecticut (*O. agilis*) Warblers overlap only partly in winter and the centres of abundance differ. In *Wilsonia* (not shown) Wilson's Warbler (*W. pusilla*)

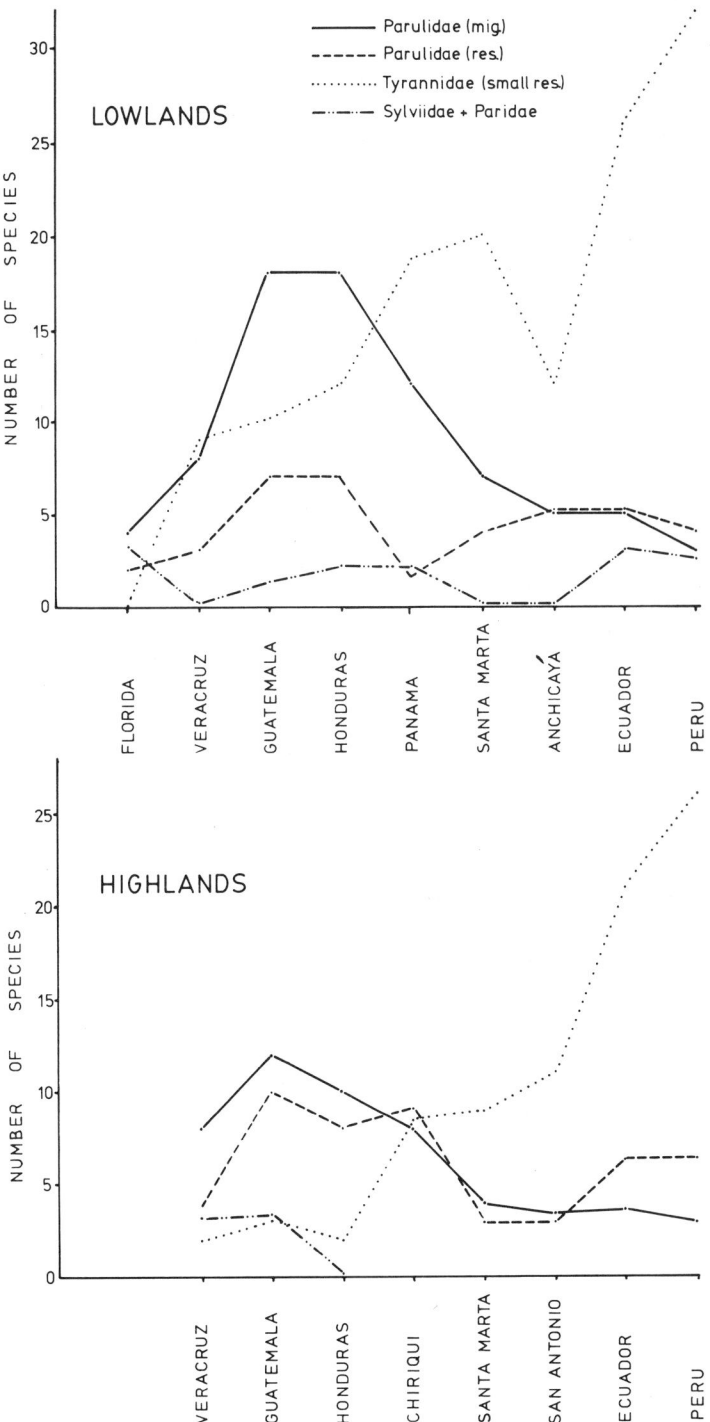

Figure 4. Numbers of species of migratory parulids, resident parulids, small tyrannids, and nearctic sylviids and parids for a series of lowland relative to highland localities at different latitudes. Anchicayá is a restricted locality.

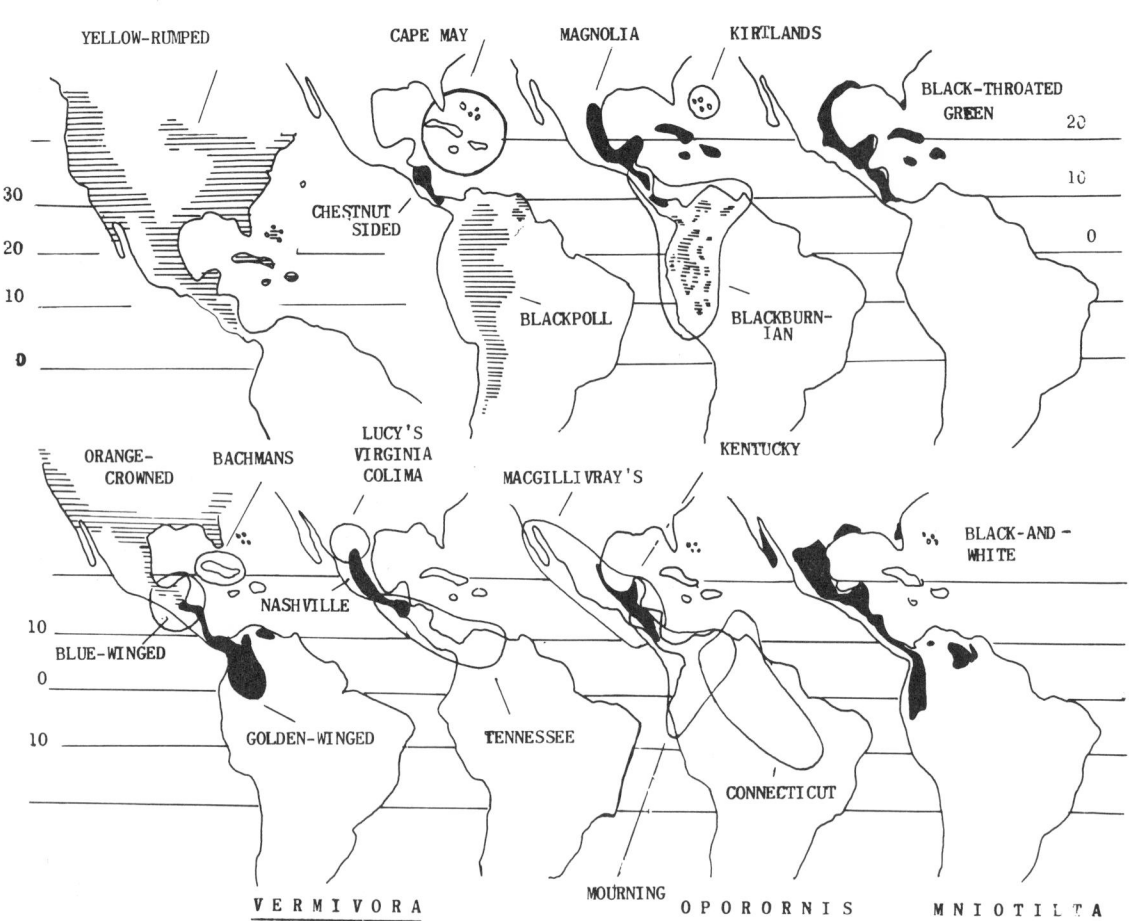

Figure 5. Winter distribution of 8 species of nearctic *Dendroica*, 9 of *Vermivora*, 4 of *Oporornis*, and the Black-and-white Warbler, *Mniotilta varia*. Allopatry of congeners is marked.

has a wide winter range in the highlands of Central America, whereas the Hooded (*W. citrina*) is confined to the northern part, and the Canada Warbler (*W. canadensis*) to South America.

Altitudinal Separation

In the Jalapa region of Veracruz, the Black-throated Green Warbler, the Ruby-crowned Kinglet, the Painted Redstart (*Myioborus picta*) and Red Warbler (*Ergaticus ruber*), and to a lesser extent Wilson's, Magnolia, and Yellow-rumped Warblers, are highland species; the Yellow Warbler (*Dendroica petechia*) and American Redstart (*Setophaga ruticilla*) lowland species, while

the Nashville Warbler occurs at a variety of altitudes (table 1). There is, however, really a third "tier" at higher altitudes, Townsend's Warbler (*Dendroica townsendi*) occurring at 2,700–3,300 m, and the Hermit Warbler (*D. occidentalis*) at 2,300–3,300 m (Loetscher 1955). In Panama the Black-throated Green and Wilson's Warblers, plus several endemics (table 1), are common in the Chiriqui Highlands, whereas the Chestnut-sided, Yellow, and Kentucky Warblers are lowland dwellers.

Do the migratory warblers vary geographically in the altitudinal zone occupied? Data from north to south are as follows:

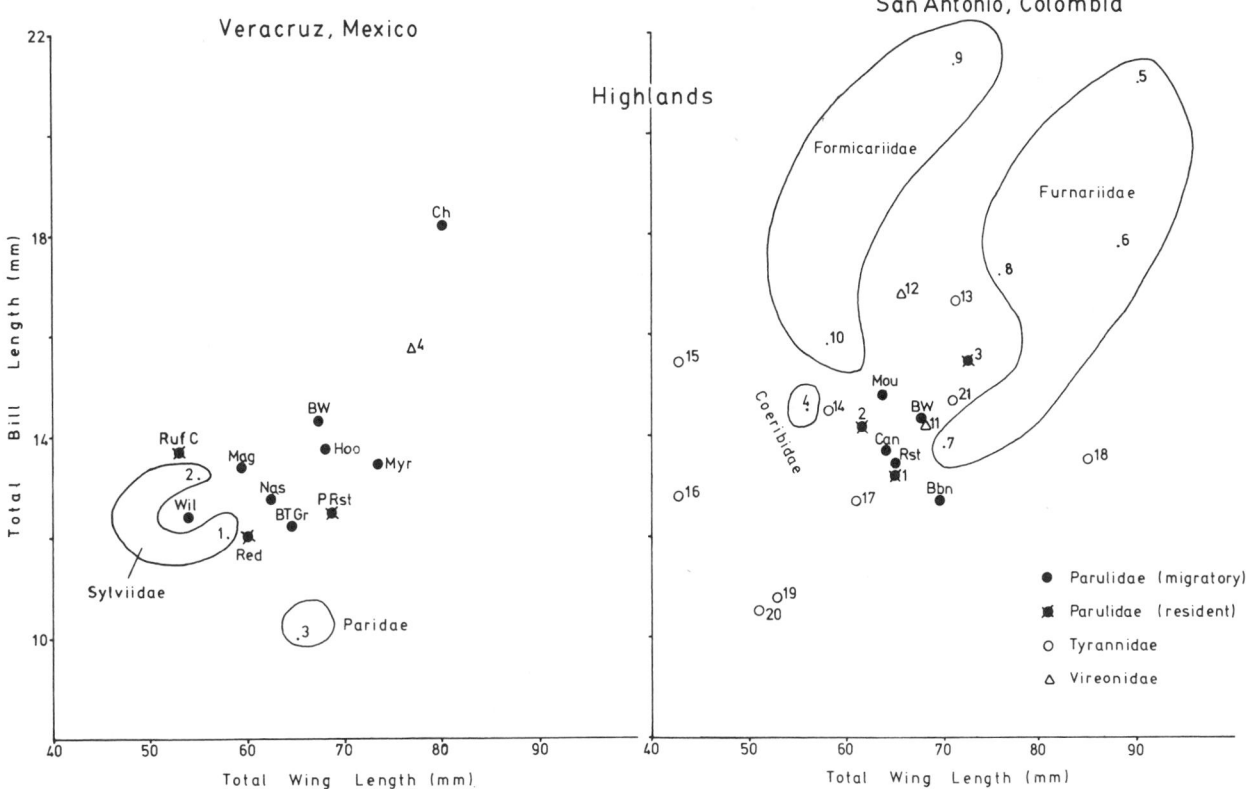

Figure 6. Bill length relative to wing length in species composing winter associations of small insectivorous birds. Veracruz, Mexico; and San Antonio, Colombia. The latter list is from Miller (1964). The bill is measured from the base of the skull to the tip and the wing length is from the angle of folded wing to the tip.

Key: Sylviidae—1—Ruby-crowned Kinglet; 2—Blue-grey Gnatcatcher; Paridae—3—Mexican Chickadee; Parulidae Wil—Wilson's Warbler; Red—Red Warbler; Ruf C—Rufous-crowned; Mag—Magnolia; Nas—Nashville; BT Gr—Black-throated Green; P. Rst—Painted Redstart; Myr—Yellow-rumped; Hoo—Hooded; BW—Black-and-white; Ch—Yellow-breasted Chat; Vireonidae 4 (triangle)—Warbling Vireo. In the San Antonio association the coerebid is the Bananaquit. The warblers are: Mou—Mourning; BW—Black-and-white; Can—Canada; Bbn–Blackburnian; Rst—American Redstart.

Parulidae	1.	*Myioborus miniatus*
	2.	*Basileuterus tristriatus*
	3.	*Basileuterus coronatus*
Coerebidae	4.	*Coereba flaveola*
Furnariidae	5.	*Syndactyla subalaris*
	6.	*Anabacerthia striaticollis*
	7.	*Xenops rutilans*
	8.	*Premnornis guttuligea*
Formicariidae	9.	*Thamnophilus multistriatus*
	10.	*Disithammus mentalis*
Vireonidae	11.	*Vireo leucophrys*
	12.	*Hylophilus semicinereus*
Tyrannidae	13.	*Empidonax virescens*
	14.	*Platyrinchus mystaceus*
	15.	*Todirostrum cinereum*
	16.	*Euscarthmornia granadensis*
	17.	*Pogonotriccus poecilotus*
Tyrannidae	18.	*Elaenia obscura*
	19.	*Camptostoma obsoletum*
	20.	*Tyranniscus chrysops*
	21.	*Mionectes striaticollis*

Table 1.   Relative percentage abundances of small arboreal insect-eaters, Veracruz and Panama sites[1]

	Veracruz Liquidamber forest	Veracruz pine highlands	Veracruz semiarid lowlands	Chiriqui highland rainforest	Panama lowland rainforest
Total of all species per km²	550	490	159	350	140
Species percentages					
Black-and-white Warbler	4	3	—	4	5
Prothonotary Warbler	—	—	—	—	8
Golden-winged Warbler	—	—	—	1	—
Tennessee Warbler	—	—	—	5	18
Flame-throated Warbler	—	—	—	7	—
Nashville Warbler	—	3	13	—	—
Tropical Parula Warbler	—	—	—	2	—
Yellow Warbler	—	—	—	—	8
Magnolia Warbler	—	4	—	—	—
Myrtle (Yellow-rumped) Warbler	—	14	—	—	—
Black-throated Green Warbler	17	36	13	13	—
Blackburnian Warbler	—	—	—	1	—
Chestnut-sided Warbler	—	—	—	—	18
Bay-breasted Warbler	—	—	—	—	13
Yellowthroat Warbler	2	—	—	—	—
Yellow-breasted Chat	—	—	8	—	—
Hooded Warbler	2	—	—	—	—
Wilson's Warbler	32	—	26	17	—
American Redstart	—	—	12	—	3
Painted Redstart	—	3	—	—	—
Slate-throated Redstart	—	—	—	13	—
Collared Redstart	—	—	—	23	—
Red Warbler	—	3	—	—	—
Golden-crowned Warbler	—	—	—	1	—
Black-cheeked Warbler	—	—	—	2	—
Chestnut-capped Warbler	5	—	—	—	—
Three-striped Warbler	—	—	—	4	—
Small tyrannids	6	—	12	7	26
Ruby-crowned Kinglet	9	21	—	—	—
Mexican Chickadee	—	13	—	—	—
Bananaquit	18	—	—	—	—
Blue-grey Gnatcatcher	—	1	12	—	—

[1] Veracruz, 26 Dec 1973–12 Jan 1974; Panama, 18–27 Feb 1975.

BLACK-AND-WHITE WARBLER

Veracruz (Loetscher 1955) throughout; El Salvador (Dickey and van Rossem 1938) sea-level to 1,300 m; Honduras (Monroe 1968) up to 700 m; Costa Rica (Slud 1964) up to 2,300 m; Panama (Ridgely 1976) primarily lowlands but up to 3,000 m; Venezuela (de Schauensee and Phelps 1978) up to 2,500 m. A wide altitudinal range is thus indicated.

PROTHONOTARY WARBLER. *Protonotaria citrea*

This is strictly a lowland species in its Central American and northern South American wintering grounds (Slud; Ridgely; de Schauensee and Phelps; S. Russell, pers. comm.).

YELLOW WARBLER

In Mexico this is a highland breeder in summer but

Allen Keast

winters in the lowlands (Blake 1953; Peterson and Chalif 1973). Farther south, northern migrants winter mainly in the lowlands; vide sea-level to 600 m in Honduras, from the coast to the central plateau in Costa Rica. It is restricted to the lowlands and lower foothills in Panama and the Santa Marta area of Colombia (Todd and Carricker 1922). It winters from sea-level to 1,000 m in Venezuela.

MAGNOLIA WARBLER

In El Salvador this species occurs up to 1,200 m but is more numerous below 700 m. In Honduras it occurs from the coast to 500 m. It is a foothills species in Costa Rica. In Panama it is quite rare but has a scattered distribution (Morton, pers. comm.).

YELLOW-RUMPED WARBLER

Occurs from sea-level up to 650 m in Honduras and 1,000–1,200 m in El Salvador. It is widespread in the Veracruz highlands and yet is not uncommon on the small offshore cays of Belize (pers. obs.).

BLACK-THROATED GREEN WARBLER

The writer found virtually none below 1,000 m, in Veracruz and 1,800 m in Panama. The vertical range in Honduras is given as 750–2,400 m; whereas it inhabits the lower mountains at 1,200–1,700 m in El Salvador and 350–2,500 m in Guatemala (Bent 1963). Slud and Ridgely both describe it as a highland bird.

BLACKBURNIAN WARBLER

This is a highland form in its wintering grounds—see Slud (1964), Todd and Carricker; R. Chipley (pers. comm.). Numbers occur also in the Silvia region (2,000 m) of the central Andes (writer's observations). In Venezuela it winters at 800–3,100 m (de Schauensee and Phelps).

CHESTNUT-SIDED WARBLER

This species winters in the lowlands (Munroe, Slud, Ridgely).

BAY-BREASTED WARBLER. *Dendroica castanea*

Winters in the lowlands (Costa Rica, Panama).

PRAIRIE AND PALM WARBLER. *Dendroica discolor* and *D. palmarum*

Both winter in the lowlands.

TENNESSEE WARBLER

This species winters over a wide vertical range, vide sea-level to 1,200 m in El Salvador, up to 700 m in Honduras; is equally abundant at high and low levels in Costa Rica and Panama and occurs up to 2,000 m in Venezuela.

GOLDEN-WINGED, BLUE-WINGED, AND FLAME-THROATED WARBLERS. *Vermivora gutturalis*

The first two of these *Vermivora* warblers are lowland dwellers, but the resident species is restricted to 1,300 m and above (Ridgely). The Golden-winged occurs at 1,000–3,000 m in Venezuela.

COMMON YELLOWTHROAT. *Geothlypis trichas*

Occurs from the coast up to 1,500 m in Honduras, up to 2,300 m in El Salvador and from sea-level to the subtropical belt in Costa Rica.

WILSON'S WARBLER

Bent (1963) credits this species as occurring from the lowlands to 3,300 m in Guatemala. It was not, however, found by the writer below about 300 m in Veracruz. In Honduras it occurs at 600–2,200 m; is conspicuous above the timberline but uncommon below 850 m in Costa Rica, and is a highland species in Panama, being common above 1,200 m.

AMERICAN REDSTART

Occurs from sea-level to 700 m in Honduras, coast to central plateau in Costa Rica, and generally below 750 m in Guatemala (Land 1970). In Venezuela, however, it may go up to 3,000 m. Resident redstarts are highland forest forms in Panama *Myioborus miniatus* (Slate-throated Redstart) occurring from 1,200–2,300 m, and *M. torquatus* (Collared Redstart) mainly above 2,000 m, but sometimes down to 1,300 m (Ridgely 1976). Altitudinal replacement of migrant by resident is also indicated in the western Andes of Colombia (Miller 1963).

Most migratory warblers thus occupy a range of altitudes. There is a tendency to go higher in the south, for example in Venezuela (but this may partly reflect available habitat). Nowhere is a species a lowland inhabitant in part of its range and a highland dweller in another. However, as noted, there are lowland and highland species. Congeners partly separate in this way, vide the Yellow, Magnolia, and Chestnut-sided Warblers relative to the Black-throated Green and Blackburnian in *Dendroica*; and Hooded and Wilson's Warblers in *Wilsonia* (Monroe 1968). In *Geothlypis* (Yellowthroats) a wide-range migrant (*trichas*) is partly replaced altitudinally and partly in habitat by endemics (e.g. *G. chiriquensis*). Lack and Lack (1972) describe a partial vertical separation of congeneric warblers in

Jamaica. (For data from Hispaniola and elsewhere, see Terborgh and Faaborg, this volume.)

Most resident parulids in Central America are, by contrast, highland dwellers. Thus, in Veracruz, *Cardellina rubrifrons* and *Myioborus pictus* are restricted to the uplands. In Honduras (Monroe 1968) two *Myioborus* occur at 1,000–2,400 m, the Fan-tailed Warbler (*Euthlypis lachrymosa*) at 300–1,800 m, the Stripe-crowned (*Basileuterus culicivorus*) at 500–1,600 m, Rufous-capped (*B. rufifrons*) at 200–1,100 m, and Golden-browed Warbler (*B. belli*) only above 1,800 m. Of the five *Basileuterus* species in Panama the Black-cheeked Warbler (*B. melanogenus*) is largely restricted to altitudes above 2,000 m; two only occur at 1,000–1,200 m and above, and two range from the lowlands upwards. In Venezuela, two of the seven *Myioborus* species occur only above 2,100 m, two others only above 1,200 m, and none extend below 600 m. In *Basileuterus*, one is restricted to 2,600–3,000 m, and six of the remaining nine species do not occur below 900 m (de Schauensee and Phelps 1977).

Separation of the Warbler Species by Habitat

The relative abundances of 14 warbler species in three habitats in the Jalapa region of Veracruz are shown in table 1 (December-January). The habitats were: 1) highland pine-oak woodland on old lava beds at 2,000–2,400 m, parklike terrain with some areas of thicket along creek channels and in depressions; 2) broad-leafed Liquidamber forest at 1,000 m on the coastal slope, a wet and mist-shrouded habitat with much lush sapling development and undergrowth; and 3) coastal lowland Caribbean dry scrub (area of Punta Nacionale).

In the highland pine areas where numbers of migrants were high, Black-throated Green Warblers made up 36 percent of the small insect-eaters; Ruby-crowned Kinglets, 21 percent; Yellow-rumped Warblers, 14 percent; Mexican Chickadees, 13 percent; Magnolia Warblers, 4 percent; Nashville, Black-and-white, Red Warblers, and Painted Redstarts, 3 percent each; and Blue-gray Gnatcatchers, 1 percent. By contrast, in the Liquidamber forest (numbers of migrants also high) Wilson's Warblers accounted for 32 percent of all individuals; Bananaquits (*Coereba flaveola*), 18 percent; Black-throated Green Warblers, 17 percent; and kinglets, 9 percent. There were small numbers of Black-and-white Warblers, Chestnut-capped Warblers (*Basileuterus delattrii*), and occasional Yellow-breasted Chats (*Icteria virens*), Yellowthroats, and Hooded Warblers. In the lowland semi-arid scrub (numbers of migrants low) Wilson's Warblers made up 26 percent of the total, Black-throated Green and Nashville Warblers, 13 percent; American Redstarts and Gnatcatch-

ers, 12 percent, and Yellow-breasted Chats, 8 percent.

Wetmore (1943) records the habitats of wintering parulids in southern Veracruz as follows: Northern Parula Warbler, scattered groves in the forest; Yellow Warbler, widespread; Magnolia Warbler, groves and woodland; Kentucky Warbler, thickets and forest; Hooded Warbler, lowland forests and thickets.

Equivalent data from Chiriqui subtropical rain forests at 2,200 m relative to lowland rain forests of the Canal Zone and Barro Colorado Island are also given in table 1. In the highlands, warbler numbers, while moderately high, did not approach those in Veracruz. In the lowlands, warblers made up only a negligible fraction of the total avifauna. At Chiriqui, Wilson's Warblers accounted for 17 percent of the total parulids; Black-throated Green Warblers, 13 percent; Tennessee Warblers, 5 percent; and Black-and-white Warblers, 4 percent. Here, however, the migrants were equalled in proportions by such residents as the Collared Redstart, 23 percent of total: Slate-throated Redstart, 13 percent; and Flame-breasted Warblers, 7 percent. In the lowland rain forests, Chestnut-sided and Tennessee Warblers accounted for 21 percent each, Bay-breasts, 15 percent, and Prothonotary Warblers, 5 percent. Small tyrannids and greenlets (*Vireonidae*) were more common in the lowlands than highlands.

Do the wintering migrants vary geographically in the kind of habitat occupied? Regional accounts provide some data on this.

BLACK-AND-WHITE WARBLER

This species occupies a range of habitats in Veracruz, as it does in Honduras (Monroe, 1968), and in Costa Rica (Slud 1974). In El Salvador, van Rossen and Dickey (1938) state that it has a preference for oaks but may also occur in mangroves and beach scrub. In the Santa Martas it occurs wherever there is forest (Todd and Carricker 1922) and in Venezuela frequents the forest edge and second growth (de Schauensee and Phelps 1978).

PROTHONOTARY WARBLER

Inhabits mangroves in the Santa Marta area, mangroves and lake edges and riverine forest in Panama, and wooded streams and mangroves in Venezuela.

YELLOW WARBLER

In the inland parts of Mexico, willows and cottonwoods bordering streams are inhabited and on the coast mangrove swamps (Blake 1953); in Guatemala, a range of habitats but especially thickets and shrubs close to water (Smythe 1966); in Honduras scrub, second-growth, semiopen areas, habitations, mangroves, being especially common close to water; Costa Rica, semiopen land, shrubbery, and scrubby vegetation; and Panama, open and semiopen areas. In northern Columbia, it lives in low growth; in Venezuela, mangroves and xerophytic vegetation.

TENNESSEE WARBLER

In Guatemala inhabits small trees and shrubs in semiopen areas (Smythe 1966) or open growth, thickets and riverside vegetation but not heavy forest (Bent 1963); open broadleaf forest, forest edge and second growth in Honduras; rain forest in Nicaragua (Howell 1972), plantations and cut-over vegetation in Costa Rica, and second-growth and mature woodland in Panama.

YELLOW-RUMPED WARBLER

Inhabits low bushes in El Salvador; pine savannah in Nicaragua; open vegetation, shrubbery, and gardens in Guatemala; lowland pine ridges and offshore keys in Belize; "any shrub or open forest situation in Honduras" (Monroe 1968:329); semiopen country, savannahs, and forest clearings in Costa Rica; and open areas in Panama.

BLACK-THROATED GREEN WARBLER

Inhabits pine-oak highlands and Liquidambar forests in Veracruz; coffee plantations and cloud forest in El Salvador; tall forest trees and clearings in Guatemala; pine-oak associations and cloud forest in Honduras; broad-leafed vegetation in forested mountain terrain in Costa Rica; and second-growth woodland in Panama where it is largely confined to the subtropical belt.

BLACKBURNIAN WARBLER

In Costa Rica, at the northern end of its range, this highland species inhabits forest edges and gaps in the forest. The habitat in Venezuela is rain and cloud forest, second growth, and dwarf forest. This is also broadly true of Colombia although here it also feeds in isolated trees in pastures (Silvia region, central Andes, pers. obs.).

CHESTNUT-SIDED WARBLER

Occurs in middle forest, at heights of 7–16 m in Nicaragua; broadleaf forest and second growth in Honduras: second-growth woodland and clearings in Costa Rica and Panama.

WILSON'S WARBLER

Inhabits low growth beneath the forest in El Salvador; wet or boggy areas with low thickets and shrubs in Guatemala; forest edge and clearings in Costa Rica. It is an inhabitant of the broad-leafed forest in the Jalapa region of Veracruz and in the Chiriqui Highlands inhabits mainly the forest edge (pers. obs.).

AMERICAN REDSTART

Inhabits broadleaf woods, second growth, or scrub, preferring open places; it avoids forests and the distribution is patchy (Slud 1964). This is also true of other central American localities. In Venezuela it inhabits mangroves, savannah, forests, and thorny thickets.

The above survey reveals that while some species keep to specific winter habitats (Yellowthroat, Prothonotary Warbler) most are fairly generalized and opportunist in habitat utilization (Black-and-white Warbler, American Redstart). Geographic variation in habitat occupied is marked in a few. All species have preferences and avoid certain habitats. In some cases, preferred habitats are somewhat similar in appearance to those of the breeding grounds (the Yellow Warbler, Yellowthroat, Kentucky's and Wilson's Warbler). Note account of breeding habitat of the last-named in Stewart (1973). In some (e.g. Chestnut-sided) the breeding and winter habitats are quite different.

Uncommonness as Factor Limiting Interspecific Competition

Prior to this symposium there has been little data on the absolute abundances of wintering migrants in different places. An exception is the Jamaica data of Lack and Lack (1972). In virtually all species, the wintering area includes a core area of high density with smaller numbers occurring over a wider area.

In all areas the warbler "community" is a mixture of numerous, moderately common, and uncommon species (table 1). Species that are uncommon will make little competitive impact. It is ecologically advantageous for a species to be "thinly spread" in its wintering grounds. Species with high populations overall cannot achieve this; they must necessarily occur in high numbers over a wide area.

Included in the wintering migrants are rare species with small winter ranges (e.g. Bachman's Warbler), moderately common ones that winter in a restricted area (Chestnut-sided), or over a wider area (Black-throated Green), and other ones that are very widely dispersed (Black-and-white Warbler). The latter winters from Florida to Ecuador but everywhere its numbers are uniformly low. The figure of one to six birds seen per morning, described by Miller (1963) for San

Table 2. Zonal feeding in small arboreal insect-eaters, pine forest,[1] Veracruz, Mexico, 2,300–2,600 m

Species	Number of individuals observed	Number of feeding observations	Pines			Deciduous Trees							
			Needles	Outer branches	Inner branches, trunks	Leaves	Twigs	Outer branches	Inner branches, trunks	Saplings	Shrubs	Ground	Air
Black-throated Green Warbler	204	730	20	—	3	30	20	18	7	3	—	—	—
Magnolia Warbler	19	89	—	—	—	15	25	15	5	40	—	—	—
Black-and-white Warbler	18	107	—	—	—	—	—	15	85	—	—	—	—
Red Warbler	15	64	—	—	—	—	—	10	5	85	—	—	—
Painted Redstart	18	80	—	16	10	—	—	25	18	5	—	—	25
Myrtle (Yellow-rumped)	21	140	—	—	—	10	10	—	—	—	60[2]	20	—
Ruby-crowned Kinglet	140	450	3	—	3	30	25	23	3	8	5	—	—

[1] 26 Dec 1973–12 Jan 1974.
[2] Taking berries.

Lorenzo, agrees well with the counts of Russell (1964) for Belize, Slud (1964) for Costa Rica, and the writer's observations in Veracruz and Panama. Probably low density and solitary feedings is associated with the trunk-feeding habit. Low densities characterize nuthatches and woodpeckers in most places.

Many parulids ensure low densities in the wintering grounds by being territorial, e.g. Schwartz (1964), Karr (1976), Morton (1976), or exhibit territorial aggressiveness (Emlen 1973). The frequency with which individual members of species return to the same place from year to year, e.g. Loftin et al (1966) and Loftin (1977) for Panama; Nickel (1968) for Belize; Diamond and Smith (1973) for Jamaica; Moreau (1966, 1972) for West Africa; Pearson (1972) for Kenya; Nisbet and Medway (1972) for Malaysia, is probably part of the mechanism that serves to keep densities low, assuming that "home range" has a territorial component.

Vertical Separation by Feeding Zone

In the highland pine-oak woodland of Veracruz the Black-throated Green Warbler and Ruby-crowned Kinglet fed in the outer leaves, twigs, and outer branches of the trees; the Nashville in the foliage; the Magnolia in the lower branches of the trees and foliage of saplings; Black-and-white on the branches and trunks; the endemic Red Warbler in the saplings and lower parts of the trees (table 2). The Painted Redstart fed aerially by fluttering at or around the branches and trunks and making sorties out between the trees. The Yellow-rumped Warbler, while occasionally feeding in trees, was more commonly seen on the open ground or seeking berries in low shrubs.

In the Liquidamber forest (table 3) the Black-throated Green Warbler fed exclusively in the outer foliage and branches of the trees, Wilson's Warbler in

Allen Keast

Table 3. Zonal feeding in small arboreal insect-eaters, Liquidamber forest,[1] Veracruz, Mexico, 1,200–1,400 m

Species	Number of individuals observed	Number of feeding observations	Feeding zone (percentages)						
			Air	Outer leaves	Outer branches	Branches and trunk	Sapling foliage	Low shrub	Ground
Black-throated Green Warbler	78	275	—	75[2]	25	—	—	—	—
Hooded Warbler	9	49	—	—	—	—	30	60	10
Black-and-white Warbler	14	68	—	—	20	60	20	—	—
Wilson's Warbler	45	180	—	15	—	—	55	20	10
Yellow-breasted Chat	80	35	—	—	—	—	—	100	—
Rufous-crowned Warbler	147	64	—	—	—	—	—	100	—
Bananaquit	28	105	—	—	—	—	60	40	—

[1] 26 Dec 1973–12 Jan 1974.

[2] 10 percent fluttering at leaves.

Table 4. Zonal feeding in parulid warblers, rainforests,[1] Chiriqui Highlands, Panama, 2,200–2,400 m

Species	Number of individuals observed	Number of feeding observations	Feeding zone (percentages)									
			Air	Outer leaves	Twigs	Outer branches	Inner branches	Trunks	Sapling foliage	Sapling branches	Low shrubs	Logs, ground
Black-throated Green	57	220	—	62	8	—	—	—	30	—	—	—
Wilson's	41	182	—	19	10	23	4	2	11	—	25	—
Tennessee	22	84	—	46	6	—	—	—	45	3	—	—
Black-and-white	11	52	—	—	—	20	30	45	10	5	—	—
Blackburnian	14	89	—	100	—	—	—	—	—	—	—	—
Tropical Parula	19	73	—	100	—	—	—	—	—	—	—	—
Flame-throated	82	109	—	70	10	—	—	10	10	—	—	—
Black-cheeked	12	52	—	—	—	—	—	—	10	—	80	10
Slaty-throated Redstart	28	142	32	16	5	12	6	—	13	10	6	—
Collared Redstart	41	178	30	—	—	4	8	12	14	7	10	15

[1] Feb–Mar 1975.

Table 5. Feeding heights of parulid warblers, rainforests,[1] 2,200–2,400 m, Chiriqui Highlands, Panama

Species	Height in m. (estimated)									
	23	20	17	13	10	7	5	3	2	Ground
Black-throated Green	10	24	8	12	16	22	7	—	—	—
Wilson's	5	17	7	12	6	8	10	14	21	—
Tennessee	6	8	22	23	23	20	8	—	—	—
Black-and-white	8	11	15	20	17	12	12	5	—	—
Blackburnian	10	40	40	10	—	—	—	—	—	—
Tropical Parula	—	8	32	37	22	—	—	—	—	—
Flame-throated	5	35	25	—	5	10	15	5	—	—
Black-cheeked	—	—	—	—	—	—	12	10	74	4
Slate-throated Redstart	—	8	18	20	15	18	10	6	4	—
Collared Redstart	—	—	—	5	8	18	14	18	26	14

[1] Feb–Mar 1975. For numbers of individual feeding observations on which this is based, see table 4.

the foliage of the saplings, and to a degree, trees and low shrubs; the Hooded Warbler in creek-edge vegetation, low shrubs, and sometimes from the ground. The Yellow-breasted Chat and resident Rufous-crowned Warbler kept to the low shrubs and thickets. the Black-and-white Warbler worked the trunks and branches. The resident Bananaquit fed in the foliage of saplings, along the creek edge, and in the low shrubbery.

There was a similar vertical separation in feeding in the semiarid lowlands, the Nashville concentrating on the outer foliage of trees and tall saplings, the Black-throated Green in the higher foliage, Wilson's in the saplings and undergrowth thickets, the Yellow Warbler in dry hillside and valley floor shrubbery, and the American Redstart and Gnatcatcher feeding aerially.

Although the species composition was different a similar vertical feeding separation characterized the warblers of the Chiriqui Highlands (table 4). There the Black-throated Green and Tennessee Warblers were the common outer foliage feeders, along with the resident Flame-throated and Tropical Parula Warblers. The Black-cheeked Warbler kept to the low shrubbery, the Three-striped Warbler to the lower middle parts of the forest. The two redstarts fed mainly from the air, by pursuit or fluttering along branches and logs, at the foliage of saplings, or over the open ground. These observations match those of other workers for these species (Slud 1964, Skutch 1967, Leck 1972; Ridgely 1976). Expressed on a vertical scale (table 5) the Black-throated Green Warbler carried out 70 percent of its feeding at heights of 10 m or more, the tropical Parula, 100 percent; Tennessee, 80 percent; and Wilson's, 50 percent. The last-named, however, did 35 percent of its feeding at heights of 3 m, or less. All of the Black-cheeked Warbler feeding was at heights of 5 m or less, as was 72 percent of that of the Collared Redstart.

In the lowland forest sections surveyed, the Tennessee Warbler foraged at all heights, the Bay-breast high up. The Northern Waterthrush fed on the ground at the edges of creeks. These observations also match those of other workers (Willis, Morton, pers. comm.).

Thus there is a broad separation of species into ground, shrub, lower to middle layer feeders, foliage, and aerial feeders.

Comparative Ecology of Resident and Migratory Parulids in Wintering Grounds

The parulids may be divided zoogeographically into several groups: 1) nearctic breeders wintering in Neotropica; 2) southern U. S.-Mexican Highlands endemics in the southern Nearctica, or undertaking only local movements. These include *Vermivora virginiae*, *V. crissalis*, *V. luciae*, *V. superciliosa*, various *Geothlypis*, chats (*Granatellus*), Red-faced Warbler (*Cardellina rubrifrons*), and pine-oak highland species, such as the Painted Redstart (*Myioborus picta*) and the Red- and Pink-headed Warblers (*Ergatus ruber* and *E. versicolor*). See also bird lists from highland and lowland pine-oak regions, such as Martin et al (1954), and Howell (1972); 3) Caribbean endemics; 4) "true" neotropical warblers of the genera *Basileuterus* and *Myioborus*. While 4 species of the former and 2 of the latter extend north to Mexico there are 19 of the former and 9 of the latter in South America proper (Meyer de Schauensee 1964). Many of these have local or very restricted ranges.

Interaction patterns between the northern migrants and resident species can, accordingly, be thought of in terms of three regional faunas.

Mexican Region

The dry and mountainous southwestern United States, the breeding area of such endemics as the Colima, Virginia's, and Lucy's Warblers, is not a significant wintering area for northern migrants, nor are parts of northern Mexico. In the pine-oak highlands of Tamilaupas, the arboreal feeding warblers are the resident Olive (*Dendroica taeniatus*), Tropical Parula, and Hartlaub's Warblers (*Vermivora superciliosa*), non-migrants (Martin et al 1954). Farther south, in Veracruz, the wintering warblers are a mixture of migrants and residents. Here, as noted, the migratory Black-throated Green, Wilson's, and Nashville Warblers, and the Ruby-crowned Kinglet, are the arboreal foliage-gleaners, and resident species (which occur in one's and two's, not flocks) feed in the low to medium stratum (Red Warbler), thickets (Rufous-crowned Warbler), or aerial feed (Painted Redstart). The resident Mexican Chickadee feeds in the outer branches and foliage although it tends to occur more in conifers than deciduous trees. Farther south in Veracruz, the neotropical parulids (one *Myioborus* and three *Basileuterus*) occur (Wetmore 1943). A northern pine-oak highland element persists south into Nicaragua where Grace's Warbler is the dominant foliage gleaner (Howell 1972).

West Indies

The West Indian parulid fauna consists of four endemic genera (*Catharopeza* on St. Vincent, *Leucopeza* on St. Lucia, *Microligea* on Hispaniola, and *Teretistris* on Cuba); there are five endemic species of *Dendroica*; and one *Geothlepis* (Bond, 1960). The endemic genera are predominantly undergrowth dwellers (Bond 1960; Andrle and Andrle 1976). By contrast, the endemic Dendroicas, which are presumably later colonizers, are arboreal although they may also feed in undergrowth (*Dendroica vitellina*, *D. pharetra*). Of the northern migrants rated as common by Faaborg and Terborg (this volume) the northern Parula, Cape May, Black-throated Blue, and, to some extent, the Palm Warblers, are largely arboreal foliage gleaners; most, however, tend to be more plastic in their feeding than on the breeding grounds. Other common migrants include the trunk-feeding Black-and-white Warbler and the

terrestrial water-thrushes and Ovenbird. The migratory Yellowthroat is a common thicket feeder. Thus while the separation is not complete, there is a broad tendency for the residents to inhabit thickets and undergrowth, and the migrants (along with the resident Dendroicas) to feed in the trees, on the ground, and from the trunks.

Lack and Lack (1972) provide a detailed analysis of ecological separation in the warblers of Jamaica. Of the 20 species occurring, 4 or 5 are rare. The warblers are distributed over five habitats; lowland arid, lowland river, middle elevation, and montane areas. Up to 14 occur in the more productive of these, but no more than 6 to 8 species exceed 2 percent of the total numbers in any place. There is both habitat and altitudinal replacement of species. Feeding zone replacement is marked with the Ovenbird (*Seiurus aurocapillus*) and the two water-thrushes (*S. noveboracensis* and *S. motacilla*), feeding on the ground. Swainson's Warbler (*Limnothlypis swainsonii*) feeds on the overgrown forest floor. The Palm Warbler is a ground feeder in open grassland and man-modified areas. Others are shrub or outer foliage feeders. There is some separation of species according to the sizes of the leaves of the shrubs in which they feed. Among the foliage gleaners the mean foraging height varies. One species, the Yellow-rumped Warbler, which was uncommon, only utilized the island for part of the winter, not arriving until January. A degree of day-to-day local wandering by warbler species occurs. Individual species differ slightly in bill length and wing length; the authors were not, however, able to ascribe any ecological meaning to this.

Terborgh and Faaborg (this volume) provide a detailed analysis of ecological separation patterns in the migratory and resident warblers on Hispaniola, and other West Indian islands. There are characteristically seven species in each of two major habitats, all belonging to different guilds.

Northern Neotropica

Assessment of the feeding zones of resident relative to migrant parulids in the Chiriqui Highlands of Panama shows the migrants to be dominant in the arboreal foliage-gleaning zone. Two resident foliage gleaners, the Flame-throated and Tropical Parula Warblers are, however, widespread. Two aerial feeding redstarts (*Myioborus torquatus* and *M. miniatus*) are dominant, the migratory American Redstart being absent. The trunk-feeding Black-and-white Warbler is a migrant. The resident Three-striped Warbler fed in the middle layers of the forest, the same zone as Wilson's Warbler; the latter, however, kept mainly to the forest edge. The resident Black-cheeked Warbler was the only species in low shrubbery in the forest proper.

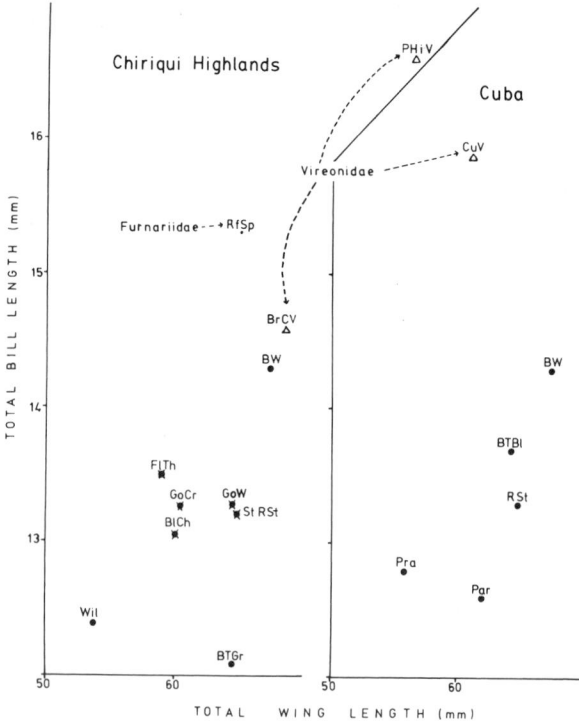

Figure 7. Bill and wing lengths of species of small insectivores occurring in mixed winter associations, Chiriqui Highlands of Panama and Cuba (later data from Eaton 1953). Migratory parulids are indicated by a black dot, resident species by a cross, and vireos by an open triangle.

Key: Wil—Wilson's Warbler; BT Gr—Black-throated Green; BlCh—Black-cheeked; GoCr—Golden-crowned; FlTh—Flame-throated; GoW—Golden-winged; St RSt—Slate-throated Redstart; BW—Black-and-white Warbler; BrCV—Brown-capped Vireo CuV—Cuban Vireo; BTBl—Black-throated Blue Warbler; Rst—American Redstart; PhiV—Philadelphia Vireo; Pra—Prairie Warbler; Par—Northern Parula Warbler; RFsp—Rufous Spinetail.

Observations in Costa Rica by Slud (1964) indicate a similar separation of migrants and residents. The foliage feeders are the migratory Tennessee, Black-throated Green, Blackburnian, and Golden-winged Warblers, and resident Tropical Parula and Flame-throated (*Vermivora gutturalis*); crowns of low trees and shrubs (migratory Chestnut-sided); second growth and scrub (Three-striped Warbler); shrubs (migratory Hooded Warbler); thickets (Yellow-breasted Chat); under-story (the endemic Striped-crowned); under-growth (migratory Kentucky and Mourning); scrubby growth to a few metres up into the trees (Chestnut-capped Warbler, *Basileuterus delatrii*); bushy under-growth (Black-cheeked Warbler).

In the Santa Marta Mountains Todd and Carriker (1922) record that the Bay-breasted, Blackburnian,

Blackpoll, and Tropical Parula Warblers feed high in the trees, the Mourning and Yellow Warblers in thickets (highland and lowland, respectively). Amongst the endemics the Yellow-crowned Redstart (*Myioborus flavivertex*) and Russet-crowned Warbler (*Basileuterus coronatus*) keep to the middle regions of the forest, flitting from shrub to shrub and through the lower branches of trees. The endemic Santa Marta Warbler (*Basileuterus basilicus*) keeps to the undergrowth (Todd and Carriker, 1922).

Thus, there are endemic neotropical parulids in all the vertical feeding zones (the River Warbler, *Phaeothlypis rivularis*, is terrestrial), except the trunk-branch feeding one. The arboreal foliage-gleaning zone is still dominated by the migrants. The residents feed mainly in two areas: 1) undergrowth and the lower levels of the forest (Munroe 1968, Honduras; Miller 1963, San Lorenzo section of Colombia; de Schauensee and Phelps; 1978, Venezuela) and 2) the aerial feeding zone. *Basileuterus* and *Euthlypis* occupy the former in Honduras, and eight species of *Basileuterus* do so in Venezuela. While the migratory Connecticut and Mourning Warblers are, of course, also undergrowth feeders, the residents are dominant in the lower and middle levels. The *Myioborus* redstarts are the common aerial feeders throughout. As noted, the American Redstart avoids dense forest and is patchily distributed (Slud 1964).

Body Dimensions Relative to Ecological Separation of Migrant and Resident Warblers and Other Small Insectivorous Species

Co-occurring species of small insectivorous birds commonly differ in bill-length or body size, which serves to channel them towards different resources (Schoener 1965). Are the mixed associations of migratory and resident warblers and other small insect-eaters, characterized by this feature?

Figure 6 plots the bill- and wing-lengths for the species comprising the highland Veracruz assemblage and for San Lorenzo, Colombia, one studied by Miller (1963). Figure 7 shows this for the Chiriqui Highland assemblages and for the Cuban one described by Eaton (1953). This latter can be used for a comparison with the Jamaica figures of Lack and Lack (1973).

In the Veracruz assemblage there is no significant difference between the migrant and resident warblers in body dimensions. The kinglet, chickadee, and gnatcatcher, however, tend to be smaller than the warblers. No significant separation occurs between migrant and resident warblers in the Chiriqui and San Lorenzo assemblages either. The single vireonid plotted in the Chiriqui group is larger than the parulids but the San

Allen Keast

Lorenzo one, and the Bananaquit (*Coereba flaveola*, Coerebidae), are in the same size range. The smaller co-occurring furnariids and formicariids, that live mostly in the denser middle and lower regions of the forest, clearly fall outside the range of the parulids.

There is some variation in warbler bill size in the case of Eaton's Cuban assemblage, but the difference is so small as to be of dubious significance. Lack and Lack (1972) provide bill- and wing-length measurements for the 20 species of parulids they studied in Jamaica. Terrestrial species (Swainson's Warbler, Louisiana Water-thrush, Northern Water-thrush, Ovenbird) have large bills, averaging 15.0, 13.2, 12.7, and 11.7 mm in length, respectively. Eleven species of foliage gleaners or sapling foliage feeders, by contrast, have bills of remarkable uniformity, with mean lengths from 9.4–10.6 mm. Only the endemic Arrow-headed Warbler (*Dendroica pharetra*), with a bill 11.3 mm in length, and Yellow-throated Warbler (*D. dominica*), 13.8 mm long, fall outside this range.

It is obvious that bill size and body size play a negligible role in the ecological separation of migratory insectivorous warblers of the genera *Dendroica* and *Vermivora*, and neotropical *Basileuterus* and *Myioborus*. At the family level, however, morphological separation of the insect eaters is relatively clear-cut.

Are Migratory Parulids Adapted by Differences in Wing Morphology for Wintering at Different Latitudes?

The distances between the breeding and wintering areas for 15 common species of warblers, 2 sylviids, and 3 vireos are shown in figures 8 and 9. In some species, the distance migrated is considerable. For example, in the Tennessee Warbler, the centers of breeding are about 50°N and wintering 10°N; in the Blackburnian, 45°N and 5°N, and in the Canada Warblers 48°N to about the equator. Distances flown may, however, be greater, or less, depending on population. At the other extreme are the Pine Warbler (*Dendroica pinus*) and Gold-crowned Kinglet. Here the distances covered in migration may be only about 10° of latitude.

Have short- and long-distance migrants different wing morphologies and hence are adapted for wintering in different areas?

Figures 10 and 11 show the relationship between wing length and the mean distance covered on migration and between wing area and distance for a series of Ontario breeding parulids. The birds measured were obtained from the banding nets at Prince Edward Point, Ontario, in late August–early September 1976.

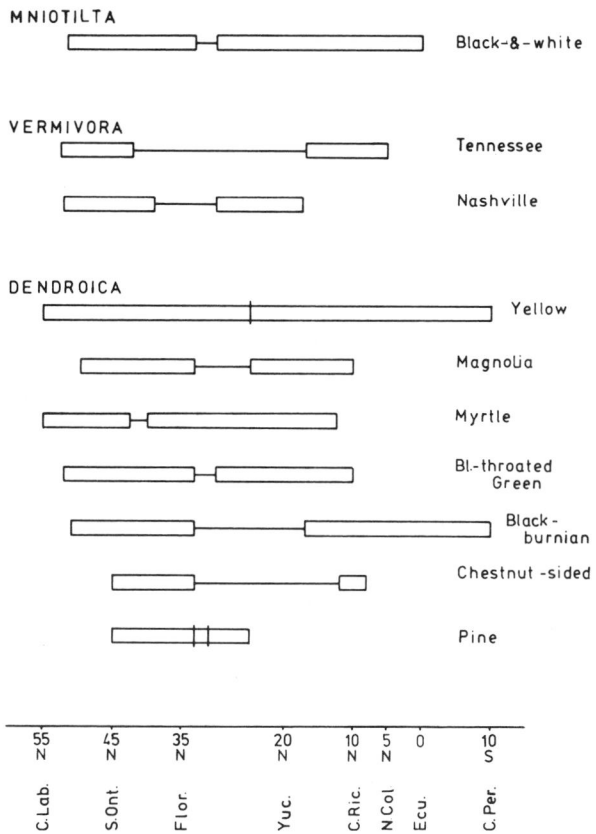

Figure 8. Breeding and wintering ranges (latitudes) compared, 7 species of *Dendroica*, 2 *Vermivora*, and *Mniotilta*.

Wing length was taken from the angle of folded wing to the tip. Wing area was obtained by outlining the outstretched wing (held at right angles from the body) onto graph paper and determining the area enclosed. While wing length can be measured precisely, only a general figure can be obtained for wing area. In each species measurements were made on eight adult specimens. The shape of the wing in five migrant and two resident parulids, the Least Flycatcher (*Empidonax satrapa*) and Gold-crowned Kinglet (*Regulus calendula*) is shown in figure 12.

There is no correlation between migration distance and wing length, shape, or area, in the *arboreal* migratory parulids, irrespective of whether they be long- or short-distance migrants. In all species the outermost

BREEDING & WINTERING RANGES
Parulidae (warblers)

SEIURUS

N. Waterthrush

SETOPHAGA

Redstart

WILSONIA

Wilson's

Canada

Hooded

Sylviidae - Regulinae (kinglets)

REGULUS

Golden-crowned

Ruby-crowned

Vireonidae (vireos)

VIREO

Solitary

Red-eyed

Warbling

55 N	45 N	35 N	20 N	10 N	5 N	0	10 S
C.Lab.	S.Ont.	Flor.	Yuc.	C.Ric.	N.Col.	Ecu.	C.Per.

Figure 9. Breeding and wintering ranges (latitudes) compared, 3 *Wilsonia*, *Seiurus noveboracensis*, and *Setophaga*, plus the 2 kinglets (*Regulus*), and 3 vireos.

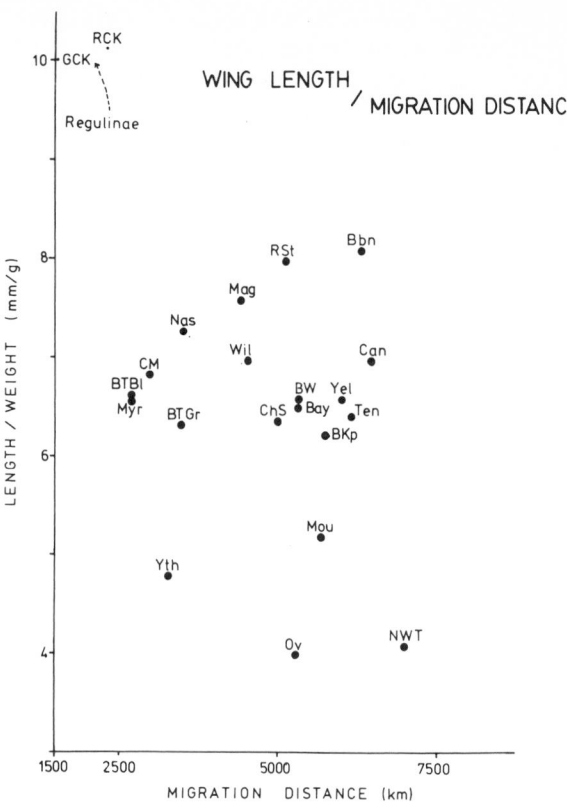

Figure 10. The relationship between wing length and "average" migration distance. Wing length is expressed relative to weight. Live birds obtained from nets, Prince Edward Point, Ontario, August-September, 1976.

Key: NWT—Northern Water-thrush; OV—Ovenbird; YTh—Yellow-throat; Mou—Mourning Warbler; Myr—Yellow-rumped; BTBL—Black-throated Blue; BT Gr—Black-throated Green; CM—Cape May; Nas—Nashville; Mag—Magnolia; Wil—Wilson's; ChS—Chestnut-sided; BW—Black-and-white; Bay—Bay-breasted; BKp—Black-poll; Ten—Tennessee; Yel—Yellow; Can—Canada; Bbn—Blackburnian; RSt—American Redstart; RCK—Ruby-crowned Kinglet; GCK—Golden-crowned Kinglet.

primary is long, equal to, or only slightly shorter than, the second outermost. However, in the terrestrial Ovenbird and Northern Water-thrush and the thicket-dwelling Mourning Warbler and Yellow-throat the wings are shorter relative to body weight than in the others. In the first three the wing is relatively smaller than in the arboreal species. These are species in which the vertical component is important in take-off. Contrasting also with the wings of the arboreal Nearctic migrants are those of two resident warblers from the Santa Marta Mountains, *Myioborus flavivertex* and *Basileuterus coronatus*. These clearly have shorter, more rounded, wings.

The wing of the small *Regulus* (Sylviidae) is relatively

long and large for the short distance migrated. The tyrannid has a somewhat rounded wing. The wing of the migratory American Redstart, equally an aerial feeder, is not however, convergent with that of *Empidonax*.

The functional morphology of the small passerine wing is only partly understood, for the selective forces acting on it are complicated. The flapping method of locomotion, used by the parulids, is the least understood method of flight, the motion being complex and involving the use of slots that can be opened or closed according to phase (Raspet 1960). In birds with short and broad wings (low aspect ratio) all parts of the

Allen Keast

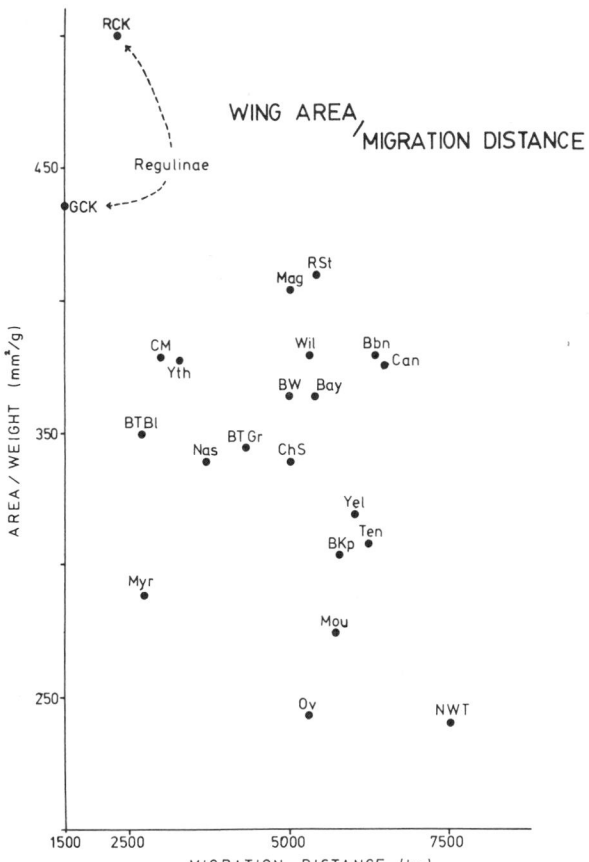

Figure 11. Wing area (area/weight) relative to "average" migration distance, fall migrating warblers, Prince Edward Point, Ontario. Same birds as figure 9.

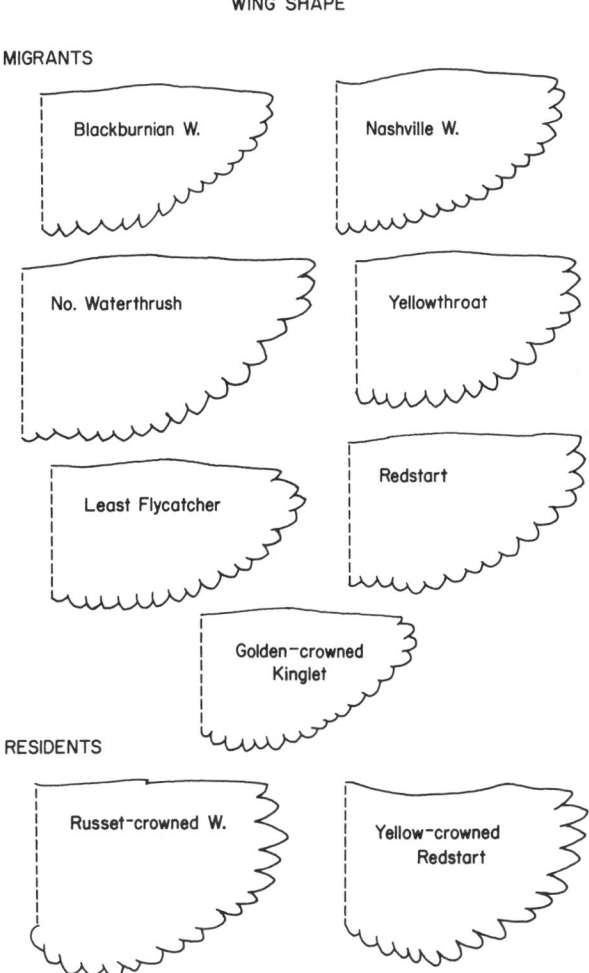

Figure 12. Wing shape of 5 migratory warblers and 2 resident Santa Marta species compared. Wings of the Least Flycatcher (*Empidonax minimus*), Tyrannidae, and Golden-crowned Kinglet (*Regulus calendula*) are included for comparison. Outlines were obtained by stretching wings of living birds at right angles from the body over graph paper. The method, that was used to obtain the wing area figures used in Figure 10, permits good comparisons but, because it is difficult to stretch the wings of different birds to the same degree, gives only general wing area figures.

wing participate in lift and propulsion. In birds with long narrow wings (high aspect ratio), the inner parts, forming a planing surface, may serve mainly to provide lift while the outer parts, particularly the primaries, function in propulsion (Salt 1967). Brown (1961) notes that the wings of small species up to 30 cm in wingspan are generally quite similar, with low aspect ratios and little emargination. It has long been known, however, that migratory races and species have more attenuation wings (longer outer primaries) than resident ones (Mayr 1942).

In summary: 1) there is a basic "migratory parulid" wing type; 2) this does not differ to any extent between long- and short-distance migrants; 3) in terrestrial and thicket-dwelling migrants, where the vertical take-off component is important, the wing is shorter relative to body weight; 4) in neotropical resident species, which undertake no seasonal movements and live in the middle sections of the forest, the wing is shorter, broader, and more rounded than in the migrant spe-

cies. Thus the wing, like the legs (Osterhaus 1962) varies somewhat with the demands placed upon it. Within the migratory species there are no differences, however, that "predispose" species to winter in different areas.

Separation Patterns in Parulids in Neotropica

Certain conclusions are very clear-cut from the preceding review. 1) The wintering migratory parulids separate out to a large extent allopatrically from the small neotropical tyrannids and greenlets (Vireonidae). Separation between migrant and resident parulids is mainly by feeding zone and behavior. Most migratory parulids winter in Guatemala-Honduras-El Salvador at the northern limits of Neotropica and north of the major center of abundance of the resident tyrannids, furnariids, formicariids, which is on the South American mainland. This suggests that the one fauna inhibits the spread of the second. 2) Within the migratory parulids there is a high degree of allopatric separation. This applies both longitudinally (central America relative to West Indies), and latitudinally (north-south), as well as altitudinally. Some species winter in limited areas; others, because of their abundance or specialized ecologies, over wide areas. 3) One of the most interesting facets of this spatial separation of the species of migrants in the wintering grounds is that it is independent of patterns on the breeding grounds. There is no tendency for birds breeding farthest north to winter at higher elevations or in the northern parts as against the southern parts of the wintering zone. Nor do co-occurring combinations of species in the south correspond to those in the north. This might have been expected if members of species combinations had evolved as an integrated unit. 4) There is a broad but incomplete separation of migratory and resident parulids in terms of feeding zone. Resident parulids are largely low shrub-thicket dwellers or are aerial feeding redstarts. The migrants are predominantly arboreal foliage feeders (one is a trunk-branch feeder), a feeding zone from which residents are largely absent (exceptions are the tropical Parula and Flame-throated Warbler). The migrants include three abundant ground feeders (Waterthrushes and Ovenbird) compared to one among the residents (the River Warbler). The single migrant redstart, while very widespread in distribution, is largely separated allopatrically and by habitat from the resident ones. Two species are represented by both migrant and resident forms. In the Yellowthroats there is a common habitat type but allopatric separation in the Yellow Warbler is mainly on habitat with the residents being in mangroves. The two species of arboreal Parula Warblers are separated spatially, just as are most congeners in other genera. 5) A number of lesser separating mechanisms operate in the migratory warblers (feeding in different zones; being somewhat nomadic). These, unimportant in themselves, no doubt further reduce the impact of so many species co-occurring. 6) While the ecologically more distinctive kinds of warblers (terrestrial Ovenbird relative to trunk-feeding Black-and-white or foliage-gleaner) differ morphologically (i.e. are morphologically adapted for different roles) there is little morphological separation in arboreal forms.

Thus, the arboreal species differ little in bill length, and species differences in wing morphology between long- and short-distance migrants are lacking.

In summary, while ecological separation of warblers in the wintering grounds is marked, it is largely spatial. Either the present cohabiting patterns are too recent for morphological differences to arise or there is strong selection pressure for maintenance of generalized structures. A high premium on adaptability is inferred (see other review in this volume). Presumably adjustment patterns continue to be worked out by the species of migrant parulid warblers, both in the wintering and breeding grounds.

Acknowledgments

The writer would like to express his thanks to the National Research Council of Canada whose funding made the present investigation possible. Miss Anne Fullerton is responsible for Figs. 5–11. I should also like to express my gratitude to Drs. Rollo and Alice Tryon who allowed me to join their field group in Veracruz, and to Dr. Steve Russell who took me to the Santa Marta Highlands.

Literature Cited

Andrle, R. F., and P. R. Andrle
1976.   Whistling Warbler of St. Vincent, West Indies. Condor 178:236–43.

Bent, A. C.
1963.   *Life Histories of North American Wood Warblers.* Two vols. New York: Dover.

Blake, E. H.
1953.   *Birds of Mexico. A Guide to Field Identification.* Chicago: Univ. of Chicago Press, 644 pp.

Blondel, J.
1969.   Sedentarité et migration des oiseaux dans une garrique meditéranienne. La Terre et la Vie 3:269–314.

Bond, J.
1960.   *Birds of the West Indies.* London: Collins, 256 pp.

Brown, R. H. J.
1961.   Flight. In *Biology and Comparative Physiology of Birds,* ed. A. J. Marshall, vol. 2, pp. 289–305, New York: Academic Press.

Chipley, R. M.
1976.   Impact of wintering migrant wood warblers on resident insectivorous passerines in subtropical Colombian oak woods. Living Bird 15:119–41.

Allen Keast

Davis, L. I.
1972.   *A Field Guide to the Birds of Mexico and Central America.* Austin, Tex.: Univ. of Texas Press, 282 pp.

De Schauensee, R. M.
1964.   *The Birds of Colombia.* Narberth, Pa.: Livingston.

De Schauensee, R. M., and W. H. Phelps.
1978.   *A Guide to the Birds of Venezuela.* Princeton, N. J.: Princeton Univ. Press, 424 pp.

Diamond, A. W., and R. W. Smith
1973.   Returns and survival of banding warblers wintering in Jamaica. Bird-Banding 44:221–29.

Dickey, D., and A. J. van Rossem
1938.   Birds of El Salvador. Field Mus. Nat. Hist., Zool. Ser. 23:1–609.

Eaton, S. W.
1953.   Wood Warblers wintering in Cuba. Wilson Bull. 65: 169–75.

Eisenmann, E.
1952.   Annotated List of Birds of Barro Colorado Island, Panama Canal Zone. Smithsonian Misc. Coll. 117: 1–62.

1957.   Wood Warblers in Panama. In *The Wood Warblers of America.* eds. L. Griscom and A. Sprunt, Jr., pp. 286–97, New York: Devin-Adair.

1962.   Notes on some Neotropical vireos in Panama. Condor 6:505–8.

Emlen, J. T.
1971.   Population densities of birds derived from transect counts. Auk 88:323–42.

1973.   Territorial aggression in wintering warblers at Bahama agave blossoms. Wils. Bull. 85:71–74.

ffrench, R.
1977.   *A Guide to the Birds of Trinidad and Tobago.* Wynnewood, Pa.: Livingston, 470 pp.

Gehlback, F. R., D. O. Dillon, H. L. Harell, S. E. Kennedy, and K. R. Wilson.
1976.   Avifauna of the Rio Corona, Tamaulipas, Mexico: Northeastern Limit of the Tropics. Auk 93:53–65.

Griscom, L.
1932.   Distribution of bird-life in Guatemala. Bull. Amer. Mus. Nat. Hist. 64:1–439.

Haverschmidt, F.
1968.   *Birds of Surinam.* Edinburgh: Oliver & Boyd, 445 pp.

Herklots, G. A. C.
1969.   *The Birds of Trinidad and Tobago.* London: Collins, 287 pp.

Howell, T. R.
1972.   Birds of the lowland pine savannah of Northeastern Nicaragua. Condor 74:316–40.

Karr, J. R.
1976.   On the relative abundance of migrants from North Temperate Zone in tropical habitats. Wils. Bull. 88: 433–58.

Keast, J. A.
1972.   Ecological opportunities and dominant families, as illustrated by the neotropical Tyrannidae (Aves). Evolutionary Biology 5:229–77.

Lack, D.
1971.   *Ecological Isolation in Birds.* Cambridge, Mass.: Harvard Univ. Press.

1976.   *Island Biology Illustrated by the Land Birds of Jamaica.* Oxford, U.K.: Blackwells.

Lack, D., and P. Lack
1972.   Wintering Warblers in Jamaica. Living Bird 11:129–53.

Land, H. C.
1970.   *Birds of Guatemala.* Wynnewood, Pa.: Livingston.

Leck, C. F.
1972.   The impact of some North American migrants at fruiting trees in Panama. Auk 89:842–50.

Leotscher, F. W., Jr.
1955.   North American Migrants in the State of Veracruz, Mexico: A Summary. Auk 72:14–54.

Loftin, H.
1977.   Returns and recoveries of banded North American birds in Panama and in the tropics. Bird-Banding 48:253–58.

Loftin, H., D. J. Rogers, and D. L. Hicks.
1966.   Repeats, returns, and recoveries of North American migrant birds banded in Panama. Bird-Banding 37: 35–44.

Martin, P. S., C. R. Robins, and W. B. Heed
1954.   Birds and biogeography of the Sierra de Tamaulipas, an isolated pine-oak habitat. Wils. Bull. 66:38–57.

Mayr, E.
1942.   *Systematics and the Origin of Species.* New York: Columbia Univ. Press.

Miller, A. H.
1963.   Seasonal activity and ecology of the avifauna of an American equatorial cloud forest. Univ. Calif. Pub. Zool. 66:1–78.

Monroe, B. L.
1968.   Distributional survey of the birds of Honduras. A.O.U. Ornith. Monogr. 7, 458 pp.

Moreau, R. E.
1952.   Place of Africa in the palaearctic migration system. J. Anim. Ecol. 21:250–71.

1966.   *The Bird Faunas of Africa and Its Islands.* New York: Academic.

1972. *The Palaearctic-African Bird Migration Systems.* New York: Academic Press.

Morton, E. S.
1976. Adaptive significance of dull coloration in Yellow Warblers. Condor 78:423.

Murray, B. G.
1965. On the autumn migration of the Blackpoll Warbler. Wils. Bull. 77:122–33.

Nickel, W. P.
1968. Return of northern migrants to tropical winter quarters and banded birds recovered in the United States. Bird-Banding 39:107–16.

Nisbet, I. C. T., and Lord Medway
1972. Dispersion, population ecology and migration of Eastern Great Reed Warblers (*Acrocephalus orientalis*) wintering in Malaysia. Ibis 114:451–94.

Osterhaus, M. R.
1962. Adaptive modifications in the leg structure of some North American Warblers. Am. Midland Naturalist 68:474–86.

Pearson, D. J.
1972. Wintering and migration of palaearctic passerines in Kampala, Uganda. Ibis 114:43–60.

Peterson, R. T., and E. L. Chalif
1973. *A Field Guide to Mexican Birds and Adjacent Central America.* Boston: Houghton Mifflin, 298 pp.

Raspet, A.
1960. Biophysics of bird flight. Science 132:191–200.

Ridgely, R. S.
1976. *A Guide to the Birds of Panama.* Princeton, N. J.: Princeton Univ. Press. 393 pp.

Russell, S. M.
1964. Distributional study of the birds of British Honduras. A.O.U. Ornith. Monogr. 1, 195 pp.

Salt, W. R.
1967. Loads lifted by homogeneous muscle in flapping flight. Canad. J. Zool. 45:73–79.

Schoener, T. W.
1965. Value of bill size differences among sympatric congeneric species of birds. Evol. 19:189–213.

Schwartz, P.
1964. The Northern Waterthrush in Venezuela. Living Bird 2:169–84.

Skutch, A. F.
1950. Nesting season of Central American birds in relation to climate and food supply. Ibis 92:185–222.

1967. Life histories of Central American highland birds. Pubs. Nuttall Ornith. Club. 7:1–213.

Slud, P.
1964. The Birds of Costa Rica. Bull. Amer. Mus. Nat. Hist. 128:1–430.

Smythe, F. B.
1966. The Birds of Tikal. Natural History Press, Amer. Mus. Nat. Hist., New York.

Stewart, R. M.
1973. Breeding behavior and life history of the Wilson's Warbler. Wils. Bull. 85:21–30.

Todd, W. E. C., and M. A. Carriker, Jr.
1922. Birds of the Santa Marta region of Colombia: a study in altitudinal distribution. Ann. Carnegie Mus. 14:1–611.

Wetmore, A.
1943. Birds of Southern Veracruz, Mexico. Proc.U.S. National Mus. 93:215–340.

Willis, E. O.
1968. Role of migrant birds at swarms of army ants. Living Bird 5:187–231.

Allen Keast

JOHN T. EMLEN
Department of Zoology
University of Wisconsin
Madison, Wisconsin, 53706

Interactions of Migrant and Resident Land Birds in Florida and Bahama Pinelands

ABSTRACT

Florida and the northern Bahama Islands experience a heavy invasion of northern land-bird migrants each winter. At a series of 13 pine forest sites in 1971 community densities (sum of all species densities) were more than doubled in Florida and nearly doubled in the Bahamas. The number of species was nearly doubled at most sites. Bird species diversity (H') remained essentially unchanged due to the low equitability of the migrant element. The proportion of migrants was higher in open habitats than in forests, higher in tree crowns than in shrubs, and higher in the aerial and ground insectivore guilds than in the granivore and bark-gleaning guilds. Migrant and resident species were similar in the amplitude of their dispersion through the habitats, compartments, and guilds.

Analyses of these distribution and abundance patterns suggest that the mixed winter assemblages of migrant and resident species represent full, integrated ecological communities and that resident species do not fill the available niche space after the migrants leave. Winter integration is considered to have evolved by selective processes of displacement and extinction; few traces of unresolved competition persist. Food shortage is probably not a critical factor in population regulation for most species and guilds. Habitat complexity is seasonally stable, a factor that may account for the stability of bird species diversity (H') in the face of marked seasonal changes in species richness and in population density.

Figure 1. Pine forest near Freeport, Grand Bahama Islands.

communities in the pine forests of Florida and the Bahama Islands (Emlen 1977; Emlen 1978) I obtained data on the population density and distribution patterns of all the migrant and resident species. In this paper, I reexamine these data in the context of interaction between the two elements. In line with the predictions of competition theory, I look particularly at 1) the density and distribution patterns of wintering migrant species for indications of avoidance of or displacement from sites and situations already heavily occupied by resident birds, 2) the density and distribution patterns of resident species for indications of ecological release or of vacant niches following the spring departure of the migrant invaders, 3) indications of seasonal changes in food abundance that might relate to the winter increases in population densities, and 4) indications of seasonal change in habitat complexity that might relate to the winter increases in community richness.

Observations were made during the winter and spring months, January through May of 1968, 1969, and 1971. In 1968, I focused on population densities and distributions within the pine forests near Freeport, Grand Bahama Islands (figure 1), and Homestead, Florida. In 1969, I compared the communities of the 7 habitat types present on Grand Bahama Island. In 1971, I made brief surveys at each of 13 pine forest sites along the Florida peninsula and on two Bahama islands. In 1975, I made a few winter and spring censuses near Georgetown, South Carolina.

Methods

Birds were censused by the count-X detectability method (Emlen 1971) along standardized transect strips traversed on foot during the first two post-sunrise hours of the day. This method provides absolute density values (detections per unit of area) for locality, season, and species comparisons and is applicable with small modifications in data processing in all seasons and in all of the vegetation types encountered in the Florida-Bahama area.

Morning censuses were run daily except in bad weather or when I was traveling between sites, and supplementary observations on foraging behavior and distribution were made whenever possible in the afternoons. Habitat structure was measured at each census site, and food abundance (foliage insects) was sampled at most sites as a basis for evaluating environmental conditions potentially significant as factors in avian distribution. Details of field procedures are described in Emlen (1977).

I obtained data on species richness, species diversity (H'), population density and, in some cases, population biomass, and used them in tracing monthly

Modern competition theory holds that bird communities are regulated in size and structure by the interaction of the member species as they partition the local resources. The familiar model generally visualizes a mosaic of contiguous or partially overlapping niches that tend to fill the available niche space of an area to its carrying capacity. Hypotheses based on this model predict that the diversity of a bird community will reflect the environmental diversity of the area and that the summed biomass of the member species will reflect its resource-based carrying capacity.

From this viewpoint the situation in neotropical and subtropical areas where the local resident populations are supplemented seasonally by large numbers of migrants from the outside is of special interest. Population densities are increased at a time when food supplies are often low, and species richness is enhanced during a period when habitat complexity is often depressed.

During the course of a three-year study of the population structure of wintering and breeding bird

John T. Emlen

changes in community structure and size and in plotting species and category distributions at four levels of ecological organization: geographic location (13 sites), habitat (7 types at 1 site), vegetation compartment (4 compartments in the pine forest at 1 site), and foraging province (10 food substrates exploited by distinctive foraging guilds in the pine forest at 1 site).

Ecological amplitude was measured for all species in terms of diversity of response (H') through the recognized habitats, compartments, and foraging provinces as an indicator of differences in levels of ecological specialization between the residents and migrants in the mixed community.

Results

Seasonal Changes in Community Structure and Size

ANNUAL CYCLE OF NUMBERS

Seasonal changes in community structure and density are graphically depicted for my principal Bahama study site in figure 2. Winter migrants in this Grand Bahama pineland community comprised 49 percent of the summed community density during January and February, then declined during the spring months to zero in mid-May by which time resident species

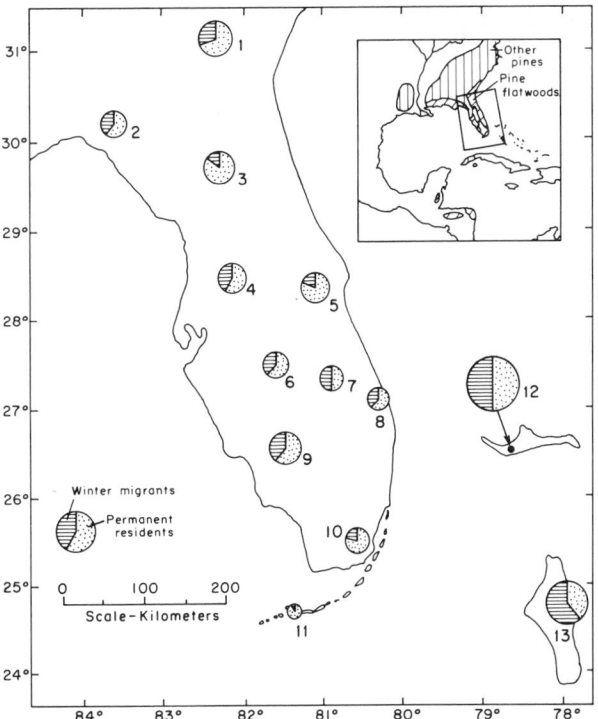

Figure 3. Migrant-resident ratios and summed densities at 13 pine flatwood sites in the Florida-Bahama area—winter 1970–71. The area of each disc reflects the summed population densities (all species) at each site; hatched shading indicates the proportion of the permanent resident birds; stippled areas, the proportion of winter migrants.

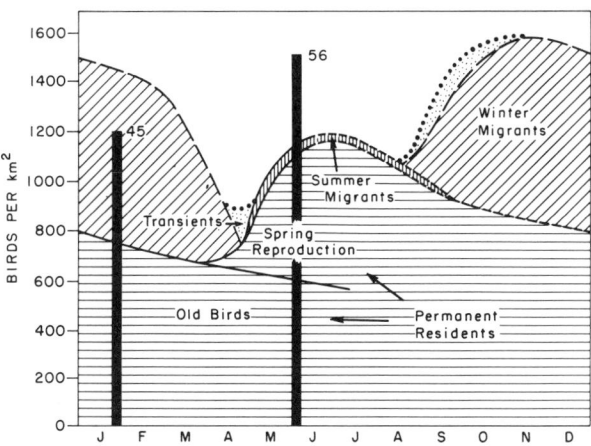

Figure 2. Annual cycle of density changes in the pine forest bird community of Grand Bahama Island. Values for January through May are based on censuses made in 1968, 1969, and 1971; values for the balance of the year are inferred by interpolation and extrapolation of these data. Spring transients, including members of species that had wintered, are arbitrarily defined as any non-resident birds present after 1 April. Fall transient values are based solely on subjective impressions and some mist-netting results by local ornithologists. Vertical bars represent indices of invertebrate food supply (standing crop) in the pine foliage in late January and late May 1971.

were reproducing, transients were moving through, and summer migrants had arrived. Extrapolating and generalizing from these winter and spring data, one can see that the midwinter density in this community was about 1.6 times as large as the late April density after the winter migrants had left, and about 1.3 times as large as the post-breeding community of adults and young in summer. The spring transient element was small but served to bridge the trough in late April and early May. The summer migrant element, present from early May to late summer, contained only two species and supplemented the resident community by only 2.7 percent. I have no data for the fall transient element.

The general picture of seasonal changes in community structure and size presented here for the Grand Bahama pine forest is apparently typical or at least representative of bird communities in the Florida-Bahama area (figure 3). The proportion of migrants in the mixed wintering communities appears to be higher here than in tropical areas to the south. Most of the data from neotropical localities have been obtained by mist-net sampling however, and caution must be exercised when comparing mist-net and transect data (Lack and Lack 1972; MacArthur and MacArthur 1974; Waide this volume).

The diversity of the Grand Bahama pine forest community also changed strongly between mid-summer and mid-winter in terms of species richness, from 28 species (24 residents plus 4 summer migrants) to 45 species (24 residents plus 21 winter migrants). Bird species diversity as measured by the information theory method ($H' = p_i log_e p_i$), however, remained essentially unchanged, even dropped a little (2.62 to 2.39). The explanation for this low winter diversity value obviously lies in the low equitability of the migrant element over 77 percent of which belonged to a single species, the Palm Warbler (*Dendroica palmarum*). I do not know whether this low equitability and seasonal stability of H' diversity is characteristic of other mixed wintering communities in the American tropics and subtropics where habitats tend to be seasonably stable. It is interesting, however, that at 10 Florida sites the mean diversity of mixed wintering communities was only slightly greater (2.63 vs 2.30) than that of the permanent resident elements. (The resident elements are roughly representative of the breeding communities in this area where the supplement of summer migrants is small).

LOCAL MOVEMENTS AND DENSITY FLUCTUATIONS

Due to irregular local movements of both migrants and resident species, the transition from winter to spring conditions may not always be as smooth as one might predict from simple migrant departure projections. For instance, the density of winter migrants apparently declined over 50 percent in the Grand Bahama pine forests during January and February of 1968 as a result of a large exodus, possibly an inter-habitat or inter-island drift, of the overwhelmingly dominant Palm Warblers; no comparable decrease occurred in 1969. Winter migrant densities increased markedly at Homestead, Florida between late January and late February 1968 (table 1) as a result, particularly, of an influx of Catbirds (*Dumetella carolinensis*) and Yellow-rumped Warblers (*Dendroica coronata*), then dropped in March in declines suggesting early phases of the regular spring emigration. But permanent residents also declined in March with conspicuous drops in such presumably sedentary species as Mockingbirds (*Mimus polyglottis*), (perhaps a local movement to more open habitats in the area) and Blue Jays (*Cyanocitta cristata*). April saw an unexpected and unexplained increase in permanent residents, especially in Blue

Table 1. Changes in bird density and proportion in the pine forest community at Homestead, Florida, mid-winter to late spring 1968[1]

Period		Density: birds/km²				
		WM	PR	Tr	SM	%WM
January	17–29	165	101	0	0	62
February	17–29	246	108	0	0	69
March	21–31	102	78	0	0	57
April	19–30	62	193	4	0	24
May	16–21	0	164	1	4	0

[1] WM = winter migrants; PR = permanent residents; TR = transients; SM = summer migrants

Jays (from 10 to 101 birds per km²!) and Red-bellied Woodpeckers (*Centurus carolinus*). Explanations for such fluctuations, and predictions of their possible recurrence on an annual basis must await the accumulation of much information on local movements of both adults and yearlings in both migrants and resident species.

Transient migrants in passage to and from winter ranges to the south, commonly an important factor in analyzing seasonal changes in population structure in the tropics, were a minor element in both the Florida and Bahama communities at least in the spring months.

Distributional Patterns

The distribution of migrant and resident populations on the shared wintering range is examined below at four levels of ecological organization: geographic, habitat, compartment, and guild.

GEOGRAPHIC DISTRIBUTION

My 1971 surveys at 11 Florida and 2 Bahama sites provide a picture of the geographic distribution of winter migrants in the area (table 2; figure 3). Both migrant and resident densities decreased southward along the Florida peninsula. The ratio of the two elements fluctuated irregularly along this north-south axis with migrants on the average constituting slightly less than half of the species (46 percent) and more than half of the summed community densities (69 percent). Both migrants and residents were much more numerous at the 2 Bahama sites than at any site in Florida. The ratios here showed migrants slightly in

John T. Emlen

Table 2. Migrant-resident composition of land bird communities at 13 Florida and Bahama pine forest sites, winter of 1970–71[1]

	Number of species			Density (detections/km²)				Bird species diversity			
	WM	PR	%WM	WM	PR	%WM	Fall Increase	H' Total	J' Total	J' WM	J' PR
Florida[2]											
1 Waycross (Ga.)	16	19	46	511	216	70	X 3.37	2.955	.831	.86	.83
2 Perry	16	17	48	266	167	61	X 2.59	2.918	.835	.83	.76
3 Gainesville	13	12	52	527	92	85	X 6.73	1.538	.491	.41	.73
4 Dade City	17	16	52	304	220	58	X 2.38	2.844	.821	.75	.82
5 Cocoa	15	15	50	433	103	81	X 5.20	2.547	.756	.75	.88
6 Highland Hammocks	13	15	46	220	134	62	X 2.64	2.597	.779	.65	.87
7 Okeechobee	16	20	44	173	164	51	X 2.05	2.968	.838	.75	.83
8 J. Dickinson State Park	10	16	38	173	103	63	X 2.68	2.505	.769	.65	.87
9 Imokalee	15	16	48	383	246	61	X 2.56	2.885	.840	.76	.89
10 Homestead	13	13	50	277	75	79	X 4.69	2.510	.771	.74	.86
11 Big Pine Key	6	2	75	122	12	91	X11.17	1.472	.708	.68	.98
Total	27	32	46	X̄-308	139	69	X̄ 3.21	2.522	.767	.71	.85
Bahamas											
12 Freeport, Grand Bahama Island	14	18	44	896	891	50	X 2.01	2.575	.743	.51	.84
13 Androstown	14	15	48	445	683	39	X 1.65	2.729	.811	.83	.73
Total	16	20	44	X̄-670	787	46	X̄ 1.85	2.652	.777	.67	.79

[1] WM = winter migrants; PR = permanent residents.

[2] The Florida sites (one in southern Georgia) are listed in sequence from north to south. Localities are shown on the map in figure 2.

the minority in both species numbers (44 percent) and summed community densities (46 percent). At a South Carolina site studied in 1975, migrants were the minority element in both species number (43 percent) and summed density (42 percent) categories. Bird species diversity (H') values for the mixed wintering communities varied between 2.51 and 2.97 at most of the sites but were markedly depressed at 2 sites where 1 or 2 very abundant migrant species dominated the community. Equitability values (J') were lower in the migrant than in the resident element in 10 of the 13 communities and averaged considerably lower ($\bar{x}$ = 0.70 vs. 0.84, p < .01, Wilcoxon signed rank test).

HABITAT DISTRIBUTION

The distribution of migrants and residents through seven habitat types on Grand Bahama Island is shown in table 3. Migrants reached highest densities in the coastal dunes and broadleaf thickets or coppets and were rather lightly represented in the pine forests that cover most of the island. They outnumbered resident birds in the four open habitats and were outnumbered by them in the three closed habitats—pine forests, young pines, and broadleaf thickets. The correlation of migrant concentrations with disturbed habitats noted in other studies (Willis 1966; Karr 1976; Waide this volume) apparently does not apply in this area where the dunes and mangrove flats with their high proportions of migrants were less modified by man than the periodically clear cut-and-burned pine forests with their relatively low migrant-resident ratios.

Ecological amplitude, determined for each species by its distributional diversity (H') through the seven habitat types, did not differ significantly between migrants and residents ($\bar{x}$ = 0.88 and 1.01, respectively).

Table 3. Numbers and distribution of winter migrants and permanent residents through 7 habitat types, Grand Bahama Island, Jan–March 1969[1]

	Dominant vegetation stratum			Number of bird species			Density detections/km²		
	Plant type	Ht. (m)	Cover %	WM	PR	WM %	WM	PR	WM %
Pine forest	Pine trees	10–12	40	14	22	39	434	573	43
Young pines	Pine trees	2–4	40	7	18	28	256	511	33
Old fields	Grass and herbs	1	98	8	12	40	751	376	67
Broadleaf thickets	Low trees	4–5	98	16	21	43	913	986	48
Marsh	Reeds and shrubs	2	100	9	10	47	633	221	74
Mangrove flats	Sparse shrubs	1	50	7	7	50	241	52	82
Coastal dunes	Grass and shrubs	<1–2	90	8	8	50	995	241	81

[1] WM = winter migrants; PR = permanent residents; TR = transients; SM = summer migrants.

COMPARTMENT DISTRIBUTION

In the winter and spring of 1968, I studied the distribution of all bird species through the vegetation layers and compartments of the pine forest on Grand Bahama Island. Densities were calculated for each of seven vegetation compartments, first in terms of number of detections per km² of transect strip, then, from vegetation measurements, for number of detections per m³ of space occupied by standing vegetation. The data for four major (combination) compartment categories are presented in table 4.

Winter migrants tended to distribute themselves where the resident populations were already most dense, the trunk and shrub compartments. Migrants were, however, better represented proportionately in the tree crowns (49 percent) and ground vegetation (41 percent) than the shrubs (39 percent) and on the trunks (30 percent).

As in the habitat distributions, there was no significant difference between the migrants and the residents in compartment specialization (mean response diversity H′ = 0.69 and 0.73, respectively). Tramer and Kemp (this volume), however, believed migrants to be less specialized than residents in Costa Rica.

GUILD DISTRIBUTION

An analysis of migrant representation in the various trophic subcommunities or definitive foraging guilds of the pine forest is shown for the Grand Bahama wintering community of 1968 in table 5. Data are presented in terms of biomass as well as density since

each definitive guild, as defined in the table, is a heterogeneous assemblage of full and part-time members representing a variety of species and size classes (Emlen 1977, 1978).

Among the major definitive guilds, the proportion of migrant participation (as measured by foraging biomass) in the mixed wintering community ranged from 34 percent in the fruit eaters and 37 percent in the flower probers to 66 percent in the aerial insect sallyers and 75 percent in the ground-insect gleaners and pouncers. More than half (58 percent) of all insect eating was by migrants while only a quarter (25 percent) of all plant material eating was by migrants.

Table 4. Numbers and distribution of winter migrants and permanent residents through the 4 major vegetation compartments of the pine forest, Grand Bahama, Jan–Mar 1978[1]

	Number of species			Density birds per million m³		
	WM	PR	WM %	WM	PR	WM %
Tree crowns	9	18	33	26	27	49
Shrubs	11	17	39	37	58	39
Ground vegetation	5	12	29	15	22	41
Trunks	3	8	27	35	82	30

[1] WM = winter migrants; PR = permanent residents; TR = transients; SM = summer migrants.

John T. Emlen

Table 5. Comparison of migrant and resident densities and foraging biomasses in 10 foraging provinces[1] of the pine forest habitat, Grand Bahama, Jan–Mar 1968 and May 1968[2]

	Winter density Detections/km^2			Winter biomass[3] g/km^2			Spring biomass g/k^2	
	WM	PR	WM %	WM	PR	WM %	PR	SM
Plant food								
Seeds on ground	1	14	7	44	795	5	1726	0
Seeds on stems	0	16	0	0	176	0	184	0
Fruits on shrubs	57	64	47	809	1580	34	2095	5
Total	58	94	38	853	2551	25	4005	5
Animal food (Arthropods)								
On ground	139	22	86	1629	550	75	762	54
In shrubs	62	52	54	651	653	50	804	26
In bark	19	41	32	236	574	29	530	0
In needles	190	202	48	1977	1634	55	1791	5
In air	52	16	76	550	279[3]	66	368	222[4]
Total	462	333	58	5043	3690	58	4255	307
Food undetermined								
In flowers	50	155	24	555	955	37	747	0
In cones	5	2	71	41	11	79	11	0
Total	55	157	26	596	966	38	758	0
Grand total	575	584	50	6492	7207	47	9018	312

[1] Foraging provinces refer to the resource bases for the recognized definitive foraging guilds. Definitive foraging guilds include all full and partial (fractions to nearest tenth) species populations foraging in a designated guild province.

[2] Values are the sums of the products of density × proportion (tenths) of observed foraging activity for each species; WM = winter migrants; PR = permanent residents; TR = transients; SM = summer migrants.

[3] Weights for most species were based primarily on live birds mist-netted locally and weighed by P. Fluck.

[4] 165 gm of Bahama Swallows that moved into the pine forest from open habitats in May are classed here as permanent residents rather than summer migrants.

The temporary and sometimes irregular concentrations of certain food resources (fruits, nectar, swarming insects) characteristic of many tropical forests and of special significance for winter migrants there (Willis 1966; Leck 1972) were relatively unimportant in the Florida-Bahama pine forests. Fruits were small and widely dispersed in the understory (no fruiting trees), and nectariferous blossoms, also restricted to the understory, were widely distributed temporally except for a concentrated blooming of agaves in late January and February. Migrants were well represented at these rich nectar and insect sources.

As with habitats and compartments, there was no significant difference between migrants and residents in dispersion through the guild provinces (mean response diversity H' = 0.34 and 0.30, respectively).

Discussion

In this discussion I will first consider the mechanisms by which migrants are absorbed into tropical habitats and communities, focusing on questions of habitat selection and of competition with resident birds already established on the scene. I will then look at the dynamics of integration and regulation in the combined resident-migrant communities, at the nature and implications of ecological segregation, and at the relation of food levels and habitat complexity to community size and structure.

Habitat and Niche Selection by Migrants on the Winter Range

The genetic and early experimental influences that shape a bird's responses to habitats and foraging substrates cannot possibly anticipate all the situations it will face as a migrant when it arrives for the first time in a strange southern land. The selection of a home site and of appropriate foraging substrates is probably determined by trial and error as the young bird discovers for itself which situations and which foraging methods are the most rewarding and efficient (Lack 1971; Partridge 1976). In turn, the particular pattern of geographic, habitat, compartment, and guild distribution that a species assumes on its winter range will depend on the behavioral responses of the individual members of the population. Natural selection presumably operates to assure viable behavior patterns and to mold responses to the special morphological and physiological requirements of the species.

Migrant species seem to fall roughly into two categories in the way they select their winter home sites, 1) "drifters," where the members remain flexible from year to year and from day to day, adjusting their distribution directly to changing circumstances, and 2) "settlers," where each individual tends to return with considerable consistency to the same winter home year after year. Adjustability to environmental changes appears to be maintained in this second group by a process of trial and error exploration during the first winter of life (Ralph and Mewaldt 1975). Both categories are represented among the winter migrants in the Florida-Bahama area. Flocking species like the Yellow-rumped Warbler (*Dendroica coronata*) tend to be drifters, and even permanent residents like the Blue Jay (*Cyanocitta cristata*) may drift extensively between localities and habitats. Trapping and mist netting reveal that many winter migrants are "settlers," (Loft in 1977; Rappole 1978; Fluck pers. comm.), but the extent of this type of behavior in neotropical wintering areas remains little known.

The factors that determine the pattern of distribution that a species population finally adopts on the winter range are beyond the scope of this paper except as they include interactions between migrant and resident species. Evidence of migrant-resident segregation and of reduced ecological overlap are discussed in a later section of this paper.

Resolution of Competition in Wintering Communities

A sudden deposition of hordes of migrants on an established resident community will inevitably produce competition. Theoretically, however, the conflicts and behavioral displacements precipitated during early stages of the confrontation will with time be resolved by selective withdrawals and redistributions until a reasonably balanced and integrated mixed community emerges with resident and migrant species

interspersed through the available niche space in patterns that minimize active competition. Such withdrawals and redistributions could occur each fall as the migrants descend on the home ranges of the residents, or they could occur as more permanent, evolutionary adjustments in the composition of the mixed wintering community. Both types of adjustment probably exist in all neotropical areas with wintering migrants. The latter type may be expected to dominate where environments and migration patterns have remained fairly stable over long periods of evolutionary time, the former where conditions change irregularly from year to year. The stage of advancement of evolutionary adjustment is important in studies of mixed community structure and dynamics in that it determines the extent to which the migrant element is integrated into the wintering community as opposed to superimposed upon the resident community. A fully integrated wintering community is presumably regulated during the period of joint occupancy in winter; a resident community with an unintegrated supplement of migrants is presumably regulated in the breeding season of reduced density and diversity.

Since the Florida-Bahama area has undoubtedly been subjected to annual invasions and withdrawals of interzonal migrants for many millennia, a reasonably stable pattern of species distributions should have been achieved in which migrants and residents are dispersed in the mixed wintering communities in patterns that minimize occasion for direct competition and behavioral displacement. A residuum of unresolved competition may persist, however, since we know very little about year to year changes in migration patterns in the area or the effect of timber cutting and other environmental disturbances on community stability.

Since I was not present to observe distributional shifts at the time of the fall arrivals, my attempts to detect traces of direct competition and behavioral displacement in the Florida-Bahama area focused on adjustments to migrant departure in the spring. These observations provided little or no evidence of direct compensatory responses in the resident species. Residents moved out of the shrub compartment in the spring, the compartment that was most strongly reduced by migrant departures. In the guild analyses, resident seed eaters, mainly doves, overcompensated, moving in from open habitats to add 930 g per km^2 to that forest guild as only 44 g per km^2 or migrants departed (table 5). Bark gleaners declined (44 g per km^2) as 236 g per km^2 of migrants departed. These and other within-habitat shifts among resident densities (table 5) cannot be satisfactorally evaluated in the absence of data on changes in food abundance, but

John T. Emlen

they obviously provide little evidence for direct compensatory responses to migrant withdrawal. For changes in habitat distribution, my observations in the spring period of migrant departure are sketchy, but the two movements noted, that of the doves cited above, and a movement of Bahama Swallows (*Callichelidon cyaneoviridis*) into the pines from open marshes, fields, and coastal dune areas accentuated rather than mitigated the habitat density inequalities in their respective guilds. Nothing was detected equivalent to the expansion of winter range into vacated woodland habitats observed by Lack and Lack (1972) for two species of warblers in Jamaica.

I conclude that the patterns of migrant-resident distribution observed in the Florida-Bahama area have been determined largely by evolutionary resolution and provide little evidence of active competition or annual behavioral displacement.

Dynamics of Integration and Regulation in Mixed Wintering Communities

In this neotropical region of annual migrant invasions the factors regulating community size and structure must operate either during the winter season of joint habitat occupancy or during the breeding season when only the resident species are present. In searching for the major regulating factors and the seasonal dynamics of their operation, I examined my Florida-Bahama data for information on levels of integration and fullness in the resident breeding and mixed wintering communities. For these examinations, I regard a community as integrated when the member species are distributed through the available niche space in a manner that minimizes interspecific competition, and as full when all the niche space is occupied. Four aspects of community structure and regulation are considered below, migrant-resident segregation in mixed wintering communities, vacant niches in resident communities, the relation of food abundance to seasonal changes in community size (biomass), and the relation of habitat complexity to seasonal changes in community diversity.

MIGRANT-RESIDENT SEGREGATION IN THE MIXED COMMUNITY

In traditional competition theory, all species in an integrated community tend to segregate themselves over time into relatively distinct and isolated ecological niches in which they are shielded from excessive interspecies competition. If winter migrants in the neotropics are incorporated into an all-inclusive integrated community, I would predict that the segregation distance between residents and migrants would

be similar to that between the various residents. If, on the other hand, they were present as supernumeraries on an integrated community of residents, I would expect, contrary to my earlier prediction (Emlen 1977), a narrower spacing relationship.

Two analyses were made to evaluate migrant-resident segregation in the Grand Bahama communities. In the first, I plotted migrant densities against resident densities through the seven habitat types, four habitat compartments, and 10 foraging guild provinces (figure 4). I predicted that if, at one extreme, the resident species occupied all the viable situations, with the migrants superimposed on them, the two distributions would be similar and the correlation coefficient would be high; if, on the other hand, the viable niche spaces were divided between the members of the two subcommunities, there would be considerable deviation from full positive correlation, perhaps even a negative correlation, as Willis (1966) thought might occur in similar situations. The diagrams presented in figure 3 show a wide scatter, indicating considerable deviation from full correlation. In the habitat distribution diagram, for instance, migrant-resident ratios varied from over 4:1 in two habitats to 0.5:1 in the young pine forest. The regression line, determined by least squares, is still positive however, indicating a basic tendency for the migrants to select the same habitats occupied

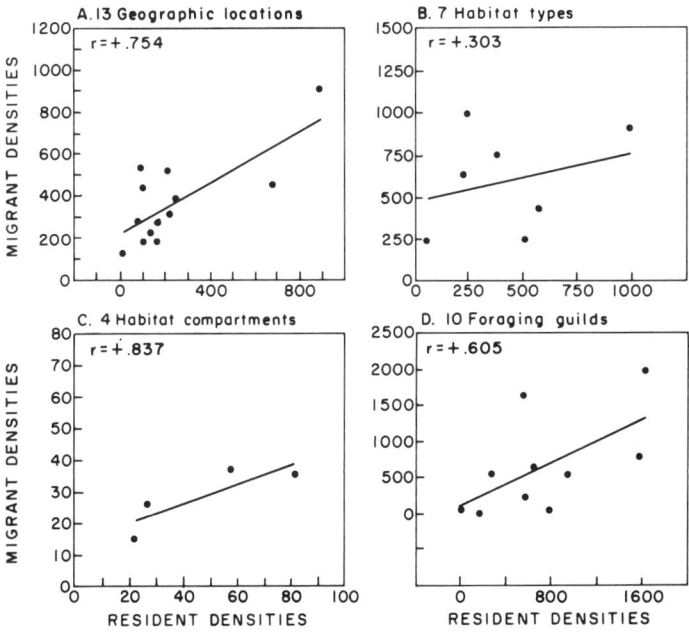

Figure 4. Plot of winter migrant densities on permanent resident densities. 3a. 13 survey sites in the Florida-Bahama area. 3b. 7 habitat types on Grand Bahama Island. 3c. 4 vegetation compartments of the Grand Bahama pine forest. 3d. 10 definitive foraging guilds in the Grand Bahama pine forest.

by residents. The interpretation of these distributions is difficult, but I tend to regard them as supporting the model of a winter-integrated community with migrant species segregated from the resident species in their niche distributions. In a comparison of the three diagrams, migrant-resident segregation appears to be more prominent in the habitat distribution ($r = +.302$) than in the guild ($+.605$) or compartment ($+.836$) distributions. This might have been predicted if Lack (1971) is correct that habitat responses are less plastic (i.e. more genetically based and hence better shielded against crisis seasons) than feeding station selection or feeding methods.

In a second test aimed at species-species interactions among migrants and residents, I calculated the ecological overlap of each species in the mixed wintering community with every other species, migrant and resident, using the index of similarity—$2W/a + b$ (Odum 1950), and then compared the mean overlap for resident-migrant pairings with that for resident-resident pairings. Assuming that extended exposure and interaction fosters ecological segregation, I predicted that resident-resident (R-R) pairings would show the least overlap (greatest segregation) in each case. Migrant-resident (M-R) overlaps would, I hypothesized, approximate these low overlap values if the two elements were well integrated and be appreciably higher if the migrants were poorly integrated. In the habitat analysis mean M-R overlap was slightly less than mean R-R overlap (35.6 percent and 40.0 percent, respectively), and in the guild province analysis it was slightly more than mean R-R overlap (16.0 percent and 12.6 percent, respectively). I interpret these data as indicating similarity and hence support for winter integration.

VACANT NICHES IN THE RESIDENT COMMUNITY

One implication of winter community integration and migrant-resident segregation is that the niches occupied by the migrant visitors in the mixed wintering community will be vacated each spring and left vacant during the entire breeding season except as residents redistribute themselves in compensatory shifts, not observed in this study, or as summer migrants move in from the south. The implied possibility that breeding communities may occupy only a fraction of the niche space in some tropical and subtropical areas has not, to my knowledge, been considered in published studies of community size and regulation in these areas.

To adequately test the proposition that there are lacunae in a resident community, one would need a control situation, a site similar to the study site in all essential respects except the seasonal occurrence of winter migrants. Unfortunately, migrant-free sites do not exist for such comparisons, and without them appraisals of vacant niches in migrant-influenced foraging guilds are difficult to identify. I can find no clear examples in my Florida and Bahama areas. Where migrants heavily dominate the winter community, however, as in the aboral insectivore guilds in Jamaica and Hispaniola, the very impoverished breeding season diversities and densities observed by Lack and Lack (1972) and Moermond (pers. comm.) could be attributed to the large number of migrants in winter.

COMMUNITY SIZE AND FOOD ABUNDANCE

Models that tie population density directly to food abundance predict that, all else being equal, the summed density (or biomass) of a community or guild will be set by the level of food abundance (standing crop) during the period of maximum population density in the breeding season except as reduced food levels may lower the carrying capacity of the environment at some time during the nonbreeding season. Under such conditions, a winter invasion of migrants could create a crisis of food shortages, especially if it occurred during a period of relatively low food abundance.

The predictions of these models were clearly not met in the Florida-Bahama pinelands where summed bird densities and biomasses for the foliage gleaning insectivores were roughly twice as high and the standing crop of foliage insects only half as high in winter as in spring. One impliction of this situation is that density and reproduction must be regulated well below the spring carrying capacity of the environment in these areas. The possibility that requirements for food are temporarily escalated during the breeding season is not supported in studies reviewed by King (1974). My observations of depressed winter food levels and those of Robinson and Robinson (1970), Foster (1973), Waide (this volume), and others also seem to suggest that resident densities are regulated during the winter season when the migrants are present. Comparisons of consumer-resource ratios in the 13 survey sites of this study (figure 5) indicate, however, that food may not be the critical limiting factor even in winter.

COMMUNITY DIVERSITY AND HABITAT COMPLEXITY

MacArthur and MacArthur (1961), Karr and Roth (1971), and others have demonstrated a strong positive correlation between habitat complexity and community diversity (species richness as well as information theory diversity) in a wide variety of temperate and tropical habitats. But, as with the community-size, food-abundance correlation discussed above, commu-

John T. Emlen

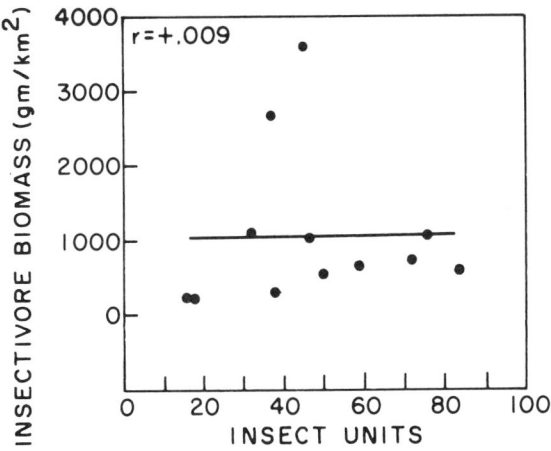

Figure 5. Plot of foliage-gleaning insectivore biomass (g per km²) on foliage insect abundance (insect units per km foliage) at 13 survey sites in the Florida-Bahama area.

nity richness in the Florida-Bahama seasonal comparisons appears to be inversely rather than positively correlated with habitat complexity. Thus, the pine forests of this area declined slightly in structural and physiognomic complexity between summer and winter while the number of species that occupied them nearly doubled. Unrecognized seasonal changes in environmental relationships could possibly be involved, or the low species equitability of the wintering communities (table 1) could somehow have obliterated the predicted effects of high species richness in effecting a nearly stable information theory (H′) diversity. Alternatively, community diversity may not be closely tied to habitat complexity in the situations under consideration.

Acknowledgments

Virginia Emlen assisted in various aspects of the field work. Many colleagues, including notably J. M. Emlen and R. Waide offered helpful suggestions on data analysis, interpretation, and presentation. Financial and logistic support for the overall project was provided by the National Science Foundation, the Wisconsin Alumni Research Foundation, the Frank M. Chapman Memorial Fund, the National Park Service and the Colonial Research Institute of Freeport, Grand Bahama.

Literature Cited

Emlen, J. T.
1971. Population densities of birds derived from transect counts. Auk 88:323–42.

1977. Land bird communities of Grand Bahama Island. A.O.U. Ornithol. Monogr. 24.

1978 Density anomalies and regulation-mechanisms in land bird populations on the Florida peninsula. Amer. Nat. 112:65–86.

Foster, R.
1973. Seasonality of fruit production and seed fall in a tropical forest ecosystem in Panama. Ph.D. Dissertation, Duke University, Durham, N. C. 156 pp.

Karr, J. R.
1976. On the relative abundance of migrants from the North Temperate Zone in tropical habitats. Wils. Bull. 88:433–58.

Karr, J. R., and R. R. Roth
1971. Vegetation structure and avian diversity in several new world areas. Amer. Nat. 105:423–35.

King, J. R.
1974. Seasonal allocation of time and energy resources in birds. In *Avian Energetics*, ed. R. A. Paynter. Nuttall Orn. Club Publ. 15.

Lack, D.
1971. Ecological isolation in birds. Oxford and Edinburgh, U. K.: Blackwell.

Lack, D., and P. Lack
1972. Wintering warblers in Jamaica. Living Bird 11:129–53.

Leck, C. F.
1972. Seasonal changes in feeding pressures of fruit and nectar eating birds in the neotropics. Condor 74:54–60.

Loftin, H.
1977. Returns and recoveries of banded North American birds in Panama and the tropics. Bird-Banding 48:253–58.

MacArthur, R. H., and J. W. MacArthur
1961. On bird species diversity. Ecol. 42:594–98.

MacArthur, R. H., and A. T. MacArthur
1974. On the use of mist nets for population studies of birds. Proc. Nat. Acad. Sci. 71:3230–33.

Odum, E. P.
1950. Bird populations of the highlands (North Carolina) plateau in relation to plant succession and avian invasion. Ecol. 31:587–605.

Partridge, L.
1976. Field and laboratory observations on the foraging and feeding techniques of blue tits (*Parus caeruleus*) and coal tits (*P. ater*) in relation to their habitats. Anim. Behav. 24:534–44.

Ralph, C. J., and L. R. Mewaldt
1975. Timing of site fixation upon the wintering grounds in sparrows. Auk 92:698–705.

Robinson, M. H., and B. Robinson
1970. Prey caught by a sample population of the spider *Argiope argentata* in Panama; a year's census data. Zool. J. Linn. Soc. 49:345–58.

Willis, E. O.
1966. Role of migrant birds at swarms of army ants. Living Bird 5:187–231.

JOHN W. TERBORGH
Department of Biology
Princeton University
Princeton, New Jersey 08540

JOHN R. FAABORG
Division of Biological Sciences
University of Missouri
Columbia, Missouri 65201

Factors Affecting the Distribution and Abundance of North American Migrants in the Eastern Caribbean Region

ABSTRACT

In the first part we evaluate several factors that could plausibly affect the abundance and distributions of overwintering populations in the eastern Caribbean region. These are: climate, distance from the North American mainland, size of landmass, density of resident species, and habitat quality.

The fraction of North American migrants in winter bird populations in the Caribbean region shows a strong inverse dependence on distance from the mainland (Florida). The mean value for a large array of censuses in Hispaniola is roughly 35 percent. The incidence of migrants drops toward the east to ca 10 percent in Puerto Rico and to 1 percent or less in more distant locations: Lesser Antilles, Trinidad, Tobago, and the Venezuelan mainland.

Area effects are difficult to factor out of the data because of the tight negative correlation between island area and distance from the mainland in the Greater and Lesser Antilles. Nevertheless, comparisons of nearby large and small islands do reveal a moderate tendency for migrants to gravitate to larger islands, although the number of comparisons is insufficient to permit a quantification of the tendency. The major factor controlling the abundance of migrants is clearly the combined effect of area and distance: the diminishing returns to be realized in flying farther and farther to reach smaller and smaller targets. The influence of the remaining factors considered, climate, habitat quality, and local density of resident species, was found to be slight or undetectable.

The second part investigates the possibility of competitive interactions between residents and migrants, and between the migrants themselves. Several lines of evidence suggest that the distributions of resident parulids in the Greater Antilles are drastically truncated by the impact of large overwintering populations of migrants. Thus, at least in the Antilles, migrants seem to exert strong pressures on resident species that are not evenly reciprocated. Interactions among the 15 species of migrant parulids that commonly winter in Hispaniola are manifested by segregation into different habitats and in the formation of stratified species complexes. Two habitats that lie near the extremes of the island's vegetation gradient, lowland rainforest and open montane pine forest, contain nonoverlapping, functionally integrated parulid complexes of 7 species each. These represent a higher level of syntopy than is normally achieved by parulids in North American habitats. If, as we predict, equivalent complexes of migrant species occur in Central and South America, their tight ecological packing will effectively exclude other species and thereby provide a mechanism for the delimitation of winter ranges. The related problem of why each species winters where it does, however, remains largely inaccessible to analysis due to our ignorance of the evolutionary history of today's migratory populations.

The location of any migratory population's wintering ground will, over time, be selected to maximize the probability of successful return to the breeding ground. Inasmuch as the necessary arduous journey and prolonged sojourn can hardly be accomplished without encountering assorted difficulties and hazards, it follows that maximizing the probability of return must entail a strategy that minimizes the combined effect of the challenges to be surmounted.

Some of these challenges are obvious to simple intuition. There is the risk of becoming lost or exhausted on the journey, a risk that can be lessened by selecting a relatively close, easy-to-find target. Then there is the challenge of surviving at the far end of the migratory route, a feat that is best realized in a low stress environment, one in which violent turns of weather, food shortages, predators, and competitors are tolerably rare. It is evident that trade-offs are involved in any overall migration strategy because longer distances must be negotiated to attain the benefits of low-risk climates. Through the redoubtable agent of selection, every migratory species solves an elaborate multi-variate optimization problem in choosing its winter range.

Our tactic in the present paper is to gain some measure of control over this problem by holding constant some of the potential variables while varying others. By this means we are able to assess the relative weights of several factors that potentially influence winter range selection by the collection of species that migrates to the eastern Caribbean region.

In the first part we examine the pattern of distribution of birds wintering in the Antilles at an aggregate level, asking simply how the proportional abundance of all migrants varies with climate, distance from the mainland, island area, habitat and density of resident species. Then in the second part, we examine several kinds of data that bear on the problem of species interactions: between migrants and residents, and among the many sympatric species of migrants themselves. Although most of the evidence is of a circumstantial nature, it suggests that the impact of migrants on residents is far greater than that of residents on migrants. The migrants are organized into tightly structured species complexes that segregate by habitat, a fact that carries major implications for the delimitation of winter ranges.

Methods

Our observations were gathered over the period of 1969 to 1976 on 11 winter trips to the region, some made separately and some jointly. Much of the analysis rests on estimates of the fraction of North American migrants in local bird populations. These estimates were obtained in two ways: by mist netting in uniform tracts of vegetation and from tallies made in Christmas Count fashion within definite habitats. Our mist-netting technique has been described in detail elsewhere (Terborgh and Faaborg 1973). Foraging heights were estimated by eye and represent independent sightings to the extent that a bird's position was recorded only once in a crown. Second and subsequent readings on an individual were taken only when it was possible to follow its progress through a series of crowns.

Factors in the Selection of a Wintering Ground

Climate

While climate is certainly a proximate, if not an ultimate cause in the phenomenon of migration itself, it can be discounted as a factor of any consequence in the distribution of migrants within the Antilles, because 1) the region lies wholly within the tropics and 2) the major pattern we shall be seeking to explain has a predominately east-west axis and hence is independent of latitude and winter climate. Moreover, the pronounced topographic diversity of many Caribbean islands assures that climatic variation within islands often greatly exceeds that between islands.

Distance from Mainland and Area of Land Mass

The longer the overwater flight a bird must negotiate, the greater its chances of encountering inclement weather, of being forced down by exhaustion, of missing its target, and other mishaps. This should be especially true for migrants taking easterly headings from the Greater Antilles toward the Lesser Antilles because of the strong prevailing northeasterly tradewinds at those latitudes. Tradewinds would not be so much of a hindrance for birds taking the transoceanic route past Bermuda to the Lesser Antilles. But radar data indicate that migrants using this route pass over the Lesser Antilles at high altitude without showing signs of stopping (Williams et al. 1977). If it is correct to infer from such negative evidence that most of the populations wintering in the West Indies embark from the vicinity of Florida, then the Lesser Antilles can properly be regarded as remote, upwind targets.

Island area may be important in two ways. A larger landmass offers 1) a better target, reducing the required precision of navigation and 2) a greater amount of living space within which locally adverse conditions can be avoided.

Separating the influences of distance and island area as they affect the abundance of overwintering populations in the Antilles proves nearly impossible. This is because of a fortuitous quirk in the geography of the archipelago such that the largest islands are all

John W. Terborgh

Table 1. Frequency of North American migrants in netted samples of winter bird populations in the Caribbean region

Locality (and area in km^2)	Distance from Miami Fla., (km)	Size of sample	Percent migrants	Number spp. migrants in sample	Number spp. residents in sample	Habitat and elevation (m)
Hispaniola (76,000)						
Pedro Sanchez	1,310	91	46.0	8	10	Rainforest (350)
Piedra Blanca	1,290	54	37.0	5	10	Montane forest (1,050)
Valle Nuevo	1,280	71	11.0	1	11	Montane forest (1,950)
Cabo Rojo	1,210	186	3.0	3	14	Xeric thorn scrub (20)
Sra. Baoruco	1,190	70	66.0	5	11	Limestone sclerophyll forest (700)
Boca de Yuma (Jan)	1,390	93	30.0	5	13	Limestone sclerophyll forest (50)
Boca de Yuma (April)	1,390	158	29.0	8	13	Limestone sclerophyll forest (50)
Isla Saona	1,390	132	25.0	5	9	Limestone sclerophyll forest (10)
Puerto Rico (10,000)						
Isla Mona (65)	1,490	399	7.0	5	6	Limestone sclerophyll scrub (30)
Guanica	1,490	1004	14.0	9	22	Limestone sclerophyll scrub (25)
Saint Kitts (180)						
Lodge Estate	1,930	108	1.0	1	11	Montane forest (500)
Lodge Estate	1,930	160	4.0	3	11	Shrubby old field (450)
Montserrat (100)	2,015	209	0.5	1	11	Montane forest (425)
Guadeloupe (1,510)						
Basse Terre (1,510)	2,070	61	2.0	1	10	Rainforest (300)
Grande Terre (1,510)	2,090	326	1.0	2	14	Secondary sclerophyll scrub (20)
Terre de Bas (6.8)	2,110	264	0.0	0	9	Secondary sclerophyll scrub (80)
Terre de Haut (4.6)	2,110	62	0.0	0	8	Primary sclerophyll scrub (60)
Marie Galante (155)	2,140	134	1.0	1	10	Secondary sclerophyll scrub (30)
La Desirade (20)	2,150	446	0.0	1	14	Secondary sclerophyll scrub (50)
Dominica (820)	2,150	48	0.0	0	10	Primary rainforest (350)
Trinidad (4,800)						
Matura	2,500	439	0.0	1	33	Primary rainforest (250)
Scotland Bay	2,450	116	0.0	0	25	Primary sclerophyll forest (30)
Scotland Bay	2,450	123	1.0	1	25	Shrubby old field (5)
Tobago (300)						
Speyside	2,250	176	2.0	1	24	Secondary sclerophyll forest (40)
Little Tobago (1.5)	2,520	127	1.0	1	14	Primary maritime forest (30)
Venezuela (∞)						
Turiamo	2,100	446	2.0	3	73	Primary deciduous forest (350)
Rancho Grande	2,100	310	0.0	0	58	Montane forest (1,150)
Guacamayo	2,100	172	0.0	0	34	Montane forest (1,900)

relatively close to the North American mainland. Not only are the largest islands (Cuba, Hispaniola, Puerto Rico) more easily reached but collectively they also form an almost continuous east-west barrier across the Caribbean for more than 2,000 km, a feature that minimizes navigational uncertainty.

That birds are in fact influenced by these purely geographical considerations in their choice of wintering grounds is suggested by the data in table 1. This gives the fraction of migrants in mist-net samples taken at 28 localities in the Greater and Lesser Antilles, Trinidad, Tobago, and Venezuela. Migrants commonly make up a third or more of the individuals in winter bird populations in Hispaniola. The value for Puerto Rico is less than half as great, and for all localities farther east and south it is on the order of 1 percent or less.

Both distance and area appear to contribute to this

result, though for the reason mentioned above, the two variables are statistically difficult to separate. Small, near islands (Saona, Mona) clearly harbor more migrants than similar-sized or much larger islands in the most distant Lesser Antilles, implicating a distance effect. The influence of area can also be examined in a crude way by comparing nearby large and small islands. Thus Eastern Hispaniola (Boca de Yuma) shows a higher (though perhaps not significantly higher) value than offshore Saona; both Hispaniola and Puerto Rico exceed Mona which lies between them; and 2 localities on the main island of Guadeloupe (Grande Terre and Basse Terre) gave higher values than any of 4 small satellite islands. (Trinidad and the South American mainland are not fairly included in the comparison because of much higher resident species densities, as will be discussed in the next paragraph.) From the merely suggested trends in these few available comparisons it would be foolhardy to attempt any quantification of area and distance effects. Suffice it to say that the combined influence of the two nearly inseparable variables is very great and can account for most of the inter-island variation in density of overwintering migrants in the Caribbean.

Interspecific Competition with Resident Species

If avoidance of inter-specific competition were a decisive factor in winter distributions, one could anticipate an inverse relationship between the abundance of migrants and the density of resident species. It might appear as if the West Indies offered ideal conditions for testing this proposition, since the archipelago contains islands with as few as 10 and as many as 80 resident land birds. Yet this proves not to be the case for two quite distinct reasons: 1) it is impossible to examine the effect of resident species number independently of that of island area because resident species number shows a roughly .9 correlation with island area (Terborgh 1973); 2) the inter-island variation in resident species number per habitat is so slight as to be inconsequential. The latter phenomenon is clearly indicated in the netting results (table 1). There are barely more resident species in the samples from Hispaniola (80 resident landbirds) than in the one from Dominica (42 resident landbirds) or the ones from La Desirade (15 species) or Terre de Bas (12 species). Thus, from the point of view of a migrant seeking to minimize its ecological interaction with resident species, the West Indian islands all appear to be roughly equivalent. Whatever slight advantage the Lesser Antilles may offer in the form of reduced density of competitors, it is apparently offset by the disadvantages of their smaller size and greater distance, as the results of the previous section suggest. In short, the

question of whether competition from residents plays much of a role in the selection of winter ranges by migrants in the West Indies is not answered by simple correlation methods. Results from the southern Caribbean are no more helpful. Although there does appear to be a good gradient in resident species density in the series Little Tobago-Tobago-Trinidad-Venezuela, the numbers of North American birds wintering in that region are so tiny as to render comparisons meaningless.

Habitat Quality

Questions about the role that habitat quality plays in winter range selection can be asked at several levels. Beginning at the most general, we can ask whether the observed variation in migrant densities over various parts of the Caribbean region are responses to degrees of suitability of the habitat? Our view is that almost certainly it is not. The opinion is based on an examination of a wide range of habitats in Hispaniola (tables 1 and 2). Wintering warblers are ubiquitous on this island, notwithstanding the remarkable range of conditions it offers. It matters little whether one censuses open stands of pine, rainforest, cloud forest, or limestone sclerophyll forest; migrants are common throughout. The one exception is xeric scrub where frequencies are decidedly lower than in other habitats.

Many species occur from sea level to over 2,000 m and appear equally at home in several conspicuously distinct vegetation formations. Indeed, a majority of the regularly occurring winter residents of Hispaniola display a substantially greater versatility with respect to habitat occupancy than they do within their breeding ranges. Thus it seems unlikely that the comparative scarcity of migrants in the Lesser Antilles, for example, could be due to an unsuitability of the vegetation there, instead of to the effects of distance and area as concluded previously. Our feeling is that the natural vegetation of any non-arid portion of the neotropics will offer appropriate conditions for several to many species of migrants, and that the factors which determine the geographical limits of species' winter ranges are often unrelated to habitat quality.

There are instances, however, in which habitat quality does appear to be the decisive factor in delimiting winter ranges. The best, and perhaps only examples among the species that winter in the West Indies are those which show a strong partiality for pines. Whereas the spruce-dwelling warblers of the north have no opportunity to select equivalent vegetation in the tropics, pine-dwelling species do. The Yellow-throated Warbler (*Dendroica dominica*) is the clearest case. It is common in pines on Hispaniola but rare in other habitats on that island and scarce to absent on islands

John W. Terborgh

Table 2. Frequency of North American migrants and resident warblers in tally censuses of winter bird populations in pine and non-pine habitats in Hispaniola

Habitat and elevation (m)	Percent migrants	Common species[1]	Percent resident warblers	Resident warbler species	Total no. resident species
Logged pine forest with remnant broadleaf understory (2,285)	28	Yel-rump, Yel-thr, Palm, Bl-thr B	38	Pine	11
Open pine forest (1,650)	42	Yel-thr, Palm, B & W, Yel-rump, C May	20	Pine	14
Open pine forest (1,140)	35	Palm, C May, Y'throat, Prairie, Yel-thr	18	Pine	11
Open pine forest (890)	33	Y'throat, C May, Palm, Prairie	7	Pine	17
Secondary pines with broadleaf understory (360)	23	Y'throat, Redst, Palm, B & W, Yel-thr	0	None	20
Montane forest (1,950)	17	Bl-th B	8	Ground	10
Limestone sclerophyll forest (760)	27	C May, Y'throat, Redst	0	None	13
Limestone sclerophyll forest (530)	14	C May, Prairie, Bl-th B, Palm	0	None	21
Secondary sclerophyll scrub (320)	45	Redst, Parula, Prairie, C May, B & W, Ovenb	2	Ground	20
Secondary deciduous forest (150)	10	Prairie, C May	9	Ground	15
Xeric thorn scrub (200)	5	Prairie	4	Ground	16
Xeric thorn scrub (180)	2	Prairie	4	Ground	19

[1] Key to abbreviations: B & W = Black and White Warbler; Parula = Parula Warbler; C May = Cape May Warbler; Bl-thr B = Black-throated Blue Warbler; Yel-rump = Yellow-rumped Warbler; Yel-thr = Yellow-throated Warbler; Prairie = Prairie Warbler; Palm = Palm Warbler; Ovenb = Ovenbird; Y'throat = Common Yellowthroat; Redst = Redstart. Species listed in order of abundance.

lacking pines. The Prairie Warbler (*Dendroica discolor*) presents a more dubious case. It is most common in pine second growth but occurs in open and semiarid vegetation on Hispaniola as well as on a good many other islands. Beyond these two examples, it would be hard to make a case on the basis of habitat for why any other species that winters in the Greater Antilles would prefer these islands to alternative locations elsewhere in the neotropics.

In sum, the pattern of variation in the aggregate abundance of North American migrants in the eastern Caribbean strongly implicates distance and island area as the decisive factors in winter range selection. Intraregional differences in climate, habitat quality and density of resident species exert little or no discernible influence. Accounting for the gross abundance of overwintering birds in a region does nothing, however, to illuminate the problem of why any given species occurs where it does. The answer to this question appears in part to lie in an understanding of the interactions that order community structure, as shall be expounded in the next section.

Interactions between Residents and Migrants

What is the nature of the interaction between resident species and migrants? Does one group have the competitive upper hand over the other, or is there a balanced reciprocity of interactive effects?

The flood of migrants that inundates Hispaniola each winter creates an opportune situation for studying these questions. Our census data show that the resident populations of that island are commonly inflated 50 percent or more by the influx of northern migrants. Moreover, the species diversity in many habitats is increased by a roughly equal factor. If we consider insectivores alone, then the population and diversity increases are greater than a factor of two. Surely community perturbations of this magnitude are not absorbed without discernible effect. We shall examine three lines of evidence that bear on this problem: the distribution of resident warblers in the Greater and Lesser Antilles, the abundance of migrants in habitats occupied by resident warblers in Hispaniola, and the degree of foraging specialization of migrant and resident species.

Table 3. Habitat utilization by resident warblers (*Parulidae*) of the Greater and Lesser Antilles

Habitats occupied

Greater Antilles (Hispaniola [H] and Puerto Rico [PR])
    Yellow Warbler (H & PR) — Mangroves
    Adelaide's Warbler (PR) — Semiarid scrub
    Pine Warbler (H) — Middle and high (but not low) elevation pine forest
    Elfin-woods Warbler (PR) — Montane elfin thickets (rare)
    Ground Warbler (H) — Montane broadleaf forest and lowland xeric scrub
    White-winged Warbler (H) — Montane thickets (rare)
Lesser Antilles (Guadeloupe [G] and Dominica [D])
    Yellow Warbler (G & D) — Mangroves, coastal thickets, semi-deciduous scrub, early second growth
    Plumbeous Warbler (G & D) — Lowland and montane forest, elfin thickets

Distribution of Resident Warblers (Parulidae) in the Greater and Lesser Antilles

Since most of the North American birds that winter in the Antilles are warblers, it is reasonable to focus on the resident members of that family as the species most likely to be affected by the seasonal invasion of migrants. The intra-island distributions of parulids in the Greater and Lesser Antilles are strikingly different (table 3). The Greater Antillean species have peripheral distributions in as much as they occupy habitats that lie at the extremities of environmental gradients: arid scrub, humid ridge-top elfin thickets, mangroves, and open pine forest. Although four species inhabit Hispaniola and three Puerto Rico, collectively they occupy only about 30 percent and 10 percent of the available habitat in the two islands, respectively. No parulids or other ecologically equivalent species occur in the predominant natural vegetation of these islands which is lowland rainforest and limestone sclerophyll forest. (The only exception is the small (11 g) endemic Flat-billed Vireo (*Vireo nanus*) which occurs locally in sclerophyll forest in Hispaniola.) Given that approximately 50 percent of the resident land birds of Hispaniola breed in one or the other of these habitats, and approximately 60 percent of those of Puerto Rico, the probability that none of the six species of warblers that occur on the two islands should do so is on the order of 0.01.

Now consider the contrasting situation in the Lesser Antilles, exemplified by Guadeloupe and Dominica. Either the Yellow Warbler (*Dendroica petechia*) or the Plumbeous Warbler (*Dendroica plumbea*) occupies virtually every available habitat on both islands: man-groves, semideciduous scrub, limestone sclerophyll forest, lowland and montane rainforest and elfin thickets. On many small low Lesser Antillean islands (La Desirade, Iles des Saintes), the Yellow Warbler can be found almost anywhere, not just in mangroves as in the Greater Antilles. That the greater habitat occupancy by resident warblers in the Lesser Antilles is causally related to the virtual absence of migrants in these islands is an appealing interpretation, though perhaps not the only one consistent with the observations.

Abundance of Migrants in Hispaniola in Habitats Occupied by Resident Warblers

Further support for the possibility that migrant warblers are squeezing their resident counterparts into ecological corners in the Greater Antilles would be gained if residents occurred preferentially in habitats that were underutilized by migrants. Although our data on this point are rather fragmentary, they do show some noteworthy patterns. Resident Pine Warblers (*Dendroica pinus*) become more numerous the higher one goes in the Dominican mountains (table 2). It is easily the most abundant species at upper elevations but is curiously absent from lowland pine forests. Migrant warblers, however, appear to be equally common at all elevations. The case of the Ground Warbler (*Microlegia palustris*), a Hispaniolan endemic, is more interesting. With respect to habitat, it shows a bimodal distribution, a pattern exceedingly rare in nature. It is a regular denizen of humid mid-elevation broadleaf forests and of lowland xeric scrub, but we have not found it in intermediate types of

John W. Terborgh

vegetation. Our three samples from montane broadleaf forest indicate normal densities of overwintering warblers in that habitat (17, 11, and 37 percent), while four samples from semiarid or arid lowland vegetation contained decidedly below average frequencies of migrants (10, 5, 2, and 3 percent). Thus the Ground Warbler does occupy a refuge from migrant competition in the latter habitat. Habitats that are intermediate between montane broadleaf forest and xeric scrub, i.e., lowland rainforest and limestone sclerophyll forest, are notably lacking any resident warbler and harbor average or above average densities of migrants (14–66 percent). In the aggregate, the evidence mildy suggests that some resident warbler populations may be localized in habitats that offer partial refuges from the deluge of northern migrants. We have no information to indicate whether this would be true of the other two resident parulids in Hispaniola, the Yellow Warbler and the White-winged Warbler (*Xenolegia montana*), as we have not censused a plot in which either was present. Yellow Warblers in Jamaica occupy mangroves exclusively during the winter but expand into nearby scrub in the spring after the migrants have departed (Lack and Lack 1972).

While tropical species are noted for having longer breeding seasons than temperate species, limited data suggest that West Indian birds (particularly insectivores) have restricted breeding seasons that tend to correspond with those of their winter resident competitors. Virtually all of the Hispaniolan insectivores studied by Bond (1943) nest in late May, June, or July. Tanagers and finches generally nest at this time but regularly expand their breeding seasons. The nectarivorous Bananaquit (*Coereba flaveola*) may be found nesting at any time. Resident insectivores may thus have adjusted their breeding seasons to the departure of the northern parulids.

Foraging Specialization of Resident and Migrant Species

Resident species might be at a competitive disadvantage with respect to migrants if their foraging habits were less specialized. A thorough assessment of this proposition would require documentation of the foraging behavior of each of the resident parulids, something we have not undertaken. We have, however, measured the foraging-height distributions of all resident and migrant species in a tract of lowland rainforest, and a striking contrast emerges in comparing the two groups of species. To facilitate the analysis we have classified the community into "guilds" of frugivores, bark feeders, nectarivores and insectivores. The Bananaquit (*Coereba flaveola*) which takes a nearly even mix of nectar and insects is included in both of the respective categories.

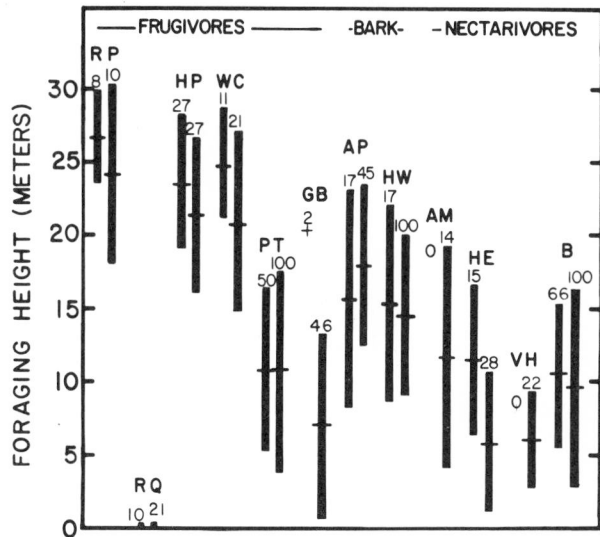

Figure 1a. Foraging heights of frugivores, bark feeders, and nectarivores in a Hispaniolan rainforest. Heavy bars indicate one standard deviation about the mean. Number of observations given over the bars. A pair of bars is shown for each species. The left bar refers to observations made in January 1970, the right bar to observations made in June 1971. Abbreviations: RP = Red-necked Pigeon (*Columba squamosa*); RQ = Ruddy Quail Dove (*Geotrygon montana*); HP = Hispaniola Parrot (*Amazona ventralis*); WC = White-necked Crow (*Corvus leucognaphalus*); PT = Black-crowned Palm Tanger (*Pharnicophilus palmarum*); GB = Greater Antillean Bullfinch (*Loxigilla violacea*); AP = Antillean Piculet (*Nesoctites micromegas*); HW = Hispaniolan Woodpecker (*Melanerpes striatus*); AM = Antillean Mango (*Anthracothorax dominicus*); HE = Hispaniolan Emerald (*Chlorostilbon swainsonii*); VH = Vervain Hummingbird (*Mellisuga minima*); B = Bananaquit (*Coereba flaveola*)

Frugivores predominate among the resident species, a condition that seems to be widespread among West Indian bird communities (Terborgh et al 1978). With respect to foraging height the frugivores subdivide into three groups: those that feed on large fruits and seeds in the canopy (a pigeon, a crow, and a parrot), those that take small fruits and seeds in the midstory (a slender-billed tanager and a heavy-billed finch) and one that scavenges fallen fruits and seeds in the leaf litter (a quail-dove, figure 1a). Like-sized species forage at the same level but have distinctly different bills and belong to different families.

There are two bark feeders, a woodpecker and a piculet, both of which forage widely in the middle and upper tiers of the forest. While the piculet is largely insectivorous, the woodpecker is strongly frugivorous. Here the main distinctions are in diet and in foraging tactics, the woodpecker preferring large trunks, the piculet smaller branches and twigs.

The four nectarivores similarly show a great deal of

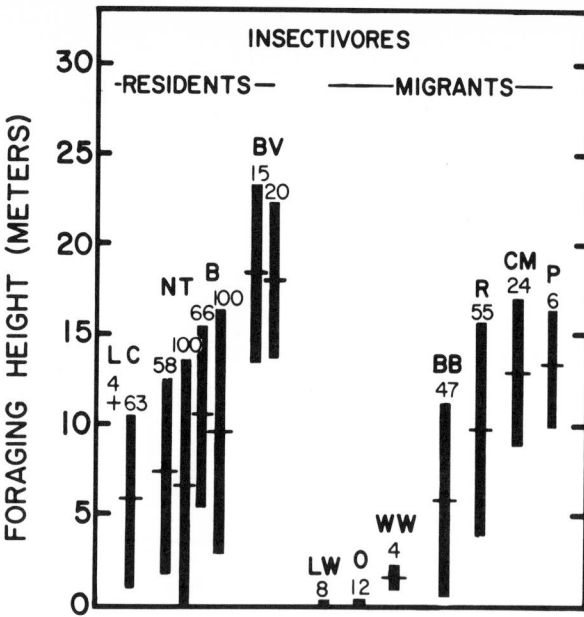

Figure 1b. Foraging heights of resident and migrant insectivores in a Hispaniolan rainforest. Heavy bars indicate one standard deviation about the mean. Number of observations are given over the bars. A pair of bars is given for each resident species. The left bar refers to observations made in January 1970, the right bar to observations made in June 1971. The single bars for migrant species refer to observations made in January 1970. Abbreviations: LC = Hispaniolan Lizard Cuckoo (*Saurothera longirostris*); NT = Narrow-Billed Tody (*Todus angustirostris*); B = Bananaquit; BV = Black-whiskered Vireo; LW = Louisiana Water-thrush; O = Ovenbird; WW = Worm-eating Warbler; BB = Black-throated Blue Warbler; R = Redstart; CM = Cape May Warbler; P = Parula Warbler.

overlap in their foraging-height distributions. They are distinguished mainly by size and bill length. A small, medium, and large hummingbird and the still larger bananaquit are all present in the study plot in the nesting season (June), but curiously, the large and small hummingbirds were absent in January.

The insectivores in this Dominican rainforest are an odd assortment of species, none of which closely fits the warbler mold (figure 1b). There is a large cuckoo, named for its lizard-eating tendencies; a tody, a tiny non-passerine with flycatcher habits; the Bananaquit, which as already mentioned feeds on nectar as much as insects; and a vireo, distinctly larger than a warbler and with a strong propensity for fruit eating, especially in the winter months. These four species differ radically from one another in size, diet, foraging tactics, and taxonomic position.

Now contrast the set of North American migrants that co-occupies the same habitat for more than half

the year. There are seven species (vs four resident insectivores); they are all primarily or exclusively insectivorous; they all engage in gleaning to some degree; and they all belong to the same family, *Parulidae*. Ecologically they differ from one another, not by the gross features of diet, size, taxonomic position that serve to distinguish resident guild-members, but by relatively subtle quantitative differences in their vertical positions in the forest and in foraging tactics. Louisiana Water-thrushes (*Seiurus motacilla*) feed along stream banks, Ovenbirds (*Seiurus aurocapillus*) on the leaf litter, Worm-eating Warblers (*Helmitheros vermivorus*) in the low understory, Black-throated Blue Warblers (*Dendroica caerulescens*) in the middle story, and Redstarts (*Setophaga ruticilla*), Cape May Warblers (*Dendroica tigrina*) and Parula Warblers (*Parula americana*) in the lower canopy. The resident Black-whiskered Vireo (*Vireo altiloquus*) forages still higher in the mid-canopy). Among the species that forage roughly at the same level, the Ovenbird and Water-thrush segregate by habitat, while the Redstart, Cape May Warbler, and Parula Warblers differ quantitatively in foraging tactics. The Redstart catches most of its prey on the wing by hover-snatching, the Parula Warbler is a methodical gleaner of leafy branch tips while the Cape May Warbler is intermediate in its behavior and displays an affinity for nectar feeding (table 4).

From even so crude an assessment of foraging behaviors as this, it is clear that the ecological packing of migrant insectivores is much tighter than that of resident insectivores, and that no resident species is as closely related ecologically to any other resident, or to any of the migrants, as the migrants are inter se. A resident warbler more generalized in its habits than the migrants would be hard pressed to fit into this community. Whether resident Antillean warblers are in fact more generalized than their migratory cousins is a question that awaits investigation.

A nearly parallel situation can be discerned in the set of warblers that frequents the open pine forests of the Hispaniolan mountains. The species separate by vertical stratification and foraging tactics (table 4). Palm Warblers (*Dendroica palmarum*) search patches of bare rocky ground, Yellow-throats (*Geothylpis trichas*) shulk in shrubs and clumps of tall grass, Prairie Warblers forage low, either in young pines or in scattered broadleaf shrubs, Yellow-rumped Warblers (*Dendroica coronata*), as elsewhere, exhibit a wide range of perch heights, but are more flycatchers than gleaners, Black-and-white Warblers (*Mniotilta varia*) creep on trunks and major limbs, Yellow-throated Warblers creep on smaller diameter branches and twigs, and resident Pine Warblers probe in the tufts of needles at branch tips. On slopes and in draws that have been sheltered

John W. Terborgh

Table 4. Foraging behavior of species comprising the Hispaniolan pine and rainforest migrant warbler complexes

Species	Foraging position	Foraging mode, substrate, etc.
Rainforest		
Louisiana Water-thrush	Terrestrial	Streams, banks
Ovenbird	Terrestrial	Gleans leaf litter
Worm-eating Warbler	Low understory	Gleans foliage, dead leaves
Black-throated Blue Warbler	Middle story	Gleans, hover-snatches in foliage
Redstart	Lower canopy	Hover-snatches, hawks
Cape May Warbler	Middle canopy	Gleans, hover-snatches in foliage, takes nectar
Parula Warbler	Middle canopy	Gleans foliage
Black-whiskered Vireo[1]	Upper canopy	Gleans foliage, takes fruit
Open pine forest		
Palm Warbler	Terrestrial, low shrubs	Hover snatches, gleans
Yellowthroat	Low thickets	Gleans in dense grass, thickets
Prairie Warbler	Middle story	Gleans, hover-snatches in outer foliage of young pines, shrubs
Yellow-rumped Warbler	Variable	Hawks, hover-snatches from exposed perches
Black-and-white Warbler	Variable	Creeps on trunks, major limbs
Yellow-throated Warbler	Crowns	Creeps, gleans in branches and trunks
Pine Warbler[1]	Crowns	Gleans needle tufts

[1] Resident species.

from fire, a broadleaf understory develops beneath the pines. Here, in addition to the species named above, one finds Black-throated Blue Warblers and Cape May Warblers using the broadleafed trees. The pine woods warbler complex is as tightly structured as the one found in lowland rainforest. Both contain seven species, more than co-occur in the nesting season in most North American Habitats. Together the pine and rainforest complexes account for all the warblers that commonly winter in Hispaniola save the Northern Water-thrush which is restricted to mangroves. The separation of foraging functions within the two sets of species conforms to such orderly patterns that one must wonder how the complexes came into being.

Discussion

We can imagine two extreme possibilities: via coadaptation or via selective screening of existing taxa for their survival in different potential wintering grounds. If coadaptation were the mode of origin, one might expect to find the same cliques of species living together at both ends of their migratory routes. But this is clearly not the case. The pine woods and rainforest complexes both contain mixes of northern and southern species that would never be found together during the nesting season. To us, the selective screening mech-

anism offers the more plausible explanation. By this interpretation, a species would tend to become common in regions where its survival was high relative to other regions. Inasmuch as competitive relationships affect survival, a species would tend to concentrate in areas where it could fit into the preexisting community with minimal ecological overlap.

Nature appears to afford ample opportunities for such a screening mechanism to operate. Winter ranges are seldom as discretely bounded as breeding ranges (Nat. Audubon Soc. 1974, 1975). An increasing number of neotropical migrants are being shown to exhibit strong philopatry for their winter locations (Loftin 1977). Individuals of many species can be found wintering tens or hundreds of miles from the main concentrations of their species. For example, Cape May, Prairie, and Black-throated Blue Warblers all occur sparingly in Florida and Central America, although their main wintering ground is in the Bahamas and Greater Antilles. Converse examples abound as well. Scattered Golden-winged, Magnolia, Black-throated Green, and Hooded Warblers winter in the Greater Antilles, while the bulk of their populations are in Central America. If the survival of any of these species were decisively better in the Antilles, one would expect to see them increase, yet there are no indications that this is happening. Clearly it is not a matter of habitat, for one can see the odd Magnolia or Black-throated Green Warbler in Hispaniola in any of a wide range of vegetation types. It seems far more reasonable to conclude that these species have a waif status in the Antilles because they fail to fit into the existing community structure because their foraging behavior too closely overlaps that of one or more of the common species. Lack and Lack (1972) arrived at a similar opinion after studying the wintering parulid populations of Jamaica.

If this view of the origin of integrated complexes is correct, it offers a means for understanding the geographical limits of certain species' winter ranges. Implicit in the notion of tightly packed, competitively closed species complexes is the existence of equivalent complexes in other habitats or in adjacent geographical regions. Hispaniola contains two such complexes. We predict that several more will be found to occur in southern Mexico where the sympatry among northern migrants reaches much higher levels than it does in the Caribbean. Additional complexes should replace one another down the Central American isthmus and in northern South America, as certain species drop out and others enter. Substitutions should commonly involve species with patently similar foraging behaviors, although more complex kinds of rearrangements may occasionally occur. In this connection, it is heartening to note Allen Keast's contribution to this symposium in which he details a number of examples of just the kind of parapatric distributions we believe to be a logical implication of the selective screening mechanism.

To summarize, the limits of winter distributions appear to be set by a variety of factors that have strong directional components. Eastern limits in the Caribbean islands and eastern and southern limits in South American are evidently established by the diminishing returns in flying farther and farther to gain incremental reductions in the density of competitors, both resident and migrant. Such limits would be expected to taper off gradually, as indeed they seem to do in the Antilles and in northern South America as well. Northern limits are clearly set by the risks posed by periods of inclement weather, as was so clearly documented in the extreme winter just past for half-hardy species such as Yellowthroat (*Geothlypis trichas*) Ruby-crowned Kinglet (*Regulus calendula*), and Carolina Wren (*Thyothorus ludovicianus*) (Smith 1977). Weather-imposed northern limits tend to taper off gradually just as do distance-imposed southern and eastern limits, except that birds become extremely selective of habitat toward their northern limits, while this does not appear to be characteristic behavior near eastern and southern range extremities.

Limits that lie somewhere in between the northern climatic and the southern distance-imposed extremes will mainly fall into two categories: those that are closely associated with a particular habitat and those that are enforced by competitive interactions. In contrast to the ill-defined boundaries imposed by weather and distance, both types of limits should be relatively abrupt. Some good examples can be found in Professor Keast's article. By our assessment, the western limits of species that are confined to the Antilles, such as the Cape May, Black-throated Blue, and Prairie Warblers, are enforced by competitive interactions with still unidentified counterparts that occupy the Central American mainland. Elucidating the competitive relationships within and between the parulid complexes of Central America presents an outstanding challenge.

But even if it were possible to deduce the mechanisms that restrain each species within its present winter range, we would have only proximate answers to the question of why any but the habitat-limited species winter where they do. The ultimate answers probably lie deep in the historical sequence of events that impelled the parulid radiation. One would need to know more about the displacements of vegetation zones that accompanied the recurrent Pleistocene glacial advances as well as facts about the numerous speciation and extinction events that no doubt took place concurrently. That we shall ever be able to reconstruct biological history in such detail seems doubtful. If not, we shall have to content ourselves with proximate answers.

Acknowledgments

We are indebted to the members of five of John Terborgh's tropical ecology classes for assistance in the field, particularly with installing and operating lines of mist nets. One or the other of us was helped on other trips by E. Balaban, H. J. Brockmann, D. Howell, J. S. Weske, and D. Willard. We wish to thank them all. We are grateful too for the abundant hospitality and good advice given us in the Dominican Republic by A. and D. Dod. Our work in the Dominican Republic was further aided by permission to enter lands under the control of Gulf and Western Corp. and Alcoa Corp. In the Lesser Antilles we were generously given access to undisturbed forest by the managers of the Syndicate Estate (Dominica), the Dannenborg Farm (Montserrat) and the Lodge Estate (St. Kitts). Mr. and Mrs. Egbert Lau, of Speyside, Tobago, also kindly granted use of their lands.

Financial support of our many trips was received from the Chapman Memorial Fund of the American Museum of Natural History and the Eugene Higgins Trust Fund of Princeton University.

John W. Terborgh

Literature Cited

Bond, J.
1943. Nidification of the passerine birds of Hispaniola. Wils. Bull. 55:115–25.

Bystrack, D.
1974. *Wintering areas of bird species potentially hazardous to aircraft*, New York: National, Audubon Society, 156 pp.

Bystrack, D., and S. R. Drennan
1975. Ten new early winter distribution maps. Amer. Birds 29:603–11.

Lack, D., and P. Lack
1972. Wintering warblers in Jamaica. Living Bird 11:129–53.

Loftin, H.
1977. Returns and recoveries of banded North American birds in Panama and in the tropics. Bird Banding 48:253–58.

Smith, K.
1977. The changing seasons. Amer. Birds 31:292–303.

Terborgh, J.
1973. Chance, habitat, and dispersal in the distribution of birds in the West Indies. Evol. 27:338–49.

Terborgh, J., and J. Faaborg
1973. Turnover and ecological release in the avifauna of Mona Island, Puerto Rico. Auk. 90:759–79.

Terborgh, J., J. Faaborg, and H. J. Brockmann
1978. Island colonization by Lesser Antillean birds. Auk. 95:59–72.

Williams, T. C., J. M. Williams, L. C. Ireland, and J. M. Teal
1977. Autumnal bird migration over the western North Atlantic Ocean. Amer. Birds 31:251–67.

JOHN R. FAABORG
Division of Biological Sciences
University of Missouri-Columbia
Columbia, Missouri 65201

JOHN W. TERBORGH
Department of Biology
Princeton University
Princeton, New Jersey 08540

Patterns of Migration in the West Indies

ABSTRACT

We begin by showing that the collection of birds that winters in the West Indies is a nonrandom subset of all North American species that migrate to the tropics. Small gleaning insectivores are strikingly overrepresented while hawking, aerial and large gleaning insectivores, frugivores and granivores are absent or conspicuously underrepresented. Most of the species that breed in the West Indies and migrate to South America for the winter are aerial or hawking insectivores or large gleaners. The pattern is consistent in the two groups of migrants, but at present it is not known whether different categories of prey (e.g., large vs small insects) vary differentially through the year.

West Indian breeding bird communities differ from mainland communities in having much higher proportions of frugivores and in having frugivore guilds that are more tightly packed than insectivore guilds. The arrival of large numbers of migrant parulids reverses this pattern in the winter.

A severe drought at Guanica, Puerto Rico, resulted in a drastic and precipitous decline of frugivores and a less extreme and more prolonged decline of insectivores. We postulate that this can be explained by a lack of buffering between climate and fruits, which are an immediate product of photosynthesis, and a substantial buffering between climate and insects, which are one or two trophic levels removed from primary production. Given the large geographic scale of climatic patterns, it may be that fruits are effectively an unreliable resource within the confined space of an island, while insects, being more buffered from perturbations, are a reliable resource that assures a high probability of survival.

There are still a number of unresolved problems in the interpretation of migratory patterns in the West Indies. We close with a brief discussion of these.

Introduction

As a locus for survival between breeding seasons, the West Indian Archipelago presents both advantages and disadvantages. The relative proximity to the North American breeding grounds, reliable weather, and low diversity resident bird communities are all conducive to high survival probabilities. Islands, however, present limited "targets" to long range migrants, offer limited land areas within which escape from unfavorable conditions may be precluded, and may provide reduced arrays of food resources relative to comparable mainland areas.

The preceding paper examined the gross pattern of distribution of overwintering birds in the West Indies and presented evidence for the role of interspecific competition in the structuring of both resident and migrant communities. Here we point out that gleaning insectivores are strikingly overrepresented in the collection of species that regularly winters in the West Indies, and then inquire into the reasons why this may be so.

Localities and Methods

Our consideration will be restricted to land birds. Data were gathered by mist-netting and observation as described in the previous article. Estimates of population densities and measurements of wing lengths, weights, and bill lengths were obtained from mist-netted specimens. Nets were operated at a site in the Guanica State Forest in Puerto Rico for four successive years to obtain indications of long-term population fluctuations and the degree of philopatry among winter residents.

Migratory Behavior in the West Indian Avifauna

To facilitate the subsequent discussion we classify the land bird species of the West Indies into four categories: 1) permanent residents—species whose populations remain throughout the year on the islands where they nest; 2) summer residents—Three behavioral types are lumped in this category: species that breed in the West Indies but which leave altogether for some portion of the winter; species that migrate from portions of their West Indian ranges but which are permanent residents in other portions; and species (or populations) in which some individuals migrate and others remain as permanent residents; 3) winter residents—Species that nest in North America and which spend the winter, in greater or smaller numbers, in the West Indies; 4) transients—Species that seasonally pass through the West Indies without breeding or lingering through the mid-winter months. This classification embraces the entire West Indian avifauna with the exception of a very few species that wander in the winter to islands outside their normal breeding ranges (e.g., Bahama Swallow). The species that fall into categories 2), 3), and 4), are listed in table 1 and assigned to broadly defined foraging/feeding guilds.

The most noteworthy feature of the lists is that nearly all species in categories 2) and 3) are insectivores. Summer residents that repair to South America for the winter are chiefly large members of the aerial and hawking guilds (nighthawk, swift, martin, flycatchers). The three gleaners that leave (two cuckoos, one vireo) are also large for their guilds. A complementary pattern is shown by the winter residents inasmuch as most of them are small gleaning insectivores. Frugivores, granivores, and aerial and hawking insectivores are curiously under-represented or absent in the set of winter residents. Only three frugivore/granivores winter on the islands, and these are all uncommon and have restricted ranges in the western Greater Antilles. The bulk of the populations of all of them winter on the neotropical mainland. No frugivore has a winter range centered on or contained wholly within the West Indies, although several insectivores do. This seems paradoxical in view of the preponderance of frugivores in the resident fauna of the archipelago.

Structure of West Indian Breeding Communities

The evolutionary structuring of West Indian breeding communities is apparent in the weight relationships within guilds (Faaborg 1975). The salient features of these relationships can be summarized as follows (and see figure 1). The frugivore and insectivore guilds of medium and large island communities contain many pairs of species whose weight ratios fall substantially below 2.0 (larger/smaller). We have shown elsewhere that in these communities of progressively smaller islands, ecological isolation becomes increasingly based on size. This happens first in the insectivorous guild. Vertical stratification disappears, and the weight ratios of adjacent sized species are all a factor of 2.0 or greater. The same pattern is repeated in the frugivore/granivore guild on still smaller islands, until on the smallest class of islands (100 km^2) all species coexist in the predominant vegetation and all guild members differ by at least a factor of two in weight. This progression holds whether one examines rainforest or scrub communities (Terborgh et al. 1978). The insular communities differ strikingly from mainland communities in at least two important respects: in having a far greater representation of frugivores and in showing tighter species packing in frugivorous than in insectivorous guilds (Diamond 1973; Terborgh 1977). It is clear from these facts that the ordering constraints on

John R. Faaborg

Table 1. Migratory birds of the West Indies[1]

Species	Freq. of occurrence[2]	Guild[3]	Range[4]	Mean weight (g)
Summer residents				
White-crowned Pigeon (*Columba leucocephala*)[5]	C	F	W	250
Mourning Dove (*Zenaida macroura*)[5]	C	F	GA	150
White-winged Dove (*Zenaida asiatica*)[5]	U	F	GA	—
Mangrove Cuckoo (*Coccyzus minor*)[6]	C	GI	W	65
Yellow-billed Cuckoo (*Coccyzus americanus*)	C	GI	GA	65
Common Nighthawk (*Chordeiles minor gundlachii*)	C	AI	GA	65
Black Swift (*Cypseloides niger*)	C	AI	W	—
Gray Kingbird (*Tyrannus dominicensis*)[6]	C	FI	W	42
Purple Martin (*Progne subis*)	C	AI	W	42
Cave Swallow (*Petrochelidon fulva*)[6]	C	AI	GA	21
Black-whiskered Vireo (*Vireo altiloquus*)[6]	C	GI	W	20
Winter residents[8]				
Chuck-Will's-Widow (*Caprimulgus carolinensis*)	C	AI	GA	—
Whip-Poor-Will (*Caprimulgus vociferus*)[7]	R	AI	Cuba	56
Belted Kingfisher (*Ceryle alcyon*)	C	P	W	—
Yellow-bellied Sapsucker (*Sphyrapicus varius*)	U	TI	wGA	42
Fork-tailed Flycatcher (*Muscivora tyrannus*)	R	FI	sLA	35
Great-crested Flycatcher (*Myiarchus crinitus*)	R	FI	wGA	35
Tree Swallow (*Iridoprocne bicolor*)	C	AI	wGA	20
Rough-winged Swallow (*Stelgidopteryx ruficollis*)	U	AI	GA	18
Barn Swallow (*Hirundo rustica*)	C	AI	W	19
Catbird (*Dumetella carolinensis*)	U	F-GI	wGA	38
American Robin (*Turdus migratorius*)	U	F	wGA	82
Gray-cheeked Thrush (*Catharus minimus*)	U	GI	GA	28
Eastern Bluebird (*Sialia sialis*)	R	F-GI	Cuba	34
Blue-gray Gnatcatcher (*Polioptila caerulea*)	U	GI	wGA	7
White-eyed Vireo (*Vireo griseus*)	C	GI	wGA	13
Black-and-white Warbler (*Mniotilta varia*)	C	GI	W	10
Prothonotary Warbler (*Protonotaria citrea*)	U	GI	W	12
Swainson's Warbler (*Limnothlypis swainsonii*)	U	GI	wGA	12
Worm-eating Warbler (*Helmitheros vermivorus*)	R	GI	GA	13
Golden-winged Warbler (*Vermivora chrysoptera*)	R	GI	GA	9
Bachman's Warbler (*Vermivora bachmanii*)	R	GI	wGA	9
Parula Warbler (*Parula americana*)	C	GI	GA	7
Magnolia Warbler (*Dendroica magnolia*)	U	GI	GA	10
Cape May Warbler (*Dendroica tigrina*)	C	GI	GA	10
Black-throated Blue Warbler (*Dendroica caerulescens*)	C	GI	W	10
Myrtle Warbler (*Dendroica coronata*)	C	GI	GA	10
Black-throated Green Warbler (*Dendroica virens*)	U	GI	GA	9
Yellow-throated Warbler (*Dendroica dominica*)	U	GI	GA	12
Prairie Warbler (*Dendroica discolor*)	C	GI	GA	7
Kirtland's Warbler (*Dendroica kirtlandii*)	R	GI	Bahamas	12
Palm Warbler (*Dendroica palmarum*)	C	GI	GA	12
Ovenbird (*Seiurus aurocapillus*)	C	GI	W	20
Northern Waterthrush (*Seiurus noveboracensis*)	C	GI	W	16
Louisiana Waterthrush (*Seiurus motacilla*)	C	GI	GA	16
Common Yellowthroat (*Geothlypis trichas*)	C	GI	GA	9

Table 1. Continued

Species	Freq. of occur-rence[2]	Guild[3]	Range[4]	Mean weight (g)
Hooded Warbler (*Wilsonia citrina*)	R	GI	GA	11
American Redstart (*Setophaga ruticilla*)	C	GI-FI	W	8
Summer Tanager (*Piranga rubra*)	R	F	wGA	28
Baltimore Oriole (*Icterus galbula*)	R	GI	wGA	30
Rose-breasted Grosbeak (*Pheucticus ludovicianus*)	R	F	W	42
Blue Grosbeak (*Guiraca caerulea*)	R	F	GA	30
Indigo Bunting (*Passerina cyanea*)	U	F	GA	13
Painted Bunting (*Passerina ciris*)	U	F	wGA	13
Savannah Sparrow (*Passerculus sandwichensis*)	U	F	wGA	18
Transients[8]				
Black-billed Cuckoo (*Coccyzus erythropthalmus*)	R	GI	GA	65
Common Nighthawk (*Chordeiles minor minor*)	C	AI	GA	65
Chimney Swift (*Chaetura pelagica*)	U	AI	GA	22
Ruby-throated Hummingbird (*Archilochus colubris*)	R	N	wGA	3
Eastern Kingbird (*Tyrannus tyrannus*)	R	FI	wGA	38
Wood Pewee (*Contopus virens*)	U	FI	wGA	15
Acadian Flycatcher (*Empidonax virescens*)	R	FI	wGA	12
Bank Swallow (*Riparia riparia*)	U	AI	W	14
Cliff Swallow (*Petrochelidon pyrrhonota*)	R	AI	GA	21
Wood Thrush (*Hylocichla mustelina*)	R	GI	wGA	45
Olive-backed Thrush (*Catharus ustulatus*)	R	GI	wGA	30
Veery (*Catharus fuscescens*)	R	GI	wGA	30
Red-eyed Vireo (*Vireo olivaceus*)	R	GI	GA	17
Blue-winged Warbler (*Vermivora pinus*)	R	GI	wGA	9
Tennessee Warbler (*Vermivora peregrina*)	R	GI	wGA	9
Cerulean Warbler (*Dendroica cerulea*)	R	GI	wGA	12
Blackburnian Warbler (*Dendroica fusca*)	U	GI	wGA	10
Chestnut-sided Warbler (*Dendroica pensylvanica*)	R	GI	wGA	11
Bay-breasted Warbler (*Dendroica castanea*)	R	GI	wGA	11
Blackpoll Warbler (*Dendroica striata*)	U	GI	W	12
Kentucky Warbler (*Oporornis formosus*)	R	GI	GA	11
Connecticut Warbler (*Oporornis agilis*)	R	GI	GA	12
Scarlet Tanager (*Piranga olivacea*)	R	F	wGA	28
Orchard Oriole (*Icterus spurius*)	R	GI	wGA	24
Bobolink (*Dolichonyx orizyvorus*)	C	GI	W	33
Dickcissel (*Spiza americana*)	R	F	wGA	23

[1] Listed are migratory species recorded regularly in the area studied. Species are listed according to migratory status (see text), with the frequency of occurrence, and the generalized foraging guild to which each belongs. General range within the West Indies is given along with an approximate mean weight. Distributional data are from Bond (1956, 1971). Weights are from Holmes and Sturges (1975) and the authors.

[2] C = common; U = uncommon; R = rare.

[3] F = frugivore; FI = flycatching insectivore; GI = gleaning insectivore; AI = aerial insectivore; TI = trunk insectivore; N = nectarivore; P = piscivore.

[4] W = widespread; GA = Greater Antilles; LA = Lesser Antilles; w = western; s = southern.

[5] These species primarily move within the West Indies during non-breeding periods.

[6] These species are permanent residents in parts of their ranges.

[7] There exists a permanent resident race in Puerto Rico.

[8] A few of the winter residents are more abundant as transients.

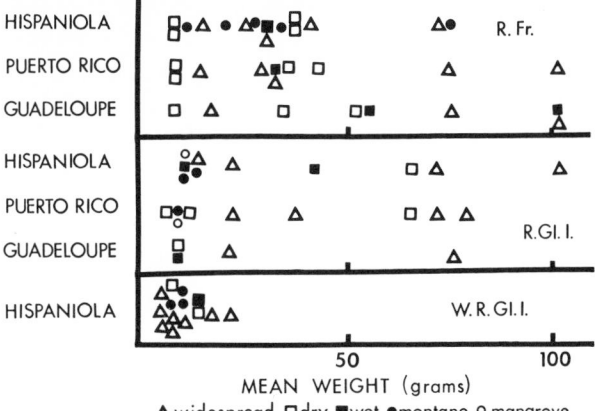

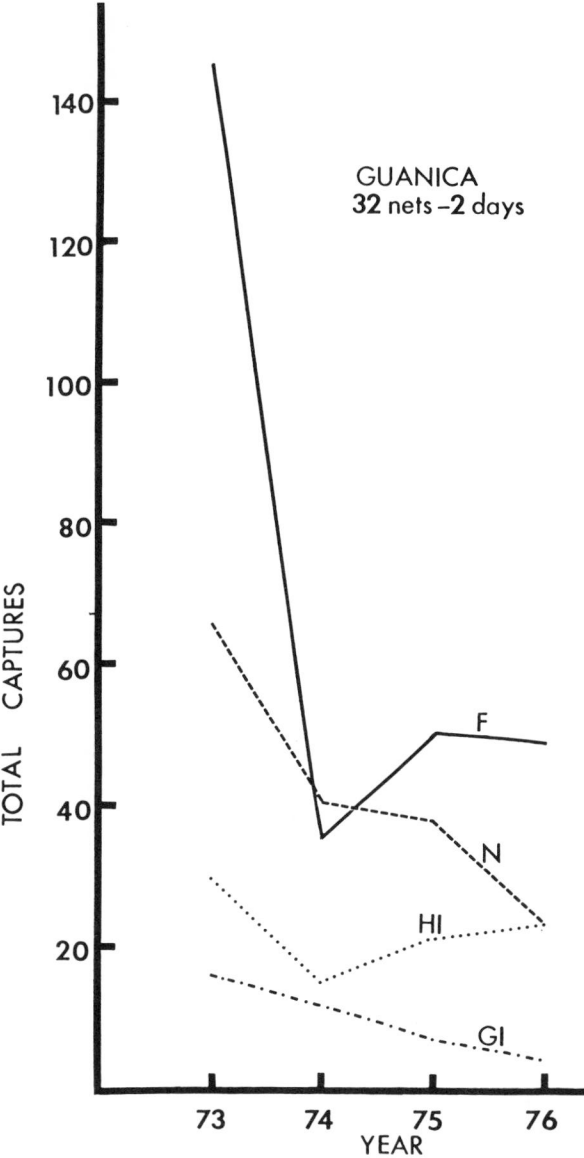

Figure 1. Size patterns of birds on selected West Indian islands. Mean weights of all island residents within the frugivorous (R.Fr.) and gleaning insectivore (R.Gl.I.) foraging guild are listed by major habitat preference along with the common winter resident gleaning insectivores (W.R.Gl.I.) of Hispaniola. Note that syntopic resident insectivores always separate by size while syntopic frugivores do so only on the smallest island shown. In contrast, size separation is a small factor in the isolation of winter resident insectivores.

the island ecosystems are very different from those that operate on the mainland, but it is not clear what significance this has for the acceptability of island habitats as wintering grounds for North American migrants.

What the migrants do, however, stands in strong contradistinction with the pattern shown by resident members of the same guild (figure 1). As many as seven or eight wintering parulids may co-occur in uniform vegetation with adjacent sized species commonly differing by 10 percent or less in weight. While this situation poses obvious questions that we are unable to answer at present, one conclusion at least seems warranted. It is that the maintenance community (the North American parulids) is able to tolerate much higher degrees of species packing than the resident community. But why should this behavior be limited to gleaning insectivores?

Differential Impact of a Drought on Avian Guilds

One of us (JF) has been conducting a long term study of population turnover at a site in the seasonal scrub vegetation of the Guanica State Forest in southwestern Puerto Rico. Over the period 1973–76, we had the fortuitous opportunity to observe the effects of a severe drought (in 1973) and the subsequent recovery of the resident bird population (figure 2). A failure of the

Figure 2. Population fluctuations during drought conditions in dry forest at Guanica, Puerto Rico. The total number of individuals captured in 32 nets over 2 full days is separated by foraging type (F = frugivore, N = nectarivore, HI = hawking insectivore, and GI = gleaning insectivore). Note the sharp drop in frugivores during the early part of the drought but slight increase with slightly improved conditions. During this same period, gleaning insectivores declined slowly but steadily.

rainfall that normally coincides with the breeding season resulted in a nearly complete suppression of nesting activity for the year. By the following winter the density of frugivorous birds in the study area had declined precipitously while that of the insectivorous guilds had undergone a conspicuous, though much less drastic reduction. The population at this time consisted almost entirely of adults, many of which had been banded the previous year. The different responses of the insectivorous and frugivorous guilds can be tentatively explained as consequences of the distinct trophic levels of their respective resources.

The advent of a drought imposes an almost immediate stress on vegetation, resulting in reduced photosynthetic activity. This in turn is more likely to be expressed as reduced flower and fruit set than as reduced leaf volume. Thus, phytophageous insects that feed on foliage will be less adversely affected than birds that feed on fruit and seeds. Moreover, many insects (and spiders) are predators or parasites of other insects and are thereby two trophic steps removed from primary production. Insectivorous birds thus depend on a resource that is substantially buffered from climatic fluctuations by being one or two trophic levels above primary production. Frugivores and granivores, on the other hand, are more directly exposed to the effects of year to year vagaries in the climate. Oscillations in frugivore numbers can thus be expected to have a large amplitude and to track a sequence of good and bad years with only minor lags. Oscillations in insectivore numbers, in contrast, should be relatively damped and should respond less rapidly to major climatic perturbations. The data in Figure 2 are consistent with this interpretation.

Discussion

If these speculations are at all valid, it is reasonable to infer that migrant frugivores and granivores shun the West Indies because their food resources are subject to marked and unpredictable fluctuations in abundance. Because climatic swings are expressed on a large geographic scale, island ecosystems probably do not afford sufficient space in which to seek pockets of locally abundant resources. Continents afford better possibilities in their greater area and heterogeneity. Thus, Dickcissels, which are granivores in the winter, move first to the Venezeulan llanos until the rice crop is harvested there, and then drift northwestward into Colombia and Central America for the remainder of the winter (Fretwell, this volume). North America provides some additional examples of nomadic wintering in birds that depend on patchily distributed resources: Rough-legged Hawks and Short-eared Owls (voles); Cedar Waxwings (berries); Crossbills and other northern finches (conifer, birch and aspen seeds). Opportunistic movements on such a scale are out of the question in the West Indies, and as a consequence, we surmise, frugivores and granivores find better pickings elsewhere.

Insectivores, on the other hand, may find a different and more propitious situation. Insects are a relatively stable, diffuse renewing resource, and they are hard to find. The latter fact means that changes in resource abundance will be manifested primarily by altered prey capture rates. In contrast to fruits, which can quickly be reduced to zero by heavy consumption pressure, insect densities fall only gradually when harvesting exceeds the renewal rate. When food begins to fail a frugivore must leave or starve, while an insectivore has the option of working harder (more hours per day) in the sure knowledge that this will maintain its energy budget at a constant level. Thus, even though insect densities appear to be lower in the West Indies than in comparable mainland sites (Janzen 1973a, 1973b), they are a sufficiently reliable resource to assure survival until the next breeding season.

Unresolved Questions

Certain aspects of the pattern of migration in the West Indies seem to be adequately explained by the rationale presented above, while others clearly are not. If fruit is an unpredictable resource, why is it, for example, that so few frugivores ever leave their home islands? If periods of fruit scarcity are unpredictable from year to year, and even as to time of year, then there might not be any alternative location that could serve as a fail-safe migratory retreat. And, if insects are so reliable a resource, why is it that the West Indian summer residents (table 1 category 2), are virtually all insectivores? We noted previously that these are all birds that feed on large and/or aerial insects. Is it that large and flying insects are predictably scarce in the West Indies in the winter while small foliage insects are not? To a degree this appears to be true over most of North America (chickadees, creepers, nuthatches, kinglets, wrens and Yellow-rumped Warblers stay, while nightjars, cuckoos, swifts, flycatchers, swallows, vireos, tanagers, orioles, etc. leave). Moreover, there are some preliminary indications that flying insects do decrease in the winter in Puerto Rico (Kepler 1972). A better understanding of these issues will require information on seasonal variation in resource levels in West Indian habitats. Today such information scarcely exists.

Studies of resource abundance also appear to be crucial to understanding why there is no small gleaning insectivore in much of the available habitat in the Greater Antilles (*cf* preceding article). If it is because such species are competitively excluded by migratory parulids, as we suggest, one would have to predict that the putatively less specialized resident gleaners require higher prey densities than do the migrants. This and other possible interpretations remain to be tested.

John R. Faaborg

Acknowledgment

We appreciate the support of the Research Council of the Graduate School, University of Missouri-Columbia.

Literature Cited

Bond, J.
1956.   *Check-list of the Birds of the West Indies.* Lancaster, Pa.: Wickersham.

1971.   *Birds of the West Indies.* Boston: Houghton-Mifflin.

Diamond, J.
1973.   Distributional ecology of New Guinea birds. *Science* 179:759–69.

Faaborg, J.
1975.   Size patterns in the structure of West Indian bird communities. Unpublished Ph.D. thesis, Princeton University, Princeton, N.J.

Holmes, R. T. and F. W. Sturges
1975.   Bird community dynamics and energetics in a northern hardwoods ecosystem. J. Anim. Ecol. 44:175–200.

Janzen, D. H.
1973a. Sweep samples of tropical foliage insects: description of study sites, with data on species abundances and size distributions. Ecol. 54:659–86.

1973b. Sweep samples of tropical foliage insects: effects of seasons, vegetation types, elevaton, time of day, and insularity. Ecol. 54:687–708.

Kepler, C. B.
1972.   Notes on the ecology of Puerto Rican swifts, including the first record of the White-collared swift *Streptoprocne zonaris.* Ibis 114:541–43.

Terborgh, J. W.
1977.   Bird species diversity on an Andean elevational gradient. Ecol. 58:1007–19.

Terborgh, J. W., J. Faaborg, and H. J. Brockman
1978.   Island colonization by Lesser Antillean birds. Auk 95:59–72.

1978.   Saturation in the West Indian avifauna.

ROBERT B. WAIDE
JOHN T. EMLEN
Department of Zoology
University of Wisconsin
Madison, Wisconsin 53706

ELLIOT J. TRAMER
Department of Biology
University of Toledo
Toledo, Ohio 43606

Distribution of Migrant Birds in the Yucatán Peninsula: A Survey

ABSTRACT

Censuses from 21 study sites show that migrants comprise a greater proportion of mixed wintering communities in the Yucatán Peninsula than they do in Central and South America. Within the peninsula, migrants are relatively more common in wetter and less populated areas. Common migrants are widely distributed geographically through the peninsula but may be restricted to a particular habitat. Different census methods are differentially effective for a given species, and bias in migrant-resident ratios may be introduced by full dependence on either mistnetting or transect counts. Insufficient data exist to evaluate seasonal or yearly changes in migrant abundance.

SUMARIO

Censos de 21 sitios muestran que aves migratorias componen una proporción más grande de comunidades invernales en la Península de Yucatán de que en otras partes de Centro y Sur America. En la península, aves migratorias son más comunes en lugares más lluviosos y menos poblados. Las aves migratorias más comunes tienen una distribución amplia en la península, pero pueden ser restringidas a habitats particulares. Diferentes métodos de censo son diferencialmente efectivos para una especie, y el uso de un sólo método puede influir en la proporción relativa de aves migratorias y residentes. Pocos datos existen para evaluar cambios estacionales o anuales en la abundancia de aves migratorias.

The Yucatán Peninsula occupies a unique geographical position with respect to the needs of migratory birds. For many autumnal trans-Gulf migrants, the north coast of Yucatán and its fringing islands are the first land masses encountered after a nonstop flight of over 650 miles. The apparent high mortality suffered by migrating birds (Paynter 1953) emphasizes the importance of the peninsula as a stopover during fall migration. Likewise in the spring, departure from Yucatán instead of points farther west or south greatly minimizes the distance traveled in a single flight and enhances the probability of successfully crossing the Gulf of Mexico.

Despite the singular role the peninsula plays in the migration patterns of numerous species, few studies have examined the distribution or ecology of migrant birds in the area. Outside of Paynter's (1955) detailed description of the avifauna of the peninsula, only Tramer (1974) has dealt with the relative abundance of migrants in different habitats. This paper is an effort to integrate these earlier data with more recent work in an overview of the distribution of wintering migrants in the Yucatán Peninsula.

Methods

Censuses have been made by the authors at 21 sites widely distributed over the Yucatán Peninsula (figure 1). Densities at Sites 1–9 were estimated by Tramer (1974) from counts of birds seen on repeated visits to plots which ranged from 6 to 40 acres in size. Waide (this volume) sampled populations at Sites 10–15 using mist nets (MacArthur and MacArthur 1974) as part of a study of the relationships of migrant and resident components of the avifauna. The populations of Sites 13 and 15 were also sampled using the count-X detectability method of Emlen (1971). Populations at Sites 16–21 were sampled by Emlen (in prep.) using this same method.

Climate and Phenology

Figure 2 shows geographic differences in mean annual rainfall in the Yucatán Peninsula. The 21 study sites cover a range of environmental conditions from very dry in the northwest part of the peninsula to moderately wet in the northeast and south. The height of the vegetation roughly parallels the moisture gradient with low scrub occurring along the north coast and semideciduous forest covering most of the rest of the peninsula. Only in extreme southern Campeche and Quintana Roo does tropical evergreen forest make an appearance. The height and composition of the forest throughout the peninsula are strongly affected by local conditions of slope, drainage, and human disturbance.

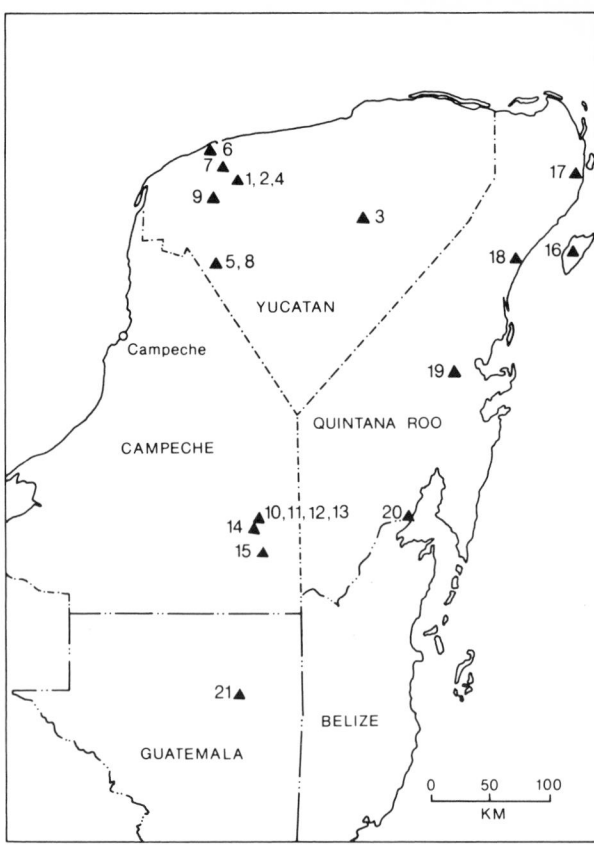

Figure 1. Map of the Yucatán Peninsula showing the location of the 21 study sites. More detailed descriptions of sites 1–9 can be found in Tramer (1974), sites 10–15 in Waide (1978), and sites 16–21 in Emlen (in prep.).

Site 1. Boulevard Paseo de Montejo, Mérida, Yucatán.

Site 2. Parque los Americas, Mérida.

Site 3. Grounds of the Hotel Mayaland, Chichen Itza.

Site 4. Abandoned sisal field with thorny shrubs and grasses less than 1 m tall, Mérida.

Site 5. Mowed lawn with shrubby undergrowth and young trees, Uxmal.

Site 6. Low thicket with low weeds near mangrove-lined bay, Progreso.

Sites 7–9. Undisturbed subevergreen forest with 9-m canopy. Site 7, Dzibilchaltun; Site 8, Uxmal; Site 9, highway 269 5 km south of Uman.

Sites 10–12. Old fields east of ruins of Becan, Campeche; Site 10, abandoned for 6 months; Site 11, for 2 yr; Site 13, for 5 yr.

Sites 13–15. Medium subevergreen forest, slightly disturbed; canopy 10–12 m; Site 13, ruins of Becan; Site 14, ruins of Chicanna; Site 15, 22 km south of village of Xpujil, Campeche.

Sites 16–21. Low to medium subevergreen forest; Site 16, southwest quadrant of Isla Cozumel; Site 17, 3 km south of Cancun; Site 18, 4 km south of Akumal; Site 19, 2 km north of Felipe Carillo Puerto; Site 20, 5 km west of Chetumal;

Site 21, Tikal, Guatemala.

Robert B. Waide

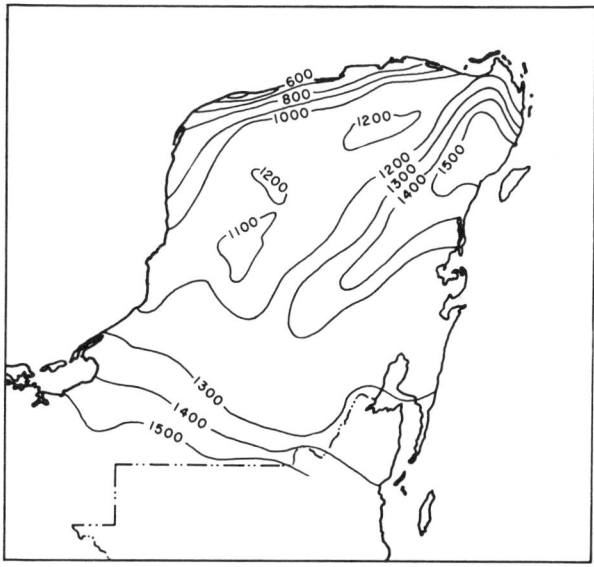

Figure 2. Distribution of rainfall in the Yucatán Peninsula. Solid lines are isohyets, rainfall in mm/yr (From Garcia 1965).

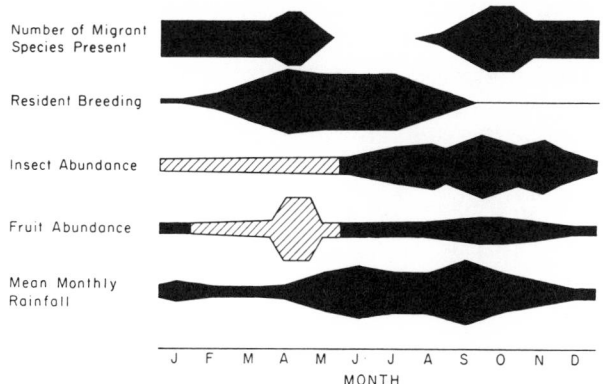

Figure 3. The phenology of rainfall, migration, breeding, and fruit and insect abundance in southeastern Campeche. The thickness of the horizontal bars in a given month is proportional to the mean monthly rainfall, the number of migrant species present or resident species breeding, and the abundance of fruit or insects. Fruit and insect abundance from February through May (hatched areas) are based on qualitative observations and values from the literature (Janzen 1967). At other times of the year, fruit and insect abundance are estimated from data collected at Sites 13 and 14. The mean monthly rainfall is based on 19 years of records from Zoh Laguna, Campeche. Breeding phenology is based on data from Paynter (1955a, b), Storer (1961), Klaas (1968) and personal observation, and migration records are from Paynter (1955a) and personal observation.

Figure 3 summarizes the phenology of bird populations and resources and the distribution of rainfall over the year at Zoh Laguna, about 10 km northeast of Sites 10–13. Migrant birds are present on the peninsula from early August through the end of April. The breeding season of resident birds overlaps with migrant presence in March and April, but most of the breeding that occurs during this period is by hummingbirds, pigeons, doves, and birds of prey, groups which interact minimally with winter residents. There is an abrupt cessation of breeding in August coinciding with the return of migrants (Waide in prep.).

Estimates of seasonal fruit and insect abundance (figure 3) were obtained at Sites 13 and 14 during 1974 and 1975 (Waide in prep.). A small fruiting peak occurred towards the end of the wet season (October–November). Although data for the latter part of the dry season are not available from Campeche, a larger fruiting peak in February–May may be inferred from information from other Central American dry forest sites (Janzen 1967). Insect abundance (determined by sweep and litter samples) was tied to rainfall, reaching its highest level in the middle of the rainy season (August–September) and trailing off in December. Thus, the period from December to February when winter residents are common is the period of lowest food supply. Although this model of food abundance is based on data from only two locations, a similar rainfall pattern holds throughout the peninsula and

there is no reason to suppose that the seasonality of fruit and insects is very different in any of the study sites.

Results and Discussion

Relative Abundance of Winter Residents

COMPARISON WITH OTHER LOCATIONS

The proportion of winter residents on study sites in the Yucatán Peninsula (mean, 27 percent; table 1) is much higher than values reported for other locations in Central and South America (10–15 percent in Colombia, Miller 1963; less than 10 percent in Panama, Karr 1976; 0–22 percent in Colombia, Orejuela et al this volume; 6 percent on Barro Colorado Island, Willis this volume), is comparable to values from Jamaica (30 percent, Lack and Lack 1972), and somewhat less than figures from the northern Bahama Islands and Florida (46 percent and 69 percent, respectively, Emlen this volume). One explanation for such a distribution might be that the increased cost of migrating longer distances forces migrants to winter as near as possible to their breeding ground (Willis 1966; Karr 1976). The fact that some species migrate

Table 1. Number and percentages of migrant and resident individuals and species from 21 study sites

Sample type and date[1]	PR[2]/km²	M[3]/km²	Percentage M	Resident species	Migrant species	Percentage migrant species
1. 40 a. plot[4] Dec–Jan 1972–73	3,307	209	6	20	12	38
2. 6 a. plot ” ”	4,856	535	10	10	5	33
3. 6 a. plot ” ”	2,875	548	16	17	4	19
4. 40 a. plot ” ”	515	25	5	14	2	13
5. 6 a. plot ” ”	3,539	617	15	14	4	22
6. ” ” ” ”	1,521	47	3	13	1	7
7. ” ” ” ”	2,387	165	6	18	2	10
8. ” ” ” ”	1,399	534	28	15	7	32
9. ” ” ” ”	1,717	303	15	15	6	29
10. Mist net Apr 1973	—	—	55	18	8	31
11. Mist net Apr 1973	—	—	57	12	11	48
12. Mist net Apr 1973	—	—	51	27	15	36
13a. Mist net Feb 1973	—	—	48	11	12	52
b. Mist net Dec 1974	—	—	50	15	11	42
c. Transect Mar 1973	366	360	50	33	13	28
d. Transect May 1973	160	—	0	20	0	—
14. Mist net Dec 1974	—	—	34	18	12	40
15a. Mist net Mar 1973	—	—	32	22	10	31
b. Transect Mar 1973	184	230	56	30	11	27
16. Transect Mar 1977	1,613	250	12	26	13	33
17. ” ” ”	540	239	31	29	8	22
18. ” ” ”	403	179	31	29	8	22
19. ” ” ”	343	283	45	28	7	20
20. ” ” ”	399	408	51	24	8	25
21. ” ” ”	419	53	11	39	4	9

[1] Descriptions of the sites can be found in the legend for figure 1.

[2] PR = permanent resident individuals.

[3] M = migrant individuals.

[4] Values for sites 1–9 were calculated from data in Tramer (1974). Because we follow Paynter (1955) in calling all individuals of *Polioptila caerulea* residents rather than migrants, our values may differ slightly from Tramer's.

over seemingly suitable areas in Central America to winter in South America indicates that other factors must also be operating.

COMPARISON AMONG PENINSULAR SITES

The proportion of migrant birds is least in the samples from the northwest part of the peninsula and increases towards wetter and less heavily populated areas in the south and east (table 1). In Tramer's samples (1–9), among which rainfall is relatively constant, the relative abundance of migrants is greatest in those sites (3, 5, 8, 9) that are distant from the urban center of Mérida (Sites 1, 2 and 4) regardless of the amount of distur-

bance in the site. This finding lends support to the suggestion that migrants are better adapted to using the mosaics of second growth and mature forest that occur in sparsely populated areas than they are to the large cleared areas that are the result of intensive agriculture and urbanization (Morton, quoted in Karr 1976).

Two exceptions to the southeasterly trend of increasing proportions of migrants are seen in the samples from Isla Cozumel (16) and Tikal (21). The low value from Tikal may reflect the beginning of a dropoff in migrant abundance correlated with the increased distance from the breeding ground or a change in the

Robert B. Waide

dominant vegetation type from deciduous to evergreen forest. Lacking further surveys from other evergreen forest sites, we are unable to evaluate these speculations. The low proportion of migrants in the Cozumel sample is interesting because previous workers have found migrants to be relatively abundant on islands (MacArthur et al 1972; Lack and Lack 1972). Actually, the absolute density of migrants on Cozumel is similar to densities from mainland Sites 17–20, and the low proportional representation of migrants on the island is the result of a resident density about four times that of the mainland (Emlen in prep.). Hence, it appears that insularity has no effect on the density of wintering migrants in this case.

COMPARISON BETWEEN YEARS

Since few data on changes in migrant abundance from year to year are available in the literature, it is interesting to note that mist-net samples from site 13 for February 1973 and December 1974 are very similar in the proportion of migrant individuals (48 vs 50 percent) and the number of migrant species (13 vs 11). There appears to be little seasonal or annual change in abundance in this site, but insufficient data exist from other sites in the peninsula to make generalizations. The importance of the Yucatán Peninsula in the migratory patterns of many species suggests that such data would be extremely valuable in furthering our knowledge of migrant species.

Population Densities of Migrant Birds

Table 2 gives the population densities of migrants at the sites sampled by the count-X detectability method together with general information on the distribution and habitat preference of migrants in the peninsula (taken from Paynter 1955a unless otherwise indicated). In most cases, common migrant species are widespread geographically throughout the peninsula, but they may be restricted to particular habitat types at a given location. A few species (*Dendroica magnolia, D. virens, Oporornis formosus, Wilsonia citrina*) are more common in wetter southern forests than in the dry forests of the state of Yucatán. Several species (*Sphyrapicus varius, Dendroica coronata, D. dominica*) were common in very disturbed habitats in the northern part of the Peninsula (Tramer 1974), but did not occur in other areas.

Comparison of Census Techniques

Differences in sampling methods prevent direct comparison of population densities among all study sites (table 1), but the proportion of migrants in each sample, the value of major interest in this study, should be relatively unaffected by technique (but see discus-

sion on mist nets below). The discrepancy in recorded densities between Sites 1–9 (plot counts) and Sites 13c, 13d, 15b, and 16–21 (sampled by the count-X detectability method) we attribute partly to the small size of Tramer's plots (6 acres in most cases) and partly to differences in census methods.

Sites 13 and 15 were sampled both by mist nets and the count-X detectability method. The number of migrant species detected by the two sampling methods was about equal, but more resident species were found by the count-X detectability method. This indicates that, compared to migrants, a relatively low proportion of resident species frequents the forest understory where the mist nets were placed. Since migrants are by no means restricted to lower levels of the forest, the data for these two sites suggest that residents may exhibit more vertical stratification than migrants. This suggestion is further supported by the high proportion of migrant species that were detected by both sampling techniques. In Site 13, 44 percent of the migrant species recorded were detected by both methods compared with 26 percent of the resident species. The corresponding figures for Site 15 were 62 percent of migrant species and 33 percent of residents.

Conclusion

The preceding discussion suggests that, in the communities considered here, mist-net and transect techniques are biased to favor understory and canopy subsets of the avifauna, respectively. Values for migrant species richness are similar regardless of census technique, but resident species lists are apparently more completely determined with transect counts. Since the proportion of migrant individuals in Site 15 is considerably greater in the transect sample than in the mist-net sample, migrant abundance may be underestimated by mist netting. Some migrant species may be sampled more effectively by mist nets, others by transect counts. For example, *Oporornis formosus* composed 26 percent of the migrant captures in Site 15 and only 2 percent of the observations. *Dendroica virens*, on the other hand, was more common in the transect census (25 percent); none were caught in mist nets. These results suggest that accurate population estimates of migrants in dense tropical forest require the use of both mist nets and visual counts, a conclusion previously advanced by Terborgh and Weske (1969) with respect to resident birds.

Acknowledgments

The senior author was supported in the field by a National Science Foundation Doctoral Dissertation Research Grant (No. GB-43852). The National Geographic Society, the Frank M. Chapman Memorial

Table 2. Abundance of migrants in Yucatán Peninsula sites sampled by the count-X detectability method[1]

Species[2]	13	15	16	17	18	19	20	21	
Empidonax spp.	21.1	9.0	3.6	0.0	11.7	6.8	8.1	0.0	Mostly *E. minimus*; more common in open habitats than in forest; widespread in peninsula.
Dumetella carolinensis	2.8	1.2	7.1	5.3	0.0	0.0	16.1	0.0	Common in thickets and old fields throughout the peninsula; more rarely in deciduous forest.
Catharus mustelina	0.0	0.0	9.5	8.3	+[3]	0.0	0.0	0.0	Common in both deciduous and rain forest. More abundant in mist net than transect samples (Waide, in prep.).
Vireo griseus	10.6	12.8	7.1	26.3	29.2	6.8	24.2	0.0	Common in both old fields and deciduous forest in Quintana Roo; apparently less abundant in Yucatán (Tramer 1974).
V. flavifrons	0.0	0.0	0.0	+	5.8	0.0	0.0	0.0	Uncommon winter resident throughout peninsula.
V. olivaceous	0.0	0.0	0.0	0.0	0.0	0.0	0.0	6.7	Transient throughout Peninsula in both spring and fall.
Mniotilta varia	23.8	49.4	24.0	64.3	15.6	45.5	64.5	0.0	Abundant in forest throughout the peninsula.
Protonotaria citrea	0.0	0.0	0.0	0.0	+	0.0	0.0	0.0	Transient and rare winter resident throughout the peninsula.
Helmitheros vermivorus	0.0	4.9	9.5	0.0	0.0	0.0	0.0	0.0	Uncommon winter resident in both deciduous and rain forest.
Vermivora pinus	6.3	0.0	0.0	0.0	0.0	0.0	0.0	0.0	Rare winter resident throughout peninsula.
Parula americana	0.0	1.5	5.0	0.0	15.6	0.0	0.0	0.0	Fairly common winter resident throughout peninsula; occasionally occurs in disturbed habitats (Tramer 1974).
Dendroica magnolia	71.4	65.1	38.0	42.9	39.1	36.4	150.5	27.3	Abundant in forests and old fields in southern part of peninsula; somewhat less common in north.
D. virens	60.8	56.1	19.0	14.3	31.3	27.3	32.2	0.0	Common in forests throughout, but more abundant in south and central parts of the peninsula.
D. dominica	0.0	0.0	5.0	0.0	0.0	0.0	0.0	0.0	Common in the vicinity of dwellings, especially in Yucatán; rare elsewhere.
Seiurus aurocapillus	0.0	0.0	11.0	0.0	0.0	0.0	0.0	13.3	Common in forest throughout the peninsula; occasionally in old fields (Waide 1978).
Oporornis formosus	1.4	3.6	0.0	0.0	0.0	0.0	0.0	0.0	Common in undergrowth of both deciduous and rain forest in southern part of peninsula; rarely seen (Waide 1978).
Icteria virens	1.7	0.0	0.0	0.0	0.0	0.0	0.0	0.0	Uncommon winter resident in second growth.
Wilsonia citrina	0.0	5.4	8.3	37.5	18.5	43.7	44.9	5.6	Forest and edge throughout, more common in south and perhaps near coast.
Setophaga ruticilla	19.4	18.0	64.0	3.6	0.0	47.4	48.4	0.0	Locally common in forest and edge throughout.
Unidentified Warblers	0.0	0.0	38.0	36.8	11.7	68.5	24.2	0.0	
Piranga rubra	5.3	0.0	0.0	14.3	0.0	0.0	0.0	0.0	Uncommon in second growth throughout (this study).
Pheucticus ludovicianus	+	0.0	0.0	0.0	0.0	0.0	0.0	0.0	Uncommon in second growth throughout.
Passerina cyanea	137.4	0.0	0.0	0.0	0.0	0.0	0.0	0.0	Extremely abundant in old fields, thickets, and heavily disturbed forests throughout.

[1] All sites were areas of low to medium subevergreen forest. Values are in individuals/km.[2] Sites 13 and 15 were sampled in Mar 1973 and all other sites in Mar 1977. Habitat information is from Paynter (1955) unless otherwise noted.

[2] Paynter (1955) records 141 species as transients or winter residents in the states of Yucatán, Campeche, and Quintana Roo. Information on migrant species not treated in this paper may be found in Tramer (1974) and Waide (1978), as well as Paynter.

[3] + sign = present but rare.

Fund, the Marsh Fund of the National Academy of Sciences, Sigma Xi, and the Davis Fund of the Department of Zoology, University of Wisconsin, also provided support. The senior author would like to thank Arquiologico Norberto Gonzalez C., Director of the Southeast Regional Center of the Instituto Nacional de Antropologia y Historia for permission to use the facilities of the Institute. Cheryl Hughes prepared the illustrations.

Literature Cited

Emlen, John T.
1971. Population densities of birds derived from transect counts. Auk 88:323–42.

Garcia, E.
1965. Distribución de la precipitación en la República Mexicana. Publicaciones del Instituto de Geografia de la Universidad Nacional de Mexico. Vol. 1.

Janzen, D. H.
1967 Synchronization of sexual reproduction of trees within the dry season in Central America. Evol. 21: 620–37.

Karr, J.
1976. On the relative abundances of migrants from the North Temperate Zone in tropical habitats. Wils. Bull. 88:433–58.

Klaas, E. E.
1968. Summer birds from the Yucatán Peninsula, Mexico. Univ. of Kansas Publ. 17:579–611.

Lack, D., and P. Lack.
1972. Wintering warblers in Jamaica. Living Bird 11:129–53.

MacArthur, R., J. Diamond, and J. Karr.
1972. Density compensation in island faunas. Ecol. 53:330–42.

MacArthur, R. H., and A. T. MacArthur.
1974. On the use of mist nets for population studies of birds. Proc. Nat. Acad. Sci. 71:3230–33.

Miller, A. H.
1963. Seasonal activity and ecology of the avifauna of an American equatorial cloud forest. Univ. Calif. Publ. Zool. 66:1–78.

Paynter, R. A., Jr.
1953. Autumnal migrants on the Campeche Bank. Auk 70:338–49.

1955a. The ornithogeography of the Yucatán Peninsula. Bull. Peabody Mus. Nat. Hist. 9:1–347.

1955b. Additions to the ornithogeography of the Yucatán Peninsula. Peabody Mus. Postilla 22, 4 pp.

Storer, Robert W.
1961. Two collections of birds from Campeche, Mexico. Occ. Paper. of the Mus. Zool. Univ. Mich. No. 621, 20 pp.

Terborgh, J. W., and J. S. Weske.
1969. Colonization of secondary habitats by Peruvian birds. Ecol. 50:765–81.

Tramer, Elliot J.
1974. Proportions of wintering North American birds in disturbed and undisturbed dry tropical habitats. Condor 76:460–64.

Willis, E. O.
1966. The role of migrant birds at swarms of army ants. Living Bird 5:187–231.

MARIO A. RAMOS
DWAIN W. WARNER
Bell Museum of Natural History
University of Minnesota
Minneapolis, Minnesota 55455

Analysis of North American Subspecies of Migrant Birds Wintering in Los Tuxtlas, Southern Veracruz, Mexico

ABSTRACT

In this paper we presented data concerning the subspecific composition of some North American migrant birds wintering in the Tuxtla Mountains of Southern Veracruz, Mexico. Eight species are included. When more than one race or population was found wintering there, their relative abundances are given. Observations concerning habitat use are also included and compared with those in the literature. Some species were found to have eastern and western races wintering together, and others just had eastern or western representatives. We conclude that the wintering grounds play an important role in the evolutionary history of the bird species, and additional efforts should be made for their conservation.

RESÚMEN

En éste trabajo presentamos datos acerca de la composición subspecifica de algunas aves migratorias de Norte America que invernan en la region de los Tuxtlas al sur de Veracrúz, México. Ocho especies son incluídas y se dan datos acerca de la abundancia relativa cuando más de una subspecie o población de la misma especie se encontraron invernando juntas. Observaciones acerca del habitat y su uso son tambien incluídas y comparadas con la literatura. Encontramos que algunas especies tienen subespecies tanto del Este como del Oeste de Norte America invernando juntas, mientras que otras solo tienen de uno o del otro lado. Concluimos que las areas de invernación juegan un papel muy importante en la historia evolutiva de las especies de aves y por lo tanto mayores esfuerzos deben hacerse para su conservación.

Introduction

The ecology of tropical birds has received considerable attention in recent years. North American migrant birds, as part of the tropical community during many months of the year, have been included in some studies (see Karr 1976, for bibliography); most of these studies have focused on the impact of North American migrants on the tropical community studying the species as a whole. Only a few studies, most of them done in the Old World tropics (Salomonsen 1955; Moreau 1972; De Roo and Deheegher 1969; Dick et al 1976), have tried to get insight into the intraspecific composition of those species of migrant birds from temperate areas wintering in tropical areas. The purpose of this paper is to analyze the subspecific composition and habitat use of some North American populations of migrants species of birds wintering in the Tuxtla Mountains of Southern Veracruz, Mexico.

Definition of Terms

SUBSPECIES.

An aggregate of local populations of a species, inhabiting a geographic subdivision of the species, and differing taxonomically from other populations of the species (Mayr 1963:348).

WINTERING BIRDS.

Although a few populations are still going through early in November, most of the North American winter residents are already settled in our study area. However, for taxonomic purposes, we have considered wintering birds to be only those North American temperate breeding birds seen, heard, netted or collected between early December and late February. Nonmigratory movements by some species occur in winter due to storms, causing birds from the highlands (indigenous and migrant winter residents) to move temporarily to the lowlands (Ramos et al unpubl. data). Species included in this study are ones that show geographic variation and have at least one subspecies wintering there and of which adequate samples for subspecific identification were obtained.

Study Area.

Our study site, on the Gulf of Mexico side of the Tuxtla Mountains, was located at approximately 18° 30′ N 95° W, in a region of humid forest that is seasonally dry; and at altitudes of 0–180 m. Annual precipitation for the Tuxtla Mountains averages 250–400 cm (Soto-Esparza 1976) and falls primarily in a rainy season that last from early June to early November. From November to late February, rain falls irreg-

ularly, and it is usually associated with nortes. The driest months are March through May. The mean annual temperature for the Tuxtla Mountains varies from 18–26° (Soto-Esparza 1976). For a detailed summary of the geology and climatology of the region see Andrle (1966) and Lot-Helgueras (1976).

The forest is the Selva Alta Perennifolia of Pennington and Sarukhan (1968:9) where the forest is more than 30 m tall and dominant trees are: *Bernoullia flammea, Lonchocarpus cruentus, Vochysia hondurensis, Brosimum alicastrum, Ficus tecolutensis, Mortoniodendron guatemalense,* and *Ceiba pentandra.*

Most of our research was conducted at six sites: Areas 1, 2, and 3, were in Selva Alta Perennifolia with variants in their composition and structure, depending mostly on the topographic changes and in the different secondary forest communities found close by. Area 1 was located on the grounds of the Estacion de Biologia Tropical de Los Tuxtlas, Veracruz. Area 4 was in one- to two-year-old second growth with a flora consisting almost entirely of dense growths of *Colvolvulus* sp., *Solanum* sp., and *Piper* sp., with a height of 2–3 m. Area 5 of 2 hectares was located approximately 2 km north of the Estacion de Biologia Tropical de Los Tuxtlas. This was secondary growth about 4–5 m tall with *Phytolaca rivinoides, Cecropia obtusifolia, Trema micrantha, Robinsonella mirandae,* and *Papaya carica* as dominant species; old stalks of *Zea mays* were also present. Area 6 was the habitat along the road from our motel on the coast to the Catemaco road a distance of 2.5 km through grazed open pasture with sparse trees, some of which are remnants of primary forest and other trees which have been cultivated such as citrus. *Solanum amazonicum* and *Acacia* sp. were common shrubs here.

Materials and Methods

Our field work was carried out from August 1973 through May 1974, and from August 1974 through May 1975. Net hours exceeded 100,000 hours.

Some of the birds caught were banded with U.S. Fish and Wildlife Service bands and colored plastic leg bands and then released; others were preserved as museum specimens. Some birds were also shot. Data on weights, amount of fat (following the method described by Helms and Drury 1960), molt, plumage, and stomach contents were also taken. Age was determined by skull ossification or plumage characters. Notes were recorded on weather, avian activity, and numbers of all migrant species.

Specimens in the following museums were used for subspecific identification of our specimens: United States National Museum, American Museum of Natural History, Delaware Museum of Natural History, and Carnegie Museum of Natural History. Color com-

Mario A. Ramos

parisons and standard measurements were used in subspecific determinations.

Results

Eight species of birds fulfilled the criteria established in the introduction, and they are considered here. Data concerning distributions were taken from the A.O.U. Check-list (1957) and the Check-list of the Birds of Mexico (1957). The behavior and social systems of migrant birds wintering in our study area are discussed by Rappole (1976) and Rappole and Warner (this volume).

Species Accounts

Dumetella carolinensis (LINNAEUS).   COMMON CATBIRD

SPECIMENS EXAMINED: 11 ♂♂, 16 ♀♀.   Three subspecies have been described with their breeding ranges defined as follows: *D. c. carolinensis* (Linnaeus), from southern Canada and the northern and eastern part of the United States; *D. c. ruficrissa* Aldrich, from the western United States and southwestern Canada; and *D. c. meridianus* Burleigh, from the southeastern and central part of the United States. The A.O.U. Check-list (1957) and the Check-list of the Birds of Mexico (1957) considered the species as monotypic, as have most of the authors who referred to winter birds. The only analysis of wintering distribution of the three described races is that of Rand and Traylor (1949) who stated that the eastern population migrates to Florida, the Greater Antilles, and the southeastern part of Mexico; the central populations winters along the Gulf Coast from Mississippi to Texas; and the western population winters in the "southwestern states and western Mexico," but Phillips (1962:341) and Phillips et. al (1964) concluded that the species does not migrate to winter in the latter region.

We examined 65 specimens from the breeding grounds of the species, and we conclude that only two races should be recognized: *D. c. carolinensis* and *D. c. ruficrissa*, and the third race, *D. c. meridianus* is not separable from *D. c. carolinensis*. Using the same criteria we identified our wintering series as: 23 specimens of *D. c. carolinensis*, 3 specimens closest to *carolinensis*, and only 1 was identified as *ruficrissa*. Subspecific characters used were the color of the crissum and upper and underparts; no size differences are appreciable between the races.

HABITAT: Specimens were collected in thickets of vegetation in forest edge (12) or open pasture, second growth in different seral stages (11) and in primary rain forest (3 specimens), where, as Rappole (1976) has stated, it is spottily distributed as are its preferred thickets.

Winter weights varied markedly. One bird (Mex 7070) collected on January 25 at 1000 hr had little fat and weighed 34.8 g. At 1600 hr a second catbird, weighing 46.4 g and with heavy fat, was shot in the same bush.

Catharus ustulatus (NUTTALL).   SWAINSON'S THRUSH

SPECIMENS EXAMINED: 13 ♂♂, 2 ♀♀.   Six races have been described, based on the coloration of the upper parts, sides of the head, sides of the body and flanks, and the size of the spots on the chest. Their breeding range is as follows: *C. u. ustulatus* (Nuttall), from the Pacific Coast of western Canada and northwestern United States; *C. u. oedicus* Oberholser from California, southwestern Oregon north along the east slopes of the cascades to northern Washington; *C. u. incanus* Godfrey from the Yukon; *C. u. almae* Oberholser from the southern Rocky Mountains area; *C. u. swainsoni* (Tschudi) from eastern Alberta eastward to Newfoundland and south in the mountains to West Virginia; *C. u. clarescens* Burleigh and Peters from Newfoundland and Nova Scotia. The A.O.U. Check-list (1957) did not recognize *almae* and *oedicus*, and the Check-list of the Birds of Mexico (1957) only recognized *ustulatus* and *swainsoni*, while the last revision of the species (Bond 1963) recognized *ustulatus, oedicus, almae* and *swainsoni*.

The winter distribution is also complex: Paynter (1968), and Dickey and van Rossem (1938) have assigned some wintering Central American specimens to *swainsoni*, whereas Griscom (1932), Miller (1963) and Phillips (1970) doubt the identification of these specimens, and Phillips adds that closer study of them would fail to show this race as wintering in Central America.

We have examined 377 specimens from the breeding grounds of the species, and we conclude that the following races are recognizable: *C. u. ustulatus, C. u. oedicus, C. u. almae, C. u. swainsoni*, and two undescribed races, one breeding in the Queen Charlotte Islands in British Columbia, and the other in the Applachian Mountains. Using the same criteria, we identified our wintering birds as 12 belonging to *C. u. ustulatus* and the other 3 to the undescribed population from the Queen Charlotte Islands.

HABITAT: Mostly primary rain forest (nine specimens), old second growth and edges of forest and open pasture (six). In Honduras, Monroe (1968) found them in broad leafed forest and pine-oak associations, but more frequently in open rain forest and cloud forest.

There is a strong correlation between weather and the presence of these birds in the lowlands. They were trapped only during "nortes" and, after cold fronts had passed, the birds disappeared. Birds banded at this time were not netted again. They probably winter higher in the mountains where Wetmore (1943) and Lowery and Dalquest (1951) collected specimens during winter.

Vireo griseus (BODDAERT).   WHITE-EYED VIREO

SPECIMENS EXAMINED: 12 ♂♂, 6 ♀♀, 5 sex?   There are six described subspecies based on the greenish coloration of the back and the yellowish green coloration of the loral areas, sides, and flanks. They are: *Vireo g. griseus* (Boddaert) found along the coast of the southeastern part of the United States; *V. g. noveboracensis* (Gmelin) found in most of the interior and eastern United States; *V. g. maynardi* Brewster in coastal and insular Florida; *V. g. micrus* Nelson in southeastern Texas and eastern Mexico (Coahuila to Puebla and northern Veracruz), and *V. g. perquisitor* Nelson in northeastern Puebla and northcentral Veracruz.

We examined 25 specimens from the southeastern breeding grounds in the United States, and we agree with the criteria followed for separating the races. Based on these criteria, our wintering specimens were identified as follows: 18 of them are *V. g. noveboracensis* and the other 5 appear to be intermediate between *V. g. noveboracensis* and *V. g. griseus*.

HABITAT: They were collected in a variety of habitats, occurring high in the primary forest canopy to second growth in different seral stages, in isolated trees in open pasture, and in mangrove forest. Russell (1964) found them along forest edges, and Griscom (1932) found them abundant in the lowland forest of Quintana Roo.

Dendroica petechia (LINNAEUS).   YELLOW WARBLER

SPECIMENS EXAMINED: 11 ♂♂, 1 ♂?, 8 ♀♀   Eight subspecies of the *aestiva* group were described based on the coloration of the upper and underparts as well as the coloration and size of the breast streaking. They are *D. p. aestiva* (Gmelin) found in most of the eastern U.S. and southeastern Canada; *D. p. amnicola* Batchelder from Newfoundland west to the prairie provinces and north to Yukon and interior Alaska; *D. p. rubiginosa* (Pallas) from southern Alaska and western British Columbia; *D. p. morcomi* Coale (including *D. p. brewsteri* Grinnell) found in the Rocky Mountains and Great Basin area; *D. p. sonorana* Brewster, found from southern Nevada, most of Arizona, south to eastern Baja California, Sonora and Zacatecas; *D. p. dugesi* Coale from the central plateau in Mexico, and *D. p. ineditus* Phillips described from transient birds of the mountains of Tamaulipas. Parkes (1968) has recently expressed the possibility that *D. p. amnicola* may be a composite of two races, one restricted to the prairie provinces of Canada (with no name), and the other located in Newfoundland and adjacent areas. Our personal observations on this species indicate that probably the undescribed race mentioned by Parkes may be, in turn, a composite one, with one population restricted to the arctic part of Alaska, and the other restricted to the Northwestern Territories and prairie provinces.

The winter range of the subspecies, though outlined by the A.O.U. Check-list (1957) and the Check-list of the Birds of Mexico (1957), is not precisely known, the main problem being the worn plumage of the specimens collected during winter. This problem has been pointed out by Griscom (1932), Zimmer (1949), Loetscher (1955), and Miller et al (1957). For this reason our analysis of wintering birds has been restricted mostly to specimens collected in December and early January.

We have examined 383 specimens from the breeding grounds of the species, and we conclude that the following races should be recognized: *D. p. aestiva* (including *ineditus* Phillips), *D. p. amnicola*, *D. p. rubiginosa*, *D. p. morcomi* (including *brewsteri*), *D. p. sonorana*, *D. p. dugesi*, and the two undescribed populations from northcentral North America, pending further analysis and recognition of both as such. Using the same criteria we identified our specimens as follows: 9 specimens of *D. p. aestiva*, 10 specimens of *D. p. amnicola* (including the prairie provinces population), and only 2 specimens are *D. p. rubiginosa*.

HABITAT: most of the specimens were collected in open areas (usually open pasture) with dispersed trees and shrubs, others in second growth and forest edges. Monroe (1968) found them in scrub, second growth, forest edges, semiopen situations, and mangroves, being especially common in the vicinity of water and around human habitations.

Remarks: Recently, Morton (1976) has proposed a possible source of selection in dull immature Yellow Warblers in the wintering grounds. A few of his points merit some comments:

1) Morton (1976:423) said: "immature northern Yellow Warblers have acquired a dull, non-yellow plumage to avoid aggression by territorial Yellow Warblers. . ." Our personal observations indicate that some of the dull plumage birds hold territories in our study area, but the possibilities of separating adult females and immature birds in the field are very limited (Chapman, 1907). So they could be adult females or immature birds (males or females).

2) Morton (loc cit) said: "they (immature birds) have lost the bright yellow color that releases aggres-

sive behavior in territorial conspecifics. . .". But to our knowledge nobody has proved yet that the bright color of Yellow Warblers elicit aggression in the wintering grounds. Dull birds in our study area hold territories.

Seiurus aurocapillus (LINNAEUS).   OVENBIRD

SPECIMENS EXAMINED: 5 ♂♂, 4 ♀♀, 1 sex?   Four races have been described based on the coloration of the upper parts (including the crown) and flanks, and the amount, size, and coloration of the streaks on the breast. Their breeding range is as follows: *S. a. aurocapillus* (Linnaeus) found in most of Canada (except Newfoundland) and central and eastern United States; *S. a. cinereus* Miller from the Rocky Mountains and Great Basin area; *S. a. furvior* Batchelder from central and southern Newfoundland, and *S. a. canivirens* Burleigh and Duvall from the southeastern United States. This last race is not recognized by the A.O.U. Check-list (1957) or by the Check-list of the Birds of Mexico (1957).

We have examined 106 specimens from the breeding grounds of the species, and we conclude that the following races should be recognized: *S. a. aurocapillus* (including *canivirens*), *S. a. cinereus* and *S. a. furvior*. Following the same criteria, we identified our wintering birds as follows: 5 are *S. a. aurocapillus* and the other 5 have intermediate characteristics between *aurocapillus* and *furvior*.

HABITAT: we found them on the ground in primary and secondary rain forest.

Seiurus noveboracensis (GMELIN).   NORTHERN

WATERTHRUSH

SPECIMENS EXAMINED: 4 ♂♂, 1 ♂?, 2 ♀♀, 1 sex?   Four races have been described based on the coloration of the upper and underparts, and amount of streaking on the breast as follows: *S. n. noveboracensis* (Gmelin) found in the northeastern part of the United States and southern Canada; *S. n. notabilis* Ridgway from Ontario westward with the exception of British Columbia; *S. n. limnaeus* McCabe and Miller found in northwestern and central British Columbia; and *S. n. uliginosus* Burleigh and Peters found in Newfoundland. Eaton (1957) considered the species as monotypic.

We have examined 43 specimens from the breeding grounds of the species, and we concluded that only two races should be recognized: *S. n. noveboracensis* (including *uliginosus*) and *S. n. notabilis* (including *limnaeus*). Using the same criteria, we identified our wintering birds as 6 belonging to *notabilis* and two are intermediate between *notabilis* and *noveboracensis*.

HABITAT: our specimens were collected in old sec-

ondary forest, usually in fairly wet places and close to pools in forest streams. This species also frequents similar habitats in Honduras (Monroe 1968), El Salvador (Dickey and van Rossem 1938), and Panama (Eisenmann 1952).

Wilsonia pusilla (WILSON).   WILSON'S WARBLER

SPECIMENS EXAMINED: 25 ♂♂, 6 ♂♂?, 20 ♀♀, 2 ♀♀?   Three races have been described based on the coloration of the upper and lower parts as well as that of the loral area. They are: *W. p. pusilla* (Wilson) from the eastern part of the breeding range; *W. p. pileolata* (Pallas) found from the northwestern part of the range south to coastal and interior British Columbia, and *W. p. chryseola* Ridgway restricted to the coast and coast range (west of the Cascades and Sierra Nevada) from southern British Columbia south to southern California.

We have examined 48 specimens from the breeding grounds of the species, and they are classified correctly by geographic origin. Using the same criteria we identified our wintering specimens as *W. p. pusilla*, 14 of them; *W. p. pileolata*, 32 of them, and the other 7 are closer to *pileolata*.

HABITAT: This was one of the most widespread wintering warblers in our study area. It was found in primary rain forest at the canopy level, in second growth at diverse seral stages, and in isolated trees and shrubs in open pasture. They sometimes frequented mangroves. There does not seem to be habitat segregation between the races; individuals belonging to *pusilla* and *pileolata* were collected at the same time in the same tree.

Passerina ciris (LINNAEUS).   PAINTED BUNTING

SPECIMENS EXAMINED: 4 ♂♂, 1 sex? Banded: 3 ♂♂, 4 ♀♀   Two races have been described based on coloration and size. They are: *P. c. ciris* (Linnaeus) found from North Carolina to Florida and Louisiana; and *P. c. pallidor* Mearns found to the west to western Texas and eastern New Mexico south to northern Chihuahua and northern Coahuila. The wintering ground of the species has been described by Storer (1951): the southeastern population winters in Yucatán, and the western population winters in Mexico (except Yucatán) and Central America.

We examined 53 specimens from the breeding grounds of the species, and we concluded that both races should be recognized. Following this criteria we identified our wintering specimens as *P. c. pallidor*.

HABITAT: All our specimens but one (Mex 1899) were collected in a small area of 2-year-old second growth

Table 1. Summary of the races described[1]

Species	1	2	3	4
D. carolinensis	carolinensis (+ meridianus)	X	X	Eastern
	ruficrissa	X	X	Western
C. ustulatus	ustulatus	X	X	Western
	oedicus	X		
	almae (+ incanus)	X		
	swainsoni (+ clarescens)	X		
	Queen Charlotte Islands		X	Western
	Appalachian Mountains			
V. griseus	griseus	X	X	Southeastern
	noveboracensis	X	X	Interior
	bermudianus	X		
	maynardi	X		
	micrus	X		
	perquisitor	X		
D. petechia	aestiva (+ ineditus)	X	X	Eastern
	amnicola	X	X	Northeastern
	rubiginosa	X	X	Northwestern
	morcomi (+ brewsteri)	X		
	sonorana	X		
	dugesi	X		
	Prairie Provinces		X	Northcentral
	Arctic Alaska			
S. aurocapillus	aurocapillus	X	X	Eastern
	cinereus	X		
	furvior	X	?	Eastern
S. noveboracensis	noveboracensis (+ uliginosis)	X	?	Eastern
	notabilis (+ limnaeus)	X	X	Western
Wilsonia pusilla	pusilla	X	X	Eastern
	pileolata	X	X	Northcentral
	chryseola	X		
P. ciris	ciris	X		
	pallidor	X	X	Western

[1] Species included in this paper = 1; races recognized by us = 2; races wintering in our study areas = 3; and their U.S. geographical breeding origins = 4.

and edge of 10-year-old second growth. The other one was collected at the edge of primary forest and a corn field.

Discussion

The subspecific composition of the eight species of birds studied is variable. There are species having just one race wintering in our study area (e.g. *Passerina ciris*), or two races present at the same time (e.g. *Dumetella carolinensis*, *Vireo griseus*, *Seiurus aurocapillus*, *Seiurus noveboracensis*, and *Wilsonia pusilla*), or even three or more races (e.g., *Dendroica petechia*). (See table 1.)

The breeding origin is also variable. If we divide North America north of Mexico in an eastern and western part at the 100th meridian, we have species with wintering races in our study area from the eastern part of the range, *Vireo griseus* and *Seiurus aurocapillus*; one that has one western race, *Passerina ciris*, and species having eastern and western races at the same time, *Dumetella carolinensis*, *Dendroica petechia*, *Seiurus noveboracensis*, and *Wilsonia pusilla* (table 1).

Salomonsen (1955) has shown that the evolutionary history of some species of birds is greatly affected by the influence of selective forces in the wintering grounds. Populations of birds of the same species wintering together in the same area, which he calls synhiemic populations, are apparently subject to the influences of the same environment during the winter months, whereas populations of the same species wintering in separate areas ("allohiemic populations") are subject to different environmental conditions during the same period of time. Then, the selective forces of the environment acting in synhiemic populations in the wintering grounds will have almost no effect on racial determination and the adaptive variation of the differences between them will arise mainly from selective influences on the different breeding grounds. In allohiemic wintering populations, selection pressures will probably be different because the different populations are isolated in different areas with different environmental conditions for longer periods of time. The wintering grounds in these groups would thus be expected to have as much or more influence on the evolutionary history of the species as a whole than the breeding grounds, probably accelerating speciation. If the wintering grounds are of this much importance for the species of birds, a greater effort should be made for the preservation of these areas. Many of these species of North American migrants winter in tropical areas, and these areas are disappearing at incredible rates and with them, all the species that inhabit them. This may lead to some extermination of selective allohiemic populations of the birds wintering there. We cannot agree with the points stressed by some in a past symposium (Buechner and Buechner 1970) that migrant birds can go elsewhere if the habitat is destroyed. Rappole (1974, 1976) and Rappole and Warner (this volume) give evidence supporting the fact that North American migrant birds are an integral part of the tropical community, and any destruction of these areas can be expected to cause destruction of the migrant bird populations.

Acknowledgments

Ramos' studies were supported by the Welder Wildlife Foundation of Sinton, Texas. We thank the late Dr.

Mario A. Ramos

Clarence Cottam, Mr. W. C. Glazener, Dr. Eric C. Bolen, and the Trustees for their support. Additional support for Ramos to visit museums was given by the Chapman Memorial Foundation of the American Museum of Natural History, and by the Dayton Fund of the Bell Museum of Natural History, University of Minnesota. Warner received support from the University of Minnesota Office of International Programs.

We thank the authorities of the Departamento de Fauna Silvestre of Mexico City for issuing us the necessary permits for our work; the authorities of the Estacion de Biologia Tropical de "Los Tuxtlas" for permission to use their facilities, and the authorities of the following museums: U.S. National Museum of Natural History, American Museum of Natural History, Delaware Museum of Natural History, and the Carnegie Museum of Natural History.

Field work assistance was given by Dr. John H. Rappole, Richard Oehlenschlager, Bruce Fall, Angel Toto, Christopher Barkan, Robert Zink, Isabel Castillo, and the personal of the Estacion de Biologia Tropical de "Los Tuxtlas."

Helpful criticisms during the subspecific identification and reading of the manuscript were given by Drs. Allan R. Phillips, John W. Aldrich, Kenneth C. Parkes, and John H. Rappole.

Our thanks also to Isabel Castillo de Ramos and Giannina Castillo Cadena for undertaking the endless task of typing the manuscript.

Literature Cited

American Ornithologists Union.
1957. *Check-list of North American Birds.* 5th ed. Baltimore, Md: A.O.U., 691 pp.

Andrle, F. F.
1954. A Biogeographical investigation of the Sierra de Tuxtla in Veracruz, Mexico. Ph.D. thesis, Louisiana State Univ., Baton Rouge, 236 p.

Bond, G. M.
1963. Geographical variation in the thrush *Hylocichla ustulata.* Proc. U. S. Nat. Mus. No. 3471, 114:373–87.
1966. North American migrants in the Sierra de Tuxtla of southern Veracruz, Mexico. Condor 68:177–84.

Buechner, H. K. and J. H. Beuchner
1970. The avifauna of northern Latin America: a symposium held at the Smithsonian Institution, 13–15 April 1966. Smithsonian Contributions to Zoology, 26:1–119.

Chapman, F.
1907. *The Warblers of North America.* New York: Appleton.

De Roo, A. and J. Deheegher
1969. Ecology of the Great Reed-Warbler, *Acrocephalus arundinaceus* (Linnaeus) wintering in the southern Congo Savanna. Gerfaut 59(2):260–75.

Dick, W. A. J.
1976. Distribution and geographical origins of Knots *Calidris canutus* wintering in Europe and Africa. Ardea, 64(1–2):22–47.

Dickey, D. R. and J. van Rossem
1938. The birds of El Salvador. Field Mus. Nat. Hist., Zool. Ser., vol 23, 609 pp.

Eaton, S.
1957. Geographic variation in *Seiurus noveboracensis* Auk, 74: 229–39.

Eisenmann, E.
1952. Annotated list of birds of Barro Colorado Island, Panama, Canal Zone. Smithsonian Misc. Coll., vol. 117. no. 5.

Griscom, L.
1932. The distribution of bird life in Guatemala. Bull. Amer. Mus. Nat. Hist., vol. 64.

Helms, C. W. and W. G. Drury
1960. Winter and migratory weight and fat field studies of some North American buntings. Bird-Banding, 31: 1–40.

Loetscher, F. W.
1955. North American migrants in the State of Veracruz, Mexico: a summary. Auk, 72:14–54.

Lot-Helgueras, A.
1976. La Estación de Biológia tropical de los Tuxtlas: pasado, presente y futuro. pp:31–51, In *Investigaciones sobre la regeneracion de Selvas Atlas en Veracruz, Mexico,* ed. A. Gomez-Pompa, Cecsa, Mexico: 679 pp.

Mayr, E.
1963. *Animal species and Evolution.* Cambridge, Mass.: Belknap Press, Harvard Univ., 797 pp.

Miller, A. H.
1963. Seasonal activity and ecology of the avifauna of an American equatorial cloud forest. Univ. Calif. Publ. Zool. 66:1–78.

Miller, A. H., H. Friedmann, Ludlow Griscom, and R. T. Moore
1957. Distributional Checklist of the birds of Mexico. Part II. Pacific Coast Avif. 33, 436 pp.

Monroe, B. L.
1968. A Distributional survey of the birds of Honduras. Amer. Ornithol. Union Monogr. 7.

Moreau, R. E.
1972. The Palearctic-African bird migration system. New York, London: Academic Press, 384 pp.

Morton, E. S.
1976. The adaptive significance of dull coloration in Yellow Warblers. Condor 78(3):423.

Parkes, K. C.
1968. Some bird records from western Pennsylvania. Wils. Bull., 80(1):100–2.

Paynter, R. A., Jr.
1955.   The Ornithogeography of the Yucatan Penninsula. Bull. Peabody Mus. Nat. Hist. 9.

Pennington, T. D. and J. Sarukhan
1968.   Arboles tropicales de Mexico. Inst. Nac. Invest. Forestales. Mexico.

Phillips, A. R.
1962.   Notas sistemáticas sobre aves mexicanas. II. An. Inst. Biol. Univ. Nac. Auton. Mex. 33(1–2):331–72.

1970.   (Review of) A Distributional survey of the birds of Honduras. In A.O.U. Ornithol. Monogr. 7, ed. Burt L. Monroe, Auk, 87(2):381–84.

1975.   Why neglect the difficult? Western Birds, 6(3):69–86.

Phillips, A. R., J. Marshall, and G. Monson
1964.   *The Birds of Arizona.* Tucson, Ariz.: Univ. Arizona Press.

Rand, A. L. and M. A. Traylor
1949.   Variation in *Dumetella carolinensis.* Auk 66:25–28.

Rappole, J. H.
1974.   Migrants and space: the wintering grounds as limiting factors. Bull. Texas Ornithol Soc., 7:2–4.

1976.   A study of evolutionary tactics in populations of solitary avian migrants. Ph. D. thesis, Univ. Minn., Minneapolis.

Russell, S. M.
1964.   A Distributional study of the birds of British Honduras. A.O.U. Ornithol. Monogr. 1.

Salomonsen, F.
1955.   The evolutionary significance of bird migration. Dan. Biol. Medd. 22(6):1–62.

Soto-Esparza, M.
1976.   Algunos aspectos climáticos de la región de los Tuxtlas, Veracruz. In *Investigaciones sobre la regeneracion de Selvas Atlas en Veracruz, Mexico.* ed. A. Gomez-Pompa, pp. 70–84. CECSA, Mexico. 676 p.

Storer, R. W.
1951.   Variation in the Painted Bunting (*Passerina ciris*) with special reference to wintering populations. Occ. Pap. Univ. Mich. Mus. Zool. 532, 12 pp.

Van Tyne, J.
1935.   The birds of southern Peten, Guatemala. Publ. Mus. Zool. Univ. Mich. 27, 46 pp.

Wetmore, A.
1943.   The birds of southern Veracruz, Mexico. Proc. U. S. Natl. Mus., 93:215–340.

Zimmer, J. T.
1949.   Studies of Peruvian birds. No. 54. Families Catamblyrhynchidae and Parulidae. Amer. Mus. Novitates. No. 1428, 59 pp.

Mario A. Ramos

RICHARD L. HUTTO
Department of Biology
University of California
Los Angeles, California 90024

Winter Habitat Distribution of Migratory Land Birds in Western Mexico, with Special Reference to Small Foliage-Gleaning Insectivores

ABSTRACT

Winter censuses were conducted in 26 sites among 13 habitat types over an elevational gradient in western Mexico. The numbers and proportions of migratory species and individuals varied considerably between habitats. There are significant inverse correlations between numbers or proportions of migrants and elevation, but more important differences between sites (particularly lowland sites) due to the level of human disturbance. Disturbed lowland sites supported greater densities (to 150/ha) and proportions (to 83 percent) of migrants than those reported by other researchers for African or Neotropical sites. Furthermore, one subset of the total migratory bird pool—small foliage-gleaning insectivores—comprised 100 percent of the wintering birds within that guild in 4 sites and averaged 95 percent over 14 lowland sites.

Within the guild of small foliage-gleaners, there seems to be little species turnover between habitats among the migrants. With the exception of only one pair of species, migrants occupy all potentially utilizable habitats and avoid those habitats which are inappropriate for reasons apparently unassociated with migrant competitors.

Although migrants appear not to influence the choice of habitats within which other migrants winter, residents and migrants seem to avoid one another in at least two respects. The small migrant and resident foliage gleaners show a degree of between-habitat avoidance since there is an inverse correlation between the numbers of migrants and residents over the 13 habitat types ($r = -.43$, $P < .05$). This same guild also shows within-habitat avoidance in 2 mature lowland habitats (mangroves and tropical evergreen forests); here the migrants are most abundant where roads, edges, or other clearings exist while the residents are least abundant in these locations. Resident bird density increases and migrant bird density decreases upon entering the interiors of these forests.

The situation is somewhat different in highland coniferous forests since an edge effect is absent, and the small insectivores join with the residents in the interior of the forests to form mixed-species flocks which are larger and more diverse than any I have seen reported for other parts of the world. As many as 30 species (more usually 17–20) and two to four times as many individuals participate in these flocks which are composed of about 30 percent migrants, on average.

After the departure of migrants during the northern summer, there is, in the small foliage-gleaner guild, an apparent ecological vacuum which remains unfilled by resident species in the lowlands; the same areas which supported 64 individuals/ha in winter harbored only 1.7 individuals/ha in summer. This "vacuum" is filled rather more effectively in the highland habitats where there may actually be more individuals/ha in summer than winter. This difference between lowland and highland habitats can be explained in part by different seasonal changes in insect densities. There is a general correspondence between the summer-to-winter changes in insect density within seven habitat types (as determined from sticky plaques) and summer-to-winter changes in the density of small foliage-gleaning insectivores. Additional non-food-related factors such as an overdispersion of nests due to predation may also contribute to the apparent underutilization of food by lowland insectivores after the departure of migrants.

Richard L. Hutto

Introduction

Very few studies of wintering migratory birds have been conducted as yet, and even fewer studies refer to migrants and their ecological role in the tropics. Many of the existing studies are limited to very small or specialized groups of migrants such as those which utilize ant raids (Willis 1966), fruiting trees (Leck 1972) or the "mist-nettable" forest understory (Britton 1974; Karr 1976) and the generality of their results is difficult to establish at this time.

Ulfstrand (1973) and Ulfstrand and Alerstam (1977) point out the lack of quantitative information related to the geographic distribution of palaearctic migrants in winter, and the situation is not much better for some parts of the New World tropics. Concerning the winter distribution of western North American migrants, little more is known than the fact that they are geographically distinct from other temperate migrants and generally occupy a relatively narrow portion of western Mexico from southern Sonora south to Guatemala (Cooke 1904; A.O.U. Check-list of North American Birds 1957; Fitzpatrick this volume). Distributional information that *is* available is misleading at times, possibly as a result of range definitions based on single records for some states. There are virtually no published studies on any part of the group of Western migrants in winter.

This study provides information on the winter habitat distributions and densities of migrant and resident land birds in western Mexico. Special emphasis was placed on one subgroup, the guild (Root 1967) of small foliage-gleaning insectivores. From the habitat distributions of migrants I attempt to answer the following questions: 1) Why do some habitats support greater densities of migrants than others? 2) How does human disturbance affect the migrant? 3) How do migrants affect one another's distributions? and 4) To what extent do the results from western Mexico appear to be unique? With additional information on the distribution of resident birds I address the following questions: 1) What is the effect of migrants on residents (and vice versa)? 2) Is the apparent effect of migrants on residents greatest where the density of migrants is greatest? 3) How, if at all, do the distributions and densities of residents in the various habitat types change during the summer absence of migrants?

Study Sites

A series of 13 habitat types, or vegetation zones, were studied. Twenty-six study sites were visited from January through mid-March 1975 and 1976, and several of these plus six additional sites were visited during late June through July 1975 and 1976. Below I give a brief description of each habitat type and list the locations and visitation dates of study sites belonging to each. All sites are (or have been) disturbed to some degree, but several sites are influenced by humans to the extent that the structure is noticeably altered and these are referred to here as "disturbed" sites. Elevations of the sites are listed in tables 1 and 3.

I periodically make the distinction between "lowland" and "highland" habitats. Lowland habitats are those which occur at or very near sea level and consist of the first eight vegetation types given below. The remaining five habitats, from oak woodland upwards in elevation, are collectively referred to as the highlands.

Lowland Habitats

DRY WASH

These include the many washes throughout the lowlands which become inundated only during the heavy summer rainstorms. The vegetation is typically a mixture of thornscrub (including *Mimosa* and *Acacia* spp.) and tropical deciduous plants (including *Ficus* and *Caesalpinia* spp.) as well as riparian elements (particularly *Salix* spp.) which reach 25 m or more in height.

SITE 21: 70 km south of Barra de Navidad, Jalisco, 24–25 February 1975, 24 February 1976. This wash was large (70 m wide at places) and ran beneath a bridge marked "Puente las Adjuntas." Both sides of the wash were censused along the 1 km stretch west of the bridge.

RIPARIAN GALLERY FOREST

Schaldach (1963) applies this name to the forest along the permanent watercourses of the lowlands. Both sites in this vegetation zone consisted of streams no wider than 10 m and were shaded by the canopies of large (15 m) trees, mainly of the genera *Salix, Ficus* and *Enterolobium.* Both also ran alongside agricultural areas and, because of the proximity and attractiveness of these fields to birds, I consider the birds of both sites to be heavily influenced by this modification.

SITE 22: 1 km south of Colima, Colima, 2–4 March 1975.

SITE 23: 7–8 km north of Colima, on the road to Coauhtemoc at the Chiapa turnoff, 26 February 1975.

MANGROVES

Mangroves line the permanent coastal and inland

waterways and consist primarily of densely tangled *Rhizophora mangle*, *Avicennia nitida* and *Conocarpus* sp. The tallest mangroves were about 12 m in height

SITE 1A: 3 km east of San Blas, near the turnoff to Matanchen from Highway 54, 10–20 February 1976. The census area was a largely undisturbed, seasonally inundated lagoon.

SITE 1B: Located west of San Blas, along the Estero del Pozo, 19 January–20 February 1975; 10–15, 24–25 July 1975; 20 January–19 February 1976. Numerous small trails and clearings had been cut by local fishermen. This site is intermediate in the level of human disturbance between sites 1a and 32.

SITE 32: An extensively cut and cleared area located 2 km south of Highway 54 off the road to Matanchen, Nayarit, 11–19 February 1976. The site is characterized by numerous areas of standing water and an abundance of water birds. An elevated dirt road provided the census route.

PLANTATIONS

Under this heading I refer exclusively to coconut plantations which consist of uniformly spaced, introduced *Cocos nucifera* and a dense leguminous undergrowth. Plantations are, of course, the result of heavy human disturbance.

SITE 2: 1 km south of San Blas, and east of Calle H. Batallón, 19 January–20 February 1975; 10–15, 25 July 1975; 20 January–19 February 1976.

SECOND GROWTH

These sites are those heavily cut areas supporting growth of mangrove, plantation, and tropical deciduous elements such as *Cocos nucifera*, *Avicennia nitida*, *Ficus continifolia* and *Randia* sp. The average vegetation height was around 5 m, but ranged from herbaceous ground cover to 15 m. Both of the sites below were apparently abandoned coconut plantations, but *Cocos* were few in number. Both were heavily disturbed sites.

SITE 36: 2 km east of Barra de Navidad, 22–23 February 1976. This site was an area which had been prepared for a housing subdivision, with cobblestone streets in place, but with each "city block" covered with second growth vegetation.

SITE 39: 1 km south of San Blas and east of Calle H. Batallón, 20 January–19 February 1976; 12 March 1976. Part of this site was beginning to be used for construction of motels in the summer of 1976. A crisscross of cobblestone streets had been in place for a number of years.

TROPICAL EVERGREEN FOREST

Pesman (1962) describes this vegetation zone and considers it intermediate between rain forest and tropical deciduous forest habitats. The common genera are *Ficus*, *Bursera*, *Cecropia*, *Sabal*, *Acacia*, *Ceiba* and *Lonchocarpus*. The tallest trees are about 49 m in height.

SITE 4: 8 km east of San Blas (1 km north of Singayta), 19 January–20 February 1975; 10–15 July 1975; 20 January–19 February 1976. The census area was along a dirt road adjacent to the forest and was heavily disturbed by man and his domesticated livestock.

THORNSCRUB

This habitat is generally only 2–3 m in height and consists primarily of *Acacia*, *Mimosa*, *Caesalpinia* and *Prosopis*. *Lamairocereus* cacti are normally present as well.

SITE 5: 1 km east of La Salada, Colima, 25–26 February 1975. A small trail out of the east end of town led through relatively undisturbed thornscrub.

SITE 6: 240 km east of Guadalajara, Jalisco, on Highway 80, 24 February 1975. The census route was along a dirt road which led to a distant ranch. Grazing pressure was light in this habitat.

SITE 26: 4 km south of Urias, Sinaloa, within a large area which was at one time cleared for the construction of high voltage lines, 30 June–1 July 1976.

TROPICAL DECIDUOUS (SHORT TREE) FOREST

This habitat normally occurs above thornscrub habitats and includes *Acacia*, *Bombax*, *Bursera*, *Caesalpinia*, *Ficus*, *Lysoloma* and *Tabebuia* species. The forest is much taller (to 20 m) than the thornscrub and one can only rarely walk through this vegetation without having to cut a trail.

SITE 25: 10 km southeast of Alamos, Sonora, 1–2 July 1976. The census area was within the heavily grazed area above the Rio Cuchujaqui.

SITE 27: 3 km northeast of Mazatlan, Sinaloa, where large tracts of relatively undisturbed forest remain, 30 June–1 July 1976.

SITE 29: 6 km north of Tepic, Nayarit, 25–26 June 1976. The study site was located in the forest surrounding the Jumatan road about 5 km west of the intersection with Highway 15.

SITE 30: 5 km north of El Avion, Sinaloa, where a dirt road exited Highway 40 and ran through essentially undisturbed forest, 19 January 1976.

Richard L. Hutto

SITE 35: 10 km south of Chamela, Jalisco, along the road which leads to the Estacion Biologica de la Universidad Autonoma de Mexico, 22–24 February 1976.

Highland Habitats

OAK WOODLAND

It is difficult to find extensive areas of pure oak (*Quercus* spp.) but fewer than 5 percent of the trees within the following sites were other than oaks. The oaks were rarely taller than 10 m, and grasses usually composed the understory.

SITE 8: 20 km south of Guadalajara, north of Highway 80, 22–23 February 1975; 17 July 1975. The census area was within the undisturbed forest above the El Palomar housing development.

SITE 40: 40 km south of Tepic, west of Highway 15, 24 July 1975; 8–9 March 1976; 28 June 1976. The oaks of this area were composed exclusively of *Quercus rugosa* and had enormous leaves 40 cm long.

SITE 9: 31 km north of Morelia, Michoacan, west of Highway 15, 9–13 March 1975; 23–24 July 1975; 24 February 1976; 1–8 March 1976. The census area was within the forest surrounding a dirt road which led to a mining area. The presence of workers on occasion and several thinned areas made this site relatively disturbed for a highland forest.

PINE-OAK WOODLAND

These woodlands are normally composed of a mixture of pines (*Pinus* spp.), oaks (*Quercus* spp.) and occasionally madrones (*Arbutus* sp.), all of which stand about 15 m high. There is generally an understory of grasses and small (1–2 m) bushes.

SITE 12: 10 km S. Carapan, Michoacan, west of Highway 37, 4–6 March 1975; 18–19 July 1975; 25–26 February 1976. The census area was located in relatively undisturbed forest beyond an agricultural field.

SITE 13: Km post 5 on the road to Tacambaro from Patzcuaro, Michoacan, 6–7 March 1975; 21 July 1975.

SITE 14: This site was located at 2,135 m elevation on the dirt road leading to the top of the Volcan de Fuego, Jalisco, 28 February–1 March 1975. The same road was used as a census route.

SITE 33: Km post 195 south of Tepic, 13 February 1976. The census area started in the forest located about 2 km west of Highway 15.

SITE 34: 50 km south of Puerto Vallarta, Jalisco, and 3.5 km east on the Unidad Cuale Road, 19–22 February 1976. The census route was along this same dirt road, which provided easy access through the steep terrain. Several small streams run through the canyons.

SITE 37: 17 km north of Guadalajara and 5 km in on El Bosque Primavera Road, 27–28 June 1976. The area is a state park, but human disturbance was very localized.

SITE 38: 20 km from Tepic on the road to El Cuarenteño, 18 February 1976; 29 June 1976. The census area was located in the forested hills just before the road descends toward the Pacific Lowlands.

PINE FOREST

Pure pine (*Pinus* spp.) forests are nearly impossible to locate within the more easily accessible areas of western Mexico. They usually consist of large (35 m) trees and little understory save a few grasses.

SITE 15: 44 km east of Uruapan, Michoacan, 10 March 1975; 20–21 July 1975; 27–28 February 1976. The census area was in the pines to the north of the Uruapan-Patzcuaro highway.

PINE-OAK-FIR FOREST

This habitat type consists of large pines (*Pinus pseudostrobus* mostly), oaks (*Quercus laurina*) which take on a pine-like growth form, and firs (*Abies religiosa*). The forests are dense, heavily shaded and typically support a low herbaceous undergrowth.

SITE 16: Located at 2,410 m elevation on the dirt road to the top of the Volcan de Fuego, 26–28 February 1975. The same road served as a census route.

SITE 18: 58 km southeast of Morelia, 7–8 March 1975; 21–22 July 1975; 29 February–March 1976. The census area was along the road leading to Mirador Atzimba.

FIR FOREST

Pure fir forests consist primarily of *Abies religiosa* and support a rather sparse herbaceous undergrowth.

SITE 19: 28 km north of Mexico City, Distrito Federal, in the fir forest west of Highway 15, 8–9 March 1975.

Methods

Censuses

Bird censuses were conducted by walking 1 km strip

transects and recording birds seen or heard approximately 20 m to either side, the precise width depending on the habitat involved. The area censused was calculated as the length times the width of the transect. This methodology was necessary in a number of habitats (mangrove, tropical evergreen forest, thornscrub, and tropical deciduous forest) where the use of preexisting roads and trails saved time (weeks) which would have been required to cut access routes for more regular plots. To be consistent, the same methods (and associated biases) were applied to all habitats so that I might establish relative densities of birds among the habitat types. More accurate estimates of bird densities which can be derived from the detectability of each species along the transect route (Emlen 1971; Järvinen and Väisänen 1975) were not attempted because of time limitations in most of the sites and because of the inappropriateness of these methods for censuses which were conducted along the edges or borders of habitats. At least three 2.5–3-hr censuses were conducted at each site and the bird densities averaged over all censuses.

The problem of trying to census rare species which may not be present on a given day is most pronounced in the tropical lowland habitats. In these habitats, it is not uncommon to see new species every day for weeks (Terborgh and Weske 1969, for example). I tried to minimize this error by conducting at least six censuses in each of several lowland habitats (mangrove, plantation, second growth, and tropical evergreen forest).

The censuses included only land birds, and densities were not estimated for aerial species or species which were most often recorded only by observing individuals fly overhead. These include vultures, hawks, falcons, parrots, swifts, swallows, ravens and crows. Nocturnal species were not censused.

Migratory Status

Distributional information from Friedmann, Griscom, and Moore (1950/1957) and comparisons of my summer and winter census data were used to determine which species were migratory. Species which breed in temperate North America and spend the winter months in Mexico were classified as long-distance migrants. Bird species which winter in one area or habitat in Mexico and breed in another Mexican locality were classified as local migrants and were determined as such from comparisons of my own summer and winter census data, from breeding census data reported in Audubon Field Notes (1951, 1954, 1964, 1968) and from Schaldach's (1963) notes on the breeding status of Colima birds. The migratory status of each bird species is given in Appendix I.

The possibility exists that most individuals of some species migrate into a habitat during winter and leave in summer but that a minority remain resident year round. This is impossible to detect from census data covering only two seasons and so migrants are labeled as such only if they were entirely absent from a habitat in summer and present in winter. I have been conservative, then, in estimating the number of migrants, especially in the highlands, where all the vireos and several warbler species were classified as residents although some individuals may have been migratory.

Food Habits

Several subgroups of the censused avifauna were defined to permit separate analyses. Birds were classified as insectivores if at least 50 percent of their diets normally consist of insect food. The diets of unfamiliar birds or their close relatives were obtained from Bent (1958, 1968) or Skutch (1954, 1960, 1969). The food habits of each species are given in Appendix I.

As defined here, small foliage-gleaning insectivores include members of the families Paridae, Sylviidae, Vireonidae and Parulidae but exclude the Black-and-white Warbler, Louisiana Waterthrush and Northern Waterthrush because of their different foraging habits. For the sake of brevity and because most of the birds belonging to this group are warblers, I sometimes refer to this group as the "warbler guild" (cf Root 1967, who defines a guild as a group of species that exploit the same class of environmental resources in a similar way).

Flock Participants

In western Mexico, insectivorous birds which participate in mixed-species flocks move together as a group, typically through the taller vegetation (although anttanager flocks in tropical evergreen forests were found exclusively in the understory). The integrated fashion of movement and frequent joining and following reactions (Moynihan 1962) provided the basis for distinguishing birds as flock participants. Ground, or brushforaging species frequently looked as if they were moving with a flock, but more careful observation revealed that they invariably moved independently of the flock and that they were most often observed alone, so they were not classified as flocking species. Lowland and highland canopy flock participants are listed in Appendix II.

Insect Densities

Insect densities were estimated from samples of flying insects which were caught on 10 × 10 cm plastic squares coated with Tanglefoot™ and hung in vege-

Richard L. Hutto

tation at 0.5 m height intervals, to 2.0 m. Twenty boards (five stations of four boards each) were left hanging for 24 hr before I counted and measured all insects to the nearest mm and were left for as many days as possible within each habitat that was sampled.

I did not expect to capture with this method, all the the kinds of food that the birds eat, but I assume that the densities of insects caught are correlated with the density of insectivorous bird food. The efficiency of sticky traps varies with meteorological conditions; particularly wind speed (Johnson 1950), may vary from one habitat to another (Southwood 1966) and varies with the aspect at which the board hangs relative to the position of vegetation (Login and Pickover 1977). It is difficult to control for these factors, but the aspect of the boards was always consistent (vertical, tangent to the "edge" of vegetation) and the boards were hung on precisely the same branches in summer and winter within a given site. I never sampled on unusually windy or overcast days. An adequate, practical method for sampling bird food simply does not exist, but this method produces striking similarities in the numbers of insects caught per board per day between stations within a given site and gives consistent day-to-day results.

Adjusted Insect Density

The number of insects caught per plaque is in itself an insufficient estimate of the density of insects available to insectivorous foliage-gleaning birds since the vegetation provides foraging substrates for gleaners/hoverers or perches for flycatchers and determines the volume of habitat space that can actually be used to capture the insects. For example, even though desert and tropical evergreen forest habitats might yield the same number of insects per board, the number of available sites from which nonaerial birds can capture them is greater in the forest, and this difference should be taken into consideration. Assuming independence of insect density and vegetation density between habitats, the number of insects per unit area of habitat (adjusted insect density) was determined by multiplying the number of insects caught per station times a measure of the density of vegetation (see below) within the habitat.

Foliage Density

I estimated the density of vegetation within a site by counting the number of times the foliage hit a 5 m extendable pole which was raised through the vegetation at 75 points (one every 25 steps) 5 m to either side of the census route. An imaginary extension for taller habitats was provided by a camera and telephoto lens.

Results

Distribution and Density of Migrants in Winter

The numbers of migratory species and individuals found to winter in each of the 13 habitat types which I censused vary rather markedly among these types (table 1). The habitats harboring the greatest number of species are the man-made or disturbed lowland habitats such as second growth forests (figure 1) and riparian gallery forests bordering cultivated fields. The fewest species occur in mangroves, thornscrub, and fir forests. In general, there is an inverse correlation between elevation and the number of wintering migrant species ($r = -.46$, $P < .05$) so that significantly more migratory species winter in the lowlands than in the highlands (figure 2). The correlation would be weakened, however, if some individuals of several of the highland species (Solitary Vireo, for example) could be shown to be migratory.

Despite natural changes in habitat type (reflected in elevational changes) which produce changes in the number of migratory species, of even greater importance is the consideration of whether or not the habitat structure has been altered by, or is a product of, human disturbance. This is particularly true for lowland habitats. All but one of the habitats which are so disturbed (figure 2, circles) have more migrant species than expected from the elevation-regression equation. Furthermore, all six relatively undisturbed lowland habitats (figure 2, squares) have fewer species than expected.

The pattern is very much the same for migrant density (number of individuals per unit area) in each of the 13 habitats (table 1). There is a trend toward fewer individuals/ha with increasing elevation ($r = -.31$, NS) and more important differences between habitats due to the presence/absence of human disturbance. The high density of migrants in one riparian gallery forest (Site 23) is due in large part to a flock of 70 Cedar Waxwings which were present. Without the waxwings, the two gallery forests support very similar numbers of individuals and still far more per unit area than any other habitat type.

Just as the numbers of wintering migratory species and individuals vary between habitats, the proportions of migratory species and individuals also vary (table 1). The number and proportion of both species ($r = .67$, $P < .001$) and individuals ($r = .41$, $P < .05$) are positively correlated. Thus, habitats which support a large number of species or individuals also support a greater proportion of migrants. Accordingly, there is a significant trend toward a decreasing proportion of migrant species ($r = -.65$, $P < .01$) and migrant individuals ($r = -.57$, $P < .01$) with increasing elevation. As much as 74 percent (mangroves) or as little as

Table 1. Some characteristics of each winter study site[1]

Habitat type	Dry wash	Gallery forest		Mangrove			Plantation	Second growth		Evergreen forest edge	Thornscrub		Tropical deciduous	
Site number	21	22	23	1a	1b	32	2	36	39	4	5	6	30	35
Area (ha)	2.0	1.0	0.6	1.6	2.0	1.9	2.7	1.6	2.0	1.6	2.4	1.4	1.0	2.0
Elevation (m)	15	460	640	0	5	15	10	10	10	20	305	460	30	30
Insect density (#/station)[2]	—	—	—	—	104	312	287	—	175	143	—	—	—	—
Adjusted insect density[2]	—	—	—	—	31.2	50.5	55.4	—	32.2	79.9	—	—	—	—
Foliage density[2]	—	—	—	—	300	162	193	—	184	559	—	—	—	—
# species	45	43	32	10	23	26	34	41	43	54	7	11	31	28
# individuals/ha	84.5	240.0	369.0	20.5	25.0	69.0	77.9	112.0	53.0	185.9	14.4	25.4	155.0	65.9
# migrant species	16	22	20	15	17	14	24	21	22	23	3	4	12	8
% migrant species	35.6	51.2	62.5	50.0	73.9	53.8	70.6	51.2	51.2	42.6	42.9	36.4	38.7	28.6
# migrant individuals/ha	35.0	154.1	256.8	15.5	20.8	56.0	39.9	70.4	31.3	89.4	8.6	14.1	27.0	16.0
% migrant individuals/ha	41.4	64.2	69.6	75.6	83.0	81.2	51.2	62.9	59.0	48.1	60.0	55.6	17.4	24.3
# local migrant species	1	2	3	0	1	2	5	3	2	5	0	0	1	1
# local migrant individuals/ha	5.8	20.0	36.3	0.0	1.3	5.0	6.8	22.5	1.2	10.5	0.0	0.0	3.0	0.5
# resident insectivorous spp	16	13	8	5	6	8	7	9	12	20	2	5	10	12
# resident insectivorous individuals/ha	20.8	60.0	72.5	5.0	4.3	10.5	16.2	15.0	12.9	59.9	1.7	6.4	33.0	24.2
# migrant insectivorous spp.	12	16	13	4	15	11	14	14	18	17	3	4	8	6
% migrant insectivorous spp	42.9	55.2	61.9	44.4	71.4	57.9	66.7	60.9	60.0	45.9	60.0	44.4	44.4	33.3
# migrant insectivorous individuals/ha	45.6	157.0	171.4	19.5	23.3	60.5	43.8	50.0	41.5	135.4	10.3	20.5	58.0	34.9
% migrant insectivorous individuals/ha	54.4	61.8	57.7	74.4	81.5	82.6	63.0	70.0	68.9	55.8	83.5	68.8	43.1	30.7
# resident warbler-guild species	4	0	1	1	1	1	0	1	1	2	1	0	0	1
# resident warbler-guild individuals/ha	1.7	0.0	1.7	2.5	2.3	1.0	0.0	0.5	0.5	2.6	0.8	0.0	0.0	1.9
# migrant warbler-guild species	11	12	10	4	12	8	10	12	13	13	3	4	8	3
% migrant warbler-guild species	73.3	100.0	90.9	80.0	92.3	88.9	100.0	92.3	92.9	86.7	75.0	100.0	100.0	75.0
# migrant warbler-guild individuals/ha	24.4	86.0	90.7	14.5	18.0	27.5	25.4	27.0	25.2	64.3	8.6	14.1	25.0	7.7
% migrant warbler-guild individuals/ha	93.7	100.0	98.2	85.3	88.9	96.5	100.0	98.2	98.0	96.1	91.3	100.0	100.0	80.0
# resident granivorous species	7	3	2	0	0	2	1	4	2	2	1	1	3	3
# resident granivorous individuals/ha	12.1	13.0	34.5	0.0	0.0	1.5	4.7	12.5	1.2	6.0	0.8	3.5	34.9	11.7
# migrant granivorous species	3	5	5	1	0	1	6	7	2	5	0	0	4	2
% migrant granivorous species	30.0	62.5	71.4	100.0	0.0	33.3	85.7	63.6	50.0	71.4	0.0	0.0	57.1	40.0
# migrant granivorous individuals/ha	8.3	52.0	41.2	1.0	0.0	1.0	9.5	35.5	2.1	11.5	0.0	0.0	20.0	6.8
% migrant granivorous individuals/ha	40.7	80.0	54.4	100.0	0.0	40.0	66.7	74.0	64.6	65.7	0.0	0.0	36.4	36.8
# insectivorous species in flocks	7	5	5	0	8	3	6	5	8	7	2	3	6	4
% insectivorous species in flocks	25.0	17.2	23.8	0.0	38.1	15.8	28.6	21.7	26.7	18.9	40.0	33.3	33.3	22.2
# insectivorous individuals/ha in flocks	15.4	39.0	47.8	0.0	10.5	2.5	12.2	13.5	8.2	23.1	8.2	6.4	20.0	8.7
% insectivorous individuals/ha in flocks	33.8	24.8	27.9	0.0	45.1	4.1	27.9	27.0	19.8	17.1	79.6	31.2	34.5	24.9

[1] Total number of species and individuals/ha censused, the percentage of migratory species and individuals, the number of resident and number and percentages of migrant species and individuals within the insectivore, warbler, and granivore guilds, and the number and percentages of insectivorous species which participate in mixed-species flocks.

[2] See methods.

Richard L. Hutto

Habitat type	Oak woodland			Pine-oak woodland					Pine forest	Pine-oak-fir forest		Fir forest
Site number	8	9	40	12	13	14	33	34	15	16	18	19
Area (ha)	1.0	2.1	3.2	3.1	2.8	3.1	3.2	2.8	3.1	3.1	2.4	3.2
Elevation (m)	1890	2286	1300	1980	2316	2135	1340	915	1770	2410	2740	2926
Insect density (#/station)[2]		41		22					11		3	
Adjusted insect density[2]		4.6		2.2					1.2		1.7	
Foliage density[2]		111		98					112		578	
# species	9	44	24	48	26	42	35	32	37	32	35	24
# individuals/ha	22.0	54.9	38.6	38.5	26.8	55.1	27.2	35.9	21.6	40.1	42.0	35.5
# migrant species	3	17	10	14	10	15	13	13	9	12	8	3
% migrant species	33.3	38.6	41.7	29.2	38.5	35.7	37.1	40.6	24.3	37.5	22.9	12.5
# migrant individuals/ha	8.0	18.1	11.4	12.2	10.6	19.9	15.4	19.6	6.8	10.1	9.7	13.0
% migrant individuals/ha	36.4	33.0	29.6	31.7	39.5	36.1	56.7	54.5	31.5	25.3	23.0	36.5
# local migrant species	0	6	4	1	0	1	0	2	0	0	0	0
# local migrant individuals/ha	0.0	7.0	4.0	2.7	0.0	1.0	0.0	1.7	0.0	0.0	0.0	0.0
# resident insectivorous species	3	17	13	26	11	17	17	16	21	13	19	14
# resident insectivorous individuals/ha	9.0	21.1	19.8	20.2	12.7	10.5	8.9	11.4	10.1	12.1	24.4	16.1
# migrant insectivorous species	3	11	6	11	9	13	9	10	8	12	7	3
% migrant insectivorous species	50.0	39.3	31.6	29.7	45.0	46.4	34.6	38.5	27.6	48.0	26.9	17.6
# migrant insectivorous individuals/ha	17.0	32.7	27.2	29.5	22.6	29.1	21.3	28.5	16.6	22.2	33.0	29.1
% migrant insectivorous individuals/ha	47.1	35.5	27.2	31.5	43.8	63.9	58.2	60.0	39.2	45.5	26.1	44.7
# resident warbler-guild species	1	7	5	9	4	6	5	5	10	7	8	7
# resident warbler-guild individuals/ha	5.0	17.2	12.7	10.0	7.8	5.5	4.0	4.0	5.5	7.2	11.5	10.5
# migrant warbler-guild species	2	8	4	9	8	10	7	8	6	10	5	2
% migrant warbler-guild species	66.7	53.3	44.4	50.0	66.7	62.5	58.3	61.5	37.5	58.8	38.5	22.2
# migrant warbler-guild individuals/ha	7.0	9.2	6.2	8.6	9.5	16.7	10.8	15.8	5.7	8.5	7.0	11.4
% migrant warbler-guild individuals/ha	58.3	34.8	32.8	46.3	55.1	75.1	72.8	79.8	50.8	54.2	37.8	52.6
# resident granivorous species	2	6	1	5	4	4	2	2	2	1	4	3
# resident granivorous individuals/ha	4.0	11.9	7.5	3.6	3.2	6.6	1.2	3.8	1.7	0.7	3.3	2.1
# migrant granivorous species	0	2	2	1	0	1	2	1	1	0	0	0
% migrant granivorous species	0.0	25.0	66.7	16.7	0.0	25.0	50.0	33.3	33.3	0.0	0.0	0.0
# migrant granivorous individuals/ha	0.0	2.2	2.2	1.7	0.0	1.0	1.6	0.2	0.3	0.0	0.0	0.0
% migrant granivorous individuals/ha	0.0	15.6	22.6	32.1	0.0	13.0	55.6	4.8	15.5	0.0	0.0	0.0
# insectivorous species in flocks	4	17	12	23	14	14	17	15	20	14	17	10
% insectivorous species in flocks	66.7	50.0	63.2	62.2	70.0	50.0	65.4	57.7	70.0	56.0	65.4	58.8
# insecitvorous individuals/ha in flocks	12.0	25.2	22.9	22.2	15.9	20.5	14.3	20.7	13.1	12.7	21.6	12.1
% insectivorous individuals/ha in flocks	70.6	77.1	84.2	75.3	70.4	70.4	67.1	72.6	78.9	57.2	65.5	41.6

[2] See methods.

Figure 1. A heavily thinned second growth habitat (Site 39) which held floral elements common to plantations (*Cocos nucifera*), tropical deciduous forests (*Ficus continifolia*, *Randia* sp.) and mangroves (*Avicennia nitida*). Thirteen migratory warbler-guild species wintered in this location and comprised 98 percent of all the warbler-guild individuals present.

13 percent (fir forests) of all species in the various habitats are winter visitors only, while as much as 83 percent (mangroves) or as little as 17 percent (tropical deciduous forest) of all individuals were found to be winter visitors. The mean percentage of migratory individuals is 57 percent for the lowland habitats and 36 percent for the highlands.

Subsets of the total pool of migrants were analyzed in the same manner. Insectivorous birds, small foliage-gleaning birds in the warbler guild, granivorous fringillids and emberizids and local migrants all show trends similar to those described for migrants in general (table 1). The data for insectivorous species are generally more complete than those for granivorous birds because I concentrated on obtaining distributional information on the former group and did not collect census data from old fields which held (at all

elevations) large numbers of seed-eaters and few insectivores. However, with the information I have, all subsets, occur in the highest densities in the disturbed lowland habitats, just as the combined results reveal. A most impressive finding is that within the small foliage-gleaner guild, some habitats had populations composed entirely of migratory birds and the average proportion of migratory foliage-gleaning insectivorous individuals in the 14 lowland sites is 95 percent (table 1).

There is a strong correlation within habitats between the number of local migrants/ha and the number of long-distance migrants/ha ($r = .93$, $P < .001$). This indicates that the local migrants cannot be distinguished from the more distant migrants in terms of the habitats within which they winter; they merely come from more locally seasonal habitats.

Richard L. Hutto

Habitat Distribution of Migrants Belonging to the Warbler Guild

If we look in more detail at migrant habitat selection within the small foliage-gleaner (warbler) guild, several species are found to be restricted to specific habitats (figure 3). For example, several warbler species occur only in pine-associated communities and several others only in open, riparian-like habitats. More strikingly, however, no fewer than eight species occupy all (or nearly all) the available habitat types. Further analysis using the densities of these eight species indicates that, for the most part, the species are distributed independently of one another. The densities of only three of the 28 possible pairs are significantly correlated, and in these cases the correlations are positive.

Association Between Migrants and Residents

By taking all migrants as a group and asking, "Do migrants avoid habitats occupied by the greatest density of residents (and vice versa)?" the answer appears to be negative. The number of resident individuals in the series of study sites is significantly positively correlated with the number of migratory individuals ($r = .67$, $P < .001$) and even more closely correlated for the insectivore subgroup ($r = .94$, $P < .001$). However, for ecologically more meaningful subgroups we discover that, while there is a significant positive correlation ($r = .68$, $P < .001$) between the numbers of individual migrant and resident granivores over all habitat types (indeed, both migrant and resident seed-eaters seem to enjoy the abundance of seeds from early successional plants and everywhere feed in mixed-species assemblages), there is a significant inverse relationship between the numbers of migrant and resident individuals belonging to the warbler guild (figure 4; $r = -.43$, $P < .05$). This relationship is due, in part, to occupancy of disturbed habitats by the migrants and complete avoidance of the same habitats by residents. After removing the disturbed habitats from the analysis, the number of migrant and resident "warblers" wintering in the remaining habitat types is still negatively correlated ($r = -.55$, $P < .05$). In other words, even in habitats which are not completely avoided by resident foliage-gleaners, the migrants are most abundant where the residents are most scarce.

These results indicate that migrant-resident avoidance may occur in some groups or guilds and not in others and that, as a group, all migrants may not reflect but may mask the patterns which various ecological subgroups might otherwise reveal.

The small foliage-gleaner guild shows an additional kind of migrant-resident avoidance within the undisturbed lowland habitats. In both mangroves and trop-

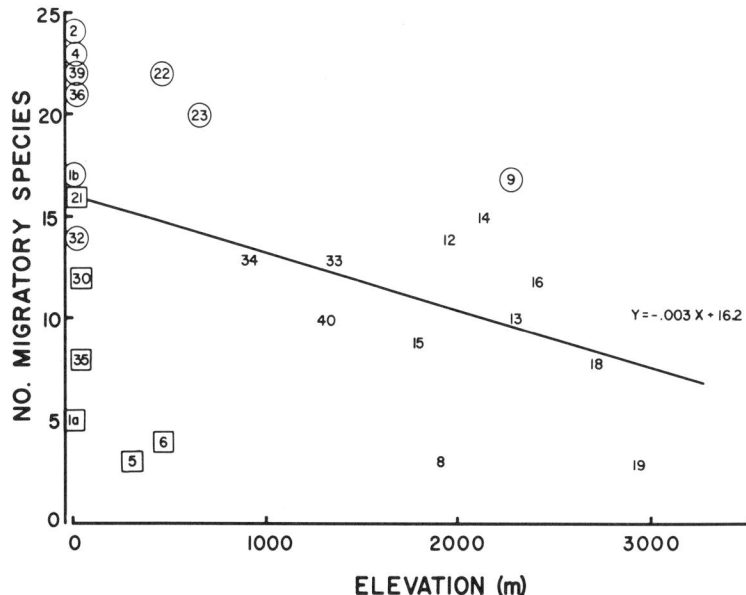

Figure 2.   The relationship between the number of migratory species which occupy different western Mexican study sites in winter vs elevation of each site. Numbers refer to site numbers given in table 1. Heavily disturbed sites are encircled, and the relatively undisturbed lowland sites are boxed. The line providing the best least-squares fit is shown.

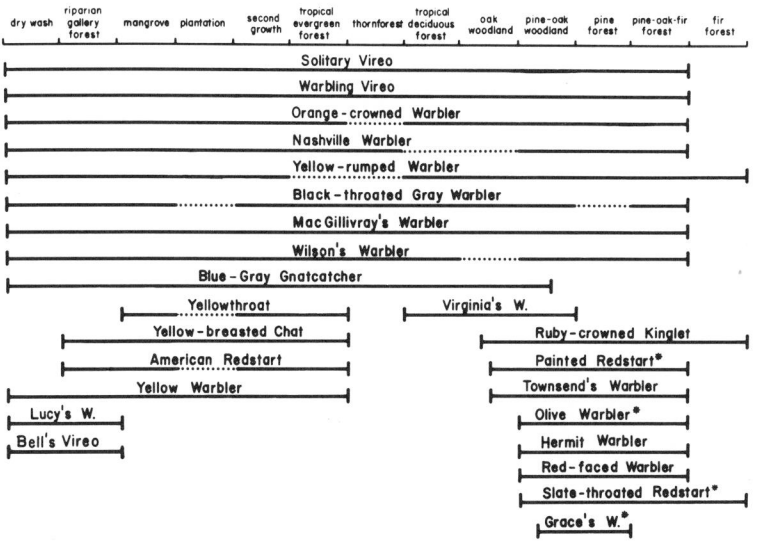

Figure 3.   Diagrammatic representation of the winter habitat distribution of migratory western North American species belonging to the warbler guild. Dotted line indicates absence from that portion of the habitat gradient. Asterisk follows the names of those permanent resident species which may contain some northern migratory individuals during the winter months.

Table 2. Numbers and densities (individuals/ha) of migrants and residents from the warbler guild[1]

Habitat type	Migrants		Residents		P[2]
	Species	Density	Species	Density	
Tropical evergreen forest					
Edge	13	64.30	2	2.62	<.05
Interior	5	13.00	3	10.00	
Mangroves					
Thinned	8	27.50	1	1.00	
Edge	10	17.50	1	2.25	>.05
Interior	4	14.50	1	2.50	
Pine-oak woodland					
Edge	9	9.01	9	8.77	>.05
Interior	9	8.64	9	9.99	

[1] Censused in winter in the interiors and edges of three habitat types.

[2] Probability that location is independent of migratory status, as determined from G-tests using the bird densities.

Table 3. Some characteristics of each summer study site, total number of species and individuals/ha censused, the number of species and individuals/ha belonging to the warbler guild

Habitat type	Man-groves	Plan-tation	Tropical Evergreen Forest	Thurn-scrub	Tropical deciduous			Oak woodland		
Site number	1b	2	4	26	25	27	29	8	9	40
Area (ha)	2.0	2.7	1.6	2.6	3.1	1.3	1.8	1.0	2.1	3.2
Elevation (m)	5	10	20	15	400	5	762	1,890	2,286	1,300
Insect density[1] (#/station)	67	164	102	—	—	—	—	—	47	—
# species	5	10	31	14	16	25	29	11	19	23
# individuals/ha	10.4	8.8	110.4	33.5	19.5	74.2	49.5	24.7	29.0	20.1
# warbler-guild species	1	1	1	1	1	2	2	1	7	4
# warbler-guild individuals	4.0	0.7	1.7	0.4	0.7	5.2	1.1	1.7	10.6	6.8

[1] See methods.

Table 4. Summer to winter change in total number of species and number of individuals/ha, number of warbler-guild species and individuals/ha, and number of insects[1]

Habitat type	Species	Indi-viduals	Warbler-guild species	Warbler-guild indi-viduals	Insects
Lowlands					
Mangroves	4.60	2.41	13.00	5.13	1.55
Plantation	3.40	8.86	10.00	38.48	1.75
Tropical evergreen forest	1.74	1.69	15.00	40.56	1.40
Thornscrub[2]	0.64	0.60	4.00	31.58	—
Tropical deciduous forest[2]	1.26	2.32	4.60	8.30	—
Highlands					
Oak woodland	1.45	1.57	2.25	3.00	0.87
Pine-oak woods	1.28	1.04	3.22	1.82	0.71
Pine forest	1.37	0.65	2.78	0.79	0.20
Pine-oak-fir	1.75	0.93	2.86	0.57	0.07

[1] Values were determined from site averages for each habitat type.

[2] Values for this habitat represent averages from different sets of summer and winter sites.

ical evergreen forests, the warbler guild migrants are most abundant (especially as individuals) along clearings and edges where the residents of the same guild are least abundant and vice versa (table 2). This trend is significant for the tropical evergreen forest habitat. The highlands differ from the lowlands in this respect. First, the residents seem to be able to use the clearings just as well as migrants and do not show an avoidance as in the lowlands since all nine resident foliage-gleaner species seen in the pine-oak interior could be found utilizing the edges in similar densities (table 2). Secondly, I did not find that edges or clearings within the pine-oak woodlands attract a great abundance of migrants as do the lowland edges (table 2). There is but a single small insectivorous species from the warbler guild which can be said to be attracted to the edge areas in large numbers (Yellow-rumped Warbler), and it spends a good deal of its time flycatching. The other migrants are as common inside the forest as out and join with the residents in large, mixed-species insectivorous flocks. These flocks are larger and more diverse than any reported in the

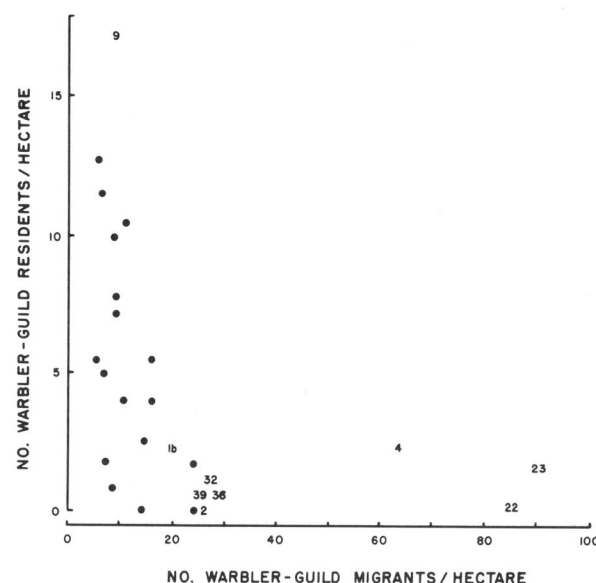

Figure 4. The relationship between the density of warbler-guild residents and migrants in each of the 26 study sites. Disturbed sites are represented by study site numbers as given in table 1.

Pine-oak woodland				Pine	Pine-oak-fir
12	13	37	38	15	18
3.1	2.8	2.8	3.1	3.1	2.4
1,980	2,316	1,525	1,400	1,770	2,740
31	—	—	—	55	43
37	22	30	27	27	20
36.0	24.8	33.6	31.4	33.1	45.3
11	6	5	5	9	7
17.2	7.8	5.5	8.8	14.2	32.6

literature to date, including Old and New World areas. They commonly include 20 species and may consist of up to 30 species and four times as many individuals (Appendix II). There is a definite elevational trend in the flocking tendency of insectivorous birds. Fewer than 40 percent of the insectivorous species in any given lowland habitat were found to participate in mixed-species flocks whereas no fewer than 50 percent of the highland insectivorous species flock (table 1).

In the absence of migrants during summer (late June–early July) one finds that the same disturbed lowland areas which held as many as 67 small insectivores/ha in winter harbor only 1.7 summer resident individuals/ha (tables 1 and 3) at this time. Vacated areas are not filled by residents, at least in the disturbed lowland sites. Table 4 shows that this is the case in general for lowland sites. There are 5 to 40 times as many small foliage insectivores in winter as in summer, depending on the habitat. The highland habitats are, again, different in this respect. On average, there are about as many individual small foliage insectivores in winter as in summer, and there is a general trend from oak woodlands up to pine-oak-fir forests where fewer and fewer individuals occur in winter relative to summer (table 4).

The summer-to-winter changes in insect densities for 7 habitat types are also shown in table 4, and it can be seen that there is a general correspondence between the summer-to-winter changes in insect density and the summer-to-winter changes in small foliage insectivore density ($r = .71$, NS). The disturbed lowland habitats have more insects during the winter (dry) season while the highland habitats, which are more like those of the temperate zones, have fewer in winter than in summer.

Discussion

Patterns of Habitat Distribution and Density of Migrants

There are a few African habitats which are reportedly avoided by migratory birds for winter residence whether disturbed or not. These include deserts (Moreau 1952; Elgood et al 1966) and montane habitats

(Moreau 1952, 1972; Elgood et al 1966; Ulfstrand 1973; Britton 1974). In the New World, the deserts and desert-like thornscrub habitats are also largely avoided for winter residence, and although montane areas may be less important in terms of the numbers of species and individuals/ha (table 1), they are certainly not "avoided" by winter residents. Brosset (1968) attributes the absence of winter residents in desert and thornscrub habitats to the unfamiliar appearance of the terrain. However, the North American deserts are preferred rather than avoided during spring migratory passages (Hutto in prep.). Surely, these desert-like habitats look no less familiar to a western North American migrant than any of the disturbed lowland tropical habitats which attract the greatest number of migrants. More likely, because these habitats produce few insects during the winter (the thornscrub and tropical deciduous habitats are virtually leafless during this period), they cannot be expected to attract insectivores, which comprise most of the north temperate migrants in western Mexico.

The discrepancy between the New and Old World migrants' use of montane habitats is coupled with the fact that montane areas in Africa support no migratory species exclusive of the lowlands (Moreau 1972) while western Mexico, and undoubtedly the rest of the neotropics, support many migratory species exclusive to the highland habitats (figure 3). Karr (1976) explains this difference by the fact that montane habitats occupy a relatively small area in Africa and a relatively greater area in the neotropics. Presumably, selection would favor utilization of the more widespread African lowland habitats if populations were limited by the extent of highland areas in winter. It would then be possible for evolution to proceed to the exclusion of migrants from the highlands if the lowland habitats did not themselves become a limiting factor. In addition, a continuity of favored montane habitat is present in the New World from the temperate breeding areas to northern Nicaragua, while Africa lacks such a continuity of montane habitat. This continuity would presumably favor an increased specialization toward its exclusive use throughout the year by pine-adapted species.

There are other habitats which harbor low densities of migrants in their virgin state but attract large densities of individuals and species along their edges or disturbed portions. These are most often lowland habitats (table 2) and include lowland tropical evergreen and rain forests (Cawkell and Moreau 1963; Elgood et al 1966; Willis 1966; Brosset 1968; Britton 1974; Tramer 1974; Karr 1976, this volume) and mangroves or pure vegetative stands such as *Cyperus* which have specialized faunas (Britton 1974, this vol-

Table 5. Winter insect densities from interior and edge situations in tropical evergreen forest and pine-oak woodland habitats

Habitat type	Insect density[1] (number/ sta.)	Adjusted density[1]
Tropical evergreen forest, interior	68	20.1
Tropical evergreen forest, edge	143	79.9
Pine-oak woodland, interior	22	2.2
Pine-oak woodland, edge	31	2.6

[1] See methods.

ume). The reason for this pattern must ultimately be related to differences in food resource abundance between the interior and edges of these habitats. Insect densities as determined from sticky plaques are in fact four times as high in edge than interior lowland forest areas (table 5). This fact in itself should lead to the preference of edges by insectivorous migrants and residents alike. Indeed, there is a strong positive correlation between numbers of migrant and resident insectivores over all sites which I censused. Cawkell and Moreau (1963) also report a preference of disturbed areas by both migrants and residents. However, for species of the warbler guild there is, superimposed on this productivity difference, a striking inverse relationship between the numbers of migrants and residents in edge and interior areas of two lowland habitats (table 2), resulting in a less even distribution of these migrants between the edges and interior than would otherwise occur. This additional feature of migrant-resident avoidance within the warbler guild will be discussed later.

There is a final set of habitats which seem to attract great numbers of migrants with apparently no substantial increase in migrant density along the edges. These include the savannah or dry woodland habitats of Africa (Elgood et al 1966), highland habitats in the neotropics (Karr 1976, this volume) and a group of habitats which are usually placed under the headings "successional," "second-growth," "disturbed," or "man-made" in both the Old and New World tropics (Cawkell and Moreau 1963; Brosset 1968; Elgood et al 1966; Willis 1966; Karr 1976; Ulfstrand and Alerstam 1977, this volume).

The substantial density of migrants in these habitats is most likely due to an interaction between the habitats' productivity and physiognomical similarity to breeding habitats. The disturbed habitats are proba-

Richard L. Hutto

bly attractive to migrants for the same reasons that edges and disturbed sections of mature forests are attractive—their productivity—while the savannah and highland habitats may be less productive but attractive because of the benefits associated with utilizing a similar habitat all year. As Tramer (1974) points out, disturbance itself may not be enough to attract migrants. The habitat type is also an important contributor to its attractiveness, particularly if a species is specialized in this respect; tropical evergreen forest edges are simply unattractive to pine-dwelling Hermit Warblers despite the habitat's productivity. The apparent lack of an edge effect in these habitats may be related in part to less of a discrepancy in insect densities from the interior to the edges (table 5). The difference in appearance between edge and interior portions may also be less pronounced in these habitats than in mature lowland forests, and this too could produce less of a discrepancy in bird use of the two portions, as will be discussed. In general, a habitat's productivity seems to be a good predictor of the density of migrant birds which winter therein (r = .93 for adjusted insect density vs warbler-guild migrant density), but exactly which species those are is another question altogether. Whether a given species winters in a given habitat at a particular latitude or not must depend on the individual's survivorship probability in that habitat relative to other options. The habitat's productivity alone is not sufficient to predict species names, only their total density.

The extreme densities of migrants in mid-winter in Africa are reported to be about 25/ha in lakeside habitats (Pearson 1972). Karr (1976) summarizes the situation for the neotropics and concludes that Smith's (1975) 150/ha in western Panama is also extreme. The western Mexican gallery forests which I censused are above either of these extremes, and the average number/ha is also much greater (205/ha). Moreau (1966) suspected such differences between African and neotropical migrant densities were simply due to the differences in the areas of the respective wintering grounds relative to the breeding grounds. Accordingly, western North American migrants utilize a wintering area which is relatively smaller than that which either the European or eastern North American migrants utilize (for reasons discussed by Hutto 1977), and we might expect an extension of Moreau's arguments to apply here as well.

The proportions of migrants which winter in most western Mexican habitats are far greater than the proportions reported to date for habitats in Indomalaysia (Karr 1976), Africa (Elgood et al 1966; Ulfstrand 1973; Britton 1974; Ulfstrand and Alerstam 1977) or the neotropics (Miller 1963; Lack and Lack 1972; Karr 1976). Karr (1976) reports an extreme value of 30 percent by individuals on Barro Colorado Island in Panama, which is below the mean values for lowland (57 percent) or highland (36 percent) habitats in western Mexico. The proportions vary with the family or guild under consideration (Morel and Bourlière 1962 and this volume), but researchers rarely subdivide their data in such a manner. Because of such differences between guilds, it is meaningless to speak of the "impact of migrants" without reference to a specific ecological group. Furthermore, as Britton (1974) points out, the impact even within a group is often misleading because frequently only the proportions of migrants by species are reported, and these are normally greater than the proportions by individuals. He continues by showing that although there are 30 percent migrants by species in Papyrus habitats, this does not mean that 30 percent of the insect food is lost to migrants since they amount to only 4 percent by individuals. Furthermore, estimates of impact by individuals may also be too high (an average of 3.7 times too high as determined from Tramer's 1974 data) since the biomass of migrants is often less than that of residents.

Since migrants and residents belonging to the warbler guild are approximately the same size, the proportions of migrants by individuals may be a reasonable estimate of the proportion of food which is lost to the winter residents. This leads to the striking conclusion that, on average, lowland migrants take 95 percent of the food harvested by small foliage-gleaners, and in four sites 100 percent of the food potentially available to this guild is utilized by the migratory segment. Why are there virtually no permanent resident foliage-gleaners in these lowland sites? One could argue that the residents have not had time to colonize the more recently disturbed sites or that nesting difficulties preclude the possibility of year round residency by small insectivores; however, these are not insurmountable difficulties since a few resident species do occur in most lowland habitats.

This rarity of small insectivorous permanent residents, or summer residents, results in apparent ecological vacuums after the migrants depart. For example, the tropical evergreen forest-edge habitat which supported 67 small foliage gleaners/ha in winter supported only 1.7/ha in summer, and the lowland sites averaged 25 times more warbler-guild birds in winter than in summer (from table 4). A partial explanation of this difference between summer and winter foliage-gleaner densities lies in the fact that the insect densities are 1.58 times higher during the mid-winter dry season than during the mid-summer wet season, as averaged over three disturbed lowland sites (table 4). Janzen

(1973) and Buskirk and Buskirk (1976) also find arthropod abundances to be higher during dry than during wet seasons. Thus, fewer individuals of a given biomass can be supported during the summer months in these lowland habitats. The seasonal difference in magnitude of insect abundances is still much smaller than the seasonal difference in magnitude of insectivore abundances (18 times less, as averaged over the same three lowland sites in table 4), and lack of food resources is probably not the entire picture.

The heavily disturbed habitats may, again, be totally inappropriate for nesting (especially plantations), and they show the largest discrepancy between summer and winter densities. On the other hand, the thornscrub and tropical deciduous habitats must certainly be appropriate for nesting but still support many fewer individuals/ha in summer, as estimated from different sets of summer and winter sites (table 3). I lack summer and winter insect data for these habitats, but I suspect the densities are many times higher in the summer when the plants are more fully vegetated, despite the rains (figure 5). This would invalidate any argument relating low densities of small foliage-gleaners in summer with a decrease in insect density and argue instead either that the birds of these two deciduous habitats are winter-limited (due to the impact of migrants?) and underutilize the summer food or that they are limited by some factor other than food in summer, such as predation, which might cause an overdispersion of nest sites. Any explanation for why these apparent ecological vacuums exist during the summer for small foliage-gleaners will certainly be habitat-dependent and probably related to factors other than simply food resources.

Patterns of Winter Distribution Within the Migratory Warbler Guild

There is very little information on the relationship between migrants during winter and whether they influence each other's distributions in an immediate, or proximate sense. In an ultimate sense, and on a broad geographic scale, there is some evidence that many European passerines use allopatry more in winter than in summer (Lack 1971), and the same may hold true for Eastern wood warblers (MacArthur 1958; Chipley this volume). This is not the case for Western wood warblers (Hutto 1977) where the degree of sympatry increases in winter.

On a more limited geographic scale, Pearson (1972) notes that in Uganda the more closely related wintering warblers show distinct habitat preferences. However, these are consistent with preferences of the species in general and removal of one species would probably not affect the others' distributions in an immediate

sense. This is not to say that competition is unimportant in segregating or maintaining segregation of species pairs as such; competition is implied with many modes of habitat segregation, but in this case competition can be only ultimately involved at best. I wish to distinguish more proximate habitat restrictions of species beyond what might be considered probable due to present day adaptations such that the removal of one species would produce a shift in the habitat distribution of another.

The only instance where such a competitive effect is probable occurs between Blue-gray Gnatcatchers and Ruby-crowned Kinglets (figure 3). In this case the 2 species are very similar ecologically and appear to replace each other altitudinally. It is difficult to imagine why either species should be restricted morphologically, behaviorally, or physiologically from occupying most of the other's elevational range. The restriction of other species to specific habitats is apparently the result of specialized use of particular features which occur only in those habitats (pine needles, marsh vegetation). Lack and Lack (1972) and Terborgh and Faaborg (this volume) point out that in Jamaica and Hispaniola, respectively, all the migratory warbler species except the two waterthrushes occupy all the available habitats. The situation is much the same for the warbler guild in western Mexico. The extreme breadth of habitats occupied by migrants is much more striking than the restricted distributions. No fewer than 8 small foliage-gleaning species occupy habitats from sea level to nearly 3,000 m elevation (figure 3). Moreover, the densities of only 3 of the 28 possible pairs of these 8 species are significantly correlated over the range of habitat types; each species is generally distributed independently of the other 7. Each species seems to utilize a habitat feature common to a variety of habitat types: Orange-crowned and Nashville Warblers use flowers and buds; Mac-Gillivray's Warbler uses low, dense shrubs; Wilson's Warbler uses primarily thick understory vegetation; Yellow-rumped Warbler uses open air space; and Warbling Vireo, Solitary Vireo, and Black-throated Gray Warbler use broad-leaved vegetation of almost any kind. Thus, each migratory species utilizes certain vegetative features either peculiar to a few habitats or common to many, and their distributions are determined accordingly.

Figure 5. A comparison of the tropical deciduous forest habitat during the dry season in February (top, Site 35) and the beginning of the heavy rains in June (bottom, Site 29). On average, this habitat supports a greater number of foliage insectivores/ha during the dry season than during the relatively lush rainy season.

Richard L. Hutto

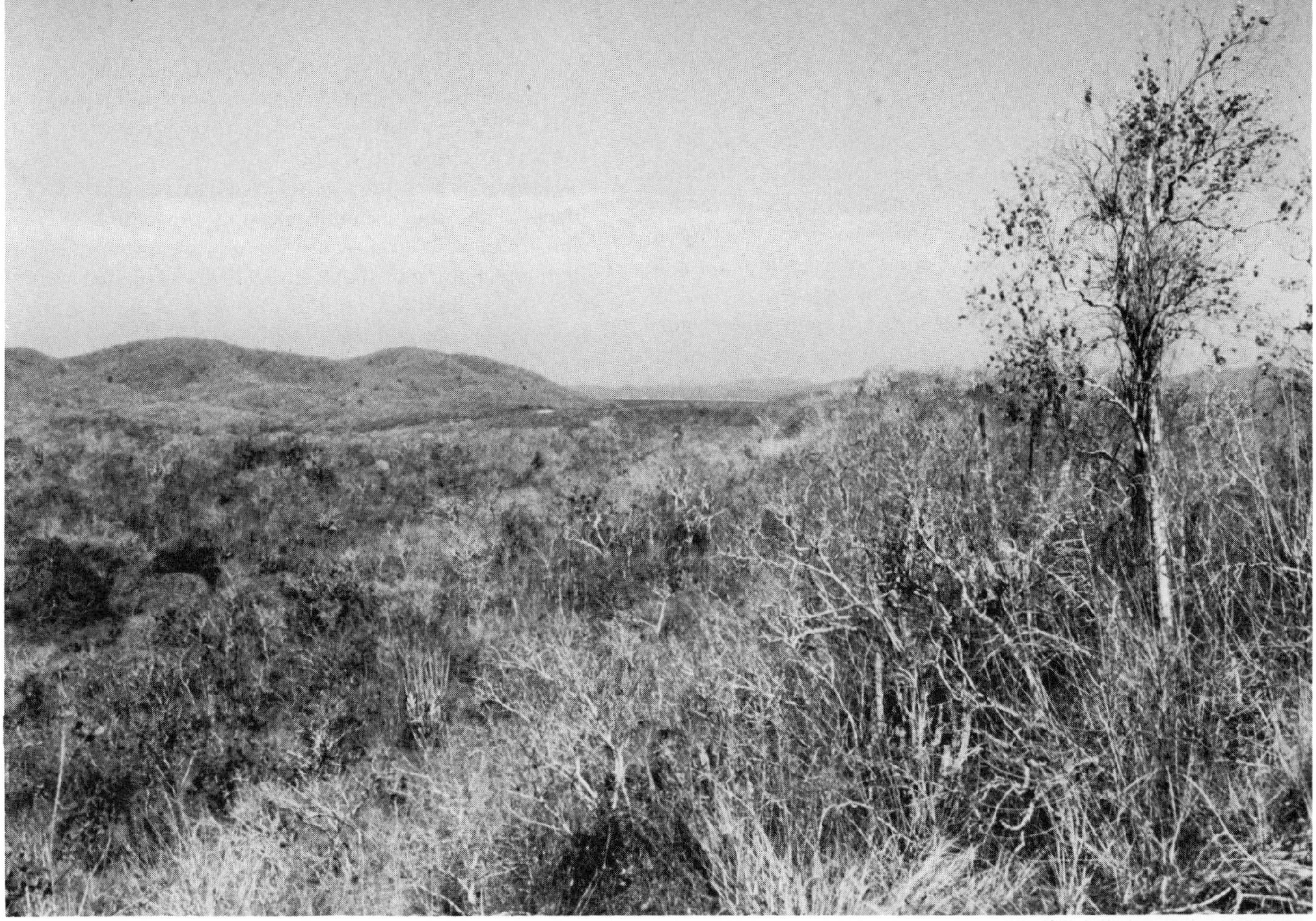

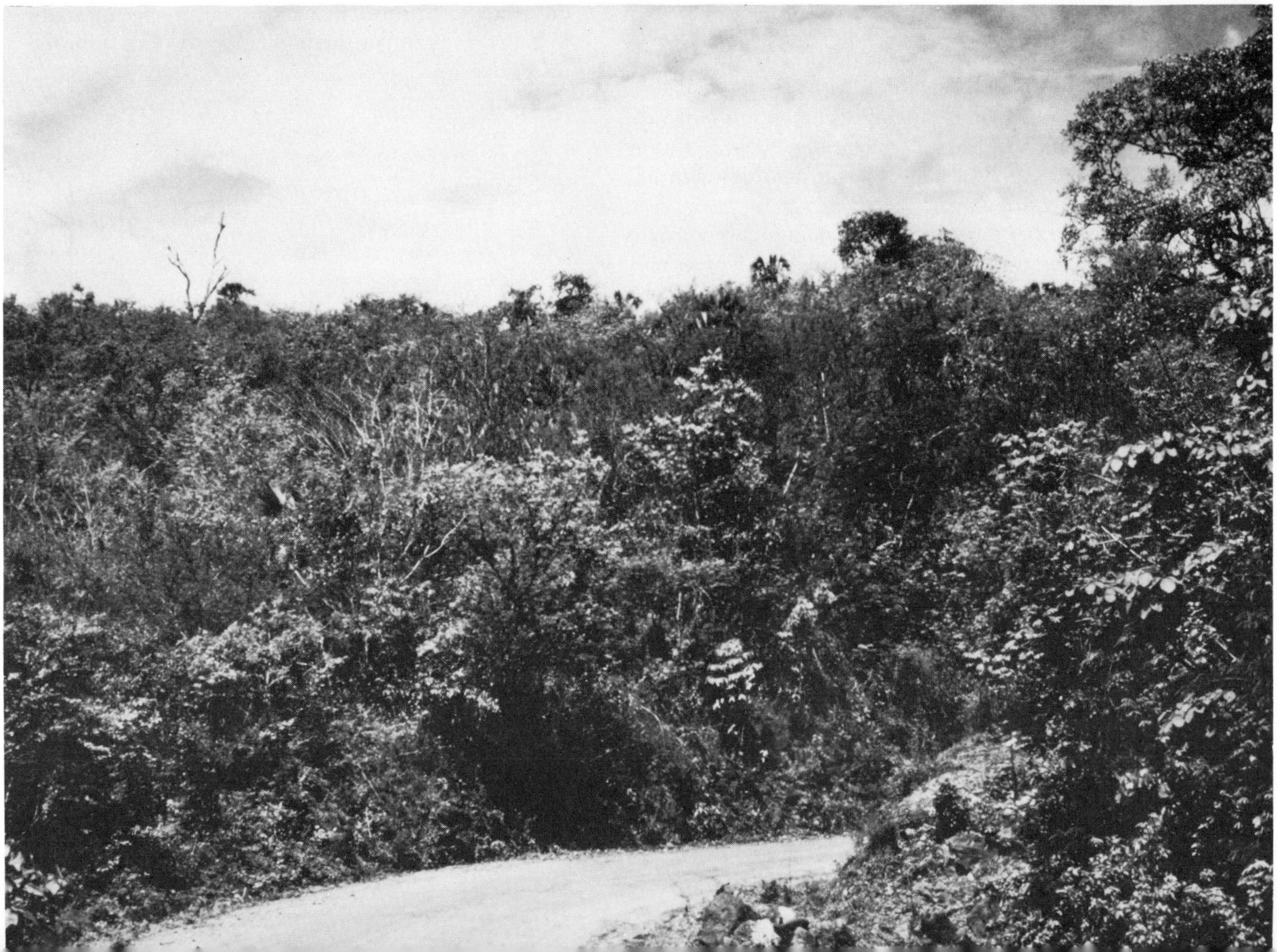

Relationship Between Migrant and Resident Distributions
and Densities

To my knowledge Moreau's (1966, 1972) analyses of the relationship between the geographic distributions of palaearctic migrants and African residents remain the only works of this sort. Anomalies in the geographic distributions of some migratory species (for example, European Swallow) might be due to migrant-resident interactions, but more definitive statements are generally unavailable. Similarly, there is a possible influence of resident neotropical insectivores on the restricted geographic distribution of migratory Western wood warblers in winter (Hutto 1977), but again this is speculative. The remaining discussion will concern a limited geographic area in an attempt to determine the influence of residents on the habitat distribution of migrants (and vice versa).

Unlike most migratory species which do not appear to have a proximate influence on the habitat selection of other migrants, I found that the habitats occupied by residents seem to be occupiable but avoided by migrants within the warbler guild and vice versa. The two groups also avoid each other by using different sections of the same lowland habitats, but this is really only a semantic difference from differential habitat selection; the edges of these habitats could be classified as separate habitats in themselves. The reason for the inverse correlation between migrant and resident densities is due at least in part to the inability of warbler-guild residents to leave mature habitats and take advantage of disturbed areas (leading to the association of high migrant densities with low resident densities) and partly to the inability of migrants to invade those habitats which are ecologically "filled" (leading to the association of high resident densities with low migrant densities).

The inability (or refusal) of resident foliage-gleaners to utilize forest clearings and second growth areas may be related to the fact that disturbed tropical forest habitat takes on such a different appearance from the undisturbed areas because of the invasion by early successional plant species. The residents avoid these areas to which they are poorly adapted and leave them open to exploitation by migrants. This "mental conservatism" (Willis 1966) of tropical forest residents is poorly understood but very real. Lack (1971) relates the fact that of 61 African rain forest bird species in Usambara, only 1 utilizes both the interior and edges. The edge areas are taboo to the other 60. In a proximate sense, Terborgh and Weske (1969) point out that several qualitative features of primary forest are missing in second growth, and primary forest birds will not colonize as a result.

The residents may also be restricted from the edges

in winter by the presence of migrants but, other than the inverse relationship between migrant and resident foliage-gleaner densities (table 2), there are no data to support or refute this contention.

Habitats which may be relatively saturated by residents of the warbler guild, possibly preventing invasion by more migrants, are the mature lowland and highland habitats. MacArthur (1972) suggested that rain forests hold few migrants because of the number of resident competitors, and I suspect such close ecological packing is the case with the highland and evergreen forest habitats in western Mexico. In these habitats, the warbler-guild migrants comprise only 54 percent of the individuals as opposed to 95 percent in other lowland areas. Pressure toward the most efficient utilization of food must be greatest in these habitats, especially in the highlands since many migrants are specialized to use pines-oaks-firs, and this is where mixed-species insectivore flocks predominate. No fewer than 50 percent of the highland insectivores flock and all species except MacGillivray's, Rufous-capped, and Golden-browed Warblers within the small foliage-gleaner guild participate in these flocks. There is also an apparent limit set by intraspecific aggression (also Jones 1977) of two to three individuals per species, suggesting a limit to the available food. Flocking may be a mechanism by which a greater number of individuals can be packed into an area given a certain resource density; note from table 1 and figure 6 that, on average, 12 times as many small foliage-gleaning insectivores occur in the highlands per unit adjusted insect density.

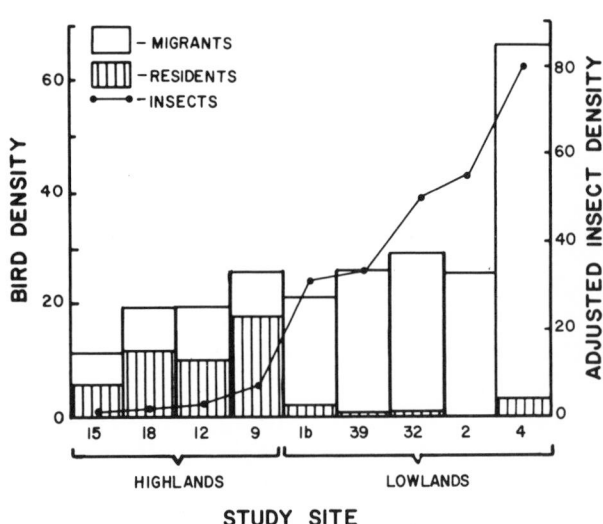

Figure 6. The relationship between bird density (number of foliage-gleaning insectivores/ha) and adjusted insect density.

Richard L. Hutto

Many disturbed lowland areas in western Mexico remain underexploited when migrants remove themselves during summer as discussed earlier. Pearson (1972) notes the same phenomenon with swallows and wagtails in Africa. In contrast, the highland areas have much more similar densities of summer and winter foliage-gleaning insectivores (table 4). This suggests first, that lowland migrants exert little immediate competitive impact on the residents. Secondly, it suggests that the migrants should be able to stay and breed successfully; why do they all leave? Concerning the first suggestion, it would be necessary to conduct an experimental removal of migrants in winter to determine whether they influence the distribution of residents since the "natural removal" (migration) of north temperate birds occurs at a time when insect densities change and breeding constraints are placed upon the residents, possibly preventing summer habitat shifts. For the same reasons, lack of foraging site shifts within a given habitat after the migrants depart cannot be taken to indicate a lack of immediate competition between migrants and residents during winter. It is, however, difficult to see how breeding constraints might prevent a resident Grace's Warbler from using a migrant Yellow-throated Warbler's foraging sites in summer as Howell (1971) discussed, and immediate competition is probably unimportant in producing differences such as these in winter.

Alternatively, the presence of habitat shifts by resident birds after the migrants leave would seem to argue more strongly that immediate competition is the major force restricting the residents in winter. Lack and Lack (1972) describe such shifts by Mangrove Warblers on Jamaica in the absence of migrants. I recognize no such shifts with the west Mexican residents and conclude that the impact of migrants on residents is probably minimal but difficult to assess, especially without knowledge about other environmental changes which may occur simultaneously with the departure of migrants.

It has been suggested (Leck 1972) that the impact of migrants is greatest in areas where the largest proportion of food is lost to migrants. Small insectivores take 100 percent of the food potentially available to that guild in some locations in western Mexico but the impact of these same species may be much greater in other areas (highlands) where they take relatively less food, but food which would probably be utilized by residents as indicated by their effective density compensation in the absence of migrants during summer.

The effect of residents on migrants is probably more substantial, and I suspect the winter removal of residents would reveal immediate shifts in the location of migrants. This is because the combined density of small migrant and resident foliage-gleaning insectivores corresponds well to the adjusted insect density over eight habitat types (figure 6; r = .79, P < .05). Since resident birds are the least likely to shift habitats, the migrants are probably responsible for density adjustments to give such a close correspondence.

North American temperate migrants from the warbler guild do not stay to breed in what appears to be underutilized habitats in the lowlands probably because the advantages of staying are greatly outweighed by the advantages of leaving to breed where resources are superabundant, despite losses due to migration. Genetic barriers preventing migratory species from staying in the nonbreeding areas are not insurmountable since there are examples of resident species in South Africa (Moreau 1966) that are presumably derived from palaearctic migrants. More definitive answers to this question are simply lacking.

Acknowledgments

This paper is based on part of a dissertation submitted to the University of California, Los Angeles in partial fulfillment of the requirements for the Ph.D. degree. I gratefully acknowledge the financial assistance provided by the National Science Foundation through Martin L. Cody, the University of California through Regent's Research Grants and the Graduate Student Patent Fund, Mr. and Mrs. Dennis M. Peacock, and my parents.

Allan Phillips and Ernest Edwards were especially helpful in providing information on potential Mexican study sites. Drs. Martin Cody, Jared Diamond, Henry Hespenheide and Thomas Howell each read and provided helpful comments on the manuscript. Financially, I wish to thank Martin Cody, Bob Montgomerie, and Brooke Stiling for their field assistance and companionship during parts of this study.

Appendix I: Bird species involved in the study

The scientific and common names, migratory status, and food habits of the bird species which were censused during the winter in various west Mexican habitats. Status represents that of the birds in the sites which I visited; different sites may produce a slightly different classification in some cases.

Scientific name	Common name	Migra-tory status[1]	Food habits[2]	Scientific name	Common name	Migra-tory status[1]	Food habits[2]
Columba fasciata	Band-tailed Pigeon	R	O	Myiarchus cinerascens	Ash-throated Flycatcher	R	I
Zenaida asiatica	White-winged Dove	LM–R	O	Myiarchus nuttingi	Nutting's Flycatcher	R	I
Scardafella inca	Inca Dove	R	O	Myiarchus tyrannulus	Brown-crested Flycatcher	R	I
Columbina passerina	Common Ground-dove	R–LM	O	Myiarchus tuberculifer	Dusky-capped Flycatcher	R	I
Columbina talpacoti	Ruddy Ground-dove	R	O	Contopus borealis	Olive-sided Flycatcher	TM	I
Leptotila verreauxi	White-tipped Dove	R	O	Contopus sordidulus	Western Wood-pewee	TM	I
Coccyzus minor	Mangrove Cuckoo	R	I	Contopus pertinax	Greater Pewee	R–TM	I
Piaya cayana	Squirrel Cuckoo	R	I	Mitrephanes phaeocercus	Tufted Flycatcher	R	I
Crotophaga sulcirostris	Groove-billed Ani	R	I	Empidonax affinis	Pine Flycatcher	R	I
Phaethornis superciliosis	Long-tailed Hermit	R	N–I	Empidonax difficilis	Western Flycatcher	TM	I
Colibri thalassinus	Green Violet-ear	R	N–I	Empidonax fulvifrons	Buff-breasted Flycatcher	R	I
Chlorostilbon canivetii	Fork-tailed Emerald	R	N–I	Empidonax spp.	Various migrant species	TM	I
Cynanthus latirostris	Broad-billed Hummingbird	R	N–I	Aechmolophus mexicanus	Pileated Flycatcher	R	I
Hylocharis leucotis	White-eared Hummingbird	R	N–I	Calocitta formosa	Black-throated Magpie-jay	R	O
Amazilia beryllina	Berylline Hummingbird	R	N–I	Cissilopha sanblasiana	San Blas Jay	R	O
Amazilia rutila	Cinnamon Hummingbird	R	N–I	Aphelocoma ultramarina	Gray-breasted Jay	R	O
Lampornis clemenciae	Blue-throated Hummingbird	R	N–I	Cyanocitta stelleri	Steller's Jay	R	O
Archilochus alexandri	Black-chinned Hummingbird	TM	N–I	Parus sclateri	Gray-sided Chickadee	R	I
Stellula calliope	Calliope Hummingbird	TM	N–I	Parus wollweberi	Bridled Titmouse	R	I
Selasphorus platycercus	Broad-tailed Hummingbird	TM–R	N–I	Psaltriparus minimus	Bushtit	R	I
Trogon mexicanus	Mountain Trogon	R	I	Sitta carolinensis	White-breasted Nuthatch	R	I
Trogon elegans	Elegant Trogon	R	I	Certhia familiaris	Brown Creeper	R	I
Chloroceryle americana	Green Kingfisher	R	P	Campylorhynchus megalopterus	Gray-barred Wren	R	I
Momotus mexicanus	Russet-crowned Motmot	R	I–F	Campylorhynchus gularis	Spotted Wren	R	I
Colaptes auratus	Common Flicker	R	I	Thryothorus sinaloa	Bar-vented Wren	R	I
Piculus auricularis	Gray-crowned Woodpecker	R	I	Thryothorus felix	Happy Wren	R	I
Dryocopus lineatus	Lineated Woodpecker	R	I	Thryomanes bewickii	Bewick's Wren	R	I
Melanerpes formicivorous	Acorn Woodpecker	R	I	Troglodytes aedon	Brown-throated Wren	R	I
Centurus chrysogenys	Golden-cheeked Woodpecker	R	I	Uropsila leucogastra	White-bellied Wren	R	I
Centurus uropygialis	Gila Woodpecker	R	I	Melanotis caerulescens	Blue Mockingbird	R	O
Sphyrapicus varius	Yellow-bellied Sapsucker	TM	I	Mimus polyglottos	Northern Mockingbird	R	O
Veniliornis fumigatus	Smoky-brown Woodpecker	R	I	Turdus migratorius	American Robin	R–LM	O
Dendrocopos villosus	Hairy Woodpecker	R	I	Turdus rufopalliatus	Rufous-backed Robin	R–LM	O
Dendrocopos scalaris	Ladder-backed Woodpecker	R	I	Turdus assimilis	White-throated Robin	R	O
Dendrocopos arizonae	Brown-backed Woodpecker	R	I	Myadestes obscurus	Brown-backed Solitaire	R	F
Xiphorhynchus flavigaster	Ivory-billed Woodcreeper	R	I	Catharus guttatus	Hermit Thrush	TM	F
Lepidocolaptes leucogaster	White-striped Woodcreeper	R	I	Catharus occidentalis	Russet Nightingale-thrush	R–LM	F
Attila spadiceus	Bright-rumped Attila	R	I–F	Catharus aurantiirostris	Orange-billed Nightingale-t.	R	F
Pachyramphus major	Gray-colllared Becard	R	I–F	Sialia sialis	Eastern Bluebird	R–LM	I–F
Platypsaris aglaiae	Rose-throated Becard	R	I–F	Sialia mexicana	Western Bluebird	R–LM	I–F
Tityra semifasciata	Masked Tityra	R	I–F	Polioptila caerulea	Blue-gray Gnatcatcher	TM	I
Pyrocephalus rubinus	Vermilion Flycatcher	R	I	Polioptila albiloris	White-lored Gnatcatcher	R	I
Tyrannus vociferans	Cassin's Kingbird	R	I	Polioptila nigriceps	Black-capped Gnatcatcher	R	I
Tyrannus melancholicus	Tropical Kingbird	R	I	Polioptila melanura	Black-tailed Gnatcatcher	R	I
Tyrannus crassirostris	Thick-billed Kingbird	R	I	Regulus satrapa	Golden-crowned Kinglet	R	I
Myiozetetes similis	Social Flycatcher	R	I	Regulus calendula	Ruby-crowned Kinglet	TM	I
Pitangus sulphuratus	Great Kiskadee	R	I	Bombycilla cedrorum	Cedar Waxwing	TM	F

Richard L. Hutto

Scientific name	Common name	Migratory status[1]	Food habits[2]
Ptilogonys cinereus	Gray Silky-flycatcher	LM–R	F
Lanius ludovicianus	Loggerhead Shrike	R	O
Vireo huttoni	Hutton's Vireo	R	I
Vireo hypochryseus	Golden Vireo	R	I
Vireo bellii	Bell's Vireo	TM	I
Vireo solitarius	Solitary Vireo	TM–R	I
Vireo gilvus	Warbling Vireo	TM–R	I
Diglossa baritula	Cinnamon Flower-piercer	R	N
Mniotilta varia	Black-and-white Warbler	TM	I
Vermivora celata	Orange-crowned Warbler	TM	I
Vermivora ruficapilla	Nashville Warbler	TM	I
Vermivora virginiae	Virginia's Warbler	TM	I
Vermivora luciae	Lucy's Warbler	TM	I
Vermivora superciliosa	Crescent-chested Warbler	R	I
Parula pitiayumi	Tropical Parula	R–LM	I
Peucedramus taeniatus	Olive Warbler	R	I
Dendroica petechia	Yellow Warbler	TM	I
Dendroica erithachorides	Mangrove Warbler	R	I
Dendroica coronata	Yellow-rumped Warbler	TM	I
Dendroica nigrescens	Black-throated Gray Warbler	TM	I
Dendroica townsendi	Townsend's Warbler	TM	I
Dendroica occidentalis	Hermit Warbler	TM	I
Dendroica graciae	Grace's Warbler	R	I
Seiurus motacilla	Louisiana Waterthrush	TM	I
Seiurus noveboracensis	Northern Waterthrush	TM	I
Oporornis tolmiei	MacGillivray's Warbler	TM	I
Geothlypis trichas	Common Yellowthroat	TM	I
Geothlypis poliocephala	Gray-crowned Yellowthroat	R	I
Icteria virens	Yellow-breasted Chat	TM	I
Granatellus venustus	Red-breasted Chat	R	I
Wilsonia pusilla	Wilson's Warbler	TM	I
Cardellina rubifrons	Red-faced Warbler	TM	I
Setophaga ruticilla	American Redstart	TM	I
Myioborus pictus	Painted Redstart	R	I
Myioborus miniatus	Slate-throated Redstart	R	I
Euthlypis lachrymosa	Fan-tailed Warbler	R	I
Ergaticus ruber	Red Warbler	R	I
Basileuterus belli	Golden-browed Warbler	R	I
Basileuterus rufifrons	Rufous-capped Warbler	R	I
Cassiculus melanicterus	Yellow-winged Cacique	R	I
Quiscalus mexicanus	Great-tailed Grackle	R	O
Icterus spurius	Orchard Oriole	TM	I–F
Icterus cucullatus	Hooded Oriole	TM–R	I–F
Icterus graduacauda	Black-headed Oriole	R	I–F
Icterus galbula	Northern Oriole	TM	I–F
Icterus sclateri	Streak-backed Oriole	R	I–F
Euphonia elegantissima	Blue-hooded Euphonia	R	F
Euphonia affinis	Scrub Euphonia	R	F
Piranga flava	Hepatic Tanager	R	I
Piranga bidentata	Stripe-backed Tanager	R	I
Piranga erythrocephala	Red-headed Tanager	R	I–F
Habia rubica	Red-crowned Ant-tanager	R	I–F
Rhodinocichla rosea	Rosy Thrush-tanager	R	I–F
Saltator coerulescens	Grayish Saltator	R	O
Pyrrhuloxia sinuata	Pyrrhuloxia	R	O
Pheucticus chrysopeplus	Yellow Grosbeak	R	O
Pheucticus melanocephalus	Black-headed Grosbeak	TM–R	O
Guiraca caerulea	Blue Grosbeak	R–LM	O
Cyanocompsa parellina	Blue Bunting	R	S
Passerina cyanea	Indigo Bunting	TM	S
Passerina versicolor	Varied Bunting	R–LM	S
Passerina ciris	Painted Bunting	TM	S
Passerina leclancherii	Orange-breasted Bunting	R	S
Sporophila torqueola	White-collared Seedeater	R	S
Sporophila minuta	Ruddy-breasted Seedeater	R	S
Volantinia jacarina	Blue-black Grassquit	LM–R	S
Atlapetes pileatus	Rufous-capped Brush-finch	R	I–O
Atlapetes virenticeps	Green-striped Brush-finch	R	I–O
Arremonops rufivirgatus	Olive Sparrow	R	S
Chlorura chlorura	Green-tailed Towhee	TM	S–O
Pipilo ocai	Collared Towhee	R	S–O
Pipilo erythrophthalmus	Rufous-sided Towhee	R	S–O
Pipilo fuscus	Brown Towhee	R	S–O
Chondestes grammacus	Lark Sparrow	TM	S
Aimophila quinquestriata	Five-striped Sparrow	R	S
Aimophila ruficauda	Stripe-headed Sparrow	R–LM	S
Aimophila rufescens	Rusty Sparrow	R	S
Aimophila ruficeps	Rufous-crowned Sparrow	R	S
Spizella passerina	Chipping Sparrow	R	S
Spizella pallida	Clay-colored Sparrow	R	S
Spizella breweri	Brewer's Sparrow	TM	S
Melospiza lincolnii	Lincoln's Sparrow	TM	S
Junco phaeonotus	Yellow-eyed Junco	R	S
Carpodacus mexicanus	House Finch	R	S
Carduelis pinus	Pine Siskin	LM–R	S
Carduelis notatus	Black-headed Siskin	LM–R	S
Carduelis psaltria	Dark-backed Goldfinch	LM–R	S

[1] TM = temperate, or long-distance migrant; LM = local migrant; R = nonmigratory. In some cases status depends on the site of habitat; for these species the more common occurrence preceeds the less common.

[2] F = fruit; N = nectar; I = insects; S = seeds; P = fish, O = omnivore. All bird species with an "I" after their name were considered insectivores in this study except for hummingbirds, which were not considered part of the insectivore guild.

Appendix II: Usual canopy species in lowland and highland mixed-species insectivorous bird flocks, winter, western Mexico

Lowland species[1]	*Highland species*[1]	*Highland species (cont.)*
Blue-gray Gnatcatcher	Ladder-backed Woodpecker	Orange-crowned Warbler
Solitary Vireo	Brown-backed Woodpecker	Nashville Warbler
Warbling Vireo	White-striped Woodcreeper	Crescent-chested Warbler
Black-and-white Warbler	Greater Pewee	Olive Warbler
Orange-crowned Warbler	Tufted Flycatcher	Yellow-rumped Warbler
Nashville Warbler	Pine Flycatcher	Black-throated Gray Warbler
Tropical Parula	Gray-sided Chickadee	Townsend's Warbler
Black-throated Gray Warbler	Bridled Titmouse	Hermit Warbler
Wilson's Warbler (rarely)	Bushtit	Grace's Warbler
	White-breasted Nuthatch	Wilson's Warbler (occasionally)
	Brown Creeper	Red-faced Warbler
	Blue-gray Gnatcatcher	Painted Redstart
	Golden-crowned Kinglet	Slate-throated Redstart
	Ruby-crowned Kinglet	Red Warbler
	Hutton's Vireo	Hepatic Tanager
	Solitary Vireo	Stripe-backed Tanager
	Warbling Vireo	Red-headed Tanager
	Black-and-white Warbler	

[1] Scientific names are given in Appendix I.

Literature Cited

American Ornithologists' Union
1957. *Check-list of North American Birds*, 5th ed., Baltimore, Md.: A.O.U., 691 pp.

Bent, A.C.
1958. Life histories of North American blackbirds, orioles, tanagers and allies. Bull. U. S. Nat. Mus. 211:1–549.

1968. Life histories of North American cardinals, grosbeaks, buntings, towhees, finches, sparrows and allies. Bull. U.S. Nat. Mus. 237:1–1889.

Britton, P. L.
1974. Relative biomass of Ethiopian and Palaearctic passerines in west Kenya habitats. Bull. Brit. Orn. Cl. 94:108–113.

Brosset, A.
1968. Localisation écologique des oiseaux migrateurs dans la forêt équatoriale du Gabon. Biol. Gabonica 4: 211–26.

Buskirk, R. E., and W. H. Buskirk
1976. Changes in arthropod abundance in a highland Costa Rican forest. Am. Midl. Natur. 95:288–98.

Cawkell, E. M., and R. E. Moreau
1963. Notes on birds of the Gambia. Ibis 105:156–78.

Cooke, W. W.
1904. Distribution and migration of North American warblers. U. S. Agriculture Biol. Survey (Bull. 18), Washington, D. C.

Emlen, J. T.
1971. Population densities of birds derived from transect counts. Auk 88:323–42.

Elgood, J. H., R. E. Sharland, and P. Ward
1966. Palaearctic migrants in Nigeria. Ibis 108:84–116.

Friedmann, H., L. Griscom, and R. T. Moore
1950/
1957. Distributional check-list of the birds of Mexico. Parts I and II. Pac. Coast Avif. 29/33.

Howell, T. R.
1971. An ecological study of the birds of the lowland pine savanna and adjacent rain forest in northeastern Nicaragua. Living Bird 10:185–242.

Hutto, R. L.
1977. The ecology of migratory Western wood warblers and the winter habitat distribution of small migratory land birds in western Mexico. Ph.D. thesis, Univ. of California, Los Angeles.

Richard L. Hutto

Janzen, D. H.
1973. Sweep samples of tropical foliage insects: Effects of seasons, vegetation types, elevation, time of day, and insularity. Ecol. 54:687–708.

Järvinen, O., and R. A. Väisänen
1975. Estimating relative densities of breeding birds by the line transect method. Oikos 26:316–22.

Johnson, C. G.
1950. The comparison of suction trap, sticky trap, and townet for the quantitative sampling of small air-borne insects. Ann. Appl. Biol. 37:268–85.

Jones, S. E.
1977. Coexistence in mixed species antwren flocks. Oikos 29:366–375.

Karr, J. R.
1976. On the relative abundance of migrants from the north temperate zone in tropical habitats. Wils. Bull. 88:433–58.

Lack, D.
1971. Ecological Isolation in Birds. Cambridge, Mass.: Harvard Univ. Press.

Lack, D., and P. Lack
1972. Wintering warblers in Jamaica. Living Bird 11:129–53.

Leck, C. F.
1972. The impact of some North American migrants at fruiting trees in Panama. Auk 89:842–50.

Login, G. R., and C. A. Pickover
1977. Sticky traps and spider prey. Carolina Tips 40:25–26.

MacArthur, R. H.
1958. Population ecology of some warblers of Northeastern coniferous forests. Ecol. 39:599–619.

MacArthur, R. H.
1972. Geographical Ecology: Patterns in the Distribution of Species. New York: Harper & Row.

Miller, A. H.
1963. Seasonal activity and ecology of the avifauna of an American equatorial cloud forest. Univ. Cal. Publ. Zool. 66:1–78.

Moreau, R. E.
1952. The place of Africa in the Palaearctic migration system. J. Anim. Ecol. 21:250–271.

1966. The Bird Faunas of Africa and Its Islands. New York and London: Academic Press.

1972. The Palaearctic-African Bird Migration Systems. New York and London: Academic Press.

Morel, G., and F. Bourlière
1962. Relations écologiques des avifaunes sédentaires et migratrices dans une savane sahélienne du bas Sénégal. La Terre et la Vie 109:371–93.

Moynihan, M.
1962. The organization and probable evolution of some mixed species flocks of Neotropical birds. Smithsonian Misc. Coll. 143:1–140.

National Audubon Society

1951 Breeding Bird Census. New York: NAS

1954 Breeding Bird Census. New York: NAS

1964. Breeding Bird Census. New York: NAS

1968. Breeding Bird Census. New York: NAS

Pearson, D. J.
1972. The wintering and migration of Palaearctic passerines at Kampala, southern Uganda. Ibis 114:43–60.

Pesman, M. W.
1962. Meet Flora Mexicana. Ariz.: Dale S. King.

Root R. B.
1967. The niche exploitation pattern of the Blue-gray Gnatcatcher. Ecol. Monogr. 37:317–50.

Schaldach, W. J., Jr.
1963. The avifauna of colima and adjacent Jalisco, Mexico. Proc. West. Found. Vert. Zool. 1:1–100.

Skutch, A. F.
1954
–69. Life histories of Central American birds I-III. Pac. Coast Avif. 31, 34, 35.

Smith, N. G.
1975. Spshing noise: Biological significance of its attraction and non-attraction by birds. Proc. Nat. Acad. Sci. 72:1411–14.

Southwood, T. R. E.
1966. Ecological Methods. London: Methuen.

Terborgh, J., and J. S. Weske
1969. Colonization of secondary habitats by Peruvian birds. Ecol. 50:765–82.

Tramer, E. J.
1974. Proportions of wintering North American birds in disturbed and undisturbed dry tropical habitats. Condor 76:460–64.

Ulfstrand, S.
1973. Proportions of Palaearctic birds in some east African habitats. Vogelwarte 27:137–41.

Ulfstrand, S., and T. Alerstam
1977. Bird communities of Brachystegia and Acacia woodlands in Zambia. J. Orn. 118:156–74.

Willis, E. O.
1966. The role of migrant birds at swarms of army ants. Living Bird 5:187–231.

EDWIN O. WILLIS
219 West Plata Street
Tucson, Arizona 85705

Ecological Roles of Migratory and Resident Birds on Barro Colorado Island, Panama

ABSTRACT

An estimate of species, individuals and biomasses of birds on forested Barro Colorado Island (14.8 km^2), Panama, indicates that migrants, even though there are many species, are only about 1 out of 16 individuals in the avifauna on an annual basis; at the October peak, migrants are 1 out of 7 birds. Migrants average one-third the weight of residents, and thus are only about 2 percent of the biomass on an annual basis and 5 percent at the October peak.

Migrants tend to concentrate in scrub patches and along the lake shore, but residents also concentrate along shore. Migrants are moderately common in young forest and uncommon in old forest, while residents decrease only slightly in old forest. However, many individual migrants (in a large area) and several migrant species use forest, so that human cutting of tropical forests can have drastic effects on migratory birds as well as resident ones.

Migrants tend to use low levels slightly more than do residents and average much less in weight on the ground and in the canopy. This is largely caused by the fact that migrants scarcely use large fruits, concentrating instead on small insects—which many small resident species and individuals (but a low biomass) also use. Resident biomass is 40 percent in heavy birds that eat large fruit on the ground or in the canopy. Directly or indirectly, large and small fruit account for the food of over half the resident biomass. Foods provided by rather than stolen from the plants thus become important in a tropical forest among residents, though not for migrants.

Migrants of the lake and clearing edge tend not to use large insects, perhaps because a large proportion of the resident birds of edge eat large insects flying out of the forest. Migrants eating large insects are few and smaller than residents, and thus form a small fraction even in the forest. However, migrants eating small insects tend to outweigh residents eating such insects.

Some cases where migrants are rare or fail to winter on Barro Colorado seem due to failure of food supplies in the dry season. Other cases may be due to competition with other migrants or residents. Migrants do seem slightly displaced from peak habitats, levels, and foods used by residents. Perhaps migrants use in fairly normal ways the most abundant foods that they can without encountering aggressive residents or problems of unpredictable fluctuations better exploited by motile resident species. They are least able to use large fruits and insects, foods relatively unavailable in temperate zones.

Introduction

Tropical forest ecosystems usually support large numbers of bird species. It has been uncertain how migrants find places in such avifaunas. Do they displace resident species (Miller 1963), go to habitats and superabundant food supplies unoccupied by domineering residents (Willis 1966a; Leck 1972a), or go to habitats like their normal ones whether or not residents are present (Brosset 1968)? A 1970 estimate (Appendix) of birds of Barro Colorado Island, Panama, gives one an opportunity to look at the roles of resident and migrant birds in a large area (14.8 km^2) in greater detail than has been possible before.

Methods and Habitats

Intensive studies of a few species of birds each year from 1960 to 1971 gave a "scale" of censused abundances (table 1) against which other species can be measured. Daily lists were kept of observed numbers of all species for comparison with censused numbers of the scale species. By 1970, calls and behavior of most species were known, and much information was available on nesting (Willis and Eisenmann ms.). Moderately accurate estimates are therefore possible for average numbers foraging on or over the island per day during the year. Great Tinamous, for instance, seemed about twice as numerous as Plain-brown Woodcreepers, but one-third as numerous as Spotted Antbirds, and hence are estimated (Appendix) to have had an average population of about 200 birds. (A bird present half the year at an average population of 200 birds is counted as 100 birds per day for the year; but a species present half the year is counted as a full species.)

Barro Colorado has several major habitats (Kenoyer 1929; Standley 1933; Eisenmann 1952; Bennett 1963; Knight 1975). Old forest, over 100 years old, covers some 705 ha, mainly on the southwest half of the island. Lighter or young forest, 50–80 years old and in general appearance rather similar to a mature summer deciduous forest in Ohio or Virginia, covers 770 ha on the northeast. Included in these areas, and about evenly divided between old and young forest, are some 0.2 km^2 of scrub, 0.3 km^2 of marshy zones, and 1.0 km^2 of lake edge (66 km long × 15 m deep) with trees or scrub overhanging the water. Small clearings surround navigation lights and the laboratory of the Smithsonian Institution: these areas total about 5 hectares of the total island area of 1,480 hectares (Areas were taken by planimeter from a 1927 map, on which I marked the boundaries between clearings, young forest, and old forest according to my revision

Table 1. Scale of abundances of birds on Barro Colorado

Species	Number on island[1]	Source
Barred Woodcreeper	4–0	Willis 1974
Ocellated Antbird	45–6	Willis 1973a
Gray-headed Tanager	50–50	Willis 1974
Plain-brown Woodcreeper	100–100	Willis 1972b
Bicolored Antbird	150–60	Willis 1967, 1974
Spotted Antbird	700–700	Willis 1972a
Chestnut-backed Antbird	800–1050	Willis and Oniki,1972
Slaty Antshrike	— –2,500	Oniki 1975

[1] First figure for early 1961, second for early 1971. Data for intermediate years often intermediate, except peak of 1,200 Chestnut-backed Antbirds in 1966.

of a preliminary map of habitats provided by Robin B. Foster. Length of the lake shore I measured directly with a string from the 1927 map.)

Birds that would be absent from the island were it not for the clearings are marked "C" in the appendix, and birds that would be absent but for the lake are marked "L"; together these are "lake and clearing species." Others are "forest species."

A minor habitat, small forest streams, includes less than 1 percent of the island surface—for the most part below the forest canopy and hence part of the forest. The air above all these habitats forms another habitat, one that derives most of its insects from the forest. The surrounding lake has some lakeshore birds eating fish or insects that eat forest products, but birds of mats of *Hydrilla* and other offshore habitats are here excluded from consideration.

Table 2 lists patchiness of species as estimated percent of the island occupied. Foods and foraging heights are based on Haverschmidt (1968), Karr (1971), Orians (1969), and my own observations. Weights of birds come from the first two authors, from Pearson (1971), Oniki (1972), and my own observations.

I call "large" any fruits over about 8 mm in diameter and any fish or arthropods over 15 mm in length. Species marked as eating large and small insects in that order eat prey about 10–25 mm for the most part, those marked as eating small and large ones in that order eat prey about 5–20 mm.

The first-listed habitats or foods are the most important for a species, and so on in sequence. For convenience in some calculations, I assume that two habitats or foods for a species are split 70:30, three are split 60:25:15, four are split 55:20:15:10, and five by 50:20:15:10:5 (the "ratio" method).

Edwin O. Willis

Table 2. Percentage of island occupied by forest species of residents and migrants

Percentage	Residents		Migrants	
	Number	Percentage	Number	Percentage
0–25[1]	17	13	3	9
26–50[1]	19	15	8	24
51–75[1]	27	20	10	29
76–100	68	52	13	38
	131	100	34	100

[1] Species with exactly this percentage in the appendix are split evenly between the given category and the next higher one.

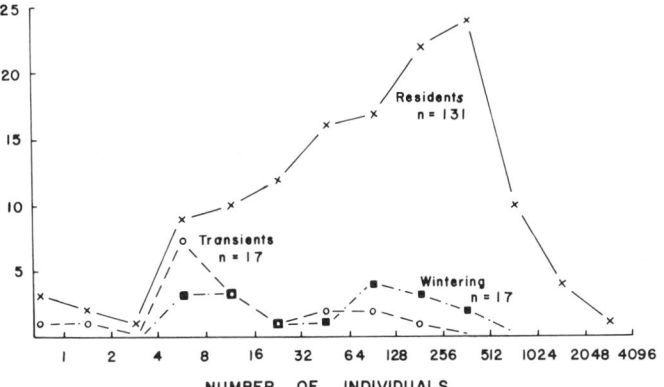

Figure 1. Number of individuals of resident, transient, and wintering migrants in the forest of Barro Colorado Island, Panama.

Results

Species: Individual Curves

Figure 1 indicates that, among forest species, residents peak at about 128–512 individuals per species, transient migrants at about 4–8, and wintering birds at about 64–128 individuals per species. The median resident species has 100 individuals, the median wintering bird 70, and the median transient 10. Since wintering birds are present half the year, their curve would be like that for residents or slightly lower if numbers present per day during that half year were counted. However, some wintering birds at their range limits are rare (see below). Transient species, present three months per year on the average, peak far lower

than wintering birds and residents even if one counts numbers per day for those three months. A few transient species, however, are common.

The curve for residents is skewed to the right, whereas curves of this type are usually not skewed (Preston 1962). Some species with low populations are on their way to local extirpation, and others have probably been eliminated (Willis 1974); the resident avifauna is in the process of "relaxation" (Diamond 1972) to the lower species number suitable for a small "island" of lowland forest. It may be that species with low numbers tend to disappear from such an island, leaving opportunities for common species to become even more common ("density compensation" of MacArthur, Diamond, and Karr 1972). To some extent, however, the Barro Colorado forest list benefits by replenishment of rare breeders from forests on the nearby mainland (as, for instance, the Collared Forest-Falcon that appeared in 1970); it may always have a number of rare but vagile species and too few moderately rare (50–100 individuals) ones. Migrants fit to some extent the left-central part of the curve, which may reflect lowered competition in this zone of abundance.

Seasonal Distribution

Figure 2 estimates numbers of migrants and of residents present at different months of the year. The average number of residents is 33,782 (2,283 per km²;

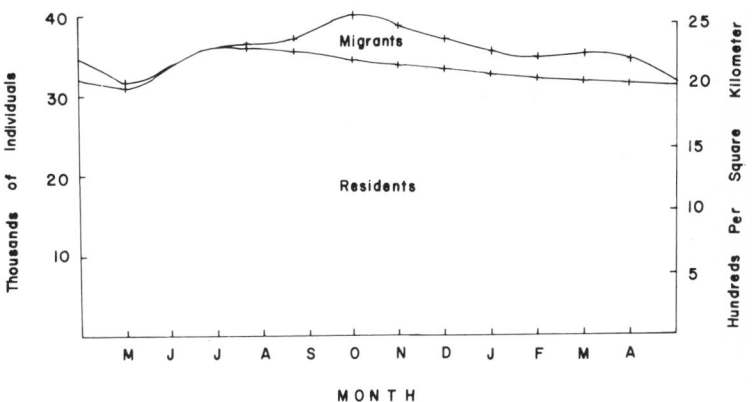

Figure 2. Number of migrants and residents present on Barro Colorado Island at different times of the year.

about 925 per 100 acres; vagrants not included). In May, slightly after the median of the starts of fledging of young for different species (from Willis and Eisenmann, ms.), the number might be 10 percent lower, or 31,000; in July, one month before the median of the

Table 3. Biomass—grams/bird

	Forest	Lake, clearing	Both
Resident (n = 33782)	62.1	145.4[1]	65.3
Vagrant (n = 25)	149.4	382.7[2]	270.7
Winter (A; n = 1778)	19.8	51.1[3]	22.5
Transient (B; n = 536)	20.2	41.3[4]	20.3
Migrant (A plus B)	19.9	50.9	22.0
Total	59.4	137.3	63.4

[1] n = 1204   [2] n = 13   [3] n = 148   [4] n = 3.

ends of fledgings of young, the number could be 10 percent higher, or 36,000. (Because some species have already stopped breeding by the time others begin, total annual fluctuations for all species are less than for individual species.) Since May to July is shorter than July to May, the annual curve should ascend steeply and descend gradually, were it not for high rates of loss of very young birds (Willis 1974). Because of high losses early in life, the descending limb of the annual curve is probably somewhat concave.

The average number of migrants is 2,314 per day over the year (156 per km,[2] or about 63 per 100 acres). Migrants thus are about 6.4 percent, or 1 out of 16, of the birds on the island. Migrants are most numerous in October, when there are some 400 per km.[2] At that time they form about 15 percent, or 1 out of 7, of some 40,000 birds on the island. Migrants are less than half as numerous in spring (Willis 1966; Leck 1972b), and even in the peak month of March form only 7.5 percent, or 1 in 13, of the 34,500 birds on the island. Migrants do not exploit increasing food supplies caused by the new rains and low numbers of resident birds in April and May, being almost gone by these months.

It seems unlikely that numbers of migrants ever exceed by much the magnitude of annual reproductive fluctuations in numbers of resident birds. Numbers of migrants of all species barely reach numbers of the most abundant resident species, the Slaty Antshrike, when averaged over the year. Migrants do cause the total number of birds on the island to surpass 36,000 in the months of September to December.

Biomass

The average biomass for migrants is one-third that for residents (table 3), so that migrants are only 2.3 percent of the avifauna of the island by weight. Probably they form about 5 percent, or 1 gram out of every 20, of the avian biomass during the October migratory peak.

The average biomass for forest residents (62.1 g) is higher than Karr (1975) estimated for "residents" in a nearby Panamanian forest (36.2 g). Barro Colorado has unusual numbers of heavy carrion-eaters for a tropical forest (see below), and perhaps unusual numbers of heavy fruit-eaters. Karr, however, lists as residents only about one-third of the species visiting his tiny study area (2 ha), for the others were seldom seen. If these rarer species had a weight distribution like the regularly seen species, it would be unimportant; but the rarer species are chiefly large birds with large home ranges. One toucan, visiting once a week, can outweigh many small regular manakins. Moreover, Karr notes that on his study area members of a hunter's club had been shooting casually at birds from the size of a Fruit-Crow on up. Karr's suggestion that a tropical forest bird weighs less than an Illinois forest bird needs reexamination, as does his thesis that small but numerous tropical birds therefore use a similar percentage of the energy input to their forest as do temperate birds. (If tropical forest birds are larger and more numerous than temperate forest birds, they use somewhat more energy per unit area per year even if large birds use less energy per gram per year than do small ones.)

Lake and clearing species consistently outweigh forest species, in part because of a few large fish-eaters (see below); vagrants outweigh others. Migrants are not just local vagrants that travel a long way, for vagrants are mainly large and migrants mainly small.

Patchiness

Lakeshore and clearing species necessarily occupy only a small fraction of the island. Forest species (table 2) can be checked to see if they are patchy in distribution, as predicted by MacArthur et al (1966). As Karr and Roth (1971) also note, there are not large numbers of patchy species among residents of this tropical forest. Many occur, some with different abundances, in over 75 percent of the forest area. However, detailed studies of individual species and areas on the island would probably show more patchiness; and surpluses of reproduction in good areas could cause the observed pattern also. Migrants are less widely distributed than residents, in part because of very low abundances of many migrants and in part because many stay out of old forest.

Distribution within Habitat

Ratios of residents to migrants vary widely in different habitats (table 4). Migrants seem relatively uncom-

Table 4. Residents, vagrants, and migrants in different habitats[1]

	Residents		Vagrants		Migrants		Ratio[2] R/Mi
	Species	Individuals/ km²	Species	Individuals/ km²	Species	Individuals/ km²	
Aerial (H = 14.8 km²)	5	3	3	0.5	6	1	3/1
Old forest (G = 6.3 km²)	41	2,081	2	0.5	4	80	26/1
Young forest (F = 6.9 km²)	71	2,500	2	0.6	22	210	12/1
Scrub (E = 0.2 km²)	3	509	2	13	1	255	2/1
Grass, trees (D = 0.1 km²)	3	738	2	38	2	90	8/1
Forest streams (C = 0.2 km²)	2	(255)	—	—	1	(389)	(0.7/1)
Lakeshore (B = 1.0 km²)	30	2,690	3	6	11	226	12/1
Marshes (A = 0.3 km²)	10	968	—	—	3	38	28/1
Total (14.8 km²)	165	2,283	14	16	50	156	14.6/1

[1] When species are recorded in more than one habitat in the appendix, the "ratio" method is used to get species or numbers in separate parts of the range (7 "GF" species with 40 individuals are counted 4.9 species and 28 individuals for "G,"etc.).

[2] R = residents; M = migrants.

mon in marshes and in old forest. These marshes are isolated and small areas, and most marsh birds winter north of Panama—perhaps temperate-zone marshes change less in winter than do land habitats because water is slow to cool or warm. Old tropical forest on Barro Colorado is a stage beyond the maximum forest stage present in temperate zones, which is more like young forest on Barro Colorado; but migrants should find places. The Chestnut-sided Warbler, a bird of scrub in summer, is on Barro Colorado a bird of young forest; it therefore should be possible for other wintering birds to move up a stage. No migrant species stays preferentially in old forest on Barro Colorado, but a number of species use both it and young forest. The number of residents is also reduced in old forest, but less reduced than is the number of migrants. Numbers of residents per square kilometer peak in young and lakeshore forests, numbers of migrants per square kilometer in scrub and lakeshore forests.

Some habitats on Barro Colorado get high ratios of migrants to residents: stream, scrub, and aerial habitats especially. Two species of warblers account for most of the stream migrants. The local tropical warbler of streams, *Basileuterus fulvicauda*, attempted colonization in 1960–61 but failed. Perhaps the small streams of the island are too variable to support breeding species. Small patches of scrub near the clearings and lake are poorly occupied by residents, but migrants are even more dense than in young forest. Migrants may move in from nearby lakeshore habitats.

The lake shore also has a high density of migrants, but because of a high density of residents is not unusual in the ratio of migrants to residents. Aerial habitats are rather sparsely inhabited, but migrants make up a high fraction (about 1 out of 4 birds). The grass and trees of the clearings attract rather low numbers of both migrants and residents, perhaps because grassy areas are so small and isolated on Barro Colorado. In the clearing, the fairly high number of vagrants per unit area suggests that "local migrants" may be more significant than in other habitats, except possibly scrub or along the lake shore.

Absolute numbers of migrants are highest in young and old forest because of the greater areas of these habitats, even though numbers per unit area and ratios of migrants to residents are lower than in edge or scrub.

Table 5 shows biomasses and percentages by weight for different habitats and food types. Average weights are strongly affected by a few large birds in some cases, such as herons in stream and marsh habitats. Average weights of lake-shore birds eating fruit or nectar are below those of birds of these types in young forest, although lake-shore birds that eat large or small arthropods average heavier than their counterparts in young forest. Birds of old forest average only slightly heavier than those of young forest, even though there are several cases where a bird of old forest weighs more than its ecological counterpart or closest relative in young forest. This is largely a result of lower average

Table 5. Average biomasses (g/bird) by food type and habitat[1]

Food	A^3 Marsh	B Edge	C Stream	D Clearing	E Scrub	F Woods	G Forest	H Air	Total
A Seeds	114	250		35.3 (30)	130				120 (30)
B Nectar		9.9 (35)		4.8 (20)	4.2 (20)	16.5	18.9		15.4 (27.5)
C Small fruit	28	16.9 (20.4)		101 (9.6)	19.3 (21)	46.1 (31.1)	38.9 (31.9)		38.3 (26.6)
D Large fruit		209 (35)		B² (30.5)	B² (30.5)	242	326		275 (32.2)
E Large arthropods	108	66.2 (34.1)	245	89.7 (25.4)	58.7 (27.1)	58.1 (33.9)	66.9 (38)	52.8 (50)	63 (34.7)
F Small arthropods	28.1 (13.3)	18.5 (16.0)	(19.4)	11.2 (12.7)	14.9 (17.6)	13.1 (14.1)	11.6 (14.1)	26.6 (31.6)	12.9 (14.7)
G Snails						270	270		270
H Small fish	188	65.5 (170)	332						170 (172)
I Large fish		444 (1077)							444 (1077)
J Herps		395				463 (350)	554 (565)	500	494 (391)
K Birds						597 (350)	760 (565)	500	650 (392)
L Mammals				420	420	565 (350)	728		643 (350)
M Carrion				1350	1350	1352	1812		1482
N Garbage				1350	1350	1350			
Total	103 (13.3)	36.8 (39.1)	283 (19.4)	934 (15.8)	313 (21.0)	63.2 (20)	67 (19.2)	36.9 (60)	65.3 (22)

[1] Residents and vagrants above; migrants (in parentheses) below; blanks = no bird use; "ratio" method used for calculations.

[2] B = limited use by Black Vultures.

[3] Letters are referred to in text.

weight for birds that eat small arthropods and small fruit in old forest, for birds of other food types average heavier in old forest.

Old forest has a somewhat low biomass percentage compared to its percentage area on Barro Colorado, and the low biomass of aerial birds is notable, but otherwise percentages by biomass (except for heavy vultures of clearings) correspond closely to percentages of area of habitats on the island. Migrant birds, however, concentrate on small arthropods in stream, aerial, edge, and young-forest habitats. Further discussion of food types follows.

Foraging Height

Table 6 indicates that many resident individuals forage high in the forest, while peak numbers of migrants forage lower. Many species of migrants, however, use high zones. Lake and clearing migrants are nearly twice as abundant compared to residents as are migrants in forest. Because vegetation is generally lower along the lake and in the clearings, both migrants and residents peak closer to the ground there than do their counterparts in forest.

Ground residents are more common along the lake

Edwin O. Willis

Table 6.   Birds foraging at different heights

| | Forest species (14 km²) | | | | | Lake and clearing species (0.8 km²)[1] | | | | |
| | Residents | | Migrants | | | Residents | | Migrants | | |
	Species	Birds/ km²	Species	Birds/ km²	R^2	Species	Birds/ km²	Species	Birds/ km²	R^2
Ground	8	77	5	16	4.8	8	172	1	12	14.0
0.2–1.2 m	7	138	3	18	7.7	9	359	3	46	8.0
1.2–5 m	16	341	5	36	9.5	6	192	4	65	3.0
5–10 m	29	675	4	39	17.0	4	397	4	53	7.5
10–25 m	40	733	9	26	28.0	2	175	1	6	29.0
25–35 m	27	359	4	19	19.0	5	234	2	4	58.0
Aerial	4	3	4	1	3.0	—	—	1	3	—
Total	131	2328	34	154	15.0	34	1505	16	190	8.0

[1] True lake and clearing species seldom penetrate more than 3 or 4 m from the 66 km of clearing and lake edge, hence the area available to them is at least 0.7 km² less than for all species along the edge (in Table 4), for which the dividing line is taken as 15 m back.

[2] "R" is the ratio between resident and migrant individuals.

shore, but ground migrants are equally common there and in forest. (However, several resident forest birds that drop to the ground from low perches are counted in Stratum B). The percentage of resident forest species that forage on the ground (Stratum A) is low on Barro Colorado, 6 percent as in Illinois forests rather than 11–15 percent as in most tropical forests (Karr 1971). Several species that forage from the ground have disappeared from Barro Colorado (Willis, 1974).

I divide the forest into six levels, while most other authors have used three to five. Splitting and recombining totals for forest residents in Table 6 so as to obtain four levels would give 8–23–49–47 species, with dividing heights at 0.2, 5, and 17 m. Seventeen percent would be at 0.2–5 m, a low percentage compared to results of other authors. Thirty seven percent would be at 5–17 m, a high fraction, and 35 percent above 17 m (normal). Graphs with more accurate height information are often necessary to detect shifts due to competition (Willis 1966b) or differing amounts of vegetation (Pearson 1971).

Table 7 shows average weights and percentages by weight for differing forest strata. As Pearson (1971) found in Peru, ground birds and birds of the canopy outweigh birds of intermediate levels. Lack of horizontal perches at intermediate levels probably causes this. Migrants are especially small compared to residents high and low, and closer to resident weights in between; but migrants also show low weights at intermediate levels. By percentage, very little resident bio-

mass is at B to D levels in the forest; but migrants distribute themselves fairly evenly from ground to canopy. On the lake shore, weights of residents are still above average up to well above the ground, probably reflecting the presence of strong horizontal branches even at middle and low levels. Percentages by biomass remain high in the B to D levels. Migrants generally weigh less than residents; the migrant peak in D is caused by assigning the Osprey to that level (its food comes from A). Vagrants along the lake shore include some heavy herons at low levels; vagrants also include some heavy canopy or aerial hawks and kites.

Foods of Individual Species

Table 8 indicates that, among both migrants and residents, many species and individuals eat small arthropods. Migrants use large insects, large and small fruits, and nectar much less than do residents. Most migrants come from summer zones where such foods are uncommon; they are usually small-beaked (Cox 1968; Schoener 1971). At the lake and clearing and in more open parts of the Canal Zone, migrants take small fruits and nectar more commonly (Leck 1972a). Leck found that migrants at fruiting trees were often small species supplanted by residents, especially in October–November when fruits were rather scarce. Competition early in the wintering season may drive migrants off Barro Colorado to parts of Panama where fruit trees are less used by residents. Many migrants

Table 7. Average biomass (g/bird[1]) and percentages by biomass for differing forest levels

| | Biomass | | | | | | | | |
| | Forest | | | Lake and clearing | | | Total | | |
	R	V	M	R	V	M	R	V	M
A[2] Ground	300.7	—	33.0	169.9	666.7	40.0	285.9	666.7	33.1
B 0.2–1.2 m	22.9	60.0	21.0	69.7	146.7	14.3	29.9	125.0	20.1
C 1.3–5 m	30.5	—	14.1	74.0	10.5	16.6	31.5	10.5	14.3
D 5.1–10 m	22.8	—	12.2	45.9	14.0	116.2	23.5	14.0	19.9
E 10.1–25 m	62.5	70.0	23.1	51.2	—	35.0	62.4	70.0	23.2
F 25.1–35 m	123.2	265.0	28.9	524.7	—	221.7	137.6	265.0	31.0
G Aerial	714.9	141.6	34.3	—	500.0	30.0	714.9	181.4	33.8
	Percentages								
A Ground	16.1	—	17.2	13.4	80.4	5.2	15.9	59.1	15.4
B 0.2–1.2 m	2.2	3.4	12.4	11.4	8.9	6.9	2.9	7.4	11.6
C 1.3–5 m	7.2	—	16.6	6.5	0.4	11.2	7.2	0.3	15.8
D 5.1–10 m	10.6	—	15.3	8.6	0.3	65.0	10.5	0.2	22.8
E 10.1–25 m	31.7	3.9	19.2	4.1	—	2.3	29.5	1.0	16.7
F 25.1–35 m	30.6	29.5	18.1	56.0	—	8.6	32.5	7.8	16.6
G Aerial	1.6	63.2	1.2	—	10.0	0.8	1.5	24.2	1.1

[1] R = resident; V = vagrant; M = migrant.

[2] Letters referred to in text.

that follow army ants are supplanted by residents in October and November (Willis 1966a); many move on to South America thereafter, when because of dry weather ant raids become scarce. However, the fact that many migrants eating small arthropods do not move off Barro Colorado, despite large numbers of residents, suggests that migrants are not at such a competitive disadvantage away from ants as over ants.

Compared with other tropical forests listed by Karr (1971) and Fogden (1972), the Barro Colorado forest totals of 60 percent insectivorous resident species, 4 percent nectarivores, and 9 percent carnivores and carrion eaters are about normal. Twenty seven percent frugivores is high. Many authors count certain species as "omnivores" rather than using a ratio method; if one assigns such species 40 percent to frugivores, 45 percent to insectivores, and 5 percent to nectarivores, the Barro Colorado frugivore totals are still high for a lowland locality and insectivore totals slightly low.

Migrant species reaching Barro Colorado are mostly insectivores, 88 percent as compared to 76 percent of a breeding avifauna in Illinois (Karr 1968). The graminivores in that avifauna mainly winter to the north

of Barro Colorado, accounting for much of the difference. Lein (1972) notes that graminivores are replaced by frugivores as one goes into the tropics.

Table 5 presents bird biomasses and Table 9 percentages by weight for differing food types and habitats. Seed-eating rails in marshes are heavy; fringillids in open areas are small. Nectarivorous hummingbirds are small, but honeycreepers and parakeets raise average weights in forests. Birds that eat large fruit are very heavy, as are hawks and others eating snails to carrion. Hawks that eat birds and mammals outweigh those that eat amphibians and reptiles. Carrion-eaters are the heaviest birds of all. Birds that eat nectar, small fruit, and small arthropods are small. (An increase in average weight of birds eating small fruit in forests is largely due to several birds that eat both large and small fruits there.) About 40 percent of the forest biomass eats large fruit. By weight, nearly half the residents eat large or small fruit. Since many of the heavy fish-eaters eat fish that are frugivorous, the biomass attributable directly or indirectly to fruit is greater here than Karr (1975) reports for some other tropical forests. (He omits, however, from his own lists

Edwin O. Willis

Table 8. Birds[1] eating various foods on Barro Colorado

| | Forest Species | | | | Lake and Clearing Species | | | |
| | Residents | | Migrants | | Residents | | Migrants | |
	Species	Number	Species	Number	Species	Number	Species	Number
Seeds (A)[3]	—	—	—	—	4	104	1	1
Nectar (B)	5	917	—	—	2	6	—	2
Small Fruit (C)	17	4803	3	131	2	142	2	33
Large Fruit (D)	18	3238	—	—	1	21	—	—
Large Arthropods (E)	41	9210	6	389	8	535	4	6
Small Arthropods (F)	36	14200	24	1638	9	226	6	103
Snails (G)	1	10	—	—	—	—	—	—
Small Fish (H)	1	7	—	—	4	93	—	1
Large Fish (I)	—	—	—	—	3	16	2	4
Amph., Rept. (J)	3	47	1	3	—	2	1	1
Birds (K)	4	21	—	1	—	—	—	—
Mammals (L)	4	65	—	1	—	—	—	—
Carrion (M)[2]	2	60	—	—	—	18	—	—
Garbage (N)	—	—	—	—	1	42	—	—
Total	131	32578	34	2163	34	1204	16	151

[1] Calculated by "ratio" method when species eats more than one food.

[2] Some migrant Turkey Vultures are counted among residents.

[3] Letters are referred in text.

of residents many heavy fruit-eaters that he saw infrequently.) Some of the high biomass of fruit-eaters may be a consequence of local extermination of such mammalian fruit-eaters as white-lipped peccaries and spider monkeys (reintroduced); but heavy macaws (*Ara* sp.) have also been exterminated.

Birds that eat large arthropods form about one-quarter the resident and migrant biomass. Carrion-eaters weigh nearly as much as do birds that eat small arthropods, an odd situation perhaps peculiar to Barro Colorado. The local Black Vultures were in part supported by a garbage dump near the laboratory until recent years. The island also has a very high population of sloths (G. Gene Montgomery and Melvin Sunquist pers. comm.) and other small mammals that, in the absence of large predators, go chiefly to carrion-eaters. Far more often than in Amazonian forests where I worked later, one sees vultures over the canopy or at carcasses in the forest. I have not seen dead fish along the few beach strips and doubt that the shore contributes much to carrion-eaters; but Black Vultures do eat iguana eggs along shore (A. S. Rand pers. comm.).

Migrants are especially small compared to residents when they eat large arthropods (and large fruit, eaten by only a few omnivorous migrants.) Lake and clearing residents eating small arthropods are larger than forest residents eating small arthropods, so that edge migrants eating small arthropods are small compared to residents, but the average forest migrant slightly outweighs the average forest resident. The slight size of forest residents using small insects perhaps results from competition from forest residents using large arthropods, but does leave migrants at a possible competitive advantage; they may dominate small residents or use medium-sized insects more efficiently. The major food type of migrants, small arthropods, supports less than 10 percent of the residents by weight. However, migrants must represent one-fourth of the local biomass eating small insects at the October peak. Along the lake shore, where residents eating large insects are very important, rather few migrants eat large insects.

Seasonal Changes among Migrants

Of 50 migrant species on Barro Colorado, only 9 (18 percent) change their foraging behavior strongly from summer to winter. Eastern Kingbirds, Red-eyed Vireos, Veery, Gray-cheeked and Swainson's Thrushes

Table 9. Percentages by weight for differing foods and habitats[1]

Food	Habitat								
	A Marsh	B Edge	C Stream	D Open	E Scrub	F Woods	G Forest	H Air	Total
A[2] Seeds	0.4	0.1	—³	0.02	0.01	—	—	—	0.5
B Nectar	—	0.1	—	0.01	0.02	0.4	0.2	—	0.7
C Small Fruit	0.0	0.7	—	0.0	0.0	5.2	2.4	—	8.3
	—	(0.04)	—	(0.0)	(0.02)	(0.1)	(0.03)	—	(0.2)
D Large Fruit	—	0.5	—	0.4	0.2	21.6	17.7	—	40.4
E Large Arthropods	0.5	1.7	0.2	0.01	0.01	13.0	11.6	0.1	27.0
	—	(0.02)	—	(0.0)	(0.01)	(0.4)	(0.2)	(0.0)	(0.6)
F Small Arthropods	0.1	0.6	—	0.0	0.02	4.2	3.2	0.1	8.2
	(0.0)	(0.1)	(0.05)	(0.0)	(0.01)	(0.7)	(0.2)	(0.02)	(1.1)
G Snails	—	—	—	—	—	0.04	0.1	—	0.1
H Small Fish	0.4	0.1	0.3	—	—	—	—	—	0.8
I Large Fish	—	0.3	—	—	—	—	—	—	0.3
	—	(0.2)	—	—	—	—	—	—	(0.2)
J Herps	—	0.1	—	—	—	0.6	0.5	0.01	1.1
	—	—	—	—	—	(0.05)	—	(0.02)	(0.07)
K Birds	—	—	—	—	—	0.4	0.3	0.02	0.7
	—	—	—	—	—	(0.02)	—	(0.01)	(0.03)
L Mammals	—	—	—	0.0	0.0	0.8	1.0	—	1.8
	—	—	—	—	—	(0.01)	—	—	(0.01)
M Carrion	—	—	—	0.6	0.3	2.4	1.8	—	5.1
N Garbage	—	—	—	1.5	0.6	0.4	—	—	2.5
Total	1.4	4.3	0.5	2.6	1.1	49.9	38.7	0.1	98.6
	(0.0)	(0.4)	(0.05)	(0.01)	(0.04)	(1.3)	(0.4)	(0.05)	(2.3)

[1] Of a total weight of 2,259.3 kilograms. Residents and vagrants outside parentheses, migrants in parentheses.

[2] Letters are referred to in text.

[3] Blanks mean food not found/used in that habitat.

eat more small fruit; and the last 3 often follow army ants. Eastern Wood Pewees move to the edges of treefall clearings; Magnolia Warblers to vine tangles, Chestnut-sided Warblers from scrub into forest, and American Redstarts up to the canopy. Most of the changes seem in the direction of unusually abundant food supplies, toward rather than away from competing residents. The Red-eyed Vireo may avoid the common local Gray-headed Greenlet by staying at the forest edge more and eating fruit more than it does in North America, but competition with the migrant Yellow-throated Vireo seems even more likely. The greenlet is smaller than the Red-eyed Vireo and seems unlikely to dominate it, whereas Yellow-throated Vireos are both large and hold winter territories.

Seasonal Changes among Residents

Of 131 species of forest residents and 6 vagrants, 11 species (3 vagrants and 8 residents) or 8 percent show seasonal movements, but none show great seasonal changes in foraging. A few White-throated Robins move to the summit of the island from higher elevations elsewhere during their nonbreeding months; Plumbeous and Swallow-tailed Kites are absent from September to February. One hummingbird (Coquette), several fruit-eating birds of the canopy (Cotinga, Scarlet-thighed Dacnis, Red-legged and Shining Honeycreepers), and two generalists of the canopy (Oropendola, Cacique) seem rare at times. These absences seem not to result from pressures by migrants. Low food supplies in the late wet season probably account for nectarivorous and frugivorous absences (Leck 1972b). There are no migrant competitors for the kites and icterids, for migrants hardly use large insects. Great Rufous Motmots spread over the island from their nesting gullies in the dry season (January–April), perhaps because their populations are high and large insects less abundant. They are then more com-

Edwin O. Willis

mon at swarms of army ants. Further studies may show other species that shift niches slightly from season to season; Slaty Antshrikes (Oniki, 1975) show several minor changes.

Of 34 species of lake and clearing residents and 8 species of vagrants, 4 of the vagrants and 6 residents (24 percent) seem to have seasonal changes, mostly local migration. Short-tailed Hawks, Great Blue and Little Blue Herons become more common in the dry season; perhaps some are migrants from the north. Three hummingbirds (Mango, Rufous-tailed, and Star-throat) and perhaps others are less common when flowering plants are less common, at the height of the rainy season (Leck, 1972b). Variable and Yellow-bellied Seedeaters are uncommon when grass seeds are rare. None of these movements seem affected by competition from migrants. Disappearance of Piratic Flycatchers and Yellow-green Vireos late in the rainy season could avoid competition from migrants; but Morton (1977) thinks they move to drier regions for fruiting seasons and thus avoid the rainy-season low in fruit on Barro Colorado. Birds of open country in the tropics commonly show local movements or seasonal changes (Karr 1971; Fry 1970) so it would not be surprising if other lake and clearing species show seasonal changes.

Ecological Isolation

The appendix shows that ecological isolation from close relatives is the rule on Barro Colorado, as in many other ecosystems. The closest competitors of a species are not always its closest relatives. Many of the species that eat large fruit on the ground are doves (tinamous and peccaries also do); but in the trees eating fruit before it falls are parrots, guans, toucans, trogons, and cotingas as well as pigeons (not to mention monkeys). Further studies are needed to delimit the niches of members of these two guilds. Small fruit is exploited by manakins, cotingas, several flycatchers, and tanagers; the first are in the forest interior and the others mainly in the canopy and forest edge.

Niches of the many birds that eat small insects seem to separate out rather better. Only among the ant-following birds are there supplantings and interspecific dominance hierarchies of the type frequent among nectar-eaters and occasional among fruit-eaters. Birds eating large insects separate out well, although some generalists like Slaty Antshrikes overlap many specialists. Vertebrate prey and carrion are mostly taken by large birds that separate rather well. Migrants of this type are not common; huge flocks of several species pass over the island without feeding. Competitive exclusion may have operated here or be operating, but the hawks are mostly so rare that studies would be difficult on Barro Colorado.

Wintering Birds and Competitive Exclusion

Eighteen of 50 migratory species winter rather commonly. Most of the 18 seem to forage like a resident species or group using abundant food supplies, but not exactly like it. Spotted Sandpipers use insects of the water edge, competing slightly with *Butorides* herons; nesting habitat is lacking for shorebirds. Ospreys fish offshore, Ringed Kingfishers inshore. Chuck-Will's Widows probably chase low insects from below, while Vermiculated Screech-Owls do so from above; the forest may be too tall and dark for native goatsuckers of the ground, except December–April when many trees lose leaves. The loss of resident Black-faced Antthrushes from Barro Colorado may have allowed Wood Thrush wintering populations to increase (Willis 1966a). The thrush may also compete with such species as Antpittas and Chestnut-backed Antbirds, but seldom finds a place in direct competition over ant swarms.

Acadian Flycatchers move to a zone heavily used by resident manakins and small flycatchers; and the Yellow-throated Vireo and Great-Crested Flycatcher frequent a canopy zone heavily used by resident insectivores. All three of these migrants are larger than their nearest relatives and competitors among the residents. These migrants may fit in between residents that eat large insects and those that eat small ones, or may dominate competitors. The roles of Bay-breasted and Chestnut-sided Warblers also need investigation, for they forage in green foliage inside the forest in ways rather like the common but smaller resident White-flanked Antwrens. Other species of antwrens split this general niche with White-flanked Antwrens in Amazonia, where there are no such migrants.

Black-and-white Warblers check limbs and high trunks, Wedge-billed Woodcreepers low on large trunks. Prothonotary Warblers and Dusky Antbirds would compete were the latter not scarce because dense cover is limited alongshore. Tennessee and Yellow Warblers occupy a lakeside zone of high resident density, but only a few small flycatchers compete directly with them. Ovenbirds and Kentucky Warblers are close to Spotted Antbirds, but forage closer to the ground (Willis 1966a, 1972a). Northern and Louisiana Waterthrushes lack close competitors, for as noted the local warbler of streams was unsuccessful at colonization. Summer Tanagers are generalists of the forest edge and canopy, overlapping with many species—especially Pied Puffbirds for insects, Palm Tanagers for cecropia and fruit, and small tanagers and *Dacnis* for berries (Leck 1972b).

Fourteen of the 50 migrants are rare in winter, usually because they lack suitable habitats on the island or are at the limits of their winter ranges. Few marshes are available for Traill's Flycatchers and

Mourning Warblers, few open areas for Zone-tailed hawks, Gray Kingbirds, Brown-chested Martins, and Dickcissels. Worm-eating, Golden-winged, and Magnolia Warblers as well as Belted Kingfishers are at the southern fringes of their winter ranges; significant resident competitors for the four are Checker-throated Antwrens, Dot-winged Antwrens, Bent-billed Flycatchers, and Amazon Kingfishers. It is doubtful that any migrant-resident pair among these eight occurs together in numbers anywhere. Whether the migratory species push out the resident species to the north and the residents push out the migrants to the south needs investigation. Baltimore Orioles and Rose-breasted Grosbeaks are rare generalists that may compete with Summer Tanagers as well as residents. Possible reasons for rarity of American Redstarts and Broad-winged Hawks are not obvious, although both overlap with several resident species.

Passage Migrants and Competitive Exclusion

Eighteen of 50 migrants pass Barro Colorado in spring or fall or both. Several seem to move on south from Barro Colorado because little food is available for them in the dry season. Competition with resident species seldom is obvious. Resident competitors are few for Lesser Nighthawks, Chimney Swifts, Olive-sided Flycatchers, Eastern Wood Pewees, Cliff Swallows, and Purple Martins. All these species use flying insects in open or semiopen areas, which in the dry period from mid-December to mid-April may produce less food than do such habitats in wetter regions to the south. Tropical swifts in particular seem to follow rain squalls about. To some extent, the Chimney Swift and Purple Martin compete with close local relatives; but there are even more species of relatives to the south where they winter, plus migrants from the south.

Sulphur-bellied Flycatchers and Eastern Kingbirds may compete directly with local relatives, although in British Honduras I have seen both species of *Myiodynastes* nesting together. January to July is the main nesting season for most of these large flycatchers in Panama, suggesting that food is abundant at a time when the Sulphur-belly and Eastern Kingbird are well south or return late and rapidly. The Eastern Kingbird is one of the few species that is more common in spring than in fall, partly because the spring fruiting of *Didymopanax* brings it through (Morton 1971). Mark Leighton (pers. comm.) has recently found it using fruits of *Trichilia cipo* in the fall.

Failure to exclude other species seems likely as a reason for a few thrushes wintering south of Barro Colorado: Veery, Swainson's, and Gray-cheeked

Thrushes are low on peck orders both at swarms of army ants (Willis 1966a) and at fruiting trees (Leck 1972a). Possibly the wintering large Wood Thrush keeps out the smaller Veery and Gray-cheeked Thrush, which are close to its niche. The wintering and dominant Yellow-throated Vireo is the most likely species (if any) to force the Red-eyed Vireo to winter farther south; the related Yellow-green Vireo returns to Panama in January, but concentrates in more open areas. Red-eyed Vireo and some tree-top warblers (Blackburnian and Cerulean) may winter to the south because tall trees tend to lose foliage on Barro Colorado in the dry months. Since there are also high populations of treetop-resident small birds, the total food available may be too low in midwinter and spring. Canada Warblers are in the undergrowth, which dries out only slightly; but they migrate late in spring as if following the wet season north. They overlap with several resident antbirds, especially Spotted Antbirds and White-flanked Antwrens (Willis 1966a). The antwren starts nesting in February, suggesting that food supplies should be high enough to permit the warbler to return earlier.

Yellow-billed Cuckoos, Orchard Orioles, and Scarlet Tanagers are rare, although the oriole winters commonly in more open parts of the Canal Zone. The tanager and cuckoo may be excluded in midwinter by the large number of puffbirds, trogons, and Slaty Antshrikes (Oniki 1975) on Barro Colorado, detecting large insects more efficiently. However, Amazonian forests where the tanager and cuckoo do winter should have more and not fewer competitors; perhaps the late-winter dry season on Barro Colorado is the problem. These migrants seem very scattered in Amazonia in winter, suggesting infiltration into very scattered local niches.

Discussion

The general picture that emerges from the study of this avifauna is that competition between migrants and residents is usually less important than over swarms of army ants or at fruiting trees (Willis 1966a; Leck 1972a). Instead, migrants move to zones abundant with residents and in habitats like those the migrants normally use. Competition from residents only pushes the migrants slightly away from peak zones and foods used by residents. In several cases, competition among migrants seems more likely than competition with residents as a reason for certain migrants' failing to winter or being rare.

Migrants scarcely use food types rare in the temperate zone. Shifts of foraging niche are also rare, so that

Edwin O. Willis

most migrant species forage rather similarly and in similar habitats all year long. Brosset (1968) seems right that many migrants go to their usual niches.

Migrants especially contrast with residents in regard to large fruits, even though the difference is unlikely to be due to competition. Over half the resident avian biomass depends on fruit, flowers, nectar, leaf litter, and other products given by the plants rather than taken from them. Migrants, however, come from habitats where much of the plant production is stolen by rather than given to insects and other organisms. This contrast between the tropical forest and extratropical habitats suggests that a direction in animal-plant evolution may be away from exploitation and toward mutualism. (Since birds that eat insects are one trophic level removed from the plants, over 90 percent of nondecomposed plant losses are stolen even in this tropical forest.)

An earlier suggestion of high densities of migrants in edge and open habitats (Willis 1966a) is confirmed—but often residents are also dense in such habitats. Where patches of habitat are very small or isolated, neither residents nor migrants are dense. Migrants do occupy some scattered habitats and less mature ones, such as scrub, better than do residents.

Migrants are indeed uncommon in tall tropical forest, where populations of resident birds dip only moderately. However, many migrants do winter in both young and old tropical forests, because these forests occupy such wide areas that even low densities per unit area add up to large totals. Moreover, several migratory species—Acadian Flycatcher, Kentucky Warbler—do not winter in patchy or open habitats. Several friends suggested, on reading my suggestion (1966a) of the tendency of migrants to be denser in disturbed or edge areas, that migrants would not be affected by the forest cutting going on everywhere in Latin America. This is not true—migrants can be affected, because the forests of the New World cover such a large area that species adapted to low-density wintering there can be lost.

Barro Colorado Island is, of course, not a representative tropical forest in several respects. It has lost 22 percent of its resident species since it was isolated from nearby forests. Moreover, several other species are declining in numbers (Willis 1974). It is thus somewhat depauperate, both in numbers of resident species and numbers of individuals. This may in part account for the large number of migrant species and individuals there. Comparable mainland forests in the nearby Canal Zone (Karr 1971 and pers. comm.) are much better for residents and slightly poorer for migrants. The lower number of migrants elsewhere may indicate

that competition between migrants and residents is important. It is also possible, however, that Barro Colorado will no longer support as many species or individuals of resident birds because of growth of the forest.

Migrants, especially small-fruit and arthropod eaters, move close to peak zones used by residents. Perhaps this is why many migrants join interspecific flocks of resident birds, such as those around army ants and at fruiting or flowering trees in the forest. (Willis [1972a] suggests that migrants may also lower predation rates by joining resident bands; but migrants are seldom intent foragers and probably gain less in safety than do intently foraging residents.) Perhaps attacks by residents and migrants, especially in October, force some migrants to move on until they find niches less occupied. If so, peak supplies of food and poor supplies of food would be occupied or not by residents, medium supplies by both migrants and residents.

Absolute fluctuations in rainfall (for example, Willis 1974) and in numbers of leaf-litter insects (Willis 1976) are highest where averages are high or intermediate. If this is generally true for food supplies, very poor supplies should be constant or predictable enough for resident species to use them. (Seasonally available foods would, of course, be open mainly to species that migrate or to species that have alternate foods to tide them over.) Very abundant foods might fluctuate but be usable by local migrations—such as those of fruit-eating or ant-following birds. Such foods would rarely "go extinct" despite fluctuations. Resident species could monopolize these foods because they could learn to recognize local predators or local patterns of food availability. Most long-distance migrants probably settle on a winter territory year after year (Schwartz 1964) and probably thus sacrifice peak foods that fluctuate temporally for less abundant but more dependable foods. Perhaps migrants use neither the most fluctuating and abundant nor the most constant and scarce foods, but rather foods at an intermediate level of availability and predictability.

Acknowledgments

The Barro Colorado studies and subsequent writing were supported by grants from the National Science Foundation, Woodrow Wilson Foundation, American Museum of Natural History, Sigma Xi, and Oberlin College. The Smithsonian Tropical Research Institute and its personnel were always helpful. I appreciate the help of my wife, Yoshika Oniki, and of many other people and organizations over the years.

Appendix. Foraging Birds of Barro Colorado in 1970 (See KEY)

	Species	Number	Per-cent/ Island	Status	Habitat	For-aging Height	Prey	Weight (grams)
Tinamidae								
Tinamou, Great	*Tinamus major*	200	95	F	FG	A	D	1000
Ardiedae								
L Heron, Great Blue	*Ardea herodius*	1	1	D	B	A	I	2500
L Green[ab]	*Butorides virescens*	20	2	F	A	A	HE	210
L Striated[ab]	*B. striatus*	50	3	F	A	A	HE	190
L Little Blue	*Florida caerulea*	5	2	D	B	A	HE	300
L Chestnut-bellied	*Agamia agami*	5	3	E	B	A	IJ	550
Tiger-Heron, Rufescent	*Tigrisoma lineatum*	10	5	E	C	A	HE	800
L Bittern, Least	*Ixobrychus exilis*	10	2	E	A	B	EH	70
Cathartidae								
Vulture, King	*Sarcoramphus papa*	10	95	F	GF	G[c]	M	3125
C Black	*Coragyps atratus*	70	50	F	DEF	F[c]	NMD	1350
Turkey[de]	*Cathartes aura*	50	100	E	FG	F[c]	M	1200
Accipitridae								
Kite, Swallow-tailed	*Elanoides forficatus*	2	95	D	GF	G	EJK	400
Plumbeous[e]	*Ictinea plumbea*	2	95	D	FG	F	E	250
Double-toothed	*Harpagus bidentatus*	30	95	F	FG	E	EJ	180
Gray-headed	*Leptodon cayanensis*	5	50	E	F	EF	KJE	450
Hook-billed	*Chondrohierax uncinatus*	10	95	E	GF	E	G	270
Hawk, Tiny[f]	*Accipiter superciliosus*	1	95	C	GF	EF	K	"100"
L Zone-tailed	*Buteo albonotatus*	1	30	A	H	F	JK	565
L Short-tailed	*B. brachyurus*	1	30	D	H	G	KJ	500
Broad-winged[e]	*B. platypterus*	5	50	A	F	E	JKL	350
White	*Leucopternis albicollis*	20	75	F	FG	E	JKL	750
Semiplumbeous	*L. semiplumbea*	20	75	F	FG	D	JKE	280
Hawk-Eagle, Black	*Spizaetus tyrannus*	10	100	F	FG	F	LK	1000
Crested	*S. ornatus*	5	75	F	GF	E	KL	950
Eagle, Crested[g]	*Morphnus guianensis*	2	75	E	G	F	LK	1750
Hawk, Crane	*Geranospiza caerulescens*	2	100	E	GF	E	JE	245
Pandionidae								
L Osprey	*Pandion haeiaetus*	3	5	A	B	D	I	1500
Falconidae								
Forest-Falcon, Collared	*Micrastur semitorquatus*	1	50	E	F	C	KE	550
Cracidae								
Guan, Crested	*Penelope purpurascens*	50	100	F	FG	E	D	1000
Chachalaca, Gray-headed	*Ortalis cinereiceps*	20	10	F	BF	D	D	540
Rallidae								
Wood-Rail, Gray-necked	*Aramides cajanea*	20	20	E	BC	A	E	420
L Crake, White-throated	*Laterallus albigularis*	40	2	E	A	A	AF	50
L Gallinule, Purple	*Porphyrula martinica*	60	5	F	AB	B	AE	250
Heliornithidae								
L Sungrebe[b]	*Heliornis fulica*	10	3	F	B	A	FH	125
L Sunbittern[g]	*Eurypyga helias*	5	3	E	B	A	EJ	240

Edwin O. Willis

	Species	Number	Percent/Island	Status	Habitat	Foraging Height	Prey	Weight (grams)
Scolopacidae								
L Sandpiper, Spotted	*Actitis macularia*	10	3	A	B	A	F	40
Columbidae								
L Pigeon, Pale-vented	*Columba cayennensis*	10	5	E	B	E	D	210
Scaled	*C. speciosa*	5	5	E	BF	F	D	300
Short-billed	*C. nigrirostris*	300	95	E	FG	EF	DC	150
C Dove, White-fronted	*Leptotila verreauxi*	6	1	F	DE	A	AC	130
Gray-chested	*L. cassinii*	400	95	F	FG	A	DC	158
Quail-Dove, Violaceous	*Geotrygon violacea*	100	30	F	F	A	DC	140
Ruddy	*G. montana*	200	70	F	GF	A	DC	125
Psittacidae								
Parakeet, Orange-chinned	*Brotogeris jugularis*	400	100	F	FG	FE	CB	60
Parrot, Blue-headed	*Pionus menstruus*	150	95	F	FG	F	CD	250
Red-lored	*Amazona autumnalis*	200	95	F	FG	FE	DC	400
Mealy	*A. farinosa*	250	95	E	GF	FE	D	650
Cuculidae								
Cuckoo, Yellow-billed	*Coccyzus americanus*	10	70	B	F	E	E	45
Squirrel	*Piaya cayana*	300	95	F	FG	F[i]	E	100
L Ani, Greater	*Crotophaga major*	50	5	F	B	C	E	170
L Smooth-billed	*C. ani*	15	2	F	A	B	E	110
Cuckoo, Pheasant	*Dromococcyx phasianellus*	5	30	E	F	D	EF	100
Strigidae								
Screech-Owl, Vermiculated[k]	*Otus guatemalae*	100	95	E	FG	D	E	124
Owl, Crested	*Lophostrix cristata*	20	50	E	GF	FE	E	"400"
Spectacled	*Pulsatrix perspicallata*	40	95	F	GF	D	LJ	750
Mottled	*Ciccaba virgata*	30	70	E	FG	C	LE	300
Black-and-White	*C. nigrolineata*	10	70	E	F	D	EL	450
C Striped[g]	*Rhinoptynx clamator*	1	1	C	ED	B	EL	420
Caprimulgidae								
Potoo, Great[k]	*Nyctibius grandis*	10	100	E	FG	E	E	550
L Nighthawk, Short-tailed	*Lurocalis semitorquatus*	5	10	E	H	F	FE	"75"
Lesser or Common	*Chordeiles acutipennis*	5	100	B	H	G	F	50
C Pauraque	*Nyctidromus albicollis*	2	1	F	D	A	E	55
Chuck-will's widow	*Caprimulgus carolinensis*	15	75	A	FG	A	E	"100"
Apodidae								
Swift, White-collared[k]	*Streptoprocne zonaris*	1	100	D	H	G	FE	83
Chimney	*Chaetura pelagica*	5	100	B	H	G	F	23
Band-rumped	*C. spinicauda*	20	100	E	H	G	F	15
species (large)		5	100	D	H	G	FE	"50"
Swallow-tailed	*Panyptila cayennensis*	10	100	E	H	G	F	22
Trochilidae								
Hermit, Long-tailed	*Phaethornis superciliosus*	60	95	F	FG	C	FB	5.5
Little	*P. longuemareus*	10	30	E	FE	B	FB	2.5
Jacobin, White-necked	*Florisuga mellivora*	60	95	F	FG	F	FB	6.3

Species	Number	Per-cent/ Island	Status	Habitat	For-aging Height	Prey	Weight (grams)
L Mango, Black-throated	*Anthracothorax nigricollis*	5	5	F	B	F	BF	7.2
Coquet, Rufous-crested	*Lophornis delattrei*	5	20	E	F	E	BF	2.5
C Emerald, Fork-tailed	*Chlorostilbon canivetii*	1	1	D	E	C	BF	4
Woodnymph, Common	*Thalurania colombica*	100	100	F	FG	CD	BF	4
Hummingbird, Violet-bellied	*Damophila julie*	100	95	F	GF	CD	FB	3.6
Blue-chested	*Amazilia amabilis*	150	25	E	F	DC	BF	3.3
C Rufous-tailed	*A. tzacatl*	5	1	F	ED	C	BF	4.8
Fairy, Purple-crowned	*Heliothryx barroti*	50	95	F	GF	E	FB	5.8
L Star-Throat, Long-billed	*Heliomaster longirostris*	1	5	D	B	D	FB	"6.5"

Trogonidae

Species	Number	Per-cent/ Island	Status	Habitat	For-aging Height	Prey	Weight (grams)
Trogon, Slaty-tailed	*Trogon massena*	200	95	F	GF	E	DE	142
Black-tailed	*T. melanurus*	6	10	F	GF	F	DE	105
White-tailed	*T. viridis*	100	60	F	F	D	DE	80
Black-throated	*T. rufus*	300	95	F	FG	C	ED	50
Violaceous	*T. violaceus*	100	95	F	FG	F	ED	50

Alcedinidae

Species	Number	Per-cent/ Island	Status	Habitat	For-aging Height	Prey	Weight (grams)
L Kingfisher, Ringed	*Ceryle torquata*	10	3	F	B	D	I	290
L Belted[b]	*C. alcyon*	2	2	A	B	C	IH	170
L Amazon[b]	*Chloroceryle amazona*	4	3	E	B	C	IH	130
L Kingfisher, Green[b]	*Chloroceryle americana*	30	5	E	B	B	HE	25
L Green-and-Rufous[b]	*C. inda*	2	1	E	BC	B	H	55
L Pigmy	*C. aenea*	20	10	F	CB	B	HE	15

Motmotidae

Species	Number	Per-cent/ Island	Status	Habitat	For-aging Height	Prey	Weight (grams)
Motmot, Broad-billed	*Electron platyrhynchum*	100	30	E	GF	D	E	57
Rufous	*Baryphthengus martii*	200	50	F	GF	C[k]	ED	170

Bucconidae

Species	Number	Per-cent/ Island	Status	Habitat	For-aging Height	Prey	Weight (grams)
Puffbird, Black-breasted	*Notharchus pectoralis*	600	95	F	GF	E[i]	E	"90"
Pied	*N. tectus*	50	50	E	FG	F	EF	25
White-whiskered	*Malacoptila panamensis*	200	75	F	FG	C[k]	E	45

Ramphastidae

Species	Number	Per-cent/ Island	Status	Habitat	For-aging Height	Prey	Weight (grams)
Aracari, Collared	*Pteroglossus torquatus*	300	95	F	FG	E	DCE	198
Toucan, Keel-billed	*Ramphastos sulfuratus*	300	95	F	FG	E	ED	370
Swainson's	*R. swainsonii*	300	95	E	GF	F	DE	650

Picidae

Species	Number	Per-cent/ Island	Status	Habitat	For-aging Height	Prey	Weight (grams)
Woodpecker, Lineated	*Dryocopus lineatus*	20	60	F	FG	E	E	200
Black-cheeked	*Melanerpes pucherani*	150	90	F	FG	FE	FD	57
Crimson-crested	*Campephilus melanoleucos*	50	95	F	GF	DE	E	260

Dendrocolaptidae

Species	Number	Per-cent/ Island	Status	Habitat	For-aging Height	Prey	Weight (grams)
Woodcreeper, Buff-throated	*Xiphorhynchus guttatus*	250	80	F	FG	DC	E	45
Black-striped	*X. lachrymosus*	500	90	F	GF	E	E	51
Wedge-billed	*Glyphorynchus spirurus*	800	95	F	GF	C	F	15
Plain-brown	*Dendrocincla fuliginosa*	100	95	F	FG	D[k]	E	42

Furnariidae

Species	Number	Per-cent/ Island	Status	Habitat	For-aging Height	Prey	Weight (grams)
Xenops, Plain	*Xenops minitus*	400	80	F	FG	D	F	12
Leafscraper, Scaly-throated	*Sclerurus guatemalensis*	150	95	F	FG	A	FE	40

Edwin O. Willis

	Species	Number	Percent/Island	Status	Habitat	Foraging Height	Prey	Weight (grams)
Tyrannidae								
Kingbird, Eastern	Tyrannus tyrannus	30	30	B	BF	F	CFE	37
L Tropical	T. melancholicus	500	20	F	BF	DEF	ECF	40
L Gray[g]	T. dominicensis	2	5	A	B	F	EF	50
L Flycatcher, Piratic	Legatus leucophaius	2	1	F	B	F	CF	22
Streaked	Myodynastes maculatus	50	30	F	BF	E	ECF	47
L Sulphur-bellied	M. luteiventris	2	10	B	B	D	CFE	47
Boat-billed	Megarhynchus pitangua	150	50	F	BF	E	E	60
L Rusty-margined	Myiozetetes cayanensis	70	5	F	AB	C	FEC	28
Social	M. similis	600	70	F	FB	ED	FEC	24.3
L Kiskadee, Lesser	Pitangus lictor	100	5	F	BA	B	EF	25
Flycatcher, Great-crested	Myiarchus crinitus	200	90	A	FG	FE	E	34
Dusky-capped	M. tuberculifer	1000	95	E	FG	E	FE	20
Olive-sided	Nuttallornis borealis	5	10	B	FG	F	FE	32
Pewee, Eastern Wood	Contopus virens	150	30	B	F	EF	FE	14
Flycatcher, Acadian	Empidonax virescens	300	95	A	FG	CD	F	14
L Traill's	E. traillii	2	3	A	A	C	F	14
Ruddy-tailed	Terenotriccus erythrurus	400	95	F	FG	DC	F	7.2
Spadebill, Golden-crowned	Platyrinchus coronatus	200	50	F	GF	CD	F	8.9
Flycatcher, Yellow-margined	Tolmomyias assimilis	500	95	F	GF	E	F	14
Flatbill, Olivaceous	Rhynchocyclus olivaceus	300	50	F	GF	D	FE	22.2
L Tody-Flycatcher, Common	Todirostrum cinereum	6	3	F	BA	D	F	7
Bentbill, Southern	Oncostoma olivaceum	400	70	F	FG	CD	F	6.5
Pygmy-Tyrant, Short-tailed	Myiornis atricapillus	300	50	F	G	ED	F	4.5
Elaenia, Forest	Myiopagis gaimardii	80	20	E	BF	EF	CF	12
C Yellow-bellied	Elaenia flavogaster	1	1	C	DE	CD	CF	25
Tyrannulet, Southern Beardless	Camptostoma obsoletum	150	20	F	BF	ED	FC	8.5
Paltry	Tyranniscus vilissimus	1000	95	E	FG	FE	CF	9
Yellow-crowned	Tyrannulus elatus	400	50	F	BF	DE	CF	7
Brown-capped	Ornithion brunneicapillum	600	95	E	GF	E	FC	"6"
Flycatcher, Ochre-billed	Pipromorpha oleaginea	100	50	F	F	CD	CF	10
Formicariidae								
Antshrike, Fasciated	Cymbilaimus lineatus	5	5	E	BF	D	E	35
Slaty	Thamnophilus punctatus	2500	95	F	FG	CD	E	23.6
Antvireo, Spot-crowned	Dysithamnus puncticeps	200	50	F	FG	D	FE	"18"
Antwren, Checker-throated	Myrmotherula fulviventris	1500	95	F	GF	D	FE	11
White-flanked	M. axillaris	2000	95	F	GF	D	F	9
Dot-winged	Microrhopias quixensis	1000	70	F	FG	D	F	8
L Antbird, Dusky	Cercomacra tyrannina	20	10	F	EB	C	FE	16.5
White-bellied	Myrmeciza longipes	5	5	E	FB	B	E	28
Chestnut-backed	M. exsul	1050	70	F	GF	B	E	27.4
Bicolored	Gymnopithys leucaspis	60	95	F	GF	B[k]	EF	33
Spotted	Hylophylax naevioides	700	90	F	FG	B[k]	FE	17.5
Ocellated	Phaenostictus meleannani	6	50	F	GF	B[k]	EF	51
Antpitta, Streak-chested	Hylopezus perspicillatus	4	5	E	GF	A	FE	42
Cotingidae								
Cotinga, Blue	Cotinga nattererii	80	95	F	FG	EF	DC	55
Attila, Bright-rumped	Attila spadiceus	50	60	E	F	DC	E	35

	Species	Number	Per-cent/Island	Status	Habitat	For-aging Height	Prey	Weight (grams)
Mourner, Speckled	*Laniocera rufescens*	30	50	E	FC	DC	E	50
Rufous	*Rhytipterna holerythra*	70	95	E	FG	EF	EC	36
Piha, Rufous	*Lipaugus unirufus*	80	60	E	FG	ED	ED	86
Tityra, Masked	*Tityra semifasciata*	300	95	F	FG	F	DE	80
Black-crowned	*T. inquisitor*	50	95	E	FG	F	ED	40
Fruit-crow, Purple-throated	*Querula purpurata*	250	90	F	GF	E	ED	100
Pipridae								
Manakin, Red-capped	*Pipra mentalis*	1000	95	F	GF	D	CF	15
Golden-collared	*Manacus vitellinus*	150	10	F	BEF	C	CF	17
Lance-tailed	*Chiroxiphia lanceolata*	1	1	E	EF	D	CF	18
Hirundinidae								
L Swallow, Rough-winged	*Stelgidopteryx ruficollis*	10	10	E	H	F	F	16
Martin, Gray-breasted[l]	*Progne chalybea*	10	100	F	H	G	FE	40
Purple	*P. subis*	1	100	B	H	G	FE	50
L Brown-chested	*Phaeoprogne tapera*	2	100	A	H	G	F	30
Swallow, Cliff	*Petrochelidon pyrrhonota*	5	100	B	H	G	F	20
Corvidae								
Jay, Black-chested	*Cyanocorax affinis*	1	5	E	F	DE	EC	220
Troglodytidae								
L Wren, Plain	*Thryothorus modestus*	20	5	E	A	B	FE	18
Turdidae								
Robin, White-throated	*Turdus assimilis*	1	10	D	FG	B	CFE	"60"
Thrush, Wood	*Hylocichla mustelina*	75	70	A	FG	A	EFC	46
Swainson's	*Catharus ustulatus*	100	90	B	FGE	C	CFE	29
Gray-cheeked	*C. minimus*	40	90	B	FG	B[k]	FCE	30
Veery	*C. fuscescens*	10	50	B[m]	F	B[k]	CFE	35
Sylviidae								
Gnatcatcher, Tropical	*Polioptila plumbea*	200	50	E	F	EF	F	7
Gnatwren, Long-billed	*Ramphocaenus rufiventris*	100	50	E	F	B	F	9.5
Vireonidae								
Shrike-Vireo, Green	*Smaragdolanius pulchellus*	10	30	E	FG	F	EF	25
Vireo, Yellow-throated	*Vireo flavifrons*	70	90	A	FG	FE	FE	23
Red-eyed[a]	*V. olivaceus*	50	70	B	BFE	ED	FC	13
L Yellow-green[ag]	*V. flavoviridis*	5	5	E	B	ED	FC	17
L Greenlet, Scrub	*Hylophilus flavipes*	5	5	E	A	C	FE	13
Gray-headed	*Hylophilus decurtatus*	1500	95	F	FG	E	F	9
Coerebidae								
Bananaquit	*Coereba flaveola*	300	60	F	BF	EF	BFC	9
Dacnis, Blue	*Dacnis cayana*	500	95	F	BFG	FE	CFB	11.5
Scarlet-thighed	*D. venusta*	40	50	F	BGF	E	F	16
Honeycreeper, Red-legged	*Cyanerpes cyaneus*	300	95	F	FGB	FE	BF	11
Shining	*C. lucidus*	50	95	E	GFB	F	FCB	11
Green	*Chlorophanes spiza*	400	95	F	FG	E	FCB	17
Parulidae								
Warbler, Black-and-White	*Mniotilta varia*	80	95	A	FG	DE	F	10
L Prothonotary	*Protonotaria citrea*	30	10	A	B	B	FC	14.5
Worm-eating	*Helmitheros vermivorus*	5	50	A	FE	C	F	13
Golden-winged	*Vermivora chrysoptera*	10	50	A	F	D	F	10
L Tennessee	*V. peregrina*	30	20	A	BED	C	CF	9.1
L Yellow	*Dendroica aestiva*	50	10	A	B	DC	F	9.5
Magnolia	*D. magnolia*	5	20	A	F	DC	F	9

	Species	Number	Per-cent/Island	Status	Habitat	Foraging Height	Prey	Weight (grams)
Cerulean	*D. cerulea*	5	50	B	F	EF	F	12
Chestnut-sided	*D. pensylvanica*	200	75	A	FG	DE	F	9
Blackburnian	*D. fusca*	2	50	B	F	E	F	11
Bay-breasted	*D. castanea*	300	95	A	FG	DC	F	14
Ovenbird	*Seiurus aurocapillus*	10	50	A	F	A	F	20
Water-thrush, Louisiana	*S. motacilla*	50	10	A	C	A	F	20
Northern	*S. noveboracensis*	75	30	A	BFC	A	F	17
Warbler, Kentucky	*Oporornis formosus*	200	60	A	FG	B	F	14
L Mourning	*O. philadelphia*	5	3	A	A	B	F	13
Canada	*Wilsonia canadensis*	100	95	B	FG	C	F	10
Redstart, American	*Setophaga ruticilla*	10	50	B	F	E	F	7.5

Icteridae

	Species	Number	Per-cent/Island	Status	Habitat	Foraging Height	Prey	Weight (grams)
Oropendola, Chestnut-headed	*Zarhynchus wagleri*	20	70	F	BFG	F	ED	140
Cacique, Yellow-rumped	*Cacicus cela*	20	70	F	FBG	FE	EFD	80
L Oriole, Baltimore	*Icterus galbula*	5	5	A	B	E	EFBCD	35
C Orchard	*I. spurius*	5	5	A	ED	DC	EFBCD	20
Yellow-backed	*I. chrysater*	40	30	F	FB	D	EFCDB	45

Thraupidae

	Species	Number	Per-cent/Island	Status	Habitat	Foraging Height	Prey	Weight (grams)
L Euphonia, White-vented	*Euphonia minuta*	2	1	E	B	DE	C	9
Fulvous-vented	*E. fulvicrissa*	1000	95	E	FGB	FE	CF.	12
Tanager, Plain-colored	*Tangara inornata*	200	50	F	BF	FE	FC	16.4
Golden-masked	*T. larvata*	100	50	F	FB	ED	FC	21
Blue-Gray	*Thraupis episcopus*	150	30	F	BF	ED	CFED	30
Palm	*T. palmarum*	100	50	F	BF	FE	CFDE	35
Summer	*Piranga rubra*	30	50	A	FBE	ED	EC	27
Scarlet	*P. olivacea*	5	50	B	FG	E	EC	35
Ant-Tanager, Red-Throated	*Habia rubica*	40	20	E	BF	C	ECDF	35
Tanager, White-shouldered	*Tachyphonus luctuosus*	100	50	E	F	E	FC	15
Sulphur-rumped	*Heterospingus rubrifrons*	500	95	E	FG	FE	FCDE	"25"

Fringillidae

	Species	Number	Per-cent/Island	Status	Habitat	Foraging Height	Prey	Weight (grams)
C Grosbeak, Rose-breasted	*Pheucticus ludovicianus*	1	1	A	ED	C	EFD	48
Slate-colored	*Pitylus grossus*	500	80	F	FG	ED	DEC	42
Blue-black	*Cyanocompsa cyanoides*	300	50	F	F	C	DCEF	31
C Dickcissel	*Spiza americana*	1	1	B	D	B	A	30
L Seedeater, Variable	*Sporophila aurita*	30	5	F	AD	B	A	10
C Yellow-bellied	*Sporophila nigricollis*	2	1	D	D	B	A	"10"

KEY

Number—average number foraging on the island per day in 1970. Birds flying over are counted only if they forage as they fly. Totals showing "1" individual represent one or less individual foraging per day.

Percent Island—Percent of island occupied.

Status—A, Winter visitor; B, Passage migrant; C, Vagrant; D, Local migrant; E, Probably breeds; F, Breeding recorded.

Foraging Height—A, Surface; B, About 1 m; C, 1–5 m; D, 5–10 m; E, 10–25 m; F, Canopy or low aerial; G, Aerial.

Habitat—A, Lake marshes or bushes; B, Lake shore; C, Forest streams; D, Grassy clearings; E, Scrub; F, Young Woodland; G, Old Forest; H, High aerial.

Food—A, Seeds; B, Nectar; C, Small Fruit; D, Large Fruit; E, Large Arthropods; F, Small Arthropods; G, Snails; H, Small fish; I, Large fish; J, Amphibians, reptiles; K, Birds; L, Mammals; M, Carrion; N, Garbage.

Weight—Weights of males and females are averaged.

[a] These species pairs are probably conspecific.

[b] Numbers have decreased greatly since 1970, due to introduction of peacock bass (*Cichla ocellaris*) into Gatun Lake and its predation on small fish.

[c] Height of foraging; prey is generally on ground.

[d] Some are migrants from the north.

[e] Large flocks of migrants, passing over without foraging, are not counted.

[f] Very rare.

[g] I have not seen these species, but reliable observers occasionally report them.

[h] Paul Schwartz reports Forest-Falcon stomachs rarely contain birds.

[i] Down to near forest floor where vine tangles or army ants.

[j] The status and foraging heights of owls, potoos, and swifts are poorly known.

[k] Most food comes from the ground.

[l] Many others forage over the lake near the island.

[m] Fall migration only.

References

Bennett, C. F., Jr.
1963. A phytophysiognomic reconnaisance of Barro Colorado Island, Canal Zone. Smithsonian Misc. Coll. 145(7):1–8.

Brosset, A.
1968. Localization écologique des oiseaux migrateurs dans la forêt équatoriale du Gabon. Biol. Gabonica 4: 211–16.

Cox, G. W.
1968. The role of competition in the evolution of migration. Evol. 22:180–192.

Diamond, J. M.
1972. Biogeographic kinetics: estimation of relaxation times for avifaunas of southwest Pacific Islands. Proc. Nat. Acad. Sci. 69:3199–3203.

Eisenmann, E.
1952. Annotated list of birds of Barro Colorado Island, Panama Canal Zone. Smithsonian Misc. Coll. 117(5):1–62.

Fogden, M. P. L.
1972. The seasonality and population dynamics of equatorial forest birds in Sarawak. Ibis 11:307–43.

Fry, C. H.
1970. Ecological distribution of birds in northeastern Mato Grosso State, Brazil. An. Acad. Brasil. Ciências 42: 275–318.

Haverschmidt, F.
1968. The birds of Surinam. Edinburgh: Oliver and Boyd 445 pp.

Karr, J. R.
1968. Habitat and avian diversity on strip-mined land in east-central Illinois. Condor 70:348–57.

1971. Structure of avian communities in selected Panamá and Illinois habitats. Ecol. Monogr. 41:207–33.

1975. Production, energy pathways, and community diversity in forest birds. Pages 161–76 in *Trends in Tropical Ecology*, eds. F. B. Golley and E. Medina, New York: Springer-Verlag.

Karr, J. R., and Roth, R. R.
1971. Vegetation structure and avian diversity in several New World areas. Amer. Nat. 105:423–35.

Kenoyer, L. A.
1929. General and successional ecology of the lower tropical rain forest of Barro Colorado Island, Panama. Ecol. 10:201–22.

Knight, D. L.
1975. A phytosociological analysis of species-rich tropical forest on Barro Colorado Island, Panama. Ecol. Monogr. 45:259–84.

Leck, C. F.
1972a. The impact of some North American migrants at fruiting trees in Panama. Auk 89:842–50.

1972b. Seasonal changes in feeding pressures of fruit and nectar eating birds in the neotropics. Condor 74:54–60.

Lein, M. R.
1972. A trophic comparison of avifaunas. Syst. Zool. 21: 135–150.

MacArthur, R. H., J. M. Diamond, and J. R. Karr
1972. Density compensation in island faunas. Ecol. 53:330–42.

MacArthur, R. H., H. Recher, and M. Cody
1966. On the relation between habitat selection and species diversity. Amer. Nat. 100:319–32.

Miller, A. H.
1963. Seasonal activity and ecology of the avifauna of an American equatorial cloud forest. Univ. Calif. Publ. Zool. 66:1–78.

Morton, E. S.
1971. Food and migration habits of the Eastern Kingbird in Panama. Auk 88:925–26.

1977. Intratropical migration in the Yellow-green Vireo and Piratic Flycatcher. Auk 94:97–106.

Oniki, Y.
1972. Some temperatures of Panamanian birds. Condor 74:209–21.

1975. The behavior and ecology of Slaty Antshrikes (*Thamnophilus punctatus*) on Barro Colorado Island, Panama Canal Zone. An. Acad. Brasil. Ciências 47:477–515.

Orians, G. H.
1969. The number of bird species in some tropical forests. Ecol. 50:783–801.

Pearson, D. L.
1971. Vertical stratification of birds in a tropical dry forest. Condor 73:46–55.

Preston, F. W.
1962. The canonical distribution of commonness and rarity. Ecol. 43:185–215.

Schoener, T. W.
1971. Large-billed insectivorous birds: a precipitous diversity gradient. Condor 73:154–161.

Schwartz, P.
1964. The northern waterthrush in Venezuela. Living Bird 3:169–84.

Standley, P. C.
1933. The flora of Barro Colorado Island, Panama. Contr. Arnold Arboretum, Harvard, 5:1–178.

Willis, E. O.
1966a. The role of migrant birds at swarms of army ants. Living Bird 5:187–231.

Edwin O. Willis

1966b. Competitive exclusion and the foraging behavior of Plain-brown Woodcreepers. Ecol. 47:667–72.

1967. The behavior of Bicolored Antbirds. Univ. Calif. Publ. Zool. 79:1–132.

1972a. The behavior of Spotted Antbirds. A.O.U. Ornith. Monogr. 10:1–162.

1972b. The behavior of Plain-brown Woodcreepers. Wils. Bull. 84:377–420.

1973. The behavior of Ocellated Antbirds. Smithsonian Contr. to Zoology 144:1–57.

1974. Populations and local extinctions of birds on Barro Colorado Island, Panamá. Ecol. Monogr. 44:153–69.

1976. Seasonal changes in the invertebrate litter fauna on Barro Colorado Island, Panamá. Rev. Brasil. Biol. 36:643–57.

Willis, E. O., and E. Eisenmann
In prep. A revised list of the birds of Barro Colorado Island, Panama.

Willis, E. O., and Y. Oniki
1972. Ecology and nesting behavior of the Chestnut-backed Antbird. Condor 74:87–98.

HENRY A. HESPENHEIDE
Department of Biology,
University of California
Los Angeles, California 90024

Bird Community Structure in Two Panama Forests: Residents, Migrants, and Seasonality During the Nonbreeding Season

ABSTRACT

Trailside censuses of birds were made in two forests in Panama over the transition from wet to dry seasons and during both (October through March) to determine the structure of nonbreeding resident communities and to observe the roles of north temperate migrants. The two forests—only about 20 miles apart—differed somewhat in vegetation structure and age, but primarily in rainfall (70 vs 105 in. per year) and the intensity of the wet and dry seasons. The drier forest was 1) dominated by a small set of common species which 2) were relatively sedentary, and 3) contained a higher proportion of North American migrants which were also more frequent in flocks. The wetter forest 1) showed no pattern of dominance by a few species and had a large number of infrequent species, 2) was characterized by mixed-species flocks which at times included most of individuals observed, and 3) contained few migrants. The term migrants includes a diversity of roles, both temporal—as transients, winter residents and extended transients—and ecological—as insectivores that are territorial, intra- or interspecific flock members, or species that change from predominantly insect to predominantly fruit or nectar diets during winter. The period of winter residency in Panama coincides with the period of minimal insect density.

Introduction

Of the few quantitative attempts to understand the structure of neotropical bird communities of moist tropical forests (Davis 1945; Howell 1971; Karr 1971a, Orians 1969) none—including the present one—has been completely successful. This has been partly due to the logistical difficulty in studying tropical systems that are relatively undisturbed, partly because in each case study of the forest community was only part of a more general study and partly due to the relative intractability of these communities to comprehension. Studies of tropical forest birds have followed those of temperate forests in their concentration on the number of species of breeding birds, with the exception of those of Davis (1945) and Buskirk (1976) who studied communities during nonbreeding seasons. Of the attempts to measure breeding densities, on the other hand, only Davis and Howell attempted to determine the breeding status of the birds. The difficulty in censusing birds in tropical forests and interpreting their status in the community have been discussed, in particular, by Orians (1969) and Howell (1971).

Ornithologists experienced with temperate bird communities tend to interpret tropical communities in terms of the classical territorial mode of dispersion of individuals in a population, although Willis (1967, 1973) and Karr (1971a) show that all-purpose, sharply bounded and carefully defended territories are not the rule among neotropical forest birds, even during the breeding season. The population structure of resident and nonresident nonbreeding birds during the nonbreeding season has rarely been considered. The present study was undertaken with the purposes of comparing the bird community structure of two climatically different lowland tropical forests during the north temperate winter, which in Panama is the period of transition from wet to dry seasons and also the nonbreeding season for most local birds, and of assessing the relative ecological importance of north temperate migrants on these two different forest communities. Both questions are important in view of Fretwell's (1972) opinion that poorer quality nonbreeding seasons may well be more critical to understanding patterns of bird diversity and abundances (and perhaps niche relationships, but see Hespenheide 1973) than are the breeding seasons with their relatively abundant food.

Methods

Two forest study sites described below were chosen in the Canal Zone of Panama and censused about every two weeks between early October 1969 and late March 1970. Censuses were taken over identical routes each time, but for lengths of time which depended on the number of birds seen—shorter for fewer birds, longer for greater numbers. Birds seen or heard were recorded in a manner similar to that of Davis (1945). Emlen (1971, 1977) and Balph et al (1977) have described how trailside censuses may be standardized to allow accurate measurement of relative densities, although this was not done for this study. As a result, conspicuous or loud birds (such as *Ramphastos* spp. and *Smaragdolanius*) are overestimated in density compared with other birds which are secretive and rarely call (*Sclerurus*). Although relative abundances will be discussed in a general way, precise estimation of densities was not the goal of this study, and the difficulties of the census method will not affect the major qualitative conclusions of the paper. In addition to differences in conspicuousness, there were some problems in field identification of several pairs of closely related tropical species. Again, these affect the details in the patterns of relative abundance, but not the general conclusions.

Study Sites

The two forests censused were chosen to differ in climatic regimes, particularly the amount of rainfall, but to be as similar as possible in structure. They also differed in plant species composition, but birds have been shown to be less responsive to plant species composition than to vegetational structure (MacArthur and MacArthur 1961; Orians 1969; Karr 1971a). The two sites are characterized as follows:

Palo Seco dry forest site: The census trail was an unpaved road (Canal Zone Road K-1B) in the Fort Kobbe U.S. Army Base that ran toward the coast from Canal Zone Road K-1, also unpaved, that joined the Palo Seco Hospital area with the Fort Kobbe Beach area. The census road ran through a disturbed forest in fairly advanced stages of regeneration. The road itself had a minimal effect on the vegetation and was under the forest canopy for more than half its censused length, a little more than 0.5 miles. Canopy trees included *Ficus*, *Sterculia* and *Bursera* and were locally mixed with apparently younger *Trema*, *Luhea* and *Cecropia*, the last at the margins of two small openings that were in the process of being overgrown. Understory plants included the spiny palm *Bactris*, *Aphylandra*, *Heliconia*, and locally dense banks of vines. Rainfall data for Balboa Heights and the Balboa Docks areas (Panama Canal Co. 1970), indicate an annual rainfall of about 70 in., with a dry season from mid- or late-December to late April, about 4.5 months. Census dates included both the average wettest and driest months (October and February).

Henry A. Hespenheide

Pipeline Road Moist Forest Site

The census trail ran through the forest study area of Karr (1971a, see for description) and beyond, along a hunting trail along a ridge to the north and east for about a 0.8 km. If one extrapolates from maps of the Panama Canal Meteorological and Hydrographic Branch (Panama Canal Co., 1970), annual rainfall is 2,667 mm annually. Data from Barro Colorado Island (11.2 km west, annual rainfall 2,692.4 mm) provide an appropriate estimate of the distribution of rainfall for the site. The length of the dry season is perhaps slightly shorter than at Palo Seco (December rainfall is less drastically lower), and the driest months (January through March) average about twice as much rainfall.

Seventeen censuses were taken in the moist forest site, compared with 16 in the dry forest. Because new species were being added with each census, and more per census in the wet than in the dry forest, this may have slightly exaggerated the difference between the two in numbers of species (see below). On the other hand, in terms of vegetation structure, the dry forest site was more heterogeneous and attracted, though only briefly, several species characteristic of second growth vegetation (*Thamnophilus doliatus, Muscivora tyrannus, Volatinia jacarina,* each seen once). Second growth vegetation—notably that around the hunt club clearing—was specifically excluded at the moist forest site. I feel therefore, that the two effects—unequal number of censuses, differences in vegetation structure—cancel each other out in affecting the number of species recorded.

Results and Discussion

Number of Species

Although the two forests were chosen to be as similar as possible in vegetation structure, and therefore might have been expected to have similar numbers of resident species by the generalizations of MacArthur and others, the moist forest area had both a higher total number of species (145 vs 107) and a disproportionately higher number of resident species (128 vs 74) than did the dry forest. On the other hand, the dry forest area had twice as many North American migrants as the moist forest (33 vs 17). Table 1 gives the numbers of species and individuals of the birds seen in the two forest sites classified into four major ecological-taxonomic categories: raptors, non-passerines, suboscine and oscine passerines. The table also gives information on the numbers of North American migrants, of species held in common between the two sites, and of birds participating in mixed species flocks, to be discussed further below. Figure 1 shows the

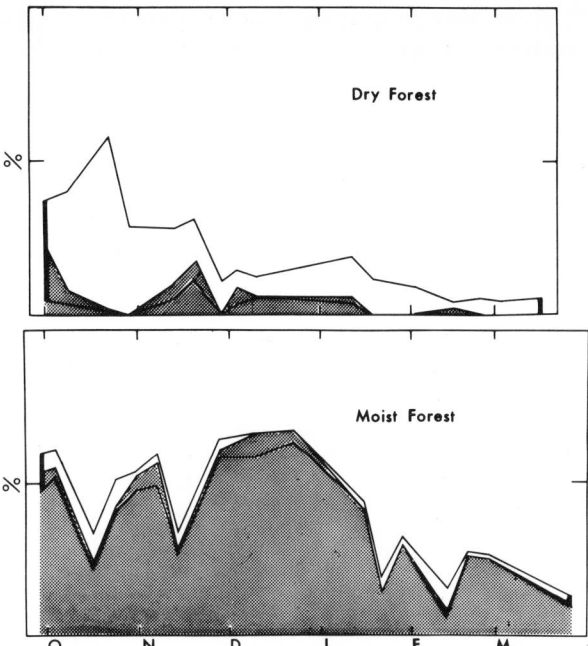

Figure 1. Seasonal distribution of migrants and mixed species flocks during census period at the dry forest (upper) and moist forest (lower) sites. Ordinate of each figure is 100 percent of a census, the abcissa the months of the censuses (October through March, with the first of each month indicated). Migrants are indicated by the center band (bounded on either end by the heavy black bar); mixed flock participants are indicated by the shaded area. Migrants are more frequent in the dry forest, whereas mixed flocks are common in the moist forest.

relative abundances of individuals as migrants and in mixed species flocks during the census period.

Although the differences in numbers of species between the two census areas is too striking to be accidental, it should be pointed out that estimating the numbers of tropical forest birds, either numbers of individuals or species, is very difficult for a variety of reasons other than methodological ones (see Methods). Among these is the fact that even repeated sampling of the same area continues to turn up species not encountered before; at times it seems almost indefinitely. One has the feeling that if one were to wait long enough in a patch of tropical forest, most of the world's birds would turn up there eventually. So, for example, the 145 species I encountered in about 100 hours of observation in the moist forest site did not include 38 species (28 residents, 10 migrants) identified by Karr (1971a) at the same site in 324 hours of observation and 2,400 mist-net hours, and I encountered 18 he did not (14 residents, 4 migrants).

Table 1. Numbers of species and individuals of birds censused at Panama dry and moist forest sites Oct–Mar 1969–70 subdivided by taxonomic/ecological group, residency status, and participation in mixed foraging flocks[1]

		Dry forest		Shared			Moist forest		Flocks Antwren-total		Antwren-dominants		Ant following		Dry forest	
		SPP	IND	IND	SPP	IND	SPP	IND	SPP	IND	SPP	IND	SPP	IND	SPP	IND
Raptors	Tot	10	148	33	4	27	10	39	—	—	—	—	—	—	—	—
	Res	9	141	33	4	27	10	39	—	—	—	—	—	—	—	—
	Mig	1	7	—	—	—	—	—	—	—	—	—	—	—	—	—
Non-passerines	Tot	26	511	266	7	115	40	396	5	5	—	—	1	1	1	3
	Res	23	434	196	6	110	38	390	5	5	—	—	1	1	1	3
	Mig	3	77	70	1	5	2	6	—	—	—	—	—	—	—	—
Suboscines	Tot	25	712	312	10	152	61	1,052	33	475	14	419	16	81	4	8
	Res	19	626	232	7	96	57	995	31	469	14	419	15	80	2	5
	Mig	6	86	80	3	56	4	57	2	6	—	—	1	1	2	3
Oscines	Tot	46	721	202	16	136	34	350	24	114	6	75	1	2	15	94
	Res	23	509	129	6	81	23	294	16	74	3	42	—	—	6	38
	Mig	23	212	73	10	55	11	56	8	40	3	33	1	2	9	56
All groups	Tot	107	2,092	813	37	432	145	1,837	62	594	20	494	18	84	20	105
	Res	74	1,710	590	23	316	128	1,718	52	548	17	461	16	81	9	46
	Mig	33	382	223	14	116	17	119	10	46	3	33	2	3	11	59

[1] Abbreviations: SPP = Number of Species; IND = Number of Individuals; TOT = Total; RES = Permanent Residents; MIG = Migrants from Temperate Zone.

One cannot, however, discuss the number of species in a community without knowing also about both the status and relative abundances of the species. A bird may be censused in low numbers either because it is a vagrant and does not "belong" there ecologically (as, for example, the second growth species recorded at the Palo Seco site) or because it is present in low densities (or is inconspicuous) even though it is characteristic of the habitat. Because the present study was specifically made during the nonbreeding season, one cannot fall back on breeding status as a means for assigning ecological importance to any given bird, but must simply define importance as proportional to abundance. This has the drawbacks that it equates resident individuals and vagrants as ecologically equivalent and is sensitive to the conspicuousness of the birds (see above), but at the same time avoids making necessarily subjective judgments about status (as do, for example, Karr 1971a and Orians 1969) Patterns in relative abundance will be considered in the following section.

Although the two forests are only about 20 miles apart, there is a surprisingly small overlap in their faunas. Of the 215 total species, only 37 (18 percent) are held in common, with a greater proportion of migrants in common (14 of 36 species, about 40 percent) than of residents (23 of 179 species, about 13 percent). The number of individuals belonging to species held in common differs for the two forests. For migrants, 97 percent of moist forest individuals are of species also recorded in the dry forest, whereas only 65 percent of dry forest individuals belonged to shared species. For residents the pattern is reversed: only 18 percent of moist forest individuals belonged to shared species, while 34 percent of dry forest individuals did.

The distribution of species among the major taxonomic-ecological groups differed for the two sites. In the dry forest, among resident species, non-passerines and oscine passerines were equally numerous, with suboscines third and raptors least numerous. In the moist forest the number of suboscine species is triple the number in the dry forest, nonpasserines almost double, oscines and raptors about the same. The dom-

Henry A. Hespenheide

inance of oscine species among the migrants, followed by suboscines and non-passerines, follows the same trend at both sites. The distribution of individuals among these groups will be further discussed below.

Patterns of Relative Abundance

Although the censusing method is sensitive to more conspicuous and vocal species, as discussed, and thereby precludes equally accurate counts of individuals for all species, a number of interesting comparisons can be made that bypass that limitation. One may compare counts of individuals between the two study sites and among the four ecological-taxonomic groups if one assumes that the distribution of conspicuous and inconspicuous species is about the same in both sites and in all four groups. This assumption seems more reasonable than its converse. Because the study is of nonbreeding populations, the question of breeding status is not important, although that of use status is. In most cases, birds present in the census areas were also using the areas ecologically (i.e., foraging), with a few exceptions mentioned below. Relative use is a function of both population size and regularity, measured respectively by the total number of individuals seen over all censuses and by the proportion of the total number of censuses in which the species was recorded. The birds of the two forests differed in both abundance and regularity.

One of the generalizations regularly made in the comparison of tropical with temperate communities is that tropical rain forests have a larger number of species present with fewer individuals of each. This generalization also holds for the comparison of moist forests with dry forests within the tropics. In the dry forest the 5 most frequently seen species account for 29 percent of all individuals recorded, the 10 most frequently seen species account for 44 percent of all individuals. In the moist forest the top 5 species account for 22 percent of all individuals seen, the top 10 species for only 33 percent. A comparison of the plots of relative abundance with relative rank for the two communities shows the dry forest with common species more common and rare species rarer than for the moist forest, in which individuals are more equitably distributed among the species.

If species ranks of the moist forest censuses of this study are compared with those of Karr (1971a) for species whose density he estimated, there are considerable differences. Although Karr does not specify how netting and observational data were combined to estimate densities, the relatively higher densities of lower understory birds in his study compared with this one indicates a heavy reliance on the mist-netting done in the lower understory. My counts indicate a larger

proportion of middle-story species and are more similar to Willis' estimates (1972) of abundances of species on Barro Colorado Island, although this may reflect my interest in mixed foraging flocks. It does not seem worthwhile to compare the two lists in detail, given the differences in census methods, seasons studied (or at least emphasized), and criteria for inclusion ("breeding" versus presence). That there are major differences merely points up the difficulty of estimating the densities of tropical birds, already discussed.

The regularity of species in the counts differs somewhat between the sites. Seven dry forest species (7 percent) were recorded in all 16 counts, whereas only 2 moist forest species (1.5 percent) were recorded in all 17 counts; 25 dry forest species (23 percent) were seen in more than 75 percent of the counts, whereas only 13 moist forest species (10 percent) were seen on more than 75 percent of the counts. This observation means that the climatically more extreme site is more predictable in terms of birds one is most likely to see there than is the climatically more benign moist forest site. Complexity has as its consequence unpredictability.

The distribution of individuals among the four ecological-taxonomic categories differs from the distribution of species, primarily in that suboscines dominate among residents in both sites numerically. In the dry forest three of the four most common species are suboscines (*Chiroxiphia linearis, Myrmeciza longipes,* and *Thamnophilus punctatus,* with *Zarhynchus wagleri*—which had a nesting colony about 75 m east of the lower end of the census route—the fourth). In the moist forest, the five most common species are suboscines (*Myrmotherula axillaris, Microrhopias quixensis, Myrmotherula fulviventris, Pipra mentalis,* and *Thamnophilus punctatus*). Oscines are next most common among residents in the dry forest and are more common than suboscines if north temperate migrants are included. If raptors are included with other non-passerines, they would become more numerous than the oscines, except that the raptors include 117 vultures (*Coragyps atratus* and *Cathartes aura*) which fed on refuse along nearby beaches and only soared above the count area because of local thermals. If the vultures are not included, the oscines still are second most common. In the moist forest non-passerines are more frequent than oscines. Both Slud (1960) and Orians (1969) discuss the dominance of suboscines in tropical forests and Orians also mentions that oscines are relatively more common in drier forests.

Mixed Species Flocks

The two forests differed radically in the dispersion patterns of the dominant species, particularly in the importance of mixed species insectivorous foraging

Table 2. Frequency of occurrence of 20 most abundant species in mixed species insectivorous foraging flocks at the moist forest site

Species[1]	Total	Individuals in flocks	Flocks[2]	Number of individuals[2]
Myrmotherula axillaris	110	108	43	106
*Microrhopias quixensis***	88	84	40	80
Myrmotherula fulviventris	77	77	36	75
*Myiobius sulphureipygius***	30	29	27	27
*Terenotriccus erythrurus***	35	17	16	16
Xenops minutus	19	18	16	16
Thamnophilus punctatus	60	24	14	21
Rhynchocyclus brevirostris	21	16	14	16
Dysithamnus puncticeps	15	15	13	15
*Hylophilus ochraceiceps**	14	14	12	13
H. decurtatus	30	15	11	14
Dendroica pensylvanica	16	14	11	13
*Thamnistes anabatinus**	15	15	9	15
Dendroica castanea	15	13	9	13
Tyranniscus vilissimus	45	9	9	9
Wilsonia canadensis	9	9	8	9
Oncostoma cinereigulare	17	8	8	8
*Microbates cinereiventris**	34	18	7	14
*Deconychura longicauda**	7	7	7	7
*Sapayoa aenigma**	8	8	6	8

[1] Symbols: * = not on Barro Colorado Island; ** = also present in army ant-following flocks

[2] Frequency of occurrence and number of individuals in 62 mixed flocks whose members were determined in some detail.

flocks (table 1). Three of the 4 most frequently encountered species of the dry forest were typically sedentary and vocal in a way that suggested territorial breeding populations. On the other hand, the moist forest was dominated by well-organized mixed flocks of two basic types: antwren flocks with the nuclear species *Myrmotherula axillaris, M. fulviventris,* and *Microrhopias quixensis* (table 2; also Jones 1977; Wiley 1971), and ant-following flocks dominated by *Gymnopithys bicolor* and *Phaenostictus mccleanni* (Willis 1966, 1972). Flocks were also found in the dry forest, but they were much less frequent, less consistent in composition, dominated by North American migrant species, and temporally restricted to the migrants' period of transience. In the moist forest, the 3 nuclear antwrens were also the most frequently recorded species in the cen-

suses, and the regular attendant *Thamnophilus punctatus* was fifth most abundant. Table 1 points out the dominance of the flocks by suboscine passerines overall: 33 of the 62 recorded species (53 percent) and 14 of the 20 most frequent species (70 percent); 80 percent of all individuals seen in flocks were suboscines, 85 percent of those of the top 20 species (table 2). Suboscines also dominate ant-following flocks: 81 of 84 individuals seen (96 percent). The role of migrants at ant-following flocks has been discussed in detail by Willis (1966); in the five ant-following flocks encountered during the censuses, single individuals of *Empidonax virescens* were seen in one flock and of *Hylocichla minima* in two.

Table 2 lists the most frequent species of 62 understory mixed foraging flocks at the moist forest site, predominantly antwren flocks (58 of 62). Wiley (1971), Willis (1972), and Jones (1977) have discussed the composition, organization and ecology of similar flocks on Barro Colorado Island. Comparison of table 2 with their lists and those lists with one another shows a number of differences.

The lack of a number of forest bird species on Barro Colorado Island (Willis 1974) leads to somewhat different composition of flocks at the Pipeline Road moist forest site. Six of the 20 most frequent species in flocks at the Pipeline Road are missing from Barro Colorado Island. From this difference over a five-mile distance one may generalize to say that, because the composition of tropical forest bird faunas changes continuously with geography, and sometimes rapidly because of steep rainfall or altitudinal gradients or topographic barriers, the composition of flocks will likewise change, even over short distances. I have observed lowland flocks in lowland forests at Rincon on the Osa Peninsula and Finca La Selva in Costa Rica, and at middle elevations in Panama (Cerro Campana) and Costa Rica (Monteverde, San Vito de Java) and can assert that flock composition varies considerably with geography and altitude. Concomitant with differences in composition, flocks have appeared to have evolved to meet a variety of ecological situations (Moriarty 1976).

The distinction of Willis (1972) between "antwren" (*Myromotherula axillaris*) and "greenlet" (*Hylophilus decurtatus*) flocks ("alliances") is insightful in view of their different foraging heights (Jones 1977) but is not an absolute one in that both species are often found together in the same flocks (Jones 1977, this volume). These and other lowland tropical flocks are worth much further study.

The participation by north temperate warblers in antwren flocks will be discussed further below. The prevalence of mixed species flocks on a seasonal basis (figure 1) is correlated with the period of minimal

Henry A. Hespenheide

insect abundance, insofar as known (see below), which, in turn, suggests the importance of flocks to the foraging efficiency of their members.

Migrants

As mentioned above, there were nearly twice as many species of migrants recorded from the dry forest as from the moist forest (table 1); there were more than three times as many individuals. Migrants appear to favor the dry forest, which is climatically harsher but which also has fewer resident birds and therefore presumably fewer competitors (Willis 1966). The tendency of north temperate migrants to use species-poor tropical bird communities (second growth, montane, and dry habitats) has been discussed by Willis (1966) and Karr (1976).

Although 14 of the 17 moist forest migrant species (table 3) were shared with the dry forest, interesting differences occur between the two sites. In the dry forest oscine migrants are about 2.5 times as common as suboscine migrants, but in the moist forest the two groups are about equally common. Among the moist forest oscines most individuals were associated with either antwren or ant-following flocks (42 of 56, or 75 percent), whereas migrant suboscines were rarely associated with flocks (7 of 57, or 12 percent), the opposite of the tendency among the residents. In the dry forest, although most mixed flock members were migrants (59 of 105, or 56 percent), these represented only a small part of all the migrants (59 of 382, or 15 percent). Of the migrants in the dry forest, the commonest was *Protonotaria citrea* which itself traveled in small groups and accounted for many of the records for mixed flocks in the dry forest (28 of 59). Of the dry forest migrants, 70 were *Chaetura pelagica* individuals which were not really foraging over the census area and which should perhaps not be included.

Of the 38 species of North American migrants seen at the two sites, only 8 can qualify as winter residents in ecologically significant numbers: *Myiarchus crinitus, Empidonax virescens, Vireo flavifrons, Protonoteria citrea, Dendroica pennsylvanica, D. castanea, Icterus galbula,* and *Piranga rubra*. Several other species are residents in very low densities (e.g., *Mniotilta varia* and *Oporornis formosus,* and species of *Seiurus*), or in other habitats, or at higher elevations (*Vermivora* spp.). In addition to winter residents, there is a small group of birds that appear to have considerable ecological impact because they occur in relatively large numbers, seem to spend a considerable length of time in transit in Panama, and "fit" into the resident communities in much the same way as do closely-related, confamilial winter residents. These birds might be called "extended transients."

The best examples are *Contopus virens*, present at both sites from the beginning of the counts, 3 October, and recorded until 29 November, and *Wilsonia canadensis,* present from the beginning of the counts and recorded until 13 November. *Contopus* sings throughout its stay in Panama, (the type 3 call of Smith, pers. comm.) as do the winter resident *Myiarchus* and *Empidonax virescens; Wilsonia* is almost invariably associated with antwren flocks at the moist forest site (table 2; see extended discussion of this species' participation in antwren flocks on Barro Colorado Island, Jones 1977) and usually in flocks at the dry forest site (11 of 16 records).

Among winter resident North American migrants there is a wide diversity of ecological roles assumed in comparison with the ecology of the same species on their breeding grounds. One group of birds is insectivorous on the breeding grounds but in winter takes primarily fruit (*Tyrannus tyrannus,* Morton 1971) or nectar (*Vermivora peregrina,* Morton, Tramer and Kemp, this volume; *Icterus galbula,* Timken 1970).

Of the species that appear not to change diet, *Myiarchus crinitus* and *Empidonax virescens* act as if they are territorial, as indicated above. Both species call throughout the winter and are found generally as isolated individuals, in some cases repeatedly at the same point on the transect. Territorial behavior on the wintering grounds has been reported elsewhere (Karr 1971b; Rappole, this volume) and now appears to be a regular phenomenon in a significant proportion of wintering species. *Vireo flavifrons* and *Piranga rubra* may also be territorial among the winter residents observed in this study. Territoriality may be combined with very low density to produce a "dilution effect" in which individuals are more widely spaced on the wintering than on the breeding range. This seems to occur in *Mniotilta varia* and *Oporornis formosus* (other authors, this volume).

Among the insectivores, several species become social in either intra- or interspecific flocks. At the dry forest site, *Protonoteria citrea* was seen regularly in monospecific flocks and was joined regularly by other transients, usually warblers, during fall migration. Similar behavior is reported by Tramer and Kemp (this volume) for *Vermivora peregrina* when not territorial at flowering trees. *Dendroica pennsylvanica* and *D. castanea,* on the other hand, regularly and perhaps usually are seen with antwren flocks, and likely with other forest understory mixed flocks of residents.

The view has been advanced that migrants from North America are excluded from tropical forest by large, resident, competitively superior faunas and that those birds which do enter the forest are behaviorally if not ecologically subordinate (Willis 1966). My ob-

Table 3. North temperate migrants in Panama Forest censuses

Species		Dry Forest					Moist Forest				
	Status[1]	Counts (WS/DS)[2]		Individuals			Counts (WS/DS)		Individuals		
				Total (WS/DS)		MSF			Total (WS/DS)		MSF
Buteo platypterus	W	6	(3/3)	7	(3/4)	—	—	—	—	—	—
B. swainsoni	T	—	—	—	—	—	1	(1/—)	1	(1/—)	—
Coccyzus americanus	T	3	(3/—)	5	(5/—)	—	—	—	—	—	—
Caprimulgus carolinensis	W?	1	(1/—)	2	(2/—)	—	1	(—/1)	1	(—/1)	—
Chaetura pelagica	T	1	(1/—)	70	(70/—)	—	1	(1/—)	5	(5/—)	—
Tyrannus tyrannus	T	1	(1/—)	2	(2/—)	—	—	—	—	—	—
T. dominicensis	W	1	(1/—)	1	(1/—)	—	—	—	—	—	—
Myiarchus crinitus	W	11	(5/6)	24	(15/9)	—	5	(3/2)	5	(3/2)	—
Nuttalornis borealis	T	3	(3/—)	3	(3/—)	—	—	—	—	—	—
Contopus virens	ET	7	(7/—)	37	(37/—)	2	8	(7/1)	26	(25/1)	5
Empidonax virescens	W	12	(7/5)	19	(14/5)	—	14	(8/6)	25	(15/10)	2
E. flaviventris	?	—	—	—	—	—	1	(1/—)	1	(1/—)	—
Petrochelidon pyrrhonota	T	1	(1/—)	1	(1/—)	—	—	—	—	—	—
Stelgidopteryx ruficollis	T	1	(1/—)	5	(5/—)	—	—	—	—	—	—
Hirundo rustica	T	3	(3/—)	7	(7/—)	—	—	—	—	—	—
Hylocichla ustulata	T	5	(4/1)	17	(16/1)	—	2	(2/—)	2	(2/—)	1
H. minima	T	1	(1/—)	1	(1/—)	—	3	(3/—)	3	(3/—)	2
H. fuscescens	T	3	(3/—)	7	(7/—)	—	—	—	—	—	—
Vireo flavifrons	W	8	(3/5)	10	(4/6)	3	1	(1/—)	1	(1/—)	1
V. olivaceus	T	5	(5/—)	13	(13/—)	3	—	—	—	—	—
Mniotilta varia	W?	1	(1/—)	2	(2/—)	2	2	(2/—)	3	(3/—)	3
Protonoteria citrea	W	14	(8/6)	77	(40/37)	28	—	—	—	—	—
Vermivora peregrina	W?	1	(—/1)	1	(—/1)	—	—	—	—	—	—
V. chrysoptera	T	—	—	—	—	—	1	(1/—)	1	(1/—)	1
Dendroica petechia	T	1	(1/—)	2	(2/—)	—	—	—	—	—	—
D. cerulea	T	+[3]	(+/—)	+	(+/—)	—	—	—	—	—	—
D. fusca	T	3	(3/—)	4	(4/—)	1	1	(1/—)	1	(1/—)	1
D. pensylvanica	W	5	(4/1)	6	(5/1)	1	10	(6/4)	16	(10/6)	14
D. castanea	W	3	(3/—)	11	(11/—)	5	6	(4/2)	15	(12/3)	13
Seiurus novaboracensis	W?	1	(1/—)	1	(1/—)	—	—	—	—	—	—
Oporornis formosus	W?	1	(1/—)	1	(1/—)	—	1	(1/—)	1	(1/—)	—
Wilsonia canadensis	ET	5	(5/—)	16	(16/—)	11	4	(4/—)	9	(9/—)	9
Setophaga ruticilla	T	+	(+/—)	+	(+/—)	—	—	—	—	—	—
Icterus spurius	T	2	(2/—)	3	(3/—)	—	—	—	—	—	—
I. galbula	W	4	(2/2)	5	(3/2)	—	—	—	—	—	—
Piranga rubra	W	4	(3/1)	5	(3/2)	—	4	(3/1)	4	(3/1)	1
P. olivacea	T	2	(2/—)	2	(2/—)	—	—	—	—	—	—
Pheucticus ludovicianus	T	2	(2/—)	15	(15/—)	—	—	—	—	—	—

[1] Status categories: T = transients; ET = extended transients (see text); W = winter resident; (?) = status uncertain because of small number of observations but best guess based on other sources.

[2] Seasonal distribution: WS = Wet Season; DS = Dry Season. December 15 is taken as the division between the seasons. In the dry forest 9 counts were taken in the wet season and 7 in the dry; in the moist forest, 9 and 8, respectively.

[3] + = presence recorded during census months but not on a census proper.

Henry A. Hespenheide

servations suggest that, although only a few species do winter in ecologically significant numbers in tropical forest in Panama, those occurring have distinct ecological roles and coexist successfully with residents. Of the eight resident species listed above, six were found at both sites: two (*Dendroica pennsylvanica, D. castanea*) were most common in the moist forest; two were in similar abundances at both sites (*Empidonax virescens, Piranga rubra*); two (*Myiarchus crinitus, Vireo flavifrons*) were more frequent in the dry forest, and two others (*Protonoteria citrea, Icterus galbula*) were found only in the dry forest. Thus, although my two census plots show that a small number of North American migrants winter successfully in moist forest that has a large resident avifauna, more winter successfully in the dry forest and among its smaller resident avifauna.

Seasonality and Resources

To my knowledge, the only attempt to relate empirically bird community structure and breeding with the availability of fruit and insect resources is that of Davis (1945, 1946; summary in figure 2). In that study, breeding was shown to be associated with high insect (mosquito) density and the occurrence of mixed species flocks with low insect density, relatively high fruit abundance, and nonbreeding. Davis' study was done in a part of Brazil where seasonal differences in temperature were substantial and correlated with seasonality of rainfall, which makes it difficult to compare with Panama.

Extensive recent light-trapping of insects (Smythe 1974; Smythe and Meyer 1973; Wolda 1978) in Panama and my own impressions from collecting insects as part of independent studies show that the peak of insect activity there is associated with the beginning of the rainy season in mid-April or early May and that minimal insect activity is associated with the transition from the rainy season to the dry season and into the first part of the dry season (December–March). The seasonal pattern differs from one group of insects to another; for example, Wolda (1978) shows that most Homoptera, Tettigoniidae, and Mantidae have minimal (light-trapped) densities for three to seven months during October through April, with the exception of the Psylloidea, which showed peak abundances in two of the four years during those months. Ricklefs (1975) shows high abundances of certain moths at lights during January, February, and March between November 1967 and August 1968, but the first two of these three months had above-average rainfall. Caterpillar abundance tends to rise sharply following the flush of new leaves after the start of the rainy season (Janzen, this volume) normally in mid-April in Panama. The abundance of bees, social Hymenoptera

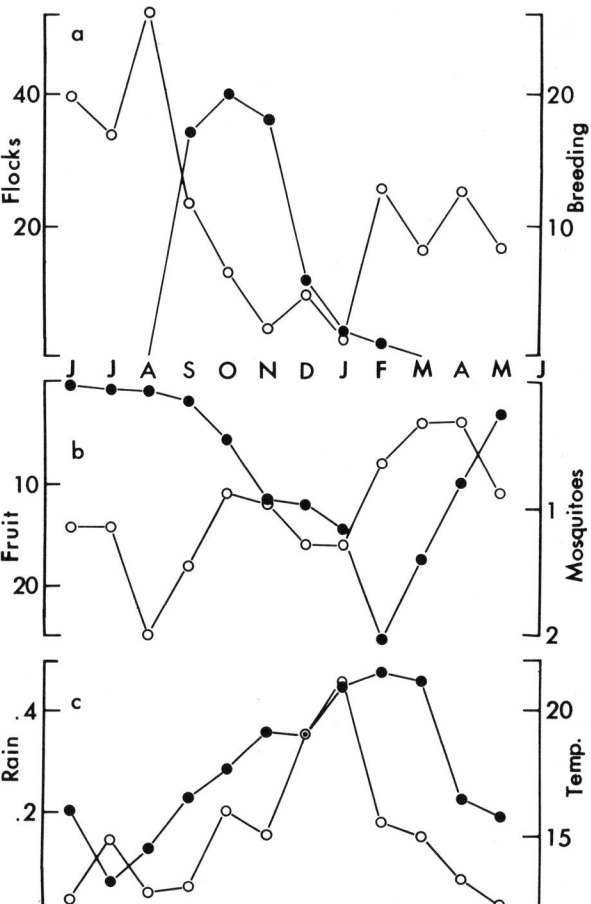

Figure 2. Seasonality of the bird community, food resources, and climatic variables at Fazenda Boa Fé, State of Rio de Janeiro, Brazil; data from Davis (1945, 1946). Upper figure shows proportion (percentage) of individuals seen in mixed species flocks (Davis 1945, table 10 and Davis 1946, Table 4; left ordinate and open circles) and number of species in breeding condition (Davis 1945, tables 7 and 8, "active" species; right ordinate and filled circles). Middle figure shows number of plant species in fruit (Davis 1945, table 4; left ordinate and open circles) and number of mosquitoes (in thousands) of 10 species captured with human bait (Davis 1945, table 6; right ordinate and filled circles). Lower figure shows mean monthly rainfall (in meters) for the city of Teresópolis (Davis 1945, figure 3, 11 years; left ordinate and open circles) and mean temperature in °C (Davis 1945, figure 3; right ordinate and filled circles).

other than ants, and other flower-visiting insects may peak during the main blooming season during the dry season (Croat 1969; Janzen 1967), and may account for the relatively early nesting of sallying flycatchers whose diets include a high proportion of larger Hymenoptera (Hespenheide, unpubl.). Overall, however, the period of winter residency for most North American migrants appears to coincide with the period of minimum abundance of insects. The same conclusion appears to hold in arid parts of Africa (Beals 1970) and in the Antilles (Emlen, this volume).

Acknowledgments

This study was conducted while the author held a Smithsonian Postdoctoral Fellowship at the Smithsonian Tropical Research Institute, Panama Canal Zone. I am indebted to STRI, and especially to Martin Moynihan and Neal G. Smith for advice and encouragement. James R. Karr introduced me to the Pipeline Road study site, and he and Robert S. Ridgely gave numerous useful pointers on field identification.

Literature Cited

Balph, M. H., L. C. Stoddart, and D. F. Balph.
1977. A simple technique for analyzing bird transect counts. Auk 94:606-7.

Beals, E.W.
1970. Birds of a *Euphorbia-Acacia* woodland in Ethiopia: habitat and seasonal changes. J. Anim. Ecol. 39: 277-97.

Buskirk, W.H.
1976. Social systems in a tropical forest avifauna. Amer. Natur. 110:293-310.

Croat, T. R.
1969. Seasonal flowering behavior in central Panama. Ann. Missouri Bot. Gard. 56:295-307.

Davis, D. E.
1945. The annual cycle of plants, mosquitoes, birds, and mammals in two Brazilian forests. Ecol. Monogr. 15: 245-95.

1946. A seasonal analysis of mixed flocks of birds in Brazil. Ecol. 27:168-81.

Emlen, J. T.
1971. Population densities of birds derived from transect counts. Auk 88:323-42.

1977. Estimating breeding season bird densities from transect counts. Auk 94:455-68.

Fretwell, S. D.
1972. Populations in a seasonal environment. Monogr. Popul. Biol. 5:xxiii + 217 pp.

Howell, T. R.
1971. An ecological study of the birds of the lowland pine savanna and adjacent rain forest in northeastern Nicaragua. Living Bird 10:185-242.

Janzen, D. H.
1967. Synchronization of sexual reproduction of trees within the dry season in Central America. Evol. 21: 620-37.

Jones, S. E.
1977. Coexistence in mixed species antwren flocks. Oikos 29:366-75.

Karr, J. R.
1971a Structure of avian communities in selected Panama and Illinois habitats. Ecol. Monogr. 41:207-33.

1971b. Wintering Kentucky warblers (*Oporornis formosus*) and a warning to banders. Bird Banding 42:299.

1976. On the relative abundance of migrants from the North Temperate Zone in tropical habitats. Wils. Bull. 88:433-58.

MacArthur, R. H., and J. W. MacArthur
1961. On bird species diversity. Ecol. 42:594-98.

Moriarty, D. J.
1976. The adaptive nature of bird flocks: a review. Biologist 58:67-79.

Morton, E. S.
1971. Food and migration habits of the Eastern kingbird in Panama. Auk 88:925-26.

Orians, G. H.
1969. The number of bird species in some tropical forests. Ecol. 50:783-801.

Panama Canal Co.
1970. Climatological Data, Canal Zone and Panama, Annual-1968. 60(1):1-49.

Ricklefs, R. E.
1975. Seasonal occurrence of night-flying insects on Barro Colorado Island, Panama Canal Zone. J. New York Entomol. Soc. 83:19-32.

Slud, P.
1960. The birds of Finca "La Selva," Costa Rica: a tropical wet forest locality. Bull Amer. Mus. Nat. Hist. 121: 53-148.

Smythe, N. G.
1974. Terrestrial studies—Barro Colorado Island. In *1973 Environmental Monitoring and Baseline Data*, ed. R. W. Rubinoff, pp. 1-110. Smithsonian Inst. Environmen. Sci. Program.

Smythe, N., and D. Meyer
1973. Terrestrial monitoring program. In *Smithsonian Tropical Research Institute Environmental Sciences Program, Progress Report, 1973*, pp. 1-27.

Timken, R. L.
1970. Food habits and feeding behavior of the Baltimore oriole in Costa Rica. Wils. Bull. 82:184-88.

Wiley, R. H.
1971. Cooperative relationships in mixed flocks of antwrens (Formicariidae). Auk 88:881-92.

Willis, E. O.
1966. The role of migrant birds at swarms of army ants. Living Bird 5:187-231.

1967. The behavior of bicolored antbirds. Univ. California Publs. Zool. 79:1-132.

Henry A. Hespenheide

1972.   The behavior of spotted antbirds. A.O.U. Ornith. Monogr. 10:1–162.

1973.   The behavior of ocellated antbirds. Smithsonian Contrib. Zool. 144:1–57.

1974.   Populations and local extinctions of birds on Barro Colorado Island, Panama. Ecol. Monogr. 44:153–169.

Wolda, H.
1978.   Fluctuations in abundance of tropical insects. Amer. Nat. 112:1017–45.

TERRY B. JOHNSON
Department of Ecology and
Evolutionary Biology
University of Arizona
Tucson, Arizona 85721

Resident and North American Migrant Bird Interactions in the Santa Marta Highlands, Northern Colombia

ABSTRACT

In a subtropical zone lower montane wet forest, North American migrant species numbers peaked in March–April and were about 1.6 times the numbers present in October. This is believed to be a result, in part, of altitudinal migration by migrants wintering in the lowlands as the highlands dry season progresses. The difference in numbers may also be a reflection of different autumn and spring migration routes, but data are presently inadequate to support this hypothesis. Migrants exhibited protracted arrival times in autumn. Numbers of species and individuals increased dramatically in spring, and departures were abrupt. Migrants contributed a higher percentage of individuals to flocks than to the non-flocking community. Migrants were subordinate in their social relations with residents in flocks. Mean numbers of individuals and species of migrants in flocks showed a tendency toward an inverse relationship to those of residents (the more residents, the fewer migrants). The competitive impact of migrants upon the resident community is believed to be small.

RESÚMEN

En un bosque bajo montano muy húmedo de la zona subtropical, los números de especies migratorias norteamericanas alcanzaron a su número máximo en Marzo y Abril y eran más o menos de 1.6 veces los que se encontraron en Octubre. Se cree que resultaba, en parte, de una migración altitudinal por las migratorias que inicialmente se lograron en las lomas, pero cuales subieron durante la estación seca. Quizás reflecione la diferencia de números una diferencia de rutas de migración entre el ontoño y la primavera, pero los datos son tan escasos que no es posible apoyar la hipótesis esta. Las migratorias mostraron unos tiempos inconsistente en llegar en el otoño. No obstante, los números de especies y individuos aumentaron muy dramáticamente por la primavera, cuando se vea que eran muy abruptos las salidas. Las migratorias contribuyeron un porcentaje más grande de individuos a las bandadas de aves que a la comunidad fuera de las bandadas. Las migratorias mostraron subordinación a los residentes en las relaciones sociales, cuando se encontraron en las bandadas. Los números promedios de individuos y de especies migratorias en bandadas mostraron una tendencia a la relación inversa al compararlos a los de las especies residentes. Se cree que el impacto en competencia de migratorias con la comunidad residente es muy pequeño.

Introduction

This report on the Santa Marta highlands is an outgrowth of an investigation of a subtropical zone avian community. From February 1972 through November 1973, data on foraging and flocking behavior were recorded for all species encountered. All flocks discussed in this paper are mixed-species foraging flocks. This paper considers mainly the period of September 1972 through May 1973 and provides information on the avian community as a whole, and on how migrant and resident species relate to each other within the community.

Study Area and Methods

The Cuchilla de San Lorenzo is a ridge on the northwest face of the Sierra Nevada de Santa Marta, approximately 25 km southeast of the city of Santa Marta, Departamento de Magdalena, Colombia. The Cuchilla rises to 2,950 m and is subject to a climatic regime heavily influenced by trade winds from the northeast. The area of principal concern in this paper is a belt of subtropical zone lower montane wet forest (Holdridge 1967) between, 1,900 m and 2,300 m on the north slope of the Cuchilla. The forest is of a fairly uniform height of about 20 m, with emergent trees to 45 m. From a forestry station at 2,250 m, down to a point at about 1,900 m (above the obvious transition into drier tropical zone forest types), a road cut allows inspection of a 4.0 km swath through the forest. Otherwise, the extreme slope and ruggedness of the mountainside make it extremely difficult to observe birds in the forest. All trees and shrubs are heavily laden with moss and epiphytes. There is lush shrub growth of melastomes, tree ferns, and the like along the road cut. There are few cecropias above 2,000 m and few palms below 2,200 m. There are no extensive clearings in the forest studied, although there are adjacent pasture lands.

Meteorological records have been kept at the Estación Experimental Forestal San Lorenzo (hereafter the Station) since 1964, with variable diligence. Mean annual rainfall is about 2,700 mm. During a dry period from January through March, about 4 percent of the mean annual precipitation falls. From June through September, about 54 percent of the year's rains fall. The two remaining periods (April–May and October–December) are transitional, and considerable variation is to be found in the onset of heavy rains in the former period and cessation of heavy rains in the latter period. A record of the rainfall during the course of this study is presented in figure 1. Temperatures at the Station range from about 6° to 20°C, with a mean annual temperature of about 13.2°C. Mornings in the

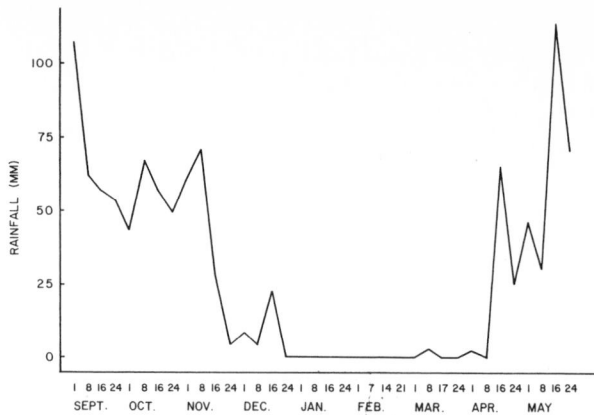

Figure 1. Rainfall (mm) in the study area during each of 4 periods per month, from 1 September 1972–31 May 1973. Monthly periods begin on date given.

study area are generally clear until around 1000 hr, when cloud cover settles to an altitude well below that of the study area. During the drier months, cloud settling is frequently delayed until 1200 hr or later. In the wet season, the sun often cannot be seen for several days at a time. Severe storms are infrequent, and the typical rain is at best a moderately heavy shower, though drearily persistent.

Periodically through the term of study, I walked the 4.0 km stretch of road from 2,250 m to 1,900 m, recording all birds seen on the walk down and various data for each individual (e.g. in flock or not, behavior, foraging behavior, social behavior.). Observations were generally initiated before 0630 hr and terminated around 1000 hr. Time spent gathering data was usually limited by weather conditions, and it was often not possible to complete the transect due to the descent of cloud cover or rain. Thus, observation periods represent varying numbers of hours and days, and cannot be quantified readily for direct comparison.

The social relationships of species in flocks were categorized in three types: 1) joining reaction, when an individual moved toward another individual from a different point of origin and landed within 1 m of the "passive" bird; 2) following actions, when an individual followed a moving bird within 15 seconds of its position change and maintained a close positional relationship; 3) supplanting actions, when an individual usurped the position of another. The methodology is similar to that of Moynihan (1962) and Leck (1971).

Results

Timing of Migration

One hundred forty-four species of birds were identified in the study area. Twenty-five (17 percent) were North

Terry B. Johnson

American migrants (table 1). Parulids were encountered more frequently than any other group. *Dendroica fusca* was the most conspicuous (=most frequently seen) and the most common (=most numerous) parulid in the study area. At lower elevations, in the coffee zone, *Vermivora peregrina* far outnumbered it. Of the nonparulids observed, *Nuttallornis borealis* was the most common species and *Buteo platypterus* the most conspicuous.

The arrival of migrants in the autumn is not so dramatic as is their spring departure. (As used in this paper, autumn refers to the period of late August–early November. Spring refers to the period of late February–early May.) Although there are August records of *Accipiter striatus* (which may be a resident species) and *Setophaga ruticilla*, most migrant species transient or wintering in the study area do not appear until September, and then only in low numbers. By October, five to eight species are encountered in a week in the study area. The number of individuals and (probably) species appear to be larger at a lower elevation, in the coffee zone.

Through the dry season, numbers of species and individuals change little until February, when some transients are seen (e.g. *Oporornis agilis*, *Piranga rubra*, *Piranga olivacea*) and when one wintering migrant begins to depart (*Mniotilta varia*). However, numbers of species and individuals increase through March and April, when up to 10 species are seen in the course of a week. *Dendroica fusca* increases sharply in numbers and becomes especially common in mixed-species flocks.

Parulid species tend to initiate departure earlier than non-parulids, although *Dendroica fusca* lingers later than other warblers. Of the non-parulids, *Buteo platypterus* is the first regularly wintering species to depart, with no records after the end of March. *Nuttallornis borealis* lingers later than other non-parulids; several individuals were observed in early June 1972. However, most wintering and transient migrants are usually gone by early May.

Patterns of Species Numbers

As can be seen from figure 2, the monthly number of different species seen in the study area peaked (14) in March and April. A drastic decrease (to 5 species) followed in May. In contrast, the autumnal peak was 9 species, in October and again in November. Comparing seasonal totals (table 1), 15 species were noted in autumn and 23 species were seen in spring. Of the 15 species seen in autumn, 2 (13 percent) were not seen again in spring; they were *Pandion haliaetus* and *Setophaga ruticilla*. Of the 23 species seen in spring, 10 (44 percent) were not seen in autumn.

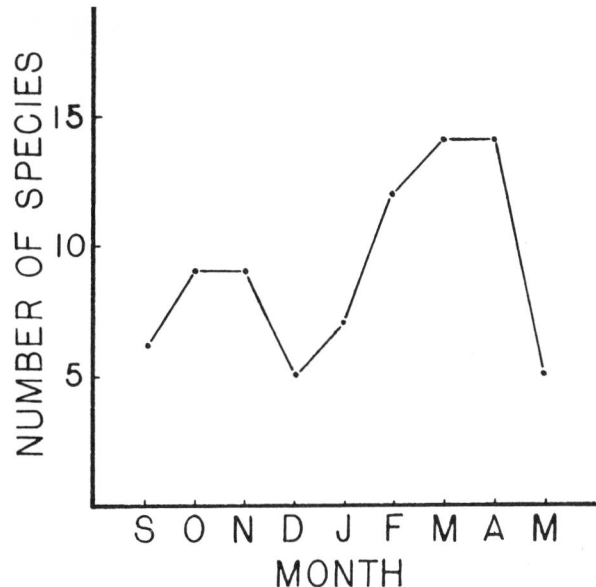

Figure 2.   Number of migrant species observed each month in the study area, September 1972–May 1973.

Composition of the Flocking Community

Table 2 defines the seasons used to aggregate data gathered during the study of flocks. The seasonal limits were derived from rainfall (figure 1) and other weather patterns during this study, rather than from previous climatic data alone. Nevertheless, climatic data sets are incomplete and thus at least partially inaccurate.

Migrant species and individuals comprise a much smaller portion of the "average" flock (n = 149) than do residents (table 2). Over all seasons, they average 1.4 individuals per flock, with a peak of 2.4 before spring departure. Migrants play a larger (greater percentage composition), if not a more significant, role in flocks than out of flocks in all seasons (figure 3).

Resident individuals per flock average higher during the wet seasons than in the dry or transition seasons. The number of resident species per flock also averages higher in the wet seasons than in dry or transition seasons, but only slightly higher. In each season, resident individuals comprise a larger percentage of total individuals observed out of flocks than in flocks.

Nine of the 25 migrant species were observed in flocks for which data were recorded (table 3). The frequency of occurrence varied from 1 individual observed in 1 flock in 1 season only (*Dendroica coronata*), to as many as 11 individuals in 1 flock and at least 1 individual in 14 flocks (58.3 percent) in 1 season (*D. fusca*). Flocking participation over all seasons varied

Table 1. Occurrence[1] of migrants in the study zone, 1972 and 1973

Species	Sept[2]				Oct				Nov				Dec			
	1	8	16	24	1	8	16	24	1	8	16	24	1	8	16	24
Accipiter striatus[3,4]																
Buteo platypterus								X	X	X	X	X	X			
Pandion haliaetus[3]		X														
Chaetura pelagica																
Tyrannus tyrannus					X											
Nuttallornis borealis					X			X	X		X	X				
Hirundo rustica																
Catharus minimus																
Catharus ustulatus																
Vireo olivaceus					X			X	X		X	X	X			
Vireo philadelphicus																
Mniotilta varia	X			X		X		X	X		X		X			
Protonotaria citrea																
Vermivora chrysoptera			X		X	X		X	X		X	X	X			
Vermivora peregrina			X		X	X		X	X							
Dendroica coronata																
Dendroica virens										X		X				
Dendroica cerulea						X										
Dendroica fusca	X	X	X	X	X	X		X	X	X	X	X	X			
Seiurus motacilla	X															
Oporornis agilis																
Setophaga ruticilla[4]																
Piranga rubra																
Piranga olivacea																
Pheucticus ludovicianus									X							
Total species observed during period	3	2	3	2	6	5	O[5]	7	8	3	6	6	5	O	O	O

[1] X = occurrence.

[2] Periods in months as in figure 1.

[3] Individuals observed may have been resident in area or region.

[4] Species observed in study area in last period of August.

[5] O indicates no days in study area during period.

for species observed in recorded flocks from 0.79 percent (*D. coronata*) to 36.9 percent (*D. fusca*) of the total number (n = 149) of flocks observed.

Eight of the 25 migrant species (*Tyrannus tyrannus, Vireo philadelphicus, Dendroica cerulea, Oporornis agilis, Setophaga ruticilla, Piranga rubra, P. olivacea,* and *Pheucticus ludovicianus*) were observed in flocks encountered while I was not recording data. All of these 8 species were much less commonly observed during this study than were the 9 flocking species discussed above.

Non-flocking Migrant Species

The remaining eight migrant species were not observed in flocks. Of these species, one (*Protonotaria citrea*) was represented by a single individual present the morning after a severe coastal storm; three are raptors (*Accipiter striatus, Buteo platypterus, Pandion haliaetus*); three are not forest dwelling species (*Chaetura pelagica, Hirundo rustica, Seiurus motacilla*) and probably are not behaviorally suited for following or joining the flocks studied; one (*Catharus ustulatus*) frequented man-made clearings with ornamental shrubs near the Station.

Terry B. Johnson

	Jan				Feb				March				April				May			
	1	8	16	24	1	7	14	21	1	8	17	24	1	8	16	24	1	8	16	24
														X						
			X		X	X	X	X	X	X	X	X								
														X						
															X					
			X		X	X		X		X	X	X	X	X		X	X		X	
														X						
															X	X	X			
															X	X				
											X	X	X	X	X					
											X			X						
			X		X	X	X		X	X				X						
			X		X	X	X	X	X	X	X			X						
			X							X	X		X							
					X	X		X	X	X	X	X	X							
			X		X	X		X	X	X						X				
										X			X							
			X		X	X	X	X	X	X	X	X	X	X	X	X	X		X	
										X	X									
							X													
							X	X	X											
						X														
					X	X		X		X										
O	O	7	O	7	9	6	7	4	7	10	9	4	10	6	6	6	0	2	0

Social Relationships Between and Among Migrant and Resident Species

There were 74 non-ambiguous social interactions involving *Dendroica fusca* over all seasons (figure 4). It was attracted to resident species far more frequently than they were to it. Summing the join-and-follow actions, 32 (52.5%) of 61 movements involved *D. fusca* joining or following resident birds, and another 20 (32.8 percent) were of *D. fusca* following members of its own species. The Supplant actions observed indicate the subordinate position of *D. fusca*; of 13 non-ambiguous cases, resident species supplanted *D. fusca*; eight times (62 percent), *D. fusca* supplanted residents twice (15 percent), and *D. fusca* supplanted other *D. fusca* three times (23 percent).

Non-ambiguous social actions were not observed often enough to allow diagrammatic presentation of the social position of any other migrant species. However, when data for all migrants other than *Dendroica fusca* are pooled, the results for the 29 non-ambiguous cases (figure 5) are generally like those of *D. fusca*. Again summing join-and-follow actions, migrants joined or followed residents 16 (76.2 percent) of 21

Table 2. Composition and seasonal distribution of mixed-species flocks

Season	Date	Number of flocks	Individuals per flock ($\bar{X}$)			Species per flock ($\bar{X}$)		
			M^1	R^2	A^3	M	R	A
Wet	1 Sept 1972– 23 Nov 1972	39	1.0	11.9	12.9	0.7	6.1	6.8
Wet-dry Transition	24 Nov 1972– 31 Dec 1972	15	1.5	7.7	9.2	1.1	5.1	6.2
Dry	1 Jan 1973– 16 Mar 1973	41	1.2	9.8	11.0	0.7	6.3	7.0
Dry-wet Transition	17 Mar 1973– 15 Apr 1973	30	1.1	9.3	10.4	0.5	6.4	6.9
Wet	16 Apr 1973– 15 May 1973	24	2.4	12.2	14.6	0.9	7.3	8.2
Total	1 Sept 1972– 15 May 1973	149	1.4	10.4	11.8	0.8	6.3	7.1

[1] M = Migrant bird species.

[2] R = Resident bird species.

[3] A = All species together.

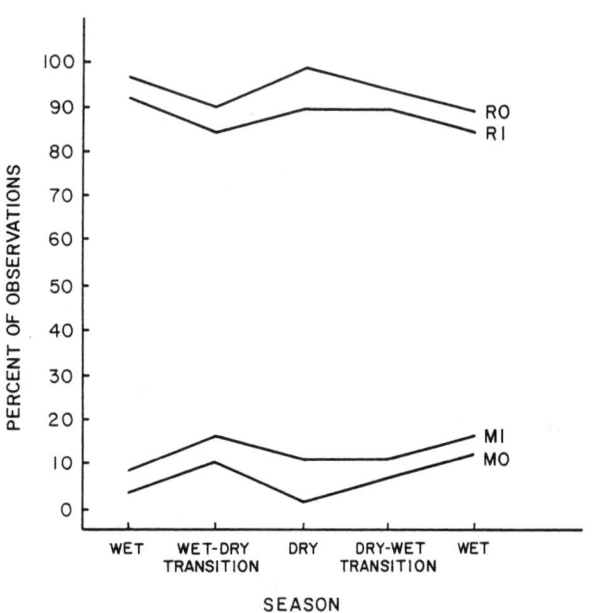

Figure 3. Percentage composition of total observations in and out of flocks for migrant and resident species in the study area. M = migrant; R = resident; I = in flocks; O = out of flocks. Seasons as in table 2. Total number of observations = 1,755 in 149 flocks, 333 out of flocks.

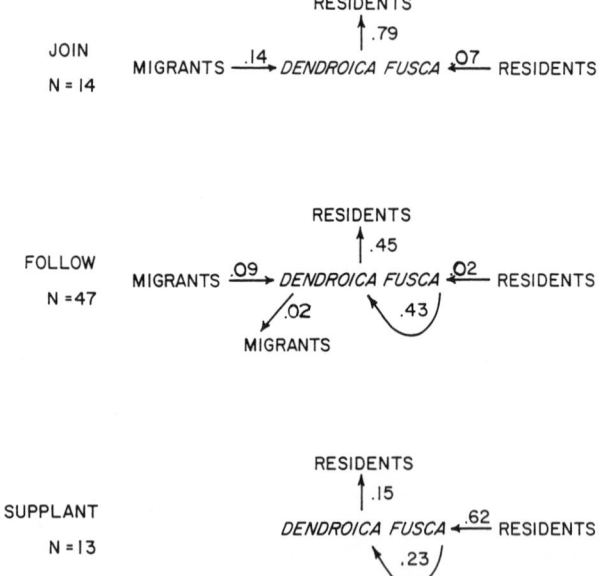

Figure 4 Social actions of *Dendroica fusca*. Arrow points from species which joined, followed, or supplanted to the species which was joined, followed, or supplanted. Decimal fractions are measures of attractive strengths. N = total number of nonambiguous cases.

Terry B. Johnson

Table 3. Seasonal occurrence of migrant birds in mixed-species flocks (percentage of flocks in which species occurs)

Species	Wet	Tran-sition	Dry	Tran-sition	Wet	All
			Season[1]			
Accipiter striatus	X^2			X		
Buteo platypterus	X	X	X	X		
Pandion haliaetus	X					
Chaetura pelagica				X		
Tyrannus tyrannus	X				X	
Nuttallornis borealis	5.1	X	X	X	4.2	2.0
Hirundo rustica				X		
Catharus minimus					16.7	2.7
Catharus ustulatus			X		X	
Vireo olivaceus	12.8	40.0		X	X	7.4
Vireo philadelphicus				X		
Mniotilta varia	12.8	6.7	12.2	X		7.4
Protonotaria citrea			X			
Vermivora chrysoptera	5.1	13.3	19.5	13.3		10.7
Vermivora peregrina	2.6		2.4	10.0		3.4
Dendroica coronata			X	3.3		0.7
Dendroica virens	X	6.7	7.3	X	8.3	4.0
Dendroica cerulea	X			X		
Dendroica fusca	35.9	40.0	3.17	26.7	58.3	36.9
Seiurus motacilla	X			X		
Oporornis agilis			X			
Setophaga ruticilla[3]						
Piranga rubra			X			
Piranga olivacea			X			
Pheucticus ludovicianus	X		X			
Overall	56.4	66.7	43.9	43.3	70.8	53.7
	(39)[4]	(15)	(41)	(30)	(24)	(149)

[1] Seasons (and dates of) as in table 2.

[2] X = species observed in study area but not in recorded flock.

[3] Setophaga ruticilla observed in late August, not in recorded flock.

[4] ( ) = number of mixed-species flocks observed during season.

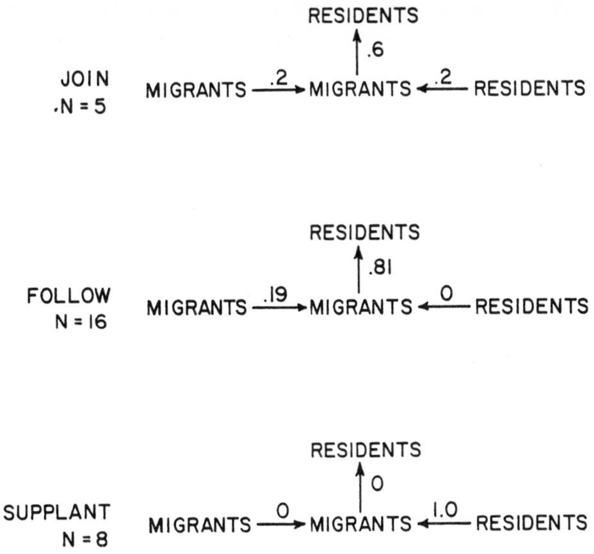

Figure 5. Social interactions involving migrants other than *Dendroica fusca*. Symbols as in figure 4.

actions, residents joined migrants once (4.8 percent), and migrants joined or followed other migrants 4 times (19 percent). Residents supplanted migrants in all (100 percent) of 8 supplant actions observed. Again, migrants assume a subordinate position to residents in flocks, in social relationships.

Discussion

North American migrants are a conspicuous and common element of the study area's species complex from September through early May. The period of occurrence is similar to that of other neotropical areas (see Karr 1976). A somewhat diffuse arrival and dramatic departure of species and individuals are characteristic here as elsewhere in the region. The percentage contribution of migrant species to the area's species list (25 of 144 = 17 percent) approximates the lower values reported by Tramer (1974) in Mexico. However, the pattern for the monthly number of species observed is quite strikingly different from patterns reported by Leck (1972) and Karr (1976). They found that peak species numbers occurred in October and were up to twice those of March–April. In the Santa Marta highlands, peak species numbers were in March–April (14 each month) and were 1.6 times those of October–November (9 each month).

Pandion haliaetus and *Setophaga ruticilla* were the only two species (of 15 total) seen in the autumn which were not seen again in spring. The single soaring individual of *P. haliaetus* seen over the study area may have been from adjacent coastal areas where the species is resident. *Setophaga ruticilla* is probably an uncommon winter resident in the coffee zone below the study area (pers. obs.) and occasional wandering of individuals into the higher forest is not unexpected.

Ten species were seen in spring but not in autumn. The presence of one (*Protonotaria citrea*) was possibly the result of a severe storm accompanied by high winds. Two species (*Chaetura pelagica* and *Hirundo rustica*) are diurnal migrants. Cloud cover and fog in autumn greatly reduce the probability that diurnal migrants will be observed over the study area. I have no lowland records for *C. pelagica* but numbers of *H.*

rustica built to hundreds along the coast in April, while numbers are very low in autumn. Three species (*Catharus minimus, Catharus ustulatus, Piranga rubra*) are uncommon to common winter residents of lower elevations in the Santa Marta region (Todd and Carriker 1922; pers. obs.), especially in the coffee zone. These species may move into the higher forested areas on the Cuchilla de San Lorenzo during the dry season, as several resident species do (Johnson, in prep.). Todd and Carriker (1922) also state that it is not clear whether *Oporornis agilis* is a transient or a winter resident in the area. I have only a single spring sighting for the species. According to Meyer de Schauensee (1966), two species (*Vireo philadelphicus* and *Dendroica coronata*) are "casual" winter visitors in Colombia. I have only two spring 1973 records for the former species, but *D. coronata* was in the study area during February–March 1972 and 1973 and in April 1972 and is undoubtedly more than "casual" (Johnson in prep.). The final species recorded in spring but not in autumn, *Piranga olivacea*, is common as a winter resident in Colombia west of the eastern Andes (Meyer de Schauensee 1966), but was not reported in the Santa Marta region by Todd and Carriker (1922). I have records of small numbers in the highlands of Santa Marta in spring.

There are several explanations for the greater number of migrant species and individuals present in spring. The difference cannot be attributed to field time, as 87 days were spent in the area in spring and 81 days in autumn. It is possible that some migrants wintering to the south reach their wintering grounds via routes which pass along the Andes, and then have different departure routes which bring them to the Santa Marta highlands in spring. Observations of *Piranga olivacea* may support this explanation, but the evidence is too sparse to do other than put forth the hypothesis. The more likely explanation, based on more consequential data, is that several species which arrive and are winter residents in the lowlands of the area, especially in the coffee zone, move into the highland forests as the dry season progresses. Resident species are known to do this (Johnson, in prep.).

During the period of their occurrence, a larger percentage (11.5 percent) of migrants are in flocks than out of them (5.1 percent). The analysis of the data reviewed in this paper suggests an interesting (but highly speculative) hypothesis. As mean number of resident species per flock increases or decreases from season to season (table 2), mean number of migrant species changes in the opposite direction in three seasons. Both increase in the fourth change (to spring wet) of season. It can be postulated that, as resident flocking species drop out of flocks in the breeding

season (December through May for many species), they leave a gap which is filled by migrant species. The migrants may forage or behave in a manner similar to the residents, thus predisposing them as potential flock members for a variety of reasons (positional strategy of the total members of a flock, predator detection, or foraging efficiency constraints).

Changes in numbers of individuals of migrants and residents are similar to the species patterns. Concomitant but opposite changes occur in two seasons (table 2); concomitant changes in the same direction occur in two seasons. This presumably reflects the departure of individuals of several species, the arrival and predeparture build up of several less common species and (mainly) the predeparture build up of large numbers of *Dendroica fusca*, which occurs in the spring wet season.

With the addition of migrant species and individuals to the flocks, the potential exists for increased competition for resources. Close comparison of foraging strategies of the appropriate species complexes is yet to be made (Johnson in prep.) to support or reject the hypothesis mentioned above in view of this consideration. However, the social interactions observed (figures 4, 5) indicate that migrants are subordinate to residents in all respects measured, placing them at a disadvantage, possibly, in a competitive situation should one exist. Also, the disproportionate representation of migrants in flocks compared to out of flocks (figure 3) leads me to believe that the advantages to be gained through association with resident birds in flocks (above; Leck 1970) must far outweigh the disadvantages (possible competition, supplanting actions) for migrant species. It seems likely that, in fact, the competitive impact of the migrant species on the resident avian community is small. A more direct measurement or comparison of competitive relationships is, of course, desirable.

Acknowledgments

Field work was made possible through a joint Peace Corps-University of Arizona program. Additional aid and living quarters were provided by El Instituto del Desarrollo de los Recursos Naturales Renovables (Inderena) as a result of the considerable efforts of Dr. Jaime Ramírez Gómez. Drs. Jorge Hernández Camacho and Stephen M. Russell provided initial information on the area, and Russell continued to aid the study throughout. I thank my wife, Sherry, for her generous help during the entire two years at San Lorenzo, and Ben Monciviaz for criticism of the Spanish abstract. In particular I thank Stephen L. Hilty for valued criticism, improvements, and encouragement offered in the development of this manuscript.

Terry B. Johnson

Literature Cited

Holdridge, L. R.
1967. *Life Zone Ecology*. Revised ed., San Jose, Costa Rica: Tropical Science Center.

Karr, J. R.
1976. On the relative abundance of migrants from the North Temperate Zone in tropical habitats. Wils. Bull. 88:433–58

Leck, C. F.
1970. The seasonal ecology of fruit and nectar eating birds in lower Middle America. Unpublished Ph.D. dissertation, Ithaca, N.Y., Cornell Univ.

1971. Measurement of social attractions between tropical passerine birds. Wils. Bull. 83:278–83.

1972. The impact of some North American migrants at fruiting trees in Panama. Auk 89:842–50.

Meyer de Schauensee, R.
1966. *The Species of Birds of South America and Their Distribution.* Narberth, Pa: Livingston.

Moynihan, M.
1962. The organization and probable evolution of some mixed species flocks of neotropical birds. Smithsonian Misc. Coll. 143, No. 7.

Todd, W. E. C., and M. A. Carriker, Jr.
1922. The birds of the Santa Marta region of Columbia: a study in altitudinal distribution. Ann. Carn. Mus., vol. 14.

Tramer, E. J.
1974. Proportions of wintering North American birds in disturbed and undisturbed dry tropical habitats. Condor 76:460–64.

STEPHEN M. RUSSELL
Department of Ecology and
Evolutionary Biology
University of Arizona
Tucson, Arizona 85721

Distribution and Abundance of North American Migrants in Lowlands of Northern Colombia

ABSTRACT

In a lowland thornscrub community, North American migrants occurred in numbers in fall when leaves were abundant. Coincident with leaf shedding and declining precipitation in December, the migrants departed. The thornscrub is dry and leafless during the time of spring migration, and migrants did not utilize it. In mangroves, *Protonotaria citrea* winters abundantly and must compete with local insectivores. On Isla San Andres, many migrants were found in April without fat reserves and were doubtless unable to complete a journey north, but local potential competitors were in good condition.

Introduction

Northern Colombia is a mosaic of varied habitats over an elevational range of nearly 6,000 m. Within short distances, migrant birds may find mangroves, thornscrub, forests (tropical, subtropical, and temperate), and many human disturbed land areas. I offer insight into the density and distribution of North American migrants in thornscrub and other lowland habitats.

Study Area

From October 1971 to May 1972, I regularly surveyed a small five-hectare plot in a rain shadow desert community near Gaira, a few miles south of Santa Marta. In northern Colombia, prevailing trade winds from the northeast produce annual rainfall of 3,800 mm on the northern slopes of the Sierra Nevada de Santa Marta but to the southwest of the mountains, rainfall may be as low as 200 mm annually. In the course of noting phenological changes in the plants and birds of the thornscrub community, records were kept of the transients seen or mist-netted.

The principal study plot at Gaira, situated in a small wash, was dominated by small, usually spiny, drought deciduous shrubs and trees. The site was about 3 km from the Caribbean coast and at an elevation of 100 m. Most plants were under 5 m in height, but some trees reached 15 m. Dominant plants included species of *Lemaireocereus*, *Pereskia*, *Prosopis*, *Acacia*, *Mimosa*, and *Lippia*; the vegetation of the area has been described by R. Schnetter (1968; Ber. Dtsch. Bot. Ges. 81:289–302). Rainfall (300 mm annually) is biseasonal, with peaks in May–June and September–October. Strong winds blow through the area almost constantly from December to April further dessicating plants and soil.

Twenty-one species of birds (18 resident, 13 passerine) nest on the Gaira plot (table 1). Most species nest between April and July, but a lesser peak occurs in October and some individuals nest in every month.

Results

Migrants have been found on the thornscrub site in May, October, and November. The plot was not visited in September but studies were conducted in all other months. Field work in this study was more extensive from October to December than in spring. Tables 2 and 3 summarize the data. Thirty percent of individuals netted in October and 18 percent in November were North American species. Seven Yellow-billed Cuckoos (*Coccyzus americanus*) were the only migrants noted in May.

Table 1. Breeding birds on 5-ha thornscrub plot near Gaira

Species	Number of pairs
Colinus cristatus	0.5
Columbina passerina	4.0
Leptotila verreauxi	4.0
Glaucidium brasilianum	1.0
Amazilia saucerotti	1.0
Hypnelus ruficollis	1.2
Centurus rubricapillus	1.0
Picumnus cinnamomeus	0.1
Xiphorhynchus picus	2.0
Sakesphorus melanotus	1.5
Formicivora grisea	2.5
Myiarchus tyrannulus	1.0
Idioptilon margaritaceiventris	2.0
Phaeomyias murina	2.0
Campylorhynchus griseus	0.5
Troglodytes aedon	1.0
Cyclarhis gujanensis	2.5
Coereba flaveola	3.0
Euphonia trinitatus	2.0
Icterus chrysater	0.4
Coryphospingus pileatus	3.0

Discussion

In fall, the maximum greenness of the vegetation occurred in October. Wilting and leaf shedding characterized November, and by mid-December nearly all plants were leafless. Insects were abundant in October and November.

Transients were most conspicuous in October, a time of abundant food supply. Even species of mesic habitats such as *Seiurus noveboracensis* and *Protonotaria citrea* foraged in the green thornscrub. Black-poll Warblers (*Dendroica striata*) foraged within inches of a nesting Pileated Finch (*Coryphospingus pileatus*) without interaction. No agonistic behavior involving any residents and transients was noted.

Coincident with the drying of the vegetation, the transients disappeared. None of the migrants were species characteristic of North American deserts, and none remained in this arid community to compete with locally adapted birds. Thus it appears the transients capitalized on temporally abundant foods and departed before interspecific competition for food became a factor. Certain resident insectivores (notably

Stephen M. Russell

Table 2. Distribution of individuals and species among residents and migrants in Colombian mist-net studies[1]

Study area	Month	Number of net hours	Total number captures	Number of captures		Number of species		Captures/ species		Percentage migrant individuals	Captures/ hour	
				R	M	R	M	R	M		R	M
Gaira	Oct	84	79	55	24	11	7	5.0	3.4	30.4	0.65	.29
(Thornscrub)	Nov	146	73	60	13	11	5	5.5	2.6	17.8	0.41	.18
	Dec	39	11	11	0	7	0	1.6	0	0	0.28	0
Salamanca	Mar	55	65	35	30	11	5	5.9	6.0	46.2	0.64	0.55
(Mangroves)												
Tayrona	Mar	95	126	118	8	30	1	3.9	8.0	6.3	1.24	0.08
(Disturbed forest)												
Isla San Andres	Apr	35	155	105	50	8	15	13.1	3.3	32.2	3.0	1.43
(Mangrove edge)												

[1] R = resident; M = migrant. Nets were 2.6 m × 12 m. Table after Karr, 1976, Wilson Bul. 88:441.

Table 3. Migrants on 5-ha thornscrub plot near Gaira

Species	October		November	
	Number netted	Additional seen	Number netted	Additional seen
Coccyzus americanus	0	2	3	0
Empidonax "trailli"	1	0	0	0
Catharus minimus	3	0	7	0
Catharus fuscescens	4	0	1	0
Vireo flavoviridis	8	1	1	0
Protonotaria citrea	2	0	0	0
Dendroica dominica	0	1	0	0
Dendroica striata	5	17	1	0
Seiurus noveboracensis	1	0	0	0

Table 4. Birds mist-netted 26 km east of Barranquilla, Mar 1972

Species	Number
Tringa solitaria	2
Actitis macularia	1
Chrysolampis mosquitus	1
Chloroceryle americana	2
Chloroceryle aenea	6
Xiphorhyncus picus	1
Certhiaxis cinnamomea	2
Fluvicola pica	5
Myiarchus ferox	1
Todirostrum cinereum	1
Sublegatus arenarum	2
Protonotaria citrea	23
Dendroica petechia (N.A.)	1
Seiurus noveboracensis	3
Coereba flaveola	7
Sporophila minuta	7

Sakesphorus, Formicivora, Idioptilon, Phaeomyias, and Troglodytes) were abundant and foraged on the same food items taken by the migrants.

December through April are dry months. Leaves do not develop until mid-May, too late to benefit transients. Migrants, except the cuckoos, were not recorded in the thornscrub in spring.

Other Localities

Mist nets were operated for a total of 55 hr at one site on 4 and 13 March 1972 in mangroves of Salamanca National Park 26 km east of Barranquilla. Three of the 16 species captured (tables 2, 4) were North American warblers. Prothonotary Warblers (Protonotaria citrea) accounted for 35 percent of all captures. Since this species winters in the mangroves at Salamanca, it is likely that it competes with *Certhiaxis cinnamomeus*, the small flycatchers, *Coereba*, and possibly *Conirostrum bicolor*. To my knowledge, this competitive situation has not been investigated.

On 8–11 March 1972 mist nets were operated for 95 net-hr at the edge of disturbed lowland tropical forest in Tayrona National Park northeast of Santa Marta (table 2). *Seiurus noveboracensis* (8 individuals) was the only migrant species among the 31 species and 126 individuals netted. All of the waterthrushes were taken along a small stream. Migrants (including *Protonotaria citrea, Mniotilta varia, Setophaga ruticilla, Pheucticus ludovicianus*) occurred in small numbers throughout the winter months in lowland forest areas east of Santa Marta, but their densities were low.

Isla San Andres, a Colombian island about 200 km east of Nicaragua, was visited in early April 1972. Mist nets were set at the edge of mangroves and a pasture and operated 35 hr. Fifteen species of migrants (50 individuals) and 8 species of resident birds (105 individuals) were captured (table 2). *Coereba flaveola* was the most frequently netted species (70 individuals). With the exception of one Gray Catbird (*Dumetella carolinensis*), which had substantial subcutaneous fat deposits, most of the migrants were emaciated. Whether these birds were in poor condition due to the effects of a drought on the island, or to other reasons, it is unlikely that many were able to reach North America. *Coereba* was abundant and nesting at the time, apparently not suffering from serious competition from migrants.

Stephen M. Russell

JORGE E. OREJUELA
Departamento de Biología,
Universidad del Valle,
Apartado Aéreo 2188, Cali, Colombia

RALPH J. RAITT
Department of Biology,
New Mexico State University
Las Cruces, New Mexico 88003

HUMBERTO ALVAREZ
Departamento de Biología,
Universidad del Valle,
Apartado Aéreo 2188, Cali, Colombia

Differential Use by North American Migrants of Three Types of Colombian Forests

ABSTRACT

Migrants' use of three Colombian forests was studied through mist netting, visual, and auditory counts. Seasonality of resources was assessed. Most migrants used the Cauca Valley and premontane forest sites. None used the lowland forest site. Differential occurrence of migrants is discussed in relation to competition in avian communities as influenced by species composition, sedentariness, and seasonality.

RESÚMEN

En un esfuerzo para adquirir una mejor comprensión de los cambios estacionales en las comunidades de aves neotropicales, nosotros comenzamos en Mayo de 1976 un estudio de algunas características de las aves que viven en 3 tipos diferentes de bosques en el departamento del Valle del Cauca, Colombia. Después de una extensa búsqueda de posibles zonas de trabajo, seleccionamos los siguientes sitios: 1) una mancha del bosque que anteriormenta cubría el piso del valle de Rio Cauca, a 950 m de elevación, cerca de la ciudad de Jamundí, clasificado como bosque seco-tropical de acuerdo con el sistema de Holdridge; 2) un bosque apreciablemente grande y bien preservado a unos 1,600 m en la ladera oriental de la cordillera occidental, llamado bosque de Yotoco de tipo premontano-húmedo, y 3) una sección del bosque húmedo-tropical del litoral pacífico, recientemente abierto y perturbado, a 40 m y situado cerca de la Estación Agroforestal del Bajo Calima a unos 20 km al nordeste de Buenaventura.

En cada sitio se demarcaron parcelas rectangulares de 2 ha en las cuales se realizaron censos de aves y estudios de vegetación en períodos trimestrales. Las aves se muestrearon de acuerdo con el método de Karr: capturas con 12 redes de nylon durante 3–4 dias sucesivos con suplementos visuales y auditivos realizados en recorridos sistemáticos y periódocos de las parcelas.

El resultado más importante fue la utilización por las aves migratorias de los bosques tropical-seco y premontano-húmedo pero no del tropical-húmedo. De un total de 78 especies observadas en Jamundí, 16 (20.5 por ciento) fueron migratorias transcontinentales. En Noviembre nosotros estimamos 33 individuos de 15 especies que se reproducen en Norte America, pero en Marzo, el número descendió a 21 individuos de 13 especies. Las aves migratorias constituyeron el 21.6 y el 14.5 por ciento de las densidades totales para los meses de Noviembre y Marzo, respectivamente. En términos de biomasa, las aves migratorias representaron 11.5 y 3.4 por ciento de los totales estimados para Noviembre y Marzo respectivamente. Las aves residentes de Jamundí están dominadas por tiránidos y las familias endémicas neotropicales están pobremente representadas.

En Yotoco, de un total de 80 especies, 11 (13.8 por ciento) anidan en Norte America. Los números de individuos migratorios estimados en Diciembre y en Marzo fueron 13 y 5, lo cual representó el 14 y el 6 por ciento de las densidades totales. De las 11 especies, 5 ocurrieron también en Jamundí. En términos de biomasa las aves migratorias representaron 9.8 y 10.8 por ciento de las densidades totales en Diciembre y en Marzo. En Yotoco los tiránidos son nuevamente importantes pero los tucanes, trogones, motmots, formicáridos y pípridos también están representados.

En Bajo Calima no se registraron aves migratorias en censos relizados en Junio, Octubre, Enero, y Marzo. Las familias neotropicales endémicas están altamente representadas y conforman el principal componente de la diversidad aviaria.

Para dar una explicación de la variación en números de individuos y especies migratorios transcontinentales entre las zonas de estudio, se examinaron características ecológicas de los diversos habitats. En términos generales hay un paralelo entre el número de aves migratorias, que es alto en Jamundí, mediano en Yotoco y nulo en Bajo Calima, y el grado de estacionalidad, insularidad, perturbación histórica de los habitats, y probablemente la impredictabilidad.

Es poco probable que estos factores tengan una incidencia directa sobre el número de aves migratorias; mas bien, estos factores pueden ejercer su efecto via los recursos alimenticios o bien, del efecto de éstos sobre el nivel de competencia que pueda ofrecer la porción de aves no-migratorias de la comunidad respectiva.

La relación inversa que se encontró entre al número de miembros locales del group de insectívoros del follaje, que puedan actual o potencialmente ofrecer competencia a los parúlidos migratorios transcontinentales y el número de tales aves migratorias ofrece apoyo a la hipótesis que la competencia limita el número de aves migratorias transcontinentales.

Otro aspecto de las comunidades aviarias que mostró variación entre las zonas de estudio, fue el grado de movilidad de las especies locales y la forma como esta movilidad pueda afectar a las aves migratorias de larga distancia. Una comparación de las avifaunas muestra a la de Jamundí como la más sedentaria y a la de Bajo Calima como la más nomádica. Estes especies tan móviles producen cambios recurrentes (renovación) en la composición de especies en Bajo Calima que bien excede el flujo de especies de Jamundí con su sustancial proporción de migratorios de larga distancia. El efecto competitivo de especialistas locales de alta movilidad sobre las aves que regresan de zonas de reproducción puede, quizás, impedir su reingreso. Pero las causas de las diferencias de grado de movilidad ya sea a nivel local ó a nivel transcontinental quedan por fijarse. Es muy probable que estén relacionados a patrones de disponibilidad de recursos alimenticios sobre los cuales sabemos todavía muy poco.

Jorge E. Orejuela

Introduction

Communities of birds vary in species diversity, species composition, relative abundance, and trophic relations to other components of the ecosystem. It is desirable to study the patterns of changes in these properties to gain an understanding of a community or a subset of it. Parallel studies of such factors as rainfall and temperature, habitat, and food may sharpen our focus on the causes of the observed changes.

The migratory bird subset of both tropical and temperate communities shows marked temporal changes in population dynamics. It is important to investigate the factors responsible for the timing of migration as well as the habitat selection by the birds.

A few published studies have looked at different aspects of migratory birds in the neotropics (Miller 1963; Willis 1966; Leck 1972; Tramer 1974; Karr 1976; Morton 1977). Karr (1976) concentrates on the problem of differential habitat occupation by migrants and attempts to estimate their densities and abundance in different habitats relative to resident birds.

We generally followed Karr's methodology in a comparative study of the organization and composition of three different southwest Colombian bird communities, in an attempt to provide comparable information on relative abundancies, temporal changes in density, and abundance of migrants relative to residents. Data gathered on climate, plant phenology, and other vegetational characteristics provide the basis for discussion of the ecological correlates of the patterns in the migrant communities, seen both within and between study areas.

Study Areas and Methods

Each of the three field sites of this study consists of two hectareś of forest; all lie within the boundaries of the Departmento del Valle del Cauca in southwestern Colombia. They encompass a variety of climatic and life-zone conditions (table 1; figure 1). The Jamundí site is located in the southern portion of the valley of the Río Cauca (3° 18′ N; 76° 33′ W, and 950 m elevation) near the junction of the Río Jamundí with the Río Cauca, near the town of Jamundí. The study area is in flat terrain in a 25-ha remnant of fairly mature secondary forest of the tropical-dry forest life zone of the Holdridge system (Espinal 1968). The average rainfall follows a bimodal pattern with a minor peak in May and a major one in October. The mean annual rainfall is 1,660 mm, a figure substantially higher than at other localities in the valley. Cali, for example, only 25 km to the north, has a mean of 950 mm. Temperature is high in Jamundí (mean annual = 23°C) and less variable than rainfall. The

Table 1. Climatic characteristics of the Jamundí, Yotoco, and Bajo Calima study areas

	Jamundí[1]	Yotoco[2]	Bajo Calima[3]
Rainfall (mm)[4]	1661 ± 385	1136 ± 161	5828 ± 1221
	23.2 (n = 6)	14.2 (n = 8)	20.9 (n = 10)
Temperature (°C)[4]	23.2 ± 0.53	18.0 ± 0.43[5]	26.6 ± 0.30
	2.3 (n = 6)	2.4 (n = 11)	1.1 (n = 8)
Life-zone[6]	Tropical-dry	Premontane dry/moist	Tropical-wet

[1] Data from Corporación Autónoma Regional del Valle del Cauca (CVC) Station El Palacio adjacent to study site.

[2] Data from CVC Station Calima-Palermo 3′ W of study site; at least both total rainfall and C.V. of rainfall at Yotoco are misleading because of effects of frequent low clouds (see text).

[3] Data from the Estación Agroforestal del Bajo Calima of the Secretaría de Fomento del Valle del Cauca.

[4] Mean ± standard deviation; coefficient of variation $\left(= \dfrac{\text{S.D. } 100}{\text{x}}\right)$; n = number of years.

[5] Data corrected for elevation difference of 150 m (0.9°C) between study area and weather station.

[6] From Espinal (1968) after Holdridge (1967).

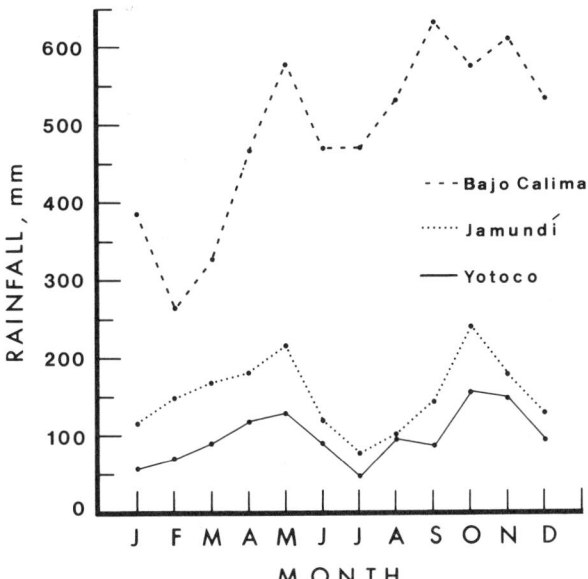

Figure 1. Long-term mean monthly rainfall at 3 southwestern Colombian study areas.

dominant tree species in this forest is *Xilopia ligustrifolia* (Annonaceae). Other important trees are *Ficus* sp. (Moraceae), *Genipa americana* (Rubiaceae), *Rheedia* sp. (Guttiferae), *Inga* sp. (Leguminosae). The canopy of the tallest trees reaches 30 m, but most trees are about 15 m. The understory is dominated by individuals of the families Myrsinaceae, Rubiaceae, Melastomaceae, and Myrtaceae. Epiphytes and parasitic plants are, relative to the other study areas, scarcely represented. The ground vegetation is dominated by grasses and ferns.

The Yotoco site (3° 52' N; 76° 33' W) is a higher (1,600 m), relatively large, natural forest preserve transitional between premontane-dry and premontane-moist forest. It is situated on the eastern slope of the Cordillera Occidental, and it has been preserved for several decades as the main watershed of the sources that serve the town of Yotoco in the Cauca Valley below. The landscape is mildly undulating from east to west, with a rather steep downgrade from south to north. The northern boundary of the study area is a mesic canyon. The rainfall follows a very similar pattern to the Jamundí site but with lower values (figure 1). The mean annual total is 1,135 mm, but this figure is misleadingly low. This forest is of the type that has often been called cloud forest. Low clouds or fog occur frequently in all seasons, causing condensation, increasing the relative humidity, and reducing evapotranspiration. As Beebe and Crane (1947) have pointed out, such effects in a cloud forest produce more mesic conditions and less seasonality than ordinary rainfall measurements would indicate. Calculated mean annual temperature is 18°C, after correction for altitudinal difference (0.9°C for 150 m) between the study site and the closest weather station (3' W). The vegetation of the Yotoco forest is closest to pristine conditions, and robust mature trees are common. The dominant trees are *Laplacea* sp. (Theaceae) and *Persea* sp. (Lauraceae), with *Ficus* sp., *Pouteria* sp. (Sapotaceae), *Hieronima* sp. (Euphorbiaceae), *Lozania* sp. (Lacistemataceae), *Casearia* sp. (Flacourtiaceae), and *Myrica* sp. (Myrtaceae) also important. The tallest trees reach 50–60 m, particularly those near the northern end of the plot of the canyon. The shrub layer is composed of Rubiaceae, Melastomaceae, Myrtaceae, and tree-ferns. Many parasites (Loranthaceae) and epiphytes (Orchidaceae and Moraceae) cover the dominant trees.

The Bajo Calima area is located in the Pacific lowlands (4° 00' N; 76° 6' W; 40 m elevation) near the Río Calima, approximately 20 km northeast of the Pacific port of Buenaventura. The study area occupied a section of partially opened tropical-wet forest about 1.5 km northeast of the Bajo Calima Forestry and Agricultural Research Station of the Secretaría de Desarrollo y Fomento del Valle. The site itself is generally flat, with a few undulations and is bordered on the eastern and western sides by small drainages. The rainfall is high during most of the year, although lower early in the year. The mean annual rainfall is 5,820 mm. Temperature is high throughout the year, the annual mean being 27°C. The most important tree species in the study are *Virola* sp. (Myristicaceae), *Dialyanthera* sp. (Myristicaceae), *Couma* sp. (Apocynaceae), *Eschweilera* sp. (Lecythidaceae), *Couratari* sp. (Lecythidaceae), and representatives of Annonaceae, Clusiaceae, Humiriaceae, and Meliaceae. Few of the trees reach 40 m, but many approach 30 m. The middle layers of the forest are dominated by a variety of Melastomaceae, Rubiaceae, Araceae, Musaceae, Araliaceae, and palms are particularly abundant. There are many bromeliads and vines. In the last quarter of the study about two-fifth of the study area was logged, resulting in a patchwork of clearings and forest with some widespread large trees.

At each site we demarcated rectangular plots of two hectares in which we made censuses of birds and studies of vegetation at approximately quarterly intervals during one year (May 1976–March 1977). The bird census methods were those suggested by Karr (pers. comm.): mist-netting for three to four consecutive days using 12 nets at ground level, supplemented by visual and auditory counts. Each day we recorded the number of birds in one or more systematic walks through the plots. The highest number of individuals seen or heard of each species on a census walk was usually taken as the best estimate of numbers present for a given census round. Care was taken to avoid counting the same individual more than once on a single walk. Birds captured in the nets were identified, weighed, individually marked, and released at the capture site.

Seasonality of resources was estimated by the seasonal distribution of rains, and approximated by the number of months with less than one-eighteenth of the annual rainfall total. The rationale for this was that if rainfall were evenly distributed throughout the year, each month would receive one-twelfth the total (Clayton and Clayton 1947).

Another estimator of seasonality of resources was the degree of synchronization of plant phenological events, or the percentage per sampling period of the total number of trees of greater than 20 cm DBH which exhibited a particular stage. Vegetational phenology from only Jamundí and Yotoco will be discussed because the Bajo Calima study area was partially destroyed. Additional supportive evidence of seasonality was the qualitative appreciation of the amount of leaves collected in mist nets during netting periods and the degree of flooding of the study areas. Resource pedictability was estimated by the coefficient of variation of mean monthly rainfall. This measure was

Jorge E. Orejuela

preferred over variation in annual rainfall as used by Cody (1974) and others because of the greater span of reproduction in the tropics.

Foliage-height profiles were measured at each site, by the method described by Pearson (1975). The profiles of the different sites were not significantly different (Wilcoxon's matched-pairs, signed ranks test, $P > 0.05$). This lack of difference indicates a general similarity in vegetation structure, but there were some subjectively apparent overall structural differences. As indices of these differences we used 1) the maximum height of the forest canopy and 2) the height of that foliage layer with the greatest frequency of foliage density. The assumption is that among these forests of similar profile a taller one and one with foliage concentration at a higher level provides a structurally more complex habitat for birds.

Results

Distribution and Abundance of Migrants

The most significant finding was the heavy use by North American migrants of the Cauca Valley and the pre-montane forests and their absence from the lowland forest (table 2). Of the 78 species observed in the Jamundí study area, 15 (19.2 percent) were north-temperate breeders and 1 was a south-temperate breeder. The most numerous migrating group was the Parulidae with 10 species. Other migrants were in the Caprimulgidae, Tyrannidae, Turdidae, Vireonidae, and Thraupidae, each with 1 species. In addition to containing the largest number of migrating species, the Jamundí area hosted the largest number of individuals (table 3). In November the estimate of migrants, both captured and sighted, was 33 individuals

Table 2. Estimated numbers of individuals (netted and/or sighted) of transcontinental migrants on Jamundí and Yotoco plots

Species	Jamundí				Yotoco			
	May	Aug	Nov	Mar	May	Oct	Dec	Mar
Coccyzus erythrophthalmus	—	—	—	—	—	1	—	—
Caprimulgus carolinensis	—	—	1	—	—	—	—	—
Nuttallornis borealis	—	—	—	—	—	1	—	—
Empidonax virescens	—	—	3	3	—	—	—	—
Empidonax euleri[1]	2	—	—	—	—	—	—	—
Catharus ustulatus	—	—	9	3	—	2	2	3
Catharus fuscescens	—	—	—	—	—	—	1	—
Vireo olivaceus[2]	—	—	—	—	—	—	—	—
Mniotilta varia	—	—	2	2	—	2	5	—
Protonotaria citrea	—	—	3	1	—	—	—	—
Vermivora chrysoptera	—	—	—	—	—	—	2	—
Vermivora peregrina	—	—	1	1	—	1	—	—
Dendoica petechia	—	—	2	1	—	—	—	—
Dendroica cerulea	—	—	—	—	—	1	—	—
Dendroica fusca	—	—	1	3	—	3	3	1
Dendroica pensylvanica	—	—	1	—	—	—	—	—
Dendroica castanea	—	—	4	2	—	—	—	—
Wilsonia canadensis	—	—	1	1	—	5	—	1
Seiurus noveboracensis	1	—	3	1	—	—	—	—
Setophaga ruticilla	—	—	2	2	—	—	—	—
Piranga rubra	—	—	—	1	—	1	—	—
Pheucticus ludovicianus[3]	—	—	—	—	—	—	—	—

[1] A South Temperate Zone breeder.

[2] A resident species but transcontinental migrants present seasonally, at Jamundí in March and probably November and at Yotoco in October.

[3] Not detected in censuses but individuals present at Jamundí in February.

Table 3. Distribution of individuals and species among resident (R) and transcontinental migrant (M) species in three study areas, Departamento del Valle, Colombia, using mist nets

Study area	Month	Net hours	Individuals captured				No. of species		Captures/ species		Captures/ hour	
			Total	R	M	Percent-age M	R	M	R	M	R	M
Jamundí	May	376	38	37	1	2.6	18	1	2.1	1.0	.10	00
	Aug	236	34	34	0	0	19	0	1.8	0	.14	00
	Nov	341	83	63	20	24.1	21	6	3.0	3.3	.18	.06
	Mar	424	65	53	12	5.4	21	7	2.5	1.7	.13	.03
Yotoco	May	297	42	42	0	0	19	0	2.2	0	.14	00
	Oct	429	82	81	7	8.5	18	4	4.5	1.8	.19	.02
	Dec	465	57	49	8	14.0	24	2	2.0	4.0	.11	.02
	Mar	432	51	47	4	7.8	21	3	2.2	1.3	.11	.01
Bajo Calima	Jun	255	78	78	0	0	23	0	3.4	0	.31	00
	Oct	282	94	94	0	0	27	0	3.5	0	.33	00
	Jan	378	88	88	0	0	27	0	3.3	0	.23	00
	Mar	301	79	79	0	0	30	0	2.6	0	.26	00

from 15 species; in March this number had declined to 21 individuals of 13 species (*Caprimulgus carolinensis* and *Dendroica pensylvanica* were absent). The migrants constituted 21.6 percent and 14.5 percent, respectively, of estimated total densities. In terms of biomass the migrants represented 11.5 percent and 3.4 percent of the totals estimated for November and March, respectively. The decline in numbers and biomass was due mostly to the departure of a sizeable number of *Catharus ustulatus*, the most numerous large migrant on the study area. The resident birds at Jamundí were dominated by tyrannids, and tropical endemic families were poorly represented.

In the Yotoco area, of a total of 80 species, 11 (13.8 percent) were North American breeders. Estimated numbers of migrant individuals in October, December, and March, respectively, were 17, 13, and 5, constituting 14 percent, 14 percent, and 6 percent of the estimated totals. Of the 11 migrant species represented, 5 were among those also at Jamundí, including the thrush and 4 parulids. In terms of biomass the migrants represented 9.8 percent and 10.9 percent of the estimated totals in December and March. Among the resident birds, flycatchers, antbirds, and manakins were important. Trogons, motmots, and toucans were also present, in contrast to their absence from Jamundí.

In both study areas, the migrant species were sig-

nificantly rarer than the residents (captures/species column of table 3), with exceptions in October (Jamundí) and December (Yotoco). These months fell in the period of peak fall migration. The high capture rates in those two samples were due in large part to the abundance of *Catharus ustulatus* at Jamundí and of *Wilsonia canadensis* at Yotoco.

No migrants at all appeared on the Bajo Calima plot, in censuses conducted in June, October, January, and March. Overall numbers and avifaunal richness at that site averaged slightly higher than at the other 2, and tropical endemic families were heavily represented.

Observations of Migrants During a Severe Dry Season

In Jamundí (Cauca Valley) the dry season of 1976 started as usual around June. However, the usual rains of September–December were restricted to a brief period in October, and dry conditions prevailed until March 1977. Observations of migrants indicated that different species responded differently to the exigencies of the habitat. During this severe dry season, some species left the habitat soon, whereas others stayed and gained weight.

Catharus ustulatus is an example of a species that left the habitat during the extended dry season. Perhaps the resources were below the maintenance level for the species. In November it was the most numerous migratory species, but we saw very few of them during the late dry season. The few individuals netted in March showed no weight increase, suggesting that maintenance costs had not permitted the fat deposition presumably necessary for the trip to the breeding grounds.

It is possible that other migrants did the opposite; that is, that they entered the forest in the dry season. Perhaps one such species was *Pheucticus ludovicianus*, which was observed at Jamundí in February. This species was only transient in the habitat, and may have used some resources opportunistically. Of the species that remained in the Jamundí forest, one *Dendroica castenea*, regularly included in its diet, in addition to insects, the small fruits of several Rubiaceae shrubs.

There is one other group of species that remained in the habitat during the dry season. This group is exemplified by *Protonotaria citrea*, which was able not only to maintain itself in the face of presumed reduction of arthropod abundance, but actually increased markedly in weight. Four individuals captured 26–27 November had a mean weight of 13.0 g, and one captured 11 March weighed 18.0 g. This figure represents a substantial (38.5 percent) increase in weight in less than 4 months.

Thus, there is not a clear picture of the extent of resource limitation of populations of migrants in tropical areas. Different species have varying abilities to exploit the changing abundance and availability of resources as well as to withstand resource depletion.

Discussion

Differential Occurrence of Migrants

For possible explanations of the variation among sites in numbers of species and individuals of transcontinental migrants, we examined between-site differences in a number of ecological characteristics; most of these are summarized in table 4. Variation in numbers of migrants from high (Jamundí) to medium (Yotoco) to nil (Bajo Calima) was paralleled by variation in degree of seasonality, insularity, historical habitat disturbance, and, probably, unpredictability. Thus, general characteristics of the sites point to several, but probably not wholly independent, explanations for the variation in migrants. The literature does not offer aid in narrowing this list, for all of the potential causative factors suggested by variation among our sites have been found by others to be correlated with migrant abundance (Willis 1966; Karr 1976).

It is, however, unlikely that any of the above factors would directly affect the number of migrants; rather, they would exert effects via effects on food resources or less directly via effects of resources on competition exerted by the nonmigrating portion of the respective

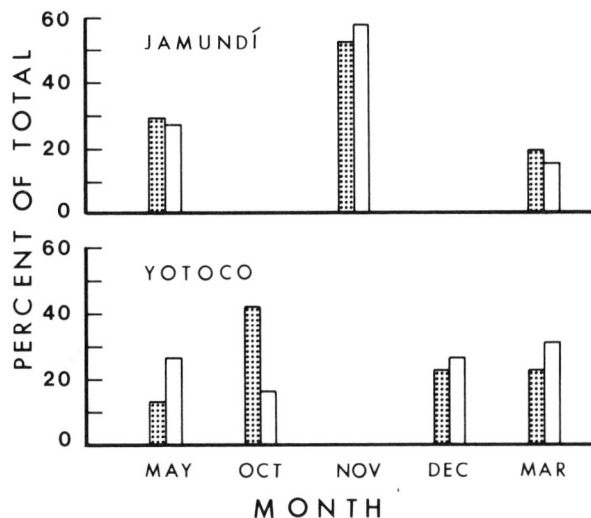

Figure 2. Percentages of trees greater than 20 cm DBH in flower (stippled bars) and in fruit (open bars) in different sampling periods at Jamundí and Yotoco study areas.

bird communities. Karr (1976), for example, attributes great importance to resources, concluding that northern migrants in the tropics rely upon "superabundant and/or sporadically available resources." Unfortunately, we were unable to make measurements of arthropod abundance, but observations of flowering and fruiting of forest trees (figure 2), indicate that these variables were more highly seasonal at Jamundí than at Yotoco. As explained earlier, because of the cutting of trees, the vegetation phenological data from Bajo Calima are not usable, but we cautiously hypothesize that the relative constancy of climatic factors at that site resulted in even less variability in fruiting and flowering than at Yotoco.

In regard to properties of the non-migrant portion of the bird communities of the three sites, Bajo Calima, as the most predictable, least seasonal habitat, should contain the most specialized avifauna, whereas more broad-niched species should occur in the other sites (Cody 1974). Indeed, such seems to be the case. Although our analysis of the trophic structure of the communities is incomplete, it is clear that the largest number of specialized guilds occurs in the Bajo Calima area. These include, at least, the army ant-following species: formicariids; the highly mobile small frugivores: many tanagers of several genera; the small clumped-fruit eaters: piprids and small tyrannids (e.g., *Mionectes olivaceus*); the medium-sized canopy fruit eaters: trogons, cotingas, and tanagers; large fruit eaters: toucans, parrots; large and small insectivores; trunk insect probers; small insect-gleaners of the canopy: parulid-like tanagers (e.g., *Erythrothlypis salmoni*) and sylviids (*Polioptila plumbea*). Many of these groups

Table 4. Ecological correlates of migrant patterns of abundance and distribution in 3 forest types, Departamento del Valle Del Cauca, Colombia

Variable estimator	Jamundí	Yotoco	Bajo Calima
Species richness			
Number of migrants	15	11	0
Total number of species	78	80	83
Density[1]			
Mean number/census round	158	118	95
Habitat complexity			
Canopy height (m)	30	50	40
Height (m) of tree level with greatest foliage frequency	15	25	20
Seasonality			
Number of months less than $\frac{1}{18}$ total annual rainfall, over 72 months	25[2]	23[2]	12[2]
		(Modified toward lesser seasonability by clouds)	
Degree of leaf drop	High	Medium	Low
Unpredictability			
Coefficient of variation, mean monthly rainfall	32.1	35.2	23.3
		(Modified toward higher predictability by clouds)	
Insularity			
Area (ha)	25	4000±	Large continuous tropical rainforest
Habitat disturbance			
Historically: (regionally)	Almost complete removal original forest	Extensive removal original forest	Extensive natural forest
Currently: (study area)	Minor logging, protected regeneration	Natural reserve	Extensive removal of forest

[1] Based on overall estimates: captures plus sightings.

[2] $P < 0.05$, Jamundí vs Bajo Calima; $P < 0.10$, Yotoco vs Bajo Calima; $P < 0.05$, Jamundí vs Yotoco; by Chi Square tests.

are characterized by a certain degree of flocking, high mobility (see beyond), and many of the species are rare in the sense of Karr (1977). Some of these guilds occur in one or both of the other two areas, but most of these that do are composed of fewer species.

A community subdivided into a number of different groups or subsets of specialized foragers probably achieves great use of total food resources. Faced with a community of birds adapted to exploit continuously changing resources, a North American breeding species might stand only a small chance of encroaching in or entering such a community.

The proposition that the absence of North American migrants from Bajo Calima was due to the fact that the residents and local migrants constitute a closed community, one that would be able competitively to exclude long-distance migrants, was examined in some detail from the point of view of the dominant North American breeding group at both other sites, the wood warblers, Parulidae. At the suggestion of J. Allen Keast we extracted data for each round of census of numbers of transcontinental migrants and residents/local-migrants belonging to the same guild as the warblers: a broadly defined foliage-gleaning guild. Included in

Jorge E. Orejuela

addition to all parulids, were all vireos, sylviids, wrens, and coerebids and certain members of the following families: Furnariidae, Formicariidae, Cotingidae, Tyrannidae, and Thraupidae (see Appendix). Criteria for inclusion of particular species were small body size and either our observations of warbler-like foraging or description of such foraging in the literature (primarily Skutch (1960) and Slud (1964). In a few cases, the decision as to inclusion was problematical. The results of this analysis are summarized in table 5. They indicate a general inverse correlation across sites between the numbers of local members of the guild and the numbers of North American breeding warblers. At Bajo Calima, where northern breeders did not appear, the numbers of locally breeding individuals and species were consistently high. At Jamundí numbers of locals were consistently low, and the total membership of the guild was approximately doubled by the migrant parulids. The case at Yotoco was more complex, but levels were generally intermediate. Thus, the data for between-site variation in numbers of local potential competitors of long-distance migrant warblers and the numbers of such migrants support the hypothesis that competition limited the numbers of long-distance migrants.

Another property of the bird communities that varied among sites was the degree of sedentariness of the member species. The principal finding discussed in this paper is the situation as regards transcontinental migrants: more of them at Jamundí, with some resident for much of the nonbreeding season and others more mobile. But what of the mobility of the locally breeding species? We had the impression of considerable flux among these also at Jamundí. In addition to being a small island of habitat, the Jamundí forest is a refuge where birds typical of plantations and open

fields seek cover and food during the hottest or driest periods of the day and year. The resident avifauna is composed primarily of common species with high densities (*Pitangus sulphuratus, Tyrannus melancholicus, Thraupis palmarum, T. episcopus, Saltator albicollis, Turdus ignobilis*). These species generally span large geographical areas and have broad niches. In addition to these resident populations, there are several opportunistic species that use the forest daily (*Columbigallina talpacoti, Volatinia jacarina, Oryzoborus angolensis*) or seasonally (*Leptotila plumbeiceps, Pionus menstruus, Aratinga wagleri, Chlorostilbon mellisugus, C. gibsoni*)

Detailed analysis, however, indicates that, compared with those of the other two areas, the avifauna of Jamundí is more sedentary. An indication of the site-fidelity of the Jamundí birds is given by the greater number of species recorded in at least three of the four rounds of censusing: 36 of 78 species (46.2 percent). In contrast, the avifaunas of Yotoco and Bajo Calima are considerably more nomadic; at Yotoco 26 of 80 (32.5 percent) and at Bajo Calima 59 of 83 (27.7 percent) species were registered in three or four of the rounds of censusing. We know virtually nothing about the nature and possible causes of the large number of nonresident but local species at Yotoco and, especially, Bajo Calima. Some were almost certainly regular, but local seasonal migrants, including altitudinal migrants (e.g., *Henicorhina leucophrys* at Bajo Calima); the apparent inconsistent occurrence of others may be a function of sampling species with large home ranges in a two-hectare plot; others are likely to have been moving opportunistically from one portion of a large tract of forest to another or into and out of the forest, in response to small-scale areal and temporal variations in food availability. In any case, these mobile species—also characteristic of Karr's (1971) Panamanian forest

Table 5. Estimated foliage-gleaning guild membership[1]

	May	June	Aug	Oct	Nov	Dec	Jan	Mar	Means
Jamundí									
Residents	17 (8)	19 (8)		17 (8)				13 (6)	16.5 (7.5)
Migrants	1 (1)	0 (0)		20 (10)				14 (9)	
Total	18 (9)	19 (8)		37 (18)				27 (15)	25.3 (12.5)
Yotoco									
Residents	31 (13)			71 (16)		37 (13)		34 (11)	43.3 (13.3)
Migrants	0 (0)			12 (5)		10 (3)		2 (2)	
Total	31 (13)			82 (21)		47 (16)		36 (13)	49.3 (15.8)
Bajo Calima									
Residents		49 (10)		45 (11)			48 (15)	62 (15)	51 (12.8)

[1] Estimated numbers of individuals (species) of residents and North American migrants (all parulids) belonging to the "foliage-gleaning guild" in each census at each of 3 Colombian forest sites.

study area—produce a flux in species composition at Bajo Calima that exceeds that at Jamundí with its substantial seasonal proportion of North American breeders. The potential competitive effect of spatially and temporally opportunistic local specialists on returning northern breeders has already been alluded to, but the question remains as to the underlying causes of differences in proportions of 1) locally mobile species and 2) those that depart to breed at great distances to the north or (in at least one case) the south. Almost certainly these causes relate to patterns of resource availability of which we know too little.

Migration Calendar and the Tropical Environment

It is usually accepted that patterns of rainfall affect changes in insect biomass and plant phenology (Janzen and Schoener 1968; Smythe 1974; Buskirk and Buskirk 1976). Thus, the analysis of rainfall patterns may yield some interesting correlations with the timing of migration.

The same overall rainfall pattern—two high and two low peaks—was observed in the two areas used by migrants. The departure of northern breeders occurred between the end of March and the beginning of May. These are months of rather high rainfall and supposedly favorable food conditions. The absence of long-distance migrants from the tropical environs considered in this study corresponds with the rainy season and periods of high food abundance and improved leaf-cover conditions (Tramer 1974; Karr 1976). Why should these birds leave during a "good season"? The answer to this question appears to be determined by events in the northern breeding grounds (Buskirk, this volume). Even though the summer of Yucatan and Panama may be a "good period," and the Colombian a "not bad" one, the north temperate summer must be "better." Furthermore, predictability (reliability) of food at this time is probably the highest of the year. The migratory birds must have historically evaluated the hazards of long distance travel against the advantage of reaching areas where food is highly reliably abundant. In addition to food, there are other advantages of North Temperate Zone residence: longer summer days and lower nest predation.

The exact departure time from tropical areas may be additionally adjusted by events in the wintering areas. For example, an unusually dry season (Cauca Valley 1976) may limit the ability of some species to accumulate the required premigratory fat, thus delaying departure time. In contrast, unusually good spring conditions may favor early departure. Relationships of the "goodness of tropical habitat" and the timing of migration would become more important as distance from breeding quarters increases.

Acknowledgments

The Fondo Colombiano de Investigaciones "Francisco José de Caldas" of COLCIENCIAS and the Research Fund of the Division of Sciences of the Universidad del Valle supported the research of the Colombian authors. Raitt's participation was made possible by a Fulbright-Hays Exchange Lectureship. We gratefully acknowledge these sources of financial support. We especially thank Biologists Hermes Cuadros, César Benalcázar, and Fabiola Silva for their active and enthusiastic participation in all phases of the study. We also thank Isidoro Cabrera for identification of plant material, Gerardo Cataño, our invaluable field assistant, and James R. Raitt for additional field assistance. We are grateful to Dr. James R. Karr for useful suggestions regarding methodology and to Dr. William Eberhard of the Universidad del Valle for criticisms of the manuscript.

Appreciation is also extended to the Facultad Nacional de Agronomía in Palmira for granting permission to work in the Yotoco forest reserve and to the Secretaría de Fomento y Desarrollo del Valle for permitting us to use the facilities at the Bajo Calima Forestry and Agricultural Research Station. Special thanks are extended to Dr. Jaime Sardi Garcés for allowing us to work on his ranch, which includes the Jamundí study area, and for extending to us many courtesies.

We also thank Ned K. Johnson, Victoria M. Dziadosz, and the Museum of Vertebrate Zoology, University of California, Berkeley, for supplying data on weights of specimens.

Appendix. Resident species assumed to be probable competitors of migrant parulids that breed in North America

Species	Study areas of occurrence		
	Jamundí	Yotoco	Bajo Calima
Furnariidae			
Synallaxis brachyura	X	—	—
Cranioleuca erythrops	X	X	—
Xenops minutus	—	X	X
Sclerurus mexicanus	—	—	X
Sclerurus guatemalensis	—	X	—
Formicariidae			
Thamnophilus punctatus	—	—	X
Dysithamnus mentalis	—	X	—
Dysithamnus puncticeps	—	—	X
Myrmotherula fulviventris	—	—	X

Jorge E. Orejuela

Appendix (cont.)

Species	Study areas of occurrence		
	Jamundí	Yotoco	Bajo Calima
Myrmotherula axillaris	—	—	X
Myrmotherula schisticolor	—	X	—
Microrhopias quixensis	—	—	X
Cercomacra nigricans	X	—	—
Myrmeciza exsul	—	—	X
Hylophylax naevioides	—	—	X
Conopophaga castaneiceps	—	X	—
Cotingidae			
Pachyramphus polychopterus	X	—	—
Tyrannidae			
Myiobius atricaudus	—	—	X
Platyrinchus mystaceus	—	X	—
Platyrinchus coronatus	—	—	X
Todirostrum cinereum	X	—	—
Todirostrum sylvia	X	—	—
Pogonotriccus ophthalmicus	—	X	—
Tyranniscus vilissimus	—	X	—
Leptopogon superciliaris	—	X	—
Mionectes olivaceus	—	X	X
Pipromorpha oleaginea	X	X	—
Troglodytidae			
Henicorhina leucosticta	—	X	X
Henicorhina leucophrys	—	—	X
Microcerculus marginatus	—	—	X
Sylviidae			
Polioptila plumbea	—	—	X
Ramphocaenus melanurus	—	—	X
Microbates cinereiventris	—	—	X
Vireonidae			
Vireo olivaceus	X	X	—
Hylophilus ochraceiceps	—	X	—
Parulidae			
Parula pitiayumi	X	—	—
Myioborus miniatus	—	X	—
Basileuterus culicivorus	X	X	—
Basileuterus rivularis	—	X	—
Coerebidae			
Coereba flaveola	X	X	—
Cyanerpes caeruleus	—	—	X
Dacnis venusta	—	—	X
Thraupidae			
Erythrothlypis salmoni	—	—	X
Tachyphonus delatrii	—	—	X

Literature Cited

Beebe, W., and J. Crane
1947. Ecology of Rancho Grande, a subtropical cloud forest in northern Venezuela. Zoologica 32:43–59.

Buskirk, R. E., and W. H. Buskirk.
1976. Changes in arthropod abundance in a highland Costa Rica forest. Amer. Midl. Natur. 95:288–98.

Clayton, H. H., and F. L. Clayton
1947. World weather records 1931–1940. Smithsonian Misc. Coll. 105:1–646.

Cody, M. L.
1974. *Competition and the Structure of Bird Communities.* Princeton, N. J.: Princeton Univ. Press.

Espinal, L. S.
1968. *Visión ecológica del Departmento del Valle del Cauca.* Cali, Colombia: Universidad del Valle.

Holdridge, L. R.
1967. *Life Zone Ecology.* San José, Costa Rica: Tropical Science Center.

Janzen, D. H., and T. W. Schoener
1968. Differences in insect abundance and diversity between wetter and drier sites during a tropical dry season. Ecol. 49:96–110.

Karr, J. R.
1971. Structure of avian communities in selected Panama and Illinois habitats. Ecol. Monogr. 41:207–33.

1976. On the relative abundances of north temperate migrants in tropical habitats. Wils. Bull. 88:433–58.

1977. Ecological correlates of rarity in a tropical forest bird community. Auk 94:240–47.

Leck, C. F.
1972. Seasonal changes in feeding pressures of fruit- and nectar-eating birds in the neotropics. Condor 74:54–60.

Miller, A. H.
1963. Seasonal activity and ecology of the avifauna of an equatorial cloud forest. Univ. Calif. Publ. Zool. 66:1–78.

Morton, E. S.
1977. Intratropical migration in the Yellow-green Vireo and Piratic Flycatcher. Auk 94:97–106.

Pearson, D. L.
1975. The relation of foliage complexity to ecological diversity of three Amazonian bird communities. Condor 77:453–66.

Skutch, A. F.
1960. Life histories of Central American birds. Pacific Coast Avifauna 34.

Slud, P.
1964. The birds of Costa Rica. Distribution and ecology. Bull. Amer. Mus. Nat. Hist. 128:1–430.

Smythe, N.
1974.   Biological monitoring—insects. In *1973. Environmental monitoring and baseline data.* ed., R. W. Rubinoff, pp. 70–115. Smithsonian Inst. Environ. Sci. Prog.

Tramer, E. J.
1974.   On latitudinal gradients in avian diversity. Condor 76:123–30.

Willis, E. O.
1966.   The role of migrant birds at swarms of army ants. Living Bird 5:187–231.

Jorge E. Orejuela

STEVEN L. HILTY
Department of Ecology and Evolutionary Biology
University of Arizona
Tucson, Arizona 85721

Relative Abundance of North Temperate Zone Breeding Migrants In Western Colombia and Their Impact At Fruiting Trees

ABSTRACT

Migrant densities are rather uniform from October through February, averaging about 8.8 percent of the total species and 5.1 percent of the total avifaunal biomass in the upper Anchicayá Valley. Densities were slightly higher in March. Some migrants were not regularly present in the upper Anchicayá Valley until December or January, and the significance of this late arrival is discussed. Migrants were more frequently encountered at a disturbed highland site than at a disturbed lowland site, and only two species were encountered frequently enough to be classified as common. Some elevational replacement of migrant species occurs on the Pacific slope; two species were recorded chiefly in the lowlands and two species chiefly in the highlands. The importance of migrants as competitors for fruit is believed minor. Only 4 of 22 species in the upper Anchicayá Valley were observed taking fruit and migrants accounted for only 1.3–4.2 percent of the total feeding visits to two species of fruiting trees.

ABSTRACTO

Un estudio acerca de las densidades de emigrantes y las explotaciónes de arboles con frutas fue realizado durante el período de Agosto de 1972 hasta Mayo de 1973 en el húmedo estacionamiento del pacífico de Colombia. Las densidades de los emigrantes fueron uniformes de Octubre hasta Febrero, promediando acerca de 8.8 por ciento del total de todas especies y 5.1 por ciento de la biomasa de la avifauna en total. El registro del número de individuos capturados mostró un período de máxima abundancia en marzo. Algúnos emigrantes no fueron presente regularmente en el Valle del Anchicayá hasta Diciembre o Enero y la significacíon de esta llega tarde del migrantes es discutida. Emigrantes fueron encontrados con más frequencia por un sitio subtropical alterado que en un sitio tropical alterado, pero la abundancia en todos los sitios parece bajo. Algún reemplazo elevacional de emigrantes fue observado por la vertiente del pacífico; 2 especies fueron registradas principalmente por una selva tropical alterada y 2 especies por una selva subtropical alterada. La importancia de los emigrantes como competidores por las frutas disponibles de arboles en una elevación mediana por la vertiente del pacífico de Colombia fue insignificante, resultando en no más de 1.3–4.2 por ciento del uso de todas las aves. Únicamente 4 de 22 emigrantes fueron observados comiendo frutas.

Introduction

The seasonal impact migrants may have on food resources in the tropics has been recognized, but quantitative information is widely scattered. This paper presents quantified information on the seasonal distribution and relative abundance of North American breeding migrants in western Colombia and assesses the seasonal impact these migrants have on the fruit resources used by resident frugivores.

Study Area and Methods

Three study areas representing three different vegetation communities were located on Colombia's Pacific slope: 1) disturbed lowlands (100 m) transitional between tropical wet forest and tropical rain forest, 2) undisturbed mid-elevation(1,050 m) premontane rain forest, and 3) disturbed highlands (1,900 m) transitional between premontane moist forest and premontane wet forest (Holdridge 1967).

The lowland forest area is located near Llano Bajo (3° 43' N, 76° 55' W), Department of Valle, Colombia, along a portion of the Old Buenaventura Road that follows the lower Anchicayá Valley. The region surveyed is predominantly disturbed forest of varying heights, including early shrub, late shrub, isolated mature trees, and isolated stands of mature trees. Rainfall data are scanty and unreliable, but annual precipitation is presumably about 6,000 mm (West 1957). Rain falls throughout the year. Mean temperature is about 26.7°C (West 1957). Most disturbance of the forest in this region has occurred within the recent 20 years.

The mid-elevation site, where most observations were made, is located in the upper Anchicayá Valley at a site known locally as Alto Yunda (3° 32' N, 76° 48' W). Steep mountain forests in the upper Anchicayá Valley received from 4,500–6,500 mm of rainfall per year, and above 1,000 m there is heavy fog much of each day. There is no well-defined dry season, but March or July (or both) usually receive less rainfall than other months (C.V.C., unpublished records, Departamento de Aguas, Cali, Colombia). The forest is predominantly green and there is no major deciduous period. Mean annual temperature is about 21.5°C. A few trees reach 30 m in height; most are somewhat less. The undergrowth is generally crowded with small palms, arums, heliconias, and melastomes. All trees are mossy and carry massive loads of epiphytes. Canopy trees indicate the area is structurally mature, but many small streams, treefalls, and landslides create an abundance of edge habitat suitable for colonization by second-growth plants. Two small clearings exist near a house.

The highland area (3° 32' N, 76° 43' W) is a steep mountain forest located about 2 km southwest of Queremal, Colombia. Rainfall is about 2,000 mm annually and trees are heavily moss-covered due to daily fog. The forest is heavily disturbed by selective logging and small clearings and consists of several seral shrub stages mixed with stands of undisturbed forest. The canopy is generally below 20 m. This region is structurally similar to the one studied by Miller (1963).

Data for this analysis were obtained during a study of seasonal availability and use of fruit resources by resident and migrant brids. In the upper Anchicayá Valley, mist nets were set from 0600 to about 1400 hr on several days each month (except September and January) from May 1972 through June 1973. Migrant and frugivorous resident birds were identified, color marked, weighed, and released at the capture site. Indices of abundance and biomass were calculated under the assumption that both migrants and residents were captured in proportion to their abundance (Karr 1976). The latter index slightly underestimates biomass for resident birds since few large resident species are captured. Analysis of the data collected allows estimation of the relative number of migrants in the "winter" avifauna in the upper Anchicayá Valley. The estimates include 1) percentages of total species, 2) percentages of total individuals, and 3) percentages of total biomass, measured as grams of live weight. For a few species where no live weight was obtained, published weights in Haverschmidt (1968), Karr (1971), or ffrench (1973) were used.

During March and April 1973, after a year of familiarity with the resident avifauna, five bird censuses were conducted in the upper Anchicayá Valley along a strip transect 1,500 m by 30 m (6.1 h). Two additional censuses conducted in May are not included since all migrants were gone. All censuses began at either 0700 or 0939 hr. All birds detected by eye and ear were recorded while the route was walked slowly once. At the lowland and highland sites, birds were censused in a similar manner between November and April by walking slowly along a nonrepeating course. At these latter two sites, the length of the routes varied with weather conditions and time available, but routes were somewhat longer than in the upper Anchicayá Valley. Data from the censuses are used to assign an index of abundance to each migrant (i.e., common, uncommon, rare) based on the number of individuals observed per hour at each of the three sites. Due to the difficulties of obtaining accurate information on density and species compostition in tropical communities with transect censuses, the data are not used to compare the density of migrants with residents.

Bird feeding use of fruit trees were studied by re-

Steven L. Hilty

cording all species and the number of feeding visits of each to trees during timed intervals lasting approximately six hours. A minimum of 30 observation hours each month, spaced over five mornings, were made from June 1972 to June 1973 at a stand of *Cecropia reticulata* growing on a steep landslide surrounded by mature forest. Varying numbers of hours were also spent observing several other species of fruiting trees. Fruit production was estimated by making biweekly counts of the number of individuals and species of trees fruiting on a 0.7 h transect. In this paper the term "migrant" refers to transient or seasonally resident birds which breed in temperate North America.

Results

Seasonal Distribution of Migrants in Pacific Colombia

I observed 22 species of migrants in the upper Anchicayá Valley (figure 1). The first migrant wood pewees (*Contopus sordidulus*) arrived in the upper Anchicayá Valley in August and the first parulids in September. Most migrants were not resident or in transit until October (figure 2). A few species such as Great Crested Flycatcher (*Myiarchus crinitus*), Bank Swallow (*Riparia riparia*), American Redstart (*Setophaga ruticilla*), and Cerulean Warbler (*Dendroica cerulea*) were seen only in October–November. These species were presumably transients only and result in a small October–November increase in the number of species (figure 2). From December through February, the number of migrants remained relatively constant. There was a sharp decline in migrant numbers in April and almost all migrants were gone before May (figures 1 and 2). Several migrants were not seen regularly until December or later. The Olive-sided Flycatcher (*Nuttallornis borealis*) was not regularly observed until January. None were observed in October, and the number of records for November and December was very small. The Rose-breasted Grosbeak (*Pheucticus ludovicianus*) was absent in October and rather sporadic during November and December. Prior to January most records were of single birds, but from January through March it was more common and often encountered in flocks ranging in size to eight or more individuals. Nine migrants (41 percent) were observed no more than twice and probably do not properly belong to the winter avifauna at this elevation (figure 1). Additionally, a Mourning Warbler (*Oporornis philadelphia*), seen infrequently in a steep grassy pasture, was probably a recent invader with the appearance of man-made clearings.

Seasonal Density of Migrants and Residents in Pacific Colombia

Due to the difficulty of reliably estimating relative abundance of birds in tropical communities by cen-

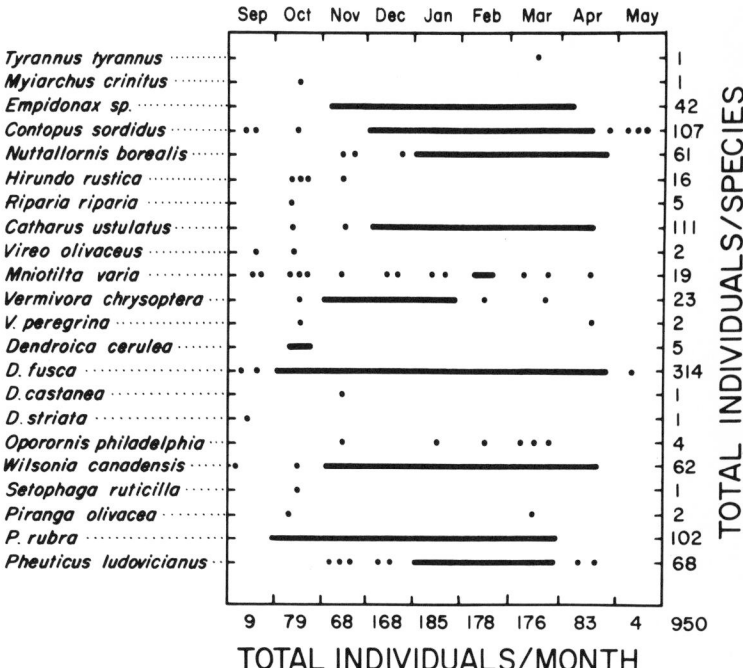

Figure 1. Seasonal occurrence of migrants in the upper Anchicayá Valley, Colombia, from September 1972 to June 1973. Solid lines = periods of continuous occurrence, with sightings on 4 or more days per month. Dots = isolated records. Each migrant record (dot) equals 1 day per individual bird (after Leck 1972). The number of observation days per month varied from 14 to 17.

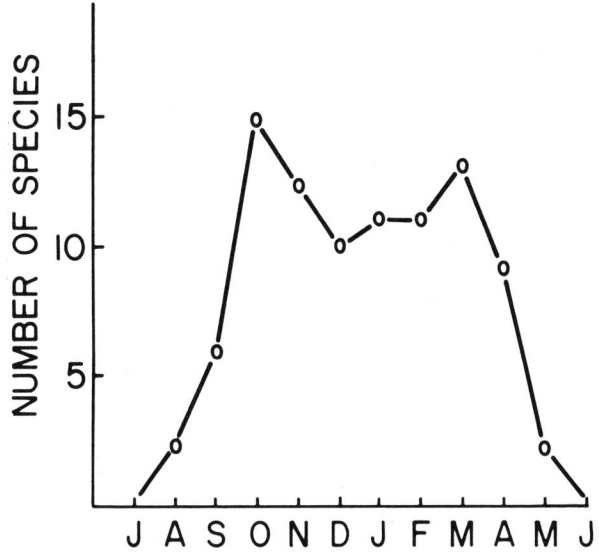

Figure 2. Number of migrant species seen in each month in the upper Anchicayá Valley, Colombia, July 1972 to June 1973.

Table 1. Distribution of migrant and resident individuals and species in mist nets in Colombia

Month	Number of net hours[1]	Total captures	Number captures		Number species		Captures/ species		Captures/ hour	
			R^2	M	R	M	R	M	R	M
Oct	291	190	180	10	56	5	3.2	2.0	.62	.03
Nov	66	55	52	3	25	3	2.1	1.0	.79	.04
Dec	103	84	81	3	38	3	2.1	1.0	.79	.03
Jan[3]	—	—	—	—	—	—	—	—	—	—
Feb	127	105	99	6	43	4	2.3	1.5	.78	.05
Mar	141	113	105	8	38	5	2.8	1.6	.74	.06
Apr	118	99	96	3	41	2	2.3	1.5	.81	.03
May	197	162	162	0	44	0	3.7	0	.82	0

[1] Net size, 2.6 m × 12 m.

[2] R = resident, M = migrant.

[3] No mist-nets set in Jan.

susing, mistnets were used to determine migrant and resident bird densities. As noted by Karr (1976) an index of relative abundance for migrants and residents can be obtained by comparing the number of captures per species for migrants and residents. These data are summarized in table 1.

The largest number of migrant captures per species was recorded in October, and the highest capture rate per hour for migrants was in March. The monthly differences are slight, however, and when compared to the number of resident captures and rate of capture, the number of migrants is insignificant. Migrants account for only a small fraction of netted individuals in all categories every month (table 1).

Table 2 summarizes the relative numbers of migrants in the upper Anchicayá Valley. The low values for the number of migrant species (October through April 8.8 percent), number of migrant individuals (October through April 5.0 percent), and migrant biomass (October through April 5.1 percent), confirm the general rarity of migrants in this premontane rain forest. Transients may contribute to slightly higher biomass values in October and March.

Some migrants probably remain resident upon arrival although actual evidence for this is slight. A female Summer Tanager (*Piranga rubra*) captured 10 October 1972 was sighted 14 November 1972 and 16 January 1973, and a male Summer Tanager captured 17 February 1973 was seen 16 March 1973. A male captured 10 October 1972 was not observed again. A single marked Blackburnian Warbler (*Dendroica fusca*)

was not observed again, and of 2 marked Canada Warblers (*Wilsonia canadensis*), 1 captured 17 February 1973 was sighted 22 March 1973.

Elevational Distribution of Migrants in Pacific Colombia

General censusing at three elevations on the Pacific slope allows an index of abundance to be calculated for each migrant species. These are summarized in table 3. The data show some elevational separation. Two species were chiefly confined to the lowlands, and 2 others chiefly to the highlands. No species was equally common, uncommon, or rare at all three elevations. Moreover, there were no large concentrations of migrants at any of the sampled elevations on the Pacific slope. Of 14 species recorded at the sites (based on a total of 62 census hr), only 2 species occurred frequently enough to be considered common. The Blackburnian Warbler, probably the most frequent migrant on the Pacific slope, was common at the two upper sites; the Golden-winged Warbler (*Vermivora chrysoptera*) was common only at the highest site. No migrants were frequent enough to be classified as common in the lowlands.

Under the assumption that migrants are about equally conspicuous and detectable at each of the three elevations, an index of relative abundance for migrants was obtained by comparing the number of migrant individuals observed per hour at each locality. The frequency of migrant encounters increases with elevation from one bird per hr in the lowlands to 2.6

Steven L. Hilty

Table 2. Relative abundance of migrants in the "winter" avifauna of the upper Anchicayá Valley, Colombia

Parameter	Month							
	Oct	Nov	Dec	Jan[1]	Feb	Mar	Apr	May
Percentage of total species	8.2	10.7	7.9	—	8.5	11.6	4.7	0
Percentage of total individuals	5.3	5.5	3.6	—	5.7	7.1	3.0	0
Percentage of total biomass	6.0	5.7	3.8	—	5.0	7.4	2.6	0

[1] No mist nets set in Jan.

Table 3. Index of abundance for migrants at 3 elevations on the Pacific Colombian slope

Species	Low-lands[1] 100 m	Inter-mediate[2] 1,000 m	High-lands[3] 1,900 m
Vireo olivaceus	U[4]		
Dendroica castanea	U		
Catharus ustulata	R	U	R
Dendroica fusca	U	C	C
Piranga rubra	R	R	U
Pheucticus ludovicianus	U	R	U
Nuttallornis borealis		U	
Contopus sordidulus		U	R
Empidonax sp.[5]		U	R
Mniotilta varia		R	
Vermivora peregrina		R	R
Wilsonia canadensis		R	C
Vermivora chrysoptera[6]			U
Oporonis philadelphia			R

[1] Near Llano Bajo, Colombia, 3 Nov 1972, 2 Feb 1973; total 14 hr.

[2] Alto Yunda, Colombia, 13 Mar, 18 Apr, 24 Apr 1973; total 12.5 hr.

[3] Near Queremal, Colombia, 1 Nov, 3 Dec 1972, 3 Mar, 30 Mar, 1 Apr 1973; total 35 hr.

[4] C = common, more than 5 birds per 10 hr; U = uncommon, 1 to 5 birds per 10 hr; R = rare, fewer than 1 bird per 10 hr.

[5] Most are probably Acadian Flycatchers, Empidonax virescens.

[6] Sparse resident at intermediate site from Nov through Jan. None observed during censuses in Mar and Apr.

Table 4. Frequency of encounter of migrants at 3 elevations in Pacific Colombia

Parameter	Low-lands[1] 100 m	Inter-mediate[2] 1,000 m	High-lands[3] 1,900 m
Number of migrants/hr	1.0	1.8	2.6

[1] Near Llano Bajo, Colombia, 3 Nov 1972, 2 Feb 1973; total 14 hr.

[2] Alto Yunda, Colombia, 13 Mar, 18 Apr, 24 Apr 1973; total 12.5 hr.

[3] Near Queremal, Colombia; 1 Nov, 3 Dec 1972, 3 Mar, 30 Mar, 1 Apr 1973; total 35 hr.

per hr in the highlands (table 4). This suggests that somewhat greater numbers of migrants are in disturbed highland habitat than in disturbed lowland habitat in Pacific Colombia.

Migrants as Competitors at Fruiting Trees in Pacific Colombia

All migrants in the upper Anchicayá Valley are chiefly insectivorous. I observed only 4 of 22 migrant species taking fruit (Swainson's Thrush, *Catharus ustulatus*, Summer Tanager, Scarlet Tanager, *Piranga olivacea*, and Blackburnian Warbler). The Scarlet Tanager was rare (two sightings) in the upper Anchicyá Valley and was not a potential food competitor. The Summer Tanager occurs chiefly in clearings, flycatching within the canopy of trees. It takes little fruit. Thus, in 28 hr of censusing at a pair of fruiting *Miconia* sp. trees growing at the edge of forest, only 2 migrants, Blackburnian Warbler and Swainson's Thrush, took fruit. Feeding visits by these migrants accounted for 4.2 percent of the total exploitation (n = 790; table 5).

At a stand of *Cecropia reticulata* surrounded by mature forest, migrant feeding pressures were even lower. From October through April only 1.3 percent of the feeding visits (n = 5923) were by migrants (table 6). Values were higher in November (1.8 percent), January (2.3 percent), and March (2.7 percent) and lower in October (0.6 percent), December (0.3 percent), and April (0.4 percent). The monthly variation suggests no seasonal relationship.

If migrants affect fruit availability for resident birds, their greatest impact probably occurs when fruit resources are lowest. Fruiting levels at Alto Yunda are

Table 5. Number and percentages of fruit feeding visits to a pair of *Miconia* sp. by residents and migrants in the upper Anchicayá Valley, Colombia[1]

Species	Number of feeding visits	Percentages of feeding visits
Residents[2]	757	95.8
Migrants[3]	33	4.2

[1] Alto Yunda, Colombia, 15 Nov–17 Dec 1972. Observation periods: 15 November, 0600–1200 hr; 21 Nov, 0600–1200 hr, 1400–1800 hr; 13 Dec, 0600–1200 hr; 17 Dec, 0600–1200 hr.

[2] Cracidae (1 species), Capitonidae (1), Cotingidae (2), Tyrannidae (3), Parulidae (1), Coerebidae (3), Thraupidae (19).

[3] Parulidae (1 species), Thraupidae (1).

Table 6. Number and percentages of fruit feeding visits to *Cecropia reticulata* by residents and migrants in the upper Anchicayá Valley, Colombia[1]

Species	Number of visits	Percentages of visits
Residents	5846	98.7
Migrants[2]	77	1.3

[1] Data gathered as in table 5. Approximately 30 observation hr each month from Oct 1972 to May 1973; 0600–1200 hr.

[2] Swainson's Thrush (most fruit feeding records were by this species), Summer Tanager, Scarlet Tanager (1 fruit feeding record).

rather constant, showing no more than a twofold seasonal increase. For fruits with bird-dispersed seeds, the lowest period occurs from June through August when migrants are absent (Hilty 1977). The results of this section suggest that the seasonal presence of migrants is of minor consequence as a factor affecting fruit availability for resident frugivores in western Colombia.

Discussion

On Colombia's Pacific slope migrants are present chiefly from October to early April. There is no October peak in migrant density similar to that found in lower Central America (Galindo and Mendez 1965; Willis 1966: Leck 1972; Karr 1976) or in Senegal (Morel 1968; Karr 1976). Monthly densities of migrants in the upper Anchicayá Valley showed a small increase only in March, probably associated with a northward movement of migrants. Several migrants were sparse or absent in October and November and were not commonly recorded until December or January. Possibly some of these migrants, arriving in lower Middle America in October and November, filter slowly southward through the Pacific Andes and do not reach southwestern Colombia until December or later. Alternatively, a few species may occupy seasonally drier areas in Colombia such as the northern coast and Cauca Valley from October to December (Russell; Orejuela et al, both this volume). With increasing drought stress and diminishing food resources, some of these migrants may shift to wetter habitats by December or January.

In disturbed habitats, migrant densities increase with elevation on the Pacific slope of Colombia. This pattern is well documented in lower Central America (Willis 1966; Leck 1972; Karr 1976) and has been subjectively appreciated in South America (Willis 1966; Chipley 1976). Miller (1963), working in a disturbed cloud forest in the western Colombian Andes, estimated nearly 15 percent of the winter avifauna was composed of migrants. Miller's estimate is higher than the values of 3.6–5.7 percent I obtained in the upper Anchicayá Valley but the latter locality is lower in elevation and virtually free of human disturbance.

Willis (1966) found few "wintering" migrants in tracts of undisturbed forest in both the highlands and lowlands of Pacific Colombia. In Willis' view, migrants are better able to exploit the temporary resources of second-growth and disturbed localities ("environmental irregularity") than the resources of mature communities. At least where migrant densities are rather low, as in northern South America, most migrants do not readily invade structurally mature and stable areas where the avifaunal complexity seems to prevent seasonal exploiters. Furthermore, the mosaic of natural edge habitat along streams, landslides, and treefalls seems to be less suitable to migrants, as in the upper Anchicayá Valley, than the extensively human-disturbed cloud forest where Miller (1963) worked.

A review of the data also supports the notion that elevational replacement of migrants occurs on the Pacific Colombian slope. Supportive data include 1) the occurrence of two species chiefly in the lowlands and two others chiefly in the highlands and 2) the lack of uniform abundance of species occurring in two or more of the three elevations surveyed. Elevational separation may play a role in diluting the competitive

Steven L. Hilty

influence of migrants among themselves and with resident species.

Migrant impact at fruiting trees is minimal in Pacific Colombia. Exploitation rates were extremely low at two species of fruiting trees widely used by residents. This conclusion is reinforced by the general observation that migrants are almost always subordinate to residents (usually migrants are smaller than residents) in interspecific encounters at food sources (Leck 1970; Hilty pers. obs.). Leck (1970) also found very low exploitation rates for migrants at fruiting trees in Panama and quantified their low dominance relationships. Leck suggested that migrant impact might be greater during periods of food shortage, i.e. late wet season in the Canal Zone. In the upper Anchicayá Valley there are no periods of severe fruit shortage, and the highest fruiting levels occur when migrants are present (Hilty 1977). Thus, their competitive impact at fruiting trees is probably minimized. Moreover, migrants seem to be neither common enough nor do they visit fruiting trees often enough to strongly affect the abundant supply of small fruit utilized by most resident frugivores on Colombia's Pacific slope.

Acknowledgments

A joint University of Arizona-Peace Corps program provided support. Ernesto Schrimpff, Eliécer Solarte, and many more people in the Corporación Autónoma del Valle del Cauca (C.V.C.), and my wife Beverly J. Hilty, helped make living and working in the Anchicayá Valley possible. I thank Terry B. Johnson for valued comments on the manuscript and Isela McKenna for assistance with Spanish translation. Stephen M. Russell aided the work in many ways.

Literature Cited

Chipley, R.
1976. The impact of winter migrant wood warblers on insectivorous passerines in a subtropical Colombian oak woodland. Living Bird 15:119–41.

ffrench, R.
1973. *A Guide to the Birds of Trinidad and Tabago*. Wynnewood, Pa.: Livingston.

Galindo, P., and E. Mendez.
1965. Banding of thrushes and catbirds at Almirante, Panama. Second year of observations. Bird-Banding 36: 233–39.

Haverschmidt, R.
1968. *Birds of Surinam*. Wynnewood, Pa.: Livingston.

Hilty, S.
1977. Food supply in a tropical frugivorous bird community. Ph.D. diss., Univ. of Arizona., Tucson.

Holdridge, L.
1967. *Life Zone Ecology*. Rev. ed. San Jose, Costa Rica: Tropical Science Center.

Karr, J.
1971. Structure of avian communities in selected Panama and Illinois habitats. Ecol. Monogr. 41:207–58.

1976. On the relative abundance of migrants from the North Temperate Zone in tropical habitats. Wils. Bull. 88:433–58.

Leck, D.
1970. The ecology of fruit- and nectar-eating birds in lower Middle America. Ph.D. diss., Cornell Univ., Ithaca, N.Y.

1972. The impact of some North American migrants at fruiting trees in Panama. Auk 89:842–50.

Miller, A.
1963. Seasonal activity and ecology of the avifauna of an American equatorial cloud forest. Univ. Calif. Publs. Zool. 66:1–78.

Morel, G.
1963. Contribution à la synécologie des oiseaux du Sahel sénégalais. Mem. ORSTOM 29, Paris. In J. Karr, 1976. On the relative abundance of migrants from the north temperate zone in tropical habitats. Wils. Bull 88:433–58.

West, R.
1957. The Pacific lowlands of Colombia. State Univ. Studies, Social Science Series, no. 8.

Willis, E.
1966. The role of migrant birds at swarms of army ants. Living Bird 5:187–231.

DAVID L. PEARSON
Department of Biology
Pennsylvania State University
University Park, Pennsylvania 16802

Bird Migration in Amazonian Ecuador, Peru, and Bolivia

ABSTRACT

Long-range migrants that breed in northern and southern temperate regions make up a small proportion of the total species occuring in western Amazonia. They appear to be able to winter in this area by 1) using secondary habitats, 2) moving within this area to take advantage of changing resource availability, and 3) using primary forest by being rare or in essence dilute in any given area. The presence of these long-range migrants is complicated by the local and/or altitudinal movement of several "resident" species. As more long-term studies are conducted, the extent and implication of these short-range migrants will likely become important in interpreting the presence or absence of long-range migrants in western Amazonia.

SUMARIO

Las aves de migraciones extensas que anidan en las regiones templadas del notre y sur forman una pequeña proporción del total de las especies que existen en la Amazonía occidental. Aparentemente pueden ellas invernar en esta area 1) usando habitats secundarios, 2) movilizándose dentro de esta area para aprovechar la disponibilidad de los cambios de recursos, y 3) usando bosques primarios siendo raras o en esencia diseminadas en cualquier área dada. La presencia de estas aves de extensas migraciones se complica con la movilización local y/o altitudinal de varias especies "residentes." A medida que se vayan efectuando estudios prolongados, la extensión e implicación de estas aves de migraciones cortas serán probablemente más importantes al interpretarse la presencia o ausencia de aves de migraciones extensas en la Amazonía occidental.

Introduction

Our knowledge of the geographical and temporal distribution of migrants in western Amazonia is much less complete than for most of the other areas discussed in this volume. However, by combining reports of early collecting expeditions and more recent accounts of relatively long-term observations from several sites, some interesting generalizations and speculations are possible.

First, using personal communications and published lists from: Amazonian Ecuador (Chapman 1926; Meyer de Schauensee 1951; Stevenson 1965; Pearson 1972, 1975a; Ortíz and Valarezo 1975; Tallman and Tallman 1977); Peru (O'Neill 1969, 1974; O'Neill and Pearson 1974; Keopcke, pers. comm.; Terborgh, pers. comm.), and Bolivia (Bond and Meyer de Schauensee 1942, 1943; Gyldenstolpe 1945; Niethammer 1953, 1956; Olrog 1963; Pearson 1975a, 1975b; J. Van Remsen, pers. comm.), I will summarize broad generalizations of latitudinal gradients in number of migrant species occurring in this part of western Amazonia and attempt some initial breakdown of the types of migrants involved, i.e., northern, southern, altitudinal, local, pioneering, and so on.

Second, based principally on my own observations, I will speculate on the possible significance of more detailed ecological patterns of temporal and spatial distribution of migrants in this area. Specifically, the impact of high-latitude breeding migrants on tropical forests has been recently discussed by several authors (Brosset 1968; Leck 1972; Tramer 1974, and others). The general conclusion of these authors was that migrants tend to select low latitude wintering habitats that either resemble nesting grounds (high altitude forest) or take advantage of areas of secondary growth where the competition from resident species is not sufficient to exclude the migrants. These authors indicate that migrants do not use lowland primary forest to any significant degree as a wintering habitat (although Karr [1976] indicated that some migrant species in Panama use primary forest regularly). I will report on the regular occurrence of migrant species in lowland primary forest as well as the ecological significance of arrival times that may be more related to species saturation of habitat than to latitude.

Geographical Zones and Study Sites

A relatively homogeneous habitat of lowland forest, palm swamps, oxbow lakes, and rivers occurs over much of western Amazonia (figure 1). For the purpose of this paper, I used the Ecuadorian-Colombian border as the northern extent of this region and the northern reaches of grasslands in Bolivia as the southern extent.

For the east-west extent of this area, I used the eastern borders of Ecuador, Peru, and Bolivia and the 300- m contour line on the eastern slope of the Andes. A north-south gradient of rainfall amount and seasonality made possible a convenient division of this region into three zones (figure 2). The northern zone included eastern Ecuador and extreme northeastern Peru, an area of high mean annual rainfall (2,500–3,000 mm) and minimal dry season. The central zone included central Peru, an area of lower annual rainfall (1,500–2,500 mm) and a definite dry season (May–September). The southern zone included extreme southeastern Peru and northeastern Bolivia, also an area of low annual rainfall (1,500–2,000 mm) and definite dry season (June–October). In addition, this zone is regularly influenced by antarctic cold fronts from July to September.

Detailed lists and concentrated studies have been carried out in at least one site within each zone. My own observations are principally from the three following sites (figure 2) and for the indicated periods: 1) Limoncocha, Ecuador, (0°24′S; 76°37′W), 3 July 1971–16 April 1972; 23 February–7 March 1977; 23–27 September 1977; 2) Yarinacocha, Peru, (8°17′S; 74°37′W), 25 May–28 August 1968, 30 May–11 September 1972; 3) Tumi Chucua, Bolivia, (11°8′S; 66°. 10′W), 14 September–15 November 1972. Details on the general bird fauna and weather patterns for each area are available elsewhere (Pearson 1972, 1975a, 1975b; O'Neill and Pearson 1974) and have been supplemented by other investigators (Tallman and Tallman 1977; Hocking, pers. comm.; Van Remsen, pers. comm.). In general, the Ecuador site had no extreme or definite dry season and as a result no synchronous fruiting season (Janzen 1967). Both the Peru and Bolivia sites had extreme dry seasons (June–September) and a synchronous fruiting season (late August–mid-September).

The primary forest available in each of these areas was extensive, but the amount of secondary forest and scrub differed considerably. The Ecuador area had only about 10 km^2 of man-made clearings and secondary growth. The Peru and Bolivia areas had hundreds of square kilometers cleared for grassland or sugar cane.

Results

Latitudinal Gradient in Number of Migrant Species

At least 61 migrant species of birds have been recorded as nonbreeding residents or transients from this region (table 1). Most of these species are totally absent from this region for 5 to 10 months of the year. Nonbreeding individuals of some migrant species, however, such as *Bibulcus ibis*, *Pandion haliaetus*, and *Actitis macularia*,

David L. Pearson

Figure 1.   Amazon forest near Limoncocha, Province of Napo, Ecuador, (el. = 300 m).

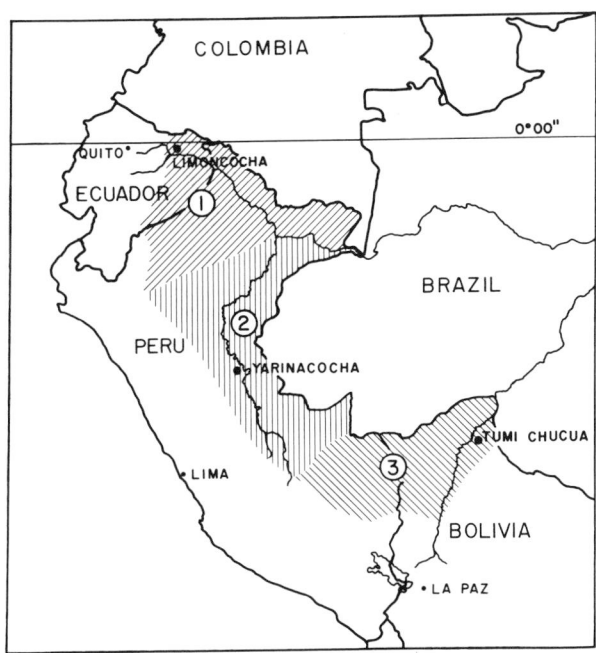

Figure 2.   Geographical zones in western Amazonia based roughly on mean annual rainfall, seasonality of rainfall, and frequency of southern cold fronts.

could be regularly found all year. The northern third of this region (Zone 1) had 61 totally migrant species, the central third (Zone 2) had 53 such species, and the southern third (Zone 3) had 45. Using lists from restricted localities in Ecuador (Pearson 1972; Tallman and Tallman 1977), Peru (Koepcke pers. comm., Terborgh pers. comm.), and Bolivia (Pearson 1975b; Van Remsen pers. comm.) these numbers of migrant species represent roughly the following percentage of total species (resident and migrant) expected in a single site of 10–25 km^2. Zone 1 = 12.7 percent; Zone 2 = 12.1 percent; Zone 3 = 10.7 percent. However, only a portion of these migrant species use each zone for wintering. The rest are present only as transients mainly during March and October. In Zone 1, 32 species (52.5 percent of migrant species and 6.7 percent of all species permanent resident and migrant) use the area for wintering. In Zone 2, 32 species (60.4 percent of migrant species and 7.3 percent of all species, permanent resident and migrant); and in Zone 3, 22 species (48.9 percent of migrant species and 5.2 percent of all species, permanent resident and migrant) use each area for wintering.

Table 1. Long-range migrants in Amazonian Ecuador, Peru, and Bolivia[1]

	Migratory status (t = transient only, w = wintering resident)[1]		
	Zone 1[2]	Zone 2[2]	Zone 3[2]
Ardeidae			
Bulbulcus ibis (nests in both northern and southern South America)	W	W	W
Anatidae			
Anas discors	W	—	—
Accipitridae			
Buteo swainsoni	T	T	T
B. platypterus	W	W	—
Pandionidae			
Pandion haliaetus	W	W	W
Rallidae			
Porzana carolina	W	W	—
Charadriidae			
Pluvialis dominica	T	T	T
Squatarola squatarola	T	*T*	T
Charadrius semipalmatus	T	*T*	T
Scolopacidae			
Arenaria interpres	T	T	T
Tringa solitaria	W	W	W
T. flavipes	W	W	W
T. melanoleuca	T	T	T
Actitis macularia	W	W	W
Calidris minutilla	T	*T*	T
C. bairdii	T	T	T
C. fusicollis	T	T	T
C. melanotos	W	W	W
C. alba	W	*W*	W
Micropalma himantopus	T	T	T
Tryngites subruficollis	T	T	T
Bartramia longicauda	T	T	T
Numenius phaeopus	T	*T*	T
Limosa haemastica	T	*T*	T
Gallinago gallinago	T	—	—
Laridae			
Larus atricilla	T	—	—
Chlidonias nigra	T	*T*	T
Sterna hirundo	T	*T*	T
Cuculidae			
Coccyzus erythopthalmus	W	W	—
C. americanus	T	W	W

David L. Pearson

	Migratory status		
	(t = transient only, w = wintering resident)[1]		
	Zone 1[2]	Zone 2[2]	Zone 3[2]

Caprimulgidae
   Chordeiles acutipennis — T — —
   C. minor — T — *T* — T

	Zone 1	Zone 2	Zone 3
Caprimulgidae			
Chordeiles acutipennis	T	—	—
C. minor	T	*T*	T
Apodidae			
Chaetura pelagica	W	—	—
Tyrannidae			
Muscivora tyrannus	W	W	W
Tyrannus tyrannus	T	W	W
Empidonomus aurantioatrocristatus	W	W	W
Myiodynastes luteiventris	T	W	W
Myiarchus swainsoni	W	W	W
Nutallornis borealis	W		
Contopus virens	W	W	W
Empidonax traillii	W	W	W
Elaenia spectabilis	W	W	T
E. parvirostris	W	W	T
E. strepera	—	W	T
Hirundinidae			
Progne subis	T	—	T
Riparia riparia	T	*T*	T
Hirundo rustica	T	T	T
Petrochelidon pyrrhonota	T	*T*	T
Turdidae			
Catharus minimus	W	W	—
C. ustulatus	W	W	W
Icteridae			
Dolichonyx oryzivorus	T	T	W
Vireonidae			
Vireo altiloquus	—	W	—
Parulidae			
Dendroica petechia	W	W	—
D. cerulea	W	W	W
D. fusca	W	W	—
D. striata	W	W	W
Seiurus noveboracensis	W	—	—
Geothylpis philadelphia	W		
Wilsonia canadensis	T	W	—
Setophaga ruticilla	W	—	—
Thraupidae			
Piranga rubra	W	W	W
P. olivacea	W	W	W
Fringillidae			
Sporophila caerulescens	—	W	W
Pheucticus ludovicianus	W	—	—

| | Migratory status | | |
| | (t = transient only, w = wintering resident)[1] | | |
	Zone 1[2]	Zone 2[2]	Zone 3[2]
Total transient species	29	21	24
Total wintering resident migrant species	32	32	22
South temperate breeding species	(5)	(7)	(4)
North temperate breeding species	(27)	(25)	(18)
Total wintering resident and transient species	61	53	46
Partially migratory populations			
Empidonax euleri	—	W	W
Empidonomus varius	W	W	W
Myiodynastes maculatus	—	W	W
Sublegatus modestus	—	W	W
Progne modesta	—	W	T
Vireo olivaceus	W	W	W

* = south temperate breeding species.

[1] *T* or *W* = migrant species for a zone in which no records are known but which has been recorded in zones to the north or south so that it undoubtedly is also found in the indicated zone.

[2] See figure 2 for delineation of Zone 1, 2, and 3.

Species from the northern hemisphere make up the bulk of migrants, both transient and wintering, in all the zones. Only seven species migrate from southern temperate areas (June–September) (table 1). Six of these species are tyrannids and one a fringillid. Of these, three are transient through Zone 3. In addition, at least six species (table 1) have resident breeding races as well as races or significant parts of the population that migrate to or through these zones. Five of these species come from southern temperate parts of their range, and one comes from the northern hemisphere.

More difficult to accurately assess were the local migrants that moved regularly within the region or were perhaps altitudinal migrants (*Elanoides forficatus*; *Graydidaculus brachyurus*; *Touit huetii*; *Amazona mercenaria*; *Pionus menstruus*; *Coccyzus melacoryphus*; *Pteroglossus mariae*; *Phaeoprogne tapera*; *Notiochelidon cyanoleuca*; *Turdus ignobilis*; *Tersina viridis*; and see Karr 1977). Some, such as the parrots and aracaris, were likely following concentrations of fruiting, and their movements were most obvious in Zones 2 and 3 where seasonality caused synchronous fruiting. The parrots *Graydidaculus brachyurus*, *Pionus menstruus*, and the aracari *Pteroglossus mariae*, for instance, were virtually absent from the Yarinacocha, Peru, area as was the parrot *Touit huetii* from the Tumi Chucua, Bolivia, area, except during the fruiting season at the beginning of the rainy season (August–September). None of these species appeared

Figure 3. Male *Tersina viridis*, Limoncocha, Ecuador, (photo by James Yost).

to nest in the above areas. Even in areas such as Limoncocha, Ecuador, where seasonality and synchrony of fruiting were much less marked, nonbreeding species such as *Amazona mercenaria* appeared regularly only a few months each year.

Insectivorous and partially insectivorous species such as *Coccyzus melacoryphus*, *Phaeoprogne tapera*, and *Tersina viridis* (figure 3) used Zone 1, and parts of Zones 2 and 3, as a wintering area and then disappeared presumably to nest in areas or altitudes yet

David L. Pearson

undetermined for these populations. *Turdus ignobilis* was the only species I know of that nested in this region and then (as least in parts of Zone 1) migrated from the area.

Another set of species made up of grassland-nesting species appeared to be at least partially migratory: (*Columbina picui*; *C. minuta*; *Milvago chimachima*; *Leistes militaris*; *Volatina jacarina*; *Tiaris olivacea*, and *Sporophila nigricollis*). Some evidence indicated that as forests were cleared these species initially nested in these newly cleared areas but then migrated to another area until the next season. Until either the populations grew sufficiently large or the newly cleared habitat became established as an adequate grassland, the migration continued. After a period of 1–10 years, depending on the species, permanent breeding populations were apparently established, and the migration was no longer apparent.

Temporal Distribution and Use of Primary Forest

Table 2 lists the number of individuals of each migrant species I saw on my three study sites and the number of individuals per hour of observation I saw in primary forest, secondary forest, and grassland (including aerial). Except for migrant cuckoos, only passerine species are included. These totals should be interpreted in light of the greater number of hours spent in primary forest than in other habitats (1,475 vs 300 hr) in the three areas, and also less total time in the Tumi Chucua area.

I found 20 migrant species at Limoncocha, 4 of which were southern or altitudinal migrants. All but 1 of the 9 species found in primary forest were northern migrants. At Limoncocha, all the northern species except *Tyrannus tyrannus*, *Myodynastes luteiventris*, *Wilsonia canadensis* and the 3 swallow species remained until March. These latter species evidently pass through to winter farther south. The arrival of most of the population of the remaining 6 northern migrants in the first week of December 1971 coincided with the arrival of the presumably altitudinal migrant *Tersina viridis* and *Phaeprogne tapera*, neither of which breeds in the area. *Coccyzus melacoryphus* used the Limoncocha area as a wintering ground and was absent from October to June. *Turdus ignobilis*, as mentioned earlier, was a common nester in the open areas and scrub from October to March but was absent the rest of the year.

I observed 19 migrant species at Yarinocoha, none of which were southern or local. A total of 7 species occurred in primary forest, and 3 of these (*Tyrannus tyrannus*, *Pyrocephalus rubinus*, *Empidonomus aurantioatrocristatus*) were seen only in the upper canopy and emergent trees. *T. tyrannus*, unlike the 2 Argentine-

nesting species, dramatically altered its foraging repertoire by feeding in intraspecific flocks (5–20 individuals) on fruit. *T. tyrannus*, however, arrived at Yarinacocha simultaneously with the annual burst of fruiting while the other 2 canopy species departed for the southern breeding grounds at this time. Several northern species (*Dendroica striata*, *Piranga rubra*) were seen regularly here in the fall three to four weeks before most individuals of these species appeared at Limoncocha, which is 700 km north of Yarinacocha.

Although the time spent at Tumi Chucua was the shortest of the three areas, I was there during the months when both northern and southern migrants should have been present (September–November). Only 10 migrant species were seen, and of these *Myiarchus swainsoni* was the sole migrant found in primary forest. Of the three areas, both the proportion of migrant individuals and species present in the primary forest at Tumi Chucua most clearly approached the observations from Mexico (Tramer 1974) and Central America (Leck 1972).

Discussion

By species numbers, migrants make up a relatively small proportion of the total avifauna in western Amazonia. If transient species are ignored, the percentage of migrant wintering species falls to about 6 percent. In addition, none of these migrant wintering species could be considered common per unit area, except perhaps for *Dolichonyx oryzivorus*, which in this study, wintered only in areas of Zone 3 cleared principally by man.

The general pattern is for populations of the wintering species to be spread out over large areas. Factors selecting for so few species wintering here could include a combination of the difficulties faced in the great distances involved moving to and from northern temperate breeding grounds and the extreme differences between breeding and wintering habitat. More subtly, the effect of resident species in this, the most species rich habitat in the world (ca 480 species/10 km^2 in Zone 1; ca 440 species/10 km^2 in Zone 2; and ca 420 species/10 km^2 in Zone 3), could be an important ultimate factor in the small number of migrant species wintering. These relatively few migrant species permit a dilution factor that could have the effect of minimizing negative interactions with the more highly specialized residents. With sufficiently few negative interactions, there would be minimal selective pressure on the resident individuals for the evolution of morphological or behavioral countermeasures that might exclude the migrant species.

By number of individuals per hour of observation (table 2), migrants were generally less common in

Table 2. Migrants at each site, months present, and number of individuals/observation hr

Limoncocha, Ecuador	Primary (800 hr)	Secondary (200 hr)	Grassland (50 hr)	Number of individuals/ observation hr
*Coccyzus melacoryphus (June–Oct)	—	.19	—	38
†Tyrannus tyrannus (Oct; April)	.05	.12	—	65
†Myiodynastes luteiventris (Oct; March)	.03	.04	—	32
Contopus virens (Oct–March)	—	.20	—	40
Empidonax traillii (Nov–April)	—	.05	—	10
*Phaeoprogne tapera (Dec–Feb)	—	.70	—	140
Riparia riparia (Nov; March)	—	—	1.00	50
Hirundo rustica (Nov; March)	—	—	6.00	300
Petrochelidon pyrrhonota (Nov; March)	—	—	3.00	150
Catharus ustulatus (Oct–March)	.03	—	—	27
†*Turdus ignobilis (Oct–March)	—	.16	—	32
Dolichonyx oryzivorous (Oct)	—	—	.10	5
Dendroica petechia (Dec–March)	—	.02	—	4
D. cerulea (Dec–March)	.01	—	—	7
D. striata (Dec–March)	.02	.21	—	53
Oporornis philadelphia (Feb)	—	.01	—	1
Wilsonia canadensis (Oct; March)	.04	.02	—	39
†*Tersina viridis (Dec–Feb)	.06	1.00	—	ca 250
†Piranga rubra (Dec–March)	.02	.02	—	18
†P. olivacea (Dec–April)	.03	.02	—	24
Total	**0.29**	**2.76**	**10.10**	**1285**

Yarinacocha, Peru	Primary (450 hr)	Secondary (100 hr)	Grasslands (25 hr)	Number of individuals/ observation hr
Coccyzus erythropthalamus (Nov–May)	—	.03	—	3
C. americanus (Nov–May)	—	.02	—	2
*Pyrocephalus rubinus (May–Oct)	.02	.20	—	31
*Muscivora tyrannus (May–Sept)	—	.12	—	12
†Tyrannus tyrannus (Oct–March)	.05	.96	—	120
*Empidonomus aurantioatrocristatus (May–Sept)	.04	—	—	16
†*Myiodynastes maculatus (June–Sept)	.06	.14	—	43
*Myiarchus swainsoni (July–Oct)	.01	—	—	5
Contopus virens (Nov–March)	—	.11	—	11
Empidonax traillii (Nov–March)	—	.24	—	24
*Elaenia spectabilis (June–Sept)	—	.18	—	18
*E. parvirostris (June–Sept)	—	.03	—	3
*Notiochelidon cyanoleuca (Aug–Oct)	—	—	9.00	225
Hirundo rustica (Nov–March)	—	—	4.00	100
Dendroica petechia (Nov–March)	—	.05	—	5
D. fusca (Nov–March)	—	.02	—	2
D. striata (Nov–March)	.01	.18	—	20
†Piranga rubra (Nov–March)	.01	.07	—	10
*Sporphila caerulescens (July–Oct)	—	—	3.72	93
Total	**0.20**	**2.35**	**16.72**	**743**

David L. Pearson

Tumi Chucua, Bolivia	Primary (225 hr)	Secondary (50 hr)	Grasslands (20 hr)	Number of individuals/ observation hr
*Pyrocephalus rubinus (April–Nov)	—	.20	—	10
*Muscivora tyrannus (April–Nov)	—	1.50	—	75
†Tyrannus tyrannus (Nov–April)	—	.10	—	5
*Myiarchus swainsoni (June–Nov)	.07	—	—	16
Progne subis (Nov; Feb)	—	—	4.00	100
Riparia riparia (Nov; March)	—	—	17.50	350
Hirundo rustica (Nov; March)	—	—	10.00	200
Petrocheliden pyrrhonota (Nov; March)	—	—	3.75	75
Dolichonyx oryzivorous (Nov–March)	—	—	3.10	62
Piranga rubra (Nov–March)	—	.06	—	3
Total	.07	1.86	38.35	896

* = southern, altitudinal, or local migrants; † = partially frugivorous.

primary forest than in secondary forest and grassland habitats. From all three plots, only six species were seen more commonly in primary forest than in secondary habitat. This overall difference in habitat use, however, if applied to the entire region can be properly interpreted only if the total area of primary forest and secondary habitats is considered. Since primary forest makes up a far greater proportion by area of the wintering habitat in this region, the total number of individuals wintering in primary forest throughout the region is likely far greater than that wintering in secondary forest and grassland habitats.

Despite the relatively brief time spent on specific study sites, some preliminary generalizations and interesting patterns concerning detailed patterns of long range migrants in Amazon lowlands also appear:

1) Migrants are more evident in some lowland primary forests, especially Limoncocha and to some extent Yarinacocha, than Leck (1972) and Tramer (1974) report from undisturbed Mexican and Central American lowland forests.

2) At Limoncocha, the simultaneous arrival of most of the populations of six northern migrants with that of the altitudinal migrant, Tersina viridis, suggests that these northern migrants spend several months (October–December) in the highlands or the southern zones before moving to the Limoncocha area.

3) The earlier arrival of several northern migrants to Yarinacocha and Tumi Chucua before the more northern areas at Limoncocha strengthens the suggestion that many of the northern migrants are initially moving south through the highlands and around the Ecuador lowlands.

One possible explanation for the pattern of migration found on these three sites is that primary forest, as suggested by Leck (1972) and Tramer (1974), is far from ideal for high latitude migrants. The Tumi Chucua area is probably too far south for most northern migrants and possibly too far south for the southern migrants as well. Antarctic cold fronts that are largely responsible for the northward movement of southern migrants regularly reach Tumi Chucua. From April to September, temperatures during these cold fronts often fall to 15°C. Combined with the driest time of year, these two factors probably force most of the south temperate migrants farther north (Willis 1976).

The Yarinacocha area received many of the same antarctic cold fronts, but they were not so extreme. Two of the southern migrants found regularly in primary forest fed in the upper canopy and emergents exclusively. This vertical stratum closely resembled their secondary scrub nesting habitat in southern South America. Most of other southern migrants did not occur in the primary forest.

The question of why the bulk of some northern species should arrive at Yarinacocha before Limoncocha may depend on several additional factors. Earlier (Pearson 1975c) I presented evidence that indicated the Limoncocha area is likely in a more saturated or equilibrium state in terms of species richness (ca 485 spp/10 km²). Yarinacocha, on the other hand, has far fewer species (ca 415 spp/10 km²). The northern migrants would be expected to move first into the areas that would present the least potential competitive resistance and thus avoid the Limoncocha area as long as possible. The movement of *Tersina viridis* indicates that the highlands do not offer sufficient resources and/or the Limoncocha area develops added resources at the same time that forces movement to lower elevations in early December. December–February is a regular season of relatively reduced rainfall at Limoncocha. These factors would likely force the northern migrants still in the highlands down, too. According to Fretwell's (1972) ideal free distribution theory, as the most ideal habitat becomes more populated, the quality of what was otherwise a suboptimal habitat becomes equivalent to the overpopulated ideal habitat. Limoncocha may become qualitatively similar to more ideal highland and lowland habitats as these latter deteriorate in relative quality either through increased population pressures of migrants, decease in some limiting resource, or increase in available resources at Limoncocha. Terborgh (pers. comm.) reports that most of the northern migrants leave the Manu National Park in southern Peru around December, which corresponds to the arrival of northern migrants at Limoncocha. Willis (pers. comm.), however, also reports that several migrant species appear to dawdle in Panama, which could explain the late influx of migrants into Limoncocha.

In addition, the extreme seasonality (three-month period with less than 200 mm mean rainfall, June–August), together with the relatively sedentary behavior of most permanent resident species at Yarinacocha, may mean that the carrying capacity of residents is largely determined by the dry months when insects and fruits are at their lowest levels. The migrants arrive at the beginning of the rainy season when insects and fruit are at their highest levels, and they use the area throughout the rainy season when resources are generally at higher levels (Pearson 1977). The migrants then leave for north temperate breeding grounds before the onset of dry season. Except for the greater distance traveled, northern migrants face a similar phenomenon and phenology of resource levels in the Tumi Chucua, Bolivia, area.

Piranga rubra is one of the few northern migrants in which adult males retain summer plumage on the wintering ground. Using this character, an additional factor is introduced by the difference in the proportion of adult male-plumage *P. rubra* individuals (these and the following data are rough estimates on unmarked birds) on the Limoncocha site and that observed on a site in Costa Rica by Powell (pers. comm.), in Panama by Morton (pers. comm.), and in Colombia by Hilty (pers. comm.). Only 2 of the 18 individuals (11 percent) I observed at Limoncocha were in adult male plumage, but Powell observed 87.5 percent adult males at Monteverde, Costa Rica; Morton observed 60 percent adult males in Panama; and Hilty observed 84.8 percent adult males in Departamento de Valle, Colombia. Rohwer (1976) has convincing evidence that during the winter in central United States, immature Harris Sparrows (*Zonotrichia querula*) are forced into the least desirable habitats. The more socially dominant adults occupy the most ideal habitats. The observed difference in the *P. rubra* proportions of adult males can be interpreted to indicate that immatures are being forced into the less ideal Limoncocha habitat. One would expect in general that the proportion of adult male northern migrants would be greatest in northern parts of the tropical wintering ground, where resources allow them the greatest chance to survive the winter and still reach the breeding grounds early enough to establish successful territories.

Many of these generalizations and speculations will likely prove to be invalid after long-term studies over several years have been included. Tallman (pers. comm.), for instance, found only a few *Tersina viridis* appearing at Limoncocha in December 1975 and some in June 1976. At present we have no way of telling which year (1971–72 or 1975–76) was "normal" or if either or both were unusual. Studies in specific habitats such as primary forests are also difficult to assess. Tallmen, who did not concentrate his studies at Limoncocha in primary forest but looked at many different habitats, came to quite different conclusions concerning the number of northern migrants in primary forest. By concentrating on a single primary forest site, I found more migrants present but perhaps have a false impression of migrants in other habitats.

In addition, simply looking at the long-range migrants is likely to be a shallow, if not misleading, approach. This region is complex, and the little evidence we do have strongly indicates that local and altitudinal migration is involved and may be much more common than anticipated. Long-term studies may well show that these less-obvious migrants have as great, if not a greater, influence on the presence and type of long-range migrants than do the sedentary residents.

Acknowledgments

My limited observations in western Amazonia were generously supplemented by observations and data from Stephen L. Hilty, the late Maria Koepcke, Eugene S. Morton, John O'Neill, Fernando Ortiz, Manuel Plenge, George Powell, J. Van Remsen, Dan and Erica Tallman, John W. Terborgh, and Edwin O. Willis. The members of the Instituto Lingüístico de

David L. Pearson

Verano at Limoncocha, Yarinacocha, and Tumi Chucua made their facilities and hospitality available to us. Nancy S. Pearson aided in all phases of the study, and a National Science Foundation grant (GB-20978) to the Department of Zoology, University of Washington, provided partial support for my research in 1971–72.

Literature Cited

Bond, J. and R. Meyer de Schauensee
1942. The birds of Bolivia. Part 1. Proc. Acad. Nat. Sci. Phila., 94:307–91.

1943. The birds of Bolivia. Part II. Proc. Acad. Nat. Sci. Phila. 95:167–221.

Brosset, A.
1968. Localisation écologique des oiseaux migrateurs dans la forêt équatoriale du Gabon. Biol. Gabonica 4: 211–16.

Chapman, F. M.
1926. The distribution of bird-life in Ecuador: a contribution to a study of the origin of Andean bird life. Bull. Amer. Mus. Nat. Hist. 55:1–784.

Fretwell S. D.
1972. Populations in a seasonal environment. Monog. in Pop. Biol. 5. Princeton, N.J.: Princeton Univ. Press.

Gyldenstolpe, N.
1945. A contribution to the ornithology of northern Bolivia. Kungl. Sv. Vet. Akad. Handl. 23:1–300.

Janzen, D. H.
1967. Synchronization of sexual reproduction of trees within the dry season in Central America. Evol. 21: 620–37.

Karr, J. R.
1976. On the relative abundance of migrants from the north temperate zone in tropical habitats. Wils. Bull. 88:433–58.

1977. Ecological correlates of rarity in a tropical forest bird community. Auk 94:240–47.

Leck, C. F.
1972. The impact of some North American migrants at fruiting trees in Panama. Auk 89:842–50.

Meyer de Schauensee, R.
1951. Notes on Ecuadorian birds. Not. Naturae, 234:1–11.

Niethammer, G.
1953. Zur Vogelwelt Boliviens. Bonn. Zool. Beitr. 4, 3–4: 195–303.

1956. Zur Vogelwelt Boliviens. Bonn. Zool. Beitr. 7, 1–3: 84–150.

Olrog, C. C.
1963. Notas sobre aves Bolivianas. Acta Zool. Lilloana, 19: 407–78.

O'Neill, J. P.
1969. Distributional notes on the birds of Peru, including twelve species previously unreported from the republic. Occas. Papers Mus. Zool., Louisiana State University 37:1–11.

1974. The birds of Balta, a Peruvian dry tropical forest locality, with an analysis of their origins and ecological relationships. Unpublished Ph.D. diss., Louisiana State University, Baton Rouge.

O'Neill, J. P., and D. L. Pearson
1974. Un estudio preliminar de las aves de Yárinacocha, Departamento de Loreto, Perú. Publ. Mus. Hist. Nat. Javier Prado, Ser. A. Zool. 25:1–13.

Ortíz-Crespo, F., and S. Valarezo-Delgado
1975. Lista de aves del Ecuador. Publ. Soc. Ecuatoriana Francisco Campos. 2:1–37.

Pearson, D. L.
1972. Un estudio de las aves de Limoncocha, Provincia de Napo, Ecuador. Boletin de Informaciones Cientificas Nacionales, Quito, 13:335–46.

1975a. Range extensions and new records for bird species in Ecuador, Peru, and Bolivia. Condor 77:96–99.

1975b. Un estudio de las aves de Tumi Chucua, Departamento del Beni, Bolivia. Pumapunku, La Paz 8:50–56.

1975c. The relation of foliage complexity to ecological diversity of three Amazonian bird communities. Condor 77:453–66.

1977. A pantropical comparison of bird community structure on six lowland forest sites. Condor 79:232–44.

Rohwer, S.
1976. The social significance of avian winter plumage variability. Evol. 29:593–610.

Stevenson, H. M.
1965. Some records of North American migrants in Ecuador. Wils. Bull. 77:407.

Tallman, D., and E. Tallman
1977. Adiciones y revisiones a la lista de la avifauna de Limoncocha, Provicia de Napo, Ecuador. Revista de la Universidad Católica, Quito 16:217–24.

Tramer, E. J.
1974. Proportions of wintering North American birds in disturbed and undisturbed dry tropical habitats. Condor 76:460–64.

Willis, E. O.
1976. Effects of cold wave on an Amazonian avifauna in the upper Paraguay drainage, Western Mato Grosso, and suggestions on Oscine-Suboscine relationships. Acta Amazonica 3:379–94.

ELLIOT J. TRAMER
and
THOMAS R. KEMP
Department of Biology
University of Toledo
Toledo, Ohio 43606

Foraging Ecology of Migrant and Resident Warblers and Vireos in the Highlands of Costa Rica

ABSTRACT

We studied habitat selection, foraging behavior, and social interactions among migrant and resident warblers and vireos at Monteverde, Costa Rica during the winter of 1976–77. Monteverde lies within a steep moisture gradient at an elevation of 1,300–1,550 m. Migrants were abundant in the drier (lower) portion of the gradient, where the dominant habitats were forest edge, parkland, pastures, and patches of mature premontane moist forest. Four residents (two vireos, the Golden-crowned Warbler, and the Slate-throated Redstart) were also restricted primarily to this zone. At higher elevations, virgin wet forest and edge comprised the major habitats. Migrants were scarce, resident vireos were absent, and Three-striped Warblers and Collared Redstarts largely replaced their congeners.

Mixed-foraging flocks were characteristic of all forest and forest-edge habitats, but their composition varied with elevation. In drier forests, flocks were led by Golden-crowned Warblers, with other warblers and vireos as frequent attendant species. In this zone, migrants often foraged alone as well as in mixed flocks. In higher wet forests, flocks were led by Three-striped Warblers and Common Bush-tanagers, with Collared Redstarts and a variety of Furnariids and Dendrocolaptids as the common attendant species. An analysis of frequencies of co-occurrence further revealed that greenlets, Philadelphia Vireos, and Tennessee Warblers frequently foraged with conspecifics, while Brown-capped Vireos, Black-and-white Warblers, and Golden-winged Warblers most commonly joined multispecies flocks.

Assessment of three components of foraging behavior (method, height, and speed) showed that migrants tended to be more variable in foraging height than residents. With the exception of Black-and-white and Golden-winged Warblers, this also appeared to hold for flexibility of feeding methods. Variations in foraging speed were generally greater in migrants, although the relationship fell just short of statistical significance. Resident warblers in wet forest flocks had less specialized foraging behavior than their congeners, suggesting the possibility that competition with migrants affected foraging of residents where migrants were common; observations when migrants are absent are needed to clarify this. There was no evidence that lone migrants foraged differently from migrants in flocks nor was there evidence of seasonal changes in foraging. Agonistic interactions involving migrants were rare, and the only territoriality observed was a small minority of Tennessee Warblers defending blooming *Erythrina* trees.

Our data suggest that at Monteverde, at least, most migrants were assimilated into the avifauna by being flexible enough to take whatever resources are most available in a given situation. The virtual lack of territoriality and the scarcity of agonistic encounters suggest that migrants are not normally experiencing food-mediated competition at this locality. Comparisons with the data of other workers suggest that the situation may be different elsewhere, especially in lowland areas with more pronounced dry seasons.

Introduction

Considerable attention has been directed to the question of how migrants interact with one another and with resident birds on their tropical wintering grounds. Data are still scanty and sometimes contradictory. In the Canal Zone, Willis (1966) and Leck (1972) found that migrants were socially subordinate to residents at ant swarms and fruiting trees, respectively. Chipley (1974) felt that migrant warblers in the Colombian highlands were neither dominant nor subordinate to residents. Studies of interactions among migrants have revealed seasonal shifts in the degree of gregariousness in some situations (Morton 1972) but intense antagonism between conspecifics throughout the winter in others (Rappole 1976). We still know very little about the roles of competition and other forces in multispecies groups of migrants.

In this paper, we treat the migrants at a highland locality in Costa Rica. Our primary purpose is to gain an understanding of the factors affecting the occurrence of migrants there, with particular emphasis on foraging ecology and the relationships of migrants with conspecifics, with other species of migrants, and with related species of resident birds. We thus fit another jagged piece into what is emerging as a very complex, spatially and temporally varying puzzle of long-range migrant biogeography.

Study Area

This study was conducted at Monteverde, a small settlement located on a high bench on the Pacific slope of the Cordillera de Tilarán in northwestern Costa Rica. Monteverde was selected because of the high diversity and abundance of migrants there, and because of the accessibility of a variety of both natural and man-altered habitats. The Monteverde bench lies within a steep moisture gradient. The lower elevations (1,300–1,400 m) experience a pronounced dry season during December–April, while slightly higher elevations (1,500 m to the crest of the divide—about 1,650 m in most places) are drenched by wind-blown mist during the "dry" months when rain is scarce. Reflecting this difference, the climax vegetation changes as one climbs the bench from a moist premontane forest (Holdridge 1967) whose vertical structure resembles a temperate zone hardwood forest, to a wet montane forest heavily laden with epiphytes.

Our study lasted from 15 December 1976 to 6 March 1977. During that time the premontane forest became progressively drier, with a noticeable increase in the amount of leaf litter on the forest floor. However, the abscission of foliage was approximately balanced by the continual appearance of new leaves, so that the total foliage volume appeared more or less constant. Mean daily low and high temperatures during our study were 15° and 23°C, respectively, with extremes of 10 and 26°. Persistent strong winds from the northeast are a feature of the Monteverde dry season; during our stay we recorded only 5 days of calm, and the wind velocity exceeded 25 miles/hr (11.25 m/sec.) on 53 of 74 days. The driving mist, foliage movement, and noise associated with these winds made observations of avian behavior difficult at times. More detailed descriptions of the climate and physiography of the Monteverde area are provided by Buskirk (1972), Buskirk and Buskirk (1976), and Powell (1977).

Procedures

We gathered three basic types of information about the migrants at Monteverde: 1) censuses of the density and species composition of migrants in the major habitats, 2) quantification of the feeding niche structure of migrants and related resident species, and 3) observations of behavioral interactions among migrants and between migrants and residents.

Major habitat types were designated as pasture, roadside edge, parkland (tracts from which approximately half of the primary forest trees and all of the undergrowth had been removed), moist premontane forest, and wet forest. Representative samples of each of these habitats were selected for censusing; these were visited at least six times each during our stay. Our visual/auditory counts were reinforced by limited mist-netting in the premontane forest, and by nonquantitative inferences gleaned in other locations in the course of our feeding and behavioral observations.

Observations of feeding ecology were conducted daily wherever warblers or vireos could be found. For each bird the following information was tape recorded in the field at the time of observation: identity of the bird, its apparent sex, type(s) of food being eaten, other birds in the immediate vicinity, social interactions with other birds, and a "play-by-play" account of the bird's foraging height, feeding method (hawk, hover, glean, etc.), and number of meters traveled through the vegetation. After each day's field work, the tapes were played back, and each observation was partitioned into number of seconds spent in various foraging behaviors, at various heights in the vegetation, and so on. At the end of our study these data were pooled to give a general picture of the feeding ecology of each species, using three niche dimensions: feeding method, foraging height, and foraging speed. No attempt was made to mark birds; therefore it was not possible to assess the variability in feeding behavior of individuals.

Elliot J. Tramer

Results

Migrants were abundant in edge, parkland, and premontane forest habitats. They were moderately common in open pastures that had a few isolated trees. Higher elevation wet forests contained few migrants. In all, 29 species of migrants were seen, of which 12 were common (see list in Appendix). Timed foraging observations sufficient for analysis were obtained for the Philadelphia Vireo (*Vireo philadelphicus*) and the following Warblers: Black-and-white (*Mniotilta varia*), Golden-winged (*Vermivora chrysoptera*), Tennessee (*V. peregrina*), Black-throated Green (*Dendroica virens*), Townsend's (*D. townsendi*), and Wilson's (*Wilsonia pusilla*). These 7 species provided the migrant data base for this paper.

Intensive timed observations were also made on six resident species: Brown-capped Vireo (*Vireo leucophrys*), Gray-headed Greenlet (*Hylophilus decurtatus*), Golden-crowned Warbler (*Basileuterus culicivorous*), Three-striped Warbler (*B. tristriatus*), Slate-throated Redstart (*Myioborus miniatus*) and Collared Redstart (*M. torquatus*). These species showed marked altitudinal segregation, with the Collared Redstart and Three-striped Warbler being restricted to wetter, higher elevations and the other four species occurring at lower, drier sites. The Slate-throated Redstart did occur rarely above 1,500 m., where it was restricted to the forest edge.

Detailed descriptions of our census plots and complete census results will be reported elsewhere. For the purpose of this paper it is important to note only the general result: that migrants were scarce in wet forests (migrants comprised less than 6 percent of the species and 5 percent of the individuals on our wet forest plot) but were a prominent feature (generally 20–30 percent) of the avifaunas on our other plots.

Mixed foraging flocks were conspicuous at Monteverde, especially in closed forests. The degree of cohesion of these flocks and their species composition varied with habitat and elevation. In edge and parkland habitats, flocks were loosely organized and might better be termed feeding aggregations. These groups usually lacked a well-defined nucleus species. They always contained migrants, with Philadelphia Vireos and Black-and-white, Black-throated Green, and Wilson's Warblers as the commonest participants. Among the residents, Slate-throated Redstarts, greenlets, and Brown-capped Vireos were frequently involved. At elevations above about 1,400 m the greenlet and both vireos were generally absent.

In the premontane forest, flocks were more cohesive and were almost always led by Golden-crowned Warblers. Greenlets, Brown-capped Vireos, Slate-throated Redstarts, and a variety of migrant warblers were

included, as well as an occasional Streak-headed (*Lepidocolaptes souleyetii*), Olivaceous (*Sittasomus griseicapillus*), or Ruddy (*Dendrocincla homochroa*) Woodcreeper. Migrant Black-and-white and Golden-winged Warblers had especially high affinity for these flocks.

The largest, most diverse, and most tightly-organized flocks occurred in the wet forests of higher elevations. The nucleus species in these flocks were the Common Bush-Tanager (*Chlorospingus ophthalmicus*) and the Three-striped Warbler, with Collared Redstarts and a variety of resident Furnariids, woodcreepers, and tanagers as the main attendant species. As mentioned above, migrants were only rarely associated with wet forest flocks. The social organization of these flocks and their possible adaptive significance has been treated by Buskirk (1976).

Table 1 gives an index of the frequency of co-occurrence for each possible pair of species. The numbers represent the ratio between the observed and expected frequencies of co-occurrence, the "expected" frequency being calculated on the assumption that pairs of birds consorted at random. Values greater than unity indicate co-occurrence more frequently than would be expected if the birds aggregated randomly; values less than unity denote co-occurrence at less-than-random frequencies. The table was derived from two pieces of raw data, the proportion of the total number of observations represented by each species, and the number of co-occurrences of each species pair.

A percentage of our observations involved birds foraging alone; these percentages are given for each species in the left-hand column of table 1. Migrant species tended to forage alone more frequently than resident species (Mann-Whitney U test, p < .01). Table 1 summarizes a great deal of information about the aggregating tendencies of the various species. Highlights of the analysis include the following:

1) The greenlet, three resident warblers, and the migrant Philadelphia Vireo and Tennessee Warbler frequently consorted with conspecifics (see descending diagonal values in table 1). The same was true to a lesser extent for the resident Brown-capped Vireo and Slate-throated Redstart. By contrast, Black-and-white, Golden-winged, and Townsend's Warblers rarely or never occurred with conspecifics. A Mann-Whitney U test showed that resident species tended to occur with conspecifics more frequently than did migrants (p < .05).

2) High indices of co-occurrence (arbitrarily, more than 3 times the "expected" frequencies) were found for 19 species pairs, involving all 13 species. Of the 19, 8 were migrant-migrant pairs, 9 were migrant-resident pairs, and 2 were resident-resident pairs. The Black-and-white Warbler was involved 6 times, the Brown-

Table 1. Ratio of observed to expected frequencies of co-occurrence for all pairs of species[1]

Species	Percentage observed alone	Ratio of observed to expected frequencies of co-occurrence											
		Brown-capped Vireo	PHILADELPHIA VIREO	*Greenlet*	BLACK-AND-WHITE WARBLER	GOLDEN-WGD WARBLER	TENNESSEE WARBLER	TOWNSEND'S WARBLER	BLACK-THR. GREEN WARBLER	WILSON'S WARBLER	*Golden-crowned Warbler*	*Three-striped Warbler*	*Slate-throated Redstart*	*Collared Redstart*
Brown-capped Vireo	13	4.0												
PHILADELPHIA VIREO[2]	29	4.0	6.1											
Gray-headed Greenlet	23	3.6	2.1	8.6										
BLACK-AND-WHITE WARBLER	28	4.0	2.7	5.2	0.7									
GOLDEN-WGD. WARBLER	33	3.2	0.9	2.9	3.7	0								
TENNESSEE WARBLER	49	3.2	4.5	1.4	2.6	0.6	8.8							
TOWNSEND'S WARBLER	48	0	2.9	0.9	1.9	4.5	0.8	0.6						
BLK.-THR. GREEN WARBLER	46	1.6	2.4	1.7	3.6	2.0	3.1	1.6	1.5					
WILSON'S WARBLER	57	2.0	2.2	1.7	3.7	2.0	1.5	4.4	3.1	1.9				
Golden-crowned Warbler	4	0	0.4	2.9	5.8	4.3	0.4	0	0.7	1.6	10.5			
Three-striped Warbler	3	0	0	0	1.8	3.1	0	0	0.4	0.9	0.4	11.7		
Slate-throated Redstart	31	0.4	0.8	1.7	2.1	1.7	0.6	2.4	1.9	3.5	1.4	1.2	3.6	
Collared Redstart	28	0	0.7	0	0	0	0.6	0	0.4	0	0	3.1	0.4	17.3

[1] Values >1 indicate that the species occurred together more frequently than would be expected if pairs of individual birds consorted at random; values <1 denote co-occurrences at less-than-random frequencies. Zeros indicate that no co-occurrences were observed.
[2] Migrant names are in CAPS.

capped Vireo and Golden-winged Warbler 5 times each, and the Wilson's Warbler 4 times.

3) Collared Redstarts and Three-striped Warblers rarely occurred with other warblers or vireos, reflecting the habitat segregation of these species.

4) Golden-crowned Warblers had high rates of co-occurrence with Black-and-white and Golden-winged Warblers (frequent attendants in flocks led by Golden-crowns), but all other migrants save Wilson's Warbler occurred with Golden-crowns at less-than-random frequencies.

Figures 1–3 summarize the results of our feeding method and foraging height analyses for the 13 species. The pie-slice diagrams depict the relative frequencies of various feeding methods, while foraging height profiles are plotted to the right of each diagram. For both these feeding niche dimensions, Shannon's index $H' = -\sum p_i \log_2 p_i$ was used to describe the degree of flexibility (niche width) of that portion of the total resource utilization strategy of each species. Number of observations and total number of seconds of observation for each species are given by n and T, respectively.

Migrant warblers varied widely in the flexibility of both feeding methods and foraging heights (figure 1). Black-and-white and Golden-winged Warblers spent most of their time gleaning (plucking arthropods from bark or leaf surfaces while perched). Tennessee and Black-throated Green Warblers were intermediate in flexibility, with the former species doing a great deal of nectar feeding. Wilson's and Towsend's Warblers were the most flexible in their feeding methods, spending considerable amounts of time hawking (taking aerial insects while on the wing) and hover-feeding (plucking food from surfaces while hovering in mid-air), as well as gleaning. Black-throated Green and

Elliot J. Tramer

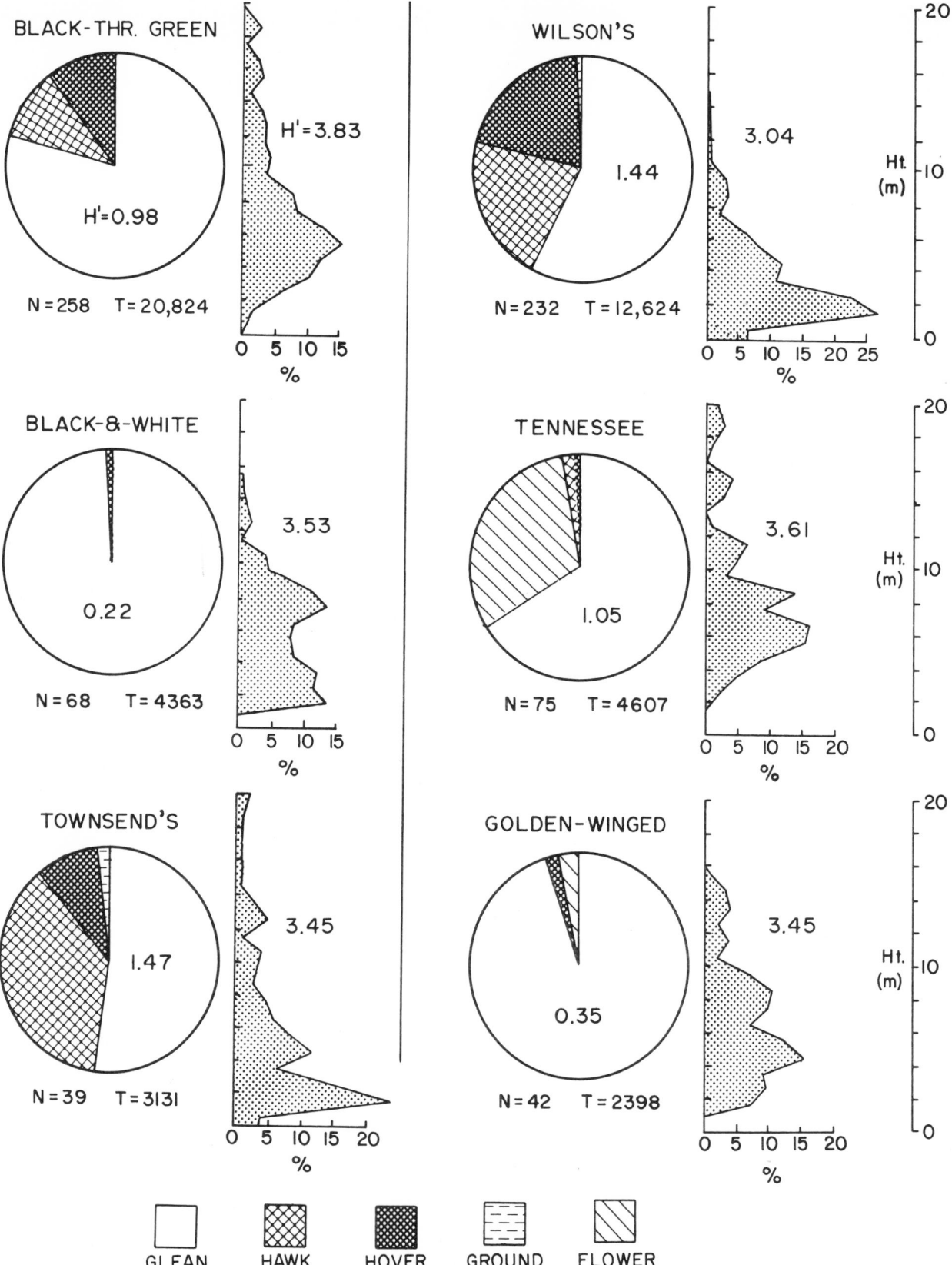

Figure 1. Relative frequency of different feeding methods (pie-slice diagrams) and foraging-height profiles for 6 migrant warblers at Monteverde, $H' = -\Sigma P_i \log_2 p_i$; where p_i represents the frequency of a given feeding method or foraging-height interval. n = number of observations; T = total number of seconds of observation.

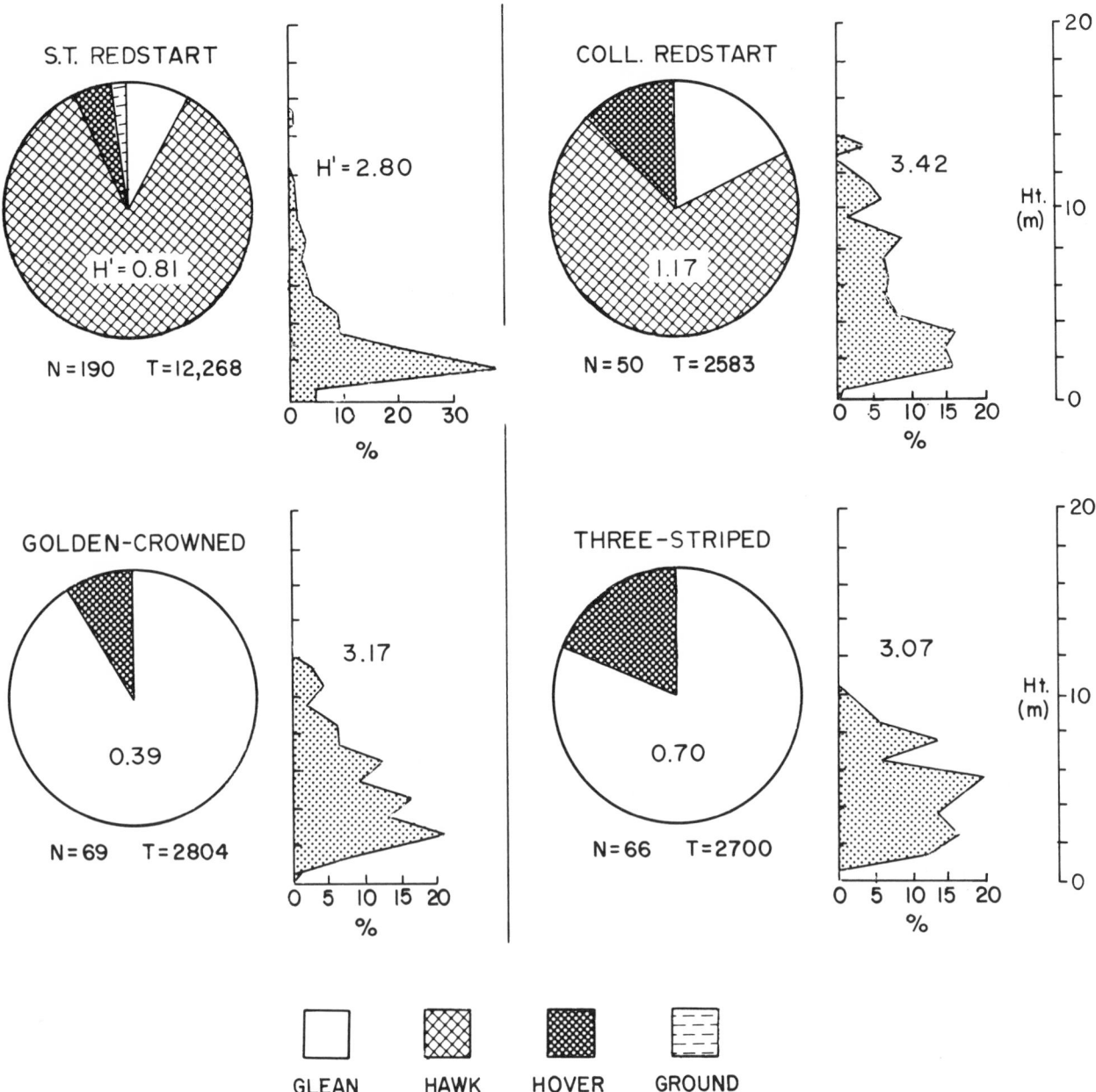

Figure 2.   Relative frequency of different feeding methods (pie-slice diagrams) and foraging-height profiles for 4 resident warblers at Monteverde. Other symbols as in figure 1.

Tennessee Warblers fed at virtually every height in the vegetation, and utilized the foliage in approximate proportion to its availability (a foliage height profile of the premontane moist forest would probably look very much like the Black-throated Green's foraging height profile). Black-and-white and Golden-winged Warblers eschewed the treetops, while Townsend's and Wilson's Warblers spent a large proportion of their time between 1 and 4 m off the ground.

Among resident warblers, the redstarts (*Myioborus* spp.) were primarily hawkers, while the *Basileuterus* species were gleaners. All four species did some hover-feeding (figure 2). The Slate-throated Redstart and the Golden-crowned Warbler exhibited more specialized feeding behavior than their wet forest congeners. The redstart also used a narrower portion of the foliage than its congener, but the two *Basileuterus* warblers had similar foraging height profiles and similar indices of

VIREOS

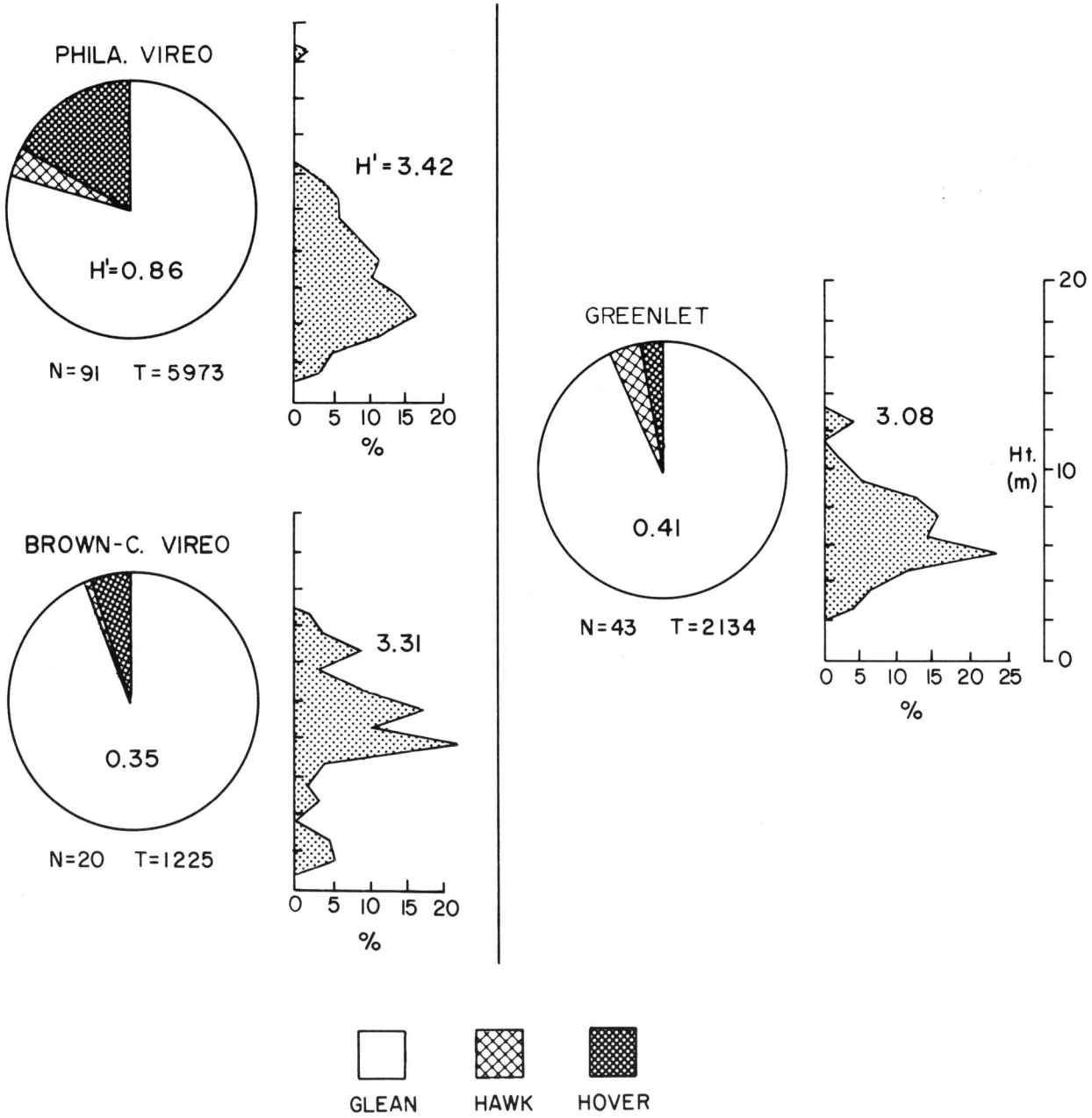

Figure 3. Relative frequency of different feeding methods (pie-slice diagrams) and foraging-height profiles for migrant and resident vireos at Monteverde. Other symbols as in figure 1.

foraging height flexibility. The *Basileuterus* warblers were exclusively birds of the forest undergrowth, while the redstarts preferred low vegetation at edges and forest clearings.

The resident greenlet and Brown-capped Vireo were more specialized in both feeding method and foraging

height diversity than the migrant Philadelphia Vireo (figure 3). The hypothesis that migrant species tended to be significantly more generalized in their foraging than residents was tested by running Mann-Whitney U tests on the ranked H′ values for feeding method and foraging height. The results were significant at p

Table 2. Foraging speeds of warblers and vireos at Monteverde, Costa Rica

Species	Number of observations	Speed (m/sec) ± standard deviations	Coefficients of variation
Brown-capped Vireo	21	0.130 ± 0.089	0.685
PHILADELPHIA VIREO[1]	90	0.093 ± 0.082	0.882
Gray-headed Greenlet	41	0.124 ± 0.112	0.903
BLACK-AND-WHITE WARBLER	68	0.122 ± 0.103	0.844
GOLDEN-WINGED WARBLER	36	0.117 ± 0.096	0.821
TENNESSEE WARBLER	60	0.089 ± 0.077	0.865
BLACK-THR. GREEN WARBLER	261	0.136 ± 0.124	0.925
TOWNSEND'S WARBLER	40	0.156 ± 0.131	0.840
WILSON'S WARBLER	232	0.157 ± 0.103	0.656
Golden-crowned Warbler	68	0.138 ± 0.065	0.471
Three-striped Warbler	66	0.152 ± 0.069	0.454
Slate-throated Redstart	182	0.272 ± 0.208	0.765
Collared Redstart	48	0.256 ± 0.135	0.527

[1] Migrants are in CAPS.

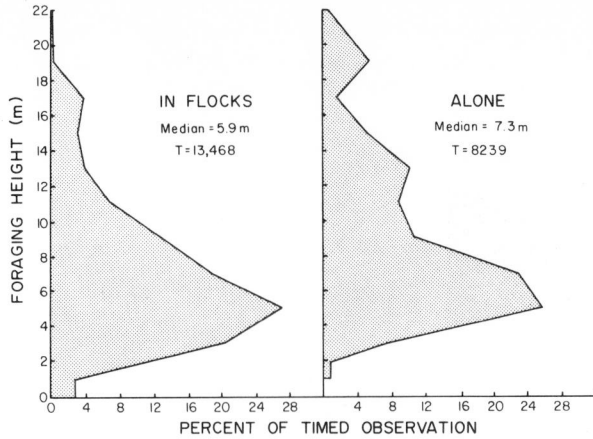

Figure 4. Foraging-height profiles for the Black-throated Green Warbler in and out of flocks.

< .05 for foraging height; the results for feeding method were not significant due to the specialized behavior of Black-and-white and Golden-winged Warblers.

Foraging speed provided another feeding niche dimension (table 2). The coefficient of variation (standard deviation/mean) provided a measure of flexibility of foraging speeds, based on the assumption that a flexible species is one that can modify its foraging speed in response to variations in substrate or in resource type and density. A Mann-Whitney U test was run on the coefficients of variation to determine whether migrant foraging speeds were significantly more variable than those of residents. The U value obtained was just beyond the threshold for statistical significance (.75 > p > .05).

The migrant foraging data were partitioned into early (mid-December–January) and late (February–early March) dry season. No seasonal shifts in foraging behavior were detected. The data were also partitioned to determine whether foraging niches were affected by the presence of other birds. Data sufficient for this analysis were available for four species: Philadelphia Vireo, Tennessee Warbler, Black-throated Green Warbler, and Wilson's Warbler. The only striking difference in feeding method appeared in the Tennessee Warbler, which did most of its flower feeding when alone. When in flocks, its flower feeding decreased from 51.7 to 17.5 percent of the total foraging time, while gleaning increased from 47.7 to 79.3 percent.

Migrant foraging height profiles were virtually identical both in and out of flocks; the Black-throated Green Warbler did appear to adjust its feeding height downward slightly when in flocks (figure 4). Mean foraging speeds in and out of flocks were not significantly different for the 4 species listed above or for the Golden-winged Warbler (t-tests).

Finally, our observations of behavioral interactions revealed the following: 1) Aggressive interactions occurred infrequently. In a total of 1,594 observations of co-occurring birds, we saw only 46 agonistic encounters (2.9 percent). 2) Agonistic encounters involved migrants far more frequently than residents. In 31 encounters both birds were migrants; migrant-resident pairs accounted for 9 agonistic interactions, while resident-resident encounters totaled only 4. In two cases one of the pair of interacting birds was not identified. 3) Some species were involved more than others. Aggressive encounters occurred during 16.6 percent of our Tennessee Warbler and 9.4 percent of our Townsend's Warbler observations, while at the other extreme, no aggressive interactions were observed for the Black-and-white Warbler, Gray-headed Greenlet, Collared Redstart, or Golden-crowned and Three-striped Warblers. 4) Twenty seven of the 46 agonistic encounters (59 percent) involved members of the same species. This figure includes 9 of 17 encounters in the Black-throated Green-Warbler, 8 of 17 for the Tennessee Warbler, 4 of 5 for Wilson's Warbler, and 2 of 2 for the Philadelphia Vireo. 5) Four of five Townsend's warbler aggressive encounters were interspecific, and in three-fourths of the cases the Townsend's was the aggressor. Black-throated Green Warblers were the aggressor in four of eight interspecific encounters, but the Tennessee Warbler was never the aggressor in any interaction with another species. In the nine migrant-resident encounters, residents were

Elliot J. Tramer

the aggressor in every case—but the only resident warbler or vireo involved was the Slate-throated Redstart (twice). The data on agonistic encounters are summarized in table 3.

Table 3. Summary of agonistic encounters

Species	N	N/T	C/N	M/N	A/N
SOLITARY VIREO[2]	1	50.0	0	100	100
PHILADELPHIA VIREO	2	1.7	100	100	0
GOLDEN-WINGED WARBLER	2	2.9	0	50.0	0
TENNESSEE WARBLER	17	16.7	47.1	70.6	0
BLACK-THROATED GREEN WARBLER	17	5.2	53.0	88.0	50.0
TOWNSEND'S WARBLER	5	9.4	20.0	80.0	75.0
WILSON'S WARBLER	5	1.6	80.0	80.0	0
Slate-throated Redstart	8	3.5	37.5	25.0	80.0

[1] N = number of agonistic encounters observed; N/T = percentage of the total number of observations in which agonistic encounters occurred; C/N = percentage of conspecific encounters; M/N = percentage of encounters in which the other individual was a migrant; A/N = percentage of interspecific encounters in which the species listed was the aggressor.
[2] Migrants are in CAPS.

Territorial behavior was observed in only one of the migrant species studied. Some Tennessee Warblers defended small feeding territories centered on flowering *Erythrina lanceolata* trees. Birds in possession of trees defended them vigorously against conspecifics, but were themselves frequently displaced by the hummingbirds *Eupherusa eximia, Amazilia saucerottei,* and *Campyloperus hemileucurus,* which also utilized the *Erythrina* flowers extensively.

Discussion

A primary goal of this investigation was to assess the importance of competition in regulating the distributions and abundances of migrants wintering at Monteverde. We infer that competition is not an important regulating factor, based on the following findings: 1) Migrants and residents foraged together frequently and with little evidence of aggressive behavior; 2) most migrants seem to forage the same way in flocks as they did alone; 3) with the exception of Tennessee Warblers at nectar sources, there was no evidence of territoriality by migrants.

These findings contrast with observations of various insectivorous migrants wintering in the neotropic lowlands—for example, Yellow Warblers (*Dendroica petechia*) everywhere, Hooded Warbler (*Wilsonia citrina*) in Veracruz (Rappole 1976) and Bay-breasted Warblers (*D. castanea*) in the Canal Zone (Morton 1972; this volume). Apparently the food supply is not a primary limiting factor for vireos and warblers wintering at Monteverde. Buskirk and Buskirk (1976) found that the Monteverde area had less pronounced seasonal changes in insect abundance than lowland sites, with

the Monteverde area had less pronounced seasonal changes in insect abundance than lowland sites, with the annual peak occurring in April–June, at the onset of the rainy season. The lack of a dry season pro-

the annual peak occurring in April–June, at the onset of the rainy season. The lack of a dry season pronounced enough to bring about marked reductions in foliage volume and insect abundance may account for the lack of seasonal changes in foraging ecology and aggressive behavior at Monteverde, in contrast with many lowland sites. On the other hand, insect levels may be generally higher in the lowlands, so that territoriality among the insectivorous migrants there may be viewed as a response to a resource that is concentrated enough to be worth defending.

Although they were generally not territorial, most migrant species at Monteverde foraged alone more frequently than residents. Among residents, greenlets, Brown-capped Vireos, and *Myioborus* warblers frequently occurred in pairs; adult birds apparently remain paired during the nonbreeding season. *Basileuterus* warblers almost always traveled in family groups (W. Buskirk pers. comm.) of from two to seven birds. The lower percentages of group foraging in migrants may also reflect the relative unfamiliarity of migrants (especially first-year birds) with the area, or, alternatively, greater migrant flexibility and opportunism. Since feeding aggregations could reliably be found in certain locations that were sheltered from the wind, it is even possible that lone migrants represented birds relegated to suboptimal foraging locations, although the lack of strong evidence for competitive stress militates against this interpretation. Exceptions to this general pattern among the migrants were the Tennessee Warbler, which frequently formed conspecific groups when insect feeding, and the Philadelphia Vireo, which often foraged in pairs.

Another interesting pattern is the tendency of migrants to be more variable than residents in at least some aspects of their feeding behavior. This difference was statistically significant for foraging height and bordered on significance for foraging speed. While it is premature to assert that migrants are "more flexible" than residents as a rule, the patterns revealed here indicate that further attention should be paid to the foraging strategies of migrants vs residents, both at Monteverde and elsewhere in the tropics. It is reasonable to expect migrants to be relatively flexible in their feeding ecologies, since they must adapt to different vegetation structures, wide variations in resource quality and quantity, and changes in competitive milieu in the course of their annual movements.

Unlike other migrants, Black-and-white and Golden-winged Warblers had specialized feeding methods. With the exception of three species of woodcreeper, all of them uncommon and quite a bit larger, the Black-and-white Warbler was the only species gleaning the trunks and large branches of trees at middle and lower elevations at Monteverde; thus its restricted feeding method may be related to its nearly exclusive domain over its preferred substrate rather than to a lack of behavioral flexibility. The Golden-winged Warbler was not especially common at Monteverde, occurring mostly as scattered singles attached to multispecies foraging flocks. It specialized on probing into clumps of dead leaves suspended in vine tangles, a behavior also noted by Morton (1972) in Panama. The absence of both species from the treetops (figure 1) may reflect the scarcity of large branches and vine tangles at high levels in the vegetation. It is interesting that the two migrants with the most specialized feeding behaviors had the highest affinity for mixed foraging flocks led by residents (table 1).

While the intensity of competition appeared to be generally low for most species, there are at least three situations that merit further study:

1) The very closely related Black-throated Green and Townsend's Warblers occurred together rather frequently. These species probably diverged from a common ancestor since the most recent glacial advance (Mengel 1964) and are morphologically quite similar. Both are forest birds while on their North American breeding grounds. At Monteverde the Townsend's stayed mainly near the ground in edge and open situations and did a great deal of hawking, while the Black-throated Green occurred at all levels in the foliage and hawked infrequently (figure 1); it was common in forest as well as edge habitats. The Townsend's was the only interspecifically aggressive migrant, engaging in agonistic encounters rather frequently and usually as the aggressor. Thus, there may be some ecological divergence on the winter grounds where these two species occur together.

2) The Tennessee warbler was unusual in many ways. It took part in agonistic interactions more frequently than any other species, it was partly nectarivorous, it was aggressive toward conspecifics while nectar feeding but when foraging for insects it was the only migrant to form conspecific flocks. In all allospecific encounters this species was subordinate, even at nectar sources. It was the subject of attacks by very similar-looking Paltry tyrannulets (*Tyranniscus vilissimus*) during late winter when the tyrannulets were beginning to establish breeding territories—an apparent case of mistaken identity. Although the Tennessee Warbler was at the bottom of the social "peck order" at Monteverde, it was very numerous and of widespread occurrence there. In terms of both diet and social behavior, it was the most plastic species at Monteverde.

3) The final situation in which competition may be exerting a significant effect is the foraging ecology of *Basileuterus* and *Myioborus* warblers occupying different forest types at Monteverde. Slate-throated Redstarts and Golden-crowned Warblers exhibited more specialized foraging than their wet forest congeners (figure 3). Habitat-related differences in the resource base may be sufficient to account for this difference. On the other hand, since Slate-throated Redstarts and Golden-crowned Warblers occupied habitats where migrants were common while their congeners did not, it is possible that their feeding niches were constricted by competition with migrants. In this vein, we note that the wet forest warblers both hover fed more frequently than their congeners. This behavior was commonly practiced by many migrants but not by any of the insectivorous Furnariids or Dendrocolaptids that flocked with wet forest warblers. If competition with migrants is responsible for this difference, competitive release may well occur when the migrants are absent. Chipley (1974) indicated that this occurs in the highlands of Colombia. Evidence for this shift would include a wider and more equitable range of foraging methods (including more hover feeding) in the Slate-throated Redstart and the Golden-crowned Warbler during the North American summer, but no concomitant shifts in the foraging ecology of the Collared Redstart and the Three-striped Warbler.

This study reconfirms the observation by many investigators that most migrants to the tropics shun humid mature forests (Karr 1976). The reasons for this pattern are unclear. In Africa, little humid forest exists relative to the large areas of savannah and dry scrub, but in the neotropics the reverse is true. At Monteverde the two most obvious explanations are 1) that most migrants are poorly adapted to wet forests or 2) that migrants are well adapted but are competitively excluded by the diversity of insectivorous birds of neotropical origin (at Monteverde mostly Denrocolaptids and Furnariids) that characterize wet forests. It is difficult to conceive of empirical tests to distinguish between these two alternatives, but the former seems more likely for two reasons. First, migrants occur commonly with resident thrushes, vireos, and warblers at Monteverde. Since there is little evidence of competitive stress among these ecologically similar species, it is doubtful that competitive exclusion is occurring between migrants and rather dissimilar suboscine species. Second, the wet forest support great volumes of epiphytic growth which may harbor a large portion of the arthropod fauna. At Monteverde, the Furnariids,

in particular, are specialized probers of this epiphytic growth. Migrants may be poorly adapted for foraging on such substrates.

Acknowledgments

Many people gave us valuable aid and encouragement during our stay at Monteverde. We are especially indebted to Jan Green, Wilford Guindon, Arnold Hoge, and Robert Lawton. The senior author also wishes to thank his wife, Flora, for her patience and understanding. The University of Toledo awarded a sabbatical leave to the senior author during the field work; support for all other aspects of this study was provided by grant DEB 76-10787 from the National Science Foundation.

Appendix. Status and habitat preferences of migrants wintering at Monteverde, Costa Rica

Sharp-shinned Hawk (*Accipiter striatus*)—Uncommon

Cooper's Hawk (*A. cooperii*)—Rare

Broad-winged Hawk (*Buteo platypterus*)—Common HE, LE, PK[1]

Yellow-bellied Sapsucker (*Sphyrapicus varius*)—Rare HE

Yellow-bellied Flycatcher (*Empidonax flaviventris*)—Rare LE

Rough-winged Swallow (*Stelgidopteryx ruficollis*)—Common PS

Wood Thrush (*Hylocichla mustelina*)—Common MF

Swainson's Thrush (*Catharus ustulatus*)—Uncommon MF, LE

Yellow-throated Vireo (*Vireo flavifrons*)—Uncommon MF, LE

Solitary Vireo (*V. solitarius*)—Rare MF

Philadelphia Vireo (*V. philadelphicus*)—Common LE, Uncommon MF, PK

Black-and-white Warbler (*Mniotilta varia*)—Common MF, LE, PK

Worm-eating Warbler (*Helmitheros vermivora*)—Uncommon MF

Golden-winged Warbler (*Vermivora chrysoptera*)—Fairly common MF, Uncommon WF

Tennessee Warbler (*V. peregrina*)—Common LE, PK, PS, Uncommon MF

Black-throated Green Warbler (*Dendroica virens*)—Abundant LE, PK, Common MF, Uncommon HE, WF, PS

Townsend's Warbler (*D. townsendi*)—Fairly common LE, Uncommon PS, PK

Chestnut-sided Warbler (*D. pensylvanica*)—Uncommon MF

Northern Ovenbird (*Seiurus aurocapillus*)—Common MF

Louisiana Waterthrush (*S. motacilla*)—Rare MF (ravines)

Kentucky Warbler (*Oporonis formosus*)—Uncommon MF

Wilson's Warbler (*Wilsonia pusilla*)—Abundant LE, PK, Common MF, Uncommon HE, WF, PS

American Redstart (*Setophaga ruticilla*)—Rare LE

Northern Oriole (*Icterus galbula*)—Common LE, PK

Western Tanager (*Piranga ludoviciana*)—Rare LE

Summer Tanager (*P. rubra*)—Fairly common LE, PK, Uncommon HE

Rose-breasted Grosbeak (*Pheucticus ludovicianus*)—Rare LE

Indigo Bunting (*Passerina cyanea*)—Uncommon LE, PK, PS

Lincoln's Sparrow (*Melospiza lincolnii*)—Rare LE

[1] Abbreviations: WF = wet forest; MF = premontane moist forest; HE = high elevation edge; LE = lower elevation edge; PK = parkland; PS = pasture.

Literature Cited

Buskirk, R., and W. Buskirk
1976. Changes in arthropod abundance in a highland Costa Rican forest. Am. Midl. Natur. 95:288–98.

Buskirk, W.
1972. Ecology of bird flocks in a tropical forest. Ph.D. diss., Univ. California, Davis.

1976. Social systems in a tropical forest avifauna. Am. Nat. 110:293–310.

Chipley, R.
1974. Wintering migrant wood warblers and their impact on resident insectivorous passerines in a subtropical Colombian oak woods. Ph.D. diss., Cornell Univ., Ithaca, N.Y.

Holdridge, L.
1967. *Life Zone Ecology.* San José, Costa Rica: Tropical Science Center.

Karr, J.
1976. On the relative abundance of migrants from the North Temperate Zone in tropical habitats. Wils. Bull. 88:433–58.

Leck, C.
1972. The impact of some North American migrants at fruiting trees in Panama. Auk 89:842–50.

Mengel, R.
1964. The probable history of species formation in some northern wood warblers (Parulidae). Living Bird 3: 9–43.

Morton, E.
1972. North American birds in the tropics. Atlantic Natur. 27:164–68.

Powell, G. V. N.
1977. Site Guide: The Monteverde cloud forest preserve, Costa Rica. Am. Birds 31:119–26.

Rappole, J.
1976. Ecological aspects of avian migrant behavior in Veracruz, Mexico. Ph.D. diss., Univ. Minnesota, Minneapolis.

Willis, E.
1966. The role of migrant birds at swarms of army ants. Living Bird 5:187–231.

Elliot J. Tramer

KERRY N. RABENOLD
Department of Biology
Bucknell University
Lewisburg, PA 17837

The Black-throated Green Warbler in Panama: Geographic and Seasonal Comparison of Foraging

ABSTRACT

I compare the foraging behavior of Black-throated Green Warblers (*Dendroica virens*) wintering in Chiriqui Province, Panama, with that of breeding populations in Maine and North Carolina. Quantitative behavioral observations of the heights and tree parts used in foraging, repertoire of techniques, directionality of flights and probing, and patchiness of habitat use indicate significant seasonal differences in foraging. Seasonal shifts in the spatial distribution of foraging are not wholly attributable to differences in the structure of the forests.

Foraging was more generalized spatially in Panama than in Maine, and all other measures of foraging showed greater generalization in Panama than in the two breeding habitats, particularly in foraging technique. Foraging was also more generalized in North Carolina than in Maine. Generalization is produced in part by greater behavioral diversity of each individual. These results, and similar observations by others, suggest that competitive pressures in diverse tropical faunas can produce niche expansion rather than contraction in wintering migrants, as compared to breeding migrants.

I suggest that a foraging optimization response to lower food availability in southern temperate and tropical systems, due to seasonal constancy and efficient consumer tracking, explains such generalization better than proposed ecological release from congeners or increased intraspecific competition. Behavioral plasticity, probably even greater in other migrants, may be favored by temporary insinuation into a diverse and stable community of tropical residents, as well as by rigors of annual colonization of the temperate zone.

Introduction

Birds that migrate from the tropics to breed in the temperate zone are opportunists on a grand scale. Because the year-round ecology of a long-distance migrant can include varied habitats and resources, the ability to exploit effectively each of several environments is as critical for the evolution of the migratory strategy as timing and orientation of migration. As annual colonists of temperate breeding grounds, migrants might be expected to be both behaviorally plastic and to have a relatively generalized foraging repertoire when compared to more sedentary species. Since migrants probably play diverse ecological roles as part-time members of several communities, questions arise concerning the degree to which they are local opportunists, and concerning the competitive effects that might occur both between migrants and residents and among migrants.

While temperate-breeding migrants are often considered temperate birds, they sometimes spend a greater part of their lives in the tropics. Temporary inclusion in complex tropical faunas can be expected to lead to strong competition, particularly if competitive ability in one habitat is compromised by the demands of others. Just as food shortage in winter has been proposed as a key factor in the regulation of resident temperate populations, migrant populations may be effectively limited in their winter habitats. If this were true, it would violate assumptions of many studies of resource partitioning among breeding birds in the temperate zone concerning food limitation and competition. It has even been suggested that ecological segregation studied in breeding birds in temperate habitats has evolved primarily because of competition in tropical wintering habitats (Holmes and Pitelka 1968; Lack 1976).

Central to all these concerns is seasonal variation in foraging behavior of tropical-temperate migrants. In spite of the expectation of behavioral plasticity in migrants (Morse 1971a), many studies have concluded that foraging behavior of migrants wintering in the tropics generally resembles the species' foraging in the temperate breeding habitat (Eaton 1953; MacArthur 1958; Schwartz 1964; Moreau 1972; Lack 1976).

However, migrants display considerable plasticity on several levels. Seasonal habitat variation, implied in the annual cycle for migrants, sometimes includes major shifts in vegetation type, as in the winter use of grassland in Panama by the Yellow-rumped Warbler (*Dendroica coronata*) that breeds in northern coniferous forests (Karr 1971). In addition, temperate-breeding migrants in both New and Old World tropics are often associated with more seasonal or less predictable habitats and often with spatially patchy and temporally irregular resources (Willis 1966; Elgood et al 1966; Moreau 1972; Karr 1976). Some migrants appear to be locally opportunistic and adept at exploiting regional heterogeneities in resources in temperate breeding habitats as well (Stewart and Aldrich 1951; Morris et al 1958; MacArthur 1958).

Moreau (1972) cites cases in Old World migrants, especially among warblers (Sylviinae), in which foraging behavior as well as habitat choice is less restricted in winter than in summer (see also Lack 1976 on New World warblers). Generalization in diet, especially to include larger proportions of plant material in the diet of insectivores, has been noted in several studies of wintering migrants. For example, Cape May Warblers (*Dendroica tigrina*) take quantities of fruit and nectar in Jamaica (Lack 1976), and Yellow-rumped Warblers (*D. coronata*) eat bayberries in winter in coastal North America (MacArthur 1958) whereas both are mainly insectivorous in summer.

Considerable shift in foraging technique is implied when migrants follow ant swarms in Panama (Willis 1966) or frequent agave blossoms in the Bahamas (Emlen 1973), as these tactics are not available on the breeding grounds. Wintering migrants have also been shown to change their foraging positions in forest foliage and possibly to use a wider range of positions compared to that used in summer (Slud 1960 in Costa Rica; Chipley 1976 in Colombia). Many of the above examples concern New World warblers (Parulidae), largely insectivorous birds that dominate northern coniferous forests in summer.

In this study, I compare the foraging behavior of Black-throated Green Warblers (Parulidae: *Dendroica virens*) wintering in Chiriqui Province, Panama, with that of breeding populations in Maine and North Carolina. Observations were designed to detect seasonal changes in foraging strategy (behavioral plasticity) and to establish whether winter foraging is more specialized or generalized than summer foraging. The Black-Throated Green warbler (BTG) has been studied previously in its breeding habitat of northern coniferous forest (MacArthur 1958; Morse 1968, 1971b) and in tropical winter habitats, but no quantitative comparison has been produced. MacArthur (1958) conducted brief, qualitative observations in Costa Rica, and concluded that foraging there generally resembled foraging in New England. Lack (1976) came to a similar conclusion based on observations in Jamaica and MacArthur's New England data. However, Slud (1960) and Tramer (pers. comm.) suggest that considerable plasticity is shown in foraging in Costa Rica.

Seasonal changes in foraging behavior could be

Kerry N. Rabenold

expressed as either greater generalization or greater specialization in the winter habitat compared with summer. While diffuse competition (MacArthur 1972; Pianka 1975) with many similar species in diverse tropical communities might favor niche contraction and specialization in the foraging of wintering migrants, at least three factors could have the opposite effect, favoring generalization. First, small ranges or narrow habitat selection in the nonbreeding season could produce higher winter population densities than summer and more intense intraspecific competition. Second, geographical or habitat separation in winter from similar species that are sympatric in summer could reduce interspecific competition and produce "ecological release." Third, low tropical food levels produced by a combination of even annual distribution of productivity and efficient utilization by the resident fauna, compared to the vernal burst of productivity in temperate systems, could favor generalization. Quantitative and multidimensional observations of foraging behavior are used in this study to evaluate these possibilities.

Study Areas and Methods

I studied the foraging behavior of the BTG at Shepherd Brook Mountain in northwestern Maine (46° 45′N elevation 475 m) and at Mount Collins in the Great Smoky Mountains National Park of North Carolina and Tennessee (35°32′ elevation 1,750 m) as part of a larger study of spruce-fir bird communities (Rabenold 1976). Both study areas are mature, probably undisturbed forests dominated by spruce (*Picea rubens*) and fir (*Abies fraseri* in North Carolina and *A. balsamea* in Maine). The stands are floristically similar and nearly identical structurally. This part of the study was carried out in May, June, and July of 1973–75. In January 1977 I gathered foraging data in the highlands of Chiriqui Province in western Panama, in montane oak (family Fagaceae) forests near Nueva Suiza and Cerro Punta (8°47′N, elevation c 2,000 m). Because this area is mainly cleared for farming, I restricted may observations to mature forest in Nueva Suiza and along the Boquete Trail above Cerro Punta.

To be sure that the Panama forest offered a structural medium for foraging similar to that of the other sites, I constructed a foliage distribution profile. Vertical distribution and type of foliage (whether tree trunk, basal, middle or distal part of a limb) were recorded at points 10m apart along an arbitrary transect using a sighting tube. This method was used at Mount Collins as well. More sophisticated photographic methods showed that Mount Collins and Shepherd Brook Mountain were structurally similar (Rabenold 1976).

I recorded the spatial distribution of foraging using 10 height classes: Ground, 0–4 ft, 5–9 ft, 10 ft intervals up to 70 ft and >70 ft (approximate metric equivalents: 0–1 m, 2–3 m, 3 m intervals up to 21 m, >21 m); and four tree-part classes: trunk, inner third, middle third, and outer third of a branch. The intersections of these classes create a two-dimensional matrix over which I calculated the spread and evenness of the distribution of foraging time using the Shannon-Wiener (Weaver) diversity index: $H_{spatial} = -\sum P_i \ln P_i$ where P_i is the proportion of foraging time in the ith cell (Shannon and Weaver 1949, see also Peet 1974 on diversity indices). In order to assess the effects of sample size on the observed distribution I constructed saturation curves of $H_{spatial}$ as a function of cumulative observation time.

I also recorded the occurrence of distinctive foraging techniques that BTGs use in addition to simple foliage gleaning for arthropod prey. The two most common of these are hawking and sallying. A sally is a rapid flight from a perch to snatch stationary prey from exposed surfaces up to 10 m away. A hawk, by comparison, is a foray out from a tree to capture flying prey. Other techniques observed are: ducking-under (quick bending of head and body down and under the level of the perch to provide access to the undersides of branches and foliage); hovering, usually accompanied by probing at small foliage tips; vertical clinging, usually on the trunk or a large vertical branch of a tree, with sideways or head-up orientation; and hanging upside-down, usually with upward probing on a small branch or twig. These distinctive techniques are probably more energetically expensive than simple upright hopping-and-gleaning, but provide access to different foliage parts and prey types. To measure behavioral diversity in foraging, I calculated the diversity index used above over the proportions of the foraging repertoire contributed by the different techniques ($H_{technique}$).

I described the continuity of the search path of foraging BTGs by recording flight lengths and comparing the frequencies of four length categories: <2 ft, 3–14 ft, 15–29 ft, and >30 ft (approximate conversions: <1 m, 1–5 m, 5–10 m, and >10 m). In this way, I was able to describe the patchiness of the birds' use of habitat. Flights between trees were also recorded so that the average time spent per tree could be calculated. The direction of movement within a tree and the direction of probing while foraging were also recorded, and I used the distributions of directions in flights and probing as additional measures of behavioral diversity. For further justification of this scheme of observation, see Rabenold (1976).

Table 1. Percentage of foliage sampled in height and tree-part classes[1]

Panama H = 3.08					North Carolina H = 3.02			
T	I	M	O		T	I	M	O
+	2	10	3	>70	+	1	2	2
+	1	5	3	60–69	+	2	3	5
+	+	4	4	50–59	+	2	4	9
+	2	3	4	40–49	1	2	4	6
+	1	3	4	30–39	+	+	3	6
+	1	3	8	20–29	1	+	+	6
+	+	3	8	10–19	+	+	2	6
+	+	2	6	5–9	+	+	3	3
		4		<5			15	
		15		GR			10	

[1] Vertical classes are in feet above ground, and horizontal classes are Trunk, Inner ⅓, Middle ⅓, and Outer ⅓ of branches. Horizontal classes are collapsed at the two lowest levels. + indicates less than 1 percent. Metric equivalents are: <1.2 m, 1.5–2.7 m, 3.1–5.8 m, 6.1–8.8 m, 9.1–11.9 m, 12.2–14.9 m, 15.2–18.0 m, 18.3–21.0 m, >21.3 m.

Results

The vertical distribution of tree parts in Panama differs somewhat from that of North Carolina, owing in part to the different geometry of individual trees. The canopy is also slightly taller in Panama but more dense in North Carolina. However, foliage profile analysis showed that an equal variety of foraging stations is presented to birds in both places (table 1). The Maine forest is also nearly identical structurally to that of North Carolina (Rabenold 1976). Differences among the three study areas in the variety of foraging stations used by birds are not attributable to the variety available.

Observations of the spatial distribution of foraging did, in fact, show striking differences both between the two breeding habitats and between breeding and nonbreeding habitats (figure 1). Although foraging is concentrated in similar parts of the forest foliage in North Carolina and Maine, it is much more generalized in the former, southern, area. In particular, lower and higher foliage strata are used much more frequently in North Carolina. Foraging in Panama occurs more often in higher and more distal parts of the forest foliage than in either breeding habitat. This shift is partly attributable to a relatively high representation of foliage above 70 ft in Panama. However, there was no scarcity in Panama of foraging stations preferred in the other two habitats. The Panama distribution is more generalized than that of Maine, and the $H_{spatial}$ values generated are significantly different p < .01, (Hutcheson's 1970 t-test). The diversity of foraging stations used in Panama as measured by $H_{spatial}$ does not differ significantly from that of North Carolina. However, the overall breadth of the distribution is greater, and the vertical spread of foraging is more even in Panama than in North Carolina (figure 1).

Females forage somewhat lower than males in all habitats, but there is no evidence that this sexual difference is more pronounced in any habitat. Saturation curves of $H_{spatial}$ against cumulative observation time show that observation effort was probably sufficient to allow meaningful comparison of these values for the three study populations (figure 2). However, the rising Panama curve indicates that further observation might have yielded a slightly higher $H_{spatial}$ value for foraging in that habitat.

BTGs show greater behavioral diversity in foraging technique in Panama than in either breeding habitat (figure 3). As shown above for spatial distribution of foraging, technique was more generalized in North Carolina than in Maine. Sallying was the dominant technique used in Maine, with some hawking and relatively few instances of ducking-under and hanging. In North Carolina, hawking was used most frequently along with sallying and hovering; ducking-under, vertical clinging, and hanging were also sometimes used. This produced a broader and more even utilization of techniques ($H_{technique}$ different, p < .01) (figure 3). In Panama, sallying, hawking and hovering were used more equally than in Maine or North Carolina, and ducking-under, vertical clinging and hanging were used relatively more frequently. The warblers, then, showed greater behavioral diversity in foraging techniques in Panama than in either breeding habitat ($H_{technique}$ different, p < .01) (figure 3). In addition, the recognized categories of techniques were used more frequently overall in Panama (1.04/min) than in either Maine (0.32/min) or North Carolina (0.49/min).

The trend toward greater generalization in both the spatial distribution of foraging and in technique in the tropical, nonbreeding habitat is based upon greater behavioral diversity in the foraging of each individual. In foraging bouts in which one individual was followed continuously for more than two minutes, the spatial diversity described was greater in Panama ($\bar{H}$ = 1.73 ± .37; N = 15) than in Maine ($\bar{H}$ = 1.52 ± .24; N = 16) (p < .05, t-test). However, the North Carolina value ($\bar{H}$ = 1.74 ± .45; N = 23) was not appreciably different from that of Panama. Individual foraging

Kerry N. Rabenold

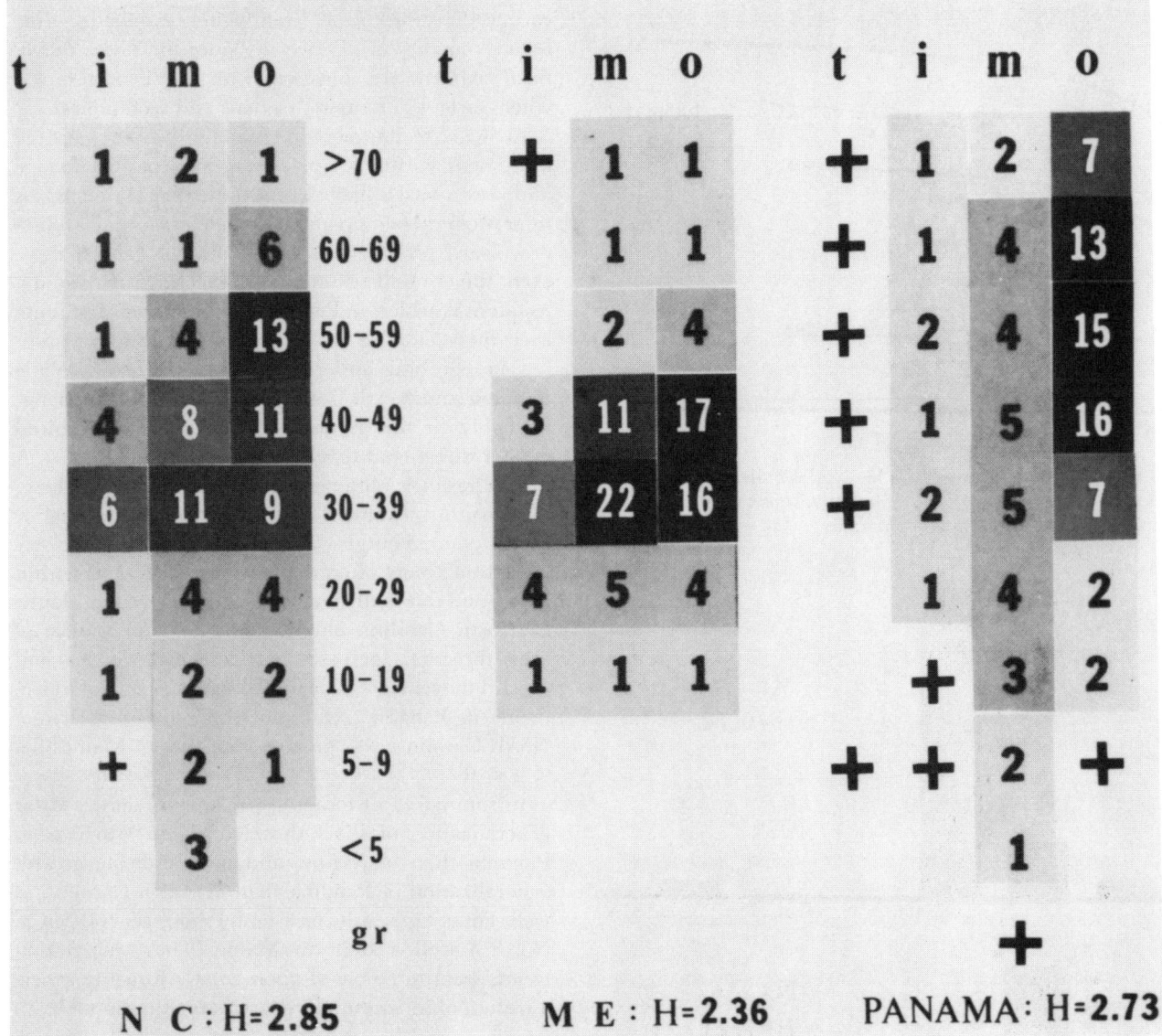

Figure 1. The spatial distribution of foraging at Mount Collins, North Carolina, Shepherd Brook Mountain, Maine, and Nueva Suiza, Chiriqui province, Panama. Vertical categories are in feet, and horizontal categories are Trunk, Inner ⅓, Middle ⅓, and Outer ⅓ of the tree. H is the diversity index calculated for each distribution. Values in the matrix represent percentage foraging time spent in the cell, with darker shades for larger values.

bouts in Panama that were long enough to contain at least one distinctive technique showed a greater variety of techniques ($\bar{X} = 3.50 \pm 1.56$; N = 14) than in either Maine ($\bar{X} = 1.86 \pm .90$; N = 7) or North Carolina ($\bar{X} = 1.80 \pm .77$; N = 20) (p < .05, t-test). Individuals in Panama may also differ from one another in foraging more than in the breeding habitats, but this was not testable without marked birds.

BTGs in Panama showed a very different movement pattern while foraging than those in either breeding habitat (figure 4). Flights of less than one meter between foraging stations occurred much more fre-

quently in Panama than in the other habitats, and flights of more than five meters were much less frequent. The ratio of the number of flights in the two shortest flight-length classes to the number in the two longest (S/L) was much higher in Panama than in North Carolina or Maine (figure 4). This indicates warblers in Panama were using the habitat in a much more continuous, fine-grained way and that they were generalizing with regard to foraging station rather than seeking out discontinuous patches (see MacArthur and Pianka 1966, MacArthur 1972). Birds also spent much longer periods of time foraging in a single

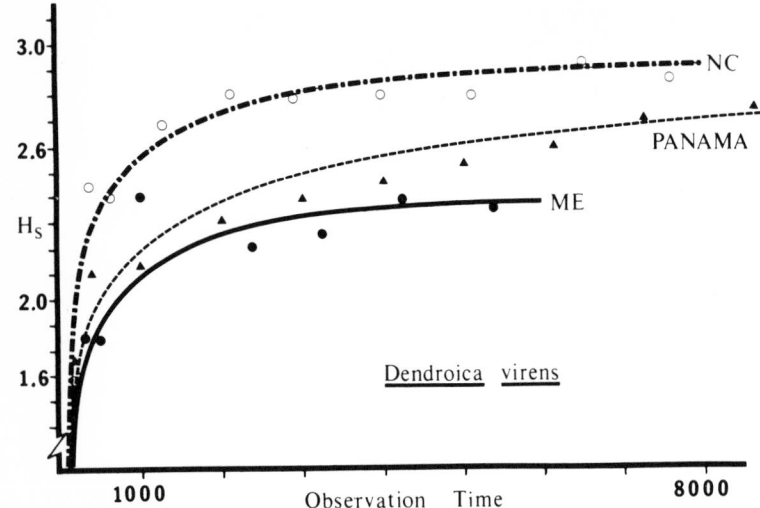

Figure 2. The relationship between the diversity of use of foraging stations, H_s, to cumulative observation time in seconds for the 3 study populations.

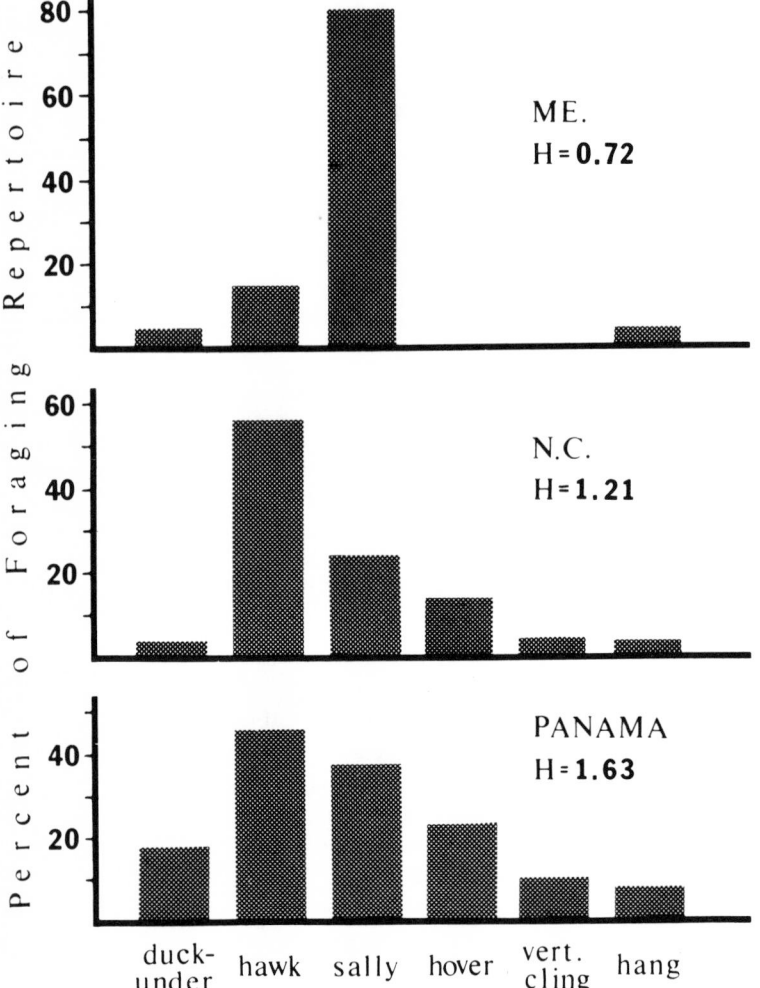

Figure 3. The distributions of techniques in foraging of the 3 study populations. See text for descriptions of techniques.

tree in Panama than in the other two habitats, indicating that they more thoroughly searched a tree before moving on (T/tree in figure 5). These movement patterns are consistent with the birds' use of a wider variety of foraging stations and techniques.

As with technique, direction of probing and of movement within a tree affects the kinds of foliage and prey a bird is likely to encounter. In Maine, BTGs most often probed up and out while in North Carolina downward probing was more common, and a more even (diverse) distribution of directions in probing resulted. Warblers in Panama used downward probing even more, adding especially down-and-under probing, i.e., probing under the level of the perch. While Panama and North Carolina birds did not differ appreciably in this parameter, both habitats showed greater directional diversity than Maine (p < .05). A similar result is obtained when considering the directionality of movement within a tree. As MacArthur (1958) pointed out, BTGs move tangentially ("across" in figure 6) more often than in other directions within a tree, and this tendency is most pronounced in Maine. In North Carolina and Panama the importance of other directions increases, particularly downward and inward movements. The directional diversity of movements in Panama, while not different from that of North Carolina, was greater than that of Maine (fig. 6, p < .05).

In summary, all foraging parameters show greater generalization of Black-throated Green Warblers in Panama than in Maine, and most indicate greater generalization in Panama than in North Carolina as well. Foraging is also consistently more generalized in North Carolina than in Maine. These population trends seem to be based upon greater foraging generalization of individual birds (see summary in table 2).

Discussion

Chipley (1976) has described the vertical distribution of foraging in Blackburnian Warblers (*Dendroica fusca*) wintering in Colombia and found generalization in this parameter when compared to MacArthur's (1958) data from New England. He attributes this generalization to the absence of congeneric species associated with the Blackburnian in summer (ecological release) and to increased intraspecific competition. Before evaluating these hypotheses as potential explanations for BTG foraging in Panama, I would like to suggest that comparisons between observers and between habitats in foraging studies can be hazardous. Even if methods are roughly similar, habitats rarely are. For instance, MacArthur (1958) conducted his studies of warblers in New England forests that are mainly second-growth or maritime spruce (*Picea*) of undescribed physiog-

Kerry N. Rabenold

nomy. My studies of the Blackburnian Warbler in a virgin spruce-fir forest in northwestern Maine show a different foraging profile from that of MacArthur, probably owing, at least in part, to different forest structure. Because of this, Chipley's Blackburnian Warblers may have shown greater stratal diversity in foraging than in MacArthur's study, but probably not greater than in mine (table 3). The shift in Colombia to lower levels is probably dictated in part by the relative scarcity of foliage at higher levels. In addition, different types and densities of foliage can seriously alter birds' observability at higher levels. Unless such varibles are controlled in comparative studies, comparisons can be seriously misleading.

The winter generalization in foraging of the BTG is probably not produced by differences in forest structure, and it is equally unlikely that the difference between the broadleaf evergreen foliage of Chiriqui and the coniferous foliage of the breeding habitats would produce such systematic generalization. Even if a shift in technique were required, generalization would not necessarily result. It is possible that a wider variety of potential arthropod prey in Panama contributed to generalization compared to the breeding habitats. While arthropods were not collected in Panama, no such difference in potential prey existed between Maine and North Carolina to explain foraging differences between those two habitats. Although the effects of foliage type and invertebrate fauna cannot be fully appreciated at this time, it is possible to consider hypotheses concerning the effects of competition on migrants in the tropics.

The BTG is separated in Panama from congeners that are sympatric during breeding, but ecological release from these species cannot adequately explain the foraging trends observed. In the Maine study area, five other parulids were sympatric with the BTG and common, three of them congeneric: the Blackburnian (*Dendroica fusca*), Bay-breasted (*D. castanea*), Yellow-rumped (*D. coronata*), and Parula (*Parula americana*) Warblers and the Ovenbird (*Seiurus aurocapillus*). The Magnolia (*Dendroica magnolia*) and Cape May (*D. tigrina*) Warblers were also present but not common. The assembly of warblers in northern coniferous forests varies, with sometimes more or fewer species, but this list is representative of mature spruce- or fir-dominated forests (see Rabenold 1976 and censuses cited).

Of the warblers listed above only the Blackburnian was common in the Panama study area. Wilson's Warbler (*Wilsonia pusilla*), which breeds in northern latitudes but is not generally sympatric with the BTG in summer, was also common. Several other migratory warblers occurred at the Panama site during the January study, including the Black-and-white (*Mniotilta*

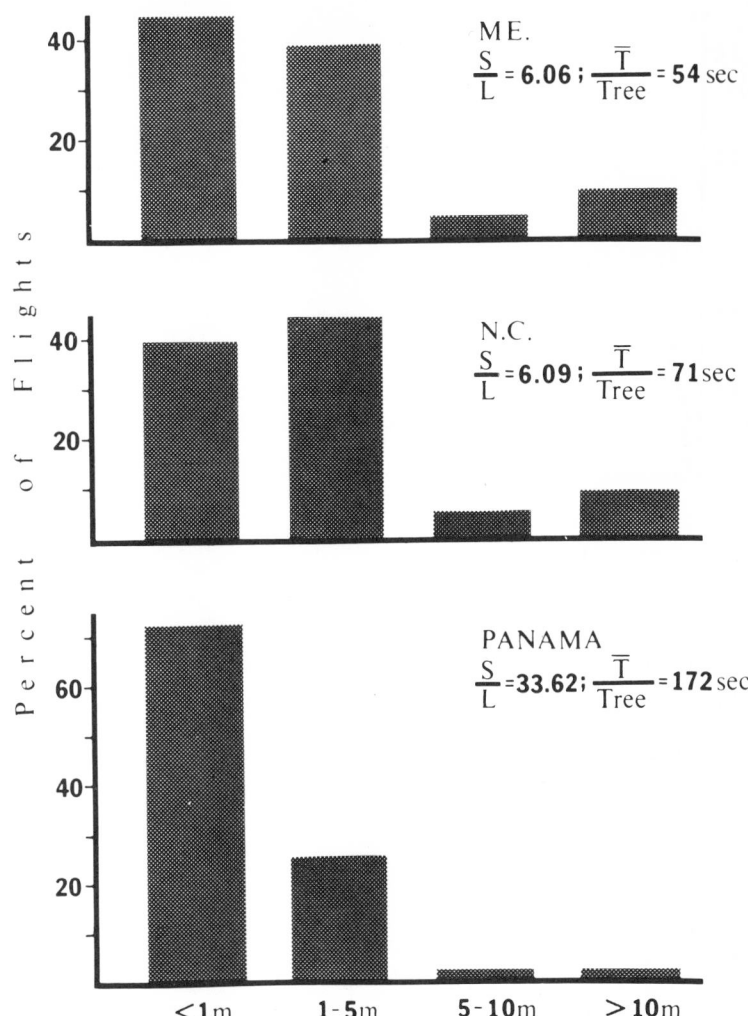

Figure 4. The distribution of flights in length classes at the 3 study sites. S/L is the ratio of the number of flights in the 2 short classes to the number in the 2 long classes.

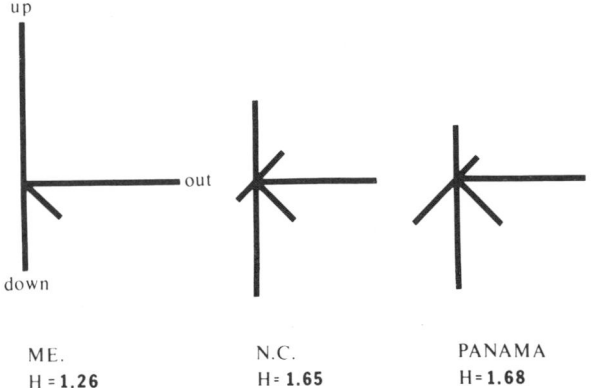

Figure 5. The directional components of probing at the 3 study sites. The length of each line is proportional to the percentage of probes in that direction.

Table 2. Parameters of foraging in the Black-throated Green Warbler in 2 breeding habitats in North America and 1 non-breeding, tropical habitat[1]

	$H_{spatial}$	$H_{technique}$	Techniques/ minute	$H_{probing}$	$H_{direction}$
Shepherd Brook Mountain, Maine	2.36	0.72	0.32	1.26	1.44
Mount Collins, North Carolina	2.85	1.21	0.49	1.65	1.55
Neuva Suiza, Chiriqui, Panama	2.73	1.63	1.04	1.68	1.52

	S/L flight ratio	Time/ tree	$H_{spatial}$/ bout	$\bar{X}$ techniques/ bout
Shepherd Brook Mountain, Maine[1]	6.06	54 sec	1.52	1.86
Mount Collins, North Carolina[1]	6.09	71 sec	1.74	1.80
Nueva Suiza, Chiriqui, Panama	33.62	172 sec	1.73	3.50

[1] See text for explanation of behavioral measures.

Table 3. Vertical distribution in feet of foraging in the Blackburnian Warbler in 3 studies

MacArthur 1958: New England spruce		Chipley 1974: Colombian oak		Rabenold 1976: Maine spruce-fir	
Height	Percentage	Height	Percentage	Height	Percentage
0–10:	0	0–10:	20.9	0–10:	1.4
10–20:	0	10–20:	27.0	10–20:	8.2
20–30:	2.6	20–30:	27.4	20–30:	14.3
30–40:	26.0	>30:	24.7	30–40:	28.7
40–50:	29.8			40–50:	25.6
50–60:	41.6			50–60:	9.6
				60–70:	7.3
				>70:	6.2

varia), Golden-winged (*Vermivora chrysoptera*), and Tennessee (*V. peregrina*) Warblers. In addition to the migrants, there were six common resident parulids: the Slate-throated Redstart (*Myioborus miniatus*), Collared Redstart (*M. torguatus*), Golden-crowned Warbler (*Basileuterus culicivorus*), Black-cheeked Warbler (*B. melanogenys*), Flame-throated Warbler (*Vermivora gutturalis*), and the Tropical Parula (*Parula pitiayumi*). This must be considered only a partial list, as more rigorous

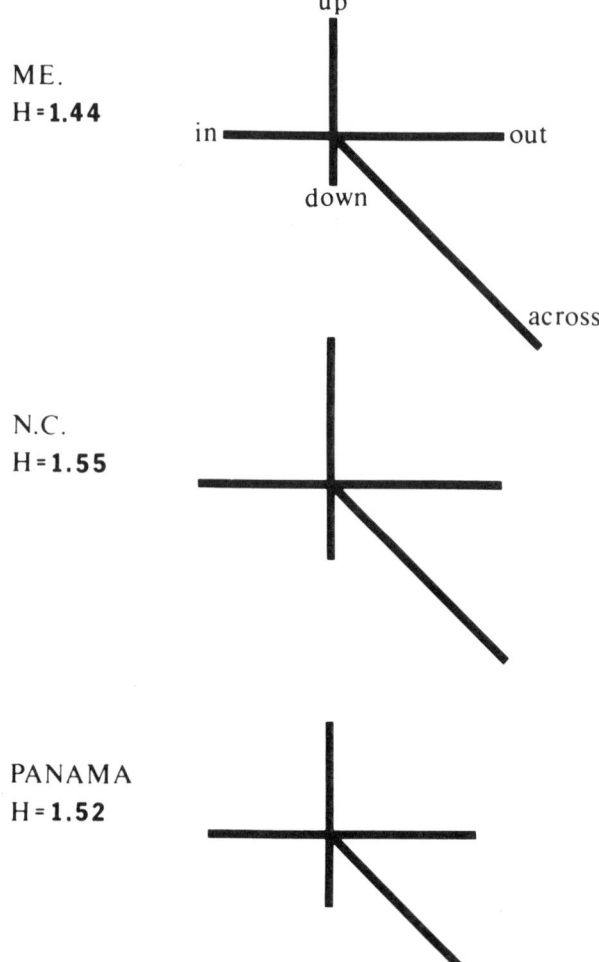

Figure 6. The directional components of flights within a tree at the 3 study sites. The length of each line is proportional to the percentage of flights in that direction.

Kerry N. Rabenold

census efforts would undoubtedly reveal more species. It should, however, be sufficient to suggest that there was no shortage of potential parulid competitors, either migrants or residents, for the BTG at the Panama site. While most are not congeneric, many are similar morphologically and behaviorally. In addition, it is artificial to limit lists of potential competitors to confamilials since the activities of similar families such as the vireos (Vireonidae) must to some degree affect the resource base available to parulids. It is hazardous to guess at competitive effects from lists of sympatric species, but it seems unlikely that the BTG would experience ecological release in Panama compared to Maine.

In North Carolina, no other warblers were commonly sympatric with the BTG. The Blackburnian, while common in censuses of similar forests, was rare in my North Carolina study. The Chestnut-sided Warbler (*Dendroica pensylvanica*) was present, but was restricted to ridge top clearings. If ecological release from congeneric species were the most important factor producing generalization in foraging in the comparison of the three habitats, generalization relative to Maine warblers would be more pronounced in North Carolina than in Panama. The foraging data show that this is not the case. In addition, the BTG has been remarkably unresponsive to potential ecological release in other studies. Morse (1971b) found that the foraging of BTGs on small islands off the coast of Maine did not appreciably differ from that on the mainland, even though the islands supported only a fraction of the similar species found on the mainland. Morse suggested that the relative "stereotypy" of the BTG is appropriate to its position as a numerical and social dominant in the mainland fauna.

High population densities and increased intraspecific competition could lead to generalization on a population level through the ecological divergence of individuals. Even if the animals were territorial, high density could lead to small territories and generalization within a territory. While it is difficult to compare censuses of singing males on the temperate breeding ground to censuses of winter populations, the population density of BTGs in Panama during this study probably fell between the densities of the other two areas: 1.1 birds/ha in Maine and 0.5 birds/ha in North Carolina. In addition, the fact that foraging in North Carolina was more generalized than in Maine, where the population was more dense, rather than vice-versa, implies that population density alone is not sufficient cause for observed behavior.

A factor that better explains the differences in foraging in the two breeding habitats as well as the tropical-temperate differences is the effect of seasonality on the abundance of food available at a partic-ular time. Pronounced climatic seasonality produces a higher peak of arthropod production in Maine than in North Carolina during the breeding season of the BTG (Rabenold 1976). Resident species in North Carolina are probably better able effectively to track the milder resource oscillations in that habitat, aided by more moderate winter conditions, resulting in a lower proportion of migrants in this community than in Maine. Although annual productivity is almost certainly higher in Panama (Lieth 1975), it is probably more evenly distributed throughout the year than in the temperate forests, owing to seasonal equitability of insolation and temperature. The diverse resident avifauna in Panama, which may contain locally opportunistic species of its own, is probably able to very effectively utilize variations in food supply that may exist.

Because of contrasts in climatic seasonality among the three areas and varying ability of residents to effectively utilize resource oscillations, food levels available to BTGs are probably highest in Maine and lowest in Panama. Others have suggested that the seasonal constancy of some tropical forests may result in keen competition and chronic food shortages even though annual productivity is high, and that this could be the reason that lowland forests are relatively little-used by migrants (Willis 1966; Karr 1976; see also Klopfer et al 1974). Lower food availability in the southern temperate and tropical study areas than in the northern area could produce generalization on an individual level as a foraging optimization response, which would result in the foraging trends presented here. Theory of optimization in foraging predicts that when food is scarce animals cannot afford to be selective, and generalization in foraging or prey selection will result (Schoener 1971; MacArthur 1972; Krebs 1973). Recent experimental tests have supported this idea (Smigel and Rosensweig 1974; Werner and Hall 1974), as have observations of individually marked temperate resident birds in winter (Rabenold in prep.).

The generality among migrants of the kind of annual cycle in foraging behavior shown here must be tested by further study of other species, as there is every reason to suppose that there exists a variety of migrant strategies. In fact, a more extensive study of a single species than has been presented here, especially along the migratory route, is required for an accurate picture of year-round economy. Future studies will undoubtedly quantify the degree of seasonal contrast in resources in various habitats, the degree of ecological similarity among potential competitors, and the degree of contrast in behavioral plasticity between migrants and residents. Studies of individually marked birds would be particularly useful, and an understanding of arthropod faunae will be essential.

In conclusion, the BTG shows considerable seasonal variation in foraging, even though it is probably one of the least behaviorally plastic species of its migratory genus. This variation is roughly as great as that found in resident temperate birds (Rabenold, in prep.). Progressive generalization occurs in several parameters of foraging from a highly seasonal northern coniferous forest to a less seasonal southern temperate coniferous forest and a relatively aseasonal tropical montane forest. This contrast is probably due to relative superabundance of food in the northern habitat and shortage in the more biologically accommodated southern habitats. This interpretation is supported by the observation that generalization on the population level is produced, at least in part, by greater behavioral diversity of each individual. These results, and similar observations by others, suggest that competitive pressures in diverse tropical avifaunas can produce niche expansion rather than contraction in wintering migrants, as compared to breeding migrants. They further suggest that competition for food can, for some migrants, be more severe in nonbreeding habitats in spite of the metabolic demands of the reproductive season and that competition for food among breeding birds in temperate habitats may sometimes be relatively insignificant for migrant populations. The increase in numbers and proportions of similar, insectivorous migrants with latitude in northern forests in the temperate zone (MacArthur 1959; Rabenold 1976, in press) is probably due to more pronounced arthropod blooms and reduced competition. Behavioral plasticity in migrants may be favored by temporary insinuation into diverse and stable communities of tropical residents, as well as by the rigors of annual colonization of the temperate zone.

Acknowledgments

This research was partially supported by the Bucknell University January Program. Earlier phases were supported by the Frank M. Chapman Memorial Fund of the American Museum of Natural History and the Curriculum in Ecology of the University of North Carolina. I would like to thank Carla Christensen, Melanie Patterson, Leslie Blackburn, and Dan Reed for help with the field work in Panama. Helmut C. Mueller, John G. Robinson, and Linda R. Cox provided critical comments, and Ranjinee Rudran typed the manuscript.

Literature Cited

Chipley, R. M.
1976. The impact of migrant warblers on resident passerines in a subtropical Colombia woodland. Living Bird 15:119–42.

Eaton, S. W.
1953. Wood warblers wintering in Cuba. Wils. Bull. 65: 169–75.

Elgood, J. H., R. E. Sharland, and P. Ward
1966. Palearctic migrants in Nigeria. Ibis 108:84–116.

Emlen, J. T.
1973. Territorial aggression in wintering warblers at Bahama agave blossoms. Wils. Bull. 85:71–74.

Holmes, R. T., and P. A. Pitelka
1968. Food overlap among coexisting sandpipers on northern Alaskan tundra. Syst. Zool. 17:305–18.

Hutcheson, K.
1970. A test for comparing diversities based on the Shannon formula. J. Theoret. Biol. 29:151–54.

Karr, J. R.
1971. Structure of avian communities in selected Panama and Illinois habitats. Ecol. Monogr. 41:207–33.

1976. On the relative abundances of migrants from the north temperate zone in tropical habitats. Wils. Bull. 88:433–458.

Klopfer, P. H., D. I. Rubenstein, R. S. Ridgeley, and R. J. Barnett
1974. Migration and species diversity in the tropics. Proc. Nat. Acad. Sci. 71:339–40.

Krebs, J. R.
1973. Behavioral aspects of predation. In *Perspectives in Ethology*, eds. P. P. G. Bateson and P. H. Klopfer, pp. 73–112. New York: Plenum Press.

Lack, D.
1976. *Island Biology*. Studies in Ecology, vol. 3. Berkeley: Univ. of California Press.

Lieth, H.
1975. Primary production of the major vegetation units of the world. In *Primary Production of the Biosphere*, eds. H. Lieth and R. H. Whittaker. New York: Springer-Verlag.

MacArthur, R. H.
1958. Population ecology of some warblers of northeastern coniferous forests. Ecology 39:599–619.

1959. On the breeding distribution pattern of North American migrant birds. Auk 76:318–25.

1972. *Geographical Ecology*. New York: Harper & Row.

MacArthur, R. H., and E. R. Pianka
1966. On optimal use of a patchy environment. Amer. Natur. 100:603–10.

Moreau, R. E.
1972. *The Palearctic-African Bird Migration Systems*. New York: Academic Press.

Morris, R. F., W. F. Cheshire, C. A. Miller, and D. G. Mott
1958. The numerical response of avian and mammalian

Kerry N. Rabenold

predators during a gradation of the spruce bud-worm. Ecol. 39:487–94.

Morse, D. H.
1968.　A quantitative study of foraging of male and female spruce-woods warblers. Ecol. 49:779–84.

1971a.　The insectivorous bird as an adaptive strategy. Ann. Rev. Ecol. Sys. 2:177–200.

1971b.　The foraging of warblers isolated on small islands. Ecol. 52:216–28.

Peet, R. K.
1974.　The measurement of species diversity. Ann. Rev. Ecol. Sys. 5:285–307.

Pianka, E. R.
1975.　Niche relationships of desert lizards. In *The Ecology and Evolution of Communites*, eds. M. L. Cody and J. M. Diamond. New York: Belknap Press.

Rabenold, K. N.
1976.　Foraging strategies, diversity, and seasonality in Appalachian spruce-fir bird communities. Ph.D. thesis. University of North Carolina, Chapel Hill, 186 pp.

In press. A reversed latitudinal diversity gradient in avian communities of eastern deciduous forests. Amer. Natur.

In prep. Seasonal variation in individual search strategies of temperate birds.

Schoener, T. W.
1971.　Theory of feeding strategies. Ann. Rev. Ecol. Sys. 2: 369–404.

Schwartz, P.
1964.　The northern waterthrush in Venezuela. Living Bird 3:169–84.

Shannon, E. C., and W. Weaver
1949.　*The mathematical theory of communication.* Urbana: U. Ill. Press.

Slud, P.
1960.　The birds of Finca "La Selva," Costa Rica: a tropical wet forest locality. Bull. Am. Mus. Nat. Hist. 121:1–148.

Smigel, B. W., and M. L. Rosenzweig
1974.　Seed selection in *Dipodomys merriami* and *Perognathus penicillatus.* Ecol. 55:329–39.

Stewart, R. E., and J. W. Aldrich
1951.　Removal and repopulation of breeding birds in a spruce-fir forest community. Auk 68:471–82.

Werner, E. E., and D. J. Hall
1974.　Optimal foraging and the size selection of prey by the bluegill sunfish. Ecol. 55:1042–52.

Willis, E. O.
1966.　The role of migrant birds at swarms of army ants. Living Bird 5:187–231.

ROBERT M. CHIPLEY
Section of Ecology and Systematics
Cornell University
Ithaca, New York 14850

Nonbreeding Ecology of the Blackburnian Warbler

ABSTRACT   Migrant warblers have been generally thought to choose the same subunits of habitat on their wintering grounds as on the breeding grounds. However, in this study of the Blackburnian Warbler in an oak woods near Popayán, Colombia, where it was particularly common from October to April, this species, which prefers the upper vegetational levels during breeding, was commonly observed at all levels. At low densities, when the vanguard arrived and the stragglers departed, it preferred the upper levels. Its use of all vegetational levels at high densities is presumably due to intraspecific competition and the absence on its wintering grounds of congeneric species with which it is sympatric during breeding. The hypothesis is presented and discussed that this species and others of its genus may avoid intrageneric competition during winter by geographical isolation from one another.

Introduction

MacArthur (1958) hypothesized that the general aspects of warbler behavior in terms of foraging height and feeding methods are nearly the same throughout the year, even though the vegetation type occupied may vary from northern spruce forest to tropical forest. Hence, the "habitat-niche" (subunit of habitat) selection may be more important to most warblers than habitat selection (Parnell 1969). MacArthur's (1958) observations of several wintering warblers in Costa Rica tended to confirm this hypothesis, although of the five breeding *Dendroica* species he studied in New England, he found only one, Black-throated Green (*D. virens*) during the nonbreeding season in Costa Rica. Skutch (in MacArthur 1958) thought that all migrant warblers in Costa Rica (with the exception of the Chestnut-sided (*D. pensylvanica*), which he felt spends more time high in trees in winter) have the same general feeding behavior and foraging height in both seasons. Lack and Lack (1972) likewise observed that the ecology of at least most of the migrant Parulidae they studied in Jamaica was similar to that of the breeding grounds. Eaton's (1953) observations in Cuba also indicated that the feeding behavior and foraging height of migrant Parulidae remains roughly the same as on the breeding grounds. Schwartz's (1964) observations of the Northern Waterthrush (*Seiurus noveboracensis*) in Venezuela also indicate similar ecology in both seasons. Two exceptions to this hypothesis are the Cape May (*Dendroica tigrina*) and Yellow-rumped (*D. coronata*) Warblers. MacArthur (1958), however, regarded the Cape May as a fugitive species whose population levels depend on outbreaks of the spruce budworm, whereas the Yellow-rumped, with its variety of winter feeding locations and enormous winter range, merely confirmed his summer observations of great behavioral flexibility. Slud (1960), however, also in Costa Rica, provided ecological notes on several migrant warblers which suggest that for some species there may be an expansion of the habitat-niche, at least in terms of feeding height, although he provided no quantitative information to allow for closer comparison. For example, in the cases of the Black-throated Green and Blackburnian (*D. fusca*) Warblers, both of which prefer the higher vegetational levels during the breeding season, Slud (1960) stated that in his lowland study area the former is encountered fairly low to fairly high in the vegetation, while the latter is found at medium to high levels, but sometimes low. Similarly, Rabenold (this volume) observed that the foraging of the Black-throated Green Warbler was more generalized spatially during the nonbreeding season in Panama than during the breeding season in Maine.

In this study it was my object to make observations on the non-breeding ecology of the Blackburnian Warbler to compare these with observations from existing studies of the bird's breeding ecology.

Study Area

This study was conducted near Popayán, Department of Cauca, Colombia at 2°27′N, 76°22′W. The study area was an oak woods of approximately 30 ha, at an elevation of about 1,800 m, lying in the subtropical zone of the western slope of the Cordillera Central of the Andes. The woods consisted of a largely homogeneous second-growth stand of the oak *Quercus humboldtii*, somewhat thinned in places by cutting. Most trees did not reach above 12 m, with a few emergents to 18 m. The scattered understory consisted largely of some stands of ferns, several species of Rubiaceae and Melastomataceae, a species of Guttiferae, and oak stumps with young shoots. Among the smaller trees were a species of Anacardiaceae and a species of *Ficus* (Moraceae). Some Araceae grew both on the ground and in the trees, but in general most trees were free of vines and epiphytes. In contrast to MacArthur's (1958) study areas, birds were relatively easy to observe in this open woods. Resident avifauna were largely widespread species characteristic of disturbed habitats (Chipley 1976). Migrant passerines were particularly common there, making up 46.4 percent of all bird observations in the woods and 50.2 percent of all passerines for the period October to April. Migrant warblers observed more than once included the Blackburnian Warbler, American Redstart (*Setophaga ruticilla*), Black-and-white Warbler (*Mniotilta varia*), Canada Warbler (*Wilsonia canadensis*), Tennessee Warbler (*Vermivora peregrina*), Golden-winged Warbler (*Vermivora chrysoptera*), and Mourning Warbler (*Oporonis philadelphia*); of these, the Blackburnian Warbler was by far the most abundant and the only one of its genus and accounted for 57.2 percent of all observations of migrants.

Procedures

As I initially observed each bird, I recorded its approximate height and the category of vegetation in which it was foraging. No two observations represented the same bird on the same perch; in fact, by moving from the area or ceasing to take foraging station data after the first observation, I attempted to maximize my observations of different individuals and insure a certain degree of independence among all observations. I estimated foraging height with a camera rangefinder and by inspection, often using a notched stick. Above 10 ft (3.05 m) I estimated height in 5-ft inter-

Robert M. Chipley

vals. A tape measure was also employed. As familiarity with the area increased, I used certain height reference points. I recorded measurements in feet rather than meters because, MacArthur (1958) used feet as a measurement, and I wished to make certain comparisons with his work.

A rough census was taken of the number of bird species and individuals seen per hour, but individual birds were not marked. Repetitions in counts were avoided by estimating populations from the maximum number of individuals seen at one time.

Observations of migrant warblers were made on the area from mid-January to early May and early September to early December 1972.

Comparative Breeding and Nonbreeding Ecology

The breeding ecology and behavior of the Blackburnian Warbler has been described in general terms by several authors (Bent 1953; Chapman 1917; Griscom 1938; Griscom and Sprunt 1957; Kendeigh 1945; Knight 1908; Palmer 1949) and has been a subject of more detailed and quantitative studies by MacArthur (1958) and Morse (1967, 1970). The consensus is that this species prefers deep evergreen forests, particularly hemlocks, where it is almost exclusively confined to the upper levels of foliage. Kendeigh (1945) records its foraging zone as 35–75 ft from the ground, while Morse (1967) found it mostly at 30–50 ft. MacArthur (1958), on the basis of 77 observations, recorded the bird at 40 ft or above 71.4 percent of the time, with no observations at 0–20 ft. Both MacArthur (1958) and Morse (1967) found that it foraged higher than any other *Dendroica* species with which it is sympatric during breeding.

The behavior and ecology of the Blackburnian Warbler during the non-breeding season is less well known. As mentioned, Slud (1960) found it at least occasionally at all levels of vegetation in lowland Costa Rica, where it appeared as a transient rather than a winter resident. Elsewhere in Costa Rica, Slud (1964) encountered isolated individuals during migration, usually accompanying mixed species foraging flocks well inside solid forest. As a winter visitant in the highlands he reported it usually singly, in tree-scattered clearings, park-like pastures, and along edges and breaks in and beside woodland. He found it active at all heights in the trees, but again provided no quantitative data on foraging height. Buskirk (1972), however, also in highland Costa Rica, found it a rare transient in his study area, and classified it as a canopy species. Skutch (in Bent 1953) found it moderately abundant in Costa Rica, mostly at 3,000–6,000 ft, both in heavy forest and among scattered tall trees. He thought it arrived

in flocks in late August or September but then dispersed throughout woodland. It showed slight sociability, but sometimes joined mixed bands of Tennessee Warblers and other small birds, high in the trees, where it is difficult to observe. In the Western Andes of Colombia, Miller (1963) found it the most common North American migrant, seen usually in crowns of forest trees but occasionally along edges and into small trees in pastures.

It is not to be expected that morphological traits and the behavioral spectrum of a species would allow massive changes in strategy between the breeding and nonbreeding seasons. Thus, my general behavioral observations for the Blackburnian Warbler in Colombia do not differ in any noticeable way from what has been recorded in New England, although it is difficult to compare the subjective observations of different observers. Thus, those I saw around Popayán frequently gleaned while perched, moving along branches and twigs, straining the neck to see prey items apparently close by, and, as noted by Knight (1908) and MacArthur (1958), searching both up and down for prey; they sometimes hovered to take prey from the bottoms of leaves, but made short rather than long flights. The most common maneuver was to take prey from the bottom of a leaf while perched (38.8 percent of 49 observations which ended in a prey capture). Second-most common was to take prey from the bottom of a leaf while making a short flight (28.5 percent), while 20.4 percent of prey captures were taken from the top of a leaf (Chipley 1974). Their preference for twigs and foliage seems most often to put them in the peripheral part of the tree. One quantified set of observations I made on this species can be compared with that made by MacArthur (1958), who, as one index by which to compare the relative foraging habits and activity of his five *Dendroica* species, measured visible wing use per unit time. When a bird landed after a flight, he began a count of seconds until it was lost from sight and during this period counted the number of visible uses of the wing. For the Blackburnian Warbler, he observed a total of 72 wing uses in 537 sec, or 0.134 wing uses per sec. Following this procedure, using a stopwatch I obtained a comparable figure of 0.112, based on 366 wing uses in 3276.4 sec. The difference between these, applying a chi-square test, is not significant. Hence, this aspect of the bird's behavior is roughly the same in both seasons. Although Moreau (1972) has estimated that migrants need only 60 percent of the intake in nonbreeding of what they need during breeding, the rate of wing use (and presumably foraging rate) is perhaps not the index by which this change can be detected.

A second set of quantified observations which can

Table 1. Hostile interactions initiated per foraging observation

Morse (1970)	Foraging obser-vations	Total inter-actions initiated	Intra-specific	Inter-specific
Black-and-white Warbler	505	.135	.038	.097
Blackburnian Warbler	198	.035	.000	.035
Canada Warbler	86	.163	.058	.105
American Redstart	68	.118	.074	.044
My Observations				
Black-and-white Warbler	202	.025	.015	.010
Blackburnian Warbler	1306	.031	.027	.003
Canada Warbler	206	.012	.012	.000
American Redstart	191	.026	.015	.011

be compared with observations on the breeding grounds deals with the rate of inter- and intraspecific agonistic encounters. Following the procedure Morse (1970) used to measure agonistic interactions for several warbler species observed on the breeding grounds, I calculated the number of agonistic encounters initiated by the species divided by the total number of foraging observations made on that species, noting also whether the encounter was inter- or intraspecific. My results and those of Morse (1970) for the species I observed are presented in table 1. The difference in these figures no doubt reflects a different physiological state, different densities and the different species complement in which the birds find themselves. For the Blackburnian Warbler, Morse (1970) found no intra-specific interactions, whereas in my study area, 34 of the 39 agonistic encounters observed for this species were intraspecific. This no doubt reflects the far higher density of the species in this woods where I frequently saw 4 or 5 at a time, than on the breeding grounds where Morse (1970) observed them. In addition, the intraspecific encounters of the Blackburnian did not seem territorial as, unlike those I observed for the American Redstart and Black-and-white Warbler, they were brief and rarely repeated, and were probably due to occasional violation of individual distance. In partial confirmation of the density effect on intraspe-cific encounters, I observed none during the period of September and late April to early May, when density was low. The low intraspecific agonistic interaction rates for the American Redstart and Black-and-white

and Canada Warblers result from the fact that these birds were very infrequently observed near one of their own species, while the Blackburnian was, as a rule, seen within sight of another of its kind. The high mutual tolerance of the Blackburnian allows the high density observed in this woods; the birds in fact seemed to form loose flocks, but generally seemed crowded rather than gregarious, since they did not show suffi-cient intraspecific attraction to make them nuclear species for mixed foraging flocks (Chipley 1974).

A third set of quantified observations deals with the foraging height preference shown by the species. The foraging height preference of the Blackburnian War-bler in this woods differs from that shown by Mac-Arthur (1958) in its spruce-forest breeding grounds in New England, chiefly in that on its wintering grounds the bird is much less narrowly confined to the upper levels. There is some evidence, however, that the upper levels are preferentially occupied first but, as density of the species increases, other levels are occupied until there is a fairly even distribution of the birds among all the 10-ft height-level categories into which I, fol-lowing MacArthur (1958), divided the habitat. Using the periods of September 10–20 and April 22–May 9 as low density, and October 1–April 21 as high density, both the Kolmolgorov-Smirnov two-tailed test and the two-tailed t-test show a tendency significant at the .001 level for a shift in foraging height between the period of low density and the period of high density; the direction is toward a lower foraging height during high density. In table 2, this information is presented in terms of percentage of total observations seen in each foraging-height category both for MacArthur's breeding data and my low and high density data from Colombia, using MacArthur's 10-ft intervals. At higher density both the standard deviation and range increase, showing the bird's tendency to utilize more foraging-height levels. These results from this woods show that, at least for the Blackburnian Warbler, MacArthur (1958) and Power (1971) are probably correct in assuming that warblers seek out the same habitat-niche in the nonbreeding season that they occupy during breeding; however, increased density complicates the problem, so that the original habitat-niche preference may become obscured. The effect of density on the ecology of a species can also be observed in reference to the Tennessee Warbler, which was infrequently encountered in this woods, usually singly but very rarely two at a time, but which is found in heavy concentrations in Costa Rica during nonbreed-ing, often in intraspecific flocks (Skutch in Bent 1953; Skutch in Griscom and Sprunt 1957; Slud 1964). Thus, although my observations show this species to forage higher than any other warbler seen in my study

Robert M. Chipley

Table 2. Foraging height preference of the Blackburnian Warbler (in feet)

New England (MacArthur, 1958)

N^1 = 77
0–10 = 0%
10–20 = 0%
20–30 = 2.6%
30–40 = 26.0%
40–50 = 29.8%
50–60 = 41.6%

Colombia

Low Density (1.21 birds/ census hr)	High Density (4.53 birds/ census hr)
N = 87	N = 1219
0–10 = 8.0%	0–10 = 20.9%
10–20 = 24.1%	10–20 = 27.0%
20–30 = 36.8%	20–30 = 27.4%
30–40+ = 31.1%	30–40+ = 24.7%
$\bar{X}$ = 26.83	$\bar{X}$ = 23.01
s = 9.41	s = 12.25
Range = 6–45	Range 0–60

[1] N = sample size.
s = standard deviation.

area (Chipley 1974), Slud (1964), who reported it usually in small to fairly large bands, found it frequently at low to medium heights, and also on the ground. It might again be noted here that one species which Skutch (in MacArthur 1958) felt differed in ecology in Costa Rica from what is known of it on its breeding grounds is the Chestnut-sided Warbler, found in great abundance in its restricted nonbreeding quarters from Nicaragua to central Panama. Comparing the warblers I observed in my study area with what is known of them elsewhere suggests to me that habitat-niche selection may be most important to widely distributed species and species at the margins of their ranges; hence, in my study area, the species that were not abundant showed no marked departure in habitat-niche from that which would be predicted from their breeding ecology.

The expansion of foraging height here by the Blackburnian Warbler, and perhaps by other warblers elsewhere, seems to be an instance of ecological release,

most frequently discussed in reference to island situations (Diamond 1970, Schoener 1967). The term describes a case in which one species, in the absence of closely related or similar species, increases the breadth of certain critical dimensions of its ecological niche (Schoener 1967). Diamond (1970), working with island avifauna in the Southwest Pacific, has described niche expansions involving type of habitat, altitudinal zone, and vertical feeding zone within a forest. Within the New Guinea forest, the foraging ranges of most bird species are vertically restricted; many species remain in the treetops, others forage primarily between 10–30 ft, while others always remain within a few feet of the ground, a situation which roughly parallels that of MacArthur's five *Dendroica* warblers. On smaller outlying islands, however, where congeners are lacking, many of these New Guinea species have a foraging range from understory to treetops (Diamond 1970). This also describes the pattern shown by the Blackburnian Warbler in my study area.

As Diamond (1970) suggests, situations in which one species is relieved from the competition of its close relatives offer the possibility of determining the extent the niche of a given species is determined by competition and by its intrinsic adaptations; in other words, which components of the niche are most plastic. In the case of the Blackburnian Warbler, foraging height seems to be the most apparent habitat-niche expansion. An extreme type of vertical shift, one requiring morphological changes, occurs when a normally arboreal bird descends to the ground (Diamond 1970). A shift in foraging height from upper to lower levels, however, requires only the ability to respond to various fluctuations in food supply or species composition and density in the woodland and is thus the type of niche expansion one would predict for the *Dendroica* warblers, where there seems to be a minimal selective advantage placed on morphological differences (Morse 1968).

Power (1971), in agreement with MacArthur (1958), believed that, in terms of vegetational strata, warblers generally select similar subunits of the habitat throughout the year, even though the vegetation type occupied may vary from northern spruce forest to tropical forest, and that therefore habitat-niche selection may be more important for most warblers than habitat selection. However, if in the more equatorial latitudes the habitat cannot be subdivided among migrants sufficiently to support all the species that co-occupy the breeding grounds, then seeking out situations where they may be ecologically released may be one strategy. If tropical avian communities are tightly organized, there may be less opportunity for the more subtle intrageneric niche partitioning that the several sympatric *Dendroica* species show in the spruce forests of New England.

Diamond (1970) suggests that the various expansions of habitat-niche, such as a shift in vertical foraging, which are characteristic of ecological release, may allow a species to occupy more space and thus, potentially, to achieve a larger population. Hence, seeking out an opportunity for ecological release may be an important device for a migrant species to maintain itself in the largest possible numbers. If this is in fact true, one might expect a certain degree of geographical isolation among congeneric warblers during the nonbreeding months.

Nonbreeding Strategy of Migrant Warblers

In the oak woods in which I worked, the Blackburnian Warbler made up almost 60 percent of all migrants and close to 30 percent of all birds observed during the period November to April (Chipley 1974). Although I spent many hours there, the only other *Dendroica* species I saw was a single Cerulean (*Dendroica cerulea*) during the fall migration. That the Blackburnian Warbler was present in high density and was the only member of its genus to be found there suggested to me that one facet of its nonbreeding strategy might be geographical isolation from others in its genus.

As Skutch (in Griscom and Sprunt 1957) has noted, there seem to be two basic wintering patterns to which most of the more common Parulidae breeding in the temperate latitudes conform. One, characterized by wide geographical dispersal, low density, and low intraspecific tolerance, including the establishment and defense of feeding territories, is seen in species such as the Black-and-white Warbler, American Redstart, Ovenbird (*Seiurus aurocapillus*), and Louisiana (*Seiurus motacilla*) and Northern Water-thrushes. The other, characterized by more narrow dispersal and, for many, instances of high density in at least part of its nonbreeding range, and intraspecific tolerance high enough to allow flocking in some species, is seen in several members of the larger genera *Dendroica* and *Vermivora*, such as the Black-throated Green in El Salvador (Dickey and van Rossem 1938), the Cape May in Hispaniola (Wetmore and Swales 1931), the Townsend's (*Dendroica townsendi*) in Guatemala (Skutch in Griscom and Sprunt 1957), the Cerulean in Peru (Cooke in Bent 1953), the Blackburnian in Colombia and Ecuador (Chapman 1917, 1926; Miller 1963; pers. obs.), the Black-throated Blue (*Dendroica caerulescens*) and Palm (*Dendroica palmarum*) in Cuba (Barbour 1943), the Chestnut-sided and Tennessee in Costa Rica (Slud 1964), the Nashville (*Vermivora ruficapilla*) in parts of Mexico (Bent 1953), and the Blue-winged (*Vermivora pinus*) in parts of Mexico and Guatemala

(Eisenmann in Griscom and Sprunt 1957). Those in the first category are either monogeneric or separated by range or habitat during breeding, while those in the second include congeners, some of which overlap during breeding. Presumably, habitat-niche division during nonbreeding is sufficient to separate the largely dissimilar species that range widely in tropical America during the northern winter; however, if it were sufficient to separate those with more restricted geographic nonbreeding ranges, then one might predict a more even dispersal of these species throughout tropical America, with as common a co-occurrence of congeners during nonbreeding as during breeding. That large concentrations of the Blackburnian Warblers, for example, occur south of the limits of the nonbreeding ranges of all its sympatrically breeding congeners indicates that this does not apply in all cases.

Salomonsen (1954) believed that related species that are separated by some feature of habitat during breeding are often isolated from one another geographically during the nonbreeding months. Thus, the limits of the nonbreeding range are conditioned in part by competition with other species. Lack (1944) also believed that closely related species that are potential food competitors have evolved geographical isolation in nonbreeding ranges as a result of differential adaptation. He suggested that closely related species are less often isolated from each other by habitat differences outside the breeding season, and that hence geographical segregation is relatively common. Working with Parulidae in Jamaica, where 18 species regularly spend the North American winter, and 12 others occur as transients, Lack and Lack (1972) suggested that the transients would not move farther if they could survive better in Jamaica than elsewhere; competition from the 18 wintering species is probably the main reason for their moving on. During breeding, MacArthur's (1958) 5 *Dendroica* species avoided competition by subtle partitioning of the same habitat rather than by use of different habitats. Since Lack and Lack (1972) found that habitat separates hardly any of the migrant warblers in Jamaica, it may be that the opportunities for subtle habitat partitioning, such as displayed by MacArthur's 5 *Dendroica*, is actually less on the nonbreeding grounds. This problem can in part be solved by geographical partitioning of habitat on different nonbreeding grounds. In addition, since migrants are also subject to competitive pressures from the resident avifauna, especially on the mainland, it might be of advantage to avoid inter-migrant competition by geographical partitioning.

MacArthur (1958), however, concluded that the 5 *Dendroica* species he studied showed no less nonbreeding range overlap than a randomly chosen group of 5

Robert M. Chipley

eastern North American warblers. He defined "significant overlap" as a case where at least half of 1 species' nonbreeding range is included in the other's. Using the nonbreeding range data from Bent (1953), he found that the 23 warbler species breeding in Maine (Palmer 1949) showed 253 significant overlaps, or 11 per species; thus, the probability that a randomly chosen pair of species of Maine warblers will show significant nonbreeding range overlap is $^{11}\!/_{23}$, or .478. For the 5 *Dendroica* species in question, MacArthur found 10 significant overlaps, or 2 per species; thus, the mean overlap is $^2\!/_5$, or .4, which is near the expected .478, suggesting that the 5 *Dendroica* overlap more or less randomly during nonbreeding. Since MacArthur's argument relies on these 10 cases of overlap, it is worth examining each in detail, and attempting a reanalysis:

1) The Cape May occupies at least half the nonbreeding range of the Yellow-rumped. This case seems unlikely, since the Cape May is found during the nonbreeding season only in the Bahamas, Greater Antilles, and to a lesser extent the Lesser Antilles, whereas the Yellow-rumped is found in the Bahamas, Greater Antilles, much of the southern and coastal United States, and Mexico to Costa Rica. Thus, the Cape May occupies less than half the nonbreeding range of the Yellow-rumped. It is further interesting to note that Wetmore and Swales (1931), who thought that Hispaniola was the "winter metropolis" of the Cape May, found it more common in the western part of the island, whereas the Yellow-rumped was seen commonly in the eastern part, and seldom if ever recorded in the west.

2) The Yellow-rumped occupies at least half the nonbreeding range of the Cape May. This seems to be true.

3) The Yellow-rumped occupies at least half the nonbreeding range of the Black-throated Green. This also seems to be true.

4) The Yellow-rumped occupies at least half the nonbreeding range of the Blackburnian. This seems very doubtful, since of the huge non-breeding range of the Yellow-rumped, only its southern limits in Costa Rica and perhaps Panama overlap with the Blackburnian, the principal nonbreeding range of which is northwestern South America to Peru (Eisenmann in Griscom and Sprunt 1957), where the Yellow-rumped is found only as an accidental (Meyer de Schauensee 1964).

5) The Black-throated Green occupies at least half the nonbreeding range of the Yellow-rumped. This seems to be true.

6) The Black-throated Green occupies at least half the nonbreeding range of the Blackburnian. This

seems doubtful. The Black-throated Green spends the nonbreeding season sparingly in the West Indies (Bond 1950), but principally from Mexico to western Panama. Dickey and van Rossem (1938) found it extremely common in El Salvador, where it made up 90 percent of the nonresident warbler population at 3,000–5,000 ft, forming flocks of 12–50 individuals. The Blackburnian overlaps the Black-throated Green only in Costa Rica; in Panama it is recorded only as a migrant (Eisenmann in Griscom and Sprunt 1957). This species is common in Colombia, where it is frequently encountered 3 or 4 or more at a time (Miller 1963; pers. obs.), and is the most common migrant warbler in Ecuador (Chapman 1926). Slud (1964) stated that as a rule he encountered the Blackburnian singly in Costa Rica, and the Black-throated Green only 1 or 2 at a time. Hence, Costa Rica seems to be the limit of the nonbreeding range for both species, and their contact is very limited. It is interesting to note that Morse (1967) regarded these 2 species as one another's most important competitors; in his study area, also in Maine, he found that the Black-throated Green was the only species of warbler that the Blackburnian frequently came into contact with and that the former foraged in a manner suggestive of the latter. He postulated that the existing ecological and behavioral relationships between 2 species were the result of a past history of intense interactions, and that the effect of the Black-throated Green on the Blackburnian was quantitatively greater than that of the Blackburnian on the Black-throated Green, probably because of the Blackburnian's lower density. It is perhaps significant that the subordinate species travel beyond the nonbreeding range of the dominant species.

7) The Blackburnian occupies at least half the nonbreeding range of the Yellow-rumped. This is doubtful; see case 4.

8) The Blackburnian occupies at least half the nonbreeding range of the Black-throated Green. This is doubtful; see case 6.

9) The Blackburnian occupies at least half of the nonbreeding range of the Bay-breasted (*Dendroica castanea*). The Bay-breasted Warbler is found during the nonbreeding season in Panama, Venezuela, and Columbia, but not south of 4°N (Meyer de Schauensee 1966); the Blackburnian is found throughout most of this range, but also in Costa Rica and south of 4°N in the Andes to Peru. Hence, the geographical overlap between the species is extensive, although it may be that the center of abundance for the Blackburnian lies south of 4°N. However, there is evidence that the two species are altitudinally isolated from one another. Phelps and Phelps (1950) reported that the Bay-breasted is found in Venezuela in forests of the tropical

zone, whereas the Blackburnian is found in forests of the subtropical zone. In Colombia, Chapman (1917) reported the Bay-breasted most frequent in the Pacific littoral; of the 9 specimens he collected, all were from the tropical zone. The Blackburnian he recorded as one of the most common of northern-breeding migrants, found in all three ranges of the Andes, mainly in the subtropical zone, but ranging upward to the temperate zone; of the 38 specimens he collected, all but 1 were taken in the subtropical zone or above. Hence, it is doubtful that the two species commonly come into contact on their nonbreeding grounds. However, because there are undoubtedly several instances of altitudinal isolation between species that are scored as overlapping in the analysis to follow, this case is conceded as significant.

10) The Bay-breasted occupies at least half the nonbreeding range of the Blackburnian. See case 9.

To reevaluate MacArthur's (1958) argument, I determined what I considered to be significant overlaps during the nonbreeding season (that is, at least half of 1 species' nonbreeding range overlapping the other) among the 23 warblers breeding in Maine (Palmer 1949), based on ranges and relative abundances as given in Bent (1953), Bond (1950), Dickey and van Rossem (1938), Friedman et al (1950), Griscom and Sprunt (1957), Land (1970), Meyer de Schauensee (1964, 1966), Monroe (1968), and Wetmore and Swales (1931). This yielded 239 significant overlaps, or about 10.4 per species; thus, the probability that a randomly chosen pair of warblers breeding in Maine would show a significant overlap during nonbreeding is $10.4/23$, or .452. For the 5 *Dendroica* species there are 5 significant overlaps or 1 per species; thus the mean overlap is $\frac{1}{5}$, or .2. As the expected probability of overlap of the 5 species with one another, I counted the overlap of the 5 species with the other 18, and the 18 with the 5, and also the overlaps of the 18 among each other, and found 234 out of a possible 486. For the overlap of the 5 species with one another, there are 5 significant cases out of a possible 20. Predicting a decreased overlap, I used a chi-square test to compare the nonbreeding range overlap of the 5 *Dendroica* and the other 18, plus the 18 among one another, with the overlap of the 5 *Dendroica* among themselves; this test showed a significantly reduced overlap among the 5 *Dendroica* at the .05 level. Thus, although this analysis is hardly conclusive, there is a distinct possibility that there is geographical partitioning of nonbreeding range among these 5 *Dendroica* species.

Acknowledgments

I wish to thank the members of my thesis committee, Drs. Douglas Lancaster, Tom Cade, and William Keeton, who offered many helpful suggestions during the preparation of this work. The project was conducted while I held a fellowship under the National Defense Education Act. This paper is an edited version of a section of a Ph.D. thesis submitted to Cornell University in August 1974.

Literature Cited

Barbour, T.
1943.   Cuban ornithology. Memoires of the Nuttall Ornith. Club 9.

Bent, A. C.
1953.   Life histories of North American wood warblers. U.S. Nat. Mus. Bull. 203.

Bond, J.
1950.   Check-list of the birds of the West Indies. Phila. Acad. Nat. Sciences.

Buskirk, W. H.
1972.   Foraging ecology of the bird flocks in a tropical forest. Univ. of Calif., Ph.D. thesis, Davis.

Chapman, F. M.
1917.   The distribution of bird-life in Colombia: a contribution to a biological survey of South America. Bull. Am. Mus. Nat. Hist. 36:1–729.

1917.   *The Warblers of North America.* 3rd ed. New York: Appleton.

1926.   The distribution of bird-life in Ecuador: a contribution to a study of the origin of Andean bird-life. Bull. Am. Mus. Nat. Hist. 55:1–784.

Chipley, R. M.
1974.   Wintering migrant wood warblers and their impact on resident insectivorous passerines in a subtropical Colombian oak woods. Unpubl. Ph.D. thesis, Cornell Univ., Ithaca, N.Y.

1976.   The impact of wintering migrant wood warblers on resident insectivorous passerines in a subtropical Colombian oak woods. The Living Bird (15th Annual): 119–41.

Diamond, J. M.
1970.   Ecological consequences of island colonization by Southwest Pacific birds. I. Types of niche shifts. Proc. Natl. Acad. Sci. 67:529–36.

Dickey, D., and A. J. van Rossem
1938.   The birds of El Salvador. Field Mus. Nat. Hist., Zool. Ser. 23:1–609.

Eaton, S. W.
1953.   Wood warblers wintering in Cuba. Wils. Bull. 65: 169–75.

Friedman, H., L. Griscom, and R. T. Moore
1950.   Distributional checklist of the birds of Mexico. Cooper Ornith. Club. Pacif. Coast Avifauna 29.

Robert M. Chipley

Griscom, L.

1938. The birds of Lake Umbagog region of Maine. Compiled from the diaries and journals of William Brewster. Bull. Mus. Comp. Zool. 66:525–620.

Griscom, L., and A. Sprunt, Jr.

1957. *The Warblers of America.* New York: Devon-Adair.

Kendeigh, S. C.

1945. Community selection in birds on the Helderberg Plateau of New York. Auk 62:418–36.

Knight, O. W.

1908. *The Birds of Maine.* Bangor.

Lack, D.

1944. Ecological aspects of species-formation in Passerine birds. Ibis 86:260–86.

Lack, D., and P. Lack

1972. Wintering warblers in Jamaica. The Living Bird (11th Annual):129–153.

Land, H. C.

1970. *Birds of Guatemala.* Wynnewood, Pa.: Livingston.

MacArthur, R.

1958. Population ecology of some warblers of northeastern coniferous forests. Ecol. 39:599–619.

Meyer de Schauensee, R.

1964. *The Birds of Colombia and Adjacent Areas of South and Central America.* Narberth, Pa.: Livingston.

1966. The species of birds of South America and their distribution. Phila. Acad. Natur. Sci.

Miller, A. H.

1963. Seasonal activity and ecology of the avifauna of an American equatorial cloud forest. Univ. Calif. Publ. Zool. 66:1–78.

Monroe, B. L., Jr.

1968. A distributional survey of the birds of Honduras. A.O.U. Ornith. Mongr. 7.

Moreau, R. E.

1972. *The Palaearctic-African Bird Migration Systems.* London: Academic Press

Morse, D. H.

1967. Competitive relationships between Parula Warblers and other species during the breeding season. Auk 84:490–502.

1968. A quantitative study of foraging of male and female spruce-wood warblers. Ecol. 49:779–84.

1970. Ecological aspects of some mixed species foraging flocks of birds. Ecol. Monogr. 40:119–68.

Palmer, R. S.

1949. Maine birds. Bull. Mus. Comp. Zool. 102: 1–656.

Parnell, H. F.

1969. Habitat relations of the Parulidae during spring migration. Auk 86:505–21.

Phelps, W. H., and W. H. Phelps, Jr.

1950. Lista de las aves de Venezuela con su distribución. Parte 2: Passeriformes. Bol. Soc. Ven. Cien. Nat. 12: 1–427.

Power, D. M.

1971. Warbler ecology: diversity, similarity, and seasonal differences in habitat segregation. Ecol. 52:434–43.

Salomonsen, F.

1954. Evolution and bird migration. Acta 11 Cong. Int. Orn., Basel, Switzerland.

Schoener, T. W.

1967. The ecological significance of sexual dimorphism in size in the lizard *Anolis conspersus.* Science 155:474–77.

Schwartz, P.

1964. The Northern Waterthrush in Venezuela. Living Bird (3rd Annual): 169:84.

Slud, P.

1960. The birds of Finca "La Selva," Costa Rica: a tropical wet forest locality. Bull. Am. Must. Nat. Hist. 121.

1964. The birds of Costa Rica. Bull. Am. Mus. Nat. Hist. 128.

Wetmore, A., and B. H. Swales

1931. The birds of Haiti and the Dominican Republic. U.S. Natl. Mus. Bull. 155:1–483.

SARA E. BENNETT
Department of Biological Sciences
Dartmouth College
Hanover, New Hampshire, 03755

Interspecific Competition and the Niche of the American Redstart (*Setophaga Ruticilla*) in Wintering and Breeding Communities

ABSTRACT

This study represents an investigation of the role of interspecific competition in the year-round ecology of a common and widely-occurring neotropical migrant, the American Redstart (*Setophaga ruticilla*). The evidence obtained, though indirect, is consistent with the hypothesis that the morphology, behavior, and distribution of this species reflect both ultimate and proximate effects of competition in both its wintering and breeding communities.

At eight sites throughout its winter and summer range, the densities and foraging characteristics of the redstart and other species in the guild of small flycatching/foliage-gleaning birds to which it belongs were quantified. From these data, redstart niche breadth and redstart niche overlap with the rest of the guild were calculated for each site. To interpret the significance of niche overlap, a technique originally suggested by Sale (1974) was used to compare the observed value of redstart overlap in each area with the expected distribution of this value among comparable, but randomly associated (and hence, competition-free), hypothetical species.

In summer sites, redstart density and redstart niche breadth were both inversely correlated with the ecological similarity (an index based on morphological and behavioral criteria) of the other species in its guild. In winter sites, redstart niche breadth, but not density, was inversely correlated with guild similarity. Total overlap in resource use between the redstart and other species was lower in the winter than in the summer, primarily because redstart densities at this time were lower. The observed overlaps of breeding

RESÚMEN

Esta investigación es un análisis del papel de competición interspecífica en la ecología de la candelita (*Setophaga ruticilla*), una especie común y extendida de ave migratoria neotropical. La evidencia obtenida, aunque indirecta, es consistente con la hipótesis de que la morfología, el comportamiento, y la distribución de esta especie reflejan efectos últimos y próximos de competición en sus comunidades de verano y también de invierno.

En ocho sitios en todas partes de su alcance, las densidades y características de forrajear de la candelita y otras especies en su gremio de papamoscas y espigadoras de follaje pequeñas estuvieron quantificadas. Con estos datos, la anchura del nicho de la candelita y la coincidencia del nicho de la candelita y de los nichos del resto del gremio estuvieron calculadas para cada sitio. En interpretando el significado de la última, una técnica sugerida originalmente para Sale (1974) estuvo empleada para comparar lo que estuvo observada en cada área con la distribución esperada de esta variable entre unas especies hipotéticas que eran comparables, pero asociadas al azar (y por tanto sin competición).

En los sitios de verano, la densidad y la anchura del nicho de la candelita eran las dos correlacionadas negativamente con la semejanza ecológica (un indice basado en criterios morfológicos y comportamentales) de las otras especies en su gremio. En los sitios de invierno, la anchura del nicho de la candelita, si no la densidad, era correlacionada con la semejanza del gremio. La coincidencia en uso de recursos entre la candelita y otras especies era menos en el invierno, prin-

redstarts were generally higher than what would be expected among randomly associated species; winter overlaps were generally lower than randomly generated overlaps. Although these trends were not statistically significant, the redstart niche is significantly more divergent from other species' in nonbreeding than in breeding communities.

Despite the evidence that the redstart experiences competition in both winter and summer situations, winter competition seems to have been more intense in both ecological and evolutionary time. The greater displacement of the redstart niche away from those of other species in its guild in winter, in conjunction with lower total overlap then, suggests that the limits to similarity between this species and those with which it coexists are greater during this season. Moreover, redstarts' flycatcher-like beaks seem most closely adapted to their winter foraging behavior: at this time, they hawk significantly more often than in summer.

cipalmente porque la densidad de la candelita era menos en este tiempo. Las coincidencias de nichos observadas de candelitas engendrandas eran en general más grande de lo que se esperaría entre especies asociadas al azar; las del invierno, menos. Aunque estas tendencias no eran significantes estadísticamente, el nicho de la candelita está significantemente más divergente de los de otras especies en comunidades invernales que en comunidades de verano.

A pesar de la evidencia que la candelita experimenta la competición en invierno y también en verano, la competición del invierno parece haber sido más intensa en tiempo ecológico y evolutivo. La desalojamiento más grande del nicho de la candelita de los de otras especies en su gremio en invierno, en conjunción con menos coincidencia de nicho luego, sugiere que los límites de semejanza entre esta especie y las con que coexiste son más grandes durante este tiempo. Además, los picos anchos y aplanados de las candelitas parecen adaptados más precisamente para su manera de forrajear en invierno, cuando se comportan más como papamoscas.

Sara E. Benne

Introduction

The American Redstart (*Setophaga ruticilla*) is a common, widely-occurring, migratory warbler which has been implicated in competitive interactions with other species in both winter and summer. Sherry (1975), for instance, attributed the frequent interspecific aggression between breeding redstarts and Least Flycatchers (*Empidonax minimus*) to competition. Morse (1973), in another breeding season study, noted that redstarts and Yellow Warblers (*Dendroica petechia*) maintain largely exclusive territories on small islands along the Maine coast and also suggested the possibility that the redstart's presence in coniferous forests may be restricted by competition from spruce-woods warblers. Observers of wintering birds have reported that competition may exist between the American Redstart and the Slate-throated Redstart (*Myioborus miniatus*) in Colombia (Chipley 1974) and, in some habitats in Puerto Rico, between it and a tody (*Todus mexicanus*, Kepler 1972). Lack and Lack (1972) stated that the wintering redstart in Jamaica has an "obviously different ecological niche from any other species," and in general felt that "competitive exclusion operates in the winter quarters (of the wood warblers)." This study was undertaken in an attempt to provide a more detailed and comprehensive analysis of the role of interspecific competition in both these seasons in the ecology of the American Redstart.

Interspecific competition among birds is difficult to demonstrate convincingly, for their populations do not lend themselves to controlled field experiments of the sort urged by Connell (1975). However, the hypothesis that interspecific competition is, or has been, an important factor in the population dynamics of a species can be tested indirectly by comparing patterns observed in natural systems with those predicted on the basis of competition theory. According to the "compression hypothesis" (MacArthur and Wilson 1967; Schoener 1974a), a species' niche should contract as the competition for resources from other species intensifies. Therefore, the populations of a species competing for resources should be least dense and most specialized in communities where the resource exploitation patterns of other species are most similar to its own. Over evolutionary time, competition among species should select for divergence among them in resource use, ultimately leading to an overdispersion of niches in niche space (Sale 1974; Schoener 1974b; Cody 1974). For instance, in a competitively structured community with a single relevant resource axis, species' utilization frequencies along that axis should be regularly spaced, with a minimum of overlap. Under these circumstances, the resource overlap observed between one species and the rest of the community will be lower than would have been predicted assuming random interactions.

My interpretation of the significance of interspecific competition to the American Redstart is based upon a comparison of this species' density, niche breadth, and niche overlap in a set of eight sites throughout its winter and summer ranges. I predicted specifically that if interspecific competition were important to the redstart in a given season, then: 1) redstart density at that time would be inversely related to the degree of potential competition from species with similar resource requirements; 2) redstart niche breadth at that time would be inversely related to the degree of potential competition; 3) the total resource overlap between the redstart and other species at that time would be lower than would be expected to result from random species interactions.

Methods

The American Redstart.

The American Redstart breeds in deciduous forests from southern Alaska to Newfoundland south to southeastern Oklahoma, central Georgia and southeastern Virginia. It winters from Mexico and the Greater Antilles to northern Peru and Brazil (A.O.U Check-list 1957; figure 1).

Redstarts are small, abundant, and conspicuous forest-dwelling parulids, which forage primarily by hawking after flying insects (figure 2), by hovering to pick them from leaf surfaces, and by gleaning them from leaves. They are apparently totally insectivorous at all times of year (Wetmore 1916; McAtee 1926). During the breeding season, pairs share defended territories; in winter, territories (or non-overlapping home ranges) are maintained by each individual (pers. obs.; Chipley 1974). They undergo a postnuptial molt in midsummer and apparently do not normally molt in winter (Bent, 1953).

Study Areas

Over a two-year period from 1975–77, I made detailed observations of the American Redstart and similar species at widely separated points throughout its range. The breeding communities I studied were located in northern New Hampshire, in the Hubbard Brook Experimental Forest (1975); in Maryland, in the Patuxent Research Refuge of the U.S. Fish and Wildlife Service (1976); in Campbell County, Tennessee, near Elk Valley (1975); and in Pend'Oreille County, Washington, near Sullivan Lake (1976). My observations at these sites were made during the

Figure 1. Summer (dashes) and winter (dots) ranges of the American Redstart and study site locations. (See table 1 for code to site name abbreviations.)

nestling and fledging stages of the redstart reproductive cycle, when its energetic demands are at an annual maximum. I observed wintering redstarts during January and February, when their energy needs are probably minimal. The nonbreeding communities in which I worked were in northeastern Puerto Rico, on the Roosevelt Roads U.S. Naval Station (1977); in Chiapas, Mexico near the town of Palenque (1976); and on the island of Grand Cayman, B.W.I. (1975).

All of the four-hectare study plots in which I gathered data were in "good redstart habitat," where the species was locally abundant, although the vegetation in each area was quite different. Beech (*Fagus grandifolia*), sugar maple (*Acer saccharum*), and yellow birch (*Betulea lutea*) dominate the northern hardwoods forest in New Hampshire (See Siccama et al 1970 and Bormann et al 1970 for detailed descriptions of the Hubbard Brook Forest). The bottomland forest on the Patuxent River floodplain in Maryland is a diverse association including beech, white ash (*Fraxinus americana*), tulip tree (*Liriodendron tulipifera*), American elm (*Ulmus americana*), sweet gum (*Liquidambar styraciflua*), and tupelo (*Nyssa aquatica*) (Hotchkiss and Stewart

1947). The Tennessee study area was in a mixed deciduous forest in which sugar maple, shagbark hickory (*Carya ovata*), and Ohio buckeye (*Aesculus glabra*) were dominant. On the floodplain of Noisy Creek, where I worked in Washington, the forest stand consisted of black cottonwood (*Populus trichocarpa*), quaking aspen (*Populus tremuloides*), white birch (*Betula papyrifera*), and alder (*Alnus* sp.).

The Mexican plot was in a tropical lower montane rainforest (Breedlove 1973) which had been selectively logged. Two of my study sites, one in Puerto Rico and one on Grand Cayman, were in virtually monospecific stands of black mangrove (*Avicennia nitida*). Logwood (*Hematoxylon compechianum*), thatch palm (*Thrinax argentea*), and red birch (*Bursera simaruba*) dominate the secondary scrub woodland in which I established another study area on Grand Cayman. Johnston (1975) provides a more complete description of the latter.

The foliage height profiles of these habitats, illustrated in figure 3, were calculated according to the methods outlined by MacArthur and Horn (1969). The foliage profile of Hubbard Brook is based on the similarly obtained data of Sherry (1975).

The Flycatching/Foliage-Gleaning Guild

The species most likely to represent direct and important competition to the redstart are those whose behavioral and morphological characteristics, and hence resource requirements, are most similar to the redstart's. Because the time available for data gathering was limited, I decided to limit the scope of this investigation to an analysis of the relationships between the redstart and the other members of its guild (Root 1967), which I term the "small flycatching/foliage-gleaning guild," and which includes other canopy warblers (Parulidae, Sylviidae) and small tyrannid flycatchers in the genera *Empidonax* and *Elaenia*. Larger tyrannids (e.g. *Myiarchus*, *Tyrannus*), vireos (Vireonidae), tanagers (Thraupidae), and grosbeaks (Fringillidae) which co-occurred with the redstart in the forest canopy were excluded from this guild on the basis of their size. My conclusions are thus dependent on the validity of the implicit assumption that diffuse competition from these larger species and from irregularly occurring birds is relatively unimportant.

Field Techniques

From about sunrise to noon each day, I mapped in detail the movements of redstarts and other guild members throughout the study area, which was marked in a 25-m² grid, and dictated into a portable tape recorder my observations of their foraging activities. For each foraging act, type of maneuver, sub-

Sara E. Bennett

Figure 2.   The American Redstart. (Illustration by Sara E. Bennett.)

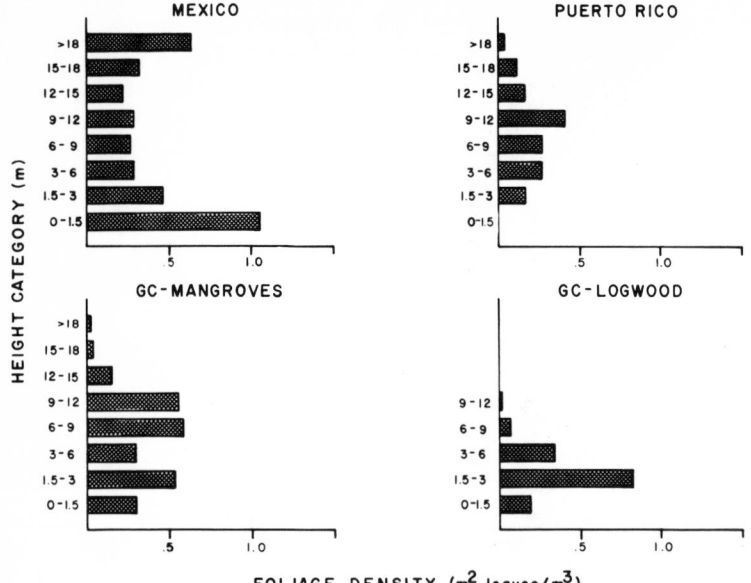

Figure 3a. Foliage height profiles of winter study sites.

Figure 3b. Foliage height profiles of summer study sites.

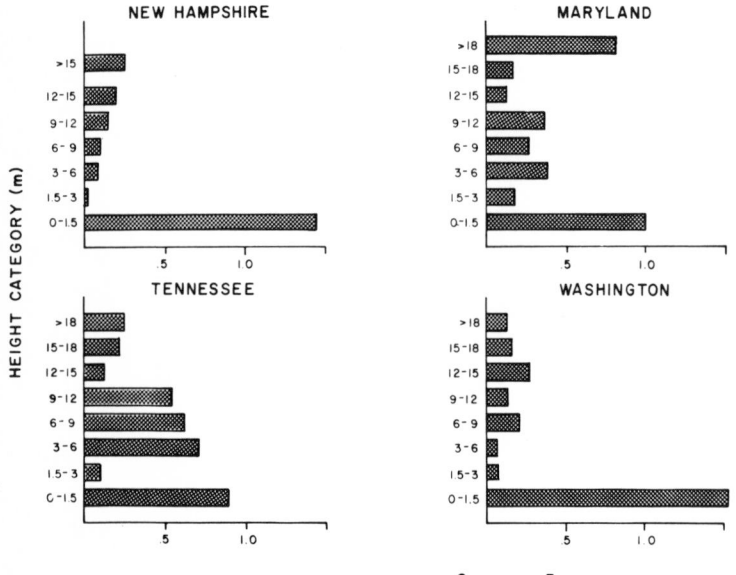

strate to which it was directed, and the estimated height at which it took place were noted. I distinguished seven log-scaled height intervals: 0–1 ft, 2–4 ft, 5–9 ft, 10–18 ft, 19–35 ft, 36–67 ft, 68+ ft (0–.3 m, .6–1.2 m, 1.5–2.7 m, 3.0–5.5 m, 5.8–10.7 m, 11.0–20.4 m, 20.7+ m).

During the breeding season, I determined species' densities from extensive observations of countersinging males and from nest locations. Winter densities were more difficult to calculate; my estimates are based on

cumulative observations of the movements of individual birds, on simultaneous observations of more than one individual of the same species, and, particularly for redstarts, on individual plumage characteristics which I could recognize.

Calculations

Redstart niche breadth was calculated for each area using Levins' (1968) index of niche width, $B = \Sigma_i (p_i^2)^{-1}$, where p_i is the proportion of observations in category i. Maneuver-substrate niche breadth and foraging-height niche breadth were calculated separately and standardized as fractions of their maximum possible values and, on the assumption that each of these represents an independent, equally important component of foraging behavior, these fractions were summed as an index of total niche breadth. (On this scale, niche breadth thus ranges from 0–2.)

Following Cody (1974), I have regarded niche overlap as the probability that members of two species are using the same resources. The index I used to measure overlap is similar to that described by him as "product alpha," the product of the separate probabilities of their joint use of horizontal space, of vertical space, and of food resources. Since there were no significant correlations among these component values, the assumption that they represent orthogonal axes seems justified.

Despite our common definition of overall niche overlap, I have defined each component of this index differently from Cody. Horizontal overlap represents here the probability of simultaneous occurrence of an individual of each species in a 25 m × 25 m quadrat (assuming that an individual is equally likely to be anywhere on its territory). Unlike Cody's analogous index, this one is a function of species' densities, as well as of the amount of area they use in common. Measured in this way, the horizontal overlap of two species which share a given area at low densities is less than would obtain if they shared the same area at higher densities. I define vertical overlap between species as the probability of their simultaneous occurrence in the same height interval, based on observed foraging height utilization patterns.

Food overlap between bird species is difficult to measure directly, not only for practical reasons but also because the appropriate criteria for identifying their food resources are not obvious. An insect in flight, for instance, may represent a different resource from the same insect at rest on a leaf. I have reasoned that the different tactics employed by foraging birds are correlated with the manner in which they perceive their resources; behavioral overlap, which I define as

Sara E. Bennett

the probability of simultaneous use of the same maneuver-substrate category, is therefore the index I have used to estimate species' overlap in prey type.

Prey size is probably another important factor determining bird diets. Hespenheide (1971) established that there is a linear relationship between the culmen length of flycatcher species and a log function of the size of their beetle prey ($Y = .028X + .384$; $Y = \log$ mean prey size, $X = $ culmen length). F-tests performed on his data indicated no significant differences among species in prey size variance (average variance = .038). (The equation and the variance were calculated from data in Hespenheide 1971.) Using this regression and published morphological information (Ridgway 1902, 1904, 1907), I constructed expected prey size utilization curves for each of the bird species I observed. My estimate of prey size overlap between the redstart and other species in its guild is a function of the area shared under the two utilization curves; it is defined as the probability that an insect eaten by either species is of a size acceptable to the other. Hence, my indirect index of overall food overlap is the product of behavioral and prey size overlap.

The number of species in the flycatching/foliage-gleaning guild in addition to the redstart varies throughout its range. Pianka (1974) has demonstrated the importance of the total group of interspecific competitors in determining patterns of niche dispersion in lizard communities; he assumed that "diffuse competition" (MacArthur 1972) was related to the number of species comprising a saurofauna. I have developed a more precise index with which to assess the resource use of the redstart in relation to the rest of its guild. "Total overlap," as I refer to this measure, represents the probability of simultaneous resource use by an individual redstart and an individual of any non-redstart species in the guild. It is defined as the sum of all pairwise overlaps between the redstart and each other guild member.

Guild similarity is defined as the probability of simultaneous use of a prey type and a height interval by a redstart and an individual of any other species in the area. It is calculated as the summation of height overlap multiplied by maneuver-substrate overlap multiplied by bill overlap between the redstart and each other species in the guild.

In order to interpret the significance of observed values of redstart total overlap, I computed for each site a set of synthetic guilds comprised of species with densities and niche breadths equivalent to those actually observed. These hypothetical species were designed to make use of resources without regard to the resource use of other species. They were created by randomly assigning observed values of species' proportional resource usages to the available resource states,

as suggested by Sale (1974). The frequency distribution of total overlap values calculated for the redstart from these synthetic arrays represents the expected distribution of this variate among randomly associated and, hence, competition-free species. (See Bennett (1978) for computer programs used.)

These randomly-generated overlap values were square-root transformed and the resulting normal distributions were standardized for comparison. Similarly transformed observed values of redstart overlap for each season were compared to the standard normal distribution by analysis of variance (Sokal and Rohlf, 1969) to test the hypothesis that they were less than could be expected in a competition-free situation.

Seasonal differences in redstart density, niche breadth, maneuver use, and total overlap were interpreted on the basis of analyses of variance. All references to correlations are based on the Spearman Rank Correlation Test (Siegel, 1956).

Results

Guild Descriptions

The habitat characteristics and species included in the small flycatching/foliage-gleaning guild at each of the eight areas are summarized in table 1. It is interesting to note that in the Mexican study site, this guild was comprised exclusively of migrant species, despite the high species diversity of other kinds of resident birds there.

The densities and foraging characteristics of these species are described by tables 2, 3, and 4. Table 5 summarizes the pair and total overlap values calculated on the basis of these observations between the American Redstart and the other members of its guild.

The Redstart Niche

There was a significant correlation between the density of breeding redstarts in the areas where I observed them and the similarity of the flycatching/foliage-gleaning guild in those areas (figure 4), which is consistent with Prediction 1. The presence and abundance of other species with comparable resource requirements may thus affect their summer dispersion directly, at least on a geographic scale. Habitat selection and distribution of redstarts on a local scale may also be influenced by the presence of other species. Howe (1974) and Ficken and Ficken (1967), for instance felt that second-year males are excluded from optimal breeding habitats by older individuals. Sherry's (1975) observation that the territories of these immature birds tended to overlap more extensively with those of Least Flycatchers suggests that the flycatchers adversely affect the quality of an area as perceived by redstarts.

Table 1a. Habitats and non-redstart members of the flycatching/foliage-gleaning guild in winter study areas[1]

Study area	Habitat	Guild members
Mexico (MEX)	Lower montane rain forest (disturbed)	Blue-gray Gnatcatcher (BGGN) Black-throated Green Warbler (GW) Hooded Warbler (HW) Least Flycatcher (LF) Magnolia Warbler (MW) Wilson's Warbler (WW)
Puerto Rico	Black mangrove swamp	Parula Warbler (PW) Yellow Warbler (YW)
Grand Cayman Mangroves (GC-M)	Black mangrove swamp	Caribbean Elaenia (E) Yellow Warbler (YW) Yellow-throated Warbler (YT)
Grand Cayman Logwood (GC-L)	Secondary scrub woodland	Blue-gray Gnatcatcher (BGGN) Cape May Warbler (CMW) Parula Warbler (PW) Vitelline Warbler (VW)

[1] Species names here and elsewhere are according to A.O.U Check-list (1957) and Bond (1971).

Table 1b. Habitats and non-redstart members of the flycatching/foliage-gleaning guild in summer study areas

Study area	Habitat	Guild members
New Hampshire (NH)	Northern hardwoods	Black-throated Blue Warbler (BW) Black-throated Green Warbler (GW) Least flycatcher (LF)
Maryland (MD)	Bottomland forest	Acadian Flycatcher (AF) Blue-gray Gnatcatcher (BGGN) Parula Warbler (PW)
Tennessee (TN)	Upland mixed deciduous	Acadian Flycatcher (AF) Blue-gray Gnatcatcher (BGGN) Cerulean Warbler (CW) Hooded Warbler (HW) Worm-eating Warbler (WEW)
Washington (WA)	Black cottonwood/quaking aspen	Traill's Flycatcher (TF) Yellow Warbler (YW) Yellow-rumped Warbler (AW)

In winter, there was also an inverse correlation between redstart density and guild similarity (figure 4), but it was not significant. These data thus do not support the hypothesis that the distribution of wintering redstarts is a function of competition from other species, but they are probably insufficient to conclusively reject it either, due to the small sample size (N = 4 sites) and to the uncontrolled and potentially confounding variables of island size and isolation, which may also influence the distribution of the redstart population at this time of year.

As shown in figure 5, redstart niche breadth was

Sara E. Bennett

Table 2a. Winter densities of the flycatching/foliage-gleaning guild[1]

	Birds/4 HA	# SQ Occupied	# SQ W/ RS
Mexico			
RS	4.0	52	—
BGGN	3.0	44	37
GW	0.5	7	5
HW	2.0	34	30
LF	1.5	29	28
MW	2.9	39	34
WW	1.6	17	16
Puerto Rico			
RS	7.0	46	—
PW	16.0	61	45
YW	16.0	61	44
GC-Mangroves			
RS	3.0	28	—
E	3.2	22	9
YT	1.0	10	7
YW	4.5	39	16
GC-Logwood			
RS	1.5	12	—
BGGN	1.0	8	3
CMW	2.0	17	4
PW	0.8	7	1
VW	2.0	18	6

[1] Each 4-ha study area consisted of 64,625-m^2 "squares" (SQ), which were scored for the presence or absence of each species. Horizontal overlaps were calculated on the basis of species densities and the number of such squares shared among them. (See table 1 for code to abbreviations of species names.)

Table 2b. Summer densities of the flycatching/foliage-gleaning guild[1]

	Birds/4 HA	# SQ Occupied	# SQ W/ RS
New Hampshire			
RS	13.0	52	—
BW	6.0	28	28
GW	4.0	30	27
LF	3.5	19	13
Maryland			
RS	8.5	49	—
AF	4.0	28	21
BGGN	2.5	23	22
PW	3.0	35	34
Tennessee			
RS	5.0	33	—
AF	4.0	26	12
BGGN	2.0	14	9
CW	4.5	21	15
HW	4.5	21	15
WEW	4.0	30	19
Washington			
RS	11.5	41	—
AW	2.5	16	13
TF	14.5	59	39
YW	5.5	23	6

[1] Each 4-ha study area consisted of 64,625-m^2 "squares" (SQ), which were scored for the presence or absence of each species. Horizontal overlaps were calculated on the basis of species densities and the number of such squares shared among them. (See table 1 for code to abbreviations of species names.)

negatively correlated with guild similarity during each season (winter: $r_s = -1.00$, $p = .05$; summer: $r_s = -1.0$, $p = .05$) and throughout the year as a whole ($r_s = -.86$; $p < .01$). In other words, redstart foraging behavior in both winter and summer appears to be directly influenced by the species composition of the communities in which it occurs. This is consistent with Prediction 2), suggesting that competition operates in both summer and winter.

An interesting seasonal difference emerges when the separate components of niche breadth are examined. In the summer, variation in redstart foraging-height niche breadth alone may account for the above pattern, for this variable was also negatively correlated with guild similarity ($p = .05$). In winter, however, maneuver niche breadth, but not foraging-height niche breadth, was negatively related to guild similar-

ity ($p = .05$). Height niche breadth was not related to total overlap in foraging height nor was maneuver niche breadth related to total maneuver multiplied by bill overlap in either season.

On the basis of these data, it thus appears that the population of the American Redstart is subject to competitive influences from other species in both breeding and wintering communities. In order to assess the relative intensity of this process at different times of year, I compared the breadth of the redstart niche, the similarity of the guilds, and the total overlap of the redstart with other species between seasons. There was no overall difference in niche breadth (figure 6) (or either of its subcomponents) or in guild similarity (figure 5) between winter and summer areas. However, the total overlap between redstarts and non-redstarts was significantly lower in nonbreeding than in breed-

Sara E. Bennett

Table 3a. Patterns of maneuver-substrate use by the fly-catching/foliage-gleaning guild in winter study areas[1]

	HK	HV-L	G-L	Nectar	Other	N
Mexico						
RS	.69	.26	.02	—	.02	164
BGGN	.41	.36	.08	—	.10	78
GW	—	.61	.32	—	.07	35
HW	.35	.15	.04	—	.27	96
LF	.18	.60	—	—	.18	65
MW	.09	.46	.28	—	.06	83
WW	.11	.59	.27	—	.02	106
Puerto Rico						
RS	.51	.36	.11	—	.02	246
PW	.01	.08	.87	—	.04	169
YW	.01	.38	.56	—	.03	109
GC-Mangroves						
RS	.45	.39	.05	—	.09	244
E	.09	.41	—	—	.09	88
YT	—	—	.38	—	.63	32
YW	.03	.17	.60	—	.15	114
GC-Logwood						
RS	.39	.50	.07	—	.04	112
BGGN	.43	.21	.21	—	.07	56
CMW	—	—	.26	.59	.15	78
PW	.03	.06	.82	.09	—	68
VW	.12	.25	.42	—	.12	170

[1] Abbreviations: Hk = Hawk; HV-L = hover at leaf surface; G-L = glean from leaf surface; N = total number of foraging maneuvers observed.

Table 3b. Patterns of maneuver-substrate use by the flycatchi[ng]/foliage-gleaning guild in summer study areas[1]

	HK	HV-L	G-L	Nectar	Other	N
New Hampshire						
RS	.35	.49	.05	—	.10	28
BW	.01	.53	.38	—	.06	11
GW	—	.52	.37	—	.11	9
LF	.16	.84	—	—	—	9
Maryland						
RS	.28	.58	.12	—	.01	16
AF	.08	.92	—	—	—	10
BGGN	.56	.28	.07	—	.05	6
PW	.02	.27	.69	—	—	9
Tennessee						
RS	.26	.56	.13	—	.06	17
AF	.05	.81	—	—	.09	4
BGGN	.56	.28	.07	—	.05	6
CW	—	.50	.50	—	—	4
HW	—	.67	.15	—	.19	6
WEW	—	—	.66	—	.34	8
Washington						
RS	.29	.59	.10	—	.02	15
AW	.12	.37	.33	—	.18	10
TF	.11	.81	—	—	.08	9
YW	.01	.38	.56	—	.03	11

[1] Abbreviations: Hk = hawk; HV-L = hover at leaf surface; G-L = glean [from] leaf surface; N = total number of foraging maneuvers observed.

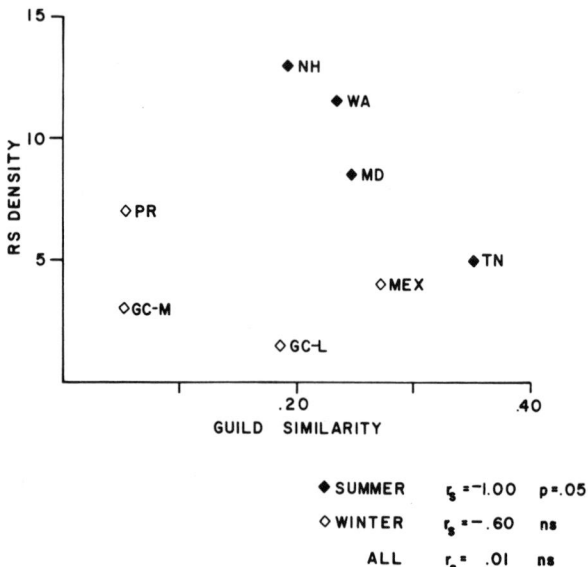

Figure 4. The relationship between redstart (RS) density and the similarity in resource use of co-occurring guild members in summer and winter.

ing communities (p = .05) (figure 7), which was probably due in large part to the significantly lower densities of this species in the winter sites (p = .06) (figure 8). This difference in density is due to the fact that wintering males and females are dispersed on individual territories whose average size is not significantly different from that of the breeding territories shared by two birds.

Baker and Baker (1973), Newton (1967), and Zaret and Rand (1971) also quantified and compared resource overlap between seasons within sets of ecologically similar species. Each of these studies found winter overlap to be less than that observed in summer. Because food was less abundant in winter, they all ascribed the low winter overlap to the effects of interspecific competition, implying that competition was less relevant to the structure of the summer communities. The energy demands of nonbreeding organisms are also lower, however. (For tropical migrants, for instance, Moreau (1972) has estimated that the energy used for self-maintenance, thermoregulation, and reproduction by a breeding bird may be equivalent to

Table 4a. Patterns of height-category use by members of the fly-catching/foliage-gleaning guild in winter study areas[1]

	0–1	2–4	5–9	10–18	19–35	36–68	>68
Mexico							
RS	—	.04	.09	.18	.47	.23	—
BGGN	—	.05	.10	.28	.36	.21	—
GW	—	—	—	—	.39	.61	—
HW	.15	.33	.48	—	.04	—	—
LF	.03	.06	.30	.21	.36	.03	—
MW	—	.12	.16	.31	.34	.07	—
WW	.07	.32	.42	.13	.06	—	—
Puerto Rico							
RS	—	—	.11	.10	.49	.30	—
PW	—	.05	.11	.17	.44	.24	—
YW	—	.17	.22	.17	.28	.17	—
GC-Mangroves							
RS	.03	.14	.17	.31	.34	.01	—
E	—	—	.14	.09	.55	.23	—
YT	.38	.63	—	—	—	—	—
YW	—	.11	.10	.22	.40	.17	—
GC-Logwood							
RS	—	.09	.05	.38	.48	—	—
BGGN	—	.04	.04	.11	.79	.04	—
CMW	—	—	—	.36	.59	.05	—
PW	—	—	—	.15	.85	—	—
VW	.02	.08	.43	.37	.10	—	—

Height (feet)

Table 4b. Patterns of height-category use by members of the fly-catching/foliage-gleaning guild in summer study areas

	0–1	2–4	5–9	10–18	19–35	36–68	>68
New Hampshire							
RS	.04	.11	.13	.22	.28	.23	—
BW	.05	.22	.16	.37	.20	—	—
GW	—	—	—	.11	.28	.61	—
LF	—	.01	.03	.06	.36	.53	—
Maryland							
RS	—	—	.03	.09	.49	.37	.02
AF	—	.04	.10	.29	.45	.12	—
BGGN	—	—	—	.09	.16	.53	.22
PW	—	—	—	.01	.10	.71	.18
Tennessee							
RS	—	.01	.01	.02	.55	.40	.01
AF	—	—	—	.24	.43	.33	—
BGGN	—	—	—	—	.03	.64	.32
GW	—	—	—	—	.36	.36	.29
HW	—	—	.34	.42	.24	—	—
WEW	—	.11	.31	.45	.14	—	—
Washington							
RS	—	.01	.06	.17	.26	.49	.01
AW	—	.02	.09	.11	.41	.38	—
TF	—	.04	.03	.11	.23	.56	.03
YW	—	.06	.18	.22	.34	.17	.03

Height (feet)

[1] See Table 3 for sample sizes.

roughly 1.6 times the energy sufficient to support the same bird on its wintering grounds.) Since overlap in resource use may indicate either the presence or absence of interspecific competition (Colwell and Futuyma 1971; Sale 1974), their explanations are plausible, but not definitive. To reduce this ambiguity, I examined redstart niche overlap in the context of the dispersion patterns of the redstart niche in winter and summer communities. Competition should select for divergence among species in characters relating to resource exploitation; the importance of competition should therefore be reflected in the extent to which species' niches are displaced from one another in the available niche space (Prediction 3).

At the traditional .05 level of significance, neither winter nor summer redstart overlaps are different from what would be expected among randomly associated species (figure 9; table 6). Nevertheless, there are trends which suggest that there may be a real seasonal difference in the way this species interacts with other guild members. The observed overlaps of breeding redstarts are generally higher than the randomly generated means (p = .17). Wintering redstarts, on the other hand, exhibited overlaps lower than the means of the random distributions (p = .11). The probability that observed winter and summer overlaps are from the same (statistical) population is .02. This apparently greater divergence of the redstart niche away from those of other species in its guild in winter sites, in conjunction with lower overall overlap in winter, suggests that this is the season in which the redstart may be most affected by the presence and behavior of other species. In other words, the limits to similarity between the redstart and the species with which it coexists appear to be greatest at this time of year.

Discussion

Many studies of avian communities have implied that interspecific competition is likely to be an important

Table 5a. Redstart overlaps with other species of the flycatching/foliage-gleaning guild in winter study areas[1]

	Horizontal	Bill	MNVR	Height	Total (X 10⁻¹)
Mexico					
BGGN	.05	.86	.38	.28	.046
GW	.01	.86	.17	.32	.005
HW	.03	.79	.28	.08	.005
LF	.03	.79	.28	.24	.016
MW	.05	.96	.19	.25	.023
WW	.03	.94	.23	.10	.006
Non-RS					.101
Puerto Rico					
PW	.26	.81	.13	.32	.088
YW	.25	.74	.14	.23	.060
Non-RS					.148
GC-Mangroves					
E	.05	.66	.20	.24	.016
YT	.02	.84	.01	.09	.0002
YW	.07	.75	.11	.24	.014
Non-RS					.030
GC-Logwood					
BGGN	.03	.86	.29	.43	.032
GMW	.04	.88	.02	.42	.003
PW	.01	.81	.10	.47	.004
VW	.06	.74	.20	.22	.020
Non-RS					.059

[1] See text for explanation.

Table 5b. Redstart overlaps with other species of the flycatching/foliage-gleaning guild in summer study areas

	Horizontal	Bill	MNVR	Height	Total (X 10⁻¹)
New Hampshire					
BW	.12	.92	.28	.18	.056
GW	.07	.86	.27	.24	.039
LF	.05	.79	.47	.24	.045
Non-RS					.140
Maryland					
AF	.06	.62	.56	.29	.060
BGGN	.05	.86	.33	.29	.041
PW	.06	.81	.25	.33	.040
Non-RS					.141
Tennessee					
AF	.06	.62	.47	.37	.065
BGGN	.04	.86	.36	.28	.035
CW	.10	.85	.35	.34	.101
HW	.08	.79	.39	.14	.035
WEW	.08	.53	.09	.09	.003
Non-RS					.239
Washington					
AW	.05	.81	.29	.32	.038
TF	.23	.62	.51	.36	.262
YW	.03	.85	.28	.22	.016
Non-RS					.316

Table 6. Observed values of square root-transformed total redstart overlap in comparison with the distributions of randomized values of this variate for each site

	Observed	Random $\bar{X}$	Standard deviation
MEX	.1005	.1121	.0149
PR	.1217	.1529	.0328
GCM	.0550	.0638	.0174
GCL	.0768	.0833	.0257
NH	.1183	.1285	.0297
MD	.1187	.0968	.0230
TN	.1546	.1331	.0355
WN	.1778	.1279	.0307

structuring force only during the season in which resources limit population growth (Lack 1944; Lack 1966; Fretwell 1972). Because of the qualitative, as well as quantitative changes in the relationship between birds and their resources in different seasons, however, it is not paradoxical to find evidence of competitive interactions in both breeding and nonbreeding situations. Survival is the currency of a bird in winter; a breeding bird's fitness depends not only on its survival, but also on its fecundity. Consequently, an individual's energetic "goals" are likely to be seasonally asymmetrical. While a wintering bird needs only to meet its fixed maintenance costs, a breeding bird should maximize its energy intake in order to maximize the number of surviving young it contributes to the next generation. Thus any decrease at all in the foraging efficiency which results from the presence of another species can be interpreted as competition in the breeding season, even if the population as a whole is limited by winter resources. In contrast, a decrease in foraging efficiency in the nonbreeding

Sara E. Bennett

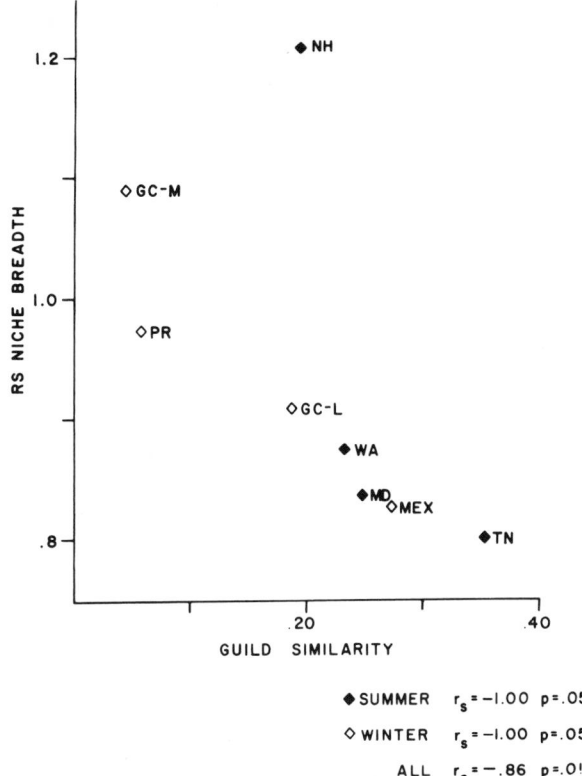

Figure 5.   The relationship between redstart niche breadth in summer and winter sites and the similarity of co-occurring guild members.

season, even if due to the presence of another species, can be interpreted as competition only when it jeopardizes an individual's probability of survival (figure 10). Where nonbreeding individuals are subject to predation during feeding, as may obtain for some wintering shorebirds (Page and Whitacre 1975; E. Mallory, pers. comm.), birds whose populations are regulated by summer resources and which appear to be in the midst of plenty could actually be undergoing intense competitive pressure. Depending on the abundance, distribution, and nature of its resources at different times of year, the extent of simultaneous demand for these resources, and the intensity of predation to which it is exposed during feeding, a species may thus experience interspecific competition in both breeding and nonbreeding seasons, in the breeding season only, in the non-breeding season only, or in neither season.

The evidence presented here for the American Redstart, which seems to place this species in the first category, can be most coherently interpreted if its population is winter-limited. Redstarts are, in general, more widely dispersed and more different from the species with which they coexist at this time than when they breed. Moreover, the apparent absence of signifi-

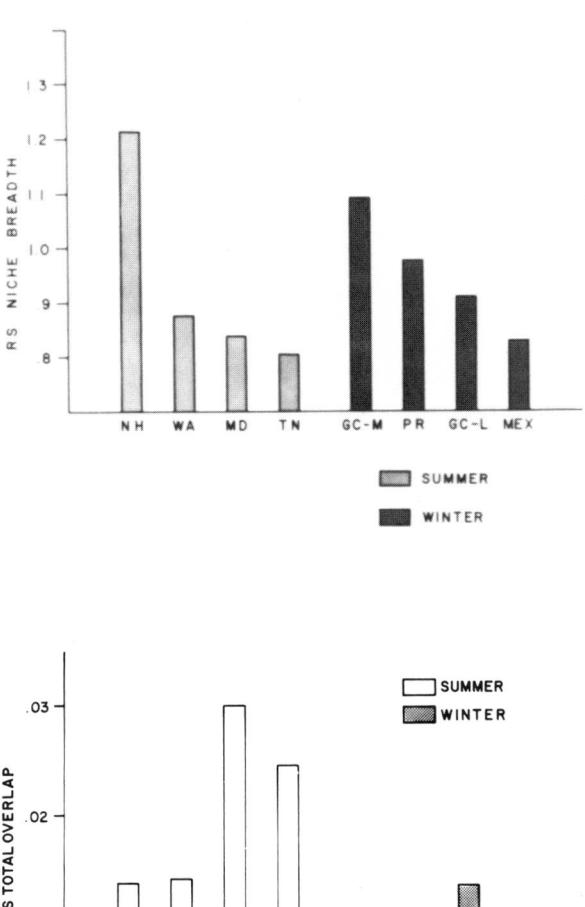

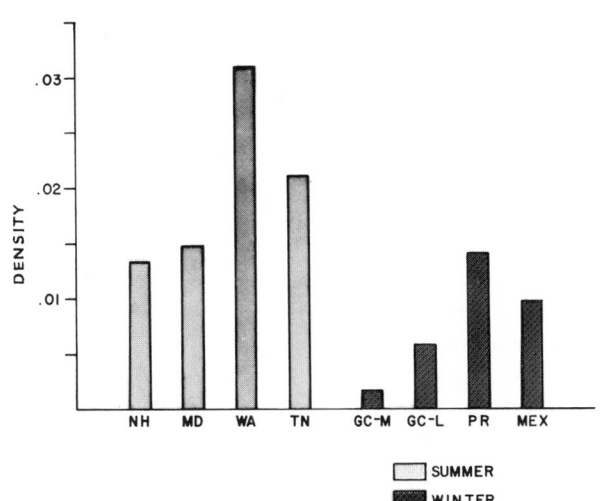

Figure 8.   Redstart density (numbers/4 ha) in summer and winter sites.

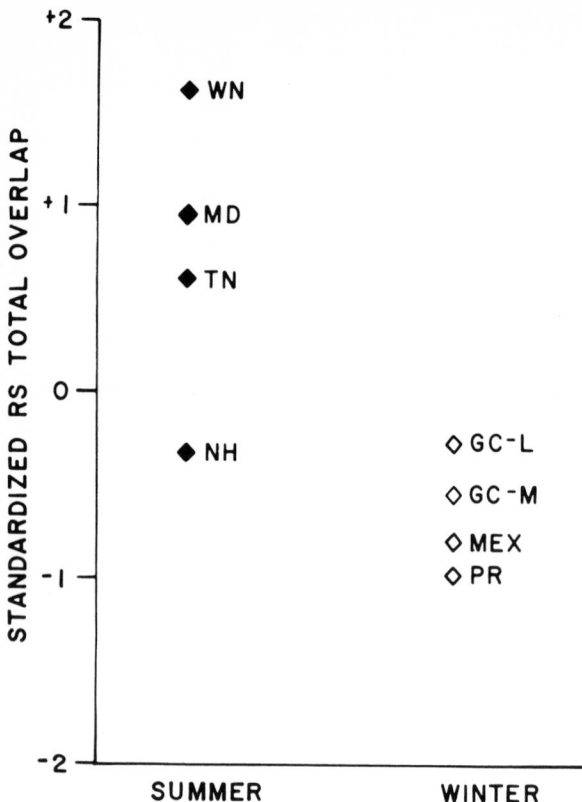

Figure 9. Observed redstart total overlap in comparison with the distribution of this variate in randomly generated guilds for each site.

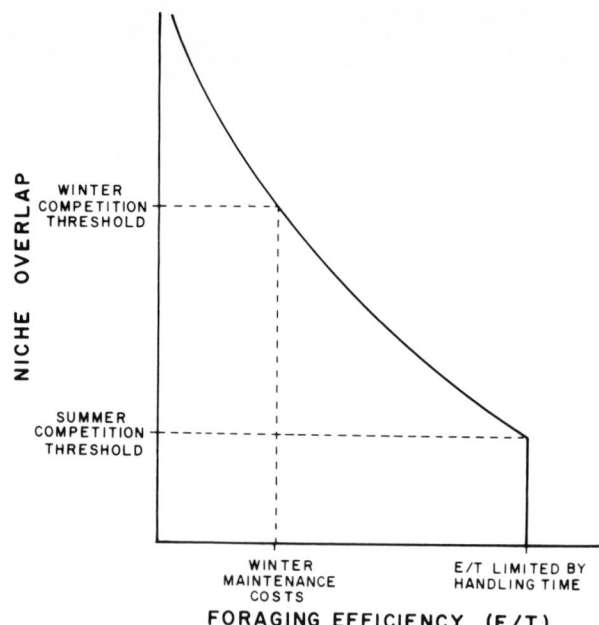

Figure 10. Competition as a function of an individual's energetic "goals." Interspecific competition in the winter (if predation is not a factor) will occur only when the presence of another species causes an individual's foraging efficiency (energy gained/unit time or E/T) to fall below the level necessary to meet its maintenance requirements. Any such decline for an energy-maximizing, breeding bird, represents interspecific competition, however.

cant displacement of the redstart niche away from those of other species in its guild in the summer, despite other evidence of direct competition, seems consistent with winter limitation. If the population persists below the potential carrying capacities of its summer habitats, as a result of regulation imposed elsewhere in time and space, interspecific competition may never become sufficiently intense to favor niche displacement.

Although Sale (1974) discussed niche dispersion in terms of evolutionary time, the actual extent of the resource overlap that I recorded between the redstart and the species with which it coexists can probably be accounted for in large part by its behavioral plasticity. To illustrate, observations by Holmes et al (1978) demonstrated that the foraging behavior of redstarts can change in the course of just a few hours in apparent response to changes in the numbers of flying insects. Because it is a flexible and opportunistic species, the variance in redstart niche breadth and niche overlap throughout its range thus most likely reflects proximate responses to local resource conditions on the part of individual birds rather than inherent behavioral differences among redstart populations.

The degree to which a species is specialized or generalized, plastic or stereotyped in its behavior (Morse 1971) will, nevertheless, be a product of selection over evolutionary time and will be subject to certain morphological constraints. Since most morphological characters cannot change on a seasonal basis, they must therefore represent the optimal compromise between winter and summer adaptations (Levins 1968; Wilson, 1975). A bird's morphology may thus reflect the exigencies of that time of year when selection intensity has been strongest for precise adaptation to environmental conditions. Selander (1965), for example, hypothesized that sexual polymorphism in body size in birds is related to competition for breeding territories and, as a result, should be more common in species limited by breeding space. The tubular tongue of the Cape May Warbler (*Dendroica tigrina*, Gardner 1925) and the conical beaks of finches seem, on the other hand, better designed to handle their winter resources of nectar (Table 3a; Lack and Lack 1972; Emlen 1973) and seeds, respectively. The wide, depressed bill and prominent rictal bristles of the redstart resemble the beak characters of the tyrannid flycatchers more than those of other parulids (figure 11),

Sara E. Bennett

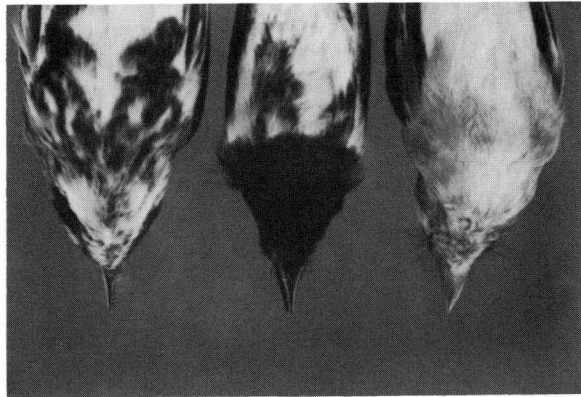

Figure 11. A comparison of the redstart beak (center) with the Least Flycatcher, a tyrannid flycatcher (right), and the Yellow-rumped Warbler (*Dendroica coronata*), another parulid warbler (left).

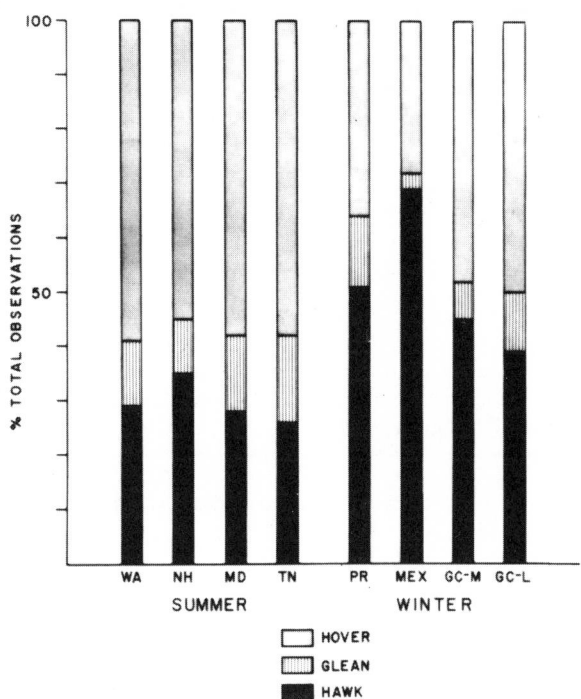

Figure 12. Frequencies of redstart foraging maneuvers in summer and winter sites.

implying that this species has been selected for efficient flycatching. An insect in flight, however, is probably a lower quality prey item than an equivalent, but stationary one, since it is most likely harder and more energetically expensive to capture. Morse's (1973) observation that unmated male redstarts in suboptimal habitats in Maine hawked significantly more often than successfully breeding males seems consistent with this conjecture. Wintering redstarts also hawk significantly more often than when they are breeding (p = .025) (figure 12). Winter conditions, including competition from other species, may thus have played a large role over evolutionary time in shaping this aspect of redstart morphology.

Conclusions

The evidence described above is indirect, but it is consistent with the hypothesis that the American Redstart, in its morphology, behavior, and distribution, reflects both ultimate and proximate effects of interspecific competition in both its wintering and breeding communities. Whether this is generally true for migratory birds is impossible to say at this point without further information on many more species. What is clear from this study of a single species, nevertheless, is that migratory birds, with their temporally, spatially, and energetically complex life cycles, pose tremendous practical and theoretical challenges to our current understanding of population and community dynamics.

Acknowledgments

The field work for this study was made possible by grants from the George D. Harris Foundation, the Frank M. Chapman Memorial Fund of the American Museum of Natural History, the National Science Foundation (to R. T. Holmes), and the Cramer Fund of Dartmouth College. The generous policy of the Kiewit Computation Center of Dartmouth College facilitated data analysis immeasurably.

I gratefully acknowledge the advice, encouragement, and guidance of Richard T. Holmes and John C. Schultz throughout all phases of this study. I am indebted to them and to W. Charles Kerfoot and Edmund W. Stiles for their critical comments on the Ph.D. thesis from which this paper is derived. My fellow graduate students, especially Thomas M. Frost, Elizabeth P. Mallory, and Philip J. Nothnagle, have helped and sometimes forced me to clarify the ideas presented here. I greatly appreciate the field assistance and moral support of my mother, Miriam L. Hoyt, in my Washington study site, the hospitality and advice of D. H. Morse and the staff of the Patuxent Research Refuge in Maryland, and the tremendous help of James W. Wiley in Puerto Rico.

My husband, Shaun M. Bennett, deserves my heartfelt thanks for all sorts of things that made this project possible.

Literature Cited

American Ornithologists' Union
1957. Check-list of North American birds, 5th ed. Baltimore, Md.: A.O.U.

Baker, M. C., and A. E. M. Baker
1973. Niche relationships among six species of shorebirds on their wintering and breeding ranges. Ecol. Monogr. 43:193–212.

Bennett, S. E.
1978. Interspecific competition and the niche of the American Redstart (*Setophaga ruticilla*) in wintering and breeding communities. Ph.D. thesis, Dartmouth College, Hanover, NH.

Bent, A. C.
1953. Life histories of North American wood warblers. Bull. U.S. Natl. Mus. 203.

Bond, J.
1971. *Birds of the West Indies.* Boston, Mass.: Houghton Mifflin.

Bormann, F. H., T. G. Siccama, G. E. Likens, and R. H. Whittaker
1970. The Hubbard Brook Ecosystem Study: Composition and dynamics of the tree stratum. Ecol. Monogr. 40: 373–88.

Breedlove, D. E.
1973. Phytogeography and vegetation of Chiapas (Mexico). In *Vegetation and Vegetational History of Northern Latin America*, ed. A. Graham, New York: Elsevier.

Chipley, R.
1974. Impact of wintering wood warblers on resident insectivorous passerines in Colombia. Ph.D. thesis, Cornell University, Ithaca, NY.

Cody, M. L.
1974. Competition and the structure of bird communities. Princeton, NJ.: Princeton Univ. Press.

Colwell, R. K. and D. J. Futuyma
1971. On the measurement of niche breadth and overlap. Ecol. 52:567–76.

Connell, J. H.
1975. Some mechanisms producing structure in natural communities: a model and evidence from field experiments. *Ecology and Evolution of Communities.* eds. M. L. Cody and J. Diamond. Cambridge, Mass.: Belknap

Emlen, J. T.
1973. Territorial aggression in wintering warblers at Bahama agave blossoms. Wils. Bull. 85:71–74.

Ficken, M. S. and R. W. Ficken
1967. Age-specific differences in the breeding behavior of the American Redstart. Wils. Bull. 79:188–99.

Fretwell, S. D.
1972. Populations in a seasonal environment. Princeton Univ. Monogr. in Population Biology. Princeton University Press, Princeton, NJ.

Gardner, L. L.
1925. The adaptive modifications and the taxonomic value of the tongue in birds. Proc. U.S. Natl. Mus. 67, 19: 1–49.

Hespenheide, H. A.
1971. Food preference and the extent of overlap in some insectivorous birds, with special reference to the Tyrannidae. Ibis 113:59–72.

Holmes, R. T., T. W. Sherry, and S. E. Bennett
1978. Diurnal and individual variability in the foraging behavior of American Redstarts (*Setophaga ruticilla*). Oecologia 36:141–49.

Hotchkiss, N. and R. E. Stewart
1947. Vegetation of the Patuxent Research Refuge, Maryland. Am. Midl. Nat. 38:1–75.

Howe, H. F.
1974. Age-specific differences in habitat selection by the American Redstart. Auk 91:161–62.

Johnston, D. W.
1975. Ecological analysis of the Cayman Islands avifauna. Bull. Fla. St. Mus. Biol. Sci. 19:235–300.

Kepler, A. K.
1972. A comparative study of todies (Aves, Todidae), with emphasis on the Puerto Rican Tody, *Todus mexicanus.* Ph.D. thesis, Cornell University, Ithaca, N.Y.

Lack, D.
1944. Ecological aspects of species formation in passerine birds. Ibis 86:260–86.
1966. *Population Studies of Birds.* Oxford, U.K.: Clarendon.

Lack, D. and P. Lack
1972. Wintering warblers in Jamaica. Living Bird 11:129–53.

MacArthur, R. H.
1972. *Geographical Ecology.* New York: Harper & Row.

MacArthur, R. H., and E. O. Wilson
1967. The theory of island biogeography. Princeton Univ. Monogr. in Population Biology.

McAtee, W. L.
1926. The relation of birds to woodlots in New York State. Roosevelt Wildlife Bull. 4:7–152.

Moreau, R. E.
1972. *The Palearctic-African Bird Migration Systems.* New York: Academic Press.

Morse, D. H.
1971. The insectivorous bird as an adaptive strategy. Ann. Rev. Ecol. Sys. 2:177–200.

Sara E. Bennett

1973. The foraging of small populations of Yellow Warblers and American Redstarts. Ecol. 54:346–55.

Newton, J.
1967. The adaptive radiation and feeding ecology of some British finches. Ibis 109:33–98.

Page, G., and D. F. Whitacre
1975. Raptor predation on wintering shorebirds. Condor 77:73–83.

Pianka, E. R.
1974. Niche overlap and diffuse competition. Proc. U.S. Natl. Acad. Sci. 71:2141–45.

Ridgway, R.
1902. The birds of North and Middle America. Bull. U.S. Natl. Mus. 50, part 2.

1904. The birds of North and Middle America. Bull. U.S. Natl. Mus. 50, part 3.

1907. The birds of North and Middle America. Bull. U.S. Natl. Mus. 50, part 4.

Root, R. B.
1967. The niche exploitation pattern of the Blue-Gray Gnatcatcher. Ecol. Monogr. 37:317–50.

Sale, P. F.
1974. Overlap in resource use, and interspecific competition. Oecologia 17:245–56.

Schoener, T. W.
1974a. The compression hypothesis and temporal resource partitioning. Proc. U.S. Natl. Acad. Sci. 71:4169–72.

1974b. Resource partitioning in ecological communities. Sci. 185:27–39.

Selander, R. K.
1965. On mating systems and sexual selection. Am. Nat. 49:129–41.

Sherry, T. W.
1975. Foraging behavior and niche relationships of breeding American Redstarts (*Setophaga ruticilla*) and Least Flycatchers (*Empidonax minimus*): the flycatcher guild in a New England hardwoods ecosystem. Master's thesis, Dartmouth College, Hanover, N. H.

Siccama, T. G., F. H. Bormann, and G. E. Likens
1970. The Hubbard Brook ecosystem study: productivity, nutrients, and phytosociology of the herbaceous layer. Ecol. Monogr. 40:389–402.

Siegel, S.
1956. *Nonparametric Statistics for the Behavioral Sciences.* New York: McGraw-Hill.

Sokal, R. H., and F. J. Rohlf
1969. *Biometry.* San Francisco: Freeman.

Wetmore, A.
1916. Birds of Porto Rico. U.S. Dept. Agr. Bull. 326.

Wilson, J. W. III
1975. Morphologic change as a reflection of adaptive zone. Amer. Zool. 15:363–70.

Zaret, T. M., and A. S. Rand
1971. Competition in tropical stream fishes: support for the competitive exclusion principle. Ecol. 52:336–42.

ROBERT B. WAIDE
Department of Zoology
University of Wisconsin
Madison, Wisconsin 53706

Resource Partitioning between Migrant and Resident Birds: The Use of Irregular Resources

ABSTRACT

Students of avian community ecology in the neotropics have suggested that wintering migrant birds avoid direct competition with resident species on their shared wintering ranges by focusing on under-exploited resources. Hypothetically, these resources are under-exploited because they occur in 1) mountaintop habitats too small to support year-round resident populations; 2) seasonal or unpredictably-shifting patches which sedentary resident birds cannot exploit; or 3) new habitat types to which residents have not yet adapted. The literature provides little support for the first and second hypotheses; data presented here from southeastern Campeche, Mexico, generally fail to support the predictions of the third. Mist-net samples of bird populations in old fields and mature forest stands reveal a positive correlation between migrant and resident abundance rather than the negative correlation predicted by the third hypothesis. In the 0–2 m level sampled by mist nets, both resident and migrant projected populations are greater in old fields than in forests. In old fields and disturbed forests, resident and migrant communities are dominated by one or two species while in less-disturbed forests species evenness is higher for both subsets of the avifauna. Ordination of the mist-net samples suggests that resident species discriminate more strongly between forests and old fields and between various stages of old field succession than do migrant species. The presence of resident species adapted to old field habitats in southeastern Campeche may be in part a result of the long history of human disturbance in the area. The proportion of migrants in

RESÚMEN

Autores anteriores han sugerido la hipótesis que las aves migratorias usan recursos que son irregulares en su distribución espacial ó temporal. Tres razones han sido propuestas para esta preferencia: 1) las aves migratorias escogen como habitat regiónes montañosas, pequeñas y aisladas dado que el número de aves residentes es relativamente escaso en estos habitats; 2) las aves migratorias, al ser más móviles, explotan recursos que son irregulares en tiempo (árboles frutales u hormigueros) más eficientemente que las aves residentes; y 3) las aves migratorias pueden explotar habitats alterados por el hombre antes que las aves residentes alcanzen a adaptarse a condiciones cambiántes. El siguiente resúmen de la literatura sugiére que las dos primeras hipótesis todavía deben ser adecuadamente comprobados. Datos obtenidos en México durante este estudio contradicen las prediccciónes de la tercera hipótesis.

En un estudio de la familia Parulidae en Jamaica, Lack y Lack (1972) descubrieron que las aves migratorias prefieron tierras bajas o de media altura a selvas montañosas. Los pocos datos que existen de Centro y Sud America no son suficientes para demonstrar un efecto claro de la elevación en la abundancía de las aves migratorias. Antes de hacer generalizaciones acerca de la relacion entre la abundancía de aves migratorias y elevación, más datos son necesarios.

Datos sobre las aves migratorias que utilizan frutas u hormiqueros sugieren que algunas especies pueden usar alimentos que son más abundantes en ciertas estaciones. Puesto que la may-

samples from Campeche forests is greater than reported from lowland rain forests in Central America. This latter result suggests that migrants may play a more important role in bird communities of tropical dry forests than they do in lowland rain forests, and that conclusions drawn from lowland forest studies may not apply to dry forest sites.

oría de las aves migratorias son insectivoras, dependen por lo tanto de alimentos que son relativamente escasos durante la temporada de Diciembre a Febrero.

La sugerencia que las aves migratorias móviles son más eficientes en explotar recursos presentes en pequeños espacios accidentales está basada en datos de un estudio aves sequidoras de hormigas en Panama (Willis 1966). Otra evidencia sugiere que tanto ambas aves migratorias y residentes usan la estrategía de migración local en condiciones apropriadas.

Datos de Campeche, Mexíco, contradicen la surgerencia que la competencia de las aves residentes relega a las aves migratorias a habitats alterados (Willis 1966). Muestreos de aves con redes en bosques y acahuales muestran que las aves migratorias usan ambos habitats alterados y naturales, y que la abundancía de aves migratorias y residentes aumenta en acahuales. En acahuales, una ó dos especies dominan ambas comunidades residentes y migratorias. Las especies residentes distinguen entre ellos. La diferencia entre estos resultados y los de otros estudios en Centro America sugiere que las aves migratorias tienen funciones diferentes en comunidades del bosque seco y húmedo.

La larga historia de perturbación humana en Campeche podría haber conducido a la acumulación de especies residentes adaptadas a acahuales. Situaciónes similares pueden existir en otras partes de Latinoamerica donde existieron grandes poblaciónes precolombianas.

Robert B. Waide

Introduction

Previous authors have hypothesized that birds that migrate to the neotropics during the north temperate winter utilize resources that are unpredictable or irregular in their spatial or temporal distribution (Willis 1966; Leck 1972; Karr 1976). Three reasons have been advanced for this preference: 1) small isolated habitats (such as might be found on mountain tops or in highland areas) that are irregularly spaced are selected by migrants because of the relative scarcity of resident birds, birds that spend the entire year in the tropics, (Willis 1966); 2) resources that are irregular in time and/or space (sporadically fruiting trees or swarming insects) result in local food superabundances that can be better exploited by mobile and opportunistic migrants than by residents; and 3) new habitats (especially man-disturbed areas), which are irregular on a greater time scale, can be exploited by migrants before residents have evolved adaptations to changing conditions (Willis 1966). Although the phenomena these hypotheses attempt to explain have received some empirical support in the literature, the hypotheses themselves have yet to be subjected to critical tests.

In particular, the idea that human disturbance of tropical habitats may have a neutral or positive effect on overwintering migrant populations (Buechner and Buechner 1970) deserves further attention because of its potential impact on conservation decisions. Disturbed areas are in general assumed to have low densities of resident birds and for this reason to present migrants with favorable competitive situations. Willis (1966) suggests that "migrants favor secondary successions, isolated patches of trees, and similarly disturbed areas where local species have not had time to move in or cannot do so because the available habitat is too small or too new a type." According to Willis' hypothesis, migrant and resident birds should respond differently to the appearance of new habitat types. Opportunistic migrants should behave like weeds, occupying and exploiting successional areas before residents become established. If this idea is correct, the distribution of migrants through a series of successional and stable habitats should be negatively correlated with resident density. Here I test this prediction by documenting the relative use of recently disturbed and relatively undisturbed habitats by resident and migrant birds in southern Campeche, Mexico.

Methods

From 1 February to 10 June 1973 I mist-netted various habitats in and around the archeological zone of Becan, in southeastern Campeche, Mexico. In 1974 (22 June–21 December) and 1975–76 (25 May–10 August; 26 December–18 January), I also worked in Becan, but my primary emphasis was in the archeological zone of Chicanna, 2 km to the southwest. Mist nets were employed for two purposes: 1) to conduct periodic censuses of the bird communities of different habitats and 2) to monitor breeding condition and stomach contents throughout the study. For censuses, I used standard 12-m NEBBA mist nets, alternating 30- and 36-mm mesh nets in a straight line along narrow lanes which had been cut through the vegetation near the center of each site. Each net sampled the space between 0–2 m above the ground. I opened the nets at dawn and closed them again just before dark. I sampled each area for seven consecutive rainless days or until the number of daily captures leveled off. To compare migrant and resident populations, I calculated projected population sizes for both migrants and residents from the regression of daily captures on cumulative captures (MacArthur and MacArthur 1974). This technique minimizes the bias resulting from differences in sampling period (Faaborg pers. comm.).

I marked each bird captured either with a colored plastic leg band or, in the case of hummingbirds, by clipping a tail feather. In addition, I recorded the time, location, and height at which the bird was captured, sex, condition of molt, amount of subcutaneous fat, breeding condition, and, when time permitted, the weight. I also measured body, wing, and tail length with a plastic ruler marked off in mm and bill length, breadth, and depth with calipers accurate to .1 mm.

Location and Ecological History of the Area

The archeological zone of Chicanna is located 7 km west of the village of Xpujil in the southeastern corner of the state of Campeche, Mexico (figure 1). The main body of ruins lies 700 m south of Federal Highway 186 and is connected to the highway by a dirt road. Becan, a more extensive zone of ruins, is located 2.5 km northeast of Chicanna (figure 2a). While areas adjacent to the highway are a mosaic of milpas and second growth resulting from the slash-and-burn agriculture practiced in the region, both archeological zones are part of the extensive forests which occur on either side of the highway.

Before Europeans arrived in the New World, the high population densities associated with the ancient Mayan civilization led to substantial deforestation on the Yucatan Peninsula. The rapid decline in indigenous populations that occurred following contact with the Spanish in the sixteenth century (Denevan 1976) allowed forests to regenerate over much of the Peninsula. Recent sources of habitat disturbance are varied.

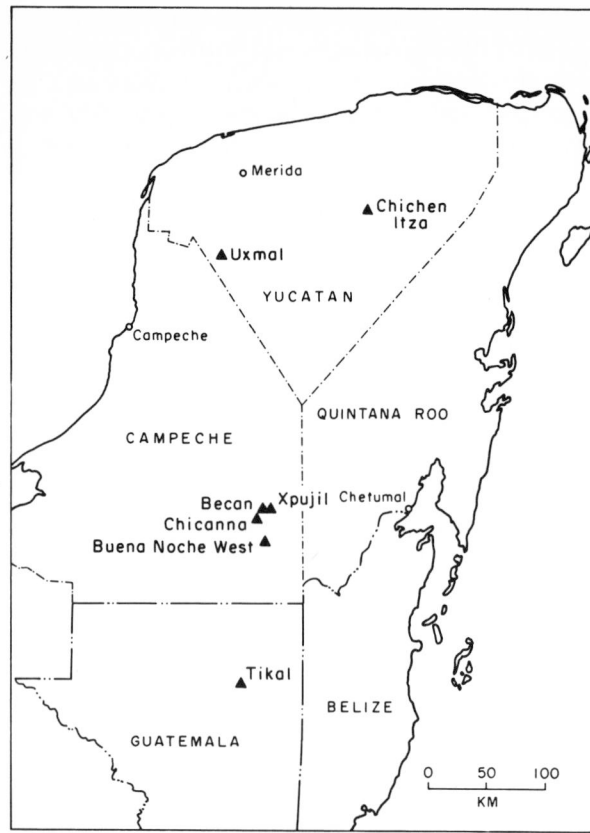

Figure 1.   Archeological zone of Chicanna, Yucatan.

Exploitation of the forests by lumber and chicle interests has caused extensive forest perturbation in the last half century. The result of this disturbance has been the almost complete removal of Spanish cedar (*Cedrela odorata*) and Honduran mahogany (*Swietenia macrophylla*) for lumber, selective removal of pucte (*Buidas buceras*) and guaya (*Talisia olivaeformis*) for railroad ties and the girdling and death of numerous sapote trees (*Manilkara achras*) in collecting the sap which is used to make chewing gum (Shepherd 1975). Although populations of shifting agriculturalists are sparse and localized in a few areas, the completion of Federal Highway 186 in 1972 and the resulting immigration into the Xpujil area have led to rapid clearing of land along the road for agricultural purposes.

Study Sites

Figure 2a shows five of the six sites sampled in the study. Sites labeled 1, 2, and 5 are areas of secondary succession lying directly east of Becan. All three areas were level with no standing or running water. Chicanna lies 2.7 km southwest of Becan, and Buena Noche West, the last site, is 22 km south of Xpujil (figure 1).

Old Field 1 (figure 2b) was an area which had been cleared of forest in early 1972 and cultivated from May to October of the same year. I sampled the site from 7–14 April 1973. The vegetation at that time (six months after abandonment) consisted mainly of weedy species interspersed with cornstalks and papaya (*Carica papaya* L.) and, except for several dead trees, was less than 2 m tall. The 8-acre (3.2 ha) site was surrounded on three sides by forest and is the most likely of the three successional habitats to suffer from an edge effect. The fourth side of the site bordered on an old field of undetermined age.

Old Field 2 (figure 2c) was an area which had been fallow for two years when I sampled its bird community. The dominant plant species was a composite (*Montonoa* sp.) which reached a height of over 2 m. Other common species included *Iresine celosia* L. (Amaranthaceae), *Elvira biflora* (Compositae), and *Viquiera dentata* (Compositae). The 10-acre (4 ha) site was bounded by a group of thatched houses to the south and the parapet surrounding the ruins of Becan on the west. A milpa lay to the north while Old Field 5 formed the eastern boundary. I sampled this study site between 19–26 April 1973.

The final successional area, Old Field 5 (figure 2d) was similar in structure to the "brambly association" described by Lundell (1937). The site, which had lain fallow for five years, contained a variety of thorny species including a bullhorn acacia (*Acacia* sp.). The vegetation was composed of small trees (<2 m) surrounded by a dense tangle of brush. A single dead tree occupied the center of the study area. Forest bordered the site on the north and east, and houses lined the southern edge. I sampled this 10-acre site on 19 April and from 23–28 April 1973.

The Mayan ruins of Becan (figure 2e, 2f) are the remains of a large Early Classic (ca A.D. 250–550) center of monumental architecture occupying a low flat hill. Within the 46 acre (18.6 ha) site, the remains of seven large ceremonial structures and their vegetative covering provide some relief in the otherwise level area. The medium subevergreen forest which currently occupies the area appears structurally intact except for a few small (.5 ha) clearings at the eastern edge of the site. As in other well-drained stands, *B. alicastrum* dominates the emergent layer, but Becan is unique in the domination of the canopy by *Croton lundelli* and in the relatively common occurrence of *Celtis trinervia* (Ulmaceae), *Hybanthus yucatanensis* (Violaceae), *Chlorophora tinctoria* (Moraceae) and *Astrocasia phyllanthoides* (Euphorbiaceae). The presence of this unique assemblage of canopy species is attributed to human disturbance within the last 20 years (Shepherd 1975).

Chicanna, a small Late Classic (ca A.D. 550–770)

center, consists of four groups of ruins surrounded by two-layered subevergreen forest (figures 2g, 2h, 2i). The emergent layer, between 12–20 m, includes *M. achras* and *B. alicastrum*, while *C. lundelli*, *D. laterifolia*, *Bursera simarouba* (Burseraceae), and *Thouinia paucidentata* (Sapindaceae) are the principal species forming a closed canopy at about 10 m. The understory is composed of saplings of the canopy species, and a sparse ground layer is present. Epiphytes and climbers are common and form dense tangles of vines at 2–4 m. The forest composition at Chicanna corresponds to that of dry-mesic sites along Shepherd's (1975) gra-

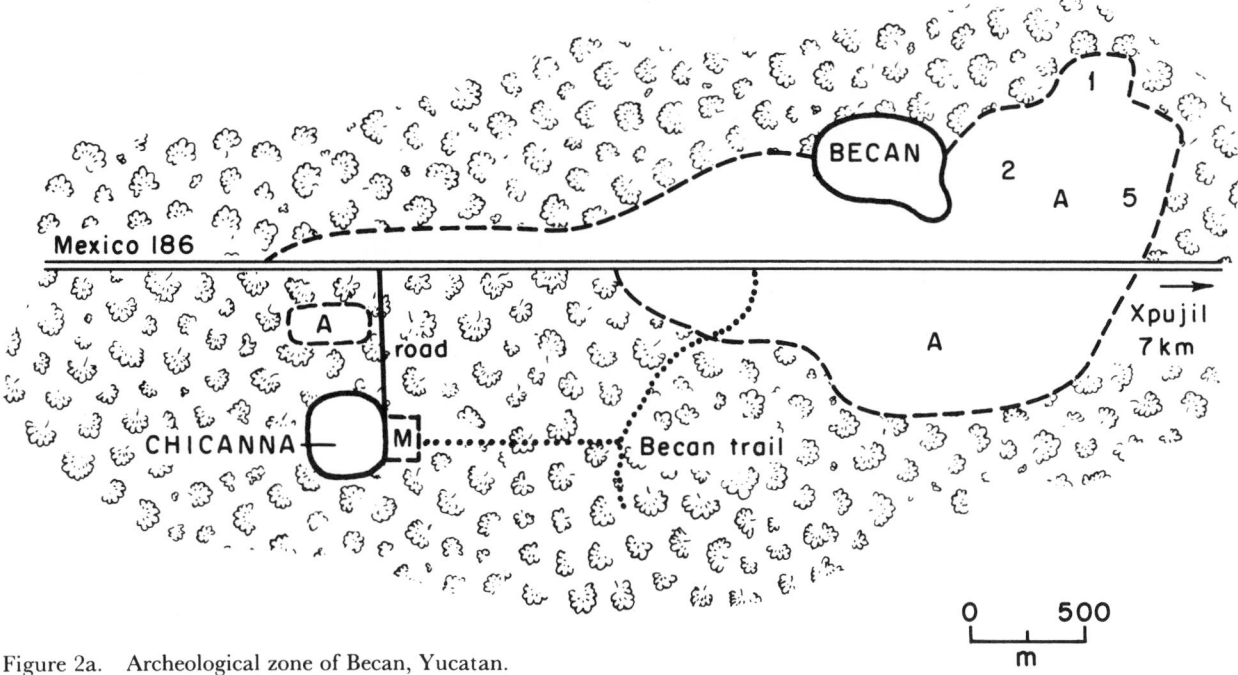

Figure 2a.   Archeological zone of Becan, Yucatan.

Figure 2b.   Old Field 1. A corn crop was harvested from this milpa 6 months before this picture was taken in April 1973, at the height of the dry season. Note the leafless appearance of the surrounding forest.

Figure 2c. Old Field 2. This field has been fallow for 2 years. The tall composite is *Montonoa* sp.; *Passerina cyanea*, *Volatinia jacarina*, and other granivores dominated the bird community.

Figure 2d. Old Field 5. Low, dense, thorny scrub occurs after a field has lain fallow for 5 years. Although *P. cyanea* was the most common migrant species in this habitat, *Vireo griseus*, *Dendroica petechia* and *D. magnolia* were also relatively abundant.

Figure 2e. Ruins of Becan (Structure IV, view from north). Compare the partially cleared section on the right with the unexcavated portion on the left. A dense cover of vegetation including tall trees makes many ruined structures unrecognizable from only a few meters.

Figure 2f. Archeological zone of Becan. Old Field 2 occupies the center of the picture. The Becan forest study site (including the partially-excavated Structure IV) can be seen on the right. (Photograph by John D. Shepherd)

Figure 2g. Chicanna study site. The forest has a dense, impenetrable appearance in the wet season.

Figure 2i. Ruins of Chicanna (Structure XX). The taller ruins provided good vantage points for observing canopy birds.

Figure 2h. Chicanna study site. During the dry season (Dec–May), much more light reaches the forest floor. Note the sapote tree (*Manilkara achras*) in the center of the picture which has been tapped for chicle.

dient, except for the presence of *C. lundelli*, a species more common on hilltops with ruins. The degree of human disturbance at Chicanna is relatively low. Topography is uniform and, as with Becan and Buena Noche West, there is no standing or running water. Although the Buena Noche West site was 23 km from the nearest settlement of any size, the area still showed some signs of disturbance by loggers, chicleros, and farmers. In addition, part of the 40-acre (16 ha) sample plot lay over the rubble of an ancient Mayan house or ceremonial mound. The sample plot was an area of medium subevergreen forest which contained two stands sampled in a concurrent phytogeographic study (Shepherd 1975). Both stands were level mesic to wet-mesic sites whose dominant emergent trees were *Manilkara achras*, *Pouteria unilocularis*, *Brosimum alicastrum*, and *Drypetes laterifolia*. While the predominant canopy species was *Nectandra salicifolia*, the common emergent species were also well represented in the canopy.

Climate

The dominant feature of the climate of the Yucatán Peninsula is the seasonal rainfall regime. Precipitation is least in the northwest corner of the peninsula and increases to the east and south. According to Garcia (1965), the Xpujil area lies in a zone of gradual transition from 1,200–1,300 mm of precipitation a year, but this classification may be modified as records accumulate from the center of the peninsula. The mean annual rainfall at Zoh Laguna, 8 km north of Xpujil, is 1,115 mm (based on 19 years of records). Comparison with data from Xpujil indicates high daily and annual variation in rainfall on a local geographic scale.

Eighty per cent of the precipitation on the Xpujil area is concentrated in the months May–October (figure 3a). The seasonal nature of the rainfall is enhanced by tropical storms which strike the peninsula from the southeast in late summer and fall bringing high winds and rain. Potential evaporation is greatest in March–June at the end of the long dry period (figure 3a), and the severe effects of this combination are evidenced by the dusty appearance of the uplands and the cracked earth of the seasonally-inundated bajos. The extreme annual fluctuation of May and June rainfall totals can result in the prolongation of the dry season, an event which occurred to different degrees in both 1974 and 1975 (figure 3b).

Results

The number of birds of each species in each of the eight samples is given in table 1. Sites with extensive human disturbance are on the left of the table, rela-

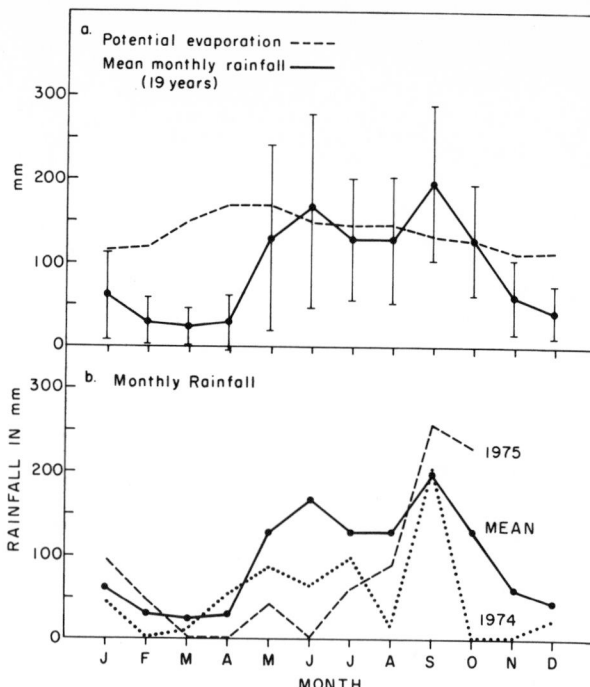

Figure 3. (a) Potential evaporation and mean monthly rainfall for 19 years. (b) Monthly rainfall during the present study.

tively undisturbed sites on the right. Note that the old fields were sampled during the spring migration while forest censuses were conducted both before and after migration. This difference in sampling period will tend to inflate the number of migrant captures in old fields relative to the number of captures in forest. However, the fact that the number of migrants captured per day decreases rapidly with the sample period suggests that transients composed a relatively small fraction of the spring samples (see discussion below and table 3). Moreover, the bias introduced by the difference in sampling date is conservative; it makes Willis' hypothesis more difficult to reject.

Table 2 summarizes estimates of the trappable population and records of the proportion, capture rate, and number of species of residents and migrants in each sample (in addition, a post-migration sample from Becan is included). Note in particular the following points:

1) Resident birds make up approximately half of the captures in old fields.

2) The number of resident species captured varies considerably between habitats, but is greatest in Old Field 5. The number of migrant species captured is about the same in all samples. Mist nets capture most of the species present in old fields, but in forest both resident and migrant species escape capture by forag-

Robert B. Waide

Table 1.   Composition of 8 samples from 6 study sites and several seasons in Southern Campeche, Mexico

Resident species[2]	Old Field 1	Old Field 2	Old Field 5	Becan Feb 1973	Becan Dec 1974	Chicanna Dec 1974	Chicanna June 1975	BNW[3] Mar 1973
Columbigallina passerina	0	0	1	0	0	0	0	0
C. minuta	0	1	0	0	0	0	0	0
C. talpacoti	0	10	2	0	0	0	0	0
Claravis pretiosa	1	0	0	0	0	0	0	0
Leptotila verreauxi	2	0	0	0	0	0	0	0
Geotrygon montana	0	0	0	3	0	0	0	0
Piaya cayana	1	0	0	0	0	0	0	0
Crotophaga sulcirostris	14	4	1	0	0	0	0	0
Glaucidium brasilianum	3	0	0	0	1	0	1	0
Campylopterus curvipennis	1	0	1	0	6	0	2	4
Chlorostilbon canivetii	0	0	4	0	0	0	0	0
Amazilia candida	0	0	1	0	0	0	0	2
A. yucatanensis	2	6	23	0	0	0	2	0
Trogon citreolus	0	0	0	0	0	1	0	0
T. violaceus	0	0	0	1	0	0	0	0
Piculus rubiginosis	0	0	0	0	0	0	0	1
Centurus aurifrons	1	0	0	0	0	0	0	0
Veniliornis fumigatus	0	0	0	0	0	2	0	0
Phloeoceastes guatemalensis	1	0	0	0	0	0	0	0
Dendrocincla anabatina	1	0	0	0	0	0	0	3
D. homochroa	0	0	0	0	0	11	2	2
Sittasomus griseicapillus	1	0	0	1	3	1	1	1
Dendrocolaptes certhia	0	0	0	0	0	0	0	1
Xiphorhynchus flavigaster	0	0	0	1	2	3	1	1
Thamnophilus doliatus	0	0	1	0	0	0	0	0
Pipra mentalis	0	0	3	1	1	0	0	0
Schiffornis turdinus	0	0	0	0	0	0	0	2
Attila spadiceus	0	0	0	1	3	1	0	2
Tyrannus melancholicus	0	0	1	0	0	0	0	0
unknown flycatcher	0	0	1	0	0	0	0	0
Myiozetetes similis	0	0	4	0	0	0	0	0
Pitangus sulphuratus	0	0	2	0	0	0	0	0
Myiarchus tuberculifer	0	0	1	0	0	0	0	0
Onychorhynchus mexicanus	0	0	0	0	1	3	0	4
Platyrinchus mystaceus	0	0	0	0	2	2	0	7
Rhynchocyclus brevirostris	0	0	0	0	0	0	0	2
Oncostoma cinereigulare	0	0	3	3	4	2	3	3
Myiopagis viridicata	0	0	1	6	0	0	0	3
Camptostoma imberbe	0	0	1	0	0	0	0	0
Pipromorpha oleaginea	0	0	1	0	0	0	0	0
Myiarchus spp.	0	1	3	0	1	0	0	0
Cissilopha yucatanica	0	0	2	0	0	3	0	0
Thryothorus maculipectus	1	3	2	0	0	1	0	3
Troglodytes musculus	4	0	0	0	0	0	0	0
Uropsila leucogastra	0	0	1	0	3	3	4	0
Polioptila plumbea	0	0	0	0	1	1	0	0
Hylophilus ochraceiceps	0	0	0	0	0	0	0	6

Table 1. (cont.)

Resident species[2]	Old Field 1	Old Field 2	Old Field 5	Becan Feb 1973	Becan Dec 1974	Chicanna Dec 1974	Chicanna June 1975	BNW[3] Mar 1973
H. decurtatus	0	0	0	0	0	0	1	0
Chamaethlypis poliocephala	0	0	0	1	0	0	0	0
Granatellus sallaei	0	0	0	0	1	3	2	1
Basileuterus rufifrons	0	1	0	0	0	0	0	0
Cassidix mexicanus	2	0	0	0	0	0	0	0
Icterus cucullatus	0	0	1	0	0	0	0	0
I. chrysater	2	0	1	0	0	0	0	0
Habia rubica	0	0	0	0	0	0	0	2
H. fuscicauda	0	0	2	0	0	4	1	6
Eucometis penicillata	0	0	0	0	0	6	0	0
unidentified	0	5	0	0	0	0	0	0
Saltator atriceps	2	0	0	0	1	0	0	0
Cardinalis cardinalis	0	3	0	0	0	0	0	0
Cyanocompsa parellina	4	0	4	30	5	2	3	3
C. cyanoides	0	1	0	0	0	0	0	0
Sporophila torqueola	0	3	6	0	0	0	0	0
Volatinia jacarina	0	147	17	0	0	0	0	0
Arremonops conirostris	1	1	8	3	1	6	2	4

Migrant species[4]

	Old Field 1	Old Field 2	Old Field 5	Becan Feb 1973	Becan Dec 1974	Chicanna Dec 1974	Chicanna June 1975	BNW Mar 1973
Archilochus colubris	4	0	2	0	0	0	0	0
Empidonax spp.	1	5	9	4	6	1	0	2
Dumetella carolinensis	0	7	3	4	0	0	0	0
Hylocichla mustelina	2	0	0	4	4	5	0	0
Catharus ustulatus	0	0	0	0	0	1	0	0
C. minimus	0	0	1	0	0	0	0	0
Vireo griseus	0	1	8	4	4	5	0	2
Mniotilta varia	0	0	1	3	4	1	0	4
Helmitheros vermivorus	0	0	0	0	1	0	0	1
Dendroica petechia	0	4	8	0	0	0	0	0
D. magnolia	2	0	9	3	3	3	0	7
D. virens	0	0	0	0	0	1	0	0
Seiurus aurocapillus	0	2	2	2	2	1	0	3
S. noveboracensis	0	0	3	1	0	0	0	0
Oporornis formosus	0	0	0	4	7	6	0	9
Geothlypis trichas	3	21	5	1	0	0	0	0
Icteria virens	0	1	0	0	0	0	0	0
Wilsonia citrina	1	0	1	3	1	3	0	4
Setophaga ruticilla	0	0	3	0	0	1	0	1
Vermivora pinus	0	0	0	0	0	1	0	0
Icterus spurius	0	30	0	0	0	0	0	0
Pheucticus ludovicianus	0	3	0	0	0	0	0	0
Passerina cyanea	37	164	44	22	2	0	0	1
P. ciris	1	14	2	1	0	0	0	0
Spiza americana	0	1	0	0	0	0	0	0

[1] Disturbed sites are on the left, stable sites on the right.

[2] Scientific names of resident species are from Eisenmann (1955).

[3] BNW = Buena Noche West.

[4] Scientific names of migrant species are from the A.O.U. Checklist of North American Birds, 5th edition (1957).

Table 2. Number of individuals and species captured and the capture rate of migrant and resident birds in 9 samples from Southern Campeche

	Old Field			Becan			Chicanna		BNW
	1 *Apr* *1973*	*2* *Apr* *1973*	*5* *Apr* *1973*	*Feb* *1973*	*Dec* *1974*	*June* *1974*	*Dec* *1974*	*June* *1975*	*Mar* *1973*
New Captures	95	441	202	108	74	3	80	26	96
Resident (%)	45	43	49	52	50	100	66	100	68
Migrant (%)	55	57	51	48	50	0	34	9	32
New capture/ net-day[a]	2.56	9.83	3.40	1.81	1.54	0.13	1.50	0.54	1.16
Residents/ net-day	1.09	3.75	1.35	0.73	0.77	0.13	0.96	0.54	0.83
Migrants/ net-day	1.47	6.08	2.05	1.08	0.77	0.00	0.54	0.00	0.33
Species	26	25	45	24	26	2	30	13	32
Resident	18	12	27	11	15	2	18	13	22
Migrant	8	11	15	13	11	0	12	0	10
Projected resident population[c]	5.2	30.6	20.8	[b]	3.6	—	6.1	3.9	4.2
Projected migrant population	9.1	30.3	10.1	7.6	4.2	—	3.4	—	3.1

[a] Based on total captures for four days of netting.

[b] Not presented because the number of captures/day increased over the first 4 days of netting. The reason for this phenomenon is not known.

[c] Individuals/net.

ing above the 0–2 m level. Transect counts in Becan revealed that 7 of the 20 migrant species (35 percent) and 23 and 34 resident species (68 percent) were never captured. In Buena Noche West, 4 of 14 migrant (29 percent) and 15 of 37 resident (41 percent) species were not captured. Hence, mist-net samples give a biased representation of forest species composition, inflating the ratio of migrant to resident species (Waide et al this volume). However, since most uncaptured resident species are relatively rare, the ratio of migrant to resident individuals is biased in the opposite direction; the proportion of migrant individuals is underestimated by mist nets (see 4 below).

3) Estimates of the trappable populations of both migrants and residents are higher in old fields than in forests.

4) The proportion of migrants in samples from old fields is 2–8 percent greater than in samples from the nearby forest (Becan). The slightly higher migrant values in the old fields are in part a reflection of the influx of spring transients not present in the winter samples at the forest site. Visual censuses confirm that the proportions of migrant in forest and old fields are very similar. Strip transect counts in the forests of Becan and Buena Noche West in March 1973 (Waide et al this volume) also yielded a high proportion of migrants (50 and 56 percent of the estimated populations, respectively). Hence, data from mist nets (which sample the bird populations of low, unstratified habitats fairly thoroughly) suggest that the proportion of overwintering migrants in old fields is close to 50 percent. The proportion of migrants in more complex forest habitats (sampled by both mist nets and transect counts) is most likely 40–50, depending on the degree of disturbance of the habitat.

5) Compared with the figures cited by Karr (1976), the proportion of migrants is high in forested areas (3 percent vs 40–50 percent).

6) In both Becan and Chicanna, resident capture rates drop after the departure of migrants. One expla-

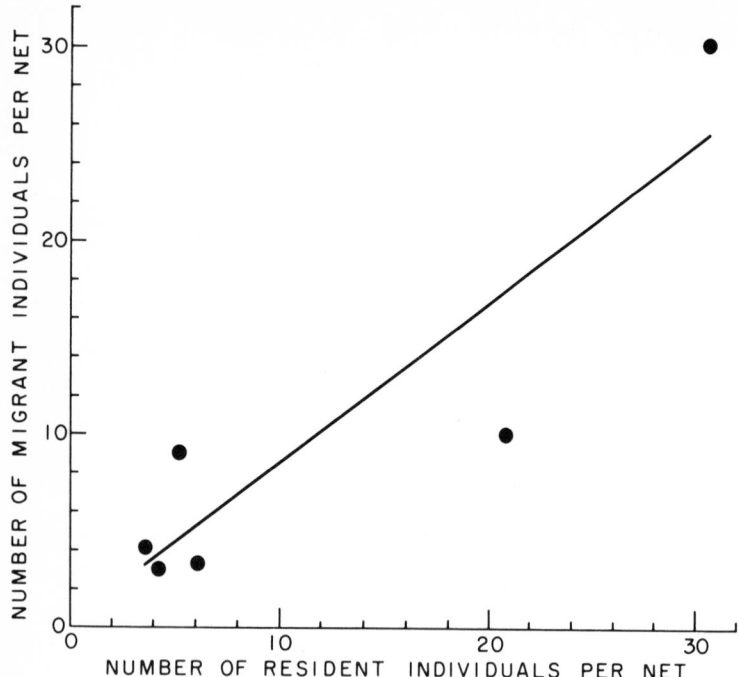

Figure 4. Numbers of migrants plotted against residents for the six study sites.

nation for this trend is that birds captured during the first sampling period remember the location of the nets and avoid them, giving a biased estimate in the second sample (Faaborg pers. comm.). The period between successive samples is quite long in both Chicanna (6 months) and Becan (16 months). Though unlikely, it is possible that net avoidance may persist for such long periods. However, transect censuses in other parts of the Becan study site in March and May 1973 confirm the decrease in resident populations during this period. The reasons for this decrease will be discussed in a subsequent paper (Waide in prep.).

Figure 4 plots projected migrant and resident populations for the six study sites. There is a strong positive correlation between the resident and migrant populations in a given site (Spearman rank correlation coefficient r = .71). This result contrasts with the negative correlation predicted by Willis' hypothesis.

The positive correlation between migrant and resident projected populations shown above is meaningful only when migrants and residents respond to differences in carrying capacity between old fields and forests to the same degree. The increase in projected populations in old fields is about fourfold for both residents and migrants (4.08 vs 4.67; p > .80). The similarity of migrant and resident responses to the

different habitats is further demonstrated by the near 45° slope of the least squares regression line of figure 4. Thus, the positive correlation between migrant and resident populations seems to reflect parallel increases in populations in old fields rather than the competitive effect predicted by Willis.

The projected population is a function of both bird density and the mean foraging radius of the captured species (Terborgh and Faaborg 1973). Mist nets will capture a smaller proportion of a population whose individuals have non-overlapping territories than of a population of free-ranging individuals. Thus, to compare projected populations, the populations sampled must be similar in the amount of intraspecific overlap in horizontal foraging range. The slope of the regression of daily captures on cumulative captures (new birds) is a measure of overlap in foraging range, with a steep negative slope indicating little overlap. Table 3 gives the slopes of the regression equations for resident and migrant subsets of each sample. After eliminating those samples where migrants and residents have significant differences in foraging-range overlap, resident and migrant projected populations still fail to show a negative correlation (r = .00). (It is interesting to note that migrants have relatively little overlap in foraging range in disturbed habitats compared to residents while the reverse is true for forest sites).

Figure 5 shows Bray and Curtis (1957) ordinations of resident and migrant subsets of the relevant mist net samples. The distance between samples in each

Table 3. Slopes of the least squares regression line of daily captures on cumulative captures

Study site	Date	Resident and migrant	Resident	Migrant
Old Field 1	Apr 1973	−.340	−.599	−.222
Old Field 2	Apr 1973	−.294	−.165	−.386[1]
Old Field 5	Apr 1973	−.259	−.086	−.464[2]
Becan	Feb 1973	−.105	−.032	−.175
Becan	Dec 1974	−.422	−.501	−.331
Chicanna	Dec 1974	−.252	−.261	−.234
Chicanna	June 1975	−.202	−.202	—
Buena Noche West	Mar 1973	−.319	−.411	−.143

[1] Migrant and resident slopes significantly different at 5 percent level.

[2] Migrant and resident slopes significantly different at 1 percent level ($F2_{(1,10)}$ = 5.14 for Old Field 2; $F2_{(1,10)}$ = 11.45 for Old Field 5).

Robert B. Waide

ordination is a measure of their dissimilarity based on the presence or absence of species. The old fields show relatively great separation in both ordinations, indicating that both residents and migrants show high species turnover rates from one early successional stage to the next. The greater separation among the early successional samples in the resident ordination suggests that residents discriminate more strongly between these disturbed habitats than do migrants. This trend is even more pronounced in ordinations which use the relativized capture data rather than presence-absence data to calculate dissimilarity. One factor that contributes to the greater similarity of migrant old-field samples is the domination of all migrant early successional communities by *Passerina cyanea* (Fringillidae). The most common resident species was different in each of the three successional communities.

The similarity between forest samples and old field samples varies in the two ordinations (figure 5). In the resident ordination, forest samples from Becan 1974, Chicanna 1974 and 1975, and Buena Noche West form a tight cluster indicating their common dissimilarity to the early successional samples. In the migrant ordination, the difference between forest samples is on the same order of magnitude as the difference between forest-old field pairs. This difference between migrant and resident avifaunas is the result of the high proportion of migrant species which occur in both forest and early successional areas (*Empidonax* sp., *Vireo griseus*, *Dendroica magnolia*, *Seiurus aurocapillus*, *Wilsonia citrina*) compared to the virtual absence of resident species with such distributions.

The sample from Becan 1973 occupies different positions relative to the other samples in the two ordinations. In the resident ordination, Becan 1973 is the forested stand which is the most dissimilar to the successional samples, while in the migrant ordination it is the most similar. The principal reason for this pattern appears to be simply a spillover of migrant species which occur in high densities in the successional areas into the adjacent forest at Becan. That the 1974 sample from the same site does not behave in a similar manner may reflect differences in migrant habitat choice between 1973 and 1974 or between December and February, when the two samples were taken.

Discussion

The results presented above show that at least in southern Campeche migrant birds do not avoid those habitats where residents are most abundant. This conclusion is the opposite of predictions from the hypothesis that migrants select a winter habitat which minimizes contact with resident birds (Willis 1966). To evaluate the significance of these findings, a brief

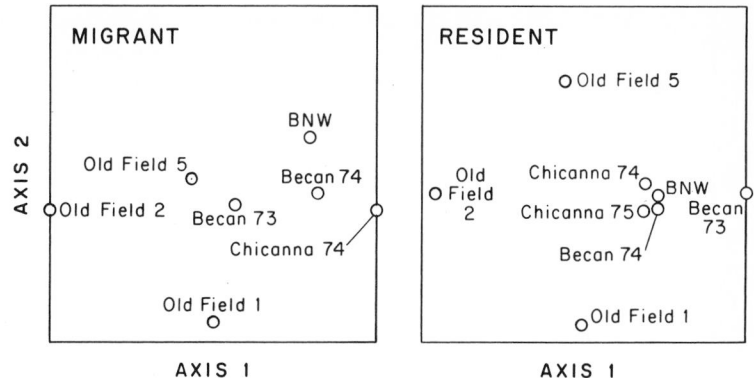

Figure 5.   Ordinations of resident and migrant subsets from mist net samples; distance between samples in each ordination is a measure of their dissimilarity based on species co-occurrence.

review of the evidence on the winter distribution and food habits of migrants is in order.

Highland Areas

The hypothesis that migrant birds favor highland areas because these habitats contain few resident competitors is based on the premise that migrants are more abundant at high elevations. Recent evidence suggests that this generalization is not universally true.

In one of the few systematic studies of the effect of elevation on migrant abundance, Lack and Lack (1972) conclude that migrant warblers winter in both lowland and montane forest in Jamaica and that some migrants are much more common in lowland forest. They found 131 migrant warblers per 10-hr census in lowland natural forest, 61 at mid-levels, and 49 in montane forests. In gardens and parkland, migrants also failed to show preference for high elevations (90, 121, and 60 individuals/10 hr from low to high elevations, respectively). (Karr's [1976] standardization of Lack and Lack's already standardized data obscures the general decrease in migrant abundance at high elevations.) In another island study, the proportion of migrants in samples from Hispaniola was independent of elevation (Terborgh and Faaborg this volume).

At Monteverde, Costa Rica, migrants were more common in the lower two-thirds of a moisture gradient from 1,300–1,550 m (Tramer and Kemp 1978). Higher elevations, where migrants were scarce, were wetter and less disturbed than the lower part of the gradient. In Panama, Leck (1972) reported that during the spring migration, migrants made 45 percent of the visits to fruiting *Leandra* shrubs at 1,800 m. During the winter, however, the importance of migrants at fruiting trees was similar at sea level and 1,200 m. Also in

Panama, Smith (1975) estimated migrant abundance at 150 per ha at 1,600 m, while Karr (1976) found that migrants comprised only about 1–3 percent of the avifauna at a lowland wet forest site.

Elsewhere, Miller (1963) estimated that migrants comprised 10–15 percent of the avifauna in a Colombian cloud forest at 2,000 m elevation. In an area of mid-elevation rain forest at Providencia on the Rio Anori in northern Antioquia, Colombia (elevation 600 m), 12 percent of the birds captured in disturbed and natural habitats from 1 September to 1 May were migrants (Waide in prep.). Hilty (this volume) found migrant abundance increased with altitude (from 100 to 1,900 m) in the Colombian Andes, while in the Cauca Valley of Colombia, migrants were more common at mid-elevations (950 m), and migrant abundance was more closely related to decreasing moisture than to elevation (Orejuela et al this volume).

The meager and conflicting evidence in the literature does not seem to justify generalization about the effect of elevation on the distribution of migrant birds. Nonetheless, several authors have stated (partly on the basis of qualitative observations) that neotropical montane and highland areas (1,000–2,500 m) have more abundant migrant populations than similar lowland sites (Miller 1963; Willis 1966; Leck 1972; Karr 1976). This conclusion must be viewed with caution until more comparative data are collected. With the information now available, the effects of elevation per se are difficult to separate from the effects of human disturbance or moisture conditions.

Seasonally or Sporadically Available Resources

On the basis of a study of migrant birds at army ant swarms in Panama, Willis (1966) has suggested that resident populations are limited at certain times of year by the availability of food. As a result, during the rest of the year there is surplus food which can be exploited by migrants. Thus, migrants exist on seasonally available food which residents cannot use because of population bottlenecks at other times of the year.

Evidence supporting this view is scanty in the literature. Leck (1972) found that frugivorous migrants tended to frequent areas of fruit superabundance in Panama. No other information is available on the relationship of migrants and seasonally abundant food in the neotropics. The meager evidence available suggests that those migrants that eat fruit or follow ant swarms may depend on seasonal food abundances at some stages of migration. Frugivores or ant-following migrant species are in the minority, however. Many migrants are leaf-gleaning or ground-feeding insectivores (Cox 1968; Leck 1972; Lack and Lack 1972), whose food may be less subject to seasonal fluctuations.

Moreover, in areas with a moderately long dry season, the season of migrant presence may be a time of food scarcity rather than abundance (Foster 1974; Waide et al this volume). The use of seasonally-abundant resources has not been demonstrated to be a general strategy of migrants.

Willis (1966) also suggests another mechanism by which migrant birds could exploit temporally fluctuating resources that are not available to residents. He hypothesizes that migrant birds are excluded from areas where ant swarms are scarce by competition from resident birds, but that migrants are able to move to other areas where local superabundances exist more easily than residents. Willis bases his hypothesis on the fact that in 1960, when ant swarms were common on Barro Colorado Island and poorly attended by residents, migrants were common. In 1961, a drier year, both ant-swarm and migrant densities were low. Willis presumes that lower migrant densities are the result of movements to more favorable areas in Panama, but he also suggests that further evidence is necessary to test the hypothesis.

Evidence on local movements of migrants and residents has accumulated very slowly. Willis' hypothesis rests on the assumption that migrants can shift their location or diet more easily than resident birds. Since many migrant species are now known to be territorial on their wintering ground (Pitelka 1942; Schwartz 1964; Rappole this volume) and many resident birds perform local movements (Ridgely 1976; Emlen this volume; pers. obs.) or change their diet (Terborgh pers. comm.) in the nonbreeding season, this assumption is of questionable validity. Although the idea also implies that fluctuating resources are unpredictable, this is true only on a local scale. The amount of fruit or insect food available at a given location may fluctuate from year to year, but the general level of any particular type of resource over a larger area must be relatively stable if any species or subset of the avifauna can specialize on it. If migrants exploit locally superabundant resources, there seems to be no reason why residents could not also do so (see Feinsinger this volume). In fact, Willis (this volume) reverses his 1966 position and suggests that resident birds monopolize abundant fluctuating food by making local migrations while migrants use less abundant but more predictable resources.

The available evidence indicates that the alternative strategies of winter territoriality and nomadism are employed by both residents and migrants. The choice of a particular strategy may be related to the distribution pattern of the preferred food of a species rather than whether or not it migrates (Morton this volume). Territoriality may be best developed in those migrant populations that face relatively little competition from

Robert B. Waide

residents. Migrant populations that encounter strong resident competition may overcome the advantage that year-round territoriality gives to residents by engaging in the scramble competition associated with nomadism.

Disturbed or Early Successional Areas

Willis (1966) and Karr (1976) found that neotropical migrants in Panama were more common in disturbed habitats than in lowland forest. On the basis of his results, Willis suggested that migrants prefer disturbed areas because resident competitors are less common there. Recently, however, he concluded that both residents and migrants are relatively common in young forest or lakeshore habitats compared to old forest (Willis this volume). Nevertheless, the ratio of migrant to resident individuals appears to be least in old forest.

This does not mean, however, that migrants are uncommon in all mature habitats. Tramer (1974) found no clear correlation between the degree of habitat disturbance and the relative proportion of migrants in nine dry forest study sites in Yucatán. He points out that two distinct avifaunas exist in the neotropics, one centered in wet lowland forest and composed mainly of tropical families and another found in montane forests, disturbed areas, and dry forests whose resident component consists of families having largely temperate distribution. Temperate migrants are a prominent part of this latter avifauna.

Although certainly an oversimplification, this dichotomy serves to point out differences in the importance of migrants in wetter and drier forests. Recent work in Costa Rica (Tramer and Kemp this volume), Panama (Hespenheide this volume), and Colombia (Orejuela et al this volume) has shown that migrants are more abundant in dry than in wet forests. In the dry forests of the Yucatán Peninsula, representatives of families endemic to the neotropics such as ovenbirds and antbirds are relatively rare (Paynter 1955), and the density of winter residents is high compared with lowland rain forests (Waide et al this volume). Previous work on migrants in the tropics has focused on lowland rain forest in Panamá (Willis 1966, this volume; Leck 1972; Karr 1976). Conclusions from these studies may be less applicable in dry forest situations where migrants seem to be a more integral part of the forest community. This is an especially important point in the formulation of management policies which seek to preserve migrant species in different parts of their winter range.

In particular, the suggestion that migrants are relegated to disturbed habitats by competition from residents (Willis 1966) is not supported by data from my dry forest sites. In southern Campeche, migrants made use of both disturbed and undisturbed habitats and migrant abundance showed a positive rather than a negative correlation with the density of resident birds. Resident and migrant densities both increased with habitat disturbance, at least in the 0–2 m level sampled by mist nets. In successional areas and disturbed forests, both resident and migrant communities were dominated by one or two species (table 1). In less disturbed forest, species evenness was higher for both residents and migrants. My results show that both migrant and resident species appeared to discriminate between different successional stages to some extent, but residents appeared to be more strongly associated with a given stage than migrants. Residents also discriminated more clearly between disturbed and undisturbed sites while migrant species were more ubiquitous.

The existence of resident species adapted to early successional stages in my study site may be due in part to the long history of human disturbance in the Yucatán Peninsula. Even though successional habitats were scarce until very recently in my study area, shifting cultivation has maintained a mosaic of mature forests and old fields in various parts of the peninsula for at least 2,000 years. This could have provided adequate time for the accumulation of resident species adapted to successional habitats. In view of the widespread habitat alteration performed by pre-Columbian populations in many parts of Latin America (Parsons 1974), the situation in the Yucatán Peninsula may be less the exception than the rule.

Acknowledgments

The major funding for this project came from a National Science Foundation Doctoral Dissertation Improvement Grant (GB 43852). The National Geographic Society, the Frank M. Chapman Fund, the Marsh Fund of the National Academy of Sciences, Sigma Xi, and the Davis Fund of the Department of Zoology, University of Wisconsin-Madison generously supported different parts of the field work. While analyzing the data, the author was supported by a Graduate Fellowship from the University of Wisconsin-Madison. ·

John Shepherd, Gail Kantak, and John Idzikowski assisted in the field work. The manuscript benefited from the comments of J. T. Emlen, E. W. Beals, T. C. Moermond, J. R. Baylis, D. B. Clark, D. A. Clark, M. DeJong and J. Faaborg. Cheryl Hughes did the illustrations, and Linda McConnell and Trish Horn typed the manuscript. Jack and Aracely Siebert and Jorge Orejuela assisted with the Spanish summary.

My special thanks go to Arquiologico Norberto Gonzales C., Director of the Southeast Regional Center of the Instituto Nacional de Antropologia E Historia, for permission to use the Institute's facilities at Xpujil, and to Felipe Osorio and Juan Briceño, guardians of Chicanna and Becan, for their considerable aid and hospitality.

Literature Cited

American Ornithologists' Union
1957.   *Check-list of North American Birds.* 5th ed. Baltimore: A.O.U.

Bray, J. R., and J. T. Curtis.
1957.   Upland forest communities of southern Wisconsin. Ecol. Monogr. 27:325–49.

Buechner, H. K., and J. H. Buechner
1970.   The avifauna of northern Latin America. Smithsonian Contrib. Zool. 26:1–119.

Cox, G. W.
1968.   The role of competition in the evolution of migration. Evol. 22:180–92.

Denevan, W. M.
1976.   *The Native Population of the Americas in 1492.* Madison: Univ. of Wisconsin Press.

Eisenmann, E.
1955.   The species of Middle American birds. Trans. Linn. Soc. of New York, vol 7., 128 pp.

Foster, Robin.
1974.   Seasonality of fruit production and seed fall in a tropical forest ecosystem in Panama. Ph.D. thesis, Duke Univ., Durham, N.C.

Garcia, E.
1965.   Distribución de la precipitación en la República Mexicana. Publicaciones del Instituto de Geografia, de la Universidad Nacional de Mexico, vol. 1.

Karr, J.
1976.   On the relative abundances of migrants from the north temperate zone in tropical habitats. Wils. Bull. 88:433–58.

Lack, D., and P. Lack
1972.   Wintering warblers in Jamaica. Living Bird 11: 129–53.

Leck, C. F.
1972.   The impact of some North American migrants at fruiting trees in Panama. Auk 89:842–50.

Lundell, C. L.
1937.   The vegetation of Petén. Carnegie Inst. Washington, D.C., Pub. 478.

Miller, A. H.
1963.   Seasonal activity and ecology of the avifauna of an American equatorial cloud forest. Univ. Calif. Publ. Zool. 66:1–78.

Parsons, J. J.
1974.   The changing nature of New World tropical forests since European colonization. In *Papers and Proceedings, The Use of Ecological Guidelines for Development in the American Humid Tropics,* Caracas. Venezuela, 20–22 Feb. 1974. International Union for the Conservation of Nature and Natural Resources. Morges, Switzerland, pp. 28–38.

Paynter, R. A., Jr.
1955.   The ornithogeography of the Yucatan Peninsula. Bull. Peabody Mus. Nat. Hist. 9:1–347.

Pitelka, F. A.
1942.   Territoriality and related problems in North American hummingbirds. Condor 44:189–204.

Rappole, J. H., and D. W. Warner
1976.   Relationships between behavior, physiology and weather in avian transients at a migration stopover site. Oecologia 26:193–212.

Ridgely, R. S.
1976.   *A Guide to the Birds of Panama.* Princeton, N.J.: Princeton Univ. Press.

Ruppert, K., and J. Denison.
1943.   Archaeological reconnaissance in Campeche, Quintana Roo, and Peten. Carnegie Inst. Washington, Pub. 543.

Schwartz, P.
1964.   The Northern Waterthrush in Venezuela. Living Bird 3:169–84.

Shepherd, J.
1975.   The phytosociology of a tropical seasonal forest in southeastern Mexico. Unpublished M.S. thesis, Univ. of Wisconsin, Madison.

Smith, N. G.
1975.   Spshing noise: Biological significance of its attraction and non-attraction by birds. Proc. Natl. Acad. Sci. 72:1411–14.

Terborgh, J., and J. Faaborg
1973.   Turnover and ecological release in the avifauna of Mona Island, Puerto Rico. Auk 90:759–79.

Tramer, Elliot J.
1974.   Proportions of wintering North American birds in disturbed and undisturbed dry tropical habitats. Condor 76:460–64.

Webster, D. L.
1974.   The fortifications of Becan, Campeche, Mexico. In *Preliminary Reports on Archaeological Investigations in the Rio Bec Area, Campeche, Mexico,* ed. R.E.W. Adams. Middle American Research Institute Pub. 31:103–146. New Orleans La.,: Tulane Univ.

Willis, E. O.
1966.   The role of migrant birds at swarms of army ants. Living Bird 5:187–231.

Robert B. Waide

JOHN H. RAPPOLE
and
DWAIN W. WARNER
Bell Museum of Natural History
University of Minnesota
Minneapolis, Minnesota 55455

Ecological Aspects of Migrant Bird Behavior in Veracruz, Mexico

ABSTRACT

Avian migrants at three primary forest sites in the Tuxtla Mountains of southern Veracruz, Mexico, were investigated during 1973–75. Mist-netting and banding were used for censusing populations and ascertaining movements of individuals within populations; observations supplemented these data for niche structure and intra- and interspecific interactions.

Individuals of both sexes of 14 non-gregarious migrant species defended separate, small (.2–.5 ha) feeding territories throughout the winter season and returned to the same territory in subsequent seasons. In populations of all species studied, some individuals of both sexes were unable to obtain territories and moved randomly through suitable habitat as floaters, assuming defense of a territory if given the opportunity. Individuals of these 14 species were able to compete for resources on a long-term basis in a primary tropical forest habitat, indicating that earlier theories describing migrants as nomadic opportunists subsisting in disturbed or marginal habitats on temporarily superabundant resources are incorrect.

Differences in resource use between migrants and permanent residents were not seen, but there were relationships between food resource distribution, social system, and use of fattening as a physiological and behavioral response to concentrated resources.

A comparison of foraging niches between migrant and resident species showed no basis for the claim that migrants are competitively inferior to permanent resident species. Migrant species occupy characteristic niches which are not used by permanent residents, even when migrants are absent.

Individuals of most migrant species took part in interspecific flocks only while the flocks were present on their territories. Presumed advantages of joining interspecific flocks are increased foraging efficiency and avoidance of predators. There was no evidence that individuals of the different species within these flocks behaved as "ecologically the same species," as has been claimed by some workers.

Although some investigators have maintained that the breeding period is the most critical part of the migrant's life cycle and others claim that winter is the critical period, there are yet no conclusive data that any one period is more important than any other. Since competition is continuous, as evidenced by the presence of floaters, the migrant must use an optimization strategy to compete well on the breeding ground, during migration and on the wintering ground.

We hypothesize that most nearctic, long distance migrants evolved from historically tropical species which were able to exploit niches common to many different forest types. With low breeding success and intense competition for resources in tropical communities, individuals of these species took advantage of reduced competition in seasonal niches in temperate areas to increase reproductive success.

Migrants use specific niches in tropical communities, a fact with important implications concerning community structure and function that has been overlooked by workers in this field. The effects of new resources, environmental stability, and community productivity are discussed in light of information on migrants and other groups not normally included in species diversity studies. We conclude that productivity is an important ultimate factor in the development of biological heterogeneity in tropical systems.

Introduction

The ecological behavior of migratory birds that occupy tropical regions for extended periods each year is little known outside the breeding season. With a few notable exceptions (Skutch in Bent 1953; Wetmore 1972; Moreau 1972; Slud 1964) literature on these species away from their breeding grounds is restricted to brief, annotated lists documenting little more than a species' occurrence within a general area. Despite this lack of behavioral and ecological information, various workers have drawn important implications concerning migrant relationships within tropical communities. Leck (1972) has stated that migrants at fruiting trees in Panama are "less efficient" than residents and maintain "low positions" in dominance hierarchies involving residents. Morel and Bourlière (1962) concluded that migrants in Senegal savannah composed a drifting population, subsisting on temporarily superabundant food sources which could not be completely exploited by resident species. Willis (1966) came to similar conclusions concerning birds exploiting swarms of army ants (*Eciton* and *Labidus*) in the neotropics.

Several studies in tropical, terrestrial communities have analyzed avian species diversity as related to structural characters of the vegetation (MacArthur et al 1966; Orians 1969; Howell 1971; Karr 1971a). The main thrust of these studies was toward gaining an understanding of resource partitioning, productivity, and energy pathways (Karr 1975). These studies all ignore migrants which occur as winter residents as members of the communities although, where reported, they make up 15–30 percent of the total avian species composition (calculated from Karr 1971a:212). This omission is presumably based on the questionable, if not totally erroneous, supposition that breeding is the only criterion of habitat usage. This idea stems from the original work relating species diversity and the structure of vegetation in temperate forests (MacArthur and MacArthur 1961). Its validity in temperate regions now seems uncertain, and we will present data which indicate that its validity in the tropics is even less likely. Migrants form a stable part of many tropical communities for most months of the year, returning year after year to the same localities (Loftin et al 1966; Nickell 1968; Schwartz 1964; de Roo and Deheeger 1969; Nisbet and Medway, 1972; and this study).

Knowledge of exactly what communities are inhabited by migrants as winter residents and the relationships between winter residents, transients and other members of these communities is necessary before theoretical work can be meaningfully developed. This knowledge is particularly urgent considering the precarious status of tropical ecosystems (Gomez-Pompa et al 1972; Russell 1973; Rappole 1974).

We obtained data on territoriality, territorial behavior, sociality, site fidelity, habitat usage, and foraging behavior of migrants in seral and climax stages of tropical forests in the Tuxtla mountains region of southern Veracruz, Mexico. These data are presented and compared to implied or stated theories in the literature concerning migrant population dynamics on the wintering grounds and are used to formulate new hypotheses concerning the role of migrants as members of tropical avian communities.

Study Area

The Sierra de Los Tuxtlas (18° 30′ N 95° W), a 4,200 km² rough, mountainous region of volcanic origin rising to 1,500 m, lies isolated by lowlands 90 km southeast of Veracruz City (figure 1). Volcanic irruptions occurred there in 1664 and 1793 (Garcia 1835), and several earth tremors were noted during our study. Annual rainfall varies from 2,500 mm to 4,500 mm depending partly on location; and mean annual temperatures range from 20°C at the highest elevations to 25°C in the lowlands (Toledo et al 1972:50, 61). A rainy season begins in late May or early June and continues through late October or early November, blending into a season of warm, clear intervals punctuated by cold, wet fronts called "nortes," three or four each month from November until March, and lasting from two to six days each. The period from March to late May becomes increasingly dry and hot. For a detailed summary of the geology and climatology of the Tuxtlas see Andrle (1964).

The original vegetation of most lower elevations was a magnificent "subformation of rainforest" (Andrle 1966). Pennington and Sarukhan (1968:5–11) refer to this vegetation type as "selva alta perennifolia" (tall, evergreen tropical forest). We refer to it as "selva" hereafter. The region also supports limited areas of cloud forest, pine-oak, pine, littoral and savannah (Andrle 1967). The selva flora is extremely rich with an estimated 2,000 plant species (Mario Sousa pers. comm.). Andrle (1966) estimated that one-half of the Sierra de Los Tuxtlas was forested in 1962. We estimated that less than one-third of the Tuxtlas remained forested by May 1975, with cutting continuing at a rapid pace.

Intensive research was conducted at five study sites 100–300 m above sea level (figure 1). Sites 1–3 were in selva (figure 2), a very heterogeneous type characterized by a multi-layered physiognomy with a canopy at 25–30 m and emergents to more than 40 m. Openings in the canopy caused by tree fall, erosion of steep

John H. Rappole

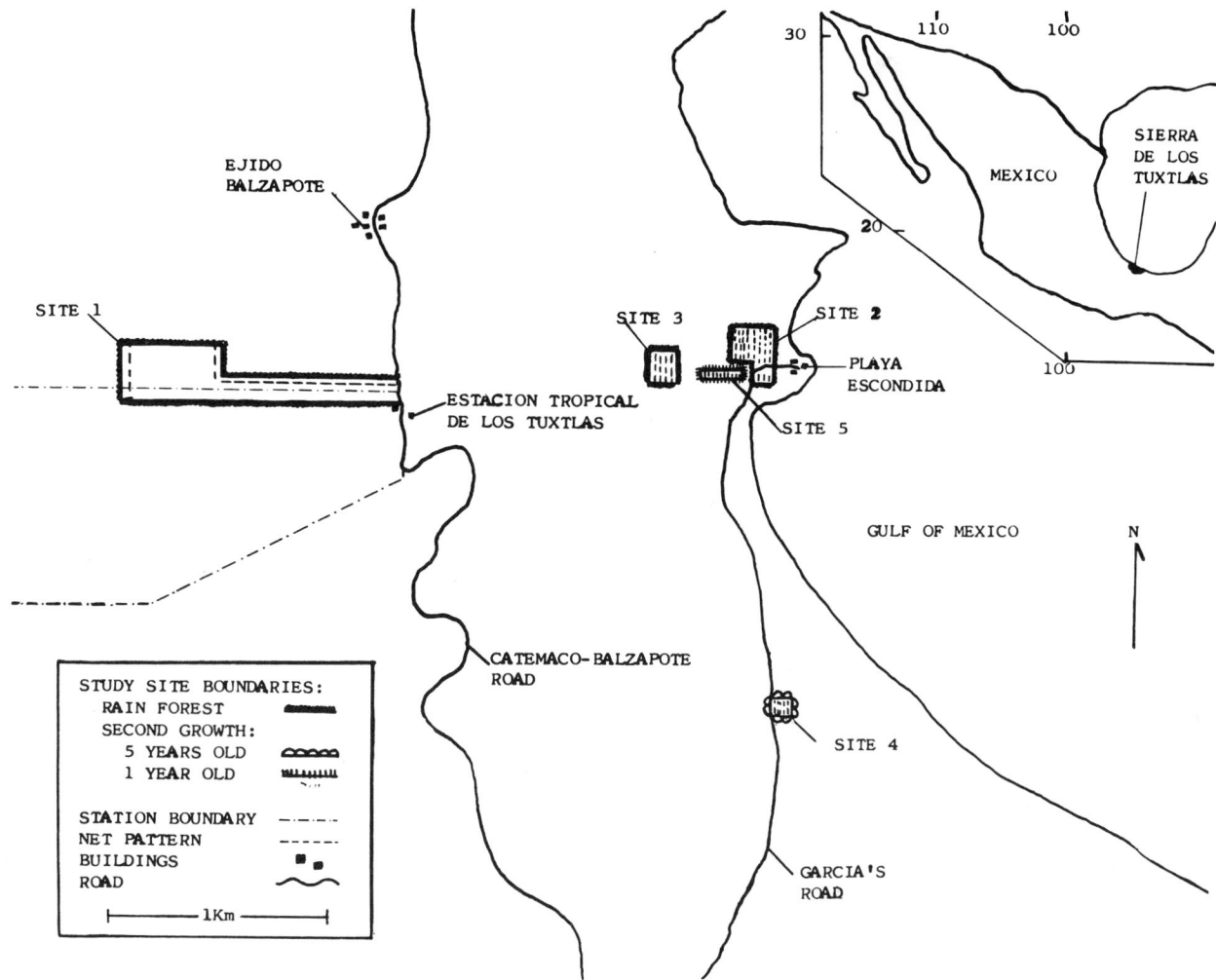

Figure 1. Location of Tuxtlas study sites.

slopes, and streams were common; and undergrowth varied from sparse to very dense. Site 4 (figure 3) was located in a five-year old second growth with a canopy 5–7 m in height and dense, fairly uniform undergrowth. Plant species diversity, dominated by species of *Cecropia*, *Piper* and *Cnidoscolus*, was greatly reduced from that of the selva. Site 5 (figure 4) was located in one-year old, grazed second growth with a flora consisting almost entirely of dense growths of *Solanum* and *Piper* with a canopy height of 2–3 m.

The bulk of the field work was done from November 1973 to March 1974 and November 1974 to March 1975. However many data utilized in this report were gathered by M. A. Ramos and R. J. Oehlenschlager from August 1973 to May 1974 and August 1974 to May 1975 working on the other ornithological studies at the same study sites, but concentrating on Site 1. Living and laboratory quarters were at the motel

Playa Escondida situated on the headlands overlooking the Gulf of Mexico 36 km north of Catemaco. Sites 2–5 were in selva and second growth near the motel while Site 1 was 1.5 km west of the motel on a portion of the 6 km² Estacion de Biologia Tropical "Los Tuxtlas," a field biology station of the University of Mexico.

Materials and Methods

Each study site was mapped using a compass and 100 m tape. Nylon nets 12 m × 2.6 m with 30 mm mesh were placed in a grid system on study Sites 2–5, spaced 15 m apart at Sites 4 and 5 and 30 m at Sites 2 and 3. Site 1 was a line of 50 nets extending 1,000 m.

Table 1 shows netting pattern, total nets, total net hours, and total observation hours for each study site; nets in primary forest were opened at 0630 hr and

Figure 2.   Selva alta perennifolia.

closed at 1600 hr; nets in second growth were closed by 1100 hr on sunny days.

Canopy nets 10–15 m above ground (similar to Whitaker 1972) in Site 2 from December 1973 to February 1974 caught few birds and were discontinued.

All birds received coded, colored plastic leg bands and North American migrants received U. S. Fish and Wildlife Service bands. For all captures, site and net number, age, sex, molt, and fat were recorded. Fat determinations followed the method described by Helms and Drury (1960). Age was determined whenever possible by skull ossification or plumage. Captives were released either in the area of capture or at release sites 1.5 km distant from area of capture. Specimens retained for molt, plumage, stomach contents, and taxonomic information are referred to by catalog number.

Notes were recorded on weather, behavior, and habitat distribution of winter resident migrants and on ecologically related permanent residents. For precise descriptions of foraging habits, coded notations were used which required a code sheet, stopwatch, binoculars, and cassette-recorder. An initial entry on foraging by an individual required about 60 sec; subsequent entries on that individual, mainly repeats of previous codes, required a few seconds each. For species less commonly observed, each observation has the statistical likelihood of representing "normal foraging behavior." Fifty-nine hr from 4 December 1974 to 20 February 1975 were spent using this method, 45 hr in selva and 14 hr in seral states. Data in the Species Accounts Section are from more than 1,000 hr of observation.

The characterization of intraspecific interactions between individuals of migrant winter residents was a major aim of the study. To increase the rate of data accumulation, we designed a series of controlled situ-

John H. Rappole

Figure 3.   Five-year-old secondary forest.

ations with caged birds, mounts or mirrors to which a free-flying individual could be expected to respond with "normal" behavior. In these experiments behavioral reactions of the free bird were recorded in detail and checked against descriptions obtained from the observations of non-manipulative interactions. Equipment used in these experiments included: a portable blind, tape recorder and parabola, 16-mm camera, 8-mm camera with intervalometer and camouflage stand, 35-mm with flash and 400-mm lens, 30 × 30 × 30-cm cage made of mist netting, mounts of the species being worked with, a mirror, notebook, binoculars, and stopwatch.

Experiments were conducted in the following fashion. The blind was placed where a study bird resided and about 10 m from the blind a conspecific individual was placed in a mist-net cage (figure 5). Response by the resident to this "stake out" was then recorded on film and in a notebook. The experimental situation was varied for measurement of responses to individuals of different age and sex. Recordings were made in the field of the calls believed to be important in displays. These were presented as vocalizations associated with the caged bird to measure the response of free-flying birds to vocalizations.

All migrants vocalized spontaneously at fairly regular intervals. To characterize this phenomenon, 50 hr were spent recording total vocalizations for all migrants within hearing range. For each species the number of territorial birds within hearing range was estimated from data on territory size and population density and divided into total vocalizations recorded for that species per hour to get an estimate of total time spent vocalizing.

Territories were mapped for all individuals of only one species, the Hooded Warbler (*Wilsonia citrina*).

Figure 4.   One-year-old secondary forest.

Boundaries of territories were determined by three methods: 1) recaptures and resightings, 2) response to playback and stake outs of intruders, 3) "territory flush technique" (Wiens 1973; see Rappole 1976 for detailed critique and description).

Territory size was determined in two ways. When territory boundaries had been determined, the size of the territory was measured. The other method was to divide the study plot area by the number of known territorial individuals by species in the manner described by Catchpole (1972). This method has the advantage of being rapid. However, a species is seldom uniformly distributed throughout a habitat so some dead space is usually included. Additional data (recapture, resighting and knowledge of preferred microhabitat) were used to modify these estimates.

Schwartz (1964) reported that defense of winter territory of the Northern Waterthrush (*Seiurus novebor-*acensis*) breaks down "during the last few weeks before they start northward . . ." To determine time, winter territories are maintained; netting continued from August to May for two years. Territoriality experiments were performed on the Hooded Warbler until 25 March 1975. The combination of recapture and territorial defense data is the basis for estimates of the time at which territory defense stopped and this species left the Tuxtlas.

Among all species of solitary (non-gregarious) migrant winter residents, floaters (i.e. non-territorial birds) continually moved through the study areas. Removal experiments were designed to find out if these birds would replace territorial individuals (Rappole 1976). Including the work of Ramos and Oehlenschlager, data were accumulated on 12,000 birds in hand.

In the following accounts of selected winter resi-

John H. Rappole

Figure 5. "Wing droop" display of a male Hooded Warbler to a caged female conspecific.

dents, we present relative abundance estimates and other data relevant to habitat use, social systems, behavior and foraging techniques, and site fidelity.

Distribution of individuals of a species on our study sites was estimated on the basis of audio-visual censusing and total captures (Rappole 1976). Based on these data we have devised the following abundance categories, which apply to normally solitary species with home ranges of less than 1 ha in size: 1) common—more than 10 occupants per 10 ha of major habitat type (extrapolated from study area size where an "occupant" is a bird living on the area for 1 or more seasons), 2) fairly common—6–10, 3) uncommon—1–5, 4) sparse—less than 1. This classification is actually a rough measure of microhabitat suitability per species for a given habitat type. The number of occupants in an area can only be determined by long-term banding projects with subsequent observation. Thus mist-netting, despite its drawbacks, is essential for an evaluation of avian community structure.

Rappole spent a total of 95 hr in a blind set in study Site 2 from 20 February 1975 to 11 March 1975 in an effort to document site attachment and stability of a small migrant community. The site was visited on 14 days of the 19 day period of observation for 3–8 hours per day.

Species Accounts

This section includes identification of preferred habitats, foraging behavior and territorial defense, and

Table 1. Forest type, size, total nets, net hours, observation hours and net pattern for the 5 study sites

Area number	Forest type[1]	Size	Total nets	Total net hours		Total observation hours		Net pattern
				73–74	74–75	73–74	74–75	
1	M	6 ha	50	34,113	28,672	35	30	1000 m line
2	M	4 ha	45	7,051	7,037	212	306	30 m grid
3	M	2 ha	37	0	7,984	5	35	30 m grid
4	S5	.7 ha	15	0	636	52	17	15 m grid
5	S1	.7 ha	16	0	390	27	15	15 m grid
Total	—	13.4 ha	163	41,164	44,719	331	403	

[1] Mature selva; S5- 5-year-old second growth; S1- 1-year-old second growth

evaluation of potential competitors for 23 species of migrants.

Migrant winter residents in the Tuxtlas used a variety of habitats (table 2). However, distribution of individuals within a habitat was not uniform. To reflect this distribution more accurately, we calculated a "homogeneity index" (H) based on the average home range or territory size for the species (X), the total size of the piece of habitat studied (Y), and the number of known individuals of each species in that area (Z_a). Dividing Y by X gives a theoretical number of indigenes (Z_t), then $\frac{Z_a}{Z_t}$ = H. If distribution is uniform for a species in an area, H = 1.00. This was true for some species, but not for others (table 2). The reason for the lack of homogeneity of distribution in some species is that preferred microhabitats are not distributed evenly, for example, in primary forest the Gray Catbird occupies only scattered dense thickets.

Variability in distribution patterns from one habitat to the next is shown by large differences in recapture percentages from one study site to the next. We consider this pattern to be due to the variability in the amount of suitable microhabitat present in each of the different study sites.

Many resident species showed a similar pattern: the Long-billed Gnatwren (*Ramphocaenus rufiventris*) occurs in thickets in both primary forest and second growth of various ages, as does the Spot-breasted Wren (*Thryothorus maculipectus*).

Yellow-bellied Flycatcher (*Empidonax flaviventris*)

PREFERRED HABITAT

Selva but also in 10–15 m second growth bordering streams in pastures as in Honduras (Monroe 1968: 266), but in dense "second growth" in Panama (Wetmore, 1972:464) and Costa Rica (Slud, 1964:254). Micro-habitat was outer margins of dense foliage.

FORAGING BEHAVIOR AND COMPETITORS

They perched 20–30 sec between foragings, flying 1–2 m and seldom returning to the same perch. Prey was as often hawked (flying out, returning to a different perch) from the surface of leaves or twigs as from the air. Angle of the bird's body at prey capture was variable, and search pattern included areas above and below the perch.

It resembles no other species in terms of foraging niche. The Oleaginous Flycatcher (*Pipromorpha oleaginea*) and Sulphur-rumped Flycatcher (*Myiobius sulphureipygeus*) are the only conceivable competitors in the sense of ecological counter-parts. The former forages higher and much slower and the latter lower and much faster; and they differ morphologically. The Yellowish Flycatcher (*E. flavescens*) was rare on Study Sites 2–5 and fairly common on Site 1. On the basis of our few observations of *E. flavescens* this species appeared to wait much longer between foraging attempts than *E. flaviventris*.

John H. Rappole

Table 2. Habitat use, distribution, abundance and sociality of wintering migrants

Species	Habitats occupied[1]	Homo-geneity of distri-bution[2]	Abun-dance[3]	Social system[4]
Empidonax flaviventris	1, 2	.53	C	T
Empidonax minimus	2, 3	.50	C	T
Dumetella carolinensis	3, 2, 1	.25	C	T
Hylocichla mustelina	1, 2	1.00	C	T, F
Catharus ustulatus	1	?[5]	U	F
Polioptila caerulea	1, 2, 3, 4	1.00	C	?
Vireo griseus	1, 2, 3	.30	C	T
Mniotilta varia	1, 2, 4	?	C	T
Helmitheros vermivorus	1, 2	?	FC	T
Vermivora celata	3, 4	.42	U	T
Dendroica petechia	4, 5	?	C	T
Dendroica magnolia	1, 2, 3	.38	C	T
Dendroica coronata	4, 5, 6	.2<	U	F
Dendroica virens	1, 2, 3	.2<	FC	T
Seiurus aurocapillus	1, 2	.26	FC	T
Seiurus novaboracensis	5	?	C	T
Seiurus motacilla	1	.2<	C	T
Oporornis formosus	1, 2, 3	.68	C	T
Geothlypis trichas	6, 3	?	C	T
Icteria virens	3, 4	1.00	C	T
Wilsonia citrina	1, 2, 3	.90	C	T
Wilsonia pusilla	1, 2, 3	?	C	T
Setophaga ruticilla	1, 2	?	C	T
Piranga rubra	1	.2<	C	T
Passerina cyanea	4	1.00	C	F
Passerina ciris	4	.50	FC	F

[1] 1 = mature selva (20 m or more in height), 2 = old second growth (10–20 m), 3 = young second growth (1–10 m), 4 = savannah or pasture with scattered clumps of trees, 5 = mangroves, 6 = marshes or wet fields.

[2] See text for explanation.

[3] C = common, FC = fairly common, U = uncommon. See text for further explanation.

[4] T = individuals of both sexes defend separate territories, F = intraspecific aggregations.

[5] ? = insufficient data.

TERRITORIALITY

Visual displays consisted of "crest raising," "wing drooping" (holding wings slightly out and down from the sides), and "wing flipping." In intense fights, a rattling "chirr" accompanied displays. The "chip" note and occasionally the "per wee" song were used to advertise the territory. Females were as effective as males in defending territory against either sex, and used the same displays and vocalizations. Territories averaged .3 ha.

Least Flycatcher (Empidonax minimus)

PREFERRED HABITAT

See Table 2; microhabitat is forest openings as on breeding grounds (Breckenridge, 1956), or second growth and forest edges.

FORAGING BEHAVIOR AND COMPETITORS

Foraging height was highly variable, 0–20 m or more depending on habitat structure, hunting was mostly by hawking and sallying (returning to same perch) about .5 m. Usually these flights were from an open area into an open pocket in broken forest. There were no species in the same microhabitat which foraged in a similar manner.

TERRITORIALITY

Both males and females advertised territories by using the "wit" call note and the "che-bec" song. The only visual display was "crest raising" (figure 6).

Figure 6. Crest-raising display in the Least Flycatcher.

Gray Catbird (Dumetella carolinensis)

PREFERRED HABITAT

Dense thickets in selva and second growth; occasionally at fruiting trees in open pasture.

FORAGING BEHAVIOR AND COMPETITORS

Invertebrates were picked from leaves and branches and occasionally from the ground. Many observations were made of their close proximity to other frugivores at fruiting trees. One group (Feb. 28) included several *Euphonia lauta*, 2 *Centurus aurifrons*, 2 *Tityra semifasciata*, and 1 *D. carolinensis*; no evidence of interspecific interaction was noted during a 10-min observation. A second Catbird stimulated an immediate reaction by the first, which attacked and chased the interloper out of sight, then returned to the tree.

Mimus gilvus is the only permanent resident species with similar habits in the Tuxtlas, and it is rare.

TERRITORIALITY

Vocalizations given at regular intervals include a "mew" or a low "chirr." Visual displays use the tail to accentuate the crest and under tail coverts. The crest is raised, under tail coverts fluffed, and wings drooped while the tail is held at a sharp angle above horizontal, straight down or moved quickly down, up, and back.

Wood Thrush (Hylocichla mustelina)

PREFERRED HABITAT

Common in selva; but reported not common in Veracruz (Loetscher 1955:36) and rare in Mexico (Edwards 1972:190).

FORAGING BEHAVIOR AND COMPETITORS

Foraging behavior is essentially as described by Dilger (1956b): the bird hops, never walks, and pokes and picks in debris on the forest floor for its food. It flies to perches 1–4 m above ground for preening, resting and calling. They followed ant swarms while swarms were on their territory but stopped at the boundaries. Food items were mostly arthropods but snails were also taken.

Willis (1966:200) has made a case for the occurrence of exclusion between the Wood Thrush and the Black-faced Antthrush (*Formicarius analis*). The antthrush is a stout, short-tailed, short-winged bird which walks with a bobbing motion rather than hops. It is roughly the same size as the Wood Thrush though proportioned quite differently. There may be some overlap in foods as both are terrestrial hunters, although the antthrush does much more rummaging in the forest floor debris. The Wood Thrush was common in all

selva sites (1–3) while the antthrush was common but unevenly distributed only on site 1, being absent or very rare at the other areas. This distribution does not support a competitive exclusion hypothesis in which the Wood Thrush is supplanted by the heavier antthrush.

TERRITORIALITY

Calls used in territorial defense included a low intensity "bup bup bup" and higher intensity "pit pit pit" calls. Territory owners called spontaneously throughout the day, but most often when light levels were low. Singing was common in March. In high intensity aggressive situations, usually on the ground, a "zeep" call was given which may be similar to the "querulous, snarling" described by Dilger (1956a:336) for the closely related genus *Catharus*.

Visual displays were studied in detail in interactions of territory owners with introduced caged conspecifics and stuffed models. At least four levels of aggression were distinguished in the display: 1) "crest raising" and "spread" (figure 7); 2) "crest raising," "wing flick" (figure 8), voice; 3) sequence of "crest raising," "wing flick" and "horizontal stretch" (figure 9); 4) sequence of "upward" (figure 10) "wing flick," and "horizontal stretch," "wing flick" and "upward." Intergradation between these types was common. These displays are similar to those described by Dilger (1956a) for *Hylocichla* on the breeding grounds, but there are some differences which may be important. Dilger reported no "horizontal stretch" or "upward" in this species, both of which are found as parts of high intensity display sequences used by both sexes on the wintering ground. Nor did he report the sequence of "upwards" and "horizontal stretches" for the Wood Thrush, although he described exactly such a sequence for the *Catharus* species which he termed "see-sawing." The status of these genera in light of these behavior patterns is being reported elsewhere.

Slud (1964:299) noted it singly or in small groups in humid forests of Costa Rica as we did in the Tuxtlas. We found that solitary birds were territorial by their sedentariness, site fidelity, and aggressiveness of color-marked individuals. The status of loose aggregations, particularly noticeable during and briefly after nortes, is unknown. Most individuals in these goups disappeared after banding, but recaptures of a few individuals showed them to be moving all over the study areas and between study areas as non-territorial individuals. Such floaters were found in all migrant species studied, but only in the Wood Thrush and Swainson's Thrush (*Catharus ustulatus*) was aggregation seen. Interactions between territorial birds and these floater groups were variable but usually involved little more

John H. Rappole

Figure 7. Crest-raising and spread displays of the Wood Thrush.

Figure 8. Wing-flick display of the Wood Thrush.

Figure 9. Horizontal-stretch display of the Wood Thrush.

Figure 10. Upward display of the Wood Thrush.

than low intensity aggression displays and calling, in contrast to the situation seen in one to one conflicts between neighbors where high intensity displays and fights took place. The association of these non-territorial birds with nortes suggests that they were temporary visitors forced to lower elevations by marked low temperatures in the higher elevations. Average territory size was about .5 ha, although one bird on Site 2 had a territory less than .2 ha which it was hard pressed to hold against three neighbors. It spent roughly 35 percent of daylight hours defending territory in February, later giving up the territory and becoming a floater.

Swainson's Thrush (Catharus ustulatus)

PREFERRED HABITAT

See table 2. It is similar to the Wood Thrush in that loose aggregations appeared in selva after nortes, but different in that it was not a consistent winter resident at our low altitude. Slud (1964:299) and Morton (1972) noted a similarly irregular pattern in Costa Rica and Panama respectively. In Colombia, where they are apparently solitary and common (Miller 1963:42–43), they may be territorial. Perhaps resources are distributed in a manner that can be efficiently defended in Colombia while in other tropical areas the food is found in dispersed clumps more suitable for exploitation by flocks. Some individuals captured in December and January in the Tuxtlas had fat loads. A strategy of hyperphagia with concomitant buildup of fat should be advantageous for individuals dependent on patchy resources. A similar pattern is seen in floaters of many species which are territorial in the Tuxtlas. While territorial individuals carried light fat loads, floaters of the same species were sometimes captured with light, moderate, and occasionally heavy fat loads. This phenomenon occurred in both winter and permanent residents. A possibility in the case of Swainson's Thrush is that the territorial and flocking populations are different subspecies. Griscom (1932: 309, 310) reports that *C. u. ustulatus* winters in Central America while *C. u. swainsoni* winters in the Andes. This is supported by Miller (1963:43) (but see Monroe [1968:307] for the records of *swainsoni* wintering in British Honduras).

DEFENSE OF TERRITORY

None observed.

Blue-gray Gnatcatcher (Polioptila caerulea)

PREFERRED HABITAT

See table 2.

FORAGING BEHAVIOR AND COMPETITORS

This is a fairly active forager in the bare topmost limbs of the canopy, hawking and gleaning, usually searching above the horizontal, taking insects from the branches as well as from the air.

No common permanent residents foraged in the same part of the canopy or in the same way. The closest possible competitor is *P. plumbea*, which is rare in the Tuxtlas, though not in other parts of *caerulea*'s range (Monroe, 1968:311). The migrant American Redstart (*Setophaga ruticilla*) often foraged in similar microhabitats where it was also an active flycatcher.

TERRITORIALITY

None observed. Intraspecific relationships were not determined. It vocalized often, giving the "pss pip pss pip pip" call as well as occasional "whisper" songs; and solitary birds were often seen, although at times two or three were seen in the same tree without apparent interaction.

White-eyed Vireo (Vireo griseus)

PREFERRED HABITAT

Common in selva. Loetscher (1955:38) listed it as "fairly common" and Andrle (1966) termed it "not common" as a winter resident in Veracruz.

FORAGING BEHAVIOR AND COMPETITORS

In selva, foraging height varied considerably, normally greater than 6 m and less than 20 m, but as high as 30 m.

A very deliberate forager, it peers from each perch before moving to the next, usually in fairly dense foliage. Individuals alternately glean, hawk or hover; and most food is insects.

The closest potential resident competitor would presumably be the two *Hylophilus* species which are roughly the same size as the White-eyed Vireo but are very different behaviorally, being more reminiscent of *Parus* than of *Vireo* both in foraging and flocking. We observed no hostile interaction between members of these or any other species with the White-eyed Vireo.

TERRITORIALITY

They vocalized at regular intervals, using both the plaintive, repeated "mew" call and song in territorial advertisement.

Playback of both song and "mew" calls elicited approach by territorial individuals. Display involved facing the opponent with feet spread apart, head and body on a plane parallel to the ground or branch with bill held open and pointed directly at CB (caged bird). Display was accompanied by whiney "chirr" notes and "mew" call notes.

Black and White Warbler (Mniotilta varia)

PREFERRED HABITAT

See table 2.

FORAGING BEHAVIOR AND COMPETITORS

All but one of 27 foraging forays was on bark, with foraging height variable but averaging, 8.8 m. It fed most often (48 percent) on trunks larger than .3 m in diameter and as often moved sideways or down, as up the tree, contrary to Slud (1964:318). No other species of similar size or anatomical configuration exploits this microhabitat.

TERRITORIALITY

Skutch noted (in Griscom and Sprunt 1957:272) that it was territorial in Panama; we also observed evidence of territoriality, however, no stylized displays occurred in these encounters other than the use of the "wesee wesee" song and attacks. The weak "tseet" call note was also given, but in general this species is quieter and less regular in its vocalizations than any other winter resident.

Worm-eating Warbler (Helmitheros vermivorus)

PREFERRED HABITAT

Fairly common in selva. Skutch noted it to be widely distributed in winter but everywhere very rare (in Bent 1953:45). Edwards (1972:204) termed it rare for Mexico although Loetscher (1955:39) called it "not rare" for Veracruz.

John H. Rappole

Foraging height averaged 3.5 m—different from that noted by Skutch (in Bent, 1953:45), Slud (1964:318), or Lack and Lack (1972:135), all of whom found it low or on the ground. It forages in dense foliage where it picks, probes, and gleans from hanging dead leaves, vine tangles, twigs, and occasionally green leaves. Rummaging among dead leaves is the most commonly observed of these activities. It searches intensively 10–15 sec in each tangle before moving on. We seldom saw it on the ground, and then it hopped rather than walked.

The most similar species in foraging behavior were the Tawny-crowned Vireo (*Hylophilus ochraceiceps*) and the Plain Xenops (*Xenops minutus*) both of which are rummagers in the lower mid-level selva. All three occurred commonly in the same foraging flocks with no evidence of aggression among them. *H. ochraceiceps* forages more often on green leaves than on dead leaves and is a gleaner rather than a prober, acrobatically hanging and searching the under sides of the large fronds of such common lower story plants as *Astrocarium mexicanum*. The xenops, although it spends more of its time exploring dead leaves than the vireo, spends most of it time tearing apart dead vine stems, for which its short, wedge-shaped bill and powerful feet are well adapted.

TERRITORIALITY

Territorial birds responded vigorously to playbacks of vocalizations and displayed to, and attacked, caged conspecifics. Frequency of its vocalizations was not determined because of the similarity of its "chewt" call to the "chip" of the more vocal Kentucky Warbler (*Oporornis formosus*).

Displays included the "bow" (figure 11) in which the bird tilts its body at a sharp angle toward the ground while facing its opponent. The effect is to emphasize the visual impact of the striped head. In this position the bird appears frozen in the act of moving from one branch to a lower one. The "gape" display (figure 12) is given in higher intensity situations. It involves facing the opponent, pointing the body on a horizontal plane and gaping. A similar display was described by Dilger (1965a:319) for the Wood Thrush as "probably a ritualized intention movement to bite."

Orange-crowned Warbler (Vermivora celata)

PREFERRED HABITAT

See table 2.

Figure 11. "Bow" display of the Worm-eating Warbler.

Figure 12. "Gape" display of the Worm-eating Warbler.

FORAGING BEHAVIOR AND COMPETITORS

Insufficient data.

TERRITORIALITY

Individuals vocalized regularly with a "chip" note and showed site fidelity.

Yellow Warbler (Dendroica petechia)

PREFERRED HABITAT

See table 2.

FORAGING BEHAVIOR AND COMPETITORS

Insufficient data.

TERRITORIALITY

Individuals vocalized regularly. Skutch (in Bent, 1953: 176) stated that "Each wintering bird appears to have its own territory. . . ."

Magnolia Warbler (Dendroica magnolia)

PREFERRED HABITAT

Common in selva contrary to Skutch (in Bent 1953: 208; Slud 1964:322; Edwards 1972:288) but in agreement with Warner and Beer (1957).

FORAGING BEHAVIOR AND COMPETITORS

No permanent resident species forage in the same portion of the canopy.

The closest possible competitor appears to be Wilson's Warbler, another migrant; they occur in the same major habitat types and both forage in the upper third of the canopy where the foliage is fairly dense and leaf size is small (6 cm or less in length). Both use twigs primarily as perches and leaves as feeding substrate. We have observed individuals of each forage close to the other, apparently in the same microhabitat in 2-m *Solanum* second growth and in 30-m selva. They show similarity in characteristics that have been used in niche overlap studies (table 3). In fact, they appear to be much more similar than examples given by Cody (1974:92–98, 256) in his study of niche overlap (e.g. Lincoln's Sparrow and Common Yellowthroat, Bridled Titmouse and Black-throated Gray Warbler, Wilson's Warbler and Yellow Warbler). Cody (1974:265) states that species similar in ". . . appearance, voice and/or morphology are apparently responding to a resource space unable to support them as separate ecological entities." He further predicts that these species should be interspecifically territorial. Yet, of the numerous occasions on which both species were

seen together, no attacks or displays were observed, although the birds sometimes passed within .5 m of one another. Both species are intolerant of conspecifics.

Can species be similar in several characteristics and yet escape competition? Cody's conclusions are based on comparisons of foraging height, morphology, habitat preference and "foraging behavior" (a measure of time between foraging attempts, average speed and distance traveled in foraging). Important ways not considered by Cody in which species may differ include foraging strategy and search area within the microhabitat. These appear to be the ways in which the Wilson's and Magnolia Warbler coexist. Wilson's searches above the horizontal plane on the underside of overhanging leaves, while the Magnolia most often searches below, peering around on the same plane on which it is standing. Furthermore, the Wilson's Warbler takes a single searching glance and then flits and picks its prey from the substrate. The Magnolia Warbler spends more time peering then gleans its prey.

The strategy of the Wilson's Warbler is that of a flycatcher; the bird takes most of its prey while in the air, although the prey may or may not be. Prey are fast and poorly camouflaged Diptera for the most part. The area searched is the undersides of the outermost leaves of the canopy. The wings are used in these short flits, although the feeding substrate is usually only 2–5 cm distant. The relatively broad bill and strong rictal bristles are further evidence of a flycatcher strategy.

The Magnolia Warbler is a quickly moving gleaner, looking for moderately fast, fairly well camouflaged prey. Bill shape and size are not adapted to catching insects on the wing but rather to snatching them quickly. Lack and Lack (1972:136) have reported that, in its hawking behavior, the Magnolia Warbler resembles the American Redstart. We found, however, that hawking and hovering combined made up less than 10 percent of total foraging attempts. Probably only larger, slower food items disturbed in gleaning are chased.

TERRITORIALITY

In all habitats, the Magnolia Warbler was solitary, and vocal, the characteristic "tszzzk" call being given by both sexes in defense of territory.

Experiments, in which males were introduced into females' territories and vice versa, proved that display patterns were the same for both sexes in defense of territory. A "wing droop" posture figure 13, similar to that seen in many other species, was given at a distance of 1–2 m from the intruder. In this position the yellow rump patch is accentuated by the darker wings, lower

John H. Rappole

Table 3. Comparison of Wilson's Warbler (*Wilsonia pusilla*) and Magnolia Warbler (*Dendroica magnolia*)

	Number	Mean bill depth[1]	Mean bill length[2]	Mean foraging height	Mean body size[3]	Mean weight	Mean wing length[4]	Number captured in selva/100 net hr[5]
Wilsonia pusilla	20	2.6 mm	6.8 mm	18.0 m	50.9 mm	6.7 g	52.6 mm	.21
Dendroica magnolia	20	2.9 mm	7.9 mm	18.2 m	52.2 mm	7.2 g	56.7 mm	.16
Ratio		.89	.86	.98	.98	.93	.93	.76

[1] At nostril

[2] Nostril to tip of bill.

[3] Total length minus exposed culmen and tail length.

[4] Chord, not flattened.

[5] Calculated as total number of individuals captured from areas 2 and 3 divided by total net hours × 100. Assuming equal probability of capture, this figure represents a relative abundance measure in selva.

rump and back feathers, as well as by the bird's continual bobbing and hopping. The "gape" display (figure 14) is similar in appearance to the "gape" display of the Worm-eating Warbler, but the visual impact of this display is different in the Magnolia Warbler as the "gape" is combined with a "stretch" that accentuates the breast streaking. The third sequence, seen in conflict situations, may or may not be a display. In this movement, the bird makes a short, fluttering horizontal flight in which the tail is held open and the bird maintains an upright position. We observed this sequence on only 4 occasions compared to over 20 for each of the other displays.

Yellow-rumped Warbler (*Dendroica coronata*)

PREFERRED HABITAT

See table 2.

FORAGING BEHAVIOR AND COMPETITORS

This is a flocking species, irregular in occurrence. Individuals usually associated in large flocks, although occasionally birds were solitary. Other authors have made similar observations (Biaggi 1970:285, Puerto Rico; Russell 1964:153, British Honduras; Slud 1964: 323, Costa Rica).

TERRITORIALITY

None observed.

Black-throated Green Warbler (*Dendroica virens*)

PREFERRED HABITAT

See table 2.

Figure 13. "Wing droop" display of the Magnolia Warbler.

FORAGING BEHAVIOR AND COMPETITORS

Foraging behavior was virtually the same as that described by Lack and Lack (1972:144), and MacArthur (1958). The bird gleans the tops of the outermost leaves of trees in canopy and subcanopy, often clambering about on terminal tufts and occasionally hovering.

There were no other species, permanent or winter resident, which normally foraged in the same part of the canopy or used similar methods.

Figure 14. "Gape" display of the Magnolia Warbler.

Both males and females vocalized at regular intervals using a "tsit" note, and they were solitary. Dickey and van Rossem (1938) reported that in El Salvador they occurred in small to medium-sized flocks.

Ovenbird (Seiurus aurocapillus)

PREFERRED HABITAT

Common in selva. It was listed as uncommon in Veracruz by Loetscher (1955:41) and rather rare in Mexico by Edwards (1972:214).

FORAGING BEHAVIOR AND COMPETITORS

Slud (1964:326) stated of the Ovenbird in Costa Rica that "It is the only migrant bird that walks about on the forest floor." This is also true in the Tuxtlas. The Kentucky Warbler spends much time on the forest floor, but contrary to authors quoted in Bent (1953: 508–509) it never walks and, in fact, seldom picks food from the ground.

The Ovenbird walks slowly and steadily over rotting logs, dead leaves, etc., almost always feeding from the substrate on which it is walking, ignoring the green leafy vegetation for the most part. The Kentucky Warbler, more active than the Ovenbird, moves by hopping and flitting, but not walking. It almost always searches above the horizontal, gleaning insects from the undersurfaces of the low herbaceous growth typical of dense humid forests. It often climbs into the lower leaves of these plants where it gleans from the under surface of the next higher layer of vegetation. A common foraging method involved making short jumps (3–4 cm) from the forest floor to snatch insects from the surface of low leafy vegetation. It will occasionally take food items from the forest floor but this was seen in less than 10 percent of observed foraging attempts.

Both a Kentucky Warbler and an Ovenbird had territories in an area under intensive study for 1.5 months. They often foraged within sight of one another, with no interaction between them or between them and any other species. There are no ground foraging permanent residents of remotely similar size, the robin-sized Streaked Cotinga (*Attila spadiceus*) and the Black-faced Antthrush (*Formicarius analis*) being the only passerines seen regularly on the forest floor.

TERRITORIALITY

Both sexes vocalized at regular intervals and Rappole heard the "teacher teacher" song once (11 February 1975). Its chip note is similar to that of the Kentucky Warbler. Both Wetmore (1916) and Skutch (in Bent, 1953:472) reported the bird silent on wintering grounds in Puerto Rico and Panama respectively, although Slud (1964:326) reported that it called often in Costa Rica.

This species did not respond strongly to introduced caged intruders. Rappole spent several hours observing birds foraging within sight of caged conspecifics without noting any signs of response. This behavior was in direct contrast to the response elicited by a free-flying intruder. On 27 February 1975, a caged intruder was placed in the territory of Ovenbird Br at 0630 hrs. Br inspected the "stake out" briefly and then ignored it. At 0710 hours an unmarked bird flew to a log within Br's territory and was immediately attacked and chased. No visual displays were seen during this sequence but a rapid bill-snapping was heard. On 11 March 1975 at 0800 hours Rappole collected Br. During the 150 hours Rappole spent in this bird's territory, it was the only individual of this species seen except for the brief encounter described above; yet by 1030 hours of the same day another ovenbird, a color-banded floater (B1) originally captured 75 m from Br's territory, had moved in and had begun vocalizing, apparently establishing a territory. On 19 April 1975 it was recaptured there.

John H. Rappole

Northern Waterthrush (*Seiurus noveboracensis*)

PREFERRED HABITAT

See table 2.

FORAGING BEHAVIOR AND COMPETITORS

Foraging behavior consists of picking insects and other small invertebrates from moist or wet soil. Like its congeners, the Northern Waterthrush is a walker, although it hops over dips, sticks, logs, etc. rather than walk around them. Bobbing is a part of its foraging motion, probably evolved to reduce time between prey sighting and capture movement. There are no other ground foraging passerines in its preferred habitat.

TERRITORIALITY

It is solitary and both sexes vocalize at regular intervals in defense of separate territories, using a loud, ringing "chink" call note. Eaton (1953) suspected this species of being territorial in winter as have others (Slud, 1964:327; Schwartz, 1964; Morton, 1971).

Louisiana Waterthrush (*Seiurus motacilla*)

PREFERRED HABITAT

See table 2.

FORAGING BEHAVIOR AND COMPETITORS

S. motacilla is very similar to *S. noveborancensis* in foraging habits. Their vocalizations are similar but distinguishable. All 3 *Seiurus* species are well separated by microhabitat preferences in the Tuxtlas; *S. noveboracensis* prefers damp, mud-floored borders, *S. motacilla*, damp or wet stream beds, while *S. aurocapillus* prefers the drier forest floor. These preferences may be accentuated through interspecific competition although Lack and Lack (1972) report seeing members of all three species foraging within 6 m of one another in Jamaica. Certainly for each of the species the other 2 are the closest competitors in the Tuxtlas.

TERRITORIALITY

Both sexes vocalize at regular intervals and show site fidelity, returning to the same territory in subsequent years. Territories are long and narrow, following stream beds closely. There were 2 territorial birds on Area 2. On 6 January one of them was collected. On 7 January another bird, unbanded, had taken over the vacant area and was patrolling it, vocalizing. On 28 February another unbanded floater was captured on the territory of 1 of the banded birds. It was banded

and released and caught on 11 March in another area, well away from the original stream.

Kentucky Warbler (*Oporornis formosus*)

PREFERRED HABITAT

Common (see table 2), although considered rare in Mexico by Edwards (1972:215).

FORAGING BEHAVIOR AND COMPETITORS

As noted in the Ovenbird account, this species forages quite differently from the Ovenbird, searching low, leafy vegetation rather than forest floor debris for food. In this behavior it resembles no other Tuxtla species.

Willis (1966:209) has made a case for competition between the Kentucky Warbler and the Spotted Antbird (*Hylophylax naevoides*) a species not found in the Tuxtlas, largely on the basis of supplanting seen at ant swarms (*Labidus praedator*). Ant swarms represent a rather special resource, where prey are localized. Under such circumstances, interspecific competition is common (Recher and Recher 1969; Chapin 1932), but it is difficult to say what, if anything, this means in terms of niche overlap between the competing species. Descriptions in Skutch (1969:245), Slud (1964:221), and Wetmore (1972:230) indicate that the antbird, while not restricted totally to ant swarms, has foraging patterns that are closely adapted to exploit this phenomenon, indicating that swarms were and probably are important to the evolution and survival of the Spotted Antbird (Leigh in Cody and Diamond 1975: 55). Swarms are not vital to the Kentucky Warbler. In the Tuxtlas, Kentucky Warblers occasionally associated with other species following ant swarms or with interspecific foraging flocks of other types, but only while these associations were on its territory. Individuals spend 60 percent or more of their foraging time on the ground while the ant bird "...drops to the ground only for the instant required to secure prey" (Slud 1964:221).

TERRITORIALITY

The bird is territorial on its wintering grounds, individuals returning to the same territory in successive seasons. Territories are advertised by a loud "chip" note. This species did not usually respond well to stake outs of caged conspecifics; but we observed three aggressive encounters between territory owners and free-flying conspecifics. Displays consisted of short, darting flights and a "gape" display similar to that of the Magnolia Warbler. Bill snapping was used during chases at intruders.

Willis (1966:208) and Karr (1971b) surmised that it might exhibit territoriality.

Common Yellowthroat (Geothlypis trichas)

PREFERRED HABITAT

See table 2.

As is the case for a few other species, cutting of rain forest can create more habitat, but only if cutover areas are wet and are allowed to grow back to short second growth.

FORAGING BEHAVIOR AND COMPETITORS

There are no resident species morphologically similar in the Tuxtlas which use the same habitat.

TERRITORIALITY

The distinctive "tsup" note is used regularly by both sexes of this species. We have no data on visual displays.

Yellow-breasted Chat (Icteria virens)

PREFERRED HABITAT

See table 2.

FORAGING BEHAVIOR AND COMPETITORS

There are no resident species morphologically similar which use the same habitat.

TERRITORIALITY

Both sexes use the hoarse "chuck" as a regular vocalization. We have no data on visual displays.

Hooded Warbler (Wilsonia citrina)

PREFERRED HABITAT

See table 2.

FORAGING BEHAVIOR AND COMPETITORS

The following summary of Hooded Warbler foraging strategy is based on general notes and on coded notes for 60 foraging attempts. The bird foraged in open to fairly dense situations. Foraging height was variable from 0–17 m but averages 2.7 m. Hawking and sallying flights for flying insects constituted 72 percent of total foraging attempts with gleaning, hovering, and rummaging being used occasionally. It is much more active than most tyrannids and probably stirs into activity much of its food. The search pattern is concentrated above the horizontal plane of the perch, and prey is captured 1.0 m from the perch on the average. Stomach contents showed mostly small (2–3 mm) weevils, fungus beetles, bark beetles, and a few Hymenoptera. Such analyses are of little value for species like the Hooded Warbler that feed largely on soft bodied prey, since hard-shelled prey take much longer to digest and therefore appear in samples in disproportionate numbers. Many individuals seemed to have "favorite" areas within their territory, such as a fallen tree or brush pile where they spent much of their time.

The Sulphur-rumped Flycatcher (*Myiobius sulphureipygius*) is the only permanent resident potential competitor for the Hooded Warbler in the Tuxtlas. Mean foraging height for the 2 species was roughly the same though less variable in the flycatcher. *Myiobius* seemed not to glean as much as the Hooded Warbler and used sallying more than hawking. Both species attended interspecific flocks while the flocks were on their territories. There are differences in micro-habitat preferences. The Hooded Warbler is common and evenly distributed in selva while *Myiobius* is common but unevenly distributed, often being seen around thickets and vine tangles. The very long (5–8 mm) rictal bristles and larger, heavier bill of *Myiobius* suggest that this species takes a different, perhaps larger, prey type.

Willis (1966:209) calls the Hooded Warbler "practically a counterpart" of the Spotted Antbird (*Hylophylax naevoides*) in foraging in British Honduras. However, Skutch (1969:245) states that few species appear to be more dependent on ant-swarms than the Spotted Antbird. The large territories (3.1 ha) of the antbird probably reflect this dependence on the ant swarms. The Hooded Warbler is not dependent on swarms. Mean prey size for the antbirds as reported by Willis (1972:106, 107) is about 10 mm with items up to 60 mm. Prey size for the much smaller Hooded Warbler (10 g to the antbird's 18 g) is usually less than 5 mm and averages less than 3 mm. This suggests differences in critical niche parameters commensurate with the considerable anatomical differences that exist between the species. Competition for food is unlikely. The Spotted Antbird is not found in the Tuxtlas.

Sex ratios in the Hooded Warbler are perplexing. Of 12 birds holding territory in selva of area 2 in 1975, 10 were males. Both birds holding territories in Area 4's secondary forest were females. In general males outnumbered females 8:1 in rain forest and females slightly outnumbered males in secondary forest. These ratios are based on specimen data as well as observations so that the skew is not caused by male-plumaged females, which, in any case, composed less than 5 percent of the female population according to specimen data. During migration both sexes were captured in an approximately equal ratio.

TERRITORIALITY

We did more work with this bird than with any other because of its abundance, visibility, and ease of cap-

John H. Rappole

ture. Visual display patterns are probably no more varied in this species than in the others described, but the bird responded well to caged intruders so that more complete descriptions and films of displays were obtained. Visual displays include: 1) "wing droop" (figure 15)—This is a basic pattern from which other displays are formed; the wings are held slightly out, the head is pulled in and the feathers fluffed so that the bird has a hunched appearance. The bird often assumes this position when landing near an intruder. It will then hop down the branch toward the intruders, maintaining this attitude. 2) "head switch" (figure 16)—This display is a variation of the "wing droop." The bird's body is turned away from the intruder and it turns its head from side to side. 3) "upward" (figure 17)—In high intensity situations the bird faces the intruder, standing close to it (10 cm), and moves up and down from this position to the "wing droop." 4) Supplanting attacks, direct attacks, and bill snapping are also included in the display repertoire. Displays seem to accentuate the gold cheek patch and black bib, yet most females do not have this pattern and are perfectly capable of defending territory against male intruders.

The Hooded Warbler was the only species for which sufficient data were gathered to allow mapping of territories. The "territory flush" technique, combined with information from recaptures, resightings, and caged intruder experiments, provided the data points for boundary determination. Average territory size was .28 ha as of 1 February 1975. Of the 12 territories shown (figure 18), 6 were occupied by birds banded during the 1973–74 season. Since 2 of the territories were in areas in which the birds were not netted the first year, this represents a return rate of 60 percent.

None of the territorial birds died of natural causes in either the 1973–74 or 1974–75 season. In February 1975 all of the area south of the road in Figure 18 was cleared. Of the birds with territories in that area, two were later captured as floaters in the area north of the road. The others disappeared.

Once territory was established, the birds became very sedentary. In over 7,000 net hr in Area 2, only twice were territorial birds captured more than 50 m from their original point of capture, with the exception of the two previously mentioned birds whose territories were destroyed.

Schwartz (1964:180) stated that territory defense by Northern Waterthrushes in Venezuela breaks down during the last few weeks before the birds start northward. To test this in Hooded Warblers, a mount was placed in a bird's territory daily in the same place at the same time. The territory owner atttacked this mount every day from 25 February until 23 March

Figure 15. "Wing droop" display of the Hooded Warbler.

Figure 16. "Head switch" display of the Hooded Warbler.

Figure 17. "Upward" display of the Hooded Warbler.

We know of no similar patterns in the winter residents of the Tuxtlas.

To test the relative importance of vocalization, color patterns, and movement, 45 experiments were performed in which different combinations of bird, voice, and mount were presented in the territory of a marked bird. Results of these experiments are presented in table 4. Responses were graded as: intense—prolonged display and attack; moderate—approach, vocalization, some visual display; light—approach and vocalization; none—no bird seen or heard. Three males and 1 female were used as the experimental birds. The results present a fairly clear pattern of the aggressive territorial response in this species. A bird sitting still was unlikely to be seen, let alone attacked. If it were seen, it was approached and investigated, sometimes displayed to and sometimes attacked. A vocalization was almost always investigated and, if a bird of the "right" color pattern were found, it was usually displayed to and attacked, often repeatedly. On a few occasions, sessions went over three hours with a territorial bird attacking a caged bird or mount at approximately one minute intervals. Once a territory owner had seen a mount or caged bird and heard an accompanying vocalization it would continue attacking and displaying whether the intruder stopped vocalizing or not.

This same pattern of interaction was seen in free-flying Hooded Warblers. On 10 March 1975, Rappole was in a blind on a territory belonging to a male Hooded Warbler banded R1Gr (# 6332). At 1115 hr a banded female Hooded Warbler (YW1, #7459) was seen on R1Gr's area. She had been captured 2 km away two days before and had not returned, indicating that she was a floater. She was silent and R1Gr was not in sight. At 1200 hr a second intruder was seen, an unbanded male (later captured and banded YWr, # 8279). Both floaters foraged in front of the blind quietly, often within 2 m of each other, with no apparent interaction. When R1Gr returned, he chased

1975 which, from recapture and resighting data, is known to be approximately their time of departure.

All species studied using caged conspecifics and playback were still defending their territories as of 14 March 1975, less than a month before most would leave. They were also heard vocalizing at regular intervals until the approximate time of departure, indicating that territories were still being maintained. It seems unlikely that selection would favor a change in social system unless there was a change in resource availability. Morton (1972) describes such a case in the Bay-breasted Warbler (*Dendroica castanea*), which is solitary and insectivorous during the early part of the winter in Panama and gregarious and frugivorous later in the winter when the dry season fruiting begins.

Table 4. Hooded Warbler (*Wilsonia citrina*) territory owner response to conspecific intruder experiments

Experiment type	Number	Intense	Moderate	Light	None
Bird − no voice	11	2	1	5	3
Bird + voice	17	10	4	3	0
Mount − no voice	6	1	2	2	1
Mount + voice	6	3	2	1	0
Voice only	5	0	0	4	1

John H. Rappole

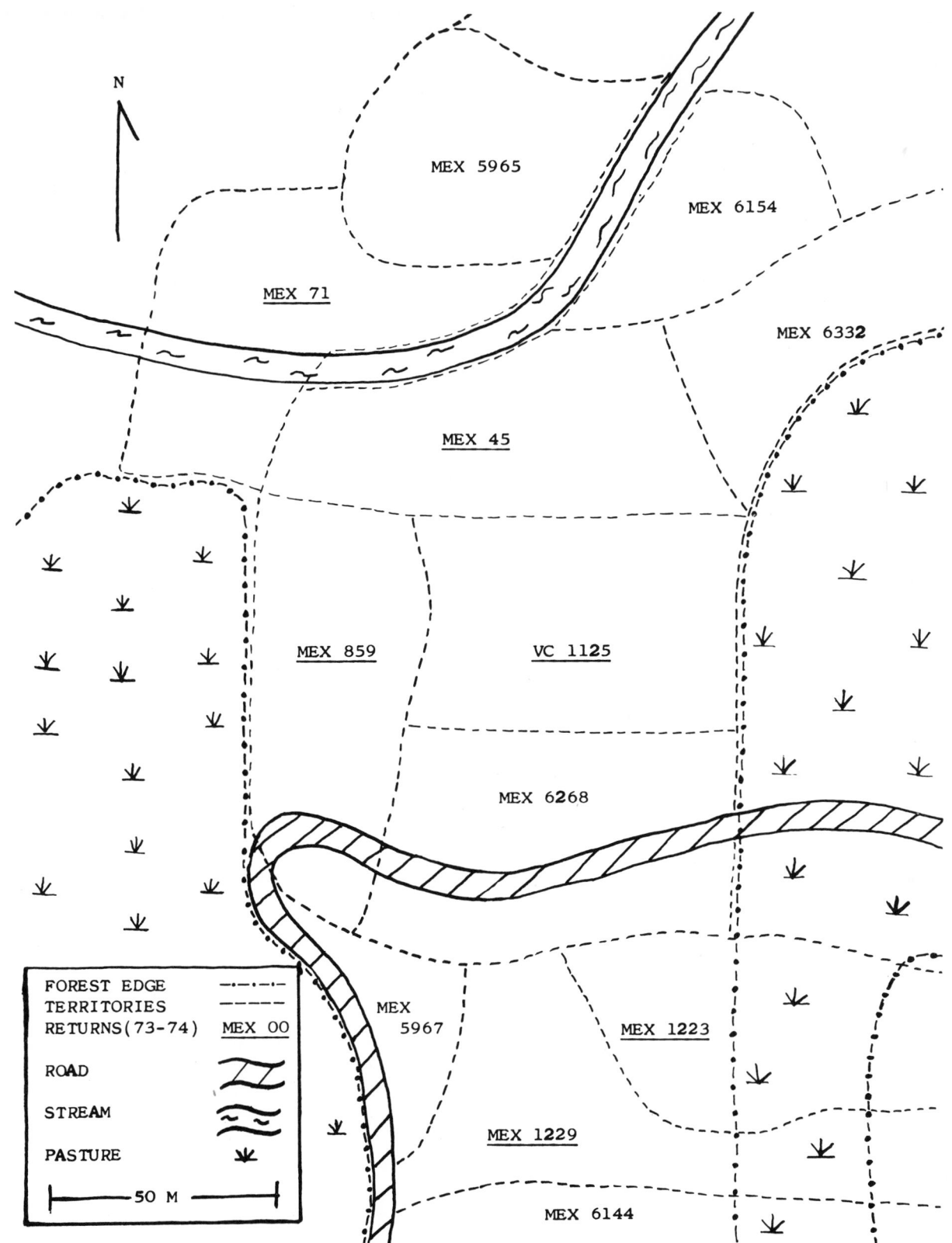

N

MEX 5965

MEX 6154

MEX 71

MEX 6332

MEX 45

MEX 859   VC 1125

MEX 6268

FOREST EDGE   —·—·—·—
TERRITORIES   — — — — —
RETURNS (73-74)   MEX 00

ROAD

STREAM

PASTURE

├——— 50 M ———┤

MEX
5967

MEX 1223

MEX 1229

MEX 6144

Figure 18.   Hooded Warbler (*Wilsonia citrina*) territories on
study Site 2.

both birds out of sight. However, they both came back as soon as he had moved to another part of his territory.

This sequence continued throughout the afternoon, the floaters being evidently unwilling to abandon a rich food source (sewage drain). Attacks were of two types. In low intensity situations, a supplanting attack was used in which the aggressor fluttered slowly in the direction of the intruder. No fighting or chasing was involved. The second type was given in response to a vocalizing intruder. About once an hour the intruder male (YWr) vocalized, giving the chip note softly. Whenever this calling occurred, R1Gr flew from wherever he was in his territory and attacked with a high intensity, rapid rush. Bill snapping accompanied this type of attack. If the intruder saw the attacker coming, the attack became a chase. If not, the intruder was hit and then chased.

At 1530 hr R1Gr was collected. The two floaters continued to forage peaceably within sight of one another for the rest of the day. The next day (11 March 1975) both floaters were again seen foraging on R1Gr's old area, and at 1230 hr the female chased an unbanded intruder male from the area. At 1730 hr the male (YWr) attacked YW1 and drove her out, taking over the territory 26 hr after R1Gr had been removed. YWr was collected at that time. When the area was checked on 12 March the female (YW1) was found to be in sole possession of the territory. In three other cases where known territorial Hooded Warblers were removed, they were replaced by birds that had previously had no territory and had shown no site fidelity. Once established on a territory they became sedentary and aggressive.

Wilson's Warbler (Wilsonia pusilla)

PREFERRED HABITAT

See table 2.

FORAGING BEHAVIOR AND COMPETITORS

The closest potential competitor for this bird appears to be the Magnolia Warbler. As described in the Magnolia Warbler account, the Wilson's Warbler forages very high in selva, at 15–20 m. They were captured in mist nets at edges or in second growth and only rarely in selva. No resident species in the Tuxtlas area resembles them in foraging microhabitat or behavior.

TERRITORIALITY

Territoriality on the wintering ground has been noted by both Skutch (in Bent 1953:634) and Moynihan (1962:96).

Caged intruder experiments gave inconclusive results. Territorial birds responded to vocalization, inspected the cage and usually left. Our only positive notes on displays were of an observation of a boundary dispute. At 1745 hr on 5 February 1975, Rappole heard a very rapid series of its chip notes and saw two birds 4 m up in a tree and about 1 m apart. The tails of both were cocked and the wings slightly down and extended in a posture similar to the "wing droop" of the Magnolia Warbler (figure 13). The birds switched back and forth very rapidly in short hops for about 60 sec, vocalizing with the harsh "tshep" call note and maintaining this "wing droop" posture. They then flew at each other and fluttered to the ground, fighting. At this point they separated to perches about 4 m up and 3 m apart, calling vigorously. Then one of them sang. The next day a Wilson's Warbler was again heard singing near the same area. They did not sing often.

American Redstart (Setophaga ruticilla)

PREFERRED HABITAT

Common in selva but noted as rather rare in Mexico by Edwards (1972:219).

FORAGING BEHAVIOR AND COMPETITORS

Foraging at canopy level involved much hawking for flying insects, although gleaning and hovering were also seen. Preferred foliage density is open, whether at the top of a 30-m canopy in primary forest or a 10-m canopy in second growth. Individuals were occasionally seen at lower levels at breaks in the forest caused by tree fall or at edges where they sometimes dropped to near ground level. MacArthur (1958:614) cited "principal feeding height" as 5–50 ft (1.5–15.2 m) in Costa Rica.

TERRITORIALITY

Both sexes responded to playback by calling and approaching, but left after inspecting "stake outs." Figure 19 shows a "wing droop" display seen in a boundary dispute between two males. In this display the wings and tail were slightly spread, exposing the bright orange areas. The body was tilted downward. The bird maintained this posture while hopping rapidly from branch to branch.

Diamond and Smith (1973) report returns of redstarts to the same wintering area in Jamaica.

Summer Tanager (Piranga rubra)

PREFERRED HABITAT

See table 2.

John H. Rappole

Foraging height was 10 m or higher in rather dense vegetation. The few foraging attempts observed involved hawking after fairly large insect prey and picking prey from leaves and branches. Slud (1964:357) states that it feeds on fruits as well as insects during the winter in Costa Rica where it is also solitary and vocal. Data are insufficient for a meaningful comparison with other species.

TERRITORIALITY

Individuals were solitary and vocalized regularly with a repeated 'chikatik." We have no data on visual displays.

Indigo Bunting (*Passerina cyanea*)

PREFERRED HABITAT

Common but irregular in open fields and pastures. Like the Yellow-rumped Warbler (*Dendroica coronata*) they would be in large flocks in a field one day and gone the next. Forest cutting is undoubtedly responsible for the movement of large numbers into the Tuxtlas. They were not always found in flocks in pastures. At times single birds or small groups were found at openings deep in selva.

FORAGING BEHAVIOR AND COMPETITORS

There were no permanent resident seed-eaters of similar size occupying the same habitats in the Tuxtlas. Blue-black Grassquits (*Volatinia jacarina*) and White-collared Seedeaters (*Sporophila torqueola*) are much smaller (8–9 gms vs 14–15 gms). Blue Buntings (*Cyanocompsa parellina*) and Rusty Sparrows (*Aimophila rufescens*) occur in different habitats. Seemingly, the closest possible competitor would be the migrant congener, the Painted Bunting (*P. ciris*).

TERRITORIALITY

Not observed.

Painted Bunting (*Passerina ciris*)

PREFERRED HABITAT

Like the Indigo Bunting it was common but irregular but not in large flocks, occurring singly or in small groups in brushy pastures. It exhibited some site fidelity. For example, a male (# 6300) captured 24 December 1974 well within primary forest in a low thicket caused by the fall of a 40 m tree, was recaptured 20 m away on 12 January 1975. The bird was recaptured a third time 2 km from the thicket in a brushy pasture on 22 February 1975.

Figure 19. "Wing droop" display of the American Redstart (*Setophaga ruticilla*).

FORAGING BEHAVIOR AND COMPETITORS

See Indigo Bunting Species Account.

TERRITORIALITY

None observed.

Territoriality

Social system structure can reveal a great deal concerning the ecology and evolution of a species (Brown 1964; Wilson 1976). Whereas most studies of sociality in birds have been on the reproductive season behavior and ecology, this study and that by Rappole and Warner (1976) have concentrated on the sociality of wintering migrants and transient migrants. Many authors have noted that individuals of some species of wintering North American passerines exhibit site fidelity and a few criteria for territoriality (Moynihan 1962; Skutch in Griscom and Sprunt 1957; Schwartz 1964; Eaton 1953; Willis 1966, Karr 1971b; Lederer 1977). However, most of these reports were based on anecedotal observations of unmarked birds. Only a few workers (e.g. Schwartz 1964) have obtained objective data on the key aspects of territoriality. We have documented these key aspects of migrant social systems in the Tuxtlas.

Site Fidelity

We define territory as a fixed area, defended against intruders. This definition includes 2 determining fac-

Table 5. Recaptures, resightings and returns of wintering migrants[1,2]

Species	Site 1[3] C	R	T	Site 2 C	R	T	Site 3 C	R	T	Site 4[3] C	R	T	Site 5 C	R	T	Totals C	R	T
Empidonax flaviventris	3	2	3	16	9	15	9	2	2	0	0	0	1	0	0	29	13	17
Empidonax minimus	1	0	0	6	2	2	0	0	0	6	3	3	1	1	1	12	6 (1)	6
Dumetella carolinensis	17	0	0	11	2	14	2	1	1	1	0	0	3	0	0	34	2	15
Hylocichla mustelina	173	40	55	72	23	77	30	7	17	2	0	0	0	0	0	277	70 (15)	149
Polioptila caerulea	1	0	0	0	0	0	0	0	0	0	0	0	0	0	0	1	0	0
Vireo griseus	15	5	6	15	5	19	5	0	0	6	2	2	6	3	4	42	16 (3)	32
Mniotilta varia	29	6	15	18	12	30	17	5	11	0	0	0	0	0	0	64	23	56
Helmitheros vermivorus	22	5	5	17	6	17	11	3	9	0	0	0	0	0	0	50	14 (1)	31
Vermivora celata	0	0	0	0	0	0	0	0	0	2	1	1	0	0	0	2	1	1
Dendroica petechia	0	0	0	1	0	0	0	0	0	2	0	0	0	0	0	3	0	0
Dendroica magnolia	19	3	5	17	7	26	10	1	1	7	4	7	4	3	7	57	18 (1)	46
Dendroica virens	6	1	1	1	0	0	1	1	1	0	0	0	0	0	0	8	2	2
Seiurus aurocapillus	6	2	6	5	2	16	7	2	2	6	3	4	2	1	2	26	8 (2)	28
Seiurus motacilla	5	2	5	4	2	2	0	0	0	0	0	0	0	0	0	9	4 (2)	8
Oporornis formosus	96	15	33	36	15	78	13	2	5	1	0	0	4	2	6	150	34 (5)	122
Geothlypis trichas	0	0	0	1	0	0	0	0	0	7	2	3	1	0	0	9	2	3
Icteria virens	0	0	0	1	0	0	0	0	0	5	4	5	1	1	3	7	5	8
Wilsonia citrina	98	10	29	39	22	146	10	6	12	7	3	6	4	1	3	158	51 (8)	196
Wilsonia pusilla	15	1	1	25	4	29	16	3	3	6	0	0	12	5	9	74	13 (1)	42
Setophaga ruticilla	4	0	0	2	1	2	1	0	0	0	0	0	0	0	0	7	1	2
Piranga rubra	5	0	0	4	1	1	5	0	0	0	0	0	0	0	0	14	1	1
Passerina cyanea	15	0	0	4	0	0	0	0	0	2	0	0	24	2	2	45	2	2
Passerina ciris	7	0	0	0	0	0	1	1	1	2	0	0	3	0	0	15	2	2
Totals																1,094	288 (39)	769

[1] C = total captured; R = individuals recaptured or resighted within 50 m of original point of capture, not including multiple recaptures of the same individuals.

[2] Numbers in parentheses denote birds captured in the 1973–74 season which were recaptured on the same territory in the 1974–75 season.

[3] Birds captured on Sites 1 and 4 had to home 2 km to return to original point of capture.

[4] T = total recaptures and resightings, including multiple recaptures and resightings of the same individual (not in same 24 hr period).

tors: site fidelity and defense. Long-term netting and observation on the 5 study sites demonstrated a high degree of site fidelity among migrants. Recapture, resighting and return data (table 5) show that: 1) 288 individuals of 22 species of migrants showed fidelity to a wintering site, 2) 124 individuals of 16 species homed to within 50 m of point of capture from release points 2 km distant and, 3) 38 individuals of 10 species captured in the 1973–74 season returned to within 50 m of point of capture in the 1974–75 season.

As the "T" columns of table 5 show, some individuals were recaptured and resighted over and over again in the same area. Table 6 is further documentation by observations of one small part of a community over a two-week period. Although only a small portion of each bird's territory was visible from the blind, the color-marked occupant birds of all six species were seen on at least 10 of 14 days of observation.

Floaters and Defense of the Territory

Both tables 5 and 6 show a large number of individuals which apparently were not sedentary occupants of a territory. Some of these birds may have been from

John H. Rappole

Table 6. Short-term dynamics of site attachment in 6 species of wintering migrants

Species	Catalog number	Date first captured	Date last seen	Total number of days on which bird was seen[1]	Total number of floaters seen
Dumetella carolinensis	6,262	23 Dec 74	11 Mar 75	11	1
Dendroica magnolia	6,153	18 Dec 74	11 Mar 75	14	1
Seiurus aurocapillus	454	23 Dec 73	11 Mar 75	13	2
Oporornis formosus	529	28 Dec 73	10 Mar 75	12	2
Wilsonia citrina	6,332	26 Dec 74	11 Mar 75	11	6
Wilsonia pusilla	5,966	13 Dec 74	11 Mar 75	10	1

[1] Total number of observation days = 14. See text for further explanation.

neighboring territories outside our netting area. Occupants occasionally were captured off their territories particularly if there were no water available on their area for drinking or bathing. Another possibility is that some of these wanderers, especially those captured in early October or late March, were migrating stragglers. A third possibility is that these wanderers were "floaters", birds without a home, still unable to defend or find a suitable area as a territory. Based on the following evidence, we conclude that most birds caught or seen on other bird's territories were floaters: 1) They were captured throughout the entire winter season, not just during migratory periods. 2) These individuals took over the territories of occupants if given the opportunity (see Species Accounts: Hooded Warbler, Ovenbird, Kentucky Warbler, Louisiana Waterthrush). 3) Movement and other behavior of these individuals were very different from that of territory owners.

The data from the species accounts, particularly those on the Hooded Warbler, Wood Thrush and Magnolia Warbler, bring into focus the relationship between territory owners and floaters. In each case where a floater was observed on the territory of another bird, it was furtive in its behavior. If the floater was seen by the owner or if it vocalized, the owner responded immediately by approach, vocalization and, if the floater did not leave, attack and chase. Yet when an owner was removed, a floater took over the area and defended it as rigorously against intruders as did the original occupant.

The response to floaters by territorial birds was not random. Rather, as described in the individual species accounts, response was a highly evolved, stylized sequence of acoustic and visual displays. In table 7, we

present a summation of response by territorial birds to caged conspecifics placed on their territories (figure 5) or to playback of taped vocalizations for 12 species of migrants. The strength of response by territorial birds to these situations varied from species to species and even among individuals of the same species. However,

Table 7. Quantification of territorial defense behavior against conspecifics for wintering migrants

Species	Field observation of territorial defense	Response to caged conspecifics			Response to playback		
		Total	+	−	Total	+	−
Empidonax flaviventris	3	1	0	1	1	1	0
Empidonax minimus	1	4	2	2	1	1	0
Dumetella carolinensis	1	3	2	1	1	1	0
Hylocichla mustelina	8	43	25	18	13	6	7
Vireo griseus	0	6	3	3	5	4	1
Helmitheros vermivorus	1	3	1	2	3	1	2
Dendroica magnolia	1	10	7	3	8	7	1
Seiurus aurocapillus	1	7	5	2	0	0	0
Oporornis formosus	3	20	11	9	11	7	4
Wilsonia citrina	15	46	38	8	55	38	17
Wilsonia pusilla	3	5	3	2	3	3	0
Setophaga ruticilla	0	0	0	0	2	2	0
Total	37	148	97	51	103	71	32

for all species tested, territory owners showed virtually the same sequence of responses to caged birds as to free-flying conspecifics. Where mounted birds or mirrors were used to mimic an intruder, these also elicited the same stylized response by the territory owner as a free-flying or caged conspecific.

In 97 of 148 staged experiments, an approach to within 5 m of the cage, speaker, or mount was recorded. Generally, approach was accompanied by vocalization and followed by visual display and attack. The species-specific displays did not vary significantly in structure from one occupant to the next of the same species, regardles of sex.

We hypothesize that floaters are an inevitable part of a territorial system. "Direction-oriented" immatures (Perdeck 1958) arrive on the wintering grounds in a random pattern of disperal. Spaces that become available due to adult mortality presumably are distributed in a random pattern as well. It is inconceivable that these two patterns should match, even if there were enough space for both immatures and returning adults. A random search through suitable habitat would seem to be the only feasible method of finding available territories.

Assuming that possession of a territory increases fitness and being a floater decreases fitness, why should an individual faced with this choice leave a territory rather than stay and fight? The answer to this question depends on the probabilities of success for each alternative. If the individual fights, are its chances of winning sufficient to offset loss of energy, physical damage or chance of death if it loses? There are a number of reasons to believe that the chance that an intruder can defeat an established owner is small: 1) The owner, in many cases, is an adult while the intruder is probably an immature. The owner is therefore likely to be a more experienced competitor and in better condition nutritionally. 2) The owner is more familiar with the area, its resources and avenues of escape. 3) An older bird represents, on the average, a superior phenotype to a younger bird, since selection has acted on it for a longer time (Mayr 1963:287).

For these reasons, the intruder is likely to lose, but it should still fight unless it has a good chance of survival if it leaves. Annual adult mortality is 40–50 percent in small passerines (Roberts 1971) so half to a third of the suitable wintering habitat will be available at the beginning of the winter season. An immature will, therefore, have a good chance of finding a territory. Even if an individual does not find an area, our data indicate that the bird can survive for some time as a floater. Removal experiments on Hooded Warblers showed that floaters were still present in early March (see Hooded Warbler Species Account).

Advertisement of the Territory

Specific descriptions of vocalizations are provided in the species accounts. For both sexes, these vocalizations were used in advertising and defending the territory from conspecifics. Song is the usual vocalization for such a function, at least for males on the breeding ground. For solitary migrants of either sex in the Tuxtlas, a much shorter, but nonetheless characteristic vocalization, the "chip note," was more often used.

Territory owners for all species of migrants studied in the Tuxtlas vocalized spontaneously at fairly regular intervals throughout the day. Mean vocalization time in seconds per hr is shown for seven common species of migrants in table 8. Often the vocalizing individual was in sight, and no obvious external stimulus for the calling could be seen. However, vocalization was also triggered by approach of a conspecific, a predator or by calling of a neighboring conspecific.

Table 8 shows that vocalization was fairly regular from dawn until 1200 hr. Calling activity then dropped off until about 1600 hr when an increase occurred. This pattern roughly parallels the general activity pattern of forest birds at this latitude.

A few species of migrants used the breeding season song throughout the winter, as well as chip notes (Yellow-bellied Flycatcher, Least Flycatcher, White-eyed Vireo). Other species did so occasionally (Ovenbird, Black-and-white Warbler, Wood Thrush). We suspected that females were singing in those species that used the song regularly. Mario Ramos was able to confirm this for two species by collecting singing females (White-eyed Vireo, Catalog 8487 and 9249; Least Flycatcher, Catalog 6037).

Establishment of Territory

Territories were established when the birds arrived on the wintering ground in the Tuxtlas and were maintained until departure in the spring (see Hooded Warbler Species Account). Early arrival and late departure dates for known wintering individuals are given in table 9.

The amount of area defended as a territory varied among individuals of the same species on our study sites (see Wood Thrush and Hooded Warbler Species Accounts). There were birds with relatively large territories, others with small territories, and floaters with no territories. Some birds remained throughout the winter on the same territory and returned there the next winter (table 5). Other birds, with apparently inadequate territories, held a territory for a time and then abandoned it, perhaps due to adverse environmental conditions, as reported for territorial Northern Waterthrushes in Venezuela by Schwartz (1964:171).

John H. Rappole

Table 8. Mean vocalization time in sec/hr for wintering migrants at Blind 1

Species	N = 4[1] 0600[2]	N = 6 0700	N = 3 0800	N = 4 0900	N = 4 1000	N = 4 1100	N = 2 1200	N = 5 1300	N = 6 1400	N = 4 1500	N = 8 1600	N = 5 1700
Empidonax flaviventris	122	23	420	180	195	195	0	0	6	45	25	20
Hylocichla mustelina	160	145	80	14	14	50	15	0	5	0	111	330
Vireo griseus	0	3	80	5	5	0	0	0	0	45	10	15
Dendroica magnolia	102	150	100	128	90	110	120	30	40	70	80	30
Oporornis formosus	20	240	60	70	167	133	20	36	27	3	23	104
Wilsonia citrina	42	69	40	66	76	105	25	52	45	13	105	114
Wilsonia pusilla	25	215	40	68	25	60	60	0	10	45	108	25
Total	471	845	820	531	572	653	240	118	133	221	462	638

[1] N = total number of hours listening during the specified time period.

[2] 0600 = 0600–0659 hr, 0700 = 0700–0759 hr, etc.

Individuals that were unable to find or defend adequate territories remained as floaters and continued to move, some throughout the winter.

Fretwell (1972:103–5) has hypothesized that territory size within habitats is a function of population density rather than competitive ability of individuals and richness of an area. According to his theory, if density is too high, a potential territory owner should leave and go to another area where density is lower but habitat is less suitable. Our observations on the behavior of territorial migrants do not support this hypothesis. This system would require a high degree of coordination between all territorial birds in a single habitat so that a potential owner could enter a single territory of this homogeneous "habitat" and receive a density cue. We have seen no evidence of coordination of this kind. Even if a cue could be evolved, it is unclear that it would be advantageous for an individual to respond. Since many habitats are fairly uniform over many square kilometers, it is difficult to perceive how the hypothetical wanderer could know the extent of the sampled "habitat" or if there was suitable habitat somewhere else into which it could fit.

Our observations indicate that territory size is determined by the amount of area a bird can economically defend (Brown 1964), dependent on an individual's competitive ability and the richness of the habitat. To find an open or weakly defended territory, an individual must move randomly through suitable habitat until it can challenge for and successfully defend an area. Schwartz (1964:171) reported unbanded newcomers in late December and January in his banded populations of territorial Northern Waterthrushes, and deRoo and Deheeger (1969) found intruders in populations of wintering, territorial Reed Warblers (*Acro-*

cephalus arundinaceus). Our data show that floaters, present throughout habitats in the Tuxtlas, continually challenged territory owners and took over defense if the owner was eliminated. We found a similar situation in territorial insectivorous passerines during migration in Texas (Rappole and Warner 1976) and on breeding grounds in Minnesota (Rappole et al 1977).

Table 9. Early and late dates for migrants known to be wintering on the basis of recapture and resighting data

Species	Earliest date[1]	Latest date
Empidonax flaviventris	—[2]	5 May
Empidonax minimus	—	26 Mar
Hylocichla mustelina	12 Oct	31 Mar
Vireo griseus	—	19 Mar
Mniotilta varia	11 Sept	20 Mar
Helmitheros vermivorus	—	27 Mar
Dendroica magnolia	21 Oct	12 Apr
Seiurus aurocapillus	—	19 Apr
Seiurus motacilla	9 Aug	9 Mar
Oporornis formosus	16 Sept	25 Mar
Geothlypis trichas	—	13 Apr
Wilsonia citrina	1 Sept	8 Apr
Wilsonia pusilla	—	19 Mar

[1] Dates are based on only a few data points for each species. March departure dates are probably too early and late Oct arrival dates are probably too late.

[2] — = insufficient data to establish a date.

Table 10. Evidence for territoriality in wintering migrants

Species	Reported by other workers	Response to playback	Site tenacity	Periodic calling	Homing	Field observation of defense[1]	Response to caged conspecific	Returned to same territory in 1974–75
Empidonax flaviventris	—	+	+	+	+	+	—	—
Empidonax minimus	—	+	+	+	+	—	+	+
Dumetella carolinensis	—	+	+	+	—	+	+	—
Hylocichla mustelina	+	+	+	+	+	+	+	+
Polioptila caerulea	—	—	—	+	—	—	—	—
Vireo griseus	—	+	+	+	+	—	+	+
Mniotilta varia	+	—	+	+	+	+	—	—
Helmitheros vermivorus	—	+	+	+	+	+	+	+
Vermivora celata	—	—	+	+	+	—	—	—
Dendroica petechia	+	—	—	+	—	—	—	—
Dendroica magnolia	—	+	+	+	+	+	+	+
Dendroica virens	—	—	+	+	+	—	—	—
Seiurus aurocapillus	—	+	+	+	+	+	—	+
Seiurus noveboracensis	+	—	+	+	—	—	—	—
Seiurus motacilla	+	—	+	+	+	—	—	+
Oporornis formosus	+	+	+	+	+	+	+	+
Geothlypis trichas	—	+	+	+	+	—	—	—
Icteria virens	—	—	+	+	+	—	—	—
Wilsonia citrina	—	+	+	+	+	+	+	+
Wilsonia pusilla	—	+	+	+	+	+	+	+
Setophaga ruticilla	—	+	+	+	—	—	—	—
Piranga rubra	—	—	+	+	—	—	—	—
Passerina ciris	—	—	+	—	—	—	—	—

[1] Chasing, fighting or visual displays in free-flying birds.

Summary of Evidence on Territoriality

Several lines of evidence indicate that the social structure of many insectivorous migrants in the Tuxtlas involves territoriality. Table 10 is a summary of the information from the species accounts and tables 4–8. This table indicates that individuals of 10 species of wintering migrants showed long-term site fidelity, returned to the same site from one year to the next, vocalized periodically and used stylized visual displays in defense of their territories against conspecifics. Definitions of territory are numerous, but most include these points (Hinde 1956; Pitelka 1959; Brown and Orians 1970).

Resource Use

How resources are used by migrants as compared with residents is vital, not only to an understanding of the ecology and evolution of migrants, but to comprehending avian community structure in the tropics.

This discussion of resource use is based on digestive tract analysis, observations of foraging strategy, behavior, prey type, and use of microhabitats.

The central questions we wish to explore are : 1) How are different resource use strategies related to migration, sociality, and fat storage? 2) Are migrants able to compete for resources with residents or must they depend on localized concentrations of food, such as fruiting trees?

Fattening and Resource Use

Birds build up subcutaneous fat reserves for various reasons: migration (Berthold 1975) molting and breeding (McNeil 1971), overnight survival (Ward 1969), and for nearly any situation that could cause energy

John H. Rappole

Table 11. Percentage of individuals with moderate fat or more by food type and residence status

Species	Number	Percent, individuals with moderate fat or more[1]	Food type[2]	Residence status[3]
Dendrocincla anabatina	30	6.6	I	P
Xiphorhynchus flavigaster	34	0.0	I	P
Pipra mentalis	14	28.5	F, I	P
Tityra semifasciata	17	17.6	F, I	P
Empidonax flaviventris	22	9.0	I	W
Myiobius sulphureipygius	36	5.5	I	P
Pipromorpha oleaginea	37	16.2	F, I	P
Henicorhina leucosticta	43	2.3	I	P
Dumetella carolinensis	49	14.3	F, I	W
Catharus ustulatus	20	10.0	F, I	W
Vireo griseus	39	15.3	F, I	W
Seiurus aurocapillus	19	0.0	I	W
Oporornis formosus	31	12.9	I	W
Icteria virens	22	13.6	F, I	W
Wilsonia citrina	36	11.1	I	W
Wilsonia pusilla	24	0.0	I	W
Basileuterus culicivorous	46	0.0	I	P
Euphonia lauta	28	10.7	F	P
Euphonia gouldi	25	24.0	F	P
Habia gutturalis	63	7.9	F, I	P
Passerina cyanea	14	21.4	S	W
Sporophila torqueola	27	22.2	S	P

[1] The fat classes are adapted from Helms and Drury (1960).

[2] F = fruit; F, I = fruit and insects; I = insects; S = seeds. Food type classification is based on stomach content analysis of the same birds used in the fat analysis. For the F, I category, neither fruits nor insects composed more than 70 percent of the food in the stomachs examined.

[3] P = permanent resident; W = wintering migrant.

Table 12. Chi square values: frequency of fat classes for species using different food types and for migrants vs residents[1,2]

	Frugivore-insectivore	Frugivore	Graminivore	Residents[3]
Insectivores	39.24**	16.01**	24.80**	—
Frugivore-insectivores	—	0.70	2.82	—
Frugivores	—	—	0.71	0.57
Migrants[2]	—	—		

[1] Data are from Table 11.

[2] Winter resident birds (Nov–Mar).

[3] Since there are no migrant frugivores in the sample, this food class is left out of the resident category for comparison with migrants.

** Significant at the .01 level

comparison of the frequencies of "moderate" and "heavy" fat classes in different resource use categories. Each class is composed of an equal number of migrants and residents.

Insectivores, most of which depend on resources that are evenly distributed in both space and time in the relatively aseasonal selva of the Tuxtlas, have a much lower frequency of individuals in the moderate and heavy fat classes than those species which depend on fruits or seeds (Chi-square, $p < .01$). Fruits and seeds represent resources that are generally clumped in space or time.

If migrants depend on temporarily abundant resources for survival in the tropics, as has been proposed by several authors (e.g., Morse 1971; Willis 1966; Karr 1976), then we would expect migrants to have a larger percentage of fat birds in any given resource-use category than residents in the same category. However, as shown in table 12, no significant differences in percentage of fat birds between migrants and resident is seen in our sample.

Food Use, Foraging Strategy and Social System

In table 13, we present data on foods used, weights, and home range size for common passerines of the Tuxtlas rain forest community. Migrants in this community depended chiefly on insects as a resource. Although a few migrants used fruits, none of the species we examined used fruit for more than 30 percent of their diet.

The major differences between groups which appear in table 13 are between members of different resource-use categories. Individuals which exploit patchy resources, such as fruits or seeds, tend to associate in

stress on the bird. If fattening is an adaptation to anticipate energy stress, we make the following prediction: birds dependent on resources clumped in space or time should show greater fat reserves on the average than those depending on resources evenly distributed in space or time.

With this prediction in mind, we present fat reserve data on specimens of both migrant and resident species in different resource-use categories (table 11). In table 12, the data from table 11 are used in a statistical

Table 13. Foods used, food distribution, average weight and estimated home range/territory size for some common passerines, Study Sites 2 and 3.

Species	Residence status[1]	Total specimens examined[2]	Food type[3]	Food distri- bution[4]	Total recaptures and resightings[5]	Estimated home range/territory size
Dendrocincla anabatina	P	30 (36.0)	I	E	7	2 ha
Xiphorhynchus flavigaster	P	30 (45.7)	I	E	7	4 ha
Automolus ochrolaemus	P	14 (46.4)	I	E	8	1 ha/pr.
Xenops minutus	P	21 (11.0)	I	E	9	.5 ha
Attila spadiceus	P	32 (46.1)	V, I, F	E	10	?[6]
Empidonax flaviventris	W	30 (10.5)	I	E	12	.3 ha
Myiobius sulphureipygius	P	30 (11.0)	I	E	11	?
Platyrinchus mystaceus	P	30 (9.5)	I	E	13	.3 ha
Rhynchocyclus brevirostris	P	30 (22.5)	I	E	1	?
Pipromorpha oleaginea	P	30 (15.0)	I	E	33	?
Thryothorus maculipectus	P	30 (15.4)	I	E	27	.5 ha/pr.
Henicorhina leucosticta	P	30 (14.3)	I	E	7	.5 ha/pr.
Dumetella carolinensis	W	14 (32.1)	F, I	E	17	.4 ha
Hylocichla mustelina	W	30 (46.0)	F, I	E	73	.5 ha
Ramphocaenus rufiventris	P	10 (9.5)	I	E	2	?
Vireo griseus	W	18 (10.4)	F, I	E	16	.3 ha
Hylophilus ochraceiceps	P	30 (10.9)	I	E	42	1 ha/flock
Hylophilus decurtatus	P	30 (9.1)	I, F	E	3	1 ha/flock
Mniotilta varia	W	26 (9.0)	I	E	32	?
Helmitheros vermivorus	W	30 (11.7)	I	E	22	?
Dendroica magnolia	W	30 (7.3)	I	E	32	.3 ha
Seiurus aurocapillus	W	30 (16.9)	I	E	23	.3 ha
Seiurus motacilla	W	16 (18.8)	I	E	5	.3 ha
Oporornis formosus	W	30 (12.8)	I	E	62	.3 ha
Wilsonia citrina	W	30 (10.0)	I	E	110	.3 ha
Wilsonia pusilla	W	30 (6.5)	I	E	28	.3 ha
Setophaga ruticilla	W	13 (7.6)	I	E	2	?
Basileuterus culicivorous	P	30 (9.5)	I	E	12	.5 ha/pr.
Euphonia lauta	P	30 (14.2)	F	P	2	1 ha/flock
Euphonia gouldi	P	30 (15.5)	F	P	5	1 ha/flock
Phlogothraupis sanguinolenta	P	22 (39.8)	F, I	?	3	?
Piranga rubra	W	15 (28.8)	F, I	?	1	?
Habia rubica	P	30 (31.2)	F, I	P	22	1.5 ha/flock
Habia gutturalis	P	30 (39.5)	F, I	P	34	1.5 ha/flock
Eucometis penicillata	P	30 (28.6)	F, I	P	6	?

[1] P = permanent resident; W = wintering migrant.

[2] Mean weights in parentheses.

[3] I = insects; F = fruits; V = vertebrates.

[4] E = evenly distributed resources, P = patchily distributed resources.

[5] These provide the basis for home range and territory size determination.

[6] ? = insufficient data.

intraspecific flocks, while species which exploit evenly distributed resources, such as insects, tend to be solitary or paired and have well-defined territories. Although few migrants exploited patchy resources in rain forest, some species of migrants did so in other habitats. For example, Indigo Buntings, Painted Buntings, and Yellow-rumped Warblers associated in intraspecific flocks and fed on seeds, fruits, and insects in savannah-like habitats of the Tuxtlas region.

Migrants and permanent residents in the same resource-use categories are basically similar in the social system evolved to exploit those resources in the Tuxtlas. The following quote from Skutch's (1960:539) description of social behavior of the Sulphur-rumped Flycatcher (*Myiobius sulphureipygius*) illustrates this similarity: "These flycatchers . . . are . . . intolerant of the presence of another of their own kind. Yet a single *Myiobius* often attaches itself to a mixed company . . . [of other species] that roam through the forest in search of food." This description could apply to many species of insectivorous migrants or permanent residents in the Tuxtlas.

From our analysis of migrant and permanent-resident feeding behavior and social systems, we have found that there are apparent relationships between resource use and social system that are independent of whether or not the species is a migrant or a permanent resident. The relationship between social system and resource use in birds has been explored for the breeding grounds by Horn (1968). He concluded that clumped resources favor a gregarious system and diffuse resources, a non-gregarious one. Ward and Zahavi (1973) come to similar conclusions. A similar pattern exists during the nonbreeding season in the Tuxtlas avian community, but with some variations:

1) Resources in disjunct clumps throughout the winter—For frugivores, graminivores, and many omnivores, this pattern is common. Social systems involve gregarious flocks of family groups or larger. We found throughout the winter individuals of these flocks with fat loads (table 11). Fretwell (1969) describes a similar situation in winter flocks of *Junco hyemalis*. In these species fattening appears to be an adaptive response to exploiting resources localized in time and space. By fattening when resources are present, individuals increase the likelihood of finding another patch of resources before their reserves are exhausted.

2) Resources mostly evenly distributed, but some disjunct clumps are available—Most insectivores and large carnivores, both migrant and permanent resident, fall into this category. They have feeding territories which cover specific areas and are fixed over time. Individuals of these species which are unable to find territories move in a random pattern in search of available space. While territorial birds seldom carry more than very light fat loads, floaters of the same species often have light fat loads and are occasionally found with moderate or heavy loads (table 11). Moreau (1972:104 and elsewhere) reports wintering insectivorous migrants with heavy fat loads in December–February. Floaters apparently are able to find clumped resources at times, which enables them to survive without a territory. When resources of this type are found, it would seem a highly adaptive physiological response to become hyperphagic and build fat reserves. The possibility thus exists that a different set of physiological responses is favored in floaters and territorial individuals of the same species.

3) Resources evenly distributed during one part of the season becoming disjunct and clumped during another part—Morton (1972) reports that Bay-breasted Warblers (*Dendroica castanea*) are solitary and aggressive (territorial?) early in the winter during the wet season in Panama when insects are plentiful and evenly distributed, but become gregarious later in the winter when fruits become abundant. Eastern Kingbirds (*Tyrannus tyrannus*) follow similar usage patterns (Morton 1971), as may Painted Buntings and some nectarivore-insectivore groups, such as trochilids and honeycreepers. These groups may be abundant at clumped resources like flowering trees during the dry season but dispersed and territorial in other seasons when nectar sources are more evenly distributed or scarce.

4) Resources evenly distributed in one region but clumped and disjunct in another—Some species of birds are reported as solitary in some parts of their winter range and gregarious in other parts (Swainson's Thrush, Black-throated Green Warbler, Yellow-rumped Warbler). Austin and Smith (1972) reported the Ruby-crowned Kinglet (*Regulus calendula*) gregarious in Arizona while Rea (1970) reported it territorial in other parts of its winter range. This dichotomy in behavior may be related to resource dispersal. Different physiological responses could be favored depending on the resource use strategy.

Swainson's Thrushes occurred in loose flocks irregularly throughout the winter on our study sites. These birds carried light to heavy fat loads. In contrast, Miller (1963:41) found members of this species to be solitary and regular on his study site in Colombia. Specimens showed only traces of fat. These observed differences in fat content and behavior may be related to different patterns of resource distribution in the two areas.

5) Resources are clumped and shift slowly over a large area—Willis' (1967, 1972, 1973) exhaustive studies of ant-following species of birds showed that most have very large home ranges or territories, which are usually defended only at resource sites (ant raids).

Possibly the large territory size of birds, such as the Ocellated Antbird (*Phaenostictus mcleannani*) (wt. 50 gm, territory size 19.5 ha), the Bicolored Antbird (*Gymnopithys bicolor*) (32 gm, 12.5 ha), and the Spotted Antbird (*Hylophylax naevioides*) (19 gm, 3.1 ha) (Willis 1974:155, 162), is correlated with the probability of an ant swarm taking place in a given area and the bird's size. Floaters occur in these species (Willis 1974:158), but there is no information on the relative amounts of fat in floaters and territorial individuals. We found that some Tawny-winged Creepers (*Dendrocincla anabatina*) had fat deposits (table 11). This species, like the antbirds, is a permanent resident with a large home range (table 13).

These points indicate that sociality and fattening are highly adaptive responses to variations in resource availability. Even within the same species radical changes in behavior from a highly structured territorial system, to floaters, to flocks can be seen, depending on individual competitive ability and resource distribution. Karr (1971a) noted a relationship between social structure and resource distribution in Panama but came to the conclusion that insectivorous species could not obtain enough food from a restricted territory in the tropics because of low insect abundance.

This hypothesis is not supported by our data on home range size for insectivorous winter or permanent residents (table 13). Almost all the passerines for which we were able to obtain recapture data, even gregarious insectivores, such as *Hylophilus decurtatus*, had small, well defined home ranges. Karr's conclusions were based partly on Willis' (1967) work with ant-following species and partly on his own recapture data. As discussed above, the large territories of ant-following species may represent special adaptations to exploitation of slowly shifting resources. There are also several reasons why recapture data can be difficult to interpret, including net shyness, floaters, and the heterogeneity of tropical forest habitat. Heterogeneity is presumably responsible for the disjunct distribution of species, such as the Long-billed Gnatwren (*Ramphocaenus rufiventris*) and the Ovenbird (*Seiurus aurocapillus*), which are restricted to patchy microhabitats in selva. Their presence in an area can be completely missed as an artifact of net placement.

Migrant–Resident Competition for Resources

Morse (1971:185, 196) has proposed that migrants subsist on irregularly abundant resources during the nonbreeding season and escape competition with permanent residents by exploiting marginal habitats. This hypothesis has also been put forward by Karr (1976). Willis (1966:222) called this the "irregularity principle" and outlined migrant strategy relative to that of permanent resident species as follows: "Migrants, by contrast (with indigens), have the high breeding rates characteristic of northern species. They can pour large numbers of individuals into situations which residents cannot safely occupy, and still end up with enough survivors to replenish the stocks the next year." He elaborates on this theory further, describing the difference in behavior between migrants and permanent residents when faced with potentially dangerous situations. Permanent residents hide while migrants remain "active and tame." The implication is that there is some sort of "species strategy" used by migrants.

There are problems with this hypothesis: 1) We find it difficult to understand how such a strategy could evolve without invoking some sort of group selection. 2) The social systems seen in many populations of wintering migrants do not fit an "irregularity principle." Most of the insectivorous species have territorial systems in which individuals stay on the same site throughout a winter season and return to the site in subsequent years. Individuals do not move around to find temporary concentrations of food as one would expect according to the "irregularity principle," unless they are floaters unable to defend or find territories. 3) Our data on migrant and indigen feeding behavior indicate that migrants are not competitively inferior to indigens. In fact, there is little evidence that migrants compete directly with indigens at all except under special circumstances, e.g. ant swarms, fruiting trees, or flowering plants (see Species Accounts). 4) If the "irregularity principle" were correct, the more "opportunistic" migrants would be expected to have a higher frequency of individuals in the moderate and heavy fat classes than indigens. We found no evidence to support this hypothesis. In fact, as table 12 shows, migrants do not differ from permanent residents in frequency of fat individuals.

Interspecific Flocks

Feeding assemblages of several species are found in both tropical and temperate habitats. Usually these flocks are organized around groups of two or three species which travel to clumps of unevenly distributed resources. We have characterized the interspecific flocking tendencies of the common migrant species of the Tuxtlas according to a classification system based on that of Moynihan (1962:68, 69). See table 14.

Moynihan (1962) concluded that the major advantages accruing to members varied according to species but that detection of predators and feeding success were important in varying degrees for all members. Buskirk (1976) reached similar conclusions although he has emphasized predation as the primary reason for flock formation.

John H. Rappole

Cody (1974:266), on the basis of data on desert finch flocks in winter, stated that interspecific groupings were the result of a shortage of food. He hypothesized that "groups of species in the flocks behave ecologically as single species" (Cody 1974:266). He further implied that a similar situation might apply to neotropical forest blocks (op. cit.).

Our results for several species which regularly took part in feeding assemblages in the Tuxtlas do not support this hypothesis. We found no evidence that species in these flocks were behaving "ecologically as single species." As discusssed in the species accounts, foraging behavior was very different for species in the community. Furthermore, members of many species, including most migrants, were intraspecifically territorial and did not follow flocks beyond the boundaries of their territories (table 14). When faced with the choice of maintaining contact with the flock or maintaining their territories, they chose the latter.

Birds in interspecific flocks, whether migrants or permanent residents, were not wanderers, as suggested by the theories of Cody (1974) and Karr (1971a). Rather, members of these species had home ranges with well-defined boundaries (table 13). We had repeated recaptures over the two-year study of individuals of such "professional" flocking species as the Grey-headed Vireo (*Hylophius decurtatus*), Tawny-crowned Vireo (*H. ochraceiceps*) and the ant tanagers (*Habia* spp.). Buskirk et al (1972) found similar results with marked flocks in Panama. The birds even used specific routes of travel in moving through their areas.

We hypothesize that food distribution, rather than food shortage, is the determining factor in flock formation for "professional" flocking species, at least in the Tuxtlas. Flocks are formed and joined to exploit food in the most economical way possible.

Competition

"Permanent" coexistence of two or more species in the same resource space is theoretically possible under rather special conditions: 1) when the resource is superabundant, 2) when species' populations are controlled by frequency-dependent mortality factors, such as predation, disease, etc. (Paine 1966; Porter 1972; Slatkin 1974), 3) when resource use by each species varies temporally (Grenney et al 1973; Stewart and Levin 1973).

How these possibilities apply to long-lived motile animals with complex life cycles, such as birds, is unknown, but before any of these explanations is necessary, it must be conclusively proven that 2 species are, in fact, competing for the same resource space. We contend that this has yet to be shown convincingly for any avian species pair, let alone for migrant species

Table 14. Interspecific flocking tendencies of migrants in the Tuxtlas

Species	Membership, interspecific flocks[1]	Species	Membership, interspecific flocks
Empidonax flaviventris	T, OA	*Dendroica virens*	T, OA
Empidonax minimus	N	*Seiurus aurocapillus*	N
Dumetella carolinensis	T, OA	*Seiurus noveboracensis*	N
Hylocichla mustelina	T, OA	*Seiurus motacilla*	N
Catharus ustulatus	OA	*Oporornis formosus*	T, OA
Polioptila caerulea	RA ?	*Geothlypis trichas*	N
Vireo griseus	T, OA	*Icteria virens*	N
Mniotilta varia	RA, T	*Wilsonia citrina*	T, OA
Helmitheros vermivorus	T, RA	*Wilsonia pusilla*	T, RA
Vermivora celata	?	*Setophaga ruticilla*	T, RA
Dendroica petechia	T, OA	*Piranga rubra*	T, RA?
Dendroica magnolia	T, OA	*Passerina cyanea*	N
Dendroica coronata	N	*Passerina ciris*	N

[1] RA = regular attendant; OA = occasional attendant; T = attendant only when the flock is on the individual's territory; N = not observed in interspecific flocks in the Tuxtlas; ? = insufficient information. (Classification modified from Moynihan, 1962:68, 69).

when paired with similar permanent-resident species or for species either migrant or resident which form interspecific flocks. Cody (1974:250) has made the best attempt to date, but our data on such pairs as the Wilson's Warbler and Magnolia Warbler and the Ovenbird and Kentucky Warbler indicate that there are parameters, unused by Cody (e.g. foraging strategy and microhabitat preferences) which are crucial in evaluating species' interactions. Theoretically, non-overlap in a single, independent parameter is sufficient to allow species with otherwise identical niche parameters to coexist in the same area without competing directly (Cody 1974:89). Cody seems to assume this, but is it not possible for species to compete intensively even though there are areas of non-overlap? What is missing from most of these studies is an independent determination of *which* niche dimensions are crucial to the coexistence of the two species

Migrants in Tropical Communities

On our primary forest study areas winter residents made up more than a third of the common passerine species. Territories and home ranges were fixed over time and space, indicating that individuals of these species were not existing on "superabundant" resources but on stable, dependable resources for which they could compete successfully, not only against members of their own species but with permanent residents as well. Although there may be shifts in feeding behavior of permanent residents coinciding with the migrant exodus, the niches migrants fill for up to nine months or more of the year, we believe, remain largely vacant during their absence, as Lack (1976) found in Jamaica. Thus, we would predict that the periodic "density compensation" (Cody in Cody and Diamond 975:226) predicted by Chipley (1976) would not take place. The reason why no permanent resident should evolve to fill these temporary niches is essentially that given by Levins (1968:11). The environment into which a potential competitor would have to evolve is changing radically at roughly six-month intervals. Any permanent resident attempting to capitalize on this situation would have to be adapted to compete in two different environments simultaneously.

Our observations of migrants indicate that these species use resources from tropical ecosystems which are, therefore, unavailable to other community members. A necessary corollary to this idea is that earlier studies of tropical avian communities which have failed to include migrants have underestimated avian species diversity. Migrants and other species which do not breed in an area have not been considered in bird species diversity (BSD) figures presumably because possession of a breeding territory is considered to be the only sure criterion of use. Thus, in MacArthur and MacArthur's (1961) original paper on the subject, members of Cathartidae, Accipitridae, Tetraonidae, Phasianidae, Strigidae, Caprimulgidae, Apodidae, and Hirundinidae are all absent from the list of bird species from forests of 5 eastern states, although these families are quite likely important in these temperate communities. In tropical communities, the problems are magnified. In Karr's (1971a) evaluation of the BSD for several Panamanian forests and grasslands, Accipitridae, Picidae, and Thraupidae are underrepresented while Cathartidae, Falconidae, Psittacidae, Strigidae, Apodidae, and all winter residents are left out completely. A similar list of missing groups can be made from works on BSD in other tropical communities (MacArthur et al 1966; Howell 1971). These omitted groups represent an important part of tropical avian communities.

The reason for omitting groups of species not known to breed in an area from community diversity calculations presumably is based on the fact that individuals of these species cannot be considered part of the productivity scheme of the community. This reasoning is incorrect. Although by excluding these species, biomass and energetics calculations are simplified, under-standing of community structure and function is obscured. Any individual that uses any resource from a community is a part of that community's food web whether it reproduces in the community or not. Migrant birds, which have determinate growth, may contribute little to net production in tropical avian communities. However, they do contribute to gross production. Similar reasoning applies to permanent residents with large home ranges, for example, members of the Psittacidae, Accipitridae, and Cathartidae. Although their impact on a community in terms of production and resource cycling is difficult to assess, it is vital to a complete understanding of community function.

Many authors have attempted to correlate BSD with structural parameters of vegetation to show that birds respond to such structural characteristics in habitats rather than other parameters, such as plant species composition. One such measure is foliage height diversity (FHD) which is a measure of foliage vertical stratification patterns. Although often used, this parameter often does not correlate well with BSD in tropical communities, even when groups of nonbreeding species are omitted from BSD calculations.

The abundance of new dependable resources (e.g. fruits and nectar) has been cited as one reason for the failure of FHD to correlate with BSD in tropical areas (Orians 1969; Karr 1971a; Lovejoy 1974). This reasoning may explain a part of the answer but, since FHD often fails to correlate with BSD in temperate zones as well, it cannot be the whole answer. A major shortcoming of FHD measurements is that, while assessing vertical diversity, horizontal diversity is ignored. Anyone walking through a "paper company" forest will notice its lack of faunal diversity. Yet such homogeneous stands can have FHDs similar to much more heterogeneous natural forests. FHD is calculated using the Shannon-Wiener formula $-\sum_i p_i \ln p_i$, where p_i is the proportion of vegetation in the i-th layer. Data from a number of points are taken for each layer, averaged, and used in the formula. The data from each point could be the same or completely different for two forests and the average could be the same.

In temperate forests of roughly equal structural heterogeneity, FHD will show a significant correlation with BSD if certain troublesome groups of species are omitted. But if strands of different structural heterogeneity are compared, the method fails (MacArthur 1964). Howell (1971) had the same problem with his plots in a tropical area (Nicaragua). FHD measurements predicted too low a BSD for the heterogeneous rain forest and too high a diversity for the homogeneous savannah.

Studies of BSD, especially those of tropical communities, have had important influences on the devel-

John H. Rappole

opment of theoretical concepts of diversity. As noted above, all diversity studies of which we are aware on tropical avian communities have overlooked migrants and various other groups as members of the communities. The inclusion of these groups has implications concerning the ultimate causes of tropical avian species diversity.

Three major equilibrium explanations of tropical vs temperate diversity have been developed by recent authors: "new resources" (Orians 1969; Karr 1971a; Lovejoy 1974), environmental stability (Lowe-McConnell 1969, Slobodkin and Sanders 1969; MacArthur 1972; MacArthur in Cody and Diamond 1975; Willson 1973) and productivity (Connell and Orias 1964). These separate theories are not necessarily exclusive nor do they exclude the possibility of other important factors.

Karr (1975) has stressed "new resources" and environmental stability as the most important factors fostering diversity in tropical communities. His arguments concerning "new resources" center on data from his 1971 paper, which show that "...70 percent of the excess tropical species exploit resources that are unavailable and/or unreliable in temperate forest" (Karr 1975:167). The "new resources" are nectar, fruit, and large insects. There are at least two problems with this analysis. First, many of those species that exploit fruits and nectar are ultimately limited by their ability to exploit small insects (Morton 1973). Secondly, as cited earlier, Karr has failed to include members of tropical communities which feed on resources that are not "new." Most of the species of wintering migrants feed on small insects or seeds, and the Falconidae and Strigidae, which were also omitted, feed on vertebrate prey. When all species using rich tropical forest are considered, the picture changes from one of an increase in new resources to one of a general increase in prey diversity (Harrison 1962). The "new resources" argument is thus a different way of saying that diversity engenders diversity. Although this statement is possibly true, it is not helpful in discerning the ultimate causes of diversity.

Karr (1975) found that tropical communities with a high BSD did not differ greatly in terms of day to day productivity measures (biomass, energy consumption), but that the physical environment in the tropical study sites underwent much less fluctuation than the physical environment in the temperate study sites. On this basis he concluded that a stable physical environment is much more important in fostering diversity in the tropics than an increased capacity for productivity. However, the fact that several groups of species have been overlooked in Karr's calculations, as noted above, makes the results questionable. Biomass and energy requirements per unit area would be increased for the

tropical communities by the inclusion of migrants, Strigidae, Falconidae, etc., revealing a considerable difference in the productivity of tropical and temperate avian communities.

An example of the importance of productivity to diversity is the tropical nonseasonal savannah. These systems are found in many parts of the world under the same climatic conditions as rain forest and, in fact, often are bordered or surrounded by rain forest (Sarmiento and Monasterio 1975). Although the physical environment is equally stable for both the forest and savannah types, productivity and species diversity are drastically reduced in the savannah due to poor soil conditions (Howell 1971; Lamotte 1975). Terborgh (1971) noted similar reductions in bird diversity along an altitudinal gradient in the Andes in an essentially nonseasonal environment. Forests at higher altitudes were exposed to conditions as stable as those at lower altitudes but, due to lower mean temperatures and longer periods of cloud cover, productivity presumably was reduced, resulting in a lower species diversity. Kikkawa (1974) provides similarly skewed BSD measurements from Australian forest of roughly equal environmental stability.

We propose that the increases in fruit, nectar, animal prey, and structural heterogeneity seen in tropical vs temperate communities are not the products of a stable physical environment per se. They are products of complex, highly productive ecosystems. Although environmental stability may be important, it is high productivity which supports these complex systems (Connell and Orias 1964).

Wintering vs Breeding Ground Adaptations of Migrants

Levins (1968:17) has stated "Over-all fitness in a heterogeneous environment depends on the fitnesses in the separate environments, but in a way which is determined by the pattern of environments." This point is particularly important in considering migratory species that must be able to compete in different environments at different times during the year. The adaptations of migrants represent compromises due to different selection pressures on their breeding grounds, wintering grounds, and migration stopover points (Rappole and Warner 1976). Grant (1966), however, implied, on the basis of tarsal length-perch stability relationships, that the Cape May Warbler (*Dendroica tigrina*) is better adapted to wintering ground habitats than to breeding habitats. Similarly, Fretwell (1972: 147) has maintained that competition for food is greatest on the wintering ground and concludes that the wintering ground is where most selection takes place. He assumes that food is not limiting on the breeding ground and that individuals of different species, breeding on his study area in North Carolina old fields, are essentially alike in their breeding ecology.

We question Fretwell's conclusions. Although the presence of floaters in all species' populations for which we had recapture and resighting data indicates that there is considerable competition for resources on the wintering ground, adaptations for the breeding ground must be important as well: 1) William (1966) has stressed the importance of balancing a maximization of reproductive effort within a single season with the probability of survival to another season. In organisms in which parental care is important (e.g. birds), the fitness of the adult depends on the number of young it can raise to maturity. Thus feeding efficiency during the breeding season has a direct effect on fitness whether food is limiting for adult survival or not.

2) Females face a considerable physiological stress in forming eggs and in spending long hours incubating with only short periods of feeding. Optimal feeding adaptations would appear to be advantageous for these birds at a time when adult female mortality may be highest (Ricklefs 1973:379).

3) A crucial point in a bird's life is immediately after achieving independence from its parents. At this time foraging adaptations are first severely tested in competition with conspecifics.

4) The fact that there are floaters in many species on the breeding grounds (Rappole et al 1977) and at migration stopover points (Rappole and Warner 1976) as well as on the wintering grounds is strong evidence for intraspecific competition.

We maintain that, to be successful, a migrant must compete well in several environments. Adaptations will be a compromise for each area. There is insufficient information at present to indicate that any one area is any more important than any other.

Evolution of Migration

Many of the migrant species found in the primary vegetation types of the Tuxtlas are also found in various types of secondary growth. This distribution is true of migrants elsewhere in the tropics as well and has been used as an argument in support of Willis' "irregularity principle" by Leck (1972) and Morse (1971:185, 186). Terbough and Weske (1969), however, found that Peruvian secondary forests also were exploited by species from different types of primary vegetation, a low riparian and a tall rain forest formation, although no migrants are members of these communities. Their data indicate that there are qualitative similarities between different vegetation types that can be used by some species. We hypothesize that migrants are found in second growth because these

habitats contain usable microhabitats similar to some found in primary vegetation types. We found that individual migrants inhabiting our secondary forest study sites held territories which they defended against intruders and to which they showed as much short- and long-term site fidelity as conspecifics with territories in primary forest.

The ability of the migrant to exploit a niche that is found in more than one forest type as opposed to the limited ability of most permanent residents is certainly not coincidental. The migrant must be able to exploit resources from a wide variety of forests in order for the tactic of migration to be at all adaptive. In some of these areas the migrant must not only be able to survive but to produce more young than it could have if it had stayed to breed in the tropics. We hypothesize that, in many species wintering in the tropics, migration evolved because of the presence of qualitative similarities between tropical, subtropical, and temperate vegetation types. These similarities were capitalized on by those tropical species whose niches were such that these species could take advantage of parallels in temperate and tropical microhabitat structure on a seasonal basis.

A major argument against the existence of parallels in microhabitat structure in summer and winter habitats for these species is the apparent differences which exist between the coniferous forests which are the summer home for many parulids and the broad-leaved tropical forests where the birds winter. Yet as Mengel (1964:10) has pointed out, some of these species also breed in deciduous, broad-leaved forests (*Dendroica tigrina, D. virens, Wilsonia candensis*), indicating that there are indeed parallels in microhabitat structure between very different types of forests. Furthermore, Eaton (1953), MacArthur (1958:615), and Lack and Lack (1972:148) have found that foraging behavior and portion of the canopy occupied is similar in summer and winter quarters for many of these species.

We hypothesize a tropical origin for most nearctic migrant passerines. Mengel (1964:38, 39) presents evidence favoring this view for Parulids, and his arguments apply to other groups as well. Reasons include: 1) There are very few Parulids, Turdids, Vireonids, or Tyrannids that winter regularly in the North Temperate Zone. 2) Many members of these families are permanent residents in the tropics. 3) The foods they exploit are not now, and probably never have been, available in temperate zones during the winter. 4) There is no convincing evidence of ecological equivalents for migrant species until the southern limit of their winter range is reached. In fact, our data on foraging behavior of both migrant and permanent-resident species indicate that migrants occupy niches

John H. Rappole

unused by permanent residents. Lack (1976) came to a similar conclusion from his studies of migrants in Jamaican communities. Cox (1968) has proposed a similar theory based on a different line of reasoning.

Cohen (1967) has proposed a very different theory. He hypothesizes that migration evolved as a strategy to maximize winter survival rather than breeding success. This hypothesis assumes a temperate origin for nearctic migrants and either "empty niches" in the tropics, which migrants could move into, or a historical displacement of tropical permanent residents by migrants. For reasons given above, neither of these occurrences appear likely. Cohen's theory further implies that organisms cannot gain any advantage by moving if survival does not change throughout the year. However, survival alone is not the key to increased fitness. Breeding success is what must be maximized.

First-year birds in saturated resident populations in the tropics, while perhaps not faced with a high probability of mortality, are faced with a low probability of breeding. Fogden (1972), in work with permanent residents of Sarawak, Borneo, reported that when the young reached independence, they were forced to disperse by the territorial behavior of their parents. Both he and Willis (1974) reported high rates of adult survivorship and low-breeding success of tropical residents (.3 young per pair annually in many cases). Given high adult longevity, low breeding success, forced dispersal, the physiological capability of building fat reserves, and the existence of qualitative similarities between temperate and tropical vegetation types, it seems inevitable that those individuals with the ability to do so would take advantage of reduced competition in seasonal niches in temperate areas to increase reproductive success.

Conclusions

Migrants are demonstrated to be important members of many tropical avian communities. Most migrant species in our study were territorial and showed long term site fidelity to their wintering areas, indicating that these species were able to compete with permanent residents for resources in primary forests and elsewhere. Some species of migrants joined interspecific flocks when the flocks entered their territories, but were not dependent on these flocks for obtaining food. There was no evidence that flock members were behaving as ecologically the same species.

We hypothesize that those migrant species whose winter ranges are in the tropics originated in the tropics and evolved a tactic of migration to temperate areas to maximize breeding potential by minimizing intraspecific and predation pressure.

Studies of tropical avian communities often have failed to include wintering migrants and other species, not known to breed on an area, in measures of community interaction. When these omitted groups are included, patterns of resource use and species diversity are changed considerably. If avian community analyses are to have maximum significance, all members of the community must be included, and the various changes in species composition understood for what they are—important shifts in the biological environment of the community.

Acknowledgments

We dedicate this work to the memory of Clarence Cottam, late Director of the Welder Wildlife Foundation, whose belief in the importance of the research made the work possible.

Rappole was generously supported by a pre-doctoral fellowship from the Welder Wildlife Foundation throughout the entire period of this study. For this assistance and for help in many other ways, we thank W. C. Glazener, Director of the Foundation; Eric G. Bolen, Assistant Director; and the Trustees.

For providing us with the permits, licenses, and other authorizations necessary for this type of study, we thank George Jonkel, Brian Sharpe and Jay Sheppard of the United States Fish and Wildlife Service, Bird Banding Laboratory; R. A. Hodgins and Wayne Adams of the United States Fish and Wildlife Service, Branch of Enforcement; and Ticul Alvarez of the Departmento de Fauna Sylvestre, Mexico.

We are indebted to Arturo Gomex-Pompa, Antonio Lot H., and Bernardo Villa R. of the University of Mexico, who were helpful on several occasions, particularly in allowing us to use the facilities of the field station of the Instituto de Biologia of the University of Mexico in the Tuxtlas.

Chris Barkan prepared the drawings from field notes and photographs, and for his excellent work we are extremely grateful.

For field assistance in Mexico, we thank Christopher P. Barkan, Bruce Fall, Robert Zink, Mario A. Ramos O., Richard Oehlenschlager, Angel Toto, Refugio Cedillo, and Elizabeth Rappole.

Helpful criticism and discussion were provided by Allan R. Phillips, Clarence Cottam, Eric G. Bolen, Mario A. Ramos O., Christopher P. Barkan, Robert J. Taylor, Thomas Boutton, Mario Sousa, Robert Zink and Elizabeth Rappole. Philip J. Regal and James R. Karr provided helpful comments on parts of the manuscript, and Daniel Janzen and Glen Woolfenden provided helpful correspondence.

Finally, we thank our families, who have shared most of the problems and few of the rewards associated with this research.

Literature Cited

Andrle, R. F.
1964   A biogeographical investigation of the Sierra de Tuxtla in Veracruz, Mexico. Ph.D. thesis, Louisiana State University, Baton Rouge, 236 pp.

1966.   North American migrants in the Sierra de Tuxtla of southern Veracruz, Mexico. Condor, 68:177–184.

1967.   Birds of the Sierra de Tuxtla in Veracruz, Mexico. Wils. Bull. 79:163–87.

Austin, G. T. and E. L. Smith.
1972.   Winter foraging ecology of mixed insectivorous bird flocks in oak woodland in southern Arizona. Condor, 74:17–24.

Bent, A. C.
1953.   Life histories of North American wood warblers. Bull. U. S. Nat. Mus., 203. 733 pp.

Berthold, P.
1975.   Migration: control and metabolic physiology. pp 77–128. In *Avian Biology*, eds. D. S. Farner and J. R. King, vol. 5. New York: Academic Press.

Biaggi, V.
1970.   *Las Aves de Puerto Rico*. San Juan: Universidad de Puerto Rico, 371 pp.

Breckenridge, W. J.
1956.   Measurements of the habitat niche of the Least Flycatcher. Wils. Bull. 68:47–51.

Brown, J. L.
1964.   The evolution of diversity in avian territorial systems. Wils. Bull. 76:160–69.

Brown, J. L., and G. Orians.
1970.   Spacing patterns in mobile animals. Ann. Rev. Ecol. Syst. 1:239–62.

Buskirk, W. H.
1976.   Social systems in a tropical forest avifauna. Am. Nat. 110:293–310.

Buskirk, W. H.; G. V. Powell., J. F. Wittenberger, R. E. Buskirk, and T. U. Powell.
1972.   Interspecific bird flocks in tropical highland Panama. Auk 89:612–24.

Catchpole, C. K.
1972.   A comparative study of territory in the Reed Warbler (*Acrocephalus scirpaceus*) and Sedge Warbler (*A. schoenobaenus*). Ibis 114:213–31.

Chapin, J. P.
1932.   The birds of the Belgian Congo, Pt. 1. Bull. Amer. Mus. Nat. Hist., lxv + 756 pp.

Chipley, R. M.
1975.   The impact of wintering migrant wood warblers on resident insectivorous passerines in a subtropical Colombian oak woods. Living Bird 15:119–41.

Cody, M. L.
1974.   Competition and the structure of bird communities. Princeton Univ. Monogr. Pop. Biol. 317 pp.

1975.   Towards a theory of continental species diversities: bird distributions over Mediterranean habitat gradients. pp. 214–57 In *Ecology and Evolution of Communities*, eds. M. L. Cody and J. M. Diamond, Cambridge, Mass.: Belknap, 545 pp.

Cohen, D.
1967.   Optimization of seasonal migratory behavior. Am. Nat. 101:5–18.

Connell, J. A. and E. Orias.
1964.   The ecological regulation of species diversity. Am. Nat. 98:399–14.

Cox, G. W.
1968.   The role of competition in the evolution of migration. Evol. 22:180–92.

De Roo, A. and J. Deheeger.
1969.   Ecology of the Great Reed Warbler (*Acrocephalus arundinaceus*) (L.) wintering in the southern Congo savanna. *Gerfaut* 59:260–75.

Diamond, A. W., and R. W. Smith.
1973.   Returns and survival of banded warblers wintering in Jamaica. Bird-Banding 44:221–24.

Dickey, D. R., and A. J. van Rossem.
1938.   The birds of El Salvador. Publ. Field Mus. Nat. Hist. Zool. 23.

Dilger, W. C.
1956a.   Hostile behavior and reproductive isolating mechanisms in the avian genera *Catharus* and *Hylochla*. Auk 73:314–53.

1956b.   Adaptive modifications and ecological isolating mechanisms in the thrush genera *Catharus* and *Hylocichla*. Wils. Bull. 68:171–99.

Eaton, S. W.
1953.   Wood warblers wintering in Cuba. Wils. Bull. 65:169–74.

Edwards, E. P.
1972.   *A field Guide to the Birds of Mexico*. Sweet Briar, Va.: E. P. Edwards, 300 pp.

Fogden, M. P.
1972.   The seasonality and population dynamics of equatorial forest birds in Sarawak. Ibis 114:307–43.

Fretwell, S. D.
1969.   Dominance behavior and winter habitat distribution in juncos (*Junco hyemalis*). Bird-Banding 40:1–25.

1972.   Populations in a seasonal environment. Princeton Univ. Monogr. Pop. Biol., 217 pp.

Garcia, J. A.
1835.   Eruption des Vulkanes von Tustla in den Jahren 1664 und 1793. Neues Jahrb. fur Minerologie, Geonosie, Geol., und Petrefaktenkunde, pp. 40–45.

John H. Rappole

Gomez-Pompa, A., C. Vazques-Yanes, and S. Guevara.
1972.   The tropical rain forest: a non-renewable resource. Science 177:762–65.

Grant, P. R.
1966.   Further information on the relative length of tarsus in land birds. Yale Peabody Mus. Nat. Hist. Postilla 98:1–13.

Grenney, W. J., D. A. Bella, and H. C. Curl, Jr.
1973.   A theoretical approach to interspecific competition in phytoplankton communities. Am. Nat. 107:405–25.

Griscom, L.
1932.   The distribution of bird-life in Guatemala. Bull. Amer. Mus. Nat. Hist. 64:425 pp.

Griscom L. and A. Sprunt, Jr.
1957.   *The warblers of America*. New York: Devin-Adair.

Harrison, J. L.
1962.   Distribution of feeding habits among animals in a tropical forest. J. Anim. Ecol. 31:53–63.

Helms, C. W. and W. H. Drury.
1960.   Winter and migratory weight and fat field studies on some North American buntings. Bird-Banding 31:1–40.

Hinde, R. A.
1956.   The biological significance of territories. Ibis 98:340–69.

Horn, H. S.
1968.   The adaptive significance of colonial nesting in the Brewer's Blackbird (*Euphagus cyanocephalus*). Ecol. 49:682–94.

Howell, T. R.
1971.   An ecological study of the birds of the lowland pine savannah and adjacent rain forest in northeastern Nicaragua. Living Bird 10:185–242.

Karr, J. R.
1971a.   Structure of avian communities in selected Panama and Illinois habitats. Ecol. Monogr. 41:207–33.

1971b.   Wintering Kentucky Warblers (*Oporornis formosus*) and a warning to banders. Bird-Banding 42:299.

1975.   Production, energy pathways, and community diversity in forest birds. In *Tropical Ecological Systems: Trends in Terrestrial and Aquatic Research*, eds. F. B. Golley and E. Medina, pp. 161–76 New York: Spinger-Verlag, 398 pp.

1976.   On the relative abundance of migrants from the north temperate zone in tropical habitats. Wils. Bull. 88:433–458.

Kikkawa, J.
1974.   Comparison of avian communities between wet and semiarid habitats of eastern Australia. Aust. Wild. Res. 1:107–116.

Lack, D.
1976.   *Island Biology*, vol. 16. Berekeley: Univ. of California Press, 445 pp.

Lack, D. and P. Lack
1972.   Wintering warblers in Jamaica. Living Bird 11:129–53.

Lamotte, M.
1975.   The structure and function of a tropical savannah ecosystem. In *Tropical Ecological Systems: Trends in Terrestrial and Aquatic Research*. eds. F. B. Golley and E. Medina, pp. 179–222 New York: Springer-Verlag, 398 pp.

Leck, C. F.
1972.   The impact of some North American migrants at fruiting trees in Panama. Auk 89:842–50.

Lederer, R. J.
1977.   Winter feeding territories in the Townsend's Solitaire. Bird-Banding 48:11–18.

Leigh, E. G.
1975.   Population fluctuations, community stability and environmental variability. In *Ecology and Evolution of Communities*, eds M. L. Cody and J. M. Diamond, pp. 51–73. Cambridge, Mass.: Belknap, 545 pp.

Levins, R.
1968.   Evolution in changing environments. Princeton Univ. Monogr. Pop. Biol. 2, 120 pp.

Loetscher, F. W.
1955.   North American migrants in the state of Veracruz, Mexico: a summary. Auk 72:14–54.

Loftin, H., D. T. Rogers, and D. C. Hicks
1966.   Repeats, returns and recoveries of North American migrant birds banded in Panama. Bird-Banding 37:35–44.

Lovejoy, T. E.
1974.   Bird diversity and abundance in Amazon forest communities. Living Bird, 13:127–91.

Lowe-McConnell, R. H., editor
1969.   Speciation in tropical environments. Biol. Jour. Linn. Soc. London 1:1–246.

MacArthur, J. W.
1975.   Environmental fluctuations and species diversity, In *Ecology and Evolution of Communities*, eds. M. L. Cody and J. M. Diamond, pp. 74–80, Cambridge, Mass.: Belknap 545 pp.

MacArthur, R. H.
1958.   Population ecology of some warblers of northeastern coniferous forest. Ecol. 39:599–619.

1964.   Environmental factors affecting species diversity. Am. Nat. 98:387–97.

1972.   *Geographical Ecology: Patterns in the Distribution of Species*. New York: Harper & Row, 269 pp.

MacArthur, R. H., and J. MacArthur
1961. On bird species diversity. Ecol. 42:594-98.

MacArthur, R. H., H. Recher, and M. L. Cody
1966. On the relation between habitat selection and bird species diversity. Am. Nat 100:319-32.

Mayr, E.
1963. *Animal Species and Evolution*. Cambridge, Mass.: Belknap, 797 pp.

McNeill, R.
1971. Lean season fat in a South American population of Black-necked Stilts. Condor 73:472-75.

Mengel, R. M.
1964. The probable history of species formation in some northern wood warblers (Parulidae). Living Bird 3: 9-44.

Miller, A. H.
1963. Seasonal activity and ecology of the avifauna of an American equatorial cloud forest. Univ. Calif. Publ. Zool. 66:1-78.

Monroe, B. L., Jr.
1968. A distributional survey of the birds of Honduras. A.O.U. Ornth. Monogr. 7.

Moreau, R. E.
1972. *The Palearctic-African Bird Migration Systems*. New York: Academic Press, 384 pp.

Morel, G. and F. Bourlière
1962. Relations écologiques des avifaunes sédentaires et migratrices dans une savane sahélienne du bas Sénégal. La Terre et la Vie 4:371-93.

Morse, D. H.
1971. The insectivorous bird as an adaptive strategy. Ann. Rev. Ecol. Syst., 2:177-200.

Morton, E. S.
1971. Food and migration habits of the Eastern Kingbird in Panama. Auk. 88:925-926.

1972. North American birds in the tropics. Atlantic Natur. 27:164-68.

1973. On the evolutionary advantages and disadvantages of fruit eating in tropical birds. Am. Nat., 107:8-22.

Moynihan, M.
1962. The organization and probably evolution of some mixed species flocks of neotropical birds. Smithsonian Misc. Coll. 143:1-140.

Nickell, W. P.
1968. Return of northern migrants to tropical winter quarters and banded birds recovered in the United States. Bird-Banding 39:107-16.

Nisbet, I. C. T. and Lord Medway
1972. Dispersion, population ecology and migration of Eastern Great Reed Warblers *Acrocephalus orientalis* wintering in Malaysia. Ibis 114:451-94.

Orians, G. H.
1969. The number of bird species in some tropical forests. Ecol. 50:783-801.

Paine, R. T.
1966. Food web complexity and species diversity. Am. Nat. 100:65-75.

Pennington, T. D., and J. Sarukhan
1968. Arboles tropicales de Mexico. Inst. Nac. Investig. Forestales, Mexico, 413 pp.

Perdeck, A. C.
1958. Two types of orientation in migrating Starlings, *Sturnus vulgaris* L., and Chaffinches, *Fringilla coelebs* L. as revealed by displacement experiments. Ardea 46: 1-37.

Pitelka, F. A.
1959. Numbers, breeding schedule, and territoriality in Pectoral Sandpipers of northern Alaska. Condor 61: 233-264.

Porter, J. W.
1972. Predation by *Acanthaster* and its effect on coral species diversity. Am. Nat. 106:487-92.

Rappole, J. H.
1974. Migrants and space: the wintering ground as a limiting factor for migrant populations. Bull. Texas Ornith. Soc. 7:2-4.

1976. A study of evolutionary tactics in populations of solitary avian migrants. Ph.D. thesis. University of Minnesota, Minneapolis.

Rappole, J. H., and D. W. Warner.
1976. Relationships between behavior, physiology and weather in avian transients at migration stopover sites. Oecologia 26:193-212.

Rappole, J. H., D. W. Warner, and M. Ramos.
1977. Territoriality and population structure in a small passerine community. Am. Midl. Nat. 97:110-119.

Rea, A. M.
1970. Winter territoriality in a Ruby-crowned Kinglet. Western Bird Bander 1970:4-7.

Recher, H. F. and J. A. Recher
1969. Some aspects of the ecology of migrant shorebirds. II. Aggression. Wils. Bull. 81:140-54.

Ricklefs, R. E.
1973. Fecundity, mortality, and avian demography. In *Breeding Biology of Birds*, ed. D. F. Farner, pp. 367-435. Nat. Academy of Sciences, Washington.

Roberts, J. O. L.
1971. Survival among some North American wood warblers. Bird-Banding 42:165-84.

Russel, S. M.
1964. A distributional study of the birds of British Honduras. A.O.U. Monograph 1.

John H. Rappole

1973. Bird conservation in Middle America. Report of the A.O.U. conservation committee 1972–73. Auk 90: 877–87.

Sarmiento, G., and M. Monasterio
1975. A critical consideration of the environmental conditions associated with the occurrence of savanna ecosystems in tropical America. pp. 223–50. In *Tropical Ecological Systems: Trends in Terrestrial and Aquatic Research*, eds. F. B. Golley and E. Medina, pp. 223–50. New York: Springer-Verlag, 398 pp.

Schwartz, P.
1964. The Northern Waterthrush in Venezuela. Living Bird 3:169–84.

Skutch, A.
1960. Life histories of Central American birds. Pacific Coast Avifauna 34:1–593.

1969. Life histories of Central American Birds. Pacific Coast Avifauna 35:1–580.

Slatkin, M.
1974. Competition and regional coexistence. Ecol. 55:128–34.

Slobodkin, L. B., and H. L. Sanders
1969. On the contribution of environmental predictability to species diversity. Brookhaven Symposia in Biology, 22:82–95.

Slud, P.
1964. The birds of Costa Rica. Bull. Amer. Mus. Nat. Hist. 128:1–430.

Stewart, F. M., and B. R. Levin
1973. Partitioning of resources and the outcome of interspecific competition: a model and some general considerations. Am. Nat. 107:171–98.

Terborgh, J.
1971. Distribution on environmental gradients: theory and a preliminary interpretation of distributional patterns in the avifauna of the Cordillera Vilcabamba, Peru. Ecol. 52:23–40.

Terborgh, J., and J. S. Weske
1969. Colonization of secondary habitats by Peruvian birds. Ecol. 50:765–82.

Toledo, V. M., A. Lot, C. Juarez, J. J. Martinez, and J. Zamacona
1972. Problemas biologicos de la region de los Tuxtlas, Veracruz. U.N.A.M., Mexico, 237 pp.

Ward, P.
1969. Seasonal and diurnal changes in the fat content of an equatorial bird. Phys. Zool. 42:85–95.

Ward, P., and A. Zahavi
1973. The importance of certain assemblages of birds as "information-centers" for food finding. Ibis 115:517–34.

Warner, D. W. and J. R. Beer.
1957. Birds and mammals of the Mesa de San Diego, Puebla, Mexico. Acta. Zoologica Mexicana 2:1–21.

Wetmore, A.
1972. Passeriformes: Dendrocolaptidae (Woodcreepers) to Oxyruncidae (Sharpbills). *The Birds of the Republic of Panama*, Part 3. Washington: Smithsonian, 631 pp.

1976. Birds of Porto Rico. U.S. Dept. Agri. Bull. 326:1–140.

Whitaker, A. H.
1972. An improved mist-net rig for use in forests. Bird-Banding 43:1–8.

Weins, J. A.
1973. Interterritorial habitat variation in grasshopper and savannah sparrows. Ecol. 54:877–84.

William, G. C.
1966. Natural selection, the costs of reproduction, and a refinement of Lack's principle. Am. Nat 100:687–90.

Willis, E. O.
1966. The role of migrant birds at swarms of army ants. Living Bird 5:187–231.

1967. The behavior of Bicolored Antbirds. Univ. of Calif. Publ. Zool. 79:1–132.

1972. The behavior of Spotted Antbirds. A.O.U. Monogr. 10.

1973. The behavior of Ocellated Antbirds. Smithsonian Contr. Zool. 144:1–57.

1974. Populations and local extinctions of birds on Barro Colorado Island, Panama. Ecol. Monogr. 44:153–69.

Williamson, M. F.
1973. Tropical plant production and animal species diversity Trop. Ecol. 14:62–65.

Wilson, E. O.
1976. Sociobiology: the new synthesis. Cambridge, Mass.: Belknap, 697 pp.

JEAN-LUC DesGRANGES
Department of Biology
McGill University Montreal, Canada
and
PETER R. GRANT
Department of Zoology
University of Michigan
Ann Arbor, Michigan 48104

Migrant Hummingbirds' Accommodation into Tropical Communities

ABSTRACT

In this study we examine seven ways in which coexistence of resident and migrant hummingbirds might be achieved. A total of eight months was spent observing hummingbird foraging patterns in four habitats of the State of Colima in Mexico. Evidence from this study suggests that the time when migrant hummingbirds are present in the tropics coincides with a seasonal abundance of food in excess of the needs of resident species. Population levels of resident hummingbirds are probably limited by food availability at times of the year when migrants are not present. Territorial behavior is widespread among both resident and migrant species, but the latter are almost always subordinate to the resident species which tend to monopolize the most favorable territories. It follows that migrants display "fugitive" behavior. They settle in a territory until displaced by a dominant species, and then search for an unoccupied territory.

RESÚMEN

En esté estudio hemos analizado siete formas de cómo puede ser consequida una coexistancia entre colibríes no migratorios y colibríes migratorios. Hemos dedicado un total de 8 meses a la observacíon de las distintas formas de alimentación de los colibríes en 4 distintos habitats del Estado de Colima en México. Los resultados de nuestro estudio nos permiten pensar que la época de estancia de los colibríes migratorios en la zona tropical coincide con una de abundancia estancional del alimento superior para las necesidades de la especie no migratoria. El nivel de poblacíon de los colibríes no migratorios puede que esté limitado por la disponibilidad del alimento en épocas de año cuando los colibríes migratorios no están presentes. La conducta territorial está extendida tanto entre la especie no migratoria como en la migratoria, pero está suele quedar casi siempre subordinada a quélla que tiende a acaparar los territorios más favorables. La especie migratoria, como resultado, presenta una conducta "de fuga." Se establece en un territorio hasta que se vea desplazada por la especie dominante y tenga que ir a la búsqueda de un territorio inocupado.

Introduction

Tropical regions of the world periodically receive a large influx of migrant birds (Elgood et al 1966; Moreau 1972; Ulfstrand 1973; Tramer 1974; Karr 1976). The reasons for the migration are clear enough; low temperatures and a small food supply in the non-growing season render the breeding area unsuitable for year-round residency (Siebert 1949; MacArthur 1959; Lack 1968; Frochot 1971). However, it is not clear how migrants can fit into tropical communities without suffering intolerable competition with the residents.

In this paper we outline, as a priori hypotheses, seven ways in which coexistence of residents and migrants might be achieved. We then test these hypotheses with data from a field study of 21 species of hummingbirds in Mexico. Hummingbirds were chosen for several reasons of convenience. They constitute a discrete feeding guild, they are easy to observe, and their principal food, nectar, is relatively easily sampled.

Methods

Volcán de Colima, Mexico (Lat. 19° N) and its surrounding region was selected for this research (figure 1). The locality contains many different habitats within a reasonable distance, and supports several hummingbird species, including five of the North American migratory species during the winter.

Data were collected in four habitats. Along the altitudinal gradient, the selected habitats are: arid thorn forest at 485 m above sea level, riparian gallery forest at 580 m, arid pine-oak forest at 2,200 m, and humid pine-oak forest at 3,300 m. The arid thorn forest is found at low elevation in relatively open situations. It consists of flowering trees, mainly legumes and cacti, scattered in a thick undergrowth of thorny vines. This forest is deciduous. Flowering occurs chief in the dry season when the branches are bare of leaves. The riparian gallery forest is found along streams at a higher altitude. It is a thin, more or less open, but heavily shaded forest of tall trees, many of which are evergreen. The arid pine-oak forest is an open, dry forest of tall pines and medium sized oaks. This habitat covers extensive areas on the Volcán at 1,500–2,500 m. Humid pine-oak forest occurs above, 2,500 m, where clouds lie against the mountain sides. It is a wetter and denser forest than the lower ones. Oaks are heavily covered with mosses.

During eight months, spread over a little more than an annual cycle (January 1975, May–July 1975, and October 1975–February 1976, table 1), the senior author spent nearly 700 hr of observation collecting some 35 hr of foraging data on 21 hummingbird species found in the study areas. The selected habitats are representative of the ones frequented by local hummingbirds. All data were gathered along 1-km transects in each habitat.

The work was divided into one-month blocks. During a typical month, one week in every habitat was spent censusing hummingbirds during the morning and late afternoon and collecting botanical data during the afternoon.

Censuses were conducted by walking slowly back and forth (three times 2 km each day) along the transects, identifying to species each hummingbird encountered. Usually a census lasted for 2.5 hr. By following movements of hummingbirds, as well as by noting location of territories, we were able to make good estimates of the number of individuals of each species found along the 1-km transects at different times of the year. The average number of birds encountered per visit in each season should then constitute acceptable measures of density. Each time a hummingbird visited a flower, the species was noted, and data were collected on habitat, height of feeding, and food eaten. Time and duration (using a stop-watch) of foraging bout and evidence of competition (i.e. aggressive and territorial behavior) were also recorded.

Table 1. Division of the total sampling period into 5 major time periods[1]

Habitats	Arrival of migrants	Mid-winter	Departure of migrants	End of dry season	Beginning of rainy season
Arid thorn forest	14 Oct–10 Dec	11 Dec– 3 Feb	4 Feb–12 Feb	18 May–18 June	19 June–19 July
Riparian gallery forest	14 Oct–10 Dec	11 Dec– 3 Feb	4 Feb–12 Feb	18 May–18 June	19 June–19 July
Arid pine-oak forest	14 Oct–11 Nov	12 Nov–21 Jan	22 Jan–12 Feb	18 May–18 June	19 June–19 July
Humid pine-oak forest	14 Oct–29 Oct	30 Oct–14 Jan	15 Jan–12 Feb	18 May–18 June	19 June–19 July

[1] Dates chosen coincided with important changes in the total number of hummingbirds in each habitat. For example, migrants are uncommon in the habitats outside the mid-winter period.

Jean-Luc DesGranges

Figure 1.   The enormous massif of twin volcanoes dominating the northern border of the State of Colima and adjacent Jalisco are known collectively as the Volcán de Colima. The higher peak is called the Volcán de Nieve (4,246 m), the lower peak, an active crater is the Volcán de Fuego (3,600 m). Photograph taken in January.

In addition, we recorded types, abundance of flowers, and distances between flowers, inflorescences, and individuals together with the color and morphology of flowers (corolla length and diameter), nectar concentration (using a pocket refractometer), the presence of insects, and volume of nectar (in flowers bagged with cheese cloth for 24 hours to prevent bird and insect visits, and in non-bagged flowers using a comparative spotting technique). This was done each month in each habitat. In most instances, the sample size was 10 flowers of each species selected nonsystematically along the transect but sometimes sample size was as large as 25 flowers. Distances smaller than 10 cm were measured with callipers while larger ones were estimated. Flower numbers were either counted along the whole 1-km transect or estimated by stratified random sampling (1 10-m transect/100-m section of the 1-km transect) when abundant. On these occasions, we counted in tens or hundreds and extrapolated from the number of flowers in a sub-sample. Methods used in this study are described in detail elsewhere (DesGranges, 1977, 1978).

Flowers and Birds

Flowering of most species was restricted to a particular season, with the long dry season having the greatest number of species in flower (figure 2).

Since most flower species change from season to season, we used a cluster analysis (Clustan lc) to group flowers that are similar in morphology, dispersion pattern, and nectar characteristics. This permits comparisons of resources at different seasons.

General characteristics of clusters are presented elsewhere (DesGranges, 1977, 1978). It is interesting to note that two clusters contain nearly 85 percent of the species. The first one groups flowers with a fairly long and more or less tubular corolla (figure 3). The flowers which are usually reddish in color produce a fair amount of nectar. The inflorescences contain relatively few flowers so that each type is rarely abundant in the habitats. We will call them tubular flowers. The second cluster groups flowers with either relatively flat, open corollas or cup-shaped corollas. The flowers which are usually whitish in color produce a small to moderate amount of nectar but their inflorescences contain large numbers of flowers so that each type is usually very abundant in the habitats. We will call them cup-shaped flowers. This paper will deal with those two types only.

Because of the synchronization of sexual reproduction of trees and shrubs within the dry season, nectar is much more plentiful during the winter than at other times. The increase in nectar from fall to winter is most pronounced in the cup-shaped group (figure 4).

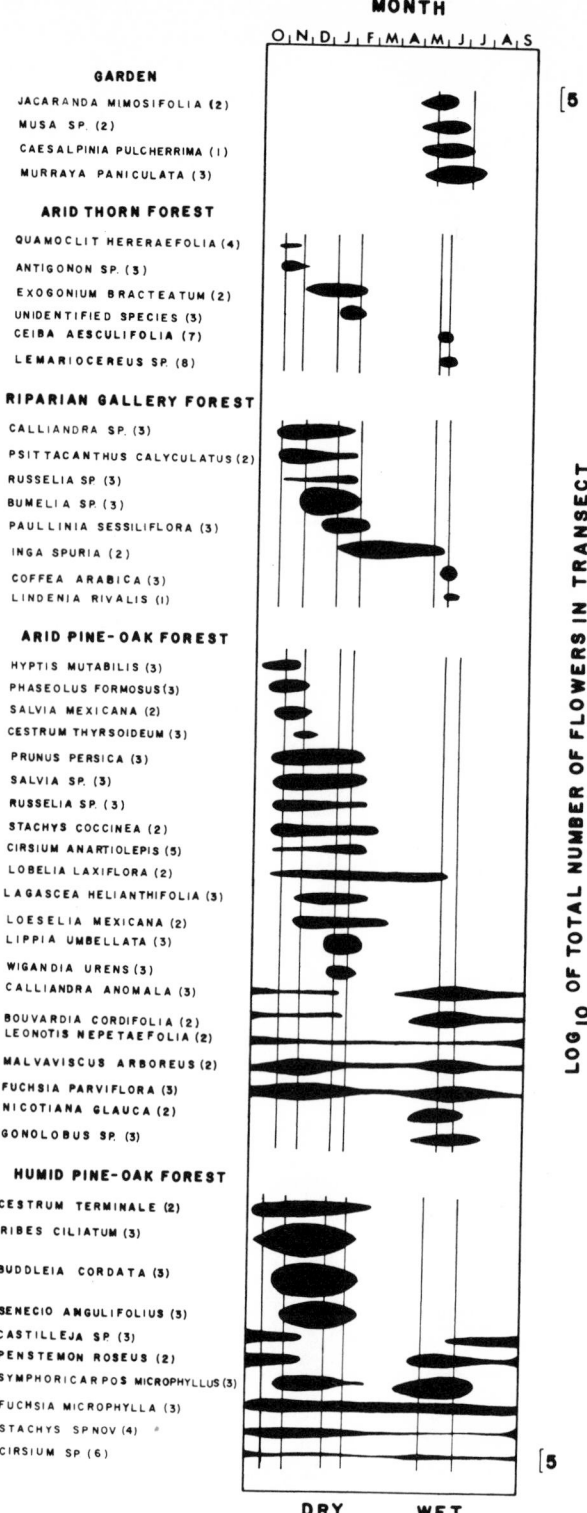

Figure 2. Blooming seasonality of plant species visited by hummingbirds. The vertical axes indicate census dates, and they show abundance as $\log_{10}$ of total number of flowers in the transect. The number in parentheses following the species name is the number of the cluster to which the species belongs. Number 2 refers to tubular flowers while 3 refers to cup-shaped flowers (See DesGranges, 1977, 1978).

Jean-Luc DesGranges

It is possible to group species of hummingbirds on the basis of their strategy of movement (table 2). A first group comprises the residents. They are tropical species which inhabit particular habitats throughout the year. They remain in these habitats even when the amount of flowers dwindles. A second group is made up of wanderers. They nest in tropical regions but unlike residents, they are not present all year long in a particular habitat but rather they visit several habitats during the year following seasonal blooms of trees and shrubs. Finally, migrants form a third group. These species breed in the north temperate regions during the summer and invade the tropical regions during winter.

Interspecific territoriality occurred in the three groups of birds. It was clear that dominant species monopolized most of the territories full of flowers although we did not collect systematic data to substantiate this phenomenon. Subordinate species defended marginal territories, if at all, with fewer flowers that were often less productive and more dispersed.

With this background information on basic biology (see DesGranges 1977 and 1978 for more details), we shall now outline the 7 hypotheses for the accommodation of migrant birds into tropical communities.

Hypotheses of Coexistence

1. Migrants Are Dominant to Residents in Social Interaction

Migrants could be dominant over the residents and thus fit into the community by monopolizing certain resources. By choosing resources (or subunits of habitats) most frequently exploited by the residents and by being physically dominant to them, they could cause ecological shifts in the resource use of the residents.

2. Migrants Are Interstitial Specialists

Because some migrants use several habitats within a year, they should exhibit greater plasticity and less specialization than the residents (Morse 1971, 1974; Ricklefs 1972). When utilizing resources of marginal value to residents, they should experience relatively greater success in exploitation competition and fit into the community as interstitial specialists (modified from Colwell 1973), especially if they are present in greater densities than the residents.

This type of accommodation differs from the previous one in that residents decrease their niche-breadth but do not change their niche-position as a consequence of competition with migrants.

3. Migrants Take Resources Neglected by the Residents

Migrants could be sequential generalists (modified from Colwell 1973). This means that they take advan-

Figure 3. *Selasphorus platycercus* feeding at *Loeselia mexicana*, a typical tubular flower.

tage of a series of seasonal resources which are neglected by the residents because these resources are unpredictable or of relatively limited value (Willis 1966; Blondel 1969; Thiollay 1973). A consequence of this hypothesis is that there should be no appreciable overlap between the niches of the migrants and the residents.

4. Migrants Defend Territories against Residents

Under the first three hypotheses, migrants and residents occupy food niches which scarcely overlap, but under the remaining four hypotheses, they share an almost identical food niche.

When resources exploited by both groups of birds are distributed in a coarse-grained fashion (Levins 1968), migrants and residents could establish territories by aggressive behavior and exclude each other from them. This strategy may seem to clash with the competitive exclusion principle (Gause 1934) if the patches occupied by the two species are very similar or identical. However, the period of coexistence, the nonbreeding season of about four months, may not be long enough for exclusion to occur.

5. Migrants Join Flocks of Residents

Migrants could join flocks of residents to form mixed-species flocks. This might be advantageous to both migrants and residents when food resources are low in quantity and variety but renewing over time. Flocks can move over the habitat in such a way that time intervals between successive visits to a particular point

Table 2 Status and abundance of hummingbird species constituting the nectarivorous bird guild in the study habitats

Species in each habitat	Vagility[1]	Territoriality[2]	Density per time period[3]					Seasonal abundance[4]				
			1	2	3	4	5	1	2	3	4	5
Garden												
Chlorostilbon canivetii	W	Tr	—	—	—	4.0	1	—	—	—	25	50
Amazilia beryllina	W	Tr	—	—	—	1.0	—	—	—	6	—	
Amazilia rutila	W	Te	—	—	—	10.0	1	—	—	63	50	
Amazilia violiceps	W	Tr	—	—	—	10.0	1	—	—	—	63	50
Arid Thorn Forest												
Chlorostilbon canivetii	W	Tr	2.0	—	—	—	—	21	—	—	—	—
Cynanthus latirostris	R	Te	3.0	6.7	9.0	2.0	1.5	31	35	36	44	100
Amazilia beryllina	W	Te	—	0.2	—	0.3	—	—	0.9	—	6	—
Amazilia rutila	W	Tr	—	0.2	0.5	—	—	—	0.9	2	—	—
Amazilia violiceps	W	Tr	—	3.3	0.5	0.8	—	—	18	2	17	—
Heliomaster constantii	R	Tr	4.0	0.8	2.0	1.5	—	42	4	8	33	—
Calothorax lucifer	W	Te	—	4.5	75	—	—	—	24	30	—	—
Archilochus sp.	M	Te	0.5	1.2	1.5	—	—	6	6	6	—	—
Selasphorus platycercus	W	Te	—	0.8	2.0	—	—	—	5	8	—	—
Selasphorus rufus	M	Te	—	1.2	2.0	—	—	—	6	8	—	—
Riparian Gallery Forest												
Phaetornis superciliosus	W	Tr	—	—	—	0.4	—	—	—	—	4	—
Chlorostilbon canivetii	R	Tr	3.5	3.2	4.0	4.0	0.7	38	20	19	40	40
Cynanthus latirostris	W	Tr	1.7	1.2	5.0	—	—	18	8	24	—	—
Amazilia beryllina	W	Te	0.1	1.5	3.0	—	—	1	10	14	—	—
Amazilia rutila	R	Te	2.5	3.0	5.0	5.5	1.0	27	20	24	56	60
Amazilia violiceps		WTr	0.1	0.2	—	—	—	1	1	—	—	—
Heliomaster constantii	W	Tr	0.2	—	—	—	—	3	—	—	—	—
Tilmatura dupontii	W	Tr	—	—	1.0	—		—	—	5	—	—
Archilochus sp.	M	Te	1.1	6.2	3.0	—	—	12	40	14	—	—
Selasphorus platycercus	W	Te	—	0.2	—	—	—	—	1	—	—	—
Arid Pine-Oak Forest												
Hylocharis leucotis	R	Te	6.8	5.5	7.0	8.0	3.0	41	27	26	65	24
Amazilia beryllina	R	Te	2.7	3.7	3.0	2.0	4.7	16	18	11	16	38
Lampornis clemenciae	W	Tr	1.0	—	—	—	—	6	—	—	—	—
Lampornis amethystinus	W	Tr	1.5	0.1	—	1.7	3.7	9	0.2	—	14	30
Eugenes fulgens	R	Tr	0.3	1.0	2.3	pe	0.3	4.5	5.0	8.0	—	3
Calothorax lucifer	W	Tr	—	0.1	0.3	—	—	—	0.4	0.9	—	—
Stellula calliope	M	Te	0.3	3.8	0.8	—	—	4.5	19	3	—	—
Atthis heloisa	W	Tr	—	—	—	0.7	0.7	—	—	5	5	—
Selaphorus platycercus	W	Te	3.3	6.0	13.5	—	—	20	27	50	—	—
Selaphorus rufus	M	Tr	0.8	0.2	—	—	—	5	0.8	—	—	—
Selaphorus sasin	M	Tr	—	—	0.3	—	—	—	—	0.9	—	—
Humid Pine-Oak Forest												
Colibri thalassinus	W	Te	—	12.8	8.0	—	—	—	20	17	—	—
Hylocharis leucotis	R	Te	9.5	7.6	8.0	5.2	4.0	81	12	17	75	100
Amazilia beryllina	W	Tr	—	—	—	0.04	—	—	—	—	0.5	—
Lampornis amethystinus	W	Tr	0.7	—	—	—	—	6	—	—	—	—
Eugenes fulgens	R	Tr	1.3	1.6	2.0	1.7	Pe	10	2	4	24	—
Stellula calliope	M	Te	—	0.4	0.5	—	—	—	0.6	1	—	—
Selasphorus platycercus	W	Te	0.3	13.8	16.7	—	—	3	22	35	—	—

Jean-Luc DesGranges

Table 2. (cont.)

Species in each habitat	Vagil-ity[1]	Territor-iality[2]	Density per time period[3]					Seasonal abundance[4]				
			1	2	3	4	5	1	2	3	4	5
Selasphorus rufus	M	Te	—	10.4	1.0	—	—	—	16	2	—	—
Selasphorus sasin	M	Te	—	0.1	—	—	—	—	0.2	—	—	—
Salasphorus sp.	M	Te	—	16.9	12	—	—	—	27	25	—	—

[1] R = resident; W = wanderer; M = migrant
[2] Te = territorial; Tr = trapliner.
[3] Density is the average number of individuals seen along a transect during a census. 1 = arrival of migrants; 2 = mid-winter; 3 = departure of migrants; 4 = end of dry season; 5 = beginning of rainy season.
[4] Seasonal abundance is the percentage of the individuals of a guild which are of a certain species.
[5] Present but not seen during the censuses.

RELATIVE SEASONAL AVAILABILITY OF NECTAR

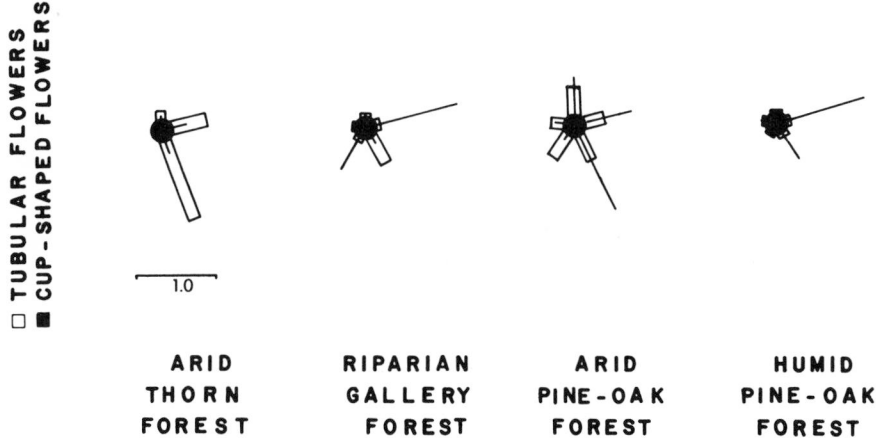

□ TUBULAR FLOWERS
■ CUP-SHAPED FLOWERS

ARID THORN FOREST   **RIPARIAN GALLERY FOREST**   **ARID PINE-OAK FOREST**   **HUMID PINE-OAK FOREST**

Figure 4. Relative seasonal availability (RSA) of nectar in tubular and cup-shaped flowers during the 5 time periods in each of the 4 habitats. RSA is the amount of nectar (A) in flower type (j) in habitat (h) during time period (t) expressed as a proportion of the maximum amount of nectar found in either of the 2 flower types in that habitat during any period of the year

$$\left(\text{i.e. } RSA_{jht} = A_{jht}/\text{maximum} \left[A_{jht} \right]^{t=1,5}_{=1,2} \right)$$

Arms of the stars represent periods of the yearly cycle with the arrival of migrants at the top and, in clockwise progression, mid-winter, departure of migrants, the end of the dry season, and the beginning of the rainy season.

in the habitat are regulated to match food renewal rates (Cody 1971). Individuals which forage independently have no knowledge of the history of prior visits to any one feeding site and thus have no way of avoiding short return times except by trial and error. Thus independent individuals would be selected against (Cody 1971).

6. Migrants Are Fugitive Species

Migrants and residents could theoretically coexist over a region of similar habitable patches if local competitive exclusion tending to favor one species is balanced by colonization of newborn patches by the other species (Levins and Culver 1971). We anticipate that the residents would be better adapted to tropical conditions and hence competitively superior to migrants but that migrants, being mobile, would be better colonists.

7. Resources Are Not Limiting

When resources used by migrant and resident birds are abundant, or when their production is rapid relative to rate of consumption, coexistence should be competition-free. This could be the case when the density of migrants is very low.

Obviously, there is room for considerable overlap between these different hypotheses, and several may

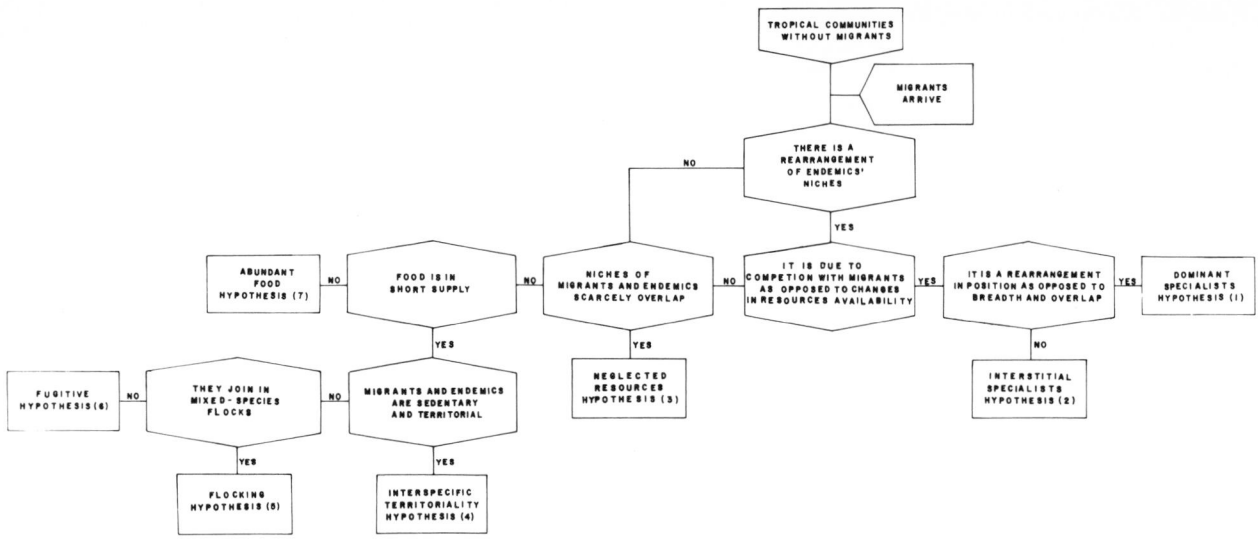

Figure 5. Operational flow chart describing a procedure for testing the ways migrant birds could fit into tropical communities. Pentagons represent input to the problem, hexagons are dichotomous questions to answer, and rectangles are the conclusions.

be acting in concert in any particular situation. For the sake of clarity, and in order to suggest tests of the various hypotheses, a dichotomous flow chart is presented in figure 5.

Testing the Hypotheses

Calculations from the Data

To move from observations on foraging patterns of the different species of hummingbirds to statements about the seasonal characteristics of their niche, we need measures of resource availability and resource use (Feinsinger 1976). Table 3 provides definitions of these measures (See Feinsinger 1976, for comparison of terms and definitions).

The proportion of foraging time a hummingbird spends feeding at a particular flower type depends upon the quantity of nectar available in that flower type (which we will call availability) as well as the nectar available in other flower types. Therefore we need an additional measure, the relative availability of nectar in a flower type, which we now define.

The relative availability of nectar in a flower type of a habitat at a time period is its availability expressed as a percentage of the sum of the availabilities of all flower types present along the transect through that habitat during this particular time period.

The utilization of a flower type by a particular hummingbird population is defined as the percentage of its observed foraging time spent feeding at that particular flower type. We assume that the 35 hr of cumulative foraging data collected in 700 hr of observation time reflects the real distribution of foraging activity among the different types of flowers by the different hummingbird species.

This measure of exploitation is a first step toward the introduction of competition with other hummingbird populations as a potential determinant of utilization of a flower type by a hummingbird population. Interference competition, both intra- and interspecific, is also important and needs to be measured.

We used an index of dominance in interspecific interactions to assess potential interference competition. From the percentage of interspecific encounters won by the different species against each other, we were able to establish a hierarchy of dominance of the different species and place them into one of five discrete groups of comparable dominance (figure 6). Species which lost most of their interspecific chases were given a dominance value of 1 while species which won most of their interspecific chases were given a value of 5. Species in the same group are about equally successful in their interspecific chases against each other, while they lose more than 60 percent of their chases with species ranked higher in the hierarchy and win more than 60 percent of their chases against species found below them in the hierarchy (DesGranges 1977, 1978).

The relative density of a species in the guild was used as a measure of potential intraspecific competition. We assume that intraspecific competition normally increases when more and more of the individuals of a guild belong to the same species. However, it is also possible that the relative density of a species increases because of the absence of intraspecific com-

Jean-Luc DesGranges

Table 3. Terms used in analyses

Term	Definition or equations
Indices	i = a hummingbird population (i = 1 to m) j a flower type (j = 1 to n) h a habitat (h = 1 to 4) t a time period (t = 1 to 5)
Availability of nectar	A_{jht} = a total amount of nectar (in ml) in a flower type at mid-day, in a habitat, during a period of the year
Relative availability	$RA_{jht} = (A_{jht}/\sum_{j=1}^{n} A_{jht}) \times 100$
Foraging time	F_{ijht} total amount of time that a hummingbird population has spent feeding at a
Utilization of a food type	$U_{ijht} = (F_{ijht}/\sum_{j=1}^{n} F_{ijht}) \times 10$
Exploitation of a food type	$E_{ijht} = (F_{ijht}/\sum_{i=1}^{m} F_{ijht}) \times 10$
Index of dominance	ID_i = 1 to 5 depending on the place of the species in a hierarchy of dominancy in interspecific interactions (see text).
Density of a hummingbird population	D_{iht} = average number of individuals of a certain hummingbird population which
Relative density	$RD_{iht} = (D_{iht}/\sum_{i=1}^{m} D_{iht}) \times 100$
Horn unweighted niche overlap	Equation 23 in Colwell and Futuyama (1971)

petition. Thus, the measure of intraspecific competition is ambiguous. Therefore, we will take into account the presence or absence of intraspecific territoriality and intraspecific aggressive encounters in the interpretation of cases where relative density of a species seems to affect the utilization of a flower type by that species.

Finally, we calculated values of the Horn unweighted niche overlap using equation 23 in Colwell and Futuyama (1971). Resources matrices consisted of total amount of time migrants and "endemics" as groups spent feeding at each of the flower species of a transect, as well as from insects during a period of the year.

Results

According to our test procedure (figure 5), "Do "endemics" modify their niches during the stay of the migrants?" is the first question we should ask. Figure 7 shows that there are major changes in the diet of the "endemic" (both the residents and the wanderers)

during the period when migrants constitute an important part of the guild.

Since the answer to our first question is yes, we should find out what caused these shifts. Is it competition with migrants or other tropical species responsible or is a change in the resource base responsible for the arrangements? A multivariate analysis enables us to describe the niches of each group of birds and shows whether change in nectar availability or competition with migrants is the better predictor of changes in the feeding niches of residents and wanderers. Thus, it enables us to test simultaneously the first two hypotheses presented in our operational flow chart.

Niche Analysis

For each one of the three goups of birds, feeding observations gathered at tubular and cup-shaped flowers were analyzed by multiple regression separately without distinction of habitats and time periods. The few observations made at other types of flowers were

Figure 6.   Plate of hummingbird species studied. They are displayed according to their status in a hierarchy of dominance in interspecific interactions. First row, very high dominance: Long-tailed Hermit ♂ (*Phaethornis superciliosus*), Cinnamon Hummingbird ♀ (*Amazilia rutila*), Amethyst-throated Hummingbird ♂ (*Lampornis amethystinus*), Rivoli's Hummingbird ♂ (*Eugenes fulgens*). Second row, high dominance: Violet-crowned Hummingbird ♀ (*Amazilia violiceps*), Berylline Hummingbird ♀ (*Amazilia beryllina*), White-eared Hummingbird ♂ (*Hylocharis leucotis*), Green Violet-ear ♀ (*Colibri thalassinus*). Third row, intermediate dominance: Plain-capped Starthroat ♂ (*Heliomaster constantii*), Broad-billed Hummingbird ♂ (*Cynanthus latirostris*), Lucifer Hummingbird ♂ (*Calothorax lucifer*), Blue-throated Hummingbird ♂ (*Lampornis clemenciae*), Rufous Hummingbird ♂ (*Selasphorus rufus*). Fourth row, low dominance: Fork-tailed Emerald ♂ (*Chlorostilbon canivetii*), Ruby-throated and Black-chinned Hummingbirds ♀ (*Archilochus colubris* and *A. alexandrii*), Broad-tailed Hummingbird ♂ (*Selasphorus platycercus*). Fifth row, very low dominance: Dupont's Hummingbird ♂ (*Tilmatura dupontii*), Bumblebee Hummingbird ♂ (*Atthis heloisa*), Calliope Hummingbird ♂ (*Stellula calliope*), Allen's Hummingbird ♂ (*Selasphorus sasin*).

Jean-Luc DesGranges

insufficient for analysis. The following variables were analyzed simultaneously: the utilization of a flower type (i.e. tubular or cup-shaped flowers) by a species of bird in a habitat during a time period was the dependent variable while independent variables were relative availability, exploitation, dominance, and relative density of each bird species.

Niches of the "Endemics"

RESIDENTS

Residents are the principal users of tubular flowers. Where utilization of this type of flower is large the exploitation of these flowers by wanderers and migrants is low (d.f. = 27, r = −.49, p < .005). Variation in utilization is principally attributable to resident species with a high dominance status. Conversely, utilization of cup-shaped flowers by resident species is negatively related to their degree of dominance (d.f. = 24, r = −.57, p < .005). These results suggest that residents appropriate tubular flowers through aggressive interaction.

Despite their competitive superiority in general, resident species which monopolize tubular flowers rarely modify their diet to feed at flowers with the most nectar. Relative availability of nectar in tubular flowers had only a moderate effect on the utilization of these flowers by the residents (d.f. = 27, r = .38, p < .05) while relative availability of cup-shaped flowers had no significant effect on the utilization of these flowers by the residents (d.f. = 24, r = .05, p < .1). It appears that resident species preferentially visit certain flowers, and they keep on feeding from them even if they are found together with flowers containing more nectar. A study of flower dispersion and hummingbird energy-budgets is necessary for an understanding of this phenomenon.

WANDERERS

Wanderers are more sensitive than residents to variation in the relative availability of nectar in tubular flowers. When they are feeding at tubular flowers, wanderers feed more at flower species containing a high proportion of the nectar available in the habitat (i.e. high relative availability) and less at flowers containing low nectar (d.f. = 29, r = .55, p < .005). While relative availability of tubular flowers was responsible for only 14 percent of the variation in utilization of tubular flowers by the residents, it is responsible for 31 percent of the variation in utilization by wanderers. Since residents are the principal users of tubular flowers and have high dominance status (DesGranges 1977, 1978), wanderers may be feeding on a nectar surplus which is not entirely controlled by residents in an aggressive fashion.

At cup-shaped flowers, relative availability of nectar is responsible for only 18 percent of the variation in the utilization of cup-shaped flowers by wanderers, while relative density of wanderers explains an extra 16 percent of the variation in a multiple regression analysis (d.f. = 23, r = .42, multiple R^2 = .34, p < .05). Their use of cup-shaped flowers, which are generally poorer energetically than tubular flowers, may be determined by aggressive interaction with residents at tubular flowers.

Niche of the Migrants

Migrants feed rarely at tubular flowers. The few observations were insufficient for analysis. They feed extensively from cup-shaped flowers. Utilization of these flowers by migrants is positively related to their relative availability (d.f. = 10, r = .51, p < .05). In addition, it is interesting to note that most data come from habitats and time periods when cup-shaped flowers were very abundant. Thus migrants draw profit from the spectacular winter bloom of cup-shaped flowers (figure 4), particularly in the riparian gallery forest and in the humid pine-oak forest (table 4). For much of the time that migrants are present, this resource is so abundant that competition cannot be important, as indicated by the small correlation coefficients between utilization of cup-shaped flowers by migrants and their relative density (r = .01), dominance (r = .05), and exploitation (r = .08).

When cup-shaped flowers are uncommon, insects are an important supplement to the diet of migrants. For example, migrants spend almost 100 percent of their time feeding on insects at their arrival in the arid thorn forest and 61 percent of their foraging time just before their departure but only 1 percent in midwinter.

Interspecific Competition

The multiple regression analysis has shown that migrants are not responsible for the variation of the feeding niches of the "endemics" (figure 7). Instead, these variations are mainly attributable to variation in relative availability of nectar in the flowers. We now consider the role of aggressive interaction among the groups of hummingbirds.

Let us say that a hummingbird species is dominant over another one at a flower species when it wins more than 50 percent of its encounters with that species at that flower type. Using this definition of dominance, we can calculate the number of flower species where hummingbird species from one group are dominant over species of another group (table 5).

In general, tropical species are dominant to mi-

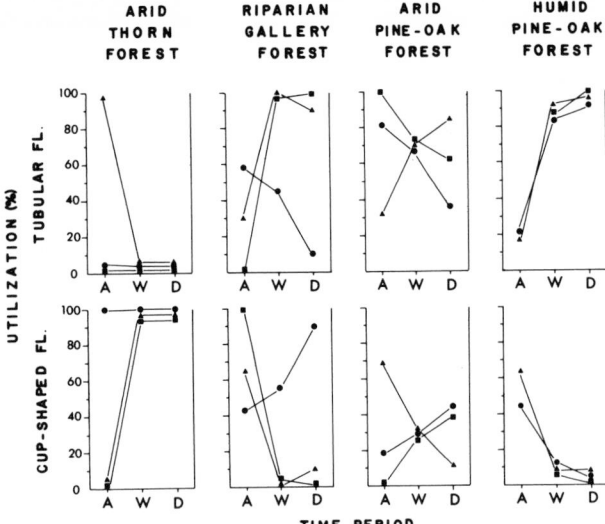

Figure 7. Utilization of tubular and cup-shaped flowers by each group of hummingbirds (■: migrants, ●: residents, ▲: wanderers) found in the 4 habitats during time periods when migrants are in the tropics (A = arrival of migrants, W = mid-winter, D = departure of migrants). Note that migrants are very uncommon in the guild at their arrival and departure. In practice, we consider that these 2 time periods frame the period during which the migrants are the most likely to have an influence on the organization of the guild.

Table 4. Comparison between daily production of nectar and daily nectar demand of hummingbirds

Habitat[1]	Observed density of humming-bird	Total volume of nectar required by these humming-birds (ml)[2]	Daily production of nectar in the whole set of flowers (ml)[3]
Riparian gallery forest	21	126	525
Humid pine-oak forest	48	288	530

[1] The 2 habitats experience a spectacular bloom of cup-shaped flowers during mid-winter while migrants are at peak abundance.

[2] Nectar demand = number of hummingbirds × 6 ml. We assume that 6 ml of nectar is the daily energetical requirement of an average hummingbird (DesGranges 1977, 1978).

[3] Daily production of nectar = $\sum_{j=1}^{n}$ {average volume of nectar in bagged flower (j) × number of flowers (j)}.

Bagged flowers are flowers which were encased in cheese cloth for a 24-hr period to prevent visitation by hummingbirds and insects. The volume of nectar they enclosed after 24 hr is an estimate of their daily production of nectar.

grants. Dominance is particularly evident at cup-shaped flowers. Residents are dominant to the two other groups of birds at most flower species. They dominate wanderers, particularly at tubular flowers, and dominate migrants, especially at cup-shaped flowers. Most of the observed chases occurred at the most common flowers. Thus, we can conclude that migrants are subordinate to tropical species and are often forced to use resources which are to some extent ignored by these endemics. Residents apparently choose to feed from the best flowers, especially tubular flowers, while wanderers have the first choice, before migrants, among flowers in excess of the residents' needs. Therefore, we reject the first two hypotheses (i.e. the dominant specialists hypothesis and the interstitial specialists hypothesis), and move to the next step on our flow chart. The question we ask now is: To what extent do the niches of migrants and endemics overlap?

Niche Overlap

Values of niche overlap are calculated from the total amount of time each species in a group of hummingbirds spent feeding at each of the flower species found in a habitat as well as from insects during a period of the year (figure 8). Niche overlap measures the degree of similarity between the niches of a pair of species. Its

value is large when the two species use similar resources in similar proportions. The maximum possible value of the Horn niche overlap is 100 percent (Colwell and Futuyma 1971). The overlap between the niches of our hummingbirds ranges from 33 percent to 99 percent, and is usually higher during the middle of winter (Fisher p < .11). Therefore, migrant and "endemics"

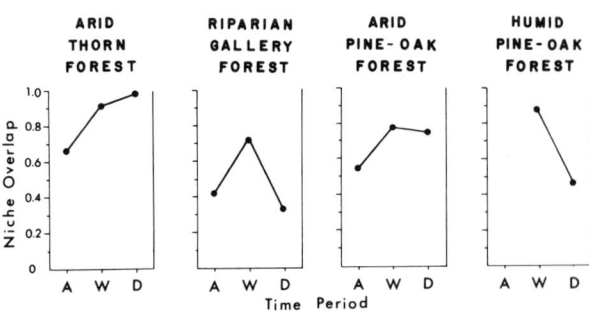

Figure 8. Values of Horn niche overlap between migrants and "endemics" found in the 4 habitats during time periods when migrants are in the tropics (symbols are the same as in figure 7).

Table 5. Number of plant species in every flower type where a hummingbird species from one group is dominant or subordinate to a species of another group[1]

	Tubular flowers				Cup-shaped flowers				Both types			
	Domi-nant	Subor-dinate	X^2	p	Domi-nant	Subor-dinate	X^2	p	Domi-nant	Subor-dinate	X^2	p
Residents against wanderers	10	3	3.8	.05	14	7	2.3	>.1	24	10	5.8	<.05
Residents against migrants	4	2		.68	8	0		.01	12	2	7.1	<.01
Wanderers against migrants	2	3		1	6	5	0.1	>.5	8	8	0.0	>.5
Endemics against migrants	6	5	0.1	>.5	14	5	4.3	<.05	20	10	3.3	>.1

[1] Binomial test is used when the expected value is less than 5 while X^2 is used in other cases

feed from several of the flower species visited by species of the other group. During winter, the two groups feed opportunistically at the most suitable flower species while each one has a particular set of "preferred" flowers at the arrival and just before the departure of migrants.

Conclusions of the Niche Analysis

We have rejected the dominant specialists and the interstitial specialists hypotheses because migrants are subordinate to "endemics," and therefore cannot be responsible for the changes we observed in the feeding niches of the tropical species during the winter. The niche-overlap study has shown that migrants occupy niches which are sometimes fairly different (e.g. overlap = 33 percent) from those of "endemics." Thus, we conclude that the neglected resources hypothesis is operating to a certain extent in the accommodation of migrant hummingbirds into tropical communities. However, often there is a high degree of overlap (i.e. more than 75 percent) between the niches of the two groups of birds. For example, both migrants and endemics are taking advantage of the spectacular winter bloom of flowers (figure 4 and table 4). Therefore, we conclude that the abundant food hypothesis is also operating in the accommodation of migrant hummingbirds. In addition, some uncommon flower species are used by both the "endemics" and the migrants." Therefore, we move to the next step on our flow chart (figure 5) and ask if migrants and "endemics" are territorial.

Territoriality

Interspecific territoriality occurred in the two groups of birds. All migrants were territorial while 7 of the 16 "endemics" were mainly territorial (DesGranges 1977, 1978). During the winter blooming peak, migrants and "endemics" were interspecifically territorial around the numerous patches which are very similar or even identical. Even though "endemics" are superior competitors in interference competition it is probable that the period of coexistence is not long enough for exclusion to occur. Therefore coexistence of migrants and "endemics" occurs in spite of interspecific territoriality and interspecific dominance.

Flocking

At their arrival and departure, as well as when they are forced by a dominant species to leave their territories, migrants need to seek out habitat patches with economically exploitable flowers. During these periods of nomadism, they often gather in large numbers around trees in full bloom. However, they were never observed to form cohesive flocks. Therefore, flocking does not play a role in the accommodation of migrant hummingbirds into tropical communities.

Fugitive Strategy

Although we did not collect systematic data to substantiate this phenomenon, it was clear that dominant species monopolized most of the good territories full of flowers while subordinate species defended marginal territories, if at all, with fewer flowers which were often less productive and more dispersed. Most migratory species have a low status of dominance. Some marked migrants (e.g. *Stellula calliope, Archilochus* sp.) were seen to be displaced by "endemics". Thus, it seems likely that at least certain migrants are "fugitive" species.

Conclusions

Our study has shown that the migration of hummingbirds coincides with a temporary abundance of food, particularly nectar in cup-shaped flowers. Tropical species are unable to consume all the nectar produced since the low carrying capacity of their environment during the summer keeps their population sizes low. Therefore, migrants, as well as "endemics," can take advantage of this abundance of food without suffering intolerable competition (abundant food hypothesis), and they can have exclusive access to resources of limited value which are neglected by tropical species because the tropical species find all the nectar they need in more suitable flowers (neglected resources hypothesis).

Despite this abundance of nectar, coexistence between migrants and "endemics" is not competition-free. The energy expended in territorial defense by hummingbirds is offset by the gain in reduced foraging time and costs (Wolf et al 1975). Therefore, migrants establish feeding territories and attempt to prevent other hummingbirds (both migrants and "endemics") from feeding in them by threatening or attacking them (interspecific territoriality hypothesis). But most migrants have a low status of dominance. Therefore several species are "fugitive." They settle first in low value territories until they are forced by dominant species to leave and seek unoccupied territories elsewhere (fugitive hypothesis).

These results are consistent with observations made on the Ruby-throated Hummingbird, *Archilochus colubris*, in Costa Rica by other workers. In general, the Ruby-throat tended to utilize either a portion of food resources which was not heavily used by the resident species or was able to fit into a complex of species using localized but very abundant food source (Wolf 1970; Feinsinger 1976).

Acknowledgments

This study has benefited from the kind help of several persons whose aid we gratefully acknowledge. We have corresponded and discussed the subject with many people including P. T. Boag, F. B. Gill, R. D. Montgomerie, and A. R. Phillips. P. Feinsinger provided many helpful suggestions on an earlier draft of the manuscript. D. Bordage and B. Houde helped with field work. R. McVaugh of the Herbarium of the University of Michigan kindly identified plant specimens. Yuk-Shan Wong of the Department of Biology, McGill, helped with nectar analysis while R. Lamarche gave considerable help with photography. Museum material was supplied by L. F. Baptista (Occidental College), J. Farrand, Jr. (American Museum), D. M. Niles (Delaware Museum), A. M. Rea (University of Arizona), and R. W. Storer (University of Michigan). I. Montpetit prepared the Spanish translation of the summary. The staff of the University of Oklahoma's Cultural Center in Colima, Mexico, helped with logistics. This research was supported by National Research Council Canada Grant A2920 to P. R. Grant.

Literature Cited

Blondel, J.
1969. Sédentarité et migration des oiseaux dans une garrigue méditérranéenne. La Terre et la Vie 23: 269–314.

Cody, M. L.
1971. Finch flocks in the Mohave Desert. Theor. Pop. Biol. 2:142–58.

Colwell, R. K.
1973. Competition and coexistence in a simple tropical community. Am. Nat. 107:737–60.

Colwell, R. K., and D. J. Futuyama
1971. On the measurement of niche breadth and overlap. Ecol. 52:567–76.

DesGranges, J. L.
1977. Interactions among resident and migrant hummingbirds in Mexico. Ph.D. thesis. McGill University, Montreal, Ontario, Canada, 123 pp.

DesGranges, J. L.
1978. Organization of a tropical nectar-feeding bird guild in a variable environment. Living Bird. 17:199–236.

Elgood, J. H., R. E. Sharland, and P. Ward.
1966. Palaearctic migrants in Nigeria. Ibis 108:84–116.

Feinsinger, P.
1976. Organization of a tropical guild of nectarivorous birds. Ecol. Monogr. 46:257–91.

Frochot, B.
1971. L'évolution saisonière de l'avifaune dans une futaie de chênes en Bourgogne. La Terre et la Vie 25:145–82.

Gause, G. F.
1934. The struggle for existence. Baltimore Md.: Williams & Wilkins, 1963 pp.

Jean-Luc DesGranges

Karr, J. R.
1976.   On the relative abundance of migrants from the North Temperate Zone in tropical habitats. Wils. Bull. 88:433–58.

Lack, D.
1968.   Bird migration and natural selection. Oikos 19:1–9.

Levins, R.
1968.   Evolution in changing environments. Princeton, N.J.: Princeton Univ. Press, 120 pp.

Levins, R., and D. Culver
1971.   Regional coexistence of species and competition between rare species. Nat. Acad. Sci. Proc. 68:1246–48.

MacArthur, R. H.
1959.   On the breeding distribution pattern of North American migrant birds. Auk 76:318–25.

Moreau, R. E.
1972.   *The Palaeartic-African Bird Migration Systems.* New York: Academic Press, 384 pp.

Morse, D. H.
1971.   The insectivorous bird as an adaptive strategy. Annu. Rev. Ecol. Syst. 2:177–200.

1974.   Niche breadth as a function of social dominance. Am. Nat. 108:818–30.

Ricklefs, R. E.
1972.   Dominance and the niche in bird communities. Am. Nat. 106:538–45.

Siebert, H. C.
1949.   Differences between migrant and non-migrant birds in food and water intake at various temperatures and photoperiods. Auk 66:128–53.

Thiollay, J. M.
1973.   Écologie des migrateurs tropicaux dans une zone pré-forestière de Côte d'Ivoire. La Terre et la Vie 27:268–96.

Tramer, E. J.
1974.   Proportions of wintering North American birds in disturbed and undisturbed dry tropical habitats. Condor 76:460–64.

Ulfstrand, S.
1973.   Proportions of palaeartic birds in some East African habitats. Die Vogelwarte 27:137–41.

Willis, E. O.
1966.   The role of migrant birds at swarms of army ants. Living Bird 5:187–231.

Wolf, L. L.
1970.   The impact of seasonal flowering on the biology of some tropical hummingbirds. Condor 72:1–14.

Wolf, L. L., F. R. Hainsworth, and F. B. Gill
1975.   Foraging efficiencies and time budgets in nectar-feeding birds. Ecol. 56:117–28.

PETER FEINSINGER
Department of Zoology
University of Florida
Gainesville, Florida 32611

Asynchronous Migration Patterns and the Coexistence of Tropical Hummingbirds

ABSTRACT

The complex vegetation of tropical mountains creates a mosaic of habitat patches among which numerous short-billed hummingbird species migrate. Calculation of "seasonal overlaps" among hummingbird populations at two Costa Rican sites, Monteverde (Feinsinger 1976) and the Cerro de la Muerte (Wolfe, Stiles, and Hainsworth 1976) demonstrates that in each patch the population density of each hummingbird species fluctuated in a unique temporal pattern. During seasons of flower scarcity, one or a few species could control all resources. Therefore, the ability of other hummingbirds to locate alternate resources through migration was crucial to their survival. I conclude that asynchronous migration patterns are instrumental in permitting the regional coexistence of large numbers of short-billed hummingbird species.

It follows that regions lacking such habitat mosaics must suffer reduced hummingbird diversity. This factor, among others, may lead to such contrasts in hummingbird diversity as that between the Andes and the Amazon Basin, between eastern and western North America, or between the tropical mainland and various islands. Data from studies in progress on Trinidad and Tobago support this reasoning. Several extensive nonforested habitats exist on Trinidad; seven short-billed hummingbird species, in particular abundant *Amazilia tobaci* and *Chrysolampis mosquitus*, travel between habitats in different spatiotemporal patterns. In contrast, Tobago has but one extensive habitat type; not only must *Chrysolampis* and *Amazilia* coexist nearly year-around, but they also migrate synchronously to exploit what flower bursts occur in peripheral habitat patches. Individuals of only two other shorter-billed species, which normally forage high in trees, enter the Tobago study sites.

The relationship between diverse migration strategies and the regional coexistence of hummingbirds follows predictions of theoretical models for fugitive species. In this sense it parallels the evolution and ecology of latitudinal migrations by other bird groups.

Introduction

Terrestrial communities in the neotropics typically support one or two resident hummingbird species with relatively short, straight bills (Feinsinger and Colwell in press). Often these "principal" species are unable to consume all available nectar, and additional species immigrate. These "secondary" birds are of two types: invaders from the principal populations in neighboring communities and chronic wanderers that follow a series of resource flushes from community to community (Wolf 1970; Feinsinger 1976; Wolf et al 1976; Karr 1977). At certain seasons, there are sufficient flowers for the principal species only. Therefore, many secondary birds must migrate among different habitats. While there are no complete data available on flower and hummingbird phenologies throughout a series of habitat patches, intensive studies on particular habitat patches (Feinsinger 1976; Wolf et al 1976) reveal cyclical shifts in the composition and diversity of hummingbird species, which implies that different species can use series of patches in different temporal (and spatial) sequences. The effects of migration opportunities on hummingbird diversity are also apparent at sites where such opportunities are few, such as in the Caribbean Islands. Finally, I will link hummingbird migration to models in theoretical ecology, and to latitudinal migration in other bird groups.

Study Sites

Cerro de la Muerte

At various times from 1966 through 1974, Wolf, Stiles, and Hainsworth (1976) investigated a high montane community (2,950–3,200 m) on the Cerro de la Muerte, Cordillera de Talamanca, Costa Rica. Their study areas contained second-growth scrub vegetation (described by Colwell 1973; Wolf et al 1976). While flower density was not quantified throughout the year, apparently dramatic peaks in flower numbers occurred annually in February–March (dry season) and August–September (wet season); flower shortages were evident May–July and November–December. Patches of many other habitat types occurred in the highly dissected topography of the surrounding region.

Monteverde

From October 1971 through May 1973, I studied a successional community at Monteverde, Cordillera de Tilarán, Costa Rica, (Feinsinger 1976). At the end of each month (December 1971–April 1973) I censused all flowers available to hummingbirds along consistent transects. Flower numbers fluctuated twentyfold in an annual cycle, from less than 3,000 in early dry season (December) or 3,600–7,700 in early wet season (June–August) to nearly 60,000 when the herb *Lobelia laxiflora* (Lobeliaceae) flowered in late dry season (April) or nearly 43,000 when the tree *Inga brenesii* (Leguminosae) flowered in late wet season (October). This community was one of a series of altitudinally zoned habitat types extending upward to the constantly moist, cool continental divide and downward to tropical dry forests.

Trinidad and Tobago

With the aid of two graduate students (Lee Ann Swarm and James A. Wolfe), I am currently investigating the comparative ecology of hummingbirds exploiting second-growth habitats on Trinidad and Tobago, West Indies. In northern Trinidad, a continental island of 4,540 km^2 some 15 km from the South American coast, there exist at least two extensive types of second-growth vegetation that are distinct relative to hummingbirds and their food plants. The mountain valleys of the Northern Range contain extensive patches of herbaceous and scrub vegetation with scattered trees. In this "Trinidad hill" habitat, where we concentrate studies along 1,000 m of transects 20-m wide, the major flowering peak occurs November–March, with a minor peak June–July. At various times, 10 hummingbird species, of which 7 have morphologically similar bills, forage here. About 8 km distant lies an extensive area of secondary scrub and natural savannah vegetation on the broad Caroni Plain. In this vegetation, where we have 300 m of transects, there is one abundant hummingbird food plant, whose prolonged flowering peak lasts April–September. To date we have noted 10 hummingbird species in this "Trinidad plains" habitat, including all 7 shorter-billed species also seen in the hills. There are several other, intergrading, types of nonforested habitat available to hummingbirds in northern Trinidad.

Tobago, a hilly island of 295 km^2 some 42 km northeast of Trinidad, has but one extensive second-growth habitat. Distributed throughout the mountains on the eastern three-quarters of the island, this "Tobago hill" habitat is similar to "Trinidad hill" habitat in terms of climate, physiognomy, and plant species. The amplitude and timing of flowering peaks on our 1,000 m of transects match those in the Trinidad hill habitat. The four shorter-billed hummingbirds that forage here also occur on Trinidad. We also have 300 m of transects in a much less extensive patch of xeric scrub that occurs on the island's western tip. In this "Tobago dry" habitat, which attracts at various times three of the shorter-billed hummingbirds, there is a single flowering peak from January through April. We have not encounterd any other distinct second-growth habitats on Tobago.

Peter Feinsinger

Data Collection and Analysis

Seasonal overlap in habitat occupancy between two hummingbird species i and j over one year is:

$$S_{ij} = \sum_{m=1}^{12} \min (a_{im}, a_{jm})$$

where a_{im} is the ratio of i's mean density in month m to the sum of its mean densities in all 12 months (see Feinsinger 1976 for fuller explanations of overlap equations). A superficial index, seasonal overlap does not take into account the finer resource partitioning that invariably develops among coexisting hummingbirds. Nevertheless, for morphologically similar species, such partitioning may be impossible at times of resource stress, and here low values for seasonal overlap, which indicate that different populations use the habitat in different seasonal patterns, must be ecologically meaningful.

I calculated seasonal overlaps from a different type of data for each study. Wolf et al (1976: figure 5) report relative population densities, on a scale of 0–10, for each species in each month May 1971–December 1972. I arbitrarily chose their first 12 months of data (May 1971–April 1972). For Monteverde, I had previously defined the monthly "effective population" of each hummingbird species as the total number of flowers that population visited on the study plots each day. This index ranged from 0 to nearly 62,300 (Feinsinger 1976). I chose the last 12 months of complete data (May 1972–April 1973). Treatment of Trinidad and Tobago data in similar fashion must await the conclusion of a lengthy analysis now in progress; instead, I use here census data collected at one point in each month by an observer spending 5 minutes on each consecutive, 20-m-long plot segment. These data are less accurate than "effective population" data, especially where rare or cryptic species are concerned (Feinsinger 1976). Nevertheless, for the two common hummingbird species on these islands we have found that censuses reflect well the relative changes in population density and impact on food resources. I chose the last 12 months of census data (April 1977–March 1978).

Results

Cerro de la Muerte

Table 1 presents seasonal overlaps between each pair of Cerro de la Muerte species, and overlaps between each species and the summed populations of the other three. *Eugenes* had the highest seasonal overlaps. But *Eugenes* also had a much longer beak than other species, foraged on flowers with long corollas, and faced little

Table 1. Seasonal overlaps[1] among hummingbird species of the Cerro de la Muerte, Costa Rica

	Overlap with:			All others	Months present
	Eugenes	*Selasphorus*	*Coilibri*		
Panterpe insignis	.71	.63	.58	.70	12
Eugenes fulgens	—	.78	.80	.86	12
Selasphorus flammula	—	—	.63	.70	9
Colibri thalassinus	—	—	—	.69	7

[1] Calculated from data in Wolf et al (1976).

competition for resources within the Cerro habitat patch (Colwell 1973; Wolf et al 1976). On the other hand, the pairs *Colibri—Panterpe* and *Selasphorus—Panterpe* overlapped considerably in the categories of flowers they preferred (Wolf et al 1976). The principal species, *Panterpe* dominated both *Colibri* and *Selasphorus*, and during scarcities of certain resource types the last two species apparently could not locate enough flowers that were unexploited by *Panterpe*. Their seasonal overlap values, which would doubtless be still lower had more sensitive population indices been possible, show that their migratory movements were temporally distinct.

Monteverde

At Monteverde (table 2), the two principal species (*Amazilia saucerottei* and *Chlorostilbon canivetti*) overlapped extensively with all other species, as would be expected, and with one another. *A. saucerottei* and *Chlorostilbon* also have similar geographic distributions in northwest Costa Rica (Feinsinger 1976), and it is possible that overall their spatiotemporal patterns of patch use are similar. These two species are adapted to exploit opposite ends of the resource density gradient, however (Feinsinger and Chaplin 1975), such that they can coexist indefinitely (Feinsinger and Colwell in press).

Colibri thalassinus and *Philodice* each subsisted for much of the year by exploiting a different set of surplus flowers, chiefly those of *Inga brenesii* and *Lobelia laxiflora*, not used by the principals. When these supplies diminished, however, each species emigrated to different habitat patches at the same or higher elevations. *Hylocharis*, an opportunist from lower elevations, also claimed many of the *Inga* and *Lobelia* flowers. Individuals of *Eupherusa*, an abundant resident of forests ad-

Table 2. Seasonal overlaps among hummingbird species[1] at Monteverde, Costa Rica

					Overlap with:									All Others	Months present
	Pb	Cc	He	Ct	Lc	Ee	Ac	Ec	Cd	At	Ch	Hc	Pl		
As	.43	.56	.30	.37	.16	.58	.17	.13	.13	.08	.21	.27	.32	.67	12
Pb	—	.21	.42	.37	.41	.14	.40	.34	.41	0	.56	0	0	.42	7
Cc	—	—	.54	.46	.07	.53	.16	.10	.03	.16	.15	.38	.17	.58	11
He	—	—	—	.54	.02	.12	.45	.39	.02	.05	.12	0	0	.36	5
Ct	—	—	—	—	.05	.20	.24	.18	.05	.26	.38	.01	0	.45	8
Lc	—	—	—	—	—	.15	0	0	.70	0	.49	.25	.17	.18	3
Ee	—	—	—	—	—	—	.12	.08	.05	.10	.10	.44	.48	.51	12
Ac	—	—	—	—	—	—	—	.83	0	0	.07	0	0	.22	4
Ec	—	—	—	—	—	—	—	—	0	0	.01	0	0	.18	4
Cd	—	—	—	—	—	—	—	—	—	0	.49	0	0	.17	1
At	—	—	—	—	—	—	—	—	—	—	0	.50	0	.08	2
Ch	—	—	—	—	—	—	—	—	—	—	—	0	0	.28	4
Hc	—	—	—	—	—	—	—	—	—	—	—	—	.17	.29	4
Pl	—	—	—	—	—	—	—	—	—	—	—	—	—	.20	1

[1] Species listed in order of annual effective population (see text). Abbreviations: *As, Amazilia saucerottei; Pb, Philodice bryantae; Cc, Chlorostilbon canivetii; He, Hylocharis eliciae; Ct, Colibri thalassinus; Lc, Lampornis calolaema; Ee, Eupherusa eximia; Ac, Archilochus colubris; Ec, Elvira cupreiceps; Cd, Colibri delphinae; At, Amazilia tzacatl; Ch, Campylopterus hemileucurus; Hc, Heliomaster constantii; Pl, Phaethornis longuemareus.*

jacent to the study habitat, regularly invaded to forage among excess flowers on a variety of plants. Individuals of *Lampornis* and *Elvira*, residents in more mesic forest less than 1 km distant, appeared during flowering bursts of particular plant species such as *Inga*. *Archilochus*, the only North American migrant, visited clumped flowers that *Amazilia saucerottei* failed to exploit, or dispersed flowers when *Chlorostilbon* was absent. *Colibri delphinae*, an especially mobile opportunist, appeared only during *Inga*'s flowering peak—which explains its high overlap with *Lampornis*. *Amazilia tzacatl*, possibly a resident in mesic communities nearby, appeared during the flowering peak of the shrub *Hamilia patens* (Rubiaceae). All 11 species possessed relatively short, straight bills (Feinsinger 1976).

Three species with distinctly shaped beaks also foraged in the study habitats. The long-billed specialist *Heliomaster* immigrated for the flowering season of one rare plant species. *Campylopterus* resided with *Eupherusa* in the nearby forest, where its long, decurved bill allowed it access to a distinct set of flowers; on its infrequent visits to the second-growth habitat, however, *Campylopterus* visited flower species also used by the shorter-billed birds. *Phaethornis*, a lower-elevation forest-edge species with a relatively short but decurved bill, entered the study habitat only twice.

In short, each species at Monteverde used habitat patches in a distinctive spatiotemporal pattern. Most converged upon flushes of one or several resource types; none but the two principals, and perhaps some *Eupherusa* individuals, could have remained in the one habitat patch year-round. It seems that all individuals I saw of 11 species, and many individuals of the other 3, depended for survival on locating resources in two or more habitat patches.

Trinidad and Tobago

Table 3 indicates a striking contrast between migration patterns on Trinidad and Tobago. *Amazilia tobaci* and *Chrysolampis mosquitus* are by far the most numerous second-growth hummingbirds on either island. On Trinidad each species acts as the principal population in a different habitat but attends resource flushes in the other. Seasonal overlap is low in each habitat. On Tobago, however, the two are forced into co-occupancy of the single extensive habitat type; not only is seasonal overlap high, but our preliminary data indicate that diet overlap within the habitat is also high. Resource flushes in peripheral habitats do not alleviate this situation; the data from the dry habitat indicate that the two species migrate in synchrony, and seasonal overlap is high there as well.

Peter Feinsinger

Discussion

Migration and Regional Coexistence

Patch use by hummingbird species fits two related models, the theoretical model for similar species competing in a heterogeneous environment (Horn and MacArthur 1972; Levin 1974, 1976) and the general model relating competition to the evolution of avian migration (Cox 1968). One application of Levin's (1974) model concerns mosaics of two or more patch types. While each patch supports but one or a few resident species, because different types favor different species the between-patch diversity of species—beta diversity (Whittaker 1975)—and the overall geographic (gamma) diversity are high. Now, if the environments in each patch type fluctuate independently, at times when competition is severe in one patch it might be relaxed in an adjacent patch, and individuals from the first patch might leak temporarily into the second (Levin 1974). Cox (1968) terms this "partial migration." Principal species of hummingbirds, then, are partial migrants; the resident population in one habitat fluctuates in size as some individuals invade resource flushes in nearby patches, then retreat when those resources decline and competition from that patch's residents increases. Patch-switching by organizer species such as *Eupherusa*, *Lampornis*, and *Elvira* (see above) increases the alpha diversity of each patch but does not add further to geographic species diversity.

Both the Levin (1974) and Cox (1968) models imply that in each patch there is a season of scarce resources when the patch can support no migrant species because residents need all resources, and outcompete migrants for them. Such seasons occur at the Cerro de la Muerte (Wolf et al 1976), at Monteverde (Feinsinger 1976), and on Trinidad (Feinsinger unpubl. data). At other times, however, the patch has resources sufficient not only for its residents and sporadic invaders from neighboring patches but also for "fugitive species" that are competitively inferior to all organizer species but adept at exploiting left-over resources. These fugitives must migrate between habitat patches and locate superfluous resources, faster than matching numbers of principals (Horn and MacArthur 1972; Levin 1974, 1976). The presence of *Colibri thalassinus* and *Selasphorus* on the Cerro (Wolf et al 1976) can be attributed to the feasibility of fugitive strategies; at Monteverde, *Colibri thalassinus*, *C. delphinae*, *Archilochus*, *Philodice*, and possibly other species pursue chronically fugitive patterns as opportunistic generalists or specialists on sporadically available resource types (Feinsinger 1976). Thus fugitive species, which depend on a series of patches in different stages, increase alpha diversity within patches and increase gamma diversity as well (Levin 1974; Levin and Pain 1974).

Thus far I have concentrated on models for morphologically similar species such as shorter-billed hummingbirds, whose migration patterns are enforced by competition (Cox 1968; Recher 1966). Morphologically unique species too must migrate, however, if the resources for which they are specialized fluctuate. While not strictly fugitive species, resource specialists such as *Eugenes* (Colwell 1973; Wolf et al 1976) or *Heliomaster* (Feinsinger 1976) follow fugitive-like migration patterns that track flushes of their resources in different communities. Therefore, these specialists are no less dependent than true fugitives on the consistency with which they can locate resources somewhere in the mosaic.

Effects of Reduced Migration Opportunities on Species Diversity

Reduced opportunities for fugitive strategies can lead to dramatic reductions in geographic species diversity (see Levin and Paine 1974, Willis 1974). Trinidad, practically a part of South America, supports at various times 16 hummingbird species, Tobago 6 (ffrench 1973). It is not surprising that the two most successful second-growth hummingbirds on Trinidad (*Amazilia tobaci* and *Chyrsolampis mosquitus*) are also successful on Tobago. But on Trinidad, each of the two species (which have similar feeding styles) resides in a separate habitat, and overflows into the other when appropriate; on Tobago they must coexist in the single extensive habitat type and migrate synchronously to any peripheral resource flushes (table 3). On both islands, nearly all nectar supplies available to shorter-billed hummingbirds are consumed daily except during sudden resource flushes (Feinsinger, Wolfe, and Swarm unpubl. data). On Trinidad this is effected by each habitat's principal species plus various combinations of the remaining six shorter-billed species, but on Tobago the two principal species alone often consume all nectar. Unless they migrated between the two islands, fugitive species on Tobago would be unable to locate superfluous resources consistently. Even *Chrysolampis*, slightly subordinate to *Amazilia* in aggressive interactions, emigrates briefly during the season of extreme resource scarcity (September–November). The only other shorter-billed species on Tobago are two large, aggressive birds (*Anthracothorax nigricollis*, typically a canopy feeder and flycatcher, and *Florisuga mellivora*, a high-elevation canopy feeder and flycatcher), which occasionally forage in the study habitats. Thus Tobago resembles the theoretical situation Levin (1974) describes, where residents migrate so freely between patches that patch boundaries are effectively obscured and the existence of additional species is endangered (see also Platt and Weis 1977); it

Table 3. Seasonal overlaps between 2 common hummingbird species on Trinidad and Tobago, April 1977– March 1978

	Months present	Total number in all months' censuses[1]	Seasonal overlap
Trinidad			
Hill habitat[2]			
Amazilia tobaci	12	233	
Chrysolampis mosquitus	3	6	0.17
Plains habitat[3]			
Amazilia tobaci	3	12	
Chrysolampis mosquitus	9	559	0.19
Tobago			
Hill habitat[2]			
Amazilia tobaci	12	693	
Chrysolampis mosquitus	9	178	0.67
Dry habitat[3]			
Amazilia tobaci	11	87	
Chrysolampis mosquitus	7	39	0.79

[1] Because these transects cover more space in the hill habitats than in the other 2, there are 3.3 times more census minutes spent in the hill habitats. See text.

[2] 1,000 m of transects.

[3] 300 m of transects.

would be impossible for fugitive species to migrate faster than the two principals (Horn and MacArthur 1972). In contrast, on Trinidad it is possible for additional species, both principals in other communities and fugitives, to sneak in and out of the two major habitat types and others.

More isolated Caribbean Islands, such as the Lesser Antilles, support but two hummingbird species per habitat (Lack 1973, 1976). There are apparently no fugitive species whatsoever; since each island in the Lesser Antilles has one, or at most two, patch types (consistent from island to island), at some seasons fugitives could locate superfluous resources only by flying vast distances. Now, gamma diversity of Antillean hummingbirds could still greatly exceed alpha diversity if there were a large species pool of hummingbirds, with initially similar competitive abilities, colonizing similar islands randomly (see Levin 1974; Levin and Paine 1974). Reef fish enter a "lottery" system where random colonization events determine each coral patch's species complement, which is then able to exclude additional species; the alpha diversity

of each patch is low, but the gamma diversity of series of patches is high (Sale 1977). Greater Antillean hummingbirds may have entered such a lottery; while each habitat has only two species, on different islands similar habitats support different combinations of species, and overall the Greater Antilles (plus the Bahamas) have 12 hummingbird species (Lack 1976). But in the Lesser Antilles every lowland habitat patch supports the same two hummingbirds; every highland habitat patch adds the same third species (except Grenada, which has instead the ecological equivalent from Trinidad and Tobago); and on two particularly mountainous islands, Dominica and Martinique, the same fourth species is added, for a grand gamma total of five species. The simplest explanation is that the isolated Lesser Antilles never had a large species pool to draw from. Given the migratory ability of hummingbirds, however, it is possible that a much larger species pool was available but that hummingbirds, like the New Guinea birds studied by Diamond (1975), follow "assembly rules" such that certain species are the best colonists of a given habitat type and can exclude, or displace other species from any patch of that type. In short, both the exclusion of species with fugitive migration strategies and the exclusion of potential residents through "assembly rules" contribute to a low geographic diversity of island hummingbirds.

Mainland sites also differ in the opportunities they offer migrant hummingbirds and, consequently, in the diversity of species they have. The extensive rain forests of the Amazon Basin support many species of hermit hummingbirds Phaethorninae, which typically have distinct bill morphologies, but contain relatively few shorter-billed species (Ridgway 1890; de Schauensee 1966). Hermit hummingbirds, whose males sometimes attend year-round leks (Hilty 1975), are quite sedentary. The environmentally heterogeneous Andes support a diverse fauna of shorter-billed species (Ridgway 1890) which apparently migrate a great deal (de Schauensee 1966; J. Terborgh pers. comm.). For example, in a single Peruvian cordillera J. Terborgh and J. S. Weske mist-netted 38 hummingbird species, 22 of which had relatively short bills (Feinsinger et al in press).

Eastern North America has 31 species of hummingbird-pollinated flowers. Excepting tropical species in peninsula Florida, these have extensive geographical distributions, leading to broad regional synchrony in resource availability (Austin 1975). In contrast, the 130 or more hummingbird-pollinated plants in western North America are patchily distributed among various montane, intermontane, desert, and coastal habitats, creating a complex mosaic of independently fluctuating resource regimes (Grant and Grant 1968; Stiles 1973). Seven hummingbird species regularly

Peter Feinsinger

breed in these habitats, and four additional species breed in the more southern areas (Grant and Grant 1968). During the breeding season each species tends to reside in a different set of habitat patches. But after breeding season there is a prolonged session of patch-to-patch migration in which different populations mingle with one another in diverse, constantly changing patterns (Cody 1966; Stiles 1973). There is evidence that certain species are competitively superior in certain patch types, and can control most flowers for brief periods (Kodric-Brown and Brown in press). Were other species unable to locate alternate resources through different spatiotemporal movements, they might face serious food shortages. In eastern North America, there is only one hummingbird species; the geographically homogeneous resources impose synchrony on migratory movements (see Austin 1975), and it is possible that the absence of opportunities for distinctive between-patch migration patterns discourages the establishment of additional species.

Parallels with Other Birds

There are striking parallels between hummingbirds migrating among tropical habitats and other birds migrating between tropical and temperate habitats. Proportionately more latitudinal migrants are found on edge habitats, where tropical residents may often leave much surplus food, than in mature tropical forest, where residents may consume most of the relatively invariant food supply year-round (Willis 1966, this volume; Leck 1972; Karr 1976a; Orejuela this volume; Hutto this volume). Like short-billed hummingbirds, latitudinal migrants tend to have broad, overlapping food preferences (Recher 1966; Willis 1966; Cox 1968; Tramer and Kemp this volume, Waide this volume). Thus they are like fugitive hummingbirds, exploiting resource flushes in one patch (temperate zone) during the summer, resource flushes in another patch (tropics) during the winter. Recher's (1966) studies of shorebirds indicate that even during the migration phase itself, distinctive temporal patterns of patch occupancy (= seasonal overlaps) alleviate potentially severe competition.

Patch-to-patch migration does not, however, seem to be crucial to year-round neotropical residents other than hummingbirds, either in the sense of maintaining particular populations or in the sense of promoting gamma diversity (although see Pearson this volume). Insect density in mature forest may remain fairly constant, and forest insectivore populations wander little (Buskirk 1976; Powell this volume). While fruit abundance fluctuates in some habitats, many species that are frugivorous switch to other foods at other seasons (Snow and Snow 1971), or migrate over restricted geographic areas in single-species or mixed-

species flocks (Terborgh and Diamond 1970; Morton 1973). Morton (1977) documents patch-to-patch migration in two tropical frugivores, but there is no evidence that their migrations are asynchronous.

Conclusions

Colwell (1974) distinguishes two components of predictibility: constancy and contingency. In terms of food resources, an environment in which the availability of each type of resource remains stable has high constancy but low contingency. An environment where resource levels vary widely, but in a consistent temporal pattern, has low constancy and high contingency. Evidently, diversity in most groups of tropical birds depends on local constancy, which allows the species in each habitat patch to subdivide food resources precisely with the assurance that there will be a steady supply of food in each resource category (MacArthur 1969, 1972; Buskirk 1976; Karr 1976b). The diversity of sedentary, morphologically specialized hermit hummingbirds in Amazonian rain forest (see above) is most likely correlated with a relatively constant environment. Habitat heterogeneity increases the beta diversity of such sedentary bird species (Janzen 1967) but does not additionally increase their gamma diversity.

In contrast, the diversity of shorter-billed hummingbird species depends on a mosaic of patches with inconstant but highly contingent resources. Local inconstancy is crucial to fugitive species; were each patch constant ("undisturbed") its organizer populations could expand in time to usurp all resources (Levin and Paine 1974; Levin 1976). At the same time, a fugitive's survival depends on its ability to locate resources in some patch or upon global constancy (see Root and Chaplin 1976 for a related example). If resource levels within each patch are highly contingent, instead of searching haphazardly for resources unpredictable in time and space fugitive hummingbirds can immigrate confidently into habitat patches in predictable, annually recurring sequence. Evidence is given above and elsewhere (Feinsinger 1976; Wolf et al 1976) that resource flushes in tropical mountains are highly contingent, and that hummingbird populations and individuals arrive at predictable times to exploit them. A final parallel can thus be drawn between tropical hummingbirds and latitudinal migrants, which require resource constancy in a truly global sense but resource inconstancy and contingency at local levels.

Acknowledgments

I am greatly in debt to Lee Ann Swarm and James A. Wolfe for the innumerable hours they have spent, are spending, and will spend collecting data on Trinidad and Tobago, where our studies are funded by National Science Foundation grant DEB76-20371. There is insufficient room here to express my gratitude to the numerous persons and agencies who contributed to the Monteverde studies; I have thanked them at length elsewhere (Feinsinger 1976). Larry L. Wolf encouraged me to use the Cerro de la Muerte data. Finally, I am grateful to Simon A. Levin for his comments on the manuscript.

Literature Cited

Austin, D. F.
1975. Bird flowers in the eastern United States. Fla. Sci. 38:1–12.

Buskirk, W. H.
1976. Social systems in a tropical forest avifauna. Am. Nat. 110:293–310.

Cody, M. L.
1968. Interspecific territoriality among hummingbird species. Condor 70:270–71.

Colwell, R. K.
1973. Competition and coexistence in a simple tropical community. Am. Nat. 107:737–60.

1974. Predictability, constancy and contingency of periodic phenomena. Ecol. 55:1148–53.

Cox, G. W.
1968. The role of competition in the evolution of migration. Evol. 22:180–92.

De Schauensee, R. M.
1966. *The Species of Birds of South America and Their Distribution.* Philadelphia: Acad. Nat. Sci.

Diamond, J. M.
1975. Assembly of species communities. In *Ecology and Evolution of Communities*, eds. M. L. Cody and J. M. Diamond, pp. 342–44. Cambridge Mass.: Harvard University Press.

Feinsinger, P.
1976. Organization of a tropical guild of nectarivorous birds. Ecol. Monogr. 46:257–91.

Feinsinger, P., and S. B. Chaplin
1975. On the relationship between wing disc loading and foraging strategy in hummingbirds. Am. Nat. 109: 217–24

Feinsinger, R., and R. K. Colwell
In press. Community organization among neotropical nectar-feeding birds. Am. Zool.

Feinsinger, P., R. K. Colwell, J. Terborgh, and S. B. Chaplin
In press. Elevation and the morphology, flight energetics, and foraging ecology of tropical hummingbirds. Am. Nat.

ffrench, R.
1973. *A Guide to the Birds of Trinidad and Tobago.* Wynnewood, Pa.: Livingston.

Grant, K. A., and V. Grant.
1968. *Hummingbirds and Their Flowers.* New York: Columbia Univ. Press.

Hilty, S.
1975. Year-around attendance of White-whiskered and Little Hermits, *Phaethornis* spp., at singing assemblies in Colombia. Ibis 117:382–84.

Horn, H. S., and R. H. MacArthur
1972. Competition among fugitive species in a harlequin environment. Ecol. 53:749–52.

Janzen, D. H.
1967. Why mountain passes are higher in the tropics. Am. Nat. 101:233–49.

Karr, J. R.
1976a. On the relative abundances of north temperate migrants in tropical habitats. Wils. Bull. 88:433–58.

1976b. Seasonality, resource availability, and community diversity in tropical bird communities. Am. Nat. 110:973–94.

1977. Ecological correlates of rarity in a tropical forest bird community. Auk 94:240–47.

Kodric-Brown, A., and J. H. Brown
In press. Influence of economics, interspecific competition, and sexual dimorphism on territoriality of migrant rufous hummingbirds. Ecol.

Lack, D.
1973. The numbers of species of hummingbirds in the West Indies. Evol. 27:326–37.

1976. *Island Biology Illustrated by the Land Birds of Jamaica.* Berkeley: Univ. of California Press.

Leck, C. F.
1972. The impact of some North American migrants at fruiting trees in Panama. Auk 89:842–50.

Levin, S. A.
1974. Dispersion and population interactions. Am. Nat. 108:207–28.

1976. Population dynamic models in heterogeneous environments. Annu. Rev. Ecol. Syst. 7:287–310.

Levin, S. A. and R. T. Paine
1974. Disturbance, patch formation, and community structure, Proc. U.S. Nat. Acad. Sci. 71:2744–47.

MacArthur, R. H.
1969. Patterns of communities in the tropics. Biol. J. Linn. Soc. 1:19–30.

1972. *Geographical Ecology: Patterns in the Distribution of Species.* New York: Harper & Row.

Morton, E. S.
1973. On the evolutionary advantages and disadvantages of fruit-eating in tropical birds. Am. Nat. 107:8–22.

1977. Intratropical migration in the Yellow-green Vireo and Piratic Flycatcher. Auk 94:97–106.

Peter Feinsinger

Platt, W. J., and I. M. Weis

1977. Resource partitioning and competition within a guild of fugitive prairie plants, Am. Nat. 111:479–513.

Recher, H. F.

1966. Some aspects of the ecology of migrant shorebirds. Ecol. 47:393–407.

Ridgway, R.

1890. The hummingbirds. U.S. Nat. Mus. Rept. 1890:253–383.

Sale, P. F.

1977. Maintenance of high diversity in coral reef fish communities. Am. Nat. 111:337–59.

Snow, B. K., and D. W. Snow

1971. The feeding ecology of tanagers and honeycreepers in Trinidad. Auk 88:291–322.

Stiles, F. G.

1973. Food supply and the annual cycle of the Anna Hummingbird. Univ. Cal. Publ. Zool. 97:1–109.

Terborgh, J., and J. M. Diamond

1970. Niche overlap in feeding assemblages of New Guinea birds. Wils. Bull. 82:29–52.

Whittaker, R. H.

1975. *Communities and Ecosystems*, 2nd ed. New York: Macmillan.

Willis, E. O.

1966. The role of migrant birds at swarms of army ants. Living Bird 5:187–231.

1974. Populations and local extinctions of birds on Barro Colorado Island, Panama. Ecol. Monogr. 44:153–69.

Wolf, L. L.

1970. The impact of seasonal flowering on the biology of some tropical hummingbirds. Condor 72:1–14

Wolf, L. L., F. G. Stiles, and F. R. Hainsworth

1976. Ecological organization of a tropical, highland hummingbird community. J. Anim. Ecol. 45:349–79.

F. GARY STILES
Escuela de Biologia
Universidad de Costa Rica
Ciudad Universitaria "Rodrigo Facio"
Costa Rica

Evolutionary Implications of Habitat Relations Between Permanent and Winter Resident Landbirds in Costa Rica

ABSTRACT

In this paper I explore distributional patterns of migrant landbirds in relation to those of permanent residents, with respect to altitude, rainfall, and habitat utilization. The latter is assessed according to a simple habitat classification based on the position and orientation of the foliage-air interface, for birds of 5 localities on the humid Caribbean slope of Costa Rica ranging from 100 to 3,000 m elevation; and for a locality in the dry Pacific lowlands at 100 m elevation. Altitudinal distributions are estimated over 10 Caribbean localities that approximate a transect from 0 to 3,500 m.

The numbers and habitat distributions of winter resident species at the five intensively studied Caribbean localities varied with altitude in the same manner as did those of permanent resident species; no consistent relation was found for fall migrants. In general, migrants occurred less frequently in forest interior and more in nonforest-edge habitats than permanent residents, but this is in part a function of taxonomic affinities: the permanent residents ecologically most similar to winter residents are also closest taxonomically. In fact, the great majority of migrants have close relatives that are tropical residents. Ecological amplitudes (in terms of number of habitat categories occupied at a site, or number of sites along an altitudinal transect at which a species is resident) of winter residents average slightly greater than those of permanent residents as a whole but are similar to those of permanent residents occurring outside the forest interior.

The striking degree of concordance between ecological distributions of permanent and winter residents suggests that the migrants are an inte-

ABSTRACTO

En este artículo se comparan las distribuciones de las aves terrestres migratorias con las de las especies residentes, con respecto a la elevación, la lluvia, y el uso del hábitat. Para esta última comparación se emplea una clasificación simple del hábitat según la posición de la interfase follaje-aire. Datos sobre uso del hábitat se presentan para las aves de 5 localidades en la vertiente del Atlántico de Costa Rica, que incluyen un rango de elevaciones de 100 a 3,000 m, y para una localidad de clima mucho más seco en la vertiente del Pacífico a 100 m de altura. Las distribuciones altitudinales se estimaron en el lado Atlántico agregando datos de 10 localidades adicionales, para tener el equivalente de un transecto desde el nivel del mar hasta 3,500 m de elevación.

Los números y distribuciones ecológicas (según la clasificación de los hábitats) varían con la elevación en la misma manera para las especies que son residentes invernales, que para los residentes permanentes, en las cinco localidades estudiados más intensivamente (Nota: en este artículo la palabra "invierno" y sus derivados se usan en el sentido del invierno o época fría de la zona templada del norte, aproximadamente Noviembre a Marzo, y no como sinónimo de la época lluviosa—Mayo a Noviembre—como se la usa corrientemente en Centroamérica). No hay ningún patrón altitudinal muy definido con respecto a estos parámetros para les especies que solamente se encuentran de paso otoñal. Por lo general, los residentes invernales se encontraron menos dentro del bosque, y más al borde o afuera del bosque, que los residentes permanentes. Sin embargo, esta diferencia se debe en gran parte a

gral part of tropical communities rather than an extraneous element superimposed upon them. Although the migrants leave the tropics for up to six months each year, the timing of their departure and return tends to preclude invasion of their niches by permanent residents. The high degree of integration of winter residents into tropical communities bespeaks a long tropical history and possibly tropical origins for many migrant taxa: they are basically tropical birds that have been able to increase breeding success by taking advantage of the summer burst of productivity at high latitudes. Given the great seasonal mobility of many "resident" tropical birds, especially canopy-edge oscines, it is difficult to draw a clear ecological distinction between "migrants" and "endemics". However one views the origin of migrant taxa, I would argue that the time is ripe for a fresh look at migration and winter residency— and at the structure of tropical bird communities—from the point of view that the migrants form an ecologically important part of these communities.

afinidades taxonómicas: las especies de residentes permanentes más parecidas ecológicamente a los residentes invernales, también son más cercanas taxonómicamente. Más bien la gran mayoría de especies migratorias tienen parientes muy cercanos entre los residentes permanentes. Las amplitudes ecológicas (en términos de los números de hábitats ocupados en un sitio, o los números de sitios ocupados a través de uns transecto altitudinal) de residentes invernales son ligeramente más grandes que las de los residentes permanentes en total, pero muy parecidas a las de las especies de éstos que no ocurren solamente adentro del bosque.

El grado de coincidencia de las distribuciones ecológicas de los residentes permanentes e invernales es muy alto, y sugiere que éstos son miembros integrales de las comunidades y no un elemento ajeno sobrepuesto en ellas. Aunque los migratorios se van de los trópicos hasta por seis meses del año, sus salidas y regresos caen temporalmente de tal manera que se dificulta mucho la invasión de sus nichos por las especies residentes. Los residentes invernales son bien integrados a las comunidades tropicales, que muy posiblemente tienen sus orígenes evolutivos en estas comunidadas. Incluso se puede llamarlos aves tropicales que han logrado aumentar el éxito de la reproducción, aprovechando la productividad grande y transitoria del verano norteño, a través de la migración. Dado el grado de movilidad de muchos "residentes" tropicales, especialmente oscines del borde y dosel del bosque, es evidente que se no sería fácil distinguir ecologicamente entre "migratorios" y "endémicos." Sea como sea el orígen de los migratorios, yo creo que es hora de reexaminar los fenómenos de la migración y la residencia invernal, desde el punto de vista de que los migratorios constituyen una parte importante de muchas comunidades tropicales.

F. Gary Stiles

Introduction

I propose to look at migrants on their tropical wintering grounds—winter residents, for want of a better term—and permanent residents ("endemics"), in terms of their respective patterns of habitat occupation. By submitting both groups to the same criteria, I hope to determine just how similar or different they are in their ecological distributions. This in turn will help to indicate to what extent we are justified in regarding winter and permanent residents as distinct ecological entities.

I emphasize that I will be dealing strictly at the level of which habitats the birds use, not with the details of how they use them. Thus, the picture I paint will be broad and somewhat superficial rather than narrow and more profound. I believe that this approach is highly justifiable in providing an overall ecological background against which migrant-resident foraging patterns, say, can be more meaningfully studied. Such a broad perspective might give an added dimension to the numerous intensive, short-term, single-site studies reported in this symposium. Furthermore, I have the impression that too many of us come to the tropics to "study migrants" instead of studying the bird communities as a whole. I hope to show that an understanding of the former requires a broader understanding of the latter.

Methods

Over the past 10 years, I have visited various Costa Rican localities with some regularity to observe and collect birds. At the conclusion of each visit, I listed the species of birds recorded, often with notes on relative abundances and habitat preferences. For this symposium, I have brought together such data from 11 sites where I feel my information on occurrence and habitat use of the birds is reasonably complete. Each site has been visited at least twice during each of the following "seasons": fall migration (September to early November), winter residency of temperate-zone breeders (December to early March) and the period when breeding populations of these species are absent (May to early August). I have delimited the "seasons" thus to permit maximum separation of migrants and winter residents, although our banding studies have shown that winter resident individuals may be present continuously in relatively restricted areas between September or October and March or early April. All but one of the sites discussed here are on the Caribbean slope of central Costa Rica, on two adjacent mountain ranges, the Cordillera Central and the Cordillera de Talamanca. At most, two or three species may occur on one mountain range and not the other, and conditions on the two ranges change similarly with altitude (Tosi 1969). Thus, these localities approximate an altitudinal transect from sea level to 3,500 m (figure 1). The other locality is Parque Nacional Santa Rosa at an elevation of 100 m in the dry Pacific lowlands of northwestern Costa Rica, which I included for comparison with the wet lowland sites, especially La Selva. For Santa Rosa, La Selva, Virgen del Socorro, Muñeco, Cerro Chompipe, and Villa Mills, I looked at patterns of habitat use of winter and permanent resident birds in more detail.

To treat habitat use I have devised a simple scheme for classifying habitats according to the position and orientation of the foliage-air interface (FAI) (figure 2). This may be a fundamental habitat parameter for many birds in that here full sunlight strikes the foliage directly, and there tends to be a concentration of primary production, flowering, fruiting, and insects. A "forest" is any vegetation with sufficient vertical differentiation that one can delimit distinct canopy and interior strata. Edge situations occur when the FAI is diagonal or vertical, nonforest situations where the FAI is at or near ground level. Perhaps the most controversial aspect of this scheme is that second

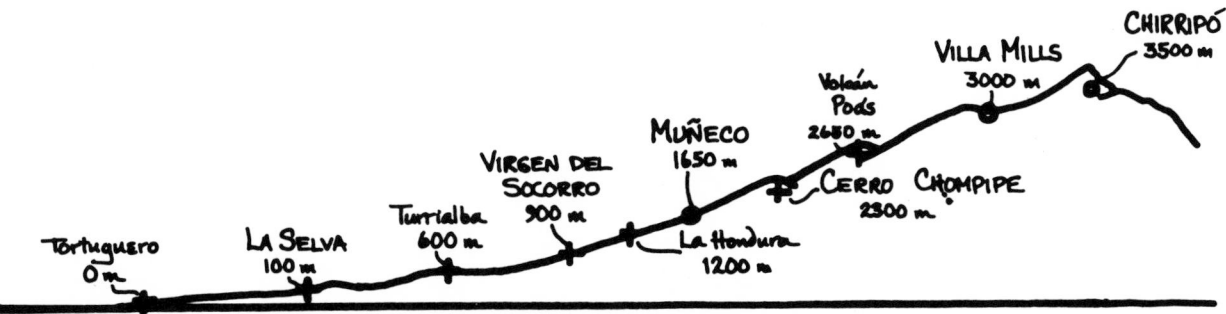

Figure 1.   Locations of 10 localities on the humid Caribbean slope of central Costa Rica along an idealized altitudinal transect. Actually, the localities are on 2 adjacent mountain ranges. + = Cordillera Central; 0 = Cordillera de Talamanca.

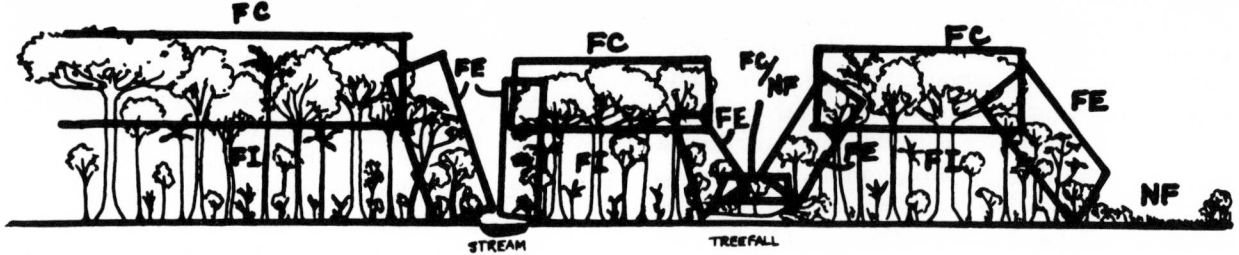

Figure 2. Idealized vegetation profile of tropical forest, and vegetation classification. Abbreviations: FI = forest interior (distinct stratum beneath canopy); FC = forest canopy (foliage-air interface overlying a distinct lower stratum); FE = forest edge (foliage-air interface vertical or inclined, or interrupted); NF = nonforest (foliage-air interface at or near ground level, no underlying stratum).

growth sufficiently advanced to have a distinct, solid canopy will be classified as forest; however, it is so treated by many forest interior birds. I should also emphasize that each of the study sites contains all four habitat types, and I have sought both migrant and permanent resident birds in each. This is important because migrants are more conspicuous, but not invariably more abundant, in secondary than in primary habitats.

As a prelude to considering the ecological affinities of migrant and resident birds, it might be useful to consider the taxonomic affinities of the two groups. For this I have used primarily the classifications of Slud (1964), recent modifications in the A.O.U. Checklist Supplements, and Mayr and Short (1970).

Results

Table 1 provides a broad overview of the Costa Rican avifauna as a whole. Comparing waterbirds (including kingfishers) and landbirds, the proportion of migrant, nonbreeding taxa is far higher in the former. Less than a third of the species of Costa Rican waterbirds breed there, although over half are "resident" in the sense of maintaining sizeable populations there year-round. This is due to the presence of nonbreeding summer residents of many species, usually—but not invariably—first-year birds. Shorebirds, herons, gulls, and terns are especially notable in this respect. The ecological significance of these summer residents will be discussed later. It is noteworthy that no migrant landbirds maintains a nonbreeding summer resident population in Costa Rica. Among the landbirds themselves, the oscines have by far the largest proportion of migrants; some 27 percent of this group are migrants breeding in North America, as opposed to ca 10 percent of the nonpasserines and suboscines (table 1). By far the largest concentration of oscine migrants is in the family Parulidae, with 35 species.

Table 1. The species of Costa Rican birds, broken down according to seasonal occurrence

Group	Permanent resident only	Breeding resident only	Resident and migrant populations	Non-breeding migrant or visitant only	Non-breeding summer population	Total number of species
Waterbirds	39	1	12	96	39+	148
Landbirds: nonpasserines	229	2	9	18	0	258
Landbirds: suboscines	151	3	2	11	0	167
Landbirds: oscines	172	1	3	66	0	242
Totals	592	7	26	190	~40	815

625 total Breeding avifauna   216: total migrant avifauna   total avifauna

F. Gary Stiles

Most migrants of all landbird groups are closely related to resident taxa: either other populations of the same species are resident, or other species in the same genus are resident (table 2). Only one family of migrants, the Mimidae, has no resident species—and only one migrant species reaches Costa Rica (*Dumetella carolinensis*). The only sizeable migrant group without congeners resident in Costa Rica is several genera of Parulidae (*Oporornis, Seiurus, Wilsonia, Mniotilta,* etc.), and this may be in part an artifact of taxonomic oversplitting at the generic level in this family (Mayr and Short 1970). In general, then, most migrants are taxonomically close to one or more resident tropical species; now we turn to ecological relationships.

The distribution of permanent and winter residents with respect to altitude and humidity is given in table 3. On the Caribbean slope, migrants comprise a rather constant 9–12 percent of the total resident avifauna until very high altitudes are reached. (I consider a species resident at a site if it occurs there regularly in five or more months per year). Numbers of both permanent and winter resident species decline linearly with increasing altitude, except for a pronounced shoulder (in both groups) at 900–1,000 m (Virgen del Socorro). The rather sharp drop in nonpasserine species among the permanent residents as one leaves the

Table 2. Affinities of migratory landbirds breeding mostly or entirely in North America

Group	Total number of species	Resident Population	Resident congener(s)	Total spp. with resident taxonomic affinities
Nonpasserines	21	6	17	18
Suboscines	12	1	12	12
Oscines	68	3	39	42
Total species	101	10	68	82

lowlands is due to the decline of such "tropical" groups as puffbirds, jacamars, and toucans; such a decline is not evident in the winter residents where these groups are not represented. Of considerably greater significance is the decline in importance of the suboscines with altitude, both among permanent and winter residents. Comparing the wet and dry lowland sites, the most striking difference is that the number of

Table 3. Numbers and percentages of permanent and winter resident species at Costa Rican localities differing in altitude and rainfall[1]

Locality	Permanent residents				Winter residents			
	NP[2]	SO	O	Total spp.	NP	SO	O	Total spp.
La Selva	96	73	66	235	3	5	24	32
	.41	.31	.29		.09	.16	.75	
Virgen del Socorro	64	62	76	202	2	2	20	24
	.32	.31	.38		.09	.09	.80	
Muñeco	42	39	52	132	2	1	10	13
	.32	.29	.39		.15	.08	.77	
Chompipe	24	18	32	74	3	0	5	8
	.34	.24	.42		.38	—	.62	
Villa Mills	18	8	23	49	1	0	2	3
	.37	.16	.47		.33	—	.67	
Chirripó	2	0	6	8	0	0	(1)	(1)
	.38	—	.62		—	—	(1.00)	
Santa Rosa	67	30	33	130	5	5	26	36
	.52	.23	.25		.14	.14	.72	

[1] Compare Figure 1.

[2] NP = nonpasserines; SO = suboscines; O = oscines.

Table 4. Occupancy of foliage categories by permanent and winter residents at 5 Costa Rican localities

Locality	Foliage categories				Total spp.
	FI	FC	FE	NF	
Permanent residents					
La Selva	77	94	166	79	235
Virgen del Socorro	66	94	150	55	202
Muñeco	42	63	106	43	132
Chompipe	25	49	61	20	74
Villa Mills	18	34	44	15	49
Totals	228	334	527	212	—
Winter residents					
La Selva	6	11	23	7	32
Virgen del Socorro	4	8	19	12	24
Muñeco	0	7	13	7	13
Chompipe	0	4	8	4	8
Villa Mills	0	2	3	2	3
Totals	10	32	66	32	—

Table 5. A comparison of habitat distributions of permanent and winter residents in tropical wet and dry forest

Locality	Number of species in:				Total number of species
	Forest interior	Forest canopy	Forest edge	Non-forest	
Permanent residents					
a). La Selva	77	94	166	79	235
b). Santa Rosa	31	62	119	66	130
Winter residents					
c). La Selva	6	11	23	7	32
d). Santa Rosa	10	14	28	14	36

Chi-square tests: a vs. b = 7.95, p < .05; c vs. d = 6.94, p < .1; a vs. c = 1.24, p > .5; b vs. d = 1.01, p > .5

migrant species, while only slightly higher absolutely at Santa Rosa, makes up nearly twice the proportion of the total resident species here as at La Selva, a highly significant difference ($X^2 = 7.28$, p < .01).

Turning now to patterns of habitat occupation (table 4), it is immediately obvious that most species occur in more than one habitat type; in fact, the modal number of habitat types occupied per species was two for both permanent and winter residents. The forest edge is the habitat with the greatest number of species in both groups. Among permanent residents the habitat with the second highest number of bird species is forest canopy at all sites; forest interior and nonforest habitats have similar but lower numbers of species. Among winter residents, forest canopy and nonforest habitats have about equal numbers of species, the forest interior the fewest. Chi-square tests for heterogeneity reveal no significant intersite heterogeneity for either winter or permanent residents ($X^2 = 7.93$, 10 d.f.—combining the three high-altitude sites p > .5; and $X^2 = 9.51$, 18 d.f., p > .9, respectively). The totals for each group may then be compared, and are significantly different ($X^2 = 13.21$, 6d.f., p < .05). Thus, there are significantly fewer winter residents in forest interior and more in nonforest habitats, as compared with permanent residents, at all elevations.

Above about 1,500 m elevation, no winter residents occupy the forest interior at all. At low elevations, the dominant group (in terms of number of species) of forest interior permanent residents are the suboscines—antbirds, furnariids, and manakins. Higher up the oscines predominate: *Catharus* thrushes, *Basileuterus* warblers, various finches. These groups are probably collectively similar enough ecologically (and in the latter case, taxonomically) to the migrants that they lower resource availability to the latter.

The habitat distributions of permanent residents differ significantly between the lowland wet and dry sites (table 5), but there is no significant difference in habitat distributions of winter residents between these sites. In fact, the overall habitat distributions of permanent residents at Santa Rosa resembles that of winter residents in humid sites with similar numbers of species in nonforest and canopy habitats and few forest interior species. This probably reflects the fact that most of the Santa Rosa forest loses its leaves during the dry season; over large areas the forest interior ceases to exist as such.

Further insight into habitat distribution patterns can be gained by asking which habitats are most likely to have bird species in common. This can be determined by calculating Sorenson's (1948) index of similarity for each pair of habitats. For both permanent and winter residents, the index is highest between canopy and edge habitats (table 6). In fact, for both groups at every site, 70–95 percent of the birds occurring in the canopy regularly follow the foliage-air interface down along edges. The index is also high for forest edge and nonforest, indicating that many spe-

F. Gary Stiles

Table 6. Coefficients of similarity[1,2] in bird species composition of different pairs of habitats at 6 Costa Rican localities

Locality	Pairs of habitats					
	FI + FC[3]	FI + FE	FI + NF	FC + FE	FC + NF	FE + NF
La Selva	.15 (.00)	.36 (.41)	.05 (.15)	.55 (.59)	.14 (.22)	.45 (.73)
Virgen del Socorro	.25 (.00)	.39 (.35)	.02 (.12)	.62 (.59)	.12 (.00)	.41 (.58)
Muñeco	.27 (−)	.31 (−)	.02 (−)	.67 (.70)	.19 (.43)	.43 (.70)
Cerro Chompipe	.27 (−)	.42 (−)	.04 (−)	.67 (.67)	.17 (.50)	.42 (.33)
Villa Mills	.27 (−)	.52 (0)	.12 (−)	.79 (.80)	.29 (.50)	.44 (.80)
Santa Rosa	.15 (.17)	.36 (.53)	.06 (.08)	.67 (.71)	.31 (.29)	.63 (.48)
Means, permanent residents	.24	.40	.05	.65	.17	.43
Means, winter resident	.10	.43	.12	.68	.31	.60

[1] Coefficient of Sorenson (1948) which runs from 0 = No species in common, to 1 = all species shared between habitats.

[2] First figure is coefficient for permanent residents, second for winter residents; − means no species occur in one of the habitats being compared

[3] FI = forest interior; FC = forest canopy; FE = forest edge; NF = non-forest.

cies, especially among the winter residents, follow the FAI up from ground level along edges as well. An appreciable proportion of species occur at the FAI all the way from ground level to the canopy in both groups. Forest interior also shared an appreciable proportion of species with forest edge in both groups, but virtually none with nonforest habitats among either winter or permanent residents (table 6).

There is a general tendency for an increase in ecological amplitude, in terms of the mean number of habitats occupied, with increasing altitude among both permanent and winter residents (table 7). The exception is Virgen del Socorro, where the mean number of habitats per species is lowest in both groups. The reasons for this shift are unknown, but it is significant that both groups show it. In all cases, the mean for winter residents tends to be slightly higher than that for permanent residents, although in no case is the difference statistically significant. Even this difference largely disappears if only the oscines are considered among the permanent residents (since the vast majority of the migrants themselves are oscines). Santa Rosa is somewhat exceptional in that here the mean number of habitats occupied by the permanent residents is slightly higher than that for the winter residents. However, the oscines in this group again approach more closely the mean for the winter residents. Thus on this basis winter and permanent residents are virtually indistinguishable in terms of their patterns of habitat occupancy. It is therefore interesting that fall migrants show no pattern of increasing habitat amplitude with increasing altitude (table 7). Fall migrants

Table 7. Mean numbers of habitat categories (out of 4) regularly occupied by species of permanent and winter residents at 6 Costa Rican localities

Locality	Mean number of sites occupied by species of:			
	Permanent oscines	Residents all species	Winter residents	Fall migrants
La Selva	1.89	1.86	1.91	2.40
Virgen del Socorro	1.80	1.78	1.88	2.03
Muñeco	1.99	1.91	2.08	2.41
Cerro Chompipe	2.08	1.96	2.13	2.40
Villa Mills	2.30	2.20	2.33	2.44
Santa Rosa	2.06	2.11	2.00	2.31

have relatively broad "habitat niches" at all altitudes; the difference from winter residents is significant at low elevations but not at high elevations, due to the increase in the means for the latter. Often the same species occurs in more habitats in fall migration than it does as a winter resident.

Another aspect of a species' habitat niche is the altitudinal range over which it occurs. As a measure of this, I take the number of sites at which a species occurs regularly, out of the 10 sites in figure 1. For this analysis I consider only passerine species, which are broken down according to habitat and taxonomic

Table 8. Mean numbers of sites along an altitudinal series of 10 sites from 0 to 3,500 m elevation on the Caribbean slope of Costa Rica where landbirds are present

Habitat(s) occupied	Number of species	Mean number of sites at which resident	Standard deviation: number of sites	Range in number of sites at which resident
Permanent resident suboscines				
Forest interior	46	2.89*	0.85	1–5
Forest canopy-edge	45	4.07	1.29	1–6
Nonforest-edge	23	3.83	1.23	2–6
Permanent resident oscines				
Forest interior	24	3.54	0.66	2–5
Forest canopy-edge	51	3.68	1.11	2–6
Nonforest-edge	42	4.10	1.55	1–7
Winter resident passerines				
Forest interior	5	4.20	1.79	2–6
Forest canopy-edge	17	4.06	1.78	1–7
Nonforest-edge	15	4.25	1.48	2–7
Fall migrant passerines (all habitats combined)	46	6.51*	2.12	2–9

* Significantly different from other means by t-test.

group. For simplicity I have eliminated the "forest edge" category, apportioning its species among the others because of the high degree of overlap: few species occur only at forest edge. This analysis is presented in table 8.

Among the resident suboscines, the mean number of localities inhabited by forest interior species is significantly lower (t-tests) than the means for canopy-edge or nonforest species. The former are mainly antbirds and furnariids, the latter largely tyrant flycatchers. Among resident oscines, forest interior species again have the narrowest altitudinal ranges. The rather low mean for the permanent resident canopy-edge oscines is influenced by the sizeable assemblage of small tanagers that occur only within a narrow altitudinal belt. There is no significant difference between any of the means among the habitat groups of permanent or winter resident oscines. Fall migrants, as a group, occur over a significantly wider altitudinal range than either group of residents. Again, a number of species occur over considerably wider altitudinal ranges as fall migrants than they do as winter residents. The only group of resident birds to show a significant difference in mean numbers of sites inhabited from any other groups is the forest-interior suboscines. This is also the group having the least in common taxonomically with the other groups.

Discussion

The major single point brought home by these data is the high degree of concordance in the broad aspects of their ecological distributions, between North American migrants on their wintering grounds and the year-round tropical "endemics"—especially when taxonomic relationships are taken into account. This strongly suggests that winter and permanent residents are subject to the same broad ecological and distributional constraints, and at this level it hardly seems justified to consider the two groups as distinct ecological entities.

There may be more overall divergence between permanent and winter residents at the level of food habits and foraging tactics. However, several papers in this symposium have pointed out a number of pitfalls in evaluating such differences, and we are still far from any clear-cut generalizations. Part of the problem lies in the fact that many migrant species change their diets between breeding and winter ranges, and we still need to know a great deal more about seasonal diet changes and movements among the tropical residents. Nevertheless, some average differences may exist between the two groups. For instance, the winter resident nonforest oscines are rather heavily weighted towards small insectivores (or omnivores), whereas permanent resident oscines in this habitat are largely graminivores or frugivores. In fact, Slud (1960) and others have suggested that migrants tend to complement the permanent residents ecologically, often fitting into niches seemingly unoccupied by the latter. My own observations are in full agreement—the forest canopy often seems much emptier in July!—and I think that this points to a rather different conclusion than that usually expressed. I would argue that the winter residents are in fact integral parts of the tropical communities in which they spend up to six to eight months of the year: they are in no sense an extraneous, foreign element superimposed upon a tropical bird community complete in and of itself. I think that the nearly perfect inverse correlation between numbers of migrant and permanent resident species in a large number of neotropical bird communities found by Slud (1976) is strong evidence that the "complete" bird communities at these sites comprise both groups. A corollary to this conclusion is that studies of tropical bird communities that pretend to describe the range of exploitation types or resource utilization strategies present, are incomplete and quite possibly biased unless winter residents are taken into account.

The contrary argument, that migrants are peripheral to tropical bird communities and/or competitively inferior to the "endemics", is supported by very little real evidence. The data of Willis (1966) are frequently cited in this connection, but he was dealing with a very special situation (migrants being subordinate to a group of highly specialized resident species at army-ant swarms; interference competition is well established among these residents, all of whom are larger than most migrants). For small foliage-gleaning insectivores, interspecific competition would probably be principally by exploitation (cf. Miller 1967); migrants could thus have a great influence on resident foraging guilds regardless of their social status. Regarding the peripheral or "marginal" position of migrants in tropical communities, the same adjective has been applied to a family of tropical passerines, the Coerebidae (Moynihan 1968), with about as little justification. Coerebids resemble many parulid warblers in various aspects of their ecology (habitats, nectarivory and omnivory, small size); like warblers, honeycreepers are regularly present in forest canopy but much more conspicuous along edges (Pearson, this volume).

Viewing the winter residents as integral parts of tropical communities makes it much easier to explain the lack of habitat expansion by permanent residents as the former leave to breed. I would suggest that very little advantage, and quite possibly some distinct disadvantages, might accrue to the resident species showing such expansion. In Central America at least, the departure of the migrants coincides very approximately with the start of the rainy season, when resources for insectivores and small frugivores will increase greatly—probably without the necessity of expansion of their foraging repertoires. Moreover, the fall migration back to the tropics follows soon after the end of breeding by many resident species, which then will have many young birds about learning to forage for themselves. The bird biomass descending upon many Central American habitats (in some years) during the fall migration far exceeds that of the winter residents: most of this biomass is concentrated in a restricted range of exploitation types. Any young resident bird learning to forage in a similar manner to many migrants will suddenly be at a great numerical disadvantage in exploitation competition. Thus one might well expect selection against any tendency to "invade the migrant niche" in the permanent residents. The competitive effect of sheer numbers of fall migrants might more than make up for the absence of the winter residents for up to five to six months of the year. It is interesting to contrast this situation with that in waterbirds, where niche expansion or diversification of permanent residents may be checked by the presence of summering populations of migrants (table 1). Thus, there might be positive selection in migrant waterbird species for first-year birds to summer in the tropics, quite apart from their possibly reduced chances of successful breeding in the north.

One might ask why the migrants leave to breed if they are so well intergrated into tropical communities. I suggest that migration might better be considered as an adaptation of a basically tropical bird to increase breeding success, rather than an adaptation of a basically temperate-zone bird to escape the harsh northern winter.

Regardless of where one supposes the migrants "originated," only in the tropics can they exist year-round, whether or not they breed there. I would suggest that we have long confused two phenomena that may not necessarily be directly related: speciation and the geographic origins of the speciating group. Speciation, by definition, requires reproductive isolation: intrinsically it has nothing to do with ecological relations on the wintering grounds, except insofar as adaptations to different breeding areas might affect ecological compatibility on wintering grounds. Thus, contra Howell (1969) and many others, I would submit that the undoubted speciation of, say, the Parulidae with the advances and retreats of the Pleistocene glaciers (Mengel 1964; Hubbard 1969) is not a valid argument that this family is North American in origin. One could envision in a single wintering population breeding over a broad expanse in North America, in which differentiation and speciation might occur in the breeding range with little effect on the winter distribution, such that eventually several closely related, morphologically similar species might occur together in winter—which in fact occurs in Central America. The sympatry of several races of *Wilsonia pusilla* in winter may represent an early stage of such a process (Ramos, this volume).

The fundamental reason for migrating to begin with is to take advantage of the huge summer burst of productivity at higher latitudes, which could permit higher nesting success (Skutch 1966) and larger clutches (Lack 1947). Given that migrant members of a population would in fact contribute more young to succesive generations than sedentary individuals, in time the genetic constitution to migrate could become fixed. Unfortunately, we still have no way of evaluating the risks of migration, nor enough data on mortality patterns to compare quantitatively the sedentary and migrant strategies. However, it should not be thought that the two are entirely separate and distinct: among supposedly "sedentary" tropical birds all degrees of altitudinal and short-to-moderate distance migration are being encountered (Pearson and Feinsinger, this volume).

The distinction between migrants and "tropical endemics" that often appears large in our minds is in part a result of a rather stereotyped notion of what constitutes a tropical bird. So often one tends to think of toucans, cotingas, antbirds, tanagers, and the like, forgetting the greenlets, warblers, seedeaters, and flycatchers, that are every bit as characteristic of tropical habitats, at least in Central America. These residents are the most similar ecologically as well as taxonomically to the bulk of the "North American" migrants. Most are canopy-edge-nonforest birds, as opposed to forest interior; many are known to be highly mobile. Many second-growth species are adapted to moving regularly from one patch to another as the second-growth in each grows up: one can mist-net *Sporophila* seedeaters regularly inside forest, but not Bicolored Antbirds in pastures. Many tropical oscines–vireos, some tanagers, and gnatcatchers occur in apparently wide-ranging canopy flocks. As different species of trees flower, fruit, and flush leaves in a diverse tropical canopy, the birds of this stratum must move about rather widely. In Costa Rica, many of these species are known to undertake pronounced altitudinal migrations (Slud 1960; pers. obs.). Thus, many canopy-edge-nonforest species in the tropics might be considered as preadapted to becoming long-distance migrants. The

taxonomic affinities of the migrants suggest that it is precisely from this segment of tropical communities that many migrant taxa have been drawn.

Migration may well have originated in different ways in different groups. However, I feel that the data presented here regarding ecological distributions of small permanent and winter resident passerines indicate strong taxonomic and ecological affinities between the two groups. This in turn suggests evolutionary affinities.

Literature Cited

Hubbard, J. P.
1969. The relationships and evolution of the *Dendroica coronata* complex. Auk 86:393–432.

Lack, D. L.
1947. The significance of clutch-size. Ibis 89:302–52.

Mayr, E., and L. L. Short
1970. Species taxa of North American birds. Publ. Nuttall Ornithol. Club 9.

Mengel, R. M.
1964. The probable history of species formation in some northern wood warblers (Parulidae). Living Bird 2: 9–43.

Miller, R. S.
1967. Pattern and process in competition. Adv. Ecol. Research 7:1–74.

Moynihan, M. H.
1968. The "Coerebini": a group of marginal areas, habits, and habitats. Amer. Natur. 102:573–581.

Skutch, A. F.
1966. A breeding bird census and nesting success in Central America: Ibis 108:1–16.

Slud, P.
1960. The birds of Finca La Selva, a tropical wet forest locality. Bull. Amer. Mus. Nat. Hist.

1964. The birds of Costa Rica: distribution and ecology. Bull. Amer. Mus. Nat. Hist.

1976. Geographical and climatic relationships of avifaunas, with special references to avian distribution in the neotropics. Smithsonian Contrib. Zool.

Sorenson, T.
1948. A method for establishing groups of equal amplitude in plant society based on similarity of species content. K. Danske Vidensk. Selsk. 5:1–34.

Tosi, J. A., Jr.
1969. *Mapa ecológico de Costa Rica*. San José, Costa Rica: Tropical Science Center.

Willis, E. O.
1966. The role of migrant birds at swarms of army ants. Living Bird 5:187–231.

F. Gary Stiles

Appendix: Status and affinities of migrant landbirds in Costa Rica

Species	Resident population in Costa Rica:		Seasonal abundance in appropriate habitat in Costa Rica:[1, 2]			Presence as winter resident at the following Costa Rican sites:[2, 3]					
	Con-specific	Con-gener	Fall	Winter	Spring	LS	VS	MU	CH	VM	SR
Turkey Vulture, *Cathartes aura*	+	+	A	C	A	+	?	—	—	—	+
White-tailed Kite, *Elanus leucurus*[4]	+	—	(A)	(A)	(A)	(+)	—	—	—	—	—
Mississippi Kite, *Ictinia mississippiensis*	—	+[5]	U	—	R	—	—	—	—	—	—
Sharp-skinned Hawk, *Accipiter striatus*	—	+	U	U	U	—	+	+	+	—	—
Cooper's Hawk, *A. cooperi**	—	+	R	R	R	—	—	—	—	+	—
Red-tailed Hawk, *Buteo jamaicensis*	+	+	R	—	R	—	—	—	—	—	—
Swainson's Hawk, *B. swainsonii*	—	+	A	R	A	—	—	—	—	—	—
Broad-winged Hawk, *B. platypterus*	—	+	A	A	A	+	+	+	+	—	+
Short-tailed Hawk, *B. brachyurus*	+	+	R	?	R	—	(+)	—	—	—	—
Marsh Hawk, *Circus cyaneus*	—	—	U	R	U	—	—	—	—	—	—
American Kestrel, *Falco sparverius*	—	+	U	U	U	?	—	—	—	—	+
Peregrine, *F. peregrinus*	—	+	R	R	R	—	—	—	—	—	—
Merlin, *F. columbarius*	—	+	R	—	R	—	—	—	—	—	—
White-winged Dove, *Zenaida asiatica*	+	+	(A)	(A)	(A)	—	—	—	—	—	+?
Mourning Dove, *Z. macroura*	+	+	(C)	(C)	(C)	—	—	—	—	—	+
Black-billed Cuckoo, *Coccyzus erythrophthalmus*	—	+	U	—	R	—	—	—	—	—	—
Yellow-billed Cuckoo, *C. americanus*	—	+	U	?	R	—	—	—	—	—	—
Common Nighthawk, *Chordeiles minor*	+	+	A	—	C	—	—	—	—	—	—
Lesser Nighthawk, *C. acutipennis*	+	+	(C)	(U)	(C)	—	—	—	—	—	—
Whip-poor-will, *Caprimulgus vociferus*	—	+	R	R	?	—	—	—	—	—	—
Chuck-will's-widow, *C. carolinensis*	—	+	U	R	R	+	—	—	—	—	—
Black Swift, *Cypseloides niger*	+	+	R	—	R	—	—	—	—	—	—

Appendix: (cont.)

Species	Resident population in Costa Rica:		Seasonal abundance in appropriate habitat in Costa Rica:[1,2]			Presence as winter resident at the following Costa Rican sites:[2,3]					
	Con-specific	Con-gener	Fall	Winter	Spring	LS	VS	MU	CH	VM	SR
Chimney Swift, *Chaetura pelagica*	—	+	U	—	U	—	—	—	—	—	—
Ruby-throated Hummingbird, *Archilochus colubris*	—	—	A	A	C	—	—	—	—	—	+
Yellow-bellied Sapsucker, *Sphyrapicus varius*	—	—	R	R	?	—	—	—	—	—	—
Eastern Kingbird, *Tyrannus tyrannus*	—	+	A	—	A	—	—	—	—	—	—
Western Kingbird, *T. verticalis*	—	+	U	U	U	—	—	—	—	—	+
Grey Kingbird, *T. dominicensis**	—	+	X	—	—	—	—	—	—	—	—
Scissor-tailed Flycatcher, *Muscivora forficata*	—	+	C	A	C	—	—	—	—	—	+
Great-crested Flycatcher, *Myiarchus crinitus*	—	+	A	C	C	+	—	—	—	—	+
Ash-throated Flycatcher, *M. cinerascens*	—	+	—	—	—	—	—	—	—	—	—
Eastern Wood Pewee, *Contopus virens*	—	+	A	R	C	+	+	—	—	—	—
Western Wood Pewee, *C. sordidulus*	+	+	U	(R?)	U	—	—	—	—	—	—
Yellow-bellied Flycatcher, *Empidonax flaviventris*	—	+	A	C	C	+	+	?	—	—	+
Traill's Flycatcher, *E. traillii (incl. alnorum)*	—	+	A	C	A	+	?	—	—	—	+
Acadian Flycatcher, *E. virescens*	—	+	U	—	U	—	—	—	—	—	—
Least Flycatcher, *E. minimus*	—	+	R	—	R	—	—	—	—	—	—
Olive-sided Flycatcher, *Contopus borealis*	—	+	C	R	C	—	—	+	+	—	—
Purple Martin, *Progne subis**	—	+	C	?	A	—	—	—	—	—	—
Cliff Swallow, *Petrochelidon pyrrhonota*	—	—	A	U	A	—	—	—	—	—	+
Tree Swallow, *Tachycineta bicolor*	—	+	U	U	U	—	—	—	—	—	+
Violet-green Swallow, *T. thalassina*	—	+	R	?	R	—	—	—	—	—	—
Rough-winged Swallow, *Stelgidopteryx ruficollis*	+	+	C	C	C	+	+	—	—	—	+
Bank Swallow, *Riparia riparia*	—	—	C	—	C	—	—	—	—	—	—

Species	Resident population in Costa Rica:		Seasonal abundance in appropriate habitat in Costa Rica:[1,2]			Presence as winter resident at the following Costa Rican sites:[2,3]					
	Conspecific	Congener	Fall	Winter	Spring	LS	VS	MU	CH	VM	SR
Barn Swallow, *Hirundo rustica*	—	—	A	A	A	+	?	—	—	—	+
Grey Catbird, *Dumetella carolinensis*	—	—	U	U	U	+	—	—	—	—	+
Wood Thrush, *Hylocichla mustelina*	—	—	C	C	C	+	+	—	—	—	+
Swainson's Thrush, *Catharus ustulatus*	—	+	A	R	A	—	—	—	—	—	+
Grey-cheeked Thrush, *C. minimus*	—	+	C	—	C	—	—	—	—	—	—
Veery, *C. fuscescens*	—	+	R	—	R	—	—	—	—	—	—
Cedar Waxwing, *Bombycilla cedrorum*	—	—	—	U	—	—	—	+	—	—	—
Red-eyed Vireo, *Vireo olivaceus*	—	+	A	R?	A	—	—	—	—	—	—
Solitary Vireo, *V. solitarius*	—	+	—	X	—	—	—	—	—	—	—
Yellow-throated Vireo, *V. flavifrons*	—	+	C	C	C	+	+	?	—	—	+
Philadelphia Vireo, *V. philadelphicus*	—	+	A	A	A	+	+	—	—	—	+
Warbling Vireo, *V. gilvus*	—	+	—		X	—	—	—	—	—	—
Black-and-white Warbler, *Mniotilta varia*	—	—	C	U	U	+	+	+	—	—	+
Prothonotary Warbler, *Protonotaria citrea*	—	—	C	C	U	—	—	—	—	—	+
Worm-eating Warbler, *Helmitheros vermivorus*	—	—	U	U	R	—	+	—	?	—	+
Golden-winged Warbler, *Vermivora chrysoptera*	—	+	C	C	C	+	+	+	+	—	—
Blue-winged Warbler, *V. pinus*	—	+	R	R	R	+	—	—	—	—	—
Tennessee Warbler, *V. peregrina*	—	+	A	A	A	+	+	—	—	—	+
Northern Parula, *Parula americana*	—	+	X	X	X	—	—	—	—	—	—
Yellow Warbler, *Dendroica petechia*	+	+	A	A	A	+	+	?	—	—	+
Magnolia Warbler, *D. magnolia*	—	+	U	U	U	+	+		—	—	—
Cape May Warbler, *D. tigrina*	—	+	R	R	R	—	—	—	?	—	—

Species	Resident population in Costa Rica:		Seasonal abundance in appropriate habitat in Costa Rica:[1,2]			Presence as winter resident at the following Costa Rican sites:[2,3]					
	Con-specific	Con-gener	Fall	Winter	Spring	LS	VS	MU	CH	VM	SR
Black-throated Blue Warbler, *D. caerulescens**	—	+		X		—	—	—	—	—	—
Black-throated Green Warbler, *D. virens*	—	+	C	C	C	—	+	+	+	+	—
Townsend's Warbler, *D. townsendii*	—	+	U	U	R	—	—	—	—	—	—
Hermit Warbler, *D. occidentalis*	—	+	—	X		—	—	—	—	—	—
Yellow-rumped Warbler, *D. coronata*	—	+	C	U	U	?	—	—	—	—	—
Cerulean Warbler, *D. cerulea*	—	+	A	—	C	—	—	—	—	—	—
Blackburnian Warbler, *D. fusca*	—	+	A	C	C	?	+	+	+	—	—
Blackpoll Warbler, *D. striata**	—	+	—	X	—	—	—	—	—	—	—
Yellow-throated Warbler, *D. dominica*	—	+	R	R	?	—	—	—	—	—	—
Chestnut-sided Warbler, *D. pensylvanica*	—	+	A	A	A	+	+	+?	—	—	+
Bay-breasted Warbler, *D. castanea*	—	+	C	I	U	+	—	—	—	—	?
Pine Warbler, *D. pinus**	—	+	X	—	—	—	—	—	—	—	—
Prairie Warbler, *D. discolor*	—	+	X	—	—	—	—	—	—	—	—
Palm Warbler, D. palmarum*	—	+	X	—	X	—	—	—	—	—	—
Northern Ovenbird, *Seiurus aurocapillus*	—	—	A	A	A	+	?	—	—	—	+
Northern Waterthrush, *S. noveboracensis*	—	—	A	A	A	+	+	—	—	—	+
Louisiana Waterthrush, *S. motacilla*	—	—	C	U	U	+	+	+	+	—	—
Kentucky Warbler, *Oporornis formosus*	—	—	C	C	C	+	+	—	—	—	+
Mourning Warbler, *O. philadelphia*	—	—	C	C	C	+	+	—	—	—	+
MacGillivray's Warbler, *O. tolmiei*	—	—	R	R	R	?	—	—	—	—	?
Northern Yellowthroat, *Geothlypis trichas*	—	+	U	R	U	—	—	—	—	—	—
Yellow-breasted Chat, *Icteria virens*	—	—	R	R	R	+	—	—	—	—	?
Wilson's Warbler, *Wilsonia pusilla*	—	—	A	A	A	?	+	+	+	+	—
Canada Warbler, *W. canadensis*	—	—	A	X	C	—	—	—	—	—	—
Hooded Warbler, *W. citrina*	—	—	R	R?	R	?	—	—	—	—	—
American Redstart, *Setophaga ruticilla*	—	—	C	U	U	?	—	—	—	—	+

Species	Resident population in Costa Rica:		Seasonal abundance in appropriate habitat in Costa Rica:[1,2]			Presence as winter resident at the following Costa Rican sites:[2,3]					
	Con-specific	Con-gener	Fall	Winter	Spring	LS	VS	MU	CH	VM	SR
Northern Oriole, *Icterus galbula*	—	+	A	C	A	+	+	—	—	—	+
Orchard Oriole, *I. spurius*	—	+	C	U	C	+?	—	—	—	—	+
Bobolink, *Dolichonyx oryzivorus*	—	—	X	?	?	—	—	—	—	—	—
Yellow-headed Blackbird, *Xanthocephalus xanthocephalus**	—	—		X	—	—	—	—	—	—	—
Scarlet Tanager, *Piranga olivacea*	—	+	U		C	—	—	—	—	—	—
Summer Tanager, *P. rubra*	—	+	C	C	U	+	+	+	—	—	+
Western Tanager, *P. ludoviciana*	—	+	C	C	C	—	—	—	—	—	+
Rose-breasted Grosbeak, *Pheucticus ludovicianus*	—	+	C	U	C	?	—	—	—	—	+
Blue Grosbeak, *Guiraca caerulea*	+	—	(C)	(U)	(C)	—	—	—	—	—	?
Indigo Bunting, *Passerina cyanea*	—	—	C	C	C	+	—	—	—	—	+
Painted Bunting, *P. ciris*	—	—	R	U?	R	—	—	—	—	—	—
Dickcissel, *Spiza americana*	—	—	A	?	U	—	—	—	—	—	—
Lincoln's Sparrow, *Melospiza lincolnii**	—	—	?	X	?	—	—	—	—	—	—
Chipping Sparrow, *Spizella passerina**	—	—	X	—	—	—	—	—	—	—	—
Total definite winter residents at localities:						32	24	13	8	3	36

* Publications documenting the occurrences of these species in Costa Rica are in press.

[1] A = abundant—many seen daily at appropriate season (in appropriate localities and habitats); C = common—1 or a few seen daily; U = uncommon—seen regularly in small numbers but usually not daily; R = rare—seen seldom, or irregularly; usually singly; X = fewer than 5 records.

[2] Values in parentheses—abundance figures may refer to both migrant and resident individuals, it being not always possible to distinguish them.

[3] +? = probably present; ? = doubtfully present.

[4] An abundant resident; increment due to migrants small at best.

[5] Plumbeous Kite, *I. plumbea*, is a breeding resident, not a permanent resident.

EUGENE S. MORTON
National Zoological Park
Smithsonian Institution
Washington, D. C. 20008

Adaptations to Seasonal Changes by Migrant Land Birds in the Panama Canal Zone

ABSTRACT Migrants that winter in the Panama Canal Zone experience about equal portions of the wet and dry seasons. At 14 study areas across the Canal Zone, changes in migrant numbers, diets, foraging behaviors, and social tolerances, were studied in relation to seasonal changes. Territorial insectivorous species initially chose the wetter habitats and microclimates such as on the ground in mature forest, mangrove swamps; being sedentary, they chose areas least affected by dry conditions. Foliage-gleaning species tended to move from young and mature forest exclusively into mature forest during the seasonal changeover in early January, then back to young as well as mature forest when fruit became available in March. Some foliage gleaners were territorial in young forest but socially tolerant in mixed species flocks in mature forest at the same time of year.

Stomach content data for Bay-breasted and Tennessee Warblers show that they eat smaller insects in the dry season relative to the wet season, even though most of their energy comes from fruit in the dry season. This is the opposite of what would be predicted from optimal foraging theory.

Food habits and social behavior of the 11 most common migrants in Panama are described. General and local effects of tropical wet and dry seasons are discussed in relation to migratory patterns.

437

Introduction

The Panama Canal Zone offers a natural experiment to augment naturalistic observations of the adaptive strategies used by North American migrants during their nonbreeding period. Migrants are present during the wet season, from their arrival to January, and the dry season, from January to May. They experience the most climatically divergent periods found in the tropics in roughly equal portions due to the Zone's 9° N. latitude. The 50-mile coast to coast width allows nearly simultaneous survey of population numbers, social behavior, and food and habitat usage by migrants.

The seasonal effects differ within the Canal Zone. The Pacific slope's dry season occurs earlier and lasts longer than the Atlantic slope's dry season (figure 1). Resident species (e.g. Clay-colored Robin, *Turdus grayi*; Yellow-green Vireo, *Vireo olivaceus flavoviridis*) may breed two months later on the Atlantic coast than the Pacific due to these seasonal differences. Migrants are "overwintering" during this time. Do they also show different regional reactions to these seasonal changes?

These reactions could take many forms of which four are obviously the most important: 1) possible numerical changes; 2) possible diet changes; 3) changes in foraging behavior, and 4) changes in social tolerance. Changes in these categories would be presumed to relate to wet/dry season differences, the natural variables provided by the Canal Zone. More generally, shifts in behavior and diet may indicate adaptation to the seasonal calendar specific to the Canal Zone.

Study Areas and Methods

Figure 2 shows the study areas, each assigned a number and listed under the current common name. These may change after most areas become formally part of the Republic of Panama. Areas 1–5, Pacific coastal locations, show the greatest dry season effects with forests composed of semi-deciduous trees. Hespenheide (this volume) refers to these as dry forest, but this is true only from January to May. Karr (1971) described my Areas 5 and 8.

The Pacific coastal forests are of two types based on edaphic factors. Upland forest contains tall emergent trees such as *Ficus insipida* and *Sterculia apetala*; lower trees form an uneven, broken canopy covered with vines but with few epiphytes. *Luehea* sp. and *Guazuma ulmifolia* are also good indicators of this habitat. Riverine forest is taller with more even canopy, abundant epiphytes, and contains the wild cashew, *Anacardium excelsum*. Riverine forest occurs along rivers and in moist valleys; its appearance changes much less with the seasons. Examples are found in Area 2, adjacent

to the Pan American Highway near the southwest Canal Zone boundary, and along the Ezra Herwitz Road near Palo Seco.

Approaching mid-Zone, near Madden Forest and the Pipeline Road (Areas 6 and 8, figure 2), second growth forest is dominated by *Didymopanax morototoni* and *Miconia argentea*, important bird fruit-producing trees. More mature forest appears structurally similar to riverine forest, described above. At about Area 10, and continuing toward the Atlantic coast, tree ferns and *Vismia* trees begin to enter the forest; they indicate wet forest with less seasonal change in leaf fall (Areas 10, 12–14, figure 2).

Each area was visited from two to six times in each season during three trips from 13 December 1973 to 12 January 1974, 2–16 March 1974, and 12–25 March 1975. Hearing and sight were used to locate and observe migrants. Forest canopy was searched carefully to avoid the bias against detecting small birds there. Noisy Lesser Greenlets (*Hylophilus minor*) in canopy attracted warblers and vireos, facilitating their detection.

Data were recorded on a Sony cassette-corder TC-66. Twenty-six species and 151 individuals were collected for stomach content analysis.

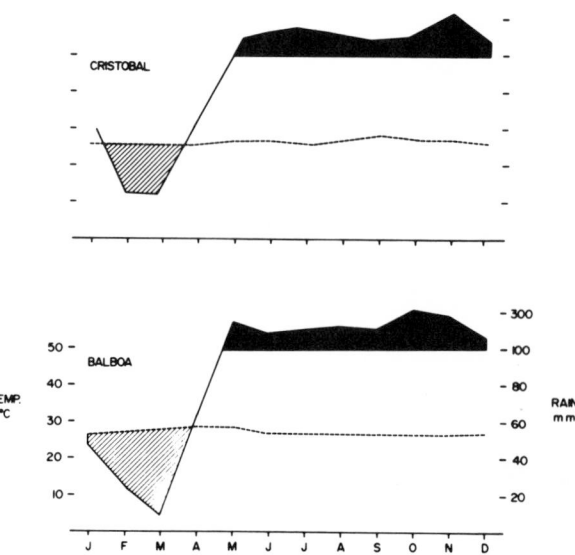

Figure 1.   Climate diagrams contrasting the drier Pacific slope (Balboa) with the Atlantic slope (Cristobal). Months are indicated on the horizontal axis; temperature and rainfall (10-year monthly averages, Anon. 1966) on the left and right vertical axes, respectively. The dashed line represents temperature; the solid line, rainfall. Temperature and rainfall axes are aligned such that a drought period (oblique lines) occurs whenever the rainfall curve drops below the temperature curve, monthly rainfall in excess of 100 mm (solid area) occurs as runoff, indicating extreme wet conditions (after Mueller-Dombois 1969).

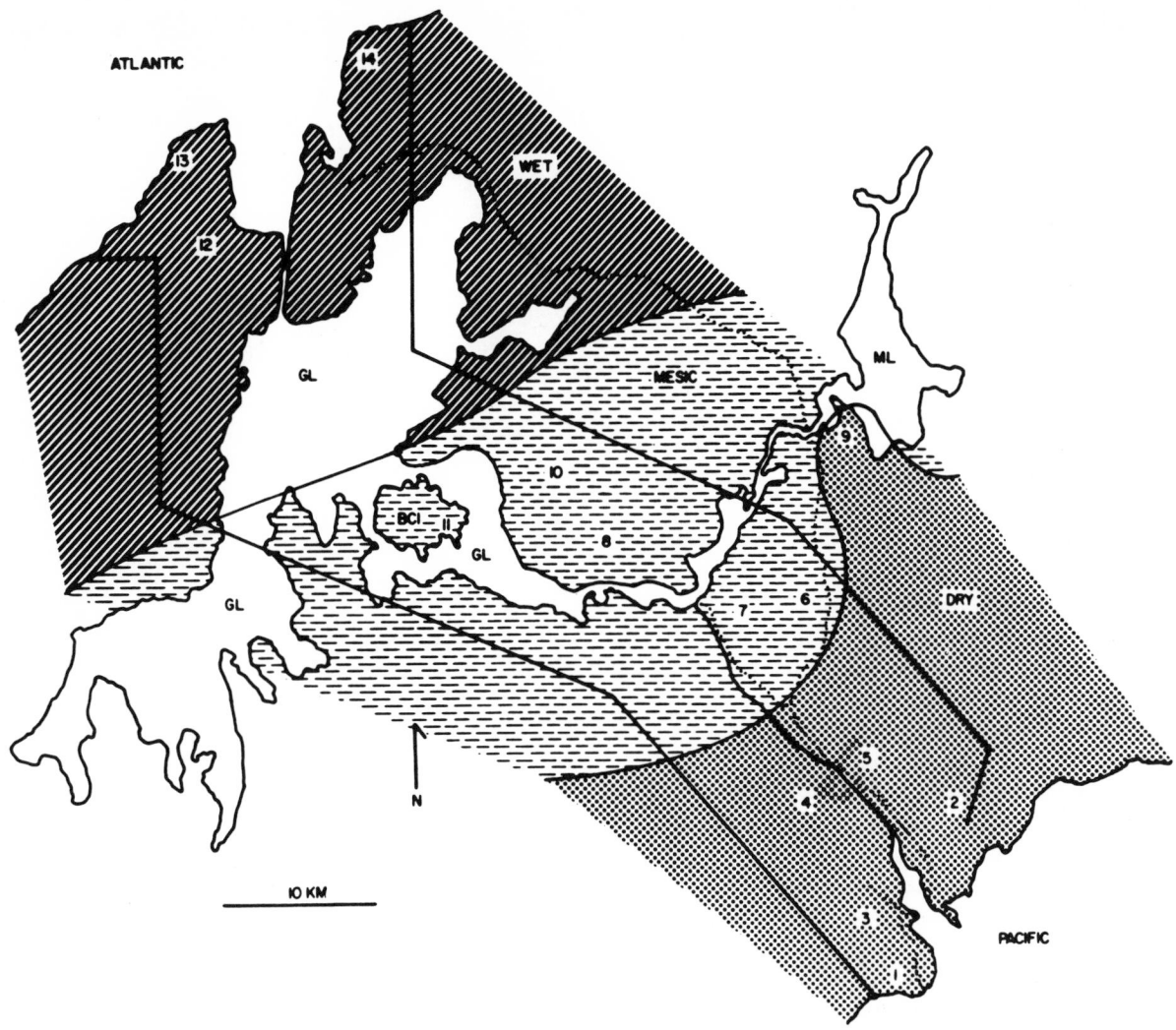

Figure 2. Map of the Canal Zone area showing study sites (numbers) and general edaphic characteristics of the Pacific and Atlantic slopes. Names of study areas are as follows: 1) Fort Kobbe, Far Fan Beach; 2) Curundu riverine and dry forest; 3) K-6 Road area, dry and riverine forest and edge; 4) Contractor's Hill and Empire Range area; 5) Chiva Chiva Road; 6) Madden Forest Preserve; 7) Summit Gardens, GH 12 Road; 8) Pipeline Road, first half; 9) Madden Lake Boy Scout Camp and watershed; 10) Pipeline Road last half; 11) Barro Colorado Island; 12) Achiote Road areas; 13) Fort Sherman, and 14) Galeta Island, mangroves and wet forest.

Species Present and Their Relative Abundance

Table 1 lists migrant land birds that remain in the Canal Zone during the December to March period, when migrating has presumably stopped. Some listed were "stragglers" to the Zone, outside their core wintering range and in small numbers (e.g. E. Wood Pewee, *Contopus virens*; Rose-breasted Grosbeak, *Pheucticus ludovicianus*; Gray Catbird, *Dumetella carolinensis*; Ovenbird, *Seiurus aurocapillus*; Blue-winged Warbler, *Vermivora pinus* and Magnolia Warbler, *Dendroica magnolia*). The remaining species are regularly present although some are rare. The Worm-eating Warbler,

Helmitheros vermivora, was not seen but is known to occur on the Atlantic slope. The 11 species noted with an asterisk (table 1) constitute 99 percent of the migrant land bird biomass, excluding the unstudied Turkey Vulture, *Cathartes aura*.

The Canal Zone is definitely part of the core nonbreeding range for the 11 species, but the distinction of "winter ranges" for other migrants is hazy. The Swainson's Thrush, *Hylocichla ustulata*, is abundant in Panama during the wet season but leaves for South America in early December (Morton 1972). Only one individual was seen by me during this study period. The Eastern Kingbird, *Tyrannus tyrannus*, bypasses Pan-

Table 1. Distribution and relative abundance of migrant land birds at 14 sites[1] in the Canal Zone (Dec–Mar)

Species	1	2	3	4	5	6
Broad-winged Hawk,* *Buteo platypterus*	1/0[2]	2/1	3/1	4/3	1/1	—
Black-billed Cuckoo, *Coccyzus erythropthalamus*	1/0	—	—	—	—	—
Eastern Kingbird, *Tyrannus tyrannus*	—	—	—	—	0/5	—
Crested Flycatcher,* *Myiarchus crinitus*	+/+	1/1	+/+	+/1	1/1	1/+
Eastern Wood Pewee, *Contopus virens*	—	—	1/0	—	—	—
Acadian Flycatcher,* *Empidonax virescens*	0/1	+/+	+/+	1/1	1/0	++/++
Barn Swallow, *Hirundo rustica*	—	—	—	—	—	—
Gray Catbird, *Dumetella carolinensis*	1/1	—	—	—	—	—
Swainson's Thrush, *Hylocichla ustulata*	1/0	—	—	—	—	—
Wood Thrush, *Hylocichla mustelina*	2/0	1/0	—	—	—	—
Cedar Waxwing, *Bombycilla cedrorum*	—	—	—	—	—	—
Yellow-throated Vireo, *Vireo flavifrons*	1/++	1/1	1/1	1/1	—	+/+
Philadelphia Vireo, *Vireo philadelphicus*	2/0	—	2/1	—	—	—
Black-and-white Warbler, *Mniotilta varia*	—	—	—	—	—	—
American Redstart, *Setophaga ruticilla*	—	—	—	—	—	—
Yellow Warbler, *Dendroica petechia*	++/++	+/+	+/+	+/+	++/++	—
Bay-breasted Warbler,* *Dendroica castanea*	1/0	+/1	++/+	+/+	++/+++	+++/++
Chestnut-sided Warbler,* *Dendroica pensylvanica*	—	1/0	+/1	1/0	1/+	++/++
Magnolia Warbler, *Dendroica magnolia*	1/0	—	2/2	—	0/1	—
Yellow-rumped Warbler, *Dendroica coronata*	0/1	—	—	—	—	—
Cerulean Warbler, *Dendroica cerulea*	—	—	—	—	—	—
Tennessee Warbler,* *Vermivora peregrina*	+++/+	+++/+	+++/+	+/+	+/+	+/+
Blue-winged Warbler, *Vermivora pinus*	—	—	—	—	—	—
Golden-winged Warbler, *Vermivora chrysoptera*	—	—	—	1/0	—	—
Kentucky Warbler,* *Oporornis formosus*	1/1	+/+	+/+	+/+	+/+	++/++
Mourning Warbler, *Oporornis philadelphia*	—	—	—	+/+	+/+	—
Northern Waterthrush,* *Seiurus noveboracensis*	++/++	+/+	+/+	+/+	+/+	+/+
Louisiana Waterthrush, *Seiurus motacilla*	—	—	—	—	—	1/0
Ovenbird, *Seiurus aurocapillus*	—	—	—	—	—	—
Orchard Oriole,* *Icterus spurius*	1/0	+/+	—	+/+++[4]	—	—
Northern Oriole,* *Icterus galbula*	+/++	+/+	+/++	++/++	+/++	—
Summer Tanager,* *Piranga rubra*	+/+	+/+	+/+	+/+	+/+	+/+
Rose-breasted Grosbeak, *Pheucticus ludovicianus*	—	—	—	—	—	—
Total species/site	17/11	14/12	15/14	15/13	12/13	10/9
Index to migrant abundance[3]	58/44	45/27	56/38	41/50	38/55	53/47
Change in index to abundance (wet minus dry season)	−14	−18	−18	+9[4]	+17	−6

* Most abundant winter residents.

[1] Sites are pictured in figure 2. a — means no birds were seen at these sites.

[2] Numbers = exact number seen; + = 2–5; ++ = 5–10; +++ = 10+; wet season to left of slash, dry season to right.

[3] Index calculated by totaling wet/dry season columns for each site with + = 3; ++ = 8; +++ = 15, with numbers added in.

[4] Index increase at this site due to flowers of *Erythrina fusca* trees attracting Orchard Orioles.

Eugene S. Morton

7	8	9	10	11	12	13	14
1/1	2/3	3/1	2/3	0/1	3/2	1/2	—
—	—	—	—	—	—	—	—
—	0/10	—	—	—	2/0	—	—
++/++	++/++	+/++	++/++	+/1	++/++	++/++	+/1
—	—	1/0	—	—	—	—	—
+/+	+++/+++	++/++	+++/+++	++/++	+++/+++	+++/+++	1/1
—	0/+++	—	—	—	—	—	—
—	—	—	—	—	—	—	—
—	—	—	—	—	—	—	—
—	1/0	—	—	0/1	—	—	—
—	0/++	—	—	—	—	—	—
+/+	++/++	+/+	++/++	1/0	+/+	+/+	1/0
—	—	—	—	—	—	0/1	—
—	—	—	—	1/0	1/1	1/1	1/1
—	—	—	—	—	—	—	1/0
—	1/1	—	—	—	—	—	++/++
++/++	++/+++	+++/++	+/+++	++/++	++/++	++/++	++/++
+/++	++/++	++/++	++/++	+/+	++/+	+/+	+/+
—	1/0	1/0	—	—	—	—	—
—	—	—	—	—	—	—	—
—	0/1	—	—	—	0/2	—	—
+/+	+/+	+/++	+/+	+/+	+/+	+/+	+/+
—	—	1/1	—	—	—	—	—
—	—	1/1	—	—	—	—	1/1
+/+	+++/+++	+++/+++	+++/+++	+/+	++/++	+++/+++	+/+
1/0	—	—	—	—	+/+	+/+	+/+
+/+	+/+	+/+	+/+	+/+	+/+	+/+	++/++
—	—	—	0/1	—	—	—	—
—	—	—	—	—	—	1/0	—
—	0/1	—	—	—	—	—	0/+
—	+/+	++/++	1/+	—	+/+	—	—
+/+	+/+	+/+	+/+	+/+	+/+	+/+	+/+
—	—	1/0	—	—	—	—	—
11/10	14/17	16/13	11/12	10/10	14/14	13/12	14/13
34/38	80/118	77/75	69/85	36/34	71/62	67/68	47/46
+4	+38	−2	+16	−2	−9	+1	−1

ama in the wet season but is abundant in dry season when fruit, its preferred food, is abundant (Morton 1971). It is unrealistic to draw a sharp distinction between these "extended transients" and those remaining in Panama for both groups use Panama extensively during their nonbreeding season.

Some species remaining in Panama may move within the country from one season to the next. Others are sedentary and hold nonbreeding territories. The small foliage-gleaning Bay-breasted Warbler, *Dendroica castanea*, Chestnut-sided Warbler, *D. pensylvanica*, Tennessee Warbler, *Vermivora peregrina*, Acadian Flycatcher, *Empidonax virescens*, and the terrestrial Northern Waterthrush, *Seiurus noveboracensis*, and Kentucky Warbler, *Oporornis formosus* are the most abundant Canal Zone species. The Broad-winged Hawk, *Buteo platypterus*, Summer Tanager, *Piranga rubra*, Great Crested Flycatcher, *Myiarchus crinitus*, Yellow-throated Vireo, *Vireo flavifrons*, are found at nearly all sites (figure 2) but in lower densities (table 1). The remaining common species are habitat restricted: Prothonotary Warbler, *Protonotaria citrea*, to riverine or mangrove forest; Yellow Warbler, *Dendroica petechia*, to mangroves, early shrub forest with scattered large trees such as *Enterolobium*, or suburban "gardens" and shrubbery; Golden-winged Warbler, *Vermivora chrysoptera*, and Black-and-white Warbler, *Mniotilta varia*, are restricted to mixed species flocks (one individual per flock); Mourning Warbler, *Oporornis philadelphia*, to dense tall grass bordering forest in damp places and to short brush along forest edge or in treefalls within forest on the Atlantic slope.

Distribution and Seasonal Changes

Marked changes in migrant density were observed in some areas but not in others (table 1). Generally, migrants withdrew from drier areas (figure 2) in late December of this study. There is also evidence that the commonest species occupied wetter habitats even before dry season effects on forest trees were apparent. On the Pacific slope, migrants concentrated in riverine forest relative to upland forest.

Bay-breasted Warblers showed both an initial wet season preference for mesic or wet areas and a decided concentration in wetter habitats in the early dry season. In addition, they shifted from using shrub habitats and forest to forest only. In early January they were relatively abundant in mature forest in Areas 6–14, nearly abandoning the drier and less mature habitats. They then shifted back to shrub and young forest habitats in March when fruit was ripening there. This will be discussed further under "Food Habits." Chestnut-sided Warblers, in contrast to their preference for shrub habitat for breeding in North America, pre-

ferred mature forest and late second growth in Panama. Most were in mature forest in areas 6–14 with few in riverine forest at Areas 3 and 5. Mesic and wet sites were preferred in both seasons. Tennessee Warblers likewise showed no seasonal changes in concentration; they occupied all areas with nectar sources. The orioles, *Icterus galbula* and *I. spurius*, preferred the drier Pacific slope where the earliest *Leuhea* flowering was followed by a succession of flowering trees. Summer Tanagers did not shift with the seasons and were widespread. Their diet of hymenopterous insects, particularly wasps and stingless bees, and fruit was probably little affected by seasonal changes. Great Crested Flycatchers preferred riverine forest on the Pacific slope but were common in all forests elsewhere.

Another group of species held nonbreeding territories during the total nonbreeding period. Northern Waterthrush defended areas in mangrove swamps on both coasts, forested streams and damp places, that changed little from wet to dry season. Kentucky Warbler territories were rare within Pacific coastal dry areas. (figure 2, 1–5) but abundant along the Pipeline Road and all moist forest areas with flat terrain. The same was true for Acadian Flycatcher territories. These territorial species chose habitats that remained less affected by dry conditions even though they arrived in Panama about 2.5 months before seasonal differences were apparent. In contrast, the Yellow Warbler defended territories in shrub and human altered landscape and mangrove swamp showing no initial preferences or shifts with the changing seasons.

Relatively few migrant species occurred in important numbers in suburban situations. Yellow Warbler, Northern and Orchard Orioles, and Summer Tanager were found. The orioles and a few Tennessee Warblers sought flowering trees and shrubs for nectar, the Summer Tanager sought fruit from exotic plants such as the Royal Palm (*Roystonea* sp.). Yellow Warblers favored hedges, shrubs, and trees in lawns. They utilize lawns as well where leafhoppers are abundant and seldom used by the larger *Myiozetetes* flycatchers that frequented the same lawns.

To summarize, insect-eating migrants prefer wetter, forested habitats; nectar and insect-eaters prefer drier areas. For territorial species, excepting the Yellow Warbler, seasonal changes constitute an important dimension of their niche as they occupy only the wettest, relatively aseasonal areas.

Foraging Behavior

There are basic motions held in common by birds feeding upon insects in foliage and the migrant and resident "foliage gleaners" used them similarly. Their goal is to survey as much leaf substrate per foraging

Eugene S. Morton

time as possible. They do this by hopping and by short flights to perches beyond hopping distance. The rate of hopping and flying is influenced by techniques used to obtain insects once the leaves are approached; the insect-locating behaviors are more important than gross foraging substrate within the foliage gleaning guild. Naturally, if the goal is to maintain a high rate of surveying unsearched foliage at close range, the distribution of that foliage in space is an important variable. *Hops* and *flights* were used only to gain access to leaves at branch tips. They were not used to approach leaves at a particular height or section of a tree nor was any species observed to prefer any particular area of a tree (contra what MacArthur 1958 showed for *Dendroica* warblers feeding in coniferous foliage in North America).

Foliage gleaners differed mainly in their way of inspecting leaves; a bird that closely scrutinizes leaf surfaces has a slower foraging rate than one moving quickly from one vantage point to another. I define the rate of foliage approach as the average number of *hops* plus *flights* per second (see table 2). *Peers* provide an index to the thoroughness of search, the higher the *peer* rate the more time spent searching foliage from a single position. *Peers* may be differentiated from more general visual searching by the motions accompanying them: the neck is stretched forward or more rarely upward, the bird appears to stretch out. *Peers* may also mean that lower leaf surfaces are inspected since they were often followed by pecks directed upwards. Among the warblers, Bay-breasted, Tennessee, and Prothonotary used *peers* more than Chestnut-sided, Yellow, and Magnolia (table 2) and had lower rates of *hops* and *flights*. This negative correlation is highly significant (r = −.8255, p < .001). Great Crested Flycatchers had the highest *peer* rate and the lowest foliage approach rate. They locate prey up to 10 m distant by visual search and do not use foliage approach behaviors for insect hunting.

Chase down occurs when prey drop from the foliage near a searching bird; the bird "flutters" quickly down after it, chasing from .5 to 10 m even to the ground. From the insect's standpoint, dropping works well for escape if there is more foliage immediately below to obscure it from the bird's view. The high use of *chase down* by foliage-gleaning birds is correlated with a preference to forage in foliage with open space below it. *Chase downs* are used frequently by all foliage gleaners with rictal bristles; *Vermivora* warblers seldom use it. Lack and Lack (1972) evidently refer to *chase down* as "flying."

Hovers are used less often than *chase downs* except for the Magnolia Warbler. The wings are used to permit access to leaf surfaces inaccessible from a perch, but it is difficult to tell if *hovers* are used to search leaves or to reach an insect already seen. *Hovers* do often precede *chase downs*.

Flycatching is seldomly used; the birds appear to concentrate on foliage to the exclusion of the surrounding airspace.

Foliage-gleaning birds, both migrant and resident, share a repertoire of prey capturing techniques. The relative frequency of their use depends on: 1) structure of substrate (openness, size of leaf, light intensity, distribution of leaves and twigs); 2) availability and use of non-insect energy sources such as nectar and fruit; 3) prey item specialization and factors related to search "thoroughness"; 4) social factors; 5) morphological differences between species, and 6) individual foraging experience, short- and long-term. Chipley and Keast (this volume) report spatial separation in winter ranges among the *Dendroica* warblers. The *Dendroica* warblers that occur together in the Canal Zone provide a contrast, a view of foraging differences that may foster co-occurrence, even though they share the same foraging behavior repertoire. The Yellow Warbler is separated from the others by habitat. The Chestnut-sided and Bay-breasted exist literally side by side but differ in the relative use of the shared repertoire. The former is a rapid forager specializing in dislodging or frightening prey: it shakes leaves. The Chestnut-sided's tail-elevated posture is indicative of this, exposing the bright white underside which may also help frighten insects (could ultraviolet reflection be involved?). The Magnolia also uses this foraging technique; it keeps the tail elevated but also opens and closes it, flashing a white patch. The Magnolia may be rare in Panama because this foliage-gleaning mode is usurped by Chestnut-sideds. The Bay-breasted Warbler is a thorough forager, defined as having more *peers* and less *hop* + *flight* moves per time. This difference probably did not evolve due to past interactions between Bay-breasted and Chestnut-sided Warblers. Their occurrence together in the Canal Zone is likely a result of competition among the *like*-foraging *Dendroicas*. It may be largely chance that the species Chestnut-sided Warbler and Bay-breasted Warbler extensively co-occur but not chance that a fast moving, tail-elevated, extensive forager is with a slower, thorough, forager.

The importance of leaf and twig distribution to foraging speed is clearly shown when ground foraging rate is compared with arboreal foraging rate in the Bay-breasted Warbler. Ten to 20 Bay-breasted and Tennessee Warblers were hopping on a gently sloping hill in sparse, short grass from which midges (Chironomidae) were picked. Since the next "perch" was not fixed by twig structure, for they were on the ground,

Table 2. Insect-foraging behaviors in some North American migrants in the Canal Zone (Dec–Mar)[1]

Species	N	Hops	Flights	Hops and flights
		Foliage approach		
Bay breasted Warbler, *Dendroica castanea*	39	.268 ± 0.1235	.062 ± .0760	.3156 ± .1291
Chestnut-sided Warbler, *D. pensylvanica*	26	.374 ± .1104	.0730 ± .0422	.4541 ± .1159
Yellow Warbler, *D. petechia*	15	.4235 ± .1985	.062 ± .0330	.4929 ± .1844
Magnolia Warbler, *D. magnolia*	4	.4631 ± .2498	.0560 ± .0534	.5188 ± .2594
Tennessee Warbler, *Vermivora peregrina*[2]	13	.2587 ± .1945	.0399 ± .0287	.3008 ± .1776
Prothonotary Warbler, *Protonotaria citrea*	8	.2477 ± .2178	.0453 ± .0278	.3263 ± .2321
Great Crested Flycatcher, *Myiarchus crinitus*	4	0	.0076 ± .0059	— —
Lesser Greenlet, *Hylophilus minor*[3]	3	.4071 ± .1918	.2557 ± .5057	— —

[1] See text for a description of foraging behaviors.

[2] Nectar feeding Tennessee Warblers are excluded from these data.

[3] A resident species most often joined by migrant Parulidae.

[4] All data are means per second ± one Standard Deviation.

the *hop* rate was .7327 ± .1296 per second (N = 3, 96 sec. of obs.), 2.3 times the *hop* + *flight* rate they use when foraging arboreally. In addition to the 2 species mentioned, 1 Northern Waterthrush and 3 Prothonotary Warblers plus 3 resident species, Royal Flycatcher (*Onychorhynchus coronatus*), Social Flycatcher (*Myiozetetes similis*), and Tropical Mockingbird (*Mimus gilvus*) were feeding on the ground. The midge abundance was caused by a septic field seepage located below the Police Lodge on the Chiva Chiva Road (Area 5, figure 2). No normally arboreal leaf-gleaning resident species were attracted to this unusual situation although several species were in nearby forest.

Other migrants, not described in table 2, are either not foliage gleaners or forage on or near the ground. Black-and-white warbler (*Mniotilta varia*), nearly restricted to the wet Atlantic coast forest and mangroves, forages by hopping along horizontal branches 2–8 cm in diameter. It was not observed using tree trunks as reported by Lack and Lack (1972). In foraging, it peers at the underside of the branches much like the resident Plain Tanager (*Tangara inornata*). Golden-winged and Blue-winged Warblers (*Vermivora chrysoptera* and *V. pinus*) forage by probing into dead, usually small (2–5 cm), tightly curled, leaves still clinging to their parent branch. Some resident species habitually use dead leaves as well (Checker-throated Antwren, *Myrmotherula fulviventris*; Rufous-breasted Wren, *Thry-*

othorus rutilis). The *Vermivora* warblers, possibly because they lack rictal bristles, are probers in dead leaves or, in the Tennessee, into flowers for nectar. Fledged Blue-winged Warbler young begin probing dead leaves before reaching independence and migrating. Families persist longer than in most warblers, perhaps due to the need for the young to acquire this leaf probing habit by example from adults (pers., obs.). They would be at a disadvantage if this behavior were not learned before reaching the tropics for Blue-winged and Golden-winged Warblers are socially intolerant there. The three migrant species considered here are what Willis (1972) called "intensive" foragers. They rely on mixed species flock members for predator warnings which in turn allows them to forage intensively, in this case to stick their heads inside dead leaves or look under branches. They occur alone, apparently treating a mixed species flock as a "territory" and excluding conspecifics. Lack and Lack (1972) note this same dead leaf probing in Worm-eating Warblers on Jamaica.

Prothonotary Warblers include dead leaf probing in their diverse foraging behaviors. Individuals may be found in mixed-species flocks, alone, in pairs, or monospecific flocks of 6–25 individuals. They probe bark, live and dead leaves, peer at branch undersides like Black-and-white Warblers, and even take nectar.

Insect foraging rates did not differ significantly

Hovers	Chase Downs	Flycatches	Peers	Pecks	Secs. of observ.
.0064 ± .0102	.0118 ± .0277	.0003	.0356 ± .0315	.0265 ± .0466	3448.1
.0067 ± .0146	.0116 ± .0177	.0022 ± .008	.0255 ± .0281	.0193 ± .0288	1900.0
.0058 ± .0113	.0124 ± .0187	.0005 ± .0018	.0273 ± .0226	.0214 ± .0210	1331.0
.0141 ± .0164	.0200 ± .0141	0	.0206 ± .0305	.0066 ± .0133	225.0
.0007 ± .0024	.0015 ± .0055	0	.0615 ± .0343	.0590 ± .0709	878.5
.004 ± .0113	.0094 ± .0088	0	.0585 ± .0843	.0482 ± .0458	676.5
.0065 ± .0030	.0076 ± .0152	0	.1528 ± .0770	0	1035.6
0	.02 .0346	0	.0633 ± .1097	No data	98

between seasons in any migrant species. However, some did take different sized insects, as described below.

Food Habits

Data from stomachs will be presented first followed by observations on foods taken.

Table 3 shows the stomach content data from 101 individuals collected while foraging. The proportions of fruit and insects in each stomach were estimated from freshly collected birds; insect lengths were taken from pickled material. The analysis was unbiased ("blind") since each stomach was identified only by a number. Insect lengths were determined to the nearest .1 mm using a microscope with a micrometer.

The three most abundant forest foliage gleaning warblers showed significant changes between the seasons. Tennessee Warblers and Bay-breasted Warblers ate significantly larger insects in the wet season. The Chestnut-sided Warbler took the same sized insects in both seasons but joined the former species in consuming more fruit in the dry season.

For Parulids in table 3, excluding the Kentucky and Golden-winged, body weight is positively correlated with the size of insect eaten in the wet season ($r = .8424$; $p < .01$) but there is no correlation in the dry season. Kentucky Warblers eat smaller insects than would be predicted from body weight and Golden-winged Warblers eat larger insects.

The warbler species that forage intensively by *peering*, contrasted with those foraging rapidly (table 2), show another correlation. *Peer* rate (table 2) regressed against the average number of larvae found per stomach (table 3) showed a significant positive correlation ($r = .8124$; $p < .05$). Apparently the "peerers," such as Tennessee, Bay-breasted, and Prothonotary Warblers, are detecting larvae more readily than the rapid foragers. Although some larvae may escape by dropping and be detected by rapidly foraging birds, intuitively it is reasonable that cryptic larvae would be found more readily through slow, intensive, foraging.

Field observations on Great Flycatchers would indicate larger prey than found in the few stomachs collected. Their "sit and wait" hunting strategy coupled with a 10-m insect detection range would select relatively large insects because these are more visible at greater distances. The "insect eggs" reported by Wilson (1976) from the stomachs collected by me do not show that Great Crested Flycatchers eat small objects; these eggs are katydid (Orthoptera) eggs, probably left over from ingestion of an adult.

The taking of smaller prey by Bay-breasted and Tennessee Warblers in the dry season seems to go against the ideas of optimal foraging theory which predicts that minimal food size accepted varies directly with energy availability (Wilson 1976). Both eat large quantities of fruit, chiefly *Didymopanax morototoni*, *Miconia argentea*, and arils of *Tetracera* sp and *Xylopia* sp, and others not identified. These species are obtaining a large portion of their energy from easily obtainable fruit and should therefore be choosing larger insects, according to theory. Other species, eating less fruit, take the same sized insects in both seasons showing that there is not a different insect size range to chose from. An alternative explanation to optimal foraging theory might include nutritional aspects. The fruit eating warblers are obtaining most of their energy

Table 3. Comparison of stomach contents in wet and dry season and taxonomic distribution of food items ($\bar{X}$ per stomach)[3]

Species						Wet season					
	$\bar{X}$ Length [1]	Range	N	Col	Dip	Hym	Hom	Hem	"Larvae"	Spiders	Misc.
Tennessee Warbler, *Vermivora peregrina*	3.16 ± .8948	1.0–8.4 mm	18	3.9	0.6	1.4	.06	0.1	2.1	0.9	27%[3]
Bay-breasted Warbler, *Dendroica castanea*	4.46 ± 1.0903	1.7–10.9	17	4.6	6.1	7.8	0.2	0.4	0.4	0.2	1.0
Chestnut-sided Warbler, *D. pensylvanica*	4.04 ± .7249	1.5–8.3	11	5.2	0.7	5.5	2.5	0.3	1.5	0.8	0.5
Yellow Warbler, *D. petechia*	4.09 ± 3.1495	1.3–8.8	4	3.8	0	8.8	0	0.3	0	0	0.3
Magnolia Warbler, *D. magnolia*	2.6 ± .5944	0.5–4.5	4	5.5	0.3	2.3	0	0.5	0.3	0	0.5
Golden-winged Warbler, *V. chrysoptera*	—	—	—	—	—	—	No data[5]	—	—	—	—
Prothonotary Warbler *Protonotaria citrea*	4.87 ± 1.5629	1.4–13.8	6	1.2	0	0.5	0.3	0	2.7	0.5	0.5 (3 Isopods; 1 snail)
Kentucky Warbler, *Oporornis formosus*	3.08 ± 1.5731	1.9–8.0	3	7	0	27	4	0	1	0	4 snails
Great Crested Flycatcher, *Myiarchus crinitus*	9.5 ± 3.2789	4.8–17.0	4	3	0	7	3	1	0	0	3 17 mm Orthopterans

from fruit but little protein from it (Morton 1973). The bird's goal therefore is to supplement the energy with protein, most readily found in insects. Smaller insects are taken since they are more abundant. By taking these, the birds are able to return to fruiting trees rapidly thereby extracting energy efficiently with no nutritional deficiencies.

Seasonal changes are important in the timing of flowering in many plants whose nectar is used by migrants. Tennessee Warblers favor *Combretum fructicosum*, flowering from early December through at least until mid-January. Pacific coast *Combretum* begin flowering about three weeks before those on the Atlantic coast, with plants in between showing a gradient in flower opening. At Far Fan (Area 1) full flowering occurred by 14 December, but plants in Area 5 were not opening flowers. Area 8 had *Combretum* flowers first on 26 December. *Combretum* is a small bush or more commonly a vine covering the crown of a tree. The flower is yellow with the calyx forming an upright cup 6.5 mm tall and 4.5–5.0 mm in diameter. From 35 to 60 flowers are clustered longitudinally along a 3-mm diameter rachis that easily supports the weight of a Tennessee Warbler (9 g). The flower contains six to eight stamens, 6.5–7.5 mm long, tipped with reddish anthers and pollin. The significance of this unusual pollin color will be discussed in the next section. One typical vine covered 57.3 m^2, contained 9,000 flower clusters with an average of 41.8 flowers per cluster, about 37,688 flowers in total. Flowers contain an average of .0143 g of nectar by 1000 h; this single plant produced a minimum of 539 g of nectar per day during a flowering period of about 14 days. The abundance of Tennessee Warblers was locally centered near or at these vines and thus changed as the *Combretum* commenced flowering with the advance of the dry season from Pacific to Atlantic coasts.

In addition to *Combretum* Tennessee Warblers took nectar from *Inga* sp., *Luehea* sp., *Calycophyllum candidissimum* and *Trichospermum*, and favored *Enterolobium* and *Pseudobombax* nectar in March. They also used extrafloral nectar from *Erythrina fusca*.

Orchard and Northern Orioles used nectar from many species, acting as pollinators in some but as nectar thieves in other species (*Tabebuia* especially) (Morton, *in press*).

Acadian Flycatchers were one of the few so-called insectivores that did indeed not eat anything but

Eugene S. Morton

Fruit² % vol.	X̄ Length	Range	N	Col	Dip	Hym	Hom	Hem	"Larvae"	Spiders	Misc.	Fruit % Vol.	P⁴
0	1.55 ± .7647	.8–3.9	3	3.0	0	1.7	0.3	0.3	1.3	1.7	1.0	71.2	<.05
2.4	3.45 ± .9969	.9–6.8	15	3.1	0	3.1	0.3	0.3	0.5	0.1	1.3	70.7	<.005
0	4.24 ± 1.2105	.9–9.1	8	3.3	0.1	11.4	0.3	0.4	0.1	0	0.9	28.8	<.4
0	3.55 ± .5972	1.2–9.6	4	6.0	0.3	3.8	0	0	1.5	0	0.3	0	N.S.⁶
0	—	—	—	—	—	—	No data⁵ —	—	—	—	—	—	—
—	6.4 ± 3.606	3.2–14.0	2	1.0	0	1.5	0	0.5	2.0	1.0	0	0	—
10	4.7 ± .6364	2.8–5.9	2	0	0	0.5	0.5	3.0	12.0	1.0	0	10	N.S.⁶
0	—	—	—	—	—	—	No data —	—	—	—	—	—	—
46.2	—	—	—	—	—	—	No data —	—	—	—	—	—	—

[1] X̄ = mean length of insects and spiders; larvae excluded.

[2] Mean % volume estimated from fresh stomachs.

[3] For Tennessee Warbler only, % volume of nectar and floral parts.

[4] P = probability that insect lengths were the same for dry and wet seasons.

[5] No food data for this species in this season shown by —.

[6] Not significant by inspection of means.

insects. This territorial species occurred in moist forest sites where it gleaned insects from leaves from .1–5 m above ground. It took insects, largely coleoptera and hymenoptera, averaging 5.78 ± 1.2933 mm in length. It never joined mixed species flocks.

Social Tolerance

Social tolerance refers to the level of aggressiveness members of one species show toward one another. High levels of aggression may result in complete exclusion of conspecifics from an area for long periods (territoriality) or temporarily from a food source such as nectar. High interspecific tolerance, exhibited when an individual joins a mixed species flock, may or may not be associated with high intraspecific tolerance. Black-and-white and Golden-winged Warblers join others but exclude conspecifics from "their" mixed species flock.

Table 4 categorizes the Canal Zone species as to social tolerance. The territorial species share some attributes. Those obligatorily territorial species tend to occupy niches that change the least from one season to another: ground or low in moist forest. Mourning Warblers and the two waterthrush also defend less abundant habitat as mentioned above. All obligatorially territorial species keep the same plumage coloration for both breeding and nonbreeding seasons. Most are sexually monomorphic. Territories are defended against all conspecifics regardless of their sex. Territorial defense now, as during the breeding season, is primarily through vocalizations. The Yellow-throated Vireo often sings, the others rely on loud species-distinctive call notes.

Tennessee Warblers have the most labile social tolerance of any migrant, equalled perhaps by the Orchard Oriole. While nectar feeding on *Combretum* they exhibit low social tolerance. Whether true territories are involved is unknown since individuals were not marked for identification. However, individuals did exclude others from *Combretum* flowers, defending areas about 1.2 × 1.2 m² by chasing intruders and through incessant loud chipping. The face and throat of successful *Combretum* defenders are soon colored reddish by the plant's pollin. This distinguishing mark stays

Table 4. Categories of social tolerance in migrants

Territorial species

Great Crested Flycatcher, *Myiarchus crinitus*[1]
Acadian Flycatcher, *Empidonax virescens*[1]
Wood Thrush, *Hylocichla mustelina*[1]
Northern Waterthrush, *Seiurus noveboracensis*[1]
Louisiana Waterthrush, *S. motacilla*[1]
Mourning Warbler, *Oporornis philadelphia*[1]
Kentucky Warbler, *O. formosus*[1]
Tennessee Warbler, *Vermivora peregrina*
Yellow Warbler, *Dendroica petechia*
Bay-breasted Warbler, *D. castanea*
Chestnut-sided Warbler, *D. pensylvanica*
Summer Tanager, *Piranga rubra*[1]
Orchard Oriole, *Icterus spurius*

JOIN MIXED SPECIES FLOCKS

Intraspecifically intolerant
Yellow-throated vireo, *Vireo flavifrons*
Black-and-white Warbler, *Mniotilta varia*
Golden-winged Warbler, *Vermivora chrysoptera*
Blue-winged Warbler, *V. pinus*

Intraspecifically tolerant
Philadelphia Vireo, *Vireo philadelphicus*
Prothonotary Warbler, *Protonotaria citrea*
Tennessee Warbler, *Vermivora peregrina*
Yellow Warbler, *Dendroica petechia*[2]
Bay-breasted Warbler, *D. castanea*
Chestnut-sided Warbler, *D. pensylvanica*
Magnolia Warbler, *D. magnolia*

FORM INTRASPECIFIC FLOCKS

Eastern Kingbird, *Tyrannus tyrannus*
Swainson's Thrush, *Hylocichla ustulata*
Prothonotary Warbler, *Protonotaria citrea*
Tennessee Warbler, *Vermivora peregrina*
Northern Oriole, *Icterus galbula*
Orchard Oriole, *I. spurius*

[1] Indicates obligate territorial species.

[2] Only juvenile Yellow Warblers of the northernmost races (see Morton 1976).

with the birds after they leave *Combretum*, perhaps for several days. It seems likely that by giving the otherwise dull-plumaged Tennessee Warbler this obvious mark of successful aggression, "war painted" warblers more easily gain access to new *Combretum* vines. This would facilitate outcrossing for the plant and thereby explain the significance of its red pollin. Only about 20 percent of Tennessee Warblers are so "war painted"

indicating successful aggressive defense by a small proportion of Tennessee Warblers. At the same time, other Tennessees are highly gregarious intra- and interspecifically. *Chips* are rarely given by these birds while foliage gleaning. Instead, soft *zeep* sounds are heard, a universally "friendly" intent is expressed. The foliage-gleaning warblers are intensive foragers, specializing in probing living leaves for larvae (see table 3). Thus their high social tolerance while foraging for insects may be related to predator avoidance (Willis 1972). Their dull coloration might facilitate the joining of mixed species flocks (Hamilton and Barth 1962; Moynihan 1962).

Bay-breasted and Chestnut-sided Warblers likewise show large variation in social tolerance. Here there is no obvious concentration of food for these insect eaters that might drive them toward territoriality. However, there was a clear relationship between their territorial behavior and habitat structure. Transect censuses on 18 December in young forest bordering the more mature forest in the Madden Preserve showed individual Bay-breasted and Chestnut-sided Warblers defending territories. The former species occurred at the rate of four birds per 100 m of transect; the latter was less common, about two birds per 100 m. The two species tolerated each other and seemed to be found close together rather than randomly distributed. This association was evident everywhere the two species were found together. The young forest here consisted of trees averaging 5–6 m in height, many covered with vines, with occasionally taller trees to 12 m. The two species were present still on 23 and 27 December but were gone from the young forest transect on 7 January. By this time the young forest was drying out and a general movement into mature forest was apparent.

Territorial behavior was identified by the reaction of the two species to playbacks of their respective sounds and natural encounters with intruding conspecifics. Reactions consisted of loud *chipping* bouts and occasional chasing. It is significant that the Bay-breasted Warbler's *chips* are entirely different from those of the Chestnut-sided Warbler's dry *chup* but not from other *Dendroicas*, such as the Yellow Warbler, which do not cohabit territories in this young forest. Apart from aggressive interactions with conspecifics, the birds here foraged actively but did not range extensively.

The relation between this forest structure and territorial behavior was remarkable. Only a few hundred meters away, in mature forest within Madden Forest Preserve, Bay-breasted and Chestnut-sided Warblers were observed only in mixed species flocks; no aggressive behavior was observed among either species. Up to 15 Bay-breasts and 5 Chestnut-sides accompanied

Eugene S. Morton

flocks ranging from near ground level up into the 30 m canopy. The species they joined in the mature forest were also present in the young forest, but no mixed species flocks formed in the young forest.

The relationship between social tolerance in these two warbler species and forest structure is likely related to food availability. Until early January the young forest contained continuous canopy with open space just below it. In mature forest the understory trees are relatively widely separated and canopy layers are uneven and thick. The structure of young forest is particularly conducive to successful *chase downs* in the capture of dislodged prey. Optimum foraging substrate is thus more densely packed in young forest than in mature; smaller, *defendible*, areas occur whereas in mature forest the birds must cover larger distances, too large to defend, to obtain foraging substrate volume equal to that of young forest. The greater light intensity within young forest may also contribute to higher food availability there.

Low social tolerance leading to aggressive exclusion of conspecifics results from a bird's ability to assess food availability. Nectar, obvious to the human observer as the source of low social tolerance in Tennessee Warblers, is the same as optimum foraging substrate for foliage gleaners. Both result in low social tolerance since resources are packed in defensibly small areas.

Observations on Bay-breasted Warblers supports this model. Territorial behavior, aggressive chasing and chipping, occurred among three Bay-breasts in rather poor habitat: scattered large trees with a mowed lawn understory. One of the Bay-breasts flew to a *Combretum* vine and sipped nectar briefly in company with Tennessee Warblers. It then flew back to one of the isolated trees, began chipping, and chased another Bay-breast away. I suspect this aggressive behavior is related to the unusual nectar feeding: this bird's assessment of resource defensibility and availability was upset by the nectar's energy such that its social tolerance was lowered. It was, in a sense "programmed" to respond this way toward conspecifics even though it did not defend the *Combretum* nectar, nor was it in a rich foliage gleaning area.

Social tolerance in Bay-breasted, Chestnut-sided, and Tennessee Warblers rose as they made increasing use of fruit during the dry season (table 3). No territorial behavior was seen. Flocks of these species occurred in young forest, late shrub, and mature forest, wherever fruit was abundant. Molt began in early March and by mid-March Bay-breasts were covered with pinfeathers (Morton 1972). Eastern Kingbirds returned from South America in great numbers at this time (Morton 1971). No attempt at defending fruit crops was seen. One striking social phenomonon was

the restricted use all species made of fruiting trees. Several *Miconia argentea* trees, equally full of fruit, would be heavily utilized while adjacent *miconia* trees would be ignored. This is undoubtedly an anti-predator behavior; it is safer to join others when the food resource is undefended and super-abundant.

Prothonotary Warblers were consistently inter- and intra-specifically socially tolerant. Intraspecific flocks of 5–28 were seen, primarily at Area 1 (figure 2). This species is unique among the Parulids in two respects. They were unique among all migrant species in that pair bonds were evident. All single birds seen (N = 23) were males, either foraging alone or in mixed species flocks. Females were either in the larger foraging groups of Prothonotaries or were foraging with a male close by but otherwise alone (N = 8). The second unique feature is that Prothonotaries roost communally, even staging in the same tree each night at dusk before flying en masse to the final roost when it is too dark to follow them visually. In this respect they are more like Orchard Orioles or other gregariously roosting icterids than warblers. All other species of warblers roosted alone; often they aggressively chased others as though good roosting sites were rare (Fretwell, this volume). Roosting occurred while strong light still prevailed, another indication that roost sites might be rare since foraging was ended long before light conditions might make it unprofitable.

Mixed Species Flocks and Interactions with Resident Species

Resident species commonly joined by migrant foliage gleaners are listed in table 5. Insect-eating species (without an asterisk) are far more commonly joined by migrants than fruit- and nectar-eating residents, except in the dry season. Then even the most commonly joined species, the Lesser Greenlet (also called Gray-headed) takes some fruit. Most migrants join residents foraging in the canopy rather than the understory.

The Lesser Greenlet, a passive nuclear species, was the focus of most mixed species flocks containing migrants (see table 4 for flock-joining migrant species). The White-shouldered Tanager and the tyrannulet species, Forest Elaenia, and Yellow-margined Flycatcher, and gnatcatcher were ubiquitous. Southern Bentbills occur alone most often and occupy habitat and elevations above ground similar to the Acadian Flycatcher. Both glean leaves, but the Bentbill's bill is specialized for gleaning by vertical flights to leaf undersides. Except for the greenlets and antwrens, all other species are represented by pairs or single birds in these flocks of insect gleaning birds.

The migrant foliage gleaners follow resident species

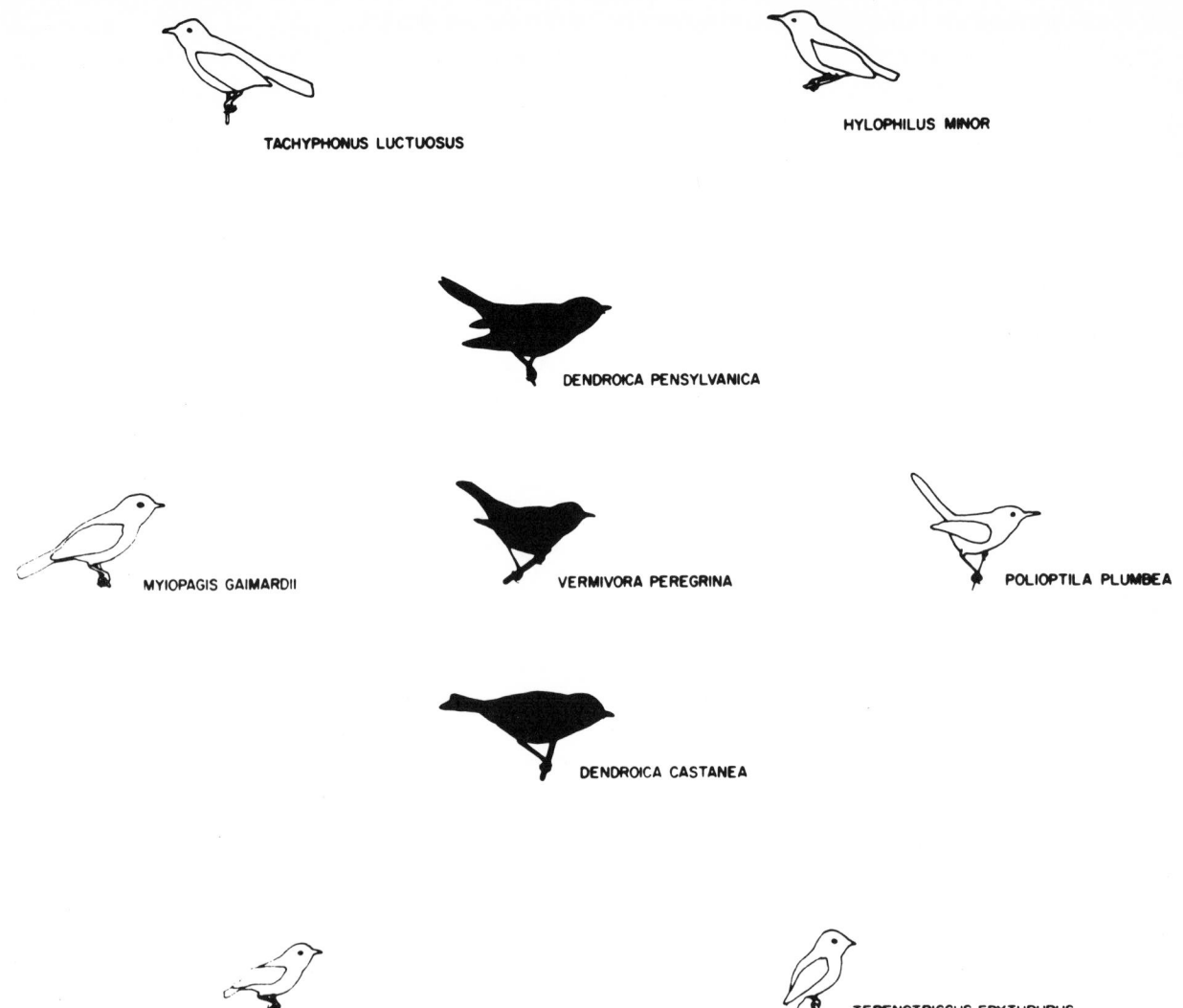

Figure 3. Three common migrants to Panama (solid figures) with a sample of the most common resident species they joined in mixed species flocks. They join residents most similar to themselves in foraging behavior, habitat preference, and foods taken.

most similar to themselves in weight, foraging methods, and foods taken (see figure 3). They are also most common where these residents are the most common, a phenomenon also reported by Waide (this volume) in Mexico.

Greenlets occur in small families (3 to 5 individuals) that defend territories year-round. They are very common, probably completely saturating all forest habitat, but their ranges are unknown. Like the Black-capped and Carolina Chickadees (*Parus atricapillus* and *P. carolinensis*), which are followed by fall migrating warblers in North America, the greenlet families are conspicuously noisy. More importantly, perhaps because they are in kin groups, they mob potential predators ac-

tively. During the period of this study, six greenlet mobbings of snakes were witnessed. Since it is of selective advantage for these kin groups to mob and to stay together during active foraging it seems likely that migrants take advantage of this behavior. By following them they, and the other residents, usurp the benefits of predator warning that evolved in the kin groups.

The White-shouldered Tanager represents a convergence in size and behavior toward the common foliage gleaner traits. It is much smaller than its congeners, none of the others are arboreal leaf gleaners, and is instead similar in size and foraging behaviors to a *Dendroica* warbler.

Eugene S. Morton

Table 5. Resident species in mixed species flocks joined by North American migrants

Species	Habitat [1]	Weight (grams)
Plain Xenops, *Xenops minutus*	FU	12.0
Checker-throated Antwren, *Myrmotherula fulviventris*	FU	10.4
White-flanked Antwren, *M. axillaris*	FU	8.5
Dot-winged Antwren, *Microrhopias quixensis*	FU	11.0
Ruddy-tailed Flycatcher, *Terenotriccus erythrurus*	FU	7.4
Yellow-margined Flycatcher, *Tolmomyias assimilis*	FC	14.2
Southern Bentbill, *Oncostoma olivaceum*	FU	6.9
Yellow-green Tyrannulet, *Phylloscartes flavovirens*	FC	7.0
Forest Elaenia, *Myiopagis gaimardii*	FC	12.0
Southern Beardless Tyrannulet, *Camptostoma obsoletum*	FC, E	6.0
Paltry Tyrannulet, *Tyranniscus vilissimus*	FC, E	7.2
Brown-capped Tyrannulet, *Ornithion brunneicapillum*	FC, E	6.5
Tropical Gnatcatcher, *Polioptila plumbea*	FC	6.7
Lesser Greenlet, *Hylophilus minor*	FC	9.3
Shining Honeycreeper, *Cyanerpes lucidus*[2]	FC, E	12.2
Red-legged Honeycreeper, *C. cyaneus*[2]	FC, E	12.0
Green Honeycreeper, *Chlorophanes spiza*[2]	FC, E	13.0
Blue Dacnis, *Dacnis cayana*[2]	FC, E	10.0
Fulvous-vented Euphonia, *Euphonia fulvicrissa*[2]	FC, E	11.5
Golden-hooded Tanager, *Tangara larvata*[2]	FC, E	20.5
White-shouldered Tanager, *Tachyphonus luctuosus*	FC	13.0

[1] FC = forest canopy, E = forest edge, FU = forest understory

[3] Fruit-eating species, or nectar-eating, joined by migrants mainly in the dry season.

Unlike the migrants, which do change in abundance with changing seasonal resources, the resident foliage gleaners are constrained by their own social behavior to remain sedentary. As Powell has shown (this volume), residents are defending territories even as they join or are joined by other species in mixed species flocks. When Bay-breasted and Chestnut-sided Warblers left their territories in young forest (see above) the same numbers of greenlets and White-shouldered Tanagers remained.

Discussion

Responses to Seasonal Changes in Panama

The kind and extent of response to Panama's wet to dry season changes is related to the interaction of social behavior and food. Insect-eating obligatorily territorial species (table 4) are restricted to areas showing the least change: mangrove swamps, mesic and wet forest or riverine forest (figure 2), forest ground and understory levels. Dry season conditions restrict them to these microhabitats even before drying occurs. These species are ecologically conservative in that they use the same microhabitat in both breeding and non-breeding areas and feed only on insects in both places. The Mourning Warbler is an exception since it uses damp tall grass bordering forests in Panama and forest edge where breeding, perhaps because its southerly breeding congener, the Kentucky Warbler, has usurped the forest ground level areas in Panama.

Omnivorous territorial species (Great Crested Flycatcher, Summer Tanager) are more widely distributed and show less response to seasonal effects in their choice of territories. Omnivorous foliage gleaners (Tennessee, Bay-breasted, Chestnut-sided Warblers) show the greatest distribution and habitat changes in response to seasonal changes.

The responses to seasonal changes by migrant species are not different in any qualitative way from those shown by resident species. Territorial insectivorous residents *and* migrants are sedentary. Ridgely (1976) notes that many resident species are restricted to the wetter Atlantic slope or the drier Pacific slope, an indication that resident species respond to seasonal changes. Omnivorous residents such as the honeycreeper, dacnis, and *Tangara* tanagers, show seasonal movements within Panama in the same direction and seasonal timing as the omnivorous migrant species. Several omnivorous Panamanian breeding species leave for South America during the late wet season (Piratic Flycatcher, *Legatus luecophaius*; Yellow-green Vireo, *Vireo o. flavoviridis*; Lesser Elaenia, *Elaenia chiriquensis* (?)). However, unlike the North American migrants which leave the driest areas, these return first to the driest areas to take advantage of fruit for breeding (Morton 1977).

Responses to Seasonal Changes in Neotropica

The geographic distribution and timing of the tropical seasons plays an important role in the evolution of winter ranges and feeding habits of migrants. As the Intertropical Convergence Zone moves north and south following the sun's perpendicular rays to the earth's surface, wet and dry seasons are produced. During the fall migration, dry season conditions prevail to the south of and near the equator. This is likely the time of greatest small, bird-dispersed, fruit production there. Some of the most abundant species that breed in eastern North America, together with the Middle American intratropical migrants, go quickly to this area: Amazonian Ecuador, Peru, and Bolivia. These include the Eastern Kingbird, Red-eyed Vireo, and Scarlet Tanager (*Piranga olivacea*). These species exhibit high social tolerance, forming intraspecific flocks that may be an adaptation to overcome territorial residents attempting to defend fruit (Moore 1977). The Eastern Kingbird goes to the southern terminus of its winter range and then moves northward with the advance of the dry season and its fruit production. The range of its "favorite" fruit-producing tree (*Didymopanax morototoni*) and the timing of its fruit production may be closely tied to the kingbirds' migration, the tree specializing on the kingbird for dispersal of its fruit.

Other migrants to South America may time their migration so as to avoid the sometimes torrential and prolonged rains that accompany the passing of the Convergence Zone. Thus the Eastern Wood Pewee and Canada Warbler (*Wilsonia canadensis*) are abundant in Panama in October but leave just before the November heavy rains occur. It is possible that the rains exclude these species, and aerial insectivores, such as the swallows and swifts, from Panama; unlike other species, there are no lowland forest congeners to offer a competition argument to explain their absence from Panama as "wintering" species.

Territorial species select habitats with the least seasonal effects. Perhaps as a consequence of this and of territorial behavior itself, these species have the largest "wintering ranges." They also show greater effects of competition-induced allopatry with closely related congeners in their nonbreeding ranges. Blue-winged and Golden-winged Warblers, for example, occupy extensive ranges in Neotropica but are allopatric. They respond more to one another than to resident species. The same is true for Solitary (*Vireo solitarius*) and Yellow-throated Vireos.

One wonders about the seasonal calendar specific to Panama relative to competitive forces in restricting the range of the Bay-breasted and Chestnut-sided Warblers to Panama or to about 9° N. Surely they change food habits, social tolerance, and undergo molt coincident with the seasonal changes, but their dependence on or adaptation to this specific calendar needs study. Attention to individuals found outside their species' core wintering range would provide the needed comparative data.

Acknowledgments

The National Geographic Society sponsored the research reported here. In Panama, The Smithsonian Tropical Research Institute provided many facilities. I am particularly grateful to Dr. Neal G. Smith for generously providing office space and for lending me equipment and providing transportation. Robert Dressler of STRI also kindly identified plants for me. The study originated through a two-year residence in Panama sponsored by fellowships from the Smithsonian Institution. I would like to thank Dr. Eugene Eisenmann for enthusiastic field companionship and Frederick Wasserman for assistance.

Literature Cited

Hamilton, T. H., and R. H. Barth
1962. The biological significance of seasonal change in male plumage appearance in some New World migratory bird species. American Naturalist 96:129–44.

Karr, J.
1971. Structure of avian communities in selected Panama and Illinois habitats. Ecol. Monogr. 41:207–33.

1976. On the relative abundance of migrants from the North Temperate Zone in tropical habitats. Wils. Bulletin 88:433–58.

Lack, D., and P. Lack
1972. Wintering warblers in Jamaica. Living Bird 11:129–53.

Moore, F. R.
1977. Flocking behaviour and territorial competitors. Animal Behaviour 25:1063–65.

Eugene S. Morton

Morton, E. S.

1971. Food and migration habits of the Eastern Kingbird in Panama. Auk 88:925–26.

1972. North American birds in the tropics. Atlantic Naturalist 27:164–68.

1973. On the evolutionary advantages and disadvantages of fruit-eating in tropical birds. American Naturalist 107:8–22.

1976. The adaptive significance of dull coloration in Yellow Warblers. Condor 78:423.

1977. Intratropical migration in the Yellow-green Vireo and Piratic Flycatcher. Auk 94:97–106.

In press. Effective pollination of *Erythrina fusca* by the Orchard Oriole (*Icterus spurius*): coevolved behavioral manipulation? Annals Missouri Botanical Garden.

Moynihan, M.

1962. The organization and probable evolution of some mixed species flocks of neotropical birds. Smithsonian Misc. Coll. 143:1–140.

Ridgely, R. S.

1976. *A Guide to the Birds of Panama*. Princeton, N.J.: Princeton University Press. 394 pp.

Willis, E. O.

1972. The behavior of Spotted Antbirds. A.O.U. Ornith. Monogr. 10, 162 pp.

Wilson, D. S.

1976. Deducing the energy available in the environment: an application of optimal foraging theory. Biotropica 8:96–103.

Implications of Over-Wintering in the Tropics

ALLEN KEAST
Department of Biology
Queen's University
Kingston, Ontario,
Canada K7L 3N6

Migratory Parulidae: What Can Species Co-occurrence in the North Reveal About Ecological Plasticity and Wintering Patterns?

ABSTRACT

In contrast with resident species that occupy one habitat throughout their lives, migrants must adapt to distinct winter and summer habitats and a variety of different living conditions while on migration. The nearctic Parulidae, the largest single group of nearctic-breeding species wintering in Neotropica average three months on the breeding grounds, two to three months on migration, and six to seven months in the wintering grounds. Each, accordingly, must exercise a strong moulding influence. This, and a variety of other aspects of the biology demand a high degree of adaptiveness and ecological plasticity. These include capacity to associate with different sets of congeners on breeding and wintering grounds, ability to fit into the neotropical communities, live in close contact with other species as members of mixed species flocks on migration and, to a degree, adjust feeding zone according to circumstances.

It is argued that migrants, although they do show the full range of "species separation" devices have somewhat different life strategies compared to residents. They are opportunists and have many of the basic characteristics of the island-colonizing species described by Rickleffs and Cox (1972), and Diamond (1975). Their fitting into the neotropical ecosystem must be viewed in this light.

Introduction

Migratory birds, in the course of a year, have to adjust to contrasting physical climates and different sets of competitor species, occupy a wide range of habitats and, if warblers, spend part of the year as members of mixed species assemblages in close association with ecologically similar congeners. This suggests that there has been a high premium on adaptability in their evolution. How versatile are migratory birds? Is versatility the key to nearctic migrants being able to overwinter in areas already "saturated" with endemic neotropical species? What can studies on the breeding grounds, and during migration, reveal about this?

The present paper attempts to analyze adaptability and ecological versatility in migratory Parulids by looking at species interaction patterns on the breeding grounds and during migration. The family, because of its dozens of species and by contributing the largest number of migrants to Neotropica, is the logical group for such a study. Relevant facets investigated are: 1) proportion of the year spent in the three phases of breeding, migration, and wintering (which exercises the strongest moulding influence?); 2) use of space by the species on the breeding grounds, how much overlap, and separation, is there in habitat and feeding zone; 3) kinds of species combinations that form migrating assemblages, how and to what extent are factors operative that might serve to reduce "interspecific completion" and 4) how much seasonal and geographic variation is there (winter compared to summer, and on migration) in the basic ecology of species, e.g. habitat used, vertical zonal feeding?

Proportions of Time Spent by the Nearctic Parulidae in Breeding, Migrating, and Overwintering

Figure 1 shows, for 14 species of Ontario breeding warblers, the proportion of the year spent in the three phases of breeding, wintering, and migrating. The "time on breeding grounds" segment is that between the spring arrival and autumn departure of migrants at Prince Edward Point, Ontario, where banding studies are carried out by the Kingston (Ontario) Field Naturalists' Club from May to October. "Time on wintering grounds" has been taken as the time of arrival in, and departure from, Panama, this being chosen as the southern reference point both because: 1) the best comparative data are available from there; and 2) it is at, or toward, the southern end of the migration of most species. Since there is a wide individual spread in each case (figures 2 and 3), an arbitrary "average" date of passage has to be set for each species. Another potential problem is that some pop-

ulations of species travel beyond these areas and hence might be credited with spending more time on the breeding grounds and less on migration than is the case. Finally, many species leave the actual breeding territory some weeks before they migrate, wandering (with their young) in the immediate local area. This can, however, still be regarded as "time on the breeding grounds."

Indication of the time lag between time of movement through Prince Edward Point and arrival and departure from the most northern breeding range limits of far-north breeding species can be gained by comparing the Ontario data discussed here with the data of Jehl and Smith (1970) and Cooke et al (1975) for Hudson Bay. The Tennessee Warbler (*Vermivora peregrina*) arrives at Churchill "by mid-June" and "departs of late August." The Yellow Warbler (*Dendroica petechia*) arrives between 9 and 14 June, and leaves by mid-August. The Yellow-rumped or Myrtle Warbler (*D. coronata*) was first noted in two years on 6 and 10 June, but there is a record for May 28; the last recorded date is 23 August. The Blackpoll Warbler (*Dendroica striata*) has an average arrival date over four years of June 10 (but at La Perouse Bay the arrival dates in three years were 20 June, 7 July, and 24 June; it leaves Churchill "by the end of August" (Jehl and Smith, p. 66). The Northern Waterthrush (*Seiurus noveboracensis*) is present at Churchill from 28 May to 15 August.

These figures indicate that the Tennessee Warbler is in the Churchill area about 9 weeks, the Yellow Warbler, 7 weeks, and the Yellow-rumped and Blackpoll Warblers, and Northern Waterthrush, 10 weeks. They are shorter only by a week or two from the Prince Edward Point arrival dates.

Figure 1. Relative proportions of the year spent on breeding grounds, wintering grounds, and on migration, by 14 common Ontario-breeding parulids. Time on breeding grounds is calculated as differences between peak arrival times in the spring and peak departure times in the fall. The former is from 1977, the latter from 1971, and is adapted from data obtained by members of the Kingston Field Naturalists' Club at the Prince Edward Point banding station, southern Ontario. Time on wintering grounds is calculated as the difference between peak fall arrival and peak spring departure times from Panama (all species except for the Northern Waterthrush and Nashville Warbler) and is taken from published and observers' records (see text). The winter data on the Waterthrush are that of Schwartz (1964) from Caracas, Venezuela, and the Nashville Warbler data (Veracruz) is estimated. Horizontal lines show spread. The presentation is generalized. It shows, however, that many species spend 7 months of the year on the wintering grounds and, commonly, 3 months on migration.

Allen Keast

WINTERING   MIGRATION   NESTING   MIGRATION   WINTERING

Black-throated Green

Chestnut-sided

Yellow-rumped

Yellow

Blackburnian

Magnolia

Black-&-white

Tennessee

Nashville   VERACRUZ

Ovenbird

Northern Waterthrush   VENEZUELA

Wilson's

Canada

Redstart

JAN   FEB   MAR   APR   MAY   JUN   JULY   AUG   SEP   OCT   NOV   DEC

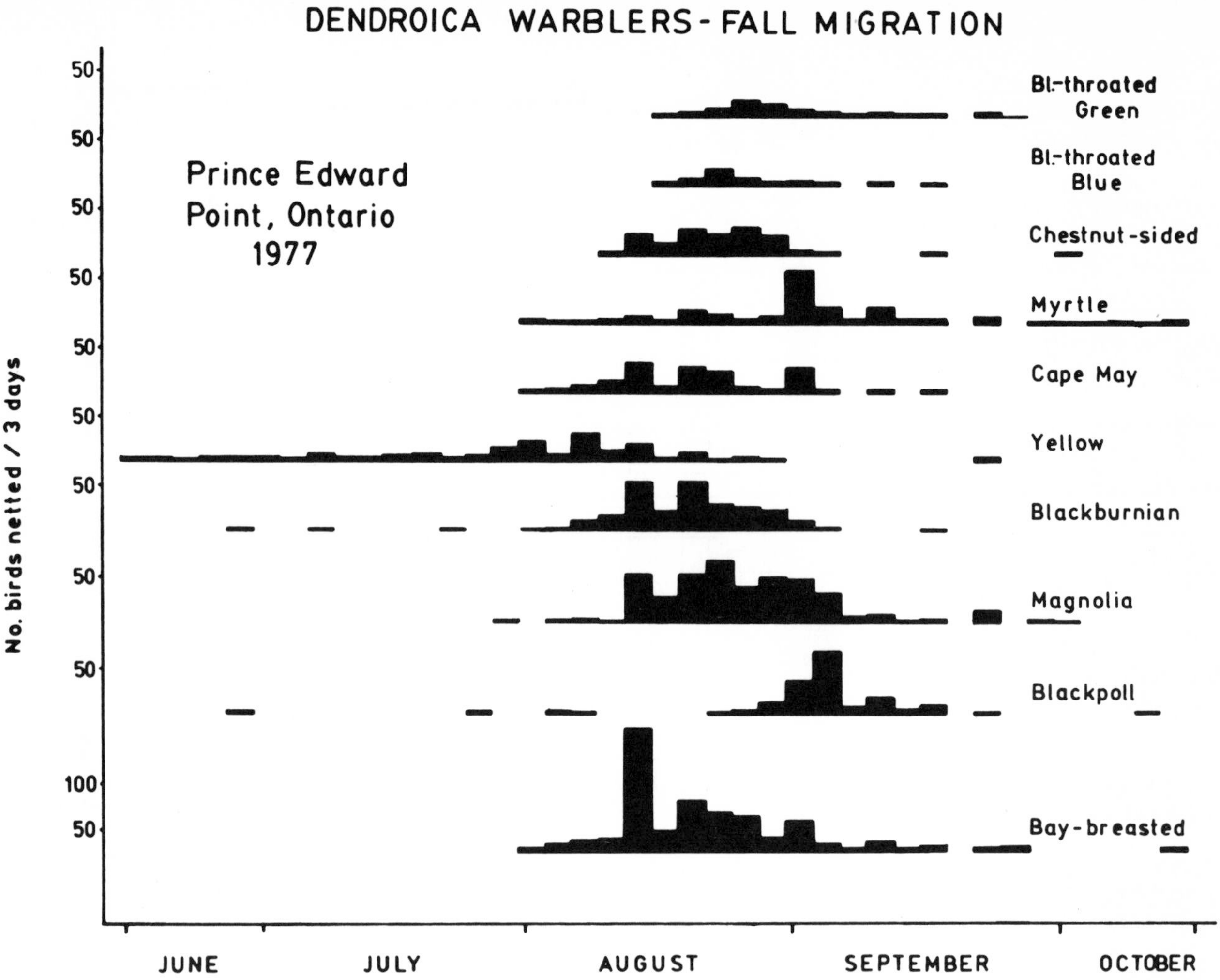

DENDROICA WARBLERS-FALL MIGRATION

No. birds netted / 3 days

Prince Edward
Point, Ontario
1977

Bl.-throated
Green

Bl.-throated
Blue

Chestnut-sided

Myrtle

Cape May

Yellow

Blackburnian

Magnolia

Blackpoll

Bay-breasted

JUNE   JULY   AUGUST   SEPTEMBER   OCTOBER

Figures 2a and 2b. Southward departure of migratory warblers in late summer and autumn, based on netting and banding of birds, June–October 1974, Prince Edward Point, Ontario. Data grouped into 3-day intervals. There is some temporal separation of species. Some species pass through quickly, others over a protracted period. The kinglets and chickadees migrate later than the warblers, although some Yellow-rumped Warblers remain in Ontario until October.

The fall migration data from Prince Edward Point are for the year 1976 and are based on net captures. For purposes of graphing, the data are grouped into 3-day intervals (figures 2a and 2b). Spring arrival information is from the year 1971, and is adapted from the studies of Weir (1972) and coworkers, who carried out day to day 2-km-long transect counts during April and May. From the original data, which are expressed in terms of quartiles (vide date of first arrival, date when 25, 50, 75, and 100 percent of birds passed through), cumulative counts were developed and these form the basis of figures 3a and 3b.

Panama arrival and departure dates have been obtained from Eisenmann (1952, 1957, and pers. comm.), H. Loftin (pers. comm.), and Ridgely (1976), and have been checked against dates given for countries to the north and south (Todd and Carricker 1922; Howell 1932; Dickey and van Rossen 1938; Miller 1963; Slud 1964; and Monroe 1968). Unfortunately, however, most authors provide only dates of first

arrivals and last departures for migrants, and ignore peak times of movement. Precise arrival and departure data are, however, available for the Northern Waterthrush in Venezuela (Schwartz 1964), and these are used in preference to Panama dates. In the case of the Nashville Warbler (*Vermivora ruficapilla*), that does not extend as far south as Panama, somewhat arbitrarily calculated data for Veracruz are used.

The 14 common parulids shown in figure 1, with the exception of the Yellow-rumped Warbler, spend only three months or less in Ontario, two to three months getting to and from the wintering grounds, and six to seven months in the south. Some of the

460   Allen Keast

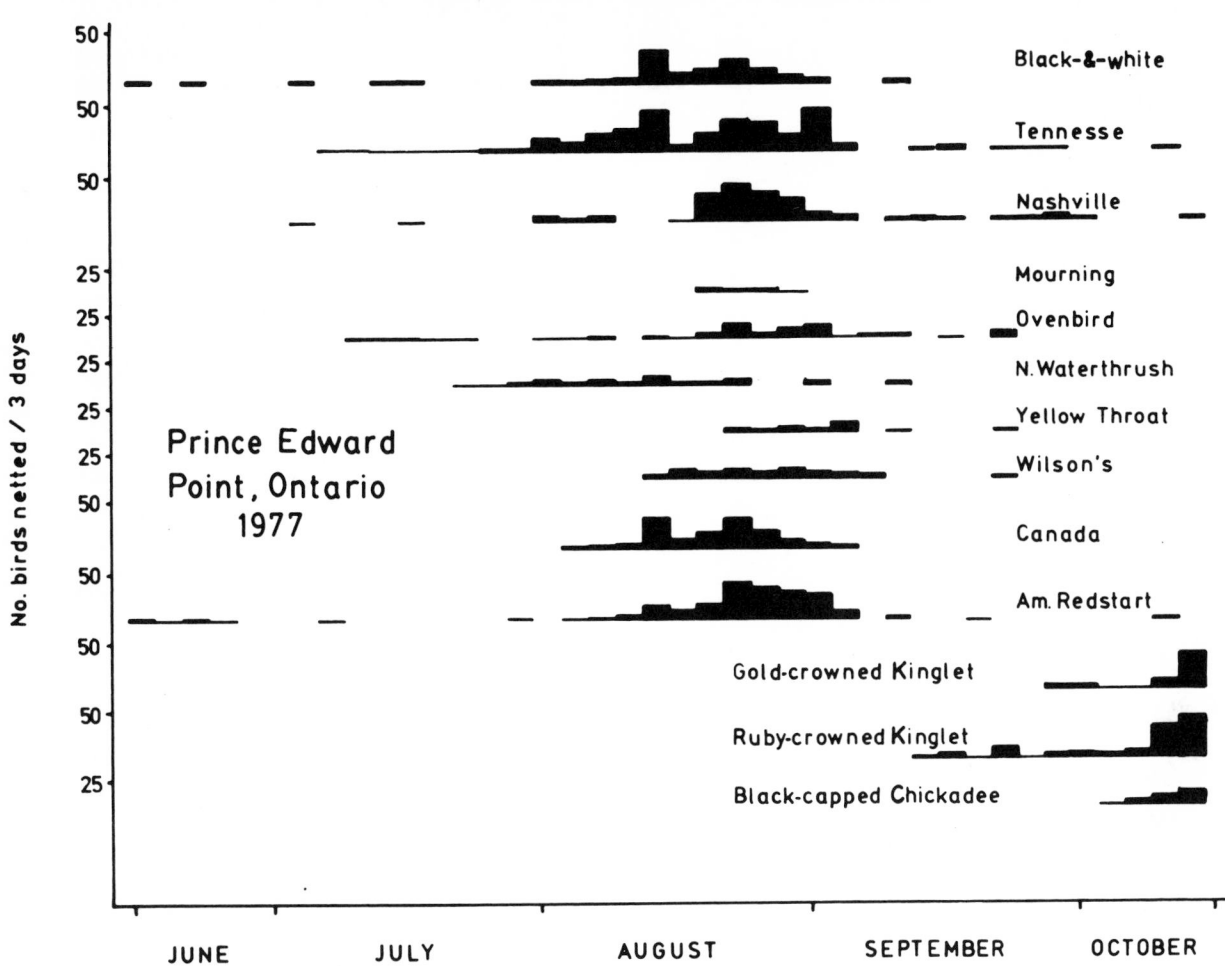

WARBLERS-FALL MIGRATION

Prince Edward
Point, Ontario
1977

No. birds netted / 3 days

Black-&-white
Tennesse
Nashville
Mourning
Ovenbird
N. Waterthrush
Yellow Throat
Wilson's
Canada
Am. Redstart
Gold-crowned Kinglet
Ruby-crowned Kinglet
Black-capped Chickadee

JUNE   JULY   AUGUST   SEPTEMBER   OCTOBER

longer-distance migrants, vide the Northern Water-thrush (Schwartz 1964) spend a full seven months on the wintering grounds. Blackburnian Warblers (*Dendroica fusca*) may arrive in Popayan, Colombia, as early as 10 September and remain as late as 9 May, a total of eight months (R. M. Chipley, this volume); other migratory species are present here from October to April, about seven months.

It is obvious from the above that the time spent by migratory warblers in each of the three phases is more than enough to exercise a major moulding influence on species ecology. The major segment of the year is spent on the wintering grounds. However, despite the brevity of the breeding season, the raising of young must make the greatest immediate demand on the environment. Interspecific competition for food should be great in the migratory mixed species associations, but little is known about this. On their northward journey in spring, this may well not be so because the birds are moving through areas of increasing produc-

tivity; at any event, it is commonly believed that the terminal phases, at least, of the spring flights are rapid (Lincoln 1950). The very generalized data in figure 1 suggest that the spring flight might be shorter than the fall one for populations in the Northern Water-thrush and Nashville Warbler but that the reverse is the case in the Yellow and Black-and-white Warblers (*Dendroica petechia* and *Mniotilta varia*).

Patterns of Spatial Separation of the Parulid Warbler Species on the Breeding Grounds and Geographic Variation in Breeding Habitat

Thirty-one species of parulid warblers breed in eastern Canada. General range maps such as those in Godfrey (1966) show some south-north species separation, particularly in terms of the coniferous relative to the deciduous forest belts. Where there are mountains, such as the Adirondacks, some forms keep to higher altitudes, for example, the Blackpoll Warbler (Palmer

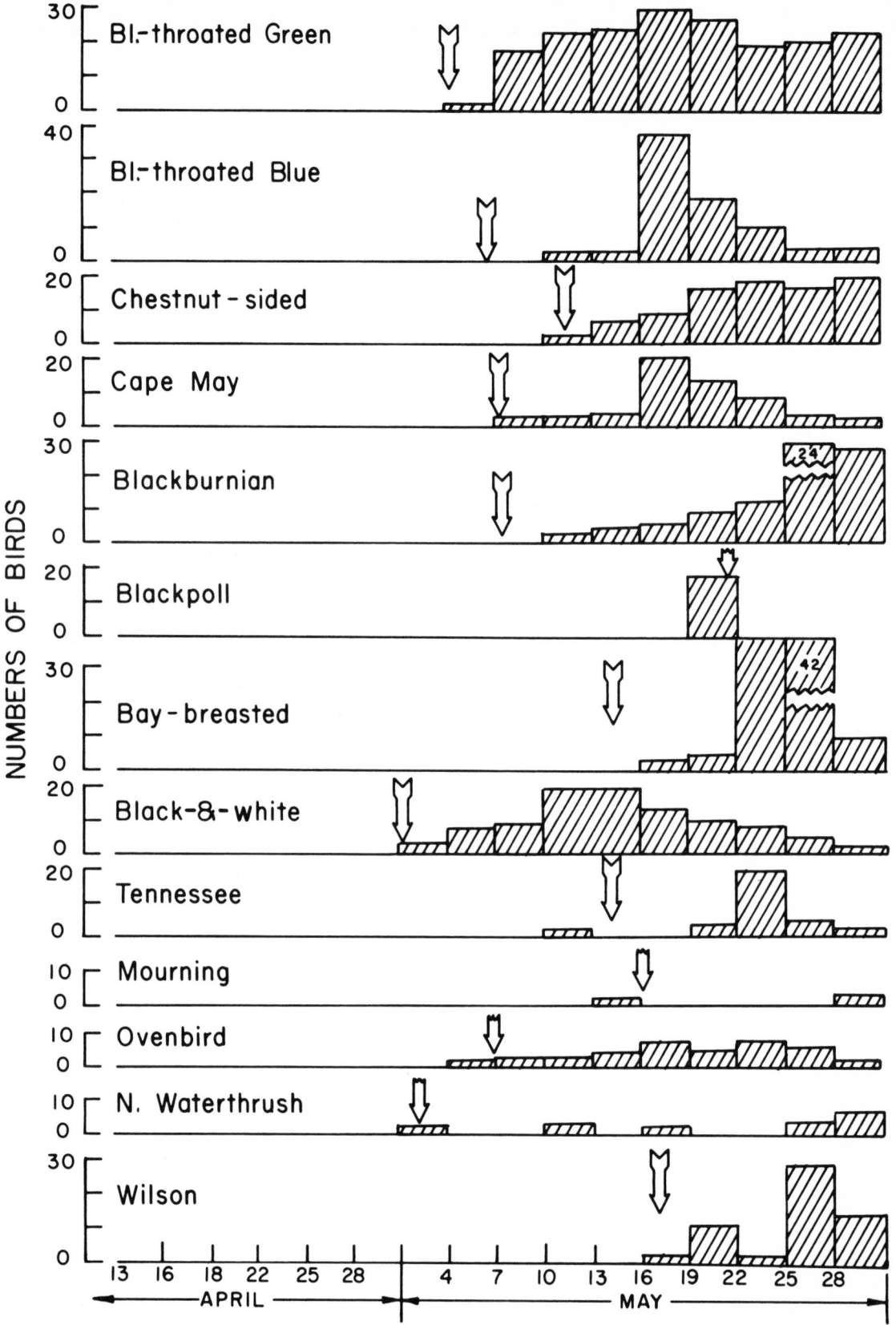

Figures 3a and 3b. Return passage of warblers in spring, Prince Edward Point, Ontario, 1971; data from Weir (1971). Developed from original data presented as "quadriles" (i.e. date of first migrant, and dates when 25, 50, 75, and 100 percent of each species arrived, by reconverting to absolute figures, accumulating, plotting, and arbitrarily diving into 3-day intervals

Allen Keast

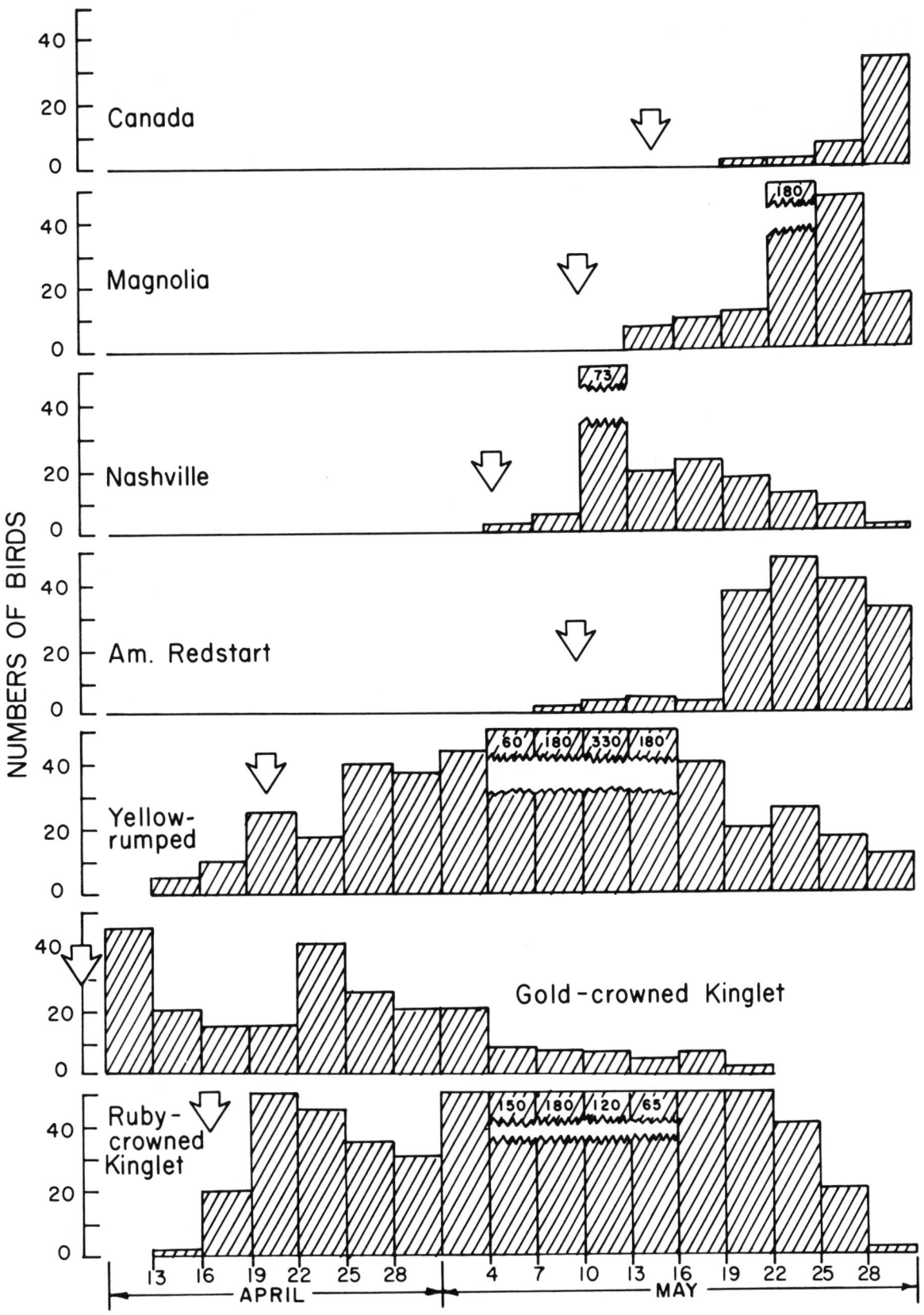

so as to produce a generalized graph equivalent to that in figure 2. White arrows show average first date of arrival of each species over the years 1960–75; data by courtesy of H. Quilliam. There is temporal separation of kinglets from the warblers during spring passage, and some separation of the warbler species. Passage is, however, much more rapid than in the fall.

1949). Some regions have a very high diversity of breeding species: 18 in Maine (Palmer 1949); 11 on the Helderberg Plateau, New York (Kendeigh 1945); 15 in Algonquin Park, Ontario (Martin 1960). Farther north in the conifer belt, 10 species breed at Eaglehead Lake and Sturgeon Lake, Ontario (Speirs 1969). The number falls to 6, however, at Hudson Bay (Jehl and Smith, 1970). Within these areas there is some separation of species by micro-habitat.

In Maine, Palmer (1949) records the breeding habitats of the species as: Black-and-white Warbler—open hardwood growth, usually lowlands, rare in spruce woods; Tennessee—arborvitae swamps, thickets of young spruces, also on higher mountains; Yellow—bushy thickets, young willows, alders; Magnolia (*Dendroica magnolia*)—edges of conifer woodland and in smaller trees along streams, in stunted spruces; Cape May (*D. tigrina*)—mature, open spaced spruces, in treetops, sometimes in spruce-grown pasture; Black-throated Blue (*D. caerulescens*)—young growth in deep mixed deciduous and evergreen woods on damp ground; Yellow-rumped—open spaced low conifers; Black-throated Green (*D. virens*)—second growth of small evergreens, tops of hemlocks in coniferous and mixed forest; Blackburnian—groves of mature hemlocks; Chestnut-sided (*D. pensylvanica*)—sprout hardwoods and brushy places in recently cut forests; Bay-breasted (*D. castanea*)—dense stands of mature firs, spruces, hemlocks; Blackpoll—areas of low dense spruce; Pine (*D. pinus*)—largely confined to areas of *Pinus strobus* and *P. rigida*; Parula (*Parula americana*)—small bogs, old brushy pastures; Yellowthroat (*Geothlypis trichas*)—cattail bogs, bush border stream; Canada (*Wilsonia canadensis*)—dense, swampy woodlands, low down in thickets; Redstart (*Setophaga ruticilla*)—alder thickets, saplings.

Confirmatory accounts of breeding habitat specializations, and separations in warblers are available for other areas, including the Helderberg Plateau, New York (Kendeigh 1945), Algonquin Park, Ontario (Martin 1960), and Utah (Whitmore 1977).

The breeding habitat of individual warbler species may vary somewhat from place to place—see Howell (1932), Kendeigh (1945), Bent (1963). A thorough comparative study has not, however, been attempted.

The habitats of six common parulids in different parts of the breeding range are as follows:

Nashville Warbler

At Eaglehead Lake, north of Lake Superior, Ontario, Speirs (1969) records the highest breeding density in black spruce forest, with slightly lower densities in balsam fir-black spruce. In northern Michigan, towards the southern limits of the breeding range, it inhabits spruce-cedar bogs and aspen-birch regeneration forest (Pitelka 1940). In New York they breed in areas of deciduous and evergreens on the forest margins and shrubby fields (Kendeigh 1945). In the Monadnock region it is common in abandoned fields and mountain pastures half smothered by small grey birches. In Idaho and California warm, dry, open forests of ponderosa pines or woodlands of oaks with a brushy understory form the habitat (Grinnell and Miller 1944; Kelgore 1971).

Yellow Warbler

The breeding habitat in Alaska is the alder-willow zone (Gabrielson and Lincoln 1969) and in the Churchill Falls area of Labrador they are largely restricted to 1.0–1.5 m-high thickets of stunted willow and alder adjacent to lakes and on hillsides (pers. obs.). North of Lake Superior it lives in the shrub layer between forest and rivers or lakes (Speirs 1969). In eastern Ontario, it is a forest edge species, especially where forest is regenerating (see also Sturm 1945, for New York) and on the coastal islands of Maine inhabits the forest edge—scrub transition zone (Morse 1971, 1973). In the southwestern United States, it inhabits shrub growth in grasslands or water-side shrub areas (Bent 1963).

Magnolia Warbler

This inhabits black spruce-balsam fir forest north of Lake Superior (Speirs 1969); *Abies-Picea* forest in Algonquin Park, Ontario (Martin 1960); hemlock and evergreen communities in New York, including forest interior, forest edge, and low second-growth trees (Kendeigh 1945), and coastal spruce forest and deciduous undergrowth in Maine (Mac Arthur 1958; Morse 1968).

Yellow-rumped Warbler

This breeds most commonly in fir-white spruce and hemlock forests in Algonquin Park, Ontario (Martin 1960); open and closed spruce forests in Maine (MacArthur 1958); spruce-poplar forest, mature spruce, and upland willow shrubbery in the Northwest Territories (Theberge 1976).

Black-throated Green Warbler

North of Lake Superior the breeding habitat is white birch-balsam fir (Speirs 1969); areas of hemlock on the Helderberg Plateau, New York, and beech-maple forests in the Catskills (Kendeigh 1945); coniferous and mixed forests in Maine (Palmer 1949); mature deciduous forest and mature *Tsuga-Acer-Fagus* forest in Algonquin Park, Ontario (Martin 1960). In the southern parts of its range it alternatively inhabits warm coastal cyprus-magnolia-oak swamps along the coast, or spruce-balsam-rhododendron and laural thickets in the highlands (Bent 1963).

Blackburnian Warbler

While in the northern part of the breeding range balsam fir-white birch forests are inhabited (Speirs 1969), the common feature of the mixed forests that form the breeding ground is the presence of hemlocks.

Thus, while some parulid species are relatively specific in their choice of breeding habitat (Yellowthroat, Blackburnian Warbler), others are plastic and readily adapt to regrowth or successional stages, or other altered habitat. The Yellow Warbler, with its northern deciduous forest edge and southern mangrove-breeding populations, is exceptionally plastic. Examples of geographic variation in habitat include the distinct highland and lowland-breeding populations of Black-throated Green (Bent 1963), and Blackpoll Warblers (Palmer 1949), the former now racially distinct. As yet no adequate information is available on the influence of one species on the habitat choice of another, but see suggestive data of Morse (1976b) on this.

In a consideration of warbler habitats, the discussion of Mengel (1964) concerning the development of habitat differences coincident with speciation in species groups of warblers should be noted. Also, Mengel postulates a southern compression of warblers in mixed deciduous-conifer habitats to the south of the ice during the glacial maxima. The relatively recent occupation of the northern breeding grounds probably explains the somewhat variable breeding habitat relationships found today.

Better quantitative data are available on feeding separations in breeding Parulidae than on habitat utilization, (MacArthur 1958; Morse 1967, 1973, 1976a and b). Morse (1967), noting that interspecific interactions are not infrequent within breeding assemblages during the incubation and nestling stages, concluded that these are a factor in delimiting species feeding zones. He also finds evidence (Morse, 1976b) for one species depressing the numbers of another. MacArthur (1958), in his studies of zonal feeding in the breeding warblers of Maine demonstrates how in this area of high species diversity the Yellow-rumped Warbler feeds in the lower reaches of the conifers, the Bay-breasted in the middle areas, the Black-throated Green on the sides, the Blackburnian towards the top, and the Cape May in the crown. Warblers may, of course, be structurally adapted for feeding in different places by their leg structure (Osterhaus 1962) although this does not apply to the strictly arboreal feeders. The finer level of zonal feeding described by MacArthur

for the Black-throated Green and Blackburnian Warblers do not, however, apply in southeastern Ontario where there are fewer species. Here, where they occupy slightly different but adjacent habitats, both are generalized arboreal foliage feeders. This confirms the observations of Morse (1971) that feeding zone is influenced by the presence/absence of a congener.

Migration Times and Temporal Separation of Migrating Species

Fall

Patterns of fall departure of 20 species of parulids from Prince Edward Point, Ontario, are shown in figures 2a and 2b, and 3a and 3b (Kingston Field Naturalists' Club data). Data are also given for Gold-crowned and Ruby-crowned Kinglets (*Regulus atrapa* and *R. calendula*), Sylviidae, and the Black-capped Chickadee (*Parus atricapillus*), Paridae, which are also arboreal insect-eaters and have somewhat similar ecologies to the Parulidae. Two warbler species, the Caerulean and Pine, which breed immediately to the north, overfly the point and are not taken in nets.

The following conclusions may be drawn about the fall migration through southern Ontario:

1) Migration begins in early July. Locally-breeding Yellow Warblers leave their breeding territories in the first two weeks of July, and birds netted at this time can be presumed to be drawn from these stocks. The early July records of Tennessee Warblers, however, must be of birds from well to the north since the species does not breed in southern Ontario.

2) The greatest amount of migration occurs in August when mixed species assemblages contain up to a dozen species.

3) The species differ somewhat in their time, or peak, of migration. Most Yellow Warblers have gone through by early August. The migration of Nashville, Black-throated Green, Mourning Warblers (*Oporornis philadelphia*), and Redstarts is concentrated into the latter half of August; and most Yellow-rumped (Myrtle), and Blackpoll, Warblers leave in early September. Ovenbirds (*Seiurus aurocapillus*) migrate later than Northern Waterthrushes.

4) The migration of some species is very protracted. Tennessee Warblers, Ovenbirds, Yellow-rumped, and Yellow Warblers, were taken in the nets for six weeks or more. In Tennessee Warblers the older birds came through first, followed by young-of-the-year. In Yellow Warblers, the later arrivals are presumably from the far northern breeding populations where egg-laying is delayed until late June. Yellow-rumped Warblers, in contrast to the other species, linger until October in southern Ontario, occurring even after the leaves have fallen.

FEEDING HEIGHTS FALL MIGRATION PARULIDAE

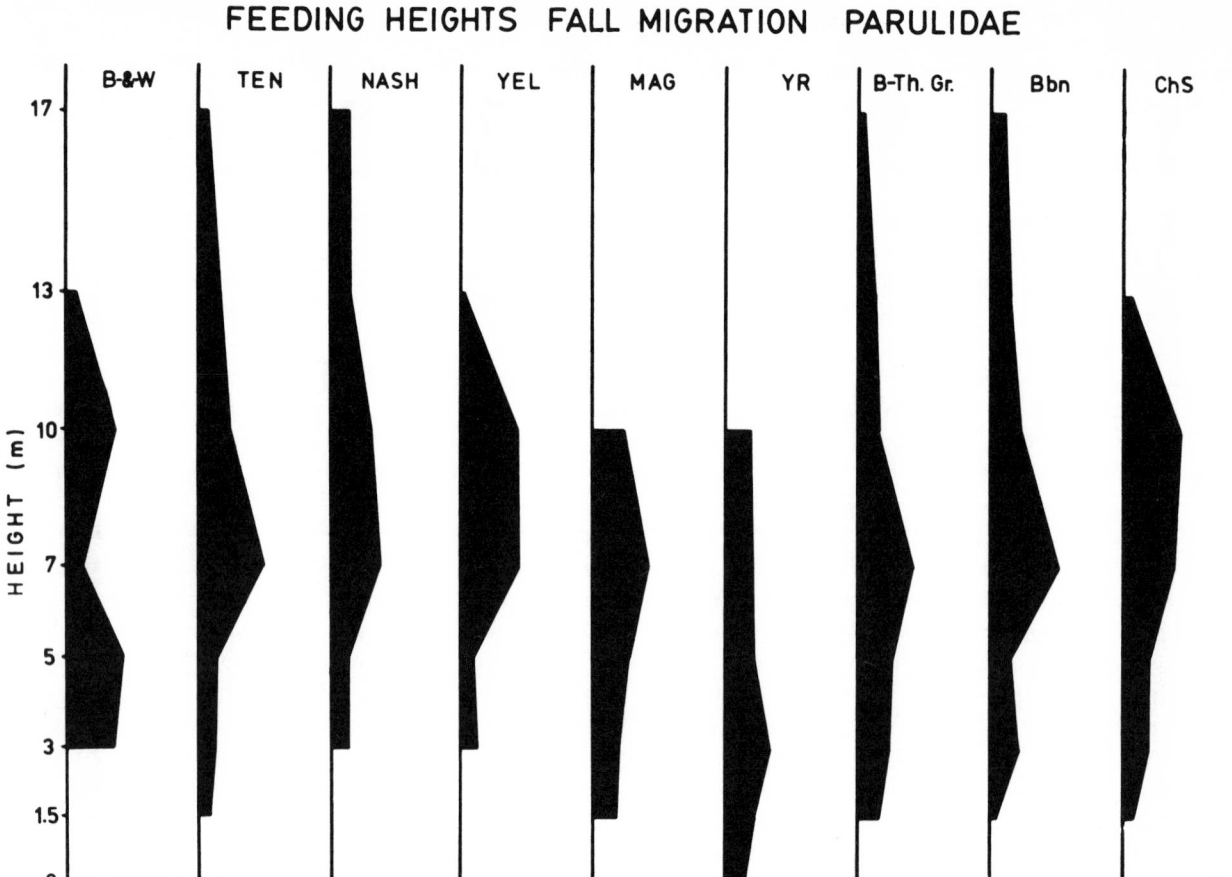

Figures 4a and 4b.   Feeding heights of migratory warblers in autumn, Lake Opinicon and Kingston, Ontario, Aug–Sept 1976 and 1977. For sample sizes see table 1. While some species fed mainly lower down and others at a wide range of heights there is marked species overlap.

5) A few species (Mourning Warbler, Black-throated Blue Warbler) are present only in small numbers and hence make little ecological impact.

6) The kinglets and chickadee pass through much later than the warblers. They also winter farther north than the warblers, only the Ruby-crowned Kinglet reaching Mexico. Their capacity to stay longer in the north (and return early in spring) presumably reflects their palearctic origin by way of the north. In the Golden-crowned Kinglet (*Regulus calendula*), the peak of female migration is 10–15 days ahead of the males (Clarke, 1976).

There is thus a degree of temporal separation of the migrating fall warblers, one effect of which must be to reduce interspecific competition for declining resources.

Spring

The return migration in spring differs from the fall one in that there are not the large numbers of young birds present. Species also pass through quicker, warbler passage being concentrated into May (figures 3a and 3b). There is again some temporal separation, some species mainly passing through in the first, and others in the last, half of the month. The kinglets appear very early in April, ahead of the warblers.

Zonal Feeding in Mixed Species Associations of Migrant Warblers

Figures 4a and 4b and table 1 show the heights and vertical zones at which the various species of migratory warblers fed during their southward migration

466

Allen Keast

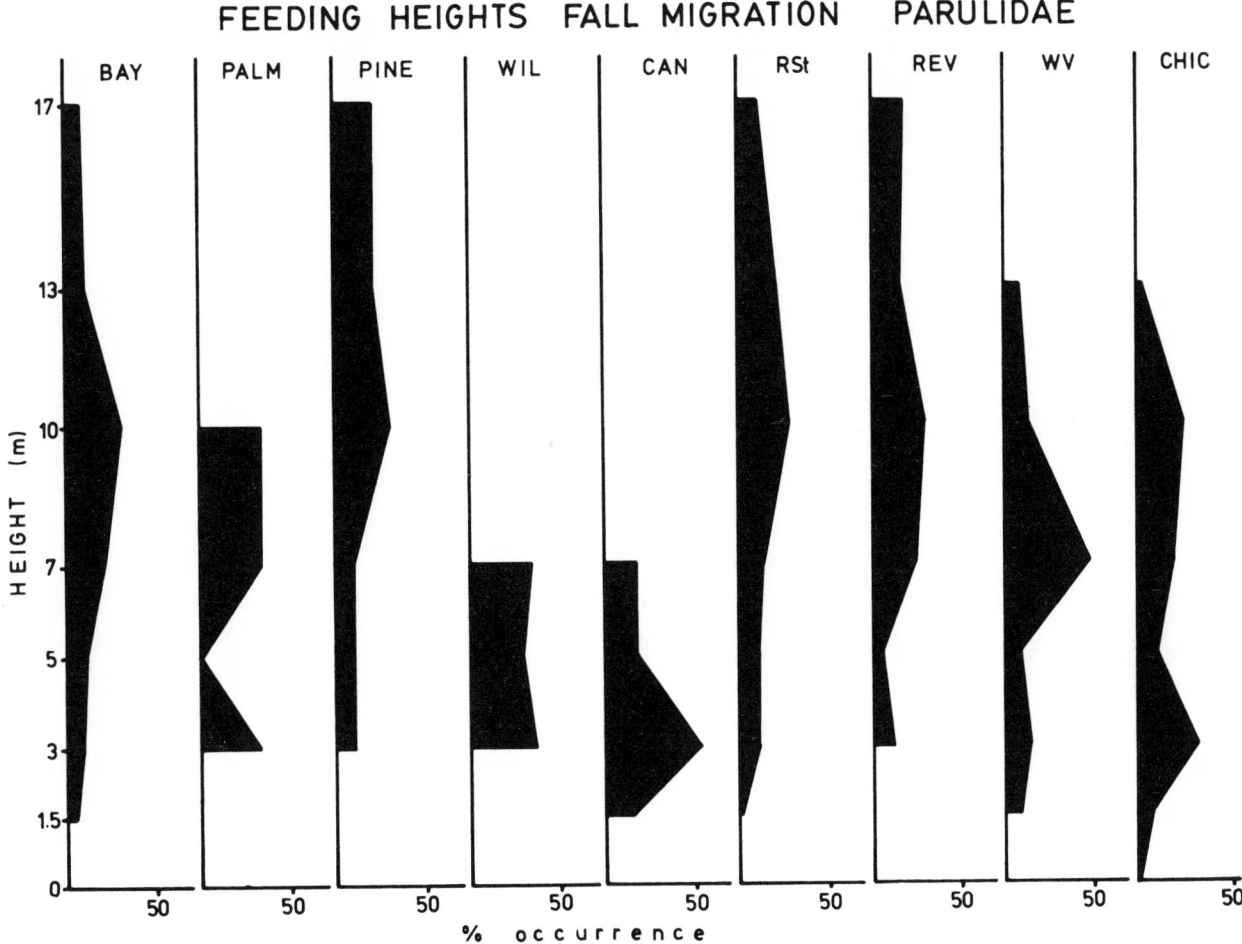

FEEDING HEIGHTS FALL MIGRATION PARULIDAE

through eastern Ontario in fall. Data from associations in the Lake Opinicon and Kingston areas between 20 August and 10 September in the years 1976 and 1977 are combined. The forest was divided into 10 vertical "feeding zones" and the relative amounts of feeding carried out by each species in each determined quantitatively. Bias was minimized by standardizing observations at 15 seconds per individual bird and a maximum of 4 minutes in any one place. Observations were made during the mornings and afternoons. In each year at least two major migratory "waves" occurred separated by periods of low numbers.

The Black-and-white Warbler fed largely on the inner branches and trunk of trees and saplings, as is characteristic. Most species fed largely in the outer foliage of trees and saplings, commonly, four or five in the same tree. The Yellow-rumped Warbler, however, fed to only a small extent in the outer foliage, concentrated mainly on the outer branches and core of the tree, and sometimes descended to the ground. The Canada Warbler fed consistently in the lower parts of the branches of saplings and spent much time in low shrubs. The radial feeding (and slower movements) of the heavier bodied species (Bay-breasted and Yellow-rumped Warblers), which approach the foliage along the branches (see MacArthur, 1958) was obvious and contrasted with the tangential feeding (alighting in the foliage from outside) of the slightly-build Tennessee Warbler. This latter sometimes hung upside down from the outer foliage. Most species fed by hopping through the outer branches, twigs, and leaves, or reaching into the foliage. Aerial pursuits of flying

Table 1. Zonal feeding in migrating warblers, Lake Opinicon and Kingston, Ontario, August–September 1976 and 1977 (data grouped), expressed as percentages of feeding in different zones

Species	Number of Indiv. from which data collected	Number of feeding actions	Air	Outer leaves	Twigs and inner leaves	Outer branches	Inner branches	Trunk	Sapling foliage	Sapling branches	Low shrubs	Ground
Black-and-white Warbler	31	230	—	—	—	8	38	25	—	29	—	—
Tennessee	92	620	5	70	9	3	—	—	6	6	—	—
Nashville	39	390	—	33	17	17	—	—	33	—	—	—
Yellow	78	440	2	53	7	2	—	—	27	4	5	—
Magnolia	121	430	—	43	8	14		—	20	10	3	—
Myrtle (Yellow-rumped)	55	330	—	21	12	12	15	—	9	10	3	18
Black-throated Green	43	390	—	46	10	10	—	—	29	—	—	—
Blackburnian	170	470	5	45	14	10	2	—	19	3	2	—
Chestnut-sided	26	180	—	67	6	6	—	—	17	3	3	—
Bay-breasted	79	410	—	32	22	29	5	2	5	2	2	—
Palm	15	89	—	33	—	—	—	—	33	34	—	—
Pine	26	290	—	44	22	11	—	—	20	—	—	—
Wilson's	31	405	—	35	—	—	18	12	35	—	—	—
Canada	19	180	—	5	—	10	25	—	13	18	25	—
American Redstart	31	340	22	11	5	17	17	—	19	11	—	—
Red-eyed Vireo	69	390	—	51	10	15	—	5	20	—	—	—
Warbling Vireo	34	290	—	49	7	15	—	—	24	7	5	—
Black-capped Chickadee	79	490	—	27	—	15	8	17	10	14	6	3

insects characterized the Redstart but occasionally occurred in the Tennessee, Yellow, Magnolia, Black-throated Green, Blackburnian, and Chestnut-sided Warblers. Pine Warblers showed some preference for conifers in their feeding.

Most species fed over a range of heights. Little groups of Tennessee, Nashville, Black-throated Green, and sometimes Blackburnian and Bay-breasted Warblers would feed part of the day at 17–18 m, then in the tops of saplings, and subsequently descend for short periods into shrubbery only 1.0–1.5 m high. Wilson's Warbler, and to a lesser extent Palm, Magnolia, and Yellow-rumped Warblers, fed at heights of 7 m or less. Yellow and Chestnut-sided Warblers fed chiefly at middle heights.

A comparable analysis of zonal feeding in southwards migrating fall warblers near Lafayette, Indiana, by Adams and Manolis (1977) confirms the existence of much overlap in these associations. They found,

however, that the species of *Dendroica* showed some variation in the proportion of time spent at different levels from year to year (? in response to a differing distribution of resources). The Redstart, Ovenbird, and Black-and-white Warbler, did not change.

Parnell (1969) analyzed spring migrating associations of warblers in North Carolina and this data have subsequently been subjected to ecological similarity studies by Power (1971). These flocks were more diversified than the fall Ontario ones, and included ground-feeding waterthrushes and Ovenbirds, as well as shrub-feeding Yellow-breasted Chats (*Icteria virens*) and Prairie Warblers (*Dendroica discolor*). The few arboreal species present fed as in the Ontario fall assemblages.

Larger-bodied Red-eyed and Warbling Vireos (*Vireo olivaceus* and *V. gilvus*), and small Black-capped chickadees (*Parus atricapillus*), were common members of the fall migratory associations in Ontario. The larger vi-

Allen Keast

Table 2. Zonal feeding in migratory warblers "grounded" by adverse weather conditions, Point Pellee, Ontario, 28–30 Apr, 1967[1]

Species	Black-and-white	Blue wing	Orange-crowned	Nash-ville	Yellow	Cape May	Bl-thr Blue	Bl-thr Green	Chest-Sided	Yellow Throat
Number of indivs. from which data collected	12	9	4	22	17	9	12	19	14	5
Number of feeding actions	60	46	25	360	250	55	45	220	130	—
FEEDING ZONE										
Aerial	—	—	—	X^2	X	X	X	X	XXX	—
Outer foliage	—	—	—	—	—	—	—	—	—	—
Bare twigs	—	50	—	25	—	50	—	60	—	—
Branches	30	—	—	15	—	40	20	20	20	—
Trunk	50	—	—	—	—	—	25	—	—	—
Sapling twigs and foliage	—	—	—	—	20	—	—	—	—	—
Sapling trunk	20	—	—	—	5	10	20	20	20	—
Low shrub	—	—	20	60	75	—	10	—	10	—
Ground, thicket	—	50	80	—	—	—	—	—	10	—
Ground, exposed	—	—	—	—	—	—	25	—	40	—
Marsh	—	—	—	—	—	—	—	—	—	XXX
FEEDING HEIGHT M.										
17 plus	—	—	—	—	—	—	—	—	—	—
13	—	20	—	20	—	40	—	50	—	—
10	20	20	—	10	—	30	15	20	10	—
7	40	10	—	10	—	20	20	10	10	—
5	20	—	—	—	10	—	30	10	10	—
3	20	—	—	—	15	10	—	10	10	—
.6–1.8	—	50	20	60	75	—	10	—	10	100
0	—	—	80	—	—	—	25	—	50	—

[1] Expressed as percentages of feeding at different levels.

[2] X means feeding zone is used; XXX = predominates.

reos fed largely in the foliage. The chickadees were generalized, taking insects from bare branch tips, trunks and the conifer needles, as well as foliage.

Changed Zonal Feeding During Times of Stress

Flocks of migrating warblers are sometimes "pinned down" in restricted areas by adverse weather fronts. One such occurence occurred at Point Pelee, Ontario, between 28 and 30 April, 1967, the birds having just crossed Lake Erie. Members of 10 species of warblers, that had advanced into cold wet weather before the trees had come into leaf showed obvious stress (table 2). Their feeding deviated from the normal; Chestnut-sided and Black-throated Blue Warblers spent much time on the open ground, and Blue-winged (*Vermivora pinus*) and Nashville Warblers in the low shrubbery. Cape May, Black-throated Blue, and Black-throated Green Warblers sought food from the bare trunks and branches alongside the Black-and-white Warblers. Aerial feeding was marked in five species, especially the Chestnut-sided Warblers. These species were apparently being forced to obtain food wherever they could get it.

Foods Eaten by Migrating Fall Warblers in Mixed Species Assemblages, Ontario

Analyses were carried out on the stomach contents of 94 warblers of 13 species, the 2 kinglets (*Regulus satrapa* and *R. calendula*), the Brown Creeper (*Certhia familiaris*), Swainson's Thrush (*Hylocichla ustulata*), Red-eyed Vireos (*Vireo olivaceus*), White-throated Sparrows (*Zonotrichia albicollis*), and Juncos (*Junco hyemalis*) killed in striking a hydro tower adjacent to Prince Edward Point, Ontario, during late August–early September 1975. Eighteen percent of the birds' stomachs were empty. Small beetles were the major food item in the stomachs of virtually all species (70 percent), especially the warblers. Four Blackpoll Warblers averaged 20 beetles of body length 5–7 mm per individual; 4 Cape May Warblers, 5 Magnolia Warblers, and 4 Ruby-crowned Kinglets about 15 beetles per individual. Two Nashville Warblers contained 66 4–5 mm-long beetles, and 11 and 13 mm-long lepidopterous larvae. Three Black-and-white Warblers averaged 25 beetles per individual, and 3 Tennessee Warblers 7. Blackburnian Warblers contained some plant material in addition to small beetles. Two Canada Warblers contained beetles and 3 1.5 mm-wide snails. The larger Red-eyed Vireos had fed on plant material, snails, and larger beetles 8–10 mm in length. The three Swainson's Thrushes contained plant remains including seeds, and the remains of beetles 12–16 mm in length. Juncos and White-throated Sparrows contained small numbers of beetles.

The predominance of beetles in the stomachs of such a diversity of species suggests that this was the only insect resource readily available to these migratory birds. The diet contrasts markedly with the one of spring breeding warblers which is characterized both by large numbers of lepidopterous larvae and a high degree of prey diversity (see accounts of the foods of Yellow and Black-throated Green Warblers in Bent 1963; data on the latter and Yellow-rumped Warblers in Morse 1976a).

The return of warblers in the spring corresponds, of course, to the major flush of caterpillars. The obtaining of food is presumably helped by the mobile nature of these migrating assemblages, remaining only a few days in any one area.

Difference Between Breeding and Wintering Habitat

The winter habitats of the migratory parulid warblers are reviewed by the writer elsewhere in this volume. No comparative studies of how the plant communities occupied in summer and winter differ in basic *structure* have been carried out, however.

In winter the northern conifer-breeding Yellow-rumped Warbler inhabits highland pine savannahs, lowland semi-open country, even sandy cays off Belize. The Blackburnian, breeding in hemlocks and mixed forests in the north, frequents subtropical rainforest and highland oak forests in South America. Wilson's Warbler, breeding in willow and dwarf birch in bogs, ponds, and along streams in the north (Godfrey 1966) inhabits the edges of mid elevation rain forests in Central America. Despite the presence of lowland, warm-adapted breeding populations in the Carolinas, the Black-throated Green Warbler is a highland inhabitant in its wintering grounds. By contrast the Maine-Ontario brush-habitat-breeding Chestnut-sided Warbler winters in the humid lowland rain forests of Panama. Another far-northern breeder, the Tennessee, winters at all elevations from sea level to over 2,000 m. Species that breed side-by-side in the northern coniferous belt may winter in very different places: Mexico (Nashville Warbler), the West Indies (Black-throated Blue and Cape May); Panamanian lowlands (Chestnut-sided); north-central South America (Blackpoll, Blackburnian Warblers).

It can be concluded that: 1) summer and winter habitats are different although structural similarities may or may not exist, and 2) there is no consistency in where species breeding in an area winter.

Parnell (1969) notes that during migration, some species of warblers are less selective of habitat than others. See also Power (1971).

Comparison of Zonal Feeding in Summer, Winter, and on Migration

Zonal feeding in five species of wood-warblers in their breeding grounds, on migration, and in winter, are compared in figure 5. The Ontario breeding data were obtained by the writer in the Leeds County area (between Kingston and Smith's Falls) and Labrador data in the Churchill Falls area. The Ontario fall migration data are those previously discussed. The spring migration data from North Carolina are those of Parnell (1969). The Veracruz Highland observations were made by the writer between 28 December 1973 and 10 January 1974 in the Jalapa region, and the Chiriqui Highland data between 18–27 February 1975. These are discussed in greater detail elsewhere in this volume. The procedure followed in obtaining the feeding zone data was as outlined earlier.

The Black-and-white Warbler shows great seasonal consistency in its feeding zone, almost exclusively utilizing the branches and trunks of saplings and trees. The Yellow-rumped Warbler, is by contrast, highly plastic. Breeding Ontario birds fed mainly in the middle and upper levels of conifers and saplings, MacArthur's Maine birds from the trunk up into the crown. During migration, both in Ontario and North Carolina, there was a major low-shrub-feeding component. During winter in Central America shrub and ground feeding predominated. On the small grassy cays off Belize, ground feeding predominated: the Yellow-rumped Warbler is here called "grassie" by the inhabitants. The species may feed on grass seeds (Bent 1963). The Yellow Warbler is mainly a shrub and sapling feeder in Ontario, with a lesser tree foliage component. The latter is absent in its alder-willow thicket habitat in Labrador, trees being absent. On fall migration in Ontario, the Yellow Warbler does much feeding in the middle parts of the trees. On spring migration through North Carolina, Parnell found that they fed mostly low-down. In the dry lowlands near Santa Marta, Colombia, the Yellow Warblers inhabit low shrubbery. Mangrove-frequenting races (e.g. on the cays off Belize) feed in the foliage of the mangrove trees, as also do some wintering northern birds.

The Black-throated Green Warbler is, consistently, a tree and sapling foliage feeder (figure 5). Note, however, feeding zone differences in the Maine, North Carolina, and Panama Highland populations studied by K. N. Rabenold (this volume), who was able to demonstrate some of the complex features of summer feeding described by MacArthur (1958). Magnolia Warblers feed mainly in the foliage and branches of saplings and medium-sized trees throughout their range, good consistency being indicated. The Blackburnian Warbler is largely a crown and inner foliage feeder, with some feeding being carried out in the outer branches and a minor amount in the canopy of saplings. There is good consistency in the sites shown. Note, however, the great broadening of the feeding zone in this species in the Popayan region of Colombia where, in winter, they feed at all heights from the trees down to low shrubbery (R. M. Chipley, this volume).

The more specialized feeders amongst the parulids like the terrestrial water-thrushes and Ovenbird, the trunk and large-branch-feeding Black-and-white Warbler, and the marsh-thicket frequenting Yellowthroat, are consistent in their feeding zones. Some of the arboreal ones are also. Other species, like the Yellow-rumped and Palm Warblers, which do much ground feeding (Lack and Lack 1974), are highly versatile. Power (1971), using the data of Parnell (1969), concluded that there is no seasonal difference in feeding zone in several warbler species.

Parulid Interaction Patterns and Ecological Plasticity, an Integration

The nearctic migratory parulids spend 2.5–3 months on the breeding grounds, 2–3 months on migration, and 6–7 months in the south. The exact amount of time spent on each phase varies with the species. Since each phase is relatively long, however, all must exercise a moulding influence on species ecology.

On the breeding grounds, the species separate out latitudinally, on habitat, and in feeding zone. There is a marked emphasis on "microhabitat" difference between species with individuals being restricted to "forest edge," "regrowth," "areas of hemlock," and so on. Such a fine degree of habitat specialization is not common in birds; it does, however, find parallels in the *Cisticola* warblers and larks in southern Africa (McLachlan and Liversidge 1978). This fine degree of separation and patchy breeding distributions of many species, plus a degree of species replacement, probably indicates that habitat separations are still evolving post-glacially.

This suggestion is supported by patterns of vertical feeding zone separation; these are fine in the high density Maine situation studied by MacArthur (1958) but relax where fewer species occur, e.g. in southeastern Ontario and in the insular situations studied by Morse.

While there are differences in morphology between terrestrial, shrubdwelling, and arboreal feeding parulids (Osterhaus 1962), the body morphology and, particularly, bill morphology of arboreal, foliage-gleaning species is remarkably similar (see other paper by writers in this volume). This could indicate that morphological separations between congeners are still developing. It is equally likely, however, that as suggested by Keast (1976), there may be an optimum bill size for small arboreal foliage-gleaning insect-eaters. As noted, counterpart species separate out spatially, not on morphology, in the parulids.

While there is some temporal separation in migration times mixed species assemblages passing through Ontario in the latter half of August and early September contain up to 15 species. Analysis shows much overlap in feeding zone in the arboreal foliage-gleaning species. The stomach contents of birds killed in late summer by collision with towers showed a common food item, adult Coleoptera, to predominate.

Notwithstanding the above some features must serve to somewhat lessen "inter-specific competition" in migrating warblers, e.g. partial temporal separation, and moving south over a broad rather than a narrow front (for example, the Yellowthroat, Taylor 1976). In this regard the direct autumn flight of the Blackpoll Warbler, from New England to South America (Drury and Keith 1962; Nesbit 1970; McClintock et al 1978), while very energy demanding, would remove it from competition for food with other migrating warblers.

Two facets of the avian annual cycle must be considered here in that they must affect food uptake rates

ZONAL FEEDING-MIGRANT WARBLERS

BLACK-AND-WHITE

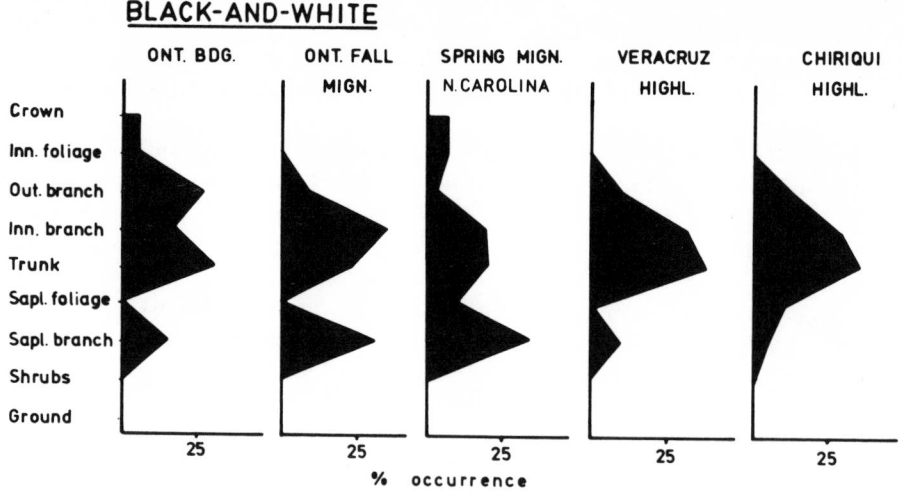

YELLOW RUMPED

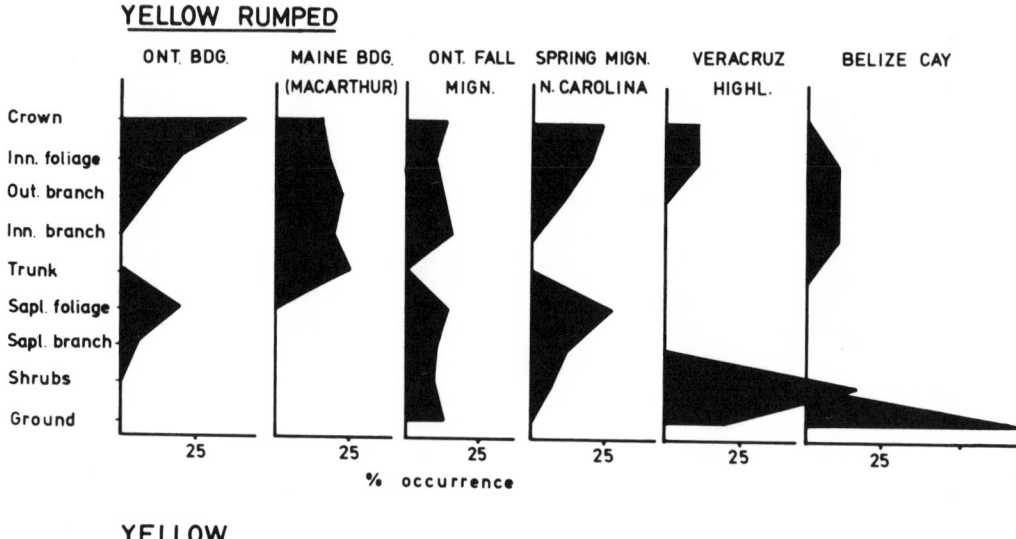

YELLOW

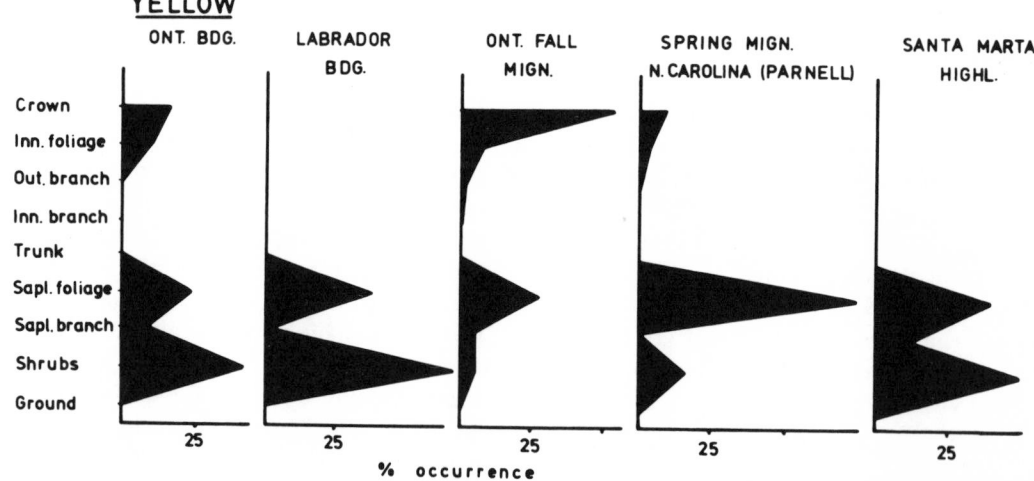

Figures 5a and 5b.   Zonal feeding in 6 species of warblers during breeding, while on fall and spring migration, and at sites in the wintering grounds. See text for sources.

ZONAL FEEDING-MIGRANT WARBLERS

BLACK-THROATED GREEN

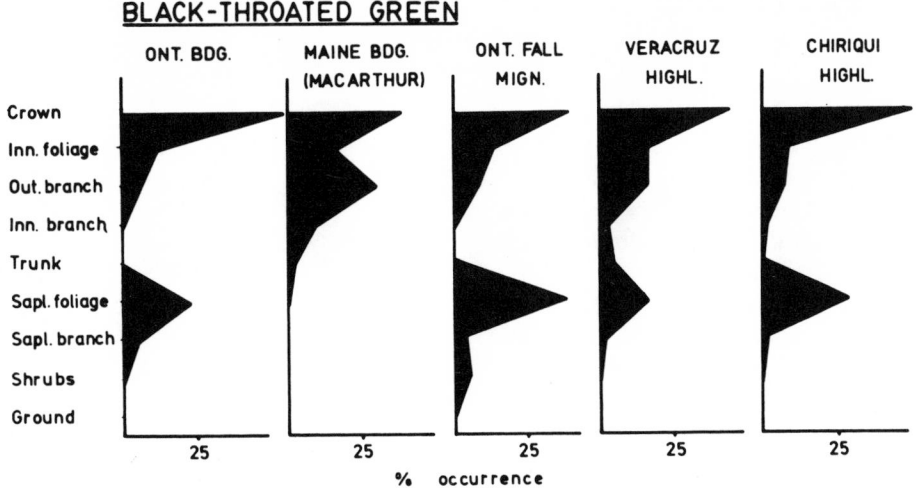

MAGNOLIA

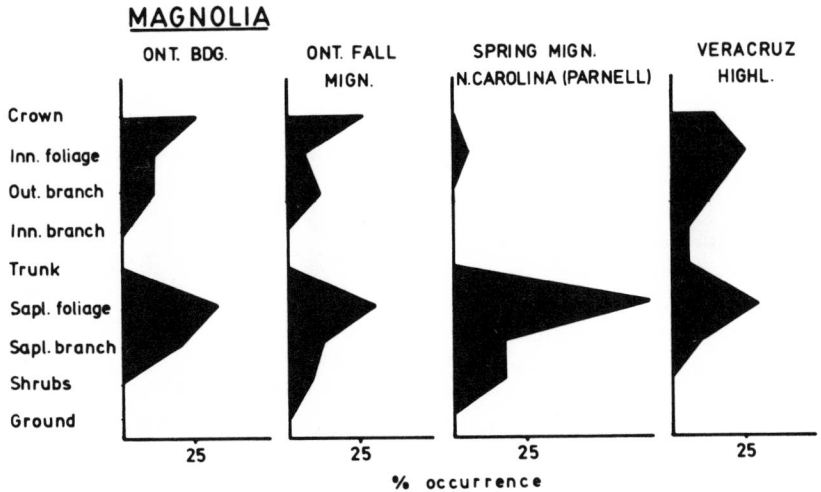

BLACKBURNIAN

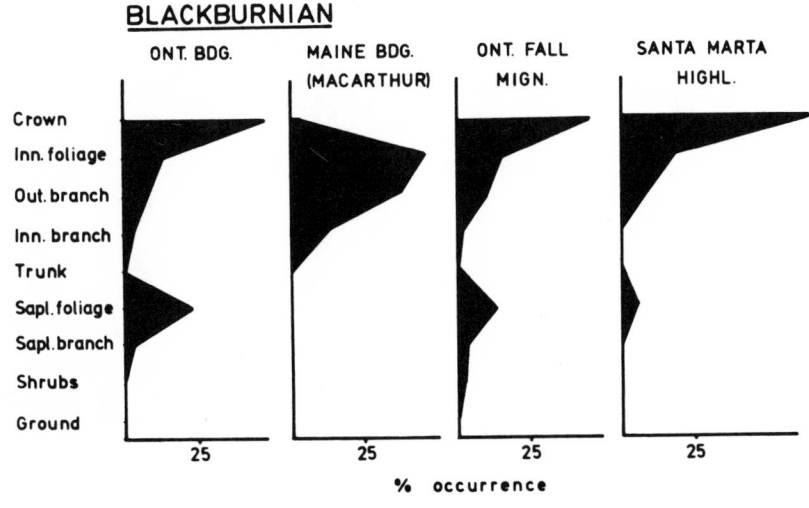

on migration, the laying down of premigratory fat as a "fuel," and moulting. Premigratory fat may equal a third of the wet weight and two-thirds of the dry weight in migrants compared to 6–7 percent at other times (Odum and Connell 1956). This is not, however, laid down prior to beginning the flight but, rather immediately prior to beginning the trans-Gulf flight (Caldwell et al. 1963). It must, accordingly, be laid down while the birds are "competing" members of mixed species migratory assemblages. The energy demanding moult is, however, completed prior to migration, i.e. before joining the mixed flocks.

It is obvious from the above that there must be a premium on adaptibility in migrant parulids. Certainly the basic species separation devices characteristic of birds occur, both between migrants and relative to residents. They differ from neotropical residents, however, in basic ways: capacity to live at different latitudes, change habitats seasonally, compete with different backgrounds of "competitor" species, physiological adaptations for migration, and larger clutch size.

An interesting analogue can be drawn between the migrant-resident situation in Central America and the insular situations depicted by Rickleff and Cox (1972) and Diamond (1975). The former writers, noting that in the West Indies the avifauna embrace the extreme types of versatile opportunist and resident forest-dweller, postulate that island colonization proceeds in a cyclical fashion with the original colonizers initially being opportunistic and adaptable and then, as they become increasingly specialized, resident forest-dwellers. Diamond finds that the inhabitants of the small southwest Pacific islands includes the distinct category of "tramps," opportunists that colonize readily and thrive in marginal habitats; they contrast again with specialized thicket or forest forms with little, or no, capacity for dispersal. In their southern winter range some migrants behave like the Rickleffs and Cox colonizing opportunists and Diamond's tramps. Not only are they mobile and diversified in their habitat choice but, as noted, some can occupy marginal and temporary habitats.

Acknowledgments

I should like to express my thanks to the members of the Kingston (Ontario) Field Naturalists' Club and Helen Quilliam for making available unpublished banding data from Prince Edward Point, Ontario, relative to the fall migration of 1976, and to Mrs. Quilliam for the average date of first arrival in the spring (mean of 15 years) for the returning spring warblers.

The diagrams were drawn by Ms. Anne Fullerton.

The work was done while the writer held a grant from the National Research Council of Canada whose support is gratefully acknowledged. Much of the autumn zonal feeding data was developed at the Queen's University Biological Station, Chaffey's Locks, Ontario.

Literature Cited

Adams, A. and T. Manolis
1977. Differences in foraging habits of migrant wood warblers in two fall seasons. Paper read at Amer. Ornith. Union Meetings, Berkeley, Calif., August 1977.

Bent, A. C.
1963. Life histories of North American Wood Warblers. 2 vols. New York: Dover.

Caldwell, L. D., E. P. Odeum, and S. G. Marshall
1963. Comparison of fat levels in migrating birds killed at a central Michigan and Florida Gulf TV tower. Wils. Bull. 75:428–34.

Clarke, L.
1976. Golden-crowned Kinglets at Prince Edward Point. In The Bluebill, Kingston Field Notes, Club 24:12–15.

Cooke, F., R. K. Ross, R. K. Schmidt, and A. J. Pakulak
1975. Birds of the tundra Biome at Cape Churchill and La Perouse Bay. Canadian Field Nat. 89:413–22.

Diamond, J. M.
1975. Assembly of species communities. In eds. M. L. Cody and J. M. Diamond, pp. 342–44. *Ecology and Evolution of Communities*. Cambridge, Mass.: Harvard Univ. Press.

Dickey, D., and A. J. van Rossem
1938. The birds of El Salvador. Field Mus. Nat. Hist., Zool. Ser. 23:1–609.

Drury, W. H. and J. A. Keith
1962. Radar studies of songbird migration in coastal New England. Ibis 104:449–89.

Eisenmann, E.
1952. Annotated list of birds of Barro Colorado Island, Panama Canal Zone. Smithsonian Miscell. Colls. 117:1–62.

Eisenmann, E.
1957. Wood warblers in Panama. In *The Wood Warblers of America*, eds. L. Griscom and A. Sprunt, Jr. New York, Devin-Adair, pp. 286–97.

Gabrielson, I. N., and F. C. Lincoln
1969. *The Birds of Alaska*. Harrisburg, Pa.: Stackpole, 922 pp.

Godfrey, W. E.
1966. *The Birds of Canada*. National Mus. Canada Bull. 203, 428 pp.

Grinnell, J. and A. H. Miller
1944. The distribution of the birds of California. Pacific Coast Avifauna 27.

Howell, A. H.
1932. Florida bird life. Florida Dept. Game and Freshwater Fish, 579 pp.

Jehl, J. R., Jr., and B. A. Smith
1970. Birds of the Churchill region, Manitoba Special Publ. No. 1, Manitoba Museum of Man and Nature, Winnipeg, 87 pp.

Kelgore, B. M.
1971. Response of breeding bird populations to habitat changes in a giant sequoic forest. Amer. Midl. Naturalist 85:135–52.

Kendeigh, S. C.
1945. Community selection by birds on the Helderberg Plateau of New York. Auk 62:418–36.

Lack, D. and Lack, P.
1972. Wintering warblers in Jamaica. Living Bird 11:129–53.

Lincoln F. C.
1950. Migration of birds. Circular 16, Fish and Wildlife Service, U.S. Dept. Interior, 102 pp.

MacArthur, R. H.
1958. Population ecology of some warblers of northeastern coniferous forests. Ecol. 39:599–619.

McClintock, C. P., T. C. Williams, and J. M. Teal
1978. Autumnal bird migration observed from ships in the western North Atlantic Ocean. Bird-Banding 49:262–77.

McLachlan, G. R., and R. Liversidge
1978. *Robert's Birds of South Africa*. Capetown, South Africa: Transvaal.

Martin, N. D.
1960. An analysis of bird populations in relation to forest succession in Algonquin Provincial Park, Ontario. Ecol. 41:126–40.

Mengel, R. M.
1964. The probable history of species formation in some northern wood warblers (Parulidae). Living Bird 3:9–44.

Miller, A. H.
1963. Seasonal activity and ecology of the avifauna of an American equatorial cloud forest. Univ. Calif. Pub. Zool. 66:1–78.

Monroe, B. L.
1968. A distributional survey of the birds of Honduras. A.O.U. Ornith. Monogr. 7, 485 pp.

Morse, D. H.
1967. Competitive relationships between parula warblers and other species during the breeding season. Auk 84:490–502.

1968. A quantitative study of foraging of male and female sprucewoods warblers. Ecol. 49:779–84.

1971. The foraging of warblers isolated on small islands. Ecol. 52:216–28.

1973. The foraging of small populations of Yellow Warblers and American Redstarts. Ecol. 54:346–55.

1976a. Variables affecting the density and territory size of breeding spruce-woods warblers. Ecol. 57:290–301.

1976b. Hostile encounters among spruce-woods warblers (*Dendroica*, Parulidae). Anim. Behav. 24:764–71.

Nesbit, I. C. T.
1970. Autumn migration of the Blackpoll Warbler; evidence for long flight provided by regional survey. Bird-Banding 4:207–40.

Odum, E. P., and C. E. Connell
1956. Lipid levels in migrating birds. Science 123:892–94.

Osterhaus, M. B.
1962. Adaptive modifications in the leg structure of some North American warblers. Am. Midl. Naturalist 68:474–86.

Palmer, R. S.
1949. Maine birds. Bull. Mus. Comp. Zool. 102, 656 pp.

Parnell, J. F.
1969. Habitat relations of the Parulidae during spring migration. Auk 86:505–21.

Pitelka, F. A.
1940. Breeding behaviour of the Black-throated Green Warbler. Wils. Bull. 52:3–18.

Power, D. M.
1971. Warbler ecology: diversity, similarity, and seasonal differences in habitat segregation. Ecol. 52:434–43.

Rickleffs, R. E. and G. W. Cox
1972. Taxon cycles in the West Indian avifauna. Am. Nat. 106:195–219.

Ridgely, R. S.
1976. *A Guide to the Birds of Panama*. Princeton, N.J.: Princetion Univ. Press, 393 pp.

Schwartz, P.
1964. The Northern Waterthrushes in Venezuela. Living Bird 2:169–84.

Slud, P.
1964. The birds of Costa Rica. Bull. Amer. Mus. Nat. Hist. 128:1–430.

Speirs, J. M.
1969. Birds of Ontario's coniferous forest region. Canadian Audubon 31:1–8.

Sturm, L.
1945. A study of the nesting activities of the American Redstart. Auk 62:189-206.

Taylor, W. K.
1976.   Migration of the common Yellowthroat with an
        emphasis on Florida. Bird-Banding 47:319–32.

Theberge, J. B.
1976.   Bird populations in the Kluane Mountains, south-
        west Yukon, with special reference to vegetation and
        fire. Canadian J. Zool. 54:1346–56.

Todd, W. E. C., and M. A. Carriker, Jr.
1922.   The birds of the Santa Marta region of Colombia: a
        study in altitudinal distribution. Carnegie Museum
        14, 611 pp.

Weir, R. D.
1972.   Spring migration at Prince Edward Point, Ontario.
        Canadian Field Natur. 68:3–16.

Whitmore, R. C.
1977.   Habitat partitioning in a community of passerine
        birds. Wils. Bull. 89:253–65.

Allen Keast

GEORGE V. N. POWELL
Department of Zoology
University of California
Davis, California 95616

Migrant Participation in Neotropical Mixed Species Flocks

Introduction

One interesting facet of resident-migrant relationships in the neotropics is their potential interaction in mixed species flocks. The ubiquitous occurrence of resident flocks in the neotropics allows most forest birds the opportunity to participate in groups irrespective of habitat selection. Flocks are found from sea level to montane forests throughout the spectrum of primary to heavily disturbed habitat. Therefore, most migrants wintering in the neotropics utilize habitat traversed by resident flocks. However, despite a universal accessability of flocks, the propensities of migrants to flock with residents varies markedly. While some migrants regularly join flocks, many follow inconsistently or ignore them completely. A few form flocks composed exclusively of migrants, but most forage singly or occasionally join into small loosely associated groups. The basis for this variation is not immediately obvious and warrants examination.

In this presentation, I use the term flock in a strict sense excluding feeding assemblages that are chance aggregations of species at resource-rich patches. Loci of aggregations include such diverse forms as fruiting trees (Leck 1971), burning grasslands (Winterbottom 1949), and army ant swarms (Willis 1972). In contrast, flocks are defined as foraging groups that are generated by intrinsic attraction between members (Morse 1970); they are identified by coordinated movement in the absence of external resource cues. Flocks may be monospecific or polyspecific in composition; they may be formed entirely by residents, or migrants, or a mixture of both.

Birds that flock presumably derive some benefit(s) from the presence of other participants. Hypothetical advantages accrued from flocking are numerous, and a complete discussion of their applicability to migrants is beyond the scope of this presentation (for a recent review of hypotheses see Morse 1977). These hypotheses are not universally applicable to all types of flocks. Some predict advantages for new arrivals that obtain information by associating with resident flocks (R), but not for flocks consisting entirely of migrants (M). Briefly, flocking is thought to enhance foraging efficiency and/or decrease the likelihood of being captured by a predator. Foraging efficiency may be enhanced by facilitating the location of food-rich areas (primarily R-type flocks, Moynihan 1962), or areas with few competitors (M and R, Morse 1970). Proximal flock members may flush prey (M and R, Belt 1874), or demonstrate the availability of new prey species (primarily R, Leck 1971). Flocking may permit more systematic resource harvesting (M and R, Cody 1971), reduce interspecific aggression (M and R, Austin and Smith 1972), or facilitate reduction of niche overlap (M and R, Morse 1967). The potential for flocks to reduce predation susceptibility is as diverse. Flocks may produce confusion or threat of physical damage for the predator (M and R, Tinbergen 1946). They may make prey more difficult to locate (M and R, Olson 1964) and surprise (M and R, Bates 1863). Following flocks may allow birds to learn the locations likely to harbor predators (primarily R, Moynihan 1962).

The advantages of flocking with residents are potentially great for migrants regardless of whether foraging enhancement or predation evasion hypotheses are invoked. As new arrivals, migrants may use resident flocks to learn local food types and abundances, to assess levels of competition, or to obtain information about types and local densities of predators. Even migrants that are returning to previous wintering sites are likely to encounter conditions sufficiently different to warrant reassessment of resource or predator status. Despite these potential benefits, migrant participation in resident flocks is limited. Only about half of approximately 40 species of migrants that regularly winter in forest habitats of Costa Rica, Panama, and

Colombia associate with resident flocks. (I have limited the discussion to this area because the most complete data were available for species wintering in these countries. Even for these countries data on migrant behavior in canopies of tall undisturbed lowland forests are essentially nonexistent. This has led me to omit tall canopy habitat from my discussion).

Information concerning migrant socioecology on their wintering grounds is sketchy at best, and until a more complete data base is available, a summary of flocking propensities can only be a coarse assessment. Migrant participation in mixed species flocks appears to be correlated with habitat type. In this regard, I have divided forest into closed and open canopy forests. Closed canopy signifies mature forest with a primarily complete canopy and a relatively open understory. Open canopy forest is used to denote disturbed, seasonally dry, or scrub forests with partial canopies and associated densely foliaged edges and openings. Seven migrant species tend to join resident flocks in closed canopy forest (table 1). Thirteen species regularly frequent flocks in forest with discontinuous canopy (table 1.). Flocks in open forest may contain large contingencies of migrants. Chipley (1976) found migrants made up 48 percent of mixed flocks in disturbed highland forest in Colombia. Approximately half the migrants on his study area were in flocks. In the highlands of Panama, migrants comprised 15 percent of mixed flock participants in open second growth habitat composed of an overgrown plantation of coffee and forest edges (Buskirk et al. 1974). Flocks along roadsides in the same area were composed of 23 percent migrants (Moynihan 1962). Migrant participation in flocks in closed canopy forests is more limited and generally restricted to single individuals of a few species. Jones (1977) studying antwren flocks on Barro Colorado Island reported only 8 percent of followers were migrants. At the same location, but later in a different winter, Wiley (1971) found migrants comprised 11 percent of individuals in flocks. At a montane site in Costa Rica migrants accounted for 3 percent of individuals in forest flocks (Powell 1977).

Review and Discussion

Several hypotheses have been suggested to explain the low propensity of migrant species to join resident flocks. Among these are two that were developed independently of the migrant-resident flock formation question. Willis (1972) suggested that species able to forage and watch for predators simultaneously are less likely to participate in flocks because of their relative immunity to predation. This is based on the premise that predators depend on surprise for successful captures of forest birds. Birds that maintain a high degree

Table 1. Flocking propensities of North American migrants in the neotropics

Species	Flocking propensity[1]	Foraging type[2]	Predation immunity[3]
Coccyzus americanus	X	½	1
Tyrannus tyrannus	S	1	1
Myiarchus crinitus	X	1	1
Empidonax flaviventris	X	1	1
E. virescens	X	1	1
E. traillii	X	1	1
E. minimus	X	1	1
Contopus virens	X	1	1
C. sordidulus	X	1	1
Hylocichla mustelina	X	0	1
Catharus ustulatus	S	0	1
C. minimus	S	0	1
C. fuscescens	X	½	0
Vireo flavifrons	O & C	½	0
V. philadelphicus	O	½	0
Mniotilta varia	O & C	0	0
Protonotaria citrea	S	½	0
Helmitheros vermivorus	C	0	1
Vermivora chrysoptera	O & C	½	0
V. peregrina	S & O	½	0
Dendroica petechia	X	½	0
D. magnolia	O	½	0
D. coronata	S	½	0
D. virens	O	½	0
D. cerulea	O	½	0
D. fusca	O	½	0
D. pensylvanica	O & C	½	0
D. castanea	O & C	½	0
Seiurus aurocapillus	X	0	1
S. noveboracensis	X	0	1
S. motacilla	X	0	1
Oporornis formosus	C	0	1
O. philadelphia	X	0	1
Wilsonia citrina	X	½	0
W. pusilla	O	½	0
W. canadensis	O & C	½	0
Setophaga ruticilla	O	½	0
Piranga rubra	O & C	½	½

[1] Divided into 4 categories: X = do not flock; S = form intraspecific flocks; O = join flocks in forest with incomplete canopy; C = join flocks in complete canopy forest.

[2] Following categorization of Willis 1966: O = intensive (examine nearby and enclosing surfaces carefully); 1 = extensive (check foliage and air at moderate or greater distances); ½ = intermediate.

[3] Following Buskirk (1977): 0 = vulnerable to predation, 1 = immune to predation.

George V. N. Powell

of alertness while they are foraging reduce the potential for undetected predator attacks. In accordance with this hypothesis, Willis divided birds into two foraging categories: "intensive," examine nearby and enclosing surfaces carefully, and "extensive," check foliage and air at moderate or greater distances. Migrants with exclusively extensive foraging habits are limited to the Tyrannidae; all of which forage independently of flocks. Beyond these species, the separation between intensive and extensive is more difficult, as most Parulidae fall in between the extremes. Some, such as *Helmitheros vermivorus* and *Seiurus aurocapillus* are relatively intensive foragers while others such as *Wilsonia pusilla* and *Setophaga ruticilla* are largely extensive foraging types. Assigning species into categories is subjective if not impossible, particularly for species with diverse foraging habits. On the basis of purely extensive (Tyrannidae) versus other foraging modes (table 1., substitute O's for ½'s), the observed propensities to flock are different than expected at the 94 percent level (Chi square, $\chi^2 = 7.54$, $P < 0.06$); intensive foragers have a higher propensity to flock. However, if migrants that forage intermediately are rated as a half in each category, the level of significance is markedly reduced (Chi square $\chi^2 = 0.25$, $P > 0.90$, table 1.).

Buskirk (1977) elaborated on the predation immunity hypothesis by redefining the extensive foraging group to include species which are difficult for a predator to "discover and approach unobserved." He considered sentinel foragers (species that spend large portions of their foraging time sitting quietly, scanning for cryptic food items or waiting for prey to approach) and terrestrial foragers as groups immune from predation. Following Buskirk's categorization, birds that he assumes to be more susceptible to predation have a higher propensity to flock while immune species, sentinel and ground foragers, tend not to flock (Chi square, $\chi^2 = 15.77$, $P < 0.01$, table 1.). However, currently there are no data to substantiate the assumption that sentinel foragers and particularly terrestrial foragers are immune to predation. Furthermore, both Buskirk and Willis ignore the threat of predation from snakes. Cryptic hide and strike snakes would not seem to be easily discovered by birds with extensive foraging behavior and certainly not by birds foraging in dense understory vegetation.

Goss-Custard (1972) suggested that flocking propensities are influenced by food resource distribution. Species that depend on clumped food supplies, particularly those that are transitory in nature, are likely to form flocks since individuals can potentially benefit from food patches discovered by other flock members. Under these circumstances, solitary foraging is presumed to be disadvantageous because solitary birds run the risk of being unable to locate new patches. In contrast, species that feed on a dispersed food resources are less likely to form flocks because flocking may increase competition for resources. Unfortunately, a lack of data on characteristics of the food supplies of most wintering migrants precludes objective testing of this hypothesis. Generally the food of insectivorous birds is asssumed to be dispersed. However, migrant concentration on patchy habitats suggests that their food may be more clumped than expected. Observations of color-banded migrants in highland Panama and Costa Rica indicate they linger in patches of dense foliage (Buskirk et al 1974; pers. obs.).

Additional hypotheses have been formulated in specific reference to the failure of migrants to associate with residents. Willis (1966) suggested that competiton with residents discouraged migrants from associating with them. While observing agonistic interactions between migrants and resident antbirds he found that residents consistently dominated the migrants. However, aside from aggregations at army-ant swarms, agonistic encounters between residents and migrants are uncommon and appear to be evenly balanced as to outcome (Chipley 1976; pers. obs.). In Costa Rica, I observed 108 interspecific agonistic interactions between flock members of which only 3 were between migrant and resident. Migrants were dominant in 2 of the 3 encounters.

Smith (1975) suggested that insectivorous migrants which set up winter territories are precluded from joining flocks by the constraints of territoriality. However, most residents that participated in mixed flocks in Costa Rica defended territories throughout the year (Powell 1977). Territory owners were restricted to associating with flocks that were in their territories so that intraspecific group size was limited to pairs or pairs with young. However, territorial behavior did not prevent flock formation. One of the most consistent flock participants on the highland Costa Rica study area, *Vermivora chrysoptera*, was intraspecifically agonistic. Its aggresion included supplanting and short-distance chasing. A single marked individual returned two years in succession to the study area. A second migrant, *Wilsonia pusilla*, which occasionally associated with mixed flocks in edge habitat, exhibited agonistic behavior against conspecifics. I had too few color-marked individuals to determine the precise nature of territoriality exercised by this species. However, they definitely excluded conspecifics from their proximity. Moynihan (1962) found *Wilsonia* to be "very territorial." My observations suggest they defend an area of several meters surrounding themselves, an extended individual space, as the shortness of typical chases did

Table 2. Foraging behavior and characteristics of flock participation of species that formed mixed species flocks in the understory[1]

Species	Foraging zone	Flocking frequency (%)	Duration of association (min)	Home range (ha)
Permanent residents				
Basileuterus tristriatus	Foliage	100	*	2.7
Premnoplex brunnescens	Stalk (S & T)	75	109	2.9
Henicorhina leucophrys	Rummage Stalk (s)	44	34	0.7
Basileuterus culicivorus	Foliage	34	65	4.1
Atlapetes brunneinucha	Ground Stalk (s)	26	22	0.8
Chlorospingus ophthalmicus	Rummage Veg	20	13	0.5
Myioborus miniatus	Aerial Foliage	19	14	0.8
Syndactyla subalaris	Rummage Stalk (T & S)	17	55	2.6
Cranioleuca erythrops	Stalk (S) Rummage	14	29	2.4
Xiphorhynchus erythropygius	Stalk (T)	13	46	3.0
Sittasomus griseicapillus	Stalk (T)	12	42	3.5
Migrants				
Mniotilta varia	Stalk (S & T)	1	11	no data
Vermivora chrysoptera	Foliage	6	18	"
Dendroica virens	Foliage	1	10	"
Oporornis formosus	Ground	5	83	"
Wilsonia pusilla	Foliage	3	8	"
Piranga rubra	Veg Aerial	1	6	"

[1] Symbols: Foraging zone (Aerial, insects captured from the air; Foliage, arthropods gleaned from foliage and branchlets; Ground, arthropods and plant materials obtained from the ground; Rummage, search through detritus and epiphytes for arthropods; Stalk, glean arthropods from surfaces of trunks and major branches, T, or smaller stems and branches, S; Veg, feed on reproductive parts of plants).

* nuclear species.

not support a conclusion of true territoriality. Other migrants on the study area gave no indication of being territorial yet failed to join flocks.

As a final hypothesis, I would like to suggest that the low propensity of migrants to join resident flocks, particularly flocks inhabiting the understory of closed canopied forests, reflects an incompatibility of spacial use patterns between migrants and permanent residents. These incompatibilities are less outstanding in open canopied forests where migrants have a greater tendency to join resident flocks. I studied understory mixed species flocks intensively for three years in a middle elevation undisturbed wet forest in western Costa Rica. At the same time, I made intermittent observations of flocks inhabiting edge and wooded pastures in the vicinity. The understory flocks were composed primarily of permanent residents that were permanently pairbonded. The nucleus or leader of the

flocks, *Basileuterus tristriatus*, occupied home ranges of 2.5–3 ha. Ten additional species that together with *Basileuterus* comprised 90 percent of individuals observed in flocks occupied territories that ranged from .5 to 4.2 ha (table 2.). At least seven of these species actively defended their territories throughout the year. Primary song was generally used to dispel frequent trespassing by conspecific neighbors. When trespassers did not retreat immediately, agonistic behavior progressed to supplanting, chasing, and physical fighting. I observed 446 agonistic encounters associated with trespassing during 700 hr of observation. Flock members therefore integrated territorial defense with foraging suggesting that movement patterns might be influenced by the need for effective territorial defense. To analyze foraging patterns, I followed flocks for periods of up to eight hours and plotted their locations every five minutes. Direction of movement was mea-

George V. N. Powell

Table 3. Directional probabilities and spatial utilization by simulated and observed mixed species flocks.[1]

Distribution	Simulated random walks[2]						
	Directional Proportions				Locations visited		
	Ahead	Right	Left	Reverse	Total	Once	Twice
standard deviation							
15	83	7	7	3	277	93	25
25	75	11	11	3	268	97	26
35	67	16	16	3	266	97	28
45	59	19	19	3	257	97	34
55	53	22	22	3	239	146	40
65	47	24	23	6	225	105	42

Month	Field data (adjusted to 400 steps)						
	Directional Proportions				Locations visited		
	Ahead	Right	Left	Reverse	Total	Once	Twice
Sept	76	8	10	6	286	93	21
Nov	82	8	7	4	304	79	13
Feb	76	9	10	5	262	97	26

[1] Observed data were collected on 4 consecutive complete days in each of 3 mos. (for explanation, see text)

[2] Simulations derived from bounded random walks of 400 steps. Means of 25 random walks for each standard deviation.

sured relative to previous movement: straight ahead = 180°, a right turn = 90°, and left = 270°. Field data were standardized for comparison with computer simulated random walks by imposing a fixed distance of 7 m (the smallest measured distance) between turns. Movements of more than 7 m in one direction were divided into 7-m increments with each increment considered a new movement straight ahead. For example, a move 17 m in one direction was considered to be three moves: 7, 7, and 3 m; the direction of the first move was relative to the previous move; directions of the second and third moves were straight ahead. By these methods, flock movements were converted to distributions that approximated circular normal distributions or equivalents of truncated normal curves extending between 0° and 360° and centered on straight ahead (180°). Comparison of these movement distributions to computer simulated walks indicates that flock movements approximate a random course with a concentration of movement ahead (table 3.). These data indicate that flocks do not follow a strategy of concentrating in or returning frequently to resource rich patches. Instead, movements throughout their

ranges are relatively uniform. A summary of four complete consecutive days of movements by a flock further demonstrates the generally uniform area visitation with flock home ranges (figure 1.). The adoption of random movement patterns and uniform territory utilization may reflect a movement scheme that sacrifices optimal foraging to facilitate the maintenance of territorial integrity. On the study area as with much of the neotropics, sufficient food resources were available to permit year-round residency. Where year-round occupancy is possible, the tendency for permanent residents to be dominant selects for permanent residency among the breeding population. Permanent residents occupy large territories which insure sufficient food resources during seasonal scarcities. Frequent trespassing, particularly by adjacent conspecifics, may cause residents to adopt movement patterns that enhance territorial defense.

Six species of migrants from North America were present on the study area between October and March (table 2.). Except for *Oporornis*, all were commonly observed in the vicinity of the study area. Two species, *Dendroica virens* and *Wilsonia pusilla* generally foraged

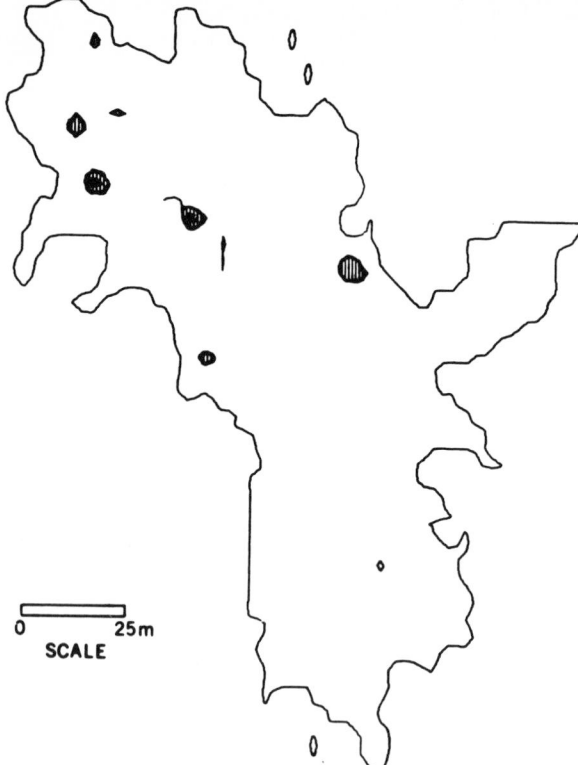

Figure 1. Pattern of spatial utilization by a mixed species flock in the understory of a closed canopied forest during 4 consecutive days in November. The flock visited quadrats bounded by the solid line from 1 to 3 times; within the solid line, quadrats visited 4 to 6 times are indicated by the hash-lined irregular circles; the 2 small solid areas within the hashed areas were visited 7 or more times. Intensity of use is thus seen to be irregular.

in dense foliage on edges and light gaps, *Oporornis formosus* frequented the forest interior where it foraged on and near the ground. *Mniotitla varia* and *Vermivora chrysoptera* were found in both edge and interior habitats with *Mniotitla* foraging primarily on trunks and large branches and *Vermivora* gleaning arthropods from foliage and branchlets. Only one migrant species, *Oporornis*, followed mixed flocks for extended periods; *Vermivora* and *Mniotitla* followed for short periods. The remaining migrants, *Dendroica virens*, *Wilsonia pusilla*, and *Piranga rubra* (which foraged extensively on Hymenoptera at nests) were occasionally found in mixed flocks on edges, but rarely in the understory.

If resident flocks sacrifice optimal foraging to include territorial maintenance in movement patterns as suggested above, then the cost to migrants joining flocks is increased. Migrants are not restricted by the need for year-round territories to secure breeding sites so they can concentrate on resource-rich patches moving to new sites as old ones are depressed. This cost is compounded for migrants that feed in patchy

habitats. Following flocks in forest understory would draw migrants away from the patches of dense foliage associated with edges and light gaps. In acccordance with this hypothesis, the greater propensity of migrants to associate with resident flocks in open forest relates to the different foraging characteristics of flocks occupying more open habitats. These flocks tend to move less rapidly (i.e., *Chlorospingus ophthalmicus* flocks moved at a rate of 1.3 m/min or less than half the rate of understory flocks). Flocks I observed in open habitat moved more irregularly and frequently lingered for long period in single trees or patches of dense foliage, and they returned more frequently to areas previously visited. Therefore, migrants could associate with these flocks without forfeiting an optimal foraging strategy.

Conclusions

A thorough discussion of migrant participation in flocks on their wintering grounds is precluded by insufficient data. Studies of neotropical flocks have generally concentrated on permanent residents with only ephemeral observations of migrant associates. There have as yet been no studies of flocks composed entirely of wintering migrants nor have there been studies of some types of resident flocks that appear to be favored by migrants (i.e., *Hylophilus* spp flocks). Migrant propensities to remain in second growth have frequently been noted, but characteristics of food supplies within this habitat, with respect to abundance and temporal distribution, remain undetermined. Little is known about the site fidelity of migrants throughout their winter residency, particularly in edge or light gap habitats. Morton (pers. comm.) reported observing a high density of migrant warblers at a site from which they were completely absent later in winter. Movements of this type suggest that migrants are opportunists, occupying temporary resources unexploitable by permanent residents. If this strategy is applicable to the migrant population in general, then the tendency for segregation of migrant and permanent-resident populations may be a manifestation of differences in habitat utilization. However, without additional data on the biology and food resources of migrants, explanations of their relative propensities to join flocks must be speculative.

Available data do not support the hypothesis that residents agonistically exclude migrants from flocks. However, this does not preclude the possibility that more efficient resident foraging might prevent migrants from utilizing habitat with large resident populations. Migrant winter territoriality should not prevent interspecific flocking since some mixed species flocks are composed almost entirely of territorial residents. Propensity of migrants to join mixed flocks

George V. N. Powell

appears to correlate with susceptibility to predation. It is suggested, therefore, that migrants able to maintain effective surveillance while feeding derive less benefit from the antipredator values of flocking. However, neither the capacity of foraging migrants to maintain surveillance nor their relative immunity to predation has been measured. The distribution of migrant food resources has been suggested as a determanent of flocking propensities. Migrants that exploit patchily distributed resources are predicted to by flockers that gain information about food types and locations from flocking residents. This hypothesis is so far untestable for lack of food distribution data. I have presented some data to suggest that migrants may avoid joining resident flocks in some habitats because the resident movement patterns compromise efficient foraging for patterns that allow territorial residents to patrol their territories. This would raise the cost of following for nonterritorial residents, particularly in understory and subcanopy habitat where flocks tend to forage over large home ranges.

Literature Cited

Austin, G. T., and E. L. Smith
1972. Winter foraging ecology of mixed insectivorous bird flocks in oak woodland in southern Arizona. Condor 74:17–24.

Bates, H. W.
1863. *The Naturalist on the River Amazons*. London: Murray.

Belt, T. W.
1874. *The Naturalist in Nicaragua*. London: Longmans.

Buskirk, W. H.
1977. Social systems in a tropical forest avifauna. Amer. Natur. 110:293–310.

Buskirk, W. H., G. V. N. Powell, J. F. Wittenberger, R. E. Buskirk, and T. U. Powell.
1972. Interspecific bird flocks in tropical highland Panama. Auk 89:612–24.

Chipley, R. M.
1976. Impact of wintering migrant wood warblers on resident insectivorous passerines in a subtropical Colombian oak woods. Living Bird 15:119–43.

Cody, M. L.
1971. Finch flocks in the Mojave Desert. Theoret. Pop. Biol. 2:142–58.

Goss-Custard, J. D.
1972. Survival on a bleak Scottish estruary. Natural History 81:68–73.

Jones, S. E.
1977. Coexistence in mixed species antwren flocks. Oikos 29:366–75.

Leck, C. F.
1971. Measurement of social attractions between tropical passerine birds. Wils. Bull. 83:278–283.

Morse, D. H.
1967. Foraging relationships of brown-headed nuthatches and pine warblers. Ecol. 48:94–103.

1970. Ecological aspects of some mixed-species foraging flocks of birds. Ecol. Monogr. 40:119–68.

Moynihan, M.
1962. The organization and probable evolution of some mixed-species flocks of neotropical birds. Smithsonian Misc. Coll. 143:1–140.

Olson, F. C. W.
1964. The survival value of fish schooling. Conseil Permanent Inter. pour l'Exploration de la Mer. J. du Conseil 29:115–16.

Powell, G. V. N.
1977. Socioecology of mixed species flocks in a neotropical forest. Ph. D. diss., Univ. of California, Davis.

Smith, N. G.
1975. "Spshing noise": biological significance of its attraction and nonattraction by birds. Proc. Nat. Acad. Sci. USA. 72:1411–14.

Tinbergen, L.
1946. De sperwer als roofvijand van zangvogels. Ardea 34:1–213.

Wiley, R. H.
1971. Cooperative roles of mixed species flocks of antwrens (Formicariidae). Auk 88:881–92.

Willis, E. O.
1966. The role of migrant birds at swarms of army ants. Living Bird 5:187–231.

1972. The behavior of spotted antbirds. A.O.U. Monogr. 10:1–162.

Winterbottom, J. M.
1949. Mixed bird parties in the tropics, with special reference to northern Rhodesia. Auk 66:258–63.

WILLIAM H. BUSKIRK
Biology Department
Earlham College
Richmond, Indiana 47374

Influence of Meteorological Patterns and Trans-Gulf Migration on the Calendars of Latitudinal Migrants

ABSTRACT   A large proportion of the birds migrating between eastern North America and the Central American tropics cross the Gulf of Mexico in spring and fall. This 1,000-km overwater flight is energy-expensive and hazardous. Selection is assumed to have optimized the calendars of trans-Gulf migration relative to the probabilities of birds encountering unfavorable flight conditions over water. The peak of spring trans-Gulf migration and the greatest frequency of high magnitude autumnal flights coincide with recognizable improvement in flight conditions during mid-April and at the beginning of October. Improved trans-Gulf flight conditions cannot be unambiguously discriminated from changes in seasonal climatic conditions in eastern North America. Yet, the coincidence of these changes in climate and the timing of migration indicate a temperate zone-based determination of the calendars of latitudinal migrants. If, however, tropical phenomena exist that influence the duration of winter residence, then the periods of April–May and September–October should be times of changing competitive pressure from permanent residents and/or changing resource abundance throughout the neotropics. That this is not the case lends support to the conclusion that migration calendars are determined by temperate-zone phenomena.

Introduction

The roles of latitudinal migrant birds in tropical ecosystems depends, among many factors, upon the duration of time that migrants spend in the tropics. Migration calendars can be expected to result from the optimization of time allocated to residence or passage in different geographical regions. The period migrants spend in the tropics may depend on conditions there. Arrivals of migrants may be timed to coincide with increased food supply or decreased competitive pressure among residents, as at the onset of reproduction. The timing of movements in and out of the tropics, however, may depend more on factors outside the tropics, along migration routes or on breeding grounds. Consideration of these extratropical influences may yield a significant perspective in the interpretation of migration calendars and therefore of migrant ecology in the tropics. This paper investigates the potential relationship between changing meteorological patterns over the Gulf of Mexico and the timing of migration between eastern North America and the Central American tropics.

Trans-Gulf Migration

The great majority of migrant species moving between the neotropics and eastern North America crosses the Gulf of Mexico (figure 1) during the spring and fall (Griscom 1945; Lowery 1946; Paynter 1953; Siebenaler 1954; Stevenson 1957; Buskirk 1968; Gauthreaux 1971, 1972). For many of these species, most of their population use the trans-Gulf route. For others, varying proportions of their populations take a circum-Gulf route through eastern Mexico (Stevenson 1957). Most spring migrants probably cross the Gulf. In the fall, however, many migrants move around the Gulf (Able 1972), and the relative magnitude of trans-Gulf versus circum-Gulf movement is not certain but appears to be less than in spring.

The 1,000-km overwater flight must constitute a significant selective factor on the migratory behavior of these birds. The trans-Gulf crossing is energy-expensive and hazardous. Vernal flights depart from the Yucatán Peninsula, during the night approximately 24 hr after departing the northern Gulf coast (Buskirk 1968). With light northerly or northeasterly winds, flight times drop to approximately 20 hr. Strong northerly, post-frontal winds reduce crossing time to as little as 12 hr. Strong opposing, southerly winds produce flight times estimated at 30 hr. In the manner of spring "fallouts," large numbers of exhausted birds land on barrier beaches in northern Yucatán during periods of strong southerly winds over the central Gulf (Buskirk 1968).

In addition to the energy demands of prolonged continuous flight, trans-Gulf migrants risk perishing in the Gulf during severe weather with precipitation and opposing or violent winds. Cases of massive mortality have been reported from shipboard, on oilrigs and reefs, and on the Gulf shores (Paynter 1953; Bullis 1954; James 1956; Gauthreaux 1971).

A migrant embarking on a trans-Gulf flight would need to be able to predict weather conditions up to 1,000-km away and 12 to 24 hr in advance to judge the likelihood of a successful crossing. While prediction of this sort may be within the abilities of trans-Gulf migrants, it has not been sufficiently accurate to avoid occasional mass mortality. Able (1972) observed that fall migrants select nights with following, northerly winds when embarking on the trans-Gulf flight. This choice assures favorable conditions for the first part of the flight but may mean that migrants will overtake frontal weather on the Gulf (Able 1972). Gauthreaux (1971) suggests that spring migrants encountering unfavorable weather soon after departure return to the southern Gulf coast.

Among other responses to selection favoring an energetically efficient and safe flight should be the adoption of a migration calendar that puts migrants in the Gulf region when the probability of high energy demand and hazard on the Gulf flight is minimal. If calendar selection has occurred, movements to staging areas near the Gulf and trans-Gulf crossings should be most frequent in periods of predictably favorable winds (southerly in spring, northerly in fall) with low likelihood of encountering adverse conditions (northerly winds in spring, southerly in fall).

In the next two sections, the timing of trans-Gulf migration and the seasonal play of weather regimes will be reviewed. Then, a discussion of their relationships and of selective factors on migration calendar follows.

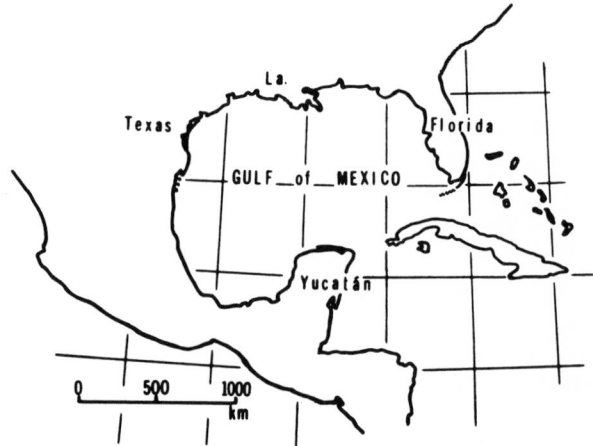

Figure 1. Map of the Gulf of Mexico region.

William H. Buskirk

Seasonal Patterns of Trans-Gulf Migration

Spring trans-Gulf migration has been well-studied (Lowery 1946; 1951; Gauthreaux 1971, 1972, and others). Migration begins in late February when Purple Martins (*Progne subis*) cross the Gulf. But it is not until mid-March that the first significant flights of passerines arrive (Gauthreaux 1968). Many of these early migrants breed in the southeastern United States. From April 1 until mid-May, trans-Gulf flights occur almost daily, with a peak in late April and early May (Newman 1957; Imhof 1965; Gauthreaux 1968). During the end of April, Gauthreaux (1968) found upwards of 80,000 birds per mile of migration front arriving on the Louisiana coast each day with little day-to-day variation in magnitude. In early April, flight densities were one-third to one-quarter that figure. Spring flights fail to arrive on the northern Gulf coast only when strong frontal weather reaches the southern Gulf (Gauthreaux 1971).

Autumnal trans-Gulf migration has not been as intensively studied as its spring counterpart. During the fall of 1967, I watched trans-Gulf migrants arriving on the north coast of Yucatán (Buskirk 1968). Using telescopic, lunar, ceilometer and flight call counts (for techniques see Lowery 1951; Lowery and Newman 1963; Buskirk 1968, and Gauthreaux 1969). I saw or heard migrants arriving from over the Gulf on 40 of 45 observation days between 2 September and 23 October. On the five dates without recorded arrivals I made only diurnal observations and migrants may have come in at night. Although fall trans-Gulf flights arrived almost daily, the magnitude of flights varied greatly and irregularly. On 21 days, the maximum number of birds recorded per hour failed to exceed 20, but on seven days peak hourly rates exceeded 200 birds. On two days, 800 or more birds per hour passed through the field of a vertically oriented 20X telescope. The largest flights of the season (29 September, 10 October, and 19 October) co-occurred with the only three periods of strong northerly, post-frontal winds across the Gulf (28–30 September, 9–10 October, and 16–19 October). Able (1972) found fall migrants departing southwestern Louisiana on trans-Gulf flights only under conditions of strong northerly, post-frontal winds. His dates for trans-Gulf flights, like the high magnitude flights in Yucatán, occurred relatively late in the season (7–8, 13–14, and 14–15 October). The only other dates for high magnitude trans-Gulf migration are those of Lowery and Newman (1966) and Siebenaler (1954) who simultaneously recorded flights originating on the nights of 2–3 and 3–4 October 1952 when post-frontal winds extended into the northern Gulf.

Almost daily arrival of at least some migrants on the north coast of Yucatán does not agree with Able's (1972) findings and suggests the Yucatán birds may have departed elsewhere on the Gulf Coast than Louisiana. As autumn winds in the Florida panhandle have northerly (northeasterly) vectors more frequently than winds west of the Mississippi Delta, Yucatán flights may originate there. A northeastern Gulf origin for Yucatán arrivals is further substantiated by my observation that large, midday flights did not reach Yucatán on 17 October 1967 when strong northerly, post-frontal winds had covered the Gulf the previous night west of a cold front passing through Mobile, Alabama, and south to Yucatán (Figure 3a, 3d). The following day, after the Florida panhandle had come under the influence of post-frontal winds on the night of 17–18 October, the heaviest flight of the fall reached Yucatán (Buskirk 1968).

The daily irregularity in magnitude of fall trans-Gulf crossings makes it difficult to identify a peak of passage. The "Summary of Seasonal Occurrences" in Lowery (1974) shows that most passerine migrants and summer residents wintering in the tropics have left Louisiana by 1 November. Migration in Louisiana peaks during the last half of September, but migrants are abundant from 1 September through 15 October. Most summer resident species depart Louisiana during the first half of October. These Louisiana birds cannot be assumed to be trans-Gulf migrants as many passerines leave Louisiana on circum-Gulf headings in fall (Able 1972). However, these migrants are in a staging area suitable for crossing the Gulf and may do so if northerly airflow begins (Able 1972). From these data, the magnitude of fall trans-Gulf migration would seem to be greatest in the first half of October.

Seasonal Patterns of Gulf Weather

Daily wind patterns over the Gulf of Mexico were characterized and tabulated for 10 years (1953–56, 1959–64). These years were selected on the basis of availability of weather maps in the California State Library and to avoid weather data for the years in which studies used to determine the seasonal pattern of trans-Gulf migration were made (Lowery and Newman 1966; Buskirk 1968; Gauthreaux 1968, 1971; Able 1972). This selection of weather data should assure its independence from the migration calendar data.

Five wind pattern categories were defined on the basis of wind direction and velocity as determined from isobar configurations on Daily Weather Maps (U.S. Department of Commerce, 1953–56, 1959–64). The spacing between isobars is related to wind speed. The steeper the barometric gradient, and therefore the

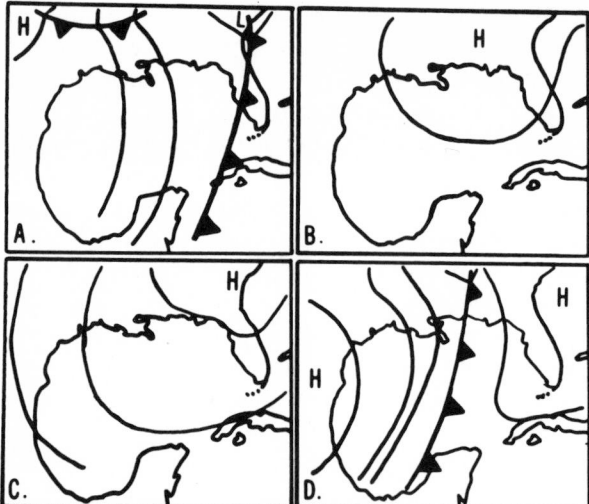

Figure 2.   Examples of Gulf meteorological conditions: A. northerly winds, 18 October 1967; B. light variable or easterly winds, 14 October 1967; C. southerly winds, 15 october 1967; and D. active front, 17 October 1967. All maps are for 0000 CST.

narrower the isobar spacing, the stronger the winds. Wind direction at 600–1,000-m altitude roughly parallels isobar orientation and blows clockwise around high pressure systems and counterclockwise around lows. The following categories of Gulf wind patterns were used:

1) Northerly winds with 75 percent or more of the Gulf under moderate to strong winds (i.e. a net gradient of 6 or more millibars across the Gulf) blowing from the north. These winds are typical of post-frontal conditions. An example of strong northerly winds is shown in figure 2A.

2) Light variable or easterly winds with 75 percent or more of the Gulf under less than a 6 millibar gradient or with moderate easterly winds. Light variable winds occur most frequently when a weak high pressure system is centered over the Gulf states region (figure 2B). Easterly winds are grouped with light variable winds as conditions not clearly expected to aid or hinder trans-Gulf migrants.

3) Southerly winds with 75 percent or more of the Gulf under moderate to strong southerly, most typically southeasterly, winds. This pattern is best developed with the presence of a strong high pressure system over the Atlantic somewhere near the northern Bahamas (figure 2c).

4) Active frontal conditions characterized by a front over the Gulf with markedly different airflow orientations before and after its passage (figure 2D). Precipitation and turbulent winds are commonly associated with fronts.

5) Other patterns with no single clearly defineable wind orientation over 75 percent of the Gulf. A variety of complex weather systems are covered by this category. Most frequently, and especially during the fall, they involve the presence of low pressure cells, tropical lows or hurricanes, in or near the Gulf.

The spring wind pattern summary shows that unfavorable conditions (fronts and northerly winds) decline in frequency through the season (figure 3). A marked improvement in flight conditions occurs in mid-April. Favorable trans-Gulf winds are most frequent in late April, in sharp contrast to their low frequency during the preceeding several weeks. By late May and early June, light variable and easterly winds dominate Gulf weather. Frontal intrusions into the Gulf and strong southerly winds are both less frequent at this time. Thus, conditions for trans-Gulf migration improve through the spring but show a marked improvement in mid-April. Thereafter, decreasing frequencies of both southerly airflow and frontal weather combine to make assesment of the relative favorableness of conditions for trans-Gulf migration difficult. No striking change in weather occurs through the end of May.

In fall, favorable post-frontal and northerly winds increase in frequency throughout the season (figure 3). Improvement in migration conditions is generally continuous, but greatest changes occur at the beginnings of September and October. Opposing, southerly winds occur at nearly constant frequency throughout the fall. Tropical storms and hurricanes are most frequent

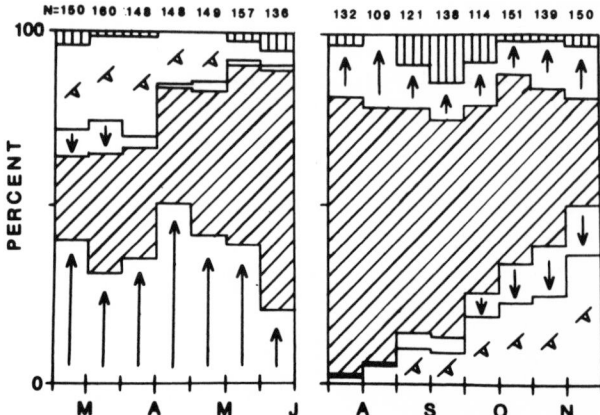

Figure 3.   Frequencies of Gulf meterological conditions, a 10-year summary. Percentage of dates with each weather type. Symbols are: toothed line, active front; downward arrow, northerly winds; cross-hatched, light variable or easterly winds; upright arrow, southerly winds; and vertical lines, undeterminable. *n* is number of dates in sample, weather maps for some dates were not available. Note shifts in position between spring and fall. Favorable conditions for trans-Gulf flight are at bottom of column, less favorable are above them.

William H. Buskirk

during September and early October in the 10-year sample considered here. Their impact on flight conditions across the Gulf is difficult to interpret. A hurricane in the eastern Gulf sends a strong surge of wind south over most of the Gulf. On the other hand, when centered in the western Gulf, winds are for the most part southerly.

Discussion

In both spring and fall, the meteorological conditions favoring rapid trans-Gulf flights with low likelihood of encountering opposing winds occur late in the season. In spring, flight conditions improve until late April then remain more or less constant through May. The peak of spring trans-Gulf migration in late April and early May corresponds to a period of strong southerly airflow with infrequent frontal activity. The frequency of southerly winds is 16 percent greater in late April than early April, and northerly winds and fronts are 16 percent less frequent. Trans-Gulf migration terminates in mid-May, before any significant change in trans-Gulf flight conditions occurs.

In fall, high magnitude trans-Gulf migrations occur under postfrontal conditions with most migrants crossing during late September and the first three weeks of October. Northerly and post-frontal winds influence the northern Gulf coast on 39 percent of early November and 51 percent of late November dates. These frequencies are 1.5 to 4 times those in early October and September. Thus, most crossings occur in advance of the periods of highest frequency of favorable winds.

In each case, migration peaks are in advance of what would be expected solely on the basis of flight conditions. Late May flight conditions are little different from those in early May, yet migration terminates in mid-May. The frequency of northerly, post-frontal winds, and particularly those penetrating to Yucatán and beyond, is greater in November than in September and early October when migration occurs.

The advanced timing of migration in both seasons suggests that other factors in addition to meteorological conditions over the Gulf of Mexico influence migration calendars. Logical arguments based on temperature zone phenomena can be made for the early migration peaks in spring and fall. Rapidly increasing food and cover abundance north of the Gulf and the selective advantages of lengthened reproductive period and early territorial establishment, can be expected to move trans-Gulf flight calendars ahead in spring. An advantage is gained by individuals reaching nesting areas as soon as they become useable. Declining food and cover supplies and deteriorating climatic conditions undoubtedly select for earlier autumnal departures.

Optimization of the Migration Calendar

Optimization of migration calendar in the context of conflicting selective pressures should result in concentrations of migration at times corresponding to marked changes in those pressures. For instance, trans-Gulf crossing should be most frequent in periods immediately following predictable improvement in meteorological conditions. Indeed, pulses of migration appear to occur following the marked improvement of trans-Gulf flight conditions in mid-April and the beginning of October. Such optimization would account also for the earlier spring migration calendars of species breeding in the southeastern United States. The advantages of an advanced flight calendar for them would be greater than for species with breeding areas that become useable later in the season. In the fall, an early migration calendar would not be as crucial for granivores and frugivores as for insectivores whose food supplies decrease earlier. Changes in the species composition of fall trans-Gulf flights demonstrate that insectivores pass earlier than frugivores and granivores. On the basis of call notes and the identification of some birds passing through the telescope field during the day, wood warblers (Parulidae) were the most abundant arrivals on the Yucatán coast through the third week of September. Thrushes (*Hylocichla*) replaced warblers as the most obvious group during the third week of September and remained prevalent into mid-October. Fringillids (mainly *Passerina*) and grey catbirds (*Dumetella carolinensis*) appeared to predominate in the flights of middle and late October (Buskirk 1968).

Clearly, changes in food and cover availability are not independent of Gulf meteorological conditions. The northward advance of spring weather across eastern North America results in part from increasingly frequent and sustained penetration of warm southerly airflow off the Gulf of Mexico. Given this lack of independence, Gulf and temperate region factors appear to be adequate to explain, in a rather precise way, the timing of migration of birds to and from the Central American tropics. This conclusion is better supported for spring migration than for fall. The implication of this conclusion is that the spring departure of migrants from Central America is not likely to be a function of tropics-based selective pressures.

A prediction resulting from this conclusion would be that the timing of neotropical departure would not necessarily correspond to profound and geographically simultaneous changes in tropical environments. April and early May, late September, and early October should not be characterized by widespread changes in food supply. In fact, geographical synchrony does not exist. In lowland Central America insect standing crop peaks in the wet months from May to November (Janzen and Schoener 1968; Robinson and Robinson 1970; Janzen 1973a, 1973b) yet in the highlands the peak occurs at other times (Janzen 1973a, 1973b; Buskirk and Buskirk 1976). Patterns of leaf flushing, flowering and fruiting in tropical trees do not show geographic synchrony (Frankie, Baker, and Opler 1974). The proposition that migrants leave the tropics to avoid unfavorable ecological circumstances there is untenable when faced with the need to explain a vast and synchronous exodus in the context of a geographic mosaic of very different departure point conditions.

Acknowledgments

I thank George H. Lowery, Jr. and Robert J. Newman for their support and discussion of my work in Yucatán while I was a student at the Louisiana State University Museum of Zoology. I have benefitted from discussions and comments from Kenneth P. Able, Sidney A. Gauthreaux, and Neal Smith. An early copy of the manuscript was reviewed by D. Levey and B. Whitney.

Literature Cited

Able, K. P.
1972.   Fall migration in coastal Louisiana and the evolution of migration patterns in the Gulf region. Wils. Bull. 84:231–42.

Bagg, A. M.
1957.   The changing seasons: a summary of spring migration. Aud. Field Notes 11:312–25.

Bullis, H. R., Jr.
1954.   Trans-Gulf migration, spring 1952. Auk 71:298–305.

Buskirk, W. H.
1968.   The arrival of trans-Gulf migrants on the northern coast of Yucatan in fall. Unpublished thesis, Baton Rouge: Louisiana State Univ.

Buskirk, R. E. and W. H. Buskirk
1976.   Changes in arthropod abundance in a highland Costa Rican forest. Amer. Midl. Nat. 95:288–98.

Frankie, G. W., H. G. Baker, and P. A. Opler
1974.   Comparative phenological studies of trees in tropical wet and dry forests in the lowlands of Costa Rica. J. Ecol. 62:881–919.

Gauthreaux, S. A., Jr.
1968.   A quantitative study by radar and telescope of the vernal migration of birds in coastal Louisiana. Unpublished Ph.D. diss. Baton Rouge, Louisiana State Univ. (Univ. Microfilms, Ann Arbor, Michigan. Diss. Abstr., 29:3538-B).

1969.   A portable ceilometer technique for studying low-level nocturnal migration. Bird-Banding 40:309–20.

1971.   A radar and direct visual study of passerine spring migration in southern Louisiana. Auk 88:343–65.

1972.   Behavioral responses of migrating birds to daylight and darkness: a radar and direct visual study. Wils. Bull. 84:136–48.

Griscom, L.
1945.   *Modern Bird Study*. Cambridge, Mass.: Harvard Univ. Press.

Imhof, T.
1965.   Spring migration: central southern region. Aud. Field Notes 19:482–85.

Janzen, D. H.
1973a.   Sweep samples of tropical foliage insects: description of study sites, with data on species abundance and size distributions. Ecol. 54:657–86.

1973b.   Sweep samples of tropical foliage insects: effects of seasons, vegetation types, elevation, time of day, and insularity. Ecol. 54:687–708.

Janzen, D. H., and T. W. Schoener
1968.   Differences in insect abundance and diversity between wetter and drier sites during a tropical dry season. Ecol. 49:96–110.

James, P.
1956.   Destruction of warblers on Padre Island, Texas, in May 1951. Wils. Bull. 68:224–27.

Lowery, G. H., Jr.
1946.   Evidence of trans-Gulf migration. Auk 63:175–210.

Lowery, G. H., Jr.
1951.   A quantitative study of the nocturnal migration of birds. Univ. Kansas Publ. Mus. Nat. Hist. 3:361–472.

1974.   Louisiana Birds. Baton Rouge: Louisiana State Univ. Press.

Lowery, G. H., Jr., and R. J. Newman.
1963.   Studying bird migration with a telescope. Spec. Publ. Mus. Zool., Louisiana State Univ.

Lowery, G. H., Jr., and R. J. Newman
1966.   A continentwide view of bird migration on four nights in October. Auk 83:547–86.

Monroe, B. L., Jr.
1968.   A distributional survey of the birds of Honduras. A.O.U. Ornithol. Monogr. 7:1–458.

Newman, R. J.
1957.   Spring migration: central southern region. Aud. Field Notes 11:350–57.

1958.   Spring migration: central southern region. Aud. Field Notes 12:358–62.

Newman, R. J., and G. H. Lowery, Jr.
1959.   The changing seasons: a summary of the 1959 spring migration and its geographic background. Aud. Field Notes 13:346–52.

Paynter, R. A.
1953.   Autumnal migrants on the Campeche Bank. Auk 70:338–49.

Robinson, M. H., and B. Robinson
1970.   Prey caught by a sample population of the spider
        Argiope argentata (Araneae: Araneidae) in Panama: a
        year's census data. Zool. J. Linn. Soc. 49:345–57.

Siebenaler, J. B.
1954.   Notes on autumnal trans-Gulf migration of birds.
        Condor 56:43–48.

Stevenson, H. M.
1957.   The relative magnitude of the trans-Gulf and cir-
        cum-Gulf spring migrations. Wils. Bull. 69:39–77.

U. S. Department of Commerce
1964.   *Daily Weather Map.* 1 March–15 June, 1 August–30
        November, 1953–1956, 1959–1964. Environmental
        Science Services, Weather Bureau.

RUSSELL GREENBERG
Museum of Vertebrate Zoology
and Department of Zoology
University of California
Berkeley, California 94720

Demographic Aspects of Long-distance Migration

Introduction

Migration is a spectacular attribute of birds. While it has attracted the attention of research probing its mechanisms, the selective bases for the evolution of migration and patterns of migration, such as partial, disjunct, leap-frog (Salomenson 1955), only recently have been given more than superficial treatment. In particular, little consideration has been given the trade-offs in demographic parameters such as productivity or adult and juvenile survivorship. Lack (1968) considered the primary trade-off to be between risk of migration and the increase in reproduction accrued to a migrant. Von Haartman (1968) viewed increase in survivorship and increase in productivity to be conflicting factors in the evolution of migration. Basically, he contended that residency in proximity to breeding range will confer certain reproductive advantages which have to be weighed against the decrease in survivorship associated with wintering in a more rigorous area. Ketterson and Nolan (1976) suggested that reproductive advantage associated with proximity to the breeding ground was one of the factors that might contribute to more northerly wintering of male than female Dark-eyed Junco (*Junco hyemalis*).

This paper reviews life history consequences of long-distance migration in birds. I concentrate on two major considerations: 1) what general demographic patterns characterize species undergoing long-distance, mainly neotropical, migrations; and 2) what changes in life history might be involved in the evolution of migratory habits. Consideration of the interplay of demographic parameters will be the basis for postulating selective forces in the evolution of migration and migratory patterns.

Survival of Migrants

Good estimates of survivorship in wild bird popula-
tions are difficult to obtain. Annual adult survivorship is far more easily determined than first-year survivorship and is more commonly presented in the literature. First year survivorship (S_j) can be calculated based on data for adult mortality (M_a) and female productivity (P) using the formula $S_j = M_a/P$ (Ricklefs 1973). Major methods for obtaining adult survivorship (S_a) are discussed below.

1) The *recapture* method involves the proportion of a population that has been previously marked; it is usually based on resightings or recaptures on the breeding ground, but on occasions winter banding studies have been used to estimate survivorship (Diamond and Smith 1965). Recapture data give a minimum estimate of survivorship and the accuracy depends on the degree of philopatry displayed by individuals in a population. In addition, survivorship may be estimated based on the frequency of recaptures of birds of different age classes (Haldane 1955; Boyd 1965; Roberts 1971).

2) The *recovery* method employs large regional banding samples. The estimate is based on the recovery of dead marked birds in different year classes. Frankhauser (1971) compares the results from recovery and recapture data and concludes that recovery data give higher and more accurate estimates, but are restricted by small sample size. This increased accuracy is because recoveries are not dependent upon the tenure of operation of banding stations.

3) The *ratio* method is generally based on the proportion of adults in a prebreeding or breeding sample of museum skins. If a population is of stable size, the proportion of adults present during the breeding season should equal the annual adult survival rate; this method has been little used (for a good discussion see Snow 1956). The technique suffers from potential collecting biases. Immatures must be unidentifiable in the field, yet distinguishable in the hand. Nonbreeding

Table 1. Adult survival in temperate zone passerines

Species	Location	Number	Status[1]	Percentage survivorship	Methods[2]	Authority
RESIDENTS AND PARTIAL MIGRANTS						
Blue Jay *Cyanocitta cristata*	E. U.S.	—	PM	55	Recov	Hickey[3]
Black-capped Chickadee *Parus atricapillus*	Brit. Col.		R	20	Recap	Smith 1973
Great Tit *Parus major*	N. Eur.	897	PM	51	Recap	Kluijver 1951
Blue Tit *Parus caeruleus*	Brit.	110	R	30	Ratio	Snow 1956
" " " "	N. Eur.	57	PM	35	Ratio	Snow 1956
" " " "	Canary I.	40	R	55	Ratio	Snow 1956
Song Thrush *Turdus philomelos*	Brit.		PM	53	Recov	Lack 1954
European Blackbird *Turdus merula*	Brit.		PM	58	Recov	Lack 1954
American Robin *Turdus migratorus*	E. U.S.		PM	52	Recap	Farner[3]
Starling *Sturnus vulgaris*	Switzer.		PM	37	Recap	Lack 1954
Starling *Sturnus vulgaris*	Holland		PM	48	Recap	Cretz[3]
Starling *Sturnus vulgaris*	Brit.		R	48	Recov	Lack 1954
Starling *Sturnus vulgaris*	E. U.S.	720	PM	43.3	Recap	Frankhauser 1971
Brown-headed Cowbird *Molothrus ater*	E. U.S.	280	PM	44.4	Recov	Frankhauser 1971
Common Grackle *Quiscalus quiscalus*	E. U.S.	734	PM	51.6	Recov	Frankhauser 1971
Red-winged Blackbird *Agelaius phoenicus*	E. U.S.	1354	PM	51.7	Recap	Frankhauser 1971
European Tree Sparrow *Passer montanus*	N. Eur.		PM	45	Ratio	
Song Sparrow *Melospiza melodia*	E. U.S.		PM	55	Ratio	Nice[3]
Purple Finch *Carpodacus purpureus*	E. U.S.	136	PM	47	Recap	Farner 1965
LONG-DISTANCE MIGRANTS						
Pied Flycatcher *Muscicapa hypoleuca*	N. Eur.		TM	41–50	Recap Ratio	von Haartman[3]
Hammond's Flycatcher *Empidonax hammondii*	W. U.S.	360	TM	60–70	Ratio	Greenberg (based on Johnson 1970)
Western Flycatcher *Empidonax difficilis*	W. U.S.	627	TM	64–73	Ratio	Greenberg (based on Johnson 1973)
"Traill's" Flycatcher *Empidonax "trailli"*	E. U.S.	53	TM	30.1	Recap	Walkinshaw 1966a
Acadian Flycatcher *Empidonax virescens*	E. U.S.	31	TM	35.4	Recap	Walkinshaw 1966b
Yellow Wagtail *Motacilla flava*	N. Eur.	31	M	53	Recap	
Orange-crowned Warbler *Vermivora celata*	N. Am.	663	TM/M	40–60	Ratio	Greenberg (based on Foster unpublished data)
Yellow Warbler *Dendroica petechia*	E. U.S.	23	TM	52.6	Recap	Roberts 1971
Kirtland Warbler *Dendroica kirtlandi*	E. U.S.		TM	60	Recap	Mayfield 1960
Massachusetts Parulidae	E. U.S.	74	TM	67.8	Recap	Roberts 1971
Ovenbird *Seiurus aurocapillus*	E. U.S.	24	TM	54.5	Recap	Hann 1937
Ovenbird *Seiurus aurocapillus*	E. U.S.	20	TM	84.5	Recap	Roberts 1971
Northern Waterthrush *Seiurus novaborensis*	E. U.S.	14	TM	72.3	Recap	Roberts 1971
Yellowthroat *Geothlypis trichas*	E. U.S.	23	TM/M	54.2	Recap	Roberts 1971

[1] PM = Partial Migrant, R = Resident, TM = Tropical Migrant.

[2] Recap = recapture; Recov = recovery.

[3] From Lack 1954.

Russell Greenberg

samples may be biased if the species has age specific migratory patterns such as found by Lack (1941).

Direct estimates of adult survivorship have been compiled and are presented in table 1; included are 19 studies of resident or partial migrants and 14 of long-distance migrants. In compiling survivorship data, it is important to remain aware of the diversity of methods employed and the possible resulting variability. Recapture data from a single population will be most sensitive to environmental variation; also, recapture is the method most likely to give severe underestimates. For example, life table calculations based on 20 percent adult survival in Black-capped Chickadee (*Parus atricapillus*) or 30–35 percent survival in "Traill's" (*Empidonax alnorum*) and Acadian flycatchers (*Empidonax virens*) give the unlikely result of first year survivorship exceeding adult survivorship. Recovery and recapture data based on regional banding records, as well as ratio estimates, tend to give estimates averaging over many seasons and large regions at the expense of community specific resolution.

Despite this variability, it is possible to draw conclusions concerning the differences between the migrant and resident groups. There is a greater proportion of high values (60 percent or greater) in the migrants, where 7 such values are indicated in 16 studies; whereas in the 18 resident studies only one value approaches 60 percent. The migrant group has significantly greater adult survivorship than the resident group (Mann-Whitney U test; U = 177, p < .025). The difference is probably not an artifact of differences in methods used in the two groups. Both groups have a similar proportion of ratio studies ($^4/_{19}$ and $^4/_{14}$) and the migrant groups have a greater proportion of recapture studies which should underestimate adult survivorship ($^{12}/_{14}$ vs $^9/_{19}$). Roberts (1971) proposed survivorship to be high in migrant parulids.

Productivity of Migrants

Results of studies of productivity of 5 resident passerines and 13 neotropical migrants are presented in table

Table 2. Productivity of temperate zone passerines

Species	Location	Number	Fledglings per female	Adult survival at S_j/S_{ad} =			Authority
				.25	.50	.75	
RESIDENTS AND PARTIAL MIGRANTS							
Great Tit *Parus major*	N. Eur		6 (3.9–14.1)	57	50	31	Kluijver 1951
Black-capped Chickadee *Parus atricapillus*	Brit. Col.		5	61	44	35	Smith 1975
European Blackbird *Turdus merula*	Brit.		4.1	66	50	40	Snow[1]
Red-winged Blackbird *Agelaius phoenicus*	E. U.S.		4.2	65	99	39	
Song Sparrow *Melospiza melodia*	E. U.S.		6.4	55	38	29	Nice[1]
LONG-DISTANCE MIGRANTS							
Acadian Flycatcher *Empidonax virescens*	E. U.S.	52	3.3	68	54	43	Walkinshaw 1966a
"Traill's Flycatcher" *Empidonax trailii*	E. U.S.	23	3.2	69	55	44	Walkinshaw 1966b
"Traill's Flycatcher" *Empidonax trailii*	E. U.S.	60	1.8	81	69	60	Holcomb 1912
Least Flycatcher *Empidonax minimus*	E. U.S.	182	2.8	74	59	49	Based on Hussell 1963
Least Flycatcher *Empidonax minimus*	E. U.S.	387	3.4	67	53	42	Based on Clench 1969
Prothonotary Warbler *Prothonotaria citrea*	E. U.S.	178	1.6	83	71	62	Walkinshaw 1953
Yellow Warbler *Dendroica petechia*	E. U.S.	12	2.0	80	66	57	Young 1949
Kirtland Warbler *Dendroica kirtlandi*	E. U.S.	154	2.2	79	64	55	Mayfield 1960
Prairie Warbler *Dendroica discolor*	E. U.S.	55	1.1	88	77	69	Nolan 1963
Ovenbird *Seiurus aurocapillus*	E. U.S.	36	2.9	73	58	48	Hann 1937
Yellowthroat *Geothlypis trichas*	E. U.S.	38	3.2	69	55	44	Hofslund 1959
Wilson's Warbler *Wilsonia pusilla*	W. U.S.	50	3.0	72	57	47	Stewart 1973
Yellow-breasted Chat *Icteria virens*	E. U.S.	37	1.2	87	76	63	Thompson and Nolan 1973

[1] From Lack 1954.

2. Annual female productivity may be determined by direct monitoring of a marked population or an examination of adult-juvenile ratios in the post-breeding season (Ricklefs 1972). Looking at ratios in banding or museum specimen samples may be severely biased if age-specific differences in migration or dispersal exists; for example, I calculated a theoretical value of 8.2 juveniles per female for productivity in the Western Flycatcher based on a fall sample presented by Johnson (1973). This high value is probably a result of the fact that, as Johnson points out, the adults migrate much earlier than the immatures. The resulting variability in productivity values does not obscure major differences between migrant and resident species. The migrants have low productivity (1–3 fledglings per female) versus the higher productivity of residents (4–6 fledglings); the two groups are significantly different ($U = O$, $p < .001$). This lower productivity is probably a result of a reduced number of clutches; the migrants listed generally lay between one and two clutches and are only rarely multibrooded. Multibroodedness is common in resident species (Ricklefs 1973). It should be noted that higher productivity was not strongly supported for the residents in the Kansas bird community analyzed by Bloom and Ricklefs (1977); while the 3 neotropical migrants have very short nesting seasons, they are not the lowest in calculated annual productivity. Two of these species were non-open nesting species which is a rare condition for neotropical migrants; this would increase survivorship to the fledgling state and thus annual productivity.

Overall Demographic Patterns of Migrants

The lower productivity found in the above analysis may be compensated for in two ways: 1) adult survivorship is higher in neotropical migrants than in residents (table 1); or 2) the disparity between first-year and adult survivorship is less in migrants. Table 2 presents calculations of necessary adult survivorships given three levels of S_j/S_a. The previously estimated S_j/S_a for resident temperate species is 25 percent (Ricklefs 1973). Given this value, the necessary adult survivorships fall between 68–89 percent for migrants and 55–65 percent for residents; these conform to the highest estimates obtained by direct calculations (table 1). An S_j/S_a of 50 percent puts the survivorship values of migrants into the range of those measured directly and gives figures comparable to those obtained for residents with S_j/S_a equalling 25 percent. From this exercise, three possibilities can be advanced: 1) first-year survivorship is one-quarter adult survivorship on both resident and migrant passerines, but adult survivorship in migrants is very high (70–90 percent); 2) adult survivorship is 50–65 percent for both migrants and residents, but first year survivorship is closer to 50 percent of adult survivorship in migrants; or 3) both adult survivorship and S_j/S_a are greater in migrants than in residents. Since 90 percent adult survivorship seems high according to current estimates, hypotheses 2) and 3) are most likely. The direct survivorship data of table 1 best fit the third hypothesis.

Risks of Migration

While the risks of migration have not been quantified, in terms of a mortality rate to an entire population, it is difficult to imagine that it is insignificant. If one subtracts the mortality of migration, it is possible that the differences on tropical versus temperate zone wintering grounds may be more dramatic than the data of tables 1 and 2 indicate. Both high adult survivorship and high S_j/S_a are characteristic of tropical residents (Snow and Lill 1974; Ricklefs 1973). It is possible that the tropics are a good place to survive and under benign conditions the disparity between adult and juvenile survivorship may be proportionally reduced.

One major cost of this increased winter survivorship may be the high risk accrued to young during their first migration. Age ratios for Western Flycatchers (*Empidonax difficilis*) indicate higher immature than adult mortality during both migrations (Johnson 1973). Several causes of this age-specific difference may be operating. Foraging efficiency may be reduced in juveniles. This may create particularly great difficulties for birds which migrate across large bodies of water or deserts. Murray (1967) found that a large proportion of Blackpoll Warblers (*Dendroica striata*) along the New Jersey coast were immature. It is possible that young birds more often find themselves over the Atlantic Ocean with insufficient reserves for the trip to the West Indies.

In immature neotropical migrants, migration is often preceded by a period of vagrancy. The evidence for a relatively rapid migration in adults is good for some species, such as Least Flycatcher (*Empidonax minimus*) (Hussell et al. 1972), Western Flycatcher (Johnson 1973), and a variety of California migrants (Stewart et al. 1972); it needs, as a general phenomenon in migrant passerines, further confirmation. If adults leave sooner and migrate more rapidly than immatures, then the young may be exposed to greater risk resulting from inclement weather.

Heavy mortality in immature resident passerines often levels off by January (Lack 1946), but this is not always the case (Klujver 1951). As the data from Western Flycatchers indicate, mortality in immature migrants may be higher than adults in both migrations. A major cause of increased mortality in young migrants may be the culling of faulty navigational

Russell Greenberg

systems. Evidence that a proportion of the young of migrants have faulty systems is that juvenile-adult ratios of fall migrants, along the outer coast and California islands, is often highly skewed towards immatures (Ralph 1971 and Stewart et al 1972). These authors suggest that a small proportion of the young, because of misorientation, are migrating along an extremely risky coastal route. Insular birds may not be oriented in a normal north-south course, and migrants are often found far out to sea where survival probabilities are essentially zero. Misorientation probably occurs in both migrations. Pitelka (1974) has found migrational overshoots occurring during the spring at Barrow, Alaska, to be almost exclusively first-year birds.

Neotropical migrants appear to glean the best of two worlds. Their trips to the tropics may bring them to a benign region to survive between breeding bouts. The tropics, however, is a difficult environment for the protection of young. Nest predation is high (Ricklefs 1973), and the requisite adaptations great for nesting in high predator environments. Further, many migrants are nomadic and employ opportunistic strategies covering large regions to locate outbreaks of food or unpredictable habitat patches. These lifestyles may not be conducive to successful reproduction. Most temperate habitats offer a short season of heavy insect productivity. The major cost of taking advantage of a productive environment for breeding and a benign winter environment may be paid by heavy juvenile mortality associated with first migrations.

Life Historical Aspects of Migration

The preceding interspecific comparisons suggest that neotropical migrants and temperate zone residents may represent two ends of a spectrum of life-history strategies. Residents may be maximizing annual productivity as opposed to migrants which are maximizing survivorship at the expense of annual productivity. This is simply a description and does not provide a mechanism relating life-history strategies to patterns of migration. Von Haartman (1968) observed the same dichotomy of migrants and residents between and within species (in partial migrants). Since the mechanism he proposed to account for it differs from the one I will propose, I will critically discuss his hypothesis. Von Haartman's hypothesis and my proposal can be designated the *Resource Competition* and *Time Allocation* hypotheses respectively.

Resource Competition

Von Haartman proposes that residents gain advantage in competition for critical nesting resources, particu-

larly nest cavities. Migrants lose the advantage of hole nesting in exchange for increased winter survivorship. He developed two lines of evidence to support this: 1) 50–70 percent of the hole nesting species in Finnish and Canadian forests are resident, whereas only 5 percent of the open nesters are resident; 2) hole-nesters always nest early and open-nesters often nest late in the season. A basic tenet of this proposal is that all species will find the critical resource, holes, equally desirable. If this were true, one would expect to find more facultative use of holes by migrants in situations where holes are not limiting. Moreover, tropical resident members of groups with neotropical migrants (such as warblers, tanagers) are also often open nesters (Skutch 1968). It is more likely that seasonal progression in nest-site selection is a consequence of seasonal progression in the initiation of breeding of birds with different foraging behaviors. Each species, then, is selecting the best nesting site for a bird with that foraging style and microhabitat. By this argument what appears to be seasonal competition for nest cavities is actually an artifact of two independent phenomena: 1) hole nesting protects nestlings and eggs from cold stress (Von Haartman 1968), and lowered predation pressure (Nice 1957) allows reduced growth rates which places less stress on the foraging rates of parents during the less productive early season. Further, slower growth rates allow increased clutch sizes (Cody 1971), but, in order to time fledging with peak insect emergence, early nesting may be necessary. 2) female incubation, found in most long-distance migrants such as tanagers, warblers and flycatchers, may restrict nest placement to localities that allow maximal foraging efficiency with minimum travel time. Morse (1968) and Williamson (1971) showed female foraging in some wood warblers and vireos to be localized around the nest. Hole nesting may be possible for birds with foraging strategies, such as those of parids, nuthatches, and wrens, and less likely for sallyers and foliage insectivores. It would be fruitful to investigate aspects of the ecology of migrant hole nesters, such as *Myiarchus* flycatchers, Prothonotary and Lucy (*Vermivora luciae*) Warblers, that distinguish them from other migrants.

Time Allocation

I propose that the critical factor behind differences in life histories of migrants and residents is the allocation of time to reproductive versus strictly survival-oriented activities. Any increase in the length of the breeding season will decrease the amount of time for occupation of the nonbreeding range. A model exploring the implication of this is graphically portrayed in figure 1. Figure 1a presents the rate of increase of fitness asso-

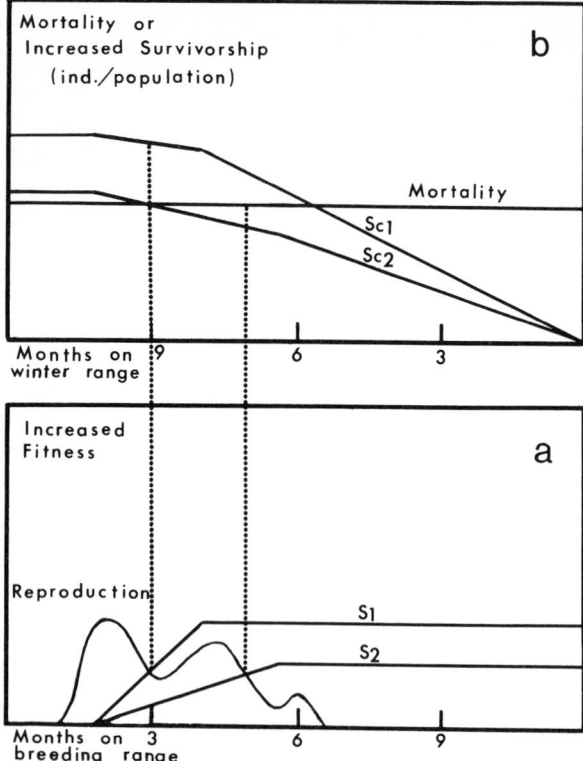

Figure 1. Optimal breeding season length, a. potential survivorship versus potential reproduction (S_1 and S_2 are survivorship rates for 2 wintering ranges); b. cumulative survivorship versus mortality of migration (S_c1 and S_c2 are cumulative survivorships for S_1 and S_2 and the dotted line connects optimal breeding season ends to S_c curves).

ciated with occupying the breeding and nonbreeding range for increasing amounts of time. It is assumed the sole component of increase for breeding range occupancy is a result of increased net productivity (productivity minus mortality associated with reproductive activities) and for nonbreeding range residency it is survivorship. The undulations in the curve for the rate of increase in reproductive output are a result of the minimum time required for the successful raising of a brood; increase between the peaks results from the possibility of replacement clutches. The survivorship curve (S) is a horizontal line, indicating constant increase, except during the best period for breeding when the increase resulting from nonbreeding range occupancy drops to zero. This is because during the peak of the breeding season, survival potential should be very high. The potential increase in fitness resulting from increased reproductive output during an increased breeding season will be weighed (through natural selection) against the potential increase in

fitness resulting from the increased occupancy of a benign nonbreeding range. Graphically, the end of the breeding season, in the absence of other factors, should be determined by the point on the survivorship line of figure 1a to the right of which all points on the line fall above all points on the reproduction line. More generally, it is the point where the area between S and reproduction is greater than the area between reproduction and S.

The complicating factor is the risk of migration. While the increment of increased survivorship depends on the length of time spent on the nonbreeding range, the risk of migration is time independent. Increases in the breeding season may reduce the total tenure of nonbreeding range residency to a point where gains in survivorship do not offset the risk of migration. This is demonstrated in figure 1 where the optimal ending point for the breeding seasons associated with two wintering ranges S_1 and S_2 (figure 1a) are connected (dotted lines) to their respective cumulative survivorship curves (figure 1b). At the point of intersection S_c1 exceeds the mortality of migration but S_c2 does not. In addition, if the reproduction curve were contracted, the optimal end points for the breeding seasons of S_1 and S_2 would shift to the left which would increase the net benefit (distance from S_c to Mortality) of migration. In this way, the seasonal potential for breeding and the relative quality of a given winter range determine whether migration to that range is a worthwhile strategy. Sharper spring peaks in prey abundance and more pronounced seasonality should favor migration by increasing the differential in survival rates between the two wintering grounds and decreasing the potential benefits of a lengthened breeding season.

Predictions and Two Tests

At higher altitudes and latitudes within the range of a single species, seasonality should be more pronounced and peaks of food abundance more precipitous. From this theory, I predict that migration to a favorable nonbreeding range should be selected over a long breeding season at higher altitudes and latitudes and, commensurate with this, survivorship should be higher in populations occupying these areas. This prediction was tested using age data from 1,350 specimens of Orange-crowned Warbler and 408 skins of Western Flycatcher. Adult survivorship was estimated using the proportion of adults in spring and breeding samples.

Adult proportions have been tabulated for four races and two additional geographic subdivisions within the (see figure 2) Orange-crowned Warbler (table 3). Mercedes Foster aged the birds based on

Table 3. Proportions of adults in samples of Orange-crowned Warblers[1]

I. Breeding	Male		Female	
	Number	Percentage adult	Number	Percentage adult
V. celata sordida	118	32	36	31.5
V. c. lutescens (south)	44	39	36	28.0
V. c. lutescens (north)	93	53	58	57.0
V. c. orestera (south)	63	50	8	50.0
V. c. orestera (north)	79	50	26	50.0
V. c. celata	67	63	35	33.0

II. Nonbreeding				
V. c. sordida (winter)	95	40	40	24.0
V. c. lutescens	212	39	121	23.0
V. c. orestera	49	50	55	31.0
V. c. celata (east)	44	67	14	71.0
V. c. celata (west)	27	28	22	21.0
V. c. celata (total)	71	52	36	47.0

[1] Data provided by Mercedes S. Foster.

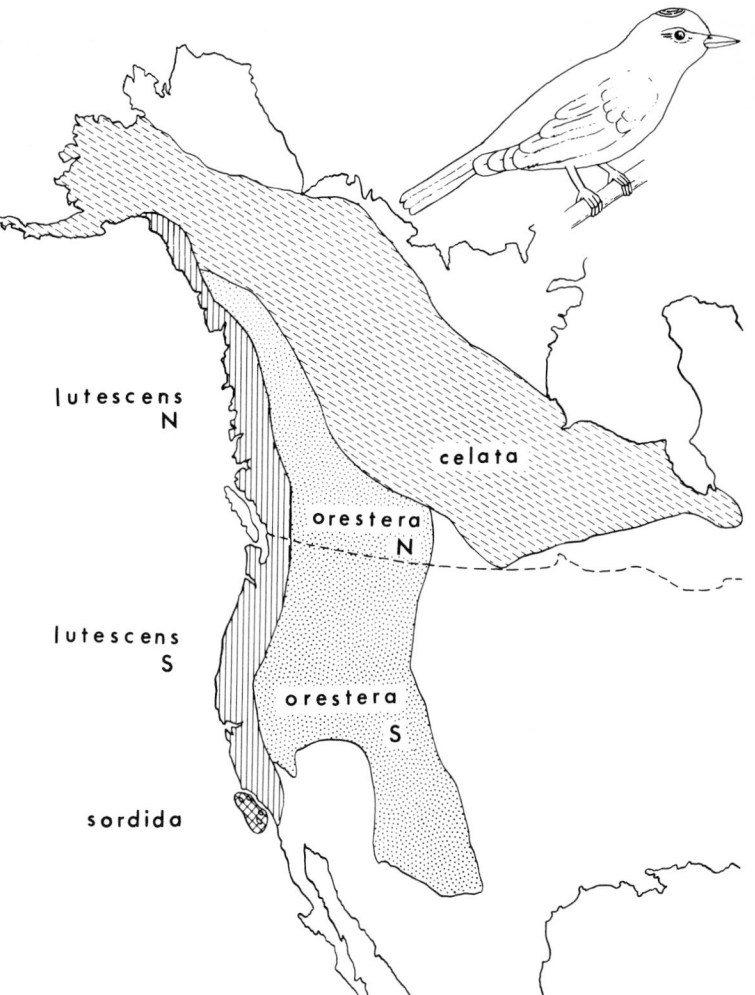

Figure 2. Breeding distribution of Orange-crowned Warbler.

criteria previously published (Foster 1967). Samples are divided into breeding or nonbreeding spring samples (March–June); breeding specimens were either determined by direct evidence or selected from a narrow range of dates for each geographic region (Foster pers. comm.). It should be noted that the geographic subdivisions examined in the breeding sample are not distinguished in the nonbreeding sample since such an ascription would be meaningless for migratory birds. The additional subdivision of eastern (east of the Continental Divide) and western (west of the divide) V. c. celata was erected because the sample seemed to be weighted heavily toward migrants from western regions, mainly California, where this race is rare (Grinnell and Miller 1944); the possibility that this biases the age ratio can be examined.

In general, the prediction of increased survivorship in populations at higher altitudes and latitudes is supported by the data. In the breeding data, survivorship is lowest in the resident V. c. sordida and increases in series from lutescens (south), orestera, lutescens (north) to celata. The major discrepancy is the sample of female celata which has a low 33 percent adult. Proportion of

adults in the nonbreeding sample increases from sordida, lutescens, orestera, to celata in both sexes; this probably corresponds to the order of increasing seasonality of the areas the races occupy. The high proportion of young in the western celata sample obscures but does not obliterate this trend. In the breeding sample, northern lutescens males and females have significantly greater proportions of adults than southern lutescens ($X^2 = 4.85$ p < .05). There is no such difference between the orestera subgroups, probably because southern orestera breed at high elevations (Grinnell and Miller 1944; Phillips et al 1964).

Data on survivorship in Western Flycatchers along the Pacific Coast of North America were similarly analyzed (based on data provided by Ned K. Johnson). The proportions of adults in breeding populations is presented in table 4 and a map of the localities of those populations presented in figure 3. A pattern of

Table 4. Proportions of adults in samples of Western Flycatchers[1]

Locality and map symbol	Male		Female	
	Number	Percentage	Number	Percentage
Alaska (AK)	22	77	12	83
Queen Charlotte Is. (QCI)	25	56	15	53
Central British Colombia (CBC)	13	92	5	80
Vancouver (Va)	29	86	15	53
Bellingham (Be)	15	66	12	58
Western Washington (Wa)	11	91	5	80
Oregon Coast (Ore)	24	71	10	40
Northwestern California (NWC)	20	70	6	83
North-central California (NCC)	18	72	5	80
San Francisco Bay Region (SF)	67	79	26	69
Channel Islands (CI)	29	86	9	78
Southwestern California Mountains (SWC)	12	100	3	66

[1] Data provided by Ned K. Johnson.

increasing adult survivorship with increasing altitude or latitude does not emerge. What appears is high survivorship throughout this portion of the species' range.

Perhaps there is only a slight gradient in the potential breeding season duration within this largely coastal nesting species. In this case a slight increase in clutch size would equal the decreased probability of double broods in more northerly populations. For example, for a five-egg clutch, an increase in clutch of one would compensate for a decrease in probability of second clutch of 0.2. In addition, a small gradient in season length would cause variability in survivorship smaller than that associated with the measurement error of the survivorship estimates. A pattern of generally high, but constant survivorship may be expected within neotropical migrants. A gradient should occur in species that span a variety of winter survivorship conditions, as well as a strong gradient in breeding range climatic regime.

Leap-frog Migration Patterns

Populations within a species and closely related species often display leap-frog migration, where more northerly breeding birds winter farther south than southerly breeding birds. Interpopulation or interspecific competition has often been implicated as the major force forming these patterns (Swarth 1920; Salomonsen

1955; Welty 1975). Moreover, competition-based winter distributions form part of the empirical core for the proposal of Cox (1968) that a driving force in the evolution of migration is geographic displacement to avoid competition. Any alternate explanation for the evolution of leap-frog migration would be critical to our understanding of the evolution of migration. Based on the theory presented here, I propose an alternate explanation.

Individuals at the northern edge of an expanding breeding population should shorten their breeding season and thereby lengthen the time available for surviving on a benign wintering ground. Not only should survivorship increase in these populations, but given certain gradients in potential survivorship and migrational risk, these populations should switch to more southerly wintering ranges. A graphic model, presented in figure 4, explores a simplified system with two possible wintering ranges. Populations can fall into three groups depending on the amount of time available for winter range occupation. Group 1 represents those populations for which migration to either wintering ground is unprofitable. It corresponds to the section of the graph where both Sc_1 and Sc_2 fall below their respective M lines. Group 2 populations should migrate to Locality 2, because the distance from Sc_2 to M_2 (Y) is greater than the distance from Sc_1 to M_1 (X) and so net survivorship would be greater. Populations in Group 3 should migrate to more distant

Russell Greenberg

localities because X is greater than Y (the point where X equals Y is indicated on the graph and is the precise boundary between Group 2 and Group 3 populations). For such a model to generate these three population types, there must be a specific relationship between S1 and S2 (the slopes of Sc1 and Sc2), M_1 and M_2. For example, figure 4 presents alternative values for S2 (reflected in the different slopes of S1' and S1"), which would not create the three groups necessary for leap-frog migration. S1' is too large, the Sc1' line crosses M_1 and Sc2 crosses M_2, and it will never be advantageous to select the closer wintering ground. S1" is too small; in a 12-month year X will never exceed Y. The M_1/M_2 critically affects the behavior of the model by setting the range of Sc_2/Sc_1 that will satisfy the conditions for leap-frog migration. The larger M_2/M_1 the greater the difference should be in survivorship and the greater the range of survivorship ratio values that will work (table 5). In qualitative terms: 1) for a given ratio of migratory risk associated with two wintering grounds, a range of value for the ratios of the two potential survivorships may exist that make residency, short migration, and long migration that most profitable strategy under different conditions; 2) under these conditions, length of time available for occupancy of winter range determines which of the three strategies is the optimum; 3) length of potential wintering season is determined by the length of the profitable breeding season which decreases at higher altitudes and latitudes. The model predicts that given certain gradients in potential survivorship and risk of migration, leap-frog migration patterns can be expected to occur.

It could be argued that the northward expansion of a breeding population also increases risk of migration to the more favorable wintering grounds. If breeding range seasonality increases very rapidly compared with risk of migration or if risk of migration is a nonlinear function of distance (such as a curve with a monotonically decreasing slope), then the model should remain valid.

Table 5. Values for survivorship ratios for given risk ratios

M_2/M_1	Minimum S_2/S_1	Maximum S_2/S_1
3.0	2.0	3.0
2.0	1.5	2.0
1.5	1.1	1.5
1.25	1.0	1.1

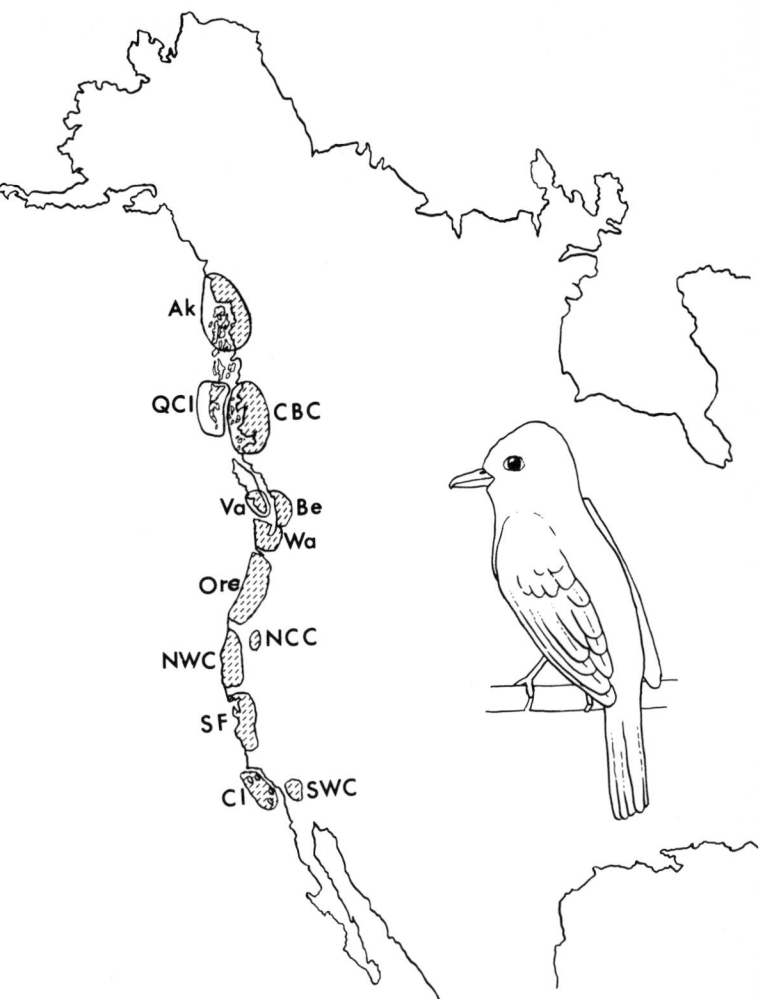

Figure 3. Distribution of populations of Western Flycatcher analyzed in table 4.

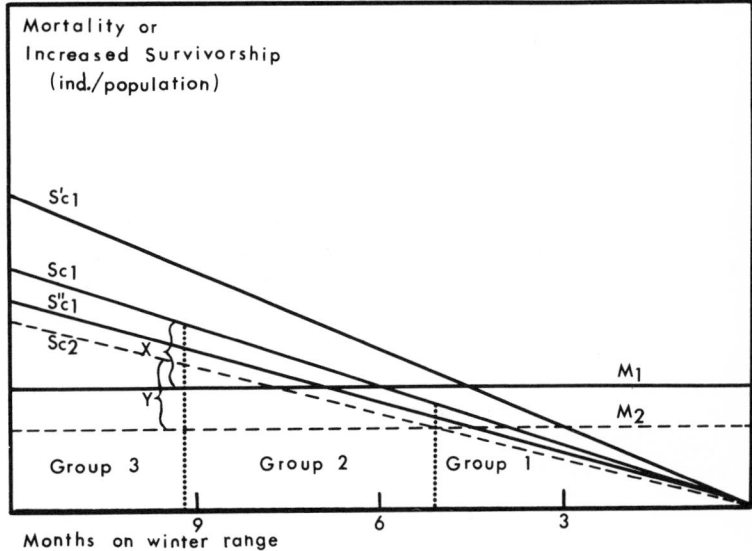

Figure 4. A model for the evaluation of leap frog migration. M = mortality of migration; Sc = cumulative survivorship; X and Y = net cumulative survivorships.

The parameters of the model do not lend themselves to direct measurement. The predictions of the model can be tested indirectly against some more easily obtained empirical data: gradients in adult survivorship. Competition-based theories should predict different patterns of adult survivorship in breeding populations than the time-allocation model presented here. In the competition model, the average individual in the new northern population will encounter a resident population that is optimally spaced with respect to competition; it cannot hope to exceed the mean survivorship of the resident population, only equal it. The distribution and resulting survivorship pattern may be viewed as a trade-off between the negative effects of increasing distance migrated and increasing competition overlaid upon an equipotential survivorship plane. The reason that there cannot be a gradient of increasing survivorship, is that the more southerly population should occupy the best possible winter range since the more northerly population is being displaced by competition. By this theory we should expect to find adult survivorship in more northerly populations, at best, equally that of southern populations. The time-allocation model would, as discussed above, predict an increase in adult survivorship in more northerly populations. The Fox Sparrow (*Passerella iliacus*), a textbook example of leap-frog migration, would be an excellent test species because there are both high latitude and high altitude races. The time-allocation model can probably better explain the high-elevation Sierra Nevada race wintering with the northerly races at the southern end of the species' winter range (Swarth 1920). Winter distribution is determined by seasonality of breeding range, not geographic location.

Acknowledgments

I am grateful to William Glanz, Ned K. Johnson and J. P. Myers for helpful comments on drafts of this manuscript, to Mercedes Foster and Ned Johnson for providing unpublished data, and to Todd and Virginia Keeler-Wolf for help in manuscript preparation. I would particularly like to thank Judy Gradwohl for her suggestions and the preparation of figures and line drawings.

Literature Cited

Anderson, K. S., and M. K. Maxfield
1967.   Warbler returns from south-eastern Massachusetts. Bird-Banding 38:218–33.

Berger, A. J., and B. E. Radabaugh
1968.   Returns of Kirtland's Warbler to the breeding grounds. Bird-Banding 34:161–86.

Boyd, H.
1962.   Mortality and fertility of European charadrii. Ibis 104:368–87.

Clench, M. H.
1969.   Additional observations on the fall migration of adult and immature Least Flycatcher. Bird-Banding 40:238–43.

Cody, M. L.
1971.   Ecological aspects of reproduction. In *Avian Biology*, eds. D. S. Farner and J. R. King, vol. 1. pp. 461–512. New York and London: Academic Press.

Cox, G.
1968.   The role of competition in the evolution of migration. Evol. 22:180–92.

Diamond, A. W., and R. W. Smith
1973.   Returns and survival of banded warblers wintering in Jamaica. Bird-Banding 43:221–25.

Ely, C. A.
1971.   Migration of Least and Traill's Flycatcher in west-central Kansas. Bird-Banding 41:190–240.

Erickson, M. M.
1938.   Territory, annual cycle, and numbers in a population of Wren-tits (*Chamaea fasciata*). Univ. Calif. Publ. Zool. 42:247–334.

Farner, D. S.
1965.   Bird Banding in the study of population dynamics. In *Recent Studies in Avian Biology*, ed. A. Wolfson, pp. 397–499. Urbana: Univ. Illinois Press.

Foster, M.
1967.   Pteriography and age determination in the Orange-crowned Warbler. Condor 69:1–12.

Frankhauser, D. P.
1971.   Annual adult survival rates in blackbirds and starlings. Bird-Banding 42:36–42.

Griscom, L., and A. Sprunt
1957.   *The Warblers of North America.* New York: Devin-Adair.

Haldane, J. B. S.
1955.   The calculation of mortality rates from ringing data. Proceedings of the Eleventh International Ornithology Congress. 1954:454–58.

Hann, H. W.
1937.   Life history of the Ovenbird in southern Michigan. Wils. Bull. 49:145–237.

Hann, N. M., and J. B. Cope
1951.   Further data on removal and repopulation of the breeding birds in a spruce-fir forest community. Auk 68:483–93.

Hofslund, P. B.
1959.   A life history study of the Yellowthroat. Proc. Minn. Acad. Sci. 27:144–74.

Russell Greenberg

Holcomb, L. C.
1972. Nest success and age-specific mortality in Traill's Flycatchers. Auk 89:537–41.

Hussell, D. J. T., T. Davis, and R. D. Montgomerie
1967. Differential fall migration of adult and immature Least Flycatchers. Bird-Banding 38:61–66.

Johnson, N. K.
1970. Fall migration and winter distribution of the Hammond Flycatcher. Bird-Banding 41:169–90.

Johnson, N. K.
1973. Spring migration of the Western Flycatcher with notes on seasonal changes in sex and age ratios. Bird-Banding 44:205–20.

Ketterson, E. D., and V. Nolan, Jr.
1976. Geographic variation and its climatic correlates in the sex ratios of eastern-wintering Dark-eyed Juncos. (*Junco hyemalis hyemalis*). Ecol. 57:679–93.

Kluijver, H. N.
1951. The population ecology of the Great Tit *Parus m. major*. Ardea 39:1–196.

Lack, D.
1941. The problem of partial migration. Brit. Birds 37:122–30, 143–50.

Lack, D.
1946. Do juvenile birds survive less well than adults? Brit. Birds 39:258–64.

1954. *The Natural Regulation of Animal Numbers*. London: Oxford Press, 343 pp.

1968. Bird migration and natural selection. Oikos 19:1–9.

MacArthur, R.
1959. On the breeding distribution pattern of North American migrant birds. Auk 76:318–25.

Mayfield, H.
1960. The Kirtland's Warbler. Cranbrook Inst. Sci. Bull. 40.

Mengel, R. M.
1964. The probable history of species formation in some northern wood warblers (Parulidae). Living Bird 3:9–43.

Morse, D. H.
1968. A quantitative study of foraging of male and female spruce-wood warblers. Ecol. 49:779–84.

Murray, B. G.
1966. Migration of age and sex classes of passerines on the Atlantic coast in autumn. Auk 83:352–60.

Nice, M. M.
1937. Studies in the life history of the Song Sparrow. Trans. Linnean Soc. New York 4:1–247.

1957. Nesting success in altricial birds. Auk 74:305–21.

Nolan, V.
1963. Reproductive success of birds in a deciduous scrub habitat. Ecol. 44:305–13.

Perrins, D. M.
1965. Population fluctuations and clutch size in the Great Tit. *Parus major*. J. Anim. Ecol. 34:601–47.

Pitelka, F. A.
1974. An avifaunal review of the Barrow region and the north slope of arctic Alaska. Arctic Alpine Research: 6:161–84.

Ralph, C. J.
1971. An age differential of migrants in coastal California. Condor 73:243–46.

Ricklefs, R. E.
1972. Latitudinal variation in breeding productivity of the Rough-winged Swallow. Auk 89:826–36.

1973. Fecundity, mortality and avian demography. p. 366–435 In *Breeding Biology of Birds*, ed. D. S. Farner. Washington: Nat. Academy of Sciences.

Ricklefs, R. E., and G. Bloom
1977. Components of Avian Breeding Productivity. Auk 94:86–97.

Roberts, J. O. L.
1971. Survival among some North American wood warblers. Bird-Banding 42:165–83.

Salomenson, F.
1955. The evolutionary significance of bird migration. Biol. Medd. (Dansk) 22:1–62.

Schrantz, F. G.
1943. Nest life of the Eastern Yellow Warbler. Auk 60:367–87.

Skutch, A. F.
1954. Life Histories of Central American Birds. Pacific Coast Avifauna 31:1–448.

Smith, S. M.
1975. Ecological aspects of dominance hierarchies in Black-capped chickadees. Auk 93:95–107.

Snow, D. W.
1956. The annual mortality of the Blue Tit in different parts of its range. Brit. Birds 49:174–77.

Snow, D. W., and A. Hill
1974. Longevity records for some neotropical landbirds. Condor 76:262–67.

Stewart, R. E.
1953. A life history of the Yellowthroat. Wils. Bull. 65:367–87.

Stewart, R. E., and J. W. Aldrich
1951. Removal and reproduction of breeding birds in a spruce-fir forest community. Auk 68:471–82.

Stewart, R. M., R. L. Mewaldt, and S. Kaiser
1974. Age ratios of coastal and inland fall migrant passerines in Central California. Bird-Banding 45:46–57.

Stewart, R. M.

1973. Breeding behavior and life history of the Wilson's Warbler. Wils. Bull. 85:21–30.

Sturm, L.

1943. A study of the nesting activities of the American Redstart. Auk 62:182–206.

Swarth, H. S.

1920. Revision of the avian genus *Passerella* with special reference to the distribution and migration of the races in California. Univ. California Pubs. Zoo. 21: 75–224.

Thompson, C. F., and V. Nolan

1973. Population biology of the Yellow-breasted Chat (*Icteria virens*) in southern Indiana. Ecol. Monogr. 43: 145–171.

Von Haartman, L.

1968. The evolution of resident versus migratory habit in birds: some considerations. Ornis Fennica 45:1–7.

Walkinshaw, L. H.

1966a. Studies of the Acadian Flycatcher in Michigan. Bird-Banding 37:227–57.

1966b. Summer biology of the Traill's Flycatcher. Wils. Bull. 78:31–46.

1953. Life history of the Prothonotary Warbler. Wils. Bull. 65:152–68.

Welty, J. C.

1975. *The Life of Birds*, 2nd ed. Philadelphia and London: Saunders.

Williamson, P.

1971. Feeding ecology of the Red-eyed vireo (*Vireo olivaceus*) and associated foliage-gleaning birds. Ecol. Monographs 41:129–52.

Young, H.

1949. A comparative study of nesting birds in a five acre park. Wils. Bull. 61:36–47.

Russell Greenberg

DOUGLASS H. MORSE
Department of Zoology
University of Maryland
College Park, Maryland 20742

Population Limitation: Breeding or Wintering Grounds?

ABSTRACT

No single explanation will account for population limitation of all neotropical migrant populations. Further, factors affecting Old World migrants differ fundamentally from those dominating in the New World.

If population limitation were initially to occur either on the breeding or wintering grounds, consequent accommodation (ecological release) of resident birds or other animals should take place in the initially limited area. Over evolutionary time, few remaining opportunities would thus occur in the previously non-limited area. This argument predicts a dynamic equilibrium between the breeding and wintering grounds, regardless of the area in which limitation initially took place and the limiting factor might be.

Contingencies encountered during migration may further affect some species, although rates of increase usually appear adequate to replenish such losses quickly. The condition of being migratory may, however, place morphological and behavioral constraints upon a bird that are not advantageous during the rest of its year, and which may compromise its performance at those times.

Man-modified habitats may have a major impact upon migratory birds. Lest we assume that presently occurring changes constitute a unique phenomenon, we should keep in mind the role that pre-Columbian Indians may have played in altering the landscape of Mexico and Central America.

Introduction

The subject of where migratory birds are limited is not a new one. On page 1 of his popular pamphlet, Lincoln (1950) asks a number of questions central to this matter: "where do they go?" [after leaving their breeding grounds]; "will the same ones return next spring to their former haunts?"; "what dangers will they face on their round-trip flight and while in their winter homes?" However, considering the intense attention paid to other aspects of migration, it seems strange that more emphasis has not been placed upon such questions, as Cox (1968) pointed out. Little direct attention is usually paid to the ecological aspects of migration (other than for energetics) in the recent *Avian Biology* series (Farner and King 1971–75). Further, several recent texts (Dorst 1974; Welty 1975; Van Tyne and Berger 1976) pay only brief attention to these ultimate factors, although they consider proximal ones (navigation, orientation) in detail.

In the basic ecological literature on neotropical migrants, one often detects the implicit assumption that populations of migratory (and other) birds are limited on their breeding grounds. This predisposition is seen in the emphasis made on fitting adaptations of migratory birds to the conditions that they experience on their breeding grounds. While Lack (1966) and Fretwell (1972) have emphasized the importance of winter in limiting bird populations, they were primarily concerned with permanent residents.

Changing Characteristics of Breeding and Wintering Areas

Most published work (Morel and Bourlière 1962; Willis 1966; Morse 1971; Moreau 1972, for example) suggests that many migratory species in the tropics do not make heavy use of extensive primary lowland forests, tending instead to frequent patches of original forest, second growth, upland areas, edge habitats, and the like. The results of this symposium do not radically change that conclusion. Therefore, given the widespread destruction of the original forest in tropical America, with part of it being replaced with second growth, numbers of migratory birds might increase, if they were previously limited on their tropical wintering grounds. That possibility seemed likely upon considering the deluge of birds (Moreau 1966) entering a wintering area not a third the size of their collective breeding range (table 1).

This hypothesis about limitation on the wintering grounds is basically dependent upon two different assumptions: that there is now more second growth in Central America and northern South America than there was recently (as opposed to concrete pavement,

Table 1. Area available to neotropical migrants on breeding and wintering grounds[1]

Category	Total area (km)^2	Ratio of breeding grounds to wintering grounds
BREEDING GROUNDS		
North America (south of tree line)	16,194,000	
WINTERING GROUNDS		
West Indies	207,000	
Tropical Mexico and Central America	1,296,000	3.96 :1
South America north of equator	2,591,000	
Total	4,094,000	

[1] From Moreau 1966.

intensively farmed cropland, and so on), and that habitat conditions on the breeding grounds are not changing. Monroe (1970) and others participating in a 1966 symposium on the avifauna of northern Latin America (Buechner and Buechner 1970) appeared confident then that the amount of second growth had recently increased in Central America (at the expense of the primary forest), so that the wintering areas for neotropical migrants as a whole had increased. This removal of the primary forest is continuing, with Bolin (1977) suggesting that primary forest in Latin America is disappearing at the rate of roughly 1 percent a year. Data from the Food and Agriculture Organization (FAO) Production Yearbooks indicate that this forest is disappearing even faster than this in Mexico, Central America, and the West Indies. Forested area declined 27.5 percent from about 1955 to 1970, while "unutilized land" (probably second growth) increased 8.4 percent (table 2).

Over the same time the forested area in North America increased slightly, and cropland remained relatively constant (table 2). It must be kept in mind that breeding areas of woodland birds have been larger in the past, since a substantial amount of once-forested North American land now is farmland. Therefore, major adjustments in relative pressure upon breeding areas have undoubtedly taken place over the past 250 years. The important point to be made is that these northern regions now appear to have stabilized in area relative to the tropics.

Douglass H. Morse

Table 2. Changes in area of cropland, meadow and pasture, and forest 1955–70[1]

Category	Locality	Area (km²), 1955	Area (km²), 1970	Percentage change
CROPLAND[2]	Canada and United States	2,289,190	2,348,230	+ 2.5
	Central America and West Indies	290,810	386,210	+24.7
PERMANENT MEADOW AND PASTURE	Canada and United States	2,781,370	2,691,780	− 3.2
	Central America and West Indies	778,630	833,670	+ 6.6
FOREST	Canada and United States	6,680,370	7,355,620	+ 9.2
	Central America and West Indies	689,630	500,000	−27.5
UNUTILIZED LAND[3]	Canada and United States	7,570,650	6,944,020	− 8.3
	Central America and West Indies	973,850	1,063,670	+ 8.4

[1] Data from FAO production yearbooks; vol. 12, table 1, pp. 3–5 (1958); vol. 27, table 1, p. 4 (1973).

[2] Arable land and land under tree crops (FAO definition).

[3] Unused but potentially productive, wasteland, and other (FAO definition).

The neotropical forests have also been modified by man before, although probably not to their present extent or with such rapidity. It is clear, however, that a sizeable population of American Indians occupied Mesoamerica prior to the Spanish Conquest (Katz 1972). Their population density, at least in some localities, greatly exceeded the populations using these areas for a few hundred years after the Conquest. Sanders (1971a) suggests, for instance, that the native population in the eastern lowlands of Mexico declined after the Conquest to about 9 percent of its previous size. It is also clear that these Indians practiced large-scale agriculture, with elaborate irrigation schemes in some locations, such as in the Valley of Mexico (MacNeish 1964). These must have involved considerable modifications of previously existing land. The capital city, Tenochtitlan, may have had a population of as many as 300,000, and the Valley region may have supported a population of 6–20 million shortly before the Conquest (Katz 1972), although others, such as Saunders (1971b), feel that the numbers in residence were considerably more modest. To what degree these conditions were duplicated elsewhere is an open question. However, many authorities believe that multiple centers of agriculture developed in the Mesoamerican region, which would have provided substantial areas of second growth and disturbed habitat comparable to that currently used by many migrants. Probably even more important than the patterns of agriculture seen in the Valley of Mexico, however, were those of the slash-and-burn techniques, which were apparently widespread through Mesoamerica. The constant clearing and abandoning of previously forested land required by this land-use pattern would insure the existence of sizeable amounts of second growth. Overall, one obtains the firm impression that second-growth forest was widespread in pre-Columbian Mesoamerica.

The point to be made is that conditions on both breeding and wintering grounds have been constantly changing for a considerable period of time, and these fluctuations should be one of a number of factors that select for a type of migrant that shows high opportunistic tendencies. This point is relevant to the attributes presently shown by neotropical migrants, even if destruction of primary habitat at present is much faster than ever before and in some places is so drastic as to make adaptation impossible.

I should parenthetically note that the pattern of land use seen in the New World does not entirely parallel that seen elsewhere. Moreau (1972), for example, suggested that numbers of European Palaearctic forest migrants are probably now only one-third of their maximum post-Pleistocene abundance, a result of man's activities on the breeding grounds. While similar changes have taken place in North America, they must be viewed as more modest than those occurring in Europe.

Comparisons of Breeding Densities over Time

If 1) neotropical migrants (or many migrants) had previously been limited on the wintering grounds, and

Table 3. Long-term population trends of breeding birds in eastern deciduous forests

Census			Pairs of neotropical migrants/ 100A (40 ha)	Pairs of others/ 100A (40 ha)	Percentage neotropical migrants	Habitat
Year	Number[1]	Census taker				
1946	27	Williams 1946	206	40	83.8	Beech-maple
1940	22	Mellinger 1940	179	43	80.5	"
1975	39	Waterhouse 1975	407	313	56.5	"
1975	36	Gough 1975	167	138	54.8	"
1946	19	Wallin 1946	192	20	90.6	Oak-hickory
1974	14	Laitsch 1974	200	93	68.2	"
1976	22	Laitsch 1977	207	39	83.8	Oak-hickory-maple
1976	31	Criswell et al. 1977	116	147	44.1	Oak-hickory
1946	10	Kendeigh 1948	96	22	81.5	Oak-maple
1975	35	Kendeigh and Eddington 1975	55	18	75.0	"
1947	23	Baldwin et al. 1947	368	149	71.1	Deciduous floodplain
1975	23	Criswell, Cramer and Gauthey 1975	182	282	38.9	"
1947	22	Stewart and Robbins 1947	349	88	80.0	Tulip-oak
1976	169	Whitcomb, Bystrak, and Whitcomb 1977	300	128	70.1	"

[1] Number of breeding-bird census in *Audubon Magazine, Bird-lore, Audubon Field Notes,* or *American Birds.*

2) if their resources have increased there, and 3) remained stable on the breeding grounds, one would predict a subsequent increase in their population density on the breeding grounds. Since conditions 2 and 3 are realistic, I attempted to test this hypothesis by comparing the breeding densities of neotropical migrants at two points in time (1940–47 and 1974–76), using breeding-bird censuses in *American Birds* and its predecessors. For this analysis, I used the few available censuses of mature "undisturbed" forests that spanned this period, and additionally matched other censuses of similar habitats from the two time periods. In each of 10 comparisons that I could make (table 3), the proportion of neotropical migrants, counter to prediction, decreased over this time (p < 0.01 in a two-tailed Wilcoxon Test). However, in all but one case it was impossible to separate this effect from an increasing island effect proposed by Whitcomb and his coworkers (Whitcomb et al 1976; Whitcomb, Whitcomb, and Bystrak 1977; Whitcomb 1977; MacClintock, Whitcomb, and Whitcomb 1977), presumably resulting

from the destruction of habitat adjacent to the census plots. The only way to test this hypothesis is to determine whether a trend has occurred among populations in large forested areas not subject to the island effect. No censuses currently available accomplish that, although one might be able to recensus mature areas studied in the 1930s and 1940s or to census carefully chosen sites closely resembling the areas studied during that time.

Integrity of Migrants' Populations on Wintering Grounds

Another way of looking at the question of limitation would be to evaluate the contingencies that local breeding populations of migratory species experience on their wintering grounds, or vice-versa. However, there probably are no populations upon which one could currently conduct such a study. Some migrants winter at the same spot year after year (Nisbet and Medway 1972; Pearson 1972; Moreau 1972), but it is

Douglass H. Morse

State	Comments
Ohio	Part of Cleveland park system
"	
"	Control (?) for study of urbanization
Indiana	
Ohio	
W. Va.	
"	
Virginia	Near beltway
Illinois	
"	Same area as 1946
Maryland	
"	Same area as 1947
Maryland	
"	Same area as 1947

unknown whether a local breeding population winters in a local area. Given the great potential for mixing that occurs in migration, this type of homogeneity seems unlikely. Some species in fact wander widely at this season (Moreau 1952; Willis 1966). Ramos' (this volume) demonstration that different geographic races of several species may winter together in a single forest in Veracruz makes it seem questionable whether such "ideal" populations will be found for study.

Evidence for Limitation on Wintering Grounds

It is, however, not difficult to present rather convincing individual cases of limitation either on the breeding or wintering grounds, although the degree to which one can generalize from these examples is open to question. Considering first the wintering grounds, perhaps the most elegant case is a massive natural experiment in the Old World, which took place between 1968 and 1974 in the Sahel (sub-Saharan Africa). Over that period, rainfall basically failed (Winstanley, Spencer,

and Williamson 1974), and numbers of migrants wintering there decreased simultaneously (Morel 1973; Morel and Morel 1974). While these birds may simply have gone elsewhere in response to these conditions, the drought was not a local one, rather being one that covered the majority of several species' wintering ranges (Moreau 1972).

Some of the species that winter in this area simultaneously experienced catastrophic decreases on their breeding grounds. The most striking example was that of the Whitethroat (*Sylvia communis*), a common breeding sylviid warbler of scrub and hedgerow throughout most of Europe (Davis 1967). Numbers of breeding Whitethroats in some parts of England decreased 77 percent between 1968 and 1969 alone (figure 1). Similar patterns appeared in other parts of its breeding range, and several other species wintering in the Sahel also showed the same trends, for example in Germany (Berthold 1973, 1974). Alternative explanations such as changed weather conditions on the breeding grounds or in migration, persistent insecticides or arboviruses do not accord with the data or are without positive evidence (Winstanley et al 1974; Bourne et al 1976).

The yearly fluctuations in numbers provided even closer correlations, making the case compelling (Winstanley et al 1974; Batten and Marchant 1977). Rainfall in the Sahel over the winter of 1969–70 ameliorated slightly, and the Whitethroat's breeding numbers stabilized that year. They subsequently decreased or remained equally low until 1975, when they showed a substantial increase, corresponding with the breaking of the drought. In the summer of 1976 they apparently increased a striking 60 percent (Batten and Marchant 1977), indicating the ability of the population to rebound from adversity.

The inescapable conclusion is that the carrying capacity of the wintering grounds was limiting the population sizes of these birds during this drought, although whether or not that was the case prior to the drought is not known. Droughts in the Sahel are certainly not unusual. Further, there have been longer-term fluctuations in this area as well (Moreau 1972). Thus, although it seems apparent that these factors can limit population numbers, we can only speculate about how often this may occur. The Whitethroat example does not demonstrate that limitation normally occurs on the wintering grounds; however, if the Sahel continues to deteriorate, the case becomes more instructive.

Other information on wintering migrants in the tropics suggests potential limitation there. Several species exhibit territoriality or other manifestations of aggressive behavior. Many of the warblers described

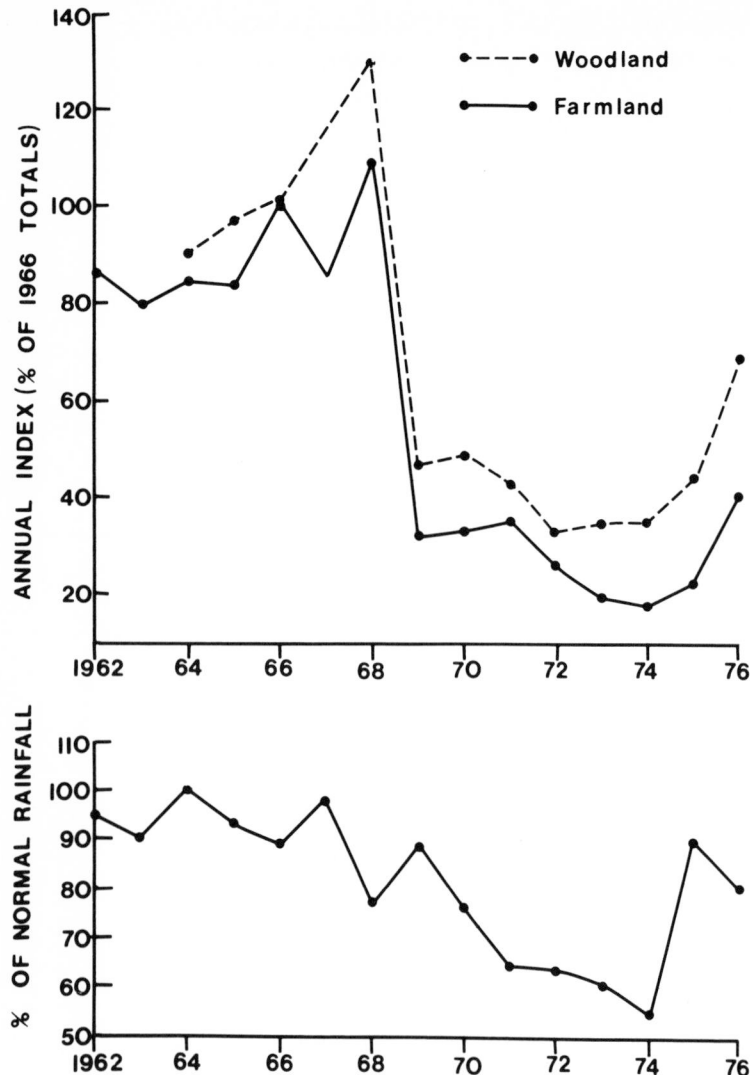

Figure 1.   Top. Annual index of Whitethroats from English Common Birds Census. Populations in 1966 form the basis for comparison. Partially redrawn from Batten and Marchant (1977), with additional data points added that were listed but not plotted in that paper.
Bottom. Mean percentage of 1931–60 May–October rainfall at Nouakchott, Atar (Mauritania), Gao, Tessalit (Mali), Agades (Niger), and Khartoum (Sudan). Data through 1972 from Winstanley et al., (1974), with subsequent data from Monthly Climatic Data for the World, Environmental Data Service, National Oceanic & Atmospheric Administration, U. S. Department of Commerce, Washington, D.C.

Dendroica petechia) Skutch distinctly indicates the existence of territoriality, and territoriality is strongly suggested by studies presented in this volume.

Where studied in company with permanent residents during the winter, the migratory species are often, though not invariably, subordinate in encounters (Willis 1966; but see Chipley 1976). Interactions between residents and wintering migrants occurred most frequently between ecologically similar species in Willis' study, which is consistent with resources being contested. Even though migrants were characterized by their subordinance, interspecific and intraspecific aggressive interactions did occur among them (Willis 1966), an important point if one is to argue strongly that the actions of the residents may have a serious impact upon the migrants. Some studies, however, have reported low frequencies of interactions among migrants (Chipley 1976; this volume), which would be consistent with, although not demonstrating, a non-limiting situation.

On the other hand, some evidence suggests that limitation may occur on the breeding grounds. During the breeding season, territoriality is the rule among migratory species. Ovenbirds (*Seiurus aurocapillus*), in fact are known to change their territory size in response to the richness of the food source available (Stenger 1958; Featherstone 1966; Zach and Falls 1975). This fluctuation has strong implications for the number of breeding individuals that can be supported, notwithstanding Lack's (1966) arguments that territoriality does not limit population size.

Nonbreeding birds also occur in many populations during the reproductive period, including those of neotropical migrants. The regular presence of such individuals also strongly suggests that conditions are limiting the numbers of individuals, at least those that will reproduce. Brown (1969) has argued that no evidence exists to justify the assumption that a surplus of both sexes capable of breeding occurs in any population. Although few studies satisfy his objection, Knapton and Krebs' (1974) work on Song Sparrows (*Melospiza melodia*), not a neotropical migrant, does, and the probable reason why few relevant data (pro or con) exist is that this factor is difficult to demonstrate. It is, however, premature to say just how important Brown's complaints really may be.

Special situations, such as those of the budworm specialists, the Cape May (*Dendroica tigrina*) and Bay-breasted (*D. castanea*) Warblers, are also strongly suggestive of periodic limitation on the breeding grounds. Numbers of these species change strikingly over time within a local or regional area (Kendeigh 1947; Morse 1978a), and these fluctuations are closely correlated with the abundance of spruce budworms

by Skutch (in Bent 1953) are, for instance, found only one to an area, which suggests that they are territorial, since they are rather common in many areas. One may find only one of a species per mixed-species flock, also, which is a condition typical of territoriality (Moynihan 1962; Morse 1970). In some cases (e.g., Yellow Warbler

Douglass H. Morse

(*Choristoneura fumiferana*). While individuals may move elsewhere when a budworm outbreak runs its course in an area, overall numbers of budworms vary dramatically from year to year, even over a large geographical area (Morris 1963). Numbers of fall migrants are known to fluctuate strikingly in concert with the budworms (Brewster in Griscom 1938; MacArthur 1958; Finch 1976), further suggesting that these species are at least sometimes resource-limited on their breeding grounds. However, these fluctuations are unusual among neotropical migrants and may not provide an appropriate model for other species.

Large buildups of these two budworm specialists are also related to the numbers of other migratory warblers. Species such as Black-throated Green (*Dendroica virens*) and Blackburnian (*D. fusca*) Warblers show population declines in areas where the specialists are abundant (Morris et al 1958). Here is further suggestion of limitation on the breeding grounds.

The information presented thus far largely considers only intraspecific factors, or factors associated with closely related groups of species. These birds form only part of the story, however, for sizeable numbers of year-round residents also occupy the breeding areas (MacArthur 1959; Willson 1976). In general, the proportions of permanent residents in forested eastern North America are considerably lower than the proportions of permanent residents in many areas of the neotropics: one-quarter or less of the individuals of eastern North American forests are permanent residents (MacArthur 1959; Willson 1976), vs up to 80–95 percent in the primary lowland neotropical forests (Karr 1976), although showing an increasing proportion as one moves southward (this volume). These data suggest that the potential effect of residents on the migrants should be greater on the wintering grounds than on the breeding grounds, even if migratory species are in part capitalizing on resources that the year-round residents cannot exploit with equal effectiveness. Northern residents might *nevertheless* prevent the migrants from expanding their influence further than they do, as I will argue in the following section.

A Dynamic Equilibrium

Evidence thus exists for limitation on both the breeding and wintering grounds. Pooling the information, one obtains the impression of a dynamic equilibrium, in which mechanisms associated with population limitation may occur in both areas, and in closely related species, if not the same species, although we can say little about the populational makeup of the individuals in question. However, if we could demonstrate widespread aggressive behavior on both the wintering and breeding grounds of any given species, it would be reasonably good presumptive evidence for such a relationship. Indeed, aggressive territorial behavior is virtually ubiquitous on the breeding grounds of these migrant birds, although it could have other functions as well, and it may also occur on the wintering grounds (Skutch in Bent 1953; this volume).

In many but not all, cases migrants appear able to intrude upon permanent neotropical residents only to a limited degree. This limitation, if real, should place an absolute ceiling on the number of individuals that could invade the north each succeeding year, and it certainly seems clear that many fewer individuals return than left the preceding fall, whatever has happened to them (Moreau 1972). Pressure upon northern permanent residents should thus be alleviated somewhat, although this impact may nevertheless be significant (Ulfstrand 1976). Under such circumstances, northern permanent residents should attain a somewhat greater abundance than they would otherwise.

Although Lack (1966), Fretwell (1972), and others have argued that high-latitude permanent residents are typically limited by the winter rather than by the breeding season, any lowered pressure during the breeding season over a substantial time span might be expected to alter life styles of the permanent residents, improving their opportunities to exploit otherwise unobtainable resources. This shift would simultaneously damp future opportunities for migrants. A similar result might obtain from initial limitation on the breeding grounds. In either case an equilibrium would result.

Unless shifts of longer duration than a year occurred in one area or the other, time might not be adequate to permit substantial permanent change, however. Populations of usually stable species may, upon occasion, decline markedly, yet they usually recoup these losses and reach their former abundance (Griscom 1941; Batten 1971). Further, short-term losses by migratory species may be temporarily compensated for by increases in other migrants, as I have seen in some breeding populations of warblers (Morse 1976).

Unfortunately, the relevant data for testing this hypothesis are currently few. However, Whitcomb et al's (1977) data (incorporating censuses of Briggs, Criswell, and others) from "island" woodlots are consistent with the equilibrium argument. They represent a longer-term change of conditions than do yearly fluctuations. In plots isolated from surrounding woodland habitats by removal of similar vegetation, neotropical migrants have decreased both in density and diversity, presumably through a variety of island effects. During the same period permanent residents have increased in some cases (Whitcomb 1977). While this increase has not by any means matched the decrease in numbers of neotropical migrants, the simplest explanation is that the permanent residents have responded to the void left by the neotropical migrants, having previously been restricted through diffuse competition with the migrants. Presumably, present shifts result from short-term ecological release. Only if a long-term permanent depression in numbers occurred would one predict appreciable evolutionary change in the permanent residents, which would permit progressively heavier exploitation of the resources present.

Other sorts of data that would provide good tests may in most instances be extremely difficult to generate. Nevertheless, other data in the literature may provide tests in the way that Whitcomb et al's work has. In a few individual cases the evidence seems good to suggest shifts in limitation patterns. In this way, the increase in abundance of Chestnut-sided Warblers (*Dendroica pensylvanica*), one of the rarest of species in Audubon's time, might be attributed to the rapid increase of second growth vegetation on its breeding grounds (Bent 1953).

The equilibrium may differ from one area to another. The number of New World migrants, along with their relatively small wintering area, combines to produce a situation quite unlike that of the European-African system, where a low proportion of migrant birds winter in a much larger area (Moreau 1966). The density of permanent residents in English woodlands is much higher than that of eastern North America, as a comparison of the English Common Birds Census (in *Bird Study*) and the North American Breeding Bird Census (in *American Birds*) will readily demonstrate. This difference probably is partially a function of the permanently available resources that the residents have available, or of the lowest point of resource availability in a year (Morse 1978b), although this remains to be proven. However, the much longer history of severe habitat despoilation there (see Moreau 1972) may have also played a role in the equilibrium. Large areas of coastal western North America, on the other hand, have higher proportions of permanent residents than does eastern North America (this volume), but have not probably suffered traditionally the degree of habitat modification seen in many parts of Europe.

Migration

Missing thus far has been any consideration of migration, which in some species occupies more than either the period spent on the breeding grounds or the wintering grounds. If little is known about the contingencies facing migrants on their wintering grounds, even less is known about the challenges that they face along the migratory lanes, although Rappole and Warner's (1976) recent paper represents an excellent start to improve this situation. However, predictability should be minimal here for the migrants. Further, real challenges are faced by these birds under the most ideal of conditions; for instance, the crossing of broad stretches of hostile environment, such as water and deserts. While it is now known that even small birds with maximum fat reserves can cross the widest ecological barriers of the world with reserves sufficient to fly hundreds of extra kilometers (Berthold 1975), this statement refers only to optimal conditions, both of weather and of the migrants' energetic condition.

For example, impressive numbers of birds cross the Gulf of Mexico (Lowery 1951), but this crossing takes place in spite of the substantial mortality that occurs in transit, even though evidence in support of this mortality usually is ·anecdotal. Webster (1974) has, however, reported one such recent catastrophe, in which some 5,000 bird carcasses washed up on Galveston Island, Texas, alone, in two days (7–8 May 1974). This mortality was associated with weather disturbances over the Gulf during the preceding few days. Emaciated individuals regularly appear at oil rigs well off the U. S. Gulf Coast (D. H. Morse, pers. obs.). One may nevertheless assume that the Gulf crossing is favored in an evolutionary sense only because these individuals' ancestors survived better than did ones traversing the arc around the west of the Gulf. If so, that in its own right testifies to the number of contingencies that may be expected around the mainland route.

Moreau (1972) discusses similar difficulties that may be experienced by palaearctic migrants, particularly those moving from central Asia to Africa. These birds must move over several thousand kilometers of largely inhospitable steppe or semidesert, reaching Africa immediately south of the Sahara at the very time that conditions there are deteriorating due to the onset of drought.

While most North American migrants do not experience this sort of drought, simply moving over unfamiliar areas, many with habitats unfamiliar to them at other times, must pay its toll. Many coniferous forest nesters migrate through areas of deciduous forests. There, their foraging patterns and habitat choices seem to match their breeding-ground preferences in many instances (Parnell 1969; Power 1971; Morse ms), although feeding in oak foliage clearly must make demands upon them that differ from those of spruce foliage.

For an extreme, I regularly find sizeable numbers of migrant spruce-forest warblers in late summer on offshore islands along the Maine Coast, where the sole

Douglass H. Morse

cover consists of savannah and rocks (D. H. Morse, unpubl. data). These birds are flying along the coast when dawn breaks and are unable or unwilling to return to the mainland at that time. The nearest-to-accustomed habitat on these islands consists of large emergent herbs, such as the tall meadow-rue (*Thalictrum polygamum*); for the most part, however, the islands are covered with a variety of grasses. It is a strange site to see Cape May Warblers, denizens of the treetops of the boreal forest, trying to forage in the rank grass associated with these islands. Yet sometimes they are the commonest land birds there. Coastal migrants may regularly encounter this type of habitat along the entire East Coast, although low, low trees or even pines may often be reasonably close at hand. Rappole and Warner (1976) have noted that migrants may leave apparently unfavorable areas, probably without feeding. However, there is a limit to how many times a bird might move on without feeding, and given the habitat predominating along much of the East Coast of the United States, it seems probable that foraging patterns of the sort seen in spruce-forest warblers on these islands are not infrequently of critical importance to them. Moving along a coastal route probably has additional hazards, in that nocturnally migrating birds may drift out into the ocean during fall migration with some regularity, although the exact nature of these movements remains a point of contention (Murray 1976).

Storms or cold weather also intervene from time to time. While the most vulnerable species generally do not migrate early (in the spring), considerable evidence indicates that success rates of early nesters often is greater than that of late nesters (Lack 1966). This factor should, in the absence of countering pressures, select for birds that progressively head northward earlier and earlier in the spring. Counteracting pressures probably are largely in the nature of infrequent cold periods, sometimes combined with snow, which during occasional springs produce catastrophic mortality. For instance, record low temperatures in May 1974 in the northeastern United States apparently killed extremely large numbers of Scarlet Tanagers (*Piranga olivacea*), Swainson's Thrushes (*Catharus ustulatus*), and several species of warblers (Finch 1975). Other recent cases include similar conditions in Manitoba during May 1974, during which a heavy dieoff occurred, including thousands of warblers washed up on the shores of Lake Manitoba (Houston and Shadick 1974); and a disaster of birds crossing the Great Lakes in May 1976, with as many as 200,000 being washed up on shore in one area of Lake Huron alone (Janson 1976).

Unfortunately, follow-ups to these disasters are largely in the nature of post-facto impressions, rather than careful censuses, and cannot eliminate the effect of other variables, such as breeding success and variation in the "visibility" of migrants as a function of varying weather patterns. However, similar to the cases of winter mortality considered above, most of the populations in question appear to recover their former densities quickly.

Migratory contingencies must thus select for individuals that are morphological generalists and that also have a high level of plasticity. These factors in their own right may compromise the extent to which adaptations for either breeding or wintering grounds may proceed. Further, characteristics favoring successful migration, such as long, narrow wings (Dilger 1956) or the ability to store large amounts of migratory fat (Odum and Connell 1956) may act against the development of highly precise adaptations to breeding or wintering grounds, either compromising efficiency or limiting the number of options available.

Conclusion

The relative importance of wintering and breeding grounds as limiting factors may differ from species to species. Additional constraints may arise from the migratory periods, even if they do not regularly reduce numbers below carrying capacity. Some evidence points to an equilibrium such that small changes on either the breeding or wintering grounds could shift the area of limitation. If real, it may result in part from interactions between the migrants and the residents, as well as among the migrants themselves. Data from the breeding grounds suggest that such shifts do occur. There, Whitcomb et al. (1977) have suggested some compensation on the part of the permanent residents when the migrants decline in numbers. Similar evidence is currently lacking from the wintering grounds.

Acknowledgments

I thank R. Fritz and R. Whitcomb for comments on an earlier draft of the manuscript.

Literature Cited

Baldwin, E.
1947. Mature deciduous flood plain forest. Audubon Field Notes 1:212–13.

Batten, L. A.
1971. Bird population changes on farmland and in woodland for the years 1968–69. Bird Study 18:1–8.

Batten, L. A. and J. H. Marchant
1977.   Bird population changes for the years 1974–75. Bird Study 24:55–61.

Bent, A. C.
1953.   Life histories of North American wood warblers. Bull. U.S. Nat. Mus. 203:1–734.

Berthold, P.
1973.   Über starken Rückgang der Dorngrasmücke *Sylvia communis* und anderer Singvogelarten im westlichen Europa. J. Ornith. 114:348–60.

1974.   Die gegenwärtige Bestandesentwicklung der Dorngrasmücke (*Sylvia communis*) und anderer Singvogelarten im westlichen Europa bis 1973. Vogelwelt 95: 170–83.

1975.   Migration: control and metabolic physiology. In *Avian Biology*, vol. 5. eds. D. S. Farner and J. R. King, pp. 77–127. New York: Academic Press.

Bolin, B.
1977.   Changes of land biota and their importance for the carbon cycle. Science 196:613–15.

Bourne, W. R. P., J. A. Bogan, and B. Johnson
1976.   Whitethroats, organochlorines and arboviruses. Bird Study 23:279–80.

Brown, J. L.
1969.   Territorial behavior and population regulation in birds. Wils. Bull. 81:293–329.

Buechner, H. K., and J. H. Buechner
1970.   The avifauna of northern Latin America. Smithsonian Contrib. Zool. 27:1–119.

Chipley, R. M.
1976.   The impact of wintering migrant wood warblers on resident insectivorous passerines in a subtropical Colombian oak woods. Living Bird 15:119–41.

Cox, G. W.
1968.   The role of competition in the evolution of migration. Evol. 22:180–92.

Criswell, J. H., W. H. Cramer, and J. R. Gauthey
1975.   Mature deciduous floodplain forest. Amer. Birds 29: 1092.

Criswell, J. H., J. M. Giusti, B. Per-Lee, and R. J. Watson
1977.   Upland oak-hickory forest. Amer. Birds 31:40–41.

Davis, P.
1967.   Migration-seasons of the *Sylvia* warblers at British bird observatories. Bird Study 14:65–95.

Dilger, W. C.
1956.   Adaptive modifications and ecological isolating mechanisms in the thrush genera *Catharus* and *Hylocichla*. Wils. Bull. 68:171–99.

Dorst, J.
1974.   *The Life of Birds*. New York: Columbia Univ. Press.

Farner, D. S. and J. R. King
1971–   *Avian Biology*, vols. 1–5. New York: Academic
1975.   Press.

Featherstone, J. D.
1966.   Effects of food supply on the utilized territory of the ovenbird, *Seiurus aurocapillus*. M.A. thesis, Univ. Toronto. (cited in Zach and Falls 1975).

Finch D. W.
1975.   The spring migration, April 1–May 31, 1974, Northeastern Maritime Region. Amer. Birds 29:125–29.

1976.   The fall migration, August 1–November 30, 1975, Northeastern Maritime Region. Amer. Birds 30:29–36.

Food and Agriculture Organization
1958.   *Production Yearbook*, vol. 12. Geneva, Switzerland: FAO.

1973.   *Production Yearbook*, vol. 27. Geneva, Switzerland: FAO.

Fretwell, S. D.
1972.   Populations in a seasonal environment. Monogr. Popul. Biol. 5:1–217.

Gough, M. R.
1975.   Beech-maple forest. Amer. Birds 29:1096.

Griscom, L.
1938.   The birds of the Lake Umbagog region of Maine compiled from the diaries and journals of William Brewster. Bull. Mus. Comp. Zool. 66:523–620.

Griscom, L.
1941.   The recovery of birds from disaster. Audubon Mag. 43:191–96.

Houston, C. S. and S. J. Shadick
1974.   The spring migration, April 1–May 31, 1974. Northern Great Plains. Amer. Birds 28:814–17.

Jansson, R. B.
1976.   The spring migration, April 1–May 31, 1976, Western Great Lakes Region. Amer. Birds 30:844–846.

Karr, J. R.
1976.   On the relative abundance of migrants from the North temperate zone in tropical habitats. Wils. Bull. 88:433–58.

Katz, F.
1972.   *The Ancient American Civilization*. Praeger: New York

Kendeigh, S. C.
1947.   Bird population studies in the coniferous forest biome during a spruce budworm outbreak. Ontario Dept. Lands Forest, Biol. Bull. 1:1–100.

1948.   Oak-maple forest and forest-edge. Audubon Field Notes 2:232–33.

Kendeigh, S. C. and J. M. Eddington
1975.   Oak-maple forest and edge. Amer. Birds 29:1095–96.

Knapton, R. W. and J. R. Krebs
1974.   Settlement patterns, territory size, and breeding density in the song sparrow (*Melospiza melodia*). Canad. J. Zool. 52:1413–20.

Lack. D.
1966.   *Population studies of birds*. Oxford, U.K.: Oxford Univ. Press.

Laitsch, N.
1974.   Maturing oak-hickory forest. Amer. Birds 28:995.

1977.   Oak-maple-hickory forest. Amer. Birds 31:37.

Lincoln, F. C.
1950.   Migration of birds. Fish and Wildl. Serv. Circ. 16:1–102.

Lowery, G. H., jr.
1951.   A quantitative study of the nocturnal migration of birds. Univ. Kansas Publ. Mus. Nat. Hist. 3:361–472.

MacArthur, R. H.
1958.   Population ecology of some warblers of northeastern coniferous forests. Ecol. 39:599–619.

1959.   On the breeding distribution pattern of North American migrant birds. Auk 76:318–25.

MacClintock, L., R. F. Whitcomb, and B. L. Whitcomb
1977.   Island biogeography and "habitat islands" of eastern forest. II. Evidence for the value of corridors and minimization of isolation in preservation of biotic diversity. Amer. Birds 31:6–12.

MacNeish, R. S.
1964.   The origins of New World civilization. Sci. Amer. 211 (5):29–37.

Mellinger, E. O.
1940.   Dense lowland beech-maple forest. Bird-lore 42:484–485.

Monroe, B. L., jr.
1970.   Effects of habitat changes on population levels of the avifauna in Honduras. Smithonian Contr. Zool. 26:1–119.

Moreau, R. E.
1952.   The place of Africa in the Palaearctic migration system. J. Anim. Ecol. 21:250–71.

1966.   *The Bird Faunas of Africa and Its Islands*. New York: Academic Press.

1972.   *The Palaearctic-African Bird Migration Systems*. New York: Academic Press.

Morel, G.
1973.   The Sahel Zone as an environment for Palaearctic migrants. Ibis 115:413–17.

Morel, G. and F. Boulière
1962.   Relations écologiques des avifaunes sédentaires et migratrices dans une savane sahélienne du bas Sénégal. La Terre et la Vie 102:371–93.

Morel, G. and M. Y. Morel
1974.   Recherches écologiques sur une savane sahélienne du Ferlo Septentrional, Sénégal: influence de la secheresse de l'année 1972-1973 sur l'avifaune. La Terre et la Vie 28:95–123.

Morris, R. F.
1963.   The dynamics of epidemic spruce budworm populations. Mem. Entomol. Soc. Can. 31:1–332.

Morris, R. F., W. F. Cheshire, C. A. Miller, and D. G. Mott
1958.   The numerical response of avian and mammalian predators during a graduation of the spruce budworm. Ecol. 39:487–94.

Morse, D. H.
1970.   Ecological aspects of some mixed-species foraging flocks of birds. Ecol. Monogr. 40:119–68.

1971.   The insectivorous bird as an adaptive strategy. Annu. Rev. Ecol. Syst. 2:177–200.

1976.   Variables affecting the density and territory size of breeding spruce-woods warblers. Ecol. 57:290–301.

1978a. Populations of bay-breasted and Cape May warblers during an outbreak of the spruce budworm. Wils. Bull. 90:404–413.

1978b. Structure and foraging patterns of tit flocks in an English woodland. Ibis: in press.

Moynihan, M.
1962.   The organization and probable evolution of some mixed species flocks of neotropical birds. Smithsonian Misc. Coll. 143 (7):1–40.

Murray, B. G., Jr.
1976.   The return to the mainland of some nocturnal passerine migrants over the sea. Bird-Banding 47:345–58.

Nisbet, I. C. T. and Lord Medway
1972.   Dispersion, population ecology and migration of eastern great reed warblers *Acrocephalus orientalis* wintering in Malaysia. Ibis 114:451–94.

Odum, E. P. and C. E. Connell
1956.   Lipid levels in migrating birds. Science 123:892–94.

Parnell, J. F.
1969.   Habitat relations of the Parulidae during spring migration. Auk. 86:505–21.

Pearson, D. J.
1972.   The wintering and migration of Palaearctic passerines at Kampala, Southern Uganda. Ibis 11:443–60.

Power, D. M.
1971.   Warbler ecology: diversity, similarity, and seasonal differences in habitat segregation. Ecol. 52:434:43.

Rappole, J. H. and D. W. Warner
1976.   Relationships between behavior, physiology and weather in avian transients at a migration stopover site. Oecologia 26:193–212.

Sanders, W. T.
1971a. Cultural ecology and settlement patterns of the Gulf Coast. In *Handbook of Middle American Indians*, eds R. Wauchope, G. F. Ekholm, and I. Bernal, vol. 11, pp. 543–57. Univ. Texas Press: Austin.

1971b. Settlement patterns in Central Mexico. In *Handbook of Middle American Indians*, eds. R. Wauchope, G. F. Ekholm, and I. Bernal, vol. 10, pp. 3–44. Univ. Texas Press: Austin.

Stenger, J.
1958.   Food habits and available food of ovenbirds in relation to territory size. Auk 75:335–46.

Stewart, R. E. and C. S. Robbins
1947.   Virgin central hardwood deciduous forest. Audubon Field Notes 1:211–12.

Van Tyne, J. and A. J. Berger.
1976.   *Fundamentals of Ornithology*, 2nd ed. New York: Wiley.

Ulfstrand, S.
1976.   Feeding niches of some passerine birds in a South Swedish coniferous plantation in winter and summer. Ornis Scand. 7:21–27.

Wallin, H. E.
1946.   Oak-hickory forest. Audubon Mag. 48:142.

Waterhouse, S.
1975.   Virgin beech-maple forest. Amer. Birds 29:1096–97.

Webster, F. S., jr.
1974.   The spring migration, April 1–May 31, 1974, South Texas region. Amer. Birds 28:822–25.

Welty, J. C.
1975.   *The Life of Birds*. Philadelphia: Saunders.

Whitcomb, B., D. Bystrak, and R. Whitcomb
1977.   Mature tulip-tree-oak forest. Amer. Birds 31:91–92.

Whitcomb, B. L., R. F. Whitcomb, and D. Bystrak
1977.   Island biogeography and "habitat islands" of eastern forest. III. Long-term turnover and effects of selective logging on the avifauna of forest fragments. Amer. Birds 31:17–23.

Whitcomb, R. F.
1977.   Island biogeography and "habitat islands" of eastern forest. I. Introduction. Amer. Birds 31:3–5.

Whitcomb, R. F., J. F. Lynch, P. A. Opler, and C. S. Robbins
1976.   Island biogeography and conservation: strategy and limitations. Science 193:1030–32.

Williams, A. B.
1946.   Climax beech-maple forest with some hemlock. Audubon Mag. 48:145 (Section II).

Willis, E. O.
1966.   The role of migrant birds at swarms of army ants. Living Bird 5:187–231.

Willson, M. F.
1976.   The breeding distribution of North American migrant birds: a critique of MacArthur (1959). Wils. Bull. 88:582–87.

Winstanley, D., R. Spencer, and K. Williamson.
1974.   Where have all the whitethroats gone? Bird Study 21:1–14.

Zach, R. and J. B. Falls
1975.   Response of the ovenbird (Aves: Parulidae) to an outbreak of spruce budworm. Can. J. Zool. 53:1669–72.

Douglass H. Morse

STEPHEN FRETWELL
Bird Populations Institute
Kansas State University
Manhattan, Kansas 66506

Evolution of Migration in Relation to Factors Regulating Bird Numbers

ABSTRACT

Our most plausible working hypothesis to answer the question "Why do some but not all birds migrate?" is: 1) birds usually leave the area where they wintered to breed elsewhere to find safe nest sites; 2) birds usually migrate from the area where they breed to winter elsewhere to find more nonbreeding season food; 3) birds are usually resident in order to maintain (through site dominance) a social advantage in contests for resources during either the breeding season or the nonbreeding season (but not necessarily both). Several untested or weakly tested predictions are offered, and some case histories are reviewed. The Field Sparrow is offered as a winter-limited species sometimes migratory to find predator free nesting habitat and sometimes resident to enhance winter survival. The Dickcissel is offered as a winter limited tropical species unable to generate sufficient site dominance to be resident and which migrates to find predator-free nesting habitats.

Introduction

My purpose in this analysis is to review the phenomenon of bird migration so as to arrive at what I believe is our most plausible working hypothesis for most American bird species. The question is: why do some but not all birds migrate? My approach differs from that of Kalela (1954) who attempts to hypothesize the step-by-step process by which migration evolved. I simply try to outline the major factors that make migration an adaptive response.

The phenomenon of bird migration has three clear elements: 1) birds leave the place in which they are spending the nonbreeding season to go breed somewhere else; 2) birds leave the place where they made their nests, and 3) some birds do neither, but stay to breed where they wintered and stay to winter where they breed. Of necessity, the birds that express 1) above also express 2) and so we mainly have to consider two kinds of birds: migrants and residents. A third kind also exist, known as erratics, which may move someplace else to winter, but will stay to breed there, and then may move someplace else to spend the next winter, or may become temporarily resident there. Red Crossbills are an example of this last category.

The question is: What are the factors which make the fitness of an individual bird higher if it migrates? How do these factors vary so that some species (or individuals) migrate and other do not?

On the surface, it is not surprising that some birds migrate. In fact, it is surprising to find that resident species occur. Most birds live in a seasonal environment, with wet seasons and dry, or hot seasons and cold. Also most birds breed only during a part of the year. When they breed, many birds change their diet, or feed their young foods different from what they eat when not breeding. Finally, the activity patterns of most birds are dramatically different for breeding and nonbreeding populations. Wanderers are tied to nests; flocks are broken up into territories. Normally secretive birds have to offer distraction displays whenever a predator passes dangerously nearby.

How unlikely, therefore, that one place, itself changing through the year, could offer conditions for survival and reproduction which would not be improved upon at another place, at least some of the year. Perhaps to other kinds of animals, the difficulties of finding the other place and of getting there diminish considerably the virtues of moving, and so migration is less plausible. But birds can fly, they have complex nervous systems, homeothermy, internal clocks, accurate perception of visual cues, and good memories. So we are forced to ask: why do they not all migrate?

To answer this question we have to answer its converse: why do migrants migrate? While we can imagine lots of possible reasons to leave (and few to stay), we still usually do not know which of all the obvious possibilities are the critical ones.

Some Examples

To give these questions substance, consider a curious example. In eastern Kansas, three wrens commonly occur in the forests: the Carolina Wren (*Thryothorus ludovicianus*), the Winter Wren (*Troglodytes troglodytes*), and the House Wren (*Troglodytes aedon*). The Carolina Wren is a resident, sedentary year round despite climatic disasters that frequently decimate the population. The other two species are total migrants, the Winter Wren occurring in winter only, the House Wren in summer only. Why is the Carolina Wren resident? Why does the House Wren not stay over winter, and why does the Winter Wren not stay to breed?

Similarly puzzling examples exist throughout both tropical and temperate bird communities. In most of the Southeast United States, Pine, Yellow-throated and Yellow-rumped Warblers inhabit pine forests. Most Pine warblers are resident year round, the Yellow-throated summer residents only, and the Yellow-rumped, winter residents only. Clearly, neither climate nor taxonomy can account for these movements: why do these similar species have such different migratory habits? Tropical communities, as other papers in this volume clearly show, provide more dramatic evidence of similar species, some of which migrate while others are resident. Only occasionally (as in arctic shorebird communities) do we encounter a situation where every species is migratory, and a climatic shift exists which is sufficiently severe that the question "Why migrate?" appears to have a trivial answer. For most communities we must be genuinely puzzled by all the comings and goings.

Which Factors Are Most Important in the Evolution of Migration?

Besides the difficulty in getting there, we recognize two separate kinds of factors affecting a given bird's choice of a habitat: 1) the intrinsic value or suitability of the different habitats and 2) the degree of crowding or competition in that habitat. The differences between habitats in their untouched state (e.g. differences in productivity or cover) are obvious, but may not play a major role in habitat selection and migration. Quality often reaches a point of diminishing returns, the asymptote of goodness being set not by the habitat, but by the organisms' ability to harvest or exploit resources. We can imagine a bird preparing to breed and surveying all possible habitats, where all

Stephen Fretwell

nabitats are completely empty of competitors, both interspecific and intraspecific. The wealth or security of many habitats could be so high, that the bird is able to raise as many young as it can produce in almost all of them. Then, the bird would settle in the closest one of the many possibilities, which might likely include the one it is leaving. Our bird, in a totally noncompetitive atmosphere, might find itself a resident.

Thus, we look with great interest at the possibility that competitive reduction in the suitability of different habitats are a part of what prompts a bird to migrate. This consideration is in fact rewarding, as Cox (1968) has shown. My discussion of this important point is largely an extension of Cox's review and analysis, and the plausibility of the argument depends largely on his work. Cox showed that land bird groups that migrate show a reduced subdivision of the niche space by factors other than space or habitat. Thus, migrants tend to be habitat segregators instead of resource segregators. Therefore, Cox argues, migration can be viewed as merely an extension of the habitat segregation whereby these species pack the niche space according to existing competitive restraints. This ingenious argument supports the idea that competitive interactions, both within and between species, are at the root of much land bird migration. Migration is viewed as evolving in species which must avoid competitive pressures by going somewhere else, instead of doing something different. For example, breeding warblers usually leave the forests in winter, but chickadees stay. The implication is that while it is clearly possible for a small insectivorous twig-gleaning bird to overwinter in these habitats, the warblers must leave for some reason. Perhaps the chickadee uses up all the resources available to this kind of bird.

I offer this discussion not to discount breeding-nonbreeding habitat changes (which are clearly important in groups such as arctic breeding shorebirds) but to emphasize the frequent importance of competition or crowding in determining the fitness of a given species in a given habitat. As long as a similar species *can* be resident, the migrants have residency as an option as well. Therefore, we can suppose that factors making migration more desirable are developed through a filling up of the habitat by competitors, which use up what a potential resident might need to stay.

The issue can be viewed another way. An empty habitat has many features affecting the fitness of the birds which might reside there. Some of these factors are used up by competition before others, so that as the habitat fills, these resources are used up, and the desirability of the habitat declines. The major influence over fitness in such a system is the one decreasing most rapidly with competition. For example, if food is

most limited, the energetic balance of the average individual in the population is likely to be farthest from the maximal energy budget possible, while its predation rate is likely to be much closer to the lowest values possible. Changing other components of fitness can alter the desirability of a given habitat a small amount—changing the component which has been reduced by crowding can sensibly alter the desirability of a given habitat. As David Lack observed (1954), each bird species has an enormous capacity to increase in population which is regularly balanced by competitive (either intra- or interspecific) reductions in either survival or reproduction. If the capacity is enormous, so must be the reductions. And if the reductions are enormous, so must be the potential for relieving the pressure of these reductions through migration.

In summary, while factors such as temperature may pose a serious challenge to the fitness of a bird, these factors can usually be overcome by evolution and adaptation. And once they are overcome, their challenging nature is permanently diminished. But if a factor which is density dependent, such as food, comes into short supply through over-exploitation, sumounting this challenge by adaptation offers only a short-lived success. If indeed a new food resource is appropriated by adaptation, the population will quickly grow until that food resource too is in short supply. Thus, density dependent-challenges are constantly maintained by population pressure, while density-independent challenges can be substantially diminished.

Which Factors Are Density Dependent in the Lives of Birds?

Food

This interesting question has not been often enough asked or answered. It is commonly assumed that food supplies, especially in the nonbreeding season are depleted through competition, until individuals die of starvation (rarely) or of starvation related disease, predation, or "stress." (See Lack 1954, for analysis, and 1966, for reviews). But there is surprisingly little evidence on this point. Lack made his strongest case for the Great Tit (*Parus major*), but when Krebs supplied a Great Tit population with additional winter food (1971) for one winter he got no increase in population. It is clear that birds, both breeding and wintering, will often go where the food is densest in microhabitat selection (for example, Goldcrests (*Regulus regulus*), and Coal Tits (*Parus ater*), Gibb 1960; ovenbirds (*Seiurus aurocapillus*), Stenger 1958) but this does not prove that food supplies are density dependent or even decrease significantly with increased consumption. Gibb's demonstration (1958) of Blut Tit (*Parus caeruleus*) use of larvae in pine cones is a clear enough case of a density-dependent reduction in a particular part of the food supply, but whether total food supply was significantly reduced over a winter still remains uncertain. More certain evidence on resource reduction does seem to exist in the studies on North American woodpeckers (Baldwin 1960) which sometimes take much more than half of the bark beetles in certain concentrated locations (Lack, 1966; 289). In none of these studies, however, is evidence presented that higher populations of birds suffered greater starvation.

Surprisingly, one clear case which is available involves the breeding food of the Great Tit. In one extraordinary year of the classic Marley Wood study (Lack 1966) the Great Tits increased their breeding numbers by 70 percent over previous population maxima. The weights of the young produced during that breeding season and the incidence of in-nest starvation both indicated that the parent birds were able to find less food than usual (or expected, if we may assume that the clutch size of the birds is adjusted to what is expected). Consistent with this evidence for significant consumption and reduction of the food supply by the breeding Great Tit population is an observed correlation between density and clutch size. At high densities, clutches are lower perhaps in anticipation of the food supplies being reduced by competitors.

In my opinion, however, this rather isolated observation does not greatly support the idea that breeding food is usually competed for by birds. The Marley Wood Great Tits commonly breed at densities which are comparable to the most abundant insectivorous North American species (warblers, titmice, vireos, or tanagers). The bird is nearly twice as big as most North American insectivorous birds, lays a clutch nearly twice as large as most, and has twice the survival rate per nest. We multiply these factors together, and arrive at the remarkable conclusion that the Marley Wood Great Tits take usually between four and eight times the insect prey to feed their young, compared with a typical warbler, sparrow, or vireo in North America. Yet with so great an increase in pressure on the food supply, a 70 percent further increase in population only reduced weights of the fledged young about 5 percent, and increased starvation about 13 percent (Lack 1966: 43). However, Lack does note that insects were less common (overexploited?) in 1961 than in any other year.

Lack's main contention (1954, 1966), which I (1972) have tried to formalize, is that it is winter food, not breeding food, that is subject to competition. This hypothesis strikes many ecologists as extremely plau-

sible, especially those who work closely with wintering populations (Jenkins, Watson, and Miller 1963; Gibb 1961; Fretwell 1972; Rohwer 1975), but is virtually untested. In no published study that I know of is it clear that a significantly greater proportion of a bird population suffered from food shortages during non-breeding seasons with higher than average population. When hungry birds are found, it seems more due to inclement weather or social stress than overpopulation.

I have argued elsewhere, however (1969, 1972) that this dearth of evidence should not discourage us. Many wintering (nonbreeding) birds face a nonrenewing resource which can not be competed for directly without severe danger of overexploitation. If a population excess exists, it means that the population alive at the beginning of the nonbreeding season contains more birds than the food supplies (seeds, over-wintering insect forms) can support. If all these birds survive until they starve, they will eat a substantial portion of the existing food supply so reducing it that the number of potential survivors is much reduced. In the extreme, the excess could survive until food supplies are reduced to the point where any bird will soon starve. Only insofar as some birds die before others, and as the resource is renewing (or defensible) will some survivors persist in a food-limited situation. Thus, it seems that winter-food limited birds are under strong evolutionary pressures to settle their population regulation through social mechanisms well before winter begins. And, indeed, it is the presence of many such mechanisms that convinces so many of us that winter food is limiting (Kalela 1954; Jenkins, Watson, and Miller 1963).

This is hardly a satisfactory discussion, but the questions of whether competition for food exists, if so, when does it happen, and how is it mediated are barely formulated properly. As Wiens (1977) wisely points out, the assumption that food is competed for is frequently made in the conduct of various niche studies (MacArthur, 1958). These studies find differences, but the finding of such differences does not greatly increase the plausibility of the competition assumption. Meanwhile we have to accept as just the most plausible working hypothesis the idea that food is competed for mainly in non-breeding populations.

Roosting Sites

Lack (1954) concludes that no other factor is likely to be density dependent in winter, but more recent studies point to roosting sites as a possible limiting factor. Kluyver (1957) noted that male Great Tits dominated roost boxes in winter, and Rohwer (1977) found a remarkable correlation between dominance status and roost site quality in Harris Sparrows and perhaps

Juncos. The evidence for roost sites is meagre in comparison to that for winter food, but it is easy to infer from Kluyver and Rohwer's work that higher populations might have trouble finding enough adequate sites. The question of when and how birds die, which is unanswered, is rather satisfactorily dealt with by supposing they die at night in their sleep.

Nest Sites

Observed for several breeding populations is a strong density dependent trend in nest predation. Lack noted it for the Great Tit in 1966, and Krebs confirmed it in 1971. I noted it in Field Sparrows (1972) and in both Red-winged Blackbirds and Dickcissels (figure 1; Fretwell, 1977). Murton (1958) noted it for the Wood Pigeon (reviewed in Lack 1966:180). It is not an easy observation to make, requiring much nest data. Therefore, to have found it in four rather dissimilar kinds of species suggests that it is a general result.

To summarize, the most plausible density-dependent factor in winter is food; roosting sites are a possibility. The most plausible strongly density-dependent factor in the breeding season is nest sites (or safety from nest predators); food is a possibility.

What Leads to the Evolution of Migration?

From the above summary and my introductory remarks, we are led to the following as a good working hypothesis for land bird migrants:

1) Birds migrate away from the breeding grounds to winter elsewhere because sufficient food (or roost sites) is (are) not available in the breeding area, to support all the birds that breed there.

2) Birds migrate away from the wintering grounds to breed elsewhere because nest predation would be too high (or food too low) where the population winters, if all the wintering birds stayed to breed.

Why Are Some Birds Resident?

I have noted that for any bird to become a resident seems to require a remarkable coincidence of the supply of diverse needs in one place. However, the foregoing discussion contained a clue to suggest otherwise. If we suppose birds are limited by winter food supply, and further accept that, in most cases this winter (nonbreeding) food supply needs to be competed for indirectly through social mechanisms, then we need to recall only one more principle to justify residence. It is a principle of some mystery, yet I daresay intuitively acceptable to every one of us. It has the name site-dominance or in aviculture, the home-cage effect. (See Maynard-Smith and Parker [1976] for a theoretical

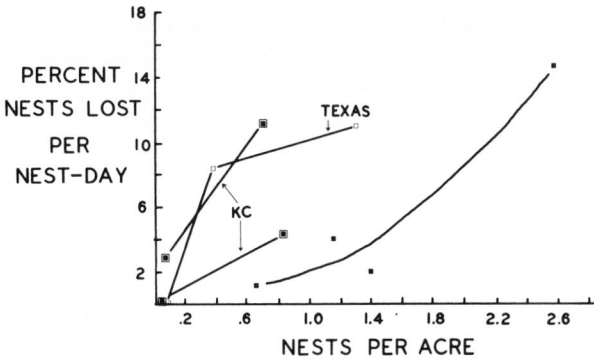

Figure 1. The rate of nest predation of Red-winged Blackbirds (*Agelaius phoeniceus*) with their nest density.

The daily rate of nest loss to predators is plotted against the number of nests per acre in upland grassland or old field habitats, for Red-winged Blackbirds. Each point represents a separate field containing 3–20 nests. The Texas data (open squares) are from 3 similar fields studied simultaneously. Four points from Kansas City, Missouri (labeled KC, enclosed solid squares) represent 2 sections of a single field in different years. The predation was higher in one of the years and higher in parts of the field where the Red-wing nests were less dense. The remaining data (solid squares) are from a central Kansas waterway where the number of nests varied through the summer. The season was divided into 4 periods of varying density, and predation rates were found to be higher during periods when many females had nests.

discussion). Almost invariably experience in a habitat contributes to dominance status there; no one known why, for sure, but site-dominance appears to be a very real effect. This effect of experience on dominance appears to be very strong in birds, which show a strong tendency to return to a defended territory year after year. Presumably, the costs of defending that territory are substantially lowered by the birds' having spent a previous summer or winter there. In any case, the tendency of migrating or dispersing males to return to territories (either wintering or breeding) is well known and is quite suggestive of the advantages of site experience in dominance exchanges.

Additional insight into site-dominance comes from the work of Rohwer and his colleagues on subadult males with female-like plumages. Rohwer presents evidence that subadult males that mimic females can often occupy and display on a territory (or nest site) from which they normally would be displaced by older males. By occupying such a site for a short time, these subadult males acquire a dominance advantage there that allows them to attract and hold mates and to breed successfully. Thus we can reasonably assume, for the sake of argument, that whenever dominance behavior is an important determinant of survival, one of the major factors determining dominance status is habitat experience. This simple fact may then play a major role in shaping the flow of migration in many birds.

I hypothesize that resident birds are commonly birds which are sacrificing a chance to move to a better habitat, in order to gain site-dominance advantages in the one of residence. If (and think this most plausible) winter food is limited and will be contested for, then a bird might breed in the wintering habitat so that, at least the bird itself and perhaps also its young have a better chance of surviving social contests the next winter. Or if breeding nest sites (for example, holes for hole nesting species) are limited, then a bird might winter where it breeds to keep its nesting site. In either case, a clear sacrifice may be necessary: the resident winterer breeding with poor success or the resident breeder barely surviving the winter.

At this point, an issue I have avoided discussing must be mentioned: whether birds are winter or breeding-season limited. Clearly, as I have shown above, there is evidence for density-dependent factors regulating at both seasons. However, it seems likely that for many species, there is an abundance of resources for either breeding or wintering because the populations are bottle necked at some other point in the annual cycle. A nonbreeding season bottleneck seems most likely for certain hole nesting and gallinaceous birds, which lay large clutches and have a great population increase through the summer. However, certain open nesting species, especially those resident in the tropics, may well find themselves so constrained by the difficulty in avoiding nest predation, that they are breeding season limited. This issue is discussed in detail elsewhere in this volume. I need to address it here because of the way it requires us to view migration. Winter-limited species may be so constrained in winter survival that greater breeding success, which sacrifices winter survival potential, may be maladaptive. For example, consider a winter-limited bird which needs to leave its wintering area to find nest sites to breed but where the first individuals to return to the wintering grounds after breeding achieve a site-dominance advantage. Although breeding grounds are available which substantially improve breeding success, these grounds may go unoccupied because they are farther from the wintering grounds. Individuals which stop and nest at a closer place are able to return more quickly to the best wintering sites, and this advantage can overwhelm the disadvantage of not going elsewhere to breed. I will show below that this is apparently the case for the Dickcissel (*Spiza americana*). Clearly, a winter-limited and a breeding-limited

species may be resident for rather different reasons, and these are reflected in the pattern of sacrifice of the residents. Breeding-limited residents will breed more successfully than would be the case if they moved. Winter (nonbreeding) limited residents will show higher survival over winter. But breeding-limited residents will show reduced winter survival rates, on which, it would seem, they could improve by migrating. The Carolina Wren may be one such example (but see Morton and Shalter 1977). Winter-limited residents will show reduced reproduction, which, it would seem, could be improved by migration. The Field Sparrow (*Spizella pusilla*) described below is an example of such a species. I think it likely that many New World open-nesting tropical birds fall into this category, since their nesting success is so very low compared to migrants (see Skutch 1949).

Winter limited migrants, as noted above, ought to show a spring migration pattern which does not optimize reproductive output, taking direct costs of migration into account. Breeding limited migrants, conversely, ought to show a fall migration pattern which does not optimize winter survival, again taking the direct costs of migration into account. Species limited at both seasons, of course, will behave more understandably in a short-term view.

It is, as I argue with residency, site-dominance that is the governing factor in all these considerations. As soon as there is an unbalancing of seasonal regulation, site-dominance becomes an urgent issue, and either residency evolves, or migration patterns are distorted.

Predictions on Species that Become Migrants

I trust the foregoing discussion strikes most readers as sufficiently plausible to merit testing. Therefore, I offer some predictions which, if unconfirmed, would require a healthy revision of these views.

1) Since nesting mortality is supposed to be more limiting than food supply in the breeding season, I predict that niche overlaps in feeding dimensions (for example both type and location of food) measured during this period ought to be greater than overlaps in nest site and morphometry.

2) Since resident bird species are presumed to be those with the greatest investment in site-dominance, I predict that there ought to be a clear separation of resident and migrants in social ecology and in habitat and population stability. In brief, species feeding on indefensible, or erratic resources, or feeding in large flocks with erratic home ranges, or feeding in apparently unstable habitats (or microhabitats) will be migrants. In general, anything precluding experience at

Stephen Fretwell

Table 1. Social system and residency in Kansas wintering birds[1]

	Residency status		
	Complete migrant	Partial migrant	Complete resident
Solitary-territorial	3	1	8
Social small flocks	2	2	1
Large flocks	8	4	0

[1] Data are from Rohwer 1975 and are number of species in each category. Winter territorial species do not migrate as frequently as winter flocking species.

one season from being useful in aggressive behavior in another will make migration a viable option. Conversely, residents will be birds which can know the individual rocks, trees, and topography of their home ranges, can use this knowledge to win aggressive contests, and which find that the appearance of their home range is unchanging. I offer table I as a cursory test of this prediction, more to stimulate a similar tropical comparison than to win converts. The data are from a paper by Rohwer (1975) on Kansas birds. He did not intend the data to be used this way, and so it is interesting how strongly they support the prediction. All the flocking species migrate, and almost all the "spaced" non-flocking and presumably territorial species are resident.

3) In winter-limited species, range extensions in winter will involve new sources of winter food (such as bird feeders). Range extensions in the breeding season will be correlated with improved conditions (food supply) on the wintering areas. In breeding-limited species, range extensions in the breeding season will involve new nest sites or habitat (such as bird boxes, marshes), or a reduction of nest predators. Range extensions in winter will involve an increase of breeding habitat.

4) Resident, winter-limited, bird species, which depend on site dominance to determine status (especially via territoriality) will not have skewed sex ratios, and will be monomorphic bright in plumage (Rohwer et al. ms) as both sexes defend territory. Migrants which regulate socially independent of site dominance will determine social status by other factors, including size and sex. Thus, females will be selectively eliminated, resulting in skewed sex ratios, sexual selection, and sexual dimorphism in plumage. In general, residents should be monomorphic bright in winter since both sexes will defend the territory then. Migrants will be monomorphic dull in winter, (or variable—see Rohwer 1975) but sexually dimorphic with bright males in summer. Breeding-season-limited species (territorial) will be monomorphic bright in summer, but dull or variable in winter.

Some Case Histories

I need to admit that the preceding arguments are an induction and generalization from my earlier studies with Field Sparrows in North Carolina (1968; 1972). I here offer a review of those studies, as an example of how the ideas work in a single species. I doubt, however, that the Field Sparrow is typical. It just happens to be the best studied example available.

Field Sparrow

The Field Sparrow in North Carolina is semi-migratory, some individuals migrating in all years, and all individuals migrating in some years. The winter distribution is largely confined to pine-broomsedge fields, but the species breeds in a wider variety of habitats. The density in the pine-broomsedge ranges up to 10 birds per acre, while breeding densities have a maximum of 4 birds per acre. Thus, there is a spring time dispersal which leaves the greatest density of Field Sparrows in the wintering habitats, with lower densities in pastures and old fields not normally occupied in winter. Presumably some of the North Carolina Field Sparows wintering population also migrate farther north; there are breeding populations from Virginia to Kansas, north to Canada, a region where few or no Field Sparrows winter.

It is remarkable density dependence in nesting predation in all wintering habitats in North Carolina which creates a situation where 60 percent of the Field Sparrow winter population has to leave to breed. Otherwise, the breeding densities and nest predation would be so high, no young would be fledged. Breeding dispersives find virtually unlimited Field Sparrow habitat outside the pine-broomsedge areas, which is occupied at such low densities that success ranges from two to three times as high as in the pine-broomsedge areas. Thus, while only 60 percent of the wintering population migrate (or disperse), probably 80 percent to 90 percent could migrate without appreciably crowding existing habitats. The 40 percent who do not leave suffer dramatically higher rates of nest mortality in order to stay (table 2).

However, the residents who stay gain some advantage, which I think is a site-dominance advantage expressed in regulatory aggression in September. They survive three times as long as the migrants (or dispersives) who breed outside the wintering habitats. The

Table 2. Life history statistics for 3 populations of Field Sparrows wintering together but breeding in different habitats[1]

	I	II	III
Winter density	10–25/ha	0–10/ha	0/ha
Breeding density	3.2/ha	2.2/ha	.74/ha
Expected life-span (years)	4.33	3.20	1.4
Offspring per year	2.64	3.45	6.23
Total lifetime productivity	11.43	11.06	8.74

[1] Fretwell 1972: 124. Permanent resident individuals have low habitat breeding productivity but higher winter survival.

net fitness of the residents is actually slightly higher than that of the migrants, but perhaps not significantly so.

Thus, some Field Sparrow individuals adopt the strategy of residence at a sacrifice in breeding success to gain in wintering survival. The migrants leave the wintering area because of intense density-dependence in nest survival. The migrants leave the breeding areas in winter because most of the seeds in the species niche then are in pine-broomsedge fields.

Dickcissel

By way of contrast, I will summarize my findings on the Dickcissel, a tropical-temperate migrant.

Dickcissels winter in Venezuela and points to the east (Trinidad) and west (Panama, north to Mexico). The species arrives in Venezuela in November and has a restricted range in the eastern part of that country until late December when the birds spread out to other parts of their range. This spreading proceeds gradually all the way into March (figure 2). In mid-April, the birds fatten for migration and fly to south Texas. From there the species spreads north (to the Dakotas), east (to Ohio), and in some cases north, east, and back south again. The males precede the females by a week in Texas but by six weeks in Kansas and points north and east. One brood is raised in each location: probably every female raises two broods in two different locations (e.g. one in south Texas in May, and one in Missouri in June–July).

The feeding areas where Dickcissels winter are weedy or tall grassy fields similar in structure to the areas where the species breed. These habitats in Trinidad, Venezuela, and Panama are densely inhabited by a variety of seedeaters and grassquits, which appear to be territorial or flocked residents, there. Although no studies of tropical nest predation are available

which investigate density dependence, my temperate studies in similar habitat convincingly show the possibility of a serious effect (figure 1; 1972, 1977). Skutch and others have repeatedly shown tropical nesting success to be low due to predation, possibly reflecting an overcrowded situation there. I showed (table 3; 1972) that the Field Sparrow nesting at high densities apparently attracted predators to other species' nests. Figure 3 shows that Dickcissel nests suffer higher predation when Red-winged Blackbirds are more dense. Presumably, similar effects would hold in the tropics. The wintering Dickcissel is a refuging species, showing highly erratic feeding habitat selection and residency. Millions of individuals roost together at night in cane fields, flying out daily to feed. Their grassland competitors are much more stable; the Blue-black Grassquit (*Volatina jacarina*) seems territorial. The other seedeaters form large roving flocks, but apparently are geographically sedentary. I suspect that the other seed-eating grassland birds, as well as the ovenbirds, blackbirds, and other tropical grassland species can develop some form of degree of site-dominance where the

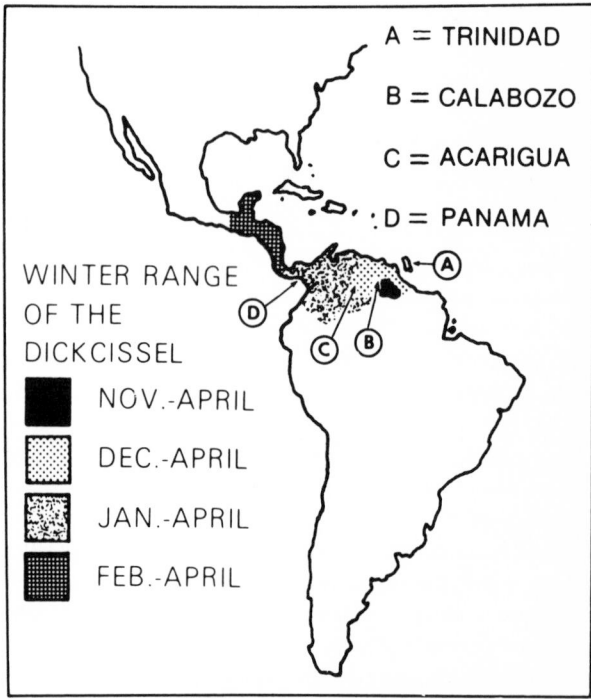

Figure 2. The winter distribution of the Dickcissel varies with the season. Dickcissels arrive in central or eastern Venezuela in November and are found there until late December when nocturnal flights out from this region occur. Birds arrive in western Venezuela in late December, in Trinidad and Panama by mid-January, and at points farther north in Central America through mid-March. The migration north begins in early April (Fretwell 1977).

Stephen Fretwell

Table 3. Relationship between nesting success of uncommon open nesting species and the density of the abundant Field Sparrow[1]

Species	Number of nests	Number success[1]	Percentage successful		Number of nests	Number success[1]	Percentage successful
Yellowthroat	10	3	30	Dickcissel	2	2	100
Prairie Warbler	5	0	00	Indigo Bunting	2	1	50
Indigo Bunting	2	0	00	Blue Grosbeak	3	2	67
Blue Grosbeak	3	0	00	Rufous-sided Towhee	1	1	100
Rufous-sided Towhee	8	1	12	Yellowthroat	3	2	67
Cardinal	5	2	40	Eastern Meadowlark	2	1	50
Total	33	6	18	Total	13	9	69
Field Sparrow	36	14	39	Field Sparrow	17	13	76

[1] Nests lost to weather excluded. Even rare species have low nest success in habitats where the combined species density is very high, showing a competitive effect.

Dickcissel cannot. The dominant individuals of these other species use their site-dominance to raise their survival rate, and so can tolerate (without migrating) densities so high that nest survival is very low. Dickcissel individuals, lacking the advantages of site dominance, cannot tolerate such low productivity and must migrate to the areas in the United States where no birds winter (for example, the ungrazed, unburned prairie).

Migrating Dickcissels arrive in the United States and settle in habitats similar to those where winter is spent. However, breeding Dickcissels occupy a broader range of habitats than do wintering individuals. The

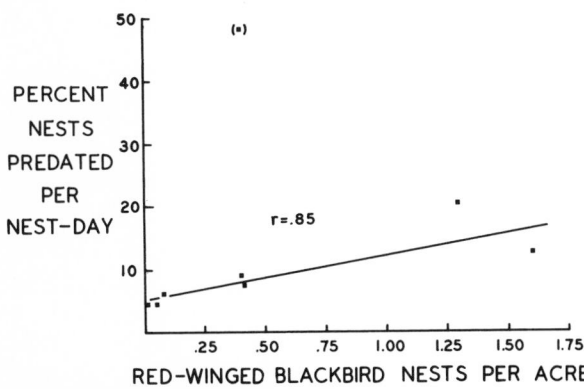

Figure 3. The rate of nest predation of Dickcissels increases as Red-winged Blackbird densities increase. The point in ( ) represents 2 nests, lost shortly after found, in a particular field. Other samples include 4–12 Dickcissel nests, which survived more reasonable periods giving more accurate estimates. The data are from the same fields as in figure 1, without dividing the data from the central Kansas waterway (highest Red-wing density point).

breeding range, from Texas to Ohio, seems set by winter limitation. Over 100 years ago, Dickcissels, commonly bred all the way to the Atlantic coast. However, in 1874, a cattle baron became dictator in Venezuela and increased the standing cattle population sevenfold, from 1.4 to 9.7 million head (Fretwell 1973). This presumably had some dramatic effects on the grasslands in the areas where Dickcissels winter and lowered the population which survived the winter. The net result was an overall decrease in breeding Dickcissel numbers, which led to a nearly complete extinction of the eastern Dickcissel population by 1880 (Rhoads 1903). This extinction has been maintained in spite of repeated colonizations of the East Coast, which are frequently quite successful reproductively (see Fretwell 1967). These eastern colonies always die out however, presumably because the advantages of extra reproduction are outweighed by some disadvantages in nonbreeding survival which accrue from the extra distance in migration from the East Coast to the tropics. Apparently, the Dickcissel is winter-limited, and the birds are at a disadvantage when they are farthest from the wintering grounds.

Thus, Dickcissels, like Field Sparrows, can be plausibly viewed as a species which belongs to (has a niche in) a certain nonbreeding bird community. However, the Dickcissel loses in the local competition for nest sites because it lacks the advantages of winter site-dominance and must migrate out of the tropical community where it winters. When the nonbreeding season begins, the Dickcissel returns to its niche because there is no other community in which it would have a competitive place. We can predict from this hypothesis, for example, that if the Dickcissels' winter niche is destroyed, the species will go extinct. If its present breeding habitats are destroyed, however, others exist which could be occupied successfully. If all other breeding habitats were destroyed, we may presume that allowing sufficient time for evolutionary adjustments, the Dickcissel could and would become a tropical resident. This transition would take place with a sufficient reduction in the wintering population that winter mortality would decrease to a level necessary to be balanced by the much lower nesting success of a resident population. The Dickcissel is thus a tropical species that migrates because it has somewhere else to breed where it has more to gain by going than it loses.

These case histories are meant to justify these speculations but not to test them. My intent in this report is simply to present to you what I believe to be the most plausible working hypothesis available and some predictions from them. My hope is that some future workers in the area of bird migration will adopt these hypotheses and test them.

Acknowledgments

I began this work while supported by National Institutes of Health GM-678 and continued it under support from National Science Foundation GB-14293. Frank Shipley and Sievert Rohwer made significant contributions to my thinking in this work, and helped in other ways as well. This is Bird Populations Institute scientific contribution #5.

Literature Cited

Baldwin, P. H.
1960. Overwintering of woodpeckers in bark beetle infested spruce-fir forests of Colorado. Proc. Int. Orn. Cong. 12:71–84.

Cox, G. W.
1968. The role of competition in the evolution of migration. Evolution 22(1):180–92.

Fretwell, S. D.
1967. Nesting success of Dickcissels breeding in North Carolina. Chat 21:68–88.

Fretwell, S. D.
1968. Habitat distribution and survival in the Field Sparrow (Spizella pusilla). Bird-Banding 39:293–306.

1969. Dominance behavior and winter habitat distribution in junco (Junco hyemalis). Bird-Banding 40:1–25.

1972. Populations in a seasonal environment. Princeton: Princeton Univ. Press. 217 pp.

1973. The regulation of bird populations on Konza Prairie: The effects of events all of the Prairie. Third Midwest Prairie Conference Proceedings, Kansas State University, Manhattan, Kansas. L. C. Hulbert ed.

1977. Is the Dickcissel a threatened species? American Birds 31:923–32.

Gibb, J.
1958. Predation by tits and squirrels on the eucosmid Ernarmonia conicolona (Heyl.). J. Anim. Ecol. 27:375–96.

1960. Populations of tits and Goldcrests and their food supply in pine plantations. Ibis 102:163–208.

1961. Bird Populations. In Biology and Comparative Physiology of Birds, ed. A. J. Marshal vol 2, pp.413–46. New York: Academic Press.

Jenkins, D., A. Watson, and G. R. Miller
1963. Population studies on Red Grouse, Lagopus lagopus scoticus (Lath.) J. Anim. Ecol. 32:317–76.

Kalela, O.
1959. Populationsokologische Geschichtspunkte zur Entstehung des Vogelzuges. Ann. Zool. Soc. 'Vanamo' 16:1–28.

Kluyver, H. N.
1957. Roosting habits, sexual dominance, and survival in the Great Tit. Cold Spring Harbor Symposium on Quantitative Biology. 22:281–85.

Krebs, J. R.
1971. Territory and breeding density in the Great Tit. Parus major L. Ecol. 52:2–22.

Lack, D.
1954. The Natural Regulation of Animal Numbers. London: Oxford Univ. Press, 343 pp.

1966. Population Studies of Birds. Oxford, U.K.: Clarendon Press, 341 pp.

MacArthur, R. A.
1958. Population ecology of some warblers of northeastern coniferous forests. Ecol. 39:598–619.

Maynard-Smith, J., and G. A. Parker
1976. The logic of asymmetric contests. Animal. Behav. 24:159–75.

Morton, E. S., and M. D. Shalter
1977. Vocal response to predation in pair-bonded Carolina Wrens. Condor 79:222–27.

Murton, R. K.
1958. The breeding of wood pigeon populations. Bird Study 5:157–83.

Rhoades, S. N.
1903. Exit the Dickcissel—a remarkable case of local extinction. Cassinia 7:17–28.

Rohwer, S. A.
1975. The social significance of avian winter plumage variability. Evol. 29:593–610.

1977. Status signaling in Harris Sparrows: some experiments in deception. Behavior 61:107–129.

Rohwer, S. A., S. D. Fretwell, and D. M. Niles
In prep. Delayed maturation in passerine plumages and the
    deceptive acquisition of resources.

Skutch, A. F.
1949. Do tropical birds rear as many young as they can
    nourish? Ibis 91:430–55.

Stenger, J.
1958. Food habits and available food of ovenbirds in rela-
    tion to territory size. Auk 75:335–40.

Svardson, G.
1957. The "invasion" type of bird migration. Brit. Birds
    50:314–43.

Wiens, J. A.
1977. On competition and variable environments. Ameri-
    can Scientist 65:599–597.

JAMES R. KARR
Department of Ecology, Ethology,
   and Evolution
University of Illinois
Champaign, Illinois 61820

Patterns in the Migration System Between the North Temperate Zone and the Tropics

ABSTRACT

Seasonal occupation of different portions of a species' range is a common phenomena and is generally associated with occupation of two distinct regions; one for breeding and the other as nonbreeding range. About 400 species have breeding ranges that are restricted to the North Temperate Zone and winter (occupy nonbreeding areas) in the tropics. Relatively wet and nonseasonal regions in the tropics (Southeast Asia and the neotropical region) host about 25 percent more nonbreeding species than drier and/or highly seasonal areas (Indian subcontient and Africa). Species richness of migrants does not seem to be correlated in any simple way with land area, vegetation type, presence of migration barriers, or migration distance. When migrant faunas are subdivided to reflect taxonomic and ecological affinities, several patterns are clear. Nonpasserine groups are more diverse in "dry" than "wet" areas while the reverse is true for passerines. When smaller geographic areas are considered, the importance of habitat type in determining number of migrant species is reinforced except in Africa where migrants favor more open habitats as wintering grounds. Among geographic areas, overlap in species composition varies significantly among taxonomic-ecological groups. In general, nonpasserine species winter over a wider geographic area than do passerine species. The complexity of migration systems in the neotropics, demonstrated by many studies in this volume, is mirrored and expanded in other tropical areas.

Introduction

Many birds occupy different portions of their range on a seasonal basis. For example, somewhat over 140 species of land birds breed in North America and winter in areas south of the Tropic of Cancer. These birds make annual round trips of great lengths as they undergo regular migrations between distant portions of their ranges. The movements of some migratory species are highly predictable (Swallows of Capistrano) while others exhibit variations in the magnitude and timing of movements.

Migrants between North America and the neotropical region winter in South America, on Caribbean Islands, and in Central America. In general, the number of migrant species (and their proportion of the fauna) declines as one moves south from Oaxaca, Mexico to Amazonia (Slud 1976). Several plausible explanations come to mind. For example, resident avifaunas are increasingly diverse from southern Mexico to Amazonia and, thus, may limit, through competition, the ability of migrants to winter successfully. Alternatively, survivorship of migrants may decline with length of migration and thereby select against long distance migration. Manipulative experiments designed to clarify the importance of these and other factors would be difficult at best. An alternate approach will be used here; I will examine patterns of movement between the North Temperate Zone and four major tropical areas. Moreau (1966, 1972) has employed this general approach in studies of the avifauna of Africa as has Slud (1976) in a study emphasizing geographic and climatic relationships in the neotropical avifauna. My objectives are to examine the geographic position, extent, and environmental characteristics of four major tropical regions as host areas for migrants that breed in the North Temperate Zone.

Although this discussion will be restricted to consideration of north temperate–tropical migration systems, many other migration patterns exist. Many species migrate wholly within the temperate zone. These may involve long-distance migrations (Rough-legged Hawk, *Buteo lagopus*; White-throated Sparrow, *Zonotrichia albicollis*) or shorter altitudinal movements (Blue Grouse, *Dendragapus obscurus*). Many permanent residents in tropical regions migrate regularly; some travel long distances (Yellow-green Vireo, *Vireo o. flavoviridis* while regular movements in others involve shorter migrations (some tropical hummingbirds). For some species, movement varies from year to year (Clay-colored Robin, *Turdus grayi*), depending on weather and other factors. While some may object to considering opportunistic movements that vary from year to

year as migration, it is clear that the movements are important to survival of individuals and therefore should be considered as one type of seasonal range occupation. Further, use of the concept of "seasonal range occupation" avoids the problem of labeling species as tropical or temperate species (Karr 1976a), which occupied so much discussion at the recent migrant symposium.

Breeding and Nonbreeding Range

Most species that make seasonal movements within their range occupy two major areas. Generally, the breeding range is occupied during late spring and summer of the temperate zone or late dry and early wet season of most tropical areas. The second portion of the range is occupied during the nonbreeding period (winter in temperate areas). The duration of residence in these two areas varies as does the proportion of the year spent traveling between them.

Some species have more complex migration patterns. Several hummingbirds seem to cycle through three geographical areas each year (Grinnell and Miller 1944; Stiles 1973). Anna's Hummingbird (*Calypte anna*) breeds in the coastal chapparal of Southern California, summers in the high mountains of California, and winters in the deserts of Arizona and Mexico (Grinnell and Miller 1944).

It seems likely that some species may not have a clearly defined nonbreeding area where individuals become more or less sedentary, although real evidence is skimpy at this time. Thrushes wintering in the neotropics seem to move slowly through Central America and into South America. About the time they reach the southern portion of their range, they turn around and move back to the northern breeding area. Evidence for this includes their prolonged period of presence in Panama (6–8 weeks) and their sudden disappearance. Marked birds are rarely recaptured, except within a few days of first capture at any location. Their major food resource in the nonbreeding season in both temperate (M. Willson pers. comm.) and tropical (pers. observ.) areas is fruit. Regular movement may be necessary to maintain access to an abundant supply of fruits. Fruiting phenologies of a number of plants seem tied to the passage period of thrushes in Illinois (Thompson and Willson 1978) and in Mexico (M. Ramos pers. comm.). Similar itinerancy has been reported for both aquatic and land birds in Africa (Moreau 1972).

In this paper, I will consider only those species that move regularly between the North Temperate Zone and tropical regions. Migration or other seasonal movements within temperate and tropical regions will

James R. Karr

not be discussed further. In addition, I will restrict my discussion to land birds, as defined by Moreau (1966). Finally, I have somewhat arbitrarily excluded species that have resident populations in the tropics and migrant populations in the temperate zone. That distinction is not particularly important in the New World where few species are excluded (for example, Turkey and Black Vultures). However, the connections between southeast Asia and the palearctic are more complex, making decisions about the status of species more difficult.

Tropical Regions—Nonbreeding Ranges

Geographically, three major land masses (Central and South America, Africa, and Indomalaysia) in the tropics are host to large numbers of birds that breed in temperate areas. They vary in size, geographic orientation, abundance of nearby island archipelagoes, and relationship to major migration barriers. Since the Indomalaysian region is divided into two distinct units, I will consider the Indian subcontinent and Southeast Asia as separate areas. I have compiled lists of birds that visit each of these areas.

In addition to considering these large areas, one or two smaller regions will be considered from each major land mass. These smaller areas were selected with two criteria in mind: first, availability of a recent compilation of species occurring in the area; second, my own experience in or near the area. Readers should keep in mind that the value of this summary is limited by sources that vary in quality and detail. Primary sources of data for this analysis, in addition to personal experience in all areas except Kerala, are as follows: 1) neotropical region—Bond 1971; Eisenmann 1955; deSchauensee 1964, 1966, 1970; Haverschmidt 1968; Peterson 1973; Slud 1964; Blake 1977; 2) Panama—Ridgely 1976; Loftin and Eisenmann 1971; 3) Ethiopian region—Moreau 1966, 1972; Mackworth-Praed and Grant 1952–73; 4) Liberia—Forbes-Watson 1970; 5) Kenya—Forbes-Watson 1971; 6) Indian subcontinent—Ali and Ripley 1968–1974; Ripley 1961; 7) Kerala—Ali 1969; 8) Southeast Asia—King and Dickinson 1975; 9) West Malaysia—Delacour 1947; Glenister 1951.

Neotropics

The geography of the neotropical region is complex. A narrow northwest-southwest isthmus connects the North American breeding grounds to the large land mass of South America. Including temperate South America the total area involved is 18.6 million km², stretching from Oaxaca and Veracruz, Mexico at about 18°N to Tierra del Fuego at 55°S. In addition,

another 230,000 km² is included in an arc of islands stretching eastward from south Florida and then southward across the Caribbean. Excluding temperate South America (Uruguay, Paraguay, Argentina, and Chile) where few north temperate breeders winter, the areas is 14.7 million km².

The region is dominated by a spine of high elevations (figure 1) beginning at the central plateau of Mexico and continuing south through Central and South America in a relatively unbroken continuum (except the Canal Zone area of Panama). West of the mountains the Pacific coastal areas are generally rather dry (figure 2). East of the mountains are extensive areas of forest—very narrow in much of Central America and broad in South America, especially in Amazonia (figure 3). A plateau in southeast Brazil is a distinctive feature as is the presence of large river systems such as the Orinoco and Amazon. Most area in the neotropics is below the 600-m elevation contour (figure 1).

Historically, the major events shaping the present neotropical region occurred in the Miocene (30 million years ago [mya]) with the uplift of mountains in western North and South America and along the developing corridor connecting the two land masses (Haffer 1974). A spate of volcanic activity in the Pliocene (10 mya) modified the mountainous areas and completed the backbone of South and Central America. Land areas have not changed much since then except as a result of changing sea levels and shifting climates due to the cooling of more northern areas. As Haffer (1969) has pointed out, changing distributions of forest and savannah habitats were significant in the Pleistocene.

Regions east of the mountains in the neotropics are dominated by lowland forest environments with scattered regions of grassland and savannah (Venezuelan llanos, Argentinian pampas), and dry and semideciduous forest (Brazilian caatinga, choco of Argentina and Bolivia). Regions west of the mountains are dominated by very dry areas in South America and by grassland and dry forest in Central America.

The neotropical subregion considered in this paper is Panama. In many respects Panama, the southernmost country of Central America, is a scale model of the neotropical region. The country is dominated by a central mountain belt with a dry coastal plain to the south of the mountains and relatively wet to the north.

Africa

Subsaharan Africa covers about the same area as the neotropical region just discussed but it is very different topographically. Northern Africa is dominated by the

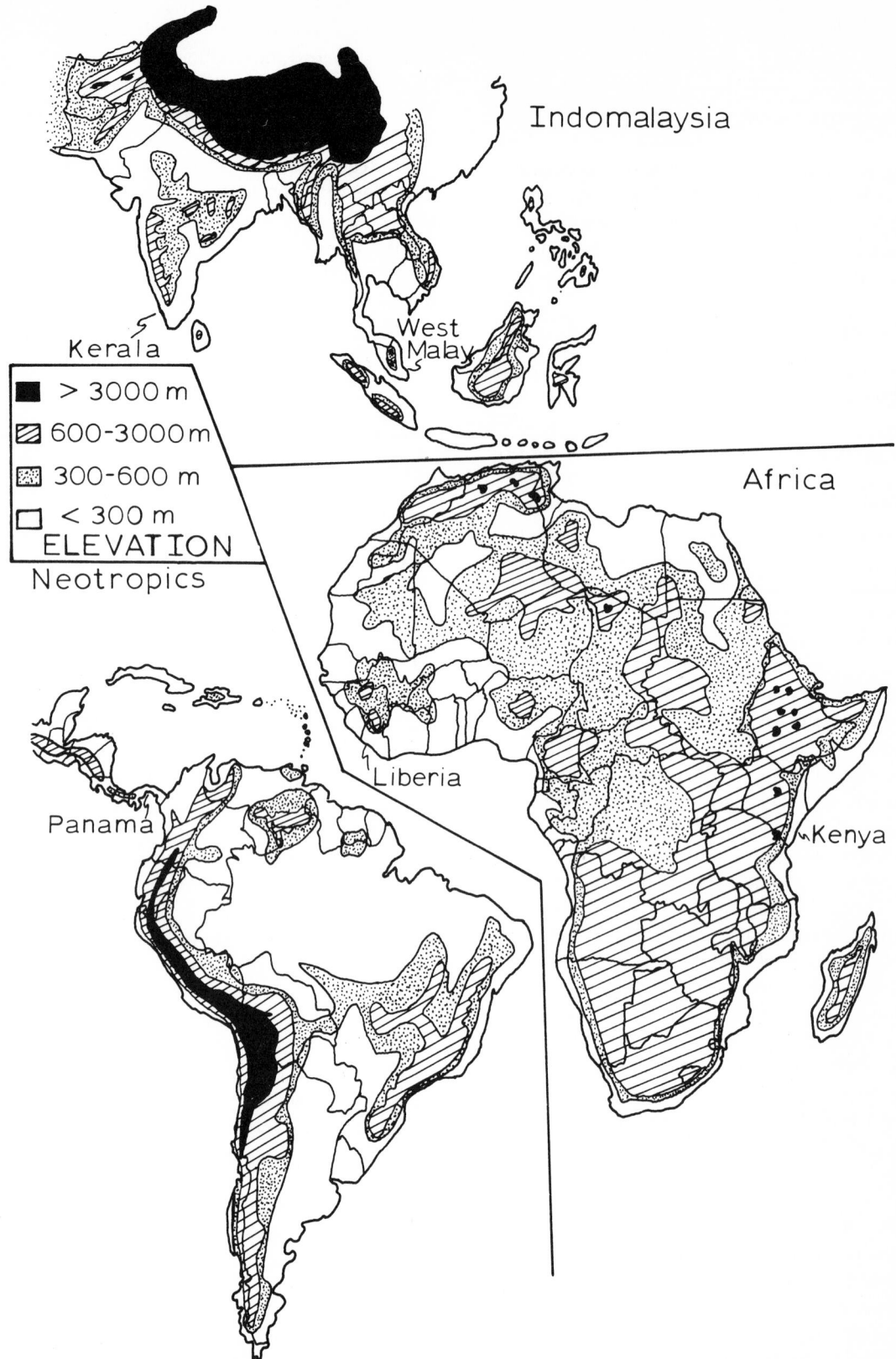

Figure 1. Topographic complexity of tropical continental areas.

James R. Karr

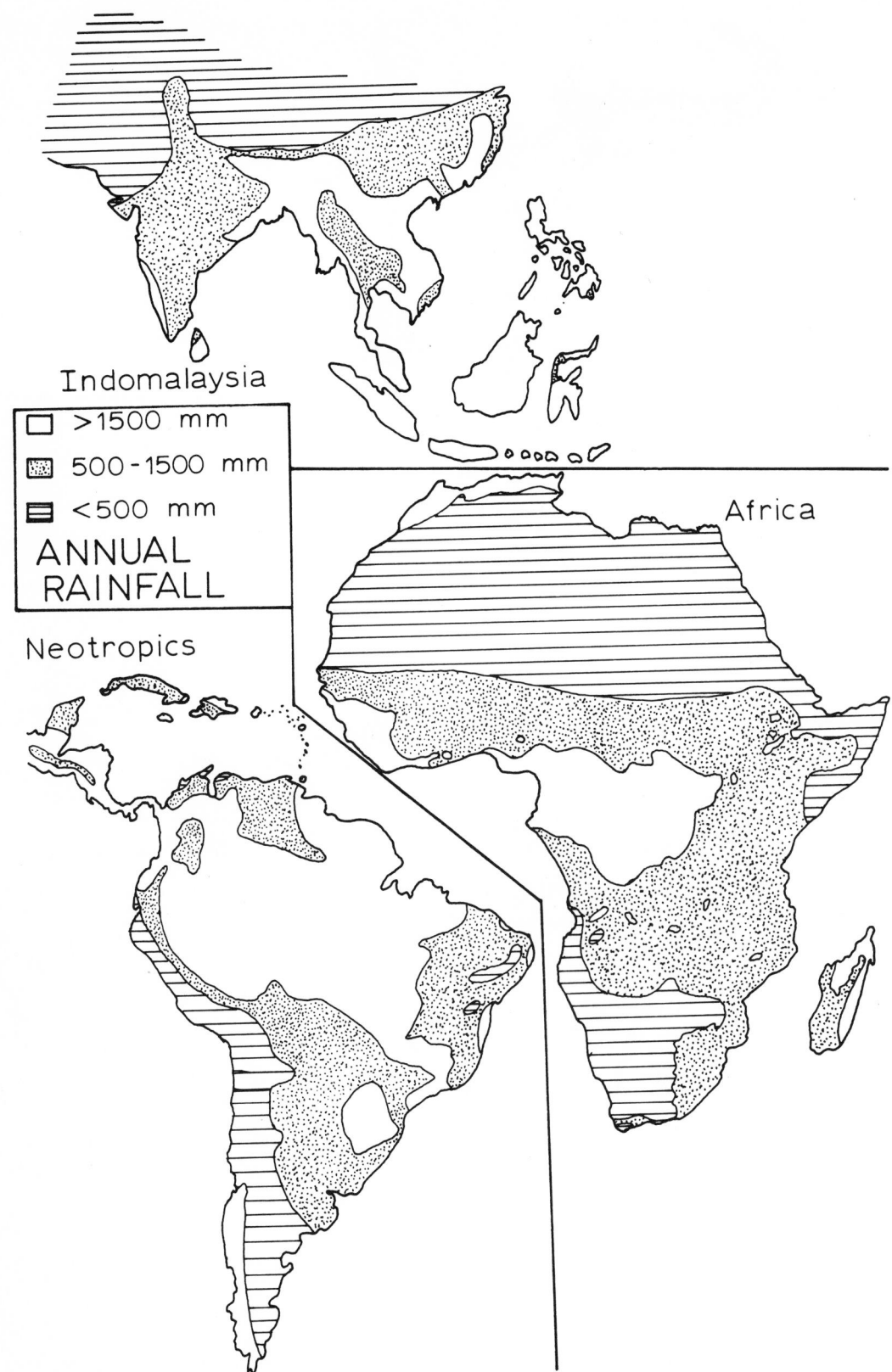

Figure 2. Average annual precipitation of tropical continental areas.

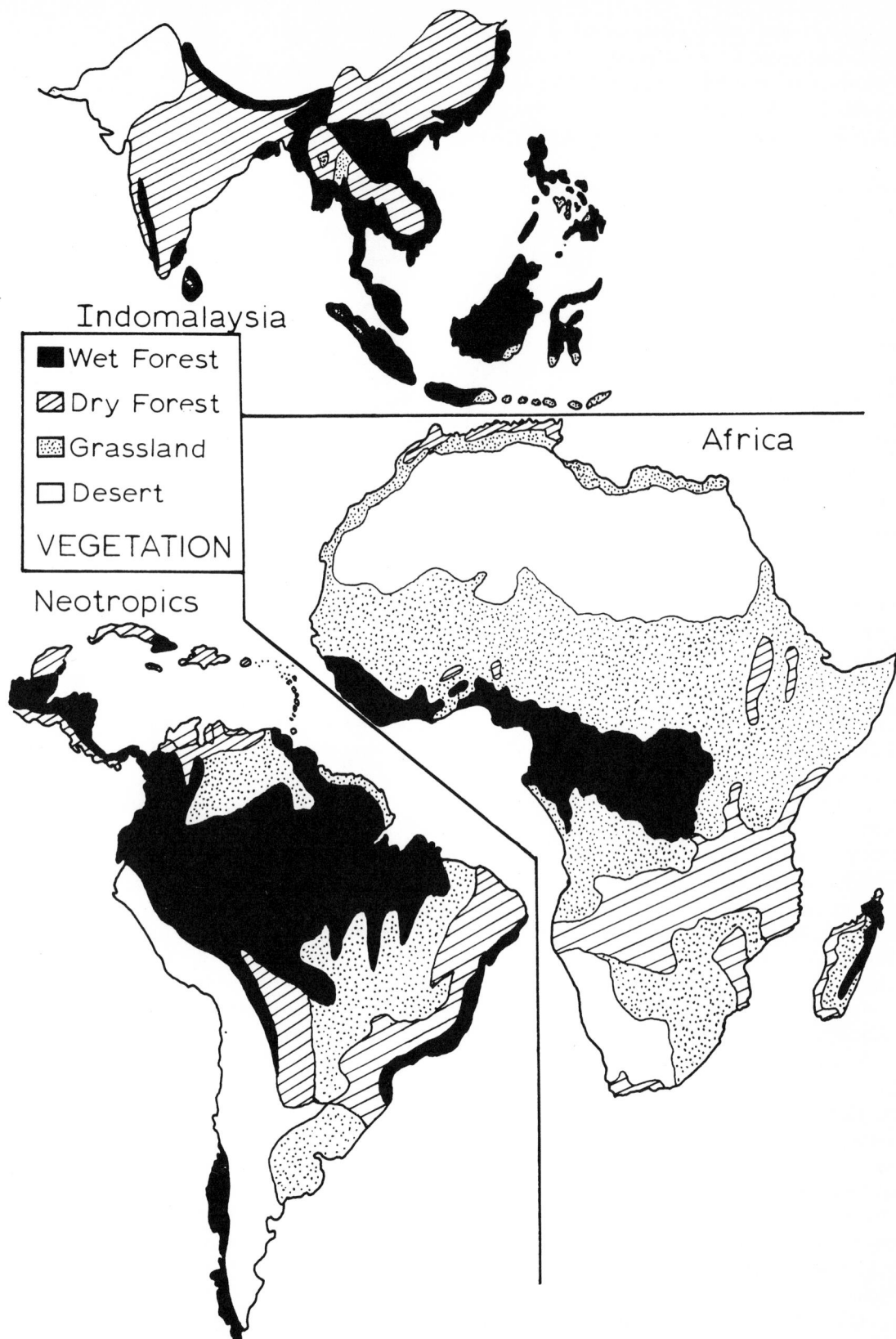

Figure 3. Major vegetation types of tropical continental areas.

James R. Karr

Sahara Desert. A broad plateau stretches from the Ethiopian highlands in the northeast to the highlands of the southern third of Africa (figure 1). The lowlands of Subsaharan Africa are restricted to a relatively narrow coastal plain on the east, the Congo Basin of equatorial Africa, and most of West Africa. The general shape of Africa has remained constant since the Eocene (50 mya). Post-Miocene movements have produced the extensive plateau and mountains of the eastern half of the continent (Moreau 1966).

The vegetation of Africa includes a centrally located area of wet forest bounded on the north and south by successive belts of woodland, grassland, and finally desert (figure 3). A similar sequence is encountered as one moves east from the Congo Basin.

Liberia and Kenya will be considered as subregions of Africa. Liberia was selected to represent the lowland regions of West Africa while Kenya represents the eastern plateau. With the exception of a small area associated with Mt. Nimba (maximum elevation 1,300 m) all of Liberia is below 600 m (most below 300 m). Most of Kenya is above 600 m, and several large mountains exceed 3,000 m. Neither Liberia nor Kenya are geographically similar to Panama with its central spine of highlands bordered by flat lowland areas.

Indian Subcontinent

The Indian Subcontinent is about 20 percent the size of Subsaharan Africa or the neotropical region. Most of peninsular India is below the 600-m contour and extensive areas are below 300 m (figure 1). The dominant geographic character of the subcontinent is the formidable mountain mass of Tibet and the Himalayas, which was uplifted as the Indian crustal plate collided with the Asian plate in the Miocene (Axelrod and Raven 1972). Although rainfall exceeds 500 mm over much of the subcontinent (figure 2), most of the subcontinent experiences a prolonged dry season. Thus, most of India is clothed in dry deciduous forest (figure 3). Exceptions include the Great Indian Desert of the northwest, mixed semideciduous forest of Bangla-Desh, and the moist and wet forest, especially on mountains, along the west coast of peninsular India.

Kerala, the southwest state of India, was selected as a small geographic area. Kerala is bordered on the west by the Arabian Sea and on the east by the Western Ghats, a string of mountains with elevations up to 2,700 m. Only a small proportion of the state is over 600-m elevation, with well over half of the state below 300 m elevation. The scattered high peaks, numerous low passes and general north-south orientation of the Ghats allows easy access to virtually all of the state for migratory birds from the north. The lowlands of Kerala are dominated by mixed deciduous forest while highland areas are rain forest.

Southeast Asia

The area considered here encompasses about 2 million km^2 including Burma, West Malaysia, Thailand, Cambodia, Vietnam, and Laos. The area is one-tenth of the area considered in Africa and the neotropics. Topographically, most of Southeast Asia is below the 600-m contour in the Malaysian peninsula, along the coastal portion of southern Burma and in the Mekong River watershed, which occupies much of the southern reaches of Thailand, Cambodia, and Vietnam. Much of Laos, Northern Thailand and Burma are topographically complex and generally above 600-m elevation (figure 1). A belt of dry-deciduous forest extends from northwest to southeast across Southeast Asia (figure 3). Two savannah areas break this belt in Burma. The rest of Southeast Asia is clothed in tropical rain forest.

The south end of the Malay Peninsula is the small region studied in Southeast Asia. Politically, this region is West Malaysia. Coastal Malaysia is lowland with central highlands up to about 2,100 m. In many respects, West Malaysia is similar to Panama, although the central highlands are more scattered (not a contiguous central spine) and not as high in Malaysia. Malaysia is larger (131,000 km^2) than Panama (75,000 km^2). Tropical rainforest is the dominant vegetation in West Malaysia. Table 1 summarizes the geographic characteristics of the study regions.

Numbers of Migrant Species

The number of species spending the nonbreeding season varies among the four areas (table 1). Despite their similar size, Africa and the neotropical region are visited by rather different numbers of species, 118 and 147, respectively. Southeast Asia, the smallest area, has a nonbreeding visitor fauna (142) slightly below that of the neotropical region, while 115 species winter in India. Clearly, geographic area is not a major factor determining number of visitors.

Migrants make up from 4.5 to 11.9 percent of the total avifauna of the tropical continents, lowest in the neotropics and highest in Southeast Asia (table 1). These differences are due to the major variation in the sizes of the total avifaunas. The neotropical region has extensive areas of forest with which high numbers of bird species are associated. Africa, on the other hand, has a relatively smaller area of wet forests and extensive areas of grassland, savannah, and dry woodland. The total avifauna of Africa is only 45 percent of that of the neotropics. The avifaunas of India and Southeast Asia are about 1,200 species. Variation in the permanent resident faunas of these areas no doubt relates to a complex set of interactions including historical factors (Karr 1976b), geographic extent and

Table 1. Geographic and avifaunal characteristics of 4 tropical continental areas

Region	Area ($\times 10^6$ km^2)	Annual rainfall (mm)	Primary altitudinal belt	Major vegetation type	Number of bird species Total	Number of bird species Migrant[1]	Percentage migrants
Southeast Asia	2.1	>1500	<1500	Deciduous and rain forest	1198	142	11.9
Indian subcontinent	4.0	500–1500	<600	Deciduous forest	1200	115	9.6
Subsaharan Africa	20.0	500–1500	300–1500	Savannah, thorn forest	1481	118	8.0
Neotropics	20.0	>1500	<600	Wet forest	3300	147	4.5

[1] Without aquatic species.

diversity of habitats (Cody 1975, Karr 1976b), topographic complexity (Diamond 1973, Terborgh 1971), and seasonality (Karr 1976c).

The only general correlation is between number of migrant species and annual rainfall and/or seasonal pattern of rainfall. Both Southeast Asia and the neotropics are dominated by areas with high and seasonally stable rainfall, while rainfall of most areas in Africa and India is either low or seasonally absent. Even high rainfall areas of India commonly have a long dry season; 95 percent of the rain at Mahabaleshwar, India, falls in one four-month period while nine months are required to accumulate 95 percent of the rainfall in central Panama (Karr 1976a). This monsoon climate (not low rainfall) in India and the tendency for birds with nonbreeding range in Africa to occupy relatively dry regions might account for the low species richnesses of these areas. Note that when areas are grouped by rainfall characteristics (Africa and India "dry"; neotropics and Southeast Asia "wet") the larger area always has the highest species richness. Virtually all of the migrants in the old world tropics (Africa, India, Southeast Asia) breed in the palearctic. High variation in number of migrants to these tropical areas suggests that breeding range is not the primary determinant of the size of a nonbreeding fauna.

Geographic Barriers to Migration

Another factor that may account for variation in the number of species spending their nonbreeding seasons in the tropical regions is the presence of major barriers to migration. By far the most imposing barrier is the extensive highland area of the Himalayas (figure 1). Most migrants to India from the palearctic pass to the west of the mountains while those bound for Southeast Asia and the East Indies move south to the east of the mountains. There is fragmentary evidence that some migrants fly directly over the Himalayan Mountains (Ali and Ripley 1968).

Migrants from the palearctic region to Africa must cross extensive desert and water barriers (Moreau 1972). A few species cross up to 4,000 km of the Indian Ocean on a flight from India. Others from Asia cross 1,600 km of the trans-Caspian desert and then face another 1,700 km of the Arabian Desert. Neither area provides many stopovers. Finally, migrants from Europe may cross as much as 1,100 km of the Mediterranean and, without a stop, 1,600 km of the most barren desert in the world, the Sahara. Migrants crossing the Sahara lose 34–44 percent of their mean body weight when they cross the desert (Ash 1960), and body fat prior to departure matches those figures closely (Ward 1963). The longest migration is that of *Phylloscopus trochilus* which may travel more than 6,000 km from eastern Siberia to Africa. As discussed by Moreau (1972), these distances suggest a myriad of questions about the navigational and energetic feats of migratory birds.

The only substantial migration barrier in the New World is the Gulf of Mexico and the Caribbean Sea. Mean fat content in migrants prior to migration is 30–40 percent also (Odum et al. 1961). A migratory journey across this area might cover up to 1,300 km, although most open-water crossings are probably shorter. A number of birds depart from eastern North America and travel in an arc over the Atlantic to the Antilles. For the Blackpoll (*Dendroica striata*) this may involve over-water migrations of over 2,400 km (Nisbet 1970). No major desert or mountain barriers similar to those in Africa or Asia occur in the neotropics.

James R. Karr

Throughout the world, many millions of birds make the journey between the breeding and nonbreeding segments of their range each year despite the presence of extensive desert, water, and mountain barriers. Although these barriers must be a problem, they do not represent insurmountable problems to migrating birds. Mortality during water crossings, and presumably desert crossings also, must be high as mariners often encounter exhausted birds. I have found dead migrants in the Bay of Panama on several occasions. In sum, my general impression is that these geographic features are difficult hurdles but not insurmountable barriers. Their impact as "funnels" to concentrate transients is clear in all tropical areas.

Ecological Characteristics of the Nonbreeding Faunas

Consideration of total number of species may obscure significant variation in the internal structure of communities (Karr 1976c). As a result, I have subdivided the nonbreeding faunas into four groups which reflect both taxonomic and ecological affiliations. The four groups are: 1) raptors—Falconiformes, Strigiformes; 2) other nonpasserines—all nonpasserine groups with migrants except raptors and aquatic birds and including the following orders: Galliformes, Columbiformes, Cuculiformes, Caprimulgiformes, Apodiformes, Coraciiformes, and Piciformes; 3) warblers—two ecologically similar but taxonomically distinct groups, Parulidae in the New World and Sylviidae in the Old World; 4) other passerines—other passerine families with temperate-tropical migrants. Throughout this discussion, I use the family designation for the Muscicapidae, Turdidae, Sylviidae (in the warbler group), but readers should recognize that there is a trend to consider these subfamilies. Similarly fringillids, ploceids, and estrildids will be lumped in a broad "finch" group.

The number of species in each family from each geographic region is listed in the Appendix.

Fewer migratory raptors spend their nonbreeding period in the neotropics than in any other area, while the largest number of raptor species visit Africa and Southeast Asia (figure 4). The number of other nonpasserines is lowest in Southeast Asia and similar in the other three areas. The lowest numbers of species occur in the two "wet" areas suggesting that migrant nonpasserines (not including raptors and waterbirds) may more commonly use savannah or dry-forest.

The number of warbler species using nonbreeding areas in the neotropics is much higher than in the other three areas. This corresponds to the recent and rather striking diversification of parulids in North

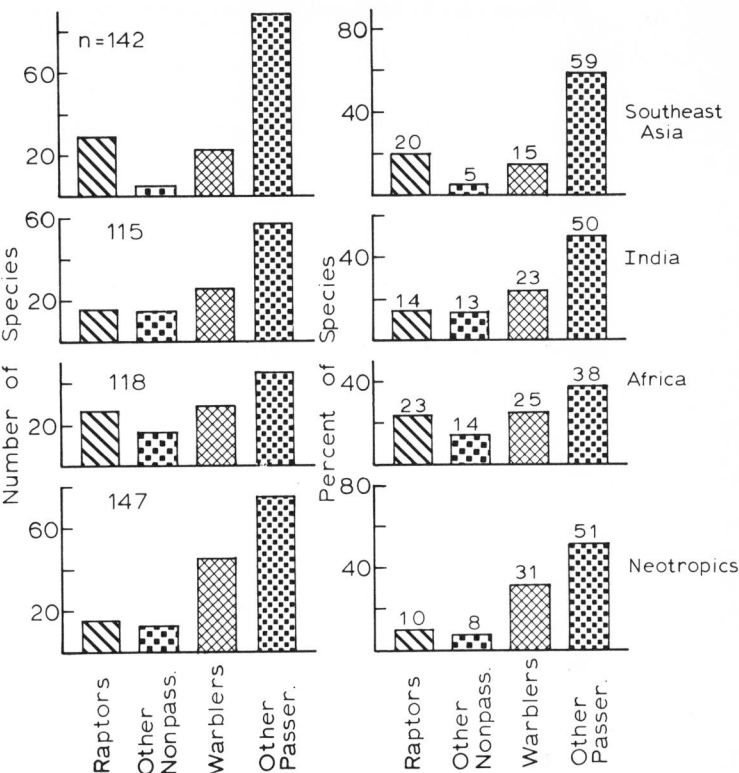

Figure 4. Number and percentage of migrant species in each of 4 taxonomic groups in continental areas.

America (Mengel 1964). The number of other passerines migrating to the "dry" areas is low (45, 58) compared to the numbers for the "wet" areas (75, 84). Species of the Turdidae (thrushes) are most abundant in the three Old World areas while the Tyrannidae (tyrant flycatchers) are represented by the largest number of species in the neotropics. Migrant thrushes in the New World are mainly fruit-eaters (see above), while Old World migrants from this family are generally insectivorous, at least in Africa. Other well-represented families include the Muscicapidae (old-world flycatchers), Motacillidae (wagtails and pipits), and several "finch" groups in the Old World and the "finches" and Vireonidae (vireos) in the New World.

The nonpasserine groups differ in their relative contribution to the migratory avifaunas. Two out of five migrant species in Africa are nonpasserines while only one of five is in the neotropics. About one in four is a nonpasserine in both Asian areas. Otherwise the general patterns among the groups are similar, whether number of species or percentage of species is examined (figure 4).

Migrant Faunas of Small Regions

All of the small areas selected for use in this comparison (West Malaysia; Kerala, India; Kenya; Liberia; Panama) are centered between the equator and 10°N. All except Kenya are located between 5° and 10°N. It is important that they be so located because both Moreau (1972) and Slud (1976) have shown a trend for decreasing numbers of migrants with decreasing latitude.

The variation in number of species among the small areas considered here is much greater (CV = 37.9 percent) than is the variation among the continental areas discussed previously (CV = 12.8 percent). The correlation between area and number of migrant species is low (r = .45, p > 0.05) showing that area is not the primary factor determining number of migrants.

Annual rainfall varies little among at least four of the five areas which generally exceed 2,000 mm per year (table 2). The exception is Kenya where average rainfall varies from 250 to 1,500 mm per year. Similarly, with the exception of Kenya, all areas are predominantly lowland and clothed in relatively wet forest (table 2).

The largest number of species visits Panama (89) while the smallest number visits Liberia, the forested African area (33). Kenya plays host to the second largest number of species (83). Malaysia has one-third

more species (63) than does Kerala (46). It is difficult to extract any ecological pattern to the number of migrant species among the five areas. The number of migrant species is not significantly correlated with the total number of land birds in the areas, but it barely misses significance at the 0.05 level (r = 0.87 vs $r_{tab,0.05}$ = 0.88). The ecological significance of this, if any exists, is obscure. However, it is more reasonable to expect this pattern than a correlation between the same factors on a continent-wide basis since habitat diversity is reduced as a variable. If migrants have a tropical origin, one might hypothesize that the number of migrants will increase as the resident fauna increases. That is, increasing faunal richness will force more species to depart to avoid highly competitive local environments. However, the percentage of migrant species varies among the areas with no general pattern emerging (table 2). Further, the pattern among the areas does not parallel that among the larger geographic areas (table 1). Migrants make up the smallest proportion of the fauna in Malaysia and Liberia at 8.7 percent and the highest proportion in Kerala (15.7 percent). Biogeographically, the high frequency of migrants in Kerala is correlated with the highly seasonal environment in peninsular India, which may limit the resident fauna (Karr 1976a). Further, depressed resident faunas are correlated with the general trend for a declining faunal and floral richness as India moved northward into the drier monsoonal belt where climates are more seasonal and continental (Axelrod and Raven 1972).

When the migrant avifaunas are subdivided on the basis of ecological and taxonomic grounds several patterns emerge (figure 5). The warblers vary more among the geographic areas than any of the other three groups. The largest number of species visits Panama. Note that the Old World warblers have the highest species richness in the driest and/or most seasonal of the paired Old World areas. This may reflect the tendency for many of these species to use nonforest habitat for breeding.

Variation in raptor numbers is also high among the areas. Both the largest and smallest number of species are found in Africa where Kenya has over four times as many species as Liberia. West Malaysia has nearly twice as many species as Kerala. The smallest number of other nonpasserines visit Kerala with the largest number in Kenya. The largest number of species from each fauna is included in the "other passerine" group with Tyrannidae, finches, Vireonidae, and Hirundinidae as the most diverse groups in Panama. Thrushes (Turdidae) are well represented in both Africa and Indomalaysia and flycatchers (Muscicapidae) are abundant in Indomalaysia. Low densities of migratory muscicapids in Africa are correlated with

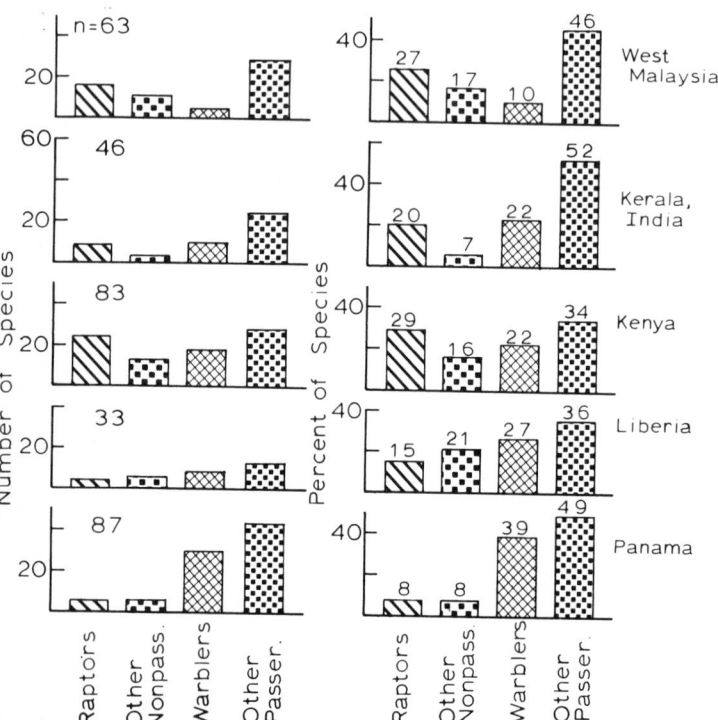

Figure 5. Number and percentage of migrant species in each of 4 taxonomic groups in "small" geographic areas.

James R. Karr

Table 2. Geographic and avifaunal characteristics of 5 "small" geographic areas

Region	Area ($\times 10^6$ km²)	Annual rainfall (mm)	Primary altitudinal belt	Major vegetation type	Number of bird species		Percentage migrants
					Total[1]	Migrant[1]	
West Malaysia	131	>2000	<300	Rain forest	727	63	8.7
Kerala, India	39	>2000	<300	Semideciduous and rain forest	293	46	15.7
Kenya	583	250–1500	300–3000	Low grass savannah	852	83	9.7
Liberia	111	>2000	<300	Rain forest	381	33	8.7
Panama	75	>2000	0–1500	Rain forest	727	87	12.2

[1] Without aquatic species.

the relative lack of flycatchers as residents in Africa (Karr 1976b).

Comparisons of the migrants visiting the two African areas (Liberia and Kenya) demonstrates that all four major groups are better represented in Kenya than in Liberia. This is correlated with the earlier conclusion (Moreau 1966, 1972; Karr 1976a) that few migrants are found in areas of mature wet forest in Africa. Most species in Africa winter in more open areas, in contrast to Asia and Panama where many species use forest habitat at least during a portion of their nonbreeding period.

Species Composition Among Areas

Discussion so far has been restricted to a number of species with little or no reference to species composi-

tion. I have determined the degree to which species compositions are similar among pairs of areas. This is most conveniently done in comparisons among areas that host migrants from the palearctic. In all cases I express similarities as number (or percentage) of species found in the smallest fauna that are also found in the largest fauna. For example, of the six migrant raptors found in Liberia, six (100 percent) are also found in Kenya.

Eighty-eight percent of the migrants that occur in Liberia also occur in Kenya and there is little variation in the percentages among the four major ecological groups (table 3). All raptors that migrate to Liberia also occur in Kenya. Of the species that visit the Indian Subcontinent only 39 percent are also found in Southeast Asia. Further, there is significant variation among the taxonomic groups. Raptors show the great-

Table 3. Overlap in species compositions between pairs of areas

Paired areas		Taxonomic groups: percentages of species				
Found in	Also in	Raptors	Other nonpasserines	Warblers	Other passerines	Total
India	Africa	75	67	27	29	40
India	Southeast Asia	81	27	46	28	39
Kerala	West Malaysia	60	50	0	12	22
Liberia	Kenya	100	83	89	83	88

est overlap (81 percent). When the two smaller areas in Asia (Kerala and West Malaysia) are compared, overlaps are even lower, averaging only 22 percent. Variation among the groups is high, ranging from zero in warblers to 60 percent in raptors.

A comparison of the Indian migrants also found in Africa is somewhat surprising. Forty percent of Indian species also visit Africa, showing that essentially the same proportion of migrants to India visit both Africa and Southeast Asia. This is surprising in light of the large distance between Africa and India relative to between Southeast Asia and India. Finally, note that the overlap is much higher for the nonpasserine groups (71 percent) than for the passerines (29 percent).

This brief analysis of affinities of migrant faunas raises a number of interesting questions. For example, what are the breeding ranges of the species in each area? The high overlap of nonpasserines between India and Africa may indicate a wide breeding range covering both eastern and western palearctic areas. However, the lower overlap between the passerine faunas may suggest that speciation events have produced sequences of species across the palearctic breeding ranges. Or, it may suggest that species with wide breeding ranges across much of the palearctic concentrate in relatively small areas of the potential tropical wintering ground. Detailed studies of areas involved in breeding and nonbreeding ranges might be very enlightening.

Discussion

While the phenomenon of migration has been recognized for millennia, most research has focused on the breeding grounds and ignored the ecological context of the wintering period. Although studies of migration are common, most are concerned with the mechanism involved in navigation and orientation. As evidenced by this volume (and references cited here), ecology of birds on the nonbreeding portion of their ranges are receiving well-deserved attention.

One of the most regrettable aspects of the upsurge of interest, however, has been the tendency to overgeneralize. Researchers have too frequently talked of a strategy of "migrants wintering in the tropics." Rather, each species has a unique way of making a living, and this may change geographically among individuals of the same species (Bennett, Hutto, Morton, Pearson, Rabenold, Terborgh this volume) or with time in the same individual (Morton this volume). Similarly, geographic variation in the characteristics of assemblages of migrant species and their environments can provide useful insights. I judiciously avoided calling the assemblages "communities" because, in general, community should be restricted to

situations where all member species have relatively high levels of interactions. Often migrant species may interact with each other (Leck 1972) and satisfy my criterion of integrated species complexes but in other circumstances interactions among sympatric nonbreeders from temperate zone may be low. For example, consider the lack of interactions between Eastern Kingbirds (*Tyrannus tyrannus*) feeding on fruits in forest canopy as they pass through Panama while Kentucky Warblers (*Oporornis formosus*) consume insects on territories in the forest undergrowth. It is important that we view migrant birds as integral components of the communities that they occupy (Terborgh this volume) and not solely in the context of sets of migrant species. Rather we must consider migrant communities when interactions among species of migrants are high but also recognize the most useful approach may be consideration of "migrant and resident" assemblages when that is ecologically sound. Further, under some circumstances communities composed of different major taxa (insectivorous birds and lizards on Caribbean islands) may be the best community units for study.

Challenges for the Future

In addition to providing studies of more carefully defined communities, this symposium has shown that we must quickly attack a number of other problems. Present recognition of the significance of nonbreeding-season ecology must be more effectively combined with knowledge of breeding season to result in consideration of species and groups of species throughout their geographic range; that is, the entire range must be considered as an ecological unit. How for example do ranges vary in breeding and nonbreeding periods? What are the energetic demands and what constraints impinge on individuals in breeding, nonbreeding, and passage portions of the geographic range? What habitats are occupied, and how are they exploited in different areas? Significant progress is being made in this area by Rabenold, Bennett, and others, but data are necessary from a wider range of species and geographic areas. In an earlier paper (Karr 1976a) I explored, albeit superficially, variation in migrant ecology in small areas throughout the tropics. This paper has emphasized intermediate- and large- (continent) scale areas. These must be more effectively integrated in the future, particularly with comparisons among regions (Mexico vs Panama vs Ecuador; Panama vs Gabon; neotropics vs Africa) and ecological groups (Parulidae vs Sylviidae; etc.). Such comparative study can yield considerable insight if developed carefully. In addition to careful development, a premium must be placed on prompt action as man accelerates the rate of destruction (or modification) of tropical environments.

James R. Karr

Acknowledgments

Support for studies in tropical regions has come from grants from the Smithsonian Tropical Research Institute and the National Geographic Society. Thanks to these agencies, their staff, and to many residents of the tropics for their financial and logistical support. T. Martin and M. Willson provided valuable comments in an early draft of the manuscript.

Appendix. Number of migrant species by family for each geographic area considered

Group	Southeast Asia	Indian sub-continent	Africa	Neo-tropics	West Malaysia	Kerala, India	Kenya	Liberia	Panama
Raptors									
Falconiformes									
Accipitridae (Hawks, Eagles)	20	9	16	7	14	7	15	3	5
Falconidae (Falcons)	5	4	8	4	2	1	2	8	1
Pandionidae (Osprey)	1	1	1	1	1	1	1	0	1
Strigiformes									
Strigidae (Owls)	3	2	2	3	1	1	2	1	0
Tytonidae (Barn Owls)	0	0	0	0	1	0	0	0	0
Other nonpasserines									
Galliformes									
Phasianidae (Pheasants)	1	1	1	0	0	0	1	0	0
Columbiformes									
Columbidae (Pigeons, Doves)	0	2	1	0	0	0	0	0	0
Cuculiformes									
Cuculidae (Cuckoos)	2	4	3	2	4	2	2	3	2
Caprimulgiformes									
Caprimulgidae (Nightjars)	0	1	3	2	1	0	1	0	2
Apodiformes									
Apodidae (Swifts)	4	3	4	2	1	0	2	1	1
Trochilidae (Hummingbirds)	0	0	0	5	0	0	0	0	1
Coraciformes									
Alcedinidae (Kingfishers)	0	0	0	0	1	0	0	0	0
Meropidae (Bee-eaters)	0	2	2	0	1	2	0	1	0
Coraciidae (Rollers)	0	1	1	0	1	0	1	0	0
Upupidae (Hoopoe)	0	0	1	0	0	0	0	0	0
Piciformes									
Picidae (Woodpeckers)	0	0	0	1	0	0	0	0	1
Jungidae (Wryneck)	1	1	1	0	0	0	1	1	0
Warblers									
Passeriformes									
Parulidae (Wood-warblers)	0	0	0	46	0	0	0	0	30
Sylviidae (Old-world warblers)	22	26	29	3	6	10	9	18	0

Appendix. Number of migrant species by family for each geographic area considered

Group	Southeast Asia	Indian sub-continent	Africa	Neo-tropics	West Malaysia	Kerala, India	Kenya	Liberia	Panama
Other passerines									
Passeriformes									
Tyrannidae (Tyrant flycatchers)	0	0	0	23	0	0	0	0	15
Pittidae (Pittas)	1	1	0	0	1	1	0	0	0
Alaudidae (Larks)	2	5	2	0	0	1	1	0	0
Hirundinidae (Swallows)	4	3	5	8	2	1	2	3	5
Campephagidae (Cuckoo-shrikes)	2	1	0	0	0	0	0	0	0
Corvidae (Crows)	1	1	0	0	0	0	0	0	0
Timaliidae (Babblers)	0	1	0	0	0	0	0	0	0
Dicruridae (Drongoes)	0	1	0	0	1	1	0	0	0
Oriolidae (Orioles)	1	1	1	0	0	1	1	0	0
Mimidae (Mimic Thrushes)	0	0	0	1	0	0	0	0	1
Cinclidae (Dipper)	1	0	0	0	0	0	0	0	0
Turdidae (Thrushes)	27	17	18	7	7	5	4	10	4
Muscicapidae (Old-world flycatchers)	10	8	3	0	8	6	2	2	0
Prunellidae (Hedge sparrows)	3	0	0	0	0	0	0	0	0
Zosteropidae (White-eyes)	2	0	0	0	0	0	0	0	0
Motacillidae (Pipits)	10	9	6	2	4	3	5	6	0
Bombycillidae (Waxwings)	0	0	0	1	0	0	0	0	1
Laniidae (Shrikes)	3	2	6	0	2	1	1	4	0
Sturnidae (Starlings)	6	2	0	0	2	1	0	0	0
Vireonidae (Vireos)	0	0	0	8	0	0	0	0	5
Ploceidae (Weaver-finches)	0	0	1	0	0	0	0	0	0
Icteridae (Troupials)	0	0	0	6	0	0	0	0	3
Thraupidae (Tanagers)	0	0	0	3	0	0	0	0	3
Fringillidae (Finches)	11	6	3	13	1	1	1	0	6

Literature Cited

Ali, S.
1969. *Birds of Kerala.* London: Oxford Univ. Press, 444 p.

Ali, S., and S. D. Ripley
1968– *Handbook of the Birds of India and Pakistan.* 10 vols.
1974. London: Oxford Univ. Press.

Ash, J. S.
1969. Spring weights of trans-Saharan migrants in Morocco. Ibis 111:1–10.

Axelrod, D. I., and P. H. Raven
1972. Evolutionary biogeography viewed from plate tectonic theory. In *Challenging Biological Problems: Directions toward their Solution.* J. A. Behnke ed. pp. 218–36. New York: Oxford Univ. Press.

Blake, E. R.
1977. *Manual of Neotropical Birds.* Vol. 1. Chicago: Univ. Chicago Press, 674 pp.

Bond, J.
1971. *Birds of the West Indies.* 2nd ed. London: Collins.

Cody, M. L.
1974. *Competition and the Structure of Bird Communities.* Princeton, N.J.: Princeton, Univ. Press, 318 pp.

Delacour, J.
1947. *Birds of Malaysia.* New York: MacMillan, 382 pp.

DeSchauensee, R. M.
1964. *The Birds of Colombia.* Narbeth Pa.: Livingston, 430 pp.

1966. *The Species of Birds of South America and Their Distribution.* Narbeth, Pa.: Livingston, 577 pp.

1970. *A Guide to the Birds of South America.* Narbeth, Pa.: Livingston, 470 pp.

Diamond, J. M.
1973. Distributional ecology of New Guinea birds. Science 179:759–69.

James R. Karr

Eisenmann, E.
1955. The species of Middle American birds. Trans. Linn. Soc. N.Y. 7:1–128.

Forbes-Watson, A.
1970. List of birds known to occur in Liberia. Mimeo report, 10 p.

1971. Skeleton checklist of East African birds. Mimeo report, 32 p.

Glenister, A. G.
1971. *The Birds of the Malay Peninsula Singapore and Penang.* Kuala Lumpur: Oxford Univ. Press, 291 pp.

Grinnell, J., and A. H. Miller
1944. The distribution of the birds of California. Pacific Coast Avifauna 27:216–25.

Haffer, J.
1969. Speciation in Amazonian forest birds. Science 165: 131–37.

1974. Avian speciation in tropical South America. Publ. Nuttall Ornith. Club 14:1–390.

Haverschmidt, F.
1968. Birds of Surinam. Edinburgh: Oliver & Boyd, 445 pp.

Karr, J. R.
1976a. On the relative abundance of migrants from the North Temperate Zone in tropical habitats. Wils. Bull. 88:433–58.

1976b. Within- and between-habitat avian diversity in African and neotropical lowland habitats. Ecol. Monogr. 46:457–81.

1976c. Seasonality, resource and availability, and community diversity in tropical bird communities. Amer. Natur. 110:973–94.

King, B. F., and E. C. Dickinson
1975. *A Field Guide to the Birds of Southeast Asia.* Boston: Houghton-Mifflin, 480 pp.

Leck, C. F.
1972. The impact of some North American migrants at fruiting trees in Panama. Auk 89:842–50.

Loftin, H., and E. Eisenmann
1971. Field Checklist of the Birds of the Panama Canal Zone Area. 2nd ed. Florida Audubon Soc. 38 pp.

Mackworth-Praed, C. W., and C. H. B. Grant.
1952– African Handbook of Birds. 6 vols. London: Long-
1973. man.

Mengel, R. M.
1964. The probable history of species formation in some northern wood warblers (Parulidae). Living Bird 3: 9–43.

Moreau, R. M.
1966. *The Bird Faunas of Africa and Its Islands.* New York: Academic Press, 424 pp.

1972. *The Palearctic-African Bird Migration Systems.* New York: Academic Press, 384 pp.

Nisbet, I. C. T.
1970. Autumn migration of the Blackpoll Warbler: Evidence for the long flight provided by the regional survey. Bird-Banding 41:207–40.

Odum, E. P., C. E. Connell, and H. L. Stoddard
1961. Flight energy and estimated flight ranges of some migrating birds. Auk 78:515–27.

Peterson, R. T.
1973. *A Field Guide to Mexican Birds.* Boston: Houghton-Mifflin, 298 pp.

Ridgely, R. S.
1976. *A Guide to the Birds of Panama.* Princeton, N.J.: Princeton Univ. Press, 394 pp.

Ripley, S. D.
1961. *A Synopsis of the Birds of India and Pakistan.* Bombay: Bombay Nat. Hist. Soc., 702 pp.

Slud, P.
1960. The birds of Finca "La Selva," Costa Rica: A tropical wet forest locality. Bull. Amer. Mus. Nat. Hist. 121:1–148.

1964. The birds of Costa Rica: Distribution and Ecology. Bull. Amer. Mus. Nat. Hist. 128:1–430.

1976. Geographic and climatic relationships of avifaunas with special reference to comparative distribution in the Neotropics. Smithsonian Contr. to Zoology 212: 1–149.

Stiles, F. G.
1973. Food supply and the annual cycle of the Anna Hummingbird. Univ. Calif. Publ. Zool. 97:1–109.

Terborgh, J. W.
1971. Distribution on environmental gradients: Theory and a preliminary interpretation of distributional patterns in the avifauna of the Cordillera Vilcabamba, Peru. Ecol. 52:23–40.

Thompson, J. N. and M. F. Willson
1978. Disturbance and the dispersal of fleshy fruits. Science 200:1161–63.

Ward, P.
1963. Lipid levels of birds preparing to cross the Sahara. Ibis 105:109–11.

DANIEL H. JANZEN
Department of Biology
University of Pennsylvania
Philadelphia, Pennsylvania 19104

Heterogeneity of Potential Food Abundance for Tropical Small Land Birds

There is no general all-purpose method of description of resources for small tropical terrestrial birds. To understand food resources for the birds in a habitat or for a particular species of bird, one has to determine what the bird(s) feed on and hand-tailor a census technique that collects data in a manner that correlates well with the actual resources taken by the bird. However, general statements about *potential* food may suggest detailed studies of birds and their resources that will produce informative close correlations. In this spirit, I offer a few brief stories about apparent severe heterogeneity of potential resources for birds in the tropics.

Rainy Season Insect Flush

In the lowland deciduous forest at Santa Rosa National Park (northwestern Guanacaste Province, Costa Rica), there is an abrupt and heavy production of new foliage at the beginning of the rainy season (May). Within two to four weeks of this flush of foliage, it is apparent that there is also a short-lived heavy peak in the biomass of moth and butterfly larvae feeding on this new foliage. Partly and entirely defoliated plants are common, and the ground is littered with caterpillar feces. A moment's inspection of vegetation produces numerous Lepidoptera larvae. Several months later, there is little trace of this event, other than the remnants of damaged leaves. A month earlier, there was no sign of caterpillars.

To quantify crudely this flush of caterpillars, four of us (P. DeVries, M. L. Higgins, G. Vega, D. H. Janzen) visually censused caterpillars on a 204-m trailside transect through deciduous forest. The vegetation was examined closely for 2 m on each side of the trail and up to 2 m in height, on sunny clear days with scudding clouds, and between 800 and 1200 hr. All caterpillars were collected into alcohol, and later sorted by morphospecies and measured (table 1). The vegetation is trail-edge and understory shrubs and saplings in old secondary deciduous forest; the trail was 1–2 m in width, and the canopy was irregularly closed overhead. The trail is the Nature Trail (Sendero Natural) from the first fork, and thence across the natural bridge to the second large rock in the trail in the guapinol grove. The following species of plants made up about half of the bulk of foliage examined: *Allophyllus occidentalis, Casearia corymbosa, Hemiangium excelsum, Acacia collinsii, Maluaviscus arboreus, Hamelia patens, Psidium* spp., *Croton* spp., *Stemmadenia donnellsmithii, Hymenaea courbaril, Calycophyllum candidissimum, Cassia* spp., *Plumeria rubra, Luehea* spp., *Tabebuia neochrysantha, Tabebuia rosea, Ficus* spp., *Bursera simaruba, Bursera graveolens, Guazuma ulmifolia, Solanum* spp., *Myrospermum frutescens, Genipa caruto, Trichilia* spp., *Guettarda macrosperma.*

By the date of the August census, the abundance of caterpillars had fallen to the level that seems to persist through the remainder of the rainy season. There are a number of traits of the caterpillars that seem particularly relevant to their potential as bird food.

1) The average length of the caterpillars (2.0–2.5 cm) did not change over the six-month period. This suggests that a bird may be confronted with the same size distribution of caterpillars early in the season as later (and visual inspection of the caterpillars suggested that this was the case). However, with the absolute number of caterpillars much higher earlier than later in the season, the number of large caterpillars available would likewise be much greater earlier than later.

2) The caterpillars ranged from very cryptic to very aposematic, and there was no conspicuous trend in change in the proportions of these two extremes of life form over the six-month period.

3) Throughout the six-month period, birds feeding on this caterpillar peak were very inconspicuous if they

Table 1. Caterpillars encountered in a 204-m census strip in deciduous forest understory in Santa Rosa National Park, Guanacaste Province, Costa Rica.

Date	Total Length of caterpillars (m)	Average length (cm)	Number of individuals	Number of species
16 June 1977	7.5	2.5	297	87
31 June 1977	2.4	2.4	101	28
15 Aug 1977	0.7	2.5	28	16
21 Nov 1977	0.3	2.0	16	7

were there at all; this was in striking contrast to the number of foraging (foliage-gleaning) birds and birds carrying larvae (to a nest) that I see regularly in the extra-tropical spring. Perhaps tropical woodland insectivorous birds forage more cryptically than do those of extra-tropical woodlots and forests, but I have no reason to suspect this to be so. There is no hint that a wave of birds moves onto the peak of caterpillars and is responsible for its demise in August. Likewise, there was no evidence that the impermanence of the high density of caterpillars was due to a build-up of arthropod predators and parasites.

4) Studies other than the census made it clear that many of the caterpillars pupated, hatched within a few weeks, and departed as adults. In the most direct sense, this was the cause of the decline in caterpillar density as the season progressed. We are left with the mystery of why the adults do not lay a second round of eggs on the remaining and replacement foliage; the answer probably has to do with increase in secondary compound content in original foliage and increased toxicity of replacement foliage but is not the subject of this paper. ·

In short, there is no hint of local avian response to the large peak in caterpillar density. Furthermore, this peak occurs almost exactly at the time of breeding of insectivorous birds in northern latitude forests. Why do these birds not migrate from intermediate elevation Costa Rica to the adjacent lowland deciduous forest to breed instead of flying all the way to Pennsylvania or elsewhere? To make the question even more puzzling, I should add that Malaise trap samples from the Santa Rosa forest show that flying insects in the 1–10 mm-length class increase dramatically in density after the rains begin and then gradually decline over the next six months.

I am hesitant to suggest such a sweeping hypothesis,

but it is marginally possible that the bulk of the caterpillars taken in the census are toxic even when not glaringly aposematic. Or at least, they may be more toxic than would be an equal bulk of forest caterpillars in Wisconsin in the spring. Three natural history facts bear on this.

1) There do appear to be more aposematic caterpillars among the Santa Rosa collection than I have seen among collections of extra-tropical spring woodland caterpillars.

2) The host plants of these caterpillars are known or suspected to contain notable quantities of highly toxic secondary compounds (in addition to tannins and other digestion inhibitors). This is not the case for many of the important caterpillar host plants in extra-tropical woodlands (e.g., *Pinus, Abies, Picea, Quercus, Fagus, Betula, Salix, Acer*).

3) Each species of Santa Rosa Caterpillar appears to be almost entirely restricted to a single species of host at this site; this suggests the presence of specialists at physiologically incorporating (or sequestering) toxic secondary compounds in their tissues. Again, the tree-foliage feeding caterpillars in northern forests tend to have several or more hosts, and there is no suggestion that a major part of their feeding physiology is the sequestering of toxins from their host plants.

If the Santa Rosa caterpillars are much more toxic than would be an equal bulk of extra-tropical caterpillars, then it may explain why there does not appear to be heavy local use of the peak in caterpillar density and why the "migrants" in the Costa Rican highlands do not settle onto this peak, but rather fly on north.

Local Movements of Insects

A large number of tropical insects in seasonal habitats move from one habitat to another, as adults, apparently in response to differential disappearance of food through drying and dormancy of food (e.g., Janzen 1973a, b). One of the most conspicuous movements is from hillsides to nearby riparian vegetation as the dry season intensifies, with subsequent movement back to the hillside with its flush of new foliage when the rainy season begins. Many species therefore pass the dry season as an active adult in a riparian refugium. This results in high concentration of adult insects in riparian vegetation during the dry season and means that the density of insects on hillsides depends on the proximity of a hillside to riparian vegetation.

In the context of this volume, how important is this local heterogeneity to the insectivorous birds? I submit that there is no way to answer without careful censusing of birds at the site concurrent with analysis of bird-gut contents *and* samples of these particular insects. At the extreme case, for birds specialized on

Daniel H. Janzen

caterpillars, neither the hillside nor riparian vegetation has enough caterpillars to feed anything during the dry season; the movements and concentrations of insects in general are largely irrelevant for this bird. Of a less extreme nature, if a bird is a specialist on small brown beetles called Bruchidae, it should forage on the dry hillside since these beetles move the opposite direction from insects in general (Bruchidae do this because they oviposit on the fruits and seeds to be found abundantly during the dry season on dry hillside sites). On the other hand, if a bird is a specialist on small foliage-inhabiting beetles in general (e.g., Chrysomelidae), the riparian vegetation is the place to forage during the dry season.

Now, what does this have to do with migrant birds? First, migrants move all sorts of distances, from 200 m to 200 miles to 200 tens of miles. How and why they move local distances should help understand why they move long distances. Second, when migrants arrive, they settle onto a very heterogeneous resource base, a heterogeneity that shifts as the year progresses. Further, there can be enormous heterogeneity among closely adjacent "similar" vegetation types, such as young second growth with different disturbance histories (Janzen 1976a). Third, there is no possible general purpose description for this heterogeneity; the heterogeneity and how it is best described will depend on what the bird desires.

Global Heterogeneity Within the Tropics

There is a strong temptation by ornithologists to divide the lowland terrestrial tropics into thorn forest, deciduous forest, evergreen forest, and second growth derived from each. Here I would like to emphasize that there can be major non-seasonal differences in the amounts of major kinds of bird food in what appear to be the same habitat in different parts of the tropics.

The most glaring examples that come to mind at present are those evident when West Malaysian lowland dipterocarp rainforest is compared with Costa Rican lowland rainforest (the remainder of this section is a direct quote from Janzen 1978a).

"At the lowland Pasoh rainforest, Negri Sembilan, Peninsular Malaysia, I censused the plants in flower that were less than 3 m tall in the understory of undisturbed forest along 3 km of narrow trail (early September 1976). I found 1 orchid, one 1.5 m tall Araliaceae, one 0.5 m tall Acanthaceae (*Lepidagathis longifolia*), and one 1 m tall *Ixora*-like Rubiaceae. In the lowlands of the national park, Taman Negara, 5.4 km of rainforest trail yielded 1 white-flowered ginger, 2 *Ixora*-like Rubiaceae, 1 Acanthaceae, 1 unknown family and two 10–20 cm tall Gesneriaceae with underground stems. In primary forest understory in the new

Corcovado National Park (20–160 m elevation, Osa Peninsula, southwestern Costa Rica), a trail-side survey of 4.3 km yielded 94 plants in flower of 18 species (20 November 1976). In other words, I averaged 1.3 plants in flower per kilometer in the Malayan rainforest understory and 21.9 plants in flower per kilometer of Costa Rican rainforest understory.

"These woefully small samples reflect accurately my general impression of the general abundance of flowers in the understory of rainforests of Peninsular Malaysia and Sarawak, as compared with those of Costa Rican rainforest of similar elevation. I was informed locally that 1976 was one of the heaviest years in memory for flower and fruit production in Peninsular Malaysia; November is the time of most reduced flower production in Costa Rican rainforest understory (and see Frankie et al 1974). In short, if one were to turn loose in Pasoh or Taman Negara the rainforest understory fauna of flower-visiting hummingbirds, butterflies, moths and bees found in the Corcovado, I predict that they would be dead of starvation in a few days. Furthermore they could not survive by moving out into secondary regeneration; Malaysian disturbed sites have a grossly lower flower abundance than any weedy wet season vegetation that I have seen anywhere in the African or Neotropical lowlands.

"Over the Malaysian transects mentioned above, I encountered 63 understory individuals in fruit (22 species) for an average of 7.5 per kilometer. In the Corcovado forest, there were 345 individuals in fruit (34 species) for an average of 78.4 per kilometer. Again, the fauna of understory birds that frequently eats small fruits in Neotropical rainforests would have a very rough go of it in the Malaysian forests.

"It is extremely interesting that after doing this and writing the above, I discovered Karr's (1976) statement that "about 80% of the canopy and understory tree species on Barro Colorado Island are dispersed by animals (Foster 1973), while only about 10 percent of the trees on Fogden's (1972) [Sarawak] study area were important as sources of fruits for birds". Furthermore, at the IV International Congress of Ecology, in Panama, Karr (March 1977) noted that "The most striking difference is the total lack of undergrowth frugivores in mist-net samples taken from Malaysia as compared with 25–33 percent of the individuals captured in undergrowth of African and Central American forest."

I would like to propose a rather sweeping hypothesis to account for this paucity of flowers and fruits on rainforest understory shrubs, a paucity which should have a very depressing affect on the biomass and species richness of the understory fauna. I need first, however, to belabor you with three facts about the lowland Malaysian rainforests in which the censuses were made.

1) They are dipterocarp forests, which means that between 50 and 80 percent of the tree crowns in the canopy belong to species of Dipterocarpaceae. The members of this family, in Malaysia and some other tropical Asian areas, mast fruit within (and between) habitats. Thus the bulk of the flower and fruit production by better than half of the upper canopy photosynthetic machinery is pulsed at 3- to 11- year intervals. Associated with this, the animal community is sufficiently satiated by the enormous numbers of seeds that a very large number survive to the seedling and small sapling stage (Janzen 1974a).

2) Malaysian rainforests, on the Malay peninsula or in Sarawak, are largely perched on sandy soils ranging from very old white sand deposits (such as in Bako National Park, Sarawak) to very sandy soils derived from weathering of granitic base rock that has not been inundated by the sea for an extremely long time. There is no volcanic overlay nor crust of weathering limestone on most of the terrain. There are many indirect measures of the relatively low ability of these soils to generate a vegetation with a high harvestable productivity for other organisms: when cleared, the second-growth vegetation is very slow to refill the site (Janzen 1974a, 1974b, and this is probably why plantation rubber is so successful on these soil types); the forest has largely remained uncut and unexploited by agrarian peoples despite their presence in the general area for many thousands of years (note that virtually all of nearby Java on volcanic soils is under agriculture); second growth vegetation of the sites has an amazingly low insect biomass as compared to that of comparable neotropical weedy sites (Janzen 1974a).

3) There are bees, butterflies, flower-visiting birds, and small fruit-eating birds present in the Malaysian rainforests. In other words, pollinators and dispersal agents can be drawn from these groups if the ecological and evolutionary opportunity is presented.

I hypothesize that the shortage of rainforest understory flowers and fruits is largely attributable to two forces operating simultaneously and synergistically. First, I hypothesize that the large pulse of dipterocarp seedlings and saplings takes up a large part of the resources that are available to neotropical understory shrubs; the dipterocarp offspring are apparently dying in large part through competition rather than through supporting a seed predator guild. Simultaneously, they are analogous to an enormous and very generalist herbivore in their impact on understory shrubs. Since dipterocarp seedlings never flower or fruit, they take a large portion of the understory resources without feeding part of it back into the flower-visitor and fruit-eater guild so conspicuous in a neotropical forest. Second, I hypothesize that as the soil conditions get progressively worse, the ability to be a reproducing individual in the light-poor understory is reduced. That is to say, irrespective of the presence of the dipterocarp seedlings, if the forest canopy is held constant, and the soil fertility is depressed, the biomass (number of individuals in general) and reproductive output per hectare by understory shrubs should fall (just as it would if soil fertility were held constant and the light were decreased). In other words, the rainforests of Malaysia sit on a poorer piece of real estate than do those of lowland Costa Rica, and the flower and fruit density in the understory reflects this.

The animals are probably woven into this matrix more firmly than I have indicated so far. I have hypothesized that the habitat-wide masting behavior of these Dipterocarpaceae is driven at present, and was selected for in the past, by the seed predators in general (Janzen 1974a). Further, I have argued that the lower the overall productivity of the site, the more likely that the animals will select for masting behavior because the less food there is for them between mast crops, the more severely they are depressed in density by masting behavior. But the scarcer they are between mast crops, the fewer understory flower and fruit crops they can (will) visit; the fewer crops they visit, the less well off will be such plants and the better off will be the dipterocarp seedlings in competition with non-dipterocarps. Why does the system not progress to where there are nothing but seedlings and saplings of overstory trees in the understory? Probably because as time passes since the last mast crop, competitive and accidental deaths clear the arena for some other species of plants, and because a number of animals that visit flowers in the understory can also go elsewhere for food; many frugivores can feed on insects and other food types when understory fruits are scarce.

The focus to this point has been largely on the biomass of flowers and fruits and associated animals. However, the species richness of plants and animals should also be negatively influenced by a reduction in harvestable productivity (Janzen 1977a). My argument involves resource partitioning and specialization on the partitions. In short, as the productivity of harvestable resources in the habitat falls, more and more resource blocks become too small to sustain a specialist. They are then taken by a more generalized harvester or by another trophic level. In the context of the example under discussion, the number of species of flower-visiting species of understory birds should decline as the soil gets poorer and as the overstory becomes progressively more synchronized at supra-annual seeding. For example, in a Costa Rican rainforest there are species and morphs (often females) of hummingbirds (e.g., *Phaethornis* spp.) that specialize on widely scattered understory individuals in flower, and species and morphs (often males) that specialize on large clumps of flowers on forest edges (Stiles 1975). From what I have seen of Malaysian lowland rainforest, a hummingbird would have to forage at all such sites and then some to stay in the game. Simultaneously the species richness of seed predators in the habitat should also decline as soils become poorer and synchrony increases, since the progressively more pulsed nature of the seed resource makes it effectively scarcer in any but the very exceptional mast year. For example, in a Costa Rican rainforest there is a large standing crop of agoutis (*Dasyprocta punctata*) and pacas (*Cuniculus paca*) that live on the rather continuous input of fruits, seeds and young seedlings (Smythe 1970). These animals are relatively sedentary. They do not have ecological analogues in Malaysian forests, and I suspect the reason to be that in most years the seed resource is not large enough to sustain them, although in mast years it is far greater than they could ever consume before the seeds germinate.

The pulsing of productivity in a rainforest can have other interesting side effects on animals. It should select for migratory or very nomadic species, which are in turn less likely to develop local regional populations than are more sedentary species. I have argued that the wind-dispersed nature of dipterocarp seed (and that of other trees that fruit as they do, such as the legume *Koompasia*) is due to their specialization to the site on which their parent grew and not being involved in escape from seed predators through dispersal (Janzen 1977b); it may also be due to an extreme shortage of biomass of frugivorous animals owing to the fact that much of the seed production by the forest is pulsed (the frugivores would be severely satiated on seeding years just as would be the seed predators). Whatever the cause, the fact that most of the canopy-level seed production is wind-dispersed eliminates a large portion of the fruit input that is an important part of the diet of many neotropical animals. For example, I doubt very much that any Malaysian forest comes anywhere close to the figures of 0.61 to 1.93 g of fruit per m^2 calculated to fall in a Panamanian rainforest by Smythe (1970). However, in closing this paragraph, I cannot help but notice that Malaysian forests have an exceptionally high number of species of squirrels for example, 19 tree squirrels in Borneo, Davis 1962). It is possible that squirrels are particularly good at dealing with a highly pulsed food input, as compared with the other animals that eat seeds and fruits (some in fact, are specialists on insects or vegetative parts of plants). In short, as harvestable productivity becomes progressively less available, there is no reason to expect all animal life forms to be depressed

at the same rate. In fact the elimination of some could quite reasonably result in an increase in others.

The ramifications of low productivity of harvestable resources by the plant community in an average year can produce a multitude of higher-order interactions. For example, in 17 days of field work and travel between field sites by boat or small car, I saw a total of three raptorial birds in Peninsular Malaysia (and none in 11 days in Bako National Park, Sarawak). The area traversed was at least 300 miles of urban, rural and forest roads, 76 miles of large river through farmland and forest reserve (Tembeling River on the way to and from Taman Negara), and about 50 hours of hiking in forest reserves. At least 80 percent of the weather was non-rainy. I should emphasize that I was not searching for raptorial birds, but rather just watching for any kind of animal. In a similar excursion up and down the similar-sized Sanaga River in Cameroun, I took photographs of 23 birds of prey and saw at least 50 more. In Ugandan and Kenyan forest-farmland and national parks, it is hard to find a moment on a clear day when a raptor or large avian scavenger is not in view somewhere (and see Janzen 1976b). In Costa Rican lowland rainforests, forest-farmland mixes, and open pasturelands, raptors and/or scavengers are seen at least once every several hours, and much more often in many circumstances.

The ornithological literature is not designed so as to provide material relevant to comments such as those above. However, a few interesting tidbits can be extracted. For example, the black or king vulture (*Torgos calvus*) is common throughout the northern part of the Malay Peninsula but is almost never seen in the southern half (rainforested portion) of the peninsula; the same may be said of the other peninsular vulture (*Pseudogyps bengalensis*) (Robinson 1927; Medway and Wells 1976). As Wells put it (pers. comm.), there is no vulture (for all practical purposes) in West Malaysia. The standard explanation for the absence of vultures is Robinson's (1927) comment that "securing their food entirely by sight, it is obvious that a heavily forested country is quite unsuited to them and it is for this reason, probably, that they do not extend to the Malay Archipelago." This seems to me to be a quite inadequate explanation. As Peninsular Malaysia has been cleared, vultures have become rarer, not more common (Robinson 1927). Furthermore, one has to ask 1) why similarly heavily forested areas in other parts of the tropics sustain vultures; 2) why the forest was not cleared for agriculture and livestock long ago as it was in other parts of the tropics, and 3) why the contemporary invasion of agricultural peoples does not bring with it adequate food for vultures? In short, I hypothesize that rainforest Peninsular Malaysian and Sarawak habitats never did generate enough carrion to keep vultures in the game and that the contemporary peoples occupying these habitats cannot raise enough livestock to generate enough spin-off carcasses for vultures to persist as the land is cleared. Central American rainforest and associated natural disturbance sites, when put into multi-use agriculture and livestock husbandry, sustain conspicuous populations of three species of vultures and two caracaras (hawks that act like vultures).

I doubt that the paucity of vultures or vulture-like birds in Malaysia is due to excessive hunting; however if there is less food for them, then even small amounts of hunting can do disproportionately more damage than if there is a large resource base. I doubt that the large varanid lizards, relatively common on river banks and in refuse dumps where not hunted, are competitively excluding the vulture-like birds. I saw 28 large (0.5–1-m snout-vent) *Varanus* along the bank of about 20 km of the Tembeling River at and below Taman Negara on one morning. Rather, I suspect that the absence of vultures allows the presence of these relatively slow scavengers; if the food is scarce and occurs at very long intervals, then a cold-blooded professional starver would be able to maintain a much higher biomass than birds. I was told by a Kuala Lumpur "pet" dealer that with water, a large varanid can live a year without food; I doubt a vulture could do the same.

The hypothesis that the natural habitats of West Malaysia generate a low density of food for large carnivorous birds is also supported by the species richness of falconids and accipiters. West Malaysia has 11 resident species of accipiters and 1 resident falcon (Medway and Wells 1976) and is about 132,000 km^2 in area; Costa Rica has at least 28 resident species of accipiters and 8 resident falcons and is 51,000 km^2 in area (Slud 1964). The tiny Costa Rican rainforest field station at Finca La Selva (6.1 km^2) has at least 9 resident accipiters and 4 resident falcons (Slud 1960).

Herons, bitterns and egrets are conspicuously scarce in fields, roadside ditches and empoundments, rice paddies, streams, marshes, and riverbanks in West Malaysia away from the sea. I did not see a single individual in the 17 day field period. More specifically, not a single one was seen along the 76 miles traversed of the Tembeling River, despite careful search for them. These birds are conspicuous in similar habitats in Africa and Central America. On the Sanaga river trip mentioned above, I photographed 7 species and saw at least 30 individuals. Such birds are a standard part of the scenery along large Central American rivers and in the kinds of habitats mentioned at the beginning of this paragraph. Inquiry of ornithologists in

West Malaysia produced two useful comments. First, "they are absent because they don't migrate here"; well, what is wrong with West Malaysian real estate so that migrating large piscivorous birds do not use it much as overwintering grounds? Second, "these birds are conspicuous in areas near the sea." For example, Medway and Wells (1976) noted that 6 of the 9 resident species of Malayan Ardeidae are associated with mangroves. If in fact West Malaysia is a poor habitat for these birds, then the mangroves and river deltas should be the best of the sites and appear disproportionately good compared to inland areas. Again, tiny Costa Rica has 14 species of resident Ardeidae (Slud 1964) to compare with 9 for Peninsular Malaysia (Medway and Wells 1976).

I hypothesize that herons, bitterns, egrets (and anhinga- and cormorant-type birds) are in short supply in the West Malaysian inlands simply because the waterways do not generate enough biomass of aquatic food for them. If the surrounding terrestrial habitats generate a reduced number of insects as well, which are an important part of the diet of many ardeids, the effect would be compounded.

There are two other non-intuitive major sources of global heterogeneity in small tropical terrestrial bird food: insularity and altitudinal gradients. In a sentence, the problem with Caribbean islands is that they have greatly reduced insect biomass overall and numbers of individuals of many insect groups as compared with Central American mainland vegetation of comparable elevation, seasonality, soil type, and disturbance history. Specifically, sweep samples (Janzen 1973b; Allan et al 1973) and visual inspection of secondary and primary forest understory vegetation on Puerto Rico, St. Thomas, Hicacos Island, Palominitos Island, Greater St. James, Gran Cayman, Providencia, and other small islands in the Virgin Islands show greatly reduced numbers and biomass of Hemiptera, Lepidoptera larvae, Orthoptera and herbivorous Coleoptera as compared with a great variety of mainland lowland sites in Costa Rica. Even more spectacularly, when the wet season arrives on a seasonal island, there does not appear to be the great increase in insect density so prominent on the Costa Rican mainland in very seasonal lowland sites, for example, Providencia Island (Janzen 1973b).

Not all groups of anthropods are equally reduced on small Caribbean Islands. Some Homoptera (aphids, scales, mealy bugs, leafhoppers, fulgorids, and flatids) are conspicuously over-represented in numbers and biomass on small islands; presumably this is due to some sort of release from predation and parasitization (Janzen 1973b). Ants, spiders and predaceous beetles are likewise proportionately (and in some cases, abso-

Daniel H. Janzen

lutely) much more abundant than in comparable mainland habitats (and see Becker 1975). This is probably related to the ability of individuals of these predaceous life forms to withstand the long starvation periods associated with a highly seasonal habitat coupled with few moist refugia to pass the dry season or from which to reinvade when there is local extinction.

I have been careful not to give or dwell on data for specific islands or habitat types on the islands. I suspect that even at low levels of insect prey there is strong inter-habitat and inter-island variation in density; even the relative lack of increase in insects in the rainy season is based on only two data points and may not be absolutely generalizable. A special word of caution is needed with respect to type of insect eaten; an aphid specialist would do extremely well on the small islands between Puerto Rico and St. Thomas. However, almost any bird depending on Orthoptera or caterpillars more than 2 cm in length would starve to death on any Caribbean Island (except Trinidad). It is imperative that the insect sampling scheme be tuned to the kinds of insects eaten by the bird of concern and that the sample be taken from the relevant habitat in the appropriate season.

In closing the subject of insularity, I should note that understanding insect densities (as food) on Caribbean Islands is relevant to more than where migrants can stack themselves. John Terborgh has pointed out to me that on Caribbean (and Pacific) islands the ratio of frugivorous and granivorous bird species to insectivorous (resident) species is the inverse of the adjacent mainland. Is this because insectivores do so poorly, because frugivores do so well on islands, or because, for instance, frugivores can find the insects they need for the very short times they are rearing young (owing to the general absence of insectivores)? This may be a ridiculous hypothesis, but I suspect that when insect and other resource densities are strongly altered compared to a mainland, we may have natural experiments that help illuminate heretofore unsuspected interactions on the mainland.

Everyone expects insect biomass numbers, sizes, etc., to change going up a tropical mountain. They do, but not quite in the way expected. In short, there is a mid-elevation bulge in insect species richness and biomass (and/or individuals). Between about 800 and 1,600 m on Costa Rican and Venezuelan mountains, sweep and visual samples in primary forest and secondary vegetation tend to produce more individuals and species of arthropods than equivalent samples from the adjacent lowlands (0–200-m elevation), and very substantially more than at higher elevations (2,000–3,500 m) (Janzen 1973b; Janzen et al 1976). To me, the most plausible hypothesis for this phenomenon is a bulge in harvestable productivity at intermediate elevations. As a dependent hypothesis, the increased productivity may be due to cooler nights at intermediate elevations coupled with only slightly reduced diurnal photosynthesis; the difference, which should be related to the harvestable productivity, is thus higher at intermediate elevations. It is those hot tropical nights. A moment's reflection should show why increased harvestable productivity from plants should result in an increase in species-richness as well as biomass in the herbivorous insect life form (with subsequent changes in the insectivores of all sorts in the habitat, and see Janzen 1977a).

I will leave the relevance of the mid-elevation bulge to insectivorous birds, migrant and resident, to the other contributors to this volume. Jim Karr has pointed out to me that it is at intermediate elevations the tropics around that take the prize for the greatest mist-net catches. Intermediate elevations have been described as "migrant heaven" (Neal Smith). Paul Slud notes that these intermediate elevations may represent a giant ecotone between upper elevation bird faunas of extra-tropical origin and lowland tropical faunas. However, the generation of migrants in evolutionary time from intermediate elevations may be one way to generate an upper elevation bird of extra-tropical origin.

Acknowledgments

This study was supported by National Science Foundation grant DEB 77-04889 and inspired by Allen Keast and Gene Morton.

Literature Cited

Allan, J. D., L. W. Barnthouse, R. A. Prestbye, and D. R. Strong
1973. On foliage arthropod communities of Puerto Rican second growth vegetation. Ecol. 54:628–32.

Becker, P.
1975. Island colonization by carnivorous and herbivorous Coleoptera. J. Anim. Ecol. 44:893–906.

Davis, D. D.
1962. Mammals of the lowland rainforest of North Borneo. Bull. Nat. Mus., Singapore, 129 pp.

Fogden, M. P. L.
1972. The seasonality and population dynamics of equatorial forest birds in Sarawak. Ibis 114:307–43.

Foster, R. B.
1973. Seasonality of fruit production and seed fall in a tropical forest ecosystem in Panama. Ph.D. diss., Duke University, Durham, N.C. 156 pp.

Frankie, G. W., H. G. Baker, and P. A. Opler

1974.   Comparative phenological studies of trees in tropical wet and dry forests in the lowlands of Costa Rica. J. Ecol. 62:881–913.

Janzen, D. H.

1973a. Sweep samples of tropical foliage insects: description of study sites, with data on species abundances and size distributions. Ecol. 54:659–686.

1973b. Sweep samples of tropical foliage insects: effects of seasons, vegetation types, elevation, time of day, and insularity. Ecol. 54:687–708.

1974a. Tropical blackwater rivers, animals, and mast fruiting by the Dipterocarpaceae. Biotropica 6:69–103.

1974b. Epiphytic Myrmecophytes in Sarawak: mutualism through the feeding of plants by ants. Biotropica 6: 237–259.

1976a. Sweep samples of tropical deciduous forest foliage-inhabiting insects: seasonal changes and inter-field differences in adult bugs and beetles. Rev. Biol. Trop. 24:149–161.

1976b. The depression of reptile biomass by large herbivores. Amer. Nat. 110:371–400.

1977a. Why are there so many species of insects? Proc. 15 International Congress of Entomology, Washington, D.C. 1976:84–94.

1977b. Seeding patterns of tropical trees. Proc. 4th Cabot Symposium, Harvard Forest, Mass.

1978a. Promising directions of study in tropical animal-plant interactions. Ann. Missouri Bot. Garden (in press).

Janzen, D. H., M. Ataroff, M. Fariñas, S. Reyes, N. Rincon, A. Soler, P. Soriano, and M. Vera

1976.   Changes in the Arthropod community along an elevational transect in the Venezuelan Andes. Biotropica 8:193–203.

Karr, J. R.

1976.   Seasonality, resource availability, and community diversity in tropical bird communities. Amer. Nat. 110:973–94.

Medway, L., and D. R. Wells

1976.   *The Birds of the Malay Peninsula.* Vol. V. London: Witherby, 448 pp.

Robinson, H. C.

1927.   *The Birds of the Malay Penninsula.* Vol. I. London: Witherby, 329 pp.

Slud, P.

1960.   The birds of Finca La Selva, Costa Rica: a tropical wet forest locality. Bull. Amer. Mus. Nat. Hist. 121: 1–148.

1964.   The birds of Costa Rica. Bull. Amer. Mus. Nat. Hist. 128:1–430.

Smythe, N.

1970.   Relationships between fruiting seasons and seed dispersal methods in a neotropical forest. Amer. Nat. 104:25–35.

Stiles, G.

1975.   Ecology, flowering phenology, and hummingbird pollination of some Costa Rican *Heliconia* species. Ecol. 56:285–301.

Daniel H. Janzen

Integrations

EUGENE S. MORTON
National Zoological Park
Smithsonian Institution
Washington, D.C. 20008

The Importance of Migrant Birds to the Advancement of Evolutionary Theory

Evolutionary Perspective

This volume brings together much descriptive information on what migrants do in the neotropics together with interpretation of ecological significance. Perhaps it is equally important to have begun a dialog over future directions for research, for the migration system as we know it may not have much time left. Ecology, as a field, has tended increasingly to assume that each species represents a fixed entity, all individuals alike, to be studied in relation to other such fixed entities. This emphasis on interspecific interactions has naturally produced a de-emphasis of evolutionary questions, since the major thrust is far from the level at which evolution operates. This vacuum has lately been filled by behavioral ecology, for only by studying intraspecific relationships can the selective forces acting upon individuals be discovered. Migrants provide perhaps the best system to illustrate the dichotomy that has grown between ecological and evolutionary approaches and also the synthesis provided by the behavioral-ecological approach.

The difficulty of applying an ecological approach to the goal of understanding evolutionary processes in migrant species is evident in this volume. One example is the so-called "plasticity" of migrants if their described roles change. Though not often explicit, this must mean that the individuals sampled have shown changes in the parameters studied, for example, between breeding and nonbreeding grounds, one part of a range from another, or perhaps even between the tropical seasons in one place. To achieve meaningfulness, "plasticity" must be discussed in relation to the sources of selection that produced the changes, for there are many migrant species that show little change and some that show great change—but both are equally adapted. Resident and migrant species show no real difference in "plasticity" anyway. The important question is why: what are the proximate and ultimate factors that produced the change or lack of change between breeding and nonbreeding ecology?

The de-emphasis on evolution in ecology has caused some fairly obvious yet important phenomena to be overlooked. One may be the most important difference between North American or intratropical migrants and some tropical residents: the importance of pair bonds. Tropical-resident insectivores are characteristically permanently pair bonded, and they defend permanent territories. About 60 percent of tropical passerine species share these attributes. In contrast, migrant species show no indication of sexual recognition. Most of the resident species they join in flocks are pair bonded; their territories are defended jointly by the bonded pair (Powell, this volume). Why has selection not favored pair bonds in the many territorial migrant species? Even "psuedo" pair bonds, that might not remain through migration into the breeding season, would give an advantage over territorial defense by single birds. However, as several authors noted, territories are defended by both sexes against all other conspecifics—sex is not recognized. The answer is that there is apparently no way that this type of cooperation can be (genetically) favored unless reproduction takes place between the cooperators. (The Prothonotary Warbler may be an exception—they seem to maintain or assume pair bonds on the wintering grounds).

What are the ecological ramifications of this lone major difference between migrants and residents? Territorial migrants and residents alike show a tendency toward habitat restriction. They choose habitat structures that best predict insect availability relative to their specific morphological and behavioral specialties. But for nonterritorial migrants and residents, or those exhibiting facultative territoriality, movements in response to local or regional changes in food availability are possible. The absence of pair bonds promotes omnivory, the most ubiquitous tropical diet, together with a loosening of foraging zones. By not breeding in the tropics, and by assiduously avoiding the recognition of sex, the evolutionary background of "plasticity" for North American migrants becomes almost a syndrome.

There is probably strong selection *against* sexual recognition. Selection might favor females that look like males, if males are larger, if only because it gave them an advantage in social conflicts. This may be the process by which the sexes of territorial migrants have become identical or similar. For example, in most Red-winged Blackbirds (*Agelaius phoeniceus*), the sexes are readily distinguishable. The sexes also forage in somewhat different habitats and in separate flocks.

The Cuban redwing is an exception in which the sexes remain together when foraging, and conflicts are frequent (pers. obs.). Here the females are black, like the males. Selection has generally favored monochromatism when winter territories are defended but sexual dichromatism when quick pair formation is of paramount importance back in North America (plus lack of female participation in territorial defense).

The evolutionary perspective will give added interest to single species studies. As Karr (this volume) points out, each migrant species represents a unique adaptation within both temperate and tropical ranges. Many of these adaptations remain unidentified due to the "fixed entity" model necessary when ecological categories larger than the species are emphasized.

How Tropical Are Migrants?

The diets of migrants while in the tropics show a convergence toward those of resident species. There is a clear trend toward omnivory through the use of plant products, one of the major reasons why the tropics support a higher species diversity than temperate areas (Karr 1971; Morton 1973; Lovejoy 1975).

North American migrants, because of their abundance and mobility relative to resident species, must exert great influence on fruiting and flowering phenology of tropical plants. The timing of fruit production in *Phytolacca* species may be largely an adaptation for fruit dispersal by Swainson's Thrush (*Hylocichla ustulata*) in both temperate and tropical areas (Karr, this volume; Ramos pers. comm.; pers. obs.). The relationship between migratory orioles (*Icterus*) to flower timing and morphology in *Erythrina* species has been discussed by Cruden and Toledo (1977) and Morton (*in press*). The timing of fruit production in *Didymopanax morototoni* and the display of the fruit (sticking up through the treecrown to be visible to overflying birds) may be adapted for the Eastern Kingbirds' (*Tyrannus tyrannus*) tropical passage (Morton 1971). In Panama, *Combretum fructicosum* is pollinated almost exclusively by the Tennessee Warbler (*Vermivora peregrina*, Morton this volume).

The diversity in behavioral ecology exhibited by migrants in the tropics points to some unsuspected complications for their conservation. Except for sedentary, territorial species, habitat requirements are not easily assessed because these vary during a single season. Bay-breasted Warblers (*Dendroica castanea*), for example, utilize young forest, late shrub, and mature forest but require mature forest for a short but critical period between wet and dry seasons. Furthermore, food-rich habitats paradoxically may not be the only critical requirements. Food-rich habitats, young forest in the wet season for Bay-breasts, may produce low

556   Eugene S. Morton

social tolerance; certain sex and age classes could be forced into mature forest habitats. The destruction of these mature habitats may cause skewed sex ratios with a reduction in breeding potential. It is not realistic to study foraging, foods, or social behavior as separate entities, for they all act synergistically. We need much more information on intraspecific competition before we can either assess the impact of habitat changes in the neotropics on migrant populations or extract scientific generalizations about tropical adaptations that migrants have to tell us.

Literature Cited

Cruden, R. W., and V. M. Toledo.
1977.   Oriole pollination of *Erythrina breviflora* (Leguminosae): evidence for a polytypic view of ornithophily. Plant Syst. Evol. 126:393–403.

Karr, J. R.
1971.   Structure of avian communities in selected Panama and Illinois habitats. Ecol. Monogr. 41:207–33.

Lovejoy, T. E.
1975.   Bird diversity and abundance in Amazon forest communities. Living Bird 13:127–91.

Morton, E. S.
1971.   Food and migration habits of the Eastern Kingbird in Panama. Auk 88:925–26.
1973.   On the evolutionary advantages and disadvantages of fruit-eating in tropical birds. Amer. Nat. 107:8–22.
1979.   Effective pollination of *Erythrina fusca* by the Orchard Oriole (*Icterus spurius*): coevolved behavioral manipulation? Ann. Mo. Bot. Garden.

ALLEN KEAST
Department of Biology
Queen's University
Kingston, Ontario
Canada K7L 3N6

Synthesis: Ecological Basis and Evolution of the Nearctic-Neotropical Bird Migration System

ABSTRACT

The original objectives of this volume were to define how nearctic-breeding species fit into the neotropical system, where the major species wintered, how their ecology compared with that of resident species, and how migrant and resident interacted. In the wider view, by bringing together a diversified team of experts in a range of areas, groups, and aspects of ecology, it was hoped to learn how northern Neotropica, a highly species-rich area presumably already "saturated" with species was able to "absorb" such vast hordes of seasonal intruders from outside. The conclusion has now come forward from many contributors that this way of looking at the situation is incorrect, that, by contrast, the migrants are part of the tropical ecosystem and that, though only present for some seven months, they retain "niches" there. Thus, Rappole and Warner hypothesize that most nearctic, long-distance migrants evolved from historically tropical species which were able to exploit niches common to many different forest types; that with low breeding success and intense competition for resources in tropical communities, individuals of these species took advantage of reduced competition in seasonal niches in temperate areas to increase reproductive success. Certainly, in the wintering grounds, there is no basis for the claim that migrants are competitively inferior to permanent resident species. Emlen, Stiles, and others find the striking degree of concordance between ecological distributions of permanent and winter residents as further evidence that they are really part of the tropical communities. Stiles sees the high degree of integration of winter residents into tropical communities as demonstrating a long tropical history. Similar views are expressed by others.

In their wintering grounds, the migrant species separate out ecologically from each other and from residents, in a range of ways: geographically, on habitat, on feeding height and behavior, etc. The nature of these separations is the same as in bird communities elsewhere. While there is ample evidence of continuing species interaction and of species' influences on each other's ecology, it must be noted that the more closely related species (congeners) tend spatially to separate out fairly clearly. Since species composition in the wintering communities is quite different from that of the summer communities, it is obvious that the two communities have developed independently and by the assemblage of groups of species that are compatible within the adaptive capacity of the individual species.

Some 150 species of land and freshwater birds that breed in North America fly south annually to winter in Central and South America and in the West Indies. This ability to seasonally exploit two very different latitudes is a typically avian phenomenon. The migrants are able to utilize the spring flushes of insects and long days of the north to raise their young. Southward migration in the winter provides them with a supportive environment the rest of the year.

Thinking about the origins and ecological basis of migration has changed drastically over the last 150 years. Several writers in this symposium, for example, argue that migrants should not be looked upon as a northern assemblage that moves southward (reluctantly?) to escape winter, an alien element fitting as best it can into neotropical habitats. Rather, by contrast, migrants and residents should be viewed as part of a common co-evolving American avifauna. The concept of these migrants being, originally, tropical birds that go north to avail themselves of seasonal opportunities in the north is not new. It was the basis of the "southern ancestral" theory of bird migration. Either way, the interaction patterns of migrant and resident on the wintering grounds today are complex and dynamic, as many papers in this symposium testify.

Origins of the Basic Elements of the Nearctic Avifauna Relative to the Development of the Migratory Habit

The Nearctic Zoogeographic Region is defined as North America plus the Mexican Plateau; Neotropica, as South America attenuating northwards to the lowland rain forests of Guatemala and Chiapas. The division, while by no means absolute, delimits a temperate avifauna adapted to deciduous forest, pine-oak, and highlands, from an avifauna of tropical rain forest and savannah. The division is reinforced by many of the more distinctive southern families (Furnariidae, Formicariidae, Dendrocolaptidae) not presently entering the Mexican highlands or continental North America. The contemporary division of Nearctica from Neotropica, nevertheless, glosses over the fact that prior to the formation of the Panamanian land-bridge North America extended southwards as a peninsula as far south as Panama, evidenced by the presence of North American fossil mammals in the Miocene (Whitmore and Stewart 1965). Accordingly, there must formerly have been a North American tropical avifauna (Mayr 1946, 1964). There is evidence, however, that this peninsula was largely covered with savannah, not rain forest (Whitmore and Stewart 1965; Mayr 1964; and other sources).

Mayr (1946, 1964), stressing that the contemporary North American avifauna are of multiple origins, has divided it into a series of elements based on the fossil record and centers of abundance. Mayr's recognition of six elements has received wide acceptance. These elements are: 1) Pantropical, 2) Panboreal, 3) Old World, 4) North American, 5) Pan-American, 6) South American, plus an aggregate element of avifauna of unanalyzed origin. This last element is made up of groups so evenly distributed between the Old and New Worlds that assessment of centers of origin is impossible. Included in this element are grebes, herons, ibises, ducks, and rallids.

The Panboreal element is small—only loons and phalaropes. The Old World element is large and, besides later colonizers, probably includes: the American quails within the Phasianidae; typical owls (Strigidae, because the related Tytonidae are clearly of Old World origin); the gnatcatchers (Polioptilinae, now included within the Sylviinae); the pigeons (because their major radiation is in the Australian part of the Old World); the Crows (Corvidae); thrushes (Turdinae); cranes, kingfishers, cardueline finches, and titmice (Paridae). These groups probably entered Nearctica progressively during the Tertiary, and some have had a very long history here. Groups that are clearly late arrivals from the Old World include the barn owls (Tytonidae), larks (Alaudidae), nuthatches (Sittidae), creepers (Certhiidae), Old World warblers and kinglets (Sylviinae), and the shrikes (Laniidae).

The North American element (endemics that originated here) is considered by Mayr to include the New World vultures (Cathartidae), turkeys (Meleagrididae), grouse (Tetraonidae), dippers (Cinclidae), and the finch subfamily Emberizinae. Mayr agrees with Lonnberg (1927) that the thrashers and mockingbirds (Mimidae), vireos (Vireonidae), wood-warblers (Parulidae), waxwings (Bombycillidae), and wrens (Troglodytidae), are basically nearctic. He notes that the parulids have 16 genera in North America (many endemic), and only 6 in South America (none endemic).

The Pan-American element, prominent in both continents, includes the Icteridae and Tyrannidae. Today, both of these families are more diversified in South America than North America.

The term neotropical element applies to groups in which the overwhelming bulk of genera are South American or are confined to Neotropica, and few if any species penetrate northwards. Included in this element are the formicariids, furnariids, dendrocolaptids, cotingids, tanagers, and hummingbirds. Most of these are obviously closely linked to the specific attributes and habitats of multi-layered tropical forest with its abundant fruit and nectar resources.

Allen Keast

From Mayr's framework, it is obvious (table 1) that migration has evolved in all groups irrespective of origin. Among the Panboreal element the phalaropes winter in the Southern Hemisphere, and within the Old World element quails, owls, gnatcatchers and thrushes are migrants. Migration is pronounced in the members of the nearctic and Pan-American elements, and the few true neotropical groups that penetrate well to the north are also migrants. Williams (1958) has developed a tabulation (table 2) in which he compares the wintering latitudes of species whose ancestors entered Nearctica from the north (i.e., species which apparently are of palaearctic origin) relative to those which entered Nearctica from the south. Half of the palaearctic species winter north of the U.S.-Mexican border, compared to 5 percent of the neotropicals. Only 1 percent of the palaearctic species penetrate into South America, compared to 36 percent of the Neotropicals.

Taxonomic Group and Ecological Category Relative to Migration Distance

Listed in table 1 are the various families of nearctic birds and the numbers of each species wintering in North America, Neotropica, or in both regions. The last category is, in part, made up of warm-temperate and subtropical forms centered in the southern United States and Central America.

The following avian families belong mainly or entirely to the group wintering in North America: loons, grebes, cormorants, grouse, quails, turkeys, cranes, woodpeckers, corvids, titmice, nuthatches, creepers and dippers, mimids, sylviids, pipits, bombycillids, and shrikes. Families in which most forms remain in Nearctica but in which there is also marked wintering in Central America include: herons, ibises, ducks, hawks, rails, pigeons and owls. Families in which wintering in Neotropica is predominant are: caprimulgids, swifts, swallows, tyrant flycatchers, vireos, parulids, and tanagers.

A number of the groups that winter both in North America and Central America, have small numbers of species that are long-distance migrants. These are: accipitres, falcons, plovers, cuckoos, hummingbirds, thrushes, orioles, and fringillids. The scolopacids have a significant proportion of very-long-distance migrants traveling to southern South America (Myers, this volume). Although only about 15 percent of icterid species winter in South America, they include one exceptionally long-distance migrant, the bobolink (*Dolichonyx oryzivorus*), that migrates to Brazil and northern Argentina. Among the 9 percent of the fringillids migrating to Neotropica are the Indigo Bunting (*Passerina cyanea*), the forest-dwelling Rose-breasted Grosbeak (*Pheucticus*

ludovicianus), and the grassland Dickcissel (*Spiza americana*).

Of the groups that are predominantly neotropical winterers, only 9 of the 30 species of tyrannids and only 14 of the 84 species of migratory parulid species winter in North America (Fitzpatrick, this volume).

The major groups that winter in Neotropica are the insect-eaters, the aerial-feeding swallows and swifts, caprimulgids, and tyrannids, and the woodland-dwelling and arboreal-feeding parulids, vireonids, and orioles. Their breeding in the north is obviously linked to the spring flushes of lepidopterous and other larvae. More data are needed, however, on the nature of the winter resource base in the south that supports the above neotropic winterers.

Where Do Migrants Winter in Neotropica?

A number of contributors to this volume provide data from north to south on the abundances of migrants relative to residents at various localities in Central America. These data are summarized by Terborgh (this volume). It shows a progressive southward drop-off in numbers of wintering species and individuals. Since the attenuation is matched by an increase in the numbers of *resident* species (as Slud [1976] and others, have noted), the impact of migrants on the system progressively diminishes southwardly.

In contrast, at the northern end of the wintering zone, *migrants* are dominant. Thus, Emlen finds that in Florida and the northern Bahamas, the number of species increases by 160–206 percent in winter; and the densities of individual birds fluctuates from about 900 per km^2 in April, after the migrants leave, to 1,600 per km^2 in mid-winter. In June with the acquisition of summer migrants, counts average 1,200 per km^2. An even more striking seasonal difference occurs in western Mexico where the tropical evergreen forest habitat that supports 67 small foliage gleaners per ha in winter supports only 1.7 per ha in summer (Hutto, this volume). The lowland sites averaged 25 times more warbler-guild birds in winter than in summer. Hutto in part ascribes the extreme difference to the fact that insect densities are 1.58 times higher in winter than in summer. In contrast with the southern nearctic localities is the situation in Ecuador, Peru and Bolivia at the southern extreme of the migrant wintering area. This area is "the most species-rich bird habitat in the world," with 420–480 species per 10 km^2. Here, wintering northern migrants make up only 5.2–7.3 percent of the species (Pearson 1975).

Terborgh tabulates the percentages of migrant individuals in the winter avifaunas of some 25 localities from Mexico through the West Indies and Central America to Bolivia. Although proportions vary with

Table 1. Seasonal migration in nearctic-breeding land and fresh-water species of birds: numbers wintering within Nearctica; Nearctica plus Neotropica; and entirely in Neotropica or the West Indies

Family	Number of nearctic breeding species	Number wintering in Nearctica	Number wintering in both Neartica and Neotropica	Number wintering in Neotropica
Gaviidae (loons)	3	3	—	—
Podicipedidae (grebes)	6	5	1	—
Pelecanidae (pelicans)	2	1	1	—
Phalacrocoracidae (cormorants)	5	4	1	—
Anhingidae (darters)	1	—	1	—
Ardeidae (herons)	13	1	12	—
Ciconiidae (storks)	1	—	1	—
Threskiornithidae (ibises, spoonbills)	5	—	5	—
Phoenicopteridae (flamingos)	1	—	1	—
Anatidae (ducks)	42	30	11	1
Cathartidae (vultures)	4	1	3	—
Accipitridae (hawks)	24	10	11	3
Pandionidae (ospreys)	1	—	1	—
Falconidae (falcons)	7	2	4	1
Cracidae (curassows)	1	—	1	—
Tetraonidae (grouse)	9	9	—	—
Phasianidae (quails)	6	6	—	—
Meleagrididae (turkeys)	1	1	—	—
Gruidae (cranes)	2	2	—	—
Aramidae (limpkins)	1	1	—	—
Rallidae (rails)	9	5	4	—
Jacanidae (jacanas)	1	—	1	—
Charadriidae (plovers)	10	3	5	2
Scolopacidae (sandpipers)	26	2	15	9
Recurvirostridae (stilts)	2	1	1	—
Columbidae (pigeons)	12	3	8	1
Psittacidae (parrots)	1	1	—	—
Cuculidae (cuckoos)	6	1	3	2
Tytonidae (Barn Owl)	17	11	6	—
Strigidae (owls)	—	—	—	—
Caprimulgidae (goatsuckers)	7	1	1	5
Apodidae (swifts)	4	—	1	3
Trochilidae (hummingbirds)	17	10	4	3
Trogonidae (trogons)	1	—	1	—
Alcedinidae (kingfishers)	2	—	2	—
Picidae (woodpeckers)	22	18	4	—
Cotingidae (cotingas)	1	—	1	—
Tyrannidae (tyrant flycatchers)	30	9	8	13
Alaudidae (larks)	1	—	1	—
Hirundinidae (swallows)	7	—	2	5
Corvidae (jays, crows)	15	13	2	—
Paridae (titmice)	14	14	—	—
Sittidae (nuthatches)	4	4	—	—
Certhiidae (creepers)	1	1	—	—

Table 1. (cont.)

Family	Number of nearctic breeding species	Number wintering in Nearctica	Number wintering in both Nearctica and Neotropica	Number wintering in Neotropica
Chamaeidae (wrentits)	1	1	—	—
Cinclidae (dippers)	1	1	—	—
Troglodytidae (wrens)	10	9	1	—
Mimidae (mockingbirds)	11	10	1	—
Muscicapidae Turdinae (thrushes)	12	9	—	3
Sylviinae (Old World warblers)	4	4	—	—
Motacillidae (pipits)	2	2	—	—
Bombycillidae (waxwings)	1	1	—	—
Ptilogonatidae (silky flycatchers)	1	1	—	—
Laniidae (shrikes)	2	2	—	—
Vireonidae (vireos)	11	3	2	6
Coerebidae (honeycreepers)	1	1	—	—
Parulidae (wood warblers)	84	14	10	30
Icteridae (orioles, etc.)	21	11	7	3
Thraupidae (tanagers)	4	—	1	3
Fringillidae (finches, sparrows)	54	44	5	5

Table 2. **Comparison of the southern extent of the wintering ranges for those birds thought to have originated either in North America (or most likely arrived from Eurasia via the Bering land bridge) to those birds which have invaded North America from southern tropical regions (from Williams, 1958)**

Southern limit of migration	Numbers of species	
	Palearctic origin	Neotropical origin
Not south of U.S.	87	8
Central Mexico	44	30
Southern Mexico	7	16
Central America	13	56
Into South America	2	63
Totals	153	173

habitat, it is apparent that for most Mexican localities, migrants are in excess of 30 percent of the population. There is a precipitous drop-off in Costa Rica and Panama (typically less than 20 percent, but only 4–7 percent at some sites). (See figures of Willis, Stiles, Tramer and Kemp, this volume.) Colombian figures are high only for a mangrove site (46 percent of individuals), a disturbed oak forest habitat in the central Andean highlands (46 percent), and a couple dry forest sites (22–24 percent). For additional sets of figures, see Waide and Tramer (this volume) who, in addition, warn of the discrepancies that may result from counts made only by netting and strip-count methods.

In the West Indies, Terborgh and Faaborg (this volume) note that the fraction of North American migrants in winter bird populations shows a strong inverse dependence on distance from the mainland (Florida). The mean value for a large array of censuses in Hispaniola is about 35 percent but drops to 10 percent in Puerto Rico and to 1 percent (or less) in more distant locations, such as the Lesser Antilles, Trinidad, and the Venezuelan mainland. This occurs even though the resident avifaunas become progressively impoverished.

Terborgh suggests that in winter half of all the migratory land birds are compressed into a segment of Mexico and the West Indies equal to 2 million km^2, compared to an area of 16 million km^2 in their North American breeding grounds. This obviously testifies to the high carrying capacity of these areas. In southern Argentina, however, Myers (this volume) records that in inland Pampas habitat, wintering migratory waders defend areas usually only one-tenth to one-hundredth the size of those defended during the breeding season, with up to 30 percent of the time being spent in territorial defense. That migrants are concentrated at such high densities is worrisome from the conservation viewpoint, suggesting that any deleterious change in these habitats will have disproportionate effects (Terborgh, this volume).

An interesting feature of winter habitat utilization by migrants is the differing abundances in the various habitats. Emlen, Hutto, Waide, Waide and Tramer, Keast, Hilty, Hespenheide, Stiles, and others, document this. Thus, on Grand Bahama, winter migrants made up: 81 and 82 percent, respectively, of all birds in the coastal dunes and mangrove flat areas; 43 percent in pine forest; but only 33 percent in pine regrowth areas. The percentages of migratory species and individuals in a range of habitats in western Mexico is given by Hutto (this volume) as follows: gallery forest, 20–22 percent (64–69 percent of individuals); mangroves, 50–74 percent (75–83 percent); second growth, 51 percent (59–63 percent); thorn scrub, 36–43 percent (55–60 percent); tropical deciduous, 28–38 percent (17–24 percent); oak woodland, 33–41 percent (29–36 percent); pine-oak woodland, 29–40 percent (31–56 percent); and pine woodland, 24 percent (31 percent). In three Colombian forest sites studied by Orejuela et al (this volume), migrants made up 20 percent of all birds in an isolated lowland valley-floor site (Jamundí), and 14 percent in an intermediate site, but were absent from a tropical wet-forest site in the Pacific lowlands (Bajo Calima). In another Colombian study which emphasizes altitudinal effects, Hilty records that the number of migrants encountered per hour was 1.0 in the lowlands (elevation, 100 m), 1.8 at 1,000 m, and 2.6 at 1,900 m.

Karr (1976b) considers the use of lowland rain forests by migrants, noting that while these forests support species in Central America, the same kind of forest in Africa is avoided. Tramer and Kemp (this volume) find that the Monteverde forests of Costa Rica are relatively little used and suggest that this is because the migrants, compared to residents, are poorly adapted for feeding on epiphytic growth. Stiles, however, suggests that the tendency for fewer migrants than residents to occupy the forest interior is merely a function of taxonomic affinities, even though the two distribution patterns are otherwise closely matched. In contrast, Rappole and Warner find that individuals of 14 migrant species were able to compete effectively in primary forest on a long-term basis. Morton (this volume) documents seasonal movements of some species to and from mature forests in Panama. Migrants occupy primary forests on Barro Colorado Island and along the Pipeline Road in the Canal Zone (Willis, Morton, this volume), and also along trails in primary forest in the Chiriqui Highlands. Regarding other forest habitats, Johnson (this volume) provides data on migrants in the subtropical lower montane forest of the Santa Marta Mountains, and Miller (1963) provides similar data relative to the Western Andes of Colombia.

In central and northern South America, some migrants are more numerous in the highlands than in the lowlands (Karr 1976; Smith 1975; and Keast, Hilty, both this volume). This does not, however, apply in Jamaica and Hispaniola (Lack and Lack 1972; Lack 1976; and Terborgh and Faaborg this volume). No author in this volume has set out to make a precise analysis of vertical abundance. Waide, however, reviews the available literature and concludes that the evidence is too conflicting to justify generalizations about the effect of elevation on the distribution of migrant birds. Altitudinal effects are difficult to separate from the effects of moisture and human disturbance. Stiles, studying migrants and residents at heights from 0 to 3,000 m in Costa Rica, finds that although the counts vary, there is no consistent relation between the migrants and residents vs elevation. Fitzpatrick (this volume) suggests that species segregation along the altitudinal gradient, while evident, is probably a byproduct of different habitats characterizing different elevations. Habitat quality, rather than altitude, may also be the major factor influencing migrant numbers.

Several authors (Terborgh, Waide, Pearson) discuss the assertion that migrants are concentrated at, or prefer, disturbed areas, second growth, marginal, patchy, and/or highly seasonal habitats (areas unused or underused by the residents) (Willis 1966; Leck 1972; Karr 1976). Alternatively, they concentrate on superabundant and/or sporadically available resources (Karr 1976). Terborgh notes that data presented by Emlen from the Bahamas, Hutto from western Mexico, Pearson from Ecuador and Bolivia, Waide from southern Yucatán and Willis from Panama, provide

Allen Keast

some support for the first assertion but that in other areas, such as the Bahamas (Emlen), Jamaica (Lack and Lack 1972), and northern Yucatán (Tramer 1974), migrants are equally common in primary and secondary vegetation. The generalization that migrants prefer second growth may also be misleading in that: 1) some migrants are actually successional stage species and 2) they may secondarily be forced to use this due to reduction of their natural habitat (Terborgh). Waide directs his study specifically to an analysis of three assertions: 1) migrants use patchy habitats (for example, mountaintops); 2) they concentrate on seasonal and unpredictable resources and, 3) they occupy new habitat types because resident species have not had time to adapt to these. The literature, he finds, provides little support for the first two hypotheses. His data fail to support the predictions of the third assertion. Thus, in the Campeche province of Mexico, while residents discriminate more strongly than migrants between forest and old fields, they nevertheless occupy old fields.

Finally, the earlier observation that the various taxonomic groups of North American birds winter in characteristic areas also applies regionally in Nearctica. The center of abundance of wintering tyrannids is southern Mexico (Fitzpatrick), and the greatest number of wintering warblers occur in the Guatemala-Costa Rica segment (Keast). No tyrannids winter in the West Indies, but good numbers of parulids do. Fitzpatrick shows that the high numbers of tyrannids in southern Mexico is due to the concentration of migrants from the western United States; eastern stocks mostly travel farther south, to southern Central America and northern South America. In a graph, Keast shows that the steep drop-off in numbers of wintering parulids from Guatemala into northern South America corresponds to an increase in numbers of such potential competitors as the small foliage-gleaning tyrannids.

Ecological Separation of Migrant-Migrant and Migrant-Resident Counterparts

The various authors of regional chapters deal comprehensively with the migrants in specific regions. Comparisons confirm that in migrant groups with many species, geographic (allopatric) replacement of species is marked. Three authors—Fitzpatrick dealing with tyrannids, Keast with parulids, and Barlow with vireos—develop species replacement in detail by the use of range maps. Keast points out that the species of the more common warbler genera such as *Dendroica*, *Oporornis*, and *Wilsonia*, show a marked degree of geographic separation. In *Dendroica*, for example, there are species that winter in northern Central America,

southern Central America, mainland South America, the West Indies, and the highlands relative to lowlands. Fitzpatrick notes that in the tyrannids geographic separation seems particularly pronounced among complexes of closely related species with similar wintering habitats. Thus, while tyrannid wintering patterns show only slight relationship to the resident community on a gross geographic scale, many wintering species sort out among themselves on a much finer scale. Ecologically dissimilar species show significant overlap on their wintering grounds. These remarks apply equally to the parulids.

Congeners also separate out on habitat. Fitzpatrick stresses that the winter habitat preferences of North American *Empidonax* flycatchers strongly resemble those of their breeding grounds. This certainly applies also to some of the parulid warblers such as *Dendroica petechia*, *Sciurus noveboracensis*, but the correlation is lacking in others.

Parulid warblers, with by far the greatest number of over-wintering migrant species, have attracted the most attention of ecologists (for example, Lack and Lack 1972; Bennett, Chipley, Rabenold, Tramer and Kemp, Keast, all this volume). Cohabiting species characteristically separate out ecologically from each other and from the resident parulids on feeding zone (Keast) and habitat, although there may be much overlap. They also differ in feeding habits, for example percentage of time spent gleaning as against hawking or fruit-eating, and several species show considerable flexibility in their feeding habits (Tramer and Kemp, this volume; Morton, this volume). This is further emphasized when feeding zones and habits in breeding and wintering grounds are compared. In fact, ecological plasticity is a basic feature of most migratory warblers (Keast).

Former workers (Lack and Lack 1972, writing of Jamaica), devoted much attention to cataloging how the various species of parulids differed ecologically from each other while in their wintering grounds. Emphasis was on habitat preferences, foraging height, and foraging habits. That each species was found to differ in one or more ways was regarded as confirmation of the competitive exclusion principle. Terborgh and Faaborg, dealing with the comparable Hispaniolan avifauna, and while also amply demonstrating these differences, have paid greater attention to evolutionary aspects. Ecological differences are considered relative to the alternative mechanisms of coadaptation (the species-developing ecological differences in response to the presence of each other) or selective screening (only species that are different can combine). They conclude that the latter is far more likely.

The papers of Feinsinger, and DesGranges and

Grant (this volume) consider the use of space and resources by migratory hummingbirds in tropical communities. Feinsinger investigates the implications of using patchily distributed resources, partial migration, and the alternative strategies of being a dominant or a fugitive species. DesGranges and Grant focus on the coexistence of resident and migrant species in four habitats in Colima, Mexico. They found that the migrants occur coincidentally with the season of superabundant nectar, food in excess of what the residents can consume. (This contrasts with the situation in the insectivorous birds.) Territorial behavior is widespread in both migrants and residents in wintertime; generally, however, the migrants are subordinate and display "fugitive" behavior. The authors conclude that the "dominant specialist," and the "interstital specialist" hypotheses are not applicable. However, migrants and residents sometimes occupy niches that are fairly different. It is obvious, accordingly, that coexistence is achieved by several mechanisms operating simultaneously. These mechanisms are broadly similar to those operative in the insectivorous parulid warblers, although the resource base is quite different.

Migrant-resident coexistence patterns in the ecologically very different shorebirds in the Buenos Aires Province of Argentina are reviewed by Myers. Local breeding species prove to be taxonomically and ecologically distinct from the migrants. In Patagonia, there is less ecological similarity between the Argentine migrants and the Patagonian residents than there is between the Argentine migrants and the North American migrants which seasonally replace them. Distributions of several potential competitors among South American breeders and North American visitors resemble geographic replacement patterns. Patterns of resource use by the migrants do not support the generalization that they depend more than residents on ephemeral resources. Aggressive interactions between migrants and residents occur repeatedly (suggesting the presence of interspecific competition). Finally, Myers believes that the high densities of residents may prevent the northern scolopacids from establishing breeding territories. There is thus strong evidence that migratory and resident shorebirds in southern Neotropica have influenced each other's evolution.

In summary, nearctic migrants wintering in Neotropica must have evolved mechanisms that reduce both the effect of migrant upon migrant, and migrant upon resident (and vice versa). This might be achieved in a limited number of ways: allopatric separation, different feeding habits, and different feeding niches. Groups as diverse as insectivorous flycatchers, parulid warblers, hummingbirds, and shorebirds, all draw on these mechanisms. The extent to which such basic

separation mechanisms (and the other lesser ones) operate, varies with the group and its resource base.

Attributes of the Neotropics Relative to the Support of Winter Migrants

A consideration of how migrants use space and separate out ecologically is, of course, only part of the problem of interpreting the nearctic-neotropical bird migration system. An understanding of how the system is able to absorb so many additional birds is basic to the problem. Do the northern neotropics have special attributes?

The subject can be considered at various levels: general biotic richness, evidence from the resident breeders (species diversity), and special features of the tropics, such as habitat diversity, production of fruit, nectar, insects, and so on.

Avian Species Diversity in the Tropics

A gradient of increasing avian species diversity extends from cold temperate North America southwards to Central America. For this aspect, see papers on within-habitat (alpha) diversity by MacArthur et al (1966), and MacArthur (1969), and earlier papers listed therein; also see Orians (1969), Karr (1971), Karr and Roth (1971), Schoener (1971), and Tramer (1974). Diversity between wider geographic regions (gamma diversity) is treated by Simpson (1964) for mammals, and by Cook (1969) for birds. Tramer (1974), in his analysis of latitudinal changes in species numbers, found that alpha diversity remains stable southwards to 20°N (which ? represents a threshold of climatic stability), then increases to the tropics. Gamma diversity, calculated as occurrences in squares with sides of 500 km, showed a striking increase in species density in winter from 20 on Hudson Bay to 80 in Massachusetts, 103 in North Carolina, 371 in Vera Cruz, and 660 in Panama. However, in summer there is a decline in gamma diversity between 45° N and the Gulf of Mexico, a feature that also puzzled Cook (1969). The western United States has a higher summer gamma diversity than the east; this has been ascribed both to the greater altitudinal diversity in the West and to proximity of source areas in Central America.

Further evidence that the migrants from North America are entering an area phenomenally rich in bird species comes from the consideration of individual regions. Thus, Costa Rica, with a land area of only 32,000 km^2, has 189 genera and 330 species of passerine birds, "in relation to its small size . . . possibly the richest bird life of any country of comparable size" (Slud 1964:22). The large country of Colombia has 328 genera and 816 species of passerines (de Schauen-

Allen Keast

see, 1964). In the Amazon segments of Ecuador, Peru and Bolivia, studied by Pearson (this volume) 420 to 480 species of birds occur per 10 km². In his study area near Belem, Brazil, Lovejoy documented over 300 species—an avian species diversity exceeding that published for any other animal or plant community, although no northern migrants occur there (Lovejoy 1974).

Avian diversity indices are high for the northern neotropics: 5.31–5.55 for lowland rain forests in Veracruz (Davis and Moroney 1953; Davis 1955); 5.67 for Belem (Lovejoy 1974); 4.38 for Barro Colorado Island (Tramer 1969); figures are calculated to the base 2. For other figures, see Orians (1969), MacArthur et al (1966), Karr (1971). Diversity indices express evenness of spread of species numbers, as well as the total number of species. Hence, while they do provide an index to the nature of the avifauna, they play down rare species; the high figures for species numbers in the tropics are in part due to the presence of many rare species. Rare species, however, are unlikely to provide competition for migrants. Karr (1971) has found that in Panama 2 percent of the species netted, accounted for 36 percent of the individuals (comparable figures for Illinois were 3.0, 13.7, and 8.2 percent). In Belem, Lovejoy (1971) found that 29.9–42.4 percent of all species were below the 2 percent level of abundance.

Migrants from Nearctica thus enter areas that have an unusually high capacity to support a diversity of bird species, as demonstrated by the rich resident avifauna. The richness, on the other hand, argues for a high degree of species saturation, hence resistance to the establishment of more species. This problem faces only migrants that enter Neotropica proper; many avoid the problem by wintering in Mexico and the West Indies. The high proportion of rare species indicates, moreover, that the system lends itself to the absorption of species at low levels of abundance. Additional species of migrants could, theoretically, be absorbed provided their numbers in any area were low.

Avian Competitors in the Neotropics: the North-South Gradient of Increasing Species Numbers

Genera of migratory passerines with resident species in Central America include *Tyrannus*, *Contopus*, *Empidonax*, *Dendroica*, *Vireo* and *Piranga*. The number of species involved is, however, small and allopatric separations are fairly clear-cut. Of greater significance are the major, or potential competitor groups among the neotropical avifauna.

All the major neotropical passerine families become increasingly diversified from Guatemala southwards. Thus, the furnariids have 13 genera and 17 species in Costa Rica compared to 26 and 68 in Colombia; the formicariids, 16 genera and 29 species to 42 and 123; the tanagers, 18 genera and 43 species to 40 and 123; the cotingids, 13 genera and 18 species to 23 and 48 (figures from Slud 1964, and de Schauensee 1964). Fitzpatrick (this volume) discusses the increasing diversity of tyrannid flycatchers from Central America southwards to the South American mainland. Keast (this volume) graphs the tapering off of numbers of wintering migratory parulids from Central America into mainland South America relative to the *increase* in the numbers of species of the small foliage-gleaning tyrannids, the parulids' ecological counterparts in South America. There is no significant difference in the numbers of genera and species of wrens (Troglodytidae), vireos and thrushes, between Costa Rica and Colombia.

It is a reasonable conclusion that 1) the increasing diversity of endemic groups from Central America southwards is a significant factor limiting the southward penetration of migratory nearctic passerines and, 2) in the longer term, furnariids, formicariids, and others have tended to restrict the morphological and ecological diversification of the parulids and others in South America.

Resource Base in Northern Neotropica during the Northern Winter

Seasonal cycles of productivity in the northern neotropics results in a heterogeneous resource base for migrants (Janzen). While the period of migrant residence is a time of peak nectar production in Mexico (DesGranges and Grant, this volume) and of insect production in Amazonian Ecuador, Peru, and Bolivia (Pearson), it is a time of reduced insect members in the Central American habitats (Janzen). Thus, in the lowland deciduous forests of Costa Rica (Santa Rosa National Park), there is a short-lived but heavy peak in biomass of moth and butterfly larvae in May, shortly after the migrants depart. These pupate, hatch within a few weeks, and depart as adults. There is no second generation, and by August caterpillar numbers are at a low level. The numbers remain low thereafter, throughout the duration of the migrants' stay. During the ensuing dry season (beginning in late September) many insects move from the drying hillsides into the riparian vegetation, resulting in relatively high numbers there during the dry season. The trend is not uniform, however; thus, while chrysomelid beetles are common in the riparian vegetation during the dry season, during this same period the bruchid beetles are the most abundant on the hillsides. Numbers of species of insects, numbers of individuals, size frequencies, weight, and taxonomic category, vary from habitat to habitat during the dry season, as earlier documented (Janzen and Schoener 1968).

In the lower montane rain forests (Monteverde, Puntarenas Province) of Costa Rica, Buskirk and Buskirk (1976) record that forest understory insects were most abundant in the late dry season and early rainy season (April through June), and lowest during the cooler, windy months (November through January). Abundance fluctuated threefold during the year. Highest Coleoptera diversity coincided with peak abundance (April–June), and average body size in the entire fauna was largest in April. Predatory groups of arthropods lagged behind others in times of peak abundance: spider populations increased in November but peaked in June. The insect cycle may vary from year to year: populations were low in the rainy season of 1970 but were high during the late dry season and early rainy season in 1971.

Buskirk and Buskirk quote several works confirming that insect abundances in northern Neotropica tend to be highest during the wet season—see Bates (1945) for mosquitoes in Colombia, Dobzhansky and Pavan (1950) for Drosophila in Brazil, and Robinson and Robinson (1970) regarding spiders in Panama. The trend is not, however, uniformly applicable—note the findings of Janzen (1973) that insect populations were much higher in the dry season in abandoned bean and corn fields in Costa Rica. Moreover, at three undisturbed lowland sites, Hutto finds that insect abundances in the mid-winter dry season average 1.58 times the abundance of the mid-summer wet season; this relatively small seasonal difference is likely due to the higher (25–35 times higher) dry season population of insectivorous birds. The finding in Costa Rica that the migrants are present when insect numbers are lower, is repeated in Emlen's findings (this volume) in Grand Bahama Island.

Also, in the savannahs of West Africa, migrants are present during the dry season when food is least abundant (Moreau 1972). Morel (1973), however, has suggested that the dry season in Africa may not be as severe on migrants, inasmuch as they have the capacity to roam widely. By contrast, in the Serengeti savannahs of Tanzania, Sinclair (1978) records that there are two insect peaks—one in November–February when the migrants are present, and a smaller one in April–May after the migrants depart and when the resident birds breed. He also notes that during their stay, migrants tend to concentrate where there has been rain.

More elaborate studies still need to be done on the seasonal aspects of the resource base in northern Neotropica, especially on the specific types of insects eaten by migrants.

Origin of Bird Migration Systems

This collection of papers the ecology of migrants in their wintering grounds is unique. Hitherto, writers have looked upon migration systems from a northern perspective, viewing southerly wintering grounds merely as alternative habitats during the season when conditions do not permit life in the north (Cooke 1888; Thomson 1936; Lincoln 1939; Wolfson 1948; Udvardy 1951; Salomonsen 1955; von Haartman 1968). But one should compare the writings of Mayr and Meise (1930), Lack (1954), and Cox (1968).

Recent years have seen a great amount of work on palaearctic migrants in their African wintering grounds, with research here proceeding faster than anything in Neotropica. This is largely due to the stimulus provided by Moreau (1952, 1966) and work begun in the Senegal (Morel and Bourliére, 1962).

Several contributors to the present Nearctica-Neotropica migrant symposium (Smith, Stiles) express indignation that we have so long looked at migration systems largely from the northern viewpoint. They note that migrants commonly spend seven months of their year in the south. (See the Keast paper that attempts to determine the actual fractions of the year spent by parulid warblers in the breeding grounds, on migration, and in the wintering grounds.) Of course, any migration system must be regarded in its entirety: its origins relative to past climatic changes, its maintenance, the ecology of species in the wintering grounds as well as breeding grounds, its energetic basic cost, and the varied adaptations of the migrants themselves.

In emphasizing ecology in wintering areas, this volume covers only part of this wider range of subjects. Fretwell reviews the evolution of migration relative to factors regulating bird numbers. He asks a series of questions (Why do some but not all birds migrate? What are the advantages of migration relative to residency?) and offers some explanatory hypotheses. Greenberg considers the demographic aspects of long-distance migration, time allocation by migrants, meaning of leapfrog migration, and other subjects. Morse considers whether population limitation in migrants occurs on the breeding or wintering grounds. Into this study, he brings habitat utilization, breeding densities over time (and evidence for population limitation both on breeding and wintering grounds), population losses during migration, and periodic disasters resulting in heavy die-offs. Buskirk considers the calendar of trans-Gulf migration relative to weather patterns. He finds that the greatest frequency of high-magnitude autumnal flights coincides with recognizable improvement in flight conditions in mid-April and at the beginning of October. He reviews the literature on seasonal resource abundance in the wintering grounds relative to the timing of migration. He finds that although the insect standing crop varies with locality, it does not occur when the migrants are present; because of this, it appears that migration calendars are determined by temperate-zone phenomena.

Theories on the Origin and Ecological Basis of Birds Migration

A brief review of the literature on bird migration is appropriate. Earlier workers were impressed with the seeming mystique of the phenomenon and considered such things as "homing instinct patterns" to be the major basis of migration (Cooke 1888;). On the other hand, workers have long recognized the importance of climatic change, both long-term and short-term, in the evolution of migration.

Prominent in discussions are the "northern ancestral home" and "southern ancestral home" theories. The first of these saw migrants as former permanent residents of the north forced southward by increasing glaciation but which annually returned as closely as possible to their original home. By contrast, the alternative idea considered them as being originally southern forms, living in the general area of their original range and annually migrating northward to exploit the exceptional conditions temporarily available to the north. Most modern workers go along with this latter explanation, at least as far as American endemics are concerned (Mengel 1964; Rappole, Smith, Stiles, all this volume). The paper of Mayr (1946) on the origins of the nearctic avifauna set the stage for Williams (1958) to put the nearctic migration system into correct perspective. He noted that species of palaearctic origin ("northerners") reflect their cold-adapted ancestry by not going far south; 87 of these species remain within the United States, and only 2 enter South America. By contrast, species derived from neotropical stocks, for the most part, winter in South America (63 species compared to only 8 wintering north of the U.S.-Mexico border). Williams suggests that latitudinal bird migration is primarily the result of seasonal climatic change combined with land distribution patterns in the two hemispheres. He attempted to explain winter ranges by postulating that northern species do not winter farther south than they were driven during the last glaciation. The winter range of southern forms, by contrast, indicates the area for which the species originally developed a locality fixation so that they return to this point annually, even though external conditions no longer force them to do so. Dorst (1962), however, correctly sees distributional changes in migratory birds as continuing (migratory populations in the Serin (*Serinus serinus*) have developed in the last hundred years), and suggests that these represented a "simple prolongation of immigration movements which followed the last glaciation" (page 190).

Some earlier workers (Mayr and Meise 1930), of course, viewed migration as not needing extreme climatic conditions but as a reaction to the existence of alternating favorable and unfavorable conditions. These authors also suggested that a biotic factor—intraspecific competition—and the need to avoid extreme crowding had had a reinforcing effect that might help explain "leapfrog" migration in which populations breeding farthest north winter farthest south. (See here the early paper by Swarth [1920] on wintering distribution in the fox sparrow, *Passerella*.)

That migration undoubtedly has a multiple origin has long been recognized (Kaleal 1954; Farner 1955). It also represented a balance between advantages and disadvantages to the bird. Thus, Lack (1954:244) wrote, "The resident habit has been evolved in those species in which, on the average, migration involves greater losses than winter residence"; thus, food shortages and low temperatures are a peril in the north, but residency has advantages—such as better opportunity to choose breeding territories. In a similar vein, Salomonsen (1955, 1970) saw migratory habits as demonstrating natural selection by the environment (with extrinsic factors operating similarly in breeding and on migration) and that selection in breeding and wintering areas may have a reinforcing effect or counteract each other. Salmonsen also states that spatial separation of bird populations in winter may ultimately lead to morphological differentiation.

Interspecific competition as a factor influencing migration patterns and winter ranges entered migration theory relatively late. Lack (1944), however, noted that each genus and species of migrant has its own wintering area and that, in many cases, the greatest differences are to be found in the most closely related species (*Anas, Larus, Anthus, Lanius, Emberiza*), and suggested that competition for food was the reason for wide dispersal. He also noted, however, that different populations commonly mixed freely in their wintering grounds. Subsequently, however, Udvardy (1951:113), reflecting the mood of the day about ecological competition as a selective force, wrote, "It has not been possible to prove in one single case that competition between species has any important influence upon the distribution ecology of European birdlife."

Later, Cox (1965) was able to develop a whole thesis

on the origins of migration relative to the need to avoid interspecific competition. Most of his ideas are still appropriate in the light of later knowledge. He postulates an evolutionary sequence of stages based on variation leading to incipient migratory movements into adjacent areas if the reduction in total competition (intraspecific and interspecific) allows greater survival or reproduction (the cost of migration being taken into consideration) than in the original range. Cox drew up a series of models illustrating sequences in the transition from resident to migrant. Possible ways in which competition between two partial migrants might be resolved include: 1) one migrant becoming a resident in an area from which it could eliminate the second, and the latter becoming a partial migrant; 2) both becoming fully migratory, and breeding and wintering in different areas, and; 3) partial competitive exclusion at one season only. Cox argued that some proof of the importance of interspecific competition in fixing different winter ranges comes from the small bill length differences between species in such nearctic migratory groups as the Parulidae and Emberizinae. Members of these groups have been less able to develop these differences as a means of ecological separation (Schoener 1965), hence must separate out allopatrically.

The kinds of sequences suggested by Cox may be invoked in the case of warblers and vireos, which have both migratory and resident populations. See Mengel (1964) for a discussion of post-glacial northward range extensions in parulid warblers. Cox's discussions of the role of interspecific competition as the factor determining winter ranges requires some modification in the light of later theoretical advances (Wiens 1977; and below).

Palaearctic-Ethiopean Bird Migration System, A Parallel with the Nearctic One

In view of the detailed treatment accorded the nearctic neotropical system in this book, it is appropriate to review in some detail the parallel palaearctic-Ethiopean system. As will be seen, it involves many similarities, and also some striking contrasts with the former (Karr 1976a, this volume, and the next section).

Moreau, in his classic paper (1952), lays out the main features of the palaearctic-Ethiopean system, with much additional data being added subsequently by Morel and Bourliére (1962), Moreau (1972), and later workers. Migration out of the palaearctic follows three main streams: birds from Western Europe wintering mainly in West Africa, birds from Central Asia migrating to East Africa, and eastern palaearctic birds concentrating in Southeastern Asia. Of the 589 species of wholly or mainly palaearctic birds, 238 leave that

region in winter, with 183 species regularly migrating to sub-Saharan Africa. Of the western palaearctic species, 29 percent find their winter quarters wholly in Africa south of the Sahara. Africa provides winter quarters for 22 percent of the central palaearctic passerines against the 24 percent which enter India, although India is much nearer. Comparable figures are not available for the Far Eastern palaearctic birds, most of which winter on the Asian continent; some 8 species, however, winter in Africa. West Africa, with a land area of over one million square miles (excluding evergreen forest), supports 61 non-passerines and 37 passerines in winter; Kenya and Uganda with about half this land area support 70 nonpasserines and 43 passerines. The difference is due to the high number of Asian forms in East Africa. Migrants cross considerable areas of desert to reach the wintering ground where they typically spend the period October–March. Most of the area between the equator and the Sahara is already dry when the migrants arrive, and it becomes drier as the winter proceeds; on the other hand, in southern Africa, the rainy season begins soon after the arrival of the migrants. Evergreen forest and desert are not utilized by the migrants. Species utilize the same feeding zone as they do in Europe, for instance, nightingales (*Luscinia*) use dense thickets, as in Europe. Migrants occupy the same areas as residents but are generally fewer in number than the latter, except along waterways. However, a few species, such as the buzzard (*Buteo b. vulpinus*) and the swallow (*Hirundo rustica*), may greatly outnumber residents in some places. In the case of smaller species, migrants and residents commonly form mixed flocks. Moreau estimated that populations of palaearctic birds were only a fraction of their present numbers at the height of the glacial maxima when habitat was greatly reduced; at that time, a maximal area of Africa would have been available to wintering migrants. The clearing of the forests in Europe in post-Roman times must also have greatly reduced the numbers of migrants. It can be inferred, accordingly, that the palaearctic-Ethiopean bird migration system has been, and is, to some degree, in a state of flux.

Morel and Bourlière (1962), in a series of studies in the lower Senegal Valley, found that for eight months of the year palaearctic migrants, which include a spectrum embracing pipits, ducks, cuckoos, hawks, swallows, and warblers, form an appreciable part of the avifauna. Numbers of migrants and residents peak at the same time, although the two seldom belong to a common genus or a closely related one, and the migrants as a whole constitute a floating population. Also, most resident birds are themselves locally nomadic.

Allen Keast

Nigerian studies (Elgood et al 1966, 1973) confirm the importance of the West African savannah zone to migrants. Here, one species in six is a palaearctic migrant. Endemic African migrants, furthermore, are also very common in the savannah zone: 120 migratory species comprise 28 percent of the avifauna here with 95 percent of the African migrants inhabiting the zone. By contrast, there are few migrants in the forests. The time of arrival of intra-African migrants corresponds with the onset of marked climatic changes elsewhere (beginning of rains, dry desert winds), and the movements would seem to be initiated by these factors.

The basis of seasonal movements in African and palaearctic migrants to West Africa have been compared for various groups: doves (Morel 1975), raptores (Thiollay 1975), and ducks (Roux et al 1978). Seven resident and one palaearctic dove species are present in the savannah only during the rainy season (June–July); three of these, however, retreat to the valley of the Senegal River when the dry season (December–February) begins.

The raptors fall into three groups: intra-tropical migrants, Palaearctic migrants, and erratically-occurring immatures of several species. Outside the vultures, half the raptors are migrants—40 percent of these raptors being palaearctics. Of the 54 species of hawks inhabiting the grasslands between the forest edge and the desert, 16 are sedentary, 6 perform regular migration (going north between March and August, and south from September to December); 14 are partial or erratic migrants; 14 are wintering palaearctic species; and the last 4 have one palaearctic and 1 Ethiopean race. Most of these hawks, which are medium to large in size, consume terrestrial vertebrates and insects in the open grasslands or along the rivers. In a subsequent paper concerned with the attributess of the migratory hawks, Thiollay (1978) records that they are morphologically adapted to feeding in open habitats, are very mobile (exploiting locally abundant but transient food sources), have high reproductive rates, are very sensitive to the dry heat of the Sahel, and, on the whole, overlap very little ecologically with resident birds of prey. The timing of migratory movements is closely correlated with the onset of the rains—the birds following the seasonal changes of the inter-tropical front, moving northward with the first rains in spring, and southward at the end of autumn. The seasonal shift in habitat is also correlated with an increase in the height of the grass cover and sometimes with flooding. There is good correlation between abundance of the migrants and that of grasshoppers, their major insect prey. The availability of drinking water is also important. African migrants generally stay in the southern savannahs

during the dry season when food is abundant, going north with the rains to utilize the food surplus left by the sparse populations of resident species. African migrants are the only ones to seasonally invade the northernmost grasslands. The southern Guinea savannahs are used by both palaerctic and African migrants during the breeding season of the resident species. However, the former, which have hunting methods and diets similar to those of the endemic migrants, never coexist with them during the dry season.

The ducks wintering in the lower Senegal (Roux et al 1978) consist of several Ethiopean species, reaching numbers of 35,000 in October when innundation is greatest, and about 120,000 palaearctic Garganey teal (*Anas querquedula*), and 100,000 pintail (*Anas acuta*). However, interspecific impact between resident and migrant is minimized by partly distinct periods of presence and habitat preference. It is suggested that the numbers of the Ethiopean species are limited by variable and adverse environmental pressures in summer; they are, in other words, underutilizing the habitat.

Studies of migrants in East Africa mainly concern a small number of passerine species. Pearson (1972) carried out a three-year trapping and banding program at Kampala, Uganda, and compiled data on 11 species, 3 of which were passage migrants en route south. Major species were: 4 species of sylviid warblers—2 *Acrocephalus*, plus *Sylvia borin* and *Phylloscopus trochilus*; the Spotted Flycatcher (*Muscicapa striata*); Yellow Wagtail (*Motacilla flava*); the Red-backed Shrike (*Lanius collurio*); and hirundines (*Hirundo rustica*, *Riparia riparia*). Most of the migrants arrived in October–November, and made their spring departure at the end of March, continuing throughout April. Half of the migrants trapped were warblers. Wet seasons were March–May and September–November, with the area tending to become parched in late winter. Migrant numbers varied greatly with habitat. In partly cultivated areas, they averaged only 1–2 per acre and were greatly outnumbered by locals. Near the lake, however, *Acrocephalus*, Yellow Wagtails and hirundines were much more numerous, and winter visitors comprised a large proportion of all birds present, averaging 10 or more per acre. In the vicinity of the lake, emergent chironomids and chaoborines were attended by equal numbers of migrant *Hirundo rustica*, *Riparia riparia*, and Ugandan swallows (*Hirundo angolensis*) in winter but, with the departure of the migrants in April and May, were dominated by sand martins (*Riparia*). Migratory warblers frequented various bush and forest-edge habitats where the principal resident species were a *Camaroptera*, a *Cisticola*, and 2 *Prinia*.

Here the migrants tended to be more unobtrusive than the locals.

Britton (1974), in a further consideration of which habitats are used by migrants in East Africa, arrived at a figure of 20 percent of individuals for overgrazed cultivation areas and 4 percent for papyrus swamp. Considering species only, however, papyrus had the greatest proportion of palaearctic birds—30 percent. Figures for introduced Lantana thickets were 25 percent of biomass for palaearctic species but only 1–11 percent for other habitats.

The review by Sinclair (1978) of the ecology of wintering palaearctic migrants in the woodlands of the Serengeti, Tanzania, provides interesting contrasts both with the West African situation and with Pearson's sites in Kenya. In contrast with West Africa where the migrants are present during the dry season (an interesting "paradox"—Moreau 1966) in the Serengeti, 14 northern migrants arrive about a month ahead of the wet season and remain through it, contemporaneous with the breeding residents. The winter visitors include 2 hawks, a stork, a roller, a bee-eater, a scolopacid, a plover, a chat, a wheatear, 2 shrikes, a flycatcher, a swallow, and a couple of sylviid warblers. The warblers keep largely to the streamside thickets. There is some obvious ecological separation of migratory and resident counterparts. Prior to the rains, both resident and migrant rollers inhabit the woodlands, but thereafter the migrants move on to the short-grass plains to feed on dung beetles. Migratory wheatears were somewhat nomadic, moving with the progress of the rains. The more abundant resident, capped wheatear (*Oenanthe pileata*) vigorously defended territories in December, presumably explaining why migrants were absent from areas of greatest resident density. The palaearctic warblers were rarely seen in the canopy frequented by residents. The migratory spotted flycatcher (*Muscicapa*) fed mainly on flying insects, while the resident species fed from the ground. The palaearctic bee-eater was larger than the endemic ones and possibly did not compete on that basis. Migrant and resident shrikes were of the same general size and occurred together; Sinclair suggests, however, that any competition was nullified by the increased food supplies following the rains.

Only a small number of palaearctic migrants penetrate to southern Africa (Moreau 1972; McLachlan and Liversidge 1978). Thus, the single warbler and flycatcher wintering in the Zambian *Brachystegia* woodland were in small numbers (Ulfstrand and Alerstam 1977), and were concentrated in disturbed habitats. In South Africa the migratory swallow, *Hirundo rustica*, occurs sometimes in very large flocks, greatly outnumbering the residents (McLachlan and Liversidge).

Palaearctic-Ethiopean and Nearctic-Neotropical Migration Systems Compared

Karr (this volume) in a comparison of the winter migrants in Africa, Neotropica, and the oriental region, gives figures of 118, 147, and 142 for the numbers of bird species wintering in each region. Thus, he concludes that available area clearly is not the main factor controlling species numbers. Rather, historical factors, geographic extent and diversity of habitats, topographic complexity, and patterns of seasonality must be invoked.

Karr tabulates the numbers of members of each family wintering in 4 major "migrant receptor" areas: Africa, the neotropics, Southeast Asia and the Indian sub-continent. Twice as many northern accipitrids and falcons migrate to Africa as to Neotropica (16 and 8 species, compared to 7 and 4). The same applies to thrushes (18 compared to 7), pipits (6 compared to 2), and swifts (4 compared to 2). However, the neotropics receive far more warblers (46 parulids compared to 29 sylviids entering Africa) and flycatchers (23 tyrannids compared to 3 muscicapids). As regards hummingbirds, vireos, and icterids, the several species of each entering the neotropics are confined to the Western Hemisphere.

Moreau (1972) outlines some of the problems facing migrants to sub-Saharan Africa: they must cross great sections of desert and in the east, must circumvent the high Himalayan Mountains. Long, direct flights are, therefore, common. No such problems face nearctic birds traveling to Neotropica, although many do make a long flight across the Caribbean. The long-distance flight of the Blackpoll Warbler (*Dendroica striata*) from Maine to South America (McClintock et al 1978) is exceptional for a nearctic breeding species. Linked to their long-distance flights, there is apparently a marked tendency for many palaearctic species to move southward in stages, pausing for weeks or even several months, before proceeding (Moreau and Dolp 1970; Pearson and Backhurst 1976). Slow migration, with intermediate stops is much less important in nearctic species, although it does occur. For example, Yellowrumped Warblers (*Dendroica coronata*) do not arrive in Jamaica until January (Lack and Lack 1972), and some migrants going to South America apparently linger in Panama (Morton, this volume).

One of the more interesting differences in the two systems is in the habitats occupied by the migrants. As many have pointed out (Moreau 1952; Morel and Bourliére 1962; Elgood et al 1966; Brosset 1968; Morel 1968; Pearson 1971; Thiollay 1970a and b; Moreau 1972; and as reviewed by Karr 1976a) most migrant species in Africa winter in savannah and dry woodland

Allen Keast

habitats. Mangroves may be much-used in West Africa (Cawkell 1964). On the other hand, besides desert areas, tropical evergreen forest is almost entirely neglected (Elgood et al 1966; Moreau 1966). Relatively few migrants use the limited highland areas (Karr 1976a). By contrast, in Nearctica the available range of habitats is basically different: highlands, pine woodlands, rain forests, and extensive areas of second growth occupy a position proximal to the northern migrant source. Grasslands are not an important wintering habitat for migrants (Karr 1976a); this may be because they are largely a secondary habitat in Central America. Just as availability determines what winter habitat is used by migrants, so do the dominant kinds of habitat and their seasons of productivity (in both north and south) determine the taxonomic kinds of birds that migrate, as noted above. Nevertheless, it is apparent that migrants forced southward by declining winter conditions must, in both areas, adapt to whatever habitat is available.

The species of passerines migrating to Africa show the same tendencies to separate out ecologically as do the nearctic ones in Neotropica. Moreau (1972) states that of 90 migrant species in six African habitats, 14 were without related native species as potential competitors, 19 were segregated by feeding site, and 32 differed significantly in size. Lack (1971) has given data for congeners in Africa as follows: 64 percent had non-overlapping ranges, 23 percent separated out on habitat, 2 percent separated out on foraging ecology, and only 10 percent had no obvious pattern of separation. Here, also see regional accounts of species separations in Pearson (1972) and Sinclair (1978).

As might be expected from the vast expanse of the Ethiopean wintering area and different regional climatic cycles, the seasonal conditions experienced by migrants in their wintering grounds vary greatly; in the Serengeti in East Africa they are present during the rainy season but in West Africa they are present during the dry season.

Interspecific Competition Relative to the Evolution of the Nearctic-Neotropical Bird Migration System

The development of species ecological specializations has long been recognized as an integral part of the speciation process (Mayr 1942). In typical systems, cohabiting species differ ecologically in one or more clearcut ways. The potential problem of interspecific competition is avoided by the occupation of different feeding zones, by differences in feeding habits, or by occupying distinct sub-habitats. A community thus consists of a group of species that either brought different adaptations with them into the system or that have developed adjustments relative to each other.

A surprising finding that emerges from this volume is that migrants belong to quite different species associations or communities in the north and in the south. Their adjustments have, accordingly, been so much greater than in resident species. Can simple "interspecific competition" be invoked as the driving force behind these ecological separations?

Weins (1977) has recently reviewed the difficulties of trying to apply the competitive exclusion principle to avian communities:

1) Obviously, it must be related to species density yet densities undergo considerable annual variation, and the magnitude of such variation differs not only among species but also among local areas. That is to say, the impact of the species on each other is *not* in the form of a constant "pressure" such that might make it highly advantageous for them to acquire rigid "separation devices."

2) Virtually all mathematical treatments of competition are based on the assumption that the system is at equilibrium. Not only the populations but also their resource functions are assumed to be at equilibrium. Natural systems, however, are highly variable seasonally and from year to year. Hence, what is optimal at one time is not optimal at another.

3) In many systems, production is concentrated into a brief growing season. Hence, variations in resource-utilization in the course of the year may be profound. Conditions of shortage may affect cohabiting species very differently.

4) Most theories of optimal foraging predict that as resources become more abundant relative to demand, individuals should progressively restrict their diets, specializing on the optimal (most profitable) prey types, or most productive habitat patches. However, general and specialist strategies both have to be incorporated into the scheme. Competition theory predicts that under conditions of high resource availability, other species may successfully invade the community. Competition will then force resource specialization and separation. Alternatively, in the absence of an invader, the population should grow to resource-defined carrying capacities; this, however, will take time in the case of slow-producing animals such as birds. Thus, populations may frequently be below the carrying capacity, invalidating the competitive exclusion argument.

Many authors in the present symposium have considered the spatial and ecological relationships of migrants in terms of interspecific competition (Emlen, Myers, Faaborg and Terborgh, Fitzpatrick, Keast). Supporting evidence for its existence, it is suggested, comes from various sources: the frequency of aggressive interactions between migrants and residents (for example, in shorebirds, Myers), habitat separation of congeners, feeding zone separations, presence of both dominant and fugitive species, and so on. At the broader evolutionary level, it is argued (Keast) that there is "resistance" by endemic groups to the southward penetration of nearctic groups like the parulid warblers. That migratory and resident species, and migrant and migrant, are interacting is undeniable. That the interaction system is a dynamic and evolving one is indicated by geographic variation in feeding ecology (compare, for example the observations of Tramer and Kemp on warbler feeding with those of Keast), such distributional anomalies as the biomodal distribution of the endemic ground warbler (*Microlegia palustris*) of Hispaniola (Terborgh and Faaborgh), and varying species combinations from place to place. On the other hand, the consistency of ecological species differences, the failure of residents to expand into niches left vacant by returning migrants, and other factors, argue that there has been a long period of co-evolution of migrants and residents.

Literature Cited

Bates, M.
1945. Observations on climate and seasonal distribution of mosquitos in Eastern Colombia. J. Anim. Ecol. 14: 17–25.

Britton, P. L.
1974. Relative biomass of European and Palaearctic passerines in West Kenya habitats. Bull. Brit. Ornith. Club 94:108–113.

Brosset, A.
1968. Localization écologique des oiseaux migrateurs dans la forêt équitoriale du Gabon. Biologia Gabonica 4: 211–26.

Buskirk, R. E. and W. H. Buskirk
1976. Changes in arthropod abundance in a highland Costa Rican forest. Am. Midl. Nat. 95: 288–98.

Cook, R. E.
1969. Variation in species density of North American birds. Syst. Zool. 18:63–84.

Cooke, W. W.
1888. Report on bird migration in the Mississippi Valley. U.S. Nat. Museum, Washington.

Cox, G. W.
1968. The role of competition in the evolution of migration. Evolution 22:180–92.

Davis, L. I.
1955. Bird census 27. Audubon Field Notes 9:425–26

Davis, L. I. and J. Moroney Jr.
1953. Bird census 31. Audubon Field Notes 7:352–53.

De Schauensee, R. M.
1964. *The Birds of Colombia and Adjacent Areas of South and Central America.* Narberth, Pa.: Livingston, 430 pp

Diamond, J. M.
1975. Distributional ecology and habits of some Bougainville birds. Condor 77:14–23.

Dobzhansky, T. and C. Pavan.
1950. Local and seasonal variation in relative frequencies of species of *Drosophila* in Brazil. J. Anim. Ecol. 19: 1–14.

Dorst, J.
1962. The Migration of Birds. Boston: Houghton Mifflin, 476 pp.

Elgood, J. H., R. E. Sharland, and P. Ward.
1966. Palaearctic migrants in Nigeria. Ibis 108:84–116.

Elgood, J. H., C. H. Fry, and R. J. Dowsett.
1973. African migrants in Nigeria. Ibis 115:1–45, 375–409.

Farner, D. S.
1955. Recent Studies in Avian Biology. Urbana: Univ. Illinois Press.

Janzen, D. H.
1973. Sweep samples of tropical foliage insects: effects of seasons, vegetation types, elevation, time of day, and insularity Ecol. 54:687–708.

Janzen, D. H. and T. W. Schoener
1968. Differences in insect abundance and diversity between wetter and drier sites during a tropical dry season. Ecol. 49:96–110.

Kalela, O.
1954. Populations—okologische gesichtspunkte zur entshung des vogelzuges. Annales Zoologica Societis Zoologisae Botanical Fennicae Vanama 1:1–30.

Karr, J. R.
1971. Structure of avian communities in selected Panama and Illinois habitats. Ecol. Monogr. 41:207–33.

1976a. Within- and between-habitat avian diversity in African and Neotropical lowland habitats. Ecol. Monogr. 46:457–81.

1976. On the relative abundance of migrants from the North Temperate Zone in tropical habitats. Wils. Bull. 88:433–58.

Karr, J. R. and R. R. Roth
1971. Vegetation structure and avian diversity in several new world areas. Amer. Nat. 105:423–36.

Keast, A.
1972. Ecological opportunities and dominant families, as illustrated by the Neotropical Tyrannidae (Aves). Evolutionary Biology 5:229–77.

Lack, D. L.
1944. The problem of partial migration. British Birds 37: 122–30; 143–50.

1954. The Natural Regulation of Animal Numbers. London: Oxford.

1971. Ecological isolation in birds. Oxford, U.K.: Blackwells.

1976. Island biology illustrated by the land birds of Jamaica. Oxford U.K.: Blackwells, 445 pp.

Lack, D. and P. Lack
1972. Wintering warblers in Jamaica. Living Bird 11:129–53.

Leck, C. F.
1972. The impact of some North American migrants at fruiting trees in Panama. Auk 89:842–50.

Lincoln, F. C.
1939. The migration of American birds. New York: Doubleday, Doran 189 pp.

Lonnberg, E.
1927. Some speculations on the origin of the North American ornithic fauna. Kungl. Svenska Vetenkapsakad. Handl. Ser. 3, 4:1–24.

Lovejoy, T. E.
1974. Bird diversity and abundance in Amazon forest communities. Living Bird 13:127–91.

MacArthur, R. H.
1969. Patterns of communities in the tropics. Biol. J. Linnaean Soc. 1:19–30.

MacArthur, R. H., J. W. MacArthur, and M. Cody
1966. On the relation between habitat selection and species diversity. Amer. Nat., 100:319–32.

McClintock, C. P., T. C. Williams, and J. M. Teal
1978. Autumnal bird migration observed from ships in the western north Atlantic Ocean. Bird-Banding 49:262–77.

McLachlan, G. R. and R. Liversidge
1978. *Robert's Birds of South Africa.* Capetown, South Africa: Cape and Transvaal Printers

Mayr, E.
1942. Systematics and the origin of species. New York: Colombia Univ. Press.

1964. Inferences concerning the Tertiary American bird faunas. Proc. Nat. Acad. Sci. 51:280–88.

1946. History of the North American bird fauna. Wils. Bull. 58:3–41.

Mayr, E. and W. Meise
1930. Theoretisches zur Geschichte des vogelsuges. Der Vogelzug (Berlin) 1:149–72.

Mayr, E. and W. H. Phelps, Jr.
1967. The origin of the bird fauna of the South Venezuelan Highlands. Bull. Amer. Mus. Nat. Hist. 136:269–328.

Mengel, R. M.
1964. The probable history of species formation in some Northern Wood Warblers (Parulidae). Living Bird 3:9–43.

Miller, A.
1963. Seasonal activity and ecology of the avifauna of American equatorial cloud forest. Univ. Calif. Publ. Zool. 68:1–78.

Moreau, R. E.
1952. The place of Africa in the Palaearctic migration system. J. Anim. Ecol. 21:250–71.

1966. The bird faunas of Africa and its islands. New York: Academic Press.

1972. The Palaearctic-African bird migration systems. New York: Academic Press, 424 pp.

Moreau, R. E. and R. M. Dolp
1970. Fat, water, weight and wing lengths of autumn migrants in transit on the northwest coast of Egypt. Ibis 112:209–28.

Morel, G.
1968. Contribution à la synécologie des oiseaux du Sahel sénégalais Mem. ORSTOM 29, Paris.

1973. The Sahel zone as an environment for Palaearctic migrants. Ibis 115:413–17.

Morel, G. and F. Bourlière
1952. Relations écologiques des avifaunes sédentaires et migratrices dans une savane sahélienne du bas Sénégal. La Terre et la Vie, 190:371:93.

Morel, M. Y.
1975. Comportement de sept espèces de Tourterelles aux points d'eau naturel et artificiels dans une sauvage sahélienne du Ferlo Septentrional Sénégal. L'Oiseau et R.F.O. 45:97–126.

Orians, G. H.
1969. The number of bird species in some tropical forests. Ecol. 50:783–801.

Pearson, D. J.
1971. Weights of some Palaearctic migrants in southern Uganda. Ibis 111:173–84.

1972. The wintering and migration of Palaearctic passerines at Kampala, Uganda. Ibis 114:43–60.

Pearson, D. J. and G. C. Backhurst
1976. The southward migration of Palaearctic birds over Ngulia, Kenya. Ibis 118:78–105.

Pearson, D. L.
1975. The relation of foliage complexity to ecological diversity of three Amazonian bird communities. Condor 77:453–66.

1977. A pantropical comparison of bird community structure on six lowland forest sites. Condor 79:232–44.

Robinson, M.H. and B. Robinson
1970. Prey caught by a sample population of the spider *Argiope argentata* (Araneae: Araneidae) in Panama: a year's census data. Zool. J. Linn. Soc. 4:345–57.

Roux, F., R. Maheo, and A. Tamisier.
1978. L'exploitation de la Basse Vallée du Sénégal (Quartier d'Hiver Tropicale) par trois espèces de canards Paléarctiques et Ethiopien. La Terre et la Vie 32: 387–416.

Salomonsen, F.
1955. The evolutionary significance of bird migration. Det Kongelige Danske Videnskabernes Selskat Biologiske Meddlelser 22:1–62.

1970. Zoogeographical and ecological problems in Arctic Birds. Pres. Add. Zoological Museum, Univ. Copenhagen, Denmark.

Schoener, T. W.
1971. Large-billed insectivorous birds: a precipitous diversity gradient. Condor 73:154–61.

Simpson, G. G.
1964. Species density of North American Mammals. Syst Zool. 12:57–73.

Sinclair, A. E. R.
1978. Factors affecting the food supply and breeding season of resident birds and movements of Palaearctic migrants in a tropical African savannah. Ibis 120: 480–97.

Slud, P.
1964. The birds of Costa Rica. Bull. Am. Mus. Nat. Hist. 128:1–430.

1976. Geographic and climatic relationships of avifaunas with special reference to comparative distribution in the Neotropics. Smith. Conf. Zoology 212:1–149

Smith, N.
1975. "Spshing noise": biological significance of its attraction and nonattraction by birds. Proc. Nat. Acad. Sci. 72:1411–14.

Smith, V. M.
1966. Autumn and spring weights of some Palaearctic migrants in central Nigera. Ibis 108:492–512.

Swarth, H. S.
1920. Revision of the avian genus *Passerella* with special reference to the distribution and migration of the races in California. Univ. California Pubs. Zoo. 21: 75–224.

Terborgh, J. and J. S. Weske
1969. Colonization of secondary habitats by Peruvian birds. Ecol. 50:765–82.

Thiollay, J. M.
1975. Les rapaces des Parcs Nationaux du Côte d'Ivoire, analyse du peuplement. L'Oiseau de la R.F. D'O. 45:241–57.

1977a. Le peuplement de Falconiformes d'une savane ongandaise L'Oiseau et la R.F. D'O 47:193–205.

1977b. Distribution saisonnière des rapaces diurnes en Afrique occidental. L'Oiseau de la R.F. D'O. 47:253–94.

1978. Les migrations de rapaces en afrique occidentale: adaptations écologiques aux fluctuations saisonnières de production des ecosystémes. La Terre et la Vie 32:89–133.

Thomson, A. L.
1936. Bird Migration: a Short Account. London: Witherby

Tramer, E. J.
1974. On latitudinal gradients in avian diversity. Condor 76:123–130.

Udvardy, M. D. F.
1951. The significance of interspecific competition in bird life. Oikos 3:98–123.

Ulfstrand, S., and T. Alerstam
1977. Bird communities of Brachstegia and Acacia woodlands in Zambia. J. Ornith. 118:156–74.

Von Haartman, L.
1968. The evolution of resident versus migratory habitat in birds: some considerations. Ornis Fennica 45:1–7.

Vuilleumier, F. and D. Simberloff.
1980. Patchy distributions in birds of the high tropical Andes. Evol. Biol. 12.

Wiens, J. A.
1977. On competition and variable environments Amer. Scientist 65:590–97.

Whitmore, F. C. Jr. and R. H. Stewart
1965. Miocene mammals and Central American Pathways. Science 148:328–29.

Williams, G. G.
1958. Evolutionary aspects of bird migration. Lida Scott Brown Lectures in Ornithology, University of California, Los Angeles.

Willis, E. O.
1966. The role of migrant birds at swarms of army ants. Living Bird. 5:187–231.

Wolfson, A.
1948. Bird migration and the concept of continental drift. D. Science 108:23–30.

Allen Keast